July 12–16, 2014
Vancouver, BC, Canada

Association for
Computing Machinery

Advancing Computing as a Science & Profession

GECCO'14

Proceedings of the 2014 Genetic and Evolutionary Computation Conference

Sponsored by:

ACM SIGEVO

Association for Computing Machinery

Advancing Computing as a Science & Profession

The Association for Computing Machinery
2 Penn Plaza, Suite 701
New York, New York 10121-0701

ISBN: 978-1-4503-3275-0 (Digital)

ISBN: 978-1-4503-3267-5 (Print)

Additional copies may be ordered prepaid from:

ACM Order Department
PO Box 30777
New York, NY 10087-0777, USA

Phone: 1-800-342-6626 (USA and Canada)
+1-212-626-0500 (Global)
Fax: +1-212-944-1318
E-mail: acmhelp@acm.org
Hours of Operation: 8:30 am – 4:30 pm ET

Printed in the USA

Welcome

On behalf of the Organizing Committee, I would like to welcome you to Vancouver for the 2014 Genetic and Evolutionary Computation Conference (GECCO 2014). This year's GECCO is comprised of 20 tracks, including the new Artificial Immune Systems and Hot Off the Press (HOP) tracks. The latter offers authors of outstanding research recently published in journals and other conferences the opportunity to present their work to the GECCO community. Under the guidance of Editor-in-Chief Christian Igel, the Track Chairs and Program Committee have selected 180 out of the 544 submissions received in all tracks (excluding HOP) for oral presentation as full papers, resulting in an acceptance rate of 33%. Close to 100 short papers will be presented in the poster session.

Highlights of the conference include keynote talks by Yoshua Bengio on "Deep Learning and Cultural Evolution", and by Dario Floreano on "Bridging Natural and Artificial Evolution", as well as an invited talk by Sumit Gulwani in the Genetic Programming track. Altogether 32 tutorials cover topics ranging from broad and introductory to specialized and at the frontier of current research. GECCO also hosts fifteen workshops, including several new ones as well as at least one that predates GECCO itself. Further high points include the 11th Annual "Humies" Awards for Human-Competitive Results, which are again generously supported by John Koza, and five competitions, ranging from Art, Design, and Creativity to the Industrial Challenge. Finally, Evolutionary Computation in Practice continues to be an important and integral part of GECCO.

I would like to thank the entire Organizing Committee for their work and dedication over the past year. Thanks also go to the Track Chairs and the Program Committee for their careful reviewing of the large number of submissions received. Finally, thanks are due to Roxane Rose and Cara Candler from *Executive Events*, who have been in charge of logistical aspects and registration, Lisa Tolles and her team at *Sheridan Communications* for the production of the proceedings, Mark Montague and his team at *Linklings* for their conference management tool and support of the reviewing process, and Gerardo Valencia for artwork and website management.

I wish you all a productive and enjoyable conference.

Dirk Arnold
General Chair

A Word from the Chair of SIGEVO

Welcome to the Proceedings of GECCO 2014, the sixteenth GECCO, the "recombination" of the 23rd International Conference on Genetic Algorithms (ICGA) and the 19th Genetic Programming Conference (GP). This year, Dirk Arnold was General Chair of GECCO 2014 acting with great diligence and care. Christian Igel, the Editor-in-Chief of GECCO-2014 has done an excellent job at coordinating the reviewing process and leading the effort to select papers for publication. The results of the effort of them and their team are presented here.

GECCO is the premiere venue for presenting papers in the area of Genetic and Evolutionary Computation worldwide. The quality of papers submitted to GECCO is very high, and GECCO has a rigorous paper selection process. This means that the best and most important work in Evolutionary Computation and on related topics is presented at GECCO. Our conference is consistently ranked at the top of Evolutionary Computation conferences, exceeding in citation counts well known journals and other venues.

If you were not able to attend GECCO 2014 in person, the Proceedings are in the ACM Digital Library; they are globally accessible and readily found, which benefits both readers and authors.

ACM SIGEVO

Members of ACM SIGEVO, sponsor of GECCO, continue to draw major benefits from joining ACM. First is a discount at SIGEVO sponsored conferences, at GECCO as much as $100 per registrant. Members have, for a fee, access to the ACM Digital Library, a large and continuously growing resource for research in computing. Another key benefit is the outstanding newsletter *SIGEVOlution* produced by Pier Luca Lanzi and his excellent editorial board. If you are accessing these proceedings and are not a member of SIGEVO, please consider joining (for the low price of $25/year for non-students, and $10/year for student members). This will help us a lot in promoting our community.

Involvement in ACM SIGEVO

SIGEVO became a Special Interest Group (SIG) of the ACM in 2005. ACM considers its SIGs as the lifeblood of the organization. We are governed by bylaws available on the SIGEVO web pages. There, you also find a list of members of the 18-member Executive Committee.

Since 2011, I serve as chair of SIGEVO, together with a team of officers: Una-May O'Reilly (Vice-Chair), Marc Schoenauer (Secretary), and Franz Rothlauf (Treasurer). The Executive, its Officers and I are dedicated to continuously improve our organization. If you have any suggestions how to make GECCO or SIGEVO better, please let us know.

Wolfgang Banzhaf
SIGEVO Chair

Table of Contents

Track: Artificial Immune Systems

Track: Artificial Life, Robotics, and Evolvable Hardware

Track: Biological and Biomedical Applications

Track: Digital Entertainment Technologies and Arts

Track: Estimation of Distribution Algorithms

Track: Evolution Strategies and Evolutionary Programming

Track: Evolutionary Combinatorial Optimization and Metaheuristics

Track: Evolutionary Machine Learning

Track: Evolutionary Multiobjective Optimization

Track: Genetic Algorithms

Track: Genetic Programming

Track: Integrative Genetic and Evolutionary Computation

Track: Parallel Evolutionary Systems

Track: Real World Applications

Track: Search Based Software Engineering

Track: Self-* Search

Track: Theory

Organizers

General Chair:	Dirk V. Arnold, *Dalhousie University*
Editor-in-Chief:	Christian Igel, *University of Copenhagen*
Publicity Chair:	Christian Gagné, *Université Laval*
Local Chair:	Elena Popovici, *Icosystem Corporation*
Students Chair:	Petr Pošík, *Czech Technical University*
Tutorials Chair:	Mengjie Zhang, *Victoria University of Wellington*
Workshops Chair:	Per Kristian Lehre, *University of Nottingham*
Competitions Chair:	Amy K. Hoover, *University of Central Florida*
Late Breaking Abstracts Chair:	Dirk Sudholt, *University of Sheffield*
Evolutionary Computation in Practice Chairs:	Thomas Bartz-Beielstein, *Cologne University of Applied Sciences* Anna I. Esparcia-Alcázar, *S2 Grupo* Jörn Mehnen, *Cranfield University*
Business Committee:	Jürgen Branke, *University of Warwick* Darrell Whitley, *Colorado State University*

Track Chairs

Anne Auger, *INRIA Saclay*

Jaume Bacardit, *Newcastle University*

Dimo Brockhoff, *INRIA Lille*

Stefano Cagnoni, *Università degli Studi di Parma*

Kalyanmoy Deb, *Michigan State University*

Benjamin Doerr, *École Polytechnique de Paris*

James Foster, *University of Idaho*

Tobias Glasmachers, *Ruhr-Universität Bochum*

Emma Hart, *Edinburgh Napier University*

Malcolm I. Heywood, *Dalhousie University*

Hitoshi Iba, *University of Tokyo*

Christian Jacob, *University of Calgary*

Thomas Jansen, *Aberystwyth University*

Yaochu Jin, *University of Surrey*

Marouane Kessentini, *University of Michigan*

Joshua D. Knowles, *University of Manchester*

William B. Langdon, *University College London*

Pedro Larrañaga, *Technical University of Madrid*

Sean Luke, *George Mason University*

Gabriel Luque, *Universidad de Málaga*

John A. W. McCall, *Robert Gordon University Aberdeen*

Marco A. Montes de Oca, *University of Delaware*

Alison Motsinger-Reif, *North Carolina State University*

Yew Soon Ong, *Nanyang Technological University*

Michael Palmer, *Stanford University*

Konstantinos E. Parsopoulos, *University of Ioanninia*

Günther Raidl, *Vienna University of Technology*

Sebastian Risi, *IT University of Copenhagen*

Guenther Ruhe, *University of Calgary*

Tom Schaul, *New York University*

Thomas Schmickl, *Karl-Franzens-Universität Graz*

Bernhard Sendhoff, *Honda Research Institute Europe*

Kenneth O. Stanley, *University of Central Florida*

Thomas Stützle, *Université Libre de Bruxelles*

Dirk Thierens, *Universiteit Utrecht*

Julian Togelius, *IT University of Copenhagen*

Carsten Witt, *Technical University of Denmark*

Christine Zarges, *University of Birmingham*

Program Committee

Abbass, Hussein, *University of New South Wales*
Abdelbar, Ashraf, *Brandon University*
Abraham, Ajith, *Machine Intelligence Research Labs*
Acampora, Giovanni, *Nottingham Trent University*
Adamatzky, Andrew, *University of the West of England*
Adami, Chris, *Michigan State University*
Affenzeller, Michael, *University of Applied Sciences Upper Austria*
Aguirre, Hernan, *Shinshu University*
Ahn, Chang Wook, *Sungkyunkwan University*
Ahrens, Barry, *Nova Southeastern University*
Aickelin, Uwe, *University of Nottingham*
Akimoto, Youhei, *Shinshu University*
Alba, Enrique, *Universidad de Málaga*
Alden, Kieran, *University of York*
Aler, Ricardo, *Universidad Carlos III de Madrid*
Alfaro-Cid, Eva, *Universidad Politécnica de Valencia*
Allmendinger, Richard, *University College London*
Alshahwan, Nadia, *University College London*
Amoretti, Michele, *Università degli Studi di Parma*
Amos, Ng, *University of Skövde*
Andrews, Paul, *University of York*
Antoniol, Giuliano, *École Polytechnique de Montréal*
Arcuri, Andrea, *Simula Research Laboratory*
Arias Montaño, Alfredo, *CINVESTAV-IPN*
Arita, Takaya, *Nagoya University*
Arredondo, Antonio D. Masegosa, *Universidad de Granada*
Arvin, Farshad, *University of Lincoln*
Avigad, Gideon, *Braude College of Engineering*
Aydin, Nizamettin, *Yildiz Technical University*
Azad, Raja Muhammad Atif, *University of Limerick*
Babovic, Vladan, *National University Singapore*
Bader-El-Den, Mohamed, *University of Essex*
Bai, Ruibin, *University of Nottingham Ningbo*
Ballester, Pedro J., *European Bioinformatics Institute*
Bandyopadhyay, Sanghamitra, *Indian Statistical Institute*
Bankovic, Zorana, *IMDEA Software Institute*
Banzhaf, Wolfgang, *Memorial University of Newfoundland*
Barbosa, Helio J. C., *National Laboratory for Scientific Computation, Brazil*
Bardenet, Remi, *University of Oxford*
Barros, Marcio, *Universidade Federal do Estado do Rio de Janeiro*
Bartz-Beielstein, Thomas, *Cologne University of Applied Sciences*
Basgalupp, Marcio, *Universidade Federal de São Paulo*
Bassett, Jeffrey K., *George Mason University*
Basseur, Matthieu, *Université d'Angers*
Bastos Filho, Carmelo J. A., *University of Pernambuco*
Batista, Lucas, *Universidade Federal de Minas Gerais*
Beal, Jacob, *BBN Technologies*
Bechikh, Slim, *University of Michigan–Dearborn*
Bennell, Julia, *University of Southampton*
Bentley, Peter J., *University College London*
Bergstra, James, *University of Waterloo*
Bernardino, Heder, *Universidade Federal de Juiz de Fora*
Bernt, Matthias, *University of Leipzig*
Berry, Rod, *University of Technology, Sydney*
Bersano, Tom, *Google Inc.*
Besada-Portas, Eva, *Universidad Complutense de Madrid*
Beyer, Hans-Georg, *Vorarlberg University of Applied Sciences*
Bezerra, Leonardo, *Université Libre de Bruxelles*
Bhanu, Bir, *University of California at Riverside*
Biazzini, Marco, *INRIA Rennes*
Bielza, Concha, *Universidad Politécnica de Madrid*
Biesinger, Benjamin, *Technische Universität Wien*
Birattari, Mauro, *Université Libre de Bruxelles*
Blackwell, Tim, *Goldsmiths, University of London*
Blekas, Konstantinos, *University of Ioannina*
Blesa, Maria J., *Universitat Politècnica de Catalunya*
Blum, Christian, *University of the Basque Country*
Bollegala, Danushka, *University of Tokyo*
Bongard, Josh, *University of Vermont*
Booker, Lashon, *The MITRE Corporation*
Bosman, Peter A.N., *Centrum Wiskunde & Informatica*
Boudjeloud, Lydia, *Université de Lorraine*
Boumaza, Amine, *Université de Lorraine*
Bouvry, Pascal, *University of Luxembourg*
Bown, Ollie, *University of Sydney*
Brabazon, Anthony, *University College Dublin*
Branke, Jürgen, *University of Warwick*
Bredeche, Nicolas, *Université Pierre et Marie Curie*
Breen, David E., *Drexel University*
Bringmann, Karl, *Max Planck Institut für Informatik*
Browne, Will N., *Victoria University of Wellington*
Brownlee, Alexander E. I., *University of Stirling*
Buarque, Fernando, *University of Pernambuco*
Bui, Lam Thu, *Le Quy Don Technical University*
Bui, Thang, *Penn State*
Bull, Larry, *University of the West of England*
Bullinaria, John A., *University of Birmingham*
Burelli, Paolo, *Aalborg University*
Burjorjee, Keki Mehernosh, *Brandeis University*
Burke, Edmund, *University of Stirling*
Butz, Martin V., *University of Tübingen*
Buzdalov, Maxim, *Saint-Petersburg National Research University of Information Technologies, Mechanics & Optics*
Buzdalova, Arina, *Saint-Petersburg National Research University of Information Technologies, Mechamics & Optics*
Cagnina, Leticia, *Universidad Nacional de San Luis*
Cairns, David, *University of Stirling*
Campelo, Felipe, *Universidade Federal de Minas Gerais*
Campo, Alexandre, *Université Libre de Bruxelles*
Cangelosi, Angelo, *University of Plymouth*
Capodieci, Nicola, *University of Modena and Reggio Emilia*
Carvalho, Andre, *Universidade de São Paulo*

Castelli, Mauro, *Universidade Nova de Lisboa*
Castellini, Alberto, *University of Verona*
Ceschia, Sara, *University of Udine*
Chakraborty, Uday, *University of Missouri*
Chang, Pei-Chann, *Yuan Ze University*
Chelly, Zeineb, *University of Tunis*
Chen, Ying-ping, *National Chiao Tung University*
Chen, Tianshi, *Chinese Academy of Sciences*
Cheong, Yun-Gyung, *IT University of Copenhagen*
Chiarandini, Marco, *University of Southern Denmark*
Chicano, Francisco, *Universidad de Málaga*
Chiong, Raymond, *University of Newcastle*
Chipperfield, Andrew J., *University of Southampton*
Chong, Siang Yew, *University of Nottingham*
Christensen, Anders, *University Institute of Lisbon*
Christensen, David Johan, *Technical University of Denmark*
Chu, Dominique, *University of Kent*
Chuang, Chung-Yao, *Carnegie Mellon University*
Clark, John, *University of York*
Clerc, Maurice
Clune, Jeff, *University of Wyoming*
Coelho, Leandro, *Pontifícia Universidade Católica do Paranà*
Coello Coello, Carlos A., *CINVESTAV-IPN*
Cohen, Myra, *University of Nebraska–Lincoln*
Colby, Mitch K., *Oregon State University*
Colmenar, J. Manuel, *Universidad Complutense de Madrid*
Colton, Simon, *Imperial College London*
Congdon, Clare Bates, *University of Southern Maine*
Connelly, Brian, *University of Washington*
Cook, Michael, *University of London*
Cordon, Oscar, *European Centre for Soft Computing*
Corns, Steven M., *Missouri University of Science and Technology*
Correia, Luís, *Universidade de Lisboa*
Costa, Lino António, *Universidade do Minho*
Costa, Ernesto, *University of Coimbra*
Cotta, Carlos, *Universidad de Málaga*
Cowling, Peter, *University of York*
Craenen, Bart G.W., *Brunel University*
Cui, Wei, *University College Dublin*
Cummins, Ronan, *University of Greenwich*
Cussat-Blanc, Sylvain, *University of Toulouse*
D'Ambrosio, David B., *University of Central Florida*
Dahal, Keshav, *University of the West of Scotland*
Dahlskog, Steve, *Malmö University*
Dahlstedt, Palle, *University of Gothenburg*
Dang, Duc-Cuong, *University of Nottingham*
Darabos, Christian, *Dartmouth College*
Das, Swagatam, *Indian Statistical Institute*
Datta, Dilip, *Tezpur University*
Datta, Rituparna, *Indian Institute of Technology Kanpur*
David, Cornforth, *University of Newcastle*
De Causmaecker, Patrick, *KU Leuven*
De Jong, Kenneth, *George Mason University*
de la Fraga, Luis Gerardo, *CINVESTAV-IPN*
de la Ossa, Luis, *University of Castilla–La Mancha*
Deakin, Anthony, *University of Liverpool*
Della Cioppa, Antonio, *University of Salerno*
Delong, Andrew, *University of Toronto*
Derbel, Bilel, *INRIA Lille*
Dhaenens, Clarisse, *INRIA Lille, CNRS*
Di Caro, Gianni, *IDSIA*
Di Gaspero, Luca, *University of Udine*
Di Penta, Massimiliano, *University of Sannio*
Diaconescu, Ada, *Télécom ParisTech*
Ding, Yongsheng, *Donghua University*
Dinh, Huy, *University of Tokyo*
Dinneen, Michael J., *University of Auckland*
Dittrich, Peter, *Friedrich-Schiller-Universität Jena*
Divina, Federico, *Pablo de Olavide University*
Doerr, Carola, *Université Pierre et Marie Curie, CNRS*
Doncieux, Stéphane, *Université Pierre et Marie Curie*
Dorin, Alan, *Monash University*
Dorronsoro, Bernabe, *Université Lille Nord de France*
Dozal, León, *Centro de Investigación Científica y de Educación Superior de Ensenada*
Drugan, Madalina, *Vrije Universiteit Brussel*
Drugowitsch, Jan, *Université de Genève*
Dubois-Lacoste, Jérémie, *Université Libre de Bruxelles*
Ebner, Marc, *Ernst-Moritz-Universität Greifswald*
El-Abd, Mohammed, *American University of Kuwait*
Emmerich, Michael T. M., *Universiteit Leiden*
Engelbrecht, Andries P., *University of Pretoria*
Epitropakis, Michael, *University of Stirling*
Eremeev, Anton V., *Sobolev Institute of Mathematics, Omsk*
Esponda, Fernando, *Instituto Tecnológico Autónomo de México*
Evelyne, Lutton, *INRIA Saclay*
Everson, Richard, *University of Exeter*
Fan, Patrick, *Virginia Tech*
Farooq, Muddassar, *Institute of Space Technology, Pakistan*
Feldt, Robert, *Chalmers University of Technology*
Fenet, Serge, *Université Lyon 1*
Ferariu, Lavinia, *"Gheorghe Asachi" Technical University of Iaşi*
Fernandez, Jose David, *Universidad de Málaga*
Fernández de Vega, Francisco, *Universidad de Extremadura*
Festa, Paola, *Universitá degli Studi di Napoli*
Fialho, Álvaro, *GE Global Research*
Fieldsend, Jonathan Edward, *University of Exeter*
Figueredo, Grazziela, *University of Nottingham*
Filipic, Bogdan, *Jožef Stefan Institute*
Finck, Steffen, *Vorarlberg University of Applied Sciences*
Fink, Andreas, *Helmut Schmidt University Hamburg*
Fischer, Asja, *Ruhr-Universität Bochum*
Fleming, Peter, *University of Sheffield*
Folino, Gianluigi, *Institute of High Performance Computing and Networking, Italy*
Fraser, Gordon, *University of Sheffield*
Freisleben, Bernd, *Universität Marburg*

Freitas, Alex A., *University of Kent*
Friedrich, Tobias, *Friedrich-Schiller-Universität Jena*
Frowd, Charlie, *University of Winchester*
Gagliolo, Matteo, *Vrije Universiteit Brussel*
Gagné, Christian, *Université Laval*
Gallagher, Marcus R., *University of Queensland*
Galvan, Edgar, *Trinity College Dublin*
Galway, Leo, *University of Ulster*
Gambardella, Luca Maria, *IDSIA*
Gamez, Jose A., *Universidad de Castilla–La Mancha*
Gandibleux, Xavier, *Université de Nantes*
Gandomi, Amir Hossein, *University of Akron*
Gao, Yang, *Nanjing University*
Garcia-Nieto, Jose, *Universidad de Málaga*
Garcia-Piquer, Alvaro, *Institute of Space Sciences, Mexico*
García-Martínez, Carlos, *Universidad de Córdoba*
García-Sánchez, Pablo, *Universidad de Granada*
Garnier, Simon, *New Jersey Institute of Technology*
Garousi, Vahid, *University of Calgary*
Garrett, Deon, *Icelandic Institute for Intelligent Machines*
Gaspar-Cunha, Antonio, *Universidade do Minho*
Geem, Zong Woo, *Gachon University*
Gelareh, Shahin, *Université d'Artois*
Gershenson, Carlos, *Universidad Nacional Autonoma de México*
Gervasi, Osvaldo, *University of Perugia*
Giacobini, Mario, *University of Torino*
Giagkiozis, Ioannis, *University of Sheffield*
Giavitto, Jean-Louis, *Institut de Recherche et Coordination Acoustique/Musique, France, CNRS*
Gießen, Christian, *Christian-Albrechts-Universität zu Kiel*
Giraldez Rojo, Raul, *Pablo de Olavide University*
Giustolisi, Orazio, *Technical University of Bari*
Goeffon, Adrien, *Université d'Angers*
Goh, Chi-Keong, *Rolls-Royce*
Goldbarg, Marco César, *Universidade Federal do Rio Grande do Norte*
Goldman, Brian W., *Michigan State University*
Gomez-Pulido, Juan A., *Universidad de Extremadura*
Gong, Wenyin, *China University of Geosciences*
Goodman, Erik D., *Michigan State University*
Grasemann, Uli, *University of Texas, Austin*
Greenfield, Gary, *University of Richmond*
Greensmith, Julie, *University of Nottingham*
Greiner, David, *Universidad de Las Palmas de Gran Canaria*
Grewal, Gary William, *University of Guelph*
Gross, Roderich, *University of Sheffield*
Grouchy, Paul, *University of Toronto*
Gu, Feng, *Kingston University London*
Guerreiro, Andreia P., *University of Coimbra*
Guinand, Frederic, *Université du Havre*
Gutjahr, Walter J., *University of Vienna*
Hagelbäck, Johan, *Blekinge Tekniska Högskola*
Hamann, Heiko, *University of Paderborn*
Hamel, Lutz, *University of Rhode Island*
Hamzeh, Ali, *Shiraz University*
Hanafi, Said, *University of Valenciennes*
Handa, Hisashi, *Kindai University*
Handl, Julia, *University of Manchester*
Hansen, Nikolaus, *IRIA Saclay*
Hao, Jin-Kao, *Université d'Angers*
Harman, Mark, *University College London*
Harvey, Inman, *University of Sussex*
Hasegawa, Yoshihiko, *University of Tokyo*
Hasle, Geir, *SINTEF ICT*
Hastings, Erin, *University of Central Florida*
Hauert, Sabine, *Massachusetts Institute of Technology*
Hauschild, Mark W., *University of Missouri–St. Louis*
He, Jun, *Aberystwyth University*
Heckendorn, Robert, *University of Idaho*
Heidrich-Meisner, Verena, *Christian-Albrechts-Universität zu Kiel*
Helbig, Marde, *Council for Scientific and Industrial Research, South Africa*
Hendtlass, Tim, *Swinburne University of Technology*
Hereford, James, *Murray State University*
Hernandez, Daniel Eduardo, *Centro de Investigación Científica y de Educación Superior de Ensenada*
Hernández-Aguirre, Arturo, *Centre for Research in Mathematics, Mexico*
Hernández-Díaz, Alfredo G., *Pablo de Olavide University*
Hidalgo, J. Ignacio, *Universidad Complutense de Madrid*
Hingston, Philip, *Edith Cowan University*
Holdener, Ekaterina, *Exegy, Inc.*
Holladay, Kenneth, *Southwest Research Institute*
Holmes, John H., *University of Pennsylvania*
Hoover, Amy K., *University of Central Florida*
Hornby, Gregory S., *University of California at Santa Cruz*
Howard, Gerard, *Commonwealth Scientific and Industrial Research Organisation*
Hsiao, Michael S., *Virginia Tech*
Hu, Bin, *Technische Universität Wien*
Hu, Jianjun, *University of South Carolina*
Husbands, Phil, *Sussex University*
Hutter, Frank, *University of Freiburg*
Iclănzan, David Andrei, *Sapientia Hungaryan University of Transylvania*
Iida, Fumiya, *ETH Zürich*
Ikegami, Takashi, *University of Tokyo*
Inführ, Johannes, *Technische Universität Wien*
Iori, Manuel, *University of Modena and Reggio Emilia*
Ishibuchi, Hisao, *Osaka Prefecture University*
Istvan, Juhos, *University of Szeged*
Jackson, David, *University of Liverpool*
Jakob, Wilfried, *Karlsruhe Institute of Technology*
Janikow, Cezary Z., *University of Missouri–St. Louis*
Jayadeva, *Indian Institute of Technology Delhi*
Jiang, Siwei, *Nanyang Technological University*
Johannsen, Daniel, *SAP Innovation Center*
Johansson, Ulf, *University of Borås*

Johnson, Colin Graeme, *University of Kent*
Jones, Ben, *University of Birmingham*
Joshi, Ayush, *University of Birmingham*
Jourdan, Laetitia, *INRIA Lille*
Joó, András, *Sapientia University*
Juarez, Reyes, *Universidad Autónoma de Baja California*
Julstrom, Bryant Arthur, *St. Cloud State University*
Kaban, Ata, *University of Birmingham*
Kaboudan, Mak, *University of Redlands*
Kampouridis, Michael, *University of Kent*
Karsai, Istvan, *East Tennessee State University*
Karthik, Sindhya, *University of Jyväskylä*
Kattan, Ahmed, *Umm Al-Qura University*
Kendall, Graham, *University of Nottingham*
Khaled Ahsan Talukder, A. K. M., *George Mason University*
Khan, Gul Muhammad, *University of Engineering & Technology Peshawar*
Khare, Vineet, *Amazon Development Centre, India*
Kirshenbaum, Evan, *HP Labs*
Kisi, Ozgur, *Canik Basari University*
Klamroth, Kathrin, *University of Wuppertal*
Klazar, Ronald, *University of Pretoria*
Knust, Sigrid, *University of Osnabrück*
Köppen, Mario, *Kyushu Institute of Technology*
Komosinski, Maciej, *Poznan University of Technology*
Kontis, Lysimachos, *University of Ioannina*
Korb, Oliver, *Cambridge Crystallographic Data Centre*
Kordon, Arthur K., *Dow Chemical*
Kotsireas, Ilias, *Wilfrid Laurier University*
Kötzing, Timo, *Max Planck Institut für Informatik*
Kovacic, Miha, *University Of Nova Gorica*
Kramer, Oliver, *University of Oldenburg*
Kratica, Jozef, *Serbian Academy of Sciences and Arts*
Krause, Oswin, *University of Copenhagen*
Krawiec, Krzysztof, *Poznan University of Technology*
Kritzinger, Stefanie, *Johannes Kepler Universität Linz*
Kronberger, Gabriel, *University of Applied Sciences Upper Austria*
Kubalik, Jiri, *Czech Technical University in Prague*
Künnemann, Marvin, *Max Planck Institut für Informatik*
Lamont, Gary Byron, *U.S. Air Force Institute of Technology*
Lampinen, Jouni, *University of Vaasa*
Landa-Silva, Dario, *University of Nottingham*
Langer, Philip, *Technische Universität Wien*
Lanzi, Pier Luca, *Politecnico di Milano*
Lara, Adriana, *CINVESTAV-IPN*
LaTorre, Antonio, *Universidad Politĕcnica de Madrid*
Lau, Henry, *University of Hong Kong*
Lau, Hoong-Chuin, *Singapore Management University*
Legrand, Pierrick, *Université Bordeaux*
Leguizamon, Guillermo, *Universidad Nacional de San Luis*
Lehre, Per Kristian, *University of Nottingham*
Leibnitz, Kenji, *National Institute of Information and Communications Technology, Japan*
Lengler, Johannes, *ETH Zürich*
Leo, Cazenille, *Université Paris Diderot*
Leon, Coromoto, *Universidad de La Laguna*
Leung, Kwong Sak, *Chinese University of Hong Kong*
Lewis, Peter R., *Aston University*
Lewis, Matthew, *Ohio State University*
Li, Ke, *City University of Hong Kong*
Li, Xianneng, *Waseda University*
Li, Bin, *University of Science and Technology of China*
Liang, Feng, *Nanyang Technological University*
Liang, Yiwen, *Wuhan University*
Liao, Tianjun, *Université Libre de Bruxelles*
Liapis, Antonios, *IT University of Copenhagen*
Lichodzijewski, Peter, *Dalhousie University*
Liefooghe, Arnaud, *Université Lille Nord de France*
Limmer, Steffen, *University of Erlangen-Nuremberg*
Ling, Ping, *Jiangsu Normal University*
Lioret, Alain, *Université de Vicennes à Saint-Denis*
Lipinski, Piotr, *University of Wroclaw*
Lissovoi, Andrei, *Technical University of Denmark*
Liu, Bo, *Chinese Academy of Sciences*
Lobo, Daniel, *Tufts University*
Lobo, Fernando G., *University of Algarve*
Loiacono, Daniele, *Politecnico di Milano*
Lones, Michael, *Heriot-Watt University*
López-Ibáñez, Manuel, *Université Libre de Bruxelles*
López-Jaimes, Antonio, *CINVESTAV-IPN*
Loshchilov, Ilya, *École Polytechnique Fédérale de Lausanne*
Louis, Sushil, *University of Nevada*
Lozano, Manuel, *Universidad de Granada*
Lozano, Jose A., *University of the Basque Country*
Lucas, Simon, *University of Essex*
Lukasiewycz, Martin, *TUM CREATE, Singapore*
Luna, Francisco, *Universidad de Extremadura*
Luna, J. M., *Universidad de Córdoba*
Luo, Wenjian, *University of Science and Technology of China*
Lust, Thibaut, *Université Pierre et Marie Curie*
Mabu, Shingo, *Yamaguchi University*
Machado, Penousal, *University of Coimbra*
Macia, Nuria, *Universitat Ramon Llull*
Madureira, Ana Maria, *Polytechnic Institute of Porto*
Majercik, Stephen, *Bowdoin College*
Malago, Luigi, *Università degli Studi di Milano–Bicocca*
Malo, Pekka, *Aalto University*
Mambrini, Andrea, *University of Birmingham*
Mancoridis, Spiros, *Drexel University*
Manderick, Bernard, *Vrije Universiteit Brussel*
Mandziuk, Jacek, *Warsaw University of Technology*
Manzoni, Luca, *Université Nice Sophia Antipolis*
Marchiori, Elena, *Radboud University Nijmegen*
Marinakis, Yannis, *Technical University of Crete*
Maringer, Dietmar, *University of Basel*
Marks II, Robert, *Baylor University*
Marmion, Marie-Eleonore, *Université Lille Nord de France*
Martin, Andrew, *University College London*
Martinez, Hector P., *IT University of Copenhagen*

Martinez, Ivette C., *Universidad Simon Bolivar*
Mascia, Franco, *Université Libre de Bruxelles*
Maslov, Igor V., *EvoCo Inc.*
Matsui, Shouichi, *Central Research Institute of Electric Power Industry, Japan*
Mauri, Giancarlo, *Università degli Studi di Milano–Bicocca*
Mayer, Helmut A., *University of Salzburg*
McDermott, James, *University College Dublin*
McEwan, Chris, *Microsoft Research*
McIntyre, Andrew Ryan, *Dalhousie University*
McKay, Bob, *Seoul National University*
McMinn, Phil, *University of Sheffield*
McPhee, Nicholas Freitag, *University of Minnesota, Morris*
Meignan, David, *University of Osnabrück*
Melab, Nouredine, *Université Lille Nord de France*
Melkozerov, Alexander, *Tomsk State University of Control Systems and Radioelectronics*
Mendes, Rui, *Universidade do Minho*
Mendiburu, Alexander, *University of the Basque Country*
Menzel, Stefan, *Honda Research Institute Europe*
Merelo-Guervós, Juan-Julián, *Universidad de Granada*
Mesejo Santiago, Pablo, *Université d'Auvergne*
Meyer, Bernd, *Monash University*
Meyer-Nieberg, Silja, *Universität der Bundeswehr, München*
Mezura-Montes, Efrén, *Universidad Veracruzana*
Miconi, Thomas, *The Neurosciences Institute*
Middendorf, Martin, *University of Leipzig*
Miettinen, Kaisa, *University of Jyväskylä*
Miikkulainen, Risto, *University of Texas, Austin*
Miklic, Damjan, *University of Zagreb*
Miller, Julian, *University of York*
Minai, Ali, *University of Cincinnati*
Minku, Leandro, *University of Birmingham*
Miramontes Hercog, Luis, *Self-Organizing Solutions*
Misir, Mustafa, *Singapore Management University*
Mitchell, George, *CCKF Ltd.*
Mjolsness, Eric, *University of California at Irvine*
Moen, Hans Jonas Fossum, *Norwegian Defence Research Establishment*
Mohan, Chilukuri K., *Syracuse University*
Montanier, Jean-Marc, *Norwegian University of Science and Technology*
Montemanni, Roberto, *IDSIA*
Moore, Jason, *Dartmouth College*
Mora, Antonio, *Universidad de Granada*
Moraglio, Alberto, *University of Birmingham*
Moses, Melanie, *University of New Mexico*
Möslinger, Christoph, *Karl-Franzens-Universität Graz*
Mostaghim, Sanaz, *Karlsruhe Institute of Technology*
Mouret, Jean-Baptiste, *Université Pierre et Marie Curie, CNRS*
Muelas, Santiago, *Universidad Politécnica de Madrid*
Müller, Christian Lorenz, *New York University*
Mumford, Christine Lesley, *Cardiff University*
Musliu, Nysret, *Technische Universität Wien*
Nagata, Yuichi, *Tokyo Institute of Technology*
Nakib, Amir, *Laboratoire LISSI*
Narukawa, Kaname, *Honda Research Institute Europe*
Nashed, Youssef, *Università degli Studi di Parma*
Naujoks, Boris, *Cologne University of Applied Sciences*
Nebro, Antonio, *Universidad de Málaga*
Neirotti, Juan, *Aston University*
Nejati, Shiva, *University of Luxembourg*
Neri, Ferrante, *University of Jyväskylä*
Neumann, Frank, *University of Adelaide*
Nguyen, Huy, *Misfit Wearables*
Nguyen Xuan, Hoai, *Hanoi University*
Nicolau, Miguel, *University College Dublin*
Nievola, Julio Cesar, *Pontifícia Universidade Católica do Paraná*
Nobile, Marco, *Universitàdegli Studi di Milano–Bicocca*
Nojima, Yusuke, *Osaka Prefecture University*
Noman, Nasimul, *University of Newcastle*
Ó Cinnéide, Mel, *National University of Ireland, Dublin*
O'Neill, Michael, *University College Dublin*
O'Riordan, Colm, *National University of Ireland, Galway*
Ochoa, Gabriela, *University of Stirling*
Ofria, Charles, *Michigan State University*
Oh, Choong Kun, *U.S. Naval Research Laboratory*
Okabe, Tatsuya, *Honda R&D Co., Ltd.*
Olhofer, Markus, *Honda Research Institute Europe*
Oliveira, Pedro N. F. P., *Universidade do Minho*
Oliveto, Pietro S., *University of Sheffield*
Oliwa, Tomasz, *University of Georgia*
Olmo, Juan Luis, *Universidad de Córdoba*
Ombuki-Berman, Beatrice, *Brock University*
Omran, Mohammed, *Gulf University for Science & Technology*
Ono, Isao, *Tokyo Institute of Technology*
Ortega, Julio, *Universidad de Granada*
Ouni, Ali, *Université de Montréal*
Özcan, Ender, *University of Nottingham*
Palafox, Leon, *University of Tokyo*
Pang, Wei, *University of Aberdeen*
Parque, Victor, *Toyota Technological Institute*
Pasquier, Philippe, *Simon Fraser University*
Pedro, Castillo, *Universidad de Granada*
Pellegrini, Paola, *Université Libre de Bruxelles*
Pereira, Francisco Baptista, *Instituto Superior de Engenharia de Coimbra*
Perez Caceres, Leslie, *Université Libre de Bruxelles*
Peña, Jose-Maria, *Universidad Polytécnica de Madrid*
Phelps, Steve, *University of Essex*
Philippides, Andrew, *University of Sussex*
Pibernat, Hugo, *King Games Inc.*
Polani, Daniel, *University of Hertfordshire*
Poles, Silvia, *EnginSoft*
Poloczek, Jendrik, *University of Oldenburg*
Pop, Petrica, *North University of Baia Mare*
Popovici, Elena, *Icosystem Corp.*
Porumbel, Daniel, *Université Lille Nord de France*

Pošík, Petr, *Czech Technical University in Prague*
Potter, Walter, *University of Georgia*
Poulding, Simon, *University of York*
Prandtstetter, Matthias, *Austrian Institute of Technology*
Prestwich, Steve, *University College Cork*
Preuss, Mike, *Technische Universität Dortmund*
Price, Kenneth
Puchinger, Jakob, *Austrian Institute of Technology*
Puente, Cesar, *Universidad Autónoma de San Luis Potosi*
Puerta, Jose Miguel, *Universidad de Castilla–La Mancha*
Punch, William F., *Michigan State University*
Purshouse, Robin, *University of Sheffield*
Qin, Kai, *RMIT University*
Randall, Marcus Christian, *Bond University*
Ranjithan, Ranji S., *North Carolina State University*
Rasheed, Khaled, *University of Georgia*
Ray, Tom, *University of Oklahoma*
Ray, Tapabrata, *University of New South Wales*
Read, Mark, *University of Sydney*
Reed, Patrick M., *Cornell University*
Reif, David, *U.S. Environmental Protection Agency*
Rhee, Phill Kyu, *Inha University*
Rhyd, Lewis, *Cardiff University*
Riff, Maria Cristina, *Universidad Técnica Federico Santa Maria*
Robert, Wille, *University of Bremen*
Robilliard, Denis, *Université Lille Nord de France*
Rohlfshagen, Philipp, *SolveIT Software*
Roper, Marc, *University of Strathclyde*
Ross, Brian J., *Brock University*
Ross, Peter, *Edinburgh Napier University*
Rothlauf, Franz, *Universität Mainz*
Rowe, Jonathan, *University of Birmingham*
Rudolph, Günter, *Technische Universität Dortmund*
Ruhul, Sarker, *University of New South Wales*
Ruiz, Ruben, *Universidad Polytécnica de Valencia*
Runkler, Thomas, *Siemens AG*
Ryan, Conor, *University of Limerick*
Sagarna, Ramon, *University of the Basque Country*
Sahin, Erol, *Middle East Technical University*
Sahraoui, Houari, *Université de Montréal*
Salem, Ziad, *Karl-Franzens-Universität Graz*
Sanchez, Luciano, *Universidad de Oviedo*
Santana, Roberto, *University of the Basque Country*
Santibáñez Koref, Iván, *Technische Universität Berlin*
Sarro, Federica, *University College London*
Sato, Hiroyuki, *University of Electro-Communications*
Sato, Yuji, *Hosei University*
Sawada, Hideyuki, *Kagawa University*
Schillaci, Massimiliano, *Dora S.p.A.*
Schoenauer, Marc, *INRIA Saclay*
Schütze, Oliver, *CINVESTAV-IPN*
Scully, Peter, *Aberystwyth University*
Segura, Carlos, *Universidad de La Laguna*
Sekanina, Lukas, *Brno University of Technology*
Semet, Yann, *Thales*
Sen, Sandip, *University of Tulsa*
Seppi, Kevin, *Brigham Young University*
Serpell, Martin, *University of the West of England*
Sevaux, Marc, *Université de Bretagne-Sud*
Shaheen, Fatima, *Loughborough University*
Shaker, Noor, *IT University of Copenhagen*
Shakya, Siddhartha, *British Telecom*
Shapiro, Jonathan Lee, *University of Manchester*
Shengxiang, Yang, *De Montfort University*
Shihab, Emad, *Rochester Institute of Technology*
Shukla, Pradyumn Kumar, *Karlsruhe Institute of Technology*
Siarry, Patrick, *Université Paris–Est Créteil*
Silva, Fernando, *Universidade de Lisboa*
Sim, Kevin, *Edinburgh Napier University*
Simões, Anabela, *Polytechnic Institute of Coimbra*
Sinha, Ankur, *Aalto University*
Sipper, Moshe, *Ben-Gurion University*
Skurikhin, Alexei N., *Los Alamos National Laboratory*
Smith, Jim, *University of the West of England*
Smith, Stephen L., *University of York*
Smith, Alice, *Auburn University*
Smyth, Tamara, *University of California at San Diego*
Snoek, Jasper, *Harvard University*
Solnon, Christine, *Institut National des Sciences Appliquées de Lyon*
Song, Andy, *RMIT University*
Sossa, Humberto, *Instituto Politécnico Nacional, México*
Souza, Jerffeson, *State University of Ceara*
Spector, Lee, *Hampshire College*
Spicher, Antoine, *Université Paris–Est Créteil*
Squillero, Giovanni, *Politecnico di Torino*
Standish, Russell, *High Performance Coders*
Stepney, Susan, *University of York*
Stibor, Thomas, *GSI Helmholtz Centre for Heavy Ion Research*
Stich, Sebastian, *ETH Zürich*
Stonedahl, Forrest, *Northwestern University*
Stouch, Daniel W., *Charles River Analytics*
Straccia, Umberto, *Istituto di Scienza e Tecnologie dell'Informazione*
Stracquadanio, Giovanni, *Johns Hopkins University*
Stradner, Jürgen, *Karl-Franzens-Universität Graz*
Sudholt, Dirk, *University of Sheffield*
Sun, Xiao-yan, *China University of Mining and Technology*
Sun, Yi, *Google Inc.*
Sun, Chaoli, *Taiyuan University of Science and Technology*
Sutton, Andrew Michael, *Friedrich-Schiller-Universität Jena*
Suzuki, Reiji, *Nagoya University*
Swan, Jerry, *University of Stirling*
Takadama, Keiki, *University of Electro-Communications*
Talbi, El-Ghazali, *INRIA Lille*
Tan, Ying, *Peking University*
Tanaka, Kiyoshi, *Shinshu University*
Tanev, Ivan, *Doshisha University*
Tang, Ke, *University of Science and Technology of China*
Tarantino, Ernesto, *Institute of High Performance Computing*

and Networking, *Italy*
Tauritz, Daniel R., *Missouri University of Science and Technology*
Tavares, Jorge, *Microsoft*
Tavares, Roberto, *Universidade Federal de São Carlos*
Taylor, Tim, *Goldsmiths, University of London*
Terashima Marín, Hugo, *Tecnológico de Monterrey*
Tettamanzi, Andrea G. B., *Université Nice Sophia Antipolis*
Teuscher, Christof, *Portland State University*
Textor, Johannes, *Universiteit Utrecht*
Teytaud, Fabien, *Université Lille Nord de France*
Teytaud, Olivier, *INRIA Saclay*
Thawonmas, Ruck, *Ritsumeikan University*
Thiele, Lothar, *ETH Zürich*
Thompson, Tommy, *University of Derby*
Timmis, Jonathan, *University of York*
Ting, Chuan-Kang, *National Chung Cheng University*
Tino, Peter, *University of Birmingham*
Tiwari, Santosh, *General Motors Company*
Tiwari, Ashutosh, *Cranfield University*
Tomassini, Marco, *Université de Lausanne*
Tonda, Alberto Paolo, *Institut National de la Recherche Agronomique, France*
Topchy, Alexander, *Nielsen Media Research*
Torres-Jimenez, Jose, *CINVESTAV-IPN*
Torresen, Jim, *University of Oslo*
Trefzer, Martin, *University of York*
Trianni, Vito, *Institute of Cognitive Sciences and Technologies, Italy*
Trujillo, Leonardo, *Instituto Tecnológico de Tijuana*
Tsang, Edward, *University of Essex*
Tuci, Elio, *Aberystwyth University*
Tufte, Gunnar, *Norwegian University of Science and Technology*
Tušar, Tea, *Jožef Stefan Institute*
Tutum, Cem Celal, *Michigan State University*
Twycross, Jamie, *University of Nottingham*
U, Man Chon, *University of Georgia*
Ugolotti, Roberto, *Università degli Studi di Parma*
Urbanowicz, Ryan, *Dartmouth College*
Urquhart, Neil, *Edinburgh Napier University*
Vašíček, Zdeněk, *Brno University Of Technology*
Van den Herik, H. Jaap, *Tilburg University*
Vanneschi, Leonardo, *Universidade Nova de Lisboa*
Vatolkin, Igor, *Technische Universität Dortmund*
Ventura, Sebastian, *Universidad de Córdoba*
Verel, Sebastien, *Université du Littoral Côte d'Opale*
Vergilio, Silvia, *Federal University of Paraná*
Viana, Ana, *Polytechnic Institute of Porto*
Vladislavleva, Ekaterina, *Evolved Analytics Europe*
Von Zuben, Fernando J., *Universidade Estadual de Campinas*
Vrahatis, Michael N., *University of Patras*
Wagner, Tobias, *Technische Universität Dortmund*
Waldock, Antony, *BAE Systems*
Walsh, Paul, *Cork Institute of Technology*
Wang, Yong, *Central South University*
Wang, Ziyu, *University of British Columbia*
Wanka, Rolf, *University of Erlangen-Nuremberg*
Weimer, Westley, *University of Virginia*
Weise, Thomas, *University of Science and Technology of China*
Werfel, Justin, *Harvard University*
Wessing, Simon, *Technische Universität Dortmund*
Whigham, Peter Alexander, *University of Otago*
White, David, *University of Glasgow*
Wilkerson, Josh, *Missouri University of Science and Technology*
Wilson, Garnett, *Afinin Labs Inc.*
Wilson, Stewart W., *Prediction Dynamics*
Wimmer, Manuel, *Technische Universität Wien*
Wineberg, Mark, *University of Guelph*
Winkler, Stephan, *University Of Applied Sciences Upper Austria*
Wong, M. L. Dennis, *Swinburne University of Technology*
Woodward, John R., *University of Stirling*
Wright, Alden H., *University of Montana*
Wrobel, Borys, *Adam Mickiewicz University*
Wu, Zheng Yi, *Bentley Systems*
Wu, Annie S., *University of Central Florida*
Xie, Huayang, *Oracle New Zealand*
Yamada, Takeshi, *NTT Communication Science Labs*
Yamamoto, Lidia, *Université de Strasbourg*
Yannakakis, Georgios, *IT University of Copenhagen*
Yeh, Wei-Chang, *National Tsing Hua University*
Yoo, Shin, *University College London*
Yu, Tina, *Memorial University of Newfoundland*
Yu, Tian-Li, *National Taiwan University*
Yu, Yang, *Nanjing University*
Zafra, Amelia, *Universidad de Córdoba*
Zahadat, Payam, *Karl-Franzens-Universität Graz*
Zaharie, Daniela, *West University of Timisoara*
Zambetta, Fabio, *RMIT University*
Zapf, Michael, *Georg Simon Ohm University of Applied Sciences Nuremberg*
Zapotecas Martínez, Saúl, *CINVESTAV-IPN*
Zell, Andreas, *Universität Tübingen*
Zexuan, Zhu, *Shenzhen University*
Zhang, Mengjie, *Victoria University of Wellington*
Zhang, Fu, *Mathworks*
Zhang, Yuanyuan, *University College London*
Zhang, Byoung-Tak, *Seoul National University*
Zhong, Yanfei, *Wuhan University*
Zhou, Aimin, *East China Normal University*

Best Paper Nominations

Track: Ant Colony Optimization and Swarm Intelligence

Track: Artificial Immune Systems

Track: Artificial Life, Robotics, and Evolvable Hardware

Track: Digital Entertainment Technologies and Arts

Track: Evolution Strategies and Evolutionary Programming

Track: Evolutionary Combinatorial Optimization and Metaheuristics

Track: Evolutionary Machine Learning

Track: Evolutionary Multiobjective Optimization

Track: Generative and Developmental Systems

Track: Genetic Algorithms

Track: Genetic Programming

Track: Parallel Evolutionary Systems

Track: Real World Applications

Track: Search Based Software Engineering

Track: Theory

Growth in Co-evolution of Sensory System and Signal Processing for Optimal Wing Control

Olga Smalikho
Technische Universität Darmstadt
Darmstadt, Germany
Olga.Smalikho@rtr.tu-darmstadt.de

Markus Olhofer
Honda Research Institute Europe
Offenbach, Germany
Markus.Olhofer@honda-ri.de

ABSTRACT

The development of adaptive systems, which react autonomously to changes in their environment, require the coordinated generation of sensors, providing information about the environment and signal processing structures, which generate suitable reactions to changed conditions. In this work we demonstrate the applicability of a concurrent evolutionary design of the optimal sensory and controller parts of a system for the example of an adaptive wing design. The focus of the work is twofold. First on the realization of developmental stages of the sensory and controlling systems design, defined as a growth process, and second on the comparison of the differences in structures of the systems developed through the presented evolutionary growth method and of evolved systems, having fixed set of sensory elements. We ascertained that the success of the realized growth process depends among others on the relation between the triggering methods and timing of the system enlargement and on parameter settings of the optimization strategy after a growth phase.

Categories and Subject Descriptors

I.2.1 [**ARTIFICIAL INTELLIGENCE**]: Applications and Expert Systems; I.2.8 [**ARTIFICIAL INTELLIGENCE**]: Problem Solving, Control Methods, and Search—*Heuristics*; I.2.6 [**ARTIFICIAL INTELLIGENCE**]: Learning—*Parameter learning*; J.7 [**COMPUTER APPLICATIONS**]: Computers in other systems—*Process control*

Keywords

Adaptive systems; co-evolution; evolutionary optimization; sensory signal processing; system growth process.

1. INTRODUCTION

During the evolution of living beings, the sensory organs as well as the body morphology co-evolve with the brain development to adjust to the changing environment and to achieve competitive advantages. Additionally the evolution process forces the development of the animals organization towards complexification. Regarding these two evolutionary aspects of the biological design of complex living systems, we assume that the design process of technical solutions with high complexity could be improved by starting the system development with an initially simple system organization while performing parallel complexification of its functional parts. In contrast to biological body-brain co-evolution, the majority of the current engineering methods adapt isolated parts of the overall structure. The design of adaptive systems implies the development of sensors as well as actuators, which allow the improvement of systems in reaction to changes in their environment according to a predefined quality measure. The developers usually design the morphological part of the system separate from the controller unit.

A variety of research on the application of evolutionary robotics to real mobile robots by optimizing of controller structure with given morphological limitations, such as fixed the number and resolution of camera system of the robot, joints angles range etc., has been carried out by Brooks [3], Dorigo and Schnepf [6], Cliff, Husband and Harvey [5], Floreano and Mondada [8], Miglino, Nafasi, Taylor [12]. However the pre-selection of sensor-actuator configuration without considering the development of a control structure limits the global optimization task to the optimization of a part of the overall structure, in the case of fixed morphological configuration to a control structure optimization. The limits of the controller performance depend, however, on the suitability and the amount of sensory information, as well as on the actuator resources. This raises the problem that in the case the sensor data is insufficient to fulfill the given task, a more complex structure of the control system is needed to compensate the lack of sensor information. The development of the complex controller, however, still does not guarantee global efficiency, when the system does not get the key information about the environment necessary to fulfill a given task. On the other hand, if the system gets too much sensor information or has a large number of actuators, the optimization of the control structure might become unfeasible. In this case the optimization might get traped in a local optimum and does not reach the global optimum, due to the large number of the optimization parameters. Based on the described problem, an optimal adaptive behavior of in a given environment seems to be a balance between the complexity of sensor, motor and control systems. The idea of a transfer of a biologically inspired growth process to a design

GECCO'14, July 12–16, 2014, Vancouver, BC, Canada.

http://dx.doi.org/10.1145/2576768.2598318.

process can give the possibility to coordinate the development of sensor and control structures without dimensional limitation of sensory setup in the early stages of structural development. Since the final system configuration is not pre-defined and is the result of the concurrent optimization process, we get an evolvable system and therefore enlarge the final search domain and potentially increase the chances of global optima detection. The found solution is expected to be globally optimal with maximal performance potential given minimal complexity. Since the growth process presents an optimization task with a regular enlargement of a search space domain, it is important to maintain a benefit solutions gained in a previous optimization step. In this way, the system growth method uses the optimal solution, found in a low dimensional search space, as an advantageous starting point for the search in a higher dimensional search space.

Gomez, Lungarella, Eggenberger, et al. [9] extended the principle of sensor-control balance to developmental enlargement of the system by simultaneously increasing the sensor resolution, the precision of motors, as well as the size of neural structure (controller). They showed with the experiments that a chosen system starting with a low-resolution sensory system, a low precision motor system, and a low complexity of controller, can learn a given task faster than a system with a complex configuration in the beginning. The coordination of the growth process was realized by internal learning mechanism where the active neural units controlling the robot were 'rewarded' or 'punished' depending on the improvement or aggravation in task fulfilling. The authors showed the advantages of concurrent optimization of the sensory and control systems as a dynamic developmental process of gradual complexification.

While the work of Gomez, Lungarella, Eggenberger et al. [9] has been done in a field of evolutionary robotics, we utilize the example of a virtual adaptive wing. Aerodynamic problems are characterized by highly complex interactions between flow body and flow field, which is, in most cases, difficult to understand in detail. Due to this fact the manual design is generally challenging. In this work we demonstrate the simultaneous evolutionary design of sensor configuration and control structure for the example of an adaptive wing configuration implemented as a structural growth process and compare the results with the optimization of the system with fixed morphological settings. We also analyze the impacts on the organization of functional structure and the final performance of the optimized outcoming system, depending on the realization of triggering methods for system enlargement. The target for the development of the adaptive wing is the reduction of the drag the airfoil generates while still creating a minimum of lift. Environmental changes are realized by changes in the angle of attack of the airflow across a wide range.

A description of the framework of the adaptive wing with a detailed explanation of the functional set-up of the sensory and controlling systems is given in section 2. In section 3 we present the results of the optimization with fixed morphological settings. In section 4 we explain implemented growth realization, summarize the results of the optimization with a fixed morphological setting and compare them with the results of the growth method. Finally, we conclude the paper with a summary of the main findings of our work.

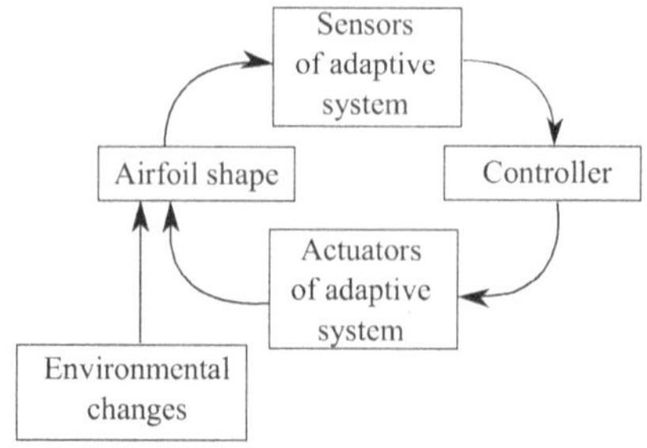

Figure 1: Framework of adaptive system

2. ADAPTIVE VIRTUAL WING SET-UP

In this work the adaptive system was implemented as a system which consists of virtual sensors, actuators and a signal processing unit. The controller of the adaptive system operates under changing environmental conditions by generating signals directed to the actuators, depending on the measured sensor values. The target is to generate a wing shape which has a minimal drag value for the actual environmental conditions. In addition a minimal lift value has to be guaranteed. In order to evaluate the airfoil shape a CFD (computational fluid dynamics) simulation is applied. The actuator signals correspond to changes of the NURBS [7] control points and define the current airfoil shape. The virtual sensors of the system have been defined as pressure sensors positioned on the airfoil surface. The values of the virtual sensors correspond to the surface pressure calculated in the CFD simulation and therefore depend on the blade's surface, the angle of attack and the speed of the air flow etc.

Fig. 1 gives a schematic overview of the system. The overall system is designed in a way that the position as well as the number of sensors and actuators can be changed freely. Therefore the system is able to adapt the wing shape optimally in reaction to environmental changes. The described setup serves a test framework for the simulation of the interactions between control structure and morphology during the operation of the control structure as well as during their evolutionary development.

In our work, we implemented the two dimensional airfoil by a non-uniform rational B-splines (NURBS) as shown in Fig. 2. The shape of the NURBS curve and with that the shape of the resulting wing profile is determined by the set of spline control points. The splines, defined by its control points C_N, result in a unique two dimensional airfoil shape. By moving the control points in the two dimensional space, a shape change of the airfoil can be achieved.

For the simulation of the aerodynamic airfoil characteristics and pressure distribution we used the computational fluid dynamic solver Xfoil[1] because of its high speed which is decisive for optimization tasks Xfoil calculates different aerodynamic characteristics for the given airfoil geometry and environmental configurations, such as angle of attack, Reynolds number etc. In the simulation we change the angle of attack to generate variations of the airfoil environment since it has a major influence on its final aerodynamical characteristics. The Reynolds number has been fixed during the optimization($Re = 10^7$). To simulate the sensors we used the distribution of the pressure coefficient over the airfoil

[1]http://web.mit.edu/drela/Public/web/xfoil/

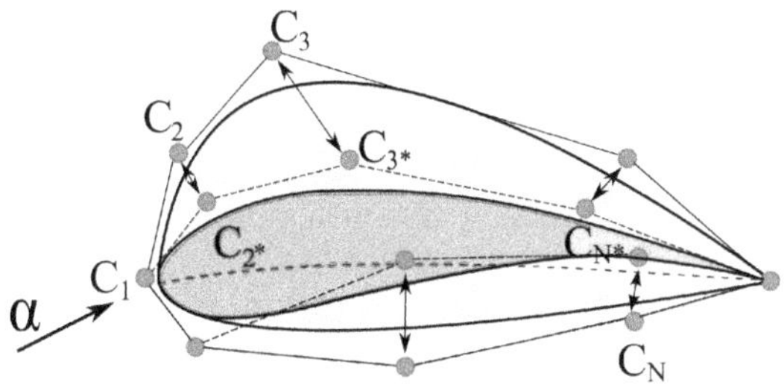

Figure 2: Example of the airfoil created with NURBS. Airfoil in white, defined by the initial positions of the spline control points. The airfoil shape change (in dark gray) results from the movements of control points

surface. The pressure coefficient, C_p is defined as following [1]:

$$C_p = \frac{p - p_\infty}{\frac{1}{2}\rho_\infty V_\infty} \quad , \tag{1}$$

where p is the gauge pressure value at the point on the airfoil at which the pressure coefficient has been calculated, p_∞ - free stream pressure value, ρ_∞ - free stream fluid density, V_∞ - free stream velocity. In comparison to a gauge pressure value at the point on the airfoil, the pressure coefficient is dimensionless and independent from effects of the density and speed of the air. We used Xfoil to calculate the profile of the pressure coefficients C_p at 160 points on the airfoil surface. A sensor placed on the airfoil returns a sensor value corresponding to the pressure coefficient at the airfoil surface.

2.1 Adaptive wing controller

The task of the neural controller is to generate suitable actuator signals in order to minimize the drag of the airfoil by morphing the airfoil surface. A wide variety of controller designs for that purpose can be found in the literature. Parker and Nathan [14] as well as Bugajska and Schutz [4] implemented a controller as a reactive system which uses "if...then" rules to control a simulated robot. Haller, Ijspeert and Floreano [10] implemented a controller inspired by the central pattern generators underlying locomotion in animals. In our previous work [16] we implemented the controller as feed forward neural network with one input layer, a single hidden layer with sigmoidal activation function and one output layer with a linear activation function. The neural controller used 20 neurons in a hidden layer and showed good performance. However the high number of neurons in the hidden layer, especially when having a high number of sensors, slowed down the optimization process considerably due to the high number of optimization parameters. Since the focus of this work is to analyze the developmental process of the system which starts with an initially simple set-up growing into a system of higher complexity, the complexity of the controller has been reduced by replacing it with a linear recurrent model. The schematic model of the controller is shown in Fig. 3

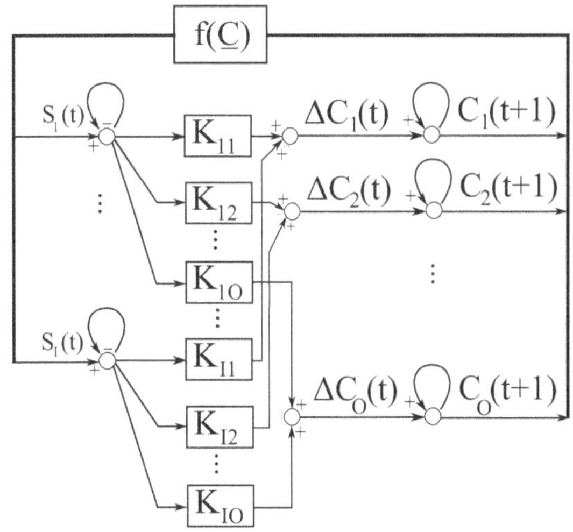

Figure 3: Model of linear recurrent controller

$$\begin{aligned} C_o(t+1) &= C_o(t) + \Delta C_o(t) \\ \Delta C_o(t) &= \sum_{i=1}^{I} (s_i(t) - s_i(t-1))K_{io} \\ s_i(t) &= f(C_1, \ldots, C_O) \end{aligned} \tag{2}$$

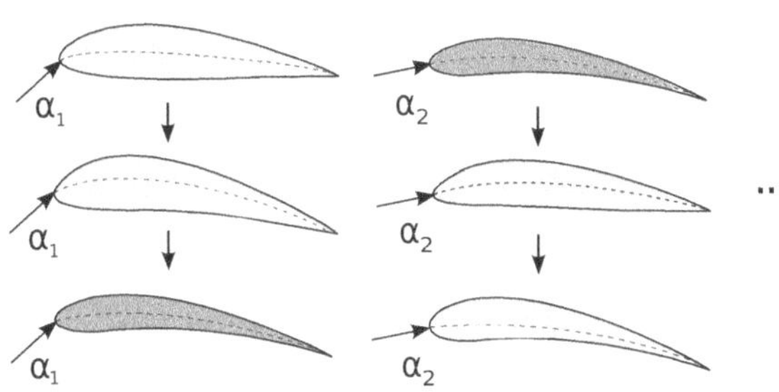

Figure 4: Example of 3 steps of controller actions for the same angle of attack

The controller input signals are the changes of the pressure coefficients s_i over one time step of controller processing. The outputs of the controller are the actuator signals C_{io} and describe the position of the virtual actuators in two dimensional space. The actuator adjustments ΔC_o are calculated as a sum of the signals of all sensors of the system multiplied with the corresponding linear controller coefficients K_{io}. The current state of the actuators C_{io} defines the pressure coefficients s_i by the nonlinear air flow function f, simulated with Xfoil solver. Three cycles of geometry change by the controller actions during the controller operation time for the same angle of attack has been implemented, in order to let the system to converge to a final state. Fig. 4 shows exemplary surface modifications during the adaptation process.

3. SENSOR-CONTROLLER CO-EVOLUTION

In this work the co-evolution process is realized by a concurrent optimization of morphological and controller structures of the described adaptive wing system. Although these two different functional units of the system are coded in a single genome, the described optimization process reflects the main aspect of co-evolutionary process, since both units are mutually co-adjusted during the entire evolutionary process. In [16] we ascertained a high correlation between the development of the sensory and the control systems. These results support the idea of the concurrent morphological and control systems development. In [16] we additionally demonstrated the existence of the optimal number of implemented pressure sensors. Due to these two main findings of our previous work we came up to the idea to transfer such an element of biological design as a growth process to the presented example of virtual adaptive wing. In work presented here we analyze the development of the system by a growth process. One of the advantages of the growth process, is a minimal requirement on the priori knowledge about the system. The growth process shows fast convergence in small search space, since it starts with an initially elementary system. Thereby we free the system from the early limitations and give it a possibility of coordinated development up to the system of minimal required complexity with maximal efficiency.

3.1 Evaluation algorithm

The system is evaluated according its ability to reduce the drag of the airfoil to its minimum while changes in the inflow angle of the air occur. Therefore the ratio in drag coefficient before C_d^1 and after C_d^2 a change of the inflow angle is evaluated. The ratio of the changed and unchanged drag values indicates the performance of the controller through actuators adjustments. Fig. 5 shows the structural diagram of individual evaluation.

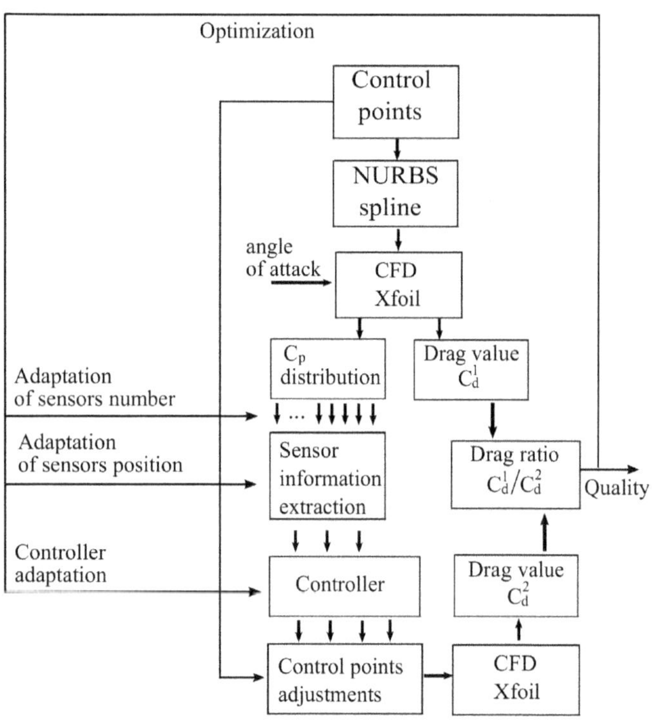

Figure 5: Overview of the system evaluation

The fitness of an individual was defined as a sum of drag value ratios over tree steps of controller actions for a single angle of attack and additionally over a cascade of angles of attack as shown in Fig. 6.

$$Fitness(Individual) = \frac{\sum_{\alpha=1}^{N}\sum_{i=1}^{M}\frac{C_d(\alpha,\text{changed airfoil})}{C_d(\alpha,\text{unchanged airfoil})}}{N * M}, \tag{3}$$

where M is a number of controller actions for the same angle of attack ($M = 3$), α is the angle of attack, N is the total number of angles of attack applied and on which the individual has been evaluated, C_d is the drag coefficient.

In order to reduce the influence of the initial condition of the wing geometry and in order to test the system for a sufficiently high number of angle changes we evaluate each system for 16 different angles, shown in Fig. 6. With that the effect of noise is removed while keeping the time necessary for the evaluation within a reasonable range. The maximal thickness of the airfoil was set to the maximal thickness of the NACA 2410 airfoil which is equal to 10% of the chord length. In addition, the constraint on the lift coefficient has

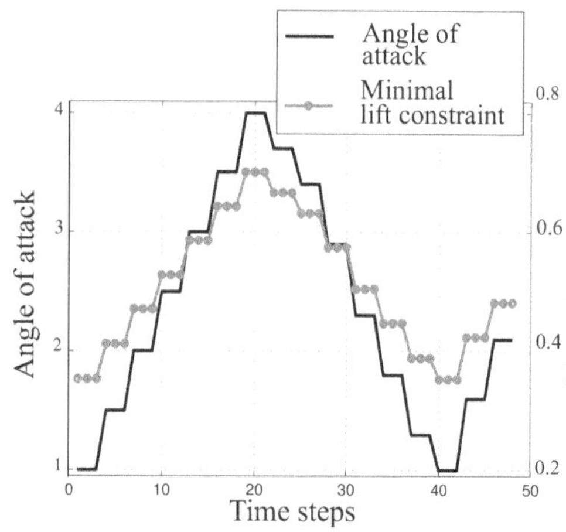

Figure 6: Training scenario of different angles of attack(in black) and lift coefficient of NACA 2410 airfoil (in gray) for the individual evaluation

been set to the lift of a standard NACA 2410 airfoil at corresponding angle of attack. The lift coefficients of the NACA 2410 airfoil are shown in Fig. 6.

3.2 Co-evolution of controller and position of sensors

To verify the functionality of the linear recurrent controller presented in 2.1 we revise the experiments with fixed morphological and controller dimensionality. The concurrent optimization of sensor positions on the airfoil surface and the optimization of controller coefficients, described above, has been implemented with a standard Evolution Strategy (ES), developed by Bienert, Rechenberg and Schwefel [15]. The implemented ES(15,100) uses two different self adapted step sizes, for the sensor positions and the controller connection weights adaptation. Although more sophisticated algorithms are available like CMA-ES [11] we stick to the comparable simple strategy which can be applied as well in the growth process. A single genome of the individual includes three chromosomes which code the position of the sensors, the controller parameters and the strategy parameters (mutation step sizes). Offsprings are the result of a single point recombination and mutation of the parent individuals with the current mutation step size. The optimization has been implemented, using SHARK[2], open-source C++ machine learning library.

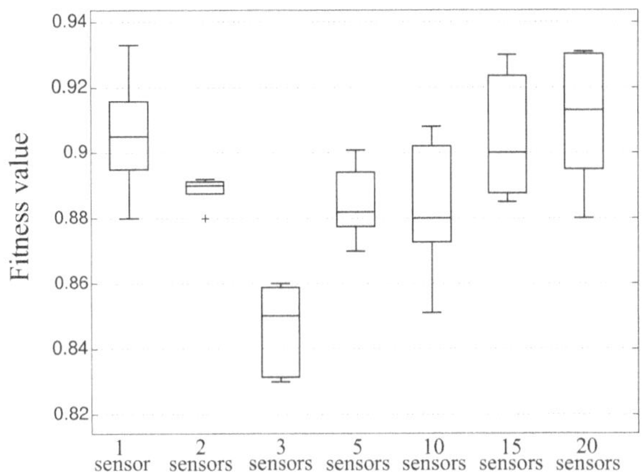

Figure 7: Final quality of the sensor-controller optimization runs after 45 generations. 10 optimization runs for each fixed number of sensors with different starting parameters.

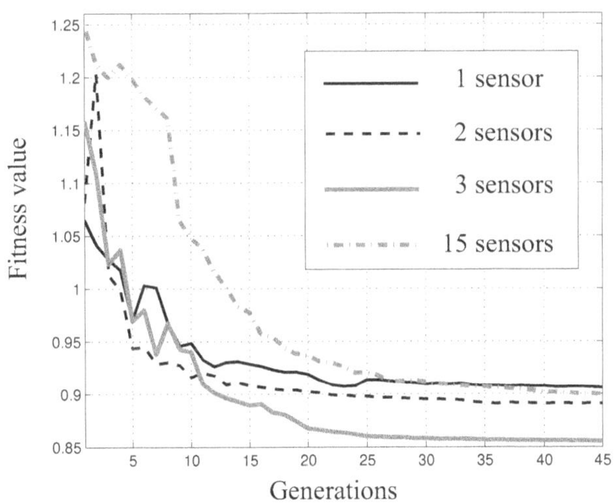

Figure 8: Averaged fitness curves of the results in Fig.7. Fitness curves has been averaged over 10 runs with different starting parameters

The optimization starts with the randomly initiated sensor positions between 0 (trailing edge, wing upper-side) and 2 (trailing edge, wing under-side) and controller coefficients, uniformly randomly initialized between -0.2 and 0.2. The trailing edge is defined as rear edge, where the airflow spited by the leading edge rejoins [1]. Two mutation step sizes are defined. One for the position of the sensors and one for the connection strengths of the controller. The parameters are initialized with 0.1 for the sensor positions, and 0.01 for the controller connections. The results of the concurrent sensor-controller optimization with different morphological dimensionality, which remain constant during the optimization process, are presented in Fig. 7 and 8. The results indicate the existence of an optimal number of sensors (3 pressure sensors) for the selected conditions of the framework and optimization strategy. Systems using one or two pressure sensors show a low performance compared with the systems using 3 sensors, due to the fact that the key information about the change of angle of attack measured indirectly through pressure sensors is missing. The relatively bad performance of the system with higher number of sensors results from the inability of the chosen optimization algorithm to optimize the resulting number of optimization parameters for the given complex aerodynamic fitness landscape. In this case the optimization is very slow or converges too early and does not reach the global optimum.

[2]http://image.diku.dk/shark/

4. DEVELOPMENT OF OPTIMAL SENSOR-CONTROLLER CONFIGURATION BY GROWTH

In this section we describe the implementation of the system growth method and specify the required conditions of the optimization set-up to find the optimal system configuration. We also compare the organization and functionality of the systems developed through the autonomous growth process with the results in 3.2.

4.1 Definition of growth process

The existence of the optimal system configuration shown in 3.2 motivated us to implement an optimization process that can detect the optimal solution for the system dimensionality during the entire optimization run. We solve this task through the system growth process which implies gradual enlargement of the initially elementary system by addition of the additional sensory and controller elements during concurrent sensor-controller optimization.

There exists a variety of approaches for the topology optimization of the processing structures in the neuro-evolutionary domain. An interesting work has been done among others by Moriarty and Miikulainen [13]. The authors implemented a new symbiotic, adaptive neuro-evolution algorithm (SANE) to optimize the topology of an artificial neural network. Stanley and Miikulainen [17],[18] developed also an approach for neural network topologies optimization named neuro-evolution of augmenting topologies (NEAT).

In this work we implement the topology optimization of the controller, realized by a linear recurrent model, as an optimization of the input dimensionality of the control structure. The input signals of the controller are fully connected with the outputs. The mentioned expected advantage of the growth process versus an optimization with a fixed number of sensory elements, is the possibility to detect the optimal number and the configuration of controller inputs as well as optimal resulting signal processing structure during the combined optimization process.

By implementing the growth process we found that the achieved quality of the final system depended strongly on the timing and the method of system enlargement as well as on the current values of the mutation step sizes at the time

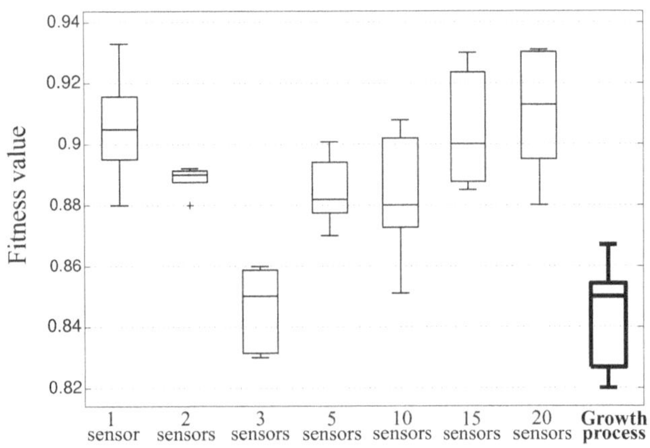

Figure 9: Comparison of the final quality of the sensor-controller optimization runs with the quality of the growth method (in bold) averaged over 10 optimization runs.

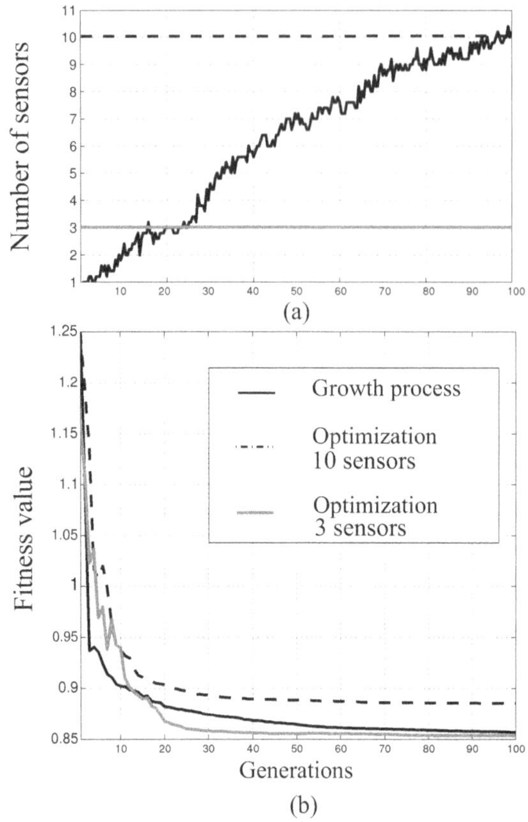

Figure 10: (a) Number of sensors during the optimization averaged over 10 runs with different starting parameters (b) Corresponding averaged quality development.

of structural changes. Since the idea of the growth process has been to use optimized solutions in the previous search dimensions as a starting point in the next searching space dimension, it is decisive to maintain benefit solution despite the structural change. To ensure a neutral system mutation we initialize the weighting coefficients of a new sensor elements with zero. Additionally a new sensor elements and the corresponding controller connections get individual mutation step sizes. This gives a new elements a possibility to develop individually while keeping the previously optimized system setup intact. We use a probability based triggering method of system enlargement. This means that each individual in a population has a fixed uniformly distributed probability to get a new sensor element. We achieved good results using a probability value of $p = 0.05$, which means that statistically 5 out of 100 individuals in the population get a new sensory input.

4.2 Experimental results of growth process

Fig. 9 shows the results of the described growth method in comparison to the optimization results with fixed morphological settings. The results demonstrate, that the systems developed with our growth method show similar good performance as the systems optimized for 3 sensors.

Fig. 10 shows the comparison of averaged development process of the systems through growth and of the systems with 3 and 10 sensory elements. The average system constructed through growth process developed 10 sensors after 100 generations and converged close to the average quality of the system using 3 sensors. In comparison to the results of the growth method, the evolved systems with fixed number of 10 sensors get trapped into local optima after 40 generations and end up with similarly bad performance of the system using 2 sensors.

The result of the growth method have been a system using 10 sensors on average. Since we expected to obtain a system with optimally placed 3 sensors, the results of the growth method has been unexpected. However, a detailed insight of the controller system organization of the systems developed by the growth method gave the explanation on the achieved results. For visualizing of controller connection strengths a Hinton diagrams has been used [2]. The size of the boxes corresponds to the value of the connection strength. The box color (gray and black) represents a positive or negative sign of the connection strength respectively. The values of the connection strengths have been scaled between minimal (no box) and maximal controller connection strength (box of maximum size). Fig. 11 and 12 demonstrate the differences in the functional controller organization and its impact on the system performance. Fig. 12 (a) and (b) compare the corresponding performance progress of two differently developed systems in Fig. 11 (a) and (c) during the optimization. The example system shown in 11 (c) has been optimized for 15 pressure sensors. We ascertained, that the controller of the system is organized in such a way that each sensor has a comparable influence on the control strategy. The organization of the control strategy of the example system developed by our growth method in Fig. 11 (a) is totally different. Due to the gradual step-wise system enlargement during the optimization, we observe a clear arrangement of the sensors according to their importance for the system, where the first sensor s_1 has the biggest and the last sensor s_{16} the smallest impact on the system performance. We also noticed, that the first 3 sensors of the system have a major impact on the system, which matches the results of the optimization in 3.2. These results confirm the applica-

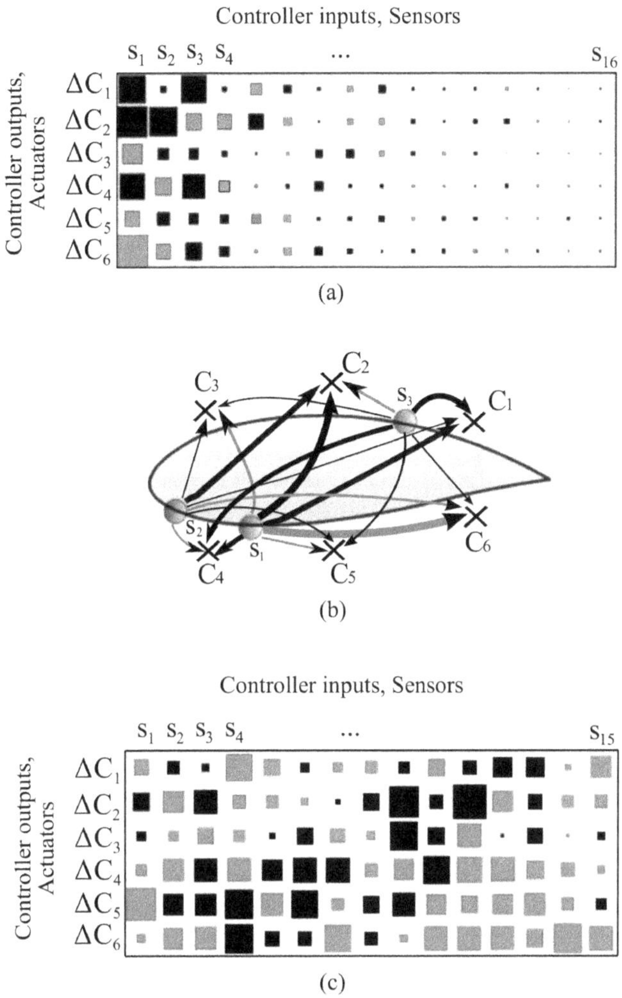

Figure 11: (a) Hinton diagram of the system controller, developed by growth process at 100th generation, (b) Schematic airfoil controller with 3 major controller connections between sensors and actuators of the system in Fig. 11 (a). Thicker lines mean a stronger connection, (c) Hinton diagram of the system controller optimized for 15 sensors at 100th generation

bility of the presented growth method for the detection of the optimal sensor and the signal processing systems.

4.3 Results validation

To get a baseline for the maximal achievable quality of the airfoils, conventional evolutionary design optimization was carried out. We used a ES(15,100) strategy to determine the optimal shapes of the airfoil for the individual angles of attack represented in Fig. 6 with a lift constraint of the lift coefficient of the NACA 2410 airfoil at corresponding angle of attack. Fig. 13 demonstrates the comparison of the baseline and NACA 2410 airfoils for 16 different angles of attack shown in Fig. 6 with the performance of the best system developed with a growth process, tested on a scenario of 100 different angles of attack, generated randomly between 1 and 4 degrees. As expected, an adaptive airfoil system developed with the growth method shows significantly better performance than a single standard NACA 2410 airfoil. It also gets close to the maximal possible quality of specialized baseline solutions, but performs less good for the marginal angles of attack.

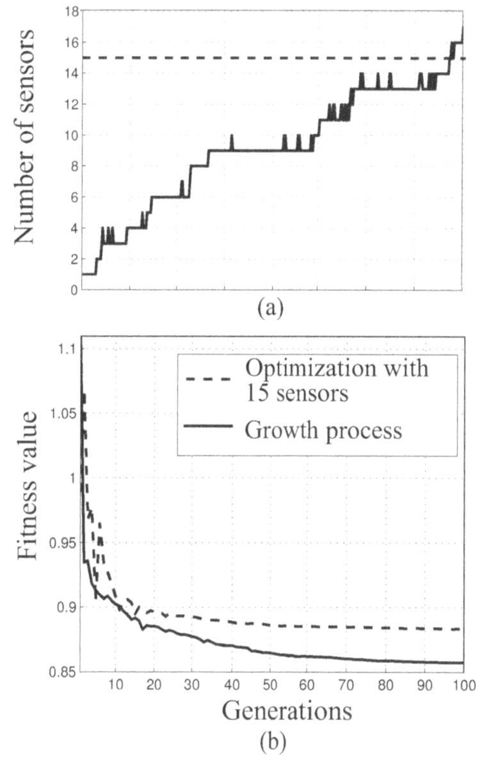

Figure 12: (a) Number of the sensors during the optimization of the systems presented in Fig. 11 (a) and (c), (b) Corresponding quality development.

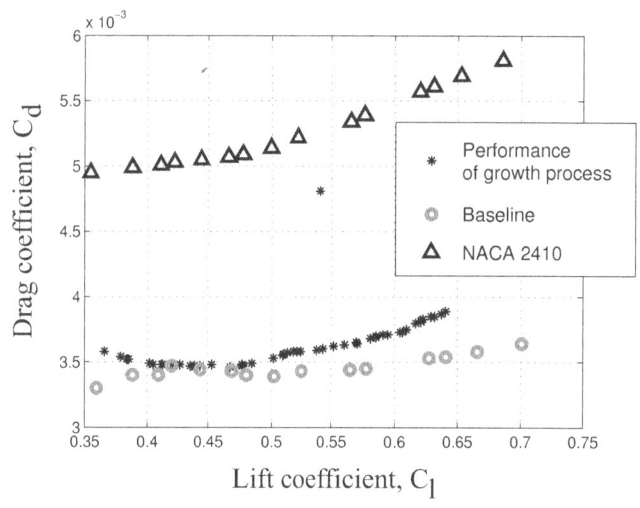

Figure 13: Performance validation: Performance of the baseline airfoils, NACA 2410 standard airfoil and system developed through growth, tested on 100 different angles of attack between 2 and 4 degrees, occurring in random sequence

5. CONCLUSIONS

This work investigates the autonomous generation of an optimal adaptive system with variable dimensionality of sensoring and signal processing structures as the overall system optimization. The adaptive system has been realized by a virtual adaptive wing, which consists of sensors and actuators as well as a related control structure. The presented adaptive wing reacts autonomously to the changes in its environment and uses the available virtual actuators to minimize the drag of the entire system. We simulated the changing environment by variating the angle in which the air is approaching the airfoil. The implemented system growth method synchronizes the design of a sensoring and a signal processing system parts during the optimization process and additionally frees the system of early structural limitations, giving it a possibility to develop autonomously to a system with an optimal number and position of the sensors and the related optimal controller. The experimental results demonstrate the expected existence of optimal dimensionality of the system and the ability of the presented growth method to detect this optimal morphological and controlling system configuration. Furthermore we ascertained, that the system development through the presented growth method results in a structured system organization, with a strong hierarchical arrangement of the elements of sensor and controller structures. Thereby, the described arranged system organization provides information about the importance of the present sensor elements of the system. We would like to emphasize, that the result of the growth process as a global system optimization depends strongly on the correct balance between the mutation rate of the initially existing and a new generated structural elements during the developmental process. New sensor and controller elements get individual strategy parameters, which values are higher than a current mutation rate of longer existent elements. This system enlargement construct gives new elements a possibility to develop individually while maintaining the overall system efficiency. Regarding our future work, we would like to include the development of the actuators of the system to the growth process, as well as to investigate a supposed trade-off relation between the number of the sensors and the complexity of the related signal processing structure.

6. ACKNOWLEDGMENTS

The authors gratefully acknowledge the support of Bernhard Sendhoff. Olga Smalikho thanks for the financial support from Honda Research Institute Europe GmbH

7. REFERENCES

[1] J. Anderson. *Fundamentals of Aerodynamics*. Anderson series. McGraw-Hill Education, 2011.

[2] F. Bremner, S. Gotts, and D. Denham. Hinton diagrams: Viewing connection strengths in neural networks. volume 26, pages 215–218. Springer-Verlag, 1994.

[3] R. A. Brooks. New approaches to robotics. *Science*, 253:1227 – 1232, 1991 1991.

[4] M. D. Bugajska and A. C. Schultz. Coevolution of form and function in the design of micro air vehicles. In *Evolvable Hardware*, pages 154–166. IEEE Computer Society, 2002.

[5] D. Cliff, I. Harvey, and P. Husbands. Explorations in Evolutionary Robotics. *Adaptive Behavior*, 2(1):73–110, 1993.

[6] M. Dorigo and U. Schnepf. Genetics-based machine learning and behaviour based robotics: A new synthesis. *IEEE Transactions on Systems, Man, and Cybernetics*, 23(1):141–154, 1993.

[7] G. E. Farin. *NURBS: From Projective Geometry to Practical Use*. A. K. Peters, Ltd., Natick, MA, USA, 2nd edition, 1999.

[8] D. Floreano and F. Mondada. Automatic creation of an autonomous agent: Genetic evolution of a neural-network driven robot. In *Proceedings of the Third International Conference on Simulation of Adaptive Behavior : From Animals to Animats 3: From Animals to Animats 3*, SAB94, pages 421–430, Cambridge, MA, USA, 1994. MIT Press.

[9] G. Gomez, M. Lungarella, P. E. Hotz, K. Matsushita, and R. Pfeifer. Simulating development in a real robot: on the concurrent increase of sensory, motor, and neural complexity, 2004.

[10] B. Haller, A. Ijspeert, and D. Floreano. Co-evolution of structures and controllers for neubot underwater modular robots. In M. CapcarrÃÍre, A. Freitas, P. Bentley, C. Johnson, and J. Timmis, editors, *Advances in Artificial Life*, volume 3630 of *Lecture Notes in Computer Science*, pages 189–199. Springer Berlin Heidelberg, 2005.

[11] N. Hansen. *The CMA Evolution Strategy: A Comparing Review*. 2006.

[12] O. Miglino, K. Nafasi, and C. Taylor. Selection for wandering behavior in a small robot. Technical Report UCLA-CRSP-94-01, Department of Cognitive Science, University of California, Los Angeles, 1994.

[13] D. E. Moriarty and R. Miikkulainen. Efficient reinforcement learning through symbiotic evolution. *Machine Learning*, (AI94-224):11–32, 1996.

[14] G. Parker and P. Nathan. Co-evolution of sensor morphology and control on a simulated legged robot. In *Computational Intelligence in Robotics and Automation, 2007. CIRA 2007. International Symposium on*, pages 516–521, 2007.

[15] I. Rechenberg. *Evolutionsstrategie '94*. Frommann, Stuttgart, 1994. Fit via Evolutionsstrategie, Routine von Volker Tuerck vorhanden.

[16] O. Smalikho and M. Olhofer. Co-evolution of sensor system and signal processing for optimal wing control. In *Proceedings of the EvoApplication Conference*. Springer, 2014.

[17] K. O. Stanley and R. Miikkulainen. Evolving neural networks through augmenting topologies. *Evolutionary Computation*, 10(2):99–127, 2002.

[18] K. O. Stanley and R. Miikkulainen. Competitive coevolution through evolutionary complexification. *Journal of Artificial Intelligence Research*, 21:63–100, 2004.

Novelty Search Creates Robots with General Skills for Exploration

Roby Velez
Evolving AI Lab
Computer Science Dept.
University of Wyoming
rvelez@uwyo.com

Jeff Clune
Evolving AI Lab
Computer Science Dept.
University of Wyoming
jeffclune@uwyo.com

ABSTRACT

Novelty Search, a new type of Evolutionary Algorithm, has shown much promise in the last few years. Instead of selecting for phenotypes that are closer to an objective, Novelty Search assigns rewards based on how different the phenotypes are from those already generated. A common criticism of Novelty Search is that it is effectively random or exhaustive search because it tries solutions in an unordered manner until a correct one is found. Its creators respond that over time Novelty Search accumulates information about the environment in the form of skills relevant to reaching uncharted territory, but to date no evidence for that hypothesis has been presented. In this paper we test that hypothesis by transferring robots evolved under Novelty Search to new environments (here, mazes) to see if the skills they've acquired generalize. Three lines of evidence support the claim that Novelty Search agents do indeed learn general exploration skills. First, robot controllers evolved via Novelty Search in one maze and then transferred to a new maze explore significantly more of the new environment than non-evolved (randomly generated) agents. Second, a Novelty Search process to solve the new mazes works significantly faster when seeded with the transferred controllers versus randomly-generated ones. Third, no significant difference exists when comparing two types of transferred agents: those evolved in the original maze under (1) Novelty Search vs. (2) a traditional, objective-based fitness function. The evidence gathered suggests that, like traditional Evolutionary Algorithms with objective-based fitness functions, Novelty Search is not a random or exhaustive search process, but instead is accumulating information about the environment, resulting in phenotypes possessing skills needed to explore their world.

Keywords

Novelty Search; Evolutionary Robotics

GECCO'14, July 12–16, 2014, Vancouver, BC, Canada.

ACM 978-1-4503-2662-9/14/07 ...$15.00.
http://dx.doi.org/10.1145/2576768.2598225.

1. INTRODUCTION

Evolutionary Algorithms (EAs) perform automated optimization and are used in many different fields, such as designing pharmaceutical drugs [16], creating stock trading agents [15], evolving gaits for robots [2, 10, 3, 7], or optimizing traffic flow in congested cities [1]. Despite often outperforming human engineers [7, 9, 6], they have the same Achilles Heel all optimization methods possess: they get stuck in local optima. The reason is because EAs typically have a user-defined objective incorporated into a fitness function that rewards solutions the closer they are to that objective (or the better they perform on that objective). The problem is that often times the path from a current solution to the global optimum is not a series of moves that are increasingly closer to the objective; problems that are *deceptive* [8] require temporarily moving away from (i.e. scoring worse on) the objective to find better solutions. A nice visual example is the "Hard Maze" from [12], wherein robot controllers are evolved to go from the Start location to the Goal (Fig. 1, upper left). A traditional, objective-driven EA results in robots stuck in the dead end just below the Goal [12]. Such local optima are present in all challenging problems [5].

Novelty Search is an EA variant that is less susceptible to local optima because it entirely ignores the objective, except as a stopping criteria [12]. It rewards agents based on how different their behaviors are from the solutions that have already been evolved, which introduces a pressure to continuously do something new. In the Hard Maze example, controllers are rewarded for reaching not-yet-explored areas of the maze [12]. By exploring all paths, Novelty Search agents solve the maze significantly more often than objective-driven EA agents [12], which tend to get stuck in the dead end just below the Goal.

Disregarding objectives in an EA is a radical idea, leading to skepticism regarding Novelty Search's ability to scale up to more challenging problem domains [4]. Because it is too easy to be novel in high-dimensional spaces, and because those spaces are so large that randomly stumbling upon the objective is exceedingly unlikely, a common objection posed to the creators of Novelty Search is that it will "simply get lost in [a] vast search space" [11].

When considering the objection that Novelty Search will get lost in a vast search space, it is important to keep in mind the distinction between the genome search space, which is usually high-dimensional, and the *behavior space*, which is usually low-dimensional by design. The behavior space, which is where the Novelty Search algorithm searches, is

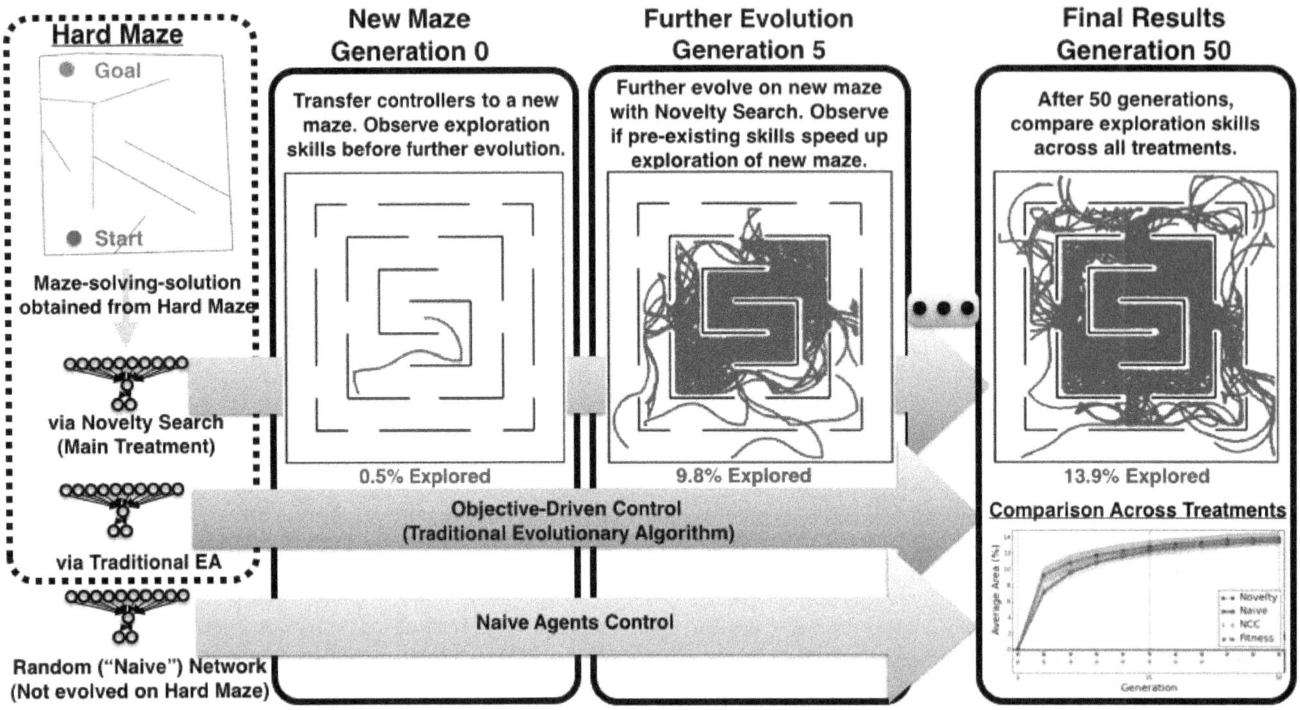

Figure 1: Experiments Designed to Test if Novelty Search Produces Exploration Skills. In the main Novelty Search treatment (blue/highest arrow), networks that solve the Hard Maze are obtained via Novelty Search. These networks are transferred into a new maze, where their initial exploration abilities are measured by quantifying the percentage of maze covered and the average distance (not pictured) from Start. The networks are then further evolved with Novelty Search to see if skills exist that speed up exploration under Novelty Search. This further evolution is stopped after 50 generations. This procedure is repeated for three control treatments: (1) a traditional, objective-driven evolutionary algorithm (middle/red arrow), (2) Naive (randomly generated) networks not evolved on the hard maze (lower/green arrow), and (3) Naive networks with the same topological complexity as Novelty Search networks (not pictured).

a user-defined description of behaviors. For example, the behavior of a robot could be described as the final location of a robot, the levers it presses, or the words it speaks. The behavior space conflates many possible genomes, phenotypes (e.g. neural networks), and actions: For example, a behavioral description might ignore an 8-legged robot's genome, the weights and topology of its neural network, and its motor commands over time, to characterize that agent just by its final location.

Novelty Search might indeed get lost in high-dimensional genome spaces, because changes in the genome due to mutations or crossover would produce new behaviors in nearly every case. However, it is not clear *a priori* that Novelty Search will get lost in low-dimensional behavior spaces, because it is non-trivial to generate new behaviors in such spaces. For example, most mutations to neural networks do not produce interesting new behaviors.

With these concepts in mind, we can return to the original objection that Novelty Search will get lost in high-dimensional search spaces. The response given by the creators of Novelty Search, is that it does not explore the search space in a random or unordered manner. Instead, to continuously produce novel behaviors, Novelty Search agents have to learn about the environment they are in and how to interact with it. As Lehman and Stanley explain:

> ...in a maze with walls, at first novel behaviors will simply crash into nearby walls, yet eventually the search must find a behavior that avoids walls to do something new. Then, once it exploits this new ability within the initial hallways, it will have to learn to go through doors to do something new. In effect, it is forced to accumulate information about the world (e.g. walls and doors) to produce novel behaviors. [11]

Over time there is constant pressure to explore even more of the environment, creating an incentive to learn general exploration skills. A key argument for Novelty Search is thus that Novelty Search causes agents to accumulate skills for exploring their environment. This paper tests that hypothesis and finds evidence that supports it.

2. NOVELTY SEARCH

Any evolutionary algorithm can be modified to perform Novelty Search by replacing the objective-based fitness function with a *novelty metric* and implementing an archive [12]. The archive contains a history of where the search has explored to prevent backtracking. In the initial Novelty Search software [11], which we conducted our experiments in, Novelty Search was implemented by replacing the objective-driven measure for the novelty metric in the fitness function of the neuroevolution of augmenting topologies (NEAT) algorithm [14]. NEAT starts with a simple neural network and adds complexity in the form of nodes and connections over evolutionary time. It also has a mechanism to promote diversity and an intelligent way of performing crossover. We made minor modifications to the original software to allow transferring maze-solving robots to new mazes. Our code and data are available at EvolvingAI.com. All parameters are identical to those in the original Novelty Search paper [12].

A traditional fitness function scores solutions based on how close they are to an objective. A novelty metric rates solutions based on how different or novel their behavior is from the current population and archive. Each robot's actions can be encoded as a vector of numbers representing important aspects of its behavior. This vector is a point in the space of all possible behaviors known as the *behavioral space*. For each agent the novelty metric computes the average distance between it and its k nearest neighbors in the behavioral space. An individual that has large distances to its neighbors is thus in an unexplored area of behavior space and is highly rewarded because it is performing a new behavior. Individuals in densely populated regions within the behavioral space have small average distances to neighbors and are less likely to be selected. In essence, the novelty metric encourages agents to explore and continuously perform new actions.

The novelty metric is computed as follows:

$$\rho(x) = \frac{1}{k}\sum_{i=0}^{k} dist(x, \mu_i) \tag{1}$$

where $dist$ is the Euclidean distance between individual x and its ith-nearest neighbor, μ_i [12].

3. METHODS

3.1 Problem Domain

The problem domain in this study is from the papers that introduce and highlight the benefits of Novelty Search: evolving wheeled robots to solve mazes [12]. The robots are controlled by artificial neural networks (ANNs). Because Novelty Search is based on NEAT, the initial population of ANNs are generated by spawning a simple, feedforward neural network. The spawning process takes the initial neural network and makes copies, each with weights drawn from a uniform, allowable range of [-1,1]. The difference between Novelty Search and NEAT is that the initial starting network, and subsequent spawned networks, start off with one hidden neuron [12] versus none [14].

In this paper we evolve robots in the "Hard Maze" from the original Novelty Search papers [12] (Fig. 1, upper left). In the Hard Maze, robots must navigate from the Start to the Goal. Each robot's behavior is represented by a two-dimensional vector holding the final x and y position of the agent. The novelty metric therefore computes the average distance, within the behavioral space, from an agent to the k closest neighbors in the population and archive. Robots are thus rewarded to explore the maze.

We conduct 50 runs of Novelty Search in the Hard Maze (Fig. 1, upper left); each run produced one *hard-maze-solving* robot, which was the first to solve the maze by reaching its finish. To test if these solutions have general exploration skills or, alternately, if they have simply memorized a trajectory that solves the Hard Maze, we transfer them to a new maze and study their exploration abilities (Fig. 1).

Our initial test for exploration skills consists of two parts. First we transfer agents into a new maze and observe their baseline exploratory abilities. Second, we further evolve the transferred agents with Novelty Search to observe the progression of their abilities over time. Two measures, Area Covered and Distance Traveled, quantify the agents' exploratory skills. For this test there is no target in the new maze and evolution is stopped after 50 generations (a predetermined number that preliminary experiments revealed to be roughly when performance stops improving).

For an additional test of exploratory skills, we evolve agents in the new maze with different Goal locations distributed around the Start position (Fig. 2). Each target location approximates conducting an experiment in a different maze, increasing the sample size from which we can draw conclusions about the abilities of transferred agents to repurpose their exploration skills in new environments. As in the original experiment [12], each run stops if an agent reaches the Goal or if 2000 generations pass.

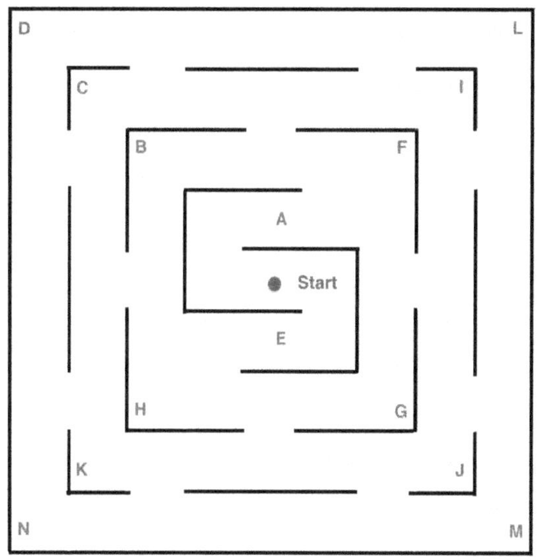

Figure 2: The Adaptation Test. The new maze, which agents are transferred into, is shown with the different Goal locations of the Adaptation Test. Novelty Search networks are transferred into this new maze and then further evolved with Novelty Search to find each Goal (in separate experiments). Each location can be considered as a separate test. If Novelty Search networks posses exploration skills, then they should find Goal locations faster than the control treatments, which are introduced in the next section.

The dimensions of the new maze, which agents are transferred into, are 450×450 (Fig. 1, 2), while those for the Hard Maze are 200×200. Since it is much larger than the Hard Maze, we refer to this new maze as the *Large Maze*. The added size provides more corridors and passageways to explore. Moreover, the Large Maze is designed so that a memorized trajectory that is successful on the Hard Maze will not lead to much exploration, since going right and up from the Start will immediately cause collisions with walls. When testing whether robots can find different Goals, the target locations are placed symmetrically around the Start position (Fig. 2) to mitigate the benefits of any memorized trajectory a transferred network may posses.

3.2 Controls

For the first control treatment, 50 randomly generated networks were obtained via the same process that generated the initial population of ANNs for the Novelty Search treatment. These *Naive* networks reveal the performance of agents that do not posses any domain knowledge or skills.

If the hard-maze-solving-networks produced by Novelty Search outperform the Naive networks, it supports the claim that Novelty Search facilitates the accumulation of exploratory skills. However, an alternate explanation exists that we would like to rule out: that the increased skill level simply results from the fact that networks evolved via Novelty Search have more complex topologies (i.e. more neurons and connections) than Naive networks. Recall that NEAT adds nodes and connections across generations and that the Novelty Search networks undergo many generations of evolution on the Hard Maze before being transferred to the new maze, whereas the Naive networks start with a single hidden neuron. To control for this explanation, we created a *network complexity control* (NCC). As with the Naive control, 50 random networks were generated. The difference is that the ith NCC network has the same number of neurons as the ith hard-maze-solving network in the Novelty treatment, where i represents the run number (for all treatments $i = 1...50$). For simplicity, the pattern of connections in the Novelty Search networks, including the presence of recurrent connections, is not mirrored in the NCC control. The initial NCC networks are all feed forward, following the convention of how initial networks are created in NEAT [14] and Novelty Search [12].

A third random control is the Random Search treatment from the original Novelty Search paper [12]: Agents were evolved with the objective-based EA, but given random fitness values. For each of 50 runs, the population evolved for E evaluations, where E is the number of evaluations it took the ith Novelty Search run to solve the Hard Maze. For each run, the agent from all of these E evaluations that got closest to the Goal became the ith member of the stock of initial networks for the Random Search treatment.

Along with Naive and NCC, the Random Search treatment is another interpretation of a random process. Because we experimentally found that this treatment performs qualitatively the same as Naive and NCC (data not shown), we do not separately report on it in the Results section.

In addition to random controls, it is informative to include in the comparison agents evolved in the original Hard Maze via a traditional, objective-driven evolutionary algorithm (EA). This *Fitness Control* sheds light on what skills exist in a process that is known to follow an information gradient (i.e. a search process that is clearly not random or exhaustive). Because objective-driven search is less likely to succeed on the Hard Maze, even if run for large numbers of generations [12], we had to conduct 306 runs of the objective-driven EA to obtain 50 hard-maze-solving-networks. Specifically, we run the objective-driven EA until an agent either solves the maze or 2000 generations pass. If the latter occurs, we start a new run. Each generation consists of N evaluations, where N is the population size. As in the original experiment, the population size is 250.

Each treatment has an initial stock of 50 networks. Each of these networks are used to seed the initial population for a Novelty Search process on the new maze.

3.3 Metrics for Measuring Skills

Each of the four treatments starts with an initial, distinct set of 50 networks. For each treatment the ith network is cloned N times to generate an initial population for each run R_i. The population for R_i is then transferred to the new maze to evaluate its inherent exploration ability prior to any further evolution (Fig. 1). Thus, any increased ability to explore in the Novelty Search networks vs. controls suggests the presence of general exploration skills that transferred from one maze to a different one. The R_i population is then further evolved on the new maze with Novelty Search for a predetermined number of generations. Since there is no Goal to cause an early stop to the evolutionary process in the new maze, each run terminates at the final generation, which is 50. Fig. 1 illustrates the entire process.

Every 5 generations, the exploration skills for each treatment are measured via two metrics: Area Covered and Distance Traveled. An example of the Area Covered metric is shown in Fig. 1. In this figure the ith Novelty Search network is first placed in the new maze to examine its baseline exploratory skills. As explained in the preceding paragraph, it is cloned N times to create the initial population for run R_i. The population for run R_i is then further evolved with Novelty Search for 50 generations. Every 5 generations the Area Covered by the N individuals within the current population is calculated.

The curved paths in Fig. 1 show the trajectories of the individuals of R_i at generation g, where g goes from 0 to 50 at intervals of 5. Each trajectory is encoded in a 2×400 vector that represents the x and y positions of a robot over 400 time steps. A 450×450 matrix, initially composed of 0's, is created to represent the Large Maze. The x and y coordinates, originally floating point values, are rounded up to whole integers. For each (x, y) point within the vector trajectories a 1 is recorded on the Large Maze matrix. The percent of 1's to 0's within the Large Maze gives a measure of the area (A_i) covered by the N individuals in the current population for run R_i at generation g. Once the A_i values for each run are calculated the median is obtained as the measure for generation g.

The Distance Traveled metric, like the Area Covered metric, is sampled every 5 generations. Like the Area Covered metric at generation g, the population for run R_i is examined. The Start position and final position for each individual are obtained and the length of the shortest path between these points is calculated. The distance traversed for all N individuals within the current population is averaged to produce D_i, which is the average distance traveled for R_i at generation g. The median D_i, over all 50 runs, is then obtained and used as the measure for generation g.

Figure 3 illustrates the procedure for obtaining the length of the shortest path for four example individuals from R_1 at generation 5. The curved lines represent the robots' trajectories and the dotted lines are the shortest path from the Start position to the final location for these agents. Each agent receives a distance score that is then averaged across all the individuals in the population to produce a single value (A_i) for the run. The A* algorithm is used to measure the shortest path. The length of the shortest path is used instead of the length of the robot trajectory, because the robot could simply go in circles within a small section of the maze. The purpose of the Distance Traveled metric is to see how far away from the Start location the agents get. Since getting away from the Start location involves avoiding collisions and navigating corridors, it is a measure of a robot's exploratory skills.

Length of paths from start location (circle) to end location (checkered flags) for each individual. Distances averaged to produce a single value for each run.

	Length
Robot1	14.4
Robot2	28.3
Robot3	17.8
. . .	
Robot250	24.6
Average	

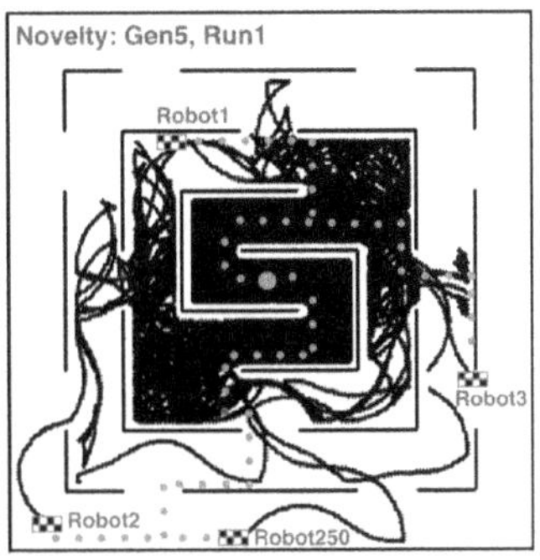

Paths are obtained via an A* algorithm. Maze and all locations were scaled from 450x450 to 90x90 to ease computation.

Figure 3: The Distance Covered Metric. Many robot trajectories (curved lines) are shown. The dotted lines represent the shortest path from the Start location to the final location (via the A* algorithm [13]) for four of the individuals within the population. A* calculates the distance traveled from Start to end so as not to count inefficient loops, while still respecting the walls of the maze (which a straight-line distance would not do). The distance values for all the individuals within the population are averaged to produce a single distance measure for this run.

Lastly to make A* computationally tractable, the maze and locations are scaled from a 450×450 maze to a 90×90 maze. This means that a matrix representing the Large Maze (0's for open space and 1's for walls) is reduced by a factor of 5 ($450 \div 90 = 5$), in the same way that images are shrunk with typical image processing. The Start and final locations for each individual are also scaled by $\frac{1}{5}$.

3.4 Adaptation Test

Aside from measuring general exploratory skills, it is interesting to measure how fast Novelty Search networks can find Goals in new mazes. If the Novelty Search agents posses exploratory skills, they should solve the new tasks faster than the Naive agents, which are starting from scratch.

As in the original experiments [12], agents are placed within a maze and evolved until they find the Goal location or a set number of evaluations elapses. Instead of evolving the treatments on a few different mazes, each with its own Goal, we conducted 14 separate experiments that involved evolving agents on the Large Maze with 14 different Goal locations (Fig. 2). The networks for each treatment begin evolution in the Large Maze for a particular Goal in the same state as they were when transferred from the Hard Maze. In other words, the results for one location do not affect the results for another. The 14 different locations allows us to generate a large sample size of data.

4. RESULTS AND DISCUSSION

4.1 Novelty Search vs. Naive

The results provide three lines of evidence showing that networks evolved with Novelty Search have greater exploration skills than Naive networks.

Second, when further evolved with Novelty Search on the new maze, Novelty Search networks explore significantly more area than Naive networks at every sampled generation (Fig. 6, Left) and travel significantly further than Naive networks in early generations (Fig. 6, Right). These results suggest that Novelty Search on the Hard Maze produces a skill set that gives networks in the Novelty Search treatment a head start for exploring the new maze. While that head start makes a significant difference for many generations, eventually the gap shrinks, suggesting that over time the Naive networks accumulate their own exploratory skills from Novelty Search and begin to catch up in terms of exploration abilities.

Third, when Novelty Search is given a specific target Goal, as in the original experiments [12], Novelty Search networks reach that Goal significantly faster ($p < 0.05$) than Naive networks for a majority of the locations: Figure 7 shows the median number of evaluations until a solution was found, for all the treatments, across 14 different Goal locations within the new maze. For this task a smaller number of evaluations is better (i.e. lower numbers on the plot are better). The Large Maze, with all the Goal locations, is shown in Figure 2 and as the inset of Figure 7.

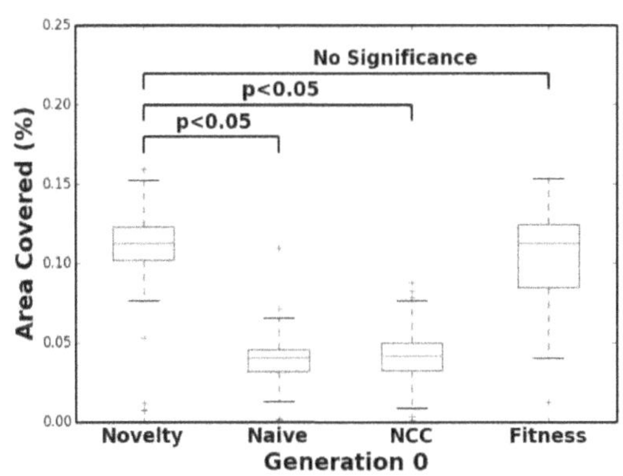

Figure 4: Area Covered on the New Maze Before Further Evolution. The data plotted show the percent area of the maze covered by the networks for the four treatments when they are evaluated in the Large Maze, prior to any further evolution on the Large Maze. Novelty Search networks explore significantly more of the maze than Naive or NCC networks. There is no significant difference in the area covered between Novelty Search networks and those evolved via a traditional, objective-driven evolutionary algorithm.

First, without further evolution, Novelty Search networks cover a significantly larger region than the Naive control (Figs. 4 and 5). Because no further evolution has occurred, and because a memorized trajectory cannot produce the diversity of paths and trajectories observed (Fig. 5), the evidence supports the claim that Novelty Search produces *general* exploration skills during evolution on the Hard Maze.

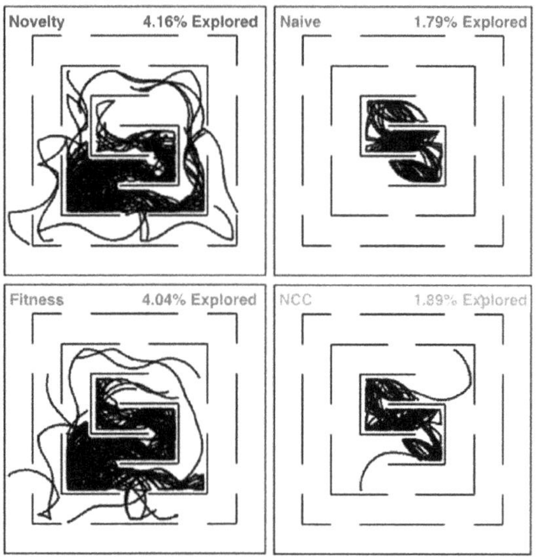

Figure 5: Paths Traveled on the New Maze Prior to Further Evolution. The networks for each treatment are run on the Large Maze without further evolution to evaluate their ability to explore a new environment. Novelty Search and Fitness networks demonstrate the capability to explore more areas of the maze, while Naive and NCC networks tend to stick to the inner sections.

The different target locations are arranged on the bottom axis from left to right, by innermost to outermost. The innermost locations (A and E) are on the far left, and the outermost locations (D, N, M, and L) are on the far right. The results reveal that the further the Goal location is from the Start position, the more evaluations are required to reach the Goal. Consistent with results described above, the longer the evolutionary process takes, the more likely the Naive treatment is to catch up to the Novelty Search treatment: Three of the four Goal locations that do not show a significant difference between Novelty Search networks and Naive networks are at the furthest reaches of the maze. The other Goal without a significant performance difference is near the Start, where substantial exploration skills are not needed to reach it.

4.2 NCC

The Novelty Search treatment significantly outperforms the NCC treatment in all but the last three sampled generations for the Area Covered metric (Fig. 6, Left), all but the last five sampled generations for the Distance Traveled metric (Fig. 6, Right), and all but three locations in the Goal tests in the new maze (Fig. 7). Novelty Search also explored a significantly larger area in the pre-evolution case (Fig. 4). That NCC networks significantly underperform Novelty Search networks is evidence that simply having more neurons and neural connections is not what gives Novelty Search networks the advantage over Naive networks.

Looking closely at the Area metric, Distance metric, and Adaptation tests it can be seen that NCC slightly outperforms Naive. This difference is only significant in generation 0 and generation 5 for the Distance metric, and location H and B in the Adaptation test (significance not shown on plots). While adding more neurons is not enough to bump up NCC's performance so that it is on par with Novelty it does seem to give a slight boost in comparison to Naive.

4.3 Novelty Search vs. Objective-Driven EA

There is no significant difference between the Novelty Search and Fitness treatments in regard to the Area Covered metric (Fig. 6, Left), initial pre-evolution test (Fig. 4), or Adaptation test (Fig. 7). For the Distance Traveled metric, Novelty Search networks significantly outperform Fitness networks at generation 10 and generation 45 (Fig. 6, Right). Since this only happens in two, non-consecutive sampled generations, it is difficult to assign any real weight to the difference. In aggregate, the data suggest that the Fitness and Novelty Search treatments are qualitatively the same (Figs. 4, 6, 7).

The Fitness treatment was created with a traditional, objective-based EA, which is regarded as an algorithm that is non-random and follows an information gradient. That the Novelty Search and Fitness treatments perform equally suggests that Novelty Search is not a random or exhaustive search, but is also encoding information about the world within its evolved solutions.

5. FUTURE WORK

The evidence presented in this paper supports the claim that Novelty Search is not random, but instead instills information (skills) in its solutions. To further test that claim, in future work we will conduct additional tests with new types of mazes. The different types of mazes (e.g. those with curved walls, narrow corridors, and other variations) will be tried both as new mazes to transfer into, new mazes to transfer from, or both. Additionally, we will conduct tests in other problem domains, including those where Novelty Search has already been shown to perform well, such as biped locomotion [12].

Another subject we will explore further is the relationship between the difficulty of domains and the exploration skills that Novelty Search develops. We hypothesize that on more difficult domains that require more skills to explore, Novelty Search will instill much more knowledge that will produce increased exploration abilities in new environments where those skills are also helpful. For example, if a robot was evolved in a house and learned to open doors, go up and down stairs, turn on faucets, etc., then those skills would also likely transfer to office buildings and possibly even to different environments like forests (where stair climbing could provide basic skills that could help on rugged, hilly terrain).

A final interesting subject we plan to study is the difference between skills acquired via Novelty Search and Fitness. It is surprising how similar the exploration skills were for networks evolved under these two very different algorithms. We plan to test whether this similarity holds, or whether there are types of problems on which the skills produced by the two algorithms differ.

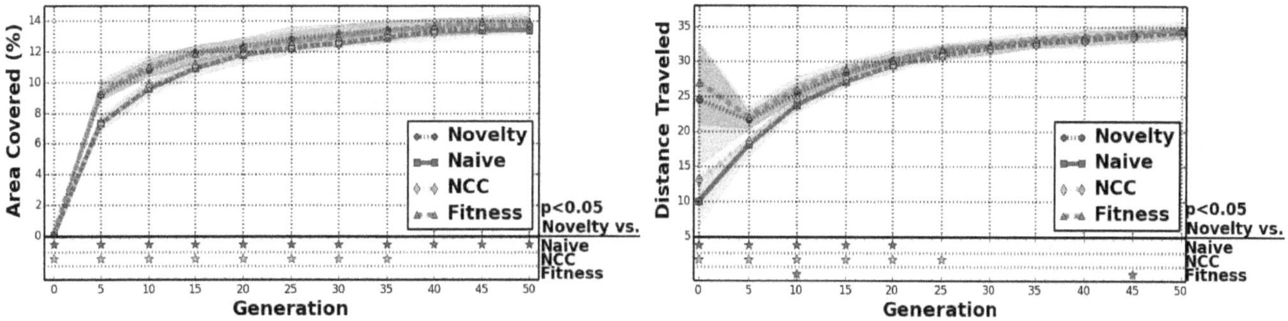

Figure 6: Novelty Search Networks Cover More Area and Travel Further Than Naive Networks. Left: Median area covered by treatments. Both the Novelty Search and Fitness treatments start off exploring more of the maze than Naive or NCC treatments. The Novelty Search treatment is significantly different than Naive for all sampled generations, and significantly different from NCC for all but the last three sampled generations. Right: Median average distance from the Start location. Both Novelty and Fitness start off traveling further than Naive and NCC. Novelty is significantly different from NCC and Naive for about half of the first sampled generations. Note the drop in distance traveled at generation 5 for the networks originally evolved with Novelty Search and the objective-driven EA (Fitness). This drop occurs because areas near the Start have not been explored yet early on, causing a temporary selective pressure to shed skills for traveling far: Recall that all treatments are being further evolved under Novelty Search, which rewards getting to all not-yet-explored places, including those near the Start. Confidence intervals represent $75th$ and $25th$ percentiles. Data are plotted every 5 generations. Asterisks indicate a significant difference ($p < 0.05$) between Novelty Search and the corresponding treatment.

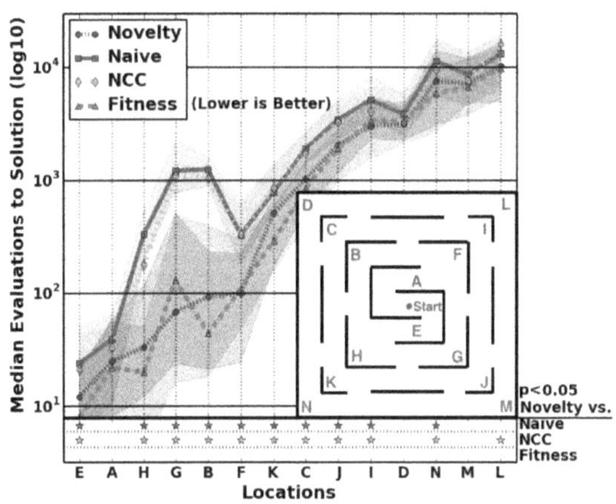

Figure 7: Adaptation Test. Median of number of evaluations for each treatment at the various locations within the Large Maze. Low values are good because it took less time for the treatment to solve the new tasks. For all locations Novelty Search solved the new locations faster than Naive. The different is also significant for all locations except A, D, M, and L. Confidence intervals represent $75th$ and $25th$ percentile.Asterisks indicate a significant difference ($p < 0.05$) between Novelty Search and the corresponding treatment.

6. CONCLUSIONS

The impetus for this study stems from concerns in regards to Novelty Search, which is an algorithm whose usefulness and popularity is slowly growing within the Evolutionary Algorithm community. Many researchers object to Novelty Search's abandonment of the objective. They argue that without a target to direct the evolutionary process, the algorithm is simply either a random search or an exhaustive search. The response by Novelty Search's creators (Lehman and Stanley), which we examine in this study, is that Novelty Search does not search randomly (or exhaustively), but instead that information (skills) relating to exploring the environment accumulate within a population evolved under Novelty Search [11]. If true, the resulting Novelty Search solutions should exhibit exploration skills that generalize to new environments where such skills are useful.

To test this claim we took successful robot controllers evolved with Novelty Search on one maze and transferred them to a different maze. We observed their general exploratory skills in the new maze. When we compared their performance to randomly generated robot controllers, we found a significant increased ability to explore in networks evolved under Novelty Search, suggesting that such agents had indeed acquired some general exploration skills.

Moreover, we compared agents evolved under Novelty Search to those evolved under an algorithm known not to be exhaustive or random, a traditional evolutionary algorithm. We found no significant difference between the two types of controllers, further suggesting that Novelty Search is following an information gradient that encodes information about the environment into its phenotypes.

Overall, our results rebut the argument that Novelty Search is similar to an exhaustive or random search process. Instead, as its creators argue, it is an interesting variant of an evolutionary algorithm well worth continued investigation.

7. ACKNOWLEDGMENTS

We thank Jean-Baptiste Mouret and the members of the Evolving AI Lab, specifically Lucas Helms, Henok Sahilu Mengistu, and Spencer Sharpe.

8. REFERENCES

[1] H. Ceylan and M. G. Bell. Traffic signal timing optimisation based on genetic algorithm approach, including drivers' routing. *Transportation Research Part B: Methodological*, 38(4):329–342, May 2004.

[2] J. Clune, B. Beckmann, C. Ofria, and R. Pennock. Evolving coordinated quadruped gaits with the HyperNEAT generative encoding. In *Proceedings of the IEEE Congress on Evolutionary Computation*, pages 2764–2771, 2009.

[3] J. Clune, K. Stanley, R. Pennock, and C. Ofria. On the performance of indirect encoding across the continuum of regularity. *IEEE Transactions on Evolutionary Computation*, 15(4):346–367, 2011.

[4] G. Cuccu and F. Gomez. When novelty is not enough. In *Applications of Evolutionary Computation*, pages 234–243. Springer, 2011.

[5] D. Floreano and C. Mattiussi. *Bio-inspired artificial intelligence: theories, methods, and technologies*. The MIT Press, 2008.

[6] G. Hornby, J. Lohn, and D. Linden. Computer-automated evolution of an x-band antenna for nasa's space technology 5 mission. *Evolutionary Computation*, 19(1):1–23, 2011.

[7] G. Hornby, S. Takamura, T. Yamamoto, and M. Fujita. Autonomous evolution of dynamic gaits with two quadruped robots. *IEEE Transactions on Robotics*, 21(3):402–410, 2005.

[8] S. Kistemaker and S. Whiteson. Critical factors in the performance of novelty search. In *GECCO*, pages 965–972, 2011.

[9] J. Koza. *Genetic programming IV: Routine human-competitive machine intelligence*. Kluwer, 2003.

[10] S. Lee, J. Yosinski, K. Glette, H. Lipson, and J. Clune. Evolving gaits for physical robots with the hyperneat generative encoding: the benefits of simulation. In *Applications of Evolutionary Computing*. Springer, 2013.

[11] J. Lehman and K. Stanley. Frequently asked questions. http://eplex.cs.ucf.edu/noveltysearch/userspage. Accessed: 2014-01-02.

[12] J. Lehman and K. Stanley. Abandoning objectives: Evolution through the search for novelty alone. *Evolutionary Computation*, 19(2):189–223, 2011.

[13] S. J. Russell, P. Norvig, J. F. Canny, J. M. Malik, and D. D. Edwards. *Artificial intelligence: a modern approach*, volume 74. Prentice hall Englewood Cliffs, 1995.

[14] K. Stanley and R. Miikkulainen. Evolving neural networks through augmenting topologies. *Evolutionary Computation*, 10(2):99–127, 2002.

[15] H. Subramanian, S. Ramamoorthy, P. Stone, and B. J. Kuipers. Designing safe, profitable automated stock trading agents using evolutionary algorithms. *Proceedings of the 8th annual conference on Genetic and evolutionary computation - GECCO '06*, page 1777, 2006.

[16] V. Venkatsubramanian. Computer-aided molecular design using neural networks and genetic algorithms. *Genetic Algorithms in Molecular Modeling*, pages 1–18, 1996.

A Continuous Developmental Model for Wind Farm Layout Optimization

Dennis Wilson
CSAIL - MIT
32 Vassar Street
Cambridge, MA 02139, USA
dennisw@mit.edu

Sylvain Cussat-Blanc
University of Toulouse
IRIT - CNRS - UMR5505
21 allée de Brienne
31042 Toulouse, France
cussat@irit.fr

Kalyan Veeramachaneni
CSAIL - MIT
32 Vassar Street
Cambridge, MA 02139, USA
kalyan@csail.mit.edu

Una-May O'Reilly
CSAIL - MIT
32 Vassar Street
Cambridge, MA 02139, USA
unamay@csail.mit.edu

Hervé Luga
University of Toulouse
IRIT - CNRS - UMR5505
21 allée de Brienne
31042 Toulouse, France
luga@irit.fr

ABSTRACT

We present DEVO-II, an improved cell-based developmental model for wind farm layout optimization. To address the shortcomings of discretization, DEVO-II's gene regulatory networks control cells that act in a continuous rather than discretized grid space. We find that DEVO-II is competitive, and in some cases, superior with respect to state-of-the-art global, stochastic search approaches when a suite of algorithms is evaluated on different wind scenarios. The modularity of the genetic regulatory network computational paradigm in terms of isolating its search algorithm, the regulatory network simulation and the cell simulation, allowed this improvement to largely focus upon cell simulation. This indicates a robustness property of the paradigm's design. As well, wind farm layout optimization highlights how developmental models can be considered more efficient than other optimization methods because of their "optimize once, use-many" adaptability.

Categories and Subject Descriptors

I.2.8 [**Artificial Intelligence**]: Problem Solving

Keywords

Layout optimization; Developmental model; Gene regulatory network; Machine learning

1. INTRODUCTION

Wind farm layout optimization is a complex problem and recent growth of large wind farms has increased demands on designers. Typically, the problem has been cast as a geometric optimization problem, usually on a discrete grid, using a power-based cost function. Direct search approaches have been employed wherein specific constraints of the problem are translated into a predefined fitness function and conditions, e.g. wind speed data and farm dimensions, are inputs. Once this configuration of the algorithm is set up by the wind farm designer, the optimization takes hours or days to converge, and must be run again if the problem changes.

We present a novel approach, DEVO-II, that facilitates wind farm optimization where, once a developmental model is evolved, results are available in a matter of seconds regardless of different constraints and conditions. In [23], we designed a discrete cell-based developmental model, DEVO-I, and obtained encouraging results. This paper, with DEVO-II, represents an improvement on DEVO-I, by casting the developmental model in a continuous space. In general, a cell-based developmental model grows a wind farm layout using cells as an analog for turbines. The cells are each controlled by a gene regulatory network which is trained using a genetic algorithm to find the best turbine efficiency and the best number of turbines. The cells respect the local and global constraints and attempt to position themselves optimally in a representation of the farm environment. To do so, each cell senses the wind coming from various directions and decides what to do: divide, reorient its division or migration heading, migrate, grow, or die. In DEVO-I our farm representation was discrete. With DEVO-II we investigate whether the continuous developmental model produces layouts with comparable quality to state-of-the-art approaches.

GECCO'14, July 12–16, 2014, Vancouver, BC, Canada.
ACM 978-1-4503-2662-9/14/07
http://dx.doi.org/10.1145/2576768.2598383.

2. WIND FARM LAYOUT OPTIMIZATION PROBLEM

The wind farm layout optimization problem is to identify turbine positions in 2-D plane, x, y coordinates, such that the energy capture is maximized while costs associated with a number of other factors are minimized. The energy capture for a turbine takes into account the following:

Wind Scenario: Wind speed, v, represented as a random variable with a Weibull distribution that is a sum-

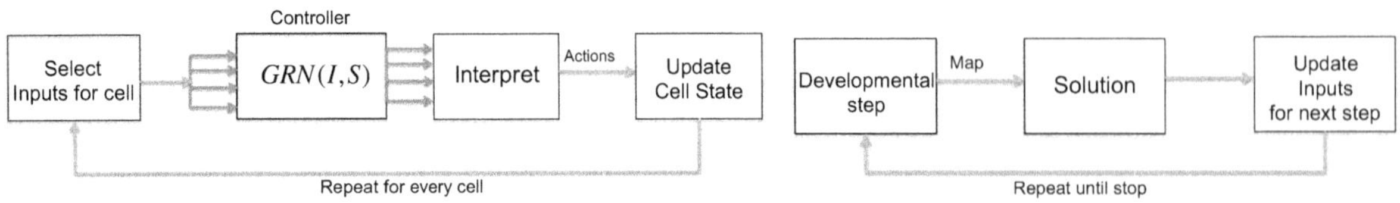

(a) A developmental step
(b) Generation of a solution

Figure 1: Two components of the developmental approach

mary of wind speed at that location for a period of time. This is given by $p_v(v;c,k|\theta)$, where c and k are Weibull shape and scale parameters and θ is a wind directional bin. The wind speed distribution is different for different directional bins, θ. Additionally, wind flows from a certain direction with some probability $p(\theta)$. Together $p_v(v;c,k|\theta)$ and $p(\theta)$ are referred to as wind resource/scenario in this paper.

Power curve: A function $\eta(v)$, known as a *power* curve, gives the power generated by a turbine for the given wind speed v. The power curve is dependent on the turbine make and model.

Wake effects: In a particular directional bin, for a given turbine i located at x_i, y_i a number of other turbines affect the wind it experiences. This is called wake effect. Given other turbines locations x_j, y_j for all $j \in \{1 \dots i-1, i+1 \dots n\}$, the turbines that affect the particular turbine is determined using a *wake* model. This is documented in [14]. If a turbine located at x_i, y_i is in the wake of another turbine located at x_j, y_j in a given direction, the wind speed distribution experienced by the turbine is modified by changing the parameter c resulting in a turbine specific $c_i|\theta$. The value $c_i < c$ is reduced in proportion to the euclidean distance between i and j.

To evaluate the energy capture the objective function calculates the *expected* value of the energy capture for a given wind resource and turbine positions. For a single turbine at position (x_i, y_i), it first determines its modified wind resource for each directional bin based on other turbine positions and then calculates its energy capture using:

$$E = \int_\theta p(\theta) \int_v p_v^\theta(v, c_i, k_i|\theta)\eta(v) \tag{1}$$

Equation 1 evaluates the overall average energy over all wind speeds for a given wind direction, and then averages this energy over all wind directions. Energy is calculated for every turbine and then summed together to give global energy capture. To implement a wake model and reproduce the results there are three options as described in [14] and [19].[1]

To evaluate the efficiency of a wind field, the energy capture is compared to the theoretical maximum energy possible by as many turbines, if they were free of energy decreasing wake effects, resulting in a wake free ratio:

[1]Software that evaluates energy capture given turbine positions and wind resource is available from `https://github.com/d9w/WindFLO`. A competition being organized at GECCO 2014 will result in an open source software release for standardized comparisons.

$$R_{wf} = \frac{E_{tot}}{E_{wf} * n} \tag{2}$$

where R_{wf} is the wake free ratio, E_{tot} is the layout energy output, E_{wf} is the theoretical maximum energy output of one turbine and n is the number of turbines in the layout.

In situations where evaluation of both the efficiency, given by the wake free ratio, and the number of turbines in a field is necessary, in this paper we use the following fitness function:

$$f = \begin{cases} R_{wf} & \text{if } 400 \le n \le 600 \\ R_{wf} * \frac{n}{400} & \text{if } n < 400 \\ R_{wf} * \frac{1200-n}{600} & \text{if } n > 600 \end{cases} \tag{3}$$

where R_{wf} is the wake free ratio of the layout and n is the number of the turbines in the layout. This could be easily replaced by an economic model that pits energy capture against turbine cost.

3. DEVELOPMENTAL APPROACH

In this paper, we develop an approach that works differently than a direct global search method. Our solution to the optimization problem $argmax_X f(X)$ consists of three components:

1. **Definition of a developmental step**: As shown in Figure 1 (a), the model is defined for entities termed *cells* as characterized by their state S. A multi-input, multi-output cell *controller* (GRN in this paper) processes a cell's current *state* information and inputs I derived for the cell to generate its outputs. The *interpreter* uses these *outputs* to create actions for the cell and updates the *state* of the *cell*. This process is repeated for every *cell* and is known as a developmental step.
2. **Generation of a solution** At the end of each *developmental step* a solution is generated and the *inputs* for the controller (on a per cell basis) are derived from the solution. The developmental steps are repeated till a stopping criterion is met. The solution at the conclusion of the last developmental step is the final solution for the design/optimization problem.
3. **Learning the controller structure and parameters**: The problem of optimization then becomes that of learning (or optimizing) the structure and parameters for the controller such that when the developmental process is run it produces the best solution for the problem. When the optimization problem is specified by its scenarios, the developmental model is run for multiple scenarios and average performance is considered when evaluating a controller's efficacy.

Once a controller is learnt, when a new instance of the optimization problem is encountered, the developmental process as described in components 1 and 2 are executed to generate a solution. Note the optimization component (3) does NOT have to be repeated. This is the computational advantage of the developmental approach over any global optimization procedure. Another advantage is that the dimensionality of the controller design problem only scales with its inputs and outputs and not with the dimensionality of the original optimization problem. The efficacy of this methodology is however dependent on the definition of the *cell, state, and its actions*, the *inputs* for the controller and its *outputs* and how they are interpreted. In this paper, we focus on developing these for the wind farm layout optimization problem.

4. LAYOUT OPTIMIZATION - DEVELOPMENTAL MODEL

As explained in the previous section, for the developmental approach we define the cell structure, the state of the cell, the inputs for the controller, the space of outputs and actions of the cells and the mapping between controller outputs and actions of the cell. In this section we describe each of these for the layout optimization problem. In next section we describe the controller followed by a methodology to learn the controller parameters and structure.

Cell definition and State: The cell is a circular structure and a turbine is placed at its center. The *state* of a cell is defined by 5 attributes - θ_m, θ_d, r, cen and b. θ_m and θ_d are continuous values between 0 and 2π that represent the migration and division directions, respectively. r is a continuous value between $R/2$ and R, where R is the minimum possible distance between any two wind turbines, called the security distance, and r represents the cell's radius. Therefore, two cells with minimum radii of $R/2$ each would be R apart and would not be within the security distance. cen is a vector of two continuous values, x_c and y_c, that represent the position of the center of the cell, and therefore the turbine, and are constrained to $[0, w]$ and $[0, h]$, respectively, where w and h are the width and height of the farm. The last state variable, b, is simply a boolean value indicating whether or not the cell is "alive". Dead cells, those with $b = False$, are removed from the layout at the end of each developmental step.

Inputs: The key elements that control the behavior of the cell (which we define below) are the inputs and outputs for the gene regulatory network (the *controller*). DEVO-II's gene regulatory network uses five inputs. For each cell, the wind energy that could be harnessed is calculated for each directional bin. Note that this is influenced by the other turbines in the field (also, positions of other cells). For each cell, the total energy captured at its center is also calculated (the sum of energy capture in all directional bins). Let max_e be the maximum energy capture for any single directional bin among all cells, and let max_E be the maximum total energy capture among all cells. The inputs for a cell are calculated as follow:

1. the maximum energy capture at cen divided by the maximum energy capture for a single directional bin found by any cell, max_e,
2. the direction with the maximum energy capture, divided by 2π,
3. the opposite direction of the maximum energy capture by 2π,
4. the total energy capture for the cell divided by the maximum total energy capture found by any cell, max_E.
5. the percentage of area covered by other cells within a circle of radius $4R$ from cen.

These input proteins are non-trivially different from their predecessors in DEVO-I because they are relative, not absolute. To compute these inputs, we use a wind model, described in §2, that takes into account the inter-turbine interferences. From the initial wind distribution provided by the wind scenario, this model computes the wake generated by the turbines and therefore their energy capture, which allows the relative quantities in 1-4 to be calculated.

Outputs and actions: For our problem we define 12 outputs for the GRN. Four actions are defined for the *cell* as shown in Figure 2. The interpreter uses the outputs and performs the following steps.

1. **Update State:**

   The cell state (orientation vectors and radius) are updated using the concentrations of the proteins o_1, o_2, o_3, o_4, o_5, o_6. o_1 and o_2 are used to update the orientation for division, θ_d, by $\theta_d = \theta_d + (o_1 - o_2)/(o_1 + o_2)$. o_3 and o_4 are used to update the orientation for migration, θ_m, by $\theta_m = \theta_m + (o_3 - o_4)/(o_3 + o_4)$. To optimize their energy capture, the cells can also modify their radii in order to compact or to expand their structure. A cell can increase or decrease its radius, r, by $r = r + (o_5 - o_6)/(o_5 + o_6)$, at each developmental step, within the radius limit $[170.5, 310]$. The minimum value corresponds to the turbine security distance. The maximum one has been chosen empirically to keep the distance between the turbines consistent. The process of updating the *state* of the *cell* is depicted in Figure 2(a).

2. **Choose an action**: 4 outputs $o_7 \ldots o_{10}$ function as cell *action* selectors. Each represents a different action and the action of the one with the highest concentration is selected. We list below the four actions.
   (a) **Divide**: if *divide* is chosen the cell creates a new cell adjacent to it $2r$ apart from its own center in the direction of the orientation θ_d (as shown in Figure 2(d)). The *state* of the new cell is the same as the current cell. When the layout is formed it is assumed that a turbine is at the center of new cell.
   (b) **Wait**: if *wait* is chosen the cell does not do anything (as shown in Figure 2(b)).

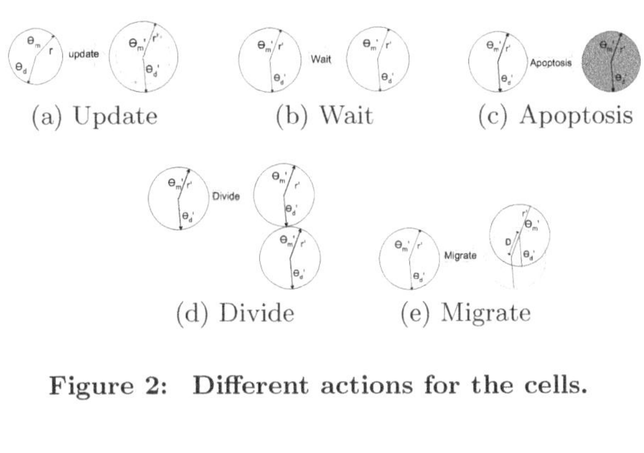

(a) Update (b) Wait (c) Apoptosis (d) Divide (e) Migrate

Figure 2: Different actions for the cells.

(c) **Apoptosis**: if *apoptosis* is chosen the value b in the state is changed to 0 implying that this cell no longer exists.

(d) **Migrate**: if *migrate* is chosen, the *cell*'s center is moved in the direction of θ_m. 2 output proteins o_{11} and o_{12} are used to determine the distance by which the *cell* is moved. It is given by v_m: $v_m = r * o_{11}/(o_{11} + o_{12})$ where r is the cell radius (as shown in Figure 2(e)).

Developmental process and stopping criteria
In each developmental step of the layout growth, each cell updates its radius (size), migration and division directions, chooses an action, and then executes that action. To ensure the turbine security constraint is not violated, a mass-spring-damper system is used [13]. When two cells overlap, a spring links their centers and the mass-spring-damper system repulses the cells along the line joining them while the dampers reduce the possible oscillatory behaviors generated by the springs.

The mass-spring-damper system is run until all constraints are resolved. Mass-spring-damper systems are often uses in artificial developmental model [8, 5, 17] because they are simple and efficient models to simulate cellular dynamics. For our problem, they help constrain the developmental process. After dampening all the cells that, either by division, migration or due to the mass-spring-damper dynamics, move into an invalid position (outside the layout or on an obstacle) are deleted from the layout. This ensures the validity of the final layout.

One last key element of the developmental model is how development is deemed to be complete. One of our stop criterions measures stability to determine the end of the developmental process. After five developmental steps which initiate cell proliferation, the developmental process continues while at least one cell is dividing or moving, either by migration or due to resizing. Another stop criterion caps development at a maximum number of steps (proportional to farm size).

5. A CELL'S CONTROLLER: GRN

As defined in the previous section, the outputs of the GRN control the functioning of an individual cell. In this section we describe the design of the $GRN(I, S)$. In nature, a gene regulatory network (GRN) is a network of proteins that controls the behavior of the cells. In a living organism, a cell has several functions described in its genome. A gene regulatory network controls their expressions by the use of external signals collected from protein sensors localized on the membrane [4]. These signals activate or inhibit the transcription of the genes, which then determines the cell's behavior.

In our model, a similar network of proteins is optimized in order to generate the simulated cells' behaviors. This kind of controller has been used in many developmental models of the literature [10, 5, 2] and to control virtual and real robots [16, 11, 3].

The GRN model used in this work is a simplified computational model of a real gene regulatory network. It has been designed for computational purposes and not to simulate protein interactions. In it, a gene regulatory network is defined as a set of interacting proteins. Each protein has the following properties:

- The protein *identifier*, encoded as an integer between 0 and ε. ε (here equal to 32) can be changed in order to control the precision of the GRN.
- The *enhancer identifier*, encoded as an integer between 0 and ε. The enhancer identifier is used to calculate the enhancing matching factor between two proteins.
- The *inhibitor identifier*, encoded as an integer between 0 and ε. The inhibitor identifier is used to calculate the inhibiting matching factor between two proteins.
- The *type*, which determines if the protein is an *input* protein, whose concentration is given by the environment of the GRN and whose regulates other proteins but is not regulated; an *output* protein, whose concentration is used as an output of the network and which is regulated but does not regulate other proteins; or a *regulatory* protein, an internal protein that regulates and is regulated by other proteins.

The dynamics of the GRN are calculated as follows. First, the affinity of a protein a with another protein b is given by the enhancing factor u^+_{ab} and the inhibiting u^-_{ab}:

$$u^+_{ab} = \varepsilon - |enh_a - id_b| \quad ; \quad u^-_{ab} = \varepsilon - |inh_a - id_b| \qquad (4)$$

where id_j is the identifier, enh_j is the enhancer identifier and inh_j is the inhibitor identifier of protein j.

Then, the proteins are compared two by two using the enhancing and the inhibiting matching factors. For each protein of the network, the global enhancing and inhibiting values are given by the following equations:

$$g_i = \frac{1}{N}\sum_j^N \phi_j e^{\beta(u^+_{ij} - u^+_{max})} \quad ; \quad h_i = \frac{1}{N}\sum_j^N \phi_j e^{\beta(u^-_{ij} - u^-_{max})} \qquad (5)$$

where g_i (resp. h_i) is the enhancing (resp. inhibiting) value for a protein i, N is the number of proteins in the network, ϕ_j is the concentration of protein j and u^+_{max} (resp. u^-_{max}) is the maximum enhancing (resp. inhibiting) matching factor observed. β is a control parameter described hereafter.

The final modification of protein i concentration is given by the following differential equation:

$$\frac{d\phi_i}{dt} = \frac{\delta(g_i - h_i)}{N_\phi} \qquad (6)$$

where N_ϕ is a function that normalizes the output and regulatory protein concentrations to sum to 1.

β and δ are two constants that set up the speed of reaction of the regulatory network. The higher these values, the more sudden the transitions in the GRN. The lower they are, the smoother the transitions.

6. LEARNING THE GRN

The GRN is encoded in a genome to be evolved by a standard genetic algorithm. The genome contains two independent chromosomes. The first is a variable length chromosome of indivisible proteins. Each protein is encoded within three integers between 0 and ε for the three different identifiers: input, output, and regulatory. The variation operators of a standard GA are redefined. *Crossover* consists of exchanging subparts of two different networks. Because proteins are indivisible, the crossover points have to be chosen between two proteins. This ensures the integrity of each

Population size	500
Mutation rate	10%
Crossover rate	75%
Selection	3-player tournament with elitism
Minimum GRN size	5 input proteins + 12 output proteins + 15 regulatory proteins
Maximum GRN size	5 input proteins + 12 output proteins + 50 regulatory proteins

Table 1: Parameters of the genetic algorithm used to train the GRN.

sub-network, and the local connectivity is maintained; only new links between the different sub-networks are created. *Mutation* is applied in three equally probable ways: *mutating an existing protein* by randomly changing one of its three integers, *adding a new protein* randomly generated or *removing one protein* randomly chosen in the network.

The coefficients β and δ presented in the dynamics model are encoded in a second independent chromosome which contains only these values. They are coded with double-precision floats in $[0.5; 2]$ (empirically chosen).

In this work, we have used a master-worker model distributed genetic algorithm in order to reduce the optimization duration. Table 1 presents the parameters used to evolve the gene regulatory network in this experience.

As the developmental process is completely deterministic, running the developmental process only once is sufficient to calculate the fitness of the corresponding wind farm layout. However, to avoid over-specialization on one scenario, this procedure is repeated on three different scenarios and the minimum fitness of all three scenarios is kept as the final fitness. The wind scenarios used to train the regulatory network are described in the supplementary materials as scenarios 1-3, and are available for download as well as part of the aforementioned open source software.

7. COMPARATIVE STUDY

We compare DEVO-II to a set of state-of-the-art layout optimization techniques: a genetic algorithm (GA), Particle Swarm Optimization (PSO), and the Turbine Distribution Algorithm (TDA). We also compare DEVO-II to DEVO-I. After briefly explaining these techniques, which are further detailed in [12, 20, 23], this section presents these comparisons.

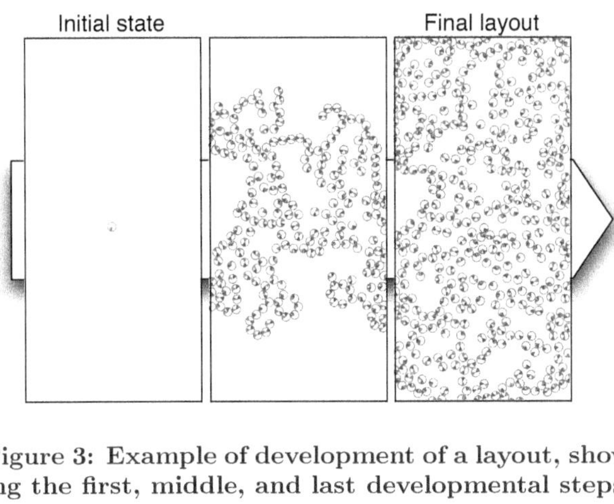

Figure 3: Example of development of a layout, showing the first, middle, and last developmental steps.

7.1 Existing approaches

7.1.1 Genetic algorithm (GA)

Genetic algorithms are commonly used to optimize wind farm layout. The farm area is discretized with a grid [15, 7, 9, 21, 6, 18, 24]. The size of each cell of the grid corresponds to the minimal security distance between 2 turbines. The genetic algorithm then optimizes a binary genome in which each gene represents the presence or absence of a turbine in each cell of the grid. This approach has the advantage of optimizing the number of turbines, but the position of the turbines is not precisely optimized as they are limited to the center of the cell. In the scope of this study, we have implemented our own genetic algorithm. The fitness function used to evaluate each layout is the one presented in equation 2. The genetic algorithm is set up with a population size of 500 individuals, a 3-player tournament selection with elitism, 20% of mutation and 70% of crossover. The genetic algorithm is run for 500 generations, which is sufficient to converge.

7.1.2 Particle swarm optimization (PSO)

In the particle swarm optimization approach, a particle represents a turbine layout by a vector of N (x, y) Cartesian coordinates, where N is the maximum number of turbines[22, 1, 19]. In other words, the PSO search space has 2N dimensions, N being the maximum possible number of turbines. The particle also maintains a memory of the global best position already found in a population of particles. For each iteration of the algorithm, the particles' velocities are calculated according to their own fitness, the position of the current best solution, and nearby particles' positions. The next positions of the particles can be immediately deduced from the velocities. A constraint-repairing algorithm, described in [19], is used to meet the security distance constraint. In this method, starting with an initial turbine, a turbine is added to a layout at position proposed by the particle only if it is not within the security distance to any existing turbine. The PSO is run with each particle on a different thread with a maximum of 1000 turbines, 20 particles, a neighborhood size of 3, and the fitness function 2. The constraint reparation mechanism causes many of the turbines to not enter the layout; 1000 as a maximum was determined empirically to place 400 turbines. The PSO is run for 100 iterations or equivalently 2000 layout evaluations, which is sufficient to converge.

7.1.3 Turbine Distribution Algorithm (TDA)

TDA uses randomized modification of turbine location starting with an initial layout [20]. At each iteration, the best layout is modified by slightly modifying a randomly chosen turbine in the layout and perturbing it to move it away from its closest neighbors in order to minimize the local interferences produced by the turbines. The new layout is compared to the previous best layout using energy output. This process is repeated a sufficient number of iterations to reach an optimal layout. This approach has the advantage of

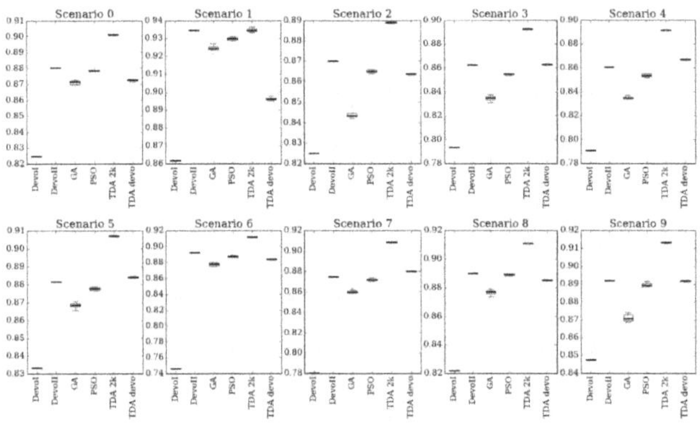

Figure 4: Results of the comparative study of layout optimization approaches. Each approach has been evaluated 8 times on each scenarios.

precisely positioning the turbines in the layout because each turbine position is computed with a high resolution but it requires a high number of layout evaluation (which is computationally expensive) and only works with a fixed number of turbines. This approach is, to our knowledge, the current best approach to optimize a layout with a fixed number of turbines. We have used the Wagner & al. implementation of TDA [20][2], with the number of turbines determined by DEVO-II. First, we run TDA for 2000 iterations, as done in [20], to determine an optimal layout. Then, we compare TDA running for the same number of evaluations as DEVO-II to provide a balanced comparison based on runtime.

7.1.4 *Discrete developmental model (*DEVO-I*)*

DEVO-I is very similar to DEVO-II: cells are controlled by a gene regulatory network to populate a 2-D layout. They use wind velocity input to decide their action: divide, rotate their division clockwise or counterclockwise, wait and die. However, instead of populating a continuous space, the cells are confined to a grid. The size of the grid cells is equal to the security distance, which keeps the layout valid during the developmental process. The GRN is also trained with a genetic algorithm in order to produce the final layout. More details are given in [23]. The GRN has been trained with the fitness function from equation 2 on the same three training scenarios than DEVO-II.

7.2 Results

To evaluate DEVO-II, we compare its results to layouts obtained using DEVO-I, GA, PSO, and TDA on 10 different wind scenarios. DEVO-I and DEVO-II were exposed to 3 of the scenarios during training, but were run without exposure to the other 7. All scenarios are available in the supplementary materials and online. As both DEVO-I and DEVO-II are deterministic once trained, the trained result was run only once on each scenario. The GA, PSO, and TDA were run 8 times on each scenario. Table 2 presents the best results for each method, and figure 4 presents the results of all runs.

First, we compare DEVO-I and DEVO-II. The gain brought by the use of a continuous space is undeniable. The layouts produced by DEVO-II are 7.9% better than the discrete ones, as the use of a continuous space allows DEVO-II to locally optimize the positions of the same number of turbines.

Then, DEVO-II and the GA are compared. With the same fitness function, DEVO-II does better on all scenarios: DEVO-II uses more turbines but has a more efficient layout, getting a higher wake free ratio. Moreover, the number of evaluations is extremely low: 250,000 evaluations for the genetic algorithm in comparison to less than 100 evaluations for DEVO-II. The PSO again displays the advantages of a continuous model when compared to the GA, where it achieves better efficiencies with at least the same number of turbines. However, most likely due to constraint repairing mechanism [19], the PSO doesn't perform as well as DEVO-II or TDA. The number of evaluations necessary for the PSO, 2000, is very costly compared to DEVO-II.

Compared to TDA with 2000 evalutions (TDA 2k), DEVO-II produces solutions with a lower quality: the wake free ratio is 2.79% lower for DEVO-II. However, DEVO-II also optimizes the number of turbines, which is simply reused by TDA to optimize the layout.

To compare DEVO-II to TDA with comparable evaluation conditions, we run TDA with the number of evaluations used by DEVO-II. As shown in the column named "TDA devo" in table 2, DEVO-II produces equivalent solutions in quality to TDA using the number of turbines optimized and the number of evaluations used by DEVO-II.

We use a t-test to compare the results of each method with all others for each scenario. In these t-tests, only two from different methods have $p > 0.05$: in scenario 1, DEVO-II and TDA 2k aren't significantly different, and in scenario 3, DEVO-II and TDA devo aren't significantly different. The t-test was performed over all 8 trials of each approach, where 2 only shows the best result from each trial.

These experiments demonstrate that DEVO-II produces layouts that can compete with TDA in comparable conditions and outperforms GA and PSO. Moreover, DEVO-II can tackle a more complex problem than TDA: the optimization of both the number of turbines and their layout. This property can be useful in the design process of wind farms. In the conclusion, we will discuss the benefits and drawbacks of this approach in the wind farm design process.

8. ADAPTATION TO THE ENVIRONMENT

In our previous work using a discrete developmental model, DEVO-I, to produce the wind farm layouts [23], we briefly show that DEVO-I was able to adapt to changes in the layout size and to obstacles without retraining. Here, we offer a detailed study of DEVO-II's ability to adapt to changes in the layout size and to obstacles.

8.1 Adaptation to the layout size

To show the capacity of DEVO-II to adapt to the layout size, we produce layouts based on the previous wind scenarios but on a small layout (6.2km by 9.61km) and a large one (9.92km by 20.15km). DEVO-II is compared to DEVO-I and TDA with 2000 evaluations. Table 3 shows the results of this study. Both DEVO-I and DEVO-II's results are deterministic, and TDA was run 8 times and the maximum fitness is showed in the table. As in the comparative study, TDA is run with the number of turbines given by DEVO-II.

The same conclusion as in §7 can be made when comparing these approaches, DEVO-I, DEVO-II, and TDA, on the

[2]Since TDA also uses Kusiak's wind model and after cross verifications, the layouts produced by TDA produce the same energy output as the layouts produced by our implementations

Scenario	DEVO-II			DEVO-I			GA			PSO			TDA 2k			TDA devo		
	R_{wf}	#t	#e	R_{wf}	#t	#e	R_{wf}	#t	#e	R_{wf}	#t	#e	R_{wf}	#t	#e	R_{wf}	#t	#e
0	0.880	403	100	0.825	399	*100*	0.873	399	*250k*	0.880	400	*2000*	0.901	*403*	*2000*	0.873	*403*	*100*
1	0.934	408	100	0.862	461	*100*	0.927	400	*250k*	0.928	400	*2000*	0.936	*408*	*2000*	0.898	*408*	*100*
2	0.870	400	100	0.825	406	*100*	0.858	400	*250k*	0.865	405	*2000*	0.890	*400*	*2000*	0.864	*400*	*100*
3	0.857	400	59	0.794	405	*100*	0.838	400	*250k*	0.855	401	*2000*	0.892	*400*	*2000*	0.863	*400*	*59*
4	0.853	399	58	0.791	466	*100*	0.837	399	*250k*	0.851	398	*2000*	0.893	*399*	*2000*	0.863	*399*	*58*
5	0.881	405	100	0.833	403	*100*	0.871	399	*250k*	0.879	404	*2000*	0.908	*405*	*2000*	0.885	*405*	*100*
6	0.892	400	100	0.781	627	*100*	0.880	400	*250k*	0.890	402	*2000*	0.912	*400*	*2000*	0.886	*400*	*100*
7	0.875	402	61	0.780	479	*100*	0.879	400	*250k*	0.871	404	*2000*	0.909	*402*	*2000*	0.881	*402*	*61*
8	0.890	409	62	0.822	523	*100*	0.879	400	*250k*	0.889	404	*2000*	0.911	*409*	*2000*	0.886	*409*	*62*
9	0.891	401	57	0.848	424	*100*	0.874	400	*250k*	0.889	404	*2000*	0.913	*401*	*2000*	0.892	*401*	*57*

Table 2: Maximum results of the comparative study of the wind farm layout optimization approaches. Italic values represents the parameters given to the algorithm, and thus not optimized. Columns are the wake free ratio R_{wf} , the number of turbines #t and the number of layout evaluation #e required to produce the layout.

small and large layouts: TDA achieves optimal results but of the same order of magnitude (on average, TDA is 2.76% better than DEVO-II). This means DEVO-II scales perfectly when the environment configuration changes; it performs the same relative to TDA as it does on the training layout. The number of evaluations is particularly crucial in this experiment, in particular on large layouts; whereas DEVO-II needs less than 4 minutes to produce the layouts, TDA 2k needs nearly one hour for each layout.

8.2 Handling obstacles

DEVO-II can naturally handle obstacles in the environment. This property is crucial since the wind farm design process has to account for possible obstacles such as lakes, roads, buildings, etc. In our approach, an obstacle is designed as a invalid position where the cells are forbidden to go. Here again, no further training is necessary to take this new constraint into consideration: the evolved GRNs can directly produce layouts optimized with the obstacles.

Sc	Size	DEVO-II			DEVO-I			TDA 2k		
		R_{wf}	#t	#e	R_{wf}	#t	#e	R_{wf}	#t	#e
0	small	0.884	248	61	0.817	275	*61*	0.907	*248*	*2000*
1	small	0.940	244	61	0.845	345	*61*	0.945	*244*	*2000*
2	small	0.871	245	41	0.804	275	*61*	0.897	*245*	*2000*
3	small	0.868	242	47	0.796	291	*61*	0.900	*242*	*2000*
4	small	0.857	254	43	0.830	230	*61*	0.893	*254*	*2000*
5	small	0.887	246	61	0.799	345	*61*	0.914	*246*	*2000*
6	small	0.895	248	61	0.772	256	*61*	0.916	*248*	*2000*
7	small	0.878	245	45	0.733	351	*61*	0.916	*245*	*2000*
8	small	0.896	246	52	0.848	254	*61*	0.918	*246*	*2000*
9	small	0.894	247	41	0.813	335	*61*	0.918	*247*	*2000*
0	large	0.879	817	205	0.813	1013	*205*	0.890	*817*	*2000*
1	large	0.922	833	205	0.865	1012	*205*	0.924	*833*	*2000*
2	large	0.860	824	205	0.796	936	*205*	0.876	*824*	*2000*
3	large	0.849	817	79	0.784	1012	*205*	0.881	*817*	*2000*
4	large	0.847	841	87	0.808	786	*205*	0.876	*841*	*2000*
5	large	0.878	817	87	0.817	1013	*205*	0.898	*817*	*2000*
6	large	0.887	824	87	0.743	1013	*205*	0.900	*824*	*2000*
7	large	0.869	819	81	0.793	1010	*205*	0.898	*819*	*2000*
8	large	0.886	814	81	0.837	900	*205*	0.903	*814*	*2000*
9	large	0.879	863	205	0.830	858	*205*	0.899	*863*	*2000*

Table 3: Results of the modification of the farm size. Italic values represent the parameters given to the algorithm, and thus not optimized.

Scenario	No obstacle			Obstacles		
	Size (km^2)	Energy per km^2	# of turb.	Size (km^2)	Energy per km^2	# of turb.
0	98	26,474	403	96.04	28,966	401
1	98	54,640	408	96.04	54,813	402
2	98	19,546	400	96.04	20,253	409
3	98	24,506	400	96.04	25,241	404
4	98	22,064	399	96.04	22,561	399
5	98	32,333	405	96.04	32,558	399
6	98	36,727	400	96.04	38,547	417
7	98	32,730	402	96.04	32,542	391
8	98	37,553	409	96.04	37,240	398
9	98	38,460	401	96.04	39,573	406

Table 4: Obstacle handling with Devo-II

To our knowledge, DEVO-I and DEVO-II are the only approaches that currently tackle this problem. Therefore, to evaluate the quality of the generated layout, we propose a comparison of the energy output per kilometer square available in the environment. We use an initial 7km x 14 km layout size in this study. Table 4 presents the results of this comparison.

The energy per km^2 is very comparable between the layout with and without obstacles. It only differs 2.4% on average on the 10 scenarios. This comparison is conclusive: DEVO-II can adapt to obstacles in environment without modifying the properties of the layout it generates.

9. CONCLUSION

The paper presents a continuous developmental model, DEVO-II, to optimize wind farm layouts. To evaluate this novel approach, we compare it to state-of-the-art techniques in layout optimization. We show that, in comparable conditions, DEVO-II generates layouts with comparable quality to those from state-of-the-art techniques. However, DEVO-II optimizes both the number of turbines and their layout, and can adapt to handle changing layout size and obstacles without retraining. These properties are crucial during the design process of a wind farm.

The main benefit of this approach is its immediate reactivity which is not found in other approaches. The developmental model only needs a few seconds to adapt to new constraints. Therefore, DEVO-II could be an helpful tool for wind farm designers, bearing in mind that the layout process requires a great deal of auxillary input guidance from engineers. DEVO-II could be used as a real-time optimization tool during this design phase. Designers could interact with the cells, constraints, etc. while the cells are optimizing the layout.

Of course, because DEVO-II doesn't currently provide the optimal layout, this tool could be used along with a standard layout optimizer. TDA could be used, for example, to precisely position the final turbines generated by DEVO-II. Our hypothesis is that TDA could optimize this layout faster and potentially better because of DEVO-II, which provides the number of turbines and an efficient starting layout.

Acknowledgement

This work was granted access to the HPC resources of CALMIP under the allocation 2013-1319

10. REFERENCES

[1] S. Chowdhury, J. Zhang, A. Messac, and L. Castillo. Unrestricted wind farm layout optimization (uwflo): Investigating key factors influencing the maximum power generation. *Renewable Energy*, 38(1):16–30, 2012.

[2] S. Cussat-Blanc, J. Pascalie, S. Mazac, H. Luga, and Y. Duthen. A synthesis of the Cell2Organ developmental model. *Morphogenetic Engineering*, 2012.

[3] S. Cussat-Blanc, S. Sanchez, and Y. Duthen. Controlling cooperative and conflicting continuous actions with a gene regulatory network. In *Conference on Computational Intelligence in Games (CIG'12)*. IEEE, 2012.

[4] E. H. Davidson. The regulatory genome: gene regulatory networks in development and evolution. *Academic Press*, 2006.

[5] R. Doursat. Organically grown architectures: Creating decentralized, autonomous systems by embryomorphic engineering. *Organic Computing*, pages 167–200, 2008.

[6] A. Emami and P. Noghreh. New approach on optimization in placement of wind turbines within wind farm by genetic algorithms. *Renewable Energy*, 35(7):1559–1564, 2010.

[7] S. Grady, M. Hussaini, and M. M. Abdullah. Placement of wind turbines using genetic algorithms. *Renewable Energy*, 30(2):259–270, 2005.

[8] P. E. Hotz. Genome-physics interaction as a new concept to reduce the number of genetic parameters in artificial evolution. In *Evolutionary Computation, 2003. CEC'03. The 2003 Congress on*, volume 1, pages 191–198. IEEE, 2003.

[9] H.-S. Huang. Distributed genetic algorithm for optimization of wind farm annual profits. In *Intelligent Systems Applications to Power Systems, 2007. ISAP 2007. International Conference on*, pages 1–6. IEEE, 2007.

[10] M. Joachimczak and B. Wróbel. Evo-devo in silico: a model of a gene network regulating multicellular development in 3d space with artificial physics. In *Proceedings of the 11th International Conference on Artificial Life*, pages 297–304. MIT Press, 2008.

[11] M. Joachimczak and B. Wróbel. Evolving Gene Regulatory Networks for Real Time Control of Foraging Behaviours. In *Proceedings of the 12th International Conference on Artificial Life*, 2010.

[12] S. A. Khan and S. Rehman. Iterative non-deterministic algorithms in on-shore wind farm design: A brief survey. *Renewable and Sustainable Energy Reviews*, 19:370–384, 2013.

[13] V. Komkov. *Optimal control theory for the damping of vibrations of simple elastic systems*. Springer-Verlag Berlin, 1972.

[14] A. Kusiak and Z. Song. Design of wind farm layout for maximum wind energy capture. *Renewable Energy*, 35(3):685–694, 2010.

[15] G. Mosetti, C. Poloni, and B. Diviacco. Optimization of wind turbine positioning in large windfarms by means of a genetic algorithm. *Journal of Wind Engineering and Industrial Aerodynamics*, 51(1):105–116, 1994.

[16] M. Nicolau, M. Schoenauer, and W. Banzhaf. Evolving genes to balance a pole. *Genetic Programming*, pages 196–207, 2010.

[17] B. Porter. A developmental system for organic form synthesis. In *Artificial Life: Borrowing from Biology*, pages 136–148. Springer, 2009.

[18] S. Şişbot, Ö. Turgut, M. Tunç, and Ü. Çamdalı. Optimal positioning of wind turbines on gökçeada using multi-objective genetic algorithm. *Wind Energy*, 13(4):297–306, 2010.

[19] K. Veeramachaneni, M. Wagner, U.-M. O'Reilly, and F. Neumann. Optimizing energy output and layout costs for large wind farms using particle swarm optimization. In *Evolutionary Computation (CEC), 2012 IEEE Congress on*, pages 1–7. IEEE, 2012.

[20] M. Wagner, J. Day, and F. Neumann. A fast and effective local search algorithm for optimizing the placement of wind turbines. *Renewable Energy*, 51(0):64 – 70, 2013.

[21] C. Wan, J. Wang, G. Yang, X. Li, and X. Zhang. Optimal micro-siting of wind turbines by genetic algorithms based on improved wind and turbine models. In *Decision and Control, 2009 held jointly with the 2009 28th Chinese Control Conference. CDC/CCC 2009. Proceedings of the 48th IEEE Conference on*, pages 5092–5096. IEEE, 2009.

[22] C. Wan, J. Wang, G. Yang, and X. Zhang. Optimal micro-siting of wind farms by particle swarm optimization. In *Advances in swarm intelligence*, pages 198–205. Springer, 2010.

[23] D. Wilson, E. Awa, S. Cussat-Blanc, K. Veeramachaneni, and U.-M. O'Reilly. On learning to generate wind farm layouts. In *Proceeding of the fifteenth annual conference on Genetic and evolutionary computation conference*. ACM, 2013.

[24] C. Xu, Y. Yan, D. Y. Liu, Y. Zheng, and C. Q. Li. Optimization of wind farm micro sitting based on genetic algorithm. *Advanced Materials Research*, 347:3545–3550, 2012.

Monotonic Functions in EC: Anything but Monotone!

Sylvain Colin
École Polytechnique
Palaiseau, France

Benjamin Doerr
Laboratoire d'Informatique (LIX)
École Polytechnique
Palaiseau, France

Gaspard Férey
École Polytechnique
Palaiseau, France

ABSTRACT

To understand how evolutionary algorithms optimize the simple class of monotonic functions, Jansen (FOGA 2007) introduced the partially-ordered evolutionary algorithm (PO-EA) model and analyzed its runtime. The PO-EA is a pessimistic model of the true optimization process, hence performance guarantees for it immediately take over to the true optimization process.

Based on the observation that Jansen's model leads to a process more pessimistic than what any monotonic function would, we extend his model by parameterizing the degree of pessimism. For all degrees of pessimism, and all mutation rates c/n, we give a precise runtime analysis of this process. For all degrees of pessimism lower than that of Jansen, we observe a $\Theta(n \log n)$ runtime for the standard mutation probability of $1/n$. However, we also observe a strange double-jump behavior in terms of the mutation probability. For all non-zero degrees of pessimism, there is a threshold $c \in \mathbb{R}$ such that (i) for mutation rates c'/n with $c' < c$ we have a $\Theta(n \log n)$ runtime, (ii) for the mutation rate c/n we have a runtime of $\Theta(n^{3/2})$, and (iii) for mutation rates c''/n with $c'' > c$ we have an exponential runtime.

To overcome the complicated interplay of mutation and selection in the PO-EA, by define artificial algorithms which provably (via a coupling argument) have the same asymptotic runtime, but allow a much easier computation of the drift towards the optimum.

Categories and Subject Descriptors

F.2.2 [**Theory of Computation**]: Analysis of Algorithms and Problem Complexity—*Nonnumerical Algorithms and Problems*

Keywords

Theory; Runtime Analysis; Evolutionary Algorithm; Monotonic Function.

GECCO'14, July 12–16, 2014, Vancouver, BC, Canada.

ACM 978-1-4503-2662-9/14/07 ...$15.00.
http://dx.doi.org/10.1145/2576768.2598338 .

1. INTRODUCTION

The intensive scientific investigation of evolutionary algorithms has greatly increased our understanding of how these algorithms work, which problems they are able to solve, and how good solutions to expect from them. Despite this, some of the very basic problems remain not well understood. One of these is how evolutionary algorithms optimize (strictly) monotonic functions. A function $f : \{0,1\}^n \to \mathbb{R}$ defined on bit-strings of length n is called monotonically increasing if $f(y) > f(x)$ whenever y can be obtained from x by flipping a positive number of zeroes to one (we say that y *dominates* x). Monotonic functions are easily optimized by hill-climbers employing 1-bit mutation (and the optimum $x^* = (1, \ldots, 1)$ is found exactly when each bit initially zero was mutated at least once). However, for evolutionary algorithms employing standard bit mutation, the situation is less clear. In fact, there are monotonic functions where the simple (1+1) evolutionary algorithm ($(1+1)$ EA), however with slightly higher than usual mutation probability $16/n$, needs an exponential time to find the optimum [4]. The reason for this counter-intuitive behavior is that monotonic fitness functions, despite being monotonic, can be (moderately) misleading. An offspring might show a superior fitness despite being further away (in terms of the Hamming distance) from the optimum. The same problem was observed for linear functions previously, however, it could be shown that here this problem only makes the analysis difficult, but not the optimization process (see Section 1.4).

We should add that an understanding of how evolutionary algorithms optimize monotonic functions is not so much desirable because anyone would actually want to do so in practice (as least not after realizing that one is regarding a monotonic function). Besides its interest as an important question of basic research, the motivation for studying this problem is rather that more complicated problems may contain monotonic optimization problems as subproblems. Hence as long as we have difficulties solving these, we have little hope to solve the big problems.

One interesting attempt towards understanding the optimization behavior of evolutionary methods on monotonic functions was made by Jansen [10], who suggested the following pessimistic version of the optimization process of the $(1+1)$ EA on a monotonic function. In this process called *partially ordered EA (PO-EA)*, a run of the $(1+1)$ EA (with standard mutation probability $1/n$) on a monotonic function is simulated. However, in the selection step the better (closer to the optimum) among parent and child is accepted only if it dominates the other. Otherwise, the worse among the two is selected (see Algorithm 1, taking $c = 1$ and $q = 1$, for the precise statement of the process). Hence this process takes the decision of which individual to select for survival to the next generation identical to the optimization process for any monotonic function when there is domination between parent and offspring (note that in this case all monotonic functions lead to the same decision). When there is no domination, there are monotonic functions leading to either decision, and consequently, this pessimistic model chooses the solution farther (in terms of Hamming distance) from the optimum to survive. It hence takes the same decision as a monotonic function that is misleading for these two search points.

For this process, Jansen shows that an expected number of $\Theta(n^{3/2})$ iterations is necessary and sufficient to find the optimum x^*. The PO-EA being a pessimistic version of the (1+1) EA, this result implies that the (1+1) EA finds the optimum of any monotonic function in $O(n^{3/2})$ iterations. No other lower bound for this problem is known than the general bound of $\Omega(n \log n)$ valid for all functions with unique optimum (see Lemma 10 in [6], note that the proof extends from linear functions to all functions having a unique optimum, or Theorem 6 in [13]). Jansen's work does hence not determine the optimization of the $(1+1)$ EA on monotonic functions. Since his analysis of the PO-EA is tight, only two alternatives remain, namely that the PO-EA is a too pessimistic model for any monotonic function, or that indeed there is a not-yet discovered monotonic function with optimization time $\Theta(n^{3/2})$.

1.1 Extending the PO-EA model.

The following simple observation can be seen as a hint that Jansen's PO-EA might be more pessimistic than any $(1+1)$ EA optimization process on a monotonic function. Recall that the PO-EA accepts the worse among parent and offspring whenever there is no domination among the two. It was already noted in [10] that there is no monotonic function leading to the fitness landscape assumed by the PO-EA. We now argue that any monotonic function f leads to a considerable number of solutions x, y such that there is no domination between x and y, y is closer to the optimum than x, and $f(y) > f(x)$. Hence there is a considerable number of pairs (x, y) for which f is not misleading, and consequently, the PO-EA is more pessimistic than the actual optimization process.

Let f be any monotonic function. Consider the three search point $x = (1, 0, 0, x_4, \ldots, x_n)$, $y = (0, 0, 1, x_4, \ldots, x_n)$, and $z = (1, 1, 0, x_4, \ldots, x_n)$. There is no domination between x and y as well as y and z, however z dominates x and consequently $f(z) > f(x)$. For this reason, we cannot have $f(y) < f(x)$ and $f(z) < f(y)$. Hence for at least one of the pairs (x, y) and (y, z), the fitness function f cannot be misleading (that is, it prefers the solution with smaller Hamming distance to the optimum $x^* = (1, \ldots, 1)$. Note that in this example, $x_4, \ldots, x_n$ can be arbitrary bit-values, hence in fact, we have proven the existence of a large number of non-misleading pairs of search points.

Based on this observation, we extend Jansen's PO-EA model by adding a parameter $q \in [0, 1]$ allowing to scale the degree of pessimism. For $q = 1$, we have exactly Jansen's pessimistic PO-EA. For $q = 0$, we have an optimistic process that always prefers the solution closer to the optimum. Note that this process occurs when the (1+1) EA optimizes the classic ONEMAX test function. For $0 < q < 1$, we interpolate between these to extremes. Hence when there is no domination, with probability q we prefer the worse search point, otherwise the one closer to the optimum. In case of domination, we always prefer the dominating solution (as done by any monotonic function). Since [4] indicates that the mutation probability is a crucial parameter when optimizing monotonic functions, we also extend the PO-EA process by allowing a general mutation probability $p = c/n$ for arbitrary $c > 0$. See Algorithm 1 for a precise statement of this process, which we shall call PO-EA(c, q).

1.2 Runtime Analysis for the PO-EA(c, q).

We conduct a rigorous runtime analysis of the PO-EA(c, q) for all $c > 0$ and $q \in [0, 1]$ leading to asymptotically sharp bounds in call cases (for exponential runtimes, we only state that they are exponential). We in particular observe the following:

(i) Whenever the degree of pessimism q is smaller than 1, then the runtime for the standard value $1/n$ of the mutation probability is $\Theta(n \log n)$. This is the same runtime that the $(1+1)$ EA has on ONEMAX. Hence this result together with our non-rigorous reasoning that Jansen's PO-EA is overly pessimistic might indicate that evolutionary algorithms with the often recommended mutation probability of $1/n$ do not have particular difficulties optimizing monotone functions.

(ii) However, for any degree of pessimism $q > 0$, there is a $c > 0$ such that the PO-EA(c, q) has an exponential runtime. Again with the caution that the PO-EA is only a model for the optimization of monotonic functions via evolutionary methods, this result might indicate that even for well-behaved monotonic functions (leading to an optimization process resembling the PO-EA with small degree of pessimism), a large mutation probability can be harmful.

More precisely, our runtime analysis shows that the parameter space of all $(c, q) \in \mathbb{R}_{>0} \times [0, 1]$ can be partitioned into three regions showing a substantially different optimization behavior. When $q < \frac{e^{-c}}{c-1+e^{-c}}$, the optimization time is $\Theta(n \log n)$, see the very end of Section 3.2 and the beginning of Section 3.3. When $q > \frac{e^{-c}}{c-1+e^{-c}}$, the optimization time becomes exponential (Theorem 10). On the thin line $q = \frac{e^{-c}}{c-1+e^{-c}}$ between these two regimes, we have an optimization time of $\Theta(n^{3/2})$, proving this is the heart of Sections 3.2 and 3.3.

Such *double-jump* behaviors (three different asymptotic behaviors touching at a single point or line) have been observed for some random processes, most notable in the evolution of random graphs [7], where the double-jump of the size of the largest component at the edge probability $p = 1/n$ is one of the most famous results (see, e.g., [16]). We are not aware of any double-jump behaviors observed so far in evolutionary computation.

1.3 Methods: Overcoming the Dependencies Imposed by the Mutation-Selection Cycle

In addition to these results, we use analysis methods that might be useful beyond this particular problem. One reason why seemingly simple mutation-based evolutionary algorithms can be surprisingly difficult to analyze are the stochastic dependencies imposed by the alternation of mutation and selection. Mutation itself is fairly simple, among others, because of the large amount of independent randomness used ("flipping each bit independently with the mutation probability p"). For this reason, extremely precise results could be obtained describing not only the expected fitness of mutants, but also higher moments and, in fact, the precise distribution (see, e.g., [2]).

What makes analyzing evolutionary algorithm so hard is the alternation of mutation and selection. The intermediate use of selection destroys the nice properties of sequences of mutation steps alone, stemming from many independent elementary actions like bit-flips. This is made worse by the fact that mutation is acting on the search space structure (bit-strings), but selection is based on the fitness, which might be misleading in the sense that search points structurally closer to the optimum (e.g., smaller Hamming distance) can have a worse fitness.

These difficulties already show up in very elementary analyses like the optimization of linear functions with positive coefficients via the (1 + 1) EA (see the related work subsection below). For optimization processes with even more misleading selection decisions like Jansen's PO-EA, things are even worse. For example, it takes around three pages of impressive calculations in [10] to estimate the expected Hamming distance of the outcome of one mutation-selection cycle (it decreases by $\Theta(z^2/n^2)$, where z is the number of zeros of the parent individual).

We overcome these difficulties by giving slightly modified variants of the PO-EA. They are provably slower or faster than the PO-EA (these proofs are short and natural), consequently lower and upper bounds on their runtime are valid for the PO-EA as well, and they have the property that the expected outcomes of one mutation-selection cycle can be easily computed (e.g., less than half a column for the proof of Theorem 5).

It should be stressed that many proofs in EA theory can be seen as diverting to a modified algorithm. A classic example is obtaining an upper bound for the runtime of the (1 + 1) EA on the OneMax test function by only regarding the effect of one-bit flips [6]. This is equivalent to regarding a modified algorithm that in each iteration with probability $(1 - 1/n)^{n-1}$ flips a single bit uniformly at random and otherwise does nothing. However, we feel that the modified mutation operator (pessimistic mutation in Algorithm 2) and selection operator (optimistic PO selection in Algorithm 3) go beyond the examples seen so far, in particular, with respect to solving the analysis problems imposed by the alternation of mutation and selection.

1.4 Related Results

That runtime analyses for basic evolutionary algorithms optimizing simple-looking problems are crucial for the understanding and the optimal use of evolutionary methods was argued for and demonstrated in [6] in a very influential way. We shall not repeat the whole history of runtime analysis here, but refer to the recent books [1, 11, 14] or the impressive almost 500 scientific works citing [6].

The intensive research on runtimes of evolutionary algorithms shows a strange dichotomy. While for several problems, including combinatorial search and optimization problems, completely satisfying runtime analyses could rigorously be conducted in a single paper, there are some innocent looking results that spurred a long sequence of works. Most prominent among these is the question how long the (1 + 1) EA needs to find the optimum of a pseudo-Boolean linear function. Note that the latter are nothing more than a OneMax function with weights attached to the bits. Despite its simplicity, this problem was investigated in a long sequence of works by various authors (see the last of these, [17], for the whole history). These works invented a number of deep analysis methods that now play a central role in the theory of evolutionary computation, in particular, drift analysis [3, 5, 8, 9]).

Since the class of linear functions is a subclass of the monotonic ones, it comes with no surprise that these are even less understood. In fact, we are not aware of any other results apart from the Jansen's work [10] described above and [4], which shows for the (1 + 1) EA (i) that all monotonic functions are optimized in time $O(n \log n)$ when the mutation probability is c/n with $c < 1$ and (ii) that there are monotonic functions such that a mutation probability of at least $16/n$ results in an exponential runtime. This last result indicates that the class of monotonic functions is more complex than the one of linear functions—for the latter, [3] for the first time showed an optimization time of $O(n \log n)$ for all mutation rates c/n, c a constant.

2. PRELIMINARIES

2.1 Definitions and Notations

For a bit string $x \in \{0,1\}^n$, we refer to the i-th bit in x as $x[i]$. When x and y are two bit strings, we write $x \leq y$ if and only if for all i, $x[i] \leq y[i]$. We write $z(x)$ to denote the number of zero entries of x.

In the study of the following evolutionary algorithms, $X^{(t)}$ refers to the random variable describing the state of the algorithm at time t, which takes its value in $\{0,1\}^n$. $z^{(t)} := z(X^{(t)})$ refers to the random variable counting the number of 0-bits in $X^{(t)}$, hence $z^{(t)}$ takes its value in $\{0, ..., n\}$.

Among the probabilistic tools we use, we remind the reader of the notion of a coupling, which in simple words means nothing more than that we squeeze two probability spaces into one common one in a suitable way. We say that one random variable X stochastically dominates another random variable Y, written as $Y \preceq X$, if for all $r \in \mathbb{R}$ we have $\Pr[Y \leq r] \geq \Pr[X \leq r]$. Note that this implies that there is a coupling such that $Y \leq X$ with probability one. We extensively use drift analysis. We call the (pointwise) drift of a sequence of real-valued random variables $X^{(t)}$ the following quantity depending on x:

$$\mathbb{E}\left[X^{(t)} - X^{(t+1)} \,\middle|\, X^{(t)} = x\right]$$

Many of our results are to be considered asymptotically. We often use inequalities only valid for sufficiently large values of n without noticing that at this point n is to be considered large enough (meaning larger than a certain constant).

2.2 Algorithms Considered

As outlined in the introduction, we extend in this work the PO-EA algorithm introduced in Jansen's article [10] by allowing a general mutation probability c/n (determined by a parameter $c > 0$) and a degree $q \in [0, 1]$ of pessimism, which is the probability that selection is done via the pessimistic PO selection of Jansen's PO-EA and not by the standard selection. See Algorithm 1 for the pseudo-code of this algorithm PO-EA(c, q). Note that PO-EA$(1, 1)$ corresponds to the original PO-EA and PO-EA$(1, 0)$ corresponds to the

(1 + 1) EA using ONEMAX as a fitness function. Later, we shall introduce a pessimistic and an optimistic version denoted by PO-EA$(c,q)^-$ and PO-EA$(c,q)^+$.

Algorithm 1: The partially ordered EA with two parameters $c > 0$ and $0 < q < 1$: PO-EA(c,q)

```
1. Initialization
t := 0. Choose x_t ∈ {0,1}^n uniformly at random.
repeat
    y := x_t

    2. Mutation
    Independently for each bit in y, flip this bit with
    probability c/n

    3. Selection
    With probability q do 3a. else do 3b.

    3.a PO selection
    if
    (y ≥ x_t) ∨ ((y ≰ x_t) ∧ (OneMax(y) ≤ OneMax(x_t))
    then
        x_{t+1} := y
    else
        x_{t+1} := x_t

    3.b Standard selection
    if OneMax(y) ≥ OneMax(x_t) then
        x_{t+1} := y
    else
        x_{t+1} := x_t

    t ← t + 1
until x_t ≠ 1^n
```

We define three domains $\mathcal{C}$, $\mathcal{L}$ and $\mathcal{D}$ to describe the different behaviors allowed by the parameters we introduced.

$$\begin{aligned}\mathcal{C} &:= \{(c,q) \in \mathbb{R}^{+*} \times [0,1] \mid q(c-1) < (1-q)e^{-c}\}\\ \mathcal{L} &:= \{(c,q) \in \mathbb{R}^{+*} \times [0,1] \mid q(c-1) = (1-q)e^{-c}\}\\ \mathcal{D} &:= \{(c,q) \in \mathbb{R}^{+*} \times [0,1] \mid q(c-1) > (1-q)e^{-c}\}\end{aligned}$$

$\mathcal{C}$, $\mathcal{L}$ and $\mathcal{D}$ form a partition of $\mathbb{R}^{+*} \times [0,1]$.

2.3 Some General Results

The following estimates will be useful in our analysis. The proofs are omitted for reasons of space.

LEMMA 1. *For all $c > 0$, there exists a constant $C > 0$ and a positive integer n_0 such that when n is greater than n_0 and z smaller than n, the following hold*

$$\left(1-\frac{c}{n}\right)^n \le e^{-c} \le \left(1-\frac{c}{n}\right)^{n-c}$$

$$\left(1-\frac{c}{n}\right)^{n-z} - e^{-c} \le C\frac{z}{n}$$

$$ce^{-c}\frac{z}{n} \le 1-\left(1-\frac{c}{n}\right)^z \le c\frac{z}{n}$$

and this means that $1-\left(1-\frac{c}{n}\right)^z = \Theta\left(\frac{z}{n}\right)$.

3. ANALYSIS OF THE RUNTIME OF THE PO-EA

We now conduct a rigorous runtime analysis of the PO-EA(c,q). For reason of space, we cannot present all proofs. Since we expect it to be most interesting for the reader to see how we overcome the difficulties of the mutation-selection alteration, we give these proofs for Jansen's original PO-EA in great detail. Naturally, this comes at the price that the remaining results can only be sketched.

3.1 A Pessimistic Version of the PO-EA

To prove an upper bound on the runtime of the PO-EA(c,q), we introduce a pessimistic version of this algorithm, PO-EA$^-(c,q)$, that uses a pessimistic mutation allowing only a single 0-bit to be flipped. We shall prove that this algorithm is slower than the PO-EA(c,q) (in a strong sense), we shall surprisingly easily compute the drift incurred by this algorithm, and from this obtain an upper bound for the runtime of the PO-EA(c,q).

Algorithm 2: The PO-EA$(c,q)^-$, a pessimistic version of the PO-EA.

```
1. Initialization
t := 0. Choose x_t ∈ {0,1}^n uniformly at random.
repeat
    y := x_t

    2. Pessimistic mutation
    for i = 1 .. n do
        if y[i] = 1 then
            Flip this bit with probability c/n
        else if no other 0-bit has been flipped so far
        then
            Flip this bit with probability c/n

    3. Selection
    With probability q do 3a. else do 3b.

    3.a PO selection
    if
    (y ≥ x_t) ∨ ((y ≰ x_t) ∧ (OneMax(y) ≤ OneMax(x_t))
    then
        x_{t+1} := y
    else
        x_{t+1} := x_t

    3.b Standard selection
    if OneMax(y) ≥ OneMax(x_t) then
        x_{t+1} := y
    else
        x_{t+1} := x_t

    t ← t + 1
until x_t ≠ 1^n
```

Algorithm 2 does not allow several 0-bits to be flipped at the same step. More precisely, when 0-bits are flipped in PO-EA(c,q), the PO-EA$^-(c,q)$ would only flip the first of these 0-bits. This seems to be a substantial difference, but we shall see that the upper bound for its runtime coincides (asymptotically) with our lower bound for the PO-EA(c,q), so the loss is not significant. The big advantage of regarding the PO-EA$(c,q)^-$ will be that we can compute two drift measures much easier than for the original PO-EA. This is made possible, among others, by the following great simplification of the selection rule.

LEMMA 2. *During the selection phase of the Algorithm 2, the offspring, y, replaces x_t if and only if one 0-bit has been flipped during mutation.*

Proof. 0-bits are given the chance to be flipped only if no other has been flipped before. Therefore at most one 0-bit can be flipped during the mutation phase. If there is one 0-bit flipped and no 1-bit flipped, the offspring dominates and replaces its parent. If there is one 0-bit flipped and more than one 1-bit flipped, $\text{ONEMAX}(y) \leq \text{ONEMAX}(x_t)$ and the offspring also replaces its parent. Reciprocally, if no 0-bit is flipped during mutation, $y \leq x_t$ and the offspring is discarded or identical to x. □

Of course, for the PO-EA$(c,q)^-$ to be meaningful, we need to show that indeed its runtime gives upper bounds for the runtime of the PO-EA(c,q) we are interested in. This is proven in the following lemma and theorem.

LEMMA 3. *Let $X^{(t)}, \tilde{X}^{(t)} \in \{0,1\}^n$ such that $z(X^{(t)}) \leq z(\tilde{X}^{(t)})$. Let $X^{(t+1)}$ be the outcome of one mutation and selection step of the* PO-EA(c,q) *applied to $X^{(t)}$. Let $\tilde{X}^{(t+1)}$ be the same for the* PO-EA$^-(c,q)$. *Then $z(X^{(t+1)})$ is stochastically dominated by $z(\tilde{X}^{(t+1)})$:*

$$z\left(X^{(t+1)}\right) \preceq z\left(\tilde{X}^{(t+1)}\right).$$

Proof. We use the following coupling of the two probability spaces. With out loss of generality, we may assume that $X^{(t)} \geq \tilde{X}^{(t)}$ (bit-wise). The coupling now consists of assuming that both algorithms try to flip the same bits, that is, we let first the PO-EA(c,q) perform its standard bit mutation (with mutation probability c/n) on $X^{(t)}$. We let then the PO-EA$^-$ perform its mutation in a way that whenever it executes the statement "flip this bit with probability c/n", it actually flips this bit if and only if the PO-EA had flipped this bit. It is easy to see that this is a valid coupling, that is, this mutation operator has the same offspring distribution as the one used in Algorithm 2.

We show that the domination claim holds both when standard selection and when PO selection is applied. For standard selection, we immediately see that $z(\tilde{X}^{(t+1)})$ dominates $z(Y)$ for the search point Y obtained from $\tilde{X}^{(t)}$ by applying standard mutation (with probability c/n). However, that $z(Y)$ dominates $z(X^{(t+1)})$ is a well-known fact (see, e.g., Lemma 6.1 of [17])—whenever the mutation probability is at most $1/2$, then the offspring of a better search point is better (in the strong sense of stochastic domination).

For the case of the PO selection, we now analyze separately three events and show in all cases that $z(X^{(t+1)}) \leq z(\tilde{X}^{(t+1)})$.

- **The PO-EA flips no 0-bits of $X^{(t)}$.** In this case, we have $X^{(t+1)} = X^{(t)}$. If $\tilde{X}^{(t)}$ has the same number of zeroes as $X^{(t)}$, meaning they are in fact equal, then also the PO-EA$^-$ rejects the offspring, that is, $\tilde{X}^{(t+1)} = \tilde{X}^{(t)}$ and thus trivially $z(X^{(t+1)}) \leq z(\tilde{X}^{(t+1)})$.

  If $\tilde{X}^{(t)}$ has more zeroes than $X^{(t)}$, then two cases can occur. If only 0-bits of $\tilde{X}^{(t)}$ are flipped, this mutation is accepted, however, this only reduces the excess zeroes $\tilde{X}^{(t)}$ has, so we still have $z(\tilde{X}^{(t+1)}) \geq z(X^{(t)}) = z(X^{(t+1)})$. If both 0-bits and 1-bits are flipped in $\tilde{X}^{(t)}$, then the PO selection accepts the worse among parent and offspring $\tilde{Y}$. Consequently, $z(\tilde{X}^{(t+1)}) = \max\{z(\tilde{X}^{(t)}), \tilde{Y}\} \geq z(\tilde{X}^{(t)}) \geq z(X^{(t)}) = z(X^{(t+1)})$.

- **The PO-EA flips only 0-bits of $X^{(t)}$, but a positive number.** In this situation, also the PO-EA$^-$ only flips 0-bits of $\tilde{X}^{(t)}$, and due to the pessimistic mutation, it flips exactly one such bit. Since both offspring are accepted, we have $z(X^{(t+1)}) \leq z(\tilde{X}^{(t+1)})$.

- **The PO-EA flips at least one 0-bit and at least one 1-bit of $X^{(t)}$.** Let $\delta_1 \geq 1$ be the number of 1-bits flipped and $\delta_0 \geq 1$ be the number of 0-bits flipped by the PO-EA in $X^{(t)}$. Let $\tilde{\delta}_1$ be the number of 1-bits the PO-EA$^-$ flips in $\tilde{X}^{(t)}$. We have $\tilde{\delta}_1 \leq \delta_1$, but $\delta_1 - \tilde{\delta}_1 \leq z(\tilde{X}^{(t)}) - z(X^{(t)})$. Note also that exactly one 0-bit of $\tilde{X}^{(t)}$ is flipped. Let $\tilde{Y}$ be the outcome of the mutation of $\tilde{X}^{(t)}$. Then we have $z(\tilde{Y}) = z(\tilde{X}^{(t)}) - 1 + \tilde{\delta}_1 \geq z(X^{(t)}) + \delta_1 - 1 \geq z(X^{(t)}) + \delta_1 - \delta_0 = z(X^{(t+1)})$. Since at least one 0-bit of $\tilde{X}^{(t)}$ was flipped, we have $\tilde{X}^{(t+1)} = \tilde{Y}$ by Lemma 2, hence $z(\tilde{X}^{(t+1)}) = z(\tilde{Y}) \geq z(X^{(t+1)})$ as just computed.

□

We easily extend this lemma to random $X^{(t)}$ and $\tilde{X}^{(t)}$, and from this obtain the following strong version of the statement that the PO-EA$^-(c,q)$ is not faster than the PO-EA(c,q).

THEOREM 4. *Consider a run of the* PO-EA(c,q) *leading to a sequence of search points $X^{(t)}_{t\in\mathbb{N}_0}$ and a run of the* PO-EA$^-(c,q)$ *leading to a sequence of search points $\tilde{X}^{(t)}_{t\in\mathbb{N}_0}$. Then for all $t \in \mathbb{N}_0$, we have $z(X^{(t+1)}) \preceq z(\tilde{X}^{(t+1)})$. Consequently, denoting the optimization times of both algorithms by T and $\tilde{T}$ respectively, we have $T \preceq \tilde{T}$. In particular, we have $\mathbb{E}[T] \leq \mathbb{E}[\tilde{T}]$.*

Proof. Lemma 3 immediately extends to random search points as follows: Let $X^{(t)}$ and $\tilde{X}^{(t)}$ be random search points such that their distribution implies $z(X^{(t)}) \preceq z(\tilde{X}^{(t)})$. Then by coupling these distributions in a way that we have $z(X^{(t)}) \leq z(\tilde{X}^{(t)})$ with probability one, we see that $z(X^{(t+1)}) \preceq z(\tilde{X}^{(t+1)})$. Since the initial search points of both algorithms PO-EA(c,q) and PO-EA$^-(c,q)$ are identically distributed, we have $z(X^{(0)}) \preceq z(\tilde{X}^{(0)})$. Consequently, by induction we have $z(X^{(t)}) \preceq z(\tilde{X}^{(t)})$ for all times $t \in \mathbb{N}_0$, our first claim.

This domination statement implies $\Pr[T \leq t] = \Pr[z(X^{(t)}) \leq 0] \geq \Pr[z(\tilde{X}^{(t)}) \leq 0] = \Pr[\tilde{T} \leq t]$ for all $t \in \mathbb{N}_0$, so $\tilde{T}$ stochastically dominates T. □

3.2 An Easy Proof for a Tight Upper Bound on the Running Time

To demonstrate the strength of this new framework most easily, we now conduct an analysis of Jansen's original PO-EA, that is, we take $c = 1$ and $q = 1$. We start by giving a very short computation for the drift of the PO-EA$^-$:= PO-EA$^-(1, 1)$ in terms of the number of zeroes. Recall that the same computation for the PO-EA in [10] was quite technical (around three pages of careful estimates).

THEOREM 5. *The drift of the number of zeroes in the* PO-EA$^-$ *is* $\Theta\left(\frac{z^2}{n^2}\right)$*:*
$\exists C_2 \geq C_1 > 0, \quad \exists n_0 \in \mathbb{N}, \quad \forall n \geq n_0, \quad \forall z \leq n,$

$$C_1 \frac{z^2}{n^2} \leq \mathbb{E}[z^{(t)} - z^{(t+1)} | z^{(t)} = z] \leq C_2 \frac{z^2}{n^2}.$$

Proof. Let $x \in \{0, 1\}^n$. We call z the number of 0-bits in x. When no 0-bit is flipped, the offspring is discarded or is identical to x and the drift is zero. Otherwise, exactly one 0-bit is flipped and by Lemma 2, the offspring is accepted. Hence

$$\begin{aligned}
&\mathbb{E}[\Delta^{(t)} | X^{(t)} = x] \\
&= \mathbb{E}[\Delta^{(t)} | X^{(t)} = x \text{ and one 0-bit is flipped}] \\
&\quad \cdot \mathbb{P}[\text{one 0-bit is flipped}] \\
&= \mathbb{E}[1 - \#\{\text{1-bits flipped}\}] \cdot (1 - (1 - 1/n)^z) \\
&= \left(1 - \frac{n-z}{n}\right) \cdot \Theta\left(\frac{z}{n}\right) = \Theta\left(\frac{z^2}{n^2}\right) .
\end{aligned}$$

□

We note that without greater difficulties, this result can be extended to PO-EA$^-(c, q)$ in the domain $\mathcal{L}$ (details omitted).

Via drift analysis, we obtain the following bound.

THEOREM 6. *For both the* PO-EA$^-$ *and the* PO-EA*, the expectation of the first time* T_k *for which the number of 0-bits reaches* k*, is* $O\left(\frac{n^2}{k+1}\right)$*:*
$\exists C_1^* > 0, \exists n_0 \in \mathbb{N}, \forall n \geq n_0, \forall k \leq n,$

$$\mathbb{E}[T_k] \leq C_1^* \frac{n^2}{k+1}.$$

In particular, when $k = \lfloor \sqrt{n} \rfloor$*, we get that the expected time for the first time,* T_s*, for which the number of 0-bits reaches* $\sqrt{n}$*, is* $O(n\sqrt{n})$*.*

Proof. By the domination result of Theorem 4, we only need to regard the PO-EA$^-$. Hence let us consider a run of the PO-EA$^-$. Let $k \in \{0, ..., n\}$. For all $t \in \mathbb{N}$, let $\chi^{(t)}$ be the random variable taking values in $\{0, ..., n-k\}$ defined by

$$\chi^{(t)} := \max\left\{0, z^{(t)} - k\right\}.$$

Furthermore, let T_k be the random variable that denotes the first point in time $t \in \mathbb{N}$ for which $\chi^{(t)} = 0$. T_k is also the first time t for which $z^{(t)}$ becomes not greater than k.

We are now going to use drift analysis on this sequence of random variables to get an estimation of T_k. The drift of $\chi^{(t)}$ is difficult to compute for the PO-EA, however for the PO-EA$^-$, we know that $z^{(t)}$ can only jump one step forward. Consequently, the drift of $\chi^{(t)}$ is the same as the drift of $z^{(t)}$, and for all $t < T_k$ and all $\chi \in \{1, ..., n-k\}$ we have

$$\begin{aligned}
&\mathbb{E}\left[\chi^{(t)} - \chi^{(t+1)} | \chi^{(t)} = \chi\right] \\
&\geq \mathbb{E}\left[z^{(t)} - z^{(t+1)} | z^{(t)} = \chi + k\right] \\
&\geq e^{-1} \frac{(\chi + k)^2}{n^2} =: h(\chi),
\end{aligned}$$

where h can be defines as a continuous and monotone increasing function $h : \mathbb{R}_0^+ \to \mathbb{R}^+$. Hence Theorem 4.6 (variable drift theorem) from Johannsen's dissertation [12] yields the following.

$$\begin{aligned}
\mathbb{E}[T_s | \chi^{(0)} = \chi] &\leq \frac{1}{h(1)} + \int_1^{\chi} \frac{1}{h(x)} \mathrm{d}x \\
\mathbb{E}[T_k | z^{(0)} = z] &\leq e \frac{n^2}{(k+1)^2} + \int_1^{\max(0, z-k)} e \frac{n^2}{(x+k)^2} \mathrm{d}x \\
&\leq en^2 \left(\frac{1}{(k+1)^2} + \int_{k+1}^{\max(k,z)} \frac{\mathrm{d}x}{x^2}\right) \\
&\leq en^2 \left(\frac{1}{(k+1)^2} + \int_{k+1}^{+\infty} \frac{\mathrm{d}x}{x^2}\right) \\
&\leq en^2 \left(\frac{1}{(k+1)^2} + \frac{1}{k+1}\right) \leq 2e \cdot \frac{n^2}{k+1}.
\end{aligned}$$

□

This result can also be extended to PO-EA$^-(c, q)$ in the domain $\mathcal{L}$ (details omitted).

As in Jansen [10], we now consider the drift in terms of the square root of the number of zeroes, that is, of the sequence of random variables $\zeta^{(t)} := \sqrt{z^{(t)}}$ taking values in $\{0, 1, \sqrt{2}, ..., \sqrt{n}\}$. Again, we shall see that computing the drift, despite the non-standard drift measure, is not overly complicated (again, the corresponding proof in [10] is quite technical).

THEOREM 7. *The drift of* $\zeta^{(t)}$ *is* $\Omega\left(\frac{1}{n\sqrt{z}} + \frac{z\sqrt{z}}{n^2}\right)$*, i.e.,*
$\exists C_3 > 0, \exists n_0 \in \mathbb{N}, \forall n \geq n_0, \forall z \leq n,$

$$\mathbb{E}[\zeta^{(t)} - \zeta^{(t+1)} | \zeta^{(t)} = \sqrt{z}] \geq C_3 \left(\frac{1}{n\sqrt{z}} + \frac{z\sqrt{z}}{n^2}\right)$$

Proof. Let us consider a run of the PO-EA$^-$. Let z be in $\{0, ..., n\}$ and $t \in \mathbb{N}$.

$$\begin{aligned}
&\mathbb{E}\left[\zeta^{(t)} - \zeta^{(t+1)} | \zeta^{(t)} = \sqrt{z}\right] \\
&= \mathbb{E}\Big[\sqrt{z} - \sqrt{z - 1 + \#\{\text{1-bits flipped}\}} \\
&\qquad\qquad | \ z^{(t)} = z \text{ and one 0-bit is flipped}\Big] \\
&\quad \cdot \mathbb{P}[\text{one 0-bit is flipped}] \\
&= \mathbb{E}\left[\sqrt{z} - \sqrt{z + X}\right] \cdot (1 - (1 - 1/n)^z),
\end{aligned}$$

where X is the random variable representing the variation of 0-bits during the mutation at the time t conditioning on the facts that $z^{(t)} = z$ and one 0-bit is flipped.

We already know that $(1-(1-1/n)^z) = \Theta\left(\frac{z}{n}\right)$, hence we focus now on the quantity $\Psi(z) = \mathbb{E}[\sqrt{z} - \sqrt{z+X}]$. We have

$$\begin{aligned}\mathbb{P}[X=-1] &= (1-1/n)^{(n-z)} < 1 \\ \mathbb{P}[X=1] &= \binom{n}{2}\left(\frac{1}{n}\right)^2 (1-1/n)^{(n-z-2)} \\ &\leq \frac{1}{2}(1-1/n)^{(n-z-1)} \\ &= \frac{1}{2(1-1/n)}\mathbb{P}[X=-1] \\ &\leq \mathbb{P}[X=-1] \qquad \text{(assuming } n \geq 2\text{)}.\end{aligned}$$

Let θ be a random variable independent from the others such that $\mathbb{P}[\theta = 1] = \frac{\mathbb{P}[X=1]}{\mathbb{P}[X=-1]} \leq 1$. We now define a particular event $\mathcal{E}$ by

$$\mathcal{E} = \{X = 1\} \cup \{X = -1 \text{ and } \theta = 1\}.$$

Then the following holds:

- $p := \mathbb{P}[X=1] = \mathbb{P}[X=-1 \text{ and } \theta = 1]$ because of the independence of the variables and the construction of θ.
- For all n and z, $e^{-1} \leq p < \frac{1}{2}$.
- Conditioning on $\mathcal{E}$, $X_{|\mathcal{E}}$ becomes a trivial random variable taking the values -1 and 1 with the same probability, $\frac{1}{2}$.
- Hence $\mathbb{E}[X|\mathcal{E}] = 0$.
- $\mathbb{E}[X|\bar{\mathcal{E}}] = \frac{\mathbb{E}[X]}{1-2p}$ deducted from law of total expectation.

Again by the law of total expectation,

$$\begin{aligned}\Psi(z) &= \mathbb{P}[\mathcal{E}] \cdot \mathbb{E}[\sqrt{z} - \sqrt{z+X}|\mathcal{E}] \\ &+ \mathbb{P}[\bar{\mathcal{E}}] \cdot \mathbb{E}[\sqrt{z} - \sqrt{z+X}|\bar{\mathcal{E}}].\end{aligned}$$

We compute

$$\mathbb{E}[\sqrt{z} - \sqrt{z+X}|\mathcal{E}] = \sqrt{z} - \frac{1}{2}\left(\sqrt{z+1} + \sqrt{z-1}\right) \geq \frac{1}{8}z^{-3/2}$$

(some details omitted).

By Jensen's inequality, we have

$$\begin{aligned}&\mathbb{E}[\sqrt{z} - \sqrt{z+X}|\bar{\mathcal{E}}] \\ &= \sqrt{z} - \mathbb{E}[\sqrt{z+X}|\bar{\mathcal{E}}] \geq \sqrt{z} - \sqrt{\mathbb{E}[z+X|\bar{\mathcal{E}}]} \\ &\geq \sqrt{z} - \sqrt{z + \frac{\mathbb{E}[X]}{1-2p}} \geq \sqrt{z}\left(1 - \sqrt{1 + \frac{\frac{n-z}{n} - 1}{z(1-2p)}}\right) \\ &= \sqrt{z}\left(1 - \sqrt{1 - \frac{1}{n(1-2p)}}\right) \geq \frac{\sqrt{z}}{n}\frac{1}{2(1-2p)},\end{aligned}$$

since $\sqrt{1+x} \leq 1 + \frac{1}{2}x$. We now have

$$\Psi(z) \geq \frac{p}{4}z^{-3/2} + \frac{1}{2}\frac{\sqrt{z}}{n} \geq \frac{1}{4e}\left(z^{-3/2} + \frac{\sqrt{z}}{n}\right)$$

and finally there exists $n_0 \in \mathbb{N}$, such that for all $n \geq n_0$ and for all $z \leq n$:

$$\mathbb{E}[\zeta^{(t)} - \zeta^{(t+1)}|\zeta^{(t)} = \sqrt{z}] \geq e^{-1}\frac{z}{n}\Psi(z) \geq \frac{1}{4e^2}\left(\frac{1}{n\sqrt{z}} + \frac{z\sqrt{z}}{n^2}\right).$$

□

This result remains valid for the PO-EA$^-(c,q)$ in the domain $\mathcal{L}$.

THEOREM 8. *The expected runtime, T, of the* PO-EA$^-$ *and the* PO-EA *on the condition that $z^{(0)} \leq \sqrt{n}$ is $O(n\sqrt{n})$.*

Proof. We first notice that the quantity $\frac{1}{n\sqrt{z}} + \frac{z\sqrt{z}}{n^2}$ is minimum for $z = \sqrt{n}$ and equals then $2n^{-5/4}$. Then, we simply use the drift analysis on the sequence of random variables $\zeta^{(t)}$ using this constant bound. We obtain that when $z \leq \sqrt{n}$,

$$\mathbb{E}[T|\zeta^{(0)} = \sqrt{z}] \leq 2e^2\sqrt{z}n^{5/4} \leq 2e^2 n\sqrt{n}.$$

This allows us to conclude that

$$\mathbb{E}[T|z^{(0)} \leq \sqrt{n}] \leq 2e^2 n\sqrt{n}.$$

□

THEOREM 9. *Theorem 6 and Theorem 8 prove that the expected runtime of* PO-EA$^-$ *and* PO-EA *are both* $O(n\sqrt{n})$.

More precisely, when n is large enough,

$$\mathbb{E}[T] \leq 2e^2\, n\sqrt{n}.$$

Details on how this result can be extended to PO-EA$^-(c,q)$ in the domain $\mathcal{L}$ are omitted for reasons of space.

Also, we only briefly note that the $O(n \log n)$ runtime bound for the PO-EA$^-(c,q)$ (and thus the PO-EA(c,q)) in the domain $\mathcal{C}$ follow easily by using multiplicative drift. This has been done for $c < 1$ and the $(1+1)$ EA optimizing monotonic functions in [4]. It is easy to see that the same arguments work for PO-EA$^-(c,q)$ once one computed its drift correctly.

3.3 Lower Bounds on the Running Time

In this section, we give several lower bounds for the expected runtime of the PO-EA(c,q) for different parameter ranges. For reasons of space, the majority of the proofs had to be omitted.

We first observe that, for all constants $c > 0$ and $q \in [0,1]$, the running time of the PO-EA(c,q) is at least $\Omega(n \log n)$. This follows from the classic argument [6] that, due to the coupon collector effect, that many iterations are necessary for the mutation operator to touch at least once each bit which initially was zero. This lower bound is sharp in the domain $\mathcal{C}$.

To prove lower bounds in the other domains, we again introduce a variation of the PO-EA(c,q) to be used as proof tool only. It differs from the original algorithm in its more optimistic selection phase. We call PO-EA$(c,q)^+$ the following Algorithm 3.

The advantage of the PO-EA$(c,q)^+$ is again that we can compute its drift much easier. In a similar vein as for the PO-EA$(c,q)^-$, with details again omitted, we compute

$$\begin{aligned}&\mathbb{E}[\Delta^{(t)}|z^{(t)} = z] \qquad (1)\\ &\leq \left[1 - \left(1 - \frac{c}{n}\right)^z\right] \cdot \\ &\quad \left[q(1-c) + 2cq\frac{z}{n} + (1-q)\frac{z}{n} + (1-q)\left(1 - \frac{c}{n}\right)^{n-z}\right].\end{aligned}$$

Algorithm 3: The optimistic approach: PO-EA$(c,q)^+$

```
1. Initialization
t := 0. Choose x_t ∈ {0,1}^n uniformly at random.
repeat
    y := x_t

    2. Mutation
    Independently for each bit in y, flip this bit with
    probability c/n

    3. Selection
    With probability q do 3a. else do 3b.

    3.a Optimistic PO selection
    if y ≤ x_t then
        x_{t+1} := x_t
    else
        x_{t+1} := y

    3.b Standard selection
    if OneMax(y) ≥ OneMax(x_t) then
        x_{t+1} := y
    else
        x_{t+1} := x_t

    t ← t + 1
until x_t ≠ 1^n
```

From this drift, we deduce an exponential lower bound in the domain $\mathcal{D}$ and an $\Omega(n\sqrt{n})$ lower bound in the domain $\mathcal{L}$ in the following two theorems.

THEOREM 10. *The expected runtime of* PO-EA$(c,q)^+$ *and* PO-EA(c,q) *is exponential in the domain* $\mathcal{D}$.

Proof. Let $(c,q) \in \mathcal{D}$. From (2), we immediately see that there exists $L > 0$ and $C > 0$ such that the drift of the PO-EA$(c,q)^+$, and thus also the PO-EA(c,q), becomes smaller than $-C\frac{z}{n}$ when $z \leq Ln$. The result then follows from the negative drift theorem in Oliveto and Witt [15]. □

THEOREM 11. *The expected runtime of* PO-EA$(c,q)^+$ *and* PO-EA(c,q) *in the domain* $\mathcal{L}$ *are* $\Omega(n\sqrt{n})$.

Proof. We consider one of these algorithms and $(c,q) \in \mathcal{L}$. We follow several steps to prove the result:

(1) First we prove that with high probability, the run of the algorithm falls at least once in the interval $[\sqrt{n}, 2\sqrt{n}]$, and in the following, only consider the run-time from this point on.

(2) We then regard a "fake" algorithm behaving exactly like the one we consider except when $z^{(t)}$ exceeds $3\sqrt{n}$ during the execution, then resets the mutation probability to zero (and thus always creates an offspring identical to the parent). By this, the $O(1/n)$ drift bound stemming from (2) for $z = O(\sqrt{n})$ extends to the whole search space. Using this drift, we deduce an $\Omega(n\sqrt{n})$ running time of the fake algorithm (using the additive drift theorem of [8]). Via Chebyshev's inequality (this seems to be a rarely used argument in runtime analysis), we turn this into the bound that with probability at least 3/4 the fake algorithm is running more than $\varepsilon n\sqrt{n}$ iterations (note that a sub-constant failure probability is not true; for the same reason, the standard Chernoff bound approach does not work here).

(3) Via a similar Chebyshev approach (and again Chernoff bounds seem not to work here), we prove that starting from $z^{(0)} \leq 2\sqrt{n}$, within $\varepsilon n\sqrt{n}$ steps $z^{(t)}$ exceeds $3\sqrt{n}$ only with probability 1/4 or less.

(4) This allows us to conclude that $\mathbb{P}[T \leq \varepsilon n\sqrt{n}] \leq 1/2$. Consequently, $\mathbb{E}[T] \geq \varepsilon n\sqrt{n} \cdot \mathbb{P}[T \geq \varepsilon n\sqrt{n}] \geq (\varepsilon/2)n\sqrt{n} = \Omega(n\sqrt{n})$. □

4. REFERENCES

[1] A. Auger and B. Doerr, editors. *Theory of Randomized Search Heuristics.* World Scientific Publishing, 2011. 360 pages.

[2] J. F. Chicano, A. M. Sutton, L. D. Whitley, and E. Alba. Fitness probability distribution of bit-flip mutation. *CoRR*, abs/1309.2979, 2013.

[3] B. Doerr and L. A. Goldberg. Adaptive drift analysis. *Algorithmica*, 65:224–250, 2013.

[4] B. Doerr, T. Jansen, C. Sudholt, C. Winzen, and C. Zarges. Mutation rate matters even when optimizing monotone functions. *Evolutionary Computation*, 21:1–21, 2013.

[5] B. Doerr, D. Johannsen, and C. Winzen. Multiplicative drift analysis. *Algorithmica*, 64:673–697, 2012.

[6] S. Droste, T. Jansen, and I. Wegener. On the analysis of the (1+1) evolutionary algorithm. *Theor. Comput. Sci.*, 276:51–81, 2002.

[7] P. Erdős and A. Rényi. On the evolution of random graphs. *Magyar Tud. Akad. Mat. Kutató Int. Közl*, 5:17–61, 1960.

[8] J. He and X. Yao. Drift analysis and average time complexity of evolutionary algorithms. *Artif. Intell.*, 127:57–85, 2001.

[9] J. Jägersküpper. Combining Markov-chain analysis and drift analysis - the (1+1) evolutionary algorithm on linear functions reloaded. *Algorithmica*, 59:409–424, 2011.

[10] T. Jansen. On the brittleness of evolutionary algorithms. In *FOGA*, pages 54–69, 2007.

[11] T. Jansen. *Analyzing Evolutionary Algorithms - The Computer Science Perspective.* Natural Computing Series. Springer, 2013.

[12] D. Johannsen. Random combinatorial structures and randomized search heuristics, 2010.

[13] P. K. Lehre and C. Witt. Black-box search by unbiased variation. *Algorithmica*, 64:623–642, 2012.

[14] F. Neumann and C. Witt. *Bioinspired Computation in Combinatorial Optimization.* Springer, 2010.

[15] P. S. Oliveto and C. Witt. Erratum: Simplified Drift Analysis for Proving Lower Bounds in Evolutionary Computation. *ArXiv e-prints*, Nov. 2012.

[16] J. Spencer. The giant component: The golden anniversary. *Not. Am. Math. Soc*, 57:720–724, 2010.

[17] C. Witt. Tight bounds on the optimization time of a randomized search heuristic on linear functions. *Combinatorics, Probability & Computing*, 22:294–318, 2013.

Adaptive-Surrogate based on a Neuro-Fuzzy Network and Granular Computing

Israel Cruz-Vega, Mauricio Garcia, Hugo Jair Escalante
Instituto Nacional de Astrofísica, Óptica y Electrónica.
Computer Science Department
Puebla, 72840, Mexico
isrcruz@ieee.org

ABSTRACT

Surrogate-based methods aim at reducing the evaluation of expensive fitness functions in optimization processes. Several surrogate-based methods for evolutionary optimization have been proposed so far, including those based on granular computing / clustering. Granular computing provides granules as an assemblage of entities arranged together by their similarity, functional or physical adjacency, indistinguishability, coherency, or the like. Techniques like this avoid multiple and unnecessary evaluations of individuals repeatedly. In this paper, with the aim of granular computing as a method of grouping data, such information is exploited to obtain knowledge of the structure and parameters of individuals and then, design a Neuro-Fuzzy network that adapts granules' parameters, providing convergence to acceptable solutions with a reduced number of evaluations of the fitness function. We implement this adaptive surrogate in a genetic algorithm and show its performance using benchmark functions.

Categories and Subject Descriptors

I.2.8 [**Artificial Intelligence**]: Problem Solving—*Heuristic methods*

Keywords

Surrogate Modeling, Neuro-Fuzzy Networks.

1. INTRODUCTION

Traditional optimization is computationally expensive and normally highly susceptible to some issues such as high dimensionality, non-differentiability, non-linearity, highly expensive function calculation, among others. Evolutionary algorithms (EAs) are bio-inspired meta-heuristics that have shown flexibility, adaptability and good performance in an important variety of difficult optimization problems, alleviating some of the above mentioned issues. One of the main drawbacks of EAs is the requirement of the repeated evaluation of the objective function. Clearly, for problems where estimating the objective function is computationally expensive, using an EA may become intractable. Surrogate modeling deals with the construction of approximation models to estimate the performance of a system, and to develop relationships between specific system inputs and outputs.

This paper introduces a surrogate modeling approach called GA - FGNFN: *Genetic-Algorithm based on Fuzzy Granulation and Neuro-Fuzzy Networks.* Under the proposed approach, reduction of fitness evaluations is performed via the construction of fuzzy granules, avoiding the use of multiple fitness evaluations on individuals of similar characteristics. The process of granules' construction provides information to be used by a Neuro-Fuzzy Network, such information includes the number of granules and their positions and widths; which is considered the basic information for training of the network. The network will update the above mentioned parameters every certain number of generations, n, so that, the genetic algorithm will converge to the optimum solution faster, and will reduce the number of fitness evaluations significantly. We evaluate the performance of the proposed method in a suite of benchmark functions. Experimental results show that the proposed approach reduces considerably the number of fitness evaluations without significantly compromising the quality of solutions.

The rest of the paper is organized as follows. Next section reviews related work. Section 3 describes a surrogate model based on fuzzy granules [1] that forms the basis for our proposal. Section 4 introduces the adaptive part of surrogate fuzzy-granules parameters. Section reports numerical results on traditional benchmark functions. Finally, Section 5, outlines conclusions and future work directions.

2. RELATED WORK

Several approaches based on surrogate modeling have been proposed so far. A popular formulation is fitness inheritance or imitation [8, 20, 22, 26], where the fitness of the individual is defined by either their parents or other individuals previously encountered along the search process (fitness is transmitted or inherited). Salami et al. proposed the "fast evolutionary strategy", in which the fitness of a child-individual is the weighted sum of the fitness values from its parents, reliability values are assigned to each new individual, and then the actual fitness function is only evaluated when the reliability value is below a certain threshold [22]. In [20] Reyes-Sierra and Coello incorporated the concept of fitness inheritance into the multi-objective particle swarm optimizer to reduce the number of fitness evaluations. How-

GECCO'14, July 12–16, 2014, Vancouver, BC, Canada.
Copyright 2014 ACM 978-1-4503-2662-9/14/07 ...$15.00.
http://dx.doi.org/10.1145/2576768.2598376.

ever, as shown in [6], the performance of parents may not be a good predictor of their children for sufficiently complex and multi-objective problems, rendering fitness inheritance inappropriate under such circumstances.

Techniques based on universal approximators, whose quality depends on the training data, are based on Artificial Neural Networks (ANN) [9, 11, 14, 17, 24, 25]. In [15], selection of centers in the RBF surrogate model, is done in an unsupervised manner with Learning Vector Quantization (LVQ) and Self-Organizing Maps, this formulation tackles the problem of good generalization, that represents an estimation of objective functions for new individuals.

Adaptive surrogates have been developed in a variety of works, for example, in [34], a hybrid surrogate modeling paradigm is developed where different surrogate models are combined (Kriging, RBF and Extended RBF), the adaptive part is done by contribution of surrogates (working as local models) providing a local measure of accuracy and defining a zone of accuracy determined on the called "crowding distance". In [13] is presented a selection-based criterion with different metrics for measuring the quality of meta-models in EAs, where the evaluation of surrogates is done with Neural Networks, an adaptive scheme is suggested for adapting the number of individuals to be evaluated using the surrogate.

In order to reduce fitness evaluations, a variety of clustering algorithms have been proposed for grouping similar patterns of data [16]. Nevertheless, in practice there are many situations in which the data could be classified as belonging to one cluster almost as well as to another one. The sense of belonging to certain clusters is used via the theory of fuzzy sets, taking advantage of the concept of membership function [4]. Some related works are presented in [2, 10]. In [10] fitness estimation models are based on fuzzy clustering, the objective is to reduce direct evaluations and to keep the diversity of the population and quality of solutions satisfactory. They use Fuzzy c-Means an the adaptive technique is Partitionary Learning Fuzzy Clustering Algorithm, which is unsupervised and able to group data to find an appropriate number of clusters. In [1], Akbarzadeh-T et al. proposed using fitness granulation, via an adaptive fuzzy similarity analysis, to reduce the number of fitness evaluations. A pool of fuzzy granules with Gaussian measures of similarity is built up and the enlargement and shrinkage of granules are adaptive each generation depending on the population fitness, but the position of granules does not change during the search process, we refer this method as GA-AFFG [1].

This paper describes a surrogate modeling approach, called GA-FGNFN, that extends GA-AFFG by incorporating a Neuro-Fuzzy Network that aims at making the granules to better adapt during the search process. As in [1], in our proposed approach reduction of fitness evaluations is performed via the construction of fuzzy granules, avoiding the use of multiple fitness evaluations on individuals of similar characteristics. Opposed to [1], we learn a model that determines how to modify the granules' parameters. In this way, we are able to further reduce the number of evaluations.

3. GA-AFFG SURROGATE MODEL

In order to reduce fitness evaluations, surrogate modeling used in this paper is based on the property of fuzzy granulation, which involves decomposition of the whole into parts [1]. An Information granule (fuzzy sets) formalizes the concept of finite precision representation of objects in real life situation, and reduces the core of an information system (both in terms of objects and features) in a granule universe drawn together by indistinguishability, similarity, proximity and functionality [33]. Granular computing concerns situations in which computation and operations are performed on information granules (clump of similar objects or points). Consequently, it leads to have both data compression and a gain in computation time, since in granular computing computations/operations are performed on granules, rather than on the individual points, so that, the computational effort is greatly reduced. The rest of this section describes a granulation-based technique for surrogate modeling that forms the base of our proposal [1].

3.1 Fuzzy Granules

In the part of granules construction, we initially have a random parent population, $P_i = \{x_1^i, x_2^i, ..., x_t^i\}$, where x_j^i is the jth individual in the ith generation. Conventional fuzzy clustering algorithms initially establish a partition of the universe of discourse with a fixed number of clusters (modifying latter the centers of granules according to the adaptive laws, and satisfying an objective function J) [4]. In this paper, following the main purpose of reducing fitness evaluations, it is desirable to explore the fitness landscape looking for individuals with similar characteristics. Hence, the base algorithm starts by finding a first cluster, and then goes to find the second one, and so on, see Figure 3. This process was introduced in [1]. For comparing new solutions to existing clusters a density function representing a data density measure is constructed; the density measure also describes a Gaussian similarity neighborhood between individuals. The density function is described by the equation,

$$\mu_k\left(x_j^i\right) = \exp\left(-\left(x_j^i - C_k\right)^2 / (\sigma_k)^2\right) \tag{1}$$

for $k = 1, 2, ..., l$ number of fuzzy granules, C_k is the vector of centers values, initially the first individual is chosen as the center of the granule. The fitness of individuals x_j^i is either calculated by computing the exact fitness function or associated with one of the existing granules, this is done according to the threshold measure of closeness[1],

$$\theta^i = \alpha \frac{\min\left\{f\left(x_1^{i-1}\right), f\left(x_2^{i-1}\right), ..., f\left(x_t^{i-1}\right)\right\}}{\bar{f}^{i-1}} \tag{2}$$

where $\bar{f}^i = \sum_{j=1}^{t} \frac{f(x_j^i)}{t}$, and $\alpha > 0$ is a constant of proportionality, $f(\cdot)$ is the real fitness evaluation, the minimal value is due to that the benchmark functions are subjected to be minimized. Then, according to θ, fitness evaluation of individuals is performed as follows,

$$f\left(x_j^i\right) = \begin{cases} f\left(C_k\right) & \text{if } \max\{\mu_k\} > \theta^i \\ f\left(x_j^i\right) & \text{computed by fitness function otherwise} \end{cases} \tag{3}$$

Radius σ_k of each granule is used to control the degree of similarity between individuals, this also determines the decision boundary of fitness evaluation of individuals, so that, the granules can shrink or enlarge in reverse proportion to their fitness,

$$\sigma_k = \gamma \frac{1}{\left(e^{f(C_k)}\right)^\beta} \tag{4}$$

[1]One should note that we have modified the expression for θ^i described in [1] in order to obtain better results.

where $\beta > 0$ is an emphasis operator, and γ is a constant of proportionality that is usually set at 1. Initially, σ_k is larger and then, as the algorithm evolves, fitness evaluations of best individuals will be evaluated in granules of reduced radius in a zone near the optimal solutions. Therefore, equation (4) adapts the width of the granules in order to have more exact fitness computed around individuals who perform very well, and fewer fitness computations around individuals who have poor performance. computational cost.

In order to prevent uncontrolled growth of fuzzy granules, only a pre-specified number of granules, with higher fitness values, will remain during each generation of the algorithm. Fig. 1 shows construction of fuzzy If-Then rules and group in granules for the case of two inputs, one output data pairs.

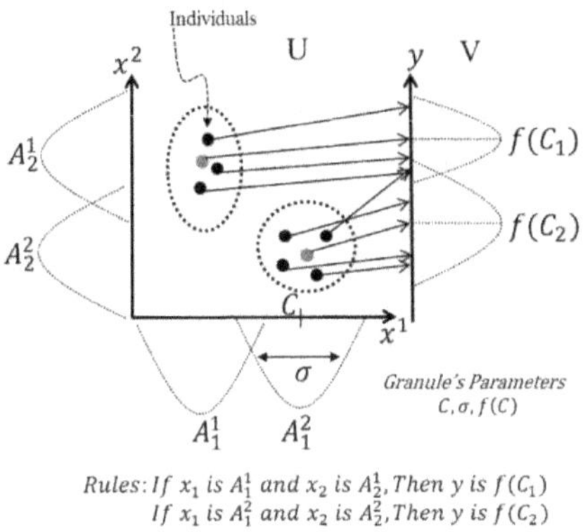

Figure 1: Construction of fuzzy granules with the respective fuzzy rules for two input, one output case

4. NEURO-FUZZY: ADAPTIVE PART

In the first part of the algorithm, using fuzzy granulation property, the number of fitness function evaluations is reduced, this step is realized by the adaptive part of the threshold of similarity between individuals and modifying the radius of each granule by an adaptive law, see Equation (2). This process suggests a reduction of computational cost changing radius of granules, but these do not change in position during the search process. Therefore, properties of mutation and crossover, which let individuals in each generation jump to optimal values, will be enclosed in granules established from the very first generations. In this paper, we propose the use of a Neuro-Fuzzy Network that will adapt free parameters of granules, these parameters are: centers, radius and fitness values of granules. The adaptive part of the granules parameters will be performed every $n-$generations, and not every generation. This is because this could cause an increase of computational time of calculus and an increase in the number of fitness evaluations.

From the last section, we have values of the granules $G = \{C_k, \sigma_k, f(C_k)\}$, where C_k is the $m-$dimensional vector of centers, σ_k is the width of membership functions of the kth fuzzy granule and $f(C_k)$ is the fitness value of granules. The fuzzy system that we are going to design has the following form,

$$f(x) = \frac{\sum_{k=1}^{M} \bar{y}^k \left[\prod_{i=1}^{n} \exp\left(-\left(x_j^i - C_k\right)^2 / (\sigma_k)^2\right)\right]}{\sum_{l=1}^{M} \left[\prod_{i=1}^{n} \exp\left(-\left(x_j^i - C_k\right)^2 / (\sigma_k)^2\right)\right]} \quad (5)$$

where $\mu_k\left(x_j^i\right) = \exp\left(-\left(x_j^i - C_k\right)^2 / (\sigma_k)^2\right)$, represents the fuzzy sets or fuzzy granules, $\bar{y}^k$ is the fitness value of the respective granule $(f(C_k))$, M is fixed and indicates the number of fuzzy rules (fuzzy granules), $\bar{y}^k, C_k$ and σ_k are free parameters. To determine these parameters in some optimal fashion, it is helpful to represent the fuzzy system of granules (5) as a feedforward network. Specifically, the mapping from the input of individuals $x \in U \subset R^n$ to the output of their desired fitness values $f(x)$ can be implemented according to the following operations: first, the input x (individual) is passed through a product Gaussian operator (granule's structure construction) to become $z^k = \prod_{i=1}^{n} \exp\left(-\left(x_j^i - C_k\right)^2 / (\sigma_k)^2\right)$; then, the z^k are passed through a summation operator and a weighted summation operator (current fitness value of the granule) to obtain $b = \sum_{k=1}^{M} z^k$ and $a = \sum_{k=1}^{M} \bar{y}^k z^k$; finally, the output of the fuzzy system is computed as $f(x) = a/b$. This three-stage operation is shown in Fig. 2 as a three-layer feedforward network.

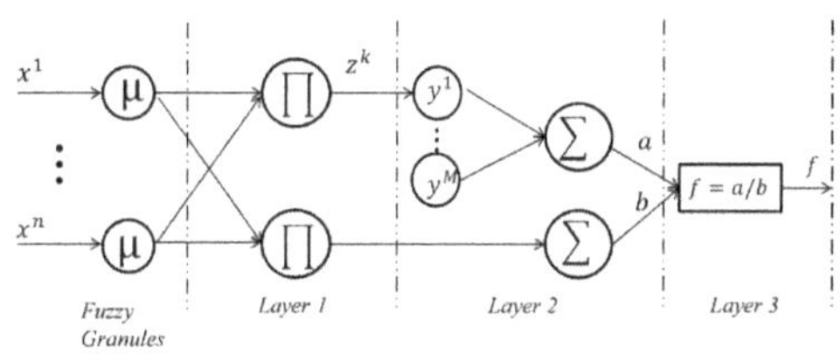

Figure 2: Three-layer feedforward network as a processing unit of fuzzy granules

4.1 Parameter update

Now, the task is updating parameters of the fuzzy granule's system (5), such that the matching error

$$e^p = \frac{1}{2}\left[f(x)^p - y^p\right]^2 \quad (6)$$

is minimized. That is, the task is to determine the parameters $\bar{y}^k, C_k$ and σ_k such that e^p of (6) is minimized. In the sequel, e, f and y will be used to denote $e^p, f(x^p), y^p$, respectively.

In this part, using a gradient descent algorithm to determine the parameters. Specifically, to determine $\bar{y}^k$, is using the algorithm

$$\bar{y}^k(q+1) = \bar{y}^k(q) - \alpha \frac{\partial e}{\partial \bar{y}^k}\Big|_q \quad (7)$$

where $k = 1, ..., M, q = 0, 1, 2, ...,$ and α is a constant step size. If $\bar{y}^k(q)$ converges as q goes to infinity, then from (7) we have $\frac{\partial e}{\partial \bar{y}^k} = 0$ at the converged $\bar{y}^k$, which means that the converged $\bar{y}^k$ is a local minimum of e. From Fig. it is seen that f (and hence e) depend on $\bar{y}^k$ only through a, where $f = a/b, a = \sum_{k=1}^{M} \bar{y}^k z^k, b = \sum_{k=1}^{M} z^k$, and $z =$

$\prod_{i=1}^{n} \exp\left(-\left(x_j^i - C_k\right)^2 / \left(\sigma_k\right)^2\right)$; hence, using the Chain Rule, we have

$$\frac{\partial e}{\partial \bar{y}^k} = (f-y)\frac{\partial f}{\partial a}\frac{\partial a}{\partial \bar{y}^k} = (f-y)\frac{1}{b}z^k \tag{8}$$

Substituting (8) into (7), we obtain the training algorithm for $\bar{y}^k$:

$$\bar{y}^k(q+1) = \bar{y}^k(q) - \alpha\frac{f-y}{b}z^k \tag{9}$$

where $k = 1, 2, ..., M$, and $q = 0, 1, 2, ...$

To determine C_k, we use

$$C_k(q+1) = C_k(q) - \alpha\frac{\partial e}{\partial C_k}|_q \tag{10}$$

we see from Fig. 2 that f (and hence e) depend on C_k only through z^k; hence, using the Chain Rule, we have

$$\frac{\partial e}{\partial c^k} = (f-y)\frac{\partial f}{\partial z^k}\frac{\partial z^k}{\partial c^k} = (f-y)\frac{\bar{y}^k - f}{b}z^k\frac{2\left(x_i^p - c^k\right)}{\sigma_k^2} \tag{11}$$

Substituting (11) into (10), we obtain the training algorithm for C_k :

$$C_k(q+1) = C_k(q) - \alpha\frac{(f-y)}{b}\left(\bar{y}^k(q) - f\right)z^k\frac{2\left(x_i^p - c^k(q)\right)}{\sigma_k^2(q)} \tag{12}$$

Using the same procedure, we obtain the training algorithm for σ_k :

$$\sigma_k(q+1) = \sigma_k(q) - \alpha\frac{\partial e}{\partial \sigma_k}|_q \tag{13}$$

$$= \sigma_k(q) - \alpha\frac{f-y}{b} \tag{14}$$

$$\left(\bar{y}^k(q) - f\right)z^k\frac{2\left(x_i^p - c^k(q)\right)}{\sigma_k(q)}$$

The training algorithm (9), (12) and (14) performs an error back-propagation procedure, that will update parameters of granules like centers, radius and fitness values, providing the genetic algorithm process fast convergence rate as well as lower computational cost.

4.2 Setting-up the training data set

The data set used in the training phase of the Neuro-Fuzzy Network, is obtained from the granules' information of the last generations. The values of centers, width and fitness values of each granule, $G = \{C_k, \sigma_k, f(C_k)\}$ (Figure 1), at generation n-1, are the initial conditions of the network. These parameters will be updated as the weights of the network with the training algorithm. Now, after n-1 generations have passed, and that genetic operations like selection, mutation and reproduction have been performed in each generation, the proposed algorithm selects automatically the best-fitted values of a certain percentage of the last generations of granules, and then, the training data set is set up. The selection of a certain percentage of the best-fitness values is above a 50% or less of the total fitness values of the granules, and is used as the target of the network. This selection of a certain percentage of best-fitness values is related with the "natural selection process" of individuals in the GA, and is realized trying to avoid falling into a local optimum value.

4.3 Algorithm

Now, general steps of the algorithm GA-FGNFN are as follows,

1. An initial random population is created:
   $P_0 = \left\{x_1^1, x_2^1, ..., x_j^1\right\}$, where x_j^i is the jth individual in the ith population

2. Structural information data are obtained from the construction of the fuzzy set of granules (fuzzy partition). The number of fuzzy granules implies the number of rules of the model.

3. Individuals within a pre-specified threshold are evaluated with the center value of the granule, otherwise, construction of a new granule is done with the respective fitness evaluation of the new center.

4. After n number of generations has passed, and genetic operations are performed each generation. Now, parameters of the fuzzy granule structure will be updated with the Neuro-Fuzzy Network and the gradient descent parameter update law. The training data of the Neuro-Fuzzy Network are the centers of granules, width of granules and fitness values of these granules. In this step, fitness function values of granules will be replaced by a certain n_i percent of the total fitness value of granules, replacing by lowest fitness function values or highest values (depending on the maximization or minimization case, respectively). This is the data generated by the granule's process, that will be used as the training data to update the parameters of the Neuro-Fuzzy system.

5. Tuning fuzzy parameters, back-propagating the error through the network and updating each one of the main parameters of granules, that is, centers, radius and fitness values.

6. Perform genetic operations and continue the genetic algorithm process for the next generations until again, update of granule's parameters is required after the pre-specified n number of generations, and until certain stop criteria or total number of generations is achieved.

We can see a flowchart of the GA-FGNFN in Figure 3, the next section reports results of experiments that aim at assessing the effectiveness of the proposed approach.

5. NUMERICAL RESULTS

This section reports experimental results that aim at showing the effectiveness of the GA-FGNFN approach. For the experimental study we considered a set of benchmark functions that comprise a variety of problems with the following characteristics: nonlinearity, unimodality, multimodality, low and high dimensionality [3, 5]. The set of benchmark functions we considered is described in Table 1.

The genetic algorithm in this paper was run with random initial populations, decimal-coded chromosomes, single-point crossover, mutation, fitness scaling, and an elitist stochastic universal sampling selection strategy. Parameters of simulations, percentage of crossover: 1, percentage of mutation: 0.01, population size: 20, and generation size: 100. In these

Function	Formulation
F_1 : De Jong	$\sum_{i=1}^{m} x_i^2$
Dimensions, range	$m = 3, -5.12 \leq x_i \leq 5.12$
F_2 :	$\sum_{i=1}^{m} x_i^4 + Gauss\,(0, 1)$
Dimensions, range	$m = 30, -1.28 \leq x_i \leq 1.28$
F_3 : Michalewicz	$-\sum_{i=1}^{m} \left(\sin(x_i) \cdot \left(\sin\left(\frac{i \cdot x_i^2}{\pi} \right) \right)^{(2 \cdot n)} \right)$
Dimensions, range	$n = 10, m = 10, 0 \leq x_i \leq \pi$
F_4 : Rastrigin	$10 \cdot m + \sum_{i=1}^{m} \left(x_i^2 - 10 \cdot \cos(2 \cdot \pi \cdot x_i) \right)$
Dimensions, range	$m = 20, -5.12 \leq x_i \leq 5.12$
F_5 : Schwefel	$\sum_{i=1}^{m} \left(-x_i \cdot \sin\left(\sqrt{\lvert x_i \rvert} \right) \right)$
Dimensions, range	$m = 20, -500 \leq x_i \leq 500$
F_6 : Griewangk	$1 + \sum_{i=1}^{m} \frac{x_i^2}{4000} - \prod_{i=1}^{m} \cos\left(\frac{x_i}{\sqrt{i}} \right)$
Dimensions, range	$m = 20, -600 \leq x_i \leq 600$

Table 1: The set of benchmark functions used for the performance evaluation of the GA-FGNFN Algorithm

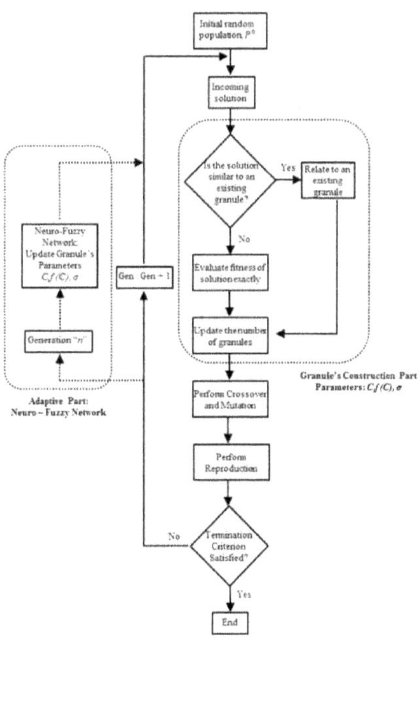

Figure 3: Flowchart of GA-FGNFN Algorithm

simulations, update of parameters of the granules is required every n generations.

We report in each of our experiments the average performance obtained by the different methods over five independent runs. Simulations are compared among the ordinary genetic algorithm (GA) of Matlab, using the same parameters above mentioned; the Genetic Algorithm with Adaptive Fuzzy Fitness Granulation (GA-AFFG) proposed in [1]; and the proposed GA-FGNFN algorithm. It is important to mention that due to the proved efficiency of the Matlab algorithm in GA, GA-AFFG and our proposed algorithm GA-FGNFN, were implemented over the Matlab-GA base algorithm. We report the average of: number of fitness function evaluations, percentage of optimal solutions reached and best fitness value. Also we report the $p-value$ obtained with a paired statistical $t-test$, comparing the performance of the standard GA algorithm and the other variants. Unless otherwise stated the learning rate parameter of the Network was fixed to: 0.1.

Average results of simulations are presented in Table 2. From this table we can see that in terms of reduction of real function evaluations (No. FFE) the proposed method obtains the best performance for all of the considered functions. The decrease of number of evaluations is of about 80% less than simulations with the GA-Matlab algorithm, and about 40% less compared with GA-AFFG. These results are obtained without degrading significantly the quality of the solutions found. The $p-$values of each one of the benchmark functions, shows that there was not a statistically significant difference.

Another point to be analyzed is the question of when to apply the Neuro-Fuzzy Network? Therefore, a comparison table of number of generations in which, when the algorithm should be applied, and reduction in fitness values is presented for the benchmark functions in the Table 3. As before, the main interest is to keep a trade-off between reduction of fitness function evaluations and quality of solutions. The results from Table 3, were obtained by running the GA-FGNFN algorithm every $n = \{5, 10, 20, 30, 50\}$ generations. In the rest of this section we analyze the performance of our method for each of the considered functions making reference to results from both Tables 2 and 3.

Function	Values	GA	GA-AFFG	GA-FGNFN
F_1	No. FFE	2000	268	220
	% Opt. Sol.	80%	80%	80%
	$p-$ value		0.35617	0.45752
	Learning Par.		$\beta = 0.1, \gamma = 1$	$\beta = 0.1, \gamma = 1$ $n = 20, n_i = 100, \mu = 0.1$
	Best-Fitness Value	0.10908	0.1092	0.1144
F_2	No. FFE	2000	730.6	509.8
	% Opt. Sol.	80%	80%	80%
	$p-$ value		0.2505	0.12681
	Learning Par.		$\beta = 0.04, \gamma = 1.7$	$\beta = 0.001, \gamma = 2$ $n = 50, n_i = 100, \mu = 0.1$
	Best-Fitness Value	0.8873	1.4667	1.0795
F_3	No. FFE	2000	750.5	209
	% Opt. Sol.	80%	80%	80%
	$p-$ value		0.17	0.123
	Learning Par.		$\beta = 0.4, \gamma = 1.85$	$\beta = 0.01, \gamma = 1.5$ $n = 50, n_i = 5, \mu = 0.1$
	Best-Fitness Value	−4.3514	−2.08	−2.967
F_4	No. FFE	2000	842	332
	% Opt. Sol.	60%	60%	60%
	$p-$ value		0.4568	0.3654
	Learning Par.		$\beta = 0.004, \gamma = 0.15$	$\beta = 0.004, \gamma = 120$ $n = 50, n_i = 100, \mu = 0.9$
	Best-Fitness Value	103.8504	126.710	109.9558
F_5	No. FFE	2000	945.33	253
	% Opt. Sol.	60%	60%	60%
	$p-$ value		0.2610	0.1456
	Learning Par.		$\beta = 0.0008, \gamma = 300$	$\beta = 0.004, \gamma = 200$ $n = 50, n_i = 100, \mu = 0.1$
	Best-Fitness Value	−3435.37	−3265.49	−3394.5
F_6	No. FFE	2000	863.53	427.6
	% Opt. Sol.	80%	80%	80%
	$p-$ value		0.69206	0.23058
	Learning Par.		$\beta = 0.00012, \gamma = 190$	$\beta = 0.009, \gamma = 100$ $n = 20, n_i = 100, \mu = 0.01$
	Best-Fitness Value	80.8125	105.1937	80.4752

Table 2: Comparison of benchmark functions with a conventional Matlab-GA algorithm, GA-AFFG and GA-FGNFN Algorithms

In the case of F_1 De Jong's and F_2 functions, which are unimodal, good results are obtained in terms of solutions' quality; F_1 is low-dimensional and the neural network can be implemented every 10 generations without modifying the computational time and the quality of solutions; however, in the case of F_2 it is not recommended to constantly apply the neural network due to its high-dimensionality, in this case, the number of evaluations in the learning process of the neural network increase considerably; therefore, we apply the learning process for F_2 each 50 generations.

The F_4 Rastrigin's function is based on De Jong's function with the addition of cosine modulation to produce many local minima, thus, it is highly multi-modal, however, the locations of the minima are regularly distributed. In this case, GA-FGNFN algorithm, presents reduction of the fitness evaluations in about 80% compared with the traditional genetic algorithm, it is recommended to apply the neural network each 50 generations due to the high-nonlinearity and high-dimensionality of the function.

The F_6 Griewangk's function is similar to Rastrigin's function, it has many widespread local minima, however, the locations of the minima are regularly distributed. In this case, the total number of optimal solutions is better in comparison with the other functions, reducing the number of fitness evaluations in a 88%, better results were obtained when the neural network is applied each 20 generations.

For F_3 Michalewicz function, if we apply the neural network each 50 generations, the best results are obtained in terms of percentage of optimal solutions and with a good number of fitness evaluations.

Summarizing, we can say that the proposed approach effectively reduces the number of fitness function evaluations without degrading the quality of solutions. The proposed method outperforms the base approach [1] in terms of reduction of evaluation of the fitness function. We would like to emphasize that in preliminary experimentation we optimized the parameters of the reference approach to have a competitive baseline for our method. Regarding our method, we have to be careful when the dimensionality of data increases, the total number of computing operations also increase and the processes of granule's construction together with the adaptive part, increase in the number of operations

Function	No. of Generations Parameters	$n=5$	$n=10$	$n=20$	$n=30$	$n=50$	GA - Matlab
F_1 :De Jong	No. FFE	1740	259	260	220	295	2000
	% Opt. Sol.	60%	80%	80%	80%	80%	80%
	Best-Fitness Value	1.654	0.1092	0.1144	1.1130	1.6506	0.10908
F_2	No. FFE	2000	460.8	569.2	455.8	440	2000
	% Opt. Sol.	80%	40%	40%	80%	80%	80%
	Best-Fitness Value	1.1706	1.0795	2.2572	1.9965	1.0182	0.8873
F_3 :Michalewicz	No. FFE	119.2	147.2	173	282	381.6	2000
	% Opt. Sol.	60%	60%	60%	40%	80%	80%
	Best-Fitness Value	−2.8510	−2.77	−2.49	−2.6287	−2.967	−4.3514
F_4 :Rastrigin	No. FFE	457	412	370	365	332	2000
	% Opt. Sol.	40%	60%	60%	60%	60%	80%
	Best-Fitness Value	128.3852	116.9746	157.8378	169.5834	109.9558	103.8504
F_5 :Schwefel	No. FFE	288	221	321	367	252.8	2000
	% Opt. Sol.	40%	40%	40%	40%	80%	80%
	Best-Fitness Value	−4786.24	−4293.34	−3987.31	−3897.3	−3394.5	−3435.37
F_6 :Griewangk	No. FFE	414	412	884	1055	964	2000
	% Opt. Sol.	60%	80%	60%	60%	60%	80%
	Best-Fitness Value	111.3852	80.4752	86.3752	105.2752	143.9852	80.8125

Table 3: Different number of generations where the GA-FGNFN was applied, percentage of optimal solutions, and best-fitness value. The last column has the values of GA-Matlab implementation

per generation. In general, we must consider, to modify parameters such as γ which modifies the shrinkage of granules and it is related to having more or less fitness evaluations on granules; the parameter μ, of the neural networks, allows to have the best approximation to the training data but also, it can cause an increase of evaluations when it is lower than the recommended value of 0.1; the last consideration is how many times do we have to apply the neural network, in general, according to the results, it is recommended to apply it 2 times per total number of generations, this is, each 50 generations in our case.

6. CONCLUSIONS

Genetic algorithms produce in each generation individuals with similar characteristics, where the objective is to try to identify those who present better conditions of adaptability and improved performance; this condition is measured by the fitness function. For some problems, estimating the fitness function can be a very time consuming process, slowing the optimization process. Surrogate modeling has been adopted for substituting the real fitness function by approximations obtained by a model.

This paper introduces a surrogate modeling approach based on granular computing and a Neuro Fuzzy Network. Granular computing leads to have data compression, gain in computation time and knowledge extraction of this individual with respective similarities between neighbors. The main idea of this paper is to take advantage of this information and use it to elaborate the structure of an adaptive network, that, according to genetic algorithms objective, will produce a reduction in fitness evaluations and, therefore, a reduction of the computational burden of the process. Our proposal extends a previous model by allowing the adaptation of granules' parameters.

Results of experiments over a suite of classical benchmark functions show the efficiency of the algorithm GA-FGNFN in reduction of fitness evaluations with at least 40 % compared with a standard genetic algorithm without compromising significantly the quality of solutions. The proposed approach also outperformed a state-of-the-art surrogate model based on granular computing. Comparative studies reveal the main importance in keeping a trade-off between reduction of fitness function evaluations and also in percentage of optimal solutions.

Future work directions include implementing a weight-decay approach in order to further improve the adaptation capabilities of our method. Also we are working on the application of the proposed surrogate for highly-complex problems from engineering applications.

7. REFERENCES

[1] M.R. Akbarzadeh-T, M. Davarynejad, and N. Pariz. Adaptive fuzzy fitness granulation for evolutionary optimization. International Journal of Approximate Reasoning, 49(3):523–538, 2008.

[2] J. C. Bezdeck, "Pattern Recognition with Fuzzy Objective Function Algorithms", Kluwer, 1981.

[3] K.A. De Jong, An analysis of the behavior of a class of genetic adaptive systems, Ph.D. Thesis, University of Michigan, 1975.

[4] J. V. De Oliveira, W. Pedrycz, Advances in Fuzzy Clustering and its Applications. John Wiley and Sons, 2007.

[5] J. G. Digalakis, K. G. Margaritis, An experimental study of benchmarking functions for Genetic Algorithms. IEEE International Conference on Systems, Man, and Cybernetics, Vol. 5, pp. 3810–3815, 2002.

[6] E. Ducheyne, B. De Baets, R. deWulf, Is fitness inheritance useful for real-world applications? Evolutionary Multi-Criterion Optimization, LNCS 2631, pp. 31–42 Springer, 2003,.

[7] Chen, S. Billings, P. Grant, Recursive hybrid algorithm for nonlinear system identification using

radial basis function networks, Int. J. Control 55 (1992) 1051–1070.

[8] J.-H. Chen, D. Goldberg, S.-Y. Ho, K. Sastry, Fitness inheritance in multiobjective optimization, in: Proceedings of the 2002 International Conference on Genetic and Evolutionary Computation Conference, pp. 319–326, 2002.

[9] M. Farina. A neural network based generalized response surface multiobjective evolutionary algorithms. IEEE Congress on Evolutionary Computation, pp. 956–961, 2002.

[10] F. M. Filho, F. Gomide, Fuzzy Clustering in Fitness Estimation Models for Genetic Algorithms and Applications, IEEE International Conference on Fuzzy Systems, pp. 1388–1395, 2006.

[11] L. Graening, Y. Jin, and B. Sendhoff. Efficient evolutionary optimization using individual-based evolution control and neural networks: A comparative study. In European Symposium on Artificial Neural Networks, pp. 273-278, 2005.

[12] A.K. Jain, M.N. Murty , and P .J. Flynn. Data clustering: A review. ACM Computing Surveys, 31(3):264-323, 1999.

[13] Jin Y., Hüsken M., Sendhoff B., Quality measures for approximate models in evolutionary computation, Proceedings of GECCO Workshops: Workshop on Adaptation, Learning and Approximation in Evolutionary Computation, pp. 170–174, 2003.

[14] I. C Kampolis, D. I. Papadimitriou, and K. C. Giannakoglou. Evolutionary optimization using a new radial basis function network and the adjoint formulation. Inverse Problems in Science and Engineering, 14:397–410, 2006.

[15] M. K. Karakasis, K. C. Giannakoglou, On the use of Surrogate Evaluation Models in Multi-Objetive Evolutionary Algorithms, European Congress on Computational Methods in Applied Sciences and Engineering, 2004.

[16] H. S. Kim and S. B. Cho, "An efficient genetic algorithms with less fitness evaluation by clustering," IEEE Congress on Evolutionary Computation, pp. 887–894, 2001.

[17] L. Ma, K. Xin, and S. Liu. Using Radial Basis Function Neural Networks to Calibrate Water Quality Model. Proceedings of World Academy of Science, Engineering and Technology, pp. 385–393, 2008.

[18] R. Myers, D. Montgomery, Response Surface Methodology, John Wiley and Sons, 1995.

[19] A. Ratle, "Kriging as a surrogate fitness landscape in evolutionary optimization,"Artif. Intell. Eng. Design Manufact., vol. 15(1):37–49, May 2001.

[20] M. Reyes-Sierra, C.A. Coello, Dynamic fitness inheritance proportion for multiobjective particle swarm optimization, Proceedings of the 8th Annual Conference on Genetic and Evolutionary Computation, 2006.

[21] J. Sacks, W.J. Welch, T.J. Michell, H.P. Wynn, Design and analysis of computer experiments, Statistical Science 4(4):409–435, 1989.

[22] M. Salami, T. Hendtlass, The fast evaluation strategy for evolvable hardware, Genetic Programming and Evolvable Machines 6(2):139–162, 2005.

[23] M. Salami, T. Hendtlass, "A Fitness Estimation Strategy for Genetic Algorithms", 15th Int. Conf. on Industrial and Engineering. Applications of Artificial Intelligence and Expert Systems, Vol. 2358, pp. 319-326, 2002.

[24] A. Schmitz, E. Besnard, and E. Vivies. Reducing the cost of computational fluid dynamics optimization using multilayer perceptrons. In IEEE 2002 World Congress on Computational Intelligence, IEEE.

[25] G. Schneider, W. Schrödl, and G. Wallukat. Peptide design by artificial neural networks and computaer-based evolutionary search. Proceedings of National Academy of Science, 95:12197-12184, 1998.

[26] R. Smith, B. Dike, and S. Stegmann, "Fitness inheritance in genetic algorithms," inProc. ACM Symp. Appl. Comput., pp. 345–350, 1995.

[27] L.X.Wang,Adaptive Fuzzy Systems and Control, Prentice-Hall, Englewood Cliffs, NJ,1994.

[28] G.S.Watson,Smooth regression analysis, Sankhya Ser. A 26 (1964) 101–116.

[29] M. Vijayalakshmi and M. Renuka Devi. A survey of different issues of different clustering algorithms used in large data sets. International Journal of Advanced Research in Computer Science and Software Engineering, 2:305–307, 2012.

[30] Y. Jin, B. Sendhoff, Reducing fitness evaluations using clustering techniques and neural networks ensembles, Proceedings of the Genetic and Evolutionary Computation Conference - GECCO, LNCS 3102 688–699, Springer, 2004.

[31] Y. Jin, "A comprehensive survey of fitness approximation in evolutionary computation,"Soft Comput., vol. 9, no. 1, pp. 3–12, Jan. 2005.

[32] Y. Jin, M. Olhofer, and B. Sendhoff, "On evolutionary optimization with approximate fitness functions," Proc. Genet. Evol. Comput. Conf., 2000, pp. 786–792.

[33] L. F. Zadeh, Toward a theory of fuzzy information granulation and its centrality in human reasoning and fuzzy logic, Fuzzy Sets and Systems, 90(2):111–127, 1997.

[34] Zhang J., Chowdhury S., Messac A., An Adaptive Hybrid Surrogate Model, Structural and Multidisciplinary Optimization, 46(2):223–238, 2012.

[35] Z. Zhou, Y. S. Ong, P. B. Nair, A. J. Keane, and K. Y. Lum, Combining global and local surrogate models to accelerate evolutionary optimization, IEEE Trans. Syst., Man, Cybern. C, 37(1):66–76, 2007.

Unbiased Black-Box Complexities of Jump Functions—How to Cross Large Plateaus

Benjamin Doerr
École Polytechnique,
Paris-Saclay, France

Carola Doerr
CNRS & Univ. Pierre et Marie Curie
Paris, France

Timo Kötzing
Friedrich-Schiller-Universität
Jena, Germany

ABSTRACT

We analyze the unbiased black-box complexity of jump functions with large jump sizes.

Among other results, we show that when the jump size is $(1/2 - \varepsilon)n$, that is, only a small constant fraction of the fitness values is visible, then the unbiased black-box complexities for arities 3 and higher are of the same order as those for the simple ONEMAX function. Even for the extreme jump function, in which all but the two fitness values $n/2$ and n are blanked out, polynomial-time mutation-based (i.e., unary unbiased) black-box optimization algorithms exist. This is quite surprising given that for the extreme jump function almost the whole search space (all but a $\Theta(n^{-1/2})$ fraction) is a plateau of constant fitness.

To prove these results, we introduce new tools for the analysis of unbiased black-box complexities, for example, selecting the new parent individual not by comparing the fitnesses of the competing search points, but also by taking into account the (empirical) expected fitnesses of their offspring.

Categories and Subject Descriptors

F.2.2 [**Theory of Computation**]: Analysis of Algorithms and Problem Complexity—*Nonnumerical Algorithms and Problems*

Keywords

Black-Box Complexity; Theory; Run Time Analysis; Evolutionary Computation

1. INTRODUCTION

The analysis of black-box complexities in evolutionary computation aims in several complementary ways at supporting the development of superior evolutionary algorithms. By comparing the run time of currently used randomized search heuristics (RSHs) with the one of an optimal black-box algorithm, it allows a fair evaluation of how good today's RSH are. With specific black-box complexity notions, we can understand how algorithm components and parameters such as the population size, the selection rules, or the sampling procedures influence the run time of RSH. Finally, research in black-box complexity proved to be a source of inspiration for developing new algorithmic ideas that lead to the design of better search heuristics.

In this work, we analyze the unbiased black-box complexity of jump functions, which are observed as difficult for evolutionary approaches because of their large plateaus of constant (and low) fitness. Our results show that, surprisingly, even extreme jump functions that reveal only the three different fitness values 0, $n/2$, and n can be optimized by a mutation-based unbiased black-box algorithm in polynomial time. We introduce new methods that facilitate our analyses. The perhaps most interesting one is a routine that creates a number of samples from which it estimates the distance of the current search point to the fitness layer $n/2$. Our algorithm thus benefits significantly from analyzing some non-standard statistics of the fitness landscape. We believe this to be an interesting idea that should be investigated further. Our hope is that it can be used to design new search heuristics.

1.1 Black-Box Complexity

Black-box complexity studies how many function evaluations are needed in expectation by an optimal black-box algorithm until it queries for the first time an optimal solution for the problem at hand. Randomized search heuristics, like evolutionary algorithms, simulated annealing, and ant colony algorithms, are typical black-box optimizers: they are typically problem-independent and as such they learn about the problem to be solved only by generating and evaluating search points. The black-box complexity of a problem is thus a lower bound for the number of fitness evaluations needed by any search heuristic to solve it.

Several black-box complexity notions covering different aspects of randomized search heuristics exist, for example the unrestricted model [12], which does not restrict in any way the sampling or selection procedure of the algorithm, the ranking-based model [8, 21], in which the algorithms are required to base their selection only on relative and not on absolute fitness values, the memory-restricted model [9, 12], in which the algorithm can store only a limited number of search points and their corresponding fitness values, and the unbiased model [17], which requires the algorithms to treat the representation of the search points symmetrically. By comparing the respective black-box complexities of a problem, one learns how the run time of RSHs is influenced by

GECCO'14, July 12–16, Vancouver, BC, Canada.

ACM 978-1-4503-2662-9/14/07 ...$15.00.
http://dx.doi.org/10.1145/2576768.2598341.

Arity	Constant Jump $\ell = O(1)$		Short Jump $\ell = O(n^{1/2-\varepsilon})$		Long Jump $\ell = (1/2-\varepsilon)n$		Extreme Jump $\ell = n/2-1$	
$k=1$	$\Theta(n \log n)$	[7]	$\Theta(n \log n)$	[here]	$O(n^2)$	[here]	$O(n^{9/2})$	[here]
$k=2$	$O(n)$	[5,7]	$O(n)$	[here]	$O(n \log n)$	[here]	$O(n \log n)$	[here]
$3 \le k \le \log n$	$O(n/k)$	[7,10]	$O(n/k)$	[here]	$O(n/k)$	[here]	$\Theta(n)$	[here]

Table 1: Known results for the unbiased black-box complexity of Jump_ℓ.

certain algorithmic choices such as the population size, the use of crossover, the selection rules, etc.

For all existing black-box models, however, the typical optimal black-box algorithm is a highly problem-tailored algorithm that is not necessarily nature-inspired. Still we can learn from such "artificial" algorithms about RSH, as has been shown in [3]. In that work, a new genetic algorithm is presented that optimizes the OneMax function in run time $o(n \log n)$, thus showing that the $o(n \log n)$ bound for the 2-ary unbiased black-box complexity of OneMax found in [5] is not as unnatural as it might have seemed at first.

Here in this work we consider unbiased black-box complexities. The unbiased black-box model is one of the standard models for analyzing the influence of the arity on the performance of optimal black-box algorithms. It was originally defined by Lehre and Witt [17] for bit string representations and has later been generalized to domains different from bit strings [6, 19]. For bit string representations, the unbiased model requires the optimizing algorithms to treat different positions of the bit strings equally, similarly with the two different possible bit contents (thus the term "unbiased"). For example, unbiased algorithms are not allowed to explicitly write a 1 or a 0 at a specific position of a bit string to be evaluated; instead, such algorithms can either sample a bit string uniformly at random, or generate one from previously evaluated solutions via operators which are unbiased (i.e., treat positions and bit contents equally). See Section 2 for a detailed description of the model.

1.2 Jump Functions

In this paper we are concerned with the optimization of functions mapping bit strings of fixed length (i.e., elements of the hypercube $\{0,1\}^n$) to real numbers; such functions are called *pseudo-Boolean*. A famous pseudo-Boolean function often considered as a test function for optimization is the OneMax function, mapping any $x \in \{0,1\}^n$ to the number of 1s in x (the *Hamming weight* of x).

Other popular test functions are the jump functions. For a non-negative integer ℓ, we define the Jump_ℓ as derived from OneMax by "blanking out" any useful information within the strict ℓ-neighborhood of the optimum (and the minimum) by giving all these search points a fitness value of 0. In other words, $\text{Jump}_\ell(x) = \text{OneMax}(x)$ if $\text{OneMax}(x) \in \{0\} \cup \{\ell+1, \ldots, n-\ell-1\} \cup \{n\}$ and $\text{Jump}_\ell(x) = 0$ otherwise. This definition is mostly similar to the two, also not fully agreeing, definitions used in [11] and [15].

Jump functions are well-known test functions for randomized search heuristics. Droste, Jansen, and Wegener [11] analyzed the optimization time of the (1+1) evolutionary algorithm on Jump functions. From their work, it is easy to see that for our definition of Jump functions, a run time of $\Theta(n^{\ell+1})$ for the (1+1) evolutionary algorithm on Jump_ℓ follows for all $\ell \in \{1, \ldots, \lfloor n/2 \rfloor - 1\}$. We are not aware of any natural mutation-based randomized search heuristic with significantly better performance (except for large ℓ, where simple random search with its $\Theta(2^n)$ run time becomes superior). For all ℓ, Jansen and Wegener [14] present a crossover-based algorithm for Jump_ℓ. With an optimal choice for the parameter involved, which in particular implies a very small crossover rate of $O(1/n)$, it has an optimization time of $O(n \log^3 n)$ for constant ℓ (this is mistakenly stated as $O(n \log^2 n \log \log n)$ on the last line of p. 60 of the paper, but it is clear from the proof that this is only a typo) and an optimization time of $O(n^{2c+1} \log n)$ for $\ell = \lceil c \log n \rceil$, c a constant.

Contrasting these results, it has been shown in [7] that for jump functions with constant ℓ, the k-ary unbiased black-box complexities are of the same order as those of the easy OneMax test function (which can be seen as a Jump function with parameter $\ell = 0$). The results in [7] are based on an intermediate result (Lemma 3 in [7]) which shows that a black-box algorithm having access to a jump function with constant ℓ can retrieve (with high probability) the true OneMax value of a search point using only a constant number of queries.

1.3 Our Results

In this work we greatly expand on the results obtained in [7] and give a much more complete picture of the unbiased black-box complexity of Jump functions.

In the regime of jump functions with super-constant jump size, we distinguish between *short*, *long*, and *extreme* jump functions. Short jump functions have ℓ values of $O(n^{1/2-\varepsilon})$; we show that the crucial Lemma 3 from [7], there only proven for constant ℓ, extends to all short jump functions. This implies that we get the same run time bounds for short jump functions as are known for OneMax.

A result like Lemma 3 in [7] is not to be expected to hold for larger values of ℓ. Nevertheless, we show that also long jump functions, where ℓ can be as large as $(1/2-\varepsilon)n$, have unbiased black-box complexities of the same asymptotic order as OneMax for arities $k \ge 3$. For $k = 2$ we get a bound of $O(n \log n)$ and for $k = 1$ we get $O(n^2)$, both surprisingly low black-box complexities. Even for the case of extreme jump functions, where $\ell = n/2 - 1$ and n even (a jump function revealing only the optimum and the fitness $n/2$), we are able to show polynomial unbiased black-box complexities for all arities $k \ge 1$.

Note that already for long jump functions, the fitness plateau that the algorithms have to cross has exponential size. For the extreme jump function, even all but a $\Theta(n^{-1/2})$ fraction of the search points form one single fitness plateau. This is the reason why none of the popular randomized search algorithms will find the optimum of long and extreme jump functions in subexponential time.

Table 1 summarizes the known black-box complexities of JUMP_ℓ and our new results.

Note that, in Table 1, the bounds for the binary and k-ary black-box complexity of the short JUMP function differ from the ones presented in [7]. The reason is that the respective bounds for ONEMAX, to which the JUMP complexities have been reduced to in [7], have been improved recently in [10].

The table clearly indicates that even without the fitness function revealing useful information for search points close the optimum, efficient optimization is still possible in the framework of unbiased black-box algorithms.

1.4 Methods

In order to show the upper bounds on the black-box complexities we give efficient algorithms optimizing the different jump functions. For arity $k = 1$, these algorithms are based on iteratively getting closer to the optimum; however we do not (and in fact cannot) rely on fitness information about these closer search points: the fitness is 0 in almost all cases. Instead, we rely on the *empirical expected fitness* of offspring. For this we use mutation operators that have a good chance of sampling offspring with non-zero fitness. We show that already a polynomial number of samples suffices to distinguish search points whose fitness differs only minimally. In order to minimize the number of samples required, we choose this number *adaptively* depending on the estimated number of 1s in the search point to be evaluated; we also allow fairly frequent incorrect decisions, as long as the overall progress to the optimum is guaranteed.

In one of our proofs we make use of an additive Chernoff bound for negatively correlated variables. This bound is implicit in a paper by Panconesi and Srivnivasan [18] and is of independent interest.

Disclaimer: For reasons of space we can present only the main proof ideas. The full version of Sections 4 and 5 along with the claimed generalization of the bounds from [7] can be found in [4].

2. THE UNBIASED BLACK-BOX MODEL

The unbiased black-box model introduced in [16] is by now one of the standard complexity models in evolutionary computation. In particular the unary unbiased model gives a more realistic complexity estimate for a number of functions than the original unrestricted black-box model of Droste, Jansen, and Wegener [12]. An important advantage of the unbiased model is that it allows us to analyze the influence of the arity of the sampling operators in use. In addition, new search points can be sampled only either uniformly at random or from distributions that depend on previously generated search points in an *unbiased* way. In this section we briefly give a brief definition of the unbiased black-box model, pointing the interested reader to [16] and [10] for a more detailed introduction.

For all non-negative integers k, a *k-ary unbiased distribution* $\left(D(\cdot \mid y^{(1)}, \dots, y^{(k)})\right)_{y^{(1)},\dots,y^{(k)} \in \{0,1\}^n}$ is a family of probability distributions over $\{0,1\}^n$ such that for all *inputs* $y^{(1)}, \dots, y^{(k)} \in \{0,1\}^n$ the following two conditions hold.

1. [$\oplus$-invariance] $\forall x, z \in \{0,1\}^n$: $D(x \mid y^{(1)}, \dots, y^{(k)}) = D(x \oplus z \mid y^{(1)} \oplus z, \dots, y^{(k)} \oplus z)$;
2. [permutation-invariance] $\forall x \in \{0,1\}^n \ \forall \sigma \in S_n$: $D(x \mid y^{(1)}, \dots, y^{(k)}) = D(\sigma(x) \mid \sigma(y^{(1)}), \dots, \sigma(y^{(k)}))$,

Algorithm 1: Scheme of a k-ary unbiased black-box algorithm

1 **Initialization:** Sample $x^{(0)} \in \{0,1\}^n$ uniformly at random and query $f(x^{(0)})$.
2 **Optimization: for** $t = 1, 2, 3, \dots$ **until** *termination condition met* **do**
3 Depending on $\left(f(x^{(0)}), \dots, f(x^{(t-1)})\right)$ choose up to k indices $i_1, \dots, i_k \in [0..t-1]$ and a k-ary unbiased distribution $D(\cdot \mid x^{(i_1)}, \dots, x^{(i_k)})$.
4 Sample $x^{(t)}$ according to $D(\cdot \mid x^{(i_1)}, \dots, x^{(i_k)})$ and query $f(x^{(t)})$.

where $\oplus$ is the bitwise exclusive-OR, S_n the set of all permutations of the set $[n] := \{1, 2, \dots, n\}$, and $\sigma(x) := x_{\sigma(1)} \cdots x_{\sigma(n)}$ for $x = x_1 \cdots x_n \in \{0,1\}^n$.

An operator sampling from a k-ary unbiased distribution is called a *k-ary unbiased variation operator*.

A k-ary unbiased black-box algorithm is one that follows the scheme of Algorithm 1 (here and in the following with $[0..k]$ we abbreviate $[k] \cup \{0\}$). The *k-ary unbiased black-box complexity*, denoted $\text{UBB}_k(\mathcal{F})$, of some class of functions $\mathcal{F}$ is the minimum complexity of $\mathcal{F}$ with respect to all k-ary unbiased black-box algorithms, where, naturally, the complexity of an algorithm A for $\mathcal{F}$ is the maximum expected number of black-box queries that A performs on a function $f \in \mathcal{F}$ until it queries for the first time a search point of maximal fitness. We let *$*$-ary unbiased black-box complexity* be based on the model in which operators of arbitrary arity are allowed.

The unbiased black-box model includes most of the commonly studied search heuristics, such as many $(\mu + \lambda)$ and (μ, λ) evolutionary algorithms (EAs), Simulated Annealing, the Metropolis algorithm, and the Randomized Local Search algorithm.

We recall a simple remark from [7] which helps us shortening some of the proofs in the subsequent sections.

REMARK 1. *Suppose for a problem P there exists a black-box algorithm A that, with constant success probability, solves P in s iterations (that is, queries an optimal solution within s queries). Then the black-box complexity of P is at most $O(s)$.*

A useful tool for proving lower bounds is Theorem 2. It formalizes the intuition that the black-box complexity of a function can only get harder if we "blank out" some of the fitness values. This is exactly the situation of the JUMP functions, whose definition we repeat here for the sake of completeness.

For all $\ell < n/2$, JUMP_ℓ is the function that assigns to each $x \in \{0,1\}^n$ fitness

$$\text{JUMP}_\ell(x) = \begin{cases} n, & \text{if } |x|_1 = n; \\ |x|_1, & \text{if } \ell < |x|_1 < n - \ell; \\ 0, & \text{otherwise,} \end{cases}$$

where $|x|_1 := \text{ONEMAX}(x) := \sum_{i=1}^n x_i$ denotes the number of 1s in x (also known as the *Hamming-weight of x*).

THEOREM 2. *For all sets of pseudo-Boolean functions C, all $k \in \mathbb{N}$, and all $f : \mathbb{R} \to \mathbb{R}$ such that $\forall g \in C$:*

$\{x \mid f(g(x))$ *optimal* $\} \subseteq \{x \mid g(x)$ *optimal* $\}$, *we have* $\mathrm{UBB}_k(C) \leq \mathrm{UBB}_k(f(C))$.

PROOF. Let C, k, and f be as in the statement of the theorem. Let A be any k-ary unbiased black-box algorithm for $f(C)$. We derive from this a k-ary unbiased black-box algorithm for C by using queries to $g \in C$ and then mapping the resulting objective value with f. Clearly, A' finds an optimum of $g \in C$ after no more expected queries than A for $f \circ g$, using the condition on the set of optimal points. Thus, the theorem follows. □

From Theorem 2 we immediately obtain a lower bound of $\Omega(n/\log n)$ for the unbiased black-box complexities of jump functions. The theorem implies that the k-ary unbiased black-box complexity of OneMax is a lower bound of that of any jump function. In general, the k-ary unbiased black-box complexity of any pseudo-Boolean function f is at least the unrestricted black-box complexity of the class of functions obtained from f by first applying an automorphism of the hypercube $\{0,1\}^n$. That the latter for OneMax is $\Omega(n/\log n)$ was shown independently in [12] and [13]. A similar line of arguments will prove the lower bound for extreme jump functions in Section 5.

3. SHORT JUMP FUNCTIONS

The key idea in [7] for dealing with jump functions of constant gap is to revert the problem to optimizing a OneMax function. The following lemma is a generalization of Lemma 3 in [7], extending it from constant ℓ to all $\ell \in O(n^{1/2-\varepsilon})$.

LEMMA 3. *For all constants* ε *and* c *and all* $\ell \in O(n^{1/2-\varepsilon})$, *there is a unary unbiased subroutine* s *using* $O(1)$ *queries to* Jump_ℓ *such that, for all bit strings* x, $s(x) = \mathrm{OneMax}(x)$ *with probability* $1 - O(n^{-c})$.

With Lemma 3 at hand, the results stated in Table 1 follow easily from the respective OneMax bounds proven in [10, 12, 16], cf. [7] for a detailed proof.

4. LONG JUMP FUNCTIONS

In this section we give bounds on long jump functions; we start with a bound on the ternary black-box complexity, followed by a bound on the unary black-box complexity. Note that the bound on the binary unbiased black-box complexity of long jump follows from the same bound on extreme jump.

4.1 Ternary Unbiased Optimization of Long Jump Functions

We show that ternary operators allow for solving the problem independently in different parts of the bit string, and then combining the partial solutions. This has the advantage that, as done in [7], we can revert to optimizing OneMax, and the missing fitness values will not show in any of the partial problems.

We start with a lemma regarding the possibility of simulating unbiased algorithms for OneMax on subsets of the bits.

LEMMA 4. *For all bit strings* $x, y \in \{0,1\}^n$ *we let* $[x,y] = \{z \in \{0,1\}^n \mid \forall i \leq n : x_i = y_i \Rightarrow x_i = z_i\}$ *(this set is isomorphic to a hypercube). Let* A *be a* k*-ary unbiased black-box algorithm optimizing* OneMax *with constant probability in time at most* $t(n)$. *Then there is a* $(k+2)$*-ary unbiased black-box subroutine* `simulateOnSubcube` *as follows.*

- *Inputs to* `simulateOnSubcube` *are* $x, y \in \{0,1\}^n$ *and the Hamming distance* a *of* x *and* y; x *and* y *are accessible as search points sampled previous to the call of the subroutine.*
- `simulateOnSubcube` *has access to an oracle returning* $\mathrm{OneMax}(z)$ *for all* $z \in [x,y]$.
- *After at most* $t(a)$ *queries* `simulateOnSubcube` *has found the* $z \in [x,y]$ *with maximal* OneMax *value with constant probability.*

This subroutine can be used to optimize Jump_ℓ blockwise. Each block is optimized by itself while we have to make sure that the correct OneMax value is available as long as only bits within the block are modified. Afterwards, the different optimized blocks are merged to obtain the optimum. As the subroutine requires an increase of the arity by two, this idea yields the following result.

THEOREM 5. *Let* $\ell \leq (1/2 - \varepsilon)n$. *For all* $k \geq 3$, *the* k*-ary unbiased black-box complexity of* Jump_ℓ *is* $O(\mathrm{UBB}_{k-2}(\mathrm{OneMax}))$.

From Theorem 5 we immediately get the following corollary, using the known run time bounds for OneMax from [10].

COROLLARY 6. *Let* $\ell \leq (1/2 - \varepsilon)n$. *Then the unbiased black-box complexity of* Jump_ℓ *is*

- $O(n \log n)$, *for ternary variation operators;*
- $O(n/k)$, *for* k*-ary variation operators with* $4 \leq k \leq \log n$;
- $\Theta(n/\log n)$, *for* k*-ary variation operators with* $k \geq \log n$ *or unbounded arity.*

Note the upper bound of $O(n \log n)$ for the ternary unbiased black-box-complexity which we will improve in Section 5 to $O(n)$. For all higher arities, the theorem presented in this section gives the best known bound.

4.2 Unary Unbiased Optimization of Long Jump Functions

When optimizing a Jump_ℓ function via unary unbiased operators, the only way to estimate the OneMax-value of a search point x (equivalently, its Hamming distance $H(x, \mathbf{1}_n)$ from the optimum), is by sampling suitable offspring that have a non-zero fitness. When ℓ is small, that is, many OneMax-values can be derived straight from the fitness, we can simply flip ℓ bits and hope that the retrieved fitness value is by ℓ smaller than $\mathrm{OneMax}(x)$. This is the main idea in [7].

When ℓ is larger, this does not work anymore, simply because the chance that we only flip 1-bits to zero is too small. Therefore, in this section, we resort to a sampling approach that, via strong concentration results, learns the expected fitness of the sampled offspring of x, and from this the OneMax-value of the parent x. This will lead to a unary unbiased black-box complexity of $O(n^2)$ for all jump functions Jump_ℓ with $\ell \leq n/2 - \varepsilon n$.

THEOREM 7. *Let* $\ell \leq (1/2 - \varepsilon)n$. *The unary unbiased black-box complexity of* Jump_ℓ *is* $O(n^2)$.

Proof outline and methods.

Since we aim at an asymptotic statement, let us assume that n is sufficiently large and even. Also, since we shall not elaborate on the influence of the constant $\varepsilon > 0$, we may assume (by replacing ε by a minimally smaller value) that ε is such that εn is even.

A first idea to optimize JUMP_ℓ with $\ell = n/2 - \varepsilon n/2$ could be to flip each bit of the parent x with probability $1/2 - \varepsilon/2$. Such an offspring u has an expected fitness of $n/2 - \varepsilon n/2 + \varepsilon\text{ONEMAX}(x)$. If ε is constant, then by Chernoff bounds $O(n \log n)$ samples are enough to ensure that the average observed fitness $n/2 - \varepsilon n/2 + \varepsilon v$ satisfies $v = \text{ONEMAX}(x)$ with probability $1 - n^{-c}$, c an arbitrary constant. This is enough to build a unary unbiased algorithm using $O(n^2 \log^2(n))$ fitness evaluations.

We improve this first approach via two ideas. The more important one is to not flip an expected number of $n/2-\varepsilon n/2$ bits independently, but to flip exactly that many bits (randomly chosen). By this, we avoid adding extra variation via the mutation operator. This pays off when x already has many ones—if $\text{ONEMAX}(x) = n - a$, then we will observe that only $O(a \log n)$ samples suffice to estimate the ONEMAX-value of x precisely (allowing a failure probability of n^{-c} as before).

The price for not flipping bits independently (but flipping a fixed number of bits) is that we have do deal with hypergeometric distributions, and when sampling repeatedly, with sums of these. The convenient way of handling such sums is to rewrite them as sums of negatively correlated random variables and then argue that Chernoff bounds also hold for these. This has been stated explicitly in [2] for multiplicative Chernoff bounds, but not for additive ones. Since for our purposes an additive Chernoff bound is more convenient, we extract such a bound from the original paper [18].

The second improvement stems from allowing a larger failure probability. This will occasionally lead to wrong estimates of $\text{ONEMAX}(x)$, and consequently to wrong decisions on whether to accept x or not, but as long as this does not happen too often, we will still expect to make progress towards the optimum. To analyze this, we formulate the progress of the distance to the optimum as a random walk and use the gambler's ruin theorem to show that the expected number of visits to each state is constant.

One key notion used in the proof of Theorem 7 is that of a p-estimator. It is used to estimate the number of zeroes in a bit string. Since the idea underlying this notion will be re-used in Theorem 14, we briefly present its definition.

DEFINITION 8. *Let f be a pseudo-Boolean function and let p be a function that maps non-negative integers to non-negative integers. Let g be an algorithm which takes as input a bit string x and a natural number α and uses $O(p(n)\alpha \log(2 + n/\alpha))$ unary unbiased queries to f. We call g a* p-estimator *using f if, for all bit strings x, $a = n - \text{ONEMAX}(x)$, and for all $\alpha \in [a/2, 3a/2]$ we have*

- $P(g(x, \alpha) \neq a) \leq \frac{a}{16n}$;
- $P(g(x, \alpha) \notin [a/2, 3a/2]) \in O(1/(p(n)n^3))$.

To prove Theorem 7 we show that there exists a p-estimator for $\text{JUMP}_{n/2-\varepsilon n}$ with $p(n)$ being a sufficiently large constant. The result then follows from the following lemma.

LEMMA 9. *Let f be a pseudo-Boolean function such that, for some p, there is a p-estimator using f. Then the unary unbiased black-box complexity of f is $O(p(n)n^2)$.*

5. EXTREME JUMP FUNCTIONS

In this section, we regard the most extreme case of jump functions where all search points have fitness zero, except for the optimum and search points having exactly $n/2$ ones. Surprisingly, despite some additional difficulties, we still find polynomial-time black-box algorithms.

Throughout this section, let n be even. We call a jump function JUMP_ℓ an *extreme jump function* if $\ell = n/2 - 1$. Consequently, this functions is zero except for the optimum (where it has the value n) and for bit-string having $n/2$ ones (where it has the value $n/2$).

The information-theoretic argument of [12] immediately gives a lower bound of $\Omega(n)$ for the unbiased black-box complexities of extreme jump functions. The intuitive argument is that an unrestricted black-box algorithm needs to learn n bits of information, but receives only a constant amount of information per query.

LEMMA 10. *For all arities k, the k-ary unbiased black-box complexity of an extreme jump function is $\Omega(n)$.*

PROOF. Since an extreme jump function takes only three values, Theorem 2 in [12] gives a lower bound of $\Omega(n)$ for the unrestricted black-box complexity of the set of all extreme jump functions. The latter is a lower bound for the unbiased black-box complexity of a single extreme jump function (cf. the end of Section 2). □

5.1 The Upper Bounds on Extreme Jump Functions

In the following three subsections, we shall derive several upper bounds for the black-box complexities of extreme jump functions.

Notice that, for an extreme jump function, we cannot distinguish between having a ONEMAX value of $n/2 + k$ and $n/2-k$ until we have encountered the optimum or its inverse. More precisely, let $x^{(1)}, x^{(2)}, \ldots$ be a finite sequence of search points not containing the all-ones and all-zeroes string. Define $y^{(i)}$ to be the inverse of $x^{(i)}$ for all i, i.e., $y^{(i)} = x^{(i)} \oplus \mathbf{1}_n$ where $\mathbf{1}_n$ denotes the all-ones string of length n. Then both these sequences of search points yield exactly the same fitness values. Hence the only way we could find out on which side of the symmetry point $n/2$ we are would be by querying a search point having no or n ones. However, if we know such a search point, we are done anyway.

Despite these difficulties, we will develop a linear time ternary unbiased black-box algorithm in the following section. In Section 5.3, we show that restricting ourselves to binary variation operators increases the black-box complexity by at most a logarithmic factor. For unary operators, the good news derived in the final subsection of this section is that polynomial-time optimization of extreme jump functions is still possible, though the best complexity we find is only $O(n^{9/2})$.

To ease the language, let us denote by $d(x) := |\text{ONEMAX}(x) - n/2|$ a *symmetricized version of* ONEMAX taking into account this difficulty. Also, let us define the *sign* $\text{sgn}(x)$ of x to be -1, if $\text{ONEMAX}(x) < n/2$, $\text{sgn}(x) := 0$, if $\text{ONEMAX}(x) = n/2$, and $\text{sgn}(x) = +1$, if $\text{ONEMAX}(x) > n/2$. In other words, $\text{sgn}(x)$ is the sign of $\text{ONEMAX}(x)-n/2$.

5.2 Ternary Unbiased Optimization of Extreme Jump Functions

When ternary operators are allowed, we quite easily obtain an unbiased black-box complexity of $O(n)$, which is best possible by Lemma 10. The reason for this fast optimization progress is that, as explained next, we may test individual bits. Assume that we have a search point u with OneMax-value $n/2+1$. If we flip a certain bit in u, then from the fitness of this offspring, we learn the value of this bit. If the new fitness is $n/2$, then the OneMax-value is $n/2$ as well and the bit originally had the value one. If the new fitness is zero, then the new OneMax-value is $n/2+2$ and the original bit was set to one. We can thus first learn the correct bit values and then copy them one by one into a bit string, creating the optimum (this is the only part of the algorithm which requires a ternary operator).

One difficulty to overcome, as sketched in Section 5.1, is that we will never have a search point where we know that its OneMax-value is $n/2+1$. We overcome this by generating a search point with fitness $n/2$ and flipping a single bit. This yields a search point with OneMax-value either $n/2+1$ or $n/2-1$. Implementing the above strategy in a sufficiently symmetric way, we end up with a search point having OneMax-value either n or 0 and in the latter case output its complement.

Theorem 11. *For $k \geq 3$, the k-ary unbiased black-box complexity of extreme jump functions is $\Theta(n)$.*

5.3 Binary Unbiased Optimization of the Extreme Jump Function

In this section, we prove that the unbiased 2-ary black-box complexity of extreme jump functions is $O(n \log n)$. With 2-ary operators only, it seems impossible to copy bits one by one, which was crucial to the strategy used in the previous subsection.

To overcome this difficulty, we follow a hill-climbing approach. We first find a search point m with d-value 0 by repeated sampling. We copy this into our "current-best" search point x and try to improve x to a new search point x' by flipping a random bit in which x and m are equal (this needs a 2-ary operation), hoping to gain a search point with d-value equal to $d(x)+1$. The main difficulty is to estimate the d-value of x', which is necessary to decide whether we keep this solution as new current-best or whether we try again.

Using binary operators, we can exploit the fact that $H(x,m) = d(x)$. For example, we can flip $d(x)-1$ of the $d(x)+1$ bits in which x' and m differ. If this yields an individual with fitness $n/2$, then clearly x' has not the targeted d-value of $d(x)+1$. Unfortunately, we detect this shortcoming only when the bit that marks the difference of x and x' is not among the $d(x)-1$ bits flipped. This happens only with probability $2/(d(x)+1)$. Consequently, this approach may take $\Theta(n)$ iterations to decide between the cases $d(x') = d(x)+1$ and $d(x') = d(x)-1$.

We can reduce this time to logarithmic using the following trick. Recall that the main reason for the slow decision procedure above is that the probability of not flipping the newly created bit is so small. This is due to the fact that the only way to gain information about x' is by flipping almost all bits so as to possibly reach a fitness of $n/2$. We overcome this difficulty by in parallel keeping a second search point y

Algorithm 2: A 2-ary unbiased black-box algorithm that for any extreme jump function f with high probability finds the optimum in $O(n \log n)$ iterations.

```
repeat
    m ← uniform();
until f(m) = n/2;
status ← failure;
while status = failure do
    x ← flipWhereEqual_1(m, m);
    y ← flipWhereEqual_1(m, x);
    status ← success;
    i ← 0;
    while (status ≠ failure) and (i ≤ √n) do
        i ← i + 1;
        u ← mix(x, y);
        if f(u) ≠ n/2 then status ← failure;
for k = 1 to n/2 − 1 do
    x' ← movefirst_k(x, y);
    y' ← movefirst_k(y, x);
    (x, y) ← (x', y');
if f(x) = n then
    return x;
else
    return y;
```

that has the same d-value as x, but is "on the other side" of m. To ease the language in this overview, let us assume that OneMax$(x) > n/2$. Let $k := d(x)$ and $H(m,x) = k$. Then we aim at keeping a y such that $d(y) = k$, $H(m,y) = k$, $H(x,y) = 2k$, and OneMax$(y) = n/2 - k$. With this at hand, we can easily evaluate the d-value of x'. Assume that x' was created by flipping exactly one of the bits in which x and y agree. Let u be created by flipping in x' exactly $k-1$ of the bits in which x' and y differ. If $d(x') = k+1$, then surely $d(u) = 2$, and thus $f(u) = 0$. If $d(x') = k-1$, then with probability $(k+2)/(2k+1) \geq 1/2$ the bit in which x' and x differ is not flipped, leading to OneMax$(u) = n/2$, visible from a fitness equal to $n/2$. Hence, with probability at least $1/2$, we detect the undesired outcome $d(x') = k - 1$. Unfortunately, there is no comparably simple certificate for "$d(x') = k+1$", so we have to repeat the previous test $2 \log n$ times to be sufficiently sure (in the case no failure is detected) that $d(x') = k+1$. Overall, this leads to an almost linear complexity of $O(n \log n)$.

This finishes a rough outline of the proof for Theorem 12. The algorithm verifying Theorem 12 is given in Algorithm 2. It uses the following unbiased operators. The first, `uniform()`, is the (0-ary unbiased) operator that samples a bit string $x \in \{0,1\}^n$ uniformly at random. $\texttt{flipWhereEqual}_1(\cdot,\cdot)$, takes two arguments and returns a bit string which is like the first argument, except that exactly one of the bits in which the first argument agrees with the second one is flipped, this bit is chosen uniformly at random; if the two strings are complements of each other, then no bits are flipped and the operator returns the first argument. The operator $\texttt{mix}(\cdot,\cdot)$ also takes two arguments; if these two arguments differ at exactly two positions, the output is exactly like the input strings where the two inputs are equal, and inherits one bit from each argument on the two positions where they differ, but if the two arguments do not differ at exactly two positions, a uniformly random bit string is returned. Finally, the algorithm also uses an unbiased subroutine $\texttt{movefirst}_k(\cdot,\cdot)$ which takes two arguments x and y and assumes $d(x) = k = d(y)$ as well as $H(x,y) = 2d$. The subroutine returns (with sufficient probability and only using unbiased operators) a bit string x' with $d(x') = k+1$ and $d(x',y) = 2k+1$.

THEOREM 12. *There is a 2-ary unbiased black-box algorithm solving the "extreme jump functions" problem in an expected number of $O(n \log n)$ queries.*

5.4 Unary Unbiased Optimization of Extreme Jump Functions

With the next theorem we show that, surprisingly, even the *unary* unbiased black-box complexity of extreme jump functions is still polynomially bounded. Note that now we cannot learn the OneMax-value of a search point x by repeatedly flipping a certain number of bits and observing the average objective value. Since $n/2$ is the only non-trivial objective value, any such average will necessarily be $n/2$ (except in the unlikely event that we encountered the optimum). The solution is to flip, depending on parity reasonings, exactly $n/2-1$ or $n/2$ bits in x and note that the probability p_a of receiving a search point with (visible) fitness $n/2$ depends on the distance $a := a(x) = \min\{|x|_1, |x|_0 := n - |x|_1\}$ of x to the optimum or its opposite. We roughly have $p_a \in \Theta(a^{-1/2})$ and $p_{a-2} - p_a \in \Theta(a^{-3/2}n^{-1}(n-2a))$. These small numbers lead to the fact that for $a \in n/2-\Theta(1)$, we will need $\Theta(n^{9/2})$ samples to estimate the a-value of x with constant probability. Since estimating becomes easier for smaller a, we are able to construct a unary unbiased black-box algorithm finding the optimum of an extreme jump function in $O(n^{9/2})$ expected fitness evaluations.

Key to proving Theorem 14 is Lemma 13, formalizing that it is possible to distinguish, in a unary unbiased manner, whether a search point x has distance $a(x) = a-1$ or $a(x) = a+1$ to the optimum (or its complement).

LEMMA 13. *There exists a unary unbiased procedure* `estimate` *that has the following properties. On arbitrary inputs $y \in \{0,1\}^n$ and $a \in [1..n/2-1]$, it performs $\Theta(a^{5/2}n^2(n-2a)^{-3/2})$ fitness evaluations. If $a(y) \in \{a-1, a+1\}$, then with probability at least $1 - \exp(-\Theta((n-2a)^{1/2}))$ the true value of $a(y)$ is returned. By choosing the implicit constant in the first statement sufficiently large, this success probability can be made arbitrary close to one.*

The algorithm certifying the desired black-box complexity stated in Table 1 is given by Algorithm 3. In this pseudocode, `uniform()` is as before, $\texttt{flip}_1(.)$ is the unary unbiased operator that, given an argument x flips in x exactly one bit, and `complement(.)` is the unary unbiased operator which outputs the bitwise complement of its argument, i.e., $\texttt{complement}(x) := x \oplus \mathbf{1}_n$ for all x.

THEOREM 14. *Let n be even and $\ell = n/2-1$. Then the unary unbiased black-box complexity of* JUMP$_\ell$ *is $O(n^{9/2})$. This is witnessed by Algorithm 3, which with constant probability finds the optimum of an extreme jump function using $O(n^{9/2})$ fitness evaluations.*

PROOF. The first sentence of the theorem follows from the second and Remark 1.

Algorithm 3: A unary unbiased black-box algorithm that for any extreme jump function f with constant probability finds the optimum in $O(n^{9/2})$ fitness evaluations.

```
repeat
    m ← uniform();
until f(m) = n/2;
x ← flip_1(m);
for a = n/2 − 1 DownTo 1 do
    status ← failure;
    while status = failure do
        y ← flip_1(x);
        if estimate(y, a) = a − 1 then
            x ← y;
            status ← success;
Sample complement(x);
```

In the analysis of Algorithm 3, let us first assume that all $\texttt{estimate}(y,a)$ calls with $a(y) \in \{a-1, a+1\}$ return $a(y)$ correctly.

Assume that we start the while-loop in Algorithm 3 with an x such that a is equal to $a(x)$. Since y is a Hamming neighbor of x, we have $a(y) \in \{a-1, a+1\}$. If $a(y) = a+1$, nothing changes. If $a(y) = a-1$, this is again correctly detected in the if-clause, and the while-loop is left with $x \leftarrow y$. Consequently, we start the following iteration of the for-loop again with $a(x) = a$. The probability of generating a y with $a(y) = a-1$ is a/n. Consequently, the while-loop is left after an expected number of n/a iterations.

The expected total number of fitness evaluations in the for-loop is now easily computed as

$$\sum_{a=1}^{n/2-1} (n/a) O(a^{5/2}n^2/(n-2a)^{3/2})$$

$$\in O(n^{9/2}) \sum_{a=1}^{n/2-1} (n-2a)^{-3/2} = O(n^{9/2}).$$

The above is true if we assume that none of the exceptional events ("failures") of Lemma 13 occurs. We now argue that in fact with constant probability, none of them occurs. To this aim, we estimate the expected number of first failures in a typical run of the algorithm (a first failure is one where all previous calls of the `estimate` procedure did not fail). Consider one iteration of the while loop. If $a \neq a(x)$, then a failure must have occurred before, hence the probability now for a first failure is zero. If $a = a(x)$, we can invoke Lemma 13 and deduce that this iteration has a failure probability of at most $\exp(-k(n-2a)^{1/2})$, where k is a sufficiently large absolute constant.

We may further assume, for the sake of this argument, that a failure is immediately corrected by some external authority. Note that this only changes the run of the algorithm after the occurrence of the first failure. So in particular, it does not change the expected number of first failures. By this, however, we may assume that the expected number of iterations done with x having a certain a-value is exactly n/a. Consequently, the expected number of first failures is at most $\sum_{a=1}^{n/2-1}(n/a)\exp(-k(n-2a)^{1/2}) = \sum_{b=1}^{n/2-1} n(n/2-b)^{-1}\exp(-k\sqrt{b}) \in O(1)$, where the implicit constant can be made arbitrarily small by the appropriate choice of k. Hence, with constant probability there is no first failure, and thus, also no failure at all. □

6. SUMMARY AND OUTLOOK

We have analyzed the unbiased black-box complexity of short, long, and extreme jump functions. Along the way, we have introduced new tools for such analyses. Our work raises a number of interesting questions for future research.

Since our focus was on deriving new ideas for the design of new search heuristics, we did not undertake in this work a complete investigation of all possible combinations of arity and jump size, but rather highlighted prominent complexity behaviors and prototypical algorithmic ideas. Still, it would be interesting to have a more complete picture than Table 1, in particular, making clear how far certain algorithmic ideas take and where certain regimes change.

Another interesting line of research would be results that are more precise than just the asymptotic order. For example, it seems reasonable that for ℓ small enough, the unary unbiased black-box complexity of JUMP_ℓ is not only of the same order as the one of ONEMAX, but equal apart from lower order terms (which might actually be surprisingly small). Note that such precise analyses for run times of given algorithms recently attracted quite some interest, see [1, 17, 20, 22] and the references therein.

Furthermore, we are optimistic that some of the algorithmic ideas developed in the previous sections can be used to design new search heuristics.

Acknowledgments

Parts of this work have been done during the Dagstuhl seminar 10361 "Theory of Evolutionary Algorithms".

7. REFERENCES

[1] S. Böttcher, B. Doerr, and F. Neumann. Optimal fixed and adaptive mutation rates for the LeadingOnes problem. In *Proc. of the 11th International Conference on Parallel Problem Solving from Nature (PPSN'10)*, pages 1–10. Springer, 2010.

[2] B. Doerr. Analyzing randomized search heuristics: Tools from probability theory. In A. Auger and B. Doerr, editors, *Theory of Randomized Search Heuristics*, pages 1–20. World Scientific Publishing, 2011.

[3] B. Doerr, C. Doerr, and F. Ebel. Lessons from the black-box: Fast crossover-based genetic algorithms. In *Proc. of the 15th Annual Genetic and Evolutionary Computation Conference (GECCO'13)*, pages 781–788. ACM, 2013.

[4] B. Doerr, C. Doerr, and T. Kötzing. Unbiased black-box complexities of jump functions—how to cross large plateaus. *CoRR*, abs/1403.7806, 2014. Available online at http://arxiv.org/abs/1403.7806.

[5] B. Doerr, D. Johannsen, T. Kötzing, P. K. Lehre, M. Wagner, and C. Winzen. Faster black-box algorithms through higher arity operators. In *Proc. of the 11th ACM Workshop on Foundations of Genetic Algorithms (FOGA'11)*, pages 163–172. ACM, 2011.

[6] B. Doerr, T. Kötzing, J. Lengler, and C. Winzen. Black-box complexities of combinatorial problems. *Theoretical Computer Science*, 471:84–106, 2013.

[7] B. Doerr, T. Kötzing, and C. Winzen. Too fast unbiased black-box algorithms. In *Proc. of the 13th Annual Genetic and Evolutionary Computation Conference (GECCO'11)*, pages 2043–2050. ACM, 2011.

[8] B. Doerr and C. Winzen. Ranking-based black-box complexity. *Algorithmica*. To appear. DOI: 10.1007/s00453-012-9684-9.

[9] B. Doerr and C. Winzen. Playing Mastermind with constant-size memory. In *Proc. of the Symposium on Theoretical Aspects of Computer Science (STACS'12)*, pages 441–452. Schloss Dagstuhl - Leibniz-Zentrum fuer Informatik, 2012.

[10] B. Doerr and C. Winzen. Reducing the arity in unbiased black-box complexity. In *Proc. of the 14th Annual Genetic and Evolutionary Computation Conference (GECCO'12)*, pages 1309–1316. ACM, 2012.

[11] S. Droste, T. Jansen, and I. Wegener. On the analysis of the (1+1) evolutionary algorithm. *Theoretical Computer Science*, 276:51–81, 2002.

[12] S. Droste, T. Jansen, and I. Wegener. Upper and lower bounds for randomized search heuristics in black-box optimization. *Theory of Computing Systems*, 39:525–544, 2006.

[13] P. Erdős and A. Rényi. On two problems of information theory. *Magyar Tudományos Akadémia Matematikai Kutató Intézet Közleményei*, 8:229–243, 1963.

[14] T. Jansen and I. Wegener. The analysis of evolutionary algorithms - a proof that crossover really can help. *Algorithmica*, 34:47–66, 2002.

[15] P. K. Lehre and C. Witt. Black-box search by unbiased variation. In *Proc. of the 12th Annual Genetic and Evolutionary Computation Conference (GECCO'10)*, pages 1441–1448. ACM, 2010.

[16] P. K. Lehre and C. Witt. Black-box search by unbiased variation. *Algorithmica*, 64:623–642, 2012.

[17] P. K. Lehre and C. Witt. General drift analysis with tail bounds. *CoRR*, abs/1307.2559, 2013. Available online at http://arxiv.org/abs/1307.2559.

[18] A. Panconesi and A. Srinivasan. Randomized distributed edge coloring via an extension of the Chernoff-Hoeffding bounds. *SIAM Journal on Computing*, 26:350–368, 1997.

[19] J. Rowe and M. Vose. Unbiased black box search algorithms. In *Proc. of the 13th Annual Genetic and Evolutionary Computation Conference (GECCO'11)*, pages 2035–2042. ACM, 2011.

[20] D. Sudholt. A new method for lower bounds on the running time of evolutionary algorithms. *IEEE Trans. Evolutionary Computation*, 17:418–435, 2013.

[21] O. Teytaud and S. Gelly. General lower bounds for evolutionary algorithms. In *Proc. of the 9th International Conference on Parallel Problem Solving from Nature - PPSN IX (PPSN'06)*, pages 21–31. Springer, 2006.

[22] C. Witt. Tight bounds on the optimization time of a randomized search heuristic on linear functions. *Combinatorics, Probability & Computing*, 22:294–318, 2013.

Runtime Analysis for Maximizing Population Diversity in Single-Objective Optimization

Wanru Gao
Optimisation and Logistics
School of Computer Science
The University of Adelaide
Adelaide, Australia

Frank Neumann
Optimisation and Logistics
School of Computer Science
The University of Adelaide
Adelaide, Australia

ABSTRACT

Recently Ulrich and Thiele [14] have introduced evolutionary algorithms for the mixed multi-objective problem of maximizing fitness as well as diversity in the decision space. Such an approach allows to generate a diverse set of solutions which are all of good quality. With this paper, we contribute to the theoretical understanding of evolutionary algorithms for maximizing the diversity in a population that contains several solutions of high quality. We study how evolutionary algorithms maximize the diversity of a population where each individual has to have fitness beyond a given threshold value. We present a first runtime analysis in this area and study the classical problems called *OneMax* and *LeadingOnes*. Our results give first rigorous insights on how evolutionary algorithms can be used to produce a maximal diverse set of solutions in which all solutions have quality above a certain threshold value.

Categories and Subject Descriptors

F.2 [**Theory of Computation**]: Analysis of Algorithms and Problem Complexity

Keywords

Runtime analysis, Single objective optimization, Diversity optimization

1. INTRODUCTION

Evolutionary algorithms have been widely used for complex optimization problems. Most evolutionary algorithms incorporate certain diversity mechanisms which ensure that the population consists of a diverse set of individuals [3, 15]. From an optimization point of view this is often beneficial to prevent premature convergence to a locally optimal solution [9]. From a design point of view, this is interesting as a diverse set of solutions gives different design choices of high quality. This is especially important as practitioners in the areas of engineering and manufacturing may have a clear preference for certain solutions even if they have similar quality according to the used fitness functions which evaluate the quality of a given solution.

With this paper, we contribute to the theoretical understanding of diversity mechanisms used in evolutionary algorithms. We study evolutionary algorithms in a rigorous way using runtime analysis [1, 8, 10]. Previous studies in the field of runtime analysis in the context of diversity have examined how different diversity mechanisms influence the ability of an algorithm to obtain an optimal solution [5, 6].

In this paper, we consider diversity from a different perspective. We are interested in how evolutionary algorithms can achieve a diverse set of solutions that all have acceptable quality. Evolutionary algorithms for the problem of maximizing the diversity of a set of solutions where each of these solution has fitness above a given threshold value v have been introduced by Ulrich and Thiele [14]. Their algorithm called NOAH iteratively improves solutions according to quality and diversity of the population. Furthermore, decision space diversity has been examined for hypervolume-based search in the context of multi-objective optimization [13].

For our theoretical investigations, we work with a fixed threshold v. Our goal is to study population-based algorithms until they have obtained a population of maximum diversity where all solutions $x \in P$ have fitness at least v. The subject of our investigations is a classical $(\mu + 1)$-EA that starts maximizing the diversity of the population after all the solutions have reached fitness v. The plain version of the $(\mu + 1)$-EA has already been studied by Witt [16] for classical problems such as *OneMax* and *LeadingOnes*. We will study these problems in the context of diversity optimization and show in a rigorous way how evolutionary algorithms are able to maximize the diversity of a population for *OneMax* and *LeadingOnes*.

The paper is organized as follows. In Section 2, we introduce the algorithm that is subject of our investigations when considering diversity maximization. Our analysis for the classical *OneMax* problem is presented in Section 3 and Section 4 shows our results for the *LeadingOnes* problem. Finally, we finish with some concluding remarks to topics for future work.

GECCO'14, July 12–16, 2014, Vancouver, BC, Canada.

http://dx.doi.org/10.1145/2576768.2598251 .

2. DIVERSITY MAXIMIZATION

In this section we introduce the basic ideas of the diversity optimization of a simple single-objective problem. We are interested in pseudo-Boolean functions $f: X \to \mathbb{R}$ that map elements of the search space $X = \{0, 1\}^n$ to real values.

There are many ways to measure the difference between different individuals. Since pseudo-Boolean functions are defined on bit-strings, we use Hamming distance

$$H(x,y) = \sum_{i=1}^{n} |x_i - y_i|,$$

where $x = (x_1, \dots, x_n), y = (y_1, \dots, y_n) \in \{0,1\}^n$, to evaluate the difference between two individuals.

According to [12, 13], a diversity measurement should have the following properties:

1. Twinning: Duplicate solutions in a population should not change the diversity.
2. Monotonicity in Varieties: Adding a new solution which is not in a population should increase the set diversity.
3. Monotonicity in Distance: $D(P') \geq D(P)$ with $|P| = |P'|$ holds, if all pairs of P' are at least as dissimilar as all pairs of P (according to some given distance function).

To fulfil the required features, the diversity of a set of solutions P is defined as the sum of Hamming distance between each pair of individuals in P. Note that in general P can be a multi-set which may include duplicates. In order to meet the twinning property, duplicates are removed when computing the diversity of a (multi-)set P based on the Hamming distance.

DEFINITION 1. *For a given population P, the population diversity is defined as* $D(P) = \sum_{\{x,y\} \in \hat{P} \times \hat{P}} H(x,y)$*, where* $\hat{P}$ *is the set with all distinct solutions in* P.

Since our aim is to find a set of solutions of different structures, we combine the classical (μ+1)-EA with diversity optimization process. The threshold v of fitness value is predefined by the decision maker. The (μ+1)-EA with solution diversity optimization is defined as (μ+1)-EA$_D$. The whole process of (μ+1)-EA$_D$ is given in Algorithm 1.

The diversity optimization is conducted until all individuals in the solution set reach the fitness requirement. Moreover, once entering the diversity optimization process, the algorithm will reject the offspring with fitness below threshold. The contribution of solution x is defined as

$$c(x) = D(P) - D(P \setminus \{x\}).$$

If an offspring of acceptable quality is produced, the individual with least contribution of diversity is eliminated from the solution set. If this solution is not unique, a solution is chosen uniformly at random among the solutions with the smallest diversity contribution. Algorithm 2 defines the *OptDiv(P)* component.

We study our algorithm in terms of the number of fitness evaluations until it has produced a population P with $f(x) \geq v, \forall x \in P$ that has the maximal diversity $D(P)$. We call this the *optimization time* of the algorithm. The *expected optimization time* refers to the expected number of fitness evaluations to reach this goal.

We first analyze the time until all individuals have fitness of at least v after having achieved such an individual for the first time. The process is similar to the take-over effect in a population and we show an upper bound of $O(\mu \log \mu)$ for a population of size μ in the following lemma. It will serve later on throughout our analysis.

Algorithm 1: (μ+1)-EA$_D$

1. Initialize P with μ n-bit binary strings which are chosen uniformly at random from $\{0,1\}^n$.
2. Choose $s \in P$ uniformly at random.
3. Produce s' by flipping each bit of s with probability $1/n$ independently from each other. Add $s'$to P.
4. Let $z \in P$ be a randomly chosen individual with the worst fitness value.
5. If $f(z) \geq v$, then execute OptDiv(P), otherwise eliminate z from P.
6. Repeat step 2 to 5 until termination criterion is reached.

Algorithm 2: Diversity optimization component OptDiv(P)

1. Choose a solution $z \in \{x \in P \mid c(x) = \min_{y \in P} c(y)\}$ uniformly at random.
2. Set $P := P \setminus \{z\}$.

LEMMA 1. *Having obtained a population with at least one individual of fitness at least* v*, the expected runtime until all individuals have fitness at least* v *is upper bounded by* $O(\mu \log \mu)$.

PROOF. Since there is already one individual which has fitness value at least v, then one possible method is making duplicates of the best solution until all μ solutions are replaced by the replicas. The probability of making a duplicate of the acceptable solution when there already exists i individuals with fitness value above the threshold in the population is

$$\frac{i}{\mu} \cdot \left(1 - \frac{1}{n}\right)^n = \frac{i}{\mu} \cdot \frac{n-1}{n} \cdot \left(1 - \frac{1}{n}\right)^{n-1} \geqslant \frac{i(n-1)}{e\mu n} \geqslant \frac{i}{2e\mu}.$$

Before entering the diversity optimization process, we need all of the μ individuals in the population set to have acceptable fitness value. The expected waiting time for this process is at most

$$\sum_{i=1}^{\mu-1} \frac{2e\mu}{i} = 2e\mu \sum_{i=1}^{\mu-1} \frac{1}{i} = O(\mu \log \mu).$$

□

3. OneMax

In this section, we investigate the classical *OneMax* problem which has been subject to numerous studies in the area of runtime analysis of evolutionary algorithms [4, 16]. Our goal is to understand how simple evolutionary algorithms can maximize the diversity of its population for this simple benchmark problem. The problem is defined as

$$OneMax(x) = \sum_{i=1}^{n} x_i.$$

We first analyze until one solution has fitness at least v. To do this, we follow the ideas of Witt [16] for the analysis of the classical $(\mu+1)$-EA.

Let v be the threshold of the fitness value, hence, the acceptable solution should have at least v 1-bits. The diversity optimization process will not begin until all of the solutions in the population have the fitness above the threshold.

We denote by $L = \max_{x \in P} OneMax(x)$ the maximal fitness value of the current population and upper bound the time to achieve for the first time a solution of fitness at least v.

LEMMA 2. *The expected time until $(\mu+1)-EA$ has obtained a solution x with $OneMax(x) \geq v$ is $O(\mu v + n \log \frac{n}{n-v})$.*

PROOF. For a certain L value, duplicates will be made from the individuals with fitness value L before L improves. Following Witt [16], we assume that L remains the same before there are $\min\{\frac{n}{n-L}, \mu\}$ duplicates of the individual with fitness L.The expected time for the population to have at least $\frac{n}{n-L}$ duplicates of one of these individuals with fitness value L is at most

$$\sum_{i=1}^{\min\{n/(n-L),\mu\}} \frac{e\mu n}{i(n-1)} = \frac{e\mu n}{n-1} \sum_{i=1}^{\min\{n/(n-L),\mu\}} \frac{1}{i} \leqslant \frac{e\mu n}{n-1} \ln \frac{en}{n-L}$$

For a population set which has i individuals with fitness value L, improvement can be made by selecting one of these individuals and flipping one of its 0-bits. The considered probability is

$$\frac{i}{\mu} \cdot \frac{(n-L)}{n} \cdot \left(1 - \frac{1}{n}\right)^{n-1} \geqslant \frac{i(n-L)}{e\mu n}$$

Therefore the expected time for the fitness value to increase is at most $\frac{e\mu n}{i(n-L)}$.

The waiting time of the (μ+1)-EA achieving the first satisfactory solution equals to the sum of expected time for each L value which includes the time for increasing L and time for duplicating individuals. The expected waiting time for the (μ+1)-EA getting the first individual with fitness v is at most

$$\sum_{L=0}^{v-1} \frac{e\mu n}{\min\{\mu, n/(n-L)\} \cdot (n-L)} + \frac{e\mu n}{n-1} \sum_{L=0}^{v-1} \ln \frac{en}{n-L}.$$

According to the Harmonic sum,

$$\begin{aligned}\sum_{L=0}^{v-1} \frac{e\mu n}{\min\{\mu(n-L), n\}} &\leqslant \sum_{L=0}^{v-1} \frac{en}{n-L} + \sum_{L=0}^{v-1} e\mu \\ &\leqslant en(\ln en - \ln(n-v)) + e\mu v \\ &= en \ln\left(\frac{en}{n-v}\right) + e\mu v\end{aligned}$$

$$\begin{aligned}\frac{e\mu n}{n-1} \sum_{L=0}^{v} \ln \frac{en}{n-L} &= \frac{e\mu n}{n-1} \ln \frac{e^v n^v}{n(n-1)(n-2)\cdots(n-v)} \\ &= \frac{e\mu n}{n-1} \ln \frac{e^v n^v (n-v-1)!}{n!}\end{aligned}$$

As stated in Stirling's Formula, $e^v n^v < \frac{e^{2v} n^v v!}{v^v \sqrt{2\pi v}}$. Hence,

$$\ln \frac{e^v n^v (n-v-1)!}{n!} < \ln\left(\frac{e^{2v} n^v}{v^v \sqrt{2\pi v} \cdot (n-v)} \cdot \frac{v!(n-v)!}{n!}\right).$$

The Binomial coefficients $\binom{n}{k}$ has the property that

$$\left(\frac{n}{k}\right)^k \leqslant \binom{n}{k}.$$

Hence, we get,

$$\begin{aligned}\frac{e\mu n}{n-1} \sum_{L=0}^{v-1} \ln \frac{en}{n-L} &< \frac{e\mu n}{n-1} \ln\left(\frac{e^{2v} n^v}{v^v \sqrt{2\pi v} \cdot (n-v)} \cdot \frac{v!(n-v)!}{n!}\right) \\ &< \frac{e\mu n}{n-1} \ln\left(\frac{e^{2v} n^v}{v^v \sqrt{2\pi v} \cdot (n-v)} \cdot \left(\frac{v}{n}\right)^v\right) \\ &= \frac{e\mu n}{n-1} \ln \frac{e^{2v}}{\sqrt{2\pi v} \cdot (n-v)} \\ &< \frac{2e\mu n v}{n-1}\end{aligned}$$

Thus, the expected waiting time of (μ+1)EA with threshold v is $O(n \log \frac{n}{n-v} + \mu v)$. □

Due to Lemma 1, we already know that after an additional phase of $O(\mu \log \mu)$ all individuals in the population have fitness at least v.

3.1 Large threshold

Firstly, we begin with a simple case where the threshold $v = n - 1$. There are $(n+1)$ possible solutions which have fitness value above the threshold. The composition of optimal solution set depends on the population size μ.

THEOREM 1. *Let $v = n-1$ and $\mu \geqslant n+1$, then the expected optimization time of (μ+1)-EA$_D$ on* OneMax *is upper bounded by $O(\mu n + \mu \log \mu + n^2 \log n)$.*

PROOF. There are $(n+1)$ different individuals that have fitness value above the threshold. When $\mu \geqslant n+1$, the optimal solution set should contain all of the $(n+1)$ different individuals. According to our definition of diversity, duplicates will not affect the diversity. Then the $(\mu - n - 1)$ other individuals have no contribution to the diversity.

As stated in Lemma 2, the expected waiting time until (μ+1)-EA has obtained a solution with fitness value above the threshold when $v = n-1$ is bounded above by $O(\mu n + n \log n)$.

After the first solution with fitness value above the threshold is produced, the algorithm will focus on producing other individuals with acceptable quality. According to Lemma 1, the expected runtime of this procedure is bounded above by $O(\mu \log \mu)$.

We now work under the assumption that all individuals have fitness at least v. Note, that (μ+1)-EA$_D$ will not accept any solution of fitness below v. In the worst case, these μ solutions are replicas, so the population diversity equals to 0 at the beginning. The diversity can be improved by producing new solutions from the replicas. Since the duplicates in the population have no contribution to the diversity, they will be replaced by the new individual which has a higher contribution to the diversity. It does not matter which individual is selected from the population to produce a new solution, since the individual with the least contribution will always be the one to be replaced. If the current population has i different individuals, the probability of creating a new solution with fitness value v is at least

$$\frac{1}{n} \cdot \frac{n-i}{n} \cdot \left(1 - \frac{1}{n}\right)^{n-2} \geqslant \frac{n-i}{en(n-1)}.$$

The 1^n solution can be produced in any stage and will stay in the population. The probability of producing the 1^n solution is

$$\frac{1}{n} \cdot \left(1 - \frac{1}{n}\right)^{n-1} \geqslant \frac{1}{en}.$$

Since the duplicated individuals in the population will not affect the diversity measurement, the diversity optimization process will not stop until the optimal diversity is reached, which means the population set contains all possible solutions that fulfil the requirement in fitness value.

The expected time for optimizing the diversity is

$$en + \sum_{i=1}^{n-1} \frac{en(n-1)}{n-i} = en + en(n-1) \sum_{i=1}^{n-1} \frac{1}{i}$$
$$\leqslant en + en(n-1)\ln(en)$$

Hence, the expected optimization of the (μ+1)-EA on *OneMax* with diversity optimization for threshold $(n-1)$ is bounded above by

$$O(\mu n + n\log n) + O(\mu \log \mu) + O(n + n^2 \log n)$$
$$= O(\mu n + \mu \log \mu + n^2 \log n).$$

□

We now study smaller population sizes such that not all different solutions of fitness at least v can be included in the population. Here the (μ+1)-EA$_D$ has to obtain of subset of μ solutions maximizing the diversity.

THEOREM 2. *Let $v = n-1$ and $\mu < n+1$, then the expected optimization time of (μ+1)-EA$_D$ on* OneMax *is upper bounded by $O(\mu n \log(\frac{n}{n-\mu}) + n\log n)$.*

PROOF. When $\mu < n+1$, the population set can not contains all possible solutions with fitness value above the threshold. Since the all 1-bit solution only has 1 bit different to other acceptable individuals which have 2 bits different to each other, it will not be in the optimal solution set. Moreover, every individual with fitness $n-1$ has the same Hamming distance to each other, therefore, it does not matter which individual is contained in the population set.

The proof for expected time of (μ+1)-EA achieving the population set with duplicates of an individual with fitness value above the threshold is the same as that in Theorem 1. The expected time is at most $O(\mu n + n\log n + \mu \log \mu)$.

It is of great possibility that the solution with all 1-bits is introduced in some stage of the diversity optimization process. When the population size is small, the probability to select the all 1-bit solution to produce the new solution is large. Since all the individuals in the population have reached the threshold, the probability of getting the 1^n solution is

$$\frac{1}{n} \cdot \left(1 - \frac{1}{n}\right)^{n-1} \geqslant \frac{1}{en}.$$

Then the expected time taken to produce the 1^n solution is less than $en = O(n)$.

After the 1^n solution is introduced, it will remain in the population until the other individuals all have different patterns. The probability of getting a new solution by flipping one 1-bit of the 1^n individual when there are i different solutions with fitness value above the threshold is

$$\frac{1}{\mu} \cdot \frac{n-i}{n} \cdot \left(1 - \frac{1}{n}\right)^{n-1} \geqslant \frac{n-i}{e\mu n}.$$

For the $\mu < n+1$ situation, all of the individuals in the expected solution population should be of different structures. Since the contribution of 1^n in diversity is smaller comparing to those of the individuals with fitness v, the 1^n solution will be replaced by a solution with fitness value v after the other $(\mu - 1)$ individuals are different from each other.

Then the waiting time for achieving a population of μ different solutions with fitness $(n-1)$ from the intermediate step is

$$\sum_{i=1}^{\mu-1} \frac{e\mu n}{n-i} = e\mu n \sum_{i=1}^{\mu-1} \frac{1}{n-i} \leqslant e\mu n(\ln n - \ln(n-\mu))$$

Having obtained μ individuals of fitness $v = n-1$, the solution 1^n is removed from the population as it has the smallest diversity contribution, and then the optimal population is achieved.

Summing up, the expected optimization time is

$$O(\mu n + n\log n + \mu\log\mu) + O(n) + O(\mu n \log(\frac{n}{n-\mu}))$$
$$= O(n\log n + \mu n \log \frac{n}{n-\mu}).$$

□

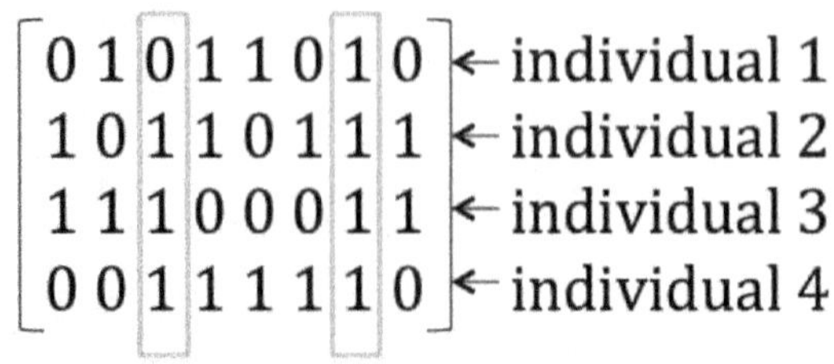

Figure 1: The $\mu \times n$ matrix represents the individuals in a population. In the example, it is a matrix for a population with 4 individuals which are all 8 bits in length. The 7th column is all-1-bit column and the 3rd column is 0-bit column as defined.

3.2 Smaller thresholds

We now consider the case where $n/2 \leq v < n-1$ holds. For convenience, we store the population in a $\mu \times n$ matrix where each individual as a row and define the column where there is no 0-bit as all-1-bit column and the column where there is only one 0-bit as 0-bit column. An example is shown in Figure 1.

The following lemma shows crucial properties of a population maximizing diversity.

LEMMA 3. *Let $\mu \leqslant \binom{n}{v}$. The matrix of a population P represents an optimal population, if the whole matrix contains $\mu(n-v)$ 0-bits and each column contains $\mu(n-v)/n$ 0-bits.*

PROOF. There are $\binom{n}{v}$ possible solutions for the *OneMax* problem with threshold v. Assuming $v \geq n/2$ implies that there have to be at least as many 1-bits as 0-bits in each individual. For $\mu \leqslant \binom{n}{v}$, we show that the optimal population should contains only individuals with fitness value v, since these individuals can make a higher contribution to the overall diversity. Then the total number of 0-bits in the population can be represented as $\mu \cdot (n-v)$, and w.l.o.g , we assume that $\mu \cdot (n-v)/n$ is an integer.

From the perspective of matrix representing the optimal population, the contribution of each column has no influence on those of other columns, so the population diversity equals to the sum of contribution of every column in the matrix. The contribution of each column should be maximized so that the population diversity is maximized. If there are m 0-bits in a column, the contribution of this column will be

$$m(\mu - m).$$

The population diversity can be calculated as

$$\sum_{i=1}^{n} m_i(\mu - m_i),$$

where m_i represents the number of 0-bits in the ith column. The constraint is that the total number of 0-bits in the population is at most $\mu(n-v)$, which can be represented as

$$\sum_{i=1}^{n} m_i \leqslant \mu(n-v).$$

When $\mu \leqslant \binom{n}{v}$, the constraint is

$$\sum_{i=1}^{n} m_i = \mu(n-v).$$

Before all columns are balanced in the number of 0-bits, there exist at least two columns that one has more 0-bits than average number and the other has less 0-bits than average number. Let i, j, k represent the number of 0-bits in columns which has 0-bits above, below and equal to the average number separately. Their relationship can be interpreted as $j < k < i$, where $i, j, k \in \mathbb{N}$. Reducing the unbalance rate by flipping a 1-bit and a 0-bit of column with i and j. Increasing j by 1 causes the diversity changed by

$$(j+1)(\mu - j - 1) - j(\mu - j) = \mu - 2j - 1.$$

Decreasing i by 1 causes the diversity changed by

$$(i-1)(\mu - i + 1) - i(\mu - i) = -\mu - 2i - 1.$$

Therefore, the overall change to diversity is

$$(\mu - 2j - 1) + (-\mu - 2i - 1) = 2(i - j - 1).$$

Since i, j and k are all natural numbers and none of them are equal as defined, $2(i-j-1)$ should be at least 2. Hence, whenever there is unbalance in the number of 0-bits in each column, there exist some columns which can be changed to gain balance and increase diversity, which implies that the population diversity is optimized only when the 0-bits are evenly distributed in each column. The number of each column is then $\mu \cdot (n-v)/n$. □

We now consider the case of a small population where $\mu \leqslant n/(n-v)$ holds. In this case the optimal population contains only individuals which have 0-bits in different positions.

THEOREM 3. *Let $\mu \leqslant \frac{n}{n-v}$, then the expected optimization time of (μ+1)-EA$_D$ on OneMax is upper bounded by $O(\mu n^2 \log \mu)$.*

PROOF. According to Lemma 1 and 2, it takes $O(\mu v + n \log \frac{n}{n-v})$ time to achieve a population with all individuals above the threshold.

Since the population size is $\mu \leqslant \frac{n}{n-v}$, the population set with optimal diversity value should contains only individuals which have 0-bits in different position with other individuals. The matrix for the population with optimal diversity value should only have all-1-bit columns and 0-bit columns.

In the worst case, there are $\mu(n-v)$ 0-bits that has duplicates in the same column. In order to achieve the optimal population, the number of columns with more than one 0-bits should be decreased to 0.

At the beginning of the diversity optimization process, the population diversity is 0 as in the worst case where there are only duplicates. The number of all-1-bit columns is v. Before the population diversity reaches the optimal value, there should exist at least one column that has more than one 0-bits. Hence, one way of improving the diversity is selecting an individual with 0-bit not in the 0-bit column and increasing its contribution to diversity. Let the number of 0-bits in ith column be represented by m_i. Then flipping one 0-bit of an individual will cause the contribution change by

$$(m_i - 1)(\mu - m_i + 1) - m_i(\mu - m_i) = -\mu + 2m_i - 1.$$

Flipping one 1-bit in the all-1-bit column will increase the contribution by $(\mu - 1)$. Therefore, flipping a pair of 1-bit and 0-bit as restricted above will change its contribution by

$$(-\mu + 2m_i - 1) + (\mu - 1) = 2(m_i - 1).$$

In order to increase the diversity, the 0-bit chosen should fulfil the condition of $m_i > 1$, which means the 0-bit to be flipped should have duplicates in the same column.

Before the diversity is optimized, there should always exist a column which has more than one 0-bit. We consider the event that selecting an individual which has an 0-bit in the column with $m_i > 1$ and flipping the certain 0-bit together with a 1-bit in one of its all-1-bit columns. According to our analysis above, this event will produce an individual that increases the diversity by at least $2(m_i - 1)$. Let the number of 0-bits with duplicates in the same column be represented by k. Then the probability for such an event described above to happen equals to

$$\frac{k}{\mu} \cdot \frac{1}{n} \cdot \frac{1}{n} \cdot \left(1 - \frac{1}{n}\right)^{n-2} \geqslant \frac{k}{e\mu n^2}.$$

The event described in the last paragraph decreases the number k by 1. When there are 2 0-bits in a column, these 2 duplicated 0-bits can be split into two 0-bit columns in one iteration. Hence, it takes $\mu(n-v) - (n-v)$ steps to get the optimal population.

Therefore the overall waiting time is

$$\sum_{k=\mu(n-v)}^{(n-v)} \frac{e\mu n^2}{k} = e\mu n^2 \sum_{k=\mu(n-v)}^{n-v} \frac{1}{k}$$
$$\leqslant e\mu n^2(\ln e\mu(n-v) - \ln(n-v))$$
$$\leqslant e\mu n^2 \ln e\mu$$

Hence, the expected optimization time is

$$O(\mu v + n \log \frac{n}{n-v}) + O(\mu n^2 \log \mu) = O(\mu n^2 \log \mu).$$

□

In the following, we study how (μ+1)-EA$_D$ is able to achieve an optimal population if μ is larger.

THEOREM 4. *Let $\mu \leqslant \binom{n}{v}$, then the expected optimization time of (μ+1)-EA$_D$ on OneMax is upper bounded by $O(\mu n^2(n - v) \log(\frac{n}{n-v}))$.*

PROOF. According to Lemma 2, the waiting time of (μ+1)-EA on *OneMax* to achieve the first individual with fitness value above the threshold v is $O(\mu v + n\log\frac{n}{n-v})$. After that, it takes $O(\mu\log\mu)$ time to obtain a solution set that contains only individuals with fitness value above the threshold as proved in the previous section.

As proved in Lemma 3, the 0-bits should be equally distributed in all columns so that the population diversity is optimized. The total number of 0-bits in the population is $\mu(n-v)$. The optimal solution set should make sure that in the corresponding matrix there are either

$$\left\lceil\frac{\mu(n-v)}{n}\right\rceil \text{ or } \left\lfloor\frac{\mu(n-v)}{n}\right\rfloor$$

0-bits in each column. Let i represent the largest number of 0-bits in a column and j represent the smallest number of 0-bits in a column. If $j \leqslant i \leqslant j+1$ is fulfilled, the population diversity is optimized. When $\mu(n-v)\%n = 0$, then the equality stands.

Before the diversity is maximized, it should be true that $i > j$. Therefore, there exists an individual that has a 0-bit in the column with i 0-bits and a 1-bit in the column with j 0-bits. Consider the event that selecting the certain individual and flipping those 0-bit and 1-bit in the same iteration. The overall change to contribution is

$$(-\mu + 2i - 1) + (\mu - 2j - 1) = 2(i - j - 1),$$

which is the same as that in Lemma 3. Since $i > j + 1$ before the diversity is optimized, such an event should lead to improvement in the diversity. The probability for such an event happen is

$$\frac{1}{\mu}\cdot\frac{1}{n}\cdot\frac{1}{n}\cdot(1-\frac{1}{n})^{n-2} \geqslant \frac{1}{e\mu n(n-1)}.$$

Hence, the expected runtime for the improvement is bounded above by $O(\mu n^2)$.

In the beginning of diversity optimization process, as the worst case, the row matrix storing the numbers of 0-bits of each column contains $(n-v)$ elements with value μ and v elements with value 0. The event mentioned above decreases the number of 0-bits in the certain column and increases the number of 0-bits in the corresponding column. As proved in Lemma 3, when $v \geqslant \mu/2$, the contribution to diversity of a column is monotonously increasing with the number of 0-bits.

In the worst case, there are $(n-v)$ columns which have μ 0-bits at the beginning. Then it takes $(n-v)$ iterations to decrease the largest number of 0-bits in a column ,which is defined as i, by 1. For a certain i, there are at least i individuals that can be chosen to produce a child by flipping a pair of 0-bit and 1-bit as stated in the previous paragraph.

Therefore the overall waiting time of (μ+1)-EA$_D$ on *OneMax* for a population with less than $\binom{n}{v}$ individuals is at most

$$\begin{aligned}
&\sum_{i=\mu}^{\frac{\mu(n-v)}{n}+1} (n-v)\cdot en(n-1)\cdot\frac{\mu}{i} \\
\leqslant\ & e\mu n^2(n-v)\sum_{i=\mu}^{\frac{\mu(n-v)}{n}+1}\frac{1}{i} \\
\leqslant\ & e\mu n^2(n-v)\ln(\frac{en}{n-v})
\end{aligned}$$

Hence, the expected optimization time is bounded above by

$$O(\mu n^2(n-v)\log\frac{n}{n-v}).$$

□

4. LeadingOnes

In this section we will discuss the expected runtime for (μ+1)-EA$_D$ on the classical *LeadingOnes* problem which has been subject to several investigations in the area of runtime analysis [2, 16]. *LeadingOnes* is defined as

$$LeadingOnes(x) = \sum_{i=1}^{n}\prod_{j=1}^{i} x_j.$$

Similar to that of *OneMax* problem, the diversity optimization on *LeadingOnes* problem can also be divided into two stages. The first one is obtaining a population of all individuals with acceptable fitness value and the second one is maximizing the population diversity.

LEMMA 4. *The expected runtime until* (μ+1)$-EA$ *on* LeadingOnes *problem has obtained a solution of fitness value above the threshold* v *is* $O(nv + \mu v\log n)$.

PROOF. Assume L represents the largest number of leading ones among all individuals in the current population and i represents the number of individuals with the fitness value L. For a certain L value, we assume it will not change until there are $\min\{n/\ln(en), \mu\}$ duplicates of the individual with fitness L as stated in Witt [16].

The probability for making a duplicate of the individual with fitness L is at least

$$\frac{i}{\mu}\cdot(1-\frac{1}{n})^n \geqslant \frac{i(n-1)}{e\mu n}.$$

The expected runtime for making $\min\{n/\ln(en), \mu\}$ duplicates is at most

$$\begin{aligned}
\sum_{i=1}^{\min\{n/\ln(en),\mu\}-1}\frac{e\mu n}{i(n-1)} &= \frac{e\mu n}{n-1}\sum_{i=1}^{\min\{n/\ln(en),\mu\}-1}\frac{1}{i} \\
&\leqslant \frac{e\mu n}{n-1}\ln\frac{en}{\ln(en)} \\
&\leqslant 2e\mu\ln(en)
\end{aligned}$$

After there exist at least $\min\{n/\ln(en), \mu\}$ duplicates, L will be improved by selecting an individual with fitness L and flipping its leftmost 0-bit. The probability for this event is

$$\frac{i}{\mu}\cdot\frac{1}{n}\cdot(1-\frac{1}{n})^{n-1} \geqslant \frac{i}{e\mu n}.$$

Since before the improvement is made, there are already

$$\min\{n/\ln(en), \mu\}$$

replicas, i is equal to $\min\{n/\ln(en), \mu\}$, which makes the expected runtime be

$$\frac{e\mu n}{\min\{n/\ln(en), \mu\}} \leqslant e\mu\ln(en) + en$$

The expected runtime of the (μ+1)-EA obtaining the first individual with fitness value above the threshold v equals to the sum of waiting time for each L value. Therefore, the overall waiting time is

$$v \cdot \left(2e\mu\ln(en) + \frac{e\mu n}{\min\{n/\ln(en), \mu\}}\right) \leqslant v(3e\mu\ln(en) + en)$$

In conclusion, the overall waiting time for $(\mu+1)-EA$ on *LeadingOnes* problem has obtained a solution of fitness value above the threshold v is $O(nv + \mu v\log n)$.

□

For a *LeadingOnes* problem with threshold v, there are 2^{n-v} different possible solutions. When $\mu > 2^{n-v}$, all of the 2^{n-v} different possible solutions should be contained in the optimal population set and there should be duplicates in the population. According to our definition of diversity, the duplicates will not affect the diversity measurement.

LEMMA 5. *The optimal solution of (μ+1)-EA*$_D$ *on LeadingOnes with threshold* v *has the population diversity* $\mu^2(n-v)/4$.

PROOF. Assume that there is a matrix which contains all individuals and each individual as a row, which is similar to the matrix for *OneMax* problem. Let m_i equal to the number of 0-bits in ith column. Then the contribution to diversity of each column can be represented as $m_i(\mu - m_i) = \mu m_i - {m_i}^2$. In the left v columns, there are only 1-bits so the contribution to diversity is 0. For the following $(n-v)$ columns, when $m_i = \mu/2$, the quadratic function reaches its maximal. The contribution of each column has no effect on those of other columns. Hence, if there is no duplicate in the population and each of the $(n-v)$ columns has $\mu/2$ 0-bits, the population diversity equals to $(\mu^2/4)\cdot(n-v) = \mu^2(n-v)/4$, which is the maximum value. □

LEMMA 6. *The expected waiting time of (μ+1)-EA*$_D$ *on LeadingOnes to achieve* μ *different solutions above the threshold, where* $\mu \leqslant 2^{\frac{n-v}{2}-1}$, *is bounded above by* $O(nv + \mu v\log n + \mu n\log\mu)$.

PROOF. After the first individual with fitness value above the threshold is achieved in $O(nv + \mu v\log n)$ time, another $(\mu-1)$ individuals with fitness value above the threshold are produced before the diversity optimization process begins. This process will take $O(\mu\log\mu)$ time as proved in Lemma 1.

Since the duplicates make no contribution to the diversity and may interfere the optimization process, we should get rid of the duplicates at the beginning of the diversity optimization process. When there is duplicates in the population, a new individual will always be accepted and replace one of the duplicates. A new individual can be produced by selecting an individual and flipped one bit to become one of its undiscovered Hamming neighbours. An upper bound for the expected number of undiscovered Hamming neighbours of a set of individuals is given in [7] as at least $n - 2\cdot r$ where $0 < |P| \leqslant 2^r$ and P is the set of discovered individuals. In the *LeadingOnes* problem, the v leftmost bits should be all $1's$. Only the $(n-v)$ other bits can be either 0-bit or 1-bit so the expected Hamming neighbours are at least $n - v - 2\cdot r$. Since $\mu \leqslant 2^{\frac{n-v}{2}-1}$, the expected number $n - v - 2\cdot r \geqslant 2$. Assume the number of non-duplicated individuals in the current population is s. Then the expected number of Hamming neighbours is equal to $(n - v - 2\log s)$. The probability of obtaining an undiscovered Hamming neighbour is at most

$$(n - v - 2\log s)\cdot\frac{s}{\mu}\cdot\frac{1}{n}\cdot\left(1-\frac{1}{n}\right)^{n-1} \geqslant \frac{s(n-v-2\log s)}{e\mu n}.$$

Therefore the total time for obtaining a population with μ different individuals is

$$\begin{aligned}\sum_{s=1}^{\mu-1}\frac{e\mu n}{s(n-v-2\log s)} &= e\mu n\sum_{s=1}^{\mu-1}\frac{1}{s(n-v-2\log s)}\\ &\leqslant e\mu n\sum_{i=1}^{\mu-1}\frac{1}{s}\\ &\leqslant e\mu n\ln(e\mu)\end{aligned}$$

Hence, it takes at most $O(\mu n\log\mu)$ time to get a population set with no duplicates in it. Taken all stages into consideration, the expected runtime of (μ+1)-EA$_D$ on *LeadingOnes* to achieve μ solutions above the threshold is bounded above by

$$\begin{aligned}&O(nv + \mu v\log n) + O(\mu\log\mu) + O(\mu n\log\mu)\\ =\ &O(nv + \mu v\log n + \mu n\log\mu).\end{aligned}$$

□

Now, we show an upper bound for *LeadingOnes* that holds for $\mu \leq 2^{\frac{n-v}{2}-1}$.

THEOREM 5. *Let* $\mu \leqslant 2^{\frac{n-v}{2}-1}$, *then expected optimization time of (μ+1)-EA*$_D$ *on LeadingOnes is upper bounded by* $O(nv + \mu v\log n + \mu n\log(\mu(n-v)))$.

PROOF. According to Lemma 4, it takes at most $O(nv + \mu v\log n + \mu n\log\mu)$ time for (μ+1)-EA$_D$ on *LeadingOnes* to get a population of μ different individuals.

After the duplicates are replaced by different solutions, if each column has $\mu/2$ 0-bits, the population diversity should equal to the maximal value $\mu^2 n/4$ as proved in Lemma 5. In the worst case, the initial value of m_i of each column is either μ or 0. In order to increase the diversity of the population, m_i value of each column should either increase or decrease to $\mu/2$. Since the duplicates does no contribution to the population diversity, in this process, it should be guaranteed that the new individual produced is not a replica of any existing individuals.

Let s_i and t_i represent the number of 0-bits and 1-bits in the ith column separately. Then $|s_i - t_i| = d_i$ can be regarded as the balance rate of 0-bits and 1-bits in the ith column. Consider the event that selecting an individual randomly and flipping one of its 0-bits or 1-bits to decrease the balance rate of the column. When $s_i < t_i$, this event will cause the contribution $s_i\cdot t_i$ change by

$$(s_i+1)(\mu - s_i - 1) - s_i(\mu - s_i) = \mu - 2s_i - 1,$$

as the contribution to diversity of other columns will not change. Since $s_i + t_i = \mu$ and $s_i < t_i$, $s_i < \mu/2$. Then the contribution change is at least 0. At the beginning of this stage, there is no duplicate in the population and in each iteration, it should be guaranteed that there is no duplicate introduced to the population. Since there is no duplicates in the parent population, there should exists at most $\min\{t_i, s_i\}$ individuals that are only different in the chosen column from any other individuals. Therefore, there exist at least $|s_i - t_i|$ individuals which have no replicas in pattern without considering the selected column , which also means there should be at least $(s_i - t_i)$ 0-bits that can be flipped without making a duplicates. The probability for such an event to happen is

$$\frac{1}{\mu} \cdot \frac{1}{n} \cdot \left(1 - \frac{1}{n}\right)^{n-1} \geqslant \frac{1}{e\mu n}.$$

In a population which is not optimized, there should be $\sum_{i=0}^{n-v} |s_i - t_i|$ different mutations that can lead to diversity improvement through the event we described in the last paragraph. At first, we assume there are either all 1-bits or all 0-bits in each column which makes the total number of feasible mutation equals to $\mu(n - v)$. After each mutation, the number of feasible mutation is decreased by 2 according to the definition of balance rate. Let $d = \sum_{i=0}^{n-v} |s_i - t_i|$, then the expected time for the improvement is at most $e\mu n/d$. For the optimized population, the balance rate of each column should be 0. Before the population diversity is maximized, one bit flipping as discussed above causes the balance rate of the certain column decreased by 2. Hence, the total waiting time for the population diversity to be maximized is

$$\sum_{d=1}^{\mu(n-v)/2} e\mu n \cdot \frac{1}{d} \leqslant \frac{1}{2} e\mu n \ln(e\mu(n - v))$$

Hence, the overall runtime of (μ+1)-EA$_\text{D}$ on *LeadingOnes* is bounded above by $O(n^2 + \mu v \log n + \mu n \log(\mu(n - v)))$. □

Conclusions

The population of an evolutionary algorithm can be used to generate a diverse set of solutions where all solutions are of good quality. We examined such approaches in a rigorous way by a first runtime analysis and studied a (μ+1)-EA$_\text{D}$ which maximizes the diversity of the population once all solutions have fitness beyond a given threshold value v. Our results for the classical benchmark problems *OneMax* and *LeadingOnes* show that the algorithm is efficiently maximizing diversity of the population.

Our investigations should set the basis for analysis of diversity maximization for classical combinatorial optimization problems and it would be an interesting topic for future work to study the investigated (μ+1)-EA$_\text{D}$ on classical combinatorial optimization problems such as the traveling salesperson problem or the vertex cover problem.

Acknowledgements

Frank Neumann has been supported by ARC grants DP130104395 and DP140103400.

References

[1] A. Auger and B. Doerr. *Theory of Randomized Search Heuristics: Foundations and Recent Developments*. World Scientific Publishing Co., Inc., 2011.

[2] S. Böttcher, B. Doerr, and F. Neumann. Optimal fixed and adaptive mutation rates for the LeadingOnes problem. In Schaefer et al. [11], pages 1–10.

[3] N. Chaiyaratana, T. Piroonratana, and N. Sangkawelert. Effects of diversity control in single-objective and multi-objective genetic algorithms. *J. Heuristics*, 13(1):1–34, 2007.

[4] S. Droste, T. Jansen, and I. Wegener. On the analysis of the (1+1) evolutionary algorithm. *Theor. Comput. Sci.*, 276:51–81, 2002.

[5] T. Friedrich, N. Hebbinghaus, and F. Neumann. Comparison of simple diversity mechanisms on plateau functions. *Theor. Comput. Sci.*, 410(26):2455–2462, 2009.

[6] T. Friedrich, P. S. Oliveto, D. Sudholt, and C. Witt. Analysis of diversity-preserving mechanisms for global exploration. *Evolutionary Computation*, 17(4):455–476, 2009.

[7] C. Horoba and F. Neumann. Benefits and drawbacks for the use of epsilon-dominance in evolutionary multi-objective optimization. In *Proceedings of the 10th Annual Conference on Genetic and Evolutionary Computation*, GECCO '08, pages 641–648, New York, NY, USA, 2008. ACM.

[8] T. Jansen. *Analyzing Evolutionary Algorithms - The Computer Science Perspective*. Natural Computing Series. Springer, 2013.

[9] Y. Leung, Y. Gao, and Z. Xu. Degree of population diversity - a perspective on premature convergence in genetic algorithms and its markov chain analysis. *IEEE Transactions on Neural Networks*, 8(5):1165–1176, 1997.

[10] F. Neumann and C. Witt. *Bioinspired Computation in Combinatorial Optimization:Algorithms and Their Computational Complexity*. Springer-Verlag New York, Inc., New York, NY, USA, 1st edition, 2010.

[11] R. Schaefer, C. Cotta, J. Kolodziej, and G. Rudolph, editors. *Parallel Problem Solving from Nature - PPSN XI, 11th International Conference, Kraków, Poland, September 11-15, 2010, Proceedings, Part I*, volume 6238 of *Lecture Notes in Computer Science*. Springer, 2010.

[12] T. Ulrich, J. Bader, and L. Thiele. Defining and optimizing indicator-based diversity measures in multiobjective search. In Schaefer et al. [11], pages 707–717.

[13] T. Ulrich, J. Bader, and E. Zitzler. Integrating decision space diversity into hypervolume-based multiobjective search. In M. Pelikan and J. Branke, editors, *GECCO*, pages 455–462. ACM, 2010.

[14] T. Ulrich and L. Thiele. Maximizing population diversity in single-objective optimization. In N. Krasnogor and P. L. Lanzi, editors, *GECCO*, pages 641–648. ACM, 2011.

[15] R. K. Ursem. Diversity-guided evolutionary algorithms. In J. J. M. Guervós, P. Adamidis, H.-G. Beyer, J. L. F.-V. Martín, and H.-P. Schwefel, editors, *PPSN*, volume 2439 of *Lecture Notes in Computer Science*, pages 462–474. Springer, 2002.

[16] C. Witt. Runtime analysis of the $(\mu + 1)$ EA on simple pseudo-boolean functions. *Evolutionary Computation*, 14(1):65–86, 2006.

Parameter-less Population Pyramid

Brian W. Goldman
BEACON Center for the Study of Evolution in Action
Michigan State University, U.S.A.
brianwgoldman@acm.org

William F. Punch
BEACON Center for the Study of Evolution in Action
Michigan State University, U.S.A.
punch@msu.edu

ABSTRACT

Real world applications of evolutionary techniques are often hindered by the need to determine problem specific parameter settings. While some previous methods have reduced or removed the need for parameter tuning, many do so by trading efficiency for general applicability. The Parameter-less Population Pyramid (P3) is an evolutionary technique that requires **no parameters** and is still broadly effective. P3 strikes a balance between continuous integration of diversity and exploitative elitist operators, allowing it to solve easy problems quickly and hard problems eventually. When compared with three optimally tuned, state of the art optimization techniques, P3 always finds the optimum at least a constant factor ***faster*** across four benchmarks (Deceptive Trap, Deceptive Step Trap, HIFF, Rastrigin). More importantly, on three randomized benchmarks (NK Landscapes, Ising Spin Glasses, MAX-SAT), P3 has a lower order of computational complexity as measured by evaluations. We also provide outlines for expected runtime analysis of P3, setting the stage for future theory based conclusions. Based on over 1 trillion evaluations, our results suggest P3 has wide applicability to a broad class of problems.

Categories and Subject Descriptors

I.2.8 [**Artificial Intelligence**]: Problem Solving, Control Methods, and Search

General Terms

Algorithms, Performance, Experimentation

Keywords

Linkage Learning; Local Search; Parameter-less

1. INTRODUCTION

Providing a good solution in reasonable time to a broad class of real world black-box problems is a fundamental goal of evolutionary computation. Achieving this goal requires an optimizer to make assumptions about the nature of the problem it is solving as no optimizer can solve all problems equally well [15]. Many genetic algorithms (GAs) introduce evolutionary parameters which provide user control of search assumptions. These parameters can have enormous impact on search efficiency [3] and can have non-obvious optimal settings which require time-consuming tuning to discover [5]. When applied to black-box problems with non-trivial evaluation functions, the tuning process can be intractable, forcing users to rely on stock values or attempt a small number of test values.

The problem of parameter tuning has encouraged work to remove parameters from user control in an effort to improve out-of-the-box GA quality. In an early example, a crossover-based GA was devised which used concurrent racing populations which removed all user specified parameters [7]. Population racing has also been paired with more advanced evolutionary system, such as Hierarchical Bayesian Optimization [10]. Without the need to set a population size, racing ensures the GA will take no more than a logarithmic factor increase in evaluations beyond optimal. While experimental evidence suggests racing is only a constant factor loss, this method explicitly trades efficiency for applicability.

In this work we shall introduce the Parameter-less Population Pyramid (P3). P3 is an iterative method for constructing a collection of populations that requires no user parameters. It leverages entropy based linkage detection to learn how to efficiently mix solutions without problem specific information beyond the evaluation function. Perhaps most importantly, unlike other parameter-less techniques it experimentally appears to be at least a constant factor ***improvement*** over comparable, optimally configured, optimization methods.

2. THE P3 ALGORITHM

Unlike many GA techniques, P3 does not have a single population of solutions. Instead P3 maintains a pyramid-like structure, such that each level of the pyramid has a population of solutions, with each level representing something akin to different generations of evolution. Figure 1 provides a high level summary of how P3 iteratively constructs these populations and utilizes them to improve randomly generated solutions through hill climbing and crossover. While P3 can be applied to any discrete value representation, we will focus on the binary domain here for simplicity.

GECCO'14, July 12–16, 2014, Vancouver, BC, Canada.
Copyright 2014 ACM 978-1-4503-2662-9/14/07 ...$15.00.
http://dx.doi.org/10.1145/2576768.2598350.

```
procedure ITERATE-P3
    Create random solution
    Apply hill climber (Section 2.1)
    if solution ∉ hashset then
        Add solution to P_0 (Section 2.2)
        Add solution to hashset
    for all P_i ∈ pyramid do
        Mix solution with P_i (Section 2.3)
        if solution's fitness has improved then
            if solution ∉ hashset then
                Add solution to P_{i+1}
                Add solution to hashset
```

Figure 1: One iteration of P3 optimization. ***pyramid*** **is an ordered set of populations and** ***hashset*** **is a set of all solutions in** ***pyramid*****.**

```
procedure CLUSTER-CREATION
    unmerged ← {{0}, {1}, {2}, ..., {N − 1}}
    useful ← unmerged
    while |unmerged| > 1 do
        C_i, C_j ← min_{C_i,C_j ∈ unmerged} D(C_i, C_j)
        unmerged ← unmerged − {C_i, C_j} + {C_i ∪ C_j}
        useful ← useful + {C_i ∪ C_j}
        if D(C_i, C_j) = 0 then
            useful ← useful − {C_i, C_j}
    Order useful based on cluster size, smallest first.
    Remove largest cluster from useful.
    return useful
```

Figure 2: Algorithm describing how clusters are created using Equation 1 for each P_i. ***unmerged*** **and** ***useful*** **are ordered sets of sets of gene loci.**

2.1 Hill Climber

We use the First Improvement Hill Climber (FIHC),[1] which acts as follows. Consider all gene loci x_i in a random order. Evaluate the solution using all possible values of x_i. If any alternative value is a strict fitness improvement over the original value for x_i, replace x_i with the improved value. Iteration of the process continues until no such change results in a strict fitness improvement.

To avoid wasting evaluations, FIHC keeps track of all loci tested since the last change was made to the solution. If the algorithm returns to the same loci without any changes, it moves on to the next loci without performing any evaluations.

FIHC solves all linear functions in $O(N)$ time, where N is the number of genes. This is in contrast to methods like Steepest Ascent Hill Climber [1, 4] which require $O(N^2)$ as changes are only accepted after all neighbor solutions are evaluated. In general, FIHC is designed to find optima using a minimum number of evaluations. Furthermore, because FIHC tests loci in a random order it does not cause any positional bias to the search.

2.2 Pyramid

As mentioned, P3 maintains a pyramid like structure of populations with more optimized solutions in higher levels. More specifically, a solution's level is one higher than its highest parent, similar to the layering done in [8].

The levels represent disjoint sets of unique solutions, such that $\forall_{i,j \in P, i \neq j} P_i \cap P_j = \emptyset$. This relationship is maintained constructively, such that new solutions can only be added to a level if they do not exist in any level of the pyramid. This uniqueness check can be achieved in constant time by maintaining a hash of all solutions in the pyramid.

Along with storing the solutions, each level also maintains a table of pairwise gene value frequencies for use by crossover. This is also built constructively, such that initially all frequencies are set to 0. Each time a solution is added to a level, all pairs of loci are queried for their gene values. The table is then updated, incrementing the count for each observed pairing. This requires $O(N^2)$ operations (no evaluations) each time a solution is added to a level of the pyramid, but is constant in the number of solutions currently in the level.

[1]We use the name FIHC for descriptive clarity. This algorithm likely already exists in the literature under various alternative names.

2.3 Crossover

P3 uses a crossover method derived from that defined for LTGA [14] (Section 3.2); P3 uses gene value entropy to construct clusters of genes that should have their values conserved during crossover. There are two steps in defining this type of crossover: *cluster creation* and *cluster usage*.

During cluster creation, P3 creates a binary tree of clusters such that the leaves represent individual gene loci and each internal node represent the subset of loci created by joining the subsets encoded in its children. Using the table of observed frequencies described in Section 2.2, Equation 1 calculates the linkage "distance" between clusters of loci using the average pairwise entropy, as given in Equation 2.

$$D(C_i, C_j) = \frac{1}{|C_i| \cdot |C_j|} \sum_{c_i \in C_i} \sum_{c_j \in C_j} 2 - \frac{H(C_i) + H(C_j)}{H(C_i \cup C_j)} \quad (1)$$

$$H(C) = -\sum_{s \in S} p_c(s) \log(p_c(s)) \quad (2)$$

Figure 2 depicts the process of agglomeratively constructing the linkage tree. Starting with each gene location in separate clusters, Equation 2 is used to find which C_i and C_j in *unmerged*, the set of gene clusters, have the tightest linkage (minimum distance). These are merged to form a new cluster $C_i \cup C_j$, and the separate pieces are removed from *unmerged* while *useful* tracks all clusters ever created in the hierarchy. This process iterates until all locations have been merged into a single cluster. With proper bookkeeping this algorithm will construct the linkage tree from the frequency table in $O(N^2)$ [6].

Not all of the resulting clusters in the linkage tree are useful for crossover. The most obvious useless cluster is one that contains all the loci. A crossover that preserves all loci in a solution cannot create a new individual. We further remove clusters that are completely contained within their direct superset, such that if $D(C_i, C_j) = 0$, C_i and C_j are not used when performing crossover. $D(C_i, C_j)$ only returns 0 when the loci in C_i perfectly predict the gene values in C_j and vice versa. From this we can conclude that the relative settings for those loci should never be disrupted. When used on particularly small populations this has the potential to greatly reduce the number of clusters used during crossover.

```
procedure CLUSTER-USAGE
    for all C_i ∈ useful do
        for all d ∈ shuffled(P_i) do
            Copy d's gene values for C_i into solution
            if solution was changed then
                if solution's fitness decreased then
                    Revert changes
                break
```

Figure 3: Algorithm describing how clusters are used to perform crossover.

For instance, if $|P_i| = 1$, no clusters exist. If $|P_i| = 2$ at most two clusters exist: one for all genes where the solutions agree and one for where they disagree.

P3 uses crossover to recombine known information in a level of the pyramid with a candidate solution as depicted in Figure 3. For each cluster C_i found by CLUSTER-CREATION, choose a random donor d from the current level such that d's gene values for at least one gene in C_i differs from the candidate solution. Copy all of d's gene values into the solution and evaluate the new solution. If the fitness of the candidate has been reduced, revert the candidate's gene values. It is important to note that candidate changes are kept in the case when the fitness is *unaffected*. This allows crossover to drift, potentially moving through fitness plateaus.

When choosing a donor, P3 ensures there is at least one gene value different between the donor and the candidate solution. This can potentially require up to $O(|C_j||P_i|)$, but empirically appears more efficient than allowing donations that do not change any gene values.

To complete a single crossover event, all of the useful clusters are tested, each requiring at most a single evaluation. Clusters are tested in smallest first order, with clusters of equal size ordered randomly. This ensures smaller building blocks are optimized before large changes are made to the genome, thus helping preserve diversity. This also helps prevent genetic hitchhikers, which may interfere with entropy calculations. As cluster building and application ordering are not dependent on the position of loci in the genome, this operator introduces no positional bias on search.

2.4 All Together

The pieces of P3 were specifically chosen to provide important complimentary capabilities. First, the hill climber provides an efficient tool for discovering pairwise linkage, as search only ends when no single bit change can be made which improves fitness. Therefore crossover, which relies on pairwise linkage, has high quality information to leverage when determining clusters.

Similarly, by starting from a random position for each new solution, P3 progressively reduces the chance of spurious linkage formation due to initialization. Furthermore, these random restarts provide exploration to balance out the hill climber and crossover's extreme exploitation. This also allows the population to grow large enough to contain enough diversity to solve the problem without having to know the optimal size beforehand.

Finally, the use of levels allows P3 to perform solution filtering without throwing away information. Once found, a local optimum is stored indefinitely, preserving both its linkage and genes for future crossovers. By splitting solutions into levels, the linkage information and the donated genes come from similar solution qualities. This prevents noise in gene linkage which only exists in low quality solutions from effecting cluster formation for high quality solutions. It also reduces the chance that optimized solutions will overwrite newer solutions, preserving search diversity.

P3 makes very weak assumptions about the search landscape. In many evolutionary systems the crossover operator assumes linked genes are collocated in the genome. This requires the user to configure genome structure based on gene linkage information they are unlikely to have. All of P3's operations ignore gene ordering, allowing the user to ignore that aspect of configuration.

In general, P3 makes two assumptions about the search landscape: local structure and non uniform gene interdependence. For the hill climber to be effective, there should be at least some correlation between a solution's fitness and the fitness of its single bit neighborhood. Stated another way, this assumes that small changes in genotype result in small changes in phenotype. The non uniform gene interdependence assumption is required by the crossover operator to perform clustering. Without this assumption, the clusters formed by crossover will detect spurious relations. The resulting donation of genes between solutions will be no better than random modification. Both assumptions are likely to hold true for real world problems and are similarly assumed by most evolutionary optimizers.

2.5 Contrasted With The Generational Model

A major advantage of P3's structure is that it avoids the need to set a fixed population size. In a generational model, the diversity contained in the initial population represents a bottleneck for future generations. This is true because in most systems, especially on deceptive problems, mutation rates are too low to create large, multi-gene substructures after initialization. As such the generational model often results in a race between decreasing diversity and increasing fitness.

Premature convergence of a population causes the generational model to have two termination conditions: out of time or out of diversity. In the former, if a smaller population size had been used, less evaluations could have been spent supporting diversity allowing more focus on exploitation. In the latter, if a larger population size had been used, more evaluations could have been performed increasing the likelihood of improving solution quality. In either case, unless the population size is correctly set, the generational model will likely result in waste.

In contrast, P3 has exploited all known information each time the top of the pyramid is reached; no evaluations are wasted on unused diversity. Similarly, because P3 does not throw away previously optimized solutions while adding diversity, it avoids waste caused by premature convergence.

2.6 Order of Complexity Per Evaluation

With the exception of crossover, P3 requires no more than $O(N)$ computations per evaluation, implying it is limited by the time required to evaluate a solution. In order to perform crossover, P3 must spend $O(N^2)$ operations updating pairwise frequencies each time a solution is added to a level of the pyramid. Similarly, it requires $O(N^2)$ time to rebuild the set of crossover clusters once the frequency table has been updated. Naïvely, this leads to the algorithm itself requiring $O(N^2)$ time. However, multiple evaluations can occur for each time a single individual is added to a population.

Each time a random restart occurs, at minimum $N + 1$ evaluations are performed. This means each time a solution is added to P_0, at least $\Omega(N)$ evaluations must be performed. This implies that the $O(N^2)$ cost of the update to P_0 can be amortized over these evaluations, making this update $O(N)$ per evaluation.

To cause an update to P_i, all of the crossovers discovered for P_{i-1} must first be applied, each causing their own evaluation. If P3 were to naïvely use all crossovers and perform an evaluation each time, this would cause $\Omega(N)$ evaluations. Again, this would result in $O(N)$ amortized cost to update P_i. However, Section 2.3 discussed how P3 will ignore some clusters and will also skip an evaluation if no change to the solution was made by a cluster. As such we are currently unable to state conclusively that updating P_i will require $O(N)$ operations per evaluation. That said, empirically it appears to be true. Furthermore, it seems counterintuitive that intentionally wasting evaluations would be considered beneficial to runtime.

There is one more operation in P3 that may not scale linearly with genome size per evaluation: finding a non-identical donor. When performing crossover P3 iteratively searches a population for a random donor with genes that differ from the current solution for the current crossover cluster. In the worst case, this operation could require $|C_j||P_i|$, where $|C_j|$ is the number of genes in the crossover and $|P_i|$ is the number of solutions in the population. However, $|P_i|$ grows very slowly. Also, in empirical evaluation, P3's wall clock time per evaluation appears to scale linearly with problem size.

3. COMPARISON ALGORITHMS

3.1 Random Restart First Improvement Hill Climber

As P3 utilizes a hill climber to perform optimization, it is necessary to show P3's added complexity is able to outperform an optimizer that uses a hill climber alone. Therefore as the first comparison we define a complete optimization method based on the First Improvement Hill Climber from Section 2.1. This definition is extended to match P3's style of restarting. Whenever the hill climber obtains a solution that cannot be improved using a single bit flip, a new solution is randomly generated and optimized.

If P3's quality relies solely on starting at random points and applying FIHC, this comparison algorithm should perform even better than P3. Like P3, the FHIC-alone algorithm is parameter-less, makes no assumptions about gene ordering, and will find the global optimum given a sufficient (potentially exponential) number of evaluations.

3.2 Linkage Tree Genetic Algorithm

The closest relative to P3 in the existing literature is the Linkage Tree Genetic Algorithm (LTGA). There have been a number of different variations proposed to LTGA since its original publication [13], so for comparison we have chosen to use the variant described in the most recent publication [14]. This algorithm is also the current state of the art, outperforming other algorithms in black-box optimization across numerous benchmarks.

LTGA works by iteratively improving a population of solutions in a generational manner. Each generation, half of the solutions (chosen using binary tournament selection) are used to construct a linkage tree just as described in Section 2.3. Each solution in the population is then crossed with the entire population using that linkage tree, with the results put into the next generation. This process continues until the population fails to change between generations, signaling convergence.

Unlike P3, this variant of LTGA does not make use of a hill climber, and there is evidence that doing so results in decreased efficiency [1]. LTGA applies clusters in least linked first order whereas P3 uses smallest first. Also, LTGA does not search for donors until one containing different genes is found. Instead, if the donated genes are identical, it simply skips the evaluation. LTGA requires a population size parameter, maintains a fixed population size across generations, and does not prevent duplicate individuals in a population. LTGA does not add new genetic information after initialization, meaning that if required diversity is not contained in the original population or lost in future generations, LTGA will fail to find the global optimum.

To ensure LTGA is able to find the global optimum quickly, we use the bisection method [4] to minimally set LTGA's population size parameter. To be considered successful, a population size must result in 100 runs without premature convergence. According to the Rule of Three [9], this bounds LTGA's failure rate to less than $\frac{3}{100+1} \approx 3\%$ with 95% confidence. Note that runs used in setting the population are considered testing and were not used during analysis. On randomized problems, training was performed on a disjoint set of problem instances.

Other variants of LTGA have more closely resembled P3 [4], but as those variants do not appear to be in active use, we did not use them for comparison. However, no LTGA variant has removed the population size parameter or fully addressed the problem of premature convergence. There have also been other model based optimization techniques that use few to no parameters. Specifically LO-LIMD [11] uses a population size of one and a parameter free algorithm to perform optimization. It relies on the existence of completely separable subproblems and noise free evaluation in order to determine if two genes are linked through perturbation of their values. While effective on this class of problems, most real world problems do not fall into this category.

3.3 $(1 + (\lambda, \lambda))$

As a final comparison we chose the $(1+(\lambda, \lambda))$ algorithm [2] which is currently the best theory based crossover method. Unlike P3 and LTGA, $(1 + (\lambda, \lambda))$ does not use a population of solutions or any model building to determine problem variable linkage. Instead it uses mutation to produce λ offspring, selecting the best to recombine with the original parent to produce λ more offspring using uniform crossover. In the original work, a method for controlling the value of λ is provided based on offspring success, meaning there are no parameters to be set in this algorithm.

In order to make $(1+(\lambda, \lambda))$ a viable method of optimizing problems with multiple local optima, we modified the original algorithm. Primarily, if during search $\lambda \geq N$, search is restarted from a random individual with $\lambda = 1$. This is done because when $\lambda \geq N$ the mutation rate is greater than or equal to 100%, nullifying search. Furthermore, this point is only reached when the algorithm has stalled for a significant number of generations.

We also made minor modifications to improve selection and to prevent wasting evaluations, as follows. If the best offspring produced in a generation is a mutant offspring, select that over any of those produced using crossover. If there is a fitness tie between the best offspring in a generation, select the one with the maximum hamming distance to the parent. This encourages drift over plateaus. While the original paper discusses a "mod" version of the λ control strategy for how to handle when offspring of equal fitness are produced, we found this conflicted with our method of restarting. As such we use the original control strategy. Finally, if an offspring produced by crossover has identical genes to either of its parents, it is not evaluated.

4. TEST PROBLEMS

All four of our optimization techniques share some interesting properties for problem equivalence. All are fitness scale invariant, in that changing the fitness values without changing the relation between solution fitnesses will not affect search. None of the methods have a bias toward creating specific gene values, in that XORing all solutions with a fixed string before evaluation will not affect search speed. All of the methods are gene order independent, in that the locations of genes in the genome can be shuffled without effecting search. Combined, these features mean that tests on apparently simple problems can be indicative of search behavior on a large class of actually complex problems.

In choosing test problems, we decided to use only benchmarks with knowable global optimum. This allows us to measure how many evaluations each method requires to converge to the global optimum, as opposed to just the highest fitness reached. This is advantageous as three of the four algorithms have no hard termination condition. The remaining algorithm, LTGA, uses a population parameter which can be increased to slow convergence while simultaneously increasing the fitness reachable before convergence. Therefore it is difficult to say how and when to declare any of the techniques converged unless the global optimum is found.

4.1 Single Instance Problems

Well defined test problem landscapes can help when performing exact analysis of algorithms. These problems can be thought of as testing the edge cases of optimizers, presenting them with unnatural but interesting problem features.

The classic example for this kind of test is the Deceptive Trap problem. For this benchmark the genome is broken up into non-overlapping "traps" of k genes, with the fitness of each trap given by Equation 3.

$$trap(t) = \begin{cases} k-1-t, & t<k \\ k, & t=k \end{cases} \tag{3}$$

In this equation t represents the sum of gene values in the trap. For each trap there is one local optimum (all bits set to 0) and one global optimum (all bits set to 1). We chose to use a trap size of $k = 7$. This problem requires exponential time to solve unless there is some method to effectively move complete traps between solutions, making this an excellent crossover test problem.

However, when using a hill climber and linkage learning, the Deceptive Trap problem may be trivially solved [4]. Thus the more difficult Deceptive Step Trap problem was defined, and is given in Equation 4.

$$step\_trap(t) = \left\lfloor \frac{(k-s) \pmod s + trap(t)}{s} \right\rfloor \tag{4}$$

This problem leverages the original Deceptive Trap problem definition, with the addition of fitness plateaus of configurable size s. This creates an enormous number of local optima and makes detection of linkages much more challenging. We chose to use a trap size of $k = 7$ with plateaus of size $s = 2$.

While both of these problems have difficult to solve subproblems, the non-overlapping nature of the solutions may not capture challenging aspects of real world problem solving. Therefore the Hierarchical If and only If (HIFF) problem is often used to test an algorithm's ability to handle these characteristics [14]. In this problem the genome is broken up hierarchically into a complete binary tree, with each gene representing a leaf, and each internal node representing the union between all genes in that node's subtree. A node in the tree contributes to the fitness only if all of the genes in its subset have the same value (IE are all 0 or are all 1). The amount contributed is equal to the number of bits in the subset. As a result this problem involves creating larger and larger blocks of single value runs which only score if the entire block is optimized.

Our final single instance problem is borrowed from the real valued optimization domain. The Discretized Rastrigin problem uses the standard Rastrigin evaluation function (Equation 5).

$$An + \sum_{i=1}^{n} \left[x_i^2 - A\cos(2\pi x_i)\right] \forall x \in [-5.12, 5.12] \tag{5}$$

This function creates a highly multimodal landscape which is completely separable and has a single global optimum. In order to apply our algorithms to this complex problem, we discretized the representation using 10 bit gray coded numbers evenly distributed on the range $[-5.12, 5.12)$.

4.2 Randomly Generated Problem Classes

By enforcing only certain characteristics of a search space while allowing others to be generated randomly, we can perform tests on *classes* of problems instead of specific instances. This can improve the generality of results as experiments then predict the expected quality over the entire class. Unlike single instance problems, the challenge with randomly generated problems is often how to know when the global optimum is reached.

NK landscapes define a class of problems such that the fitness of a single gene's value is dependent on k other genes in the genome. Finding the solution which maximized fitness on an arbitrary NK landscape requires exponential time, and are therefore a good candidate for heuristic techniques. Nearest Neighbor NK landscapes are a subset of NK landscapes such that each gene is dependent on the k genes following it in the genome. The advantage of this subset is that they can be solved in polynomial time [16]. For our experiments we used wrapping neighborhoods, such that genes near the end of the genome depend on genes at the start of the genome. We chose to set $k = 5$.

Ising Spin Glasses are another large class of NP-Hard problems: Given a graph describing the interactions between vertices, set the signs of all vertices to minimize interactions.

Similar to NK landscapes, there is a polynomially solvable subset of Ising problems known as $2D\pm J$ Ising Spin Glasses. This subset restricts graph interactions to a toroidal two dimensional grid with edge weights of $\{-1, +1\}$. This subset can be solved in polynomial time [12], and there are existing tools for solving arbitrary instances.[2]

Our final class is a subset of the Maximum Satisfiability (MAX-SAT) problem. This problem consists of a series of disjunctive clauses, such that each clause contains three problem variables, some of which are negated. While MAX-SAT requires exponential time to solve, we have devised a method of generating only satisfiable instances. First, a random target solution is generated. For each clause, set the signs of each term ensuring the target solution satisfies that clause. To ensure there is no bias to term signs in the generated problem, there is a $\frac{1}{6}$ probability all clause signs match the target, a $\frac{1}{6}$ probability two of the three signs match, and a $\frac{4}{6}$ probability only one sign matches. Note that it's possible for there to be other solutions that also satisfy all clauses. We chose the standard clause to variable ratio of $r = 4.27$.

5. EXPERIMENTAL RESULTS

In total, our experiments performed 100 runs of each optimization algorithm across 7 benchmark problems, with each run limited to 100 million evaluations. In performing data collection, we performed over 150,000 runs, totaling approximately 1.5 trillion evaluations. Of these, approximately 100,000 runs were used to optimally set the population size of LTGA. Note that these runs are considered a training phase, and therefore all results for LTGA use independent runs to create a testing phase. This was the only algorithm that received tuning. As such, LTGA should have a significant advantage over the others in that it has pre-learned the correct population size. All of the code used to perform our experiments as well as individual run results and analysis scripts are available from our website.[3] The results are summarized in Figure 4 and Table 1.

On all 7 problems, the First Improvement Hill Climber and the $(1 + (\lambda, \lambda))$ optimizers appear to have a higher growth complexity than P3. On all of the problems except MAX-SAT they are also worse than LTGA. This makes sense as all of the benchmarks are deceptive in some sense, and neither of these techniques is designed to handle deceptive landscapes. The inability for the iterative hill climber to quickly solve the problems indicates that P3's success is more than just performing local search.

Figure 4 does provide one misleading exception for $(1 + (\lambda, \lambda))$ on the Deceptive Trap problem, where it appears to level out at high genome sizes. This is entirely an artifact of the extremely high variance of this algorithm on this problem. Note that many of the large problem sizes failed to find the optimum for the majority of runs (no data element shown for that size).

The behavior of P3 and LTGA on the four single instance problems appears very similar, with P3 generally being lower by a constant factor. This makes sense as LTGA's tuning allows it to determine a single population size sufficient to solve that instance. However, because it uses a fixed population size, it must set the that size large enough to ensure all random initializations of its population contain enough diversity to reach the global optimum. By comparison, P3 is able to iteratively increase the population size, stopping once enough diversity has been generated. As such we would expect P3 to do better, but not a lot better than tuned LTGA.

	Median	Confidence Interval
Deceptive Trap, N=805, Speedup=2.936		
LTGA	1,807,127	1,805,039 .. 1,808,718
P3	615,503	577,000 .. 653,504
Deceptive Step Trap, N=805, Speedup=1.107		
LTGA	14,106,751	14,102,987 .. 14,109,910
P3	12,742,411	11,951,148 .. 13,777,090
HIFF, N=2048, Speedup=3.1278		
LTGA	1,847,077	1,845,662 .. 1,848,951
P3	590,519	570,739 .. 608,160
Discretized Rastrigin, N=800, Speedup=1.1854		
LTGA	244,086	242,815 .. 245,189
P3	205,908	201,012 .. 210,913
Nearest Neighbor NK, N=600, Speedup=4.408		
LTGA	37,620,027	37,244,617 .. 37,990,772
P3	8,533,322	7,315,275 .. 9,481,271
Ising Spin Glass, N=784, Speedup=20.403		
LTGA	12,677,619	12,601,917 .. 12,761,798
P3	621,347	568,100 .. 667,236
MAX-SAT, N=60, Speedup=942.50		
LTGA	21,130,960	17,576,126 .. 28,314,680
P3	22,420	14,363 .. 29,161

Table 1: Comparison of the median evaluations to success for LTGA and P3. Includes the 95% bootstrapped confidence interval around the median, as well as the speedup factor for P3 over LTGA.

When applied to the randomly generated problem classes, P3 appears to outperform LTGA by an order of complexity. We suspect some of the cause is LTGA's need to fix a single population size. Specifically, during tuning LTGA must set its population size large enough to solve all of the random instances of that class. Therefore all instances which could be solved more efficiently with a smaller population size are penalized. P3 on the other hand grows with problem difficulty. As such its median evaluation time better reflects the median difficulty of a class, whereas LTGA's evaluation time reflects the maximum difficulty of a class.

Of the experiments where LTGA was successful in the median run, it failed to find the optimal solution 109 times, or 0.8%. By comparison, P3 failed to find the optimum 3 times. All three where on Nearest Neighbor NK, two at size 550 and one at size 600. Also, P3 was able to reliably find the optimum on Nearest Neighbor NK $N = 650$, $N = 700$ and MAX-SAT $N = 65$, $N = 70$ while LTGA was not.

Table 1 provides a detailed look at the largest problem sizes in which LTGA was able to find the global optimum reliably in less than 100 million evaluations. For each, we performed a pairwise Mann-Whitney U test, all resulting in p-values less than 10^{-22}, with the exception of Deceptive Step Trap which resulted in 0.00025. As such these results are highly significant. The amount of speedup as compared to optimally tuned LTGA ranged from 1.1 on Deceptive Step

[2]`http://www.informatik.uni-koeln.de/spinglass/`
[3]`https://github.com/brianwgoldman/Parameter-less_Population_Pyramid`

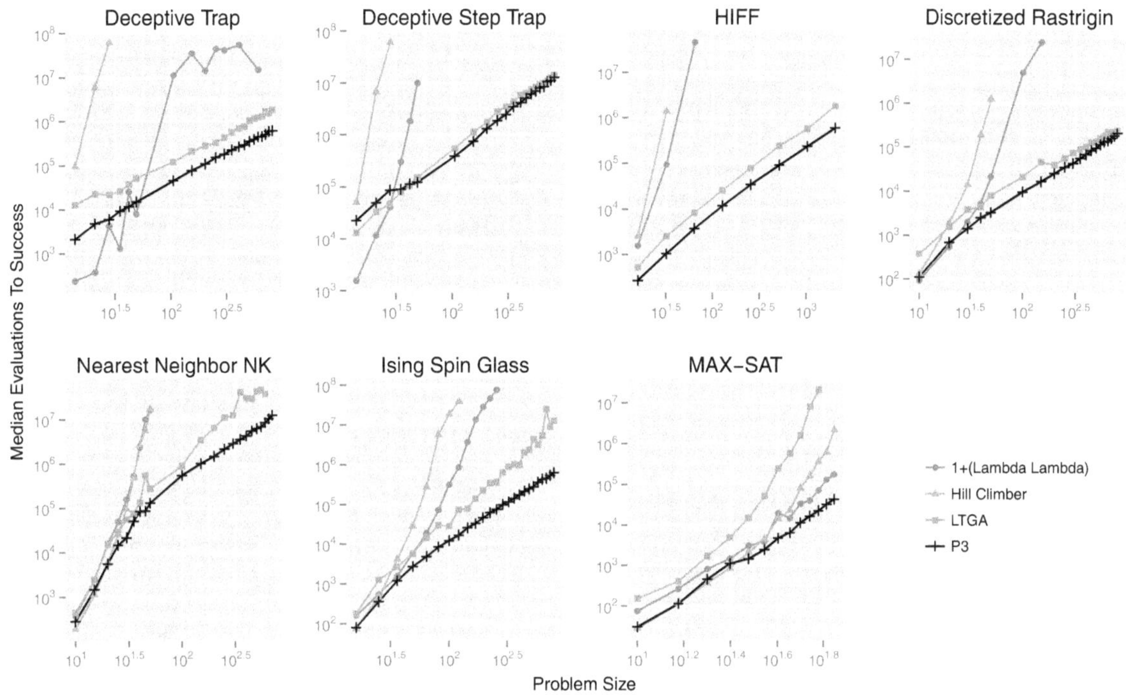

Figure 4: Comparison of the median number of evaluations to reach the global optimum for the four different optimization methods with respect to problem size. If the median run did not reach the global optimum no data element is shown. Results given on a log-log scale.

Trap to 942 on MAX-SAT, but in all cases P3 outperformed LTGA and all other comparison techniques.

As verification that our tuning for LTGA is valid, we refer to [14], which tested the same variant of LTGA that we used. In the section on Child Node filtering, they reported approximately 200,000 mean evaluations to success on the HIFF problem using $N = 512$. Our result of 239,365 is of comparable quality, with P3 solving the same problem using an average of 92,129 evaluations. The discrepancy is likely due to the cited work using their tuning runs in their average.

6. PROMISING THEORY

Due to P3's persistent integration of random solutions, it always has a non zero probability of reaching the global optimum. Because of this (and unlike LTGA), it is possible to derive expected running times for P3 on a number of problems. While we do not present a rigorous solution to any particular problem here, we wish to illuminate potential avenues for future proofs.

The traditional One Max class, as well as all linear functions, will be trivially solved by the hill climber in at most $N+1$ evaluations. These come from the initial evaluation of the random solution, plus the N evaluations required to test each gene for improvement. While more difficult to bound, any unimodal search space without fitness plateaus will be solved by a single application of the hill climber. Notably we expect a bound on Leading Ones of $O(N^2)$ evaluations.

Unlike many theory based algorithms, we believe P3 can achieve bounds on more complex and interesting landscapes. Consider this proof sketch on the Deceptive Trap problem. Each restart will require at most $2N$ evaluations to evaluate the random individual and optimize it to a local optimum using the hill climber. In P_0 each trap in all solutions will either have all 1s or all 0s. As a result $D(C_i, C_j) = 0$ if all C_i and C_j come from the same trap. Therefore all crossover clusters will move only complete traps between solutions, and once there is sufficient diversity in the population there will be a cluster for each individual trap. When performing a crossover of a single trap there can only be a single alternative value, meaning if the candidate solution has all 0s the donor must have all 1s, or vice versa. Therefore if P_i contains the optimum solution for a trap in at least one individual and has a cluster that identifies that trap, all solutions produced by crossing P_i with a candidate solution will have the optimized value of that trap. Extending to all traps we can say that once any P_i has at least one solution with the optimized version of a trap for all traps the very next crossover with P_i will produce the global optimum. The only remaining portion of the proof is to determine how many evaluations are required to reach this point.

Using relaxed requirements, this can likely be extended to any arbitrary, fully decomposable, problem. Assuming that for sufficiently large population sizes the entropy between bits in a single subproblem is lower than the entropy of bits between subproblems, P3 will construct a cluster capable of moving exactly one subproblem's gene values during crossover. As crossover cannot decrease the fitness of a solution each crossover will have a greater than zero probability of improving subproblem solution quality. The probability of low fitness local optima for a subproblem reaching high pyramid levels is therefore low, which increases the probability of donors only having high quality solutions to subproblems. Combined, this is expected to create a runtime potentially exponential in subproblem size, but polynomial in problem size.

This proof sketch can also be extended to the HIFF problem with minor modifications. Each application of the hill climber ensures all subproblems of size 2 will be solved. Once P_0 has a sufficient number of solutions it will correctly cross all subproblems of size 2 independently, such that all future solutions crossed with P_0 will have all subproblems of size 4 solved. While P_1 can contain solutions that do not correctly solve some 2 bit subproblems (added before P_0 reached critical mass), the probability of these solutions being selected as donors decreases rapidly (solutions added after P_0 reaches critical mass). As such each level effectively serves to optimize the next largest subproblem size, leading to convergence using a logarithmic number of levels.

7. CONCLUSIONS AND FUTURE WORK

While many parameter-less techniques trade the potential quality of optimal tuning for general effectiveness, P3 appears to robustly outperform all of the comparison, state of the art, techniques across a diverse set of benchmark problems. This is because, unlike other parameter-less techniques, P3 does not duplicate effort running multiple populations, nor does it throw away learned information like many evolutionary techniques. By striking a balance between continuously adding diversity and the extreme exploitation provided by the multiple evaluation crossover, P3 is able to solve easy problems quickly and hard problems eventually without any problem specific tuning.

Even when compared against LTGA, the closest relative to P3 in current literature, P3 performs better. This is even after LTGA was extensively tuned to each problem class, an unrealistic proposition on any real world problem.

P3's ability to efficiently optimize not just single problem instance classes, but randomly generated problem classes, without parameter tuning makes it an ideal candidate for real world applications. Its focus on exploiting all known information before spending time increasing diversity makes it a great "stop anytime" algorithm.

While not yet complete, we feel that future work will be able to provide a strong theoretical foundation for the design of P3.

Currently, our results are limited to single objective, noiseless, discrete valued problems. In future work we plan to extend (or show no modification is necessary for) P3 to handle problems from these classes. Doing so will help make P3 more applicable to a wider range of real world problems.

8. REFERENCES

[1] P. A. N. Bosman and D. Thierens. The roles of local search, model building and optimal mixing in evolutionary algorithms from a bbo perspective. In *Optimization by building and using probabilistic models (OBUPM-2011)*, pages 663–670, Dublin, Ireland, 12-16 July 2011. ACM.

[2] B. Doerr, C. Doerr, and F. Ebel. Lessons from the black-box: fast crossover-based genetic algorithms. In *GECCO '13: Proceeding of the fifteenth annual conference on Genetic and evolutionary computation conference*, pages 781–788, Amsterdam, The Netherlands, 6-10 July 2013. ACM.

[3] D. E. Goldberg, K. Deb, and J. H. Clark. Genetic algorithms, noise, and the sizing of populations. *COMPLEX SYSTEMS*, 6:333–362, 1991.

[4] B. W. Goldman and D. R. Tauritz. Linkage tree genetic algorithms: variants and analysis. In *GECCO '12: Proceedings of the fourteenth international conference on Genetic and evolutionary computation conference*, pages 625–632, Philadelphia, Pennsylvania, USA, 7-11 July 2012. ACM.

[5] J. Grefenstette. Optimization of control parameters for genetic algorithms. *IEEE Trans. on Systems, Man, and Cybernetics*, SMC-16(1):122–128, 1986.

[6] I. Gronau and S. Moran. Optimal implementations of UPGMA and other common clustering algorithms. *Information Processing Letters*, 104(6):205–210, 2007.

[7] G. Harik and F. Lobo. A parameter-less genetic algorithm. Technical Report IlliGAL 99009, Illinois Genetic Algorithms Laboratory, University of Illinois at Urbana-Champaign, Urbana, IL, 1999.

[8] G. S. Hornby. ALPS: the age-layered population structure for reducing the problem of premature convergence. In *GECCO 2006: Proceedings of the 8th annual conference on Genetic and evolutionary computation*, volume 1, pages 815–822, Seattle, Washington, USA, 8-12 July 2006. ACM Press.

[9] B. D. Jovanovic and P. S. Levy. A look at the rule of three. *The American Statistician*, 51(2):137–139, May 1997.

[10] M. Pelikan and T.-K. Lin. Parameter-less hierarchical BOA. In *Genetic and Evolutionary Computation – GECCO-2004, Part II*, volume 3103 of *Lecture Notes in Computer Science*, pages 24–35, Seattle, WA, USA, 26-30 June 2004. Springer-Verlag.

[11] P. Pošík and S. Vaníček. Parameter-less local optimizer with linkage identification for deterministic order-k decomposable problems. In *GECCO '11: Proceedings of the 13th annual conference on Genetic and evolutionary computation*, pages 577–584, Dublin, Ireland, 12-16 July 2011. ACM.

[12] L. Saul and M. Kardar. The 2d±j ising spin glass: exact partition functions in polynomial time. *Nuclear Physics B*, 432(3):641–667, 1994.

[13] D. Thierens. The linkage tree genetic algorithm. In *Parallel Problem Solving from Nature, PPSN XI*, pages 264–273. Springer, 2010.

[14] D. Thierens and P. A. N. Bosman. Hierarchical problem solving with the linkage tree genetic algorithm. In *GECCO '13: Proceeding of the fifteenth annual conference on Genetic and evolutionary computation conference*, pages 877–884, Amsterdam, The Netherlands, 6-10 July 2013. ACM.

[15] D. H. Wolpert and W. G. Macready. No free lunch theorems for optimization. *IEEE Transactions on Evolutionary Computation*, 1(1):67–82, 1997.

[16] A. H. Wright, R. K. Thompson, and J. Zhang. The computational complexity of N-K fitness functions. *IEEE Transactions on Evolutionary Computation*, 4(4):373–379, Nov. 2000.

Genetic Algorithm for Sampling from Scale-free Data and Networks

Pavel Krömer

University of Alberta
ECERF, 9107 - 116 Street
Edmonton AB T6G 2V4, Canada
pavel.kromer@ualberta.ca

VŠB - Technical University of Ostrava
17.listopadu 15
708 33 Ostrava-Poruba, Czech Republic
pavel.kromer@vsb.cz

Jan Platoš

VŠB - Technical University of Ostrava
17.listopadu 15
708 33 Ostrava-Poruba, Czech Republic
jan.platos@vsb.cz

ABSTRACT

A variety of real-world data and networks can be described by a heavy-tailed probability distribution of its values, vertex degrees, or other significant properties, that follows the power law. Such a scale-free data and networks can be found in both natural phenomena such as protein interaction networks and gene regulation networks and man-made structures like the Internet, language, and various social networks. An efficient analysis of large scale data and networks is often impractical and various heuristic and metaheuristc sampling techniques are deployed to select smaller subsets of the data for analysis and visualisation. A key goal of data and network sampling is to select such a subset of the original data that would accurately represent the original data with respect to selected attributes. In this work we propose a novel genetic algorithm for scale-free data and network sampling and evaluate the algorithm in a series of computational experiments.

Categories and Subject Descriptors

I.2.8 [**Artificial Intelligence**]: Problem Solving, Control Methods, and Search

General Terms

Algorithms

Keywords

Genetic algorithms, data, networks, power law, sampling

1. INTRODUCTION

Sampling is an important step of data and network processing that enables practical analysis, mining, and for example visualisation of real-world data which usually comes in large quantities and cannot be handled directly. This *scale-down* objective of data sampling is different from the *back-in-time* objective which aims at finding accurate snapshots of earlier stages of dynamic data and networks [19]. In order to obtain results that are valid for both, the data sample and the original data set, it is necessary to find samples that represent the original data set well in terms of selected key attributes [29]. Moreover, it has been shown that methodology used to produce data sample affects the result in terms of properties which are often in some way biased [1, 18].

It is now well-known that scale-freeness is a property that can be frequently found in both natural and artificial data and networks [5, 6, 12, 15, 16, 17, 20, 23]. Scale-free networks contain very small fraction of nodes with very high degree and a large number of nodes with small degree. The probability distribution of node degrees in scale-free networks follows the power law. Due to their abundance, the analysis of both static and dynamic scale-free data and networks is of great interest, especially since previous and ongoing research has produced large volumes of scale-free data.

Popular and inexpensive methods for data and network sampling include basic (uniform) random sampling and random walk sampling. However, it has been shown that networks randomly sampled from scale-free networks are not scale-free themselves [29, 18], even though some topological properties of the networks randomly sampled from networks with degree distribution exponent $\alpha \leq 3$ are similar to those of the original networks. The difference in parameters has been found increasing with the difference of sample size and original network size [32]. Random walk sampling has been shown more accurate when it comes to scale-free network sampling [22, 32].

In this work, we propose and evaluate a novel efficient yet simple genetic algorithm for data and network sampling that finds samples of given size with respect to degree distribution parameters estimated for the original data using the analytical method introduced in [9].

The rest of this paper is organized in the following way: in section 2, the basics about scale-free data and networks are summarized. The analytical method for power law parameter estimation that is used as the basis of the fitness function of the proposed genetic algorithm is is discussed as well. Section 3 briefly introduces genetic algorithms as the metaheuristic technique used in this work to sample representative subsets from larger data sets and networks.

GECCO'14, July 12–16, 2014, Vancouver, BC, Canada.

http://dx.doi.org/10.1145/2576768.2598391.

Related work on network and data sampling by genetic algorithms is also reviewed in this section. The genetic algorithm proposed in this work is detailed in section 4 and numerical experiments are shown in section 5. Finally, conclusions are drawn and future work is outlined in section 6.

2. SCALE-FREE DATA AND NETWORKS

Scale-free data and scale-free networks can be characterized by the fact that the probability distribution of their values or node degrees can be for each $x > x_{min}$ described by the power law [5, 6, 20]:

$$p(x) \propto x^{-\alpha} \tag{1}$$

where α is a *scaling parameter*.

Examples of scale free networks include collaboration and coauthorship networks [7, 12], technological networks including the World Wide Web, and the Internet [6], and biological networks such as gene regulatory networks, genomic quantities, DNA sequences [17], and pedigree graphs [23] to name just a few.

Apart from their prevalence in nature and technology, scale-free networks have some interesting properties [20]. They are not random (their growth can be controlled), but have larger entropy than small worlds and regular networks. They contain nodes with extremely high degree (hubs). Moreover, they are robust and less vulnerable to attacks than other types of networks [6].

Due to their properties and because more real-world networks follow power law distribution than any other probability distribution [20], the analysis of scale-free networks is a hot topic. Due to the large volumes of real-world data and networks, a sampling method that would preserve the properties of value/degree probability distribution is needed.

2.1 Analytical method for power law distribution estimation

Clauset et al. [9] introduced in 2009 a statistical framework for the detection and parameter estimation of power law distribution in general empirical data. The method uses goodness-of-fit statistics based on the Kolmogorov-Smirnov test and likelihood ratios to detect the presence of power law distribution in the data and maximum-likelihood fitting to estimate both parameters (α, x_{min}) of the distribution. The algorithm presented in [9] allowed the estimation of power law presence and distribution parameters from both continuous and discrete data. In this work we use the discrete variant of the algorithm to estimate the parameters of power law distribution of an original data set (either a series of empirical values or a graph vertex degrees) and subsequently to estimate the same parameters for samples taken from the original data set. The estimate is used as a basis for a fitness function employed by the genetic algorithm used for data and network sampling.

3. GENETIC ALGORITHMS

Genetic algorithms (GA) form a family of well known population-based metaheuristic soft optimization methods [24]. GAs solve complex optimization problems by programmatic evolution of an encoded population of candidate problem solutions. The solutions are ranked using a problem specific fitness function. The artificial evolution is implemented by iterative application of genetic operators and leads to discovery of above average solutions. The basic workflow of a simple steady state GA [24] is shown in fig. 1.

Problem encoding is an important part of the genetic search. It translates candidate solutions from the problem domain (phenotype) to the encoded search space (genotype) of the algorithm and

```
Define objective (fitness) function and problem encoding;
Encode initial population P of possible solutions as fixed length strings;
Evaluate chromosomes in initial population using objective function;
while Termination criteria not satisfied do
    Apply selection operator to select parent chromosomes for reproduction:
    sel(P_i) → parent1, sel(P_i) → parent2;
    Apply crossover operator on parents with respect to crossover probability
    to produce new chromosomes:
    cross(pC, parent1, parent2) → {offspring1, offspring2};
    Apply mutation operator on offspring chromosomes with respect to
    mutation probability: mut(pM, offspring1) → offspring1,
    mut(pM, offspring2) → offspring2;
    Create new population from current population and offspring
    chromosomes: migrate(offspring1, offsprig2, P_i) → P_{i+1};
end
```

Figure 1: A summary of genetic algorithm

defines the internal representation of the problem instances used during the optimization process. The representation specifies chromosome data structure and a decoding function[10]. The data structure defines the actual search space, its size and shape.

Crossover operator is the main operator of genetic algorithms distinguishing it from other population-based stochastic search methods [24]. Crossover is primarily a creative force in the evolutionary search process. It is supposed to re-combine parent chromosomes in a stochastic manner and propagate building blocks (low order, low defining-length schemata with above average fitness) from one generation to another and create new (higher order) building blocks by combining low order building blocks. It is intended to introduce to the population large changes with small disruption of building blocks [30]. In contrast, mutation is expected to insert new material to the population by random perturbation of chromosome structure. As a result, new building blocks can be created or old ones disrupted [30].

Genetic algorithms and its derivatives have been successfully used to solve non-trivial multimodal optimization problems including data mining, classification, and prediction problems [28, 31]. They inherit the robustness of emulated natural optimization processes and excel in browsing huge, potentially noisy problem domains. In this work we propose a new genetic algorithm for data and graph sampling. Suitable encoding, mutation and crossover operators as well as a fitness function that enable efficient execution of the algorithm are defined.

3.1 Related work

According to authors' knowledge, there is no previous GA designed specifically for data or network sampling. The objective of sampling is, however, to some extent similar to the goals of genetic subgraph selection (subgraph is a sample picked from the original graph), genetic community detection (community is a sample picked from the network), and certain variants of genetic clustering (cluster representatives are sampled from the network). Related work from these areas is outlined in this section.

3.1.1 Genetic subgraph selection

Genetic subgraphs selection is a broad class of combinatorial optimization problems that includes some very well-known problems such as the travelling salesman problem, the minimum spanning tree problem [27], the maximum clique problem [11], and the minimum-label spanning tree problem [25]. Generally speaking, the search for an optimum subgraph usually involves a search for an ordering (permutation) of graph vertices or a path connecting all vertices in the graph. Different variants of the problems exist for weighted and unweighted graphs. Besides, subgraph selection problems with various constraints are defined [27]. Pure genetic approaches are often not very successful when it comes to subgraph selection problems, so special operators, greedy steps [25], local search, and problem-specific heuristics are being deployed [11, 25].

3.1.2 Genetic community detection

Genetic algorithms for community detection are of uppermost interest of social network analysis and network analysis in general. The aim of GA for community detection is to discover structure hidden in a network, i.e. to find an optimum network division (with respect to some criteria) [26]. The problem is complicated due to the nature of community relationships which are often overlapping and not clearly bounded and due to the dynamic nature of social networks [21]. The complexity and specific properties of the problem represent an opportunity for advanced genetic approaches such as multiobjective GA [21, 26].

3.1.3 Medoid-based genetic clustering

The main goal of genetic clustering is to find meaningful clusters in data with the help of genetic algorithms. There are multiple types of clustering representations used by genetic and evolutionary clustering algorithms. Among them, the *integer encoding* [14] with the notion of medoids yields algorithms similar to the GA for sampling proposed in this work. The representation of a clustering consists of a sequence of medoids, i.e. objects that represent individual clusters in encoded partitioning [14]. The search for good medoids can be seen as a sampling of the original data set or network. However, the main challenges of genetic clustering are different from those of genetic sampling and include automated selection of the number of clusters (whereas the size of sample is fixed for genetic sampling) and efficient formation and evaluation of the clustering induced by the medoids (whereas sampling does not require further processing of selected samples). Relevant works from the area of genetic clustering include approaches by Hruschka et al. [13], Alves et al. [3], and Bandyopadhyay [4].

The three related areas summarized above have something in common: all of them define problem specific representations and special genetic operators to facilitate efficient GA-based search for optimal solutions. Many of them handle the network as a whole and seek for a re-ordering or hidden structure of the whole network. However, none of them is really suitable for the goals of genetic sampling in which only a single small subset of all values/vertices needs to be selected from the original data set or network. Therefore, a new GA for sampling is proposed in section 4 of this paper.

4. GA FOR SCALE-FREE DATA AND NETWORK SAMPLING

In order to design an efficient genetic algorithm for sampling from scale-free data and scale-free networks, we define the chromosome encoding, genetic operators, and fitness function. The encoding and operators were designed with the aim to use compact chromosomes, to exploit both crossover and mutation, and to avoid the creation of invalid individuals in course of the evolution.

4.1 Chromosome encoding

A valid sample of exactly k positions/vertices can be defined by the indices of the k positions/vertices selected from the full data set or network of N positions/vertices. No position/vertex can appear in the sample more than once in order to achieve the required sample size of k. The natural encoding of a sample is based on the indices of selected positions/vertices, i.e. chromosome c can be defined by eq. (2).

$$c = (c_1, c_2, \dots c_k), \quad \forall (i,j) \in \{0, \dots N\} : c_i \neq c_j \tag{2}$$

However, such encoding would be prone to the creation of invalid individuals in case traditional genetic operators such as the 1-point crossover or uniform mutation were applied. A few examples of the creation of invalid individuals from valid ones are given in fig. 2 (conflicting genes are shown in **bold**). To avoid the creation of such

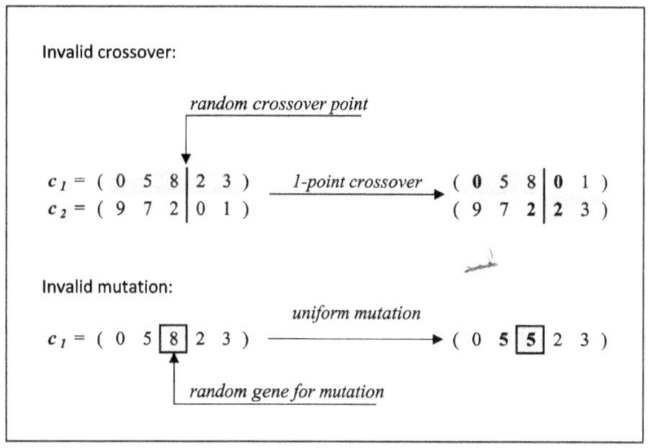

Figure 2: Examples of the creation of invalid individuals.

invalid individuals, we slightly modify the encoding by sorting the indices within each chromosome, i.e. the encoding of a sample of k positions/vertices from N is defined by (3).

$$c = (c_1, \dots c_k), \ \forall (i,j) \in \{0, \dots N\} : i < j \implies c_i < c_j \tag{3}$$

With such modified encoding, the generation of random sampling individuals involves two steps. First, k unique positions/vertices out of all N possible positions/vertices are selected. Then, the indices in each individual are sorted in increasing order. However, the ordering of the indices within the chromosome still requires the use of modified mutation and crossover operators that respect the encoding and do not generate invalid individuals. We note that the encoding differs from that used for permutation-based combinatorial optimization problems and thus traditional order-type crossover operators (e.g. order crossover, partially matched crossover, uniform partially matched crossover, etc. [8]) are not suitable.

4.2 Genetic operators

The genetic operators used by the GA for sampling are based on traditional mutation and crossover operators that were modified with respect to chromosome encoding so that they do not break the ordering of the chromosomes and do not create invalid offspring.

4.2.1 Order-preserving mutation

The order-preserving mutation replaces ith gene c_i in chromosome c with a value from the interval defined by its left and right neighbour as defined in (4):

$$mut(c_i) = \begin{cases} urand^*(0, c_{i+1}), & \text{if } i = 0 \\ urand(c_{i-1}, c_{i+1}), & \text{if } i \in (0, N-1) \\ urand(c_{i-1}, N), & \text{if } i = N-1 \end{cases} \tag{4}$$

where $i \in \{0, \dots, N\}$ and $urand(a,b)$ selects a uniform pseudo-random integer from the interval (a,b) (whereas $urand^*(a,b)$ selects a uniform pseudo-random integer from the interval $[a,b)$). This mutation operator guarantees that the ordering of the indices within the chromosome remains valid. However, the order-preserving mutation of ith gene has no effect on chromosomes for which it holds that $(c_{i-1}+1) = c_i = (c_{i+1}-1)$.

4.2.2 *Order-preserving crossover*

The order-preserving crossover is based on the traditional one-point crossover operator [2, 24]. It selects a random position i in parent chromosomes $c1$ and $c2$, which is inspected for suitability to be a crossover point. A position i is suitable for crossover iff eq. (5) is true.

$$c1_i < c2_{i+1} \wedge c2_i < c1_{i+1} \tag{5}$$

If eq. (5) does not hold for i, the remaining positions in the chromosomes are scanned in the search for a suitable crossover point (i.e. a position for which eq. (5) holds). It should be noted that an order-preserving crossover between 2 chromosomes might not always be possible. Examples of the use of the order-preserving crossover in various situations are shown in fig. 3.

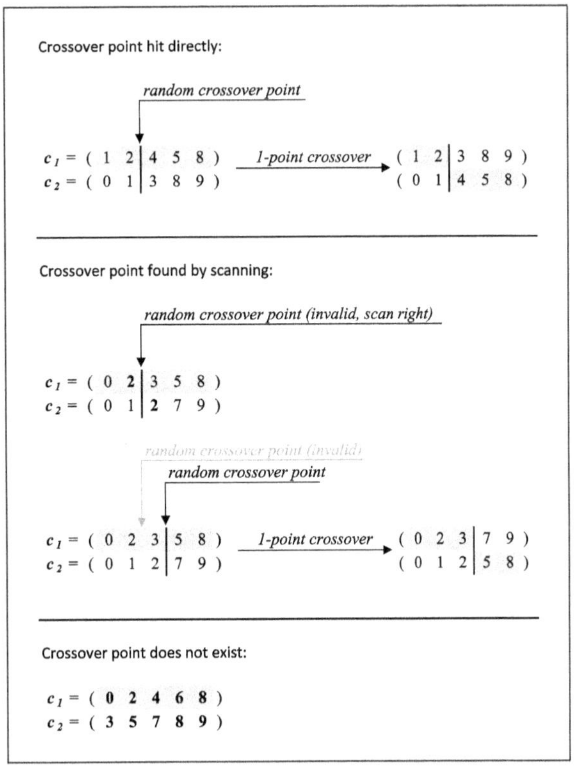

Figure 3: Examples of order-preserving crossover scenarios.

4.3 Fitness function

The fitness function used in this work utilizes the power law distribution estimation algorithm by Clauset et al. [9] described in section 2.1. It minimizes the difference between estimated power law distribution parameters in the original data and sampled data:

$$fit(c) = \frac{1}{2}\left(\sqrt{(\alpha^o - \alpha^c)^2} + \sqrt{(x^o_{min} - x^c_{min})^2}\right) \tag{6}$$

where α^o and x^o_{min} are the scaling parameter and x_{min} estimates from the original data and α^c and x^c_{min} are estimates from the sample defined by chromosome c. Obtaining the estimates can be costly for large data. However, it becomes less computationally intensive when the samples are rather small.

Table 1: Sampling GA parameters.

Parameter	Value
GA type	Steady state GA with gen. gap 2 (parents are replaced by offspring)
Population size	400
No. of generations	50000
Crossover probability	0.9
Mutation probability	0.8

Optionally, the values of α^o and x^o_{min} can be scaled down according to the size of the sample and a penalty can be placed for every sampled vertex with degree 0.

The fitness function is *minimized* by the proposed GA.

5. EXPERIMENTS

In order to verify the ability of the proposed GA to sample from scale-free data and networks, a series of computational experiments was performed. The experiments involved sampling from empirical data, artificial scale-free networks, and real-world scale-free networks. A steady state GA featuring the proposed chromosome encoding, genetic operators, and fitness function was implemented in C++ and used to select samples from the test data. The parameters of the algorithm are shown in table 1. They were selected on the basis of initial trials and previous experience with the algorithm. The mutation probability is high due to the fact that it mutates only one gene and might not have effect every time it is applied.

In all experiments, the GA was used to select a sample of the size $k = 20$ from various data sets and networks. The results were compared to the results of random sampling (RS) in terms of accuracy of power law parameters of obtained samples (when compared to power law parameters of the original data sets). The values presented for random sampling were collected as an average of 10400 random samples which corresponds to the number of fitness function evaluations performed by the GA.

5.1 Sampling from empirical data

Several data sets from the collection used by Clauset et al. [9] were downloaded from authors website[1] and used to evaluate the efficiency of sampling from empirical data. Interesting properties of the data sets are summarized in table 3. The following data sets were used [9]:

- the *blackouts* data set that consists of the numbers of customers affected by electrical blackouts in the United States between 1984 and 2002.
- the *flares* data set that contains peak gamma-ray intensity of solar flares between 1980 and 1989.
- the *names* data set that captures the frequencies of occurrence of US family names in the 1990 US Census.
- the *terrorism* data set that contains the number of deaths caused by terrorist attacks worldwide from February 1968 to June 2006.
- and the *words* data set that captures the frequency of occurrence of unique words in the novel Moby Dick by Herman Melville.

[1] http://tuvalu.santafe.edu/~aaronc/powerlaws/data.htm

Table 3: Properties of test data sets.

Data set	No. of records	Param. estimate α	x_{min}
blackouts	212	2.20327	200000
flares	12774	1.78706	323
surnames	2754	2.19721	14922.6
terrorism	9102	2.33988	10
words	18856	1.95223	7

The results of computational experiments are shown in table 2 in terms of average α and x_{min}. It can be seen that the GA has found for all data sets samples with more accurate average α and x_{min} with smaller standard deviation than random sampling.

5.2 Sampling from networks

The second series of experiments focused on sampling from scale-free networks. A set of artificial scale-free networks generated using the SNAP platform[2] and several real-world networks obtained from the CCNR website[3] were used to test the ability of the proposed GA to find good network samples.

The real-world networks included protein interactions in the *yeast* Saccharomyces cerevisiae [15] and three cellular networks of Aquifex Aeolicus (*AA*), Synechocystis Sp. (*CY*), and Methanobacterium Thermoautotrophicum (*TH*) [16]. The generated networks had fixed number of nodes and fixed α. However, the network generation procedure was approximate since it used the configuration model (function *GenRndPowerLaw*) for network generation. The properties of all test networks are summarized in table 4.

In this set of experiments, a penalty was applied for each vertex with degree 0 found in the sample and the value of target x_{min} was scaled down according to the size of the sample). The comparison to random sampling is not available this time because no scale-free random samples were found during the experiments and hence no meaningful α and x_{min} were estimated.

The results of network sampling are shown in table 5. It can be seen that the GA has found samples with good average accuracy of both α and x_{min}. The average accuracy of α lies between 99.99% and 93.10% for all networks with $\alpha \in [2,3]$, however, it falls to 57.71% with increasing α. We can also observe that the GA failed to find scale-free sample during some runs for some networks with $\alpha \in [4,5]$. This is due to much larger probability of sampling disconnected vertices from networks with large α and large number of nodes.

A few visual examples of sampled networks are shown in fig. 4.

6. CONCLUSIONS

A novel genetic algorithm for scale-free data and network sampling was introduced in this work. The algorithm was defined in terms of the chromosome encoding, genetic operators, and fitness function. It was designed memory efficient and fast. The size of chromosomes is bound to the size of required sample and independent on the size of original data. The algorithm does not waste time by creating and/or fixing invalid candidate solutions and it also does not need to maintain any hash/lookup tables or bitmaps to check whether a position was already sampled or not.

The algorithm was evaluated in a series of computational experiments and it was shown that it can find samples from empirical data and networks with required parameters. The results of computational experiments also confirm that the complexity of the sampling problem grows with growing probability distribution exponent α and the GA in some experimental runs failed to find scale-free samples of networks with larger α during the 50000 generations for which the evolution was executed. Nevertheless, the results of sampling by GA were better than the results of random sampling which could not find scale-free samples of test networks at all.

Chromosome encoding and operators proposed in this work were used to find scale-free samples of scale-free data and networks. However, they can be used to search for any type of data or network sample according to any criteria expressed by the fitness function. Other types of genetic operators (e.g. 2-point crossover) can be also modified in order to be used with sorted chromosomes.

Our future work will include further evaluation of the proposed algorithm, comparison with advanced sampling heuristics, and applications of the proposed algorithm to tasks such as community detection and subgraph mining.

[2] `https://snap.stanford.edu/`

[3] `http://www3.nd.edu/~networks/resources.htm`

Table 4: Properties of test graphs.

Network	No. of vertices	No. of edges	Param. estimate α	x_{min}
sf-5000-2	5000	15634	2.04737	3
sf-5000-3		4785	3.14119	2
sf-5000-4		3521	4.24039	2
sf-5000-5		3088	5.16554	2
sf-10000-2	10000	32348	2.05370	2
sf-10000-3		9623	3.08339	2
sf-10000-4		7012	4.25569	2
sf-10000-5		6173	5.37180	2
sf-30000-2	30000	108840	2.07844	3
sf-30000-3		28798	3.23898	2
sf-30000-4		21264	4.23796	3
sf-30000-5		18427	5.96999	2
sf-50000-2	50000	193159	2.08324	2
sf-50000-3		47726	3.18743	3
sf-50000-4		35389	4.49424	2
sf-50000-5		30854	5.82852	2
yeast	2115	4480	3.03945	5
AA	1113	2572	2.04031	9
CY	1491	3528	2.21631	8
TH	1124	2705	2.11660	9

7. ACKNOWLEDGMENTS

This work was partially supported by the Grant of SGS No. SP2014/110, VŠB - Technical University of Ostrava, Czech Republic, by the European Regional Development Fund in the IT4Innovations Centre of Excellence project (CZ.1.05/1.1.00/02.0070) and by the Bio-Inspired Methods: research, development and knowledge transfer project, reg. no. CZ.1.07/2.3.00/20.0073 funded by Operational Programme Education for Competitiveness, co-financed by ESF and state budget of the Czech Republic. The University of Alberta supported this work via the Helmholtz-Alberta Initiative and TECTERRA.

Table 2: Results of sampling from empirical data.

Data set	Algo- rithm	Average values α (stddev)	Average values x_{min} (stddev)	Average accuracy (in %) α (stddev)	Average accuracy (in %) x_{min} (stddev)
blackouts	GA	2.83 (0.10)	185928 (43864.7)	99.09 (04.43)	92.96 (21.93)
flares		1.78 (0.02)	313.7 (50.4547)	99.78 (01.20)	97.12 (15.62)
surnames		2.26 (0.31)	16249.1 (7618.09)	97.16 (14.27)	91.11 (51.05)
terrorism		2.25 (0.19)	8.5 (3.3541)	96.32 (08.33)	85.00 (33.54)
words		1.95 (0.05)	6.2 (2.03961)	99.93 (02.72)	88.57 (29.14)
blackouts	RS	2.40 (1.12)	132224 (120392)	91.15 (50.99)	66.11 (60.20)
flares		2.30 (0.79)	75.5334 (121.37)	71.71 (44.01)	23.38 (37.58)
surnames		2.57 (0.84)	18825.9 (12787.8)	83.30 (38.12)	73.84 (85.69)
terrorism		2.17 (0.52)	1.583 (1.48)	92.87 (22.10)	15.83 (14.82)
words		2.07 (0.54)	2.216 (2.97)	93.96 (27.56)	31.66 (42.48)

Table 5: Results of graph sampling.

Network	Not found	Average values α (stddev)	Average values x_{min} (stddev)	Average accuracy (in %) α (stddev)	Average accuracy (in %) x_{min} (stddev)
sf-5000-2	0	2.04733 (0.000223607)	1 (0)	99.99 (0.01)	100.00 (0.00)
sf-5000-3	0	3.14888 (0.0672555)	1 (0)	99.76 (2.14)	100.00 (0.00)
sf-5000-4	15	3.53164 (0.0487621)	1 (0)	83.29 (1.15)	100.00 (0.00)
sf-5000-5	25	3.27841 (0)	1 (0)	63.47 (0.00)	100.00 (0.00)
sf-10000-2	0	2.05365 (0.000665242)	1 (0)	99.97 (0.03)	100.00 (0.00)
sf-10000-3	0	3.12388 (0.0796578)	1 (0)	98.69 (2.58)	100.00 (0.00)
sf-10000-4	10	3.42227 (0.143855)	1 (0)	80.42 (3.38)	100.00 (0.00)
sf-10000-5	20	3.31783 (0.144845)	1 (0)	61.76 (2.70)	100.00 (0.00)
sf-30000-2	0	2.04475 (0.000762139)	1 (0)	98.38 (0.04)	100.00 (0.00)
sf-30000-3	0	3.01537 (0.0779567)	1 (0)	93.10 (2.41)	100.00 (0.00)
sf-30000-4	0	3.36689 (0.152172)	1 (0)	79.45 (3.59)	100.00 (0.00)
sf-30000-5	20	3.31857 (0)	1 (0)	61.78 (0.00)	100.00 (0.00)
sf-50000-2	0	2.03088 (0.000892669)	1 (0)	97.49 (0.04)	100.00 (0.00)
sf-50000-3	0	3.21401 (0.191168)	1 (0)	99.17 (6.00)	100.00 (0.00)
sf-50000-4	10	3.47811 (0.0508097)	1 (0)	77.39 (1.13)	100.00 (0.00)
sf-50000-5	20	3.3636 (0.085185)	1 (0)	57.71 (1.46)	100.00 (0.00)
yeast	0	3.03471 (0)	1 (0)	99.84 (0.00)	100.00 (0.00)
AA	0	2.04268 (0.00732238)	1 (0)	99.88 (0.36)	100.00 (0.00)
CY	0	2.21792 (0.0025737)	1 (0)	99.93 (0.12)	100.00 (0.00)
TH	0	2.11597 (0.00521358)	1 (0)	99.97 (0.25)	100.00 (0.00)

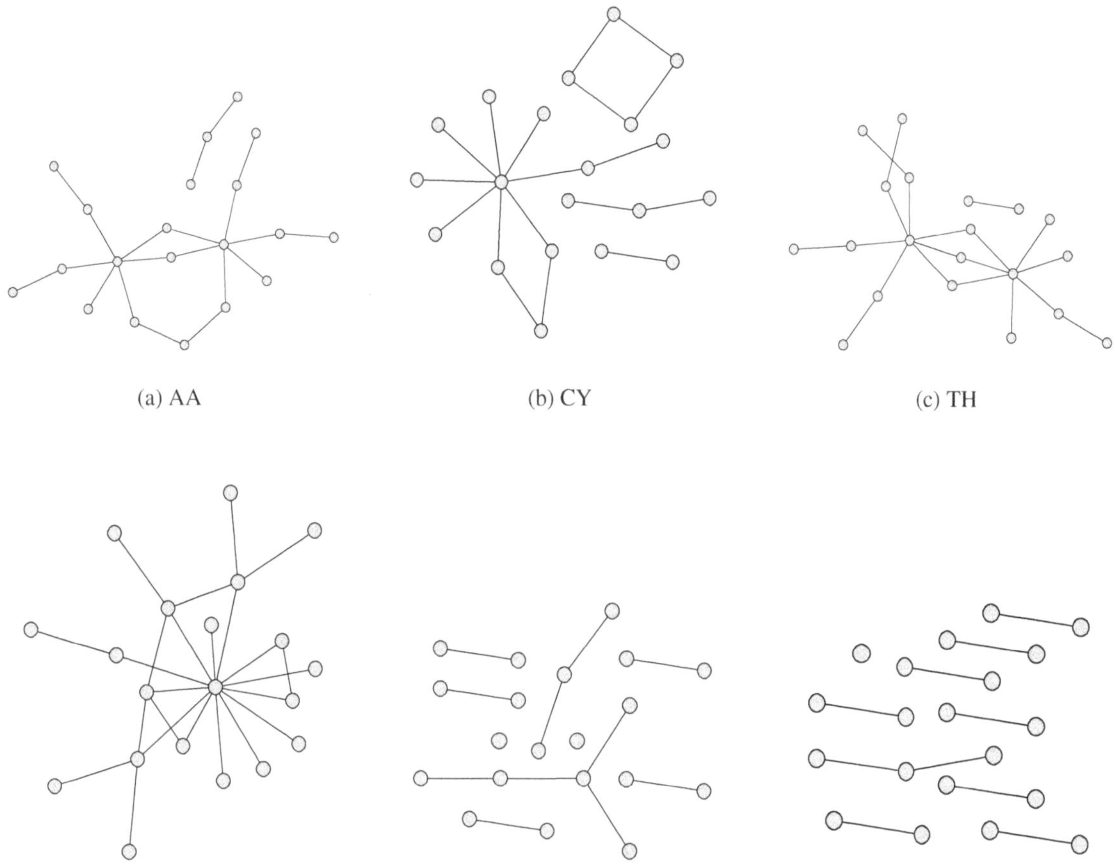

(a) AA (b) CY (c) TH

(d) sf-50000-2 (e) sf-50000-3 (f) sf-50000-4

Figure 4: Examples of sampled networks.

8. REFERENCES

[1] D. Achlioptas, A. Clauset, D. Kempe, and C. Moore. On the bias of traceroute sampling: Or, power-law degree distributions in regular graphs. *J. ACM*, 56(4):21:1–21:28, July 2009.

[2] M. Affenzeller, S. Winkler, S. Wagner, and A. Beham. *Genetic Algorithms and Genetic Programming: Modern Concepts and Practical Applications*. Chapman & Hall/CRC, 2009.

[3] V. Alves, R. Campello, and E. Hruschka. Towards a fast evolutionary algorithm for clustering. In G. G. Yen, S. M. Lucas, G. Fogel, G. Kendall, R. Salomon, B.-T. Zhang, C. A. C. Coello, and T. P. Runarsson, editors, *Proc. of the 2006 IEEE Congress on Evolutionary Computation*, pages 1776–1783, Vancouver, BC, Canada, 16-21 July 2006. IEEE Press.

[4] S. Bandyopadhyay. Genetic algorithms for clustering and fuzzy clustering. *Wiley Interdisciplinary Reviews: Data Mining and Knowledge Discovery*, 1(6):524–531, 2011.

[5] A.-L. Barabasi. *Linked - The new Science of Networks*. Perseus Publishing, 2002.

[6] A.-L. Barabasi. Scale-free networks: A decade and beyond. *Science*, 325(5939):412–413, 2009.

[7] A. L. Barabási, H. Jeong, Z. Néda, E. Ravasz, A. Schubert, and T. Vicsek. Evolution of the social network of scientific collaborations. *Physica A: Statistical Mechanics and its Applications*, 311(3-4):590 – 614, 2002.

[8] V. A. Cicirello. Non-wrapping order crossover: An order preserving crossover operator that respects absolute position. In *Proc. of the 8th Annual Conference on Genetic and Evolutionary Computation*, GECCO '06, pages 1125–1132, New York, NY, USA, 2006. ACM.

[9] A. Clauset, C. R. Shalizi, and M. E. J. Newman. Power-law distributions in empirical data. *SIAM Rev.*, 51(4):661–703, Nov. 2009.

[10] A. Czarn, C. MacNish, K. Vijayan, and B. A. Turlach. Statistical exploratory analysis of genetic algorithms: The influence of gray codes upon the difficulty of a problem. In *Australian Conf. on Artificial Intelligence*, pages 1246–1252, 2004.

[11] D.-C. Dang and A. Moukrim. Subgraph extraction and metaheuristics for the maximum clique problem. *Journal of Heuristics*, 18(5):767–794, 2012.

[12] E. Elmacioglu and D. Lee. On six degrees of separation in dblp-db and more. *SIGMOD Rec.*, 34(2):33–40, June 2005.

[13] E. R. Hruschka, R. J. Campello, and L. N. de Castro.

Evolving clusters in gene-expression data. *Information Sciences*, 176(13):1898 – 1927, 2006.

[14] E. R. Hruschka, R. J. G. B. Campello, A. A. Freitas, and A. C. P. L. F. De Carvalho. A survey of evolutionary algorithms for clustering. *Trans. Sys. Man Cyber Part C*, 39:133–155, March 2009.

[15] H. Jeong, S. Mason, A. Barabasi, and Z. Oltvai. Lethality and centrality in protein networks. *Nature*, 411:41–42, May 2001.

[16] H. Jeong, B. Tombor, R. Albert, Z. N. Oltvai, and A. L. Barabasi. The large-scale organization of metabolic networks. *Nature*, 407(6804):651–654, October 2000.

[17] E. Koonin, Y. Wolf, and G. Karev. *Power Laws, Scale-Free Networks and Genome Biology*. Molecular Biology Intelligence Unit. Landes Bioscience/Eurekah.com, 2007.

[18] S. H. Lee, P. J. Kim, and H. Jeong. Statistical properties of sampled networks. *Phys Rev E Stat Nonlin Soft Matter Phys*, 73(1 Pt 2):016102, Jan 2006.

[19] J. Leskovec and C. Faloutsos. Sampling from large graphs. In *Proc. of the 12th ACM SIGKDD international conference on Knowledge discovery and data mining*, KDD '06, pages 631–636, New York, NY, USA, 2006. ACM.

[20] T. G. Lewis. *Network Science: Theory and Practice*. Wiley Publishing, 2009.

[21] C.-C. Lin, W.-Y. Liu, and D.-J. Deng. A genetic algorithm approach for detecting hierarchical and overlapping community structure in dynamic social networks. In *Wireless Communications and Networking Conference (WCNC), 2013 IEEE*, pages 4469–4474, 2013.

[22] J. Lu and D. Li. Sampling online social networks by random walk. In *Proc. of the First ACM International Workshop on Hot Topics on Interdisciplinary Social Networks Research*, HotSocial '12, pages 33–40, New York, NY, USA, 2012. ACM.

[23] S. Maenhout, B. De Baets, and G. Haesaert. Graph-based data selection for the construction of genomic prediction models. *Genetics*, 185(4):1463–1475, 2010.

[24] M. Mitchell. *An Introduction to Genetic Algorithms*. MIT Press, Cambridge, MA, 1996.

[25] J. Nummela and B. A. Julstrom. An effective genetic algorithm for the minimum-label spanning tree problem. In *Proc. of the 8th Annual Conference on Genetic and Evolutionary Computation*, GECCO '06, pages 553–558, New York, NY, USA, 2006. ACM.

[26] C. Pizzuti. A multi-objective genetic algorithm for community detection in networks. In *Tools with Artificial Intelligence, 2009. ICTAI '09. 21st International Conference on*, pages 379–386, 2009.

[27] G. R. Raidl, G. Koller, and B. A. Julstrom. Biased mutation operators for subgraph-selection problems. *Trans. Evol. Comp*, 10(2):145–156, Sept. 2006.

[28] M. Sabeti, R. Boostani, and T. Zoughi. Using genetic programming to select the informative eeg-based features to distinguish schizophrenic patients. *Neural Network World*, 22(1):3–20, 2012.

[29] M. P. H. Stumpf, C. Wiuf, and R. M. May. Subnets of scale-free networks are not scale-free: Sampling properties of networks. *Proc. of the National Academy of Sciences*, 102(12):4221–4224, 2005.

[30] A. S. Wu, R. K. Lindsay, and R. Riolo. Empirical observations on the roles of crossover and mutation. In T. Bäck, editor, *Proc. of the Seventh Int. Conf. on Genetic Algorithms*, pages 362–369, San Francisco, CA, 1997. Morgan Kaufmann.

[31] J. B. Yao, B. Z. Yao, L. Li, and Y. L. Jiang. Hybrid model for displacement prediction of tunnel surrounding rock. *Neural Network World*, 22(3):263–275, 2012.

[32] S. Yoon, S. Lee, S. H. Yook, and Y. Kim. Statistical properties of sampled networks by random walks. *Phys Rev E Stat Nonlin Soft Matter Phys*, 75(4 Pt 2):046114, Apr 2007.

Stochastic Tunneling Transformation during Selection in Genetic Algorithm

Benjamin E. Mayer
Technische Universität Darmstadt
AG Computational Biology & Simulation
Germany, 64287 Darmstadt
Schnittspahnstr. 10
mayer@cbs.tu-darmstadt.de

Kay Hamacher
Technische Universität Darmstadt
AG Computational Biology & Simulation
Germany, 64287 Darmstadt
Schnittspahnstr. 10
hamacher@bio.tu-darmstadt.de

ABSTRACT

Genetic Algorithms (GA) combine mutational and recombination operators to then select between individuals. Thereby, competition becomes the driving force to improve solutions. Now, this naive approach to biological evolution often assumes a static fitness function, e.g., co-evolutionary effects cannot easily be leveraged.

Here, we introduce a fitness landscape transformation inspired by Monte-Carlo-based optimization schemes. In the Stochastic-Tunneling (STUN) framework fitness values are non-linearly transformed under preservation of the relative ranking of optima. The "base line" of the STUN-transformation can be set based on different memory mechanisms – from current to full history.

This STUN-based GA-variant allows to include co-evolution and history into the GA. Based on analytic arguments we can show that the non-linearity of the transformation generates high population densities in areas of interest.

We numerically simulated small, controllable, and well understood test instance: replicas of Ising-spin glasses. For these systems the STUN-GAs have shown significant improvements in terms of relative error for given computational effort. In addition, we introduce an empirical measure of selection to discuss the improved convergence behavior.

Categories and Subject Descriptors

G.1.6 [**Numerical Analysis**]: Optimization—*Global Optimization*; G.3 [**Probability And Statistics**]: Probabilistic algorithms ; J.2 [**Physical Science and Engineering**]: Physics

Keywords

Genetic Algorithm; Metaheuristic; Ising spin-glass; Stochastic Tunneling

1. INTRODUCTION

The problem of global optimization occurs in almost all fields of natural sciences and engineering. The difficulty in real-world applications arises for objective functions – also referred to as potential energy surfaces (PES) – with a high roughness of the PES and the associated high number of local minima. These lead to the empirical finding that many local optimizers get trapped in local minima only and will therefore terminate early, without finding the global minimum.

While the "no free lunch"-theorem [17] guarantees that no algorithm will be distinguishably more efficient *averaged over all* optimization problems, there are specialized problem-dependent algorithms which perform better on their respective problem[1].

1.1 Previous work

1.1.1 Monte-Carlo based approaches & STUN

A rather general approach for a broad range of optimization problems are randomized algorithms which offer a compromise between reliability and computational cost. One such randomized algorithm, from the class of Monte-Carlo-algorithms, is the Simulated Annealing (SA) algorithm. In SA the temperature corresponds to the ability to move out of local minima. A "cooling schedule" is used to slowly reduce this ability until convergence to the global minimum [8]. However, if the temperature is reduced too fast, the search process almost always gets trapped in a local minimum.

The Stochastic Tunneling (STUN) approach has been proposed to overcome this problem [14]. It is essentially a Monte-Carlo process working on a transformed PES. The PES transformation has the effect that the Markov chain of the search process cannot get trapped in local minima. It reduces barriers that might hinder movements of the Markov chain exploring the PES. The reduction is always gauged with respect to the best minimum found so far. Eventually, the optimization process incorporates knowledge about already visited minima and thus has history – effectively destroying the Markov property and "coupling" Markov walkers.

1.1.2 Genetic algorithms

In contrast to the sole "runner" in SA and STUN that explores the PES, genetic algorithms (GA) are population based, randomized optimization schemes. The algorithm iterates operators like "mutation" and "recombination" over a population and selects individuals in the population based on their (relative) fitness [9, 18].

Additional choices in the GA implementation are, e.g., the encoding of individuals, which in most cases is just a simple binary encoding [1]. This will be used in our study, too.

While *transformations in the coding space* were previously investigated [5], such steps influence the action of mutation and re-

[1]and worse for other to maintain the average performance

GECCO'14, July 12–16, Vancouver, BC, Canada.

ACM 978-1-4503-2662-9/14/07 ...$15.00.
http://dx.doi.org/10.1145/2576768.2598243.

combination operators due to potential new encodings or coordinate transformations and such.

Some restricted sets of *transformations of the objective function* were also studied [13]. There, however, the authors were concerned with conceptual arguments on what they coined "neutral transformations". Basically, those transformations do not change the overall behavior in a sense of efficiency classes.

Here, we will, however, focus on a concrete and measurable, real-world algorithm and not on conceptual classifications. In the following section we detail our contribution.

1.2 Our Contribution

Here, we investigate how the STUN-"coupling" via the best known minimum (Section 1.1.1) is an alternative approach to exploit co-evolution in GAs (Section 1.1.2). This offers performance improvements as there is – indeed – free lunch in *co*-evolution [16, 15]. We show that for a complex optimization problem, namely finding the ground-state of so called Ising spin glasses, this is the case.

Furthermore, we introduce and apply in our STUN-GA setting a measure of selective pressure in GAs. While mutation and recombination are the mechanism how a GA "moves" in search space, the selection stage is the main driving force that can render GAs efficient.

2. A COMPLEX TEST INSTANCE

We focus our empirical performance evaluation on a well-known NP-hard global optimization problem: the so-called Ising spin-glass. The problem is stated as finding the combinatorial solution to the minimization of the following Hamiltonian

$$\mathcal{E} = -\frac{1}{2} \sum_{<i,j>} s_i s_j J_{ij} \,. \qquad (1)$$

where the s_i are Ising spin variables $s_i \in \left[-\frac{1}{2}; \frac{1}{2}\right]$ and the coupling parameters J_{ij} are chosen from a distribution

$$\rho(J_{ij}) = \frac{1}{\sqrt{2\pi}} \exp\left(-\frac{J_{ij}^2}{2}\right) \,. \qquad (2)$$

The summation over the index pair $< i, j >$ in Equation (1) is performed over those spins that are direct neighbors in a topology. Here, we use a regular grid in 2D with periodic boundary conditions (cmp. Figure 1).

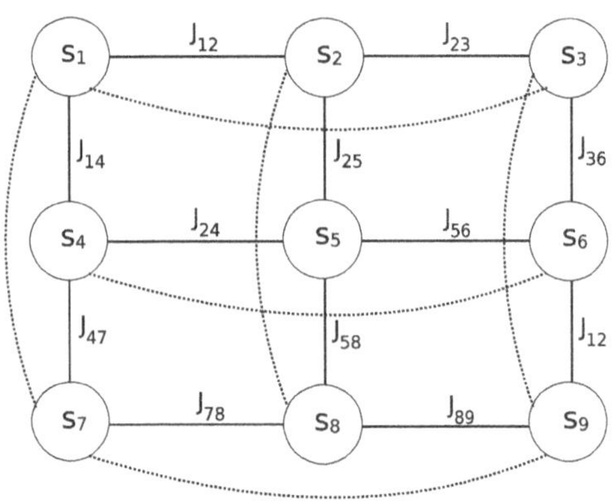

Figure 1: Cartoon picture of the coupling topology $< i, j >$ of Equation (1). Each node represents a spin variable, while the lines represent couplings J_{ij}. The dashed lines represent the couplings resulting from the periodic boundary conditions.

This geometry inherits certain features allowing the application of a graph algorithm [11] to find the minimal energy states. We use these as reference values for the quality of the solutions produced by our GA variant. To be more precise, for the exact solution E_{sol} from [11], a found value of E_{ga} is mapped to a relative error

$$\Delta E_{\text{rel}} = \left| \frac{E_{\text{ga}} - E_{\text{sol}}}{E_{\text{sol}}} \right| \,. \qquad (3)$$

This will allow us to average the ϵs over several instances of Ising spin glasses and thus several "replicas", that is various drawings of the J_{ij} from the distribution of Equation (2).

3. THE TRANSFORMED POTENTIAL ENERGY SURFACE

The general idea of the STUN transformation [14] is that any randomized optimization algorithm searching for the global minimum on a PES should be able to "tunnel" through barriers separating (local) minima. In particular, those minima, whose value are larger or equal to the best solution found so far, are irrelevant for the search and thus can be ignored. Therefore, STUN transforms the PES in such a manner that such minima will become less and less influential on the search dynamics. As the transformation is strictly monotonous the relative ranking of minima will be maintained. Furthermore, it is mandatory to maintain the location of minima in search space. One among several potential transformations which fulfill these requirements [6] is

$$f_{\text{trans}}(E) = 1 - \exp\left[-\gamma\left(E - E_0\right)\right] \,, \qquad (4)$$

where E_0 is the best (deepest) local minimum encountered so far, while $\gamma \in \mathbb{R}^+$ is a free parameter of the transformation. For our GA running on a transformed PES there are also other possible choices for E_0. For example, instead of using the best minimum found so far, it would also be possible to use only the best minimum within the current population, or – more general – the best minimum found within the m generations of the GA population.

For our Ising system, however, the effect of m was not analyzed, as performance results did not differ between $m = 0$ (best E_0 within current population) and m =current iteration (E_0 taken from the full evolutionary history).

To illustrate the effect of the transformation in Equation (4) we show in Figure 2 the results for two different choices of E_0 in the function[2]

$$I(x) = I_0 \left(\frac{\sin\left(\frac{k}{2} b \sin(x)\right)}{\frac{k}{2} b \sin(x)} \right)^2 \cos\left(\frac{k}{2} a \sin(x)\right)^2 + c \cdot x^2 \,. \quad (5)$$

As can be easily verified a major advantage of the transformation Equation (4) is that every function value above the E_0 is mapped into $[0; 1)$ and thus we do not need to control for units or scales.

3.1 Fitness function in STUN

In our GA we compare tournament [3] and roulette selection [7]. While tournament selection just uses rankings of fitness values, the roulette selection scheme requires positive fitness values. We implement this by using a mapping of the form

$$f(E) = |\max(E)_P - E| \,, \qquad (6)$$

where $\max(\circ)_P$ is the maximum of the E-values over the current population. For our STUN-transformed energy/objective func-

[2] A function inspired by optics/quantum mechanics with many minima, the parameters are: $k = \pi$, $a = 2\pi$, $b = \pi/3$, $I_0 = 1$ and $c = 0.03$

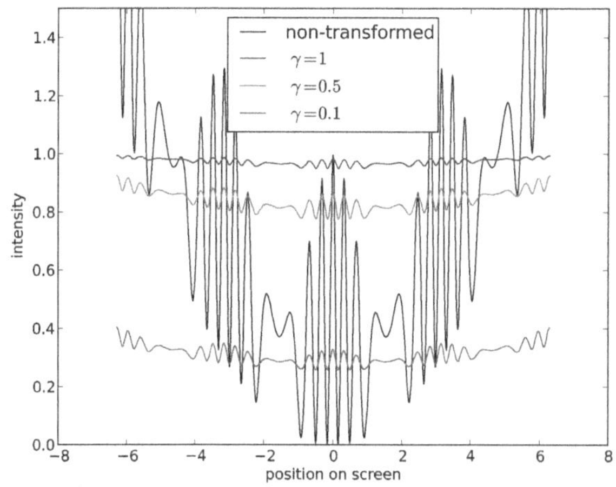

Figure 2: Illustration of the STUN transformation of Equation (4) on a function with many minima given by Equation (5). We have set $E_0 = I(-3)$ as a reference in Equation (5). Clearly the barriers between the multiple minima are reduced and can now more easily be traversed.

tion we therefore obtain the effective fitness in our GA given by $f(f_{\text{trans}}(E))$.

3.2 Implementation details

As we are interested in studying the effects of transformations in the objective function values, that is the fitness landscape, we have decided to use the most generic procedure for mutation and recombination in spin systems:

- mutation is implemented as single-spin flips: $s = 1/2 \stackrel{\text{mut.}}{\longrightarrow} s = -1/2$ and $s = -1/2 \stackrel{\text{mut.}}{\longrightarrow} s = 1/2$ with a mutation rate μ.

- recombination is implemented as a one-point crossover with probability ν as illustrated by the following scheme

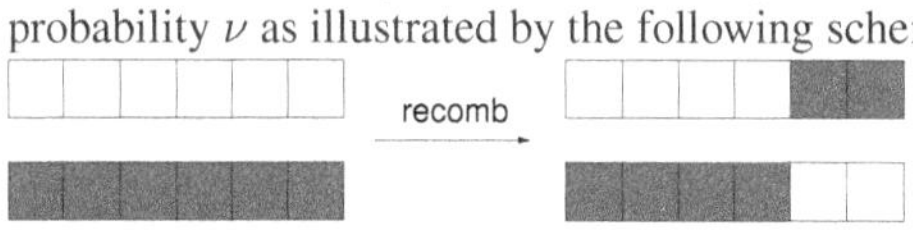

4. RESULTS

4.1 Performance comparison

In Figure 3, performance results from 60 independent GA runs over 49 replicas each for 6×6 Ising systems are presented[3]. We compare the time-course of the relative error of Equation (3) over the generation count [4].

[3]Note, that we always report and analyze the behavior of any GA variant with respect to the real energies in the subsequent parts of this study, rather than the transformed values. The transformed values are only used internally in our simulation software during selection, never in the analysis and presentation of final results.

[4]which is a strictly monotonous function of the number of calls to the object function for fix sized populations. We argue that the number of calls to the objective function as a "time measure" as it is the relevant resource measure: typically, the evaluation of the objective function is the dominant and time-consuming step.

In Figure 3 we compare tournament with roulette selection and a roulette selection approach based on our STUN transformation for $\gamma \in \{10^1, 10^0, 10^{-1}, 10^{-2}\}$.

First, it is noteworthy that we replicate previous results on the relative merit of tournament selection over generic roulette wheel selection: without additional improvements the average performance of the tournament variant is superior to the classical roulette wheel scheme [4].

Clearly, however, the tournament selection based GA is entering a phase of saturation after its initial success.

Now for STUN-GA, we see a major improvement for $\gamma = 10$ over both, the tournament selection scheme and the classical roulette selection idea (note the logarithmic scale for ΔE_{rel}).

Furthermore, our regular grid of $\log(\gamma)$ in Figure 3 shows the monotonic improvement for increasing γ, that is, for "stronger" transformation: the larger γ, the higher the non-linearity of the STUN-transformation in Equation (4).

In contrast, the choice $\gamma = 10^{-2}$ provides for a more or less linear mapping as can be seen if the STUN-transformation of Equation (4) is developed in a Taylor series around $\kappa := \gamma \cdot (E - E_0)$:

$$\begin{aligned} f_{\text{trans}}(E) &= 1 - \exp[-\gamma(E - E_0)] \\ &= 1 - e^{-\kappa} \\ &= 1 - \sum_{n=0}^{\infty} \frac{(-\kappa)^n}{n!} \\ &\approx 1 - (1 - \kappa) + O(\kappa^2) \\ &= \kappa = \gamma \cdot (E - E_0) \end{aligned}$$

and the final formula is just a rescaled and shifted objective function value. Therefore, small γ can only have small effects via Equation (6) of the order $O(\gamma^2)$.

To analyze this further, we give a detailed overview over the reached ΔE_{rel} for some selected generations in Figure 4. The plots give a graphical overview of some of the statistical evidence, that in fact the $\gamma = 10$ STUN-GA variant is not only superior *on average*, but also that the distribution of the ΔE_{rel} is much narrower and thus the application of "strong" STUN-transformations also increases the likelihood of obtaining low minima or even the global optimum.

Note, how the outliers for initial generation in Figure 4 have quite some outliers to smaller energy values. The classical and the STUN-roulette selection are able to "compress" the distribution so that only a few or no bad outliers occur after some generations, while tournament selection is still featuring a high number of those high-energy outliers.

4.2 Selective pressure

To quantify how strong selection acts on the corresponding population an empirical selective pressure can be defined analogous to [2]

$$I_{\text{emp}} := \frac{\mu_{t+1} - \mu_t}{\sigma_t}, \qquad (7)$$

where μ_t and σ_t are population mean and the variance of relative error of Equation (3) at a particular generation t.

Therefore, I_{emp} quantifies the reduction or increase in average quality of solutions within the population from one generation to the other. This (potential) improvement is then expressed in units of the standard deviation as a measure of dispersion of objective function values within the population. Note, that I_{emp} uses the population means μ_t and therefore will – upon convergence of the GA – return different values for a random sample compared to any subset of best individuals in our non-elitist setup.

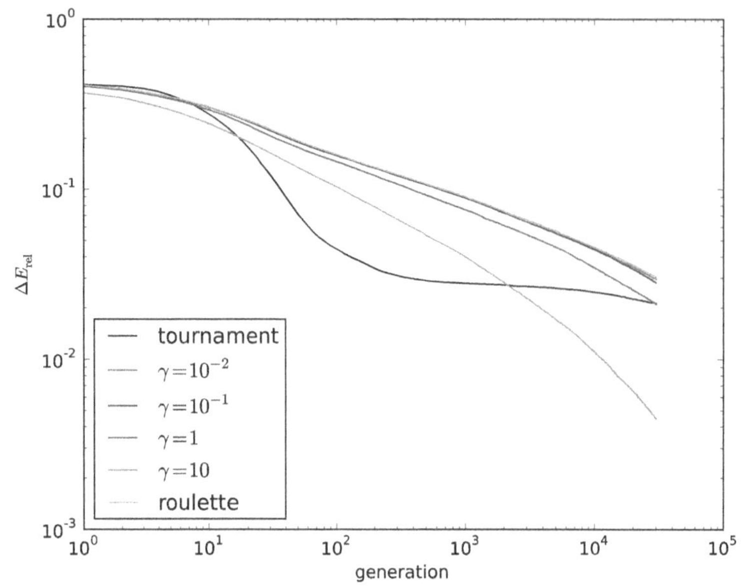

Figure 3: Averaged relative error in the found minima for various selection schemes and transformation strengths in the used GA. We let the GA run with 1,000 individuals per generation, a mutation rate of $\mu = 0.08$, and a recombination rate of $\nu = 0.41$. The averaging was done over $49 \cdot 60 = 2,920$ independent runs. The separation of points on the x-axis is smaller than line size and justifies the usage of lines.

We want to stress that we use this as an *empirical* selection measure in our real-world scenario, while [2] derived it for restricted, but analytically solvable GA-versions on simplified PES.

As is evident from Figure 5 the selection pressure for roulette wheel selection is especially strong in the early generations but decays rapidly. In contrast, the selective pressure for the tournament selection declines over far greater time scales. This can explain the superior convergence behavior of tournament selection in Figure 3 compared to classical roulette wheel selection: up to some $5 \cdot 10^3$ generations the selection step contributes more to the dynamics of the tournament-based GA than to the roulette one.

Eventually, this compares well with the restricted setting of [2]: where tournament selection showed a constant selective pressure for the trivial problems [2] while the selective pressure of a roulette wheel was found to vanish as the algorithm reaches the (global) optimum [10].

Now, for the STUN-GA variants in our study, we also find higher empirical selective pressures. Early on, the selective pressure is much higher for the STUN-GA working on the transformed PES with the large value $\gamma = 10$. This is in good agreement with our findings in Section 4.1 and our discussion on the empirical selective pressure for tournament vs. roulette selection from above.

Figure 5 also explains why we found in Section 4.1 that the tournament variant leveled out in a saturation regime: the selective pressure for the tournament GA despite of being maintained far longer than the selective pressure for roulette wheel selection, eventually falls beneath the pressure for the roulette wheel GAs.

We confirmed this divergent behavior between roulette, tournament, and STUN-GAs for larger systems of 9×9 Ising spins but fewer replicas by extrapolation from the initial phase to more than one order of magnitude more generations [data not shown].

Clearly, the distinction between the tournament selection approach with very low average values of I_{emp} in Figure 5, the modest values of I_{emp} for the classical or low-transformation STUN-GAs and the much larger variety and diversity indicated by the high values of I_{emp} for $\gamma = 10$-STUN-GA can be seen. The monotonous tendency to improve solutions with increasing γ shows the usefulness of non-linear transformations.

This shows, again, that the STUN-transformation contributes to a more efficient search dynamics; with larger diversity, more selective pressure, *on average* better performance, and a better *worst-case* performance.

5. CONCLUSION

This study has motivated and introduced a transformation technique in the selection step of genetic algorithm (GA) – in contrast to previous ideas [5] of transforming the search space topology and thus affecting the mutation and recombination operators.

With the STUN-transformation we eventually included *co*-evolutionary effects into the GA dynamics. As was previously discussed [16] such *co*-evolutionary synergies in optimization might resolve the "no free lunch" phenomena.

With our complex test problem of Ising spin glasses we were able to show that, indeed, the STUN-transformation provides for higher efficiency in terms of relative error in predicted optima.

Furthermore, we were able to explain these performance findings based on an empirical measure of selective strength. In our simulations we found that the STUN-transformation maintains the selective pressure over a longer simulation time than the non-transformed, classical roulette scheme. Furthermore, the saturation of tournament selection can be understood as a deprivation of the pool of diversity and the implied selective pressure.

6. ACKNOWLEDGMENTS

KH acknowledges financial support by the Deutsche Forschungsgemeinschaft under grant no. HA 5261/3-1.

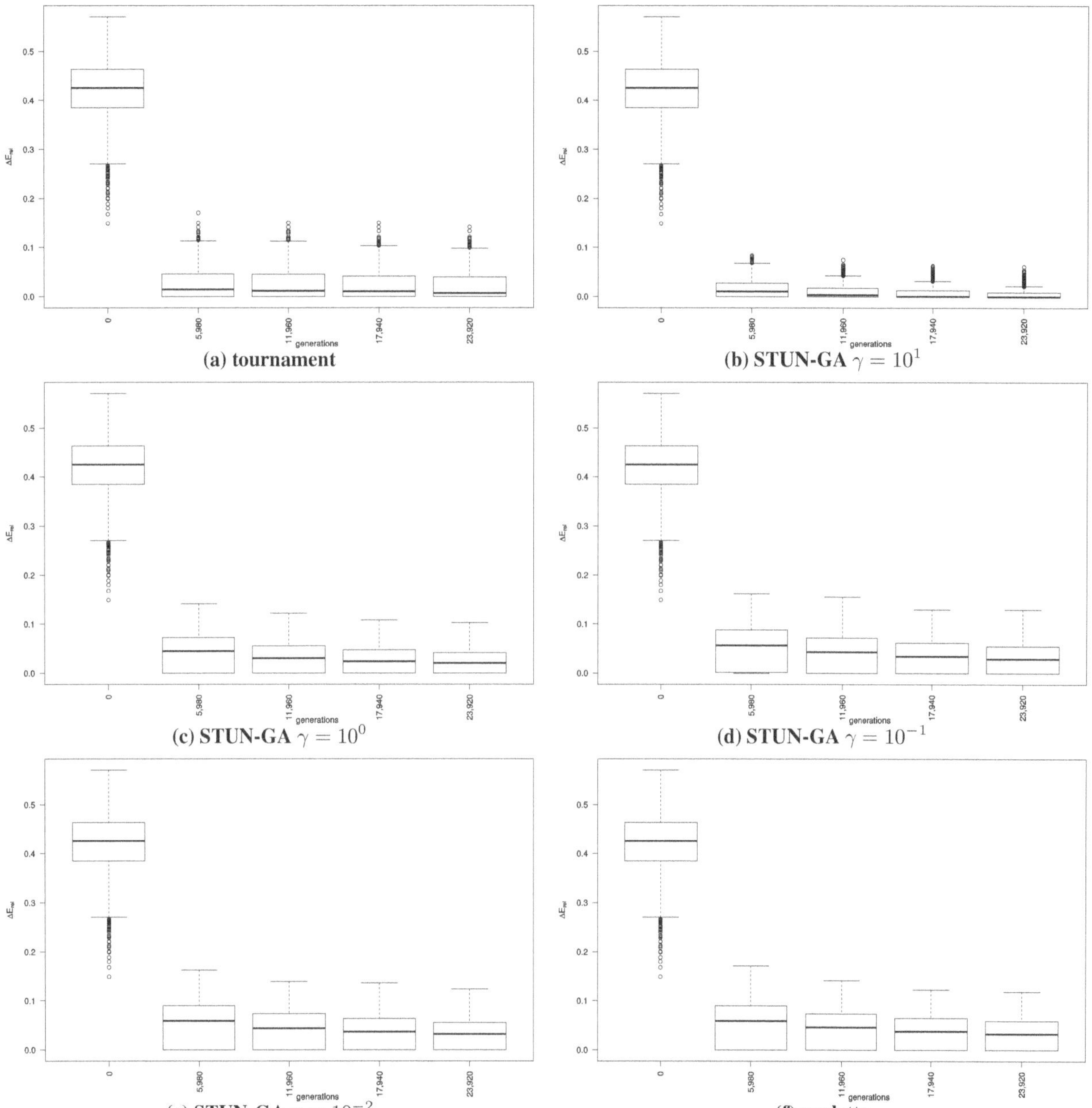

(a) tournament

(b) STUN-GA $\gamma = 10^1$

(c) STUN-GA $\gamma = 10^0$

(d) STUN-GA $\gamma = 10^{-1}$

(e) STUN-GA $\gamma = 10^{-2}$

(f) roulette

Figure 4: Detailed analysis of the distribution of relative errors ΔE_{rel} for some number of generations and all the selection schemes of this study. The boxplots show by the thick, horizontal line at the median of ΔE_{rel}; The upper and lower box boundaries are the first and third quartiles of the distribution of the $2,940$ ΔE_{rel}-values at each generation; the whiskers from the boxes indicate the 1.5-fold interquartile range, and the open circles outliers of the data points beyond the whiskers. Plots were done with the statistical software R [12].

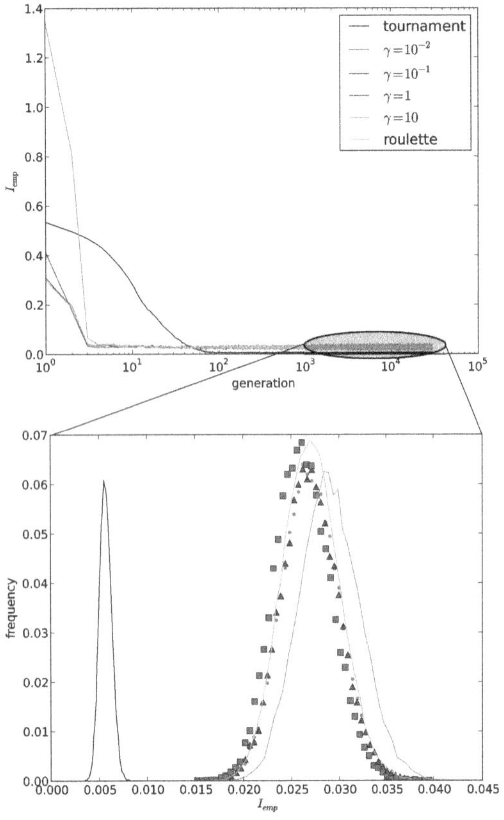

Figure 5: Empirical selective pressure for the GA variants. The values were obtained for 60 independent runs for 49 replicas of a 6×6 Ising spin-glass system (thus $60\cdot49 = 2,940$ independent samples). The second plot in the bottom shows histograms of I_{emp} averaged over the latest parts of the trajectory (indicated by the zooming elipsis); colors as above.

7. REFERENCES

[1] H. J. C. Barbosa and A. C. C. Lemonge. A genetic algorithm encoding for a class of cardinality constraints. In *GECCO'05*, pages 1193–1200, 2005.

[2] T. Blickle and L. Thiele. A comparison of selection schemes used in genetic algorithms. Technical report, Swiss Federal Institute of Technology (ETH) Zurich, Computer Engineering and Communications Networks Lab (TIK), 1995.

[3] T. Blickle and L. Thiele. A mathematical analysis of tournament selection. In *Proceedings of the Sixth International Conference on Genetic Algorithms*, pages 9–16. Morgan Kaufmann, 1995.

[4] D. E. Goldberg and K. Deb. A comparative analysis of selection schemes used in genetic algorithms. In G. J. E. Rawlins, editor, *Foundations of Genetic Algorithms*, pages 69–93. San Francisco, CA: Morgan Kaufmann, 1991.

[5] J. A. M. H. Search space modulation in genetic algorithms: evolving the search space by sinusoidal transformations. In *GECCO*, pages 1559–1560, 2005.

[6] K. Hamacher. Adaptation in stochastic tunneling global optimization of complex potential energy landscapes. *Europhys. Lett.*, 74(6):944–950, 2006.

[7] J. H. Holland. *Adaptation in natural and artificial systems*. MIT Press, Cambridge, MA, USA, 1992.

[8] P. J. Laarhoven and E. H. Aarts. Simulated annealing. In *Simulated Annealing: Theory and Applications*, volume 37 of *Mathematics and Its Applications*, pages 7–15. Springer Netherlands, 1987.

[9] M. Mitchell. *An Introduction to Genetic Algorithms (Complex Adaptive Systems)*. A Bradford Book, 1998.

[10] H. Mühlenbein and D. Schlierkamp-Voosen. Predictive models for the breeder genetic algorithm – I. continuous parameter optimization. *Evol. Comp.*, 1:25–49, 1993.

[11] G. Pardella and F. Liers. Exact ground states of large two-dimensional planar ising spin glasses. *Phys. Rev. E*, 78:056705, Nov 2008.

[12] R Development Core Team. *R: A Language and Environment for Statistical Computing*. R Foundation for Statistical Computing, Vienna, Austria, 2011. ISBN 3-900051-07-0.

[13] T. Storch. On the impact of objective function transformations on evolutionary and black-box algorithms. *Genetic Programming and Evolvable Machines*, 7(2):171–193, June 2006. GECCO'05.

[14] W. Wenzel and K. Hamacher. Stochastic tunneling approach for global minimization of complex potential energy landscapes. *Phys. Rev. Lett.*, 82:3003–3007, Apr 1999.

[15] R. P. Wiegand and K. A. De Jong. Understanding coevolution - theory and analysis of coevolutionary algorithms: Preface. In A. M. Barry, editor, *GECCO 2002: Proceedings of the Bird of a Feather Workshops, Genetic and Evolutionary Computation Conference*, page 228, New York, 8 July 2002. AAAI.

[16] D. Wolpert and W. Macready. Coevolutionary free lunches. *IEEE Trans. Evol. Comp.*, 9(6):721–735, Dec 2005.

[17] D. H. Wolpert and W. G. Macready. No free lunch theorems for optimization. *IEEE Trans. Evol. Comp.*, 1(1):67–82, 1997.

[18] X. Yu and M. Gen. *Decision Engineering: Introduction to Evolutionary Algorithms*. Springer, 2010.

A Fixed Budget Analysis of Randomized Search Heuristics for the Traveling Salesperson Problem

Samadhi Nallaperuma
Optimisation and Logistics
School of Computer Science
The University of Adelaide
Adelaide, Australia

Frank Neumann
Optimisation and Logistics
School of Computer Science
The University of Adelaide
Adelaide, Australia

Dirk Sudholt
Dept. of Computer Science
The University of Sheffield
Sheffield, United Kingdom

ABSTRACT

Randomized Search heuristics are frequently applied to NP-hard combinatorial optimization problems. The runtime analysis of randomized search heuristics has contributed tremendously to their theoretical understanding. Recently, randomized search heuristics have been examined regarding their achievable progress within a fixed time budget. We follow this approach and present a first fixed budget runtime analysis for a NP-hard combinatorial optimization problem. We consider the well-known Traveling Salesperson problem (TSP) and analyze the fitness increase that randomized search heuristics are able to achieve within a given fixed budget.

Categories and Subject Descriptors

F.2 [**Theory of Computation**]: Analysis of Algorithms and Problem Complexity

Keywords

Traveling Salesperson Problem; fitness gain; theory

1. INTRODUCTION

Randomized Search heuristics (RSH) such as randomized local search, evolutionary algorithms and ant colony optimization have become very popular in recent years to solve a wide range of hard combinatorial optimization problems. Regarding them as classical randomized algorithms [11], a lot of progress has been made in recent years on their theoretical understanding [1, 6]. Initially, most of the studies were focused on simple example functions [4]. Gradually, the analysis on combinatorial optimization [10, 12, 14] problems was also established. We refer the textbook of Neumann and Witt [13] for a comprehensive presentation on the runtime analysis of randomized search heuristics for problems from combinatorial optimization.

All these studies on analyzing of time complexity were based on a single perspective, the expected optimization time. There were slight variations on this considering the number of iterations/generations or fitness evaluations. Jansen and Zarges [7] and Zhou et al. [18] pointed out that there is a gap between the empirical results and the theoretical results obtained on the optimization time. Theoretical research most often yields asymptotic results on finding the global optimum while practitioners concern more about achieving some good result within a reasonable time budget. Furthermore, it is beneficial to know how much progress an algorithm can make given some additional time budget. Experimental studies on this topic have been carried out in the domain of algorithm engineering [15] and the term fixed budget runtime analysis has been introduced by Jansen and Zarges [8].

So far, the fixed budget analysis has been conducted for very simple test functions, on which the considered randomized search heuristics such as randomized local search and the (1+1) EA follow a typical search trajectory [3, 7, 8] with high probability. This implies that on these functions the development of the best fitness over time forms an almost deterministic curve that describes the algorithm's typical behavior. Given such a strong relation between fitness and time, and the availability of upper and lower tail bounds, it is then possible to derive tight upper and lower bounds on the expected fitness increase over any given period of time.

The goal of obtaining tight upper and lower bounds is only feasible for functions where randomized search heuristics show a typical search trajectory and tail bounds are available to bound deviations from this trajectory. This usually does not apply to hard combinatorial problems like the Traveling Salesperson Problem, and currently no fixed-budget analysis is available for such problems. We argue that for these problems fixed budget results can be obtained by relaxing the above goal towards only considering *lower bounds* on the expected fitness gain. Lower bounds can be determined based on the expected minimum improvement made in an iteration. In this manner there is no requirement for obtaining tail bounds, which drastically widens the scope of problems that can be tackled with this approach. Even though lower bounds on the expected fitness gain may not be tight, they provide proven guarantees on the progress made by a RSH. The aim of this approach is to establish guarantees on the expected fitness gain for various kinds of RSH, hence providing guidance for choosing, designing, and tuning RSH such that they find high-fitness solutions in short time.

This study provides a starting point for fixed-budget analysis of randomized search heuristics for combinatorial optimization problems. In particular, we consider random-

GECCO'14, July 12-16, 2014, Vancouver, BC, Canada.
Copyright 2014 ACM 978-1-4503-2662-9/14/07...$15.00.
http://dx.doi.org/10.1145/2576768.2598302

ized local search (RLS) and (1+1) Evolutionary Algorithm ((1+1) EA) on the famous Traveling Salesperson Problem (TSP). We analyze TSP instances on Manhattan and Euclidean instances in the setting of smoothed complexity [16]. Smoothed analysis provides a generic framework to analyze algorithms like 2-Opt for TSP with the capability to interpolate between average and worst case analysis. This analysis was first proposed by Spielman and Teng [16] focusing on the simplex algorithm to explain the discrepancy between its exponential worst case runtime and the fast performance in practice. The probabilistic model proposed by Englert et al. [5] is a reminiscence of the original smoothed analysis model. Later, these results were refined by Manthey and Veestra [17]. Here, we will adhere to the initial analysis by Englert et al. [5] as our major focus is on transferring these results to a fixed budget analysis of RSH.

We build on the analysis of Englert et al. [5] for 2-Opt which allows to get bounds on the expected progress of a 2-Opt operation in the smoothed setting. First, we obtain fixed budget results based on the minimum improvement that RLS and (1+1) EA can make in one iteration. We further improve these results, following [5], by analyzing a sequence of consecutive 2-Opt steps together to identify linked pairs. Interestingly, considering only single improving steps gives a constant lower bound on the progress achievable in each of the t iterations whereas the analysis of a sequence of consecutive 2-Opt steps gives a larger expected progress per step if t is large.

The organization of the paper is as follows. Section 2 describes problem context and the considered algorithms. Section 3 and section 4 contain the analysis for Manhattan and Euclidean instances respectively. Finally, Section 5 concludes with highlights and future directions.

2. PRELIMINARIES

The Traveling Salesperson problem (TSP) is one of the most famous NP-hard combinatorial optimization problems. Given a set of n cities $\{1, \ldots, n\}$ and a distance matrix $d = (d_{ij})$, $1 \leq i, j \leq n$, the goal is to compute a tour of minimal length that visits each city exactly once and returns to the origin.

A TSP instance is considered to be metric if its distance function is in metric space. Metric space satisfies reflexivity, symmetry and triangle inequality conditions. A pair (V, d) of a nonempty set V and a function $d : V \times V \to R^+$ is called a metric space if for all $x, y, z \in V$ the following properties are satisfied:

- $d(x, y) = 0$ if and only if $x = y$,
- $d(x, y) = d(y, x)$
- $d(x, z) \leq d(x, y) + d(y, z)$.

We consider the case where the n cities are given by points (x_i, y_i), $1 \leq i \leq n$, in the plane and distances are given according to the L_1 or L_2 metric. For a distance metric L_p the distance of two points $p_i = (x_i, y_i)$ and $p_j = (x_j, y_j)$ is

$$d_p(p_i, p_j) = (|x_i - x_j|^p + |y_i - y_j|^p)^{1/p}.$$

L_1 and L_2 are called Manhattan and Euclidean metric, respectively.

2.1 RLS and Simple Evolutionary Algorithm

We consider simple randomized search heuristics and analyze them with respect to the progress that they make within a given time budget.

We investigate Randomized Local Search (RLS) (Algorithm 1) and variants of the (1+1) EA (Algorithm 2). All algorithms work with a population size of 1 and produce 1 offspring in each iteration. A basic mutation is given by the well-known 2-Opt operator. The 2-Opt operator selects two edges $\{u_1, u_2\}$ and $\{v_1, v_2\}$ from the tour such that u_1, u_2, v_1, v_2 are distinct and appear in this order in the tour, and it replaces these edges by the edges $\{u_1, v_1\}$ and $\{u_2, v_2\}$.

RLS performs one 2-Opt step in each iteration to produce an offspring. (1+1) EA chooses an integer variable s drawn from the Poisson distribution with expectation 1 in each mutation step and performs sequentially $s+1$ 2-Opt operations. In case $s + 1 = 1$, we speak of a singular mutation, or a singular generation.

The reason we are studying the (1+1) EA is that it can simulate a 2-Opt step in singular generations, which occur with probability $1/e$, $e = \exp(1)$. Moreover, it has a positive probability of generating a global optimum in every generation through executing the right number and sequence of 2-Opt steps. So it is guaranteed to find a global optimum in finite time, though this time may be exponential in n.

Note that in our algorithms we consider the notion of fitness with regard to the minimization of the tour-length. As evolutionary algorithms often maximize fitness, we use the term *fitness gain* to describe fitness improvements, that is, the decrease of the tour length.

Algorithm 1 RLS

```
x ← a random permutation of [n]
repeat
    y := x
    y ← apply a 2-Opt step chosen uniformly to y.
    if f(y) ≤ f(x) then
        x ← y
    end if
until forever
```

Algorithm 2 (1+1) EA

```
x ← a random permutation of [n]
repeat
    s from a Poisson distribution with unit expectation
    y := x
    for s + 1 times do
        y ← apply a 2-Opt step chosen uniformly to y.
    end for
    if f(y) ≤ f(x) then
        x ← y
    end if
until forever
```

We study our algorithms regarding the expected progress that they make within a given number of t iterations. We consider the algorithms on random instances in the setting of smoothed analysis [5, 16].

In this model, n points are placed in a d-dimensional unit hypercube $[0, 1]^d$ for $d \geq 2$. Each point v_i, $i = 1, 2, \ldots, n$, is chosen independently according to its own probability density function $f_i : [0, 1]^d \to [0, \phi]$ for some parameter $\phi > 1$. To model worst-case instances, it is assumed that these densities are chosen by an adversary who is trying to create the most difficult random instances possible. By adjusting the parameter ϕ, one can tune the power of this adversary and hence interpolate between worst and average case. For example, for $\phi = 1$ there is only one valid choice for the densities, and every point is chosen uniformly at random from the unit hypercube. The larger ϕ, the more concentrated the probability mass can be, hence the adversary becomes more powerful in creating a worst case, and the analysis gets closer to a worst-case analysis.

This model covers a smoothed analysis also with a slight modification. There the adversary determines the initial distribution of points and then a slight perturbation is applied to each position, adding a Gaussian random variable with small standard deviation σ. There ϕ has to be set as $1/\sigma^2$. The two types of instances are called ϕ-perturbed Manhattan instances and ϕ-perturbed Euclidean instances.

Analyzing our algorithms in this setting, we may assume that any two different tours have different function value. Hence, both algorithms always accept strict improvements.

2.2 Minimum Improvement of a 2-Opt Step

We now summarize results by Englert et al. [5] on the minimal improvement of a 2-Opt step. These results will later on be used in our analysis of the randomized search heuristics. We denote the random variables Δ that describes the fitness gain obtained in one iteration and Δ_t the fitness gain in t iterations. Based on the smallest improvement of any 2-Opt step we can find the expected improvement made in t iterations of (1+1) EA. The interval $(0, \varepsilon]$ is determined by an adversary. Let us first consider a fixed 2-Opt step in which the edges e_1 and e_2 are exchanged with the edges e_3 and e_4. This 2-Opt step decreases the length of the tour by $\Delta(e_1, e_2, e_3, e_4) = d(e_1) + d(e_2) - d(e_3) - d(e_4)$.

Let $\Delta_{\min}$ denote the smallest possible improvement made by any improving 2-Opt step:

$$\Delta_{\min} = \min\{\Delta \mid \Delta > 0\}.$$

Inspired by the original ideas of Kern [9], Chandra et al. [2] bounded the probability that this smallest improvement lies within the interval $(0, \varepsilon]$ with a high probability for the uniform distribution.

We will make use of the following theorem by Englert et al. [5] which gives an upper bound on the probability that an improving 2-Opt step gives an improvement of at most ε for the Manhattan metric.

THEOREM 1 (MANHATTAN METRIC [5, THEOREM 7]). *For the Manhattan metric and any $\varepsilon > 0$, it holds*

$$\Pr(\Delta_{\min} \leq \varepsilon) \leq 4!^2 \varepsilon n^4 \phi.$$

Based on this result we get a lower bound on the probability that the smallest improvement is greater than any given ε.

Similar to the Manhattan instances, for the Euclidean instances also, the minimum improvement per a 2-Opt step is inspired by the original ideas of Kern [9]. Based on this, the expected runtime was proved polynomial for uniform distribution by Chandra et al. [2]. This was later extended for a more generalized setting having any probability distribution by Englert et al. [5].

LEMMA 2 (EUCLIDEAN METRIC [5, LEMMA 18]). *For the Euclidean metric and any $\varepsilon > 0$, it holds*

$$\Pr(\Delta_{\min} \leq \varepsilon) \leq n^4 \cdot \varepsilon \cdot \log(1/\varepsilon) \cdot \phi^3.$$

In case the considered algorithms reach a local optimum, we cannot guarantee a steady fitness gain. So instead we use the fact that local optima have a good approximation ratio. The approximation ratio for the worst local optimum with regard to 2-Opt was proven originally in Chandra et al. [2] for the uniform distribution. This was later generalized by Englert et al. [5] for any probability distribution with a given density function ϕ.

THEOREM 3 ([5, THEOREM 4]). *Let $p \in \mathbb{N} \cup \{\infty\}$. For ϕ perturbed L_p instances the expected approximation ratio of the worst tour that is locally optimal for 2-Opt is $O(\sqrt[d]{\phi})$, where d represents the dimension*

As a consequence, for Manhattan and Euclidean instances the expected approximation ratio is at most $O(\sqrt{\phi})$ as we consider instances in a 2 dimensional unit hypercube $[0, 1]^2$.

3. ANALYSIS FOR MANHATTAN INSTANCES

In this section, we first present the analysis for RLS and (1+1) EA based on the minimum possible improvement for a single 2-Opt step. We later extend the analysis for the improvement in a sequence of consecutive 2-Opt steps.

3.1 Analysis of a Single 2-Opt Step

We start by showing a lower bound on the fitness gain achievable by RLS.

THEOREM 4. *In t iterations, RLS achieves an expected fitness gain of $\Omega(t/(n^6\phi))$ or reaches a local optimal solution with expected approximation ratio $O(\sqrt{\phi})$.*

Proof. Based on Theorem 1, we get

$$\Pr(\Delta_{\min} > \varepsilon) \geq 1 - 4!^2 \varepsilon n^4 \phi = 1 - 576 \varepsilon n^4 \phi$$

as a lower bound on the probability that the minimum improvement is at least ε.

Let Δ_{imp} denote the random variable describing the fitness gain obtained in a single improving 2-Opt step. This is obviously no less than the minimum possible improvement $\Delta_{\min}$. For any fixed $\varepsilon > 0$, the expected fitness gain per one improving 2-Opt step can be lower bounded as follows:

$$\begin{aligned} E(\Delta_{\text{imp}}) &= \int_{\Delta_{\text{imp}}} \Pr(\Delta_{\text{imp}}) \cdot \Delta_{\text{imp}} \\ &\geq \Pr(\Delta_{\text{imp}} \geq \varepsilon) \cdot \varepsilon \\ &\geq \Pr(\Delta_{\min} \geq \varepsilon) \cdot \varepsilon \\ &= (1 - 576 \varepsilon n^4 \phi) \cdot \varepsilon \end{aligned}$$

Setting $\varepsilon = 1/(2 \cdot 576 n^4 \phi)$ we get

$$\Pr(\Delta_{\min} \geq \varepsilon) \geq 1/2$$

and accordingly

$$E(\Delta_{\text{imp}}) \geq 1/(2304 n^4 \phi).$$

The number of mutations occurring in one iteration is 1 and the probability for an improving 2-Opt step is at least $1/\binom{n}{2} \geq 2/n^2$ if the current solution is not locally optimal. Therefore, the expected value for the fitness gain Δ in any 2-Opt step can be lower bounded as

$$E(\Delta) \geq 1/(1152 n^6 \phi).$$

Hence, the expected value for the fitness gain in t iterations if no locally optimal solution has been obtained in between can be derived as $E(\Delta_t) \geq t/(1152n^6\phi)$.

By Theorem 3, a locally optimal solution has expected approximation ratio $O(\sqrt{\phi})$ which completes the proof. □

THEOREM 5. *In t iterations (1+1) EA achieves an expected fitness gain of $\Omega(t/(n^6\phi))$ or reaches a local optimal solution with expected approximation ratio $O(\sqrt{\phi})$.*

Proof. The expectation for the fitness gain in an improving 2-Opt step can be derived similar to the above proof in Theorem 4

$$E(\Delta_{\text{imp}}) \geq 1/(2304n^4\phi).$$

The probability of singular mutation occur in a generation is $1/e$ due to the Poisson distribution with unit expectation. The probability of an improving 2-Opt step is therefore at least $2/(en^2)$. Thus the expected value for the fitness gain Δ in any 2-Opt step is

$$E(\Delta) \geq 1/(1152en^6\phi).$$

Hence, the expected value for the fitness gain in t iterations can be derived as $E(\Delta_t) \geq t/(1152en^6\phi)$.

By Theorem 3, a locally optimal solution has expected approximation ratio $O(\sqrt{\phi})$ which completes the proof. □

3.2 Analysis of Linked Steps for RLS

The lower bound for the expected fitness gain presented in previous section is based on the minimum improvement a single 2-Opt step can make. This bound can be improved further by considering the improvement made in a sequence of consecutive 2-Opt steps.

The analysis of consecutive steps in Englert et al. [5] is based on the number of disjoint pairs of 2-Opt steps linked by an edge, such that in one step an edge is added and in the other it is removed. Different types of linked pairs of 2-Opt steps are considered as follows. Let $\{v_1, v_2\}$ and $\{v_3, v_4\}$ be the edges that are replaced by $\{v_1, v_3\}$ and $\{v_2, v_4\}$ in the first 2-Opt step, and $\{v_1, v_3\}$ and $\{v_5, v_6\}$ be replaced by $\{v_1, v_5\}$ and $\{v_3, v_6\}$ in the second 2-Opt step.

Following [5], we consider three different types of steps:

type 0: $|\{v_2, v_4\} \cap \{v_5, v_6\}| = 0.$

type 1: $|\{v_2, v_4\} \cap \{v_5, v_6\}| = 1.$

type 2: $|\{v_2, v_4\} \cap \{v_5, v_6\}| = 2.$

As explained in [5], it is important to limit the number of occurrences of type 2 as no guarantee on the fitness gain made by type 2 steps is available. We need to show that there is a sufficient number of linked pairs of type 0 and 1 as for linked pairs of type 0 and 1 a good progress can be guaranteed.

Due to [5, Lemma 9] there are at least $t/6 - 7n(n-1)/24$ such pairs in a sequence of t consecutive 2-Opt steps. The analysis in [5] considers all 2-Opt steps $S_1, \ldots, S_t$ in sequence and constructs disjoint linked pairs (of any type) in a greedy fashion. When processing some step S_i, we search for steps S_j and S'_j, where the two edges inserted by S_i are being removed again, if such steps exist. If either S_j or S'_j exist, the respective pair (S_i, S_j) or (S_i, S'_j) is being added to a list of disjoint linked 2-Opt steps, and both S_j and S'_j are being removed from the list to ensure disjointness of pairs. The proof of [5, Lemma 9] then shows that when removing all pairs of type 2 from this list, at least $t/6 - 7n(n-1)/24$ pairs of type 0 or 1 remain.

We further improve this bound, considering the fact that the possible number of pairs excluded is constrained by the number of edges in the final tour.

LEMMA 6. *Let u be the total number of linked pairs in an improving 2-Opt sequence. Then the number of linked pairs v of type 0 or 1 in that sequence is at least $u/2 - n/4$.*

Proof. Following the argument in the proof of [5, Lemma 9] there cannot be a type 2 linked pair that associates with another type 2 linked pair. Therefore, each of the type 2 pairs (S_i, S_j) can be associated with at most two different pairs (S_j, S_ℓ) and $(S_j, S_{\ell'})$ of type 0 or 1, unless the steps S_ℓ or $S_{\ell'}$ are undefined. This happens if the edges added to the tour in S_j are never removed. Since the final tour contains n edges, at most $n/2$ pairs are excluded due to this. If we consider the number of type 2 pairs as x then the total number of pairs of type 0 or 1 must be at least $x - n/2$. This implies $u \geq x + (x - n/2)$ and $x \leq u/2 + n/4$. The number of good pairs is therefore $u - x \geq u/2 - n/4$. □

Using the same argument, we can improve [5, Lemma 8] on the total number of disjoint linked pairs. There, the authors show that for each processed 2-Opt step S_i at most two other steps S_j S'_j are excluded from being processed if j or j' is defined. Hence, for a sequence of t steps there are at least $t/3$ pairs, from which we have to subtract the number of steps S_i where neither j nor j' are defined. Englert et al. [5, Lemma 8] argue that we need to subtract a number of $n(n-1)/4$ steps. However, this number can be improved from $n(n-1)/4$ to $n/2$ considering that the number of edges in the final tour is exactly n, and S_i can only be excluded if both edges inserted in the tour are never removed again. Therefore, the total number of disjoint pairs is at least $u = t/3 - n/2$. Combining the result of above Lemma 6 to this we obtain the number of disjoint pairs of type 0 and 1.

LEMMA 7. *In every sequence of t consecutive 2-Opt steps, the number of disjoint pairs of 2-Opt steps of type 0 or 1 is at least $t/6 - n/2$.*

Due to above Lemma 7 there are at least $t/6 - n/2$ such pairs in a sequence of t consecutive 2-Opt steps. Here we consider the probability of both 2-Opt steps in a linked pair having improvement at least ε.

LEMMA 8 ([5, LEMMA 10]). *In a ϕ perturbed L1 instance with n vertices, the probability that there exists a pair of type 0 or 1 in which both 2-Opt steps are improvements by at most ε is bounded by $O(n^6 \cdot \varepsilon^2 \cdot \phi^2)$.*

Based on the above Lemmas (7 and 8), we can bound the fitness gain for a given number of t iterations. Note that the Theorem requires a lower bound on the number of iterations as only for large enough t we can guarantee that linked 2-Opt steps of type 0 or 1 do exist.

THEOREM 9. *In $t \geq cn^3$ iterations, $c > 3/2$ constant, RLS obtains an expected fitness gain of $\Omega(t/(n^5\phi))$ unless it reaches a local optimum. In that case, expected approximation ratio of the solution is $O(\sqrt{\phi})$.*

Proof. Let $\Delta_{\min}$ denote the minimum possible improvement made by any pair of type 0 or 1. Using above result in Lemma 8,

$$\Pr(\Delta_{\min} > \varepsilon) \geq 1 - n^6 \cdot \varepsilon^2 \cdot \phi^2.$$

Let Δ be the random variable describes the fitness gain obtained in a pair of linked 2-Opt steps of type 0 or 1. For any $\varepsilon > 0$, the expected fitness gain $E(\Delta)$ can be bounded as follows.

$$\begin{aligned} E(\Delta) &= \int_{\Delta} \Pr(\Delta) \cdot \Delta \\ &\geq \Pr(\Delta \geq \varepsilon) \cdot \varepsilon \\ &\geq (1 - n^6 \cdot \varepsilon^2 \cdot \phi^2) \cdot \varepsilon. \end{aligned}$$

Setting $\varepsilon = 1/(2\sqrt{(n^6 \cdot \phi^2)})$ we get $\Pr(\Delta > \varepsilon) \geq 1/2$ and as a consequence

$$E(\Delta) \geq 1/(4\sqrt{(n^6 \cdot \phi^2)}) \geq 1/(4n^3\phi).$$

The expected number of improving 2-Opt steps made in t iterations is at least $2t/n^2$. Let t^* be the number of improving steps. By Lemma 7 we know there are at least $t^*/6 - n/2$ type 0 or 1 pairs in a sequence of t^* improving steps. As $t \geq cn^3$ for $c > 3/2$, we have $2t = (2-3/c) \cdot t + 3t/c \geq (2-3/c) \cdot t + 3n^3$ and

$$E(t^*/6 - n/2) \geq \frac{2t}{6n^2} - \frac{n}{2} \geq \frac{(2-3/c) \cdot t}{6n^2} = \Omega(t/n^2).$$

A lower bound for the expected fitness gain for t iterations is therefore

$$E(\Delta_t) = E(\Delta) \cdot \Omega(t/n^2) \geq \Omega(t/(n^5\phi)).$$

By Theorem 3, a locally optimal solution has expected approximation ratio $O(\sqrt{\phi})$ which completes the proof. □

3.3 Analysis of Linked Steps for (1+1) EA

The challenge for analyzing the (1+1) EA instead of RLS lies in the fact that the (1+1) EA can execute multiple 2-Opt steps in one generation. For RLS Englert et al. [5] showed that certain pairs of improving 2-Opt steps yield a large fitness increase on perturbed instances, with high probability. Executing multiple 2-Opt steps in one generation complicates this argument, as some of these mutations may not be improving. As such, they might interfere with the mentioned pairs, and prohibit a large fitness increase. In the following, we show that there are sufficiently many linked 2-Opt operations that take place in generations where only one 2-Opt step is executed.

To this end, we consider a slightly modified variant of the (1+1) EA, which we call (1+1) EA* (see Algorithm 3). The (1+1) EA* will exclude generations containing multiple 2-Opt steps where an edge e is being inserted in one of these 2-Opt steps and being removed in a later 2-Opt step of the same generation.

The purpose of this modification is to enable a theoretical analysis as some of the excluded steps are difficult to handle. (1+1) EA and (1+1) EA* show identical behavior most of the time; it is easy to show that the probability of removing an edge that was inserted in the same generation is at most $O(1/n)$. So (1+1) EA and (1+1) EA* are identical most of the time, apart from a vanishingly small fraction of steps.

Algorithm 3 (1+1) EA*

```
x ← a random permutation of [n]
repeat
    Choose s from a Poison distribution with unit expectation
    for s + 1 times do
        y ← Mutate(x)
    end for
    if f(y) ≤ f(x) then
        check whether one of the above mutations has removed
an edge that was inserted in the same generation
        if so, reject y. Otherwise, x ← y
    end if
until forever
```

Note that, when the (1+1) EA* does behave differently from the (1+1) EA, it rejects a new offspring that would otherwise improve the current tour. We therefore believe that we are being pessimistic by considering the progress of the (1+1) EA* instead of that of the (1+1) EA.

LEMMA 10. *In every sequence of t generations of the (1+1) EA*, the expected number of disjoint pairs of 2-Opt steps, both of which are singular, is at least*

$$\frac{t}{3e^2n^2} - n/2,$$

unless a local optimum is reached beforehand.

Proof. We call a 2-Opt step *improving* if it does not decrease the current fitness. A 2-Opt step is called *singular* if it is the only 2-Opt step executed in that generation.

We adapt the proof of Lemma 8 in [5] to take into account steps that are rejected by the (1+1) EA*, and the fact that the (1+1) EA* can accept non-improving 2-Opt steps in generations with multiple 2-Opt steps.

Let $\mathcal{S} = S_1, S_2, \ldots$ be a list of all 2-Opt steps executed in t generations. Then we process this list to create a list $\mathcal{L}$ of linked 2-Opt steps, both of which are singular.

The probability of the (1+1) EA* making an improving 2-Opt step is at least $1/\binom{n}{2} \geq 2/n^2$, so long as no local optimum has been reached. The probability that an improving step takes place in a singular generation is $1/e$ due to the Poisson distribution. So, the probability of having an improving and singular step is at least $2/(en^2)$.

Let S_i be such an improving and singular 2-Opt step, and assume w. l. o. g. that edges e_1, e_2 are exchanged with the edges e_3, e_4. Then we process S_i to try to find a linked operation, which is both improving and singular. More precisely, let S_j be the next 2-Opt step where e_3 is being removed and the outcome of that generation is accepted, if such a step exists. Let S'_j be the next 2-Opt step where e_4 is being removed and the outcome of that generation is accepted, if such a step exists. If either S_j or S'_j exists and if one of these steps is singular, we add the corresponding pair (S_i, S_j) or (S_i, S'_j) to $\mathcal{L}$ and remove both S_j and S'_j from $\mathcal{S}$ to ensure disjointness of pairs. Otherwise, we proceed with the next improving and singular 2-Opt step following S_i.

We estimate the probability of a step S_j occurring and being a singular step. Let $A(e_3)$ denote the event that an accepted generation contains an improving 2-Opt step where e_3 is being removed from the tour.

Let $R(e_3)$ denote the set of all edges e such that a 2-Opt move removing e_3 and e results in a strict fitness improvement. Let x_ℓ denote the search point of the (1+1) EA* at time ℓ, and let us regard x_ℓ as a set of edges in the tour. Note that then $|R(e_3) \cap x_\ell|$ describes the number of improving 2-Opt moves where e_3 is being removed from the tour.

Let ℓ be the index of the first 2-Opt step in a new generation, and let $S+1$ be the random number of 2-Opt steps being executed in that generation. If $S=0$, that is, only one 2-Opt step is executed, the conditional probability of $A(e_3)$ is given by

$$\Pr(A(e_3) \mid S=0) = \frac{|R(e_3) \cap x_\ell|}{\binom{n}{2}} := p.$$

If $S+1>1$ operations are being executed in that generation, the probability of $A(e_3)$ is bounded by the union bound:

$$\Pr(A(e_3) \mid S=s) \leq \sum_{k=0}^{s} \frac{|R(e_3) \cap x_{\ell+k}|}{\binom{n}{2}}.$$

Note that $|R(e_3) \cap x_\ell|$ might increase if edges from $R(e_3)$ are being inserted into the tour. However, the additional selection criterion on the (1+1) EA* implies that, if a following step removes e_3 and one of the edges inserted previously, in the same generation, this sequence of 2-Opt steps will be rejected. Thus, only $|R(e_3) \cap x_\ell|$ edges can cause $A(e_3)$ and

$$\Pr(A(e_3) \mid S=s) \leq \sum_{k=0}^{s} \frac{|R(e_3) \cap x_\ell|}{\binom{n}{2}} = (s+1) \cdot p.$$

Note that, using the union bound for $S+1$ trials,

$$\begin{aligned} \Pr(A(e_3)) &= \sum_{s=0}^{\infty} \frac{1}{es!} \cdot \Pr(A(e_3) \mid S=s) \\ &\leq \sum_{s=0}^{\infty} \frac{1}{es!} \cdot (s+1)p = 2p. \end{aligned}$$

Combining this with Bayes' Theorem, we get

$$\begin{aligned} \Pr(S=0 \mid A(e_3)) &= \frac{\Pr(A(e_3) \mid S=0) \cdot \Pr(S=0)}{\Pr(A(e_3))} \\ &\leq \frac{p \cdot 1/e}{2p} = \frac{1}{2e}. \end{aligned}$$

It follows that the probability of finding a linked pair (S_i, S_j) or (S_i, S'_j) is at least $1/(2e)$, if one of the steps S_j or S'_j exists.

Recall that the expected number of singular and improving steps S_i in t generations is at least $2t/(en^2)$. Each processed element S_i excludes at most 2 other elements of $\mathcal{S}$. This leaves an expected number of $2t/(3en^2)$ processed elements S_i, each of which has a probability of $1/(2e)$ for pairing with some S_j or S'_j, if one of them exists. A processed element S_i is excluded if neither S_j nor S'_j exist. This only happens if both edges are never removed from the tour. Since the final tour contains n edges, at most $n/2$ steps S_i are excluded. Hence, the resulting expected number of pairs is at least

$$\frac{t}{3e^2n^2} - n/2.$$

□

The following Theorem now gives a lower bound on the expected fitness gain of the (1+1) EA*.

THEOREM 11. *In $t \geq cn^3$ generations, $c > 3e^2$ constant, (1+1) EA* obtains an expected fitness gain of $\Omega(t/(n^5\phi))$ unless it reaches a local optimum. In that case, expected approximation ratio of the solution is $O(\sqrt{\phi})$.*

Proof. As in the proof of Theorem 9, we have

$$E(\Delta) \geq 1/(4n^3\phi).$$

From Lemma 10 we know that the expected number of disjoint pairs of 2-Opt steps, both of which are singular, is at least

$$u := \frac{t}{3e^2n^2} - \frac{n}{2}.$$

Lemma 7 implies that among these there are at least

$$\frac{u}{2} - \frac{n}{4} = \frac{t}{6e^2n^2} - \frac{n}{2} = \frac{(1-3e^2/c)t}{6e^2n^2} = \Omega(t/n^2)$$

type 0 or 1 pairs. The expected fitness gain in t generations, $E(\Delta_t)$, is therefore at least

$$E(\Delta) \cdot \Omega(t) \geq \Omega(t/(n^5\phi)).$$

The expected approximation ratio is proved in Theorem 3.

□

4. ANALYSIS FOR EUCLIDEAN INSTANCES

We now turn our attention to the Euclidean instances. First we obtain the expected progress based on a single 2-Opt step for RLS and (1+1) EA, later improve these results by analyzing a sequence of consecutive 2-Opt steps.

4.1 Analysis of a Single 2-Opt Step

THEOREM 12. *In t iterations RLS achieves an expected fitness gain of $\Omega(t\log(n\phi)/(n^6\phi^3))$ unless it reaches a local optimum. In that case, expected approximation ratio of the solution is $O(\sqrt{\phi})$.*

Proof. Due to Theorem 2, we have

$$\Pr(\Delta_{\min} < \varepsilon) \leq n^4 \cdot \varepsilon \cdot \log(1/\varepsilon) \cdot \phi^3.$$

Let Δ_{imp} denote the random variable that describes the fitness gain in an improving 2-Opt step. Then similar to the proof for the Manhattan instances (Theorem 4), we get

$$E(\Delta_{\text{imp}}) \geq (1 - (n^4 \cdot \varepsilon \cdot \log(1/\varepsilon) \cdot \phi^3)) \cdot \varepsilon.$$

Setting $\varepsilon = c\log(n^4\phi^3)/(n^4\phi^3)$, $c > 0$ a constant such that $\Pr(\Delta_{\text{imp}} > \varepsilon) \geq 1/2$, we get

$$E(\Delta_{\text{imp}}) \geq c\log(n^4\phi^3)/(2n^4\phi^3).$$

The number of mutations occurring in one iteration is 1 and the probability for an improving 2-Opt step is at least $1/\binom{n}{2} \geq 2/n^2$. Therefore, the expected value for the fitness gain Δ in any 2-Opt step is

$$E(\Delta) \geq c\log(n^4\phi^3)/(n^6\phi^3).$$

The expected value for the fitness gain in t iterations is

$$\begin{aligned} E(\Delta_t) &\geq \Omega(t\log(n^4\phi^3)/(n^6\phi^3)) \\ &= \Omega(t\log(n\phi)/(n^6\phi^3)). \end{aligned}$$

Having obtained a locally optimal solution during the run implies an expected approximation ratio of $O(\sqrt{\phi})$ according to Theorem 3. □

THEOREM 13. *In t generations (1+1) EA achieves an expected fitness gain of $\Omega(t\log(n\phi)/(n^6\phi^3))$ unless it reaches a local optimum. In that case, the expected approximation ratio of the solution is $O(\sqrt{\phi})$.*

Proof. Similar to the above proof on RLS in Theorem 12 the expected fitness gain for an improving singular generation can be derived as

$$E(\Delta_{\mathrm{imp}}) \geq c\log(n^4\phi^3)/(2n^4\phi^3).$$

The probability of a single step mutation occur in a generation is $1/e$. This minimum fitness gain is due to any accepted singular steps. Therefore, we consider only singular steps. And the waiting time for the correct mutation is at most $2/n^2$. Hence, the expected fitness gain $E(\Delta)$ for any generation is

$$E(\Delta) \geq c\log(n^4\phi^3)/(en^6\phi^3).$$

The expected value for the fitness gain in t generations is derived accordingly:

$$\begin{aligned} E(\Delta_t) &\geq (2/(en^2))\varepsilon t = \Omega(t\log(n^4\phi^3)/(n^6\phi^3)) \\ &= \Omega(t\log(n\phi)/(n^6\phi^3)). \end{aligned}$$

Having obtained a locally optimal solution during the run implies an expected approximation ratio of $O(\sqrt{\phi})$ according to Theorem 3. □

4.2 Analysis of Linked Steps for RLS

The above lower bounds are based on the minimum possible improvement a single 2-Opt step can make. We can further improve this bound considering the improvement made in a sequence of consecutive steps. Similar to the analysis on the consecutive steps for Manhattan instances in section 3 here also we consider the set of linked pairs of type 0 and 1. In a sequence of t iterations, there are at least $t/6 - n/2$ such pairs due to Lemma 7. Here we consider Lemma 14 in Englert et al. [5] related to the probability of existence of each of the two types of linked pairs in a sequence of consecutive steps for Euclidean instances. Based on these we can bound the expected fitness gain made in t iterations.

LEMMA 14 ([5, LEMMA 14]). *For ϕ perturbed L_2 instances, the probability that there exists a pair of type 0 and 1 in which both 2-Opt steps are improvements by at most $\varepsilon \leq 1/2$ is bounded by $O(n^6\cdot\phi^5\cdot\varepsilon^2\cdot\log^2(1/\varepsilon)) + O(n^5\cdot\phi^4\cdot\varepsilon^{3/2}\log(1/\varepsilon))$.*

THEOREM 15. *In $t \geq cn^3$ iterations, $c > 3/2$ constant, RLS achieves an expected fitness gain of $\Omega(t\sqrt{\log(n\phi)}/(n^5\phi^{5/2}))$ unless it reaches a local optimum. In that case, the expected approximation ratio is $O(\sqrt{\phi})$.*

Proof. Using Lemma 14, the probability that the improvement $\Delta_{\min}$ in a linked 2-Opt step of type 0 or 1 is less than ε is at most

$$\Pr(\varepsilon) = O(n^6\cdot\phi^5\cdot\varepsilon^2\cdot\log^2(1/\varepsilon)) + O(n^5\cdot\phi^4\cdot\varepsilon^{3/2}\cdot\log(1/\varepsilon)).$$

Following the proof ideas of Theorem 9 on the consecutive 2-Opt steps for Manhattan instances, the expected fitness gain $E(\Delta)$ for a pair of linked 2-Opt steps of type 0 or 1 can be bounded from below as

$$E(\Delta) \geq (1 - \Pr(\varepsilon))\cdot\varepsilon.$$

We set $\varepsilon = c'\sqrt{\log(n^6\phi^5)}/\sqrt{n^6\phi^5}$ for a constant $c' > 0$ such that $\Pr(\Delta > \varepsilon) \geq 1/2$. This implies

$$E(\Delta) \geq c'\sqrt{\log(n^6\phi^5)}/(2n^3\phi^{5/2}).$$

The expected number of improving 2-Opt steps made in t iterations is at least $2t/n^2$. Let t^* be the number of improving steps. By Lemma 7 we know there are at least $t^*/6 - n/2$ type 0 or 1 pairs in a sequence of t^* improving steps. As $t \geq cn^3$ for $c > 3/2$, we get

$$E(t^*/6 - n/2) = \frac{2t}{6n^2} - \frac{n}{2} = \frac{(2-3/c)t}{6n^2} = \Omega(t/n^2).$$

A lower bound for the expected fitness gain for t iterations is therefore

$$\begin{aligned} E(\Delta_t) = E(\Delta)\cdot\Omega(t/n^2) &\geq \Omega(t\sqrt{\log(n^6\phi^5)}/(n^5\phi^{5/2})) \\ &= \Omega(t\sqrt{\log(n\phi)}/(n^5\phi^{5/2})). \end{aligned}$$

The bound on the expected approximation ratio in the case that a locally optimal solution has been obtained holds according to Theorem 3. □

4.3 Analysis of Linked Steps for (1+1) EA

We improve the current results for (1+1) EA with the analysis for consecutive 2-Opt steps in a similar way to the analysis presented in the previous section. Again, we consider the (1+1) EA* but conjecture that the expected fitness gain in the (1+1) EA is no smaller than that for the (1+1) EA*. Based on our arguments on the number of type 0 or 1 linked pairs from Lemmas 10 and 7 and the stated Lemma 14 of [5] on the probability of the existence of a pairs of both improving steps we can bound the expected fitness gain in t generations.

THEOREM 16. *In $t \geq cn^3$ generations, $c > 3e^2$ constant, (1+1) EA* achieves an expected fitness gain of $\Omega(t\sqrt{\log(n\phi)}/(n^3\phi^{5/2}))$ unless it reaches a local optimum. In that case, the expected approximation ratio is $O(\sqrt{\phi})$.*

Proof. Following the proof ideas in above Theorem 15 we get for a $c' > 0$

$$E(\Delta) \geq c'\sqrt{\log(n^6\phi^5)}/(2n^3\phi^{5/2}).$$

From Lemma 10 we know that the number of disjoint pairs of 2-Opt steps, both of which are singular, is at least

$$u := \frac{t}{3e^2n^2} - \frac{n}{2}.$$

Lemma 7 implies that among these there are at least

$$\frac{u}{2} - \frac{n}{4} = \frac{t}{6e^2n^2} - \frac{n}{2} = \frac{(1-3e^2/c)t}{6e^2n^2} = \Omega(t/n^2)$$

type 0 or 1 pairs.

The expected fitness gain in t generations, $E(\Delta_t)$, is therefore at least

$$\begin{aligned} E(\Delta)\cdot\Omega(t/n^2) &\geq \Omega(t\sqrt{\log(n^6\phi^5)}/(n^5\phi^{5/2}) \\ &= \Omega(t\sqrt{\log(n\phi)}/(n^5\phi^{5/2}). \end{aligned}$$

Having obtained a locally optimal solution with respect to the 2-Opt neighbourhood implies the bound on the expected approximation ratio according to Theorem 3. □

Metric	RLS		(1+1) EA	
	Single Step (any t)	Consecutive Steps ($t \geq 3/2 \cdot n^3$)	Single Step (any t)	Consecutive Steps ($t \geq 3e^2/2 \cdot n^3$)
Manhattan	$\Omega(t/(n^6\phi))$	$\Omega(t/(n^5\phi))$	$\Omega(t/(n^6\phi))$	$\Omega(t/(n^5\phi))$
Euclidean	$\Omega(t\log(n\phi)/(n^6\phi^3))$	$\Omega(t\sqrt{\log(n\phi)}/(n^5\phi^{5/2}))$	$\Omega(t\log(n\phi)/(n^6\phi^3))$	$\Omega(t\sqrt{\log(n\phi)}/(n^5\phi^{5/2}))$

Table 1: Expected fitness gain in t iterations for RLS and (1+1) EA for Manhattan and Euclidean instances due to single-step and consecutive-steps analysis. The former applies for any time span t; the latter requires $t = \Omega(n^3)$. The consecutive-steps analysis was formally proven for the (1+1) EA* and transfers to the (1+1) EA if, as conjectured, the latter does not perform worse. All fitness gains assume that no local optimum is reached. otherwise the expected approximation ratio is $O(\sqrt{\phi})$.

5. CONCLUSIONS

We have carried out a fixed budget analysis of randomized local search (RLS) and variants of the (1+1) EA on the well-known Traveling Salesperson Problem (TSP). Our analysis allows to estimate the progress, or fitness gain, that these algorithms make within a given number of t iterations. This is, in particular, useful as it gives a guarantee to practitioners on the progress that such algorithms can make when deciding between stopping the algorithm or giving it additional running time.

We analyzed the algorithms in the setting of smoothed complexity for the Manhattan and Euclidean metric. We provided lower bounds on the expected fitness gain based on the minimum improvement the algorithms (RLS and (1+1) EA) can make in an iteration. The results show that for any number of iterations both algorithms gain a fair improvement based on single 2-Opt steps. We further improved these results by analyzing a sequence of consecutive 2-Opt steps together to identify linked pairs. Table 5 summarizes these results. It is observed that a larger improvement can be obtained considering the consecutive steps, for this however, the number of iterations t needs to be at least $\Omega(n^3)$.

The variant of the (1+1) EA ((1+1) EA*) analyzed for the linked steps accepts fewer solutions than the classical (1+1) EA and therefore we expect (1+1) EA* to be slower than (1+1) EA. Proving this is an interesting technical open problem and would give additional insights into the advantages of mutations that make multiple changes at the same time.

Acknowledgments: This research has been supported by the European Union Seventh Framework Programme (FP7/2007-2013) under grant agreement no 618091 (SAGE) and by the Australian Research Council through grants DP130104395 and DP140103400. We thank Joseph Kempka and Anh Quang Nguyen for early discussions, and the participants and organizers of Dagstuhl seminar 13271 "Theory of Evolutionary Algorithms", where this research started.

References

[1] A. Auger and B. Doerr. *Theory of Randomized Search Heuristics: Foundations and Recent Developments.* World Scientific Publishing Co., Inc., 2011.

[2] B. Chandra, H. Karloff, and C. Tovey. New results on the old k-Opt algorithm for the TSP. In *Proc. of SODA'94*, pages 150–159, 1994.

[3] B. Doerr, T. Jansen, C. Witt, and C. Zarges. A method to derive fixed budget results from expected optimisation times. In *Proc. of GECCO'13*, pages 1581–1588. ACM, 2013.

[4] S. Droste, T. Jansen, and I. Wegener. On the analysis of the (1+1) evolutionary algorithm. *Theoretical Computer Science*, 276(1–2):51–81, 2002.

[5] M. Englert, H. Röglin, and B. Vöcking. Worst case and probabilistic analysis of the 2-Opt algorithm for the TSP. *Algorithmica*, 68(1):190–264, 2014.

[6] T. Jansen. *Analyzing Evolutionary Algorithms - The Computer Science Perspective.* Natural Computing Series. Springer, 2013.

[7] T. Jansen and C. Zarges. Analysis of evolutionary algorithms: From computational complexity analysis to algorithm engineering. In *Proc. of FOGA '11*, pages 1–14. ACM, 2011.

[8] T. Jansen and C. Zarges. Fixed budget computations: a different perspective on run time analysis. In *Proc. of GECCO'12*, pages 1325–1332, 2012.

[9] W. Kern. A probabilistic analysis of the switching algorithm for the euclidean TSP. *Mathematical programming: Series A*, 44(1-3):213–219, 1989.

[10] J. Lässig and D. Sudholt. Analysis of speedups in parallel evolutionary algorithms for combinatorial optimization. In *Proc. of ISAAC'11*, pages 405–414. Springer, 2011.

[11] R. Motwani and P. Raghavan. *Randomized Algorithms.* Cambridge University Press, 1995.

[12] F. Neumann and I. Wegener. Randomized local search, evolutionary algorithms, and the minimum spanning tree problem. In *Proc. of GECCO'04*, pages 713–724, 2004.

[13] F. Neumann and C. Witt. *Bioinspired Computation in Combinatorial Optimization: Algorithms and Their Computational Complexity.* Springer, 2010.

[14] P. S. Oliveto, J. He, and X. Yao. Time complexity of evolutionary algorithms for combinatorial optimization: A decade of results. *International Journal of Automation and Computing*, 4(3):281–293, 2007.

[15] P. Sanders and D. Wagner. Algorithm engineering. *Informatik-Spektrum*, 36(2):187–190, 2013.

[16] D. A. Spielman and S.-H. Teng. Smoothed analysis of algorithms: Why the simplex algorithm usually takes polynomial time. *J. ACM*, 51(3):385–463, May 2004.

[17] B. M. R. Veenstra. Smoothed analysis of the 2-Opt heuristic for the TSP: Polynomial bounds for gaussian noise. In *Proc. of ISAAC'13*, 2013.

[18] D. Zhou, D. Luo, R. Lu, and Z. Han. The use of tail inequalities on the probable computational time of randomized search heuristics. *Theoretical Computer Science*, 436(0):106 – 117, 2012.

From Fitness Landscape to Crossover Operator Choice

Stjepan Picek
Digital Security Group - ICIS
Radboud University Nijmegen
The Netherlands
stjepan@computer.org

Domagoj Jakobović
Faculty of Electrical Engineering and Computing
University of Zagreb
Croatia
domagoj.jakobovic@fer.hr

ABSTRACT

Genetic algorithms are applied to numerous problems that demonstrate different properties. To efficiently solve these problems, during the years a significant number of variation operators have been and still are created. It is a problem by itself how to correctly choose between those operators, i.e. how to find the most suitable operator (or a set) for a given problem. In this paper we investigate the choice of the suitable crossover operator on the basis of fitness landscape. The fitness landscape can be described with a number of properties, so a thorough analysis needs to be done to find the most useful ones. To achieve that, we experiment with 24 noise-free problems and floating point encoding. The results indicate it is possible to either select a suitable operator or at least to reduce the number of adequate operators with fitness landscape properties.

Categories and Subject Descriptors

I.2.8 [**Artificial Intelligence**]: Problem Solving, Control Methods, and Search—*heuristic methods*

General Terms

Algorithms, Experimentation

Keywords

Heuristic Methods, Fitness Landscape, Crossover Operator, Genetic Programming, Automatic Classification

1. INTRODUCTION

Evolutionary algorithms play an important role in solving many difficult problems. To be able to solve different problems, in the last decades numerous versions of algorithms and operators have emerged that can be readily applied. Naturally, different algorithms were necessary since the "No Free Lunch" theorem states that there is no single best algorithm for all the problems [29].

GECCO'14, July 12–16, 2014, Vancouver, BC, Canada.

http://dx.doi.org/10.1145/2576768.2598320

However, this diversity of the algorithms, as much as it is advantageous, is often also a pitfall. It is not an easy task to choose the optimal algorithm and its parameters without a combination of experience and extensive testing. Therefore, it would be useful to have a method that can help in the choice of the parameters. In this work, we concentrate our attention to genetic algorithms with floating point encoding applied to continuous optimization. Furthermore, we are interested only in the differences in the behavior of the algorithm with respect to the choice of the crossover operator. We point out, even with this simplification, that there is still a plethora of options; for instance, in [9] there are descriptions of 89 floating point crossover operators.

To be able to give an insight about the choice of crossover operators, we analyze fitness landscape properties. The most common motivation for fitness landscape analysis is to get a better understanding of algorithm performance on a certain problem [19]. However, we approach the problem from the opposite point fo view, where we investigate fitness landscape in order to reach conclusion about the choice of the appropriate operator and, in consequence, the performance of the algorithm as a whole.

Of course, there is a question of the relative importance of crossover operator in genetic algorithms. Here, we regard crossover operator as the vital part of GA and refer to literature for a further discussion about the importance of crossover operator [18].

1.1 Related Work

In existing literature the fitness landscape analysis is used mainly for the determination of optimization problem hardness for evolutionary algorithms and other optimization algorithms, such as deterministic local search. Authors in [8] formally define fitness landscapes, provide an in-depth look at basic properties and give detailed explanations and examples of existing fitness landscape analysis techniques. A survey of the literature on fitness landscape analysis for local search is given in [26]. Fitness analysis of landscape for the n-queens problem is conducted in [13]. The distribution of local optima in this instance is uniformly random and scattered over the search space. The landscape is rugged and there is no significant correlation between fitness and distance of solutions. Landscape analysis for benchmark fitness functions: Sphere, Rastrigin, Rosenbrock and Ackley functions is performed in [14]. To better understand the influence of genetic representations and associated variation operators when solving a combinatorial optimization problem (the Optimal Golomb Ruler problem) various landscape analysis techniques are used in [24]. The fitness landscape analysis for mutation reveals that indirect encodings have a good fitness distance correlation and distance to the optimum.

Herrera et al. apply a hybrid scheme in crossover, where each reproduction produces offspring using different crossover operators, and different parent and children selection mechanisms are used [11]. The operators are tested on 13 real-valued functions with 8 crossover operators and their pairs; performance was evaluated for individual problems, but the overall efficiency was difficult to predict [11].

1.2 Our Contribution

There are two main contributions in this paper. First, we correlate the choice of the crossover operator with the fitness landscape properties. As far as we are aware, this is the first application of fitness landscape analysis in such a way. Although there is a significant body of work about fitness landscape, usually its properties are investigated post-hoc to get a better insight in the performance of the algorithm. The second contribution is the usage of genetic programming for automatic classification of crossover eligibility on the basis of fitness landscape properties.

The rest of the paper is organized as follows: in Section 2 we give preliminary information on crossover operators and benchmark functions we consider. Additionally, we present fitness landscape properties used in this research. In Section 3 we describe experimental results on the benchmark functions. Also, we give preliminary analysis on the correlation between fitness landscape properties and the choice of operators. In Section 4 we present a genetic programming approach to classify operators on a basis of fitness landscape and a discussion about achieved results and possible avenues for future work. Finally, in Section 5 we give a conclusion.

2. PRELIMINARIES

In this section we present the crossover operators used in the experiments, the employed benchmark functions and fitness landscape properties we consider in the experiments.

2.1 Crossover Operators

We consider only crossover operators for a two-parent case. Naturally, there are many crossover operators and the question is why we chose the following ones. When conducting the experiments we wanted to use as small as possible representative set of operators. Therefore, we chose the operators that are designed with various objectives in mind and that are widely accepted.

If n denotes the dimensionality of the individual, for all crossover operators presented here holds that parents $\beta^{f_1} = \beta_1^{f_1}, \beta_2^{f_1}, ..., \beta_n^{f_1}$ and $\beta^{f_2} = \beta_1^{f_2}, \beta_2^{f_2}, ..., \beta_n^{f_2}$ form a child $\beta^s = \beta_1^s, \beta_2^s, ..., \beta_n^s$, where f_1 and f_2 are the parents' fitness values and s child's fitness value. In some operators, a parameter α is used as a weighting factor whose value is chosen at random over $[0, 1]$, if not specified otherwise.

2.1.1 Arithmetic Crossover

This is probably the most commonly used operator (also called whole arithmetic crossover), which takes the weighted sum of two parental alleles for each gene with the same α [5]:

$$\beta^s = \alpha \cdot \beta^{f_1} + (1 - \alpha) \cdot \beta^{f_2}. \tag{1}$$

2.1.2 Arithmetic Simple Crossover

In this operator a recombination point k is chosen uniformly. Then the first k float values of a random chosen parent are taken and copied into the child. The rest is the arithmetic average of parents 1 and 2 [5]. The arithmetic average is obtained via:

$$\beta^s = \alpha \cdot \beta^{f_1} + (1 - \alpha) \cdot \beta^{f_2}. \tag{2}$$

2.1.3 Arithmetic Single Crossover

In arithmetic single crossover first a random allele k is chosen. At that position the child assumes the arithmetic average of two parents. All other points are copied from a single randomly chosen parent. The expression for the arithmetic average is the same as for the simple arithmetic crossover [5].

2.1.4 Local Crossover

Local crossover is the same as arithmetic crossover, except that the value α is randomly selected for each gene location [4].

$$\beta_i^s = \alpha_i \cdot \beta_i^{f_1} + (1 - \alpha_i) \cdot \beta_i^{f_2}. \tag{3}$$

2.1.5 Average Crossover

Average crossover is whole arithmetic crossover with $\alpha = 0.5$. Two parents β^{f_1} and β^{f_2} generate offspring β^s in the following way [17]:

$$\beta_i^s = (\beta_i^{f_1} + \beta_i^{f_2})/2. \tag{4}$$

2.1.6 BGA Crossover

In BGA crossover two parents β^{f_1} and β^{f_2} generate offspring β^s. Let β^{f_1} be the parent with better fitness. In that case, the offspring has genes calculated in the following way:

$$\beta_i^s = \beta_i^{f_1} \pm rang_i \cdot \gamma \cdot \lambda_i, \tag{5}$$

where λ equals

$$\lambda = \frac{\beta^{f_2} - \beta^{f_1}}{\|\beta^{f_1} - \beta^{f_2}\|}. \tag{6}$$

The sign "-" is selected with 0.9 probability and $rang_i = 0.5 \cdot (\beta^{f_1} - \beta^{f_2})$. Parameter γ equals

$$\gamma = \sum_{k=0}^{15} \alpha_k \cdot 2^{-k}, \tag{7}$$

where $\alpha_i \in 0, 1$ is randomly generated with $p(\alpha_i = 1) = \frac{1}{16}$ [16, 18, 21].

2.1.7 BLX-α Crossover

Blend-α crossover combines two parents β^{f_1} and β^{f_2} to generate offspring β^s by sampling a new value in the range $[min - I \cdot \alpha, max + I \cdot \alpha]$. Here, min and max equal minimum and maximum values respectively for interval $(\beta_i^{f_1}, \beta_i^{f_2})$. I equals $max - min$ [7, 12]. For the α we use value of 0.5.

2.1.8 BLX-α-β Crossover

Blend-α-β operator creates a new offspring by selecting a random value from the interval between the two alleles of the parent solutions β^{f_1} and β^{f_2}. The interval is increased in direction of the solution with better fitness by the factor α, and into the direction of the solution with worse fitness by the factor β [6, 12]. The value for α is 0.75, and for β

0.25. In the case that $\beta_i^{f_1} \leq \beta_i^{f_2}$, random value is sampled from the interval:

$$[\beta_i^{f_1} - I \cdot \alpha, \beta_i^{f_2} + I \cdot \beta], \tag{8}$$

otherwise is sampled from:

$$[\beta_i^{f_2} - I \cdot \beta, \beta_i^{f_1} + I \cdot \alpha]. \tag{9}$$

2.1.9 Discrete Crossover

In discrete crossover an offspring β^s is created from parents β^{f_1} and β^{f_2}, where the allele value for each gene i is given by $\beta_i^s = \beta_i^{f_1}$ or $\beta_i^s = \beta_i^{f_2}$ with equal likelihood [25].

2.1.10 Flat Crossover

Flat crossover generates offspring whose genes are sampled randomly from the interval $min(\beta_i^{f_1}, \beta_i^{f_2}), max(\beta_i^{f_1}, \beta_i^{f_2})$ [18, 20]. This crossover is the same as BLX-α crossover when α = 0.

2.1.11 Heuristic Crossover

In heuristic crossover (Wright's heuristic crossover), given two parents β^{f_1} and β^{f_2}, assume that the first parent (β^{f_1}) has a smaller value on current allele [12, 30]. Then the offspring β^s is created as

$$\beta_i^s = \alpha \cdot (\beta_i^{f_2} - \beta_i^{f_1}) + \beta_i^{f_1}, \tag{10}$$

where α is chosen uniformly at random from interval $[0, 1]$.

2.1.12 One Point Crossover

In one point crossover the descendant is created in the same way as in the one point crossover for a binary coded GA. First, choose a random point k. Two parents β^{f_1} and β^{f_2} generate offspring β^{s_1} and β^{s_2}. The first offspring copies allele values from the first parent up to the point k, and from the second parent from that point on. For the second offspring the procedure is analogous [15].

2.1.13 Simulated Binary Crossover

Simulated binary crossover is devised to simulate the effect of one point binary crossover [2, 18]. Two parents β^{f_1} and β^{f_2} generate offspring β^{s_1} and β^{s_2} in the following way:

$$\beta_i^{s_1} = \frac{1}{2}\left[(1 + B_k)\,\beta_i^{f_1} + (1 - B_k)\,\beta_i^{f_2}\right] \tag{11}$$

and

$$\beta_i^{s_2} = \frac{1}{2}\left[(1 - B_k)\,\beta_i^{f_1} + (1 + B_k)\,\beta_i^{f_2}\right], \tag{12}$$

where $B_k \geq 0$ is obtained from the random number source having density

$$B_k(u) = \begin{cases} (2 \cdot u)^{\frac{1}{\eta+1}} & \text{if } u \leq \frac{1}{2} \\ \left(\frac{1}{2 \cdot (1-u)}\right)^{\frac{1}{\eta+1}} & \text{if } u > \frac{1}{2} \end{cases}. \tag{13}$$

Distribution index η is any non-negative real number [3].

2.2 Benchmark Functions

The test problems originate from the COCO platform (COmparing Continuous Optimisers) [10], which has been extensively used in the last few years. Of the functions available we use 24 noise-free real-parameter single-objective problems. The dimensionality D of all the functions is set to 30, which matches a medium-sized optimization problem. The test functions are implemented so the global minimum has the value of zero. The problems can be differentiated on the basis of their modality, where functions 1, 2, 5, 6, 7, 10-14 are unimodal and 3, 4, 8, 9, 15-24 are multimodal.

2.3 Fitness Landscape Properties

Here we present only the properties we used in the correlating fitness landscape and crossover operators. Naturally, there are other properties we could have chosen and indeed adding more properties will be a future goal. Due to the lack of space we do not give discussion about fitness landscape but rather refer to the literature. Likewise, for explanations of the influence of some property to the landscape shape refer to [19, 23]. Fitness landscape can be defined as a set of two functions f and d that define the fitness value and the distance between encoded solutions in the landscape [19].

The diameter of the population P is the maximum distance between the elements of the population [23]:

$$d(P) = max_{s,t \in P} dist(s, t), \tag{14}$$

where $dist(s, t)$ represents L_1 distance [28].

Average distance of the population P is defined as [23]

$$dmm(P) = \frac{\sum\limits_{s \in P} \sum\limits_{t \in P, t \neq s} dist(s, t)}{|P| \cdot (|P| - 1)}. \tag{15}$$

Indicator δ_{dmm} represents the variation of the average distance of the initial population and population after local search algorithm [23]:

$$\delta_{dmm} = \frac{(dmm(U) - dmm(O))}{dmm(U)}, \tag{16}$$

where U is the initial population, and O is population after local search.

Amplitude $Amp(P)$ represents distribution of solutions in objective space, i.e. the difference between the best and worst solution [23]:

$$Amp(P) = \frac{|P| \cdot (max_{s \in P} f(s) - min_{s \in P} f(s))}{\sum\limits_{s \in P} f(s)}. \tag{17}$$

Relative variation of the amplitude Δ_{Amp} of initial and final population [23] is defined as

$$\Delta_{Amp} = \frac{Amp(U) - Amp(O)}{Amp(U)}. \tag{18}$$

The average length of walk $Lmm(P)$ represents the average number of steps needed for the convergence of a solution [23]:

$$Lmm(P) = \frac{\sum\limits_{p \in P} l(p)}{|P|}. \tag{19}$$

Autocorrelation function measures the correlation of the solutions that have distance d [27]:

$$\rho(d) = \frac{\sum\limits_{s,t \in S \times S, dist(s,t) = d} (f(s) - \bar{f})(f(t) - \bar{f})}{n \cdot \sigma_f^2}. \tag{20}$$

Here, n is the number of pairs with distance d. In our experiments we use distance that equals 1.

Correlation length is defined in the following way [22]:

$$l = \frac{1}{ln(|\rho(1)|)}. \tag{21}$$

Autocorrelation coefficient is a normalized measure of autocorrelation function [1].

$$\xi = \frac{1}{1-\rho(1)}. \qquad (22)$$

There are many other properties one could choose and indeed we experimented with other properties. The previous properties were chosen on a basis of the variance of their values for the benchmark functions; e.g. if a property gives roughly the same value for every test function, then it is not a good choice for further experiments. Nevertheless, additional properties can be easily added to the analysis as input variables in genetic programming (in Section 4).

3. CORRELATING CROSSOVER AND FITNESS LANDSCAPE

In this section we first compare individual operators on the set of all problems. Then we try to discern whether there are statistically significant differences between the operators in regards to the specific functions. Finally, we try to correlate between individual crossover operator efficiency on a given function and fitness landscape properties of that function.

3.1 Experimental Setup

In all the experiments with crossover operators, the same selection method and parameter values are used for all the operators. The evolutionary algorithm is a steady-state GA with a tournament selection operator. In every iteration, k individuals are randomly selected for tournament (k is set to 3). The worst of k individuals is identified and replaced with a new individual. The new individual is obtained by crossing the two parents remaining from the tournament. This selection scheme was applied in part because it avoids the use of crossover probability, giving all the operators a fair treatment. Additionally, it has produced the best overall results in different optimization domains in our previous experience.

Mutation is also applied to the new individual with a given mutation rate (0.3 in our experiments). The mutation operator is a simple random change of a random solution variable within the given bounds. We are aware that the influence of mutation may be even more pronounced than with the selection mechanism and crossover. We believe that the differences between crossover operators, if they are significant, should hold even with other mutation operators. On the other hand, conducting experiments without mutation is not in accordance with realistic application conditions.

The population size was set to 100, and the termination criteria is defined as reaching 10^6 fitness evaluations (some operators require an additional evaluation that was accounted for). This number of evaluations allows the algorithm a stable convergence for this problem size (30 variables), which should be a requirement for operator performance comparison. Each combination of benchmark function and operator was tested in 50 runs, and the average (mean) error of the 50 best solutions is recorded.

3.2 Crossover Operator Performance

The obtained results for each operator and each problem are aggregated in Tables 5 and 6. The tables show *normalized error*, where the worst performing operator has the value of 1, and the optimal solution is denoted with zero.

Table 1: Average rankings of the operators (Friedman) and average normalized error

Algorithm	Ranking	$\bar{e}_N$
Arithmetic	6.2917	0.42
Arithmetic Simple	7.0417	0.45
Arithmetic Single	8.3333	0.58
Average	6.875	0.42
BGA	5.625	0.44
BLX-α	8.3333	0.71
BLX-α-β	7.8333	0.69
Discrete	6.625	0.45
Flat	8.4583	0.71
Heuristic	7.625	0.68
Local	5.9167	0.40
One point	7.2917	0.53
SBX	4.75	0.39

From these results, we are interested in discovering significant differences between the operators, which are regarded as different optimization algorithms. Since the resulting values are not normally distributed (the analysis is omitted), we rely on nonparametric methods to reveal if there are significant differences. This is achieved with the Friedman test, which calculates the *average rank* of each algorithm and determines the corresponding P-value. The Friedman results are given in Table 1, and the P-value is equal to 0.016 which means there are significant differences with level of significance $\alpha = 0.05$. The last column in the previous Table gives the *normalized average error* ($\bar{e}_N$), which is defined as the mean normalized error over all the problems.

3.3 Landscape Properties and Crossover Efficiency

The described landscape properties of benchmark functions are obtained with the following: a random population of 1000 individuals is generated within the defined boundaries ($[-50, 50]$ for each variable) and the same initial population is used on every function. A local search algorithm was executed in parallel for every starting point in the population; the algorithm used is based on Hooke-Jeeves directed pattern search. The local search algorithm is run for every starting point until convergence, which was determined with precision of 10^{-6}. After the convergence, the final population is recorded and fitness landscape properties are calculated for each function. The obtained values are given in Table 2.

Just by visually inspecting these values, it is not easy to reach a conclusion whether one can choose the crossover operator on a basis of those data. For instance, it seems there is a correlation between data for functions 2, 6 and 19. In functions 2 and 6 the properties have similar values and BGA crossover performs good, while Flat, BLX-α and BLX-α-β perform poorly. However, for function 19 BGA operator performs poor and Flat, BLX-α and BLX-α-β perform good. For the function 19 we see that fitness landscape properties are consistently different than for functions 2 and 6. We believe that inspecting the properties only visually it is hard to see correlations if they are not obvious, and especially to quantify the impact of those differences.

Table 2: Fitness landscape properties

Problem	d(P)	dmm(P)	Δ_{dmm}	Amp(p)	Δ_{Amp}	Lmm(P)	$\rho(1)$	l	ξ
1	0.000016	0.000003	1	1.618034	-0.034137	64.811	-0.001	0.144765	0.999001
2	0.000009	0.000002	1	2.169216	-0.386414	76.649	-0.001	0.144765	0.999001
3	232.181431	60.475268	0.878971	2.209141	-0.411932	57.769	0.5094	1.482532	2.03832
4	122.409501	32.98095	0.933995	2.608001	-0.666856	59.466	0.519048	1.524952	2.079211
5	650.35941	181.643388	0.636478	1	0.360868	32.475	0.999	999.499917	1000
6	140.178412	6.770292	0.986451	37.165919	-22.753912	2035.275	0.092841	0.420721	1.102342
7	713.30565	93.711719	0.812455	8.515323	-4.442412	160.959	0.313675	0.862516	1.457035
8	8.729045	0.568895	0.998861	8.275631	-4.289217	875.903	0.564717	1.749994	2.297356
9	295.068994	7.855163	0.984279	41.967988	-25.823066	1594.981	0.080365	0.39664	1.087388
10	22.557226	1.041349	0.997916	138.077539	-87.249712	3292.147	0.015926	0.241559	1.016184
11	20.28115	3.482909	0.99303	9.276794	-4.929092	5779.649	0.17005	0.564441	1.204892
12	520.334509	8.894347	0.9822	362.252363	-230.526916	2268.188	0.005114	0.189547	1.00514
13	27.766903	2.906121	0.994184	7.946438	-4.07882	162.833	0.478247	1.355699	1.916617
14	0.493758	0.113324	0.999773	2.49133	-0.592288	632.568	-0.001	0.144765	0.999001
15	391.415693	85.361853	0.829166	2.517099	-0.608758	144.773	0.572866	1.794999	2.341186
16	489.009861	141.624098	0.716568	3.020404	-0.930435	77.137	0.492803	1.413134	1.971619
17	1997.479698	337.798776	0.323965	748.42151	-477.339803	10952.256	0.001762	0.15769	1.001765
18	2175.891213	408.295428	0.18288	853.344799	-544.399588	12795.219	0.001371	0.151686	1.001372
19	877.58457	93.438758	0.813001	3.272264	-1.091407	140.494	0.415787	1.139494	1.711704
20	88.67771	22.475023	0.955021	1.434853	0.08294	218.525	0.000047	0.100428	1.000047
21	158.902852	48.15173	0.903634	2.952137	-0.886804	82.297	0.841152	5.780901	6.29531
22	132.732042	44.09263	0.911758	2.838727	-0.81432	80.208	0.715527	2.987425	3.515267
23	345.344015	90.238947	0.819405	3.86982	-1.473324	86.339	0.424284	1.16638	1.736966
24	159.542561	41.711814	0.916522	1.919647	-0.226907	94.761	0.54411	1.643105	2.193511

4. INFERRING PERFORMANCE WITH A GP-BASED CLASSIFIER

In this section we try to address the following questions: firstly, are the derived fitness landscape properties sufficient to distinguish between suitable and inefficient crossover operators for a specific function? Secondly, is it possible to predict crossover performance based on landscape features in a general case?

4.1 Crossover Operator Classes

To answer the first question, the crossover operators in this work are manually classified into three classes for each function: "good", "average" and "bad" crossovers. The classification is entirely subjective and is based on average operator error (Tables 5 and 6). The main goal here is to discern between the operators, rather than to give a formally justified classification.

The selection is made with the following guidelines: operators belong to different groups if their performances differ by at least a factor of two; if there are no three discernible groups, the "good" and "average" classes are populated first. For instance, for the second function in the benchmark, the division is made as follows: the BGA crossover is the only one considered "good", arithmetic, arithmetic simple, average, local and SBX are considered as "average", while the rest are classified as "bad". On the other hand, for functions 5, 17 and 22 all operators are considered "good" because there is no (significant) difference in their average error.

4.2 A Simple GP-based Classifier

Based on the described layout and available fitness landscape properties, we define a simple classifier based on symbolic regression (more advanced techniques are being investigated). A classifier of the same form is constructed independently for *each* crossover operator, so the final result is a family of classifiers where each is trained and tested separately. The GP classifier uses all landscape properties as terminals and the arithmetic operators (+, -, *, /) to build a tree that produces a value for a given function. Additionally, random constants (ERCs) in $[-1, 1]$ are added to the terminal set. The absolute tree output value is used to determine the operator class: value in $[0, 1]$ corresponds to "good", $[1, 10]$ to "average" and greater values to "bad".

The classifier is trained to minimize the penalty (not entirely equivalent to classification error), which is accumulated for every function. If the operator is classified correctly, the penalty is zero; if the resulting class is different, the penalty is 1 for adjacent classes (e.g. good operator classified as "average") and 3 for opposite classes (e.g. a bad operator classified as "good"). The GP parameters are of secondary importance, but we used a population of 2000 and a stopping criteria of 50 generations without improvement.

4.3 Classification Results

When all the test cases (24 functions) are used as a learning set, the GP is able to produce classifiers for every operator that succeed in obtaining a correct class for every function (i.e. the total penalty is zero). This provides the answer to the first question of whether the landscape properties are correlated with operator performance. A detailed analysis of relevant properties for each operator was not conducted at this stage, but it is to be expected that not every property is equally important for every operator.

The answer to the second question remains a greater challenge. Since this is a preliminary investigation, no specific measures are undertaken to increase the generalization ability of the employed classifier - both the learning model, termination condition and additional test cases are devoted to future research. In this work a simple 4-fold cross-validation is performed on the available set of functions, so that 18

Table 3: Average rankings of the algorithms (Friedman)

Algorithm	Ranking
Arithmetic	7.0208
Arithmetic Simple	7.875
Arithmetic Single	9.2083
Average	7.7708
BGA	6.1458
BLX-α	9.0208
BLX-α-β	8.6042
Discrete	7.375
Flat	9.3125
Heuristic	8.2917
Local	6.6458
One point	8.0417
SBX	5.2708
Learned crx	4.4167

Table 4: Post-hoc analysis (control operator: learned crossover)

i	algorithm	unadjusted p	$p_{Hochberg}$
1	Flat	0.00005	0.000654
2	Arithmetic Single	0.000073	0.00087
3	BLX-α	0.000138	0.001513
4	BLX-α-β	0.000525	0.005252
5	Heuristic	0.001333	0.011996
6	One point	0.002684	0.021472
7	Arithmetic Simple	0.004186	0.029304
8	Average	0.005478	0.032866
9	Discrete	0.014296	0.071481
10	Arithmetic	0.031048	0.124193
11	Local	0.064903	0.194709
12	BGA	0.152176	0.304353
13	SBX	0.479369	0.479369

functions are used for training and the remaining 6 for evaluation in each fold.

For any number of test cases (functions), the maximum penalty would equal to 3 times the number of functions, which corresponds to a 100% normalized penalty. In the cross-validation, penalties on the *evaluation* set on unseen functions for every operator and every fold are recorded. The average penalty of the evaluation set is 17%, which for individual operators varies from 12% to 22%. The achieved values are not spectacular, but we believe that a carefully designed classification process can enhance the quality of these initial results.

4.4 Constructing an Efficient Operator

To test the efficiency of the classifiers, we constructed an artificial algorithm that uses the "recommended" operator for each test function. This method may be considered a hyperheuristic, where a machine learning technique is used to construct the suitable optimization algorithm. For each function, only the operators that classify to "good" are considered; out of these, the operator with the closest to true average rank is selected (the rank is previously available from experimental results in Table 1). For instance, if three operators are classified as "good" for a given function, the one with the true rank closest to average among those three is selected.

The efficiency of such *learned crossover* is compared with individual crossover operators, and the results in terms of average rank are shown in Table 3. The normalized average error ($\bar{e}_N$) obtained for this operator amounts to 0.33, which is the best among the individual crossover operators (Tables 5 and 6).

Based on the Friedman test results in Table 3, a post-hoc statistical analysis is performed to determine where the significant differences are. The analysis is performed by taking the operator with the best rank (which is the learned crossover) as a *control operator* and comparing it with the other operators. The Table 4 presents the results obtained with the Hochberg test; for the level of significance $\alpha = 0.05$, we can conclude that the learned crossover operator is significantly better than the first eight operators from the table (with p-value less than α). For the remaining operators, a statistically significant difference cannot be proven, but the learned operator still provides the best normalized average error.

5. CONCLUSIONS

This paper describes how fitness landscape properties can be used to assess the crossover operator efficiency. The results show that the differences between the operators can be correlated with appropriate landscape properties. A preliminary investigation is performed which shows the potential of fitness landscape properties for operator classification in optimization.

Several issues need to be further investigated in this context. A more diverse set of classifiers (such as decision trees based on information gain) will be employed to enhance the learning and generalization. Also, additional test functions should be investigated, as well as their variations (e.g. rotations, translations, different number of variables).

Various local search algorithms are available for fitness landscape determination that should be investigated. This is especially important in terms of their time complexity, since a very large number of evaluations may be needed for convergence, which can negate the performance gain in a suitable crossover choice.

6. REFERENCES

[1] E. Angel and V. Zissimopoulos. Autocorrelation coefficient for the graph bipartitioning problem. *Theoretical Computer Science*, 191:229–243, 1998.

[2] K. Deb and R. B. Agrawal. Simulated binary crossover for continuous search space. *Complex System*, 9:115–148, 1994.

[3] K. Deb, S. Karthik, and T. Okabe. An introduction to genetic algorithms. In *Sadhana*, pages 293–315. John Wiley & Sons, Inc, 1999.

[4] D. Dumitrescu, B. Lazzerini, L. C. Jain, and A. Dumitrescu. *Evolutionary Computation.* CRC Press, Florida, USA, 2000.

[5] A. E. Eiben and J. E. Smith. *Introduction to Evolutionary Computing.* Springer-Verlag, Berlin Heidelberg New York, USA, 2003.

[6] L. J. Eshelman, K. E. Mathias, and J. D. Schaffer. Crossover operator biases: Exploiting the population distribution. In *ICGA*, pages 354–361, 1997.

[7] L. J. Eshelman and J. D. Schaffer. Real-coded genetic algorithms and interval-schemata. In L. D. Whitley, editor, *FOGA*, pages 187–202. Morgan Kaufmann, 1992.

[8] J. C. Fodor, R. Klempous, and C. P. S. Araujo, editors. *Recent Advances in Intelligent Engineering Systems*, volume 378 of *Studies in Computational Intelligence.* Springer, 2012.

[9] T. D. Gwiazda. *Genetic Algorithms Reference.* Tomasz Gwiazda, 2006.

[10] N. Hansen, S. Finck, R. Ros, and A. Auger. Real-parameter black-box optimization benchmarking: Noiseless functions definitions. Technical Report RR-6829, INRIA, 2009.

Table 5: **Normalized error of crossover operators (functions 1-12)**

Operator	1	2	3	4	5	6	7	8	9	10	11	12
Arithmetic	0.0000	0.0290	0.0003	0.0054	0.0000	0.1787	0.4661	0.0595	0.1028	0.1182	0.0994	0.0001
Arithmetic Simple	0.0002	0.0682	0.0011	0.0061	0.0000	0.5278	0.4996	0.0719	0.2203	0.2839	0.2185	0.0003
Arithmetic Single	0.0010	0.3350	0.0107	0.0185	0.0000	1.0000	0.5840	0.1182	0.5585	1.0000	0.9503	1.0000
Average	0.0004	0.1194	0.0042	0.0155	0.0000	0.2040	0.4914	0.1002	0.1063	0.1006	0.0675	0.0001
BGA	0.0000	0.0011	0.0004	0.0011	0.0000	0.0085	0.4515	0.0607	0.2472	0.2852	0.2109	0.0021
BLX-Alpha	0.9717	0.5809	1.0000	0.9977	0.0000	0.3473	0.9833	1.0000	1.0000	0.5270	0.0737	0.0663
BLX-Alpha-Beta	1.0000	0.5437	0.9833	1.0000	0.0000	0.3150	0.9286	0.7809	0.7769	0.5611	0.0785	0.0778
Discrete	0.0021	0.5679	0.0193	0.0240	0.0000	0.4549	0.4197	0.1220	0.3948	0.7851	0.9467	0.0029
Flat	0.9786	0.7980	0.9892	0.9810	0.0000	0.3158	1.0000	0.7865	0.8453	0.5768	0.0780	0.1021
Heuristic	0.9156	0.4816	0.9662	0.9831	0.0000	0.3324	0.9824	0.6980	0.8785	0.4558	0.0753	0.0924
Local	0.0000	0.0411	0.0006	0.0036	0.0000	0.2193	0.4736	0.0794	0.0977	0.0869	0.1038	0.0000
One point	0.0028	1.0000	0.0186	0.0234	0.0000	0.8855	0.4551	0.1348	0.3992	0.9174	1.0000	0.0450
SBX	0.0000	0.0183	0.0000	0.0002	0.0000	0.0322	0.3848	0.0532	0.0715	0.0939	0.1698	0.0000

Table 6: **Normalized error of crossover operators (functions 13-24)**

Operator	13	14	15	16	17	18	19	20	21	22	23	24
Arithmetic	0.0421	0.0137	0.9631	0.4760	0.9406	0.9298	0.7300	0.4999	0.9658	0.7409	0.7778	1.0000
Arithmetic Simple	0.0549	0.0188	0.9311	0.6340	0.9118	0.9193	0.6315	0.4763	0.8489	0.6901	0.8031	0.8812
Arithmetic Single	0.0755	0.0237	0.8939	0.8006	0.7455	0.7623	0.7941	0.3571	0.6217	0.8869	0.6860	0.6483
Average	0.0712	0.0215	0.9535	0.3941	1.0000	0.9492	0.6234	0.4928	0.8744	0.8337	0.6431	0.9218
BGA	0.0271	0.0037	0.8493	1.0000	0.7726	0.7191	1.0000	0.3922	0.9356	0.7610	1.0000	0.8656
BLX-Alpha	0.9905	0.8047	0.5726	0.2982	0.8222	0.7628	0.4735	0.9062	0.8657	0.9249	0.4530	0.5071
BLX-Alpha-Beta	0.9938	1.0000	0.5470	0.2959	0.8540	0.7427	0.4789	0.8845	0.8267	0.9349	0.4363	0.5004
Discrete	0.0563	0.0189	0.6670	0.5874	0.6839	0.5918	0.6409	0.3125	0.5065	0.8468	0.6215	0.6030
Flat	0.9621	0.8230	0.5858	0.3047	0.8700	0.7543	0.5006	1.0000	0.8098	1.0000	0.4391	0.4945
Heuristic	1.0000	0.7828	0.5812	0.2973	0.8368	0.7038	0.4738	0.9014	0.9029	0.9170	0.4473	0.4981
Local	0.0393	0.0137	1.0000	0.3466	0.8813	1.0000	0.6469	0.5310	0.8176	0.8916	0.5649	0.7811
One point	0.0555	0.0201	0.6345	0.7267	0.6432	0.6549	0.9526	0.3101	0.7536	0.7615	0.6421	0.5908
SBX	0.0261	0.0085	0.8301	0.5889	0.8882	0.9155	0.5217	0.4993	1.0000	0.7979	0.7630	0.7468

[11] F. Herrera, M. Lozano, and A. Sánchez. Hybrid crossover operators for real-coded genetic algorithms: an experimental study. *Soft Computing*, 9(4):280–298, 2005.

[12] F. Herrera, M. Lozano, and A. M. Sánchez. A taxonomy for the crossover operator for real-coded genetic algorithms: An experimental study. *International Journal of Intelligent Systems*, 18:309–338, 2003.

[13] E. Masehian, H. Akbaripour, and N. Mohabbati-Kalejahi. Landscape analysis and efficient metaheuristics for solving the n-queens problem. *Comp. Opt. and Appl.*, 56(3):735–764, 2013.

[14] G. Merkuryeva and V. Bolshakovs. Benchmark fitness landscape analysis. *International Journal of Simulation*, 12(2), 2011.

[15] Z. Michalewicz. *Genetic algorithms + data structures = evolution programs (3rd ed.)*. Springer-Verlag, London, UK, UK, 1996.

[16] H. Mühlenbein and D. Schlierkamp-Voosen. Predictive Models for the Breeder Genetic Algorithm I. Continuous Parameter Optimization. *Evol. Comput.*, 1(1):25–49, Mar. 1993.

[17] T. Nomura. An analysis on crossovers for real number chromosomes in an infinite population size. In *Proceedings of the Fifteenth international joint conference on Artifical intelligence - Volume 2*, IJCAI'97, pages 936–941, San Francisco, CA, USA, 1997. Morgan Kaufmann Publishers Inc.

[18] D. Ortiz-Boyer, C. Hervas-Martinez, and N. Garcia-Pedrajas. Improving crossover operators for real-coded genetic algorithms using virtual parents. *Journal of Heuristics*, (13):265–314, 2007.

[19] E. Pitzer and M. Affenzeller. A comprehensive survey on fitness landscape analysis. In J. Fodor, R. Klempous, and C. Suárez Araujo, editors, *Recent Advances in Intelligent Engineering Systems*, volume 378 of *Studies in Computational Intelligence*, pages 161–191. Springer Berlin Heidelberg, 2012.

[20] N. J. Radcliffe. Equivalence class analysis of genetic algorithms. *Complex System*, 2(5):183–205, 1991.

[21] D. Schlierkamp-voosen and H. Mühlenbein. Strategy adaptation by competing subpopulations. In *Parallel Problem Solving from Nature (PPSN III*, pages 199–208. Springer-Verlag, 1994.

[22] P. F. Stadler. Landscapes and their correlation functions. *Journal of Mathematical Chemistry*, 20(1):1–45, 1996.

[23] E.-G. Talbi. *Metaheuristics - From Design to Implementation*. Wiley, 2009.

[24] J. Tavares and F. B. C. Pereira. Golomb rulers: A fitness landscape analysis. In *IEEE Congress on Evolutionary Computation*, pages 3695–3701. IEEE, 2008.

[25] H.-M. Voigt, H. Mühlenbein, and D. Cvetkovic. Fuzzy recombination for the breeder genetic algorithm. In *Proc. Sixth Int. Conf. on Genetic Algorithms*, pages 104–111. Morgan Kaufmann Publishers, 1995.

[26] J.-P. Watson. *An Introduction to Fitness Landscape Analysis and Cost Models for Local Search*, volume 146, chapter 20, pages 599–623. Springer US, Boston, MA, 2010.

[27] E. Weinberger. Correlated and uncorrelated fitness landscapes and how to tell the difference. *Biological Cybernetics*, 63(5):325–336, 1990.

[28] S. Willard. *General Topology*. Dover Publications, 2004.

[29] D. H. Wolpert and W. G. Macready. No free lunch theorems for optimization. *IEEE Transactions on Evolutionary Computation*, 1(1):67–82, April 1997.

[30] A. H. Wright. Genetic algorithms for real parameter optimization. In *Foundations of Genetic Algorithms*, pages 205–218. Morgan Kaufmann, 1991.

Evolving QWOP Gaits

Steven Ray
CSU Sacramento
stevenlray@gmail.com

V. Scott Gordon
CSU Sacramento
gordonvs@ecs.csus.edu

Laurent Vaucher
Google, Inc.
laurentvaucher@gmail.com

ABSTRACT

QWOP is a popular Flash game in which a human player controls a sprinter in a simulated 100-meter dash. The game is notoriously difficult owing to its ragdoll physics engine, and the simultaneous movements that must be carefully coordinated to achieve forward progress. While previous researchers have evolved gaits using simulations similar to QWOP, we describe a software interface that connects directly to QWOP itself, incorporating a genetic algorithm to evolve actual QWOP gaits. Since QWOP has no API, ours detects graphical screen elements and uses them to build a fitness function. Two variable-length encoding schemes, that codify sequences of QWOP control commands that loop to form gaits, are tested. We then compare the performance of SGA, Genitor, and a Cellular Genetic Algorithm on this task. Using only the end score as the basis for fitness, the cellular algorithm is consistently able to evolve a successful scooting strategy similar to one most humans employ. The results confirm that steady-state GAs are preferred when the task is sensitive to small input variations. Although the limited feedback does not yet produce performance competitive with QWOP champions, it is the first autonomous software evolution of successful QWOP gaits.

Categories and Subject Descriptors

I.2.6 [**Learning**]: Artificial Intelligence – *learning.*

Keywords

Genetic algorithms; games

1. INTRODUCTION

QWOP is a simple online game in which a human player controls a graphical representation of an Olympic sprinter. The player wins by successfully guiding the sprinter to the finish line. The only inputs are the keystrokes Q, W, O, and P, which control particular muscles in the sprinter's legs. For a game with only four inputs, the game has proven to be a difficult, unintuitive task for humans.

We attempt to evolve successful gaits using a genetic algorithm. We do this by building an API for QWOP, a genetic encoding for keystroke sequences, looping such sequences in real-time, and using the resulting score as the fitness function. We then test the efficacy of various evolutionary models on this application.

GECCO'14, July 12–16, 2014, Vancouver, BC, Canada.

ACM 978-1-4503-2662-9/14/07...$15.00.
http://dx.doi.org/10.1145/2576768.2598248

2. BACKGROUND

2.1 QWOP

QWOP is a popular computer game developed in Adobe Flash by Bennett Foddy, and is available for free on his site Foddy.net [3]. In QWOP, the player takes control of an Olympic sprinter running a 100-meter race. Upon reaching the 100-meter mark, the player wins the game. If the runner's head or one of his hands touches the ground at any point along the way, QWOP considers him fallen, and the game is over. The game quickly became notorious for its difficulty, despite what seems like a simple task. Playing QWOP well has been described as "a ballet of tiny corrections, any of which is likely to throw off the player's timing and may result in a fatal error" [11]. QWOP's difficulty is largely a function of two factors: the *control scheme* and the *physics engine*.

QWOP gets its name from the game's control scheme. To play a game of QWOP, the user controls the runner using only the Q, W, O, and P keys on the keyboard, each of which controls a specific muscle group in the runner's legs. Q and W move forward the runner's left and right thighs respectively. The O and P keys each map to his left and right calves. Achieving a realistic bipedal gait in QWOP is often soon abandoned by new players, who tend to resort to finding a repeatable pattern of inputs sufficient enough to scoot the sprinter to the finish line.

The QWOP website states: *"QWOP is a game where ... you need to regain something many of us take for granted: the ability to walk."* Thus the game forces us to work out mechanically a task that most of us perform every day yet to which we do not devote much active thought. Users are precluded from relying on their own experience and knowledge of balancing and walking on two legs, because QWOP reroutes the motor skill of synchronized leg muscle manipulation to the user's fingers via the game controls. Players are also limited with regard to the amount and type of relevant sensory feedback available to tell how well they are doing and make necessary adjustments to their runner's gait, as the only available sensory feedback is the visual state of the runner.

The second factor that complicates QWOP is its *ragdoll physics engine*. Ragdoll physics is a method for procedurally animating characters based on a skeletal configuration of rigid bodies connected by joints and muscles in a simulated physical environment [6]. The physics system is an approximation but reasonably realistic simulation of a real runner's body with regard to physical laws like gravity, friction, and inertia. The player must constantly work not only to complete the race, but also to keep the runner from falling over with each step. Every slight movement of the runner's legs carries with it consequences of momentum and velocity compounded by the game world's gravity and friction. As a result, achieving QWOP's seemingly simple goal becomes extremely difficult, as the game is unforgiving to imprecise and even slightly poorly-timed movements.

2.2 Genetic Algorithm Models

Genetic algorithms (GA) are search algorithms based loosely on the principles of natural genetic evolution. They have been useful mainly for optimization, by applying simplified notions of selection, crossover, mutation, and survival of the fittest to an artificial population of encoded candidate solutions. Each member of the population is evaluated by a fitness function, and the GA iterates the genetic operations through generations until it reaches some terminating condition, such as a sufficiently optimized solution or a fixed number of generations.

The Simple Genetic Algorithm (SGA) is a *generational* model described by Holland [5], in which the entire population is replaced by a new population of individuals at each iteration.

A *Steady-state* GA does not follow a generational model, instead creating only a few new individuals at a time, which replace weaker individuals. In some versions, a few individuals are selected at random, using the strongest of those as parents, and the offspring replace the weakest only if they have higher fitness. The steady-state model has been shown to have advantages over the generational model in many problem spaces [12].

In a *Cellular* GA, each individual in a population selects a mate from those in its local proximity. This mechanic simulates isolation by distance within the population, and promotes niches of subpopulations that can improve diversity and help to prevent premature convergence [7]. Our version is based on a CGA described in a previous study [4].

2.3 Evolving Gaits

GAs have been explored for learning and optimizing gaits in hexapod [8], quadruped [2], and biped robots [13]. Biped robotic gait learning offers a slightly different problem domain from learning for robots with more than two legs, as walking with only two legs necessarily involves periods of time during which the robot is supported entirely by only one leg. Thus, bipedal gaits require more careful balance than gaits in which multiple legs are supporting the robot at any given moment. Most research on evolving bipedal gaits uses either physical or simulated robots with relatively high degrees of freedom compared to QWOP's runner, which has only four degrees of freedom.

Brodman and Volstad used reinforcement learning to achieve bipedal gaits in a stick-figure simulation of QWOP. Their program took a multi-dimensional feedback approach that moved the runner and adjusted his various limbs based on their horizontal, vertical and angular velocities, the body's calculated center of mass, and whether or not at least one foot was touching the ground. Their learning approach was able to achieve both a stable "shuffle-like" gait and a less stable but faster more standard gait, depending on the reinforcement learning model used [1].

3. Qwopper INTERFACE

In March of 2011, Vaucher implemented and described a Java-based controller program that could play QWOP through a web browser [10]. Unlike the work of Brodman and Volstad, which uses a model of QWOP, Vaucher's program attempts to play QWOP itself. Vaucher's QWOP controller program, named "Qwopper", uses the java.awt.Robot class to interact with the screen and play QWOP. It captures screen images and compares them with screenshots and known patterns and colors found in the QWOP interface to locate the game window. Once the game window is located, Qwopper gives it focus by sending a mouse event to the game. Once the game window has focus, QWOP is played entirely using keyboard commands sent by Qwopper. Qwopper monitors the current game score, consisting of the current distance traveled by the runner, by periodically capturing a rectangular image of the location on the game screen where the score is displayed. Qwopper then applies a thresholding function that converts the image to black and white, tokenizes each character in the image, and then compares against a set of reference images of each character to parse the score for each runner. If the runner falls over, Qwopper sends a spacebar command to restart the game [10].

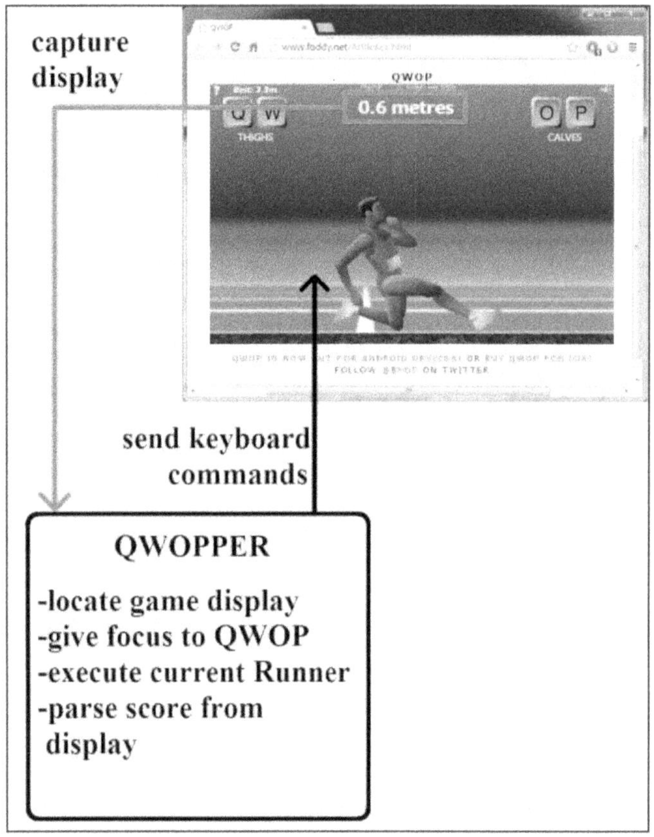

Figure 1. QWOPPER system interface

We use Vaucher's Qwopper software to evaluate the fitness of each runner in a GA population, by decoding each individual in the population into a sequence of runner keystrokes, and then playing QWOP according to each runner's genetic sequence, which is looped until the runner crashes, reaches the time limit, or wins the game. Generations of runners evaluated by Qwopper are evolved using a genetic algorithm and logged for analysis.

4. QWOP GAIT EVOLUTION

4.1 Genetic Encoding

Two different encodings were explored. The first encoding was described by Vaucher [10]. A second encoding was developed for this project to address disruptive effects of crossover and mutation discovered to be particular to QWOP gaits. The two methods are dubbed "encoding 1" and "encoding 2", respectively.

Vaucher's original encoding (*Encoding 1*) encodes a sequence of QWOP inputs as a string of characters. Each character represents either a key press, a key release, or a delay. An example individual is shown in Figure 2:

```
QO+qPW+wpo+QPW+wO+qp+P+Q+++
qp+QPW+wo+qp+POQ+q+W+Qp+qwo
```

Figure 2. Example runner using Encoding 1

A capital letter represents pressing that key on the keyboard, a lowercase letter represents a key release, and the '+' represents a delay in which the current state of inputs is maintained for a set length of time. The individual in the above figure translates to "Press Q and O, hold them for 150ms, release Q, press P and W, hold for 150ms, release W, P and O, wait..." and so on. An advantage of Encoding 1 is that it is easy to read and understand the sequence of inputs represented by the solution candidate.

Encoding 1 proved problematic when crossover and mutation were introduced, because the control state at any given point on an individual using this encoding is highly dependent on its context within the sequence. Crossover and mutation operations on individuals defined with Encoding 1 resulted in producing "non-coding DNA" or redundant commands such as consecutive capitals or lower-case letters. Encoding 1 was designed such that each letter indicates a change in the current input state. Each crossover and mutation operation had a high probability of rendering one or more characters in the chromosome redundant, which often dramatically altered the input sequence.

The second genetic encoding explored (Encoding 2) encodes input sequences using a 16-character alphabet, each letter of which represents one of the possible input combinations in QWOP. In order to describe Encoding 2, we must first describe the alphabet it uses, shown in Figure 3.

QWOP uses only four buttons, so there are 16 possible input combinations that comprise QWOP's input space. Each letter in Encoding 2 maps to one of these 16 input combinations. Unlike Encoding 1, input sequences built with this alphabet assume a small delay between each letter's execution, since each letter defines a distinct input state for all four control keys. Encoding 2 does not suffer from the context-dependence of letters in Encoding 1, since each letter here represents a distinct input state for *all four* keys. As seen in Figure 3, a key value of 0 indicates a key release command, and the key value 1 indicates a command to press the key. Redundant sequential press commands for a given key will simply continue to hold the pressed key continuously, while redundant release commands will just continue to refrain from pressing that key.

An example individual defined using Encoding 2 is shown in Figure 4. Each letter in the sequence is separated by an implied wait period of 150ms, like Encoding 1, during which the current input state is maintained, meaning that any keys pressed according to the current letter are held until a letter is encountered that releases that key. The individual in Figure 4 translates to "press Q and O, hold for 150ms, press P and release O while continuing to hold Q, wait for 150ms, release Q and O and press W, hold for 150ms, release W and press O, wait..." and so on.

Alphabet	Q	W	O	P
P	0	0	0	0
D	0	0	0	1
C	0	0	1	0
J	0	0	1	1
B	0	1	0	0
I	0	1	0	1
H	0	1	1	0
N	0	1	1	1
A	1	0	0	0
G	1	0	0	1
F	1	0	1	0
M	1	0	1	1
E	1	1	0	0
L	1	1	0	1
K	1	1	1	0
O	1	1	1	1

Figure 3. Encoding 2 Alphabet with Input States

```
FGBCHFELMIEFNGJCLHLEMCLJKJLNEKGHDGJDAJLE
```

Figure 4. Example runner using Encoding 2

The *mutation operator* used throughout the project, for both genetic encodings, was to randomly select and alter a single character in every child runner.

We tested two different crossover strategies: *single-point "cut-and-splice"* crossover, and standard *two-point* crossover. The "cut-and-splice" strategy selects a different crossover point for each parent, allowing for varying chromosomal lengths to be produced in offspring. The motivation for this approach was that the appropriate length of a good input loop in QWOP is not at all obvious, and we anticipated that this strategy could increase the search power of the algorithm with regard to the length of looped input sequences. By contrast, the two-point crossover strategy selects two crossover points for each parent at the same location on both parent chromosomes, thus maintaining chromosomal length in children and throughout all generations.

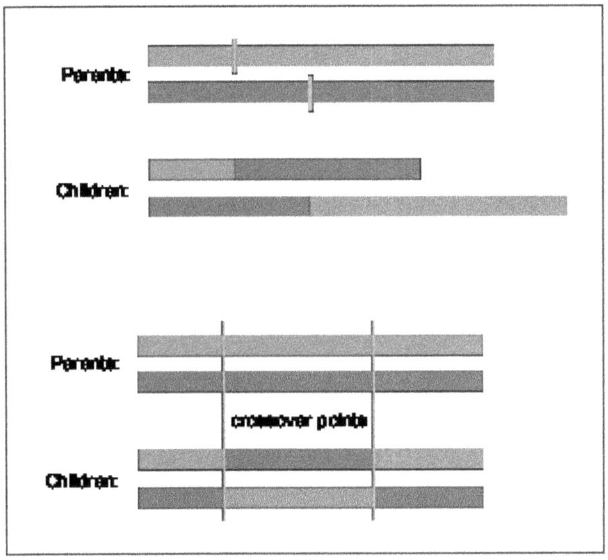

Figure 5. One-point "Cut-and-splice" crossover (above), and standard two-point crossover (below).

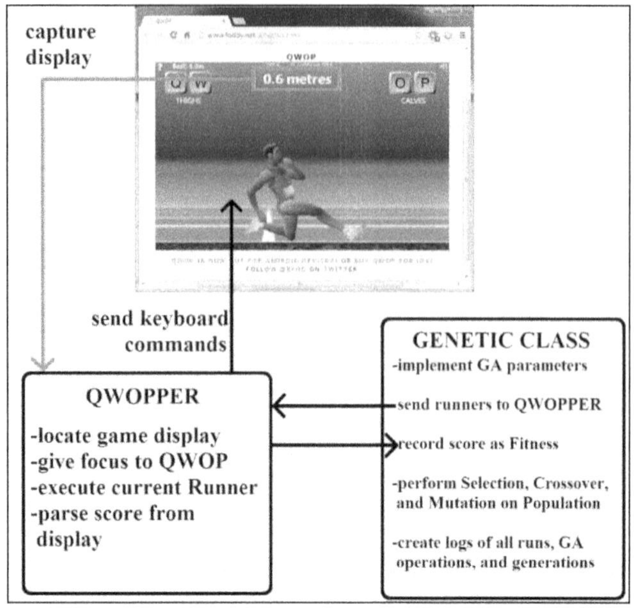

Figure 6. Genetic Algorithm real-time QWOP interface

4.2 Genetic Algorithm

We tested two different implementations of the evolutionary model: a standard generational model (SGA, described earlier) and a cellular model.

Our cellular GA implementation uses a local selection strategy that restricts the pool of potential mates for a given runner to those nearest to it in the population. Local selection was realized using a two-dimensional borderless "wrap-around" grid structure so that each individual has the same number of neighbors. Local selection was introduced to prevent, or at least slow considerably, premature convergence on a suboptimal solution due to loss of genetic diversity in the population. Children are only allowed to advance to the next generation (i.e., replace their parents) if they perform better than their parents. This both guarantees that average population fitness can only increase, and also introduces a form of elitism, whereby good solutions that outperformed their children would continue survive to the next generation.

In our cellular configuration, each runner is allowed to mate only with its fittest neighbor. The cellular configuration is synchronous, meaning that the algorithm proceeds from the top left individual through each row until every individual has mated. A temporary population is used to store the best runners produced for each index. After the entire population has mated, the current generation is replaced with the new temporary population.

The fitness function uses two parameters collected by Qwopper. The first is the final state at the end of a run, that is, either *stopped* or *crashed*. If the runner falls over, Qwopper considers the final state *crashed*, and in that case we assign a fitness of 0.0 (regardless of the distance achieved before crashing). If the run ends for any other reason, such as the time limit being reached or the race having been completed, the final state is *stopped*, and in that case we assign a fitness equal to the second parameter, which is the final score, in particular the *distance*, achieved when the game is stopped. Other combinations were explored through experimentation, but are not reported here.

The population was initialized in one of two ways. In the first method, a collection of hundreds of random runners were generated and fitness-tested. Each random runner played QWOP for 60 seconds or until it fell down. Generation 0 was then seeded with the best performing randomly generated runners. In the second method, Generation 0 was populated completely with untested randomly generated runners.

We used a population size of 16 individuals for the SGA implementation, and a population size of 30 for the CGA implementation.

5. RESULTS

The combination of the physics engine and restrictive control scheme make falling over in QWOP very easy, both for humans and, as it turned out, also for the GA implementations described. It is critically important for the player to achieve a stable gait. While the fitness function also selects for speed, this can only evolve after stability is achieved. Compounding the difficulty is the fact that some amount of randomness exists when the Qwopper program plays QWOP. Because of the ragdoll physics system, when the game starts, the runner is first initialized to a standing state, and then the physics rules are immediately applied, causing his body to "settle in" due to gravity. To illustrate the runner's instability, one can simply start a game and not press any buttons, then watch as the runner eventually begins to wobble and fall forward as the physics calculations appear to create a feedback loop that increases the wobble. This introduces some amount of random variability in the performance of *any* given solution sequence played by the Qwopper program. A single sequence of inputs, run multiple times, will rarely result in the exact same score. It was often observed in early generations that the same runner could score well in one trial and crash in the next. This is evident in the run logs, as many populations were initialized to the same generation of runners, and in each trial these runners achieved different scores. This inconsistency increases the importance of a stable gait, as the best surviving gaits were necessarily those that crashed the least despite this variability.

It is therefore no surprise that the primary trait that emerged was a sort of "stability gene," usually expressed as an opening sequence that resulted in a stable stance. There were two button combinations that almost always came to dominate the population. Namely, to simultaneously press Q and O or to simultaneously press W and P.

The 'QO' combination moves the left thigh backward and extends the right calf forward, causing the runner to step forward and drop to his left knee with the right leg extended in front. The 'WP' opening performs the inverse operation of bending the right leg back and extending the left leg forward, which drops the runner to his right knee. In both openings, the runner lowers his center of gravity and spreads his legs wide, as if trying to do the splits. Figure 7 illustrates both combinations.

Figure 7. Opening moves 'QO' (above) and 'WP' (below)

The 'QO' and 'WP' openings dominated populations, even when using a local selection policy in a large population to slow premature convergence.

Notably, the opening consistently used by the fastest human QWOP scores documented is instead 'WO', which causes the runner to push off with the back foot and raise the knee of the other leg, as shown in Figure 8. The GA always evolves away from this opening because following it with a stable gait is likely impossible without the visual sensory feedback that the fastest human players enjoy, and that is not yet a part of Qwopper. Our GA implementation, which uses an essentially "blind" input loop, is inherently unable to react to visual feedback to adjust its gait during a run like a skilled and sighted human player can, so the 'WO' gene is quickly bred out of the population in favor of solutions with more stable openings.

Figure 8. The 'WO' opening stride and resulting stance

Our best-evolved solutions transitioned from one of the two stable openings shown in Figure 7, into a gait that scooted forward while largely maintaining the runner's stable stance. Later generations gave way to the transition from scooting forward to more of a hopping gait. In these gaits, the runner would typically hop on one knee while kicking his free leg out in front of him to increase forward momentum. Even in the hopping gait, the legs remained spread apart, maintaining stability. Figure 9 shows the runner engaged in this evolved hopping gait. The gait is able to complete the QWOP race in about 2 minutes.

We posted a video of the evolved gaits, starting with some initial unsuccessful gaits and ending with the evolved hopping gait, at `http://www.youtube.com/watch?v=eWxFI3NHtT8`.

Figure 9. Gait involving hopping on one knee while kicking forward with the free leg.

5.1 Algorithm Performance

Three configurations of the GA models and parameters described earlier are tested. The first configuration uses a generational model, encoding 1, 3:2 tournament selection (three individuals are selected at random, the best two of which serve as parents), single-point cut-and-splice crossover, and a population consisting of the 16 best-performing runners from a pool of 390 randomly-generated individuals. As seen in Figure 10, this configuration fails to evolve solutions that played QWOP any better than the best randomly generated ones. This lack of improvement was attributed to a consistently observed high rate of failure in children (>50%). Because this GA configuration used a naïve succession policy wherein every child produced was guaranteed to succeed to the next generation, this high failure rate precluded the gene pool from improving with any significance.

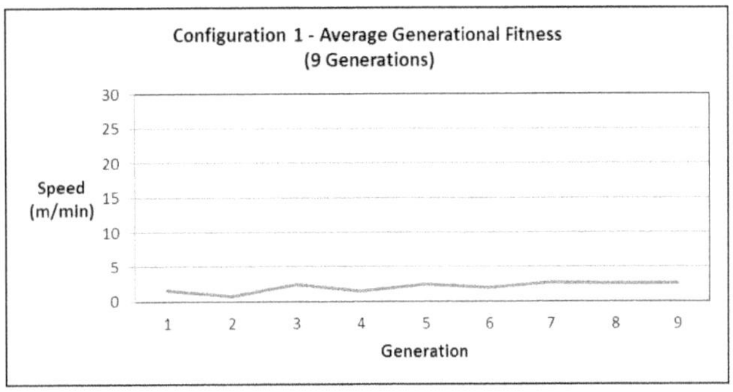

Figure 10. Fitness improvement in Generational GA model

The second configuration tested is identical to the first (including the same initial population), except that it uses a succession policy similar to that of the steady-state model. In this configuration, children only survive to the next generation if they outperform the worst of the three potential parents selected. This single modification results in a GA that produces positive results, as shown in Figure 11.

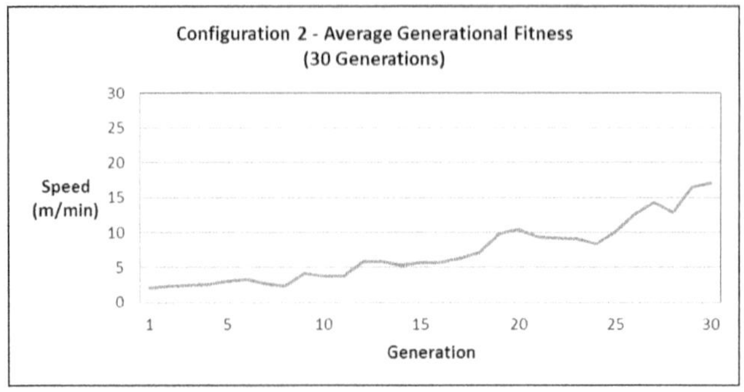

Figure 11. Fitness improvement in Steady-State model

Note that average generational fitness does not always improve, because offspring are not required to be better than their parents.

The third configuration, and the one that yields the most stable and consistently efficient gaits, uses the CGA model, encoding 2, two-point crossover and a population size of 30 individuals. This population is initialized with the best individuals from a pool of 500 randomly-generated runners. Figure 12 shows the relative performance of configurations 2 and 3.

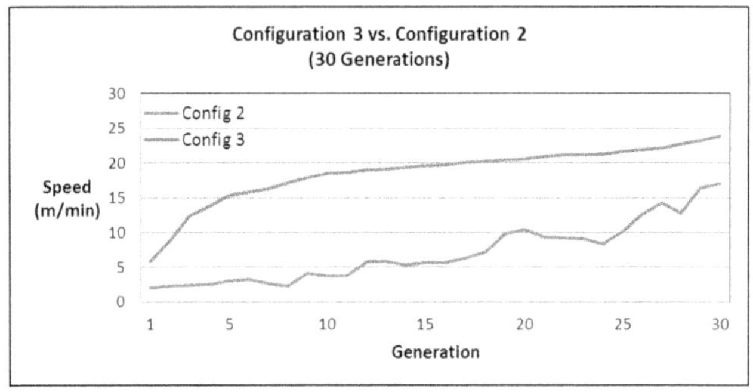

Figure 12. Fitness improvement in Config. 2 vs. Config 3

We took a closer look at the two encoding methods (Vaucher's original keystroke encoding, and the newer alphabet of keystroke combinations) to determine to what extent the quality of the initially-generated populations might be influencing the results. To this end, two pools of random runners were generated, one for each encoding method, and compared. Although the vast majority of randomly-generated runners for both methods crashed at or near the starting line, the top 30 runners from a pool of 500 using encoding 2 traveled, on average, over twice as far as the best 16 runners from a pool of 390 using encoding 1. The average fitness of the 30 fastest random runners from encoding 2 was 5.767 meters per minute, while encoding 1 averaged 2.033 meters per minute in its 16 fastest random runners.

To control for this performance gap between the best random runners generated by the two different encodings, Configuration 3 was further tested using a different initial population of random runners, all of which had crashed outright when first tested by Qwopper. Despite a low average fitness of this initial population at 1.3 meters per minute, the average generational fitness accelerated just as quickly in early generations as did the population seeded with high quality random candidates. Regardless of the fitness of the initial population, Configuration 3 consistently performed better than Configuration 2, suggesting that the other GA parameters were largely responsible for the algorithm's accelerated evolution toward faster runners compared to the previous configurations.

The performance of configuration 3, initialized with fit versus unfit randomly-generated individuals, is shown in Figure 13.

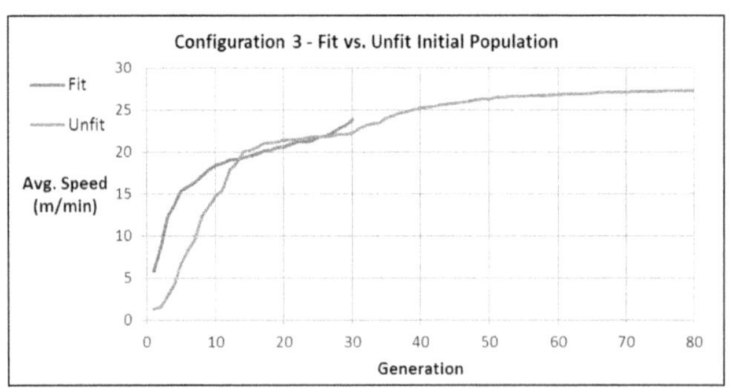

Figure 13. performance, fit vs. random initial populations

6. CONCLUSIONS

This project experimented with and compared many different flavors of the genetic algorithm and its components on the task of evolving QWOP gaits. Some of configurations were demonstrably better suited to solving this particular problem than others. This experiment found the greatest success with a Cellular GA.

The results confirm that steady-state evolutionary models outperform generational models when the fitness of potential solutions is highly sensitive to small changes in their encoding. This is intuitive considering the high failure rate of children observed throughout this experiment. Maintaining successful individuals and only replacing the weak ones with children of higher quality was critical to evolving successful gaits.

Through repeated trials we observed that certain traits, particularly traits that conferred a greater degree of gait stability, consistently emerged and eventually came to dominate the population. This observation held true even in a Cellular GA implementation which used a local selection policy in conjunction with a larger population size. If an argument can be made that the GA prematurely converged toward only solutions with the most stable opening moves, it is likely a consequence of requiring the system to learn to play QWOP without the ability to react to dynamic sensory feedback.

The results suggest methods that might evolve even better solutions to QWOP. Clearly the GA would benefit from a fitness function that provided more sensory information, such as the physical configuration of the legs or body of the runner at a given time. Another possible improvement would involve separating the opening stage from the looped stage, since it is possible that an optimal input loop may not contain the same sequence that starts the runner from his initial standing position, which is only needed once at the beginning of the race. There is also room for further exploration with regard to solving QWOP using other variations of the genetic algorithm that were not explored here.

One factor that limited the amount of experimentation we were able to do is the time that it takes to evaluate the fitness of an individual. Qwopper is a bot that must run each individual in a browser window in real time; a typical population of size 30, evolving for only 30 generations, often required over 20 hours of uninterrupted execution. Fortunately, the steady-state GA models that we used (including the CGA) have already been shown to be highly parallelizable [4], representing another potential avenue for improving the results.

Interestingly, the best solutions ultimately found by the CGA bear a striking resemblance to the way many people actually play the game. Most people who play QWOP do not post speed-run videos on YouTube and compete for the world record, which is currently held by Roshan Ramachandra at 51 seconds [9]. Finding a repeatable pattern and scooting to the finish line is a commonly-recommended strategy in online discussions about how to beat QWOP, which is the same type of solution that the GA consistently achieves.

Considering QWOP's volatile ragdoll physics system, its limited control scheme, and the fact that the GA has no mechanism for direct sensory feedback with which to respond and make adjustments, the gaits achieved by the GA implementations described in this paper serve as a proof of concept for robotic gait learning in a complex space with minimal inputs and feedbacks.

7. ACKNOWLEDGMENTS

We wish to thank Bennett Foddy for granting us permission to use the images of QWOP that appear in this paper.

8. REFERENCES

[1] Brodman, G. and Voldstad, R. (2012). *QWOP Learning*. Department of Computer Science CS 229 class project, Stanford University, 2012. Retrieved 4/13/2014 from http://cs229.stanford.edu/projects2012.html

[2] Clune, J., Beckmann, B., Ofria, C., and Pennock, R. (2009). *Evolving Coordinated Quadruped Gaits with the HyperNEAT Generative Encoding*. Proceedings of the 2009 IEEE Congress on Evolutionary Computation (CEC '09).

[3] Foddy, B. *QWOP* [Flash Game] (2008). Retrieved 11-6-13 from http://www.foddy.net/Athletics.html

[4] Gordon, V. and Whitley, D. (1993). *Serial and Parallel Genetic Algorithms as Function Optimizers*. Proceedings of the 5th Int. Conf. on Genetic Algorithms (ICGA-93).

[5] Holland, J. (1975). *Adaptation in Natural and Artificial Systems*, University of Michigan Press, ©1975.

[6] Jakobsen, T. (2001). *Advanced Character Physics*. Proceedings of the Game Developers Conference (GDC-01).

[7] Mahnig, T. and Muhlenbein, H. (2002). *A Comparison of Stochastic Local Search and Population Based Search*. Proceedings of the 2002 Congress on Evolutionary Computation (CEC '02).

[8] Parker, G., Braun, D., and Cyliax, I. (1997). *Evolving Hexapod Gaits Using a Cyclic Genetic Algorithm*. Proceedings of the IASTED International Conference on Artificial Intelligence and Soft Computing (ASC '97).

[9] Ramachandra, R. (2013). *Fastest 100m run, QWOP (flash game)*. Guinness World Records. Retrieved 11-6-13 from http://challengers.guinnessworldrecords.com/challenges/160-fastest-100m-run-qwop-flash-game

[10] Vaucher, L. (2011). *Genetically Engineered QWOP (Part 1)*. Slow Frog Blog [blog]. Retrieved 11-6-13 from http://slowfrog.blogspot.com/2011/03/genetically-engineered-qwop-part-1.html

[11] Wheeler, C. (2012). *QWOP and Simulation Design, Pt. 2. The Rules on the Field* [blog]. Retrieved 11-6-13 from http://therulesonthefield.com/2012/07/10/qwop-and-simulation-design-pt-2/

[12] Whitley, D. (1989). *The GENITOR Algorithm and Selection Pressure: Why Rank-Based Allocation of Reproductive Trials is Best*. Proceedings of the Third International Conference on Genetic Algorithms (ICGA-89).

[13] Wolff, K. and Nordin, P. (2002). *Evolution of Efficient Gait with an Autonomous Biped Robot Using Visual Feedback*. Proceedings of the 8th Mechatronics Forum International Conference (Mechatronics-2002).

Search for Maximal Snake-in-the-Box Using New Genetic Algorithm

Kim-Hang Ruiz
International MIS
1065 Waltons Pass
Evans, GA 30809
kimhangruiz@aol.com

ABSTRACT

The "Snake-In-The-Box" (SIB) problem is a challenging combinatorial search problem to find the longest constrained open path (k-spread snake) in n-dimensional hypercube (Q_n). In addition to constructive techniques, many search algorithms such as Depth First Search (DFS), Genetic Algorithm (GA), hybrid Evolutionary Computation algorithm (EC), and Nested Monte-Carlo Search (NMCS) have been used to tackle this problem. To get better results and to speed up the process, these techniques often used a long snake as the starting point for the search (priming/seeding).

This paper reviews the hypercube fundamentals, then presents a new search technique, Mitosis Genetic Algorithm (MGA), which was applied in search for the four different spread snakes (spread 2 to 5) in seven different dimensional hypercubes (Q_6 to Q_{13}). The MGA found three new record-breaking 3-spread snakes in Q_{10}, Q_{11} and Q_{13}, all the previously known optimal snakes from spread 2 to spread 5, and the best previous known maximal 3-S_9 snake of length 63. It is remarkable that it found those within minutes to hours without priming, significantly shorter than days to weeks needed in the other techniques.

Categories and Subject Descriptors

I.2.8 [**Artificial Intelligence**]: Problem Solving, Control Methods, and Search – *backtracking, graph and tree search strategies, heuristic methods, plan execution, formation, and generation.*

General Terms

Algorithms, Theory

Keywords

Genetic Algorithm, Mitosis Genetic Algorithm, Heuristics, Snake, Hypercube

GECCO '14, July 12 –16, 2014, Vancouver, BC, Canada.

ACM 978-1-4503-2662-9/14/07…$15.00.
http://dx.doi.org/10.1145/2576768.2598296

1. INTRODUCTION

The n-dimensional hypercube Q_n is a graph whose vertices consist of all binary strings $b_{n-1} \ldots b_1\ b_0$ where each vertex connects to n adjacent vertices. Two vertices are adjacent if and only if their binary strings differ by exactly one bit. By definition a k-spread snake is an induced path in an undirected graph G, such that every pair of vertices of a least distance k in the path are also at a least distance k in graph G. The "Snake-in-the-Box" (SIB) problem, to find the longest k-spread snakes in Q_n (k-S_n), has been a challenge for researchers over the past fifty years.

The properties of the SIB have been applied in error-detecting codes, in analog-to-digital encoders and converters [5, 7], modulation schemes in multi-level flash memories [16], efficient resource distributions in high speed computer clusters [11], and in identifying gene regulation networks in embryonic development [17]. The accuracy of error detection in certain analog-to-digital conversion systems increases as the length of the snake increases; the greater the spread, the greater is the error-detection capability. Accordingly, there has been much interest in finding the longest maximal k-S_n.

When a snake cannot be extended at either end, it is maximal. The number of maximal snakes vary with the hypercube dimension and the spread. The longest maximal k-S_n is the optimal. Many mathematicians have suggested several constructive techniques [1, 2, 12, 15] to build the longest maximal k-S_n. Other scholars have either applied heuristic search such as GA [2, 13], EC hybrids [3], and NMCS [8], or exhaustive search such as DFS [6, 10] to find the optimal or the longest maximal k-S_n. These search techniques can find the optimal in the small dimensional hypercubes Q_n; but not in the large ones. Most record-breaking k-S_n (for large Q_n) reported in literature have not been proven to be the optimal. The GA holds the record in finding the maximal 2-S_8 of length 98 [2] and the NMCS in 2-S_{10}, 2-S_{11} and 2-S_{12} of lengths 370, 695 and 1274 respectively [8]. Only constructive techniques and DFS were used to build or to search for snakes with spreads higher than 2. To get better results and to speed up the search process, a longer snake is often used as the starting point for search (priming) in these techniques.

This paper reviews the hypercube fundamentals in section 3 and then introduces a new search technique: Mitosis Genetic Algorithm (MGA) in section 4. The MGA implementation and how the experiment was set up in search for the longest maximal k-S_n snakes are described in section 5. The search results for the four different spread snakes (spread 2 to 5) in seven different dimensional hypercubes (Q_6 to Q_{13}) are discussed in section 6 and section 7. The MGA found three new record-breaking 3-S_{10}, 3-

S_{11} and 3-S_{13} of lengths 125, 158, and 509, longer than the best previously known value, 103, 157 and 493 respectively [6]. It also found all the previously known optimal snakes from spread 2 to spread 5; and the known longest 3-S_9 snake of length 63 without priming. It is remarkable that the search times to find these optimal and longest maximal k-S_n snakes took minutes or hours, significantly shorter than the days to weeks required by the other techniques. A list of transition sequences of three record-breaking snakes is provided in an appendix (section 9).

2. TERMINOLOGY AND DEFINITIONS

The following standard abbreviations and terms are used in this paper.

2.1 Terminology

k	spread
k-S_n	n-dimensional k-spread snake, e.g 3-S_8 denotes 8-dimensional 3-spread snake. In the literature S_n is used for 2-S_n.
n	number of dimensions.
Q_n	n-dimensional hypercube, e.g Q_9 denotes 9-dimensional hypercube.
$O(n)$	search space.
$O_{GA}(t)$	search time for each Genetic Algorithm in the MGA.
$O(t)$	search time for the Mitosis Genetic Algorithm.
$O_k(t)$	search time for k-spread snakes.
$O_{k-1}(t)$	search time for (k-1)-spread snakes

2.2 Definitions

- ***Available nodes*** are nodes that have distances at least equal to spread k from any snake node except (k-1) nodes from the tail (or the head).
- ***Available transition*** is the transition that leads to an available node.
- ***Canonical form*** of a snake is a type that requires each transition number to first appear in a transition sequence only after all smaller transition numbers have appeared. For example, the transition sequence 01203123 is in canonical form but the transition sequence 10321032 is not.
- ***Chromosomes*** represent possible solutions to the genetic algorithm problem at hand.
- ***Free neighbors*** are neighbors that are available nodes.
- ***Fitness*** is the evaluation of a chromosome as a solution to the given genetic algorithm problem.
- An ***induced path*** in an undirected graph G, is a sequence of nodes P, where every pair of non-consecutive vertices in P are non-adjacent in G.
- A ***maximal*** snake is not a subsequence of any other snake, which cannot be extended at either end without violating the non-chord constraint.
- The ***n-dimensional k-spread snake k-S_n*** is an open induced (chord free) path in an undirected graph G such that every pair of vertices at distance at least k in the path are also at distance at least k in G.
- A ***node sequence*** of a k-S_n snake is the sequence of n-code-words which consist of all binary strings $b_{n-1}\ldots b_1\ b_0$ and two words are adjacent if and only if their binary strings differ by exactly one bit.
- The ***optimal*** snake is the longest maximal snake proven.
- ***Population*** is a collection of chromosomes in a genetic algorithm problem.
- ***Spread k*** is the distance between two nodes that are at least k units apart.
- A ***transition sequence*** of a k-S_n snake is the sequence of integers ranging from 0 to (n-1), which corresponds to the bit positions (index) in which successive n–code-words differ.
- The ***Vicinity V_k*** consists of all nodes in Q_n that have a distance k from the snake path.
- ***Unavailable nodes*** are nodes that have distances less than k units from any snake node (in the vicinity V_1 or $\ldots V_{k-1}$).
- ***Unavailable transition*** is the transition that leads to an unavailable node.

2.3 Font Style

- *Italic* font represents variable name in programming or in calculating the search space and the search time of the algorithm.
- ***Bold underlined italic*** font represents definitions.

3. HYPERCUBE FUNDAMENTALS

One of the most important properties of the hypercube is that the number of vertices in Q_n is always twice as much as in Q_{n-1}. Figure-1 shows how the sole node in Q_0 duplicates itself by translating in coordinate 0 (transition 0), to form a line in Q_1 which continues to duplicate in transitions 1, 2, and 3 to form Q_2, Q_3, and Q_4 respectively.

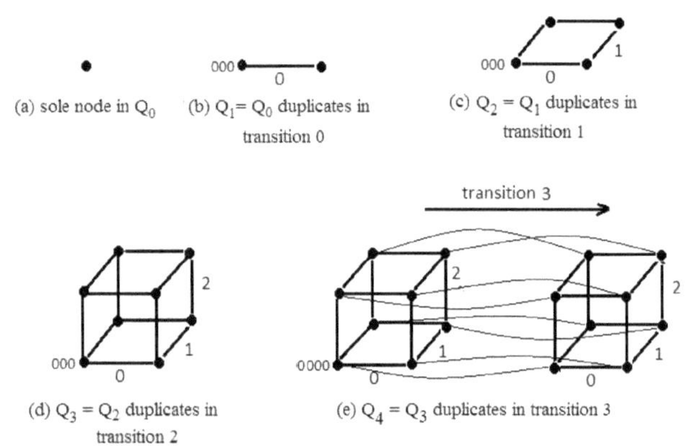

Figure 1. Formation of Q_n by duplicating Q_{n-1} in transitions (n-1)

Each vertex in Q_n connects to n other vertices. If there is no induced path in the graphs, every vertex has an equal chance to be selected as a snake node based on the isomorphic symmetries of the hypercube. If, however, there is an induced path (snake) in the graph already, only some nodes can be selected to extend the path. The conditions for a node to be selected are that, it must be available and adjacent to the end nodes (tail or head). For example, an induced path 3-S_6 in Q_6 with transition sequence 0123 is illustrated with the thick black line in Figure-2. Red circle vertices represent unavailable nodes in vicinity V_1 that are one distance away from snake nodes. Green triangle vertices are unavailable nodes in vicinity V_2. Black square vertices are available nodes that can be added to the path. There are 26 available nodes in Figure 2 but only 3 of them (marked e0, e4, and e5) are adjacent to the tail and can extend the path. Thus the next transition for the induced path (snake) can only be either 0, 4 or 5.

The left half of the graph can be considered as Q_5 (Q_{n-1}) where the most significant bit of all nodes is equal to 0. The right half of the graph is also considered Q_5 (Q_{n-1}) with the most significant bit equal to 1. Some of the unavailable nodes can be connected to form some paths which replicate part of the snake path. Notice that:

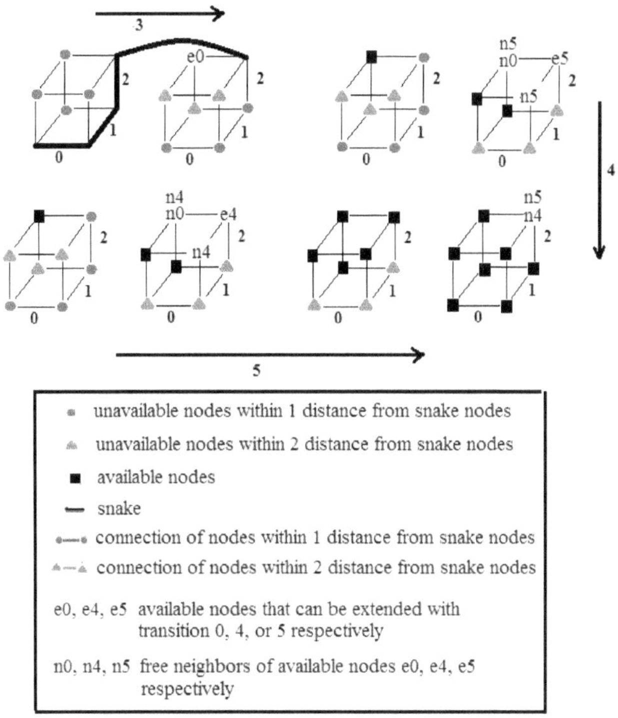

Figure 2. available nodes that a 3-S6 can extend to

1) Path of unavailable nodes in vicinity V_1 (red lines connecting red circles) on the right half of figure replicates the snake path on the left half minus 1 node.
2) Paths of unavailable nodes in vicinity V_2 (green lines connecting green triangles) on the right half of figure replicates the path of unavailable nodes in vicinity V_1 in the left half of figure minus 1 node.
3) There are no unavailable nodes on the right half figure corresponding to the unavailable nodes in vicinity V_2 on the left half. This is because the nodes on the right half are in vicinity V_3 which are available nodes according to the definition of 3-S_n.
4) There is one available node in the right half figure corresponding to each available node in the left half figure.

The first two notices indicate that a tight k-S_{n-1} snake with less unavailable nodes in vicinity V_1 would be more likely to produce a longer k-S_n snake. The third notice indicates that the number of unavailable nodes in vicinity V_{k-1} can be used to distinguish the ability of a k-S_{n-1} snake in extending into a longer k-S_n snake. If two snakes k-S_{n-1} have the same length but different number of unavailable nodes in vicinity V_{k-1}, the snake with the larger number would have higher ability to extend into a longer snake (since nodes in V_{k-1} will become available nodes in Q_n). The fourth notice indicates that there are 2 available nodes in Q_n for every available node in Q_{n-1}. These important properties will be incorporated in calculating the fitness function in the MGA.

The replication of the snake path and unavailable paths in the left half of the hypercube (Q_{n-1}) into the right half, in preparing for extending k-S_n snakes in Q_n is analogous to the natural mitosis process in biology where DNA replicates to prepare for cell duplication. A cell with good DNA grows into many more cells with good DNA. Imitating this natural process, Mitosis Genetic Algorithm (MGA) was developed with the assumption that a long k-S_{n-1} can extend into a long k-S_n.

4. MITOSIS GENETIC ALGORITHM

Mitosis Genetic Algorithm is a heuristic search technique applying a series of Genetic Algorithms to many parts of the problem at hand to find the optimal or near optimal solutions for each part which will then be combined or extended to ultimately find the optimal solution to the problem. Genetic Algorithms are heuristic search methods modeled from the theory of natural evolution. The process in GA involves generating a population of chromosomes (possible solutions to the problem) which will then be modified by the genetic operators, namely, selection, crossover, and mutation, to create a new generation. This evolutionary process is repeatedly carried out a predetermined number of times for each GA.

4.1 Encoding Schemes

Depending on the nature of the given problem, many encoding techniques can be used. Normally, the chromosomes in the population can be represented as strings of binary digits, integers, real numbers, or ordered list. The bit string representations are more commonly used because they are simple to create and easy to manipulate. It is recommended that the representations in all GA's are the same to ease the later process of combining or extending partial solutions into the solution of the problem.

4.2 Objective Function

Objective Function is a formula used to evaluate the fitness of a chromosome as a solution to the problem at hand. The formula can be mathematical or non-mathematical depending on the problem. Choosing an appropriate and effective objective function in each GA is very crucial for MGA to find the efficient solution of any given problem.

4.3 Selection

Based on the fitness which is evaluated by the objective function, individual chromosomes with a higher value will have a better chance to be selected as a parent to produce offspring of the next generation. There are many different methods to select, the two most common are: weighted Roulette-Wheel, and Tournament. In Roulette-Wheel selection, the probability of a member being selected is proportional to its fitness. In Tournament selection, four or six members in the current population are randomly selected; and the one "best fitted" will become parent (Tournament-4 or Tournament-6). Two selected parent chromosomes may or may not be replaced back to the current population. If it is, the selection is with replacement, otherwise, selection without replacement. In the selection with replacement, the fitness of the parent is unchanged after being selected. In the selection without replacement, the fitness of the parent is set to 0 to eliminate the chance to be selected again. It is also recommended that the selection types in all GA's be the same.

4.4 Crossover

Each time two parents are selected, their chromosomes are interchanged to generate new chromosomes that are different but retain some of their characteristics (crossover operator). A number from 0 to 1 is randomly generated and the crossover operator is then carried out only if the generated number is smaller than the predetermined crossover probability. There are two basic crossover techniques: one-point crossover and two-point crossover, which can be utilized by MGA. Depending on the type of crossover, one or two numbers between 1 and chromosome's length are randomly selected as the crossover point or points. In one-point crossover, two parent chromosomes beyond the crossover point are swapped, rendering two children. In two-point crossover, the part of the chromosome between the two crossover points are swapped to create two children. The two children chromosomes will then be copied to the new population. If the crossover operation is not carried out, the two parent chromosomes will be copied instead. The type of crossover can be different for each GA. Using two-point crossover in MGA tends to find the efficient solution to the problem more often than using one-point crossover.

The predetermined crossover probability can be different in each GA, but it is often set to be the same.

4.5 Mutation

A common single point mutation is used in MGA. It involves a probability that an arbitrary gene in the chromosomes of the new population will be changed from its original state. Each gene in the chromosomes of the new population is visited by the algorithm, and a number from 0 to 1 is randomly generated. If the generated number is smaller than the predetermined mutation probability, the gene will be replaced with a different gene. The predetermined mutation probability can be different in each GA; but it also is often set to be the same.

4.6 Repeating Time

Since the random function is called on many times in GA's procedures, it is likely to produce a different solution in every run. In order to increase the reliability of producing the same result and the chance to get the optimal solution, the MGA procedure was set to repeat a predetermined number of runs. The best solution found in each run is stored in a variable local-best. The best of all the local-best values is the solution. For example, if the repeating time is set to 5 and the local best values are 46, 47, 48, 47, and 49, then the solution is 49. Thus the higher is the repeating time, the higher is the reliability, but the longer is the searching time.

A hypercube Q_n consists many lower dimensional hypercubes, thus finding the optimal k-spread snake in Q_n can be viewed as finding many optimal k-spread snakes in many lower dimensional hypercubes Q_{n-2} or Q_{n-1} which will then be combined or extended to obtain the optimal k-spread snake in Q_n. Thus MGA is well suited to tackle SIB problem.

5. MGA IMPLEMENTATION

Figure 3 illustrates the MGA procedure in searching for the longest maximal k-S_n. First, an initial population of transition sequences of k-S_{n-1} is generated. The GA is applied to it to find a population of near optimal k-S_{n-1} which will then be replicated and extended to form an initial population of transition sequences of k-S_n. The GA will be applied again to this new initial population to find the longest maximal k-S_n, the solution to the problem. The first initial population can be from any lower dimensional hypercube that is different than Q_{n-1}. For example, a series of GA can be applied to an initial population of transition sequences of k-S_{n-2} instead. In this case, the replications and extensions must be repeated twice and the GA must be applied three times to evolve the populations of transition sequences of k-S_{n-2}, k-S_{n-1} and k-S_n.

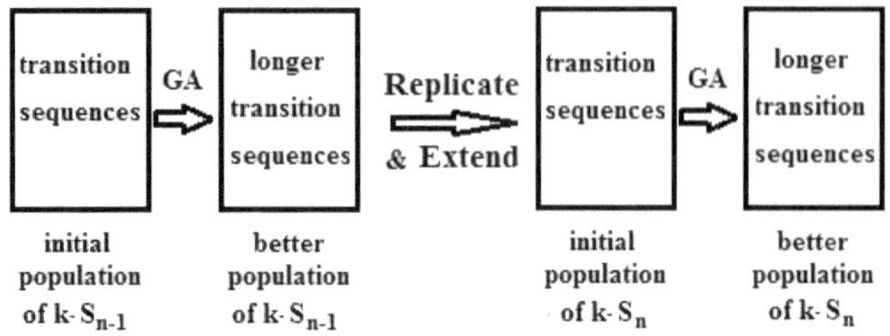

Figure 3. The procedure of Mitosis Genetic Algorithm

5.1 Representation

To avoid adjacency violations during crossover and mutation operators, the transition sequence is used as the representation for each individual chromosome in the population. Each transition sequence is stored in a one-dimension array whose length is at least 5 units longer than the best previously known value. For example, the best previously known values for 3-S_8 and 4-S_8 snakes are 35 and 19, thus the length of chromosomes for these snakes are set at 40 and 24 respectively. When a new record-breaking k-S_n is found, the number of available nodes will be determined. If there are m available nodes left, the array length for this k-S_n will be reset to the sum of the length of the longest found maximal plus m. For example, the array length for 3-S_{10} is initially set at 108. When a maximal with length 108 is found, there are 17 available nodes left. Thus the array length is reset to 125 and the MGA is rerun with the same settings.

5.2 Initial Population

By definition a k-spread snake is an induced path in an undirected graph G such that every pair of vertices of at least distance k in the path are also at least distance k in G. This indicates that if C is the transition sequence for a k-S_n snake with length $L > 2k$, then all the numbers in every block of $(k + 1)$ consecutive numbers of C are distinct (Douglas' Remark [4]). For example, the four transitions of the 3-S_6 snake in Figure 2 are 0123, the integer that can be assigned to the fifth gene can only be either 0, 4, or 5. If the integer 0 is chosen for the fifth, then the integer that can be assigned to the sixth must be either 4, or 5. Let's assume that the transition sequence 012304 is formed. It can be seen that every four consecutive numbers in the transition sequence are distinct. Thus the following procedure is used to generate each chromosome in an initial population of snakes in canonical form.

1) Assign integers from 0 to k to the first $(k + 1)$ genes.
2) Randomly assign an integer that is different than k previous genes for the next gene.
3) Repeat step 2 until all genes are assigned.

5.3 GA Operators

In this study, both Tournament-4 and Tournment-6 selections with and without replacement are used. Both one-point crossover and two-point crossover are utilized. Since the representation of the chromosome is the transition sequence, there is no special works needed to perform during or after the crossover operators to keep the node adjacency intact. Single point mutation is used.

There are two different procedures to carry out these GA operators. First procedure uses the selection with replacement, and all GA operators are carried out repeatedly until the entire new population is created. Second procedure uses the selection without replacement to select members from the current population and then directly copied them to the first sixty percent of the new population. The single point mutation is then applied to this part of the new population. After that, each pair of mutated members will be selected in order from the top down to be crossed over and copied to the remaining 40 percent of the new population. For example, the crossover will be carried out on the first and the second members in the new population to create the 61st and 62nd members. Ultimately, the fitness function is carried out before and after crossover as well as mutation in the second procedure.

5.4 Fitness Function

After a new population is created, a transition sequence of each member is mapped to node sequence before calculating snake length. The function to calculate the snake length is outlined below:

1. Set one-dimensional array *Status* of length 2^n to zero which represents available nodes.
2. Mark *Status* of the first node in the chromosome as *n* which represents snake nodes. Set variable *count* that represents snake length to 0.
3. Check whether *Status* of the next node in the chromosome is available. If it is not, return *count*; otherwise, increase *count*.
4. Mark *Status* of the next node as *n* (represents snake node) and of its neighbors within (k-1) distances to an integer that represents its distance from the snake node, e.g. mark 1 for 1 distance, … (k-1) for (k-1) distances
5. Return to step 3.

The snake length calculation stops when the next transition in the chromosome leads to an unavailable node. Since the subject of this study is to find the longest maximal $k\text{-}S_n$ snake, an extension procedure will be applied to the snake to determine whether it could be extended and if so what the extended length would be. The extension procedure begins with the calculation of the number of available transitions from the snake tail. If the number of available transitions is zero, the snake is maximal (can't be extended), and the length of the maximal $k\text{-}S_n$ snake can be reported in the fitness function. If the number of available transition is greater than zero, replace the unavailable transition with an available transition. Either one of four extension procedures listed below can be used to select an available transition:

- Extension F: selects the available transition that has the lowest number of free neighbors.
- Extension H: selects the available transition that has the highest coordinate.
- Extension L: selects the available transition that has the lowest coordinate.
- Extension R: randomly selects one available transition from the set of available transitions.

For example, the snake with the transition sequence 0123 in Figure 2 can only be extended with either the available transition 0, 4 or 5. The available transition 0 has the lowest index (coordinate) and the transition 5 has the highest index. If the snake is extended with the extension L, the transition 0 will be selected. If the snake is extended with the extension H, the transition 5 will be selected. If the snake is extended with the extension R, either 0, 4 or 5 will be selected (based on a generated random number). The transition 0 leads to the node e0 that has 2 free neighbors n0, both transitions 4 and 5 lead to nodes e4 and e5 that have 3 free neighbors n4 and n5 respectively. Thus if the snake is extended with the extension F, the transition 0 will be selected since it has the lowest free neighbors.

The variable *count* increases by an increment each time an available transition is selected. The extension stops when available transition is no longer found and the value of the variable *count* is reported as length L in the fitness function.

Since the MGA is a series of GA applied to different populations of $k\text{-}S_{n-1}$ and $k\text{-}S_n$ transition sequences in search for the longest maximal $k\text{-}S_n$, the fitness function for each GA will be different. Depending on the population where the GA is applied to, either one of the two fitness functions below is used:

$$\text{Fitness} = \text{length} + E \qquad (1)$$

$$\text{Fitness} = \text{length} \qquad (2)$$

Where E is the least potential extended snake nodes in the next-higher-dimensional hypercube.
Function (1) is used in GA's to evolve $k\text{-}S_{n-1}$ populations in lower dimensional hypercubes, which will be used further to extend into $k\text{-}S_n$ population. Thus this function must account for the ability of $k\text{-}S_{n-1}$ to extend into $k\text{-}S_n$. Each time that one more node is added to the snake path in the extension procedure, (n-k)*(k-1) nodes will become unavailable. Based on the notices in the hypercube fundamentals above, the total available nodes in Q_n is equal to the sum of all unavailable nodes in vicinity V_{k-1} plus two times the available nodes in Q_{n-1}. The least potential extended snake nodes in the next higher dimensional hypercube E roughly equals to the ratio of the total available nodes in Q_n over (n-k)*(k-1). Therefore

$E = (2 * \text{available nodes} + \text{unavailable nodes in } V_{k-1}) / [(n-k)*(k-1)]$

Function (1) will distinguish between two equal-length $k\text{-}S_{n-1}$ snakes that can extend into two different length $k\text{-}S_n$ snakes by using E.

Function (2) is used in the last GA to evolve the $k\text{-}S_n$ population which contains the solution to SIB problem. Thus Function (2) only utilizes the length of the longest maximal $k\text{-}S_n$.

5.5 Experiment Settings

In this study, the population sizes were initially set at 500, 1000, 1500, 2500, and 3000; and the number of generations at 50, 70, 80, 90, 110, 120, and 150. When the length of the $k\text{-}S_n$ being searched for is found to be shorter than the best previously known value, the population size were increased to 5000, 10000, 20000, and 30000; and the number of generations to 170, 200, and 300 in an attempt to extend few more nodes. This action was taken based on the assumption that the larger the population and the number of generations, the better is the chance to find the longest maximal. The crossover probability was set at 0.6 and 0.8. The mutation probabilities were set at 0.02, 0.01, 0.005, 0.009, and 0.0001. The number of generations was set to 50 in GA's in search for better $k\text{-}S_{n-1}$ populations (partial solutions). The repeating time was initially set at 20, 50, 100 and 200. Later, only the repeating time of 20 is used in high $Q_{n,}$ (n>10).

The MGA was written in VB.net (using Microsoft Visual Studio 2008 package) and run on five processors with 2.0 GHz Pentium Dual-Core CPU.

6. RESULTS

A summary of the results is given in Table 1, where the lengths of the best known k-S_n values for dimension $n \leq 13$ and spread $k \leq 5$ are listed. The values in parentheses are the best previously known values published in [2, 6, 8, and 15].]. Recent tests at http://ai.uga.edu/sib/sibwiki/doku.php/records discover longer 2-S_{11}, 2-S_{12} and 2-S_{13} but results have not been published yet.

Table 1. Longest known k-S_n snakes. (Best previously known values in parentheses)

Dimension n	Spread K 2	3	4	5
6	(26*)	(13*)	(8*)	(7*)
7	(50*)	(21*)	(11*)	(9*)
8	(98)	(35*)	(19*)	(11*)
9	(190)	(63)	(28*)	(19*)
10	(370)	125 (103)	(47*)	(25*)
11	(695)	158 (157)	(68)	(39*)
12	(1274)	(286)	(104)	(56)
13	(2466)	509 (493)	(181)	(79)

* optimal value

The Mitosis Genetic Algorithm found three new record-breaking 3-S_{10}, 3-S_{11} and 3-S_{13} of lengths 125, 158 and 509 within 7, 17 and 87 minutes of search time respectively. The previous best known values are 103, 157 and 493 which were found by starting from a longest known coil and backtracking for seven days [2]. It is worth noting that the MGA was able to find these records relatively quick without seeding. A list of transition sequences of these three record-breaking snakes is provided in the appendix.

The MGA also found all the previously known optimal k-S_n snakes and the best previously known maximal 3-S_9 of length 63. Any optimal snake of length shorter than 26 was found within a few seconds and longer ones within a few minutes. DFS took only few milliseconds to find the former and days to find the latter [2, 8]. The MGA found the optimal 2-S_7 of length 50 within 5 minutes, much shorter than the days needed by the GA in [13]. These results indicate that the DFS is best suited in search for the optimal(s) shorter than 27 and the MGA for the optimal and longest snakes longer than 26.

The MGA found the nearest values to the best previous known maximal 2-S_8, 4-S_{11}, 4-S_{12}, 5-S_{10}, 5-S_{11}, 5-S_{12} within minutes to hours. In the attempt to reach the best previously known value, the search for these snakes were repeated with much larger population sizes and larger numbers of generations. The results showed that the snake lengths did not improve and in some cases were actually shorter. Thus, the assumption that the larger the population size and the number of generations, the better is the chance to find the longest maximal is not always true, especially in the excessively large population sizes. This might have been due to the convergence in the selection operator. When the population size is too large, duplicate members are more likely to happen. Duplicate "better fit" members will quickly flood the next population which causes premature convergence, and the snake closest to the longest will consequently be found instead of the longest. This phenomenon happens more often in the selection with replacement than the selection without replacement, and especially in high dimensional Q_n.

Even though the MGA found the optimal 2-S_7 of length 50 and the maximal 2-S_8 of length 97 within 5 minutes, it could not find the maximal 2-$S_{n>8}$ snakes near the previously known records. It found 2-S_9, 2-S_{10}, 2-S_{11}, 2-S_{12} and 2-S_{13} of lengths 185, 350, 595, 1033, and 1887 while the previously established records are 190, 370, 695, 1274, and 2466 respectively. This indicates that in order to be more effective in search for these 2-spread snakes, the parameter settings in GA's, the fitness functions and/or the MGA procedure should be modified.

7. DISCUSSION

It is noticed that the extension type, the length of chromosomes, the number of replication, the population size, the number of generations, the probability of crossover and mutation, all affect the MGA's ability to find the longest k-S_n snakes.

7.1 The Effect of the Extension Types

The results show that different extension procedures have different effects in finding the longest snakes in different spreads. Extension R (randomly selects an available transition to extend) can find longer 2-S_8 snakes than the other extensions can. However, for Q_n with $n > 8$, the extension F (extending with the available transition that has the lowest number of free neighbors) can find longer 2-spread snakes than the others can.

Extension L or H (extending with the available transition that has the lowest or highest index respectively) can find much longer 3-S_n snakes than Extension F or R can. The record-breaking 3-S_{10} was found by either using Extension L or H. The record-breaking 3-S_{11}, and 3-S_{13} were found by using Extension L only. It is noticed that a special repeating pattern (a _ b _ a _ b) occurs in the transition sequences of the 3-S_{10}, and 3-S_{13} produced by Extension L and H, but does not occur by Extension F and R (where $a \neq b$ and the underscore _ is different than a, and b).

Similar effect of the extension types on spread-2 was found on spread-4: Extension R can find longest 4-S_n snakes in low Q_n and Extension F in high Q_n. In all cases, the extension R tends to find longer 5-S_n snakes than the other extensions can.

In summary, Extension F works best for spread-2 and spread-4, H and L extensions for spread-3, and Extension R best for spread-5 in the search for the longest maximal k-spread snakes in high Q_n.

In most cases, Extension H tends to find shorter k-S_n snakes than the others, except in searching for 3-S_n. To understand why, let's examine the snake with the transition sequence 0123 in Figure 2. If the extension H is applied, transition 5 will be selected and the next extending node will be e5 which has 3 free n5 neighbors. One of these n5 nodes (marked n5 and n4) will subsequently become a snake node in the next extension and the other two nodes will become unavailable. Similarly, if the snake is extended with Extension L or F, transition 0 will be selected and the next extending node will be e0 which has 2 free n0 neighbors. One of these n0 nodes (marked n0 and n4) will subsequently become a snake node and the other will become an unavailable node. At this state, two 3-S_n snakes have the same length but different number of available nodes. The snake extended with H has one less available node than the others. If the extension repeats many times as often happens in high dimensional Q_n, H will end up with much less available nodes. Thus, the snake repeatedly extended by H will more likely be shorter since the snake's ability to extend depends on the amount of available nodes.

7.2 The Effect of the Number of Replications

In this experiment, the optimal 2-S_6 of lengths 26 and the optimal 2-S_7 of lengths 50 can only be found when the number of replications is set to 0 and 1 respectively. The maximal 2-S_8 of length 97 and 2-S_9 of length 185 can only be found when the number of replications is set to 2. This correlation between the number of replications and the length of the snake being searched for are also observed in other spread. In general, in order to find the optimal, or the longest maximal k-S_n snakes, the number of replications should be set based on the length of the snake being searched for. Zero should be set for lengths less than 26, one for lengths between 27 and 65, and greater than one for lengths greater than 65.

7.3 Search Time

In general, the search time for k-S_n snakes is longer than the search time for k-S_{n-1} snakes because the length of k-S_n snakes are longer and the number of vertices in Q_n is twice as much as Q_{n-1}. However, the results show that the search time for k-S_{n-1} snakes with large population size is generally longer than the search time for k-S_n snakes with lower population size. The results also show that for the same settings, the search time for k-S_n snakes is more than double the search time for k-S_{n-1} snakes, even though the number of vertices in Q_n is twice as much. For example, with setting of population size at 5000 and number of generations at 180, the search time [$O(t)$] for finding 2-S_{13} is about 15 hours, while the search time for finding 2-S_{12} is 4 hours. It is almost four times more.

Let's look at the search space and the search time of the MGA to understand why. The search space is clearly proportional to the population size p, the number of generation g, and the repeating time r. Thus

$$O(n) = pgr$$

Each time a new generation is built, the selection, crossover and mutation operators in the GA are carried out, therefore the search time in the GA can be formulated as followed:

$$O_{GA}(t) = prg(s+c+m)$$

Where p is the population size.
g is the number of generation.
r is the repeating time.
s is the search time during the selection operator.
c is the search time during the crossover operator.
m is the search time during the mutation operator.

If the selection is Tournament-6, the operator will locate the best fit chromosome out of six randomly selected chromosomes. Thus the search time for the selection is

$$s = 6p$$

Accordingly, $s = 4p$ for Tournament-4 selection.

During the crossover operator, each gene in two parent chromosomes will be copied to the next generation despite the type of crossover operator. Thus the search time for c is proportional with the length of the chromosome l and the population size p.

$$c = lp$$

During mutation, each gene is determined whether to be mutated or not, therefore the search time for m also is proportional to the length of the chromosome l and to the population size p.

$$m = lp$$

Replace s, c and m in $O_{GA}(t)$

$$O_{GA}(t) = prg\ (6p + lp + lp)$$
$$O_{GA}(t) = prg\ (6p + 2lp)$$
$$O_{GA}(t) = 2p^2rg\ (3 + l)$$

When l is large, $3 + l \sim l$, *thus*

$$O_{GA}(t) = 2rgp^2l$$

The MGA repeats the GA operations R times (R represents the number of replications). Since the number of generations is usually set to 50 for any dimension less than n, the search time for the MGA is

$$O(t) = (50*R + g)\ 2rp^2l \qquad (3)$$

For any Q_n, the maximum length of k-S_n snakes must be less than the depth of the search tree, $2^n/k$. Thus

$$O(t) < (50*R + g)\ 2rp^2(2^n/k)$$
$$O(t) < (50*R + g)\ rp^2(2^{n+1}/k) \qquad (4)$$

Functions (3) and (4) indicate that the MGA search time is linearly proportional to the number of generations, the repeating time, the length of the chromosomes, and the square of the population size, and grows exponentially with n. Thus, when n is raised by one increment, the number of vertices double and the search time grows exponentially with n (not double).

The results show that the real search time for 4-S_{10} is 35 minutes, much longer than the search time for 2-S_7 of 5 minutes, even though the length of chromosome representing 4-S_{10} (52) is slightly shorter than the length of chromosome representing 2-S_7 (55) and the population size in the search for 4-S_{10} (3000) is smaller than the population size in the search for 2-S_7 (5000). The search time functions above did not include the run time needed to mark unavailable nodes each time a snake node is assigned or extended in the chromosome. In general, the higher the spread, the more unavailable nodes need to be marked. The number of unavailable nodes that need to be marked in the MGA are:

(n - 1) for spread-2,
(n - 1)*(n - 2) / 2 for spread-3,
(n - 1)*(n - 2)*(n - 3) / 4 for spread-4, and
(n - 1)*(n - 2)*(n - 3)*(n - 4) / 8 for spread-5.

Thus for the approximately same length of chromosomes

$$O_k(t) = (n - k - 1) / 2\ O_{k-1}(t)$$

Where $O_k(t)$ and $O_{k-1}(t)$ are search time for k-spread snakes and (k-1)-spread snakes respectively. Thus, the search time for higher-spread snakes is much longer than the search time for the lower spread snakes even though the length of the higher-spread snakes is slightly shorter than the lower spread snakes.

The facts discussed in this section have been utilizing to modify the MGA procedure and/or alter the experiment settings to improve the speed as well as the results in search for k-S_n snakes which is the subject of another paper. For example, by applying Function (3), the search time for 2-S_8 snake of length 97 can be improved from 5 minutes to 1 minute by changing the settings of the population size from 5000 to 500 and of the number of generations from 150 to 400. Preliminary results are promising but more tests need to be done.

7.4 Advantages of Using MGA

MGA is a very versatile genetic algorithm. It has many advantages over other GA's. It functions the same as GA when the number of replications is set to 0, while GA cannot function as MGA. In solving the same optimization problem such as SIB, MGA can utilize many fitness functions in different parts of the problem to get better results in a relatively quick run time. To find the optimization solution to the problem, GA can use only one fitness function for the whole search. Generally, the use of GA requires longer processing times and may achieve the same results as in MGA.

8. CONCLUSIONS

The MGA found three new record-breaking 3-spread snakes in Q_{10}, Q_{11} and Q_{13}, all the previously known optimal snakes from spread 2 to spread 5, and the known longest maximal 3-S_9 snake of length 63. It is remarkable that it found those within minutes to hours without using any longest previously known snake to seed. This proves that MGA is a very effective technique in tackling SIB problem. Modifications to the MGA procedure or settings have been researched to improve its search for 2-spread snakes in dimensions higher than 8. Preliminary results are promising but more tests need to be done before those results can be reported.

9. APPENDIX

The transition sequence for each new record discovered by this study is listed below. The symbols for transition sequence are from 0 to 9 for the bit positions 0 to 9, and A to C for the bit positions 10-13.

A 3-spread snake of length 125 in Q_{10} is presented below:

81748675837486728175847683758470827684738576847182738
67485738679817486758374867281758476837584708276847385
7684718273867485738

A 3-spread snake of length 158 in Q_{11} is presented below:

01234015206130281072401320516024103290152701320416250
13208140271032501426013291A0241032801742013251420612
30917201530241056201328041720132504236029150271032410

A 3-spread snake of length 509 in Q_{13} is presented below:

07120513041205160712031504120319061502140315021 70A15
041203150418071205130412051607120315041203190615021 40
31502170615041203150 41B071205130412051607120315041203
18061502140315021 70A15041203150419071205130412051607
12031504120318061502140315021706150412031504 1C0712051
3041205160712031504120319061502140315021 70A150412031
50418071205130412051607120315041203190615021403150217
06150412031504 1B071205130412051607120315041203180615 0
21403150217 0A15041203150419071205130412051607120315 0
412031806150214031502170615041203150

10. REFERENCES

[1] Abbott, H. L. and Katchalski, M., On the construction of snake in the box codes, *Utilitas Mathematica*, 40, (1991), 97–116.

[2] Carlson, B. P. and Hougen, D. F., Phenotype feedback genetic algorithm operators for heuristic encoding of snakes within hypercubes, in *Proceedings of GECCO'10, Portland, Oregon, ACM*, (2010), 791–798.

[3] Casella, D. and Potter, W., New lower bounds for the snake-in-the-box problem: Using evolutionary techniques to hunt for snakes and coils, in *Proceedings of the Florida Artificial Intelligence Research Society Conference*, (2005).

[4] Douglas, R. D., Some Result on the Maximum Length of Circuits of Spread K in the d-Cube, *Journal of Combinatorial Theory 6*, (1969), 323-339.

[5] Hiltgen, A. P. and Paterson, K. G., Single-track circuit codes, IEEE Transactions on Information Theory, 47, (2000), 2587–2595.

[6] Hood, S., Recoskie, D., Sawada, J., and Wong, C., Snakes, coils, and single-track circuit codes with spread k, *Journal of Combinatorial Optimization* (May 2013).

[7] Kautz, W. H., 'Unit-distance error-checking codes'. *IRE Trans Electronic Computers*, (1958), 179–180,.

[8] Kinny, D., A New Approach to the Snake-In-The-Box Problem, *European Conference on Artificial Intelligence (ECAI)*, (2012).

[9] Klee, V., The use of circuit codes in analog-to-digital conversion. In *Graph Theory and its Applications. B. Harris, Ed. New York: Academic*, (1970).

[10] Kochut, J., Snake-in-the-box codes for dimension 7, *Combinatorial Mathematics and Combinatorial Computations*, 20, (1996), 175–185.

[11] Livingston, M. and Stout, Q. Distributed resources in hypercube computers. In *Proceedings 3rd Conference on Hypercube Concurrent Computers and Applications*, ACM, (1988), 222-231.

[12] Paterson, K. G. and Tuliani, J. Some new circuit codes, *IEEE Transactions on Information Theory*, 44(3), (May 1998), 1305–1309.

[13] Potter, W., Robinson, R., Miller, J., Kochut, K., and Redys, D. Using the genetic algorithm to find snake-in-the-box codes. In *Proceedings of the 7th International Conference on Industrial & Engineering Applications of Artificial Intelligence and Expert Systems*, (1994) 307-314.

[14] Rajan, D. and Shende, A. Maximal and reversible snakes in hypercubes. *24th Annual Australasian Conference on Combinatorial Mathematics and Combinatorial Computation*, 1999.

[15] Wynn, E., Constructing circuit codes by permuting initial sequences, *arXiv:1201.1647v*, (Jan. 2012).

[16] Yehezkeally. Y., and Schwartz, M., Snake-in-the-box codes for rank modulation, (2011). Available at http://arxiv.org/abs/1107.3372

[17] Zinovik, I., Chebiryak, Y. and Kroening, D., Periodic orbits and equilibria in glass models for gene regulatory networks, *IEEE Transactions on Information Theory*, 56(2), (Feb 2010), 805–820.

Feedback Control for Multi-modal Optimization using Genetic Algorithms

Jun Shi
Carnegie Mellon University
Pittsburgh, PA
jshi1@andrew.cmu.edu

Ole J. Mengshoel
Carnegie Mellon University
Moffett Field, CA
ole.mengshoel@sv.cmu.edu

Dipan K. Pal
Carnegie Mellon University
Pittsburgh, PA
dipanp@andrew.cmu.edu

ABSTRACT

Many optimization problems are multi-modal. In certain cases, we are interested in finding multiple locally optimal solutions rather than just a single optimum as is computed by traditional genetic algorithms (GAs). Several niching techniques have been developed that seek to find multiple such local optima. These techniques, which include sharing and crowding, are clearly powerful and useful. But they do not explicitly let the user control the number of local optima being computed, which we believe to be an important capability.

In this paper, we develop a method that provides, as an input parameter to niching, the desired number of local optima. Our method integrates techniques from feedback control, includes a sensor based on clustering, and utilizes a scaling parameter in Generalized Crowding to control the number of niches being explored. The resulting Feedback Control GA (FCGA) is tested in several experiments and found to perform well compared to previous approaches. Overall, the integration of feedback control and Generalized Crowding is shown to effectively guide the search for multiple local optima in a more controlled fashion. We believe this novel capability has the potential to impact future applications as well as other evolutionary algorithms.

Categories and Subject Descriptors

G.3 [**Probability and Statistics**]: Markov Processes, Probabilistic algorithms including Monte-Carlo; I.2.8 [**Artificial Intelligence**]: Problem Solving, Control methods, Search methods—*Heuristic methods*

Keywords

FCGA; Genetic Algorithms; Generalized Crowding; Feedback Control; Multi-modal Optimization

GECCO'14, July 12–16, 2014, Vancouver, BC, Canada.

ACM 978-1-4503-2662-9/14/07$15.00.
http://dx.doi.org/10.1145/2576768.2598231.

1. INTRODUCTION

Multi-modal problems have multiple local optima in their solution landscape. In many cases it is desirable to obtain multiple distinct and locally optimal solutions to such problems. One reason for such a requirement is that some of the local optima may be surrounded by a steep fitness landscape, while other local optima may not be. The latter case might be preferred if a more stable solution is needed. Obtaining multiple solutions is also useful in situations where there is considerable uncertainty about the fitness function or important problem aspects are not fully captured in it.

Different niching techniques including sharing and crowding have been developed to converge to multiple solutions [1, 2, 3, 4, 5]. Based on Deterministic [1] and Probabilistic Crowding [6], a new Generalized Crowding method which integrates these two original ideas has been developed [5]. A so-called *scaling factor* is the key parameter in Generalized Crowing which allows us to simulate both Deterministic and Probabilistic Crowding. The existence of a scaling factor of course raises the question of designing schedules for varying it. Recently, several schedules have been investigated including a constant schedule; an exponentially-decaying schedule; a diversity-adaptive schedule based on population entropy; and a self-adaptive schedule [5, 7]. Although these approaches work well, there is no explicit control of the number of local optima, multiple distinct solutions, or niches explored or found.

More broadly, investigating the trade-off between exploration and exploitation is one of the central themes of evolutionary algorithms (EAs). In particular, exploration is emphasized in niching techniques, where the goal is to improve diversity or increase the number of local optima explored. Surprisingly, to the best of our knowledge, the literature has not discussed how to directly control the number of local optima found by niching algorithms. In this paper, we investigate this problem.

Specifically, we use the desired number of distinct niches (number of local optima) to be explored as the set-point in a feedback control loop. This enables the user to directly control, using the set-point, the number of niches explored in a Feedback Computing GA (FCGA) run. A set-point represents external constraints associated with a user or a computational process using an FCGA. In other words, the set-point may not have anything to do with the number of local optima in the fitness function, as long as we make the reasonable assumption that the set-point is less than or equal to the number of local optima.

Before summarizing our approach, we highlight a few situations in which better user control of the number of local optima, through a set-point, promises to be powerful:

- It might be useful in a design process to create diverse physical prototypes of candidate solutions. Clearly, there might exist time and budget constraints for developing such prototypes (e.g. 3D printing). In this case, the FCGA set-point would be the number of distinct physical prototypes to be created.
- When software is evolved, one might require that the candidate solutions be tested extensively. While running computer programs might seem relatively inexpensive, there are always time and budget constraints given the complexity often found in software. In this case, the FCGA set-point would be the number of distinct software prototypes to be evolved.
- A computer screen may visualize candidate solutions being evolved, for example for the purpose of interactive design of shapes [8] or interactive optimization of robot controllers [9]. In this case, the user's FCGA set-point would be the number of diverse shapes or robot controllers that can be meaningfully visualized.

In this paper, we consider applying feedback control on the scaling factor ϕ in Generalized Crowding to better achieve the desired number of locally optimal solutions as defined by the user. We apply simple proportional control, and analyze the impact of control parameters and also compare the resulting performance with existing scaling factor schedules.

The rest of this paper is organized as follows. In Section 2, related research on crowding, self-adaptation, and feedback computing is discussed. Section 3 presents our feedback control approach to EAs, the Feedback Control GA, and defines the components of the control loop in a GA context. In Section 4, we present experimental results for several test functions. Finally, we conclude with Section 5 and outline future research directions.

2. RELATED RESEARCH

2.1 Niching Techniques

Niching techniques in Evolutionary Algorithms (EAs) are often motivated by multi-modality in the objective function. Niching techniques include sharing [10] and crowding [11, 1, 6, 5]. Crowding, which we focus on in this paper, was introduced as a technique for preserving population diversity [11]. It is perhaps interesting to consider the mechanism of crowding using a biological perspective. Even when the whole population is derived from the same species, individuals mostly compete with each other within a niche. This results in the preservation of sub-populations in distinct niches, corresponding to local optima and their neighborhoods in the fitness function.

Technically, crowding techniques are applied in the survival stage of GAs. There are two phases in the crowding process: The Grouping Phase, used to pair up individuals according to a similarity metric, and the Replacement Phase, in which competitions are held within each pair to decide the winner [4]. In most crowding approaches the similarity metric used is genotypic distance.

The replacement rule plays an important role in crowding. Depending on how replacement is performed, several rules have been identified, including Deterministic Crowding [1] and Probabilistic Crowding [6]. Deterministic Crowding is an exploitative replacement rule since the winner of a competition is always the one with a higher fitness [1]. One shortcoming of Deterministic Crowding, however, is that it may lead to premature convergence. In Probabilistic Crowding, an individual wins a competition with a probability proportional to its fitness. This approach is more exploratory than Deterministic Crowding, but similar to Deterministic Crowding the selection pressure is not adaptive.

Subsequently, these two techniques were generalized by introduced a scaling factor ϕ, creating *Generalized Crowding* [5]. In Generalized Crowding the exploration-exploitation trade-off is parametrized through ϕ. This is similar, to some extent, to the use of temperature in simulated annealing [12, 13]. Intuitively, high temperature and high scaling factor give exploration, while low temperature and low scaling factor give exploitation. A key difference between simulated annealing and Generalized Crowding is that the latter is a population-oriented technique, while the former is not. Generalized Crowding and other EAs thus lend themselves more naturally to multi-modal optimization.

2.2 Adaptation and Self-adaptation

The idea of self-adaptation, including self-adaptive parameter control, has been extensively performed by EAs. Evolution strategies [14, 15] self-adapts the mutation step sizes throughout the search process. Mutation [16] as well as crossover rates [17] have been self-adapted. Generalized Crowding has been augmented with diversity-adaptive and self-adaptive methods [7]. In diversity-adaptive Generalized Crowding, the scaling factor ϕ is changed according to population diversity. In self-adaptive Generalized Crowding, ϕ is added to the chromosome, and undergoes crossover, mutation, and selection along with it.

2.3 Feedback Computing

Feedback control, both theory and practice, has traditionally been applied to physical systems governed by Newtonian mechanics. More recently, feedback control is starting to be applied to computing hardware and software; this is known as feedback computing [18]. Examples of feedback computing include: control of HTTP servers [19, 20], email servers [21], quality of service assurance [22], and Internet traffic control [23]. While computing systems are clearly different from traditional feedback control applications, many techniques have carried over.

3. FEEDBACK COMPUTING GA (FCGA)

Although the various crowding techniques and their corresponding replacement rules have been proven to work well with multi-modal optimization problems, one drawback is that they provide no direct user control over the number of niches (or local optima) being explored. We seek to attack this problem by adopting techniques from feedback control. Our novel idea of integrating feedback control with evolutionary computation is illustrated in Figure 1. Crucially, the user now has direct control over a set-point $r(t)$. This set-point represents how many niches, with local and diverse optima, a user wants to find using the GA.

We call this feedback computing pattern, where the computational process is a GA operating on a population $\pi(t)$ at time $t \geq 0$, a Feedback Control GA (FCGA). Similar

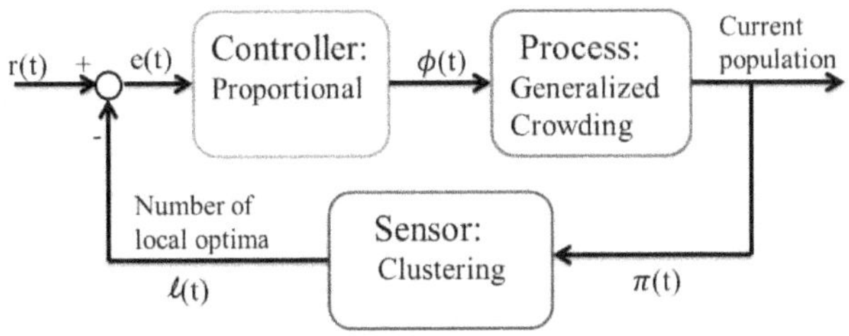

Figure 1: Feedback control loop of the Feedback Computing GA (FCGA) with a Generalized Crowding GA as the *process*. A proportional *controller* is used, while clustering is used as a *sensor*.

to more traditional feedback control loops, there are three important components.

- **Process** $P : \phi(t) \times \pi(t-1) \rightarrow \pi(t)$. The process to be controlled is a GA, currently a Generalized Crowding GA. The (multi-modal) fitness function f and the population $\pi(t)$ are also part of this computational process. The population consists of M individuals $\pi(t) = (\pi_1(t), \pi_2(t), ..., \pi_M(t))$.
- **Sensor** $S : \pi(t) \rightarrow l(t)$. The objective of the sensor is to measure the current process status. In our case, the number of niches (or local optima) in the current population is the statistic $l(t)$ to be sensed. This number is then sent to the controller.
- **Controller** $C : e(t) \rightarrow \phi(t)$. The controller is a mathematical function that maps the error $e(t)$ between the current number of local optima $l(t)$ and the set-point $r(t)$ to the scaling factor $\phi(t)$. The controller sends a signal to manipulate the GA process by adjusting the scaling factor $\phi(t)$. We use $r(t)$ to capture potential variation of the set-point through time t, however, it might be kept constant $r(t) = r$.

Now, we discuss the **Process**, the **Sensor**, and the **Controller** in more detail.

3.1 Process: Generalized Crowding

Various methods have been developed to avoid premature convergence in GAs and to find multiple solutions. Crowding is one such method developed by De Jong [11] and later modified by Mahfoud [1]. Crowding attempts to prevent premature convergence to a single local optimum by trying to distribute individuals across niches. Generalized Crowding introduces a scaling factor ϕ [5], which is the "knob" being controlled in FCGA.

The replacement rule for Generalized Crowding is expressed as follows. Assume that parent $p \in \pi(t)$ and child $c \in \pi(t)$ are paired in the grouping phase. Let $f(c)$ and $f(p)$ be the fitness of the child and the parent, respectively. We let P_c be the probability that child c replaces parent p:

$$P_c = \begin{cases} \frac{f(c)}{f(c)+\phi \times f(p)} & \text{if } f(c) > f(p) \\ 0.5 & \text{if f(c)=f(p)} \\ \frac{\phi \times f(c)}{\phi \times f(c)+f(p)} & \text{if } f(c) < f(p). \end{cases}$$

Putting $\phi = 0$ results in Deterministic Crowding, which mostly exploits the niches already found and does not usually result in the discovery of new niches. On the other hand, putting $\phi = 1$ results in Probabilistic Crowding which is biased more towards exploration and finding new niches. Using $0 < \phi < 1$ allows for a combination of such effects while $\phi > 1$ provides even more exploration than Probabilistic Crowding does.

A larger scaling factor ϕ leads to a greater probability of the less fit individual surviving a competition, on average. This results in more extensive exploration of less fit parts of the search space, including less-fit niches. Control over the scaling factor ϕ enables FCGA to *dynamically vary* the balance between exploration and exploitation. In FCGA, a time index $t \geq 0$ is added to ϕ, and $\phi(t)$ is varied by FCGA's controller.

3.2 Sensor: Clustering

A key component of the FCGA control loop is a reliable sensor. An unreliable sensor would make incorrect estimates of the current process status, which may mislead the controller to make poor adjustments to $\phi(t)$. The statistic that we would like to sense from the population is the number of local optima explored (niches). Hence, a natural way to arrive at such a sensor would be to employ a clustering algorithm.

Clustering solves the problem of finding clusters in a set of data points, given an assumption about the number of clusters. Specifically, the k-means clustering algorithm requires as input the number of clusters $k(t)$. The algorithm therefore does not directly solve our problem, namely estimating the number of sub-populations $l(t)$ in $\pi(t)$. However, there are methods to use a clustering algorithm, such as k-means, to estimate the number of clusters. One such method, which we use in this paper, is to find $l(t)$ through estimating the change in the k-means objective function (see below).

Since FCGA calls the clustering algorithm multiple times during each FCGA generation, we need clustering to be computationally efficient. This justifies our use of k-means clustering, which is linear in the number of data points in each iteration, as the basis for our sensor. The pseudo-code for clustering using k-means in the context of a GA population is presented as follows:

- **Given**: GA population $\pi(t)$ and the number of clusters $k(t)$.
- **Initialize**: Use random initialization, and then compute and store $k(t)$ centriods.
- **Iterate**: While there exists an individual $(\pi_i(t))$ which is not well clustered (an individual is closest to a cluster centroid to which it does not currently belong):
  - Reassign the mis-classified individual to its nearest cluster centroid
  - Recalculate the centroid of each cluster
- **Output**: Population $\pi(t)$ partitioned into $k(t)$ clusters.

We now describe the algorithm used in FCGA to estimate $l(t)$ using k-means. k-means minimizes an objective function (within-cluster sum-of-squares) for a given k. Thus, one can specify different k and measure the objective function. As we increase k, we would see a decrease in the objective function since we allow for greater model complexity. Now, when k approaches the "correct" number of clusters, the objective function might observe a sharp decrease for well-defined clusters. The decrease is much smaller after this point, since adding more complexity does not help as the data is well-clustered using a smaller k. Using Occam's razor, the smallest k after the drop in the k-means objective function is chosen as the estimate for $l(t)$ for the tth generation.[1]

3.3 Controller: Proportional Control

Inspired by the successful integration of adaptive control and feedback control with Bayesian network computation [26, 27], FCGA uses a simple Proportional-Integral-Derivative (PID) controller. The PID controlled is arguably the most widely used controller in industrial applications due to it being simple and well-suited in most situations. Although it has problems in dealing with non-linear systems and obtaining optimal control strategies, its advantages often dominate. Furthermore, the process to be controlled in our study is hard to model. Thus, another reason to use a proportional controller is that it can work without an explicit model of the process.

In our FCGA method using Generalized Crowding, we explore a simplified application of PID control. The parameter that we control in Generalized Crowding is the scaling factor ϕ, which has a direct impact on the exploration/exploitation trade-off. If we desire to increase the number of niches (local optima) found, we would desire a higher ϕ whereas in order to decrease the number of niches, we would decrease ϕ. This leads us to the following control strategy:

$$\Delta\phi(t) = \begin{cases} \gamma(r(t) - l(t)) & \text{if } l(t) \neq r(t) \\ 0 & \text{if } l(t) = r(t) \end{cases}$$

for some $\gamma > 0$, which we call the *control rate*. Although there exist analytical methods to determine γ, their application to the case in which the process is a Generalized Crowding GA is non-trivial. Thus we have explored a range of values for γ, optimizing it empirically (see Table 2).

FCGA currently uses proportional control to adjust the scaling factor based on the difference between the current number of clusters $l(t)$ and the set-point $r(t)$:

$$\phi(t+1) = \phi(t) + \Delta\phi(t).$$

There are three cases possibly needing control:

- $l(t) < r(t)$: In this case, the current number of niches $l(t)$ is less than desired and therefore we need to explore more niches. Thus we *increase* the scaling factor $\phi(t)$ proportional to the error $e(t) = r(t) - l(t) > 0$, to enable more exploration and less exploitation.
- $l(t) = r(t)$: When the current number of niches equals its set-point, we keep the scaling factor *constant* at its current value.
- $l(t) > r(t)$: In this case, the current number of niches $l(t)$ is greater than desired and therefore we need to lose some niches. Thus we *decrease* the scaling factor $\phi(t)$ proportional to the error $e(t) = r(t) - l(t) < 0$, to enable less exploration and more exploitation.

[1]There are alternative methods for estimating the number of clusters, such as X-means [24] and G-means [25]. A detailed study of these methods versus our method of estimating k through a change in the objective function is left for future research.

Table 1: Parameters used for FCGA experiments unless specified otherwise. Bold indicates defaults.

GA parameter	Value
Population size	$M \in \{25, \mathbf{100}, 400\}$
Mating	Random
Crossover (Uniform)	$P_c = 1$
Mutation (Uniform)	$P_m \in \{0.0125, 0.025, \mathbf{0.3}\}$
Survivor Selection	Generational
Scaling Parameter	Initially $\phi = 1$
Generations per run	$G = 500$
Number of runs	$N = 100$
Control rate	$\gamma \in \{0.1, \mathbf{1}, 10, 100\}$

3.4 Discussion

The idea of integrating feedback control and computing, or feedback computing, is not new [18]. However, we believe that feedback computing for the purpose of controlling an EA process—which is what we do in this paper—is new. We hypothesize that this amalgamation of evolutionary algorithms, feedback computing, and clustering can potentially bring substantial benefit to multi-modal optimization by means of genetic algorithms. While multi-modal optimization using genetic algorithms is well-established, it has so far lacked the capability of controlling the number of local optima being searched for by the algorithm. In hindsight, this appears to be a small but crucial limitation of previous work, since the number of local optima as well as the local optima themselves are of considerable interest to the EA user. Our introduction of a desired number of niches or local optima (a high-level parameter) as a set-point in a feedback control loop is key, and distinguishes the present work from previous efforts.

4. EXPERIMENTAL RESULTS

In this section, we present experimental results using the FCGA with Generalized Crowding. Our aim is to validate the behavior of FCGA when faced with the problem of achieving a user's desired number of niches in the population. Before discussing experimental results, we present the experimental setting, test functions, and metrics that we use for evaluation.

4.1 Experimental Setting

For all experiments, we simulate 100 runs of all GAs. For FCGA we explore different set-points $r(t)$ to illustrate the versatility of the algorithm. For each experiment, we look at the mean number of niches present in the population as generations progress. Further, unless specified otherwise, the initial scaling factor ϕ for FCGA is set to 1. Table 1 showcases the GA parameters that are used in all experiments unless specified otherwise. Generally, these values are close to those used in previous studies [4, 7].

4.2 Fitness Functions

Experiments are concerned with maximizing multi-modal fitness functions. We consider m-dimensional real-valued[2] fitness functions $f : \mathbb{R}^m \to \mathbb{R}$. Normalized versions of the 1D functions we use are shown in Figure 2. Both functions

[2]For the GA implementation used in all experiments in this paper, we use Java doubles to represent reals in $\mathbb{R}$. Doubles are 64-bit double precision floats that follow the IEEE 754 standard. This is the highest precision available in Java.

are representative of multi-modal problems. They also enable comparison as they have been used in several previous studies. Note that we add 1000 to the Schwefel function to make it positive for the range we focus on.

We also experiment with the 2D version of the Schwefel function:

$$f(x, y) = x \sin(\sqrt{|x|}) + y \sin(\sqrt{|y|}) + 2000,$$

where $x, y \in [-500, 500]$.

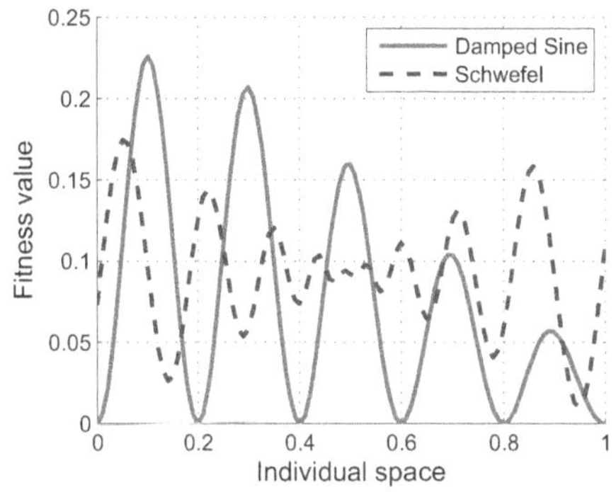

Figure 2: Normalized versions of the 1D Damped Sine function $f(x) = e^{-2(ln2)(\frac{x-0.1}{0.8})^2} \sin^6 5\pi x$ and the Schwefel function $f(x) = x \sin(\sqrt{|x|}) + 1000$.

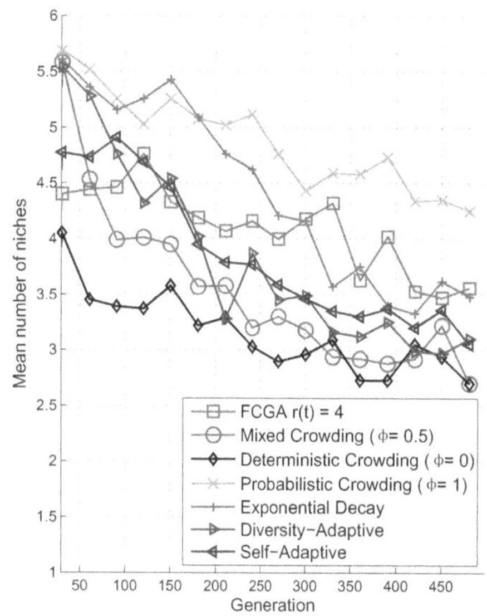

Figure 4: Mean number of niches for different algorithms on the 2-dimensional Schwefel function ($P_m = 0.3$ and $\gamma = 1$).

4.3 Metrics

It is desirable to not only find the required number of niches but also to have the most fit solutions as evaluated by the fitness function f. In order to measure the overall quality of solutions, we report a statistic which is computed by dividing the mean of the sum total fitness of the best fit individuals in each desired niche (say, the top $r(t)$ niches) over all runs by the ideal value. The ideal value for some $r(t)$ is the total optimal fitness value attainable within the best $r(t)$ number of niches. This statistic, which we term the *Solution Quality Coefficient* (*SQC*), lies between 0 and 1, and would ideally be 1. If the complete search space is denoted by Ω, then $\Omega = \bigcup_{i=1}^{Z} \omega_i, \forall i = 1, ..., Z$, where ω_i is the ith partition of Ω (i^{th} niche) such that each ω_i contains just one local optimum of fitness f_i. If $\{\omega_j | j = 1, ..., \lambda\}$ is the set of partitions of Ω containing the top $r(t)$ local optima as measured by the fitness function, then $\{f_j | j = 1, ..., \lambda\}$ is the set of the corresponding fitness values. Further, $\left\{\widehat{f}_j | j = 1, ..., \lambda\right\}$ is the set of the fitness values for the solutions found in each of $\{\omega_j | j = 1, ..., \lambda\}$. Then for set-point $r(t)$, SQC=mean($\sum_{j=1}^{\lambda} \widehat{f}_j / \sum_{j=1}^{\lambda} f_j$), with the mean taken over the individual SQC values of all runs. Note that this does not measure any statistic of non-desired niches and that this SQC metric changes as we change the set-point.

We use another metric to effectively measure the total deviation of the number of niches from the set-point. We term this metric ρ, and define it as $\rho = \sum_{i=1}^{N} (W(i) - r(t))^2$, where $W(i)$ is the number of niches present at the end of the ith run out of the N runs. A low ρ signifies that the distribution of niches present in the population over multiple runs is not only sharp but is actually close to the desired ideal distribution as expressed by the set-point.

4.4 Feedback Control for Crowding

In this experiment, we develop a broader understanding of FCGA. We explore $r(t) = 3$ and $r(t) = 5$ for the Damped Sine function, and for the Schwefel function we set $r(t) = 2$ and $r(t) = 4$. We choose these set-points so that other algorithms do not converge to this many niches on average. This illustrates the control that we introduce in FCGA.

Varying Control Rate: We first vary γ to study its effect on the behavior of FCGA for the Damped Sine function. The left part of Table 2 shows the SQC values for feedback control on every generation. While SQC values vary along with generations, we always report the SQC value at the end of the run (for the last generation). We also report the standard deviation of the number of niches across the end of the 100 runs. A lower deviation reflects a better control through a sharper distribution of the number of niches. However, this statistic does not measure how close the distribution is to the desired $r(t)$ which is measured by ρ. Figure 3 showcases a number of scaling factor schedules affecting the number of niches as generations progress. We see that reasonable control of the actual number of niches is only possible with FCGA, wherein the mean number of niches present in the population closely matches the set-point $r(t)$.

Here we briefly examine the effect of varying γ-values on the convergence towards the set-point for feedback control. We choose to focus on the Damped Sine function for this study and vary the control rate γ through 0.1, 1, 10 and 100 for the set-points $r(t) = 3$ and $r(t) = 5$. Figure 5 shows the results for this study. Generally, the converge properties are not very different for the different γ-values, while $\gamma = 0.1$

	SQC: Control every generation								SQC: Control every 5th generation							
	$\gamma = 0.1$		$\gamma = 1$		$\gamma = 10$		$\gamma = 100$		$\gamma = 0.1$		$\gamma = 1$		$\gamma = 10$		$\gamma = 100$	
r	μ	σ	μ	σ	μ	σ	μ	σ	μ	σ	μ	σ	μ	σ	μ	σ
3	0.94	0.53	0.95	0.83	0.79	1.25	0.59	1.56	0.95	0.69	0.94	0.85	0.70	1.18	0.61	1.39
5	0.92	1.57	0.85	2.13	0.77	2.44	0.74	2.34	0.95	0.82	0.89	1.72	0.86	2.23	0.80	2.15

Table 2: Mean μ and standard deviation σ of measured SQC values for FCGA with control on every generation (left in table) or every five generations (right in table) for the Damped Sine function. This is for varying setpoints r and control rates γ with $P_m = 0.3$.

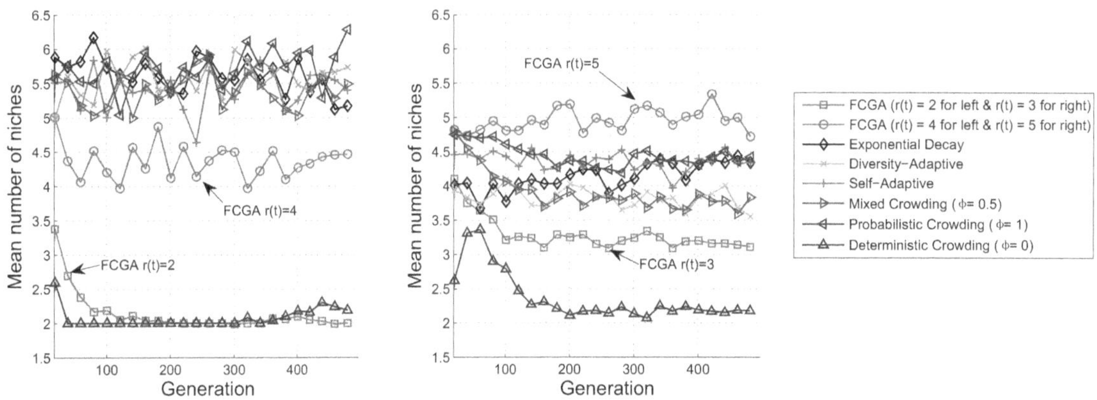

Figure 3: Mean number of niches for different algorithms evaluated on the 1D Schwefel function (left) and the 1D Damped Sine function (right). FCGA, using varying $r(t)$, allows us to converge to a desired number of niches, making the algorithm more versatile than previous niching methods ($P_m = 0.3$ and $\gamma = 1$).

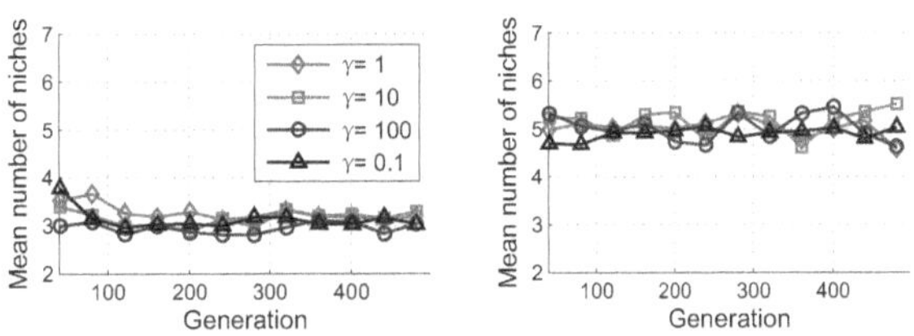

(a) $r(t) = 3$ (b) $r(t) = 5$

Figure 5: Effect of varying γ on FCGA's performance using different set-points $r(t)$ for the Damped Sine function ($P_m = 0.3$ and $\gamma = 1$).

and $\gamma = 1$ perform the best overall as measured by the SQC in the left part of Table 2.

Immediate versus Delayed Control: Since GAs are inherently stochastic, once we change the scaling factor ϕ, the effects in the population might not be immediate. In fact, it might take a few generations to reflect change, during which time an estimate $l(t)$ would not be very accurate since the population would have "not settled" in distinct clusters after the last change. In order to compensate, we explore a minimal gap of $t_{\min}$ generations between each control attempt. A control attempt is estimation of $l(t)$, using k-means clustering, followed by a potential change in $\phi(t)$.

We now briefly explore the effect of immediate control versus delayed control. In immediate control, control attempts are made on every generation and in delayed control, they are made more sparingly. In this study, we examine $t_{\min} =$ 0 (immediate control) and $t_{\min} = 5$ (delayed control). We set γ=1 for this experiment. Figure 6 shows the mean number of niches for the two cases. Table 2 shows results where also γ is varied. Overall, varying γ has a bigger impact than varying $t_{\min}$, and using $\gamma = 0.1$ or $\gamma = 1$ is reasonable for both immediate and delayed control.

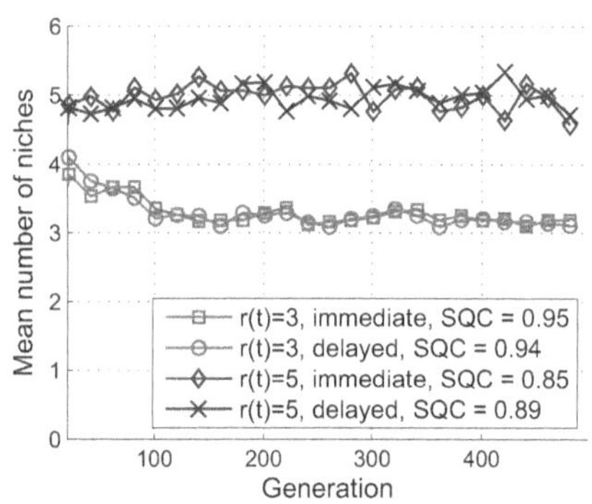

Figure 6: Effect of control attempts at every generation (immediate control) versus every 5th generation (delayed control) for FCGA, using varying $r(t)$, on the Damped Sine function. SQC is reported for the last generation ($P_m = 0.3$ and $\gamma = 1$).

4.5 Varying GA Parameters

We now conduct a study of the effect of varying the population size M and the mutation rate P_m when FCGA eval-

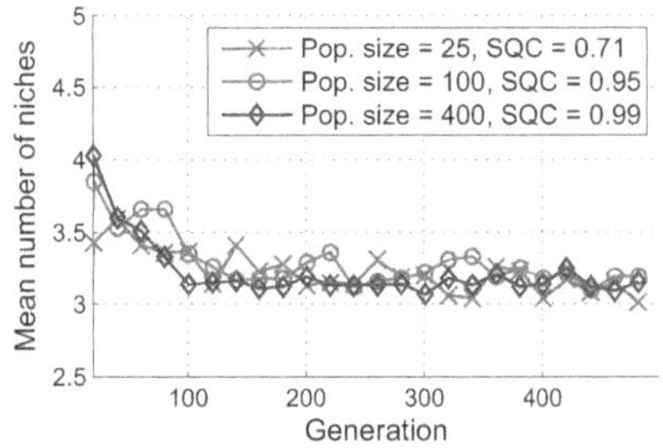

Figure 7: Effect of varying the size of the GA population on FCGA for the 1D Damped Sine function. SQC value is reported for the last generation ($P_m = 0.3$ and $\gamma = 1$).

uates the Damped Sine function. We examine population sizes $M \in \{25, 100, 400\}$ and mutation probabilities $P_m \in \{0.0125, 0.025, 0.3\}$ while keeping $r(t) = 3$ and $\gamma = 1$. Figure 7 and Table 3 show the results of these studies. While using a larger population has a higher computational cost, it seems to provide better solutions in terms of SQC, as expected. Regarding varying the mutation probability P_m, we observe in Table 3 that FCGA performs competitively over a broad range of mutation probabilities.

4.6 Changing the Set-point Mid-run

We now investigate the impact of a mid-run change of the FCGA set-point. In particular, we change $r(t) = 3$ to $r(t) = 5$ at $t = 500$ generations while keeping $\gamma = 1$. Figure 8 shows how changing the set-point $r(t)$ mid-run has a drastic and desired effect on the number of niches in the population. This experiment validates that the PID controller works, at least in this case.

In addition, this experiment illustrates an FCGA user's meaningful control over the exploitation/exploration tradeoff through the set-point $r(t)$. Such control is not offered by previous niching methods when applied to multi-modal optimization. A use case for such a mid-run change is when an FCGA user wants to see a larger (and more diverse) set of candidate solutions starting at $t = 500$.

4.7 Different Scaling Factor Schedules

We now experiment with different scaling factor schedules. The schedules that we compare against FCGA are the following. **Fixed Generalized Crowding** [5] uses a constant scaling factor ϕ. For $\phi = 0$ this becomes Deterministic Crowding and for $\phi = 1$ it becomes Probabilistic Crowding. We also experiment with $\phi = 0.5$ (Mixed Crowding). **Exponentially-Decaying Scaling** decreases the scaling factor, following an exponentially decaying function [7]. **Diversity-Adaptive Scaling** is a scheme where the population entropy is computed and the scaling factor is varied accordingly [7]. **Self-Adaptive Scaling** embeds the scaling factor in each individual's chromosome and the GA changes it adaptively in each generation [7].

We run all schedules with 100 individuals for 500 generations. Only for FCGA do we expect to see a change in the mean number of niches in response to a change in the set-point. Figure 3 shows the mean number of niches for multiple scaling factor schedules for the 1D Damped Sine

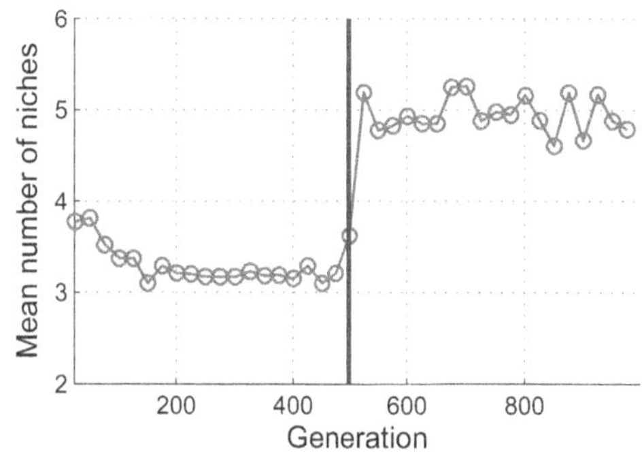

Figure 8: Effect of changing the set-point, at generation $t = 500$, from $r(t) = 3$ to $r(t) = 5$ on FCGA for the 1D Damped Sine function. The vertical line signifies the point of the set-point change ($P_m = 0.3$ and $\gamma = 1$).

and the Schwefel functions. Figure 4 showcases the means for the same scaling factor schedules for the 2D Schwefel function. As we see, all schedules other than FCGA seem to converge to an arbitrary mean number of niches. On the other hand, FCGA is able to converge quite reliably to the user defined set-point $r(t)$. Thus, FCGA allows us to have reasonable control over the number of niches, which opens up a new dimension in versatility for GAs.

Table 4 shows the run statistics for the 1D Damped Sine and Schwefel functions. For FCGA, we used the control loop at every 5th generation with $\gamma = 0.1$ and ϕ was initialized at 1 for the comparison. For the Damped Sine function in Table 4, we find that feedback control performs the best for $r(t) = 5$. For $r(t) = 3$, it performs very competitively while keeping the number of niches very close to the set-point. For the Schwefel function in Table 4, we see that FCGA performs the best overall for $r(t) = 2$, however, the Schwefel function presents a more challenging scenario for $r(t) = 4$. Here we see that though FCGA returns a lower SQC, it provides a better distribution of niches close to that defined by $r(t)$ as seen by ρ being relatively smaller. Even though Deterministic Crowding seems to obtain a more ideal distribution (a lower ρ), it fails at achieving a high SQC.

5. CONCLUSION AND FUTURE WORK

This paper formulates and develops a Feedback Control GA (FCGA) with Generalized Crowding as the GA. The FCGA algorithm is used to better control the number of niches that a user wants the GA to explore. Thus, the algorithm is able to allocate more resources to exploring desired niches, resulting in a higher-quality and more directed search. The FCGA sensor is designed using k-means clustering while the controller uses proportional control. In experiments, FCGA reliably controls the number of niches and finds high-quality solutions as evaluated by the fitness function.

This work brings to the table many questions which we leave for further investigation. One of the key steps in FCGA is using k-means to determine the number of niches in the population. However, determining the "optimal" number of clusters in a population is still an active area of research

	Control every generation						Control every 5th generation					
	$P_m = 0.0125$		$P_m = 0.025$		$P_m = 0.3$		$P_m = 0.0125$		$P_m = 0.025$		$P_m = 0.3$	
r	μ	σ	μ	σ	μ	σ	μ	σ	μ	σ	μ	σ
3	0.98	1.18	0.98	0.98	0.95	0.83	0.96	1.09	0.99	1.08	0.94	0.85
5	0.90	1.75	0.95	1.60	0.85	2.13	0.92	1.32	0.95	1.28	0.89	1.72

Table 3: Mean μ and standard deviation σ of measured SQC values for FCGA with control on every generation (left in table) or every five generations (right in table) for the 1D Damped Sine function for varying values of P_m and r; here $\gamma = 1$.

	Damped Sine Function						Schwefel Function					
	Setpoint $r(t) = 3$			Setpoint $r(t) = 5$			Setpoint $r(t) = 2$			Setpoint $r(t) = 4$		
Schedule	SQC	σ	ρ	SQC	σ	ρ	SQC	σ	ρ	SQC	σ	ρ
FCGA ($r(t)$ varies)	0.95	0.69	6.92	0.95	0.82	8.24	1.00	0.40	4.00	0.75	2.38	23.91
Exponential Decay	0.87	1.33	18.08	0.85	1.33	15.32	0.98	2.66	44.77	0.82	2.66	31.00
Self-Adaptive	0.90	1.22	17.83	0.88	1.22	14.07	0.99	2.76	42.52	0.82	2.76	30.19
Diversity Adaptive	0.83	1.39	17.94	0.81	1.39	16.03	0.96	2.64	43.10	0.80	2.64	32.26
Deterministic Crowding	0.38	0.92	11.61	0.30	0.92	28.61	1.00	0.81	8.18	0.54	0.81	20.37
$\phi = 0.5$	0.99	0.89	12.00	0.75	0.89	14.96	0.98	2.85	43.78	0.81	2.85	31.38
Probabilistic Crowding	0.98	1.16	18.16	0.92	1.16	13.03	0.93	2.64	44.66	0.83	2.64	30.83

Table 4: Experimental results for different scaling factor schedules, including FCGA with varying setpoints, for the Damped Sine and Schwefel functions ($P_m = 0.3$ and $\gamma = 1$).

in machine learning. Also, although we show that the simple approach of proportional control works reasonably well, more sophisticated control schemes might bring substantial improvements. Further improvements can only help make FCGA more effective as a multi-modal optimization scheme. Finally, interesting results are expected from having setpoints for parameters other than the number of niches and also exploring the control perspective for evolutionary algorithms other than crowding.

6. REFERENCES

[1] S. W. Mahfoud. Crowding and preselection revisited. In *Parallel Problem Solving from Nature 2 (PPSN-II)*, pages 27–36. Elsevier, 1992.

[2] G. R. Harik. Finding multimodal solutions using restricted tournament selection. In *Proc. of the 6th International Conference on Genetic Algorithms*, ICGA'95, pages 24–31, 1995.

[3] P. J. Ballester and J. N. Carter. Real-parameter genetic algorithms for finding multiple optimal solutions in multi-modal optimization. In *Proc. of the Genetic and Evolutionary Computation Conference*, GECCO'03, pages 706–717, 2003.

[4] O. J. Mengshoel and D. E. Goldberg. The crowding approach to niching in genetic algorithms. *Evolutionary Computation*, 16(3):315–354, 2008.

[5] S. F. Galán and O. J. Mengshoel. Generalized crowding for genetic algorithms. In *Proc. of the Genetic and Evolutionary Computation Conference 2010 (GECCO-10)*, pages 775–782, 2010.

[6] O. J. Mengshoel and D. E. Goldberg. Probabilistic crowding: Deterministic crowding with probabilistic replacement. In *Proc. of the Genetic and Evolutionary Computation Conference*, GECCO'99, pages 409–416, Orlando, FL, July 1999.

[7] O. J. Mengshoel, S. F. Galán, and A. De Dios. Adaptive generalized crowding for genetic algorithms. *Information Sciences*, 258:140–159, 2014.

[8] G. S. Hornby and J. C. Bongard. Accelerating human-computer collaborative search through learning comparative and predictive user models. In *Proc. of the 14th Annual Conference on Genetic and Evolutionary Computation*, GECCO'12, pages 225–232, 2012.

[9] J. C. Bongard and G. S. Hornby. Combining fitness-based search and user modeling in evolutionary robotics. In *Proc. of the 15th Annual Conference on Genetic and Evolutionary Computation*, GECCO'13, pages 159–166, 2013.

[10] D. E. Goldberg and L. Wang. Adaptive niching via coevolutionary sharing. *Genetic Algorithms and Evolution Strategy in Engineering and Computer Science*, pages 21–38, 1997.

[11] K. A. De Jong. *Analysis of the behavior of a class of genetic adaptive systems*. PhD thesis, University of Michigan, 1975.

[12] S. Kirkpatrick, C. D. Gelatt, and M. P. Vecchi. Optimization by simulated annealing. *Science*, 220:671–680, 1983.

[13] E. Aarts, J. Korst, and W. Michiels. Simulated annealing. In *Search Methodologies*, pages 187–210. Springer, 2005.

[14] I. Rechenberg. Evolution strategy: Natures way of optimization. In *Optimization: Methods and applications, possibilities and limitations*, pages 106–126. Springer, 1989.

[15] H.-P. Schwefel. *Numerical optimization of computer models*. John Wiley, 1981.

[16] T. Back. Self-adaptation in genetic algorithms. In *Proc. of the First European Conference on Artificial Life*, pages 263–271, 1992.

[17] S. Meyer-Nieberg and H.-G. Beyer. Self-adaptation in evolutionary algorithms. In *Parameter setting in evolutionary algorithms*, pages 47–75. Springer, 2007.

[18] J.L. Hellerstein, Y. Diao, S. Parekh, and D. M. Tilbury. *Feedback Control of Computing Systems*. Wiley, 2004.

[19] T. F. Abdelzaher and N. Bhatti. Adaptive content delivery for Web server QoS. *Compututer Networking*, 31:1563–577, 1999.

[20] Y. Diao, N. Gandhi, J. L. Hellerstein, S. Parekh, and D. M. Tilbury. Using MIMO feedback control to enforce policies for interrelated metrics with application to the Apache Web server. In *Proc. of Network Operations and Management Symposium (NOMS-02)*, pages 219–234, Florence, Italy, 2002.

[21] S. Parekh, N. Gandhi, J. Hellerstein, D. Tilbury, T. Jayram, and J. Bigus. Using control theory to achieve service level objectives in performance management. *Real-Time Systems*, 23(1/2):127–141, July 2002.

[22] C.-Z. Xu, B. Liu, and J. Wei. Model predictive feedback control for QoS assurance in webservers. *Computer*, 41:66–72, March 2008.

[23] C. Hollot, V. Misra, D. Towsley, and W. Gong. On designing improved controllers for AQM routers supporting TCP flows. In *Proc. of IEEE INFOCOM*, pages 1726–1734, 2000.

[24] D. Pelleg and A. W. Moore. X-means: Extending k-means with efficient estimation of the number of clusters. In *Proc. of the Seventeenth International Conference on Machine Learning*, ICML'00, pages 727–734, 2000.

[25] G. Hamerly and C. Elkan. Learning the k in k-means. In *Neural Information Processing Systems*, 2003.

[26] E. Reed, A. Ishihara, and O. J. Mengshoel. Adaptive control of Bayesian network computation. In *Proc. of 2012 - 5th International Symposium on Resilient Control Systems*, Salt Lake City, UT, August 2012.

[27] O. J. Mengshoel, A. Ishihara, and E. Reed. Reactive Bayesian network computation using feedback control: An empirical study. In *Proc. of BMAW-12*, Catalina Island, CA, August 2012.

A Bilevel Optimization Approach to Automated Parameter Tuning

Ankur Sinha, Pekka Malo, Peng Xu, Kalyanmoy Deb*
Department of Information and Service Economy
Aalto University School of Business
PO Box 21220, 00076 Aalto, Helsinki, Finland
Firstname.Lastname@aalto.fi

ABSTRACT

Many of the modern optimization algorithms contain a number of parameters that require tuning before the algorithm can be applied to a particular class of optimization problems. A proper choice of parameters may have a substantial effect on the accuracy and efficiency of the algorithm. Until recently, parameter tuning has mostly been performed using brute force strategies, such as grid search and random search. Guesses and insights about the algorithm are also used to find suitable parameters or suggest strategies to adjust them. More recent trends include the use of meta-optimization techniques. Most of these approaches are computationally expensive and do not scale when the number of parameters increases. In this paper, we propose that the parameter tuning problem is inherently a bilevel programming problem. Based on this insight, we introduce an evolutionary bilevel algorithm for parameter tuning. A few commonly used optimization algorithms (Differential Evolution and Nelder-Mead) have been chosen as test cases, whose parameters are tuned on a number of standard test problems. The bilevel approach is found to quickly converge towards the region of efficient parameters. The code for the proposed algorithm can be accessed from the website `http://bilevel.org`.

Categories and Subject Descriptors

G.1.6 [**Numerical Analysis**]: Optimization—*Nonlinear programming, Stochastic programming*; I.2.2 [**Artificial Intelligence**]: Automatic Programming—*Automatic analysis of algorithms*

Keywords

Bilevel optimization, evolutionary algorithms, parameter tuning, automatic algorithm configuration

1. INTRODUCTION

When conventional solution procedures fail and exhaustive search is impractical, heuristic approaches like evolutionary algorithms are often used to optimize difficult problems. Over the past few decades, such approaches have been successful in solving a number of practical optimization problems. This has led to the design and development of problem-specific evolutionary algorithms to handle problems that are otherwise difficult to solve. Most of the heuristic procedures involve parameters that often require tuning during the design and development phase. The choice of parameter values has a significant influence on the performance of the algorithms. The task is particularly challenging when the algorithm to be tuned is stochastic in nature.

Parameter tuning is a necessary step during the algorithm design phase. Though a number of strategies have been proposed, most of the techniques become computational very expensive when the number of parameters increases. Common strategies that researchers often use for parameter tuning are grid search and random search. These procedures are brute-force approaches that are applicable only when the number of parameters to be optimized is small. Researchers working on automated parameter tuning have proposed some structured search techniques based on grid search like Full factorial design [30]. Attempts have also been made towards more efficient techniques, such as model based methods [15, 34] and meta-evolutionary algorithms [17, 21]. Although considerable progress has been in this direction, there is still a significant need for more efficient strategies.

In this paper, we propose an evolutionary strategy for automated parameter tuning that can be used to tune both deterministic and stochastic optimization algorithms. The method differs from existing approaches as it draws insights from the domain of bilevel optimization. The contributions of the paper can be summarized as follows:

1. Formulating the automated parameter tuning task as a bilevel optimization problem
2. Proposing an algorithm based on bilevel optimization for automated parameter tuning
3. Suggesting a termination criterion for stochastic optimization problems.

The paper is organized as follows. In Section 2 we provide a literature survey of the parameter tuning approaches proposed in the past. We also discuss about the relevant studies on bilevel optimization. In Section 3 we provide a brief description of bilevel optimization problem. This is followed by the bilevel formulation of the parameter tuning problem in Section 4. In Section 5 we propose the algorithm based on the bilevel approach to handle parameter tuning problems. Thereafter, we create the test cases for evaluating our approach in Section 6, and provide the results of the approach in Section 7. Finally, we conclude the paper in Section 8.

*Kalyanmoy Deb is a Professor at the Department of Electrical and Computer Engineering, Michigan State University, East Lansing, MI, USA (Kdeb@egr.msu.edu).

GECCO'14, July 12–16, 2014, Vancouver, BC, Canada.
Copyright 2014 ACM 978-1-4503-2662-9/14/07 ...$15.00.
http://dx.doi.org/10.1145/2576768.2598221 .

2. PAST STUDIES

In this paper, we show that the parameter tuning problem is inherently a bilevel optimization task. Although the problem of parameter tuning has been handled as a two layer optimization task, a direct link between parameter tuning and bilevel optimization has not been established. Therefore, we highlight the past studies on parameter tuning and bilevel optimization separately. This section has been divided into two parts. In the first part, we discuss the prior research on automated parameter tuning. In the second part, we highlight some of the past studies on evolutionary bilevel optimization.

2.1 Parameter Tuning

The parameter tuning problem has been widely studied and a number of different techniques have been proposed to find suitable parameters. In this section, we provide a brief survey of these techniques. For a detailed overview, we refer the readers to a study by Eiben and Smit [14], which also provides a conceptual framework for parameter tuning along with categorizations for the existing approaches.

One of the early approaches for parameter tuning is full factorial design, which is a straightforward technique for a comprehensive search. However, due to its computational expense it is often avoided and many of the new algorithms in the domain of evolutionary computing still rely on individual parameter-wise search to obtain suitable parameters. One way to reduce the computational expense in full factorial design is Graeco-latin square [30]. In this method, a few combinations are taken in order to allow a wide exploration in the factor range. Even though this dimensionality reduction diminishes the search effort, such a square still gets computationally expensive for larger number of parameters. Further, dimensionality reduction lowers the search potential by not accounting for possible interactions between parameters. Another method relying on a similar strategy is CALIBRA [1] that acts iteratively by refining and re-sampling in the area with better performance measures.

Model-based techniques are also used for computationally expensive problems. In these techniques, the target is to create a surrogate model that imitates the original problem. Since finding optimal parameters is a computationally expensive problem, a number of model-based techniques have been proposed. In these techniques a model is generated that approximates the performance measures for a given parameter vector without solving the corresponding optimization problem. Some of the model-based approaches are Least Square and Gradient Methods [22], Gaussian Models [15], and Logistic Regressions [34]. A natural extension of the technique would be to follow an iterative model construction to converge to the best parameter vector that has been proposed by Coy [9]. There also exist a number of screening methods [23, 7] that attempt to select the best parameter vector with as few simulations as possible.

Meta-evolutionary techniques have also been employed to optimize the parameters. These procedures follow a nested structure where an evolutionary algorithm at the meta-level acts on the parameters of another evolutionary algorithm that operates at a lower level. This is a classic example of a brute-force technique to solve bilevel optimization problems, and is a common strategy in the evolutionary bilevel optimization field. One of the first studies on meta-evolutionary algorithms was performed by Mercer and Sampson in 1978 [29] that optimized the genetic parameters. The study by Mercer and Sampson was preliminary and presented the results only from a single run. Greffenstette [17] did a more extensive study on meta-evolutionary algorithm by providing the experimental results from multiple runs of a genetic algorithm (GA). The performance of the GA was evaluated using two metrics, online and offline performances [12]. Some new extensions of the techniques in meta-optimization have been addressed in FocusedILS [21] and ParamILS [20].

2.2 Bilevel Optimization

We briefly highlight some of the studies in classical and evolutionary optimization literature on bilevel optimization. Bracken and Mcgill [6] introduced bilevel programming to the domain of mathematical programming in the early seventies. Since then a number of studies have been conducted on bilevel programming [8, 41, 13].

Researchers in the classical optimization community have attempted to solve bilevel programming problems using the Karush-Kuhn-Tucker approach [5, 19], branch-and-bound approach [4], and the use of penalty functions [2]. Commonly, the methodologies are suitable for problems adhering to simplifying assumptions of smoothness, linearity or convexity. One often needs to resort to other approaches like evolutionary techniques when bilevel problems get complex.

Many of the proposed evolutionary bilevel optimization algorithms are nested strategies [28, 45, 26, 39, 3], that is, they solve the lower level optimization problem completely for any given upper level decision. For instance, in [28, 45, 26] the upper level optimization task is handled using an evolutionary algorithm and the lower level is handled using a classical approach. In [39, 3] both levels are handled using an evolutionary technique. Researchers in the evolutionary community have also used the Karush-Kuhn-Tucker conditions at the lower level [42, 25, 27] to convert bilevel optimization into a single level constrained optimization task. Co-evolutionary approaches to handle bilevel optimization problems have been attempted in [32, 24]. Studies where mathematical insights have been successfully used with evolutionary algorithms to handle bilevel problems are [43, 44, 38]. Researchers have also worked on multi-objective extensions of bilevel optimization. Some of the studies in this direction are [18, 36, 11, 37, 35, 46].

3. A BRIEF DESCRIPTION OF BILEVEL OPTIMIZATION

Bilevel optimization involves two levels of optimization tasks with one level nested within the other. The outer optimization task is commonly referred as the upper level optimization task, and the inner optimization task is commonly referred as lower level optimization task. The nested structure of the problem puts a constraint that only the optimal solutions to the lower level optimization task may be acceptable as possible feasible candidates to the upper level optimization task. There are two kinds of variables in a bilevel optimization problem: the upper level variables x_u, and the lower level variables x_l. Optimization at the lower level is performed with respect to the lower level variables x_l, while the upper level variables x_u act as parameters. An optimal lower level vector and the corresponding upper level vector x_u constitute a feasible upper level solution, provided that the pair also satisfies the upper level constraints. Below, we provide two equivalent formulations for a general bilevel optimization problem:

DEFINITION 1 (BILEVEL OPTIMIZATION PROBLEM). *Let $X = X_U \times X_L$ denote the product of the upper level decision space X_U and the lower level decision space X_L, i.e. $x = (x_u, x_l) \in X$, if $x_u \in X_U$ and $x_l \in X_L$. For the upper level objective function $F : X \to \mathbb{R}$ and the lower level objective function $f : X \to \mathbb{R}$, a* *general bilevel optimization problem is given by*

$$\begin{aligned} \underset{x \in X}{Min} \quad & F(x), \\ s.t. \quad & x_l \in \underset{x_l \in X_L}{\operatorname{argmin}} \left\{ f(x) \mid g_i(x) \geq 0, i \in I \right\}, \\ & G_j(x) \geq 0, j \in J. \end{aligned} \tag{1}$$

where the functions $g_i : X \to \mathbb{R}$, $i \in I$, represent the lower level constraints and $G_j : X \to \mathbb{R}$, $j \in J$, is the collection of upper level constraints.

The above formulation requires that a member $x^{(0)} = (x_u^{(0)}, x_l^{(0)})$ can be considered feasible at the upper level if it satisfies the upper level constraints and $x_l^{(0)}$ be an optimal solution to the lower level problem corresponding to $x_u^{(0)}$. Therefore, in a bilevel program the lower level problem appears as a parameterized constraint to the upper level problem. Next, we provide an equivalent formulation of the bilevel optimization problem by replacing the lower level optimization problem with a set-valued function that maps the given upper level decision vector to the corresponding set of optimal lower level solutions.

DEFINITION 2 (ALTERNATIVE DEFINITION). *Let a set-valued function $\Psi : X_U \rightrightarrows X_L$, denote the optimal-solution set mapping of the lower level problem, i.e.*

$$\Psi(x_u) = \underset{x_l \in X_L}{\operatorname{argmin}} \left\{ f(x) \mid g_i(x) \geq 0, i \in I \right\}.$$

A general bilevel optimization problem (BLOP) is then given by

$$\begin{aligned} \underset{x \in X}{Min} \quad & F(x), \\ s.t. \quad & x_l \in \Psi(x_u), \\ & G_j(x) \geq 0, j \in J. \end{aligned} \tag{2}$$

where the function Ψ may be a single-vector valued or a multi-vector valued function depending on whether the lower level function has multiple global optimal solutions or not.

4. BILEVEL FORMULATION FOR PARAMETER TUNING

To the best knowledge of the authors, there does not exist a well-defined mathematical formulation of the parameter tuning problem. A close look at the bilevel optimization formulation reveals the "nested" connection between the parameter tuning problem and a bilevel optimization problem. Given this similarity, it is possible to write the parameter tuning problem as a bilevel program. Such formulation would allow bilevel solution approaches to be applicable for parameter tuning. Consider that $\mathcal{A}_\mathcal{P}$ represents an algorithm $\mathcal{A}$ operating on a problem $\mathcal{P}$ for which the algorithm parameters θ are supposed to be optimized. The performance of the algorithm is given by γ that follows an unknown distribution $\mathcal{D}_{\mathcal{A}_\mathcal{P}}$. The problem of finding the optimal set of parameters θ can be written as the following bilevel optimization problem:

$$\begin{aligned} \underset{\theta \in \Theta}{\text{minimize}} \quad & F(\gamma, \theta) = E[\gamma|\theta] \\ \text{subject to} \quad & \gamma = \mathcal{A}_\mathcal{P}(\theta), \end{aligned}$$

The problem $\mathcal{P}$ on which the algorithm $\mathcal{A}$ operates is given as follows:

$$\begin{aligned} \underset{z \in Z}{\text{minimize}} \quad & f^p(z) \\ \text{subject to} \quad & g_k^p(z) \leq 0, k \in K. \end{aligned}$$

where f_p represents an objective function to be optimized with respect to vector z subject to the constraints g_k^p. The above bilevel formulation for parameter tuning is a special case of Definition 1, where $x_u = \theta$ and $x_l = \gamma$.

5. ALGORITHM DESCRIPTION

In this section, we provide a description for the parameter tuning algorithm under the bilevel framework. The algorithm is motivated by a recently proposed bilevel evolutionary algorithm based on quadratic approximations (BLEAQ) [38] that bears similarities with the iterative model-based strategies attempted in the automated parameter tuning literature. In this paper we extend BLEAQ so that it can be applied to the problem of parameter tuning. The extended approach is referred as Bilevel Automated Parameter Tuning (BAPT) Algorithm.

The BAPT optimization strategy is based on quadratic approximation of the lower level optimal vector as a function of the upper level vector. In other words, the approach attempts to approximate the Ψ-mapping in the bilevel optimization case. However, the lower level optimization task in this case is noisy leading to different performance values in different runs of $\mathcal{A}_\mathcal{P}$ for a fixed θ. Therefore, multiple executions may be required for any given θ to be able to compute the expectation at the upper level. A high number of executions to compute the expectation might make the algorithm very expensive and a low number of executions would lead to a large noise causing problems in determining the fitness of solutions at the upper level. In the proposed BAPT approach we avoid large number of runs at the lower level and at the same time suppress noise arising from the lower level runs.

The operation of the BAPT algorithm can be summarized as follows. To begin with, we initialize an upper level population of size N with random θ_i, $i \in \{1, \dots, N\}$. For each θ_i, q lower level optimization runs of $\mathcal{A}_\mathcal{P}$ are executed leading to an array of performance values given as $\gamma_{i,j}, j \in \{1, \dots, q\}$. Let these performance values[1] be collectively represented as γ_i. An expectation over $\gamma_{i,j}$ ($F_i = \frac{1}{q}\Sigma_{j=1}^q \gamma_{i,j}$) leads to the upper level objective value for (θ_i, γ_i). Based on these results we construct a quadratic approximation of F (or $E[\gamma|\theta]$) using θ. The approximation step serves a dual purpose in the algorithm. First, the quadratic approximation is used to determine F (or $E[\gamma|\theta]$) for θ when $\mathcal{A}_\mathcal{P}$ is not executed leading to savings in the executions of $\mathcal{A}_\mathcal{P}$. Second, the quadratic approximation is used to assign fitness values (Fit_i) to upper level population members that leads to a reduction in noise. Below we provide a step-by-step procedure for the BAPT algorithm.

S. 1 Initialize a random population of θ_i vectors of size N. For each $\theta_i, i \in \{1, \dots, N\}$ execute $\mathcal{A}_\mathcal{P}$ q times and store $\gamma_{i,j}, j \in \{1, \dots, q\}$.

S. 2 Compute upper level function $F(\gamma_i; \theta_i) = \frac{1}{q}\Sigma_{j=1}^q \gamma_{i,j}$ value for all $i \in \{1, \dots, N\}$. Tag all the population members as 1.

S. 3 Copy all the population members (θ_i, γ_i), $i \in \{1, \dots, N\}$ into an archive A.

S. 4 Perform a localized quadratic approximation of F (or $E[\gamma|\theta]$) over θ about each population member by choosing $\frac{(dim(\theta)+1)(dim(\theta)+2)}{2} + dim(\theta)$ closest members [2] from the

[1] In the later part of this paper, we will propose $q = 1$, thus producing a single performance value for a given θ_i. This avoids multiple computations at the lower level for a given θ_i leading to savings in computation.

[2] At least $\frac{(dim(\theta)+1)(dim(\theta)+2)}{2}$ points are required for a quadratic approximation. Extra points are chosen to avoid over-fitting.

archive A. Use the value of the quadratic function to assign fitness to the respective population and archive members.

S. 5 Given the current population, choose the best member by fitness as one of the parents. Choose $\mu - 1$ more parents by performing a tournament selection among $2(\mu - 1)$ members randomly chosen from the population.

S. 6 Perform crossover among the chosen parents by using the best parent as an index parent. Create λ offspring from the crossover operation.

S. 7 Assign fitness to the λ offspring using a quadratic approximation in a similar manner as in Step 4..

S. 8 If the number of tag 1 members in the population is less than $\frac{N}{2}$, then execute $\mathcal{A}_{\mathcal{P}}$ q times on the offspring and compute the objective function value for the offspring; tag the offspring as 1 and copy them to the archive. If the number of tag 1 members in the population is greater than or equal to $\frac{N}{2}$ then assign fitness from quadratic approximation as the objective function value for the offspring; tag the offspring as 0 and do not copy them to the archive.

S. 9 Choose r members from the parent population. Form a pool of chosen r members and λ offspring. The best r members (in terms of fitness) from the pool replace the chosen r members from the population. A termination check (refer Subsection 5.4) is performed and the algorithm moves to the next generation (Step 4) if the termination check is false.

5.1 Constraint handling

In the current setting, there are no equality or inequality constraints. The formulation contains only box constraints that are taken care by assigning the boundary value if one or more of the upper level variables (θ) violate it. However, there could be situations when the user might like to have a functional dependence between two or more variables at the upper level. This could give rise to equality or inequality constraints. In such situations we use the constraint handling procedure proposed in [10]. The overall constraint violation for any solution is the summation of the violations of all the equality and inequality constraints. A solution $x^{(i)}$ is said to 'constraint dominate' a solution $x^{(j)}$ if any of the following conditions are true:

1. Solution $x^{(i)}$ is feasible and solution $x^{(j)}$ is not.
2. Solution $x^{(i)}$ and $x^{(j)}$ are both infeasible but solution $x^{(i)}$ has a smaller overall constraint violation.
3. Solution $x^{(i)}$ and $x^{(j)}$ are both feasible but the objective value of $x^{(i)}$ is less than that of x^{j}.

5.2 Parameters

The parameters in the algorithm are fixed as $\mu = 3$, $\lambda = 2$ and $r = 2$. The crossover and mutation probabilities are fixed as 0.9 and 0.1 respectively. The upper level population size N is fixed as 50 and the number of lower level executions q for a given parameter vector is fixed as 1.

5.3 Crossover Operator

The crossover operator used in the algorithm is similar to the PCX operator proposed in [40] with minor modifications. The operator creates a new solution from $\mu = 3$ parents as follows:

$$c = x^{(p)} + \omega_\xi d + \omega_\eta \frac{p^{(2)} - p^{(1)}}{2} \qquad (3)$$

The terms used in the above equation are defined as follows:

- $x^{(p)}$ is the *index* parent which is always the best parent in this algorithm
- $d = x^{(p)} - g$, where g is the mean of μ parents
- $p^{(1)}$ and $p^{(2)}$ are the other two parents
- $\omega_\xi = 0.1$ and $\omega_\eta = \frac{dim(x^{(p)})}{||x^{(p)} - g||_1}$ are the two parameters.

Parameters ω_ξ and ω_η, describe the extent of variations along the respective directions.

5.4 Termination

In this paper, we suggest a termination criterion inspired by [16], which is commonly used with Markov chain Monte Carlo (MCMC) algorithms. The criterion is used to determine the stationarity of a time variant chain. It is noteworthy that the stochasticity at the lower level causes the mean of the population at the upper level to vary from one generation to the other. At every generation of the algorithm we extract the population means (say θ^m) from the past g_l generations. The criterion is based on the analysis of two parts (usually start and end) of the extracted chain. A z-score from two parts of the chain, say p_1 and p_2, is computed as follows:

$$z_{12} = \frac{\bar{\theta}^m_{p_1} - \bar{\theta}^m_{p_2}}{\sqrt{Var(\bar{\theta}^m_{p_1}) + Var(\bar{\theta}^m_{p_2})}}$$

Note that the terms in the numerator represent the means of the two parts of the chain while the terms in the denominator represent the asymptotic variances of $\bar{\theta}^m_{p_1}$ and $\bar{\theta}^m_{p_2}$. The asymptotic variances are estimated from the spectral density at zero.

In this paper we choose $g_l = 100$ and divide the chain as $p_1 = (1, 10), p_2 = (11, 20), p_3 = (21, 30), p_4 = (31, 40), p_5 = (41, 50)$ and $p_6 = (51, 100)$. Five different z-scores, $z_{16}, z_{26}, z_{36}, z_{46}$ and z_{56} are computed, and if all the absolute z-scores are smaller than 0.0125 then we terminate the algorithm.

6. TEST CASES

To evaluate the BAPT procedure, we construct 2 different test cases. Each test case represents an algorithm whose parameters we want to optimize. Within each test case there are 8 test problems for which we optimize the parameters of the algorithms. The algorithms that we have used in this paper are: Differential Evolution (DE) [33] and Nelder-Mead (NM) [31]. Table 1 provides a brief description for the basic versions of the algorithms and their parameters that are optimized using the BAPT approach on the chosen set of 8 test problems. The test problems on which the parameters of these algorithms are optimized are given in Table 2. The chosen test problems are small dimensional unconstrained optimization tasks.

7. RESULTS

In this section, we present the results obtained from BAPT for the two test cases i.e. DE and NM. For each test case, when executed on a specific test problem, we provide the mean and the standard deviation for the optimal parameter values obtained from 21 runs of BAPT. To evaluate the algorithm performance we consider grid search as the baseline. At each grid point we perform 101 optimization runs with DE and NM for every test problem. We provide the results for the test cases separately in the following sub-sections.

Table 1: Description of the chosen algorithms and their parameters to be optimized. The bounds chosen for the parameters to be optimized in this study are also provided.

Algo.	Description	Parameters to be optimized
DE	Differential evolution is a population based search heuristic that uses vector differences to proceed towards the optimum. In differential evolution, at each generation of the algorithm a mutant vector is constructed for different members in the population. In a simple DE algorithm, the mutation operation is based on adding differences between randomly selected members to another member, though other variants are also possible. This is followed by a recombination operation where a trial vector is constructed using the initial member and the mutant vector. The trial member competes with the current population members in order to enter the population. A number of variants are possible for DE by varying the mutation and the recombination operation. In this paper, we use DE/rand/1/bin variant, which means that the mutation vector is constructed by choosing the members randomly from the population, a single difference is used to arrive at the mutant vector, and the crossover type is binomial.	Differential Weight: $F \in [0, 2]$ Crossover Probability: $CR \in [0, 1]$
NM	Nelder-Mead method is a non-linear derivative-free optimization technique to find the local minimum of a function. For a function with d dimensions or variables, the method starts with a simplex that is a polytope with $d + 1$ vertices in the hyperspace. It is a heuristic based on pattern search that compares the function values at the vertices and updates the simplex. The method involves the steps of reflection, expansion and contraction to converge towards a minimum. The simplex gets updated at each of these steps based on the respective coefficients that appear as parameters in the Nelder-Mead algorithm. We use the basic version of the Nelder-Mead algorithm proposed in [31] in our computations.	Reflection Coefficient: $\alpha \in [0, 2]$ Expansion Coefficient: $\gamma \in [1, 4]$ Contraction Coefficient: $\rho \in [0, 1]$ Shrink Coefficient, σ, has not been considered in this study.

Table 2: Description of the selected test problems (TP1-TP8).

Problem	Formulation	Optimal Solution
TP1 (Sphere) $dim(z) = 2$	$\underset{z}{\text{Min}}\ f^p(z) = z_1^2 + z_2^2.$	$f^p = 0.0, z = (0.0, 0.0).$
TP2 (Himmelblau) $dim(z) = 2$	$\underset{z}{\text{Min}}\ f^p(z) = (z_1^2 + z_2 - 11)^2 + (z_1 + z_2^2 - 7)^2.$	$f^p = 0.0, z = (3.0, 3.0),$ $f^p = 0.0, z = (3.58439, -1.84813),$ $f^p = 0.0, z = (-3.77934, -3.28317),$ $f^p = 0.0, z = (-2.80512, 3.13134).$
TP3 (Schwefel) $dim(z) = 2$	$\underset{z}{\text{Min}}\ f^p(z) = \Sigma_{i=1}^2 \left(\Sigma_{j=1}^i z_j\right)^2.$	$f^p = 0.0, z = (1.0, 1.0).$
TP4 (Bohachevsky) $dim(z) = 2$	$\underset{z}{\text{Min}}\ f^p(z) = z_1^2 - 0.3\cos(3\pi z_1) + 2z_2^2 - 0.4\cos(4\pi z_2) + 0.7.$	$f^p = 0.0, z = (0.0, 0.0).$
TP5 (Goldstein-Price) $dim(z) = 2$	$\underset{z}{\text{Min}}\ f^p(z) = \left(1 + a(z)^2 b(z)\right)\left(30 + c(z)^2 d(z)\right),$ where $a(z) = z_1 + z_2 + 1.0,$ $b(z) = 19 - 14z_1 + 3z_1^2 - 14z_2 + 6.0z_1z_2 + 3z_2^2,$ $c(z) = 2z_1 - 3z_2,$ $d(z) = 18 - 32z_1 + 12z_1^2 + 48z_2 - 36z_1z_2 + 27z_2^2.$	$f^p = 3.0, z = (0.0, -1.0).$
TP6 (Mckinnon) $dim(z) = 2$	$\underset{z}{\text{Min}}\ f^p(z) = \begin{Bmatrix} \alpha\beta\lvert z_1\rvert^\tau + z_2(1.0 + z_2) & z_1 \leq 0 \\ \alpha z_1^\tau + z_2(1.0 + z_2) & z_1 > 0 \end{Bmatrix}.$ where $\alpha = 6, \tau = 2, \beta = 60.$	$f^p = -0.25, z = (0.0, -0.5).$
TP7 (Beale) $dim(z) = 2$	$\underset{z}{\text{Min}}\ f^p(z) = \left(1.5 - z_1(1 - z_2)\right)^2 + \left(2.25 - z_1(1 - z_2^2)\right)^2 + \left(2.625 - z_1(1 - z_2^3)\right)^2$	$f^p = 0.0, z = (3.0, 0.5).$
TP8 (Powell) $dim(z) = 4$	$\underset{z}{\text{Min}}\ f^p(z) = \left(z_1 + 10z_2\right)^2 + \left(z_3 - z_4\right)^2 + \left(z_2 - 2z_3\right)^2 + \left(z_1 - z_4\right)^2.$	$f^p = 0.0, z = (0.0, 0.0, 0.0, 0.0).$

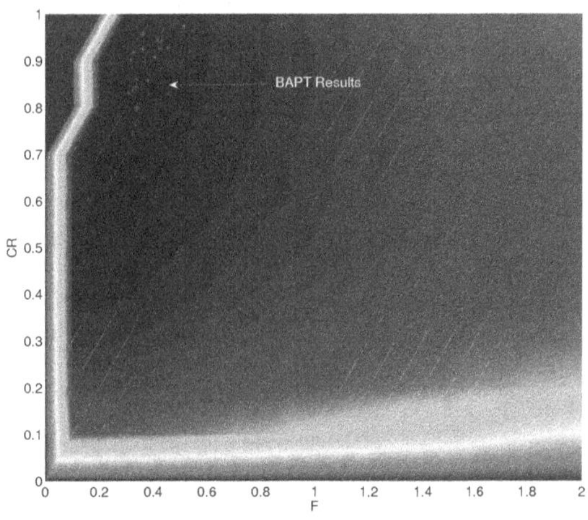

Figure 1: Performance of different DE parameters obtained using grid search is shown with contours when the DE is executed on sphere. The good parameters obtained using BAPT from 21 runs for DE-Sphere are shown as points in the flat valley.

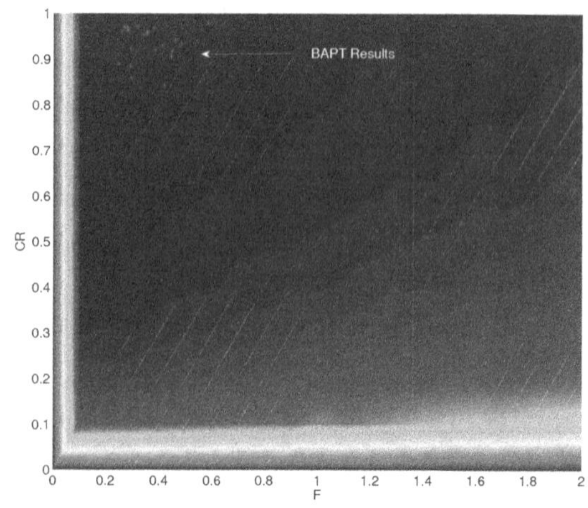

Figure 2: Performance of different DE parameters obtained using grid search is shown with contours when the DE is executed on schwefel. The good parameters obtained using BAPT from 21 runs for DE-Schwefel are shown as points in the flat valley.

7.1 DE Results

The results of the BAPT approach, when used to optimize the parameters of differential evolution, are presented in Table 3 for individual test problems. The table shows the mean value and the standard deviation of the best parameters obtained from 21 runs of BAPT for each test problem. The small standard deviations suggest that the BAPT approach converges in the same region in most of its runs. The results have been contrasted with the grid search approach that has an accuracy of $(\pm 0.1, \pm 0.1)$. It can be seen that the mean result obtained from the algorithm lies close to the result obtained from grid search. To give a better idea of the performance of BAPT, we have plotted the best parameter values obtained from 21 runs for Sphere and Schwefel functions in Figures 1 and 2 respectively. The contours in the figures represent the average performance of the parameters obtained using a fine-grained grid search at equally spaced points in the 2-D plane. The dark region represents better performaing parameters and the lighter region represents worse performing parameters. It can be observed that the good parameter region is a flat valley suggesting a range of possible parameters that would perform well on the problems. Our approach converges close to the optimal region in all of the 21 runs.

7.2 NM Results

Nelder-Mead algorithm requires a few starting points equal to one more than the number of dimensions of the test problem being solved. In the experimental runs we initialized the starting points randomly in a cubic polyhedron (size 1) about the optimum. The results of the BAPT approach for Nelder-Mead algorithm are presented in Table 4. For this test case as well the standard deviations suggest that the BAPT algorithm converges with respect to α, γ and ρ. Once again the optimal landscape is expected to be a stochastic flat valley. The results have once again been compared with grid search. The accuracy of grid search in this case is $(\pm 0.2, \pm 0.2, \pm 0.2)$. The number of lower level calls required by BAPT to optimize DE and NM on respective test problems is given in Table 5.

7.3 Algorithm Analysis

One of the important aspects to be analyzed is the number of lower level runs, q, that should be performed for any given parameter vector. Keeping all the other aspects in the algorithm fixed, we varied q as $\{1, 3, 5, 10, 20\}$ for DE-Sphere and DE-Schwefel in order to determine the appropriate number of lower level runs that should be performed for a given parameter vector. For each q we determined the accuracy (with respect to fined grained grid search) and total number of lower level optimization calls required to optimize the problem. The normalized average results are given in Figure 3, where surprisingly $q = 1$ performed significantly better than any other q. One of the reasons for this is that performing a large number of runs at a single point in a region provides the algorithm an accurate performance estimate at that point. However, performing the same number of runs at different points in the same region may lead to more information, i.e. it provides an approximate performance estimate for the region and it also provides an indication to the algorithm of the direction in which further search should be performed. For example, at the start of the algorithm, if a number of parameter vectors in a particular region perform poorly in single runs, then the region is quickly eliminated without wasting computational effort for computing accurate performance values.

8. CONCLUSIONS

In this paper, we have formulated the parameter tuning problem as a stochastic bilevel optimization problem. An algorithm (BAPT) has been proposed that draws ideas from the domain of bilevel optimization and automated parameter tuning to solve the parameter tuning problem. A new termination criterion is also suggested that can be used for evolutionary algorithms operating on stochastic problems. The results using the BAPT approach has been provided on two test cases and have been contrasted with grid search. The

Table 3: Parameter values obtained using BAPT and grid search for Differential Evolution.

	Differential Evolution				Grid Search	
	mean		std.			
TP	F	CR	F	CR	F	CR
1	0.3703	0.8760	0.0531	0.0657	0.4	1
2	0.3903	0.9199	0.0472	0.0611	0.4	1
3	0.3622	0.9331	0.0880	0.0389	0.3	1
4	0.3502	0.8584	0.0236	0.0693	0.4	0.8
5	0.4168	0.9586	0.0559	0.0290	0.5	0.9
6	0.4537	0.8627	0.0525	0.0671	0.4	0.9
7	0.4544	0.9488	0.0620	0.0347	0.5	1
8	0.5109	0.9142	0.0405	0.0487	0.5	0.9

Table 4: Parameter values obtained using BAPT and grid search for Nelder-Mead.

	Nelder-Mead						Grid Search Results		
	mean			std.					
TP	α	γ	ρ	α	γ	ρ	α	γ	ρ
1	1.1627	2.6741	0.3984	0.1958	0.2582	0.0474	1.0	2.8	0.4
2	1.1053	2.7099	0.4086	0.1493	0.3272	0.0352	1.0	3.0	0.4
3	1.0238	2.5320	0.3233	0.1082	0.3484	0.0830	1.2	2.0	0.2
4	1.4371	2.7394	0.5249	0.1550	0.4335	0.0677	1.0	2.8	0.4
5	1.3602	2.4991	0.4896	0.1443	0.3673	0.0743	1.2	3.8	0.4
6	0.9580	2.6641	0.4483	0.1161	0.3699	0.0543	0.8	2.8	0.4
7	1.1833	2.5826	0.4271	0.1612	0.3797	0.0663	1.0	2.2	0.4
8	1.0380	2.4765	0.5223	0.0546	0.3251	0.0461	1.0	2.4	0.4

Table 5: Number of lower level optimization calls required by the BAPT approach.

TP	Differential Evolution			Nelder-Mead		
	min	median	max	min	median	max
1	360	588	1034	500	790	1088
2	374	634	1000	486	752	960
3	380	494	996	458	696	1026
4	310	572	944	914	1038	1192
5	372	740	1096	488	936	1172
6	334	632	1062	466	778	1068
7	480	906	1104	538	638	1054
8	340	620	1008	294	790	1128

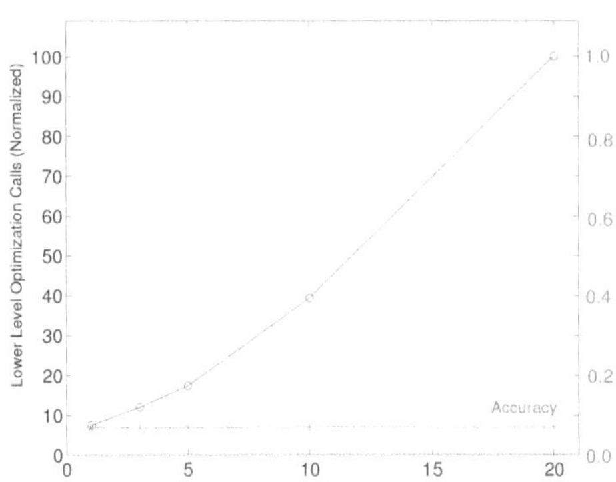

Figure 3: Computational expense and accuracy (distance from the best grid search point) against number of lower level runs q for a given parameter vector.

algorithm is found to converge close to the best parameter for most of the cases.

9. REFERENCES

[1] B. Adenso-Diaz and M. Laguna. Fine-tuning of algorithms using factional experimental designs and local search. *Operations Research*, 54:99–114, 2006.

[2] E. Aiyoshi and K. Shimizu. Hierarchical decentralized systems and its new solution by a barrier method. *IEEE Transactions on Systems, Man, and Cybernetics*, 11:444–449, 1981.

[3] J. Angelo, E. Krempser, and H. Barbosa. Differential evolution for bilevel programming. In *Proceedings of the 2013 Congress on Evolutionary Computation (CEC-2013)*. IEEE Press, 2013.

[4] J. Bard and J. Falk. An explicit solution to the multi-level programming problem. *Computers and Operations Research*, 9:77–100, 1982.

[5] L. Bianco, M. Caramia, and S. Giordani. A bilevel flow model for hazmat transportation network design. *Transportation Research Part C: Emerging technologies*, 17(2):175–196, 2009.

[6] J. Bracken and J. McGill. Mathematical programs with optimization problems in the constraints. *Operations Research*, 21:37–44, 1973.

[7] J. Branke, E. Chick, and C. Schmidt. New developments in ranking and selection: an empirical comparison of the three main approaches. In *WSC 2005: Proceedings of the 37th conference on Winter simulation*, pages 708–717. Winter Simulation Conference, 2005.

[8] B. Colson, P. Marcotte, and G. Savard. An overview of bilevel optimization. *Annals of Operational Research*, 153:235–256, 2007.

[9] S. P. Coy, B. L. Golden, G. C. Runger, and E. A. Wasil. Using experimental design to find effective parameter settings for heuristics. *Journal of Heuristics*, 7:77–97, 2001.

[10] K. Deb. An efficient constraint handling method for genetic algorithms. *Computer Methods in Applied Mechanics and Engineering*, 186(2–4):311–338, 2000.

[11] K. Deb and A. Sinha. An efficient and accurate solution methodology for bilevel multi-objective programming problems using a hybrid evolutionary-local-search algorithm. *Evolutionary Computation Journal*, 18(3):403–449, 2010.

[12] K. A. DeJong. *An Analysis of the Behavior of a Class of Genetic Adaptive Systems*. PhD thesis, Ann Arbor, MI: University of Michigan, 1975. Dissertation Abstracts International 36(10), 5140B (University Microfilms No. 76-9381).

[13] S. Dempe, J. Dutta, and S. Lohse. Optimality conditions for bilevel programming problems. *Optimization*, 55(5–6):505–524, 2006.

[14] A. E. Eiben and S. K. Smit. Parameter tuning for configuring and analyzing evolutionary algorithms. *Swarm and Evolutionary Computation*, 1:19–31, 2011.

[15] M. El-Beltagy, P. Nair, and A. Keane. Metamodeling techniques for evolutionary optimization of computationally expensive problems: promises and limitations. In W. Banshaf, J. Daida, E. Eiben, M. H. Garzon, V. Honavar, M. Jakiela, and R. E. Smith, editors, *Proceedings of the Genetic and Evolutionary Computation Conference*, pages 196–203. Morgan Kaufmann, 1999.

[16] J. Geweke. Evaluating the accuracy of sampling-based approaches to the calculation of posterior moments. *In Bayesian Statistics 4 (eds. J.M. Bernardo, J. Berger, A.P. Dawid and A.F.M. Smith)*, pages 169–193, 1992.

[17] J. Greffenstette. Optimisation of control parameters for genetic algorithms. *IEEE Transactions on Systems, Man and Cybernetics*, 16:122–128, 1986.

[18] W. Halter and S. Mostaghim. Bilevel optimization of multi-component chemical systems using particle swarm optimization. In *Proceedings of World Congress on Computational Intelligence (WCCI-2006)*, pages 1240–1247, 2006.

[19] J. Herskovits, A. Leontiev, G. Dias, and G. Santos. Contact shape optimization: A bilevel programming approach. *Struct Multidisc Optimization*, 20:214–221, 2000.

[20] F. Hutter, H. H. Hoos, K. Leyton-Brown, and T. Stützel. Paramils: an automatic algorithm configuration framework. *Journal of Artificial Intelligence Research*, 36:267–306, 2009.

[21] F. Hutter, H. H. Hoos, and T. Stützle. Automatic algorithm configuration based on local search. In *IN AAAI 2007: Proc. of the Twenty-Second Conference on Artificial Intelligence*, pages 1152–1157, 2007.

[22] Y. Jin. A comprehensive survey of fitness approximation in evolutionary computation. *Soft Computing*, 9:3–12, 2005.

[23] S.-H. Kim and B. L. Nelson. A fully sequential procedure for indifference-zone selection in simulation. *ACM Transactions on Modeling and Computer Simulation*, 11:251–273, 2001.

[24] F. Legillon, A. Liefooghe, and E.-G. Talbi. Cobra: A cooperative coevolutionary algorithm for bi-level optimization. In *2012 IEEE Congress on Evolutionary Computation (CEC-2012)*. IEEE Press, 2012.

[25] H. Li and Y. Wang. A genetic algorithm for solving a special class of nonlinear bilevel programming problems. In Y. Shi, G. Albada, J. Dongarra, and P. Sloot, editors, *Computational Science AI ICCS 2007*, volume 4490 of *Lecture Notes in Computer Science*, pages 1159–1162. Springer Berlin Heidelberg, 2007.

[26] H. Li and Y. Wang. A hybrid genetic algorithm for solving nonlinear bilevel programming problems based on the simplex method. *International Conference on Natural Computation*, 4:91–95, 2007.

[27] H. Li and Y. Wang. An evolutionary algorithm with local search for convex quadratic bilevel programming problems. *Applied Mathematics and Information Sciences*, 5(2):139–146, 2011.

[28] R. Mathieu, L. Pittard, and G. Anandalingam. Genetic algorithm based approach to bi-level linear programming. *Operations Research*, 28(1):1–21, 1994.

[29] R. Mercer and J. Sampson. Adaptive search using a reproductive metaplan. *Kybernetes*, 7:215–228, 1978.

[30] R. Myers and E. R. Hancock. Empirical modelling of genetic algorithms. *Evolutionary Computation*, 9:461–493, 2001.

[31] J. A. Nelder and R. Mead. A simplex method for function minimization. *Computer Journal*, 7:308–313, 1965.

[32] V. Oduguwa and R. Roy. Bi-level optimization using genetic algorithm. In *Proceedings of the 2002 IEEE International Conference on Artificial Intelligence Systems (ICAIS 2002)*, pages 322–327, 2002.

[33] K. V. Price, R. Storn, and J. Lampinen. *Differential Evolution: A Practical Approach to Global Optimization*. Springer-Verlag, Berlin, 2005.

[34] I. Ramos, M. Goldbarg, E. Goldbarg, and A. Neto. Logistic regression for parameter tuning on evolutionary computation. In *IEEE Congress on Evolutionary Computation*, Edinburgh, UK, 2005. IEEE Press.

[35] S. Ruuska and K. Miettinen. Constructing evolutionary algorithms for bilevel multiobjective optimization. In *Evolutionary Computation (CEC), 2012 IEEE Congress on*, pages 1–7, june 2012.

[36] X. Shi. and H. S. Xia. Model and interactive algorithm of bi-level multi-objective decision-making with multiple interconnected decision makers. *Journal of Multi-Criteria Decision Analysis*, 10(1):27–34, 2001.

[37] A. Sinha and K. Deb. Towards understanding evolutionary bilevel multi-objective optimization algorithm. In *IFAC Workshop on Control Applications of Optimization (IFAC-2009)*, volume 7. Elsevier, 2009.

[38] A. Sinha, P. Malo, and K. Deb. Efficient evolutionary algorithm for single-objective bilevel optimization. *CoRR*, abs/1303.3901, 2013.

[39] A. Sinha, P. Malo, A. Frantsev, and K. Deb. Finding optimal strategies in a multi-period multi-leader-follower stackelberg game using an evolutionary algorithm. *Computers & Operations Research*, 41:374–385, 2014.

[40] A. Sinha, A. Srinivasan, and K. Deb. A population-based, parent centric procedure for constrained real-parameter optimization. In *2006 IEEE Congress on Evolutionary Computation (CEC-2006)*, pages 239–245. IEEE Press, 2006.

[41] L. N. Vicente and P. H. Calamai. Bilevel and multilevel programming: A bibliography review. *Journal of Global Optimization*, 5(3):291–306, 2004.

[42] G. Wang, Z. Wan, X. Wang, and Y. Lv. Genetic algorithm based on simplex method for solving linear-quadratic bilevel programming problem. *Comput Math Appl*, 56(10):2550–2555, 2008.

[43] Y. Wang, Y. C. Jiao, and H. Li. An evolutionary algorithm for solving nonlinear bilevel programming based on a new constraint-handling scheme. *IEEE Transactions on Systems, Man, and Cybernetics, Part C: Applications and Reviews*, 32(2):221–232, 2005.

[44] Y. Wang, H. Li, and C. Dang. A new evolutionary algorithm for a class of nonlinear bilevel programming problems and its global convergence. *INFORMS Journal on Computing*, 23(4):618–629, 2011.

[45] Y. Yin. Genetic algorithm based approach for bilevel programming models. *Journal of Transportation Engineering*, 126(2):115–120, 2000.

[46] T. Zhang, T. Hu, Y. Zheng, and X. Guo. An improved particle swarm optimization for solving bilevel multiobjective programming problem. *Journal of Applied Mathematics*, 2012.

Learning the Structure of Large-scale Bayesian Networks using Genetic Algorithm

Fatemeh Vafaee
Charles Perkins Centre
The University of Sydney
Sydney, NSW 2050, Australia
fatemeh.vafaee@sydney .edu.au

ABSTRACT

Bayesian networks are probabilistic graphical models representing conditional dependencies among a set of random variables. Due to their concise representation of the joint probability distribution, Bayesian Networks are becoming incrementally popular models for knowledge representation and reasoning in various problem domains. However, learning the structure of the Bayesian networks is an NP-hard problem since the number of structures grows super-exponentially as the number of variables increases. This work therefore is aimed to propose a new hybrid structure learning algorithm that uses mutual dependencies to reduce the search space complexity and recruits the genetic algorithm to effectively search over the reduced space of possible structures. The proposed method is best suited for problems with medium to large number of variables and a limited dataset. It is shown that the proposed method achieves higher model's accuracy as compared to a series of popular structure learning algorithms particularly when the data size gets smaller.

Categories and Subject Descriptors

I.2.8 [**Artificial Intelligence**]: Problem Solving, Control Methods, and Search—*Graph and tree search strategies*; *Heuristic methods*; I.2.6 [**Artificial Intelligence**]: Learning

Keywords

Bayesian networks; structure learning; genetic algorithms

1. INTRODUCTION AND RELATED WORK

Bayesian networks (BNs) are probabilistic graphical models that provide a powerful formalism for representing and reasoning under uncertainty. They represent the joint probability distribution among the variables of interest by exploiting conditional independencies allowing a compact and natural representation of the domain's knowledge. Bayesian networks have become increasingly popular for modeling knowledge in a variety of domains such as computational biology and bioinformatics [41, 43], medicine[18, 18], information retrieval [13], semantic search [19], image processing [30], security [42] , etc.

GECCO'14, July 12–16, 2014, Vancouver, BC, Canada.

ACM 978-1-4503-2662-9/14/07 ...$15.00.
http://dx.doi.org/10.1145/2576768.2598223.

A Bayesian network $B(G, \Theta)$ is characterized by a structure and a set of parameters: the structure $G = (V, E)$ is a *directed acyclic graph* (DAG) whose vertices $V = \{X_i\}$ corresponds to random variables $\mathbf{X} = (X_1, \ldots, X_n)$ of the problem domain. The conditional dependencies among the variables are represented by the edges $E = \{e_{i,j}\}$ where a directed edge $e_{i,j}$ connects a parent node X_i to a child node X_j. The set of parameters Θ quantifies the graph edges by specifying local conditional probabilities over $\mathbf{X}$, i.e., $p(X_i|Pa(X_i, G))\, \forall X_i$, where $Pa(X_i, G)$ is the set of parents of node X_i in graph G. Bayesian networks therefore decompose the joint probability distribution for $\mathbf{X}$ into the product of conditional probability distributions over each variable given its parents:

$$p(X_1, \ldots, Xn) = \prod_{i=1}^{n} p(X_i|Pa(X_i, G)) \tag{1}$$

In order to use BNs to model domain variables and their relationships from empirical observations or sampled data, one has to first learn the underlying DAG structure and then estimate the conditional probability distributions. The focus of this paper is on the BN structure learning rather than the parameter estimation.

Learning the structure from data is an NP-hard problem [7] as the number of possible structures grows super-exponentially by the number of variables n, i.e., $O(n!2^{\binom{n}{2}})$ [34]. This makes the use of exact methods infeasible for any domain, regardless of the size of the data [7]. BN structure learning thus requires either sub-optimal heuristic search algorithms or algorithms that are optimal under certain assumptions. These approximate structure learning algorithms are usually categorized into two groups of *constraint-based* (CB) and *search-and-score* (S&S) approaches.

CB algorithms rely on a number of conditional independency (CI) tests (e.g., χ^2 test or information-theory based tests) to determine whether two variables are independent given a set of conditioned variables. They usually construct DAGs in two consecutive stages by first learning the associations between variables resulting in an undirected graph structure, and then directing the edges by employing the orientation rules. The first stage requires a number of CI tests growing exponentially with the number of nodes, which makes CB methods incorporating different assumptions or strategies to restrict the size of the condition set. Some widely known examples of CB approaches are Inductive Causation (IC) by Pearl [31], PC by Spirtes *et al* [38], and Three Phase Dependency Analysis (TPDA) by Cheng *et al.* [6]. More recent examples of CB algorithms include the Grow-Shrink (GS) Markov Blanket algorithm [32], and the Recursive Anatomy Identification (RAI) algorithm

[33]. CB approaches are generally asymptotically correct [6, 38], and have a well-defined stopping criterion [11].

The more popular S&S approach involves a strategy for searching through the space of possible structures and a scoring function measuring the fitness of each structure to the data. The idea here is to try and maximize the score by moving from one structure to another by employing some variation operators (e.g., deletion or addition of a link between two nodes) and then evaluating the overall effect of the move, and iterating this process until an optimal score is found or a stop-criterion is met. Several works have been done in proposing score functions as well as search algorithms for BN structure learning.

The scoring metrics are commonly categorized into two major classes of *Bayesian* and *information-theoretic* scoring functions.

The general idea of Bayesian scoring functions is to compute the posterior probability distribution of a graph G, given the Data $\mathcal{D}$ as shown by Equation 2, where $p(G)$ is the prior probability on different graph structures, and $p(\mathcal{D}|G)$ is the parameter prior that puts a probability on different parameters Θ given a graph G.

$$p(G|\mathcal{D}) = \frac{p(\mathcal{D}|G)p(G)}{p(\mathcal{D})} \propto p(\mathcal{D}|G)p(G) \quad (2)$$

Following the Bayes' theorem, $p(\mathcal{D}|G) = \int_\theta p(\mathcal{D}|G,\theta)p(\theta|G)d\theta$, which is the marginal likelihood that averages the probability of the data $\mathcal{D}$ over all possible parameter assignments to G. Major examples of Bayesian scoring functions include Bayesian Dirichlet (BD) scoring function [17] and its variants (i.e., BDe [17] and BDeu [40]).

Information-theoretic metrics are based on the compression that can be achieved over the data with an optimal code induced by the Bayesian network (Shannon's source coding theorem establishes the limits to the possible data compression). Minimum description length (MDL) scoring function [23, 23], Akaike Information Criterion (AIC) [1], Bayesian Information Criterion (BIC), a score based on Schwarz Information Criterion [37] and mutual information test (MIT) score [12], are well-known examples of information-theoretic scoring metrics for BN structure learning. As empirically investigated by [5], Bayesian scores generally perform better in terms of the classification accuracy for learning over large data. Interested readers are referred to [5, 44] for an overview of different scoring functions and their empirical evaluation in BN model selection.

On the other hand, there has also been a good deal of works on proposing combinatorial search strategies to effectively explore the huge space of possible DAGs. These approximate methods either adhere to some assumptions to reduce the effective size of the search space or employ heuristics. The popular K2 algorithm proposed by Cooper and Herskovit [10], for instance, assumes an ordering on the nodes. Chow and Liu [9] proposed a method derived from the maximum weight spanning tree (MWST) algorithm to learn a tree structure. They therefore restricted the search space to the tree space which is poorer than the DAG space. Friedman *et. al* [15] also reduce the search space by iteratively restricting the parents of each variable to belong to a small subset of candidates.

Besides, various heuristics have been developed to produce suboptimal solutions in a reasonable time frame. Examples include hill climbing [3], simulated annealing [2] and the Metropolis-Hastings algorithm , which is a Markov Chain Monte Carlo (MCMC) based meta-heuristic method [28, 39]. Genetic algorithms (GAs) have been also previously used for BN structure learning (e.g., [24], [20], and [4]). One of the pioneering works in using GAs for BN structure learning is K2GA proposed by Larranaga *et al.* [24] who used the genetic algorithm to search for an optimal ordering of the nodes that is passed on to the K2 algorithm. To reduce the time complexity of K2GA, Kabli *et al.* [20] then proposed a chain-model GA which relies on chain structures for the evaluation of node orderings. The chain model is used to evolve a small number of orderings using the genetic algorithm that are then injected into the K2 algorithm to search for an optimal structure. More recently, Carvalho [4] proposed a cooperative coevolutionary genetic algorithm that decomposes the problem of BN structure learning into two sub-problems of finding an ordering of the nodes, and an optimal connectivity matrix. GAs are generally powerful candidates for S&S structure learning as they maintain and improve a population of solutions, and thus, comparing to the single-solution search algorithms such as simulated annealing and hill climbing, they better explore the search space, and have a lower chance of trapping into local optima.

In spite of the diversity of the methods proposed for the problem of the Bayesian network structure learning, many of the existing methods fail to cope with large scale problems due to their memory and/or time complexity. In order to manage the memory required for conditional probability tables (CPTs),[1] some algorithms undergo arbitrary constraints (e.g., limiting the number of parents to an arbitrary number). To handle the algorithmic time complexity, on the other hand, some algorithms make impractical assumptions (e.g., the ordering of the nodes, which is not usually known a priori in real problems). Besides the scale of the problem, the size of the data is another issue in learning BN models. For example, when data size is limited, constraint-based methods become unreliable in performing CI tests as the condition sets enlarge [10, 38]. The aim of this work is therefore to propose a solution for learning medium to large scale Bayesian networks in the presence of relatively small training data. Accordingly, a hybrid algorithm is proposed which uses a *constraint-based* approach to narrow the search space for the genetic algorithm which is used as an effective *search-and-score* method of Bayesian network structure learning.

The remainder of this paper is organized as follows: Section 2 provides a detailed description of the proposed method and the underlying ideas. In Section 3, the benchmark problems, the compared algorithms, and the experimental results are presented. Finally, Section 4 briefly summarizes the proposed algorithm.

2. STRUCTURE LEARNING OF BAYESIAN NETWORK USING A GA

The proposed algorithm uses a hybrid strategy for BN structural learning by first performing a series of conditional independence tests to narrow the search space, and then incorporating the genetic algorithm to efficiently explore the reduced space of Bayesian networks. By the first stage, an undirected "super-graph" $\mathbb{G} = (V, \mathbb{E})$ is constructed, where vertices correspond to the domain's random variables $V = \{X_i, \ldots, X_j\}$, and the undirected edges $\mathbb{E} = \{a_{i,j}\}$ represent mutual dependencies among the variables. Then, at the second stage, GA is responsible for finding a highly-scored directed acyclic graph which is a subgraph of the original super-graph. So, each edge in $\mathbb{G}$ can be either removed in G, or instantiated to one of the two possible directions (given that G does not hold any directed cycle). GA therefore is used here to tackle the optimization problem of the type

$$\max\{f(G)|G \text{ is a DAG } \& \ G \text{ is a subgraph of } \mathbb{G}\},$$

where $f(G)$ is the score of the Bayesian network G obtained from the scoring mechanism of interest (Bayesian scoring function in

[1]In learning over discrete variables, the size of the CPT for each node grows exponentially with the number of node's parents.

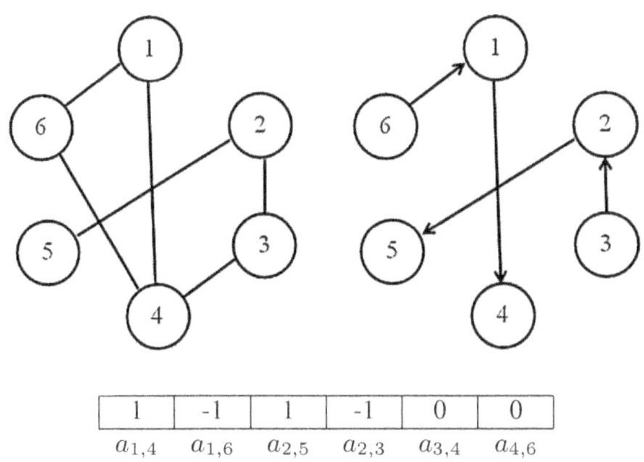

Figure 1: An example of a hypothetical super-graph $\mathbb{G}$ (left), a sample graph G (right) which is a directed sub-graph of $\mathbb{G}$, and the corresponding string representation of G.

these experiments). Bayesian networks are particularly useful models in problems where the underlying relations are relatively sparse, and thus the joint distribution can be efficiently expressed by the BN graphical model. In such cases, we expect $|\mathbb{E}| \ll O(n^2)$ implying that the reduction phase exponentially narrows the search space providing a more directed landscape for GA to explore. Next subsection discusses the details of the proposed algorithm, which is henceforth referred to as *HSL-GA* standing for *Hybrid Structure Learner using Genetic Algorithm.*

2.1 HSL-GA Algorithm (Pseudo-code)

In order to apply GA to the problem of interest, it is first required to select an appropriate representation of the individual solutions. Here, each individual (which encodes a graph G) is represented by a ternary string of length $l = |\mathbb{E}|$, $x_i = \langle x_{i,0}, \ldots, x_{i,l} \rangle$, where each ternary digit $x_{i,j}$ corresponds to a specific edge, say $a_{u,v}$, in $\mathbb{G}$ such that:

$$x_{i,j} = \begin{cases} 1 & \text{if there is an edge from } X_u \text{ to } X_v \text{ in } G \\ -1 & \text{if there is an edge from } X_v \text{ to } X_u \text{ in } G \\ 0 & \text{if the edge } a_{u,v} \text{ is removed in } G \end{cases}.$$

Figure 1 shows a toy example of a super-graph $\mathbb{G}$, an instantiation of $\mathbb{G}$ and its corresponding ternary string representation.

The overall framework of the proposed algorithm has been shown in Figure 2. The algorithm starts by extracting mutual dependencies among random variables—i.e., constructing the super-graph $\mathbb{G} = (V, \mathbb{E})$—and then randomly initializing a population of size m individuals each encoding an acyclic directed sub-graph of $\mathbb{G}$. Then, following the inherent mechanism of evolutionary algorithms, HSL-GA main evolutionary cycle—lines 5 to 9 in Figure 2—incorporates two primary operations of *selection* and *reproduction* as follows:

At each iteration of the main evolutionary loop, the best individual in the current population s_t is first determined and saved as $x^*(s_t)$ (line 5). Then, a population consisting of better individuals in s_t are selected to go under the reproduction phase (line 6). Every individual in the selected population s'_t then experiences mutation and crossover resulting in a new population s''_t (line 7). Finally, upon the termination of generation t, the reproduced population s''_t is examined to check whether its best individual has a lower (i.e., worse) fitness value than $x^*(s_t)$. If that would be the case, $x^*(s_t)$ replaces the worst individual in s''_t (line 8), and the resultant population proceeds to the next generation.

```
Algorithm: Hybrid Structure Learning using Genetic Algorithm
Given: Data D, number of variables n, population size m,
       significance level α, and fitness function f(...)

1. t ← 0
2. 𝔼 ←MUTUAL-DEPENDENCIES(D, α, d)
3. s0 ←INITIAL-POPULATION(n, m, 𝔼)
4. repeat
5.    x*(st) ←GET-ELITE(st)
6.    s't ←SELECTION(st)
7.    s''t ←REPRODUCTION(s't, pm, pc, 𝔼)
8.    st+1 ←PLACE-ELITE(s''t, x*(st))
9.    t ← t + 1
10. until not stop
```

Figure 2: HSL-GA algorithm

The line-by-line description of the HSL-GA pseudo-code is given below:

Line 2: **MUTUAL-DEPENDENCIES**$(\mathcal{D}, \alpha, d)$
Given the CI threshold (i.e., significance level) α, the CI order d, and the data matrix $\mathcal{D}$ (with m rows and n columns), this function performs χ^2 conditional independence tests to find the set of all undirected edges whose corresponding random variables are conditionally dependent given any parent set S of size d. More formally, the function returns the set $\mathbb{E} = \{a_{i,j}\}$, where an undirected edge $a_{i,j}$ connects random variables X_i and X_j such that:

$$X_i \not\perp X_j | S \quad \forall\ S \subseteq V \text{ and } |S| = d$$

In our experiments, we assumed that the data size is only enough for performing reliable zero-degree CI tests, i.e., $S = \emptyset$.

Line 3: **INITIAL-POPULATION**$(n, m, \mathbb{E})$
This function generates an initial population consisting of m random ternary strings of length l, each encoding a directed graph—i.e., an instantiation of the super-graph $\mathbb{G}$. Once the initial population is instantiated, a call to the MAKE-DAG routine is made to ensure the validity of the instantiated individuals. The pseudo-code of MAKE-DAG function is shown in Figure 3, and its general idea is discussed below:

MAKE-DAG$(\mathbb{E}, x)$
Since random instances of $\mathbb{G}$ may contain directed cycles, an auxiliary algorithm is required to convert each invalid instance x—encoding a cyclic graph G—to a corresponding DAG, preferably with the minimum number of changes to the original graph. This brings up the problem of *minimum feedback arc set*: the feedback arc set (FAS) of a graph G, is a set of edges that when removed from G, leaves a DAG. Finding the minimum number of edges to remove is called the minimum feedback arc set problem, which is an NP-hard problem [21], and thus heuristics should be employed. Eades *et. al* [14] proposed a fast and yet effective heuristic for the FAS problem that executes in linear time with close-to-optimal asymptotic performance bound in sparse graphs. In this work, a slightly-modified version of this algorithm, displayed in Figure 3, has been used to maintain the validity of all the individual solutions. The minimum FAS problem is equivalent to the problem of determining a vertex sequence $v_1, v_2, \ldots, v_n$ such that the number of leftward arcs $v_i v_j$, $i > j$, (i.e., feedback arcs) is minimized [14]. Accordingly, the algorithm shown in Figure 3 first finds a (quasi-) optimal vertex sequence S^*, and then removes the corresponding backward edges from G resulting in a DAG.

```
function: MAKE-DAG(E, x) returns
    inputs: Edge set E and individual string x
    returns: the corresponding DAG of x
    Notations: d^-(v): indegree of vertex v, d^+(v): outdegree of vertex v

G ← BUILD-GRAPH(E, x)        // build the adj.matrix of x given E
S1 ← ∅; S2 ← ∅
while G ≠ ∅
    while G contains v s.t. d^+(v) = 0        // v is sink
        S2 ← v S2
        G ← G − v
    while G contains v s.t. d^-(v) = 0        // v is source
        S1 ← S1 v
        G ← G − v
    v ← arg max_{v∈G} (d^+(v) − d^-(v))      // random tie-breaking
        S1 ← S1 v
        G ← G − v
S* ← S1 S2
return G_dag ← REMOVE-BACKARCS(G, S*)
```

Figure 3: Minimum Feedback Arc Set algorithm

Line 5: **GET-ELITE**(s_t)
By this function the best individual in population s_t is determined and saved as $x^*(s_t)$. More formally,

$$x^*(s_t) = \arg\max_{x_i^t}\{f(x_i^t) | x_i^t \in s_t\},$$

where x_i^t for $i \in \{1, \ldots, m\}$ refers to the ith individual in population s_t, and $f(x_i^t)$ corresponds to its fitness. Notice that a *copy* of the best individual in s_t is saved as $x^*(s_t)$. Thus, the original version still exists in the population and undergoes selection and reproduction as other members of the population do.

Line 6: **SELECTION**(s_t)
This function uses the *rank selection* by which the individuals in population s_t are first ranked according to their fitness values such that the worst individual receives rank 1 and the best one receives rank m. These ranks are then treated as individuals' fitness values and fitness-proportional selection is used by which the selected population s_t' is determined through m independent random experiments. The probability that individual $x_i^t \in s_t$ is selected from s_t to be a member of population s_t' at each experiment is given by

$$P\{x_i^t \ is \ selected\} = \frac{rank(x_i^t)}{\sum_{j=1}^{m} rank(x_j^t)} = \frac{rank(x_i^t)}{m(m+1)/2}$$

Line 7:**REPRODUCTION**(s_t', p_m, p_c)
The conventional uniform mutation and single-point crossover have been employed to maintain the genetic diversity. The mutation unary operator replaces every digit of each individual string with a random value in $\{-1, 0, 1\}$, with a small probability of p_m. As for the binary operator, crossover, each individual x_i^t is first paired up with a random mate from the population, a single crossover point is then randomly selected, and the sub-strings beyond that point are swapped between the two parents. Then, one of the offspring at random replaces x_i^t with the probability of p_c. To ensure the validity of the reproduced population, the perturbed individuals undergo the MAKE-DAG function.

Line 8: **PLACE-ELITE**$(s_t'', x^*(s_t))$
If the best individual in the reproduced population s_t'' has a lower fitness than $f(x^*(s_t))$, this function places $x^*(s_t)$ into s_t'' by replacing the *worst* individual in s_t''. Thus, the fitness value of the best individual contained in the population s_{t+1} which proceeds to the next generation, is at least as good as the best individual in the current population s_t.

3. EXPERIMENTS AND RESULTS

The proposed method has been implemented within the BNT Structure Learning Package (BNT-SLP) [25], which is developed on top of the Bayes Net Toolbox for Matlab [29], and it is aimed to provide a comprehensive tool for structure learning methods.

3.1 Compared Algorithms

HSL-GA performance is compared with a series of well-known and widely-used structure learning algorithms implemented in BNT-SLP. In order to include a GA-based structure learner in the comparison, we also implemented Chain-GA algorithm [20] within the BNT-SLP package. Compared algorithms are briefly explained as follows:

Maximum weight spanning tree (MWST) [9] associates a weight to each edge based on the mutual information between the corresponding variables. Once the weight matrix is created, a typical *maximum weight spanning tree* algorithm (e.g., Kruskal algorithm) builds up an undirected tree, which is then oriented given a chosen root (i.e., first node by default).

K2 [10] is a greedy search algorithms. Given a topological node ordering, K2 starts with an empty ancestor set for each node and incrementally adds edges which maximizes the score of the resulting structure until no more ancestor node addition improves the score.

Hill climbing (HC) [3], which is an iterative search-and-score algorithm that starts with an arbitrary DAG, examines all its neighboring configurations by making all DAGs that differ from the current graph by a single edge deletion, addition or reversal. A neighbor DAG with the highest score whose score is improved as compared to current DAG is then selected to move to the next iteration. The process is repeated until no further improvement can be found.

Greedy Equivalent Search (GES) [8], which is a greedy search in Markov equivalent space[2] based on the idea that a greedy search in this space is more likely to converge as compared to the DAGs space [27]. Using *Completed Partially Directed Acyclic Graphs* (CPDAG) [3] to represent Markov equivalent classes, GES first starts with an empty graph, and adds edges until the score cannot be improved. It then further improve the overall score by removing some irrelevant edges.

Chain-model genetic algorithm (Chain-GA) [20] uses genetic algorithm to search over the space of node orderings and then recruits K2 algorithm to reconstruct a full network given the best-found ordering of the nodes. Similar to the previously-developed K2GA algorithm, Chain-GA is aimed to release K2 reliance on the initial node ordering while compensating for the K2GA inefficiency by evolving a population of chain structures rather than searching over the the space of full networks.

Causality search algorithm (PC) [38] is a constrained-based structure learning algorithm that computes many conditional indepen-

[2]Two DAGs are said to be Markov equivalent if they entail the same set of conditional independencies.
[3]the space of CPDAGs is defined as the set of PDAGs which have only undirected arcs and irreversible directed arcs.

Table 1: End-of-run results achieved by different algorithms for different problem settings

Method	ASIA (Small)		ALARM (Medium)		HEPAR-II (Large)	
	score	F1	score	F1	score	F1
HSL-GA	-130.67 (10.02)	**0.3910** (0.261)	-1016.70 (65.98)	**0.4340** (0.071)	-3515.78 (49.09)	**0.1541** (0.033)
Chain-GA	-130.41 (10.56)	0.2823 (0.177)	-1046.93 (44.93)	0.2796 (0.046)	-3484.53 (46.97)	0.1047 (0.029)
HC	-128.94 (10.81)	**0.3573** (0.208)	1238.66 (61.14)	0.2168 (0.055)	-3655.05 (48.22)	0.0262 (0.0179)
GES	-146.79 (13.01)	0.2629 (0.052)	runs out of memory		runs out of memory	
K2	-129.78 (10.70)	0.3162 (0.140)	-1052.79 (49.47)	0.2560 (0.056)	-3487.05 (53.27)	0.1016 (0.023)
MWST	-152.42 (17.99)	0.1077 (0.143)	-1110.14 (100.40)	0.2932 (0.080)	-3628.23 (50.81)	**0.1504** (0.025)
PC	-162.08 (13.39)	0.1548 (0.137)	runs out of time		runs out of time	

dence tests, and combines these constraints into a PDAG which should be then instantiated to a DAG. PC worst-case time complexity is $O(n^k)$, where n is the number of variables and k is the maximum in-degree.

3.2 Benchmark Bayesian Networks

As for the benchmark problems, three Bayesian networks of different sizes have been chosen from Bayesian Network Repository [35]. Based on the BN Repository categorization, we selected a small BN (ASIA, $n = 8$), a medium BN (ALARM, $n = 37$) and a large BN (HEPAR-II, $n = 70$) as the benchmark problems. Since the Bayes nets in BN Repository are given in Bayes net Interchange Format (BIF), they were first converted to the BNT format which is readable by BNT-SLP package using the bif2bnt program developed by Ken Shan [36]. The `sample-bnet` function implemented in Bayes Net Toolkit [29], is then used to generate datasets of 50, 70, and 100 random cases for ASIA, ALARM, and HEPAR-II networks, respectively.

3.3 Simulation Settings

Free parameters in HSL-GA are set as follows: maximum number of iterations is set to 300, the population size is 50, the CI significance level $\alpha = 0.01$, the crossover rate $p_c = 0.6$, and the mutation rate is set to the conventional value of $1/l$, where l is the string length (i.e., $l = |\mathbb{E}|$). Likewise, for Chain-GA, the maximum number of iterations and the population size are set to 300 and 50, respectively. To preserve the node ordering structure of individual solutions, Chain-GA makes use of cycle crossover with the rate of 0.9, and displacement mutation with the rate of 0.1; similar settings were applied in here. The parameters in the rest of compared algorithms are all set to their defaults values (see [26] for details).

To have a feasible running time and a fair comparison across different methods, the iterative methods HC, GES, Chain-GA and HSL-GA are slightly adjusted to stop when either their default stop criteria are met (e.g., maximum number of iterations is reached, no further improvement can be made, or the population is converged), or when the maximum allotted CPU time T is reached, whichever occurs the first. Based on our resources (CPU of i7-3.40 GHz, and RAM of 32.0 GB), T is set to 200, 4000 and 12000 seconds for ASIA, ALARM, and HEPAR-II networks, respectively. K2 and MWST are fast algorithms, and thus no constraint on running time is required. PC method requires major adjustments to adhere to the time constraint. To preserve the method's original implementation, PC is left to run until its default stop condition is met.

Last but not least, the fitness function being used is the Bayesian score (i.e., the marginal likelihood of the model) as implemented by the BNT-SLP package and discussed by Equation 2.

3.4 Results and Analysis

HSL-GA is aimed to model Bayesian networks in presence of relatively high number of variables and limited number of samples (as it is usually the case in biological and medical applications). Accordingly, relatively few number of cases were generated for each benchmark BN, and thus in order to adjust for the stochasticity effect of these small-sized datasets, and to obtain more reliable performance measures, for each benchmark problem, all algorithms were run on 20 different random samples of identical sizes. The averaged performance measures were then reported for each algorithm.

As for the performance measures, besides the best-found Bayesian scores, we used F1-score as a measure of model's accuracy. F1-score considers both the *precision* and the *recall* to evaluate the classifier performance. In this context, precision is the number of correctly found directed edges divided by the number of all edges in the the predicted BN. Recall, on the other hand, is the number of correctly found directed edges divided by the number of edges in the actual benchmark BN. F1-score is then the harmonic mean of precision and recall values (Equation 3).

$$F_1 = 2 * \frac{precision * recall}{precision + recall} \tag{3}$$

Table 1 lists for each algorithm, the end-of-run F1 scores and the best-found Bayesian scores averaged over 20 independent runs (i.e., samples) for each of the benchmark problems. Statistics in parentheses are the standard deviations of the means. The highest Bayesian scores in each of the benchmark problems are underlined

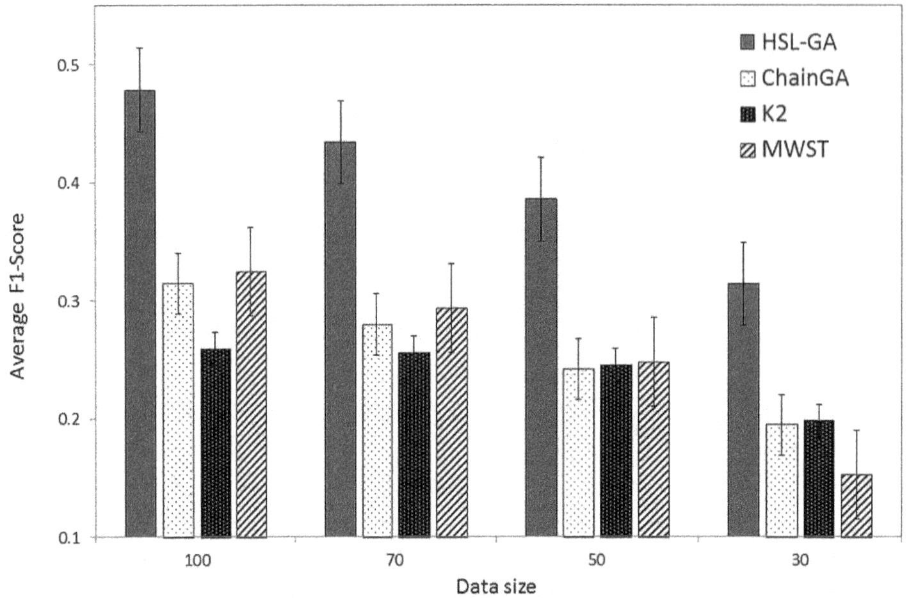

Figure 4: Average F1-scores of different algorithms in problems of variable data sizes (ALARM network)

in Table 1. Cases where more that one value are underlined imply that the differences are not statistically significant based on the nonparametric Wilcoxon signed-rank test (significance level $\alpha =$ 0.01). Similarly, the bold F1-scores are those with the highest values as well as values whose difference with the highest F1-score is statistically insignificance.

According to the results displayed in Table 3, HSL-GA can find highly-scored BNs while preserving relatively high model accuracy. In other words, in all the three problems, HSL-GA is among the best-performing algorithms in maximizing the Bayesian score, while at the same time, it achieves the highest F1-score when compared to other algorithms.

Chain-GA does not significantly improve the performance of the K2 algorithm. Note that Chain-GA equips K2 with a GA-based optimizer to search for an optimal chain structure model of node orderings prior to commencing the K2 structure learner. However, neither the Bayesian score nor the F1-score is significantly enhanced by Chain-GA when compared to K2 with random initial node orderings. The Bayesian score's standard deviation, however, is slightly decreased in Chain-GA as compared to K2, implying that the score of the predicted networks over different samples are less deviated from the mean, and thus possibly less affected by the initial node orderings.

HC is well-performing in ASIA problem, but performs poorly in medium and large-scaled problems. According to our computational resources, GES ran out of memory in medium and large problems. PC, on the other hand, suffers from excessive time complexity. In medium and large problems, PC is forced to stop after 24 hours spent on a single run.

K2 and Chain-GA can efficiently optimize the Bayesian scores, but the optimized structures have comparatively lower F1-scores. On the contrary, MWST is the second best-performing algorithm in terms of the model accuracy, but it performs poorly in regards to the Bayesian scores. This confirms the previous findings [16, 22] that a structure having a higher score does not necessarily have a higher classification accuracy.

In order to study the effect of the dataset size on the algorithmic performance, datasets of different sizes are sampled from ALARM network, and the average F1-scores over 20 samples generated at each size, were plotted in Figure 4. Notice that only F1-score statistic has been selected, as the magnitude of Bayesian scores negatively correlates with data size—i.e., the scores sharply decreases as the data size increases. Therefore, Bayesian scores across different datasets are not comparable, while F1-scores always vary between 0 and 1. Furthermore, the ultimate goal of a model is to provide a closer representation of the reality, and thus accuracy is a better metric to evaluate the performance of a model. Figure 4 draws the mean F1-scores of HSL-GA as compared to MWST, Chain-GA and K2 (which are the second and the third best performing algorithms in terms of the model accuracy) on datasets of 100, 70, 50, and 30 cases. As the bar charts show, HSL-GA outperforms the compared methods regardless of the data size. MWST is the most sensitive one to the data size, and its performance suddenly collapses when the dataset becomes very small (similar behavior was observed in HEPAR-II network as well). K2's accuracy is rather robust to the data size, but it is comparatively low, particularly in smaller data sizes. Chain-GA outperforms K2 in datasets of 100 and 70 cases, but similar to MWST, its performance significantly deteriorates as data cuts down.

4. SUMMARY

This work was concerned with proposing a hybrid structure learning algorithm, referred to as HSL-GA, which makes use of the capacities of both constraint-based and search-and-score approaches: HSL-GA performs a series of conditional independency tests to restrict the search space and then incorporates a genetic algorithm to effectively search over this reduced space. GA is a population-based S&S algorithm that can more effectively explore the space as compared to the single-solution heuristics such as the hill climbing algorithm.

HSL-GA is designed for medium to large scale problems where many of the existing powerful methods fail to function due to memory and/or time complexity (e.g., GES and PC). As compared to a series of well-known existing methods, HSL-GA can more accurately model the domain's knowledge specifically when data is limited. It shows a robust performance over datasets of different sizes.

HSL-GA, however, is not recommended for real-time learning problems, or time critical applications. In such cases, MWST and K2 are recommended according to our experiments. MWST is a suitable choice in time critical applications when enough data is also available. K2, on the other hand, is robust to the data size, but it has the drawback of being very sensitive to the initial node ordering and thus should be used with care in problems when the node ordering is not known a priori.

As for the future plans, following our overall research theme in modeling complex cellular processes, we intend to apply the proposed method in reconstructing the gene regulatory network of early adipocyte differentiation, as well as inferring the signaling network topology in oxidative stress-induced insulin responsive cells. In both of these applications, we are dealing with a relatively large number of genes/proteins and a small data size, for which we expect HSL-GA to be a powerful modeling candidate.

5. REFERENCES

[1] H. Akaike. A new look at the statistical model identificatione. *IEEE Transactions on Automatic Control*, 19, 1974.

[2] R. R. Bouckaert. Bayesian belief networks: From construction to inference. *PhD thesis, University of Utrecht*, 2, 1995.

[3] W. Buntine. Operations for learning with graphical models. *Journal of Artificial Intelligence Research*, 2, 1994.

[4] A. Carvalho. A cooperative coevolutionary genetic algorithm for learning bayesian network structures. *In Proceedings of the 13th annual conference on Genetic and evolutionary computation. ACM*, 2011.

[5] A. M. Carvalho. Scoring functions for learning bayesian networks. *Inesc-id Tec. Rep*, 2009.

[6] J. Cheng, D. Bell, and W. Liu. Learning bayesian networks from data: An efficient approach based on information theory. *In Proceedings of the 6th ACM International Conference on Information and Knowledge Management*, 1997.

[7] D. Chickering, D. Heckerman, and C. Meek. Large-sample learning of bayesian networks is NP-hard. *Journal of Machine Learning Research*, 5, 2004.

[8] D. M. Chickering. Optimal structure identification with greedy search. *The Journal of Machine Learning Research*, 3, 2003.

[9] C. Chow and C. Liu. Approximating discrete probability distributions with dependence trees. *IEEE transactions on Information Theory*, 14, 1968.

[10] G. Cooper and E. Herskovits. A bayesian method for the induction of probabilistic networks from data. *Machine Learning*, 9, 1992.

[11] D. Dash and M. Druzdzel. Robust independence testing for constraint-based learning of causal structure. *In Proceedings of the 19th Conference on Uncertainty in Artificial Intelligence*, 2003.

[12] L. M. de Campos. A scoring function for learning bayesian networks based on mutual information and conditional independence tests. *Journal of Machine Learning Research*, 7, 2006.

[13] L. M. de Campos, J. M. Fernández-Luna, and J. F. Huete. Bayesian networks and information retrieval: an introduction to the special issue. *Information Processing and Management (Elsevier)*, 40(5):727–733, 2004.

[14] P. Eades, X. Lin, and W. F. Smyth. A fast and effective heuristic for the feedback arc set problem. *Information Processing Letters*, 47(6):319–323, 1993.

[15] N. Friedman, I. Nachman, and D. Peer. Learning bayesian network structure from massive datasets: The "sparse candidate" algorithm. *In Uncertainty in Artificial Intelligence*, 1999.

[16] D. Grossman and P. Domingos. Learning bayesian network classifiers by maximizing conditional likelihood. *In Proceedings of the 21th International Conference on Machine Learning*, 2004.

[17] D. Heckerman, D. Geiger, and D. M. Chickering. Learning bayesian networks: The combination of knowledge and statistical data. *Machine Learning*, 20(3):197–243, 1995.

[18] S. M. Hill, Y. Lu, J. Molina, L. M. Heiser, P. T. Spellman, T. P. Speed, J. W. Gray, G. B. Mills, and S. Mukherjee. Bayesian inference of signaling network topology in a cancer cell line. *Bioinformatics*, 28(21):2804–2810, 2012.

[19] L. Huang, J. Nan, L. Guo, and Q. Lin. A bayesian network approach in the relevance feedback of personalized image semantic model. *Advances in Multimedia, Software Engineering and Computing, Springer Berlin Heidelberg*, 1, 2012.

[20] R. Kabli, F. Herrmann, and J. McCall. A chain-model genetic algorithm for bayesian network structure learnings. *In Proceedings of the 9th annual conference on Genetic and evolutionary computation. ACM*, 2007.

[21] R. M. Karp. *Reducibility among combinatorial problems.* Springer, 1972.

[22] P. Kontkanen, P. Myllymaki, T. Sliander, and H. Tirri. On supervised selection of bayesian networks. *In Proceedings of the 15th Conference on Uncertainty in Artificial Intelligence*, 1999.

[23] W. Lam and F. Bacchus. Learning bayesian belief networks: An approach based on the MDL principle. *Computational intelligence*, 10(3):269–293, 1994.

[24] P. Larranaga, C. Kuijpers, and R. Murga. Learning bayesian network structures by searching for the best ordering with genetic algorithms. *IEEE Transactions on System, Man and Cybernetics*, 26:87–493, 1996.

[25] P. Leray and O. Francois. *BNT structure learning package: Documentation and experiments.* Technical Report FRE CNRS 2645. Laboratoire PSI, Universitè et INSA de Rouen, 2004.

[26] P. Leray and O. Francois. *Source Code: BNT Structure Learning Package.* https://code.google.com/p/bnt/source/browse/trunk/SLP/, Last visited on 28, January 2014.

[27] P. Munteanu and M. Bendou. The EQ framework for learning equivalence classes of bayesian networks. *In Proceeding of the 1st IEEE International Conference on Data Mining*, 2002.

[28] K. Murphy. Active learning of causal bayes net structure. *Norsys, Netica*, 2001.

[29] K. Murphy. The bayes net toolbox for matlab. *Computing science and statistics*, 33(2):1024–1034, 2001.

[30] S. Nikolopoulos, G. T. Papadopoulos, I. Kompatsiaris, and I. Patras. Evidence-driven image interpretation by combining implicit and explicit knowledge in a bayesian network. *IEEE Transactions on Systems, Man, and Cybernetics, Part B: Cybernetics*, 41(5):1366–1381, 2011.

[31] J. Pearl. *Causality: Models, Reasoning, and Inference*. Cambridge University Press, 2000.

[32] J. Pellet and A. Elisseeff. Using markov blankets for causal structure learning. *The Journal of Machine Learning Research*, 9:1295–1342, 2008.

[33] Y. Raanan and B. Lerner. Bayesian network structure learning by recursive autonomy identification. *The Journal of Machine Learning Research*, 10:1527–1570, 2009.

[34] R. Robinson. Counting labeled acyclic digraphs. *Combinatorial mathematics V. Springer Berlin Heidelberg*, 5, 1977.

[35] M. Scutari. Bayesian network repository. *http://www.bnlearn.com/bnrepository/*, Last visited on 28, January 2014.

[36] C. Shan. Converting bayes nets from bif format to bnt format: bif2bnt program. *http://www.cs.rutgers.edu/ ccshan/*, Last visited on 28, January 2014.

[37] Y. M. Shtarkov. Universal sequential coding of single messages. *Problems of Information Transmission*, 23(3):3–17, 1987.

[38] P. Spirtes, C. Glymour, and R. Scheines. *Causation, Prediction and Search*. MIT Press, 2nd edition, 2000.

[39] O. Woodberry, A. Nicholson, K. Korb, and C. Pollino. Parameterising bayesian networks. *In Australian Conference on Artificial Intelligence*, 2004.

[40] B. Wray. Theory refinement on bayesian networks. *In Proceedings of the Seventh conference on Uncertainty in Artificial Intelligence*, 1991.

[41] J. Xia, R. Neapolitan, M. M. Barmada, and S. Visweswaran. Learning genetic epistasis using bayesian network scoring criteria. *BMC bioinformatics*, 12(1):89, 2011.

[42] G. Yan, R. Lee, A. Kent, and D. Wolpert. Towards a bayesian network game framework for evaluating ddos attacks and defense. *In Proceedings of the 2012 ACM conference on Computer and communications security, ACM*, 2012.

[43] C. Zhang, M. A. Frias, A. Mele, M. Ruggiu, T. Eom, C. B. Marney, H. Wang, D. D. Licatalosi, J. J. Fak, and R. B. Darnell. Integrative modeling defines the nova splicing-regulatory network and its combinatorial controls. *Science*, 329(5990):439–443, 2010.

[44] L. Zhifa, B. Malone, and C. Yuan. Empirical evaluation of scoring functions for bayesian network model selection. *BMC bioinformatics*, 13(Suppl 15):S14, 2012.

Among-site Rate Variation: Adaptation of Genetic Algorithm Mutation Rates at each Single Site

Fatemeh Vafaee
The University of Sydney
Sydney, NSW 2009, Australia
fatemeh.vafaee@sydney.edu.au

György Turán
University of Illinois at Chicago
Chicago, IL 60607, USA, and
MTA-SZTE Research Group on Artificial Intelligence
gyt@uic.edu

Peter C. Nelson and Tanya Y. Berger-Wolf
University of Illinois at Chicago
Chicago, IL 60607, USA
{nelson,tanyabw}@uic.edu

ABSTRACT

This paper is concerned with proposing an elitist genetic algorithm which makes use of a new mutation scheme aimed to tackle both explorative and exploitative responsibilities of genetic operators. The proposed mutation scheme follows an approach similar to motif representation in biology, to derive the underlying pattern of highly-fit solutions discovered so far. This pattern is then used to derive mutation rates specified for every site along the encoded solutions. The site-specific rates are amended for every individual to balance the required explorative and exploitative power. The Markov chain model of the proposed method is also derived and used to analyze its convergence properties.

Categories and Subject Descriptors

I.2.6 [**Artificial Intelligence**]: Learning—*Parameter learning*; I.2.8 [**Artificial Intelligence**]: Problem Solving, Control Methods, and Search—*Heuristic methods*

Keywords

Genetic Algorithms, mutation rate adaptation, Markov chain models of Genetic Algorithms

1. INTRODUCTION AND RELATED WORK

Evolutionary Algorithms belong to the family of stochastic generate-and-test search algorithms which achieve their power from the two sources: *exploration* of the search space and *exploitation* of the already found promising information [11]. Exploration is the ability of a search algorithm to discover unseen regions of the search space, and to avoid convergence to local optima. On the other hand, exploitation is defined as "*the ability of an algorithm to step into the direction of the desired improvement*" [2] or the capability of the "*good use of good information*" [11]. A search algorithm with well-adjusted exploitative power can improve the possibility of generating "better" solutions from already found "good" ones. A widespread opinion is that exploration and exploitation are opposite forces. Therefore, the success of a search algorithm resides in a reciprocal balance of the two [32]. It is well understood that excessive exploratory power usually leads to the discovery of the global optimum, but critically slows down the convergence rate. Conversely, the excessiveness of the exploitation rapidly results in the convergence to a local optima. In Genetic Algorithms (GAs), variation operators are known to be major sources which are supposed to introduce the required explorative and exploitative power into GAs, and to retain their mutual balance.

There has been a considerable amount of discussion and sometimes contradictory studies on the usefulness, or lack thereof, of the crossover and mutation operators in solving different problems. Spears [28], for instance, demonstrates that increasing the number of peaks in a fitness landscape has a deleterious effect on the performance of GA with crossover, while mutation-only GAs are unaffected by the number of peaks. Hordijk and Manderick [13] also conclude that crossover is ineffectual on uncorrelated NK-landscapes, but useful when high peaks are near one another. Furthermore, it is argued by Richter *et al.* [23] that GAs with crossover require exponential optimization time on Ignoble Trail functions, while mutation based genetic algorithms optimize them efficiently.

On the contrary, there is some evidence in the form of theoretical arguments or empirical studies that crossover speeds up GAs' optimization time for some functions—e.g., all-pairs shortest path problem, [21] and coloring problems by the Ising model [29].

Besides, the mutual effect of mutation and crossover is discussed in [17] showing that GAs with crossover perform a convex search on the population, i.e., compressing the convex hull of the population generation by generation until it eventually collapses to a single point. Mutation, instead, can randomly extend the convex hull by generating new points outside the present one, and the interaction of these conflicting operators leads to an equilibrium state.

The bottom line, however, is that retaining the balance of exploration vs. exploitation is necessary to GA performance, and it should be done by means of the variation operators either mutation, crossover, or both. In this work, we propose a new mutation scheme with both explorative and exploitative capabilities. The proposed mutation operator assigns specific rates to different sites (loci) of individuals in the population. The rates are derived in such a way that good individuals are exploited, while bad individuals are freely disrupted to allow a vast exploration of the search space. Furthermore, in order to retain the reciprocal balance of exploration and exploitation, we *adaptively* control the mutation rates throughout the evolution. In this regard, our proposed method can be suited within the parameter control Evolutionary Algorithms in which the parameters are subject to change *during* the algorithm run (as opposed to parameter tuning methods which set the parameter values *before* a run).

GECCO'14, July 12–16, 2014, Vancouver, BC, Canada.

ACM 978-1-4503-2662-9/14/07 ...$15.00.
http://dx.doi.org/10.1145/2576768.2598216.

Parameter control techniques can be divided into two major categories, referring to the taxonomy introduced by [10]: *self-adaptive* and *adaptive* approaches. In the self-adaptive paradigm, the parameters are encoded into the representation of the individual solutions and undergo mutation and recombination. The intuition is that the parameter values (e.g., the genetic operator rates) have a chance to co-evolve with problem solutions to hopefully (near)-optimal settings; see, for instance, [27] and [18].

On the other hand, in an adaptive scheme, the direction and/or magnitude of the parameters are determined based on some form of feedback (e.g., the quality of solutions) from the search. Among different parameters, adapting operator probabilities is known to be a worthy path toward improving the performance of Evolutionary Algorithms; e.g., [33], [20], [35], [4], and [3].

The mutation operator proposed in this paper fits into the category of adaptive parameter control Evolutionary Algorithms. Accordingly, we selected a series of adaptive and self-adaptive operator rate control methods, and compared them with our suggested method over a set of benchmark problems with different levels of "difficulty" (the notion of "difficulty" is defined in Section 5).

Henceforth, we refer to the method proposed in this paper as *SiRG* which stands for *Site-specific Rate Genetic-algorithm.* It is worth mentioning that the idea of attributing specific mutation rates to different sites has a root in biological models of evolution. The concept of "among-site rate variation" which indicates that the rate of nucleotide substitution varies among different sites of a DNA strand has long been introduced in phylogenetic and molecular evolutionary studies. Several among-site rate variation models—e.g., gamma-distributed and site-specific rates (SSR) models [31]—have emerged to properly describe the evolutionary behavior of nucleotide substitutions. Even though SiRG has not been directly inspired by such evolutionary models, we made use of the *Site-specific Rate* phrase in naming our proposed method since the idea of deriving mutation rates at single gene level came to us once we encountered the SSR model of evolution.

The remainder of this paper is organized as follows: Section 2 provides a detailed description of the SiRG algorithm and the underlying ideas. In Section 3 the Markov chain model of SiRG is derived and its convergence properties are analyzed. Experiments and results are presented in Section 4. Finally, Section 5 briefly summarizes the proposed algorithm.

2. A GA WITH AN EXPLORATIVE AND EXPLOITATIVE MUTATION

Exploration in GAs can be simply achieved by a random perturbation of individuals (e.g., uniform mutation is intrinsically an explorative operator). However, achieving an exploitative power, and then, retaining its balance with the required exploration are properties which are not readily attainable. As it is formerly mentioned, exploitation is *good use of good information to move the search towards the desirable improvements.* However, what is good information, and how can it be extracted and used for further improvements?

In non-deceptive environments, the underlying pattern of already found highly fit individuals seems to be a reliable source of the currently available good information. To learn such patterns, we make use of a revised version of *motif representation* in biology. Roughly speaking, motifs are biologically important patterns frequently recurring in different DNA sequences.

Once the pattern of good individuals has been derived, it is used to compute mutation rates specified to each site of every individual. As we will discuss later, these site-specific mutation rates are designed to explore the unseen regions, and equivalently, exploit already found promising regions of the search space.

To better understand the proposed motif-based approach, we first make a very brief detour into DNA motif representation. We then continue by describing the SiRG core ideas on extracting the underlying patterns of the currently available good individuals. Finally, we end this section by demonstrating the SiRG pseudo-code and explaining its functionality.

2.1 A Brief Detour into DNA Motif Representation

In genetics, a DNA *motif* is defined as a nucleotide acid sequence pattern that is widespread and has some biological significance [5]. Given a set of m DNA sequences, the problem of *motif discovery* can be roughly defined as finding a set of m subsequences $\mathcal{X} = \{x_1, x_2, \ldots, x_m\}$, one from each input sequence, that maximizes a predefined scoring criterion. The set of discovered patterns is usually represented as a *consensus sequence* or in a *matrix* form.

In the consensus approach, the patterns (subsequences) are lined up by their starting positions and at each site, the nucleotide basis with the highest frequency is recorded. Consider for instance, the following example of four DNA subsequences of length $l = 5$:[1]

x_1:	ACCTG
x_2:	TCGTG
x_3:	ACGTC
x_4:	ACGTA
Consensus:	ACGTG

An alternative to consensus, is matrix representation usually referred to as *position frequency matrix* (PFM). Considering n subsequences of length l and $b = 4$ nucleotide bases, a PFM is a matrix $F = (f_{i,j})$ of size $b \times l$, where $f_{i,j}$ is the frequency of the occurrence of nucleotide basis b_i at site j of all n sequences. For instance, the matrix representation of the four sequences of the previous example would be of the form

	nucleotide site				
basis	1	2	3	4	5
A	3	0	0	0	1
C	0	4	1	0	1
T	1	0	0	4	0
G	0	0	3	0	2

Matrix representation, in general, carries more information since the consensus representation simply neglects the occurrence of nucleotide bases with lower frequencies. Matrix representation, on the other hand, preserves all available information. Additionally, the consensus sequence can be easily derived by a PFM, but not the other way around.

2.2 SiRG Algorithm (Basic Ideas)

In our framework, highly fit individuals can be thought of as motifs since they are "important" sequences in a sense that they possibly carry the underlying patterns of promising solutions. Assume that out of a population of n binary solutions, $m(\leq n)$ individuals have been drawn based on the superiority of their fitness values. Intuitively, we interpret the underlying pattern of (available) promising solutions as the possibility of the occurrence of each allele (i.e., '0' and '1') appearing at each site of high-quality individuals selected out of the current population.

[1]Note that on its most elementary level, the structure of DNA sequence can be thought as a long succession of four letters—A, C, G, and T—representing the four nucleotide bases of a DNA strand.

```
Algorithm: Site-specific Rate Genetic-algorithm (SiRG)
Given: String length l, population size n ≥ 1,

1. t ← 0
2. s_0 ←INITIAL-POPULATION(n, l)
3. repeat
4.    x*(s_t) ←GET-ELITE(s_t)
5.    s'_t ←SELECTION(s_t)
6.    s''_t ←SiRG-MUTATION(s'_t)
7.    s_{t+1} ←PLACE-ELITE(s''_t, x*(s_t))
8.    t ← t + 1
9. until stop condition is met
```

Figure 1: SiRG algorithm

```
function: SiRG-MUTATION(s'_t) returns mutated population
   inputs: (fitness-proportional) Selected population s'_t

1. E_t ←FORM-ELITE-GROUP(s'_t)
2. PWM_t ←CONSTRUCT-PWM(E_t)
3.    for each individual x^t_k = ⟨x^t_{k,0}, ..., x^t_{k,l-1}⟩ ∈ s'_t do
4.       for each site j = 0, ..., l − 1 do
5.          μ^t_{k,j} ←COMPUTE-SiRG-MU(x^t_k, j, PWM_t)
6.          if rand(0, 1) ≤ μ^t_{k,j} do
7.             x^t_{k,j} ← x^t_{k,j} ⊕ 1
8. return s'_t
```

Figure 2: Site-specific Rate Mutation scheme

To derive such a pattern, we can construct a revised version of position frequency matrix, denoted as $PFM' = (f'_{i,j})$ in which each component $f'_{i,j}$ corresponds to the *probability* of the occurrence of allele $i \in \{0, 1\}$ at site j.

Notice that PFM' representation suffers from an important drawback: all chosen individuals have an identical effect on determining the pattern of promising solutions. However, intuitively, better individuals should play a more important role in the procedure.To resolve this problem, we further refine the representation by constructing a *position weight matrix*, $PWM = (w_{i,j})$, wherein the individuals are weighted by their fitness values based on:

$$w_{i,j} = \frac{\sum_{k=1}^{m} f(x_k).\delta(x_{k,j} = i)}{\sum_{k=1}^{m} f(x_k)}, \tag{1}$$

where $f(x_k)$ is the fitness of individual x_k. PWM is then used to derive site-specific mutation rates. These rates are gauged for every individual to control the exploration and exploitation of the search space.

2.3 SiRG Algorithm (Pseudo-code)

The overall framework of the proposed SiRG algorithm has been sketched in Figure 1. The algorithm starts by randomly initializing a population of n individuals. Then, following the inherent mechanism of evolutionary algorithms, SiRG main evolutionary cycle—lines 4 to 7 in Figure 1—incorporates two primary operations of *selection* and *reproduction*. As for the selection mechanism, SiRG employs a modified version of the canonical *elitist*[2] *fitness-proportional* selection [8]. The reproduction operation is then accomplished by means of the newly proposed mutation operator. SiRG generally works as follows:

At each iteration of the SiRG main evolutionary loop, the best individual in the current population s_t is first determined and saved as $x^*(s_t)$ (line 4). Then, a population consisting of better individuals in s_t are selected to go under the reproduction phase (line 5). Every individual in the selected population s'_t then experiences mutation resulting in a new population s''_t (line 6). The proposed mutation scheme is discussed in the next subsection. Finally, upon the termination of generation t, the reproduced population s''_t is examined to check whether its best individual has a lower (i.e., worse) fitness value than $x^*(s_t)$. If that would be the case, $x^*(s_t)$ replaces the *worst* individual in s''_t (line 7), and the resultant population proceeds to the next generation.

[2]In elitist selection, the best individual survives with probability 1.

2.4 Site-specific Rate Mutation Scheme

Figure 2 gives the detailed pseudo-code of the proposed mutation scheme. As the Figure shows, the SiRG-MUTATION function begins by forming an elite set containing highly-fit individuals selected out of the population s'_t. An individual $x^t_k \in s'_t$ is eligible for being selected if $f(x^t_k) \geq \alpha f_{max}$, where $\alpha \in [0.5\ 1]$ is a reduction factor, and f_{max} is the best individual in the current population which is also the best individual ever found as SiRG is elitist (i.e., maintains the best solution discovered so far).

The selected individuals are then considered as the currently available promising solutions to construct the position weight matrix (PWM) according to Equation (1). The resultant PWM gives the *weighted* probability of occurrence of each allele at every site of high-quality individuals. This has been considered as the underlying pattern of the promising solutions discovered so far.

Accordingly, for each site $j = 0, \ldots, l-1$ of every individual $x^t_k \in s'_t$, a distinct mutation rate $\mu^t_{k,j}$ is computed (COMPUTE-SiRG-MU function in line 5 of Figure 2), and used to mutate site j of individual x^t_k.

$\mu^t_{k,j}$ is computed according to Equation (2), where ε is a small positive number to avoid zero probabilities. Furthermore, $w_{i,j}$ is the (i, j)th element of matrix PWM where $i = x^t_{k,j}$ is the allele number (i.e., either 0 or 1 corresponding to alleles '0' and '1') appearing in site j of individual x^t_k.

$$\begin{aligned} \mu^t_{k,j} = \quad & \left[\varepsilon + (1-\varepsilon)(1 - f(x^t_k)/f_{max})\right] * \\ & \left[\varepsilon + (1-\varepsilon)(1 - w^t_{i,j})\right]. \end{aligned} \tag{2}$$

Notice that using the above equation, the mutation rate at each site is gauged based on the following two criteria: 1) The probability of having the corresponding allele at that site based on the PWM constructed out of high-quality individuals. Since the pattern of good solutions is somehow represented by a PWM, being in conformity with this pattern should give rise to lower rates of mutation and vice versa. 2) The fitness of the individual which is about to get mutated; in general better individuals are more probable to carry more valuable information, and thus, they need to be modified more carefully. In other words, assigning them high mutation rates is rather risky and may cause destruction of useful information.

We have already claimed that our proposed mutation scheme retains the exploitation and exploration reciprocal balance. How can this claim be justified?

As we mentioned earlier, exploitation is defined to be the *good use of good information*. The exploitatory power in this framework is achieved by mutating highly-fit individuals. These individuals are not radically disrupted by mutation since besides their high fitness which lessens the mutation rates, they usually show more conformity with the pattern of good individuals represented by the PWM. Even though only a few number of genes are usually perturbed across good individuals, that small fraction of perturbation mostly occurs on sites which are not in accordance with the general pattern of best found solutions. That is how good information concealed in good-quality individuals is used to wisely reproduce new individuals and consequently exploit the promising solutions.

On the other hand, the exploratory power of the proposed mutation scheme is achieved by mutating low-fit individuals. These individuals in contrast are subject to high disruption which results in the discovery of possibly new regions of the search space.

3. MARKOV CHAIN MODEL OF SIRG

A finite Markov chain model is a probabilistic trajectory over a finite space state $\mathcal{S}$, where the states are usually numbered from 0 to $|\mathcal{S}|-1$, with the property that the next state depends only on the current state. Any (homogeneous)[3] Markov chain can be fully described by its state space and the corresponding $\mathcal{S}\times\mathcal{S}$ *transition matrix* $\boldsymbol{P}=(p_{ij})$, where $p_{ij}\in[01]$ is the probability of transitioning from state $i\in\mathcal{S}$ to state $j\in\mathcal{S}$, and $\sum_{j=0}^{\mathcal{S}-1}p_{ij}=1$.

Historically, it was quite natural to view GAs as Markov chain processes in which the current population corresponds to the current state of the process [8, 6]. The characteristics of the population trajectories from randomly generated initial populations can be then modeled as Markovian transitions over the state space of all possible populations. The majority of the prior GA Markov chain models were proposed based upon infinite-population assumption and target to characterize the steady-state behavior of the process [7, 34, 25, 30]. Among the many papers on Markov Models of GAs, Nix and Vose model [22] has been the most widely used one as it assumes no constraints on population size and its trajectories. This model serves as a basis to derive the SiRG Markov model presented in this section.

Markov chain models have been widely used to analyze the dynamic behavior of evolutionary algorithms. Deriving the convergence rate [30, 12], the steady state distribution [34, 22, 26], and the expected short-term behavior of evolutionary algorithms [9, 28] are some examples of the problems addressed within the framework of Markov chain models.

Markov chain models have been also traditionally used to analyze the convergence of genetic algorithms to the global optima as time approaches to infinity [26, 30]. It has been formerly proved by [24] that *elitist* genetic algorithms converge to global optima.In Section 3.3, we derive the same fact from the Markov chain model, in order to illustrate the potential use of this model to obtain more detailed information. The Markov chain model of SiRG should be more intensively used in our future work in order to analyze the short-term and asymptotic behavior of our proposed method.

3.1 Nix & Vose Markov Chain Model of GAs

Let Ω be the set of all possible strings of length l, i.e. $\Omega=\{0,1\}^l$, and $r=|\Omega|=2^l$ be the number of possible strings of such a space. A population s of size n is a multiset of n elements from Ω. The number of possible populations of size n, denoted by N is given by: $N=\begin{pmatrix} n+r-1 \\ n \end{pmatrix}$ [22].

The possible populations are described by an $r\times N$ matrix Z with the ith column $\phi_i=\langle z_{0,i},\ldots,z_{r-1,i}\rangle^T$ corresponding to the incidence vector of the ith population, s_i. In other words, $z_{y,i}$ is the number of occurrences of string y in s_i, where y is the integer representation of the binary string.

Now, the goal is to construct the $N\times N$ transition matrix of the model, P, where each entry $p_{i,j}$ represents the conditional probability of being in state s_j in the next generation given that the current state is s_i.

Let $q_i(y)$ be the probability of producing string y in the next generation knowing that the current population is s_i. To produce population s_j we need to get exactly $z_{y,j}$ copies of the string y for $y=0,\ldots,r-1$. The probability of this joint event can be then written as a multinomial distribution with success probabilities $q_i(y)$ for $y=0,\ldots,r-1$:

$$p_{i,j}=\frac{n!}{z_{0,j}!z_{1,j}!\ldots z_{r-1,j}!}\prod_{y=0}^{r-1}(q_i(y))^{z_{y,j}} \tag{3}$$

To calculate the conditional probability $q_i(y)$, Nix and Vose used two mathematical operators [34], $\mathcal{F}$ and $\mathcal{M}$, known as *selection scheme* and *mixing scheme*, respectively. Operator $\mathcal{F}$ is determined from the fitness function and captures the effect of the selection pressure. Operator $\mathcal{M}$ models the recombination (mixing) process and depends on the mutation rate, the crossover rate, and the form of the crossover and mutation operations.

More specifically, if v would be a vector with its yth component equal to the number of occurrence of individual y in the current population, $\mathcal{F}(v)$ returns a vector whose y^{th} element corresponds to the probability of selecting y for recombination. Subsequently, if v is a vector with y^{th} component equal to the probability of selecting y for recombination, $\mathcal{M}(v)$ is a vector whose y^{th} element is the expected proportion of y in the next generation. Clearly, with $\mathcal{F}$ and $\mathcal{M}$ defined, $q_i(y)$ can be exactly derived from $\mathcal{M}(\mathcal{F}(\phi_i))_y$.

Through the next section, precise formulations of $\mathcal{F}$ and $\mathcal{M}$ operators for SiRG are first derived, and then, a revised version of Equation (3) which captures the elitist property of the SiRG selection mechanism has been devised .

3.2 Markov Chain Model of SiRG

According to the SiRG algorithm displayed in Figure 1, elite is placed in the population after the completion of the selection and reproduction procedures. Thus, we can simply put aside the elitist property of SiRG for a while, and merely focus on deriving the selection and the mixing schemes based on the corresponding functions appearing in lines 5 and 6 of the SiRG pseudo-code. Note that the notation introduced in the previous subsection are also adopted throughout the rest of this paper.

Using the *fitness-proportional* selection, the selection scheme, $\mathcal{F}$, is defined by Equation (4), where f is a row vector of individuals' fitness values, and v is the incidence vector of a population.

$$\mathcal{F}(v)=\frac{diag(f)v}{fv} \tag{4}$$

The mixing operator in our framework depends on the current population since, as it is discussed in Section 2.4, the Position Weight Matrix, and consequently the mutation rates, are derived based on the individuals contained in the currently selected population, s'_t. To derive the mixing operator of the current population $\mathcal{M}_t$, we need to construct an $r\times r$ *mixing matrix* $M_t=(m^t_{y,x})$, where $m^t_{y,x}$ corresponds to the probability that string y is the child of mutating parent string x, given that the current population is s_t. If we define $\acute{\mu}^t_{y,x,j}$ as

$$\acute{\mu}^t_{y,x,j}=\begin{cases}\mu^t_{x,j} & \text{if } y_j\neq x_j\\ 1-\mu^t_{x,j} & \text{otherwise}\end{cases}, \tag{5}$$

[3] A Markov chain is said to be *homogenous* if the transition probabilities are independent from time.

where $\mu^t_{x,j}$ is the mutation rate of individual x at site j (refer to Equation (2)), $m^t_{y,x}$ would be simply derived by

$$m^t_{y,x} = \prod_{j=0}^{l-1} \dot{\mu}^t_{y,x,j}. \quad (6)$$

Having mixing matrix M_t on hand, the mixing operator is defined by Equation (7), where v is an r-dimensional column vector whose components correspond to the proportions of different individuals in the selected population. $\mathcal{M}_t(v)$ would give then the expected proportions of different individuals in the next (intermediary) population s''_t.

$$\mathcal{M}_t(v) = M_t v \quad (7)$$

Once $\mathcal{F}$ and $\mathcal{M}_t$ are defined, the conditional probability $q_t(y)$ in Equation (3)—the probability of producing string y in the next (intermediary) population (i.e., s''_t) given that the current population is s_t—is derived by

$$q_t(y) = \mathcal{M}_t(\mathcal{F}(\phi_t))_y, \quad (8)$$

where ϕ_t is the incidence vector of population s_t.

Now, we are ready to encounter the elitist property of SiRG applied in line 7 of Figure 1. For the ease of representation and subsequent analysis, without loss of generality, we assign a label $k \in \{0, 1, \ldots, r-1\}$ to each individual in the *descending* order of $f(k)$ where individuals with equal fitness values are numbered according to a predetermined tie-breaking rule. Furthermore, we label every population a number $i \in \{0, 1, \ldots, N-1\}$ according to the *descending* order of $f(x^*(i))$, where $x^*(i)$ is the best individual contained in the population labeled as i. Similarly, a predetermined tie-breaking rule should be applied when more than one population have the same $f(x^*(i))$.

Assume that by adopting the above-mentioned numbering strategy, s_t (the population of the current generation), s'_t (the *selected* temporary-population), s''_t (the *mutated* temporary-population), and s_{t+1} (the population of the next generation) are respectively labeled as i, k, m, and $j \in \{0, 1, \ldots, N-1\}$.

$p^e_{i,j}$ is then interpreted as the transition probability from the current population labeled as i to the population of the next generation labeled as j under the elitist mechanism adopted by SiRG. The superscript e stands for *elite*, and is to distinguish the elitist transition probability from the non-elitist one $p_{i,j}$ in Equation (3). Since regular transitions of states based on selection and mutation operators are restricted by PLACE-ELITE function, the formulation of the transition probabilities $p_{i,j}$ appeared in Equation (3) should be redefined. Notice that the probabilities of transitioning to states containing fitter individuals than the best individual in the current population i is unaffected. Furthermore, SiRG never performs a transition to a population whose best individual is worse than $x^*(i)$. Therefore, the SiRG transition probability $p^e_{i,j}$ can be formally defined as

$$p^e_{i,j} = \begin{cases} 0 & \text{if } f(x^*(j)) < f(x^*(i)) \\ p_{i,j} & \text{if } f(x^*(j)) > f(x^*(i)) \\ \tilde{p}^e_{i,j} & \text{otherwise} \end{cases}. \quad (9)$$

We are now only left with the calculation of $\tilde{p}^e_{i,j}$ which is the transition probability from state i to j by the next generation when the best individuals in both populations i and j have identical fitness values. Note that every mutated temporary-population m whose best individual is *worst* than $x^*(i)$, would be converted by PLACE-ELITE function to a new population j. Population j is identical to population m except for the number of occurrences of the worst individual in m, denoted as $\breve{x}(m)$, which would be reduced by 1 in j, and the number of occurrences of $x^*(i)$ which is increased to 1 in j. More formally, the incidence vector of population j would be of the form[4]

$$\begin{aligned} &z_{y,j} = z_{y,m} \text{ for } y \in \{0, \ldots, r-1\} - \{\breve{x}(m), x^*(i)\}, \\ &z_{\breve{x}(m),j} = z_{\breve{x}(m),m} - 1, \text{ and} \\ &z_{x^*(i),j} = 1. \end{aligned}$$

Therefore, the transition probabilities to populations containing: only one occurrence of individual $x^*(i)$, no individual which is better than $x^*(i)$, and no *distinct* individual which is as good as $x^*(i)$, can *not* be determined directly from Equation (3) since PLACE-ELITE function converts any population "worse"[5] than the current population to a population of these forms. The transition probabilities $\tilde{p}^e_{i,j}$ could be accordingly written as

$$\tilde{p}^e_{i,j} = \begin{cases} p_{i,j} & \text{if } z_{x^*(i),j} > 1 \text{ or } x^*(j) \neq x^*(i) \\ p_{i,j} + \sum_{j'} p_{i,j'} & \text{otherwise} \end{cases}, \quad (10)$$

where $p_{i,j'}$ is a (non-elitist) transition probability to any population j' whose incidence vector is identical to j's for all components except for $x^*(i)$th component where $z_{x^*(i),j'} = 0$, and for a component $y \in \{x^*(i)+1, \ldots, r-1\}$ for which $z_{y,j'} = z_{y,j} + 1$.[6]

Now, we further investigate the structure of SiRG transition matrix $P^e = (p^e_{i,j})$, which can be useful for further analysis of the algorithm's properties (e.g., convergence analysis).

Let us define $N_{[ab]}$ be the number of populations containing *at least* one individual from set $\{a, a+1, \ldots, b-1\}$, assuming that $b > a$, and including no individual whose label is less than a (note that the lower the label is, the higher the fitness would be).

THEOREM 1.

$$N_{[ab]} = \binom{n+r-a-1}{n} - \binom{n+r-b-1}{n} \quad (11)$$

PROOF. We define $N_{[a-]}$ to be the number of populations that have no individual with label below a. $N_{[a-]}$ contains all the populations counted in $N_{[ab]}$ plus the populations having no solution with label less than b, that is, $N_{[b-]}$. Therefore, $N_{[a-]} - N_{[b-]}$ is exactly the number of populations having at least one solution in $[a\ b)$, which is $N_{[ab]}$.

Notice that $N_{[a-]} = \binom{n+r-a-1}{n}$ is simply the n-combinations with replacement of all the possible individuals except those with label lower than a, i.e., $r-a$ individuals. □

Furthermore, suppose the objective function for all r individuals, has $h \leq r$ *distinct* values. Assuming that these h values are descendingly *ranked* (i.e., sorted), we define r_k to be the number of individuals whose fitness rank is *at most* $k \in \{1, \ldots, h\}$. Thus, r_1 is the number of individuals with the highest possible fitness (i.e., optimal solutions), and r_h refers to all possible individuals. Accordingly, $N_{[r_k r_{k+1}]}$ for $k = 0, \ldots, h-1$, where $r_0 = 0$, refers to the number of populations possessing at least one individual from $\{r_k, \ldots, r_{k+1}-1\}$ and no individual from the set $\{0, \ldots, r_k - 1\}$.

[4]Notice that according to our labeling strategy, $x^*(i)$ and $\breve{x}(m)$ now correspond to two numbers in $\{0, 1, \ldots, r-1\}$.

[5]Population a would be worst than population b if $f(x^*(a)) < f(x^*(b))$.

[6]Without loss of generality, assume that $x^*(i)$ has the highest label among all individuals possessing identical fitness value as $f(x^*(i))$.

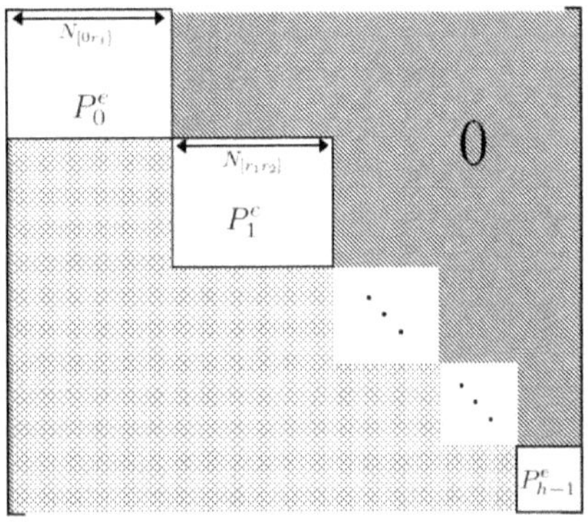

Figure 3: SiRG transition matrix

In other words, $N_{[r_k r_{k+1}]}$ corresponds to the number of possible populations whose best individuals' fitness is ranked as $k+1$. The following property on the sum of all $N_{[r_k r_{k+1}]}$'s should rationally hold:

THEOREM 2.

$$\sum_{k=0}^{h-1} N_{[r_k r_{k+1}]} = N = \begin{pmatrix} n+r-1 \\ n \end{pmatrix}. \tag{12}$$

PROOF. It is simply derived by the fact that each population is counted exactly once in one of the $N_{[r_k r_{k+1}]}$ terms. □

Using the above definitions and theorems, we are now ready to expose the structure of the SiRG transition matrix.

THEOREM 3. *The SiRG transition Matrix $P^e = (p^e_{i,j})$, as it is depicted in Figure 3, has h diagonal sub-matrices P^e_k of size $N_{[r_k r_{k+1}]} \times N_{[r_k r_{k+1}]}$ for $k = 0, \ldots, h-1$. Furthermore, all components to the upper right of the diagonal matrices are zeros, all components at the lower left of the diagonal matrices are computed based on the non-elitist transition probability formula $p_{i,j}$ (Equation (3)), and the diagonal matrices' components are themselves derived according to the elitist transition probability $\tilde{p}^e_{i,j}$ (Equation (10)).*

PROOF. Considering our labeling strategy, the above theorem trivially holds since: 1) any diagonal sub-matrices P^e_k includes all transition probabilities among the populations which their best individuals have an identical fitness; thus, they should be computed based on $\tilde{p}^e_{i,j}$ derived according to Equation (10), 2) all components to the upper right of the diagonal matrices correspond to the transition from a population i to population j where $f(x^*(j)) < f(x^*(i))$; therefore they are all 0, and 3) all components to the lower left of the diagonal matrices correspond to the transition from a population i to population j where $f(x^*(j)) > f(x^*(i))$. Thus, they are not affected by the elitist strategy and derived by the non-elitist transition probability formula $p_{i,j}$ displayed by Equation (3). □

3.3 Convergence Analysis using SiRG's Markov Model

Even though SiRG converges to global optima due to its elitist nature, in order to provide a simple example of applying Markov chain theories in the analysis of SiRG's properties, we followed the traditional approach of using the Markov model to prove the convergence [26].

The convergence of a genetic algorithm to global optimum is defined by [26] as follows:

Let $\mathcal{X}_t = max\{f(x)|x \in s_i^{(t)}\}$ denote the best fitness within a population represented by state s_i at timestamp t. A genetic algorithm is then said to converge to the global optimum, if and only if

$$\lim_{t\to\infty} P\{\mathcal{X}_t = f^*\} = 1 \tag{13}$$

where $f^* = max\{f(x)|x \in \Omega\}$ is the global optimum of the maximization problem under study.

The convergence of any genetic algorithm can be analyzed based on the limit behavior of its underlying Markov chain. Since the limit distribution of the Markov chain depends on the structure of the transition matrix, it is quite useful to first review the following classification of transition matrices:

An $n \times n$ square matrix $A = (a_{ij})$ is said to be ***nonnegative***, if $a_{i,j} \geq 0$ for all $i, j \in \{0, \ldots, n-1\}$, ***positive***, if $a_{i,j} > 0$ for all $i, j \in \{0, \ldots, n-1\}$, ***primitive***, if A is nonnegative and there exists a $k \in \mathbb{N}$ such that A^k is positive, ***stochastic***, if A is nonnegative and $\sum_{j=0}^{n-1} a_{ij} = 1$ for all $i = 0, \ldots, n-1$, ***stable***, if A is stochastic and as k gets large, A^k approaches a fixed matrix, the fixed matrix is called the stable matrix of A, and ***reducible***, if A is nonnegative and by applying the same permutation to rows and columns, it can be brought into the form

$$\begin{pmatrix} C & 0 \\ R & T \end{pmatrix}, \tag{14}$$

where C and T are square matrices.

THEOREM 4 ([15], P. 126). Let P be an $n \times n$ reducible stochastic matrix written in the form of Equation (14), where C is an $m \times m$ primitive stochastic matrix and $R, T \neq 0$. Then

$$P^\infty = \lim_{k\to\infty} P^k = \begin{pmatrix} C^\infty & 0 \\ R^\infty & 0 \end{pmatrix}$$

is a stable stochastic matrix with $P^\infty = \mathbf{1}^T p^\infty$, where $p^\infty = p^0 P^\infty$ is unique regardless of the initial distribution p^0, and p^∞ satisfies: $p_i^\infty > 0$ for $1 \leq i \leq m$ and $p_i^\infty = 0$ for $m < i \leq n$.

Refereing to the structure of SiRG transition matrix sketched in Figure 3, Theorem 4 can be used to simply prove the convergence of SiRG to globally optima.

THEOREM 5. *SiRG converges to populations containing globally optimal solutions.*

PROOF. The SiRG transition matrix P^e as it is depicted by Figure 3 and described by Theorem 3, is clearly a reducible matrix. The sub-matrix $P^e_0 > 0$ gathers the transition probabilities for states containing at least one optimal solution. P^e_0 is positive, so it would be primitive. Furthermore, P^e_0 is stochastic because P^e is stochastic, and thus, $\sum_{j=0}^{N-1} p^e_{i,j} = 1$ for all $i = 0, \ldots, N-1$. However, $p^e_{i,j} = 0$ for $i = N_{[0,r_1]}, \ldots, N-1$. Therefore,

$$\sum_{j=0}^{N_{[0r_1]}-1} p^e_{i,j} = 1 \text{ for } i = 0, \ldots, N_{[0,r_1]-1},$$

which means that P^e is stochastic. Additionally, R and T both contain positive-valued elements as the mutation rates are non-zero; therefore, $T, R \neq 0$. Hence, Theorem 4 guarantees that the probability of staying in any population containing no globally optimal solution converges to zero, while the probability of being in some populations possessing a global optimal solution converges to one. Thus, the limit of $P\{\mathcal{X}_t = f^*\}$ converges to one as $t \to \infty$. □

4. EXPERIMENTS AND RESULTS

4.1 Problem Formulation

In this work we used the multimodality test-problem generator proposed by [28]. In general, test-problem generators can create random problems from certain classes of problems with user-controllable characteristics. We selected a controllable multimodal framework in order to investigate how well SiRG can explore the landscape and exploit true optima as the number of peaks in the search space varies. Furthermore, it has been shown that the multimodality of a search space is an important characteristic for determining the utility of crossover in an evolutionary algorithm [28]. Therefore, the chosen test-problem generator can provide a good framework to compare the performance of our method equipped with an exploitive mutation with GAs using the traditional crossover operator.

In the multimodality problem generator employed in this paper, the number of peaks $\mathcal{P}$ (the degree of multimodality) can be controlled easily and systematically by the experimenter. The idea is to randomly generate $\mathcal{P}$ peaks each represented by an l-bit string in the space. To evaluate an arbitrary binary string, the nearest peak (in Hamming space) is first located. Its fitness is then the number of bits the string has in common with that nearest peak, divided by l. Formally, the fitness of an arbitrary string j denoted by f_j is derived from the following formula:

$$f_j = \frac{1}{l} \max_{i=1}^{\mathcal{P}} \{l - \text{HAMMDIST}(j, peak_i)\} \quad (15)$$

4.2 Compared Algorithms

The performance of SiRG has been compared to the canonical GA as well as some evolutionary algorithms formerly designed to control the rates of variation operators. We have selected the following adaptive/self-adaptive evolutionary algorithms:
1) canonical genetic algorithm (CGA), 2) credit-based adaptive genetic algorithm (CAGA) [20], 3) ranked based genetic algorithm (Rank-GA) [4], 4) auto-tuning based genetic algorithm (atGA) [19], 5) adaptive genetic algorithm based on fuzzy mechanism (FuzzyAGA) [14], and 6) self-adaptive genetic algorithm (SAGA) [1].

The compared algorithms are either recently devised and shown to outperform some of the former mutation rate heuristics, or they are pioneer works in this context, frequently cited, and seem to be well-matured benchmark algorithms. Due to the space limitation, we refer readers to the corresponding references for the description of the selected EAs.

4.3 Simulation Settings

We assessed different algorithms using problems with different levels of "difficulty."[7] To gauge the difficulty of the problem, we changed the length of the individuals l and the population size n. Clearly, as l increases the problem becomes more challenging since the state space is exponentially extended as the length of individuals grows. Increasing the population size, however, reduces the chance of premature convergence to non-optimal values, and increases the possibility of finding better solutions at the end of the optimization process [16].

We set up different levels of problem difficulty by setting the parameter pair (l, n) to (50,30), (100,50), and (150,100). Additionally, to investigate the optimization performance in multimodal landscapes, we separately applied each of the three problem settings on search spaces with different degrees of multimodality by setting the total number of peaks $\mathcal{P}$ to 1, 5, and 10. Each peak is represented by a randomly generated l-bit binary string which determines the location of the peak in the search environment. Maximum number of iterations is set to 100. Furthermore, due to the stochastic nature of genetic algorithms, the performance of all algorithms over each problem setting is evaluated based on statistics obtained from 50 independent runs. Free parameters in compared EAs are set according to their authors' suggestions. In canonical GA, mutation and crossover rates are set to 0.1 and 0.8, respectively. In SiRG, reduction factor α is set to 0.9.

[7]Here the problem difficulty is defined in terms of the size of the search space and the availability of the resources (i.e., the population size), rather than the deceptiveness of the fitness landscape.

4.4 Simulation Results and Analysis

The detailed simulation results including the average and the standard deviation (in parentheses) of the best-found fitness values over 50 trials are listed in Table 1. The average best fitness is calculated from all of the end-of-run best fitness values which are either obtained when the maximum number of generations is encountered, or if a perfect solution is found. Any bold average value indicates that the corresponding algorithm outperforms the rest for the given parameter setting. Additionally, the underlined average values are those with the smaller corresponding standard deviations. Smaller standard deviations represent steadier and consequently more reliable ultimate solutions. Thus, a bold and underlined average value indicates that the corresponding algorithm provides both more accurate and more consistent final results.

As the statistics displayed in Table 1 demonstrate, in all experiments, SiRG clearly outperforms all the compared algorithms. in order to test the statistical significance of the differences between the performance of SiRG and the compared algorithms, as the sample distributions *do not* follow Normal distribution, we have run the Wilcoxon non-parametric statistical hypothesis test. The obtained statistics confirmed the significance of the differences at confidence level of 0.01 (i.e., p-value < 0.01) for all problem settings.

Rank-GA is the second best-performing algorithm. Even though Rank-GA performs well as compared to other benchmark algorithms, it suffers from excessive fitness evaluations and run time complexity. Rank-GA sorts the individuals according to their fitness values prior to applying the mutation and crossover operators. Therefore, comparing to SiRG and other benchmark algorithms, the number of fitness evaluations are doubled per generation. In addition, sorting the population two times at every iteration further raises the algorithmic time complexity.

Furthermore, as the results displayed in Table 1 show, the performance of SiRG is perfectly robust with respect to the number of peaks. The performance of the compared algorithms slightly varies, though not statistically significantly, as the number of peaks increases. Intuitively, as the number of desirable peaks (i.e., true optima) increases the possibility of randomly finding one of them grows. Hence, the performance of stochastic search methods which are meant for finding *an* optimum (not *all* optima) should be naturally improved by the growth of the number of the true optima. In our experimental settings, however, as l is always set to high values, the higher number of peaks does not show significant improvement of the optima's reachability in such a huge search space.

5. SUMMARY

In this paper we proposed an elitist genetic algorithm, called SiRG, augmented by a new mutation scheme that is capable of exploring the unseen regions of the search space, and simultaneously exploiting the already-found promising elements. SiRG adaptively specifies different mutation rates for different sites of an encoded solution based on the underlying pattern of highly-fit solutions, and

Table 1: End-of-run results achieved by different algorithms for different problem settings

Peak No.	(l, n)	SiRG	atGA	CAGA	CGA	FuzzyAGA	Rank-GA	SAGA
$\mathcal{P} = 1$	(50,30)	**0.996** (0.008)	0.896 (0.065)	0.661 (0.035)	0.669 (0.039)	0.808 (0.066)	0.972 (0.025)	0.730 (0.051)
	(100,50)	**0.939** (0.016)	0.783 (0.048)	0.612 (0.021)	0.697 (0.031)	0.681 (0.040)	0.921 (0.021)	0.663 (0.040)
	(150,100)	**0.907** (0.016)	0.736 (0.037)	0.603 (0.018)	0.604 (0.016)	0.652 (0.035)	0.897 (0.016)	0.634 (0.030)
$\mathcal{P} = 5$	(50,30)	**0.997** (0.008)	0.808 (0.058)	0.685 (0.027)	0.690 (0.034)	0.799 (0.067)	0.967 (0.024)	0.752 (0.051)
	(100,50)	**0.937** (0.015)	0.721 (0.035)	0.641 (0.018)	0.688 (0.041)	0.688 (0.037)	0.903 (0.024)	0.685 (0.041)
	(150,100)	**0.903** (0.011)	0.678 (0.027)	0.625 (0.019)	0.624 (0.018)	0.656 (0.026)	0.886 (0.020)	0.655 (0.022)
$\mathcal{P} = 10$	(50,30)	**0.996** (0.008)	0.785 (0.060)	0.670 (0.028)	0.699 (0.025)	0.822 (0.068)	0.964 (0.020)	0.770 (0.044)
	(100,50)	**0.936** (0.014)	0.713 (0.035)	0.653 (0.019)	0.674 (0.028)	0.695 (0.034)	0.908 (0.023)	0.700 (0.039)
	(150,100)	**0.899** (0.014)	0.678 (0.027)	0.632 (0.015)	0.633 (0.014)	0.668 (0.036)	0.886 (0.018)	0.672 (0.026)

adjusts them to every single individual to retain the required balance of exploration vs. exploitation. To evaluate SiRG's performance, we applied it to a range of test problems and compared the results to a series of (self-)adaptive EAs. The results demonstrated the superiority of the proposed method over the compared algorithms. We also derived the SiRG's Markov chain model. We then showed the reducibility of its transition matrix which leads to the convergence proof of SiRG. Here, the aim of the convergence analysis was to exemplify a simple use of SiRG's Markov model in obtaining more detailed information. A more practical question, however, would be about the time complexity of the algorithm to achieve the globally optimal solution. Deriving the upper-bound of the SiRG convergence would be of our future plans.

6. REFERENCES

[1] T. Back and M. Schutz. Intelligent mutation rate control in canonical genetic algorithms. *In Foundations of Intelligent Systems, Springer*, pages 158–167, 1996.

[2] H. G. Beyer. On the "explorative power" of ES/EP-like algorithms. *Proc. of the 7th Annual Conf. on Evolutionary Programming, , Lecture Notes in Computer Science. Springer, Berlin*, 1998.

[3] S. Bottcher et al. Optimal fixed and adaptive mutation rates for the leadingones problem parallel problem solving from nature. *In Proc. of the 11th international Conf. on Parallel Problem Solving from Nature (PPSN XI), Springer*, 2010.

[4] J. Cervantes and C. R. Stephens. Limitations of existing mutation rate heuristics and how a rank GA overcomes them. *IEEE Trans. on Evolutionary Computation*, 13(2):369–397, 2009.

[5] M. K. Das and H.-K. Dai. A survey of DNA motif finding algorithms. *BMC Bioinformatics*, page 8(Suppl 7):S21, 2007.

[6] E. David et al. Finite Markov chain analysis of genetic algorithms. *In Grefensttete 1987 (Ed.), ICGA89*, pages 1 – 8, 1987.

[7] T. E. Davis and J. C. Principe. A simulated annealing like convergence theory for the simple genetic algorithm. *In: R.K. Belew, L.B. Booker (Eds.), ICGA91*, pages 174–181, 1991.

[8] K. A. DeJong. Analysis of the behavior of a class of genetic adaptive systems. *Ph.D. thesis, University of Michigan, Ann Arbor, MI*, 1975.

[9] K. A. DeJong, W. M. Spears, and D. F. Gordon. Using Markov chains to analyze GAFOs. *In Foundations of Genetic Algorithms 3*, pages 115–137, 1995.

[10] A. Eiben et al. Parameter control in evolutionary algorithms. *IEEE Trans. on Evolutionary Computation*, 3(2):124–141, July 1999.

[11] A. E. Eiben and C. A. Schipper. On evolutionary exploration and exploitation. *Fundamenta Informaticae*, 35:35–50, 1998.

[12] L. J. Fogel. Evolving artificial intelligence. *Ph.D. dissertation, Univ. of California, San Diego*, 1992.

[13] W. Hordijk and B. Manderick. The usefulness of recombination. *In Proc. of the 3rd Int. Conf. on Artif. Life*, 929:908–919, 1995.

[14] X. B. Hu and S. F. Wu. A self-adaptive genetic algorithm based on fuzzy mechanism. *IEEE Congress on Evolutionary Computation*, pages 4646–4652, 2007.

[15] M. Iosifescu. *Finite Markov Processes and Their Applications.* Wiley, 1980.

[16] J. Koljonen and J. T. Alander. Effects of population size and relative elitism on optimization speed and reliability of genetic algorithms. *In Proc. of the 9th Scand. Conf. on Artif. Intel.*, pages 25–27, 2006.

[17] T. Kotzing et al. How crossover helps in pseudo-boolean optimization. *In Proc. of the 13th annual Conf. on Genetic and evolutionary computation (GECCO 11), ACM*, 2011.

[18] R. Li et al. On the log-normal self-adaptation of the mutation rate in binary search spaces. *In Proc. of the 13th annual Conf. on Genetic and evolutionary computation (GECCO 11), ACM*, 2011.

[19] L. Lin and M. Gen. Auto-tuning strategy for evolutionary algorithms: balancing between exploration and exploitation. *Soft Computing, Springer*, 13:157–168, 2009.

[20] F. Nadi and A. T. Khader. A parameter-less genetic algorithm with customized crossover and mutation operators. *In Proc. of the Genetic and Evolutionary Computation (GECCO 2011).*

[21] F. Neumann and M. Theile. How crossover speeds up evolutionary algorithms for the multi-criteria all-pairs-shortest-path problem. *In Proc. of the 11th international Conf. on Parallel Problem Solving from Nature (PPSN XI), Springer*, 2010.

[22] A. Nix and M. D. Vose. A Markov chain analysis on a genetic algorithm. *Annals of Mathematics and Artificial Intelligence*, 5:79–88, 1992.

[23] J. N. Richter et al. Ignoble trails-where crossover is provably harmful. *In Proc. of the 10th international Conf. on Parallel Problem Solving from Nature (PPSN X), Springer*, 2008.

[24] G. Rudolph. *Convergence Properties of Evolutionary Algorithms.* Verlag Dr. Kovac, Hamburg, Germany.

[25] G. Rudolph. Massively parallel simulated annealing and its relation to evolutionary algorithms. *Evolutionary Computation*, 4(1):361–383, 1993.

[26] G. Rudolph. Convergence analysis of canonical genetic algorithms. *IEEE Trans. on Neural Networks*, 5(1):96–101, 1994.

[27] J. Smith and T. Fogarty. Self adaptation of mutation rates in a steady state genetic algorithm. *In Proc. of congress on evolutionary computation*, pages 318–323, 1996.

[28] W. M. Spears. Evolutionary algorithms, the role of mutation and recombination. *Natural Computing, Springer-Verlag, Berlin*, 2000.

[29] D. Sudholt. Crossover is provably essential for the ising model on trees. *In Proc. of the 7th annual Conf. on Genetic and evolutionary computation (GECCO 05), ACM*, 2005.

[30] J. Suzuki. A Markov chain analysis on simple genetic algorithms. *IEEE Trans. on Sys., Man, and Cyber.*, 25(4):655–659, 1995.

[31] D. L. Swofford et al. *Phylogenetic inference.* Sinauer Associates, Massachusetts.

[32] S. Tsutsui et al. A real coded genetic algorithm with an explorer and an exploiter populations. *In Proc. of the 73th Int. Con. on GAs*, pages 238–245, 1997.

[33] F. Vafaee and P. C. Nelson. An explorative and exploitative mutation scheme. *In Proc. of IEEE Conf. on Evolutionary Computation*, 2010.

[34] M. D. Vose and G. E. Liepins. Punctuated equilibria in genetic search. *Complex Systems*, 5:31–44, 1991.

[35] S. Y. Yuen and C. K. Chow. A genetic algorithm that adaptively mutates and never revisits. *IEEE Trans. on Evolutionary Computation*, 13(2):454–472, April 2009.

Efficient Global Optimization for Combinatorial Problems

Martin Zaefferer, Jörg Stork, Martina Friese,
Andreas Fischbach, Boris Naujoks, Thomas Bartz-Beielstein
Cologne University of Applied Sciences
51643 Gummersbach, Germany
[firstname].[lastname]@fh-koeln.de

ABSTRACT

Real-world optimization problems may require time consuming and expensive measurements or simulations. Recently, the application of surrogate model-based approaches was extended from continuous to combinatorial spaces. This extension is based on the utilization of suitable distance measures such as Hamming or Swap Distance. In this work, such an extension is implemented for Kriging (Gaussian Process) models. Kriging provides a measure of uncertainty when determining predictions. This can be harnessed to calculate the Expected Improvement (EI) of a candidate solution. In continuous optimization, EI is used in the Efficient Global Optimization (EGO) approach to balance exploitation and exploration for expensive optimization problems. Employing the extended Kriging model, we show for the first time that EGO can successfully be applied to combinatorial optimization problems. We describe necessary adaptations and arising issues as well as experimental results on several test problems. All surrogate models are optimized with a Genetic Algorithm (GA). To yield a comprehensive comparison, EGO and Kriging are compared to an earlier suggested Radial Basis Function Network, a linear modeling approach, as well as model-free optimization with random search and GA. EGO clearly outperforms the competing approaches on most of the tested problem instances.

Categories and Subject Descriptors

G.1.6 [**Mathematics of Computing**]: Optimization—*Global Optimization*; G.2.1 [**Discrete Mathematics**]: Combinatorics—*Combinatorial Algorithms*

General Terms

Algorithms, Experimentation

Keywords

Genetic Algorithm, Surrogate Model-Based Optimization, Efficient Global Optimization, Kriging, Gaussian Processes, Distance Measure

GECCO'14, July 12–16, 2014, Vancouver, BC, Canada.

ACM 978-1-4503-2662-9/14/07 ...$15.00.
http://dx.doi.org/10.1145/2576768.2598282.

1. INTRODUCTION

Surrogate models are well established tools for cost reduction of time consuming or expensive simulation and optimization runs in the continuous domain. Surrogate models, as employed in methods like Efficient Global Optimization (EGO) [15] or Sequential Parameter Optimization (SPO) [3] offer several advantages. They reduce the number of function evaluations, give information on the shape of the optimized landscape and estimate effects and interactions between parameters.

Combinatorial optimization problems arise in many real-world settings. Examples for expensive combinatorial problems are scheduling or sequencing problems that depend on time consuming simulations (e.g., [30]). The application of surrogate-models to combinatorial problems is scarce. It is desirable to extend successful approaches from continuous optimization to combinatorial spaces.

The generalization of distance-based models to combinatorial spaces was earlier proposed by Moraglio and Kattan [20]. The core idea is to replace continuous distance measures (e.g., Euclidean) with distance (or similarity) measures native to a combinatorial problems representation, e.g., Hamming Distance (HD) or various edit distances. Relevant previous studies and similar work are reviewed in Sec. 2.

Moraglio and Kattan [20] use Radial Basis Function Networks (RBFN) in their studies, but also suggest to employ more complex models like Kriging. Kriging may provide an error estimate for each prediction, which can be exploited to calculate the Expected Improvement (EI) of a candidate solution. Thus, EGO can be applied to combinatorial optimization problems.

The following topics will be addressed in this paper:

1. extension of Kriging to combinatorial problems,
2. determination of the optimization performance of a Kriging-supported Genetic Algorithm (GA), and
3. investigation of the applicability of EGO to combinatorial optimization problems.

Methods to deal with these topics are introduced in Sec. 3. Numerical tests, which are performed on standard test problems, are described in Sec. 4. Experimental results are presented in Sec. 5 and discussed in Sec. 6. Finally, Sec. 7 gives a summary and an outlook.

2. PREVIOUS RESEARCH

2.1 Surrogate Models in Optimization

Generally speaking, a surrogate model $\widehat{\mathcal{M}}$ is a (coarse grained or cheap) model that replaces a (fine grained or expensive) model $\mathcal{M}$ with higher complexity. The reader may consider a Computational Fluid Dynamics (CFD) model that replaces a real-world problem. This CFD model itself can be replaced by a simplified analytical model. In the former case, CFD models are considered as surrogates, whereas in the latter, they are considered as fine grained models that are replaced by a surrogate.

In this paper, however, the term surrogate is restricted to data-driven models. They replace the simulation model $\mathcal{M}$, which is given by a function f, see Algorithm 1. Here, it is assumed that function evaluations clearly dominate the time consumption (or cost), i.e., most time is spent in line two and six of Algorithm 1. Stopping criteria can be a given budget of function evaluations, a specified time limit or a fitness value to be reached. The set A_p contains all underlying parameters of Algorithm 1, e.g., number of initial solutions, type and parameterization of the search strategy (line 5) or the type of surrogate model.

Algorithm 1: Surrogate model-based optimization

Input: Function f, stopping criteria, parameter set A_p
Output: Best solution found y^*, final model $\widehat{\mathcal{M}}^*$

```
1 Create initial solutions (randomly or with design of
  experiment);
2 Evaluate solutions with f;
3 while Stopping criteria not reached do
4     Build/update M̂;
5     Find best solution(s) predicted by M̂;
6     Evaluate solution(s) with f;
7 end
```

Surrogate models can be Artificial Neural Networks, Linear Models, Kriging, Multivariate Adaptive Regression Splines, Random Forests, and many more. Jones et al. [15] introduced EGO, which uses the predicted mean and variance provided by a Kriging surrogate to compute the Expected Improvement (EI) of a candidate solution. Without loss of generality, we will consider the case of minimization. Following the notation in [10], we consider an expensive function f and a related surrogate of f, denoted $\hat{f}$. Gaussian process models allow the determination of the mean squared error $\hat{s}^2(\mathbf{x})$ as described in [26]. Let y^* denote the best found function evaluation so far, $\Phi(\cdot)$ and $\phi(\cdot)$ denote the cumulative distribution function and probability density function, respectively. If $\hat{s}(\mathbf{x}) > 0$, then the expected improvement can be determined as

$$\mathrm{EI}(\mathbf{x}) = (y^* - \hat{y}(\mathbf{x}))\Phi\left(\frac{y^* - \hat{y}(\mathbf{x})}{\hat{s}(\mathbf{x})}\right) + \hat{s}\phi\left(\frac{y^* - \hat{y}(\mathbf{x})}{\hat{s}(\mathbf{x})}\right),$$

otherwise $\mathrm{EI}(\mathbf{x}) = 0$. EI determines how much improvement can be expected from the candidate solution to be predicted. Thus, EGO uses EI instead of the mean prediction to determine a promising candidate solution in line 5 of Algorithm 1. Besides saving evaluations of the expensive function f, this approach also provides an infill criterion (i.e., EI) that balances exploitation versus exploration. For a more detailed summary on surrogate model-based numerical optimization we refer to the overview by Jin et al. [13]. A statistical framework for model-based optimization is provided by the Sequential Parameter Optimization [3].

2.2 Surrogate Models in Combinatorial Optimization

Combinatorial surrogate models are a relatively new research topic [14]. Data-driven surrogate models were used in combination with GA or Ant Colony Optimization (ACO), however, mostly for optimization of continuous vectors, where classical models are applicable. Methods like Estimation of Distribution Algorithms or ACO can also be understood to use models [32], e.g., the Bayesian network model in the Bayesian Optimization Algorithm [23] or the pheromone model in ACO.

Another branch of combinatorial surrogate-model applications comprehends solvers for specific problem representations and specific applications. Voutchkov et al. [30] optimize a welding sequence. To represent the combinatorial problem, a signed permutation is used. The surrogate model replaces an expensive Finite Element (FE) model by estimating the influence of each individual element in the sequence, based on the observations made in previously tested sequences. Their surrogate model uses not only the resulting fitness values. It also exploits intermediate results that reflect impact of individual elements, depending on their position in the sequence. Exploiting such intermediate results will give this model a clear advantage over the more simple, fitness-value driven approaches. On the other hand, the applicability of this model is restricted to this specific setup and cannot be transferred to other application areas.

Fonseca et al. [9] defined Similarity-Based Models (SBM) as models that keep a memory of solutions and estimate the performance of new samples by comparing them to that memory. Fonseca et al. list Fitness Inheritance [29], Fitness Imitation [18, 13] and k-Nearest Neighbor (k-NN) [2] as examples. They test a GA supported by a k-NN model on a set of numerical, continuous test functions. Bernardino et al. [5] perform similar tests with Artificial Immune Systems. In both cases Hamming and Euclidean Distance are used as measures of similarity, showing that this approach does not depend on a specific problem representation. In this study, we do not employ the SBM variants suggested by Fonseca et al. [9], because the proposed models are not suited to predict a new optimum. For example, the k-NN model would never predict that a candidate solution has better performance than the best known solution. The k-NN model may be useful in a model management algorithm [9, 5]. However, it is not useful in a framework as outlined in Algorithm 1.

More suited towards our goal are the approaches of Li et al. [19] and Moraglio and Kattan [20]. They use distance-based models, which are able to predict promising, new solutions. Section 2.3 will review related results. Also, we introduce a model similar to k-NN but more suited to the given purpose in Sec. 3.2.

2.3 Applying Continuous Surrogates in Combinatorial Search Spaces

Li et al. [19] proposed RBFN models for optimization in non-Euclidean spaces by replacing the employed distance measure. Their RBFN models were applied to mixed-integer problems, using a mixed integer evolution strategy. Another approach to a mixed problem is taken by Hutter [12], who describes a Kriging model based on a weighted Hamming distance to model categorical variables for algorithm tuning. In a very similar way, Moraglio and Kattan [20] suggested a generalization of distance-based models from continuous to combinatorial spaces.

The core idea is to employ distance measures, which are inherent to the combinatorial problem representation (e.g., Edit Distance). Such problem representations can be binary strings (e.g., binary knapsack problem, NK-Landscapes) permutations (e.g., assignment and scheduling problems) trees (e.g., symbolic regression) or any non-standard combinatorial problem representation.

Moraglio and Kattan [20] demonstrated this with a RBFN adapted to arbitrary distance measures to solve instances of NK-Landscapes (NKL). This RBFN-based approach has also been applied to the Quadratic Assignment Problem (QAP) [22], package-deal negotiation [8] and tree-based problems from Genetic Programming (GP) [21]. GP has also been coupled with the RBFN-based approach to evolve better discrete surrogate models [16]. All those works employ some form of RBFN based on arbitrary distance measures, thus adapted to combinatorial spaces. As Moraglio and Kattan [20] indicate, this can also be done with other models, e.g., with Kriging.

The key issue is to replace the Euclidean (RBFN) or per-variable (Kriging) distances by distance measures, which directly work for the inherent problem representation. Depending on the model type under consideration, other changes may become necessary. For instance, in the context of arbitrary distance measures, there is no guarantee that a given distance matrix will be invertible, as required by RBFN. Therefore, Moraglio and Kattan [20] suggested to replace the matrix inversion with the pseudoinverse. This issue is revisited in the following description of the Kriging model employed in the herein described work.

3. METHODS

3.1 Kriging for Combinatorial Problems

Kriging is a method for interpolation and regression based on Gaussian process modeling. The following notation is adopted from Forrester et al. [10]. Given a set of n solutions $\boldsymbol{X} = \{\mathbf{x}^{(i)}\}_{i=1\ldots n}$ in a k-dimensional continuous search space with observations $\mathbf{y} = \{y^{(i)}\}_{i=1\ldots n}$, Kriging is a method to find an expression for a predicted value at an unknown point by interpreting the observed responses $\mathbf{y}$ as if they are realizations of a stochastic process. The following set of random vectors $\boldsymbol{Y} = \{Y(\mathbf{x}^{(i)})\}_{i=1\ldots n}$ is used to define this stochastic process. The random variables $Y(\cdot)$ are correlated as follows [10]:

$$\mathrm{cor}\left[Y(\mathbf{x}^{(i)}), Y(\mathbf{x}^{(l)})\right] = \exp\left(-\sum_{j=1}^{k}\theta_j |x_j^{(i)} - x_j^{(l)}|^{p_j}\right). \quad (1)$$

Equation (1) defines a non-Euclidean distance measure, which uses a weighted per-element distance. The weights θ_j and the shape parameter p_j have to be estimated. The matrix that collects correlations of all pairs $\{(i,l)\}$ is called the correlation matrix $\boldsymbol{\Psi}$. It is used in the Kriging predictor

$$\hat{y}(\mathbf{x}) = \hat{\mu} + \boldsymbol{\psi}^T\boldsymbol{\Psi}^{-1}(\mathbf{y} - \mathbf{1}\hat{\mu}), \quad (2)$$

where $\hat{y}(\mathbf{x})$ is the predicted function value of a new sample $\mathbf{x}$, $\hat{\mu}$ is the maximum likelihood estimate of the mean and $\boldsymbol{\psi}$ is the vector of correlations between training samples $\boldsymbol{X}$ and the new sample $\mathbf{x}$. The error of the prediction can be estimated with

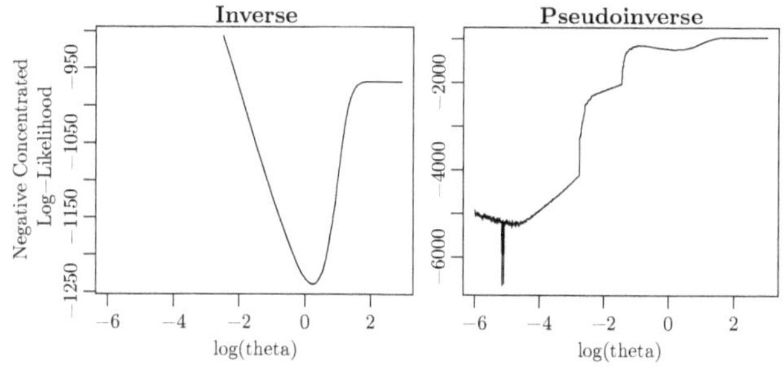

Figure 1: Negative concentrated log-likelihood plotted versus $\log(\theta)$. Likelihood landscape for a Kriging model, based on 200 randomly sampled solutions of a $N = 10$, $K = 2$ NKL-Landscape. Standard matrix inversion is compared to pseudoinverse. Values not plotted in the left plot represent (close to) singular correlation matrices. Both plots show a (local) optimum at $\log(\theta) \approx 0.24$.

$$\hat{s}^2(\mathbf{x}) = \hat{\sigma}^2(1 - \boldsymbol{\psi}^T\boldsymbol{\Psi}^{-1}\boldsymbol{\psi}^T), \quad (3)$$

where $\hat{\sigma}^2$ is a model parameter to be estimated. The (usually small) contribution of error due to estimation of $\hat{\mu}$ is omitted.

The width parameter $\boldsymbol{\theta}$ determines how far the influence of each sample point $\mathbf{x}$ spreads. If the correlation structure differs in different directions of the search space, fitting different θ_j values for each direction of the search space is desirable. This is the so-called anisotropic case. Isotropic models are better suited for combinatorial search spaces, because direction is a vague concept for combinatorial optimization problems. Therefore, Eq. (1) is transformed to become isotropic, i.e., with scalar θ and p, i.e.:

$$\mathrm{cor}\left[Y(\mathbf{x}^{(i)}), Y(\mathbf{x}^{(l)})\right] = \exp(-\theta \mathrm{d}(\mathbf{x}^{(i)}, \mathbf{x}^{(l)})^p), \quad (4)$$

where $\mathrm{d}(\cdot)$ can be any distance measure for the given problem representation. Now, the samples $\mathbf{x}$ are not restricted to continuous values and may consist of various types, e.g., binary strings, permutations, or trees.

Maximum Likelihood Estimation (MLE), which comprehends an optimization procedure, is used to determine the model parameters, i.e., θ, p, $\hat{\sigma}$ and $\hat{\mu}$. MLE requires a matrix inversion (also later in the prediction step, see (2)), which can usually be performed directly or via Cholesky decomposition. A non degenerated or positive-semidefinite matrix is required for this inversion. Moraglio and Kattan [20] state that it can not be guaranteed that such matrices will still be invertible if they are based on an arbitrary distance measure. Therefore, they replace the matrix inversion in their RBFN model with the pseudoinverse.

In case of Kriging, this can introduce a new global optimum into the MLE landscape. Selecting θ based on such an optimum may lead to a poor prediction at new sample points. This situation is exemplified in Fig. 1. Here, a Kriging model is built, based on 200 random samples from a NK-Landscape ($N = 10$, $K = 2$), see Sec. 4.1. The Hamming distance (HD) metric is employed as a distance measure. The likelihood is calculated once with standard matrix inversion, once with the pseudoinverse. The figure shows the dependency of the estimated likelihood value on the θ parameter. Clearly, when θ becomes too small, the correlation matrix will become close to singular. Hence, no values are plotted for this region (Fig. 1, *left*). In practice, a penalty function is used to handle this problem. The pseudoinverse generates extremely good likelihood values in this region.

While both plots have an optimum at approx. 0.24, it is a local one when using pseudoinverse. Thus, it is disregarded during MLE with pseudoinverse. Instead, very small θ values would be chosen. As mentioned earlier, θ will control how far the influence of each observation will spread in the search space. With very small θ, all observations affect the whole search space equally. Here, this leads to very bad predictive performance. On the other hand, the local optimum ($\theta \approx 0.24$) results in a surrogate model $\widehat{\mathcal{M}}$ that is highly correlated with the expensive model $\mathcal{M}$ at unseen sample points. This example shows that standard matrix inversion works well with HD, while pseudoinverse does not. This is not surprising, as the HD metric was successfully applied in related contexts (e.g., [24, 25]).

Of course, there may be distance measures where the situation is more complicated. If a distance measure does not yield valid (i.e., non-degenerate or even positive-semidefinite) correlation matrices, two solutions are possible. First, MLE may be replaced with a cross-validation approach. This may increase the computational burden. Second, the correlation function (4) or the distance measure may be adapted to guarantee that the correlation matrix is valid. As a first step, this paper only relies on the assumption that all employed distance measures are valid.

3.2 A Linear Model

As a simple base-line comparison, a Linear, distance-based Model (LM) is introduced. To predict the quality of a new solution, all existing samples are sorted according to their distance to the new sample. The average of the observations at the smallest and second smallest distance can be used to estimate a linear trend, i.e., slope and intercept. The intercept is the prediction for the utility value of the new sample. This approach may be compared to a k-NN model with $k = 2$, with the difference that the prediction is not based on the mean of the two nearest neighbors, but rather on a linear trend estimated from these. Thus, it may suggest new optimal solutions, which k-NN can not.

3.3 Radial Basis Function Network

The employed RBFN model is based on the description by Moraglio and Kattan [20], with the predictor,

$$\hat{y}(\mathbf{x}) = w_0 + \sum_{i=1}^{K} w_i \exp\left(-\beta \mathrm{d}(\mathbf{x}, c^{(i)})^2\right)$$

where K is the number of centers $\mathbf{c}$ (here: all samples in $\boldsymbol{X}$ are centers), $\mathrm{d}(\cdot)$ is an arbitrary distance measure and w_0 is the mean of all observations. The weights $\mathbf{w}$ are determined with the pseudoinverse, $\mathbf{w} = \boldsymbol{G}^{+}(\boldsymbol{y} - \mathbf{1}w_0)$. Here, the matrix $\boldsymbol{G}$ has the elements $g_{ij} = \exp\left(-\beta \mathrm{d}(\mathbf{x}^{(i)}, \mathbf{x}^{(j)})^2\right)$. Furthermore, D denotes the maximum distance and $\beta = 1/2D^2$. The RBFN will also be used in an EGO framework (hence called EGOR). To that end, we can get a rough error estimate in a similar way as done with Kriging, i.e., from Eq. (3), where $\boldsymbol{\Psi}$ is replaced by $\boldsymbol{G}$ and $\hat{\sigma}$ is replaced by the standard deviation of the observations.

4. EXPERIMENTAL SETUP

4.1 Test Problems

The experiments in this paper are based on those in two previous studies [20, 22]. All experiments are performed using the free software environment for statistical computation, `R`. Function evaluations are assumed to be expensive, dominating the cost of the optimization process. This assumption is made to justify the large computational overhead of surrogate model training and exploitation. Hence, strictly limited budgets are imposed during the experiments.

NK-Landscapes (NKL), as proposed by Kauffman [17], are fitness landscapes based on binary strings. The fitness of a string is the sum of fitness contributions of N string elements, each impacted by K other elements. The fitness of a binary string is therefore given by (cf. [1])

$$f(\mathbf{x}) = \frac{1}{N} \sum_{i=1}^{N} g_i(x_i; x_{i1}, ...x_{iK}), \tag{5}$$

where x_i is the i-th bit of the string $\mathbf{x}$, and $x_{i1}, ...x_{iK}$ are the bits that influence the contribution of x_i. A cyclic order is used, i.e., x_1 follows x_N. For each string element, a function g_i assigns a real-valued weight to each possible combination of the element and its neighbors, typically sampled uniformly from $[0; 1]$. This results into N lookup tables of $2^{(K+1)}$ values. In this paper, the K neighbors that impact the contribution of the i-th element x_i are given by the sequence $(x_{i+1}, ..., x_{i+K})$.

The **Quadratic Assignment Problem** (QAP) [6] describes a permutation problem, where N facilities have to be assigned to N locations. Assignment cost is minimized, based on flow between facilities (a) and distance between locations (b). The optimization problem is to find an optimal permutation π of length N from the set of all permutations Π_N, that is

$$\min_{\pi \in \Pi_N} \sum_{i=1}^{N} \sum_{j=1}^{N} a_{ij} b_{\pi(i), \pi(j)}. \tag{6}$$

The instances `nug30`, `tho30` and `kra32` from the QAP Library (QAPLIB) [7] were chosen in [22]. Here, instance (`nug12`) was added to incorporate smaller search spaces.

Unimodal (UNI) problems were suggested by Moraglio et al. [22] as simple and transparent test cases. Here, the fitness of a permutation is its distance to the fixed reference permutation $\pi = 1, 2, 3, ..., 30$. Both HD and Swap Distance (SD) are used, each forming a different UNI instance (`unih30`, `unis30`).

Because the look-up tables are randomly generated, our results differ from previous results presented in [20, 22]. Also, the exact distribution of the K neighbors may differ. The UNI problems depend on the chosen reference permutation. The QAP instances should be identical, thus yielding the most comparable results. All problems are of a low or moderate sizs, e.g., the permutations are no longer than 32 elements. Of course, larger problems may be handled as well. Still, larger problems would require much more data to build reasonable models. In practice, even small problem instances may be hard to solve when evaluation becomes expensive, e.g., Voutchkov et al. [30] only consider signed permutations of length six. Hence, we chose rather small or medium sized problem instances.

4.2 Surrogate Models

Three surrogate models are employed in the experiments, RBFN, Kriging, and LM. No tuning of model parameters is performed. EGO will be performed with Kriging or RBFN (EGOR). The Kriging implementation is based on the original Matlab code by Forrester et al. [10], as reimplemented in the SPOT R package. It is adapted to combinatorial spaces as described in Sec. 3.1. The parameter p is fixed at a value of one, all others are estimated with MLE. RBFN and LM are implemented in R, according to their description in Sec. 3.2 and 3.3.

4.3 Optimization Algorithms

Two model-free optimization algorithms are employed, Random Search (RS) and GA. RS will only be employed to optimize the test functions, namely QAP, NKL, and UNI. This provides a reference performance which should be beaten by any more sophisticated algorithm. The GA will be used on all problems and with all surrogate models.

In all cases, the crossover rate is 0.5, the mutation rate $\frac{1}{N}$. Tournament selection is performed with a tournament size of two and a probability 0.9. For NKL, bitwise mutation and uniform crossover are used. In case of the permutation problems (UNI, QAP) interchange mutation (i.e., interchange of arbitrary elements) and cycle crossover are chosen.

When the NKL instances are optimized directly, the population size is N. When a NKL surrogate model is optimized, population size is $10N$. For QAP and UNI, the population size is set to 10 (direct) and 20 (surrogate), respectively. The number of function evaluations for NKL is N^2 (direct) and $100N^2$ (surrogate), respectively, and the number of function evaluations for UNI and QAP is set to 100 (direct) and $10,000$ (surrogate), respectively.

The GA is combined with five different model-based approaches (RBFN, LM, Kriging, EGO with Kriging and EGOR with RBFN). For RBFN, LM and Kriging, the exploration strategy used by Moraglio and Kattan [20] is employed: a random solution is selected for evaluation, if the model does not predict a value better than the best known solution. The EGO variants do not need this explicit exploitation mechanism, because they use a natural way to balance between exploration and exploitation.

To enable a more coherent experimental setup, the use of a memetic GA with a two-opt step to optimize the surrogate model for QAP and UNI (cf. [22]) is omitted in our setup. Preliminary experiments indicated that additional local search does not improve the results significantly. This may be due to the accuracy of the surrogate models. Since their prediction is not perfectly exact, exhaustive local search may be unprofitable. Also note, that duplicates are avoided, with respect to the restricted budgets.

Of course, the rather simple GA is a potentially weak competitor, the RS even more so. Future work may replace the model-free GA with a more potent, state-of-the-art competitor. Still, a state-of-the-art approach may be hard to find for the case of strictly limited budgets.

4.4 Distance Measures

Several distance measures are discussed in the literature. Schiavinotto and Stützle [27] compared several distance metrics for search landscape analysis, concerning permutations. A different set is reviewed by Sevaux et al. [28] for their usefulness in a diversification strategy of a memetic algorithm. As shown for QAP, even phenotype information can be used for calculating distances [4]. For the purpose of measuring distance between binary strings or permutations, we consider the following distance measures.

Hamming Distance (HD) The number of unequal elements between two strings $\mathbf{x}$ and $\mathbf{y}$, i.e.,

$$HD(\mathbf{x},\mathbf{y}) = \sum_{i=1}^{n} a_i \text{ where } a_i = \begin{cases} 0 & \text{if } x_i = y_i, \\ 1 & \text{otherwise} \end{cases} \quad (7)$$

The Hamming distance fulfills the conditions of a metric on the vector space of the words of length n. It can quickly determined, especially for binary strings and is therefore used in the NKL experiments. It is expected that the HD works well when modeling NKL data, as it very much resembles the distance measure usually used in RBFN or Kriging for continuous problems. In detail, $\sum_{i=1}^{n} |x_i - y_i|$ yields values identical to Eq. (7) if the two binary strings $\mathbf{x}$ and $\mathbf{y}$ are interpreted as numerical vectors containing zeros or ones. Equation (7) can be used to measure the distance between arbitrary strings of equal length. Hence, it can also be applied to permutations. There, two other distance measures are employed in the experiments.

Swap Distance (SD) A swap operation is the interchange in position of two adjacent elements in a permutation. SD counts the minimal number of swaps necessary to transform one permutation into another. For the calculation of this measure, we use the algorithm as described by Schiavinotto and Stützle [27]. Moraglio et al. [22] report that SD performed poorly. This may be due to the fact, that SD only concerns adjacent elements, while interchanging two arbitrary elements may be a more reasonable smallest step. This gave the inspiration to add an additional distance measure to our portfolio.

Interchange Distance (ID) An interchange operation is the interchange in position of two arbitrary elements in a permutation. ID counts the minimal number of interchanges required to transform one permutation into another. Schiavinotto and Stützle [27] provide an algorithm to calculate this measure, which is employed in this work. They also performed experiments to measure correlation between different distance measures and report a high correlation between HD and ID, whereas the correlations between HD and SD, as well as between SD and ID are low. Based on this information, ID is an interesting candidate in our portfolio. It has to be noted that HD has the lowest computational complexity. In case of equal performance, HD should be selected.

5. RESULTS

Experimental results are visualized by boxplots in Fig. 2, 4 and 5. The inner box indicates the 25 and 75 % quartiles and the bold line is the median. Circles are outliers, and the outmost lines specify the range of values exluding these outliers. For the two instances with $K = 2$, EGO finds the optimum in all of the 20 runs. EGOR (with RBFN) performs similarly well, but does not find the optimum in every run on the $K = 2, N = 25$ instance. In General, EGO outperforms EGOR. For $N = 25$, $K = 5$, only EGO and EGOR ever solve the problem, but not in all runs (EGO: 7 of 20, EGOR: 1 of 20). EGO is clearly best on all NKL instances but the instance with $N = 10$, $K = 5$. To analyze this behavior further, the runs with $N = 10$, $K = 5$ are extended to 300 function evaluations. The corresponding results are visualized in Fig. 3. Here, no decision can be made for small budgets. EGO performs better for budgets > 100. The model-free GA is clearly outperformed on the NKL instances by RBFN and EGO. LM fails to outperform

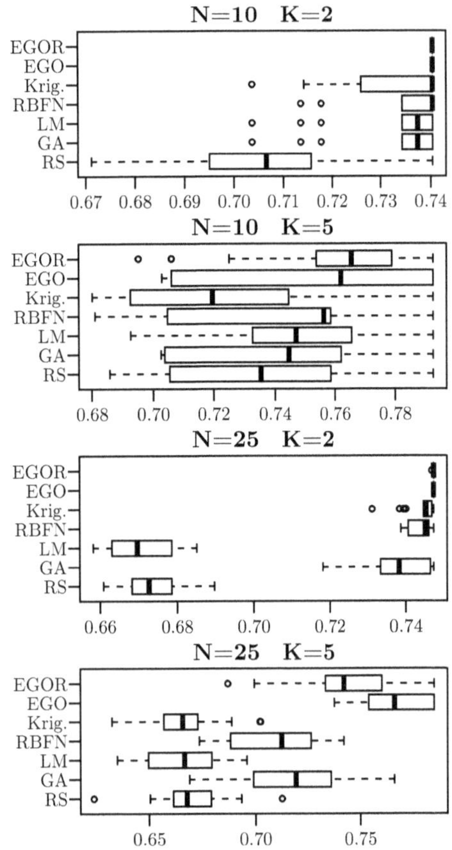

Figure 2: Boxplot of NKL results. All modeling approaches employ HD only. Larger values are better.

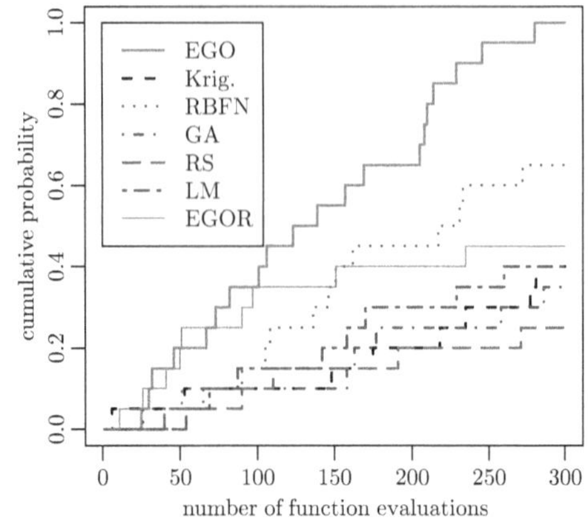

Figure 3: Empirical runtime distribution plot for the NKL instance ($N = 10, K = 5$). Y-axis shows the fraction of the 20 runs which reached the optimum.

the basic RS for the two larger NKL instances. Optimization with Kriging mean predictions often performs worse than RBFN or LM, with the exception of the $N = 25$, $K = 2$ NKL instance.

EGO is best on all QAP instances, but only with HD. Other distance measures may or may not lead to performance that is worse than the model-free GA, which often ranks second best to EGO. On the QAP instances, SD is sometimes better than ID, sometimes vice-versa.

For `unis30` the GA outperforms only RS and LM, as well as Kriging with HD. For `unih30`, GA is outperformed by EGO, EGOR and RBFN with HD. HD seems to work best on all tested permutation problems, with exception of `unis30`. Optimization with Kriging mean predictions performs better than RBFN for `unis30`. With EI, on the other hand, Kriging (EGO) performs nearly always better than RBFN (EGOR).

Overall, EGO clearly performs best, often (but not always) followed by RBFN or EGOR. Of the model-based approaches without EI, RBFN is best, although it is outperformed by the model-free GA several times. None of the permutation problems are ever solved with the given budgets, although EGO comes very close for `unis30` and `nug12`.

6. DISCUSSION

The surrogate model-based approaches work very well for NKL with $K = 2$. Results in general were much better than for the permutation problem experiments. Two reasons for this excellent performance can be given. First, the search space of the tested NKL instances is much smaller than that of the permutation problems. E.g., the largest NKL ($n = 25$) has $2^n \approx 3.36 \times 10^7$ possible combinations, whereas the smallest QAP problem (n=12) has $n! \approx 4.79 \times 10^8$. Second, the choice of distance measure (HD) is not only natural to this problem, but is a measure which is similar to the distance measures used in continuous domains.

Relative to RS, performance of most algorithms decreased with larger K. This has to be expected to some extent, since such landscapes are clearly more rugged and difficult. That is, the larger K is, the more fitness contributions change when one single bit is flipped. Clearly, this does not only make the optimization more difficult, but also the modeling, since the correlation between neighboring solutions decreases.

For $N = 10$ and $K = 5$, the results showed large variances and the worst EGO performance. Additionally, the GA performance was not significantly better than RS. This can be attributed to the more rugged fitness landscape. The high variance in the performance of all approaches also suggests that more function values are required, which can be supported by earlier work on NKL. The dynamic programming algorithm proposed by Weinberger [31] solves the NKL in $O(2^K N)$ steps. That is, it needs 40 ($N = 10, K = 2$), 320 ($N = 10, K = 5$), 100 ($N = 25, K = 2$) or 800 ($N = 25, K = 5$) steps. As can be seen, all but the $N = 10$ and $K = 5$ instance received budgets rather close to these numbers, which may be a reason for the observed performance. Longer runs with 300 evaluations revealed that after sufficient evaluations, EGO would outperform the other approaches and reliably solve the instance.

For the permutation problems, EGO is the best working optimization approach, and HD the most suitable distance measure. It is interesting to observe that SD sometimes outperforms ID, although ID was reported to have larger correlation with HD, which worked best. This result should be investigated further. In contrast to results from Moraglio et al. [22], the model-free GA often outperforms the RBFN-supported GA on the permutation problems. The performance of the RBFN model seems to be very similar to the performance reported earlier. Thus, the difference may be in the choice of settings for the basic, model-free GA, which performs better than reported in the earlier study. E.g., the choice of using tournament over truncation selection may be

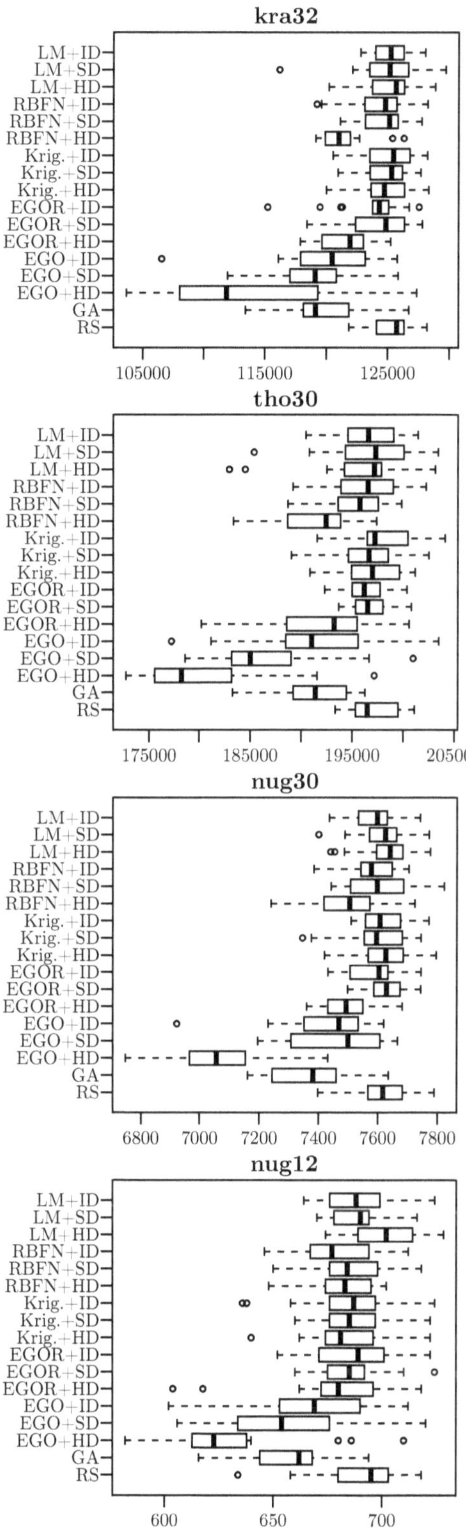

Figure 4: Boxplot of QAP results. Smaller values are better.

the reason. Or else, there may be differences due to the mutation operator, as interchange mutation was used instead of swap mutation. This result stresses the need for a future study on tuning of the applied approaches.

A further difference to earlier results [22] is the performance observed for the unimodal functions. Here, the best

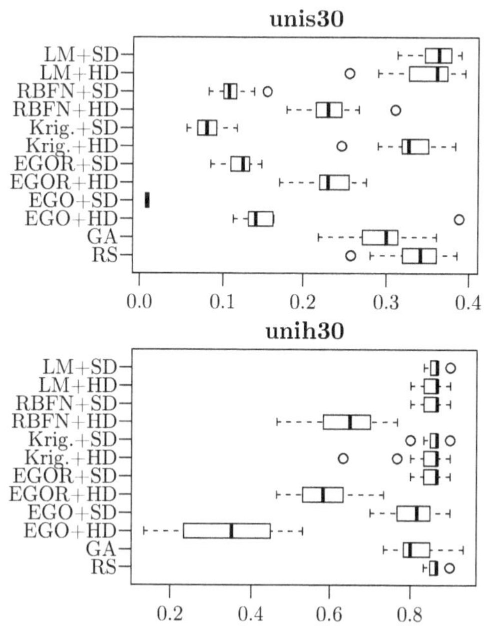

Figure 5: Boxplot of results for the artificial, unimodal test instances. Smaller values are better.

working distance measure is always that which is used in the instance itself. That is, HD works best with `unih30` and SD works best with `unis30`. The bad overall performance on `unih30` may be caused by the larger number of non-unique fitness values. Our results indicate that HD is clearly the best metric for the given problems. But the results on `unis30` show that the choice of distance measure can be affected by the problem type. This warrants further research with problem instances of larger variety. For other permutation problems, completely different measures may be preferable.

7. SUMMARY AND OUTLOOK

We demonstrated that EGO can be successfully applied to combinatorial optimization problems and that this Kriging-based approach was able to outperform a model-free GA. However, EGO does not make approaches like GA superfluous, because GAs are very useful for the proposed extension of EGO to combinatorial spaces. Searching for the solution with largest EI takes usually place in a multi-modal landscape. EI depends on the variance estimate which is zero at known samples. In between samples, this will often create local optima. Finding the global optimum solution of the EI landscape requires a surrogate-optimizer that is able to escape such local optima. Stochastic, population-based methods like GA are most suitable for this purpose.

Besides EGO and GA, model-based searches with Kriging (without EI), RBFN and LM were included in the comparison. All model-based approaches were outperformed by EGO, in some cases even by the model-free GA. It was also observed that RBFN does hold on very well to the basic Kriging model, as long as they are not used in EGO. Kriging outperformed the more simple RBFN when it was employed in EGO. The exploration/exploitation balancing of EGO in combination with the more powerful Kriging predictor and a well chosen distance measure seem to make the difference. As other model types do not provide an error estimate, heuristics may be examined in future research. E.g., variance estimated from distances to known samples, or by using some form of cross-validation.

Furthermore, the permutation distance measures were revealed to have a strong impact on the results. With one exception, Hamming Distance worked best for all problem instances. For other problems, the situation may be different. At the same time, the number of possible distance measures is much larger than the set used in this work. This issue will again occur, when tree-based representations or more exotic representations are concerned. Hence, the question of choosing a distance measure will remain an important issue. Distance measures were previously used for several tasks, e.g., diversity preservation in GAs or fitness landscape analysis. On the other hand, considering expensive problems yields different limitations than those encountered in earlier studies. For example, measures previously disregarded because of their complexity [28] may be of use in contexts where overall time consumption is dominated by the expensive target function. The interaction of distance measure, the correlation functions, and other parameters of the model are of interest for further investigation. The following topics will also be subject of our future research:

- performing a detailed study on parameter tuning of all compared approaches, to guarantee a fair comparison and understanding interactions of parameters
- implementing Co-Kriging [11] for combinatorial spaces, to include cheaply available data into the optimization process.

Acknowledgments.

This work has been kindly supported by the Federal Ministry of Education and Research (BMBF) under the grant CIMO (FKZ 17002X11).

8. REFERENCES

[1] L. Altenberg. *NK Fitness Landscapes*, chapter B2.7.2, pages B2.7:5–B2.7:10. IOP Publishing Ltd and Oxford University Press, 1997.

[2] N. S. Altman. An introduction to kernel and nearest-neighbor nonparametric regression. *The American Statistician*, 46(3):175–185, Aug 1992.

[3] T. Bartz-Beielstein, C. Lasarczyk, and M. Preuß. Sequential parameter optimization. In B. McKay et al., editors, *Congress on Evolutionary Computation (CEC'05), Proceedings*, pages 773–780. IEEE, 2005.

[4] A. Beham, E. Pitzer, and M. Affenzeller. A new metric to measure distances between solutions to the quadratic assignment problem. In *International Symposium on Logistics and Industrial Informatics (LINDI'11), Proceedings*, pages 45–50. IEEE, 2011.

[5] H. S. Bernardino, L. G. Fonseca, and H. J. C. Barbosa. *Surrogate-Assisted Artificial Immune Systems for Expensive Optimization Problems*, chapter 10, pages 179–198. InTech, Oct 2009.

[6] R. E. Burkard. Quadratic assignment problems. *European Journal of Operational Research*, 15(3):283 – 289, 1984.

[7] R. E. Burkard, S. E. Karisch, and F. Rendl. QAPLIB – a quadratic assignment problem library. *Journal of Global Optimization*, 10(4):391–403, 1997.

[8] S. Fatima and A. Kattan. Evolving optimal agendas for package deal negotiation. In N. Krasnogor et al., editors, *Genetic and Evolutionary Computation Conference (GECCO'11), Proceedings*, pages 505–512. ACM, 2011.

[9] L. Fonseca, H. Barbosa, and A. Lemonge. A similarity-based surrogate model for expensive evolutionary optimization with fixed budget of simulations. In *Congress on Evolutionary Computation*, pages 867–874. IEEE, 2009.

[10] A. Forrester, A. Sobester, and A. Keane. *Engineering Design via Surrogate Modelling*. Wiley, 2008.

[11] A. I. Forrester, A. Sóbester, and A. J. Keane. Multi-fidelity optimization via surrogate modelling. *Proceedings of the Royal Society A: Mathematical, Physical and Engineering Sciences*, 463(2088):3251–3269, Dec 2007.

[12] F. Hutter. *Automated configuration of algorithms for solving hard computational problems*. PhD thesis, University of British Columbia, 2009.

[13] Y. Jin. A comprehensive survey of fitness approximation in evolutionary computation. *Soft Computing*, 9(1):3–12, 2005.

[14] Y. Jin. Surrogate-assisted evolutionary computation: Recent advances and future challenges. *Swarm and Evolutionary Computation*, 1(2):61 – 70, 2011.

[15] D. R. Jones, M. Schonlau, and W. J. Welch. Efficient global optimization of expensive black-box functions. *Journal of Global Optimization*, 13(4):455–492, 1998.

[16] A. Kattan and E. Galvan. Evolving radial basis function networks via gp for estimating fitness values using surrogate models. In *Congress on Evolutionary Computation (CEC'12), Proceedings*, pages 1–7. IEEE, 2012.

[17] S. A. Kauffman. *The Origins of Order: Self-Organization and Selection in Evolution*. Oxford University Press, USA, 1993.

[18] H.-S. Kim and S.-B. Cho. An efficient genetic algorithm with less fitness evaluation by clustering. In *Congress on Evolutionary Computation (CEC'01), Proceedings*, volume 2, pages 887–894. IEEE, 2001.

[19] R. Li, M. T. M. Emmerich, J. Eggermont, E. G. P. Bovenkamp, T. Bäck, J. Dijkstra, and J. Reiber. Metamodel-assisted mixed integer evolution strategies and their application to intravascular ultrasound image analysis. In *Congress on Evolutionary Computation*, pages 2764–2771. IEEE, 2008.

[20] A. Moraglio and A. Kattan. Geometric generalisation of surrogate model based optimisation to combinatorial spaces. In *Proceedings of the 11th European Conference on Evolutionary Computation in Combinatorial Optimization*, EvoCOP'11, pages 142–154, Berlin, Heidelberg, 2011. Springer-Verlag.

[21] A. Moraglio and A. Kattan. Geometric surrogate model based optimisation for genetic programming: Initial experiments. Technical report, University of Birmingham, 2011.

[22] A. Moraglio, Y.-H. Kim, and Y. Yoon. Geometric surrogate-based optimisation for permutation-based problems. In N. Krasnogor et al., editors, *Genetic and Evolutionary Computation Conference (GECCO'11), Companion*, pages 133–134. ACM, 2011.

[23] M. Pelikan, D. E. Goldberg, and E. Cantu-Paz. BOA: The bayesian optimization algorithm. In W. Banzhaf et al., editors, *Genetic and Evolutionary Computation Conference*, pages 525–532. Morgan Kaufmann, 1999.

[24] J. C. Platt, C. J. Burges, S. Swenson, C. Weare, and A. Zheng. Learning a gaussian process prior for automatically generating music playlists. In *NIPS*, pages 1425–1432, 2001.

[25] P. A. Romero, A. Krause, and F. H. Arnold. Navigating the protein fitness landscape with gaussian processes. *Proceedings of the National Academy of Sciences*, 110(3):E193–E201, 2013.

[26] J. Sacks, W. J. Welch, T. J. Mitchell, and H. P. Wynn. Design and analysis of computer experiments. *Statistical Science*, 4(4):409–435, 1989.

[27] T. Schiavinotto and T. Stützle. A review of metrics on permutations for search landscape analysis. *Computers & operations research*, 34(10):3143–3153, 2007.

[28] M. Sevaux, K. Sörensen, et al. Permutation distance measures for memetic algorithms with population management. In *Metaheuristics International Conference*, 2005.

[29] R. E. Smith, B. A. Dike, and S. A. Stegmann. Fitness inheritance in genetic algorithms. In *Proceedings of the 1995 ACM Symposium on Applied Computing*, SAC '95, pages 345–350, New York, NY, USA, 1995. ACM.

[30] I. Voutchkov, A. Keane, A. Bhaskar, and T. M. Olsen. Weld sequence optimization: The use of surrogate models for solving sequential combinatorial problems. *Computer Methods in Applied Mechanics and Engineering*, 194(30-33):3535–3551, Aug 2005.

[31] E. D. Weinberger. Np completeness of kauffman's n-k model, a tuneable rugged fitness landscape. Working Papers 96-02-003, Santa Fe Institute, Feb. 1996.

[32] M. Zlochin, M. Birattari, N. Meuleau, and M. Dorigo. Model-based search for combinatorial optimization: A critical survey. *Annals of Operations Research*, 131(1-4):373–395, 2004.

Multiple Regression Genetic Programming

Ignacio Arnaldo
Massachusetts Institute of Technology, CSAIL
Cambridge, MA
iarnaldo@mit.edu

Krzysztof Krawiec*
Institute of Computing Science
Poznan University of Technology
60965 Poznan, Poland
krawiec@cs.put.poznan.pl

Una-May O'Reilly
Massachusetts Institute of Technology, CSAIL
Cambridge, MA
unamay@csail.mit.edu

ABSTRACT

We propose a new means of executing a genetic program which improves its output quality. Our approach, called Multiple Regression Genetic Programming (MRGP) decouples and linearly combines a program's subexpressions via multiple regression on the target variable. The regression yields an alternate output: the prediction of the resulting multiple regression model. It is this output, over many fitness cases, that we assess for fitness, rather than the program's execution output. MRGP can be used to improve the fitness of a final evolved solution. On our experimental suite, MRGP consistently generated solutions fitter than the result of competent GP or multiple regression. When integrated into GP, *inline* MRGP, on the basis of equivalent computational budget, outperforms competent GP while also besting *post-run* MRGP. Thus MRGP's output method is shown to be superior to the output of program execution and it represents a practical, cost neutral, improvement to GP.

Categories and Subject Descriptors

I.2.2 [**Artificial intelligence**]: Automatic Programming

Keywords

Genetic Programming, Multiple Regression

1. INTRODUCTION

In principle Genetic Programming (GP), given enough time, should be capable of simultaneously identifying and combining useful program subexpressions to yield an overall program that maximizes fitness. In reality, our existing GP algorithm designs often fall short of this capability. While there has been prior work on building block identification, promotion and aggregation, in this contribution we take a new tact toward fitness maximization. We decouple program subexpressions and combine them linearly via regression on the target variable. Our regression yields an alternate output for a GP program: the prediction of the resulting multiple regression model. It is this output, over many fitness cases, that we assess for fitness, rather than the program's execution output. We call our approach Multiple Regression Genetic Programming (MRGP) because it hybridizes GP with multiple regression.

In GP's current paradigm, selection pressure is not explicitly on a program's subexpressions but is instead on the entire program. Because a program's final output determines its fitness, not the intermediate outputs of its subexpressions, expressions are only optimized indirectly. This may lead to suboptimal fitness maximization because an explicit focus on the evolution of good building blocks is missing. We posit that it is possible to improve subexpression contribution to fitness without resorting to selection on the unit of a subexpression. We propose to optimize a program prior to selection by changing the way its output is calculated, i.e. by optimizing the fitness contributions of its subexpressions. We decouple the subexpressions from their nesting in the program after we have saved their outputs during execution. We then linearly combine them by means of a multiple linear regression which regresses the target variable on the saved outputs from every fitness case. This method basically places optimal coefficients in front of each subexpression within a linear model in an attempt to improve the overall combination of subexpressions. It thus acts as a surrogate for direct selection on them.

Our contribution is primarily to change how a program's output is derived so that this new output provides a more reliable fitness signal (one amenable to evolutionary selection and variation) and, overall, so that the ability of GP to evolve highly fit programs improves. Specifically we propose two variants of MRGP and compare them, based upon testing performance, to multiple regression (MR) directly on the input variables and to a competent GP that uses multiobjective optimization based upon accuracy and complexity. In the *post-run* approach we simply use MRGP on the best solution of a run. We experiment with regressing 5 alternate sets of subexpressions. We find that, for a suite of 6 symbolic regression problems, at least one of these optimizations is always superior to our competent GP and MR. Given the low cost of trying all variants and the option to also apply them to other programs at the end of a run, MRGP appears to offer a viable post-run optimization. Its Success confirms the basic proposal that a program can be improved

*research conducted during K. Krawiec's stay at the ALFA Group, Computer Science and Artificial Intelligence Laboratory (CSAIL), MIT

GECCO'14, July 12–16, 2014, Vancouver, BC, Canada.

ACM 978-1-4503-2662-9/14/07 ...$15.00.
http://dx.doi.org/10.1145/2576768.2598291.

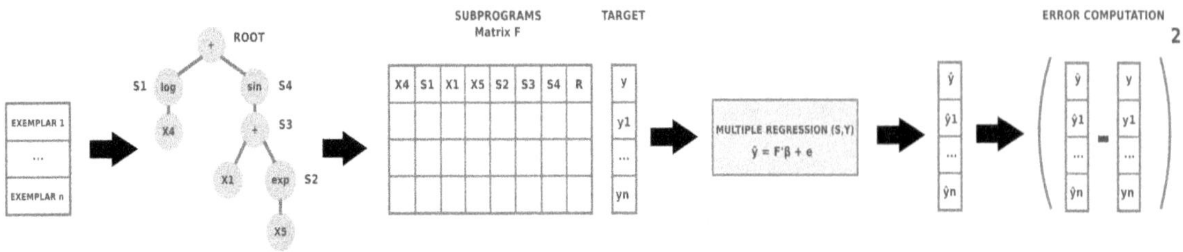

Figure 1: The outline of regressing program subexpressions.

by targeting its subexpressions explicitly for tuning within a linear framework. It also sets up the question of whether inlining multiple regression of subexpressions, within GP's evolutionary cycle is helpful. Our experiments provide a positive response: *inline* MRGP is superior even to *post-run* MRGP and is cost-neutral vs competent GP. By cost-neutral, we mean that, if we fix the optimization time, *inline* MRGP is superior despite using fewer fitness evaluations.

We proceed as follows: We describe the general approach in Section 2. In Sections 3 and 4 we respectively describe the *post-run* variant and empirically examine its effectiveness. In Sections 5 and 6 we respectively describe the *inline* variant and empirically examine its effectiveness. We describe related work in Section 7 and then conclude and mention future work in Section 8.

2. THE MRGP APPROACH

2.1 Terminology

The objective in a regression task is to find a *model* that maps one or more *input variables* onto a single *target variable* (desired output). When solving such a task using GP-based symbolic regression, models are instantiated by *programs* (expression trees in case of tree-based GP), where *program inputs* (*terminals*, *leaves*) map to the input variables' values, and *program output* (the expression's value when the root node is executed) maps to the target variable's value.

2.2 Subexpression Multiple Linear Regression

MRGP differs from conventional GP primarily in eliminating direct comparison of the final program output against the target variable, y. Instead, we substitute a new calculation of a program's output which is based on the linear combination of subexpression behavior as regressed against the target variable. We assume that all subexpressions of a program can be tuned in linear combination with respect to the target output. We also expect the resulting regression model to be superior over program output because it disregards the nested order in which subexpressions are considered in program execution to arrive at the final program output. We compare the target variable y to the output of the regression model.

Given a dataset D (also known as a set of fitness cases) composed of m columns of input variables and n rows of example values and a target vector y with target values for each example, we proceed as follows:

1. We step by step execute the program (with the conventional inorder tree parse) and store the output of each subexpression after it is executed. For tree-based GP, this means pausing the program execution process at each tree node (including leaves and the root node) and storing the value calculated at that node. By doing this for each training example, we obtain an $n \times k$ matrix of subexpressions F, where k is the size of the GP tree and n is the number of exemplars of D.

2. We map the values of F onto the desired output y using multiple linear regression (MR), which produces an optimal linear combination that minimizes the prediction error of $\hat{y}$. Multiple regression determines the vector of coefficients β that minimizes the sum of squares of residuals e of mapping the k subexpressions (predictors) onto the desired output y:

$$y = F'\beta + e$$

where F' is a $n \times (k+1)$ matrix obtained from F by prepending it with an additional column of ones, so that the corresponding coefficient β_1 implements the intercept of the linear model.

3. To assess the quality of the regressed model, we compute its output as $\hat{y} = F\beta$ and compare it to the original targets of the dataset in a conventional way, i.e., as $(y - \hat{y})^T(y - \hat{y}) = e^T e$.

Fig. 1 outlines this process for tree-based GP.

2.3 Enlisting Least Angle Regression

Major challenges with multiple regression can arise because the least squares approach fails if the matrix F is not of full rank. This may happen when the number of features k is large with respect to the number of exemplars n or if some of the columns of F are not linearly independent. The former circumstance will occur whenever a GP tree size exceeds the number of examples. Given GP tree size parameters and bloat, it should be anticipated. The former circumstance occurs when the outputs of different subexpressions are correlated. This correlation arises from one of the following scenarios:

- a subexpression appears multiple times in the GP tree.
- two or more subexpressions are syntactically different but semantically equivalent, i.e., present the exact same output. For instance, the subprograms X_2 and *exp* lnX_2 produce identical outputs,
- two subexpressions are linearly dependent, e.g., $(x_1 + x_2)$ and $(x_1 + x_2) * (x_1 + x_1)/x_1$.

To deal with these challenges, we employ the Least Angle Regression (LARS) algorithm presented by Efron et al. [4]. LARS is a stepwise process in which the variables are added one by one to the *active set* while the model's coefficients are continuously moved toward its least-square value until all the variables are included in the model. At the end of the process, the obtained model is the full least-squares fit. The steps involved in the LARS algorithm are listed below as presented in [6]:

1. Standardize the predictors to have zero mean and unit norm. Set the initial coefficients to 0, $\hat{\beta}_1, \hat{\beta}_2, ..., \hat{\beta}_p = 0$. The error or residual is then $r = y - \hat{y} = y$.
2. Initialize the active set with the variable x_i that is most correlated with r (equivalent in this first iteration to the target vector y).
3. Move $\hat{\beta}_i$ from 0 towards its least-squares coefficient $\langle x_i, r \rangle$, until another variable x_j is as correlated with the current residual as x_i. Add x_j to the active set.
4. Move $\hat{\beta}_i$ and $\hat{\beta}_j$ in the direction defined by their joint least squares coefficient of the current residual on (x_i, x_j), until some other competitor x_l has as much correlation with the current residual. Add x_l to the active set.
5. Repeat step 4 until all k predictors have been added to the active set.

The LARS algorithm is efficient since it takes k steps to get to the full least squares estimates and can be adapted [2] to solve the family of regression problems written as follows:

$$\min_{\beta} \frac{1}{2}||X\beta - y||_2^2 + \lambda_1||\beta||_1 + \frac{1}{2}\lambda_2||\beta||_2^2$$

where β is the vector of regression coefficients. We set $\lambda_1 = 0$ and $\lambda_2 = 0$ so the solution is unregularized and we ensure the active set includes all input variables. Without loss of generality we refer to this as multiple regression (MR).

3. POST-RUN REGRESSION OF PROGRAMS EVOLVED BY COMPETENT GP

The *post-run* multiple regression strategy consists of applying MR to programs evolved by a competent implementation of GP. Our goal is to determine whether GP programs, when 'behaviorally re-interpreted' in various ways by MR, have better fitness than when interpreted in the conventional way. Note that, in this case, GP does not receive any feedback from the outcomes of MR, i.e., the evolutionary process is not *driven* by MRGP (contrary to the approach studied in Section 5). We propose 5 strategies of the *post-run* variant (see Figure 2):

(a) Root: root node only (in which case the MR problem collapses to the simple univariate regression problem).

(b) Root and leaves: the leaves of the GP tree and the outputs of the root node are included in F.

(c) Subexpressions: the outputs of all the nodes of the tree (including the root node and leaves) are in F.

(d) Root and variables: matrix F contains outputs of the root and all the explanatory variables of the problem.

(e) Subexpressions and variables: F contains the outputs of all subexpressions and all the explanatory variables.

Note that in strategies (d-e) the explanatory variables are added to the matrix F even if they do not appear in the program tree. This is justified for high-dimensional problems, where GP trees would need to be very large to reference all the variables of a problem.

4. POST-RUN MRGP EVALUATION

We now compare the performance of the *post-run* multiple regression to a competent GP and multiple regression solely on the problem's explanatory variables.

4.1 Evaluation Problems

Table 1 summarizes the five symbolic regression problems used in this study. We chose problems of various sizes (number of explanatory variables and training set size) and characteristics. Energy problems (datasets ENH and ENC) come from simulation experiments while the NOX emissions dataset is a collection of real power plant data. For the Wine Quality Datasets, both red and white, the input variables are physical measurements, but the dependent variable is the median score of human 'sensory assessors', expressed on a scale from 0 (very bad) to 10 (excellent). In the case of the NOX dataset, the train/test split was fixed beforehand. To obtain the training and test sets of the remaining datasets, we performed random 0.66/0.33 splits.

To provide comparability of results across the benchmarks, their target variables are normalized to the interval $[0, 1]$.

4.2 Competent GP

We compare MRGP and MR to our "competent" GP system. It performs multi-objective optimization based on Non-Dominated Sorting Genetic Algorithm II (NSGA-II) [3] working with two minimized objectives: model error and model complexity. In the experiment reported in this section, the former is simply the error of the (normalized) program output with respect to target (calculated using L2 metric), while the latter is the Subtree Complexity measure introduced in [18].

We run 10 replicas of each experiment. Therefore, a total of 50 GP runs (5 datasets × 10 replicas) are performed to analyze the suitability of the different *post-run* multiple regression strategies. In each run, we select the solution presenting the lowest error and apply the five different post-run linear regression strategies introduced in Section 3 and depicted in Fig. 2, namely Root, Root and Leaves, Subexpressions, Root and variables, Subexpressions and variables. Table 2 presents the settings of the essential evolutionary parameters, most of which remain constant throughout the rest of this paper (unless otherwise stated). We execute each GP replica for 15 minutes, computing however many generations fit into this deadline.

4.3 Regression process

The data derived from GP subexpressions, before undergoing regression by the LARS algorithm (Section 2.3), requires the following preprocessing. First, if a given subexpression's output list contains not-a-number (NaN) values (resulting from, e.g., numerical over- or underflow), they are replaced by median value of that output list. If a subexpression's outputs are exclusively NaN values, it is discarded altogether as an input variable to the multiple regression (equivalently as a column of F). Subexpressions with constant outputs are also removed.

Once the regression model is induced, we adopt the following policy when applying it to data (either training or testing): if the model's prediction is beyond the interval $[-0.5, 1.5]$ (i.e., 0.5 below or above the assumed $[0, 1]$ range of target variable), it is clamped/trimmed to that value. This avoids contaminating the results with outlier predic-

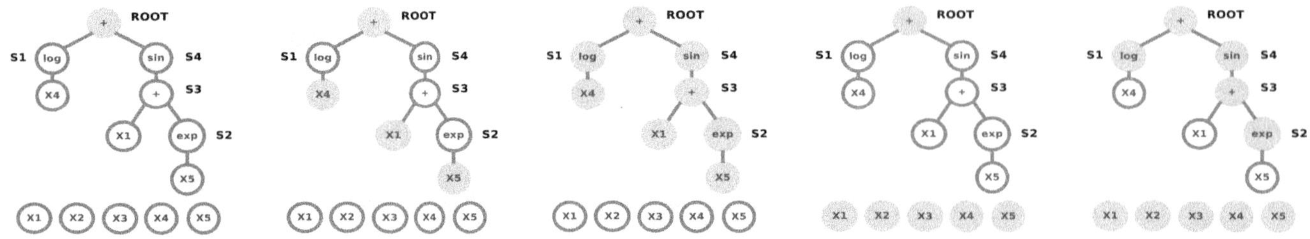

(a) Root (b) Root and leaves (c) Subexpressions (d) Root and Variables (e) Subexpressions and variables

Figure 2: Post-run multiple regression strategies for the expression $logX_4 + sin(X_1 + exp(X_5))$. Outputs of blue colored nodes are included in the multiple regression.

Acronym	Description	Number of attributes	Number of instances			Reference
			Total	Training	Test	
ENC	Energy efficiency, cooling load	8	768	512	256	[17]
ENH	Energy efficiency, heating load	8	768	512	256	[17]
NOX	NOX	18	5227	4017	1210	[20]
WIR	Wine quality assessment, red wine	11	1559	1066	533	[1]
WIW	Wine quality assessment, white wine	11	4898	3265	1633	[1]

Table 1: Benchmark datasets.

Parameter	Value
pop size	1000
selection	NSGAII with crowded Tournament
crossover	Single Point Crossover
mutation	Subtree mutation
MSE	Normalized tree output
Complexity	Subtree Complexity
stop criterion	15 minutes

Table 2: Parameters settings of our competent GP.

tions from degenerate models which may happen to be induced from, e.g., very small GP trees, or GP trees producing many NaNs. For fairness of comparison, we adopt this interpretation policy for all considered methods, including MR and GP.

4.4 Post-Run MRGP Results

Table 3 presents the mean square error (MSE) on the test set returned by the compared methods. The striking observation is that GP fails to outperform the baseline MR on all benchmarks, both on train set and test set. This indicates that evolutionary search was not effective enough at finding useful subexpressions and assembling them into expressions, at least within the selected computational budget.

More importantly however, almost all variants of *post-run* MRGP reduce the error rate when compared to standard GP and MR. Interestingly, the only exception is the 'root' case, where MRGP typically attains error in between that of MR and GP. Thus, we can expect that applying regression to the root node's outputs results in less error than when that output is directly compared to the target. However, this regression is not sufficient (at least for this benchmark suite) to outperform MR; that becomes possible only when more features, collected from various subexpressions, are used of predictors in a MR process.

The practical upshot is that providing the *post-run* regression process of end-of-run GP outcomes with additional predictors derived from program subexpressions is always worth trying. The extra computation incurred is marginal, while there may be significant gains in prediction accuracy. Moreover, as this experiment shows, the improvements on the training and testing set are usually correlated: if additional predictors lower the error on the training set, then it is very likely that they will do so also for the test set. Therefore, a recommended practice could be to first verify whether performing multiple regression on the subexpressions of the best-of-run GP program improves accuracy on the training set, and adopt it for the testing set if it does, otherwise falling back to the pure, non-augmented GP model.

This result also prompts the question as to whether it would be advantageous to apply MRGP to each program during a GP run, i.e. inline with evolution. Hypothetically evolutionary pressure on fitness arising from considering a different output from a program might be favorable. Thus, we next propose *inline* MRGP.

5. GUIDING EVOLUTIONARY SEARCH USING INLINE MRGP

In the inline approach, we integrate multiple regression into fitness evaluation in the GP flow. This substantially changes the evolutionary dynamics: programs are not forced anymore to produce execution outputs that are useful since the signal used for the fitness of a given program is the output of the model regressed as a linear combination of its subexpressions.

In proceeding, we anticipate that evolutionarily selecting programs solely on the basis of multiple regression error may be ill-advised. In particular, programs of different sizes have different quantities of subexpressions and, in turn, lead to models of different sizes (vector $\hat{\beta}$ varies in length from program to program). Given more subexpressions (many of

Table 3: Testing-set mean absolute error (MAD) of models considered in **post-hoc analysis**. The best result in each column is highlighted. 0.95-confidence intervals provided in smaller font.

Method	ENC	ENH	NOX	WIR	WIW
MR	0.0612 —	0.0541 —	0.0773 —	0.1012 —	0.0992 —
GP	0.0909 0.0358	0.1278 0.1109	0.0832 0.0034	0.1084 0.0131	0.1048 0.0050
leaves+root	0.0515 0.0079	0.0320 0.0108	0.0799 0.0039	0.0999 0.0019	0.1001 0.0009
leaves+FEFs	0.0584 0.0523	0.0497 0.0613	0.0802 0.0044	0.1049 0.0039	0.0990 0.0012
root	0.0809 0.0291	0.0727 0.0504	0.0834 0.0035	0.1045 0.0058	0.1028 0.0019
vars+root	0.0513 0.0077	0.0320 0.0108	0.0759 0.0011	0.0989 0.0017	0.0985 0.0006
vars+FEFs	0.0585 0.0523	0.0488 0.0580	0.0755 0.0021	0.1036 0.0043	0.0977 0.0011

them potentially uncorrelated), regression is likely to regress a better fitting model with lower overall error. This may bias the search towards programs that yield more subexpressions, i.e. larger trees, and hence contribute to program bloat.

To combat the anticipated bloat, similarly to the *post-run* approach, we rely on two-objective selection based on NSGA-II algorithm. In this case, the first objective is the error of the regression model induced from the outputs collected from tree subexpressions, and the second objective is model complexity. However, it is far from obvious how to measure the complexity of the compound model that involves both *symbolic* GP execution and *numeric* MR transform. To address that, we consider four different complexity measures.

GP Tree complexity (TC). This measure is simply the number of subexpressions, which coincides with program tree size, a criterion often used in GP to prefer smaller programs and lessen program bloat.

Sum of t-statistics (Sum-t). One may argue assessing model complexity by simply counting the number of subexpressions (or columns of F) is too crude. First, k is discrete, so ties between programs are likely, particularly for small programs. Secondly, and more importantly, k is insensitive to the impact of specific subexpressions. One may expect that among the subexpressions within a program, the outputs of only some of them will serve as useful predictors for the target output. In an extreme case, regression may build a perfect model using a single subexpression and neglecting all the remaining ones. Thus, two equally sized program trees may give rise to models that involve different numbers of significant parameters.

Following this observation, we define our second complexity measure as:

$$c(\hat{\beta}) = \sum_{i=2}^{k} \left|\frac{\hat{\beta}_i}{SE(\hat{\beta}_i)}\right| \tag{1}$$

where $SE(\hat{\beta}_i)$ is the standard error of the sample coefficient $\hat{\beta}_i$. The $\frac{\hat{\beta}_i}{SE(\hat{\beta}_i)}$ term in Formula (1) is the t-statistic that reflects the significance of $\hat{\beta}_i$. The greater its absolute value, the more it is likely that the corresponding predictor is a significant element of the model. Thus, $c(\hat{\beta})$ penalizes the models that use large number of significant predictors. Note that the summation in Eq. (1) starts from $i = 2$, so models are not penalized for using intercepts. Including $\hat{\beta}_1$ in the complexity measure would promote MR models that use no intercept, and compensate for its absence by engaging other predictors.

Minimum Description Length (MDL). In [16], Stine, following the work by Elias [5] and Rissanen [13], proposes a complexity measure of regression models that takes into account the significance of particular model parameters. Based on those findings, we define the complexity of a multiple regression model as the total *description length* of its parameters, i.e.,

$$c(\hat{\beta}) = \sum_{i=2}^{k} lu(\frac{\hat{\beta}_i}{SE(\hat{\beta}_i)}) \tag{2}$$

where $lu(x)$ is an idealized length of the universal code of number x [5, 13]:

$$lu(x) = 2 + \log_2|x| + 2\log_2\log_2|x|$$

where we set $\log_2(x) \equiv 0$ for $|x| < 1$.

Derivation of this measure is beyond the scope of this paper; it is however worth noting that the t-statistic of $\hat{\beta}_i$ is also present in this metric, thus penalizing models with many significant predictors. Moreover, because $lu(t)$ is concave, a model that involves a single variable is favored over a model that uses two variables that are 'half as significant', i.e., $lu(t) < 2lu(\frac{t}{2})$.

Saturated Minimum Description Length (SMDL). This measure is an extension of MDL in which the encoding length for large t-statistics are saturated. The motivation is that models that use very useful predictors (high t) should not be excessively penalized. The Saturated Minimum Description Length is computed as follows:

$$c(\hat{\beta}) = \sum_{i=2}^{k} slu(\frac{\hat{\beta}_i}{SE(\hat{\beta}_i)}) \tag{3}$$

where

$$slu(x) = \begin{cases} lu(x) & |x| < 2.626 \\ lu(2.626) & otherwise \end{cases}$$

where 2.626 is a critical value of t-statistics for significance level 0.01.

6. EXPERIMENT WITH INLINE MRGP

The experiment reported below has two primary goals: (i) to analyze whether *inline* MRGP attains better predictive accuracy than MR, conventional GP, and *post-run* MRGP, and (ii) to compare the suitability of different complexity measures to drive the *inline* MRGP process.

The inline MRGP implements a multi-objective approach based on NSGA-II. In this case, the targeted objectives are *multiple regression error* (see Section 2.2) and one of the complexity measures introduced in the previous section, namely TC, Sum-t, MDL, or SMDL. Therefore, we consider four different MRGP configurations:

(a) MRGP-TC: MR error and TC complexity

(b) MRGP-SumT: MR error and Sum-t complexity

(c) MRGP-MDL: MR error and MDL complexity

(d) MRGP-SMDL: MR error and SMDL complexity

We compare these four configurations to MR, conventional GP, and to an additional method called Root Regression GP (RRGP). RRGP represents the simplest inline MRGP strategy and consists of regressing only the program's output onto the target variable. In this sense, it is the inline version of the 'root' variant of *post-run* GP (cf. Table 3). In contrast to GP's conventional approach where program output y_p is directly compared to the target y, RRGP runs simple linear regression on y_p (and intercept) and assume that the resulting predicted values $\hat{y}$ constitute the final output. This approach finds the best linear mapping between y_p and y and is thus closely linked to using correlation coefficient to assess program quality, which has been used in the past [11, 15]. Note however that it is *not* equivalent to scaling of y_p and y to the same interval, a technique often practiced in symbolic regression.

Table 4 presents the settings of the essential evolutionary parameters of inline MRGP. MRGP presents a higher cost per fitness evaluation than conventional GP. As a result, given that we will execute with a fixed time budget, a lower number of generations will be executed. However, we anticipate that multiple regression provides a finer discrimination between subexpressions modifying the exploration/exploitation balance involved in GP search. To investigate how this balance impacts the inline MRGP process, we consider two population sizes, namely 100 and 1000.

In summary, a total of 400 MRGP runs (4 configs $\times$ 5 datasets $\times$ 10 replicas $\times$ 2 population sizes) were performed to investigate the search dynamics involved in MRGP. We assume that the final outcome of an evolutionary run is the lowest-error model found in the last generation of a run.

6.1 The results

Table 5 compares the mean absolute deviation (MAD) error on the test set, for the models evolved using the above variants of MRGP. We present there also the MAD of conventional linear regression applied to the original features (MR) and standard GP (GP).

The hybrid methods quite consistently outperform MR, and often do so by a large margin. This is not surprising, given the rich repertoire of nonlinear transformations available to GP which MR, being a linear technique, cannot model. The relative size of the gap between the evolutionary techniques and MR is problem dependent: it is rather small for the test sets of WIR and WIW, substantial for NOX, and

Parameter	Value
pop size	100,1000
selection	NSGAII with crowded Tournament
crossover	Single Point Crossover
mutation	Subtree mutation
MSE	Multiple regression error
Complexity	Subtree Complexity
stop criterion	15 minutes

Table 4: Parameters settings of the inline MRGP strategy.

dramatic for ENC and ENH. As expected, some problems may require more sophisticated models, while others not.

Concerning the different MRGP variants with a population size of 1000, TC, SumT and MDL outperform MR and GP on four out of five benchmarks, while on WIR they are worse. On the other hand, MRGP-SMDL presents a significantly higher average error for the ENC and ENH problems. Moreover, this last approach has also great variance between runs.

Similar remarks apply to the runs performed with a population size of 100 individuals. In fact, no significant differences can be noticed with respect to the setup considering a larger population. The TC, SumT, and MDL variants still outperform MR and GP, while SMDL fails to provide satisfactory results for the ENC and ENH problems. MRGP thus shows to be robust since its results seem insensitive to population size.

Overall, there is no clear winner among the MRGP variants. However, MGRP-SumT seems most reliable. It often produces the smallest or the close-to-smallest error, and for many benchmarks its error varies the least across evolutionary runs (see the confidence intervals shown in smaller font). Also, for the challenging WIR benchmark, where all GP-based methods (except RRGP) behave badly, MGRP-SumT is worse than MR only by $\sim$10% for population size 1000 and even by a smaller margin for population size 100. On the other hand, on ENC it halves the test-set error of MR, and on ENH it yields a test-set error four times smaller than MR. Apparently, the fine-grained model complexity assessment implemented by this method proves effective as a second objective of the search. Nevertheless, MRGP-TC also often attains quite good results, despite its discrete nature (Section 5). The possible reason for this is computational overhead: calculating program size (MRGP-TC) is much faster than computing t-statistics (MRGP-SumT), so the former method has the chance to evaluate more individuals and execute more generations.

Except for the WIR benchmark, MRGP variants are almost always better than RRGP. This corroborates the rationale for intra-execution behavioral evaluation: the regression process provided with insight into internal program behavior (MRGP), rather than only into program output (RRGP), has the chance to build better predicting models and thus helps guide the evolutionary search process more efficiently.

The general observation resulting from this experiment follows from comparison of the results of *post-run* analysis (Table 3) with the inline approach (Tables 5). With a few exceptions, the inline approach provides lower regression error. Given that the same execution time budget was available to all methods, we may conclude that using partial program outcomes for fitness evaluation is most often beneficial. Postponing the usage of partial outcomes till the end of evolutionary runs (as the *post-run* approach does) still brings some improvements compared to conventional approaches (Table 3), but not as substantial as for the inline approach. Apparently the redefined selection pressure is capable of guiding the evolutionary search toward better performing candidate solutions, despite making fewer fitness evaluations due to computational overhead introduced by multiple regression. In fact, for a fixed time budget, MRGP yields better results than conventional GP, even if less generations are executed or a reduced population is considered.

Table 5: Test-set mean absolute error (MAD) of models evolved using standard GP, RRGP, and four variants of MRGP, averaged over 10 evolutionary runs, for population sizes 1000 and 100. MR marks the result for multiple regression of original problem variables. Two best results in each column are highlighted. 0.95-confidence intervals provided in smaller font.

Population size	Method	ENC		ENH		NOX		WIR		WIW		Avg. rank
	MR	0.0612	—	0.0541	—	0.0773	—	0.1012	—	0.0992	—	6.7
1000	GP	0.0909	0.0358	0.1278	0.1109	0.0832	0.0034	0.1084	0.0131	0.1048	0.0050	9.2
	RRGP	0.0497	0.0358	0.0193	0.0111	0.0826	0.0037	0.1012	0.0017	0.1094	0.0187	6.5
1000	MRGP-TC	0.0536	0.0288	0.0115	0.0005	0.0710	0.0015	0.1172	0.0046	0.0958	0.0008	4.4
	MRGP-SumT	0.0300	0.0037	0.0123	0.0010	0.0704	0.0023	0.1115	0.0026	0.0959	0.0005	3.0
	MRGP-MDL	0.0365	0.0098	0.0982	0.1247	0.0724	0.0018	0.1120	0.0037	0.0960	0.0009	6.4
	MRGP-SMDL	0.2549	0.2453	0.2028	0.1931	0.0732	0.0012	0.1347	0.0425	0.0961	0.0004	9.1
100	MRGP-TC	0.0325	0.0082	0.0128	0.0028	0.0692	0.0018	0.1085	0.0059	0.0961	0.0004	3.7
	MRGP-SumT	0.0307	0.0023	0.0237	0.0245	0.0718	0.0015	0.1076	0.0030	0.0963	0.0007	4.6
	MRGP-MDL	0.0739	0.0526	0.0140	0.0044	0.0705	0.0009	0.1030	0.0025	0.0964	0.0009	5.0
	MRGP-SMDL	0.1176	0.1434	0.0868	0.1222	0.0720	0.0012	0.1080	0.0037	0.0968	0.0011	7.4

7. RELATED WORK

In the past literature, there were relatively many attempts to hybridize linear regression with GP. An early example is STROGANOFF by Iba *et al.* [7], where multiple regression was used to tune the *internal* parameters of GP programs (the weights of inputs of particular program instructions). However, program fitness was defined in a conventional way, no attempt was made to map the behavior of entire program onto target, and model complexity was not considered there.

McKay et al. [12] used continuum regression (a generalization of multiple regression, principal component regression, and partial least squares) in combination with GP to build nonlinear models. The regression algorithm iterates over latent variables, and for each of them invokes an independent GP run aimed at matching that variable (this may be likened to, e.g., cascade correlation learning algorithms developed for neural networks).

Keijzer proposed to use univariate (simple) symbolic regression to map program output onto the desired output, in every act of fitness evaluation independently. Apart from demonstrating the usefulness of this approach in practice [9], Keijzer provided also theoretical evidence that evaluating GP individuals in this manner leads to programs that are on average better than programs evolved using conventional GP [10]. Similarly to McKay *et al.*'s work, only the program output is used as a predictor variable in regression. This method is equivalent to RRGP considered in Section 6.

The approach proposed by Sobester *et al.* in [14] is similar to [9] in also using regression within fitness evaluation. In particular, GP was used there to evolve 'intervening variables' for linear regression. Interestingly, for multivariate problems a basis function was evolved for every dimension independently, by means of cooperative coevolution. However, only final program outcomes were taken into account. Also, model complexity was not considered.

By linearly combining program components, MRGP becomes distantly related to approaches that optimize constants in programs. One of the earliest examples is here the work by Jiang and Wright [8], who used the Levenberg-Marquardt algorithm for this purpose. The same algorithm is used for that purpose in a purely deterministic search method proposed in [19]. However, such algorithms implicitly assume that the structural form of a GP program being tuned is correct, and that its performance can be improved by adjusting the constants. MRGP, as argued in Introduction, is based on fundamentally different premises, viz. that the arrangement of program components can be inappropriate, and thus deteriorate program fitness, and that the hidden yet valuable program components can be detected by a MR analysis.

In the context of past studies, MRGP remains novel in (i) exploiting multiple features generated by program subexpressions, (ii) taking into account model complexity, and (iii) using state-of-the-art stage-wise least-angle regression to avoid rank deficiency problem harassing conventional multiple regression.

8. SUMMARY AND FUTURE WORK

We have introduced Multiple Regression Genetic Programming, a new means of executing a genetic program that provides a practical and cost-neutral improvement to GP. MRGP hybridizes GP with multiple regression by decoupling program's subexpressions and linearly combining them via regressing their outputs on the target variable. The use of Least Angle Regression, a stepwise linear regression algorithm, was important for the success of the approach, since it deals with the ways using GP subexpression outputs in this manner could trip up regression.

When applied in a *post-run* fashion, MRGP always improves the output of the programs obtained with a competent GP system and, as a consequence, often outperforms MR. In this mode, multiple regression only needs to be applied once, to the best-of-run individual. We consider these to be strong arguments to systematically employ MRGP *after every GP run.*

MRGP turns out to be even more beneficial when performed *inline*, i.e., when the feedback provided by the multiple regression process drives the evolutionary process. In this case, the search algorithm is provided with more robust and more reliable information on the value of individual's genetic code, which captures a complete decomposition of the program's behavior, rather than only its output. Compared to post-run MRGP, it introduces a higher cost for each fitness evaluation but when evaluated on an equal execution duration it yields substantial improvement of predictive accuracy. In this sense, both these usage scenarios (post-run and inline) complement each other.

We have analyzed the impact of considering different complexity measures corresponding both the complexity of genetic programs and that of the retrieved linear models. Inline MRGP has shown to be robust to this parameter, outperforming MR, GP, and post-run MRGP.

As a future work, we plan to extend the post-run MRGP approach so that the final linear model combines features retrieved from *multiple models*. With this approach, we expect to obtain a wider variety of features, many of them possibly uncorrelated, and increase the accuracy of the final regressed linear model. Apart from that, we would like to consider use of *regularized* linear regression, which would automatically promote simpler linear models and thus possibly impose qualitatively different selection pressure on the population of evolving programs.

9. ACKNOWLEDGMENTS

This work was supported by the Li Ka Shing Foundation. The authors would like to thank Dr. Kalyan Veeramachaneni for his contributions to this paper. Krzysztof Krawiec acknowledges financial support from Fulbright Commission and grants no. 91-543 and DEC-2011/01/B/ST6/07318.

10. REFERENCES

[1] P. Cortez, A. Cerdeira, F. Almeida, T. Matos, and J. Reis. Modeling wine preferences by data mining from physicochemical properties. *Decision Support Systems*, 47(4):547 – 553, 2009. Smart Business Networks: Concepts and Empirical Evidence.

[2] R. R. Curtin, J. R. Cline, N. P. Slagle, W. B. March, P. Ram, N. A. Mehta, and A. G. Gray. MLPACK: A scalable C++ machine learning library. *Journal of Machine Learning Research*, 14:801–805, 2013.

[3] K. Deb, A. Pratap, S. Agarwal, and T. Meyarivan. A fast and elitist multiobjective genetic algorithm: NSGA-II. *Evolutionary Computation, IEEE Transactions on*, 6(2):182 –197, apr 2002.

[4] B. Efron, T. Hastie, I. Johnstone, and R. Tibshirani. Least angle regression. *The Annals of statistics*, 32(2):407–499, 2004.

[5] P. Elias. Universal codeword sets and representations of the integers. *Information Theory, IEEE Transactions on*, 21(2):194–203, 1975.

[6] T. Hastie, R. Tibshirani, and J. Friedman. *The elements of statistical learning: data mining, inference and prediction.* Springer, 2 edition, 2009.

[7] H. Iba, T. Sato, and H. de Garis. Numerical genetic programming for system identification. In J. P. Rosca, editor, *Proceedings of the Workshop on Genetic Programming: From Theory to Real-World Applications*, pages 64–75, Tahoe City, California, USA, 9 July 1995.

[8] M. Jiang and A. H. Wright. An adaptive function identification system. In *Proceedings of the IEEE/ACM Conference on Developing and Managing Intelligent System Projects, Vienna, Virginia, USA*, pages 47–53, Mar. 1993.

[9] M. Keijzer. Improving symbolic regression with interval arithmetic and linear scaling. In C. Ryan, T. Soule, M. Keijzer, E. Tsang, R. Poli, and E. Costa, editors, *Genetic Programming, Proceedings of EuroGP'2003*, volume 2610 of *LNCS*, pages 70–82, Essex, 14-16 Apr. 2003. Springer-Verlag.

[10] M. Keijzer. Scaled symbolic regression. *Genetic Programming and Evolvable Machines*, 5(3):259–269, Sept. 2004.

[11] S.-Y. Liong, T. R. Gautam, S. T. Khu, V. Babovic, M. Keijzer, and N. Muttil. Genetic programming: A new paradigm in rainfall runoff modeling. *Journal of American Water Resources Association*, 38(3):705–718, June 2002.

[12] B. McKay, M. Willis, D. Searson, and G. Montague. Non-linear continuum regression using genetic programming. In W. Banzhaf, J. Daida, A. E. Eiben, M. H. Garzon, V. Honavar, M. Jakiela, and R. E. Smith, editors, *Proceedings of the Genetic and Evolutionary Computation Conference*, volume 2, pages 1106–1111, Orlando, Florida, USA, 13-17 July 1999. Morgan Kaufmann.

[13] J. Rissanen. A Universal Prior For Integers And Estimation By Minimum Description Length. *Annals Of Statistics*, 11(2):416–431, 1983.

[14] A. Sobester, P. B. Nair, and A. J. Keane. Evolving intervening variables for response surface approximations. In *10th AIAA/ISSMO Multidisciplinary Analysis and Optimization Conference*, number AIAA 2004-4379 in , pages 1–12, Albany, New York, USA, 30-Aug. 1-Sept. 2004.

[15] K. Stanislawska, K. Krawiec, and Z. W. Kundzewicz. Modeling global temperature changes with genetic programming. *Computer & Mathematics with Applications*, 64(12):3717–3728, 2012.

[16] R. A. Stine. Model Selection Using Information Theory and the MDL Principle. *Sociological Methods Research*, 33(2):230–260, Nov. 2004.

[17] A. Tsanas and A. Xifara. Accurate quantitative estimation of energy performance of residential buildings using statistical machine learning tools. *Energy and Buildings*, 49(0):560 – 567, 2012.

[18] E. Vladislavleva. *Model-based Problem Solving through Symbolic Regression via Pareto Genetic Programming.* PhD thesis, Tilburg University, Tilburg, the Netherlands, 2008.

[19] T. Worm and K. Chiu. Prioritized grammar enumeration: symbolic regression by dynamic programming. In C. Blum, E. Alba, A. Auger, J. Bacardit, J. Bongard, J. Branke, N. Bredeche, D. Brockhoff, F. Chicano, A. Dorin, R. Doursat, A. Ekart, T. Friedrich, M. Giacobini, M. Harman, H. Iba, C. Igel, T. Jansen, T. Kovacs, T. Kowaliw, M. Lopez-Ibanez, J. A. Lozano, G. Luque, J. McCall, A. Moraglio, A. Motsinger-Reif, F. Neumann, G. Ochoa, G. Olague, Y.-S. Ong, M. E. Palmer, G. L. Pappa, K. E. Parsopoulos, T. Schmickl, S. L. Smith, C. Solnon, T. Stuetzle, E.-G. Talbi, D. Tauritz, and L. Vanneschi, editors, *GECCO '13: Proceeding of the fifteenth annual conference on Genetic and evolutionary computation conference*, pages 1021–1028, Amsterdam, The Netherlands, 6-10 July 2013. ACM.

[20] F. Xue, R. Subbu, and P. Bonissone. Locally weighted fusion of multiple predictive models. In *Neural Networks, 2006. IJCNN '06. International Joint Conference on*, pages 2137–2143, 2006.

GPU–Parallel SubTree Interpreter for Genetic Programming

Alberto Cano
Department of Computer Science
and Numerical Analysis
University of Cordoba, Spain
acano@uco.es

Sebastián Ventura
Department of Computer Science
and Numerical Analysis
University of Cordoba, Spain
sventura@uco.es

ABSTRACT

Genetic Programming (GP) is a computationally intensive technique but its nature is embarrassingly parallel. Graphic Processing Units (GPUs) are many-core architectures which have been widely employed to speed up the evaluation of GP. In recent years, many works have shown the high performance and efficiency of GPUs on evaluating both the individuals and the fitness cases in parallel. These approaches are known as *population parallel* and *data parallel*. This paper presents a parallel GP interpreter which extends these approaches and adds a new parallelization level based on the concurrent evaluation of the individual's subtrees. A GP individual defined by a tree structure with nodes and branches comprises different depth levels in which there are independent subtrees which can be evaluated concurrently. Threads can cooperate to evaluate different subtrees and share the results via GPU's shared memory. The experimental results show the better performance of the proposal in terms of the GP operations per second (GPops/s) that the GP interpreter is capable of processing, achieving up to 21 billion GPops/s using a NVIDIA 480 GPU. However, some issues raised due to limitations of currently available hardware are to be overcomed by the dynamic parallelization capabilities of the next generation of GPUs.

Categories and Subject Descriptors

D.1.3 [**Programming Techniques**]: Concurrent Programming—*Parallel programming*; I.2.6 [**Artificial Intelligence**]: Learning—*Concept Learning*

General Terms

Algorithms, Performance, Experimentation

Keywords

Genetic Programming; Graphic Processing Units; Parallelism

GECCO'14, July 12–16, Vancouver, BC, Canada.

ACM 978-1-4503-2662-9/14/07 ...$15.00.
http://dx.doi.org/10.1145/2576768.2598272.

1. INTRODUCTION

Genetic Programming is an evolutionary-based paradigm that creates and optimizes computer programs as solutions to a given problem [13]. It is a well-established and effective machine learning approach which has been applied to many optimization problems and data mining tasks [9, 18]. However, its computational complexity has been a limiting factor when solving large and complex problems or datasets [20]. Its high computational complexity is due to the evaluation function to compute the fitness of the solutions. Typically, each individual of the population is run repetitively over a large number of fitness cases along generations.

On the other hand, Genetic Programming is usually considered as *embarrassing parallel* [1] and can take advantage of the parallel capabilities of modern hardware. First, every individual of the population can be evaluated independently (*population parallel* approach). Second, the evaluation of an individual on each of the fitness cases is also an independent computation that can be run in parallel (*data parallel* approach). These approaches have been widely used to speed up the fitness computation using Graphic Processing Units (GPUs) [4, 8, 16]. GPUs are high-performance and many-core devices comprising thousands of compute cores and fast memory. The application of GPUs to compute Genetic Programming is not new but there is much work to be done to increase the performance and efficiency of Genetic Programming implementations on GPUs.

The *population parallel* approach is useful to speed up the evaluation when the population size (number of individuals) increase, whereas the *data parallel* approach speeds up the computation when the number of fitness cases increase, e.g. when solving very large datasets. Both approaches combined have demonstrated to achieve high performance on solving different machine learning problems [4, 5, 10, 16]. However, these approaches do not take into account the length of the Genetic Programming individuals. There are problems which may require very long individuals to appropriately solve the given task. For example, when learning classification rules on high-dimensional datasets, algorithms may need to learn very long rules comprising a high number of conditions to perform accurate classification. Therefore, effective performance is decreased due to the increasing time devoted to compute the the high number of tree nodes encoded on large individuals.

The cornerstone of a program–interpreted Genetic Programming evaluator is the program interpreter. The Genetic Programming individuals are created and manipulated as reverse polish (RPN) expressions, which are evaluated via a stack in single pass. Traditional stack-based interpreters are limited due to the dependencies between the tree nodes, i.e., a parent node cannot be evaluated until its children nodes have been evaluated. This nature limits the performance of the interpreter, especially when evaluating long individuals. Nevertheless, it is straightforward to see that the evaluation of each of the children nodes is an independent operation and consequently, they could be computed in parallel.

In this work we present a GPU-based parallel approach for evaluating independent subtrees of Genetic Programming individuals. This approach complements the *population parallel* and *data parallel* approaches in order to develop a massively parallel model for Genetic Programming. The proposed model addresses the parallel evaluation of the subtrees of the individuals by means of the concurrent computation of independent tree branches. The Genetic Programming interpreter is modified to make parallel computation of multiple subtrees at once. Therefore, it can be treated as a cube of work to be done [*population, individual's subtrees, fitness cases*]. This allows for reducing the total amount of time required for evaluating an individual, especially when its length increases.

An experimental study has been carried out to evaluate the performance and efficiency of the proposal as compared with the traditional Genetic Programming interpreter on the GPU. Multiple experimental configurations have been tested to analyze the performance variation when changing the population size, the length of the individuals, and the number of fitness cases. The experimental results advocate for the better performance of the proposal in terms of the number of Genetic Programming operations per second (GPops/s) it is capable of computing.

The remainder of this work is organized as follows. The next section reviews related works on the application of GPUs to Genetic Programming. Section 3 presents the proposed approach for parallel subtree evaluation. Section 4 describes and discusses the experiments carried out. Finally, Section 5 presents some concluding remarks.

2. RELATED WORK

This section reviews the related work available in the literature about GPU-based parallel implementations of Genetic Programming approaches. NVIDIA introduced in 2007 the Compute Unified Device Architecture (CUDA)[22] framework to facilitate the application of GPU computing for general purpose computation (GPGPU). Since then, the use of GPUs and CUDA has been widely employed to speed up many scientific researches involving parallel computation, and in particular, Genetic Programming.

Chitty [7], and Harding and Banzhaf [11] first developed an implementation of the Genetic Programming fitness function on GPUs, which is known to consume most of the computation time of the evolutionary algorithm. They followed a *data parallel* approach achieving high speedups, but they used an individual-compiled approach rather than individual-interpreted [12].

Langdon and Banzhaf [17] proposed a reverse polish notation (RPN) stack-based Genetic Programming interpreter to efficiently compute GP individuals on GPUs. Moreover, Langdon applied the GPU-parallel interpreter to a large scale bioinformatics problem [14], seeking for the scalability of the implementation to large population and data sizes. Langdon also defined a metric for measuring the speed of a Genetic Programming implementation known as Genetic Programming Operations per Second (GPops/s) [15].

Robilliard et al. [23, 24, 25] presented a *population parallel* and *data parallel* approach whereby the population was distributed across the multiprocessors of the GPU whilst the fitness cases were parallelized on the stream processors within each multiprocessor. This approach provides millions of active threads in which the interpreter allows all the fitness cases associated with a single program to be run on the same multiprocessor, avoiding the threads divergence, which is a major cornerstone for achieving maximum performance. Specifically, they reported a maximum performance of up to 4.7 billion GPops/s using a NVIDIA G80 GPU.

Maitre et al. [19] focused on achieving significant speedups even when using small number of fitness cases by using hardware scheduling. Seeking the scalability of the models to both low and high dimensionality problems is as important as achieving high speedup values. Cano et al. [5] also presented a *population parallel* and *data parallel* approach to speed up the evaluation of Genetic Programming algorithms applied to classification problems, including algorithms with Pittsburgh-style encoding [6]. Both authors gave special attention on achieving speedups even for small fitness cases.

Augusto and Barbosa [2] proposed a parallelization of the Genetic Programming evaluation using the OpenCL programming platform, whose advantage is its applicability to CPUs and GPUs from different vendors. They evaluated the performance on the symbolic regression and data classification domains achieving up to 13 billion GPops/s using a NVIDIA GTX 285 GPU.

Wilson and Banzhaf [26] presented an optimized methodology for deploying the Genetic Programming application on multiple architectures. Their work described the considerations necessary to maximize available CPU and GPU usage, and for the first time, an Xbox 360 implementation that uses its GPU for fitness evaluation. Implementations on different platforms were benchmarked on the basis of execution time for an established Genetic Programming regression benchmark problem.

There are many other related works which applied similar GPU–parallel approaches to other evolutionary-based paradigms [3, 10] achieving promising results. The high number of recent related works in the literature shows the increasing interest and attention of the scientific community on the application of GPU computing for solving Genetic Programming problems.

3. PROPOSED APPROACH

This section presents the parallel approach for subtree evaluation which extends the *population parallel* and *data parallel* approaches. First, the basis of the Genetic Programming interpreter are presented to identify parallelization opportunities. Finally, the proposal is introduced.

The Genetic Programming tree interpreter is a function that receives a genetic program encoded in an individual, and executes the instructions stored on the tree's nodes in a flow given by the tree's structure (parent-children). An interpreter is commonly implemented as a stack-based procedure in which the partial results coming from the children

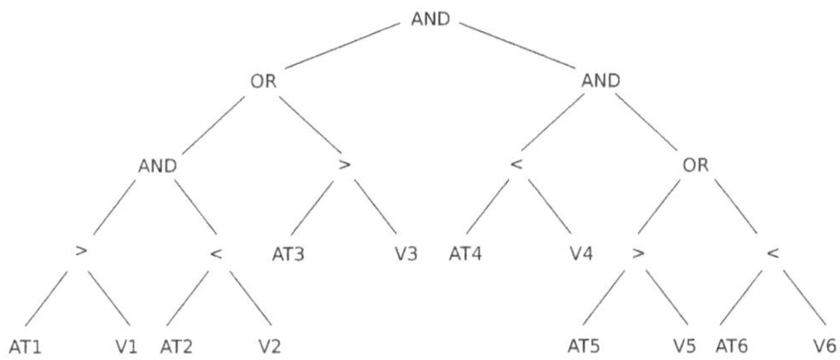

Figure 1: Tree structure of a GP program.

nodes are pushed into a stack and pulled back when a parent operator needs the accumulated result.

Figure 1 shows a sample Genetic Programming individual with its tree structure, which is composed by logical AND/OR operations and attribute–value comparions. This kind of individuals are commonly used in Data Mining for classification and association rule mining tasks. The aforementioned individual can be written in an array using the RPN notation as:

```
RPN individual: (V6 AT6 < V5 AT5 > OR V4 AT4 < AND
V3 AT3 > V2 AT2 < V1 AT1 > AND OR AND)
```

The interpreter reads the individual from the left to the right, performing push and pop operations when necessary. The number of push and pop operations increases with the length of the individual. The code of the traditional stack-based interpreter is shown in Algorithm 1. Its computational complexity increases as the population size, the number of fitness cases, and the length of the individuals increase.

Algorithm 1 Traditional stack-based GP interpreter.

```
for program in population do
  for instance in dataset do
    for op ← 0 to program_size do
      switch (program[op])
        case AND:
          PUSH(POP() && POP());
        case OR:
          PUSH(POP() || POP());
        case NOT:
          PUSH(!POP());
        ...
        case GREATER:
          PUSH(POP() > POP());
        case LESS:
          PUSH(POP() < POP());
        ...
        case ATTRIBUTE:
          PUSH(dataset[instance][attribute]);
        case VALUE:
          PUSH(value);
      end switch
    end for
  end for
end for
```

The traditional implementation of the GPU interpreter addresses both the *data parallel* and *population parallel* approaches. First, the *data parallel* approach handles as many threads as the number of fitness cases. When the interpreter reads an attribute node, each thread is responsible for reading its corresponding instance–attribute value based on its thread identifier (avoiding the *for instance in dataset* loop in Algorithm 1). Second, the *population parallel* approach performs similarly, running in parallel the interpretation of each of the individuals within the population (avoiding the *for program in population* loop in Algorithm 1). Consequently, a 2D matrix of threads is used to compute concurrently the individuals and fitness casses. As pointed by Robilliard [25], it is necessary to guarantee that individuals should be run on different GPU multiprocessors to avoid threads divergence, which eventually significantly impacts on the efficiency. This way, non-divergent threads are implicitly synchronous along the compute code, and ideally, they also satisfy memory coalescence requirements.

The implementation of a prefix or postfix interpreter requires to employ a stack memory and every operand/operator performs push/pop operations. Thus, the number of reads and writes over the stack increases with the length of the individual. However, seeking for an efficient implementation on GPUs is not straightforward. GPUs are not especially designed for stack-based memory operations. Therefore, we propose to employ an intermediate representation to minimize the number of operations over the stack. For instance, the attribute–value conditions can be computed in a single pass with a single push operation and they can be internally represented in prefix notation whereas the rest of the individual is written in postfix. The sample individual can be rewritten as:

```
Individual: (< AT6 V6 > AT5 V5 OR < AT4 V4 AND
> AT3 V3 < AT2 V2 > AT1 V1 AND OR AND)
```

This representation allows the interpreter performance to speed up, and minimizes the number of push and pop operations on the stack. When the interpreter finds an attribute–value comparison it directly computes the operation without pushing the operands first. For instance, to compute the sample individual from Figure 1, the RPN representation requires 23 push and 22 pop operations whereas the mixed representation requires only 11 push and 10 pop operations, which reduces memory accesses and increases interpreter performance.

Nevertheless, the main aim of this work is to speed up the interpreter by means of the concurrent computation of subtrees. Analyzing the structure of a Genetic Programming tree, multiple independent subtrees can be identified by means of the depth of the branches. First, all the attribute–value comparisons ([operator attribute value] chain) are considered leaf nodes and independent operations. Consequently, we could define a parallel model in which they can be computed concurrently. Second, as we climb the tree to the root, each of the independent branches can be also computed in parallel. Therefore, we may propose an interpreter which computes concurrently multiple subtrees based their depth. For instance, using the sample tree from Figure 1, we can compute the whole tree in as many steps as the longest branch depth. This is very important since the deepest branch determines the maximum number of steps that the interpreter must iterate. Therefore, the computational complexity of evaluating a Genetic Programming tree is reduced from $\mathcal{O}(tree\ size)$ to a complexity relying on the maximum tree depth $\mathcal{O}(longest\ tree\ branch)$. Moreover, the arity of the nodes (number of children of a node) and the degree of

		synchronization barrier	synchronization barrier	synchronization barrier
$Thread_4$	< AT6 V6	OR stk[3] stk[4]		
$Thread_3$	> AT5 V5	> AT4 V4		
$Thread_2$	< AT2 V2	> AT3 V3	AND stk[3] stk[4]	
$Thread_1$	> AT1 V1	AND stk[1] stk[2]	OR stk[1] stk[2]	AND stk[1] stk[2]
Time	T_1	T_2	T_3	T_4

Figure 2: Concurrent computation of subtrees for the sample individual.

Algorithm 2 Parallel subtree GP interpreter.

```
instance ← dataset[tid_x]
program ← population[tid_y]
for depth ← 0 to max_depth(program) do
  sp ← program[tid_z + depth];
  switch (program[sp])
   case AND:
    op1 ← stack[program[sp+1]];
    op2 ← stack[program[sp+2]];
    stack[tid_z] ← op1 && op2;
   case OR:
    op1 ← stack[program[sp+1]];
    op2 ← stack[program[sp+2]];
    stack[tid_z] ← op1 || op2;
   case NOT:
    stack[tid_z] ← !stack[program[sp+1]];
   ...
   case GREATER:
    op1 ← instance[program[sp+1]];
    op2 ← program[sp+2];
    stack[tid_z] ← op1 > op2;
   case LESS:
    op1 ← instance[program[sp+1]];
    op2 ← program[sp+2];
    stack[tid_z] ← op1 < op2;
   ...
  end switch
  __syncthreads();
end for
```

balance of the tree structure determine the opportunities for parallelization.

The implementation of the model extends the 2D interpreter function kernel [population,fitness cases] with a new dimension to handle concurrent operations for multiple subtrees. The pseudo-code of the proposed parallel Genetic Programming interpreter is shown in Algorithm 2. It computes multiple threads based on the 3D thread identifier tid_{xyz}. The full code detailed with comments is available at the website in[1]. This interpreter employs the mixed representation to minimize the number of push and pop operations as well as it runs concurrent subtrees whenever the tree structure allows. Figure 2 shows a timeline in which the sample tree from Figure 1 is disposed for concurrent subtrees computation in 4 steps from T_1 to T_4. Threads from $Thread_1$ to $Thread_4$ cooperate to compute independent branches of the individual via stack-based shared memory $stk[thread]$. Each thread only requires a single-value stack element that is shared using the GPU's shared memory, which is a fast access memory visible by all the threads in the thread block. At first step, the leaf nodes of the longest tree branches are computed and their results are stored in shared memory (memory addresses are directly related to the threads identifiers). At the following steps, the interpreter climbs the tree computing the nodes and reading/writing partial results from/to shared memory. Every time, synchronization must be controlled with barriers to guarantee that results are correctly stored in memory prior to utilization in further computations on following steps (read-after-write hazard). The `__syncthreads()` call is responsible for the synchronization within the scope of all threads in the same block. This is very important since the synchronization barrier guarantees the correct and parallel interpretation of the individual's subtrees while it does not limit the execution of other thread blocks computing other individuals in different compute units. At the last step, the root node is computed and the final result is returned.

The parallelization chances and the number of concurrent operations available decrease as the interpreter reaches the root node. For clarification, let us define a complete binary tree whose depth is d. The tree has $2^{d+1} - 1$ nodes and there are 2^d nodes at level d. When evaluating this tree, the number of concurrent operations starts with 2^d, and it is divided by two at each level until we reach the root node. The complete binary tree is a best-performance tree where the feasible concurrency is maximal. However, trees usually obtained in real-world machine learning problems are not necessarily complete, balanced, nor binary, yet this parallel evaluation model is feasible for any tree structure and node's cardinality, taking advantage of parallelism whenever the tree structure allows.

Moreover, the proposed model is scalable to multiple GPU devices by means of the distribution of the population into several GPUs, following a similar multi-GPU approach as presented in [5]. This allows for the scalability of the interpreter to very large population sizes, and large-scale and high-dimensional datasets.

4. EXPERIMENTS

This section presents the experiments run to evaluate the performance of the proposed model as compared with the previous GPU *population parallel* and *data parallel* approach.

[1] The source code and the datasets are fully described and publicly available at the website:

http://www.uco.es/grupos/kdis/kdiswiki/GPevaluation

		Tree size	31			63			127		
		Population size	32	64	128	32	64	128	32	64	128
Dataset	Instances	Atts.									
fars	100968	29	7.23	7.24	7.24	7.31	7.31	7.31	7.34	7.33	7.33
glass	214	9	7.02	8.39	10.39	11.07	15.06	18.24	14.66	16.62	18.14
heart	270	13	7.75	9.70	11.41	13.18	15.23	18.41	14.18	15.66	18.37
ionosphere	351	33	7.44	8.19	9.23	8.19	8.76	9.53	8.54	9.00	9.28
iris	150	4	5.69	7.82	9.67	10.11	13.55	16.78	12.03	15.08	16.68
kddcup	494020	42	6.67	6.67	6.68	6.75	6.75	6.76	6.75	6.76	6.77
mushroom	8124	22	14.21	14.45	14.48	14.66	14.65	14.71	14.60	14.77	14.74
penbased	10992	16	13.08	13.23	13.35	13.40	13.45	13.52	13.53	13.56	13.55
pima	768	8	9.58	11.11	12.35	18.48	20.04	20.76	18.23	19.00	19.32
satimage	6435	36	7.10	7.17	7.22	7.25	7.33	7.34	7.36	7.38	7.38
shuttle	58000	9	16.19	16.58	16.77	19.32	19.41	19.48	19.69	19.69	19.71
sonar	208	60	6.50	7.79	9.41	7.89	8.93	10.45	8.87	9.05	10.31
texture	5500	40	7.14	7.24	7.26	7.35	7.38	7.38	7.38	7.43	7.42
thyroid	7200	21	10.31	10.40	10.53	10.65	10.61	10.63	10.67	10.63	10.66
vowel	990	13	11.28	12.79	14.24	15.23	17.01	17.93	16.28	17.61	17.93

Table 1: Performance of the traditional GP interpreter (billion GPops/s).

		Tree size	31			63			127		
		Population size	32	64	128	32	64	128	32	64	128
Dataset	Instances	Atts.									
fars	100968	29	16.37	16.66	16.90	19.69	19.71	19.71	21.74	21.76	21.77
glass	214	9	9.80	12.86	12.04	14.73	17.14	19.25	15.06	17.17	20.84
heart	270	13	10.44	12.82	16.37	14.49	17.25	19.21	15.10	17.52	19.25
ionosphere	351	33	8.03	9.62	11.41	15.53	18.24	18.71	16.52	18.05	20.81
iris	150	4	7.50	11.04	13.78	11.09	14.57	17.35	13.93	16.24	18.12
kddcup	494020	42	16.86	16.93	17.00	19.69	19.70	19.70	21.78	21.78	21.78
mushroom	8124	22	14.18	15.18	15.76	19.60	19.73	19.78	21.33	21.64	21.78
penbased	10992	16	15.28	16.03	16.27	19.58	19.64	19.68	21.44	21.63	21.71
pima	768	8	14.21	16.48	19.24	16.96	18.29	20.63	18.58	19.99	21.33
satimage	6435	36	13.59	15.28	15.92	19.48	19.58	19.64	21.20	21.48	21.61
shuttle	58000	9	16.99	17.02	17.03	19.55	19.57	19.59	21.83	21.84	21.85
sonar	208	60	6.72	8.63	10.75	13.07	16.22	18.63	15.20	17.06	17.93
texture	5500	40	13.62	14.52	16.19	19.44	19.55	19.61	21.16	21.46	21.62
thyroid	7200	21	14.08	15.21	16.27	19.52	19.62	19.64	21.32	21.51	21.66
vowel	990	13	14.30	16.49	17.24	18.62	19.10	19.38	19.25	20.19	21.06

Table 2: Performance of the parallel subtree GP interpreter (billion GPops/s).

4.1 Experimental setup

The experiments were run on a machine equipped with an Intel Core i7 quad-core processor running at 3.0GHz and 12 GB of DDR3-1600 host memory, NVIDIA GeForce 480 GTX video card equipped with 1.5GB of GDDR5 video RAM, 15 multiprocessors and 480 CUDA cores clocked at 1.4 GHz. The host operating system was GNU/Linux Ubuntu 13.10 64 bit along with CUDA runtime 5.5, NVIDIA drivers 331.20, and GCC compiler 4.6.4 (O3 optimization level).

The experiments measure the runtime devoted for evaluating a series of Genetic Programming individuals on a set of 15 datasets. The datasets were collected from the UCI machine learning repository [21], and they represent a wide variety of dataset complexities with different number of instances and attributes. This will allow us to evaluate the performance of the interpreter with regards of the dataset size, analyzing the scalability to larger data problems. The runtime employed to evaluate a Genetic Programming individual on a dataset with multiple fitness cases is used to build a performance measure known as Genetic Programming operations per second (GPops/s). This measure, proposed by Langdon [15], directly evaluates the runtime as related with the number of operations computed by the interpreter. Therefore, we report performance in such terms.

In order to carry out a fair comparison of the performance of the classical GPU interpreter and the subtree parallel model proposed, exactly the same GP individuals are run in both interpreters. Both approaches follow a mixed individual representation to minimize push and pop operations, so that only the sequential tree interpretation vs the parallel subtree evaluation performance difference is measured.

4.2 Results

Table 1 shows the performance of the traditional GPU-based interpreter, following a *population parallel* and *data parallel* approach. Rows represent different datasets, each one having different number of instances and attributes. Columns are grouped by the tree size (the number of nodes of the tree, i.e., the length of the encoded individual), whereas different population sizes are also evaluated for each tree

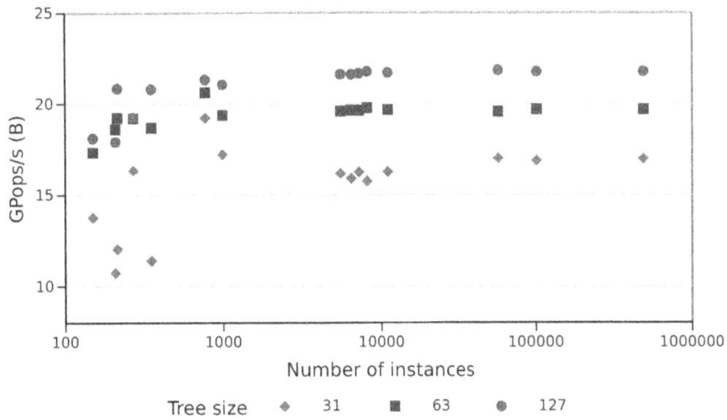

Figure 3: Performance with regards of the tree size and dataset size.

size. The combination of the population size and the dataset size determine the 2D configuration of the compute grid on the GPU and the number of threads of the evaluation process. The experimental results for the traditional GPU-based interpreter report a performance as low as 5 billion GPops/s and as high as 20 billion GPops/s. On the one hand, the lowest performance is achieved on the *iris* dataset when using the smaller population size. This can be explained because of the lower number of threads due to the small number of instances and population size. Therefore, there is less computational intensity and less parallelizability under these conditions, and the GPU compute units are not fully occupied. On the other hand, best performance is achieved when increasing the population size. It can be observed the higher number of GPops/s when the population size is increased for each of the datasets.

Table 2 shows the performance of the proposed GPU-based parallel interpreter, following a *subtree parallel*, *population parallel* and *data parallel* approach. Now, the combination of the population size, the dataset size, and the tree size determine the 3D configuration of the compute grid on the GPU and the number of threads of the evaluation process. The experimental results for the proposed subtree parallel GPU-based interpreter report a performance as low as 6 billion GPops/s and as high as 21 billion GPops/s. On the one hand, lower performances are also achieved on the *ionosphere*, *iris*, and *sonar* datasets when using the smaller population size. This behaviour can be also explained because of the lower number of threads due to the small number of instances and population size. On the other hand, best performance is achieved when increasing the population size and the tree size, as shown in Figure 3. It can be observed the higher number of GPops/s when the population size or the tree size is increased for a dataset. Specifically, it is also noted the lower performance when the tree size and the dataset size is very small, achieving performance lower than 15 billion GPops/s. Under such conditions, there is less parallelization opportunities due to the less computational complexity of evaluating small individuals on small data and therefore, the GPU compute capability is not fully occupied and it cannot demonstrate its high performance. However, as soon as the tree size or the dataset size are big enough to provide many parallelization chances, the performance increases to higher levels.

4.3 Limitations of the current proposal

Even the high performance achieved by the proposed model, it is necessary to point out the limitations of the proposal. The current approach requires threads synchronization between each of the depth levels of the tree, which inevitably introduces a small delay into the evaluation process. The longer the deepest tree branch, the higher number of synchronization barriers to be executed. Therefore, increasing even further the tree size would not impact in practice the real performance of the currently proposed interpreter. Moreover, the current approach suffers from threads divergence within the thread block, which significantly impacts in the effective performance. Specifically, as the depth level to be evaluated raises to the tree root, it implies higher number of threads to be idle waiting for active threads to complete their respective nodes computation for the current level.

Nevertheless, these issues can be overcome using modern NVIDIA GPUs based on the compute capability 3.5 or higher. New NVIDIA GPUs allow for dynamic parallelism in CUDA, which enables a CUDA kernel to create and synchronize dynamic nested kernels. Therefore, we can overcome the issues of the proposed Genetic Programming interpreter by defining a dynamic parallel kernel in which each of the depth levels are dynamically parallelized with regards of the exactly number of threads necessary to compute, avoiding to create unnecessary idle threads and threads divergence. The adaptation of the current proposal to take advantage of dynamic parallelism is straightforward. However, we were not able to get GK110-based GPUs to evaluate the performance of the Genetic Programming interpreter using the dynamic parallelism capability. It is our aim to adapt the proposed model for dynamic parallelism as future work.

5. CONCLUSIONS

In this work we presented a GPU-parallel approach for evaluating independent subtrees of Genetic Programming individuals. The proposal extended the *population parallel* and *data parallel* approaches in order to develop a massively parallel model for Genetic Programming on GPUs. The proposed model addressed the parallel evaluation of the subtrees of the individuals by means of the concurrent computation of independent tree branches based on the their depth level. This approach resulted in a 3D cube of compute threads that is defined by the number of instances, the population size and the tree size. The computational complexity of evaluating a Genetic Programming tree was reduced from linear complexity $\mathcal{O}(tree\ size)$ to a complexity relying on the maximum tree depth $\mathcal{O}(longest\ tree\ branch)$.

Experimental results showed the better performance of the proposal in terms of the number of Genetic Programming operations per second that the interpreter is capable to compute, achieving a performance up to 21 billion GPops/s using a NVIDIA GTX 480 GPU. However, there were some limitations to the currently proposed model that prevented its performance to effectively increase on very large tree sizes. Nevertheless, these issues were discussed to be solved by taking advantage of the dynamic parallelism capabilities of modern GPUs. This was aimed as future work as we are able to get a GK110-based GPUs.

6. ACKNOWLEDGMENTS

This research was supported by the Spanish Ministry of Science and Technology, project TIN-2011-22408, and by FEDER funds. This research was also supported by the Spanish Ministry of Education under FPU grant AP2010-0042.

7. REFERENCES

[1] D. Andre and J. R. Koza. A parallel implementation of genetic programming that achieves super-linear performance. *Information Sciences*, 106(3-4):201–218, 1998.

[2] D. A. Augusto and H. J. Barbosa. Accelerated parallel genetic programming tree evaluation with OpenCL. *Journal of Parallel and Distributed Computing*, 73(1):86–100, 2013.

[3] W. Banzhaf and S. Harding. Accelerating evolutionary computation with graphics processing units. In *Proceedings of the 14th Annual Conference Companion on Genetic and Evolutionary Computation*, GECCO '09, pages 3237–3286, 2009.

[4] W. Banzhaf, S. Harding, W. B. Langdon, and G. Wilson. Accelerating genetic programming through graphics processing units. In *Genetic Programming Theory and Practice VI*, Genetic and Evolutionary Computation, pages 1–19. Springer US, 2009.

[5] A. Cano, A. Zafra, and S. Ventura. Speeding up the evaluation phase of GP classification algorithms on GPUs. *Soft Computing*, 16(2):187–202, 2012.

[6] A. Cano, A. Zafra, and S. Ventura. Parallel evaluation of pittsburgh rule-based classifiers on GPUs. *Neurocomputing*, 126:45–57, 2014.

[7] D. M. Chitty. A data parallel approach to genetic programming using programmable graphics hardware. In *Proceedings of the 12th Annual Conference Companion on Genetic and Evolutionary Computation*, GECCO '07, pages 1566–1573, 2007.

[8] D. M. Chitty. Fast parallel genetic programming: multi-core cpu versus many-core GPU. *Soft Computing*, 16(10):1795–1814, 2012.

[9] P. G. Espejo, S. Ventura, and F. Herrera. A Survey on the Application of Genetic Programming to Classification. *IEEE Transactions on Systems, Man, and Cybernetics, Part C Applications and Reviews*, 40:121–144, 2010.

[10] M. A. Franco, N. Krasnogor, and J. Bacardit. Speeding up the evaluation of evolutionary learning systems using GPGPUs. In *Proceedings of the 15th Annual Conference Companion on Genetic and Evolutionary Computation*, GECCO '10, pages 103–110, 2010.

[11] S. Harding and W. Banzhaf. Fast genetic programming on GPUs. In *Proceedings of the 10th European Conference on Genetic Programming*, pages 90–101, 2007.

[12] S. L. Harding and W. Banzhaf. Distributed genetic programming on GPUs using CUDA. In *Workshop on Parallel Architectures and Bioinspired Algorithms*, pages 1–10, 2009.

[13] J. R. Koza. *Genetic Programming: On the Programming of Computers by Means of Natural Selection*. MIT Press, 1992.

[14] W. B. Langdon. Large scale bioinformatics data mining with parallel genetic programming on graphics processing units. In *Parallel and Distributed Computational Intelligence*, pages 113–141. 2010.

[15] W. B. Langdon. A many threaded CUDA interpreter for genetic programming. In *Proceedings of the 13th European Conference on Genetic Programming*, volume 6021 of *Lecture Notes in Computer Science*, pages 146–158, 2010.

[16] W. B. Langdon. Graphics processing units and genetic programming: an overview. *Soft Computing*, 15(8):1657–1669, 2011.

[17] W. B. Langdon and W. Banzhaf. A SIMD interpreter for genetic programming on GPU graphics cards. In *Proceedings of the 11th European Conference on Genetic Programming*, volume 4971 of *Lecture Notes in Computer Science*, pages 73–85, 2008.

[18] W. B. Langdon and S. M. Gustafson. Genetic programming and evolvable machines: Ten years of reviews. *Genetic Programming and Evolvable Machines*, 11(3-4):321–338, 2010.

[19] O. Maitre, N. Lachiche, and P. Collet. Fast evaluation of GP trees on GPGPU by optimizing hardware scheduling. In *Proceedings of the 13th European Conference on Genetic Programming*, volume 6021 of *Lecture Notes in Computer Science*, pages 301–312, 2010.

[20] F. Neumann. Computational complexity analysis of multi-objective genetic programming. In *Proceedings of the 17th Annual Conference Companion on Genetic and Evolutionary Computation*, GECCO '12, pages 799–806, 2012.

[21] D. J. Newman and A. Asuncion. UCI Machine Learning Repository, University of California, Irvine, School of Information and Computer Sciences, 2007.

[22] NVIDIA Corporation. NVIDIA CUDA Programming and Best Practices Guide, 2013.

[23] D. Robilliard, V. Marion, and C. Fonlupt. High performance genetic programming on GPU. In *Proceedings of the Workshop on Bio-inspired Algorithms for Distributed Systems*, BADS '09, pages 85–94, 2009.

[24] D. Robilliard, V. Marion-Poty, and C. Fonlupt. Population parallel GP on the G80 GPU. In *Proceedings of the 11th European Conference on Genetic Programming*, volume 4971 of *Lecture Notes in Computer Science*, pages 98–109, 2008.

[25] D. Robilliard, V. Marion-Poty, and C. Fonlupt. Genetic programming on graphics processing units. *Genetic Programming and Evolvable Machines*, 10(4):447–471, 2009.

[26] G. Wilson and W. Banzhaf. Deployment of CPU and GPU-based genetic programming on heterogeneous devices. In *Proceedings of the 14th Annual Conference Companion on Genetic and Evolutionary Computation*, GECCO '09, pages 2531–2538, 2009.

Kaizen Programming

Vinícius Veloso de Melo
Institute of Science and Technology (ICT)
Federal University of São Paulo (UNIFESP)
São José dos Campos, SP, Brazil
vinicius.melo@unifesp.br

ABSTRACT

This paper presents Kaizen Programming, an evolutionary tool based on the concepts of Continuous Improvement from Kaizen Japanese methodology. One may see Kaizen Programming as a new paradigm since, as opposed to classical evolutionary algorithms where individuals are complete solutions, in Kaizen Programming each expert proposes an idea to solve part of the problem, thus a solution is composed of all ideas together. Consequently, evolution becomes a collaborative approach instead of an egocentric one. An idea's quality (analog to an individual's fitness) is not how good it fits the data, but a measurement of its contribution to the solution, which improves the knowledge about the problem. Differently from evolutionary algorithms that simply perform trial-and-error search, one can determine, exactly, parts of the solution that should be removed or improved. That property results in the reduction in bloat, number of function evaluations, and computing time. Even more important, the Kaizen Programming tool, proposed to solve symbolic regression problems, builds the solutions as linear regression models - not linear in the variables, but linear in the parameters, thus all properties and characteristics of such statistical tool are valid. Experiments on benchmark functions proposed in the literature show that Kaizen Programming easily outperforms Genetic Programming and other methods, providing high quality solutions for both training and testing sets while requiring a small number of function evaluations.

Categories and Subject Descriptors

I.2.2 [**Artificial Intelligence**]: Automatic Programming, Program Synthesis, Program Modification; D.1.2 [**Programming Techniques**]: Automatic Programming

Keywords

Symbolic regression, Linear regression, Evolutionary algorithm, Collaborative problem solving, Genetic programming

GECCO'14, July 12–16, 2014, Vancouver, BC, Canada.
Copyright 2014 ACM 978-1-4503-2662-9/14/07 ...$15.00.
http://dx.doi.org/10.1145/2576768.2598264.

1. INTRODUCTION

Genetic programming (GP) [8] is an evolutionary computation algorithm, inspired by the Genetic Algorithm (GA) [3], which evolves computer programs to solve a particular task. GP has been employed to automatically produce codes to solve (see [13]): curve-fitting, data modelling, symbolic regression, image and signal processing, financial trading, time series, industrial process control, bioinformatics, among others. Despite its successful application in several domains, there are some known issues with GP and related algorithms [11, 7], for instance, bloat, lack of heuristics, slow speed (large population size), and low success rate.

One of the main reasons for those issues is that the methods perform blind/random search. The only guide, or at least the most important, is pressure selection, which selects the best solutions to be mixed and to continue in the population. On the other hand, recombination and mutation are, in general, simple guesses: select two *random* sub-trees for swapping, generate a *random* sub-tree, generate a *random* ephemeral constant. The evolutionary process is done expecting that a new *random* solution presents a better fitness than the current solution. According to Korns [7], these characteristics make automated design algorithms hard to be accepted in the industry.

This paper presents a novel approach in order to overcome some of the presented drawbacks. The purpose of this paper is to improve the mechanism that guides the search, resulting in the reduction in bloat, population size, and number of function evaluations while increasing solution quality. The proposed method is called Kaizen Programming and is based on the Japanese methodology of Continuous Improvement of solutions in a collaborative problem solving approach.

2. RELATED WORKS

Some related works that try to improve tools for symbolic regression are presented next.

Moraglio et al. [10] presented the geometric crossover that searches directly the space of the underlying semantics of the programs. The operator transforms the syntax of an individual in order to perform a ball mutation on the semantic space. Consequently, any random improvement moves the current solution towards the optimum. Thus, as they pointed out in their paper, all random codes can be used, resulting in huge black-box solutions.

Korns [6] stated that all current approaches needed serious improvements. In the last years, he proposed several modifications in order to increase the quality of Genetic Programming and created an engine where numerical constants are replaced by abstract constants, which are optimized by continuous meta-heuristics such as Particle Swarm Optimization and Differential Evolution.

Pennachin et. al [12] proposed the improvement of both performance and robustness of GP by the use of Affine Arithmetic to estimate the output range of expressions given their inputs over the training data. Estimated outputs with values too far from the desired output range are identified and the corresponding trees are discarded from the solutions. That strategy avoided extreme errors on the testing data.

The present work may be more related to ensembles of trees [14], a method in which several models (trees) are independently evolved, and then combined to provide a better forecast. The final fused prediction may be the average of the individual predictions, a weighted average, or another statistic. However, the technique proposed herein employs a distinct strategy, as will be presented in the next sections.

All these approaches improve solution quality, but bloat and the number of evaluations are still high, except for the works of Korns, who employs user specified goal expressions. With Kaizen Programming, this can be reduced because it can identify the contribution of parts of the solution. The Kaizen methodology is presented next.

3. THE KAIZEN METHODOLOGY

The Japanese word Kaizen means "Good Change," and is adopted as a philosophy of work [4] which means continuous improvement. Kaizen Event is the term given to an event consisting of a team (of workers and managers) working together for a brief period to find effective solutions to identified business problems. In an industry, for instance, it could be cycle time reduction, waste reduction, speed improvement, or any other problem.

Kaizen teams are usually small groups of about five individuals who spend their time for a few days until a particular issue is solved or a significant improvement is achieved according to the mission statement. The individuals are selected by their knowledge in the area where the issue is present or because they work elsewhere, but are also impacted by the issue. This way, different aspects of the problem may be analyzed in order to identify the effects of the proposed changes.

In a kaizen event, the team of experts meets for instructions. During the meeting, the experts discuss critical issues, do a brainstorming of ideas to provide solutions for the problem, and develop action plans. In general, the Plan-Do-Check-Act (PDCA [2]) methodology is employed to guide the continuous improvement process.

In PDCA, actions are planned, executed, checked, and new actions are taken based on the results. The cycle is repeated until the mission is complete. At each cycle, more knowledge on the problem is gained and every action can be evaluated according to its effectiveness in helping solving the issue. Therefore, at each cycle, the experts have more information to avoid bad actions and guide the search towards the solution. One of the interesting aspects is that complex actions that do not provide significant improvement may be discarded, reverting back to old simple yet not so efficient procedures.

4. KAIZEN PROGRAMMING

Kaizen Programming (KP), proposed herein, is a novel evolutionary tool based on the concepts of the Kaizen methodology. KP is a computational implementation of a Kaizen event with PDCA.

In usual evolutionary algorithms such as GP, an individual is a mapping of the problem's solution (a complete solution), and different individuals are different solutions for the same problem. That creates diversity for the search mechanism and gives the user the possibility of choice among the final best solutions.

When compared to GP, KP may be seen as a new paradigm for automated design of algorithms because KP individuals are not complete solutions, but part of it. Consequently, evolution becomes a collaborative approach instead of an egocentric one.

In KP, a team of experts is formed to propose ideas to solve a problem, then are joined to become a solution. The quality of the solution is how good it solves the problem, and the quality of an idea is a measurement of its contribution to the solution. Therefore, differently from general GP and other evolutionary algorithms that perform trial-and-error search, in KP one can determine, exactly, which parts of the solution should be removed or improved. Consequently, KP is a collaborative problem-solving approach and that the experts have to contribute by providing better ideas at each cycle. Such property results in a reduction in bloat, smaller population sizes, and lower number of function evaluations.

Not all experts may provide useful contributions all the time, but their knowledge is shared with the group to improve everyone's ideas. Algorithm 1 presents a high-level KP algorithm, and Figure 1 presents a flowchart.

Algorithm 1 The Kaizen Programming algorithm.

1. Create a team of experts;
2. Define target and set it as not achieved;
3. Do
   (a) PLAN: the team performs a brainstorming and each expert proposes an idea to solve part of the problem;
   (b) DO: the current ideas and the new ones (created from the second iteration) are applied to the problem and joined to become a complete solution;
   (c) CHECK: evaluate the solution then each single idea (old and new) is analyzed and its contribution to solve the problem is measured;
   (d) ACT: if the solution is improved, then the best ideas are selected and become the new standard, which is presented to the team along with each contribution, improving the knowledge of the problem. Create another kaizen event with a new team if the current one gets stuck in a local optimum;
4. Loop while target is not achieved;
5. Return the ideas with significant contribution and the final solution.

In this paper, KP is employed to solve symbolic regression problems. As mentioned before, KP will build solutions as linear regression models, where each variable of the model is called a *regressor*. The next subsections explain, in more detail, the PDCA cycle of KP.

4.1 PLAN

In this phase KP has to generate ideas, which are proposed by the team of experts to solve parts of the problem.

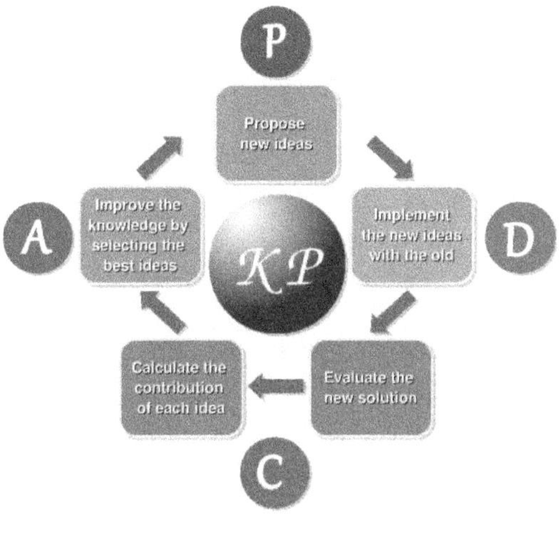

Figure 1: Basic Kaizen Programing flowchart.

Since the problem is new to all experts there are no initial standard and no initial knowledge. After the first cycle, a standard is established and the team acquires knowledge on the problem, improving it over the cycles.

For the symbolic regression problem, an idea from an expert is a mathematical expression that will be implemented and transformed into a *new* regressor ($K_j, j = 1, ..., t$) of the model. Therefore, the team size (t) corresponds to the *new* number of regressors. If the original problem has only one regressor (x) and KP is configured with a team of three experts, then one may have, for example, $K_1 = x^2$; $K_2 = sin(x)$; $K_3 = -x + 3/x$.

4.2 DO

After all experts present their ideas these are individually applied to the problem (calculated). Therefore, the result is a matrix $TRIAL_{n,w}$, where n is the number of observations in the sample dataset used for training and w is the new number of regressors. The new ideas are joined with the current standard $STD_{n,t}$ and all of them will be used to build a new model. The solution quality and the contributions of the current standard can be changed for better or worse. Below there is an example of regressors matrix $K_{n,(t+w)}$, where t and w may have different values as explained later.

$$K = \begin{bmatrix} STD_{11} & \dots & STD_{1t} & TRIAL_{11} & \dots & TRIAL_{1w} \\ \vdots & \dots & \vdots & \vdots & \dots & \vdots \\ STD_{n1} & \dots & STD_{nt} & TRIAL_{n1} & \dots & TRIAL_{nw} \end{bmatrix}.$$

4.3 CHECK

In this phase KP creates a linear model using K and the set of expected outputs for the problem (y), and optimizes it using Ordinary Least-Squares (OLS). OLS is a statistical tool that minimizes the sum of the squared residuals, which are the squared vertical distances between the observed responses in the sample dataset and the responses predicted by the linear model. Using the previous example with K_1, K_2, and K_3, the model is created in the form:

$$\hat{y}_i = \hat{\beta}_1 K_{i,1} + \hat{\beta}_2 K_{i,2} + \hat{\beta}_3 K_{i,3}, \qquad (1)$$

where $\hat{y}_i, i = 1, ..., n$ is the calculated output for an and $\hat{\beta}_1$, $\hat{\beta}_2$, and $\hat{\beta}_3$ are the coefficients estimated by OLS using

$$\hat{\beta} = (K^T K)^{-1} K^T y. \qquad (2)$$

Therefore, it is easy to notice that all models generated by KP are linear *in the parameters* since $\hat{\beta}_i$ are *never* within the regressors (K_i) generated by the experts. Also, one can notice that Eq. 1 does not explicitly contain the intercept. In fact, one of the regressors can be a constant generated by KP.

The linear model is used not only to perform the linear scaling and evaluate the solution, but also to guide the search for better ideas. Hence, it is important to be clear that the estimated parameters are *not* included in the solution during the search, *only* in the final solution.

In order to guide the search one must check the contribution of each regressor to the model, that is, the contribution of each idea to the solution. Hence, the quality of an idea (*fitness*) is not the sum of residuals.

The contribution is measured as the $p{-}value$ of the regressor, calculated using $p = 2 * (1 - T(df, |t|))$, where T is the cumulative distribution of the studentâĂŹs t-distribution, df is the residual degrees of freedom, and $|t|$ is the absolute value of the observed t-statistic. If $p{-}value$ is not significant ($p{-}value > \alpha$), then the idea was not useful to solve the problem and may be discarded in the next cycle. Furthermore, if the $p{-}value$ of a regressor K_j is significant, but the absolute value of the corresponding coefficient $\hat{\beta}_j$ is lower than a predefined threshold θ, then K_j is considered not significant because $\hat{\beta}_j K_j \approx 0$. Thus, K_j is penalized and set to 1.0. The penalty also applies to duplicated ideas, for which OLS calculates the coefficient as NA.

The use of the contribution is a very important characteristic of the method to automatically act as bloat control. On the other hand, if an idea is improved it can automatically replace the old one.

$$contrib(K_j) = \begin{cases} 1.0, & if\ p{-}value(K_j) = NA \\ 1.0, & if\ p{-}value(K_j) > \alpha \\ 1.0, & if\ |\hat{\beta}_j| < \theta \\ p{-}value(K_j), & otherwise \end{cases}. \qquad (3)$$

The solution (model) quality is given by a goodness of fit measure by comparing how much the initial variation in the sample dataset can be reduced by regressing onto K. In statistics, the coefficient of determination R^2 is the proportion of variability in the dataset that is accounted for by a statistical model. While R^2 is a goodness of fit measure, adjusted R^2 is a comparative measure of suitability of models with distinct sets of regressors. R^2 may increase just because the number of regressors increased. On the other hand, adjusted R^2 increases only if the new regressor improves the model more than would be expected by chance. Since KP generates distinct models with different number of regressors (selected according to their contribution) each cycle, adjusted R^2 can be used to compare the models and select the one that presents higher value without being mistaken by the number of regressors. Adjusted R^2 is calculated as follows, where p is the number of regressors:

$$Adj.R^2 = 1 - (1 - R^2)\frac{n-1}{n-p-1} = R^2 - (1 - R^2)\frac{p}{n-p-1}, \qquad (4)$$

Adjusted R^2, which was used to stop the search, can be easier to interpret than RMSE, for instance, because it is scale-free, w.r.t. the response values of the problem, and the result of this statistic is in the range [0, 1] where 1 means a perfect fit. Actually, negative values may occur but are not expected and correspond to a very low-quality model. The corresponding algorithm of this phase is presented in Algorithm 2.

Algorithm 2 The Check phase of KP.

Input: K, y, α, θ, *MAXVALUE //the penalty*
Output: *Fit*, *Contrib //the Contributions*

1. Build the model
2. Calculate the contribution of the regressors
3. If there are no significant regressors
   (a) Set *Fit* as MAXVALUE and the *Contrib* as in Eq. 3
4. Else
   (a) Build a new model using only the significant regressors
   (b) Calculate the contribution of the regressors
   (c) Calculate *Fit* as the goodness-of-fit (Adjusted R^2)

4.4 Act

In this stage, the experts will propose new ideas to solve the problem, based on the knowledge acquired in the Check phase due to the contributions of the current ideas in the standard. The new solution replaces the standard *only* if it is better.

To generate a new idea, the expert may combine his current idea with the idea proposed by another expert, and then improve the combined solution with another new information. However, not all experts have to present new ideas every cycle. That procedure works in a similar fashion as crossover and mutation of a GP algorithm.

An additional characteristic of KP is that it uses a small number of experts and works as a hill-climbing method. Thus, it is necessary to use a restarting procedure to escape from a local optimum if the standard is stagnated (remains the same) for a period defined by the user. That means that the investigated issue was underestimated and it is necessary to create a new Kaizen event with a different and larger team. Hence, the restart procedure saves the current standard, increases the number of experts by EF (expansion factor), and generates new random ideas ignoring the old ones. The method restarts the PDCA cycle until some stopping criterion is achieved. The best standard discovered out of all restarts is returned as the final solution.

4.5 Resulting solution

The resulting solution (standard) is an additive function that approximates the regressors on the response variable. It is not expected that the exact function which generated the response will be found (because KP generates a composite function). For instance, take the following example function:

$$f(x_0, x_1, x_2, x_3, x_4) = -5.41 + 4.9 \frac{x_3 - x_0 + \frac{x_1}{x_4}}{3x_4}, \quad (5)$$

where $x_i = U(-50, 50)$. The best solution found by a KP is shown in Figure 2.

$$\begin{aligned} f_{found}(x_0, x_1, x_2, x_3, x_4) = \\ (0.261141430577 \\ *(-1 * ((1/((-1 * (((1/(-1 * (x0))) \\ *(1/-6.2545928837239835)))) \\ *(-1 * (x4))))))) \\ +(-1.63333333333 \\ *(-1 * ((1/((-1 * (((1/(x4 * x3)) * x4))) \\ *(-1 * (x4))))))) \\ +(-1.63333333333 \\ *(-1 * ((1/((-1 * (((1/x1) * x4))) \\ *(-1 * (x4))))))) \\ +(0.6446225282 \\ *(-1 * ((1/(1/8.3925084267666))))) \end{aligned}$$

(a)

$$\begin{aligned} f_{simplified}(x_0, x_1, x_2, x_3, x_4) = \\ -1.6333333333324 * \tfrac{x_0}{x_4} \\ +1.63333333333 * \tfrac{\frac{x_1}{x_2}}{x_4} \\ +1.63333333333 * \tfrac{x_3}{x_4} \\ -5.41000000000209 \end{aligned}$$

(b)

Figure 2: (a) the best solution found by a KP run; (b) the simplified expression.

That set of ideas can be plot with random x_i values as in Figure 3(a), whereas the final calculated outputs $\hat{y}$ and the expected real outputs are shown in Figure 3(b). The calculated output (dashed line) is exactly inside the expected output (solid line), meaning that the exact function was found besides in a different form.

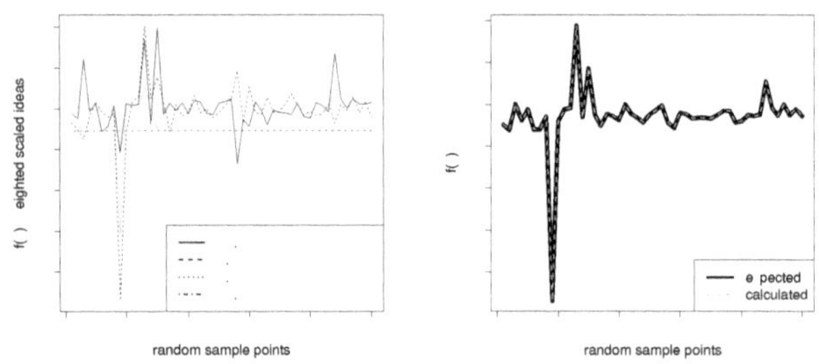

(a) (b)

Figure 3: (a) Plot of significant ideas; (b) Expected (Eq. 5) and calculated (Fig 2(b)).

Next section presents experimental results of Kaizen Programming to solve symbolic regression problems.

5. EXPERIMENTAL RESULTS

This next section presents a comparison of Kaizen Programming against related methods in solving a set of well-known symbolic regression benchmark functions.

5.1 Benchmark functions

The functions tested in this work, whose definitions one can see in Table 1, were taken from [9]. The description of the table, as shown in [9] is: variable names are, in order, x, y, z. Some benchmarks intentionally omit variables from the function. U[a,b,c] is c uniform random samples drawn from a to b, inclusive, for the variable. E[a,b,c] is a grid of points evenly spaced (for this variable) with an interval of c, from a to b inclusive. Testing and training sets are independent.

In order to compare to other methods, tests were also performed in the well-known Nguyen benchmark functions shown in Table 2

5.2 Implementation and configuration of the algorithms

GP was implemented using DEAP (Distributed Evolutionary Algorithms in Python, [1]), an evolutionary computation framework for rapid prototyping and testing of ideas.

Table 1: Symbolic regression functions (Keijzer functions) and the datasets as proposed in [9].

Function	Training data	Testing data
$keijzer1(x) = 0.3xsin(2\pi x)$	E[-1, 1, 0.1]	E[-1, 1, 0.001]
$keijzer2(x) = 0.3xsin(2\pi x)$	E[-2, 2, 0.1]	E[-2, 2, 0.001]
$keijzer3(x) = 0.3xsin(2\pi x)$	E[-3, 3, 0.1]	E[-3, 3, 0.001]
$keijzer4(x) = x^3e^{-x}cos(x)sin(x)(sin^2(x)cos(x) - 1)$	E[0, 10, 0.05]	E[0.05, 10.05, 0.05]
$keijzer5(x) = (30xz)/((x - 10)y^2)$	x,y: U[-1, 1, 1000] z: U[1, 2, 1000]	x,y: U[-1, 1, 10000] z: U[1, 2, 10000]
$keijzer6(x) = \sum_i^x 1/i$	E[1, 50, 1]	E[1, 120, 1]
$keijzer7(x) = lnx$	E[1, 100, 1]	E[1, 100, 0.1]
$keijzer8(x) = \sqrt{x}$	E[1, 100, 1]	E[1, 100, 0.1]
$keijzer9(x) = arcsinh(x)$	E[1, 100, 1]	E[1, 100, 0.1]
$keijzer10(x) = x^y$	U[0, 1, 100]	E[0, 1, 0.1]
$keijzer11(x) = xy + sin((x - 1)(y - 1))$	U[-3, 3, 20]	E[-3, 3, 0.01]
$keijzer12(x) = x^4 - x^3 + y^2/2 - y$	U[-3, 3, 20]	E[-3, 3, 0.01]
$keijzer13(x) = 6sin(x)cos(y)$	U[-3, 3, 20]	E[-3, 3, 0.01]
$keijzer14(x) = 8/(2 + x^2 + y^2)$	U[-3, 3, 20]	E[-3, 3, 0.01]
$keijzer15(x) = x^3/5 + y^3/2 - y - x$	U[-3, 3, 20]	E[-3, 3, 0.01]

Table 2: Symbolic regression functions (Nguyen functions) and the datasets as proposed in [9].

Function	Training/Testing data
$nguyen1(x) = x^3 + x^2 + x$	x: U[-1, 1, 20]
$nguyen2(x) = x^4 + x^3 + x^2 + x$	x: U[-1, 1, 20]
$nguyen3(x) = x^5 + x^4 + x^3 + x^2 + x$	x: U[-1, 1, 20]
$nguyen4(x) = x^6 + x^5 + x^4 + x^3 + x^2 + x$	x: U[-1, 1, 20]
$nguyen5(x) = sin(x^2)cos(x) - 1$	x: U[-1, 1, 20]
$nguyen6(x) = sin(x) + sin(x + x^2)$	x: U[-1, 1, 20]
$nguyen7(x) = log(x + 1) + log(x^2 + 1)$	x: U[0, 2, 20]
$nguyen8(x) = \sqrt{x}$	x: U[0, 4, 20]
$nguyen9(x) = sin(x) + sin(y^2)$	x, y: U[-1, 1, 100]
$nguyen10(x) = 2sin(x)cos(y)$	x, y: U[-1, 1, 100]

DEAP provides a complete GP implementation, with several operators and flexibility for improvements.

KP was also implemented using GP modules from DEAP. Therefore, the same modules used in the GP implementation were used in KP, which means that KP was not privileged by a better implementation of the genetic operators. The statistical parts of KP (the OLS method, Adjusted R^2, $p-values$, among others) used the lm (linear model) function from R programming language. The connection between Python and R was performed by the Rpy2 Python package.

For the tests using *Keijzer* functions, the methods were configured as shown in Table 3 with the function set proposed in [9].

Table 3: Run and evolutionary parameter values for *Keijzer* functions.

Parameter	Value (KP/GP50/GP500)
Initial Experts/Population size	8/50/500
Ideas/Population generator	GP Ramped
Generations	2000/500/50
Stagnation	25% of the generations
Factor (EF) to increase experts/population	ceiling (10% of popsize)
Tournament Selection	1/3/3
Crossover probability	1.0/0.9/0.9
Idea combinator/crossover operator	One-point
Mutation probability	1.0/0.05/0.05
Idea improver/mutation operator	90% GP Uniform Mutation 10% GP ERC Mutation
Max. depth	2/15/15
Non-terminals	$+$, $\times$, $\frac{1}{n}$, $-n$, $\sqrt{n}$,
Terminals	x, Constants (ERC) are random values from $N(\mu = 0, \sigma = 5)$.
Solution quality/fitness	$Adjusted\, R^2/R^2/R^2$
Value-to- reach (VTR)	$1 - fitness < 1e - 5$
Trials	50
θ (for KP Check)	$1e - 4$
α (for KP Check)	0.05

For the test using *Nguyen* functions, KP was configured as shown in Table 4 with the function set proposed in [5].

Table 4: Modified run and evolutionary parameter values for *Nguyen* functions. The configuration of the other parameters are in Table 3.

Parameter	Value (KP)
Maximum number of node evaluations	100.000
Stagnation	25% of the generations
Max. depth	8
Non-terminals	$+$, $\times$, $-$, $/(protected)$, sin, cos, exp, $log(protected)$
Terminals	x, Constant 1 (*nguyen1* to *nguyen8*), y (*nguyen9* and *nguyen10*)
Hit	when the solution has an absolute error < 1e-2 on a fitness case
Successful run	when the solution scores hits on all fitness cases
Trials	100

5.3 Evaluation

A descriptive analysis of the results obtained in the experiments is presented with the median best values for each benchmark function and statistical comparison between KP and GP50 (GP with popsize of 50 individuals), and KP and GP500 (GP with popsize of 500 individuals). The Wilcoxon Mann-Whitney test at a significance level $\alpha = 0.01\%$ was performed using the RMSE Testing results of 50 trials. No statistical comparison was performed for the Training results.

5.4 Results

Regarding the *Keijzer* benchmark functions, Table 5 presents the results of the training set whereas Table 6 presents the results of the testing set.

The *Nguyen* benchmark functions use the same interval for training and testing, but the sets of points are distinct. For these tests, it was employed the same methodology presented by Karaboga et al. in [5]. The descriptive analysis is shown in Table 7 and the comparison with other methods is shown in Table 8.

5.5 Discussion

One can notice in Table 3 that, as suggested in [9], not all operators employed in the benchmark functions (see Table 1) are available in the function set. Therefore, the exact solution can be hard or impossible to find. Thus, it is expected that KP fails for some runs.

In this work, the generation of ideas is performed using the same well-known evolutionary operators employed by GP: population initialization, crossover, mutation, and selection. KP guides the search by identifying the partial solutions to be improved, but the search is still random as in GP.

Given that both methods can restart when stagnation is detected, i.e the best solution does not change during a period, the number of function evaluations (NFEs) can vary. For KP, at each cycle the current ideas have to be reevaluated because they will be part of a new solution with the new ideas. Therefore, at each generation there are 16 evaluations instead of 8. However, the number of generations was set to provide similar NFEs as presented in Table 5. GP was configured with populations 50 and 500 as commonly used in related works in the literature.

Table 5: **Training Results using *Keijzer* benchmark functions (descriptive analysis).**

		KP			GP50			GP500		
Function	**Statistic**	**Adj.R^2**	**RMSE**	**NFEs**	R^2	**RMSE**	**NFEs**	R^2	**RMSE**	**NFEs**
	Min	9.996e-01	1.926e-06	328	1.404e-01	4.833e-02	25050	4.123e-01	8.001e-02	26700
keijzer1	Median	**1.000e+00**	**2.210e-04**	9492	4.144e-01	8.969e-02	25050	4.144e-01	8.969e-02	30450
	Max	1.000e+00	2.279e-02	32260	8.300e-01	1.087e-01	25050	5.340e-01	8.985e-02	32170
	Min	1.252e-01	5.419e-04	2880	3.439e-02	1.031e-01	25050	5.502e-02	2.174e-01	28460
keijzer2	Median	**8.994e-01**	**6.747e-02**	32190	1.957e-01	2.159e-01	25050	1.392e-01	2.234e-01	30550
	Max	1.000e+00	2.194e-01	32380	8.165e-01	2.366e-01	25050	1.844e-01	2.341e-01	32310
	Min	1.259e-01	9.983e-02	32100	0.000e+00	2.469e-01	25050	3.263e-02	3.346e-01	28300
keijzer3	Median	**3.830e-01**	**2.654e-01**	32170	1.064e-01	3.437e-01	25050	7.050e-02	3.506e-01	30300
	Max	9.132e-01	3.359e-01	32260	5.389e-01	3.636e-01	25050	1.530e-01	3.576e-01	31950
	Min	5.120e-01	3.533e-02	32180	0.000e+00	2.517e-01	25050	0.000e+00	3.155e-01	25500
keijzer4	Median	**7.408e-01**	**1.631e-01**	32330	7.186e-03	3.164e-01	25050	1.489e-03	3.174e-01	25500
	Max	9.887e-01	2.658e-01	32540	3.725e-01	3.186e-01	25050	1.383e-02	4.051e-01	26550
	Min	1.000e+00	8.122e-04	368	5.197e-02	1.918e-02	25050	8.050e-01	8.048e-02	28760
keijzer5	Median	**1.000e+00**	**1.524e-03**	2180	8.988e-01	1.756e-01	25050	8.582e-01	2.036e-01	32020
	Max	1.000e+00	9.060e-03	27180	9.987e-01	5.428e-01	25050	9.797e-01	2.417e-01	32740
	Min	1.000e+00	6.985e-16	56	1.000e+00	9.899e-01	51	1.000e+00	9.899e-01	501
keijzer6	Median	1.000e+00	**9.216e-16**	56	1.000e+00	9.899e-01	51	1.000e+00	9.899e-01	501
	Max	1.000e+00	1.179e-14	14510	1.000e+00	9.899e-01	51	1.000e+00	9.899e-01	501
	Min	1.000e+00	2.964e-06	56	9.391e-01	6.074e-02	25050	9.955e-01	1.049e-01	28590
keijzer7	Median	**1.000e+00**	**4.613e-04**	80	9.978e-01	1.747e-01	25050	9.977e-01	1.813e-01	30660
	Max	1.000e+00	1.776e-02	224	9.997e-01	9.258e-01	25050	9.992e-01	2.512e-01	32480
	Min	1.000e+00	7.911e-16	56	1.000e+00	0.000e+00	51	1.000e+00	0.000e+00	501
keijzer8	Median	1.000e+00	3.499e-15	56	1.000e+00	**0.000e+00**	51	1.000e+00	**0.000e+00**	501
	Max	1.000e+00	1.340e-02	160	1.000e+00	0.000e+00	101	1.000e+00	0.000e+00	501
	Min	1.000e+00	9.773e-06	56	9.479e-01	8.466e-02	25050	9.694e-01	1.118e-01	25500
keijzer9	Median	**1.000e+00**	**1.587e-03**	88	9.985e-01	1.714e-01	25050	9.991e-01	1.354e-01	30300
	Max	1.000e+00	2.912e-02	248	9.996e-01	1.006e+00	25050	9.994e-01	7.704e-01	32050
	Min	1.000e+00	2.057e-03	2616	9.361e-01	4.198e-02	25050	9.297e-01	9.039e-02	30760
keijzer10	Median	**1.000e+00**	**2.998e-03**	32210	9.565e-01	1.562e-01	25050	9.575e-01	1.526e-01	32870
	Max	1.000e+00	1.946e-02	32330	9.968e-01	1.887e-01	25050	9.863e-01	1.917e-01	32870
	Min	9.709e-01	8.244e-02	32090	8.980e-01	3.121e-01	25050	8.862e-01	4.060e-01	31930
keijzer11	Median	**9.936e-01**	**1.934e-01**	32160	9.577e-01	6.452e-01	25050	9.597e-01	6.359e-01	32680
	Max	9.985e-01	4.542e-01	32230	9.906e-01	7.936e-01	25050	9.899e-01	7.766e-01	32870
	Min	9.999e-01	3.960e-15	328	8.275e-01	1.028e+00	25050	8.650e-01	1.373e+00	30220
keijzer12	Median	**1.000e+00**	**2.628e-02**	2692	9.751e-01	3.527e+00	25050	9.802e-01	3.565e+00	31190
	Max	1.000e+00	7.772e-01	32220	9.985e-01	1.204e+01	25050	9.981e-01	9.722e+00	32300
	Min	8.947e-01	8.033e-02	32120	1.926e-01	6.009e-01	25050	1.368e-01	1.645e+00	28340
keijzer13	Median	**9.765e-01**	**3.482e-01**	32190	4.064e-01	2.217e+00	25050	3.895e-01	2.261e+00	31190
	Max	9.990e-01	8.525e-01	32310	9.626e-01	3.090e+00	25050	6.765e-01	2.889e+00	32870
	Min	9.890e-01	2.354e-03	7976	6.821e-01	8.574e-02	25050	6.858e-01	2.988e-01	28860
keijzer14	Median	**9.984e-01**	**5.319e-02**	32180	8.358e-01	5.821e-01	25050	7.935e-01	6.968e-01	30890
	Max	1.000e+00	1.294e-01	32310	9.955e-01	1.031e+00	25050	9.333e-01	9.405e-01	32740
	Min	1.000e+00	8.585e-16	272	4.192e-01	4.882e-01	25050	4.722e-01	9.975e-01	29910
keijzer15	Median	**1.000e+00**	**3.923e-15**	2732	7.752e-01	1.520e+00	25050	7.609e-01	1.705e+00	32200
	Max	1.000e+00	3.308e-02	11000	9.804e-01	2.387e+00	25050	9.398e-01	2.542e+00	32870

The stopping criteria are the maximum number of generations or the value-to-reach (VTR). VTR was set as a high-quality model ($R^2 > 0.99999$) instead of a small RMSE because R^2 is scale-free with a maximum value of 1.0. KP uses Adj.R^2 because the number of regressors can change during the process because only the significant ideas are used to build the model. Also, Adj.R^2 tends to be lower than R^2, thus a high Adj.R^2 can be better than a high R^2.

For the 15 functions, the training results show that KP achieved the highest values of R^2 for 12 functions, with two ties (*keijzer*6 and 8), but the RMSE value of KP in *keijzer*6 is largely better. KP found very high-quality models (median Adj.$R^2 > 0.99$) for 11 functions, whereas GP50 and GP500 achieved such quality for only four functions.

For several functions KP required a much lower NFEs (median) than GP (see *keijzer*1, 5, 9, 12, 15). In fact, KP is much faster in finding good models, but the final adjustments can take time because it uses the same random evolutionary procedures employed by GP. Lower quality models (Adj.$R^2 > 0.95$) were found by KP using just hundreds of evaluations.

In the first experiment, the goal was to verify if KP could outperform GP, thus the statistic tests were carried out as KPxGP50, and KPxGP500. With respect to the testing results (see Table 6), one can see that KP showed statistically inferior quality results for functions *keijzer*3, 8, 11, 13, and 14. For the functions with very large values (say $> 1e5$) it was detected that the solution found by KP included the operator $\frac{1}{n}$. When n approaches zero, the result increases exponentially. If the training dataset does not include small values for n, then KP can not treat this extreme behavior, thus resulting in an over-fitted model.

For functions *keijzer*1, 2, 5, 6, 7, 10, and 15, KP errors were smaller by one order of magnitude or more. GP50 and GP500 presented similar results to each other, with GP500 having smaller variance.

The second experiment, using Nguyen benchmark functions, provides the comparison of KP against state-of-the-art techniques recently presented in the literature [5]. For these problems, the method has to perform curve-fitting where the maximum absolute error for any of the points (fitness cases) is lower than 0.01, therefore, resulting in a successful run.

Table 6: Testing Results using *Keijzer* benchmark functions. KP x GP50 and KP x GP500. Signal "=" means that the results of KP and GP are statistically equal, "<" that the results of GP are statistically better, and ">" that are statistically worse.

Function	Statistic	KP	GP50	GP500
	Min	1.067e-05	4.528e-02	7.876e-02
*keijzer*1	Median	**4.360e-04**	8.260e-02	8.199e-02
	Max	5.737e+06	2.423e+03	1.304e+00
	P-value	-	>	>
	Min	6.858e-04	1.729e-01	2.089e-01
*keijzer*2	Median	**6.849e-02**	2.391e-01	2.217e-01
	Max	8.229e+00	2.345e+01	1.002e+00
	P-value	-	>	>
	Min	9.673e-02	2.950e-01	3.412e-01
*keijzer*3	Median	2.065e+00	3.889e-01	**3.526e-01**
	Max	9.984e+01	9.999e+08	2.710e+00
	P-value	-	=	<
	Min	3.541e-02	2.516e-01	3.155e-01
*keijzer*4	Median	**1.612e-01**	3.165e-01	3.174e-01
	Max	2.656e-01	9.736e+00	5.835e+00
	P-value	-	>	>
	Min	8.298e-04	1.946e-02	7.827e-02
*keijzer*5	Median	**1.604e-03**	1.928e-01	2.076e-01
	Max	1.042e-02	2.236e+08	2.327e-01
	P-value	-	>	>
	Min	5.490e-16	9.958e-01	9.958e-01
*keijzer*6	Median	**8.808e-16**	9.958e-01	9.958e-01
	Max	8.030e-14	9.958e-01	9.958e-01
	P-value	-	>	>
	Min	3.888e-04	7.352e-02	1.063e-01
*keijzer*7	Median	**1.272e-02**	2.040e-01	1.711e-01
	Max	4.491e+02	9.995e+09	5.502e+08
	P-value	-	>	>
	Min	1.232e-15	0.0	0.0
*keijzer*8	Median	6.077e-15	**0.0**	**0.0**
	Max	1.628e+00	0.0	0.0
	P-value	-	<	<
	Min	4.739e-03	1.452e-01	1.393e-01
*keijzer*9	Median	**1.026e-01**	3.650e-01	1.513e-01
	Max	3.823e+09	9.995e+08	Inf
	P-value	-	>	>
	Min	2.000e-03	3.179e-02	2.375e-01
*keijzer*10	Median	**5.642e-02**	3.492e-01	3.480e-01
	Max	1.496e+01	3.570e-01	3.574e-01
	P-value	-	>	>
	Min	8.528e-01	6.091e-01	5.943e-01
*keijzer*11	Median	1.223e+13	**6.425e-01**	6.749e-01
	Max	8.597e+41	4.624e+26	1.016e+13
	P-value	-	<	<
	Min	7.485e-15	1.024e+00	1.123e+00
*keijzer*12	Median	**1.274e-01**	1.342e+01	4.010e+00
	Max	2.037e+13	7.184e+42	1.895e+01
	P-value	-	>	>
	Min	9.516e-01	1.985e+00	1.834e+00
*keijzer*13	Median	4.634e+12	8.184e+00	**4.693e+00**
	Max	1.319e+43	5.658e+42	1.572e+42
	P-value	-	<	<
	Min	1.269e-01	9.317e-01	1.064e+00
*keijzer*14	Median	1.455e+13	2.094e+01	**1.242e+00**
	Max	2.578e+41	1.803e+28	4.805e+13
	P-value	-	<	<
	Min	1.084e-15	8.889e-01	1.409e+00
*keijzer*15	Median	**1.481e-02**	3.559e+00	3.098e+00
	Max	5.055e+13	5.868e+13	9.610e+13
	P-value	-	>	>

The results of KP, shown in Table 7, are averaged over 100 trials. One can observe that the maximum average error is lower than 0.01 for all problems, the raw fitness (sum of the absolute errors for all fitness cases) is low considering the number of points (see Table 4), RMSE for the training is also very low, and RMSE for testing is not too high. Therefore, one can conclude that the fitted curve is close to the real curve.

The other important analyses are the number of objective function and node evaluations. For functions *nguyen*1-8, the average number of function evaluations was lower than 100. That number corresponds to less than 12 generations (starting with 8 experts, but not all ideas may be included in the final solution) to find a model with the desired accuracy. The number of node evaluations is also small, which means that the ideas generated to compose the final solutions used few functions and, more importantly, the mechanism the KP uses to guide the search was extremely effective.

Just for the sake of comparison, the results shown in [5] used the limit of 15×10^6 node evaluations as stopping criterion to terminate the methods. That number is four to five orders of magnitude higher than the average required by KP to achieve the expected solution quality. In fact, this number is ever higher when one analyses the number of successful runs shown in Table 8. Not only KP required a substantially smaller number of function evaluations to discover high-quality models, but also did this for all runs and all problems, easily outperforming all methods used in the comparison.

Another important issue is the comparison against ensembles of trees [14]. Ensembles usually rely on the model performance, therefore, the best models are selected to generate a fused prediction. That means that all models must have a high-quality prediction and thus similar behavior. That also means that one can not expect that the models complement each other, that is, that a model is evolved to fill the gaps left by the other models. That behavior is exactly the opposite of what KP does. One of KP's strengths is that it fuses high-quality models (for example, $f(x) = x^4$ and $f(x) = x^3 + x^2$) with poor quality models (for instance, $f(x) = x$) to compose the correct model ($f(x) = x^4 + x^3 + x^2 + x$).

6. SUMMARY AND CONCLUSIONS

Kaizen Programming (KP) proposed in this work is an evolutionary algorithm that uses a collaborative problem solving approach in which partial solutions are joined to result in a complete solution. The partial solutions are created by the experts, that generate ideas based on knowledge obtained from the problem during the improvement process. The knowledge increases because the ideas have their contribution to the problem measured when a complete solution is evaluated. Thus, one can know, exactly, which ideas are useful for the next improvement cycle. With this approach, the guessing, and consequently the bloat, are decreased when compared to Genetic Programming (GP), making KP less art and more science.

The search used by KP showed effective, but the creation of new ideas is still random, which limits KP's performance. Besides that, KP was significantly superior in the tested benchmark functions when compared to the results of GP and other methods.

Given that KP returns a solution in the form of a linear regression model, it can be easier to interpret than a solution found by GP. One can separately investigate the behavior of each component of the solution because it is an additive function. Moreover, the model is based on strong mathematical and statistical foundations, it is largely described and employed in the literature and also to solve real world problems. The linear model allows the posterior use of several other statistical tools such as model selection (AIC, BIC, among other), calculate prediction and confidence intervals, perform residual analysis, among others. Therefore, KP is a promising tool to be used in computer science, statistics, engineering, and any other field of study that make use of linear models.

Table 7: Results of KP (averaged of 100 trials) using *Nguyen* benchmark functions as in [5]. The raw fitness is the sum of absolute error on all fitness cases.

Problem	Maximum Error	Raw Fitness	RMSE Training	Func. Eval.	Node Eval.	RMSE Testing	Succ. Runs
nguyen1	0.00168	0.01256	0.00075	62.72	148.98	0.11654	100
nguyen2	0.00256	0.02013	0.00117	71.44	183.57	0.01779	100
nguyen3	0.00268	0.01992	0.00119	78.80	216.17	0.01753	100
nguyen4	0.00284	0.02211	0.00130	90.00	246.35	0.01988	100
nguyen5	0.00211	0.01613	0.00095	66.80	160.09	0.01863	100
nguyen6	0.00311	0.02356	0.00139	75.44	190.91	0.10314	100
nguyen7	0.00138	0.01037	0.00062	59.04	146.23	0.98138	100
nguyen8	0.00301	0.02075	0.00126	76.56	199.86	0.29934	100
nguyen9	0.00777	0.17801	0.00235	1,792.27	10,682.74	0.00437	100
nguyen10	0.00588	0.04586	0.00271	1,178.51	5,461.95	0.03762	100

Table 8: Number of successful runs using *Nguyen* benchmark functions (F1-F10) as in [5].

Method	F1	F2	F3	F4	F5	F6	F7	F8	F9	F10
KP	**100**	**100**	**100**	**100**	**100**	**100**	**100**	**100**	**100**	**100**
ABCP	89	50	22	12	57	87	58	37	33	21
SC	48	22	7	4	20	35	35	16	7	18
NSM	48	16	4	4	19	36	40	28	4	17
SAC2	53	25	7	4	17	32	25	13	4	4
SAC3	56	19	6	2	21	23	25	12	3	8
SAC4	53	17	11	1	20	23	29	14	3	8
SAC5	53	17	11	1	19	27	30	12	3	8
CAC1	34	19	7	7	12	22	25	9	1	15
CAC2	34	20	7	7	13	23	25	9	2	16
CAC4	35	22	7	8	12	22	26	10	3	16
SBS31	43	15	9	6	31	28	31	17	13	33
SBS32	42	26	7	8	36	27	44	30	17	27
SBS34	51	21	10	9	34	33	46	25	26	33
SBS41	41	22	9	5	31	34	38	25	19	33
SBS42	50	22	17	10	41	32	51	24	24	33
SBS44	40	25	16	9	35	43	42	28	33	34
SSC8	66	28	22	10	48	56	59	21	25	47
SSC12	67	33	14	12	47	47	66	38	37	51
SSC16	55	39	20	11	46	44	67	29	30	59
SSC20	58	27	10	9	52	48	63	26	39	51

Acknowledgments

We thank the anonymous reviewers for their careful reading of this manuscript and their many insightful comments and suggestions. This paper was supported by CNPq (Universal) grant (486950/2013-1).

7. REFERENCES

[1] F.-A. Fortin, F.-M. De Rainville, M.-A. Gardner, M. Parizeau, and C. Gagné. DEAP: Evolutionary algorithms made easy. *Journal of Machine Learning Research*, 13:2171–2175, jul 2012.

[2] H. Gitlow, S. Gitlow, A. Oppenheim, and R. Oppenheim. *Tools and Methods for the Improvement of Quality*. Irwin series in quantitative analysis for business. Taylor & Francis, 1989.

[3] D. E. Goldberg. *Genetic Algorithms in Search, Optimization, and Machine Learning*. Addison-Wesley, 1989.

[4] M. Imai. *Kaizen (Ky'zen), the key to Japan's competitive success*. McGraw-Hill, 1986.

[5] D. Karaboga, C. Ozturk, N. Karaboga, and B. Gorkemli. Artificial bee colony programming for symbolic regression. *Information Sciences*, 209(0):1 – 15, 2012.

[6] M. F. Korns. Abstract expression grammar symbolic regression. In *Genetic Programming Theory and Practice VIII*, volume 8 of *Genetic and Evolutionary Computation*, chapter 7, pages 109–128. Springer, Ann Arbor, USA, 20-22 May 2010.

[7] M. F. Korns. Abstract expression grammar symbolic regression. In *Genetic Programming Theory and Practice VIII*, volume 8 of *Genetic and Evolutionary Computation*, pages 109–128. Springer New York, 2011.

[8] J. R. Koza. *Genetic programming - on the programming of computers by means of natural selection*. Complex adaptive systems. MIT Press, 1993.

[9] J. McDermott, D. R. White, S. Luke, L. Manzoni, M. Castelli, L. Vanneschi, W. Jaskowski, K. Krawiec, R. Harper, K. A. D. Jong, and U.-M. O'Reilly. Genetic programming needs better benchmarks. In T. Soule and J. H. Moore, editors, *GECCO*, pages 791–798. ACM, 2012.

[10] A. Moraglio, K. Krawiec, and C. G. Johnson. Geometric semantic genetic programming. In C. A. C. Coello, V. Cutello, K. Deb, S. Forrest, G. Nicosia, and M. Pavone, editors, *PPSN (1)*, volume 7491 of *Lecture Notes in Computer Science*, pages 21–31. Springer, 2012.

[11] M. O'Neill, L. Vanneschi, S. Gustafson, and W. Banzhaf. Open issues in genetic programming. *Genetic Programming and Evolvable Machines*, 11(3-4):339–363, 2010.

[12] C. L. Pennachin, M. Looks, and J. A. de Vasconcelos. Robust symbolic regression with affine arithmetic. In *GECCO '10: Proceedings of the 12th annual conference on Genetic and evolutionary computation*, pages 917–924, Portland, Oregon, USA, 7-11 July 2010. ACM.

[13] R. Poli, W. Langdon, and N. McPhee. *A field guide to genetic programming*. Lulu Enterprises Uk Ltd, 2008.

[14] K. Veeramachaneni, O. Derby, D. Sherry, and U.-M. O'Reilly. Learning regression ensembles with genetic programming at scale. In *Proceedings of the 15th Annual Conference on Genetic and Evolutionary Computation*, GECCO '13, pages 1117–1124, New York, NY, USA, 2013. ACM.

On Size, Complexity and Generalisation Error in GP

Jeannie Fitzgerald
BDS Group
CSIS Department
University of Limerick, Ireland
jeannie.fitzgerald@ul.ie

Conor Ryan
BDS Group
CSIS Department
University of Limerick, Ireland
conor.ryan@ul.ie

ABSTRACT

For some time, Genetic Programming research has lagged behind the wider Machine Learning community in the study of generalisation, where the decomposition of generalisation error into *bias* and *variance* components is well understood. However, recent Genetic Programming contributions focusing on complexity, size and bloat as they relate to over-fitting have opened up some interesting avenues of research. In this paper, we carry out a simple empirical study on five binary classification problems. The study is designed to discover what effects may be observed when program size and complexity are varied *in combination*, with the objective of gaining a better understanding of relationships which may exist between solution size, operator complexity and variance error. The results of the study indicate that the simplest configuration, in terms of *operator complexity*, consistently results in the best average performance, and in many cases, the result is significantly better. We further demonstrate that the best results are achieved when this minimum complexity set-up is combined with a less than parsimonious permissible size.

Categories and Subject Descriptors

I.2.2 [**Artificial Intelligence**]: Automatic Programming

Keywords

Genetic Programming, Generalisation, Classification

1. INTRODUCTION

In this paper we carry out an empirical study on potential impacts on generalisation error when program size and operator complexity are varied. For the current study we choose to focus on numerical binary classification problems using tree based GP.

The decomposition of generalisation error into *bias* and *variance* components as shown in Equation 1 is well known in Machine Learning (ML) literature [13]. Where bias error represents the extent to which the *average* prediction over all data sets differs from the desired target, and variance error measures the extent to which the solutions for individual data sets *vary* around their average, and hence variance measures the extent to which the model is sensitive to the particular choice of data set [4]. Noise is the unavoidable component of the error, incurred independently of the learning algorithm [9].

$$generalisation\ error = bias + variance + noise \quad (1)$$

Arguably the most widely accepted theoretical view of the bias and variance of a learner in ML is the unified approach put forward by Domingos [9]. In that work, Domingos outlined a decomposition of bias and variance that could be applied to both regression and classification problems, which catered for both variable cost and zero-one loss functions for classification. The underpinnings of the theoretical conclusions arrived at in this, and other related works, depend on having a large (possibly infinite) number of datasets of the same size, where a potentially different classifier is trained on each dataset. For zero-one loss functions, the researchers approach was to define the bias of a learner (for an example x) as the loss incurred by the *main prediction* relative to the *optimal prediction*, where the main prediction is the class most frequently predicted by the various classifiers for that example x. In this approach variance is the *average* loss incurred by predictions relative to *the main prediction*. Bias and variance could be averaged over all examples to produce average bias and average variance.

In practice we do not have an infinite number of datasets available for experimentation. Nor do we have an infinite number of models from which we can extract prediction statistics for comparison purposes. In GP, we generally work with a training set and a test set and want to compare performance of our best models or the average performance across a population of models, over many runs.

We propose to apply the decomposition outlined by Domingos [9] to our practical study by defining the average bias of a single model to be the zero-one loss (classification accuracy) on *the training set* divided by the number of training instances, and the average bias of a set of models to be the average of these average biases. We define the average variance of a single model to be the difference between the average bias of the model, and the zero-one loss on the test set divided by the number of test instances. Where a positive value for average variance indicates that the loss on the

GECCO'14, July 12–16, 2014, Vancouver, BC, Canada.

ACM 978-1-4503-2662-9/14/07 ...$15.00.
http://dx.doi.org/10.1145/2576768.2598346 .

test set is greater than the loss on the training set. Similarly, the average variance of a set of models is the average of the average variances.

In taking this vastly simplified approach we acknowledge that we cannot claim, or rely on, any of the theoretical guarantees or conclusions outlined in Domingos [9]. However, such simplifications may prove useful in understanding generalisation error in GP and other learning algorithms.

The remainder of this paper is laid out as follows: Section 2 provides some background on impacts of size and complexity on generalisation performance, Section 3 explains the set-up of the empirical study and details the results, and Section 4 outlines conclusions and future work.

2. BACKGROUND

In ML, approaches to improving generalisation, as it may be influenced by complexity or size, usually involve *regularisation* [3] or *Minimum Description Length*(MDL) strategies [15, 25]. Regularisation is concerned with minimising some notion of complexity while at the same time optimising fitting of the data and generally involves the application of a complexity penalty.

A common interpretation of the MDL principle says that the best hypothesis for a given set of data is the one that leads to the largest compression of the data, and such strategies often involve setting the inductive bias in a system to favour smaller models.

The concept of the bias variance trade-off as it might be applied to regression problems in GP was introduced by Keijzer and Babovic [17]. Important conclusions arising out of their work are that larger programs effectively handle bias error, and that ensemble approaches can eliminate variance error such that the total error of the average model is then reduced to the bias term. Unfortunately, since that work appeared there has been little new research, that we are aware of, in further investigating the presented ideas as they might apply to the GP paradigm.

Typically, in the GP community, variance error as described here, is referred to as "over-fitting", and topics of bloat, size, complexity, over-fitting and generalisation have, for some time, been tightly coupled in GP research. In studying some of this previous work in GP it is sometimes difficult to differentiate the treatment of aspects such as size and complexity, as several researchers seem to take the view that large programs are by definition complex, see for example [7] and [12]. If this were the case, then an obvious approach to minimising complexity is to reduce program size. To this end Gagné et al. [12] demonstrated that controlling program size with *parsimony pressure* lead to improvements in generalisation. However, in contrast, Soule and Foster [28] showed that the application of parsimony pressure could have a negative effect on performance when the technique was applied to every individual in the population.

Rosca [26] in an analysis of generality versus size in GP, concluded that smaller programs do tend to generalise better but that methods which control the *effective size* are more likely to be beneficial in promoting generalisation than approaches which apply a generalised size penalty. Their results indicated that small, generalisable solutions may be difficult to find when a simple size penalty is applied. Rosca defines effective code as *any code that is executed at least once.*

Nikolaev and Iba [21] proposed an adapted "Stroganoff" GP system which encouraged small solutions and applied a regularisation penalty to reduce variance in the semantics. They applied their method to data mining and time series data and reported that their approach eliminated complex solutions from the population and resulted in programs that were "parsimonious, accurate and predictive". More recently, Vladislavleva et al. [31] proposed *order of nonlinearity* as a complexity measure, which they used to encourage simpler model *behaviour* without limiting the complexity of the model *structure*. They applied the method on a number of synthetic symbolic regression problems and reported that the generated models exhibited significantly better extrapolative abilities.

Paris et al. [22] carried out an empirical study comparing the over-fitting behaviour of three versions of GP: standard GP, GP using *size fair crossover* [18], and GP that was boosted [11]. They concluded that, all other things being equal, smaller populations of smaller programs were less likely to over fit than larger populations of larger programs. Overall, they found that boosted GP was the least likely to over fit and noted a general rule of thumb: increased computational effort increases the likelihood that the system will over fit the training data.

Gomez et al. [14] investigated *behavioural complexity* in reenforcement learning, where the concept of behavioural complexity recognised that programs with very similar structure may exhibit quite different behaviour when they interact with the problem environment. The researchers noted that, in general, when training fitness was low - high behavioural complexity had a beneficial effect on generalisation, but as training fitness improved, behavioural complexity was negatively correlated with generalisation.

For some time, the accepted wisdom in the GP community was that smaller programs may generalise better. This *appeared* consistent with the general principle of Occam's razor, and its formalisation in the MDL principle. However, in the last few years, the link between bloat and over-fitting has become controversial. Recent work by Vanneschi et al. [30] which set out to define the concepts of bloat, over fitting and complexity, and to investigate relationships that may exist between them, suggests that somewhat contrary to popular belief, these phenomena may be independent to some degree. Azad and Ryan [1] explained that a small GP tree is not necessarily simple: for example, $sin(x)$ is more complex than a larger GP tree encoding $x+x+x+x$. Related work of Castelli et al. [6] tentatively suggested that functional complexity, or the lack thereof, may play a more important role in generalisation than bloat does.

In the wider ML context Domingos [8] talks about two different interpretations of the principle of Occam's razor: the first suggests preferring the simpler of two models with the same generalisation error because simplicity is a goal in itself, and the second favours the simpler of two models with the same training-set error because this will lead to lower generalisation error. Domingos [8] empirically demonstrated that the latter interpretation is false, and in doing so cited numerous instances where simple solutions underperformed and many others where complex methods were superior. In that research Domingos suggested that a more realistic technique for reducing over-fitting is to incorporate domain knowledge in the learning algorithm. Another suggested strategy proposed by Jensen and Cohen [16] is to reduce the number of hypotheses considered, which in the case of GP implies that smaller populations may result in solutions which are less likely to over-fit than those originating from larger ones.

Program growth without (significant) return in terms of fitness [24] is a widely accepted definition of the term *bloat* as used in the GP community. The phenomenon of bloat is inconvenient for several reasons, including computational expense, increased run times, deterioration in program comprehensibility and a likely dilution of program semantics. Naturally, the topic has been an area of intense and prolific research since the behaviour came to the notice of the GP research community, see for example [20] and [27] for reviews of current bloat theories and methods of controlling or preventing it.

While it is important to solve the problem of bloat for reasons already outlined, the close coupling of bloat and program size for the purpose of analysing variance error/over-fitting may be something of a "red herring". Given the definition of bloat as previously provided by Poli et al., we can imagine that is it quite possible to have small programs which are bloated and large ones which are not. It might be beneficial to focus on bloat, size and complexity separately as sources of over-fitting.

Much of the previous work concerned with a possible relationship between *functional* complexity and generalisation has focused on symbolic regression problems [6, 30] where the term *functional complexity* usually refers to model/solution complexity. That is to say, the complexity aspect relates to the relative complexity of the function encoded in the solution. This is a point of view that may be particularly useful when considering symbolic regression tasks, but may not be quite so relevant to binary classification problems, which we focus on in this paper.

The previously mentioned *order of non-linearity* complexity measure [31] differentiated *size complexity* from *expressional complexity*. Similarly, for the current study, we define complexity in terms of the *complexity of the function set available to encode possible solutions*: the simplest function set contains operators such as addition and subtraction, whereas a more complex function set may contain trigonometric operators such as *sin* and *cos*. From now on, we refer to this concept as *operator complexity*.

3. INVESTIGATING SIZE, COMPLEXITY AND GENERALISATION

Whigham [32] introduced the concept of *language bias*, which when applied to GP refers to inductive bias associated with the function and terminal sets. He also introduced the terms *search bias* and *selection bias* where search bias refers to the the way in which the learning system *transforms* one hypothesis into another and selection bias refers to the method used to *select* one hypothesis over another. In GP the former relates to such things as genetic operators and permissible tree size, and the latter relates to aspects such as the fitness function. We contend that these biases expressed as algorithmic and parameter choices in GP influence the bias and variance components of generalisation error in GP.

In this study we choose to investigate language bias in terms of function sets together with aspects of search bias introduced through parameters which control *permissible* program size. We choose this combination because of the historical tight coupling of size and complexity in GP terminology around the topic of generalisation. We carry out a simple empirical study designed to discover what effects on generalisation may be observed when program size and operator complexity are *varied in combination*.

3.1 Experiments

Here we outline the various experiments carried out for this investigation. GP parameters are detailed in Table 2, experimental configurations are shown in Tables 4 and 3. For this study we use several well known datasets from the UCI repository [2], as outlined in Table 1, as between them they offer good variety in the numbers of attributes and instances together with differing levels of class imbalance.

Table 1: Data Sets [2]

Data Set	Acronym	Features	Instances	%Minority
Bupa Liver	BUPA	7	345	42
Caravan	CAR	85	5946	6
Ecoli	ECO	7	332	10
Habermans Survival	HS	4	306	36
Ionosphere	ION	34	348	36

Table 2: GP Parameters. Details of depth constraints and function sets are shown in Table 3.

Parameter	Value
Strategy	Steady State
Initialisation	Ramped half-and-half
Selection	Tournament
Tournament Size	2
Crossover	70
Mutation	20
Reproduction	10
Initial Min Depth	Various
Initial Max Depth	Various
Max Depth	Various
Function Set	Various
Population	500
Max Gen	60

Table 3: Size Constraints

Size	Init Min	Init Max	Max Depth
TINY	1	2	8
SMALL	1	4	10
MED	2	6	16
LARGE	4	8	20
HUGE	8	16	32

3.2 Experimental Configurations

For this study we investigate the effects of varying both size and operator complexity with tree based GP on a variety of binary classification tasks. We use relative terms such as "tiny" and "huge", which while they do not have an intrinsic scientific meaning, provide a description of the relative values of each, and are easily understood for discussion purposes. Table 3 details size constraints used for the experiments: parameter values for initialisation minimum depth, initialisation maximum depth and maximum depth permissible, in five different configurations. Obviously, there are numerous combinations of depth parameters which could be used. We have chosen these to provide a range of initial minimum, initial maximum and overall maximum allowable values. Table 4 outlines four different function sets facilitating varying degrees of operator complexity, as the term is defined in Section 2. For each task, identical random seeds were used and two thirds of the data was allocated for training and one third for testing with random selection preserving class ratios.

Table 4: Operator Complexity Configurations

Config.	Functions
MIN	+ −
LOW	* /
MID	+ − * /
HI	+ − * / *sin cos*

From now on, we refer to the various configurations either by the acronyms outlined in Tables 3 and 4 or by a conjunction of these, in size complexity order. For example TINYMIN uses the TINY size constraints combined with the least complex function set.

Table 5: ECO Training & Test Accuracy

		Training		Test					
Size	Complexity	Avg Accuracy	Best Accuracy	Avg Accuracy	Best Accuracy	Std. Dev.	% OverFit	AUC	Best AUC
Tiny	MIN	77.15	80.91	52.85	78.57	18.67	24.28	0.69	0.90
	LOW	90.06	90.45	88.36	88.40	0.17	1.70	0.17	0.90
	MID	82.04	90.00	74.30	83.93	10.91	7.94	0.79	0.90
	HI	83.85	89.09	74.86	83.92	10,91	8.90	0.76	**0.93**
Small	MIN	79.52	80.91	71.64	80.35	12.61	7.88	0.84	0.90
	LOW	90.19	90.45	88.25	88.39	0.33	1.94	0.50	0.90
	MID	84.64	90.91	76.05	84.82	10.81	8.58	0.75	0.90
	HI	84.77	91.81	74.35	84.82	14.24	10.40	0.75	0.90
Med	MIN	80.28	81.36	76.84	80.36	2.80	3.44	0.88	0.89
	LOW	71.46	90.45	68.14	88.39	31.40	3.32	0.56	0.91
	MID	87.56	91.82	77.42	84.82	8.24	10.14	0.73	0.89
	HI	86.08	92.27	75.14	84.82	10.94	9.77	0.74	0.90
Large	MIN	81.05	81.81	78.84	80.36	1.79	2.18	**0.89**	0.89
	LOW	79.18	80.90	79.34	82.19	1.53	-0.16	0.77	0.90
	MID	89.61	92.27	78.12	83.93	7.01	11.50	0.71	0.89
	HI	87.68	92.73	77.51	84.82	6.79	10.16	0.74	0.90
Huge	MIN	81.26	81.82	78.81	80.36	1.79	2.46	**0.89**	0.89
	LOW	82.61	88.63	71.73	82.14	7.49	10.88	0.65	0.87
	MID	90.01	93.18	76.46	83.92	6.82	13.55	0.72	0.89
	HI	88.95	93.18	77.91	84.82	5.07	11.04	0.73	0.89

3.3 Results and Discussion

We report experimental results in two categories: the first subsection 3.3.2 outlines and discusses results for classification accuracy and over-fitting (variance error), and the second subsection 3.3.3 details results relating to program size. All results reported relate to the fifty best-of-run individuals for each configuration for each data set.

3.3.1 Area Under the ROC Curve (AUC)

Originating from World War II where it was initially used to evaluate the performance of radio personnel at accurately reading radar images, the *Receiver Operating Characteristic* (ROC) is a tool which may be used to measure the performance of medical tests, radiographers, and classifiers. The area under the ROC curve, known as the *AUC* is a scalar value which captures the accuracy of the entity under scrutiny. The AUC is a non-parametric measure representing ROC performance independent of any threshold [5]. A perfect ROC will have an AUC of 1, whereas the ROC plot of a random classifier will result in an AUC of approximately 0.5.

There are various ways to calculate the AUC and we have chosen the Wilcoxon Mann Whitney approximation as it is easy to calculate and has the advantage that it facilitates the estimation of confidence intervals [29].

3.3.2 Training and Test Accuracy, AUC and Over-fitting

We firstly report results for average and best % accuracy on training and test data, together with the average and best AUC score on test data. We also report the degree of over-fitting in each case. The measure of over-fitting used here is simply the difference between training fitness and test fitness for the best of run individuals as shown in Equation 2.

$$avgOverfit = \frac{\sum_{i=1}^{n}(BOR_i(TrainAcc) - BOR_i(TestAcc))}{n} \quad (2)$$

Where BOR_i is the best of run individual of the ith run, n is the number of runs, $BOR_i(TrainAcc)$ is the training accuracy of the best of run individual and $BOR_i(TestAcc)$ is the test accuracy of the best of run individual.

For this study, the most important measure of classification performance is the AUC score for each configuration. However we are also very interested in over-fitting, accuracy and variability. See Ling et al. [19] for a detailed explanation of why AUC should be preferred to accuracy as a measure of classifier performance.

Looking at results for the *BUPA* data set in Table 6 we see that the set-up with the best overall average AUC was the simplest function set used with the large size constraints. In fact, for each size configuration, the least complex function set produced the best average AUC result. The high complexity setting exhibited both the greatest variability in accuracy and the highest degree of variance error. The MIN complexity settings did not exhibit any over-fitting, while for the more complex MID and HI complexity settings over-fitting was present and *tended to increase with size.* The LOW complexity configuration (* /) produced very weak results for classification accuracy and AUC on both training and test data for several of the problems. .

The results for the *HS* data, shown in Table 7, illustrate how important it is to use a performance measure such as AUC for classification tasks even on relatively balanced data sets. Even though we have used *average* accuracy as our fitness measure, both the MID and HI complexity configurations had poor accuracy on the minority class which resulted

Table 6: BUPA Training & Test Accuracy

Size	Complexity	Training: Avg Accuracy	Training: Best Accuracy	Test: Avg Accuracy	Test: Best Accuracy	Std. Dev.	% OverFit	AUC	Best AUC
Tiny	MIN	70.63	73.68	72.77	75.43	2.15	-2.14	0.77	0.80
	LOW	43.42	43.42	43.00	43.86	0.12	0.42	0.40	0.52
	MID	70.90	75.87	68.96	76.31	6.20	1.93	0.71	**0.83**
	HI	68.41	72.81	65.61	76.31	7.94	2.80	0.69	0.79
Small	MIN	72.69	74.12	73.75	76.31	1.37	-1.06	0.78	0.80
	LOW	43.45	43.85	43.00	43.86	0.12	0.42	0.40	0.53
	MID	71.53	75.43	70.15	78.07	5.76	1.38	0.72	**0.83**
	HI	70.33	75.43	67.73	77.19	7.00	2.60	0.70	0.81
Med	MIN	72.93	74.12	73.22	77.19	1.58	-0.28	0.78	0.80
	LOW	43.56	44.29	43.19	43.86	0.38	0.37	0.44	0.70
	MID	72.78	76.75	69.61	78.07	5.67	3.17	0.71	0.81
	HI	70.61	75.87	66.70	76.31	6.68	3.91	0.70	0.79
Large	MIN	73.12	74.56	73.71	77.19	1.53	-0.60	**0.79**	0.80
	LOW	43.79	44.30	43.31	43.85	0.55	0.41	0.47	0.74
	MID	72.40	77.19	68.57	76.31	5.37	3.82	0.68	0.81
	HI	70.60	75.43	66.52	77.19	5.94	4.07	0.69	0.79
Huge	MIN	73.03	74.56	74.01	78.07	1.48	-0.98	0.78	0.80
	LOW	46.58	69.29	44.84	60.52	4.45	1.74	0.40	0.71
	MID	72.25	78.07	66.70	77.19	5.65	5.66	0.67	0.80
	HI	69.72	75.87	57.19	78.07	8.90	12.53	0.59	0.77

Table 7: HS Training & Test Accuracy

Size	Complexity	Training: Avg Accuracy	Training: Best Accuracy	Test: Avg Accuracy	Test: Best Accuracy	Std. Dev.	% OverFit	AUC	Best AUC
Tiny	MIN	61.87	62.06	65.49	65.69	0.97	-3.61	0.71	0.72
	LOW	57.14	57.14	60.78	60.78	0	-3.64	0.62	0.63
	MID	72.28	75.76	75.25	78.43	3.03	-2.96	0.64	0.76
	HI	71.37	76.35	71.31	79.41	4.30	0.07	0.61	0.75
Small	MIN	62.10	62.10	64.04	65.69	0.14	-3.55	0.71	0.72
	LOW	57.14	57.14	60.78	60.78	0	-3.64	0.62	0.63
	MID	72.92	77.34	75.67	78.43	3.12	-2.74	0.62	0.75
	HI	72.21	78.32	71.98	78.43	4.15	0.23	0.61	**0.77**
Med	MIN	63.76	70.44	66.29	77.45	3.27	-2.53	0.72	0.73
	LOW	57.14	57.14	60.78	60.78	0	-3.64	0.61	0.63
	MID	73.65	77.34	74.66	78.43	2.40	-1.01	0.64	0.76
	HI	71.79	77.83	72.17	78.43	3.63	-0.38	0.65	0.76
Large	MIN	69.14	70.44	77.45	77.65	1.43	-8.30	**0.73**	0.73
	LOW	57.14	57.14	60.78	60.78	0	-3.64	0.61	0.63
	MID	74.01	78.32	74.45	78.43	2.30	-0.43	0.63	0.76
	HI	73.37	78.81	72.35	78.43	3.90	1.02	0.64	0.74
Huge	MIN	69.00	69.45	77.27	77.45	0.87	-8.27	**0.73**	0.73
	LOW	57.78	58.13	60.78	60.78	0	-3.60	0.52	0.62
	MID	75.45	78.82	72.90	78.43	2.56	3.32	0.62	0.74
	HI	73.27	80.09	66.58	77.45	6.28	6.68	0.61	0.75

in low average AUC scores in spite of apparently superior overall classification accuracy. This data set is relatively balanced, having a minority class percentage of 36%. The higher overall accuracy of the MID and HI configurations is a result of the learner classifying most of the instances as belonging to the majority class.

For this data set the best average AUC score is shared by a configuration which involve the least complex function set combined with either the large or huge size constraints. Again, the most complex function set resulted in the greatest variability and most over-fitting. However the SMALLHI set-up had the best individual AUC score. For variance error, the simplest function set delivered test results that were actually better than the corresponding training results and tended to improve with size. In contrast, over-fitting increased as the allowed size increased for the more complex configurations.

For the *ION* data set shown in Table 8, we note again that the *best overall* individual AUC result was achieved using the more complex function sets. The best average AUC resulted from the MEDMIN set-up and, as with several of the other data sets, increased operator complexity resulted in greater variability in training and test accuracy. For this data set, some over-fitting was apparent for each experimental set-up, and this *tended to increase as size was permitted to increase.*

The *CAR* dataset has a relatively large number of features (86) and instances (5822) and is quite imbalanced. The best average AUC score resulted from a configuration using MIN complexity combined with either medium or large size constraints. Again, the simplest in terms of complexity had the best average AUC over all of the size configurations. Excluding the tiny configuration, the least complex function set exhibited the least variability in training and test accuracy. The best overall AUC result of 0.76 was shared between MIN combined with Large and High combined with Huge. In the latter case, the difference in the best score of 0.76 and the average of 0.65 illustrates the degree of variability in performance when solutions using the most complex function set were applied to the test data. Overall, there was no evidence of over-fitting on this data set.

The ECO data set is different to others used in this investigation, as it was originally a multi-class data set consisting of seven classes. We have collapsed six classes into one, resulting in an unbalanced data set. For almost half of the runs of the TINYMIN set-up the system consistently converged on a seven node solution which had very poor accuracy on test data. In constructing the training and test sets, we maintained the same ratio of the two classes in each set, however we did not ensure that for the majority class, the same balance of the underlying, original six classes was in place. This may explain the high level of over-fitting and variability for this configuration. The best average AUC result for this data set again resulted from one of the configurations which combined the simplest function set with either the large or huge set-up.

3.3.3 Solution Size

In this this section we examine size data for each configuration and each data set. Table 9 provides information for the CAR dataset on population average size and standard deviation at the final generation, average size of best-of-run trained individual and size of the individual with the best AUC score on test data. Tables of results for the other datasets are similar but not included for space reasons.

For the BUPA data set, with the exception of the TINY set-up the MIN complexity setting resulted in the largest population average program size. This is probably not surprising, as semantics that are encoded using addition and subtraction operators will naturally result in a bigger expression that if multiplication and division are employed.

Comparing the average size of the best-of-run individuals with the population average program size, we note that

Table 8: ION Training & Test Accuracy

		Training		**Test**					
Size	Complexity	Avg Accuracy	Best Accuracy	Avg Accuracy	Best Accuracy	Std. Dev.	% OverFit	AUC	Best AUC
Tiny	MIN	87.30	89.65	82.31	91.37	3.42	4.99	0.81	0.92
	LOW	86.34	87.50	83.58	87.07	2.34	2.76	0.82	0.93
	MID	87.17	90.09	85.48	90.51	3.40	1.68	0.82	0.90
	HI	87.26	90.94	86.27	93.10	3.31	0.99	0.83	0.90
Small	MIN	88.78	90.95	83.79	92.24	3.25	4.99	0.83	0.92
	LOW	86.50	89.22	83.34	89.65	2.72	3.15	0.73	0.91
	MID	89.50	93.10	86.00	94.83	4.02	3.44	0.79	**0.97**
	HI	89.07	93.10	86.58	95.69	3.86	2.50	0.81	0.93
Med	MIN	89.81	91.38	82.84	87.93	2.82	6.96	**0.84**	0.90
	LOW	86.97	90.08	82.53	87.07	2.41	4.43	0.68	0.88
	MID	90.17	93.96	85.56	92.24	4.54	4.60	0.77	0.88
	HI	89.43	92.67	85.24	92.24	3.68	4.20	0.82	0.92
Large	MIN	90.50	92.67	83.50	91.37	2.41	6.99	0.82	0.91
	LOW	87.82	89.65	82.05	89.65	3.11	5.77	0.66	0.91
	MID	90.53	93.96	86.08	91.37	4.11	4.44	0.77	0.92
	HI	89.73	93.53	85.27	93.10	4.59	4.46	0.82	**0.97**
Huge	MIN	90.28	92.24	83.20	89.65	3.68	7.07	0.82	0.90
	LOW	88.12	92.24	83.08	89.65	3.45	5.03	0.67	0.83
	MID	88.01	93.10	81.67	92.24	8.21	6.34	0.73	0.89
	HI	89.60	93.10	83.06	90.51	4.50	6.53	0.82	0.94

Table 9: CAR Size Data

Size	Complexity	Pop Avg Size	Std Dev	BOR Avg Size	Best AUC Size
Tiny	MIN	15	6.68	17	21
	LOW	16	7.02	18	15
	MID	16	7.0	19	21
	HI	16	7.03	15	11
Small	MIN	21	9.78	24	57
	LOW	27	11.52	27	11
	MID	32	12.12	35	19
	HI	27	11.52	30	17
Med	MIN	180	44.26	167	247
	LOW	71.09	26.09	114	147
	MID	119	36.72	110	95
	HI	71	26.09	74	40
Large	MIN	518	100.41	473	475
	LOW	131	41.30	230	151
	MID	239	65.22	230	263
	HI	131	41.30	115	84
Huge	MIN	4714	395.26	3871	1745
	LOW	363	108.39	584	391
	MID	607	175.05	584	821
	HI	363	108.39	334	277

in general for many of the datasets, these are broadly similar. In contrast, the size of the individual with the best AUC score *on test data*, is generally much smaller than the population average with the exception of HS. This does not always hold true for the TINY and SMALL size constraints, and a possible explanation for this is that the average population size may not be quite big enough to encode a satisfactory solution.

For several of the datasets, including the CAR dataset in Table 9, the population average size for the HUGEMIN experiments is very large. Looking at the underlying run data, we observe that these large average values are a result of a small number of extremely big outliers.

This simple study delivers some interesting results regarding size and operator complexity in GP for binary classification tasks. For the problems investigated, the following observations can be made from a study of the experimental results:

1. The simplest configuration in terms of complexity consistently results in the *best average AUC* score and in many cases the result is appreciably better. Best results are achieved when this MIN complexity set-up is combined with a MED LARGE or HUGE potential size.

2. The simplest configuration *almost always* produces programs with the least variability *regardless of size* whereas, in general, greater complexity results in greater variability;

3. In four of the five data sets, the MIN complexity configurations had negative or no over-fitting whereas the more complex set-ups showed evidence of over-fitting, and this *increased as size was permitted to increase*;

4. With some explainable exceptions, the size of the best overall individual with respect to AUC on test data was *significantly smaller* than the population average size whereas the size of the best trained individual in terms of classification accuracy was broadly in line with the average population size.

3.3.4 Statistical Significance

A Friedman plot of the results for average AUC shown in Figure 1 clearly illustrates that an approach which uses the simplest function set is most successful. With regard to size, all but the TINY configuration perform well when combined with MIN complexity, however the Large set-up is clearly superior. Post hoc analysis established that results for configurations which combined MIN operator complexity with Small, Medium, Large or Huge size constraints are significant at the 95% level when compared with the LOW set-ups. We also analysed results separately by size and by operator complexity. Again, results for the MIN complexity are highly significant when compared with the LOW setting, with a p-value of 0.001. Results for the Large size set-up are significant at the 90% level when compared with Tiny.

4. CONCLUSIONS

Experimental results from this study provide some evidence of the effects of selected sources of search and language bias i.e. *program size* and *operator complexity*, to bias and variance error components of generalisation error for binary classification tasks. Against this background we can tentatively suggest the following heuristics for tackling classification problems with GP:

1. A simple function set consisting only of addition and subtraction may be suitable if consistent results are required, where system performance on training data is likely to provide a reliable indication of possible test performance.

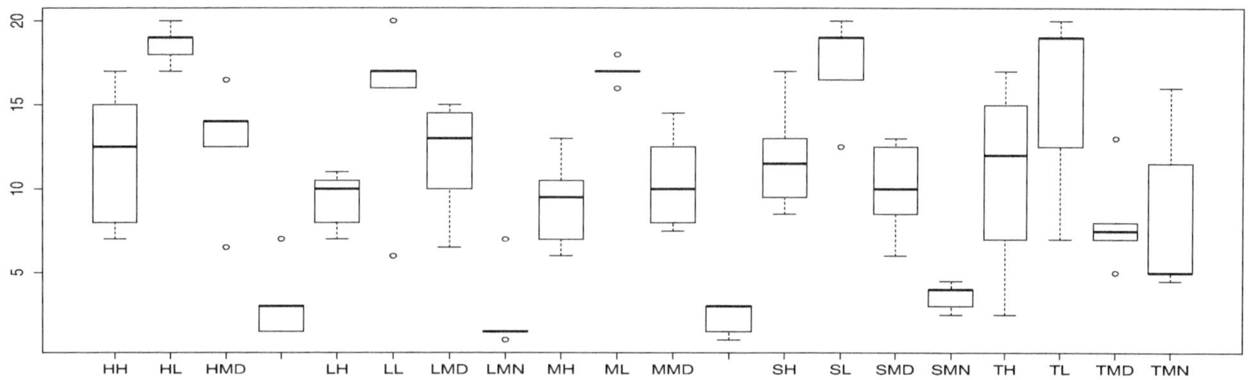

Figure 1: Friedman plot of algorithm ranking across datasets, where 1 is highest. H=Huge, L=Large, M=Med, S=Small, T=Tiny. MN=MIN, L=LOW, MD=MID, H=HI. E.g HH = HUGEHI.

Table 10: CAR Training & Test Accuracy

		Training		Test					
Size	Complexity	Avg Accuracy	Best Accuracy	Avg Accuracy	Best Accuracy	Std. Dev.	% OverFit	AUC	Best AUC
Tiny	MIN	62.99	74.46	64.56	76.30	6.47	-1.58	0.67	0.74
	LOW	70.91	73.54	71.70	74.19	3.40	-0.79	0.46	0.63
	MID	64.31	78.27	65.41	78.97	6.46	-1.10	0.62	0.74
	HI	63.35	72,61	64.63	73.31	5.15	-1.27	0.59	0.71
Small	MIN	65.08	71.94	66.58	73.57	3.82	-1.49	0.70	0.74
	LOW	69.78	73.18	70.58	73.67	3.80	-0.79	0.47	0.60
	MID	65.01	72.66	65.56	74.70	4.01	-0.54	0.63	0.72
	HI	64.26	77.24	65.04	77.69	5.06	-0.77	0.62	0.74
Med	MIN	67.95	73.33	68,62	74.81	2.61	-0.67	**0.73**	0.75
	LOW	66.71	75.21	67.04	76.40	3.61	-0.33	0.52	0.60
	MID	67.74	76.96	67.97	77.22	3.20	-0.23	0.63	0.74
	HI	66.57	79.41	67.11	77.79	3.84	-0.54	0.62	0.73
Large	MIN	67.35	71.81	68.09	72.69	2.76	-0.74	**0.73**	**0.76**
	LOW	65.90	72.40	66.19	72.38	3.32	-0.29	0.51	0.60
	MID	67.28	72.97	67.80	72.85	3.43	-0.52	0.66	0.75
	HI	66,57	74.88	67.33	74.24	3.09	-0.76	0.63	0.73
Huge	MIN	67.05	75.52	67.74	76.20	2.74	-0.68	0.72	0.75
	LOW	65.55	73.56	65.79	74.09	4.27	-0.23	0.50	0.62
	MID	66.34	77.32	66.57	76.98	3.62	-0.23	0.66	0.73
	HI	64.76	72.35	65.73	71.61	3.07	-0.97	0.65	**0.76**

2. A more complex function set may be more appropriate if we are seeking to evolve the best individual possible, and are prepared to tolerate high variability together with some over-fitting.

3. Solutions which generalise well may tend to be relatively small and simple but the evolution of these solutions may be more successful in an environment which facilitates medium to large programs.

Is it the case that small, simple solutions generalise better, or that solutions which generalise well will tend to be simple and smaller than average? The results would seem to suggest that the latter is closest to the truth: given that the MED LARGE or HUGE configurations delivered the best average AUC where the size of the individual with the best overall AUC score was in many cases smaller than the population average.

Intuition tells us that it is not surprising that the set ups with the MIN complexity option should exhibit the smallest variance error, as the evolved solutions are by definition simple and thus less likely to closely fit any idiosyncrasies in the data. However, this lack of over-fitting may also be related to the *low variation* in the quality of the solutions generated using the simple function set. This view is consistent with that expressed by Elkan [10]: "the danger of over-fitting is not reduced just because a learning algorithm outputs a model with only a few parameters. For the risk of over-fitting to be lessened, *all* models that the algorithm *could have* output must be equally simple".

Some of the results in this study emphasise that generalisation is not all about variance error, we should also concern ourselves with bias error. For example, in the CAR data set there is no evidence of over-fitting, yet there is significant variation in average AUC score across configurations. Also, in the ION experiments, several of the configurations which had the most over-fitting also had the best average AUC score. We conclude from these preliminary results that the availability of larger solutions reduces bias error whereas simpler function sets improve variance, and the combination of these provides a balance from the perspective of the bias variance trade-off. We further suggest that language and search biases [32] inherent in parameter choices relating to size and operator complexity, may have a significant influence on the generalisation capability in terms of bias and variance error, of GP for binary classification tasks.

Future work should examine a wider range and larger set of problems to determine if findings in this preliminary work have more general applicability.

References

[1] R. Muhammad Atif Azad and Conor Ryan. Abstract functions and lifetime learning in genetic programming for symbolic regression. In Juergen Branke et al., editors, *GECCO '10: Proceedings of the 12th annual conference on Genetic and evolutionary computation*, 2010.

[2] Bache, K. and Lichman, M. (2013). UCI machine learning repository.

[3] Chris M Bishop. Training with noise is equivalent to tikhonov regularization. *Neural computation*, 7(1):108–116, 1995.

[4] Christopher M Bishop and Nasser M Nasrabadi. *Pattern recognition and machine learning*, volume 1. springer New York, 2006.

[5] Brown, C. D. and Davis, H. T. (2006). Receiver operating characteristics curves and related decision measures: A tutorial. *Chemometrics and Intelligent Laboratory Systems*, 80(1):24–38.

[6] Mauro Castelli, Luca Manzoni, Sara Silva, and Leonardo Vanneschi. A quantitative study of learning and generalization in genetic programming. In Sara Silva et al., editors, *Proceedings of the 14th European Conference on Genetic Programming, EuroGP 2011*, volume 6621 of *LNCS*, pages 25–36, Turin, Italy, 27-29 April 2011. Springer Verlag.

[7] Michael J Cavaretta and Kumar Chellapilla. Data mining using genetic programming: the implications of parsimony on generalization error. In *Evolutionary Computation, 1999. CEC 99. Proceedings of the 1999 Congress on*, volume 2. IEEE, 1999.

[8] Pedro Domingos. The role of occam's razor in knowledge discovery. *Data mining and knowledge discovery*, 3(4):409–425, 1999.

[9] Pedro Domingos. A unified bias-variance decomposition. In *Proceedings of 17th International Conference on Machine Learning. Stanford CA Morgan Kaufmann*, pages 231–238, 2000.

[10] Charles Elkan. Magical thinking in data mining: lessons from coil challenge 2000. In *Proceedings of the seventh ACM SIGKDD international conference on Knowledge discovery and data mining*, pages 426–431. ACM, 2001.

[11] Yoav Freund and Robert E. Schapire. Experiments with a new boosting algorithm. In *Thirteenth International Conference on Machine Learning*, pages 148–156, San Francisco, 1996. Morgan Kaufmann.

[12] Christian Gagné, Marc Schoenauer, Marc Parizeau, and Marco Tomassini. Genetic programming, validation sets, and parsimony pressure. In Pierre Collet et al., editors, *Proceedings of the 9th European Conference on Genetic Programming*, volume 3905 of *Lecture Notes in Computer Science*, pages 109–120, Budapest, Hungary, 10 - 12 April 2006. Springer.

[13] Stuart Geman, Elie Bienenstock, and René Doursat. Neural networks and the bias/variance dilemma. *Neural computation*, 4(1):1–58, 1992.

[14] Faustino J Gomez, Julian Togelius, and Juergen Schmidhuber. Measuring and optimizing behavioral complexity for evolutionary reinforcement learning. In *Artificial Neural Networks–ICANN 2009*, pages 765–774. Springer, 2009.

[15] Peter Grünwald. The minimum description length principle and non-deductive inference. In *Proceedings of the IJCAI Workshop on Abduction and Induction in*, page http://www.mpeg.org/, 1997.

[16] David D Jensen and Paul R Cohen. Multiple comparisons in induction algorithms. *Machine Learning*, 38(3):309–338, 2000.

[17] Maarten Keijzer and Vladan Babovic. Genetic programming, ensemble methods and the bias/variance tradeoff - introductory investigations. In Riccardo Poli, et al., editors, *Genetic Programming, Proceedings of EuroGP'2000*, volume 1802 of *LNCS*, pages 76–90, Edinburgh, 15-16 April 2000. Springer-Verlag.

[18] W. B. Langdon. Size fair tree crossovers. In Eric Postma and Marc Gyssen, editors, *Proceedings of the Eleventh Belgium/Netherlands Conference on Artificial Intelligence (BNAIC'99)*, pages 255–256, Kasteel Vaeshartelt, Maastricht, Holland, 3-4 November 1999.

[19] Charles X Ling, Jin Huang, and Harry Zhang. Auc: a better measure than accuracy in comparing learning algorithms. In *Advances in Artificial Intelligence*, pages 329–341. Springer, 2003.

[20] Sean Luke and Liviu Panait. A comparison of bloat control methods for genetic programming. *Evolutionary Computation*, 14(3):309–344, 2006.

[21] Nikolay Y Nikolaev and Hitoshi Iba. Regularization approach to inductive genetic programming. *Evolutionary Computation, IEEE Transactions on*, 5(4):359–375, 2001.

[22] Gregory Paris, Denis Robilliard, and Cyril Fonlupt. Exploring overfitting in genetic programming. In Pierre Liardet, et al., editors, *Evolution Artificielle, 6th International Conference*, volume 2936 of *Lecture Notes in Computer Science*, pages 267–277, Marseilles, France, 27-30 October 2003. Springer.
Revised Selected Papers.

[23] Riccardo Poli. A Simple but Theoretically-Motivated Method to Control Bloat in Genetic Programming. pages 43–76. 2003.

[24] Riccardo Poli, W B Langdon, and Nicholas Freitag McPhee. *A Field Guide to Genetic Programming*. Lulu.com, March 2008.

[25] Jorma Rissanen. Modeling by shortest data description. *Automatica*, 14(5):465–471, 1978.

[26] Justinian Rosca. Generality versus size in genetic programming. In John R. Koza, et al., editors, *Genetic Programming 1996: Proceedings of the First Annual Conference*, pages 381–387, Stanford University, CA, USA, 28–31 July 1996. MIT Press.

[27] Sara Silva and Ernesto Costa. Dynamic limits for bloat control in genetic programming and a review of past and current bloat theories. *Genetic Programming and Evolvable Machines*, 10(2):141–179, 2009.

[28] Terence Soule and James A Foster. Effects of code growth and parsimony pressure on populations in genetic programming. *Evolutionary Computation*, 6(4):293–309, 1998.

[29] Stober, P. and Yeh, S.-T. (2007). An explicit functional form specification approach to estimate the area under a receiver operating characteristic (roc) curve. *Available at http://www2. sas. com/proceedings/sugi27/p226–227. pdf Accessed March*, 7.

[30] Leonardo Vanneschi, Mauro Castelli, and Sara Silva. Measuring bloat, overfitting and functional complexity in genetic programming. In *Proceedings of the 12th annual conference on Genetic and evolutionary computation*, GECCO '10, pages 877–884, New York, NY, USA, 2010. ACM.

[31] Ekaterina J. Vladislavleva, Guido F. Smits, and Dick Den Hertog. Order of nonlinearity as a complexity measure for models generated by symbolic regression via pareto genetic programming. *Trans. Evol. Comp*, 13:333–349, April 2009.

[32] Peter A Whigham. Search bias, language bias and genetic programming. In *Proceedings of the First Annual Conference on Genetic Programming*, pages 230–237. MIT Press, 1996.

Asynchronously Evolving Solutions with Excessively Different Evaluation Time by Reference-based Evaluation

Tomohiro Harada
The University of Electro-Communications
W6-309, 1-5-1 Chofugaoka, Chofu, Tokyo, Japan
Research Fellow of the Japan Society for the Promotion of Science DC1
harada@cas.hc.uec.ac.jp

Keiki Takadama
The University of Electro-Communications
W6-309, 1-5-1 Chofugaoka, Chofu, Tokyo, Japan
keiki@inf.uec.ac.jp

ABSTRACT

The asynchronous evolution has an advantage when evolving solutions with excessively different evaluation time since the asynchronous evolution evolves each solution independently without waiting for other evaluations, unlike the synchronous evolution requires evaluations of all solutions at the same time. As a novel asynchronous evolution approach, this paper proposes Asynchronous Reference-based Evaluation (ARE) that asynchronously selects good parents by the tournament selection using reference solution in order to evolve solutions through a crossover of the good parents. To investigate the effectiveness of ARE in the case of evolving solutions with excessively different evaluation time, this paper applies ARE to Genetic Programming (GP), and compares GP using ARE (ARE-GP) with GP using $(\mu+\lambda)$ selection ($(\mu+\lambda)$-GP) as the synchronous approach in particular situation where the evaluation time of individuals differs from each other. The intensive experiments have revealed the following implications: (1) ARE-GP greatly outperforms $(\mu+\lambda)$-GP from the viewpoint of the elapsed unit time in the parallel computation environment, (2) ARE-GP can evolve individuals without decreasing the searching ability in the situation where the computing speed of each individual differs from each other and some individuals fail in their execution.

Categories and Subject Descriptors

I.2.8 [**Problem Solving, Control Methods, and Search**]: Heuristic methods

General Terms

Algorithms

Keywords

Asynchronous evolution, Genetic Programming

GECCO'14, July 12–16, 2014, Vancouver, BC, Canada.
Copyright 2014 ACM 978-1-4503-2662-9/14/07 ...$15.00.
http://dx.doi.org/10.1145/2576768.2598330.

1. INTRODUCTION

Recently, a parallel computation technique to quickly compute using many distributed computer nodes has attracted attention. In the evolutionary computation community, many researches have studied to parallelize an evolution process for efficiently searching solutions [12, 3]. In general, Evolutionary Algorithms (EAs) typified as Genetic Algorithm (GA) [5] and Genetic Programming (GP) [7] evolve individuals (solutions) by repeating a *generation* step. This approach waits for evaluations of all individuals in a population and generates a next population through the parent selection and the individual deletion depending on the evaluations of all individuals. This requires that all individuals be evaluated at the same time, i.e., requires waiting for an individual with the slowest evaluation, where the evaluation time of individuals differs from each other. This causes to consume a computational time. Such situation easily occurs in the parallel computation, for example, because of (1) the difference of property of individuals and (2) the difference of computing speed of distributed computer notes. Additionally, in some case, evaluations of some individuals could never complete, for example, because of the communication error between computer notes or an infinite loop in the case of evolving computer programs in GP. When some individual do not complete their evaluation, in general, EAs cut off the evaluation of an individual that exceeds a certain limitation and evaluate its fitness as the minimum value. However, since it is difficult to determine an ideal limitation, it is hard for conventional EAs to efficiently evolve individuals in such situation.

To tackle this problem, *asynchronous* approaches are recently proposed [8, 4], that evolves individuals independently, i.e., individuals do not have to wait for the evaluations of other individuals. The asynchronous evolution can continue to evolve individuals without waiting for other individuals such as slower one, which enables to efficiently evolve individuals without wasting the computational time. However, when some individual do not complete their evaluation, these methods [8, 4] also require the execution time limitation as same as the synchronous EAs. In contrast to this, we have proposed GP employing the asynchronous approach, named as TAGP (Tierra-based Asynchronous Genetic Programming) [6], as one kind of machine-code GP based on the idea of a biological simulator, Tierra [11]. An advantage of TAGP is that it can continue to evolve individuals (programs) without any limitation even if some of them do not complete their evaluation. Our previous research [6] reported that TAGP could asynchronously evolve the machine-code programs even if they include loop structure. However, TAGP has the following two essential problems: (1) Unlike general EAs, TAGP do not guarantee to select the good individuals as parents from a population, which prevents from improving its performance; and (2) since TAGP selects individuals as parents or deletes them depending on a threshold based on an absolute evaluation, it is difficult to properly evolve individuals in the case that settings of a fitness function and a threshold are not proper.

To overcome these problems, this paper proposes a novel asynchronous reference-based evaluation (named as ARE) for asynchronous EA, which not only inherit the advantage of TAGP but also overcome its weak points. Concretely, in ARE, the *archive* mechanism is employed to preserve good individuals for improving the performance, and the parent selection and the individual deletion are asynchronously executed to evolve individuals through a comparison of two parents with the *tertiary* parent randomly selected from the archive as a *reference* individual. This is called as a *reference-based evaluation* as a relative evaluation, which does not require any threshold like TAGP.

To investigate the effectiveness of ARE, this paper applies it to the Linear GP (LGP) [1, 2] problems and compares GP using ARE (ARE-GP) with GP using $(\mu + \lambda)$ selection ($(\mu + \lambda)$-GP) as the synchronous GP. Experiments simulate the following situations: (1) The computing speed of each individual differs from each other; and (2) some individuals do not complete (fail in) their evaluations.

This paper organized as follows. Section 2 introduces TAGP that is the base method of ARE and explains its problems. Section 3 proposes the novel asynchronous reference-based evaluation for asynchronous EAs. Section 4 shows the experimental settings and cases, and Section 5 shows the experimental results. The experiment is firstly conducted in situation where all individuals have the same evaluation time, and then, is conducted in situation where each individual has the different evaluation time and some individuals do not complete their evaluations. Section 6 discusses the experimental results, and finally, our conclusion is given in Section 7.

2. TIERRA-BASED ASYNCHRONOUS GENETIC PROGRAMMING

2.1 Overview

TAGP (Tierra-based Asynchronous Genetic Programming) [6] is one kind of machine-code GP employing the asynchronous approach. TAGP is based on the idea of a biological simulator, Tierra [11]. To apply Tierra to evolving programs that solves given tasks, TAGP introduces *fitness* into Tierra and executes the parent selection and the individual deletion mechanisms depending on fitness.

2.2 Algorithm

Fig 1 illustrates the image of TAGP, which simple flow is shown in Algorithm 1. In Algorithm 1, *ind* indicates an individual just after evaluation, $ind.f$ and $ind.f_{acc}$ indicate the fitness and an *accumulated* fitness of *ind* respectively, f_{max} indicates the maximum fitness, and N_p indicates the maximum population size. All individuals are stored in a queue named as *reaper queue*. Firstly, each individual is evaluated

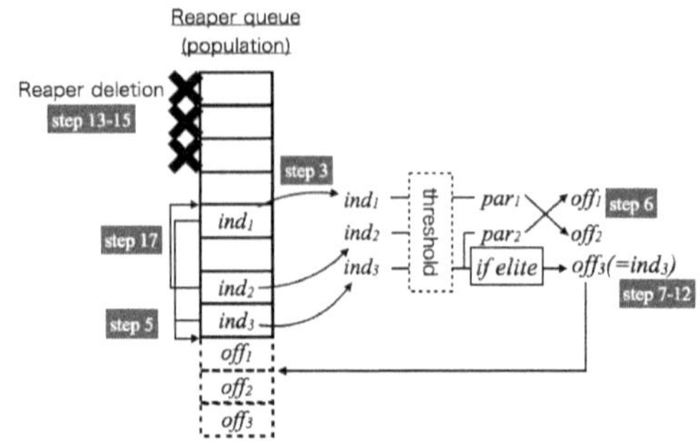

Figure 1: An illustration of TAGP

Algorithm 1 An algorithm of TAGP

```
1: Evaluating fitness of ind (ind.f)
2: ind.f_acc ← ind.f_acc + ind.f
3: if ind.f_acc ≥ f_max then
4:     ind.f_acc ← ind.f_acc − f_max
5:     Shifting the position of ind toward lower
6:     Generating offspring of ind
7:     if Population size>MAX_POP then
8:         Removing the individual at the top of the queue
9:     end if
10: else
11:     Shifting the position of ind toward upper
12: end if
```

in (pseudo-)parallel (step 1), and it accumulates its fitness to $ind.f_{acc}$, when its evaluation completes (step 2). Because of the use of the accumulated fitness, the fitness function is designed as the maximizing function. If its accumulated fitness exceeds a certain threshold (e.g., f_{max} in Algorithm 1), the threshold is subtracted from the accumulated fitness and it generates offspring (step 3-6). For example, if the accumulated fitness of ind_1 and ind_3 exceed the threshold (f_{max}), they generate offspring in the genetic operators as shown in Fig. 1. Depending on whether an individual can generate offspring or not, its position in the queue changes. If an individual generate offspring, its position in the queue shifts toward lower (step 5), otherwise its position shifts toward upper (step 11). For example, in Fig. 1, positions in the reaper queue of ind_1 and ind_3 that generate their offspring shift toward lower, while one of ind_2 that cannot generate offspring shifts toward upper. If the population size exceeds N_p, the individuals located at the top in the reaper queue are removed (step 7-9). For example, when three offspring are added as shown in Fig. 1, three individuals at the top of the reaper queue are removed.

The main feature of TAGP is summarized as follows: (1) Each individual in TAGP can be asynchronously evolved without waiting for other evaluation because the parents are selected to evolve their offspring only depending on their accumulated fitness, i.e., such parent selection is executed when the accumulated fitness of an individual exceeds a certain threshold; and (2) the reaper queue mechanism in TAGP can remove an individual that requires huge evaluation time or does not complete its evaluation (e.g., because of an infinite loop) *before* completing its evaluation.

3. ASYNCHRONOUS REFERENCE-BASED EVALUATION

This paper proposes a novel *asynchronous reference-based evaluation* (named as ARE) for an asynchronous EA, which not only inherits the advantages of TAGP but also overcomes the problems of TAGP. In this section, we firstly explain the main concept of ARE, and then we describe its algorithm.

3.1 Concept

The main concept of ARE is based on (1) the good individuals preservation (i.e., *archive*) and (2) the deletion of bad individuals with quick evaluation with the *relative* evaluation which does not require a threshold as an *absolute* evaluation like in TAGP. Regarding (1) the good individuals preservation, it is generally difficult to guarantee to preserve the good individual in a population due to an asynchronous manner, which means that good individuals are not always to be selected as parents for an evolution. In ARE, the *archive* mechanism is employed to preserve good individuals.

Regarding (2) the deletion of bad individuals with quick evaluation with the *relative* evaluation, what should be noted here is that, in the asynchronous evaluation, the individuals that quickly complete their evaluation preferentially get selection chance as parents regardless of its fitness. This causes to fill the population with offspring generated by such individuals, and it is easy to fall into local optimal through this kind of an evolution. To avoid such a situation, in ARE, all individuals are compared with the *tertiary* one that has already completed its evaluation with high fitness, which is named as *reference individual.* If they are worse than the reference individual, they are not selected as parents. This contributes to selecting the good individuals by excepting for bad individuals with quick evaluation. In ARE, an evaluation based on a comparison with a reference individual is called as *relative* evaluation, which does not require a threshold as an *absolute* evaluation. Concretely, the parent selection and the individual deletion are asynchronously executed to evolve individuals through a comparison of the offspring with the *reference* individual.

Finally, the main difference between ARE and TAGP is summarized as follows: (1) TAGP requires the accumulated fitness and the selection threshold, while ARE does not require these conditions, i.e., any fitness function in ARE can be employed like general EAs. This means that ARE can be applied to the problems where an optimal solution is unknown; and (2) ARE has the archive mechanism to guarantee to maintain the good individuals in the population, unlike TAGP does not have such mechanism. This mechanism also contributes to selecting better individuals for an evolution by excepting for bad individuals.

3.2 Algorithm

Fig. 2 illustrates the image of ARE, which flow is shown in Algorithm 2. In Algorithm 2, *ind* indicates an individual just after evaluation. All individuals are stored in either the reaper queue or the archive. As same as TAGP, in ARE, the individuals are evaluated in (pseudo-)parallel (step 1). The parent individuals are selected when two individuals complete their evaluations (here we call them *temporally selected individuals*). As a unique point of ARE, the parent selection is done by the tournament selection from the temporally selected individuals (T in Algorithm 2) and the reference individual (ind_{ref} in Algorithm 2) that randomly selected from the archive (step 4-5). This mechanism guarantees to mate with the individuals that have a high fitness in the genetic operators. After the parent selection, two offspring are generated from two selected parents (step 6), and they are added into the bottom of the reaper queue (step 7).

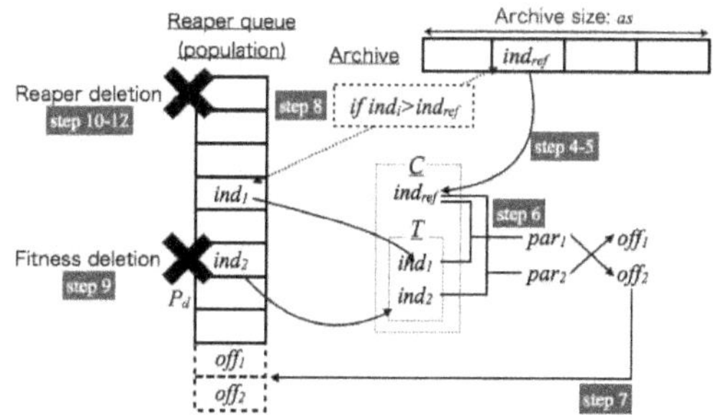

Figure 2: An illustration of ARE

Algorithm 2 An algorithm of ARE

1: Evaluating fitness of *ind* (*ind.f*)
2: $T \leftarrow ind$
3: **if** $|T| = 2$ **then**
4:   Randomly selecting ind_{ref} from archive
5:   $C \leftarrow T \cup \{ind_{ref}\}$
6:   Selecting two individuals from C and generating offspring
7:   Adding offspring into the bottom of the reaper queue
8:   Replacing ind_{ref} with an individual in T that is better than ind_{ref}
9:   Removing individuals in T from the population that is worse than ind_{ref} in the probability P_d
10:   **if** Population size>MAX_POP **then**
11:     Removing individuals depending on the reaper queue
12:   **end if**
13:   $T \leftarrow \phi$
14: **end if**

As the other unique point of ARE, the archive mechanism preserves good individuals, while the deletion mechanism keeps the number of the archive size. In order to determine the individuals that should be archived or should be deleted, the temporally selected individuals are compared with the reference individual. If one of the temporally selected individuals is better than the reference individual, it is archived and the reference individual change its position to the bottom of the reaper queue alternatively (step 8). To maintain the diversity of the individuals in the archive, if the better temporally selected individual already exists in the archive and the reference individual is unique in the archive, they are not replaced each other. For example, if ind_1 is better than ind_{ref}, ind_1 is archived and ind_{ref} is added to the bottom of the reaper queue as shown in Fig. 2. This mechanism guarantees to preserve the good individuals in the archive. On the other hand, if the temporally selected individuals are worse than the reference individual, they are removed from the reaper queue with a certain probability P_d (step 9). Afterward this deletion is called *fitness deletion*, and the probability P_d is called *fitness deletion probability*. For ex-

Table 1: Functions employed in symbolic regression problems

Ex. 1	$f(x) = x^4 + x^3 + x^2 + x$
Ex. 2	$f(x) = x^6 - 2x^4 + x^2$
Ex. 3	$f(x) = sin(x^2) \times cos(x) - 1$
Ex. 4	$f(x) = ln(x+1) + ln(x^2+1)$

ample, if ind_2 is worse than ind_{ref}, ind_2 is removed from the reaper queue with the probability P_d as shown in Fig 2.

If the temporally selected individuals are not removed and the population size exceeds the maximum population size, the reaper queue mechanism removes the individual located at the top of the reaper queue (step 10-11). Afterward this deletion is called *reaper deletion*. For example, when two offspring are added but only one individual (ind_2) is removed as shown in Fig. 2, one individual at the top of the reaper queue is additionally removed.

What should be noted here is that the fitness deletion probability P_d determines the ratio between the fitness deletion and the reaper one. Concretely, when P_d is high, the fitness deletion is increasingly executed, while the reaper deletion is decreasingly executed. On the other hand, when P_d is low, the fitness deletion is decreasingly executed, while the reaper deletion is increasingly executed. Since many individuals are removed before their evaluations completes if the reaper deletion increases, P_d can control how long the reaper deletion waits for the individuals that require long evaluation time.

4. EXPERIMENTS

4.1 Overview

To investigate the effectiveness of ARE, this paper applies ARE to Linear GP (LGP) [1, 2]. This experiment employs symbolic regression problem that is a general benchmark program in LGP, and employs four functions shown in Table 1 [10]. Eight instructions $\{+, -, \times, /, sin, cos, exp, ln\}$ and constant value $\{1, \cdots, 9\}$ can be used. Each program has eight registers (variables). The number of training data is 100 in all problems. The mean square error represented in Eq. (1) is used as the fitness function, where $\hat{y}$ and y^* respectively indicate the output of a program and the target value.

$$fitness = \frac{1}{n}\sum_{i=1}^{n}(\hat{y} - y^*)^2 \quad (1)$$

In this experiment, GP using (μ+λ) selection ((μ+λ)-GP) is employed as the synchronous GP because its evolution process can be easily parallelized.

4.2 Settings

The common parameter is shown in Table 2. In ARE-GP, the settings of the archive size $as = 5$ and the fitness deletion probability $P_d = 0.5$ are used. Each case executes 20 independent runs and the average of the minimum fitness in the population is evaluated.

4.3 Cases

This experiment simulates the situation where (**Case1**) all computing nodes have same speed, (**Case2**) the computing speed of each individual differs from each other, (**Case3**) some individuals do not complete (fail in) their evaluations in the parallel computation environment, and (**Case4**) both of Cases 2 and 3 occurs. These details are described below.

Table 2: Parameters

Maximum #instructions	256insts.
Population size	100
Crossover rate	0.7
Mutation rate	0.1
Insertion rate	0.1
Deletions rate	0.1
#executable instructions per unit time	100insts.

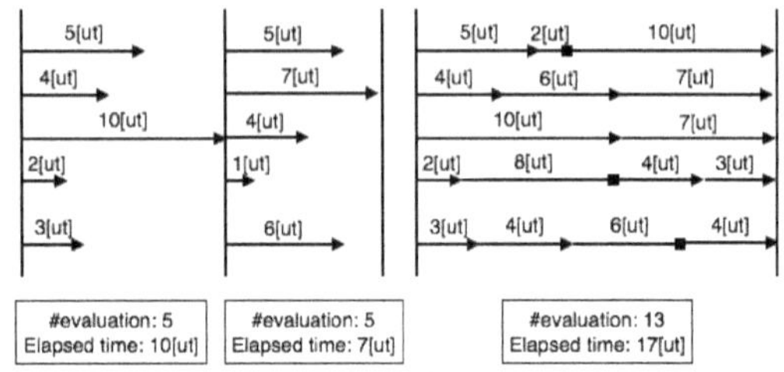

(a) Synchronous evolution (b) Asynchronous evolution

Figure 3: An image of elapsed time in this experiment (*ut*=unit time)

Case1: Same computing speed

In Case1, all individuals execute the same number of instructions (100 instructions) per unit time and can certainly complete their evaluation. Note that the number of executable instructions per unit time means how many instructions can be executed in one unit time. For example, when 100 instructions are executable per unit time and an individual (program) has 100 instructions, it can execute all 100 instructions in one unit time. Since the number of the training data is set as 100 in this experiment, this individual can complete its evaluation with 100 unit time. Since this experiment simulates the parallel evaluation of 100 individuals, ($\mu + \lambda$)-GP requires the maximum number of required unit time in a population in one generation (shown in Fig. 3(a)). While ARE-GP spends the parallel evaluation time including a termination of an evaluation due to the reaper deletion (shown in Fig. 3(b)).

Case2: Different computing speed

Unlike Case1 where all individual execute 100 instructions per unit time, in Case2, the number of executable instructions of each individual differs from each other as shown in Table 3. Concretely, 3, 3, 20, 43, and 31 individuals in 100 individuals respectively execute 20, 40, 60, 80, and 100 instructions per unit time. This setting is used in [8]. In this setting, the slowest individual requires five times longer evaluation time than the fastest one. Since the synchronous evolution needs to wait the slowest individual, five times longer evaluation time elapse in one generation cycle. This simulates the situation where each computer node has different computing speed.

Table 3: Difference of the number of executable instructions per unit time in Case2

#executable instruction	#individual
20	3
40	3
60	20
80	43
100	31

Case3: Evaluation failure

Unlike all individuals in Case1 complete their evaluations, some individuals in Case3 do not complete their evaluation with the certain probability of the evaluation failure P_f. This experiment set $P_f = 0.05$, in other words, 5% of the evaluations do not complete. Since the synchronous evolution requires all evaluation of individuals in a population at the same time, it needs to determine the execution time limitation to terminate the evaluation. This environment simulates the situation where evaluations of some individuals do not complete due to the communication error between computer notes or an infinite loop of a computer program.

In Case3, $(\mu+\lambda)$-GP cuts off the evaluation of an individual if its execution time exceeds the limitation (described in Section 5.3) and calculates its fitness as $-\infty$.

Case4: Both of Case2&3

In Case4, both situations of Case2 and Case3 occur. In particular, the number of executable instructions is set as shown in Table 3, while P_f is set as 0.05.

5. RESULTS

5.1 Case1: Same computing speed

Fig. 4 shows the change of the average fitness of ARE-GP and $(\mu + \lambda)$-GP from the viewpoint of the number of evaluations until 1.0×10^6 evaluations in Case1. In Fig. 4, the horizontal axis indicates the number of the evaluations, while the vertical axis indicates the average fitness of 20 independent runs. The solid line with circles shows the result of ARE-GP, while the dash line shows one of $(\mu + \lambda)$-GP. Fig. 4 indicates the ARE-GP requires the larger number of evaluations than $(\mu + \lambda)$-GP in the early term, while ARE-GP and $(\mu + \lambda)$-GP have the equivalent fitness value after the maximum number of evaluations.

On the other hand, Fig. 5 shows the change of the average fitness of ARE-GP and $(\mu + \lambda)$-GP from the viewpoint of the elapsed unit time until 1.0×10^7 unit time in Case1. In Fig. 5, the horizontal axis indicates the elapsed unit time, while the vertical axis indicates the average fitness of 20 independent runs. The solid line with circles shows the result of ARE-GP, while the dash line shows one of $(\mu + \lambda)$-GP. From the viewpoint of the elapsed unit time, ARE-GP outperforms $(\mu + \lambda)$-GP in all test problems regarding both of the convergence speed and the final fitness value. This is because $(\mu + \lambda)$-GP needs to wait the latest evaluation (i.e., the largest program in the population) to generate the next population, it causes to waste a lot of evaluation time, while ARE-GP can asynchronously generate a lot of offspring by efficient use of the evaluation time since ARE-GP needs not to wait for other evaluation of individuals.

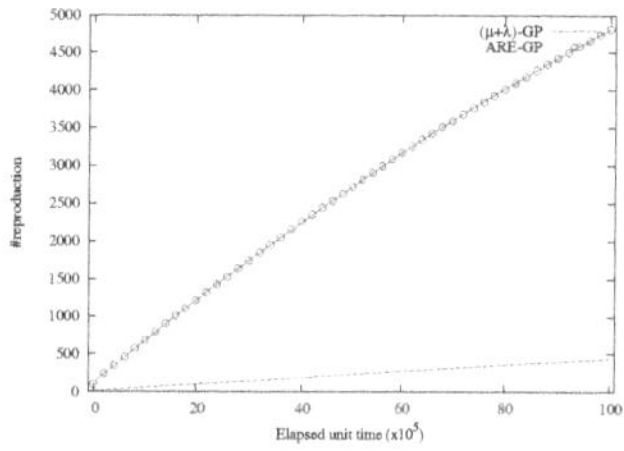

Figure 6: Case1 - Accumulated number of evaluations per unit time (Ex. 1)

Fig. 6 shows the accumulated number of generation of offspring in Ex. 1 in Case1. In Fig. 6, the horizontal axis indicates the elapsed unit time, while the vertical axis indicates the accumulated number of generation of offspring. The solid line with circles shows the result of ARE-GP, while the dash line shows one of $(\mu + \lambda)$-GP. Note that although Fig. 6 only shows the result of Ex. 1, we confirm same trend in other test problems. As shown in Fig. 6, ARE-GP can execute ten times generation of offspring than $(\mu + \lambda)$-GP. This indicates that ARE-GP can generate many offspring in one unit time, which contributes to improve its searching ability.

From these results, it is revealed that although ARE-GP is not better than $(\mu+\lambda)$-GP from the viewpoint of the number of evaluations, ARE-GP greatly outperforms $(\mu + \lambda)$-GP from the viewpoint of the elapsed unit time in the parallel computation environment.

5.2 Case2: Different computing speed

Fig. 7 shows the change of the average fitness of ARE-GP and $(\mu + \lambda)$-GP from the viewpoint of the elapsed unit time until 1.0×10^7 unit time in Case2. Axes and lines in Fig. 7 have the same meaning as Fig. 5. From the result of $(\mu + \lambda)$-GP, the convergence speed decreases from Case1 where all individuals have the same computing speed in all test problems. This is because $(\mu + \lambda)$-GP elapses five times longer unit time in one generation than Case1 since the synchronous evolution needs to wait the slowest evaluation that can execute only 20 instructions per unit time. In particular, in this experiment, a few slow computer nodes causes to waste many computer resources despite the number of the slowest computer notes is very few (only three nodes). On the other hand, ARE-GP achieves the equivalent convergence speed and the final fitness value as Case1 and outperforms $(\mu + \lambda)$-GP in all test problems.

These results reveal that ARE-GP can evolve individuals in the situation where the computing speed of each individual differs from each other without decreasing the searching ability.

5.3 Case3: Evaluation failure

Fig. 8 shows the change of the average fitness of ARE-GP and $(\mu + \lambda)$-GP from the viewpoint of the elapsed unit time until 1.0×10^7 unit time in Case3. Axes and lines in Fig. 8 have the same meaning as Fig. 5. In this case, since the maximum number of instructions, the number of executable instructions per unit time, and the number of training data is respectively set as 256 instructions, 100 instructions, 100, the ideal execution time limitation is 256 unit time. In all test problems, the execution time limitation is set as 256

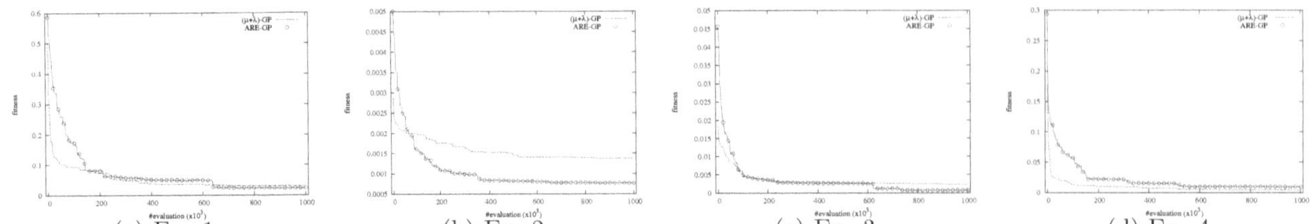

(a) Ex. 1 (b) Ex. 2 (c) Ex. 3 (d) Ex. 4

Figure 4: Case1 - Change of the average fitness from the viewpoint of the same number of evaluations

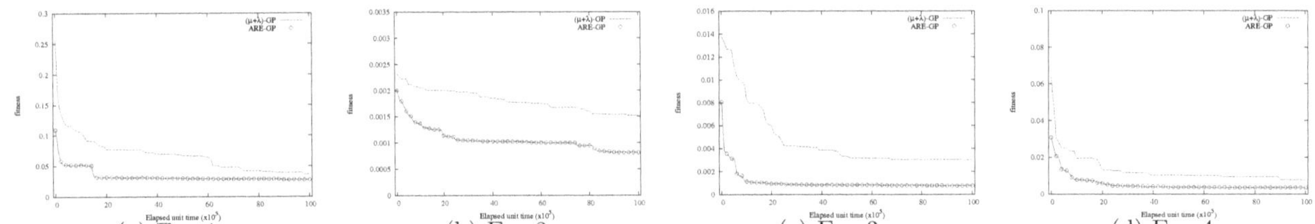

(a) Ex. 1 (b) Ex. 2 (c) Ex. 3 (d) Ex. 4

Figure 5: Case1 - Change of the average fitness from the viewpoint of the same elapsed unit time

and 2560 unit time, the former value is ideal while the latter one is 10 times larger than the ideal value, which result is additionally shown as the dotted line in Fig. 8.

The comparison of the different time limitation indicates that the searching ability of $(\mu+\lambda)$-GP decreases depending on the setting of the execution time limitation. From this result, it is verified that the setting of the execution time limitation affect to the searching ability of $(\mu+\lambda)$-GP. It is, however, difficult to determine the ideal time limitation because the properties of the solved problem are generally unknown, so that it is difficult to keep the searching ability of $(\mu+\lambda)$-GP in such situation. On the other hand, the results of ARE-GP indicate that it outperforms $(\mu+\lambda)$-GP with the ideal time limitation, and achieves the equivalent convergence speed and the final fitness value as Case1. What should be noted here is that ARE-GP can achieve this performance *without* the time limitation unlike $(\mu+\lambda)$-GP.

These results reveal that ARE-GP can evolve individuals in the situation where some individuals do not complete their execution and do not require the execution time limitation, which is required in the synchronous evolution.

5.4 Case4: Both of Case2&3

Fig. 9 shows the change of the average fitness of ARE-GP and $(\mu+\lambda)$-GP from the viewpoint of the elapsed unit time until 1.0×10^7 unit time in Case4 that includes the both situations of Case2 and Case3. Axes and lines in Fig. 9 have the same meaning as Fig. 5. In this case, since the slowest evaluation requires five times longer than the fastest one, the ideal value of the execution time limitation is 1280 ($= 256\times 5$) unit time, and $(\mu+\lambda)$-GP employs this limitation in all test problem.

In contrast to the convergence speed of $(\mu+\lambda)$-GP greatly decreases as same as the result of Case2 and Case3 in all test problems, ARE-GP achieves the equivalent convergence speed and the equivalent final fitness value as Case1.

These results reveal that ARE-GP can also evolve individuals in the situation where each individual has the different computing speed and some individuals do not complete their evaluation without decreasing the searching ability, unlike the searching ability of the synchronous evolution greatly decreases in such situation.

Table 4: The ratio of the elapsed unit time when ARE-GP achieves the average fitness that $(\mu+\lambda)$-GP finally achieves

	Ex. 1	Ex. 2	Ex. 3	Ex. 4
Case1	0.15	0.06	0.06	0.14
Case2	0.02	<0.01	0.04	0.10
Case3	0.06	0.01	0.11	0.36
Case4	0.03	0.02	0.01	0.02

6. DISCUSSION

ARE-GP can evolve individuals without any setting in the situation of the different evaluation time, and achieves efficient search and better performance than $(\mu+\lambda)$-GP. Table 4 shows the ratio of the elapsed unit time when ARE-GP achieves the average fitness that $(\mu+\lambda)$-GP finally achieves. Table 4 indicates that ARE-GP needs less than 10% elapsed time to achieve the equivalent performance as $(\mu+\lambda)$-GP. To check the statistically difference between ARE-GP and $(\mu+\lambda)$-GP, the non-parametric *Mann-Whitney U test* [9] is conducted with the level of significance $\alpha = 0.05$ regarding the fitness achieved after 10^7 unit time. Table 5 shows the p value in all cases and all test problems. This result reveals that the significant difference between ARE-GP and $(\mu+\lambda)$-GP is found in all cases and all test problems, which means ARE-GP significantly outperforms $(\mu+\lambda)$-GP.

As the interesting feature of ARE-GP, in some cases of the different evaluation time, the convergence speed and the final average fitness improve in the comparison with the situation of the same evaluation time. To confirm this insight, Figure 10 shows the change of the ratio that is calculated as $r(t) = f_{Case4}(t)/f_{Case1}(t)$, where $f_{Case1}(t)$ and $f_{Case4}(t)$ indicate the average fitness in Case1 and Case4 respectively when t unit time elapsed. This indicator explains whether

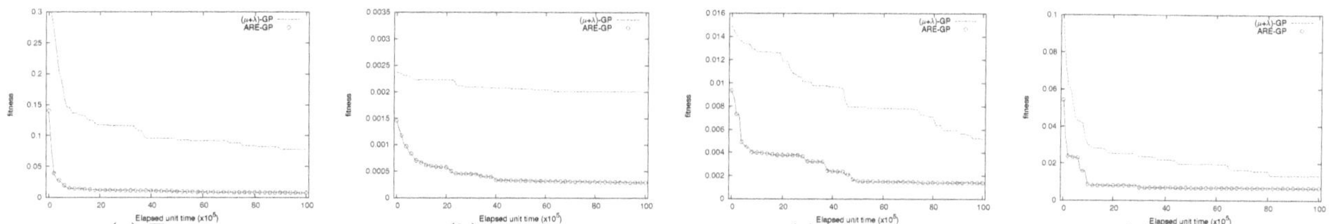

(a) Ex. 1 (b) Ex. 2 (c) Ex. 3 (d) Ex. 4

Figure 7: Case2 - Change of the average fitness from the viewpoint of the same elapsed unit time

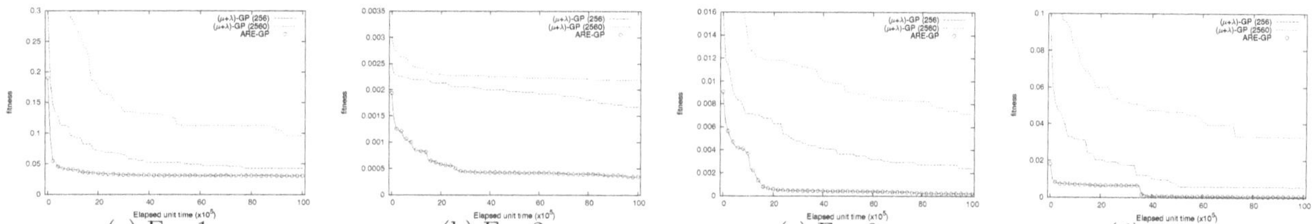

(a) Ex. 1 (b) Ex. 2 (c) Ex. 3 (d) Ex. 4

Figure 8: Case3 - Change of the average fitness from the viewpoint of the same elapsed unit time

Table 5: The p values given by the comparison of ARE-GP and $(\mu+\lambda)$-GP with the Mann-Whitney U test

	Ex. 1	Ex. 2	Ex. 3	Ex. 4
Case1	1.16×10^{-5}	1.11×10^{-2}	6.80×10^{-5}	1.31×10^{-3}
Case2	4.48×10^{-6}	4.20×10^{-6}	2.84×10^{-6}	8.24×10^{-4}
Case3	3.29×10^{-3}	7.01×10^{-6}	4.78×10^{-6}	2.49×10^{-6}
Case4	9.51×10^{-5}	4.18×10^{-7}	9.01×10^{-6}	2.63×10^{-4}

the fitness of Case1 is better (smaller) than Case4 at t unit time. If $r(t)$ is grater than 1, i.e., the results are plotted over the dotted line in Figure 10, the fitness of Case1 is smaller than one of Case4 at t unit time, in other words, Case1 outperforms Case4 at t unit time. While if $r(t)$ is less than 1, i.e., the results are plotted under the dotted line in Figure 10, the fitness of Case4 is smaller than one of Case1 at t unit time, in other words, Case4 outperforms Case1 at t unit time. In Figure 10, the horizontal axis indicates the elapsed unit time with the logarithmic scale, while the vertical axis indicates $r(t)$. The solid line shows with circles the result of ARE-GP, while the dash line shows one of $(\mu+\lambda)$-GP. As shown in Figure 10, the results of ARE-GP with the different evaluation time in Case4 outperforms one with the same evaluation time in Case1 in all problems but Ex. 3, while ARE-GP shows the same performance in these cases in Ex. 3. Unlike these results, $(\mu+\lambda)$-GP becomes worse with the different evaluation time in all problems. Since the required evaluation time in GP is determined depending on the size of a program and ARE-GP selects parents when an individual completes its evaluation, in the situation of the same evaluation time, the small size program can get a lot of chance of a parent selection. In contrast to this, due to the difference of the evaluation time, the selection turn in ARE-GP is not determined depending on the program size because the large program can get the selection chance if its evaluation time is shorter than others. It is considered that this contributes to increase the diversity of selected parents and to improve the searching ability.

7. CONCLUSIONS

This paper proposed Asynchronous Reference-based Evaluation (ARE) that is a novel asynchronous EA to evolve each individual independently, unlike the synchronous EAs requires the evaluations of all individuals at the same time. Concretely, ARE asynchronously evolve individuals through a comparison with only three of individuals (i.e., two parents and one *reference* individual as the tertiary parent) unlike a synchronous evolution through a comparison with all of them in general EAs, and ARE improves its performance by archiving good individuals as the *reference* individual. To investigate the effectiveness of ARE in the situation where the evaluation time of each individual differs from each other, ARE is applied to Linear GP (LGP) and is compared with GP using $(\mu+\lambda)$ selection ($(\mu+\lambda)$-GP). The experiments employs the symbolic regression problems which is well known benchmark problem in GP, and simulates the situation where (1) the computing speed of each individual differs from each other, and (2) some individuals do not complete their evaluations. The intensive experiments have revealed the following implications: (1) In the situation of the same evaluation time, although ARE-GP has slower convergence speed than $(\mu+\lambda)$-GP from the viewpoint of the number of evaluations, ARE-GP greatly outperforms $(\mu+\lambda)$-GP from the viewpoint of the elapsed unit time in the parallel computation environment; (2) ARE-GP can evolve individuals without decreasing the searching ability in the situation where the computing speed of each individual differs from each other and some individuals do not complete their execution without the execution time limitation, even in the situation including both of them; and (3) ARE-GP has probability to improve the search performance in the situation of the different evaluation time in comparison with the same evaluation time environment.

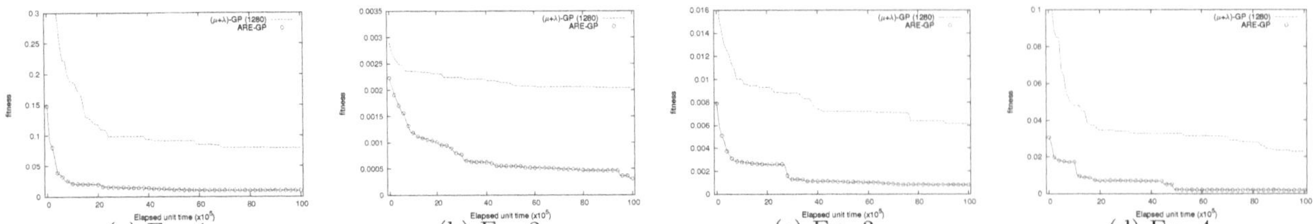

(a) Ex. 1 (b) Ex. 2 (c) Ex. 3 (d) Ex. 4

Figure 9: Case4 - Change of the average fitness from the viewpoint of the same elapsed unit time

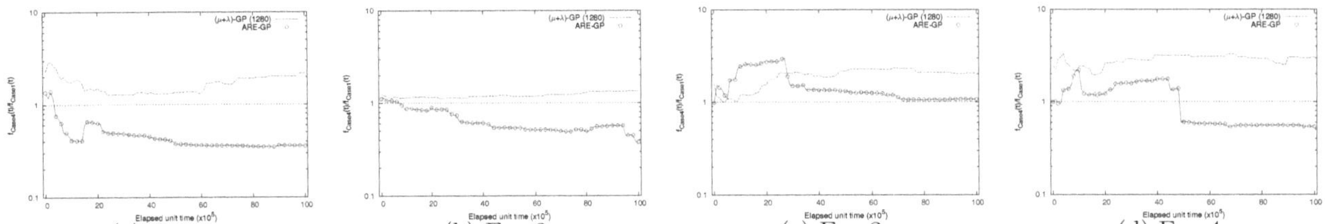

(a) Ex. 1 (b) Ex. 2 (c) Ex. 3 (d) Ex. 4

Figure 10: The change of the ratio between the fitness of Case1 and the one of Case4

What should be noticed here is that these implications have only been obtained from one type of problem, i.e., Linear GP. Therefore, further careful qualifications and justification, such as an analysis of results using other general LGP problems such as symbolic regression or classification problem, are needed to extend the range of application of ARE to other EA domain. Such important directions must be pursued in the near future in addition to the following future research: (1) a verification of the validity of ARE on the actual parallel computing environment because some overheads are considered in the actual environment; and (2) an adaptation of the fitness deletion rate P_d and the archive size depending on the evolution degree or the diversity of the population because these parameters gives a big influence to the performance of ARE.

8. ACKNOWLEDGMENTS

This work was supported by Grant-in-Aid for JSPS Fellows Grant Number 249376.

9. REFERENCES

[1] W. Banzhaf, F. D. Francone, R. E. Keller, and P. Nordin. *Genetic programming: an introduction: on the automatic evolution of computer programs and its applications.* Morgan Kaufmann Publishers Inc., San Francisco, CA, USA, 1998.

[2] M. F. Brameier and W. Banzhaf. *Linear Genetic Programming.* Springer, 2007.

[3] J.-F. Chang, S.-C. Chu, J. F. Roddick, and J.-S. Pan. A parallel particle swarm optimization algorithm with communication strategies. *Journal of Information Science and Engineering*, pages 809–818, 2005.

[4] T. Glasmachers. A natural evolution strategy with asynchronous strategy updates. In *Proceeding of the fifteenth annual conference on Genetic and evolutionary computation conference*, GECCO '13, pages 431–438, New York, NY, USA, 2013. ACM.

[5] D. E. Goldberg. *Genetic Algorithms in Search, Optimization and Machine Learning.* Addison-Wesley Longman Publishing Co., Inc., Boston, MA, USA, 1 edition, 1989.

[6] T. Harada and K. Takadama. Asynchronous evaluation based genetic programming: Comparison of asynchronous and synchronous evaluation and its analysis. In K. Krawiec, A. Moraglio, T. Hu, A. Etaner-Uyar, and B. Hu, editors, *Genetic Programming*, volume 7831 of *Lecture Notes in Computer Science*, pages 241–252. Springer Berlin Heidelberg, 2013.

[7] J. Koza. *Genetic Programming On the Programming of Computers by Means of Natural Selection.* MIT Press, 1992.

[8] A. Lewis, S. Mostaghim, and I. Scriven. Asynchronous multi-objective optimisation in unreliable distributed environments. In A. Lewis, S. Mostaghim, and M. Randall, editors, *Biologically-Inspired Optimisation Methods*, volume 210 of *Studies in Computational Intelligence*, pages 51–78. Springer Berlin Heidelberg, 2009.

[9] H. B. Mann and D. R. Whitney. On a test of whether one of two random variables is stochastically larger than the other. *The Annals of Mathematical Statistics*, 18(1):50–60, 03 1947.

[10] J. McDermott, D. R. White, S. Luke, L. Manzoni, M. Castelli, L. Vanneschi, W. Jaskowski, K. Krawiec, R. Harper, K. A. D. Jong, and U.-M. O'Reilly. Genetic Programming Needs Better Benchmarks. In *GECCO*, pages 791–798, 2012.

[11] T. S. Ray. An approach to the synthesis of life. *Artificial Life II*, XI:371–408, 1991.

[12] D. Tasoulis, N. Pavlidis, V. Plagianakos, and M. Vrahatis. Parallel differential evolution. In *Evolutionary Computation, 2004. CEC2004. Congress on*, volume 2, pages 2023 – 2029 Vol.2, june 2004.

Word Count as a Traditional Programming Benchmark Problem for Genetic Programming

Thomas Helmuth
Computer Science
University of Massachusetts
Amherst, MA 01003
thelmuth@cs.umass.edu

Lee Spector
Cognitive Science
Hampshire College
Amherst, MA 01002
lspector@hampshire.edu

ABSTRACT

The Unix utility program wc, which stands for "word count," takes any number of files and prints the number of newlines, words, and characters in each of the files. We show that genetic programming can find programs that replicate the core functionality of the wc utility, and propose this problem as a "traditional programming" benchmark for genetic programming systems. This "wc problem" features key elements of programming tasks that often confront human programmers, including requirements for multiple data types, a large instruction set, control flow, and multiple outputs. Furthermore, it mimics the behavior of a real-world utility program, showing that genetic programming can automatically synthesize programs with general utility. We suggest statistical procedures that should be used to compare performances of different systems on traditional programming problems such as the wc problem, and present the results of a short experiment using the problem. Finally, we give a short analysis of evolved solution programs, showing how they make use of traditional programming concepts.

Categories and Subject Descriptors

I.2.2 [**Artificial Intelligence**]: Automatic Programming—*Program synthesis*

Keywords

genetic programming; traditional programming; PushGP; benchmark; lexicase selection

1. INTRODUCTION

The Unix utility wc is a command that prints the newline, word, and character counts in one or more specified files[1]. For each given file, wc's first output counts the newlines in the file, which can be as low as zero if all characters are on the same line. Its second output gives the number of words in the file, defined as contiguous runs of non-whitespace characters separated by whitespace characters (spaces, tabs, and newlines). Its third output gives the number of characters in the file.

We would like to investigate automatic program synthesis techniques such as genetic programming (GP), in particular their ability to solve traditional programming problems such as replicating the the behavior of the wc utility. Automatically synthesizing a wc program presents a variety of challenges tackled routinely by software programmers but not handled well by most GP systems. In this paper we will present the wc problem as a challenging but solvable GP problem, for which programs that duplicate the wc utility can be synthesized without knowledge beyond a data set of desired behavior tests consisting of example input/output pairs.

The GP community has recently discussed the need for better benchmarks [5, 18]. These discussions provide recommended benchmarks for some problem domains, but not for traditional programming problems (which they call "algorithmic programming" problems), despite the traditional programming category receiving the second most votes in a community survey asking what types of problems a GP benchmark suite should contain [18]. Traditional programming problems mimic the programming of human programmers, requiring multiple data types, control flow, and a large instruction set. Automating human programming tasks has long been a goal of GP, as articulated in Koza's first book [4] for example. The absence of traditional programming problems among current recommended benchmarks is unfortunate and should be addressed.

The wc problem can be used as a traditional programming benchmark problem with many desirable qualities. Since this problem requires one to find a program that performs a task available as a Unix utility command, it shows that GP can be used to solve a useful problem. The wc problem is solvable yet non-trivial using GP, which we will show with an experiment. Relative to currently existing program synthesis technology, it strikes a good compromise between difficulty and the ability to perform many runs quickly; we were able to perform 200 GP runs per condition in a reasonable amount time using a small cluster. The problem is open source, representation independent, and easily implemented; we have done so in the PushGP system, which is available for free[2]. This paper provides a precise definition of the wc problem, including recommendations for computational resources, instruction sets, and training and test data. We

[1]See, e.g. `http://www.linuxmanpages.com/man1/wc.1.php`

[2]`https://github.com/lspector/Clojush`

GECCO'14, July 12–16, 2014, Vancouver, BC, Canada.

ACM 978-1-4503-2662-9/14/07 ...$15.00.
http://dx.doi.org/10.1145/2576768.2598230.

also make recommendations for comparing the performance of different systems on this problem.

In the next Section we describe the PushGP genetic programming system, which we used to conduct the experiments described in Section 5. Following this we give a detailed description of the proposed wc benchmark problem, including the data set and instruction set we recommend. Section 4 discusses performance measures and statistical procedures appropriate for comparing GP systems on the wc problem. We then present our experimental results and conclusions.

2. PUSH AND PUSHGP

The experiments described in Section 5 use the PushGP genetic programming system, which evolves programs in the Push programming language. Push was designed specifically for use in GP systems as the language in which evolving programs are expressed [11, 17, 15]. Push is a stack-based programming language similar in some ways to others that have been used for GP (e.g. [8]). Although any general purpose GP system could be applied to the wc problem, Push provides many tools important for traditional programming problems, such as multiple types, control flow, and the ability to return multiple outputs. We chose to use PushGP in our experiments because of its ease of use for traditional programming problems; much of PushGP was designed with this type of problem in mind. The experiments we present in Section 5 are simply an example of using the wc benchmark; since they are not the focus of the paper, the choice of the GP system has little bearing on our analysis of the benchmark and will not be discussed further.

Push is a postfix, stack-based programming language. Interpreted Push programs push literals onto data stacks, and instructions act on stack data, returning their results to stacks. A separate stack is used for each data type; instructions take their arguments (if any) from stacks of the appropriate types and leave their results (if any) on stacks of the appropriate types. This use of multiple stacks allows instructions and literals to be freely intermixed regardless of type while still ensuring type safety. Instructions that find insufficient data on the relevant stacks act as "no-ops"—that is, they do nothing.

"Code" is itself a Push data type, and Push programs can easily (and often do) manipulate their own code as they run; this permits the expression of complex and novel control structures. The execution of a Push program is interpreted on the exec stack, and instructions that manipulate the exec stack can change the program itself as it runs. Various exec stack instructions allow for the concise expression of iteration, recursion, and conditional statements. Blocks of code can be hierarchically structured with parentheses, allowing exec-stack-manipulating instructions to affect larger chunks of code.

Push and PushGP implementations now exist in Clojure, Java, C++, JavaScript, Python, Ruby, Scheme, Common Lisp, and Scala. Many of these are available for free download from the Push project page[3].

3. WC PROBLEM

We wish to automatically create a program that replicates the functionality of the wc utility using a general-purpose program synthesis system that has not been tailored to this specific problem. We would like our program synthesis system to create such a program based entirely on examples of the desired input/output behavior. The evolved program should take a file as input and should output three integers representing the number of newlines, words, and characters in the file. An evolved solution should produce the correct results for any file between 0 and 100 characters in length; we chose 100 characters as a maximum length to ensure reasonable execution times when evaluating programs.

Our requirements for a successful program differ slightly from the full functionality of the wc utility command. In particular, the wc command prints the outputs, where we just require the program to use output instructions to return the results. Additionally, the wc command can take multiple file inputs and print the output for each, along with summed totals across the files. Of course, a human programmer could take an evolved solution to the wc problem and use it as the core functionality of a program to perfectly replicate the full wc command. This would only require a loop over the input files which calls the evolved program and formats the results. If a fully evolved wc command was desired, we could likely evolve the iteration and printing part of the utility separately, which would use the evolved newline, word, and character counting function (presented as the primary objective here) as a subroutine. A reasonable avenue of future work could use this extension to show how complete software can be evolved based on high-level descriptions of the modularity of the software and behavioral examples for each module.

A GP problem is defined primarily by the labeled data set it uses to evaluate evolved programs and the instructions used in random code generation. The following section defines the data set to be used with the wc problem, and Section 3.2 presents the instructions we recommend for the wc problem.

3.1 Data set

The goal of the wc problem is to find a program that correctly outputs the number of newlines, words, and characters in any given file containing 100 characters or fewer. We chose to limit the available characters to non-whitespace ASCII characters (i.e. those with decimal values between 33 and 126) along with newline, space, and tab. In order to guide GP toward a solution program, we require a set of labeled training data. Additionally, we would like a set of labeled test data that the GP algorithm never sees in order to test the generality of evolved solutions.

From a set of file inputs we can produce the labeled data by running an existing word count function on each file and storing integers representing the numbers of newlines, words, and characters in the file. In our GP runs, we produce three error values (newlines, words, characters) for each test case, each the absolute difference between the expected output and the output of the program. These three errors could be combined into a single error per test case, but we keep them separate since some parent selection mechanisms treat errors across test cases differently. Since we can create correct outputs given an input, our task is reduced to deciding which files to use as training and test inputs.

The number of files containing 100 or fewer of the allowed characters far outnumbers the number of files we can use as training and test data. We must therefore either provide

[3] `http://hampshire.edu/lspector/push.html`

Table 1: Data domains for the wc problem.

Type	Train	Test
Random string	200	500
Random string ending in newline	20	50
Edge cases (see Table 2)	22	0

a data set of prescribed files or a method of creating randomly generated files as data. We use a combined method, holding some data constant across every run while randomly generating other data.

In order to facilitate this creation of training and test data for the wc problem and other traditional programming problems, we designed a general system for automatic data generation based on data domains. A "data domain" D is a set of program inputs described by either a list of inputs or a random input generator function. The sets {"hi", "hello", "howdy", "hey"} and $\{s | \text{"}zoo\text{" is a substring of } s; \text{len}(s) <= 100]\}$ are examples of data domains, where the former is an enumerated set of four inputs and the latter is a large set containing all strings of length less than or equal to 100 that contain the substring "zoo". Along with each data domain D, the user must provide the integers $train(D)$ and $test(D)$ that indicate the number of training and test cases respectively to generate from D.

To generate training and test data from a set of data domains $\{D_1, D_2, ..., D_n\}$, we simply take each domain and create the required number of cases. If the domain D_i is an enumerated list of inputs, we select $train(D_i)$ and $test(D_i)$ of them at random, without replacement within the training cases or test cases. If the domain is described by a random input generator, we run it $train(D_i)$ and $test(D_i)$ times (with replacement) to create the data. This automatic data generation system allows for the generation of training and test cases for a wide range of problems.

Table 1 summarizes the data domains we recommend for the wc problem. The first data domain, from which we draw the most training and test cases, creates random strings between 0 and 100 characters long. This random string generator first chooses a random size uniformly from the range $[0, 100]$ inclusive. It then creates a string of random characters, biasing each character selection to choose a space 35% of the time, newline 10% of the time, tab 5% of the time, and any other character 50% of the time. This bias, although somewhat arbitrary, seems to result in a good variety of whitespace and non-whitespace characters to cover a range of inputs. This random string generator has a higher percent of newlines and tabs compared to English text and program language code; still, it empirically does a good job of covering many interesting types of files.

The second data domain in Table 1 uses a random string generator identical to the first data domain, except that it ensures that the last character in the string is a newline. In our initial exploration of this problem, we did not always require some data cases that end in a newline. In those runs, we noticed that a number of evolved solution programs did not generalize to file inputs ending in newlines, so we added a relatively small set of them to ensure evolution sees this type of input.

Although the randomly generated strings created by the first two data domains usually cover a wide range of inputs, they often omit specific edge cases. Exploratory GP runs evaluated on random inputs often resulted in solutions that did not generalize, particularly to very small inputs and inputs with many newlines or words. Our third data domain in Table 1, expanded in Table 2, addresses this issue by ensuring that every run includes a set of training cases that covers these problem edge cases. The first 11 of these inputs represent short files containing limited characters. The last 11 edge cases are long strings that have 100 characters each, and include files with many more lines and words than most randomly generated inputs. The inclusion of these edge cases in the training data seems to improve our system's ability to evolve general solutions.

Table 2: This table contains the 22 edge case training cases used in our wc problem runs. Each case attempts to cover a possibly tricky input that may not be exemplified in the random string inputs. Here \n represents a newline, \t represents a tab, and ␣ represents a space.

1	""
2	"A"
3	"␣"
4	"\t"
5	"\n"
6	"5"
7	"#"
8	"A\n"
9	"␣\n"
10	"\t\n"
11	"\n\n"
12	"\n" repeated, 100 characters
13	"␣" repeated, 100 characters
14	"\t" repeated, 100 characters
15	"A" repeated, 100 characters
16	"\nA" repeated, 100 characters
17	"\n\nB" repeated, 100 characters
18	"CD\n" repeated, 100 characters
19	"E␣" repeated, 100 characters
20	"F\t" repeated, 100 characters
21	"x\ny␣" repeated, 100 characters
22	"␣\n" repeated, 100 characters

Overall, we recommend the use of 242 training cases and 550 withheld test cases. These numbers seem to strike a reasonable balance between providing enough training data to guide evolution toward a general solution while not requiring the evaluation of evolving programs on an unreasonable number of training cases.

Note that GP practitioners need not use every training case during every program evaluation; they may choose to use a subset of the training cases for some or all evaluations. Some recent GP techniques such as co-evolved fitness predictors [9, 10] and spatial co-evolution [2] require fewer training cases per evaluation. Others may wish to use fewer training cases in order to lessen the number of program evaluations required, possibly increasing the performance of GP compared to the number of evaluations. In any case, the training cases used for evaluation should be taken exclusively from the training data set, which should remain static throughout the GP run even if its subset used for evaluation does not. Also, practitioners using fewer evaluations per program must take care when reporting results, as we discuss in Section 4. Finally, no matter what subset of the training set is used for evaluating programs, the entire training and test sets should be used to verify the generalization of evolved solutions.

3.2 Instruction Set

Traditional programming problems require much larger and more diverse instruction sets than many other problems solved by GP. As such, we do not want to specify a particular instruction set that should be used for the wc problem, but instead give some guidelines as well as the instruction set we use in our experiments. This allows others to compare results using different representations and instruction sets.

Most typical instructions from programming languages, whether designed for GP or general purpose programming, are allowable. This list could include control flow instructions for looping or conditionals, functional instructions such as mapping and filtering, or string manipulation instructions. We encourage researchers working on the wc problem to use their best judgment when choosing instruction sets, noting only that one should obviously not include instructions that have been tailored specifically to this problem. To give an extreme example, instructions that return the newline count, word count, or character count in a file would immediately solve most of the problem and should obviously be avoided.

The wc problem, unlike many problems in GP, requires programs to read input from files. The input instructions should give the evolving programs enough power to solve the task without making it trivial. They should also be reasonably similar to input instructions in modern high-level programming languages. For example, providing a `file_readword` instruction that reads the file until the next whitespace character seems inappropriately powerful, especially considering such an instruction does not exist in most programming languages. We also elected to omit an instruction that reads the entire file, since it seems to provide too much power when combined with other string manipulation instructions, although an argument could be made for its inclusion.

Table 3 gives the Push instructions we include in our instruction set. The "Input" row gives the file input instructions. The `file_readchar` and `file_readline` instructions read a single character and a single line from the file respectively, keeping track of the location in the file. They both do nothing if the end of the file has been reached. These instructions are similar to those found in many higher-level languages. The `file_EOF` instruction pushes true onto the Boolean stack if the end of the file has been reached, and false otherwise. Finally, `file_begin` moves the file "cursor" to the beginning of the file. In our implementation, the input instructions actually just manipulate and read sections of a string instead of an actual file, but we could easily change those instructions so that an evolved program actually reads a file from the disk.

The wc problem requires programs to output three integers, one each for the character count, word count, and newline count. One approach, which we employ, is to use output instructions that store a return value. It is less clear what the best approach is for a fully functional language, whose programs traditionally only produce one value. Our three output instructions in the second row of Table 3 each take the top value on the integer stack and store it in a variable, which is later used as the output at the end of execution. If an output instruction is called multiple times during the execution of a program, each execution overwrites the previous, meaning that the value stored during the final execution is the one given as output.

Table 3: Push instructions included in our instruction set.

Input	`file_readchar, file_readline, file_-EOF, file_begin`
Output	`output_charcount, output_wordcount, output_linecount`
Exec	`exec_pop, exec_swap, exec_rot, exec_dup, exec_yank, exec_yankdup, exec_shove, exec_eq, exec_stack-depth, exec_when, exec_if, exec_-do*times, exec_do*count, exec_-do*range, exec_y, exec_k, exec_s`
Tag ERCs	`tag_exec, tag_integer, tag_string, tagged`
String	`string_split, string_parse_to_chars, string_whitespace, string_contained, string_reverse, string_concat, string_take, string_pop, string_-eq, string_stackdepth, string_rot, string_yank, string_swap, string_-yankdup, string_flush, string_-length, string_shove, string_dup`
Integer	`integer_add, integer_swap, integer_-yank, integer_dup, integer_yankdup, integer_shove, integer_mult, inte-ger_div, integer_max, integer_sub, integer_mod, integer_rot, integer_-min, integer_inc, integer_dec`
Boolean	`boolean_swap, boolean_and, boolean_-not, boolean_or, boolean_frominte-ger, boolean_stackdepth, boolean_dup`
ERC	Integer from [-100, 100] {"\n", "\t", "␣" } $\{x \mid x$ is a non-whitespace character$\}$

The exec instructions given in the third row of Table 3 provide the ability to define and execute arbitrary control structures within a Push program, and make the language Turing-complete. Each of these instructions manipulates the top of the exec stack, thus changing what instruction will be executed next. The first nine exec instructions simply allow for normal stack manipulations. `exec_when` and `exec_if` provide conditional execution of the following parenthesized block(s) of code. The next three instructions provide explicit looping. Finally, the last three instructions are combinators that allow for recursion (see [15]).

Tagging provides for another method for manipulating control flow in Push [16]. The `tag_exec`, `tag_integer`, and `tag_string` ERCs (ephemeral random constants) create instructions, each of which has a name that specifies an associated integer tag. For example, the instruction `tag_string_-392` specifies the tag 392. Each instruction created by one of these ERCs takes the top item from the indicated stack and tags it with the associated tag. For example, `tag_-string_392` takes a string from the string stack and tags it with 392. The `tagged` ERC creates instructions that retrieve tagged items by closest tag match[4] and push the retrieved items onto the exec stack. For example, after tagging a string with 392, the instruction `tagged_344` would push the tagged string onto the exec stack, assuming no other data had been tagged with a tag between 344 and 392. Since tagging instructions can tag code from the exec stack, tags can be used to create subroutines that become available to the rest of the program. The inexact matching used in tag-based retrieval allows the number of tags used in programs to grow incrementally over evolutionary time [13].

The wc problem obviously requires significant string manipulation to count newlines, words, and characters in files. The string stack instructions in Table 3 provide diverse string manipulations without making the problem trivial. The instruction `string_split` takes a string argument and splits it on whitespace characters, returning the results to the string stack. `string_parse_to_chars` takes a string and pushes each individual character string onto the string stack. `string_whitespace` returns the boolean true if the string argument consists entirely of whitespace characters, and false otherwise. The remaining string instructions consist of standard string manipulation instructions and stack instructions.

The integer and boolean instructions we provide in our instruction set are all normal stack manipulation instructions or integer/boolean operators. Integer instructions are necessary, since the outputs for the problem are integers from the integer stack. The exec stack instructions that allow for conditional expressions rely on the boolean stack for their arguments.

We provide three ERCs that create random constants during random code generation. The first creates integers in the range $[-100, 100]$. The second randomly selects a single whitespace character string: newline, tab, or space. The third creates a string with a single non-whitespace character.

4. WC PERFORMANCE MEASURES

The primary goal of a benchmark problem is to compare the characteristics, in particular performance, of different methods or algorithms on problems with similar traits to actual applications of those methods. As such, we must determine how to measure the performance of GP systems on the wc problem.

The most frequently used performance metrics in GP papers include success rate, computational effort, and mean best fitness. Success rate measures the percent of runs performed that find a successful program (sometimes called an "ideal solution"). Computational effort extends success rate to estimate the number of program evaluations necessary to find a successful program with high probability [4]. The best fitness of a run is simply the best fitness achieved by a program during the run; the mean best fitness of a set of runs is the mean of the best fitnesses found in the runs.

Recent discussions of benchmarks in GP have criticized the use of success rate and computational effort, instead recommending either best fitness of run or testing with a withheld generalization data set [5, 18]. The main criticisms cited are that success rate and computational effort "measure how well a method solves trivial problems" and that they have "poor accuracy and statistical invalidity" [5]. Although we agree that computational effort may be statistically problematic, we believe that for the wc problem and many other traditional programming problems success rate remains the best method for measuring performance, especially when used in conjunction with a withheld test set.

The goal of the wc problem is to find a program that *perfectly* counts the numbers of newlines, words, and characters in a file. If a GP system finds a program that returns the correct outputs except for when the input file contains the character `Q`, it is of little importance even if it otherwise achieves good fitness. In essence, no one cares about incremental improvements in discovered programs unless one is found that perfectly passes all of the training cases. Therefore, when measuring performance of a GP system on the wc problem, best fitness contributes little useful information.

The success rate of a set of GP runs gives more information than best fitness about how well the system performs on the wc problem, since it measures how often the system finds perfect programs. We do agree that programs that achieve perfection on the training data should be tested on withheld generalization data, which we describe for the wc problem in Section 3.1. A program should only count as a successful program if it achieves zero error on both the training data and the test data. The success rates we report only include programs that have perfect error on the training and test data, although we also note the numbers of programs that achieve perfect error on the training data only.

We argue more generally that the ability to solve a traditional programming benchmark problem perfectly does not indicate the triviality of the problem. If our goal is to someday have GP evolve complex software that performs important functionality without having to be coded by humans, we would hope that such a system would pass all of its tests before going into use. The purpose of traditional programming benchmark problems is to compare the performances of GP methods on traditional programming problems; as such, we would expect GP to be able to solve them in order to have a hope of solving real programming problems. Although the wc problem is simpler than almost all software systems of real value, it is useful enough to be included as a Unix utility, and offers more interesting requirements than other suggested traditional programming problems such as list sorting.

4.1 Computational Budget

When comparing success rates of different GP methods, one must be careful to ensure each method receives similar amounts of computation. Using CPU time or wall time as a proxy for computational requirements has many flaws, including differing greatly for the same computation based on the machine used, the machine's load, and the optimization of the GP system. Instead, since program evaluations often dominate the runtime of GP algorithms, most comparisons in the literature use a unit related to program evaluation to measure the computation used by the system. The computational effort measurement tries to take this into account by taking the population size and generation of found solutions into account, but we would like to avoid using computational effort. Another approach prescribes a budget of some sort to limit the computation of the GP system. Options for computation budgets offered by the community survey in [18] include, in increasing level of granularity: number of

[4]The closest match for a reference to tag t_{ref}, among all tags t_{val} that have been used to tag values, is the tag t_{val} for which $t_{val} - t_{ref}$ is minimal if at least some $t_{val} \geq t_{ref}$, or maximal if all $t_{val} < t_{ref}$ [13].

generations, number of program fitness evaluations, number of fitness case evaluations (i.e. number of times any program is executed), and number of node evaluations.

Using the number of generations as the computational budget is equivalent to using the number of program fitness evaluations if the population size is also prescribed, except that it does not allow for testing varying population sizes. The number of program fitness evaluations provides a good level of control, assuming that each GP system tests every fitness case during every program evaluation. But, as mentioned in Section 3.1, some recent GP techniques require a small subset of the fitness cases be used during each program evaluation [9, 2]. These techniques would be at a disadvantage if they must adhere to numbers of program evaluations equivalent to techniques that use every fitness case during evaluation. In fact, both of these papers report results relative to the number of fitness case evaluations in order to make the comparisons fair. The number of node evaluations seems too fine of a measurement that could vary largely based on the GP system and how high-level the language is in which programs evolve. This method may be more accurate than using number of fitness case evaluations when using a single GP system with the same instruction set, but likely includes too much variation when comparing different GP systems.

Of these options, we recommend using a maximum budget based on the number of fitness case evaluations to limit the computation of the compared GP methods. This method allows for flexibility in many areas of algorithm design while ensuring systems receive similar computation. For the wc problem, we use the 242 training cases given in Section 3.1 for every program evaluation. We use a maximum of 300 generations with a population size of 1000, giving us at most 72,600,000 fitness case evaluations per run. To produce results that could be compared against those provided here, we recommend using a similar limit.

4.2 Statistical Procedure

In order to determine the statistical significance and reliability of the difference in success rates found by different GP methods, we recommend the use of both Fisher's exact test and confidence intervals of the difference in success rates.

Fisher's exact test tests the null hypothesis that there is no association between two compared methods and their number of successes. This test returns a p-value, which can indicate a rejection of the null hypothesis if it is below a prespecified significance level, usually 0.05. This test behaves similarly to the chi-squared test, except that it is much more accurate when the number of successes or failures for either of the compared methods is near zero; if the number of successes and failures for each method is sufficiently large, the chi-squared test is also acceptable.

There has recently been increasing criticism of null hypothesis significance testing in the sciences, for example [1], which instead recommends the use of confidence intervals to indicate the reliability and precision of results. To supplement Fisher's exact test, we recommend reporting the difference in success rates along with a confidence interval of the difference. If each method produces at least 10 successes and failures, the large-sample confidence interval for comparing two proportions can be used. Otherwise, Moore and McCabe recommend the use of the plus four confidence interval for comparing two proportions, by adding one success and one failure to the observed results for each method [7]. This correction is effective as long as there are at least 5 runs from each method.

Table 4: PushGP parameters used in our experiment.

Parameter	Value
Runs Per Condition	200
Fitness Evaluations Budget	72,600,000
Population Size	1000
Max Generations	300
Max Program Size	1000
Max Initial Program Size	400
Max Node Evaluations	2000
Genetic Operator	ULTRA (100%)
ULTRA Mutation Rate	0.01
ULTRA Alternation Rate	0.01
ULTRA Alignment Deviation	10

5. EXPERIMENTAL RESULTS

We would like to show that the wc problem can be solved within the constraints we've recommended, without being too easy. We designed a simple experiment using PushGP comparing two parent selection methods, primarily to show the utility of the wc problem as a benchmark. The source code for our experiment is available freely online[5]. In this experiment, we will compare traditional tournament parent selection, with tournament size 7, to a recent selection algorithm called lexicase selection [12].

When lexicase selection is used, parent selection is not based on the total error of individuals aggregated over fitness cases, as it is in tournament selection and most other traditional parent selection methods, but rather case-by-case errors considered in random order. To select a parent, the lexicase selection procedure first randomly shuffles the fitness cases and creates a pool of candidate parents that initially includes the entire population. It then removes from the pool any individuals that do not have the best error in the pool on the first fitness case in the random ordering. Assuming more than one candidate for selection survives, this process is iterated with the second fitness case, and so on, until either a single individual remains or all fitness cases have been used (in which case a random remaining candidate is selected).

Lexicase selection tends to select individuals that are very good on a subset of the fitness cases, even if they perform poorly on other fitness cases. Recent results suggest that this selection pressure allows GP to find perfect solutions to difficult problems more often than tournament selection [3], suggesting an experiment that investigates its performance on the wc problem.

Table 4 presents the PushGP parameters used in our experiment. We allow a maximum of 72,600,000 fitness evaluations, as we recommend when using the wc problem as a benchmark. In all runs we used ULTRA ("Uniform Linear Transformation with Repair and Alternation") as the only genetic operator [14]. ULTRA takes two parents and creates one child by applying uniform crossover and mutation operations. In this study we use a variation of ULTRA that does not allow mutation to add or remove parentheses, al-

[5]`http://thelmuth.github.io/GECCO_2014_WC_Materials/`

Table 5: This 2 x 2 table presents the numbers of successes and failures for 200 PushGP runs using either tournament selection with size 7 tournaments or lexicase selection. A program is counted as a success if it achieves zero error on the training data as well as the withheld test data.

Selection Method	Successes	Failures	Success Rate
Tournament	0	200	0
Lexicase	11	189	0.055

though parentheses may nonetheless be added or removed via ULTRA's crossover and repair steps.

Table 5 presents the results from our runs comparing tournament selection and lexicase selection. The runs using tournament selection found no programs that achieved perfect error on the training data. Runs using lexicase selection found 17 programs that achieved perfect error on the training data, 11 of which were also perfect on the withheld test data. Based on this data, Fisher's exact test gives a p-value of 0.001, so we can reject the null hypothesis at the 0.05 significance level that there is no association between the selection method used and the number of successes. The difference in success rate between these methods is 0.055, with a 95% confidence interval of $[0.020, 0.088]$. This confidence interval uses the plus four estimate of the difference in proportions, since, as described in Section 4.2, the large-sample confidence interval does not apply because tournament selection resulted in zero successes.

For our experiment, Fisher's exact test tells us that there is likely an association between the selection method and the number of successes in our runs. The confidence interval for the difference in success rate between lexicase selection and tournament selection shows it is likely that the difference is small but meaningful. We interpret these results to mean that lexicase selection improves PushGP's ability to find solutions to the wc problem over tournament selection. We further find it important that PushGP found zero solutions when using tournament selection, showing that the system seems to need selection pressure different from what tournament selection provides to solve the wc problem, at least given our other parameters. This also shows that the wc problem is challenging, making it more interesting that PushGP was able to solve it using lexicase selection

Why can lexicase selection find solutions while tournament selection fails? We believe that the main difference lies in the ways in which these selection algorithms focus attention on certain characteristics of errors across fitness cases. Tournament selection aims to select individuals with the lowest total error across all fitness cases, and will therefore rarely select an individual with the lowest error in the population on many fitness cases but a few very bad errors. Instead, it will often select individuals with many mediocre-to-good errors. For problems like wc where the goal is an individual with zero error, we think that often an individual that does really well on many cases but poorly on others is in some sense closer in the evolutionary space to a perfect solution than an individual with better total error but not as many elite fitness cases. Lexicase selection may be taking advantage of this effect by selecting individuals that are very good on the fitness cases that randomly appear at the start of the shuffled fitness case list. It appears that this selection pressure helps GP to find solutions on the wc problem, and it seems reasonable to hypothesize that it will also help to solve other traditional programming problems in which it is necessary to perform perfectly on every fitness case. The selection pressure given by lexicase selection is in some ways related to that given by implicit fitness sharing [6], though unlike implicit fitness sharing it gives advantages to individuals that are good at combinations of cases rather than single cases; this suggests a comparison of the two as a future avenue of study.

We also analyzed the 11 evolved successful programs to see if they make good use of traditional programming techniques. We first simplified each program to remove instructions that had no effect on its outputs, and then counted the occurrences of types of instructions remaining in the simplified programs[6]. We found moderate uses of iteration and recursion in some of the programs, although others seemed to use brute force looping by repeating the same instruction many times sequentially. Conditional statements were also used occasionally, although not as frequently as we had expected. Tagging instructions occurred very infrequently, meaning that our programs did not use tags to implement subroutine-like modularity. Every program made use of strings, integers, and booleans; some programs also used string and integer literals, with `"\n"` appearing most often. Every solution used multiple outputs, as required by the problem definition. Overall evolution made decent use of PushGP's available traditional programming techniques, but success rates may be raised by improving GP's ability to evolve solutions that use iteration, conditional constructs, and modular subroutines.

6. CONCLUSIONS AND FUTURE WORK

This paper introduces wc as a traditional programming benchmark problem for genetic programming systems. Our demonstrations show that genetic programming can indeed solve this problem, and that it provides a sufficiently difficult and useful benchmark in the context of current technology. We also give guidance to researchers who wish to use wc as a benchmark in future work, with respect to both experimental design (e.g. instruction sets) and performance analysis.

We conducted experiments using PushGP comparing two parent selection algorithms, tournament selection and lexicase selection, in order to assess the relative strengths of these algorithms on the task of automatically synthesizing wc programs. The results clearly favored lexicase selection, which is itself an interesting finding, but the larger point is that the wc problem is a suitable traditional programming problem for conducting such experiments.

The most obvious direction for future work is to attempt to solve the wc problem, as described here, with other genetic programming systems using comparable computational resources. Analysis of the relative performance of different genetic programming systems on this problem may help us to advance the state of the art for applying genetic programming to traditional programming problems.

Another direction for future work is to consider other common UNIX utilities as possible traditional programming problem targets for genetic programming. Many such util-

[6]The simplified Push source code of the 11 successful evolved programs is available online: `http://thelmuth.github.io/GECCO_2014_WC_Materials/`

ities will probably be beyond the reach of current genetic programming techniques, but work on such problems may bring us closer to achieving the long-term goal of using genetic programming to automate programming tasks usually undertaken by human programmers. Additionally, the full wc command, including the handling of multiple input files and the printing of results, could be evolved in pieces as described in Section 3. This method of human-guided evolution of software seems like an avenue for evolving entire complex software systems.

The wc problem provides a starting place for traditional programing benchmarks for genetic programming. We would like to see the inclusion of the wc problem and other traditional programming problems in recommended genetic programming benchmark suites. Benchmark problems provide more information when techniques are compared on multiple problems. Such benchmark suites may be composed of problems from different classes in order to test general genetic programming systems, or entirely composed of traditional programming problems to test systems more specifically aimed at traditional program synthesis.

7. ACKNOWLEDGMENTS

Thanks to the members of the Hampshire College Computational Intelligence Lab, Yuriy Brun, and David Jensen for discussions that helped to improve the work described in this paper, to Josiah Erikson for systems support, and to Hampshire College for support for the Hampshire College Institute for Computational Intelligence. This material is based upon work supported by the National Science Foundation under Grants No. 1017817 and 1129139. Any opinions, findings, and conclusions or recommendations expressed in this publication are those of the authors and do not necessarily reflect the views of the National Science Foundation.

8. REFERENCES

[1] G. Cumming. The new statistics: Why and how. *Psychological Science*, 25(1):7–29, 2014.

[2] R. Harper. Spatial co-evolution: quicker, fitter and less bloated. In *GECCO '12: Proceedings of the fourteenth international conference on Genetic and evolutionary computation conference*, pages 759–766, Philadelphia, Pennsylvania, USA, 7-11 July 2012. ACM.

[3] T. Helmuth and L. Spector. Evolving a digital multiplier with the pushgp genetic programming system. In *GECCO '13 Companion: Proceeding of the fifteenth annual conference companion on Genetic and evolutionary computation conference companion*, pages 1627–1634, Amsterdam, The Netherlands, 6-10 July 2013. ACM.

[4] J. R. Koza. *Genetic Programming: On the Programming of Computers by Means of Natural Selection.* MIT Press, Cambridge, MA, USA, 1992.

[5] J. McDermott, D. R. White, S. Luke, L. Manzoni, M. Castelli, L. Vanneschi, W. Jaskowski, K. Krawiec, R. Harper, K. De Jong, and U.-M. O'Reilly. Genetic programming needs better benchmarks. In *GECCO '12: Proceedings of the fourteenth international conference on Genetic and evolutionary computation conference*, pages 791–798, Philadelphia, Pennsylvania, USA, 7-11 July 2012. ACM.

[6] R. I. B. McKay. Fitness sharing in genetic programming. In *Proceedings of the Genetic and Evolutionary Computation Conference (GECCO-2000)*, pages 435–442, Las Vegas, Nevada, USA, 10-12 July 2000. Morgan Kaufmann.

[7] D. Moore, G. McCabe, and B. Craig. *Introduction to the Practice of Statistics.* W.H. Freeman, 2009.

[8] T. Perkis. Stack-based genetic programming. In *Proceedings of the 1994 IEEE World Congress on Computational Intelligence*, volume 1, pages 148–153, Orlando, Florida, USA, 27-29 June 1994. IEEE Press.

[9] M. D. Schmidt and H. Lipson. Co-evolving fitness predictors for accelerating and reducing evaluations. In *Genetic Programming Theory and Practice IV*, volume 5 of *Genetic and Evolutionary Computation*, pages 113–130. Springer, Ann Arbor, 11-13 May 2006.

[10] M. D. Schmidt and H. Lipson. Coevolution of fitness predictors. *IEEE Transactions on Evolutionary Computation*, 12(6):736–749, Dec. 2008.

[11] L. Spector. Autoconstructive evolution: Push, pushGP, and pushpop. In *Proceedings of the Genetic and Evolutionary Computation Conference (GECCO-2001)*, pages 137–146, San Francisco, California, USA, 7-11 July 2001. Morgan Kaufmann.

[12] L. Spector. Assessment of problem modality by differential performance of lexicase selection in genetic programming: a preliminary report. In *1st workshop on Understanding Problems (GECCO-UP)*, pages 401–408, Philadelphia, Pennsylvania, USA, 7-11 July 2012. ACM.

[13] L. Spector, K. Harrington, B. Martin, and T. Helmuth. What's in an evolved name? the evolution of modularity via tag-based reference. In *Genetic Programming Theory and Practice IX*, Genetic and Evolutionary Computation, pages 1–16. Springer, Ann Arbor, USA, 12-14 May 2011.

[14] L. Spector and T. Helmuth. Uniform linear transformation with repair and alternation in genetic programming. In *Genetic Programming Theory and Practice XI*, Genetic and Evolutionary Computation. Springer, Ann Arbor, USA, 2013.

[15] L. Spector, J. Klein, and M. Keijzer. The push3 execution stack and the evolution of control. In *GECCO 2005: Proceedings of the 2005 conference on Genetic and evolutionary computation*, pages 1689–1696, Washington DC, USA, 2005. ACM Press.

[16] L. Spector, B. Martin, K. Harrington, and T. Helmuth. Tag-based modules in genetic programming. In *GECCO '11: Proceedings of the 13th annual conference on Genetic and evolutionary computation*, pages 1419–1426, Dublin, Ireland, 12-16 July 2011. ACM.

[17] L. Spector and A. Robinson. Genetic programming and autoconstructive evolution with the push programming language. *Genetic Programming and Evolvable Machines*, 3(1):7–40, Mar. 2002.

[18] D. R. White, J. Mcdermott, M. Castelli, L. Manzoni, B. W. Goldman, G. Kronberger, W. Jaśkowski, U.-M. O'Reilly, and S. Luke. Better GP benchmarks: community survey results and proposals. *Genetic Programming and Evolvable Machines*, 14(1):3–29, Mar. 2013.

Evolving "Less-myopic" Scheduling Rules for Dynamic Job Shop Scheduling with Genetic Programming

Rachel Hunt
School of Mathematics, Statistics and Operations Research
Victoria University of Wellington
PO Box 600
Wellington, New Zealand
Rachel.Hunt@msor.vuw.ac.nz

Mark Johnston
School of Mathematics, Statistics and Operations Research
Victoria University of Wellington
PO Box 600
Wellington, New Zealand
Mark.Johnston@msor.vuw.ac.nz

Mengjie Zhang
School of Engineering and Computer Science
Victoria University of Wellington
PO Box 600
Wellington, New Zealand
Mengjie.Zhang@ecs.vuw.ac.nz

ABSTRACT

Job Shop Scheduling (JSS) is a complex real-world problem aiming to optimise a measure of delivery speed or customer satisfaction by determining a schedule for processing jobs on machines. A major disadvantage of using a dispatching rule (DR) approach to solving JSS problems is their lack of a global perspective of the current and potential future state of the shop. We investigate a genetic programming based hyper-heuristic (GPHH) approach to develop "less-myopic" DRs for dynamic JSS. Results show that in the dynamic ten machine job shop, incorporating features of the state of the wider shop, and the stage of a job's journey through the shop, improves the mean performance, and decreases the standard deviation of performance of the best evolved rules.

Categories and Subject Descriptors

I.2.8 [**Artificial Intelligence**]: Problem Solving—*Scheduling*

Keywords

Genetic Programming, Scheduling, Hyper-heuristics

1. INTRODUCTION

Job shop scheduling (JSS) is a common and difficult scheduling problem. Scheduling is a decision making process which deals with the allocation of resources over time, in order to complete a number of tasks, subject to given constraints and optimising one or more objectives [9]. Scheduling is important in manufacturing and service industries [23]. JSS involves determining a schedule for processing jobs on machines to optimise some measure of delivery speed or customer satisfaction. Each job consists of a sequence of one or more operations in a specified processing order, and each operation has a specified processing time on a certain machine [3]. The development of more effective scheduling methods could significantly decrease costs and increase throughput, increasing profitability in the many job shops world-wide [13]. JSS problems have been widely studied in the academic literature over the past 50 years [9, 24], due in part to their real-world applicability combined with the computational challenge of creating a schedule in such environments (JSS is *NP*-hard [3]).

The majority of current research into JSS lies at two extremes: a global approach through optimisation methods where an entire schedule is constructed and, at the other extreme, local approaches using dispatching rules. A dispatching rule (DR) is a mathematical function of the attributes of queued jobs, machines and the shop. The DR calculates a priority value for each job awaiting processing at a given machine and the job with the highest priority value is scheduled next on the machine [7]. DRs are probably the most commonly used heuristics for solving JSS problems in practice. This is because of the ease with which they can be implemented, their low time complexity, easy interpretability by shop floor (human) operators, and the ability to cope with dynamic environments [3].

However, a major disadvantage of dispatching rules is a lack of a global perspective [4]. Dispatching rules are generally myopic (short-sighted) and only take into account the local and current conditions [1, 7], i.e., rules look at one machine and the queue of jobs awaiting processing at that machine at that moment in time. Decisions are made at machines independently, without considering the flow of jobs from one machine to another, and the negative impact a decision might have on these subsequent machines in the future [22].

A "less-myopic", i.e., less short-sighted, approach to scheduling would take into account the current state of more than just one machine and its queue ("less-myopic" in *space*), or more than just the current state of the job, e.g., it could also include an approximation of a priority value for the next operation, and corresponding machine, in its specified processing order ("less-myopic" in *time*).

GECCO'14, July 12–16, 2014, Vancouver, BC, Canada.

ACM 978-1-4503-2662-9/14/07 ...$15.00.
http://dx.doi.org/10.1145/2576768.2598224.

Gere [8] proposed several heuristics which were used in conjunction with priority rules. One heuristic, the "look ahead" heuristic, checks if there is a critical job due to reach the machine at a future time, but before the scheduled job is finished processing. If there is such a critical job this can replace the scheduled job. Results showed that combining look-ahead heuristics which consider the future state of the shop with dispatching rules improved schedules significantly.

There has been recent research into using genetic programming (GP) to evolve DRs for JSS problems [11, 12, 17, 19, 20, 21, 18, 25]. However rules evolved by most approaches still lack a global perspective as the features of the jobs, machines and the shop used are mainly limited to the current state of the current machine and its queue. A schedule is *non-delay* if a machine cannot be idle while there is an operation awaiting processing [23]. Dispatching rules generally create non-delay schedules. Some works [18, 10] incorporate "look-ahead" in which a machine is notified that a job will be arriving once it is finished its current operation. When the jobs in the queue at the machine are evaluated, if the job which has not yet arrived has the highest priority then the machine is able to enforce idle time, and wait for the job to arrive.

Nguyen et al. [18] develop the GP method to learn iterative dispatching rules (IDRs) for static JSS problem. IDRs are functions of not only the properties of a machine and the job queued there, but also of the recorded properties of the schedule obtained previously. This allows the IDR to potentially correct mistakes that have been made in previous iterations. The evolved IDRs perform better than benchmark DRs. Evaluation may take longer in the proposed GP method than existing GP. A look-ahead strategy component was also investigated, and results showed it to "play a very important role to enhance the performance of IDRs and the proposed method can effectively evolve suitable look-ahead strategies to deal with specific JSS problems." Look-ahead allows consideration of active or hybrid schedules, not only non-delay schedules.

Hildebrant et al. [10] developed dispatching rules for the dynamic ten machine job shop, with the minimise mean flow time objective. They used two less-myopic terminals in their GP terminal set. These were the processing time of the next operation in the job, and work in next queue (WINQ). WINQ estimates the waiting time before the job could begin processing on the next machine using the sum of the processing times of jobs waiting in the queue already. They compared the approach of changing the problem instances used for the simulations at each generation throughout evolution with using the same problem instances at every generation throughout evolution. Their results suggested that changing the problem instances at every generation gives the most improved performance. The results with the look-ahead incorporated had a high variance. In some runs only "rather bad" solutions were found, yet the best performing rule outperformed the best found without using look-ahead.

The challenge we are addressing is to find "local, decentralized rules which result in a good global performance of a given complex manufacturing system" [4]. We consider using a genetic programming based hyper-heuristic (GPHH) approach to developing less-myopic scheduling rules. In a ten machine job shop we will incorporate features from the wider shop system, to see if the rules evolved that are less-myopic give improved performance. We want to find robust DRs which perform well in job shops where jobs have different properties so we will compare training with problem instances where all jobs have four operations, and training with problem instances where all jobs have eight operations to see which provides the better environment for DRs with good generalisation. The overall goal of this paper is to develop less-myopic scheduling rules through a GPHH approach.

The rest of this paper is organised as follows: Section 2 gives a background of JSS, GPHH and existing work using GPHH for JSS; Section 3 explains the proposed approach; Section 4 presents the results; and Section 5 presents the conclusions and suggests future work.

2. BACKGROUND

2.1 Job Shop Scheduling Problem

In this paper we focus on the ten machine dynamic job shop. In a dynamic job shop, jobs arrive according to a stochastic process, and no information is known about a job until its arrival into the shop.

Let N_j be the number of operations of job j; $\sigma_{j,i}$ be the ith operation of job j; O_j be the sequence of operations of job j; $p(\sigma)$ be the processing time of operation σ; $m(\sigma)$ be the machine required to process operation σ; w_j be the weight of job j; d_j be the due date of job j; and r_j be the release date (arrival time) of job j. Then let C_j be the completion time of job j and T_j be the tardiness of job j, i.e., $T_j = \max\{0, C_j - d_j\}$.

Each job j arrives at time r_j with a set of N_j operations ($N_j \in \{1, \ldots, n\}$), $O_j = (\sigma_{j,1}, \ldots, \sigma_{j,N_j})$, in a predefined route. Upon a job's arrival into the shop it joins the queue at the first machine on its route, $m(\sigma_{j,1})$. A DR or scheduling rule is used to select the next job to be processed from among those waiting in the queue using various properties of the job, machine and shop. Once an operation σ has completed its processing time $p(\sigma)$ on a machine it is moved to the next machine on its route, or if the entire job is completed then it is delivered to the customer. We do not allow recirculation, i.e., a job cannot have multiple operations which require the same machine.

There are many different objectives that can be optimised in JSS. In this paper we are interested in minimising the total weighted tardiness,

$$TWT = \sum w_j T_j. \tag{1}$$

There are many existing DRs for dynamic JSS in the literature, including the following popular DRs. *First In First Out (FIFO)* processes jobs in the order that they arrive at the machine. *Weighted Shortest Processing Time (WSPT)* orders jobs by increasing weighted processing time at the machine [7], i.e., the job that has the maximum weighted shortest processing time, $w_j/p(\sigma)$, is processed next. The minimum slack of job j is defined by $MS_j = d_j - \sum_{l=h}^{N_j} p(\sigma_{j,l}) - t$ where t is the ready time R_m of the machine, i.e., the time that the scheduling decision must be made and the next job dispatched. In the *Minimum Slack (MS)* rule the job with the minimum slack is processed next. *Cost over Time (COVERT)* [2] and *Apparent Tardiness Cost (ATC)* [26] are two other DRs for dynamic JSS.

2.2 Genetic Programming based Hyper-heuristics for JSS

Hyper-heuristics are "automated methodologies for selecting or generating heuristics to solve hard computational search problems" [5]. Hyper-heuristics search the search space of heuristics (rather than searching the solution space directly), with an aim to increase the robustness of search methods [6].

The suitability of genetic programming as a hyper-heuristic was explored by Burke et al. [6]. The advantages offered include variable length encoding (GP tree depth is allowed to vary between minimum and maximum depths), and an executable data structure as output of a GP run. Humans are also able to identify the problem domain, search space, and potential terminal and function sets. There are also disadvantages to using GP for hyper-heuristic evolution. Multiple GP runs are needed to establish what quality of heuristics the approach can produce, as each GP run may give a different best-of-run heuristic. Another issue with GP is the large number of parameter values which must be selected.

There have been various applications of GPHH to JSS. Jakobović and Marasović [12] used priority functions evolved through GP within a meta-algorithm for a given environment to form a scheduling heuristic. The meta-algorithm was designed manually. Results showed that the evolved heuristics performed comparably or better than human-made heuristics for given environments. Miyashita [17] compared three approaches to evolving rules for JSS: a homogeneous agent model, where every machine uses the same rule evolved by a single GP process; a distinct agent model, where every machine learns a distinct rule; and a mixed agent model, where a bottleneck agent and a non-bottleneck agent learn rules. A bottleneck is a resource with high demand from many operations. A set of benchmark problems with five machines and ten jobs (of five operations each), and one or two bottleneck machines was used. The mixed agent model is limited in that it requires the bottleneck machines to be identified a priori. Results show that the mixed agent model learnt good heuristics quicker than the distinct agent model, and outperformed both the homogeneous and distinct agent models as well as well-known DRs. Tay and Ho [25] used GP to evolve composite dispatching rules (heuristic combinations of single existing dispatching rules) for the multi-objective flexible job shop problem with the aim of greater scalability and flexibility. Results showed that the evolved rules outperformed single dispatching rules and composite dispatching rules from the literature.

3. PROPOSED METHOD

We implement a GPHH system using ECJ20 [15] for evolving DRs; this is a heuristic generation approach. The fitness of a DR (individual) in the current GP population is evaluated using discrete-event simulations of problem scenarios of a job shop. The objective of interest to be minimised, TWT, is calculated for each problem instance, and the average over all problem scenarios used is the fitness of the DR. The best DR evolved is then tested on independent test problem scenarios.

We randomly create problem scenarios with ten machines. The processing times for machines follow a discrete uniform distribution with mean μ. In each problem instance, jobs arrive stochastically according to a Poisson process with rate λ. Equation (2) is used to set λ so that the machines have a desired expected utilisation (ρ),

$$\lambda = \frac{\rho \times p_M}{(1/\mu)}, \tag{2}$$

where p_M is the proportion of jobs that need to be processed at machine M. For example, with ten machines, if each job has two operations, $\lambda = \rho/(1/\mu) \times (2/10)$. Due dates are set using Equation (3),

$$d_j = r_j + h \times \sum_{l=1}^{N_j} p(\sigma_{j,l}), \tag{3}$$

where h is a due date tightness parameter, randomly chosen from the choices available for each job. Jobs are given weight 1, 2 or 4, with probability (0.2, 0.6, 0.2) [19]. A warm up period of 500 jobs is used, and we collect data from the next 2000 jobs to arrive ($N = 2000$), however new jobs keep arriving in the system until the 2500th job is completed. The two configurations used for training, and the four used for testing are shown in Table 1. In training we use either four operations in every job (4op training), or eight operations in every job (8op training). Two training scenarios are used for evaluation at each generation of evolution, T1 and T2. The average TWT from these is used as the fitness for the individual. In testing we also vary the number of operations in each job, using each configuration for a scenario where the number of operations is 4, 6, 8, 10, and where the number of operations in each job varies randomly between 2 and 10 (with equal probability). This gives 20 test scenarios.

Table 1: Simulation properties for training and testing.

		μ	ρ	h
Training	T1	25	0.85	{3,5,7}
	T2	25	0.95	{3,5,7}
Testing	P1	25	0.90	{2,4,6}
	P2	50	0.90	{2,4,6}
	P3	25	0.97	{2,4,6}
	P4	50	0.97	{2,4,6}

Genetic Programming System.

All terminals used are shown in Table 2. `RJ` is the release time of the job, or the time its last completed operation finished. The wider looking properties, `NPR`, `NNQ` and `NQW` all return zero if the job does not have an operation after the current operation. If less than five jobs have visited a machine, then `NQW` and `AQW` return the average wait time of the jobs which have visited. We will consider GP using two different feature sets. NGP consists of the terminals listed under job properties and machine properties only in Table 2. The second, LMGP, uses a feature set consisting of all the features in Table 2. By including `NNQ` and `NQW` the DR has access to the same information about the next machine the job visits (if there is one) as it does about the machine it is currently at. Including `AQW`, a rule is able to approximate the total time a job has remaining in the system.

The function set is {+, −, ∗, %, `if>0`, `max`, `min`}. The arithmetic operators take two arguments. The first three arithmetic operators, +, − and ∗, have their usual meanings. The % operator is protected division, returning zero if dividing by zero. The `if>0` function takes three arguments;

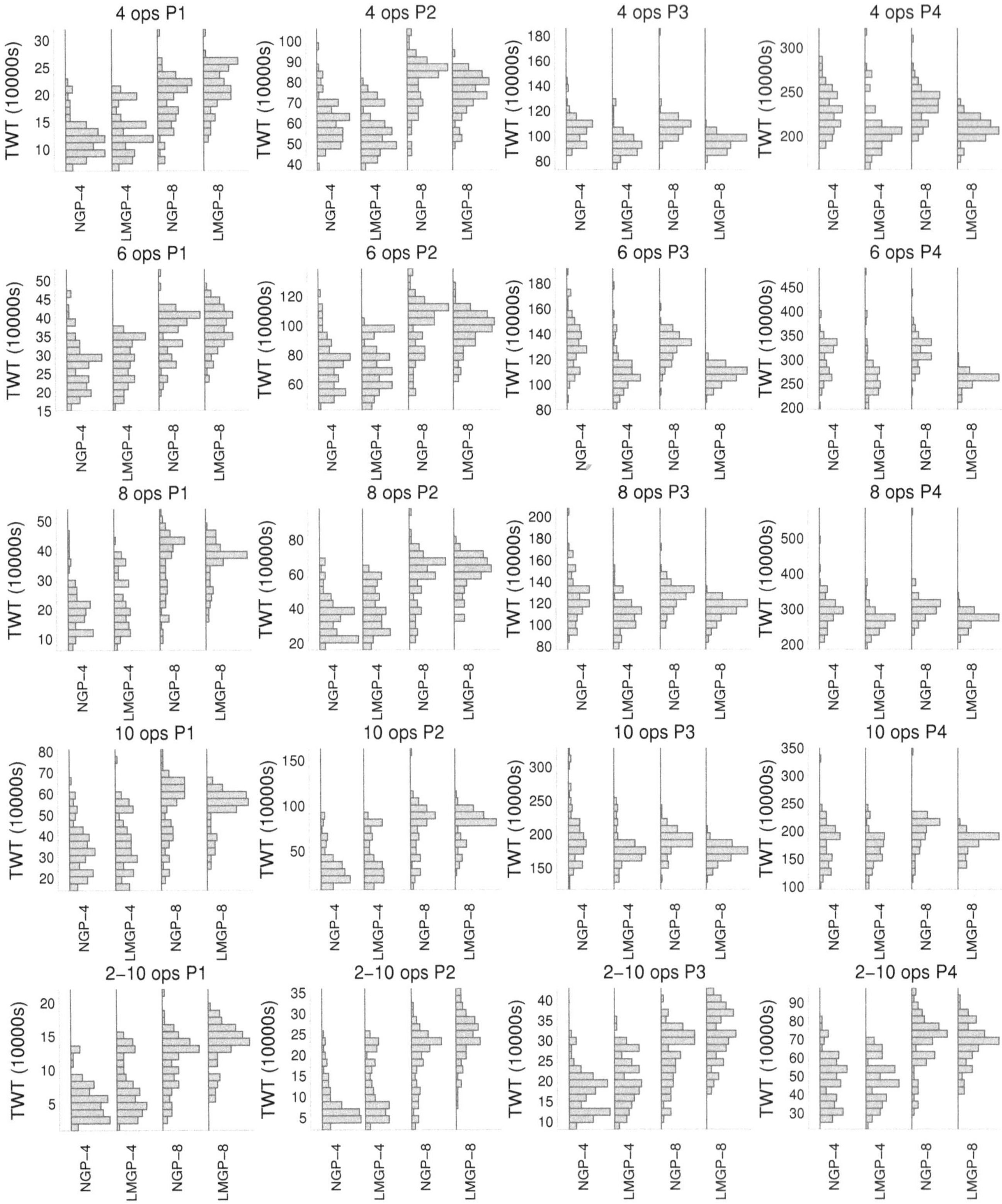

Figure 1: Histograms presenting results (TWT) of test scenarios for NGP-4op, LMGP-4op, NGP-8op and LMGP-8op. Note that the vertical axis scales are different in each subfigure.

Table 2: Terminal set used in GPHH system.

Feature	Symbol
Job Properties	
Processing time of operation	PR
Remaining processing time of job	RT
Remaining number of operations	RO
Ready time of job	RJ
Due date of job	DD
Weight of job	W
Machine Properties	
Ready time of machine	RM
Number of jobs in queue	NQ
Average wait time of last five jobs processed	QW
Current time	CT
Wider Looking Properties	
Next operation's processing time	NPR
Number of jobs in queue at the next machine job visits	NNQ
Average wait time of last five jobs processed at the next machine job visits	NQW
Average wait time of last five jobs processed across all machines in the shop	AQW

if the first argument is greater than 0 then it returns the second, else the third is returned. The `max` and `min` functions take two arguments and return the maximum and minimum of their arguments respectively. The initial population is generated using the ramped-half-and-half method [14]. The population size is 1024 and evolution is for 50 generations. GP trees have a maximum depth of eight. For the genetic operators crossover, mutation and elitism, we use rates of 85%, 10% and 5% respectively. Tournament selection with a tournament size of seven is used to select individuals for genetic operators. This is a common setting that has been previously used [20].

4. EXPERIMENTAL RESULTS

Here we present the results of using NGP and LMGP. We also compare training in a job shop where every job has four operations (NGP-4op and LMGP-4op), with training in one where every job has eight operations (NGP-8op and LMGP-8op). For each we performed 90 GP evolutionary runs, using 90 common random seeds.

4.1 Performance on Test Scenarios

Figure 1 shows the results on the 20 test scenarios by the 90 best-of-run evolved DRs from both NGP and LMGP, trained with four and eight operations in every job respectively. Each graph presents the results for one test scenario, with a rotated histogram showing the distribution of TWT attained for each method. Table 3 gives the corresponding mean and standard deviation of TWT.

Figure 1 shows that on the P1 and P2 test scenarios, with the lower expected utilisation, NGP evolves better performing DRs, as there is a greater number of DRs with low values of TWT. However we performed Mann-Whitney U tests, which showed that the difference in means between NGP and LMGP is not statistically significant at the 5% level.

On the other hand, if we consider the P3 and P4 test scenarios with higher expected utilisation (except for 2-10ops P3), LMGP now evolves more DRs that attain low TWT values, and fewer DRs with very high TWT. The difference in means is statistically significant at the 5% significance level. These have a higher utilisation rate than P1 and P2, so it seems logical that it would be more important to take into consideration values of shop features that look further than the current machine, as there are likely to be longer queues at machines. From Table 3 we observe that on these test scenarios the standard deviation is always smaller using LMGP, except for P4 with 4ops and 6ops. Further LMGP-8op has smaller standard deviation than LMGP-4op on all but one problem instance.

The methods with four operations in every job through evolution, NGP-4op and LMGP-4op outperform their eight operation counterparts, NGP-8op and LMGP-8op respectively, on all the P1 and P2 scenarios as well as P3 and P4 2–10ops scenarios. On scenarios with P3 and P4 (except 2–10ops) there is not a statistically significant difference in performance between NGP-4op and NGP-8op, or between LMGP-4op and LMGP-8op. Also note that the best (lowest) values for the worst performance (highest TWT) are achieved by either LMGP-4op (7/20) or LMGP-8op (9/20) on the majority of the test scenarios.

Table 4 shows the mean of both the mean and standard deviation of the number of jobs waiting in machine queues for each of the 20 scenarios and methods. LMGP-8op gives the lowest mean value of both mean and standard deviation on almost all of the scenarios. LMGP-4op also improves on the values of NGP-4op and NGP-8op although is not as good as LMGP-8op. We see through these results that the improvements offered by using LMGP can be partly attributed to reducing the expected number of jobs in queues, and evening out the queue lengths at the different machines in the shop. The results of 2-10ops show a trend of increasing TWT in the order NGP-4op, LMGP-4op, NGP-8op, LMGP-8op. DRs evolved by LMGP-4op achieved the lowest TWT of the runs from the four methods on 15 of the 20 test scenarios, rules evolved by NGP-4op achieved the lowest TWT on five of the test scenarios.

Table 5 gives the mean and standard deviation of the evolution time, in minutes, and the total testing time (for all twenty test scenarios), in milliseconds. The evolution time is lowest for LMGP-4op, followed by NGP-4op and LMGP-8op. The LMGP methods have smaller standard deviations. NGP-8op has the longest average evolution time and the largest standard deviation. Table 5 shows that the time taken for testing is less with NGP-4op than LMGP-4op and less with LMGP-8op than NGP-8op, and that the standard deviation is smaller for LMGP methods. LMGP-8op has the quickest mean test time of approximately five seconds.

4.2 Analysis of Evolved DRs

To analyse why the evolved DRs work well, we choose some of the best performing evolved rules and present them as trees. We have simplified the DRs shown in Figures 2, 3 and 4 slightly, though more simplification is likely possible.

Figure 2 shows a dispatching rule evolved using LMGP with four operations in every job throughout evolution represented as a tree. The shaded boxes highlight the additional terminals introduced to incorporate features of the wider shop. This rule achieved the minimum TWT on ten of the twenty test scenarios (4 ops P1–P4, 6 ops P1–P2, 8 ops P3–P4 and 2-10 ops P3–P4). A useful fragment appearing in this DR is DD−CT which will be greater than 0

Table 3: Mean and standard deviation of total weighted tardiness.

	NGP-4op		LMGP-4op		NGP-8op		LMGP-8op	
	Mean	Stdev	Mean	Stdev	Mean	Stdev	Mean	Stdev
4op P1	120172.5	33713.9	132827.9	40220.4	186254.1	45523.5	213017.1	40265.6
4op P2	609428.6	106118.5	567201.3	103795.7	791073.6	127464.0	745190.8	93795.2
4op P3	1047035.8	110560.0	938599.6	101976.7	1082094.3	108418.2	953673.6	56345.8
4op P4	2293114.6	228424.1	2066391.2	266909.5	2341840.0	194269.7	2087059.3	127766.1
6op P1	269921.7	66253.0	282273.7	58291.5	354181.9	64643.3	370473.2	54555.4
6op P2	725696.5	167233.0	720926.5	162954.5	986275.5	193743.1	968679.7	129534.8
6op P3	1315468.2	187315.2	1098321.7	157045.8	1300713.8	110167.3	1076417.4	67398.8
6op P4	3014284.4	385778.8	2664289.2	439610.0	3177282.4	318888.0	2581677.5	161812.9
8op P1	195380.9	79044.8	221547.0	92390.7	345605.5	109825.0	359346.5	71551.5
8op P2	350297.3	122288.6	397849.5	127321.7	563303.3	160031.4	604046.8	105535.6
8op P3	1246104.3	211054.5	1089119.8	145542.8	1261017.9	126742.9	1138713.4	94253.0
8op P4	2952357.0	440151.6	2662941.8	334695.1	3036016.6	422340.0	2705169.8	217867.8
10op P1	335583.7	119002.2	367515.3	133399.7	516456.2	147864.5	522800.0	98694.9
10op P2	340658.7	197556.3	436121.4	243389.1	727692.5	282219.5	775795.2	184660.3
10op P3	1953376.9	389473.6	1783788.0	244557.9	1902701.9	181351.4	1725990.5	132300.5
10op P4	1774315.8	373340.2	1681015.9	307575.2	1977866.0	321441.9	1795461.9	188845.4
2-10op P1	55414.0	26754.2	74944.3	38934.3	111282.9	40278.4	136343.9	33206.0
2-10op P2	84530.2	51780.8	119492.9	68779.4	189420.1	69929.7	243571.9	58095.2
2-10op P3	170812.8	52019.7	202734.2	61293.8	264444.8	67687.0	314177.2	64653.1
2-10op P4	478764.0	134874.8	476843.5	121796.3	680624.5	144670.0	678257.5	110070.6

Table 4: Mean of average and mean of standard deviation of queue length.

	NGP-4op		LMGP-4op		NGP-8op		LMGP-8op	
	Mean	Stdev	Mean	Stdev	Mean	Stdev	Mean	Stdev
4op P1	2.56	0.08	2.43	0.12	2.52	0.09	2.37	0.09
4op P2	3.53	0.15	3.17	0.19	3.48	0.14	3.08	0.13
4op P3	5.97	0.20	5.14	0.31	5.87	0.22	4.88	0.22
4op P4	6.75	0.24	5.85	0.39	6.61	0.25	5.61	0.25
6op P1	3.06	0.12	2.86	0.16	2.98	0.11	2.73	0.10
6op P2	3.16	0.13	2.94	0.17	3.07	0.11	2.79	0.11
6op P3	6.37	0.28	5.50	0.36	6.14	0.25	5.14	0.22
6op P4	6.93	0.41	5.96	0.41	6.70	0.27	5.65	0.27
8op P1	2.54	0.11	2.41	0.14	2.52	0.09	2.34	0.08
8op P2	2.29	0.11	2.19	0.13	2.23	0.09	2.10	0.07
8op P3	4.89	0.21	4.40	0.29	4.74	0.18	4.15	0.16
8op P4	5.48	0.41	4.67	0.29	5.27	0.24	4.45	0.24
10op P1	2.78	0.16	2.64	0.19	2.74	0.12	2.54	0.09
10op P2	2.31	0.12	2.21	0.15	2.26	0.10	2.12	0.06
10op P3	5.44	0.25	4.92	0.30	5.30	0.20	4.69	0.16
10op P4	3.71	0.18	3.44	0.21	3.72	0.13	3.36	0.10
2-10op P1	1.75	0.07	1.71	0.09	1.72	0.06	1.66	0.06
2-10op P2	1.64	0.07	1.61	0.09	1.60	0.06	1.57	0.05
2-10op P3	2.60	0.11	2.48	0.13	2.59	0.09	2.45	0.09
2-10op P4	2.82	0.12	2.64	0.16	2.76	0.11	2.53	0.09

Table 5: Mean and standard deviation of training and testing times.

	NGP-4op		LMGP-4op		NGP-8op		LMGP-8op	
	Mean	Stdev	Mean	Stdev	Mean	Stdev	Mean	Stdev
Evolution time (min)	364.6	369.8	359.8	246.2	598.5	461.1	423.3	215.6
Test time (ms)	6026.3	4444.5	6162.8	3491.2	7442.2	5137.8	5075.6	2336.4

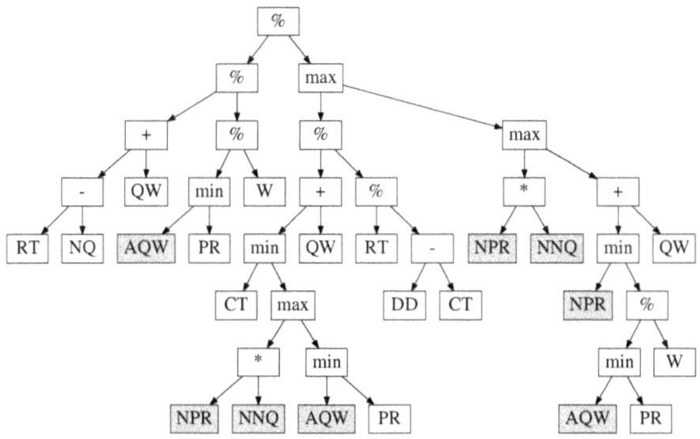

Figure 2: One of the best performing LMGP-4op DRs on the test scenarios.

if the job is not overdue, further this appears in the DR as RT/(DD − CT), which is a ratio of the remaining time to the time until due. In Figure 4 we note a similar fragment to that observed in the DR of Figure 2, RT/(DD − RM). In this DR we also observe the presence of the WSPT rule.

In Figure 3 one of the best performing rules from LMGP-8op is presented as a tree. It is interesting to note the appearance of the inverse of the WSPT rule in the two places in the rule, both times in the left branch of a `min` operator. It occurs as (AQW ∗ PR)/(CT ∗ W). It is interesting to observe that if there are no operations after the current operation this DR will return 0.

It is interesting that all of the DRs presented are smaller than what they could potentially be, hence it may be promising to restrict the depth to seven, or less, and compare the behaviour of the DRs evolved under that constraint.

In the evolved DRs (trees) we frequently see a count (e.g., RO, NQ or NNQ) compared to a length of time (e.g., PR) compared to an absolute time (e.g., DD). The comparisons between counts and local measures using + and − make little sense as we try to interpret the DR, however comparisons using ∗ and % are acceptable.

5. CONCLUSIONS

The goal of this paper was to develop a GPHH approach to evolve less-myopic scheduling rules for the dynamic ten machine job shop environment. To achieve this we introduced four additional terminals to the terminal set, which captured more information about the current state of the job shop beyond the current machine.

Results showed that the inclusion of these less-myopic terminals led to the evolution of better DRs in terms of total weighted tardiness across the test simulation scenarios with high utilisation. On these scenarios the difference in means was statistically significant at the 0.05 level, with the LMGP evolved DRs having lower mean and smaller standard deviations, as well as shorter evolution and test times. Increasing the terminal set leads to a great increase in the size of the search space of possible GP trees; despite the larger search space, LMGP outperformed NGP.

Across all twenty test scenarios LMGP-4op and LMGP-8op decreased the average queue length in comparison to NGP-4op and NGP-8op. In terms of mean queue length LMGP-8op $<$ LMGP-4op $\leq$ NGP-8op $\leq$ NGP-4op. The mean standard deviation of queue length was generally less under LMGP methods than NGP methods. Further the time for testing was less with LMGP-8op than NGP-8op. On 18/20 test scenarios the four operations methods outperformed their eight operation counterparts.

In future work we will see if the additional less-myopic terminals continue to offer improved performance as the scale of the job shop increases. We will also investigate additional terminals which capture further properties of the job shop's current and potential future states, and incorporate a look-ahead element.

We will also develop evolved rules with greater interpretability by constraining the search through using a grammar or strongly typed GP [16]. This will enable us to reduce the comparisons which do not make sense and enable better understanding of what information effective rules are capturing from the shop system.

6. REFERENCES

[1] H. Aytug, M. A. Lawley, K. McKay, S. Mohan, and R. Uzsoy. Executing production schedules in the face of uncertainties: A review and some future directions. *European Journal of Operational Research*, 161(1):86–110, 2005.

[2] K. Bhaskaran and M. Pinedo. Dispatching. *Handbook of Industrial Engineering*, pages 2184–2198, 1992.

[3] J. Blazewicz, W. Domschke, and E. Pesch. The job shop scheduling problem: Conventional and new solution techniques. *European Journal of Operational Research*, 93(1):1–33, 1996.

[4] J. Branke and C. Pickardt. Evolutionary search for difficult problem instances to support the design of job shop dispatching rules. *European Journal of Operational Research*, 212(1):22–32, 2011.

[5] E. Burke, M. Hyde, G. Kendall, G. Ochoa, E. Ozcan, and J. R. Woodward. A classification of hyper-heuristic approaches. In M. Gendreau and J.-Y. Potvin, editors, *Handbook of Meta-Heuristics*, pages 449–468. Kluwer, 2010.

[6] E. K. Burke, M. R. Hyde, G. Kendall, G. Ochoa, E. Ozcan, and J. R. Woodward. Exploring hyper-heuristic methodologies with genetic programming. In C. Mumford and L. Jain, editors, *Computational Intelligence*, volume 1 of *Intelligent Systems Reference Library*, pages 177–201. Springer, 2009.

[7] C. Geiger, R. Uzsoy, and H. Aytug. Rapid modeling and discovery of priority dispatching rules: an autonomous learning approach. *Journal of Scheduling*, 9(1):7–34, 2006.

[8] W. S. Gere, Jr. Heuristics in job shop scheduling. *Management Science*, 13(3):167–190, 1966.

[9] E. Hart, P. Ross, and D. Corne. Evolutionary scheduling: a review. *Genetic Programming and Evolvable Machines*, 6:191–220, 2005.

[10] T. Hildebrandt, J. Heger, and B. Scholz-Reiter. Towards improved dispatching rules for complex shop floor scenarios: a genetic programming approach. In *GECCO '10: Proceedings of the 12th Annual Conference on Genetic and Evolutionary Computation*, pages 257–264, 2010.

[11] D. Jakobovic, L. Jelenkovic, and L. Budin. Genetic programming heuristics for multiple machine scheduling. In *EuroGP'07: Proceedings of the 10th*

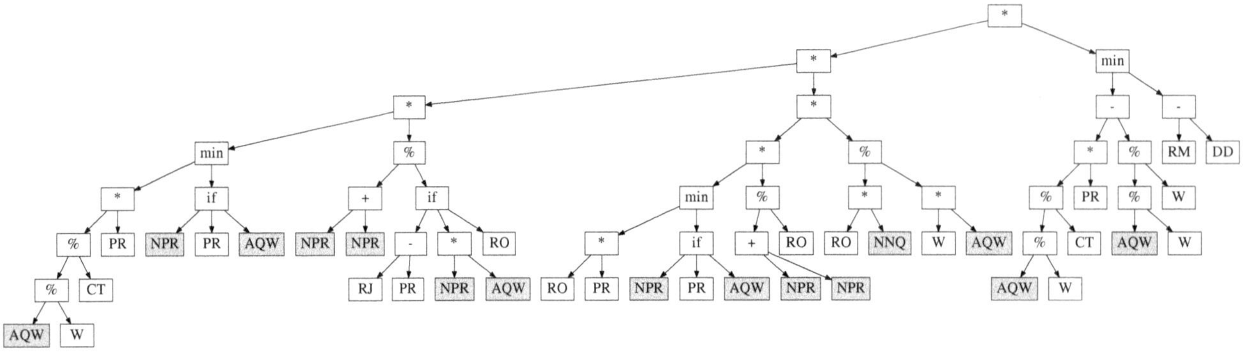

Figure 3: One of the best performing LMGP-8op DRs on the test scenarios.

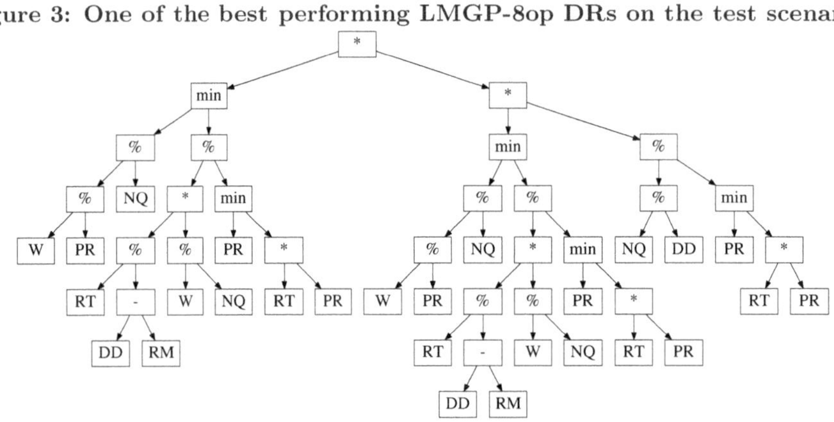

Figure 4: One of the best performing NGP-8op DRs on the test scenarios.

European Conference on Genetic programming, pages 321–330, 2007.

[12] D. Jakobović and K. Marasović. Evolving priority scheduling heuristics with genetic programming. *Applied Soft Computing*, 12(9):2781–2789, 2012.

[13] A. Jones and L. C. Rabelo. Survey of job shop scheduling techniques. Technical report, National Institute of Standards and Technology, Gaithersberg, 1998.

[14] J. R. Koza. *Genetic Programming: On the Programming of Computers by Means of Natural Selection.* MIT Press, Cambridge, MA, USA, 1992.

[15] S. Luke. *Essentials of Metaheuristics.* Lulu, second edition, 2013. Available for free at http://cs.gmu.edu/∼sean/book/metaheuristics/.

[16] R. I. McKay, N. X. Hoai, P. A. Whigham, Y. Shan, and M. O'Neill. Grammar-based genetic programming: a survey. *Genetic Programming and Evolvable Machines*, 11(3–4):365–396, 2010.

[17] K. Miyashita. Job-shop scheduling with GP. In *GECCO'00: Proceedings of the Genetic and Evolutionary Computation Conference*, pages 505–512, 2000.

[18] S. Nguyen, M. Zhang, M. Johnston, and K. Tan. Learning iterative dispatching rules for job shop scheduling with genetic programming. *The International Journal of Advanced Manufacturing Technology*, 67(1-4):85–100, 2013.

[19] S. Nguyen, M. Zhang, M. Johnston, and K. C. Tan. A coevolution genetic programming method to evolve scheduling policies for dynamic multi-objective job shop scheduling problems. In *Proceedings of the 2012 IEEE Congress on Evolutionary Computation*, pages 1–8, 2012.

[20] S. Nguyen, M. Zhang, M. Johnston, and K. C. Tan. A computational study of representations in genetic programming to evolve dispatching rules for the job shop scheduling problem. *IEEE Transactions on Evolutionary Computation*, 17(5):621–639, 2013.

[21] Nguyen Su, Zhang Mengjie, Johnston Mark, and Tan Kay Chen. Genetic programming for evolving due-date assignment models in job shop environments. *Evolutionary Computation*, 22(1):105–138, 2013.

[22] C. W. Pickardt, T. Hildebrandt, J. Branke, J. Heger, and B. Scholz-Reiter. Evolutionary generation of dispatching rule sets for complex dynamic scheduling problems. *International Journal of Production Economics*, 145(1):67–77, 2013.

[23] M. L. Pinedo. *Scheduling: Theory, Algorithms, and Systems.* 3rd edition, Springer, 2008.

[24] C. Potts and V. Strusevich. Fifty years of scheduling: a survey of milestones. *Journal of the Operational Research Society*, 60(S1):41–68, 2009.

[25] J. C. Tay and N. B. Ho. Evolving dispatching rules using genetic programming for solving multi-objective flexible job-shop problems. *Computer & Industrial Engineering*, 54:453–473, 2008.

[26] A. Vepsalainen and T. Morton. Priority rules for job shops with weighted tardiness costs. *Management Science*, 33:1035–1047, 1987.

Behavioral Programming: A Broader and More Detailed Take on Semantic GP

Krzysztof Krawiec*
Institute of Computing Science
Poznan University of Technology
60965 Poznan, Poland
krawiec@cs.put.poznan.pl

Una-May O'Reilly
CSAIL
Massachusetts Institute of Technology
Cambridge, MA
unamay@csail.mit.edu

ABSTRACT

In evolutionary computation, the fitness of a candidate solution conveys sparse feedback. Yet in many cases, candidate solutions can potentially yield more information. In genetic programming (GP), one can easily examine program behavior on particular fitness cases or at intermediate execution states. However, how to exploit it to effectively guide the search remains unclear. In this study we apply machine learning algorithms to features describing the intermediate behavior of the executed program. We then drive the standard evolutionary search with additional objectives reflecting this intermediate behavior. The machine learning functions *independent of task-specific knowledge* and discovers potentially useful components of solutions (subprograms), which we preserve in an archive and use as building blocks when composing new candidate solutions. In an experimental assessment on a suite of benchmarks, the proposed approach proves more capable of finding optimal and/or well-performing solutions than control methods.

Categories and Subject Descriptors

I.2.2 [**Artificial Intelligence**]: Automatic Programming—*Program synthesis*; I.2.8 [**Artificial Intelligence**]: Problem Solving, Control Methods, and Search—*Heuristic methods*

Keywords

program synthesis; genetic programming; program semantics; behavioral evaluation; search operators; archive; multi-objective evolutionary computation

1. MOTIVATION

Most of the algorithms developed in the field of evolutionary computation (EC) obstinately insist on using an objective function directly associated with the given task as their central, if not the only, gauge of candidate solutions. If no additional performance information is available (i.e., the objective function is a black-box), and there is no access into the internal structure of candidate solutions, this is indeed necessary. However, in many domains there is much more information available about the problem solving nature of a candidate solution as well as access to its internal structure. This is particularly true in genetic programming (GP), where the objective function is typically an aggregate calculated over a set of fitness cases while the candidate solutions are programs that are both syntactically and semantically decomposable. As a consequence, nothing precludes scrutinizing program output for particular fitness cases, or examining program behavior on the level of particular program components (subprograms). In such cases, relying exclusively on the original objective function is a mere artifact of researchers' habits and conventions, rather than necessity.

This habit may be crippling because one cannot expect difficult learning and optimization problems to be efficiently solved by heuristic algorithms that are driven by a scalar objective function which provides low-information feedback. For example, consider the domain of Boolean function synthesis, a common benchmark suite for GP. Given a programming language with k binary instructions and m input variables, there are programs composed of n instructions, where $cat(n)$ is the nth Catalan number. Thus, even for the relatively simple multiplexer-11 benchmark ($m = 11$) and instruction set of $k = 4$ binary instructions, the number of 'minimal' programs that can *potentially* solve this problem (i.e., fetching every input variable only once) is a staggering 2.93×10^{11}. To believe that *any* heuristic search algorithm can efficiently traverse such a big space using an objective function with a range of only $2^{11} = 2048$ values (and thus conveys only 11 bits of information) is very optimistic, if not naive. The problem is general. Symbolic regression, despite having a continous objective function, which is arguably more fine grained, also falls victim. By shaving off diminishing fractions of error, evolution often chases the noise in data and ends up overfitting to it.

This problem becomes even more grave when a search quickly converges to solutions of high quality, all of which have very similar or even identical fitness. The selective pressure ceases to be able to differentiate them, the search gradient is lost, and random search becomes the only way to improve. This partially explains why, though attempts have been made to address the above problem from a few angles and GP is capable of solving some complex problems

*Research conducted during K. Krawiec's stay at the ALFA Group, Computer Science and Artificial Intelligence Laboratory (CSAIL), MIT.

GECCO'14, July 12–16, 2014, Vancouver, BC, Canada.
Copyright 2014 ACM 978-1-4503-2662-9/14/07 ...$15.00.
http://dx.doi.org/10.1145/2576768.2598288 .

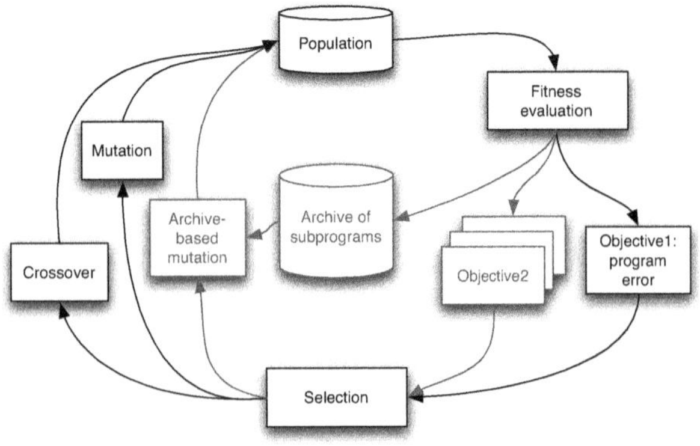

Figure 1: Conventional genetic programming workflow (in black) and the components added by behavioral programming (in blue).

at a reasonable computational expense, it does not scale well with problem size.

From a wider evolutionary perspective, the reliance on a task-oriented fitness function alone is coherent with *gradualism*, the cornerstone of classical Darwinism. However, even if we assumed that gradualism drives biological evolution (though it has been questioned many times), we posit that it is *not necessarily most appropriate for problem solving* (in a broad meaning of this term, i.e., including search, optimization, and learning). Humans rarely solve problems gradually, case by case. Instead, they inductively and deductively reason to be able to identify regularities and perform conceptual leaps. They need to reason about how they achieved their goals, not simply whether or not they achieved them.

Our general claim is thus that we should seek *search drivers* based on the general problem solving ability *of intermediate behavior* in order to make learning and optimization metaheuristics more 'intelligent' and, in effect, possibly more efficient. We therefore propose *behavioral programming*, which conceptually fits under the umbrella of semantic genetic programming. It consults both the semantics of GP outputs (like existing semantic GP variants) and intermediate behavior, with the help of task-agnostic machine learning. In this paper, we demonstrate the underlying conceptual framework of behavioral programming by embedding an implementation of it within conventional tree-based genetic programming (GP) in a system we call BPGP. BPGP retrieves detailed, intra-execution information on program behavior and uses it to (i) 'multiobjectivize' [8] the search space, (ii) identify the potentially valuable pieces of code, and (iii) reuse them later in search using an archive. Our experimental analysis shows that this 'better-informed' search algorithm attains radically better performance when compared to methods driven by conventional objective functions alone.

2. BEHAVIORAL PROGRAMMING

Behavioral programming extends the workflow of conventional GP adding three components (see Fig. 1): behavioral evaluation, archiving of useful subprograms, and an archive-based search operator. The former two execute in the fitness evaluation phase, while the archive-based search operator is used in the breeding phase (possibly along the conventional search operators like mutation or crossover). We detail these components in the following sections.

2.1 Behavioral evaluation

Behavioral evaluation, preliminary version of which has been proposed under the name of PANGEA (Pattern-Guided Evolutionary Algorithm) in [9], can be conveniently presented as an extension of conventional fitness evaluation.

In standard tree-based GP, the fitness function iterates over a set of fitness cases of the form (x, y), where x is *program input* (typically one or more input variable), and y is the *desired output* for x. The input x is fed into the program p (i.e., made available to its leaves), and p is executed, which consists of traversing p's tree nodes in an inorder sequence, and propagating the partial results upwards in the tree. Upon completion, execution produces *program output* $\hat{y}$. This process, repeated over all tests, results in a vector of program outputs $\hat{\mathbf{y}}$, which is subsequently compared to the vector of desired outputs $\mathbf{y}$ (the *target*). This is typically done using some form of metric $|\,|$, so that p ultimately receives fitness

$$f(p) = |\mathbf{y}, \hat{\mathbf{y}}|. \tag{1}$$

As evolution proceeds, programs represented as trees often experience excessive growth (a.k.a. bloat), which increases evaluation cost and makes the search process less effective. In response to that, program size is taken into account. In the simplest case, this boils down to calculating program length (size):

$$s(p) = |p| \tag{2}$$

where $|p|$ is simply the number of tree nodes. This measure can be used to make decisions at various stages of the evolutionary loop, e.g., for resolving ties on f in tournament selection, or as another objective. In the latter case, the program is characterized by a *multiobjective fitness*

$$(f(p), s(p)) \tag{3}$$

where both objectives are minimized.

Behavioral evaluation does not affect the above process (and thus has no impact on $f(p)$ nor $s(p)$), but rather works *with* it. Prior to running the program on a given input x, an empty list l is created. Then, as execution traverses the program tree, the output produced by every visited program node is appended to l. When the program terminates, the resulting list gathers all intermediate outcomes of execution and so forms the *trace* of program p for a given test. If the considered programs are expressions, free of conditional statements and loops (as we assume in this paper), the nodes of program tree are visited in the same order for every fitness case, and the lists l have the same length n for every fitness case. Let l_i denote the trace obtained for the ith test. The traces resulting from evaluation on particular fitness cases are gathered in a *trace table* of the following structure:

$$\begin{matrix} l_1[1] & l_1[2] & \dots & l_1[n] & y_1 \\ l_2[1] & l_2[2] & \dots & l_2[n] & y_2 \\ \vdots & \vdots & & \vdots & \vdots \\ l_t[1] & l_t[2] & \dots & l_t[n] & y_t \end{matrix} \tag{4}$$

where $l_i[j]$ denotes the jth element of a list for the ith test, and t is the number of tests.

The trace table is subsequently treated as inputs that can be passed to a machine learning algorithm, where the last column plays the role of the label (dependent variable), while the preceding columns are *features* (independent variables).

If the original desired output y is categorical, y_i's are *class labels* and the task is *classification*; if y is continuous, it is a *response variable* and the task is *regression*.

In either case,the learning algorithm is trained on the data of the trace table (4), which results in a *model* $M(p)$ of the data, which indirectly reveals a *behavioral description* of the program's intermediate execution. This description can be characterized by two measures: *error* $e(M(p))$ on the training data (goodness of fit) and *complexity* $c(M(p))$ denoting M's complexity.

The technical definitions of these measures may vary depending on domain and application, but there is a central motivation for adopting them as additional program characteristics. If a program produces output $\hat{\mathbf{y}}$ that is far from the desired output $\mathbf{y}$ (which implies an inferior score on f), or is excessively large (inferior score on s), it may still host subprograms that can turn out to be useful when, e.g., re-arranged/composed in a different way, and/or used in other programs. The machine learning process is intended to discover such subprograms among the population by analyzing the trace data and using behavioral features (columns in table (4)) that relate to the desired output of the program (the dependent variable of the learning task (4)). If a program exhibits such features, the resulting model M is likely to achieve low error e. However, sometimes a model may attain low error even without particularly good features at hand, i.e., by overfitting to the training data or even by rote learning in an extreme case. This is where model complexity c comes into picture: its role is to promote succinct models in the hope of evolving general subprograms..

The tuple gathering all characteristics derived from p, i.e.,

$$(f(p), s(p), c(M(p)), e(M(p)) \tag{5}$$

is the final result of behavioral evaluation. By analogy to bi-objective evaluation (Eq. (3)), the elements of the above tuple are treated as search objectives, and reported to the multiobjective evolutionary search process. Other ways of exploiting this information are conceivable, but remain future work.

2.2 Archiving useful subprograms

Behavioral evaluation results in two measures of the behavioral model $M(p)$ derived from the evaluated program p, which provide more information on p (compared to the conventional single- or two-objective evaluation). However, those measures are still only scalar values, while the model itself captures even more information about program behavior and the prospective utility of its components.

It is thus natural to seek means of directly exploiting the information contained in the behavioral model, rather than only characterize it quantitatively. For this we assume that the model can explicitly reveal *which* trace features it uses to make predictions (of all the features gathered from all program tree nodes). For models represented as classification (or regression) trees, which we employ in this paper, we retrieve that information by traversing the decision tree and gathering the features used by decision nodes. However, model representation is largely irrelevant, and the fact that we deal with program *trees* and examine models represented as decision/regression *trees* is incidental (and those two should not be confused). For many other 'white-box' (i.e., more or less symbolic) algorithms (e.g., decision rules, Bayesian nets) such information is equally available, and even the 'blackbox' representations (like linear regression models or artificial neural networks) do not preclude such possibility.

As the features used by a model correspond one-to-one to subprograms in the evaluated tree, the knowledge of whether they are included in the model immediately allows us to pinpoint the *useful subprograms* in the program tree and collect them into a set $U(p)$. Subsequently, we gather these useful subprograms of all individuals in population in a global *archive* A, a prioritized queue of a fixed length, maintained throughout the entire evolutionary run. The priority is based on a measure we associate with a useful subprogram, p' called its *utility*, u:

$$u(p') = \frac{1}{(1 + e(p))|U(p)|} \tag{6}$$

Useful subprograms are added to the archive until it reaches capacity. At that point the archive is reset and re-populated by utility-proportional selection. Subprogram utility helps promote subprograms that contribute to good models (low error $e(p)$) and from within compact models (low $U(p)$).

2.3 Reusing useful subprograms: archive-supplied mutation

The ultimate goal of archiving useful subprograms is their reuse in new candidate solutions. For compatibility with the EC conceptual toolkit, we implement this component as a mutation-like search operator.

Given a parent program tree p, the operator picks at random a node in p and replaces it (and the subtree rooted in it) with a subprogram drawn at random from the archive A. Here, the subprograms are selected from archive in exactly the same manner that determines their survival in the archive (Section 2.3), i.e., proportional to utility (Eq. 6). Therefore, subprograms of higher utility are more likely to become components of other programs.

This operator, though applied to a single parent program and in this sense mutation-like, can be considered as a form of crossover, because it outfits the offspring with a piece of code that has been previously retrieved from another individual (in the current or previous generations). As a result, the archive-supplied mutation cannot use arbitrary subprograms, in particular cannot use instructions other than those currently present in archive. For this reason, we use conventional mutation side-by-side with this operator (Section 4).

3. RELATED WORK

The closest counterpart to BPGP or behavioral programming in GP literature is semantic GP, where, rather than assessing program quality aggregated over all tests (i.e., conventional fitness), program output is scrutinized for every test individually. This avenue of GP research was initiated by McPhee *et al.*, who studied the impact of crossover on program semantics and semantic building blocks [14], although earlier work on implicit fitness sharing paved its way [13]. The more contemporary studies [15, 16] reason about the geometry of semantic space. Behavioral programming can be seen as semantic GP pushed one level of detail deeper, i.e., not limited to program output, but to program behavior over its entire execution. Also, from start to finish in terms of behavior.

Other past works employ alternative search objectives, even if not explicitly framed in that way. The concept of multiobjectivization by Knowles *et al.* [8] was an early forerunner of the idea that additional objectives can, paradoxically, sometimes make the problem easier. However, Knowles *et al* and similar studies assumed that the additional objectives would be proposed by the experimenter because then task-specific sub-goals could be expressed. In contrast, behavioral programming discovers subsolutions autonomously (i.e., it induces behavioral models from program traces without explicitly formulating what is the desired intermediate behavior of a program). Behavioral programming can be seen thus as an intermediate approach between conventional single-objective search and novelty search [10], where the task-driven objective is discarded altogether.

With respect to the use of archive, behavioral programming can be likened to methods that maintain repositories of code pieces. Automatically defined functions can be seen as such repositories of subprograms, albeit only local (i.e. attached to an individual) and devoid of any directed maintenance (i.e., the content of the repository is controlled only by evolution). A more similar approach is implemented in *run transferable libraries* [18] that collect program fragments throughout a GP run and reuse them in separate evolutionary runs applied to other problems. Rosca and Ballard [17] create and use an analogous library within a single evolutionary run, with sophisticated mechanism for assessing subroutine utility, and entropy for deciding when a new subroutine should be created. Haynes [4] integrated a distributed search of genetic programming-based systems with 'collective memory', albeit only for redundancy detection. Other approaches involving some form of library include reuse of assemblies of parts within the same individual [6] and explicit expert-driven task decomposition using layered learning [1]. None of these methods however analyze program behavior to make a decision about which subprograms should be archived, and only some of them associate utility with a subprogram.

4. EXPERIMENTAL ANALYSIS

Behavioral programming involves behavioral evaluation (Section 2.1) and manipulation of subprograms (Sections 2.2 and 2.3). From practical perspective, it is worth asking whether and how these components affect the efficiency of evolutionary search, and if there is any synergy between them. To answer these questions, we conduct a thorough cross-domain comparative assessment of various configurations of BPGP, using certain configurations of conventional GP as baselines.

4.1 The problems

Table 1 presents the 35 benchmark problems used in our experiment, which come from three domains we characterize by different data types: Boolean (8 benchmarks), categorical (10 benchmarks), and regression (17 benchmarks). Table 1 summarizes the problems, listing the instruction set used for each, and for every problem, the number of variables, tests, and the cardinality of the search space (where countable). Note that none of the instruction sets contains constants.

The targets for particular **Boolean problems** are defined as follows. For an v-bit comparator *Cmp v*, a program is required to return *true* if the $\frac{v}{2}$ least significant input bits encode a number that is smaller than the number represented by the $\frac{v}{2}$ most significant bits. In case of the majority *Maj v* problems, *true* should be returned if more that half of the input variables are *true*. For the multiplexer *Mul v*, the state of the addressed input should be returned (6-bit multiplexer uses two inputs to address the remaining four inputs, 11-bit multiplexer uses three inputs to address the remaining eight inputs). In the parity *Par v* problems, *true* should be returned only for an odd number of *true* inputs.

The **categorical problems** come from Spector *et al.*'s work on evolving algebraic terms [20] and dwell in the ternary domain: the admissible values of program inputs and outputs are $\{0, 1, 2\}$. The peculiarity of these problems consists of using only one binary instruction in the programming language, which defines the underlying algebra. For instance, for the a_1 algebra, the semantics of that instruction (a1 in Table 1) is defined as follows:

a_1	0	1	2
0	2	1	2
1	1	0	0
2	0	0	1

For brevity, we refer the reader to [20] for the definition of the remaining algebra problems.

For each of the five algebras considered here, we consider two tasks (of four discussed in [20]). In *discriminator term* tasks (*D-** in Table 1), the goal is to synthesize an expression (using only the one given instruction) that accepts three inputs x, y, z and is semantically equivalent to

$$t^A(x, y, z) = \begin{cases} x & if\, x \neq y \\ z & if\, x = y \end{cases} \tag{7}$$

Given three inputs and ternary domain, this gives rise to $3^3 = 27$ fitness cases for these benchmarks.

The second task defined for each of algebras (*M-** in Table 1), consists in evolving a so-called *Mal'cev term*, i.e., a ternary term that satisfies

$$m(x, x, y) = m(y, x, x) = y \tag{8}$$

This condition specifies the desired program behavior only for the indicated combinations of inputs. In other words, the desired value for $m(x, y, z)$, where x, y, and z are all distinct, is not determined. As a result, there are only 15 fitness cases in our Mal'cev tasks, the lowest of all considered benchmarks.

The **regression problems** considered here come from [12] and include both univariate and multivariate target functions. The univariate ones (*Keij1*, *Keij4*, *Nguy3..7* and *Sext*) use 20 tests uniformly distributed in the $[-1, 1]$ interval, except for the *Keij4* benchmark which uses the $[0, 10]$ interval. The remaining problems are predominantly bivariate, and involve $5 \times 5 = 25$ fitness cases uniformly distributed on the two-dimensional grid. The only exception is *Keij5*, which hosts three input variables, with $4 \times 4 \times 4 = 64$ fitness cases distributed equidistantly in the cube. For other details on these benchmarks, see [12][1].

4.2 Configurations

Conceptually, there are two main aspects in which BPGP differs from conventional GP: the behavioral evaluation and manipulation of subprograms. To determine how the presence of these components impacts search performance, we

[1]The original formulation of some of these benchmarks in [12] assumes random drawing of fitness cases from variables' domains. However, to assure reproducibility of results we employ deterministic equidistant grid.

Table 1: The benchmarks. v – number of input variables, m– the number of tests, k – number of unique program semantics.

	Instr. set	Problem	v	m	k
Boolean	and, nand, or, nor	Cmp6	6	64	2^{64}
		Cmp8	8	256	2^{256}
		Maj6	6	64	2^{64}
		Maj8	8	256	2^{256}
		Mux6	6	64	2^{64}
		Mux11	11	2,048	2^{2048}
		Par6	6	64	2^{64}
		Par8	8	256	2^{256}
Categorical	$a_1(x,y)$	D-a1	3	27	3^{27}
	$a_2(x,y)$	D-a2	3		
	$a_3(x,y)$	D-a3	3		
	$a_4(x,y)$	D-a4	3		
	$a_5(x,y)$	D-a5	3		
	$a_1(x,y)$	M-a1	3	15	3^{15}
	$a_2(x,y)$	M-a2	3		
	$a_3(x,y)$	M-a3	3		
	$a_4(x,y)$	M-a4	3		
	$a_5(x,y)$	M-a5	3		
Regression	$+, -, *,$ %, sin, cos, log, exp, $-x$	Keij1,Keij4	1	20	–
		Nguy3,Nguy4	1		
		Nguy5,Nguy6	1		
		Nguy7,Sext	1		
		Keij5, Keij11	2		
		Keij12, Keij13	2		
		Keij14, Nguy9	2		
		Nguy10, Nguy12	2		
		Keij15	3		

design 3 configurations. In BPGP4 and BPGP4A there are 4 objectives, (see Formula 5 and the latter configuration uses an archive). BP2A uses two objectives and an archive. GP1 is the standard single-objective GP. We employ generational GP with tournament selection. For single-objective configurations (GP1, GP1L), tournament selection with the conventional tournament size 7 is used. For multiobjective setups, e.g.GP2, we employ Non-Dominated Sorting Genetic Algorithm II (NSGA-II, [2]) at the selection stage, an *ipso facto* standard of multiobjective evolutionary optimization.

As BPGP can perform quite well with small population, we set population size to 100. However, this may be inconvenient for conventional GP, which is know to require larger populations. To make comparison fair, we consider additional configuration GP1L that uses population size 1000. Because the maximal number of generations is the same in all configurations, GP1L's computational budget (max. number of evaluations) is ten times greater than for the other configurations.

Search operators. We employ three search operators: (i) subtree-replacing mutation, present in all setups and engaged with probability 0.1, (ii) subtree-swapping crossover, and (iii) archive-supplied mutation (Section 2.3). To eliminate the interference of other factors, operators (ii) and (iii) proceed in the same way, except only for the source of subprograms. While the conventional subtree mutation plants a randomly generated subtree at the selected locus, the archive-based operator uses for that purpose a subprogram drawn at random from the archive, as described in Section 2.3.

Table 2: Configurations. For search operators, the numbers denote the probability at which an operator is being engaged (blanks are zeros).

	Setup	GP1	GP1L	GP2	BPGP4	BP2A	BPGP4A
Objectives	f	✓	✓	✓	✓	✓	✓
	s			✓	✓	✓	✓
	c				✓		✓
	e				✓		✓
Operators	Mutation	0.1	0.1	0.1	0.1	0.1	0.1
	Crossover	0.9	0.9	0.9	0.9		
	A-Mutation					0.9	0.9
	Pop. size	100	1000	100	100	100	100
	Tourn. size	7	7	4	4	4	4

Node selector. To lessen potential bloat, rather than using a conventional method for drawing mutation and regression loci in programs, we employ 'home brewed' *uniform depth node selector.* This selector calculates tree depth d, draws uniformly a random number d' from the interval $[0, d]$, and returns a randomly chosen loci at depth d' in the tree. In this way, the probability of node selection does not grow exponentially with node depth (as it is the case in the conventional methods). Mutations and crossovers close to the root node become more likely, and bloat is thus partially constrained. We employ this node selection method in all search operators. Preliminary experiments have shown that it is beneficial for standard GP.

Behavioral model. We chose REPTree [3] as the algorithm for deriving behavioral models, which we motivate twofold. Firstly, REPTree can induce both classification as regression trees, so it can handle problems from all three domains we consider in this paper without any adjustments or parametrization. Secondly, certain technical tricks make it remarkably faster than other decision tree inducers.

Though REPTree can post-prune (simplify) the induced decision trees, we disable this option, and make it always grow maximal trees (i.e., it always splits a decision node if any gain in entropy can be achieved). In this way, we expect the size of the induced classifier reflect the complexity of the underlying training data.

Archive. Archive capacity is set to 50. N.B. this is the only parameter of BPGP.

Objectives. NSGA-II resolves ties between solutions in the same tier of ranking by resorting to *sparsity* measure [2], which involves calculating the Euclidean distance between the points on the Pareto front. This requires the objectives to range in the same interval, so that particular objectives have on average the same impact on sparsity. To that aim, we define the objectives (Eq. 5) as follows:

		Boolean	*Categorical*	*Regression*
Program error	f	$d_h(\mathbf{y}, \hat{\mathbf{y}})/t$		$1 - \frac{1}{1+d_c(\mathbf{y}, \hat{\mathbf{y}})}$
Program size	s	$1 - 1/\lvert p \rvert$		
Model complexity	c	$1 - 1/\lvert M \rvert$		
Model error	e	$d_h(M, \hat{\mathbf{y}})/t$		$1 - \frac{1}{1+d_c(M, \hat{\mathbf{y}})}$

where d_h and d_c denote respectively Hamming and city-block distance, t is the number of tests, $|p|$ denotes the length of program p (number of nodes in its tree), and$|M|$ is the number of nodes in REPTree M.

The objectives defined in this way are minimized and assume values from interval $[0, 1]$. We handle numerical imprecision in regression problems by assuming that $|y_i - \hat{y}_i| = 0$ whenever $|y_i - \hat{y}_i| < 10^{-15}$.

Termination. A run is terminated when an ideal solution is found ($f = 0$) or the maximum number of 250 generations has elapsed. We assume that the final outcome of an evolutionary run is the individual that attained the best fitness (lowest f) at any stage of the run. All data reported below characterize such individuals, averaged over 30 independent evolutionary runs for every setup and benchmark; a total of 30 ×35 benchmarks ×6 configurations = 6300 runs has been conducted.

Let us emphasize that, except for the elements of the setup that have to differ across domains because of their different natures, all benchmarks from all domains use the same parameter settings. For parameters not mentioned here we assume their default values in the ECJ library [11].

4.3 The results

Success rate. We first assume the strong-AI perspective and consider our benchmarks as *search problems*. In that case, the objective is to find an ideal solution to the problem, and any other outcome is considered a failure. The appropriate performance measure for this type of problems is success rate, i.e., the percentage of runs that produced an ideal individual.

Because of the large total number of benchmarks (35), we present the detailed results in a separate Table 3, while in the following we report and discuss the aggregated outcomes. We report the outcome of the Friedman's test for multiple achievements of multiple subjects [7]. Compared to ANOVA, it does not require the distributions of variables in question to be normal (which we cannot assume for most of the performance indicators considered here). It is then worth pointing out that the results presented below are very conservative in terms of statistical significance, i.e., many insignificant differences could become significant given larger pool of benchmarks.

Before passing to the pairwise comparisons, we report the average ranks of the methods (the lower, the better):

BPGP4A	GP1L	BP2A	BPGP4	GP1	GP2
2.43	3.10	3.36	3.43	**3.86**	**4.83**

The p-value for Friedman test is $\ll 0.001$, which strongly indicates that at least one method performs significantly different from the remaining ones. We conducted post-hoc analysis using symmetry test [5]: bold font above marks the methods that are outranked at 0.05 significance level by the *first* method in the ranking (BPGP4A in this case).

The BPGP4A variant ranks the best, outperforming conventional GP methods, including even the GP1L configuration, which has ten times greater number of evaluations at its disposal. For GP1L, the difference is statistically insignificant but the difference in ranking might signal significance if it holds over more benchmarks.

BPGP methods managed to solve (at least once in 30 evolutionary run) five problems that remained unsolved by GP algorithms. These are (see Table 3): D-a1, D-a4, D-a5, Keij4, and Par8. On the other hand, the only benchmark that they could not solve while GP could is Nguy5.

Error rate. In this section we treat the benchmarks as *optimization problems*. In that case, the objective is to minimize the error, and the appropriate performance measure is the error (f) of the best-of-run program.

We report the results for this performance measure in an analogous way to the previous section. The Friedman test is conclusive, and methods' ranks are as follows:

BPGP4A	GP1L	BP2A	BPGP4	GP1	GP2
2.17	2.21	**3.31**	**3.71**	**3.79**	**5.8**

Again, BPGP4A ranks the best, and this time even beats the BPGP configurations that miss one of the components: behavioral evaluation (BP2A) and subprogram archive (BPGP4).

Predictive accuracy. For the Boolean and categorical problems considered in this paper, the training sets contain all fitness cases, so predictive accuracy cannot be assessed. However, it is possible for the regression problems. To this aim, we calculate the error of best-of-run individuals on 10,000 tests drawn at random from the same domain (hypercube) as for the training set. The ranking according to this performance measure is:

BPGP4	BPGP4A	BP2A	GP1	GP1L	GP2
2.65	3.35	3.47	3.47	3.59	4.47

The BPGP-based methods rank best again, but the differences in ranks are less prominent, and, as a result, the Friedman test is inconclusive. However, its p-value is relatively low (0.142), which makes it likely that BPGP superiority would become significant on a larger repertoire of problems.

Run time. Behavioral evaluation and maintenance of an archive impose additional computational costs. To assess their impact, we measure the total run time of every algorithm (which terminates if ideal solution is found or when the number of generation elapses). Methods ranked according to runtime are (see detailed results in Table 3):

GP1	GP2	BPGP4	BPGP4A	BP2A	GP1L
1.09	**3.11**	**3.77**	**3.97**	**4.09**	**4.97**

Expectantly, conventional GP running with small population is much faster than all the other methods. However, it performs much worse on the other measures considered above.

It is interesting to see that the BPGP-based methods are faster than GP1L. In combination with the results on other measures, this allows us to conclude that B4A does not only find better solutions that GP1L, but also does it at a lower computational expense.

Program size. The ranking of configurations according to the size of the best-of-run program is as follows:

GP2	BPGP4	BP2A	BPGP4A	GP1	GP1L
1.26	**2.57**	**2.89**	**3.91**	**4.81**	**5.56**

GP2 wins on this measure, which may be attributed to the fact that (i) it uses program size s as one of the objectives (contrary to GP1 and GP1L), and (ii) s is the only additional objective (other than program error f) that it employs (as opposed to BPGP4 and BPGP4A that also use yet another two objectives, c and e). As a result, s is a very important objective in this configuration, and allows is to produce very compact programs. However, given the poor performance of GP2 on the other measures, one may argue that the impact of this objective in this particular configuration is detrimental (as opposed to BPGP4 and BPGP4A, where it acts as only as one of four objectives).

The above ranking takes into account the best-of-run individuals of all evolutionary runs, whether successful or not. For the successful runs only, the outcome is

BPGP4	GP2	BP2A	BPGP4A	GP1	GP1L
1.35	2.35	3.2	4.1	**4.9**	**5.1**

It turns out then that BPGP4 is able to provide ideal solutions that are on average even smaller than those of GP2 (though the difference is not statistically significant).

4.4 Experiment summary

The experimental results clearly indicate that BPGP is more likely to find an ideal solution than the traditional GP methods, proves capable of solving problems that GP struggles with, produces programs that commit smaller error and generalize better, requires moderate computational effort, and in some configurations (BPGP4) yields smaller ideal solutions.

Another important outcome is that combining behavioral evaluation with an archive-based search operator (in BPGP4A) seems to be beneficial, particularly for success rate and program error. This corroborates the hypothesis posed earlier, that these two components can complement each other and lead to synergy. However, this does not mean that behavioral evaluation or archive-based search operator alone have no virtues: for instance, BPGP4 seems a viable method for finding compact programs that generalize very well.

5. CONCLUSION

The gathered evidence suggests that behavioral programming is a promising methodology for evolutionary synthesis of programs. BPGP, a method that represents this approach, provides superb results for many problems from various domains, is universal by not requiring any adjustments to a domain or problem, is almost parameterless (except for archive size), and can employ any suitable machine learning technique as a generator of behavioral models.

Another appeal of behavioral programming is that the additional 'search drivers' are in a sense *invented* by the search algorithm. By relying on ML-induced behavioral models, behavioral programming can autonomously detect behavioral regularities/patterns that reveal potentially useful candidate solutions (via behavioral evaluation) and parts thereof (via manipulation of subprograms). No background knowledge or human ingenuity is necessary for that purpose: the experimenter is not required to, e.g., specify, in addition to providing an objective function, which properties/qualities of subsolutions are desirable. This makes behavioral programming attractive when compared to, e.g., some reinforcement learning methods in which the additional search drivers have to be explicitly provided [19].

One might wonder why could such search drivers be more useful than the original objective function? In the end, it is the objective function that comes as a part of problem formulation and ultimately characterizes solution quality. Unfortunately, as demonstrated in countless studies on fitness-distance correlation, in problems with complex fitness landscapes, with intricate neighborhood structure, plateaus, and local optima, there is absolutely no guarantee that the objective function correlates with the amount of computational effort it will take to solve the problem. Therefore, it is justified to suppose that other objectives (or a combination thereof, as in this study) may lead a given search algorithm more efficiently. As odd as it sounds, the objective function can be sometimes precisely the *worst possible* search driver, as it is the case in deceptive problems.

On a higher level of discourse, we anticipate that behavioral programming is capable of joining a new *paradigm* for program evolution/synthesis, that is based upon semantics, a.k.a. behavior. The particular realization of behavioral programming in this study, BPGP was embedded in conventional tree-based genetic programming. However, nothing precludes applying it to other program representations, or in combination with other search mechanisms.

Acknowledgments. The authors thank the members of the ALFA Group. Krzysztof Krawiec acknowledges financial support from Fulbright Commission and grant no. DEC-2011/01/B/ST6/07318. Una-May O'Reilly acknowledges support from the Li Ka Shing Foundation. Both authors thank Faustynka, Dominika and Michasia Krawiec for verifying Table 3.

6. REFERENCES

[1] A. Bajurnow and V. Ciesielski. Layered learning for evolving goal scoring behavior in soccer players. In *Proceedings of the 2004 IEEE Congress on Evolutionary Computation*, pages 1828–1835, Portland, Oregon, 20-23 June 2004. IEEE Press.

[2] K. Deb, A. Pratap, S. Agarwal, and T. Meyarivan. A fast and elitist multiobjective genetic algorithm: NSGA-II. *Evolutionary Computation, IEEE Transactions on*, 6(2):182–197, apr 2002.

[3] M. Hall, E. Frank, G. Holmes, B. Pfahringer, P. Reutemann, and I. H. Witten. The weka data mining software: An update. *SIGKDD Explor. Newsl.*, 11(1):10–18, Nov. 2009.

[4] T. Haynes. On-line adaptation of search via knowledge reuse. In J. R. Koza, K. Deb, M. Dorigo, D. B. Fogel, M. Garzon, H. Iba, and R. L. Riolo, editors, *Genetic Programming 1997: Proceedings of the Second Annual Conference*, pages 156–161, Stanford University, CA, USA, 13-16 July 1997. Morgan Kaufmann.

[5] M. Hollander and D. Wolfe. *Nonparametric Statistical Methods*. A Wiley-Interscience publication. Wiley, 1999.

[6] G. S. Hornby and J. B. Pollack. Creating high-level components with a generative representation for body-brain evolution. *Artif. Life*, 8(3):223–246, 2002.

[7] G. Kanji. *100 Statistical Tests*. SAGE Publications, 1999.

[8] J. D. Knowles, R. A. Watson, and D. Corne. Reducing local optima in single-objective problems by multi-objectivization. In *EMO '01: Proceedings of the First International Conference on Evolutionary Multi-Criterion Optimization*, pages 269–283, London, UK, 2001. Springer-Verlag.

[9] K. Krawiec and J. Swan. Pattern-guided genetic programming. In C. Blum, et al., editors, *GECCO '13: Proceeding of the fifteenth annual conference on Genetic and evolutionary computation conference*, pages 949–956, Amsterdam, The Netherlands, 6-10 July 2013. ACM.

[10] J. Lehman and K. O. Stanley. Abandoning objectives: Evolution through the search for novelty alone. *Evolutionary Computation*, 19(2):189–223, Summer 2011.

Table 3: Detailed characteristics of best-of-run individuals, averaged over 30 evolutionary runs. Bold marks the best result for each benchmark and performance indicator (not necessarily statistically significant).

	Success rate (×100)						Average error						Average run time [seconds]						Average program size [nodes]					
	GP1	GP1L	GP2	BP2A	BP4A	BP4	GP1	GP1L	GP2	BP2A	BP4A	BP4	GP1	GP1L	GP2	BP2A	BP4A	BP4	GP1	GP1L	GP2	BP2A	BP4A	BP4
Cmp06	43	77	0	**100**	**100**	97	.015	.007	.089	**.000**	**.000**	.001	48	418	140	68	**15**	64	351	392	**15**	80	156	52
Cmp08	3	57	0	60	**100**	20	.020	.005	.139	.019	**.000**	.025	233	2587	279	825	**220**	933	466	643	**11**	108	242	70
D.A1	0	0	0	13	**47**	0	.216	.212	.222	.131	**.026**	.074	**2**	19	50	128	136	117	8	21	**1**	35	134	48
D.A2	0	10	0	7	**70**	7	.190	.181	.222	.128	**.014**	.059	**5**	53	49	128	95	124	71	74	**1**	33	202	58
D.A3	20	53	0	47	**97**	47	.085	.062	.222	.052	**.001**	.021	**14**	131	49	97	36	94	192	233	**1**	69	152	47
D.A4	0	0	0	0	**23**	0	.222	.222	.222	.211	**.060**	.109	**1**	6	49	104	180	142	**1**	**1**	**1**	6	196	83
D.A5	0	0	0	7	**80**	20	.222	.222	.222	.191	**.011**	.056	**1**	7	50	110	96	126	**1**	**1**	**1**	13	168	68
Keij1	0	0	0	0	0	0	.125	**.073**	.257	.275	.234	.278	**26**	567	99	129	151	116	189	447	**34**	36	60	51
Keij11	7	7	3	10	**33**	20	.659	.604	.882	.212	**.110**	.322	**14**	243	104	160	151	118	90	177	36	29	**27**	34
Keij12	0	0	0	0	0	0	.802	**.661**	.966	.932	.929	.902	**31**	504	103	140	173	135	181	296	**37**	65	112	78
Keij13	10	10	17	7	0	**30**	.231	**.125**	.607	.245	.346	.214	**28**	505	88	139	166	92	161	280	**26**	37	38	34
Keij14	0	0	0	0	0	0	.708	**.657**	.855	.683	.683	.774	**19**	339	86	122	143	113	100	207	**20**	32	35	37
Keij15	0	0	0	0	0	0	.721	.597	.846	**.576**	.613	.697	**24**	412	128	193	213	156	141	295	**45**	64	59	57
Keij4	0	0	0	**3**	0	0	.358	**.249**	.508	.281	.265	.272	**29**	585	93	144	160	127	187	390	**46**	62	85	68
Keij5	0	0	0	0	0	0	.362	**.246**	.759	.479	.583	.569	**43**	783	200	376	468	316	129	243	**26**	40	49	46
M.A1	**83**	**83**	0	40	**83**	43	.013	**.011**	.242	.040	**.011**	.038	**4**	36	66	82	41	61	181	173	**14**	53	142	40
M.A2	50	63	0	50	**97**	30	.053	.038	.187	.047	**.002**	.064	**9**	70	75	64	21	74	184	181	**18**	61	160	44
M.A3	83	90	3	77	**97**	33	.011	.007	.262	.016	**.002**	.044	**8**	49	59	47	27	66	240	253	**13**	67	104	38
M.A4	27	37	0	23	**100**	43	.102	.073	.269	.129	**.000**	.044	14	147	68	92	**9**	65	255	240	**13**	40	115	43
M.A5	77	**100**	13	93	**100**	90	.018	**.000**	.171	.007	**.000**	.007	**4**	21	65	28	14	29	132	146	**19**	57	74	37
Maj06	83	90	3	90	**100**	90	.003	.002	.048	.002	**.000**	.002	**21**	145	203	71	36	132	361	365	**35**	149	280	79
Maj08	23	53	0	47	**93**	0	.013	.005	.051	.010	**.001**	.032	**329**	3170	1156	1769	2019	1834	687	938	**94**	295	563	145
Mux06	**100**	**100**	17	**100**	**100**	87	**.000**	**.000**	.090	**.000**	**.000**	.011	**3**	**3**	132	13	10	38	169	169	**19**	68	117	39
Mux11	53	97	3	93	**100**	10	.020	.001	.200	.005	**.000**	.056	**1391**	3809	6757	9713	9780	13362	481	496	**32**	193	303	70
Nguy10	50	53	30	**60**	43	57	.050	**.026**	.171	.054	.079	.105	**8**	120	82	88	121	76	47	98	**22**	25	27	**22**
Nguy12	0	0	0	0	0	0	.301	**.262**	.436	.335	.314	.289	**17**	246	86	123	164	132	90	152	**13**	41	51	49
Nguy3	**23**	**23**	**23**	3	0	13	.101	**.035**	.255	.127	.136	.286	**15**	310	76	133	145	89	122	245	**22**	49	52	25
Nguy4	7	7	3	3	10	**13**	.130	**.045**	.328	.172	.138	.219	**17**	404	92	122	123	91	119	350	**27**	52	47	37
Nguy5	**3**	**3**	**3**	0	0	0	.019	**.007**	.062	.032	.026	.021	**15**	340	95	115	132	107	104	291	**19**	25	**19**	20
Nguy6	43	43	50	83	**93**	80	.034	.020	.105	.005	**.002**	.024	**9**	213	64	46	39	53	71	183	18	19	17	**15**
Nguy7	**7**	**7**	0	3	0	3	.052	**.023**	.156	.037	.040	.134	**16**	315	101	125	142	104	110	255	**25**	70	87	29
Nguy9	47	50	33	73	87	**100**	.147	.117	.082	.027	.002	**.000**	**8**	104	73	77	78	14	50	85	9	10	15	**7**
Par06	0	13	0	23	**100**	13	.155	.075	.429	.133	**.000**	.137	**118**	2065	188	466	233	404	677	1018	**24**	128	356	108
Par08	0	0	0	0	**40**	0	.309	.207	.486	.374	**.115**	.326	**365**	7359	648	2081	3792	2845	696	1343	**23**	138	581	168
Sext	**3**	**3**	0	0	0	**3**	.029	**.019**	.089	.031	.041	.048	**22**	436	105	137	151	118	164	372	**34**	36	37	45

[11] S. Luke. ECJ evolutionary computation system, 2002. (http://cs.gmu.edu/eclab/projects/ecj/).

[12] J. McDermott, D. R. White, S. Luke, L. Manzoni, M. Castelli, L. Vanneschi, W. Jaskowski, K. Krawiec, R. Harper, K. De Jong, and U.-M. O'Reilly. Genetic programming needs better benchmarks. In T. Soule, et al., editors, *GECCO '12: Proceedings of the fourteenth international conference on Genetic and evolutionary computation conference*, pages 791–798, Philadelphia, Pennsylvania, USA, 7-11 July 2012. ACM.

[13] R. I. B. McKay. Fitness sharing in genetic programming. In D. Whitley, D. Goldberg, E. Cantu-Paz, L. Spector, I. Parmee, and H.-G. Beyer, editors, *Proceedings of the Genetic and Evolutionary Computation Conference (GECCO-2000)*, pages 435–442, Las Vegas, Nevada, USA, 10-12 July 2000. Morgan Kaufmann.

[14] N. F. McPhee, B. Ohs, and T. Hutchison. Semantic building blocks in genetic programming. In M. O'Neill, L. Vanneschi, S. Gustafson, A. I. Esparcia Alcazar, I. De Falco, A. Della Cioppa, and E. Tarantino, editors, *Proceedings of the 11th European Conference on Genetic Programming, EuroGP 2008*, volume 4971 of *Lecture Notes in Computer Science*, pages 134–145, Naples, 26-28 Mar. 2008. Springer.

[15] A. Moraglio, K. Krawiec, and C. G. Johnson. Geometric semantic genetic programming. In C. A. Coello Coello, V. Cutello, K. Deb, S. Forrest, G. Nicosia, and M. Pavone, editors, *Parallel Problem Solving from Nature, PPSN XII (part 1)*, volume 7491 of *Lecture Notes in Computer Science*, pages 21–31, Taormina, Italy, Sept. 1-5 2012. Springer.

[16] A. Moraglio and A. Mambrini. Runtime analysis of mutation-based geometric semantic genetic programming for basis functions regression. In C. Blum, et al., editors, *GECCO '13: Proceeding of the fifteenth annual conference on Genetic and evolutionary computation conference*, pages 989–996, Amsterdam, The Netherlands, 6-10 July 2013. ACM.

[17] J. P. Rosca and D. H. Ballard. Discovery of subroutines in genetic programming. In P. J. Angeline and K. E. Kinnear, Jr., editors, *Advances in Genetic Programming 2*, chapter 9, pages 177–201. MIT Press, Cambridge, MA, USA, 1996.

[18] C. Ryan, M. Keijzer, and M. Cattolico. Favorable biasing of function sets using run transferable libraries. In U.-M. O'Reilly, T. Yu, R. L. Riolo, and B. Worzel, editors, *Genetic Programming Theory and Practice II*, chapter 7, pages 103–120. Springer, Ann Arbor, 13-15 May 2004.

[19] S. Singh, R. L. Lewis, A. G. Barto, and J. Sorg. Intrinsically motivated reinforcement learning: An evolutionary perspective. *IEEE Trans. on Auton. Ment. Dev.*, 2(2):70–82, June 2010.

[20] L. Spector, D. M. Clark, I. Lindsay, B. Barr, and J. Klein. Genetic programming for finite algebras. In M. Keijzer, et al., editors, *GECCO '08: Proceedings of the 10th annual conference on Genetic and evolutionary computation*, pages 1291–1298, Atlanta, GA, USA, 12-16 July 2008. ACM.

Utilization of Reductions and Abstraction Elimination in Typed Genetic Programming

Tomáš Křen[*†]
tomkren@gmail.com

[*]Faculty of Mathematics and Physics
Charles University in Prague
Malostranské náměstí 25, 11000,
Prague, Czech Republic

Roman Neruda[†]
roman@cs.cas.cz

[†]Institute of Computer Science
Academy of Sciences of the Czech Republic
Pod Vodárenskou věží 2, 18207,
Prague, Czech Republic

ABSTRACT

Lambda calculus representation of programs offers a more expressive alternative to traditional S-expressions. In this paper we discuss advantages of this representation coming from the use of reductions (beta and eta) and a way to overcome disadvantages caused by variables occurring in the programs by use of the abstraction elimination algorithm. We discuss the role of those reductions in the process of generating initial population and propose two novel crossover operations based on abstraction elimination capable of handling general form of typed lambda term while being a straight generalization of the standard crossover operation. We compare their performances using the even parity benchmark problem.

Categories and Subject Descriptors

I.2.2 [**Artificial Intelligence**]: Automatic Programming—*Program synthesis*; F.4.1 [**Mathematical Logic and Formal Languages**]: Mathematical Logic—*Lambda calculus and related systems*

General Terms

Experimentation, Languages, Theory

Keywords

genetic programming; lambda calculus

1. INTRODUCTION

Genetic programming (GP) represents an efficient method for automatic generating of programs by means of evolutionary techniques [5, 6]. Early attempts to enhance the GP approach with the concept of types include the seminal work [9] where the ideas from Ada programming language were used to define a so-called strongly typed GP. Usage of types naturally opens door to enriching S-expressions, the traditional GP representation of individuals, with concepts from lambda calculus, which is a simple yet powerful functional, mathematical and programming language extensively used in type theory [11].

One of the motivations for using lambda calculus is that it is backed by a considerable theoretical background. From this background we can utilize several useful concepts such as reductions, normalization or abstraction elimination, and use them to enhance the standard GP algorithm. We use normalization to reduce the size of the search space of program trees and the abstraction elimination to prevent the difficulties caused by the presence of variables in program trees.

In our system we use a simply typed lambda calculus. Since abstraction elimination and reductions do not involve many type related issues it seems to us as a sufficient choice of a type system. Techniques described here would be analogous for a more sophisticated type system and can be directly applied to such systems as the Hindley–Milner type system.

In this paper we present an approach to typed GP over lambda calculus capable of operating with the full array of notions given by a simply typed lambda calculus while being a direct generalization of standard GP [5]. We discuss the advantages of generating lambda terms in their long normal form and present two novel crossover operations for simply typed lambda terms. Compared to the approach to typed GP over lambda calculus proposed by Yu [11], it uses more general term representation which is not restricting the use of outer local variables in the body of an anonymous function. Compared to the purely combinator approach by Briggs and O'Neill [4], it has the advantage of reducing the size of the search space in the term generation phase.

The rest of the paper is organized as follows: The next section briefly discusses related work in the field of typed GP, while section 3 introduces necessary notions. The body of the paper is presented in sections 4 and 5; the former discusses the term generating procedure and its relations with reductions, the latter describes several approaches to lambda term crossover, and how they solve the variable problem. Section 6 examines those ideas on the even parity benchmark problem, while the paper is concluded by section 7.

GECCO'14, July 12–16, 2014, Vancouver, BC, Canada.

ACM 978-1-4503-2662-9/14/07 ...$15.00.
http://dx.doi.org/10.1145/2576768.2598361.

2. RELATED WORK

Yu presents a GP system utilizing polymorphic higher-order functions and lambda abstractions [11]. An important point of interest in the work is the use of `foldr` function as a tool for *implicit recursion*, i.e., recursion without explicit recursive calls. The terminal set for constructing lambda abstraction subtrees is limited to use only constants and variables of that particular lambda abstraction, i.e., outer variables are not allowed to be used as terminals in this work. This is a significant difference from our approach since we permit all well-typed normalized λ-terms. This difference also causes the need for different crossover operators.

Briggs and O'Neill present a technique utilizing typed GP with combinators [4]. The difference between the approach presented in their work and our approach is that they generate terms in a straightforward way directly from the library of combinators, without any use of lambda abstractions. They use the Hindley–Milner type system. They also present an interesting concept of *Generalized genetic operator* based on term generation. The combinator based genetic algorithm has the advantage of avoiding the need of dealing with variables.

Binard and Felty use an even stronger type system, the (*System F*) [3]. But with the increasing power of the type system also comes an increasing difficulty of term generation. For this reason, the evolution in this work takes interesting and nonstandard shape (fitness is associated with *genes* which are evolved together with *species* which together participate in creation of individuals). This differs from our approach which tries to be a straightforward generalization of the standard GP[5].

In contrast to the above mentioned works, our approach uses a very simple type system (the simply typed lambda calculus) and concentrates on process of generation able to generate all possible well-typed normalized lambda terms. In order to do so we use technique based on *inhabitation machines* described by Barendregt[2].

3. PRELIMINARIES

In this section, several notions necessary to build a typed GP based on lambda calculus are introduced. First, let us describe a programming language, in which the GP algorithm generates individual programs — the so called λ-terms.

DEFINITION 1. *Let V be infinite countable set of variable names. Let C be set of constant names, $V \cap C = \emptyset$. Then Λ is set of λ-terms defined inductively as follows.*

$$x \in V \cup C \Rightarrow x \in \Lambda$$
$$M, N \in \Lambda \Rightarrow (M\ N) \in \Lambda \qquad \textit{(Function application)}$$
$$x \in V, M \in \Lambda \Rightarrow (\lambda\, x\, .\, M) \in \Lambda \qquad \textit{(λ-abstraction)}$$

Function application and *λ-abstraction* are concepts well known from common programming languages. For example, in JavaScript, $(M\ N)$ translates to expression M`(`N`)` and $(\lambda\, x\, .\, M)$ translates to expression `function(`x`){return` M`;}`. In other words, the function application corresponds to the act of supplying a function with an argument, and the λ-abstraction is equivalent to *anonymous function*[1].

[1]Apart from JavaScript, anonymous functions are common e.g. in Python and Ruby, they were recently introduced to C++, and they are expected to be supported in Java 8.

To ensure better readability, $M_1\ M_2\ M_3\ \ldots\ M_n$ will be an abbreviation for $(\ldots((M_1\ M_2)\ M_3)\ \ldots\ M_n)$. And $\lambda\, x_1 x_2 \ldots x_n\, .\, M$ for $(\lambda\, x_1\, .\, (\lambda\, x_2\, .\, \ldots (\lambda\, x_n\, .\, M) \ldots))$.

3.1 Reductions

In order to perform computation, there must be some mechanism for term evaluation. In λ-calculus there is a β-reduction procedure for this reason.

A term of a form $(\lambda\, x\, .\, M)N$ is called *β-redex*. A β-redex can be β-reduced to term $M[x := N]$. This fact is written as *relation* $\rightarrow_\beta$ of those two terms:

$$(\lambda\, x\, .\, M)N \rightarrow_\beta M[x := N] \qquad (1)$$

It is also possible to reduce *subterm β-redexes* which can be formally stated as:

$$P \rightarrow_\beta Q \Rightarrow (R\ P) \rightarrow_\beta (R\ Q)$$
$$P \rightarrow_\beta Q \Rightarrow (P\ R) \rightarrow_\beta (Q\ R)$$
$$P \rightarrow_\beta Q \Rightarrow \lambda\, x\, .\, P \rightarrow_\beta \lambda\, x\, .\, Q$$

In other words, β-reduction is the process of insertion of arguments supplied to a function into its body.

Another useful relations are $\twoheadrightarrow_\beta$ and $=_\beta$ defined as follows.

1. (a) $M \twoheadrightarrow_\beta M$
   (b) $M \rightarrow_\beta N \Rightarrow M \twoheadrightarrow_\beta N$
   (c) $M \twoheadrightarrow_\beta N, N \twoheadrightarrow_\beta L \Rightarrow M \twoheadrightarrow_\beta L$
2. (a) $M \twoheadrightarrow_\beta N \Rightarrow M =_\beta N$
   (b) $M =_\beta N \Rightarrow N =_\beta M$
   (c) $M =_\beta N, N =_\beta L \Rightarrow M =_\beta L$

We read those relations as follows.

1. $M \twoheadrightarrow_\beta N$ — "M β-reduces to N."
2. $M \rightarrow_\beta N$ — "M β-reduces to N in one step."
3. $M =_\beta N$ — "M is β-convertible to N."

Similarly as for β-reduction we can define η-reduction except that now it is defined as follows.

$$(\lambda\, x\, .\, (M\ x)) \rightarrow_\eta M \qquad \textbf{if } x \notin FV(M)$$

Analogically, a term of a form $(\lambda\, x\, .\, (M\ x))$ is called *η-redex*.

Relation[2] $\rightarrow_{\beta\eta} = \rightarrow_\beta \cup \rightarrow_\eta$. Similarly as for $\twoheadrightarrow_\beta$ and $=_\beta$ we can define relations $\twoheadrightarrow_\eta$, $=_\eta$, $\twoheadrightarrow_{\beta\eta}$ and $=_{\beta\eta}$.

The η^{-1}-reduction (also called η-expansion) is the reduction converse to η-reduction. It is defined as follows.

$$M \rightarrow_{\eta^{-1}} (\lambda\, x\, .\, (M\ x)) \qquad \textbf{if } x \notin FV(M)$$

3.2 Normal forms

DEFINITION 2.

1. *A λ-term is a β-normal form (β-nf) if it does not have a β-redex as subterm.*
2. *A λ-term M has a β-nf if $M =_\beta N$ and N is a β-nf.*

A normal form may be thought of as a result of a term evaluation. Normalization of the term M is the process of finding normal form of M. Similarly we can define *η-nf* and *$\beta\eta$-nf*.

[2]Relation $R = \{\ (a, b) \mid a\ R\ b\ \}$.

3.3 Types

A λ-term as described above corresponds to a program expression with no type information included. Now we will describe *types* (or *type terms*).

DEFINITION 3. *Let A be set of atomic type names. Then $\mathbb{T}$ is set of types inductively defined as follows.*

$$\alpha \in A \Rightarrow \alpha \in \mathbb{T}$$
$$\sigma, \tau \in \mathbb{T} \Rightarrow (\sigma \to \tau) \in \mathbb{T}$$

Type $\sigma \to \tau$ is type for functions taking as input something of a type σ and returning as output something of a type τ. $\tau_1 \to \tau_2 \to \ldots \to \tau_n$ is an abbreviation for $\tau_1 \to (\tau_2 \to (\ldots \to (\tau_{n-1} \to \tau_n)\ldots))$. The system called *simply typed λ-calculus* is now easily obtained by combining the previously defined *λ-terms* and *types* together.

DEFINITION 4.

1. *Let Λ be set of λ-terms. Let $\mathbb{T}$ be set of types. A statement $M : \sigma$ is a pair $(M, \sigma) \in \Lambda \times \mathbb{T}$. Statement $M : \sigma$ is vocalized as "M has type σ". The term M is called the subject of the statement $M : \sigma$.*
2. *A declaration is a statement $x : \sigma$ where $x \in V \cup C$.*
3. *A context is set of declarations with distinct variables as subjects.*

Context is a basic type theoretic concept suitable as a typed alternative for terminal, and function set in standard GP. Notation $\Gamma, x : \sigma$ denotes $\Gamma \cup \{(x : \sigma)\}$ such that Γ does not contain any declaration with x as subject. We also write $x : \sigma \in \Gamma$ instead of $(x, \sigma) \in \Gamma$.

DEFINITION 5. *A statement $M : \sigma$ is derivable from context Γ (notation $\Gamma \vdash M : \sigma$) if it can be produced by the following rules.*

$$x : \sigma \in \Gamma \;\Rightarrow\; \Gamma \vdash x : \sigma$$
$$\Gamma \vdash M : \sigma \to \tau\,,\; \Gamma \vdash N : \sigma \;\Rightarrow\; \Gamma \vdash (M\ N) : \tau$$
$$\Gamma, x : \sigma \vdash M : \tau \;\Rightarrow\; \Gamma \vdash (\lambda x\,.\,M) : \sigma \to \tau$$

Our goal in term generation is to produce terms M for a given pair $\langle \tau; \Gamma \rangle$ such that for each M is $\Gamma \vdash M : \tau$.

3.4 Long normal form

DEFINITION 6. *Let $\Gamma \vdash M : \sigma$ where $\sigma = \tau_1 \to \ldots \to \tau_n \to \alpha, n \geq 0$.*

1. *Then M is in long normal form (lnf) if following conditions are satisfied.*
   (a) *M is term of the form $\lambda\, x_1 \ldots x_n\,.\, f\ M_1\ \ldots\ M_m$ (specially for $n = 0$, M is term of the form f).*
   (b) *Each M_i is in lnf.*
2. *M has a lnf if $M =_{\beta\eta} N$ and N is in lnf.*

As is shown in [2], *lnf* has following nice properties.

PROPOSITION 1. *If M has a β-nf, then it also has an unique lnf, which is also its unique $\beta\eta^{-1}$-nf.*

PROPOSITION 2. *Every B in β-nf has a lnf L such that $L \twoheadrightarrow_\eta B$.*

3.5 Abstraction elimination

Abstraction elimination is a process of transforming an arbitrary λ-term into λ-term that contains no lambda abstractions and no bound variables. The newly produced λ-term may contain function applications, free symbols from former λ-term and some new symbols standing for combinators **S**, **K** and **I**.

Those combinators are defined as:

$$\mathbf{S} = \lambda\, f\, g\, x\,.\, f\, x\, (g\, x)$$
$$\mathbf{K} = \lambda\, x\, y\,.\, x$$
$$\mathbf{I} = \lambda\, x\,.\, x$$

Let us describe transformation AE performing this process.

$$\mathrm{AE}[x] = x$$
$$\mathrm{AE}[\,(M\,N)\,] = (\mathrm{AE}[M]\ \ \mathrm{AE}[N])$$
$$\mathrm{AE}[\lambda\, x\,.\, x] = \mathbf{I}$$
$$\mathrm{AE}[\lambda\, x\,.\, M] = (\mathbf{K}\ \ \mathrm{AE}[M])\ \textbf{if}\ x \notin \mathrm{FV}(M)$$
$$\mathrm{AE}[\lambda\, x\,.\,(\lambda\, y\,.\, M)] = \mathrm{AE}[\lambda\, x\,.\ \mathrm{AE}[\lambda\, y\,.\, M]]\ \textbf{if}\ x \in \mathrm{FV}(M)$$
$$\mathrm{AE}[\lambda\, x\,.\,(M\,N)] = (\mathbf{S}\ \ \mathrm{AE}[\lambda\, x\,.\, M]\ \ \mathrm{AE}[\lambda\, x\,.\, N])$$
$$\textbf{if}\ x \in \mathrm{FV}(M) \vee\ x \in \mathrm{FV}(N)$$

As is stated in [10], the biggest disadvantage of this technique is that the translated term is often much larger than in its lambda form — the size of the translated term can be proportional to the square of the size of the original term. But the advantage is also tempting — no need to deal with variables and lambda abstractions.

The algorithm presented here is a simple version of this process. More optimized version (used in our *hybrid* crossover described below), by means of the size of resulting term and its time performance is presented in [10].

4. GENERATING AND REDUCTIONS

This section is focused on the individual generating method producing terms in their long normal form, which can be understood as a straight generalization of S-expressions into lambda calculus. We discuss the relation between terms in *lnf* with beta and eta reductions, the advantages of such representation and we also show how to easily transform such terms into short $\beta\eta$-*nf*.

4.1 Grammar producing λ-terms in *lnf*

In [2], the following term generating 2-level grammar[3] for generating all possible terms in their *long normal form* is described.

If we want to generate a term M satisfying $\Gamma \vdash M : \tau$, then the initial non-terminal is (τ, Γ).

For every $\alpha \in A$ and context Γ and f such that $(f : \rho_1 \to \ldots \to \rho_m \to \alpha\ ) \in \Gamma$ we have a rule of the first form:

$$(\alpha, \Gamma) \longmapsto (\ f\ (\rho_1, \Gamma)\ \ldots\ (\rho_m, \Gamma)\ )$$

[3] 2-level grammar (unlike a standard grammar) can have infinitely many non-terminals and its rule is better described as *rule schema*. The original grammar described in [2] has $(\sigma \to \tau, \Gamma) \longmapsto (\ \lambda\ x\ .\ (\tau; \Gamma, x : \sigma)\ )$ as second rule, but our grammar is equivalent – it packs consecutive uses of this rule into our rule.

In other words, one possible way to construct a term of the atomic type α from the building symbols Γ is to take a function symbol f from Γ with the return type α (or if $m = 0$ a constant of the type α), put it into the root of the term and to generate a subtrees of appropriate types for each of f's arguments from the building symbols Γ.

For every atomic type α, context Γ and types $\tau_1, \ldots, \tau_n$ (where $n > 0$) we have a rule of the second form:

$$(\tau_1 \to \ldots \to \tau_n \to \alpha, \Gamma)$$
$$\longmapsto (\ \lambda\ x_1\ \ldots\ x_n\ .\ (\alpha; \Gamma, x_1 : \tau_1, \ldots, x_n : \tau_n)\ )$$

In other words, the way to construct a term of the function type $\tau_1 \to \ldots \to \tau_n \to \alpha$ from the building symbols Γ is to create an anonymous function with fresh variables $x_1, \ldots, x_n$ in its head whose body is constructed as a term that has type α and is constructed using symbols from Γ enriched with those new variables $x_1, \ldots, x_n$, which are associated with appropriate types.

Long normal form is a generalization of S-expressions into lambda calculus: Let Γ be a context satisfying the closure requirement, then only the first rule will be applicable. (α, Γ) rewrites to $(\ f\ (\alpha, \Gamma)\ \ldots\ (\alpha, \Gamma)\ )$. One can see that f stands for the root node and that each (α, Γ) will produce a direct subtree.

For a context containing at least one higher order function (or if the desired type of generated terms is a function type) we get special kind of root node containing lambda head with one direct subtree standing for body of the lambda function. Local variables defined in the lambda head may also appear in this body.

Discussion of what is the best strategy for browsing the search space given by above described grammar in order to generate *lnf* terms is beyond the scope of this paper. Standard *ramped half-and-half* strategy can be used for this purpose, or some other, which we discuss in [7]. In our experiments we use the *geometric* strategy proposed in [7].

4.2 Benefits of generating λ-terms in *lnf*

By generating λ-terms in *lnf* we avoid generating λ-terms M,N such that $M \neq N$, but $M =_{\beta\eta} N$. This means that M,N correspond to two programs with different source codes, but both perform the same computation.

Every λ-term M such that $\Gamma \vdash M : \sigma$ has its unique *lnf* L, for which $L =_{\beta\eta} M$. Therefore, the computation performed by λ-term M is not omitted, because it is the same computation as the computation performed by λ-term L.

Generating λ-terms in *lnf* is even better than generating λ-terms in β-*nf*. Since *lnf* is the same thing as $\beta\eta^{-1}$-*nf*, every λ-term in *lnf* is also in β-*nf*.

This comes straight from the definition of $\beta\eta^{-1}$-*nf*, but one can also see it by observing the method for generating terms in β-*nf*. As shown in [2], this method is obtained by the following 2-level grammar.

$$(\pi, \Gamma) \longmapsto (\ f\ (\rho_1, \Gamma)\ \ldots\ (\rho_m, \Gamma)\ )$$
$$(\sigma \to \tau, \Gamma) \longmapsto (\ \lambda\ x\ .\ (\tau; \Gamma, x : \sigma)\ )$$
$$\textit{where} \quad (f : \rho_1 \to \ldots \to \rho_m \to \pi) \in \Gamma$$

This grammar differs from the grammar for *lnf* only in the first rule[4]. Specifically, it differs in that f's type is no longer needed to be fully expanded ($\pi \in \mathbb{T}$ instead of $\alpha \in A$). This makes the grammar less deterministic, resulting in a bigger search space. The new rule is generalization of the old one, thus all terms in *lnf* will be generated, along with many new terms in β-*nf* that are not in *lnf*.

By generating λ-terms in *lnf* we avoid generating λ-terms M,N such that $M \neq N$ and $M =_\eta N$; but generating in β-*nf* does not have such a property.

The disadvantage of the *lnf*, as the name suggests, is that it is long. Terms in *lnf* are said to be *fully η-expanded* [2]. A relevant property of η-reduction is that it always shortens the term that is being reduced by it. And conversely, η-expansion prolongs.

$$(\lambda\, x\, .\, (M\ x)) \to_\eta M \qquad \textbf{if } x \notin FV(M)$$

Now we show that for every λ-term M, every sequence of η-reductions is finite and it leads to a unique η-*nf* N.

1. Every application of η-reduction shortens the term. Since every term has finite size, this process must end at some point. Thus every λ-term has η-*nf*.
2. Since η-reduction is *Church–Rosser*, η-*nf* is unique (see [1]).

So we can take every generated λ-term M in *lnf* and transform it to shorter term in η-*nf*. The question is whether it remains in β-*nf*, thus being in $\beta\eta$-*nf*. The answer is yes; it can be proven by showing that no new β-redex is created by η-reduction.

PROPOSITION 3. *Let P be in β-nf and $P \to_\eta Q$. Then Q is in β-nf.*

PROOF. For better clarity let us show the η-reduction and β-redex using @-trees (a λ-term representation derived from the definition of λ-terms where @ stands for *function application*).

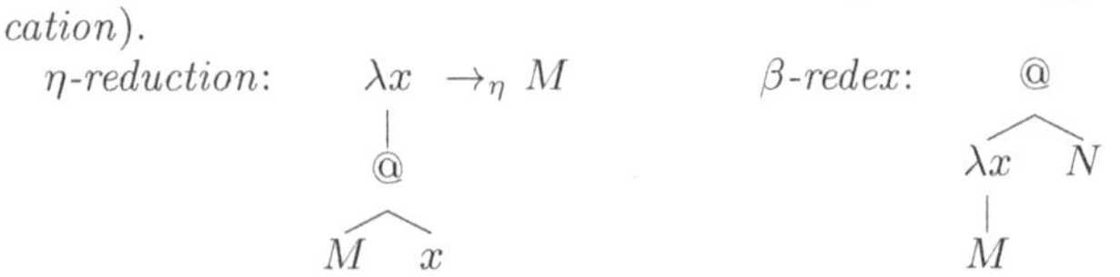

Let us assume that $P \to_\eta Q$ creates a new β-redex B in Q. Since η-reduction only destroys and never creates *function applications* (i.e. @), the root @ of B must be present in P. But since P contains no β-redex, the left subterm L of this root @ is not λ-abstraction. Only possible way for L to be changed by $\to_\eta$ into a λ-abstraction is that L is the reduced subterm (so that L is changed for its subterm). But that is in contradiction with P not containing any β-redex, because it would cause L be a λ-abstraction. □

Notable property of *lnf* and $\beta\eta$-*nf* is that there is *bijection* (i.e. one-to-one correspondence) of the set of simply typed λ-terms in *lnf* and the set of simply typed λ-terms in $\beta\eta$-*nf*.

PROPOSITION 4. *Reduction to η-nf is bijection between the set of simply typed λ-terms in lnf and the set of simply typed λ-terms in $\beta\eta$-nf.*

PROOF. Since reduction to η-*nf* always leads to an unique term, it is a function. In previous proposition is shown that η-reduction of *lnf* leads to a term in $\beta\eta$-*nf*.

In order to show that a function is bijection it is sufficient to show that it is both *injection* and *surjection*.

[4]We use a different second rule for *lnf* grammar, but as is mentioned in footnote above, it also works with this second rule.

Suppose it is not injection.

So there must be M_1, M_2 in *lnf* such that $M_1 \neq M_2$ and N in $\beta\eta$-*nf* such that $M_1 \twoheadrightarrow_\eta N$, $M_2 \twoheadrightarrow_\eta N$. Therefore $M_1 =_\eta M_2$, so $M_1 =_{\beta\eta^{-1}} M_2$. This contradicts with M_1, M_2 being distinct *lnf*s.

Every M in β-*nf* has a *lnf* N such that $N \twoheadrightarrow_\eta M$ (proposition from 3.4). Term M in $\beta\eta$-*nf* is in β-*nf*, thus it has desired *lnf* N which reduces to it.

Therefore it is surjection. □

Suppose we have a systematic method (i.e. gradually generating all terms, but no term is generated twice) for generating terms in *lnf*, we may transform it to a systematic method for generating terms in $\beta\eta$-*nf* by simply reducing each generated term to its η-*nf*.

5. CROSSOVER OPERATOR

The design goal behind our approach to the crossover operation is to try to generalize the standard tree swapping crossover.

The crossover operation in standard GP is performed by swapping randomly selected subtrees in each parent S-expression. For typed lambda terms two difficulties arise: Types and variables.

As in standard GP, our crossover will be performed by swapping two subtress of the same type.

Variables bring more difficulties then types do. The problem arises from variables that are free in subterms corresponding to swapped subtrees.

The following example illustrates the problem. Let us have these two parent trees with selected nodes in bold.

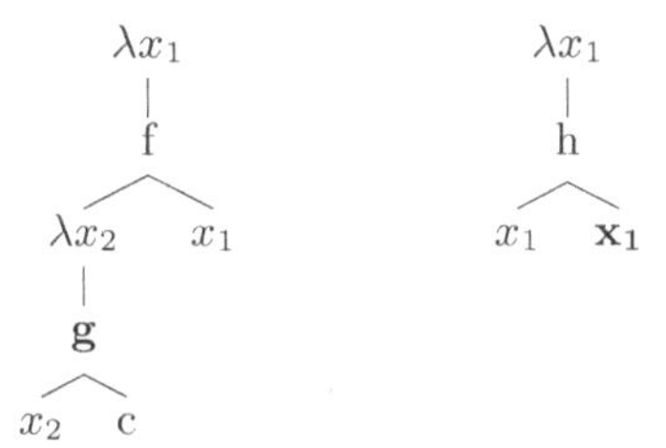

The swap of subtrees results in following trees:

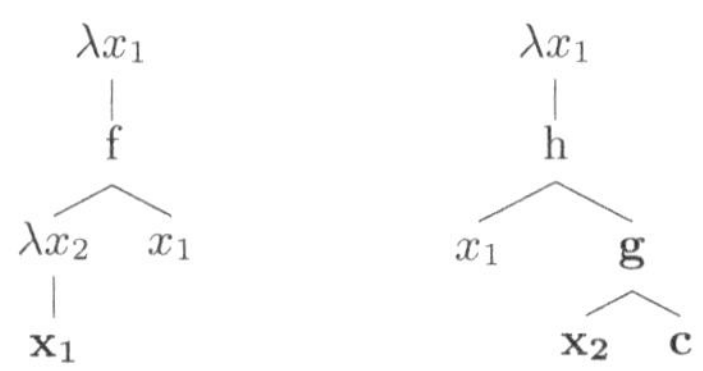

The problem is that variable x_2 in second tree is not bound by any λ-head and since it is not element of Γ, the second tree is not well-typed λ-term.

Generally speaking, the variable problem is caused by the fact that the local variable is not defined in the new place, or the variable is defined in the new place, but has a different type. Let us list some possible approaches to solving this problem.

One option is to choose a less general representation of lambda terms. Such approach is successfully used in [11] where the terminal set for constructing lambda abstraction subtrees is limited to use only constants and variables of that particular lambda abstraction, and an appropriate variable naming convention is used in order to prevent troubles with variables. We choose not to follow such approach because we do not want to lose the opportunity to represent every possible well-typed term in its normal form.

Another option is to overlook the variable problems and to correct the defects when they occur. Such correction can be performed by renaming the problematic variable to some other variable defined in the new local scope of swapped subtree. Or, if there is no suitable candidate, to replace its occurrence with a newly generated term of the required type. This approach seems to us as a very unwieldy one – there are clearly problems for which such collisions would occur very often and when there is no suitable rename candidate the generation of new term brings the unnecessary element of a mutation. Such solution seems to be useful only as a last resort.

There is an elegant way to overcome the problem with variables by getting rid of them. This is possible thanks to the abstraction elimination algorithm described above. It turns a λ-term into a λ-term that contains no lambda abstractions and no variables, instead, it contains additional function symbols standing for polymorphic combinators (i.e. **S**, **K** and **I** in the simple case of the algorithm). When there are no variables we can freely swap the subtrees of the same type.

We also use a little trick; if the type of the individual is a function type it is not necessary to abstract out the input variables (and to them associated lambda heads) of the function since all the individuals share them. (This is illustrated by the figure 2 bellow, where the root lambda head λx is still on the trees and so is the variable x in the leafs.)

We identified two approaches that utilize abstraction elimination.

5.1 Hybrid crossover

The first one converts all the generated terms at the end of the population initialization phase. We call this approach to lambda term crossover *hybrid*, because it can be understood as hybrid of the lambda calculus representation and the purely combinator representation used in [4]. The advantage of generating terms as *lnf* lambda terms instead of generating them directly as combinator terms is that it reduces the search space, because there is more than one way to represent a *lnf* lambda term as a combinator term (this can be seen considering that *lnf* term $(\lambda x \,.\, x)$ is equivalent to both **I** and **SKK**), but every combinator term has only one unique *lnf* form. Unfortunately, one disadvantage is also important; the abstraction elimination can cause up to a quadratic increase in the term size. It is reasonable to suspect that combinator terms generated directly may be smaller than those mechanically translated by the abstraction elimination. The act of producing a small normalized term and translating it immediately to a bulky combinator form can be seen as a wasteful behavior.

5.2 Unpacking crossover

Thus, we propose the following crossover operator in order to be able to analyze the above mentioned issues, which we call the *unpacking* crossover. Unlike the *hybrid* it operates over λ-terms and produces λ-term offspring in $\beta\eta$-*nf*. When two parent λ-terms are about to be crossed, they are both converted to combinator terms using the elimination abstraction algorithm. After the trees are swapped, the offspring terms are again normalized to the $\beta\eta$-*nf* λ-terms containing no temporary combinators added during the abstraction elimination. This normalization is achieved by replacement of all occurrences of temporary combinators by their respective definitions (e.g. $\mathbf{K}$ is replaced by $(\lambda xy\,.\,x)$) followed by beta and eta normalization. We believe that the property of increasing the term size is advantageous for the *unpacking* crossover. This belief is based on the fact that larger terms have more crossover points and on the observation that higher number of crossover points is beneficial for crossover operation, this observation will be discussed in more detail in the subsequent subsection. The difference between the *unpacking* and *hybrid* crossover is that in the case of the *unpacking* this increase is only in the temporary stage, which is reversed by the normalization. The most notable disadvantage of this crossover approach is that it is more time consuming than the simple one.

5.3 Typed subtree swapping in greater detail

The first thing to do in a standard subtree swapping crossover is to select random node in the first parent.

We modify this procedure so that we allow selection only of nodes with such a type that there exists a node in the second parent with the same type.

The standard subtree swapping crossover selects whether the selected node will be inner node (usually with probability $p_{ip} = 90\%$) or leaf node (with probability 10%).

We are in a more complicated situation, since one of those sets may be empty, because of allowing only nodes with possible "partner" in the second parent. Thus we do this step only if both sets are nonempty.

After selecting a node in the first parent we select node in the second parent such that the type of that node must correspond to the type of the first node. Again, this may eliminate the "90-10" step of first deciding whether the selected node will be internal node or leaf node.

When both nodes are selected we may swap the trees.

If the abstraction elimination was performed, then since the trees are of the same type, and there are no variables to be moved from their scope, the offspring trees are well typed.

Both sexpr-tree and @-tree are able to be crossed by this mechanism. But @-tree has more possibilities than sexpr-tree. This comes from the fact that every subtree of the sexpr-tree corresponds to a subtree of @-tree, but there are subtrees of @-tree that do not correspond to a subtree of a sexpr-tree.

The following example should clarify this:

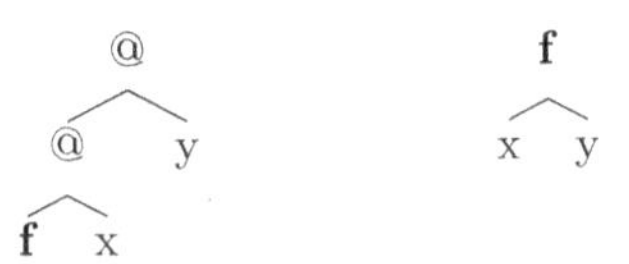

In the @-tree, **f** is leaf, thus it is a subtree, whereas in sexpr-tree it is an internal node and thus not a subtree. Those favorable properties of @-tree are also reported in [12].

Another nice property of sexpr-trees with no lambdas is that they are the same representation as S-expressions used by standard GP.

Again, similarly to standard GP, a maximum permissible depth $D_{created}$ for offspring individuals is defined (e.g. $D_{created} = 17$). If one of the offspring has greater depth than this limit, then this offspring is replaced by the first parent in the result of the crossover operator. If both offspring exceed this limit, then both are replaced by parents.

For @-tree the $D_{created}$ must be larger since @-tree (without lambdas) is a binary tree. Then this enlargement is approximately proportionate to average number of function arguments. We use generous $D_{created} = 17 \times 3$.

6. EXPERIMENTS

In this section we demonstrate our approach on the well-known even parity problem. More extensive experimental evaluation will be a subject of future work. We made two experiments, in the first we have used the *hybrid* crossover, while in the second we have used the *unpacking* crossover.

Each experiment consisted of 50 independent runs of GP algorithm. Each run had a limit of 51 generations, and the population size was 500 individuals. In the experiments we analyze the fitness of the best individual, the average size of an individual, the ability of the system to produce a correct solution, and computational cost estimates throughout generations. For the last two metrics we use the popular measurement methods within the GP field — the *performance curves* described in [5] — $P(M, i)$ (cumulative probability of success) and $I(M, i, z)$ (the total number of individuals that must be processed to yield a correct solution with probability $z = 99\%$). Difference of those two crossover methods is statistically analyzed by the Welch t-test by comparing the fitness values of the best individuals of the run. Graphs showing mean values of the fitness of the best individual and the average size of an individual throughout generations contain error bars representing the standard error of the mean (SEM).

The even parity function is a boolean function taking as inputs N boolean values and returning *True* if an even number of inputs are *True*. For odd number it returns *False*. This problem has been used by many researchers as a benchmark for GP. We compare our results with that presented in [11, 4]. We use very similar set of *building symbols* as in [11].

$$
\begin{aligned}
\tau &= [Bool] \to Bool \\
\Gamma &= \{and : Bool \to Bool \to Bool, \\
&\quad or : Bool \to Bool \to Bool, \\
&\quad nand : Bool \to Bool \to Bool, \\
&\quad nor : Bool \to Bool \to Bool, \\
&\quad foldr : (Bool \to Bool \to Bool) \\
&\qquad \to Bool \to [Bool] \to Bool, \\
&\quad head' : [Bool] \to Bool, \\
&\quad tail' : [Bool] \to [Bool]\}
\end{aligned}
$$

The type $[Bool]$ stands for *list of Bools* and for purpose of this problem is considered atomic. Unlike in [11], we use specific instance of polymorphic function `foldr`. And modifications of functions `head` (returning the first element of the list) and `tail` (returning the list without the first element) are used; making them total by returning default value *False* and `[]`, respectively. We use the same fitness function as in [11]. The fitness function examines the individual by giving it all possible boolean lists of length 2 and 3.

Figure 1 shows results of this experiments. Table 1 summarizes statistical analysis of the fitness values of the best individuals of the run (*p-value* = 0.7323). According to

Figure 1: Graphs for Even parity problem.

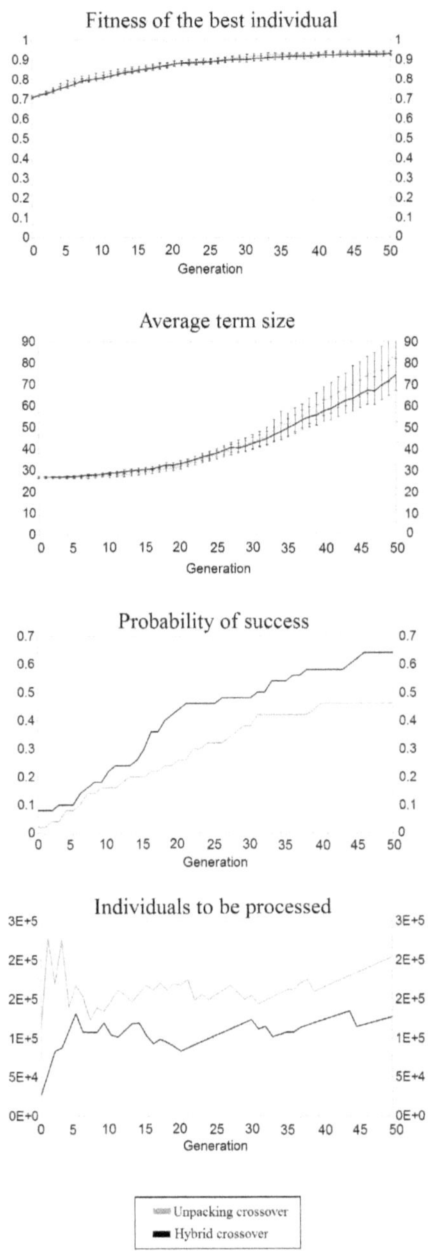

this analysis both crossovers performed about the same; by conventional criteria, this difference is considered to be not statistically significant.

The *unpacking* crossover scored 23/50 (46%) success rate. Minimal $I(M, i, z)$ was in generation 0 with 114,000 individuals to be processed. The average individual size for generation 50 was 83.1.

The *hybrid* crossover scored 32/50 (64%) success rate. Minimal $I(M, i, z)$ was in generation 0 with 28,000 individuals to be processed. The average individual size for generation 50 was 74.3.

Comparison with other results taken from literature is summarized in table 2. Concerning the time complexity,

	Unpacking	Hybrid
Mean	0.935000	0.930000
SD	0.066768	0.078490
SEM	0.009442	0.011100
N	50	50
t-value	0.3431	$\alpha = 0.05$
p-value	0.7323	**Not statistically significant**

Table 1: Statistical analysis.

GP approach	$I(M, i, z)$
PolyGP	14,000
Our approach (hybrid)	**28,000**
GP with Combinators	58,616
GP with Iteration	60,000
Our approach (unpacking)	**114,000**
Generic GP	220,000
OOGP	680,000
GP with ADFs	1,440,000

Table 2: Results comparison.

both experiments were run under same conditions on a fairly standard machine with 4 core 3.3 GHz processor and 4 GB RAM. The first experiment took 388 minutes while the second one took 33 minutes.

We have also analyzed ratio of failed crossovers due to exceeding the maximal permissible depth. Only around 0.5% of offspring created by the unpacking crossover fail due to exceeding the limit and 0.2% for the hybrid crossover. Thus we conclude that the case of crossover failure does not have a significant effect on the performance of the operators.

In order to illustrate how the individuals actually look like and how the crossover works, figure 2 depicts creation of the correct solution by the hybrid crossover in one particular run of the system.

The found correct solution can be rewritten as:

$$\lambda\, x\ .\ foldr\ (\mathbf{S}(\mathbf{S}(\mathbf{K}\ \mathbf{S})(\mathbf{S}(\mathbf{K}(\mathbf{S}(\mathbf{K}\ nor)))and))nor)$$
$$(nor\ (head'\ x)\ (head'\ x))\ \ (tail'\ x)$$
$$=_{\beta\eta}$$
$$\lambda\, x\ .\ foldr\ (\lambda\, y\ z\ .\ nor\ (and\ y\ z)\ (nor\ y\ z))$$
$$(nor\ (head'\ x)\ (head'\ x))\ \ (tail'\ x)$$

Which is equivalent to:

$$\lambda\, x\ .\ foldr\ xor\ (not\ (head'\ x))\ \ (tail'\ x)$$

7. CONCLUSIONS

In this paper we presented a generalization of standard GP based on simply typed lambda calculus trees. We discussed the advantages of generating lambda terms in their long normal form and presented two novel crossover operations for this system.

The first one — the *hybrid* crossover — transforms all generated individuals into combinator terms at the end of generation phase. The second crossover approach — the *unpacking* crossover — uses the lambda term representation during the whole run, except for the temporary phases during the crossover. We have compared their relative performance on even parity problem; the first one is performing the same or better in all observed metrics. Since the use of

Figure 2: Hybrid crossover example.

the *unpacking* crossover brings a significant computational overhead while its performance is the same or worse than the performance of the *hybrid* crossover we conclude that the *hybrid* crossover is better suited for the job.

According to comparison of "individuals to be processed" metric our GP approach is performing better than the GP system presented in [4] and worse than the one presented in [11]. By observation of typical solution which is often some modification of `foldr xor True inputList` one sees that an important task for GP here is to create `xor` function. This is the advantage for the more specialized term representation used in [11], which restricts the use of outer variables.

It is also fair to say, that this popular metric (in which the comparison data are available) is somehow problematic, since it is prone to have large variation across various instances of the same experiment [8]. As is also visible from our results; both our approaches scored best in generation 0 thus the result shown in table 2 depended only on the generation method which those two approaches shared, yet the individuals to be processed estimates are quite different.

In the future work, we would like to support our theoretical results concerning relations of generating procedure and reductions described in this paper with substantially extended experimental results.

In this paper we touched varied aspects of the two lambda calculus concepts – reductions and abstraction elimination – in the hope that it will shed some more light on the promising intersection of lambda calculus and genetic programming.

8. ACKNOWLEDGMENTS

Tomáš Křen has been partially supported by the project GA ČR P202/10/1333 and by the SVV project number 260 104. Roman Neruda has been partially supported by The Ministry of Education of the Czech Republic project COST LD 13002.

9. REFERENCES

[1] H. Barendregt. *The Lambda Calculus: its Syntax and Semantics, revised ed.* North-Holland, 1984.

[2] H. Barendregt, W. Dekkers, and R. Statman. *Lambda Calculus With Types.* Cambridge University Press, 2010.

[3] F. Binard and A. Felty. Genetic programming with polymorphic types and higher-order functions. In *Proceedings of the 10th annual conference on Genetic and evolutionary computation*, pages 1187–1194. ACM, 2008.

[4] F. Briggs and M. O'Neill. Functional genetic programming and exhaustive program search with combinator expressions. *International Journal of Knowledge-Based and Intelligent Engineering Systems*, 12(1):47–68, 2008.

[5] J. R. Koza. *Genetic programming: on the programming of computers by means of natural selection.* MIT Press, Cambridge, MA, USA, 1992.

[6] J. R. Koza. *Genetic Programming IV: Routine Human-Competitive Machine Intelligence.* Kluwer Academic Publishers, Norwell, MA, USA, 2003.

[7] T. Křen and R. Neruda. Generating lambda term individuals in typed genetic programming using forgetful A*. In *Proceedings of the Congress on Evolutionary Computation.* IEEE Computer Press, 2014. (in print).

[8] S. Luke and L. Panait. Is the perfect the enemy of the good? In *GECCO*, pages 820–828, 2002.

[9] D. Montana. Strongly typed genetic programming. *Evolutionary computation*, 3(2):199–230, 1995.

[10] S. L. Peyton Jones. *The Implementation of Functional Programming Languages (Prentice-Hall International Series in Computer Science).* Prentice-Hall, Inc., Upper Saddle River, NJ, USA, 1987.

[11] T. Yu. Hierarchical processing for evolving recursive and modular programs using higher-order functions and lambda abstraction. *Genetic Programming and Evolvable Machines*, 2(4):345–380, 2001.

[12] T. Yu and C. Clack. PolyGP: A polymorphic genetic programming system in haskell. *Genetic Programming*, 98, 1998.

Improving 3D Medical Image Registration CUDA Software with Genetic Programming

William B. Langdon, Marc Modat, Justyna Petke, Mark Harman
Dept. of Computer Science, University College London Gower Street, WC1E 6BT, UK
W.Langdon@cs.ucl.ac.uk

ABSTRACT

Genetic Improvement (GI) is shown to optimise, in some cases by more than 35%, a critical component of health-care industry software across a diverse range of six nVidia graphics processing units (GPUs). GP and other search based software engineering techniques can automatically optimise the current rate limiting CUDA parallel function in the Nifty Reg open source C++ project used to align or register high resolution nuclear magnetic resonance NMRI and other diagnostic NIfTI images. Future Neurosurgery techniques will require hardware acceleration, such as GPGPU, to enable real time comparison of three dimensional in theatre images with earlier patient images and reference data. With millimetre resolution brain scan measurements comprising more than ten million voxels the modified kernel can process in excess of 3 billion active voxels per second.
Categories and Subject Descriptor I.2.8 [search]: heuristic

Categories and Subject Descriptors

I.2.2 [**Artificial Intelligence**]: Automatic Programming; D.2.8 [**Software Engineering**]: Metrics—*complexity measures, performance measures*

Keywords

SBSE; GPGPU; Medicine; Software engineering

1. INTRODUCTION

Future brain surgery techniques will require comparison of current images with images of the same patient taken earlier and also with reference data, e.g. from medical atlases. To be used in theatre, the system must be real time [8], ruling out cloud and other off-site solutions. And yet even a simple task of superimposing today's data with pre-surgery data is computationally heavy. The currently favoured solution is to take advantage of the impressive parallel processing abilities of high-end graphics processing units. Such GPUs can easily be placed physically near the surgeon to reduce latency and offer affordable tera-flop performance.

GECCO'14, July 12–16, 2014, Vancouver, Canada.

ACM 978-1-4503-2662-9/14/07 ...$15.00.
DOI http://dx.doi.org/10.1145/2576768.2598244 .

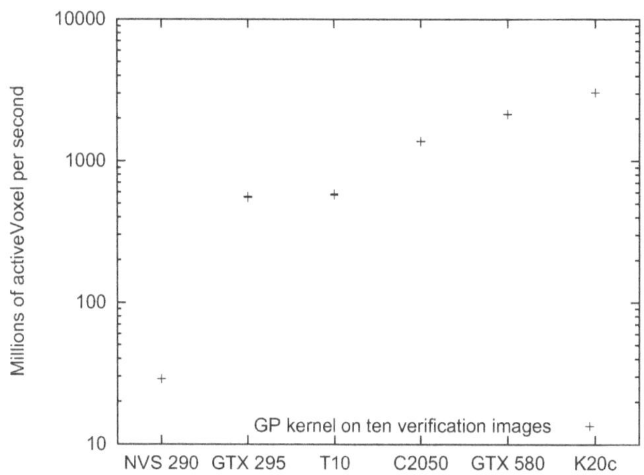

Figure 1: Performance of modified `reg_spline_getDeformationField3D` CUDA kernel after optimisation by GP, bloat removal and with optimal block size and `-arch`.

The need to compare or align noisy real-world high resolution three dimensional data occurs widely in industry. Here we concentrate upon the medical domain since this is the target of the open source Nifty Reg software[1]. To take advantage of the cost effectiveness of general computing on graphics processing units GPGPU [10], parts of Nifty Reg have been ported to nVidia's CUDA system. Indeed many CUDA kernels are included in the SourceForge download. However GPGPU programming is acknowledged to be difficult and so only parts of the Nifty Reg tool set can take advantage of GPUs. Even those parts which have been ported to CUDA impose a high software maintenance load and are not necessarily able to make the best use of more recent hardware or software.

Nifty Reg has twin goals of both providing tools and of creating a library of routines which are available to other C++ programmers. These are somewhat in conflict. Tool users want the best tool for what they are doing now and using the hardware they have. Whilst a programmer wants a library which is generic and can be used for many things to support many future users whose aims and environments can only be estimated. Accordingly Nifty Reg has been flexibly coded.

[1]`http://sourceforge.net/projects/niftyreg/`

Table 1: GPU Hardware. Second column is CUDA compute capability level (as can be used with nvcc's -arch). Each GPU chip contains a number of identical and more or less independent multiprocessors (column 3). Each MP contains a number of stream processors (cores, column 4) whose clock speed is given in column 6. Measured data rate (ECC enabled) between the GPU and its on board memory is in the last column.

GPU	Capability	MP ×	cores		GHz	Bandwidth
NVS 290	1.1	2 ×	8 =	16	0.92	4 GB/s
GTX 295	1.3	30 ×	8 =	240	1.24	92 GB/s
Tesla T10	1.3	30 ×	8 =	240	1.30	72 GB/s
Tesla C2050	2.0	14 ×	32 =	448	1.15	101 GB/s
GTX 580	2.0	16 ×	32 =	512	1.54	161 GB/s
Tesla K20c	3.5	13 ×	192 =	2496	0.71	140 GB/s

The Nifty Reg toolset makes heavy use of traditional convex optimisation techniques to find the optimal match between three dimensional images. Since these are based on derivatives, they require many exact calculations. With high resolution images, the basic image calculation may need to be done hundreds of thousands of times. Each one processing millions of voxels. With millimetric resolution NMR images becoming common place this presents a growing need for fast 3D registration. At present this can be met off-line by coarse grained bulk parallel processing in high performance super computer clusters either locally or in the cloud. Such "embarrassingly parallel" approaches work slowly per image but gain performance when each image can be treated independently. However such approaches are not suitable for real-time processing of data for a single patient.

During image registration, with typical hardware and images containing ≈ten million voxels, Nifty Reg is able to fully load a single GPU. In some cases more than 70% of the elapsed time is taken by a single CUDA kernel. We have used search based engineering to improve both the code within the kernel and hardware parameters used to control its parallel running. In so doing we have deliberately traded some of the generic nature of the original code, instead automatically producing code which is tailored to each of six very different graphics cards (see Figure 1 and Table 1).

2. NIFTY REG KERNEL

Next we describe the existing CUDA kernel which, even though running in parallel, typically dominates run time and then describe its efficient data access pattern. `reg_spline_getDeformationField3D` is typically used as part of an interactive cycle. Each time it is used it takes the current deformation expressed as a δx, δy, δz vector at regularly spaced grid control points and returns the corresponding deformation (again as δx, δy, δz vectors) for every active voxel in the image. For a typical 217^3 (10 218 313 voxel) image there are $47^3 = 103\,823$ grid control points. (47 being 217/5 plus allowance for up to three neighbouring grid points lying outside the image.) Each individual deformation vector is given by a cubic spline calculation involving 4 control points in each of the three dimensions (a total of $4 \times 4 \times 4 = 64$ neighbouring control points). The calculation of each active voxel requires ≈600 (single precision) floating point calculations.

The original code allowed complete flexibility, with the calling code able to specify any separation of the grid control points. However, in practice, grid control points are not chosen irrationally, instead they often align with voxels. We chose the most popular spacing (each grid point lies every fifth voxel) to demonstrate the effect of using simple integer or half integer spacings. The intention is to support a few popular spacings and that the Nifty Reg library revert to its original non-optimised code if the user chooses others.

Notice this means the 64 distances from each voxel to each of its 64 neighbouring control points now becomes one of a small set (5) of discrete values. Since the 64 spline coefficients depend only on these distances, instead of calculating each on the fly they can be precalculated and stored. By using the fact that the x, y and z components are independent only twenty (4×5) values need to be stored.

In addition to the 103 823 grid control points, the other large input to the kernel is the list of active voxels for which it must calculate their δx, δy, δz displacements. The active voxel list is stored as a vector of integer values, which makes it easy for the kernel to process each in parallel. The 32-bit integer values are decoded into the x,y,z location of the output voxel. This location also readily gives the locations of each of the neighbouring 64 control points.

As an efficiency measure, instead of each integer referring to a single voxel it actually represents a $1 \times 5 \times 5$ volume of 25 voxels, with y,z corners lying at grid control points and thus having the same 64 neighbouring control points. Thus an individual warp (32 threads) calculates 25 voxels in parallel. Despite discarding 7 threads of every 32, considerable performance gain is made as all the data for the 25 voxels is read once, rather than being read individually 25 times. This also reduces the size of the list of active voxels by a factor of 25. At the boundary of the region of interest the lower resolution ($1 \times 5 \times 5$ instead of $1 \times 1 \times 1$) means there is a small increase in the total number of active voxels.

A potential future enhancement would be to use $5 \times 5 \times 5$ volumes all having the same 64 neighbouring control points. So perhaps using 128 threads to calculate 125 active voxels. This has not been tried, partly because the GPU lays data along the x-axis so neighbouring data are more likely to be pre-fetched or to remain in cache.

Each of the twenty five active voxels needs data from the same 64 control points. In fact since they share the same x-location, these reduce to just 16 values. These are calculated in parallel by 16 (of 32) threads and stored in on-chip fast shared memory.

These 16 values are combined with different (but pre-calculated) spline co-efficients to give the 25 output values that are written simultaneously in parallel by 25 threads. Each output is represented as a `float4`, so 400 bytes are written in one go. Since these are consecutive, the GPU hardware can do this fairly efficiently. (In fact several 32-thread warps are grouped together into blocks so the writes to global memory are even more efficient.)

3. EVOLVING CUDA C++ CODE VIA A BNF GRAMMAR USING GP

The CUDA C++ code for the kernel is automatically converted into a BNF grammar of 255 rules. See Figure 2. Essentially each rule represents a line of code. Of these 198 are fixed. Twenty five grammar rules represent ordinary lines of code, six more are C++ `#define` configuration macros, and four are for C++ `if` statements. Although not used in the final solutions, for completeness we next describe the more exotic grammar rules.

There are two BNF rules to control CUDA `#pragma` loop unrolling compiler directives (plus a further 12 rules to control choosing `#pragma` arguments). `#pragma` may have been unsuccessful since the kernel contains nested `for` loops and it appears nvcc may not support `#pragma` with nested loops.

The CUDA nvcc compiler uses the C++ `__restrict__` qualifier, which allows some optimisations. The grammar was automatically generated to include a rule which allows evolution to control the use of `__restrict__`. Since the kernel has only one argument, which is not read-only, `__restrict__` was not expect to have an impact.

The final group of rules control the use of the CUDA `__launch_bounds__` qualifier on the kernel. With a further six allowing evolution to control its parameters. Although documented, `__launch_bounds__` is fairly obscure. It is thought to have been introduced as an aid to the compiler's register allocation strategy but as the compiler heuristics have improved, newer hardware supports more registers and the CUDA driver overrides the compiler's choices at run time, `__launch_bounds__` has fallen out of favour.

3.1 Configuration Macros

3.1.1 `c_UseBSpline` *and* `c_controlPointVoxelSpacing`

In the Nifty Reg code these variables are passed to the kernel via CUDA `__constant__` memory. However, as we have evolved efficient kernels for fixed values of `c_UseBSpline` and `c_controlPointVoxelSpacing`, they are no longer variable but instead their values are known at compile time. (They are respectively, true and 5). The two grammar rules, `c_UseBSpline` and `c_controlPointVoxelSpacing`, give evolution the option of replacing the corresponding variables with their constant values.

3.1.2 BNF rules controlling conditional compilation

There are four C++ macros which control conditional compilation. These enable evolution to individually control whether code options are enabled. As with `c_UseBSpline` and `c_controlPointVoxelSpacing`, the idea is that such code may be beneficial in some cases. This follows some of the ideas in [9], in that the source code is made more generic and we leave it to some later optimisation stage to decide on the exact parameters. However, Merrill et al. [9] were thinking of deterministic optimisation rather than more powerful search based techniques [2].

`constantBasis` directs the compiler to read pre-calculated spline coefficients from `__constant__` memory rather than fetching them from the texture cache. It also forces the use of pre-calculated values for the x dimension. (It may have been better to separate these two aspects into two separated genes.)

Two dimensional arrays or textures are used to store the pre-calculated spline coefficients. Typically the efficiency with which the hardware accesses arrays depends (in an arcane way) on how the array is laid out and how this matches the underlying storage hardware. To avoid thinking deeply about this, the `BasisA` gene allows evolution to determine which of the two indexes should appear first.

As voxels with multiple y and z coordinates are calculated together, y and z use pre-calculated spline coefficients. Since only one x is in use, the old Nifty Reg code to calculate the associated spline coefficients was left. However the `directxBasis` option allows evolution to read pre-calculated spline coefficients for x as well as y and z. (The compiler may be able to spot that the results of the x-calculation are not used and so optimise away their calculation.)

It is often claimed that division and modulus operations are very expensive on nVidia GPUs. Accordingly the `RemX` configuration macro was introduced to allow the calculation of $x\%5$ to be done just once. However it requires the storage (in new variable `int remx`) of $x\%5$. It is not clear the reduced calculation justifies the extra storage. `RemX` is typically used by more than a third of the final population and usually appears in the best of them. However, except in the optimised C2050 kernel, `RemX` is always removed along with the bloat.

3.2 Linear Genetic Representation

The GP works with a linear variable length genome which specifies (via the grammar) changes to the kernel. I.e., the GP evolves not complete programs but changes or patches to programs.

Each genome is stored as a line of text. (See examples on the RHS of Table 4.) The genome is split into genes by spaces. The genes are processed in left right order. Each gene represents one of the 3 fundamental types of mutation: 1) a gene is the name of a BNF rule, meaning that rule, and hence the corresponding line of code, is deleted. 2) a pair of BNF rules, meaning the first rule is replaced by a copy of the second. Typically meaning the first line of code is replaced by the second. 3) As 2) but the pair of BNF rules are separated by a `+`. This means instead of replacing the first rule, the second rule is inserted before the first. I.e. inserting a copy of the second line of code before the first.

There are several BNF rule types. Where a gene is composed of two rules, they must be of the same type. For example, `#pragma` rules can only be substituted by other `#pragma` rules and `if` condition expressions by other `if` conditions. Similarly, plain lines of code can be replaced by other simple lines of code.

A new GPU mutant kernel is created by applying the chromosome in left-right order to the BNF grammar and then inverting the modified grammar to create the complete source code of the new kernel. Although all this manipulation is done in plain text, typically it takes less than a second to create a new population and generate 300 new kernels from it. This it is negligible compared to the time taken by nvcc to compile them.

3.3 Gentic Operators

3.3.1 Initialisation

The initial population is composed of 300 different individuals each being exactly one gene. In subsequent generations evolution is free to create duplicate individuals. For each member of the breeding pool one child is created by mutation and one by crossover.

In the rare cases where the number of acceptable parents in the breeding pool is less than half the population size, the missing children are created from scratch by uniformly

Example of grammar rules used to connect GP with C++ code for configuration control parameter `c_UseBSpline` Section 3.1.1

```
<Kkernel.cu_17>          ::= <def_Kkernel.cu_17>
<def_Kkernel.cu_17>      ::= "#define c_UseBSpline 1\n"
```

Grammar rules for code at the start of CUDA kernel function. Also showing grammar for the substitutable conditional expression within an `if` statement.

```
<Kkernel.cu_164>         ::= "//each warp processes 25 z values\n"
<Kkernel.cu_165>         ::= "const int thread = (threadIdx.x & 31); //each warp acts independently\n"
<Kkernel.cu_166>         ::= "const unsigned int tid= (blockIdx.y*gridDim.x+blockIdx.x)*blockDim.x/32+threadIdx.x/32;\n"
<Kkernel.cu_167>         ::= " if" <IF_Kkernel.cu_167> " {\n"
<IF_Kkernel.cu_167>      ::= "(tid<c_ActiveVoxelNumber)"
```

Fragment of grammar rules covering `for` loop and automatically inserted compiler pragma to control loop un-rolling

```
<Kkernel.cu_289>         ::= <pragma_Kkernel.cu_289> "for(c=0;c<4;c++) {\n"
<pragma_Kkernel.cu_289>  ::= ""
<pragma_K0>              ::= "#pragma unroll \n"
<pragma_K1>              ::= "#pragma unroll 1\n"
<pragma_K2 ··· 11>       ::= "#pragma unroll 2 ··· 11\n"
<Kkernel.cu_290>         ::= <pragma_Kkernel.cu_290> "for(b=0;b<4;b++) {\n"
<pragma_Kkernel.cu_290>  ::= ""
```

Fragment of grammar rules covering a simple substitutable line of code, the end of nested `for` loops and code which writes the kernel's output to the GPU's off-chip global memory

```
<_Kkernel.cu_294>        ::= "displacement.z += tempDisplacement(c,b).z * basis;"
<Kkernel.cu_295>         ::= "}\n"
<Kkernel.cu_296>         ::= "}\n"
<Kkernel.cu_298>         ::= "" <_Kkernel.cu_298> "\n"
<_Kkernel.cu_298>        ::= "positionField[tid2] = displacement;"
```

Figure 2: Fragments of the 255 rule BNF grammar describing the human coded image registration graphics card function which is evolved by GP to create optimised CUDA C++ code.

randomly selecting from all the possible mutations (i.e., in the same way as those in the initial population).

3.3.2 Mutation

Half the new population is created by simply appending another random mutation.

3.3.3 Crossover

We use two point crossover. In each of the parents two cut points are randomly chosen. The child is created from the genes at the start and end of the first parent with those from the middle of the second parent inserted between them. Duplicate genes are removed from the offspring and crossovers producing empty children are discarded.

In the very rare cases where, after five trials, crossover is unable to find a legal offspring, its child is created by mutation.

3.4 Ensuring for Loop Termination

The kernel code includes two loops, each of which cycle between 0 and 3. To ensure, even badly mutated, kernels always terminate, the GP was prevented from mutating the `for` loop headers or modifying the loop control variables inside the loops.

3.5 Protecting Array Indexes

Almost all access to arrays is done via CUDA textures. Textures provide hardware protection against array indexes going out of legal ranges. Only in the case of new GPUs and then only in one case, which accesses on-chip shared memory, was it necessary to provide array bounds protection. This was done by preventing GP from moving lines of code accessing shared memory from inside `for` loops to after them. Inside (and indeed before) the `for` loops the indexes have legal values, problems only arrive in code after the `for` loops, where the loop control values are undefined.

3.6 Ensuring Compilation, C++ Scope

To ensure every kernel compiles, GP mutation and crossover are prevented from copying lines of code to parts of the kernel where variables it might contain might be out of scope. Typically this means moving lines of code down the source code is ok. To increase the flexibility allowed to GP, the variable declarations and their initialisation were moved *by hand* to the top of kernel. This increased flexibility increases the search space.

The mutated code causes the nvcc C++ compiler to generate many warnings but the code always compiles, runs, terminates and produces a fitness value.

3.7 Efficient Operation of Evolutionary Search

Considerable efficiencies were achieved by compiling and running every member of the GP population together rather than individually. Typically the nVidia compiler (CUDA 5.0) processes in the region of 500 lines of C++ code per second when more than 50 kernels are compiled together. However the curve is fairly flat and nvcc also gives good performance if given more lines of code. Thus, for simplicity, the complete population was compiled in one go [3]. Similarly running the whole population in one image avoids start/stop process overheads. It also makes for easy comparison with both the reference algorithm (i.e. CPU, for correctness) and (for timing) the reference kernel (no mutations). However care must be taken to isolate all read-write data so later mutations cannot take advantage of results created by earlier ones. Omitting all index bounds and loop over run checks, means that to get accurate timings, each kernel need only be run once. I.e., there is no need to run with protection enabled (which has a performance impact, so rendering fitness measurements unusable [7]) and then run successful mutants a second time normally. Typically on a 4GB 2.66GHz desktop it takes about 50 seconds to compile the population and about 30 seconds to run it. The bulk of the runtime being the fitness function which is run on the CPU and compares every answer generated with the correct answer.

3.8 Error and Execution Time Based Fitness

Each generation a new random image is created and each GPU kernel is run on it. Fitness is firstly given by the number of GPU clock ticks taken. To avoid overflow, the number of ticks is divided by ten. Notice fitness is minimised. Kernel execution times run from 48 626 to 185 678 246 ticks.

The Nifty Reg CPU code is used to create the ideal correct answer. Typically it contains about 1.7 million active voxels. Each answer created by each GPU kernel is checked against the CPU's. There may be a small discrepancy due to floating point operations. The GP accepts errors smaller than 0.001 without penalty. However if the worst voxel is more than 0.001 from its CPU calculated value a severe penalty is added to the fitness: $213\,748\,364 \times (\text{error} + 0.1)$, subject to not exceeding 213 748 364. In a very small number of cases the mutated kernel may fail to set an answer, in which case there is a penalty of 213 748 364×the fraction of voxels without an answer. If any error exceeds 0.1, it attracts a penalty of 213 748 364×the fraction of wrong voxels. Each of these penalties is added to the original fitness based on the kernel's elapsed time. Since typically Nifty Reg uses the kernel's answer immediately on the same GPU, we use the elapse time on the GPU, excluding any host-GPU interaction time.

3.9 50% Truncation Selection

We use 50% truncation selection, with the best half of the population getting two children each and the rest none.

At the start of each generation the original unmutated kernel is run on the current test image. This serves firstly as a sanity check that the GPU is actually running ok and secondly it gives a reference fitness which any improved mutated kernel should beat. Even on the GPU, elapse times are subject to some random variation, therefore when we impose the rule that to be a parent a mutant must be faster than the reference kernel we allow a ten percent tolerance. Once evolution is underway, mutation and crossover typically have no difficulty in generating 150 children which make no errors and take no more than 10% longer than the original kernel. In each case in the initial random population at least 140 random mutants were fast enough to become parents.

4. OPTIMISING NIFTY REG KERNELS

4.1 Random Fitness Test Cases

Typical high resolution NMR brain scans are represented in the nifti format as $217 \times 217 \times 217$ 1 millimetre 3D images with the brain in the centre. We need only processes the region of interest (e.g. the brain). For purposes of testing the software, we can represent the region of interest as a squashed ball.

An effectively unlimited number of test cases can be generated at random. The images are simply deformed spheres of white noise with a diameter of 140 approximately centred in a cube of side 217. The exact radius, centre and degree of compression along each dimension can vary by 5% and each is chosen independently at random. On average 1 700 000 of the 10 218 313 voxels are active. Note each image contains ≈1.7 million test examples, each of which must be correct.

Table 2: CUDA compiler options. Optimal block size before GP and used during GP runs (column 2). After GP was run and bloat removed block size was re-optimised (column 3) and the best nvcc `-arch` chosen (column 4). The final column gives the run time of the optimised kernels on a 217 cube image.

GPU	Block size pre-GP	post-GP	`-arch`	typical mS
Quadro NVS 290	128	256	sm_11	62.40
GeForce GTX 295	64	512	sm_13	3.22
Tesla T10	64	480	sm_13	3.09
Tesla C2050	128	160	*none*	2.06
GeForce GTX 580	64	160	*none*	0.84
Tesla K20c	128	128	*none*	0.71

Table 3: Genetic Programming for Nifty Reg

Representation:	Variable list of replacements, deletions and insertions into BNF grammar
Fitness:	Compile modified CUDA code. Run on about 1.7 million active voxels. Compare its answers with CPU implementation and compare its run time with that of original kernel on the same hardware.
Population:	Panmictic, non-elitist, generational. 300 members. New randomly chosen training image each generation.
Parameters:	Initial population of random single mutants. 50% truncation selection. 50% two point crossover, 50% mutation. No size limit. Stop after 50 generations.

4.2 Pre-Evolution Parameter Tuning

The kernel was written with one warp per block (i.e. a block size of 32). It is well known that 1) block size plays a critical role in GPU performance and 2) it is almost impossible to calculate the optimal block size from first principles. Thus: for each of the six GPUs, the kernel was individually compiled and run with all sensible legal values of block size. The one giving the fastest elapsed time was chosen and used during evolution. In detail the block size was set to the next multiple of 32 until either the architecture defined limit on block size (which varies between GPUs) or a resource limit, such as number of registers or limit on on-chip shared memory, was exceeded. The used block sizes are given in Table 2.

The GP was run with a population of 300 for fifty generations on each of the six GPUs (see Table 3).

4.3 Post Evolution Clean Up and Re-Tune

As expected [11] in all cases the population bloats with rapid approximately linear increase in number of genes per individual. In part this may be due to our mutation operator which increases the length of the child w.r.t. its parent. However since we want the GP to explore different code it is reasonable for it to increase the number of changes it makes. Since these changes include code deletion, increase in GP individual size need not lead to increase in source

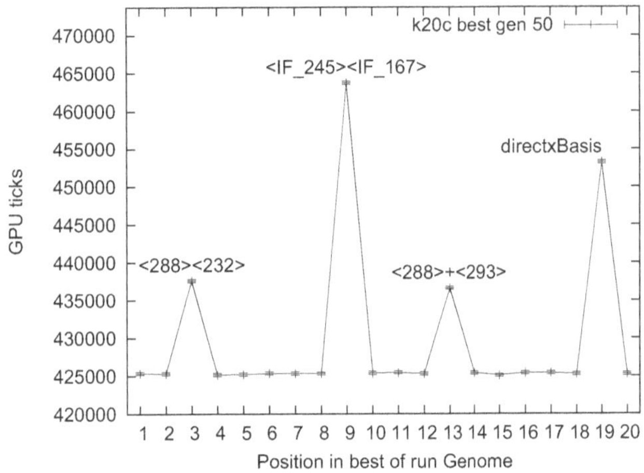

Figure 3: Example of post-evolution clean up, showing performance of GP evolved Nifty Reg kernel as genes are knocked out. (Tesla k20c). The four spikes correspond to the four of the 19 genes that are vital to its performance. Error bars indicate noise tolerance. Numbers in < > are line numbers in the kernel source code. Line in the left < > is replaced by that in right. < >+< > says insert rather than replace.

code size, and since nvcc is an optimising compiler, and, especially since we are actively selecting for faster programs, bloat need not lead to an increase in executable GPU code. However in all cases such bloat proved unnecessary for the final solution. We use a simple gene knock out strategy to determine which parts of the best program from the last generation are needed.

The genome of the bloated GP individual is processed one gene at a time in left right order. At each step the next gene is removed; the modified chromosome is applied to the BNF grammar, the grammar reversed to give a new CUDA kernel, which is compiled and run. For repeatability, the same random image is used. The speed of the new kernel is compared against that of the evolved kernel. If it is worse, the gene is retained. If there is no difference the gene is excluded permanently. We then proceed to the next gene, until the whole genome has been processed. In all cases, this leads to a considerable reduction in mutant genome size. To allow for measurement noise, a gene is excluded if it is less than 3.0 standard deviations of the GPU clock measurement noise. See Figure 3.

Finally the optimal block size was determined again (using the technique described in the previous section). Until this point the compiler default architecture setting had been used. This is the setting used by Nifty Reg. In the final step the compiler was run both without the `-arch` switch and with it set appropriately to the target GPU. Surprisingly in some cases, with CUDA 5.0, `-arch` actually produced a slower kernel.

4.4 Validation

The final speeds quoted for each GPU are given by running the final kernels on ten configurations not used in the pre- post- or evolutionary stages. In total these amount to 16 816 875 test cases. In all cases the optimised kernel had an error of 0.000107 or less. On the newest GPU, the optimised kernel is more than two thousand times faster than the host CPU (K20c Tesla v. 2.67GHz Intel server).

There is little evidence of over fitting with performance on the unseen examples being close to those used to train the GP population.

Depending upon GPU the genetically improved kernel is from 7 to 39 percent faster than the human code (See Figure 4).

Table 4: Post-GP Best program length (column 2). After bloat removal length (column 3). Column 4 contains the final automatically generated patch to the manual code.

GPU	GP	len	Optimised Program
NVS 290	39	8	<291>+<285> <283>+<249> `constantBasis` `directxBasis` <249>+<255> <288>+<283> <249>+<251> <248>+<288>
GTX 295	25	1	`constantBasis`
T10	38	1	`constantBasis`
C2050	26	10	<230>+<283> <252>+<251> `c_UseBSpline` <230>+<291> `RemX` <237>+<292> <IF_245><IF_167> <288>+<293> <IF_239><IF_167> <238><249>
GTX 580	39	3	`constantBasis` <251>+<283> <IF245><IF167>
K20c	19	4	<288><232> <IF245><IF167> <288>+<293> `directxBasis`

4.5 Evolution of Genes and their Phenotypes

For space, we limit our discussion to common mutations used in the final kernels. `constantBasis` (Section 3.1.2) prospers in all the sm_1x GPUs occurring in almost all members of the final GP populations. However both the later GPUs prefer fetching from textures and `constantBasis` is removed from most of their GP individuals. With the NVS 290, GTX 295, GTX 580 and Tesla T10, `constantBasis` is part of the best of run individual and survives the bloat cull process (Section 4.3) to give a speed up in the optimised kernel (see Table 4).

Except in the case of the C2050 Tesla, `directxBasis` is strongly preferred by evolution and appears in most GP individuals by the last generation, including the best of run individual. (Despite our high mutation rate, `directxBasis` is extinct in the last C2050 population.) With the two powerful high clock rate sm_1x GPUs, `directxBasis` is removed with the bloat by the post evolution clean up phase and only figures in the kernel optimised for the least powerful or slowest clocked GPUs (NVS 290 and K20c Tesla).

4.6 Evolved Code and its Implications

The following sections describe in detail the impact of all the mutations that survive the bloat removal stage (see Table 4) and thus (as single genes) have a beneficial impact. Much of the explanation is devoted to why a change does not cause errors. However there are cases (e.g. in Section 4.6.4) where evolution found surprising ways to improve the parallel code.

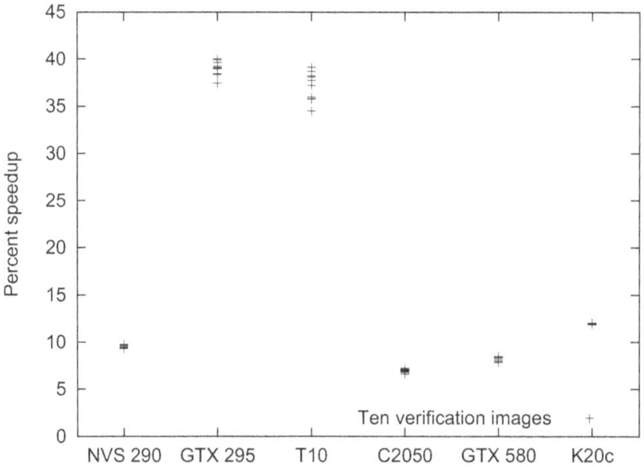

Figure 4: Speedup of CUDA kernel after optimisation by GP, bloat removal and with optimal block size and -arch compared to hand written kernel with default block size (192) and no -arch. Unseen data.

4.6.1 Quadro NVS 290

Inserting additional copies of line 283 before line 283 has no effect since they always set the variable `remz` to the same value. Clearing variable `displacement` multiple times (by inserting copies of line 288) before its first use on line 292 has no effect. Line 251 sets variable `indexXYZ` to its correct value. After line 251 it is used and updated multiple times. However setting its value (by inserting copies of line 251) before line 251 has no effect. Variable `nodeCoefficientD` is set by reading from a texture on line 255 after which its value is used multiple times.

As long as there is one instance of line 249 (at or before line 249) inserting additional copies has no effect as they always overwrite variable `indexYZ` with the same value. Inserting copies of line 249 and line 283 before line 288 has no effect since in both cases the efected variables (indexYZ and remz) are over written with their current values. Inserting another copy of line 285 before line 291 has no effect (it over writes variable tid2 with its current value).

4.6.2 GeForce GTX 295

The GTX 295 is actually a twin CPU (approximately two GTX 280s in a single board). However each of its halves is programmed and used separately. Therefore we report figures for just one half of it. After bloat removal the kernel optimised for the GTX 295 only uses the `constantBasis` configuration control gene (Section 3.1.2).

4.6.3 Tesla T10

Again we report figures for a single GPU, although physically four GPUs are co-located. After bloat removal the kernel optimised for the Tesla T10 only uses the `constantBasis` configuration control gene (Section 3.1.2).

4.6.4 Tesla C2050

The `c_UseBSpline` and `RemX` genes are both used by the optimised C2050 kernel. They were described in Section 3.1.2. `c_UseBSpline` is only used in one place, in an `if`. Telling the nvcc compiler it will always be true, means it does not have to generate code for the branch itself or for the `else` condition. `c_UseBSpline` appears in between a quarter and three quarters of the final GP populations and in most of the best of run individuals. However, its advantage seems to be quite small since it is removed along with the bloat in all but the C2050.

As above, since the original code to set a variable (`basis` or `remz`) is retained copying the line of code which write to it before it is used has no effect. Evolution used interacting genes to insert multiple lines of code before line 230. It is not clear if this is why our anti-bloat program simplifier was unable to remove these duplicates or if indeed there is some other effect, such as interaction with the hardware or the nvcc optimising compiler's register allocation, that causes the more verbose code to be more efficient.

Inserting a copy of line 292 before line 237 has no effect since the variable (`displacement.x`) is reset by the original code before it is used.

Line 238 `relative=relative>0?relative:0.f;` is designed to ensure that `float relative` is never negative. However the line above will ensure it never is. Hence removing line 238 improves the code. The mutation which deletes it (`<238><249>`) also adds a copy of line 249 in place of line 238. However this has no deleterious effect since the variable `indexYZ` it writes to is reset (by the original code) before `indexYZ` is used.

Replacing the `if` condition on line 245 with that on line 167 is a really innovative optimisation. Firstly line 245 is inside the conditional code controlled by the if on line 167 and therefore the condition must have been true at line 167 (and in fact the compiler can see that it must still be true on line 245). Hence in the mutant, the compiler can remove the code to test the condition. The original condition `(threadIdx.x & 31) < 16` is false half the time. It was designed to use 16 threads to calculate 16 values and store them in on-chip shared memory. It was intentional that the other 16 threads (per warp of 32) do nothing. But if the condition is removed, all threads run in synchrony (which is actually cheaper than having half of them idle) and calculate the 16 values twice. When the 32 threads all try to write to 16 shared locations, it is defined that only 16 will succeed. But 16 threads will write the correct values to the 16 shared locations. (The writes from the other 16 threads will simply be discarded.) I.e., GP has removed an operation (`(threadIdx.x & 31) < 16`) and also made the following 23 lines of code slightly more efficient.

The `if` on line 239 is always true. It appears evolution has repeated its trick of replacing it with another conditional which must also be true (again copied from line 167) and thus allowing the compiler to remove it. However the `c_UseBSpline` gene is also used which has the same effect. It's not clear why the post-evolution bloat removal retained both.

The mutation <252>+<251> makes a copy of line 251 setting variable `indexXYZ` to exactly the same value. Doubtless nvcc can spot this and optimise it away but again it is unclear why the bloat removal stage did not remove it itself.

Mutation <288>+<293> adds updating `displacement.y` immediately before it is set to 0.0f. So it obviously has no effect and hopefully nvcc sees this and removes it. But yet again we would have hoped the anti bloat system would have removed it.

4.6.5 *GeForce GTX 580*

Pre-calculated spline coefficients are read from `__constant__` memory rather than read from textures (`constantBasis`, Section 3.1.2).

Evolution has again used the trick of removing `(threadIdx.x & 31) < 16`. (Described in detail for the C2050 optimised kernel, Section 4.6.4.)

`<251>+<283>` creates a copy of `remz = thread/5;` before `remz` is used. It is not clear why this is beneficial, perhaps it reduces warp divergence since the copy is executed by all 32 threads, rather than just 25.

4.6.6 *Tesla K20c*

The `directxBasis` configuration control (see Section 3.1.2) gene is enabled.

Evolution has again used the trick of removing `(threadIdx.x & 31) < 16`. (Described in detail for the C2050 optimised kernel, Section 4.6.4.)

Evolution has used two genes <288><232> <288>+<293> to insert a copy of line 293 in place of line 288. Variable `displacement` is initialised when it is declared and so evolution has spotted clearing it again on line 288 is not needed. However it has been partially replaced by an expression which updates only its `y` component. This appears to be safe only because variable `basis` is zero. Inserting a copy of line 232 is safe since it recalculates the same value. However since its output `nodeAnte.z` is not used after line 232 the nvcc compiler will probably spot this and remove the redundant code. Possibly the change is not removed by the post evolution clean up as there are two genes involved.

5. DISCUSSION

Performant parallel programming remains difficult [4]. After several decades of compiler development, it is widely accepted that completely automatic parallelisation using compiler technology is infeasible. Instead nVidia's parallel compiler throws the main tasks of parallel algorithm design and implementation back onto the user. Some in nVidia [9] have advocated this approach be taken further and suggest instead of the programmer coding a solution they should aim to use C++ templates to code generic solutions which the compiler or other tools can tailor, either at compile or run time, to the available hardware. Indeed in future this might take the form of a JIT "just-in-time" approach which dynamically adjusts the code to actual usage [1]. However instead of easing the already insurmountable load on the human programmer a further level of indirection makes it worse.

Ryan [12] and ourselves [6] have shown with very different approaches, that starting with sequential code GP may be able to generate parallel code. We have previously shown GP may substantially improve existing code [5] by tailoring it for a specific task and maintain legacy software for new hardware [7]. Here, instead of creating parallel code from scratch, we use GP to improve existing parallel code. There are some similarities with [9] in that our grammar exposes key parameters to the evolutionary process.

6. CONCLUSIONS

A combination of genetic programming acting via a simple automatically produced BNF grammar in combination with simple post evolution bloat removal and tuning of two key compile time CUDA parameters (block size and compute level) can tune state of the art hand coded critical components of medical imaging C++ software. During evolution GP discovered novel and interesting optimisations which may be applied (either automatically or directly) by other software engineers (Section 4.6.4). The resulting graphics card software has been both specialised to the problem and tuned to get the best from a wide range of nVidia hardware (spanning five years since they were launched and more than two orders of magnitude in processing power). The improvement on manual coding varies with GPU type but can exceed 35% on out of sample tests. The evolved and optimised kernels have been run on many millions of tests, all of their answers have been compared to the "gold standard" of running the original Nifty Reg code on the CPU. The difference is always within expected floating accuracy.

Acknowledgements

I am grateful for the assistance of the anonymous reviewers. Tesla donated by nVidia. Funded by EPSRC grant EP/I033688/1. Code etc. in http://www.cs.ucl.ac.uk/staff/W.Langdon/ftp/gp-code/niftycuda.tar.gz

7. REFERENCES

[1] HARMAN, M., LANGDON, W. B., JIA, Y., WHITE, D. R., ARCURI, A., AND CLARK, J. A. The GISMOE challenge: Constructing the Pareto program surface using genetic programming to find better programs. In *ASE 2012*, ACM, pp. 1–14.

[2] HARMAN, M., LANGDON, W. B., AND WEIMER, W. Genetic programming for reverse engineering. In *WCRE*, (Koblenz, Germany, 14-17 Oct. 2013), IEEE.

[3] HARRIS, C. *An investigation into the Application of Genetic Programming techniques to Signal Analysis and Feature Detection.* PhD thesis, UCL. 1997.

[4] LANGDON, W. Creating and debugging performance CUDA C. In *Parallel Architectures and Bioinspired Algorithms*, F. Fernandez de Vega, J. I. Hidalgo Perez, and J. Lanchares, Eds., Springer, 2012, ch. 1, pp. 7–50.

[5] LANGDON, W. B., AND HARMAN, M. Optimising existing software with genetic programming. *IEEE Transactions on Evolutionary Computation.* Accepted.

[6] LANGDON, W. B., AND HARMAN, M. Evolving a CUDA kernel from an nVidia template. In *WCCI* (Barcelona, 18-23 July 2010), IEEE, pp. 2376–2383.

[7] LANGDON, W. B., AND HARMAN, M. Genetically improved CUDA C++ software. In *EuroGP 2014*.

[8] LIU, Y., AND SUVRANU, D. CUDA-based real time surgery simulation. *Studies in Health Technology and Informatics 132* (2008), 260–262.

[9] MERRILL, D., GARLAND, M., AND GRIMSHAW, A. Policy-based tuning for performance portability and library co-optimization. In *Innovative Parallel Computing (InPar), 2012*, IEEE.

[10] OWENS, J. D., HOUSTON, M., LUEBKE, D., GREEN, S., STONE, J. E., AND PHILLIPS, J. C. GPU computing. *Proc. of the IEEE 96*, 5 (2008), 879–899.

[11] POLI, R., LANGDON, W. B., AND MCPHEE, N. F. *A field guide to genetic programming.* Published via `http://lulu.com` and freely available at `http://www.gp-field-guide.org.uk`, 2008.

[12] RYAN, C. *Automatic Re-engineering of Software Using Genetic Programming.* Kluwer, 1999.

Grammar-Based Genetic Programming with Dependence Learning and Bayesian Network Classifier

Pak-Kan Wong
Department of Computer Science and Engineering
The Chinese University of Hong Kong
Hong Kong
pkwong@cse.cuhk.edu.hk

Leung-Yau Lo
Department of Computer Science and Engineering
The Chinese University of Hong Kong
Hong Kong
lylo@cse.cuhk.edu.hk

Man-Leung Wong
Department of Computing and Decision Sciences
Lingnan University
Tuen Mun
Hong Kong
mlwong@ln.edu.hk

Kwong-Sak Leung
Department of Computer Science and Engineering
The Chinese University of Hong Kong
Hong Kong
ksleung@cse.cuhk.edu.hk

ABSTRACT

Grammar-Based Genetic Programming formalizes constraints on the solution structure based on domain knowledge to reduce the search space and generate grammatically correct individuals. Nevertheless, building blocks in a program can often be dependent, so the effective search space can be further reduced. Approaches have been proposed to learn the dependence using probabilistic models and shown to be useful in finding the optimal solutions with complex structure. It raises questions on how to use the individuals in the population to uncover the underlying dependence. Usually, only the good individuals are selected. To model the dependence better, we introduce Grammar-Based Genetic Programming with Bayesian Network Classifier (GBGPBC) which also uses poorer individuals. With the introduction of class labels, we further propose a refinement technique on probability distribution based on class label. Our results show that GBGPBC performs well on two benchmark problems. These techniques boost the performance of our system.

Categories and Subject Descriptors

I.2 [**Artificial Intelligence**]: Automatic Programming

General Terms

Algorithms

GECCO'14, July 12–16, 2014, Vancouver, BC, Canada.

ACM 978-1-4503-2662-9/14/07...$15.00.
http://dx.doi.org/10.1145/2576768.2598256.

Keywords

Genetic programming, grammar-based genetic programming, Bayesian network, classifier

1. INTRODUCTION

Genetic Programming (GP) evolves programs from the given terminal set and function set. To relax the constraint of closure requirement, Grammar-Based Genetic Programming (GBGP) [1] has been introduced to use grammar in the GP formalism. In the early works of GBGP, context-free grammar is often used. This suffers from the problem of dependence in the context.

To tackle this problem in canonical Genetic Algorithm (GA), GP or GBGP, Probabilistic Model-Building Genetic Algorithm (PMBGA) [2] and Probabilistic Model-Building Genetic Programming (PMBGP) [3] focus on estimating a probabilistic distribution of good solutions. They weaken the context-free assumption in the grammar by overlaying probabilistic models. As a result, the grammar becomes more context sensitive. Probabilistic models are learnt from individuals in the past generation. In each generation, individuals are generated from the current estimate of distribution. Part of them are selected based on fitness for improving the estimate. PMBGP approach is attractive because the estimate of distribution may also describe the general principles to generate good solutions when an optimal good solution is found.

One of the limitations commonly found in the current PMBGP approaches is that only the promising solutions are used to construct the probabilistic model. The ignored less fit individuals, however, may also improve the model. One way is to utilize a probabilistic model based classifier which can differentiate well between different classes of individuals. The problem is that only limited number of classes of individuals can lead to a fitter individual if we follow the distribution strictly in the generation of individuals. If we know what the underlying classes are, we may refine the distribution according to the semantics of a given class. In short, we utilize the discrimination power of probabilistic classifier and knowledge on the class in order to generate fitter individuals. This can be viewed as a way to increase the diversity.

In this paper, a new PMBGP framework, called Grammar Based Genetic Programming with Bayesian Network Classifier (GBGPBC), is proposed for the purpose of learning the dependence to boost the performance of PMBGP. GBGPBC learns the local dependence from both good and poor individuals through Bayesian network (BN) classifiers. Each BN classifier aims at discriminating these two classes of individuals by using the non-terminals as the attributes. GBGPBC also generates individuals using two different schemes. Our approach is scalable to large problem and efficient.

This paper is organized as follows. Section 2 summarizes existing works related to PMBGP approaches and BN classifiers. Then our grammar model is formalized in Section 3. The details on the work flow of the whole system are discussed in Section 4. We apply our system in two benchmark problems and the results are shown in Section 5. Finally, we discuss the performance and the potentials of the new GBGPBC.

2. RELATED WORKS

Since our framework is closely related to probabilistic model-building genetic programming and applies BN classifier, the related works in these areas are summarized.

2.1 PMBGAs and PMBGPs

The objective of Probabilistic Model-Building Genetic Algorithm (PMBGA) or Estimation of Distribution Algorithm (EDA) [4] is to describe a population of optimal solutions of a problem using a probability distribution. Individuals sharing the same components are also assumed to be correlated in their fitnesses [5]. The probabilistic model can either be univariate, bivariate or multivariate (BOA [6], EBNA [7], LDFA[8]). Some works apply non-statistical model learning methods inspired by LEM [9]. SI3E uses decision trees [10]. EBCOA applies some Bayesian classifier models to account for the differences in fitness values between individuals [11]. COIN utilizes both good and not-good solutions [12] and updates the generator using reward and punishment.

Probabilistic model can also be applied on GP. Many Probabilistic Model-Building Genetic Programming (PMBGP) approaches have been realized in two classes of models: probabilistic prototype tree (PPT) model-based method and probabilistic grammar (PG) model-based method. The former method operates on a fixed-length chromosome, which is essentially a tree structure, and utilizes probabilistic models. PIPE [13], being the first PMBGP, introduced PPT and adopted a univariate model, which has been subsequently used and extended by EDP [14], eCGA [3], BOAP [15], POLE [16, 17], POLE on binary encoded PPT [18] and POLE-BP [19].

PG model-based method incorporates probabilistic context-free grammar (PCFG) [20]. Stochastic CFG (SCFG) is a simple PCFG and adds weights on each derivation rule while the weights on the rules having the same non-terminal are normalized to sum to 1. Stochastic grammar-based GP (SG-GP) [21] combines PBIL [22] with GGGP [1] and has been shown to resist bloating. PEEL [23] extends SG-GP and allows the use of depth and the relative location in the tree. GMPE [24] modifies the grammar to describe the search space by applying stochastic hill-climbing search to find a good merging of the non-terminals of the production rules of SCFG scored by the Minimum Description Length (MDL) [25]. GT-EDA [26] is similar to GMPE but it learns from expression trees. PAGE [27] employs PCFG with Latent Annotations (PCFG-LA) to weaken the context free assumption. PAGE-EM uses expectation-maximization (EM) algorithm [28] to estimate the annotations from promising individuals. Variational Bayes (VB) learning [29] is also introduced to PAGE to learn the annotations and infer their quantity from the learning data. Unsupervised PAGE (UPAGE) [30] utilizes PCFG-LA mixture model to deal with local dependencies and global contexts. BAP [31] applies a learnt BN on top of a fixed size chromosome and generates new individuals using the BN. Tanev's work [32] relies on probabilistic context-sensitive grammar (PCSG), which extends PCFG by assigning the probability according to the predefined context.

Other models have also been proposed. N-gram GP [33] evolves linear GP. AntTAG [34] evolves programs using an ant colony optimization algorithm and estimates the dependencies in tree structures using the pheromone matrix. Infeasible individuals are collected to extract useful substructures in the Probabilistic Model Building Genetic Network Programming [35].

Contrary to the aforementioned PMBGP approaches, we introduce a new PCSG model to maintain the syntactical correctness and overlay each derivation rule with a BN classifier to raise the scalability. These BN classifiers can discriminate good and poor individuals in the previous generation. Since the grammar and class give the semantics of the parse tree, we propose and employ a novel method that performs semantic refinement on the probability distributions. From the best of our knowledge, it is the first attempt to apply multiple BN classifiers as well as semantic refinement on GBGP.

2.2 Bayesian Network Classifier

A BN is a graphical model to define probability distributions among variables [36]. Consider a set of random variables $\mathbf{X} = (X_1, X_2, ..., X_n)$ and their assignment of states is $\mathbf{x} = (x_1, x_2, ..., x_n)$. The joint probability $p(\mathbf{X} = \mathbf{x})$ can be factorized into a set of conditional probability distributions encoded in a BN, which is a directed acyclic graph. In the network, nodes and edges represent the variables and the conditional dependencies respectively. Each node X_i is associated with a conditional distribution $p(x_i|\mathbf{pa}(x_i))$, where $\mathbf{pa}(x_i)$ is the configuration of the parents of X_i in the network. If all the variables in the BN are discrete, a conditional probability table can store the conditional distribution for every node. The product of conditional probabilities is equal to the joint distribution for $\mathbf{X}$, i.e. $p(\mathbf{X} = \mathbf{x}) = \prod_{i=1}^{n} p(x_i|\mathbf{pa}(x_i))$.

BN has been applied for supervised classification problem: given a vector $\mathbf{x} = (x_1, x_2, ..., x_n)$, assign it to one of the classes. The best assignment to the sample $\mathbf{x}$ is the class with the highest posterior probability $\arg\max_c p(c|\mathbf{x})$. The simplest form of BN classifier is Naïve Bayes classifier in which the class node is the only parent of all other predictors. All predictors are conditionally independent given the class variable. Selective Naïve Bayes approach groups some original predictor variables into new variables. Tree Augmented Naïve Bayes (TAN) [37] approach weakens the

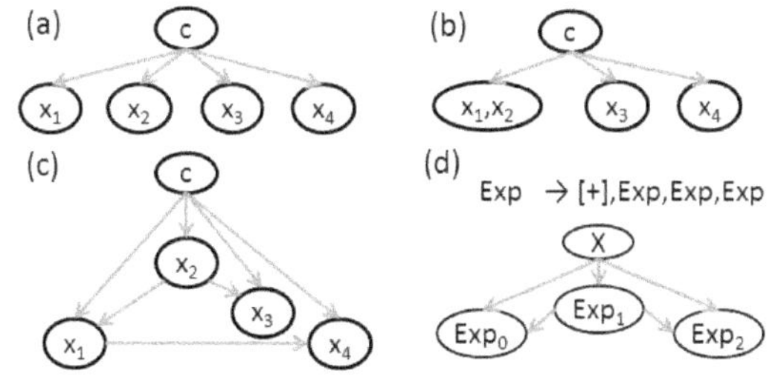

Figure 1: Several types of Bayesian network classifier. (a) Naïve Bayes (b) Selective naïve Bayes. (c) Tree augmented naïve Bayes. (d) The Bayesian network classifier in Rule 2.0.

conditional independence assumption using a tree structure on the predicator attributes. TAN can be generalized to use a k-tree in which each attribute has at most k attribute nodes as parents. It uses conditional mutual information between attributes given the class variable as the weights and constructs a maximum weighted spanning tree. It balances the use of information in the network and the network complexity giving a competitive classification power [37]. The structures of these BN classifiers are depicted in Figure 1. With these attractive features, our system has adopted multiple TANs in learning the conditional probabilities in the PCSG.

3. GRAMMAR MODEL

Our PCSG formulation differs from previous works in the introduction of the class labels and combining grammar rules with Bayesian network classifiers. Formally, a PCSG $\mathcal{G}$ is defined by 7-tuple:

1. A set of non-terminal symbols N
2. A set of terminal symbols T
3. A start non-terminal symbol $S \in N$
4. A set of derivation rules $R \subset N \times (N \cup T)^*$
5. A set of context elements C
6. A set of class labels X
7. A set of derivation probabilities D containing the probabilities $p(w, c, x|r)$, where $r \in R$ and r contains non-terminal in its right-hand side, $L_i^r = \{s \in R : LHS(s) = i^{th}$ element in $RHS(r)\}$, $L^r = L_1^r \times L_2^r \times ... \times L_{|RHS(r)|}^r$, $w \in L^r$, $c \subseteq C$ and $x \in X$. In other words, L_i^r contains all the possible ways to derive the ith non-terminal and L^r contains all valid combinations for the whole rule r. $p(w, c, x|r)$ gives the *joint* distribution of the context elements, the class label and the expansion choices of the non-terminals for a rule r.

A right-hand side function $RHS : R \to N^*$ is defined to obtain an ordered set of non-terminals on the right-hand side of a derivation rule. Similarly, a left-hand side function $LHS : R \to N$ gives the left-hand side of a derivation rule. Assuming there are only two classes labelled as p (poor) and g (good), the formalized version of an example of the PCSG for the Deceptive Max Problem [17] is depicted in Table 1. We use a pair of square brackets (e.g. [0.95]) to enclose the terminals while the non-terminals (e.g. $Exp, Start$) are not enclosed by them. Since each rule is associated with a BN classifier, there are in total five BN classifiers representing $p(w, c, x|r)$. When the set of context elements C is empty, we may use $p(w, x|r)$ to represent $p(w, \emptyset, x|r)$ for notational simplicity.

Table 1: Formalized PCSG for the DMax problem.

N	$\{Start, Exp\}$
T	$\{*, +, 0.95, \lambda\}$
S	$Start$
R	$\{r_0, r_1, r_2, r_3, r_4\}$, where $r_0 = Start \to Exp$ $r_1 = Exp \to [*]\ Exp\ Exp\ Exp$ $r_2 = Exp \to [+]\ Exp\ Exp\ Exp$ $r_3 = Exp \to [0.95]$ $r_4 = Exp \to [\lambda]$
C	$\emptyset$
X	$\{g, p\}$
D	Initial probability distributions for the rules $p(w, \emptyset, x\|r_0) = 1/(4 \times 2)$, where $w \in \{r_1, r_2, r_3, r_4\}, x \in X$ $p(w, \emptyset, x\|z) = 1/(4^3 \times 2)$, where $w \in \{r_1, r_2, r_3, r_4\}^5, z \in \{r_1, r_2\}, x \in X$

Given the grammar, we can derive an individual from the start symbol S by choosing the derivation rules for each non-terminal. Previous works on PMBGP applied different probabilistic models for the variables (e.g. PIPE: a position-dependent model; POLE: a global dependence model for all nodes in a parse tree). They did not use classifier nor did they learn the model using the poor individuals. In contrast, GBGPBC applies a BN classifier for each rule that encodes the choice dependency (i.e. $p(w, c, x|r)$) and modifies the distributions based on the class label.

4. PROPOSED ALGORITHM

In this section, we present the details in GBGPBC. The whole process of GBGPBC involves seven steps.

1. Initialize a BN classifier with independent uniform distribution for each derivation rule.
2. Produce a population of individuals from the grammar following the (refined) probabilities specified in the BN classifiers given the class label which is randomly chosen along the generation.
3. Select the fitter individuals and the poorer individuals based on the fitness values and label the respective parse tree as "good" (g) and "poor" (p) accordingly.
4. Collect the usage counts of class label and derivation choices for each rule from the selected individuals.
5. For each production rule in the grammar, check if the number of samples accumulated exceeds a predefined threshold, if so, its BN classifier is reconstructed and the samples are then cleared.
6. Refine the probability distributions in the BN classifier based on the class labels so as to reduce the probability of generating poor individuals.
7. Repeat from step 2 and the selected good individuals survive to the next generation.

Step 2 to step 7 are repeated until certain criteria, such as reaching the maximum number of generation, are satisfied.

4.1 Initialization of Bayesian Networks

Initially, all variables are assumed to be independent and the joint probability distribution is uniform. Therefore, no edge can be found between any nodes in the BN classifiers.

4.2 Individual Generation

An individual is essentially a tree satisfying the language defined in the grammar. We construct a tree starting from the only rule with the start symbol S. Then we choose a class label x from $\{g,p\}$ with a probability $prob_g$ and $prob_p$ respectively, where g and p represent the class of "good" and "poor" individuals respectively; $prob_g + prob_p = 1$. The rules for deriving all non-terminals on the right-hand side of it will be chosen according to the probability distribution $p(w,x|r)$ of the starting rule. For any newly derived non-terminals, we recursively apply this procedure until no more non-terminal needs to be instantiated.

To illustrate the derivation procedure, an example is shown in Figure 2. We focus on the derivation of the Exp_0 node (circled in dotted line) under the $Start$ node. At first, we instantiate the rule $r = Exp \rightarrow [+]\ Exp_0\ Exp_1\ Exp_2$ according to a topological order in the BN classifier (a TAN classifier) B_r, (i.e. $X\ Exp_1\ Exp_0\ Exp_2$ in the Figure 1d), where the subscript distinguishes the three Exp non-terminals in the RHS. In a TAN classifier, Exp_0, Exp_1 and Exp_2 must form a tree structure. Then we choose a class label x from $\{g,p\}$ with a fixed probability $prob_g$ and $prob_p$ respectively, say g. Next, we choose the state for Exp_1. It has four possible states representing the four rules (i.e. 2.0, 2.1, 2.2, 2.3) of Exp respectively. To instantiate Exp_1, we choose a state according to the distribution $p(Exp_1|g)$, say state 3, so the derivation rule 2.3 of Exp is picked. After that, we instantiate Exp_0 according to the distribution $p(Exp_0|Exp_1, g)$ and obtain 2. We follow the same procedure for Exp_2 to get 1. Therefore, the states are $(2,3,1)$ which means the rule is derived to $(2.2, 2.3, 2.1)$. The chosen rules can then be recursively expanded to produce a parse tree. The chosen rule by the non-terminal will be as shown in the individual i_4 in Figure 2, where $\#n$ in the circles represent the instantiated choice of state for that non-terminal is n.

4.3 Learning Bayesian Network Classifier

After generating and evaluating all the individuals in a population, the individuals are sorted according to their fitness values. The number of individuals selected depends on the selection rate r_{select} and $n_{select} = r_{select} \times pop$, where pop is the population size. The first n_{select} of individuals are labelled as g. Another parameter $pivot$ ranging from 0 to $1 - r_{select}$ is for locating the position of $poor$ samples. The n_{select} of individuals starting at $pivot \times pop$ are labelled as p. With the categorized selected individuals as training examples, BN classifiers are learnt.

Since each node in the parse tree records the rule choice, it is possible to acquire the set of applied rules in constructing an individual. In the example in Figure 2, we know that the $Start$ symbol applies the rule 1.0, and the children Exp is in turn instantiated to state 1 and the non-terminals of the right-hand side of the rule $r_{2,1}$ are being instantiated to states $(2,3,1)$. We collect the derivation events together with the class label of the respective parse tree, and construct a table for each derivation rule (See Figure 2). With this table of cases, BN classifiers can be used to model the relations of variables in the network. In this work, the TAN classifier learning algorithm is chosen to learn the structures of the BN classifiers for the variables to classify the class labels given the derivation events. Since the population will gradually bias to the optimal solutions, the classifiers have to be reconstructed from time to time based on a parameter *accumulation-size*. They are reconstructed only when there are at least *accumulation-size* number of cases. It is encouraged to start with a small *accumulation-size*, say 15, when applying this system to a new problem.

4.4 Context Elements during Derivation

The proposed grammar model allows us to add extra contextual information to the conditional probabilities. In the BN classifier, a new predictor variable corresponding to each context element will be inserted (preceding the nodes for the non-terminals). Two context elements are introduced to improve the performance of GBGPBC.

Depth: The substructure of the solution may change across different tree depth. Therefore, it may be helpful to learn the dependence between the non-terminals and the depth of the current level. As an illustration, in Figure 3, the state of $Depth$ context is 2 for the bottom layer of non-terminals so the choices of the three Exp non-terminals will be conditioned on $Depth = 2$.

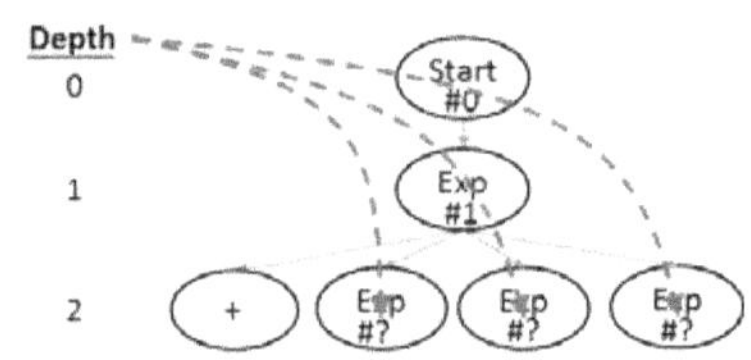

Figure 3: Tree depth context.

Caller: During the derivation of a parse tree, not only the derivation can be affected by other non-terminals within the same rule, but also affected by whom (the parent rule) calling the rule. Consider a non-terminal symbol s and the subset of rules $Z \subseteq R$ containing s in their RHS. We index these rules (starting from 0 to $|Z|$-1) by their order of occurrence in the grammar. Then, we subsequently annotate the non-terminals having symbol s on the right-hand side of each rule in Z using the index, namely the $caller$ value. For example, considering the Exp symbol in Figure 4, Rule 1.0, Rule 2.0 and Rule 2.1 are indexed by 0,1 and 2 respectively with respect to the symbol. Next, the Exp non-terminals on the right-hand side of Rule 1.0 (having index 0) are annotated by 0 as shown using superscript in Exp^0 and similarly for other rules. We repeat this for all the non-terminal symbols on the right-hand side in the grammar. Subsequently, each non-terminal is associated with a *caller* value.

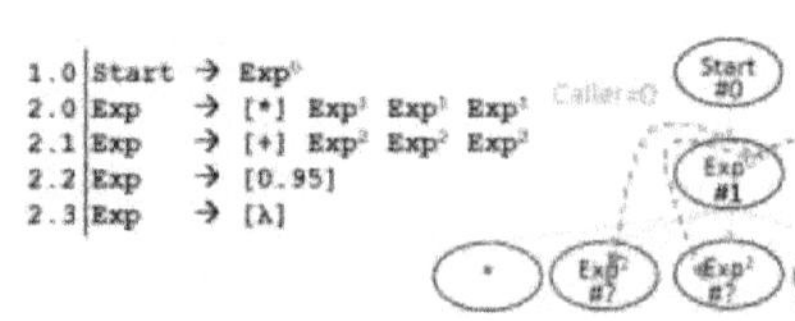

Figure 4: Caller context.

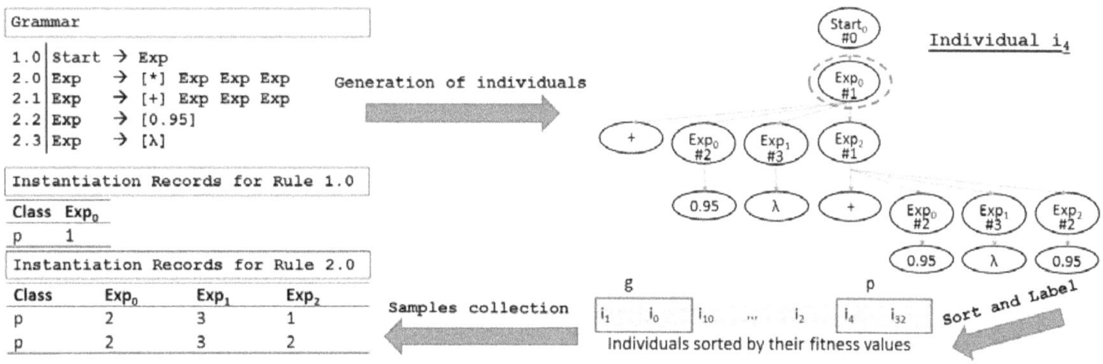

Figure 2: A valid parse tree on the Deceptive Max grammar

4.5 Class Dependent Refinement

A BN classifier contains the original joint distribution of class p, but we do not follow it to generate individuals because it very likely leads to poor individuals. Therefore, we heuristically alter the probability distribution in the classifiers based on class type so as to raise the chance of generating useful structures of an individual to improve the fitness in the next generation. Now we propose a generation scheme to generate less poor ones as follows.

When we are about to derive a rule given the conditional distribution $p(w_i|p, r, \mathbf{pa}(w_i))$, we set the most probable entry(ies) to a very small number (say 10^{-6}) and renormalize. Then, we sample from the renormalized conditional distribution. An example is shown in Table 2. This makes sense as the distribution is learnt from poor individuals and we can avoid it by suppressing the likelihood. This modification procedure can be applied to any types of problem in general if the semantics of the class label is known.

Table 2: Probability refinement assuming $\epsilon = 10^{-6}$

Exp_2	Exp_0	$p(Exp_2\|Exp_0, p)$	$p'(Exp_2\|Exp_0, p)$
...	...	...	...
0	1	0.30	ϵ
1	1	0.30	ϵ
2	1	0.15	0.375
3	1	0.25	0.625
...	...	...	...

5. COMPARATIVE EXPERIMENTS

To demonstrate the effectiveness of our algorithm, we have implemented GBGPBC and tested it with two benchmark problems: the deceptive maximum (DMax) problems and the asymmetric royal tree (ART) problems. It was compared with three state-of-the-art GP methods: POLE[16, 17], PAGE-EM [27], and PAGE-VB[27]. These three approaches were shown to be superior to univariate model (PIPE), adjacent model (EDP model) and simple GP [27]. The parameters and their values of configuration on different problems are shown in Table 3. Due to time constraints, we assume an approach fails if the highest non-optimal fitness value of the individuals in the population keeps constant for ten generations or it cannot obtain the optimal solution in 200,000 fitness evaluations. We label GBGPBC with *depth* when depth context variable is used and similarly for other variables. Besides, '-' is used if more than one variable is used. For example, *caller-depth* indicates that *caller* and *depth* variables are used. If none of the context variables is used, we call it a *plain* GPGPBC.

5.1 Deceptive Max

The DMax problem [17] is a modified version of the original Max problem [38]. Given a terminal set and a function set, the goal is to find a program which returns the maximum value within a depth limit. The DMax problem adds deceptiveness by introducing complex number in the terminal set but maximizing only the real part of the output of a program. Interaction between sub-trees must be considered in order to achieve this goal. Formally, the DMax problem has a function set $\{+_m, \times_m\}$ and a terminal set $\{0.95, \lambda\}$, where $\lambda^r = 1$. We use the notation *DMax(m,r)* to represent this class of problems. The grammar of $DMax(3, r)$ is shown in Figure 4. DMax(5,3) and DMax(3,2) are also called strong DMax and weak DMax respectively [27]. In this paper, we have tested four DMax problems with different combination of m and r (see Table 3). We follow the procedures in previous works [18][27] and report the average number of fitness evaluations needed to obtain the optimal solution with a probability of at least 90% in 50 independent runs under different configurations in Table 4.

It is observed that GBGPBC performs quite well in the DMax problems with *depth* and *caller* context elements. Its number of fitness evaluations is almost half of the second best approach PAGE-EM in DMax(3,2). For DMax(3,5) and DMax(3,4), GBGPBC performs slightly better than PAGE-EM and vice versa for DMax(5,3). The search performance of PAGE-VB is poorer than GBGPBC (being almost three times faster) at depth 5 because it needs to estimate the annotation size. Canonical GBGP cannot solve the DMax problems as the chance for obtaining an optimal solution drops by means of crossover and mutation. Using *depth* context element, GBGPBC is faster than POLE by at least two times. It also shows the importance of context elements in GBGPBC because the plain version fails to solve the DMax problem at a higher level when it does not consider where the derivation takes place. This is because the *Exp* in Rule 2.0 has to be derived using both Rule 2.0 or Rule 2.1.

5.2 Asymmetric Royal Tree Problem

This is a variation of the traditional royal tree problem [39] where all the siblings of a node in the perfect tree have to be the same. Therefore, the optimal choice of a node depends only on the parent. In order to test the

Table 4: **Results for Deceptive Max Problem. The table shows the statistics of the number of fitness evaluation needed under different configurations in 50 runs. For PAGE-EM, only the best results were shown. Numbers enclosed in brackets mean it fails to obtain the optimal solution with a probability of at least 90% in 50 independent runs. 'X' means none of the runs succeeds. '-' means results are unavailable.**

	DMax(3,2)				DMax(3,5)				DMax(3,4)		DMax(5,3)	
	Level 4		Level 5		Level 4		Level 5		Level 5		Level 4	
	μ	σ	μ	σ	μ	σ	μ	σ	μ	σ	μ	σ
GBGPBC												
-plain	6,697	2,273	(141,979)	(25,347)	(10,178)	(1,919)	x	x	x	x	65,689	15,62
-depth	3,640	1,155	13,017	5,729	9,453	27,700	20,702	3,134	18,306	4,098	26,827	6,172
-caller	4,592	1,273	(155,842)	(20,977)	(7,069)	(5,186)	x	x	x	x	32,586	6,748
-depth-caller	3,487	1,214	8,977	2,096	4680	1122	14,535	2,438	12,996	2,273	20,089	4,192
GBGP	(39,098)	(6,922)	x	x	x	x	x	x	x	x	x	x
POLE	9,800	1,160	33,333	3,231	7,960	605	285,652	95,023	73,723	2,223	119,572	4,295
PAGE-EM	5,756	743	15,851	1,250	6,400	606	18,040	1,814	16,521	1,473	16,043	1,189
PAGE-VB	8,304	939	24,622	3,967	8,304	940	43,733	15,611	39,022	3,361	18,293	1,688

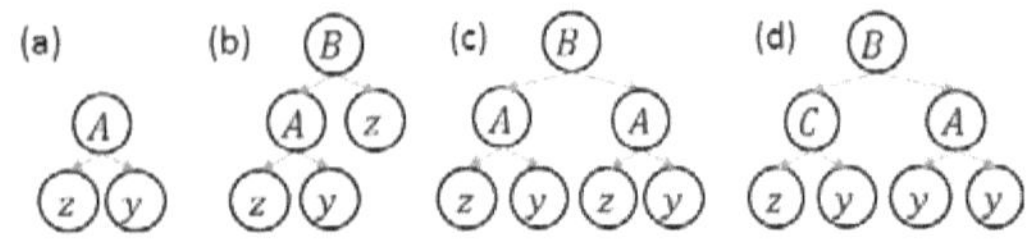

Figure 5: Examples of asymmetric royal tree. (a) A perfect tree at level A. Fitness= $2\times(2\times1+2\times1)=8$**. (b) A perfect tree at level B. Fitness=** $2\times\{2\times(2\times(2\times1+2\times1))+2\times1\}=36$**. (c) Imperfect tree at level B. Fitness=** $2\times8+2\times8=32$**. (d) Imperfect tree at level B. Fitness=** $\frac{1}{3}\times(\frac{1}{3}\times1+\frac{1}{3}\times1)+(2\times1+2\times1)\approx4.222$

ability to learn dependency among sub-trees, we propose a new variation of royal tree problem: asymmetric royal tree (ART). It again has a set of functions labelled by symbols from A to Z and two terminals y and z. Each function has arity of two and the arguments are interchangeable, i.e. $f(x,y)=f(y,x)$. Define an ordered list of symbols $L=(y,z,A,B,C,D,...,Z)$, and $Prec(\alpha)$ is the preceding symbol of α in L, e.g. $Prec(A)=z$.

A perfect sub-tree with a root node labelled α must have $Prec(\alpha)$ and $Prec(Prec(\alpha))$ as the children of α and the sub-trees rooted at each child must be a perfect sub-tree as well. For the base case, when α is A, $Prec(\alpha)$ and $Prec(Prec(\alpha))$ are z and y respectively. This corresponds to the function $A(z,y)$. When α is D, $Prec(\alpha)$ and $Prec(Prec(\alpha))$ will be C and B respectively. Therefore, the optimal choice of a sub-tree depends on its sibling and parent.

We define the term *perfect children* of a node R to be the set of the immediate child nodes found in the perfect sub-tree of R. Under our settings, perfect children of A, B and C are $\{y,z\}$, $\{A,z\}$ and $\{A,B\}$ respectively.

Some examples of ARTs are shown in Figure 5. Table 5 shows the best ART at different depth in S-expression.

To calculate the score for each individual, we evaluate the structural difference between the proposed individual and the goal from the deepest nodes to the root using the formula $Score(X_p)=b_p\sum_j(a_{pj}\times Score(X_{pj}))$, where X_p is the current node for evaluation, X_{pj} is the jth children node of X_p, b_p is the bonus for the node X_p which can be equal to *full bonus* (which is 2) if X_p has the whole set of perfect children); otherwise, its value is 1. a_{pj} is the bonus for the child node X_{pj} of X_p. Its value can be either *full bonus* (2), *partial bonus* (1) or *penalty* (1/3). If X_{pj} is in the perfect children of X_p and X_{pj} is perfect, a_{pj} is equal to the *full bonus*; when X_{pj} is in the perfect children of X_p but X_{pj} is not perfect, a_{pj} is equal to the *partial bonus*; a_{pj} is *penalty* if X_{pj} is not in the perfect children of X_p. And $Score(y)=Score(z)=1$.

Results in Table 6 show excellent performance of GBGPBC. It can be observed that only GBGPBC and POLE can complete the task in all 50 runs while the performance of PAGE-EM and PAGE-VB drops dramatically in depth E. In the best case, the number of evaluations for GBGPBC is only half of that of POLE. It is suspected that PAGE algorithm cannot handle the dependence specified in the asymmetric royal tree. In PAGE, it is assumed that all the right-hand side non-terminal symbols have the same annotation in order to make the number of parameters tractable. Therefore, using a distribution to encode two viable choices may pose a challenge. Because POLE uses a global BN to model the dependence, it still has a reasonably good performance in some runs. The traditional GBGP system can still obtain a global optimal solution which may be due to the large number of optimal solutions in the search space and the fact that the children of a perfect sub-tree are interchangeable.

6. DISCUSSION AND CONCLUSION

From the experiments, GBGPBC has been shown to be competitive among the tested approaches in the problems requiring strong dependence. It has several advantages when compared with the previous approaches in the following ways.

6.1 Classification on Individuals

Our method combines probabilistic classification (the TAN classifier) with PMBGP approach. The probability models are learnt from the selected *good* individuals for discovering the frequently occurred substructures in the good individuals, but these substructures may not be useful as some of them may commonly appear in both good individuals and poor individuals. In other words, discriminative substructures are more preferred. Rather than discarding the poor individuals, we select part of them to train the BN classifiers and store the discriminative information between the two classes of individuals. When we have the BN classifiers, it is easy to produce a good individual based on the joint distribution by conditioning on the *good* class. In this work, we only explore the use of good and poor classes, and it is possible to extend our approach by having other ways to classify the individuals.

Table 3: Problem specific configuration.

Parameter	Value
Depth	DMax(3,2), DMax(3,5): 4, 5 DMax(3,4): 5 DMax(5,3): 4 ART: 5 (Level D), 6 (Level E)
GBGP Configuration	
Parameter	**Value**
Population size	1000
Generation	1000
Crossover rate	0.9
Mutation rate	0.09
POLE Configuration	
Parameter	**Value**
Population size	1000 (DMax Level 4, ART) 4000 (DMax Level 5)
Parent range	2
Selection rate	0.1
Elite rate	0.005
PAGE-EM Configuration	
Parameter	**Value**
Population size	1000
Annotation size	8, 16
Selection rate	0.1
Elite rate	0.1
PAGE-VB Configuration	
Parameter	**Value**
Population size	1000
Annotation to explore	{1,2,4,8,16}
Annotation exploration range	2
Selection rate	0.1
Elite rate	0.1
GBGPBC Configuration	
Parameter	**Value**
Population size	250
Accumulation size	25
Context variables tested	Depth, Caller
Class labels	good, poor
Selection rate	0.1
$prob_p$	0.05 (DMax level 4) 0.02 (DMax level 5) 0.1 (ART)
$prob_g$	$1 - prob_p$
pivot	0.8

6.2 Semantic Refinement on Distribution

Previous works such as EBCOA [11] generate individuals directly using the BN classifier learnt from both good and poor individuals. But, if we follow the distribution of poor individuals, it is likely to generate a poor one, so we modify the distribution to avoid the generation of poor individuals. In essence, the generation procedure of a given class should be refined according to the meaning of the class label.

6.3 Derivation Order Learning

Non-terminals in a derivation rule are usually inter-dependent. Tanev's approach [32] accumulates context information using the derived terms but sampling enough data can be a problem. Besides, it implicitly assumed that the derivation is in a specific order (say in a depth-first search manner and from left-to-right). On the contrary, GBGPBC decides the order from the dependence of instantiating the non-terminals. Some non-terminals can be instantiated first if it does not depend on other non-terminals. Subsequently, other non-terminals can be instantiated.

Table 5: Optimal structure from depth 2 to 6 in the Asymmetric Royal Tree Problem

Depth	S-expression	Score
2	(A y z)	8
3	(B (A y z) z)	36
4	(C (B (A y z) z) (A y z))	176
5	(D (C (B (A y z) z) (A y z)) (B (A y z) z))	848

Table 6: Results for Asymmetric Royal Tree Problem. It shows the statistics of the number of fitness evaluation in 50 runs. Column *Suc.* is the number of successful runs.

	Level D			Level E		
	Suc.	μ	σ	Suc.	μ	σ
GBGPBC						
-plain	50	1,755	402	50	3,955	970
-depth	50	1,915	587	50	8,650	5,666
-caller	50	2,130	1,000	50	7,430	3,072
-depth-caller	50	2,800	583	50	9,610	7,953
GBGP	48	11,249	2,240	22	19,960	3,138
POLE	50	8,360	1,998	50	9,420	6,204
PAGE-EM	21	6,048	1,987	13	20,846	10,915
PAGE-VB	50	15,060	9,079	5	63,000	33,586

6.4 Future Works

Our novel integration with BN classifiers and GBGP together with semantic refinement gives a new insight of PMBGA and PMBGP research to handle the dependence issues. To extend our approach, it may be interesting to apply other kinds of BN classifiers, especially those which can discover latent classes in the training samples. Furthermore, we would also like to develop problem specific semantic refinement in the future by identifying key features of a program in a certain class. Applying our GBGPBC system to real world problems will be promising. It is fast and scalable to large optimization problems in which the structure of solution can be defined using grammar.

7. ACKNOWLEDGMENTS

This research has been supported by General Research Fund LU310111 from the Research Grant Council of the Hong Kong Special Administrative Region.

8. REFERENCES

[1] P. A. Whigham, "Grammatically-based genetic programming," in *Proc. of the workshop on genetic programming: from theory to real-world applications*, vol. 16, no. 3, 1995, pp. 33–41.

[2] M. Pelikan and D. E. Goldberg, *Bayesian optimization algorithm: From single level to hierarchy*. University of Illinois at Urbana-Champaign Urbana, IL, 2002.

[3] K. Sastry and D. E. Goldberg, "Probabilistic model building and competent genetic programming," in *Genetic Programming Theory and Practice*. Springer, 2003, pp. 205–220.

[4] P. Larrañaga and J. A. Lozano, *Estimation of distribution algorithms: A new tool for evolutionary computation*. Springer, 2002, vol. 2.

[5] K. Kim, Y. Shan, X. H. Nguyen, and R. McKay, "Probabilistic model building in genetic programming: a critical review," *Genetic Programming and Evolvable Machines*, pp. 1–53, 2013.

[6] M. Pelikan, "Bayesian optimization algorithm," in *Hierarchical Bayesian Optimization Algorithm*. Springer, 2005, pp. 31–48.

[7] R. Etxeberria and P. Larranaga, "Global optimization using bayesian networks," in *Second Symposium on Artificial Intelligence (CIMAF-99)*, 1999, pp. 332–339.

[8] H. Mühlenbein and T. Mahnig, "FDA-A scalable evolutionary algorithm for the optimization of additively decomposed functions," *Evolutionary computation*, vol. 7, no. 4, pp. 353–376, 1999.

[9] R. S. Michalski, "Learnable evolution model: Evolutionary processes guided by machine learning," *Machine Learning*, vol. 38, no. 1-2, pp. 9–40, 2000.

[10] X. Llora and D. E. Goldberg, "Wise breeding ga via machine learning techniques for function optimization," in *GECCO 2003*, 2003, pp. 1172–1183.

[11] T. Miquélez, E. Bengoetxea, and P. Larrañaga, "Evolutionary computation based on bayesian classifiers," *International Journal of Applied Mathematics and Computer Science*, vol. 14, pp. 335–349, 2004.

[12] W. Wattanapornprom, P. Olanviwitchai, P. Chutima, and P. Chongstitvatana, "Multi-objective combinatorial optimisation with coincidence algorithm," in *Proc. IEEE Congr. Evol. Comput.* IEEE, 2009, pp. 1675–1682.

[13] R. Salustowicz and J. Schmidhuber, "Probabilistic incremental program evolution," *Evolutionary Computation*, vol. 5, no. 2, pp. 123–141, 1997.

[14] K. Yanai and H. Iba, "Estimation of distribution programming based on bayesian network," in *Proc. IEEE Congr. Evol. Comput.*, 2003, pp. 1618–1625.

[15] M. Looks, B. Goertzel, and C. Pennachin, "Learning computer programs with the bayesian optimization algorithm," in *Proc. of GECCO*, 2005, pp. 747–748.

[16] Y. Hasegawa and H. Iba, "Estimation of bayesian network for program generation," in *Proc. 3rd Asian-Pacific Workshop on Genetic Programming*, 2006, p. 35.

[17] ——, "A bayesian network approach to program generation," *IEEE Trans. Evol. Comput.*, vol. 12, no. 6, pp. 750–764, 2008.

[18] T. Yanase, Y. Hasegawa, and H. Iba, "Binary encoding for prototype tree of probabilistic model building GP," in *Proc. of GECCO 2009*, 2009, pp. 1147–1154.

[19] H. Sato, Y. Hasegawa, D. Bollegala, and H. Iba, "Probabilistic model building GP with belief propagation," in *Proc. IEEE Congr. Evol. Comput.*, 2012, pp. 1–8.

[20] T. L. Booth and R. A. Thompson, "Applying probability measures to abstract languages," *Computers, IEEE Trans. on*, vol. 100, no. 5, pp. 442–450, 1973.

[21] A. Ratle and M. Sebag, "Avoiding the bloat with stochastic grammar-based genetic programming," in *Artificial Evolution*. Springer, 2002, pp. 255–266.

[22] S. Baluja, "Population-based incremental learning. a method for integrating genetic search based function optimization and competitive learning," DTIC Document, Tech. Rep., 1994.

[23] R. Shan, R. McKay, H. Abbass, and D. Essam, "Program evolution with explicit learning," in *Proc. IEEE Congr. Evol. Comput.*, 2003, pp. 1639–1646.

[24] Y. Shan, R. I. McKay, R. Baxter, H. Abbass, D. Essam, and H. Nguyen, "Grammar model-based program evolution," in *Proc. IEEE Congr. Evol. Comput.*, 2004, pp. 478–485.

[25] R. Solomonoff, "Complexity-based induction systems: comparisons and convergence theorems," *IEEE Trans. on Information Theory*, vol. 24, no. 4, pp. 422–432, 1978.

[26] P. A. Bosman and E. D. de Jong, "Grammar transformations in an EDA for genetic programming," *UU-CS*, no. 2004-047, 2004.

[27] Y. Hasegawa and H. Iba, "Latent variable model for estimation of distribution algorithm based on a probabilistic context-free grammar," *IEEE Trans. Evol. Comput.*, vol. 13, no. 4, pp. 858–878, 2009.

[28] A. P. Dempster, N. M. Laird, and D. B. Rubin, "Maximum likelihood from incomplete data via the EM algorithm," *Journal of the Royal Statistical Society. Series B (Methodological)*, pp. 1–38, 1977.

[29] H. Attias, "Inferring parameters and structure of latent variable models by variational bayes," in *Proc. of the Fifteenth conf. on Uncertainty in artificial intelligence*. Morgan Kaufmann Publishers Inc., 1999, pp. 21–30.

[30] Y. Hasegawa and S. Ventura, "Programming with annotated grammar estimation," *Genetic Programming-New Approaches and Successful*, pp. 49–74, 2012.

[31] E. N. Regolin and A. T. R. Pozo, "Bayesian automatic programming," in *Genetic Programming*. Springer, 2005, pp. 38–49.

[32] I. Tanev, "Incorporating learning probabilistic context-sensitive grammar in genetic programming for efficient evolution and adaptation of snakebot," in *Genetic Programming*. Springer, 2005, pp. 155–166.

[33] R. Poli and N. F. McPhee, "A linear estimation-of-distribution GP system," in *Genetic Programming*. Springer, 2008, pp. 206–217.

[34] H. A. Abbass, X. Hoai, and R. I. Mckay, "AntTAG: A new method to compose computer programs using colonies of ants," in *Proc. IEEE Congr. Evol. Comput.*, vol. 2. IEEE, 2002, pp. 1654–1659.

[35] X. Li, S. Mabu, and K. Hirasawa, "Use of infeasible individuals in probabilistic model building genetic network programming," in *Proc. of GECCO*, 2011, pp. 601–608.

[36] D. Heckerman, *A tutorial on learning with Bayesian networks*. Springer, 2008.

[37] N. Friedman, D. Geiger, and M. Goldszmidt, "Bayesian network classifiers," *Machine learning*, vol. 29, no. 2-3, pp. 131–163, 1997.

[38] J. R. Koza, *Genetic Programming: vol. 1, On the programming of computers by means of natural selection*. MIT press, 1992, vol. 1.

[39] W. F. Punch, "How effective are multiple populations in genetic programming," *Genetic Programming*, vol. 98, pp. 308–313, 1998.

Neuro-evolutionary Topology Optimization of Structures by Utilizing Local State Features

Nikola Aulig
Honda Research Institute Europe GmbH
Carl-Legien-Straße 30
63073 Offenbach/Main, Germany
nikola.aulig@honda-ri.de

Markus Olhofer
Honda Research Institute Europe GmbH
Carl-Legien-Straße 30
63073 Offenbach/Main, Germany
markus.olhofer@honda-ri.de

ABSTRACT

In this paper we propose a novel method for the topology optimization of mechanical structures, based on a hybrid combination of a neuro-evolution with a gradient-based optimizer. Conventional gradient-based topology optimization requires problem-specific sensitivity information, however this is not available in the general case. The proposed method substitutes the analytical gradient by an artificial neural network approximation model, whose parameters are learned by an evolutionary algorithm. Advantageous is that the number of parameters in the evolutionary search is not directly coupled to the mesh of the discretized design, potentially enabling the optimization of fine discretizations. Concretely, the network maps features, obtained for each element of the discretized design, to an update signal, that is used to determine a new design. A new network is learned for every iteration of the topology optimization. The proposed method is evaluated on the minimum compliance design problem, with two different sets of features. Feasible designs are obtained, showing that the neural network is able to successfully replace analytical sensitivity information. In concluding remarks, we discuss the significant improvement that is achieved when including the strain energy as feature.

Categories and Subject Descriptors

I.2.6 [**ARTIFICIAL INTELLIGENCE**]: Learning;
I.2.8 [**ARTIFICIAL INTELLIGENCE**]: Problem Solving, Control Methods, and Search—*Heuristic methods*;
J.6 [**COMPUTER-AIDED ENGINEERING**]: Computer-aided design (CAD)

Keywords

Cma-es; hybrid algorithm; local state features; minimum compliance; neuro-evolution; topology optimization

GECCO'14, July 12–16, 2014, Vancouver, BC, Canada.

ACM 978-1-4503-2662-9/14/07 ...$15.00.
http://dx.doi.org/10.1145/2576768.2598314.

1. INTRODUCTION

Neuro-evolution is the field of designing artificial neural networks by using evolutionary algorithms [30, 11]. Inspired by its application to numerous problems like classification [9], pole-balancing [25, 13] or computer games [23, 24] we propose to apply a neuro-evolutionary process to the task of topology optimization. Concretely, we propose a method that uses neuro-evolution as part of a hybrid algorithm, combining it with a mathematical topology optimization algorithm.

In the field of structural optimization, the target of topology optimization is to provide an engineer or designer with an initial concept of a mechanical structure. This task is addressed by algorithms, which find the layout of a design by optimizing the distribution of material within a given design space, resulting in a geometrical layout defined by void and material regions.

Topology optimization algorithms operate on a cell mesh representation, in which each element is a discrete variable that can be empty or filled with material, subject to a constraint on the total mass. An example for a two-dimensional topology optimization design space for a structure with a static load and supports in the corners is given in Fig. 1. In the literature, mathematical methods [8, 10] and a variety of population-based methods are proposed for topology optimization, see [1, 22, 4, 29, 17] for some examples. In our work we combine aspects of both fields, therefore both are briefly introduced.

In density-based approaches [8] the binary problem is relaxed into a continuous problem by a material interpolation scheme. The relaxed problem is then solved by using rigorously derived adjoint sensitivities and specialized optimizers like the method of moving averages [28] or optimality criteria methods. Those approaches are computationally efficient and deal well with the typically very high dimensionality of topology optimization problems in industrial applications. In Fig. 1 an example for the minimum compliance structure obtained with the state of the art gradient-based topology optimizer from [2] for a mass fraction of 40% is shown. However, although efficient, the gradient-based topology optimization is only applicable when the required problem-specific knowledge, i.e. the analytical adjoint sensitivties are available for the considered objective function.

Topology optimization methods which rely on stochastic search algorithms can attempt to directly optimize the discrete problem. In approaches using genetic algorithms the design is in the simplest cases encoded as a bit-array in which each bit represents one element of the mesh [18, 5, 29]. Ex-

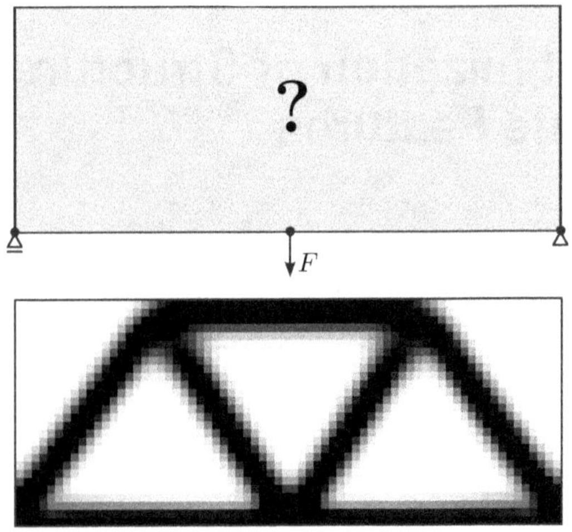

Figure 1: Example of gradient-based topology optimization of a structure from [2]; top: design space with applied force and supports; bottom: result of the topology optimization with 40% mass fraction.

tensions of the bit-array representation combine it with a skeleton geometry representation [4] or utilize a random tree encoding [17]. Recently a solid geometry based topology optimization [1] was proposed in which a geometry is obtained by a super-position of bars defined by triangulating a set of nodes. Other approaches use more sophisticated indirect encodings of the design based on cellular growth models [22, 26, 27].

The population-based methods are able to perform a global search and provide a solution to the discrete problem. However, algorithms based on a bit-array representation are not efficient when the number of parameters is very large, which is the case for finely discretized design spaces. Other approaches introduce more elaborate representations, instead of operating directly on the cell mesh. Although thereby the number of optimization parameters is reduced, this usually reduces the set of possible solutions.

Nevertheless evolutionary approaches do not require extensive previous knowledge, like explicit gradient information and can therefore be applied to the optimization of complex objective functions. Assumptions on the objective function are only made implicitly by the choice of representation and variational operators. This universality is an important advantage over gradient-based methods.

Independently of the topology optimization method, the analysis of the design provides state information at all nodes and elements within the discretized design space, like e.g. local displacement, strain or energy values. Currently existing population-based methods neglect this information and rely on random variation (sometimes augmented with self-adaptation) of the solution.

An exception is the work of Kaveh et.al. [16] who optimize a minimum compliance design with an ant colony optimization methodology that uses the elemental local strain energy for determining the amount of pheromone that is placed on the elements. However, the algorithm is specialized to minimum compliance problems and does not preserve the generality of a population-based method. Another exception is [3], in which a more generic approach was proposed. Instead of specializing the topology optimization algorithm to the objective function, for example by manually determining gradients, a neuro-evolution is used for this task. Concretely, a directly encoded neural network model that provides a design update rule is optimized. Local displacement and densities are processed by the network and an update signal for each design variable is provided. This update signal is used instead of true analytical sensitivities in a gradient-based topology optimization algorithm. In this way the generality of evolutionary optimization is combined with the established methods from mathematical topology optimization. As the evolutionary optimization is operating on the network parameters, it is not facing an increased problem dimensionality when the mesh size is increased, respectively when a more fine grained structure is required. The method aimed for a general model, respectively a general rule for a class of problems. It was evaluated on the minimum compliance problem, however, in several cases the optimization converged to local optima and results on the generality of the model were not published.

Similar to [3] we propose a combination of neuro-evolution and a gradient-based topology optimization algorithm. However, our approach is scaled to achieve a single topology optimization of a design, by optimizing a unique neural network for each design update.

The next section briefly presents a standard gradient-based topology optimization method for the minimum compliance problem. Section 3 introduces the neuro-evolutionary topology optimization algorithm, followed by the concept of local state features in Sect. 4. In Sect. 5 experiments and results are described. The paper is concluded in Sect. 6.

2. MINIMUM COMPLIANCE TOPOLOGY OPTIMIZATION

A relevant problem in the field of topology optimization, which is frequently used as benchmark problem is to minimize the compliance of a structure. It is a suitable test problem for our algorithm since it is possible to evaluate our results with respect to a well established baseline and analytical sensitivity information. Furthermore, the nonlinear relation between the elemental displacements and the analytical sensitivity will show to provide a challenging task for the learning of the neural network.

Besides from that, the implementation of the minimum compliance optimization is facilitated by the availability of efficient algorithm and solver implementations available in literature [2]. In this section the required concepts for a gradient-based topology optimization are introduced, as described in [8], where a density-based material distribution approach is applied.

We consider to minimize the compliance c (i.e. maximizing the stiffness) of a structure subject to a mass constraint in a two-dimensional rectangular design space. The design space is discretized in $N = N_x \times N_y$ uniform square finite elements. N_x and N_y define the number of elements in horizontal and vertical direction, respectively. For relaxing the problem a continuous density $x_i \in [x_{\min}, 1]$ is assigned to each element i of the mesh in the originally binary problem. The minimum density $x_{\min} = 0.001$ is introduced in order to avoid numerical problems. The SIMP (solid isotropic material with penalization) scheme [7] determines the Young's modulus $E_i(x_i)$ of the material in element i according to:

$$E_i(x_i) = x_i^p E_0, \tag{1}$$

with E_0 the Young's modulus of the full material and a penalization p. The penalization renders the use of intermediate densities inefficient and drives the structure towards a discrete design.

The minimum compliance topology optimization problem in its finite element formulation subject to a mass constraint can be stated as [8]:

$$\begin{aligned} \min_x c(\mathbf{x}) &= \mathbf{u}^T \mathbf{f} \\ \text{s.t. : } & \mathbf{K}(\mathbf{x})\mathbf{u} = \mathbf{f}, \\ & V(\mathbf{x}) = V_f, \\ & 0 < x_{\min} \leq x_i \leq 1, \ i = 1, \cdots, N. \end{aligned} \tag{2}$$

The vectors $\mathbf{u}$ and $\mathbf{f}$ are the global displacements and the forces vector, respectively, and $\mathbf{K}$ is the global stiffness matrix. A volume constraint V_f is imposed, specifying the proportion of design space which can be filled with material.

Problem (2) can be solved by a standard optimality criteria method (OC-update). A heuristic update scheme that redistributes material among the design variables and maintains the volume constraint is [8]:

$$x_i^{\text{new}} = \begin{cases} \max(x_{\min}, x_i - m) \\ \quad \text{if } x_i B_i^\eta \leq \max(x_{\min}, x_i - m), \\ \\ \min(1, x_i + m) \\ \quad \text{if } \min(1, x_i + m) \leq x_i B_i^\eta, \\ \\ x_i B_i^\eta \text{ else,} \end{cases} \tag{3}$$

with the move-limit m, damping coefficient η, and

$$B_i = \frac{\partial c}{\partial x_i} / \Lambda, \tag{4}$$

with the adjoint sensitivity $\frac{\partial c}{\partial x_i}$ and subject to the assumption that every element has a unit volume. The Lagrangian multiplier $\Lambda > 0$ is found using a bi-sectioning algorithm, which tunes the material redistribution in (3) such that the volume constraint holds. Based on the sensitivities the optimizer increases or decreases the design variables, respectively the material in the element. For the considered case, the analytical compliance sensitvities are given as:

$$\frac{\partial c}{\partial x_i} = -p x_i^{p-1} \mathbf{u}_i^{\mathrm{T}} \mathbf{k}_0 \mathbf{u}_i, \tag{5}$$

where $\mathbf{k}_0$ is the elemental stiffness matrix and $\mathbf{u}_i$ is the elemental displacement vector. This information is only used for comparison, since in our work the replacement of this analytic information by an evolved model is investigated.

In order to impose a minimum length scale and prevent numerical instabilities like checkerboard patterns a sensitivity filtering scheme is applied. The sensitivities $\frac{\partial c}{\partial x_i}$ are filtered according to:

$$\widehat{\frac{\partial c}{\partial x_i}} = \frac{1}{x_i \sum_{j \in N_i} H_{ij}} \sum_{j \in N_i} H_{ij} x_i \frac{\partial c}{\partial x_i} \tag{6}$$

where N_i is the set of elements whose center lies within the radius $r_{\min}$ around the center of element i. H_{ij} is defined as

$$H_{ij} = r_{min} - \operatorname{dist}(i, j) \tag{7}$$

where $\operatorname{dist}(i, j)$ is the center to center distance of elements i and j. In essence, the filter averages the elemental sensitivities over the neighboring elements within the radius $r_{\min}$.

The density-based topology optimization starts with an initial design guess, e.g. a homogenous distribution of density $x_i = V_f$, and involves the following iterative steps:

1. Design evaluation by solving the state equation in (2)
2. Computation of sensitivities (5)
3. Filtering of sensitivities (6)
4. Optimality criteria update (3)
5. If not converged, repeat from 1.

In the following section this algorithm is augmented by a neuro-evolutionary learning process in order to address objective functions with unknown sensitivities. Note that the OC-update and the filtering of sensitivities can be generally utilized, in contrast to the compliance objective function, which is only a specific test case.

3. NEURO-EVOLUTIONARY TOPOLOGY OPTIMIZATION

In this section we introduce the proposed Neuro-Evolutionary Topology Optimization (NETO) algorithm as a generic method for topology optimization based on material redistribution. The topology optimization algorithm from [2] presented in the preceding section is an efficient approach, however it requires analytic sensitivities which can be difficult to obtain in the general case. This paper explores the possibility of heuristically substituting these analytical sensitivities by a regression model. The parameters of the model are optimized by an evolutionary strategy before its output is applied to determine a new structural design. The hybrid combination of a population-based method with gradient-based topology optimization provides the advantage that some well established methods like SIMP, problem regularization and the optimizers can be used. Algorithms that combine a global search with a local search are often called memetic algorithms [20]. Our approach is such a combination, however conventionally the local search is applied to enhance the global search. The NETO algorithm instead uses the global optimizer in order to provide a direction in a local, gradient-based search for an optimal design topology. In the next paragraph the choice of a neural network and the evolutionary optimizer are motivated.

The choice of a neural network as approximation model does not constitute an incorporation of previous knowledge on the considered problem. This is relevant since the target of NETO is to provide a generic topology optimization method. When applied to the optimization of directly encoded artificial neural network models, the covariance matrix adaptation evolutionary strategy (CMA-ES) [12] has shown to be a competitive approach [13]. Additionally in [3] first insights have been gained on applying neural networks for the task of representing update signals in topology optimization. Therefore, as a first attempt to address the issue of model choice we propose to use a fully connected feed-forward multi-layer perceptron (MLP) with one hidden layer with sigmoidal activation functions and a linear output neuron. The inputs of the MLP are features obtained

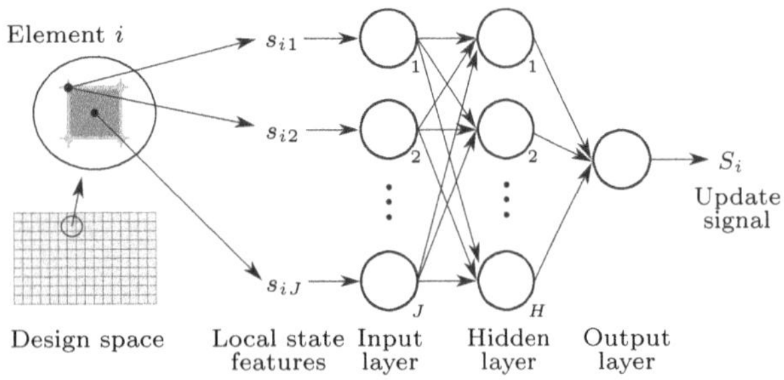

Figure 2: A feed-forward network with one hidden layer, processing local state features.

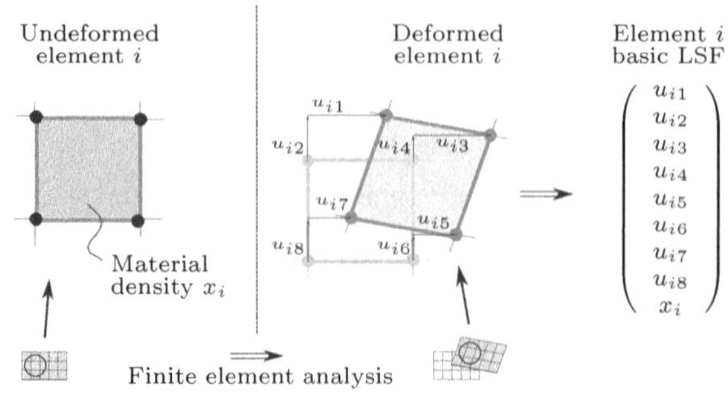

Figure 4: Basic local state features: elemental material density and displacements of element nodes after a finite element analysis was performed.

from the analysis of the design and are described in detail in Sect. 4. An illustration of the MLP and its inputs is depicted in Fig. 2. We designate the model output as S_i and the model inputs s_{ij} for $i = 1, \ldots, N$ and $j = 1, \ldots, J$, with J the number of features. The parameters subject to CMA-ES optimization are hidden weights and biases, and output weights. For the evolutionary optimization these parameters are directly encoded sequentially as a vector of real values. It is important to distinguish between the topology of the neural network model and the topology of the design. Since the neurons and connections within the network are fixed, the topology of the network does not change. With the term "topology" we only refer to the topology of the design (i.e. the mechanical structure) which is to be optimized.

The gradient-based topology optimization, as described in the previous section and the NETO algorithm are depicted on the right and left side of Fig. 3, respectively. For NETO, two optimization loops can be distinguished. The outer loop is the actual topology optimization, which is closely related to the gradient-based topology optimization. However, instead of computing analytical sensitivities, the inner loop with the CMA-ES optimization of the MLP is started. The quality (respectively fitness) of a MLP is defined as the reduction in compliance - respectively in the general case the improvement of the objective of the topology optimization. This quality is obtained by emulating a single topology optimization step, consisting of filtering, OC-update and design evaluation. In this update, the sensitivities are substituted by the MLP output. Formally, $\frac{\partial c}{\partial x_i}$ is replaced by the model output S_i, in the equations of the preceding section. In the filtering scheme (6) and the OC-update (3) the MLP output is then treated exactly as analytical sensitivities would be. The better the MLP substitutes the analytical sensitivities the more the compliance of the new design is reduced. The best MLPs are selected as parents and a new set of MLP candidates is provided by the variational operators of the CMA-ES optimizer. This inner loop is repeated until a convergence criterion is met. Then the optimized MLP is used in the outer topology optimization loop to perform a persistent design update. Identical to the inner loop the update is performed using the MLP output as substitute for sensitivities. In this way, the outer loop in every iteration performs a CMA-ES search followed by a design update, until a convergence criterion is met.

4. LOCAL STATE FEATURES

In this section we will introduce the inputs of the MLP, respectively the features used. In topology optimization, evaluating the structure not only yields its performance, but at the same time a detailed state information. The mathematical approaches often utilize this state information to compute the adjoint sensitivities of the objective function, revealing that these data contain valuable information for optimization. Some examples are compliance minimization, eigenvalue maximization, thermal conductivity maximization or compliant mechanism synthesis [8]. Accordingly, the state contains valuable information on how beneficial increasing or decreasing an elemental material density is.

This fact is also used by biologically-inspired approaches that use state information for heuristically conducting a topology optimization. In [6, 19] the stress within an element is used as basis for topology optimization inspired by the natural growth processes in trees. The bi-directional evolutionary structural optimization approach [14], which despite the name is not mimicking Darwinian evolution, uses an elemental "sensitivity number" computed from state information. Based on this, material in elements is discretely switched on or off. In the field of crashworthiness design, in which sensitivity information is difficult to obtain, Patel [21] uses a hybrid-cellular automata algorithm which operates on the elemental internal energy density for material distribution.

State information is characteristically defined locally for every element and the corresponding nodes in the discretized mesh. We therefore term the model inputs Local State Features (LSF). The choice of LSF is critical to the performance of NETO, since for weak LSF, which contain little information, the learning task can be very challenging, and on the other hand for strong LSF the learning task can be relatively easy. Depending on the objective function and the type of analysis, different LSF are available. For the minimum compliance problem, the most basic LSF are naturally those variables computed by the solver, which for a (displacement-based) finite element solver are the nodal displacements $\mathbf{u}$. In the considered two-dimensional problem, each element is defined by four nodes, which can be displaced horizontally and vertically. For element i an eight-dimensional displacement vector $\mathbf{u}_i = [u_{i1}, \ldots, u_{i8}]^{\mathrm{T}}$ results. Another very basic LSF is the material density in an element x_i i.e. the design variable. These basic LSF are illustrated in Fig. 4. Furthermore, it is possible to post-process those basic LSF to obtain stronger features which represent some physical information, as for example elemental strains, stresses or energy. This is a possibility to incorporate expert knowledge, depending on the problem and the solver used.

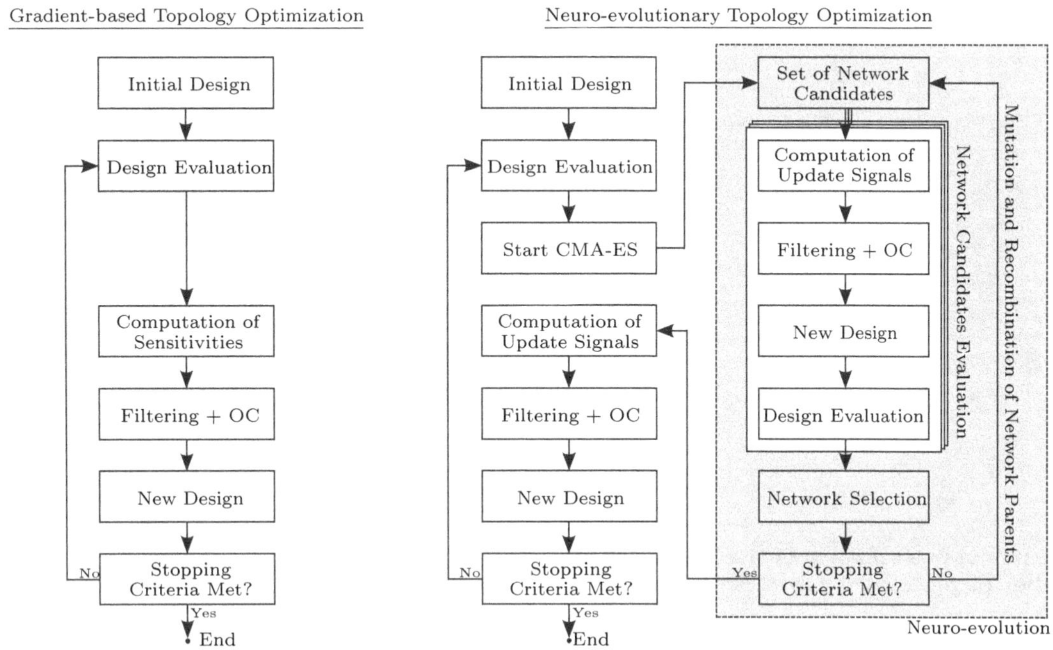

Figure 3: Comparison of the computational flow for gradient-based topology optimization (left) and neuro-evolutionary topology optimization (right).

For the minimum compliance problem, the elemental strain energy can be considered as a valuable higher level feature. It can be constructed from the basic features according to:

$$W_i = x_i^p \mathbf{u}_i^{\mathrm{T}} \mathbf{k_0} \mathbf{u}_i. \tag{8}$$

Previous knowledge on the problem is incorporated implicitly by choosing this feature over other physical information (like e.g. elemental strains or stresses) and explicitly since the computation of the stiffness matrix requires the material constants and the element type to be known.

5. EXPERIMENTS

5.1 Setup

In this section the performed experiments are described. The problem of designing a two-dimensional structure as in Fig. 1 was chosen as test problem for evaluating the neuro-evolutionary topology optimization. The design space is discretized with a mesh size of $N = 70 \times 28 = 1960$ elements with an element size of 1mm $\times$ 1mm, a load of $F = $ 1N, and a target volume fraction $V_f = 0.4$ is chosen. Young's modulus and Poisson's ratio are set as $E_0 = 1\mathrm{N/mm}^2$ and $\nu = 0.3$ respectively. The radius of the sensitivity filter is set to $r_{\min} = 2.5$mm. Intermediate densitities are penalized with $p = 3$. A homogenous distribution of material ($x_i = V_f, i = 1, \cdots, N$) is used as initial design guess. The resulting design, when applying the optimizer from [2] is shown in Fig. 1.

For our experiment two sets of LSF are chosen. LSF set I consists of the basic LSF i.e. the elemental displacement vector and the elemental density as introduced in section 4. Accordingly for LSF set I it holds

$$s_{ij}^{\mathrm{I}} = \begin{cases} u_{ij} & \text{for } j = 1, 2, \dots, 8, \\ x_i & \text{for } j = J^{\mathrm{I}} = 9. \end{cases} \tag{9}$$

This set of features does not include additional previous knowledge about the problem and is generally available when a displacement-based finite element solver is applied for analyzing the design.

LSF set II is meant to demonstrate how additional expert knowledge can be utilized to enhance the method. It consists of the same features as LSF set I extended by the strain energy absorbed by the element:

$$s_{ij}^{\mathrm{II}} = \begin{cases} u_{ij} & \text{for } j = 1, 2, \dots, 8, \\ x_i & \text{for } j = 9, \\ W_i & \text{for } j = J^{\mathrm{II}} = 10. \end{cases} \tag{10}$$

As approximation model we apply a MLP with ten hidden neurons. The number of hidden neurons was chosen based on a set of preceding test runs. This yields a search dimension for the CMA-ES optimization of 110 (LSF set I) and 120 (LSF set II) dimensions, respectively. Based on the recommendations from [12], the parent population size was chosen as $\mu = 9$ (aiming for a slightly more explorative behavior) and the offspring population size was chosen as $\lambda = 18$.

A maximum number of iteration was chosen as convergence criteria. For LSF set I the outer topology optimization is run for 60 iterations, and each inner CMA-ES is run for 500 iterations. For LSF set II the outer topology optimization is run for 30 iterations and each inner CMA-ES is run for 100 iterations, since in test runs a much faster convergence was observed for this LSF set.

The initial step size of the CMA-ES is chosen as 0.01 and the MLP parameters of the first inner loop are initialized between -0.01 and 0.01. For any but the first inner loop, the optimized MLP parameters and the covariance matrix from the previous CMA-ES run are used as starting point. Only the global step size of the CMA-ES is reset.

As the OC-update can only deal with negative sensitvities any positive model output is replaced by zero. For infeasi-

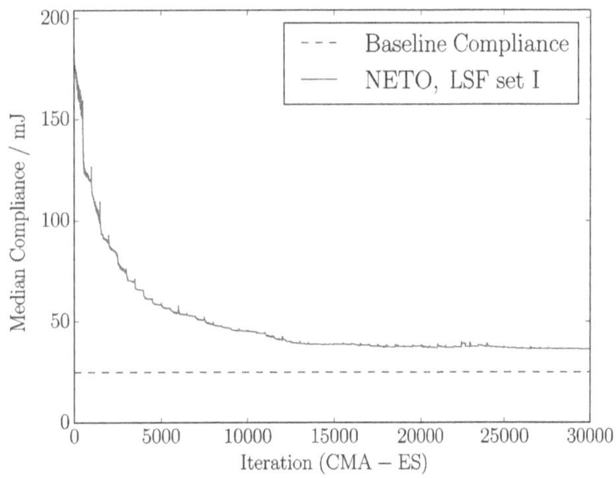

Figure 5: The median compliance of the best design over the number of performed CMA-ES iterations, for LSF set I.

ble weights the MLP may provide output which renders a design update impossible - for example when outputs for all elements are identical. In such cases the model candidate is assigned a high objective value. The inputs of the MLP are normalized to zero mean and to the range between −1 and 1, based on the numberss obtained from the initial design.

The implementation from [15] for the CMA-ES and the Python implementation from [2] for the topology optimizer and design analysis are used, respectively. Each run was started for 20 different random seeds. An overview of the results in terms of compliance is given in Tab. 5.1. In the following the results for the two feature sets are presented separately.

	Compliance/mJ		
Baseline	25.011		
NETO	Best	Median (± std)	Worst
LSF set I	27.258	34.499 (±5.593)	50.619
LSF set II	23.684	23.877 (±0.439)	25.737

Table 1: Compliance of best structures obtained by NETO using LSF set I and II, in each case based on 20 runs with different random seeds, and the baseline compliance.

5.2 Results LSF set I

Fig. 5 shows the median compliance over the number of performed CMA-ES iterations. Peaks in the compliance can be observed. These result from the update of the design and the restart of the inner CMA-ES optimization. On the new design the MLP initially performs worse than on the preceding design. This indicates that the MLP optimized for the previous design, is not valid for the new design and needs to be adapted. It can be seen that the optimization is to the most part converged after roughly 30 design updates (i.e. 1.5×10^4 CMA-ES iterations), but there are still small fluctuations towards the end.

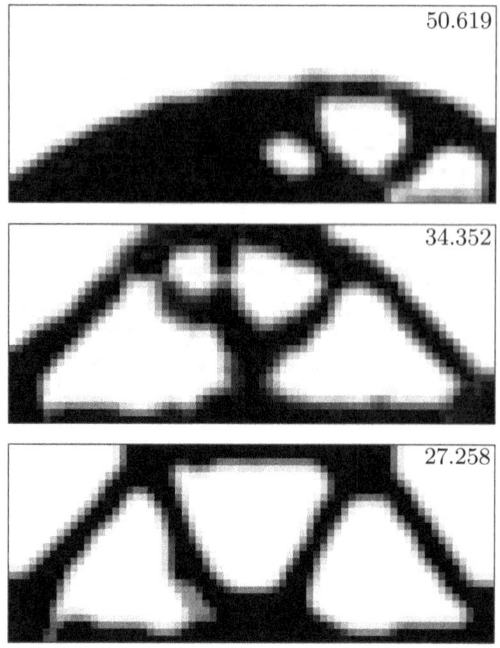

Figure 6: Best designs and compliance / mJ obtained for NETO for LSF set I from top to bottom: For the worst run, for the run closest to the median performance and for the best run.

Fig. 6 shows the best design of the best and worst run, and the best design of the run closest to the median performance. Similar as in Tab. 5.1 from the compliance value, it can be noticed visually that there is a high variance in the solutions. The best design has in essence the same layout as the baseline solution in Fig. 1, although with less straight boundaries. It can be interpreted as the same concept. In the sense that topology optimization yields a concept for a new structure, the generic update signal has successfully replaced the analytical sensitivities. Also the design obtained by the run closest to the median is showing similar characteristics as the baseline solution and might consist a valuable design concept. However, the structure is less symmetric and has even less straight connections. In the case of the worst run, the solution is not utilizing the full design space and quite different from the targeted baseline.

5.3 Results LSF set II

From Tab. 5.1, a clear improvement in the quality and a strong reduction of the variance is obtained for LSF set II. Fig. 7 shows the median compliance over the number of performed CMA-ES iterations. Clear steps reducing the compliance are visible for some of the iterations. In these iterations the MLP is applied to a new design and is instantly performing well. This is different to the compliance curve of LSF set I in Fig. 5. It indicates that the MLP using the strain energy feature can be generalized from one design to the next. A convergence can be observed after approximately 25 design updates (i.e. 2.5×10^3 CMA-ES iterations).

Fig. 8 shows the best design of the best and worst run, and the best design of the run closest to the median performance. As indicated by the small variance in the compliance value, also the designs show little variation. Best and me-

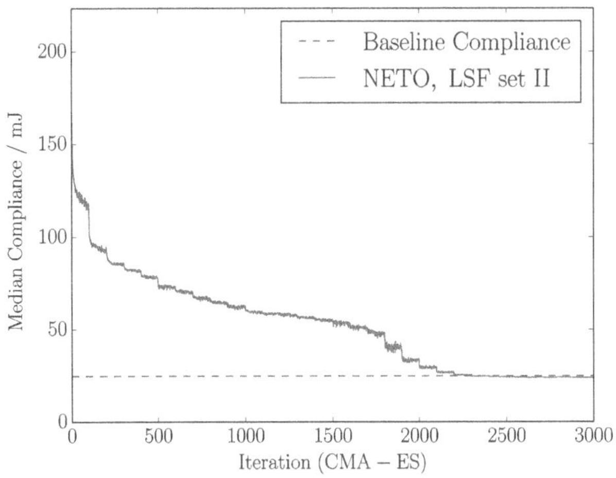

Figure 7: The median compliance of the best design over the number of performed CMA-ES iterations, for LSF set II.

dian design are visually extremely similar to the baseline in Fig. 1. Even the worst run yields a design, from which the same layout of the baseline can be easily identified. This shows, that for LSF set II, NETO is capable of successfully substituting the analytical sensitivities.

5.4 Discussion

A large difference in the performance of the two feature sets can be observed. NETO with LSF set II performs extremely well compared to LSF set I. There is a clear convergence to a constant value, in about 10% of the time. All obtained design concepts are very similar to the baseline. LSF set II extends the basic features by the elemental strain energy and minimizing compliance is defined by minimizing the energy absorbed by the design. Therefore an improvement can be expected for including the strain energy as LSF. When comparing the strain energy in (8) with the true compliance sensitivity in (5) a strong correlation is intuitive. This demonstrates that the NETO algorithm offers the possibility to include expert knowledge in the form of analytical or semi-analytical gradient information - and that the results can significantly benefit from it. From Tab. 5.1 it can be seen that the median compliance is even slightly better than that of the baseline, however considered from a conceptual level this improvement is not significant. This unexpected observation could result from a lack of tuning of the baseline algorithm, but it is also thinkable that the optimization of the complete design update step yields a slightly better design.

NETO can even provide the engineer with a sensible design concept when LSF set I is used. This result is especially interesting from the generalization point of view. Since a strong feature like the strain energy might not be available for other objective functions, it is important to note that the MLP is able to sufficiently substitute the non-linear relation of basic features and the analytical sensitivity in (5). That this is a challenging optimization task is indicated by the high solution variance.

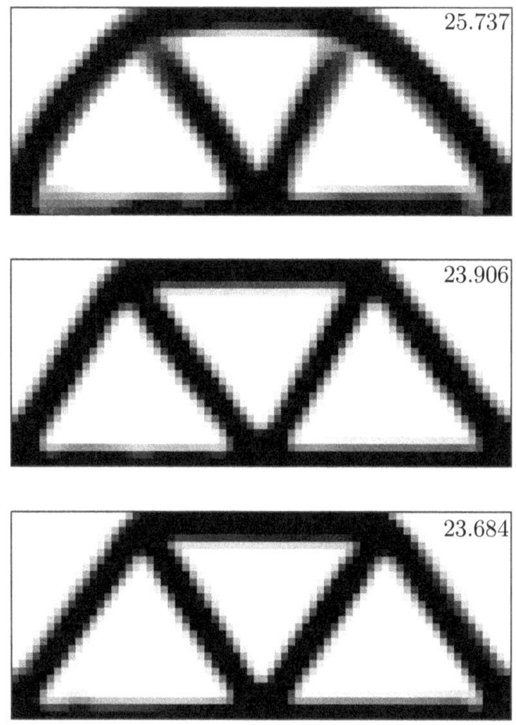

Figure 8: Best designs and compliance / mJ obtained for NETO for LSF set II from top to bottom: For the worst run, for the run closest to the median performance and for the best run.

The choice of features depends on the problem and on the available expert knowledge. From the experiments, we recommend to use the potentially strongest LSF, especially when these represent analytical or semi-analytical sensitivity information. Our results indicate that if no such features are available, this can partially be compensated by a higher computational effort.

6. CONCLUSIONS

A novel approach for the topology optimization of structures, is proposed in this paper. NETO is a hybrid algorithm combining a neuro-evolution with methods from gradient-based topology optimization. We see the main potential for our method in an application to objective functions for which mathematical gradients are difficult to obtain. However, in order to perform a statistical evaluation and a baseline comparison, NETO was applied to a minimum compliance problem. The algorithm is able to provide feasible designs even when only basic features are used. When including the elemental strain energy as feature, a significant improvement can be observed both in convergence and solution quality.

7. ACKNOWLEDGMENTS

The authors thank Dr. Martina Hasenjäger from the Honda Research Institute Europe GmbH for providing her neural network Python implementation.

8. REFERENCES

[1] F. Ahmed, B. Bhattacharya, and K. Deb. Constructive solid geometry based topology optimization using evolutionary algorithm. In J. C. Bansal, P. K. Singh, K. Deep, M. Pant, and A. K. Nagar, editors, *Proceedings of Seventh International Conference on Bio-Inspired Computing: Theories and Applications (BIC-TA 2012)*, volume 201 of *Advances in Intelligent Systems and Computing*, pages 227–238. Springer India, 2013.

[2] E. Andreassen, A. Clausen, M. Schevenels, B. Lazarov, and O. Sigmund. Efficient topology optimization in matlab using 88 lines of code. *Structural and Multidisciplinary Optimization*, 43(1):1–16, 2011.

[3] N. Aulig and M. Olhofer. Evolutionary generation of neural network update signals for the topology optimization of structures. In *Proceeding of the Fifteenth Annual Conference Companion on Genetic and Evolutionary Computation Conference Companion*, GECCO '13 Companion, pages 213–214, New York, NY, USA, 2013. ACM.

[4] R. Balamurugan, C. Ramakrishnan, and N. Swaminathan. A two phase approach based on skeleton convergence and geometric variables for topology optimization using genetic algorithm. *Structural and Multidisciplinary Optimization*, 43(3):381–404, 2011.

[5] R. Balamurugan, C. V. Ramakrishnan, and N. Singh. Performance evaluation of a two stage adaptive genetic algorithm (TSAGA) in structural topology optimization. *Appl. Soft Comput.*, 8(4):1607–1624, 2008.

[6] A. Baumgartner, L. Harzheim, and C. Mattheck. SKO (soft kill option): the biological way to find an optimum structure topology. *International Journal of Fatigue*, 14(6):387 – 393, 1992.

[7] M. Bendsøe. Optimal shape design as a material distribution problem. *Structural optimization*, 1:193–202, 1989.

[8] M. Bendsøe and O. Sigmund. *Topology Optimization Theory, Methods and Applications*. Springer Verlag Berlin, 2nd edition edition, 2004.

[9] A. Chandra and X. Yao. Ensemble learning using multi-objective evolutionary algorithms. *J. Math. Model. Algorithms*, 5(4):417–445, 2006.

[10] J. Deaton and R. Grandhi. A survey of structural and multidisciplinary continuum topology optimization: post 2000. *Structural and Multidisciplinary Optimization*, 49(1):1–38, 2014.

[11] D. Floreano, P. Dürr, and C. Mattiussi. Neuroevolution: from architectures to learning. *Evolutionary Intelligence*, 1(1):47–62, 2008.

[12] N. Hansen and A. Ostermeier. Completely derandomized self-adaptation in evolution strategies. *Evolutionary Computation*, 9(2):159–195, 2001.

[13] V. Heidrich-Meisner and C. Igel. Neuroevolution strategies for episodic reinforcement learning. *J. Algorithms*, 64(4):152–168, 2009.

[14] X. Huang and Y. Xie. *Evolutionary Topology Optimization of continuum structures*. John Wiley & Sons, 2012.

[15] C. Igel, V. Heidrich-Meisner, and T. Glasmachers. Shark. *Journal of Machine Learning Research*, 9:993–996, 2008.

[16] A. Kaveh, B. Hassani, S. Shojaee, and S. Tavakkoli. Structural topology optimization using ant colony methodology. *Engineering Structures*, 30(9):2559 – 2565, 2008.

[17] J. Madeira, H. Pina, and H. Rodrigues. GA topology optimization using random keys for tree encoding of structures. *Structural and Multidisciplinary Optimization*, 40(1-6):227–240, 2010.

[18] J. A. Madeira, H. Rodrigues, and H. Pina. Multi-objective optimization of structures topology by genetic algorithms. *Advances in Engineering Software*, 36(1):21 – 28, 2005. Evolutionary Optimization of Engineering Problems.

[19] C. Mattheck. *Design in Nature Learning from Trees*. Springer-Verlag Berlin Heidelberg, 1998.

[20] F. Neri and C. Cotta. Memetic algorithms and memetic computing optimization: A literature review. *Swarm and Evolutionary Computation*, 2(0):1 – 14, 2012.

[21] N. M. Patel, B.-S. Kang, J. E. Renaud, and A. Tovar. Crashworthiness design using topology optimization. *Journal of Mechanical Design*, 131:061013, 2009.

[22] H.-T. C. Pedro and M. H. Kobayashi. On a cellular division method for topology optimization. *International Journal for Numerical Methods in Engineering*, 88(11):1175–1197, 2011.

[23] J. Reisinger, E. Bahçeci, I. Karpov, and R. Miikkulainen. Coevolving strategies for general game playing. In *CIG*, pages 320–327. IEEE, 2007.

[24] K. O. Stanley, R. Cornelius, and R. Miikkulainen. Real-time learning in the NERO video game. In R. M. Young and J. E. Laird, editors, *AIIDE*, pages 159–160. AAAI Press, 2005.

[25] K. O. Stanley and R. Miikkulainen. Evolving neural networks through augmenting topologies. *Evolutionary Computation*, 10(2):99–127, 2002.

[26] T. Steiner, Y. Jin, and B. Sendhoff. A cellular model for the evolutionary development of lightweight material with an inner structure. In *Proceedings of the Genetic and Evolutionary Computation Conference (GECCO 2008)*, New York, 2008. ACM.

[27] T. Steiner, J. Trommler, M. Brenn, Y. Jin, and B. Sendhoff. Global shape with morphogen gradients and motile polarized cells. In *Proceedings of the 2009 IEEE Congress on Evolutionary Computation, Trondheim*. IEEE, 2009.

[28] K. Svanberg. The method of moving asymptotes - a new method for structural optimization. *Int. J. Numer. Meth. Engrg.*, 24:359–373, 1987.

[29] C.-Y. Wu and K.-Y. Tseng. Topology optimization of structures using modified binary differential evolution. *Structural and Multidisciplinary Optimization*, 42(6):939–953, 2010.

[30] X. Yao. Evolving artificial neural networks. *Proceedings of the IEEE*, 87:1423–1447, 1999.

Evolutionary Algorithms and Artificial Immune Systems on a Bi-Stable Dynamic Optimisation Problem

Thomas Jansen
Department of Computer Science
Aberystwyth University
Aberystwyth, SY23 3DB, UK
t.jansen@aber.ac.uk

Christine Zarges
School of Computer Science
University of Birmingham
Birmingham B15 2TT, UK
c.zarges@bham.ac.uk

ABSTRACT

Dynamic optimisation is an important area of application for evolutionary algorithms and other randomised search heuristics. Theoretical investigations are currently far behind practical successes. Addressing this deficiency a bi-stable dynamic optimisation problem is introduced and the performance of standard evolutionary algorithms and artificial immune systems is assessed. Deviating from the common theoretical perspective that concentrates on the expected time to find a global optimum (again) here the 'any time performance' of the algorithms is analysed, i. e., the expected function value at each step. Basis for the analysis is the recently introduced perspective of fixed budget computations. Different dynamic scenarios are considered which are characterised by the length of the stable phases. For each scenario different population sizes are examined. It is shown that the evolutionary algorithms tend to have superior performance in almost all cases.

Categories and Subject Descriptors

F.2.2 [**Analysis of Algorithms and Problem Complexity**]: Nonnumerical Algorithms and Problems

General Terms

Algorithms, Design, Performance, Theory

Keywords

Dynamic environments, evolutionary algorithms, artificial immune systems, theory

1. INTRODUCTION

In static environments optimisation means finding a global optimum as quickly as possible. In dynamic environments optimisation does not only require locating an optimum but also tracking an optimal solution over time. Many real-world problems are subject to changing conditions over time and thus, dynamic optimisation is an important area of application for evolutionary algorithms (EAs) and other randomised search heuristics (RSHs) [16]. While RSHs are applied very successfully in this domain, their theoretical investigations are lagging behind considerably. This becomes even more apparent when comparing the current body of results with analyses for RSHs in static domains, which has rapidly grown in recent years [4, 10]. Consequently, theoretical analysis of RSHs in dynamic environments has been identified as an important future research direction [16, Chap. 9]. Clearly, due to the additional dynamics imposed by the dynamic problem such analysis constitutes a very challenging area of research.

Previous theoretical work in dynamic optimisation investigated, e. g., the ability of the (1+1) EA to track a target bitstring moving at different speed [1, 2, 13]. Jansen and Schellbach [5] later analysed a (1+λ) EA for a simple lattice problem. Investigations of the influence of magnitude and frequency of change were executed by Rohlfshagen et al. [12]. Parts of their analysis were later picked up by Oliveto and Zarges [11], who analysed different diversity mechanisms for optimisation in dynamic environments with low frequencies of change. Kötzing and Molter [9] compared the performance of a simple ant colony optimisation system with that of the (1+1) EA. All these analyses concentrate on the time needed to (re-)discover a global optimum and ignore the level of performance in the time where an optimum is not yet found or lost again.

In this paper, we take a new perspective on the theoretical analysis of RSHs in dynamic environments inspired by fixed budget computation [7]. The idea is to assess the performance of an RSH at any time during a run instead of concentrating on the time needed to reach some predetermined optimisation goal.

We introduce a novel dynamic example problem that exhibits several important properties of dynamic optimisation and we feel is suitable to serve as a new benchmark problem. It is characterised by phases of stable behaviour that interchange with phases of rapid change. It is motivated by characteristics of practical problems in, e. g., pharmaceutical design [14]. It differs from other example functions that have been used in theoretical analyses by having stable phases where the optimum does not move (different from a dynamic OneMax [1] or the lattice function [5]) while the optimum is actually moving at times (different from the function introduced by Rohlfshagen et al. [12]).

We investigate the performance of two different types of RSHs on this novel problem, namely an EA and an artifi-

GECCO'14, July 12–16, 2014, Vancouver, BC, Canada.
Copyright 2014 ACM 978-1-4503-2662-9/14/07 ...$15.00.
http://dx.doi.org/10.1145/2576768.2598344.

cial immune system (AIS). Contrary to previous theoretical work we do not only adopt the notion of 'any time performance' (i. e., the perspective of fixed budget computations) but we also take into account the speed of the execution platform for the RSHs as potentially different from the rate of change of the objective function. This allows us to relate the performance of the RSHs to the speed of the execution platform indicating where investing in a more performant computer pays off when dealing with a dynamic problem with a dynamic that is influenced by external parameters and consequently independent of the speed of the computer that is used to solve the problem.

We introduce our example problem in the next section. Section 3 contains formal definitions of the EA and AIS we consider (both well-known from numerous previous publications) and of the performance measure we will be using. Our analytical results are contained in Section 4 where we present complete characterisations of the performance of both algorithms for short, long and very long stable periods of the example functions, slow, fast and very fast execution platforms and small and large offspring population sizes. We conclude and point out future research directions in Section 5.

2. A BI-STABLE PROBLEM

We introduce a bi-stable optimisation problem that on the one hand has a simple structure that facilitates analysis and understanding and on the other hand has properties that we hope are perceived as natural in a vague sense. At any point in time the problem can be described as a generalised version of the well-known example problem OneMax where the function value is n for the unique global optimum and all other search points have function values that are decreased by their Hamming distance to the unique global optimum. For the classical OneMax problem that unique global optimum is the all ones bit string, in a generalised version the unique global optimum may be any search point. Our bi-stable optimisation problem comes with two parameters $o \in \{0,1\}^n$ and $\tau \in \mathbb{N}$. The search point o is the unique global optimum for a duration of τ steps. After that the global optimum shifts gradually in a random but orderly fashion towards the bit-wise complement of o. The bit-wise complement of o, denoted by $\overline{o}$, is the unique global optimum for a duration of τ steps. After that the global optimum shifts back towards the original optimum o, again. After this the cycle repeats itself. During the shifting from one global optimum to the other in each step one bit is changed so that the other stable optimum is reached after n changes. Thus, the bi-stable optimisation problem has a period of length $\Pi = 2(\tau + n - 1)$.

We use the well-known notation for the concatenation of letters for the definition of the bi-stable optimisation problem. For a letter $b \in \{0,1\}$ and a length $i \in \mathbb{N}$ we define b^i as the concatenation of i copies of b, e. g., $1^3 = 111$. Note that for $i = 0$ we get the empty word, i. e., $b^0 = \varepsilon$. As usual $b^1 = b$ holds. We allow the concatenation of such expressions, e. g., $1^0 0^3 1^2 0^4 = 000110000$.

For two bits $x, y \in \{0,1\}$ let $x \oplus y$ denote the exclusive OR of x and y, i. e., $x \oplus y = 1$ if $x \neq y$. For two bit strings $x, y \in \{0,1\}^n$ let $x \oplus y$ denote the bit-wise exclusive OR of x and y, e. g., $010 \oplus 110 = 100$.

For two bit strings $x, y \in \{0,1\}^n$ let $\mathrm{H}(x,y)$ denote the Hamming distance of x and y, i. e., $\mathrm{H}(x,y) = \sum\limits_{i=1}^{n} |x[i] - y[i]|$.

Definition 1. *Let $n \in \mathbb{N}$, $\tau \in \mathbb{N}$, and $o \in \{0,1\}^n$ be given. To define the bi-stable optimisation problem $\mathrm{BSO}_{o,\tau}\colon \{0,1\}^n \times \mathbb{N}_0 \to \mathbb{N}_0$ we later define $x^*(t) \in \{0,1\}^n$, the unique global optimum at time step t. Given this the function is defined by $\mathrm{BSO}_{o,\tau}(x,t) := n - \mathrm{H}(x, x^*(t))$.*

We define the cycle length $\Pi := 2(\tau + n - 1)$ and, for the shifting between the two stable optima, transition masks that define the random transition from o to $\overline{o}$ and back. The transition masks are $M_s^c \in \{0,1\}^n$ (for $s \in \{0,1,\ldots,n-2\}$) where $c \in \mathbb{N}_0$ denotes the number of the cycle (so that the random transition is potentially different in each cycle). When we define $M_s^c \in \mathcal{M}$ for some set $\mathcal{M}$ this means that M_s^c is selected uniformly at random from $\mathcal{M}$.

We define $M_0^c \in \{0^i 1 0^{n-i-1} \mid i \in \{0,1,\ldots,n-1\}\}$.

For $s \in \{1,2,\ldots,n-2\}$ and $c \in \mathbb{N}_0$ we define

$$M_s^c \in \begin{cases} \{0^{i-1}1^{s+1}0^{n-i-s}, & \text{if } M_{s-1}^c \in \{0^i 1^s 0^{n-i-s} \\ \ 0^i 1^{s+1} 0^{n-i-s-1}\} & \mid i \in \{1,2,\ldots,n-s-1\}\}, \\ \{1^{i+1}0^{n-s-1}1^{s-i}, & \text{if } M_{s-1}^c \in \{1^i 0^{n-s} 1^{s-i} \\ \ 1^i 0^{n-s-1} 1^{s-i+1}\} & \mid i \in \{0,1,\ldots,s\}\}. \end{cases}$$

Using these transition masks we define the global optimum at time step t as

$$x^*(t) := \begin{cases} o & \text{if } t' \in [0, \tau-1], \\ o \oplus M_{t'-\tau}^{\lfloor t/\Pi \rfloor} & \text{if } t' \in [\tau, \tau+n-2], \\ \overline{o} & \text{if } t' \in [\tau+n-1, 2\tau+n-2], \\ \overline{o} \oplus M_{t'-(2\tau+n-1)}^{\lfloor t/\Pi \rfloor} & \text{if } t' \in [2\tau+n-1, \Pi-1], \end{cases}$$

where $t' = t \bmod \Pi$.

The masks are designed such that the bits where o and $o \oplus M_s^c$ differ are always in one contiguous block that may be 'wrapping around', i. e., ending at the end and being continued at the beginning. We provide a tiny example for Definition 1 to avoid any misunderstanding. We consider the example for $n = 3$, $o = 110$ and $\tau = 4$. We consider the location of the unique global optimum for each step of the first cycle, i. e., for each $t \in \{0,1,2,\ldots,11\}$. In order to do that we first fix the random transition masks and decide on $M_0^0 = 001$, $M_1^0 = 101$, $M_2^0 = 111$ (where the first two masks are actual 'random' choices). We depict the sequence of unique global optima in Figure 1.

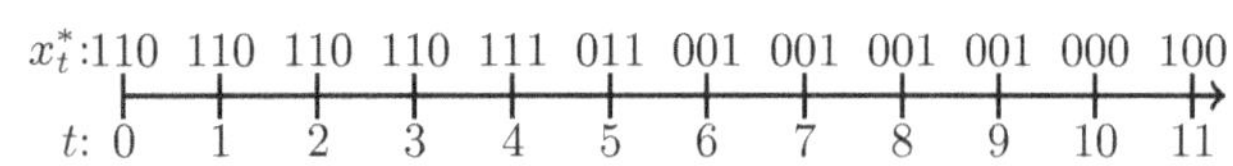

Figure 1: Example: Sequence of unique global optima for $\mathrm{BSO}_{110,4}$ with 'random' transition masks $M_0^0 = 001$, $M_1^0 = 101$, $M_2^0 = 111$.

Using the same visualisation as in Figure 1 we depict an abstract version of the way the unique global optimum moves in Figure 2.

3. ALGORITHMS

We consider one evolutionary algorithm and one artificial immune system, both well-known and extensively studied in previous publications. The EA is known as $(\mu+\lambda)$ EA, uses a population of size μ, uniform selection for reproduction, generates λ independently identically distributed offspring

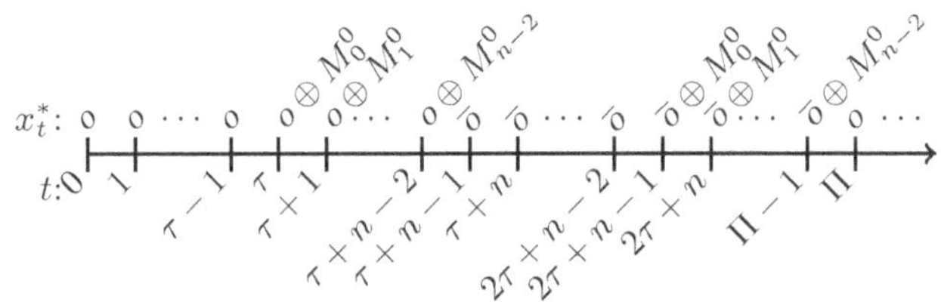

Figure 2: Sequence of unique global optima for $\text{BSO}_{o,\tau}$ for bit string length n, first cycle and first global optimum of second cycle.

by means of standard bit mutations with mutation probability $1/n$ (and no crossover) and employs plus-selection to select the population for the next generation (see, e. g., [4]). A formal description is given as Algorithm 2. The artificial immune system is the B-cell algorithm as introduced by Kelsey and Timmis [8]. It uses a population of size μ, generates λ clones for each member of the population and applies somatic contiguous hypermutations to all and standard bit mutation to one of them. It applies plus-selection between each member of the population and its clones. A formal description is given as Algorithm 1.

For the algorithms we assume that whenever a fitness value $f(x)$ is computed this is automatically translated to the appropriated evaluation $\text{BSO}_{o,\tau}(x,t)$ with parameters o and τ and correct current time step t without the need for the algorithm to be aware of the values of o, τ and t. We keep track of 'time' inside the algorithms by means of a generation counter g.

Algorithm 1: The B-Cell Algorithm (BCA)

Let $g := 0$ and choose $x_1^{(g)}, \ldots, x_\mu^{(g)} \in \{0,1\}^n$ independently uniformly at random (u. a. r.);
repeat
  Set $g := g+1$;
  for $i \in \{1, \ldots, \mu\}$ `// Clonal expansion`
    for $j \in \{1, \ldots, \lambda\}$ Set $y_{i,j} := x_i^{(g-1)}$;
  for $i \in \{1, \ldots, \mu\}$ `// Standard bit mutation`
    Select $j \in \{1, \ldots, \lambda\}$ u. a. r.;
    for $k \in \{1, \ldots, n\}$
      With probability $1/n$, invert the bit $y_{i,j}[k]$;
  for $i \in \{1, 2, \ldots, \mu\}$ `// Hypermutation`
    for $j \in \{1, 2, \ldots, \lambda\}$
      Select $p \in \{0, 1, \ldots, n-1\}$ u. a. r.;
      Select $l \in \{0, 1, \ldots, n\}$ u. a. r.;
      for $k \in \{0, 1, \ldots, l-1\}$
        Invert the bit $y_{i,j}[1 + ((p+k) \bmod n)]$;
  for $i \in \{1, 2, \ldots, \mu\}$ `// Selection`
    if $f(x_i^{(g-1)}) \le \max\{f(y_{i,1}), \ldots, f(y_{i,\lambda})\}$ **then**
      Set $x_i^{(g)} := y_{i,j}$ where $f(y_{i,j}) = \max\{f(y_{i,1}), \ldots, f(y_{i,\lambda})\}$, break ties u. a. r.;
    end
    else Set $x_i^{(g)} := x_i^{(g-1)}$;
until *some termination criterion is met*;

When considering dynamic problems the rate of change plays an important role. This rate of change needs to be measured against the speed of the execution platform of the algorithms since it determines how many steps an algorithm can make before the fitness landscape may change and all previous function evaluations may become obsolete. In the definition of the dynamic problem we consider (Definition 1) we have defined that time passes in discrete time steps and that the fitness landscape may change at each step (but it does not actually change during the stable intervals of length τ time steps). We measure the speed of the execution platform by means of a value $\sigma \in \mathbb{N}$ that gives the number of fitness evaluations that can be carried out in one time step. To avoid complications with the fitness landscape during a single generation we demand that the algorithms need to be parameterised such that one generation can be carried out within one time step. We state this formally in the following definition.

Algorithm 2: $(\mu+\lambda)$ EA

Let $g := 0$ and choose $x_1^{(g)}, \ldots, x_\mu^{(g)} \in \{0,1\}^n$ independently uniformly at random (u. a. r.);
repeat
  Set $g := g+1$;
  for $i \in \{1, 2, \ldots, \lambda\}$ `// Variation` **do**
    Select $y_i \in \{x_1^{(g-1)}, \ldots, x_\mu^{(g-1)}\}$ u. a. r.;
    for $j \in \{1, 2, \ldots, n\}$ **do**
      With probability $1/n$, invert the bit $y_i[j]$
    end
  end
  Selection: Sort $x_1^{(g-1)}, \ldots, x_\mu^{(g-1)}, y_1, \ldots, y_\lambda$ descending according to fitness, break ties by sorting $y_1, \ldots, y_\lambda$ in front of $x_1^{(g-1)}, \ldots, x_\mu^{(g-1)}$, break remaining ties u. a. r.. Set $x_1^{(g)}, \ldots, x_\mu^{(g)}$ to the first μ elements from this sorted sequence.
until *some termination condition is met*;

Definition 2. *Let $\sigma \in \mathbb{N}$ be the number of function evaluations that can be carried out between time steps t and $t+1$, i. e., before a potential change of the unique global optimum of $\text{BSO}_{o,\tau}$.*

Algorithms are unaware of the time steps and do not know when the fitness function values may change. The execution platform makes sure that one round of an algorithm is executed in one time step of the fitness function so that the values of search points do not change during one round. To allow for this the number of function evaluations per round needs to be bounded above by σ.

Saying that the algorithms need to be parameterised such that one generation can be carried out within one time step means that we need to have $\mu(\lambda+1) \le \sigma$ for the BCA (Algorithm 1) and $\mu+\lambda \le \sigma$ for the $(\mu+\lambda)$ EA (Algorithm 2) as these are the numbers of function evaluations per generation for the two algorithms.

We classify the performance of the algorithms on $\text{BSO}_{o,\tau}$ broadly into four categories. Remember that the function value at time step t is given as $\text{BSO}_{o,\tau}(x) = n - \text{H}(x, x^*(t))$. Obviously, we can expect to have

$$\max\left\{\text{BSO}_{o,\tau}\left(x_i^{(g)}\right) \mid i \in \{1, 2, \ldots, \mu\}\right\} = \Theta(n)$$

at almost any time for any useful algorithm since even a single search point selected uniformly at random has expected fitness $n/2 = \Theta(n)$. Therefore, it makes more sense to concentrate on the current distance to the global optimum, i. e., $n - \text{BSO}_{o,\tau}$. We use this perspective to classify the performance of an algorithm in time step t.

Definition 3. *For $g, t \in \mathbb{N}_0$, we introduce the shorthand $M(g) := \min\left\{n - \text{BSO}_{o,\tau}\left(x_i^{(g)}, t\right) \mid i \in \{1, 2, \ldots, \mu\}\right\}$ assuming that the fitness function is in time step t and generation g. We say that an algorithm (either Algorithm 1 or Algorithm 2) has* perfect *performance in generation g if $M(g) = 0$ holds. We say that its performance is* good *in generation g if it does not perform perfectly but $M(g) = O(1)$ holds. We say that its performance is* mediocre *in generation g if its performance is neither perfect nor good but $M(g) = o(n)$ holds. We say that its performance is* bad *in generation g if $\mathrm{E}(M(g)) = \Theta(n)$ holds.*

4. ANALYSIS

We analyse the performance of the EA and the BCA on $\text{BSO}_{o,\tau}$. Note that due to symmetry reasons the choice of o has no influence on the performance. We analyse the performance in terms of the external clock t that is given by the time steps of the dynamic problem. It is important to realise that this is different from the internal clock of the algorithms. If the speed of the execution platform σ is sufficiently large it is possible to make many function evaluations in one clock tick of the external clock. In these situations one may wonder if it makes more sense to perform many generations with small population and offspring population sizes or few generations with large population and offspring population sizes.

We will consider the two extreme cases with respect to the offspring population size. On the one hand we consider the case $\lambda = 1$ where we perform a maximal number of generations. On the other hand we choose λ as large as possible so that only one generation can be performed.

We do not consider the choice of the population size and restrict our interest to the case $\mu = 1$. Since our test problem is OneMax-like we do not expect to see significant benefits due to the introduction of a larger population (see [15]). This will only change if one introduces measures to increase and maintain the population's diversity. Including such measures into the analysis is beyond the scope of this paper. Note that $\mu = 1$ has the advantage that the EA and the BCA are very similar. In each generation, the EA performs $\mu + \lambda$ function evaluations and only 1 selection. The BCA performs $\mu + \mu\lambda$ function evaluations and μ selections. With $\mu = 1$ the number of function evaluations and selections per generation are equal facilitating a fair comparison.

We consider three different durations of the stable phases τ and deal with each of them in one of the following subsections. The smallest duration we consider sensible is $\tau = n$ since the phases of rapid transition have also length n. As an example of a significantly longer stable phase we consider $\tau = n^{3/2}$ (here and in the following we assume that values are silently rounded down where integer values are needed, e. g, we assume that $\tau = n^{3/2}$ is silently replaced by $\tau = \lfloor n^{3/2} \rfloor$). The significance of $\tau = n^{3/2}$ in comparison to $\tau = n$ is that the first is significantly longer than the expected time the EA with $\mu = \lambda = 1$ needs to locate the optimum of OneMax whereas the second is significantly shorter [3]. As an example of a very long stable phase we consider $\tau = n^3$. Note that the significance of $\tau = n^3$ in comparison to $\tau = n^{3/2}$ is the same as before but for the BCA with $\mu = \lambda = 1$: the first is significantly longer than the expected time the BCA needs to optimise OneMax whereas the second is significantly shorter [6].

4.1 Short Stable Intervals

We consider a short stable period $\tau = n$ and start with the case where the execution platform is not on a much faster clock than the objective function, i. e., $\sigma = \Theta(1)$. Since we assume that one generation can be carried out in one time step this implies $\mu = \Theta(1)$ and $\lambda = \Theta(1)$. We show that both algorithms fail to catch up with the global optimum.

Theorem 4. *For $\tau = n$ and $\sigma = 2$, with $\mu = 1$ and $\lambda = 1$, the BCA (Algorithm 1) and the EA (Algorithm 2) are both always bad in the first $n^{O(1)}$ steps with probability converging to 1.*

Proof. After initialisation both algorithms have search points with Hamming distance $\Theta(n)$ to the optimum with probability exponentially close to 1. First, we consider the EA and the situation during a phase of stability of length τ, i. e., while the optimum does not move. Let d denote the current Hamming distance to the optimum. The expected decrease in distance in one generation is bounded above by $(d/n)(1-1/n)^{n-d}$. For $d < n/2$ we have that $(1-1/n)^{n-d} < c < 1$ for some appropriately chosen constant $c \in (0, 1)$. We see that the expected decrease in distance in n generations is bounded above by $(d/n)c \cdot n = cd < d$. Application of Chernoff bounds yields that the probability to decrease the distance by at least $c(1+\varepsilon)d$ is bounded above by $e^{-\Omega(d)}$ for all positive constant ε. We can choose $\varepsilon = (1-c)/(2c)$ which guarantees that $\varepsilon > 0$ and $c(1+\varepsilon)d < d$ both hold. For $d = \Theta(n)$ the probability is exponentially small and the claim follows. Outside the stable phases the optimum is moving. If the optimum is moving away from the current search point it is even more unlikely to decrease the Hamming distance to $o(n)$. For the case where it moves towards the current search point assume that the optimum moves from o to $\bar{o}$ (the other case is symmetric). We consider all points with equal distance from the search point o. Due to symmetry reasons all these points have equal probability to become current search point. The moving global optimum will hit exactly one of these points. Since the current search point has linear Hamming distance to o there are exponentially many such search points and it is exponentially unlikely that the global optimum decreases the Hamming distance to the current search point below $c'n$ for some sufficiently small constant $c' > 0$. This concludes the proof for the EA. For the BCA we observe that the probability for any specific mutation is $\Theta(1/n^2)$. This implies that the probability to decrease the Hamming distance to the global optimum by any constant is significantly smaller than for the EA. Since the initial search point is selected uniformly at random the probability that the Hamming distance can be decreased by $\omega(\log n)$ is superpolynomially small. When optimising OneMax this does not change significantly (see [6]). This implies that the BCA performs at most as well as the EA. □

We visualise the results by presenting the results of experiments in Figure 3 (left diagram). All experiments entail 30 independent runs for both algorithms for $n = 100$. We display averages and standard deviation. Note that the x-axes display time steps as defined by the dynamic problem, not generations or function evaluations. We see that both algorithms are bad all the same as predicted by Theorem 4, neither able to reduce the distance to 20 or below (corresponding to fitness 80 or above). We see that the EA gets clearly closer to the global optimum in the stable phases and, consequently, has worse fitness when the optimum moves rapidly. Note that our results are too coarse to reveal these differences.

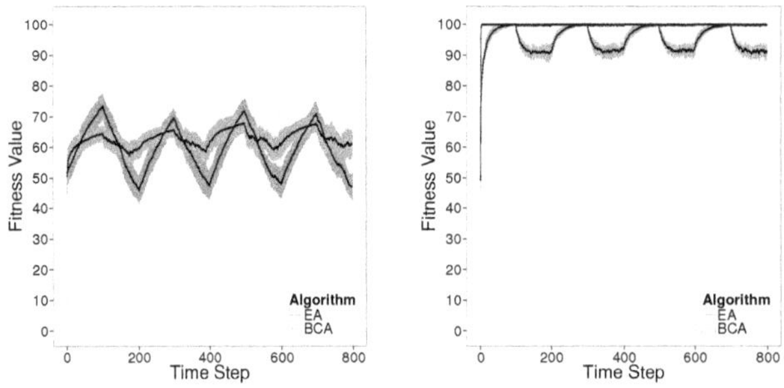

Figure 3: Visualisation of experiments showing averages and standard deviation over 30 independent runs for both algorithms on $\mathrm{BSO}_{o,\tau}$ for $n = 100$, on the left matching Theorem 4 with $\tau = 100$, $\mu = \lambda = 1$ and $\sigma = 2$; on the right matching Theorems 5 and 6 with $\tau = 100$, $\mu = \lambda = 1$ and $\sigma = 1001$.

We stick to the case $\mu = \lambda = 1$ and analyse what happens if a considerably faster execution platform is used for the RSHs. We start with $\sigma = n^{3/2} + 1$, i.e., in one step of the external clock $n^{3/2} + 1$ fitness evaluations can be performed.

THEOREM 5. *For $\tau = n$ and $\sigma = n^{3/2} + 1$, with $\mu = 1$ and $\lambda = 1$, the EA (Algorithm 2) is always perfect after the first step for $n^{O(1)}$ steps with probability converging to 1.*

PROOF. It is well known that the expected optimisation time of Algorithm 2 with $\mu = \lambda = 1$ on ONEMAX is $\Theta(n \log n)$ and that the probability not to be finished in $O\left(n^{3/2}\right)$ generations is exponentially small [4]. This implies that the EA performs perfectly after one step with overwhelming probability. After this it will remain perfect while the optimum does not move. When the optimum moves it changes by 1 bit in each step. In a single step the EA generates $\lfloor \sigma/2 \rfloor$ offspring by means of standard bit mutation. The probability that none of these equals the new optimum is bounded above by $\left(1 - (1/n)(1 - 1/n)^{n-1}\right)^{\Theta(n^{3/2})} = e^{-\Omega(n^{1/2})}$. Thus, the probability to be always perfect for the next $n^{O(1)}$ steps is $1 - n^{O(1)} \cdot e^{-\Omega(n^{1/2})} = 1 - e^{-\Omega(n^{1/2})}$. □

THEOREM 6. *For $\tau = n$ and $\sigma = n^{3/2} + 1$, with $\mu = 1$ and $\lambda = 1$, the BCA (Algorithm 1) becomes perfect after $O\left(n^{1/2} \log n\right)$ steps, remains perfect for the remaining $\Theta(\tau)$ steps of the stable phase and becomes bad again in the next n steps with probability converging to 1. This behaviour is repeated in the next $n^{O(1)}$ steps with probability converging to 1.*

PROOF. In each step the BCA performs $\Theta(\sigma) = \Theta\left(n^{3/2}\right)$ generations. In the beginning we have a stable phase and $\mathrm{BSO}_{o,\tau}$ is ONEMAX-like for τ steps. It is known that the BCA optimises this function on average and with probability very close to 1 in $O(n^2 \log n)$ generations [6]. Thus, it reaches the optimum in a stable phase within the first $O\left(n^{1/2} \log n\right)$ steps with probability converging to 1. The second part of the statement follows from the proof of Theorem 4. When the optimum starts moving the probability to decrease the Hamming distance by 1 in 1 generation is $O(1/n^2)$. Thus, the BCA remains perfect only with probability $O\left(1/n^{1/2}\right)$. Remember that also for larger Hamming distances the expected decrease in distance is bounded by $O(\log(n)/n^2)$. Thus, with probability converging to 1, the Hamming distance becomes linear in n steps. □

We visualise this result again by presenting results of experiments in Figure 3 (right diagram; using the same parameters and method as before). We observe that the results match the rough predictions made in Theorems 5 and 6.

Now we consider an even faster execution platform by considering $\sigma = n^3 + 1$.

THEOREM 7. *For $\tau = n$ and $\sigma = n^3 + 1$, with $\mu = 1$ and $\lambda = 1$, the BCA (Algorithm 1) and the EA (Algorithm 2) are both always perfect after the first step for the next $n^{O(1)}$ steps with probability converging to 1.*

PROOF. The result for the EA is direct consequence of Theorem 5 since increasing the speed σ cannot decrease the performance of the algorithm. For the BCA's performance after the first step and during the stable phase it suffices to remember that the expected optimisation time of the BCA with $\mu = \lambda = 1$ on ONEMAX is $O(n^2 \log n)$ and that the probability not to be finished in $O(n^3)$ generations is exponentially small [6]. Analogously to the proof of Theorem 5 the probability that no offspring equals the new optimum is bounded above by $\left(1 - (1/(n^2 + n))(1 - 1/n)^n\right)^{\Theta(n^3)} = e^{-\Omega(n)}$. Thus, the probability to be always perfect in for the next $n^{O(1)}$ steps is $1 - n^{O(1)} \cdot e^{-\Omega(n)} = 1 - e^{-\Omega(n)}$. □

We now investigate the influence of larger offspring population sizes. Our execution platform needs to be fast enough to execute at least one complete iteration of the two respective algorithms. Since both algorithms we consider execute $1 + \lambda$ fitness evaluations per iteration, we set $\lambda = \sigma - 1$ in the following. We start with $\lambda = n^{3/2}$. Note that standard bit mutation does not flip any bit with probability $(1 - 1/n)^n = \Theta(1)$. Thus, to simplify our arguments for the BCA, we only consider contiguous hypermutations. As all our results are asymptotic, ignoring standard bit mutations for one offspring does not cause any changes here. We have also performed experiments for subsequent settings where all parameters are $o(n^3)$. All results matched our theoretical findings. Details are omitted due to space restrictions.

THEOREM 8. *For $\tau = n$ and $\sigma = n^{3/2} + 1$, with $\mu = 1$ and $\lambda = n^{3/2}$, the EA (Algorithm 2) is always perfect after the first $O(n)$ steps for the next $n^{O(1)}$ steps with probability converging to 1.*

PROOF. We consider the situation directly after initialisation and denote with d the current Hamming distance to the optimum. Clearly, $d \leq n$ holds. The probability to decrease the Hamming distance by at least 1 in a single generation of the EA with $\lambda = n^{3/2}$ is at least

$$1 - \left(1 - \frac{1}{n} \cdot \left(1 - \frac{1}{n}\right)^{n-1}\right)^{n^{3/2}} = 1 - e^{-\Omega(\sqrt{n})}$$

and the probability to see up to $d \leq n$ such decreases in d subsequent generations is at least $1 - d \cdot e^{-\Omega(\sqrt{n})} = 1 -$

$e^{-\Omega(\sqrt{n})}$. Thus, after at most n generations, the EA is perfect. Since the EA executes n generations within the first $\tau = n$ steps, i. e., before the optimum starts moving, the first claim follows.

Outside the stable phases the optimum is moving, however, in each step only a single bit of the current optimum changes. Thus, again with probability $1 - e^{-\Omega(\sqrt{n})}$, the EA is able to catch up with this change and the probability to be always perfect for the next $n^{O(1)}$ steps is $1 - n^{O(1)} \cdot e^{-\Omega(\sqrt{n})} = 1 - e^{-\Omega(\sqrt{n})}$. □

THEOREM 9. *For $\tau = n$ and $\sigma = n^{3/2} + 1$, with $\mu = 1$ and $\lambda = n^{3/2}$, the BCA (Algorithm 1) is always bad in the first $n^{O(1)}$ steps with probability converging to 1.*

PROOF. After initialisation the Hamming distance to the global optimum is $\Theta(n)$ with probability exponentially close to 1. Consider l consecutive bits that contain m more bits different from the global optimum than equal to it. We can bound the contribution of these bits to the expected decrease in Hamming distance by $O(m \cdot l^2/n^2)$. Initially the expected decrease is $O(\sqrt{n})$ (since we have $m = O(\sqrt{n})$ and $l = O(n)$). It decreases over time. Consider the situation when the Hamming distance is $(n/2) - dn$ with some constant $0 < d < 1/4$. Since the expected decrease in function value is always $O(\sqrt{n})$ such a d exists with overwhelming probability. Consider l consecutive bits. Since the bit string is random the expected number of 0-bits equals $l((1/2) - d)$. By application of Chernoff bounds we have more 0-bits than 1-bits with probability $e^{-\Omega(l((1/2)-d)\cdot(2d/(1-2d))^2)} = e^{-\Omega(l)}$. The BCA mutates an interval of length l with probability $1/(n+1)$ for each $l \in \{0, 1, \ldots, n\}$. This implies an expected decrease in Hamming distance of $O(\sqrt{n}/n) = O(1/\sqrt{n})$. Thus, it is at most $O(\sqrt{n})$ within $\tau = n$ steps of a stable phase. Let $c\sqrt{n}$ (c some appropriately chosen constant) denote this decrease. Chernoff bounds yield that the probability to decrease the distance by at least $2c\sqrt{n}$ is $e^{-\Omega(\sqrt{n})}$. Therefore, a Hamming distance $\Theta(n)$ at the beginning of a stable phase it is not decreased to $o(n)$ during the phase with probability converging to 1. For steps outside the stable phase, we use the same argumentation as in Theorem 4. □

We increase the offspring population size further and consider $\lambda = n^3$ (and consequently $\sigma = n^3 + 1$).

THEOREM 10. *For $\tau = n$ and $\sigma = n^3 + 1$, with $\mu = 1$ and $\lambda = n^3$, the BCA (Algorithm 1) and the EA (Algorithm 2) both are always perfect after the first $O(n)$ steps for the next $n^{O(1)}$ steps with probability converging to 1.*

PROOF. The result for the EA is a direct consequence of Theorem 8 since increasing the speed σ (and the offspring population size λ accordingly) cannot decrease the performance of the algorithm.

For the BCA we follow the argumentation of Theorem 8 for the EA and observe that the probability to decrease the Hamming distance by at least 1 in a single generation of the BCA is at least

$$1 - \left(1 - \frac{1}{n \cdot (n+1)}\right)^{n^3} \geq 1 - e^{-\Omega(n)}.$$

Consequently, the BCA is perfect after $O(n)$ steps and stays perfect for the next $n^{O(1)}$ steps with probability $1 - n^{O(1)} \cdot e^{-\Omega(n)} = 1 - e^{-\Omega(n)}$. □

4.2 Long Stable Intervals

We consider a longer stable period $\tau = n^{3/2}$ and start with the case of $\mu = \lambda = 1$ and the execution platform being not on a much faster clock than the objective function, i. e., $\sigma = \Theta(1)$ analogously to the previous subsection.

COROLLARY 11. *For $\tau = n^{3/2}$ and $\sigma = 2$, with $\mu = 1$ and $\lambda = 1$, the BCA (Algorithm 1) is always bad in the first $n^{O(1)}$ steps with probability converging to 1.*

PROOF. The statement follows from the proof of Theorem 4. There we have argued that the expected decrease in distance for the BCA is $O(\log(n)/n^2)$ per generation. Thus, the expected decrease in $O\left(n^{3/2}\right)$ generations is bounded above by $O\left(\log(n)/n^{1/2}\right)$ and the result follows since in the phases where the optimum moves it is increased with probability converging to 1 as shown in the proof of Theorem 6. □

THEOREM 12. *For $\tau = n^{3/2}$ and $\sigma = 2$, with $\mu = 1$ and $\lambda = 1$, the EA (Algorithm 2) becomes perfect after $O(n \log n)$ steps, remains perfect for the remaining $\Theta(\tau)$ steps of the stable phase and becomes bad again in the next n steps with probability converging to 1. This behaviour is repeated in the next $n^{O(1)}$ steps with probability converging to 1.*

PROOF. The statement about the repeating behaviour is a direct consequence of the first statement when applying the union bound. We see that the EA becomes perfect after $O(n \log n)$ steps and remains perfect as long as the optimum does not change as we did in the proof of Theorem 5. Now consider the subsequent n steps where the optimum changes by 1 bit in each of the steps. If the Hamming distance to the global optimum and the current search point is d the probability that the EA is able to decrease the Hamming distance is bounded above by d/n. We see that in n steps a Hamming distance $d = \Theta(n)$ is reached with probability exponentially close to 1. After the global optimum has reached either o or $\bar{o}$ we are in a simulation very similar to the one after initialisation and we can repeat the argument. □

Now we investigate what happens with faster execution platforms. We begin with speed $\sigma = n^{3/2} + 1$.

COROLLARY 13. *For $\tau = n^{3/2}$ and $\sigma = n^{3/2} + 1$, with $\mu = 1$ and $\lambda = 1$, the EA (Algorithm 2) is always perfect after the first step for the next $n^{O(1)}$ steps with probability converging to 1.*

PROOF. The statement is a direct consequence from the proof of Theorem 5 since making the stable phase longer by a polynomial number of steps is not a significant change in this setting. □

THEOREM 14. *For $\tau = n^{3/2}$ and $\sigma = n^{3/2} + 1$, with $\mu = 1$ and $\lambda = 1$, the BCA (Algorithm 1) becomes perfect after $O\left(n^{1/2} \log n\right)$ steps, remains perfect for the remaining $\Theta(\tau)$ steps of the stable phase and becomes mediocre or bad in the next n steps with probability converging to 1. We call this a phase. In the next $p(n) = n^{O(1)}$ phases this behaviour is repeated in $p(n) - o(p(n))$ phases with probability converging to 1.*

PROOF. The proof is similar to the proof of Theorem 12. The bound of $O\left(n^{1/2}\log n\right)$ for the time needed to become perfect follows from the expected optimisation time $O(n^2 \log n)$ of the BCA on ONEMAX [6] and the fact that the BCA performs $n^{3/2}$ generations per time step. The probability to reduce the Hamming distance by d is bounded by $O(d/n^2)$. The probability to see such an event in n steps before the Hamming distance is $\Omega(n)$ is bounded above by $n \cdot o(n/n^2) = o(1)$. The expected number of phases where we see this behaviour when considering $p(n)$ phases is bounded below by $(1-o(n))\,p(n)$. Application of Chernoff bounds yields the result. □

Even faster execution platforms improve the performance further as we see for $\sigma = n^3 + 1$.

COROLLARY 15. *For $\tau = n^{3/2}$ and $\sigma = n^3+1$, with $\mu = 1$ and $\lambda = 1$, the BCA (Algorithm 1) and the EA (Algorithm 2) are both always perfect after the first step for the next $n^{O(1)}$ steps with probability converging to 1.*

PROOF. The result is a direct consequence of the proof of Theorem 7. Making the stable phase longer by a polynomial number of steps is not a significant change in this setting. □

We again investigate the influence of larger offspring population sizes, set $\lambda = \sigma - 1$ and consider $\lambda = n^{3/2}$ and $\lambda = n^3$. We observe that the results for the EA with $\lambda = n^{3/2}$ and all results for $\lambda = n^3$ carry over immediately since longer stable intervals cannot decrease the performance of the algorithms.

COROLLARY 16. *For $\tau = n^{3/2}$ and $\sigma = n^{3/2}+1$, with $\mu = 1$ and $\lambda = n^{3/2}$, the EA (Algorithm 2) is always perfect after the first $O(n)$ steps for the next $n^{O(1)}$ steps with probability converging to 1.*

PROOF. This is a direct consequence of Theorem 8. □

COROLLARY 17. *For $\tau = n^{3/2}$ and $\sigma = n^3+1$, with $\mu = 1$ and $\lambda = n^3$, the BCA (Algorithm 1) and the EA (Algorithm 2) both are always perfect after the first $O(n)$ steps for the next $n^{O(1)}$ steps with probability converging to 1.*

PROOF. This is a direct consequence of Theorem 10. □

For the BCA with $\lambda = n^{3/2}$ the behaviour changes considerably. We start with deriving an upper bound on the expected optimisation time for this algorithm on ONEMAX.

LEMMA 18. *The BCA with $\mu = 1$ and $\lambda = n^{3/2}$ (Algorithm 1) finds the optimum of ONEMAX in expected $\mathrm{E}(T) = O(n)$ iterations.*

PROOF. Let d denote the Hamming distance of the current search point to the global optimum. Then, a single contiguous hypermutation decreases the Hamming distance with probability $d/(n\cdot(n+1))$. The probability that at least one of the $\lambda = n^{3/2}$ offspring decreases the Hamming distance is $1-(1-d/\left(n(n+1)\right))^{n^{3/2}} \geq 1-e^{-d/(2\sqrt{n})}$. Using standard fitness-level argument and $\exp(x)/(\exp(x)-1) \leq 1+1/x$ we derive an upper bound on $\mathrm{E}(T)$:

$$\mathrm{E}(T) \leq \sum_{d=1}^{n} \frac{1}{1-\exp\left(-d/(2\sqrt{n})\right)} = \sum_{d=1}^{n} \frac{\exp\left(d/(2\sqrt{n})\right)}{\exp\left(d/(2\sqrt{n})\right)-1}$$

$$\leq \sum_{d=1}^{n}\left(1+\frac{1}{d/(2\sqrt{n})}\right) = n + 2\sqrt{n}\cdot\sum_{d=1}^{n}\frac{1}{d} = n + 2\sqrt{n}H_n$$

where H_n is the n-th Harmonic number. With $H_n \leq \ln n + 1$ we get $\mathrm{E}(T) \leq n + 2\sqrt{n}\ln(n) + 2\sqrt{n} = O(n)$. □

THEOREM 19. *For $\tau = n^{3/2}$ and $\sigma = n^{3/2}+1$, with $\mu = 1$ and $\lambda = n^{3/2}$, the BCA (Algorithm 1) becomes perfect after $O(n)$ steps, remains perfect for the remaining $\Theta(\tau)$ steps of the stable phase and becomes mediocre in the next n steps with probability converging to 1. This behaviour is repeated in the next $n^{O(1)}$ steps with probability converging to 1.*

PROOF. The first part of the theorem follows direct from Lemma 18 since the first $\tau = n^{3/2}$ steps after initialisation are stable and the underlying problem corresponds to ONEMAX. Once the BCA is perfect in a stable phase, it remains stable until the end of the stable phase.

After the stable phase the optimum is moving and in each step the Hamming distance of the new global optimum to the global optimum in the stable phase is increased by 1. Let d denote the Hamming distance after d such steps. As in the proof of Lemma 18 the probability to decrease the Hamming distance by at least 1 is $1-\exp(-d/(2\sqrt{n}))$. For $d = \omega(\sqrt{n})$ this is $1-o(1)$ and thus, with probability converging to 1, d will not increase beyond $o(n)$ between two stable phases.

We repeat the above argumentation to conclude the theorem. □

4.3 Very Long Stable Intervals

Finally, we consider the same settings as before but now with very long stable intervals, concrete with $\tau = n^3$. It does not come as a surprise that the in settings where an algorithm was already good this continues to be the case here. Moreover, the longer stable phases allows the BCA to catch up with the global optimum whereas the stable phase of length $n^{3/2}$ could be too short for this. All results here are quite direct consequence from results in the earlier subsections. Due to space restrictions we omit the proofs.

COROLLARY 20. *For $\tau = n^3$ and $\sigma = 2$, with $\mu = 1$ and $\lambda = 1$, the EA (Algorithm 2) becomes perfect after $O(n\log n)$ steps, remains perfect for the remaining $\Theta(\tau)$ steps of the stable phase and becomes bad again in the next n steps with probability converging to 1. This behaviour is repeated in the next $n^{O(1)}$ steps with probability converging to 1.*

COROLLARY 21. *For $\tau = n^3$ and $\sigma = 2$, with $\mu = 1$ and $\lambda = 1$, the BCA (Algorithm 1) becomes perfect after $O(n^2\log n)$ steps, remains perfect for the remaining $\Theta(\tau)$ steps of the stable phase and becomes mediocre or bad in the next n steps with probability converging to 1. We call this a phase. In the next $p(n) = n^{O(1)}$ phases this behaviour is repeated in $p(n) - o(p(n))$ phases with probability converging to 1.*

COROLLARY 22. *For $\tau = n^3$ and $\sigma = n^{3/2}+1$, with $\mu = 1$ and $\lambda = 1$, the EA (Algorithm 2) is always perfect after the first step for the next $n^{O(1)}$ steps with probability converging to 1.*

COROLLARY 23. *For $\tau = n^3$ and $\sigma = n^{3/2}+1$, with $\mu = 1$ and $\lambda = 1$, the BCA (Algorithm 1) becomes perfect after $O\left(n^{1/2}\log n\right)$ steps, remains perfect for the remaining $\Theta(\tau)$ steps of the stable phase and becomes mediocre or bad in the next n steps with probability converging to 1. We call this a phase. In the next $p(n) = n^{O(1)}$ phases this behaviour is repeated in $p(n) - o(p(n))$ phases with probability converging to 1.*

Corollary 24. *For $\tau = n^3$ and $\sigma = n^3 + 1$, with $\mu = 1$ and $\lambda = 1$, the BCA (Algorithm 1) and the EA (Algorithm 2) are both always perfect after the first step for the next $n^{O(1)}$ steps with probability converging to 1.*

As before we investigate the influence of larger offspring population sizes, set $\lambda = \sigma - 1$ and consider $\lambda = n^{3/2}$ and $\lambda = n^3$. We see that all results can be carried over from previous theorems since longer stable intervals cannot decrease the performance of the algorithms.

Corollary 25. *For $\tau = n^3$ and $\sigma = n^{3/2} + 1$, with $\mu = 1$ and $\lambda = n^{3/2}$, the EA (Algorithm 2) is always perfect after the first $O(n)$ steps for the next $n^{O(1)}$ steps with probability converging to 1.*

Corollary 26. *For $\tau = n^3$ and $\sigma = n^3 + 1$, with $\mu = 1$ and $\lambda = n^3$, the BCA (Algorithm 1) and the EA (Algorithm 2) both are always perfect after the first $O(n)$ steps for the next $n^{O(1)}$ steps with probability converging to 1.*

Corollary 27. *For $\tau = n^3$ and $\sigma = n^{3/2} + 1$, with $\mu = 1$ and $\lambda = n^{3/2}$, the BCA (Algorithm 1) becomes perfect after $O(n)$ steps, remains perfect for the remaining $\Theta(\tau)$ steps of the stable phase and becomes mediocre in the next n steps with probability converging to 1. This behaviour is repeated in the next $n^{O(1)}$ steps with probability converging to 1.*

5. CONCLUSIONS

We have introduced a novel benchmark for dynamic optimisation, $\text{BSO}_{o,\tau}$, a bi-stable problem where the unique global optimum moves rapidly between o and $\overline{o}$ and remains in these two points for a stable phase of duration τ. We have analysed the any time performance of two randomised search heuristics, an evolutionary algorithm and an artificial immune system, on this benchmark problem. We have considered different durations of the stable phase (short, long and very long) and analysed the performance of the algorithms also depending on the speed of the execution platform, explicitly decoupling the clock tick as introduced by the dynamic of the objective function from the clock tick as introduced by the speed of the execution platform. Where the execution platform is sufficiently fast we have compared small offspring population sizes (allowing for many generations per external clock tick) with large offspring population size (allowing for only one generation per external clock tick). The performance of both algorithms tends to improve with longer stable phases and on faster execution platforms. Using our rough measures the EA often outperforms the AIS and never performs worse.

This work is another step on the way to a better understanding of randomised search heuristics in dynamic optimisation. The most important aspects are the introduction of the benchmark function, the explicit decoupling of the rate of change of the dynamic problem from the speed of the execution platform and using the perspective of fixed budget computations to assess the performance at any time and not only with respect to (re-)discovering a global optimum.

Many questions remain for future research. Our analysis distinguishes only between bad, mediocre, good and perfect performance. A more detailed study of the exact performance will reveal that there are phases in which we characterised the performance of both algorithms as bad where the AIS actually outperforms the EA. We have only considered extreme choices for the offspring population size and three different values for the duration of the stable phase. Results for the whole range of possible parameter settings are desirable. We have ignored the role populations can play and how diversity mechanisms influence the performance of the algorithms, a vital aspect in dynamic optimisation. Getting more precise results for all these aspects will ultimately improve our understanding and guide us in the design of better search heuristics for dynamic optimisation.

6. REFERENCES

[1] S. Droste. Analysis of the (1+1) EA for a dynamically changing OneMax-variant. In *Proc. of CEC'02*, pages 55–60. IEEE Press, 2002.

[2] S. Droste. Analysis of the (1+1) EA for a dynamically bitwise changing OneMax. In *Proc. of GECCO '03*, LNCS 2723, pages 909–921. Springer, 2003.

[3] S. Droste, T. Jansen, and I. Wegener. On the analysis of the (1+1) evolutionary algorithm. *Theor. Comput. Sci.*, 276:51–81, 2002.

[4] T. Jansen. *Analyzing Evolutionary Algorithms. The Computer Science Perspective.* Springer, 2013.

[5] T. Jansen and U. Schellbach. Theoretical analysis of a mutation-based evolutionary algorithm for a tracking problem in the lattice. In *Proc. of GECCO '05*, pages 841–848. ACM Press, 2005.

[6] T. Jansen and C. Zarges. Analyzing different variants of immune inspired somatic contiguous hypermutations. *Theor. Comput. Sci.*, 412(6):517–533, 2011.

[7] T. Jansen and C. Zarges. Performance analysis of randomised search heuristics operating with a fixed budget. *Theor. Comput. Sci.*, 2014. To appear. http://dx.doi.org/10.1016/j.tcs.2013.06.007.

[8] J. Kelsey and J. Timmis. Immune inspired somatic contiguous hypermutations for function optimisation. In *Proc. of GECCO '03*, pages 207–218, 2003.

[9] T. Kötzing and H. Molter. ACO beats EA on a dynamic pseudo-Boolean function. In *Proc. of PPSN'12*, LNCS 7491, pages 113–122. Springer, 2012.

[10] F. Neumann and C. Witt. *Bioinspired Computation in Combinatorial Optimization – Algorithms and Their Computational Complexity.* Springer, 2010.

[11] P. S. Oliveto and C. Zarges. Analysis of diversity mechanisms for optimisation in dynamic environments with low frequencies of change. In *GECCO*, pages 837–844. ACM, 2013.

[12] P. Rohlfshagen, P. K. Lehre, and X. Yao. Dynamic evolutionary optimisation: an analysis of frequency and magnitude of change. In *Proc. of Gecco '09*, pages 1713–1720. ACM Press, 2009.

[13] S. A. Stanhope and J. M. Daida. (1+1) genetic algorithm fitness dynamics in a changing environments. In *CEC*, pages 1851–1858. IEEE, 1999.

[14] R. M. Tifenbach. A combinatorial approach to nearly uncoupled Markov chains I: Reversible Markov chains. *Electronic Transactions on Numerical Analysis*, 40:120–147, 2013.

[15] C. Witt. Runtime analysis of the (μ+1) EA on simple pseudo-Boolean functions. *Evolutionary Computation*, 14(1):65–86, 2006.

[16] S. Yang and X. Yao, editors. *Evolutionary Computation for Dynamic Optimization Problems.* Springer, 2013.

Derivative Free Optimization using a Population-based Stochastic Gradient Estimator

[Track: Integrative Genetic and Evolutionary Computation]

Azhar Khayrattee
Intersil Corporation
akhayrat2001@my.fit.edu

Georgios C. Anagnostopoulos
Florida Institute of Technology
150 W. University Blvd
Melbourne, FL 32901-6975
georgio@fit.edu

ABSTRACT

In this paper we introduce a derivative-free optimization method that is derived from a population based stochastic gradient estimator. We first demonstrate some properties of this estimator and show how it is expected to always yield a descent direction. We analytically show that the difference between the expected function value and the optimum decreases exponentially for strongly convex functions and the expected distance between the current point and the optimum has an upper bound. Then we experimentally tune the parameters of our algorithm to get the best performance. Finally, we use the Black-Box-Optimization-Benchmarking test function suite to evaluate the performance of the algorithm. The experiments indicate that the method offer notable performance advantages especially, when applied to objective functions that are ill-conditioned and potentially multi-modal. This result, coupled with the low computational cost when compared to Quasi-Newton methods, makes it quite attractive.

Categories and Subject Descriptors

G.1.6 [**Numerical Analysis**]: Optimization—*Global Optimization*; I.2.8 [**Artificial Intelligence**]: Problem Solving, Control Methods, and Search—*Heuristic methods*

General Terms

Algorithms

Keywords

Stochastic Gradient, Derivative Free Optimization, Stochastic Optimization

GECCO'14, July 12-16, 2014, Vancouver, BC, Canada.

ACM 978-1-4503-2662-9/14/07 ...$15.00.
http://dx.doi.org/10.1145/2576768.2598365.

1. INTRODUCTION

Stochastic optimization (SO) is a class of algorithms that attempts to optimize stochastic objectives and/or employ stochastic iterates in the optimization process. SO techniques have become an important paradigm in a wide range of optimization areas such as adaptive filtering, control systems and machine learning [20].

SO algorithms can be categorized in two major groups, those which use random variables (or functions) in the formulation of the problem or those which introduce randomness into the search-process to accelerate progress. One of the earliest algorithms that falls under the first group is the SO method described by Robbins-Monro (RM) in [15]. Similar approaches include stochastic gradient descent, finite difference stochastic approximation([10], [1]), simultaneous perturbation stochastic approximation [19] and, more recently, accelerated stochastic optimization [11]. All these algorithms have analytically-shown convergence. Such algorithms are commonly used in situations, where the function cannot be measured directly, *i.e.* it can only be estimated. Recently, they have been applied to many real world applications, where the function values are not readily available, such as online optimization or control systems.

SO also encompasses algorithms that are based on metaheuristics and inspired from nature, *e.g.* simulated annealing and population-based methods, such as evolutionary algorithms, differential evolution, and Particle Swarm Optimization (PSO). The randomness in these algorithms can make them less sensitive to noise and are, hence, less prone to getting trapped in local minima.

In this paper, we propose a derivative-free SO method that is suited for optimizing objective functions, whose gradients may be too expensive to compute. The particular form of the stochastic gradient estimator employed is shown to have certain desirable characteristics in Sections 2.1 and 2.2. In specific, we show that, on average, the search direction is indeed a descent direction and the convergence rate of the difference between the expected function value and the optimum is exponentially decreasing for strongly convex functions. In Section 2.4, we experimentally investigate how to tune the algorithm for best performance and evaluate it using the Black Box Optimization Benchmarking [2, 6, 7] (BBOB) framework. Moreover, in Section 3, we show that this method is very competitive when compared to the Covariance Matrix Adaptation Evolution Strategies (CMA-ES) method and hybrid algorithms namely Differential Evolution

Broyden-Fletcher-Goldfarb-Shanno (DE-BFGS) and Particle Swarm Optimization Broyden-Fletcher-Goldfarb-Shanno (PSO-BFGS). It outperforms Broyden-Fletcher-Goldfarb-Shanno (BFGS), New Unconstrained Optimization Algorithm (NEWUOA) and Separable Natural Evolution Strategies(SNES) methods. We also compare it to state-of-the-art population-based methods such as BI Population CMA-ES (BIPOP-CMA-ES).

Overall our algorithm was able to reach the optimum within an accuracy level of 10^{-8} across all dimensions over the majority of the test functions ($> 85\%$).

2. PROPOSED SO ALGORITHM

In this section, we present an outline of our algorithm followed by an overview of the gradient estimator along with its convergence analysis. Finally, we conclude the section by experimentally tuning the parameters of the presented algorithm. Note that, in this paper, we consider unconstrained single-objective problems, whose objective $f : \mathbb{R}^D \to \mathbb{R}$, depends on a parameter vector $\mathbf{x} \in \mathbb{R}^D$.

2.1 Overview

The basic framework for the algorithm is outlined in Algorithm 1. Starting from an initial solution $\mathbf{x}_o \in \mathbb{R}^D$, the algorithm randomly draws N *i.i.d.* samples from a D-variate Gaussian distribution with mean the current solution $\mathbf{x}_k$ and covariance matrix $\mathbf{S}_k \in \mathbb{R}^{D\times D}$. After evaluating the objective function on these samples, an estimate $\hat{\mathbf{g}}(\mathbf{x}_k)$ of the function's gradient is computed, as described shortly, a direction vector $\mathbf{p}_k$ is generated and a new candidate solution is tested. If the latter solution decreases the objective function value, the step length α_k is increased and the current solution is updated. Otherwise, the step length is decreased and the best sample drawn becomes the current solution. In the sequel, the covariance matrix is updated in manner that will be described later on and the whole scheme is iterated until a convergence criterion is met. For the purpose of our algorithm, we consider the estimate $\hat{\mathbf{g}}(\mathbf{x})$ of $\mathbf{g}(\mathbf{x}) \triangleq \frac{\partial f(\mathbf{x})}{\partial \mathbf{x}}$ to be of the form

Algorithm 1 Pseudo-code for Stochastic GD

Initialize parameters N, $\mathbf{S}_0 \leftarrow \mathbf{I}$, $\alpha_0 \leftarrow 0.1$, $k \leftarrow 0$, and $\mathbf{x}_0 \in \mathbb{R}^D$
while convergence tolerance not reached **do**
  Sample $\boldsymbol{\delta}_k^n \overset{\text{i.i.d}}{\sim} \mathcal{N}_D(\mathbf{0}, \mathbf{S}_k)$ for $n = 1...N$
  $\mathbf{X}_{sample} \leftarrow \mathbf{x}_k + \boldsymbol{\delta}_k^n$
  Evaluate $f(\mathbf{X}_{sample})$
  Calculate estimated gradient $\hat{\mathbf{g}}(\mathbf{x}_k)$ using Equation (1) and compute search direction $\mathbf{p}_k$
  Set point $\mathbf{x}_{trial} \leftarrow \mathbf{x}_k - \alpha_k \mathbf{p}_k$
  if $f(\mathbf{x}_{trial}) < f(\mathbf{x}_k)$ **then**
    $\mathbf{x}_{k+1} \leftarrow \mathbf{x}_{trial}$
    $\alpha_{k+1} \leftarrow 2\alpha_k$
  else
    $\mathbf{x}_{k+1} \leftarrow \mathbf{arg}\min_n f(\mathbf{x}_k + \boldsymbol{\delta}_k^n)$ for $n = 1...N$
    $\alpha_{k+1} \leftarrow \alpha_k/2$
  end if
  Update $\mathbf{S}_{k+1}$
  $k \leftarrow k+1$
end while

$$\hat{\mathbf{g}}(\mathbf{x}) \triangleq \frac{1}{N}\sum_{n=1}^{N}\left(f(\mathbf{x}+\boldsymbol{\delta}_n) - f(\mathbf{x})\right)\boldsymbol{\delta}_n \quad (1)$$

where $\boldsymbol{\delta}_n \overset{\text{i.i.d.}}{\sim} \mathcal{N}_D(\mathbf{0}, \mathbf{S})$ for $n = 1, \ldots, N$. Note that, obviously, for all n

$$\mathbb{E}\{\boldsymbol{\delta}_n\} = \mathbf{0} \quad (2)$$

$$\mathbb{E}\left\{\boldsymbol{\delta}_n\boldsymbol{\delta}_n^T\right\} = \mathbf{S} \quad (3)$$

2.2 Expectation of estimated gradient

We shall show that Equation (1) always yields a descent direction, when the $\boldsymbol{\delta}_n$'s are *i.i.d.* normally distributed. Taking expectations, from Equation (1) we have

$$\mathbb{E}\{\hat{\mathbf{g}}(\mathbf{x})\} \triangleq \frac{1}{N}\sum_{n=1}^{N}\left(\mathbb{E}\{f(\mathbf{x}+\boldsymbol{\delta}_n)\boldsymbol{\delta}_n\} - f(\mathbf{x})\mathbb{E}\{\boldsymbol{\delta}_n\}\right) \quad (4)$$

Using the assumption of Equation (2) in conjunction with Equation (3), we obtain that

$$\mathbb{E}\{\hat{\mathbf{g}}(\mathbf{x})\} = \mathbb{E}\{f(\mathbf{x}+\boldsymbol{\delta})\boldsymbol{\delta}\} \quad (5)$$

Now, assuming that f is convex and differentiable, there are $\mu, M \geq 0$ such that

$$\begin{aligned} f(\mathbf{x}) + \mathbf{g}^T(\mathbf{x})\boldsymbol{\delta} + \frac{\mu}{2}\boldsymbol{\delta}^T\boldsymbol{\delta} \leq f(\mathbf{x}+\boldsymbol{\delta}) \leq \\ f(\mathbf{x}) + \mathbf{g}^T(\mathbf{x})\boldsymbol{\delta} + \frac{M}{2}\boldsymbol{\delta}^T\boldsymbol{\delta} \end{aligned} \quad (6)$$

Multiplying both sides with $\boldsymbol{\delta}$, taking expectation of all terms and using Equation (6) and Equation (3), yields

$$\begin{aligned} \mathbb{E}\left\{\boldsymbol{\delta}^T\boldsymbol{\delta}\right\}\mathbf{g}(\mathbf{x}) + \frac{\mu}{2}\mathbb{E}\left\{\boldsymbol{\delta}\boldsymbol{\delta}^T\boldsymbol{\delta}\right\} \preceq \mathbb{E}\{\hat{\mathbf{g}}(\mathbf{x})\} \preceq \\ \mathbb{E}\left\{\boldsymbol{\delta}^T\boldsymbol{\delta}\right\}\mathbf{g}(\mathbf{x}) + \frac{M}{2}\mathbb{E}\left\{\boldsymbol{\delta}\boldsymbol{\delta}^T\boldsymbol{\delta}\right\} \end{aligned} \quad (7)$$

Based on the definition in Equation (3), and the fact that the probability density function is radial, $\mathbb{E}\left\{\boldsymbol{\delta}\boldsymbol{\delta}^T\boldsymbol{\delta}\right\} = \mathbf{0}$. Thus, $\mathbf{S}\mathbf{g}(\mathbf{x}) \preceq \mathbb{E}\{\hat{\mathbf{g}}(\mathbf{x})\} \preceq \mathbf{S}\mathbf{g}(\mathbf{x})$ and we have

$$\mathbb{E}\{\hat{\mathbf{g}}(\mathbf{x})\} = \mathbf{S}\mathbf{g}(\mathbf{x}) \quad (8)$$

Since $\mathbf{S}$ is positive definite, the previous result immediately implies that $\mathbb{E}\left\{\mathbf{g}^T(\mathbf{x})\hat{\mathbf{g}}(\mathbf{x})\right\} > 0$ for all non-stationary points of f, *i.e.*, $\mathbb{E}\{\hat{\mathbf{g}}(\mathbf{x})\}$ is an ascent direction.

2.3 Convergence Analysis

Next, we shall show that a more basic variant of our algorithm, which uses $\mathbf{p}_k = \hat{\mathbf{g}}(\mathbf{x}_k)$, always performs the step $\mathbf{x}_{k+1} \leftarrow \mathbf{x}_{trial}$ and appropriately scales $\mathbf{S}_k$, converges in the mean square sense for strongly convex, differentiable objective functions that are Lipschitz-continuous and have Lipschitz-continuous gradients. Note that, in what follows, $\|\cdot\|$ represents the ordinary Euclidean norm for $\mathbb{R}^D$. Now, if we let

$$\mathbf{e}_k \triangleq \hat{\mathbf{g}}(\mathbf{x}_k) - \mathbf{g}(\mathbf{x}_k) \quad (9)$$

then the update step can be expressed as

$$\mathbf{x}_{k+1} = \mathbf{x}_k - \alpha_k\left(\mathbf{g}(\mathbf{x}_k) + \mathbf{e}_k\right) \quad (10)$$

Taking conditional expectations on Equation (9) and using Equation (8), we have the following

$$\mathbb{E}\left\{\mathbf{e}_k|\mathbf{x}_k\right\} = (\mathbf{S}_k - \mathbf{I})\mathbf{g}(\mathbf{x}_k) \quad (11)$$

where $\mathbf{S}_k$ is the covariance matrix at iteration k used for sampling possible solutions. Also, $\mathbf{I}$ denotes the identity matrix. It is assumed that $\mathbf{S}_k$ is appropriately scaled (to be discussed shortly) and is updated in a manner that preserves its positive definiteness. The expectation of the norm squared of the error term is given by

$$\begin{aligned}\mathbb{E}\left\{||\mathbf{e}_k||^2|\mathbf{x}_k\right\} &= \mathbb{E}\left\{||\hat{\mathbf{g}}(\mathbf{x}_k) - \mathbf{g}(\mathbf{x}_k)||^2|\mathbf{x}_k\right\} = \\ &= \mathbb{E}\left\{||\hat{\mathbf{g}}(\mathbf{x}_k)||^2 - 2\hat{\mathbf{g}}^T(\mathbf{x}_k)\mathbf{g}(\mathbf{x}_k) + ||\mathbf{g}(\mathbf{x}_k)||^2|\mathbf{x}_k\right\}\end{aligned} \quad (12)$$

Next, we need an expression for $\mathbb{E}\left\{||\hat{\mathbf{g}}(\mathbf{x}_k)||^2|\mathbf{x}_k\right\}$. Since f is assumed Lipschitz-continuous, there is a constant $L' > 0$, such that $|f(\mathbf{x} + \boldsymbol{\delta}_n) - f(\mathbf{x})| \leq L'||\boldsymbol{\delta}_n||$ for all $\mathbf{x}$ and $\boldsymbol{\delta}_n$, which, in conjunction with Equation (1), yields

$$\begin{aligned}||\hat{\mathbf{g}}(\mathbf{x}_k)|| &\leq \frac{1}{N}\sum_{n=1}^{N}|f(\mathbf{x}_k + \boldsymbol{\delta}_k^n) - f(\mathbf{x}_k)|||\boldsymbol{\delta}_k^n|| = \\ &= \frac{L'}{N}\sum_{n=1}^{N}||\boldsymbol{\delta}_k^n||^2\end{aligned} \quad (13)$$

Using Equation (13), we have that

$$\mathbf{E}\left\{||\hat{\mathbf{g}}(\mathbf{x})||^2|\mathbf{x}_k\right\} \leq \frac{L'^2}{N^2}\sum_{n=1}^{N}\sum_{m=1}^{M}\mathbf{E}\left\{||\boldsymbol{\delta}_{m,k}||^2||\boldsymbol{\delta}_k^n||^2|\mathbf{x}_k\right\} \quad (14)$$

The summand of Equation (14) can be expanded as follows

$$\begin{aligned}&\mathbf{E}\left\{||\boldsymbol{\delta}_{m,k}||^2||\boldsymbol{\delta}_k^n||^2|\mathbf{x}_k\right\} = \\ &= \begin{cases} n = m & \mathbf{E}\left\{||\boldsymbol{\delta}_k^n||^4|\mathbf{x}_k\right\} \\ m \neq m & \mathbf{E}\left\{||\boldsymbol{\delta}_{m,k}||^2|\mathbf{x}_k\right\}\mathbf{E}\left\{||\boldsymbol{\delta}_k^n||^2|\mathbf{x}_k\right\}\end{cases}\end{aligned} \quad (15)$$

Expanding the terms and simplifying we get

$$\begin{aligned}&\mathbf{E}\left\{||\hat{\mathbf{g}}(\mathbf{x}_k)||^2|\mathbf{x}_k\right\} \leq \\ &\leq \frac{L'^2}{N}\left[(2N-1)\mathrm{trace}^2(\mathbf{S}_k) + 2N\mathrm{trace}(\mathbf{S}_k^2)\right]\end{aligned} \quad (16)$$

Now, let Λ_k be the maximum eigenvalue of $\mathbf{S}_k$. Due to the inequalities $\mathrm{trace}(\mathbf{S}_k) \leq N\Lambda_k$ and $\mathrm{trace}(\mathbf{S}_k^2) \leq N\Lambda_k^2$, we can simplify Equation (16) to

$$\mathbf{E}\left\{||\hat{\mathbf{g}}(\mathbf{x}_k)||^2|\mathbf{x}_k\right\} \leq L'^2N(2N+1)\Lambda_k^2 \quad (17)$$

Next, assume that $\mathbf{S}_k$ is scaled, such that $\Lambda_k^2 = C||\hat{\mathbf{g}}(\mathbf{x}_k)||^2$, for some $C > 0$. Then we obtain

$$\mathbf{E}\left\{||\mathbf{e}_k||^2|\mathbf{x}_k\right\} \leq \gamma_k||\mathbf{g}(\mathbf{x}_k)||^2 \quad (18)$$

where $\gamma_k \triangleq CL'^2N(2N+1)\Lambda_k^2$. We can, thus, upper-bound Equation (12) as

$$\mathbf{E}\left\{||\mathbf{e}_k||^2|\mathbf{x}_k\right\} \leq (\gamma_k - 2\Lambda_k + 1)||\mathbf{g}(\mathbf{x}_k)||^2 \quad (19)$$

For objective functions f, which have a Lipschitz-continuous gradient, we have that for all $\mathbf{x}$ and $\mathbf{y}$ in $\mathbb{R}^D$,

$$f(\mathbf{y}) \leq f(\mathbf{x}) + \mathbf{g}^T(\mathbf{x})(\mathbf{y} - \mathbf{x}) + \frac{L}{2}||\mathbf{y} - \mathbf{x}||^2 \quad (20)$$

Substituting $\mathbf{x} = \mathbf{x}_k$, $\mathbf{y} = \mathbf{x}_{k+1}$ from Equation (9), we obtain

$$\begin{aligned}f(\mathbf{x}_{k+1}) &\leq f(\mathbf{x}_k) - \alpha_k(1 - \alpha_k L/2)||\mathbf{g}(\mathbf{x}_k)||^2 - \\ &\alpha_k(1 - \alpha_k L)\left\langle\mathbf{g}(\mathbf{x}_k), \mathbf{e}_k\right\rangle + (\alpha_k^2 L/2)||\mathbf{e}_k||^2\end{aligned} \quad (21)$$

Taking expectations on Equation (21) and using Equation (10) and Equation (19), we have that

$$\begin{aligned}\mathbb{E}\left\{f(\mathbf{x}_{k+1})|\mathbf{x}_k\right\} &\leq f(\mathbf{x}_k) - \alpha_k(1 - \alpha_k L/2)||\mathbf{g}(\mathbf{x}_k)||^2 - \\ &-\alpha_k(1 - \alpha_k L)\left\langle\mathbf{g}(\mathbf{x}_k), (\mathbf{S}_k - 1)\mathbf{g}(\mathbf{x}_k)\right\rangle + \\ &+(\alpha_k^2 L/2)(\gamma_k - 2\Lambda_k + 1)||\mathbf{g}(\mathbf{x}_k)||^2\end{aligned} \quad (22)$$

After simplifications we arrive at

$$\begin{aligned}&\mathbb{E}\left\{f(\mathbf{x}_{k+1})|\mathbf{x}_k\right\} \leq \\ &\leq f(\mathbf{x}_k) - \alpha_k\left(\Lambda_k - \alpha_k L\gamma_k/2\right)||\mathbf{g}(\mathbf{x_k})||^2\end{aligned} \quad (23)$$

Equation (23) shows that, if $\mathbf{x}_k$ is not a minimizer, then the descent step is expected to decrease f for any step size satisfying

$$0 < \alpha_k < \frac{2\Lambda_k}{L\gamma_k} \quad (24)$$

Moreover, for strongly convex functions, we have that

$$f(\mathbf{x}) \geq f(\mathbf{x}) + \mathbf{g}^T(\mathbf{x})(\mathbf{y} - \mathbf{x}) + \frac{\mu}{2}||\mathbf{y} - \mathbf{x}||^2 \quad (25)$$

for some $\mu > 0$. Minimizing Equation (25) w.r.t $\mathbf{y}$ and substituting $\mathbf{x} = \mathbf{x}_k$, we get

$$-||\mathbf{g}(\mathbf{x}_k)||^2 \leq -2\mu\left[f(\mathbf{x}_k) - f(\mathbf{x}^*)\right] \quad (26)$$

Substituting Equation (26) into Equation (23) and assuming that the step sizes α_k obey Equation (24), we get

$$\mathbb{E}\left\{f(\mathbf{x}_{k+1})|\mathbf{x}_k\right\} \leq f(\mathbf{x}^*) - \beta_k\left[f(\mathbf{x}_k) - f(\mathbf{x}^*)\right] \quad (27)$$

where $\beta_k \triangleq 2\mu\alpha_k\left(\Lambda_k - \alpha_k L\gamma_k/2\right)$. Subtracting $f(\mathbf{x}^*)$ from Equation (27) and taking expectations results in

$$\mathbb{E}\left\{f(\mathbf{x}_{k+1})\right\} - f(\mathbf{x}^*) \leq (1 - \beta_k)\left[\mathbb{E}\left\{f(\mathbf{x}_k)\right\} - f(\mathbf{x}^*)\right] \quad (28)$$

Applying the previous inequality recursively, we finally obtain

$$\mathbb{E}\left\{f(\mathbf{x}_k)\right\} - f(\mathbf{x}^*) \leq \left[f(\mathbf{x}_0) - f(\mathbf{x}^*)\right]\prod_{i=1}^{k}(1 - \beta_i) \quad (29)$$

As long as $\beta_k < 1$ for all k, which is equivalent to $\alpha_k > \frac{\Lambda_k}{L\gamma_k} + \sqrt{\frac{\Lambda_k^2}{L^2\gamma_k^2} - \frac{1}{\mu L\gamma_k}}$, Equation (29) implies that

$\lim_{k\to+\infty} \mathbb{E}\{f(\mathbf{x}_k)\} = f(\mathbf{x}^*)$. Furthermore, again using the strong convexity assumption, based on what has been derived so far, it is straightforward to show that

$$\mathbb{E}\left\{||\mathbf{x}_{k+1} - \mathbf{x}^*||^2\right\} \leq \frac{2}{\mu}(1-\beta_k)\left[\mathbb{E}\{f(\mathbf{x}_k)\} - f(\mathbf{x}^*)\right] \quad (30)$$

and, following a similar rationale as before, as long as $\frac{2}{\mu}(1-\beta_k) < 1$ for all k, we conclude that $\lim_{k\to+\infty} \mathbb{E}\left\{||\mathbf{x}_k - \mathbf{x}^*||^2\right\} = 0$, *i.e.*, the sequence of $\mathbf{x}_k$'s generated by our algorithm converges to the minimum $\mathbf{x}^*$ in the mean square sense.

2.4 Search & Covariance Matrix Adaptation

In this section, we explore practical choices for $\mathbf{p}_k$ and choices for adapting $\mathbf{S}_k$. Note that the $\mathbf{x}_{k+1}$ update on line 12 of Algorithm 1 still satisfies the form of Equation (5) because for any differentiable convex function, we can find a positive definite matrix, $\mathbf{A}$, such that $\mathbf{x}_k - \mathbf{x}_{k+1} = \mathbf{A}\mathbf{g}(\mathbf{x}_k)$. Thus, the error term defined by Equation (9) still applies and the convergence analysis still holds. Also, for the purpose we used set N equal to the problem dimension. Possible choices for the search direction are as follows

$$\mathbf{p}_k = \hat{\mathbf{g}}(\mathbf{x}_k) \quad (31)$$

$$\mathbf{p}_k = \mathbf{S}_k\hat{\mathbf{g}}(\mathbf{x}_k) \quad (32)$$

The second choice aims to use a covariance matrix that, potentially, approximates the inverse Hessian of the objective function at the current solution, thus, yielding an approximate Newton step. Regarding the covariance matrix, a simple choice is to decrease it by a factor γ_k as follows

$$\mathbf{C}_{k+1} = \gamma_k \mathbf{I} \quad (33)$$

such that $\sum_k \gamma_k = \infty$ and $\sum_k \gamma_k^2 < \infty$. Another approach is to adaptively change the distribution such that it is more likely to sample points along the direction which yields the best points. The method we propose was adapted from the CMA-ES [8] algorithm which, in summary, updates it covariance matrix by using a weighted mean of the current matrix, a rank-one update using the difference in mean vector and a rank-μ update . In our case, we shall use a rank-one update of $\mathbf{S}_{k+1}$ by an outer product change in position vector, $\mathbf{x}_{k+1} - \mathbf{x}_k$. Additionally, in order to maintain a balance between exploration and exploitation, we shall use the following heuristic to update the covariance matrix, which provides an additional dampening factor.

$$\mathbf{D}_{k+1} \leftarrow (1-c_1)\mathbf{D}_k + c_1(\mathbf{x}_{k+1} - \mathbf{x}_k)(\mathbf{x}_{k+1} - \mathbf{x}_k)^T \quad (34a)$$

$$\mathbf{S}_{k+1} \leftarrow (1-c_2)\mathbf{S}_k + c_2\mathbf{D}_{k+1} \quad (34b)$$

where $\mathbf{D}_0 = 0$. It should be noted that the update method in Equation (34) ensures that if no better point is found, the width of the covariance matrix is decreased to better exploit the landscape since $\mathbf{D}_{k+1} = 0$.

We shall also investigate the effect of using $\boldsymbol{\delta}_k^n$ s.t. $f(\mathbf{x}_k + \boldsymbol{\delta}_k^n) < f(\mathbf{x}_k)$ (i.e. only the points better than the current one) in the calculation of the estimated gradient using Equation (1).

Applying the above mentioned variations to Algorithm 1, we get the variations listed in Table 1

The algorithms are benchmarked using the BBOB suite using functions $1, 2, 5-14$. More details about the experimental setup are given in the Section 3. The results are displayed in Figures 1, 2, 3, and 4. They represent the bootstrapped empirical cumulative distribution of the number of objective function evaluations divided by dimension (FEvals/D) for 50 targets in $10^{[-8..2]}$ for all functions. The "best 2009" line corresponds to the best Expected Running Time (ERT) observed during BBOB 2009 for each single target. From Figures 1, 2, 3, and 4, firstly, it is very obvious that the variants using Equation (33) suffer from poor performance which is to be expected since the new population is sampled from a uniform distribution and thus is affected by ill-conditioned or rotated functions. On the other hand, the covariance matrix update scheme defined by Equation (34)

Table 1: Algorithm test versions

Name	Options
v1	eqn. 31, eqn. 34, eqn. 1 using best points
v2	eqn. 31, eqn. 33, eqn. 1 using best points
v3	eqn. 31, eqn. 34, eqn. 1 using all points
v4	eqn. 31, eqn. 33, eqn. 1 using all points
v5	eqn. 32, eqn. 34, eqn. 1 using best points
v6	eqn. 32, eqn. 33, eqn. 1 using best points
v7	eqn. 32, eqn. 34, eqn. 1 using all points
v8	eqn. 32, eqn. 33, eqn. 1 using all points

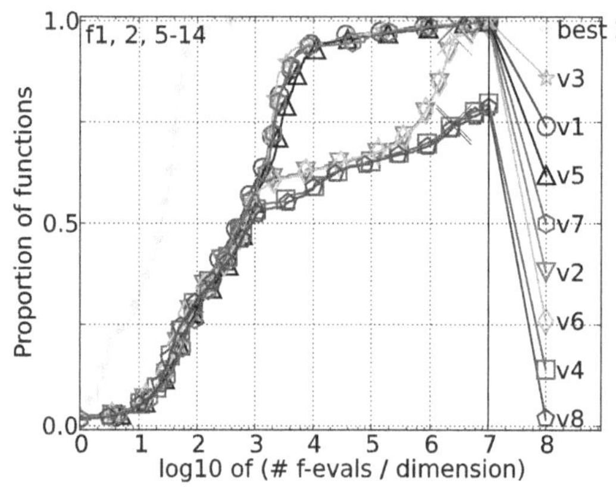

Figure 1: Performance in 2–D

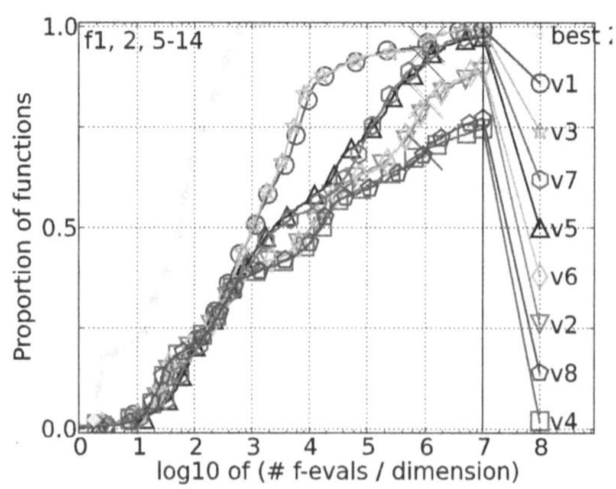

Figure 2: Performance in 5–D

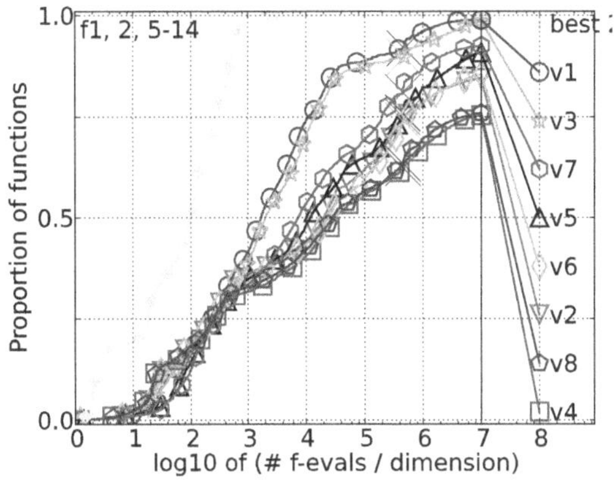

Figure 3: Performance in 10−D

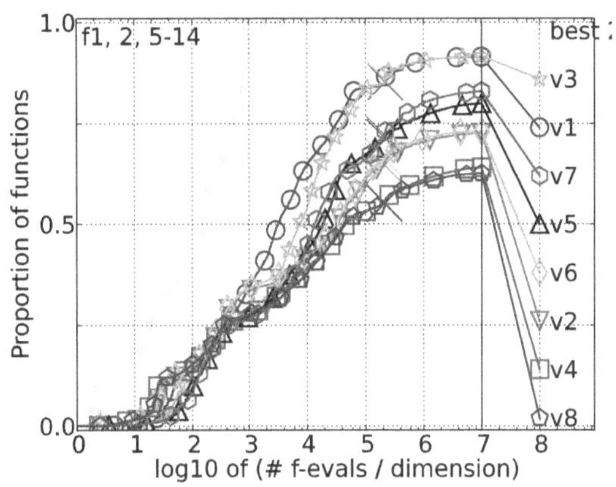

Figure 4: Performance in 20−D

offers better performance because it incrementally updates the matrix so that its major eigenvalue is aligned with the step taken.

Secondly, the results show that the descent direction based solely on the gradient estimator (Equation (31)) slightly outperforms the option defined by Equation (32) as the number of dimensions increases. We believe this is the case since the expectation of Equation (32) expands to $\mathbf{S}^2\mathbf{g}(\mathbf{x}_k)$. Thus, if $\mathbf{S}$ approximates the inverse Hessian, the step length is either being increased or decreased from the Quasi-Newton step depending on its eigenvalues. Equation (31) offers competitive performance because its expected value represents the Quasi-Newton step *if* the covariance matrix represents the inverse Hessian.

Finally, it seems that the choice of the points (i.e., either all or only the best points) used to estimate the gradient using Equation (1) does not affect performance.

In the light of above analysis, we shall define $\mathbf{x}_k$ as in Equation (31), $\mathbf{S}_{k+1}$ as in Equation (34) and finally use all points (i.e. $\boldsymbol{\delta}_n$ for $n = 1...N$) to evaluate Equation (1).

Line 7 of Algorithm 1 is based on the step update equation for the RM algorithm. IN out case, ι_k represents the stochastic gradient estimator. One difference is that we use the best of the population (on line 12), if the estimator does not yield a better point whereas the RM always uses the next point. When compared to CMA-ES algorithms, the key difference is that we use the gradient estimator to determine where to move the population as opposed to the change in the mean of the population. The similarity is in the adaptation of the covariance matrix. Assuming that the gradient estimator points towards the global optimum, it is reminiscent of a Particle Swarm Optimization (PSO) algorithm, without the momentum and local best components.

3. EXPERIMENTAL ASSESSMENTS

3.1 Setup

Results from the experiments according to the BBOB test suite [2, 5, 6] are presented in Figures 5, 6, 8, 9 and 7. The following set of functions are used as benchmark: $f1$-Sphere Function, $f2$-Ellipsoidal Function, $f5$-Linear Slope, $f6$-Attractive Sector, $f7$-Step Ellipsoidal, $f8$-Rosenbrock, $f9$-Rotated Rosenbrock, $f10$-Ellipsoidal, $f11$-Discus, $f12$-Bent Cigar,$f13$-Sharp Ridge, $f14$-Different Powers. They were chosen because they offer various levels of difficulty with some being non-differentiable. The **expected running time (ERT)**, used in the figures, depends on a given target function value, $f_t = f_{\text{opt}} + \Delta f$, and is computed over all relevant trials as the number of function evaluations executed during each trial while the best function value did not reach f_t, summed over all trials and divided by the number of trials that actually reached f_t [5, 14]. **Statistical significance** is tested with the rank-sum test for a given target Δf_t (10^{-8} as in Figure 7) using, for each trial, either the number of needed function evaluations to reach Δf_t (inverted and multiplied by -1), or, if the target was not reached, the best Δf-value achieved, measured only up to the smallest number of overall function evaluations for any unsuccessful trial under consideration.

3.2 Benchmark Algorithms

The algorithms described in this section were chosen as comparison as they encompass both numerical (BFGS and New Unconstrained Optimization Algorithm (NEWUOA)) and stochastic methods (CMA-ES, BIPOP-CMA-ES, Natural Evolution Strategies (NES)). We also have hybrid algorithms such as DE-BFGS and PSO-BFGS.

The standard BFGS algorithm is implemented as described in [16] by using the MATLAB built in function *fminunc* which uses numerical gradient *i.e.* a variation of the finite difference method. This also gives an idea how out estimator compares to the finite difference method of approximating the true gradient.

We also compare the algorithm with the NEWUOA [13] since it is also a Derivative-Free Optimization (DFO) algorithm. Its basis is a quadratic approximation of the trust region. It performs a truncated conjugate gradient minimization of the surrogate model in the trust region and then updates either the current best point or the radius of the trust region, based on the a posteriori interpolation error. The time complexity of the algorithm is $\mathcal{O}(m^2n)$ in the worst case but in practice closer to $\mathcal{O}(mn)$, where m is the number of interpolation points used for the determination of the model and n is the dimension of the search space.

The other algorithm used in the comparison is CMA-ES [8]. It has been heavily studied since it was introduced. It is available in numerous variations and has been combined with various other stochastic optimization strategies in an

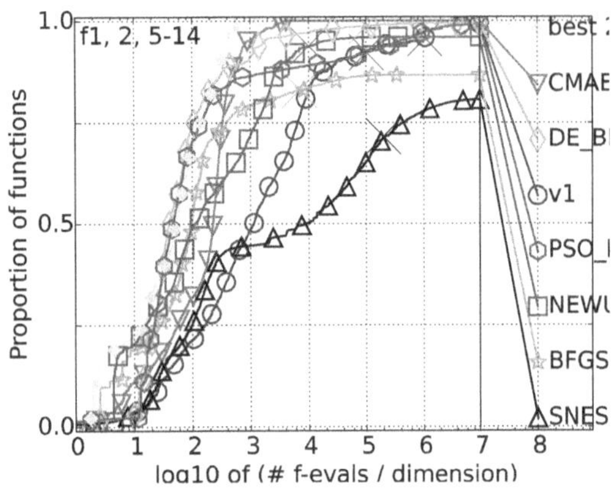

Figure 5: Performance in 5−D

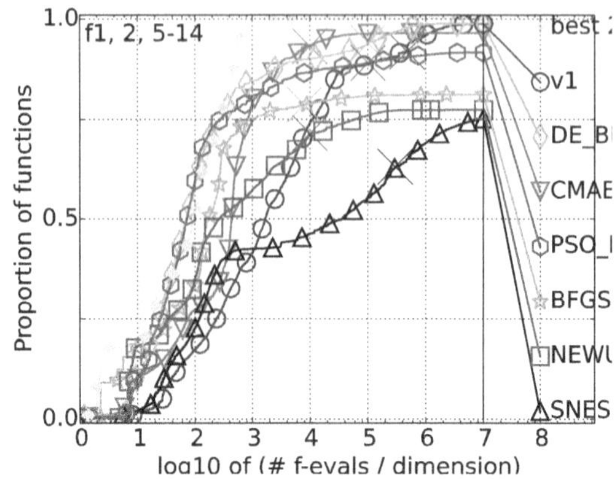

Figure 6: Performance in 10−D

attempt to improve performance and robustness. We will use both the original version and BIPOP-CMA-ES [3, 4] which attempts to overcome the local search of the original CMA-ES by utilizing two schemes to enhance global search. The first scheme starts with a default population size and applies two interlaced multi-start regimes, each equipped with a function evaluation budget accounting for the so far conducted function evaluations. Depending on which budget value is smaller, a complete run of either one or the other strategy is launched. During each restart, the population size is increased by a factor of two. The second scheme utilizes a multi-start regime with small population size. A maximum number of function evaluations of half of the recent large budget is enforced. The second multi-start regime is launched, if and only if its recent budget is smaller than the one for the first regime with increasing populations. Note that BIPOP-CMA-ES is referenced as *best 2009* in Figures 5, 6, 8, 9 and 7

The NES [21] class of algorithms aim at a higher level of generality, providing a procedure to update the search distribution's parameters for any type of distribution, by ascending the gradient towards higher expected fitness. Further, it has been shown [18] that following the natural gradient to adapt the search distribution is highly beneficial, because it appropriately normalizes the update step with respect to its uncertainty and makes the algorithm scale-invariant. Separable Natural Evolution Strategies (SNES) [17], is a variant which scales linearly with problem dimension and are particularly appropriate for large, separable problems.

Finally, we also use hybrid algorithms which combine the stochastic nature of Differential Evolution (DE) and PSO along with BFGS namely DE-BFGS [9] and PSO-BFGS [12]

3.3 Results

Note that due to space constraints we shall summarize the performance assessment figures and tables. Figures 5, 6, 8, and 9 display the bootstrapped empirical cumulative distribution of the number of objective function evaluations divided by dimension (FEvals/D) for 50 targets in $10^{[-8..2]}$ for all functions. The "best 2009" line corresponds to the best ERT observed during BBOB 2009 for each single target, which is the BIPOP-CMA-ES. It gives an idea about the computational cost (in terms of FEvals/D) involved in reaching the solution. Figure 7 measures the ERT to reach the solution within 10^{-8} across dimensions, which gives an idea on how the algorithm scales with dimension. From Figures 5, 6, 8, and 9 it can be observed that the performance of the gradient estimation technique used by our algorithm consistently outperforms BFGS, NEWUOA and SNES across all the benchmarked dimensions. When compared to CMA-ES, it offers a slight performance improvement. Also, from these figures, it can also be observed that our algorithm takes a slightly longer time to adapt to the problem but the overall performance is better with roughly 85% of the functions successfully solved. When compared to BFGS, the advantages of our method becomes clear as our algorithm has a higher success rate. Note that BFGS is very robust in adapting the inverse Hessian exactly which is obvious in Figure 7. We can observe that BFGS solves the problems with low to moderate conditioning faster. However, on functions with moderate to high conditioning, such as $f6 - f7$, and $f10 - f13$, we can observe that it fails to reach the optimum within 10^{-8} accuracy level. On the other hand, our algorithm is successful at solving all problems in low dimensions albeit loosing some performance on high conditioned functions in high dimensions for $f13$ and $f14$. It should be noted that these functions are very deceptive to algorithms because of their landscape is composed of a narrow flat valley with steep edges. This shows that our gradient estimate (1) is sensitive to such landscapes. This can be expected if the covariance matrix is not aligned with the contours of the problem, the resulting estimate will be poor. One reason behind this is that we do not have a method that increases the width of the distribution. The updates from Equation (34) works best if the step taken is along the descent direction. Increasing the number of points might help in sampling more points in the direction of the optimum, but doing so will increase the number of function evaluations. Note that in our experiments, our algorithm eventually converges but at a very slow rate and a high cost in terms of function evaluations. Another property of our algorithm that is apparent from Figure 7 is that it is rotation invariant. This can be observed for $f8$ and $f9$ (which are represent two orientation of the Rosenbrock function), where the performance of the algorithm is similar. Comparing the figures, we can observe that our algorithm linearly scales with dimension for 4 problems ($f1$, $f5$, $f6$, $f11$). For the Rosenbrock functions ($f8$, $f9$), the scaling is linear for $D = 5$ through $D = 40$. For the other functions,

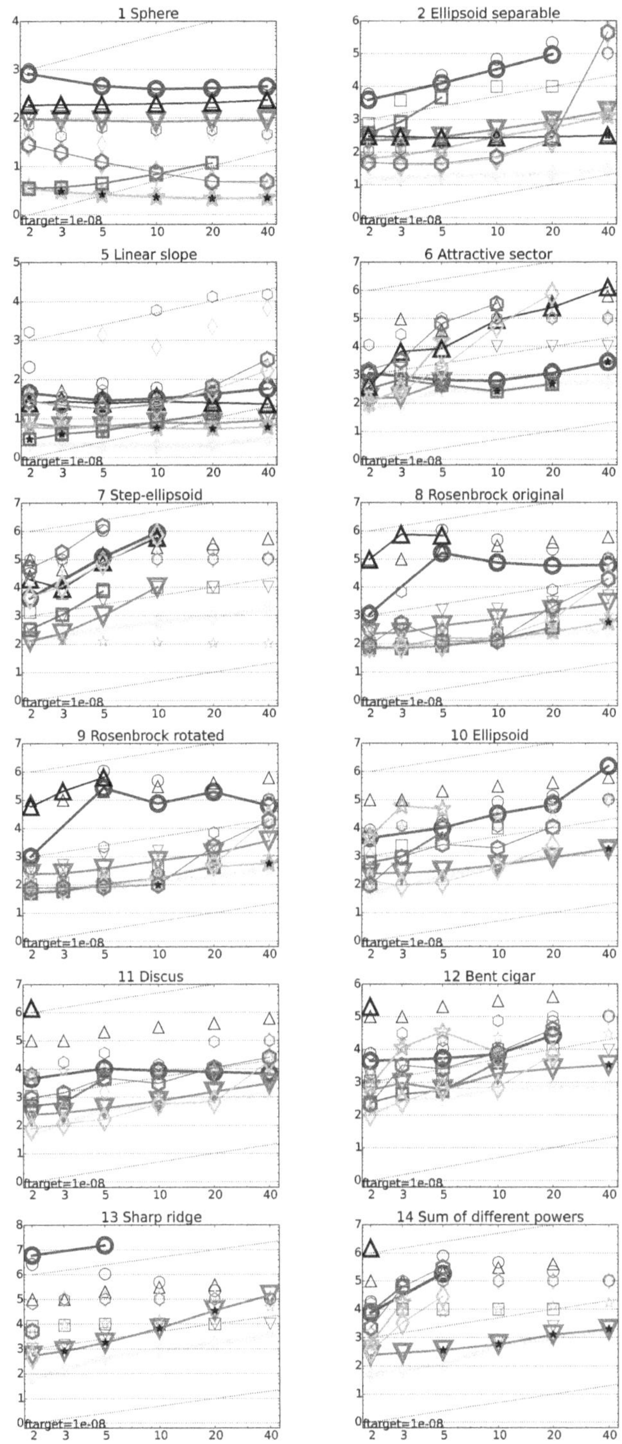

Figure 7: Expected running time (ERT in number of f-evaluations) divided by dimension for target function value 10^{-8} as $\log_{10}$ values versus dimension. Different symbols correspond to different algorithms given in the legend of f_1 and f_{24}. Light symbols give the maximum number of function evaluations from the longest trial divided by dimension. Horizontal lines give linear scaling, slanted dotted lines give quadratic scaling. Black stars indicate statistically better result compared to all other algorithms with $p < 0.01$ and Bonferroni correction number of dimensions (six). Legend: ○:v1, ▽:BFGS, ☆:CMAES, □:NEWUOA, △:SNES, :DE_BFGS, ⬡:PSO_BFGS

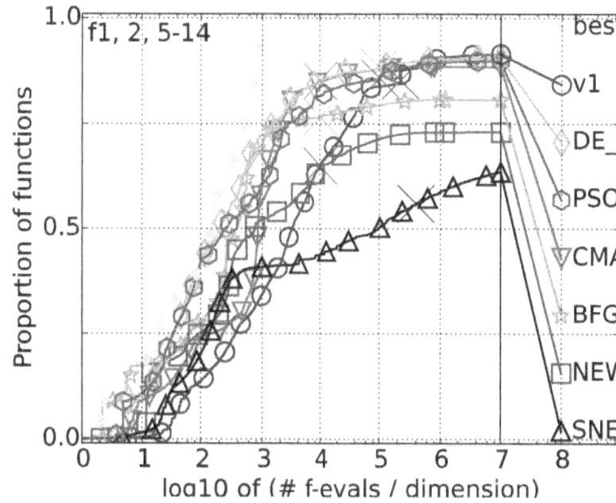

Figure 8: Performance in 20−D

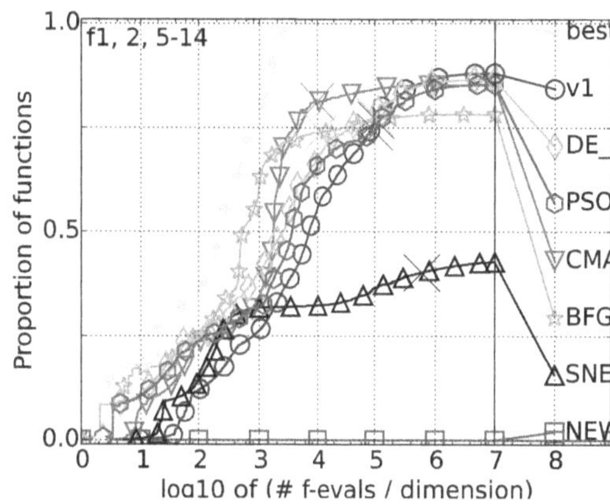

Figure 9: Performance in 40−D

the scaling is quadratic and is slightly higher for $f7$, the step ellipsoid which consists of many plateaus of very small gradient. Finally, when compared to BFGS which uses the Hessian update, our scheme in Equation (34) is less computationally intensive.

4. CONCLUSIONS

In this manuscript we have developed a stochastic gradient estimation technique that uses a population whose distribution is adaptive. We have analytically shown that the direction of the estimator is always a descent direction thus increasing the likelihood of finding the optimum. We have also shown that the convergence rate of the difference between the expected function value and the optimum on strongly convex functions decreases exponentially and that the expected distance between the current point and the optimum has an upper bound. We have used the popular BBOB test suite and benchmarked some state-of-the-art algorithms as well as the BFGS method and another quadratic model based algorithm (NEWUOA) to assess the performance of our algorithm. The key observations are that the algorithm clearly outperforms BFGS on functions with moderate to high conditioning. Overall, it is very competitive with CMA-ES, PSO-BFGS and DE-BFGS. Moreover, it is able to reach the optimum across all dimensions over the majority of the functions. However, there are a few problems that are open for future research. For example, on severely ill conditioned functions, the algorithm has difficulty converging to the optimum with the budget number of functions evaluations. We believe an update to the adaptation of $\mathbf{C}_{k+1}$ might solve the issue.

5. ACKNOWLEDGMENTS

G. C. Anagnostopoulos acknowledges partial support from US National Science Foundation (NSF) grant No. 1263011. Any opinions, findings, and conclusions or recommendations expressed in this material are those of the authors and do not necessarily reflect the views of the NSF.

References

[1] M. Broadie, D. Cicek, and A. Zeevi. General bounds and finite-time improvement for the kiefer-wolfowitz stochastic approximation algorithm. *Operations Research*, 59(5):1211–1224, Sept. 2011.

[2] S. Finck, N. Hansen, R. Ros, and A. Auger. Real-parameter black-box optimization benchmarking 2009: Presentation of the noiseless functions. Technical Report 2009/20, Research Center PPE, 2009. Updated February 2010.

[3] N. Hansen. Benchmarking a BI-population CMA-ES on the BBOB-2009 function testbed. In *Workshop Proceedings of the GECCO Genetic and Evolutionary Computation Conference*, pages 2389–2395. ACM, July 2009.

[4] N. Hansen. Benchmarking a BI-population CMA-ES on the BBOB-2009 noisy testbed. In *Workshop Proceedings of the GECCO Genetic and Evolutionary Computation Conference*, pages 2397–2402. ACM, July 2009.

[5] N. Hansen, A. Auger, S. Finck, and R. Ros. Real-parameter black-box optimization benchmarking 2012: Experimental setup. Technical report, INRIA, 2012.

[6] N. Hansen, S. Finck, R. Ros, and A. Auger. Real-parameter black-box optimization benchmarking 2009: Noiseless functions definitions. Technical Report RR-6829, INRIA, 2009. Updated February 2010.

[7] N. Hansen, S. Finck, R. Ros, and A. Auger. Real-parameter black-box optimization benchmarking 2009: Noisy functions definitions. Technical Report RR-6869, INRIA, 2009. Updated February 2010.

[8] N. Hansen and A. Ostermeier. Completely derandomized self-adaptation in evolution strategies. *Evol. Comput.*, 9(2):159–195, June 2001.

[9] R. Khanum and M. Jan. Hybridization of adaptive differential evolution with bfgs. In M. Bramer and M. Petridis, editors, *Research and Development in Intelligent Systems XXIX*, pages 441–446. Springer London, 2012.

[10] J. Kiefer and J. Wolfowitz. Stochastic estimation of the maximum of a regression function. *The Annals of Mathematical Statistics*, 23:462–466, 1952.

[11] G. Lan. An optimal method for stochastic composite optimization. *Mathematical Programming*, 133(1-2):365–397, 2012.

[12] S. Li, M. Tan, I. W. Tsang, and J. T.-Y. Kwok. A hybrid pso-bfgs strategy for global optimization of multimodal functions. *IEEE Transactions on Systems, Man, and Cybernetics, Part B*, 41(4):1003–1014, 2011.

[13] M. Powell. The newuoa software for unconstrained optimization without derivatives. In G. Pillo and M. Roma, editors, *Large-Scale Nonlinear Optimization*, volume 83 of *Nonconvex Optimization and Its Applications*, pages 255–297. Springer US, 2006.

[14] K. Price. Differential evolution vs. the functions of the 2nd iceo. In *Evolutionary Computation, 1997., IEEE International Conference on*, pages 153–157, Apr 1997.

[15] H. Robbins and S. Monro. A Stochastic Approximation Method. *The Annals of Mathematical Statistics*, 22(3):400–407, 1951.

[16] R. Ros. Benchmarking the bfgs algorithm on the bbob-2009 function testbed. In *Proceedings of the 11th Annual Conference Companion on Genetic and Evolutionary Computation Conference: Late Breaking Papers*, GECCO '09, pages 2409–2414, New York, NY, USA, 2009. ACM.

[17] T. Schaul. Benchmarking separable natural evolution strategies on the noiseless and noisy black-box optimization testbeds. In *Proceedings of the fourteenth international conference on Genetic and evolutionary computation conference companion*, GECCO Companion '12, pages 205–212, New York, NY, USA, 2012. ACM.

[18] T. Schaul. Natural evolution strategies converge on sphere functions. In *Proceedings of the Fourteenth International Conference on Genetic and Evolutionary Computation Conference*, GECCO '12, pages 329–336, New York, NY, USA, 2012. ACM.

[19] J. C. Spall. Multivariate stochastic approximation using a simultaneous perturbation gradient approximation. *IEEE Transactions on Automatic Control*, 37(3):332–341, mar 1992.

[20] S. W. Wallace and W. T. Ziemba, editors. *Applications of stochastic programming*. MPS-SIAM series on optimization. Society for Industrial and Applied Mathematics, Philadelphia, PA, 2005.

[21] D. Wierstra, T. Schaul, J. Peters, and J. Schmidhuber. Natural evolution strategies. In *Evolutionary Computation, 2008. CEC 2008. (IEEE World Congress on Computational Intelligence). IEEE Congress on*, pages 3381–3387, June 2008.

A Novel Population-based Multi-Objective CMA-ES and the Impact of Different Constraint Handling Techniques

Sílvio Rodrigues
Delft University of Technology (TUDelft)
Delft, The Netherlands
s.m.fragosorodrigues@tudelft.nl

Pavol Bauer
Delft University of Technology (TUDelft)
Delft, The Netherlands
p.bauer@tudelft.nl

Peter A.N. Bosman
Centrum Wiskunde & Informatica (CWI)
Amsterdam, The Netherlands
peter.bosman@cwi.nl

ABSTRACT

The Covariance Matrix Adaptation Evolutionary Strategy (CMA-ES) is a well-known, state-of-the-art optimization algorithm for single-objective real-valued problems, especially in black-box settings. Although several extensions of CMA-ES to multi-objective (MO) optimization exist, no extension incorporates a key component of the most robust and general CMA-ES variant: the association of a population with each Gaussian distribution that drives optimization. To achieve this, we use a recently introduced framework for extending population-based algorithms from single- to multi-objective optimization. We compare, using six well-known benchmark problems, the performance of the newly constructed MO-CMA-ES with existing variants and with the estimation of distribution algorithm (EDA) known as iMAMaLGaM, that is also an instance of the framework, extending the single-objective EDA iAMaLGaM to MO. Results underline the advantages of being able to use populations. Because many real-world problems have constraints, we also study the use of four constraint-handling techniques. We find that CMA-ES is typically less robust to these techniques than iAMaLGaM. Moreover, whereas we could verify that a penalty method that was previously used in literature leads to fast convergence, we also find that it has a high risk of finding only nearly, but not entirely, feasible solutions. We therefore propose that other constraint-handling techniques should be preferred in general.

Categories and Subject Descriptors

G.1.6 [**Optimization**]: Global optimization

General Terms

Algorithms, Performance, Experimentation

Keywords

CMA-ES, Estimation-of-Distribution Algorithms, Mixture Distributions, Multi-Objective Optimization

GECCO'14, July 12–16, 2014, Vancouver, BC, Canada.

http://dx.doi.org/10.1145/2576768.2598329.

1. INTRODUCTION

Many real-world problems have more than one conflicting objective that need to be optimized simultaneously. Moreover, many problems require taking a black-box optimization (BBO) perspective, i.e. assume that (virtually) nothing is known about the problem at hand (e.g. complex simulation based real-world models). Studying and understanding algorithms to tackle optimization problems under such conditions is therefore important.

For single-objective (SO) real-valued optimization problems, the Covariance Matrix Adaptation Evolution Strategy (CMA-ES) is a well-known, state-of-the-art algorithm, especially in black-box settings. Several multi-objective (MO) extensions of CMA-ES exist [1, 2, 3, 4]. However, none incorporates a key component of the most robust and general CMA-ES variant [5]: the association of a population with each Gaussian distribution to drive optimization. In the first MO extension of CMA-ES [1], a $(1+\lambda)$-MO-CMA-ES is introduced. In this approach, each parent generates one or more offspring solutions. Thereafter, parents and offspring solutions are selected based on non-dominated sorting. The search strategy parameters are updated based on a direct comparison between offspring and respective parents. However, there is no information-sharing mechanism for different individuals, even if they are in similar search space areas. In the second proposed MO-CMA-ES variant, in each generation only one parent is selected to generate one offspring [2]. The parent may be randomly selected from the entire population or, in a greedy approach, from the subset with the lowest non-dominated rank. In another MO-CMA-ES variant, a notion of continuity of the optimization problem was assumed [3]. Successful offspring then update their covariance matrix taking into consideration information not only from their parent but also from all the successful offspring solutions of that generation. In the latest MO-CMA-ES variant, a new success criterion was introduced: an offspring is considered successful if it is present in the next parent population. This criterion is broader since offspring are not compared only with their respective parent, but rather, how well they perform in the entire population is also evaluated.

All existing MO-CMA-ES extensions are based on the $(1+\lambda)$-MO-CMA-ES which use populations of size one. Using larger populations could be beneficial however, since an increased spread and coverage of the Pareto front would be expected. Moreover, if all the population information content is used to drive optimization, the algorithm is less prone to getting stuck in sub-optimal local minima [1].

Many real-world problems have constraints, making the performance of BBO algorithms under different constraint-handling techniques important. All MO-CMA-ES variants previously introduced use a penalty term to handle box constraints. This approach lead to fast convergence speeds for certain benchmark problems [1, 2, 3, 4]. However, this approach has drawbacks. For example, it only performs well with box constraints since these, differently from general problem constraints, allow an easy mapping to the feasible space. Furthermore, infeasible solutions may be accepted in the elitist archive with this constraint handling technique.

The main objectives of this paper stem from the fact that all existing MO-CMA-ES variants use populations of size one and that only the penalty approach was used to handle constraints. Our first goal is to study the benefits of having a population-based MO-CMA-ES. To do so, we study a combination between a multi-objective optimization framework that was recently introduced [6] with the most general SO version of CMA-ES [5]. Our second goal is to assess the performance and robustness of the previously introduced MO-CMA-ES variants, the novel population-based MO-CMA-ES and the iMAMaLGaM algorithm [6] under different and more general constraint handling techniques.

The remainder of this paper is organized as follows: Section 2 briefly introduces the key concepts in MO optimization. Then, Section 3 describes the most popular MO-CMA-ES variants. Subsequently, in Section 4 a recently introduced general framework for extending population-based algorithms from single- to multi-objective optimization is described. Thereafter, iMAMaLGaM is described in Section 5. The novel population-based MO-CMA-ES is introduced in Section 6. Subsequently, the different constraint-handling techniques are briefly discussed in Section 7. The performance of the algorithms is tested in Section 9 on 6 benchmark problems and with different constraint-handling techniques. A discussion of the results is given in Section 10, while final conclusions are presented in Section 11.

2. MULTI-OBJECTIVE OPTIMIZATION

We assume to have m objective functions $f_i(\boldsymbol{x})$, $i \in \{1, 2, \ldots, m\}$ and, without loss of generality, we assume that the goal is to *minimize* all objectives. A solution $\boldsymbol{x}^1$ is said to (Pareto) *dominate* a solution $\boldsymbol{x}^2$ (denoted $\boldsymbol{x}^1 \succ \boldsymbol{x}^2$) if and only if $f_i(\boldsymbol{x}^1) \leq f_i(\boldsymbol{x}^2)$ holds for all $i \in \{1, 2, \ldots, m\}$ and $f_i(\boldsymbol{x}^1) < f_i(\boldsymbol{x}^2)$ holds for at least one $i \in \{1, 2, \ldots, m\}$. A *Pareto set* of size n is a set of solutions $\boldsymbol{x}^j$, $j \in \{1, 2, \ldots, n\}$ for which no solution dominates any other solution, i.e. there are no $j, k \in \{1, 2, \ldots, n\}$ such that $\boldsymbol{x}^j \succ \boldsymbol{x}^k$ holds. A *Pareto front* corresponding to a Pareto set is the set of all m-dimensional objective function values corresponding to the solutions, i.e. the set of all $\boldsymbol{f}(\boldsymbol{x}^j)$, $j \in \{1, 2, \ldots, n\}$. A solution $\boldsymbol{x}^1$ is said to be *Pareto optimal* if and only if there is no other $\boldsymbol{x}^2$ such that $\boldsymbol{x}^2 \succ \boldsymbol{x}^1$ holds. Further, the *optimal Pareto set* is the set of all Pareto-optimal solutions and the *optimal Pareto front* is the Pareto front that corresponds to the optimal Pareto set. We denote the optimal Pareto set by $\mathcal{P}_{\boldsymbol{S}}$ and the optimal Pareto front by $\mathcal{P}_{\boldsymbol{F}}$.

3. MO-CMA-ES

The four MO-CMA-ES variants used for testing are briefly explained here. For more in-depth explanations, the interested reader is referred to the original works [1, 2, 3, 4].

The so-called generational MO-CMA-ES was the first attempt to construct a MO CMA-ES [1]. A $(1+1)$-CMA-ES was used to this end. The idea is to maintain a population of λ_{MO} elitist $(1+1)$-MO-CMA-ES instances which are subjected to selection based on non-dominated sorting. The hypervolume measure, defined as the Lebesgue measure of the union of hypercubes in the objective space [7], was used as second level sorting criterion to rank individuals with the same level of non-dominance.

The so-called Steady-State Selection MO-CMA-ES was the second attempt. Although, this approach is very similar to the generational variant, in each generation, only one parent solution generates one offspring [2]. This variant is computationally more demanding than the generational variant since all the necessary computations to update the parent pool are performed for each new offspring.

The so-called Recombination MO-CMA-ES [3] was the first attempt to transfer information between successful offspring. Each individual adapts its own covariance matrix considering not only its parent but also all successful offspring generated in the same generation. The underlying idea is that individuals that are close in the search space are likely to be similar if a notion of continuity is assumed. Nonetheless, the influence of successful offspring is weighted by their distance to the solution to be updated.

In the Improved Step MO-CMA-ES [4], an offspring is said to be successful if it is present in the next parent population. This not only reduces computational complexity, but it also improves performance since the success criterion is broader since a solution is compared to a set of solutions instead of solely with the individual from which it originated.

4. MO OPTIMIZATION FRAMEWORK

A general framework for extending population-based algorithms from single- to multi-objective optimization was introduced in [6]. An overview of the multi-objective optimization framework is depicted in Figure 1. Next, a description of each step of the framework is given.

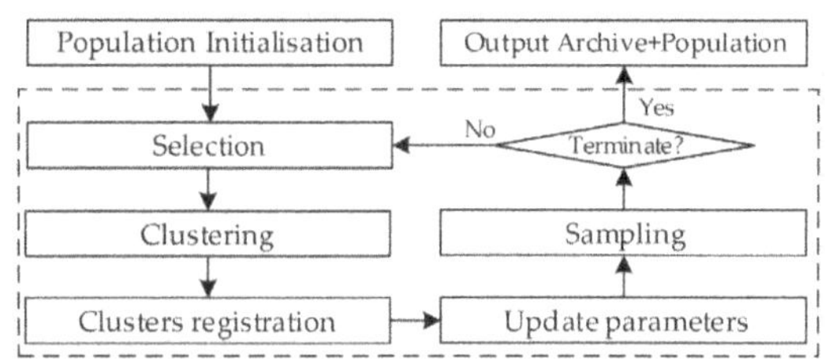

Figure 1: Flowchart of the multi-objective optimization framework.

4.1 Selection

Given a population of size n, $\lfloor \tau n \rfloor$ ($\tau \in [\frac{1}{n}, 1]$) solutions with the lowest domination ranks are selected. From the rank that crosses the boundary of $\lfloor \tau n \rfloor$ solutions a subset must be chosen. For this, the same nearest-neighbor heuristic is used as for selecting cluster leaders (see below).

4.2 Clustering

A nearest-neighbor heuristic is used to select $k - m$ cluster leaders, that are spread as well as possible, from the selection set. The first leader is chosen as a solution with a maximum value for a randomly chosen objective. For all remaining solutions, the nearest-neighbor distance is computed to the first leader and the most distant solution is chosen as the next leader. The distances for the remaining solutions are updated by checking whether the distance to the new leader is smaller than the currently stored nearest-neighbor distance. This procedure is repeated until all the necessary cluster leaders are selected.

Next, the distance from each solution in the selection set to the cluster leaders is computed. These leaders serve as initial cluster centroids in the subsequent application of the k-means clustering algorithm. After running k-means clustering, for each cluster, the c closest solutions are to the final cluster centroid assigned to it, ensuring that each cluster consists of exactly c solutions.

Because the final assignment is done independently for each cluster, some solutions may be assigned to multiple clusters whereas other solutions may not be assigned at all. The probability of this happening can be reduced by increasing the probability that the clusters will overlap by setting $c > \frac{1}{k}\lfloor \tau n \rfloor$. Specifically, we use $c = \frac{2}{k}\lfloor \tau n \rfloor$ as proposed in [6], resulting in substantial expected overlap between neighboring clusters. This increases the expected density in the usual void between the boundaries of clusters in the objective space, thereby increasing the probability of finding a good, uniform spread of solutions faster.

To ensure that spatial separation of the search bias is obtained in the objective space, clustering is performed on the basis of objective values. Specifically, the distances are based on *normalized* objective values to remove the influence of differently scaled objectives. To this end, first the minimum $f_i^{\min}$ and maximum $f_i^{\max}$ values for each objective i are computed from all selected solutions. A point in objective space $f(\boldsymbol{x})$ is then scaled linearly to the observed ranges, i.e. $(f(\boldsymbol{x}) - f_i^{\min})/(f_i^{\max} - f_i^{\min})$.

4.3 Cluster registration

An important part of state-of-the-art variation operators are adaptive mechanisms that span multiple generations such as the Anticipated Mean Shift (AMS) [6] approach in estimation of distribution algorithms (EDAs) and the evolution path and the estimation of the covariance matrix based on the mean shift in CMA-ES [5]. The performance of these mechanisms strongly depends on a correlation between the solution sets in subsequent generations. By re-applying clustering each generation however, in principle, there is no spatial relation between clusters in subsequent generations, i.e. the final enumeration of clusters does not guarantee that cluster i in generation $t-1$ is near cluster i in generation t.

To obtain a smooth evolution of clusters and their paths over subsequent generations, a registration between clusters in subsequent generations that minimizes the distance of the matched clusters is computed [6]. To do so, a matching of clusters is computed in subsequent generations that minimizes the distance between the matched clusters. Firstly, the distances between clusters in generations t and $t-1$ are calculated. The distance between two clusters is taken to be the sum of the smallest pair-wise distance between the cluster's solutions. Furthermore, the cluster distances are computed between the clusters in generation t and between the clusters in generation $t-1$. Then, $r \leq k$ clusters, from each generation, are repeatedly selected to be registered. To this end, first the two still-unregistered clusters in generation t are determined that are the farthest apart. One of these two clusters is randomly selected, as well, as the still-unregistered cluster in generation $t-1$ that is closest to it. The $r-1$ nearest neighbors of these clusters are then determined in the set of still-unregistered clusters of their respective generations, leading to two subsets of r clusters to be registered. To register subsets of clusters, all possible $r!$ permutations for the set of clusters in generation t are considered. The permutation for which the sum of the distances between the matched clusters is minimal, is selected. Subset registration is repeated until all clusters are registered. The reason for using subset registration with $r \leq k$ instead of $r = k$ is that subset registration is performed by enumerating permutations. As this number grows factorially fast, exhaustive optimization by enumeration can only be done for small values of r.

4.4 Parameter estimation

After explicit cluster registration, depending on the optimization algorithm being combined with the framework, the parameters that span multiple generations are updated.

4.5 Elitism

An elitist archive is maintained with all currently non-dominated solutions. If the objectives are real-valued, there will be infinitely many non-dominated solutions possible. To prevent the archive from growing to extreme sizes, the objective space is discretized into hypercubes. Only one solution per hypercube is allowed in the archive. Newly generated solutions are compared to the solutions in the archive. If a new solution is dominated by any archive solution, it is not entered. If a new solution is not dominated, it is added to the archive if the hypercube that it resides in does not already contain a solution or if it dominates that particular solution. When a new solution is entered all archive solutions that are dominated by it are removed.

Keeping elitist solutions in the population can improve convergence. Therefore, each solution in the elitist archive is associated with its nearest cluster. The distance is computed between the cluster mean to the archive solution. For each cluster, at most $\frac{1}{k}\lfloor \tau n \rfloor$ of its associated elitist solutions are copied to the population. If there are more elitist solutions, the same nearest-neighbor heuristic is used as in selection. Finally, each cluster generates equally many solutions. Depending on how many elitist solutions were copied to the population, at least $n - \lfloor \tau n \rfloor$ new solutions are generated.

4.6 New aspects

In this work several changes are made to the optimization framework presented in [6]. The modifications are as follows:

- The k-means algorithm is not used because the clusters means tend to drift "inwards" in the selection set, leading to reduced search effort in the vicinity of the Pareto extremes. Instead, the clusters are grown directly around the leaders chosen from the selection set;
- The previous framework included m external, independent SO optimizers whose best solutions were infused into the MO population. Instead, m clusters are added to the MO population that are constructed by selecting solutions from the population in a single-objective manner. This effectively keeps SO pressure on the Pareto extremes while ensuring that this pressure in terms of solutions overlaps with the MO population.

With external SO optimizers there is a larger probability of the Pareto extremes becoming fully disconnected from the population and Pareto front as governed by the MO population;

- An adaptive gridding technique was employed for the elitist archive [8]. The main advantage of this is that only a target size for the elitist archive needs to be specified while all the gridding details are automatically handled. Initially, all solutions are accepted in the archive. After an upper bound size is crossed, a grid adaptation process is triggered to ensure that the number of elitist solutions stays in the vicinity of the target size. This method provides the same convergence guarantee as the static grid approach, only potentially losing convergence properties when the grid is redefined. Furthermore, as shown in [8] grid adaptations do not occur often during a run and no loss in performance was observed in experiments;
- Solutions that share an elitist hypercube and do not dominate the already existing solution found there but further extend the front are accepted. Such solutions were previously discarded. This feature guarantees that the front is always extended since the granularity of the grid plays no part in the process.

5. IMAMALGAM

The following is a brief description of the MO-EDA that we compare our results to. The MO-EDA follows the above framework and was previously called iMAMaLGaM-X$^+$, indicative of being an extension of an earlier version called iMAMaLGaM-X and the SO-EDA iAMaLGaM (the internal mechanisms of which are used in each cluster in the multi-objective framework). For a more in-depth explanation the interested reader is referred to literature [6, 9]. In the remainder however, for simplicity, we shall generally use the acronym iMAMaLGaM to indicate the framework-leveraged MO version of iAMaLGaM. Moreover, we shall use iMAMaLGaM^{Old} to denote the use of the previously existing framework without the above mentioned new aspects.

After clustering and explicit cluster registration, a Gaussian distribution is estimated in each of the clusters and adapted using the combination of AMS, SDR and AVS as in [6]. The AMS is computed as the difference between the means of subsequent generations, i.e. $\hat{\boldsymbol{\mu}}^{\text{Shift}}(t) = \hat{\boldsymbol{\mu}}(t) - \hat{\boldsymbol{\mu}}(t-1)$. If the AMS-altered solutions violate box constraints, a shrinking factor is used to keep the solution feasible. Specifically $\alpha 100\%$ of the newly sampled solutions are moved in the direction of the AMS: $\boldsymbol{x} \leftarrow \boldsymbol{x} + 2\hat{\boldsymbol{\mu}}^{\text{Shift}}(t)$. The rationale is that solutions so changed are further down the slope. Selecting those solutions as well as solutions not changed by AMS aligns the distribution estimate better with the direction of improvement. In a population of size n where $\lfloor \tau n \rfloor$ solutions are selected, n^{elitist} solutions are maintained and $n - n^{\text{elitist}}$ new solutions are generated, proportioning the selected solutions perfectly between unaltered and AMS-altered solutions requires $\alpha(n - n^{\text{elitist}}) = \frac{1}{2}\tau n$ and thus $\alpha = \frac{1}{2}\tau \frac{n}{n - n^{\text{elitist}}}$.

By estimating the distribution only using the selected solutions of the current generation, the density contours can become aligned with directions in which only solutions of similar quality can be found. Methods that only adaptively scale the covariance matrix, such as SDR-AVS, do no help much as it almost solely increases search effort in the futile direction perpendicular to the direction of improvement. In SDR-AVS, a distribution multiplier $c^{\text{Multiplier}}$ is maintained by which the covariance matrix is multiplied in each generation. This multiplier is scaled up if improvements are found that are more than standard deviation away from the mean and scaled down if no improvements are found.

In iMAMaLGaM memory decay is used in estimating the covariance matrix and the AMS in generation t as follows:

$$\hat{\boldsymbol{\Sigma}}(t) \quad = (1-\eta^{\boldsymbol{\Sigma}})\hat{\boldsymbol{\Sigma}}(t-1) + \eta^{\boldsymbol{\Sigma}} \tfrac{1}{|\boldsymbol{\mathcal{S}}|} \textstyle\sum_{i=0}^{|\boldsymbol{\mathcal{S}}|-1} (\boldsymbol{\mathcal{S}}_i - \hat{\boldsymbol{\mu}}(t))(\boldsymbol{\mathcal{S}}_i - \hat{\boldsymbol{\mu}}(t))^T$$

$$\hat{\boldsymbol{\mu}}^{\text{Shift}}(t) = (1-\eta^{\text{Shift}})\hat{\boldsymbol{\mu}}^{\text{Shift}}(t-1) + \eta^{\text{Shift}} (\hat{\boldsymbol{\mu}}(t) - \hat{\boldsymbol{\mu}}(t-1)).$$

Values for the learning-rate parameters $\eta^{\boldsymbol{\Sigma}}$ and η^{Shift} were determined empirically [9]. The cluster sizes computed from the selected solutions were set according to guidelines from recent literature on SO [9]: $n^{cluster} = \tau 10 l^{0.5}$.

6. POPULATION-BASED MO-CMA-ES

A novel population-based MO-CMA-ES was obtained by combining the most robust and general CMA-ES variant [5], $(\mu/\mu_W, \lambda)$-CMA-ES, with the MO optimization framework. For the solutions in the single-objective clusters, domination ranks are assigned in a linear way, with the best solution getting assigned rank one, similar to the $(\mu/\mu_W, \lambda)$-CMA-ES strategy. For the remaining clusters, the ranks are determined through a non-dominated sorting scheme per cluster.

The size of each individual cluster is an important parameter. Since recombination may smooth the effect of selecting erroneous solutions, increasing solely λ is inferior to randomly generating new solutions, whereas increasing both μ and λ are superior [5]. The cluster size was defined as two times larger than the default value of the population size of the single objective $(\mu/\mu_W, \lambda)$-CMA-ES:

$$\text{cluster size} = \lfloor 2\tau \times (4 + \lfloor 3 \ln n \rfloor) \rfloor \qquad (1)$$

This was done to maintain the cluster size similar to the population size given as guideline [5] since $\tau = 0.5$. Moreover, all the remaining internal parameters of CMA-ES were also kept the same as the standard guidelines [5].

7. CONSTRAINT HANDLING

Four different constraint handling techniques were implemented in order to assess their impact on the performance of the algorithms under study:

- Resampling [10]: a newly generated solution is resampled if it lies outside the variables boundaries. After 100 trials, a new solution is randomly generated;
- Constraint domination: for each constraint, a measure of the amount by which the constraint is violated, is used. The total constraint-violation value is the sum over all constraints. For box constraints, the constraint-violation value is the distance to the closest feasible solution. Solutions are then ranked using constraint-domination ranking whereby a solution with a smaller constraint violation is always preferred. If two solutions are both feasible, the one with the lowest domination rank is performed;
- Penalty term: if a solution violates box constraints, the closest feasible solution is evaluated. A penalty

term is then added to the fitness value. This has been the constraint handling technique of choice in previous MO-CMA-ES tests [1, 2, 3, 4].

- Global Competitive Ranking [11]: this ranking approach aims to create a balance between objective values and constraint violations, allowing both feasible and infeasible solutions to preside in the population. In this way, the algorithm may approach the optimal front from both the feasible and the infeasible sides, leading, in theory, to faster convergence speeds. A weighing factor, P_f, sets the relevance of one ranking scheme compared to the other. If $P_f = 0$, this scheme behaves as constraint domination, whereas if $P_f = 1$ the constraint violations are neglected and ranking is purely based on fitness. A value of $P_f = 0.45$ was used since it is known to provide good results [11].

The boundary repair technique, by which variables are set to their closest bound, in case they fall outside of the allowed range, was not considered. Key reason is that some of the artificial benchmark functions that we consider have optimal Pareto fronts which are obtained by setting all variables to one of the bounds while only one variable defines the front size and shape. In this way, if boundary repair is carried, infeasible solutions may be altered and placed automatically in the optimal front, biasing the results.

8. EXPERIMENTS

For all benchmark problems the algorithms were allowed one million function evaluations (per objective). However, if the distance to the front, as measured using the performance indicator introduced in 8.2, does not improve at least 10^{-10} after 50 generations, the algorithm is stopped and convergence is deemed to be too slow.

Twenty clusters were used in iMAMaLGaM since it was previously found to provide good results [6]. For registration, two subsets of seven clusters ($r = 7$) and one of six clusters ($r = 6$) were used. A similar number of clusters was used for the population-based MO-CMA-ES. The cluster sizes of the population-based MO-CMA-ES were 10 and 14 for problem dimensions of 10 and 30, respectively. For iMAMaLGaM the cluster sizes were 11 and 19, respectively.

For all the MO-CMA-ES instances from literature, the population size was set to $\lambda = 20$ and the offspring number was set to one per population. The population size was chosen to lead to a similar number of estimated distributions, per generation, in all algorithms. In the case of the steady-state algorithm, the variant where all the population members are potential parents was selected [2].

The selection percentile was set to $\tau = 0.35$ for iMAMaLGaM. For the population-based MO-CMA-ES a value of $\tau = 0.5$ was used since it is the SO-$(\mu/\mu_W, \lambda)$-CMA-ES guideline, which corresponds to a maximal step-size for a given λ [12].

The desired archive size was set to 1000 solutions.

8.1 Test suite

The definitions of the problems in our test suite are presented in Table 1. We used the well-known problems ZDT_i, $i \in \{1, 2, 3, 6\}$. The IRs of the ZDT_i problems are also constraints. For more details about these functions, see [13]. The final two problems are labeled BD_i, $i \in \{1, 2\}$ and were taken from [6]. Both problems make use of the Rosenbrock function. Premature convergence on this function is likely without proper induction of the structure of the search space. Function BD_2 is harder than BD_1 since the objective functions overlap in all variables instead of only in x_0. Furthermore, the IR of x_0 in function BD_1 is also a constraint. Finally, we have scaled the objectives of BD_2 to ensure that the optimum of all problems is in approximately the same range. By doing so, using the same value-to-reach for the $\boldsymbol{D}_{\boldsymbol{\mathcal{P}_F} \to \mathcal{S}}$ indicator (explained in the next Section) corresponds to a similar front quality on all problems.

Name	Objectives	IR
ZDT_1	$f_0 = x_0, \quad f_1 = \gamma\left(1 - \sqrt{f_0/\gamma}\right)$ $\gamma = 1 + 9\left(\sum_{i=1}^{l-1} x_i/(l-1)\right)$	$[0;1]^{30}$ $(l = 30)$
ZDT_2	$f_0 = x_0, \quad f_1 = \gamma\left(1 - (f_0/\gamma)^2\right)$ $\gamma = 1 + 9\left(\sum_{i=1}^{l-1} x_i/(l-1)\right)$	$[0;1]^{30}$ $(l = 30)$
ZDT_3	$f_0 = x_0, \quad f_1 = \gamma\left(1 - \sqrt{f_0/\gamma} - (f_0/\gamma)\sin(10\pi f_0)\right)$ $\gamma = 1 + 9\left(\sum_{i=1}^{l-1} x_i/(l-1)\right)$	$[0;1]^{30}$ $(l = 30)$
ZDT_6	$f_0 = 1 - e^{-4x_0}\sin^6(6\pi x_0), \quad f_1 = \gamma\left(1 - (f_0/\gamma)^2\right)$ $\gamma = 1 + 9\left(\sum_{i=1}^{l-1} x_i/(l-1)\right)^{0.25}$	$[0;1]^{10}$ $(l = 10)$
BD_1	$f_0 = x_0, \quad f_1 = 1 - x_0 + \gamma$ $\gamma = \sum_{i=1}^{l-2}\left(100(x_{i+1} - x_i^2)^2 + (1 - x_i)^2\right)$	$[0;1]\times$ $[-5.12;5.12]^9$ $(l = 10)$
BD_2^{s}	$f_0 = \frac{1}{l}\sum_{i=0}^{l-1} x_i^2$ $f_1 = \frac{1}{l-1}\sum_{i=0}^{l-2}\left(100(x_{i+1} - x_i^2)^2 + (1 - x_i)^2\right)$	$[-5.12;5.12]^{10}$ $(l = 10)$

Table 1: The MO problem test suite.

8.2 Measuring performance

We consider the Pareto set that can be computed from the elitist archive combined with the population upon termination to be the approximation set, denoted $\mathcal{S}$. To measure performance, the $\boldsymbol{D}_{\boldsymbol{\mathcal{P}_F} \to \mathcal{S}}$ performance indicator is computed. This performance indicator computes the average distance over all points in the optimal Pareto front $\boldsymbol{\mathcal{P}_F}$ to the nearest point in $\mathcal{S}$:

$$\boldsymbol{D}_{\boldsymbol{\mathcal{P}_F} \to \mathcal{S}}(\mathcal{S}) = \frac{1}{|\boldsymbol{\mathcal{P}_F}|} \sum_{\boldsymbol{f}^1 \in \boldsymbol{\mathcal{P}_F}} \min_{\boldsymbol{f}^0 \in \mathcal{S}} \{d(\boldsymbol{f}^0, \boldsymbol{f}^1)\} \qquad (2)$$

where $\boldsymbol{f}$ is a point in objective space and $d(\cdot,\cdot)$ computes Euclidean distance. A smaller $\boldsymbol{D}_{\boldsymbol{\mathcal{P}_F} \to \mathcal{S}}$ value is preferable and a value of 0 is obtained if and only if the approximation set and the optimal Pareto front are identical. This indicator is useful for evaluating performance if the optimum is known because it describes how well the optimal Pareto front is covered and thereby represents an intuitive trade-off between the diversity of $\mathcal{S}$ and its proximity (i.e. closeness to the optimal Pareto front). Even if all points in $\mathcal{S}$ are on the optimal Pareto front the indicator is not minimized unless the solutions in the approximation set are spread out perfectly. Because the optimal Pareto front may be continuous, there are infinitely many solutions possible on the optimal Pareto front. Therefore, we computed 5000 uniformly sampled solutions along the optimal Pareto front to use as a discretized version of $\boldsymbol{\mathcal{P}_F}$ for a high-quality approximation.

For the problems in our test-suite, given the ranges of the objectives for the optimal Pareto front configurations, a value of 0.01 for the $\boldsymbol{D}_{\boldsymbol{\mathcal{P}_F} \to \mathcal{S}}$ indicator corresponds to fronts that are close to the optimal Pareto front.

9. RESULTS

The results are averaged over 100 independent runs and shown in Figure 2. For each algorithm, averages are shown both for successful and unsuccessful runs, giving double occurrences of lines if some runs were unsuccessful. All combinations of algorithms and constraint-handling techniques are shown, except for iMAMaLGaM^{Old} for which results are only shown with resampling. The differences between the old and new versions of iMAMaLGaM have a positive, but small effect in terms of convergence, leading to similar differences when other constraint-handling techniques are used and making resampling sufficiently illustrative of the impact of the new aspects described in Section 4.6.

9.1 Unconstrained problems

None of the MO-CMA-ES implementations from literature were able to solve unconstrained problem BD_2^{s} as the algorithms were able to find only one of the Pareto extremes, solving the Sphere function. Because solving Sphere is much simpler than solving Rosenbrock, the population is pulled quickly toward one end of the Pareto front. Due to the lack of pressure to extend the Pareto front at the edges, i.e. pressure toward improving individual objectives as is present in the MO framework from which population-based MO-CMA-ES and the iMAMaLGaM variants are derived, it is hard for existing MO-CMA-ES implementations to find the other Pareto extreme, resulting in a very low convergence speed which led to an early stop of the optimization run. The population-based MO-CMA-ES and the iMAMaLGaM variants did solve BD_2^{s}.

9.2 Constrained problems

Besides BD_2^{s}, all benchmark functions are constrained due to the existence of box constraints.

9.2.1 Resampling

None of the MO-CMA-ES algorithms were able to converge to the optimal Pareto front of any of the benchmark functions with this constraint-handling technique. An important factor here is that MO-CMA-ES does not have the iMAMaLGaM mechanism that employs a shrinking factor when AMS is applied to better approach constraints. Consequently, MO-CMA-ES has intrinsic difficulties to approach variable boundaries without triggering resampling, whereby a randomly generated solution is created and all its internal parameters are set to guideline values. The knowledge previously gathered during the optimization run is discarded, leading to very slow convergence speeds and/or, as in this case, high failure rates.

The population-based MO-CMA-ES demonstrated to be more robust than the MO-CMA-ES instances from literature, obtaining better results on all problems with exception for the BD_1 problem. Moreover, it was able to converge faster than iMAMaLGaM on ZDT_1.

iMAMaLGaM with the new aspects presented convergence speeds at least as good as the old version in all problems. Furthermore, iMAMaLGaM was the only algorithm able to solve all problems.

9.2.2 Constraint domination

No MO-CMA-ES variant obtained successful runs in any of the problems with this constraint-handling technique, as opposed to iMAMaLGaM, which was again able to solve all problems. iMAMaLGaM did present convergence speeds when compared to the use of resampling. This may explained by the fact that, with constraint domination, the shrinking factor of the AMS technique was not applied since the variables were considered to be unbounded. Moreover, iMAMaLGaM algorithm presented some unsuccessful runs for 3 problems.

9.2.3 Penalty function

All the algorithms converged to the ZDT optimal fronts extremely fast. This is in agreement with previous literature studies [1, 2, 3, 4]. For all ZDT problems, the solutions on the optimal front have their variables set at their lowest boundary, besides the first variable which dictates the size and shape of the optimal front. With the penalty function, the benchmark functions are not evaluated with infeasible solutions but rather the closest feasible solution in parameter space is evaluated. Therefore, this strategy brings advantages to the algorithms to approach the optimal Pareto front in these test problems. However, for all ZDT problems and algorithms, the final elitist archives were filled with mostly infeasible solutions. The reason for this is that all variables have box constraints and, once again, it is only the first variable that sets the size and shape of the Pareto front. In this way, solutions with all negative variables besides the first will be evaluated in the optimal Pareto front, entering, in this way, in the elitist archive.

Regarding then the only other constrained problem in our test suite, BD_1, none of the MO-CMA-ES instances from literature were able to solve it. Differently from the ZDT problems, only the first variable is bounded. In this way, if a solution is infeasible, the evaluated solution will not be placed in the optimal Pareto front since only the first variable is altered. The population-based MO-CMA-ES and iMAMaLGaM variants demonstrated to be more robust and were able to solve all problems. Moreover, the final elitist archives were mostly filled with feasible solutions when BD_1 was solved. The first variable is the only one that has box constraints and it is also the only variable that sets the size and shape of the optimal Pareto front. Infeasible solutions present in the final elitist archive of a successful run, are always mapped only to one of the optimal Pareto extremes. Therefore, the first variable, in the elitist archive solutions, has to vary along its entire range.

9.2.4 Global Ranking Procedure

The results were found to be similar to constraint domination. None of the MO-CMA-ES variants were able to solve any of the benchmark functions. iMAMaLGaM performed better with this constraint-handling technique than with constrained domination on ZDT_1 since all runs were considered successful. On the other hand, similar to constraint domination, some unsuccessful runs for both ZDT_2 and ZDT_3 problems were found.

10. DISCUSSION

The CMA-ES-based MO algorithms that we experimented with, showed a higher susceptibility to non-smooth search-space adaptations created by the constraint domination and global ranking approaches to constraint handling. From the results that we obtained, we can conclude that these constraint-handling techniques do not suit CMA-ES-based approaches very well.

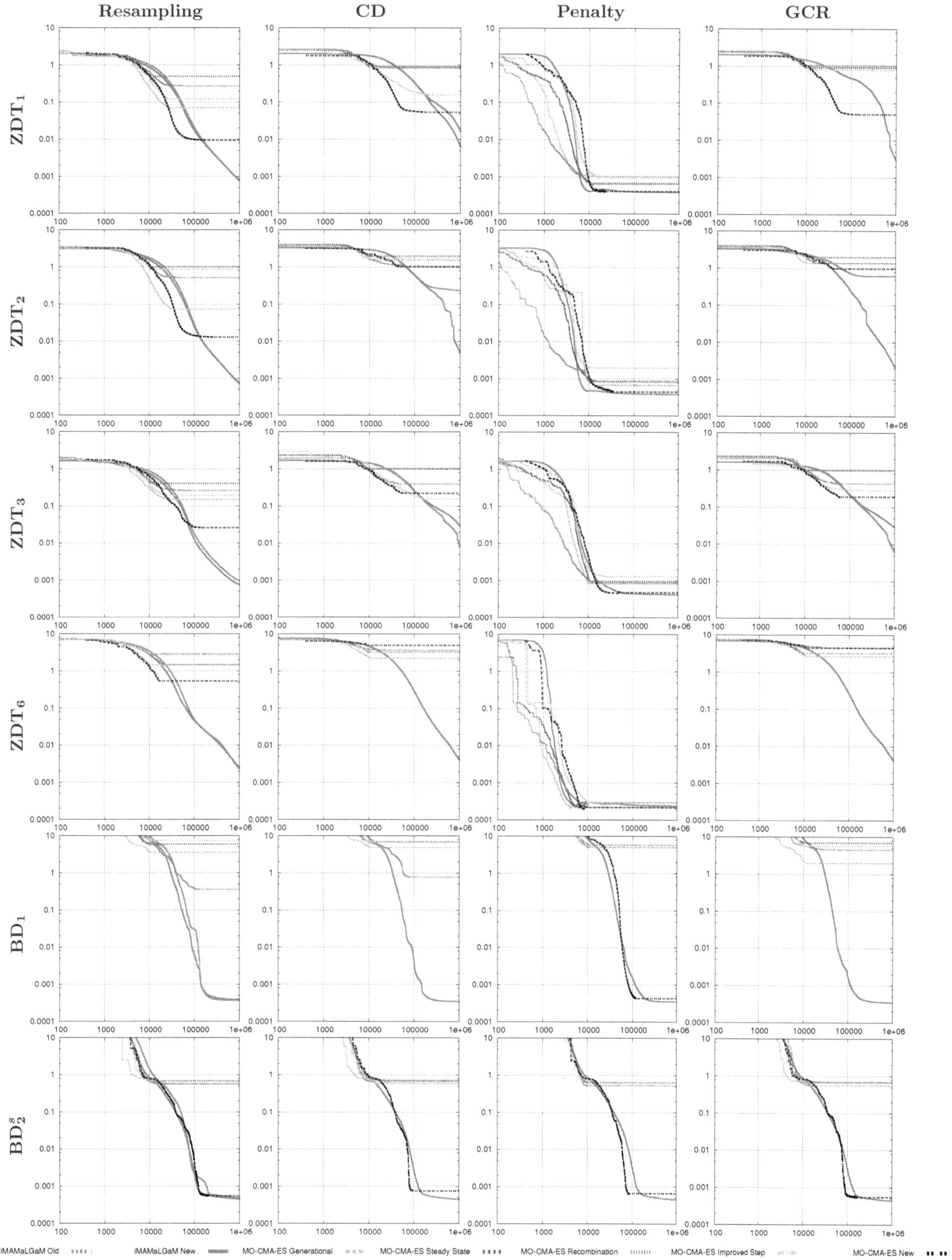

Figure 2: Convergence of all algorithms and all constraint-handling techniques on all problems, averaged over 100 runs. Horizontal axis: number of evaluations (both objectives per evaluation). Vertical axis: $D_{\mathcal{P}_F \rightarrow \mathcal{S}}$.

When the penalty term approach was used, all CMA-ES-based algorithms presented very fast convergence speeds for all ZDT problems. This may explained by the fact that this constraint-handling technique does not alter the smoothness of the functions. It is known that CMA-ES is a very powerful SO optimizer for smooth functions [5]. The final elitist archives contained almost only infeasible solutions, however. Although the solutions were slowly moving toward to the feasible area of the search space, it was very difficult to actually enter it. The same holds for iMAMaLGaM, clearly making this a property of the penalty term approach itself. Therefore, if an elitist archive filled with only feasible solutions is desired, this technique is not advised.

The constraint domination and the penalty term techniques enforce different ways in which the search process approaches the optimal Pareto front. With constraint domination, the front is approached from the feasible side, whereas with the penalty term the front is approached from the infeasible side. The global competitive ranking approach is an interesting technique since it allows the algorithms to approach the optimal front from both sides. However, our results do not support any substantial performance improvement over the use of constraint domination alone.

Although in the cluster registration procedure the distance between clusters in subsequent generations is minimized, it is not guaranteed that the cluster means, in subsequent generations, are close to each other. Such phenomenon demonstrated to be counterproductive for the proposed population-based MO-CMA-ES for the benchmark function BD_1. Since the update of the internal parameters, covariance matrix and sigma, depend on the mean shift in subsequent generations, high values may be obtained for these parameters, resulting in erratic behavior. Overall however, the novel population-based MO-CMA-ES was found to be more robust than existing MO-CMA-ES variants.

The population-based MO-CMA-ES presented faster convergence speeds than iMAMaLGaM on smooth functions. This was expected since for single-objective optimization of smooth functions, CMA-ES outperforms iAMaLGaM. However, iMAMaLGaM was found to be able to reach smaller distances to the optimal Pareto fronts. It is therefore debatable which algorithm performs best. If the number of evaluations are the most important criterion and a non-disruptive constraint-handling technique can be designed and used, one might say that population-based MO-CMA-ES is preferable, whereas otherwise iMAMaLGaM can be preferred.

For future work it would be interesting to extend the shrinking factor in the AMS technique to also work with the more general case of constraint domination. One goal in this paper was to test the multi-objective CMA-ES-based algorithms with the same number of distributions as the iMAMaLGaM variants. As future work, it would be interesting to also assess the performance impact if larger population sizes are used. Furthermore, problems with than two objectives should be used in future work and the correlation between the number of objectives and required number of clusters should be assessed.

11. SUMMARY AND CONCLUSIONS

In this paper we introduced a novel population-based MO-CMA-ES algorithm. Experimental results demonstrate that the proposed approach is, in general, more robust when compared to the multi-objective extensions of CMA-ES that were previously introduced in literature.

The performance of several evolutionary multi-objective optimization algorithms under different constraint-handling techniques was assessed. The algorithms based on CMA-ES demonstrated to be very sensitive to the technique applied. On the other hand, iMAMaLGaM showed to be more robust since it was able to solve all problems with all constraint handling techniques.

12. REFERENCES

[1] C. Igel, N. Hansen, and S. Roth, "Covariance matrix adaptation for multi-objective optimization," *Evolutionary Computation*, vol. 15, no. 1, pp. 1–28, 2007.

[2] C. Igel, T. Suttorp, and N. Hansen, "Steady-state selection and efficient covariance matrix update in the multi-objective cma-es," in *Proceedings of the Fourth International Conference on Evolutionary Multi-Criterion Optimization*, Springer, Ed., 2007, pp. 171–185.

[3] T. Voß, N. Hansen, and C. Igel, "Recombination for learning strategy parameters in the mo-cma-es," in *Fifth International Conf. on Evol. Multi-Criterion Optimization (EMO 2009)*. Springer-Verlag, 2009, pp. 155–168.

[4] T. Voß, N. Hansen, and C. Igel, "Improved step size adaptation for the mo-cma-es," in *Proceedings of the 12th annual conference on Genetic and Evol. Comp.* Portland, United States: ACM, 2010, pp. 487–494.

[5] N. Hansen and S. Kern, "Evaluating the cma evolution strategy on multimodal test functions," in *Parallel Problem Solving from Nature (PPSN VIII)*, ser. LNCS, X. Yao *et al.*, Eds., vol. 3242. Springer, 2004, pp. 282–291.

[6] P. A. N. Bosman and T. Alderliesten, "Incremental gaussian model-building in multi-objective edas with an application to deformable image registration," in *Proceedings of the Genetic and Evolutionary Computation Conference - GECCO-2012*. New York: ACM Press, 2012, pp. 241–248.

[7] E. Zitzler and L. Thiele, "Multiobjective optimization using evolutionary algorithms - a comparative case study," in *Parallel Problem Solving from Nature (PPSN-V)*. Springer Berlin Heidelberg, 1998, vol. 1498, pp. 292–301.

[8] N. Luong and P. A. N. Bosman, "Elitist archiving for multi-objective evolutionary algorithms: To adapt or not to adapt," in *Parallel Problem Solving from Nature (PPSN XII)*. Berlin: Springer-Verlag, 2012, pp. 72–81.

[9] P. A. N. Bosman, "On empirical memory design, faster selection of bayesian factorizations and parameter-free gaussian edas," in *Proceedings of the Genetic and Evolutionary Computation Conference - GECCO-2009*. New York: ACM Press, 2009, pp. 389–396.

[10] A. Oyman, K. Deb, and H.-G. Beyer, "An alternative constraint handling method for evolution strategies," in *Evolutionary Computation, 1999. CEC 99. Proceedings of the 1999 Congress on*, vol. 1, 1999.

[11] T. P. Runarsson and X. Yao, "Constrained evolutionary optimization - the penalty function approach," 2002.

[12] H.-G. Beyer, "Evolutionary algorithms in noisy environments: theoretical issues and guidelines for practice," *Computer Methods in Applied Mechanics and Engineering*, vol. 186, no. 24, pp. 239–267, 2000.

[13] E. Zitzler, K. Deb, and L. Thiele, "Comparison of multiobjective evolutionary algorithms: Empirical results," *Evol. Comput.*, vol. 8, no. 2, pp. 173–195, Jun. 2000.

Use of Explicit Memory in the Dynamic Traveling Salesman Problem

Renato Tinós
Department of Computing and Mathematics
University of São Paulo
Ribeirão Preto, SP, Brazil
rtinos@ffclrp.usp.br

Darrell Whitley
Department of Computer Science
Colorado State University
Fort Collins, CO, USA
whitley@cs.colostate.edu

Adele Howe
Department of Computer Science
Colorado State University
Fort Collins, CO, USA
howe@cs.colostate.edu

ABSTRACT

In the dynamic traveling salesman problem (DTSP), the weights and vertices of the graph representing the TSP are allowed to change during the optimization. This work first discusses some issues related to the use of evolutionary algorithms in the DTSP. When efficient algorithms used for the static TSP are applied with restart in the DTSP, we observe that only some edges are generally inserted in and removed from the best solutions after the changes. This result indicates a possible beneficial use of memory approaches, usually employed in cyclic dynamic environments. We propose a memory approach and a hybrid approach that combines our memory approach with the elitism-based immigrants genetic algorithm (EIGA). We compare these two algorithms to four existing algorithms and show that memory approaches can be beneficial for the DTSP with random changes.

Categories and Subject Descriptors

I.2.8 [**Artificial Intelligence**]: [Problem Solving, Control Methods, and Search]

Keywords

Dynamic Environments, Traveling Salesman Problem, Memory Schemes, Evolutionary Algorithms

1. INTRODUCTION

In the last decade, interest has been increasing in the area of evolutionary dynamic optimization (EDO) (Cruz et al. [4] and Nguyen et al. [14] offer excellent surveys). In a dynamic optimization problem (DOP), the fitness landscape may be modified at intervals, and as a consequence, the dynamic problem can be viewed as a sequence of stationary instances of an optimization problem [14].

One of the benchmark problems for EDO algorithms is a dynamic version of the traveling salesman problem (TSP). An instance of the static TSP is defined by a complete weighted graph $G(V, E)$, where $V = \{v_1, v_2, \ldots, v_n\}$ is a set of n vertices (representing cities in the classic TSP) and E contains edges between every pair of vertices in V. An undirected graph defines a symmetric TSP, while a directed graph defines an asymmetric TSP. Each edge $e_{i,j} \in E$ between vertices $v_i, v_j \in V$ is associated with a weight $w_{i,j} \in \mathbb{R}^+$, indicating, in the classic TSP, the distance or travel cost between two cities. Only Hamiltonian cycles in G are allowed as solutions for the TSP. Considering v_{x_1} as the fixed start and final vertex, then the evaluation of a particular solution $\mathbf{x} = [x_1, x_2, \ldots, x_n]^{\mathrm{T}} \in X$, specifying a permutation on $n-1$ vertices, is given by:

$$f(\mathbf{x}) = w_{x_n,x_1} + \sum_{i=1}^{n-1} w_{x_i,x_{i+1}} \tag{1}$$

The objective of optimization for the static TSP is to find $\mathbf{x} \in X$ such that $f(\mathbf{x})$ is minimized.

In the dynamic TSP (DTSP), the set of vertices V and/or the weight matrix $\mathbf{W}$ can be modified while optimization is ongoing. In some research (e.g., [5, 10, 17, 13, 12]), only $\mathbf{W}$ is modified. For example, in [5], $w_{i,j}$ indicates the automotive travel time between cities v_i and v_j and the changes in $\mathbf{W}$ are caused by traffic. Simões and Costa [17] present a DTSP based on the scheme proposed in [21], where an edge of the best current solution is increased and then decreased by a given factor. In this case, the DOP has the time-linkage property, i.e., knowing the current best solution influences the future dynamics of the problem [14]. In [10], the DTSP arises from a network routing configuration problem with $n-1$ land-based stations and one artificial satellite with known periodic orbit. In this case, $w_{i,j}$ represents the distance between points v_i and v_j, which can be a land-based station or the artificial satellite, and the dynamism of the problem is caused by changing the position of the satellite, i.e., only the edges related to the vertex representing the satellite are changed during the optimization procedure.

Other research (e.g., [7, 21, 11]) allows the set of vertices V also to be modified. For example, in [11], the number of vertices or the weights between two vertices can change with a fixed probability.

Because changes in the DTSP are detectable, we ask: Can we consider the DTSP as a series of unrelated static instances and use efficient algorithms already developed for the static TSP? In other words, because the DTSP can be viewed as a sequence of static instances of the TSP (Figure 1), we ask if it is better to restart the optimization process after each change instead of using the knowledge

GECCO'14, July 12–16, 2014, Vancouver, BC, Canada.
Copyright 2014 ACM 978-1-4503-2662-9/14/07 ...$15.00.
http://dx.doi.org/10.1145/2576768.2598247.

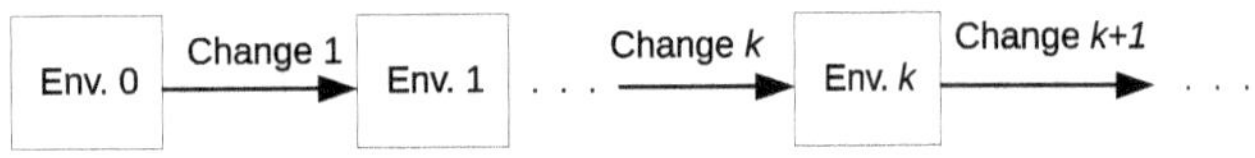

Figure 1: The DTSP as a sequence of static instances of the TSP, where each environment is created by changing the previous environment.

obtained before the change, which is usually done by most of the EDO algorithms. Section 2 explores this issue.

In Section 3, we investigate two types of changes in the DTSP. From simulations of a state-of-art heuristic for the static TSP applied to DTSP for both types of changes, we observe an interesting behavior: only some edges, from all possible edges, are inserted in and removed from the best solutions after the changes.

We hypothesize that explicit memory, which is used often by algorithms developed for dynamic environments in the case of cyclic changes, can be useful for the DTSP even in the case of random changes. A memory approach for the DTSP is then proposed in Section 4. A related issue is how to store and retrieve past solutions when the vertices of the TSP change. We propose a mechanism for this issue in Section 4. Section 5 presents an experimental comparison of memory approaches and other approaches for DOPs.

2. THE DYNAMIC TSP (DTSP)

In the DTSP, if the change is considerable, we can treat the landscapes before and after the change as two unrelated static instances of the TSP. However, if the change is small, the two graphs representing the problem before and after the change are similar and the knowledge obtained before the change can be employed to search for the solutions of the problem after the change.

The interval between changes in the DTSP leads to the following trade-off: Is it better to restart a new optimization process after the change in the problem or to continue the optimization process with the knowledge previously obtained? To address our question, it is important to check if the interval between the changes is adequate to find a good solution and whether information about good solutions can profitably be carried over to the changed problem.

If the application is the *classic TSP* (the lowest cost circuit for a vehicle around a set of cities or physically disparate locations), the restart approach with methods currently used for the static TSP is the best option. The reasons are: i) Current exact methods to solve TSPs, e.g., Concorde [3], are capable of finding a global optimum for instances of the symmetric TSP with hundreds of cities *in seconds*. In fact, some GPS devices incorporate exact solvers for the TSP with a few points [3]. ii) The change interval is generally large, when compared to the optimization time, for the classic TSP. For example, Google Maps updates traffic data generally every 15 minutes, which is clearly less than is needed by Concorde to find the new best solution even for problems with hundreds of cities. iii) Real-world classic TSPs like pick-ups and deliveries problems are small-scale TSPs [3]. Thus, EDO seems to be more appropriate for other dynamic vehicle routing problems (VRPs) where routes for more than one vehicle should be found.

However, DTSP can also encompass applications, such as robotics and telecommunication, where the change interval is short relative to the computational time required by exact solvers. For example, in [6], TSP algorithms are used to optimize the order in which a robotic manipulator inspects points in an object. The *atex* instances of the asymmetric TSP [2] derive from robotic motion planning. In [1], methods to solve the TSP are applied to minimize communication costs and energy consumption among sensors where each edge of the graph represents the average number of transmissions required to successfully complete a delivery. TSPLIB [15] also presents asymmetric TSPs which could have rapidly changing dynamic versions, such as scheduling and sequencing problems. Soler et al. [18] present a polynomial transformation of the VRP with time windows and time-dependent weights into an asymmetric TSP; an exact solver is then used to find the optimal solutions, which requires hours or days of computation for some instances.

We consider two types of the DTSP. In both, because the weight matrix $\mathbf{W}$ is assumed to be available, we can detect when and where the change occurs and identify the solutions that are affected by the changes. This important property does not hold in several of the DOPs presented in the literature.

For example, Mavrovouniotis et al. [13] present a benchmark problem generator that is used in the *IEEE WCCI-2014 Competition on Evolutionary Computation for Dynamic Optimization Problems*. In the DTSP produced by this generator, some vertices of the TSP are swapped at every change point, producing a permutation of the weight matrix $\mathbf{W}$. In this way, the generator supports setting the change frequency (by the number of fitness evaluations between changes) and severity (by the percentage of swapped cities); also the global optimum is known during the optimization process, what is very useful for comparing EDO algorithms. However, the authors concede that the dynamism produced by this benchmark generator does not necessarily reflect situations in real-world TSPs [13]. If one knows how the weight matrix $\mathbf{W}$ is permuted when the problem changes, it is not difficult to develop algorithms that efficiently exploit this property by correctly permuting past best solutions.

In a real situation, the changes in the weight matrix are known because $\mathbf{W}$ is used to compute the fitness of the solutions, and this knowledge can be explored in the analysis of the fitness landscape changes of the problem and when developing algorithms for the DTSP.

3. DTSP TYPES

Two components of the graph representing the TSP can change: the weights on the edges and the set of vertices.

3.1 DTSP with Weight Changes

Def. 1: DTSP with Weight Changes incurs at least one modification to $\mathbf{W}$ during the optimization process.

As depicted in Figure 2(a), all the weights of a subset of $\lfloor \rho n \rfloor$ vertices are randomly modified at each change point. Thus, the parameter ρ controls the change severity by defining the percentage of weights modified each time. At each change point, a subset of edges is randomly chosen according

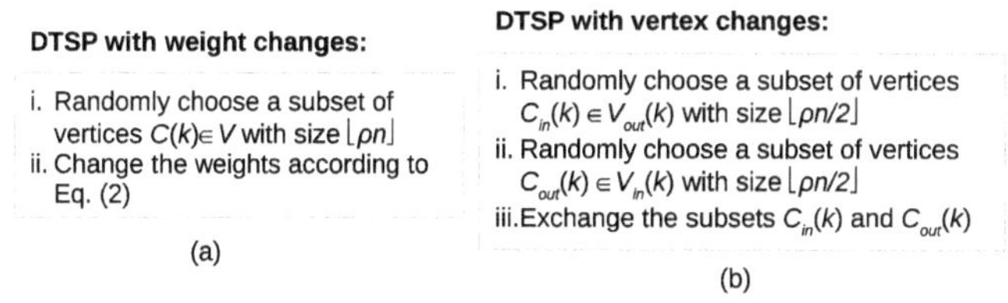

Figure 2: Types of DTSP: a) DTSP with weight changes: for each change k, the weights of the edges of a random subset of vertices $C(k) \in V$ are modified according to Eq. 2. b) DTSP with vertex changes: in environment k, the set of vertices V is split into two subsets ($V_{in}(k)$ and $V_{out}(k)$) with equal size. The graph for environment k is defined only by the vertices in $V_{in}(k)$. Each change k removes a random subset of vertices $C_{out}(k)$ from $V_{in}(k)$ and inserts another random subset of vertices $C_{in}(k) \in V_{out}$.

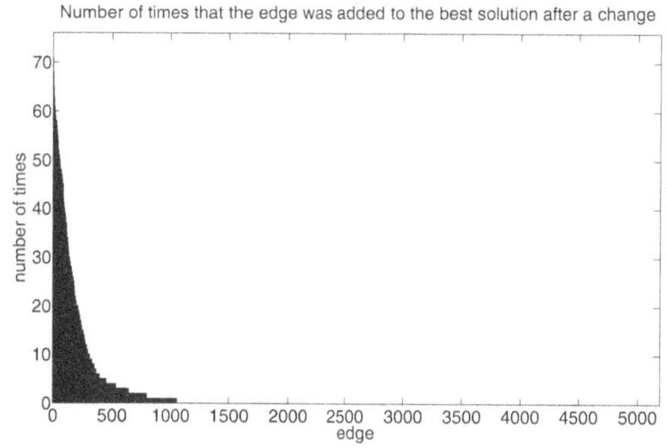

Figure 3: Modifications in the best solution found by LKH after changes in the weights of static instance *atex5* for $\rho = 0.1$.

to a uniform distribution, while the weights of this subset of vertices are randomly modified according to a normal distribution. In this way, the fitness of all solutions of the search space is modified. In the DTSP with weight changes, it is possible that the best solution may remain the same. However, as more edges are modified, it becomes less likely that the same solution will be best before and after the changes.

The changes in the weights are given by:

$$w_{ij}(k+1) = \begin{cases} w_{ij}(0) + p_{ij}(k), & \text{if } v_i \in C(k) \\ w_{ij}(k), & \text{otherwise} \end{cases} \qquad (2)$$

where $p_{ij}(k)$ is a random number generated from a normal distribution with zero mean and standard deviation equal to $0.2 * w_{ij}(0)$ at change k, $w_{ij}(0)$ is the weight between vertices v_i and v_j for the static instance of the TSP used to generate the DTSP (i.e, in environment 0), and the subset $C(k)$ contains $\lfloor \rho n \rfloor$ vertices randomly chosen at change k.

If the change frequency is not high, i.e., the time between changes is not small, state-of-the-art static TSP heuristics can be effectively applied to each environment of the DTSP (Figure 1). To test this conjecture, we applied the well known LKH heuristic [8] to environments generated by following the process in Figure 2. LKH is a state-of-art heuristic for the TSP, capable of producing very impressive results both for symmetric and asymmetric TSPs [8, 9]. The environments were generated by 500 consecutive applications of changes to the asymmetric static instance *atex5* [2] in environment 0 with $\rho = 0.1$; *atex5* has $n = 72$ vertices.

To show how the best solutions change with the weight changes, Figure 3 presents the number of times that each possible edge of the TSP was added to the best solution found by LKH after a change, i.e., the edge was not present in the best solution for environment $k-1$, but was present in the best solution for environment k (the results were sorted from the edge that was included the most times to the edge that was included the fewest times).

From Figure 3, we can observe that only a small part of all possible edges were added to the best solutions after the changes. Some edges were included (after being removed) in the best solution more than 50 times. Most of the possible edges were not added to the best solution after any change. This occurs because some expensive edges overly degrade the evaluation of the solutions and so, are never (or rarely) found in the local and global optima. Very similar results were reached in symmetric TSP instances using Concorde (this result is not shown in this paper due to space limitations).

Based on these observations, we hypothesize that past best solutions can effectively inform solutions in the current environment, i.e., in the fitness landscape after a change. Thus, memory approaches, which are used often by algorithms developed for dynamic environments with cyclic changes, can be applied to the DTSP even with random changes. This hypothesis is tested in Section 5.

3.2 DTSP with Vertex Changes

Def. 2: DTSP with vertex changes inserts or deletes at least one vertex during the optimization process.

As in [12], we consider the case where, after a change, $\lfloor \rho n/2 \rfloor$ of the vertices are removed, while $\lfloor \rho n/2 \rfloor$ other vertices not previously present are inserted into the TSP. For the k-environment, the set of vertices V of the static instance of the TSP is split into two subsets with equal size ($n/2$): one subset ($V_{in}(k) \in V$) with vertices that are present in the graph of the current environment and one subset ($V_{outn}(k) \in V$) with the remaining vertices. When a change occurs, $\lfloor \rho n/2 \rfloor$ randomly chosen vertices of the current graph are replaced by the same number of vertices randomly chosen from the subset of vertices currently not used. Thus, the size of the graph is equal for all environments, and ρ controls the severity of the change. Figure 2(b) summarizes the process.

When LKH is applied to the DTSP generated from changing the vertices of static instance *atex5* for $\rho = 0.05$, similar results are obtained (Figure 4), i.e., only a small part of all possible edges were added to the best solutions after the changes. In this case, some edges of the best solution are always removed after the changes.

The results presented in Figure 4 reinforces our hypothesis that, in DTSPs, knowing solutions previously found in past environments can be useful to find the solution in the current environment. However, in this case, solutions from the memory (i.e., past solutions) cannot be directly inserted into the new environment because some of the vertices of the problem are different. A strategy to solve this problem is presented in Section 4.

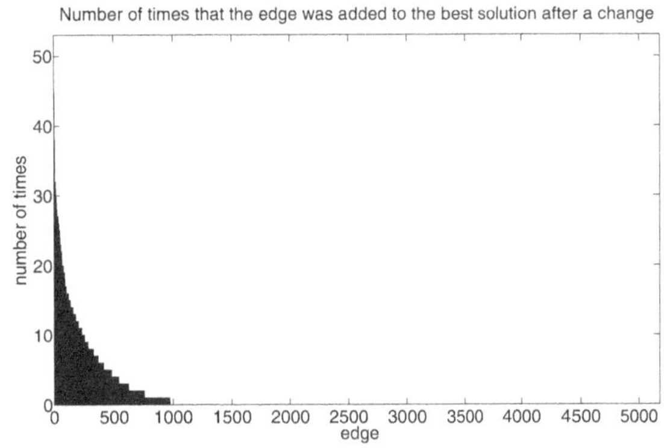

Figure 4: Modifications in the best solution found by LKH after changes in the vertices of static instance *atex5* for $\rho = 0.05$.

Algorithm 1 Memory approach for the DTSP with weight changes

---

initialize population P and memory M;
while termination condition is not satisfied **do**
  if change detected **then**
    M=updateMemory(P,M);
    re-evaluate the individuals in P and M
  end if
  Q=selectForReproduction(P,M);
  Q=Reproduction(Q);
  P=Q;
end while

COMMENTS:
i) M=updateMemory(P,M): *insert* $\mathbf{x_b}$ *(the current best solution of P) in M if* $\mathbf{x_b}$ *is better than the solution in M that is most similar to* $\mathbf{x_b}$
ii) Q=selectForReproduction(P,M): *each individual in Q is obtained by selecting an individual from M or P*

---

4. MEMORY APPROACH

One of the common approaches to EDO is the use of implicit or explicit memory where past solutions (or parts of them) are stored and retrieved according to different strategies. The basic idea is that solutions found in the past can be useful in subsequent environments. This is particularly true in cyclic DOPs, where past environments often reappear, sometimes slightly modified, during the optimization.

One of these memory approaches is the memory-enhanced genetic algorithm (MEGA) [20], where some of the best solutions found are explicitly stored in a memory M with size N_m, i.e., the memory contains N_m individuals found in past generations (in general $N_m < N$, where N is the size of P). When the problem changes, the current population (P) and the memory (M) are re-evaluated, and the best individuals among them form the new population P.

In this paper, we propose a different approach. Instead of directly inserting the individuals of memory M into population P as in MEGA, the individuals of M (or parts of them) can only be inserted into P after crossover. Thus, parts of the solutions in memory can be reintroduced, using crossover, in any generation of the optimization process.

The pseudo-code for the proposed approach for the DTSP with weight changes is presented in Algorithm 1. Individuals can be selected from the current population P or the memory M for crossover. In this way, the crossover can occur between one solution in the memory and another in the current population, or between two solutions in memory, or between two solutions in the current population. Crossover supports recombination of parts of past solutions with current solutions of the TSP, which may prove to be useful even after the changes in the problem. As in MEGA, when the memory is updated, one solution of M is removed before inserting the current best solution, $\mathbf{x_b}$, of P. The replacement strategy is: i) find the solution $\mathbf{x_s} \in M$ that is most similar to $\mathbf{x_b}$; ii) if the fitness of $\mathbf{x_b}$ is better than the fitness of $\mathbf{x_s}$, then $\mathbf{x_b}$ replaces $\mathbf{x_s}$ in the memory.

For the DTSP with vertex changes, the solutions must be modified when a change occurs because some vertices are removed and others are added to the subset of vertices used to evaluate the solutions. Also, as the subsets of vertices in different environments are not the same, a solution from memory cannot be directly recombined with solutions from the population as in Algorithm 1. Thus, two memories are employed. The first (M_1), which is similar to the memory used in Algorithm 1, contains solutions created in different environments, i.e., solutions with different encodings. The second (M_2) is created by repairing the individuals of M_1 according to the subset of vertices used in the current environment. As M_2 contains solutions mapped to the current environment, these solutions can be recombined with the solutions in the current population. Algorithm 2 shows the proposed memory approach for the DTSP with vertex changes.

The repair process for M_2 occurs in two steps. First, the indices of the solutions in the original environment are mapped to the new environment. This is made possible by recording information about the subset of vertices used in the current environment and in the environment where the solution was generated. When the solution is repaired, the recorded subset of vertices are used to map the solution in the new codification according to the same order of vertices in the original solution. Since some vertices are removed, the new intermediate solution has less vertices than the original solution. Then, the new vertices are inserted in the solution, i.e., the vertices that are not present in the subset of vertices in the original environment but are now present.

The insertion of the vertices occurs according to the insertion heuristic presented in [16], where the edge (x_i, x_{i+1}) in the current solution that minimizes $w_{x_i,m} + w_{m,x_{i+1}} - w_{x_i,x_{i+1}}$ is removed and the edges (x_i, m) and (m, x_{i+1}) are inserted, where v_m is the vertex that should be inserted in the solution. This process is repeated for all vertices that were not present in the subset of vertices of the original environment, but are now present after the change.

5. EVALUATION

To evaluate our approaches, we compare the performance of the following Genetic Algorithms (GAs):

Alg. 1: Standard GA (SGA)

Alg. 2: Random immigrants GA (RIGA), where in every generation rN randomly chosen individuals of the current population are replaced by randomly generated individuals. The parameter r ($0 \leq r \leq 1$) controls the percentage of the population to be replaced by random immigrants;

Algorithm 2 Memory approach for the DTSP vertex changes

```
initialize population P and memories M1 and M2;
while termination condition is not satisfied do
  if change detected then
    M1=updateMemory(P,M1);
    P=repairSolutions(P);
    M2=repairSolutions(M1);
    re-evaluate the individuals in P and M2
  end if
  Q=selectForReproduction(P,M2);
  Q=Reproduction(Q);
  P=Q;
end while
```

COMMENT:
i) M_2=repairSolutions(M_1): *for each individual in M_1, the vertices that were present in the environment where the individual was created, but are not present in the current environment, are removed from the solutions, while the vertices that were not present in the environment where the individual was created, but are now present, are inserted according to the heuristic presented in [16].*

Alg. 3: Elitism-based immigrants GA (EIGA) [20], where in every generation rN randomly chosen individuals of the current population are replaced by individuals generated by mutation of the current best solution of the population;

Alg. 4: Memory-enhanced GA (MEGA) [20];

Alg. 5: Proposed memory approach presented in Section 4;

Alg. 6: Hybrid approach combining the proposed memory approach (Alg. 5) with EIGA. The algorithm is the same as Alg. 5, but rN randomly chosen individuals of the current population are replaced by individuals generated by mutation of the current best solution of the population, as in Alg. 3.

RIGA is a traditional algorithm employed for DOPs, while EIGA and MEGA are state-of-art EDO algorithms. While the first three algorithms (SGA, RIGA, and EIGA) are not based on memory, algorithms 4, 5, and 6 explicitly store best individuals found in past generations.

For our DTSP comparison, changes occur after a fixed number of fitness evaluations (τ). Thus, τ controls the interval of the changes. Besides the evaluations of the new individuals generated by crossover and mutation, evaluations are also counted each time an individual is re-evaluated after a change. The follow additional evaluations are counted: i) for RIGA, $r * N$ evaluations for the new random individuals each generation; ii) for EIGA, evaluations resulting in the mutation of $r * N$ individuals (immigrants) in each generation; iii) for MEGA and Alg. 5, N_m evaluations resulting in the re-evaluation of the individuals in the memory after each change; iii) for Alg. 6, N_m evaluations resulting in the re-evaluation of the individuals in the memory after each change and evaluations resulting in the mutation of $r * N$ individuals each generation.

For each DTSP generated from a static instance of an asymmetric TSP, 50 changes occur during each run. To test a range of DTSPs, we vary the change type (weights or vertices), change frequency (τ = 2000 or 6000), and change severity (ρ = 0.1 or 0.3 for the DTSP with weight changes and 0.05 or 0.1 for the DTSP with vertex changes). The results of 25 runs for each combination are presented here. The reduced number of evaluations between changes (τ) considered here does not allow the application of the restart approach with LKH employed in the experiments presented in Section 3; LKH needs many more evaluations for each environment created in the DTSPs.

For all algorithms, tournament selection (where the best solution between two random solutions are chosen with probability 0.8) and elitism are used. The Generalized Asymmetric Partition Crossover (GAPX) [19] is applied to the solutions selected by tournament selection, and, if the solution is not improved, mutation is applied. When a solution is selected for mutation, it is modified by 3opt in 30% of the cases, by 2opt in 10% of the cases, and by local search using 3opt and "don't look bits", as in [19] but limited to a total of 2 evaluations per individual, in the remaining cases. While 3opt keeps the order of the edges in the original solution, 2opt allows the inversion of sub-paths of the tour given by the solution. To compute the fitness of the individuals generated by 2opt and 3opt, we do not need to evaluate the entire individual. For example, each time 2opt is applied, only 2 edges of the solution are replaced (in this way, the mutated individual has fitness equal to the fitness of the original individual plus the difference caused by exchanging 2 edges). The proportional values of the evaluations are added to the total number of evaluations when 2opt and 3opt are applied. The initial population in each run is generated by local search using 3opt [19].

As in [20], the population size is N = 100 individuals, the parameter r is equal to 0.2 when the immigrants approaches are utilized and the memory size is equal to 20% of the population size (i.e., $N_m = 0.2N$). The static asymmetric instances used to generated the DTSPs are instances with less than 400 vertices of TSPLIB and the *dc* and *atex* instances from [2]. These asymmetric static instances do not represent the classic TSP (i.e., with vehicles) and were used in the *8th DIMACS TSP Challenge.*

As the performance metric, the mean best fitness in each environment is recorded for each run, i.e.:

$$F(run) = \frac{1}{n_k} \sum_{k=1}^{n_k} f^*(k, run) \quad (3)$$

where n_k is the number of changes in a run and $f^*(k, run)$ is the best fitness found in environment k for the run.

Tables 1 and 2 show the results for each of the two DTSP types. Each column compares a pair of algorithms, e.g., the first column is between Alg. 5 and Alg. 3 [1]. To test statistical significance, the Wilcoxon signed-rank test with significance level 0.01 was used. The comparison between algorithms 5 and 3 contrasts the memory approach (Alg. 5) against the non-memory approach with the best performance (Alg. 3).

For the DTSP with weight changes, the memory approach performed better for the instances *atex*, *ft* and *p43*. In such instances, only a small part of all possible edges are added to the best solution after the changes, as observed in Section 3.1. As a consequence, the insertion of parts of good solutions (subpaths of the tours) found in past environments is shown to be beneficial to performance, i.e., finding good solutions faster.

[1]Tables with the results of average $F(run)$ and the source codes are available as supplementary material.

However, the memory approach performed worse in most of the cases for instances *dc*, *rbg*, and *td* in Table 1. Figure 5 shows a simulation of the DTSP generated from the asymmetric static instance *dc112* where 500 consecutive changes occur with $\rho = 0.1$ and LKH is used to find the best solutions after each change (as in the simulation presented in Section 3). When compared to Figure 3, we can observe that more edges are used in the best solutions for *dc112*. This is likely because many solutions in the fitness space for instances *dc* (and for the instances *rbg* and *td*) present close (or even equal) evaluation. Thus, when the problem changes, the algorithm finds a different solution for the new environment, but with similar values of fitness (this can also be observed when we analyze the weight matrices $\mathbf{W}$). In such cases, the memory approaches do not perform best because new edges (not found in the past solutions) need to be explored. We did not observe this effect in the DTSP with vertex changes (Table 2), except for the instances *rbg*, because the redundancy of the solutions is partially reduced by the fact that only 50% of the vertices are present in each environment each time. The simulation presented in Figure 6 indicates that a smaller subset of the possible edges are inserted in the best solutions when LKH is used to find the best solutions after the changes in the vertices for instance *dc112*. The memory approach performed better than EIGA (Alg. 3) for the DTSP with vertex changes, with the exception of instances *rbg*.

The hybrid approach (Alg. 6) exploits both memory (Alg. 5) and elitism-based immigrants (Alg. 3). Even when its performance is inferior, it behaves similarly to Alg. 5 when this is the best approach, and to Alg. 3 when this is the best approach. This behavior can be seen in Figure 7, which shows the averaged fitness in each environment for the DTSP with weight changes generated from instance *dc112* for $\tau = 2000$ and $\rho = 0.1$. In this DTSP, Alg. 3 presents the best results (Table 1). However, in Figure 7, the results for algorithms 6 and 3 present similar behavior, clearly different from the behavior of the other algorithms.

Alg. 6 showed very good performance, when compared to the other algorithms, for both types of DTSP (tables 1 and 2). The averaged results for $F(run)$ differ when the frequency (τ) and severity (ρ) of the changes are modified (tables in the supplementary material). However, the observations concerning the comparison between Alg. 6 and the other algorithms are practically the same for different combinations of τ and ρ.

6. CONCLUSIONS

The DTSP has been used by many authors to test EDO algorithms. In this paper, we argue that developing new EDO algorithms for the dynamic version of the *classic TSP* is not relevant from a practical point of view. However, instances of the DTSP in domains where the changes can be fast when compared to the optimization time required by the solver exist, as in robotics and telecommunication, and in such cases, EDO algorithms present an interesting approach.

From simulations of the LKH heuristic applied to environments generated by the DTSP, an interesting behavior is observed: only some edges, from all possible edges, are inserted and removed from the best solutions after the changes. This phenomenon occurs because some edges increase the fitness of the solution too much and, then, are never (or rarely) found in the best solutions. Thus, memory approaches can be effective for the DTSP. In this paper, a memory approach

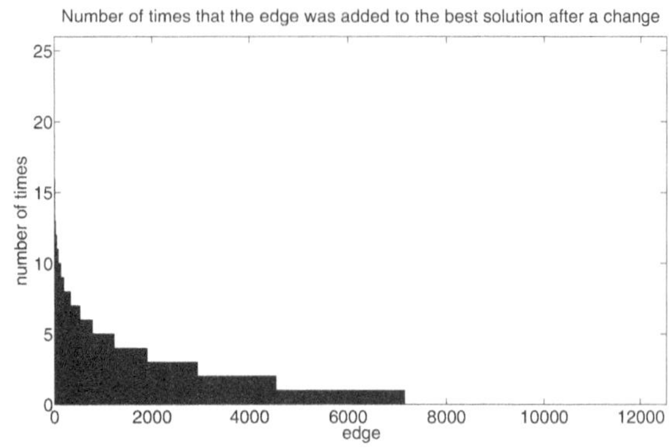

Figure 5: Modifications in the best solution found by LKH after changes in the weights of static instance *dc112* for $\rho = 0.1$.

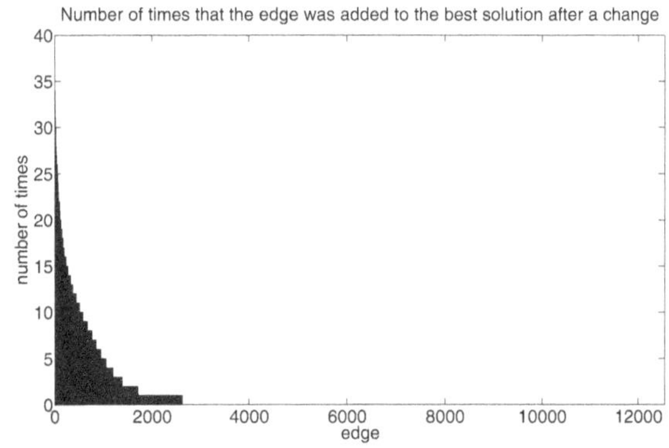

Figure 6: Modifications in the best solution found by LKH after changes in the vertices of static instance *dc112* for $\rho = 0.05$.

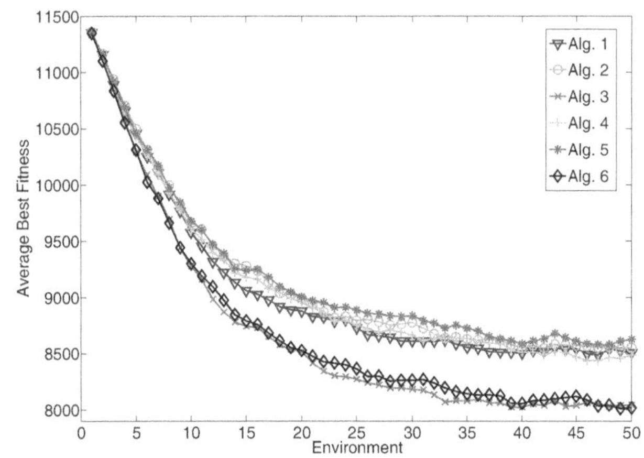

Figure 7: Averaged results (for 25 runs) of the best fitness in each change cycle for the DTSP with weight changes for instance *dc112* for $\tau = 2000$ and $\rho = 0.1$.

for the DTSP is proposed, as well as a method to store and retrieve past solutions for the case where the set of vertices of the DTSP changes.

The experiments support our hypothesis that memory of past solutions can be beneficial for the DTSP with random changes in the weight matrix or in the set of vertices. In instances of DTSP generated from static instances of TSP with redundancy in the solutions, an elitism-based immigrants approach produces better performance. A hybrid approach using memory and elitism-based immigrants produces the best overall performance on our generated problems, when compared to the other algorithms.

The DTSP instances employed here were generated from static instances of the asymmetric TSP and are not real-world instances of the DTSP. Thus, the obvious next step is to investigate how our observations generalize to real-world DTSPs. Investigating the adaptation of the memory size during the run and the effects of the insertion order for the new vertices in the proposed algorithms are also possible future directions.

7. ACKNOWLEDGMENTS

Renato Tinós was a visiting researcher in the Department of Computer Science at CSU. The visit of the researcher was made possible by the support provided by FAPESP (under grant 2012/22200-9), USP, and CSU. This research was sponsored by the Air Force Office of Scientific Research, Air Force Materiel Command, USAF (under grant FA9550-11-1-0088). The U.S. Government is authorized to reproduce and distribute reprints for Governmental purposes notwithstanding any copyright notation thereon.

8. REFERENCES

[1] D. Apiletti, E. Baralis, and T. Cerquitelli. Energy-saving models for wireless sensor networks. *Knowledge and Inf. Systems*, 28(3):615–644, 2011.

[2] J. Cirasella, D. S. Johnson, L. A. McGeoch, and W. Zhang. The asymmetric TSP: algorithms, instance generators, and tests. In *Algorithm Engineering and Experimentation*, pages 32–59. Springer, 2001.

[3] W. Cook. *In pursuit of the traveling salesman: mathematics at the limits of computation.* Princeton University Press, 2011.

[4] C. Cruz, J. González, and D. Pelta. Optimization in dynamic environments: a survey on problems, methods and measures. *Soft Computing*, 15:1427–1448, 2011.

[5] C. J. Eyckelhof, M. Snoek, and M. Vof. Ant systems for a dynamic TSP: Ants caught in a traffic jam. In *Ant Algorithms : Third International Workshop (LNCC2463)*, pages 88–99. Springer Verlag, 2002.

[6] L. B. Gueta, R. Chiba, J. Ota, T. Arai, and T. Ueyama. A practical and integrated method to optimize a manipulator-based inspection system. In *Proc. of the IEEE Int. Conf. on Robotics and Biomimetics*, pages 1911–1918, 2007.

[7] M. Guntsch, M. Middendorf, and H. Schmeck. An ant colony optimization approach to dynamic TSP. In *Proc. GECCO'2001*, pages 860–867, 2001.

[8] K. Helsgaun. An effective implementation of the Lin-Kernighan traveling salesman heuristic. *European Journal of Operational Research*, 126(1):106–130, 2000.

[9] K. Helsgaun. LKH results for Soler's ATSP instances. http://www.akira.ruc.dk/ keld/research/LKH/, April 2012.

[10] L. Kang, A. Zhou, B. McKay, Y. Li, and Z. Kang. Benchmarking algorithms for dynamic travelling salesman problems. In *Proc. of the 2004 IEEE Cong. on Evolut. Comp.*, volume 2, pages 1286–1292, 2004.

[11] W. Li. A parallel multi-start search algorithm for dynamic traveling salesman problem. In *Experimental Algorithms (LNCC6630)*, pages 65–75. Springer Berlin Heidelberg, 2011.

[12] M. Mavrovouniotis and S. Yang. Ant colony optimization algorithms with immigrants schemes for the dynamic travelling salesman problem. In S. Yang and X. Yao, editors, *Evolutionary Computation for Dynamic Optimization Problems*, pages 317–341. Springer Berlin Heidelberg, 2013.

[13] M. Mavrovouniotis, S. Yang, and X. Yao. A benchmark generator for dynamic permutation-encoded problems. In *Parallel Problem Solving from Nature XII (LNCC7492)*, pages 508–517. Springer Berlin Heidelberg, 2012.

[14] T. T. Nguyen, S. Yang, and J. Branke. Evolutionary dynamic optimization: A survey of the state of the art. *Swarm and Evolutionary Computation*, 6:1–24, 2012.

[15] G. Reinelt. TSPLIB 95. http://www.iwr.uni-heidelberg.de/groups/comopt/software/TSPLIB95/, 1995. Interdisziplinäres Zentrum für Wissenschaftliches Rechnen (IWR), Heidelberg.

[16] D. J. Rosenkrantz, R. E. Stearns, and P. M. Lewis, II. An analysis of several heuristics for the traveling salesman problem. *SIAM Journal on Computing*, 6(3):563–581, 1977.

[17] A. Simões and E. Costa. CHC-based algorithms for the dynamic traveling salesman problem. In *Applications of Evolutionary Computation (LNCC6624)*, pages 354–363. Springer Berlin Heidelberg, 2011.

[18] D. Soler, E. Martínez, and J. C. Micó. A transformation for the mixed general routing problem with turn penalties. *Journal of the Operational Research Society*, 59(4):540–547, 2007.

[19] R. Tinós, D. Whitley, and G. Ochoa. Generalized asymmetric partition crossover (GAPX) for the asymmetric TSP. In *Proc. of GECCO'2014*, 2014.

[20] S. Yang. Genetic algorithms with memory-and elitism-based immigrants in dynamic environments. *Evolutionary Computation*, 16(3):385–416, 2008.

[21] A. Younes, O. Basir, and P. Calamai. A benchmark generator for dynamic optimization. In *Proc. of the 3rd Int. Conf. on Soft Computing, Opt., Simulation and Manufacturing Syst.*, 2003.

Table 1: Results for the DTSP with weight changes. Column $A - B$ compared algorithms A and B, where $+$ and $-$, respectively, indicate that the results of Alg. A were statistically better ($+$) or worse ($-$) than Alg. B, while $=$ indicates that the results were statistically similar. For each static instance of the TSP, four instances of the DTSP were generated for the four combinations of τ and ρ settings.

Problem	τ	ρ	5-3	6-1	6-2	6-3	6-4	6-5
	2000	0.1	+	+	+	+	+	=
atex1		0.3	+	+	+	+	+	=
n=16	6000	0.1	+	+	=	+	=	=
		0.3	+	+	+	+	+	=
	2000	0.1	+	+	+	+	=	=
atex3		0.3	+	+	+	+	+	=
n=32	6000	0.1	+	=	+	+	=	=
		0.3	+	+	+	+	+	=
	2000	0.1	+	+	+	+	=	=
atex4		0.3	+	+	+	+	+	=
n=48	6000	0.1	+	+	+	+	+	=
		0.3	+	+	+	+	+	=
	2000	0.1	+	=	+	+	=	-
atex5		0.3	+	+	+	+	+	=
n=72	6000	0.1	+	+	+	+	=	=
		0.3	+	+	+	+	+	=
	2000	0.1	-	+	+	-	+	+
dc112		0.3	-	+	+	-	+	+
n=112	6000	0.1	-	+	+	-	+	+
		0.3	-	+	+	-	+	+
	2000	0.1	-	+	+	=	+	+
dc126		0.3	-	+	+	-	+	+
n=126	6000	0.1	-	+	+	=	+	+
		0.3	-	+	+	-	+	+
	2000	0.1	-	+	+	=	+	+
dc134		0.3	-	+	+	=	+	+
n=134	6000	0.1	-	+	+	=	+	+
		0.3	-	+	+	-	+	+
	2000	0.1	-	+	+	=	+	+
dc176		0.3	-	+	+	-	+	+
n=176	6000	0.1	-	+	+	=	+	+
		0.3	-	+	+	-	+	+
	2000	0.1	-	+	+	=	+	+
dc188		0.3	-	+	+	-	+	+
n=188	6000	0.1	-	+	+	-	+	+
		0.3	-	+	+	-	+	+
	2000	0.1	+	+	+	+	=	=
ft53		0.3	+	+	+	+	=	-
n=53	6000	0.1	+	+	+	+	=	=
		0.3	+	+	+	+	=	=
	2000	0.1	+	+	+	+	+	=
ft70		0.3	+	+	+	+	+	+
n=70	6000	0.1	+	+	+	+	+	=
		0.3	+	+	+	+	+	+
	2000	0.1	+	+	+	=	=	=
p43		0.3	+	+	+	+	=	=
n=43	6000	0.1	+	=	=	=	=	=
		0.3	+	+	+	+	=	=
	2000	0.1	-	+	+	=	+	+
rbg323		0.3	+	+	+	+	+	+
n=323	6000	0.1	-	+	+	-	+	+
		0.3	-	+	+	=	+	+
	2000	0.1	-	+	+	=	+	+
rbg358		0.3	+	+	+	+	+	+
n=358	6000	0.1	-	+	+	=	+	+
		0.3	-	+	+	+	+	+
	2000	0.1	-	+	+	=	+	+
td100.1		0.3	-	+	+	=	+	+
n=101	6000	0.1	-	+	+	=	+	+
		0.3	-	+	+	=	+	+
	2000	0.1	-	+	+	=	+	+
td316.10		0.3	+	+	+	+	+	+
n=317	6000	0.1	-	+	+	-	+	+
		0.3	-	+	+	+	+	+

Table 2: Results for the DTSP with vertex changes. Here, ρ indicates the percentage of vertices modified by each change.

Problem	τ	ρ	5-3	6-1	6-2	6-3	6-4	6-5
	2000	0.05	+	+	+	+	-	=
atex1		0.1	+	+	+	+	-	=
	6000	0.05	+	+	-	+	=	=
		0.1	+	+	-	+	=	=
	2000	0.05	+	+	+	+	=	=
atex3		0.1	+	+	+	+	=	=
	6000	0.05	+	+	+	+	=	=
		0.1	+	+	+	+	=	=
	2000	0.05	+	+	+	+	=	=
atex4		0.1	+	+	+	+	+	-
	6000	0.05	+	+	+	+	+	=
		0.1	+	+	+	+	+	=
	2000	0.05	+	+	+	+	=	=
atex5		0.1	+	+	+	+	+	-
	6000	0.05	+	+	+	+	+	=
		0.1	+	+	+	+	+	=
	2000	0.05	+	+	+	+	+	=
dc112		0.1	+	+	+	+	+	=
	6000	0.05	+	+	+	+	=	=
		0.1	+	+	+	+	+	=
	2000	0.05	+	+	+	+	+	+
dc126		0.1	+	+	+	+	+	=
	6000	0.05	+	+	+	+	-	+
		0.1	+	+	+	+	-	=
	2000	0.05	+	+	+	+	-	=
dc134		0.1	+	+	+	+	-	=
	6000	0.05	+	+	+	+	+	=
		0.1	+	+	+	+	+	=
	2000	0.05	+	+	+	+	=	=
dc176		0.1	+	+	+	+	=	=
	6000	0.05	+	+	+	+	-	=
		0.1	+	+	+	+	+	=
	2000	0.05	+	+	+	+	=	=
dc188		0.1	+	+	+	+	=	=
	6000	0.05	+	+	+	+	+	+
		0.1	+	+	+	+	+	=
	2000	0.05	+	+	+	+	=	-
ft53		0.1	+	+	+	+	+	=
	6000	0.05	+	+	+	+	+	=
		0.1	+	+	+	+	+	=
	2000	0.05	+	+	+	+	=	=
ft70		0.1	+	+	+	+	+	=
	6000	0.05	+	+	+	+	=	=
		0.1	+	+	+	+	+	=
	2000	0.05	+	+	+	+	=	=
p43		0.1	+	+	+	+	=	=
	6000	0.05	+	+	+	+	+	=
		0.1	+	+	+	+	+	=
	2000	0.05	-	+	+	=	+	+
rbg323		0.1	=	+	+	+	+	+
	6000	0.05	-	+	+	=	+	+
		0.1	-	+	+	=	+	+
	2000	0.05	-	+	+	+	+	+
rbg358		0.1	+	+	+	+	+	+
	6000	0.05	-	+	+	=	+	+
		0.1	-	+	+	+	+	+
	2000	0.05	+	+	+	+	=	=
		0.1	+	+	+	+	+	-
td100.1	6000	0.05	+	+	+	+	+	=
		0.1	+	+	+	+	+	-
	2000	0.05	+	+	+	+	+	+
td316.10		0.1	+	+	+	+	+	+
	6000	0.05	=	+	+	+	+	+
		0.1	=	+	+	+	+	+

Solving GA-Hard Problems with EMMRS and GPGPUs

J. Ignacio Hidalgo
hidalgo@ucm.es

J. Manuel Colmenar
jmcolmenar@ajz.ucm.es

Jose L. Risco-Martín
jlrisco@ucm.es

Carlos Sánchez-Lacruz
carlos.muaddib@gmail.com

Juan Lanchares
julandan@ucm.es

Oscar Garnica
ogarnica@ucm.es

Adaptive and Bioinspired Systems Group (ABSys)
Facultad de Informática
Universidad Complutense de Madrid (Spain)

ABSTRACT

Different techniques have been proposed to tackle GA-Hard problems. Some techniques work with different encodings and representations, other use reordering operators and several, such as the Evolutionary Mapping Method (EMM), apply genotype-phenotype mappings. EMM uses multiple chromosomes in a single cell for mating with another cell within a single population. Although EMM gave good results, it fails on solving some deceptive problems. In this line, EMMRS (EMM with Replacement and Shift) adds a new operator, consisting on doing a replacement and a shift of some of the bits within the chromosome. Results showed the efficiency of the proposal on deceptive problems. However, EMMRS was not tested with other kind of hard problems. In this paper we have adapted EMMRS for solving the Traveling Salesman Problem (TSP). The encodings and genetic operators for solving the TSP are quite different to those applied on deceptive problems. In addition, execution times recommended the parallelization of the GA. We implemented a GPU parallel version. We present here some preliminary results proving that Evolutionary Mapping Method with Replacement and Shift gives good results not only in terms of quality but also in terms of speedup on its GPU parallel version for some instances of the TSP problem.

Categories and Subject Descriptors

I.2.8 [**Artificial Intelligence**]: Problem Solving, Control Methods, and Search—*Heuristic methods*; G.1.6 [**Numerical Analysis**]: Optimization—*Global optimization*

Keywords

GAs, Hard problems, genotype and phenotype mapping

1. INTRODUCTION AND MOTIVATION

Although GAs are very powerful algorithms capable of successfully solve a lot of complex optimization problems, there are some problems which remain difficult to solve and are named GA-Hard problems. Liepins and Vose [10] named 4 main reasons that make a GA fail in the search of optimal solutions: (1) the domain is not appropriate; (2) sampling error is too large; (3) crossover destroys good schemata; (4) the problem is deceptive.

The term deceptive was introduced, using other previous works, by Goldberg [5] [7] to test the limitations of the Genetic Algorithms (GAs). Deceptive problems are a particular kind of problems, and when being solved with GAs, they exploit the weakness of the coding of the chromosomes [15]. The problem stems from classical encodings. Normally, a particular codification scheme of binary numbers is chosen to transfer each binary sequence to the corresponding numeric value (or other type of information) of the parameter. Different techniques have been proposed to tackle deceptive problems. Among them, some papers presented techniques that work with different encodings and representations. There are also some theoretical works about genotype-phenotype mappings and some variations on Whitley and Goldberg works. For example, Shackleton et al[14] show the potential use of redundant genotype-phenotype mappings to improve evolutionary algorithms. In [1] Chow proposes a new encoding technique, the Evolutionary Mapping Method (EMM), to tackle some deceptive problems. Chow uses multiple chromosomes in a single cell for mating with another cell within a single population. As he claimed, the mapping from genotype-to-phenotype is explicitly evolved and maintained. Although this works improved previous reported results, it fails on solving some deceptive problems and the method does not assure a 100 % of optimal solutions for all of the tests solved.

Using Chow's ideas, Risco et al. presented also a new method to solve deceptive problems by modifying the Evolutionary Mapping Method [12]. The method, EMMRS (EMM with Replacement and Shift) adds a new operator to traditional crossover and mutation operators, consisting on doing a replacement and a shift of some of the bits within the chromosome. Experimental results showed the efficiency of the proposal on deceptive problems, obtaining 100 % of optimal solutions in less number of generations for the first set of experiments used in [1] and a significant improvement of previous results for other deceptive problems. However EMMRS was not tested with other kind of hard problems like discrete or combinatorial problems. In general, it is not an easy task to determine whether a problem is deceptive or not [3], so having a good method which works reasonably well on different kind of GA-Hard Problems (deceptive or not) it would be of interest for the community.

In this paper we have adapted EMMRS for solving the Traveling Salesman Problem (TSP). Given a set of cities and the cost of traveling between each pair of cities, the TSP problem formulation tries to find the cheapest way of visiting all the cities and returning to your starting point, visiting each city once and only once. The adaptation is not easy since the encodings and genetic operators

GECCO'14, July 12–16, 2014, Vancouver, BC, Canada.
Copyright 2014 ACM 978-1-4503-2662-9/14/07 ...$15.00.
http://dx.doi.org/10.1145/2576768.2598219 .

for solving the TSP are quite different to those applied in [12]. In addition, when trying to solve big TSP instances, the high execution time recommends the parallelization of the GA. We choose a GPGPU for implementing the parallel version and we have solved several issues in its implementation.

The main contributions of this paper are

- We present the EMMRS method for permutational representations
- We have implemented EMMRS on a GPU. EMMRS is not directly parallelizable, so we explain here some important issues of the parallelization process.

We present here some preliminary results proving that Evolutionary Mapping Method with Replacement and Shift gives good results not only in terms of quality but also in terms of speedup on its GPU's parallel version. In addition we have tested a shuffling algorithm for preserving the diversity of random numbers on the GPU.

The rest of the paper is organized as follows. In section 2 a brief review of the literature on deceptive problems and evolutionary algorithms is performed. Section 3 introduce the TSP instances solved in this paper. Section 4 describes EMMRS and Section 5 explains some details an the adaptation of EMMRS to the TSP and of the GPU parallelization. We present the experimental results on Section 6. Finally Section 7 gives some conclusions and ideas for future work.

2. RELATED WORK

As we have mentioned, there are some problems which are GA-Hard Problems. Of course a lot of effort has been made during the last years for improving the quality of the solutions obtained by GA-based methods on those problems. Some papers presented techniques that work with different encodings and representations. One reference paper was presented by Whitley in 1991 [15]. Here, the author presents several theorems about deception and proves that the problems which are interesting for GA optimization involve some degree of deception. Whitley proposed the use of tags to specify the phenotypic bit location, in addition to each binary chromosome.

Goldberg and Bridges also presented an analytical study of reordering operators in [6]. The main drawback of those approximations is the need of a double search. There are also some theoretical works about genotype-phenotype mappings and some variations on Whitley and Goldberg works. For example, Shackleton et al. [14] need a double search to obtain optimal gene positions (instead of bit positions) to preserve building blocks. Igel and Toussaint worked on the design of neutral encodings to improve the efficiency of evolutionary algorithms[8]. A similar approximation is used by Dasgupta in [2]. He presents other approach for solving deceptive problems, implementing what he called the *structured genetic algorithm*. The structured GA uses a two-level hierarchical encoding in its over-specified chromosomal representation. Finally, Rothlauf designed practical representations for genetic and evolutionary computation in [13]. These works allow to better understand representation issues in this kind of algorithms.

In [1] Chow proposes EMM (see Section 4), to tackle some deceptive problems with evolved mapping chromosomes. However EMM failed on solving some deceptive problems and the method does not assure a 100 % of optimal solutions. Motivated by this lack of results of EMM and as a continuation of Chow's work, Risco et al. proposed EMMRS [12] which incorporates a replacement and shift operator explained also in detail on Section 4. EMMRS solved efficiently a set of deceptive problems, obtaining up to 100 % of optimal solutions in less number of generations than EMM. However, EMMRS was not tested with other kind of hard problems like TSP, the minimum spanning tree problem ("MST") or other combinatorial problems.

Table 1: TSP instances used in this study.

Instance	Number of Cities	Optimal Solution
Gr48	48	5046
Pr76	76	108159
kroA100	100	21282
kroB100	100	22141
kroC100	100	20749
kroD100	100	21294
kroE100	100	22068

Given that techniques like EMMRS obtain good results for typical deceptive problems, the aim of our paper is to apply the same ideas to a well-known hard problem like the Traveling Salesman Problem (TSP). Many methods have been applied to solve the TSP, however the purpose of this work is not to compete with them. Our aim is to test the performance of the EMMRS algorithm (and its GPU version) when solving not only deceptive problems but also a real combinatorial problem with a high complexity, like the TSP.

3. TSP

In this work we have used several instances of the Traveling Salesman Problem (TSP). We have selected the TSP because is one of the most intensively studied problems in computational mathematics and it also has a lot of applications in real world problems. This work was made under a project which considers logistic problems. We should highlight that the propose of this work was to test that EMMRS works not only on deceptive continuous problems but also in discrete combinatorial optimization problem. Future work will include harder instances of the TSP.

Given a set of cities, and known distances between each pair of cities, the TSP problem is to obtain a tour that visits each city exactly once returning to the starting point and that minimizes the total distance traveled. If we represent the cities as the vertexes of a graph and the connections between cities as edges, we can formally define the problem as: Given an undirected graph, and a cost for each edge of that graph, find a Hamiltonian circuit of minimum total cost.

The TSP instances used in this study belong to TSPLIB[1] library and are listed on Table 1 including the number of cities and the optimal tour length of each instance.

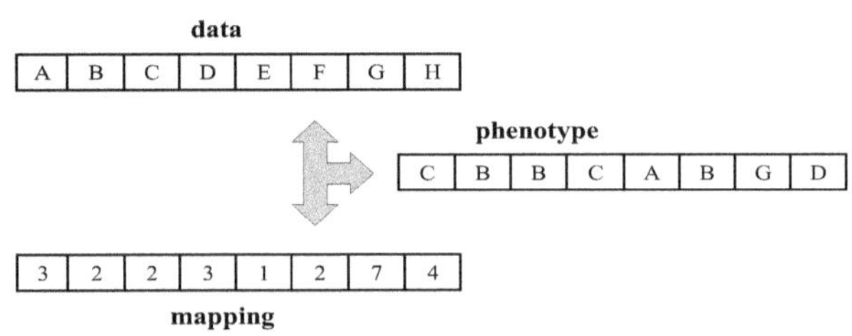

Figure 1: EMM example.

[1] http://comopt.ifi.uni-heidelberg.de/software/TSPLIB95/

Figure 2: EMMRS. Genetic operators.

4. EVOLUTIONARY MAPPING WITH REPLACEMENT AND SHIFT (EMMRS)

The encoding implemented in this paper is based on the method of double codification presented by Chow. To improve it, Risco et al. proposed EMMRS in [12]. They added a new genetic operator called replacement and shift (R&S) that is applied after the mutation operator in EMM. In this paper we adapt the EMMRS to the TSP problem and propose a parallel implementation to run in GPU. Thus, in this section we first review the EMM, second we explain EMMRS and finally we detail our EMMRS code implementation.

In [1] Chow proposes a double encoding technique, the Evolutionary Mapping Method (EMM), to tackle deceptive problems. According to this method, each individual is represented by two chromosomes: a data chromosome, which stores the genotype for the optimization function, and a mapping chromosome which stores the location of each data as integer values. Each pair of data and mapping chromosomes form a so called cell. Figure 1 represents an example of the EMM codification.

The major advantage of EMM is that decoupling the genotype and the mapping process permits the possibility of capturing useful schemes in hard problems~[1]. The operators that are applied to both chromosomes are those habitually used in GAs. The proposal in that paper is to apply a traditional two points crossover operator and a mutation operator, which is an integer operator that randomly alters a gene in one of the positions of bits.

Hence, the basis of EMM are: (1) the data chromosomes are forced to concentrate themselves on the exploration and survival in the genotypic space where the genomic materials constantly suffer construction and destruction of schemes; (2) the mapping chromosomes concentrate themselves on the effort to obtain an optimal mapping between the genotype and the phenotype.

Therefore given that the number of chromosomes is twice the number of individuals, and genetic operators work over both elements, the amount of work to be done is higher in EMM versus a classical GA. Therefore, a parallel implementation should be proposed in order to speed up the execution.

Risco et al. presented in [12] an R&S operator which is applied to the mapping chromosome after crossover and mutation on an EMM approach. They named this method as EMMRS (which stands for EMM with Replacement and Shift). The authors proved that the R&S operator reduces the number of evaluations needed to find the global optimum. Figure 2 depicts the genetic operators applied to the mapping chromosome under the EMMRS approach. As in [1], a 2-point integer crossover and an integer mutation operator are applied. After them, the R&S operator is applied, which randomly picks up two genes at random positions i and j, and makes $m[j] = m[i]$, where m is the mapping array. Next, it moves j to follow i, shifting the rest along to accommodate. Mutation and R&S probabilities alter each gene independently with probabilities P_m and $P_{R\&S}$.

```
EMMRS::main() {
    Initialize population pop
    t = 0;
    While ((t < maxGenerations) and (Not Optimum Found))
        {
        parent1 = tournamentSelection(pop);
        parent2 = tournamentSelection(pop);
        children = crossover(parent1, parent2);
        children.genotype.mutate(probMutation);
        children.mapping.mutate(probMutation);
        children.mapping.replacementAndShift(probRS);
        t = t + 1;
    }

EMMRS::replacementAndShift(prob) {
    i = 0;
    While (i < mapping.length) {
       If (randFloat(0,1) < prob) {
          pos2 = randInteger(0, mapping.length)
          posMin = min(i, pos2);
          posMax = max(i, pos2);
          mapping[posMin+2 .. posMax] = mapping[posMin+1
               .. posMax-1]
          mapping[posMin+1] = mapping[posMin]
       }
       i = i + 1;
    }
```

Figure 3: Proposed EMMRS algorithm implementation.

G	1	3	4	2	7	9	8	5	6
M	9	8	5	6	7	4	3	1	2
T	5	6	8	9	4	2	7	3	1

Figure 4: Individual for 9 cities. G is the genotype chromosome, M is the mapping chromosome and T is the tour.

As is stated in the paper by Chow, once a subschema is explicit formed, the change of one genotypic bit may trigger the changes of multiple defining bits on the phenotype. Hence, the Hamming distance between two hyper-planes is shortened. The inclusion of the R&S operator obtains another reduction of the Hamming distance between hyper-planes because of two reasons. First, replacement reinforces the movement from one schema to another schema in the mapping chromosome. Second, shifting bits takes into account the relative order of the mapping bits and therefore, the relative order of bits in the phenotype, which recalls the partial schemas reached at that point. Thus, as stated in [12], the search in EMMRS is able to get away from a deceptive attractor and go towards a global optimum faster than in EMM, specially in those problems where the global optimum is far away (in terms of Hamming distance) from the deceptive attractor. Therefore, all the benefits described before lead us to select EMMRS as the scheme to tackle the TSP problem.

Hence, we have made an implementation of EMMRS as shown in Figure 3. Given that the kernel of the algorithm is a traditional GA, we have defined the `main` function following its typical approach. Initially, a random population is created. Next, we iterate until the termination condition is satisfied. The loop executes the genetic operators, where selection and crossover are applied using both the data and the mapping chromosomes. The mapping chromosome is needed in selection to obtain the phenotype and the fitness value. Crossover operator is applied to data and mapping chromosomes, generating two offsprings (`children`). After that, the mutation operator is applied over the offspring. Notice that mutation is executed independently twice: one for the data chromosome and the other for the mapping chromosome. This requires the generation of two random numbers in order to decide if mutation is applied on each chromosome. Finally, the R&S operator is applied. Figure 3 shows the code implementation of this operator in the `replacementAndShift` function, which performs the operator as described above.

5. IMPLEMENTATION OF EMMRS IN TSP

In this section we explain some decisions that have been made about the concepts presented previously in relation to the design of the evolutionary algorithm. First we focus on the adaptation of EMMRS and TSP and then we will review some important concepts of the parallel implementation on the GPU.

5.1 Representation

We employed a permutation representation of theividuftals, which is the most natural way of representing problems based on scheduling or sequencing. In permutation encodings if there are X variables of the problem (jobs, cities, etc..), then the representation is performed using a list of X integers, each of which appears exactly once in the chromosome. EMMRS needs two chromosomes, thus each individual is represented by two chromosomes of N integers (where N is the number of cities) with values between 1 and N. A chromosome of genotype (G) and chromosome of mapping (M) . The advantage is that EMM and EMMRS were designed for dealing with permutations, since the mapping operation is necessarily a permutation of the number of genes of the chromosome. Chromosomes are stored separately, in two vectors of $N * S_{pop}$ dimensions, where S_{pop} is the size of the population of individuals. This way of storing the information meets the requirements for allowing a correct memory coalescing when threads access the population stored in the global memory of the GPU. Figure 4 shows an example of an individual for 9 cities, where G is the Genotype chromosome, M is the mapping chromosome and T is the resulting Tour which is represented by the pair of chromosomes. It is important to note that the permutational nature of the solutions of the TSP slightly changes the mapping process. Unlike original EMM and EMMRS implementations, we are allowed to map only once each tour. We will see on the experimental results, that EMMRS works also fine with this evolutionary mapping.

5.2 Initial Population

When generating the initial population it is necessary to have in mind both the problem and the parallel architecture. We have applied the algorithm showed in Figure 5. The process uses an auxiliary vector l_{aux} for storing the elements still available for filling the chromosome (G or M)without repetition. This process is repeated twice for each individual, one for the G chromosome and another for the M chromosome.

The main advantage of the algorithm above is that we do not need to check what components of the l_{aux} vector have been already written, reducing the computational time of the process. This is very important, specially having in mind that we works with up to 4092 individuals per population.

5.3 Operators

The method chosen for the crossover operator in this work is known as PMX (Partially Mapped Crossover) [4] which has been extensively applied for TSP evolutionary algorithms. The operator is applied separately for genotype chromosomes (G) and for mapping chromosomes (M) of both parents. Figure 6 shows an example

```
void Chromosome_init (int* Chromosome, const int N){
    //N= Number of cities
    unsigned int  r=0;
    int* l_aux;
    l_aux=(int*)malloc((N)*sizeof(int));
    for (int i=0; i<N; i++){
        l_aux[i]=i+1;
    }
    for (int i=0; i<N-1; i++){
        r=rand()\%(N-i-1);
        Individual [i] = l_aux[r];
        l_aux[r] = l_aux[N-i-1];
    }
    Individual [N-1] = l_aux[0];
    free (l_aux);
  }
```

Figure 5: Algorithm to initialize a chromosome.

with two Individuals using Genotype and Mapping chromosomes and 7 cities. Parent 1 is represented by M_{P1} and G_{P1} and Parent 2 by M_{P2} and G_{P2}. PMX works by first randomly selecting two points within each Pair of chromosomes: a_m and b_m for M_{P1} and M_{P2} and a_g and b_g for G_{P1} and G_{P2} obtaining 3 sections; *Initial-Medium-Final.*

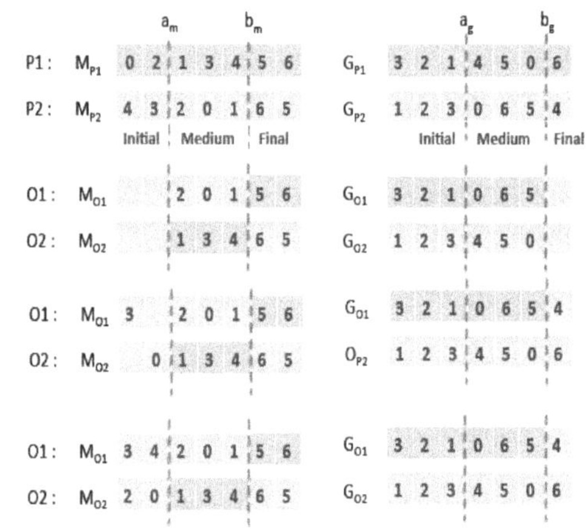

Figure 6: PMX crossover example with Mapping an Genotype chromosomes

Then, PMX interchanges the *Medium* segments of both parents (genes from a_i to b_i) to generate two new individuals Offspring1 represented by M_{O1} and G_{O1} and Offspring 2 by M_{O2} and G_{O2}. The rest of the chromosomes of the Offsprings are filled as much as possible with the same parent elements placed in the same position. The only condition is to respect the permutation encoding. After this step if still there are free genes, those are positioned according to the position of the replaced allele in the other parents. In other words PMX solves permutational constraints problem by establishing relationships between genes exchanged. Mutation and R&S operators were explained in section 4 and the selection is a tournament selection of two individuals, which is a good selection operator for parallel implementations on the GPU, since we can perform the tournaments in parallel.

5.4 Improving random numbers

The quality of random numbers is a very important issue when implementing a non-deterministic optimization algorithm. There

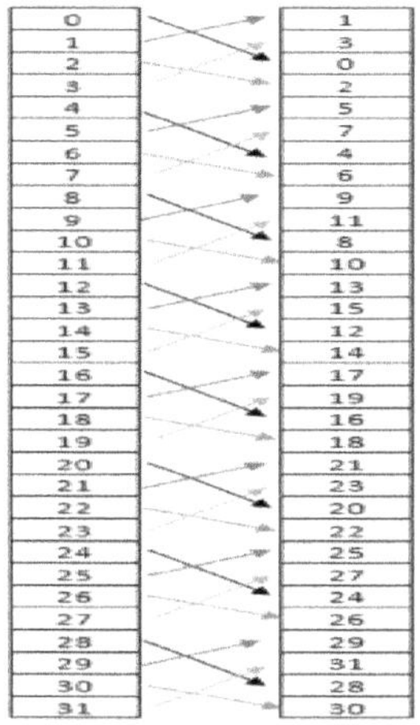

Figure 7: The shuffler process

are a plethora of applications and recipes for the implementation of random number generators on a CPU. However, on a GPU there are additional factors which make more difficult to implement a good generator without degradation on the GPU performance. In this paper we propose to use a simple method for refreshing random numbers on the GPU, in order to improve the quality of the solutions of Parallel Evolutionary Algorithms without performance reduction. It is well known that the bandwidth between the GPU and the CPU is very limited so this communication channel should be used with caution.

In the early versions of our algorithm, random numbers were recomputed from the CPU on each generation and then copied to the GPU. Obviously this greatly slowed the process. Although we did some preliminary tests with *Curand ()* function and the Park & Miller generation methods [11], we found little improvement in both execution times and quality of solutions. While trying to fix the bugs with those, widely tested, methods, we thought on several solutions, and finally, we chose the option of generating a small *Random Number Shuffler (RNS)* within the GPU. This shuffler has the property of being easily paralelizable. RNS is just to shuffle random vectors in the global memory. In this way we only have to communicate with the Host once every two migration.

Figure 7 explains the shuffler process. The threads of a block work in groups of 32, reading one position of the random numbers vector and writing them in the next 32 positions, but displaced in groups of four threads according to the sequence +2, -1, +1, -2 as Figure 7 shows . Threads copy their values into registers and then those are sent to the global memory displaced in GPU block and position as explained. Registers belonging to the following block store also their values before to the write of the new values, so we have no problem of missing values and hence we do not need additional or auxiliary memory structures. Anyway, this should not be a problem, since random number within a block have no dependencies, and changing one value from the random number list will have little effect on the performance of the algorithm. In order to have a control of the process we perform all the necessary $syncthreads$ operations. We tested the correctness of the process by checking that the same seed produces always the same numbers on each generation. We implemented this process to solve some problems with the quality of the obtained solutions, however we think that it is necessary a deeper study and a more exhaustive comparison with other well tested methods presented in the literature [9].

5.5 Parallel Implementation

As we have mentioned GPU computing on the parallelization under the CUDA architecture have been applied. GPU computing consists of using the GPU to perform general purpose computations. CUDA (Compute Unified Device Architecture) is a Single Instruction Multiple Thread (SIMT) computing platform and programming model developed by NVIDIA. Broadly speaking, it allows to use Graphics Processor Units (GPUs) for general purpose computation in a simplified way without a deep knowledge of the underlying architecture. Architectures compatible with the CUDA programming model are typically referred to as General Purpose Graphics Processor Units (GPGPUs). However, the CUDA platform presents several implementation constraints that might impact the final performance of a GPGPU applications.

The population level parallelism can be exploited with the implementation of an island model in which disjoint sets of individuals evolve independently with the exception of infrequent migrations (exchanges of individuals). The evaluation of individuals of the same population can be performed simultaneously through the implementation of a Master-Worker model. We have implemented several configurations of the parallel algorithm reported in Table 2. On it we can see the name of the Configuration (*CONFIG*), the number of individuals per island (*IND/ISL*), the number of islands (*ISLANDS*), the frequency of migration in number of generation (*F*) and the number of total migrations(*ERAS*). The *CONFIG* name will be used in section 6 to identify them. In this way $EMMRS_E$ denoted that we run $EMMRS$ algorithm on 64 islands with 64 individuals per island with a migration frequency of 30 generations an a total number of $(30 \cdot 600) = 9000$ generations.

Table 2: Configurations.

CONFIG	IND/ISL	ISLANDS	F	ERAS
A	32	128	30	600
B	32	128	40	450
C	32	256	30	300
D	32	256	40	225
E	64	64	30	600
F	64	64	40	450
G	64	128	30	300
H	64	128	40	225
I	32	256	40	4000
J	64	128	40	4000

5.6 EMMRS on the GPU

Host (CPU) and device (GPU) have different memory spaces. This means that the device memory cannot be directly accessed from the host and vice-versa. Thus, memory transfers are necessary to perform data exchanges between CPU and GPU. The programmer has to be aware of the complex GPU memory hierarchy. Note that accessing on-chip memories is two orders of magnitude faster than off-chip memory accesses. Thus, an appropriate use of both registers and shared memory is crucial to obtain the maximum performance from GPUs. The efficiency of those accesses is determined by the configuration in terms of threads Blocks.

There are several important kernels in our GPU implementation. Selection kernel is in charge of finding the best individuals and proceed with the tournament selection. This kernels launch as many Blocks as islands and a Block has as many threads as individuals per island. The fitness values of the individuals of an island are stored in the shared memory. Then one thread obtains the two best individuals on each Block. This is the less parallel part of the kernel.

Addresses of the best individuals of each island are stored in global memory. Tournament kernel follows a similar grid organization.

Crossover Kernel performs three operation: Crossover, Mutation and Replacement and Shift. This kernel will have the population, the vector of random numbers and the selection vector as inputs. The output of the kernel is a vector of offspring population. The structure of this kernel is the most unusual as it has as many blocks as crossover operations (population divided by 2) and each block has as many threads as genes has the chromosomes (i.e. number of cities). Each block of the crossover operator manages a crossover and each thread is responsible for copying only 1 gene. However, in the repair phase, PMX operator does not allow thread level parallelization so a lot of computing time is lost there. Offspring are sent from shared memory to global memory at the end of the kernel.

6. EXPERIMENTAL RESULTS

In this section we present four kind of results. First we justify the election of the value of the probability of the Replacement and Shift. Then, in order to check the utility of the Replacement and Shift operator on discrete problems, we have performed a set of experiments on several TSP instances listed on Table 1. We will contrast the results with those of [1] and [12]. This was the main motivation of the work. As we have also explained we have also parallelized the algorithm on the GPU, thus we present also the results of a profiling of the algorithm, which is used to select the functions to parallelize. Finally we present some results in terms of Speedup comparing the CPU and the CPU-GPU implementation.

All the experiments were carried out in a dedicated Intel Core-i5 machine, a 4-core processor, running at 2.80 GHz with 8 GB of RAM under a Linux operating system, NVIDIA GeForce GTX 570. After several tests, the crossover and mutation rates for all the algorithms were set to 0.7 and 0.2, respectively. The RS probability was set to 0.4, as determined by the experiments shown in the following Section.

6.1 Study of the value of the probability of the Replacement and Shift.

Before to start testing EMMRS with the TSP instances we should select a value for the probability of the R&S operador. We made several test with Gr48 and Pr76 instances and we made 100 runs of 10 configurations. This is not the objective of this paper, however we think it is important to highlight an extract of this study. For instance, one of the best configuration in terms of the number of optimal solutions reached is: 4096 individuals, organized in islands of 32, with a migration frequency of 30 generations and a total of 18000 generations.

We have varied the R&S probability ($P_{R\&S}$) from 0 to 1 in steps of 0.05. Table 3 shows the % of averaged approximation to the optimal solution (Avg,) of 100 runs of Configuration 1 for the most significative results, i.e probability which reach to optimal solutions. All the configurations obtained the best results for values of R&S between 0.3 and 0.6, and in most cases around 0.4. We fixed then, R&S probability to 0.4. As we have said, it would be necessary a more exhaustive statistical analysis of these experiments.

6.2 TSP Results

Experimental results are shown in Table 4, Table 5 and Table 6. These tables present the % of averaged approximation to the optimal solution (Avg,), the standard deviation (Std.) and the number of optimal solutions (#Opt) obtained in runs of the best configuration of three algorithms; a GA with EMMRS, a GA with EMM, and a simple GA. Each run stops when the maximum number of evaluations is achieved. Although it seems clear that EMMRS is better than GA and EMM for the selected TSP instances, we have use a statistical analysis. We have used Kolmogorov-Smirnov test to check normality. We obtained a p-value much less than 0.05 for all the dataset, thus we need a non-parametric test. We can perform a Wilcoxon sign ranked test, however in this case it is not necessary since EMMRS is better than EMM and GA for all the instances of Table 1. An interesting result is that on Table 5 and Table 6, results of GA are better than the ones of EMM. We need more research on this fact, but it seems that EMM alone is not positive for discrete problems.

Table 3: Study of the value of the probability of the Replacement and Shift.

Configuration 1			
$P_{R\&S}$	Avg	Std Dev	# Opt
0.15	98.031	1.399755045	2
0.2	98.594	0.970789525	6
0.25	98.971	0.903708026	10
0.3	99.214	0.723249687	16
0.35	99.353	0.58194348	19
0.4	99.47	0.468225062	26
0.45	99.461	0.491970213	21
0.5	99.496	0.397107748	23
0.55	99.358	0.567018556	20
0.6	99.314	0.554906403	15
0.65	99.316	0.513764949	13
0.7	99.056	0.708178284	6

Table 5: Results for Gr48 instance.

Instance	Gr48		
Algorithm	Avg.	Std	#Opt
$EMMRS_A$	99.513	0.457	14
$EMMRS_B$	99.346	0.538	11
$EMMRS_C$	99.124	0.660	5
$EMMRS_D$	98.865	0.646	1
$EMMRS_E$	99.240	0.645	6
$EMMRS_F$	99.118	0.678	8
$EMMRS_G$	99.190	0.639	3
$EMMRS_H$	99.076	0.731	5
EMM_A	81.898	3.914	0
EMM_B	81.369	3.867	0
EMM_C	82.250	2.754	0
EMM_D	80.502	3.376	0
EMM_E	81.178	4.626	0
EMM_F	80.278	4.214	0
EMM_G	83.574	3.554	0
EMM_H	81.861	2.889	0
GA_A	85.478	3.550	0
GA_B	85.531	3.687	0
GA_C	85.242	3.295	0
GA_D	83.023	3.190	0
GA_E	83.491	4.286	0
GA_F	83.905	3.822	0
GA_G	86.390	4.215	0
GA_H	85.302	3.118	0

Table 4: Results 100 cities for "kro" instances.

Algorithm	$EMMRS_I$	$EMMRS_J$	EMM_I	EMM_J	GA_I	GA_J
Instance	kroA100					
Avg.	98.343	98.238	61.840	61.180	62.499	61.043
#Opt	0	1	0	0	0	0
StdDev	1.144	1.125	3.968	4.214	3.486	4.355
Instance	kroB100					
Avg.	97.516	97.451	63.029	62.459	65.569	63.094
#Opt	0	0	0	0	0	0
StdDev	1.116	0.975	3.255	3.065	4.667	4.625
Instance	kroC100					
Avg.	98.641	97.736	60.255	59.982	61.470	59.576
#Opt	2	1	0	0	0	0
StdDev	1.055	1.408	3.961	3.971	3.958	3.460
Instance	kroD100					
Avg.	98.044	97.570	62.834	61.655	63.387	62.546
#Opt	1	0	0	0	0	0
StdDev	0.955	1.237	3.762	3.046	4.078	4.633
Instance	kroE100					
Avg.	98.036	97.875	62.013	62.038	64.052	62.808
#Opt	1	1	0	0	0	0
StdDev	0.888	1.164	3.066	3.956	3.702	4.063

6.3 Analysis of the parallel algorithm

In most GPGPU scenarios, a segment of the code is still executed in the CPU in a sequential manner while the GPU is used to accelerate those parts of the code presenting a higher computational cost. Thus, the GPU is mainly used as a co-processor in charge of executing only some specific tasks. It is important to note that launching a kernel is an order of magnitude slower than calling a CPU function. Therefore, the obtained speedup must be high enough to hide the overhead caused the kernel call and the memory transfers between CPU and GPU. Figure 8 shows the percentage of the total time spent on each part of the Parallel Algorithm. As was expected, Fitness evaluation and PMX are the most time consuming parts. This is due to the distances matrix, which has the information of the cities and paths, does not fit in the shared memory so we do the addition of the distances by the global memory of the GPU.

Figures about Shuffle operator and migration are also of interest. As we can see, Shuffle time is negligible (0.814 %) when compared with the cost of copying random numbers from the CPU (4.287 %). Migration operations percentages are also very small (0.043 %).

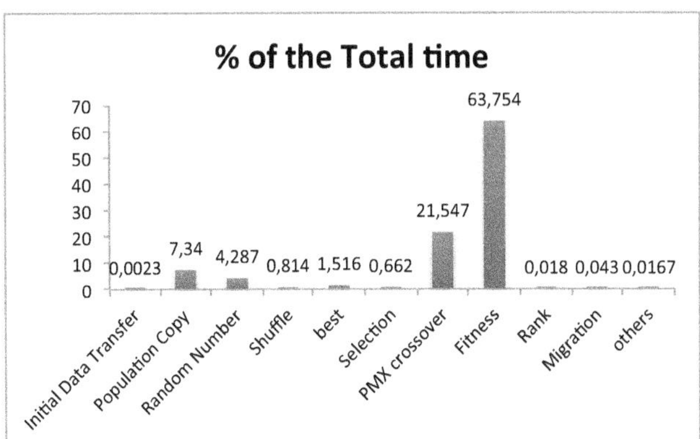

Figure 8: Execution time of each part of the algorithm

6.4 Speedup Results

Regarding running times we made two different comparatives. The first one is a comparison of the average execution time among EMMRS, EMM and GA on the GPU. We can confirm what was expected; EMMRS need more time than EMM (5 % to 8 % more, depending of the instance) and than GA (25 % to 30 % more). Of course the main and only reason is the implementation of the R&S operator, which is also the main contributor to the improvement of the quality of the solutions. The lower execution time of the GA is justified by the use of half the number of chromosomes than EMM and EMMRS. Although important, this increase in total times seems reasonable because we get solutions 15 % better for Gr48, 25 % better for Pr76 and more than 35 % for the five 100-cities instances of the TSP tested.

The second study compares the time needed by EMMRS on both the GPU and the CPU for the same number of generations. We observed an speedup of 24, computing the speedup as:

$$Speedup = \frac{T_{CPU}(16K_{gen})}{T_{GPU}((16K_{gen})}$$

where $T_{CPU}(16K_{gen})$ and $T_{GPU}(16K_{gen})$ are the execution time for 160000 generations on the CPU and on the CPU-GPU respectively. This figure is important also if we think (1) about the difficulty of the parallel implementation (on the GPU) of the crossover operator when dealing with permutational encodings (as is the case here with the TSP), and (2) When computing the fitness value on the GPU, we need a high amount of data transfers with the global Memory of the GPU, since we didn't store the information of the distances on the shared memory. The former should be improved in future work when dealing with bigger TSP instances.

7. CONCLUSIONS

In this paper we have checked the utility of the EMMRS algorithm not only with deceptive functions but also with the TSP problem. The main motivation of the paper was to show that the Replacement and Shift favors the search in several regions of the space. It works on a way similar to a mutation operator, however it is not

Table 6: Results for Pr76 instance

Instance	Pr76		
Algorithm	Avg.	Std	#Opt
$EMMRS_A$	98.460	0.805	3
$EMMRS_B$	98.548	0.956	6
$EMMRS_C$	98.935	0.712	8
$EMMRS_D$	98.939	0.744	9
$EMMRS_E$	98.135	1.018	3
$EMMRS_F$	98.319	1.133	5
$EMMRS_G$	98.444	0.868	3
$EMMRS_H$	98.358	0.893	3
EMM_A	70.942	3.561	0
EMM_B	70.766	4.366	0
EMM_C	72.966	3.144	0
EMM_D	72.765	3.349	0
EMM_E	69.785	4.482	0
EMM_F	70.830	3.690	0
EMM_G	72.562	3.099	0
EMM_H	72.902	3.283	0
GA_A	71.318	3.953	0
GA_B	72.237	3.870	0
GA_C	76.042	3.546	0
GA_D	74.763	3.397	0
GA_E	70.778	3.620	0
GA_F	71.792	4.663	0
GA_G	74.148	3.965	0
GA_H	74.170	3.769	0

so aggressive in terms of the translation through the search space. We think that applied with a medium probability allows to combine both exploration and exploitation. As a final conclusion we put together results from [12] and our new results. Although we need not only more experimental study, but also a theoretical analysis, we extract from the experimental results that the R&S is good for problems so different as those presented in Table 7.

Acknowledgements

ABSys group is supported by Spanish Government grants INNPACTO-IPT-2011-1198-430000 and TIN 2008-00508.

8. ADDITIONAL AUTHORS

Josefa Díaz (Universidad de Extremadura, GEA Group, email: mjdiaz@unex.es).

9. REFERENCES

[1] R. Chow. Evolving genotype to phenotype mappings with a multiple-chromosome genetic algorithm. *GECCO 2004*, vol. 3102 of *LNCS*, pages 1006–1017. Springer, 2004.

[2] D. Dasgupta. Handling Deceptive Problems Using a Different Genetic Search. In *International Conference on Evolutionary Computation*, pages 807–811, 1994.

[3] S. Forrest and M. Mitchell. What Makes a Problem Hard for a Genetic Algorithm? Some Anomalous Results and Their Explanation. *Machine Learning*, 13:285–319, 1993.

[4] D. Goldberg and R. L. Alleles. Loci and the traveling salesman problem. In *International Conference on Genetic Algorithms*, 1985.

[5] D. E. Goldberg. Genetic Algorithms and Walsh Functions Part II: Deception and its Analysis. *Complex Systems*, 3:129–152, 1989.

Table 7: default

Problem	GA %	GA Avg.	EMM %	EMM Avg.	EMMRS %	EMMRS Avg.
f4	100 %	1690	100 %	916	100 %	179
f8	0 %	n/a/	78 %	8291	100 %	1040
fU40	0 %	n/a	100 %	1593	100 %	105
fU60	0 %	n/a	100 %	2739	100 %	253
fB40	0 %	n/a	100 %	4578	100 %	380
fB60	0 %	n/a	64 %	9353	100 %	550
fS	83 %	3756	74 %	1874	82 %	2137
fR	0 %	n/a	0 %	n/a	100 %	3105
Gr48	0 %	n/a/	0 %	n/a/	28 %	13468
Pr76	0 %	n/a/	0 %	n/a/	18 %	57911
kroA100	0 %	n/a/	0 %	n/a/	2 %	124703
kroB100	0 %	n/a/	0 %	n/a/	0 %	n/a
kroC100	0 %	n/a/	0 %	n/a/	4 %	85784
kroD100	0 %	n/a/	0 %	n/a/	2 %	64893
kroE100	0 %	n/a/	0 %	n/a/	2 %	34296

[6] D. E. Goldberg and C. L. Bridges. An analysis of a reordering operator on a GA-hard problem. *Biological Cybernetics*, 62:397–405, 1990.

[7] D. E. Goldberg and J. Richardson. Genetic algorithm with sharing for multimodal function optimization. In *Proceedings of the Second International Conference on Genetic Algorithms*, pages 41–49, Hillsdale, NJ, 1987. Lawrence Erlbaum Associates.

[8] C. Igel and M. Toussaint. On classes of functions for which No Free Lunch results hold. *Information Processing Letters*, 86:317–321, 2003.

[9] W. B. Langdon. Graphics processing units and genetic programming: an overview. *Soft Computing*, 15:1657–1669, 2011.

[10] G. E. Liepins and M. D. Vose. Deceptiveness and genetic algorithm dynamics. In G. J. E. Rawlins, editor, *FOGA*, pages 36–50. Morgan Kaufmann, 1990.

[11] S. K. Park and K. W. Miller. Random number generators: good ones are hard to find. *Communications of The ACM*, 31:1192–1201, 1988.

[12] J. L. Risco-Martin, J. I. Hidalgo, J. Lanchares, and O. Garnica. Solving discrete deceptive problems with EMMRS. In *Genetic and Evolutionary Computation Conference*, pages 1139–1140, 2008.

[13] F. Rothlauf. *Representations for genetic and evolutionary algorithms*, volume 104 of *Studies in Fuzziness and Soft Computing*. Springer, 2002.

[14] M. Shackleton, R. Shipma, and M. Ebner. An investigation of redundant genotype-phenotype mappings and their role in evolutionary search. In *IEEE Congress on Evolutionary Computation*, 2000.

[15] L. D. Whitley. Fundamental Principles of Deception in Genetic Search. In *Foundations of Genetic Algorithms*, pages 221–241, 1990.

Towards Highly Optimized Cartesian Genetic Programming: From Sequential via SIMD and Thread to Massive Parallel Implementation

Radek Hrbacek
Brno University of Technology, Czech republic
Faculty of Information Technology
ihrbacek@fit.vutbr.cz

Lukas Sekanina
Brno University of Technology, Czech republic
Faculty of Information Technology
sekanina@fit.vutbr.cz

ABSTRACT

Most implementations of Cartesian genetic programming (CGP) which can be found in the literature are sequential. However, solving complex design problems by means of genetic programming requires parallel implementations of search methods and fitness functions. This paper deals with the design of highly optimized implementations of CGP and their detailed evaluation in the task of evolutionary circuit design. Several sequential implementations of CGP have been analyzed and the effect of various additional optimizations has been investigated. Furthermore, the parallelism at the instruction, data, thread and process level has been applied in order to take advantage of modern processor architectures and computer clusters. Combinational adders and multipliers have been chosen to give a performance comparison with state of the art methods.

Categories and Subject Descriptors

B.6.0 [**Hardware**]: Logic Design—*General*; I.2.8 [**Computing methodologies**]: Artificial intelligence—*Problem Solving, Control Methods, and Search*

Keywords

Cartesian Genetic Programming, Parallel Computing, SIMD, AVX, Cluster, Combinational Circuit Design

1. INTRODUCTION

The evolutionary design conducted by means of genetic programming (GP) is a very computationally demanding design method. In order to reduce the design time, various accelerators of genetic programming have been proposed. The accelerators are typically developed to speed up the main components of the method – the search algorithm and the fitness evaluation procedure. While the former case is usually investigated in the field of parallel and distributed evolutionary algorithms, the latter one typically involves accelerating an application specific simulator in which every candidate phenotype has to be evaluated. The most famous parallel approaches to GP are represented by Koza's Beowulf-style parallel cluster [10] and recently, an approach developed for the cloud environment [17].

As CGP has been accelerated on GPUs [6] and FPGAs [20], in this contribution, the parallelism at the instruction, data, thread and process level has been applied in order to take advantage of modern processor architectures and computer clusters. The goal of this paper is to provide a set of parallel CGP implementations that can be used on these widely accessible parallel computers. The proposed implementations will be compared and evaluated in the task of adder and multiplier evolutionary design. The reason for choosing these two problems is that the literature includes several case studies that can be used for comparative purposes.

Another important assumption of this study is that CGP starts with a randomly generated initial population and the objective is to find a fully functional solution, i.e. an n_i-input/n_o-output circuit which provides $n_o \cdot 2^{n_i}$ correct output bits when all possible input combinations are evaluated. In other words, the goal is not in minimizing the number of gates, delay or other criteria. Note that for the evolutionary circuit optimization, in which CGP starts with a fully functional solution and the goal is to minimize the number of gates, efficient and fast fitness calculation methods based on formal functional equivalence checking algorithms have already been proposed [21]. While such methods are capable of optimizing circuits having hundreds of inputs and thousands of gates, only relatively small circuits (with ten to fifteen inputs and less than 100 gates) have been evolved so far in the proposed scenario. Finally, this work does not take into account advanced methods such as divide and conquer [18, 16] or self-modifying CGP [7] which allow for reducing the problem complexity and consequently applying the standard CGP on sub-problems. Therefore, all techniques reported in this paper operate on the whole circuit.

Parallel CGP implementations are usually focused on an efficient phenotype evaluation, which is the most time critical operation of CGP due to the fact that the circuit evaluation time grows exponentially with the number of circuit inputs. In order to accelerate a candidate circuit evaluation, one can apply a parallel evaluation of multiple training vectors by means of bit-level instructions [14], circuit precompilation techniques or streaming SIMD extensions (SSE) of modern processors [22].

GECCO'14, July 12-16, 2014, Vancouver, BC, Canada.
Copyright 2014 ACM 978-1-4503-2662-9/14/07 ...$15.00.
http://dx.doi.org/10.1145/2576768.2598343

On the other hand, the search algorithm used in the standard CGP is a simple (1+λ) evolution strategy. A natural approach to accelerating the search is evaluating λ offspring on λ processors in parallel. A few attempts were made to introduce more advanced operators into this search method, but only a small improvement was reported in [3]. However, a noticeable improvement can be obtained when the standard CGP is replaced by parallel coevolutionary CGP [9].

The rest of the paper is organized as follows. Section 2 introduces CGP and its usage as combinational circuit design method. The implementation of several sequential solutions is discussed in Section 3. Section 4 deals with the CGP parallelisation. Section 5 is dedicated to experiments and the achieved results. Final conclusions can be found in Section 6.

2. CARTESIAN GENETIC PROGRAMMING

Cartesian genetic programming has been introduced by Miller [12] as a branch of genetic programming. Unlike GP which uses tree representation, an individual in CGP is represented by a directed acyclic graph which enables the candidate solution to have multiple outputs and automatically reuse intermediate results. This makes CGP very suitable for design of various kinds of digital circuits, such as arithmetic and logic circuits, digital filters, etc. [13].

CGP uses a cartesian grid of $n_r \times n_c$ programmable elements (nodes) interconnected by a feed-forward network (Figure 1). Each node's input (usually each node has a fixed number of inputs $n_{ni} = 2$) can be connected either to one of n_i primary inputs or to a node output in the preceding l columns. By setting the l-back parameter and the grid size, one can control the area and delay of the circuit. Each node can be programmed to perform one of n_{ni}-input functions defined in the set Γ (let $n_f = |\Gamma|$). The n_o primary circuit outputs are connected either to the primary inputs or nodes. The output connectivity can be optionally restricted by the o-back parameter.

Since all the CGP parameters are fixed, each chromosome is encoded using a fixed-sized array of $n_r \cdot n_c \cdot (n_{ni} + 1) + n_o$ integers. Each primary input is assigned a number from $\{0, ..., n_i - 1\}$ and the nodes are assigned numbers from $\{n_i, ..., n_i + n_r \cdot n_c - 1\}$. The genotype is of fixed length, whereas the phenotype is of variable length depending on the number of inactive nodes, i.e. nodes whose output is not used by any other node or primary output. Hence, the genotype-phenotype mapping is not injective. The existence of genotypes with the same fitness is usually referred to as neutrality. The role of neutrality has been intensively studied [24] and it was shown that for certain problems the neutrality significantly reduces the computational effort and helps to find more innovative solutions [11].

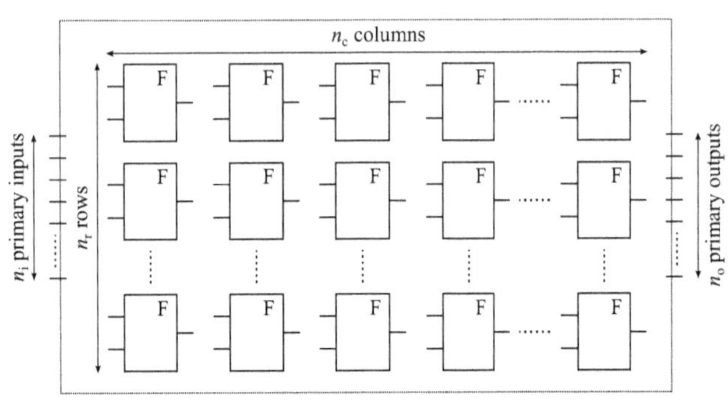

Figure 1: Cartesian genetic programming scheme.

In CGP, a simple mutation based (1 + λ) evolutionary strategy is used as a search mechanism. The population size $1 + \lambda$ is usually very small, typically, λ is between 1 and 15. The initial population is constructed either randomly (evolutionary design) or by mapping of a known solution to the CGP chromosome (evolutionary optimization) [21]. In each generation, a randomly selected individual with the best fitness value is passed to the next generation unmodified and its λ offspring individuals are created by means of point mutation operator which modifies m randomly selected genes of the chromosome. The mutation rate m is usually set to modify up to 5 % of the genes. Despite numerous attempts, no useful crossover operator has been introduced. For some problem classes (e.g. symbolic regression problem), special crossover operators have been investigated [3], however, in the case of digital circuits design, none of them has been confirmed as useful.

In the case of combinational circuit evolution, the fitness function corresponds to the quality of the candidate circuit measured as the number of correct output bits compared to a specified truth table. In order to obtain a fully working circuit, all combinations of input values have to be evaluated. For a circuit with n_i inputs and n_o outputs, 2^{n_i} test vectors need to be fetched to the primary inputs and $n_o \cdot 2^{n_i}$ output bits have to be verified so as to compute the fitness value.

3. SEQUENTIAL IMPLEMENTATION

Every CGP implementation must process all the 2^{n_i} test vectors on the whole phenotype for the entire population of individuals and compare all the n_o outputs to the desired ones. This requirement directly implies the presence of 3 independent nested loops – the test vector loop, the loop over all nodes and the population loop. The order of these 3 loops is crucial for the performance and the optimal choice varies among different implementations. In a very naive implementation, one can process each test vector separately on all nodes no matter if they are active or not. However, in order to take advantage of modern superscalar out-of-order processors, the parallelism at various levels has to be employed and special attention to memory access policy has to be paid.

The most fundamental optimization we can apply is the bit-level parallelism. Instead of separate test vector processing, up to 64 test vectors can be processed in parallel on 64-bit processors thanks to bitwise operations. Furthermore, by introducing the data-level parallelism using SIMD instructions, 128 or even 256 test vectors can fit into the SSE or AVX registers respectively.

One of the most commonly used optimization in CGP is the detection of inactive nodes. Before processing each individual, the genotype is traversed in the reversed order and the nodes whose output is never used are marked as inactive. While processing, all inactive nodes are skipped and thus only the phenotype is treated.

3.1 Interpreted implementation

The *interpreted* implementation is very simple, yet for smaller circuits very efficient. The principle is shown in Algorithm 1. At the beginning, an initial population is created randomly just like in any other implementation. Then, in

```
randomly create and evaluate initial population;
while termination condition is false do
    for i in 1 to P do
        if i = best_ind then
            continue;
        end
        copy ind[best_ind] chromosome to ind[i];
        mutate ind[i];
        analyze ind[i];
        foreach node do
            foreach test vector do
                compute node output value;
            end
        end
        foreach primary output do
            ind[i].fit += number of wrong bits;
        end
        if ind[i].fit > ind[best_ind].fit then
            best_ind := i;
        end
    end
end
```

Algorithm 1: Interpreted implementation

every generation, the evaluation of the population is going on as follows: For each individual not being the best individual from the previous generation, the chromosome of the best individual is copied and mutated. After that, the chromosome is analyzed in order to find the inactive nodes. For each active node, all test vectors are processed according to the node function. The test vector loop is put inside the node loop because of the overhead of the `switch` statement the node function is based on. Besides the overhead, by putting the test vector loop inside, the compiler is able to optimize this loop by unrolling. After computing each node's output value, the primary outputs are checked against desired values and the number of wrong bits is accumulated. This can be done very efficiently just by `XOR`ing the actual output value and the expected value and counting the number of ones. Since SSE 4.2, a special instruction `POPCNT` exists which allows to count the number of ones with the latency of 3 clock cycles (on the Intel Sandy Bridge microarchitecture) [4].

Since all of the intermediate results for all test vectors have to be kept in memory during the evaluation, the memory usage of the interpreted implementation is not optimal (up to $n_r \cdot n_c \cdot 2^{n_i}/8$ bytes), but it is still efficient for small circuits, until the required memory size exceeds the cache size.

3.2 Native implementation

By introducing the *native* implementation, both the memory requirements and the `switch` statement overhead can be significantly reduced. The principle can be seen from Algorithm 2. Just like in the interpreted implementation, each individual except the previous best one is copied, mutated and analyzed. The difference lies in the evaluation process

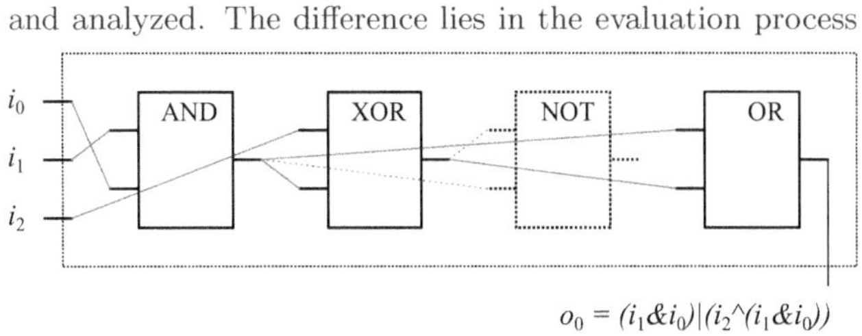

Figure 2: CGP individual example.

```
randomly create and evaluate initial population;
while termination condition is false do
    for i in 1 to P do
        if i = best_ind then
            continue;
        end
        copy ind[best_ind] chromosome to ind[i];
        mutate ind[i];
        analyze ind[i];
        compile ind[i];
    end
    foreach test vector do
        for i in 1 to P do
            if i = best_ind then
                continue;
            end
            ind[i].fit += run compiled code;
        end
    end
    for i in 1 to P do
        if ind[i].fit > ind[best_ind].fit then
            best_ind := i;
        end
    end
end
```

Algorithm 2: Native implementation.

– instead of traversing the chromosome and computing the node outputs directly, the chromosome is compiled at first. The compiled program is then executed on each test vector for each individual in the population. This technique was first introduced in [22] and the implementation presented in this paper further improves this principle by introducing subroutine parameters, native fitness calculation and by utilizing AVX instructions. Moreover, the native implementation uses slightly less memory since there is no need to keep the intermediate results for all test vectors.

Figure 2 depicts a very simple circuit with $n_i = 3$ primary inputs, $n_o = 1$ primary output and $n_c = 4$ nodes. Listing 1 shows the compiled chromosome from Figure 2 in 64-bit version. The compiled subroutine has 4 parameters passed on in the 64-bit registers `RDI`, `RSI`, `RDX` and `RCX` [15] – the pointers to the primary inputs filled by corresponding test vectors, node outputs, desired primary outputs and spe-

Listing 1: Native 64b implementation example.

```
push    %rbx                ; store RBX

mov     0x08(%rsi),%rbx     ; node n0
and     0x00(%rsi),%rbx     ; AND
mov     %rbx,0x18(%rdi)     ; n0 := i1 AND i0

mov     0x10(%rsi),%rbx     ; node n1
xor     0x18(%rdi),%rbx     ; XOR
mov     %rbx,0x20(%rdi)     ; n1 := i2 XOR n0

mov     0x18(%rdi),%rbx     ; node n3
or      0x28(%rdi),%rbx     ; OR
mov     %rbx,0x30(%rdi)     ; n3 := n0 OR n2

xor     %rax,%rax           ; RAX := 0

mov     0x30(%rsi),%rbx     ; output 00
xor     0x0(%rdx),%rbx
and     0x0(%rcx),%rbx      ; mask m0
popcnt  %rbx,%bdx           ; error count
add     %rbx,%rax           ; accumulate

pop     %rbx                ; restore RBX
retq                        ; return RAX
```

cial masks.[1] For each node, the first input value is loaded from the memory to the RBX register and the desired operation is performed (optionally, the second input value is loaded).[2] The node output is then stored back to the memory. After processing all active nodes, the number of wrong output bits is accumulated in the RAX register. For each primary output, the corresponding node output is loaded from the memory and XORed with the desired value. After applying the mask, the number of incorrect bits is computed using the POPCNT instruction and accumulated in the RAX register. The register RAX is used for integer return values [15], thus the subroutine returns the number of wrong bits for a given test vector.

The same example compiled in the AVX version can be seen in Listing 2. Here, the calling convention is the same and the register RAX has the same purpose as in the 64-bit version. The intermediate results are computed in the YMM0 register. The register YMM1 contains just ones and serves for computing the NOT operation using XOR, since there is not an AVX instruction for this purpose. Compared to the 64-bit version, the error computation is more complicated as there is only a 32-bit and 64-bit POPCNT instruction available.

[1]After XORing the actual and desired output value, the result is ANDed with this mask, which enables to specify which output bits are not considered (we don't care about their values).

[2]There is no need to avoid the output dependency thanks to hardware register renaming.

Listing 2: Native AVX implementation example.

```
push      %rbx                          ; store RBX

mov       0xXXXXXXXX,%rax               ; RAX := &avx_ones
vmovdqa   0x0(%rax),%ymm1               ; YMM1 := 111..111

vmovdqa   0x20(%rsi),%ymm0              ; node n0
vandps    0x0(%rdi),%ymm0,%ymm0         ; AND
vmovdqa   %ymm0,0x60(%rdi)              ; n0 := i1 AND i0

vmovdqa   0x40(%rsi),%ymm0              ; node n1
vxorps    0x60(%rdi),%ymm0,%ymm0        ; XOR
vmovdqa   %ymm0,0x80(%rdi)              ; n1 := i2 XOR n0

vmovdqa   0x60(%rdi),%ymm0              ; node n3
vorps     0xa0(%rdi),%ymm0              ; OR
vmovdqa   %ymm0,0xc0(%rdi)              ; n3 := n0 OR n2

xor       %rax,%rax                     ; RAX := 0

mov       0xc0(%rsi),%rbx               ; output o0[0]
xor       0x0(%rdx),%rbx
and       0x0(%rcx),%rbx                ; mask m0[0]
popcnt    %rbx,%rbx                     ; error count
add       %rbx,%rax
mov       0xc8(%rsi),%rbx               ; output o0[1]
xor       0x8(%rdx),%rbx
and       0x8(%rcx),%rbx                ; mask m0[1]
popcnt    %rbx,%rbx                     ; error count
add       %rbx,%rax
mov       0xd0(%rsi),%rbx               ; output o0[2]
xor       0x10(%rdx),%rbx
and       0x10(%rcx),%rbx               ; mask m0[2]
popcnt    %rbx,%rbx                     ; error count
add       %rbx,%rax
mov       0xd8(%rsi),%rbx               ; output o0[3]
xor       0x18(%rdx),%rbx
and       0x18(%rcx),%rbx               ; mask m0[3]
popcnt    %rbx,%rbx                     ; error count
add       %rbx,%rax

pop       %rbx                          ; restore RBX
retq                                    ; return RAX
```

The native implementation enables to introduce more optimizations than the interpreted implementation. The fitness computation can be stopped after exceeding the number of wrong bits matching the best individual. Both native and interpreted implementations can detect neutral mutations and skip recomputing fitness values for individuals affected only by neutral mutations [5].

The efficiency of the native implementation lies in exploiting the instruction-level parallelism offered by modern superscalar out-of-order processors by reducing branch mispredictions and cache misses and increasing the arithmetic intesity.

4. PARALLEL IMPLEMENTATION

Until the beginning of the 21st century, the aim of the processor architects was to increase the single threaded performance by means of extracting more instruction-level parallelism (ILP) and utilizing superscalar out-of-order execution, sophisticated branch predictors, multi-level cache hierarchy, etc. However, growing power consumption and limited ILP extractable from common sequential code together with increasing transistor density led to the introduction of multiprocessors [8]. Since then, special attention has to be paid to parallel computing in order to make use of modern processor architectures.

4.1 Thread parallelism

The purpose of the thread-level parallelism (TLP) in CGP is to speed up the whole evolutionary process – both the fitness calculation and the genetic operators. Both interpreted and native parallel implementations are discussed in this subsection; the OpenMP library has been used for managing the threads.

Algorithm 3 shows the scheme of the interpreted parallel implementation, very similar to the corresponding sequential variant. The outer population loop has to be scheduled dynamically, because if it were scheduled statically, the thread responsible for the previous best individual would have less work than the others resulting in poor load balancing.

The parallelization of the native implementation is some-

```
randomly create and evaluate initial population;
while termination condition is false do
    #pragma omp for schedule(dynamic)
    for i in 1 to pop_size do
        if i = best_ind then
            continue;
        end
        copy ind[best_ind] chromosome to ind[i];
        mutate ind[i];
        analyze ind[i];
        foreach node do
            foreach test vector do
                compute node output value;
            end
        end
        foreach primary output do
            ind[i].fit += number of wrong bits;
        end
        #pragma omp critical
        if ind[i].fit > ind[best_ind].fit then
            best_ind := i;
        end
    end
end
```

Algorithm 3: Parallel interpreted implementation.

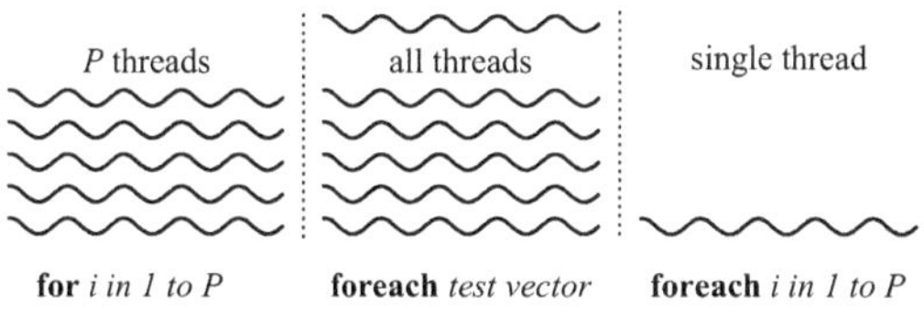

Figure 3: Parallel native implementation threading.

```
randomly create and evaluate initial population;
while termination condition is false do
    #pragma omp for
    for i in 1 to P do
        if i = best_ind then
            continue;
        end
        copy ind[best_ind] chromosome to ind[i];
        mutate ind[i];
        analyze ind[i];
        compile ind[i];
    end
    foreach i in 1 to P do
        fit[i] = 0;
    end
    #pragma omp barrier
    #pragma omp for nowait
    foreach test vector do
        foreach i = 1 to P do
            if i = best_ind then
                continue;
            end
            fit[i] += run compiled code;
        end
    end
    foreach i in 1 to P do
        #pragma omp atomic
        ind[i].fit += fit[i];
    end
    #pragma omp barrier
    #pragma omp single
    for i in 1 to P do
        if ind[i].fit > ind[best_ind].fit then
            best_ind := i;
        end
    end
end
```

Algorithm 4: Parallel native implementation.

what more complicated, since it consists of three separate loops, each having a different number of iterations. Figure 3 depicts the threading scheme. At first, a new population has to be created using up to P threads, then the evaluation can utilize all the threads (if there are enough test vectors) and at the end, the new best individual has to be found, unfortunately by a single thread.

Algorithm 4 shows the overall parallel implementation principle. A special attention had to be paid for the fitness accumulation across test vectors treated by different threads. Each thread has its own partial fitness values which are finally atomically accumulated to the total fitness values doing a manual reduction over the fitness values (OpenMP offers only reduction over scalar variables).

4.2 Process parallelism (inter-population)

Spatially structured evolutionary algorithms have been intensively studied in the past and a variety of approaches differing in the used evolutionary algorithm or communication topology has emerged [19, 2]. By introducing multiple populations evolving in parallel, one can increase the population

```
seed := randomly generated individual;
while termination condition is false do
    run evolutionary design starting with seed;
    exchange best individuals among islands;
    if global best fitness is higher than local then
        seed := global best individual;
    end
end
```

Algorithm 5: Isolated islands model.

diversity and thus make the EA more explorative leading to a higher probability of finding the global optimum for particular problems.

The combinational circuit design is a very complex problem, the search space is generally rugged containing lots of local optima and thus the potential of exploiting parallel EA is high. Unfortunately, the absence of a crossover operator in CGP is a very limiting factor since most parallel models take advantage of combining genotypes from different isolated populations. Nevertheless, the model of isolated islands with migration of the best individuals in each population can be applied to this problem.

Algorithm 5 describes the parallel evolutionary process. At the beginning, each population starts with a randomly generated initial population. Until a perfectly working circuit is found, the evolutionary process is executed on each island and after specified number of generations, the best individual from each island is broadcasted to the other islands. If the global best individual has higher fitness value than the local best individual, the island is seeded by the global best one.

After migration, each isolated population is evolving independently and can explore different areas in the search space. This makes the search algorithm more effective and speeds up the evolutionary process.

The implementation is based on the Open MPI library and can be executed on computer clusters of arbitrary size as well as on a single multiprocessor giving a great scalability to the evolutionary design process.

5. EXPERIMENTAL RESULTS

In this section, experiments regarding the implementation performance are presented and the scalability of the implementation is demonstrated on selected combinational circuit design problems. All experiments were performed on a computer cluster of 112 nodes with the following hardware configuration: 2× 8-core Intel E5-2670, 128 GB RAM, 2× 600 GB 15 k scratch hard disks, connected by gigabit Ethernet and Infiniband links.

The implementations have been examined by means of the common metrics: *speedup*, defined as the ratio of the sequential implementation execution time to the parallel execution time, and *efficiency*, the ratio between the achieved speedup and the number of threads.

5.1 Sequential implementation efficiency

The performance of the sequential implementations has been measured in the task of a combinational adder design. Table 1 and Figure 4 summarize the mean evolution times obtained from 100 independent runs for individual sequential implementations. The CGP parameters were set as follows: population of 5 individuals, $n_c = 100$ nodes, mutation rate 5 %, $\Gamma = \{\texttt{BUF}, \texttt{NOT}, \texttt{AND}, \texttt{OR}, \texttt{XOR}, \texttt{NAND}, \texttt{NOR}, \texttt{XNOR}\}$. The goal was not to find a fully functional solution, the evolu-

Table 1: Sequential implementation performance (combinational adders, 10 000 generations).

width	evolution time [s]			
	interpreted		native	
	64b	256b	64b	256b
1 × 1	0.00382	-	0.00477	-
2 × 2	0.00908	-	0.02168	-
3 × 3	0.01994	-	0.04954	-
4 × 4	0.02442	0.02398	0.05497	0.07092
5 × 5	0.04681	0.03215	0.07076	0.08550
6 × 6	0.11488	0.08280	0.11168	0.11109
7 × 7	0.97894	0.40800	0.28149	0.21899
8 × 8	6.27716	2.14536	0.88332	0.55520
9 × 9	32.64657	9.84838	3.63436	2.21870
10 × 10	154.38932	47.59685	14.99801	8.75244

Table 2: Sequential implementation speedup (combinational adders, 10 000 generations).

width	speedup [-]		
	interpreted	native	
	256b	64b	256b
1 × 1	-	0.80084	-
2 × 2	-	0.41882	-
3 × 3	-	0.40250	-
4 × 4	1.01835	0.44424	0.34433
5 × 5	1.45599	0.66153	0.54749
6 × 6	1.38744	1.02865	1.03412
7 × 7	2.39936	3.47771	4.47025
8 × 8	2.92592	7.10633	11.30612
9 × 9	3.31492	8.98276	14.71428
10 × 10	3.24369	10.29399	17.63957

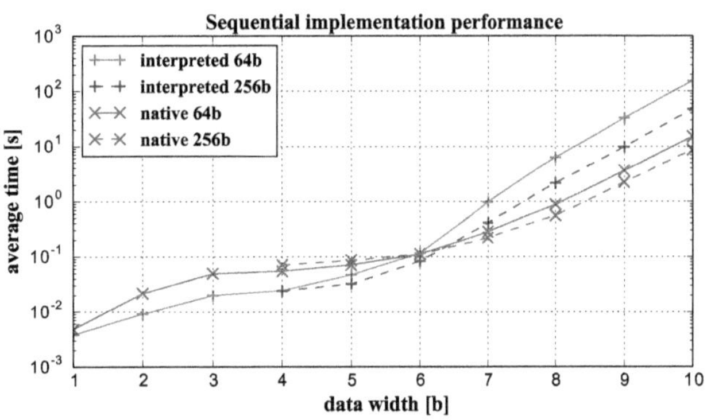

Figure 4: Sequential implementation performance (combinational adders, 10 000 generations).

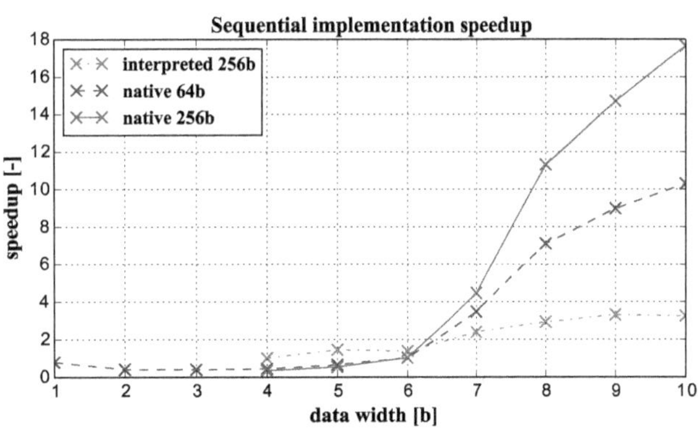

Figure 5: Sequential implementation speedup (combinational adders, 10 000 generations).

tion has been stopped after reaching 10 000 generations. The achieved speedup relative to the 64b interpreted implementation can be seen in Table 2 and Figure 5. The experimental results indicate that for small circuits, the best implementation is the 64b interpreted implementation. Starting with 8 primary inputs, the number of test vectors goes over the limit of 256 test vectors and the AVX implementation comes to the foreground. The native AVX implementation needs even larger circuits to overcome the compilation overhead and to be sufficiently efficient, however, the achieved speedup is significant.

5.2 Parallel implementation efficiency

The sequential implementation performance is not substantially dependent on the number of nodes, which is not the case of the parallel implementation efficiency. Therefore, in order to evaluate the parallel speedup and efficiency, a more complex circuit has been chosen for the experiment, namely the combinational multiplier with $n_c = 800$ nodes. The population size was 5 individuals, the evolutionary process was stopped after 100 000 generations in the case of data widths 4–6 bits, 10 000 otherwise. Table 3 summarizes

Table 3: Parallel implementation efficiency.

width	threads	time [s]	speedup [-]	efficiency [%]
4 × 4	1	1.092	-	-
	2	0.705	1.550	77.484
	3	0.683	1.598	53.277
	4	0.490	2.227	55.677
5 × 5	1	1.409	-	-
	2	0.857	1.644	82.213
	3	0.837	1.683	56.094
	4	0.567	2.486	62.149
6 × 6	1	3.616	-	-
	2	2.048	1.766	88.295
	3	1.950	1.855	61.827
	4	1.226	2.950	73.751
7 × 7	1	0.584	-	-
	2	0.372	1.571	78.554
	3	0.295	1.983	66.103
	4	0.247	2.361	59.033
	5	0.212	2.755	55.101
	6	0.198	2.947	49.119
	7	0.202	2.899	41.410
	8	0.196	2.985	37.312
8 × 8	1	1.663	-	-
	2	0.925	1.797	89.872
	3	0.678	2.452	81.745
	4	0.539	3.082	77.044
	5	0.448	3.710	74.202
	6	0.399	4.163	69.385
	7	0.380	4.370	62.424
	8	0.347	4.786	59.831
9 × 9	1	6.108	-	-
	2	3.251	1.879	93.945
	3	2.202	2.774	92.466
	4	1.717	3.556	88.908
	5	1.422	4.294	85.879
	6	1.230	4.964	82.730
	7	1.105	5.529	78.990
	8	0.985	6.199	77.482
10 × 10	1	25.825	-	-
	2	13.455	1.919	95.972
	3	9.070	2.847	94.912
	4	7.077	3.649	91.231
	5	5.840	4.422	88.440
	6	4.905	5.265	87.758
	7	4.363	5.919	84.553
	8	3.842	6.722	84.029

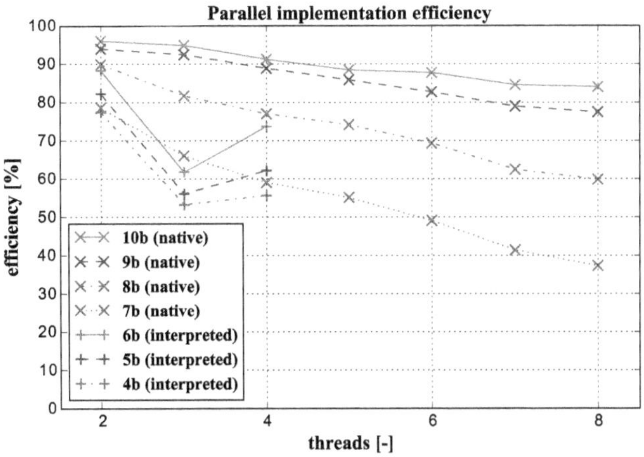

Figure 6: Parallel implementation efficiency.

the results. For each input data width, 100 independent runs were performed and the mean evolution time has been calculated.

The interpreted parallel implementation is limited to λ threads since each thread treats its own individual. Besides that, the number of threads should divide λ for the best load balancing. This is not the case of the native parallel implementation, however, sufficiently many test vectors need to be evaluated to fully utilize all eight cores of the E5-2670 processor (Figure 6).

The parallel efficiency is affected by the dynamic frequency scaling which is present in Intel's processors. In real deployment, when all processor cores are fully loaded, the sequential implementation evinces slightly worse performance due to lower frequency, hence the parallel efficiency is better. Especially on multi-socket systems, one must mind the affinity of the threads, preferably by binding individual threads to specific processor cores, to reduce cache misses and keep the memory access time as low as possible.

5.3 Test problems

Three different configurations of the evolutionary algorithm have been examined – standard single-population CGP optionally parallelized, multi-population CGP with few isolated islands and massively parallel CGP exploiting tens of islands. The performance of these approaches has been evaluated in the task of a combinational adder and multiplier design, in the literature generally considered as very difficult tasks [23, 18]. The evolutionary design was stopped after finding a fully functional solution.

Table 4: Combinational adder design performance.

width	nodes $n_r \times n_c$	hosts/ threads	time [s] mean	median	std
6 × 6	1 × 100	1/6	39.4644	31.713	27.87117
		6/1	12.3851	10.620	7.966
		60/1	3.259	2.871	1.608
7 × 7	1 × 150	1/6	142.419	103.722	139.862
		6/1	53.479	44.286	37.883
		60/1	17.569	16.410	7.864
8 × 8	1 × 200	1/6	367.915	307.545	254.455
		6/1	129.546	106.111	76.887
		60/1	57.961	48.986	44.527
9 × 9	1 × 250	1/6	3085.891	2802.061	1548.292
		6/1	1607.212	1413.261	795.004
		60/1	525.032	462.648	250.616

Table 5: Combinational multiplier design performance.

width	nodes $n_r \times n_c$	hosts/ threads	time [s] mean	median	std
2 × 2	1 × 50	1/1	0.00451	0.00333	0.00385
3 × 2	1 × 100	1/1	0.0451	0.0338	0.0319
3 × 3	1 × 200	1/1	1.897	1.469	1.605
		6/1	0.530	0.417	0.403
4 × 3	1 × 400	1/4	10.365	8.427	8.726
		6/1	5.106	3.979	3.991
		60/1	2.457	2.210	1.140
4 × 4	1 × 800	1/4	817.689	874.075	148.275
		6/1	538.058	458.494	310.345
		60/1	191.175	154.922	141.206
5 × 4	1 × 1200	60/1	761.327	700.151	303.906
5 × 5	1 × 1600	60/2	16452.75[3]		

Table 4 shows the statistics for combinational adders of data widths 6–9 bits calculated on a set of 100 independent runs for each experimental setup, namely the mean evolution time, median and standard deviation. In the case of the multi-population approaches, the migration of the best individuals occurred every 100 000 generations. It can be observed that the multi-population approach even with few isolated islands significantly reduces the time requirements on the design process compared to the single-population CGP using the same computational capacity (6 threads vs. 6 processes). By increasing the number of islands, the evolution time decreases and according to the standard deviation, the convergence becomes more stable. The stalling effect in the fitness function, commonly observed when using other approaches [18, 1], is mitigated as a consequence of a more explorative search.

The evolutionary design of combinational multipliers is an even more complex task. No satisfactory results related to techniques operating on the whole circuit without decomposition have been published so far. While paper [23] reports only a single complete run for the 4-bit multiplier, with the aid of the proposed highly optimized CGP implementation, we can routinely design 4-bit multipliers and moreover, 5-bit multipliers are feasible as well (Table 5).

6. CONCLUSIONS

In this paper, highly optimized CGP implementations have been presented. Starting with several sequential versions, the paper thoroughly examines miscellaneous implementation aspects and gives detailed performance comparisons of the proposed approaches. Parallelism at various levels has been applied in order to speed up the evolutionary design process. The native implementation based on compilation of the genotype into machine code exploits the instruction-level parallelism by reducing program branching and increasing the arithmetic intensity. A large amount of test vectors can be evaluated in parallel thanks to the use of AVX instructions. Besides a thread-parallel version, a process-parallel implementation based on the isolated islands model has been proposed.

The performance and scalability has been demonstrated on the task of combinational adders and multipliers design which is believed to be a very complex task. No additional knowledge has been introduced into the design process. All

[3]Due to the very high computational effort, only a single experiment has been executed for the 5-bit multiplier.

experiments started from a randomly generated initial population. In comparison with the previously published results regarding similar evolutionary design approaches, much more complex circuits are feasible to be designed with the proposed CGP implementation.

Note that the absence of a crossover operator in CGP is a potential limiting factor and by inventing a suitable one, more efficient parallel evolutionary approaches could be applied. In our future research, we will focus on investigating more sophisticated spatially structured evolutionary algorithms with the aim of designing even more complex combinational circuits on computer clusters.

7. ACKNOWLEDGMENTS

This work was supported by the Czech Science Foundation project 14-04197S. The access to the CERIT-SC computing and storage facilities provided under the programme Center CERIT Scientific Cloud, part of the Operational Program Research and Development for Innovations, reg. no. CZ. 1.05/3.2.00/08.0144 is highly appreciated.

8. REFERENCES

[1] T. Aoki, N. Homma, and T. Higuchi. Evolutionary synthesis of arithmetic circuit structures. *Artif. Intell. Rev.*, 20(3-4):199–232, Dec. 2003.

[2] E. Cantu-Paz. *Efficient and Accurate Parallel Genetic Algorithms*. Kluwer Academic Publishers, Norwell, MA, USA, 2000.

[3] J. Clegg, J. A. Walker, and J. F. Miller. A new crossover technique for cartesian genetic programming. In *GECCO '07: Proceedings of the 9th annual conference on Genetic and evolutionary computation*, volume 2, pages 1580–1587, London, 7-11 July 2007. ACM Press.

[4] A. Fox. Instruction tables: Lists of instruction latencies, throughputs and micro-operation breakdowns for intel, amd and via cpus. `http://agner.org/optimize/instruction_tables.pdf`, 2013.

[5] B. W. Goldman and W. F. Punch. Reducing wasted evaluations in cartesian genetic programming. In *Proceedings of the 16th European Conference on Genetic Programming*, EuroGP'13, pages 61–72, Berlin, Heidelberg, 2013. Springer-Verlag.

[6] S. Harding and W. Banzhaf. Implementing cartesian genetic programming classifiers on graphics processing units using gpu.net. In *13th Annual Genetic and Evolutionary Computation Conference, GECCO 2011, Companion Material Proceedings, Dublin, Ireland, July 12-16, 2011*, pages 463–470. ACM, 2011.

[7] S. Harding, J. F. Miller, and W. Banzhaf. Self modifying cartesian genetic programming: Parity. In *2009 IEEE Congress on Evolutionary Computation*, pages 285–292. IEEE Press, 2009.

[8] J. Hennessy and D. Patterson. *Computer Architecture: A Quantitative Approach*. The Morgan Kaufmann Series in Computer Architecture and Design. Elsevier Science, 2011.

[9] R. Hrbacek and M. Sikulova. Coevolutionary cartesian genetic programming in fpga. In *Advances in Artificial Life, ECAL 2013, Proceedings of the Twelfth European Conference on the Synthesis and Simulation of Living Systems*, pages 431–438. MIT Press, 2013.

[10] J. R. Koza, M. A. Keane, M. J. Streeter, W. Mydlowec, J. Yu, and G. Lanza. *Genetic Programming IV: Routine Human-Competitive Machine Intelligence*. Kluwer Academic Publishers, 2003.

[11] J. Miller and S. Smith. Redundancy and computational efficiency in cartesian genetic programming. *Evolutionary Computation, IEEE Transactions on*, 10(2):167–174, 2006.

[12] J. Miller and P. Thomson. Cartesian genetic programming. In *Genetic Programming*, volume 1802 of *Lecture Notes in Computer Science*, pages 121–132. Springer Berlin Heidelberg, 2000.

[13] J. F. Miller, editor. *Cartesian Genetic Programming*. Natural Computing Series. Springer Verlag, 2011.

[14] R. Poli and J. Page. Solving high-order boolean parity problems with smooth uniform crossover, sub-machine code gp and demes. *Genetic Programming and Evolvable Machines*, 1(1-2):37–56, Apr. 2000.

[15] R. Seyfarth. *Introduction to 64 Bit Intel Assembly Language Programming for Linux*. CreateSpace Independent Publishing Platform, 2012.

[16] A. P. Shanthi and R. Parthasarathi. Practical and scalable evolution of digital circuits. *Appl. Soft Comput.*, 9(2):618–624, Mar. 2009.

[17] D. Sherry, K. Veeramachaneni, J. McDermott, and U.-M. O'Reilly. Flex-gp: Genetic programming on the cloud. In *Applications of Evolutionary Computation - EvoApplications 2012*, volume 7248 of *LNCS*, pages 477–486. Springer, 2012.

[18] E. Stomeo, T. Kalganova, and C. Lambert. Generalized disjunction decomposition for evolvable hardware. *Trans. Sys. Man Cyber. Part B*, 36(5):1024–1043, Oct. 2006.

[19] M. Tomassini. *Spatially Structured Evolutionary Algorithms: Artificial Evolution in Space and Time (Natural Computing Series)*. Springer-Verlag New York, Inc., Secaucus, NJ, USA, 2005.

[20] Z. Vasicek and L. Sekanina. Hardware accelerator of cartesian genetic programming with multiple fitness units. *Computing and Informatics*, 29(6):1359–1371, 2010.

[21] Z. Vasicek and L. Sekanina. Formal verification of candidate solutions for post-synthesis evolutionary optimization in evolvable hardware. *Genetic Programming and Evolvable Machines*, 12(3):305–327, 2011.

[22] Z. Vasicek and K. Slany. Efficient phenotype evaluation in cartesian genetic programming. In *Proc. of the 15th European Conference on Genetic Programming*, LNCS 7244, pages 266–278. Springer Verlag, 2012.

[23] V. K. Vassilev, D. Job, and J. F. Miller. Towards the automatic design of more efficient digital circuits. *Evolvable Hardware, NASA/DoD Conference on*, 0:151, 2000.

[24] T. Yu and J. Miller. Finding needles in haystacks is not hard with neutrality. In *Genetic Programming*, volume 2278 of *Lecture Notes in Computer Science*, pages 13–25. Springer Berlin Heidelberg, 2002.

GPU-accelerated Evolutionary Design of the Complete Exchange Communication on Wormhole Networks

Jiri Jaros
Faculty of Information Technology
Brno University of Technology
Bozetechova 2
612 66 Brno, Czech Republic
jarosjir@fit.vutbr.cz

Radek Tyrala
AT&T Mobility
Palachovo namesti 7262
625 00 Brno, Czech Republic
radek.tyrala@att.com

ABSTRACT

The communication overhead is one of the main challenges in the exascale era, where millions of compute cores are expected to collaborate on solving complex jobs. However, many algorithms will not scale since they require complex global communication and synchronisation. In order to perform the communication as fast as possible, contentions, blocking and deadlock must be avoided. Recently, we have developed an evolutionary tool producing fast and safe communication schedules reaching the lower bound of the theoretical time complexity. Unfortunately, the execution time associated with the evolution process raises up to tens of hours, even when being run on a multi-core processor. In this paper, we propose a revised implementation accelerated by a single Graphic Processing Unit (GPU) delivering speed-up of 5 compared to a quad-core CPU. Subsequently, we introduce an extended version employing up to 8 GPUs in a shared memory environment offering a speed-up of almost 30. This significantly extends the range of interconnection topologies we can cover.

Categories and Subject Descriptors

C.1.2 [**Processor architectures**]: Multiple Data Stream Architectures—*Interconnection architectures, Parallel processors, multiple-data-stream processors (SIMD)*
D.2.2 [**Software engineering**]: Design Tools and Techniques—*Evolutionary prototyping*

General Terms

Algorithms, Performance, Design.

Keywords

Complete exchange communication; Collective communications; Communication scheduling; Evolutionary design; GPU-based acceleration; Multi-GPU systems.

GECCO'14, July 12–16, 2014, Vancouver, BC, Canada.
Copyright 2014 ACM 978-1-4503-2662-9/14/07 ...$15.00.
http://dx.doi.org/10.1145/2576768.2598315 .

1. INTRODUCTION

A recent trend in high performance computing (HPC) has been towards the use of parallel processing to solve computationally-intensive problems. Nowadays, with the enormous transistor budgets of 32-nm and 22-nm technologies on a silicon die, it is feasible to place large CPU clusters on a single chip (System on Chip, SoC). Such systems are based on both x86 compute cores (Intel Xeon Phi[1]) and ARM based cores (Paralella[2], Calxeda[3], etc). The memory of many-core systems is physically distributed among computing nodes that communicate by sending data through a Network on Chip (NoC) [5]. With an increasing number of processor cores, memory modules and other hardware units in the latest chips, the importance of communication among them and of related interconnection networks is steadily growing.

Communication operations can be either point-to-point, with one source and one destination, or collective, with more than two participating processes. Some embedded parallel applications, like network or media processors, are characterized by independent data streams or by a small amount of inter-process communications [6]. However, many general-purpose parallel applications display a bulk synchronous behaviour: the processing nodes access the network according to a global, structured communication pattern.

The performance of these collective communications (CC) has a dramatic impact on the overall efficiency of parallel processing. The most efficient way to switch messages through the network connecting multiple processing elements makes use of pipelined wormhole (WH) switching [12]. Wormhole switching reduces the effect of the path length on the communication time, but if multiple messages exist in the network concurrently (as it happens in CCs), contention for communication links may be a source of congestion and waiting times. To avoid congestion delays, it is necessary to organize CC into separate steps in time and to put into each step only such pair-wise communications whose paths do not share any links. The contention-free scheduling of CCs is therefore important.

In our previous work, we developed an evolutionary tool capable of creating optimal communication schedules for various communication patterns on wide range of interconnection network topologies with the size of up to 256 nodes [7]. The only exception was the complete exchange (CE) pattern where we had been unsuccessful even on small meshes with 32 nodes. This was given by the overwhelming run time requirements on the order of days even when running on a quad-core CPU. Since the CE is very widely used in iterative finite difference methods, fast Fourier transformations, numeric PDE solvers, linear algebra and many other, we de-

[1] http://www.intel.com/
[2] http://www.parallella.org/
[3] http://www.calxeda.com/

cided to harness the potential of massive parallel architectures such as GPUs to accelerate the evolution and produce optimal schedules in more realistic times.

The rest of this paper is organised as follows. The section continues with discussing the main characteristics of GPUs and provides fundamental concepts for writing fast codes. Section 2 describes the problem of scheduling the complete exchange communication pattern, the evolutionary algorithm, and defines the solution encoding followed by the fitness function. Section 3 introduces the accelerated version of the EA, presenting the key design decisions. The experimental results are presented in section 4 for two different GPU cards and a multi-GPU system. Finally, a summary and directions for the future work are provided in the Conclusions.

1.1 GPU Architecture and Programming

Graphics Processing Units (GPUs) are massively parallel accelerators primarily targeted on speeding up the computer graphics with millions of independent polygons and pixels. Their architecture is therefore adapted for executing relatively simple algorithms on big datasets in parallel. Nevertheless, GPUs have become key part of many supercomputing systems (Titan in Oak Ridge) and the trend in their employment steadily grows. There are two basic APIs commonly used for writing the GPU-accelerated applications, namely CUDA[4] and OpenCL[5]. Roughly speaking they are more or less the same. In this work, we decided to implement the codes in OpenCL to be able to support a wider range of GPU cards (we intend to deploy the code on Intel Xeon Phi cards in the future), however, porting it on CUDA would be trivial.

As we mainly targeted the proposed code on NVIDIA GTX 580 cards, we are going to provide the fundamental architecture basics of the Fermi architecture in this subsection. The graphics card is divided into a graphics chip (GPU) and 1.5GB of main memory. Main memory, acting as an interface between the host CPU and GPU, is connected to the host system using a PCI-Express 2.0 bus. This bus can easily become a bottleneck as its bandwidth is only a fraction of what both GPU and CPU memories provide [9].

The GPU main memory is optimized for block transactions and stream processing providing very high bandwidth but also high latency. Hiding this latency is very important for keeping GPU executions units busy. The GTX 580 offers 768KB of fast on-chip L2 cache to allow reordering of the memory requests as well as on-chip shared memory, and large register fields to get the working data as close the execution units as possible. The GTX580 processor consists of 16 independent Streaming Multiprocessors (SM), each of which is further divided into 32 CUDA cores. SMs are based on the Single Instruction, Multiple Thread (SIMT) concept allowing them to execute exactly the same instruction over a batch of 32 consecutive threads (referred to as a warp) at a time. This concept dramatically reduces the control logic of SMs, but on the other hand, dictates strict rules on thread cooperation and branching. A few consecutive warps form a thread block that is the smallest resource allocation unit of SM. In order to fully exploit the potential of a given GPU, a few concepts must be kept in mind [13]:

- Thousands of threads are necessary to be executed concurrently on the GPU to hide memory latency.
- All the threads within a warp should follow the same execution path minimizing the thread divergence.
- All memory requests within a warp should be coalesced reading data from consecutive addresses.
- Synchronization and/or communication among threads can be done quickly only within a thread block.
- Working data set should be partitioned to fit on-chip shared memory to minimize main memory accesses.
- Data transfers between CPU and GPU memories can easily become a bottleneck given the low PCI-Express bandwidth.

[4]https://developer.nvidia.com/cuda-downloads

[5]http://www.khronos.org/opencl/

2. EVOLUTIONARY DESIGN

The selection of Evolutionary Algorithms (EA) for the scheduling problem has been justified already in [7]. Although the proposed methodology of designing near-optimal CC schedules is independent of the particular evolutionary algorithm, we restricted ourselves in this work only to a simple EDA evolutionary algorithm without gene dependencies (UMDA).

Univariate Marginal Distribution Algorithm (UMDA) [11] is a very simple EDA [10] (Estimation of Distribution Algorithm) which does not reflect any interaction between genes (variables/solution parameters). The main advantages of this algorithm are better mixing of genetic material than it is possible in standard GA [4], very simple implementation and much faster execution than more complex EDAs like BOA (Bayesian Optimization Algorithm [10]) algorithms. Of course, any other EA could be employed. Basic comparison of a success rate and execution time of other types of EA applied to CC scheduling problem can be found in [7].

2.1 Complete Exchange Communication

The Complete Exchange (CE) communication pattern, also referred to as all-to-all scatter (AAS) or personalised all-to-all broadcast is one of the most complex collective communication (CC) routine present in many parallel algorithms, such as BLAS, FFT, island model of EA and many others. This communication is often aligned with matrix transposition where the data is originally distrusted over processing elements by rows and after applying the operation by columns.

The complete exchange algorithm is usually defined in terms of a group of processes. In this case, we have P communication processes each of which is sending and receiving a message to all its $P-1$ partners. To complete one complete exchange, $P(P-1)$ point-to-point message transfers have to be carried out.

The simplest time model of point-to-point communication in direct Wormhole (WH) networks takes the communication time composed of a fixed start-up time t_s at the beginning (SW and HW overhead of a sender and a receiver), a serialization delay, i.e. the transfer time of m message units (words or bytes), and of a component that is a function of distance h (the number of channels on the route or hops a message has to do)

$$t_{p2p} = t_s + mt_1 + ht_r \tag{1}$$

where t_1 is per unit-message transfer time and t_r includes a routing delay, switching and inter-router latency. A relatively small dependence on h may be taken into account by including $h_{max}t_r$ into t_s, so that only two parameters t_s and mt_1 are sufficient.

In the rest of the paper we assume that all collective communication (CC) including CE in WH networks proceeds in synchronized steps. In one step of CC, a set of simultaneous packet transfers takes place along complete disjoint paths between source and destination node pairs. If the source and destination nodes are not adjacent, the messages go via some intermediate nodes, but processors in these nodes are not aware of it; the messages are routed automatically by the routers attached to processors.

Complexity of collective communication is determined in terms of the number of communication steps or equivalently by the number of "start-ups" τ_{CC} (upper bound). Provided that the term $h_{max}t_r$ is included in t_s and excluding contention for channels, CC time can be obtained approximately as the sum of start-up delays plus associated serialization delays $m_i t_1$ in individual communication steps

$$\tau_{CC} = \sum_{i=1}^{\tau_{CC}} (t_s + m_i t_i) = \tau^{CC}[t_s + mt_1]. \quad (2)$$

The above expression assumes that the nodes can only re-transmit/consume original messages, so that the length of messages $m_i = m$ remains constant in all communication steps. This is true in the so called non-combining model of communication; on the contrary, in the combining model the nodes can combine/extract partial messages with negligible overhead. The combining/non-combining model influences CC performance and either one can outperform the other in some cases. Further on we will consider the non-combining model only. Possible synchronization overhead involved in communication steps, be it hardware or software-based, should be included in the start-up time t_s. Let us note that with uniform messages and a single clock signal domain, one barrier synchronization before CC might be sufficient to synchronize the whole CC. Communication steps would then follow in the lockstep. According to frequency of CCs and an amount of interleaved computation (BSP model) in a certain application, efficiency of parallel processing can be estimated.

The lower bound of the time complexity (number of communication steps) for complete exchange can be obtained considering that half the messages from each processor cross the bisection, whereas the other half do not. There will be altogether $\lceil 2(\frac{P}{2})^2/BC \rceil$ of such messages in both ways, where BC is the channel bisection width [2]. Sometimes a stronger lower bound may be obtained considering the count of channels from all sources to all destinations (Σ) and the limited count Σ_1 of channels available for one step. In regular networks with constant node degree such as hypercube and torus $\Sigma_1 = Pk$, where k is the number of output channels in each node. In irregular networks such as mesh, as each node has to accept $P-1$ distinct messages, $\lceil (P-1)/min(k) \rceil$ bound has to be also obeyed.

2.2 Input Data Structure and Preprocessing

The input data structure maintains a description of the network topology, the definition of CC and sets of transmitters, receivers and intermediate routers. The topology description is saved in the form of node neighbour lists, where the nodes are considered to be neighbours only if they are connected by a simple direct link.

After the input file is loaded, the data have to be preprocessed. In the first phase, the preprocessor divides the set of all nodes V^* into a set of transmitters T and a set of receivers R. Then, a set of terminal nodes $V \subseteq V^*$ is determined as the union $T \cup R$. The terminal nodes can inject/consume messages to/from the network, while the non-terminal nodes (routers) can only retransmit the messages. Finally, all the sets are ordered based on the node index.

The preprocessor generates all the shortest paths (the set R_{xy}) between all transmitter-receiver pairs $x, y \in V$ and saves them into a specific data structure in the operating memory during the second phase. This task is performed by a modified well known Breadth-First Search (BFS) algorithm [3].

2.3 Solution Encoding

Let us define the chromosome encoding for the complete exchange communication. Considering CE communication between M transmitters from set T and N receivers from set R:

1. The complete exchange can be defined as a set CC of pair-wise transfers src, dst originating in $src \in T$ and terminating in $dst \in R$, where $src \neq dst$.

$$CC = \{p2p_{src,dst} : src \in T, dst \in R, src \neq dst\} \quad (3)$$

2. A direct encoding can be designed for the CE schedules (i.e. an exact description of the schedule is stored in a chromosome). Chromosome can be formalized as n-tuples of genes:

$$chr = \begin{pmatrix} gene_{0,0} & \dots & gene_{0,N-1} \\ \vdots & \ddots & \vdots \\ gene_{M-1,0} & \dots & gene_{M-1,N-1} \end{pmatrix}, \quad (4)$$

where M is the number of transmitters and N is the number of receivers while n is the total number of genes. Notice that

$$M, N \leq P \wedge n = M \cdot N. \quad (5)$$

3. A gene $gene_{i,j}$ represents a single message transfer from the transmitter $x_i \in T$ to the receiver $x_j \in R$, where $x_i \neq x_j$. The source and the destination are identified by the genes' indexes i and j. A gene is the ordered couple:

$$\begin{aligned} & gene_{i,j} = [l_{i,j}, s_{i,j}], 0 \leq i < M, 0 \leq j < N, i \neq j \\ & l_{i,j} \in R_{i,j} \\ & 0 \leq s_{i,j} < Steps \end{aligned} \quad (6)$$

The first component $l_{i,j}$ represents a chosen path from the transmitter x_i to the receiver x_j stored in the set $R_{i,j}$. The second component $s_{i,j}$ determines a selected time slot (communication step) of the transfer. The total number of time slots is given as the predefined parameter $Steps$.

4. The (shortest) path is defined as an ordered set of unidirectional channels:

$$l_{i,j} = \{c_1, c_2, c_3, \dots, c_L\}, c_i = [a, b] \in V^* \times V^* \quad (7)$$

where $c_1 = [a_1, b_1] \wedge a_1 = x_i$ and $c_L = [a_L, b_L] \wedge b_L = x_j$.

5. Next, consider a set G containing all the genes included in a chromosome chr:

$$G = \{gene_{i,j} : 0 \leq i < M, 0 \leq j < N, i \neq j\}. \quad (8)$$

6. Finally, we can define bijective mapping f from set G into set CC meaning that each gene corresponds to a unique pair-wise transfer and also vice versa:

$$\begin{aligned} f : gene_{i,j} \in G \mapsto p2p_{src,dst} \in CC \iff \\ x_i = src, x_j = dst. \end{aligned} \quad (9)$$

2.4 Conflict-based Fitness Function

This section proposes a formal description of the fitness function.

1. Let SS (Same Slot/Step) be a binary relation on the set G. Let $a, b \in CC$ be message transfers represented by $gene_{i,j}$ and $gene_{k,l}$, then

$$gene_{i,j} SS gene_{k,l} \iff s_{i,j} = s_{k,l}. \quad (10)$$

Thus, two transfers are in relation SS if and only if they are executed during the same time slot.

Now, we show that SS is an equivalence relation:

(a) SS is reflexive, since no transfer can be performed in more than one time slot.

(b) SS is clearly symmetric considering $s_{i,j} = s_{k,l}$, then $s_{k,l} = s_{i,j}$.

(c) SS is transitive. Let a, b, c be elements of G. Whenever $aSSb$ and $bSSc$, then also $aSSc$ (a is executed during the same slot as c whenever a is executed during the same slot as b and b is executed during the same slot as c).

Thus SS is an equivalence relation.

2. The equivalence relation SS induces the partition on set G. Each equivalence class $[g_s]$ includes all transfers performed in the same slot s.

3. Let $E_{a,b}$ be a set of all channels shared by two transfers a, b represented by genes $gene_{i,j}, gene_{k,l} \in G$ going over paths $l_{i,j}$ and $l_{k,l}$. Then

$$E_{a,b} = l_{i,j} \cap l_{k,l}. \tag{11}$$

The number of conflicts between a and b can be obtained as the cardinality of the set $E_{a,b}$.

4. Define a multiset E_s including channels shared by all transfers within a given time slot, then

$$E_s = \bigcup_{a,b \in [g_s], a \neq b} E_{a,b}. \tag{12}$$

5. The multiset E, covering all shared channels within the whole CC, can be obtained as a union over all equivalence classes. Thus

$$E_s = \bigcup_{[g_s] \in G/SS} E_s. \tag{13}$$

6. The total number of conflicts can be obtained as the cardinality of multiset E. Thus

$$Fitness = |E|. \tag{14}$$

The valid communication schedule for a given number of communication steps must be conflict-free. Valid schedules are either optimal (the number of steps equals the lower bound) or suboptimal. Evolution of a valid schedule for the given number of steps is finished up as soon as fitness (number of conflicts) drops to zero. If it does not do so in a reasonable time, the prescribed number of steps must be increased.

2.5 Execution Time on Small Networks

In our previous work we have applied this approach on a wide range of network topologies targeted on networks on a chip with up to 256 nodes. However, the results for the complete exchange have not been satisfactory. Table 1 shows the time complexity of the evolved communication plans in term of communication steps followed by the lower bound. It can be seen that for bigger topologies (36 nodes and more) the EA was not successful and produced only suboptimal solutions. The table also shows the average runtime of the EA to find such a solution. It can be seen that the run time grows significantly, reaching the order of days for as low as 36 nodes. The optimisation of bigger networks was thus impractical.

Table 1: The time complexity of best schedules discovered and the theoretical lower bounds for the complete exchange communication along with the evolution time on a quad-core CPU.

Topology	Number of time steps	Time to solution
Mesh 3x3	6/6	2s
Mesh 4x4	16/16	22m 7s
Mesh 5x5	32/32	9h 20m
Mesh 6x6	56/54	3d 20h
Cube 3D	4/4	1s
Cube 4D	9/9	10m
Cube 5D	16/16	2d 8h
Cube 6D	35/32	2d 18h
Torus 3x3	4/4	1s
Torus 4x4	9/8	19m
Torus 5x5	16/15	7h
Torus 6x6	30/24	1d 12h

3. GPU ACCELERATION

The main disadvantage of the CPU implementation is the compute time required to find an optimal solution (a conflict-free plan with minimal number of time steps) that makes optimisation of more complex communication plans impractical. Thus, we decided to accelerate the evolution by Graphics Processing Units (GPU).

There are several strategies how to port the EA on the GPU platform with different difficulty and attainable speed-up [8]. Thus, we first profiled the original CPU implementation using the GNU profiler `gprof` on typical topologies. The flat profile (Fig. 1) reveals that almost 93% of the execution time is consumed by the fitness calculation, 2% are consumed by the random number generator, another 2% by the UMDA model building and sampling, and the rest can be attributed to support routines.

Taking into account the effort necessary to port the whole evolutionary algorithm on the GPU, the limits imposed on the EA by the GPU, and the negligible overhead of the EA in our case, we decided to only offload the fitness calculation onto the GPU. This makes the design much easier, allows to simply exchange the EA engine (e.g. GAUL[6] or NSGA-II[7]) and preserves the quality of the solution (many GPU-accelerated EAs need to make compromises to get good performance). On the other hand, the simple fitness offload limits the accessible speed-up. According to the Amdahl's law [1] with the non-accelerated part of the algorithm $\alpha = 0.07$, the theoretical speed-up is bounded by 14. Practically, the speed-up factor will be even lower because of the overhead of uploading the chromosomes for evaluation onto the GPU and downloading the fitness values back. Fortunately, the use of asynchronous transfers can hide this overhead by overlapping the calculation of the actual chromosome with transferring the following one.

3.1 Global Data Representation on GPU

In order to offload the fitness function evaluation on the GPU, we have to accommodate the global data on the GPU as well. This dataset maintains the list of all shortest paths between all transmitter-receiver pairs (R_{xy}). The preprocessor orders this set into a list of 4-tuples $T \times R \times R_{xy} \times l_{ij}$ stored in the CPU memory as a sparse 4D array. Since allocation, transfer and access to sparse multidimensional arrays are very inefficient on GPU, the array was restructured into a form of a simple 1D array with the size of $|T| * |R| * max(|R_{xy}|) * max(|l_{ij}|)$ and the shortest paths copied into it.

[6]http://gaul.sourceforge.net/

[7]http://www.iitk.ac.in/kangal/codes.shtml

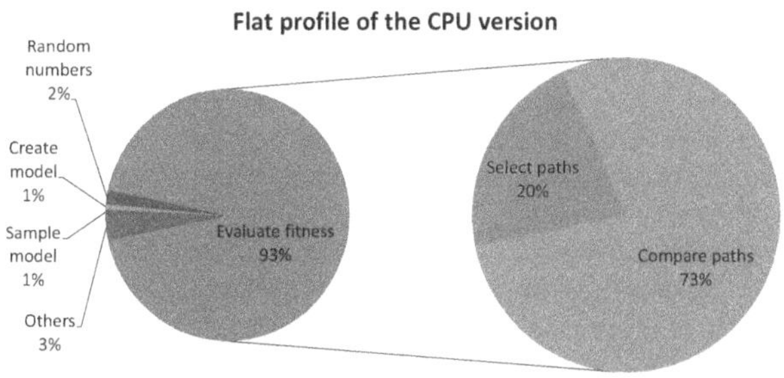

Figure 1: The flat profile of the CPU version of the code captured for a 7x7 2D mesh topology and 128 individuals in the EA population. The fitness evaluation takes more than 93 % of the execution time.

Considering that neither all shortest paths are of the same length nor there are the same number of shortest paths between all T-R pairs, this data layout introduces a non-negligible memory overhead that limit the maximum topology size to 192-256 nodes.

3.2 Fitness Evaluation on GPU

The fitness function evaluation consists of two phases. First, the path used in the G are partitioned into the equivalence classes $[g_s]$ using the equivalence relation SS in eq. (10). Second, the number of conflicts in each equivalence class is counted up and eventually summed up into the fitness function value.

Looking at Fig. 1, the path partitioning takes about 20% of the execution time while the search for conflicts does almost 80%. The CPU code for partitioning G traverses through the chromosome and classifies the path's ID into a particular equivalence class (C++ vector). Although this is a trivial operation, it requires dynamic memory allocation because it is not a priori known how many paths belongs into a given class $[g_s]$. Moreover, doing so in parallel implies the use of mutual exclusion (memory locks) when adding a path into a given class. Both these features have very limited support on GPUs and are always strongly performance penalised. Thus, this part of the fitness function evaluation is better to be processed on the CPU. The second phase, comparing the pairs of paths and seeking for conflicts, is completely data independent not requiring any dynamic memory allocation and/or synchronisation. That's why it is a good candidate for GPU acceleration.

The basic idea of the GPU-accelerated fitness function evaluation is as follows:

1. The CPU partitions the paths in G into equivalence classes and stores them in separate memory arrays.
2. The CPU uploads an equivalence class on the GPU.
3. The GPU mutually compares all path pairs within the class in parallel and stores the number of conflicts for each pair.
4. The GPU performs a parallel reduction to get the total number of conflicts within a given equivalence class.
5. The CPU downloads the number of conflicts for $[g_s]$ and adds them to the total sum from other equivalence classes.
6. The previous steps are repeated until all equivalence classes have been processed.

3.3 GPU Thread Model

The thread model describes how the work is distributed over many thousands of lightweight GPU threads. Ideally, the work should be evenly distributed, minimising the need for communication and synchronisation and maximising the data reuse. For identifying all path conflicts (shared channels), all path pairs have to be mutually compared. Having N paths in a given class $[g_s]$ yields $N(N-1)/2$ path comparisons. Considering the global exchange communication pattern, and a topology with $P = |T| = |R|$ nodes, $P^2(P^2-1)/2$ path comparisons have to be performed in the worst case. Considering even a small 4x4 mesh topology, this stands for 32 640 path comparisons.

This finding suggests that each thread could be assigned one pair of paths to compare since there are enough path pairs in larger topologies to employ hundreds of GPU threads. The GPU thread can be identified by a 1D index (ID) within a GPU kernel function. The ID determines which pair of paths from $[g_s]$ is assigned to the thread as follows:

$$\begin{array}{ll} \text{1st path:} & \text{ID mod } |[g_s]| \\ \text{2nd path:} & (\text{ID} + \frac{\text{ID}}{|[g_s]|} + 1) \text{ mod } |[g_s]| \end{array} \tag{15}$$

The threads are then grouped into thread blocks of a specific size (usually 512 or 1024).

3.4 On-chip Memory Utilisation

As the path comparison involves no floating point operations and only a tiny amount of fixed point arithmetic (comparisons and indexing), the GPU kernel is strongly memory bound. Moreover, the memory access patter is not regular but scattered. Therefore, the memory accesses must be carefully designed to get reasonable performance.

Let's recall the path is stored as list of network nodes the message goes through on the way from the transmitter to the receiver, see Eq. (7). Every thread is assigned a path pair and processes it channel by channel, see Fig. 2. Since the threads are grouped into warps executed in the SIMT (Single Instruction Multiple Thread) fashion, a thread warp processes 32 path pairs simultaneously. Thus, when reading the first component of the channel (say path1[i]), the GPU actually reads first components of 32 different paths from distant places scattered over the global memory. This breaks one of the fundamental rules of the SIMT processing (neighbour threads read from neighbour memory locations), see Fig. 2.

The second issue is that the second path is read multiple times. Since there are no or very small caches on GPU, it is almost sure that all accesses will be served by global memory, which further decreases the performance.

```
for (int i = 0; i < path1Size - 1; i++)
{
  for (int j = 0; j < path2Size - 1; j++)
  {
    if ((path1[i] == path2[j]) &&
        (path1[i+1] == path2[j + 1])
       )
       conflicts[threadID]++;
  }
}
```

Figure 2: Code snippet of the conflict seeking GPU kernel on a pair of paths. To detect conflicts, all channels has to be mutually compared.

One way how to lighten the GPU memory load would be to use shared on-chip memory to rearrange memory accesses and reuse the second path data. The idea is to use multiple threads to load a path from main memory exploiting the SIMT-friendly coalesced memory access pattern. After all paths are loaded, call a barrier and then redistribute the paths stored in shared memory to threads for processing. Although looking promising, this idea holds many problems. First, since the paths are not of the same size, a mapping function to decide what threads are assigned to load particular paths would be necessary. This would require an expensive parallel prefix sum. Second, the paths wouldn't squeeze into the small shared memory. Considering even a small 4x4 mesh, the longest shortest path has a length of 7. Having 1024 threads in a thread block would require 2*28KB of shared memory, which is more than current GPUs can offer. Reducing the number of threads would lead to low occupancy and reduced performance. Considering all these obstacles, we concluded it would be better not to use shared memory as we did not want to limit the size of the topology optimised.

The memory bandwidth can yet be reduced by proper use of registers to hold the segments of the path for the time they are needed and not to read them from the global memory repeatedly. According to the principle of path comparing, every segment of the first path (two nodes) is compared with all segments of the second path. Thus, it will be read only once, stored in a pair of registers and compared with all segments of the second path. When moving to the flowing segment of the first path, we preserve the endpoint of the previous channel, declare it as the start point of the following channel and read only the endpoint from the maim memory. This sort of software pre-fetching reduces the memory bandwidth by 40%. The same node pre-fetching can be then applied on the second path, which further reduces the memory bandwidth down to 30%. The code snippet can be seen in Fig. 3.4.

```
node1_1 = path1[0];

for (int i = 0; i < path1Size - 1; i++)
{
  node1_2 = path1[i + 1];
  node2_1 = path2[0];

  for (int j = 0; j < path2Size - 1; j++)
  {
    node2_2 = path2[j + 1];
    if ((node1_1 == node2_1) &&
        (node1_2 == node2_2)
       )
         conflicts[threadID]++;

    node2_1 = node2_2;
  }
  node1_1 = node1_2;
}
```

Figure 3: Code snippet of the optimised conflict seeking GPU kernel on a pair of paths. The paths are loaded using software pre-fetching and stored in registers.

The numbers of conflicts identified by particular threads are stored in a shared on-chip memory array. The array has the same size as the thread block (usually 1024). Then, the parallel reduction kernel is used to sum the number of conflicts within the thread block. Finally, the first thread of the blocks adds its value to the others' one in global memory using an atomic add operation.

3.5 Multidimensional Kernel Organisation

The use of 1D GPU kernels and thread blocks imply that that a chromosome is processed in multiple stages, each communication slot and its class $[g_s]$ in one stage. Although this enables fine-granularity, the PCI-E transfers are too small to efficiently use the PCI-E bandwidth since only path indices are transferred (a few KBs). Moreover, the kernels have only a little work and has to be started many times, which introduced additional overhead.

To alleviate the overhead associated with the kernel launch and PCI-E transfers, the GPU kernels were redesigned to be multidimensional. The first dimension is associated with the paths within one communication slot $[g_s]$. The second dimension allows to process multiple communication slots. If necessary, the third dimension can be used to process multiple chromosomes at once. This introduces a high degree of freedom and allows for better workload balancing.

3.6 Multi-GPU Processing

Since many high-end desktops and supercomputer nodes can house multiple GPU accelerators, we investigated the possibility of employing multiple GPUs. Fortunately, both OpenCL and CUDA have simple extensions to support this feature.

The population of candidate solutions is divided into small batches, each of which including one or more chromosomes. Then, the CPU code spawns as many CPU threads as GPUs in the system and links each CPU thread with a single GPU. After that, two processing streams are opened on each GPU. These are used for double-buffering. When one work batch is processed using the first stream, another batch is uploaded on the GPU using the second stream, and vice-versa. This virtually hides the overhead associated with the data transfers and allows good scaling.

4. EXPERIMENTAL RESULTS

The proposed GPU implementation was tested on two machines. First, a standard desktop equipped with a quad-core Intel i7-920 CPU and 12GB of RAM was used to run the parallel CPU implementation and provide a reference point. This machine housed two NVIDA GPUs; GTX 285 - a high-end graphics of the pre-Fermi architecture released in 2009 and GTX 580 - a high-end graphics card of the Fermi architecture released in 2011. The main differences between these two cards are the presence of L2 cache and twice as high raw performance in the case of the GTX580. The memory bandwidth, the expected limitation of the proposed implementation, is comparable. The second machine was a single node of a GPU cluster equipped with two hex-core Xeons X5660 and eight NVIDIA GTX580 GPU cards. This machine served as a platform for multi-GPU tests.

Several instances of the most common topologies were used to evaluate the benefit of using the GPU accelerated implementation. We selected 2D meshes, 2D tori and multidimensional hypercubes topologies with the number of nodes varying from 4 to 64, see Table 1. The parameters of evolutionary algorithms were carefully set in our previous work as follows: the population consisted of 256 individuals, the model of the UMDA algorithm was built using 50% of the population selected by the binary tournament selection, 50% of new individuals were generated and evaluated every generation. Although not typical in EDA algorithms, a small amount of mutation was used to preserve population diversity. Let's mention that bigger populations could offer more work for GPU and thus a higher speed-up, however the population would converge slower [7]. This implies that unnecessary work would be done.

4.1 Tuning the Block and Grid Layout

In order to obtain the best possible performance we investigated the suitable thread block and grid layout and size. The performance evaluation was done on the most complex topology we had, a 2D mesh with 49 nodes containing the longest shortest paths (up to 13 hops). To spawn enough thread blocks on the GPU, we used a 2D grid layout where multiple multiple communication steps ($[g_s]$ of a

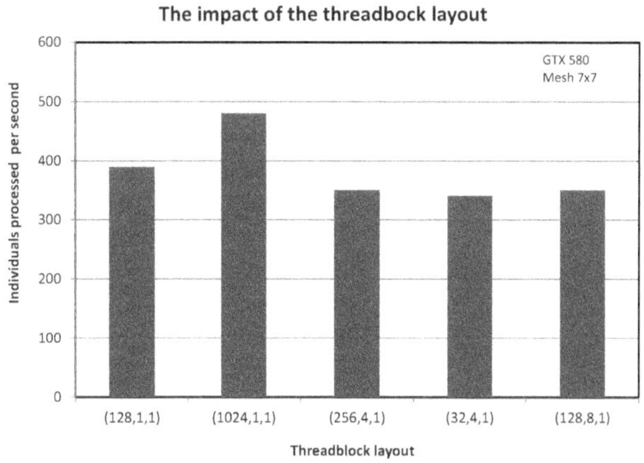

Figure 4: The influence of the GPU thread block layout on the performance on an NVIDIA GTX580 and Mesh 7x7. The fastest configuration seems to be a 1D thread block with 1024 threads.

Table 2: The number of individuals processed per second on various topologies (speed-up factor vs. CPU) using an NVIDIA GTX 285 and 580 GPUs.

Topology	GPU GTX 285	GPU GTX 580	CPU i7 920
Mesh 2x2	92,692 (0.16x)	537,895 (0.93x)	581,530
Mesh 3x3	48,369 (0.54x)	113,188 (1.26x)	89,572
Mesh 4x4	16,741 (1.05x)	22,981 (1.44x)	15,930
Mesh 5x5	3,810 (1.06x)	7,563 (2.11x)	3,588
Mesh 6x6	750 (1.49x)	2,372 (4.71x)	504
Mesh 7x7	108 (0.96x)	539 (4.81x)	112
Cube 3D	52,454 (0.36x)	85,384 (0.59x)	145,077
Cube 4D	18,621 (0.72x)	23,456 (0.91x)	25,845
Cube 5D	1,835 (1.34x)	4,152 (3.03x)	1,369
Cube 6D	51 (0.78x)	222 (3.42x)	65
Torus 4x4	18,619 (0.95x)	23,551 (1.21x)	19,498
Torus 5x5	6,336 (1.71x)	8,353 (2.26x)	3,695
Torus 6x6	1,230 (1.84x)	2,709 (4.06x)	677
Torus 7x7	351 (1.99x)	725 (4.11x)	176

single solution were being evaluated simultaneously and two GPU streams were feeding the GPU with data and overlapping communication and computation.

The question we addresses here is whether it is better to use a 2D thread block, where multiple communication steps are processed simultaneously or keep only one communication step per block. Fig. 4 shows that the best performance is obtained when the biggest possible 1D thread block of 1024 threads is used. The most likely cause of this behaviour the only one parallel reduction calculated in the 1D thread block while there are multiple reductions in 2D thread blocks. When smaller 1D thread blocks are used, the GPU is not fully exploited, and the parallel reduction with logarithmic time complexity plays a key role here. The performance of all tested 2D block configurations is comparable. We can thus conclude that a 1D thread block of 1024 threads is the best layout and this will be used in future tests.

4.2 Evolution Time on Single GPU

When the computation was optimally distributed over GPU threads and blocks, the acceleration of the EA was investigated using a number of different topologies. Table 2 shows the number of individuals processed per second. This covers not only the fitness function evaluation but the whole run of the UMDA algorithm including all the GPU-CPU transfers. The number of generations per second can thus be obtained by dividing numbers in the table by the value of 128 (the number of individuals evaluated per generation).

The first general observation says the bigger the topology the higher the performance benefit. This is natural, given by the substance of massively parallel architectures like GPUs. Hence, accelerating the communication on a 2x2 mesh cannot bring any speed-up and must deteriorate the performance. Here, there are only 16 communications and the longest path only has two hops, which gives us 120 comparisons. A speed-up factor of as low as 0.16 can be seen on a GTX 280. However, what was a congenial surprise was the performance of GTX 580 which almost met a quad-core CPU.

The achieved performance on GTX 285 was quite modest. The peak speed-up observed was about 2. On the other hand, GTX 580 showed its potential and reached a speed-up of almost 5. We suppose that the main reason was the presence of L2 cache memory that helps in reorganizing the scattered memory accesses and offers better buffering of the path. When accessing the first element of the path, the cache buffers the whole memory transaction of 128B. This is usually enough to store 32 elements of the path for long enough. The following memory accesses are thus served much faster.

There is also a notable variation in the speed-up observed on different topologies. The best one was measured for 2D meshes, followed by 2D tori and finally by n-dimensional hypercubes. It is believed that this is given by the topology diameter. The bigger the diameter is, the longer paths must be compared and the more work per thread is available reducing the overhead associated with offloading the fitness function evaluation.

When comparing the observed speed-up factors with the theoretical asymptotic ones, we can conclude that reaching 5 out of 14, considering a part of the fitness function still remains on the CPU although partially overlapped with the GPU work, is significant and helps a lot. Please remember that whole evolutionary runs for a topology with 64 nodes used to take couple of days.

4.3 Evolution Time on Multiple GPU

This section investigates the sustainable performance of a multi-GPU server under the proposed evolutionary toolkit. The parameters of the EA remained the same as in the previous section but the UMDA model was constructed and sampled by twelve CPU threads. This offered about three times higher performance than the desktop machine (the both CPUs run at the same frequency). The newly sampled individuals were then uniformly distributed over up to 8 GPUs for fitness evaluation.

Fig. 5 shows the strong scaling of the multi-GPU implementation (the population size is fixed). The performance scaling is almost ideal up to 4 GPUs. Beyond, the saturation of the system can be observed and the performance stagnates. There are three main reasons for this behaviour. First, the population is really small. When having 8 GPUs, a GPU has only 16 individuals assigned for evaluation in every generation. This decreases the possibility of pipelining and communication hiding. Second, the PCI-E subsystem gets congested by so many data transfers. It should be also mentioned that two GPUs share one PCI-E link to the CPU. Third, 12 CPU cores may not be enough to feed 8 hungry GPUs.

We anticipate that having more complex topologies would have led to much better scaling. To comment on the absolute performance provided by a single 8-GPU machine, we now have at our

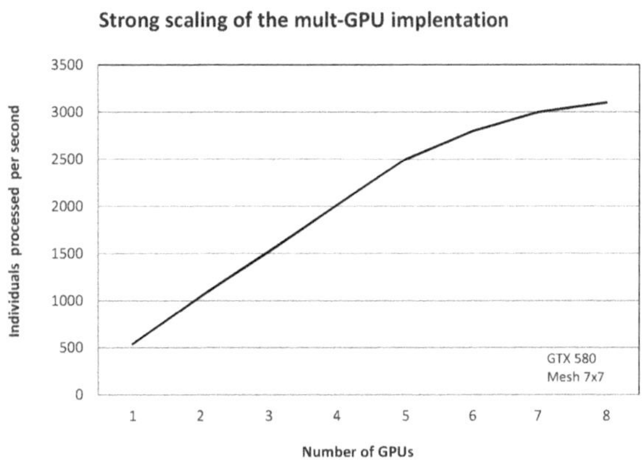

Figure 5: The strong scaling of the multi-GPU implementation tested on an 8-GPU machine equipped wit NVIDIA GTX 580 graphics cards. The GPUs are being fed by two hex-core Xeons here.

disposal a machine that accelerates the original EA algorithm running on a quad-core CPU by a factor of almost 30 (10 times compared to a two hex-core CPUs).

5. CONCLUSIONS

The importance of fast collective communications on interconnection networks of parallel computers steadily grows. Evolutionary design has been proven to be efficient in optimising the communication schedules on small scale networks, targeted mainly on networks on chips. However, the execution time necessary to evolve high quality communication schedules is still a limiting factor preventing the deployment of the evolutionary design on networks with more than 64 nodes [7].

In this paper, we have been investigating the possibility of accelerating the evolution by the use of Graphics Processing Units (GPUs). After profiling the original multi-thread CPU code, it was decided to only offload the most time consuming part of the fitness function and keep the rest of the algorithm on the CPU side. This allows us to simply exchange the evolutionary core by more advanced algorithms. On the other hand, the maximum attainable speed-up is limited due to the data transfers between CPU and GPU. Therefore, the best effort was made to hide the memory transfers and overlap them with computing.

The experimental measurements were divided into two sets. First, we investigated the performance of two NVIDIA GPU cards (GTX 285 and GTX 580). While GTX 285 showed quite poor performance, the GTX 580 reached a speed-up factor of almost 5. This reduces the typical evolutionary run on networks with 36 nodes from 30-50 hours down to 6-10. Second, we deployed the code on a multi-GPU server with 8 NVIDIA GTX 580 GPUs. Here, when supported by two hex-core Xeons, the speed-up factor reached almost 30. This reduces the execution time down to 1.5 hours, which is significant.

Let us point out the GPU acceleration has no influence on the quality of communication schedules found due to same evolutionary technique used. Naturally, the faster execution runs allow to run the evolution for longer time periods and find fast communication plans of the complete exchange pattern even for topologies we have not been successful on so far (64 nodes and more). The faster evolution also gives us a possibility to generate libraries of many irregular communication plans such as meshes/tori/cubes in faulty states where one or more links are broken in a reasonable time.

In the future work, we would like to focus on accelerating the evolution using the island model to employ a distributed GPU cluster that currently maintains 192 GPUs. We would also like to refactor the code to work with 8b integer values only, which is enough for topologies up to 256 nodes. This could reduce the memory requirements and memory bandwidth four times.

6. ACKNOWLEDGMENTS

This work was supported by the research project "Architecture of parallel and embedded computer systems", Brno University of Technology, FIT-S-14-2297, 2014-2016.

7. REFERENCES

[1] G. M. Amdahl. Validity of the single processor approach to achieving large scale computing capabilities. In *Proceedings of the April 18-20, 1967, Spring Joint Computer Conference*, AFIPS '67 (Spring), pages 483–485, New York, NY, USA, 1967. ACM.

[2] J. Duato and S. Yalamanchili. *Interconnection Networks - An Engineering Approach*. Morgan Kaufman Publishers, Elsevier Science, 2003.

[3] S. Gill. Parallel programming. *The Computer Journal*, 1:2–10, 1958.

[4] D. Goldberg. *Genetic algorithms in search, optimization, and machine learning*. Addison-Wesley, Reading, MA, 1989.

[5] A. Ivanov and G. D. Micheli. Guest editorsâĂŹ introduction: The network-on-chip paradigm in practice and research. In *Proceedings of IEEE Design&Test of Computers*, pages 399–403. IEEE Los Alamitos CA, 2000.

[6] A. Jantsch and H. T. (Eds.). *Networks on Chip*. Kluwer Academic Publishers, 2003.

[7] J. Jaros. *Evolutionary Design of Collective Communications on Wormhole Networks*. Publishing house of Brno University of Technology VUTIUM, Brno, 2010.

[8] J. Jaros. Multi-gpu island-based genetic algorithm solving the knapsack problem. In *2012 IEEE World Congress on Computational Intelligence*, pages 217–224. Institute of Electrical and Electronics Engineers, 2012.

[9] J. Jaros, B. E. Treeby, and A. P. Rendell. Use of Multiple GPUs on Shared Memory Multiprocessors for Ultrasound Propagation Simulations. In J. Chen and R. Ranjan, editors, *Australasian Symposium on Parallel and Distributed Computing (AusPDC 2012)*, number AusPDC, pages 43–52, Melbourne, Australia, 2012. ACS.

[10] P. Larranaga and J. Loazano. *Estimation of Distribution Algorithms, A New Tool for Evolutionary Computation*. Kluwer Academic Publishers, 2002.

[11] H. Muhlenbein and G. Paas. From recombination of genes to the estimation of distributions i. binary parameters. In *Lecture Notes in Computer Science 1411: Parallel Problem Solving from Nature - PPSN IV*, pages 178–187, 1996.

[12] L. Ni and P. McKinley. A survey of wormhole routing techniques in direct networks. *Computer*, 26:62–76, 1993.

[13] NVIDIA. Cuda c best practices guide. Technical Report March, 2011.

MapReduce-based Optimization of Overlay Networks using Particle Swarm Optimization

Simone A. Ludwig
Department of Computer Science
North Dakota State University
Fargo, USA
simone.ludwig@ndsu.edu

ABSTRACT

An overlay network is a virtual network that is built on top of the real network such as the Internet. Cloud computing, peer-to-peer networks, and client-server applications are examples of overlay networks since their nodes run on top of the Internet. The major needs of overlay networks are content distribution and caching, file sharing, improved routing, multicast and streaming, ordered message delivery, and enhanced security and privacy. The focus of this paper is the optimization of overlay networks using a Particle Swarm Optimization (PSO) approach. However, since the ever growing need for more infrastructure causes the number of network nodes to grow significantly, the parallelization of the PSO approach becomes a necessity. In this paper, the MapReduce concept, proposed by Google, is adopted for the PSO approach in order to be able to optimize large-scale networks. MapReduce is easy to implement since it is based on the divide and conquer method, and implementation frameworks such has Hadoop allow for scalability and fault tolerance. Experiments of the MapReduce based PSO algorithm are performed to investigate the solution quality and scalability of the approach.

Categories and Subject Descriptors

I.2.8 [**Artificial Intelligence**]: Problem Solving, Control Methods, and Search

Keywords

Evolutionary computation, overlay network optimization

1. INTRODUCTION

Overlay networks are networks that are built on top of the physical network and rely on basic networking functions such as routing and forwarding of the physical network. The nodes of an overlay network are connected via logical links, and these can span over multiple physical links. The nodes of the overlay network are expected to meet the following requirements [1]:

- Provide the infrastructure to support the execution of one or more distributed application(s).
- Support high-level routing and forwarding tasks necessary in a network. The overlay network should provide data-forwarding capabilities that are different from the ones that are part of the Internet.
- Deployment should be across the Internet to allow third parties to participate in the organization and operation of overlay networks.

The main properties of overlay networks are adaptability and robustness. These two features are the major driving force behind the research of overlay networks. The aim of this paper is the optimization of an overlay network in terms of cost, performance, and reliability. In particular, the main focus of the optimization is the application of data mirroring.

Optimization of overlay networks has received significant attention. For example, the design of Service Overlay Networks (SON) is optimized by keeping reliability constraints in mind [2]. Two subfunctions, maximum profit and minimum cost are optimized using Lagrange multipliers.

Considering the scalability of an overlay network configuration, exact techniques are only applicable to solve very small sizes of overlay networks. Among a broad set of modern heuristic and metaheuristic methods for optimization, nature-inspired methods have emerged as promising techniques. For example, network design problems are solved by nature-inspired techniques since they are able to compute approximate solutions within a reasonable amount of time [3].

An Ant Colony Optimization approach is applied to the AntNet routing protocol [4]. Agents are used to concurrently explore the network and exchange collected information in the same way as ants explore the environment. It is the ants indirect communication capability depositing pheromone that is being exploited for the routing optimization.

A multi-objective evolutionary algorithm called NSGA-II was used in [5] to optimize a multicast overlay network. The aim is to minimize the total end to end delay of a multicast tree, and to maximize the link utilization.

A multi-swarm approach for neighbor selection in peer-to-peer overlay networks is described in [6]. A multi-swarm interactive pattern is introduced to match the dynamic nature of P2P networks.

The reconfiguration of the topology and link capacities of an operational network using genetic algorithms is de-

GECCO'14, July 12–16, 2014, Vancouver, BC, Canada.
Copyright 2014 ACM 978-1-4503-2662-9/14/07 ...$15.00.
http://dx.doi.org/10.1145/2576768.2598269.

scribed in [7]. The reconfiguration is done in order to adapt to changes of its operational conditions. For example, nodes and links might become unavailable, the traffic patterns might change, and the quality of service requirement and priorities of different users and applications might change suddenly.

Another genetic algorithm approach for the reconfiguration in autonomic computing systems was proposed in [8]. The genetic algorithm approach, called Plato, uses evolutionary processes to automate the decision-making process of an autonomic system. Plato dynamically evolves target reconfigurations at run time, and at the same time, balances the trade-offs between functional and non-functional requirements to changes in environmental requirements and conditions. In particular, Plato is designed for the reconfiguration of a collection of remote data mirrors for diffusing data, and minimizing operational costs, and maximizing data reliability and network performance.

This paper closely follows the Plato approach, however, instead of using a genetic algorithm approach, a Particle Swarm Optimization (PSO) approach is implemented and evaluated. In an earlier study [9, 10], we showed that PSO outperforms the Genetic algorithm-based approach. However, since the scalability of the overlay network optimization is limited by the computational capability of the computer the algorithm is running on, a new parallelization approach is needed in order to enable the optimization of very large overlay networks.

The growth of the internet has challenged researchers to develop new ideas to deal with the ever increasing amount of computing infrastructure. The number of networking nodes is steadily increasing and therefore, more scalable algorithms need to be developed. Parallelization of the optimization algorithms is such option. Classic parallel applications that were developed in the past either used message passing runtimes such as MPI [11] or PVM (Parallel Virtual Machines) [12]. Both concepts utilize a rich set of communication and synchronization constructs, however, these need to be explicitly programmed. In order to make the development of parallel applications easier, Google introduced a programming paradigm called MapReduce that uses the *map* and *reduce* primitives that are present in functional programming languages. The MapReduce implementation enables large computations to be divided into several independent map functions. MapReduce provides fault tolerance since it has a mechanism that automatically re-executes *map* or *reduce* tasks that have failed.

The MapReduce model works as follows. The input of the computation is a set of key-value pairs, and the output is a set of output key-value pairs. The algorithm to be parallelized needs to be expressed as *map* and *reduce* functions. The *map* function takes an input pair and returns a set of intermediate key-value pairs. The framework then groups all intermediate values associated with the same intermediate key and passes them to the *reduce* function. The *reduce* function uses the intermediate key and set of values for that key. These values are merged together to form a smaller set of values. The intermediate values are forwarded to the Reduce function via an iterator. More formally, the *map* and *reduce* functions have the following types:

$map(k_1, v_1) \rightarrow list(k_2, v_2)$
$reduce(k_2, list(v_2) \rightarrow list(v_3)$

The main focus of this paper is to adapt Google's MapReduce paradigm for our Particle Swarm Optimization algorithm applied to the optimization of overlay networks in order to be able to optimize large-scale networks by making use of parallel computing. This enables large-scale networks above sizes of 500 nodes and 124750 links to be optimized. Previous experiments revealed that it is possible to run the optimization on a single computer for a network size of 500, however, for a 550-node network the algorithm did not execute anymore.

The paper is outlined as follows. Section 2 describes related work in the area of optimization for which MapReduce was adopted. In Section 3, the MapReduce-based PSO overlay optimization approach is described. Section 4 describes the experimental setup, and in Section 5 the results obtained are outlined. Section V contains the conclusions of this study.

2. RELATED WORK

The MapReduce paradigm has found widespread use in many fields of study. For example, it has been applied in the areas of spatial data processing, information retrieval, machine learning, data mining, bioinformatics, etc.

Since our paper addresses an optimization problem we review related work in the area of optimization for which MapReduce has been adopted. For example, MapReduce has been applied to a differential evolution algorithm in [13]. The authors demonstrate how easily MapReduce can be applied by parallelizing the fitness evaluation of the algorithm, which is the most time-consuming portion of the algorithm. Two alternative approaches were investigated - population based and data based. The experimental results suggested that even though the population based approach is the better way to proceed due to simplicity reasons, however, the extra cost of I/O operations and system overhead significantly reduces the benefits of parallelism.

In [14], MapReduce is applied to a variety of learning algorithms including locally weighted linear regression, k-means, logistic regression, naive Bayes, support vector machine, independent component analysis, principal component analysis, gaussian discriminant analysis, EM, and backpropagation. The authors' experimental results show a near to linear speedup with increasing numbers of processors.

An asynchronous implementation of MapReduce was investigated in [15]. The paper investigates partial synchronizations for iterative MapReduce applications to overcome global synchronization overheads. The approach applies a locality-based partitioning method. Local computations with relatively frequent local synchronizations and with less frequent global synchronizations are executed as mapper tasks. The performance gains are demonstrated for PageRank, shortest path and k-means.

The following related work is with regards to MapReduce applied to nature-inspired algorithms. Since nature-inspired algorithms are population-based algorithms for which all individuals in the population are evaluated by a fitness function that can be executed in parallel, this makes nature-inspired algorithms perfect candidates for parallelization. [16] shows how genetic algorithms can be modeled with the MapReduce paradigm. The experiments conducted showed the convergence and scalability of the approach on the OneMax optimization [17] problem for up to 10^5 variables.

Another Genetic algorithm based MapReduce approach is presented in [18]. The authors argue since a genetic algorithm is iterative in nature, an extension to the MapReduce model is necessary using a hierarchical reduction phase in order to speed up the computation further.

A MapReduce Particle Swarm Optimization approach is implemented to solve benchmark functions in [19]. The paper describes how MapReduce is adopted without explicitly addressing the parallelization details such as communication and synchronization. Their approach is applied on a benchmark function and the authors note that the MapReduce concept is not appropriate for easy benchmark functions since the parallelization overhead is outweighing the speedup gain obtained by parallelizing the function evaluations.

An intrusion detection system based on a parallel particle swarm optimization clustering algorithm using the MapReduce methodology is proposed in [20]. Particle swarm optimization is used for the clustering task and it shows that the sensitivity problem of initial cluster centroids as well as premature convergence are avoided. The experimental results on a real intrusion data set show that the proposed intrusion detection system scales very well with increasing data set sizes. In addition, close to linear speedup is achieved by improving the intrusion detection and false alarm rates.

The focus of this paper is to investigate the scalability of a MapReduce implemented Particle Swarm Optimization approach that is applied to the optimization of overlay networks. In particular, the scalability is investigated in terms of increasing network sizes, increasing numbers of available computational nodes, and increasing numbers of particles (i.e., population).

3. MAPREDUCE-ENABLED OVERLAY NETWORK OPTIMIZATION USING PSO

3.1 Overlay Network Optimization Formulation

The optimization in this paper is based on the dynamic reconfiguration of a collection of remote data mirrors. Data copies of critical data, in remote data mirroring, is stored at one or more secondary site(s) that prevent the protected data from failures that may affect the primary copy [21]. Two design criteria for remote data mirroring are given; the choice of the type of network link connection to the mirrors, and the choice of the remote mirroring protocol. Each link in the network is associated by the cost, throughput, latency and loss rate in order to determine the overall remote mirror design performance [21]. Furthermore, there are two types of remote mirroring protocols that affect the network performance and data reliability, namely synchronous and asynchronous propagation protocols.

The optimization design criteria are the same as for Plato [8]. The main goal is the construction of an overlay network for the data to be distributed to all nodes within the following constraints: (1) Overlay network must remain connected at all times; (2) Overlay network should never succeed the allocated monetary budget; (3) The data should be distributed as efficiently as possible, meaning the amount of bandwidth consumed when diffusing data should be minimized.

The author of this paper has implemented three optimization algorithms to evaluate and compare their performances.

Table 1: Link Propagation Methods

Time interval	Avg. data batch size in GB
0	0
1 min	0.0436
5 min	0.2036
1 hr	2.091
4 hr	6.595
12 hr	15.12
24 hr	27.388

An implementation of Genetic Algorithms as used in the Plato implementation [8], an implementation of the network selection algorithm inspired by Artificial immune systems, and an implementation of a discrete Particle Swarm Optimization approach have been implemented [20]. Since the PSO-based implementation showed the best performance, it is used in this study for the parallelization using MapReduce. However, we first describe details about the algorithm as well as the problem description of the overlay network optimization task before moving on to the description of the MapReduce adoption.

The fitness function that is used as a measure is slightly modified compared to the Plato approach [8]. The differences are that normalization of the overall fitness value is done as to obtain a value between 0 and 1, as well as the sum of weights for each part of the fitness function is 1.

The fitness function consists of three parts (as in Plato); the first part evaluates the overlay network in terms of cost, the second in terms of performance, and the third part evaluates the reliability of the overlay network. The overall fitness function (Equation 1) is the weighted average of all three fitness portions. Please note that the sum of the weights needs to sum up to 1 (Equation 2).

$$F_{overall} = w_1 * F_{cost} + w_2 * F_{perf} + w_3 * F_{rel} \tag{1}$$

$$\sum_{i=1}^{3} w_i = 1 \tag{2}$$

Looking at the different fitness sub-functions, the fitness sub-function for cost is given as:

$$F_{cost} = 1 - \frac{cost}{budget} \tag{3}$$

where *cost* is the sum of operational expenses of all active links, and *budget* is a user supplied value on the maximum amount of money for an operating overlay network. The sub-function for the performance consists of two parts: latency and bandwidth as given below:

$$F_{perf} = 0.5 * (1 - \frac{latency_{avg}}{latency_{wc}}) + 0.5 * (\frac{bandwidth_{sys} - bandwidth_{eff}}{bandwidth_{sys}} + bound) \tag{4}$$

where $latency_{avg}$ is the average latency over all active links, and $latency_{wc}$ is the largest latency value measured over all links in the underlying network; $bandwidth_{sys}$ is the total available bandwidth across the overlay network given the active links, and $bandwidth_{eff}$ is the total effective bandwidth across the overall network after data has been coalesced, and *bound* is a limit on the best value that can be achieved throughout the network.

The last fitness sub-function measures the overlay network in terms of reliability consisting of two parts as given below:

$$F_{rel} = 0.5 * (\frac{links_{used}}{links_{max}}) + 0.5 * (1 - \frac{dataloss_{pot}}{dataloss_{max}}) \quad (5)$$

where $links_{used}$ is the number of active links, and $links_{max}$ is the maximum number of possible links given the network structure; and $dataloss_{pot}$ is the total amount of data that could be lost during write coalescing using the propagation methods as given in Table 1, and $dataloss_{wc}$ is the amount of data that could be lost during write coalescing using the propagation method with the largest time window.

3.2 Particle Swarm Optimization Implementation

Particle Swarm Optimization (PSO) as introduced in [22], is a swarm based global optimization algorithm. The algorithm is inspired by the behavior of bird swarms searching for an optimal food source. There are two standard kinds of PSO variants: global best PSO and local best PSO. Since we are using global best PSO, the movement of a single particle is influenced by its last movement, its knowledge, and the swarm's knowledge. PSO's basic equations are the following:

$$x_i(t+1) = x_i(t) + v_{ij}(t+1) \quad (6)$$

$$\begin{aligned} v_{ij}(t+1) = w(t)v_{ij}(t) + c_1 r_{1j}(t)(y_{ij}(t) - x_{ij}(t))) \\ + c_2 r_{2j}(t)(\hat{y}_j(t) - x_{ij}(t))) \end{aligned} \quad (7)$$

where x represents a particle, i denotes the particle's number, j the dimension, t a point in time, and v is the particle's velocity. y_{ij} is the best location the particle ever visited (the particle's knowledge), and $\hat{y}_j$ is the best location any particle in the swarm ever visited (the swarm's knowledge). w is the inertia weight and used to weigh the last velocity, c_1 is a variable to weigh the particle's knowledge, and c_2 is a variable to weigh the swarm's knowledge. r_1 and r_2 are uniformly distributed random numbers between zero and one. The pseudo code of the global best PSO is given in Algorithm 1 [23].

Since the overlay network optimization is a discrete problem, and PSO was designed for continuous problems, several operations have to be defined. This discrete implementation follows in part the implementation for solving the traveling salesman problem as described in [24]. First, a swarm of particles is initialized. A single particle represents one overlay network, i.e., every particle's position in the search space has to correspond to a possible overlay network. Velocities are implemented as lists of changes that can be applied to a particle (its vector) and that moves the particle to a new position (a new overlay network). Changes are exchanges of values of the overlay network. Furthermore, the difference between two matches (particles), multiplication of a velocity with a real number, and the addition of velocities have to be defined. The difference is implemented as a function of particles which returns the velocity containing all changes that have to be applied to move from one particle's position to another in the search space. Multiplication randomly deletes single changes from the velocity vector if the real number to be multiplied is smaller than one. If the real number is one, no changes are applied. For a real number larger than one, random changes are added to the velocity vector. Table 2 shows the specific parameters chosen for the PSO implementation as identified by preliminary experiments.

Algorithm 1 PSO Algorithm

```
Initialize an n_x-dimensional swarm S
repeat
    for each particle i = 1, ..., S.n_s do
        if f(S.x_i) < f(S.y_i) then
            S.y_i = S.x_i
        end if
        if f(S.y_i) < f(S.ŷ) then
            S.ŷ = S.y_i
        end if
    end for
    for each particle i = 1, ..., S.n_s do
        updateVelocity()
        updatePosition()
    end for
until stopping criterion is satisfied
```

Table 2: PSO parameters

Parameter	Value
Number of particles	100
Number of iterations	500
Inertia weight	0.001
Weight of local knowledge	0.5
Weight of global knowledge	0.5

3.3 MapReduce-based PSO Implementation

For the experiments in this paper, we are making use of Apache Hadoop [25], which is the commonly used MapReduce implementation. It is an open source framework that supports data-intensive distributed applications and enables applications to work with thousands of computational independent computers and petabytes of data. Hadoop Distributed File System (HDFS - storage component) and MapReduce (processing component) are the main core components of Apache Hadoop. HDFS allows high-throughput access to the data while maintaining fault tolerance by creating multiple replicas.

As mentioned before, a MapReduce implementation consists of three parts, the main, *map* and *reduce* functions. The main function first reads the overlay network parameters that are being used by the fitness function and writes it to the HDFS in order to be used by the *reduce* function. It then initializes the swarm by randomly initializing particles. Then the iteration loop of the algorithm starts by going through each particle and the Hadoop framework calls and executes the *map* and *reduce* functions, respectively. The pseudo code in Algorithm 2 shows the main function.

MapReduce's main operations are the *map* function and the *reduce* function. As shown in Algorithm 3, the *map* function reads the global best network from the HDFS. Given the global best network, the PSO update portion is applied in order to generate a modified network. This network, which

Algorithm 2 Main Function

```
procedure MAIN(maxIteration)
    network = readsOverlayNetworkParametersFromFile()
    writesOverlayNetworkParametersToHDFS(network)
    particles[] = initializeSwarm()
    iteration = 0
    while iteration ≤ maxIteration do
        for all particles do
            hadoopCallsAndExecutesMapFunction()
            hadoopCallsAndExecutesReduceFunction()
        end for
    end while
end procedure
```

is the particle including the particle ID, is then emitted and can be used by the *reduce* function.

Algorithm 3 Map Function

```
procedure MAP(Key: ParticleID, Value: Particle)
    particleID=Key
    particle=Value
    readGlobalBestFromHDFS()
    applyDiscretePSOUpdates(particle)
    emit(particleID, particle)
end procedure
```

The *reduce* function reads the global best network from the HDFS first. Then, the network parameters are read from the HDFS, and the particle's fitness is calculated. Afterwards, the fitness value is then compared to the global best fitness value. If the particle's fitness is greater than the current best, the particle is written to the HDFS, i.e., the network is written to the HDFS. At the end, the particle ID and the particle are emitted to be used in the next iteration.

Algorithm 4 Reduce Function

```
procedure REDUCE(Key: ParticleID, ValueList: Particle)
    particleID=Key
    particle=Value
    globalBestFitness = readGlobalBestFromHDFS()
    network = readNetworkParametersFromHDFS()
    fitness = calculateFitness(particle,network)
    if fitness ≤ globalBestFitness then
        globalBestFitness = fitness
        writeGlobalBestToHDFS(particle)
    end if
    emit(particleID, particle)
end procedure
```

4. EXPERIMENTAL SETTINGS

In this section, we describe the experimental setup of the MapReduce based PSO overlay optimization algorithm. First, the computing environment used is described, followed by a description of the different networks used for the experiments.

4.1 Computing Environment

The experiments were conducted on the Longhorn Hadoop cluster hosted by the Texas Advanced Computing Center (TACC)[1]. The TACC cluster consists of 48 nodes containing 48GB of RAM, 8 Intel Nehalem cores (2.5GHz each) which results in 384 compute cores with 2.304 TB of aggregated memory. Hadoop version 0.21 was used for the MapReduce framework, and Java runtime 1.7 for the system implementation. Furthermore, in order to provide a constant level of parallelization, the number of mapper and reducer tasks were set to the maximum, which are 8 per node since each node contains 8 cores.

[1]https://portal.longhorn.tacc.utexas.edu/

Table 3: Different networks used for scaling experiments

Number of nodes	Number of links	File size
100	4,950	187KB
200	19,900	775KB
300	44,850	1.8MB
400	79,800	3.1MB
500	124,750	4.9MB
600	179,700	7.1MB
700	244,650	9.7MB
800	319,600	12.7MB
900	404,550	16.1MB
1,000	499,500	19.1MB

4.2 Network Sizes

Table 3 shows the different network characteristics used for the scaling experiments. The number of nodes, number of links, and the file size are listed.

5. RESULTS

This section shows the results obtained from the experiments. Three different experiments were performed, the first investigated the fitness and running time when the number of iterations are scaled, the second looked at the fitness and running time when the number of network nodes are scaled, and the third investigated the running time and speedup when different numbers of computing nodes are used. All measurement points shown in the graphs are average values of 25 independent runs.

5.1 Scaling of number of iterations

First of all, experiments were run to capture the solution quality and the running time of the algorithm per iterations, as shown in Figures 1 and 2, respectively. A 300-node network was used, and the particle size was set to 100 using the fitness equation with equal weights (as shown in Equation 1). Two computation nodes of the TACC environment were used for these experiments. Figure 1 shows that the optimization converges after around 270 iterations to the optimum value of 8.33.

As for the running time, as expected we can see that each iteration takes roughly the same amount of time resulting in a linear trend (with only slight variations) for increasing iterations.

5.2 Scaling of number of network nodes

The next set of experiments investigated again the solution quality and running time, however, this time not the number of iterations were increased but the network sizes were increased. The number of iterations was fixed to 500, and network sizes between 100 to 1,000 with increments of 100 were used. The number of computational nodes used was 2 for this experiment. In terms of fitness, the values up to network sizes of 400 produce the optimal fitness of

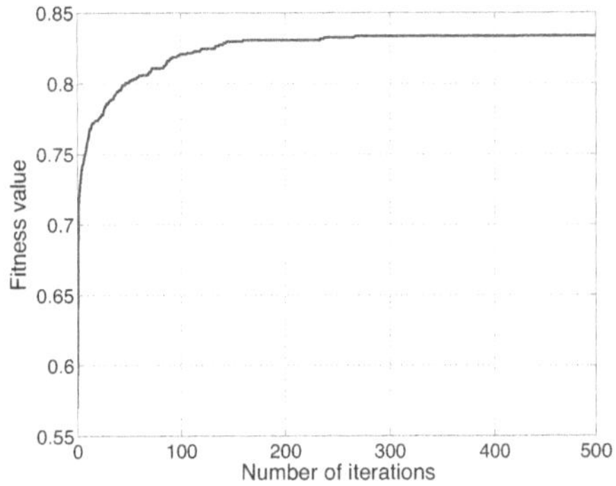

Figure 1: Fitness value versus number of iterations

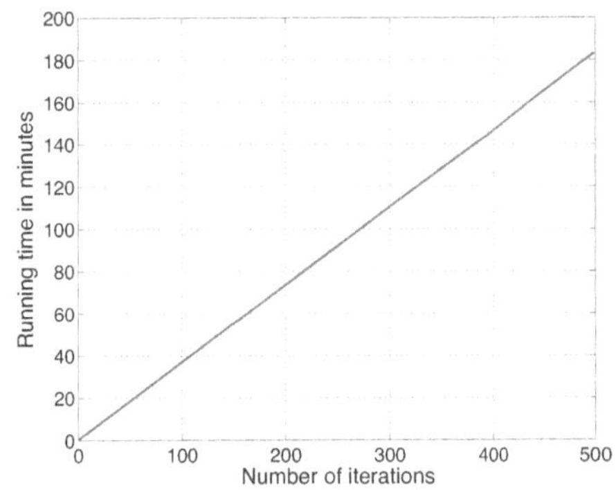

Figure 2: Running time versus number of iterations

0.833, however, for larger network sizes the fitness reduces as shown in Figure 3. In order to achieve the optimal fitness value the number of iterations would need to be increased for networks of size 500 and higher.

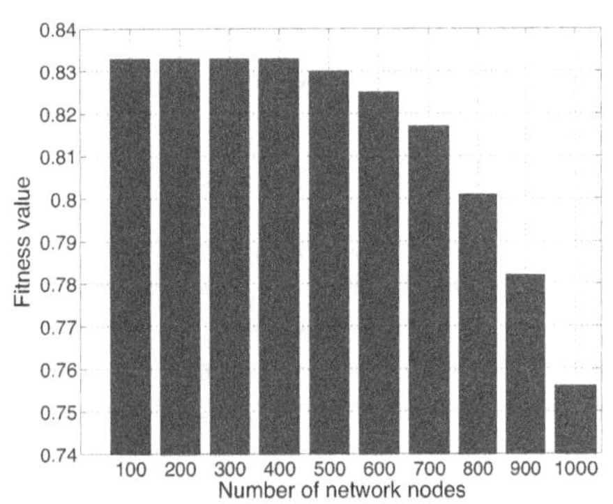

Figure 3: Fitness value versus number of nodes

In terms of running time, we can see the effect of increasing numbers of network sizes in Figure 4. An exponential trend is observed measuring 5.3 minutes and 195.2 minutes for a network of 100 nodes and 1,000 nodes, respectively.

5.3 Scaling of number of computational nodes

Since speedup is the measure to evaluate parallel algorithms, we used the following speedup equation:

$$Speedup = \frac{T_2}{T_n} \tag{8}$$

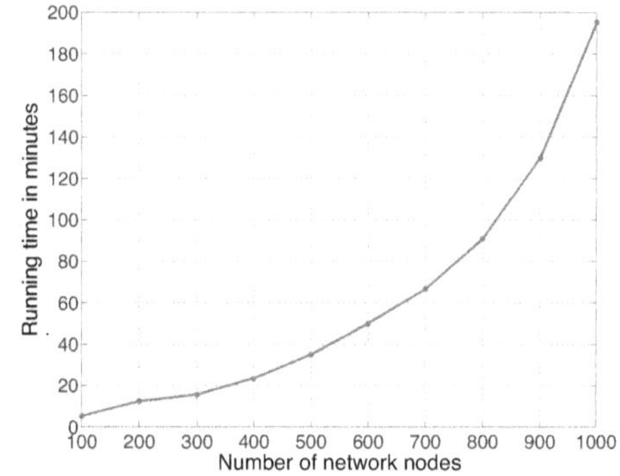

Figure 4: Running time versus number of nodes

where T_2 is the running time using 2 nodes, and T_n is the running time using n nodes, where n is a multiple of 2.

For these sets of experiments, we increased the number of computational nodes by 2 starting from 2 compute nodes up to 16 compute nodes. The running time is measured and the speedup is calculated by Equation 8. Experiments were run for a 500-node network using 200, 400, and 600 particles, respectively. The number of iterations were kept constant with 500. The black line in all speedup figures shows the ideal speedup. The closer the measured speedup gets to the line, the better the utilization of the parallel computing nodes is. Figure 5 shows the results. As can be seen from the figure, the speedup is worse for fewer numbers of particles achieving a speedup of around 6.5 for 200 particles, a speedup of around 10 for 400 particles, and a speedup of around 12 for 600 particles. This demonstrates that the utilization of the Hadoop framework is better when larger numbers of particles are used. This implies that the fitness evaluations of the particles that are partitioned onto the different compute nodes is more efficient when more computation is necessary. Therefore, the control and communication overhead of the Hadoop framework does not have as large as an effect for larger numbers of particles.

Figure 6 shows similar behavior of running time and speedup (please note that the running times are this time in hours and not in minutes as in Figure 5). However, a 1,000-node network was used and initial experiments with the same numbers of particles as for the 500-node network did produce poor results. Therefore, the particle sizes of 400, 800, and 1,200 were used for this set of experiments. The interesting observation, as seen in the figure, is that the speedup in all cases turn out to be better as compared to the 500-node network. Again, this can be explained with a better utilization of the Hadoop framework resulting in higher speedup gains when larger particle sizes are used. A speedup of around 10 is achieved with 400 particles, a speedup of almost 12 is obtained when 800 particles are used, and the speedup for 1,200 particles is close to 14.

6. CONCLUSION AND FUTURE WORK

The focus of this paper was the parallelization of a Particle Swarm Optimization (PSO) approach for the optimization of overlay networks. For the parallelization, the MapReduce paradigm was exploited. A MapReduce based PSO overlay network optimization algorithm was implemented and extensive experiments were conducted to evaluate the solution

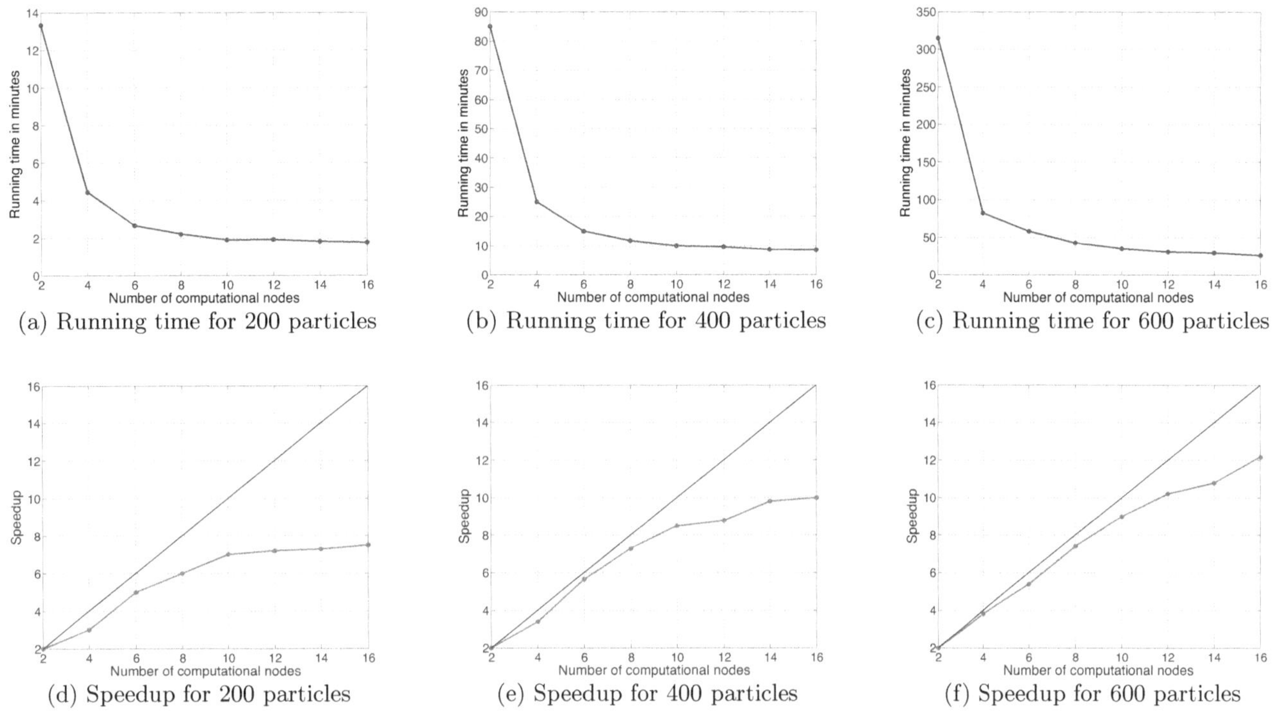

(a) Running time for 200 particles (b) Running time for 400 particles (c) Running time for 600 particles

(d) Speedup for 200 particles (e) Speedup for 400 particles (f) Speedup for 600 particles

Figure 5: Running time and speedup results for network of 500 nodes with 200, 400, and 600 particles

quality, running time and speedup for increasing numbers of network nodes. Networks consisting of 100 up to 1,000 nodes were investigated. The results revealed that the utilization of the Hadoop framework increased with increasing network sizes as well as with increasing numbers of particles used. A general recommendation can be made that the larger the network to be optimized, the larger the number of particles used within the PSO algorithm has to be. Reflecting on the particular speedup measurements conducted, good speedups can be achieved using 10 or 12 computational nodes.

Further work includes the investigation of how long each function per iteration runs in order to find out which of the three portions (main, map, or reduce function) of the code runs the longest. In addition, larger sizes of networks over 1,000 nodes could be optimized, however, running times of several days are expected.

Acknowledgments

The author acknowledges the support of the NDSU Advance FORWARD program sponsored by NSF HRD-0811239 and ND EPSCoR through NSF grant EPS-0814442. This work would have not been possible without the Extreme Science and Engineering Discovery Environment (XSEDE) infrastructure, which is supported by the National Science Foundation under grant number OCI-1053575.

7. REFERENCES

[1] S. Tarkoma, "Overlay Networks: Toward Information Networking", CRC Press, Auerbach Publications, ISBN: 978-1-4398-1371-3, 2010.

[2] N. Lam, Z. Dziong, L. G. Mason, "Service Overlay Network Design with Reliability Constraints", Proceedings of IEEE 7th International Workshop on the Design of Reliable Communication Networks, Washington, D.C., USA, 2009.

[3] T. Baeck, D. Fogel, and Z. Michalewicz, "Handbook of Evolutionary Computation", IOP Publ. Ltd., Bristol, UK, 1997.

[4] G. D. Caro, M. Dorigo, "AntNet: distributed stigmergetic control for communications networks", J. Artif. Int. Res. 9, 1 (December 1998), 317-365, 1998.

[5] J. Montoya, Y. Donoso, E. Montoya, D. Echeverri, "Multiobjective model for multicast overlay networks over IP/MPLS using MOEA", Proceedings of International Conference on Optical Network Design and Modeling, 1-6, 2008.

[6] A. Abraham, H. Liu, Y. Badr, C. Grosan, "A multi-swarm approach for neighbor selection in peer-to-peer networks", Proceedings of the 5th international conference on Soft computing as transdisciplinary science and technology (CSTST '08), ACM, New York, NY, USA, 178-184, 2008.

[7] D. Montana, T. Hussain, T. Saxen, "Adaptive reconfiguration of data networks using genetic algorithms", Proceedings of the Genetic and Evolutionary Computation Conference, pp. 1141-1149, San Francisco, CA, USA, 2002.

[8] A. J. Ramirez, D. B. Knoester, B. H. C. Cheng, P. K. McKinley, "Plato: A Genetic Algorithm Approach to Run-Time Reconfiguration in Autonomic Computing Systems", Journal of Cluster Computing, 2010.

[9] S. A. Ludwig, "Nature-Inspired Reconfiguration of Overlay Networks", Proceedings of Third World Congress on Nature and Biologically Inspired Computing (NaBIC), Salamanca, Spain, 2011.

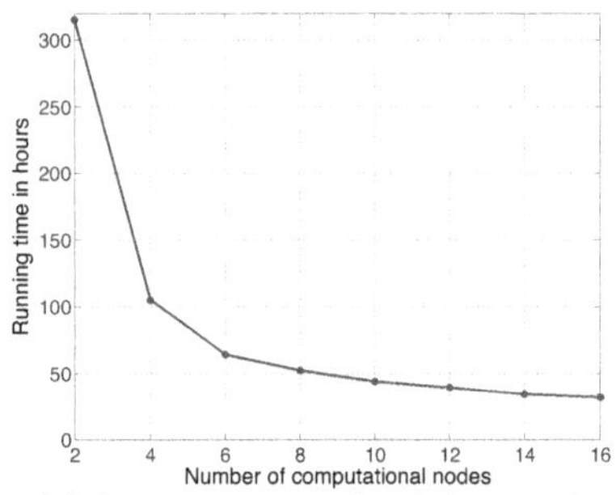

(a) Running time for 400 particles

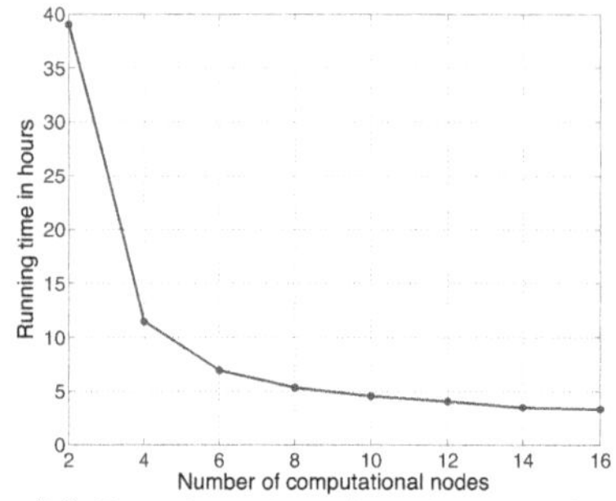

(b) Running time for 800 particles

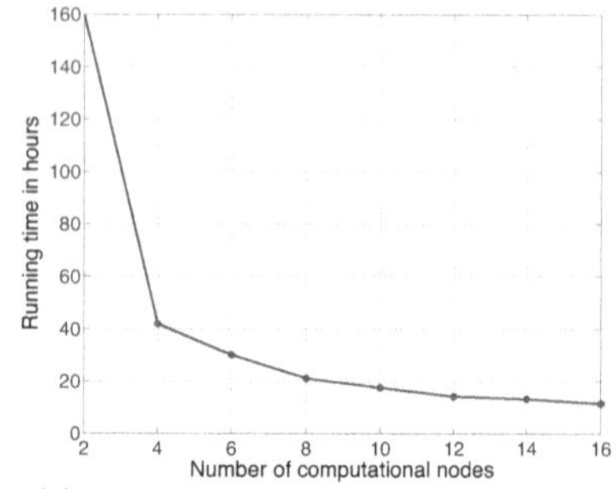

(c) Running time for 1,200 particles

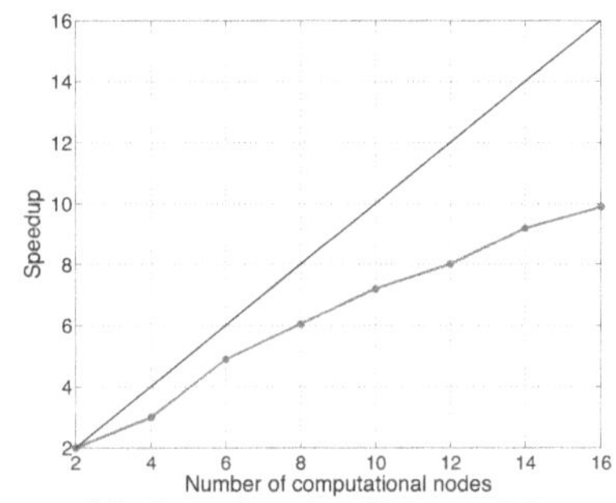

(d) Speedup for 400 particles

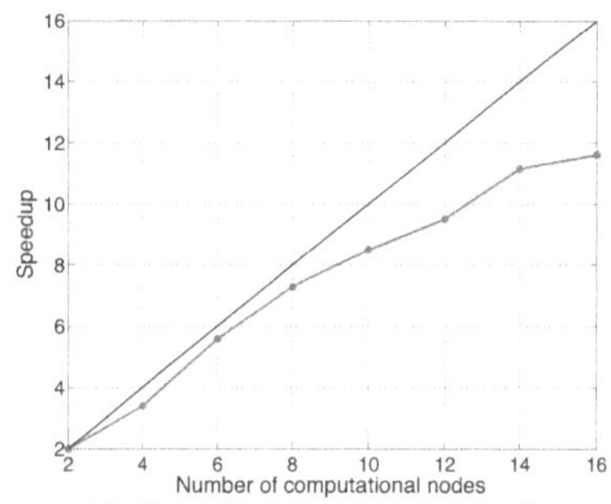

(e) Speedup for 800 particles

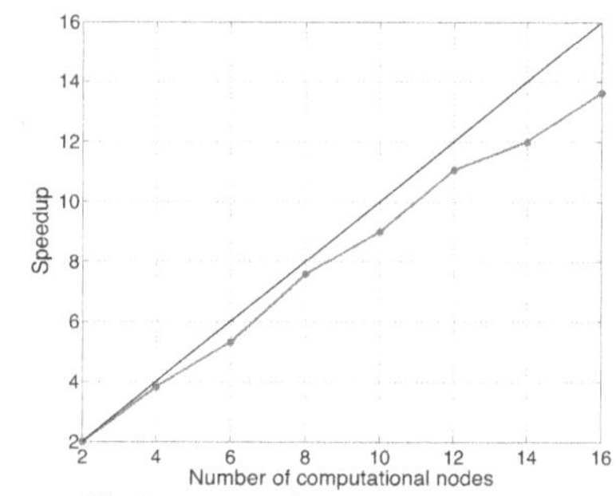

(f) Speedup for 1,200 particles

Figure 6: Running time and speedup results for network of 1,000 nodes with 400, 800, and 1,200 particles

[10] S. A. Ludwig, "Scalability Analysis: Reconfiguration of Overlay Networks Using Nature-Inspired Algorithms", in Advances in Intelligent Modelling and Simulation: Artificial Intelligence-based Models and Techniques in Scalable Computing, Studies in Computational Intelligence series, vol. 422, pp. 137-154, Springer, 2012.

[11] MPI (Message Passing Interface), 2014, `http://www-unix.mcs.anl.gov/mpi/`.

[12] PVM (Parallel Virtual Machine), 2014, `http://www.csm.ornl.gov/pvm/`.

[13] C. Zhou, "Fast parallelization of differential evolution algorithm using MapReduce", Proceedings of the 12th annual conference on Genetic and evolutionary computation, 2010.

[14] C. T. Chu, S. K. Kim, Y. A. Lin, et al., "Map-Reduce for Machine Learning on Multicore", In NIPS (2006), pp. 281-288 by edited by Bernhard Schoelkopf, John C. Platt, Thomas Hoffman.

[15] K. Kambatla, N. Rapolu, S. Jagannathan, and A. Grama, "Asynchronous Algorithms in MapReduce", Proceedings of the 2010 IEEE International Conference on Cluster Computing (CLUSTER '10), Washington, DC, USA, 245-254, 2010.

[16] A. Verma, X. Llora, D. E. Goldberg, and R. H. Campbell, "Scaling Genetic Algorithms Using MapReduce", Proceedings of the 2009 Ninth International Conference on Intelligent Systems Design and Applications (ISDA '09), Washington, DC, USA, 2009.

[17] J. Schaffer and L. Shelman, "On Crossover as an Evolutionary Viable Strategy", In R. Belw and L. Booker, editors, Proceedisn of the 4th International Conference on Genetic Algorithms, Morgan Kaufmann, 1991.

[18] C. Jin, C. Vecchiola, R. Buyya, "MRPGA: An Extension of MapReduce for Parallelizing Genetic Algorithms", Proceedings of IEEE Fourth International Conference on eScience, 2008.

[19] A. W. McNabb, C. K. Monson, K. D. Seppi, "Parallel PSO using MapReduce", Proceedings of Congress of Evolutionary Computation (CEC), 2007.

[20] I. Aljarah and S. A. Ludwig, "MapReduce Intrusion Detection System based on a Particle Swarm Optimization Clustering Algorithm", Proceedings of the 2013 IEEE Congress on Evolutionary Computation, Cancun, Mexico, June 2013.

[21] K. Keeton, C. Santos, D. Beyer, J. Chase, J. Wilkes, "Designing for disasters", Proceedings of the 3rd USENIX Conference on File and Storage Technologies, pp. 59-62. Berkeley, CA, USA, 2004.

[22] J. Kennedy, R. Eberhart, "Particle swarm optimization", Proceedings of IEEE International Conference on Neural Networks, Perth, Western Australia, 1995.

[23] A. Engelbrecht, "Computational Intelligence - An Introduction", 2nd Edition, Wiley, 2007.

[24] M. Clerc, "Discrete particle swarm optimization - illustrated by the traveling salesman problem". New Optimization Techniques in Engineering, In Studies in Fuzziness and Soft Computing, Springer, 2004.

[25] Apache Software Foundation, Hadoop MapReduce, 2011. `http://hadoop.apache.org/mapreduce`.

Enhancing Parallel Cooperative Trajectory Based Metaheuristics with Path Relinking

Gabriel Luque
Universidad de Málaga, Andalucía Tech
E.T.S.I. Informática, Campus Teatinos,
29071 Málaga (España)
gabriel@lcc.uma.es

Enrique Alba
Universidad de Málaga, Andalucía Tech
E.T.S.I. Informática, Campus Teatinos,
29071 Málaga (España)
eat@lcc.uma.es

ABSTRACT

This paper proposes a novel algorithm combining path relinking with a set of cooperating trajectory based parallel algorithms to yield a new metaheuristic of enhanced search features. Algorithms based on the exploration of the neighborhood of a single solution, like simulated annealing (SA), have offered accurate results for a large number of real-world problems in the past. Because of their trajectory based nature, some advanced models such as the cooperative one are competitive in academic problems, but still show many limitations in addressing large scale instances. In addition, the field of parallel models for trajectory methods has not deeply been studied yet (at least in comparison with parallel population based models). In this work, we propose a new hybrid algorithm which improves cooperative single solution techniques by using path relinking, allowing both to reduce the global execution time and to improve the efficacy of the method. We test here this new model using a large benchmark of instances of two well-known NP-hard problems: MAXSAT and QAP, with competitive results.

Categories and Subject Descriptors

F.2 [**Theory of Computation**]: Analysis of Algorithms and Problem Complexity; G.1.0 [**Mathematics of Computing**]: General—*Parallel algorithms*

General Terms

Algorithms

Keywords

parallelism, trajectory based metaheuristics, path relinking

1. INTRODUCTION

Metaheuristics are general heuristics that provide suboptimal solutions in a reasonable time for various optimization problems [10]. According to the number of solutions they manage during optimization process, they fall into two categories: trajectory based methods and population based techniques. On the one hand, a population based metaheuristic makes use of a randomly generated population of solutions. The initial population is enhanced through a natural evolution process. At each generation of the process, the whole population or a part of the population is replaced by newly generated individuals (often the best ones). On the other hand, a trajectory based algorithm starts with a single initial solution which, at each step of the search, is replaced by another (often better) solution found in its neighborhood.

Although the use of metaheuristics allows to significantly reduce the temporal complexity of the search process, the exploration remains time-consuming for many industrial and engineering problems. In this context, parallelism emerges as a useful strategy to reduce the computational times down to affordable values. The point is that the parallel versions of metaheuristics allows not only to speed up the computations, but also to improve the quality of the provided solutions [1, 16]. For both trajectory-based and population-based metaheuristics, different parallel models have been proposed in the literature. In general, these parallel models are mostly oriented to study parallel population-based algorithms, but it actually exists a gap in the studies about parallel models for single solution methods from which something could be gained for other researchers.

The focus of this paper is on parallel trajectory-based metaheuristics. Usually, three major parallel models for this kind of algorithms exist: the parallel exploration of the neighborhood, the parallel evaluation of each solution, and the multi-start model. The two first models speed up the execution of the method without changing the semantics of the algorithm in comparison with a sequential exploration. The last one is maybe more interesting from the algorithmic point of view since it can change the behavior of the method with respect to its serial counterpart. The multi-start model lies in launching in parallel several independent or cooperative homo/heterogeneous algorithms. Usually, in its cooperative mode, subalgorithms of the parallel multi-start model exchange information (solutions) during execution and when the target subalgorithm receives a solution, it continues the search using the previous one or the newly received one according to a selection scheme. The problem of this cooperative model is that some interesting information is lost since either the new solution is discarded (it is not chosen by the selection scheme) and no new information is incorporated, or it is accepted and the previous historical information of the subalgorithm is lost.

GECCO'14, July 12–16, 2014, Vancouver, BC, Canada.

ACM 978-1-4503-2662-9/14/07 ...$15.00.
http://dx.doi.org/10.1145/2576768.2598337.

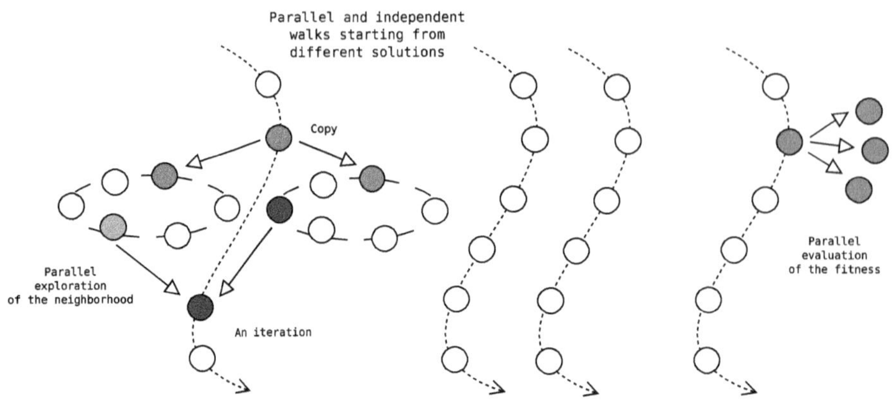

Figure 1: Parallel models for trajectory based methods: parallel exploration of the neighborhood (left), the multi-start model (center), and the parallel evaluation of each solution (right).

This work proposes a new parallel yet simple model that extends the cooperative multi-start model to avoid the aforementioned flaw. In this case, when a solution is received, we use the path relinking technique to generate a set of new candidate solutions which combine the information of the new solution and the previous tentative solution of the target subalgorithm. Therefore, the subalgorithm incorporates new information but, at the same time, it keeps information of its own search. The utilization of path relinking opens some design alternatives: which subalgorithms cooperate, which solution of the set generated by path relinking will be selected to continue the search, ... Then, the main goal of this paper is to propose a new cooperative scheme and study the different design alternatives. This parallel model has been evaluated with two well-known NP-hard problems: MAXSAT and QAP problems [15].

This paper is organized as follows. The next section (Section 2) introduces some background information about parallel trajectory based methods and path relinking. Section 3 presents our proposed parallel model. Then we describe the experimental design used in this paper. Later, we discuss experimental results in Section 5 and finally we summarize the conclusions and give some hints on the future work.

2. BACKGROUND

In this section, we present some background information about the basic techniques that we use to design our new proposal described in this paper.

2.1 Trajectory based techniques

Trajectory based methods, illustrated in Algorithm 1, are single solution-based metaheuristics dedicated to the improvement only one solution in its neighborhood. They start their exploration process from an initial solution randomly generated or provided by another metaheuristic. This solution is then updated during a certain number of steps. At each step, the current solution is replaced by another (often the better) one found in its neighborhood. These methods are mainly characterized by: an internal memory storing the state of the search, a strategy for the selection of the initial solution, a generator of candidate solutions i.e. the neighborhood, and a selection policy of the candidate moves. Three major trajectory based algorithms are largely used: Hill Climbing (HC) [15], Simulated Annealing (SA) [13], and Tabu Search (TS) [11].

Generate($s(0)$);
$t := 0$;
while not Termination_Criterion($s(t)$ **do**
  $m(t)$:= SelectAcceptableMove($s(t)$);
  $s(t+1)$:= ApplyMove($m(t)$,$s(t)$);
  $t := t+1$;
end while

Algorithm 1: Trajectory based technique skeleton pseudo-code

Although these technique allows to obtain very accurate results for a large number of problems, some advanced mechanisms have to be used to tackle with the high requirements of the industrial problems. One of these mechanisms is the utilization of parallel models. In the literature are usually identified three major parallel distributed models of this kind of method [2]: the parallel exploration of the neighborhood, the multi-start model, and the parallel evaluation of each solution (see Figure 1).

- **Parallel multi-start model**: The model consists in launching in parallel several independent or cooperative homo/heterogeneous single solution method. Each subalgorithm is often initialized with a different solution. The independent approach is widely exploited because it is natural and easy for the user. In this case, the semantics of the model is the same as the serial execution. That is to say the results obtained with N parallel independent methods is the same as that provided by N algorithms performed in a serial way on a single machine. The parallelism allows to efficiently enhance the robustness of the execution.

  In its cooperative mode, subalgorithms of the parallel multi-start model exchange information during execution. Usually that information is a solution.

- **Parallel exploration of the neighborhood model**: This parallel model is a kind of farmer/worker model allowing to speed up the exploration of the possible moves without changing the semantics of the algorithm in comparison with a sequential exploration. At the beginning of each iteration of the algorithm, the farmer sends the current solution to a pool of workers. Each worker explores some neighboring candidates, and returns back the results to the farmer.

- **Parallel evaluation of solution model**: The fitness of each solution is evaluated in a parallel centralized way. This kind of parallelism could be efficient if the evaluation function is CPU time-consuming and/or IO intensive.

In the literature, we can found parallel versions of the most popular trajectory based metaheuristics such as parallel SA [8, 4], parallel VNS [17, 7], parallel TS [3, 6], ... But most of them are focused on the application to be solved and they use classical parallel models. The aim of this paper is the parallel model itself, our goal is to provide a new mechanism to build more efficient and accurate parallel solution-based techniques.

The two last models uses the parallel platform to speedup the search procedure but they don't change the behavior of the method. On the contrary, the first parallel model using cooperation modify the dynamics of the technique. In this work, we focus in this kind of methods.

2.2 Path Relinking

Path relinking (PR) [12] was originally proposed into the context of scatter search by extension of its basic philosophy. PR is based on the generation of paths between high quality solutions. This leads to a broader conception of the meaning of creating combinations of solutions. Such combinations may be conceived to arise by generating paths between and beyond selected solutions in neighborhood space, rather than in Euclidean space. This conception is reinforced by the fact that a path between solutions in a neighborhood space will generally yield new solutions that share a significant subset of attributes contained in the parent solutions, in varying "mixes" according to the path selected and the location on the path that determines the solution currently considered. The character of such paths is easily specified by reference to solution attributes that are added, dropped or otherwise modified by the moves executed in neighborhood space. To generate the desired paths, it is only necessary to select moves that perform the following role: upon starting from an initiating solution, the moves must progressively introduce attributes contributed by a guiding solution (or reduce the distance between attributes of the initiating and guiding solutions). In Figure 2, we can observe the scheme followed for this technique to obtain new solutions.

3. OUR PROPOSED MODEL

Our goal is to design a new parallel model for trajectory based metaheuristics which allows to reduce the global execution time but, at the same time, it also improves the efficacy of the exploration of the search space. A number of papers has been devoted to this topic for parallel approaches involving population based methods (some of them also involving trajectory-based ones) but it is not a very studied field for pure parallel trajectory based metaheuristics.

Since we want to improve the efficacy of the resulting parallel algorithm, we focus on the multi-start cooperative paradigm (the other two models do not change the dynamics of the method with respect to the serial version). As discussed in the introduction, a problem in classical approaches of multi-start models for trajectory-based metaheuristics is the lost of information. Indeed, when a subalgorithm receives a solution from other subalgorithm, it has to choose whether it continues the search either with the current one or the newly received one, loosing the stored information in the discarded solution.

We propose a new model in which we do not have to choose between the two solutions, but generate a new solution with the main features of both solutions. With this aim, we can use some mechanisms, similar to the recombination operator of population based method, which combine both solutions [14]. But, in this work, we propose the utilization of a more advanced technique such as path relinking. We run this technique to generate some paths using the current solution and the incoming solution as initial points. The generated path provides the parallel technique of a set of candidate solutions to continue the search, and therefore, a selection scheme is needed to chose one.

Several important design issues arise from the general model proposed in this work:

- **Cooperation scheme:** it indicates what and how subalgorithms cooperate each other.

- **Selection scheme:** it refers what solution is selected from the set of candidate ones generated by PR.

For each design feature we have proposed some alternatives. In the previous existing multi-start models, the features of the incoming solution were not very important rather than it fitness value, but now, this issue can provoke an important impact in the search behaviour. Different possible cooperation schema are analyzed here:

- **Predefined**: in this case, each subalgorithm receives a single solution (the sending island is defined by the topology). Therefore, any subalgorithm only receives a single solution which is combined with the local one.

- **Depending of the fitness value (best)**: in this case, each subalgorithm receives a solution from each subalgorithm which composes the global method. Now, the subalgorithm has to select one solution from this set of candidate solutions, that will be combined with the current one. In this strategy, the selection mechanism is based on the fitness value of the incoming solutions. In this study, we select the solution with the best fitness.

- **Depending of the features of the solution (distance)**: as in the previous one, each subalgorithm receives several solutions (one per subalgorithm) and it has to select one. In this case, the selection will be performed by using a genotypic distance (a diversity measure) among the solutions and we select the farthest one. This distance depends on how the solution are represented in the algorithm.

- **Random**: as in the previous scenarios, each subalgorithm receives several solutions (one per subalgorithm) but in this strategy, random one is selected from all the incoming solutions.

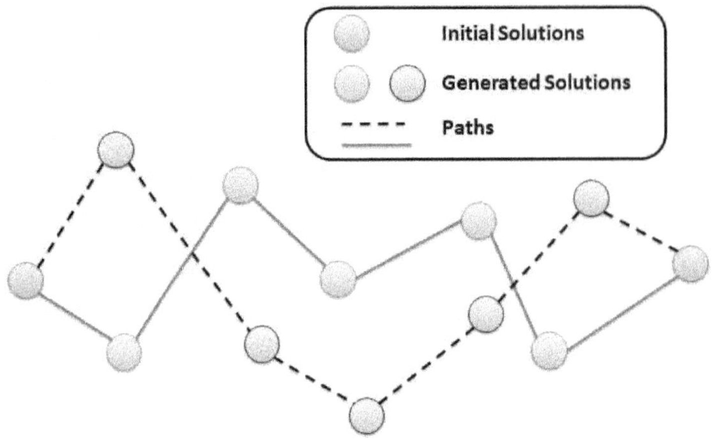

Figure 2: Path relinking scheme.

Using one of the these strategies, our proposed technique obtains the second initial solution (the first initial one is the current point of the subalgorithm) and then, we can apply the path relinking to generate a path. That path provides some new candidate solutions and the method has to select one of them to replace the current one and continue the search process. To choose the new solution we also take into account some alternatives:

- **Best**: the algorithm selects the best solution in the generated path:
$$max_{s \in S}(f(s)), \quad (1)$$
where S is a set of solution composed by the points visited during the path generated by PR and f is the fitness function (assuming the maximization case).
- **Most shared information**: in this case, the subalgorithm selects the solution sharing more information from initial solutions. To do this, we calculate the genotypic distance among the solutions and then we apply the next equation:
$$min_{s \in S}(max(dist(s,s'), dist(s,s''))), \quad (2)$$
where S is a set of solution composed by the points visited during the path generated by PR, s' and s'' are the initial solutions and $dist$ is the genotypic distance between two solutions. With this process we simultaneously minimize the distance of the new solution with respect to the two initial ones.
- **Random**: in this case, the subalgorithm select a random solution from the path without taking into account its quality or any other feature.

In the experimental section we study the behaviour and the performance of each strategy.

4. EXPERIMENTAL DESIGN

In this section, we describe the experimental design followed in this work. First, we present the problems and the instances used in the experiments. Later, we explain the algorithm used to test our parallel model. Finally, we present the methodology and parameters used in the experiments.

4.1 Benchmark

In order to make more relevant contribution, we have selected a wide set of instances from two very different problems: MAXSAT and QAP.

MAXSAT: The satisfiability (SAT) problem is commonly recognized as a fundamental problem in computer science, automated reasoning, mathematical logic, and related fields. The MAXSAT is a variant of this general problem.

Formally, the SAT problem can be formulated as follows. Let $U = \{u_1, \ldots, u_n\}$ be a set of n Boolean variables. A truth assignment for U is a function $t : U \to \{true, false\}$. Two literals, u and $\neg u$, can match with each variable. A literal u (resp. $\neg u$) is true under t if and only if $t(u) = true$ (resp. $t(\neg u) = false$). A set C of literals is called a clause and it represents the disjunction (*or* logical connective). A set of clauses is called a formula. A formula f is interpreted as a formula of the propositional calculus in conjunctive normal form (CNF) so that a truth assignment t satisfies a clause C iff at least one literal $u \in C$ is true under t. Finally, t satisfies f iff it satisfies every clause in f. The SAT problem consists of a set of n variables $\{u_1, \ldots, u_n\}$ and a set of m clauses $C_1, \ldots, C_m$. The goal is to determine whether there exists or not an assignment of truth values to variables that makes the formula $f = C_1 \wedge \cdots \wedge C_m$ in CNF satisfiable. Among the extensions to SAT, MAXSAT [9] is probably the most known one. In this case, a parameter K is given and the problem is to determine whether there exists an assignment t of truth values to variables such that at least K clauses are satisfied. SAT can be considered as a special case of MAXSAT when K equals the number m of clauses.

In the experiments we use five instances from standard benchmark SATLIB[1]. We use the instances: *uf250-01.cnf* - *uf250-05.cnf*. Each instance has 250 variables and 1065 clauses, and all them are in the transition phase.

QAP: The Quadratic Assignment Problem (QAP) is a well-known NP-hard combinatorial optimization problem, which is the core of many real-world optimization problems [9]. QAP models many applications in diverse areas. In par-

[1] `http://www.cs.ubc.ca/~hoos/SATLIB/benchm.html`

ticular the following problems can be formulated as special cases of the QAP: the Traveling Salesman Problem (TSP), the Fragment Assembly Problem (FAP), Scheduling problems, the Facility Layout Problem, among others.

Let P be a set of n facilities and L a set of n locations. For each pair of locations i and j, an arbitrary distance is specified r_{ij} and for each pair of facilities p and q, a flow is specified w_{pq}. The QAP consists of assigning to each location in L one facility in P in such manner that the total cost of the assignment is minimized. Each location can only contain one facility and all facilities must be assigned to one location. For each pair of locations, the cost is calculated as the product of the distance between the locations and the flow associated with the facilities in the locations. The total cost is the sum of all the costs associated with each pair of locations. One solution to this problem is a bijection between L and P, that is, $x : L \rightarrow P$ such that x is bijective. Without loss of generality, we can just assume that $L = P = \{1, 2, ..., n\}$ and each solution x is a permutation in S_n, the set permutations of $\{1, 2, ..., n\}$.

The cost function to be minimized can be formally defined as:

$$f(x) = \sum_{i,j=1}^{n} r_{i,j} \cdot w_{x(i),x(j)} \quad (3)$$

We chose the five most complex QAP instances of QAPLIB Library[2]. The complexity of the QAP instances is given by their size and autocorrelation length ℓ [5]. In consequence, we selected esc128, tho150, tai100b, tai150b, and tai256c instances that are described in Table 1.

Table 1: The five most complex instances of QAPLIB.

Instance	*Size*	ξ	ℓ	*Lowest Known Cost*
esc128	128	32	32	64
tho150	150	41.19	44.174	8.13E+06
tai100b	100	35.472	39.613	1.19E+09
tai150b	150	40.458	42.947	4.99E+08
tai256c	256	64	64	4.48E+07

4.2 Algorithm

We have used the well-known simulated annealing algorithm to test our parallel model. Simulated annealing (SA) [13] is a stochastic optimization technique, which has its origin in statistical mechanics. It is based upon a cooling procedure used in industry. This procedure heats the material to a high temperature so that it becomes a liquid and the atoms can move relatively freely. The temperature is then slowly lowered so that at each temperature the atoms can move enough to begin adopting the most stable configuration. In principle, if the material is cooled slowly enough, the atoms are able to reach the most stable (optimum) configuration. This smooth cooling process is known as *annealing*. Algorithm 2 shows a scheme of SA. First at all, the parameter T, called the temperature, and the solution, are initialized. The solution $s1$ is accepted as the new current solution if $\delta = f(s1) - f(s0) < 0$. Stagnations in local optimum are prevented by accepting also solutions which increase the objective function value with a probability $exp(-\delta/T)$ if $\delta > 0$. This process is repeated several times to obtain good sampling statistics for the current temperature. The number of such iterations is given by the parameter $Markov\_Chain\_length$, whose name alludes the fact that the sequence of accepted solutions is a Markov chain (a sequence of states in which each state only depends on the previous one). Then the temperature is decremented and the entire process repeated until a frozen state is achieved at T_{min}. The value of T usually varies from a relatively large value to a small value close to zero.

```
t = 0
initialize(T)
s0 = Initial_Solution()
v0 = Evaluate(s0)
repeat
  repeat
    t = t + 1
    s1 = Generate(s0,T)
    v1 = Evaluate(s0,T)
    if Accept(v0,v1,T) then
      s0 = s1
      v0 = v1
    end if
  until t mod Markov_Chain_length == 0
  T = Update(T)
until 'loop stop criterion' satisfied
```

Algorithm 2: Scheme of the Simulated Annealing(SA) Algorithm.

In order to apply SA to solve our problems, we have to define how a solution in the neighborhood is generated (function Generate in Algorithm 2). Since we use a bitstring to represent a solution for MAXSAT, we use the standard bit-flip operator (it change a single bit from 0 to 1 or from 1 to 0) to generate a neighbor from the current solution. In the QAP case, we use an integer permutation in order to represent a solution inside the algorithm and the swap operator (the values of two positions are interchanged) is the selected mechanism to build a new solution from the current one.

In our parallel approach we run eight independent instances (subalgorithms) of SA which asynchronously cooperate every 50 iterations. As cooperation scheme, we use the four alternatives presented in Section 3. When a new solution arrives to the target subalgorithm, the PR method is applied to generate a path. To build this path, first, it analyzes the component which are different between the two initial solutions, and then, each visited point in the path is generated by changing one of these components.

This way of building the path allows us to obtain efficient implementations of the selection scheme (see Section 3). For example, we do not need to build the whole path when we want to select a random solution from the path or when we plan to use a solution which maximizes the shared information, since they can be calculated *a priori* only generating a single solution. However, to obtain the best solution of the path, all the visited points should be generated and evaluated. In order to the reduce the computation cost of this last strategy, we will use partial evaluations instead of a complete evaluation of the solution. This allows to reduce the computational cost of the resulting algorithm. For example,

[2]`http://www.seas.upenn.edu/qaplib/`

in the MAXSAT problem, when the variation operator only modify a single logic variable, we only have to analyze the effect on a low percentage (2-5%) of clauses in the instance. Also, in the QAP problem, we can reduce the computational complexity of the evaluation of a solution from $O(n^2)$ (a complete evaluation) to $O(n)$ (when a partial evaluation is performed).

4.3 Methodology

This subsection provides the reader with the details of the experiments performed to evaluate the new parallel model proposed for trajectory-based metaheuristics. We have analyzed 12 different variants (three selection strategies and four cooperation schema). We use the terminology **SA_X_Y**, where **X** is the selection mechanism and **Y** is the cooperation strategy. The possible values for **X** are: **rnd** for random, **bst** for best, and **inf** for maximizing the shared information scheme. The possible values for **Y** are: **pre** for the predefined topology, **bst** for the best solution, **dst** for the strategy based on the distance, and **rnd** for the random one. We will also compare our proposed model with a parallel version using the multi-start no-cooperative model, also known as independent run model (**iSA**) , and a parallel version using the classical multi-start cooperative model (**cSA**), in which incoming solutions just replace the current one. In order to perform fair comparisons, the stopping condition is to find the optimal solution.

The experiments have been executed on a Intel Pentium IV 2.8GHz with 512MB running SuSE Linux 8.1. Because of the stochastic nature of the algorithms, we perform 30 independent runs of each test to gather meaningful experimental data and apply statistical confidence metrics to validate our results. First, we use the Kolmogorov-Smirnov test to check whether the data follows a normal distribution or not. If so, then we carry out an ANOVA test to compare the means; otherwise, a Kruskal-Wallis test is used to compare the medians. In each case, a confidence level of 99 % is used.

5. ANALYSIS OF THE EXPERIMENTS

In this section we analyze the results of the different variants of our proposed model. First, we study the accuracy of the methods and then, we discuss their computational cost.

5.1 Accuracy

Let's first compare the accuracy of the different algorithms. Since there are many different problem instances and analyzing them thoroughly would hinder us from drawing clear conclusions, we have summarized in Table 2 the results. In this table we only study the accuracy of the techniques. Since the stopping criterion is to find the optimal solution (if it is possible since some variants get stuck in a local one), to measure the accuracy we use the number of instances solved by the method (the algorithm was able to find the optimum). We use two different values: the first one is the number of instances in which the algorithm found the optimal solution in at least one run; and the second one is the number of instances in which the algorithm found the optimal solution in *robust* way (this means the algorithm find the optimum in at least 25 out 30 independent runs). The range of both values is between 0 and 10 (5 instances of QAP plus 5 instances of MAXSAT)

From Table 2, we can obtain several interesting conclusions. First, we can note that cooperative schema significantly outperform to non-cooperative ones. In fact, **iSA** is not able to find the solution to any instance in a robust way. A second important conclusion is that all the variants of our model outperform traditional parallel models for trajectory based methods. This results shows that the exploration scheme induced by our model is more accurate than the other parallel algorithms in the context of this problem.

Cooperation scheme	Selection scheme		
	bst	**rnd**	**inf**
pre	9 - 5	7 - 3	8 - 3
bst	**10 - 10**	**10** - 6	**10** - 8
rnd	**10** - 6	8 - 3	**10** - 4
dst	**10 - 10**	9 - 4	**10** - 8
iSA	5 - 0		
cSA	7 - 2		

Table 2: Accuracy of the algorithms.

Analyzing the different variants of the proposed model, it can be seen that the models that make use of some information from the incoming solutions (fitness, distance or shared information) outperform the variants which are based on other features (random or predefined topologies). This is an expected result since the utilization of additional information during the process allows the method to have more elements to guide its search.

In concrete, we can see that cooperation strategies using the best incoming solution or the farthest solution are the best variants. This is a quite surprising result, since these techniques promote very different search behaviours (the **bst** strategy favors the intensification while the **dst** scheme promotes the diversification) but both methods get very high-quality solutions. A similar behaviour can be observe when we analyze the different selection method: the **bst** (which promotes intensification) and **inf** (which promotes diversification) strategies obtain equivalent results. Although the result are similar, we can notice a clear trend toward the techniques which favor the intensification. In fact, **SA_bst_bst** and **SA_dst_bst** are the only ones which can solve all the instances in all the runs.

5.2 Computational cost

Now, we focus on the computational cost: numerical performance (number of partial evaluations) and wall-clock time (in seconds). In order to perform a fair comparison, we only consider the algorithms which get similar results. In concrete, we compare **SA_bst_bst**, **SA_bst_inf**, **SA_dst_bst** y **SA_dst_inf** using the instances which are robustly solved by these methods. In Figure 3, we show the numerical performance (left figure) and the runtime (right figure). Both values are normalized with respect to the value obtained by **SA_dst_inf**.

From Figure 3, we can distinguish three different behaviours according to the statistical analysis (all the results are statistically different with the exception of **SA_X_inf** models) . The first behaviour is the presented by **SA_dst_bst** which is the variant with the highest computational cost. This is expected since the initial solutions selected by **dst** cooperation strategy are very different and therefore the generated path are longer and it also has to evaluate all the generated solution to find the best solution in the path (**bst** selection scheme). The second behaviour

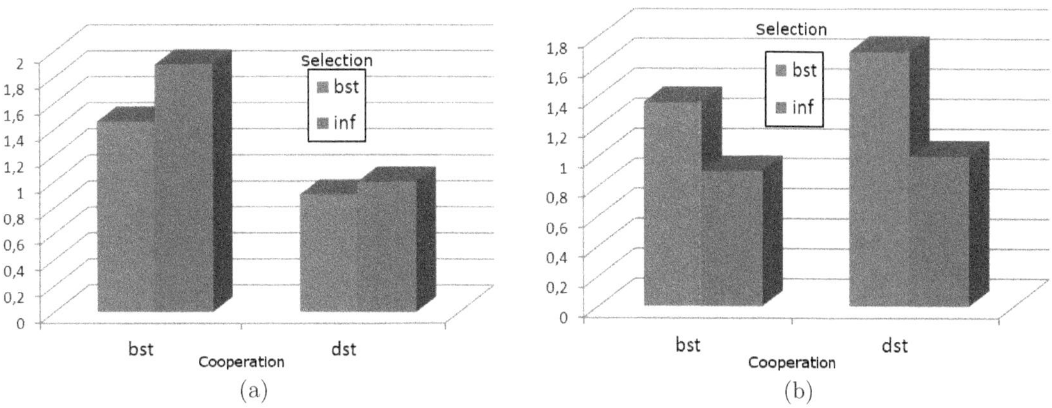

Figure 3: (a) Numerical performance (number of partial evaluations) and (b) execution time (seconds).

is the provoked by **SA_bst_bst** which is the second variant with a higher computational cost. This high cost is due to the utilization of **bst** selection scheme, in which the variant has to evaluate all the solutions in the path, although in this case the path are usually shorter than in the previous variant (**SA_dst_bst**). Finally, the last behaviour is the presented by **SA_X_inf** strategies which need less runtime to find the solution. This is mainly due to the **inf** selection scheme only need to evaluate a single solution in the path.

Summarizing we can conclude that variants using the best solution in the path obtain the best accurate results but they need more execution time to find these high-quality solutions. By contrast, strategies using the shared information between solutions are faster but the solution obtained are slightly worse.

6. CONCLUSIONS AND FUTURE WORKS

In this paper, we have developed a new parallel model for trajectory based methods, which improves the cooperation phase by means of adding path relinking technique. The utilization of this last technique allow to generate a wide set of candidate solutions to continue the search. This set is composed by solutions which include information from the current solution of the subalgorithm and also information from the incoming solution.

The results show that our proposed method is more accurate and efficient than the existing one. We have studied different design alternatives such as the several cooperation schema or different mechanism to select the next solution from the set of solutions generated by path relinking. Each variant has its own advantages and drawbacks. For example, we saw that using the best solution of the path, the algorithm obtains very accurate solution but the computation cost is higher.

As future work, we plan to extend this study to other problems or other trajectory based methods for generalizing the conclusion of this paper. In this paper, we have observed that the evaluation of the point visited by the path generated by PR is a quite high-consuming process, then we want to analyze different alternatives to perform that process (maybe using some theoretical results about the search space) and then speed up the search.

Acknowledgments

The authors acknowledge funds from the Spanish Ministry of Sciences and Innovation European FEDER, under contract TIN2011-28194 (roadME http://roadme.lcc.uma.es), Andalucía Tech, and from the project number 8.06/5.47.4142 in collaboration with the VSB-Technical University of Ostrava.

7. REFERENCES

[1] E. Alba, editor. *Parallel Metaheuristics: A New Class of Algorithms.* Wiley, 2005.

[2] E. Alba, G. Luque, and S. Nesmachnow. Parallel metaheuristics: recent advances and new trends. *International Transactions in Operational Research*, 20(1):1–48, 2013.

[3] W. Bożejko, J. Pempera, and C. Smutnicki. Parallel tabu search algorithm for the hybrid flow shop problem. *Computers & Industrial Engineering*, 65(3):466–474, 2013.

[4] Y.-L. Chang, K.-S. Chen, B. Huang, W.-Y. Chang, J. A. Benediktsson, and L. Chang. A parallel simulated annealing approach to band selection for high-dimensional remote sensing images. *Selected Topics in Applied Earth Observations and Remote Sensing, IEEE Journal of*, 4(3):579–590, 2011.

[5] F. Chicano, G. Luque, and E. Alba. Autocorrelation measures for the quadratiec assignment problem. *Applied Mathematics Letters*, 25(4):698–705, 2012.

[6] J.-F. Cordeau and M. Maischberger. A parallel iterated tabu search heuristic for vehicle routing problems. *Computers & Operations Research*, 39(9):2033–2050, 2012.

[7] M. Eskandarpour, S. H. Zegordi, and E. Nikbakhsh. A parallel variable neighborhood search for the multi-objective sustainable post-sales network design problem. *International Journal of Production Economics*, 145(1):117–131, 2013.

[8] A. Ferreiro, J. García, J. López-Salas, and C. Vázquez. An efficient implementation of parallel simulated annealing algorithm in gpus. *Journal of Global Optimization*, 57(3):863–890, 2013.

[9] M. Garey and D. Johnson. *Computers and Intractability: A Guide to the Theory of NP-Completeness.* W. H. Freeman, 1979.

[10] M. Gendreau. *Handbook of metaheuristics*, volume 146. Springer, 2010.

[11] F. Glover. Tabu Search, part I. *ORSA, Journal of Computing*, (1):190–206, 1989.

[12] F. Glover, M. Laguna, and R. Martí. Fundamentals of scatter search and path relinking. *Control and cybernetics*, 39(3):653–684, 2000.

[13] S. Kirkpatrick, C. Gellatt, and M. Vecchi. Optimization by Simulated Annealing. *Science*, 220(4598):671–680, 1983.

[14] G. Luque, F. Luna, and E. Alba. A new parallel cooperative model for trajectory based metaheuristics. In *Distributed Computing and Artificial Intelligence*, pages 559–567. Springer, 2010.

[15] C. Papadimitriou. *The Complexity of Combinatorial Optimization Problems*. Master's thesis, Princeton University, 1976.

[16] E.-G. Talbi. *Parallel combinatorial optimization*, volume 58. John Wiley & Sons, 2006.

[17] M. Yazdani, M. Amiri, and M. Zandieh. Flexible job-shop scheduling with parallel variable neighborhood search algorithm. *Expert Systems with Applications*, 37(1):678–687, 2010.

Design and Analysis of Adaptive Migration Intervals in Parallel Evolutionary Algorithms

Andrea Mambrini
School of Computer Science
University of Birmingham
Birmingham B15 2TT, United Kingdom

Dirk Sudholt
Department of Computer Science
University of Sheffield
Sheffield S1 4DP, United Kingdom

ABSTRACT

The migration interval is one of the fundamental parameters governing the dynamic behaviour of island models. Yet, there is little understanding on how this parameter affects performance, and how to optimally set it given a problem in hand. We propose schemes for adapting the migration interval according to whether fitness improvements have been found. As long as no improvement is found, the migration interval is increased to minimise communication. Once the best fitness has improved, the migration interval is decreased to spread new best solutions more quickly. We provide a method for analysing the expected running time and the communication effort, defined as the expected number of migrants sent. Example applications of this method to common example functions show that our adaptive schemes are able to compete with, or even outperform, the optimal fixed choice of the migration interval, with regard to running time and communication effort.

Categories and Subject Descriptors

F.2.2 [**Analysis of Algorithms and Problem Complexity**]: Nonnumerical Algorithms and Problems

Keywords

Parallel evolutionary algorithms, island model, migration interval, runtime analysis, theory

1. INTRODUCTION

Evolutionary algorithms (EAs) have given rise to many parallel variants [13, 20] fuelled by the rapidly increasing number of CPU cores and the ready availability of computation power through GPUs and cloud computing. Parallelization provides a cost-effective approach to solving problems in real time and for tackling large-scale problems.

There are many variants of parallel evolutionary algorithms, from parallelising function evaluations on multiple processors to fine-grained models such as cellular EAs and coarse-grained EAs such as island models [20, 13]. In the latter approach, multiple populations evolve independently for a certain period of time. Every τ generations, for a parameter τ called *migration interval*, individuals migrate between islands to coordinate their searches. Communication takes place according to a spatial structure, a topology connecting populations. Common topologies include rings, two-dimensional grids/toroids, hypercubes, or complete graphs.

Island models are popular optimisers for several reasons:

- Multiple communicating populations can make the same progress as a single population in a fraction of the time, speeding up computation.
- Small populations can be simulated faster than large populations, reducing execution times [1].
- Periodic communication only requires small bandwidth, leading to low communication costs.
- Solution quality is improved as different populations can explore different regions of the search space.

The usefulness of parallel populations has been demonstrated in thousands of successful applications ranging from language tagging, circuit design, scheduling and planning to bioinformatics [13, 3].

However, designing an effective parallel evolutionary algorithm can be challenging as the method and amount of communication needs to be tuned carefully. Too frequent communication leads to high communication costs, and it can compromise exploration. Too little communication means that the populations become too isolated and unable to coordinate their searches effectively. There is agreement that even the effect of the most fundamental parameters on performance is not well understood [13, 3].

We make a contribution towards finding good values for the migration interval, the parameter describing the frequency of migration. We propose adaptive schemes that adjust the migration interval, depending on whether islands have managed to find improvements during the last migration interval or not. The goal is to reduce communication, while not compromising the exploitation of good solutions. The main idea is: if an island has improved its current best fitness, migration is intensified to spread this solution to other islands. Otherwise, islands decrease the frequency of migration in order to avoid large communication costs.

Two different adaptive schemes are proposed. In both of them islands have individual migration intervals which are adapted throughout the run. In Scheme A if an island has not improved its current best fitness during the last migration interval, its migration interval is doubled. Once an

GECCO'14, July 12–16, 2014, Vancouver, BC, Canada.

ACM 978-1-4503-2662-9/14/07 ...$15.00.
http://dx.doi.org/10.1145/2576768.2598347.

improvement is found, the migration interval is set to 1 to communicate this new solution quickly. In Scheme B an island also doubles the migration interval when no improvement was found, while when an improvement is found, it halves τ at the end of the current migration interval.

We show that doubling the migration interval guarantees for elitist EAs that the number of migrations from an island is logarithmic in the time this island spends on a certain fitness level, i. e. for any value of the current best fitness.

We contribute a rigorous analytical framework that yields upper bounds on the expected optimisation time and the expected communication effort, defined as the total number of migrants sent. This is done for fixed migration intervals in Section 3, Scheme A in Section 4, and Scheme B in Section 5. Our adaptive schemes are then compared in Section 6 against the best fixed values of the migration interval for classical test problems. The results reveal that our adaptive schemes are able to match or even outperform the best fixed migration intervals with regard to the expected parallel time and the expected communication effort.

1.1 Related Work

This paper is in line with recent theoretical research on the running time of parallel EAs. Lässig and Sudholt [8] presented a method for analysing speedups in island models, and applications to combinatorial problems [10]. Neumann, Oliveto, Rudolph, and Sudholt [15] considered the benefit of crossover during migration for artificial problems and instances of the VERTEX COVER problem. Mambrini, Sudholt, and Yao [14] studied the running time and communication effort of homogeneous and heterogeneous island models for finding good solutions for the NP-hard SET COVER problem.

Skolicki and De Jong [19] investigated the impact of the migration interval and the number of migrants on performance, while different migration policies were compared by Araujo and Merelo [4]. Bravo, Luque and Alba [5] studied the effect of the migration interval when tackling dynamic optimization problems.

Alba and Luque [2] analysed growth curves and takeover times based on migration intervals and migration topologies, showing how quickly good solutions spread in an island model. Theoretical analyses were presented by Rudolph [18].

Lässig and Sudholt [11] presented a theoretical analysis and a problem where island models excel over both panmictic populations as well as independent runs. This requires a delicate choice of the migration interval, and performance degrades drastically when suboptimal parameter values are being used. This again emphasises the importance of this parameter for the performance of island models.

Hong, Lin, Liu, and Lin [6] and Lin, Hong, and Lin [12] presented a fitness-based adaptive migration scheme: each island compares its increase of its best fitness over the last migration interval with the same quantity from the migration interval before. If the new fitness increase is larger than the old one, the migration interval is increased by some constant value. Otherwise, it is decreased by the same constant value. A preliminary experimental study on random 0/1 knapsack problem instances showed that the adaptive scheme can lead to a better final fitness [6].

The difference in our scheme is that we adapt the migration interval in opposite directions: we decrease the migration interval in case of good fitness gains and increase it otherwise. Furthermore, our changes to the migration interval are most drastic than their additive changes.

Osorio, Luque, and Alba [17, 16] presented adaptive schemes for the migration interval, which aim for convergence at the end of the run (for runs of fixed length). The migration interval is set according to growth curves of good individuals and the remaining number of generations; migration intensifies towards the end of a run. They obtained competitive performance results, compared to optimal fixed parameters, for MAX-SAT instances [16]. Our perspective is different as we do not optimise for fixed-length runs.

Finally, Lässig and Sudholt [9] presented schemes for adapting the number of islands during a run of an island model (and offspring populations in a (1+λ) EA). Scheme A doubles the number of islands if no improvement was found in a generation. Otherwise, the number of islands drops to one island. Scheme B also doubles the number of islands when no improvement is found, and halves it otherwise. Both schemes achieve optimal or near-optimal parallel running times, while not increasing the total number of function evaluations by more than a constant factor. Our schemes for adapting the migration interval are inspired by this work.

2. PRELIMINARIES

We define the parallel EAs considered in this work, which contain our adaptive schemes. Our analytical framework is applicable to all kinds of elitist EAs: EAs that do not lose their current best solution. We define our schemes for maximisation problems.

Scheme A (Algorithm 1) maintains a migration interval τ_i for each island. As soon as the current best fitness on an island has improved, the migration interval for that island drops to 1, so that the island will communicate this solution to its neighbouring islands at the end of the generation. If no improvement of the current best fitness is found after τ_i generations, the migration interval τ_i doubles.

Algorithm 1 Elitist parallel EA with adaptive Scheme A

Initialize λ islands $P_1^1, \dots, P_1^\lambda$ uniformly at random and let $\tau_i := 1$ for each island.
Let f_i^* be the best fitness value for each island $P_1^1, \dots, P_1^\lambda$.
for $t := 1$ to ∞ **do**
  for all $1 \le i \le \lambda$ in parallel **do**
    Simulate one generation of the EA and create a new population P_{t+1}^i.
    Update P_{t+1}^i by selecting a new population from P_{t+1}^i and all immigrants, keeping the best individuals.
    Let $f_i^{*\prime}$ be the best fitness value for P_{t+1}^i.
    if $f_i^{*\prime} > f_i^*$ **then**
      Let $\tau_i := 1$
      Let $f_i^* := f_i^{*\prime}$
    else
      Let $\tau_i := \tau_i \cdot 2$
    end if
    if $t \bmod \tau_i = 0$ **then**
      Send a copy of a fittest offspring in P_{t+1}^i to all neighbouring islands.
    end if
  end for
end for

For the purpose of a theoretical analysis, we assume that all islands run in synchronicity: the t-th generation is executed on all islands at the same time. However, this is not a restriction of our adaptive scheme as it can be applied in asynchronous parallel architectures using message passing for implementing migration.

Inspired by [9], we also consider a Scheme B where the migration interval is being halved once an improvement has been detected. Thus line 9 in Algorithm 1 is replaced with "Let $\tau_i := \tau_i/2$". The advantage of Scheme B is that it uses less communication than Scheme A, and if there is a good region in the parameter space of τ, our hope is that it will maintain a good parameter value in that region over time.

We provide general methods for analysing the expected parallel time and the expected communication effort for arbitrary elitist EAs that migrate copies of selected individuals (the original individuals remain on their island). The parallel time is defined as the number of generations until a global optimum is found and denoted T^{par}. The communication effort T^{com} is defined as the total number of individuals migrated until a global optimum is found. For simplicity and ease of presentation, we assume that each migration only transfers one individual; if $\nu > 1$ individuals migrate, the communication effort has to be multiplied by ν.

In order to demonstrate and illustrate this approach, we consider one simple algorithm in more detail: following [9], the parallel (1+1) EA is a special case where each island runs a (1+1) EA.

In terms of communication topologies, for Scheme A we consider general graphs on λ vertices and the following common graphs. A unidirectional ring is a ring with edges going in one direction. A grid graph contains undirected edges with vertices arranged on a 2-dimensional grid. A torus can be regarded a grid where edges wrap around horizontally and vertically. A hypercube graph of dimension d contains 2^d vertices. Each vertex has a d-bit label, and vertices are neighboured if and only if their labels differ in exactly one bit. The complete graph contains all possible edges. For Scheme B we only consider complete topologies as on sparse topologies migration intervals may adapt too slowly (see Section 5). Then all islands use the same migration interval.

The diameter $\text{diam}(G)$ of a graph G with λ vertices is defined as the largest number of edges on any shortest path between two vertices. The unidirectional ring has the largest diameter of λ. The diameter of any grid or torus graph with side lengths $\sqrt{\lambda} \times \sqrt{\lambda}$ is at most $2\sqrt{\lambda}$. The diameter of a $(\log \lambda)$-dimensional hypercube is $\log \lambda$, and that of a complete topology is 1.

3. FIXED MIGRATION INTERVALS

In order to compare our adaptive schemes against fixed migration intervals, we first need to investigate the latter. Lässig and Sudholt [8, 11] presented general upper bounds for the parallel optimisation time of island models with different topologies. Their method is based on the so-called fitness-level method, also known as fitness-based partitions [21].

Throughout this work, we use a special case of this method: without loss of generality consider a problem with fitness values $1, \dots, m$. Consider fitness-level sets $A_1, \dots, A_m$ such that A_i contains all points with fitness i. In particular, A_m contains all global optima. We further assume that, if the current best individual of a population is in A_i, there is a lower bound s_i for the probability of finding a higher fitness level $A_{i+1} \cup \dots \cup A_m$ in one generation. It is easy to show that then $\sum_{i=1}^{m-1} 1/s_i$ is an upper bound for the expected running time of an elitist EA.

Lässig and Sudholt [8, 10] showed how upper bounds on the parallel optimisation time can be derived through general functions on these success probabilities $s_1, \dots, s_{m-1}$. They considered migration in every generation ($\tau = 1$) [10] as well as probabilistic migration, where every island independently decides for each neighbouring island whether migration occurs, and the probability for a migration is a fixed parameter p [11]. The following theorem is an adaptation of their results for periodic migration with migration interval τ [11]. The results for the expected communication effort on a topology with edge set E follow from multiplying the expected parallel time by $|E|/\tau$, as this term reflects the average number of migrated individuals across the topology in one generation. The upper bounds on the expected parallel time can be derived as in [11]. We do not give a formal proof due to space restrictions.

THEOREM 1. *Consider an island model with λ islands where each island runs an elitist EA. Every τ iterations each island sends a copy of its best individual to all neighbouring islands. Each island incorporates the best out of its own individuals and its immigrants. For fitness-level sets $A_1, \dots, A_m$, A_i containing all points of the i-th fitness value, let s_i be a lower bound for the probability that in one generation an island in A_i finds a search point in $A_{i+1} \cup \dots \cup A_m$. Then the expected parallel optimization time $\mathrm{E}(T^{\text{par}})$ and the expected communication effort $\mathrm{E}(T^{\text{com}})$ are at most*

$$\mathrm{E}(T^{\text{par}}) \leq 2\tau^{1/2} \sum_{i=1}^{m-1} \frac{1}{s_i^{1/2}} + \frac{1}{\lambda} \sum_{i=1}^{m-1} \frac{1}{s_i}$$

$$\mathrm{E}(T^{\text{com}}) \leq 2\lambda\tau^{-1/2} \sum_{i=1}^{m-1} \frac{1}{s_i^{1/2}} + \frac{1}{\tau} \sum_{i=1}^{m-1} \frac{1}{s_i}$$

for every unidirectional ring,

$$\mathrm{E}(T^{\text{par}}) \leq 3\tau^{2/3} \sum_{i=1}^{m-1} \frac{1}{s_i^{1/3}} + \frac{1}{\lambda} \sum_{i=1}^{m-1} \frac{1}{s_i}$$

$$\mathrm{E}(T^{\text{com}}) \leq 12\lambda\tau^{-1/3} \sum_{i=1}^{m-1} \frac{1}{s_i^{1/3}} + \frac{4}{\tau} \sum_{i=1}^{m-1} \frac{1}{s_i}$$

for an undirected grid or torus with side lengths $\sqrt{\lambda} \times \sqrt{\lambda}$,

$$\mathrm{E}(T^{\text{par}}) \leq \tau m + \tau \sum_{i=1}^{m-1} \log\left(\frac{1}{\tau s_i}\right) + \frac{1}{\lambda} \sum_{i=1}^{m-1} \frac{1}{s_i}$$

$$\mathrm{E}(T^{\text{com}}) \leq \lambda(\log \lambda) m + \lambda(\log \lambda) \sum_{i=1}^{m-1} \log\left(\frac{1}{\tau s_i}\right) + \frac{\log \lambda}{\tau} \sum_{i=1}^{m-1} \frac{1}{s_i}$$

for the $(\log \lambda)$-dimensional hypercube, and

$$\mathrm{E}(T^{\text{par}}) \leq m\tau + m + \frac{1}{\lambda} \sum_{i=1}^{m-1} \frac{1}{s_i}$$

$$\mathrm{E}(T^{\text{com}}) \leq \lambda(\lambda - 1)m + \frac{\lambda(\lambda - 1)m}{\tau} + \frac{\lambda - 1}{\tau} \sum_{i=1}^{m-1} \frac{1}{s_i}$$

for the complete topology K_λ.

These bounds match the ones from [7] for the case of probabilistic migration, if we compare τ against a migration probability of $p = 1/\tau$; the constant factors here are even better. The constants for probabilistic migration are higher to account for the variation in the spread of information. Periodic migration is more reliable in this respect since information is guaranteed to be spread every τ generations.

4. ADAPTIVE SCHEME A

In this section we analyse Scheme A on different topologies, including those from Theorem 1. Note that whenever an island improves its current best solution, a copy of this solution is being spread to all neighbouring islands immediately. Thus, good fitness levels spread in the same way as a migrating in every generation would do, i. e., using a global parameter $\tau = 1$. This means that the upper bounds from Theorem 1 apply for $\tau = 1$.

THEOREM 2. *For Scheme A on topologies from Theorem 1, the expected parallel optimisation time is bounded from above as in Theorem 1 with* $\tau = 1$.

Note that the bounds on the expected parallel time from Theorem 1 are minimised for $\tau = 1$. This implies that we get upper bounds on the expected parallel time equal to the best upper bounds for any fixed choice of the migration interval. In case these bounds are asymptotically tight, this means that our adaptive Scheme A never increases the expected parallel running time asymptotically.

The intended benefit of Scheme A comes from a reduced communication effort as all islands decrease communication while no improvement is encountered through either variation or immigration. The expected communication effort is bounded from above in the following theorem. The main observation is that for each fitness level, the number of migrations from an island is logarithmic in the time it remains on that fitness level. For an upper bound we consider the expected worst-case time spent on a fitness level A_i, where the worst case is taken over all populations with its best individual in A_i.

THEOREM 3. *Consider Scheme A on an arbitrary communication topology* $G = (V, E)$ *with diameter* $\mathrm{diam}(G)$. *Let* $\mathrm{E}(T_i^{\mathrm{par}})$ *be (an upper bound on) the worst-case expected number of generations during which the current best search point in the island model is on fitness level i. Then the expected communication effort is at most*

$$\mathrm{E}(T^{\mathrm{com}}) \le |E| \sum_{i=1}^{m-1} \log\left(\mathrm{E}(T_i^{\mathrm{par}}) + \mathrm{diam}(G)\right).$$

Proof. Initially, and after improving its current best fitness, an island will double its migration interval until its current best fitness improves again. If the current best fitness does not improve for t generations, the island will perform at most $\log t$ migrations.

Consider an island v after reaching fitness level i for the first time, either through variation or immigration. If no other island has found a better fitness level, the random parallel time for some island finding such an improvement is given (or bounded) by T_i^{par}. Then this solution (or another solution of fitness better than i) will be propagated through the topology, advancing to neighbouring islands in every generation. Hence, some solution on a better fitness level than i will eventually reach v within the following $\mathrm{diam}(G)$ generations. The latter also holds if some island has already found a better fitness level than i at the time v reaches fitness level i. In any case, the total time v will spend on fitness level i is at most $T_i^{\mathrm{par}} + \mathrm{diam}(G)$.

An island v in the topology with outdegree $\deg^+(v)$ will send $\deg^+(v)$ individuals during each migration. Hence, the total number of migrated solutions in t generations on fitness level i is at most

$$\sum_{v \in V} \deg^+(v) \cdot \log t = |E| \log t.$$

The expected communication effort, therefore, is at most

$$\begin{aligned}
\mathrm{E}(T^{\mathrm{com}}) &= \sum_t \Pr\left(T_i^{\mathrm{par}} + \mathrm{diam}(G) = t\right) \cdot |E| \log t \\
&= |E| \cdot \mathrm{E}\left(\log(T_i^{\mathrm{par}} + \mathrm{diam}(G))\right) \\
&\le |E| \cdot \log\left(\mathrm{E}(T_i^{\mathrm{par}} + \mathrm{diam}(G))\right) \\
&= |E| \log\left(\mathrm{E}(T_i^{\mathrm{par}}) + \mathrm{diam}(G)\right),
\end{aligned}$$

where the inequality follows from Jensen's inequality and the fact that log is a concave function. □

The communication effort is proportional to the logarithm of the expected time spend on each fitness level. For functions that can be optimised by the island model in expected polynomial time, and for polynomial λ (note $\mathrm{diam}(G) \le \lambda$), this logarithm is always at most $O(\log n)$. Then Theorem 3 gives the following upper bound.

COROLLARY 1. *Consider a fitness function f with m fitness values, such that f is being optimised by the island model in an expected polynomial number of generations, for every initial population. If also* $\lambda = n^{O(1)}$, *we have*

$$\mathrm{E}(T^{\mathrm{com}}) \le O(|E| m \cdot \log n).$$

The expected parallel time on a fitness level can be smaller than a polynomial: if sufficiently many islands are being used, and the topology spreads information quickly enough, it can be logarithmic or even constant. For specific topologies we get the following results by combining Theorem 3 with bounds on the parallel time from Theorem 1.

THEOREM 4. *Given success probabilities* $s_1, \dots, s_{m-1}$ *as in Theorem 1, the expected communication effort for Scheme A is bounded from above for certain topologies with* λ *islands as follows:*

1. $\lambda \sum_{i=1}^{m-1} \log\left(\frac{1}{s_i^{1/2}} + \frac{1}{\lambda s_i} + \lambda\right)$ *for a unidirectional ring,*
2. $4\lambda \sum_{i=1}^{m-1} \log\left(\frac{1}{s_i^{1/3}} + \frac{1}{\lambda s_i} + 2\sqrt{\lambda}\right)$ *for every undirected grid or torus with side lengths* $\sqrt{\lambda} \times \sqrt{\lambda}$,
3. $\lambda(\log \lambda) \sum_{i=1}^{m-1} \log\left(\log\left(\frac{1}{s_i}\right) + \frac{1}{\lambda s_i} + \log \lambda\right)$ *for the* $(\log \lambda)$*-dimensional hypercube,*
4. $\lambda(\lambda - 1) \sum_{i=1}^{m-1} \log\left(2 + \frac{1}{\lambda s_i}\right)$ *for the complete graph.*

We demonstrate the application of this theorem in Section 6.

5. ADAPTIVE SCHEME B

Scheme A resets the migration interval of an island to 1 every time an improvement is found. We propose Scheme B which halves this value instead. This may be advantageous if there is a "Goldilocks region" of good values for the migration interval. In contrast to Scheme A, Scheme B should be able to maintain a value in that region over several fitness levels.

When improvements are being found with probability p, good parameter values are close to $\tau \approx 1/(\lambda p)$, as then we find one improvement in expectation. If the current migration interval is much smaller, chances of finding an improvement are small, and τ is likely to increase. Likewise, if τ is large, the island will find an improvement with high probability and halve τ. Thus, the migration interval will reach an equilibrium state close to $1/(\lambda p)$.

Scheme B might have a smaller communication effort as it does not reset the migration interval to 1, where communication is most frequent. This, however, only holds if Scheme B does not lead to an increase in the parallel time. In fact, for sparse topologies G such as the unidirectional ring there is a risk that improvements may take a very long time to be communicated. If, say, all islands had the same migration interval τ, and one island found a new best solution, it may take up to $\text{diam}(G) \cdot \tau$ generations for this information to arrive at the last island.

Scheme B therefore makes more sense for dense topologies such as the complete graph, where $\text{diam}(G) = 1$ and decreases of τ quickly propagate to all islands.

We follow the analysis of Scheme B for adapting the number of islands in [9]. In both approaches over some time span a resource is being doubled and halved, depending on whether an improvement of the best fitness has been found. In [9] this resource is the number of islands, and hence the number of function evaluations executed in one generation. Here it is the number of generations within one migration period. The time span in [9] is just one generation, leading to the parallel time in [9] as performance measure. In our case the time span is the current migration interval, leading to the communication effort as performance measure.

For $\lambda = 1$ the parallel time in our work equals the sequential time in [9], and the communication effort in this work equals the parallel time in [9]. However, a difference emerges for $\lambda > 1$ as in our scenario an island has $\lambda\tau$ trials to find an improvement, so the resources for finding improvements are by a factor of λ higher, compared to [9].

We adapt the analysis from [9] to accommodate this difference. The following lemma is a straightforward adaptation of parts of [9, Lemma 1], hence a proof is omitted. It estimates the expected communication effort for finding a single improvement, based on a given initial migration interval τ_0. We abbreviate $\max\{x, 0\}$ by $(x)^+$.

LEMMA 1. *Assume an island model with a complete topology starts with a migration interval of τ_0 and that in each generation each island finds an improvement over the current best individual with probability at least p. Let T^{com} be the random number of individuals migrated between islands. Let τ^* be the migration interval at this time (before it is halved). Then for every $\alpha \in \mathbb{N}_0$*

1. $\Pr\left(\log(\tau^*) - \log(\tau_0) > (\log(1/(\lambda p)) - \log(\tau_0))^+ + \alpha\right) \leq \exp(-2^\alpha)$,
2. $\text{E}\left(T^{\text{com}}\right) \leq \lambda(\lambda - 1) \cdot \left((\log(1/(\lambda p)) - \log(\tau_0))^+ + 2\right)$.

The expected number of migrations is expressed as the difference between logarithms of the ideal value $1/(\lambda p)$ and the initial value τ_0. If the initial migration interval is larger, $\tau_0 \geq 1/(\lambda p)$, the expected number of migrations is just 2.

This fact is reflected in the following Theorem. The upper bound on the communication effort only contains values $\log(1/(\lambda s_j))$ when the migration interval needs to be increased, i. e. $s_j < s_{j-1}$. For the special case where fitness levels get progressively harder, $s_1 \geq s_2 \geq \cdots \geq s_{m-1}$, the bound simplifies significantly.

THEOREM 5. *Given success probabilities $s_1, \ldots, s_{m-1}$ as in Theorem 1, for Scheme B we have*

$$\text{E}\left(T_B^{\text{par}}\right) \leq 3m + \frac{3}{2\lambda} \sum_{i=1}^{m-1} \frac{1}{s_i} \quad \textit{and}$$

$$\text{E}\left(T_B^{\text{com}}\right) \leq \lambda(\lambda-1)\cdot \left(3m + \log\left(\frac{1}{\lambda s_1}\right) + \sum_{j=2}^{m-1}\left(\log\left(\frac{1}{\lambda s_j}\right) - \log\left(\frac{1}{\lambda s_{j-1}}\right)\right)^+\right).$$

For $s_1 \geq s_2 \geq \cdots \geq s_{m-1}$ the latter simplifies to

$$\text{E}\left(T_B^{\text{com}}\right) \leq \lambda(\lambda-1)\cdot \left(3m + \log\left(\frac{1}{\lambda s_{m-1}}\right)\right).$$

The upper bound for the expected parallel time is only by a factor of $3/2$ larger than the upper bound for Scheme A. Hence, both upper bounds are asymptotically equal. In other words, the reduced communication in Scheme B does not worsen the running time, for problems where the upper bounds for Schemes A and B are asymptotically tight.

We give an informal argument to convey the intuition for this result. Assume that Scheme B has raised the migration interval from 1 to some large value $\tau^* = 2^i$ before an improvement is found. Then Scheme B has spent $1 + 2 + 4 + \cdots + 2^i = 2^{i+1} - 1$ generations leading up to this value. In the worst case, the new migration interval $\tau^*/2 = 2^{i-1}$ is too large: improvements are found easily, and then the algorithm has to idle for nearly $\tau^*/2$ generations before being able to communicate the current best fitness. The total time spent is around $3/2 \cdot (2^{i+1} - 1)$, whereas Scheme A in the same situation would spend $2^{i+1} - 1$ generations. So, in this setting Scheme B needs at most $3/2$ as many generations as Scheme A.

A formal argument was given in [9] to derive an upper bound for the parallel time of Scheme B, which is $3/2$ that for Scheme A. The bound on the expected communication effort follows from similar arguments and applying our refined Lemma 1. We refrain from giving a formal proof here as it can be obtained with straightforward modifications from the proof of Theorem 3 in [9].

6. PERFORMANCE ON COMMON EXAMPLE FUNCTIONS

The analytical frameworks for analysing fixed migration intervals and our two adaptive schemes can be applied by simply using lower bounds on success probabilities for improving the current fitness. We demonstrate this approach, and how to use the results from the previous sections to analyse the parallel time and the communication effort on common test problems.

We provide an analysis for the maximisation of the same pseudo-Boolean test functions investigated in [7]. For a search point $x \in \{0,1\}^n$, $x = x_1 \dots x_n$, we define $\text{OneMax}(x) := \sum_{i=1}^{n} x_i$ as the number of ones in x, and $\text{LO}(x) := \sum_{i=1}^{n} \prod_{j=1}^{i} x_i$ as the number of leading ones in x. We also consider the class of unimodal functions taking d fitness values $f_1, \dots, f_d$. A function is called unimodal if every non-optimal search point has an Hamming neighbour with strictly larger fitness. Finally for $1 \leq k \leq n$ we consider

$$\text{Jump}_k := \begin{cases} k + \sum_{i=1}^{n} x_i, & \text{if } \sum_{i=1}^{n} x_i \leq n-k \text{ or } x = 1^n , \\ \sum_{i=1}^{n}(1-x_i) & \text{otherwise} . \end{cases}$$

Where a "jump", a mutation flipping k specific bits at the same time, has to be made. The parameter k tunes the difficulty of this function.

6.1 Fitness partition and success probabilites

In order to apply Theorems 1, 4, 5, it is just necessary to define probability s_i to move from the fitness level A_i to a better one. Recall that s_i is a lower bound on the probability of one island finding a search point of strictly higher fitness, given that the population has current best fitness i.

For the simple (1+1) EA, these values are easy to derive:

- For OneMax, a search point with i ones has $n-i$ zeros. The probability of a mutation flipping only one of these zeros is $s_i \geq (n-i)/n \cdot (1-1/n)^{n-1} \geq (n-i)/(en)$.
- For LO, it is sufficient to flip the first 0-bit, which has probability $s_i \geq 1/n \cdot (1-1/n)^{n-1} \geq 1/(en)$.
- For unimodal functions the success probability on each fitness level is at least $s_i \geq 1/n \cdot (1-1/n)^{n-1} \geq 1/(en)$ as for any non-optimal point there is always a better Hamming neighbour.
- For Jump_k with $k \geq 2$, it is possible to find an improvement to an individual having up to $n-k$ 1-bits just increasing the number of ones, thus the s_i with $i < n-k$ are equal to the ones for OneMax. A similar argument applies to levels $n-k < i < n$. From an individual with $n-k$ 1-bits an improvement is found by generating as offspring a specific bitstring having Hamming distance k from the parent, which has probability $s_{n-k} \geq \left(\frac{1}{n}\right)^k \cdot \left(1-\frac{1}{n}\right)^{n-k} \geq \left(\frac{1}{n}\right)^k \cdot \left(1-\frac{1}{n}\right)^{n-1} \geq \frac{1}{en^k}$.

6.2 Fixed scheme

Given Theorem 1 it is possible to bound the parallel time and the communication effort for fixed migration intervals similarly to [7]. For example, for OneMax and the complete topology we get an expected parallel time of $\mathrm{E}(T^{\text{par}}) = O\left(n\tau + \frac{n \log n}{\lambda}\right)$ and an expected communication effort of $\mathrm{E}(T^{\text{com}}) = O\left(\lambda^2 n + \frac{\lambda n \log n}{\tau}\right)$.

For fixed λ, the value of τ yields a trade-off between upper bounds for the parallel time and that of the communication effort. In our example, for say $\lambda = O(1)$, we get $\mathrm{E}(T^{\text{par}}) = O(n\tau + n \log n)$ and $\mathrm{E}(T^{\text{com}}) = O\left(n + \frac{n \log n}{\tau}\right)$. We can notice how a large τ always minimises the bound for the communication effort, while a small one (i. e. $\tau = 1$) minimises the bound for the parallel time.

Given a fixed number of islands λ, we define the best τ as the largest τ that does not asymptotically increase the bound for the parallel time (compared to $\tau = 1$). This assures good scalability while minimising the communication effort. For the example proposed the best τ is $\tau = \Theta(\frac{\log n}{\lambda})$. This leads to $\mathrm{E}(T^{\text{par}}) = O(\frac{n \log n}{\lambda})$ and $\mathrm{E}(T^{\text{com}}) = O(\frac{|E|}{\tau} \cdot \mathrm{E}(T^{\text{par}})) = O(\frac{\lambda^2}{\tau} \cdot \mathrm{E}(T^{\text{par}})) = O(\lambda^2 n)$. The results for other topologies and problems are summarised in Table 1. Notice that fixing τ to its best value is possible, provided that the number of island is small enough. Particularly for the example proposed the number of islands must be $\lambda = O(\log n)$ for the best τ to be defined ($\tau \geq 1$).

6.3 Adaptive scheme

In order to calculate the parallel time for the adaptive Scheme A we can refer to the results for the fixed scheme when $\tau = 1$, as shown in Theorem 2. For example, our Scheme A running on a complete topology solves OneMax in time $O(\frac{n \log n}{\lambda} + n)$. Scheme B has asymptotically the same parallel time of Scheme A, as shown in Theorem 5.

We only consider values of λ that lead to a linear speedup as defined in [11]: the expected parallel time for λ islands is by a factor of λ smaller than the expected optimisation time of a single island, in an asymptotic sense. In this setting an island model thus makes the same expected number of function evaluations, compared to a single island. In the example proposed linear speedup is achieved for a number of islands up to $\lambda = O(\log n)$, in fact for a larger number of islands the upper bound on the parallel time would be $O(n)$ regardless of λ. The bounds on λ limit the best upper bound on the parallel time achievable with our analytical framework. Table 1 shows the bound on λ for different problems and topologies and the best achievable parallel time bound.

In order to calculate the communication effort we use Theorem 4 and 5 for Schemes A and B, respectively. We first get a general bound for every λ included in the linear speedup bound, and then we calculate it for the maximum value of λ, thus providing the communication effort for the value of λ leading to the best achievable parallel time. Table 1 shows all results derived in this manner.

6.4 Evaluation of Results

Recall that Table 1 only shows results for linear speedups, hence all parallel times are equal, but the range of λ values varies between topologies. Comparing the communication efforts for the best fixed value of τ against our adaptive schemes, for OneMax on all topologies the communication effort is by a small $O(\log \log n)$ term larger for the adaptive schemes, compared to the best fixed τ. The latter varies according to the topology: it is $\tau = ((\log n)/\lambda)^2$ for the ring, $\tau = ((\log n)/\lambda)^{3/2}$ for the grid, and $\tau = (\log n)/\lambda$ for the hypercube and the complete graph. So, the additional $O(\log \log n)$ factor is a small price to pay for the convenience of adapting τ automatically.

For LO and the general bounds for unimodal functions, Scheme A on the ring has a communication effort of $O(n^{3/2} \log n)$ compared to $O(n^2)$, and for the grid it is $O(n^{5/3} \log n)$ versus $O(n^2)$. These significant improvements show that decreasing the migration interval is an effective strategy in lowering the communication costs, without harming the parallel running time. For the hypercube the communication effort is lower by a factor of $O(\log(n)/\log \log n)$, whereas for the complete graph no differences are visible in the upper bounds.

For Jump there are no differences for the complete graph, while on the hypercube Scheme A is by a $O(\log \log(n^{k-1}))$ factor worse than the best fixed value. For rings and grids the adaptive scheme is better; the performance gap even grows with k and hence the difficulty of the function.

Comparing Schemes A and B, both achieve similar results. For LO we see an advantage of Scheme B over Scheme A: the general bound for the communication effort of Scheme A is $O(\lambda^2 n \log(n/\lambda))$, whereas that for Scheme B is $O(\lambda^2 n)$. This makes sense as the probability for finding an improvement in one generation is of order $\Theta(\lambda/n)$ for the considered λ, and the ideal value for the migration interval is in the region of $\Theta(n/\lambda)$. Scheme A needs to increase the migration interval around $\log(n/\lambda)$ times to get into this range, which is precisely the performance difference visible in our upper bounds. The difference disappears for $\lambda = \Theta(n)$.

The same argument also applies to the more general function class of unimodal functions.

7. CONCLUSIONS

We have presented two adaptive schemes for adapting the migration interval in island models. Both schemes have been accompanied by analytical frameworks that yield upper bounds on the expected parallel time and the expected communication effort, based on probabilities of fitness improvements in single islands running elitist EAs. The results show that our schemes are able to decrease the communication effort without significantly compromising exploitation. For arbitrary topologies, we got upper bounds on the expected parallel time no larger than those for maximum exploitation, that is, migration in every generation.

Example applications to common example functions revealed that, in the realm of linear speedups and comparing against the best fixed choice of the migration interval, the expected communication effort was larger by a tiny $O(\log \log n)$ term for OneMax and similarly for the hypercube on Jump, but significantly smaller on LO, for a general analysis of unimodal functions, and for rings and grids on Jump. Both schemes are able to match the performance of the best fixed migration interval up to doubly logarithmic factors, or they can perform significantly better by polynomial factors.

Acknowledgments: The authors would like to thank Joseph Kempka and the participants of Dagstuhl seminar 13271 "Theory of Evolutionary Algorithms" for fruitful discussions. Andrea Mambrini was partially funded by EPSRC (Grant No. EP/I010297/1). The research leading to these results has received funding from the European Union Seventh Framework Programme (FP7/2007-2013) under grant agreement no 618091 (SAGE).

8. REFERENCES

[1] E. Alba. Parallel evolutionary algorithms can achieve super-linear performance. *Information Processing Letters*, 82(1):7–13, 2002.

[2] E. Alba and G. Luque. Theoretical models of selection pressure for dEAs: topology influence. In *Proc. of IEEE CEC 2005*, pages 214–221, 2005.

[3] E. Alba, G. Luque, and S. Nesmachnow. Parallel metaheuristics: Recent advances and new trends. *International Transactions in Operational Research*, 20(1):1–48, 2013.

[4] L. Araujo and J. J. M. Guervós. Diversity through multiculturality: Assessing migrant choice policies in an island model. pages 456–469, 2011.

[5] Y. Bravo, G. Luque, and E. Alba. Influence of the migration period in parallel distributed GAs for dynamic optimization. In *Proc. of LION*, pages 343–348, 2012.

[6] T.-P. Hong, W.-Y. Lin, S.-M. Liu, and J.-H. Lin. Experimental analysis of dynamic migration intervals on 0/1 knapsack problems. In *Proc. of IEEE CEC 2007*, pages 1163–1167, 2007.

[7] J. Lässig and D. Sudholt. General upper bounds on the running time of parallel evolutionary algorithms. *Evolutionary Computation*. In press. Available from `http://www.mitpressjournals.org/doi/pdf/10.1162/EVCO_a_00114`.

[8] J. Lässig and D. Sudholt. General scheme for analyzing running times of parallel evolutionary algorithms. In *Proc. of PPSN 2010*, pages 234–243. Springer, 2010.

[9] J. Lässig and D. Sudholt. Adaptive population models for offspring populations and parallel evolutionary algorithms. In *Proc. of FOGA 2011*, pages 181–192. ACM Press, 2011.

[10] J. Lässig and D. Sudholt. Analysis of speedups in parallel evolutionary algorithms for combinatorial optimization. In *Proc. of ISAAC 2011*, pages 405–414. Springer, 2011.

[11] J. Lässig and D. Sudholt. Design and analysis of migration in parallel evolutionary algorithms. *Soft Computing*, 17(7):1121–1144, 2013.

[12] W.-Y. Lin, T.-P. Hong, S.-M. Liu, and J.-H. Lin. Revisiting the design of adaptive migration schemes for multipopulation genetic algorithms. In *Proc. of TAAI 2012*, pages 338–343, 2012.

[13] G. Luque and E. Alba. *Parallel Genetic Algorithms–Theory and Real World Applications*. Springer, 2011.

[14] A. Mambrini, D. Sudholt, and X. Yao. Homogeneous and heterogeneous island models for the set cover problem. In *Proc. of PPSN 2012*, pages 11–20. Springer, 2012.

[15] F. Neumann, P. S. Oliveto, G. Rudolph, and D. Sudholt. On the effectiveness of crossover for migration in parallel evolutionary algorithms. In *Proc. of GECCO 2011*, pages 1587–1594. ACM Press, 2011.

[16] K. Osorio, E. Alba, and G. Luque. Using theory to self-tune migration periods in distributed genetic algorithms. In *Proc. of CEC 2013*, pages 2595–2601, 2013.

[17] K. Osorio, G. Luque, and E. Alba. Distributed evolutionary algorithms with adaptive migration period. In *Proc. of ISDA*, pages 259–264, 2011.

[18] G. Rudolph. Takeover time in parallel populations with migration. In *BIOMA 2006*, pages 63–72, 2006.

[19] Z. Skolicki and K. De Jong. The influence of migration sizes and intervals on island models. In *Proc. of GECCO 2005*, pages 1295–1302. ACM, 2005.

[20] M. Tomassini. *Spatially Structured Evolutionary Algorithms: Artificial Evolution in Space and Time*. Springer, 2005.

[21] I. Wegener. Methods for the analysis of evolutionary algorithms on pseudo-Boolean functions. In R. Sarker, X. Yao, and M. Mohammadian, editors, *Evolutionary Optimization*, pages 349–369. Kluwer, 2002.

Table 1: Overview of expected parallel optimisation times and expected communication efforts for island models with λ islands running a simple (1+1) EA on common example functions, derived using Theorems 1, 2, 3, and 5. As explained in Sections 6.2 and 6.3, the table shows restrictions on λ to yield linear speedups and fixed values for τ leading to the best upper bounds for the communication effort, while not increasing the parallel running time. For both parallel time and communication effort we show bounds for general λ in the realm of linear speedups, and the best parallel time $\mathrm{E}(T^{\mathrm{par}}_{\mathrm{best}})$ achieved by using the largest such λ, along with the corresponding communication effort $\mathrm{E}(T^{\mathrm{par}}_{\mathrm{best}})$ for the same λ. For Jump$_k$ we assume $3 \leq k = O(n/(\log n))$.

Problem	Topology and Scheme	λ	$\mathrm{E}(T^{\mathrm{par}}) \rightsquigarrow \mathrm{E}(T^{\mathrm{par}}_{\mathrm{best}})$	$\mathrm{E}(T^{\mathrm{com}}) \rightsquigarrow \mathrm{E}(T^{\mathrm{com}}_{\mathrm{best}})$
OneMax	Complete, Scheme A	$O(\log n)$	$O\left(\frac{n}{\lambda}\log n\right) \rightsquigarrow O(n)$	$O(\lambda^2 n) \rightsquigarrow O(n\log^2(n))$
	Complete, Scheme B	$O(\log n)$	$O\left(\frac{n}{\lambda}\log n\right) \rightsquigarrow O(n)$	$O(\lambda^2 n) \rightsquigarrow O(n\log^2(n))$
	Complete, $\tau = \Theta\left(\frac{\log n}{\lambda}\right)$	$O(\log n)$	$O\left(\frac{n}{\lambda}\log n\right) \rightsquigarrow O(n)$	$O(\lambda^2 n) \rightsquigarrow O(n\log^2(n))$
	Ring, Scheme A	$O(\log n)$	$O\left(\frac{n}{\lambda}\log n\right) \rightsquigarrow O(n)$	$O(n\lambda\log\lambda) \rightsquigarrow O(n\log(n)\log\log(n))$
	Ring, $\tau = \Theta\left(\left(\frac{\log n}{\lambda}\right)^2\right)$	$O(\log n)$	$O\left(\frac{n}{\lambda}\log n\right) \rightsquigarrow O(n)$	$O\left(\frac{\lambda^2 n}{\log n}\right) \rightsquigarrow O(n\log(n))$
	Grid, Scheme A	$O(\log n)$	$O\left(\frac{n}{\lambda}\log n\right) \rightsquigarrow O(n)$	$O(n\lambda\log\lambda) \rightsquigarrow O(n\log(n)\log\log(n))$
	Grid, $\tau = \Theta\left(\left(\frac{\log n}{\lambda}\right)^{3/2}\right)$	$O(\log n)$	$O\left(\frac{n}{\lambda}\log n\right) \rightsquigarrow O(n)$	$O\left(\frac{\lambda^{3/2} n}{\log^{1/2}(n)}\right) \rightsquigarrow O(n\log(n))$
	Hypercube, Scheme A	$O(\log n)$	$O\left(\frac{n}{\lambda}\log n\right) \rightsquigarrow O(n)$	$O(n\lambda\log(\lambda)\log\log(\lambda))$ $\rightsquigarrow O(n\log(n)\log\log(n)\log\log\log(n))$
	Hypercube, $\tau = \Theta\left(\frac{\log n}{\lambda}\right)$	$O(\log n)$	$O\left(\frac{n}{\lambda}\log n\right) \rightsquigarrow O(n)$	$O(n\lambda\log\lambda) \rightsquigarrow O(n\log(n)\log\log(n))$
LO	Complete, Scheme A	$O(n)$	$O\left(\frac{n^2}{\lambda}\right) \rightsquigarrow O(n)$	$O\left(\lambda^2 n\log\left(\frac{n}{\lambda}\right)\right) \rightsquigarrow O(n^3)$
	Complete, Scheme B	$O(n)$	$O\left(\frac{n^2}{\lambda}\right) \rightsquigarrow O(n)$	$O\left(\lambda^2 n\right) \rightsquigarrow O(n^3)$
	Complete, $\tau = \Theta\left(\frac{n}{\lambda}\right)$	$O(n)$	$O\left(\frac{n^2}{\lambda}\right) \rightsquigarrow O(n)$	$O\left(\lambda^2 n\right) \rightsquigarrow O(n^3)$
	Ring, Scheme A	$O(n^{1/2})$	$O\left(\frac{n^2}{\lambda}\right) \rightsquigarrow O(n^{3/2})$	$O(\lambda n\log\left(\frac{n}{\lambda}\right)) \rightsquigarrow O(n^{3/2}\log n)$
	Ring, $\tau = \Theta\left(\frac{n}{\lambda^2}\right)$	$O(n^{1/2})$	$O\left(\frac{n^2}{\lambda}\right) \rightsquigarrow O(n^{3/2})$	$O(\lambda^2 n) \rightsquigarrow O(n^2)$
	Grid, Scheme A	$O(n^{2/3})$	$O\left(\frac{n^2}{\lambda}\right) \rightsquigarrow O(n^{4/3})$	$O(\lambda n\log\left(\frac{n}{\lambda}\right)) \rightsquigarrow O(n^{5/3}\log n)$
	Grid, $\tau = \Theta\left(\frac{n}{\lambda^{3/2}}\right)$	$O(n^{2/3})$	$O\left(\frac{n^2}{\lambda}\right) \rightsquigarrow O(n^{4/3})$	$O(n\lambda^{3/2}) \rightsquigarrow O(n^2)$
	Hypercube, Scheme A	$O\left(\frac{n}{\log n}\right)$	$O\left(\frac{n^2}{\lambda}\right) \rightsquigarrow O(n\log n)$	$O\left(\lambda\log(\lambda)n\log\left(\frac{n}{\lambda}\right)\right) \rightsquigarrow O(n^2\log\log n)$
	Hypercube, $\tau = \Theta\left(\frac{n}{\lambda\log n}\right)$	$O\left(\frac{n}{\log n}\right)$	$O\left(\frac{n^2}{\lambda}\right) \rightsquigarrow O(n\log n)$	$O(\lambda\log(\lambda)n\log(n)) \rightsquigarrow O(n^2\log n)$
unimodal f with d f-values	Complete, Scheme A	$O(n)$	$O\left(\frac{dn}{\lambda}\right) \rightsquigarrow O(d)$	$O(\lambda^2 d\log\left(\frac{n}{\lambda}\right)) \rightsquigarrow O(n^2 d)$
	Complete, Scheme B	$O(n)$	$O\left(\frac{dn}{\lambda}\right) \rightsquigarrow O(d)$	$O(\lambda^2 d) \rightsquigarrow O(n^2 d)$
	Complete, $\tau = \Theta\left(\frac{n}{\lambda}\right)$	$O(n)$	$O\left(\frac{dn}{\lambda}\right) \rightsquigarrow O(d)$	$O(\lambda^2 d) \rightsquigarrow O(n^2 d)$
	Ring, Scheme A	$O(n^{1/2})$	$O\left(\frac{dn}{\lambda}\right) \rightsquigarrow O(dn^{1/2})$	$O\left(\lambda d\log\left(\frac{n}{\lambda}\right)\right) \rightsquigarrow O(dn^{1/2}\log n)$
	Ring, $\tau = \Theta\left(\frac{n}{\lambda^2}\right)$	$O(n^{1/2})$	$O\left(\frac{dn}{\lambda}\right) \rightsquigarrow O(dn^{1/2})$	$O(\lambda^2 d) \rightsquigarrow O(dn)$
	Grid, Scheme A	$O(n^{2/3}))$	$O\left(\frac{dn}{\lambda}\right) \rightsquigarrow O(dn^{1/3})$	$O\left(\lambda d\log\left(\frac{n}{\lambda}\right)\right) \rightsquigarrow O(dn^{2/3}\log n)$
	Grid, $\tau = \Theta\left(\frac{n}{\lambda^{3/2}}\right)$	$O(n^{2/3}))$	$O\left(\frac{dn}{\lambda}\right) \rightsquigarrow O(dn^{1/3})$	$O(\lambda^{3/2} d) \rightsquigarrow O(dn)$
	Hypercube, Scheme A	$O\left(\frac{n}{\log n}\right)$	$O\left(\frac{dn}{\lambda}\right) \rightsquigarrow O(d\log n)$	$O\left(\lambda\log(\lambda)d\log\left(\frac{n}{\lambda}\right)\right) \rightsquigarrow O(dn\log\log n)$
	Hypercube, $\tau = \Theta\left(\frac{n}{\lambda\log n}\right)$	$O\left(\frac{n}{\log n}\right)$	$O\left(\frac{dn}{\lambda}\right) \rightsquigarrow O(d\log n)$	$O(\lambda\log(\lambda)d\log(n)) \rightsquigarrow O(dn\log n)$
Jump$_k$	Complete, Scheme A	$O(n^{k-1})$	$O\left(\frac{n^k}{\lambda}\right) \rightsquigarrow O(n)$	$O(\lambda^2 n) \rightsquigarrow O(n^{2k-1})$
	Complete, Scheme B	$O(n^{k-1})$	$O\left(\frac{n^k}{\lambda}\right) \rightsquigarrow O(n)$	$O(\lambda^2 n) \rightsquigarrow O(n^{2k-1})$
	Complete, $\tau = \Theta\left(\frac{n^{k-1}}{\lambda}\right)$	$O(n^{k-1})$	$O\left(\frac{n^k}{\lambda}\right) \rightsquigarrow O(n)$	$O(\lambda^2 n) \rightsquigarrow O(n^{2k-1})$
	Ring, Scheme A	$O(n^{k/2})$	$O\left(\frac{n^k}{\lambda}\right) \rightsquigarrow O(n^{k/2})$	$O(n\lambda\log\lambda) \rightsquigarrow O(kn^{k/2+1}\log n)$
	Ring, $\tau = \Theta\left(\frac{n^k}{\lambda^2}\right)$	$O(n^{k/2})$	$O\left(\frac{n^k}{\lambda}\right) \rightsquigarrow O(n^{k/2})$	$O(\lambda^2) \rightsquigarrow O(n^k)$
	Grid, Scheme A	$O\left(n^{2k/3}\right)$	$O\left(\frac{n^k}{\lambda}\right) \rightsquigarrow O(n^{k/3})$	$O(n\lambda\log\lambda) \rightsquigarrow O(kn^{2k/3+1}\log n)$
	Grid, $\tau = \Theta\left(\frac{n^k}{\lambda^{3/2}}\right))$	$O\left(n^{2k/3}\right)$	$O\left(\frac{n^k}{\lambda}\right) \rightsquigarrow O(n^{k/3})$	$O(\lambda^{3/2}) \rightsquigarrow O(n^k)$
	Hypercube, Scheme A	$O(n^{k-1})$	$O\left(\frac{n^k}{\lambda}\right) \rightsquigarrow O(n)$	$O(n\lambda\log(\lambda)\log\log(\lambda))$ $\rightsquigarrow O(kn^k\log(n)\log\log(n^{k-1}))$
	Hypercube, $\tau = \Theta\left(\frac{n^{k-1}}{\lambda}\right)$	$O(n^{k-1})$	$O\left(\frac{n^k}{\lambda}\right) \rightsquigarrow O(n)$	$O(n\lambda\log\lambda) \rightsquigarrow O(kn^k\log n)$

An Implicitly Parallel EDA Based on Restricted Boltzmann Machines

Malte Probst
University of Mainz
Dept. of Information Systems and Business Administration
Mainz, Germany
probst@uni-mainz.de

Franz Rothlauf
University of Mainz
Dept. of Information Systems and Business Administration
Mainz, Germany
rothlauf@uni-mainz.de

Jörn Grahl
University of Mainz
Dept. of Information Systems and Business Administration
Mainz, Germany
grahl@uni-mainz.de

ABSTRACT

We present a parallel version of RBM-EDA. RBM-EDA is an Estimation of Distribution Algorithm (EDA) that models dependencies between decision variables using a Restricted Boltzmann Machine (RBM). In contrast to other EDAs, RBM-EDA mainly uses matrix-matrix multiplications for model estimation and sampling. Hence, for implementation, standard libraries for linear algebra can be used. This allows an easy parallelization and leads to a high utilization of parallel architectures. The probabilistic model of the parallel version and the version on a single core are identical. We explore the speedups gained from running RBM-EDA on a Graphics Processing Unit. For problems of bounded difficulty like deceptive traps, parallel RBM-EDA is faster by several orders of magnitude (up to 750 times) in comparison to a single-threaded implementation on a CPU. As the speedup grows linearly with problem size, parallel RBM-EDA may be particularly useful for large problems.

Categories and Subject Descriptors

D.1.3 [**Software**]: Programming Techniques—*Parallel programming*; I.2.6 [**Artificial Intelligence**]: Learning—*Neural Networks*; I.2.8 [**Artificial Intelligence**]: Problem Solving, Control Methods, and Search—*Heuristic methods*

Keywords

Parallelization; Restricted Boltzmann Machines; Estimation of Distribution Algorithms; Machine Learning; Combinatorial Optimization Problems; GPU; Neural Networks

1. INTRODUCTION

As most computing power of modern systems comes from multi-core CPUs and Graphics Processing Units (GPUs), parallelization of algorithms has become an important topic in optimization. We present a parallel version of RBM-EDA, an Estimation of Distribution Algorithm (EDA) which uses a Restricted Boltzmann Machine (RBM). RBMs are a special type of neural network. EDAs use a population of solutions and capture dependencies between problem variables in a probabilistic model. Subsequently, they use this model to sample new solutions, which compete with the existing population, based on their fitness [see e.g. 14, 10]. RBM-EDA uses an RBM as its model.

In [24], we analyze the performance of RBM-EDA for different combinatorial optimization problems such as Onemax, concatenated deceptive traps and NK-landscapes and compare it to the state-of-the-art Bayesian Optimization Algorithm (BOA [22]). RBM-EDA can solve complex combinatorial optimization problems with a number of fitness evaluations that grows polynomial in the problem size. At the same time, the computational complexity is lower that that of BOA. That is, a single-threaded RBM-EDA can build its probabilistic model for large, complex problems significantly faster, leading to lower total run times.

An RBM can capture complex multivariate dependencies. Nevertheless, the effort for implementing a parallel RBM-EDA is comparatively low. The parallel implementation is flexible and can be ported to different hardware environments (e.g. a multi core CPU system, an ARM device, a system using GPUs). The reason for the simplicity lies in the nature of an RBM. As a neural network, it is implicitly parallel. That is, most operations necessary to build the model and to sample from it are independent of each other. Formally, almost all operations are either matrix multiplications or element-wise matrix operations. Those operations can be implemented using standardized Basic Linear Algebra Subprogram (BLAS) libraries. Parallelization of the whole optimization algorithm essentially means using a parallel BLAS library.

As a consequence, the algorithm can make efficient use of parallel resources if the BLAS library is implemented efficiently. Furthermore, the sequential and parallel versions of the probabilistic model are identical and model quality is not affected by parallelization.

Our experiments indicate that the parallel version comes with massive speedups. For example, the GPU version can solve large concatenated trap problems up to 750× faster than a single-threaded CPU version. Also, the speedup grows with problem size.

The layout of the paper is as follows: Section 2 introduces EDAs and RBMs and shows how to use RBMs in EDAs. In Section 3, we discuss basic parallelization techniques for EDAs and show how RBM-EDA can be parallelized using

GECCO'14, July 12–16, 2014, Vancouver, BC, Canada.
Copyright 2014 ACM 978-1-4503-1964-5/14/07 ...$15.00.
http://dx.doi.org/10.1145/2576768.2598273.

Algorithm 1 Pseudo code for main EDA loop

Initialize Population P
while not converged **do**
  $P_{parents} \leftarrow$ **Select** high quality solutions from P based on their fitness
  $M \leftarrow$ **Build** a model estimating the (joint) probability distribution of $P_{parents}$
  $P \leftarrow$ **Sample** new candidate solutions from model M
end while

BLAS libraries. Section 4 introduces the benchmark problem, concatenated deceptive traps, presents our experimental setup and shows the speedups RBM-EDA achieves using BLAS on a CPU or GPU. We discuss results and implications in Section 5.

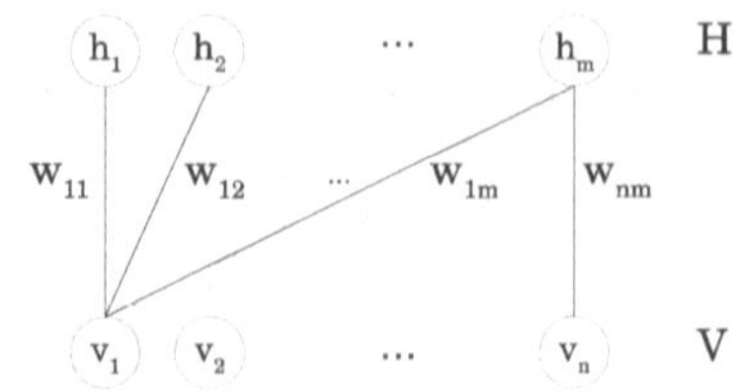

Figure 1: Restricted Boltzmann Machine, visualized as a graph. The visible neurons v_i ($i \in 1..n$) can hold a data vector of length n from the training data. The hidden neurons h_j ($j \in 1..m$) represent m features. Weight w_{ij} connects v_i to h_j. In the EDA context, V represents the decision variables

2. PRELIMINARIES

We review the basic concept of EDAs. We introduce RBMs, describe the relevant elements Gibbs sampling and contrastive divergence [4, 6], and show how an RBM can be used in an EDA.

2.1 Estimation of Distribution Algorithms

EDAs are well-established tools for solving combinatorial optimization problems [see e.g. 14, 10]. The basic structure of EDAs is given by Algorithm 1. In a nutshell, they select promising individuals from a population, build a probabilistic model of this population and then use this model to sample new individuals. These new individuals are evaluated and usually form the new population. This loop continues until the population has converged. The underlying assumption is that a model, which has captured the essence of the old population, is able to sample new, unknown individuals that possess the same high-quality structure, thereby searching the solution space efficiently.

EDAs differ in their choice of the model. Simple models use a vector with activation probabilities for each variable of the problem, while neglecting dependencies between the variables [e.g. UMDA, see 14]. Slightly more complex models use pairwise dependencies modeled as trees or forests [23]. More complex dependencies can be captured by models with multivariate interactions, like ECGA, BOA or DEUM [5, 22, 26]. Multivariate models are better suited for complex optimization problems, as univariate models can cause an exponential growth of the required number of fitness evaluations for growing problem sizes [22, 21]. Many algorithms use probabilistic graphical models with directed edges, i.e. Bayesian networks, or undirected edges, i.e. Markov random fields [9]. Hence, model building consists of finding a network structure that matches the problem structure and estimating the model's parameters. Usually, the computational effort to build the model rises with model complexity and representational power. Hence, parallelization is particularly useful for complex models.

2.2 Restricted Boltzmann Machines in EDAs

A Restricted Boltzmann Machine is a stochastic neural network where connections between neurons form a bipartite graph [28]. An RBM forms a Markov random field, as all connections are undirected. We can use an RBM as a model within an EDA, because it can be trained to model a probability distribution and it is possible to draw samples from this model [24]. Figure 1 illustrates the structure of an RBM. The input or visible layer V holds the input data represented by n binary variables $v_i, i = 1, 2, \ldots, n$. The m binary neurons $h_j, j = 1, 2, \ldots, m$ of the hidden layer H are called feature detectors as they are able to model patterns in the data. A weight matrix W holds weights $w_{i,j} \in \mathbb{R}$ between all neurons v_i and h_j. Each neuron in the visible as well as hidden layer makes a stochastic decision whether to be active after collecting inputs from all connected neurons. The weights W determine the strengths of the influence. An RBM encodes a joint probability distribution $P(V, H)$, which is the probability of sampling a joint configuration of V and H [28]. In the training phase, the weights are adapted in such a way that the marginal probability $P(V)$ of the training data is maximized. Training and sampling are tractable because of the bipartite structure of an RBM.

2.2.1 Sampling

Sampling new values for the visible neurons V is straightforward, if the activations of the hidden layer H are known. The v_i are independent of each other. The conditional probability $P(v_i = 1|H)$ that the visible neuron v_i is active is calculated as

$$P(v_i = 1|H) = sigm\left(\sum_j w_{ij} h_j\right), \tag{1}$$

where $sigm(x) = \frac{1}{1+e^{-x}}$ is the logistic function.[1] Analogously, for a given vector V, the conditional probability $P(h_j = 1|V)$ for the hidden neurons H is calculated as

$$P(h_j = 1|V) = sigm\left(\sum_i w_{ij} v_i\right). \tag{2}$$

Unfortunately, sampling from the joint probability distribution $P(V, H)$ is much more difficult than sampling from the conditional distributions as it usually requires integrating over one of the joint distributions. An alternative is *Gibbs sampling* which approximates the joint distribution $P(V, H)$ from the conditional distributions $P(V|H)$ and $P(H|V)$.

[1]In addition, all neurons are connected to a special "bias" neuron, which is always active and works like an offset to the neuron's input. Bias weights are treated like normal weights during learning. Due to brevity, we omit bias terms throughout the paper. For details, see [7].

Gibbs sampling starts by assigning random values to the visible neurons. Then, it iteratively samples from $P(H|V)$ and $P(V|H)$, respectively, while assigning the result of the previous sampling step to the non-sampled variable. The iterative sampling of V and H ($V \rightarrow H \rightarrow V \rightarrow ...$) forms a Markov chain, whose stationary distribution is identical to the joint probability distribution $P(V, H)$ [4]. The higher the number of sampling steps, the better the approximation of the joint probability distribution $P(V, H)$. When starting Gibbs sampling with a V that is close to the stationary distribution, only a few sampling steps are necessary to obtain a good approximation.

2.2.2 *Training*

The joint probability distribution $P(V, H)$ of an RBM is encoded in its weights W. An effective approach for learning $P(V, H)$ by adjusting the weights of an RBM is contrastive divergence (CD) learning [6]. CD learning maximizes the log-likelihood of the training data under the model $P(V, H)$ by performing a stochastic gradient ascent. The main element of CD learning is Gibbs sampling.

For each data point V in a training sample, CD learning updates w_{ij} in the direction of $-\frac{\partial log(P(V))}{\partial w_{ij}}$, where $P(V)$ is the probability of V. It can be shown that this partial derivative is the difference of two terms usually referred to as positive and negative gradient, Δ_{ij}^{pos} and Δ_{ij}^{neg} [6]. Consequently, the total gradient Δw_{ij} becomes

$$\begin{aligned} \Delta w_{ij} &= \Delta_{ij}^{\text{pos}} &&- \Delta_{ij}^{\text{neg}} \\ &= < v_i \cdot h_j >^{\text{data}} &&- < v_i \cdot h_j >^{\text{model}}, \end{aligned} \quad (3)$$

where $< >$ denotes expectation. Δ_{ij}^{pos} is the expected value of $v_i h_j$ when setting the visible layer V to a data vector from the training set and sampling H according to (2). Δ_{ij}^{pos} increases the probability of a configuration V. In contrast, Δ_{ij}^{neg} is the expected value of a configuration sampled from the joint probability distribution $P(V, H)$, which is approximated by Gibbs sampling. If $P(V)$ is equal to the distribution of the training data, in the expectation, the positive and negative gradient equal each other and the total gradient becomes zero.

Calculating Δ_{ij}^{neg} exactly is infeasible, as the number of required Gibbs sampling steps until the RBM is sampling from its stationary distribution is high. Hence, contrastive divergence usually uses a much lower number N of sampling steps (CD-N). For CD-N, Δ_{ij}^{neg} is approximated by initializing the visible neurons with a data vector from the training set and performing only N Gibbs sampling steps.

Algorithm 2 summarizes the functionality of CD-1 ($N = 1$). For each training vector, V is initialized with the training vector and H is sampled according to (2). This allows calculating Δ_{ij}^{pos} as $v_i h_j$. Then, two more sampling steps are carried out: First, we calculate the "reconstruction" $\hat{V}$ of the training vector as in (1). Subsequently, we calculate the corresponding hidden probabilities $P(\hat{h}_j = 1|\hat{V})$. Now, we can approximate Δ_{ij}^{neg} as $\hat{v}_i \cdot P(\hat{h}_j|\hat{V})$ and obtain Δw_{ij}. Finally, we update the weights as

$$w_{ij} := w_{ij} + \alpha \cdot \Delta w_{ij} \quad (4)$$

where $\alpha \in (0, \ldots, 1)$ is a learning rate defined by the user.

Algorithm 2 Pseudo code for a training epoch using CD-1

for all training examples **do**
 $V \leftarrow$ set V to the current training example
 $H \leftarrow$ sample $H|V$, i.e. set h_j to 1 with $P(h_j = 1|V)$ from (2)
 $\Delta_{ij}^{\text{pos}} = v_i h_j$
 $\hat{V} \leftarrow$ sample "reconstruction" $\hat{V}|H$, using (1)
 $\hat{H} \leftarrow$ calculate $P(\hat{H}|\hat{V})$ as in (2)
 $\Delta_{ij}^{\text{neg}} = \hat{v}_i \cdot P(\hat{h}_j|\hat{V})$
 $\Delta w_{ij} \leftarrow$ calculate all Δw_{ij} as in (3)
 $w_{ij} \leftarrow$ update all weights according to (4)
end for

2.2.3 *Using RBMs in EDAs*

RBM-EDA uses an RBM as its model to capture the probability distribution of the population. In each generation of the EDA, the individuals surviving the selection step are used as training data for the RBM. Using contrastive divergence learning, the weights of the RBM are updated until a termination criterion has been reached. A simple termination criterion is the convergence of the reconstruction error, i.e. the degree to which the RBM is able to reconstruct the training data after one Gibbs sampling step $V \rightarrow H \rightarrow \hat{V}$. After training, the RBM is used to sample new individuals, which are then incorporated into the population.

In contrast to other EDAs using Markov random fields like DEUM [26], it is not necessary to specify a network structure in advance. The bipartite nature of the RBM makes Gibbs sampling a feasible means for approximating samples from the fully connected model's equilibrium distribution.

3. PARALLELIZATION OF EDAS

We discuss approaches to parallelize EDAs and the major challenges. We then show how to parallelize RBM-EDA.

3.1 Basic concepts and challenges

Parallelization has been done for many EDAs, including the above mentioned UMDA, ECGA and BOA [see e.g. 27, 8, 17, 19, 15, 13, and others]. Parallel versions usually result in significant speedups compared to the single-core versions. Often, there are moderatly diminishing returns on increasing the number of cores.

It is straightforward to parallelize fitness evaluation. Furthermore, simple EDA models like UMDA can be parallelized easily, as all parts of the model (i.e. all variables) are independent. In contrast, parallel building and sampling become more difficult for complex models with multivariate dependencies [18]. When distributing tasks of unknown, and potentially different, sizes to multiple processors, job scheduling and load balancing mechanisms are required to maximize utilization [see e.g. 20, 13].

In multivariate EDAs, interdependent parts of the model may have to exchange information. To facilitate efficient parallelization, this communication can be reduced by using sub-populations or islands [11]. Alternatively, it is sometimes possible to introduce additional assumptions to render separate parts independent of each other. For example, the parallelization approaches for BOA assume a predetermined order of nodes in the dependency graph.

Depending on the hardware platform, specific restrictions must be considered to maximize the utilization of the parallel resources. For example, when running in a cluster environment, the parallelization scheme must consider latencies between nodes. When using Graphics Processing Units (GPUs), there is only a limited amount of very fast shared memory available and memory access to slower global memory has to be done in a coalesced fashion to maximize the utilization of the memory bandwidth [see e.g. 15].

Thus, parallelization itself and subsequent tuning for maximum hardware utilization may pose a significant challenge. Sometimes, the necessary algorithmic changes also result in slightly reduced model quality. For example, the parallel version may need larger populations to match the quality of its sequential counterpart [see e.g. 27]. Hence, besides parallelization being complicated, there is often a trade-off involved: maximizing the utilization of the hardware does not always entail maximizing the model quality, and vice versa.

3.2 Parallelization of RBM-EDA

It is simple and efficient to parallelize the training and sampling of RBM-EDA. Also, parallelization can be achieved without changes to the model itself. The reason is that, due to their bipartite structure, RBMs are implicitly parallel. Furthermore, the actual implementation can use standard libraries for most of the computational steps.

3.2.1 Implicit parallelism

The RBM's bipartite structure factorizes the distributions of both visible and hidden layer. That is, a visible neuron v_i is independent of all other visible neurons $v_{j \neq i}$, given the activation of the m neurons of the hidden layer, and vice versa. Hence, the activation of all v_i can be calculated by n independent threads. This holds for training and sampling.

Furthermore, contrastive divergence, which is used for training, is a stochastic gradient ascent algorithm and usually implemented in a mini-batch fashion. That is, we simultaneously calculate Δw_{ij} in (4) for each training example in a mini-batch of size B, and subsequently use the average to update w_{ij}. This reduces sampling noise and makes the gradient more stable [1, 7]. The initial population in an EDA is usually random. Thus, the signal-to-noise ratio is low and the batch size B can be even larger than in classical, well structured training tasks.

Hence, when training with mini-batches of batch size B, the activation of $B * m$ independent neurons has to be calculated to perform a single Gibbs sampling step $V_b \rightarrow H_b$ for all $b = 1, 2, \ldots, B$ using Equation 2. Accordingly, to perform a single Gibbs sampling step $H_b \rightarrow V_b$, the activation of $B * n$ independent neurons is calculated using (1). Thus, for training, the number of independent neurons grows linearly with the problem size n, given that m is some fixed fraction of n. When sampling new candidate solutions, all individuals are independent, so B is equal to the number of new individuals. Hence, for sampling, the number of independent neurons grows linearly with the problem size *and* with the population size.

Recall that, unlike other EDA models based on probabilistic graphical models, RBM-EDA does not separate the search for a suitable network structure from parameter estimation. During training, the connectivity of the RBM remains unchanged. Only the strength of the connections are adjusted. Hence, there is no need for mechanisms balancing unequal workloads due to different subproblem sizes.

3.2.2 Usage of BLAS libraries

Formally, calculating a single sampling step $V_b \rightarrow H_b$ consist of two steps: first, we perform one vector-matrix multiplication $V \times W$. Subsequently, we apply the sigmoid function to each element of the result vector. The same applies to the calculation of $H_b \rightarrow V_b$. When performing mini-batch learning or sampling, we combine all B vector-matrix multiplications into a single matrix-matrix multiplication.

Efficient implementations of matrix-matrix operations are part of Basic Linear Algebra Subprogram (BLAS) libraries with standardized high-level interfaces [see e.g. 3]. These libraries are available for almost every platform (e.g. ATLAS, ATLAS for ARM, CUBLAS, Intel MKL, and others). Using a BLAS library comes with two major benefits: first, BLAS libraries are usually optimized to use the full potential of a single core. For example, modern BLAS libraries can make use of the processor's hardware extensions such as SSE (Streaming SIMD Extensions). Here, identical instructions that have to be be carried out many times on multiple data items can be processed simultaneously in parallel registers of a single CPU core. Second, there are numerous parallel BLAS libraries, which can make use of multiple cores or use special hardware, like GPUs. As the interface is standardized, switching to different parallelization platform can be as easy as - technically spoken - changing the "#import" statement which specifies the used library. As most of the operations to train and sample an RBM are covered by BLAS libraries, the amount of custom code for the parallelization is very low (see Section 4.2).

4. EXPERIMENTS

This section introduces the test problem, concatenated deceptive traps, and presents our experimental setup. We then show the speedups of the single-threaded BLAS and the GPU version of EDA-RBM in comparison to a naive serial implementation.

4.1 Test Problem

We evaluate the speedup on a standard benchmark problem for EDAs - concatenated deceptive traps. Concatenated deceptive traps are tunably hard, yet decomposable test problems [2]. Here, a solution vector x is divided into l subsets of size k, with each one being a deceptive trap. Within a trap, all bits are dependent on each other but independent of all other bits in x. Thus, the fitness contribution of the traps can be evaluated separately and the total fitness of the solution vector is the sum of these terms[2]. In particular, the assignment $a = x_{i:i+k-1}$ (i.e. the k bits from x_i to x_{i+k-1}) leads to a fitness contribution F_l as

$$F_l(a) = \begin{cases} k & \text{if } \sum_i a_i = k, \\ k - (\sum_i a_i + 1) & \text{otherwise.} \end{cases}$$

The fitness of a single trap increases with the number of zeros, except for the optimum of all ones.

[2]In general, the k variables assigned to trap l do not have to be adjacent but can be at any position in x. Due to easier visualization, however, we assume in the remainder of this paper that they are adjacent. This goes without loss of generality, because the model does not assume any neighborhood relation between adjacent x_i.

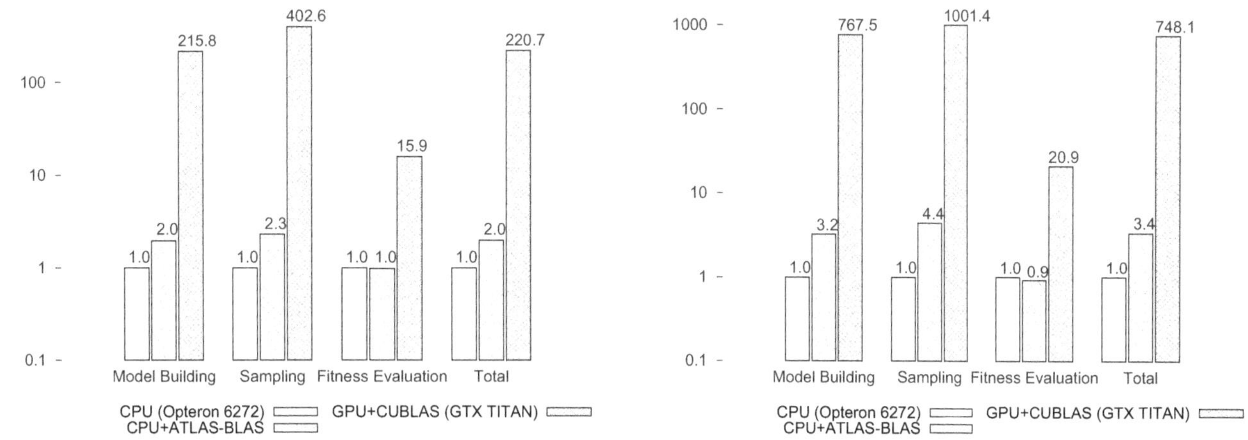

Figure 2: Speedups for solving concatenated trap-5 problems. Left hand side: $l = 20$ concatenated traps; right hand side: $l = 70$ concatenated traps

4.2 Experimental Setup

We test three versions of the EDA implemented in C++. The base version, henceforth referred to as *CPU* version, is a single threaded RBM, which performs all operations sequentially. That is, all matrix operations are carried out in nested for-loops. Second, we test a version of RBM-EDA which uses an optimized ATLAS BLAS library for all linear algebra operations, but is still restricted to one CPU core. Hence, model building and sampling operations utilize the SIMD extensions of the CPU core. The third version uses CUBLAS, the BLAS library of CUDA, the general purpose programming language for NVIDIA GPUs. We run the GPU code on an NVIDIA GeForce GTX TITAN GPU with 2,688 cores.

In the ATLAS and CUBLAS versions, all matrix multiplication operations necessary for model building and sampling are covered by the BLAS libraries. For all other operations, i.e. mainly the sigmoid function in (1) and (2), and the stochastic activations, we wrote approximately 20 lines of custom CUDA/C++ code. The first two versions do not use any parallel code for evaluating the fitness of the population. The GPU version performs parallelized model building, sampling and fitness evaluations. Here, we wrote problem-specific CUDA code. Like in other methods, device-specific restrictions have to be considered. For example, when using GPUs, the number of solutions that can be evaluated in parallel on each of the GPUs streaming multiprocessors (SM) is limited by the shared memory of the device. All together, the code for the GPU parallelization makes up for as little as 2% of the total application code.

From an algorithmic perspective, all three versions of RBM-EDA are identical. If we use the same pseudo random number generator to initialize the population and for the stochastic activation of neurons, they produce the same results, except for hardware-specific floating point rounding errors.

Also, the parametrization of all versions is identical. The number m of hidden neurons is half of the number n of visible neurons (i.e. half the problem size). Before training the model, we use the normalization scheme of [29]. We set the batch size B to 1024 and use CD-1 as learning algorithm. When sampling the k'th individual of the new generation, we initialize V to the k'th individual previous generation and perform 25 Gibbs sampling steps between V and H. We choose the initial learning rate α to be 0.5 and a *momentum* of $m = 0.5$ [see 25]. As in [24], we automate the training process to decrease α and increase m towards the end of the training, and stop training upon convergence.

4.3 Results

We test the different versions of RBM-EDA with concatenated deceptive traps with trap sizes of $k = 4$ and $k = 5$ for various sizes l. First, we report the respective speedups for model building, sampling, fitness evaluations and the total speedup when solving the respective problem to optimality. Subsequently, we analyze to what extent the parallelization can make use of the implicit parallelism of the RBM. The results for solving problems with a trap size of $k = 4$ and $k = 5$ are qualitatively equivalent. Hence, for brevity, we only report the results for $k = 5$. Initial sanity checks with other problem types such as MAXSAT also support the findings. All results are statistically significant ($p < 10^{-5}$ for BLAS results, $p < 10^{-16}$ for CUDA results).

4.3.1 *Speedups for solving trap problems*

We choose the EDA's population size such that 20 out of 20 runs find the global optimum of the respective problem.

Figure 2 (left hand side) shows the results for a trap problem with $k = 5$ and $l = 20$. That is, the length of the overall solution vector is 100. Using the ATLAS BLAS library speeds up model building, i.e. the application of the contrastive divergence training algorithm, by a factor of approx. 2.0, while still utilizing only one core. This is due to the use of the CPUs SIMD (single instruction, multiple data) units by the BLAS library.

When sampling new individuals, the ATLAS BLAS version is 2.3× faster than the nested loop version. The reason for the higher speedup is the larger matrix size: Model building is performed with a mini-batch size of 1024. Hence, the input matrix size for the calculation of Equation 2 is 1024×100 (i.e. 1024 rows holding one individual of length 100 each). During sampling, mini-batches are not necessary and all individuals are encoded in one large matrix. With larger input matrices, the underlying BLAS library is able to distribute the work to the parallel resources more efficiently.

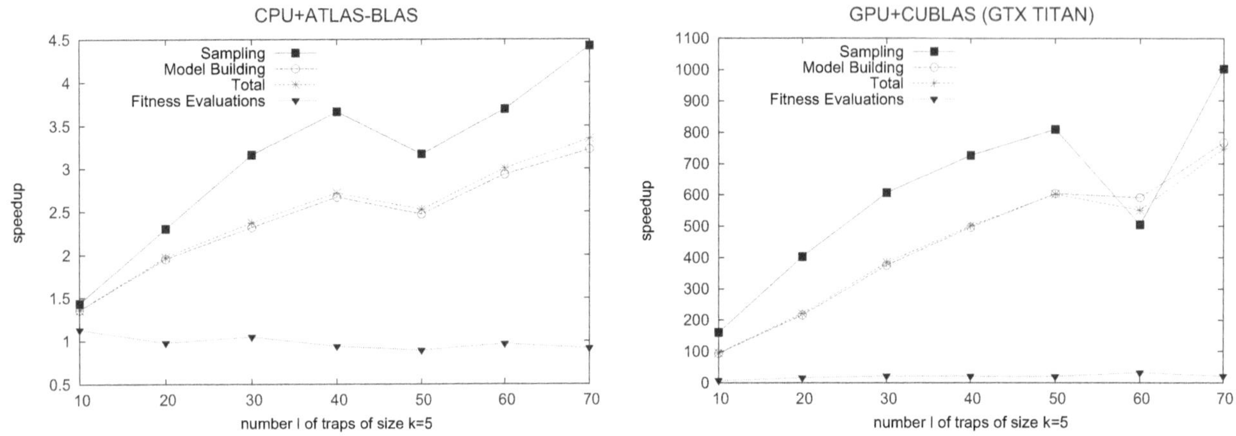

Figure 3: Speedups for for solving concatenated trap-5 problems of various sizes l, compared to nested loop CPU version. Left hand side: ATLAS BLAS version; right hand side: CUBLAS version on GPU

The CPU version and the BLAS version are identical in terms of the fitness evaluations, hence there is no speedup. As the total time is dominated by model building, the total speedup of the BLAS version is approximately 2.0.

The GPU version shows a similar speedup pattern for model building and sampling, however on a much higher level. Model building and sampling are approx. 216× and 402× faster than the nested-loop version. Fitness evaluations are performed approximately 16× faster on the GPU. Compared to the model-related speedups, the gain for fitness evaluations is small. This is due to the small amount of on-chip shared memory, which limits the number of individuals, that can be processed simultaneously on the streaming multiprocessors of the GPU. However, the overall effort for fitness evaluations is low, compared to model building and sampling. Thus, a trap-5 problem of with $l = 20$ traps can be solved approximately 220× faster using a GTX TITAN GPU. Figure 2 (right hand side) shows the results for an increased problem size of $l = 70$ traps. The benefit of using the BLAS libraries increases. Due to the growing matrix sizes, the libraries utilize the parallel resources much better. Using ATLAS now yields speedups of 3.2 and 4.4 for model building and sampling, respectively. The total speedup grows to 3.4×. Using the GPU, it is possible to achieve a speedup of approximately 768 for model building and $1,001$ for sampling. The total speedup of using the GPU instead of a nested loop implementation on the CPU is approximately 748-fold.

Figure 3 summarizes the speedups for the ATLAS BLAS and GPU implementations for solving trap-5 problems of different sizes. As with other parallel implementations (e.g. [20]), the speedup grows with problem size, as the matrix sizes increase. Both the graphs for ATLAS and CUBLAS show a pronounced dent in the speedup at problem sizes of $l = 50$ and $l = 60$, respectively. Here, especially the speedup for sampling is lower than for smaller problem sizes. However, a saw tooth-like pattern is common in speedup charts for parallel matrix multiplications and most likely related to the device utilization (see e.g. [16]). On a GPU, threads working on independent subproblems are usually launched in thread blocks containing a fixed number of threads each. If there are 1024 subproblems, and the block size is 1,024, launching a single block of threads will utilize the GPU optimally. If there are 1,025 subproblems, two blocks of threads will be launched, and in one of those blocks 1,023 of 1,024 threads will be idle. The same logic applies if the number of required thread blocks does not match the number of SMs. If we launch 15 thread blocks on a GPU with 14 SMs, the 15th block will be processed on one of the SMs after the other blocks have finished. While block 15 is running, the other SMs are idle, assuming that they cannot proceed with other tasks, which is often the case if some order of execution is required.

4.3.2 Scalability of model building and sampling

The previous subsection reports speedups for solving trap problems with varying l. We now assess the scaling behavior of the model building and sampling steps in the CUBLAS version of EDA-RBM. We analyze if the CUBLAS implementation makes efficient use of the implicit parallelism of an RBM. Keep in mind that the number of independent neurons rises linearly with the *problem* size for sampling and training and, additionally, linearly with the *population* size for sampling (see Section 3.2.1). Thus, an efficient implementation should be able to distribute these independent calculations to the parallel resources without introducing significant overhead.

The number of calculations required to determine all activations within the layers V and H grows quadratically with the problem size n, as each neuron collects input from all neurons of the other layer according to (1) and (2), respectively. Hence, the run time of the CPU version is quadratic in the problem size. In theory, efficient parallelization distributes the quadratic number of steps onto a linear number of independent threads, as the number of independent neurons grows linearly. This would yield a run time that grows linearly (instead of quadratically) with the problem size. We define speedups as $\text{runtime}_{\text{CPU}}/\text{runtime}_{\text{GPU}}$. Consequently, the speedup of an efficient parallel implementation increases linearly with the problem size. This should be true until the hardware is fully utilized. We test this hypothesis as follows. We run a single EDA generation. We train the RBM for 50 epochs with contrastive divergence. Subsequently, we sample a new generation of individuals, using 25 Gibbs sampling steps. All results are averaged over 20 independent runs.

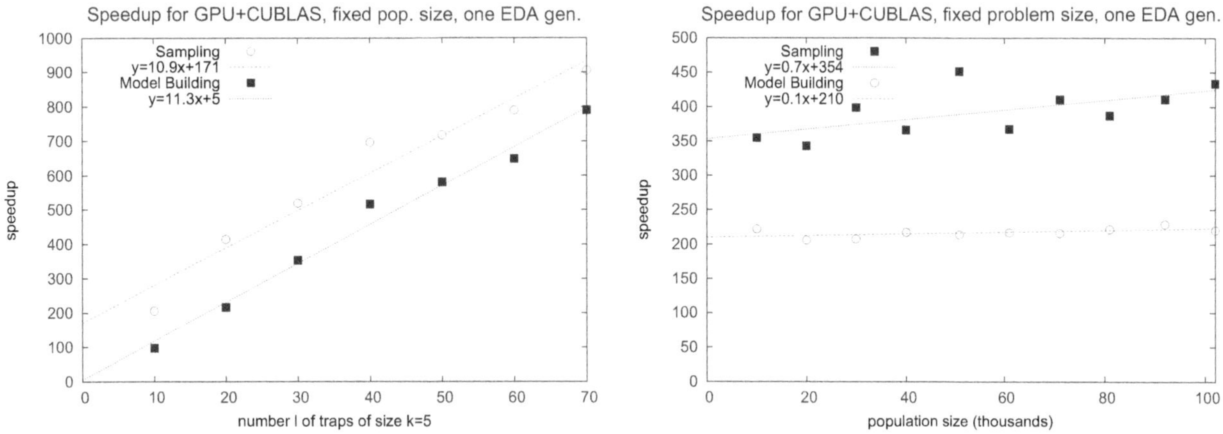

Figure 4: Speedups for the GPU version of RBM-EDA for a single EDA generation. Left hand side: fixed population size of 25,600; right hand side: fixed problem size of 100 ($l = 20, k = 5$)

In a first analysis we fix the population size to 25,600 and measure the speedups of the CUBLAS version compared to the single core CPU version for growing problem sizes ($l = 10, 20, ..., 70$). Figure 4, left hand side, shows the speedups for increasing problem sizes, and the corresponding approximations derived by linear regression. As predicted, the relationships for sampling and model building are about linear. For model building, the linear approximation goes almost exactly through the origin. If the input size doubles, we observe twice the speedup. In a second analysis we set the problem size to 100 ($l = 20$). Figure 4, right hand side, shows the speedups for various population sizes. The speedup for model building is unrelated to the population size for mini-batch learning. The underlying trend for sampling is linear. The vertical offset of the linear approximation is high and the familiar saw-tooth pattern is much stronger.

This indicates that the CUBLAS implementation uses the GPU resources efficiently. The speedup for the model building and sampling steps grow linearly with the problem size.

The previous results show that for *solving* trap-5 problems, the speedups for sampling already converge towards a maximum value (Figure 3, right hand side). As the problem size grows, the required population size also increases. For sampling, the utilization of the GTX TITAN is already close to the theoretical maximum. The clock speed of each GPU core is at 837 MHz, which is around 40% of the CPU clock speed of 2,100 MHz. Assuming a similar number of instructions per clock cycle, the 2,688 GPU cores should be able to process $\approx 40\% \times 2,688 = 1,070$ times as fast as a single CPU core not using its SIMD extensions. The speedups for sampling in our experiments are just slightly smaller than this upper bound. In turn, it is reasonable to assume that larger problem sizes will further increase the speedup for model building towards the upper bound.

5. DISCUSSION AND CONCLUSION

RBM-EDA appears to be particularly suited for parallelization. Because of the bipartite structure of the RBM most neuron-related calculations required for training and sampling are independent of each other. Hence, they can be processed in parallel. Many of these calculations can be expressed as linear algebra operations, namely matrix multiplications. They can be implemented using standardized BLAS libraries, which are available for many parallel architectures.

In practice, the parallel GPU version of RBM-EDA can use much of this theoretical potential for parallelization of RBMs. For a fixed population size, the speedups for both sampling and model building grow linearly with the problem size. This yields massive speedups when solving combinatorial optimization problems like concatenated deceptive traps. For a trap-5 problem with 70 concatenated traps, the parallel version using a NVIDIA GTX TITAN GPU is approximately 750× faster than a "plain vanilla" CPU implementation.

Furthermore, when using a BLAS library, RBM-EDA is able to utilize the parallel resources available in modern CPUs. Despite the restriction to a single CPU core, the ATLAS BLAS version can achieve significant speedups of up to 3.4× compared with the non-BLAS CPU version.

Fortunately, the large speedups come without much additional complexity of the implementation. The interface of BLAS libraries is standardized. Hence, it is easy to switch the underlying library, e.g. when porting RBM-EDA to another platform, or if a more efficient BLAS library is available. This allows us to use the library that utilizes the given hardware the best. Second, the parallelization is implicit to an RBM, i.e. the model itself is unaffected. Hence, it is not necessary to make significant changes to the code structure. Only 2% of our code is parallelization-specific. Moreover, the majority of this code is required for the parallelization of the fitness evaluations. It is not specific to the RBM.

In sum, RBM-EDA is particularly interesting for parallel architectures. The implementation effort is comparatively low, achieved speedups are large, and portability is high.

The basic principles of the parallelization could potentially be applied to other EDAs as well. Algorithms using models which factorize due to latent variables, like, for example, the growing neural gas network, have been used in EDAs and show a similar structure with implicit parallelism [12]. It may be more difficult for EDAs based on directed graphical models. This is an interesting area for future research.

Acknowledgments

We would like to thank the anonymous reviewers for their valuable comments on a previous version of this paper.

References

[1] C. M. Bishop. *Pattern Recognition and Machine Learning*. Information Science and Statistics. Springer, 2006.

[2] K. Deb and D. E. Goldberg. *Analyzing deception in trap functions*. University of Illinois, Department of General Engineering, 1991.

[3] J. J. Dongarra, J. Du Croz, S. Hammarling, and I. S. Duff. A Set of Level 3 Basic Linear Algebra Subprograms. *Transactions on Mathematical Software*, 16(1):1–17, Mar. 1990.

[4] S. Geman and D. Geman. Stochastic Relaxation, Gibbs Distributions, and the Bayesian Restoration of Images. *IEEE Transactions on Pattern Analysis and Machine Intelligence*, PAMI-6(6):721–741, 1984.

[5] G. Harik. Linkage Learning via Probabilistic Modeling in the ECGA. *Urbana*, 51(61):801, 1999.

[6] G. E. Hinton. Training Products of Experts by Minimizing Contrastive Divergence. *Neural Computation*, 14:1771–1800, 2002.

[7] G. E. Hinton, S. Osindero, and Y.-W. Teh. A Fast Learning Algorithm for Deep Belief Nets. *Neural Computation*, 18:1527–1554, 2006.

[8] J. M. Lanza-Gutierrez, J. A. Gomez-Pulido, M. A. Vega-Rodriguez, and J. M. Sanchez-Perez. A Parallel Evolutionary Approach to Solve the Relay Node Placement Problem in Wireless Sensor Networks. In *Proceedings of the Fifteenth Annual Conference on Genetic and Evolutionary Computation Conference*, GECCO'13, pages 1157–1164. ACM, 2013.

[9] P. Larrañaga, H. Karshenas, C. Bielza, and R. Santana. A Review on Probabilistic Graphical Models in Evolutionary Computation. *Journal of Heuristics*, 18(5):795–819, 2012.

[10] P. Larrañaga and J. A. Lozano. *Estimation of Distribution Algorithms: A New Tool for Evolutionary Computation*. Genetic Algorithms and Evolutionary Computation, 2. Kluwer Academic Pub, 2002.

[11] J. Madera, E. Alba, and A. Ochoa. A Parallel Island Model for Estimation of Distribution Algorithms. In J. Lozano, P. Larrañaga, I. Inza, and E. Bengoetxea, editors, *Towards a New Evolutionary Computation*, volume 192 of *Studies in Fuzziness and Soft Computing*, pages 159–186. Springer Berlin Heidelberg, 2006.

[12] L. Martí, J. García, A. Berlanga, and J. M. Molina. Introducing MONEDA: Scalable Multiobjective Optimization with a Neural Estimation of Distribution Algorithm. In *Proceedings of the 10th annual conference on Genetic and evolutionary computation*, pages 689–696. ACM, 2008.

[13] A. Mendiburu, J. A. Lozano, and J. Miguel-Alonso. Parallel Implementation of EDAs based on Probabilistic Graphical Models. *Evolutionary Computation, IEEE Transactions on*, 9(4):406–423, 2005.

[14] H. Mühlenbein and G. Paaß. From Recombination of Genes to the Estimation of Distributions I. Binary Parameters. In H.-M. Voigt, W. Ebeling, I. Rechenberg, and H.-P. Schwefel, editors, *Parallel Problem Solving from Nature - PPSN IV*, volume 1141 of *Lecture Notes in Computer Science*, pages 178–187. Springer Berlin Heidelberg, 1996.

[15] A. Munawar, M. Wahib, M. Munetomo, and K. Akama. Theoretical and Empirical Analysis of a GPU-based Parallel Bayesian Optimization Algorithm. In *2009 International Conference on Parallel and Distributed Computing, Applications and Technologies*, pages 457–462. IEEE, 2009.

[16] NVIDIA. Speedup Charts for CUBLAS Matrix Multiplications, see https://developer.nvidia.com/cuBLAS, 2014.

[17] J. Očenášek and J. Schwarz. The Parallel Bayesian Optimization Aalgorithm. In *The State of the Art in Computational Intelligence*, pages 61–67. Springer, 2000.

[18] J. Očenášek, Jiří, E. Cantú-Paz, M. Pelikan, and J. Schwarz. Design of Parallel Estimation of Distribution Algorithms. In *Scalable Optimization via Probabilistic Modeling*, pages 187–203. Springer, 2006.

[19] J. Očenášek, Jiří and J. Schwarz. The Distributed Bayesian Optimization Algorithm for Combinatorial Optimization. *EUROGEN-Evolutionary Methods for Design, Optimisation and Control, CIMNE*, pages 115–120, 2001.

[20] J. Očenášek, Jiří, J. Schwarz, and M. Pelikan. Design of Multithreaded Estimation of Distribution Algorithms. In *Proceedings of the 2003 International Conference on Genetic and Evolutionary Computation*, GECCO'13, pages 1247–1258. Springer, 2003.

[21] M. Pelikan. Bayesian Optimization Algorithm. In *Hierarchical Bayesian Optimization Algorithm*, volume 170 of *Studies in Fuzziness and Soft Computing*, pages 31–48. Springer Berlin / Heidelberg, 2005.

[22] M. Pelikan, D. E. Goldberg, and E. Cantu-Paz. BOA: The Bayesian Optimization Algorithm. In *Genetic and Evolutionary Computation Conference*, pages 525–532, 1999.

[23] M. Pelikan and H. Mühlenbein. The Bivariate Marginal Distribution Algorithm. *Advances in Soft Computing-Engineering Design and Manufacturing*, pages 521–535, 1999.

[24] M. Probst, F. Rothlauf, and J. Grahl. Scalability of Using Restricted Boltzmann Machines to Solve Problems of Bounded Difficulty. Technical report, Information Systems and Business Administration, Universität Mainz, 2014.

[25] N. Qian. On the Momentum Term in Gradient Descent Learning Algorithms. *Neural Networks*, 12(1):145–151, 1999.

[26] S. Shakya and J. McCall. Optimization by Estimation of Distribution with DEUM Framework based on Markov Random Fields. *International Journal of Automation and Computing*, 4(3):262–272, 2007.

[27] C.-Y. Shao and T.-L. Yu. Speeding Up Model Building for ECGA on CUDA Platform. In *Proceedings of the Fifteenth Annual Conference on Genetic and Evolutionary Computation Conference*, GECCO'13, pages 1197–1204. ACM, 2013.

[28] P. Smolensky. *Parallel Distributed Processing: Explorations in the Microstructure of Cognition*, volume 1, chapter Information Processing in Dynamical Systems: Foundations of Harmony Theory, pages 194–281. MIT Press, Cambridge, MA, USA, 1986.

[29] Y. Tang and I. Sutskever. Data Normalization in the Learning of Restricted Boltzmann Machines. Technical Report UTML-TR-11-2, Department of Computer Science, University of Toronto, 2011.

Playing Regex Golf with Genetic Programming

Alberto Bartoli
DIA - University of Trieste
Italy
bartoli.alberto@units.it

Andrea De Lorenzo
DIA - University of Trieste
Italy
andrea.delorenzo@phd.units.it

Eric Medvet
DIA - University of Trieste
Italy
emedvet@units.it

Fabiano Tarlao
DIA - University of Trieste
Italy
fabiano.tarlao@phd.units.it

ABSTRACT

Regex golf has recently emerged as a specific kind of code golf, i.e., unstructured and informal programming competitions aimed at writing the shortest code solving a particular problem. A problem in regex golf consists in writing the shortest regular expression which matches all the strings in a given list and does not match any of the strings in another given list. The regular expression is expected to follow the syntax of a specified programming language, e.g., Javascript or PHP.

In this paper, we propose a *regex golf player* internally based on Genetic Programming. We generate a population of candidate regular expressions represented as trees and evolve such population based on a multi-objective fitness which minimizes the errors and the length of the regular expression.

We assess experimentally our player on a popular regex golf challenge consisting of 16 problems and compare our results against those of a recently proposed algorithm—the only one we are aware of. Our player obtains scores which improve over the baseline and are highly competitive also with respect to human players. The time for generating a solution is usually in the order of tens minutes, which is arguably comparable to the time required by human players.

Categories and Subject Descriptors

I.5.4 [**Pattern Recognition**]: Applications—*text processing*; H.4.1 [**Information Systems Applications**]: Office Automation—*word processing*

Keywords

Regular Expressions, Genetic Programming, Programming by Example, Machine Learning

GECCO'14, July 12–16, 2014, Vancouver, BC, Canada.

http://dx.doi.org/10.1145/2576768.2598333.

1. INTRODUCTION

Regex golf has recently emerged as a specific kind of code golf, i.e., unstructured and informal programming competitions aimed at writing the shortest code solving a particular problem. A problem in regex golf usually consists in writing the shortest regular expression which matches all the strings in a given list and does not match any of the strings in another given list. Examples of such lists could be the names of all winners of an US presidential election and of the names of all losers (the specific constraints on the contents of these lists will be clarified later, e.g., their intersection must be empty). A trivial way for generating systematically a regular expression with these requirements consists in building a disjunction of all the desired matches—i.e., all the matches glued together by the | character which, in common regex syntax, means "or". To reward non trivial solutions, the *score* assigned to a given solution is higher for more compact expressions.

There has recently been a growing interest toward regex golf in the programmers' communities, motivated more by the challenge itself than by the actual utility of any given problem. Such interest has been fueled further by a blog post of a famous researcher—Peter Norvig—in which a simple yet powerful algorithm for solving regex golf problems systematically is proposed [16]. Norvig points out that problems of this sort are related to set cover problems, which are known to be NP-hard, and describes a greedy algorithm which is very efficient and works well in a number of cases, while at the same time identifying the fundamental trade-offs made in his proposal.

In this paper, we propose a methodology based on Genetic Programming (GP) for generating solutions to regex golf problems—a *regex golf player*. We generate a population of candidate regular expressions represented as trees and constructed with carefully selected regular expression operators and constants. We evolve such population based on a multi-objective fitness which maximizes the correct handling of the provided matches and unmatches while minimizing the length of the regular expression represented by the individual.

We implemented our proposal and assessed its performance on a recently proposed suite of 16 regex golf problems which is very popular. We used as baseline the algorithm proposed by Norvig—the only one we are aware of—and an existing GP-based system for generating regular expressions for text extraction tasks by examples [3]. Our proposal compares very favorably to the baseline and obtains the highest score on the full suite. We also attempted the construct a baseline based on scores obtained by human players, which is difficult because no structured collections of human players results are available: however, we collected several results by crawling the web and found that our proposal is ranked in the top positions.

A prototype of our regex golf player is available at `http://regex.inginf.units.it/golf`.

2. RELATED WORK

The only algorithm explicitly designed for solving regex golf-related problems which we are aware of is the one by Peter Norvig mentioned in the introduction. We used this algorithm as baseline for our proposal.

Several proposals for learning regular expressions from examples exist for *text extraction* problems [18, 13, 1, 12, 5, 2, 3]. Text extraction from examples is radically different from regex golf in several crucial points. First, regex golf assumes an input stream segmented so that the input strings listed in the problem specification are processed by the solution one segment at a time. Text extraction requires instead the ability to identify and extract specific portions from a longer stream. In other words, regex golf consists in binary classifying input strings whereas text extraction requires the identification in the input string of the boundaries of the substring(s) to extract, if any. Second, a regex golf problem places no requirements on how strings not listed in the problem specification will be classified. Text extraction requires instead a form of generalization, i.e., the ability of inducing a general pattern from the provided examples. Third, text extraction requires the ability to identify a context for the desired extraction, that is, a given sequence of characters may or may not constitute a match depending on its surroundings. A requirement of this form is not meaningful in regex golf.

For example, a regex golf problem requiring the match of all winners of US presidential elections and no loser may be solved with a disjunction of `ls` and several short regexes [16]. Such a regular expression is not useful for the text extraction problem, because applying it to a superstring of a winner would provide no information about the substring which actually identifies the winner. Furthermore, any string containing the substring `ls` will thus be matched by the regex. On the other hand, a regex generated for text extraction might be applied to regex golf but it would be largely suboptimal: the solution generation process must induce a general pattern and there is clearly no syntactical pattern capable of predicting the names of future US presidents. In other words, learning approaches tailored to text extraction purposefully attempt to prevent any overfitting of the examples which is instead a necessity in regex golf.

Our proposal builds on the text extraction method in [3], which we modified and specialized by taking the specific requirements of regex golf into account. We included the cited method in the baseline because, although it was designed for a different problem, it is available as a webapp[1] and its inclusion demonstrates that solving regex golf effectively calls for a specialized solution.

Another proposal for learning regular expressions from examples is [6], but this work considers a problem whose requirements are a mix of regex golf and text extraction. On the one hand, the problem consists in merely classifying input strings without the need of identifying the boundaries of the matching substrings. On the other hand, the problem assumes input streams not necessarily segmented in advance at the granularity of the desired matches and unmatches. Moreover, and most importantly, the cited work aims at inferring a general pattern capable of solving the desired task beyond the provided examples.

Since a regular expression may be obtained from a deterministic finite automata (DFA), approaches for learning a DFA from labelled examples and counterexamples could be used (e.g., [14, 4]; see [7] for a survey). On the other hand, such proposals assume the number of states of the target DFA is known and, most importantly, they are not concerned with minimizing the length of the regular expression corresponding to the generated DFA. While approaches of this form may deserve further investigation, they do not appear to match the specific requirements of regex golf. Similar remarks may be applied also to proposals for induction of non-deterministic finite automata (NFA) from labelled examples [10, 17].

Finally, regex golf might be seen as a problem in the broader category of *programming by examples* (PBE), where a program in a given programming language is to be synthesized based on a set of input-output pairs. Notable results in this area have been obtained recently for problems of string manipulation [11, 15] and some of the corresponding algorithms have been included in the latest release of Microsoft Excel (Flash-Fill functionality). While such approaches are able to deal with *context-free grammars* and are thus potentially able to solve classification problems of the form encountered in regex golf, they use an underlying language which is much richer than regular expressions and thus may not generate solutions useful for regex golf.

3. THE PROBLEM

While the term "regex golf" may indicate any challenge requiring the generation of a regular expression, its usual meaning is the one described in the introduction and formalized as follows.

We consider strings constructed over a large alphabet $\alpha =$ UTF-8. Strings may potentially include arbitrary characters in the alphabet, including spaces, newline and so on. A problem instance is defined by $\mathcal{I} = (M, U)$, where M and U are sets of strings whose intersection is empty.

The problem consists in generating a regular expression which:

1. matches all strings in M;
2. does not match any string in U; and,
3. is shorter than the regular expression constructed as a disjunction[2] of all strings in M.

Note that, for a given problem instance, it might not be known whether a regular expression satisfying the above requirements actually exists. Furthermore, given a solution r' satisfying the three requirements, it might not be known whether there exists a shorter solution r'' satisfying requirements 1 and 2.

[1] `http://regex.inginf.units.it`

[2] More precisely, the disjunction of all strings in M, where each string is prefixed by the "start of string" anchor `^` and postfixed by the "end of string" anchor `$`.

Solutions may satisfy requirements 1 and 2 in part. That is, a solution might fail to match one or more strings in M and/or match one or more strings in U. Solutions are thus given a *score* quantifying their behavior in terms of the desired matches and unmatches, as well as their compactness.

We use the score definition in **`http://regex.alf.nu`**, from which we have also collected the suite of problem instances for our experimental evaluation. The definition is as follows. Let r be a candidate solution, let n_M and n_U denote the number of elements in M and U, respectively, which are matched by r. The score of r on instance $\mathcal{I} = (M, U)$ is:

$$w_{\mathcal{I}}(n_M - n_U) - \text{length}(r)$$

where $w_{\mathcal{I}}$ is a statically defined value which is meant to weigh the "difficulty" of the problem instance $\mathcal{I}$. Note that the numerical value of the score, as well as the range of possible values, is problem instance-dependent and that a solution may obtain a negative score.

4. OUR APPROACH

The system requires a description of the problem instance $\mathcal{I} = (M, U)$ and generates a Javascript-compatible regular expression. A prototype is available at **`http://regex.inginf.units.it/golf`**.

Our proposal builds on the text extraction method in [3], which we modified and specialized by taking the specific requirements of regex golf into account. We will summarize the differences at the end of this section.

Every individual of the GP search process is a tree τ, where labels of leaf nodes are taken from a specified *terminal set* and labels of internal nodes from a specified *function set* as follows.

The function set consists of the following regular expressions operators (the central dot · represents a placeholder for a child node): *possessive quantifiers* (`·*+`, `·++`, `·?+` and `·{·,·}+`), *group* `(·)`, *character class* `[·]` and *negated character class* `[^·]`, *concatenator* `··`—a binary node which concatenates its children—and *disjunction* `·|·`. We did not include greedy or lazy quantifiers [9] because, as indicated in [3], these operators lead to execution times which are not practically acceptable.

The terminal set consists of a set of terminals which do not depend on the problem instance $\mathcal{I}$ and other terminals which depend on $\mathcal{I}$. Instance independent terminals are: the alphabetical *ranges* `a-z` and `A-Z`, the start of string *anchor* `^` and the end of string anchor `$`, and the *wildcard character* `.`. Instance dependent terminals are: all characters appearing in M, *partial ranges* appearing in M, and *n-grams*.

Partial ranges are obtained as follows. We (i) build the sequence C of all characters appearing in M (without repetitions), sorted according to natural order; (ii) for each maximal subsequence of C which includes *all* characters between subsequence head c_h and tail c_t, build a partial range c_h-c_t. For example, if $M = \{$`bar`, `den`, `foo`, `can`$\}$, then the partial ranges are `a-e` and `n-o`.

n-grams are obtained as follows. We (i) build the set N of all n-grams occurring in M and U strings, with $2 \leq n \leq 4$; (ii) give a score to each n-gram as follows: $+1$ for each string in M which contains the n-gram and -1 for each string U which contains the n-gram; (iii) sort N according to descending score and (iv) select the smallest subset N' of all top-scoring n-grams such that the sum of their scores is at least $|M|$ and each individual score is positive. For example, if $M =$

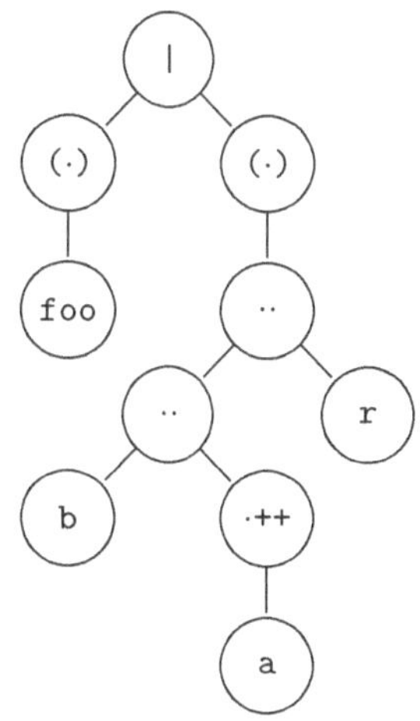

Figure 1: Tree representation of the regular expression `(foo)|(ba++r)`.

$\{$`can`, `banana`, `and`, `ball`$\}$ and $U = \{$`indy`, `call`, `name`, `man`$\}$, then the n-grams are `an` and `ba`, as they are the two top-scoring n-grams and the sum of their scores is $2 + 2$.

A tree τ is transformed into a string r_τ which represents a regular expression by means of a depth-first post order visit—Figure 1 shows an example of a tree and the corresponding regular expression (in the caption). In our implementation, each regular expression is evaluated by the Java regular expression engine, which works with possessive quantifiers. However, the regex golf competition being considered accepts only Javascript-compatible regular expressions and Javascript regular expression engine does not work with possessive quantifiers. Hence, we further transform r_τ into a Javascript-compatible regular expression by means of a mechanical transformation [9].

The initial population is generated as follows. Let $n_P = 500$ be the size of the population to be generated. For each string s in M, we generate an individual corresponding to s, built using only the concatenator node and single characters of s as terminals. We generate the remaining $n_P - |M|$ individuals randomly, with the ramped half-and-half method and depth of 1–5 levels.

We drive the evolutionary search based on two fitness indexes associated with each individual. Let r be an individual and let n_M and n_U be the number of elements in M and U, respectively, which are matched by r. The two fitness indexes are: $n_M - n_U$, which has to be maximized (the upper bound being $|M|$), and the length of r (in the Javascript-compatible version), which has to be minimized. We use the *Non-Dominated Sorting Genetic Algorithm II* (NSGA-II) [8] to rank individuals according to their fitness values.

We evolve the population for a number of generations $n_g = 1000$, according to the following iterative procedure. Let P be the current population. We generate an evolved population P' as follows: 10% of the individuals are generated at random, 10% of the individuals are generated by applying the genetic operator "mutation" to individuals of P, and 80% of the individuals are generated by applying the genetic operator "crossover" to a pair of individuals of P. We select individuals for mutation and crossover with a *tournament* of size 7, i.e., we pick 7 individuals at random and then select the best individual in this set, according to NSGA-

Table 1: **Salient information for the 16 problems.**

<table>
<tr><th></th><th>Problem name</th><th>$|M|$</th><th>$|U|$</th><th>$w_\mathcal{I}$</th><th>Ideal score</th><th>Best human score</th><th>Best human solution</th></tr>
<tr><td>1</td><td>Plain strings</td><td>21</td><td>21</td><td>10</td><td>210</td><td>207</td><td><code>foo</code></td></tr>
<tr><td>2</td><td>Anchors</td><td>21</td><td>21</td><td>10</td><td>210</td><td>208</td><td><code>k$</code></td></tr>
<tr><td>3</td><td>Ranges</td><td>21</td><td>21</td><td>10</td><td>210</td><td>202</td><td><code>^[a-f]*$</code></td></tr>
<tr><td>4</td><td>Backrefs</td><td>21</td><td>21</td><td>10</td><td>210</td><td>201</td><td><code>(...).*\1</code></td></tr>
<tr><td>5</td><td>Abba</td><td>21</td><td>22</td><td>10</td><td>210</td><td>193</td><td><code>^(?!.*(.)(.)\2\1)</code></td></tr>
<tr><td>6</td><td>A man, a plan</td><td>19</td><td>21</td><td>10</td><td>190</td><td>177</td><td><code>^(.)[^p].*$</code></td></tr>
<tr><td>7</td><td>Prime</td><td>20</td><td>20</td><td>15</td><td>300</td><td>286</td><td><code>^(?!(..+)\1$</code></td></tr>
<tr><td>8</td><td>Four</td><td>21</td><td>21</td><td>10</td><td>210</td><td>199</td><td><code>(.)(.\1){3}</code></td></tr>
<tr><td>9</td><td>Order</td><td>21</td><td>21</td><td>10</td><td>210</td><td>199</td><td><code>^.5[^e]?$</code></td></tr>
<tr><td>10</td><td>Triples</td><td>21</td><td>21</td><td>30</td><td>630</td><td>596</td><td><code>00($|3|6|9|12|15)|4.2|.1.+4|55|.17</code></td></tr>
<tr><td>11</td><td>Glob</td><td>21</td><td>21</td><td>20</td><td>420</td><td>397</td><td><code>ai|c$|^p|[bcnrw][bnopr]</code></td></tr>
<tr><td>12</td><td>Balance</td><td>32</td><td>32</td><td>10</td><td>320</td><td>289</td><td><code>^(<(<(<(<<?>?>|.9)>)>)>)$</code></td></tr>
<tr><td>13</td><td>Powers</td><td>11</td><td>11</td><td>10</td><td>110</td><td>93</td><td><code>^(?!(.(..)+)\1*$)</code></td></tr>
<tr><td>14</td><td>Long count</td><td>1</td><td>20</td><td>270</td><td>270</td><td>254</td><td><code>((.+)0 \2?1){7}</code></td></tr>
<tr><td>15</td><td>Long count v2</td><td>1</td><td>21</td><td>270</td><td>270</td><td>254</td><td><code>((.+)0 \2?1){7}</code></td></tr>
<tr><td>16</td><td>Alphabetical</td><td>17</td><td>17</td><td>20</td><td>340</td><td>317</td><td><code>.r.{32}r|a.{10}te|n.n..</code></td></tr>
<tr><td></td><td>Total</td><td></td><td></td><td></td><td>4320</td><td>4072</td><td></td></tr>
</table>

II. Finally, we generate the next population by choosing the individuals with highest fitness among those in P and P'. The size of the population is kept constant during the evolution. Upon generation of a new individual, we check the syntactic correctness of the corresponding expression: if the check fails, we discard the individual and generate a new one.

In order to generate a solution for a problem instance $\mathcal{I}$, we evolve $n_e = 32$ independent populations, with different random seeds, obtaining 32 candidate regular expressions. Finally, we choose the regular expression with the highest score.

We remark the key features of our proposal (w.r.t. [3]):

1. a method for constructing the terminal set based on the problem instance $\mathcal{I}$, rather than being defined once and for all;
2. a method for initializing the population based on the problem instance $\mathcal{I}$, rather than being completely random;
3. a different functions set which includes, in particular, a disjunction operator—which is difficult to use in text extraction because it tends to promote overfitting;
4. fitness definitions based on the number of examples handled correctly—definitions proven to be inadequate for text extraction [3];
5. usage of all learning information for synthesizing candidate solutions, that is, without reserving any partition as validation set for assessing the generalization capabilities of those solutions.

5. EXPERIMENTAL EVALUATION

We considered the 16 problem instances along with the accompanying scores proposed in **http://regex.alf.nu**. Salient properties of these instances are summarized in Table 1. The table shows, for each problem instance, the ideal score—i.e., the score equal to $w_\mathcal{I}|M|$ which could be obtained with a zero-length regular expression matching all strings in M and no strings in U. The table also shows, for each problem instance, the highest score obtained by (different) human players[3].

5.1 Baseline

We used as baseline the algorithm by Peter Norvig, which we call Norvig-RegexGolf, and the system for generating regular expressions for text extraction presented in [3], which we call GP-RegexExtract.

We provide a brief outline of Norvig-RegexGolf below. Full details, including the (partially for fun) motivations and design trade-offs can be found in [16]. The solution for a given problem instance $\mathcal{I} = (M, U)$ is obtained as a disjunction of a set of *components*, a component being a short regular expression which matches at least one string in M and does not match any string in U. Initially, a pool of components is built with several heuristics, including the generation of a component for each n-gram of each string in M (up to n=4) and, for each such component, the generation of a component for every possible substitution of a single character with the dot character (meaning "match any" in regular expression syntax). Next a set of components from that pool is built, such that each string in M is matched by at least one component in the set. Components in the resulting set are then glued together by the or regular expression operator `|`.

Concerning GP-RegexExtract, we reimplemented the algorithm according to the details presented in [3] (see also Section 2). We set those parameters which determine the computational weight of GP to the same values for GP-RegexExtract and GP-RegexGolf, in order to allow a fair comparison of the results w.r.t. computational weight: $n_e = 32$, $n_g = 500$ and $n_P = 500$. Note that GP-RegexExtract requires that examples are partitioned in a training set and a validation set: while using it as a regex golf player, we chose to use half of M and half of U strings as training set, and the remaining string as validation set.

5.2 Results

[3]The information is obtained from **https://gist.github.com/jonathanmorley/8058871**.

We executed each of the algorithms on each problem instance and computed the score of the corresponding solution. Table 2 summarizes the resulting scores, which are presented as absolute value and as the percentage of the ideal and the best human score associated with each problem instance. Table 3 shows the regular expressions generated by GP-RegexGolf for each problem.

It can be seen that GP-RegexGolf outperforms both Norvig-RegexGolf and GP-RegexExtract: 3090 vs. −665 and 249, respectively. In particular, considering individual problem instances, GP-RegexGolf performs better than Norvig-RegexGolf in 6 problems, worse in 8 problems and obtains the same score in 2 problems. Despite obtaining a better score in 8 problems, Norvig-RegexGolf obtains a negative score on the full suite because on three problems (7, 12 and 13) it is not able to generate a non trivial solution: in these problems, the regular expression generated by Norvig-RegexGolf is the disjunction of all the M strings. Our algorithm, on the contrary, generates non trivial solutions for these problems. Concerning GP-RegexExtract, both its score on the full suite and its score on individual instances make it clear that this approach does not the requirements of regex golf.

Table 2 lists also, for each algorithm, the *competitive ratio* of the solutions [16], defined as the ratio between the length of a trivial solution (disjoining all the strings in M) and the length of the corresponding solution. Note that this index does not take matches or unmatches into account. It can be seen that both Norvig-RegexGolf and GP-RegexGolf generate solutions which are much shorter than the trivial solution for several problems: regular expressions generated by GP-RegexGolf are shorter than those of Norvig-RegexGolf in 9 problems, longer in 5 problems and with the same length in 2 problems.

Table 4 shows the time required by GP-RegexGolf and GP-RegexExtract for generating a solution. It is similar for all the problems (around 50 min) with the exception of 13, 14 and 15. For the latter problems, in which M is composed by very long strings, GP-RegexExtract attempts to generate a regular expression which extracts (rather than just matching) the each M string entirely: this leads to a population composed by very long regular expressions which require long times to be evaluated. The time required by Norvig-RegexGolf is practically negligible (less than a second per problem). All the experiments have been performed on a quad core Intel Xeon E5-2440 (2.40GHz) with 4 GB of RAM.

We wanted to investigate whether our approach can achieve better scores at the expense of increased computational weight. To this end, we repeated the experiments by setting $n_P = 1000$ and $n_P = 1500$, i.e., with an enlarged population: Table 5 shows the results in terms of score and competitive ratio. It can be seen that the full score does improve for larger values of n_P. Moreover, with $n_P = 1500$, the number of problems for which GP-RegexGolf score is not worse than Norvig-RegexGolf score is 11 vs. 8 with $n_P = 500$. The computation time for the full suite goes from 820 min for $n_P = 500$ to 1551 min and 2611 min for $n_p = 1000$ and $n_p = 1500$, respectively. As expected, with higher values for n_P GP-RegexGolf takes longer to generate a solution: yet, it is fair to claim that even such longer times may be acceptable for playing to a game of this kind.

Finally, we attempted to assess the performance of our proposal with respect to scores of highly skilled human players. We remark that there are several caveat concerning the

Table 4: Execution times of GP-RegexGolf and GP-RegexExtract algorithms in minutes.

Problem	GP-RegexGolf	GP-RegexExtract
1	53	51
2	52	52
3	53	65
4	38	25
5	34	18
6	20	23
7	33	43
8	19	27
9	46	21
10	45	25
11	44	47
12	56	71
13	71	269
14	94	289
15	95	173
16	66	64
Total	820	1262

Table 5: Scores and competitive ratio (C.R.) of GP-RegexGolf with different values for n_P.

	$n_P = 1000$		$n_P = 1500$	
Problem	Score	C.R.	Score	C.R.
1	207	66.3	207	66.3
2	208	105.5	208	105.5
3	196	11.5	197	12.4
4	146	5.2	147	6.5
5	188	12.5	186	11.5
6	142	6.0	151	4.3
7	188	24.1	188	24.1
8	183	11.7	180	10.5
9	190	8.7	190	8.7
10	456	10.5	354	27.2
11	355	28.2	522	3.2
12	36	7.3	223	26.5
13	65	46.2	40	29.7
14	191	1.0	191	1.0
15	191	1.0	191	1.0
16	259	21.1	237	10.4
Total	3201	-	3412	-

Table 2: Results of the three algorithms as score, score %, score % w.r.t. to best human score and competitive ratio (C.R., see text). For each problem, the score of the best algorithm is shown in bold.

	Norvig-RegexGolf				GP-RegexGolf				GP-RegexExtract			
Problem	Score	Score %	Hum. %	C.R.	Score	Score %	Hum. %	C.R.	Score	Score %	Hum. %	C.R.
1	**207**	98.6	100.0	66.3	**207**	98.6	100.0	66.3	170	81.0	82.1	5.0
2	**208**	99.1	100.0	105.5	**208**	99.1	100.0	105.5	185	88.1	88.9	8.4
3	191	91.0	94.6	8.5	**195**	92.9	96.5	10.7	107	51.0	53.0	7.0
4	**175**	83.3	87.0	8.0	138	65.7	68.7	6.7	−70	<0	<0	4.0
5	**186**	88.6	96.4	11.5	184	87.6	95.3	17.2	77	36.7	39.9	4.4
6	**157**	82.6	88.7	5.1	136	71.6	76.8	7.0	−246	<0	<0	0.7
7	−398	<0	<0	1.0	**188**	35.3	37.0	24.1	−52	<0	<0	13.4
8	**192**	91.4	96.5	17.5	183	87.1	92.0	11.7	−45	<0	<0	7.0
9	**190**	90.5	95.5	8.7	186	88.6	93.5	7.3	−39	<0	<0	4.5
10	**589**	93.5	98.8	6.1	430	68.3	72.2	12.6	−106	<0	<0	2.4
11	**392**	93.3	98.7	25.2	340	81.0	85.6	17.7	−163	<0	<0	4.3
12	−1457	<0	<0	1.0	**130**	40.6	45.0	11.1	−85	<0	<0	20.9
13	−1969	<0	<0	1.0	**51**	46.4	54.8	109.4	−47	<0	<0	44.2
14	189	70.0	74.4	1.0	**191**	70.7	75.2	1.0	**191**	70.7	75.2	1.0
15	189	70.0	74.4	1.0	**191**	70.7	75.2	1.0	**191**	70.7	75.2	1.0
16	**294**	86.5	92.7	18.8	132	38.8	41.6	8.0	181	53.2	57.1	11.0
Total	−665	-	-	-	**3090**	-	-	-	249	-	-	-

Table 3: Regular expressions generated by GP-RegexGolf.

Problem	Regular expression
1	`foo`
2	`k$`
3	`(^..[a-f][a-f])`
4	`v|[^b][^o][^p]t|ngo|lo|[n]o|rp|rb|ro|ro|rf`
5	`z|.u|nv|st|ca|it`
6	`oo|x|^k|ed|^m|ah|^r|v|^t`
7	`^(?=((?:x[A-Zx])+))\1x`
8	`ell|j|W|ele|o.o|Ma|si|de|do`
9	`ch|[l-p]o|ad|fi|ac|ty|os`
10	`24|55|02|54|00|95|17`
11	`lo|ro|^p|(?=((c)+))\1r|en|^w|y.|le|^p|rr`
12	`((?=((?:<<\>\>\>)*))\2(?=((?:<<<(?=(<*))\4\>\><<<<)*))\3(?=((?:<<<<<\>\>\>(?=(<*))\6\>\>\>)*))` `\5(?=((?:<<<<<<)*))\7^(?=((?:<<\><<)*))\8(?=((?:<<<\>\>\>)*))\9<<)`
13	`^(?=(((x|^)x)+))\1$`
14	`0000 0001 0010 0011 0100 0101 0110 0111 1000 1001 1010 1011 1100 1101 1110 1111`
15	`0000 0001 0010 0011 0100 0101 0110 0111 1000 1001 1010 1011 1100 1101 1110 1111`
16	`tena|[^et][^etren](?=((?:(?:ren|eren.(?=((?:(?:ren|[^ren]))+))\2|eren.(?=((?:(?:ren|` `[^ren]))+))\3))+))\1|eas`

assessment of the results obtained by human players. The web site hosting the challenge does not, at the time of this writing, provide a score ranking computed on the full suite of problems—on the other hand, there exists a collection of "Best possible answers collected so far for regex golf" (see Table 1) which shows, for each problem, the best solution. Results by human players are advertised on web forums by players themselves, often without providing any actual evidence of their results. On the other hand, there are players which do make some very good solutions publicly available, thereby simplifying the job of other players, which may either attempt to improve those solutions further or may use them for the corresponding problem instance while focusing their efforts on the remaining instances. In other words, the score obtained by a given player may actually result from efforts by multiple players. Finally, human players generally do not care to indicate the time they spent for generating a solution.

We collected several human players scores on the full suite from different web locations (including Reddit, Hacker News, Github) which we obtained by querying Google and Twitter with the search string "regex golf". Table 6 shows the 10 best scores we found, along with the total ideal score (i.e., the sum of ideal scores on the 16 problems), the best human score (i.e., the sum of the highest human player scores on the 16 problems) and the score of the three considered algorithms.

It can be seen that GP-RegexGolf would rank from 6th to 8th among human players (with $n_P = 1500$ and $n_P = 500$, respectively), whereas the scores of the other two algorithms are significantly lower than those of human players. In other words, leaving aside any caveat about how we gathered human scores, GP-RegexGolf is in the top ten of worldwide regex golf players.

6. CONCLUDING REMARKS

We have proposed and assessed experimentally an approach based on Genetic Programming for playing regex golf automatically, i.e., for generating automatically solutions to challenges which have recently become popular in the programmers' communities. The challenges consist in writing

Table 6: Total scores obtained by the 10 best humans and by the three algorithms.

	Player	Score
	Total ideal score	4320
	Best human score	4072
1	geniusleonid	4006
2	k_hanazuki	3785
3	bisqwit	3753
4	AlanDeSmet	3736
5	adamhiker	3693
	GP-RegexGolf ($n_P = 1500$)	3412
	GP-RegexGolf ($n_P = 1000$)	3201
6	adamschwartz	3181
7	flyingmeteor	3171
	GP-RegexGolf ($n_P = 500$)	3090
8	jpsim	3060
9	ItsIllak	2939
10	bg666	2683
	GP-RegexExtract	249
	Norvig-RegexGolf	−665

the shortest regular expression that matches all strings in a given list and does not match any string in another given list.

Our approach collects a score that is highly competitive against human players and improve significantly over a challenging baseline including a recently proposed algorithm tailored to this specific problem class and a recent proposal for automatic generation of regular expressions tailored to text extraction tasks. The time for generating a solution is in the order of tens of minutes and a prototype is available at `http://regex.inginf.units.it/golf`.

We think that our work shows how a GP-based approach running on modern IT machinery may deliver results, at least for this task, which are practically useful and can compete with humans.

7. REFERENCES

[1] D.F. Barrero, David Camacho, and M.D. R-Moreno. Automatic Web Data Extraction Based on Genetic Algorithms and Regular Expressions. *Data Mining and Multi-agent Integration*, pages 143–154, 2009.

[2] A. Bartoli, G. Davanzo, A. De Lorenzo, M. Mauri, E. Medvet, and E. Sorio. Automatic generation of regular expressions from examples with genetic programming. In *International Conference on Genetic and evolutionary computation*, pages 1477–1478. ACM, 2012.

[3] A. Bartoli, G. Davanzo, A. De Lorenzo, E. Medvet, and E. Sorio. Automatic synthesis of regular expressions from examples. *Computer*, Early Access Online, 2013.

[4] Josh Bongard and Hod Lipson. Active coevolutionary learning of deterministic finite automata. *The Journal of Machine Learning Research*, 6:1651–1678, 2005.

[5] Falk Brauer, Robert Rieger, Adrian Mocan, and W.M. Barczynski. Enabling information extraction by inference of regular expressions from sample entities. In *ACM International Conference on Information and knowledge management*, pages 1285–1294. ACM, 2011.

[6] Ahmet Cetinkaya. Regular expression generation through grammatical evolution. In *International Conference on Genetic and evolutionary computation*, GECCO, pages 2643–2646, New York, NY, USA, 2007. ACM.

[7] Orlando Cicchello and Stefan C Kremer. Inducing grammars from sparse data sets: a survey of algorithms and results. *The Journal of Machine Learning Research*, 4:603–632, 2003.

[8] K. Deb, A. Pratap, S. Agarwal, and T. Meyarivan. A fast and elitist multiobjective genetic algorithm: Nsga-ii. *IEEE Transactions on Evolutionary Computation*, 6(2):182 –197, apr 2002.

[9] Jeffrey Friedl. *Mastering Regular Expressions.* O'Reilly Media, Inc., 2006.

[10] Pedro García, Manuel Vázquez de Parga, Gloria I. Álvarez, and José Ruiz. Universal automata and {nfa} learning. *Theoretical Computer Science*, 407(1–3):192 – 202, 2008.

[11] Sumit Gulwani. Automating string processing in spreadsheets using input-output examples. In *Proceedings of the 38th Annual ACM SIGPLAN-SIGACT Symposium on Principles of Programming Languages*, POPL '11, pages 317–330, New York, NY, USA, 2011. ACM.

[12] Efim Kinber. Learning regular expressions from representative examples and membership queries. *Grammatical Inference: Theoretical Results and Applications*, pages 94–108, 2010.

[13] Yunyao Li, Rajasekar Krishnamurthy, Sriram Raghavan, Shivakumar Vaithyanathan, and Ann Arbor. Regular Expression Learning for Information Extraction. *Computational Linguistics*, (October):21–30, 2008.

[14] Simon M Lucas and T Jeff Reynolds. Learning deterministic finite automata with a smart state labeling evolutionary algorithm. *IEEE Transactions on Pattern Analysis and Machine Intelligence*, 27(7):1063–1074, 2005.

[15] Aditya Menon, Omer Tamuz, Sumit Gulwani, Butler Lampson, and Adam Kalai. A machine learning framework for programming by example. In *Proceedings of the 30th International Conference on Machine Learning (ICML-13)*, pages 187–95, 2013.

[16] Peter Norvig. xkcd 1313: Regex golf. `http://nbviewer.ipython.org/url/norvig.com/ipython/xkcd1313.ipynb`, January 2014.

[17] Wojciech Wieczorek. Induction of non-deterministic finite automata on supercomputers. *Journal of Machine Learning Research-Proceedings Track*, 21:237–242, 2012.

[18] Tianhao Wu and W.M. Pottenger. A semi-supervised active learning algorithm for information extraction from textual data. *Journal of the American Society for Information Science and Technology*, 56(3):258–271, 2005.

The Tradeoffs between Data Delivery Ratio and Energy Costs in Wireless Sensor Networks: A Multi-Objective Evolutionary Framework for Protocol Analysis*

Doina Bucur
University of Groningen
Nijenborgh 9, 9747 AG
Groningen, The Netherlands
d.bucur@rug.nl

Giovanni Iacca
INCAS[3]
Dr. Nassaulaan 9, 9401 HJ
Assen, The Netherlands
giovanniiacca@incas3.eu

Giovanni Squillero
Politecnico di Torino
C.so D. d. Abruzzi 24, 10129
Torino, Italy
giovanni.squillero@polito.it

Alberto Tonda
INRA UMR 782 GMPA
1 Av. L. Brétignières, 78850
Thiverval-Grignon, France
alberto.tonda@grignon.inra.fr

ABSTRACT

Wireless sensor network (WSN) routing protocols, e.g., the Collection Tree Protocol (CTP), are designed to adapt in an ad-hoc fashion to the quality of the environment. WSNs thus have high internal dynamics and complex global behavior. Classical techniques for performance evaluation (such as testing or verification) fail to uncover the cases of extreme behavior which are most interesting to designers. We contribute a practical framework for performance evaluation of WSN protocols. The framework is based on multi-objective optimization, coupled with protocol simulation and evaluation of performance factors. For evaluation, we consider the two crucial functional and non-functional performance factors of a WSN, respectively: the ratio of data delivery from the network (DDR), and the total energy expenditure of the network (COST). We are able to discover network topological configurations over which CTP has unexpectedly low DDR and/or high COST performance, and expose full Pareto fronts which show what the possible performance tradeoffs for CTP are in terms of these two performance factors. Eventually, Pareto fronts allow us to bound the state space of the WSN, a fact which provides essential knowledge to WSN protocol designers.

Categories and Subject Descriptors

C.2.2 [**Computer-Communication Networks**]: Network Protocols—*Protocol verification, Routing protocols*; C.4 [**Performance of Systems**]: [Design studies]; G.1.6 [**Numerical Analysis**]: Optimization—*Global optimization*

General Terms

Performance, Algorithms

Keywords

Evolutionary Algorithms; Multi-objective Optimization; Wireless Sensor Networks; Collection Tree Protocol; Performance Evaluation; Ad-hoc Routing; Data Delivery Ratio; Energy Consumption

*All authors contributed equally and their names are presented in alphabetical order.

GECCO'14, July 12–16, 2014, Vancouver, BC, Canada.
Copyright 2014 ACM 978-1-4503-2662-9/14/07 ...$15.00.
http://dx.doi.org/10.1145/2576768.2598384.

1. INTRODUCTION

Wireless sensor networks (WNSs) are distributed, energy-constrained – often battery powered – self-organizing systems most often employed for autonomous data collection in challenging communication environments, as part of monitoring applications in nature or industry. WSNs are paradigmatic examples of complex systems embedded in the environment: while each node in the network is a constrained embedded system, the global behavior of the network depends upon the physical *topology* of the network (i.e., the set of viable wireless communication links) and upon the *environmental conditions* (e.g., the pattern of added environmental noise which can impede wireless communication between nodes). It is important to understand precisely which type of topology combined with which type of environmental conditions may cause a WSN infrastructure to fail at its task.

The performance evaluation of WSN routing protocols is extremely difficult, since protocol designers have very limited information about the cause of any malfunction which occurred in a remote deployment: "We frequently failed to understand performance results and could not determine who was to blame (i.e., the testbed characteristics, or the routing layer?)" [17]. Some WSN protocols which performed well in controlled environments had as low as 2% data delivery in the field [9, 26]. An inability to reproduce faulty scenarios was also stated: "it is unclear why collection performs well in controlled situations yet poorly in practice, even at low data rates" [14].

This lack of understanding is not surprising. WSN testing is often done on indoor WSN testbeds [4, 14], which form well-connected networks unlikely to reproduce the type of communication interruptions encountered later in environmental deployments. Furthermore, "experimental results obtained on a single testbed are very difficult to generalize" [17]. Since worst-case scenarios are statistically rare events in the state-space of the problem, non-exhaustive methods, such as testbed analysis [14, 22] or random testing, are likely to miss them.

A semi-automatic method to generate worst-case data-throughput scenarios for a *model* of the IEEE 802.11 MAC protocol was proposed in [3]. The approach is based on a search algorithm through the state-space of an abstract model in state-machine syntax; the modeling makes some simplifying assumptions for some system features, which is a disadvantage of the method. On the other hand, using formal verification for analyzing full *implementations* of protocols is computationally prohibitive, and has met with limited success [21, 27]. At best, it succeeds in identifying unsafe behavior of a WSN protocol in a few concrete, small-size WSN topologies, which makes it impossible to generalize the cause of the behavior.

Recently, Evolutionary Algorithms (EAs) were proven to be an effective technique for protocol analysis in WSNs, as a means to create the network configurations required for exploiting simulation-based techniques [1, 2, 5, 6]. In [5, 6], WSNs were analyzed against a single performance metric: the lifetime of a WSN routing protocol. This metric was used as evaluator for the "interestingness" of network configurations, and served to generate sets of interesting examples of critical WSN topologies with unexpectedly low lifetime. Earlier, [1] presented a seminal work on the use of an evolutionary algorithm for generating a critical test case for a simplified TCP/IP network. In [2], the authors do a search of the state space of a particular WSN application for fire detection, using a fitness function designed such that it guides the search algorithm towards WSN situations in which not only the system fails to detect a fire, but does so because of a minimal number of node failures caused by the environment.

Applying evolutionary computation to verification and testing has also been explored in other domains. Preliminary experiments in [25] suggest that stochastic meta-heuristics are effective in locating the most promising parts of the search space to test complex software modules. A flight system software is verified in [23], where a genetic algorithm outperforms classical random testing. In [13], the operating system of a mobile phone prototype is tested with evolved keyboard inputs, uncovering several power-related bugs.

This work extends the scope of EA-guided WSN performance evaluation by considering multiple fitness values to uncover multi-dimensional performance bounds, and using a *Multi-Objective Evolutionary Algorithm* (MOEA) to solve the associated optimization problem. Such analysis deepens the practical lessons to be learned by WSN designers compared to the single-metric cases previously found in the literature, by providing a complex, heterogeneous set of misbehaving network topologies.

Our experiments focus on the Collection Tree Protocol (CTP) [14] and its mainstream full implementation in the TinyOS [19] embedded operating system; while analyzing the implementation of the protocol, rather than an abstract model of it, adds to the complexity of the problem, it has the great advantage that the results of the analysis can immediately be translated into practical knowledge. To evaluate the performance of CTP, we consider two fitness functions, namely (1) the ratio of data packets delivered successfully by the network (i.e., the most important functional requirement of a WSN), and (2) the energy consumed from the nodes' batteries in the process (i.e., the most important non-functional requirement). By obtaining WSN configurations which maximize or minimize both metrics at the same time, we can draw practical conclusions about the *performance tradeoffs* of the network.

The remaining of this paper is organized as follows: Section 2 summarizes WSN concepts, Section 3 presents the design of our multi-objective search framework, and experimentation is reported in Section 4. Conclusions and future work are outlined in Section 5.

2. WSN DESIGN AND ANALYSIS

This section gives an overview of the design, complexity, and performance factors of the WSN data collection protocol under study.

2.1 Data collection with WSNs

In a WSN, each node is a small, wireless embedded system with limited memory, computation power, communication bandwidth, and available energy. The physical topology of the wireless network typically exhibits heavy link dynamics due to various changes in the environmental conditions. The nodes are deployed at locations of interest and will sense, store and forward data wirelessly to a *sink* node. The sink node has a more reliable connection to data storage, and will forward all collected data.

For successful data collection, WSNs employ ad-hoc collection routing protocols, which form the basic underlying infrastructure to many WSN applications. WSN collection routing aims at adaptively organizing the nodes for data collection into a multi-hop, cycle-free spanning tree rooted in the sink node. In order to design adaptive routing, all nodes broadcast to their immediate neighbors *beacon* messages containing the nodes' local routing knowledge, thus allowing these neighbors to (i) update their estimation of the quality of communication links in the neighborhood, and (ii) extend their routing knowledge with that of the neighbors. On the basis of this, a protocol will then do adaptive route selection, i.e., will choose the route to forward packets based on the current quality of known routes to sink.

Among the distance-vector collection routing mechanisms applied to WSNs, CTP [14] is the de facto standard: it builds on the concept of combining the basic distance-vector, beacon-based mechanism by adding adaptive beacon intervals, designed to broadcast beacons more often in order to quickly reconstruct the routing tree when the network is changing. The combination of heavy link dynamics, continuous link-quality estimation, adaptive beaconing, and adaptive route selection makes CTP a quite complex subject suitable for our analysis. Given that CTP is widely deployed in battery-powered testbeds for environmental, medical or infrastructure monitoring [7, 16, 26], it is also of practical importance that its performance tradeoffs be known.

2.2 Quality metrics for WSN data collection

A number of performance metrics are crucial when analyzing a WSN collection protocol in any environmental configurations. *Functional* performance metrics assess the overall ability of the protocol to deliver all the data packets to the sink node; *non-functional* metrics evaluate how efficiently (in terms of, e.g., delay or energy consumption) data collection is done. Here, we select two critical quality metrics:

1. The *data delivery ratio* (DDR) is the main functional performance metric. This metric is calculated as the fraction of unique data packets sent by all nodes which are received successfully at the sink node.
2. The *total energy cost* (COST) spent in (a) organizing and maintaining a routing tree using beacon messages, and (b) forwarding data packets towards the sink. This is the basic non-functional metric, and is evaluated here via a roughly equivalent heuristic: the total number of network messages sent and received on the network during the interval of experimentation.

In order to uncover novel worst cases for the performance of CTP, we aim to find not only the single worst possible values for DDR or COST, but also more elusive information about the interplay between these performance factors:

- Does DDR generally correlate positively with COST, as intuitively expected from routing protocols, where heavier network communication is expected to lead to better data delivery?
- For an observed value of DDR, what are the upper and lower bounds of COST values over all possible real-world network situations?

To answer these questions, we need to search for those extreme network topologies and environmental conditions which give a performance tradeoff between the network energy consumption and the data delivery ratio. In effect, we need to obtain the *bounds* of the *two-dimensional state space* created by these performance metrics. As we will show in Section 3, this problem can be intuitively formulated in terms of multi-objective optimization, thus representing a natural, yet unconventional, application of MOEAs.

2.3 WSN simulation: stochasticity, topology, and noise injection

We use the open-source simulator TOSSIM [20] to evaluate CTP over different WSNs. TOSSIM is a discrete-event simulator which allows the definition of a controlled WSN environment. It guarantees high-fidelity simulations, from the level of hardware interrupts up to application-level events. Also, it provides a complete Python API which allows full control over the simulation, as well as the collection of the statistics needed for our performance analysis.

In Table 1, we summarize the configuration we use for simulation. We consider dense topologies of 20 nodes booting at simulation time 0; there is randomness in the network stack purposely designed for concurrent boots not to cause network collisions due to synchronicity. Each topology is simulated for 200 seconds, i.e., much longer than the time needed for CTP to form a routing tree (which is less than 1 second [14]), and data packets to be routed to sink. In particular, each node samples an on-board sensor every second, and after bundling 5 readings, forwards them to the sink.

A viable link between two nodes is that which assumes any value above -110 dBm (a threshold particular to the modelling of radio-frequency communication in TOSSIM). We thus have two intervals of interest for the quality (i.e., signal gain) of any network link:

- *strong link*, with a signal gain between -100 and 0 dBm;
- *no link*, modeled with a fixed gain of -200 dBm.

WSNs are affected by a number of stochastic effects, including *noise* on the radio frequencies used for communication, interference among the nodes themselves, packet collision, etc. TOSSIM provides an accurate model of the mainstream radio stack. In addition to that, to further improve the realism of the simulation (e.g., taking into account bursts of interference) it is possible to add a statistical *noise model* over the original links' signal gains. This model is generated automatically from a trace measured experimentally in real-world testbeds, with the generation algorithm based on Closest Pattern Matching [18]. In our experiments, we used two noise traces: one of *light*, and one of *heavy* noise (the `meyer-short` trace available with TOSSIM).

Table 1: Configuration of simulation variables.

Simulation setting	Value
Network size, density	20 nodes, 50%
Sink node	node 0
Simulation time	200 seconds
Rate of data packets	every 5 seconds

A noise model is injected into a simulation by TOSSIM as described in Fig. 1: while a link between two given nodes will be modelled with a fixed signal gain value, a given noise pattern is superimposed to all the links in the network. If the amplitude of the noise gain is higher than that of the signal gain for any time interval, then for that interval the data link becomes unusable. The heavy noise model that we use has peaks of amplitude reaching -40 dBm.

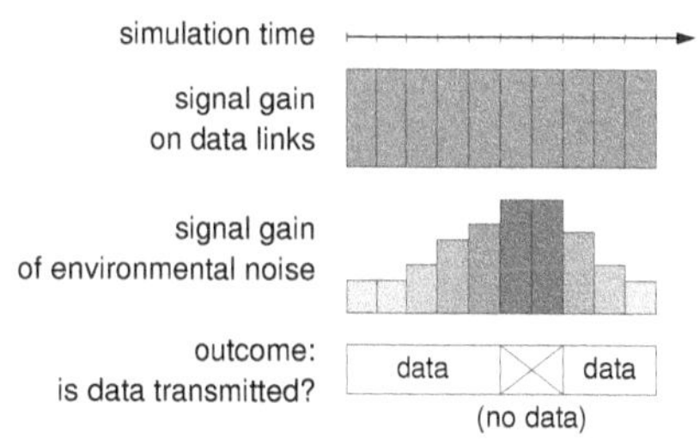

Figure 1: TOSSIM technique for simulating noise on radio frequencies.

Due to these stochastic effects, in order to compute a statistically meaningful value for the WSN performance factors, each evaluated WSN topology is simulated multiple times with different random seeds. Since the standard error of the mean of an n-dimensional sample whose variance is σ is $\sigma/\sqrt{n}$, and applying the central limit theorem to approximate the sample mean with a normal distribution, a sample size $n = 16\sigma^2/W^2$ guarantees a 95% confidence interval of width W. Thus, in order to guarantee confidence interval $W = \sigma$ regardless of the actual value of σ (which is not constant in the search space) we always run $n = 16$ simulations per each WSN evaluation.

2.4 The size of the search space

For WSNs of 20 nodes with a 50% density of strong links, the search space of our problem is defined by the variables listed in Table 2.

Table 2: Variables used and their definition domain.

Variables	Domain of definition for each
380 links	{strong links, no links}
190 strong links	{0} or {-100, -80, -60, -40, -20, 0} dBm
noise model	{light, heavy}

We thus estimate the size of the search space as follows: 10^{113} different combinations exist of choosing 190 strong links out of the total 380 possible links in the network; this is thus the size of the state space for networks with a single gain value for strong links, and with light noise. In the experiments where we inject heavy communication noise, we need to multiply this number by the 6 different gain values which may be given to any strong link (see subsection 3.1).

3. A MULTI-OBJECTIVE PERSPECTIVE

Many real-life optimization problems have more than one aspect to be considered at the same time, i.e., more than one objective to be minimized or maximized. A possible solution (the *scalarization* approach) is to aggregate all objectives into a single function, e.g., through a weighted sum. As an alternative (the *lexicographical* approach), a domain expert might prioritize the objectives according to some order of preference, so that these objectives are evaluated following that predefined order. In both cases, however, an implicit bias is introduced in the problem, that might be harmful, especially if the objectives are conflicting. Moreover, such approaches are not usually able to provide a full set of tradeoff solutions, but rather they tend to offer a few solutions (perhaps only a single solution), which are often not homogeneously distributed in the objective space.

Unlike the fitness scalarization and lexicographical approaches, Multi-Objective Evolutionary Algorithms [10] are based on the assumption that all the objectives of a problem should be considered at the same time. In other words, in order to capture the complexity of the search space of two conflicting objectives, an algorithm cannot provide a single optimal solution, but rather should generate a *Pareto front*, that is, a set of *non-dominated* solutions such that none of the objective functions can be further improved without degrading some other objective value. The user is thus presented a set of optimal solutions, each one corresponding to a different tradeoff between different, conflicting goals. Due to their versatility, EAs have proven a valid tool for solving many hard, real-world multi-objective problems [8].

3.1 Individual description

In our problem, an individual (depicted in Fig. 2) represents a candidate topology of the WSN, encoded as a square matrix $N \times N$, with $N = 20$ the number of nodes in the network. Each position i, j in the matrix holds the gain of the signal between nodes i and j, expressed in dBm units. It is to note that, given the nature of wireless transmitters and receivers, the matrix should not be symmetrical in the general case. In Fig. 2, in the noiseless case, strong links have 0 dBm gain (green cells, gray in print); absent links are assigned -200 dBm (white cells). In the noisy case, strong links take a gain value from a set (green scale, gray scale in print, with darker cells being higher gains). The diagonal elements (node self-connectivity) are not part of the model.

Since we are also interested into investigating the effect of noise on the link performance, we further discretize the sets of possible gain values, depending on the presence of noise in the network. More specifically, in absence of noise, we assign to strong links a fixed, ideal signal gain of 0 dBm: this can be explained considering that links, in the absence of noise, will have the same relative performance regardless of their actual gain value. On the other hand, in the noisy case, we discretize the set of possible signal gains as {-100, -80, -60, -40, -20, 0} dBm: in this case, depending on the link noise generated by the noise model (as described in subsection 2.3) at a point in time, the link performance will strictly correlate to its gain.

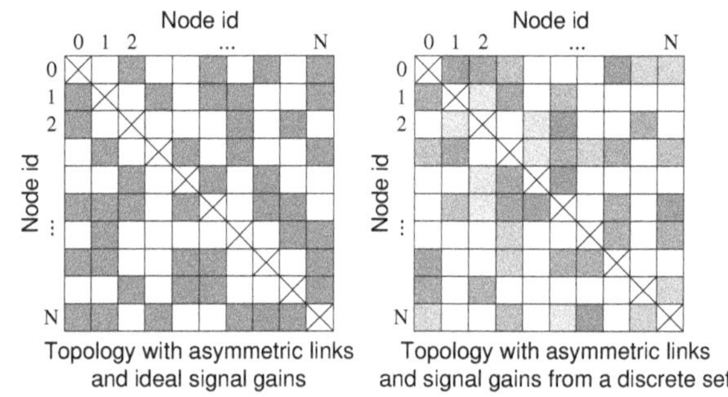

Figure 2: Visual representation of individual encoding. Noiseless case (left); noisy case (right). Shades of green (grey in print) model signal gain values of strong links; white models the absence of links.

From an evolutionary perspective, this kind of encoding translates into the fact that individuals (i.e., candidate network topologies) present two different *alleles* for each *gene* in their genome, i.e., two possible (sets of) values for each link gain value, corresponding respectively to either strong or no links. Mutation operators (see subsection 3.3) can either (a) switch a gene from one allele to the other or, (b) in the case of a finite set of possible gain values (for noisy strong links), tune the allele selecting one of those values. Thus, an individual with a strong link at a given matrix position is *close* (in the parameter search space) to an individual without a link at the same position, regardless of the actual gain of the link. Moreover, an individual without a link contains in its genome the value of the strong link as non-coding material, thus *remembering* it.

Additionally, a user-defined occurrence probability is associated to each allele, so that it is possible to design an initial population where each individual is characterized by a predetermined percentage of strong links.

3.2 Experimental framework

The framework used for the experiments is summed up in Fig. 3: the evolutionary core creates candidate network topologies for TOSSIM. All events of interest on each node (i.e., the sending and receiving of beacons and data packets at each node), are logged during the simulation, and the logs are then processed to obtain the COST and DDR values.

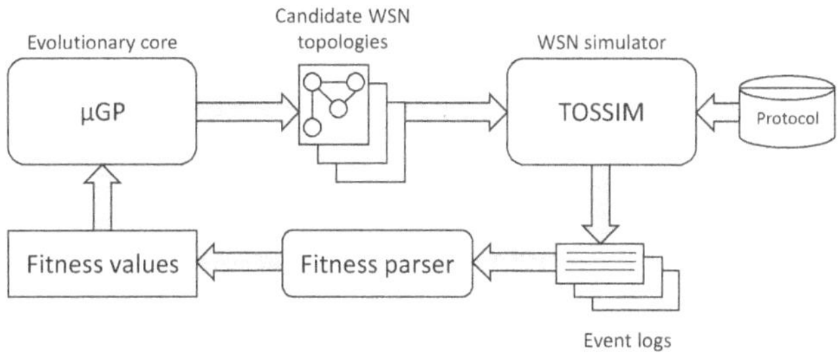

Figure 3: Conceptual scheme of the proposed evolutionary approach.

For our experiments, we specialize a general-purpose MOEA, μGP [24]. Three interesting properties influence our choice: first, since μGP's individuals are represented as a succession of macros with a tunable probability of appearance, it is possible to describe an individual structure such as the one presented in subsection 3.1[1]; second, this EA is capable of managing complex genetic structures, with constant values, integers and reals; and third, the μGP framework can be easily coupled with an external evaluator, which makes the integration with a WSN simulator straightforward.

μGP features built-in support for two or more fitness values, which can be evaluated either in lexicographical order or with a multi-objective approach. The MOEA algorithm makes use of a *crowding distance* metric similar to NSGA-II [12] in order to push the exploration of the Pareto front: for each individual, the closest neighbours are located on the same front in the fitness space; such neighbours are then used as vertices to compute the hypervolume of the resulting cuboid; individuals associated with larger hypervolumes will be favored for reproduction. The underlying idea is that individuals that are the farthest from others are positioned on segments of the Pareto front not yet well explored. By favoring such individuals, an even exploration of the Pareto front is promoted.

3.3 Evolutionary process

The MOEA is executed with the parameter settings shown in Table 3, and the genetic operators listed in Table 4, namely two standard crossover operators (`one-point` and `two-point`), and two mutation operators that act at the level of a single gene. As explained in subsection 3.1, one mutation operator, namely `replacement mutation`, switches one or more genes from one allele to the other (so that an absent link becomes a strong link, and vice versa). On the other hand, `alteration mutation` perturbs on or more genes corresponding to strong links modifying their gains, i.e. selecting one of the other possible values in the predefined range.

[1]It should be noted that such a complex individual structure (characterized by predefined discrete sets for each allele, each one with a user-defined occurrence probability) makes difficult the application of general-purpose state-of-the-art MOEAs, such as NSGA-II [12] or its recent variant NSGA-III [11, 15]. Indeed, although it would be possible to implement such individual structure within NSGA-II/III, these algorithms do not provide natively this kind of flexible encoding, that is crucial to this problem. On the other hand, μGP offers off-the-shelf various encoding schemes, thus requiring a much smaller coding effort on the algorithm implementation, and allowing users to focus on applications rather than algorithmic details.

The latter mutation is effective only in noisy cases, where strong links are associated to a range of 6 possible values (see Table 2).

In addition to that, the algorithm uses a self-adaptation mechanism able to tune the activation of the different genetic operators, and to determine the strength of a mutation operator, thus effectively balancing exploration and exploitation during the evolution. The evolutionary algorithm is configured in such a way that a μ+λ evolution strategy is used. Selection is performed resorting to tournament selection with tournaments of size τ. Each evolutionary process is allotted a computational budget of 1,000 generations.

Table 3: MOEA parameters used.

Param.	Description	Value
μ	population size	40
λ	no. of operators applied at every step	5
τ	size of tournament selection	2
stop	no. of generations allotted	1000

Table 4: Genetic operators used.

Operators	Description
`alteration mutation`	Change one or more integer values to different integer values (strong links, noisy case)
`replacement mutation`	Substitute one or more integer values (strong links) with the constant value modeling an absent link, or vice versa
`one-point crossover`	Standard one-point crossover
`two-point crossover`	Standard two-point crossover

4. EXPERIMENTAL EVALUATION

In order to obtain the bounds of the state space of CTP with regard to the two performance factors, we laid down the possible configurations for the MOEA: since both the DDR and the COST objectives may be either maximized (denoted ↑) and minimized (denoted ↓) in an experiment, four experimental configurations are possible. Two of these configurations uncovered rich, informative Pareto fronts, while the other two yielded legitimate, but trivial Pareto fronts of few distinct points, due to the shape of the state space. In what follows, we report on the informative experiments.

For each of the two informative configurations, we set up two experiments: without and with heavy radio-frequency noise injection. The resulting list of experiments performed is shown in Table 5.

4.1 Parallelization and runtimes

All experiments have been performed on a 32-core Linux machine (Intel(R) Xeon(R) CPUs, 2.00GHz, 128GB RAM), running Ubuntu 12.04.1 LTS. In order to exploit the inherent parallelism of the objective evaluation (for which every simulation is repeated 16 times with different random seeds, as motivated in Section 2.3), we ran pairs of experiments in parallel, each one using 16 cores, so that each individual evaluation was parallelized. The values for COST and DDR obtained from the 16 simulation repetitions were then averaged and passed to the MOEA.

Furthermore, we assessed the repeatability of results by rerunning each experiment configuration (not reported here

Table 5: Configuration of the experiments considered in this study.

Fitness functions maximized (↑) or minimized (↓)	Noise model	Network size	Model for strong links: discrete set of gains (dBm)	% of strong links	No of generations	No of evaluations	Runtime
COST ↑ – DDR ↑	light	20	{0}	50%	1000	5123	~ 18h
COST ↓ – DDR ↓	light	20	{0}	50%	1000	5164	~ 18h
COST ↑ – DDR ↑	heavy	20	{-100, -80, -60, -40, -20, 0}	50%	1000	6652	~ 33h
COST ↓ – DDR ↓	heavy	20	{-100, -80, -60, -40, -20, 0}	50%	1000	6551	~ 20h

due to lack of space) and observing the statistical equivalence of the Pareto fronts obtained on repeated experiments.

With regard to the runtime of the experiments, it should be noted that the runtime of each experiment depends on (a) the signal gain model for strong links, (b) the noise model, (c) the number of topologies thus evaluated in an experiment, and, significantly, (d) it is higher for topologies with high final COST and DDR values, as these are the cases in which the network will generate large numbers of logged events. Hence, COST ↓ – DDR ↓ experiments show shorter runtimes than COST ↑ – DDR ↑, due to the lower number of packets generated by each simulation. On the other hand, experiments with heavy injected noise have longer runtimes than the corresponding noiseless ones, because of the additional overhead introduced by the noise generation. This can be seen also at individual level, where the duration of each single simulation ranges from approximately 18 seconds (heavy noise, COST ↑ – DDR ↑) to $11 - 12$ seconds (remaining cases). Obviously, the individual runtime scales up with the network size: however, since in this study we focused only on 20-nodes networks, we were not interested in studying simulation runtime scalability.

Another important aspect that should be noted is that, in the experiments with heavy injected noise, a higher number of topologies was evaluated. This is due to the stochastic activation of the genetic operators from Table 4 during each generation: indeed, while the number of operators activated per generation is fixed, the type of operators is variable, so that a higher number of crossover activations will generate a higher number of individuals. Moreover, due to the self-adaptation scheme embedded within μGP, the activation probability changes across generations. The MOEA tends to use the crossover operators more intensively in the noisy experiments than the corresponding noiseless experiments, thus generating more individuals. This can be easily explained since the fitness landscape is likely more rugged in the presence of noise, and the fine-tuning caused by mutations may be less effective.

4.2 Pareto fronts for collection routing

The Pareto fronts obtained, for each experimental configuration (after various numbers of generations, including the final count of 1000 generations) are reported in Figures 4 and 5. To be able to answer the question whether a stopping condition at 1000 generations is sufficient to find Pareto fronts, we illustrate not only the final front, but also the first, randomly selected generation, and also the Pareto fronts found after every 100th generation in the experiment.

The figures also show the combined Pareto fronts obtained in the COST ↑ – DDR ↑ and COST ↓ – DDR ↓ experiments for both light (Fig. 4) and heavy injected noise (Fig. 5), so as to give a visual depiction of how all tradeoff topologies are spread over the two search spaces, and thus delineate the search spaces features. It can be seen, for example, that noisy links have a stronger influence on the upper bounds of COST and DDR, while the lower-bound Pareto front for COST and DDR is more robust against noise.

4.3 Practical implications of this study

The importance of our results for WSN protocol designers is manifold. By finding bounds to the two-dimensional performance of CTP, we are able to prove that – surprisingly – this protocol for collection routing has strongly unintuitive performance trends, which may be summarized and used by practitioners as follows:

1. COST and DDR will, in general, *correlate negatively* for CTP.
2. The upper bound of the energy COST in WSN situations with *low* DDR is one order of magnitude *higher* (rather than lower, as expected) than that of WSN situations with near-perfect data delivery ratios. This statement is true regardless of the amplitude of the injected noise.
3. WSN situations which allow for high DDR can only exhibit few COST values from a small interval. On the other hand, WSN situations where DDR is low can exhibit a staggering amount of COST variation.

These results can be an important tool for WSN practitioners: by having this quantitative *model* of the performance bounds for the protocol across the entire space of possible topologies and communication conditions, practitioners can:

- Predict the worst possible performance for a completely uncontrolled WSN testbed; not only can DDR fall to zero, but also the total energy COST of the testbed can rise to an average of 30 radio events per node per second, a number on the basis of which a worst-case lifetime can be predicted for the network.
- Gain visibility into the effect of a network problem in the field. E.g., a practitioner who sees a current global DDR over 95% calculated at the sink can be certain that the current energy COST of the network is under a relatively low average of 7.5 radio events per node per second; on the other hand, if the DDR at the sink is close to zero, there is a possibility that the total COST has currently risen to the upper bound of 30 radio events per node per second, which may require corrective intervention over the testbed.

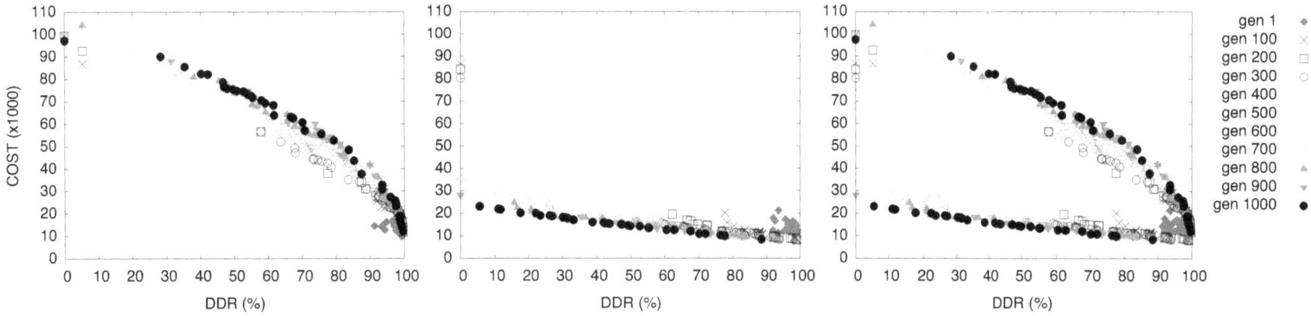

Figure 4: Pareto fronts obtained for CTP with light noise, for the configurations COST $\uparrow$ – DDR $\uparrow$ (left), COST $\downarrow$ – DDR $\downarrow$ (center), and the combination of the two fronts (right).

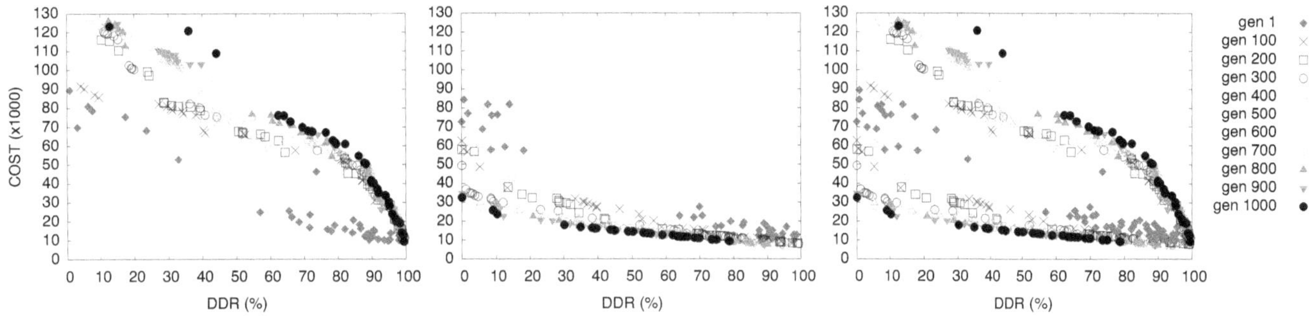

Figure 5: Pareto fronts obtained for CTP with heavy noise, for the configurations COST $\uparrow$ – DDR $\uparrow$ (left), COST $\downarrow$ – DDR $\downarrow$ (center), and the combination of the two fronts (right).

Furthermore, the experiments yielded a large number of WSN situations which exhibit interesting performance; a detailed analysis of topologies was partially done in [6] (only for topologies of high COST), partly left as future work. In Fig. 6, we show two such top individuals; dashed links are links which are strong in only one direction.

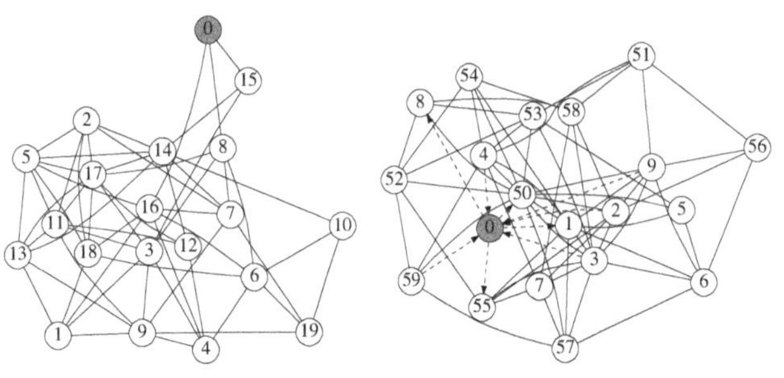

Figure 6: (Left) topology with DDR=0.99%, COST=12000; (right) topology with DDR=0%, COST=97000; both with light noise.

The WSN topology in Fig. 6 (left) (shown as an undirected topology, i.e., disregarding, for readability, all links which are not strong in both directions) is an extremely well-behaved topology, with near-perfect values for both DDR and COST under noiseless conditions. This shows that bidirectional connectivity of the topology graph can be crucial to good performance. On the other hand, the topology of the top individual in Fig. 6 (right) is such that the topology is still connected, yet partially through directional links. While the protocol is still expected to function using these directional links, even if no node is bidirectionally connected to the sink node, the protocol delivers an unexpected DDR value of zero, and also causes a one order of magnitude increase in the COST. This energy is spent by the protocol in an effort to, unsuccessfully, build the routing tree, even in the presence of only light noise. The low DDR demonstrates a vulnerability of the CTP design or configuration, complicated further by the adaptive beacon intervals, which also add an excessive amount of network traffic to the problem.

5. CONCLUSIONS

In this paper, we presented recent developments on an evolutionary methodology to analyze routing protocols in WSNs. The underlying idea is to use an evolutionary core to generate individuals, i.e. candidate WSN topologies, showing unexpected network performances. We analyzed the behavior of a target protocol, CTP, on the generated topologies evaluating two metrics that relate with undesired protocol behaviors: data delivery ratio, and total energy cost. With the proposed approach, we were able to explore in feasible time the highly multidimensional network state space, uncovering full sets of Pareto-efficient topologies characterized by tradeoff values of the two metrics. Essential to the success of the approach was the use of a MOEA toolkit able to handle the complex description of the individuals.

Future works will focus on performing additional experiments with more configurations and on other protocols, in order to further explore the capabilities of the proposed evolutionary framework. From an algorithmic point of view, we are also interested in extending the capabilities of μGP, enriching it with more sophisticated multi-objective search operators and archiving methods.

6. ACKNOWLEDGMENTS

INCAS[3] is co-funded by the Province of Drenthe, the Municipality of Assen, the European Fund for Regional Development and the Ministry of Economic Affairs, Peaks in the Delta.

7. REFERENCES

[1] M. Baldi, F. Corno, M. Rebaudengo, and G. Squillero. GA-based performance analysis of network protocols. In *Proc. Ninth IEEE International Conference on Tools with Artificial Intelligence, 1997*, pages 118–124, 1997.

[2] I. Bate and M. Fairbairn. Searching for the minimum failures that can cause a hazard in a wireless sensor network. In *Proceeding of the Fifteenth Annual Conference on Genetic and Evolutionary Computation Conference*, GECCO '13, pages 1213–1220, New York, NY, USA, 2013. ACM.

[3] S. Begum, A. Helmy, and S. Gupta. Modeling and test generation for worst-case performance evaluation of mac protocols for wireless ad hoc networks. In *IEEE International Symposium on Modeling, Analysis Simulation of Computer and Telecommunication Systems (MASCOTS)*, pages 1–10, 2009.

[4] A. Boukerche. Performance evaluation of routing protocols for ad hoc wireless networks. *Mob. Netw. Appl.*, 9(4):333–342, Aug. 2004.

[5] D. Bucur, G. Iacca, G. Squillero, and A. Tonda. An evolutionary framework for routing protocol analysis in wireless sensor networks. In A. I. Esparcia-Alcázar, editor, *Applications of Evolutionary Computation*, volume 7835 of *Lecture Notes in Computer Science*, pages 1–11. Springer Berlin Heidelberg, 2013.

[6] D. Bucur, G. Iacca, G. Squillero, and A. Tonda. The impact of topology on energy consumption for collection tree protocols: An experimental assessment through evolutionary computation. *Applied Soft Computing*, 16(0):210–222, 2014.

[7] O. Chipara, C. Lu, T. C. Bailey, and G.-C. Roman. Reliable clinical monitoring using wireless sensor networks: experiences in a step-down hospital unit. In *Proceedings of the 8th ACM Conference on Embedded Networked Sensor Systems*, SenSys '10, pages 155–168, New York, NY, USA, 2010. ACM.

[8] C. A. C. Coello, G. B. Lamont, and D. A. Van Veldhuisen. *Evolutionary algorithms for solving multi-objective problems.* Springer, 2007.

[9] P. Corke, T. Wark, R. Jurdak, W. Hu, P. Valencia, and D. Moore. Environmental wireless sensor networks. *Proceedings of the IEEE*, 98(11):1903 -1917, nov. 2010.

[10] K. Deb. *Multi-Objective Optimization Using Evolutionary Algorithms.* Wiley, 2001.

[11] K. Deb and H. Jain. An Evolutionary Many-Objective Optimization Algorithm Using Reference-point Based Non-dominated Sorting Approach, Part I: Solving Problems with Box Constraints. *IEEE Transactions on Evolutionary Computation*, PP(99):1–1, 2013.

[12] K. Deb, A. Pratap, S. Agarwal, and T. Meyarivan. A fast and elitist multiobjective genetic algorithm: NSGA-II. *IEEE Transactions on Evolutionary Computation*, 6(2):182–197, 2002.

[13] S. Gandini, W. Ruzzarin, E. Sanchez, G. Squillero, and A. Tonda. A framework for automated detection of power-related software errors in industrial verification processes. *Journal of Electronic Testing*, 26(6):689–697, 2010.

[14] O. Gnawali, R. Fonseca, K. Jamieson, M. Kazandjieva, D. Moss, and P. Levis. CTP: An Efficient, Robust, and Reliable Collection Tree Protocol for Wireless Sensor Networks. *ACM Transactions on Sensor Networks (TOSN)*, 10(3), 2014.

[15] H. Jain and K. Deb. An Evolutionary Many-Objective Optimization Algorithm Using Reference-point Based Non-dominated Sorting Approach, Part II: Handling Constraints and Extending to an Adaptive Approach. *IEEE Transactions on Evolutionary Computation*, PP(99):1–1, 2013.

[16] J. G. Ko, T. Gao, and A. Terzis. Empirical study of a medical sensor application in an urban emergency department. In *Proceedings of the Fourth International Conference on Body Area Networks*, BodyNets '09, pages 10:1–10:8, ICST, Brussels, Belgium, Belgium, 2009.

[17] K. Langendoen. Apples, oranges, and testbeds. In *In Proc. IEEE International Conference on Mobile Adhoc and Sensor Systems (MASS '06)*, pages 387–396, 2006.

[18] H. J. Lee, A. Cerpa, and P. Levis. Improving wireless simulation through noise modeling. In *Proceedings of the 6th international conference on Information processing in sensor networks*, IPSN '07, pages 21–30, New York, NY, USA, 2007. ACM.

[19] P. Levis, D. Gay, V. Handziski, J.-H. Hauer, B. Greenstein, M. Turon, J. Hui, K. Klues, C. Sharp, R. Szewczyk, J. Polastre, P. Buonadonna, L. Nachman, G. Tolle, D. Culler, and A. Wolisz. T2: A second generation OS for embedded sensor networks. Technical Report TKN-05-007, Technische Universität Berlin, 2005.

[20] P. Levis, N. Lee, M. Welsh, and D. E. Culler. TOSSIM: Accurate and scalable simulation of entire TinyOS applications. In *Proceedings of the ACM conference on Embedded Networked Sensor Systems (SenSys)*, pages 126–137, 2003.

[21] L. Mottola, T. Voigt, F. Österlind, J. Eriksson, L. Baresi, and C. Ghezzi. Anquiro: Enabling efficient static verification of sensor network software. In *Workshop on Software Engineering for Sensor Network Applications (SESENA) ICSE(2)*, 2010.

[22] D. Puccinelli, O. Gnawali, S. Yoon, S. Santini, U. Colesanti, S. Giordano, and L. Guibas. The impact of network topology on collection performance. In *Proc. 8th European Conference on Wireless Sensor Networks (EWSN)*, pages 17–32, 2011.

[23] G. Sacco, K. Barltrop, C. Lee, G. Horvath, R. Terrile, and S. Lee. Application of genetic algorithm for flight system verification and validation. In *Aerospace conference*, pages 1–7. IEEE, 2009.

[24] E. Sanchez, M. Schillaci, and G. Squillero. *Evolutionary Optimization: the μGP toolkit.* Springer Publishing Company, Incorporated, 1st edition, 2011.

[25] W. Shyang, C. Lakos, Z. Michalewicz, and S. Schellenberg. Experiments in applying evolutionary algorithms to software verification. In *IEEE World Congress on Computational Intelligence (CEC)*, pages 3531–3536. IEEE, 2008.

[26] G. Werner-Allen, K. Lorincz, J. Johnson, J. Lees, and M. Welsh. Fidelity and yield in a volcano monitoring sensor network. In *Proceedings of the 7th symposium on Operating systems design and implementation*, OSDI '06, pages 381–396. USENIX Association, 2006.

[27] M. Zheng, J. Sun, Y. Liu, J. Dong, and Y. Gu. Towards a model checker for nesc and wireless sensor networks. In S. Qin and Z. Qiu, editors, *Formal Methods and Software Engineering*, volume 6991 of *Lecture Notes in Computer Science*, pages 372–387. Springer Berlin Heidelberg, 2011.

Automated Vibrational Design and Natural Frequency Tuning of Multi-Material Structures

Nicholas Cheney, Ethan Ritz, Hod Lipson
Creative Machines Lab
Cornell University
Ithaca, NY
nac93@cornell.edu, etr38@cornell.edu, hod.lipson@cornell.edu

ABSTRACT

Natural frequency tuning is a vital engineering problem. Every structure has natural frequencies, where vibrational loading at nearby frequencies excite the structure. This causes the structure to resonate, oscillating until energy is dissipated through friction or structural failure. Examples of fragility and distress from vibrational loading include civil structures during earthquakes or aircraft rotor blades. Tuning the structure's natural frequencies away from these vibrations increases the structure's robustness. Conversely, tuning towards the frequencies caused by vibrations can channel power into energy harvesting systems. Despite its importance, natural frequency tuning is often performed ad-hoc, by attaching external vibrational absorbers to a structure. This is usually adequate only for the lowest ("fundamental") resonant frequencies, yet remains standard practice due to the unintuitive and difficult nature of the problem. Given Evolutionary Algorithms' (EA's) ability to solve these types of problems, we propose to approach this problem with the EA CPPN-NEAT to evolve multi-material structures which resonate at multiple desired natural frequencies without external damping. The EA assigns the material type of each voxel within the discretized space of the object's existing topology, preserving the object's shape and using only its material composition to shape its frequency response.

Categories and Subject Descriptors: J.6 [**Computer-Aided Engineering**]:Computer-aided design
General Terms: Algorithms, Design, Experimentation
Keywords: Genetic Algorithms, Design Automation, Frequency Tuning, Vibration Analysis, Structural Optimization

1. INTRODUCTION

In engineering mechanics, the response of a structure to vibrational loads is of acute interest and importance. Every object will exhibit some motion when excited with any periodic load – such as vibrations. But vibrations at certain frequencies will excite certain objects with greater intensity. The natural frequencies of each object dictate the frequencies of vibrations which exhibit particularly intense responses. In many cases, this type of loading is harmful to the system – larger responses put more stress on the structure. The energy trapped in the structure through these oscillating motions is not efficiently dissipated into the surrounding environment in these cases, leading to weakening or even failure over time (Fig. 1).

GECCO'14, July 12–16, 2014, Vancouver, BC, Canada.

ACM 978-1-4503-2662-9/14/07 ...$15.00.
http://dx.doi.org/10.1145/2576768.2598362.

Figure 1: *(left)* **Resonant vibrations are a common source of fragility in natural objects. Here a glass fails in the presence of an acoustic wave at resonance.** *(right)* **On a larger scale, structural failure through periodic loading of the Broughton Suspension Bridge caused its collapse in 1831 due to the resonance of the solders marching in lockstep [14].**

Large arch dams in earthquake prone areas are one example of antagonistic periodic loading, where oscillations at resonance encourage cracking and rupture through brittle concrete [1]. Wind turbine blades are another instance of this, where rotation at a resonant frequency may cause tip deflection that stresses the blades and lowers their effectiveness [15]. In aerospace applications, or other vehicles producing massive propulsive loads, the vibrations caused can be particularly damaging [6].

On the other hand, some applications may benefit from increased oscillatory response. Oscillations of larger magnitude contain more energy, which are ideal for power harvesting mechanisms such as microelectromechanical systems (MEMS) like piezoelectric microcantilevers. In this case, the lack of energy dissipation from structures with resonant frequencies close to the frequency of the vibrations enhances the efficiency of these energy harvesting systems [3, 22].

However, the process of tuning structures to have specific resonant frequencies remains largely unintuitive – changes to the material properties at one point in a structure often lead to non-linear effects on its vibrational response, both near and far from the point of change. Thus existing methods usually change the shape of the structure, often involving the addition of mass dampers to the system or requiring significant structural modifications. In cases where weight and size are at a premium, such as aerospace or remote sensing, these solutions are unsatisfying. Additionally, many of these damping strategies are only useful for the first ("fundamental") resonant frequency.

In many cases, important structures must interface into a pre-existing system, be robust (free from fragile additions), or serve aesthetic purposes. In existing structures the topology has often already been optimized, such as airfoils tuned for aerodynamic efficiency. In these cases, it would be advantageous to perform vibrational optimization of structures which preserves the overall shape of the object while also giving it desirable vibrational properties.

Muti-material design involves the use of different material types within a given shape to produce overall object properties outside of those available to the given shape composed of a single material. By optimizing a structure's vibrational response though multi-material design within an existing envelope, we open new doors towards the study and implementation of vibrational optimization of these fixed topology structures. Additionally, with current advances in multi-material additive manufacturing, we now have the ability to specify the placement and interwovenness of individual material droplets with vastly different properties during the manufacturing of a given structure, making such designs physically realizable today.

In this study, we optimize the two dimensional projection of a fixed-free cantilevered beam, with the first ten natural frequencies optimized to reproduce a randomly chosen resonant frequency profile. This is a particularly difficult and unintuitive problem because the material properties at each voxel are coupled (often non-linearly, and non-locally) with the material properties at every other voxel to produce the vibrational response of the object as a whole. Furthermore, this static topology responds differently to vibrations at different frequencies, making ad-hoc tuning of more than one or two natural frequencies exceptionally challenging.

Due to the unintuitive nature of the problem, we use evolutionary computation to traverse this design space – specifically the evolutionary algorithm CPPN-NEAT. We choose this because the Compositional Pattern Producing Network (CPPN) genome provides a compact and evolvable representation of the discretized physical design space necessary for this problem. We use this EA to optimize the placement of two materials (stiff and soft) at each discretized voxel of the structure's original shape envelope. We optimize towards randomly chosen frequency profiles (which specify the first ten natural frequencies of a structure), and show the promise of this approach to become an automated design platform for structural vibration optimization going forward.

2. BACKGROUND

Controlling system performance through the frequency domain is a classical idea [18], but conventional engineering strategies have remained largely unchanged since the early 20th century. In many cases, harmful vibrations are attenuated by directing energy away from the most sensitive parts of the system, to another auxiliary system. This is done through the addition of tuned vibrational absorbers (TVA) [17, 25, 26]. However these systems come with the tradeoff of increasing the mass and complexity of the original structure. This typically involves augmenting the system with spring-mass element or small cantilever with a first resonant frequency tuned to that of the undesired excitation, where the undesirable energy is contained within oscillations of this auxiliary structure until it is dissipated though friction.

This process is not only inefficient, but fails to fully explore the design space - as the attachment location and parameters of these devices are often chosen through intuition and physical guess-and-check iterations by the engineers, and are thus biased by the engineer's assumptions and training. Additionally, the amount of energy that can be absorbed by these types of systems is limited. As the TVA becomes large, its own dynamics begin coupling with the original system. This not only produces harmful vibrations within the original structures, but also changes its resonance profile and further complicates design. Furthermore, volume constraints of the system, such as inside the fairing of a rocket in launch, inherently restrict the size and shape of a TVA.

Some work has examined changing the system's topology to have a desired frequency profile without the addition of other components. Many of these strategies optimize the placement or parameter settings of a few predetermined basic structures, such as rods or trusses [13, 23, 7]. Duhring et al. studied the automatic design of structures with desired natural frequencies using homogenization [10]. However, this method could only optimize for a single frequency band, trying to maximize or minimize the frequency response between a set of frequency borders. This strategy also involved the generation of structures with complex and unpredictable shapes, rather than optimizing the response of an existing structure's topology. Du and Olhoff used topological optimization to automate the design of a voxelized plate structure with a binary material array to minimize sound power flow [9]. However, their designs were also constrained to the optimization of just a single frequency.

Our system expands upon these strategies by allowing us to optimize an arbitrarily large number of natural frequencies of a structure. Additionally, any number of material values can be used for any geometry. Since our search of the design space is topology-preserving; the final product will still have the shape of the original design, ensuring it will have the same functionality and maintain previous topology optimization, with only natural frequencies changed.

3. METHODS

Our method involves tuning the natural frequencies of a structure, which for lightly damped systems well approximates the resonant frequencies (where vibrational energy resonates to create sustained oscillations). First, the user specifies a design geometry. In many practical cases this is a pre-existing object shape, in this study we simply use a 2D projection of a cantilever beam, fixed on one end. Next the user produces a list of n desired natural frequencies. These frequencies are again dependent on the specific application; vibration in the environment can be found by measuring excitation loads with an accelerometer and applying the Discrete Fourier Transform [8]. Here, we select the frequency profile randomly (Sec. 3.4). Finally a selection of materials from which to construct the object is necessary. These depend on the additive manufacturing capabilities and supplies

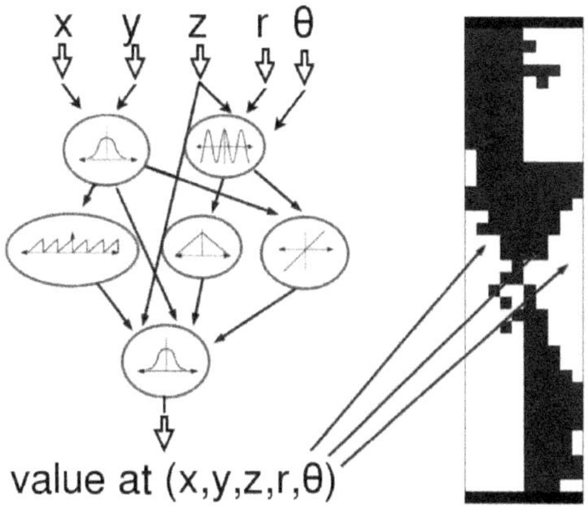

Figure 2: The CPPN genome iterates through each voxel in the discretized design space, placing either a soft or stiff voxel at each location to produce the phenotype structure it encodes (Sec. 3.2)

available to the user, and in this case is simply represented by two idealized materials, one an order of magnitude stiffer than the other. The structure to be optimized is meshed in a uniform voxelized grid. In this study, the beam is discretized into a 40x10x1 set of uniform cubic voxels. Each of these voxels is assigned a material according to the phenotype described by its associated Compositional Pattern Producing Network (CPPN) genome (Sec. 3.2). The natural frequencies of the structure are calculated (Sec. 3.1), and used to determine the individual's fitness (Sec. 3.3). Individuals who best minimize the error between the calculated and desired natural frequency profile are disproportionally favored to reproduce (and are subject to both genetic mutations and crossover in this process), creating the next generation to again iterative this evolutionary process.

3.1 Approximating Natural Frequencies with FEM

Determining the harmonic behavior of an object is equivalent to solving for the eigenvalues of the matrix representing the FEM mesh of the structure. The shape and material of the system will govern the frequency at which each of the n desired natural frequencies lie. There is one natural frequency per degree of freedom of the system, but typically the number of nodes required for accurate simulation far exceeds the number of natural frequencies in an engineering range of interest. In this case of the 40x10 discretized voxels, the 400 voxels are approximated by 1301 nodes, with 8 nodes per quadrilateral element (many nodes are shared between adjacent elements). This is more than adequate to approximate the first 10 natural frequencies. These are computed using a generalized conjugate residual method, to a residual error $< 10^{-8}$. For this computation we employ Elmer, a popular open source finite element software for multiphysical problems, developed and maintained by the CSC - IT Center for Science [19].

3.2 CPPN-NEAT Evolutionary Algorithm

CPPN-NEAT has been repeatedly described in detail [24, 5, 4, 12], so we only briefly summarize it here. A Compositional Pattern Producing Network (CPPN) is similar to a neural network, but its nodes contain one of multiple mathematical functions (sine, cosine, Gaussian, sigmoid, linear, square, or positive square root). CPPNs evolve according to the NEAT algorithm, which is largely based on: complexification of genomes over time, speciation within the genotypic space for diversity maintenance, and tournament selection within species [24].

The CPPN produces a spacial output pattern that is built up from these functions' geometric transformations of the input gradients (changing values of each input coordinate over the space). Because the nodes have regular mathematical functions, the output patterns tend to be regular (e.g. a Gaussian function can create symmetry and a sine function can create repetition). In this paper, each voxel has x, y, and z coordinates, polar coordinates (r and θ) in each of the x, y, and z planes, and a measure of the voxel's distance from the center of the search space (d), which are all input in the range $[-1, 1]$, describing the relative location of each voxel in this geometric design space. The single output of this network is interpreted as either a stiff material present in that voxel's location for a value above zero, or a soft material present for a value less than or equal to zero.

Alternate experiments were conducted with the value of the output node ($[-1, 1]$) representing a mixture of the stiff and soft materials with a compliance representative of an interpolation between the maximally stiff or soft materials at each endpoint. While the real valued compliance affords more flexibility in the design space, the problem of physically mixing materials during the additive manufacturing process is not yet a solved problem [16].

In order to produce a structure from a CPPN, each voxel in the discretized design space is iterated though. At each iteration through this space, the voxel's coordinate are input into the network, which is then undergoes it's update function to produce an output value. The value out this output determines the type of voxel which is placed at this location. A positive output stipulates the placement of a stiff voxel (denoted by to a Young's Modulus (E) of 10 gigapascal (GPa), and Poisson's ratio of 0.3), while a negative output value produces a soft voxel at this location (resulting in a Young's Modulus of 1 GPa, and the same Poisson's ratio of 0.3). After iterating through each voxel within the design space, the CPPN genome has produced a phenotypic description of the structure, which can then be analyzed to find it's natural frequencies, or sent to a 3D printer for fabrication. This iterative process is outlined in Fig. 2.

3.3 Fitness Function

The quality (fitness) of each structure's ability to match a desired frequency profile of n frequencies is described by:

$$\frac{1}{\Sigma_{i=1}^{n}(\frac{n-i+1}{n})E(i)^2}$$

Where n is the number of frequencies being optimized, and $E(i)$ is the relative error in matching the ith frequency. The linear weighting factor $\frac{n-i+1}{n}$ is to place more weight on the primary frequencies than the later ones, which contribute less significantly to the behavior of real world systems. For example: for frequency 1 of 10, $\frac{n-i+1}{n} = \frac{10-1+1}{10} = 1$, thus the first frequency contributes to the fitness penalty with a weight of 1. For frequency 6 of 10, this weighting factor becomes $\frac{10-6+1}{10} = 0.5$, so the 6th frequency is discounted such that it's relative error is only counted by half of that belonging to the first frequency. Similarly, the 10th frequency has a discount factor of 0.1, meaning that it's relative error contributes to the overall fitness only one tenth the amount which the error of the 1st frequency does.

The motivation for using the weighted sum of the squared errors is simply a standard practice to negate the sign of the error terms, and to more heavily penalize larger deviations from the desired frequencies.

3.4 Producing Random Target Frequencies

In order to optimize a structure to match a given frequency profile, such a profile must exist within the limits of the structure's realizable material properties. Thus to produce random frequency profiles to be used as targets for the optimization process, we use the following:

$$f_n = \frac{f_n^{\mathbf{stiff}} + f_n^{\mathbf{soft}}}{2} + \frac{f_n^{\mathbf{stiff}} - f_n^{\mathbf{soft}}}{2} * rand(-0.5, 0.5)$$

For frequency number $n = 1, 2, ..., 10$. Where $f_n^{\mathbf{stiff}}$ is the nth frequency of a beam fully populated with maximally stiff voxels (and conversely with soft voxels for $f_n^{\mathbf{soft}}$). Thus the above equation produces a random number from the middle 50% of the range between these minimum and maximum frequencies. Much like the fact that a primary frequency above or below that of the fully stiff or soft beams is not physically realizable with the chosen materials, the frequencies at (or near) the edge of this allowable range necessitate beams that are (almost) entirely filled with stiff/soft voxels, and thus may or may not be realizable in a case where more than a single frequency is being optimized for. For this proof of concept we conservatively constrain ourselves to the middle 50% of this range, where we feel a balance of both materials is likely to produce a vast array of frequency responses from the relative positions of voxels rather than the proportion of voxel types themselves. Future work will experimentally examine how optimization success drops off as these goals become less and less physically realizable with the expansion of the allowable target frequency range.

After all 10 frequencies are chosen, the values are then sorted from smallest to largest, as natural frequencies must occur in a monotonically increasing order. The 10 target frequencies for four random seeds are given in Fig 3, as well as those of the beams fully populated with stiff or soft voxels.

n	Full Soft	Full Stiff	Rand. #1	Rand. #2	Rand. #3	Rand. #4
1	0.782	1.596	1.215	1.062	1.044	1.315
2	4.666	9.549	7.994	7.279	6.858	6.613
3	11.973	24.894	18.592	16.059	17.447	19.177
4	12.220	25.087	15.594	17.749	21.404	20.691
5	22.080	45.475	30.026	29.250	33.929	38.461
6	33.513	69.209	49.484	52.985	52.274	49.015
7	35.868	74.574	51.903	59.555	55.862	58.415
8	45.964	95.121	65.639	76.686	59.337	69.871
9	59.072	122.436	84.398	79.505	77.530	97.132
10	59.598	123.911	105.121	87.085	85.164	97.485

Figure 3: The first 10 natural frequencies (in MHz) for beams with all soft voxels or all stiff voxels gives the boundaries for the creation of 4 random frequency target profiles (Sec 3.4).

3.5 Control Treatment

In order to test the validity of the evolved structures, a control method was devised. To isolate the effects of the optimization towards natural frequency matching structures, the control groups consist of the same 32 independent runs of 30 CPPN genomes evolving for 1000 generations. This negates any natural advantage that the genomic representation of the CPPN might have in this domain, as well as the complexification of the NEAT algorithm over time. In the control setup, however, no preferential reproduction is afforded to those individuals who more closely match the desired frequency profile, but rather this selection happens at random. At the end of the 1000 generations of this evolutionary drift, the resulting structure are still compared to each of the four Random Frequency Profiles and their effectiveness is measured in the same manner as with the experimental treatments.

4. RESULTS

All treatments below consist of 32 independent runs, with populations of 30 individuals evolved for 1000 generations.

4.1 Statistical Measures

The data resulting from the control conditions pass the Shapiro-Wilk test for normality [21] (with $p<0.0329$ for all 10 frequencies), and thus error bars are used to describe this data in the following plots. However, the experimental treatments routinely fail the Shapiro-Wilk test for normality, with many of the 10 frequencies for each random frequency profile falling above the $p=0.05$ confidence cutoff for the normality of the distribution. Given that the shape these distributions are unknown, we employ bootstrapping to produce 95% confidence intervals to graphically describe the experimental data [11]. Given that at least one distribution for any statistical tests will be an experimental treatment, we employ the Mann-Whitney U test, as it does not require the assumption of normality of the data, yet performs almost as well as the student's t-test on normally distributed data (such as the control data) [20].

4.2 Statistical Data

4.2.1 *Optimization for Random Frequency Profiles*

We optimize the material makeup of our 40x10x1 voxel beam to set its natural frequencies to resonate with Random Frequency Profile #1. This is done for 32 independent trials, using a "soft" material (Young's Modulus(E) of 1 gigapascal(GPa), and Poisson's ratio of 0.3), and a "hard" material (Young's Modulus of 10 GPa, and Poisson's ratio of 0.3) as the material library. We compare the relative error for the task of matching with Random Frequency Profile #1 with the control conditionfor each of the $n = 10$ desired frequencies, resulting in 10 different p-values. A one-sided U test is employed in order to test the hypothesis that optimized structures will produce lower errors than the control structures. All of these 10 measures fall below the 95% confidence threshold, as $max(\text{p-values}) < 1.008 * 10^{-5}$, showing statistical significance that our system can effectively optimize all of the first 10 frequencies of this desired frequency profile.

In order to test the sensitivity of this analysis on this randomly generated target frequency profile, three additional desired frequency sets are randomly produced. These each

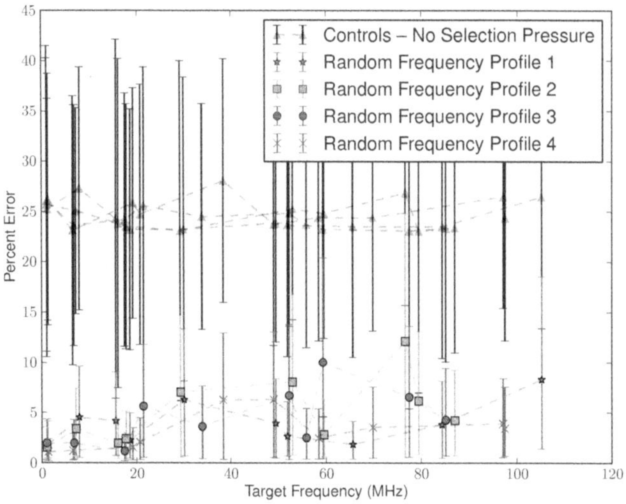

Figure 4: Examination of the effect of particular random frequency profile targets on the resulting optimization process. Structures are optimized to match (*red stars*) Random Frequency Profile #1, (*blue squares*) #2, (*green circles*) #3, or (*magenta crosses*) #4. While it is not possible to compare the responses to the same frequencies across treatments here, since no two treatments optimize towards the same frequency, we can compare each Random Profile to a control treatment (without selection pressure), plotted as *black triangles*). In all 10 frequencies for all 4 runs, the optimized structures outperform their control counterparts against the same frequencies (with all p-values $< 1.008 * 10^{-5}$), suggesting the ability of this technique to effectively evolve structures for various frequency profiles.

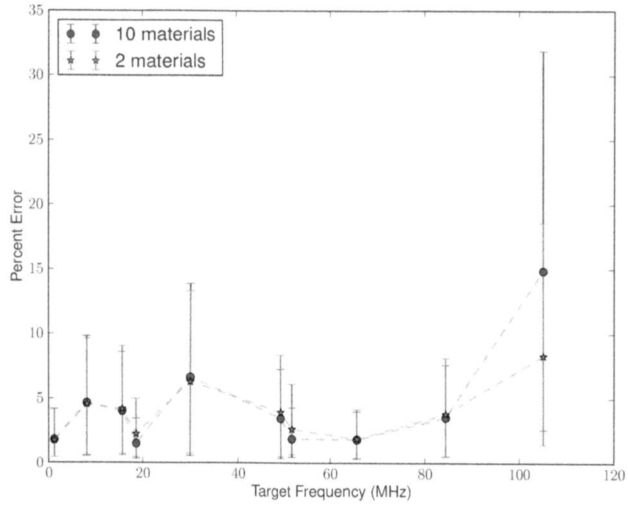

Figure 5: Examination of the effect of number of materials used on the performance of optimized structures. Both data sets use the same random seeds and target frequency (Random Frequency Profile #1). (*red stars*) Optimized structures from a combination of the maximally stiff or maximally soft voxels only (2 materials). (*blue circles*) Each voxel can take on one of 10 intermediate material properties (including the two endpoints in the previous treatment). A two-sided Mann-Whitney U test lacks significant at the 95% confidence level with p-values > 0.0745 for all frequencies except: $n = 4$ (15.594 MHz) with p-value < 0.029, and $n = 10$ (105.121 MHz) with p-value < 0.0005. This suggests that for most frequencies (besides $n = 4, 10$) the addition of intermediate material properties often does not significantly impact the frequency matching ability of the resulting structures.

consist of $n = 10$ desired natural frequencies, but each of these frequencies differs from those in Random Frequency Profile #1, so a comparison coupled by desired frequency (in MHz) is no longer possible. One could imagine instead coupling by frequency number, and comparing the accuracy of $n = 1$ for each of the four frequency profiles, then comparing $n = 2$ for all four, and so on. However, actual frequencies between desired profiles can greatly differ: even when comparing with the equivalent frequency number (for example 15.594 MHz for Random Profile #1 is the 4th desired natural frequency of the system, which has the value 21.404 MHz for Random Profile #3 – a value 37% higher). Additionally, with the highly non-linear nature of the frequency tuning domain, the effects of differences in other frequencies may play a major role in the overall structural evolution strategy and influence desired frequencies that do happen to be closely coupled by both n and frequency value (in MHz). Instead, we attempt to compare "apples-to-apples" but assessing each of the optimized structures against control structures evolved through a random walk. These rancom control structures are then compared to the same target frequencies for each of the Random Frequency Profiles. As seen in Fig 4, each of these four independently generated random frequency profiles show a statistically significant improvement over their associated control treatments (with the max p-value of the Mann-Whitney U test $> 1.008 * 10^{-5}$).

4.2.2 10 Materials vs. 2 Materials

Fig. 5 shows the effect of intermediate materials. In this setup, we optimize structures via the same method as in Sec. 4.2, where the CPPN genome specifies the material present in each voxel of the structure by again choosing from one of two materials – either stiff (E=10 GPa) or soft (E=1 GPa). To explore the impact of this assumption of two available materials, we compare this to another treatment in which there are 10 material choices, representing materials of intermediate compliances (between and including the endpoints of the fully stiff and fully soft voxels as before). Materials 2-9 are assigned a Young's Modulus (E) of 2- 9 GPa, respectively, with a constant Poisson's ratio of 0.3. The results of a two-sided Mann-Whitney U test show that 8 of the 10 desired frequencies showed no significant difference (min(p-value) > 0.0745. The exceptions to this rule were the frequencies of 15.594 MHz ($n = 4$), which had a p-value < 0.029, and 105.121 MHz ($n = 10$) with p-value < 0.0005. In the case of the final ($n = 10$) frequency of the group, the 10 material structures actually performed worse than their 2 material counterparts. Thus, in general, we believe that using 10 intermediate materials does not typically produce significantly better optimized structures than those made with just the two extreme materials.

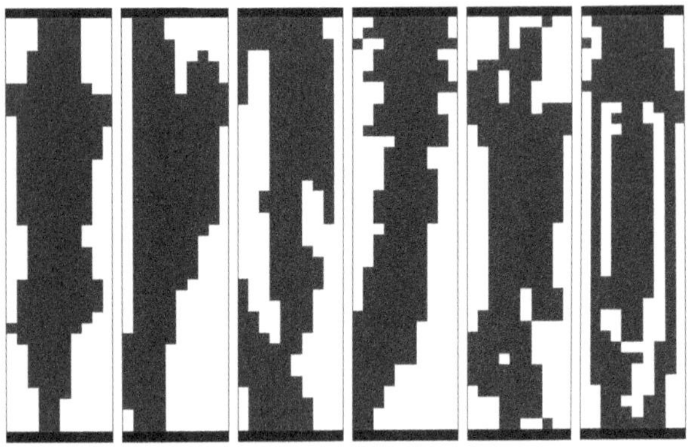

Figure 6: Six examples of stereotypical structures evolved for Random Frequency Profile #1. Black pixels represent stiff material, while white pixels represent soft material. Optimized structures often consist of one or two large continuous regions. They often span all or nearly all of the design space allocated in both width and length. They also often display minor branching structures off of this primary long-spanning structure.

4.2.3 Optimization for the First Natural Frequency

In the course of the work, we also explored other fitness function setups. Of particular interest is the one which rewards only (or disproportionately more) for the matching of the first natural frequency to its desired target. This is of particular interest because the optimization of the first natural frequency alone is considered state of the art in frequency tuning via external damping, and we would like to show that our approach also can be compared directly to traditional approaches. In this case, the following data comes from a quadratic-scaling fitness function. This is a variation on the fitness function described in Sec. 3.3, with the $\frac{n-i+1}{n}$ term squared, such that the primary natural frequency now accounts for 100 times as much weight as the 10th natural frequency does (as opposed to 10 times more in the linear scaling scenario above). In this scenario (not plotted here), the 32 independent runs shows a mean of 0.106% error for the primary natural frequency, with a 95% bootstrapped confidence interval of $[0.104\%, 0.110\%]$ error. One could also imagine this trend being even more extreme should the entire weight be placed on the primary frequency.

4.3 Vibrationally Optimized Beam Examples

Fig. 6 shows a representative sample of interesting beams evolved to match Random Frequency Profile #1. The top end has a fixed boundary condition, where the bottom is free; white and black voxels correspond to the soft and stiff materials, respectively. These beams tend to feature a long vertical primary structures (or two connected shorter beams spanning the length of the beam), often with horizontal protrusions acting as secondary structures.

Fig. 7 shows beams which are stereotypical of the structures evolved in response to Random Frequency Profile #2. These structures tend to exhibit greater curvature, exhibiting circular patterns from the center of the beam, which presumably rely heavily on the gradients caused by the polar coordinate inputs to the CPPNs. These structures seem more likely than Fig. 6 to include material discontinuities

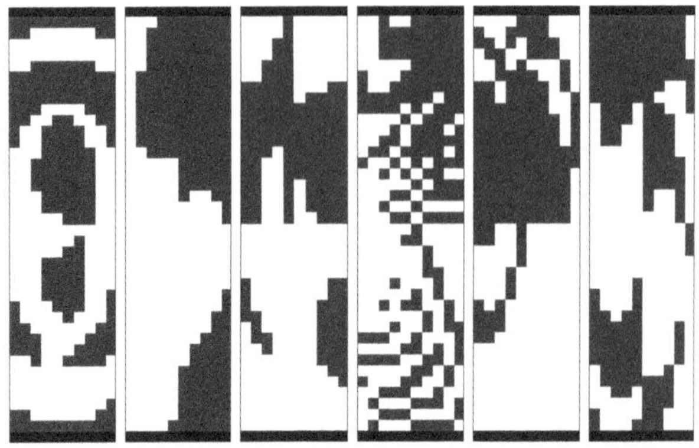

Figure 7: Six examples of stereotypical structures evolved for Random Frequency Profile #2. These structures appear to favor sweeping curvature in their designs, often with repeating or symmetric motifs. This group is shows more use of thinly (or non-)connected areas of stiff material than group #1.

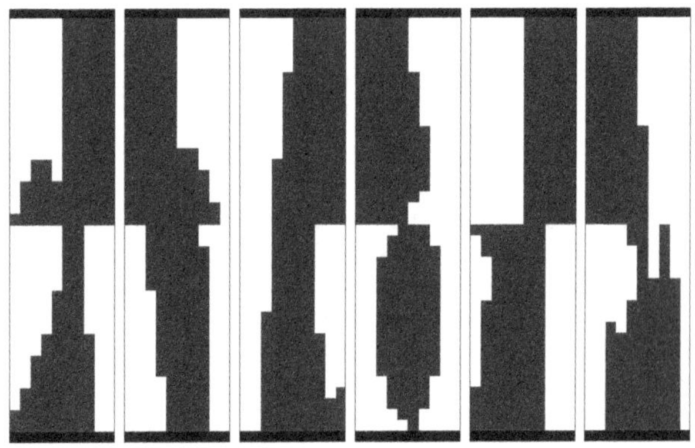

Figure 8: Typical structures evolved to match the natural frequencies of Random Frequency Profile #3 display very simple structures with long vertical motifs, often displaying symmetry or repetition along the midpoint of the vertical axis, where a thin strip of stiff voxels connects the top and bottom features.

and have multiple floating sections of continuous material instead of a single one than spans the length of the beam.

Figs. 8 and 9 display structures optimized for the remaining target frequency profiles. In Fig. 8, the results of optimization towards Random Frequency Profile #3 display simple vertical structures, often with a repetition or separation point along the mid-line between top and bottom halves of the structures. While in Fig. 9, structures evolved for Random Frequency Profile #4 display a distinct pattern of stiff material near the center of the beam, with mostly soft voxels at the top and bottom edges of the structures. These unique structural types, recurring frequently within treatments, but rarely for treatments optimizing towards another random frequency profile, provide further evidence of the algorithm's ability to produce multi-material placements suited for specific vibrational optimization problems.

Alternatively, Fig. 10 showcases the beams created from a process without the selection pressure to optimize towards a specific frequency profile. These structures appear more

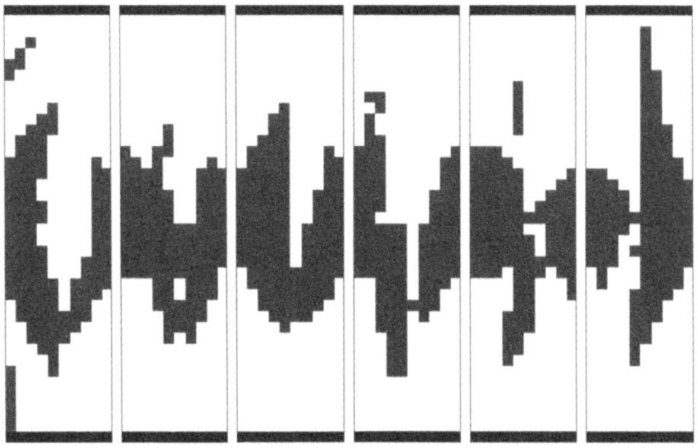

Figure 9: The top six performing structures optimized for Random Frequency Profile #4. This frequency profile tends to drive the evolution of structures with stiff voxels concentrated around the center, with near-symmetric "wings" stretching vertically from the primary horizontal structure.

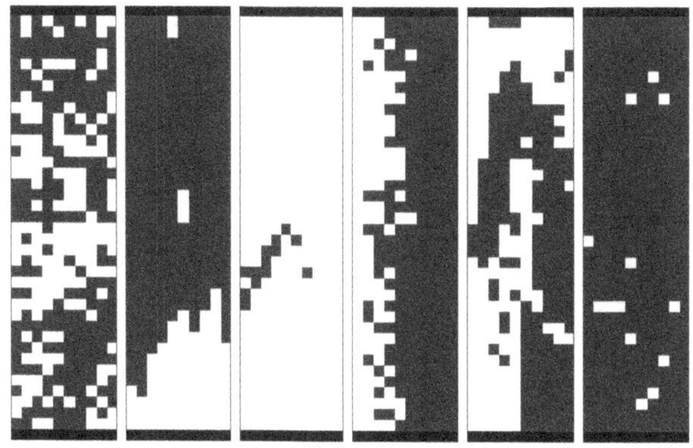

Figure 10: Six examples of stereotypical structures from the control group that features a random walk through the genotypic space in lieu of selection pressure towards high performing structures. The resulting structures appear to be much noisier, with many unconnected single pixels. This suggests that the continuous shapes from the previous trials are preserved because of their vibrational advantages.

pixelated, featuring isolated single, or small groups of, voxels. These structures tend to display very broad divisions, such as a single fuzzy line splitting stiff and soft sides of a beam. The presence of these structures implies that the CPPN itself complexifying over time is not in itself sufficient to produce the crisp lines, solid patches, and features such as symmetry and repetition found in Figs. 6-9. But suggests that selection towards specific frequencies, combined with the apparent vibrations benefit of such features for these specific cases, is required to produce these motifs.

4.4 Fabricated Structures

While these structures are evolved in simulation, the optimized beams are easily produced via additive manufacturing. Fig. 11 shows two optimized structures in simulation, and their fabricated counterparts. While the simulated materials in this study were not modeled after any real-world materials, and thus the printed structures were not tested for their actual natural frequencies, future and ongoing work will demonstrate both of these features.

5. DISCUSSION

The above describes a system in which vibrational properties of an existing topological design are optimized through the placement of soft and stiff voxels according to an evolved Compositional Pattern Producing Network. The culmination of the results presented previously implies that this new system is indeed capable of producing structures which are optimized to match a predetermined set of natural frequencies. Furthermore, the system is fairly robust to the specific natural frequencies, and their relations to each other – at least within the limited space we explored between range of frequencies existing in single material (all stiff or all soft) beams. We compared the results of these beams to those created from a random evolutionary walk to show the ability of the system to optimize for many natural frequencies simultaneously, since there have not existed previous studies which optimize as many as 10 natural frequencies which we could compare our results to. Existing structural optimization methods such as homogenization allow for the optimization of one or few frequencies, but rely heavily on spatially-local gradients or properties which do not capture the highly coupled relationships across a structure that occur when optimizing for multiple frequencies. The employment of an evolutionary algorithm helps to remove the top-down design from this difficult problem, and the use of a CPPN genome creates correlated global mutations which evidently is helpful in optimizing the spacial coupling which made this problem previously unsolvable. In order to compare to the state of the art single frequency optimization, we show that our method can move an object's natural frequency to the order of a tenth of a percent error, without having to affect it's existing topology or augment it with dampers.

Arguably the most interesting of all, are the examples of optimized topologies in Figs. 6-9. The differences between the strategies in designing these structures, at such a basic level that it is immediately obvious to the eye, display the flexibility and creativity of design which evolutionary algorithms have previously made their acclaim [2]. The ability to produce structures that are inherently and consistently different in their fundamental layout and design strategy, attuned to each new scenario (as opposed to minor variations on a preexisting paradigm) provide the hope that future work with this system will demonstrate the ability to produce effective and realizable solutions specifically designed for the many real-world applications of vibrational analysis.

6. FUTURE WORK

Given the novelty of this work, the potential for future work is nearly limitless. We are currently upgrading this system to produce 3D structures which include boundary conditions outside of classical beams, running experiments on a larger number of frequencies and on a less restricted set of desired frequency profiles, and exploring the effect of finer resolution on this design paradigm.

It is also not yet clear how the system will approach demands to push natural frequencies away from wide frequency bands, rather than pushing them towards specific targets (though these two problems are highly related). The fitness function employed in this work was chosen logically, though

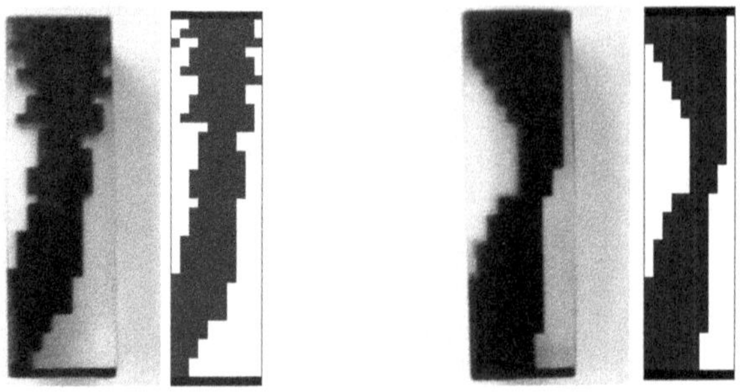

Figure 11: Optimized designs printed on an Objet Connex 500. Shown here are voxels of 0.9mm for visualization purposes, though the resolution on this 3D printer would allow voxels as small as 16 microns.

not rigorously, and further experiments will take place to provide evidence of it's effectiveness in relation to others. Specifically, this applies to multi-objective fitness functions. One could easily imagine other desirable function properties of a real world system, such as the minimization of deflection in a fixed-free beam, which needs to be optimized in parallel with the structures vibrational properties.

Given the ability the system's consistent ability to match all 10 frequencies, it is unknown where the limits of this paradigm fall. In future work, we push this system to failure, exploring its limitations on number of frequencies optimized.

7. CONCLUSION

In this work, we approached the tuning of an object's natural frequencies without the use of external damping or changing the shape envelope of the existing object topology. This problem is of vital engineering importance to produce parts, objects, and structures with are robust to the structural weakening and eventual failures caused by vibrations in many domains such as civil or aerospace engineering. The inverse case is also an important problem, where systems that collect energy and drive oscillations of a piezoelectric beam represent a significant advance in the efficiency of energy harvesting. Despite the difficulty of this problem, we show here that we are capable of producing structures which can optimally place their natural frequencies to match one of multiple desired resonant frequency profiles of 10 frequencies. We do so by optimizing the placement of multiple materials within an existing topology with the evolutionary algorithm CPPN-NEAT. The demonstrated ability to optimize many frequencies simultaneously, as well as the fundamental differences in structures optimized across multiple target frequency profiles show promise for this technique to soon be a design automation platform for the vibrational optimization of important real-world structures.

8. ACKNOWLEDGMENTS

This work was supported by DARPA Open Manufacturing Grant W911NF-12-1-0449 and NASA Space Technology Research Fellowships NNX13AL37H for Nicholas Cheney and NNX13AL39H for Ethan Ritz.

9. REFERENCES

[1] A. M. Abdel-Ghaffar and R. F. Scott. Analysis of earth dam response to earthquakes. *Journal of the Geotechnical Engineering Division*, 105(12):1379–1404, 1979.

[2] P. J. Bentley and D. W. Corne. *Creative evolutionary systems*. Morgan Kaufmann, 2002.

[3] V. R. Challa, M. Prasad, Y. Shi, and F. T. Fisher. A vibration energy harvesting device with bidirectional resonance frequency tunability. *Smart Materials and Structures*, 17(1):015035, 2008.

[4] J. Clune and H. Lipson. Evolving three-dimensional objects with a generative encoding inspired by developmental biology. In *Proc. Conf. Artificial Life*, pages 144–148, 2011.

[5] J. Clune, K. O. Stanley, R. T. Pennock, and C. Ofria. On the performance of indirect encoding across the continuum of regularity. *IEEE Trans Evol. Comp.*, 15(4):346–67, 2011.

[6] F. E. Culick. Acoustic oscillations in solid propellant rocket chambers. *Astronautica Acta*, 12(2):113–126, 1966.

[7] A. de Ávila Borges, L. Miguel, and L. Miguel. Size and shape optimization of structures by harmony search. 2013.

[8] C. H. Dowding. *Blast vibration monitoring and control*, volume 297. Prentice-Hall Englewood Cliffs, 1985.

[9] J. Du and N. Olhoff. Minimization of sound radiation from vibrating bi-material structures using topology optimization. *Structural and Multidisciplinary Optimization*, 33(4-5):305–321, 2007.

[10] M. B. Dühring, J. S. Jensen, and O. Sigmund. Acoustic design by topology optimization. *Journal of sound and vibration*, 317(3):557–575, 2008.

[11] B. Efron and R. Tibshirani. Bootstrap methods for standard errors, confidence intervals, and other measures of statistical accuracy. *Statistical science*, pages 54–75, 1986.

[12] J. Gauci and K. O. Stanley. Generating large-scale neural nets through discovering geometric regularities. In *Proc. of the Genetic & Evol. Comp. Conf.*, pages 997–1004, 2007.

[13] Z. Hadas, J. Kurfurst, C. Ondrusek, and V. Singule. Ai based optimization for vibration energy harvesting apps. *Microsystem technologies*, 18(7-8):1003–14, 2012.

[14] C. Hales and S. Gooch. *Managing Eng Design*. Springer, 04.

[15] M. Hansen. Improved modal dynamic wind turbines avoid stall-induced vibrations. *Wind Energy*, 6(2):179–95, 2003.

[16] J. Hiller and H. Lipson. Tunable digital material properties for 3d voxel printers. *Rapid Prototyping Journal*, 16(4):241–7, 2010.

[17] C. Q. Howard, C. H. Hansen, and A. C. Zander. Noise reduction of a rocket payload fairing using tuned vibration absorbers with translational and rotational dofs. In *Proc. Australian Acoustical Society*, pages 165–71, 2005.

[18] D. J. Inman. Engineering vibrations. *Prentice-Hall*, 2010.

[19] M. Lyly, J. Ruokolainen, and E. Järvinen. Elmer–a finite element solver for multiphysics. *CSC-report on scientific computing*, 2000:156–159, 1999.

[20] H. B. Mann and D. R. Whitney. On a test of whether one of two random variables is stochastically larger than the other. *The annals of mathematical statistics*, 18(1):50–60, 1947.

[21] S. S. Shapiro and M. B. Wilk. An analysis of variance test for normality. *Biometrika*, 52(3):591–611, 1965.

[22] D. Shen, J.-H. Park, J. Ajitsaria, S.-Y. Choe, H. C. Wikle III, and D.-J. Kim. The design, fabrication and evaluation of a mems pzt cantilever with an integrated si proof mass for vibration energy harvesting. *Journal of Micromechanics and Microengineering*, 18(5):055017, 2008.

[23] B. K. Stanford and P. D. Dunning. Optimal topology of aircraft rib and spar structures under aeroelastic loads.

[24] K. O. Stanley. Compositional pattern producing networks: A novel abstraction of development. *Genetic Programming and Evolvable Machines*, 8(2):131–162, 2007.

[25] J. Sun, M. R. Jolly, and M. Norris. Passive, adaptive and active tuned vibration absorbers - a survey. *Journal of mechanical design*, 117:234, 1995.

[26] Y. Tarng, J. Kao, and E. Lee. Chatter suppression in turning operations with a tuned vibration absorber. *Journal of materials processing technology*, 105(1):55–60, 2000.

Hierarchical Simulation for Complex Domains: Air Traffic Flow Management

William Curran
Oregon State University
Corvallis, Oregon
curranw@onid.orst.edu

Adrian Agogino
NASA AMES Research Center
Moffet Field, California
adrian.k.agogino@nasa.gov

Kagan Tumer
Oregon State University
Corvallis, Oregon
kagan.tumer@oregonstate.edu

ABSTRACT

A key element in the continuing growth of air traffic is the increased use of automation. The Next Generation (Next-Gen) Air Traffic System will include automated decision support systems and satellite navigation that will let pilots know the precise locations of other aircraft around them. This Next-Gen suggestion system can assist pilots in making good decisions when they have to direct the aircraft themselves. However, effective automation is critical in achieving the capacity and safety goals of the Next-Gen Air Traffic System. In this paper we show that evolutionary algorithms can be used to achieve this effective automation.

However, it is not feasible to use a standard evolutionary algorithm learning approach in such a detailed simulation. Therefore, we apply a hierarchical simulation approach to an air traffic congestion problem where agents must reach a destination while avoiding separation violations. Due to the dynamic nature of this problem, agents need to learn fast. Therefore, we apply low fidelity simulation for agents learning their destination, and a high fidelity simulation employing the Next-Gen technology for learning separation assurance. The hierarchical simulation approach increases convergence rate, leads to a better performing solution, and lowers computational complexity by up to 50 times.

Categories and Subject Descriptors

I.2.11 [**Distributed Artificial Intelligence**]: Intelligent Agents

General Terms

Algorithms, Performance, Experimentation

Keywords

Aerospace Industry, Simulation Optimization, Multi-agent Systems, Co-evolution

GECCO'14, July 12–16, Vancouver, BC, Canada.

http://dx.doi.org/10.1145/2576768.2598385.

1. INTRODUCTION

Automation is becoming an important aspect of air traffic control. Decision support systems, computer-based information acquisition, trajectory planning systems, and advisory systems are considered to be automation components related to Next Generation (Next-Gen) airspace [15]. With the addition of these systems, learning becomes computationally intractable and approximations need to be made, but with more approximations the learned policy becomes less representative of the real application. To resolve this issue, we develop an approach that use both high and low fidelity simulations. The high fidelity simulations include complex computation and are used during separation assurance, while the low fidelity simulation solves high level problems and are used for reaching a destination. Both fidelities are needed to fully understand the system.

Typical methods to alleviate computational complexity in complex systems have been applied during learning, one such example is transfer learning [12]. Transfer learning has been shown to alleviate computational complexity by learning in a simple domain, and transferring that knowledge to a more complex domain. In transfer learning there are three key research questions: What to transfer, how to transfer and when to transfer. Each of these questions are difficult to answer and all are completely domain dependent. When the source domain and the target domain are loosely or not related, straight forward transfer learning does not work, and can lead to worse performance [12]. Lastly, transfer learning requires a computable mapping from the source domain to the target domain, which isn't always easily achieved.

Other methods have been applied to the simulation as a whole [16]. An approximation of a high fidelity simulator can greatly speed up computation time, but subtle, yet important, details can be approximated or removed from the system. In complex domains, these important details are needed, but are no longer available or are approximated, adding error into the system. Over time this error can propagate throughout the system, invalidating results and leading to suboptimal learning. An example of this is air traffic simulation. Two popular approaches to simulating air traffic in the United States had been to develop Lagrangian models of each aircraft's dynamics, or to create aggregate models of the National Airspace (NAS) [4, 10, 11]. When the aircraft's dynamics are taken into account, the simulation is accurate, but also time-intensive and complex. On the other hand, aggregate models can be used as an approximation of the Lagrangian models. When using only a low fidelity simulation, a lot of pertinent information is lost, but when using

using a high fidelity simulator, such as the Lagrangian model simulations, the simulation cost becomes high.

Coordinating aircraft is also a critical and difficult task. Cooperative Coevolutionary Algorithms (CCEAs) are well suited for evolving multiple populations simultaniously and evaluating fitness based on an individuals interactions with other agents in the system. Additionally, CCEAs are well suited for multiagent domains where robustness is a desirable quality, and agents need to succeed or fail as a team [13]. The population member assignment generates a robustness well suited for the Next-Gen system, as a solution needs to be able to withstand sudden changes that are frequent in air traffic. Although robustness is nice, the key advantage of this multiagent approach is each agent only has to search a subspace of the entire state space.

Our motivation for this work borrows from the field of Economics. Macroeconomics studies the impact of national economic policies on growth, inflation and unemployment, where microeconomics studies the behavior of individual households and businesses. Microeconomics exists because macroeconomics cannot adequately explain the decision making of an individual, and macroeconomics exists because analyzing an individual cannot explain large scale effects on the economy. The same is true for low fidelity and high fidelity simulators. The low fidelity simulation is on a macro scale. It is a useful tool when analyzing the performance of many agents as a whole, but it does not detail an individual. On the other hand, high fidelity simulation is on a micro scale, and is a very useful tool when learning requires fine grained detail of an individual agent. They are both required in order to fully understand the system, and if one is used to attempt to understand the environment as a whole, useful information can be lost.

In this work we apply our hierarchical simulation evolutionary approach to an air traffic control congestion domain. In our domain agents must reach their destination quickly while simultaneously avoiding separation violations. A low fidelity simulator is used for reaching the destination quickly, while the high fidelity simulation takes advantage of the advanced Next-Gen [15] technologies, namely Automatic Dependent Surveillance-Broadcast (ADS-B). ADS-B is a satellite-based technology that provides aircraft information of other aircraft, such as position and velocity, and can be used to avoid separation violations. We find that combining a low fidelity and high fidelity simulator leads to faster convergence rate and faster computation time.

The remainder of this paper is organized as follows. Section 2 describes the related work in hierarchical methods, multiagent coordination and fitness function shaping, and prior work in air traffic control. In Section 3 we describe the domain we use, and in Section 4 we explain our approach in detail by developing a low fidelity simulator and high fidelity simulator and combine the two. Experimental results are then provided in Section 5, followed by the conclusion in Section 6.

2. BACKGROUND

To motivate our approach, we introduce previous work performed in the field of agent-based simulation techniques and hierarchical methods, describe the fitness function shaping technique used in this work, and include a description and overview of the air traffic problem.

2.1 Simulation Techniques

Many simulation techniques leverage the concept of simultaneous use of multiple fidelity models. In general, they partition the environment and run a different model in each partition. Anh et al. [3] and Stylianou et al. [17] applied such a model toward pedestrian simulation. Anh et al. used low fidelity flow and distribution models to steer nonvisible agents along a network of nodes that describe the accessible areas of a city. They also use a high fidelity simulation to perform collision avoidance. Stylianou et al. applied a top-down approach where the movement of the pedestrians was computed using a low fidelity simulation, taking a global view of the model. This information is used for guiding a more detailed and realistic high fidelity simulation when the user zooms in to a specific region, thus maintaining the consistency. Both of these approaches focused on consistency and speed of the results, showing that a mixed fidelity simulation can be as accurate as a high fidelity simulation. Additionally, both works require a preprocessed environment and predefined transition functions between the agents models while switching fidelities.

An alternative to simultaneous fidelity models is to approximate the high fidelity simulation [14, 16]. In the work by Sóbester et al. they employ parallel updates by searching an expected improvement surface generated from a radial basis function model [16]. They find that this is an accurate approximation of the high fidelity model. Proper et al. on the other hand replaced a high fidelity air traffic simulation entirely with an event-based air traffic model [14]. In complex domains approximations introduce small errors, which over time can propagate throughout the system, deteriorating performance.

In this work, we employ the simultaneous use of multiple fidelity models in multiagent learning for coordination. In this problem, transition functions between the fidelity models cannot be found, the environment is generalized, and agent interactions cannot be predicted and must be learned.

2.2 Hierarchical Learning

Hierarchical methods decompose large problems into smaller ones, overcomes partial observability, and re-uses subtasks. This organizational structure leads to many benefits, such as faster learning and learning from fewer trials. MAXQ by Dietterich et al. [7] decomposes a Markov Decision Process (MDP) into a hierarchy of smaller MDPs and decomposes the value function of the target MDP into an additive combination of the value functions of the smaller MDPs. Our work similarly decomposes a large task into many semi-independent smaller tasks, essentially simultaneously solving many smaller, and therefore easier problems.

Similar to hierarchical methods, task-based decomposition decomposes large problems into many smaller, more task-specific problems. Agents are grouped together in teams that are specialized for a specific task. An agent can explore more parts of the state relevant to its current task rather than exploring the entire state space, and therefore learn faster [8, 20]. Task-based decomposition has been previously applied in robotics for cellular manufacturing [18], where the complexity of the manufacturing process is too large for a straightforward multiagent approach. Task-based decomposition has also been used in pattern recognition [9] to simplify image classification through the use of decomposing pattern classification problems based on the task required.

This work can be seen as a mixture of hierarchical methods and task-based decomposition. Task-based decomposition typically uses the same agent throughout learning, and hierarchical methods don't use different fidelity levels in their simulations. In this work, multiple agents control each aircraft and hand over control. Essentially this approach employs one agent per fidelity level per aircraft, meaning the lower fidelity simulations have agents that can learn much faster, receiving state information useful only to their specific task.

2.3 Fitness Function Shaping

Multiagent coordination is an important aspect of many domains, such as air traffic control [2], Robocup soccer [1] and power plant operations [5]. A learning or evolutionary algorithm will often convert a once computationally intractable search problem into a feasible guided search.

In learning algorithms fitness function design is important in keeping convergence time low while keeping performance high. In many multiagent coordination domains there is a difference between maximizing the system-level fitness and maximizing a single agent's fitness. If an agent always takes the locally-optimal action, it does not always maximize the system-level fitness.

The difference evaluation function [2] is evaluated such that each agent's fitness is related to the individual's contribution to team performance, therefore the signal-to-noise ratio is improved considerably. This leads to final better policies at an accelerated convergence rate, as well as overcoming the Tragedy of the Commons. The difference evaluation function is defined as:

$$D_i(z) = G(z) - G(z - z_i + c_i) , \quad (1)$$

where z is the system state, z_i is the system state with agent i, and c_i is a counterfactual replacing agent i. This counterfactual offsets the artificial impact of removing an agent from the system. For example, removing an aircraft from the system always artificially decreases the amount of congestion, which would provide a inaccurate fitness if a counterfactual is not used.

The difference evaluation function provides a compact encapsulation of the agent's impact on the system. It reduces the noise from other agents in the fitness function signal and has outperformed both system-level and local fitness functions in many congestion domains [1, 2, 5].

2.4 Air Traffic Control

The Next Generation (Next-Gen) Air Traffic System will replace the system in place by the FAA. For decades aircraft have been flying indirect routes over radar towers, causing increased delay and adding congestion to highly traveled intersections. Next-Gen is the upgrade to a satellite-based technology. Automatic Dependent Surveillance-Broadcast (ADS-B) navigation is part of this Next-Gen technology and will let pilots know the precise locations of nearby aircraft. However, pilots cannot directly comprehend all of the data for each nearby aircraft. Adding an evolutionary agent as a suggestion system for the pilot is an ideal way show the pilot only pertinent navigation information. This allows more aircraft in the sky while enhancing the safety of travel.

Two popular approaches to simulating the Air Traffic Flow Management Problem (ATFMP) had been to develop Lagrangian models of each aircraft's dynamics, and to create aggregate models of the NAS [4, 10, 11]. In the Lagrangian model approaches, typically the trajectories of each aircraft are taken into account and either collision-avoidance or congestion-reduction is performed [10]. This is an accurate and fine-grained approach to the ATFMP, but also time-intensive and complex. Aggregate models have been shown to simplify the NAS and therefore are a much simpler approach to the ATFMP. The aggregate models have been used in conjunction with linear programming to find solutions to air traffic flow [4], and linear algorithms to analyze departure, enroute and arrival delays [11].

In this work we chose to use a Lagrangian model of the NAS, receiving the benefits of a more detailed simulation. Each aircraft is simulated relative to their velocity, yaw, and pitch.

3. DOMAIN

This paper demonstrates the usefulness of the hierarchical simulation approach in an important air traffic congestion problem. Therefore, we discuss the aircraft traffic congestion problem first, and then show how to apply our approach with respect to that optimization problem. This section describes how we formulated a multiagent congestion problem by defining the scenarios and agents and developed an appropriate system evaluation function.

3.1 Scenario

We test our approach in two scenarios. In both scenarios, aircraft are lined up on the final approach to their destination. Each aircraft is 100 units above ground and 25 units from the aircraft arriving before and after themselves. Initial orientations of each aircraft are assigned to be toward the destination airport and initial starting locations begin at 125 units away from the destination airport. An amount of gaussian noise ($\sigma = 5$, $\mu = 0$) is then added to the starting location of each aircraft. Lastly, the speed of each aircraft is held statically at 1 unit.

In the first scenario, there are two airports, and a set of 6 aircraft arriving at each airport. In this scenario there is one intersection point where aircraft flying a direct route trajectory can reach potential separation violations. The goal in this scenario is to show our approach adequately optimizes the delay to the aircraft's destination while incurring no separation violations.

In the second scenario there are 6 airports with 10 aircraft arriving at each airport. Again, the aircraft are lined up on a final approach vector. In this scenario each aircraft must go through three intersection points, with a total of 9 intersection points on the map. Our goal in this scenario is to see what issues occur in later intersections when an aircraft must switch many times between a low fidelity and high fidelity simulation. We also would like to see how our approach scales to larger systems.

We measure the performance in each scenario by computing the overall delay and congestion of all aircraft:

$$P(z) = \sum_{a \in A} (\tau_{opt,a} - \tau_a) - C(z) \quad (2)$$

where $C(z)$ is the separation violation penalty (Equation 6), and $\tau_{opt,a}$ is the optimal time taken by aircraft a to land as if it took a straight-line route from its starting location to its destination and τ_a is the actual time taken by aircraft

a to land. If an aircraft does not land, the negative of the total number of time steps is used, in this case -600.

3.2 Agent Definition

Agents actions are continuous and they may choose to change yaw by up to 1 radian in a positive or negative direction and change their pitch by up to 2 radians positively or negatively for one time step. Each aircraft's speed is held static, therefore the steeper it ascends or descends the slower it moves toward its destination. Agents dynamics are modeled according to the equations:

$$\begin{aligned} dx &= |cos(pitch)| * cos(yaw) \\ dy &= |cos(pitch)| * sin(yaw) \\ dz &= sin(pitch) \end{aligned} \tag{3}$$

Each agent receives a state relative to their current simulation fidelity. Agents in the low fidelity simulations simply receive a state representing the aircraft relative to its destination, and agents in the high fidelity simulations receive a state that include the positions of nearby aircraft and the low fidelity state. This is explained in far more detail in Section 4.

3.3 Agent Policies

Agents developed policies using traditional cooperative coevolutionary algorithms (CCEAs) evolving weights for neural networks. In CCEAs, each population member of an agent is randomly assigned with population members of other agents to create a team. Fitnesses assigned to population members are based on the interactions within a given team. This team is evaluated and each population member is given a fitness. Once all population members have been assigned to a team, evolutionary subsampling is performed. For this evolutionary algorithm, we use 50 population members per agent for 2000 generations.

3.4 Fitness Evaluation

It is extremely important for pilots to keep a safe distance from other aircraft, therefore our goal in this work is to remove all separation violations, while simultaneously incentivizing aircraft to get to their destination in a timely manner. Therefore, the system-level fitness evaluation we developed focuses on the cumulative delay (δ) and congestion (C) throughout the system:

$$G(z) = (\delta(z) + -C(z)) , \tag{4}$$

where $\delta(z)$ represents the delay in the system, and $C(z)$ is the total penalty for congestion violations.

The delay is defined by the sums of the difference between the straight-line distance to the goal during the last time step and the straight-line distance to the goal the current time step, such that the maximum value for each sum is the speed of aircraft a:

$$\delta(z) = \sum_{a \in A} \eta(a_{t-1}, a_{dest}) - \eta(a_t, a_{dest}) , \tag{5}$$

where $\eta(a_t, a_{dest})$ is the distance from aircraft a at time t and aircraft a's destination.

The total congestion penalty is the summation of violations per time step:

$$C(z) = \sum_{a_1 \in A} \sum_{a_2 \in A} -\omega * \theta(\eta(a_1, a_2)) , \tag{6}$$

where $\theta(\eta(a_1, a_2))$ is a step function that is 1 if aircraft a_1 and a_2 are close enough to cause a violation, and 0 otherwise, and ω is the weight placed upon congestion, 1000 for our setup.

4. HIERARCHICAL SIMULATION

The hierarchical simulation requires three main steps for agents to learn well-developed policies: formulating the low fidelity simulation, formulating the high fidelity simulation, and combining the two. This section will describe how to properly develop and combine these simulations with respect to the aircraft optimization problem.

4.1 Low Fidelity Simulation

Our low fidelity simulation includes very little detail of the environment, and is therefore very computationally inexpensive. Environment information for each agent includes only the location of its aircraft and the location of the aircraft's destination airport. Due to this minimal representation, agents in this simulation receives a simple state space and fitness function.

The agents in the low fidelity simulation are given a state that only includes the $\Delta heading$ to their destination, and the fitness function calculated as the change in distance to their destination (Equation 5). Since the low fidelity simulation includes all of the agents, many actions simultaneously impact the system environment, causing the fitness for a specific agent to become noisy with the actions of other agents. An agent would have difficulty evolving to an optimal solution using such a noisy fitness evaluation signal. A difference evaluation function reduces much of this noise (Equation 1), and is easily derived from the system-level delay function (Equation 5):

$$D_i(z) = \delta(z) - \delta(z - z_i + c_i) , \tag{7}$$

where $\delta(z)$ is the delay fitness function with all agents and $\delta(z - z_i + c_i)$ is the delay fitness function with agents i removed from the system and replaced with counterfactual agent c_i. This counterfactual represents the aircraft taking a locally optimal action toward it's destination.

4.2 High Fidelity Simulation

Our high fidelity simulation takes advantage of the advanced Next-Gen [15] technologies, namely Automatic Dependent Surveillance-Broadcast (ADS-B). ADS-B is a satellite-based technology that provides aircraft information of other aircraft, such as position and velocity.

ADS-B technology provides pilots information of other aircraft nearby, but pilots (and agents) cannot use all of this information, as the state space would become too large. For this reason, we model this limitation by only allowing agents to observe x, y and z locations of aircraft within 10 units.

Since the ADS-B technology is not currently implemented, different approaches of using ADS-B is a current area of research. Yildiz et al. [19] modeled the pilot as being able to observe a limited section of the space in front of them, essentially discretizing the space in front of the agent into regions, and including 8 additional binary states, one for each region. This approach worked well in a 2D environment, but with a 3D environment the state space would need to be increased to at least 24 regions, 8 in front, 8 above and 8 below.

Our ADS-B approach is simplified. It simply includes the relative x, y and z location of the nearest aircraft within its simulation. This approach involves a much smaller state representation than Yildiz et al. since it only includes the aircraft closest to the agent and the distance discretized into 10 bins. It also covers a larger area of the environment, which we predict will allow the agent to make more informed decisions.

The fitness function for the high fidelity simulation includes penalties for violations and incentives for arriving at the airport quickly:

$$G(z) = \delta(z) + -C(z) \, , \tag{8}$$

where $C(z)$ is Equation 6 and $\delta(z)$ is Equation 5.

We use the global evaluation function in the high fidelity simulations because only a few agents are using the high fidelity simulation at one time (This is explained further in the next section). Additionally, the difference evaluation function heavily biases the evolutionary search. If an agent takes an action that prevents a violation, that population member receives a very high fitness, and future mutations will search around that area of the state space. It was often during preliminary analysis that particular part of the state space had a high chance of being efficient at avoiding a violation in one particular orientation, but performed poorly at reaching its destination, or avoiding aircraft in other orientations, therefore we did not use the difference evaluation.

4.3 Applying Hierarchical Simulation

A key part of this research is how the high and low fidelity simulation interact. Each simulator contains its own set of agents, so when one simulator takes over, the aircraft that are switching fidelity levels are now being controlled by different agents. The differences between the low fidelity and high fidelity agents are the state inputs and fitness evaluation functions. These two sets of agents must learn to cooperate together in order for this approach to be viable.

To switch from the low fidelity simulation to the high fidelity simulation, an aircraft needs to be within 10 units of another aircraft. At this point those two aircraft switch to a high fidelity agent and are ran in the same high fidelity simulation independently of other agents. If another aircraft enters within 10 units of one of these two aircraft, they are also added to the same high fidelity simulation as the original two. Independent simulations allowed us to calculate a global fitness relative to agents within that simulation (See Figure 1). This greatly reduces the noise of other aircraft during learning.

Since the state for the low fidelity agents involves simply the angle from the aircraft to their destination, the agent has no knowledge of when the high fidelity agents are going to take over. During preliminary analysis of this approach, we discovered interesting emergent behavior when the high fidelity and low fidelity agents learned simultaneously. Since the high fidelity agents learned slower, due to a larger state space, they led the aircraft to a highly suboptimal location during early learning. Once the low fidelity simulation took over again, the aircraft was in an unexplored part of the state space, and the agent was required to learn how to lead the aircraft to its destination. Additionally, the low fidelity simulation can learn how to lead an agent to its destination much faster than the high fidelity simulation, due to the simpler state space. This ultimately led to the high fidelity simulation to have caused the low fidelity simulation to receive a worse fitness.

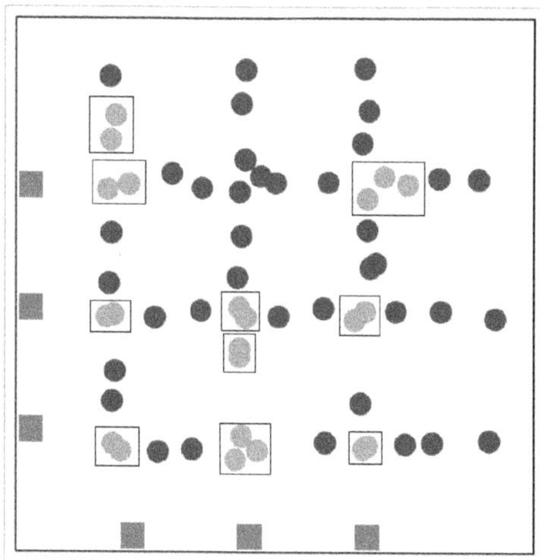

Figure 1: Aircraft within boxes are in independent high fidelity simulations, aircraft not in boxes are in the same low fidelity simulation, and squares are airports. Note that the environment is in 3D, so agents look like they are within a separation violation, but are actually above or below each other. This situation is during the 60 aircraft scenario.

Since the agents in the low fidelity simulation received a lower fitness due to the actions taken by the high fidelity simulator, the agents in the low fidelity simulation "learned" to avoid situations where the high fidelity simulation took over. Due to the high fidelity simulator only taking over the agent when a potential conflict is detected, the low fidelity agent indirectly began learning to avoid violations. Indirectly teaching agents on the simulation level is an interesting emergent behavior and is a topic in future work.

Due to this emergent behavior, we do not train the high fidelity and low fidelity agents simultaneously. Instead, we borrow from the field of transfer learning. We first train a set of low fidelity agents to convergence in a large set of simple environments. We vary the starting location and orientation of each aircraft, and train the agent to reach its destination. Once trained, these agents are capable of always reaching their destination from any starting location and orientation. Low fidelity agents are held static, and used in our scenarios while we trained high fidelity agents in our scenarios.

Since agents were are active during every time step, their fitness functions need to be slightly modified. If agent a is active for 400 time steps, and receives the same fitness as agent b, who was active for 300 time steps, agent b performed better than agent a. We solve this problem by dividing each agent's fitness by their number of active time steps, assigning each agent their average fitness per time step.

5. RESULTS

In this section we test our simulation hierarchy approach in the air traffic domain and compare it to the performance of using a high fidelity only approach. We show general benefits of using a simulation hierarchy, including faster convergence and faster computation. Lastly, we show that due to the low fidelity and high fidelity separation, the simulation hierarchy approach is very robust to noise. All graphs in this

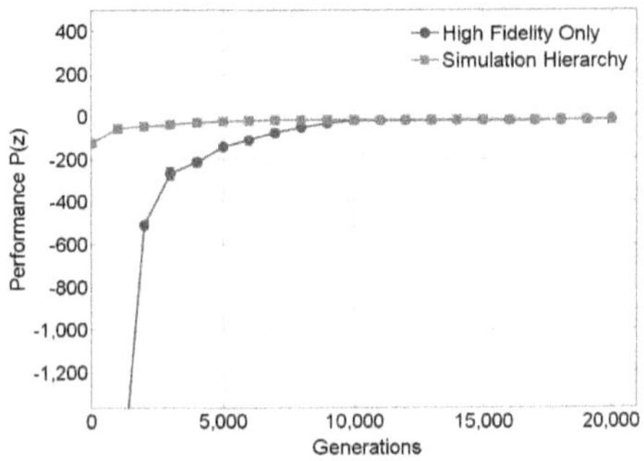

Figure 2: The simulation hierarchy approach and high fidelity only approach converged to the same performance. However, the simulation hierarchy approach reached that level of performance much faster, and with less computation.

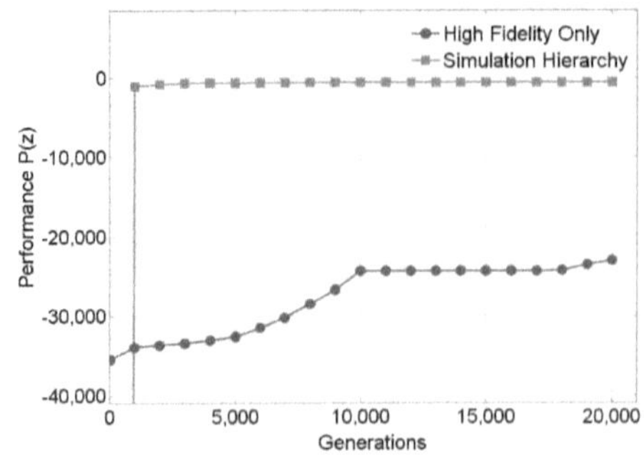

Figure 3: The simulation hierarchy approach outperformed the high fidelity only approach due to a less noisy fitness function and transfer learning. Since each high fidelity simulation is treated independently of each other, the global fitness function accurately encapsulates how each agent affects the environment.

section were computed using 10 statistical runs, and error bars are included.

5.1 Performance

The key benefit of using a simulator hierarchy is the increased speed of convergence. Agents in the low fidelity simulation are only concerned with reaching their destination. In this domain, this is a trivial problem to solve, and agents converge very fast to optimal. When adding in violation constraints, the problem becomes much harder. Agents are required to coordinate with each other to avoid separation violations. If only one fidelity simulator is being used, this problem becomes more difficult. Agents using only a high fidelity simulator will need to learn how to reach the destination while simultaneously learning to coordinate. If one agent evolves to a policy that allows an aircraft to reach the destination faster, but that policy leads to a separation violation, another agent must also have evolved to coordinate with that agent, all within the same simulation. This makes policies that perform separation coordination and reach their destination difficult to find.

When using a simulation hierarchy, the agents in the low fidelity simulation can quickly learn how to reach their destination, while the high fidelity agents only turn on when a separation violation might occur. This means the high fidelity agents need only care about a very small portion of the state space, and will also learn much faster. This also means that we can easily perform transfer learning since the low fidelity aircraft are not coordinating. As long as the low fidelity agents can learn how to reach their destination from any location, which again is an easy problem to solve, they do not need to learn further. Only the high fidelity agents compute their fitness during each time step they are active.

As mentioned in Section 4.2, the difference evaluation function can't be used in the high fidelity simulation, and we have to use a global fitness evaluation function. The global evaluation function is easily computable, but does not perform well with many agents in a congestion domain [1, 5, 2]. This isn't a problem when we use simulation hierarchies. Each group of agents within a high fidelity simulator are treated independently of each other, so the global fitness function represents only a few agents at a time. The global fitness function is a very good learning signal when only a few agents are included. When using only the high fidelity simulator, every agent receives the same global fitness function, and is therefore given a noisier global fitness function.

This increased convergence rate makes it much easier to scale to larger systems, since well performing policies become much easier to find. As you can see from Figure 2, using a hierarchical simulation in the smaller scenario leads to a much faster convergence rate to an equally performing solution. In this scenario, we apply transfer learning in the low fidelity simulation, which gives it a much higher starting performance. This scenario is not complex enough for the simulation hierarchy approach to see any performance benefits over the high fidelity only approach. However, the high fidelity only approach takes much more computation to reach that same level of performance, as will be discussed in the next section.

In the higher complexity scenario, the simulation hierarchy approach is able to converge to a well performing solution very quickly (Figure 3). This is due to the high fidelity simulations being treated independently of each other, and the low fidelity transfer learning. The high fidelity only approach should theoretically eventually reach the performance of the simulation hierarchy, but at a huge cost of computation.

In these experiments, transfer learning was not used for the high fidelity only approach due to the noise in the global fitness function. In both approaches, once an agent transferred to a larger environment, it was able to reach its destination, but not without incurring violations. The global fitness function in the high fidelity only approach was too noisy for agents to learn to avoid these violations, and therefore have a much worse performance than if transfer learning was not used. In the hierarchical simulation approach, the fitness function is less noisy, and agents are able to quickly learn to avoid violations.

5.2 Speed

Decreasing the computational complexity of a simulator is extremely useful in learning. When performing hundreds of thousands of trials, even a small speedup of one simulation step can impact overall computation time by magnitudes. In complex domains this decreased computation time leads to an ability to scale to larger systems, add more agents, or use more accurate physical models.

Scenario	Simulation time (s) No Penalty	Penalty	HF calls	LF calls
12-HF+LF	0.02	2.94	146	1702
12-HF	0.05	39.23	1959	0
60-HF+LF	0.1	11.68	579	21789
60-HF	0.25	617.21	30848	0

Table 1: The amount of computation time required per simulation step was much smaller when using the simulation hierarchy approach both with and without the penalty to the high fidelity simulation.

When using only the high fidelity simulation, computing the high fidelity state requires each agent to compute a larger state: x, y and z of the closest aircraft, and the degree between the aircraft and the destination. In addition, due to the more complex state space and additional neural network inputs, a larger neural network is needed to fully learn the system, further increasing computation time.

In a high fidelity simulator, it is common for systems to need to sacrifice speed to compute additional useful information, such as querying 3rd party software or performing additional computation. In this scenario, this additional information is through the use of the ADS-B system, which is used in the high fidelity simulator to compute the relative location of nearby aircraft. Note that the ADS-B system data received will be 1 MB, with a 50MB/s signal [6]. Therefore, we added an additional computational cost of 0.02 second when using the ADS-B technology to give a more realistic computational complexity analysis the high fidelity simulator.

When using the hierarchical simulation approach, agents are required to compute the full state a small number of time steps. Agents are in the low fidelity simulation unless a potential separation violation can occur. Table 1 shows the computation time per simulation step of the different scenarios. During learning we call the simulation 200,000 times, for 600 time steps each, therefore even a small speed up here leads to an extremely large time savings.

When using the simulation hierarchy approach without penalties to the high fidelity simulation, the computation time required per simulation step was about half of when using the high fidelity only approach. This is due to the fast computational speed of the low fidelity simulation, and only switching to the slower, yet more detailed, high fidelity simulation to perform collision avoidance. When adding in the penalties for the ADS-B system, the simulation hierarchy approach was 13x faster per simulation step in the smaller scenario, and 52x faster in the larger scenario. This is one of the key benefits of using the simulation hierarchy approach.

In an application that uses the difference evaluation function, the computational speed up would be even greater. The difference fitness function is a useful tool for accurately evaluating a policy, but it is often computationally expensive, especially when resimulation is required. This approach can speed up the difference fitness function computation in a high fidelity simulation, since the number of agents in each independent high fidelity simulation is very small. This can easily turn a once intractable problem into a tractable one.

5.3 Accuracy

One of the key concerns of using a simulator hierarchy is whether or not the simulation as a whole is accurate enough for the agents to learn a well performing policy. We argue that as long as the correct fidelity transition function is used, a simulation hierarchy is as accurate as simply using a high fidelity simulator, except with a much faster convergence rate and at less computational complexity. As shown in Figure 2, the high fidelity only approach eventually reaches the performance of simulation hierarchy approach, but at a much slower convergence rate. Additionally, as shown in Table 1, the high fidelity only approach is much more computationally expensive.

We further analyze the robustness of the simulator hierarchy approach by adding noise to the low fidelity simulation. There is an interesting cost-benefit study here. If the mechanism deciding which fidelity an agent uses is centralized, and therefore noiseless, adding noise to the low fidelity system state will hardly hurt performance. This is because if an agent is within the fidelity transition function criteria, the high fidelity simulation takes over and insures there will be no separation violations. This centralized approach is ideal, but comes with the typical problem of centralized approaches. If this decision mechanism has an error, or breaks down, all of the aircraft in the system will be at risk.

If the fidelity transition function is included in the agent design, it becomes decentralized and doesn't suffer from a system wide break down if one mechanism incurs an error. However, since the fidelity transition function is on a per-agent basis and is included in the agent definition, it must include the noise that the agent receives. If the noise is greater than the fidelity transition function criteria, agents may be in a low fidelity simulation when they should be attempting to avoid a violation. The agent is in a low fidelity simulation and does not realize it is close to another agent. This issue does not occur if the noise is less than the fidelity transition function criteria, as the high fidelity simulation will take over before a violation can occur.

We simulate this by adding a static amount of noise modified by a normal distribution noise model to the low fidelity simulation:

$$\eta = N(0,1) \pm r \tag{9}$$

where $N(0,1)$ is a normal distribution with $\mu = 0$ and $\sigma = 1$, and r is a static value representing a constant noise being added or removed from the Gaussian distribution.

Adding Gaussian noise to the x, y, and z locations during each time step introduced noise in both the state information and the fidelity transition function. As shown in Figure 4, this noise introduction affects performance negatively, but this approach is still very robust to noise.

6. CONCLUSION

This paper introduces the simulation hierarchy approach, an approach that uses both a high and low fidelity simulation and receives benefits from both. High fidelity simulation leads to higher quality learning due to a more detailed state space, but at a large cost of computation. On the other hand, low fidelity simulation has a less detailed state space, but is computationally inexpensive.

In this work, we show that the simulation hierarchy approach leads to a faster convergence rate while simultaneously reducing the computational complexity of running

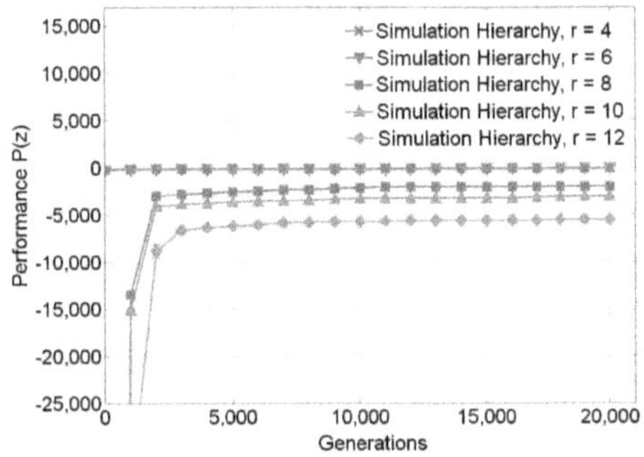

Figure 4: Adding/subtracting up to 6 units for noise while adding $N(0,1)$ Gaussian noise only slightly affected performance. Performance was largely affected when the total noise could potentially become greater than the fidelity transition function criteria.

simulations. Learning using simulation hierarchies leads to a similar performing solution in the low complexity scenario at a 13x reduction in time complexity. In the higher complexity scenario, learning with simulation hierarchies leads to a much better performing solution at a 52x reduction in time complexity. When using simulation hierarchies, treating each high fidelity simulation as an independent simulation led to this increase of performance, while switching between the high and low fidelity simulation led to the decrease in computation time and robustness to noise, resulting in a fast, robust, and well performing approach.

7. REFERENCES

[1] Noa Agmon and Peter Stone. Leading ad hoc agents in joint action settings with multiple teammates. In *Proc. of 11th Int. Conf. on Autonomous Agents and Multiagent Systems (AAMAS 2012)*, June 2012.

[2] A. K. Agogino and K. Tumer. A multiagent approach to managing air traffic flow. *Autonomous Agents and MultiAgent Systems*, 24:1–25, 2012.

[3] Nguyen Thi Ngoc Anh, Zucker Jean Daniel, Nguyen Huu Du, Alexis Drogoul, and Vo Duc An. A hybrid macro-micro pedestrians evacuation model to speed up simulation in road networks. In *Proceedings of the 10th international conference on Advanced Agent Technology*, AAMAS'11, pages 371–383, Berlin, Heidelberg, 2012. Springer-Verlag.

[4] Dimitris Bertsimas and Sarah Stock Patterson. The air traffic flow management problem with enroute capacities. *Oper. Res.*, 46(3):406–422, March 1998.

[5] Mitchell Colby and Kagan Tumer. Shaping fitness functions for coevolving cooperative multiagent systems. In *Proceedings of the 11th International Conference on Autonomous Agents and Multiagent Systems*, 2012.

[6] ADS-B In Aviation Rulemaking Committee. Recommendations to define a strategy for incorporating ads-b in technologies into the national airspace system. Technical report, U.S. Department of Transportation, Federal Aviation Administration, 2011.

[7] Thomas G. Dietterich. Hierarchical reinforcement learning with the MAXQ value function decomposition. *Journal of Artificial Intelligence Research*, 13:227–303, 2000.

[8] John A. Doucette, Peter Lichodzijewski, and Malcolm I. Heywood. Hierarchical task decomposition through symbiosis in reinforcement learning. In *Proceedings of the fourteenth international conference on Genetic and evolutionary computation conference*, GECCO '12, pages 97–104, New York, NY, USA, 2012. ACM.

[9] Bao-Liang Lu and M. Ito. Task decomposition and module combination based on class relations: a modular neural network for pattern classification. *Neural Networks, IEEE Transactions on*, 10(5):1244–1256, 1999.

[10] David McNally and Chester Gong. Concept and laboratory analysis of trajectory-based automation for separation assurance. In *AIAA Guidance, Navigation and Control Conference and Exhibit*, Keystone, CO.

[11] Eric R. Mueller and Gano B. Chatterji. Analysis of aircraft arrival and departure delay characteristics. In *AIAA Aircraft Technology, Integration and Operations (ATIO) Conference*, Los Angeles, CA.

[12] Sinno Jialin Pan and Qiang Yang. A survey on transfer learning. *IEEE Trans. on Knowl. and Data Eng.*, 22(10):1345–1359, October 2010.

[13] Liviu Panait and Sean Luke. Cooperative multi-agent learning: The state of the art. *Autonomous Agents and Multi-Agent Systems*, 11(3):387–434, November 2005.

[14] Scott Proper and Kagan Tumer. Modeling difference rewards for multiagent learning. In *Proceedings of the 11th International Conference on Autonomous Agents and Multiagent Systems - Volume 3*, 2012.

[15] Corker K. M. Sheridan, T. B. and E. D. Nadler. Final report and recommendations on human-automation interaction in the next generation air transportation system. Technical report, U.S. Department of Transportation, Research and Innovative Technology Administration., 2006.

[16] A. Sóbester, S.J. Leary, and A.J. Keane. A parallel updating scheme for approximating and optimizing high fidelity computer simulations. *Structural and Multidisciplinary Optimization*, 27(5):371–383, 2004.

[17] Soteris Stylianou and Marios M. Fyrillas. Scalable pedestrian simulation for virtual cities. In *In ACM VRST*, 2004.

[18] E.S. Tzafestas. Agentifying the process: task-based or robot-based decomposition? In *Systems, Man, and Cybernetics, 1994. Humans, Information and Technology., 1994 IEEE International Conference on*, volume 1, pages 582–587 vol.1, 1994.

[19] Yildiz Yildiray, Adrian Agogino, and Guillaume Brat. Predicting pilot behavior in medium scale scenarios using game theory and reinforcement learning. Technical report, AIAA Modeling and Simulation Technologies Conference, 2013.

[20] Lasheng Yu, Fei Hong, PengRen Wang, Yang Xu, and Yong Liu. Influence graph based task decomposition and state abstraction in reinforcement learning. In *Young Computer Scientists, 2008. ICYCS 2008. The 9th International Conference for*, pages 136–141, 2008.

Using an Adaptive Invasion-based Model for Fast Range Image Registration

Ivanoe De Falco
ICAR–CNR
Via P. Castellino, 111
Naples, Italy
ivanoe.defalco@na.icar.cnr.it

Antonio Della Cioppa
University of Salerno
Via Ponte Don Melillo, 1
Fisciano (SA), Italy
adellacioppa@unisa.it

Domenico Maisto
ICAR–CNR
Via P. Castellino, 111
Naples, Italy
domenico.maisto@na.icar.cnr.it

Umberto Scafuri
ICAR–CNR
Via P. Castellino, 111
Naples, Italy
umberto.scafuri@na.icar.cnr.it

Ernesto Tarantino
ICAR–CNR
Via P. Castellino, 111
Naples, Italy
ernesto.tarantino@na.icar.cnr.it

ABSTRACT

This paper presents an adaptive model for automatically pair–wise registering range images. Given two images and set one as the model, the aim is to find the best possible spatial transformation of the second image causing 3D reconstruction of the original object. Registration is effected here by using a distributed Differential Evolution algorithm characterized by a migration model inspired by the phenomenon known as biological invasion, and by applying a parallel Grid Closest Point algorithm. The distributed algorithm is endowed with two adaptive updating schemes to set the mutation and the crossover parameters, whereas the subpopulation size is assumed to be set in advance and kept fixed throughout the evolution process. The adaptive procedure is tied to the migration and is guided by a performance measure between two consecutive migrations. Experimental results achieved by our approach show the capability of this adaptive method of picking up efficient transformations of images and are compared with those of a recently proposed evolutionary algorithm. This efficiency is evaluated in terms of both quality and robustness of the reconstructed 3D image, and of computational cost.

Categories and Subject Descriptors

I.2.8 [**Artificial Intelligence**]: Problem Solving, Control Methods, and Search—*heuristic methods*; I.4.3 [**Image Processing and Computer Vision**]: Enhancement—*Registration*

GECCO'14, July 12–16, 2014, Vancouver, BC, Canada.
Copyright 2014 ACM 978-1-4503-2662-9/14/07 ...$15.00.
http://dx.doi.org/10.1145/2576768.2598340.

Keywords

Distributed Differential Evolution, adaptive control parameter setting, range image registration.

1. INTRODUCTION

Range Image Registration (RIR) is a crucial task in computer vision used for integrating information acquired under diverse viewing angles (multi–view analysis). Over the years, several multi–view RIR techniques have been developed [21, 29, 17, 30] to tackle many practical applications, such as 3D modeling ranging from medical imaging, remote sensing, digital archeology, restoration of historic buildings, virtual museum, artificial vision, reverse engineering and computer–aided design (CAD) [27].

Since a physical object cannot be completely scanned with a single image due to the limited field of view of a sensor, a set of images taken from different positions is required to supply the information needed to build the whole 3D model. To avoid manually producing such a model by means of error–prone CAD–based techniques, multiple images are acquired by using range scanners [2] and joined together by a registration algorithm. The registration strategy can differ according to whether all range views of the objects are registered at the same time (multi–view registration) or only a pair of adjacent range images is processed in every execution (pair–wise registration). This paper is focused on the pair–wise registration of range images. As a consequence, starting from two views, i.e., the model and the scene, the objective of our registration process consists in finding the best spatial transformation that, when applied to the scene, aligns it with the model in a common coordinate system.

Image registration is usually formulated as an optimization problem solved by iterative procedures. Among these, examples are Iterative Closest Point (ICP) methods [28], centered on the point–to–point and point–to–plane correspondences. However, as a drawback, the majority of these iterative algorithms requires to provide either a rough or a near–optimal prealignment of the images to avoid being trapped in local optima. Unfortunately, an exhaustive exploration of the search space of all the candidate solutions becomes impracticable in case of absence of constraints for the possible transformations. Moreover, most of the computation time is spent in finding the closest point in the model image to every point in the aligned image. Thus stochastic optimization algorithms, such as Evolutionary Algorithms (EAs) [1], capable of providing a solution acceptably close to the global optimum in a reasonable time, have been successfully applied to complex real–world problems in computer vision and image registration [3, 8, 11, 12, 20, 26, 30]. Although these methods constitute an interesting alternative because they do not necessitate a good prealignment of the views to converge to the global optimum, they require a careful tuning of many control parameters. The setting of these parameters can strongly affect the performance of the algorithms [15] and is a very time–consuming task. Therefore, automatic procedures for efficiently setting these crucial control parameters for dealing with complex optimization problems are highly recommended. Moreover, the computation time to find the closest point in the model image can be significantly reduced by applying a Grid Closest Point (GCP) transformation [37] before the registration process.

With the aim to overcome the above drawbacks, within this paper we examine the ability of a recently proposed adaptive model for distributed Differential Evolution (DE) [25] to perform automatic pair–wise image registration by exploiting a distributed implementation of GCP without any *a priori* knowledge of the pose of the views. The distributed adaptive model is characterized by a migration model inspired by the phenomenon known as biological invasion [34] and is endowed with two updating schemes for automatically setting DE control parameters. Hereinafter, this adaptive algorithm is referred to as Adaptive Invasion–based migration Model for distributed DE (AIM–dDE) [7].

The adaptive procedure occurs at each migration time and is based on two steps. Firstly a local performance measure related to the average fitness improvement for each subpopulation is computed between two consecutive migration steps. Secondly, a specific updating scheme based on these measures takes place to update the control parameter values of some subpopulations.

The evolutionary system has been tested by means of a set of eight widely used 3D range images. To further estimate its effectiveness, it is also compared with a Self–adaptive Evolutionary Optimization algorithm, named SaEvO, recently proposed by Santamaria et al. [33] for facing RIR problems. The experimental results demonstrate the ability of the proposed adaptive approach in facing these RIR problems.

Paper structure is as follows: Section 2 describes the state of the art. Section 3 contains a brief description of AIM–dDE algorithm and illustrates the application of our system to the registration task defining the encoding and the fitness of the related optimization problem. Section 4 reports the results achieved by our tool. The last section contains final remarks and future works.

2. STATE OF THE ART

Several surveys on RIR are available in literature. A complete study focused on pair–wise registration is presented in [5], while different techniques for both pair–wise and multi–view registration, and a new classification, can be found in [29].

In the last two decades, EAs have been extensively applied to the image registration problems. Differently from methods based on the ICP algorithm, EAs can work with images without any kind of prealignment. An extensive review of evolutionary image registration methods is reported in [30].

He and Narayana [16] propose a real coding scheme that makes use of arithmetic crossover and uniform mutation operators within an elitist generational model including a restart mechanism. The evolutionary method uses a real–coded Genetic Algorithm (GA) to estimate the rigid transformation and a local search procedure to refine the obtained preliminary solution.

Chow et al. [3] still propose the use of real–coded GA considering a rigid transformation but introduce a crossover operator that randomly selects the number of genes to be swapped and a different sophisticated restart mechanism.

Silva et al. [35] face the pair–wise registration problem of range images captured by 3D laser range scanner by means of a parameter–based approach for rigid transformations. The proposed technique is inspired to the steady–state evolutionary scheme of GAs. Tournament selection, uniform crossover, and random selection mutation operator are used together with a hill–climbing algorithm in order to improve the precision of the results.

In [20] a new method for the pair–wise registration is introduced. The novelty is represented by the inclusion of a degree of overlapping parameter in the solution vector and the utilization of the trimmed square metric as objective function to be minimized.

Cordón et al. [4] present a Scatter Search [18] EA adopting a matching–based approach while Santamaria et al. propose different memetic–based image registration techniques to deal with 3D reconstruction of forensic objects [31, 32].

As regards the adaptive approaches, De Falco et al. [10] propose a novel adaptive updating scheme based on chaos theory for setting the control parameters for a DE algorithm to tackle pair–wise registration problem. Moreover, Santamaria et al. [33] illustrate a self–adaptive memetic evolutionary optimization algorithm, named SaEvO, for facing real–world RIR problems.

3. ADAPTIVE INVASION–BASED MODEL

Among EAs, DE has proven fast and reliable to face several multivariable optimization tasks in many applications [6, 24]. As underlined in Section 1, one of the ways to improve the DE chance to generate solutions with higher quality is to devise suitable control parameter adaptive strategies. Based on these considerations we introduced AIM–dDE, a novel adaptive distributed model endowed with updating schemes for setting the values of mutation and crossover parameters.

Our model is different from the others in literature relative to dDEs in the following aspects:

- the control parameter updating is strictly tied to the migration process in order to balance exploration and exploitation in the parameter space;
- the choice of the subpopulations which update the parameter values is driven by a performance measure related to the average fitness improvements of each subpopulation between two consecutive migration times;

- the subpopulations involved by the parameter changing are unknown *a priori*, in that they are selected based on the performance feedback coming from the same subpopulations.

AIM–dDE is based on IM–dDE [9], a previous distributed invasion–based model proposed by us, with the addition of an adaptive strategy for the DE control parameters. Therefore, in the next subsections we firstly report a brief description of our IM–dDE, and then we present the associated adaptive schemes.

3.1 The IM–dDE algorithm

IM–dDE is a stepping–stone dDE using a migration inspired by the biological invasion process instead of the canonical exchange mechanism. The model makes use of a locally connected topology where each node p hosts an instance of a DE, and is connected to its neighboring nodes.

At each generation t, the subpopulation $P_p(t)$ of each node p performs a sequential DE until t equals $t_{\max}$ generations.

At every $\mathcal{T}$ generations, $\mathcal{T}$ being an algorithm parameter named *invasion interval*, neighboring subpopulations exchange individuals. Hence, at a generic *invasion time* $t = k\mathcal{T}$, with $k \in \{1, \ldots, \lfloor \frac{t_{\max}}{\mathcal{T}} \rfloor\}$ and $t_{\max}$ the maximum number of generations, the set of individuals each subpopulation $P_p(t)$ sends to its neighbors, i.e., the *propagule*, is indicated as $\mathcal{M}_{P_p(t)}$ and is determined by collecting the individuals of $P_p(t)$ which are fitter than its current average fitness $\langle \Phi_p(t) \rangle$:

$$\begin{aligned}\mathcal{M}_{P_p(t)} &= \left\{ x_i^p(t) \in P_p(t) \;\middle|\; \Phi(x_i^p(t)) \succ \langle \Phi_p(t) \rangle \right\} \\ \text{with } \langle \Phi_p(t) \rangle &= \frac{1}{l} \sum_{j=1}^{l} \Phi(x_j^p(t)), \\ t &= k\mathcal{T}, k \in \left\{ 1, \ldots, \lfloor \frac{t_{\max}}{\mathcal{T}} \rfloor \right\}\end{aligned} \tag{1}$$

where $\Phi(x_i^p(t))$ is the fitness associated to the individual $x_i^p(t)$ and "$\succ$" is a binary relation stating that the left member is fitter than the right member.

All of the chosen individuals are sent to all of the neighboring subpopulations $P_{\tilde{p}}(t)$, with $\tilde{p}$ belonging to the set of neighbors of the node p. Then, at each invasion time, each subpopulation receives a total number of $\sum_{\tilde{p}} \left| \mathcal{M}_{P_{\tilde{p}}(t)} \right|$ elements where $\left| \mathcal{M}_{P_{\tilde{p}}(t)} \right|$ is the cardinality of the set $\mathcal{M}_{P_{\tilde{p}}(t)}$.

Afterwards, in each node, a *founding subpopulation*, formed by both native and exogenous individuals, is constructed by adding this massive number of invading individuals to the local subpopulation. Hence, the founding subpopulation constitutes a source of heterogeneity exploitable by the algorithm to improve its ability to search new evolutionary paths.

Subsequently, a fitness–proportionate selection mechanism is applied to the founding subpopulation to generate the new subpopulation $P'_p(t)$.

3.2 Adaptive Strategy

If, without loss of generality, minimization problems are considered, the procedure on which the adaptive model is based occurs in three steps as follows:

1. At the beginning of the evolution for each subpopulation random values for mutation and crossover parameters are sampled from two independent sequences of an uniform distribution $U(0.1, 1.0)$. This distribution has been used in the following each time a parameter is randomly generated.
2. At a generic invasion time $t = k\mathcal{T}$, with k as above, and before the new founding subpopulations have been created on all the nodes, for each subpopulation the local improvement $\Delta\langle \Phi_p(t) \rangle$ of the average fitness is evaluated as the difference between the average fitness values after the last invasion and at the current generation (for the first invasion time only, the initial generation is taken into account as 'last invasion'):

$$\begin{aligned}\Delta\langle \Phi_p(t) \rangle =& \langle \Phi_p(t - \mathcal{T}) \rangle - \langle \Phi_p(t) \rangle, \\ & \text{with } t = k\mathcal{T}, k \in \left\{ 1, \ldots, \lfloor \frac{t_{\max}}{\mathcal{T}} \rfloor \right\}.\end{aligned} \tag{2}$$

3. According to a predefined updating scheme a set of subpopulations is chosen and the values of their control parameters are changed.

As concerns the step 3, several updating schemes can be devised in order to select the set of subpopulations on which the adaptive setting of control parameters has to take place. To this end, we propose two updating schemes, i.e., *RandAvg* and *ChAvg*.

- *RandAvg*. According to this scheme, the average of all the local improvements, i.e., the global average improvement $\langle \Delta\langle \Phi_p(t) \rangle \rangle$ is computed:

$$\begin{aligned}\langle \Delta\langle \Phi_p(t) \rangle \rangle =& \frac{1}{\mathcal{N}} \sum_{p=1}^{\mathcal{N}} \Delta\langle \Phi_p(t) \rangle, \\ & \text{with } t = k\mathcal{T}, k \in \left\{ 1, \ldots, \lfloor \frac{t_{\max}}{\mathcal{T}} \rfloor \right\}.\end{aligned} \tag{3}$$

  The control parameter values of each subpopulation for which $\Delta\langle \Phi_p(t) \rangle < \langle \Delta\langle \Phi_p(t) \rangle \rangle$ are randomly replaced. Then the control parameter values of all the subpopulations are kept constant until next invasion when the procedure takes place again.

- *ChAvg*. At each invasion time, the mutation and the crossover parameter values of all the subpopulations are generated according to a chaotic series. The control parameter values of each subpopulation for which $\Delta\langle \Phi_p(t) \rangle < \langle \Delta\langle \Phi_p(t) \rangle \rangle$ are updated as follows:

$$\begin{cases} F_{t+1} &= \mu \cdot F_t \cdot (1 - F_t) \\ CR_{t+1} &= \mu \cdot CR_t \cdot (1 - CR_t) \end{cases} \tag{4}$$

  Then the control parameter values of all the subpopulations are kept constant until next invasion when the procedure takes place again. The *ChAvg* scheme is based on one of the simplest and most commonly used dynamic systems evidencing chaotic behavior known as the logistic map [23] which is described by the following quadratic recurrence equation:

$$y_{t+1} = \mu \cdot y_t \cdot (1 - y_t), \text{ with } t = 1, 2, 3, \ldots \tag{5}$$

Algorithm 1 Pseudo-code of AIM–dDE on a generic node p with $p \in \{1, ..., P_{\mathcal{N}}\}$

$t = 0$
randomly initialize a subpopulation $P_p(t) = \{\mathbf{x}_1^p(t), \cdots, \mathbf{x}_l^p(t)\}$
evaluate the fitness $\Phi(\mathbf{x}_i^p(t)),\ \forall i \in \{1, \ldots, l\}$
randomly initialize the values for F and CR from two independent $U(0.1, 1.0)$
while halting conditions are not satisfied **do**
  $t = t + 1$
  update the subpopulation $P_p(t)$ using the evolutionary operators of the DE
  evaluate the fitness $\Phi(\mathbf{x}_i^p(t)),\ \forall i \in \{1, \ldots, l\}$
  if $((t \bmod \mathcal{T}) = 0)$ **then**
    create the propagule $\mathcal{M}_{P_p}(t)$ for the current subpopulation
    send the propagule $\mathcal{M}_{P_p}(t)$ to the neighboring subpopulations
    receive the propagules $\mathcal{M}_{P_{\bar{p}}}(t)$ from the neighboring subpopulations
    construct the founding subpopulation $\Pi_p(t)$
    select l individuals in $\Pi_p(t)$ through a fitness–proportionate selection mechanism
    insert the l selected individuals into a new subpopulation $P'_p(t)$
    replace the subpopulation $P_p(t)$ with $P'_p(t)$
    set the values for F and CR according to the chosen updating scheme
  end if
end while

---

where μ is a positive constant sometimes known as *biotic potential*. The behavior of the system is greatly affected by the value of μ which determines whether y stabilizes at a constant size, oscillates among a limited sequence of sizes, or behaves chaotically in an unpredictable pattern. A very small difference in the initial value y_1 causes large differences in the long–time dynamic behavior [19]. Eq. (5) exhibits chaotic dynamics with values within the range $[0, 1]$ at μ approximately 3.57. Beyond $\mu = 4$ and $y_1 \neq 0, 0.25, 0.50, 0.75, 1$, the values eventually leave the interval $[0, 1]$ and diverge for almost all initial values.

Depending on the specific scheme selected, we have two algorithms for AIM–dDE, namely AIM–dDE–*RandAvg* and AIM–dDE–*ChAvg*.

The pseudo–code of the AIM–dDE model for a generic node, regardless of the specific updating scheme chosen, is reported in Algorithm 1.

3.3 Encoding and Fitness

Given two input images, named scene $I_S = \{\vec{p}_1, \ldots, \vec{p}_n\}$ and model $I_M = \{\vec{p}'_1, \ldots, \vec{p}'_m\}$ with n and m points respectively, RIR aims to find the best possible Euclidean motion f for I_S determined by the rotation R_θ of an angle θ around an axis A and the translation $\vec{t} = (t_x, t_y, t_z)$. Then the transformed points are denoted as: $f(\vec{p}_i) = R_\theta(\vec{p}_i) + \vec{t},\ i = 1, \ldots, n$. Actually unit quaternions are used to manage rotations in order to avoid singularities and discontinuities, e.g. gimbal lock. In this notation $R_\theta = (\theta, A_x, A_y, A_z)$.

The pair–wise RIR problem can then be seen as a numerical optimization problem in which solutions are encoded as seven–dimensional vectors of real values $\mathbf{x} = (\theta, A_x, A_y, A_z, t_x, t_y, t_z)$. The aim is to search the Euclidean transformation f^* achieving the best alignment of both $f(I_S)$ and I_M based on the chosen similarity metric Φ to optimize:

$$f^* = \arg\min_f \Phi(I_S, I_M; f) \tag{6}$$

Due to its robustness in presence of outliers (i.e., acquired noisy range images), the similarity metric Φ usually considered in 3D modeling is the median square error (*MedSE*) [27]. It can be formulated as:

$$\Phi(I_S, I_M; f) = MedSE(d_i^2),\ \forall i = \{1, \ldots, n\} \tag{7}$$

where *MedSE* corresponds to the median value of all the squared Euclidean distances, $d_i^2 = ||f(\vec{p}_i) - \vec{p}'_j||^2$ $(j = 1, \ldots, m)$, between the transformed scene point, $f(\vec{p}_i)$, and its corresponding closest point, $\vec{p}'_j$, in the model view I_M.

To speed up the computation of the closest point the GCP transform is used. It is important to remark here that, although performed only once before the registration, such a computation is the most time–consuming part of the RIR problem. In fact, the amount of time needed for this computation strongly depends on the discretization of the physical space into which the object is, and on the number of points composing the two images to register. In a sequential environment this computation can last even hours, before evolution can start and a suitable transformation is found. Yet, the computation of the GCP can highly profit from a distributed approach as the one we are proposing. In fact, it can be easily and completely parallelized without introducing any parallel overhead: each image can be divided into slices along one of the axes, and each slice can be assigned to a different core. In this way, this task can be completed in an amount of time depending on the quantity of hardware available, the higher the number of processing units the higher the number of slices and, consequently, the lower the computation time.

4. EXPERIMENTAL RESULTS

To investigate the behavior of AIM–dDE in the RIR field, a set of benchmarks from the image repository [22] collected at Signal Analysis and Machine Perceptron Laboratory (SAMPL) at the Ohio State University has been taken into account. From that repository, the following eight objects have been considered: Angel, Bird, Buddha, Bunny, Duck, Frog, Lobster, and Teletubby. For each of them the pair of images taken at angles 0 and 40 degrees has been chosen as exemplary instances for pair–wise RIR.

The parallel algorithms, which use the Message Passing Interface (MPI) [36], are written in C language. All the experiments have been carried out on an Apple iMac that is equipped with an Intel Core i7 Quad–core, each core running at 3.4 GHz.

Throughout the experiments we have made use of a DE/*rand*/1/*bin* strategy. After a preliminary tuning, for the whole experimental phase the parameter setting has been chosen as follows: number of subpopulations $\mathcal{N}$ equal to 16, size of each subpopulation $l = 10$, the value for the migration interval $\mathcal{T}$ equal to 30. Finally, AIM–dDE has been executed for each of the two updating schemes. For the logistic map, we have used $\mu = 4$ and $y(1) =]0, 0.5[-\{0.25\}$.

As concerns the number of generations for our distributed algorithm, its exact value has been set after making a great deal of careful consideration. In fact, to assess in a fair way

Table 1: RIR results in terms of best and average values, and standard deviations obtained over 25 runs.

Algorithm		Angel	Bird	Buddha	Bunny	Duck	Frog	Lobster	Teletubby
AIM–dDE–*RandAvg*	Φ_b	0.5550	0.2274	0.6571	0.2015	0.2245	0.2364	0.3886	0.1723
	$\langle\Phi\rangle$	0.5622	**0.2279**	0.6592	0.2025	0.2262	0.2399	0.3949	0.1746
	σ_Φ	**0.0045**	**0.0005**	0.0046	**0.0007**	**0.0012**	**0.0025**	0.0034	0.0022
AIM–dDE–*ChAvg*	Φ_b	0.5524	0.2274	0.6524	0.2015	0.2240	**0.2362**	0.3926	0.1707
	$\langle\Phi\rangle$	0.5611	0.2280	0.6541	0.2030	**0.2261**	**0.2396**	0.3950	**0.1732**
	σ_Φ	0.0049	**0.0005**	**0.0018**	0.0008	**0.0012**	0.0026	**0.0021**	**0.0017**
SaEvO	Φ_b	**0.3493**	**0.2028**	**0.3990**	**0.0712**	**0.1585**	0.2536	**0.2505**	**0.1050**
	$\langle\Phi\rangle$	**0.4983**	0.4451	**0.6120**	**0.1800**	0.2355	0.3991	**0.3787**	0.1911
	σ_Φ	0.2175	0.3052	0.1224	0.2052	0.1135	0.1963	0.1984	0.1667

the quality of the results achieved, in this paper we also wish to compare our results against those obtained by the best–so–far algorithm used in the literature to perform range image registration over the same eight objects, i.e., SaEvO described in [33]. The fitness function used in that paper is the same as in ours, so comparisons in terms of averaged final fitness values are sensible.

Unfortunately, in that paper the exact number of fitness evaluations performed to achieve those results is not given, rather their sequential algorithm is allowed an execution time of 20 seconds for evolution over an Intel Pentium IV 2.6 GHz processor, and then evolution is stopped.

Therefore, to carry out an as–fair–as–possible comparison, we need to carefully set for our distributed algorithm an execution time for evolution that is equivalent to that of their sequential one, and we should also take into account the differences in the number and types of processors used and in their clock rates.

Since we use four 3.4 Ghz cores, the following equality has to hold: $20 \cdot 2.6 = (4 \cdot \tau) \cdot 3.4$ where τ is the execution time for the evolution of our distributed program over each core. This equality yields $\tau = 3.824$ seconds. Furthermore, we wish to run our distributed algorithm over 16 subpopulations, that means that each core should run four subpopulations. Therefore, the actual time for the evolution of each subpopulation is 0.956 seconds.

The images of the eight test objects contain different numbers of points, ranging from a minimum of 5,612 up to a maximum of 14,258. Depending on the different numbers of points, different times would be needed to carry out the computation of the quality of each registration proposed by the evolutionary algorithm over the objects, so different numbers of fitness evaluations could be carried out for the different problems in the 0.956 seconds allowed.

Following [33] we randomly sample the points composing the images by means of a uniform distribution, and choose 5,000 points for each image, exactly as in that paper.

In this way, by running our distributed code we see that over each core we can execute 30 generations for each of the four there allocated subpopulations in a time equal to 42.61 milliseconds. The number of 30 generations has been chosen due to the value assigned to the migration interval, so as to include in this time also that needed to carry out migration. Therefore, in the time allowed to each subpopulation, we can carry out a number of generations equal to $0,956 \cdot 30/0.04261 = 673.08$. This, multiplied by the population size and by the number of subpopulations, yields a total number of fitness evaluations equal to 107,693.

Actually, we have decided to use a number of fitness evaluations lower than the one computed above, because we wish to take into account also other issues, including, among others, the fact that the Intel Pentium IV used in the reference paper has several features that are no longer up–to–date, which are reflected in an execution a bit slower than the one that can be achieved with our more modern processors. Therefore, we have limited that number to 100,000. This latter figure results in 625 generations.

As regards the GCP, our distributed approach allows strongly reducing the computation time to just some minutes. As examples, for the image with the lowest number of points, i.e., Teletubby, the sequential time for the GCP is 3,077 s, whereas the distributed is 87 s. The corresponding times for the image with highest number of points, i.e., Buddha, are 8,489 s and 272 s respectively. This is a noticeable by-product offered by a distributed approach such as ours.

For each algorithm and for each problem Table 1 reports the best final value Φ_b achieved in 25 runs, the average value $\langle\Phi\rangle$ over the 25 final values, and the related standard deviation σ_Φ. With reference to each such index, the table shows in bold the algorithm with the best value for each problem.

As a first remark, the superiority of one algorithm with respect to the others in terms of performance is not evident. In fact, SaEvO outperforms the other methods in terms of Φ_b, whereas the average results achieved by all the methods are at first glance comparable. On the other hand, AIM–dDE shows an evident superiority as far as σ_Φ is accounted. In fact, on all the eight problems both the adaptive versions of AIM–dDE show lower values for σ_Φ with respect to SaEvO, meaning that the adaptive invasion model is very robust. Nevertheless, it should be noted that the standard deviation values shown by SaEvO are very high and of the same magnitude of the average values.

As an example of the results obtained by AIM–dDE, Fig. 1 shows the outcome for Angel object, while Fig. 2 shows the registered images. It is worth noting that the differences between the aligned images by AIM–dDE–*RndAvg* and AIM–dDE–*ChAvg* are barely perceivable as evidenced by the numerical results.

4.1 Statistical analysis

To compare the algorithms from a statistical point of view, a classical approach based on nonparametric statistical tests has been carried out, following [13, 14]. To do so, the ControlTest package [14] has been used. It is a Java package freely downloadable at *http://sci2s.ugr.es/sicidm/*, developed to compute the rankings for these tests, and to carry out the related post–hoc procedures and the computation of the adjusted p–values.

The results for the one–to–all analysis are reported in the following. Table 2 contains the results of the Friedman, Aligned Friedman, and Quade tests in terms of average rankings obtained by the three algorithms. The last two

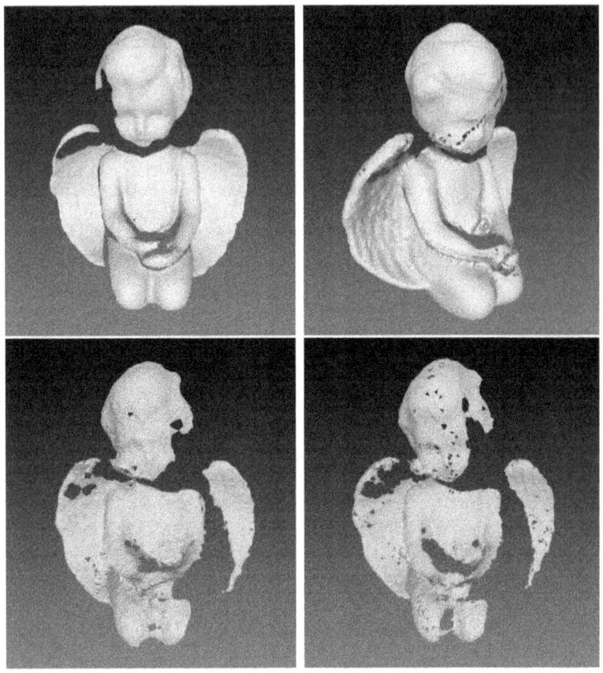

Figure 1: Some examples of results for Angel problem. Top left: original model image at zero degrees. Top right: original scene image at forty degrees. Bottom left: the best transformation of the scene image achieved by AIM–dDE–*RandAvg*. Bottom right: the best transformation of the scene image achieved by AIM–dDE–*ChAvg*.

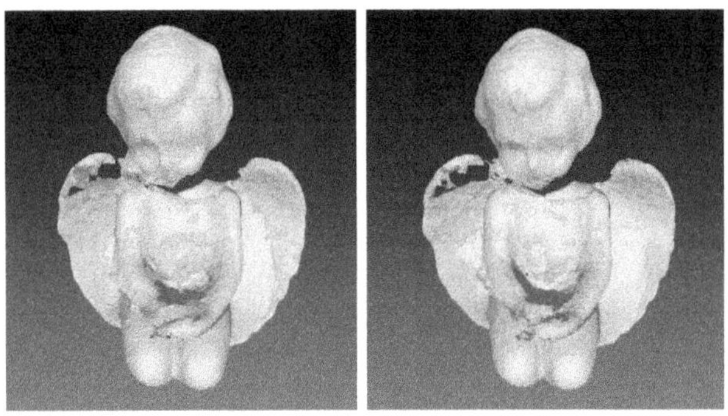

Figure 2: Reconstructed objects. Left pane: AIM–dDE–*RndAvg*. Right pane: AIM–dDE–*ChAvg*.

Table 2: Rankings of the algorithms.

Algorithm	Friedman	Aligned Friedman	Quade
AIM–dDE–*ChAvg*	1.875	12.000	1.861
AIM–dDE–*RandAvg*	2.125	12.250	2.083
SaEvO	2.000	13.250	2.056
test statistic	0.250	5.968	0.082
p–value	0.896	0.051	0.921

rows show the statistic and the p–value for each test, respectively. For Friedman and Aligned Friedman tests the statistic is distributed according to chi–square with 2 degrees of freedom, whereas for Quade test it is distributed according to F–distribution with 2 and 14 degrees of freedom.

In each of the three tests, the lower the value for an algorithm, the better the algorithm. AIM–dDE–*ChAvg* turns out to be the best in all of the three tests. Among the other algorithms, SaEvO is the second in Friedman and Quade, whereas AIM–dDE–*RandAvg* is the second in Aligned Friedman.

Furthermore, with the aim to examine if some hypotheses of equivalence between the best performing algorithm and the other ones can be rejected, the complete statistical analysis based on the post–hoc procedures ideated by Holm, Hochberg, Hommel, Holland, Rom, Finner, and Li has been carried out following [14]. Moreover, the adjusted p–values have been computed by means of [14].

Table 3 reports the results of this analysis performed at a level of significance $\alpha = 0.05$. The level of significance represents the maximum allowable probability of incorrectly rejecting a given null hypothesis. In our case, $\alpha = 0.05$ means that if an equivalence hypothesis is rejected, there is a 5% probability of making a mistake in rejecting it, so a 95% that we are correctly rejecting it.

In this table the other algorithms are ranked in terms of distance from the best performing one, and each algorithm is compared against this latter to investigate whether or not the equivalence hypothesis can be rejected. For each algorithm each table reports the z value, the unadjusted p–value, and the adjusted p–values according to the different post-hoc procedures. The variable z represents the test statistic for comparing the algorithms, and its definition depends on the main nonparametric test used. In [14] all the different definitions for z, corresponding to the different tests, are reported. The last row in each sub–table contains for each procedure the threshold value Th such that the procedure considered rejects those equivalence hypotheses that have an adjusted p–value lower than or equal to Th.

Summarizing the results of these tables, in each of the three tests AIM–dDE–*ChAvg* is for all the post–hoc procedures statistically better than the third classified algorithm, whereas statistical equivalence hypothesis cannot be rejected with the runner up.

5. CONCLUSIONS AND FUTURE WORKS

In this paper an adaptive distributed Differential Evolution technique based on invasions has been investigated to optimize a 3D rigid transformation for automatic pair–wise registration of range images without considering any previous knowledge of the pose of the view. A parallel version of Grid Closest Point has been used to speed up the computation of the closest points. The experimental phase, carried out on a set of benchmark range images, shows that our AIM–dDE with the adaptive scheme based on chaos theory is at least statistically equivalent the best–so–far algorithm from literature in terms of performance, while it performs better in terms of robustness of the reconstructed 3D image, and of computational cost. If computational costs are considered, our approach has two positive features. Firstly, the time for the computation of GCP has been strongly reduced, which is very useful when large images are to be registered. Secondly, the time for the evolution has been decreased from 20 s to 3.824 s.

Although promising, there is plenty of work still to do to further evaluate the effectiveness of our system, and its limitations as well.

Firstly, a wide tuning phase will be carried out to investigate if other chaotic parameter settings for AIM–dDE–*ChAvg* are, on average, more fruitful than others. Moreover, the use of other chaotic maps will be investigated.

6. REFERENCES

[1] Bäck, T., Fogel, D., Michalewicz, Z.: Handbook of Evolutionary Computation. IOP Publishing Ltd. (1997)

[2] Campbell, R.J., Flynn, P.J.: A survey of free-form object representation and recognition techniques. Computer Vision and Image Understanding 81(2), 166–210 (2001)

[3] Chow, K.W., Tsui, T.: Surface registration using a dynamic genetic algorithm. Pattern Recognition 37, 105–117 (2004)

[4] Cordón, O., Damas, S., Santamaría, J., Martí, R.: Scatter search for the point-matching problem in 3D image registration. Informs J. on Computing 20(1), 55–68 (2008)

[5] Dalley, G., Flynn, P.: Pair-wise range image registration: a study in outlier classification. Computer Vision and Image Understanding 87(1–3), 104–115 (2002)

[6] De Falco, I., Della Cioppa, A., Iazzetta, A., Tarantino, E.: An evolutionary approach for automatically extracting intelligible classification rules. Knowledge and Information Systems 7(2), 179–201 (2005)

[7] De Falco, I., Della Cioppa, A., Maisto, D., Scafuri, U., Tarantino, E.: An adaptive invasion–based model for distributed differential evolution. Information Sciences (2014), http://dx.doi.org/10.1016/j.ins.2014.03.083

[8] De Falco, I., Della Cioppa, A., Maisto, D., Scafuri, U., Tarantino, E.: Satellite image registration by distributed differential evolution. In: Lecture Notes in Computer Science, vol. 4448, pp. 251–260. Springer–Verlag (2007)

[9] De Falco, I., Della Cioppa, A., Maisto, D., Scafuri, U., Tarantino, E.: Biological invasion–inspired migration in distributed evolutionary algorithms. Information Sciences 207, 50–65 (2012)

[10] De Falco, I., Della Cioppa, A., Maisto, D., Scafuri, U., Tarantino, E.: Adding chaos to differential evolution for range image registration. In: Lecture Notes in Computer Science, vol. 7835, pp. 344–353. Springer–Verlag (2013)

[11] De Falco, I., Della Cioppa, A., Maisto, D., Tarantino, E.: Differential evolution as a viable tool for satellite image registration. Applied Soft Computing 8(4), 1453–1462 (2008)

[12] De Falco, I., Maisto, D., Scafuri, U., Tarantino, E., Della Cioppa, A.: Distributed differential evolution for the registration of remotely sensed images. In: 15th EUROMICRO International Conference on Parallel, Distributed and Network-based Processing. pp. 358–362. IEEE (2007)

[13] Demšar, J.: Statistical comparisons of classifiers over multiple data sets. Journal of Machine Learning Research 7, 1–30 (2006)

[14] Derrac, J., García, S., Molina, D., Herrera, F.: A practical tutorial on the use of nonparametric statistical tests as a methodology for comparing evolutionary and swarm intelligence algorithms. Swarm and Evolutionary Computation 1, 3–18 (2011)

[15] Eiben, A.E., Hinterding, R., Michalewicz, Z.: Parameter control in evolutionary algorithms. IEEE Transactions on Evolutionary Computation 3(2), 124–141 (1999)

[16] He, R., Narayana, P.A.: Global optimization of mutual information: application to three–dimensional retrospective registration of magnetic resonance images. Comput. Med. Imag. Grap 26, 277–292 (2002)

[17] Kurogi, S., Nagi, T., Yoshinaga, S., Koya, H., Nishida, T.: Multiview range image registration using competitive associative net and leave-one-image-out cross-validation error. In: Neural Information Processing. pp. 621–628. Springer (2011)

[18] Laguna, M., Martí, R., Martí, R.C.: Scatter search: methodology and implementations in C, vol. 24. Springer (2003)

[19] Liu, J., Lampinen, J.: A fuzzy adaptive differential evolution algorithm. Soft Computing-A Fusion of

Table 3: Results of post–hoc procedures for Friedman(top), Aligned Friedman (center), and Quade (bottom) tests over all tools (at $\alpha = 0.05$).

i	Algorithm	$z = (R_0 - R_i)/SE$	p	Holm/Hochberg/Hommel	Holland	Rom	Finner	Li
2	AIM–dDE–*RandAvg*	0.500	0.617	0.025	0.025	0.025	0.025	0.010
1	SaEvO	0.250	0.803	0.050	0.050	0.050	0.050	0.050
Th				0.025/–/0.025	0.025	0.025	0.025	0.010

i	Algorithm	$z = (R_0 - R_i)/SE$	p	Holm/Hochberg/Hommel	Holland	Rom	Finner	Li
2	SaEvO	0.354	0.724	0.025	0.025	0.025	0.025	0.003
1	AIM–dDE–*RandAvg*	0.071	0.944	0.050	0.050	0.050	0.050	0.050
Th				0.025/–/0.025	0.025	0.025	0.025	0.003

i	Algorithm	$z = (R_0 - R_i)/SE$	p	Holm/Hochberg/Hommel	Holland	Rom	Finner	Li
2	AIM–dDE–*RandAvg*	0.396	0.692	0.025	0.025	0.025	0.025	0.014
1	SaEvO	0.347	0.729	0.050	0.050	0.050	0.050	0.050
Th				0.025/–/0.025	0.025	0.025	0.025	0.014

Foundations, Methodologies and Applications 9(6), 448–462 (2005)

[20] Lomonosov, E., Chetverikov, D., Ekárt, A.: Pre-registration of arbitrarily oriented 3D surfaces using a genetic algorithm. Pattern Recognition Lett. 27(11), 1201–1208 (2006)

[21] Matsuda, T.: Log–polar height maps for multiple range image registration. Computer Vision and Image Understanding 87(1–3) (2009)

[22] Ohio State University: SAMPL image repository, http://sampl.eng.ohio-state.edu/ sampl/database.htm (2009)

[23] Peitgen, H.O., Jürgens, H., Saupe, D.: Chaos and Fractals: New Frontiers of Science. Springer Verlag (2004)

[24] Price, K., Storn, R., Lampinen, J.: Differential Evolution: A Practical Approach to Global Optimization. Natural Computing Series, Springer–Verlag (2005)

[25] Price, K., Storn, R.: Differential evolution. Dr. Dobb's Journal 22(4), 18–24 (1997)

[26] Robertson, C., Fisher, R.: Parallel evolutionary registration of range data. Computer Vision and Image Understanding 87(1), 39–50 (2002)

[27] Rodrigues, M., Fisher, R., Liu, Y.: Introduction: Special issue on registration and fusion of range images. Computer Vision and Image Understanding 87, 1–7 (2002)

[28] Rusinkiewicz, S., Levoy, M.: Efficient variant of the icp algorithm. In: Third International Conference on 3–D Digital Imaging and Modeling. pp. 145–152 (2001)

[29] Salvi, J., Matabosch, C., Fofi, D., Forest, J.: A review of recent range image registration methods with accuracy evaluation. Image and Vision Computing 25(5), 578–596 (2007)

[30] Santamaría, J., Cordón, O., Damas, S.: A comparative study of state–of–the–art evolutionary image registration methods for 3d modeling. Computer Vision and Image Understanding 115(9), 1340–1354 (2011)

[31] Santamaría, J., Cordón, O., Damas, S., Aleman, I., Botella, M.: A scatter search-based technique for pair-wise 3d range image registration in forensic anthropology. Soft Computing-A Fusion of Foundations, Methodologies and Applications 11(9), 819–828 (2007)

[32] Santamaría, J., Cordón, O., Damas, S., García-Torres, J.M., Quirin, A.: Performance evaluation of memetic approaches in 3d reconstruction of forensic objects. Soft Computing-A Fusion of Foundations, Methodologies and Applications 13(8), 883–904 (2009)

[33] Santamaría, J., Damas, S., Cordón, O., Escámez, A.: Self–adaptive evolution toward new parameter free image registration methods. IEEE Transactions on Evolutionary Computation 17(4), 545–557 (2013)

[34] Shigesada, N., Kawasaki, K.: Biological invasions: theory and practice. Oxford University Press, USA (1997)

[35] Silva, L., Bellon, O.R.P., Boyer, K.L.: Precision range image registration using a robust surface interpenetration measure and enhanced genetic algorithms. IEEE Transactions on Pattern Analysis 27(5), 762–776 (2005)

[36] Snir, M., Otto S, Huss-Lederman, S., Walker, D., Dongarra, J.: MPI: The Complete Reference – The MPI Core, vol. 1. MIT Press, Cambridge, MA, USA (1998)

[37] Yamany, S.M., Ahmed, M.N., Heyamed, E.E., Farag, A.A.: Novel surface registration using the grid closest point (cgp) transform. In: Int. Conf. on Image Processing. vol. 3, pp. 809–813. IEEE Press (1998)

Recognizing Planar Kinematic Mechanisms from a Single Image Using Evolutionary Computation

Matthew Eicholtz
Department of Mechanical Engineering
Carnegie Mellon University
Pittsburgh, PA 15213
meicholt@andrew.cmu.edu

Levent Burak Kara
Department of Mechanical Engineering
Carnegie Mellon University
Pittsburgh, PA 15213
lkara@cmu.edu

Jason Lohn
Department of Electrical and Computer Engineering
Carnegie Mellon University - Silicon Valley
Moffett Field, CA 94035
jlohn@ece.cmu.edu

ABSTRACT

In this paper, a method is presented that automatically recognizes kinematic mechanisms from textbook images using an evolutionary algorithm to complement computer vision techniques for object detection. Specifically, a nondominated sorting genetic algorithm (NSGA-II) is used to optimize the number and position of mechanical joints in an image and corresponding joint connections (i.e. rigid bodies) such that Pareto front solutions maximize image consistency and mechanical feasibility. A well-known object detector is used as an example method for locating joints, and local image features between pairwise detected joints are used to predict likely connections. The performance of the algorithm using these specific vision techniques is compared to a parameterized detection scheme in order to decouple the efficacy of the object detector from the evolutionary algorithm. Experiments were performed to validate this approach on selected images from a custom dataset, and the results demonstrate reasonable success in both accuracy and speed.

Categories and Subject Descriptors

G.1.6 [**Numerical Analysis**]: Optimization—*Constrained optimization*; I.4.8 [**Image Processing and Computer Vision**]: Scene Analysis—*Object Recognition*

Keywords

computer vision; evolutionary multiobjective optimization; kinematic simulation; object recognition

1. INTRODUCTION

Visualizing the motion characteristics of a multibody mechanical system is an important step in design analysis and synthesis [8]. Often, engineers use mental simulations to infer mechanical behavior [16], but this can be difficult for complex problems [15] or for individuals with low spatial ability [17]. Alternatively, computer simulations can be generated using specialized software [1, 20], but this task is often time-consuming, which limits its usefulness in certain situations (e.g. students solving a dynamics problem, engineers brainstorming potential design concepts), and may require advanced software skills, which hinders novice users.

In the present work, we propose a method for quickly generating simulation models by automatically identifying the underlying mechanical structure in single images. Researchers have briefly studied the automatic recognition of mechanical systems from sketches [7, 12, 13], but these approaches typically involve clean images, well-defined part templates, and sometimes make use of temporal information to aid recognition. Raw textbook images of kinematic mechanisms, on the other hand, are often noisy, may contain extraneous information from other graphics, and do not always contain well-defined part models.

To our knowledge, the automatic recognition of kinematic mechanisms from textbook images is a novel problem in both computer vision and evolutionary computation, and it has many interesting challenges. One of the primary challenges in tackling this problem is determining the best mechanism representation for recognition. Typical vision-based detection methods treat an object as a single part and learn a model using low-level image features [6, 19], but this technique would not work well for mechanical linkages, which may vastly differ in appearance from one to the next. More recent vision approaches use part-based models [5, 10, 11], which treat the object of interest as a collection of parts to be recognized. While this is more in line with the structure of mechanisms, which can be viewed as a collection of rigid bodies connected by joints that constrain their motion, these methods require learned spatial relationships (deformable models) between the parts. In the present domain, this is impractical given that there are an infinite number of possible mechanism configurations. The problem is compounded by the fact that model parameters of a mechanism, in general, are unknown *a priori*; the number of joints, type of joints, number of bodies, and configuration can all vary.

With this in mind, we propose solving the problem of mechanism identification in two stages. The system takes as input a raw textbook image containing a single, planar, kinematic mechanism of unknown structure. In the first stage, joints are detected using a conventional object detector, and low-level image features are used to predict the likelihood of

GECCO'14, July 12–16, 2014, Vancouver, BC, Canada.

http://dx.doi.org/10.1145/2576768.2598354.

joint connections (i.e. rigid bodies). In the second stage, we use a multiobjective evolutionary algorithm (MOEA) to optimize the detected parts, while simultaneously evolving structures that are mechanically feasible. The result is a small set of feasible mechanisms that can be easily integrated into engineering software packages for kinematic simulation and analysis.

The remainder of the paper is structured as follows: section 2 highlights related work in object detection and evolutionary computation. Specific algorithm details are provided in section 3. Experiments and concluding remarks are given in sections 4 and 5, respectively.

2. RELATED WORK

Object detection is an important task for computer vision that has been widely studied in recent years. A typical approach is to generate a large number of training images containing the object of interest, extract salient features from those images [2, 6, 19], train a model on those features, and then scan test images using the model to locate the object. One of the primary challenges when designing an object detector is determining which features are most relevant. In this paper, histogram of oriented gradients (HOG) is used [6]. This popular feature descriptor was originally developed for human detection and has been utilized in numerous applications since. The basic steps for computing HOG features are as follows: color normalization *(if desired)*, compute gradients over entire image, compute weighted histograms over small cells, merge and normalize overlapping blocks of cell histograms (each cell typically contributes to 4 block normalizations), and collect features *(vectorize if needed)*. In the original work, HOG features were computed on a set of training images and used to train a soft ($C = 0.01$) linear support vector machine (SVM), which attempts to find the most discriminative hyperplane in feature space to separate the two classes (human/no human). The present study implements this method as an initial step to identifying mechanism structure.

The task of recognizing underlying structure in images is not a new one. Research on structured prediction spans a breadth of applications including face recognition [29], human pose estimation [28], and 3D surface estimation [24]. The key difference between existing applications and our present domain is that mechanisms do not have well-defined structural or spatial dependencies. While it is expected in pose estimation, for example, that the head is always connected to the neck rather than the foot, it is less clear in mechanism identification if a specific kinematic joint is connected to another.

There is a growing body of research in the area of multiobjective evolutionary algorithms (MOEAs), especially in regard to real-world applications. Many well-known MOEAs are based on Pareto dominance [9, 27, 30], which states that a given solution dominates another solution if it is at least as good on all objectives and better on at least one objective. Arguably the most popular MOEA of this type and the one used in this present work is the nondominated sorting genetic algorithm (NSGA-II) [9], which has been successful largely due to fast computation of nondominated fronts, preservation of elitist solutions, and lack of a user-specified sharing parameter.

The nondominated sorting genetic algorithm was first introduced almost 20 years ago (NSGA, [27]) and improved 8 years later (NSGA-II, [9]). The two identifying characteristics of NSGA-II are nondominated sorting and crowding distance. Nondominated sorting involves locating the Pareto front (all nondominated solutions), assigning those solutions a rank of 1, and iteratively assigning higher ranks to each Pareto front level, ignoring all previously detected levels. Crowding distance measures the local spread of solutions and is used to preserve diversity in the population. These parameters are used during the selection process as follows. When sorting a set of solutions, any solution with lower rank goes before solutions with higher rank. Inevitably, there will be cases when the desired number of survivors cuts through one of the Pareto ranks. In this case, the solutions with that rank are sorted with preference to higher crowding distances. This algorithm has been shown to have success when the number of objectives is small, so it should be a suitable approach for the problem presented in this paper.

3. TECHNICAL DETAILS

The proposed approach to mechanism identification in images combines vision strategies for object detection with a popular multiobjective evolutionary algorithm for optimization. In this section, specific details are provided for each component of the algorithm.

3.1 Vision-based Detection of Mechanical Components

In this work, the key to identifying the true mechanism contained in an image lies in the ability to accurately detect two classes of objects: joints and rigid bodies. While previous works in parts-based detection might suggest we learn detectors for each class separately [10], the present domain is ill-suited for this approach because rigid bodies exhibit high variance in image features such as size, shape, and color, making the task of learning a reliable rigid body detector difficult. Instead, we make use of the fact that knowing the location of likely joints in an image greatly reduces the space of likely rigid body locations because all rigid bodies must be connected to at least two joints[1]. With this in mind, the general pipeline for the vision portion of the algorithm is as follows: (i) detect likely locations of mechanical joints; then (ii) evaluate the likelihood of a rigid body between each pair of joints.

3.1.1 Detecting mechanical joints

The first step in the vision pipeline is to identify the locations of each joint type[2] in an input image. We accomplish this task by running a sliding window over the entire image and classifying each patch using a linear SVM. The SVM is trained over HOG features [6] computed on a set of example images.

The training data comprises positive and negative image patches extracted from selected images. The positive examples contain the joint type of interest and are taken from hand-labeled images of mechanisms, while the negative examples are randomly selected from the same images, mak-

[1]One exception to this rule is a pendulum, for which a rigid body has only one joint connection, but this case is excluded from the current domain of interest due to lack of complexity

[2]For all experiments described in this paper, we limit the domain exclusively to revolute joints, but in theory, incorporating additional joint types (e.g. prismatic joints) would simply require training a new detector.

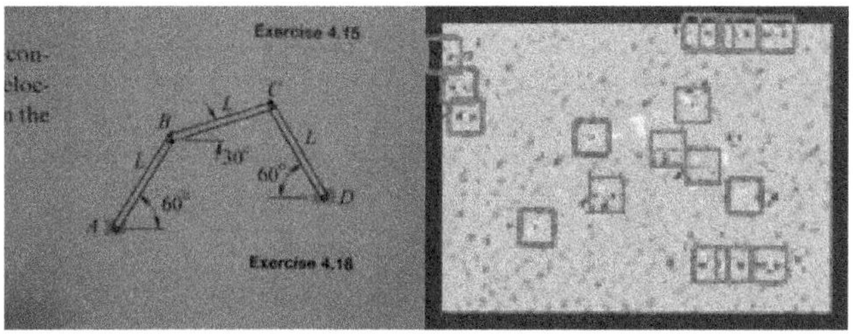

(a) (b)

Figure 1: (a) An example image and (b) the heat map of joint detections, where color represents detection strength and rectangles highlight local maxima.

ing sure they do not overlap with positive examples. Similar to previous work on supervised learning algorithms [12], we augment the training set by applying a series of simple transformations to each positive example: reflection about the vertical or horizontal axis, and rotation by 90, 180, and 270 degrees. This effectively increases the positive training data by a factor of 5, which likely improves the discriminative power of the joint detector. In addition, we follow the approach of Dalal and Triggs [6] to improve classification accuracy by mining hard negatives from an initially trained SVM. This is especially critical for our problem domain because most of the background in textbook images is blank, and therefore the initial set of negative training examples may not accurately reflect the diversity of the negative image space.

After training, the SVM can be used on a test image to classify the image patch centered at each pixel. The result is a heat map, in which distance from the decision boundary (hyperplane) encodes detection strength. In our method, we apply the mean shift procedure [4] to isolate local maxima and then discard extrema with strength less than zero (negative distance to the hyperplane indicates the patch is more likely to *not* contain a joint). Figure 1 illustrates this concept on an example image. The remaining detected joint locations and strengths are then passed to later stages of the algorithm.

3.1.2 Detecting rigid bodies

As mentioned previously, rigid bodies are not explicitly recognized using a sliding window detector; rather, they are identified by the local image features that exist between pairs of detected joints. Specifically, we use a normalized measure of geodesic time to determine the strength of a pairwise joint connection (see Figure 2). The geodesic time [25] between any pair of pixels (p, q) in a grayscale image is defined as

$$t_g(p, q) = \min\{t_g(P) | P \text{ links } p \text{ to } q\} \quad (1)$$

and the geodesic time of a given path P of length n connecting two pixels is given by

$$t_g(P) = \frac{I_{p_0}}{2} + \frac{I_{p_n}}{2} + \sum_{i=1}^{n-1} I_{p_i} \quad (2)$$

where I_{p_j} is the pixel intensity of the jth pixel on the path. Without loss of generality, let us assume we want to maximize geodesic time (i.e. true joint connections should have high values). In a typical mechanism, there generally exists a path through darker regions for pairs of joints that are located on the same rigid body (especially along solid boundary lines). With this in mind, we invert the grayscale image so that dark regions in the raw image have higher values of geodesic time. Then, we normalize the result using the Euclidean distance transform with one of the joints in question acting as the seed location. Without this normalization, the algorithm would strongly bias connections between joints that are far away from each other, even if the connection is false.

One strength of this metric is its ability to identify rigid bodies of varying shape and size. However, due to the nature of kinematic chains, it also tends to misclassify false connections for joints that are on neighboring bodies. To overcome this challenge, we increase the pixel intensity in the grayscale image of each patch surrounding the detected joints, proportional to SVM strength. This has the effect of decreasing geodesic time for paths between joints that intersect other joints. Also, to accommodate small errors in the location of detected joints, which may undesirably decrease geodesic time, we artificially darken a small region (e.g. 16-pixel radius) surrounding the joint center to ensure the beginning of all paths emanating from that joint are equally strong.

3.1.3 Parameterized detection scheme

While the aforementioned vision-based detection scheme is likely a good practical solution to the problem of mechanism recognition, it may lead to a misleading evaluation of the evolutionary algorithm, since the two processes are not independent. In order to decouple the performance of the computer vision and evolutionary computation aspects of our approach, we propose the parameterization of detection results as follows,

1. Precision (Pr): $Pr = n_{tp}/(n_{tp} + n_{fp})$
2. Difference in mean strength ($\Delta\mu$): $\mu_{fp} - \mu_{tp}$
3. Standard deviation of true positive strength (σ_{tp})
4. Standard deviation of false positive strength (σ_{fp})

where n is a detection count, and the subscripts tp and fp refer to true positives and false positives, respectively.

In theory, these parameters could apply to any object detector. For the present work, detection of joints and connections are coupled, such that precision is only defined once, yielding a 7-dimensional parameter space (4 for joints, 3 for rigid bodies). Given any 7-tuple corresponding to these parameters, we can artificially generate strength values for positive and negative examples of joints and connections, without regard to actual image features or the spatial characteristics of joints. In this manner, the efficacy of the evolutionary computation can be evaluated without specifying a specific vision-based algorithm for object detection.

3.2 Evolutionary-based Optimization

Given the output from the object detection pipeline, which is a set of strength values associated with detected joints and pairwise joint connections, the problem becomes one of constrained multiobjective optimization. Specifically, we seek to find a hypothesis of a mechanism that is strongly consistent with what has been detected in the image as well

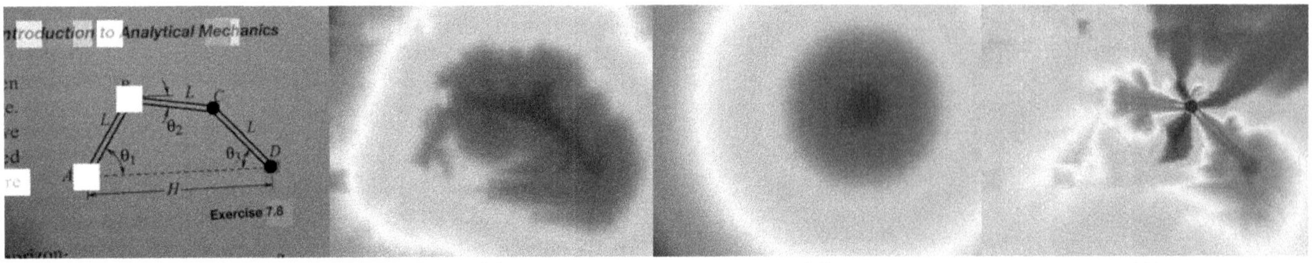

(a) (b) (c) (d)

Figure 2: Computation of normalized geodesic time. (a) A sample grayscale image, with the pair of joints in question identified by black circles and all other joint lightened proportional to their detection strength. The inverse of (b) geodesic time transform divided by (c) Euclidean distance transform yields (d) normalized geodesic time. Stronger values are more red while weaker values are more blue.

as reasonable in terms of kinematic simulation. To that end, we employ the nondominated sorting genetic algorithm (NSGA-II) introduced by Deb *et al.* [9]. This algorithm was selected for several reasons, including its well-known success in solving real-world applications, its ability to quickly find a diverse set of good solutions for multiple conflicting objectives, and the unique opportunities it provides for handling constraints. Notable details specific to the present domain are outlined below.

3.2.1 Representation

We represent a mechanism using a graph structure, similar to [18], but with nodes representing joints and edges corresponding to rigid bodies. There are several interesting properties of this representation. In particular, the presence of an edge indicates that the pair of joints associated with the connecting nodes are located on the same rigid body. It is not always true, however, that all edges correspond to unique bodies; in fact, any body containing more than two joints will contribute a fully connected subgraph comprising multiple nodes and edges. In addition, we relax the constraint that multiple pins fixed to the ground must share an edge because a typical image may not exhibit strong visual cues that grounded pins are on the same body. Consequently, the graph representation for a given mechanism is not necessarily unique; also, multiple mechanisms can be represented by the same graph.

Figure 3 illustrates the phenotype-genotype mapping for our problem. The genotype is a vectorized transformation of the mechanism graph, and it consists of two parts: (i) a bit-string of length N to indicate the presence of a joint in an individual hypothesis, where N is the number of detected joints; and (ii) a bit string of length $N(N-1)/2$, which encodes the presence of pairwise edges. The latter part is derived from the upper triangular matrix of the adjacency matrix, which is symmetric. It should be noted that the genotype does not explicitly include any information regarding the spatial layout of detected joints. Also, this representation allows an edge to exist in the absence of one or more of its connecting nodes. To deal with this issue, the bit-string that encodes nodes (joints) is used to virtually mask "invalid" edges (connections) for the purpose of fitness evaluation. However, the true value of those edges is retained during crossover and mutation so that there is no internal bias toward solutions with fewer edges.

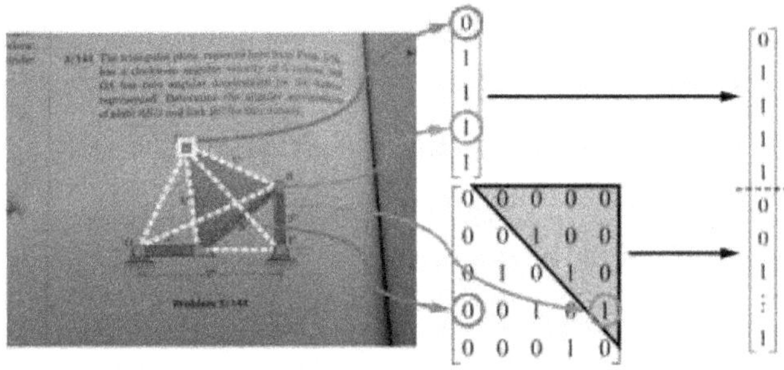

Figure 3: Abstracting the mechanism into a graph, then mapping the graph to a bit-string, where the first part of the chromosome identifies which joints exist in a solution, and the second part dictates the presence of connections between those joints.

3.2.2 Fitness criteria

The goal of our recognition algorithm is to find the mechanism topology graph that optimizes a series of objectives, which can be broadly categorized as relating to image consistency and mechanical feasibility. More specifically, we seek to maximize the image-based strength of joints and connections used in a solution, to minimize the strength of unused image information, and to maximize the likelihood that the mechanical behavior of the optimal solution is meaningful.

1. The *joint likelihood* (f_1) is the average detection strength of joints present in a given hypothesis (H), or

$$f_1(H) = \frac{\sum_{i=1}^{N} S_{j,i}}{\sum_{i=1}^{N} h_i} \tag{3}$$

where $S_{j,i}$ is the strength of the ith joint and h_i is the (Boolean) value of the ith gene.

2. Similarly, the *joint connection likelihood* (f_2) for a given hypothesis is computed as the average connection strength,

$$f_2(H) = \frac{\sum_{i=N+1}^{L} S_{c,i}}{\sum_{i=N+1}^{L} h_i} \tag{4}$$

where $S_{c,i}$ and L are the strength of the ith connection and the chromosome length, respectively.

3. *Residual image data* refers to the average strength of unused joints (f_3) and connections (f_4) in an individ-

ual solution. These two objectives are critical for enabling the detection of complex mechanisms; without them, a four-bar linkage (the simplest mechanism in our domain) will *always* be preferred unless additional nodes and edges improve the strength of f_1 or f_2.

4. A series of binary *mechanical constraints* are evaluated to estimate the kinematic feasibility of solutions. The percentage of constraints that are satisfied make up the final objective (f_5); for a feasible mechanism, this will have a value of 1. No constraint is more important than the others, and the feasibility objective contributes to nondominated sorting in the same way as the other fitness criteria. We chose this method (as opposed to approaches that always prefer feasible solutions [9, 3]) to allow infeasible, yet strong, solutions to persist because they are likely to be near the constraint boundaries.

   While a full kinematic simulation would arguably provide the best insight regarding feasibility, it is simply too computationally expensive. Instead, we found through trial-and-error that simple heuristics yield a reasonable estimate of feasibility without the lag in computational speed. The current set of constraints used by our algorithm include: (i) the degrees of freedom[3] (DOF) should be 1, (ii) each joint must have at least one connection, (iii) there must be at least four rigid bodies, including the frame, and (*iv*) all joints must be a minimum distance away from each other (e.g. 15-30 pixels).

3.2.3 *Dealing with uncertainty*

Uncertainty exists in the image consistency fitness criteria due to the nature of learned detector models and noise in the images. Comparing the distance to the SVM decision boundary for two joints may not always accurately reflect the true relative strength of those joints, especially when the relative distance is small. Similarly, minor illumination changes may induce small errors in the geodesic time calculations that dictate connection strength. These discrepancies can cause the true solution to be dominated by other solutions with similar, but unequal, strength. We implement two measures to combat this shortcoming. First, we add Gaussian noise ($\mu = 0, \sigma = 0.02$) to the raw strength values on each generation. This increases the probability that two similar solutions remain on the same nondominated front, allowing "less fit" solutions to survive in the short term. Second, we do not require that the "best" solution be in the Pareto-optimal set; if the true solution exists in the population at the end of a run, there is a chance to recover it during post-processing.

3.2.4 *Post-processing*

The output of a typical multiobjective evolutionary algorithm is a set of Pareto-optimal solutions. In our application, however, only one solution[4] is truly optimal. To reduce the final population in an effort to identify the true solution, we use the following procedure. First, all infeasible hypotheses are discarded. Next, duplicate solutions are identified via graph matching and subsequently removed. The remaining set is sorted based on a priority of objectives; currently, we prioritize connection strength because it seems to have greater discriminative power than joint detection.

[3]The *degrees of freedom* is the number of independent variables required to fully characterize the configuration of a mechanism.

[4]Or a very small set of solutions (see section 3.2.1)

Table 1: General NSGA-II parameters

Parameter	Symbol	Value
population size	μ	$200N^\dagger$
number of offspring	λ	μ
maximum number of generations	n	20
crossover method	–	uniform
crossover probability	p_c	0.9
mutation method	–	uniform
mutation probability	p_m	0.1
tournament size	k	0.02μ

$^\dagger N$ refers to number of detected joints (section 3.1.1)

4. EXPERIMENTS

4.1 MECH135 Dataset

A custom dataset was created comprising 135 images from 5 textbooks [14, 21, 22, 23, 26] (see Figure 6 for examples). Each image shows a closed, planar mechanism containing only revolute joints. No assumptions were made regarding position, scale, or orientation of the mechanism, although it is assumed the entire mechanism is included in the image. Images were not processed (e.g. cropping, filtering), so they may contain noise, illumination changes, and extraneous information such as text, annotations, pencil markings, or partial components from other mechanisms.

4.2 Methods

Two experimental studies were conducted on sample images from the MECH135 dataset to investigate the effectiveness of our approach. The first study aims to isolate the performance of the evolutionary algorithm from the vision aspects of the problem by creating artificial data for the image consistency fitness criteria based on generalized detection characteristics. The second study focuses on a practical implementation of the full system using the vision-based methods outlined in section 3.1. Both experiments were performed using the same general settings listed in Table 1, and only differ in the ways outlined in the following paragraphs. The implementation has been developed in MATLAB [20], and all experiments were performed on an Intel(R) quad-core 3.30GHz CPU with 8GB RAM.

4.2.1 *Parameterized Detection*

Two images containing nonisomorphic mechanisms were selected for this study. The performance of joint and body detection was explored independently. For each case, all combinations of the applicable parameter values (Table 2) were used to generate artificial detection strength data. The remaining parameters were fixed to their lowest values. For every 7-tuple, 5 random sets of strength values were generated, and 2 independent runs were executed on each set; this amounts to 3,240 total runs. Success rate is measured based on whether or not the true solution is found in the pruned and sorted population at the end of a run.

Table 2: Parameterization of detection performance

Parameter	Symbol	Values
1	Pr	$\{0.5, 0.7, 0.9\}$
2	$\Delta\mu_j$	$\{-0.4, -0.2, 0\}$
3	$\sigma_{tp,j}$	$\{0.1, 0.2, 0.3\}$
4	$\sigma_{fp,j}$	$\{0.1, 0.2, 0.3\}$
5	$\Delta\mu_c$	$\{-0.4, -0.2, 0\}$
6	$\sigma_{tp,c}$	$\{0.1, 0.2, 0.3\}$
7	$\sigma_{fp,c}$	$\{0.1, 0.2, 0.3\}$

4.2.2 *Vision-based Detection*

A set of 15 images (3 per textbook) containing 1-DOF mechanisms was hand-selected for testing. Considerable effort was made to include examples with varying rigid body abstraction, shape, and configuration as well as differing levels of extraneous noise. The remaining 120 images were used to train a linear SVM using HOG features. Joint detection strength and rigid body likelihood were calculated according to the techniques in section 3.1. For each test image, 100 independent runs were performed using NSGA-II. See Figure 6 for an overview of this experiment.

4.3 Results and Discussion

4.3.1 *Parameterized Detection*

Figure 4 illustrates algorithm performance for the parameterized detection scheme described in previous sections. The goal of this study was to characterize the accuracy of our method in correctly identifying the underlying mechanical structure in an image for a generalized joint and rigid body detector. As expected, the success rate varies significantly depending on the parameters. In general, good performance is achieved when precision is high, the false positive joints are weaker than true positives, and the standard deviation of peak values remains low. It is clear from the figure that small changes in the parameters related to joint connection strength have the greatest impact on success rate. While the results may not look promising in this case, post-processing of our object detectors reveal that we are operating in the redder regions of the image. Figure 5 shows the normalized sensitivity of success rate to each of the seven parameters and confirms that joint connection performance is critical to accuracy. Also, the mean peak of the false positives relative to true positives is important for both types of detection. The important outcome of this study is the ability to predict the performance of a detection scheme when you only know the general quality of the detector as defined by this parameterization.

4.3.2 *Vision-based detection*

An overview of this experiment is provided in Figure 6, and relevant performance measures are summarized in Table 3. The algorithm was able to find the correct solution at least once for all images and nearly 80% of the time on average. But perhaps the more important performance measure is *where* the solution was found. The top-N accuracy refers to the percentage of successful runs in which the true solution was at least in the top N solutions.

4.3.3 *Limitations*

Despite the promising results presented in this paper, our method has some limitations. For example, the algorithm operates under the assumption that all true joints are at least weakly detected; in the presence of a false negative, the method presented in this paper will never find the correct solution. Correcting this deficiency would require either a different representation of the hypothesis space or relaxation of joint detection thresholds. Another limitation is the narrow domain employed here; to fully assess how this algorithm generalizes, the scope of mechanisms must be increased.

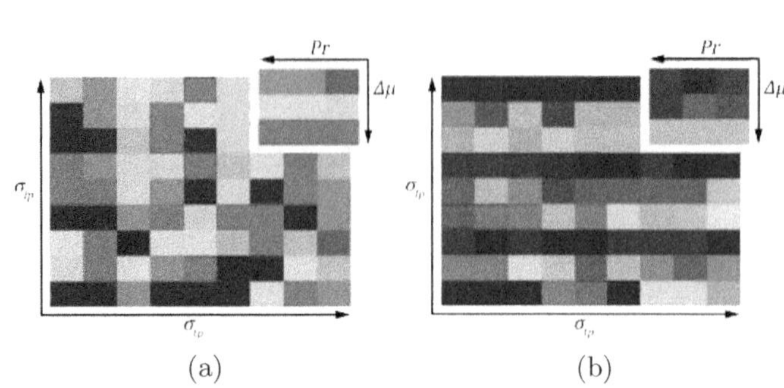

Figure 4: Parameterization results for (a) joint detection and (b) connection likelihood. Each pixel represents the average success rate (20 runs/pixel) for the subset of parameter vectors defined by the 4-tuple $<Pr, \Delta\mu, \sigma_{tp}, \sigma_{fp}>$, normalized by the maximum accuracy. Blue values are low and red values are high.

Table 3: Vision-based experimental results

Performance Measure	Result
average success rate	77.0%
top-1 accuracy	63.6%
top-3 accuracy	77.2%
top-5 accuracy	87.2%
average time	5.41 ± 5.14 sec
average time per gene	0.166 ± 0.014 sec

5. CONCLUSIONS AND FUTURE WORK

Our approach leverages the well-understood computer vision methods for object recognition with the optimizing power of evolutionary computation. The efficacy of this method has been demonstrated on a diverse series of textbook images, with the true solution being found in the top 5 optimal solutions 87% of the time. Another contribution of this work is the creation of a custom dataset comprising textbook images of planar mechanisms, which may serve as a benchmark for future approaches to solving this problem.

The algorithm has room for improvement in terms of accuracy, speed, and scalability. In the future, it is critical to investigate how well this method generalizes to more complex mechanisms (e.g. various joint types, spatial kinematics) and more difficult images (e.g. less abstract graphics, natural images of real systems); such robustness and scalability would make this a very practical computational tool for engineering design and analysis. For now, we have demonstrated a successful framework for mechanism recognition that can be easily adapted to new object detection schemes and optimization objectives.

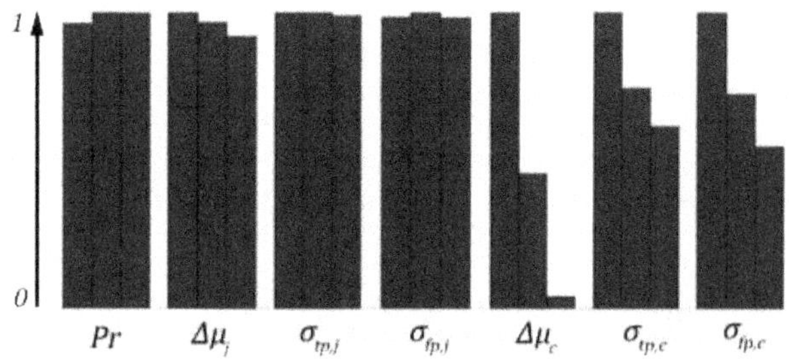

Figure 5: Normalized sensitivity, given by the average success rate for all corresponding runs.

6. ACKNOWLEDGMENTS

This material is based upon work supported by the National Science Foundation under Grant Nos. CMMI-0846730, CMMI-1031703, DUE-1043241, and GRFP-0946825. The authors kindly thank Aniruddha Basak for useful discussions on evolutionary algorithms.

7. REFERENCES

[1] Adams. *version 2013.2.* MSC Software Corporation, Newport Beach, California, 2010.

[2] M. Calonder, V. Lepetit, C. Strecha, and P. Fua. Brief: Binary robust independent elementary features. In *Computer Vision–ECCV 2010*, pages 778–792. Springer, 2010.

[3] C. A. Coello Coello. Theoretical and numerical constraint-handling techniques used with evolutionary algorithms: a survey of the state of the art. *Computer methods in applied mechanics and engineering*, 191(11):1245–1287, 2002.

[4] D. Comaniciu and P. Meer. Mean shift: A robust approach toward feature space analysis. *Pattern Analysis and Machine Intelligence, IEEE Transactions on*, 24(5):603–619, 2002.

[5] D. Crandall, P. Felzenszwalb, and D. Huttenlocher. Spatial priors for part-based recognition using statistical models. In *Computer Vision and Pattern Recognition (CVPR), 2005 IEEE Conference on*, volume 1, pages 10–17. IEEE, 2005.

[6] N. Dalal and B. Triggs. Histograms of oriented gradients for human detection. In *Computer Vision and Pattern Recognition (CVPR), 2005 IEEE Conference on*, volume 1, pages 886–893. IEEE, 2005.

[7] R. Davis. Magic paper: sketch-understanding research. *Computer*, 40(9):34–41, 2007.

[8] J. G. De Jalon and E. Bayo. *Kinematic and dynamic simulation of multibody systems.* Springer-Verlag New York, USA, 1994.

[9] K. Deb, A. Pratap, S. Agarwal, and T. Meyarivan. A fast and elitist multiobjective genetic algorithm: Nsga-ii. *Evolutionary Computation, IEEE Transactions on*, 6(2):182–197, 2002.

[10] P. F. Felzenszwalb, R. B. Girshick, D. McAllester, and D. Ramanan. Object detection with discriminatively trained part-based models. *Pattern Analysis and Machine Intelligence, IEEE Transactions on*, 32(9):1627–1645, 2010.

[11] P. F. Felzenszwalb and D. P. Huttenlocher. Pictorial structures for object recognition. *Int J Comput Vis*, 61(1):55–79, 2005.

[12] L. Fu and L. B. Kara. Recognizing network-like hand-drawn sketches: a convolutional neural network approach. ASME, 2009.

[13] L. Fu and L. B. Kara. From engineering diagrams to engineering models: Visual recognition and applications. *Computer-Aided Design*, 43(3):278–292, 2011.

[14] J. Ginsberg. *Engineering Dynamics.* Cambridge University Press, New York, New York, 2008.

[15] M. Hegarty. Mental animation: inferring motion from static displays of mechanical systems. *Journal of Experimental Psychology: Learning, Memory, and Cognition*, 18(5):1084, 1992.

[16] M. Hegarty. Mechanical reasoning by mental simulation. *Trends in cognitive sciences*, 8(6):280–285, 2004.

[17] M. Hegarty and V. K. Sims. Individual differences in mental animation during mechanical reasoning. *Memory & Cognition*, 22(4):411–430, 1994.

[18] H. Lipson. Evolutionary synthesis of kinematic mechanisms. *AI EDAM*, 22(3):195, 2008.

[19] D. G. Lowe. Distinctive image features from scale-invariant keypoints. *Int J Comput Vis*, 60(2):91–110, 2004.

[20] MATLAB. *version 8.1.0.604 (R2013a).* The MathWorks Inc., Natick, Massachusetts, 2013.

[21] D. J. McGill and W. K. King. *Engineering Mechanics: An Introduction to Dynamics.* Tichenor Publishing, Bloomington, Indiana, 2003.

[22] J. L. Meriam and L. G. Kraige. *Engineering Mechanics, Volume 2.* John Wiley and Sons, Inc., Singapore, 1993.

[23] J. L. Meriam and L. G. Kraige. *Engineering Mechanics: Dynamics.* John Wiley and Sons, Inc., Hoboken, New Jersey, 2007.

[24] S. Ross, D. Munoz, M. Hebert, and J. A. Bagnell. Learning message-passing inference machines for structured prediction. In *Computer Vision and Pattern Recognition (CVPR), 2011 IEEE Conference on*, pages 2737–2744. IEEE, 2011.

[25] P. Soille. Generalized geodesy via geodesic time. *Pattern Recognition Letters*, 15(12):1235–1240, 1994.

[26] E. Soylemez. *Mechanisms.* Middle East Technical University, Ankara, Turkey, 1993.

[27] N. Srinivas and K. Deb. Muiltiobjective optimization using nondominated sorting in genetic algorithms. *Evolutionary computation*, 2(3):221–248, 1994.

[28] Y. Yang and D. Ramanan. Articulated pose estimation with flexible mixtures-of-parts. In *Computer Vision and Pattern Recognition (CVPR), 2011 IEEE Conference on*, pages 1385–1392. IEEE, 2011.

[29] A. L. Yuille. Deformable templates for face recognition. *Journal of Cognitive Neuroscience*, 3(1):59–70, 1991.

[30] E. Zitzler and L. Thiele. Multiobjective evolutionary algorithms: A comparative case study and the strength pareto approach. *Evolutionary Computation, IEEE Transactions on*, 3(4):257–271, 1999.

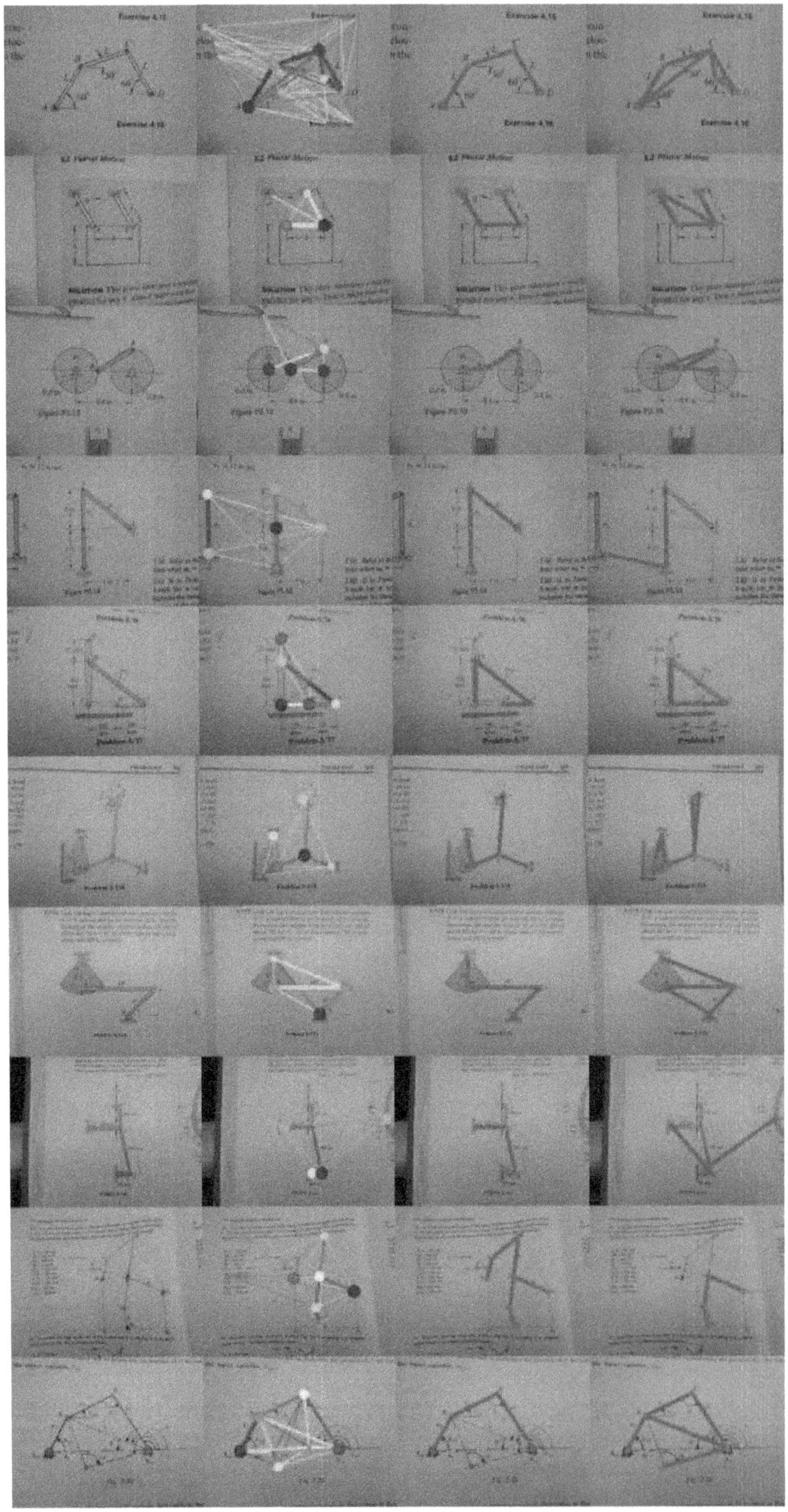

(a) (b) (c) (d)

Figure 6: Example results on MECH135 dataset. (a) Raw images. (b) Strength of joint detections and pairwise connections; higher values indicated by darker (red) color, thicker lines, and larger markers. (c) Correct solution found by the algorithm. (d) An incorrect solution on the Pareto front.

Passive Solar Building Design Using Genetic Programming

M. Mahdi Oraei Gholami
Brock University
Dept. of Computer Science
500 Glenridge Ave.
St. Catharines, Ontario
L2S 3A1, Canada
mahdi.oraei@gmail.com

Brian J. Ross
Brock University
Dept. of Computer Science
500 Glenridge Ave.
St. Catharines, Ontario
L2S 3A1, Canada
bross@brocku.ca

ABSTRACT

Passive solar building design considers the effect that sunlight has on energy usage. The goal is to reduce the need for artificial cooling and heating devices, thereby saving energy costs. A number of competing design objectives can arise. Window heat gain during winter requires large windows. These same windows, however, reduce energy efficiency during nights and summers. Other model requirements add further complications, which creates a challenging optimization problem. We use genetic programming for passive solar building design. The EnergyPlus system is used to evaluate energy consumption. It considers factors ranging from model construction (shape, windows, materials) to location particulars (latitude/longitude, weather, time of day/year). We use a strongly typed design language to build 3D models, and multi-objective fitness to evaluate the multiple design objectives. Experimental results showed that balancing window heat gain and total energy use is challenging, although our multi-objective strategy could find interesting compromises. Many factors (roof shape, material selection) were consistently optimized by evolution. We also found that geographic aspects of the location play a critical role in the final building design.

Categories and Subject Descriptors

I.2.2 [**Artificial Intelligence**]: Automatic Programming—*Program synthesis*

General Terms

Experimentation

Keywords

passive solar performance; energy efficiency; evolutionary design; genetic programming

GECCO'14, July 12–16, 2014, Vancouver, BC, Canada.
Copyright 2014 ACM 978-1-4503-2662-9/14/07 ...$15.00.
http://dx.doi.org/10.1145/2576768.2598211.

1. INTRODUCTION

Evolutionary design is well established in the field of architecture [2, 26]. Genetic algorithms have been used to design external shapes [25, 24, 6], internal floor plans [16, 12], and structurally sound forms [28].

Of particular relevance in today's world of climate change is the application of evolutionary algorithms towards energy-efficient building design. Some examples are as follows. Caldas applies evolutionary design towards a number of energy-related design problems, such as window placement, and building and roof design, in order to minimize energy use [7]. Turrin *et al.* evolve large roof structures that provide thermal and lighting comfort using passive solar techniques [27]. Malkawi *et al.* address the placement of windows and air ducts to maximize ventilation and satisfy thermal criteria [18]. Marin *et al.* create 3D building designs that maximize sunlight exposure during winter [19]. Harrington *et al.* evolve structures that maximize sun exposure in summer, and minimize it in winter [14]. Yu considers human occupancy factors, which helps in efficiently using lighting and mechanical heating and cooling systems [30]. Bouchlaghem designs building envelopes using energy considerations [5]. Wright *et al.* use a genetic algorithm to design the HVAC (heating, ventilating, and a/c) system for a multi-story building [29].

This paper uses genetic programming (GP) to evolve buildings using energy efficiency considerations.[1] A strongly typed design language denotes all aspects of the building to be evolved, including model geometry, window definitions, roof shape, and construction materials. Experiments focus on simple cuboid structures with optional roof shapes and open-area floor plans. The two main energy factors investigated are winter window heat gain and annual energy usage. These factors are usually at odds with each another. Passive solar heating in winter requires windows to collect the mid-day solar radiation. This reduces the need for artificial heating, which in turn saves energy costs. It is also ecologically responsible. But these same windows are poor insulators at night, and also can cause overheating during warmer weather. One goal is to see how well evolution balances these competing factors in the solutions produced. We introduce other model requirements into fitness measurements, which pertain to model shape and window usage. We use multi-objective analysis to evaluate these multiple, often conflicting, requirements.

[1]See [13] for more details about this research.

Another goal is to explore the effects of location geography on the model designs. Fitness evaluation uses the EnergyPlus simulation software to perform energy simulations. This comprehensive system considers a wealth of factors, such as model shape and size, windows, and materials used. It also considers environmental information about the location, for example, weather conditions, latitude/longitude, time of year and day, and many others. This results in a very detailed and precise analysis of energy usage.

The paper is organized as follows. Section 2 reviews the EnergyPlus system, and discusses basic issues regarding energy analyses and evolutionary design. Our system's design language and sum of ranks multi-objective technique are described in Section 3. Section 4 presents results for two experiments. The first examines a single-story building designed for 5 diverse world locations. The second case investigates a multi-story building, evolved using 5 fitness objectives pertaining to shape and energy factors. Comparisons with related work are made in Section 5. Concluding remarks end the paper in Section 6.

2. ENERGY EFFICIENCY AND EVOLUTIONARY DESIGN

2.1 EnergyPlus

A green building is a sustainable resource-efficient building, that minimizes negative impact on the environment [15]. Over 70% of green building research was focused on energy and atmosphere research [1]. Therefore, in most cases when designing a green building, architects and engineers try to minimize fossil fuel energy and electricity usage. One way to do this is by using passive and active solar techniques for heating during the winter, and not overheating in the summer.

There are many building analysis systems available for thermal simulation and energy usage analysis. One popular free system is EnergyPlus [23]. EnergyPlus uses a sophisticated and detailed simulation that considers load calculation, building and energy performance, heat and mass balance, water use, energy flow, and other factors. To analyze a building model, EnergyPlus will consider the structure's geometry and construction (e.g. materials, windows, doors, roof shape), and environmental information about the location (latitude and longitude, weather, time of year, time of day, and many others). The result is a precise and comprehensive analysis, useful for performing detailed investigations about many aspects of energy use of the building. More than 2000 international weather files are available.

We use EnergyPlus to perform energy analysis during fitness evaluation. Our GP system (implemented in ECJ [17]) communicates with EnergyPlus via multi-threaded processes. GP generates an input file for EnergyPlus, containing all evolved aspects of the building to analyze, including model geometry, location of windows and doors, and material information for all components. A weather file will supply the relevant geographic and environmental information for the building's location. Results of EnergyPlus's analysis will then be used to establish energy performance. Final results of analyses, including 3D model views, are readable with Sketchup[2], a free 3D design and visualization tool. All the 3D images in this paper are rendered with Sketchup.

[2]http://www.sketchup.com/

2.2 Preliminary Insights

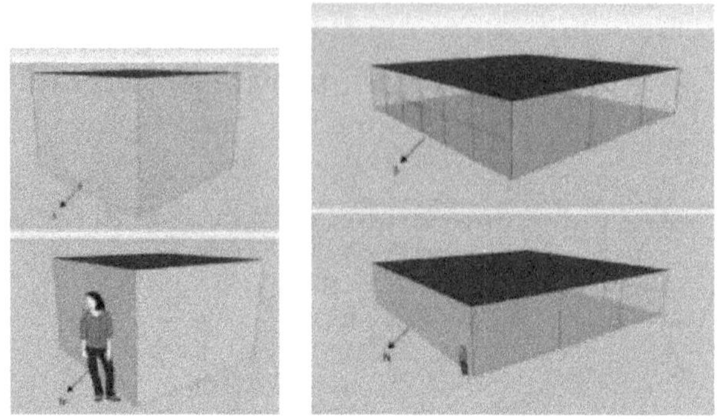

(a) (b)

Figure 1: Evolved results using (a) minimize winter energy usage, and (b) maximize solar heat gain from windows.

Preliminary experiments gave useful insights into the nature of energy evaluation and evolutionary design. We quickly learned that the most energy-efficient buildings may also be undesirable ones. Early experiments used single fitness criteria, for example, minimize annual energy usage in winter, or maximize solar heat gain from windows. Figure 1 shows the inevitable results. Figure 1(a)'s small insulated shack with no windows and door is very efficient to heat and cool. Figure 1(b) maximizes sun intake with its walls of windows on the east, south, and west sides. The north wall of the building has no windows at all.

Practical designs require balancing energy efficiency and functional necessities. With respect to the window creation, there are two strategies that can be used. One approach is to enforce window creation with design language, to guarantee window generation via the genotype itself. Another strategy, which we follow in this paper, is to use energy usage as a major influence on window creation. In this case, evolutionary pressure will indirectly encourage window inclusion, by including window heat gain as a fitness requirement. This promotes passive solar heating during winter daytime, which should promote lower energy consumption during winter. However, these windows also result in heat leakage during winter nights, and higher air conditioning costs in the summer, both of which increase energy consumption. It will be a task for GP to balance these competing factors, which are clearly evident in the cases shown in Figure 1.

Other design trends were seen. Skylights are energy leakers, and GP always discards them. Similarly, flat roofs were always preferred. Because we did not incorporate insulated attics, any non-flat roof would needlessly enlarge the building's interior, adding to energy use. These insights notwithstanding, gabled roof shapes and skylights were always available for use, although we expected evolution to ignore them.

The architectures examined are based on basic cuboid structures, with roof variations (Fig. 2). We do not consider room layouts (floor plans), but instead treat each floor as an open space. EnergyPlus can handle either case, and both affect its energy simulations. Note that, in the case of open areas, EnergyPlus will not accurately simulate floor levels whose footprints have concavities.

(a) Gabled roof 1.

Gabled roof 2.

(c) Overhangs and skylights.

(d) Gabled Skylight roof.

Figure 2: Roof, overhangs, skylights.

3. SYSTEM DETAILS

3.1 Design Language

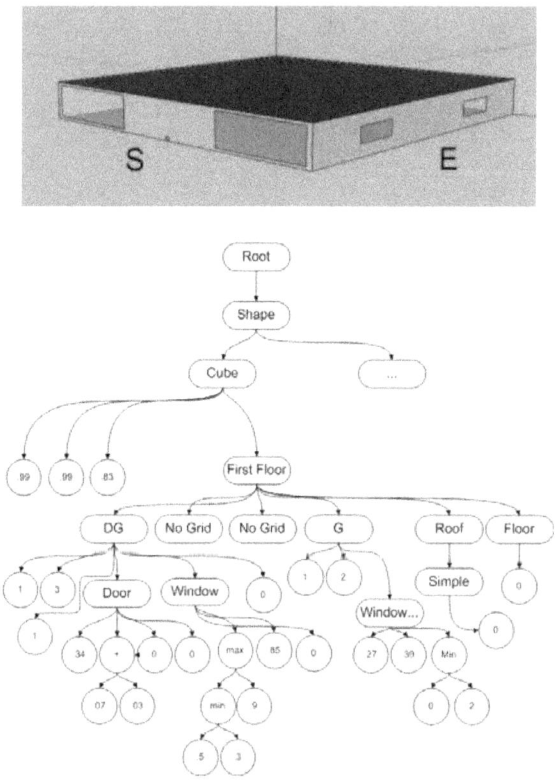

Figure 3: Building model and its grammar tree.

Our GP design language encodes a tree structure which, when interpreted, creates a 3D model. The GP tree structure parallels that of a CFG-based grammar-guided GP system [20]. Explicit mappings are made between the GP tree expressions and models being designed. Figure 3 shows a GP tree, along with the corresponding building structure. Each modeling requirement (cubic model with 3 walls, 1 wall with a door, floor, roof,...) is encoded directly in the tree. Other GP functions likewise refine the requirements of walls, doors, windows, and skylights.

Table 1: Design language.

Type	Function
R	Add Root(S)
S	Add Cube(D,D,D,FF), Add Cube(D,D,D,F)
FF	First Floor(DG,G,G,G,R2,I)
F	Add Floor(G,G,G,G,R2,I)
DG	Add Door Grid(I,I,I,D,W,I)
G	Add Grid(I,I,W,I), Add Empty Grid(I)
DR	Add Door(D,D,I,I)
W	Add Window(D,D,I)
W	Add Window Overhang(D,D,D,D,D,I)
R2	Add Simple Roof(I), Add Skylight(G)
R2	Add Gabled Roof(I,G,G,D)
R2	Add Gabled Roof2(I,G,G,D)
D (& I)	avg(D,D), max(D,D), min(D,D), Mul(D,D), Div(D,D), IfElse(D,D,D,D), ERC
D	half(D), halffwd(D)
I	inc(I), dec(I)

Table 1 shows our design language we used in Section 4.1. We use the ECJ GP system [17], and the design language is implemented with ECJ's strong typing [21]. Strongly typed functions denote CFG rule instances, and function arguments denote CFG production rule bodies. Eleven data types are used, which represent numbers (double D, int I), and abstract types for the grammar rules (window W, door D, door grid DG, first floor FF, etc.). Most functions create instances of components in the 3D model. To do this, many functions are inspired by the ideas used in split grammars, as found in the CityEngine system[3] [22]. For example, the DG function

$$Add\ Door\ Grid(I_1, I_2, I_3, D, W, I_4)$$

subdivides a wall into an $I_1 \times I_2$ grid, locates the door at position I_3, uses expression D to define the door, W to define the windows, and I_4 to define the wall material. D and W are sub-trees of type D (door) and W (wall) respectively, and I_i are integer expressions. Further iterative refinement on these grid elements could be undertaken (although we did not explore this here). Please see [13] for complete descriptions of other functions in Table 1.

Different construction materials with varying energy efficiency properties are available to the grammar. Wall and window materials are shown in Table 2. U-factor is the overall heat transfer coefficient. Lower U-factors means better insulation. SHGC (sun heat gain coefficient) measures the solar energy transmittance of glass. A high SHGC means solar energy (heat) is more easily transferred through the glass. The total number of materials were 5 walls , 3 roofs, 2 floors, 6 windows, and 3 doors.

3.2 Multi-objective Fitness Evaluation

Given the multiple, heterogeneous factors used in fitness evaluation, we treat this as a multi-objective problem (MOP) [9]. This avoids the complexities and biases involved with a single-objective, weighted sum approach. We use the sum of ranks (average rank) scoring strategy. It was originally used for high-dimensional MOP [3, 11], since Pareto ranking is increasingly ineffective with 4 or more objectives. Unlike

[3] http://www.procedural.com/

Table 2: Wall and window materials. LG=low emissivity glass.

Name	Material	U-Factor
Wall_1	wood, fiberglass, plaster board	0.516
Wall_2	wood, plywood, insulation, gypsum	0.384
Wall_3	gypsum, air (0.157 TR), gypsum	1.978
Wall_4	gypsum, air (0.153 TR), gypsum	1.994
Wall_5	brick, insulation, concrete, gypsum plaster	0.558

Name	Material	U-F.	SHGC
Win_1	3mm glass, 13mm air, 3mm glass	2.720	0.764
Win_2	3mm glass, 13mm argon, 3mm glass	2.556	0.764
Win_3	6mm glass, 6mm air, 6mm glass	3.058	0.700
Win_4	6mm LG, 6mm air, 6mm LG	2.371	0.569
Win_5	3mm glass	5.894	0.898
Win_6	6mm glass	5.778	0.819

Table 3: Example different rankings for a minimization problem. Best in each ordering labelled *.

Fitness	Wt-Sum	Pareto Rank	Ranks	NRS
(33,0,125,39)	197	1*	(3,1,6,3)	2.27
(30,24,38,18)	110	1*	(2,3,3,2)	1.4
(0,47,43,18)	108*	1*	(1,4,4,2)	1.73
(78,62,2,0)	142	1*	(6,6,1,1)	1.37*
(43,19,20,79)	161	1*	(4,2,2,4)	1.47
(55,55,89,80)	279	2	(5,5,5,5)	2.67

Pareto, sum of ranks does not commonly result in outlier solutions that are strong in a minority of objectives [4].

Sum of ranks is computed as follows. Given a minimization problem in k objectives, a population member i has a raw objective vector $(o_1^i, ..., o_k^i)$. Next, each objective 1 through k is assigned a rank relative to the rest of the population, resulting in a rank vector $(r_1^i, ..., r_k^i)$. The normalized sum of ranks is then:

$$Fitness_i = \sum_{j=1}^{k} \frac{r_j^i}{max_j}$$

where max_j is the maximum rank value for objective j. Lower fitness scores are preferred.

Table 3 shows example rankings for a minimization problem of 4 objectives. The weighted sum tallies the raw scores using a weight of 1 for all. This is followed by the Pareto rank. Finally, the normalized sum of ranks is shown, using the above procedure.

To promote diversity, when 2 individuals have identical raw fitness vectors, a penalty value is added to their ranks. This discourages copies of the same individual.

4. EXPERIMENTS AND RESULTS

4.1 Experiment: Geography

Table 4: Average daily temperature (C) for 5 cities.

Location	Description	Jan.	July
Anchorage, USA	northern subarctic	-2	14
Eldoret, KE	equatorial, tropical	17	17
Las Vegas, USA	subtropical, hot desert	9	32
Melbourne, AU	southern hemisphere, temperate	18	8.5
Toronto, CA	humid continental	-6	21

Table 5: GP Parameters

Parameter	Value
Number of runs per city	10
Generations	100
Population size	300
Initialization	ramped half&half
Grow tree depth range	2-6
Full tree depth range	5-12
Max tree depth	17
Tournament size	3
Crossover/mutation rates	90%/10%
Prob. function node selection	90%
Elitism	2
Diversity penalty	2

A single-story building suitable as a public facility (pool, library) or small business (offices, store) is to be designed. Table 4 lists 5 cities to be separately considered. The goal is to see how their geographic locations and weather affects the resulting designs. Files containing weather data and other geographic information for the cities were obtained from [23], and used by EnergyPlus.

The modeling grammar in Table 1 is used. Only single floor models are considered. A variety of roof shapes are possible, as well as skylights and window overhangs. Walls, windows, doors and floors are constructed from materials, as described in Section 3. Reasonable size ranges for floors, walls, doors, and roofs are specified. For example, floors are between 10 to 20 meters in length and width.

The fitness objectives are: (i) Window heat gain in winter (maximize); (ii) Annual energy consumption (minimize); (iii) At least 25% window area per wall. The first two objectives are measured by EnergyPlus. Temperatures below 20C invoke heating, and those above 24C activate air conditioning. Window area is evaluated by proportionally penalizing wall window areas below 25%. Other GP parameters are shown in Table 5. Many values were established during earlier runs, and are not necessarily optimal.

4.1.1 *Results*

Figure 4 (a-e) shows the top ranked solution for each city's 10 runs, and an additional Toronto solution (f). They were selected by collecting the top ranked solution of each of the 10 runs per city, and re-ranking using the sum of ranks. The resulting top score is designated the top-ranked solution (which does not necessarily mean they have the minimal energy efficiency, since energy usage is but one of the 3 objectives considered).

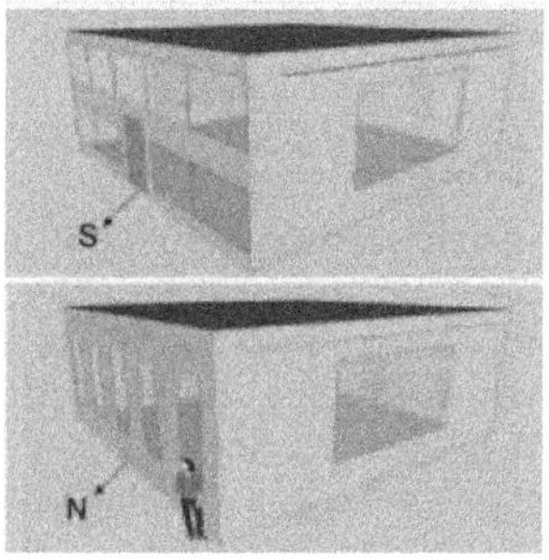

(a) Anchorage, USA

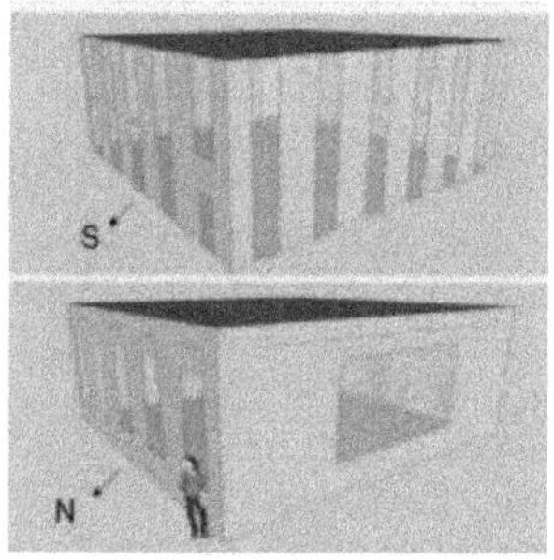

(b) Eldoret, Kenya

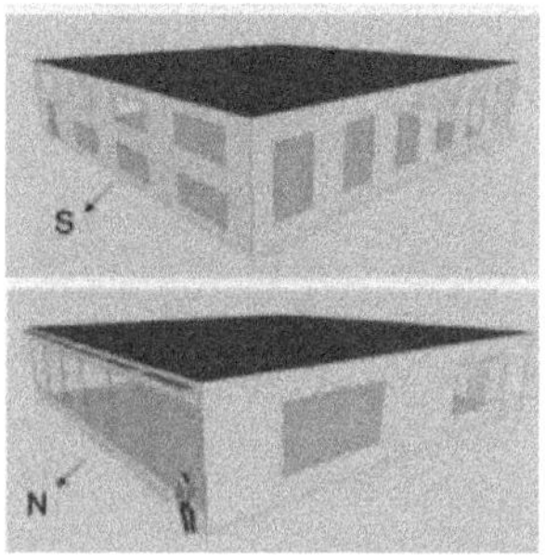

(c) Melbourne, Australia

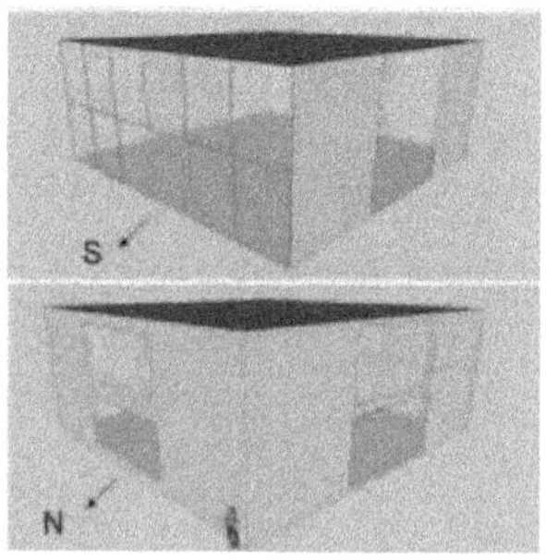

(d) Las Vegas, USA

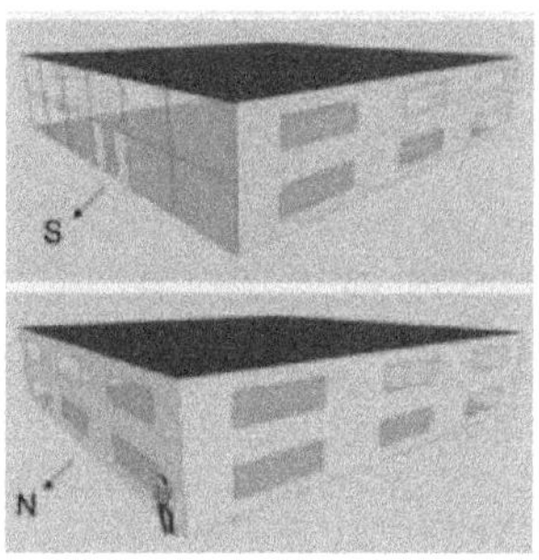

(e) Toronto, Canada

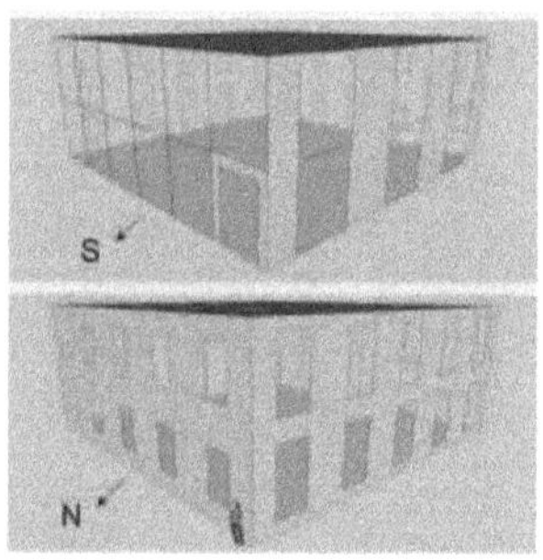

(f) Least efficient Toronto solution ("a")

Figure 4: Top ranked solution for each location.

Some design trends can be seen. Energy considerations meant that all models have flat roofs. Alternate roof shapes do not contribute to window heat gain, and so the greater volumes they introduce are detrimental. Skylights never appear, as they reduce energy efficiency (they are poor insulators). Window awnings are missing or very small. Larger awnings reduce heat gain, and so they are discarded.

All northern cities (a, d, e, f) have a wall of windows facing south for solar heat gain, while Melbourne's (c) is facing north. Eldoret's equatorial location means that window heat gain is omnidirectional. Windows on the other walls are often minimally over the desired 25% target. Many Eldoret, Melbourne, and Toronto models tended to have larger window areas on the east compared to the west. Perhaps this warms the building in the morning, after a cold night. Table 6 summarizes the window areas for the top solutions.

Most building footprints expanded to the maximum area. The exception to this was Anchorage, whose models were smaller than the others. Because of the weak sub-arctic sun, window heat gain has less impact, and so smaller building sizes are preferred for heating.

Table 6: Window area of top solutions.

Location	South	West	North	East
Toronto	94	27.5	24	35
Las Vegas	87	28	25	28
Eldoret	45	52.5	27.5	55
Anchorage	89	26	22.5	28
Melbourne	25	29	81.5	38

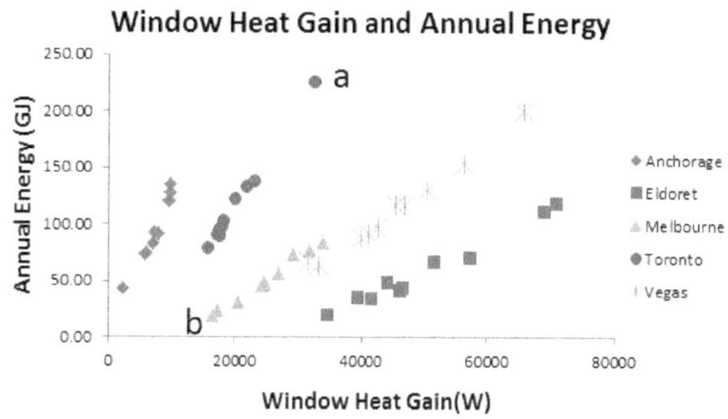

Figure 5: Energy usage scatter plot of top-ranked solutions. Each point is top scoring solution from one run.

Figure 5 is an energy vs window heat gain scatter plot of the solutions. Each city's set of solutions occupies a distinct niche, with only Melbourne and Las Vegas partially coinciding. Note that heat gain is proportional to annual energy usage: greater sun exposure for heat gain requires increased window area. But these windows are poor insulators during winter nights, and also increase cooling costs during the summer. Anchorage models have the least window heat gain. Conversely, the intense sunlight at Eldoret and Las Vegas give them the highest heat gain. The most efficient model was a Melbourne model (**b**), while an outlying Toronto solution (**a**) was the least efficient. Curiously, the majority of plotted solutions reside on Pareto fronts: 8 solutions for Eldoret, Toronto and Las Vegas sets are Pareto nondominated, as are 9 for Anchorage and Melbourne.

The annual energy usage in Figure 5 spans a significant range. The average home energy usage in Canada ranges between 94-129 GJ[4], and so our energy range is reasonable. Note that domestic houses are much smaller than the buildings in Fig. 4, and do not have empty, open floor plans as our models have. In the GP runs, energy efficiency competed equally with window heat gain and minimum window area, and the solutions indicate varying degrees to which these criteria were satisfied. Besides factors in material selection (discussed below), the main criteria for comparing and selecting between solutions for each city is to determine the preferred balance between heat gain and energy use. The top-ranked Toronto solution in Figure 4(e), also happens to be the most energy efficient of the Toronto models. An alternative Toronto solution shown in Figure 4(f) is the least energy efficient Toronto solution ("a" in Figure 5) The difference between these solutions' scores – and most solutions for all cities – is due to this classic trade-off between energy

[4]http://www.statcan.gc.ca/pub/11-526-s/2010001/part-partie1-eng.htm

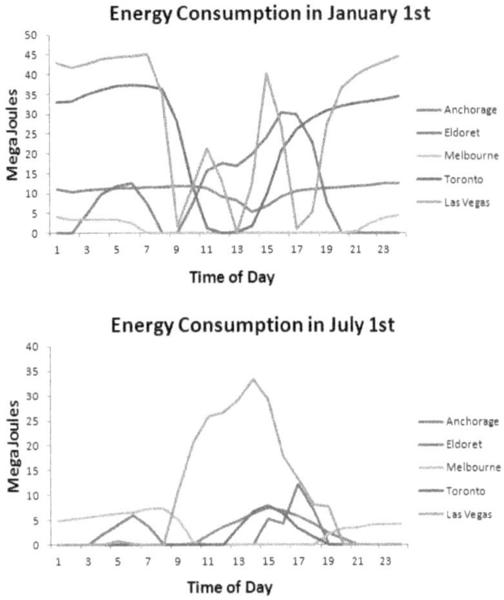

Figure 6: Energy consumption of the top-ranked model for each city, January 1 and July 1.

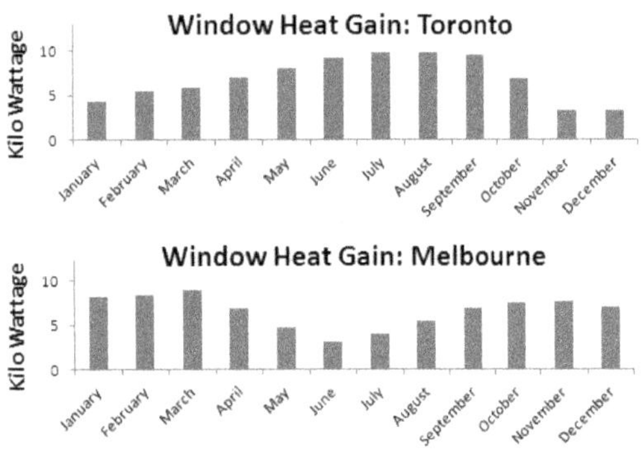

Figure 7: Annual window heat gain: Toronto and Melbourne

use and window heat gain. The model in (f) has the largest roof height, and hence largest southern window area. This optimizes window heat gain, but also increases energy use on the whole. The model in (e) has the smallest height of all the Toronto models. Hence it has lower heat gain, and uses less energy.

Figure 6 shows the hourly energy consumption of the top-ranked models for each city, during January 1 and July 1. Melbourne has consistently low energy use. Las Vegas, however, is an energy hog during winter nights and summer days. Toronto also requires heating energy during winter nights.

The effect of latitude is illustrated in Figure 7. Toronto's heat gain peaks in August, while Melbourne's peaks in March.

Consistent use of energy-efficient materials could be seen in the solutions. Walls always used an energy-efficient material definition composed of brick, insulation, concrete, and gypsum plaster ($Wall_5$ in Table 2). A window glass (Win_2) having a balance of good U-factor and high SHGC was used in almost all cities. Anchorage results, however, sometimes used Win_4, which sacrifices SHGC efficiency for higher insulating properties.

4.2 Experiment: Multi-floor Building

Here, we create a 5-floor office building to be built in Toronto, Canada. Five fitness objectives measuring energy efficiency and model design are defined: (i) Window heat gain in winter (maximize). (ii) Annual energy usage (minimize). (iii) Each wall should have 35% window area. (iv) Each floor should have 15% smaller area than the floor below it. (v) The sum of floor level volumes should be 10000 m^3. Items (i) and (ii) use the evaluations as used in Section 4.1. Sum of errors squared is used for (iii) and (iv), and the absolute volume error is used in (v). The GP language in Table 1 is used, except that *Add Root* permits 5 floors. The parameters in Table 5 are used, except the maximum generations is increased to 80.

4.2.1 Results

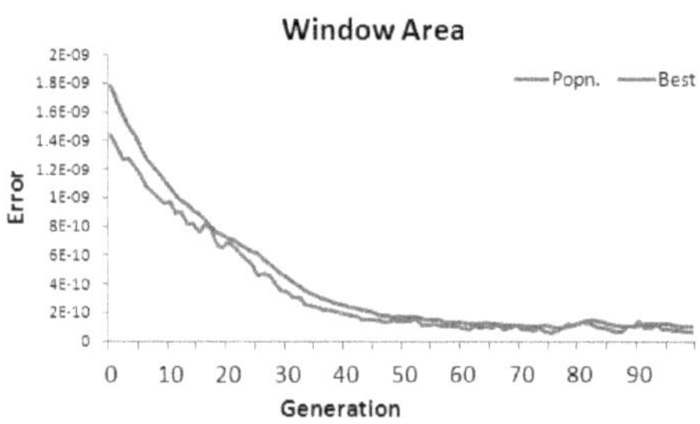

Figure 8: Window sum of errors. Average 10 runs.

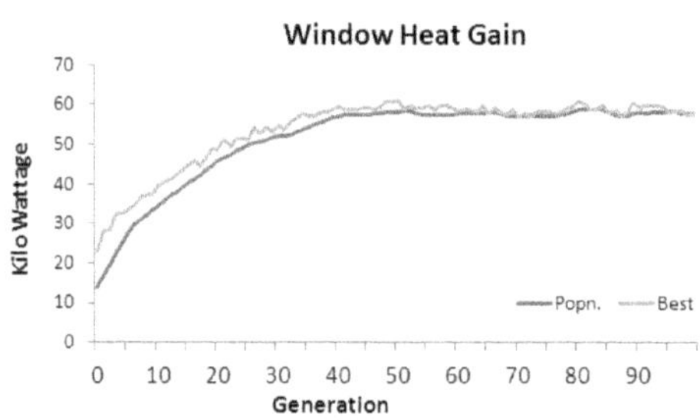

Figure 9: Window heat gain. Average of 10 runs.

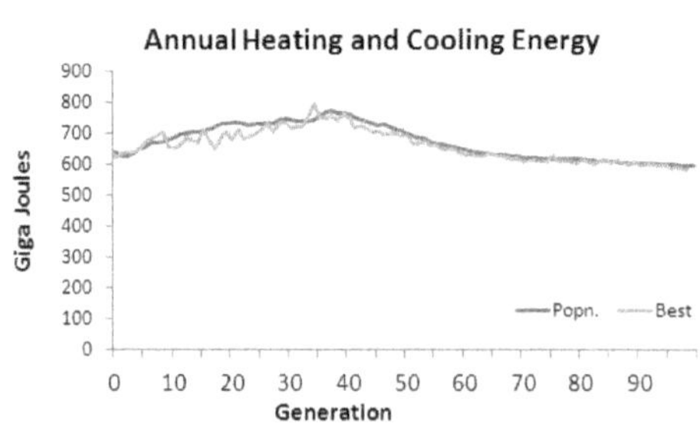

Figure 10: Annual energy. Average of 10 runs.

Figure 8 shows the performance of the 10 runs for the window objective (volume and floor area graphs are similar). The plots of the energy objectives are in Figures 9

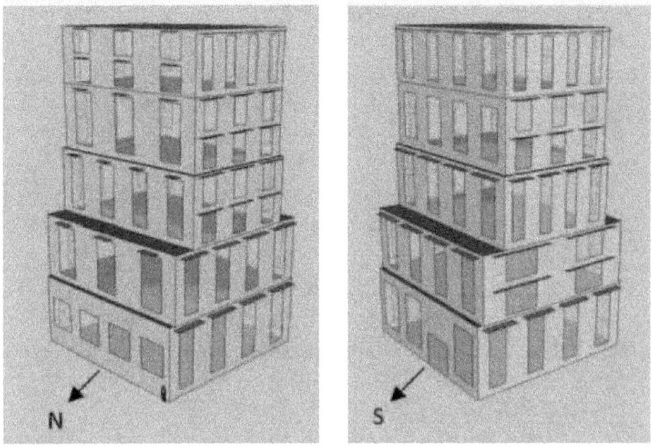

Figure 11: Best model of 10 runs for multi-floor experiment

and 10. Due to the stringent geometry criteria used, energy improvements were more difficult to optimize. Window heat gain steadily improves, until it plateaus at generation 45. This coincides with the time when window areas have reached their 35% goal (Fig. 8). Thus, window heat gain can only improve by reducing the window objective score. Hence, a balance has been reached between them.

Looking at the annual energy plot, a slow increase in energy consumption occurs up to generation 40. At that point, there is a gradual improvement to the score until the end of the run. This phenomenon often arises with sum of ranks scoring. Improvements to one objective can be delayed, to allow for improvements in other objectives. It is a democratic distribution of benefits to the population as a whole.

Figure 11 shows the top ranked solution of the 10 runs (again determined by using sum of ranks on the 10 top-scoring solutions). Its window areas are 32.3% (N), 33.5% (E), 36.4% (W), and 36.4% (S). The total volume is 9950 m^3. The same wall and window materials were selected as used in the majority of cities in Section 4.1. Some very small window awnings appeared in the model. Larger awnings reduce solar heat gain during the winter.

5. COMPARISON TO RELATED WORK

Caldas's research using evolutionary computation towards energy efficient building design (reviewed in [7]) is the most related to ours in many respects. In [8], she uses multi-objective Pareto ranking to reconcile two objectives: maximize daylight use and minimize energy consumption. She examines Pareto nondominated solutions to show trade-offs between these conflicting objectives. Whereas a single run with Pareto ranking can produce multiple candidate solutions, we obtain a similar effect in Section 4.1.1 with multiple runs using the sum of ranks. (We did not examine multiple solutions from a single run.) An advantage of sum of ranks over Pareto is that its solutions tend to perform well in multiple objectives, whereas Pareto solutions can often be outliers, with a good score in only one objective. For evolutionary design problems [4], including those examined here, such solutions are often of little value. Furthermore, Pareto ranking becomes ineffective with 5 or more objectives, as found in our multi-floor building experiment. Sum of ranks was originally suggested for high-dimensional multi-objective problems [3, 11], and is quite suitable for the size of problems examined here.

Caldas uses the DOE2 simulation software to evaluate energy usage. DOE2 is a forerunner of EnergyPlus, and uses many of the same factors we use (material, model shape, windows, etc.). Since she uses a genetic algorithm, her chromosome has fixed fields for denoting the evolved model parameters required in DOE2 simulations. Our grammar is more flexible for denoting variable-sized, complex structures. Although we did not exploit split grammar operations to generate complex building shapes, we were easily able to denote varying forms of roofs, skylights, and multiple floors.

Whereas our GP system was entirely automated, many researchers use semi-automated methods for energy-efficient building design. Turrin *et al.* evolve roofs using an interactive GA [27]. The user will consider the roof aesthetics, along with energy simulation results, to interactively evaluate results. Similarly, Malkawi *et al.* use a GA to evolve energy efficient rooms using a combination of energy simulation and user interaction [18]. Marin *et al.* also incorporate results of energy evaluation with human judgements to evolve building envelopes (shapes) [19]. We feel that user interaction is the next natural direction for our system, as it would permit aesthetic judgements to be included. Although we did not examine complex building envelopes, aesthetics would definitely be useful for that, as well as for evaluating the window design and placement that arose in our models

Our grammar is inspired by the split grammar of Muller *et al.* [22], and later used by Coia *et al.* with GP [10].

6. CONCLUSIONS

This paper applied GP towards the energy-oriented design of building architectures. By using the sum of ranks analysis, multiple diverse and conflicting design objectives were considered. Results show that solutions from different runs present trade-offs of the design goals. In particular, because we treated annual energy use and winter heat gain with equal priority, solutions usually indicate a trade-off of these two factors: winter heat gain improvements come at the expense of annual energy usage. In future work, it would be worth examining different preferential targets for energy use and heat gain. One intriguing idea is to consider seasonally-adaptable window awnings. Furthermore, EnergyPlus is capable of accounting for an enormous range of factors besides those that we examined, including ventilation models, various HVAC design factors, floor plans, human factors (clothing), staged zone thermostats, and a host of others. Another important consideration is monetary cost, since the most efficient design concepts may be prohibitively expensive. All these factors can be considered in evolutionary design.

We found our CFG implementation using the strongly typed GP tree language to be practical for the problems examined. Any aspect of the building architecture (size, shape, material, window placement,...) was quickly incorporated into the grammar. Furthermore, candidate structures were usually sensible. This would not be the case if a more general design grammar (e.g. L-system) were used. Although we focused exclusively on simple cuboid structures with different roof choices, future work should consider more complex building layouts and envelopes. In order for EnergyPlus simulations to be accurate, however, complex footprints will require floor plan definitions. Automated floor plan design is a significantly complex problem [16, 12].

Our experiments never considered the aesthetic merits of the evolved structures. Although the cuboid structures permit little design variation, window placement could be evaluated with respect to aesthetics. For this purpose, a symmetry analysis might be included. Alternatively, permitting user interaction with the system, as done by other researchers (Section 5), is worth considering.

7. ACKNOWLEDGEMENTS

Thanks to Beatrice Ombuki-Berman, Sheridan Houghten and Tina Yu for their advice, and Cale Fairchild for his assistance with systems issues. This research is partially supported by NSERC DG 138467.

8. REFERENCES

[1] U. E. P. Agency. Green building basic information, October 2010. http://www.epa.gov/greenbuilding/pubs/about.htm.

[2] P. Bentley and D. Corne. *Creative Evolutionary Systems*. Morgan Kaufmann, 2002.

[3] P. J. Bentley and J. P. Wakefield. Finding acceptable solutions in the pareto-optimal range using multiobjective genetic algorithms. In *Soft Computing in Engineering Design and Manufacturing*, pages 231–240. Springer, 1998.

[4] S. Bergen and B. Ross. Evolutionary Art Using Summed Multi-objective Ranks. In *Genetic Programming - Theory and Practice VIII*, pages 227–244. Springer, May 2010.

[5] N. Bouchlaghem. Optimising the design of building envelopes for thermal performance. *Automation in Construction*, 10(1):101–112, 2000.

[6] J. Byrne, M. Fenton, E. Hemberg, J. McDermott, M. O'Neill, E. Shotton, and C. Nally. Combining structural analysis and multi-objective criteria for evolutionary architectural design. In *Applications of Evolutionary Computation*, volume 6625 of *LNCS*, pages 204–213. Springer, 2011.

[7] L. Caldas. Generation of energy-efficient architecture solutions applying gene_arch: An evolution-based generative design system. *Advanced Engineering Informatics*, 22(1):59–70, 2008.

[8] L. G. Caldas and L. K. Norford. Shape generation using pareto genetic algorithms: integrating conflicting design objectives in low-energy architecture. *Intl. Journal of Architectural Computing*, 1(4):503–515, 2003.

[9] C. A. C. Coello, G. B. Lamont, and D. A. Van Veldhuisen. *Evolutionary Algorithms for Solving Multi-objective Problems*. Springer, 2007.

[10] C. Coia and B. Ross. Automatic evolution of conceptual building architectures. In *Proc. CEC*, pages 1140–1147. IEEE, 2011.

[11] D. Corne and J. Knowles. Techniques for highly multiobjective optimisation: Some nondominated points are better than others. In *Proc. GECCO 2007*, pages 773–780. ACM, 2007.

[12] R. Flack and B. Ross. Evolution of architectural floor plans. In *Proc. App. of Evolutionary Computation (EvoStar)*, volume 6625 of *LNCS*, pages 313–322. Springer-Verlag, 2011.

[13] M. M. O. Gholami. Passive solar building design using genetic programming. Master's thesis, Brock University, 2013.

[14] A. Harrington and B. Ross. Generative representations for artificial architecture and passive solar performance. In *Proc. CEC 2013*, pages 537–545. IEEE, June 2013.

[15] Y. Ji and S. Plainiotis. *Design for sustainability*. China Architecture & Building Press, Beijing, 2006.

[16] D. Lobos and D. Donath. The problem of space layout in architecture: A survey and reflections. *arquiteturarevista*, 6(2):136–161, 2010.

[17] S. Luke. Ecj. Last accessed Mar 24, 2014.

[18] A. M. Malkawi, R. S. Srinivasan, Y. K. Yi, and R. Choudhary. Decision support and design evolution: integrating genetic algorithms, cfd and visualization. *Automation in Construction*, 14(1):33–44, 2005.

[19] P. Marin, J.-C. Bignon, and H. Lequay. Generative exploration of architectural envelope responding to solar passive qualities. In *Design & Decision Support Systems in Architecture and Urban Planning*. Eindhoven U of Tech, 2008.

[20] R. McKay, N. Hoai, P. Whigham, Y. Shan, and M. O'Neill. Grammar-based Genetic Programming: a Survey. *Genetic Programming and Evolvable Machines*, 11:365–396, 2010.

[21] D. J. Montana. Strongly typed genetic programming. *Evolutionary Computation*, 3(2):199–230, 1995.

[22] P. Muller, P. Wonka, S. Haegler, A. Ulmer, and L. V. Gool. Procedural modeling of buildings. In *Proc. SIGGRAPH*, pages 614–623, New York, 2006. ACM.

[23] U. D. of Energy. Energyplus energy simulation software, October 2012. http://apps1.eere.energy.gov/buildings/energyplus/.

[24] M. O'Neill, J. McDermott, J. M. Swafford, J. Byrne, E. Hemberg, A. Brabazon, E. Shotton, C. McNally, and M. Hemberg. Evolutionary design using grammatical evolution and shape grammars: Designing a shelter. *International Journal of Design Engineering*, 3(1):4–24, 2010.

[25] U.-M. O'Reilly and M. Hemberg. Integrating generative growth and evolutionary computation for form exploration. *Genetic Programming and Evolvable Machines*, 8(2):163–186, 2007.

[26] P. Steadman. *The Evolution of Designs*. Routledge, 2008.

[27] M. Turrin, P. von Buelow, R. Stouffs, and A. Kilian. Performance-oriented design of large passive solar roofs. In *Proc. ECAADE*. ETH, 2010.

[28] P. von Buelow. *Genetically Engineered Architecture*. VDM, 2007.

[29] J. A. Wright, H. A. Loosemore, and R. Farmani. Optimization of building thermal design and control by multi-criterion genetic algorithm. *Energy and Buildings*, 34(9):959–972, 2002.

[30] T. Yu. Modeling occupancy behavior for energy efficiency and occupants comfort management in intelligent buildings. In *Proc. ICMLA*, pages 726–731. IEEE, 2010.

Quantum Inspired Genetic Algorithm for Community Structure Detection in Social Networks

Shikha Gupta
Department of Computer Science
University of Delhi
New Delhi, India
shikha.gupta.cs.du@gmail.com

Sheetal Taneja
Dayal Singh College
University of Delhi
New Delhi, India
sheetaltaneja1@gmail.com

Naveen Kumar
Department of Computer Science
University of Delhi
New Delhi, India
nk.cs.du@gmail.com

ABSTRACT

Community detection is a key problem in social network analysis. We propose a two-phase algorithm for detecting community structure in social networks. First phase employs a local-search method to group together nodes that have a high chance of falling in a single community. The second phase is bi-partitioning strategy that optimizes network modularity and deploys a variant of quantum-inspired genetic algorithm. The proposed algorithm does not require any knowledge of the number of communities beforehand and works well for both directed and undirected networks. Experiments on synthetic and real-life networks show that the method is able to successfully reveal community structure with high modularity.

Categories and Subject Descriptors

D.2.2 [**Design Tools and Techniques**]: [Top-down programming]; H.3.3 [**Information Storage and Retrieval**]: Information Search and Retrieval—*clustering*

Keywords

Social Network; Community detection; Quantum-inspired genetic algorithm; Modularity; Normalized mutual information; Hierarchical divisive strategy; Modularity

1. INTRODUCTION

The problem of community detection has captured the interest of many researchers [1, 12, 17, 29, 33]. Girvan and Newman [14] introduced the famous divisive hierarchical GN algorithm that uses edge betweenness measure to identify and remove the edges lying between communities, leading to isolation of communities. The algorithm was extended in [26] (GN-Fast) by introducing *network modularity* as a measure of partition quality. High modularity values indicates strong community structure, that is, dense connections between the nodes within communities and sparse connections between nodes in different communities. The algorithm computes the modularity for each split of the network and selects the set of communities that maximizes the modularity value. Based on the notion that a high modularity value represents a good community structure, Newman [25] suggested a greedy agglomerative hierarchical community detection approach (Newman-Fast) that optimizes modularity value over all possible partitions of the network. Clauset et al. [7] gave a faster version of the Newman-Fast algorithm (CNM). Duch and Arenas [11] proposed a community detection algorithm (DA) that uses the concept of extremal optimization to optimize modularity. Pons and Latapy [34] proposed a modularity based agglomerative hierarchical algorithm (PL) centered on the idea that random walks tend to get trapped in densely connected parts of the graph. Tasgin and Bingol [38] introduced one of the earliest genetic algorithms (GATHB) that optimizes modularity as the fitness function for the problem of community detection. A more recent genetic algorithm (MOGA-Net) [32], optimizes *community score* [30], along with the modularity value.

In this paper, we propose a novel two-phase algorithm for community detection considering community detection as an optimization problem. The proposed algorithm assumes that the communities in the social network are non-overlapped and uses network modularity as the objective function to measure the goodness of the communities formed. For each node i, first phase marks a set of nodes for inclusion in the community to which i belongs.

Community detection problem being an NP-hard problem [26], most of the available algorithms do not scale well for large networks [10]. Further, most of these algorithms require knowledge of structure of the entire network at all times and are classified as *global algorithms* as opposed to *local algorithms* that work with a subset of the network at any given point in time. Gargi et al. [13] points out that whereas global algorithms do not scale well for large and dynamic networks, local algorithms [2, 4, 6, 28] may work better. [2] points out that social networks exhibit considerable variations in the local density and a global methodology for community detection may either fail to detect communities present in sparse areas of the network or may discover irrelevant communities. A hybrid approach [31, 37] comprising of a local search phase that captures the local variations in density in conjunction with global search on a reduced network structure may be more effective.

In the second phase, we adopt a global hierarchical divisive strategy that repeatedly divides the network into two halves while maximizing the network modularity (Q). This phase deploys a variant of quantum-inspired genetic algorithm (QIGA) [15]. Quantum-inspired computing is characterized by the use of a quantum-inspired computational method, inspired by principles of quantum mechanics, to generate candidate solutions, followed by the use of a classical algorithm to check these candidate solutions [23]. QIGA works with quantum population comprising of chromosomes. Each chromosome is represented as a string of qubits with the advantage that it can represent a linear superposition of states in search space prob-

GECCO'14, July 12–16, 2014, Vancouver, BC, Canada.

ACM 978-1-4503-2662-9/14/07 ...$15.00.
http://dx.doi.org/10.1145/2576768.2598277 .

abilistically. Whereas a classical chromosome with n bits can store one value out of 2^n, a quantum chromosome can be in a superposition of all 2^n values. Further, whereas an operation applied to the classical chromosome produces one result, an operation applied to the quantum chromosome produces a superposition of all possible results in the form of *quantum parallelism* and serves as a basis for parallelization of quantum-inspired algorithms. Thus, evolutionary computing with qubit representation has a better characteristic of population diversity than classical representation [36]. As the system evolves, property of diversity disappears gradually as the qubit probabilities approach the value 1 or 0 and the quantum chromosome converges to a single state [15]. A detailed survey of extensions and applications of QIGA may be found in [41]. The rest of the paper is organized as follows: section 2 gives the problem definition and notations used, section 3 presents the solution strategy, section 4 covers the experiments conducted and the results obtained, and section 5 concludes the paper.

2. PROBLEM DEFINITION AND NOTATIONS

A social network S can be modeled as a graph $G = (V, E)$, where $V = 1, \ldots, n$ is the set of vertices or nodes representing the users in S and $E = (E_{ij})$, $i, j \in V$ is the set of edges that connect elements of V. The graph G may be directed or undirected, depending on the nature of the social network. $n = |V|$ denotes the number of nodes in G and $m = |E|$ denotes the number of edges in G. A graph G may be represented as an n x n adjacency matrix $A = (A_{ij})$, for $i, j \in V$, where,

$$A_{ij} = \begin{cases} 1 & \text{if there is an edge from i to j,} \\ 0 & \text{otherwise.} \end{cases} \quad (1)$$

and the number of edges (m) may be expressed as follows,

$$m = \begin{cases} \frac{1}{2}\sum_{i,j} A_{ij} & \text{for undirected graphs,} \\ \sum_{i,j} A_{ij} & \text{for directed graphs.} \end{cases} \quad (2)$$

The problem of finding communities in G may be described as the problem of finding cohesive sub-graphs of G. Newman [24] describes community structure as groups of nodes that have a high density of edges within them, with a lower density of edges between groups. The community detection problem may be formulated as the problem of finding subgraphs (of G), C_l, $l = 1, \ldots, k$, satisfying the following inequation,

$$\sum_{i,j \in C_l} A_{ij} > \sum_{i \in C_l, j \notin C_l} A_{ij}$$

The proposed strategy measures the goodness of the communities formed in the network using *network modularity* (Q). Network modularity is defined as follows:
Let D be the modularity matrix [20],
for directed networks,

$$D_{ij} = \frac{1}{m}(A_{ij} - \frac{d_i^{out} d_j^{in}}{m}) \quad i, j = 1, \ldots, n \quad (3)$$

for undirected networks,

$$D_{ij} = \frac{1}{2m}(A_{ij} - \frac{d_i^{out} d_j^{in}}{2m}) \quad i, j = 1, \ldots, n \quad (4)$$

Then,

$$Q = \sum_{i,j}^{n} D_{ij}\, \delta_{ij} \quad i, j = 1, \ldots, n \quad (5)$$

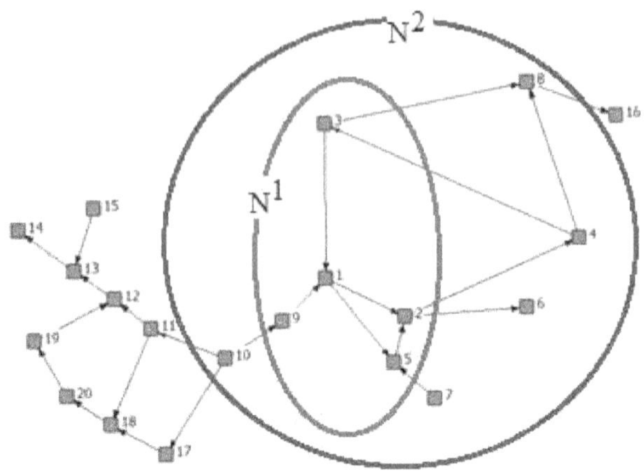

Figure 1: The 1-neighborhood of node 1 comprises of all the nodes in the inner circle, $N^1(1)$ = 1, 2, 3, 5, 9. 2-neighborhood of node 1 comprises of all the nodes in the outer circle, $N^2(1)$ = 1, 2, 3, 4, 5, 6, 7, 8, 9, 10.

where,

$$d_i^{out} = \sum_j A_{ij}, \; d_j^{in} = \sum_i A_{ij}$$

$$\delta_{ij} = \begin{cases} 1 & \text{if nodes i and j belong to the same community,} \\ 0 & \text{otherwise.} \end{cases}$$

3. SOLUTION STRATEGY

The process of community detection is organized in two phases: a local-search preprocessing phase and a global-search phase that deploys a quantum-inspired genetic algorithm.

3.1 Phase-I: Preprocessing

This phase, given in procedure *preprocessing*, groups together those nodes of social network S, that have a high chance of falling in a single community. The output of this phase is a higher abstracted network S' where a node in S' corresponds to a community formed in S. The first step of this phase is an agglomerative algorithm. It starts by initializing every node i in its own community and identifies nodes that are at a maximum distance of two edges from the node i. This is based on the intuition that the nodes that are separated by at most one node in the chain of interactions have a naturally high propensity of being in the same community. We define *p-neighborhood* of node i as the set of all nodes that are at a distance p (in the corresponding undirected graph) with respect to node i. Then, 1-neighborhood (N^1) and 2-neighborhood (N^2) of node i (example in figure 1) may be formulated mathematically as,

$$N^1(i) = \{i\} \cup \{j \mid A_{ij} \neq 0\} \cup \{j \mid A_{ji} \neq 0\}$$

$$N^2(i) = N^1(i) \cup \{j \mid \exists k \in N^1(i), (A_{jk} \neq 0 \vee A_{kj} \neq 0)\}$$

Jaccard coefficient (J_{ij}), given in (7), is used to compute the neighborhood overlap. A node j is added to the community of node i if J_{ij} exceeds a certain multiple of the average overlap for node i (J_i), given in (8), that is if,

$$J_{ij} > \alpha\, J_i \quad (6)$$

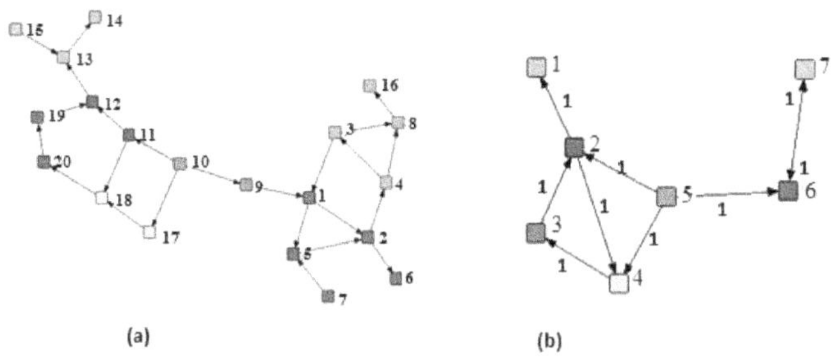

Figure 2: (a) Communities formed after preprocessing phase, (b) Communities in graph *(a)* abstracted as nodes

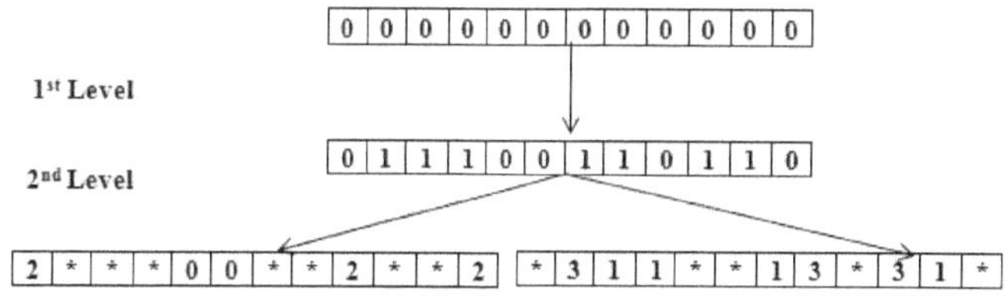

Figure 3: Example of hierarchical bi-partitioning. * indicates the nodes that are not of interest for the split. All the nodes are initialized to community 0. At the first level, nodes are split into communities 0 and 1. At the second level, nodes in community 0 are split into communities 0 and 2 while nodes in community 1 are split into communities 1 and 3.

Procedure Preprocessing

Input: Adjacency matrix A of size $n \times n$, Vertex list V
Output: Adjacency matrix B for abstracted graph
  step1:
  for $i \leftarrow 1, \ldots, n$ **do**
    compute 2-neighborhood $N^2(i)$
    for $j \leftarrow 1, \ldots, n$ **do**
      compute Jaccard coefficient J_{ij}
    end for
    compute average Jaccard J_i
    determine community $C_i \leftarrow \{j \in N^2(i) \mid J_{ij} > \alpha J_i\}$
  end for
  $C \leftarrow \{C_1, \ldots, C_n\}$
  // Pruning- Remove redundancies
  for $C_i \in C, i \leftarrow 1, \ldots, n$ **do**
    remove communities that consist of ≤ 2 nodes
    combine communities that differ by single node or are subsets
  end for
  // Let $C \leftarrow \{C_1, \ldots, C_{r_1}\}$ be the resulting set of communities
  repeat
    $C_{old} \leftarrow C$
    compute multi-way Jaccard similarity J_M for all $C_j \in C$
    find the community $C_j \in C$ with largest non-zero J_M
    for all $C_i \in C, i \neq j$ **do**
      if $C_i \subset C_j$ **then**
        remove C_j from C
      else
        $\forall v \in C_j$, remove v from all other communities in C
      end if
    end for
  until $C_{old} = C$
  for every node i not included in any community **do**
    assign i to its own community
  end for
  compute abstracted adjacency matrix $D \leftarrow (D_{ij}),\ i, j \in [1, r_2]$
  where $D_{ij} \leftarrow \sum_{p \in C_i, q \in C_j} A_{pq}$, r_2 =no. of communities in C
  step2:
  each node in D is assigned to its own community
  compute modularity gain matrix, $\triangle Q \leftarrow (\triangle Q_{ij})\ \forall i, j \in [1, k]$
  for $i \leftarrow 1, \ldots, k$ **do**
    add i to community of j where

$$j \leftarrow \arg\max_j \triangle Q_{ij}$$

  end for
  let $k \leftarrow$ number of communities in C
  compute abstracted adjacency matrix $B \leftarrow (B_{ij}),\ i, j \in [1, k]$
  where $B_{ij} \leftarrow \sum_{p \in C_i, q \in C_j} D_{pq}$

---

where value of *threshold parameter* α was decided through experimentation for various datasets and the value was found to lie in the range (2, 3) in each case,

$$J_{ij} = \frac{N^1(i) \cap N^1(j)}{N^1(i) \cup N^1(j)},\ j \in N^2(i) \tag{7}$$

$$J_i = \frac{1}{|N^2(i)|} \sum_j J_{ij} \tag{8}$$

Since degree distribution in social networks follows power-law [3] (that is, number of nodes with very high degree is very small while most nodes have small degree), expected time to compute pair-wise Jaccard (7) is not very high. Thus, we form n communities C_i, $i = 1, \ldots, n$, one for each node i in the graph G, each containing the node i itself. The following types of communities are considered redundant and removed: communities consisting of 2 nodes or less, communities that are proper subsets of other communities, and communities that differ only in one node. Multi-way Jaccard similarity coefficient [2] is then computed for each remaining community to get the neighborhood overlap between all the nodes of a community. Communities with high, non-zero multi-way Jaccard similarity value are accepted. The algorithm works in a pessimistic way finding islands of nodes with a high chance of being in the same community. Once a community consisting of a node j is finalized, node j is removed from all other subgraphs, that is, node j is considered only in that community where it shows highest cohesiveness. Each community so formed is abstracted into a node for the next step of the preprocessing phase as shown in figure 2. This step is computationally expensive due to the requirement of multi-way Jaccard computation, but not prohibitive as the algorithm performs only a single iteration.
In the second step of preprocessing, we further merge the communities by maximizing local modularity [4]. The preprocessing step is formally described in step 2 of preprocessing algorithm.

3.2 Quantum-Inspired Genetic Algorithm for Community Detection Problem

The second phase of the community detection procedure begins by assigning all the nodes to the same community. It repeatedly bi-partitions the existing communities until no more new communities are formed. Bi-partitioning is achieved by calling a quantum-inspired genetic algorithm (procedure *QIGA*), first implemented by Han and Kim [15]. A quantum-inspired genetic algorithm is an evolutionary algorithm that uses the fundamental notions in quantum mechanics and quantum computing like quantum bits (qubits), superposition, and unitary transformations of quantum states. The smallest unit of information stored in two-state quantum system

Procedure QIGA

Input: Graph $G = (V, E)$
Output: Best solution B
  $t \leftarrow 0$
  initialize quantum population $Q(t) \leftarrow \{q_1^t, q_2^t, \ldots, q_{pop}^t\}$ (q_i^t, as in (10)): $a_i^t \leftarrow 1/\sqrt{2}, b_i^t \leftarrow 1/\sqrt{2}, i \leftarrow 1, \ldots, n$
  determine $P(t)$ by measuring $Q(t)$ (procedure Measure)
  evaluate $P(t)$- $\forall$ chromosomes, compute fitness (modularity)
  store the best solution (positive gain in network modularity) in B
  while not termination condition **do**
    $t \leftarrow t+1$
    determine $P(t)$ by measuring $Q(t-1)$
    evaluate $P(t)$
    for all chromosome in $Q(t)$ and $P(t)$ **do**
      mutate the chromosome (procedure Mutate)
      modify $Q(t)$ using Q-gates (procedure Update)
      update B with the best solution among $P(t-1)$ and $P(t)$
    end for
  end while

is called a qubit which may be in "1" state, "0 "state, or in any superposition of "1" and "0" states. The state of a qubit can be represented as follows:

$$|\Psi>= a\,|0> +b\,|1> \tag{9}$$

where a and b are complex numbers that specify the probability amplitudes of the corresponding states. $|a|^2$ and $|b|^2$ denote the probabilities that the qubit may be found in states 0 and 1 respectively. The condition $|a|^2 + |b|^2 = 1$ guarantees normalization.
In a quantum-inspired genetic algorithm, a chromosome encoding binary representation of the solution uses a representation based on qubits where a qubit is defined using a pair of complex numbers (a, b) , represented by the vector, $[a\ b]^T$. Thus, n qubits may be used to represent a *quantum chromosome* of size n as follows,

$$q = \left[\begin{array}{c|c|c|c} a_1 & a_2 & \ldots & a_n \\ b_1 & b_2 & \ldots & b_n \end{array}\right]$$

For example, consider the following 3-qubit chromosome with three pairs of amplitudes,

$$q = \left[\begin{array}{c|c|c} \frac{1}{\sqrt{2}} & \frac{\sqrt{3}}{2} & \frac{-1}{\sqrt{2}} \\ \frac{1}{\sqrt{2}} & \frac{1}{2} & \frac{1}{\sqrt{2}} \end{array}\right].$$

Here, the states are in superposition and can be represented as,

Procedure Measure

Input: Quantum population $Q(t)$
Output: Classical Population $P(t)$
  for all quantum chromosomes $q_j \leftarrow (|\Psi_1>, |\Psi_2>, \ldots, |\Psi_n>), j \leftarrow 1, \ldots, pop$ **do**
    for all qubits $|\Psi_i> \leftarrow a_i\,|k_0> + b_i\,|k_1>, i \leftarrow 1, \ldots, n$ **do**
      if random[0, 1) $< |a_i|^2$ **then**
        $x_i \leftarrow 1$
      else
        $x_i \leftarrow 0$
      end if
    end for
    chromosome $X_j \leftarrow \{x_1, x_2, \ldots, x_n\}$ is added to $P(t)$
  end for

$|\Psi>= \frac{-\sqrt{3}}{4}|000> + \frac{\sqrt{3}}{4}|001> - \frac{1}{4}|010> + \frac{1}{4}|011> - \frac{\sqrt{3}}{4}|100> + \frac{\sqrt{3}}{4}|101> - \frac{1}{4}|110> + \frac{1}{4}|111>$. This implies that states $|000>$, $|001>$, $|010>$, $|011>$, $|100>$, $|101>$, $|110>$, and $|111>$ occur with probabilities 3/16, 3/16, 1/16, 1/16, 3/16, 3/16, 1/16, and 1/16 respectively. A system of n-qubits can represent 2^n states at the same time but each qubit collapses to a single state 0 or 1 when measured, resulting in a classical binary chromosome. For example, a 12-qubit chromosome $a_1|0> +b_1|1>, a_2|0> +b_2|1>, \ldots, a_{12}|0> +b_{12}|1>$ when measured may yield a binary chromosome such as,

0	1	1	1	0	0	1	1	0	1	1	0

Thus, by the above explanation, the second phase of the proposed strategy begins by allocating all the nodes in the graph to community 0 (assuming that the community IDs to be assigned are 0, 1, ...). The first bi-partitioning step divides the network into two communities 0 and 1. In this context, the values 0 and 1 in the above chromosome may be interpreted as a community IDs associated with the corresponding nodes. Thus, the above chromosome may be interpreted as,

Node no.	1	2	3	4	5	6	7	8	9	10	11	12
Community ID	0	1	1	1	0	0	1	1	0	1	1	0

That is, nodes 1, 5, 6, 9, and 12 belong to the community 0 while nodes 2, 3, 4, 7, 8, 10, and 11 belong to the community 1.

Example 1
Considering an example network of size n = 12. A chromosome in the initial quantum population $Q(t)$ (3.2.1) will appear as:

$$q = \left[\begin{array}{c|c|c|c} \frac{1}{\sqrt{2}} & \frac{1}{\sqrt{2}} & \ldots & \frac{1}{\sqrt{2}} \\ \frac{1}{\sqrt{2}} & \frac{1}{\sqrt{2}} & \ldots & \frac{1}{\sqrt{2}} \end{array}\right]$$

where a qubit is of the form $|\Psi> = 1/\sqrt{2}\,|0> + 1/\sqrt{2}\,|1>$. On measuring q, string such as the following will appear:

0	1	1	1	0	0	1	1	0	1	1	0

In the next step of the hierarchical divisive method, community 0 is further subdivided into communities 0, 2 and the corresponding qubit is of the form $|\Psi> = a'\,|0> + b'\,|2>$. Similarly, community 1 is further subdivided into communities 1, 3 and the corresponding qubit is of the form $|\Psi> = a''\,|1> + b''\,|3>$. In general, a qubit may be written as $|\Psi> = a\,|k_0> + b\,|k_1>$. On measuring this quantum population $Q(t)$, string such as the following appears:

2	3	1	1	0	0	1	3	2	3	1	2

The fitness function (network modularity) is computed after every split and the split is accepted if it increases the modularity. At the next level in hierarchical bi-partitioning, nodes in community 0 are split into communities 0 and 2 while nodes in community 1 are split into communities 1 and 3 . The process terminates when no further increase in the modularity is possible. This is shown in figure 3 and described in the Example 1.

3.2.1 Algorithm

Procedure QIGA [15] maintains a quantum population $Q(t)$ of quantum chromosomes, that is, $Q(t) = q_1^t, q_2^t, \ldots, q_{pop}^t$ where t denotes the generation number and pop is the size of the population. The quantum chromosome q_j^t, $j = 1, \ldots, pop$ is defined as,

$$q_i^t = \left[\begin{array}{c|c|c|c} a_1^t & a_2^t & \ldots & a_n^t \\ b_1^t & b_2^t & \ldots & b_n^t \end{array}\right] \tag{10}$$

Procedure Mutate

Input: Quantum chromosome $q \leftarrow (|\Psi_1>, |\Psi_2>, \ldots, |\Psi_n>)$ where $|\Psi_i> = a_i\, |k_0> + b_i\, |k_1>$, corresponding classical chromosome $X \leftarrow (x_1, \ldots, x_n)$
Output: Mutated quantum chromosome $q' \leftarrow (|\Psi'_1>, |\Psi'_2>, \ldots, |\Psi'_n>)$
  for $i \leftarrow 1, \ldots, n$ **do**
    if $random[0,1) < 1/n$ **then**
      compute change in modularity, $\triangle Q_i$
      if $\triangle Q_i > 0$ **then**
        if $x_i \leftarrow 0$ **then**
          $x_i \leftarrow 1$
        else
          $x_i \leftarrow 0$
        end if
        //exchange the probabilities of the states in i^{th} quantum qubit
        $|\Psi'_i> \leftarrow b_i\, |k_0> + a_i\, |k_1>$
      else
        $|\Psi'_i> \leftarrow |\Psi_i>$
      end if
    end if
  end for

where the size of the chromosome (n) is the number of nodes in the graph. The algorithm starts by initializing the quantum population $Q(t)$ such that a^t_i and b^t_i, $i = 1, \ldots, n$ of q^t_j, $j = 1, \ldots, pop$ are all initialized with value $1/\sqrt{2}$. That is, initially, each possible state of a quantum chromosome occurs with equal probability $1/2$. Measurement step (procedure *Measure*) generates the corresponding initial classical binary population $P(t)$ by observing states of quantum chromosomes in $Q(t)$ where,

$$P(t) = \{x^t_1, x^t_2, \ldots, x^t_{pop}\}$$

x^t_j is a classical binary chromosome of length n, each bit of which is selected on the basis of the probability of the corresponding qubit. The value stored in the jth bit of x^t_j represents the community ID to which the node j is assigned. Each solution x^t_j is evaluated for its fitness. The best solution among $P(t)$ is stored in B. At every generation t, population $P(t)$ is obtained by measuring $Q(t-1)$ and B is the best chromosome among $P(t-1)$ and $P(t)$. Exploration of the solution search space is achieved in the proposed algorithm using a variant of the quantum mutation operator (procedure *Mutate*) [21], and a quantum rotation gate (procedure *Update*) [15]. Mutation is performed in the chromosome of classical population $P(t)$ and in the quantum chromosome of quantum population $Q(t-1)$ at the mutation rate of $1/n$ [27]. If the mutated gene in $P(t)$ increases the modularity, then the mutation is accepted by interchanging the probabilities of the states of the corresponding qubit. Qubits in $Q(t)$ are modified by applying quantum rotation gate,

Procedure Update

Input: Quantum chromosome $q \leftarrow (|\Psi_1>, |\Psi_2>, \ldots, |\Psi_n>)$ where $|\Psi_i> = a_i\, |k_0> + b_i\, |k_1>$, corresponding classical chromosome $X \leftarrow (x_1, \ldots, x_n)$, best solution chromosome B
Output: Updated quantum chromosome $q' \leftarrow (|\Psi'_1>, \ldots, |\Psi'_n>)$ where $|\Psi'_i> = a'_i\, |k_0> + b'_i\, |k_1>$
  for $x_i \in X$ **do**
    determine $\triangle\theta_i$ from the lookup table (Table 1)
    calculate

$$\begin{pmatrix} a'_i \\ b'_i \end{pmatrix} \leftarrow U(\triangle\theta_i) \begin{pmatrix} a_i \\ b_i \end{pmatrix}$$

  end for

Table 1: Lookup table for quantum rotation gate, applied to qubit $|\Psi> = a\, |k_0> + b\, |k_1>$

x_i	B_i	$f(x) \geq f(B)$	$\triangle\theta_i$
0	0	false	0
0	0	true	0
0	1	false	$\begin{cases} -0.05\pi & if(a,b) > 0, \\ 0.05\pi & otherwise. \end{cases}$
0	1	true	0
1	0	false	0
1	0	true	$\begin{cases} 0.05\pi & if(a,b) > 0, \\ -0.05\pi & otherwise. \end{cases}$
1	1	false	0
1	1	true	0

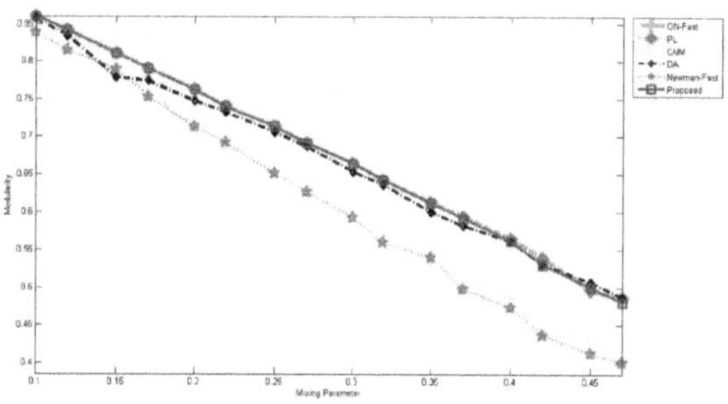

Figure 4: Comparison of modularity values obtained by Newman-Fast, GN-Fast, CNM, PL, DA, and Proposed algorithms for LFR benchmark datasets when mixing parameter, $\mu \in [0.1, 0.5)$.

$$U(\triangle\theta_i) = \begin{pmatrix} cos(\triangle\theta_i) & -sin(\triangle\theta_i) \\ sin(\triangle\theta_i) & cos(\triangle\theta_i) \end{pmatrix} \tag{11}$$

where, $\triangle\theta_i$, $i = 1, 2, \ldots, n$ is the rotation angle of the qubit q_i, towards the fitter state. For the purpose of community detection problem, the values for $\triangle\theta_i$ given in the Table 1 were obtained experimentally. B_i is the ith bit of the best solution (B) achieved so far. The magnitude of $\triangle\theta_i$ has an effect on the speed of convergence, but for very large values, the solutions may diverge or converge prematurely to a local optimum.

4. EXPERIMENTAL RESULTS

We evaluate the effectiveness of the proposed solution strategy on synthetic and real data sets and compare the results obtained with those of Newman-Fast [25], GN-Fast [26], CNM [7], PL [34], DA [11], GATHB [38], and MOGA-Net [32] algorithms. We use the catastrophe operation to avoid premature convergence [39]. In all cases, we show that the proposed algorithm successfully detects the community structure in the network.

The proposed algorithm was implemented in MATLAB on a Pentium Intel Core I3 processor, operating at 2.10 GHz, having 3 GB RAM and 512 GB HDD. Netdraw [5], R [35] with igraph library [8] and MATLAB softwares were used to draw the graphs. We make use of implementations of Newman-Fast as in [19], GN-Fast, CNM, and PL algorithms as in igraph library [8], and DA algorithm

Table 2: Comparison of the modularity (Q) values obtained by the Proposed algorithm and genetic algorithms - MOGA-Net, GATHB.

Algorithm	Zachary	Dolphins	Football
Proposed	0.4188	0.5265	0.603
MOGA-Net	0.416	0.505	0.515
GATHB	0.402	0.522	0.551

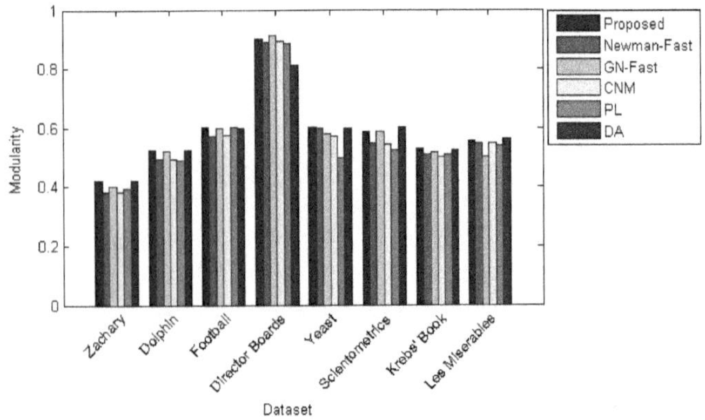

Figure 5: Comparison of modularity values obtained by the Proposed, Newman-Fast, GN-Fast, CNM, PL, and DA algorithms for Zachary karate club, Dolphins, Football, Directors board, Yeast, Scientometrics, Krebs' books, and Les Miserables networks.

as in Radatools software (http://deim.urv.cat/ sgomez/radatools.php). The modularity values for GATHB and MOGA-Net algorithms (Table 2) are reported from literature.

4.1 Synthetic Datasets

In order to check the ability of the proposed algorithm to successfully detect the community structure of a network, we use the benchmark proposed by Lancichinetti et al. [18], which is an extension of the GN benchmark [14] and is considered a harder test. LFR benchmark is characterized by the mixing parameter, $\mu = z_{out}/(z_{in} + z_{out})$ where z_{in} and z_{out} are the internal and external degrees of a node with respect to its community. The authors have shown that while communities are not strong for $\mu \geq 0.5$, they are well defined for $\mu \in [0.1, 0.5)$, and a good algorithm should discover them.

We have evaluated the performance of the proposed algorithm on LFR benchmark for unweighted and undirected networks for values of $\mu \in [0.1, 0.5)$ with 1000 nodes, average node degree: 20, maximum node degree: 50, exponent of degree distribution: -2, and exponent of community size distribution: -1. We compute Normalized Mutual Information (NMI) [9] to measure the similarity between the found and known partitions and modularity to evaluate the global goodness of the communities obtained. Results of experimentation on LFR datasets are summarized in table 3 and figure 4. It is evident from table 3 that the proposed algorithm is able to detect the community structure successfully. For $\mu \leq 0.4$, the proposed algorithm gives better or comparable performance than all the other compared algorithms in terms of modularity values obtained (figure 4).

4.2 Real-World Datasets

We compare the results of the proposed algorithm with those of Newman-Fast, GN-Fast, CNM, PL, and DA algorithms (figure 5) on two real-world benchmark networks, Zachary Karate Club network [40], Bottlenose Dolphins social network [22] and six other real-world networks, American college football network [14], Directors board network [31], Scientometrics network [31], Yeast network [32], network of books on American politics, compiled by V. Krebs (unpublished http://www.orgnet.com/), and Les Miserables Network [16]. We noted that for networks of small size, the preprocessing step was not useful.

Table 3: Modularity (Q) and number of communities (NC) for different values of the mixing parameter (μ) in the labeled LFR datasets are compared with corresponding values generated by the proposed algorithm. NMI values measure the similarity between the partitions found by the proposed algorithm and the known partitions of the label.

μ	Proposed Algorithm		Label		NMI
	Q	NC	Q	NC	
0.1	0.8599	34	0.8599	34	1
0.12	0.8413	29	0.8413	29	1
0.15	0.8112	31	0.8112	31	1
0.17	0.7906	30	0.7906	30	1
0.2	0.7628	33	0.7628	33	1
0.22	0.7404	28	0.7404	28	1
0.25	0.7134	32	0.7134	32	1
0.27	0.6909	30	0.6909	30	1
0.3	0.6637	31	0.6644	32	0.9944
0.32	0.6423	29	0.6423	29	1
0.35	0.6113	31	0.6135	31	0.9947
0.37	0.5915	29	0.5937	30	0.991
0.4	0.5615	29	0.5654	31	0.9818
0.42	0.5297	24	0.5407	27	0.9611
0.45	0.5002	23	0.5128	30	0.9353
0.47	0.4804	27	0.4941	30	0.9561

Zachary karate club network consisting of 34 nodes and 78 edges was generated by observing the members of a karate club over a period of two years. During this period, due to disagreements, the club divided in two groups almost of same size. If we cut the dendrogram generated by our solution strategy at 2 communities, we are able to obtain two communities (each having 17 nodes), and NMI and modularity values of 0.7324 and 0.3718 respectively. But since the algorithm attempts to maximize the modularity, it produces 4 communities (figure 6) with a better modularity value of 0.4188 and a corresponding NMI value of 0.5538. Newman-Fast finds 3 communities with NMI value of 0.6467, GN-Fast finds 7 communities with NMI value of 0.6718, while CNM, PL, and DA algorithms find 4 communities each with NMI values of 0.6467, 0.5288, and 0.5538 respectively.

Lusseau generated the Bottlenose Dolphins network by observing the behavior of 62 bottlenose dolphins (figure 7) living in Doubtful Sound, New Zealand, over a period of seven years. The network consisting of 159 edges split naturally into two groups. The proposed, Newman-Fast, and DA algorithms find 4 communities each with NMI values of 0.8496, 0.7033, and 0.8496 respectively. GN-Fast finds 6 communities with 0.9122 as NMI value while CNM and PL algorithms find 5 communities each with 0.7033 and 0.6329 as NMI values.

The American College Football network comes from the United States college football. The network represents the schedule of Division I games during the 2000 season. The network consists of 115 nodes and 616 edges grouped in 12 teams.The teams were divided in conferences where, on an average, every team played four interconference matches and seven intra-conference matches. Directors board is an affiliation network among the Spanish top directors board with 1130 nodes and 6647 edges. Scientometrics is a cita-

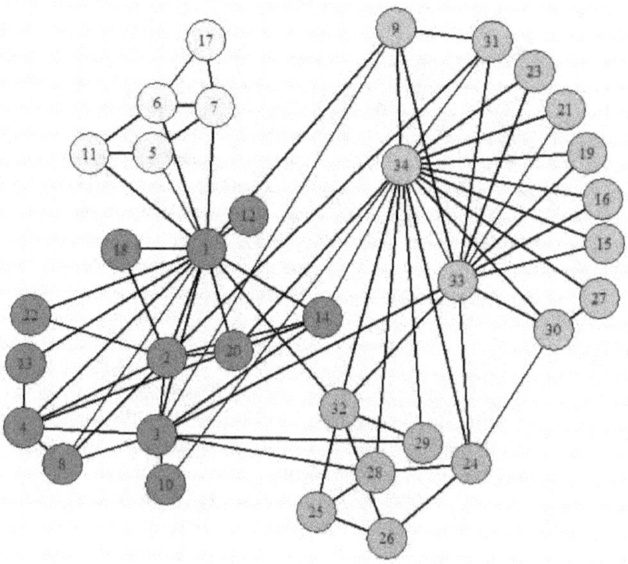

Figure 6: Community structure detected by the proposed algorithm for Zachary Karate network

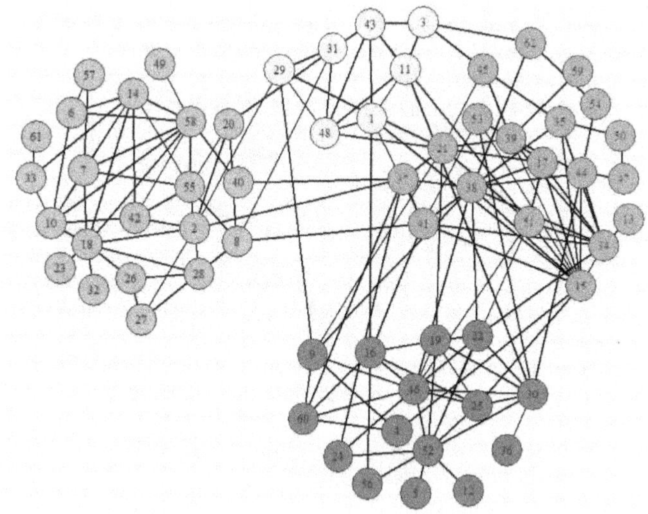

Figure 7: Community structure detected by the proposed algorithm for Dolphins network

tion network with 2678 nodes and 10368 edges. Yeast Network of protein-protein interactions in budding yeast has 7182 interactions (edges) among 2361 proteins (nodes). Krebs books is a network of political books containing 105 nodes and 441 edges. The nodes represent the recent books on American politics brought from Amazon.com and edges join pairs of books frequently purchased by the same buyer. Les Miserables is a network of co-appearances of 77 main characters in the famous novel of the same name written by Victor Hugo. Nodes in the network represent the characters and edges connect any pair of characters that appear in the same chapter of the book.

Figure 5 compares the modularity value results of the proposed algorithm with those of Newman-Fast, GN-Fast, CNM, PL, and DA algorithms corresponding to the real-world networks. Table 2 compares the proposed algorithm with the genetic algotihms MOGA-Net and GATHB. The proposed algorithm works better than all the algorithms for all the datasets except in the case of Scientometrics and LesMiserables datasets where the DA algorithm performs marginally better.

5. CONCLUSION AND FUTURE WORK

The paper presents a novel two-phase strategy that employs a preprocessing step followed by use of a quantum-inspired genetic algorithm for community detection in social networks. The strategy obviates the need to know the number of communities in advance and successfully detects the community structure in the network. Experiments on synthetic and real life networks show that the proposed approach is promising.

In future, the algorithm may be extended for overlapping and dynamic social networks. We also intend to explore a parallel implementation of the algorithm with a view to reduce the computation time as the quantum-inspired algorithms lend themselves naturally to parallel computation. The local search in preprocessing step also has scope for parallelizing for different sub-graphs. Further, one can also explore the use of several metrics and reformulate the community detection task as a multi-objective optimization problem. It is evident from table 3 that the proposed algorithm is able to detect the community structure successfully. For $\mu \leq 0.4$, the proposed algorithm gives better or comparable performance than all the other compared algorithms in terms of modularity values obtained (figure 4). One may investigate the behaviour of the proposed algorithm for μ exceeding 0.4 when the community structure becomes weak. It needs to be investigated further though, why the modularity results are not consistent as the mixing parameter (μ) value approaches the value of 0.5, that is, as the communities become weak.

6. ACKNOWLEDGEMENTS

The work is supported by University of Delhi research grant no. DRCH/R&D/2013-14/4155. The authors thank Rattan K. Datta, Mohyal Educational and Research Institute of Technology, Delhi, India, Natwar Modani, IBM Research, India, S. K. Gupta, Indian Institute of Technology, Delhi, India, and Subhash Bhalla, University of Aizu, Japan for their useful insights and suggestions. We also thank Clara Pizzuti, National Research Council of Italy, Rende, Italy for quickly responding to our request for datasets.

7. REFERENCES

[1] C. C. Aggarwal, editor. *Social Network Data Analytics*. Springer, 2011.

[2] C. C. Aggarwal, Y. Xie, and S. Y. Philip. Towards community detection in locally heterogeneous networks. In *SDM*, pages 391–402, 2011.

[3] A.-L. Barabási and R. Albert. Emergence of scaling in random networks. *science*, 286(5439):509–512, 1999.

[4] V. D. Blondel, J.-L. Guillaume, R. Lambiotte, and E. Lefebvre. Fast unfolding of communities in large networks. *Journal of Statistical Mechanics: Theory and Experiment*, 2008(10):P10008, 2008.

[5] S. P. Borgatti. Netdraw: Graph visualization software. *Harvard: Analytic Technologies*, 2002.

[6] A. Clauset. Finding local community structure in networks. *Physical review E*, 72(2):026132, 2005.

[7] A. Clauset, M. E. J. Newman, and C. Moore. Finding community structure in very large networks. *Phys. Rev. E*, 70:066111, Dec 2004.

[8] G. Csardi and T. Nepusz. The igraph software package for complex network research. *InterJournal*, Complex Systems:1695, 2006.

[9] L. Danon, A. Diaz-Guilera, J. Duch, and A. Arenas. Comparing community structure identification. *Journal of Statistical Mechanics: Theory and Experiment*, 2005(09):P09008, 2005.

[10] N. Du, B. Wu, X. Pei, B. Wang, and L. Xu. Community detection in large-scale social networks. In *Proceedings of the 9th WebKDD and 1st SNA-KDD 2007 workshop on Web mining and social network analysis*, pages 16–25. ACM, 2007.

[11] J. Duch and A. Arenas. Community detection in complex networks using extremal optimization. *Physical review E*, 72(2):027104, 2005.

[12] S. Fortunato. Community detection in graphs. *Physics Reports*, 486(3):75–174, 2010.

[13] U. Gargi, W. Lu, V. S. Mirrokni, and S. Yoon. Large-scale community detection on youtube for topic discovery and exploration. 2011.

[14] M. Girvan and M. E. Newman. Community structure in social and biological networks. *Proceedings of the National Academy of Sciences*, 99(12):7821–7826, 2002.

[15] K.-H. Han and J.-H. Kim. Genetic quantum algorithm and its application to combinatorial optimization problem. In *Evolutionary Computation, 2000. Proceedings of the 2000 Congress on*, volume 2, pages 1354–1360. IEEE, 2000.

[16] D. E. Knuth. *The Stanford GraphBase - a platform for combinatorial computing*. ACM, 1993.

[17] A. Lancichinetti and S. Fortunato. Community detection algorithms: a comparative analysis. *Physical review E*, 80(5):056117, 2009.

[18] A. Lancichinetti, S. Fortunato, and F. Radicchi. Benchmark graphs for testing community detection algorithms. *Physical Review E*, 78(4):046110, 2008.

[19] E. Le Martelot and C. Hankin. Multi-scale community detection using stability as optimisation criterion in a greedy algorithm. In *Proceedings of the 2011 International Conference on Knowledge Discovery and Information Retrieval*, pages 216–225, 2011.

[20] E. A. Leicht and M. E. Newman. Community structure in directed networks. *Physical review letters*, 100(11):118703, 2008.

[21] B. Li and Z.-q. Zhuang. Genetic algorithm based-on the quantum probability representation. In *Proceedings of the Third International Conference on Intelligent Data Engineering and Automated Learning*, pages 500–505. Springer-Verlag, 2002.

[22] D. Lusseau. The emergent properties of a dolphin social network. *Proceedings of the Royal Society of London. Series B: Biological Sciences*, 270(Suppl 2):S186–S188, 2003.

[23] A. Narayanan and M. Moore. Quantum-inspired genetic algorithms. In *Evolutionary Computation, 1996., Proceedings of IEEE International Conference on*, pages 61–66. IEEE, 1996.

[24] M. E. Newman. The structure and function of complex networks. *SIAM review*, 45(2):167–256, 2003.

[25] M. E. Newman. Fast algorithm for detecting community structure in networks. *Physical review E*, 69(6):066133, 2004.

[26] M. E. J. Newman and M. Girvan. Finding and evaluating community structure in networks. *Physical Review*, E 69(026113), 2004.

[27] G. Ochoa. *Error thresholds and optimal mutation rates in genetic algorithms*. PhD thesis, 2000.

[28] Y. Pan, D.-H. Li, J.-G. Liu, and J.-Z. Liang. Detecting community structure in complex networks via node similarity. *Physica A: Statistical Mechanics and its Applications*, 389(14):2849–2857, 2010.

[29] S. Papadopoulos, Y. Kompatsiaris, A. Vakali, and P. Spyridonos. Community detection in social media. *Data Mining and Knowledge Discovery*, 24(3):515–554, 2012.

[30] C. Pizzuti. Ga-net: A genetic algorithm for community detection in social networks. In *Parallel Problem Solving from Nature–PPSN X*, pages 1081–1090. Springer, 2008.

[31] C. Pizzuti. Boosting the detection of modular community structure with genetic algorithms and local search. In *Proceedings of the 27th Annual ACM Symposium on Applied Computing*, pages 226–231. ACM, 2012.

[32] C. Pizzuti. A multiobjective genetic algorithm to find communities in complex networks. *Evolutionary Computation, IEEE Transactions on*, 16(3):418–430, 2012.

[33] M. Plantié and M. Crampes. Survey on social community detection. In *Social Media Retrieval*, pages 65–85. Springer, 2013.

[34] P. Pons and M. Latapy. Computing communities in large networks using random walks. *Journal of Graph Algorithms and Applications*, 10(2):191–218, 2006.

[35] R Core Team. *R: A Language and Environment for Statistical Computing*. R Foundation for Statistical Computing, Vienna, Austria, 2013.

[36] B. Rylander, T. Soule, J. Foster, L. Spector, E. D. Goodman, A. Wu, W. Langdon, H.-M. Voigt, and M. Gen. Quantum evolutionary programming. In *Genetic and Evolutionary Computation, Proceedings of Conference on*, pages 1005–1011. Morgan Kaufmann, 2001.

[37] R. Shang, J. Bai, L. Jiao, and C. Jin. Community detection based on modularity and improved genetic algorithm. *Physica A: Statistical Mechanics and its Applications*, 2012.

[38] M. Tasgin and H. Bingol. Community detection in complex networks using genetic algorithm. In *ECCS '06: Proc. of the European Conference on Complex Systems*, Apr. 2006.

[39] L. Wang, H. Wu, F. Tang, and D.-Z. Zheng. A hybrid quantum-inspired genetic algorithm for flow shop scheduling. In *Advances in Intelligent Computing*, pages 636–644. Springer, 2005.

[40] W. W. Zachary. An information flow model for conflict and fission in small groups. *Journal of anthropological research*, pages 452–473, 1977.

[41] G. Zhang. Quantum-inspired evolutionary algorithms: a survey and empirical study. *Journal of Heuristics*, 17(3):303–351, 2011.

Evolved Spacecraft Trajectories for Low Earth Orbit

David W. Hinckley Jr.
Mechanical Engineering
University of Vermont
Burlington, VT 05405 USA
dhinckle@uvm.edu

Karol Zieba
Computer Science
University of Vermont
Burlington, VT 05405 USA
kzieba@uvm.edu

Darren L. Hitt
Mechanical Engineering
University of Vermont
Burlington, VT 05405 USA
dhitt@uvm.edu

Margaret J. Eppstein
Computer Science
University of Vermont
Burlington, VT 05405 USA
maggie.eppstein@uvm.edu

ABSTRACT

In this paper we use Differential Evolution (DE), with best evolved results refined using a Nelder-Mead optimization, to solve complex problems in orbital mechanics relevant to low Earth orbits (LEO). A class of so-called 'Lambert Problems' is examined. We evolve impulsive initial velocity vectors giving rise to intercept trajectories that take a spacecraft from given initial positions to specified target positions. We seek to minimize final positional error subject to time-of-flight and/or energy (fuel) constraints. We first validate that the method can recover known analytical solutions obtainable with the assumption of Keplerian motion. We then apply the method to more complex and realistic non-Keplerian problems incorporating trajectory perturbations arising in LEO due to the Earth's oblateness and rarefied atmospheric drag. The viable trajectories obtained for these difficult problems suggest the robustness of our computational approach for real-world orbital trajectory design in LEO situations where no analytical solution exists.

Categories and Subject Descriptors

I.2.m [**Artificial Intelligence**]: Differential Evolution; J.2 [**Physical Sciences and Engineering**]: Engineering; Aerospace

Keywords

Orbital Mechanics; Lambert's Problem; Differential Evolution; Orbital Trajectory Planning; Low Earth Orbit

1. INTRODUCTION

The planning of orbital maneuvers and/or trajectories for spacecraft represents a design optimization problem that is associated with multiple engineering constraints (e.g., time of flight, fuel consumption, and positional accuracy). Due to the inherently nonlinear equations of classical orbital motion, analytical approaches to most trajectory optimization problems are generally not available and numerical optimization is required. This is especially true in the case of modern problems of practical interest for designing low Earth orbits (LEOs), which are further complicated by various sources of non-Keplarian perturbations that become significant near to the Earth such as planetary oblateness, atmospheric drag, and solar radiation pressure among others.

Owing to the multiple objectives and system complexity, various evolutionary approaches for trajectory optimization have been explored over the past decade. Cacciatore & Toglia [2] considered minimum fuel orbital trajectories resulting from a finite series of impulsive thrusts using a genetic algorithm (GA). Lee et al. [13] also used GAs to evolve orbital elements (semi-major axis, eccentricity, inclination) instead of an initial trajectory velocity. As such, their approach was necessarily limited to the idealized two-body problem of Keplerian theory and lacks the ability to incorporate perturbations that arise in LEO scenarios. Bessette & Spencer [1] used both DE [18] and Covariance Matrix Adaptation Evolution Strategy (CMA-ES) [8] approaches to optimize multi-objective Keplerian orbital transfers in LEO; in their study, the optimal trajectory was based on the simultaneous considerations of fuel consumption and time of flight. Sentinella and Casalino [17] used both GA and DE approaches to examine interplanetary orbit trajectory optimization (e.g., as opposed to LEO maneuvers) involving intermediate planetary fly-by gravitational assists. Englander [5] posed the problem of choosing a sequence of fly-bys as an integer programming problem that was solved using a GA approach, and nested DE and particle swarm optimization inside a GA to reproduce solutions to the Galileo and Cassini missions [6]. Izzo et al. [11] utilized DE to design a highly complex trajectory among the Galilean moons of Jupiter that optimized observational conditions at time of spacecraft at the time of flyby. However, all of these prior efforts assumed idealized physics for the governing equations of motion and, as such, are not sufficient for trajectory planning for LEO.

In the present study, differential evolution is used to solve a class of 'Lambert-type' orbital trajectory problems (Figure 1). We incorporate orbital perturbations due to planetary oblateness and atmospheric drag that are necessary for accurate planning of LEO trajectories. In the classical Lambert problem (i.e., without perturbations) a trajectory is sought that takes a spacecraft from an initial orbit location $\boldsymbol{P_1}$ to a new position $\boldsymbol{P_2}$ during some time interval Δt [4]. The end condition of the arrival at $\boldsymbol{P_2}$ may involve a simple positional requirement (intercept trajectory) or a positional and velocity requirement (rendezvous trajectory). Multiple objectives may include minimizing positional accuracy of the trajectory endpoint (i.e., relative to $\boldsymbol{P_2}$), fuel consumption, and time-of-flight accuracy. In particular, the fuel constraint has historically represented a key limitation in orbit planning. In this work we combine these objectives into a single weighted fitness function, with various weights depending on the particular problem being solved. The resulting fitness function thus represents a

GECCO'14, July 12–16, 2014, Vancouver, BC, Canada.
Copyright 2014 ACM 978-1-4503-2662-9/14/07 ...$15.00.
http://dx.doi.org/10.1145/2576768.2598246 .

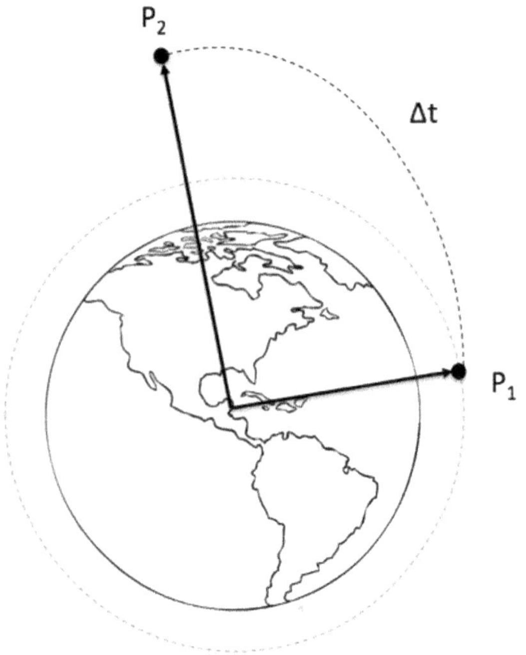

Figure 1: Schematic diagram of the classical Lambert problem involving the orbital transfer from an initial position P_1 to a new location P_2 with a prescribed time-of-flight Δt.

trajectory optimization problem. The solution sought in this class of problems is ultimately the initial velocity vector at $\boldsymbol{P_1}$ that initiates the transfer trajectory; from this initial velocity vector, all orbital elements of the of the trajectory may be determined (e.g., [4]).

This investigation consists of two essential parts. In the first part, we show that it is possible to recover classic solutions to Lambert's problem for either (1) a specified time-of-flight or (2) a minimum energy orbital transfer, thus validating the evolved trajectories against known analytical results. In the second part, we evolve trajectories in the presence of orbital perturbations arising from the oblateness of the Earth and from rarefied atmospheric drag, for which there are no known analytical solutions. Both of these effects are most pronounced in LEO (~100-400 km), which is the altitude range occupied by the new generation of small satellites ('cubesats', 'nanosats') being developed by NASA, the European Space Agency, and universities [9]. The ability to automate the optimization of these nonlinear problems offers real-world benefits for designing LEO trajectories.

2. OVERVIEW OF GOVERNING PHYSICS

2.1 Newtonian Gravitational Potential

A Newtonian gravitational potential is the canonical model used in orbital mechanics. In this model, gravity is a assumed to be a spherically-symmetric, attractive force that is inversely proportional to the square of the distance between the centers of mass between two bodies. For problems involving a spacecraft and the Earth, the mass of the spacecraft is inconsequential and the gravitational constant is given by $\mu = GM_e$ where G is the universal gravitational constant and M_e is the mass of the Earth. The governing equation for the spacecraft motion relative to a frame centered at the Earth is given by

$$\frac{d^2\mathbf{r}}{dt^2} = -\frac{\mu}{|\mathbf{r}|^3}\mathbf{r} \tag{1}$$

where $\mathbf{r}$ is the position vector of the spacecraft from the Earth's center and μ is the gravitational parameter defined above.

2.2 Classical Lambert Problem

As the perturbation-free, classical Lambert Problem will be used for validation of the numerical simulations, a brief overview of the analytical solution is warranted. The Lambert problem is a boundary value problem in time for the governing differential equation for the spacecraft motion. The solution represents a trajectory that takes a spacecraft from an initial position $\boldsymbol{P_1}$ to a new position $\boldsymbol{P_2}$ in a specified time interval Δt (see Figure 1). According to Lambert's Theorem [15], the time-of-flight depends only on the geometry of the space triangle formed between $\boldsymbol{P_1}$, $\boldsymbol{P_2}$ and the central body center of gravity, and the semi-major axis a of the elliptical path connecting the initial and final positions. This analytical result is expressed as

$$\sqrt{\frac{\mu}{a^3}}\,\Delta t = \alpha - \beta - (\sin\alpha - \sin\beta) \tag{2}$$

where μ is a gravitational constant and a is the semi-major axis of the transfer ellipse. The angles α, β are defined by

$$\sin\frac{\alpha}{2} = \sqrt{\frac{s}{2a}}, \qquad \sin\frac{\beta}{2} = \sqrt{\frac{s-c}{2a}} \tag{3}$$

Here, s is the semi-perimeter of the space triangle defined by $\boldsymbol{P_1}$, $\boldsymbol{P_2}$ and the Earth's center, c is the chord length of the segment $\boldsymbol{P_1P_2}$, and a is the semi-major axis of the elliptical path from $\boldsymbol{P_1}$ to $\boldsymbol{P_2}$. It is known that a is *inversely proportional* to the total mechanical energy of the trajectory and thus is linked with the fuel requirements for the maneuver. An important corollary to Lambert's Theorem is the existence of a minimum energy trajectory for which:

$$a_{\min} = \frac{s}{2} \tag{4}$$

For a given semi-major axis a of the ellipse, the corresponding initial velocity vector $\mathbf{v}_1$ can be determined according to [15]:

$$\mathbf{v}_1 = \sqrt{\frac{\mu}{4a}}\left[\left(\cot\frac{\alpha}{2} + \cot\frac{\beta}{2}\right)\frac{\boldsymbol{P_2} - \boldsymbol{P_1}}{c} + \left(\cot\frac{\beta}{2} - \cot\frac{\alpha}{2}\right)\frac{\boldsymbol{P_1}}{|\boldsymbol{P_1}|}\right] \tag{5}$$

The inherent utility of Eq. (5) for this study is that the vector components of the evolved initial velocities for Classical Lambert problems can be validated against these exact analytical results. For example, if a solution is sought that emphasizes positional accuracy and time-of-flight constraints (i.e., no consideration given to energy costs) one expects to recover the classical Lambert solution given by subsituting Eq. (3) into Eq. (2), solving nonlinearly for a, and substituting a into Eq. (5) to solve for the initial velocity vector v_1 (note that in this case Δt, $\boldsymbol{P_1}$, and $\boldsymbol{P_2}$ are specified, so by the geometry of the problem s and c are also known). Alternatively, if one seeks to emphasize positional accuracy and minimize energy consumption (i.e., no consideration given to time-of-flight), the minimum energy transfer orbit with a_{min} given by Eq. (4) results. One can then substitute Eq. (4) into Eq. (5) to solve for the initial velocity vector v_1. In this case, Δt can be solved for using Eqs. (2) and (3), given a_{min}.

In reality, LEO trajectories are subject to non-negligible perturbative effects – including gravitational variations due to planetary oblateness and rarefied atmospheric drag – that result in non-Keplerian motion. The details and forms of these perturbations are described below. A consequence of the non-Keplerian motion is that the analytical results for the Lambert Problem are no longer valid.

2.3 Perturbation from Earth's Oblateness

A correction to the Newtonian gravitational potential is required to account for the fact that the Earth is actually an oblate spheroid, as a consequence of its axial rotation. This oblateness gives rise to an axisymmetric gravitational potential that can be formally expressed in terms of a series expansion of zonal spherically harmonics [16]. For the Earth, the oblateness perturbation can be well modeled by the addition of a single correction term, called the second zonal harmonic J_2, to the spherically symmetric Newtonian potential. The corresponding perturbative acceleration $\mathbf{a}_{\text{oblate}}$ is given by [16]:

$$\mathbf{a}_{\text{oblate}} = \frac{3}{2}\frac{J_2 \mu R_E^2}{|\mathbf{r}|^5}\left[x\left(5\frac{z^2}{|\mathbf{r}|^2} - 1\right)\mathbf{i} + y\left(5\frac{z^2}{|\mathbf{r}|^2} - 1\right)\mathbf{j} + z\left(5\frac{z^2}{|\mathbf{r}|^2} - 3\right)\mathbf{k}\right] \quad (6)$$

where R_{E} is the equatorial radius of the Earth and $\mathbf{i}, \mathbf{j}, \mathbf{k}$ are unit vectors aligned in the directions of the coordinate axes. The magnitude of this perturbation is zero at the equator and increases with latitude; further, the magnitude is seen to diminish with the fourth-power of the altitude. Therefore, its effect is most pronounced for LEO scenarios and especially those with high-latitude inclinations. A dynamical consequence of this perturbation is that a slow precession of the orbit results – that is, the orbit is no longer closed as in Keplerian motion. Although the precession rate is typically no more that a few degrees per orbit, over the span of many orbits the impact of this perturbation effect becomes significant.

2.4 LEO Atmospheric Drag

The so-called 'Karman line', defined to be at an altitude of 100 km above the Earth, is commonly regarded as the boundary between the Earth's atmosphere and space. In reality, the density of the Earth's atmosphere undergoes a significant decay beginning at an altitude of 20 km and a highly rarefied vestige of the atmosphere extends well beyond the Karman line and into the region of LEO [19], as illustrated in Figure 2. As a consequence, spacecraft in very low orbits are subject to a ballistic drag force from the residual atmosphere. While small in magnitude, the effect of atmospheric drag is to reduce the velocity of an orbiting object and, given sufficient time, leads to an orbital decay and eventual atmospheric reentry. A model of ballistic drag $\mathbf{a}_{\text{drag}}$ is typically employed to describe this effect and is given by [19]:

$$\mathbf{a}_{\text{drag}} = -\frac{1}{2}\frac{\rho}{B}|\mathbf{v}|^2\mathbf{v} \quad (7)$$

where ρ is the altitude-dependent atmospheric density, $\mathbf{v}$ is the instantaneous velocity vector and B is the ballistic coefficient for the spacecraft geometry. As this effect is a retarding force, the acceleration is always negative and in the direction opposite of the current velocity.

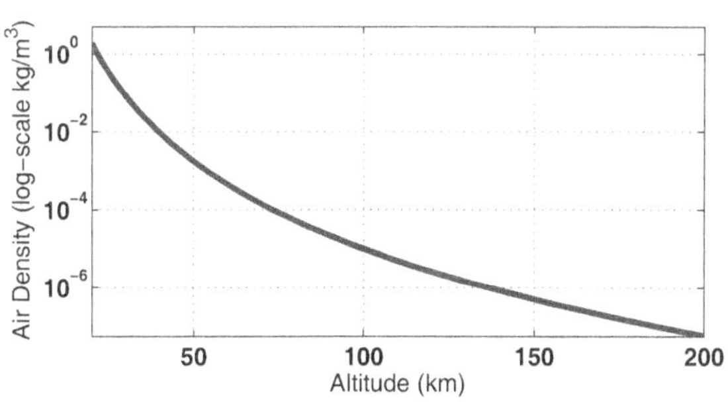

Figure 2: A power law fit of atmospheric density data showing the density decay with altitude.

3. METHODS

3.1 Hybrid Evolutionary Approach

We initially considered both CMA-ES [8] and DE [18], since both are well-suited for evolving real-valued genomes. In preliminary experimentation, we found that both methods were often successful. When CMA-ES was able to find a correct solution, it was able to do so more quickly than DE. However, DE more consistently found correct solutions whereas CMA-ES had a greater tendency to become trapped in local minima. Moreover, DE has been used successfully for other types of space mission planning, as reviewed in Section 1. Thus, for the remainder of this study we opted to use DE (Matlab implementation available at `http://www1.icsi.berkeley.edu/~storn/code.html`).

For all experiments reported here we used DE/rand/1/bin [18]. For each solution vector in the current population (x_i) a new vector (v_i) is created as $v_i = x_{r_0} + F(x_{r_1} - x_{r_2})$ where x_{r_0}, x_{r_1}, and x_{r_2} are distinct random vectors from the population. Next, a new trial vector u_i is formed by performing crossover, randomly selecting each allele from either v_i or x_i based on a crossover probability C_r (a separate binomial trial is performed for each allele). The target vector x_i is replaced by u_i in the next generation, if the fitness of the latter is better than or equal to the fitness of the former.

In this work, DE was used to find solutions in the correct basin of attraction of the global optimum. Once DE had terminated, we then refined the single best solution from the DE run using Matlab's fminsearch (a Nelder-Mead unconstrained nonlinear optimization method). The use of the gradient-based solver permitted more rapid convergence to an accurate solution once a potential solution was in the correct basin of attraction.

3.2 Fitness Function

The final position of the spacecraft $\hat{\mathbf{P}}_2$ is estimated by integrating the governing equations using Matlab's ode45 based on the evolved intial velocity vector $\hat{\mathbf{v}}_1$ and the prescribed or evolved time-of-flight $\Delta\hat{t}$. Because the fitness function is necessarily based on this simulation of flight trajectories, the time required to evaluate fitness is proportional to the time of flight of the trajectory being simulated, which varies for different individuals in the population. We created a single objective fitness function f to be minimized by weighting multiple objectives as follows:

$$f = w_1\|(\hat{\boldsymbol{P}}_2 - \boldsymbol{P}_2)\| + w_2\|(\hat{\boldsymbol{v}}_1 - \boldsymbol{v_p})\|^2 + w_3 \min(\boldsymbol{C}, 0) \quad (8)$$

In the above, w_i are the weights for each term and $\|...\|$ denotes the 2-norm of the vector (Euclidean distances between estimates and targets). $\|(\hat{\boldsymbol{P}}_2 - \boldsymbol{P}_2)\|$ represents the positional error relative to the target location $\mathbf{P_2}$. The square of the necessary change in velocity relative to the initial velocity $\|(\hat{\boldsymbol{v}}_1 - \boldsymbol{v_p})\|^2$ is proportional to the amount of energy required to change the velocity of the spacecraft for the new trajectory. The final term is a crash penalty, where $\boldsymbol{C}$ is the maximum depth of $\hat{\mathbf{P}}_2$ below the surface of the Earth (this term is only non-zero when the aircraft has crashed, and helps provide a gradient back to the feasible region). The values of the three weights w_i vary with the particular test problem (and are sometimes 0), as described in Section 3.4.

3.3 Test Problems

A set of four test problems were identified for the application of the evolutionary algorithm. Described below, these problems consist of both Keplerian motion, for which analytical solutions exist and non-Keplerian motion:

Problem 1: Classical Lambert Problem for a Given Time of Flight. In this problem only Newtonian physics are considered and the goal is to minimize positional error at $\boldsymbol{P}_2$ for some prespecified time of flight. Only the initial velocity vector is evolved. The exact analytical solution for this problem is known.

Problem 2: Classical Lambert Problem with Minimum Energy. As above, only Newtonian physics are considered, however in this case the goal is to minimize the amount of energy necessary to reach $\boldsymbol{P}_2$. In this case, the time of flight along the desired trajectory is unknown in advance, so both the initial velocity vector and the time of flight are evolved. The exact analytical solution for this problem is known.

Problem 3: Intercept Trajectory Accounting for Oblateness and Drag. In this non-Keplerian problem, perturbations are introduced through the inclusion of the J_2 correction for non-spherical oblateness of the Earth (Eq. (6)) as well as the correction for atmospheric drag (Eq. (7)). The time of flight is specified, so only the initial velocity vector is evolved. The goal is to minimize positional error at $\boldsymbol{P_2}$ for some prespecified time of flight. No analytical solution exists for this problem.

Problem 4: Multi-Orbit Intercept Trajectory Accounting for Oblateness. In this problem, the Keplerian orbit is perturbed through the inclusion of a J_2 gravitational correction for non-spherical oblateness of the Earth (Eq. (6)). A pre-specified time of flight is imposed that will require the spacecraft to complete multiple orbits of the Earth before reaching the target position. While perturbations due to atmospheric drag could be included as incorporated as in Test Problem 3, when drag is present it is impossible to guarantee that a trajectory exists that will reach the target without entering the Earth's atmosphere. Thus, in this proof-of-concept study where we wish to quantify how often we can find a correct solution, we neglected perturbations due to atmospheric drag for this problem to ensure that a solution existed. The time of flight is specified, so only the initial velocity vector is evolved. The goal is to minimize positional error at $\boldsymbol{P_2}$ for some prespecified time of flight. No analytical solution exists for this problem.

3.4 Experiments

For all experiments reported here, we used the same initial and final locations. Centering a 3-dimensional Cartesian coordinate system at the center of the Earth, the initial position was specified to be $\boldsymbol{P_1} = \langle 6500, 0, 0\rangle$ km. This places the spacecraft approximately 122 km above the surface of the Earth, a realistic value for a LEO. The final position was specified to be $\boldsymbol{P_2} = \langle -3591.7, 4024.3, 4024.3\rangle$ km, which has a simple Classical Lambert solution of $\boldsymbol{v_1} = \langle 0, 5.6, 5.6\rangle$ km/s, assuming a time of flight $\Delta t = 30$ min (as specified for test problems 1 and 3). For test problem 4, $\Delta t = 479.895$ min, which forces the trajectory to orbit the Earth 5 times before arriving at the target location $\boldsymbol{P_2}$. For test problem 2, $\mathbf{v_p}$ is specified as $\langle 0, 1, 1\rangle$ ($\mathbf{v_p}$ is not needed for the other 3 test problems) and the evolving Δt is prevented from going negative. Parameter values used for each of the four test problems are summarized in Table 1. Appropriate values for the weights w_i were determined empirically, since accurate normalization of the ranges of the terms is not possible. Note that we have set some weights to zero so that not all terms are used in all test problems.

Table 1: Parameter Values for the 4 Test Problems (NA = not applicable).

Problem	M	Δt (min)	w_1	w_2	w_3
1	3	30	10	0	0
2	4	NA	1	25	0
3	3	30	100	0	1E+08
4	3	479.895	100	0	1E+08

The four test problems were each run for 12 repetitions from different initial random populations. DE runs were terminated after a maximum of 20 min of CPU time (on an HP Pavilion g7 with an intel core i3 processor), but were allowed to terminate early if either (i) the maximum absolute error of any dimension in the evolving estimate of the intial velocity vector $\hat{\boldsymbol{v}}_1$ was less than 0.01 km/s (for those cases where the true v_i was known) or (ii) fitness f fell below 1e-9. We then applied fminsearch to the best evolved solution for 200 iterations (with all tolerances and other options left at the default settings). A trial was considered successful if the final best solution was within 1 m of the target location (this is a very conservative criterion for real LEO missions).

For the DE, we used a scaling parameter $F = 0.85$, a crossover rate of $C_r = 0.8$, and population size of $N = 5 \times M$, where M is the number of objective variables. These parameter settings were chosen based on limited preliminary experimentation using recommended ranges in [18]. For example, we experimented with crossover rates between 0.1 and 1.0 in increments of 0.1 and found that $C_r = 0.8$ performed the best for this problem (gave lower fitnesses in a shorter amount of time). We also experimented with population sizes N based on using either 5 or 10 individuals per gene, but did not see appreciable differences in resulting fitnesses and so went with the smaller population sizes.

4. RESULTS

Upon examination of the results, three types of results were apparent: (i) infeasible trajectories that ended up at $\boldsymbol{P_2}$ but that intersected the Earth (this occurred only once, for test problem 1), (ii) trajectories that ended up hundreds or thousands of km from $\boldsymbol{P_2}$ (this occurred in 7 of the 12 trials of the difficult mulit-orbit test problem 4), and (iii) feasible trajectories that ended close to the target location $\boldsymbol{P_2}$ (in all but one case these were much less than 1 m from the target and were considered successful trials).

Histograms of the positional error $\|(\hat{\boldsymbol{P}}_2 - \boldsymbol{P_2})\|$ are shown in Figure 3 for all solutions after DE (before fminsearch) within 50 km of the target, and in Figure 4 for all solutions within 1 m of the target after refinement using fminsearch. Quantitative results for all successful runs of DE + fminsearch are summarized in Table 2. Positional errors represent the average Euclidean distance (in m) between $\hat{\boldsymbol{P}}_2$ and $\boldsymbol{P_2}$ for all successful runs.

For test problems 1,2, and 3, we were able to find successful solutions in all but two trials (Table 2). In the one unsuccessful trial for problem 1, the solution was in a local optimum that sent the spacecraft on a trajectory through the Earth (note that this could have been precluded if we had explicitly formulated the fitness function to guard against such trajectories, but we opted to check for this in post-processing rather than further slow down the fitness function). In the one trial considered unsuccesful for problem 2, the final positional error was still only 4.6 m from the target; this level of error may actually be within tolerance, depending on the mission, and probably could have been further

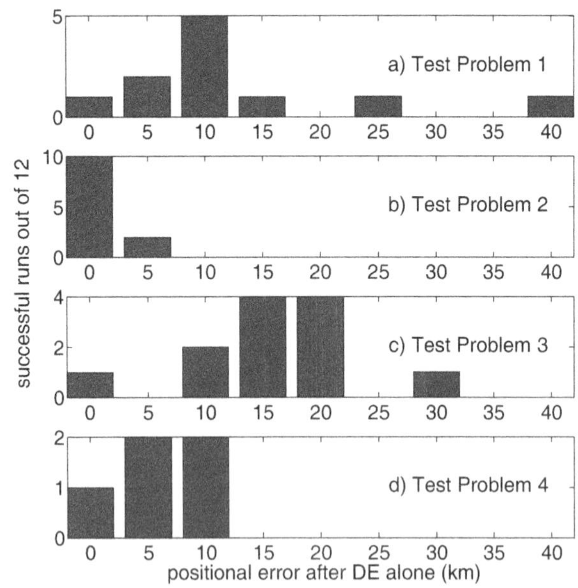

Figure 3: Histograms of the positional error $\|(\hat{P}_2 - P_2)\|$ (in km) after DE but before refinement with fminsearch, for all trials that were within 50 km of the target after DE (out of 12 trials for each of the four test problems.

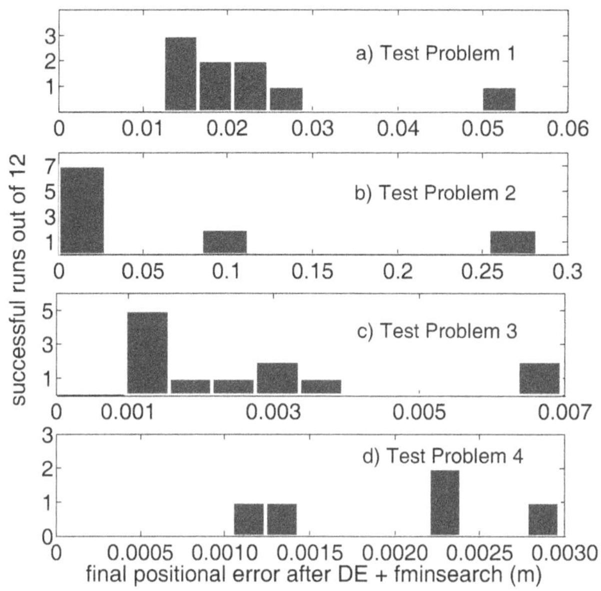

Figure 4: Histograms of the positional error $\|(\hat{P}_2 - P_2)\|$ (in m) after DE followed by refinement with fminsearch, for all trials that were within 1 m of the target after DE + fminsearch (out of 12 trials for each of the four test problems).

reduced with additional iterations of fminsearch, although we did not try the latter. For the more difficult test problem 4, we were still able to find successful solutions in 5 out of 12 trials (Table 2).

If one views the 12 trials as restarts, the best solutions found are quite impressive, as summarized in the rightmost column of Table 2. Here, it can be seen that final positional errors of the best solutions found were negligible. For test problem 1 the analytical solution for the initial velocity was recovered to within 9 decimal places of accuracy (in km/s), and for test problem 2 the analytical solution for the optimal time-of-flight was recovered to within 4.8s.

Table 2: Number of successful trials (out of 12), average positional of successful trials, positional error of best trial out of 12.

Test Problem	Successful Trials	Avg Pos Err (m)	Best Pos Err (m)
1	11	0.023	9.3e-3
2	11	0.071	6.7e-6
3	12	0.003	9.6e-4
4	5	0.002	1.0e-3

The trajectories for all successful runs for Test Problems 1, 2, and 3 are shown in Figures 5, 6, and 7, respectively. In some cases trajectories lie on top of each other and are not visually distinguishable. For Test Problem 4 we show all 5 orbits of only the single best trajectory in Figure 8; note the precession of the orbits toward the target point $\boldsymbol{P_2}$. The right-hand panels of Figures 5-8 show close-ups of the successful trajectories after DE but before refinement with fminsearch (note the zoomed in scales of the axes). After refinement with fminsearch, the successful trajectories are all < 0.3 m from the target (Figure 4), so they would appear indistinguishable on these figures.

5. DISCUSSION

The focus of this study has been to investigate the utility of a DE-based approach for spacecraft trajectory planning under the realistic orbital conditions that would be present in the LEO environment. With this in mind, it is appropriate to examine both the performance and limitations of the present model within the context of actual mission planning performed by space agencies such as NASA.

5.1 Traditional Mission Planning Approaches

Historically, the computational design of mission trajectories has been based on problem-specific algorithms that employed classical numerical approaches for orbital mechanics (e.g. boundary-value problems [7]). Within the past decade or so, however, there has been an effort to develop more generalized and robust trajectory design approaches including optimization. Johnson et al. [12] developed the *Copernicus* program for NASA Johnson Space Center that incorporated many existing case-specific NASA trajectory codes into a single mission design and optimization tool. Beginning in the 1990s, modern dynamical systems approaches using invariant manifolds were introduced for mission planning in perturbed systems [10]; this approach was realized in mission planning for the NASA Genesis mission launched in 2001 [14]. Most recently, NASA Goddard Space Flight Center has introduced the Evolutionary Mission Trajectory Generator software which designs and optimizes complex interplanetary trajectories involving multiple planetary flybys using a GA [5]. However, to date these methods have largely focused on planning orbital trajectories for problems where near-Earth perturbations are negligible.

With the recent increase in small satellites in LEO, such as 'cubesats' and 'nanosats', it is important to extend automated design approaches to include realistic LEO perturbations. The current study serves as proof-of-concept that DE can be effective in automating accurate LEO trajectory planning, which represents a new contribution to the current astrodynamics literature.

5.2 Trajectory Accuracy

In real LEO maneuvers, the required positional accuracy for modern trajectory plannign is on the order of meters (Jacob Englander, personal communication). Of course, the specific error tolerance is necessarily dependent on the particular mission. In the results presented here, all succesful runs had positional errors of less than 0.3 m (with best runs out of 12 trials within 0.01 m of the target position) for all four problems (Table 2); these positional errors are well within the required tolerances for LEO missions.

5.3 Opportunities for Model Improvement

Although the computational model presented in this work has incorporated a number of realistic and important perturbations for LEO maneuvers, there remain opportunities for further improvement, including: (a) incorporating additional perturbations; (b) solving more difficult LEO problems, such as multi-impulse, trajectories, continuous thrust trajectories, and multi-spacecraft swarm trajectories; and (c) evolving Pareto sets of non-dominated solutions with respect to the multiple objectives. We discuss these three areas below.

There are two particular sources of perturbation that are not accounted for in the present model. The first is the effect of solar radiation (photon) pressure, which can either accelerate or decelerate the spacecraft depending on its orientation. For very low orbits, this effect is small compared to atmospheric drag; however, for higher orbits the reverse is true. The second source of perturbation is caused by gravitational effects of the Moon. This effect is negligible for LEO scenarios but is relevant for higher orbits (e.g., geosynchronous orbits, GEO). Therefore, to extend the capabilities of the current framework beyond LEO, the inclusion of lunar gravity will be required.

The current version of the model is restricted to trajectories produced by a single initial impulse. While this is acceptable for preliminary orbit design, it excludes the possibility of mid-course correction(s) to account for perturbative effects. A more flexible and realistic approach would be to allow for a finite number of impulses during the trajectory. One could also allow for the possibility of a continuous thrust trajectory, where the spacecraft produces a thrust during the entire maneuver. Continuous thrust maneuvers are consistent with spacecraft utilizing electric propulsion systems (e.g., ion engines) as well as solar sails.

Another area of interest is the design of trajectories of small swarms of LEO spacecraft flying together; these spacecraft must not only reach a particular target area, but must also remain within certain distances of each other and, in some cases, maintain specific formations (as in the Magnetosspheric Multiscale (MMS) mission `http://mms.gsfc.nasa.gov/`). We have recently begun work on this challenging problem.

In the current approach we chose to combine the multiple objectives into a single weighted fitness function, and have emphasized trajectory planning where the primary objective is either time-of-flight or fuel considerations. Realistic mission planning could benefit from a multi-objective version of DE (e.g., [3]) that returns a relatively uniformly spaced set of non-dominated solutions. Mission planners could then consider the trade-offs between the various objectives and constraints in selecting an appropriate trajectory to implement.

In the proof-of-concept study described here, we implemented the model in Matlab and allowed each trial of DE to evolve solutions for 20 minutes each on a laptop computer. In the context of real mission planning, this is an insignificant amount of computation, especially given the computational capabilities at places such as NASA Goddard. However, there is no doubt that the efficiency of the code could also be improved dramatically in numerous ways, such as converting from Matlab to C or C++. Moreover, for real mission planning one should use a higher fidelity forward trajectory simulator, such as the publically available GMAT code (`http://gmat.gsfc.nasa.gov/`), and a higher order ordinary differential equation solver.

6. CONCLUSIONS

In this study, Differential Evolution (DE) was investigated as a tool for the design of intercept and rendezvous problems in low Earth orbit (LEO). The accuracy of the technique was demonstrated in two test cases involving Keplerian orbits that could be benchmarked against known solutions. The method was then applied to two cases involving non-Keplerian orbits due to two types of realistic perturbations encountered in LEO. The DE was found to be very robust in that it was rarely trapped in local optima and was often able to get very close enough to the global optimum that subsequent refinement with Nelder-Mead optimization was able to reduce final positional errors to within less than 0.3 m, which is well within the acceptable tolerance for real LEO mission planning. More challenging problems, such as the multi-orbit problem studied here, may require multiple restarts. However, even in this difficult problem we were successful in 5 out of 12 trials. Because we only evolve the initial velocity (and possibly time of flight), additional complex physics effects can be readily incorporated into fitness evaluation without affecting the remainder of the evolutionary code. We conclude that a hybrid method using DE to find the global basin of attraction, followed by refinement with a local optimization method such as Nelder-Mead to hone in on the global optimum, is a promising approach to mission design and optimization of LEO trajectories.

7. ACKNOWLEDGEMENTS

This work was partially supported by the Vermont Space Grant under NASA Cooperative Agreement # NNX10AK674. We thank Jacob Englander (NASA Goddard) for helpful discussions that improved this manuscript.

8. REFERENCES

[1] C. Bessette and D. Spencer. Optimal space trajectory design: a heuristic-based approach. *Adv. Astronaut. Sci*, 124:1611–1628, 2006.

[2] F. Cacciatore and C. Toglia. Optimization of orbital trajectories using genetic algorithms. *Journal of Aerospace Engineering, Sciences and Applications*, 1(1):58–69, 2008.

[3] K. J. Chichakly and M. J. Eppstein. Improving uniformity of solution spacing in biobjective evolution. In *Genetic and Evolutionary Computation Conference (GECCO)*, pages 87–88, 2013.

[4] H. Curtis. *Orbital mechanics for engineering students.* Butterworth-Heinemann, 2009.

[5] J. Englander. Automated trajectory planning for multiple-flyby interplanetary missions. *Ph.D. Thesis, University of Illinois*, 2013.

[6] J. A. Englander, B. A. Conway, and T. Williams. Automated mission planning via evolutionary algorithms. *Journal of Guidance, Control, and Dynamics*, 35(6):1878–1887, 2012.

[7] R. W. Farquhar, D. P. Muhonen, C. R. Newman, and H. S. Heubergerg. Trajectories and orbital maneuvers for the first libration-point satellite. *Journal Of Guidance Control And Dynamics*, 3(6):549–554, 1980.

[8] N. Hansen, S. D. Müller, and P. Koumoutsakos. Reducing the time complexity of the derandomized evolution strategy with covariance matrix adaptation. *Evolutionary Computation*, 11(1):1–18, 2003.

[9] H. Helvajian and S. W. Janson. *Small satellites: past, present, and future.* Aerospace Press, 2008.

[10] K. Howell, B. Barden, and M. Lo. Application of Dynamical Systems Theory to Trajectory Design for a Libration Point Mission. *Journal of Astronautical Sciences*, 45(2):161–178, 1997.

[11] D. Izzo, L. F. Simões, M. Märtens, G. C. de Croon, A. Heritier, and C. H. Yam. Search for a grand tour of the jupiter galilean moons. *Genetic and Evolutionary Computation Conference (GECCO)*, 1(1):1301–1308, 2013.

[12] G. Johnson, S. Munoz, and J. Lehman. Copernicus: A generalized trajectory design and optimization system. *UT Austin Engineering Communication ASE 333T, available online*, 2003.

[13] S. Lee, P. von Ailmen, W. Fink, A. Petropoulos, and R. J. Terrile. Design and optimization of low-thrust orbit transfers. In *Aerospace Conference, 2005 IEEE*, pages 855–869. IEEE, 2005.

[14] M. Lo, B. Williams, W. Bollman, D. Han, r. Corwin, P. Hong, K. Howell, B. Barden, and R. Wilson. Genesis Mission Design. *AIAA Paper 98-4468*, pages 1–13, 1998.

[15] J. E. Prussing, B. A. Conway, and J. E. Prussing. *Orbital mechanics*, volume 57. Oxford University Press New York, 1993.

[16] H. Schaub and J. L. Junkins. *Analytical mechanics of space systems.* AIAA, 2003.

[17] M. R. Sentinella and L. Casalino. Cooperative evolutionary algorithm for space trajectory optimization. *Celestial Mechanics and Dynamical Astronomy*, 105(1-3):211–227, 2009.

[18] R. Storn and K. Price. Differential evolution–a simple and efficient heuristic for global optimization over continuous spaces. *Journal of global optimization*, 11(4):341–359, 1997.

[19] J. Wong, H. Reed, and A. Ketsdever. University micro-/nanosatellite as a micropropulsion testbed. *Micropropulsion for Small Spacecraft*, 187:25, 2000.

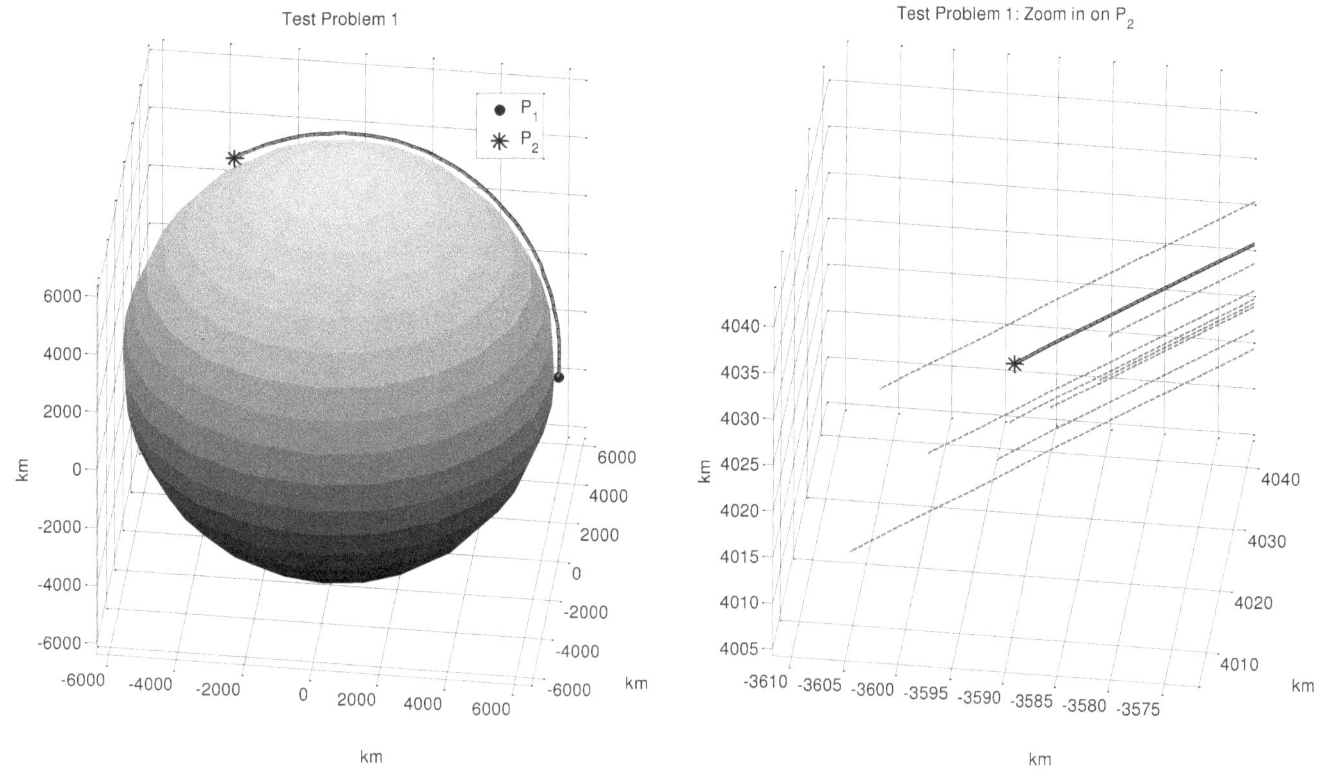

Figure 5: Trajectories of the 11 successful runs for Test Problem 1. The analytical trajectory is shown in black. Left: Earth scale view. Right: Close up of the best solutions from DE (before fminsearch) near target

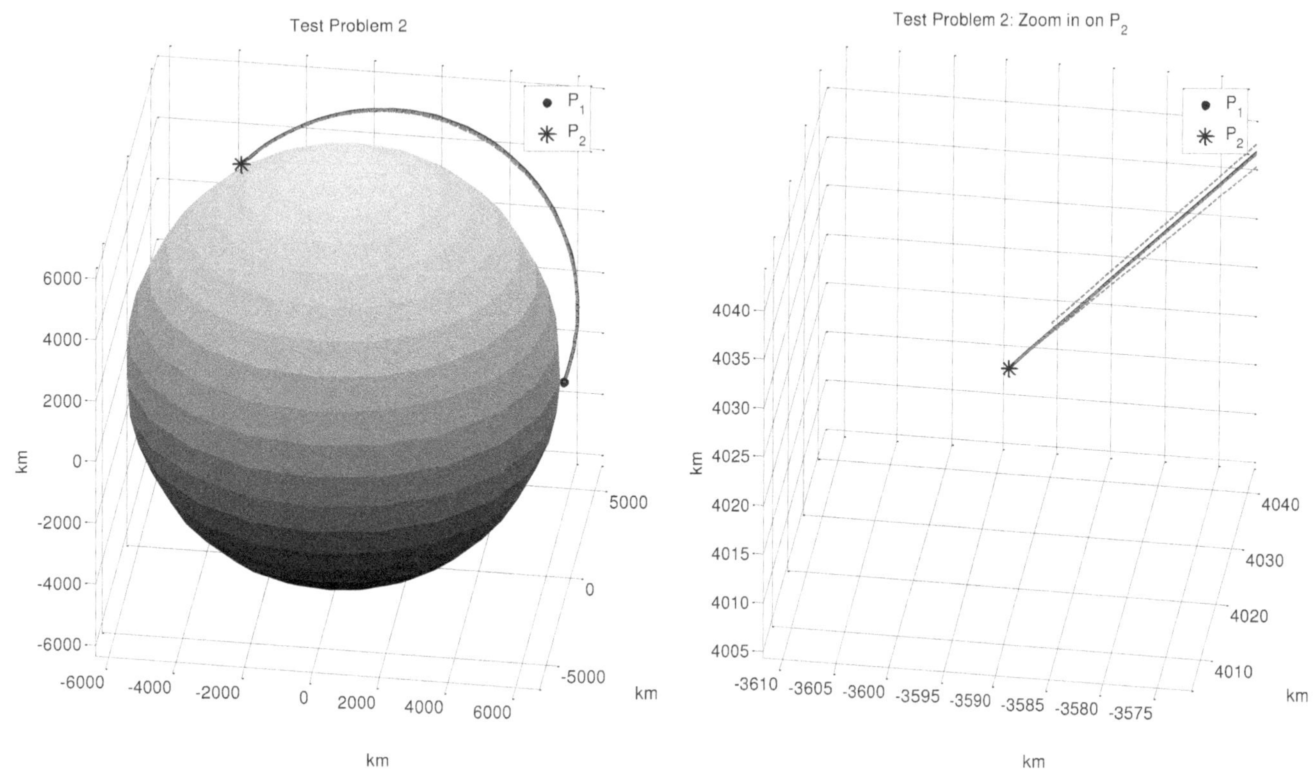

Figure 6: Trajectories of the 11 successful runs for Test Problem 2. The analytical trajectory is shown in black. Left: Earth scale view. Right: Close up of the best solutions from DE (before fminsearch) near target P_2.

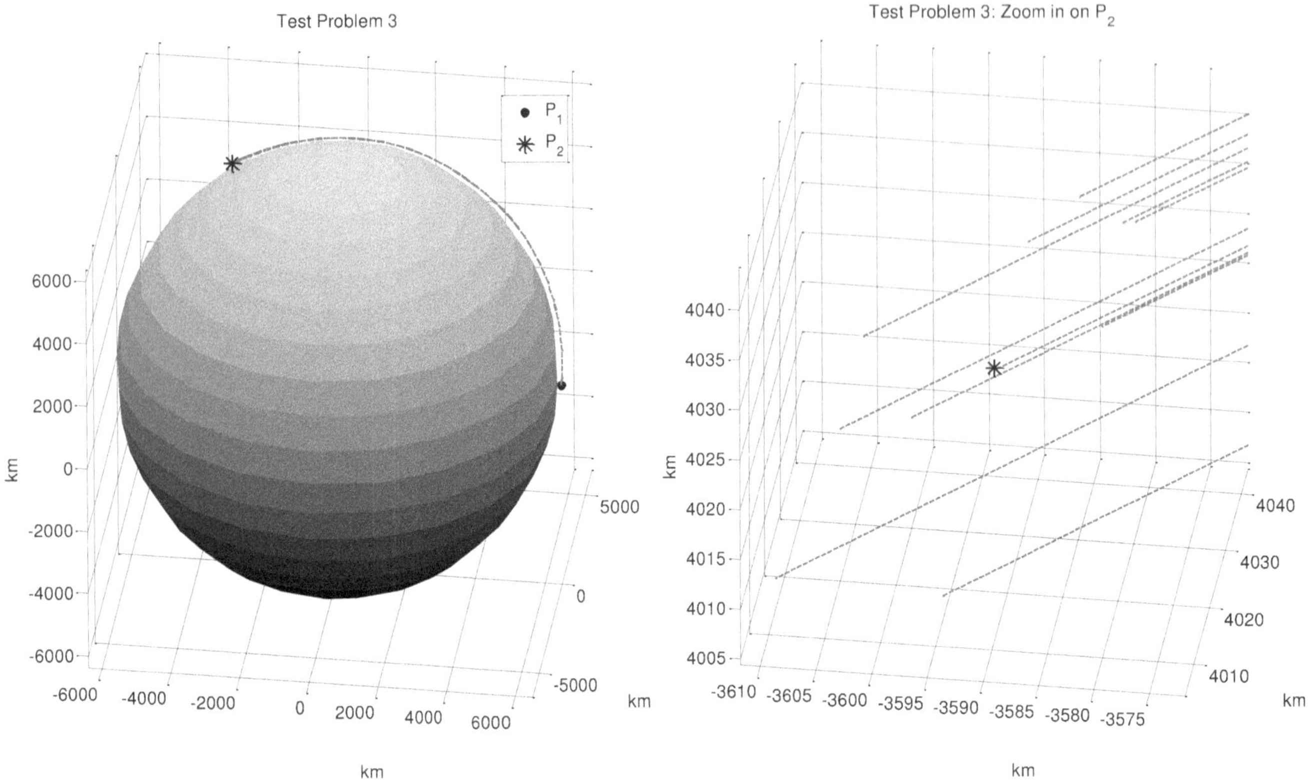

Figure 7: Trajectories of the 12 successful runs for Test Problem 3. Left: Earth scale view. Right: Close up of the best solutions from DE (before fminsearch) near target P_2.

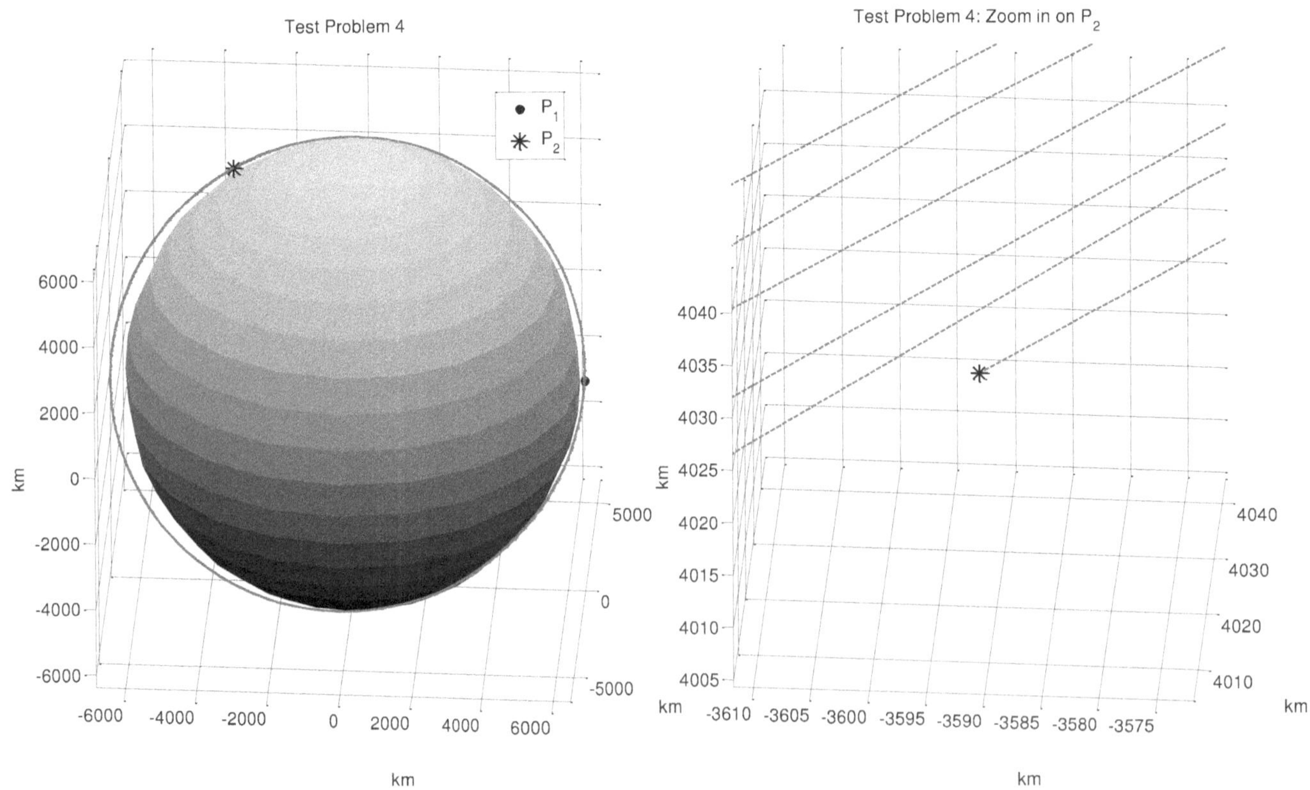

Figure 8: Trajectory of most successful run for Test Problem 4. To avoid confusion, only the 5 orbits of the most successful trial are shown. Left: Earth scale view. Right: Close up of the best solution from DE (before fminsearch) near target P_2.

Dynamic Multi-Dimensional PSO with Indirect Encoding for Proportional Fair Constrained Resource Allocation

Jonathan Hudson
University of Calgary
2500 University Dr. NW
Calgary, Canada
jwhudson@ucalgary.ca

Majid Ghaderi
University of Calgary
2500 University Dr. NW
Calgary, Canada
mghaderi@ucalgary.ca

Jörg Denzinger
University of Calgary
2500 University Dr. NW
Calgary, Canada
denzinge@ucalgary.ca

ABSTRACT

Dynamic particle swarm optimization (PSO) problems are generally characterized by the exhaustively examined issues of the changing location of optima, the changing fitness of optima, and measurement noise/errors. However, the challenging issue of continuously changing problem dimensionality has not been similarly examined. Given that in anytime dynamic resource allocation it is necessary to maintain a high quality solution, we argue that, rather than restarting the PSO algorithm, a more appropriate approach is to design an algorithm that robustly handles changing problem dimensionality. Specifically, we propose an indirect particle encoding scheme specifically designed for a dynamic multi-dimensional PSO algorithm for proportional fair constrained resource allocation. This PSO algorithm is implemented for the proportional fair allocation of power and users to channels within a simulation of an Orthogonal Frequency-Division Multiple Access (OFDMA) wireless network with mobile users switching cells as they traverse the simulation environment. The proposed PSO algorithm is evaluated using simulations, which demonstrate the ability of the proposed indirect encoding scheme to maximize the overall proportional fair optimization goal, without unfairly penalizing the individual components of the solution related to newly introduced problem dimensions.

Categories and Subject Descriptors

G.1.6 [**Optimization**]: Constrained optimization;
C.2.1 [**Network Architecture and Design**]: Wireless communication

General Terms

Algorithms, Performance, Experimentation

Keywords

Dynamic Particle Swarm Optimization, Multi-Dimensional, Constrained Resource Allocation, Proportional Fair, OFDMA

GECCO'14, July 12–16, Vancouver, BC, Canada.
Copyright 2014 ACM 978-1-4503-2662-9/14/07 ...$15.00.
http://dx.doi.org/10.1145/2576768.2598387.

1. INTRODUCTION

Real-world optimization problems are often dynamic in nature, due to alterations in the search space resultant from environmental or system changes. These changes require optimization to be continuous in some manner, through either restarting the optimization, or adapting the current optimization attempt on the fly. Depending on the application, restarting the optimization attempt is often undesirable due to the loss of discovered information and reduplication of effort. This is especially true, if the search space of the new problem is highly similar to that of the previous problem. However, the method of adapting the previous optimization attempt faces the challenge that the new optimization may remain stuck in a previously found optimum and therefore be unable to transition to find new local optima.

In particle swarm optimization (PSO) for dynamic optimization problems there are a number of sources of change for the search space. These include noise, location of optima, changes in fitness of optima, and changes in problem dimensionality. Noise in the problem is generally the result of stochastic influences on the fitness function, such as measurement or discretization errors [15]. Nickabadi et al. observed the following types of changes in optima: Type I as a change in optimum location, Type II as a change in optimum fitness with a fixed location, and Type III as a change of both optimum fitness and location [13]. These changes are subject to temporal severity (change occurs quickly) and/or spatial severity (local optima move a large distance in the search space as defined by the fitness function). These first three problems have been addressed in a wide variety of manners depending on the optimization problem's requirements, while the problem of dimensionality has not been explored to the same extent.

The problem of dimensionality changing has been examined by Kiranyaz et al. [9]. However, Kiranyaz et al. formulate the multi-dimensional problem with the range of dimensionality being a component of the search space. This means that the algorithm searches for both the optimal solution within a number of dimensions and which number of dimensions is optimal. However, multi-dimensionality is not always a component of the current working optimization search space. For example, the search space may be associated with a shared resource allocation problem for a certain number of agents. If new heterogeneous agents and their unknown constraints and relationship to current agents are entered into the search problem during optimization, then the dimensionality of the problem changes. More importantly, this possibility cannot be represented within the previous search space and therefore Kiranyaz et al.'s method does not apply.

The challenge addressed in this paper is to dynamically incorporate new search space dimensions by adapting the current PSO optimization attempt. This challenge is addressed for the problem of proportional fair allocation of shared resources in a cellular network with mobile users. The most common solution for the majority of dynamic search space changes is to maintain diversity within the PSO swarm's population such that the algorithm does not get trapped in local optima. However, in constrained proportional fair resource allocation there is a high dependency between the new dimensional values and current values, due to their relationship sharing a constrained resource (e.g. transmission power). This means there is high spatial severity and depending on the time requirements, temporal severity, in the impact of dimensional changes on the locations of local optima.

This paper develops a continuous dynamic PSO solution for the problem of changing dimensionality within optimizing the proportional fair distribution of shared and constrained resources in a cellular network employing OFDMA [18]. This solution takes the challenge of high dependency between new/existing values and through a unique indirect encoding method turns it into an advantage for robustly handling the changing dimensionality of the problem. More particularly, through the indirect encoding the proportional fair nature of the resource allocation problem is exploited to enable the incorporation of new dimensional values gracefully into the particle and fitness function. This inclusion is accomplished in a manner that the initial values of the new dimensions represent a relatively good start in regards to finding more optimal values. Importantly, the developed method allows for previous population and solution to be utilized in the subsequent optimization within the new search space, improving the quality and efficiency of the continuous optimization. Additionally, the PSO solution has the anytime property, quickly finding a valid, yet approximate and possibly suboptimal, solution and improving on it continuously for as long as required [26].

The rest of the paper is organized as follows. Section 2 examines the background of dynamic PSO. Then, Section 3 introduces the general method of continuous dynamic PSO optimization for the problem of proportional fair constrained resource allocation under the associated conditions of changing dimensionality. An application of this indirect encoding to continuous wireless OFDMA resource allocation with mobile users is outlined in Section 4. Numerical evaluations of the general method, through the application to OFDMA resource allocation, are completed in Section 5 demonstrating the ability of the method to robustly handle the changing dimensions of the search space. The evaluations demonstrate that the method is beneficial to the overall fitness of the problem and the individual components of the fitness related directly to the new dimensions. Finally, Section 6 concludes by examining the contributions of this paper and possible future work.

2. DYNAMIC PSO

Particle swarm optimization is a stochastic optimization method exploiting the concept of swarm intelligence [10]. The population for a PSO algorithm consists of a swarm of particles where each n-dimensional particle corresponds to a prospective solution within the current search space. In each iteration, every particle is updated using its velocity, its personal best position, and the swarm's global best position, along with a random influence. The swarm's global best encourages convergence towards a global optimum, the personal best influences convergence towards local optima, and the randomness acts as a stochastic influence. In each iteration of the algorithm, every particle is evaluated using the chosen fitness function in order to determine the particle's fitness value for its current location in the search space. If a better particle position in the search space has been found, then using this value the particle's personal and global best are updated.

Our PSO algorithm is designed to maintain a valid solution for a resource allocation problem at all times (anytime property [26]). To accomplish this, each dimension is limited strictly within the chosen valid boundary values. Consequently, the PSO consists of a swarm W of m particles P of n dimensions in length, and the swarm's global best $gbest = (gb_1, ..., gb_n)$ such that $W = (P_1, \ldots, P_m, gbest)$.

Each particle P is a 3-tuple, $P_i = (X_i, V_i, pbest_i)$, consisting of the particle's position $X_i = (x_1, ..., x_n)$, velocity $V_i = (v_1, ..., v_n)$, and personal best $pbest_i = (pb_1, ..., pb_n)$. The particle's dimensions are bounded as within a range with $x_j, pb_j, gb_j \in [0, 1]$, and velocity is bounded as $v_j \in [-0.1, 0.1]$.

The PSO algorithm begins with a swarm W consisting of particles with randomly initialized positions and velocities. For each next iteration $k+1$ from the current iteration k, each particle is updated according to the following equations:

$$V_i^{k+1} = w \cdot V_i^k + c_1 \cdot rand() \cdot (pb_i - X_i^k) + c_2 \cdot rand() \cdot (gb_i - X_i^k).$$

The velocity is changed based upon the previous velocity V_i^k and an inertial weight w, as well as the difference between the current position and the particle's personal best influenced by a learning factor c_1 and a random number in the range $[0, 1]$, and the difference between the current position and the particle's neighborhood best influenced by a learning factor c_2 and a random number in the range $[0, 1]$. This new velocity is limited such that each $v_j \in V_i^{k+1}$ is bounded by $v_j \in [-0.1, 0.1]$ with excess velocity beyond the bounds being discarded.

Next, the position is changed using the new velocity as described by the following equation:

$$X_i^{k+1} = X_i^k + V_i^{k+1}.$$

This new position is limited such that each $x_j \in X_i^{k+1}$ is bounded by $x_j \in [0, 1]$ with excess dimensional values beyond the bounds being discarded.

The basic PSO algorithm, as described by Eberhart et al., is unsuited for dynamic problems. Issues such as outdated memory as the search space changes (as stored in the global best of the swarm and personal best of the particles), lack of search space change detection, and the loss of diversity over time limit this base PSO algorithm to static problems [3]. Outdated memory is addressed in this paper using the common method of re-evaluating the fitness function of the personal and global best as the search space changes, such as in [8]. A common solution for search space change detection is sentry particles [6]. However, this is unnecessary in this paper as we know the problem changes quickly and continuously and therefore our solution requires no such trigger.

Diversity loss is a more complex challenge and the chosen technique for addressing it relies on the circumstances of the given problem. The general techniques as listed in [22] are: multi-population approaches, memory-based methods, and to increase population diversity after change. The first multi-population method is suited for multiple moving optima [14], while memory-based techniques are useful for problems with recurring search space states [23]. Our problem deals with a single optimum which is altered by a search space change with limited to no recurrence, and thus can be dealt with the random immigrants technique [20] which adds diversity (new particles) after a search space change.

One unaddressed area for PSO, which is explored in this paper, consists of dynamic optimization problems in which the dimensionality of the problem changes along with the other changes in the search space. Note, this is different from what was done by Kiranyaz et al. in [9] where it was possible to search within a known range of dimensionality of a specific search space. In the work of Kiranyaz et al. finding the optimal solution to a specific problem also consisted of simultaneously searching for an associated optimal number of dimensions. This paper deals with a dynamic search space in which the dimensionality of the problem will change indeterminately over time, resulting in unpredictable changes in the search space.

In the following section, an abstract continuous dynamic PSO solution to the problem of changing dimensionality is described. This solution tackles the challenge of a high dependency between existing and new dimensional values as the result of attempting proportional fair distribution of a constrained shared resource. The dynamic PSO solution is unique as it utilizes an indirect particle encoding method to incorporate new dimensions and their associated values within a particle into the existing solution. This is done in such a way that the new values are a relatively good starting point in regards to finding more optimal values, allowing for previously found populations and solutions to be utilized in the subsequent optimization.

3. PROPORTIONAL FAIR CONSTRAINED RESOURCE ALLOCATION

In this section, first the resource allocation problem and the associated assumptions necessary for the given solution are defined, then this paper's unique indirect encoding of this problem as a PSO particle is described.

3.1 Problem Definition

We are solving a constrained shared resource allocation problem with the assumptions that:

- We have a set $R = \{r_0, \ldots, r_{n_{res}-1}\}$ of n_{res} shared resources where each resource $r_j \in R$ has a constrained resource quantity $r_j^{quant} > 0$.
- We want to determine a proportionally fair allocation of the shared resources by determining a set $S = \{s_0, \ldots, s_{n_{sh}-1}\}$ of n_{sh} where each share $(port_i, r_j) = s_i \in S$ consists of a portion $port_i \in [0, r_j^{quant}]$ of a resource $r_j \in R$.
- The total of all portions $port_i$ related to the same resource r_j is equal to r_j^{quant}. That is, every resource represented by at least one share is allocated completely between all referencing shares.
- It is expected that at least two shares may reference (share) the same resource during optimization.
- Every resource does not need to be allocated to a share, but every share needs a resource even if the portion is assigned zero as an amount.
- Most importantly, the set S of shares is dynamic and the number of shares n_{sh} will increase and decrease over the continuous optimization process.

The optimization goal is the sharing of the resources R in a proportionally fair manner by determining assignments of the shares in S. It is important to note that this is proportionally fair in regards to the fitness function, which may value equal portions of a share differently depending on the entity/agent/system resource/etc. associated with that share. Therefore, a fair solution will not necessarily be the division of every resource equally between all the shares. For example, each share s_i has a logarithmic utility U of benefit, weighted by w_{r_j}, to the end user for utilizing the portion $port_i$ of resource r_j such that $U(port_i) = log(w_{r_j} \cdot port_i)$. The fitness function applied to a particle representing a resource allocation solution maximizes the summation of these utilities.

$$fit(X) = fit(S) = \sum_{s_i \in S} U(port_i)$$

In addition to the constrained OFDMA resource allocation problem considered in this paper [4,5], some examples of constrained resource allocations problems include: resource constrained multi-robot allocation which assigns robots to solve tasks given resource constraints [7], the allocation of constrained resources within a grid system to satisfy the performance requirements of the user's and system [12], and the constrained allocation of energy within data centers to maximize task completion [25].

3.2 PSO Indirect Encoding Solution

A solution to a constrained shared resource allocation problem consists of an assignment of resources from R to the shares in S. Each resource allocation solution is encoded as a particle in the PSO swarm in the following manner.

Every share $s_i \in S$ can be defined in one of two ways: with a known resource which does not need to be searched for during optimization, or an unknown resource that must be searched for during optimization. The most efficient method to encode a resource allocation solution as a particle in a PSO swarm is to encode a single dimension for every share s_i with a known resource (this dimension represents the portion $port_i$ of that resource), and two dimensions for every share with an unknown resource (these dimensions represent the resource r_j and the portion $port_i$ of that resource). However for simplicity of presentation in the following encoding definition, two dimensions x_{2i} and x_{2i+1}, and their accompanying velocities, will be encoded for each share s_i. A resource allocation solution

s_0	s_1	$\ldots$	$s_{n_{sh}-1}$

is expanded to

$r_{j'}$	$port_0$	$r_{j''}$	$port_1$	$\ldots$	$r_{j'''}$	$port_{n_{sh}-1}$

with $r_{j'}, r_{j''}, r_{j'''} \in R$ and is mappable one-to-one with

x_0	x_{0+1}	x_2	x_{2+1}	$\ldots$	$x_{2(n_{sh}-1))}$	$x_{2(n_{sh}-1)+1}$

To determine the resource referenced by a share with an unknown resource the particle value $x_{2i} \in X$ associated with the share's resource must be converted into a resource reference. The range [0, 1] of the dimension of x_{2i} is consequently divided into equally sized segments for each resource r_j valid for the share s_i. The share's assigned resource is determined by which segment the value x_{2i} falls within. This is done using the following equation $r_j = r_{\lfloor x_{2i} \cdot |R^{s_i}| \rfloor}$ where $R^{s_i} \subseteq R$ consists of the valid resources in R for share s_i.

Now that the resources referenced by all shares are known, the portion $port_i$ for each share s_i can be determined by converting the value $x_{2i+1} \in X$ associated with the share's portion into a portion value $port_i$. We will consider the determined resource of a given share to be r_j. This portion is equal to the quantity of the resource r_j^{quant}, multiplied by the fraction of the current share's portion value x_{2i+1}, divided by the sum total of the portion values for every share sharing the current share's resource. That is

$$port_i = r_j^{quant} \cdot \frac{x_{2i+1}}{\sum_{r_j \equiv r_k} x_{2k+1}}$$

In each regular iteration of the PSO, all particles in the swarm will be updated according to the standard PSO algorithm defined in the previous section. In order to evaluate the fitness function, each particle is then converted via this encoding into a resource allocation solution and the fitness function is used to determine the value of the particle's location in the search space. The optimization process is never reset, rather diversity is maintained by adding new random immigrants periodically.

If a new share is created, n_{sh} is incremented and a new share $s_i = s_{n_{sh}-1}$ is added to S and the dimensions, x_{2i} and x_{2i+1} required to represent it, are added to every particle/velocity in the swarm, including the global/personal best, with new random values. If a share s_i is removed, then n_{sh} is decremented and the dimensions, x_{2i} and x_{2i+1} relating to the share, are similarly removed. At either of these times the fitness values of the particles and global/personal best are re-evaluated.

The chosen indirect encoding ensures that when dimensions for a new share are added, then the share is already referencing some resource r_j and is being given a portion $port_i$ of it. By determining this portion by utilizing a fraction of the summation of portions referencing the same resource, this initial portion is taken proportionally from all of the other shares. This may not exactly be the optimal proportionally fair solution, especially in regards to the utility function U, but it is often a good initial value such that the agent/entity/etc. associated with the new share is not unfairly penalized by being new to the problem.

To demonstrate these claims, the following section implements this particle encoding method for the problem of OFDMA cellular bandwidth allocation with mobile users entering and leaving the service of cell towers.

4. OFDMA CELLULAR BANDWIDTH ALLOCATION

In order to validate the described continuous dynamic PSO for proportional fair multi-dimensional search, this paper applies it to the problem of proportional fair Orthogonal Frequency-Division Multiple Access (OFDMA) resource allocation. Many high-rate wireless data services, such as the 4G cellular services standard Long Term Evolution (LTE), employ OFDMA to allocate radio resources to users, based on channel condition, in order to improve the overall performance of the cellular system.

The dynamic multi-user OFDMA literature generally divides optimization techniques into two classes: margin adaptive (MA) [2] and rate adaptive (RA) [17] techniques. MA schemes attempt to minimize overall transmit power, while RA schemes attempt to maximize the total data rate. Of particular interest for this paper are existing RA applications of well performing heuristic techniques such as simulated annealing [4], game theoretic [11], genetic algorithm [21], and particle swarm optimization (PSO) [2, 16, 17, 24] approaches. Unlike MA algorithms, which have free capacity for users, RA algorithms have to redistribute resources (i.e. power, time) away from other users to handle an increase in load resulting in a high dependency between users' resource allocations.

PSO techniques have been applied rather successfully to the problem. However, the papers utilizing RA PSO techniques do so in a static setting, which does not address the issue of solving the continuous dynamic optimization problem caused by user mobility [17,24]. As users leave/enter the coverage of a cell, so do the user's accompanying resource allocation requirements. Therefore, it is desirable for the network to gracefully incorporate the additional load of new mobile users while maintaining appropriate data rates for existing users. Additionally, it is important that the system maintains an appropriate valid solution such that users are always provided cellular service (i.e. the anytime property).

4.1 OFDMA Model

A static version of the dynamic rate adaptive OFDMA model used in this paper, which ignores the difficulty of user mobility and hand-off between cells, can be found in [4]. In our dynamic OFDMA model, let K denote the set of separately managed wireless cells. In this paper, each individual cell's resource allocation problem is optimized separately. Let, M and N denote, respectively, the set of users and channels (sub-carriers) each cell has available. Each user $i \in M$ has a proportional fair throughput utility function $U(Rate_i) = \log(Rate_i)$. Proportional fairness among users is then achieved by maximizing the summation of the logarithm of individual users' throughputs $\sum_{i \in M} U_i(Rate_i)$.

In order to determine this rate, the resource of transmission power at each cell is allocated to available cell channels and the users are allocated each to a single channel for a portion of time. First, each cell $k \in K$ allocates a portion of power P_{jk} to channel $j \in N$ under its maximum total transmit power p_k^{max} such that $\sum_{j \in N} P_{jk} \leq p_k^{max}, \forall k \in K$. Second, $\tau_{ijk} \geq 0$ is the time portion granted by a cell to user $i \in M$ on channel $j \in N$ for cell $k \in K$ with $\sum_{i \in M} \tau_{ijk} \leq 1, \forall j \in N, \forall k \in K$.

The total throughput $Rate_i$ that is achieved by user $i \in M$ is therefore

$$Rate_i = \sum_{j \in N} \sum_{k \in K} q_{ik} \cdot \tau_{ijk} \cdot C(S_{ijk}).$$

The variable $q_{ik} \in \{0, 1\}$ indicates if a user $i \in M$ is assigned to a cell $k \in K$ where each user is served by a single cell such that $\sum_{k \in K} q_{ik} = 1, \forall i \in M$. The Shannon-Hartley capacity formula $C(S_{ijk}) = \log(1+S_{ijk})$ is used to determine the feasible transmission rate based on the signal to noise ratio (SINR) S_{ijk} of user $i \in M$ served by cell $k \in K$ on channel $j \in M$ [19]. The Signal-to-Interference-plus-Noise-Ratio (SINR) of user $i \in M$ being served by cell $k \in K$ on channel $j \in M$ is $S_{ijk} = \frac{G_{ik}P_{jk}}{\eta + \sum_{l \neq k} G_{il}P_{jl}}$, with η being the thermal background noise power. Additionally, G_{ik} is the power gain of user $i \in M$ for cell $k \in K$, with each cell having a strict finite communication range resulting in a gain of zero if the user is outside the cell's range.

4.2 PSO for OFDMA

OFMDA resource allocation has typically been approached as a static problem, relying on the optimization to be reset when the problem search space changes. OFDMA resource allocation is a continuous problem, with the changing environment conditions and mobile user demands resulting in both the dimensions and the search space of the problem to be in flux. The following three problems must be dealt with for proportional fair OFDMA dynamic resource allocation: (1) the algorithm should not get stuck in local optima as the search space changes, (2) it is undesirable to restart the search every time a user leaves/enters service, and (3) it is undesirable that users are disproportionally penalized when they change between serving cells.

The first of these problems will be addressed by maintaining diversity through regularly introducing random immigrants into the swarm's population [20] to avoid unwanted homogeneity and retain flexibility during the search. The second problem is addressed through the expandable multi-dimensional nature of the particle in this paper's PSO. The particle expands with two new dimensions for every new user, and contracts similarly by deleting the two dimensions referenced by a leaving user. Every time this occurs the old personal and global bests, are re-evaluated, as in [8].

The final problem is addressed by the interpretation of the particle values as shares in the resource allocation solution. An arriving user is assigned two new dimensions with random values. Given the interpretation method, this portion of time on the assigned channel is taken equally from each of the other users already assigned to the channel. This allows for the transitioning user to receive an initial acceptable level of service, without requiring the other users served by the cell to sacrifice their own service unfairly. Similarly, a leaving user's time is redistributed to the remaining users. From this state, the search algorithm will continually optimize towards possible better solutions, shifting users among channels, changing channel power levels, and user time portions.

The remaining parts of this subsection describe the formal application of the abstract PSO solution from the previous section to the problem of dynamic constrained OFDMA resource allocation with mobile users. First, an OFDMA resource allocation particle encoding is described as an implementation of the general resource allocation encoding. Then, an example is given to demonstrate a particle's interpretation.

4.2.1 OFDMA Encoding

Our resources R consist of a resource of transmission power and a set of channels $|N|$. Our set of shares S consists of a share for every channel that the power (known resource) will be split between, and a share for every user that requires service from the cell on some channel (unknown resource). The OFDMA encoding for a single cell $k \in K$ has to include three parts: (1) the fraction of the total power P^k_{max} assigned to each channel $j \in N$, (2) the channel resource for each served user, and (3) the time portion for each served user on his assigned channel. Note, a cell k serves a set of users O where $O \subseteq M$ is a subset of all users.

An n-dimensional vector therefore consists of two portions: (1) a static portion of $|N|$ shares which maps to assignments of the known power resource to a channel $j \in N$, and (2) a dynamic portion of $2 \cdot |O|$ shares which maps two vector values for each user to a portion of time on a single channel resource. Therefore, the size of a vector is $n = |N| + 2 \cdot |O|$, which dynamically changes as users are added and removed from a cell. The vector encoding is defined

pow_0	...	$pow_{|N|-1}$	$user_0$	...	$user_{|O|-1}$

with the unknown resource user $i \in O$ shares defined

$user_i =$

$chan_i$	$time_i$

This encoding can be interpreted as an OFDMA resource allocation solution. First, the power p_{jk} for each channel $j \in N$ is determined via

$$p_{jk} = P^k_{max} \cdot \frac{pow_j}{\sum_{l \in N} pow_l}.$$

That is the power for each channel is found by totaling the power values in the vector and determining the portion of that total which consists of the channel's power value. This portion is multiplied by the total available power P^k_{max} to get the power assigned to the channel. Second, the channel $j \in N$ of the user $i \in O$ is $\lfloor chan_i \cdot |N| \rfloor$.

The range $[0, 1]$ is divided into an equal portion for each channel, and which portion the vector's user channel value falls within is the user's assigned channel. Finally, the time fraction of the user $i \in O$ on channel $j \in N$ is

$$\tau_{ijk} = \frac{time_i}{\sum_{chan_j \equiv chan_l} time_l}.$$

That is the time for the user on his assigned channel is found by totaling the time values in the vector for all users on the same channel. Then the portion of that total, given by the individual's time value, is determined. This portion is the time allocated to the user on his assigned channel.

4.2.2 Example

Consider the following example of a vector:

pow_0	pow_1	$user_0$		$user_1$		$user_2$	
0.25	0.25	0.33	0.45	0.66	0.30	0.70	0.20

For this example there are two channels, i.e. $|N| = 2$, and there are three users, i.e. $|O| = 3$. The total possible power in each cell is 16 W.

The following is how to interpret the encoding. First, the power p_{0k} for channel 0 is $p_{0k} = 16 \cdot \frac{pow_0}{\sum_{l \in N} pow_l} = 16 \cdot \frac{0.25}{0.5} = 8$. As well, the power p_{1k} for channel 1 is $p_{1k} = p_{0k} = 8$. Second, the channel of the user 0 is channel $\lfloor chan_0 \cdot 2 \rfloor = \lfloor 0.33 \cdot 2 \rfloor = 0$. The channel of the user 1 is channel $\lfloor chan_1 \cdot 2 \rfloor = \lfloor 0.66 \cdot 2 \rfloor = 1$. The channel of the user 2 is channel $\lfloor chan_2 \cdot 2 \rfloor = \lfloor 0.7 \cdot 2 \rfloor = 1$. Finally, the time fraction of the user 0 on channel 0 is $\tau_{00k} = \frac{time_0}{\sum_{chan_0 == chan_l} time_l} = \frac{0.45}{0.45} = 1$. The time fraction of the user 1 on channel 1 is $\tau_{11k} = \frac{time_1}{\sum_{chan_1 == chan_l} time_l} = \frac{0.3}{0.5} = 0.6$. The time fraction of the user 2 on channel 1 is $\tau_{21k} = \frac{time_2}{\sum_{chan_2 == chan_l} time_l} = \frac{0.2}{0.5} = 0.4$.

5. EXPERIMENTS

In this section, the evaluations completed to examine the OFDMA implementation of the PSO for proportional fair constrained resource allocation with changing dimensions are presented. It is important to mention that we know of no other **dynamic** OFDMA resource allocation methods to compare our method to. This is primarily because the existing developments for OFDMA resource allocation have focused on the static version of the problem. Therefore, to use one of these static techniques for the dynamic variant would require additional research to create a new dynamic development of a given static technique. Additionally, it would be an unproductive evaluation to compare the initial solutions of static techniques, which are made suboptimal and unsuitable as time passes and users move between cells, to the dynamic and continuously relevant solution created by our dynamic technique. First, Subsection 5.1 outlines the parameters of the OFDMA wireless model and the experimental configurations. Then, Subsection 5.2 describes the results of evaluating the performance of our indirect vector encoding for dynamic OFDMA resource allocation

5.1 Parameters

In this subsection, the parameters of the simulation environment, PSO algorithm, and wireless OFDMA model are described as used in the experimental evaluations.

5.1.1 Environment Parameters

The environment for the experiments is constructed similar to the environment in [4]. There are $|K| = 4$ cell sites located in a rectangular coverage area of $X_0 = 4$ km by $Y_0 = 4$ km. Each cell has a circular coverage diameter of 2.5 km. The edges of the environment are connected in a toroidal 'wrap-around' manner to avoid boundary effects. The cell sites are arranged in a diamond pattern in the environment to maximize coverage. The model is tested with three amounts of $|M| = 64$, 128, or 256 users, which are distributed at random across the coverage area. These users are each given a random static directional vector of (x, y) environmental movement velocity with a speed of at most 100 km/h. Additionally, the model is tested with three different counts of channels $|N| = 16$, 128, or 1024.

5.1.2 PSO Parameters

A cell is assigned a swarm of 25 particles, which every 100 iterations has 5 particles replaced by new random immigrant particles to maintain diversity. The learning factors are $c_1 = 1.0$ and $c_2 = 1.0$. At the beginning of an evaluation, users are randomly assigned to any cell which currently covers them for service. When a user leaves a coverage area, his associated particle dimensions are removed from the cell's swarm they are leaving and two new random dimensions are added and assigned to the user in the swarm of the cell they are arriving at. Each PSO swarm operates continuously and independently in its own thread. Similarly, the users' positions are updated independently by a thread which evaluates their current location every 0.1 seconds. In order to facilitate comparison between varying numbers of users, the fitness function (aggregate throughput utility) for the PSO is normalized by the number of users, obtaining the average throughput utility per user: $\frac{1}{|M|}\sum_{i=1}^{M}\log(Rate_i)$.

5.1.3 Wireless Parameters

The assumptions concerning channel gains are broadly consistent with the standard 3GPP propagation models [1]. In particular, the channel gain value from cell site k to user i is $G_{ik} = H(D_{ik})$, with D_{ik} the distance between cell site k and user i (in km), and $H(d) = 10^{h_0} \cdot d^{-\kappa}$, i.e. $H(d) = 10 \cdot h_0 - 10 \cdot \kappa \cdot log_{10}(d)$ (dB), with a path loss exponent $\kappa = 3.5$ and $h_0 = -14.4$. The thermal background noise is $\eta = -174$ dBm (Hz^{-1}), and the bandwidth per frequency is 1 MHz. Each cell site has a maximum total transmit power budget of $P_k^{max} = 16$ W. The feasible transmission rate as a function of SINR s is given by $C(s) = c_0 \cdot \log_2(1+s)$ (Kbps), with $c_0 = 1000$.

5.2 Numerical Evaluations

In order to complete the evaluations a simulator was developed. Four cells in a diamond pattern with overlapping coverage areas were simulated. In total, nine evaluations of 3 minutes in length were completed, each consisting of a unique combination of the user and channel counts stated in the previous subsection. We examine the results, first to see if the overall throughput of cell service was maintained, and second to see how the throughput of individual users was maintained as mobile users transit the environment and shift between cells. Finally, we examine the impact of changing the PSO parameters that maintain diversity and how the algorithm performs at different rates of user mobility.

Figure 1 examines the overall service by reporting the average user throughput utility and served users for the 4 cells with 64 users and 16 channels. The other results for the remaining combinations are omitted as they show the same behavior with a slightly higher or lower convergence of average user throughput utility. Summarizing across all nine evaluations, an increase in channels available to a cell in general increases the ability of the cell to share and utilize available bandwidth, resulting in, on average, higher user throughput utility. This convergence is higher the more channels and less users being served per cell. Additionally, cross-referencing (a) and (b) in Figure 1 shows that the average user throughput utility of a cell is inversely correlated to the number of users being served by the cell.

Figures 2 and 3, of low and then high user load per channel, report the user throughput utility and serving cell for 4 selected users which switch between the 4 cells during the evaluation period. Each time a user transfers between cells the transfer is indicated by an additional point on the horizontal Elapsed Time axis. The graphs are combinations of 64/256 total users and 16/1024 channels. The other results are omitted as they do not provide as much detail as the chosen examples of more extreme combinations of low and high user per channel load.

In the case of low load usage the existence of unused channels, as in Figure 2, means that the initial random channel assignment for a user on a particular cell may be completely unpowered. This unpowered condition can be seen in User 0 and 1 who each transfer between cells and are assigned to an initial random unpowered channel and resultantly have no throughput. However, when this event happens the algorithm immediately rectifies the lack of power in the next update. This boundary case may be rectified easily in future algorithm development by limiting initial random channel assignment for new users to only channels with power. This is not a problem with high load usage, such as in Figure 3,

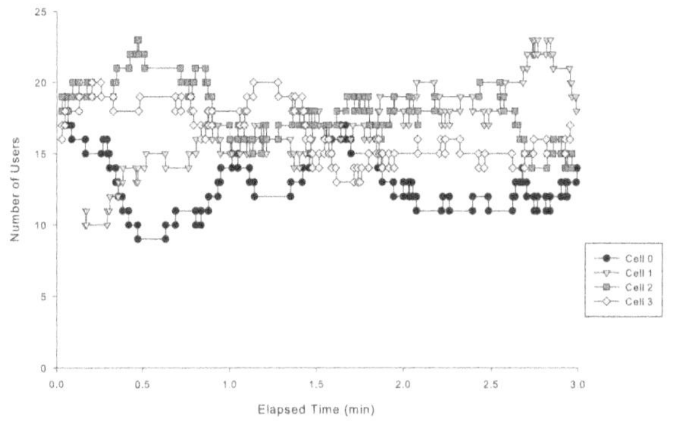

(a) Number of Users Served by each Cell

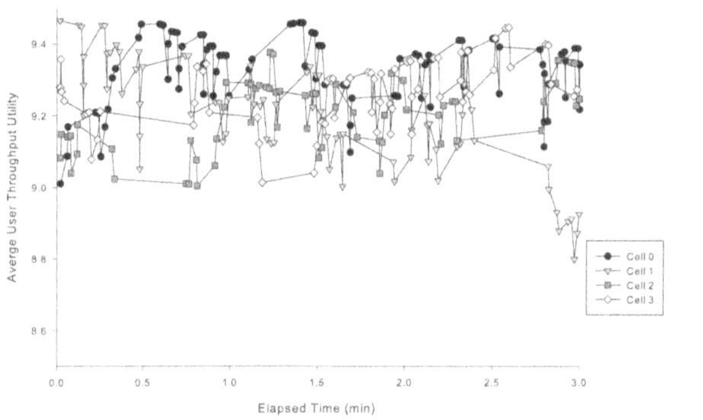

(b) Average User Throughput Utility for each Cell

Figure 1: Cell Service (64 Users, 16 Channels)

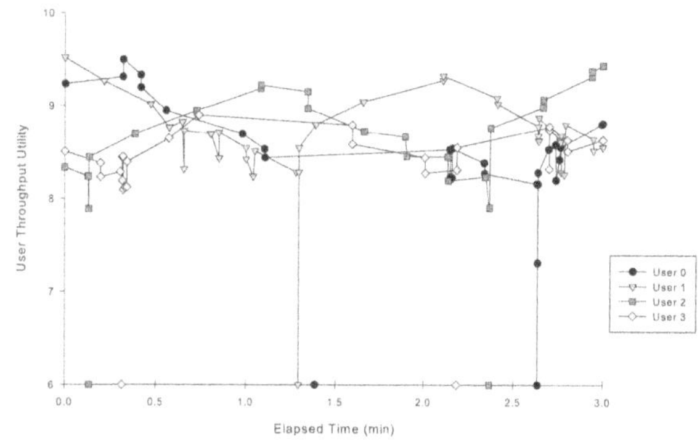

Figure 2: Low Load - 1 User per 16 Channels (64 Users, 1024 Channels)

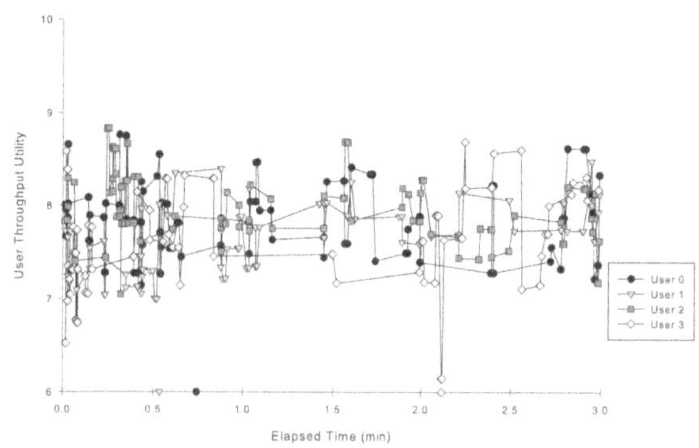

Figure 3: High Load - 16 Users per 1 Channel (256 Users, 16 Channels)

when there are more users than channels, as all channels are always powered.

In the case of high load usage, such as Figure 3, there is much more volatility to an individual user's transfer rate. This is because in most cases a user is sharing a channel with other users. Therefore, as the users' channel conditions change as they move around the environment, when the algorithm attempts to change the user's time portion on a channel it not only affects the user's own throughput but that of the other users on the same channel. A user transferring between cells can also experience additional volatility when the user's new time portion assignment on a channel is much lower than those of the other users sharing the channel. This is the case for user 1 in Figure 3. This may be rectified in future algorithm development by caching an average user portion for each channel which is assigned to newly arriving users instead of a completely random value. Volatility is not a problem with low load usage, such as in Figure 2, where after a user moves to a new cell their throughput is more stable, increasing as the user moves closer towards the cell center then decreasing as the user subsequently moves away.

Figure 4 examines the impact of changing the PSO diversity parameters. In the previous evaluations these parameters replaced 5 random particles in the PSO every 100 iterations to maintain the diversity of the swarm. This diversity is desirable as it means the PSO can avoid being unable to find the desired solution to the current problem because it has become too homogenous and is trapped in past local optima. In these evaluations the impact of variable rates of diversity change on the average throughput utility of a cell is reported for a single cell of the 4 for 64 users on 16 channels. The different chosen rates include never updating the diversity, or replacing a single particle every 10, 100, 1000, and 10000 iterations of swarm. All the different rates face very short term drops in the average throughput rate, which is the expected result of the changing problem. However, never updating, or updating too rarely, result in longer periods around the 2 minute mark where the algorithm remains stuck in an old local optima and is unable to transition to the better solution found by the more diverse algorithms.

In summary, outside of the identified rectifiable edge cases, the algorithm maintains good initial rates for users switching between cells and the service level of existing users as new users arrive. The identified issues, with low channel load users being assigned to an unpowered channel and with high channel load users getting inadequate initial time portions, should be solvable with the described additions to the algorithm's behavior. The algorithm's diversity is an important factor in allowing the algorithm to provide relevant solutions to even challenging problems with highly mobile users.

6. CONCLUSION

This paper introduced a proportional fair constrained resource allocation PSO algorithm for dynamic multi-dimensional optimization problems and implemented it for rate adaptive OFDMA resource allocation with mobile users. This imple-

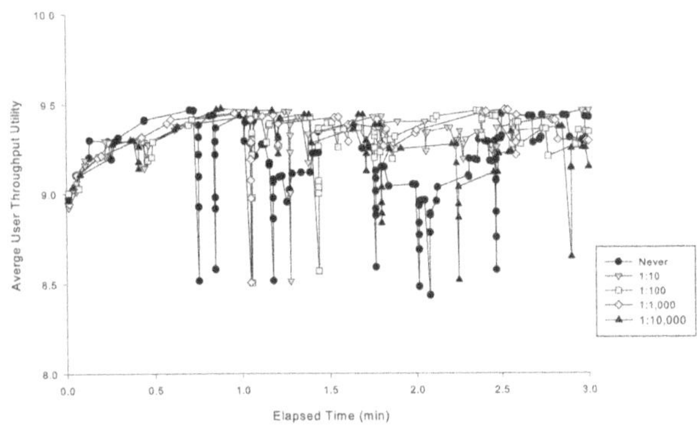

Figure 4: Diversity Maintenance (64 Users, 16 Channels)

mentation demonstrated, over a continuous period of operation, the ability to gracefully optimize the proportional fair allocation of resources within a cell as user load moved between cells. This load management optimization benefited both the overall cellular system's performance, as well as the data rates experienced by individual cellular users switching between cells. The implementation demonstrated the ability of the PSO algorithm to allocate a constrained and shared set of resources in a proportional fair manner for a dynamic problem with quickly changing dimensionality. However, the evaluations also indicated addressable boundary case weaknesses. First, when low load resulted in initial assignments of users to unpowered channels. Second, when high load resulted in volatility due to inadequate initial time portion assignment on shared channels. In the future, providing more considerations on the initial resource portion, such as a cached average instead of random value, may provide the ability to suppress this volatility.

7. REFERENCES

[1] "3GPP." Internet: *www.3gpp.org*. [Jan. 29, 2013].

[2] I. Ahmed and S. Majumder. Adaptive Resource Allocation Based on Modified Genetic Algorithm and Particle Swarm Optimization for Multiuser OFDM Systems. In *Proc. ICECE*, 211–216, 2008.

[3] T. Blackwell. *Particle Swarm Optimization in Dynamic Environments*. Springer, 2007.

[4] S. Borst, M. Markakis, and I. Saniee. Distributed Power Allocation and User Assignment in OFDMA Cellular Networks. In *Proc. Allerton*, 1055–1063, 2011.

[5] F. Brah, L. Vandendorpe, and J. Louveaux. OFDMA Constrained Resource Allocation with imperfect Channel Knowledge. In *Proc. COM/VT*, 1–5, 2007.

[6] A. Carlisle and G. Dozler. Tracking Changing Extrema with Adaptive Particle Swarm Optimizer. In *Proc. WAC*, vol.13, 265–270, 2002.

[7] Chen et. al. Resource Constrained Multirobot Task Allocation with A Leader-Follower Coalition Method . In *Proc. IROS*, 5093–5098, 2010.

[8] X. Hu and R. Eberhart. Adaptive Particle Swarm Optimization: Detection and Response to Dynamic Systems. In *Proc. CEC*, vol.2, 1666–1670, 2002.

[9] T. Ince, S. Kiranyaz, and M. Gabbouj. A Generic and Robust System for Automated Patient-Specific Classification of Electrocardiogram Signals. *IEEE Trans. Bio-Med. Eng.*, 56(5):1415–1426, May 2009.

[10] J. Kennedy and R. Eberhart, "Particle Swarm Optimization," in *Proc. ICNN*, 1995, pp. 1942–1948.

[11] Z. Liang, Y. Chew, and C. Ko. Decentralized Bit, Subcarrier and Power Allocation with Interference Avoidance in Multicell OFDMA Systems using Game Theoretic Approach. In *Proc. MILCOM*, 1–7, 2008.

[12] Y. Liu, K. Han, and D. Zhang. Consumer Sharing Policy Constrained Resource Allocation Method for Grid System . In *Proc. ISCIT*, 721–725, 2009.

[13] A. Nickabadi, M. Ebadzadeh, and R. Safabakhsh. DNPSO: A Dynamic Niching Particle Swarm Optimizer for Multi-Modal Optimization. In *Proc. CEC*, 26–32, 2008.

[14] D. Parrott and X. Li. A Particle Swarm Model for Tracking Multiple Peaks in a Dynamic Environment using Speciation. In *Proc. CEC*, vol.1, 98–103, 2004.

[15] K. Parsopoulos and M. Vrahatis. Recent approaches to global optimization problems through Particle Swarm Optimization. *Natural Computing*, 1:235–306, 2002.

[16] S. Sadeque, I. Ahmed, and R. Vaughan. Impact of Individual and Joint Optimizations in Multi-user OFDM Resource Allocation by Modified PSO. In *Proc. CCECE*, 1233–1237, 2011.

[17] Sharma et. al. On the use of particle swarm optimization for adaptive resource allocation in orthogonal frequency division multiple access systems with proportional rate constraints. *Info. Sci.*, 182(1):115–124, 2012.

[18] T. Starr, J.M. Cioffi, P.J. Silverman. *Understanding Digital Subscriber Line Technology*. Prentice Hall PTR, 1999.

[19] D. Tse, P. Viswanath. *Fundamentals of Wireless Communications*. Cambridge University Press, 2004.

[20] H. Wang, D. Wang, and S. Yang. Triggered Memory-Based Swarm Optimization in Dynamic Environments. In *Proc. the EvoCOP*, 637–646, 2007.

[21] Y. Wang, F. Chen, and G. Wei. Adaptive Subcarrier and Bit Allocation for Multiuser OFDM System Based on Genetic Algorithm. In *Proc. ICC*, vol.1, 242–246, 2005.

[22] S. Yang. Population-Based Incremental Learning with Memory Scheme for Changing Environments. In *Proc. the GECCO*, 711–718, 2005.

[23] S. Yang and X. Yao. Population-Based Incremental Learning With Associative Memory for Dynamic Environments. *IEEE Trans. Evol. Comput.*, 542–561, October 2008.

[24] Y. Yi, Z. Yu, and W. Ye. Modified Particle Swarm Optimization and Genetic Algorithm Based Adaptive Resources Allocation Algorithm for Multiuser Orthogonal Frequency Division Multiplexing System. *Information Technology*, 10(5):955–964, 2011.

[25] Young et. al. Energy-Constrained Dynamic Resource Allocation in a Heterogeneous Computing Environment. In *Proc. ICPPW*, 298–307, 2011.

[26] S. Zilberstein and S. Russell. Approximate Reasoning Using Anytime Algorithms. In S. Natarajan, editor, *Imprecise and Approximate Computation*, 43–62. Springer US, 1995.

Genetic Algorithms and Deep Learning for Automatic Painter Classification

Erez Levy
Dept. of Computer Science
Bar-Ilan University
Ramat-Gan 52900, Israel
erezlevy@gmail.com

Omid E. David
Dept. of Computer Science
Bar-Ilan University
Ramat-Gan 52900, Israel
mail@omiddavid.com

Nathan S. Netanyahu*
Dept. of Computer Science
Bar-Ilan University
Ramat-Gan 52900, Israel
nathan@cs.biu.ac.il

ABSTRACT

In this paper we describe the problem of painter classification, and propose a novel hybrid approach incorporating genetic algorithms (GA) and deep restricted Boltzmann machines (RBM). Given a painting, we extract features using both generic image processing (IP) functions (e.g., fractal dimension, Fourier spectra coefficients, texture coefficients, etc.) and unsupervised deep learning (using deep RBMs). We subsequently compare several supervised learning techniques for classification using the extracted features as input. The results show that the weighted nearest neighbor (WNN) method, for which the weights are evolved using GA, outperforms both a support vector machine (SVM) classifier and a standard nearest neighbor classifier, achieving over 90% classification accuracy for the 3-painter problem (an improvement of over 10% relatively to previous results due to standard feature extraction only).

Categories and Subject Descriptors

I.2.6 [**Artificial Intelligence**]: Learning—*Parameter learning*

General Terms

Algorithms

Keywords

Genetic Algorithms, Deep Learning, Painter Classification, Restricted Boltzmann Machines, Deep Belief Network

1. INTRODUCTION

Art forgery, which dates back more than two thousand years, has played a key role in the development of painting authentication. This task has been usually performed manually by art experts who have dedicated their lives to this profession. Their expertise amounted to using various characteristics other than what the human eye can see, including chemical analysis, spectrometry, and infrared or X-ray imaging. The infamous Vermeer forgery [14] attests, perhaps, most vividly to the challenges presented by painting authentication. Han van Meegeren used historical canvasses and managed to deceive art experts into believing that his painting was an authentic Vermeer. Only after being charged with treason and sentenced to death for selling another (forged) Vermeer, did he confess and was forced to create another painting to prove himself innocent of treason. A more recent case of painting authenticity involves the Pollock paintings found a decade ago in a storage locker in Wainscott, NY. The authenticity of these paintings was compromised on the basis of computer analysis of the paintings' fractal dimension [21]. This claim was subsequently disputed by analyzing childlike drawings that supposedly have the same fractal dimension as the Pollock paintings [8].

In this paper we address the closely related problem of painting classification, i.e., the task of assigning a specific artist to a given painting (from a dataset of paintings by several artists). Note that the image authentication problem can be viewed as a binary image classification problem (i.e., determine whether or not a given painting was painted by a certain artist). Recent developments for both problem types have focused on preprocessing techniques of reducing the high dimensionality of visual data to low-dimensional representations which can be manipulated towards image understanding. This process is essentially accomplished upon the transition from image space to feature space. That is, painting classification consists of two main stages: (1) Performing feature extraction on the painting (i.e., obtaining a low-dimensional vector of feature values for each image), and (2) performing supervised classification given the feature vectors.

Levy *et al.* [13] applied feature extraction to paintings using generic image processing (IP) functions (e.g., fractal dimension, Fourier spectra coefficients, texture coefficients, etc.), followed by genetic algorithms (GA)-based learning of the weights of a weighted nearest neighbor (WNN) classifier [18]. Their approach achieved 80% accuracy for the 3-painter classification problem.

In recent years *deep learning* (DL) methods, in particular, deep *restricted Boltzmann machines* (RBM) [6] have proven highly successful in unsupervised feature extraction

*Nathan Netanyahu is also with the Gonda Brain Research Center at Bar-Ilan University, and the Center for Automation Research, University of Maryland, College Park, MD 20742 (email: nathan@cfar.umd.edu).

GECCO'14, July 12–16, 2014, Vancouver, BC, Canada.
Copyright 2014 ACM 978-1-4503-2662-9/14/07 ...$15.00.
http://dx.doi.org/10.1145/2576768.2598287 .

tasks, improving the state-of-the-art of numerous classification problems in image processing and computer vision [11].

In this paper we present the problem of painter classification and briefly survey recent research that has been conducted in the field. We then describe our approach which combines feature extraction due to standard image processing techniques and deep RBMs, and compare several classification methods which use the augmented set of extracted features as input. Specifically, we compare support vector machine (SVM), standard nearest neighbor (NN), and GA-based weighted nearest neighbor (WNN) classifiers. The results presented here show that the GA-based WNN classifier using features extracted by standard IP, as well as deep RBMs outperforms the other classifiers; specifically, it achieves over 90% classification accuracy, improving previous results in [13] by over 10%.

2. BACKGROUND

Image authentication is the task of determining whether or not a given painting was painted by a specific artist. The related task addressed by us, though, is image classification, i.e., the task of determining the artist of a given painting (from a certain group of artists). The input to our problem consists of painting images of the group of artists (several paintings of each artist), and our objective is to automatically classify a given painting. One of the difficulties in solving this problem is that we cannot define a certain set of rules that the painting has to conform to in order to classify it to the subgroup corresponding to the correct artist. For this reason, computer vision techniques which are capable of identifying shapes and objects in an image are not sufficiently effective for solving the problem.

Formerly there have been attempts to harness the strength of image analysis tools to classify historical art paintings into categories of artists or genres. Levy *et al.* [13] used GA-based WNN with a set of 78 prevalent image features for classifying paintings by Rembrandt, Renoir, and van Gogh, obtaining 80% classification accuracy. Herik and Postma [22] surveyed image features relevant to the historic art domain and concluded that neural network techniques combined with domain knowledge were most suitable to the task of automatic image classification. Under-drawing strokes in infrared reflectograms were analyzed by Kammerer *et al.* [9] in order to classify how and by what tools paintings are painted. Natural language processing techniques using a naive-Bayes classifier and the coefficients of a discrete cosine transform (DCT) were used by Keren [10] in order to classify local features in an image. Kroner *et al.* [12] classified drawings by using image histograms and pattern recognition methods.

The above past research focused on specific image processing features tailored for specific datasets (such as ink paintings, infrared reflectograms, or black and white sketches). This domain-specific knowledge facilitates the exploitation of various characteristics of the painting-specific domain. In the next section we present our generic approach which does not rely on any domain-specific knowledge. Specifically, the features are extracted using both generic image processing functions (not specialized for paintings) and deep RBM neural networks.

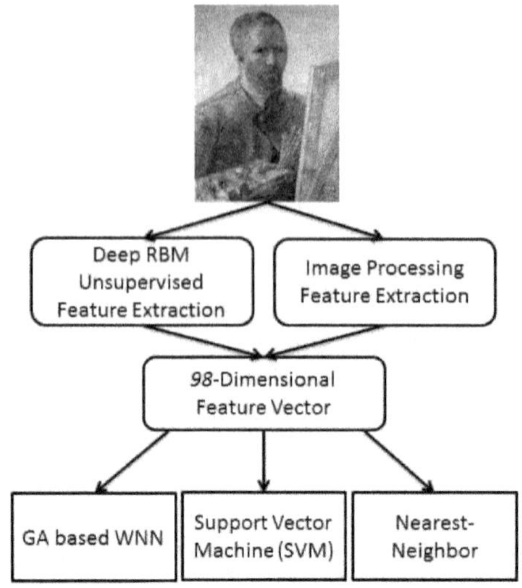

Figure 1: Basic structure of the research conducted, feature extraction techniques used and the learning methods compared.

3. FEATURE EXTRACTION

In this section we describe two feature extraction methods, using (1) generic IP functions and (2) deep RBM neural networks. The number of features extracted by these methods is 78 and 20, respectively. Namely, our module extracts a total of 98 features for each painting. Section 4 describes, in detail, the GA-based WNN module using these 98 features for painter classification.

3.1 Feature Extraction Using Image Processing Functions

We use 78 features extracted by standard IP techniques, as described in [13]. These features include also color uniqueness features, defined in terms of unique color values in the two color representations considered. We review below some of these feature types.

3.1.1 Fractal Dimension and Texture Features

Fractal dimension measures essentially the self similarity of an image, and is an index for characterizing fractal patterns or sets by quantifying their complexity as a ratio of the change in detail to the change in scale. A common approximation to the fractal dimension is the Hurst exponent [16, 17], which is related to the fractal dimension by $D = 2 - H_E$, where D is the fractal dimension and H_E is the Hurst exponent. Fractal dimension is widely used in various areas of applied mathematics (e.g., fractals and chaos theory), biophysics, hydrology, etc.

Additionally, we extract texture features, which are important when identifying objects or regions in an image. The texture of an image can be captured by a gray level co-occurrence matrix which provides the distribution of co-occurring values for a given offset. Haralick's texture features (defined in [5]) are extracted and used in our experiments.

3.1.2 Statistical Descriptors

Statistical descriptors are among the most trivial features that may be extracted in the preprocessing stage. Nonetheless, they may be highly valuable to painter classification. Specifically, we employ various standard statistical descriptors, e.g., standard deviation, skewness, kurtosis, and the minimum, maximum, mean and median values for each of the values of the RGB and HSV representations, and of the amplitudes of the Fourier transform.

Let $I(x, y)$ denote an image value (at a particular pixel) of an $N \times M$ image, for all of the image bands considered (i.e., gray-scale, as well as RGB and HSV bands). We compute the following parameters:

$$mean = \bar{I} = \frac{\sum_{x=1}^{N} \sum_{y=1}^{M} I(x,y)}{NM} \quad (1)$$

$$stddev = \sigma = \frac{\sqrt{\sum_{x=1}^{N} \sum_{y=1}^{M} (I(x,y) - \bar{I})^2}}{NM - 1} \quad (2)$$

$$skewness = \frac{\sum_{x=1}^{N} \sum_{y=1}^{M} (\frac{I(x,y)-\bar{I}}{\sigma})^3}{NM} \quad (3)$$

$$kurtosis = \frac{\sum_{x=1}^{N} \sum_{y=1}^{M} (\frac{I(x,y)-\bar{I}}{\sigma})^4}{NM} - 3 \quad (4)$$

3.1.3 Steerable Filters and Color Histograms

A steerable filter is an orientation-selective convolution kernel used for image enhancement and feature extraction. It can be expressed via a linear combination of a small set of rotated versions of itself. A steerable Gaussian filter evaluates the first directional derivative of an image. The filter was implemented as outlined in [4] with successive angles separated by 15°, with an expectation that the angles contain the data of the brush strokes used by the painter while painting.

Additionally, color histograms were extracted separately for six image bands (i.e., red, green, blue, hue, saturation, value) using 256 depth sized bins. Afterwards, statistical descriptors were applied to the histogram vectors, producing feature values. RGB values were translated to HSV representation as outlined in [19].

3.1.4 Fourier Spectra

Fourier's transform is one of the most applied transformations in signal processing. Upon transforming an image matrix, the transform produces a spectral representation of frequencies that form the image. Sine waveforms of amplitudes and phases constitute an image when joined together, and can be inversely transformed to the original image. The transform and its inverse for a vector of length N are computed by:

$$X(k) = \sum_{j-1}^{N} x(j)\omega_N^{(j-1)(k-1)} \quad (5)$$

$$x(j) = (1/N) \sum_{k=1}^{N} X(k)\omega_N^{-(j-1)(k-1)} \quad (6)$$

where $\omega_N = e^{(-2\pi i)/N}$ is an N-th root of unity. Amplitudes for the transform are computed by applying an absolute operator on the transformation's matrix.

3.2 Feature Extraction Using Deep RBMs

Deep learning, in general, and deep RBMs, in particular, have proven recently rather effective in several machine learning and computer vision benchmarks [3]. The idea is to enable learning via deep networks in a manner that was not possible before (due to the learning complexity of these deep networks). The concept of using restricted Boltzmann machines and stacking them on top of each other in order to learn one layer at a time, was proved to be quite effective for unsupervised feature extraction.

We now provide a brief overview of RBMs, and describe how they are used to provide the 20 additional features (to the 78 features extracted due to standard IP functions).

3.2.1 Restricted Boltzmann Machines

An RBM uses a network of stochastic binary units arranged in two layers; a visible layer and a hidden one. Units $\mathbf{v}$ in the visible layers are fully connected via weights W to units $\mathbf{h}$ in the hidden layer. There are no connections within the visible layer or the hidden layer (the only connections are between the layers). The configuration of visible and hidden units has the energy:

$$E(\mathbf{v}, \mathbf{h}) = -\sum_{i \in visible} a_i v_i - \sum_{j \in hidden} b_j h_j - \sum_{i,j} v_i h_i w_{ij} \quad (7)$$

where v_i and h_j are the states of visible and hidden units i and j, w_{ij} denotes the weight between visible unit i and hidden unit j, and a_i and b_j are bias terms. The network assigns probabilities to all pairs of a visible and a hidden units via the function:

$$p(\mathbf{v}, \mathbf{h}) = \frac{1}{Z} e^{-E(\mathbf{v},\mathbf{h})} \quad (8)$$

where the partition function Z is calculated by summing all possible pairs of visible and hidden vectors, i.e.,

$$Z = \sum_{\mathbf{v},\mathbf{h}} e^{-E(\mathbf{v},\mathbf{h})} \quad (9)$$

Since RBMs lack connections between units within a layer, the conditional distributions $p(\mathbf{h}|\mathbf{v})$ and $p(\mathbf{v}|\mathbf{h})$ have a convenient form:

$$p(h_j = 1|\mathbf{v}) = \sigma(b_j + \sum_i w_{ij} v_i) \quad (10)$$

$$p(v_i = 1|\mathbf{h}) = \sigma(a_i + \sum_j w_{ij} h_j) \quad (11)$$

where $\sigma(x)$ is the logistic sigmoid function:

$$\sigma(x) = \frac{1}{1 + e^{-x}} \quad (12)$$

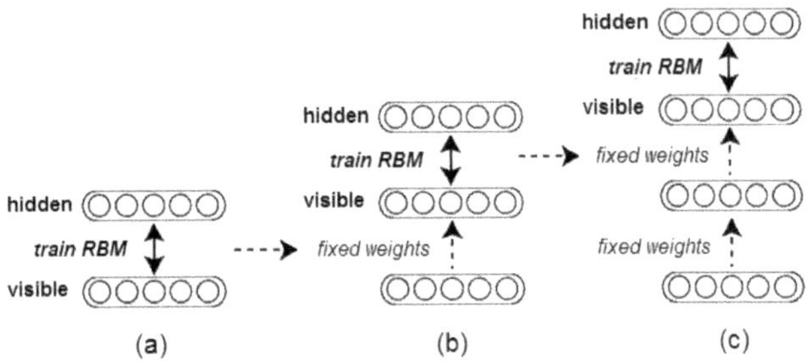

Figure 2: Composition of a 3-layer deep network subsequent to learning stacks of RBMs: (a) One layer of RBM is trained, (b) learned weights are fixed (can no longer be modified) and new RBM layer is added on top of previous one, and (c) weights of second layer are fixed, and a third RBM layer is added.

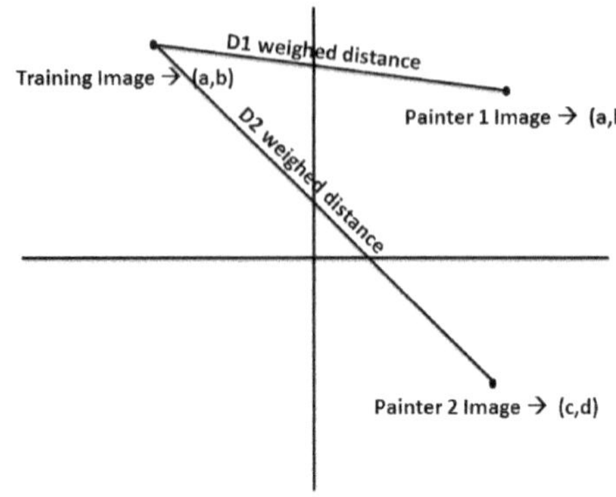

Figure 3: Simplified two-dimensional feature space, illustrating the notion of weighted distance between a (point representing a) training image and two points representing images by two painters.

The weights w_{ij} and the biases a_i and b_j can be updated during training using the so-called contrastive divergence algorithm of Hinton *et al.* [6].

3.2.2 Deep RBMs

RBMs can be stacked on top of each other to form a deep neural network (so-called *deep belief network*), as proposed by Hinton *et al.* [6]. The idea is to train, one layer at a time, a stack of RBM, after which the entire stack can be viewed as a single probabilistic model. This is achieved by first learning the initial RBM layer, then freezing the values of the weights (can no longer be modified), and finally adding another layer on top of the current one. Thus, the output values of the first layer form the input values for the next layer in the hierarchy (see Figure 2). We implemented deep RBMs using *dropouts* [7, 2, 20], which regularize the network and prevent overfitting by randomly disabling some neurons in the hidden layer during training. The deep RBM network provides 20 features in our implementation (see Figure 4).

4. PROPOSED CLASSIFICATION APPROACH

We now map the classification of the data acquired during preprocessing (i.e., feature extraction due to standard IP and deep RBMs) to GA-based learning of the weights of a WNN classifier. As mentioned previously, each painting in the dataset, which consists of $(3 \times 40 =)$ 120 images, is represented by a $(78 + 20 =)$ 98-dimensional feature vector. The 78 features (due to standard IP) consist of $(5 \times 6 =)$ 30 values of the mean, median, maximum, minimum and the number of histogram bins with non-zero frequency of each band of the RGB and HSV color representations, $(4 \times 2 =)$ 8 values of the standard deviation, skewness, kurtosis and mean of the gray-scale and FFT images, as well as the number of unique RGB color triplets, the Hurst exponent, 24-bin histogram of directional derivatives, and Haralick's texture features (in the gray-scale image).

Adding the 20 features produced by the deep RBM to the above 78 features, we obtain chromosomes of 98 real-valued weights. We then train the GA-based scheme on these weight vectors to produce the best chromosome, i.e., to evolve the best weights for the WNN classifier. The above chromosome weights are tested during validation and the overall performance of this hybrid approach is evaluated. The basic framework is as follows:

1. Produce 98-feature vectors values for each painting in the dataset.
2. Initialize vectors to be used with the nearest neighbor algorithm.
3. Train a genetic algorithm using a fitness function based on the previously produced vectors and the weighted nearest neighbor algorithm.
4. Compare the performance of the best chromosome to that of an ordinary (unweighted) nearest neighbor algorithm and an SVM classifier.

Our training is divided to $(36 \times 3 =)$ 108 training images and $(4 \times 3 =)$ 12 validation images (one tenth of the dataset, as in 10-fold cross-validation). Additionally, the image subset for training is divided to $(5 \times 3 =)$ 15 paintings used for NN classification (as explained in the next subsection), and $(31 \times 3 =)$ 93 paintings used to train the GA. We have tested a 3-way classification for paintings of Rembrandt, Renoir, and van Gough. We elaborate below on each of the above stages.

4.1 Feature Vector Extraction

As previously discussed, 78 features are extracted due to standard IP techniques. Additionally, a network of stacked RBMs is trained in an unsupervised manner using the dataset images. Running these images through the stacked RBMs produces 20 additional features for a total of 98 features per image. The structure of the deep RBM network (see Figure 4) consists of $(35 \times 35 \times 3 =)$ 3675 nodes in the visible layer. Note that each image is resized to 35×35 pixels (per each color band). The hidden layers contain 2000, 1000, 500, 250, 100, 50, and 20 nodes. Each layer was trained for 1000 epochs, during which the weights were tuned.

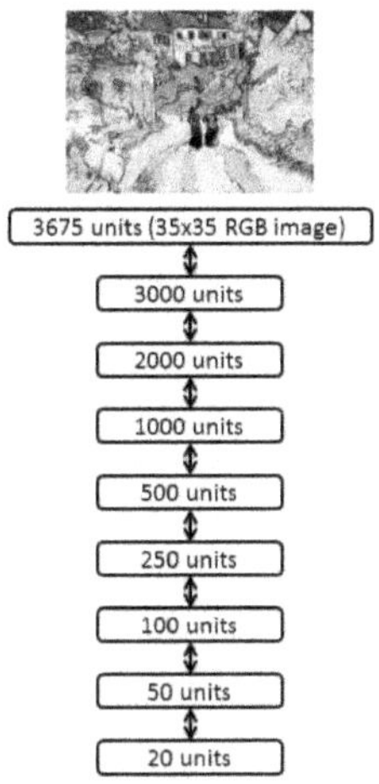

Figure 4: Structure of RBM network: Visible layer is of size $35 \times 35 \times 3$ (for RGB representation). Number of nodes in each hidden layer is indicated. Final 20-node layer provides 20 features for each image representation.

```
initialize population randomly
evaluate fitness of each chromosome
repeat
        select best-ranked individuals to reproduce
        mate pairs at random
        apply crossover operator
        apply mutation operator
        evaluate fitness of each chromosome
until enough generations have passed
```

Figure 5: Pseudo-code of genetic algorithm.

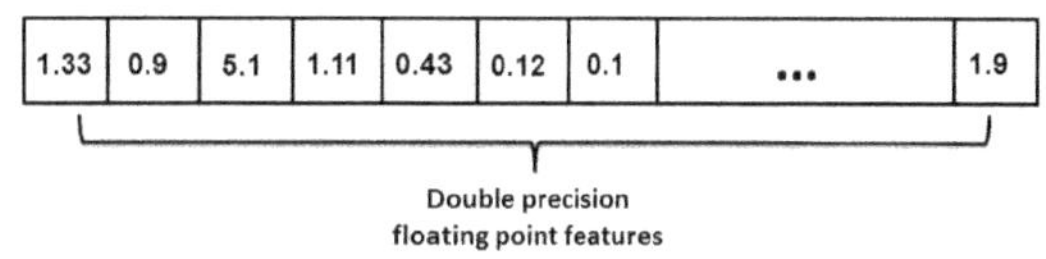

Figure 6: An example of a chromosome containing 98 feature values. Every cell contains the coefficient of its appropriate feature, and the 98-value chromosome is a solution for the classification weights applied by the weighted nearest neighbor method.

4.2 Nearest Neighbor Initialization

A portion of the training data is used for an initialization of vectors that are used by the nearest neighbor algorithm. A simple two-dimensional example is depicted in Figure 3. Suppose that the vectors, "Painter 1 Image" and "Painter 2 Image", are added to the feature space and are subsequently utilized in the fitness evaluation of the chromosomes and in the verification stage. During this process, weighted distances with respect to a given chromosome are calculated between the initialized vectors and image vectors used to train the GA.

The nearest neighbor algorithm is a special case of the general k-nearest neighbor algorithm (where $k = 1$). It is a method for classifying objects based on the closest training examples in feature space. The training stage consists of storing labeled training vectors, and the classification is accomplished by calculating which vector label is the most frequent among the k closest vectors to a feature vector in question. Based on our experiments, we chose k to be 1, using Euclidean distance as a distance metric.

4.3 Training of Genetic Algorithm

The training phase of the genetic algorithm employs the representation of the problem as a chromosome, and the definition of several evolutionary operators that are used during the genetic simulation performed by the genetic algorithm. These operators include crossover and mutation (see below). Also, the evolution is customized by fine-tuning parameters and flags such as crossover/mutation rates and elitism.

A chromosome represents double precision values that are vector components in feature space. Upon calculating the fitness for each chromosome we insert it into the nearest neighbor algorithm discussed earlier, and calculate weighted distances (according to Eq. (13)). Based on the weighted distances calculated, the nearest neighbor algorithm classifies the paintings. The classification accuracy is used as the chromosome's fitness value. The weighted distance is dependent on the chromosomes' parameters as weights, and is defined by:

$$NN_w = \sqrt{\sum_{i=1}^{d} w_i (y_i - z_i)^2} \tag{13}$$

where $Y = (y_1, y_2, ..., y_d)$ and $Z = (z_1, z_2, ...z_d)$ are painting representations in feature space, and $w_i (i = 1, .., d)$ are the weights corresponding to a given chromosome ($d = 98$ in our case). Figure 6 illustrates a chromosome structure, which consists of the various weights used by the nearest neighbor classifier.

Additional GA properties used are double-point location crossover operator, Gaussian additive mutation operator, 80% crossover occurrence, 40% mutation rate and elitism.

```
int calculate_fitness (chrom, training_data){
   fitness = 0;
   for each (image in training_data){
      weighted_vec = get_weighted_vec(img, chrom);
      if (check_nearest_neighbor(weighted_vec))
          fitness += 1;
   }
   return fitness;
}
```

Figure 7: Pseudo-code of fitness evaluation during training.

4.4 Performance Validation

Subsequent to the training phase of the genetic algorithm, validation (and cross-validation) is performed on $(4 \times 3) = 12$ images of the dataset by applying the best chromosome obtained, i.e., the one with the highest fitness value after 40 generations. Each vector (chosen for validation) is compared against all of the vectors in the dataset (stored during the initialization phase), by applying the weights of the best chromosome to find the vector's (weighted) nearest neighbor. The vector is classified according to its (weighted) nearest neighbor label. We can thus classify all of the "validation vectors" and evaluate the performance according to the number of correctly classified vectors.

Aside from evaluating the GA-based WNN and deep RBM-based classification, we compare its performance to that of a GA-based WNN classifier without the features produced by deep learning (i.e., just the module described by Levy *et al.* [13]), and a standard (unweighted) nearest neighbor classifier. Additionally, we compare all the results to those obtained by using an SVM classifier.

5. EXPERIMENTAL RESULTS

The dataset for the conducted experiments is identical to that used by Levy *et al.* [13] in their experiments. It consists of $(3 \times 40 =)$ 120 digital reproductions of paintings by Rembrandt, Renoir, and van Gough, downloaded from the Webmuseum [15]. The acquisition process is uniform across the images, ensuring that the classification is based on painter characteristics rather than artifacts of electronic devices or the digitization process. Artifacts due to JPEG compression are uniform across all images and are relatively negligible. Thus, they do not pose a problem. The images have 24-bit color depth with varying resolutions averaged approximately at 1000×1000 pixels, and compressed as JPEG formatted files. We have resampled the images and normalized them to 35×35 pixels for the deep RBM learning process. The Appendix contains the painting titles of the images used in our experiments.

We have implemented our scheme using [1] as a platform for the genetic algorithm and MATLAB as an infrastructure for calculating feature values. Additionally, deep RBM learning was implemented in Python. As described in Section 3, 98 feature values were calculated for each image. The dataset experimented with consists of $(40 \times 3) = 120$ images of paintings by Rembrandt, Renoir, and van Gough. 10 random runs were invoked, where each run was restarted with random initial chromosomes. The best chromosome over these 10 runs was chosen for a given subset of the training images. Additionally, cross-validation was conducted by shuffling (at random) the role of the images and averaging the results, i.e., images previously used for training were used for validation in a subsequent run and vice versa. This way we utilized effectively our dataset.

The experiments were conducted using three feature subsets: 78 features due to standard IP, 20 features due to deep RBMs, and the augmented set of 98 features due to both. The classification algorithms tested were a basic NN classifier, an SVM classifier, and the GA-based WNN classifier. Using only standard IP features, these classifiers achieved, respectively, 65.71%, 68.33%, and 78.33% accuracy.

The accuracy results obtained by the above classifiers using only the 20 features (from the deep RBMs) were 64.41%, 77.50%, and 73.92%, respectively. However, for the entire feature set the accuracy results were 68.71%, 71.66%, and 90.44%, respectively. Namely, the improvement obtained by the GA-based WNN classifier is substantial with respect to the 80% accuracy reported by Levy *et al.* [13]. Examining the output chromosome reveals that every feature is crucial for the painter classification, as small feature values are rarely encountered in practice. The graph in Figure 8 presents the fitness function (classification accuracy) associated with the best and average chromosomes in a single run over 40 generations. The evolutionary improvement is clearly evident.

Table 1 provides a summary of the classification performance obtained using different methods and features. IP, DL, and IP + DL stand for features obtained due to standard IP techniques, deep learning, and the combination of both, respectively.

	IP	DL	IP & DL
GA-based WNN	78.33%	73.92%	90.44%
Basic NN	65.71%	64.41%	68.71%
SVM	68.33%	77.50%	71.66%

Table 1: Classification accuracy for GA-based WNN, basic NN, and SVM, using features due to standard IP, deep learning (DL), and the combination of both (IP + DL).

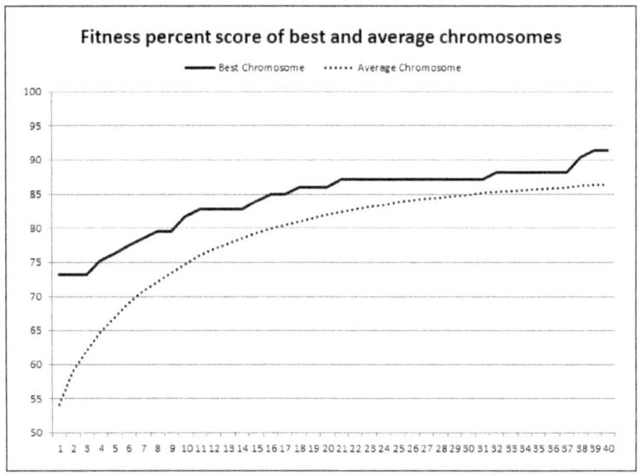

Figure 8: Accuracy scores of best and average chromosomes over 40 generations: The vertical axis represents the fitness score (classification accuracy) in each generation and the horizontal axis represents the generation number; a chromosome's fitness is defined as the classification accuracy using that chromosome's weights.

6. CONCLUSION

Automatic painter classification has gained much attention over the past decades, and much progress has been made with regards to both relevant preprocessing techniques and classification algorithms. Still, the problem of painter classification remains a complex task that requires more sophisticated techniques.

Deep learning techniques, in particular, those based on deep RBMs have gained popularity in recent years as powerful tools for unsupervised feature extraction. These methods have proven successful in improving the state-of-the-art of numerous classification tasks in computer vision..

The results presented in this paper show that deep learning methods can yield substantial improvements when integrated with standard, existing techniques. While the classification rate (using either standard IP features or deep learning features) does not exceed 80%, employing the augmented set of features due to both methods results in an enhanced performance of over 90% accuracy.

Additionally, during the supervised classification we observed that while SVM performs well on a smaller feature set, its performance deteriorates on a larger number of features (98 in our case). Also, while the basic NN classifier is consistently inferior to SVM, the performance of its weighted version improves dramatically (from 68.71% to over 90% accuracy) by evolving the feature weights due to GA. This attests to the power of genetic algorithms for parameter tuning. The hybrid IP+DL for unsupervised feature extraction and GA+NN (WNN) for supervised classification underlines the vast potential in combining several methods, resulting in a hybrid approach which substantially outperforms each method separately.

The presented hybrid approach is generic, and does not rely on any domain-specific assumptions. As such, it may be ported easily to additional classification domains.

7. REFERENCES

[1] S. Adcock. Gaul - Genetic Algorithms Utility Library. `http://gaul.sourceforge.net`, 2000.

[2] J. Ba and B. Frey. Adaptive dropout for training deep neural networks. In *Advances in Neural Information Processing Systems*, pages 3084–3092, 2013.

[3] L. Deng and D. Yu. *Deep learning: Methods and applications*. Now Publishers, 2014.

[4] W.T. Freeman and E.H. Adelson. The design and use of steerable filters. *IEEE Transactions on Pattern Analysis and Machine Intelligence*, 13(9):891–906, 1991.

[5] R.M. Haralick, K. Shanmugam, and I.H. Dinstein. Textural features for image classification. *IEEE Transactions on Systems, Man and Cybernetics*, (6):610–621, 1973.

[6] G.E Hinton, S. Osindero, and Y.W. Teh. A fast learning algorithm for deep belief nets. *Neural computation*, 18(7):1527–1554, 2006.

[7] G.E Hinton, N. Srivastava, A. Krizhevsky, I. Sutskever, and R. Salakhutdinov. Improving neural networks by preventing co-adaptation of feature detectors. *arXiv preprint arXiv:1207.0580*, 2012.

[8] K. Jones-Smith and H. Mathur. Fractal analysis: revisiting Pollock's drip paintings. *Nature*, 444(7119):E9–E10, 2006.

[9] P. Kammerer, M. Lettner, E. Zolda, and R. Sablatnig. Identification of drawing tools by classification of textural and boundary features of strokes. *Pattern Recognition Letters*, 28(6):710–718, 2007.

[10] D. Keren. Painter identification using local features and naive Bayes. In *Proceedings of the IEEE International Conference on Pattern Recognition*, volume 2, pages 474–477, 2002.

[11] Alex Krizhevsky, Ilya Sutskever, and Geoff Hinton. Imagenet classification with deep convolutional neural networks. In P. Bartlett, F.C.N. Pereira, C.J.C. Burges, L. Bottou, and K.Q. Weinberger, editors, *Advances in Neural Information Processing Systems 25*, pages 1106–1114, 2012.

[12] S. Kroner and A. Lattner. Authentication of free hand drawings by pattern recognition methods. In *Proceedings of the IEEE 14th International Conference on Pattern Recognition*, volume 1, pages 462–464, 1998.

[13] E. Levy, O.E. David, and N.S. Netanyahu. Painter classification using genetic algorithms. In *IEEE Congress on Evolutionary Computation*, pages 3027–3034, 2013.

[14] D. Phillips. How do forgers deceive art critics? *The Artful Eye*. R. Gregory, J. Harris, P. Heard, and D. Rose, Eds., Oxford University Press, pages 372–388, 1995.

[15] N. Pioch. Webmuseum. `http://webmuseum.meulie.net/wm/`, 1994.

[16] J.C. Russ. Surface characterization: Fractal dimensions, Hurst coefficients, and frequency transforms. *Journal of Computer-Assisted Microscopy*, 2(3):161–183, 1990.

[17] B. Schiele and J. Crowley. Object recognition using multidimensional receptive field histograms. *In Proceedings of the European Conference on Computer Vision*, pages 610–619, 1996.

[18] W. Siedlecki and J. Sklansky. A note on genetic algorithms for large-scale feature selection. *Pattern Recognition Letters*, 10(5):335–347, 1989.

[19] A.R. Smith. Color gamut transform pairs. In *ACM Siggraph Computer Graphics*, volume 12, pages 12–19, 1978.

[20] N. Srivastava. *Improving neural networks with dropout*. PhD thesis, University of Toronto, 2013.

[21] R.P. Taylor, R. Guzman, T.P. Martin, G.D.R. Hall, A.P. Micolich, D. Jonas, B.C. Scannell, M.S. Fairbanks, and C.A. Marlow. Authenticating Pollock paintings using fractal geometry. *Pattern Recognition Letters*, 28(6):695–702, 2007.

[22] H.J. van den Herik and E.O. Postma. Discovering the visual signature of painters. *Future Directions for Intelligent Systems and Information Sciences*. N. Kasabov, Ed., Physica-Verlag, Heidelberg, pages 129–147, 2000.

APPENDIX

This appendix lists the $(40 \times 3) = 120$ titles of the paintings experimented with by van Gogh, Rembrandt, and Renoir.

#	van Gogh	Rembrandt	Renoir
1	bandaged-ear	abraham	apres-bain
2	berceuse	anslo	baigneuses
3	cordeville	aristotle-homer	bathers-1887
4	corridor-asylum	artemis	bathers-1918
5	cypress-star	bathing-river	bougival
6	cypresses	bathsheba	canoeist
7	flower-beds-holland	belshazzar	chocquet
8	green-vineyard	children	city
9	green-wheat-field	danae	country
10	house-ploughman	david	dancer
11	mme-trabuc	descent	durieux
12	mr-trabuc	emmaus	flowers
13	old-mill	hendrickje	gabrielle
14	old-vineyard	holy-family	girl-seated
15	olive-alpilles	jan-six	jugglers
16	olive-trees	magn-glass	lady-piano
17	orchard-bloom-poplars	meditation	laundress
18	orchard-plum-trees	mill	loge
19	poppies	music-party	lucie-berard
20	red-vineyard	nicolaes-tulp	near-lake
21	reminiscences	old-man	fournaise
22	road-menders	ostrich	horsewoman
23	roulin	potiphar	meadow
24	self-1	prodigal-son	moulin-galette
25	self-2	raising-lazarus	nini
26	self-easel	.1640	parapluies
27	self-gauguin	.1661	premiere-sortie
28	self-orsay	.1669	promenade
29	self-whitney	.night-watch	ride
30	skull-cigarette	return-prodigal-son	romain-lacaux
31	sun-cloud	ruts	sisley-wife
32	threatening-skies	samson	women
33	trees-asylum	scholar	seashore
34	trees-ivy-asylum	self-1629	seated-bather
35	village-stairs	self-1634	sewing
36	wheat-field	self-1660	sisley
37	wheat-rising-sun	slaughtered-ox	swing
38	willows	staalmeesters	terrace
39	peasant	stofells	watercan
40	woman-arles	tobias	woman-veil

Lithology Discrimination Using Seismic Elastic Attributes: A Genetic Fuzzy Classifier Approach

Eric da S. Praxedes, Adriano S. Koshiyama, Douglas M. Dias, Marley M. B. R. Vellasco and Marco A. C. Pacheco
Pontifical Catholic University of Rio de Janeiro
Dept. of Electrical Engineering
Rio de Janeiro, Brazil
[praxedes,adriano,douglasm,marley,marco]@ele.puc-rio.br

Elita S. Abreu
University of Houston
Dept. of Earth and Atmospheric Sciences
Houston, TX, United States of America
elitadeabreu@gmail.com

ABSTRACT

One of the most important issues in oil & gas industry is the lithological identification. Lithology is the macroscopic description of the physical characteristics of a rock. This work proposes a new methodology for lithological discrimination, using GPF-CLASS model (Genetic Programming for Fuzzy Classification) a Genetic Fuzzy System based on Multi-Gene Genetic Programming. The main advantage of our approach is the possibility to identify, through seismic patterns, the rock types in new regions without requiring opening wells. Thus, we seek for a reliable model that provides two flexibilities for the experts: evaluate the membership degree of a seismic pattern to the several rock types and the chance to analyze at linguistic level the model output. Therefore, the final tool must afford knowledge discovery and support to the decision maker. Also, we evaluate other 7 classification models (from statistics and computational intelligence), using a database from a well located in Brazilian coast. The results demonstrate the potentialities of GPF-CLASS model when comparing to other classifiers.

Categories and Subject Descriptors

I.2.1 [**Computing Methodologies**]: Artificial Intelligence—*Application and Expert Systems*

General Terms

Experimentation

Keywords

Oil & Gas Industry, Fuzzy Classification Systems, Genetic Programming

GECCO'14, July 12–16, Vancouver, BC, Canada.

http://dx.doi.org/10.1145/2576768.2598319 .

1. INTRODUCTION

One of the most important activities in the oil & gas industry is the lithological identification. Lithology is the macroscopic description of the physical characteristics of a rock such as color, texture, grain size, and mineral content [27, 30] Based on this description, and knowing the location of each type of rock in the well, it is possible to infer where are the three principal formations necessary for the occurrence of a petroleum system: source rock, seal/trap and, reservoir.

One of the main sources of information to support the lithological identification is the well logs. Well logs consists of detailed records of the geological formations through physical measurements collected by tools taken downhole into the well. Since logging tools measure properties at subsurface, their records are intrinsically correlated with geological properties [8].

Traditionally, statistical techniques are used to provide lithological identification by studying the logs. A common used technique is the discriminant analysis [5]. More recently, computational intelligence techniques have been used with relative success, such as Neural Networks, Support Vector Machine and Fuzzy Inference Systems [24, 26, 20, 25]. However, in most studies, the logs used in lithological identification, such as gamma ray, neutron porosity and resistivity, can just be directly obtained from the wells. Outside the wells, the only available records from the subsurface are volumes with attributes derived from seismic survey, such as amplitude, phase and impedance.

In order to apply lithological identification models outside the wells, it is necessary to correlate characteristics present in the wells with the seismic data. Wells where the lithology is known from conventional logs can be used to generate and train models as well to assess its accuracy. These models can be applied on seismic volumes and the quality of its result is evaluated by a geologist or geophysicist.

However, these models should provide not just more accuracy than the standard approach (Linear Discriminant Analysis) but also a robust geological interpretation of the results. Models based on the use of Genetic Fuzzy Systems [7, 13], have been applied with success once results have shown accuracy and good understanding of the linguistic classifications to the users.

This work proposes a new methodology for lithological discrimination, using GPF-CLASS model (Genetic Programming Fuzzy Inference System) a Genetic Fuzzy System based on Multi-Gene Genetic Programming. The main advantage of our approach is the possibility to identify, through seismic patterns, the rock types in new regions without well control. The GPF-CLASS (Genetic Programming for Fuzzy Classification) model was chosen due to its good results in a benchmark set, compared to other Fuzzy-Genetic Systems present in the literature [18]. We also compare its results with statistical and computational intelligence techniques.

This paper is organized as follows: the next section describes notions of rock physics and presents in detail the problem addressed. Section 3 provides the GPF-CLASS model methodology suitable for the classification problem set out in Section 2. Section 4 talks about other classification models, evaluation metrics, experimental procedure and the results and discussions. Finally, Section 5 presents conclusions and future work.

2. UNDERSTANDING ROCK PHYSICS AND PROBLEM ADDRESSED

Rock physics theory is the geophysics area which provides relationships between elastic seismic attributes, measured from the surface of the Earth, well-logs or in the laboratory data, with the petrophysical properties of rocks [1]. It provides understanding and theoretical/empirical models to improve the characterization based on elastic data.

The sensitivity of seismic signatures to the reservoirs parameters has been known for many years. Improvements on acquisition and data processing requires a more quantitative interpretation in order to detect hydrocarbons, reservoir characterization and monitoring. Empirical equations have been published by several authors relating petrophysical properties with elastic attributes in a quantitative way. An example is Han equations [11], which relate compressional and shear velocity to the volume of clay and the porosity.

Among seismic elastic attributes, one of the most used is the acoustic impedance, both compressional (IP) and shear (IS). Impedance is defined as the product of density and velocity (compressional or shear) in a medium [29] and can be calculated from laboratory measurements, well logs and seismic volumes. In the well, it can be calculated by the product of the density log and the transit time logs which measures the time of compressional and shear transit. On seismic volumes it is possible to produce a volume of impedance values, obtained from a process called seismic elastic inversion that uses the Aki-Richards equation and angle-gathers [1]. Using the compressional and shear impedances, it is possible to create a model based well data to classify lithology and extrapolate it to the seismic data.

For this work, the data came from a well located in the eastern Brazilian margin. The stratigraphical unit chosen for this study was a mixed carbonate-siliciclastic system of the Albian age. The lithology found in this well was interpreted by an expert geologist, who has used the conventional well logs like gamma ray, density, photoelectric factor and compressional sonic, in addition to the petrographic description of sidewall cores thin sections and image logs (resistive and acoustic). In this lithological interpretation seven different types of rocks were found as follows: sandstone, carbonate sandstone, calcarenite, mudstone, packstone, sandy claystone and shale. The seven rock types were grouped

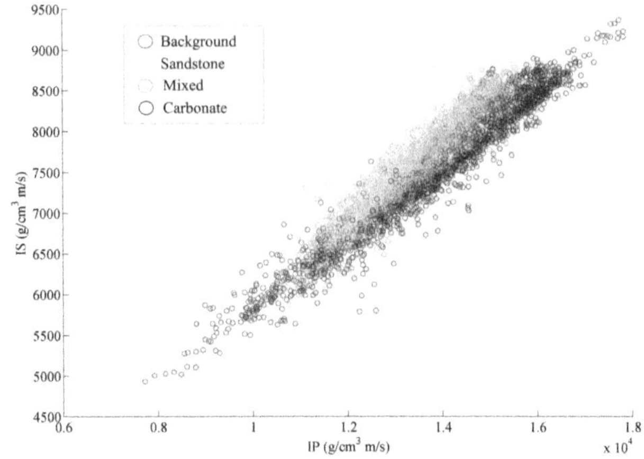

Figure 1: Relationship between IP and IS and the rock class types.

into four different classes since the characteristics that distinguish the rocks of the same class are not detected in the seismic scale. Table 1 presents the groups performed to create the four classes.

To perform this classification, in addition to direct values of the impedances (IP and IS), two others seismic attributes calculated from them were used. The first attribute is the difference impedance (IP - IS), and the second is the Poisson's ratio (PR): $PR = \frac{(IP^2 - 2IS^2)}{2(IP^2 - IS^2)}$. These attributes were choosen based on the study of the rock physics which indicated that both are good lithological discriminators [11, 6]

Figure 1 shows a graphic between IP and IS of the well data. The four classes are identified by the colors yellow = Sandstone, red = Background, light blue = Mixed and dark blue = Carbonate. It can be seen that when the two impedances are used together, all the data are located along a narrow and extremely simple trend in accordance with previous work [11, 6], difficulting the identification of the different lithology..

The goal of this work is to obtain a model that can infer, from the behavior of IP, IS, IS-IP and RP features, the lithologies in question: Sandstone, Mixed, Carbonate or Background, so we can extrapolate it to the seismic volumes. The great advantage of GPF-CLASS, to be described in the next section, is the possibility to offer such interpretation at linguistic level and still allow the specialist to decide the type of rock from the degree of relevance of a seismic

Table 1: Types of lithology and grouping made in the well under examination.

Lithology	Class	Patterns	Freq.
Sandstone	Sandstone	1991	33.21%
Carbonate Sandstone	Mixed	1803	30.08%
Calcarenite Mudstone Packstone	Carbonate	1480	24.69%
Sandy Claystone Shale	Background	721	12.03%

sample. The next section presents the GPF-CLASS model applied to the problem addressed.

3. GPF-CLASS MODEL

This section presents GPF-CLASS model [18]. We primarily describe the main concepts regarding Multi-Gene Genetic Programming [28, 14] Then, we present GPF-CLASS model focused on lithology discrimination task.

3.1 Multi-Gene Genetic Programming

Genetic Programming (GP) [19, 23] belongs to the Evolutionary Computation field. Typically, GP uses a population of individuals, each denoted by a tree structure that codifies a mathematical equation, which describes the relationship between the output Y and a set of input terminals X_j ($j = 1, ..., J$) (features, in the current work). Multi-Gene Genetic Programming (MGGP) [28, 14, 10] denotes an individual as a structure of trees, also called genes, that receives X_j and tries to predict Y (Figure 2). Each individual is described by a set of functions of size D ($d = 1, ..., D$).

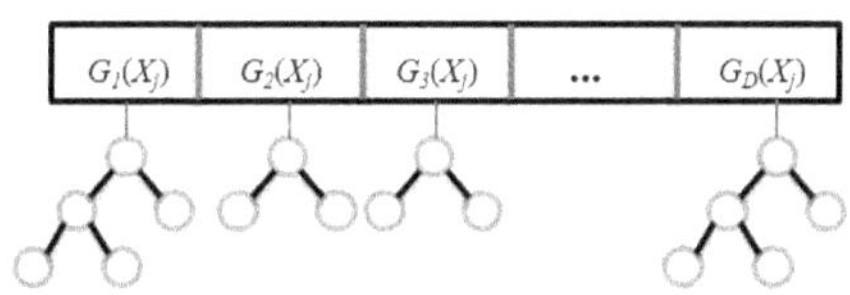

Figure 2: Example of a multi-gene individual.

In relation to the genetic operators, the mutation operation in MGGP is similar to that in GP. As for crossover, the level at which the operation is performed must be specified: it is possible to apply crossover at high and low levels. Figure 3 presents a multi-gene individual with five equations ($D = 5$) accomplishing a low-level crossover, while Figure 4 exhibit the mutation operation.

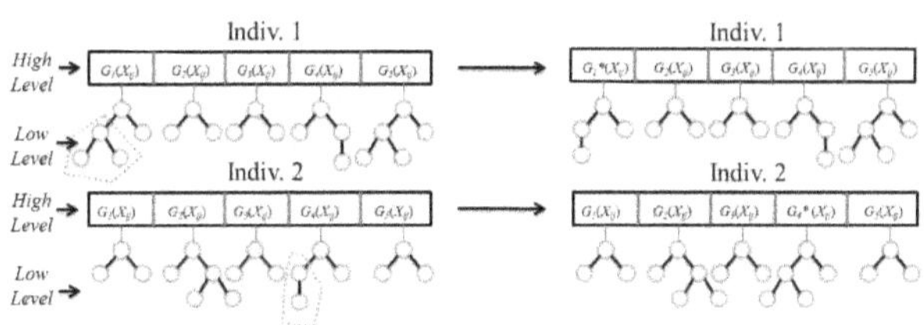

Figure 3: Low-level crossover in a individual.

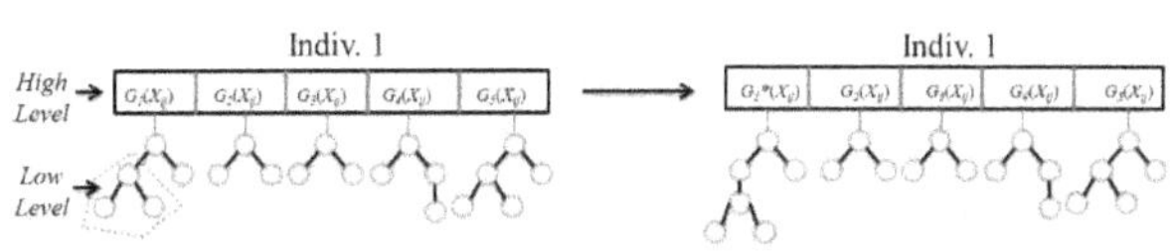

Figure 4: Mutation operation in a individual.

The low-level is the space where it is possible to manipulate the structures (terminals and functions) of equations presented in an individual. In this case, both operations are similar to those performed in GP.

The high-level, on the other hand, is the space where the expressions can be manipulated in a macro way. An example of high level crossover is displayed in Figure 5. As can be observed, from two random cutting points (black dashed line), the equations were switched from an individual to the other (violet dashed line). This cutting point can be symmetric, ie., exchanging the same number of equations between individuals, or asymmetric. Intuitively, the resulting output is more affected by high-level crossover than by low-level crossover or mutation.

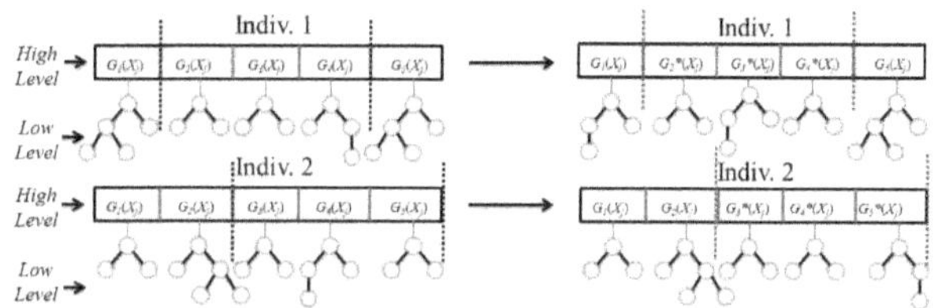

Figure 5: High-level crossover in a multi-gene individual.

3.2 Model Description

GPF-CLASS model has four sections: fuzzification, inference, decision and evaluation. The inference procedure begins with the fuzzification of the seismic patterns. After that, the functions of each individual are synthesized through MGGP and a decision is made about which class a seismic pattern belongs to. This solution is evaluated and the process is repeated until a solution that fulfills a certain criterion is achieved. The diagram below (Figure 6) illustrates the GPF-CLASS model.

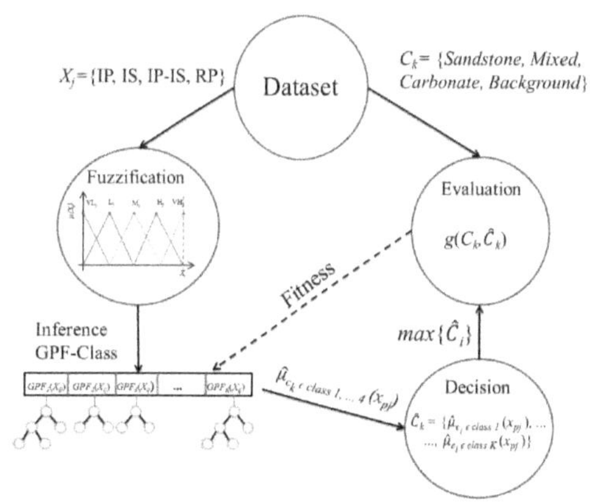

Figure 6: GPF-CLASS model.

3.2.1 *Fuzzification*

Consider X_1, X_2, X_3 and X_4 features that represent IP, IS, IP-IS and RP, respectively. Thus, let $C_k = \{Sandstone, Mixed, Carbonate, Background\}$ the set of class labels. Then, X_j denotes the j-th feature ($j = 1,2,3,4$) and C_k the k-th class ($k = 1,2,3,4$). Also, consider the presence of n patterns in the data base ($p = 1, ..., n$).

Fuzzification procedure consists on mapping each $x_{pj} \in X_j$ in membership degrees to each fuzzy set of X_j. In standard GPF-CLASS model, these fuzzy sets are displayed uniformly and 2-juxtapose (strong fuzzy partition), as exhibited in Figure 7. Each linguistic term assigned to each fuzzy set is denoted by: VL = Very Little, L = Little, M = Mean, H = High, VH = Very High.

The shape outlined is very common in the fuzzy systems literature [4, 2] From the expert point of view, after several discussions about its linguistic properties, this format was choose to use in GPF-CLASS model.

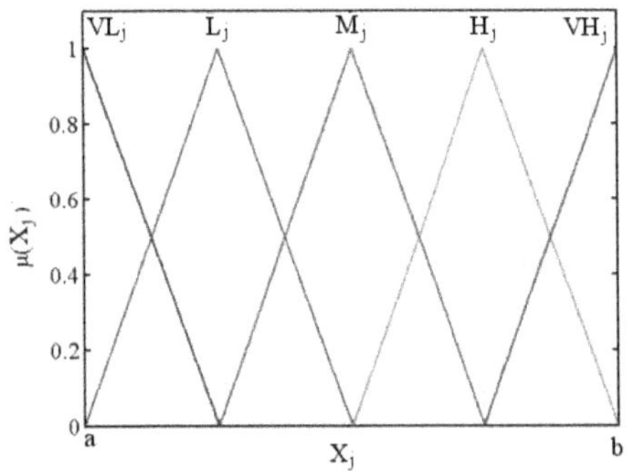

Figure 7: Strong fuzzy partition for each X_j

Therefore, let $A_{mj} = \{VL_j, L_j, M_j, H_j, VH_j\}$ the collection of fuzzy sets ($m = 1,, 5$) associated to each j-th feature. For example, A_{11} refers to VL of IP attribute. Consequently, $\mu_{A_{mj}}(x_{pj})$ represent the membership degree of p-th pattern of j-th feature in m-th fuzzy set.

3.2.2 *Inference GPF-CLASS and Decision*

GPF-CLASS establishes how the membership functions of the features are associated with the output class. In other words, how many and with which sense the linguistic concepts of each feature are linked to a class label. There are different representations for binary and multi-class classification. In our case of multiple classes, the GPF-CLASS can be described by:

$$C_1 = f_1(\mu_{A_{mj}}(x_{pj})) + \varepsilon_1 = \mu_{C\in 1}(x_{pj}) + \varepsilon_1 \quad (1)$$
$$C_2 = f_2(\mu_{A_{mj}}(x_{pj})) + \varepsilon_2 = \mu_{C\in 2}(x_{pj}) + \varepsilon_2 \quad (2)$$
$$C_3 = f_3(\mu_{A_{mj}}(x_{pj})) + \varepsilon_3 = \mu_{C\in 3}(x_{pj}) + \varepsilon_3 \quad (3)$$
$$C_4 = f_4(\mu_{A_{mj}}(x_{pj})) + \varepsilon_4 = \mu_{C\in 4}(x_{pj}) + \varepsilon_4 \quad (4)$$

where C_k is a binary value: $C_k = 1$ when C is class k, and $C_k = 0$ otherwise, $\mu_{C\in k}(x_{pj})$ is the predicted membership degree of x_{pj} to class k and ε_k is the model classification error. The f_k are mapping functions to be found by MGGP. As $\mu_{C\in k}(x_{pj}) \in [0, 1]$, define $\hat{C}_k = \{\mu_{C\in 1}(x_{pj}), \mu_{C\in 2}(x_{pj}), \mu_{C\in 3}(x_{pj}), \mu_{C\in 4}(x_{pj})\}$. The input pattern class is given by max($\hat{C}_k$), ie., the pattern belongs to the class to which it shows to be more compatible. In case of $\mu_{C\in 1}(x_{pj}) = ... = \mu_{C\in 4}(x_{pj})$, the class is undefined and a heuristic can be applied to define to which class this pattern belongs (or a non-specific class may be simply imposed).

Considering the estimated $\hat{C}_k$ and observed classes C_k, the individual in MGGP population is evaluated by:

$$MPCE = \frac{\sum_p (|C_k - \hat{C}_k|)}{n} \quad (5)$$

where MPCE is the mean percentage classification error and n is the number of patterns in the database. The individual which best selects $\mu_{A_{mj}}(x_{pj})$ and fits the expression is the one that minimizes MPCE.

To establish f_k it is necessary to define a functional form and choose which membership function may remain in each mapping. This decision is complex, since it involves many possibilities regarding functional form (linear or nonlinear; identical for all equations or different for some) and the selection of membership functions (which, how many and to which output mappings fk they may be linked to). Besides, the compromise between accuracy and interpretability must not be forgotten. Since an individual in MGGP represents a set of programs, it is possible to assume that each individual owns a number of programs to produce a number of outputs necessary to fill the class labels. In case of four output classes, four trees per individual are needed, with symmetric high-level crossover and initialization of strictly four programs in order to create always a valid solution.

To synthesize equation (1-4), for example, consider the sets of terminals (membership functions) and function set (fuzzy operators) shown in Table 2.

Table 2: Terminals and Function Set to GPF-CLASS model.

Terminals	Function Set
$\mu_{VL_j}(x_{pj})$,$\mu_{L_j}(x_{pj})$, $\mu_{M_j}(x_{pj})$, $\mu_{H_j}(x_{pj})$ and $\mu_{VH_j}(x_{pj})$	max, times and classical negation operator

The terminals set is represented by five membership functions for each feature (a total of 20 inputs) and the function set consists of several fuzzy logic operators, such as max (t-conorm), times (t-norm) and a classical negation operator [17]. These type of operators are special, because they preserve the interpretability and the constraint that $\mu_{C\in k}(x_{pj}) \in [0, 1]$. Based on these operators, each membership function is combined, in order to best describe the lithology type using seismic features.

Based on these descriptions, next section describes the case studies and evaluates the results.

4. CASE STUDIES

4.1 Experiment Description

In addition to GPF-CLASS model, we fitted statistical models, such as Linear Discriminant Analysis, and computational intelligence techniques. Table 3 presents each classifier and also their parameters. It's worth to mention that the choice of each parameter was based on several preliminary tests, in order to select the best configuration. Also, it has been applied a Pittsburgh-type Genetic Fuzzy Rule Based Classification System (Pitt-GFS) based on GP [3]. In order to perform an almost fair comparison with GPF-CLASS, we considered the same GP parameters and number of membership functions for every feature.

It has been gathered 5995 patterns from the oil well under analysis (Table 1). In order to verify each classifier quality, it has been applied a 10-fold cross validation procedure (10-fold-cv), placing in each fold a total of 5394 train and 601 test patterns. We used two performance measures: classification accuracy and precision [9]. The great advantage of precision is due to the account of the classes imbalance

Table 3: **Classifiers and parameters used.**

Model	Parameters
GPF-CLASS	Table 4
Pittsburgh type Genetic-Fuzzy System (Pitt-GFS) [3]	Table 4
Naive Bayes (NB) [22]	-
KNN [22]	2-nearest-neighbour, euclidean distance
Classification Tree (CART) [22]	-
Linear Discriminant Analysis (DISC) [15]	-
Multi-Gene Genetic Programming	Table 4
Multi-Layer Perceptron (MLP) [12]	One hidden layer, sigmoid transfer function (hidden) and step function (output), 10 neurons

(Sandstone have more patterns than Background, for example) and, therefore, penalize classifiers that favors the lithology with more patterns. All results are an average of 3 executions.

Table 4 exhibits parameters set in GPF-CLASS model. In case of MGGP the procedure is similar of [16], relative to the treatment of multi-class problem as binary classes. In this sense MGGP is run 4 times, splitting the number of evaluations and producing in each execution a discriminant function for each class label. Finally, all discriminant functions are assembled and the test patterns are classified. All analysis were performed in MATLAB R2010a [21].

Table 4: Main Configuration of Genetic Programming based models.

Parameters	Values
Pop Size	100
Generations	200
Tournament Size	5
High level Crossover Rate*	50%
Low level Crossover Rate	80%
Mutation Rate	20 %
Elitism Rate	2 %
Maximum tree depth	9

* Only applied to MGGP based models.

4.2 Results and Discussions

Table 5 exhibits the results regarding to the accuracy of all classifiers. It can be seen that GPF-CLASS obtained the higher accuracy in average, about 4 % more than the second best model (MLP). In comparison, Pitt-GFS achieved worst results than GPF-CLASS and NB method. The standard approach - DISC - performed poorly when compared to GPF-CLASS. Table 6 present the precision of each model. Still, GPF-CLASS obtained the best results, providing 6.98% more classification precision than NB, the second best classifier in this case.

When compared to the expert Linear Discriminant Analysis, the results of GPF-CLASS showed two important properties: better results when taking account the number of patterns correct labeled (accuracy) and correctly weighing its efforts to maximize the matched patterns for distinct classes (precision). It is worth to mention that NB approach, which demands little computational effort, also achieved competitive results and could be useful in situations that require fast learning and decision processing.

Both results indicate that GPF-CLASS behaves well in situations that occur low imbalance of classes, when comparing to other standard classifiers. An explanation for this can be found when analyzing the Fuzzy Rule Base (Table 7) on Figure 1. For example, consider the Background lithology. It can be seen that the first rule, R1, states that if IS is little (L) then the seismic pattern belongs to Background. Also, R2 and R3 when jointly evaluated state that if IP is little and IS is little, with IP-IS is medium to high, then the seismic pattern belongs to Background. In summary, we can see that R1 and R2 delimit the region that many patterns from Background appear: little values of IP and IS (Figure 1); R3 cooperates with R2 in order to focus more on patterns that reside on that region, and some near of IP and IS medium values. Through this best description of the discriminant region, GPF-CLASS can successfully label patterns concerned to classes with few patterns.

Figure 8 provides the discriminant region of GPF-CLASS best accuracy model. It can be seen that the seismic pattern related to the background lithology belongs to medium to low values of IP and IS . When a seismic pattern has higher values of IP and IS, accordingly to GPF-CLASS, it is labeled as Carbonate lithology. Finally, suppose a seismic pattern with IP about 14000 $g/cm^3m/s$ and IS of 8200 $g/cm^3m/s$. After computing IP-IS and PR, we can evaluate using GPF-CLASS model that the membership degree of this seismic pattern to each lithology is: Background=0, Carbonate=0.02, Sandstone = 0.6 and Mixed = 0.398. An expert can interpret this result in two ways: (i) define the pattern as Sandstone, using the class most compatible; (ii) states that the pattern have about 60.00% of Sandstone, 39.80% of Mixed and traces of Carbonate (maybe occurred by noise measurements), due to the lack of homogeneity of the seismic pattern (e.g., big areas, or with distinct topologies). These two types of interpretability are very useful and are possible by applying a Fuzzy Classifier System, in this case GPF-CLASS model.

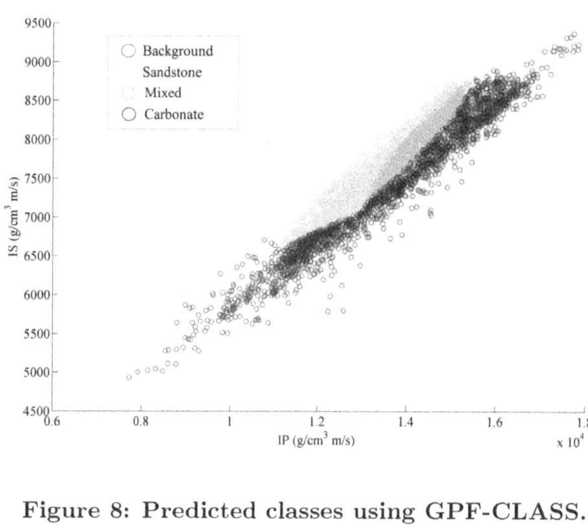

Figure 8: Predicted classes using GPF-CLASS.

5. CONCLUSIONS

This work presented an investigation of lithology discrimination using seismic patterns. We applied several classifiers, such as statistical based (e.g., Naive Bayes, Linear Discriminant Analysis) and computational intelligence techniques (Multilayer Perceptron, Genetic Fuzzy Rule Based Classification System, just to name a few). We found that Genetic Programming for Fuzzy Classification (GPF-CLASS) model performed better than others methods. Due to the imbalanced classes, it has been provided an insight of why GPF-CLASS obtained a fair performance, using the Fuzzy Rule Base for this task. Finally, two distincts interpretation of the results were presented.

Future works should explore preprocessing techniques, such as oversampling/undersampling methods to reduce the effects of the imbalanced distribution of patterns between the classes. Other approach is to use ensemble classifiers to improve the overall performance for this task, and evaluate the methodology proposed in this work to wells in others sites.

6. REFERENCES

[1] P. Avseth and T. M. G. Mavko. *Quantitative Seismic Interpretation: Applying Rock Physics Tools to Reduce Interpretation Risk.* Cambridge University Press, Cambridge, 2005.

[2] E. K. Aydogan, I. Karaoglan, and P. M. Pardalos. hga: Hybrid genetic algorithm in fuzzy rule-based classification systems for high-dimensional problems. *Applied Soft Computing*, 12(2):800–806, 2012.

[3] A. Bastian. Identifying fuzzy models utilizing genetic programming. *Fuzzy Sets and Systems*, 113(3):333–350, 2000.

[4] F. J. Berlanga, A. J. Rivera, M. J. del Jesús, and F. Herrera. Gp-coach: Genetic programming-based learning of compact and accurate fuzzy rule-based classification systems for high-dimensional problems. *Information Sciences*, 180(8):1183–1200, 2010.

[5] J. M. Busch, W. G. Fortney, and L. N. Berry. Determination of lithology from well logs by statistical analysis. *Society of Petroleum Engineers Formation Evaluation*, 2:412–418, 1987.

[6] J. P. Castagna, M. L. Batzle, and T. K. Kan. Rock physics: The link between rock properties and avo response. *Investigations in Geophysics*, 8:135–171, 1993.

[7] O. Córdon, F. Herrera, F. Hoffmann, and L. Magdalena. *Genetic Fuzzy Systems: Evolutionary Tuning and Learning of Fuzzy Knowledge Bases.* World Scientific, Singapore, 2001.

[8] J. H. Doveton. The geological application of wireline logs: A keynote perspective. *AAPG Methods in Exploration*, 13:115–122, 2002.

[9] T. Fawcett. An introduction to roc analysis. *Pattern recognition letters*, 27(8):861–874, 2006.

[10] A. H. Gandomi and A. H. Alavi. A new multi-gene genetic programming approach to nonlinear system modeling. part i: materials and structural engineering problems. *Neural Computing and Applications*, 21(1):171–187, 2012.

[11] D. Han. *Effects of porosity and clay content on acoustic properties of sandstone and unconsolidated sediments.* PhD Thesis, Stanford University, Stanford.

[12] S. Haykin. *Neural networks and learning machines.* Prentice-Hall, New York, 2009.

[13] F. Herrera. Genetic fuzzy systems: taxonomy, current research trends and prospects. *Evolutionary Intelligence*, 1(1):27–46, 2008.

[14] M. Hinchliffe, H. Hiden, B. McKay, M. Willis, M. Tham, and G. Barton. Modelling chemical process systems using a multi-gene. In *Late Breaking Papers at the Genetic Programming*, pages 56–65, Stanford, June 1996. Stanford University.

[15] R. A. Johnson and D. W. Wichern. *Applied multivariate statistical analysis.* Prentice-Hall, New Jersey, 5 edition, 2002.

[16] J. K. Kishore, L. M. Patnaik, V. Mani, and V. K. Agrawal. Application of genetic programming for multicategory pattern classification. *IEEE Trans. Evol. Comput.*, 4(3):242âĂŞ258, 2000.

[17] G. J. Klir and B. Yuan. *Fuzzy sets and fuzzy logic.* Prentice Hall, New Jersey, 1995.

[18] A. Koshiyama, T. Escovedo, D. M. M. Vellasco, and R. Tanscheit. Gpf-class: A genetic fuzzy model for classification. In *Congress on Evolutionary Computation*, pages 3275–3282, Cancun, June 2013. IEEE.

[19] W. B. Langdon and R. Poli. *Foundations of genetic programming.* Springer, Heidelberg, 2002.

[20] V. R. C. Leite. *An Classification Analysis of Lithology using SVM, MLP and Ensemble Methods.* Master Thesis. Department of Informatics, Pontifical University of Rio de Janeiro, 2012.

[21] MATLAB. *MATLAB 7.10.0 (R2010a).* The MathWorks Inc., Massachusetts, 2010.

[22] T. M. Mitchell. *Machine learning.* McGraw Hill, Burr Ridge, 1997.

[23] R. Poli, W. B. Langdon, and N. F. McPhee. *A field guide to genetic programming.* Lulu, Raleigh, 2008.

[24] S. J. Rogers, J. H. Fang, C. L. Karr, and D. A. Stanley. Determination of lithology from well logs using a neural network. *AAPG Bulletin*, 76(5):731–739, 1992.

[25] M. M. Saggaf and E. L. Nebrija. A fuzzy logic approach for the estimation of facies from wire-line logs. *AAPG Bulletin*, 87(7):1223–1240, 2003.

[26] R. Santos, M. Vellasco, F. Artola, and S. D. Fontoura. Neural net ensembles for lithology recognition. In T. Windeatt and F. Roli, editors, *Multiple Classifier Systems.* 2003.

[27] Schlumberger. *Schlumberger Oilfield Glossary.* http://www.glossary.oilfield.slb.com/Display.cfm?Term=lithology, 2013.

[28] D. Searson, M. Willis, and G. Montague. Coevolution of nonlinear pls model components. *Journal of Chemometrics*, 21(12):592–603, 2007.

[29] W. M. Telford, L. P. Geldart, and R. E. Sheriff. *Applied Geophysics.* Cambridge University Press, Cambridge, 2 edition, 2005.

[30] U.S. Geological Survey. *Earthquake Glossary.* http://earthquake.usgs.gov/learn/glossary/?term=lithology, 2013.

Table 5: **Average accuracy of three runs by cross-validation folder in test phase.**

Fold	MLP	Pitt-GFS	GPF-CLASS	MGGP	DISC	NB	CART	KNN
I	69.11%	57.22%	69.17%	47.17%	61.00%	**69.50%**	46.83%	48.33%
II	66.33%	57.15%	**68.73%**	57.48%	57.26%	57.76%	52.25%	53.92%
III	55.87%	54.09%	55.98%	44.69%	44.07%	**60.43%**	44.74%	45.74%
IV	60.60%	59.04%	63.44%	53.20%	46.74%	**69.95%**	45.58%	41.90%
V	51.53%	54.42%	**68.78%**	54.65%	50.25%	68.61%	56.09%	53.26%
VI	**62.99%**	55.04%	61.83%	56.82%	61.10%	51.92%	44.91%	46.91%
VII	46.52%	34.17%	**65.55%**	50.81%	40.57%	35.06%	43.57%	45.58%
VIII	51.78%	**52.06%**	49.83%	47.56%	46.67%	46.50%	41.17%	47.00%
IX	54.44%	54.22%	**58.50%**	58.22%	45.67%	51.33%	41.67%	45.67%
X	**57.79%**	49.81%	55.57%	52.63%	39.43%	46.26%	44.43%	48.25%
Average	57.70%	52.72%	**61.74%**	52.32%	49.28%	55.73%	46.12%	47.66%

Table 6: **Average precision of three runs by cross-validation folder in test phase.**

Fold	MLP	Pitt-GFS	GPF-CLASS	MGGP	DISC	NB	CART	KNN
I	60.16%	47.95%	**64.10%**	44.66%	61.30%	61.38%	41.35%	44.23%
II	60.05%	54.64%	**66.66%**	49.73%	60.84%	53.63%	47.00%	49.62%
III	56.95%	53.65%	60.05%	38.49%	51.95%	**61.47%**	46.57%	47.90%
IV	58.20%	58.39%	65.39%	46.33%	54.11%	**70.26%**	45.97%	44.07%
V	43.67%	56.44%	**69.66%**	50.23%	55.69%	67.89%	57.84%	56.08%
VI	58.22%	51.65%	61.64%	50.08%	**63.16%**	51.00%	42.31%	45.85%
VII	43.47%	34.39%	**64.47%**	42.79%	46.62%	36.11%	40.45%	41.95%
VIII	49.23%	52.99%	52.21%	43.10%	**52.50%**	46.70%	38.71%	46.11%
IX	48.43%	49.69%	**54.49%**	50.16%	44.82%	47.49%	38.37%	41.22%
X	**50.43%**	44.19%	48.87%	46.94%	36.66%	41.73%	39.20%	43.41%
Average	52.88%	50.40%	**60.75%**	46.25%	52.77%	53.77%	43.78%	46.04%

Table 7: **Fuzzy Rule Base of the best individual of GPF-CLASS model.**

Rule	Antecedent	Consequent
R1	If IP is not L or M and IP-IS is H and PR is H	Sandstone
R2	If PR is not H	Sandstone
R3	If IP-IS is VH	Sandstone
R1	If IP is M and PR is H and IP-IS is not L or M	Mixed
R2	If IS is H and IP-IS is M or H or VH	Mixed
R1	If IS is VH and IP-IS is M	Carbonate
R2	If IP is H and PR is M	Carbonate
R3	If IS is H and PR is M	Carbonate
R4	If IP-IS is not M and PR is not H	Carbonate
R1	If IS is L	Background
R2	If IP is L and IP-IS is not M	Background
R3	If IP is not VH and IS is L and IP-IS is not VH	Background

Evolutionary Parameter Estimation for a Theory of Planned Behaviour Microsimulation of Alcohol Consumption Dynamics in an English Birth Cohort 2003 to 2010

Robin C. Purshouse
Department of Automatic Control & Systems Engineering
University of Sheffield
Sheffield, UK
r.purshouse@sheffield.ac.uk

Abdallah K. Ally
School of Health & Related Research
University of Sheffield
Sheffield, UK
a.k.ally@sheffield.ac.uk

Alan Brennan
School of Health & Related Research
University of Sheffield
Sheffield, UK
a.brennan@sheffield.ac.uk

Daniel Moyo
Department of Automatic Control & Systems Engineering
University of Sheffield
Sheffield, UK
d.moyo@sheffield.ac.uk

Paul Norman
Department of Psychology
University of Sheffield
Sheffield, UK
p.norman@sheffield.ac.uk

ABSTRACT

This paper presents a new real-world application of evolutionary computation: identifying parameterisations of a theory-driven model that can reproduce alcohol consumption dynamics observed in a population over time. Population alcohol consumption is a complex system, with multiple interactions between economic and social factors and drinking behaviours, the nature and importance of which are not well-understood. Prediction of time trends in consumption is therefore difficult, but essential for robust estimation of future changes in health-related consequences of drinking and for appraising the impact of interventions aimed at changing alcohol use in society. The paper describes a microsimulation approach in which an attitude-behaviour model, Theory of Planned Behaviour, is used to describe the frequency of drinking by individuals. Consumption dynamics in the simulation are driven by changes in the social roles of individuals over time (parenthood, partnership, and paid labour). An evolutionary optimizer is used to identify parameterisations of the Theory that can describe the observed changes in drinking frequency. Niching is incorporated to enable multiple possible parameterisations to be identified, each of which can accurately recreate history but potentially encode quite different future trends. The approach is demonstrated using evidence from the 1979-1985 birth cohort in England between 2003 and 2010.

GECCO'14, July 12–16, 2014, Vancouver, BC, Canada.
ACM 978-1-4503-2662-9/14/07.
http://dx.doi.org/10.1145/2576768.2598239.

Categories and Subject Descriptors

I.6 [**Simulation and Modeling**]: Model Validation and Analysis

General Terms

Experimentation

Keywords

Simulation optimization; Social science; Genetic algorithms; Multiple solutions / niching

1. INTRODUCTION

Alcohol consumption is regarded as a major public health issue internationally, with alcohol recognised as a risk factor across a wide range of diseases, including neuropsychiatric disorders, gastrointestinal disease and cancer, and both intentional and unintentional injuries. The World Health Organization estimates that 4.5% of the global burden of disease and injury in 2004 was attributable to alcohol [31]. As a result, policies that aim to reduce the harms caused by alcohol are under consideration in many jurisdictions, including population-level interventions to reduce the affordability of alcohol to consumers (such as introducing a floor price for alcoholic beverages), e.g. [28]. With an increasing societal demand for such interventions to be *evidence-based*, policymakers are increasingly commissioning mathematical models that aim to appraise the likely impact of policy options across a range of criteria, drawing on input assumptions based on relevant data – see, for example, [22].

The current state-of-the-art methods for model-based appraisal are grounded in neoclassical economics, where the effects of an intervention are estimated *ceteris paribus* – in other words, a static approach where the dynamics of the system are ignored [24]. However, since alcohol consumption in a society is a complex system driven by many causal

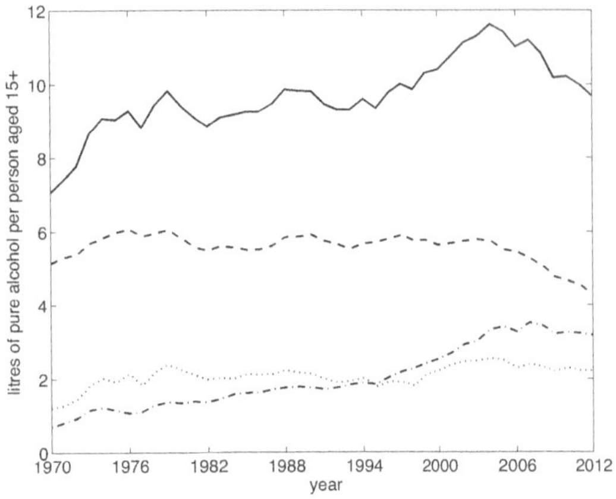

Figure 1: Alcohol consumption in the UK (litres of ethanol per person aged 15 and over): —— all alcohol; – – – beer and cider; – · – wine; · · · spirit and ready-to-drink [4].

factors [17, 25, 26], patterns of drinking in a population tend not to be in stasis, but rather to be varying in ways that are not fully understandable or predictable (see Figure 1, showing 42 years of change in estimated UK per capita consumption).

In this setting, the *ceteris paribus* assumptions of neoclassical models may lead to incorrect estimates for intervention effects, and also make validation of the models on observed data exceptionally difficult to perform. Such concerns have foundation, but have become increasingly distorted by ideologically-driven libertarian critics of population-level interventions, who now question the very basis of using models for prediction of policy effects, claiming for example, "There is no shame in saying that we simply do not know." [10, p. 12], despite the portfolio of evidence available for analysis.

To overcome these unconstructive yet influential critics of model-based appraisal, we need new methods that account for alcohol as a dynamic factor in a complex system, that are underpinned by theory that supports a causal argument, that can reproduce historical data and that provide credible intervals around predictions of future impacts. This is an agenda that has been recognised by sociologists for over 50 years, including the early cybernetics work on drivers of change (*morphogenesis*) and stasis (*morphostasis*) in social systems by Walter Buckley [5] and, more recently, the vision of British sociologist David Byrne:

> "...to identify historical dynamics of particular socio-spatial systems — with models of how such systems might have been different at this point in time — coupled with forward projections ... This is a new kind of 'social engineering science', a rational programme not of assertion based on absolute prediction, but of social action based on specification of the multiple but not limitless range of ... options ... We have the possibility of qualitative representations of alternative futures." [6, p. 166-7]

Despite the apparent strong potential of complex systems methods for modelling alcohol consumption dynamics, disappointingly little progress has been made to date. The few

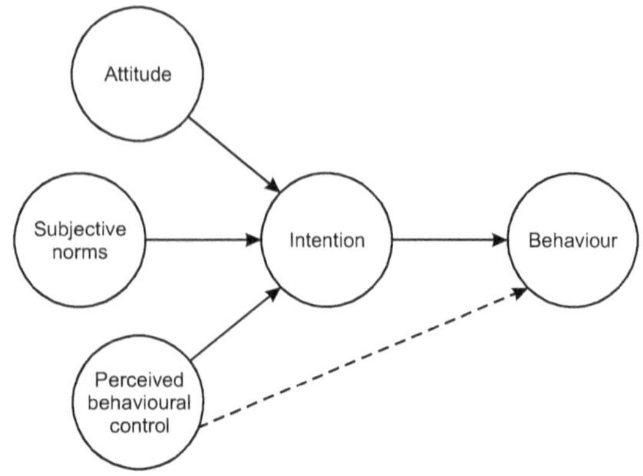

Figure 2: Schematic of the Theory of Planned Behaviour: —— link; – – – potential link.

studies available either lack an appropriate theoretical basis, lack any empirical validation of results, or suffer from both these issues [12, 13, 15].

In this paper, we set out a new approach to dynamic complex systems modelling of alcohol consumption that is underpinned by theory, is able to reproduce historical observations, and includes uncertainty estimates in its predictions.

The remainder of the paper is organised as follows. In Section 2, the proposed complex systems modelling methodology for the purposes of describing and predicting drinking behaviours over time is introduced. Results are shown in Section 3 for an exemplar population sub-group in England. Section 4 concludes with a comparison of the findings to existing knowledge, a discussion of strengths and limitations of the proposed methodology, and research directions.

2. METHOD

2.1 The Theory of Planned Behaviour

The theory selected for investigation in the study is the *Theory of Planned Behaviour* (TPB), which is a well established social psychological model [2]. The TPB has been previously used with some success in the prediction of alcohol consumption behaviours in field studies [7]. As shown in Figure 2, the theory posits that *behaviour* (for example, consuming alcohol or drinking to intoxication) is driven by the immediate antecedent *intention* (i.e. decision) to perform that behaviour, and that the intention is itself driven by three psychological factors:

- *Attitude* – The extent to which an individual positively values the behaviour to be predicted.
- *Subjective norms* – An individual's perception over whether other people who are important to her would approve or disapprove of her performing the behaviour.
- *Perceived behavioural control (PBC)* – An individual's perception of her level of control over engaging in the behaviour and her perceived ability to perform the behaviour. If an individual has accurate perceptions of actual control, PBC may also directly affect behaviour.

To construct a quantitative model of the TPB process, population weightings are assigned to indicate the relative importance of attitude, subjective norms and perceived behavioural control. When combined with individual data on these factors, the weightings produce an overall intention score. The score is compared to some threshold to determine whether or not the individual is predicted to perform the behaviour. In our implementation, we define behaviour as frequency of drinking an alcoholic drink on an ordinal categorical scale $y \in \{y_1 =$ `once a month`; $y_2 =$ `2-3 times a month`; y_3 = `once or twice a week`; $y_4 =$ `most days`$\}$. We then determine the probability that an individual i will engage in drinking category j according to a cumulative logit model [1]:

$$\text{logit}[P(Y \leq j \mid \mathbf{x}_i)] = \alpha_j - \boldsymbol{\beta}^{\mathrm{T}}\mathbf{x}_i \tag{1}$$

where $\boldsymbol{\beta}$ is a set of population weightings relating to both TPB variables and demographic variables. The values of these exogenous variables for each individual are denoted by $\mathbf{x}_i$. The α_j in (1) are intercepts that determine the logarithmic odds of an individual drinking at a level less than or equal to j for the reference case $\mathbf{x} = 0$.

The set of exogenous variables used in the model is constrained by data availability. In the study, we were restricted to secondary analysis of existing datasets; the most promising we found that had TPB-like measures together with an indication of drinking was the *Offending, Crime and Justice Survey* (OCJS) from 2003 [18]. This is a cross-sectional survey of the UK population aged 10-65 with a sample size of 6,892[1]. In our study, we restricted the analysis to persons aged 18 and over in England. We used the following data from OCJS to populate $\mathbf{x}$ for a baseline year in the model:

Attitude: The survey invites respondents to indicate the level to which they agree or disagree with the following statements related to alcohol consumption: "Drinking alcohol makes me feel relaxed"; "Drinking makes me forget my problems"; "Drinking makes me feel more friendly and outgoing"; "I drink to get drunk".

Subjective norms: Specific questions on an individual's perceptions of drinking norms are not included in the survey. Therefore, we use a question that invites respondents to indicate the types of people they usually drink with – i.e. "by self, parents, spouse/partner, girl/boyfriend, friends, siblings, other relatives, work colleagues, others" – and count the number of types selected by the respondent as a proxy measure of perceived social pressure to drink.

Perceived behavioural control: Again, specific questions on perceived control are not included in the survey. We use a question that invites respondents to indicate the types of location where they usually drink – i.e. "own home, other's home, pub/bar, nightclub/disco, restaurant, party, youth/community club, street/park/outdoors, elsewhere" – and count the number of types selected by the respondent as a proxy measure of facilitating factors that may increase perceptions of control. We also include a count of the number of social roles held by the individual, in terms of parenthood (having a dependent child aged under 18), partnership (cohabitation within a relationship) and paid labour (holding a salaried job).

[1]OCJS also has a major longitudinal component from 2003-2006, but this is limited to persons aged under 25, with no repeated measures on alcohol consumption or attitudes to drinking.

Demographics: Data is available on the sex and age of the respondent and the highest level of education attained. Responses to the latter are mapped on to the UK National Qualifications Framework (NQF) [21].

2.2 Microsimulation of the Theory

The TPB model is embedded within a wider microsimulation which aims to describe the dynamics of drinking in a population over time. The microsimulation is an agent-based model (ABM) designed according to object-oriented principles. In the ABM, agent objects represent 1,845 individual respondents to the OCJS survey and encode both TPB properties and demographics (i.e. an agent i encodes properties $\mathbf{x}_i$). Agent frequency of drinking is then evaluated using (1) to identify probabilities of being in each possible drinking state. The actual drinking state y is then selected via a uniform random number generator.

Dynamics are introduced into the microsimulation by allowing certain agent properties to vary over time – specifically, in this first version of the ABM, age and the three social roles (parenthood, partnership and paid labour). An annual update cycle, t, is chosen, such that (1) is extended to a dynamic form:

$$\text{logit}[P(Y(t) \leq j \mid \mathbf{x}_i(t))] = \alpha_j - \boldsymbol{\beta}^{\mathrm{T}}\mathbf{x}_i(t) \tag{2}$$

Social role trajectories are defined for each agent as exogenous inputs to the ABM. Trajectories are extracted from a separate longitudinal study, the *British Household Panel Survey* (BHPS) which has tracked the lives of over 10,000 individuals in Great Britain since 1991 [29]. Trajectories for parenthood, partnership and paid labour are constructed for 7,309 English individuals who were aged 18-65 in 2003, for the period 2003-2009 (the latest available data). A simple trend analysis is used to estimate trajectory development for 2010. At initialisation, agents in the ABM are matched to samples from the BHPS, enabling social role trajectories to be imputed. Agents are matched using sex, age, education and social role states at baseline.

The microsimulation is implemented in Python v2.7.5. Code is available from the authors.

2.3 Evolutionary Parameter Estimation

The TPB weights, $\boldsymbol{\beta}$, and thresholds, $\boldsymbol{\alpha}$, are estimated via an optimization process. In addition to identifying parameterisations that can reproduce observed time trends in the frequency of drinking, the optimizer is designed to find diversity in such parameterisations.

An evolutionary algorithm (EA) has been selected as the optimization engine since it can handle non-differentiable cost functions, provides an element of robustness to the stochastic nature of the ABM, and can be extended to include mechanisms that promote a search for diverse, high quality, solutions. The overall structure of the EA is given by:

$$\mathcal{P}[g+1] = s_s\left(v\left(s_v\left(\mathcal{P}[g]\right)\right), \mathcal{P}[g]\right) \tag{3}$$

where $\mathcal{P}[g]$ is the population of candidate solutions (i.e. a collection of particular configurations of $\boldsymbol{\alpha}$ and $\boldsymbol{\beta}$) at iteration g of the algorithm, s_v is the selection-for-variation operator, v is the variation process, and s_s is the selection-for-survival operator. The components of the EA are described in more detail below.

Table 1: EA parameter settings

Parameter	Setting
Population size, N	100
Generations, G	200
SBX crossover probability, p_c	1
SBX exchange probability, p_e	0.5
SBX crossover strength, η_c	15
Polynomial mutation probability, p_m	1/13
Polynomial mutation strength, η_m	20

2.3.1 *Representation*

Each candidate solution, $\mathbf{p}$, represents a particular choice of TPB parameters – $\mathbf{p} = [\beta_{a1}, \beta_{a2}, \beta_{a3}, \beta_{a4}, \beta_{n1}, \beta_{p1}, \beta_{p2}, \beta_{d1}, \beta_{d2}, \beta_{d3}, \alpha_1, \alpha_2, \alpha_3]$ – where the definition of each of the 13 components in the chromosome is given in Table 2. Each component is represented by a real number within the range $[-10, +10]$.

2.3.2 *Cost Function*

A time series of drinking frequency for 2003-2010 is extracted from a repeated cross-sectional survey, the *Health Survey for England* (HSE), which has included a variety of questions on drinking for individual respondents aged 16 and over in England since the inception of the survey in 1991 [20]. Sample size varies between 4,645 and 15,102, depending on year, over the analysis period. The time series is expressed as a sequence of counts, $c_{\text{actual},j}(t)$, of the number of HSE respondents in each drinking state y_j at time t.

To construct a cost function for a candidate solution, the HSE-derived time series $\mathbf{c}_{\text{actual}}$ is compared to the estimates of the same time series coming from the microsimulation when parameterised with $\mathbf{p}$. Here, the sequence of counts $c_{\text{model},j}(t)$ relate to the number of agents in each drinking state y_j over time t. For each year, the HSE and ABM counts are formulated as a contingency table, $\mathbf{C}(\mathbf{p}, t)$, as shown in (4). The similarity of the two distributions is then assessed using a chi-square test of independence, where the output used in the cost function is the chi-square test statistic, χ^2. The total cost for the candidate solution is obtained by taking the mean of the test results for every year of the time series, as shown in (5), where $T = 7$ is the total number of years of data.

$$\mathbf{C}(\mathbf{p}, t) = \begin{bmatrix} c_{\text{actual},j=1}(t) & \cdots & c_{\text{actual},j=J}(t) \\ c_{\text{model}(\mathbf{p}),j=1}(t) & \cdots & c_{\text{model}(\mathbf{p}),j=J}(t) \end{bmatrix} \quad (4)$$

$$e(\mathbf{p}) = \frac{1}{T}\sum_{t=1}^{T} \chi^2 \left[\mathbf{C}(\mathbf{p}, t)\right] \quad (5)$$

Since smaller values of χ^2 indicate better matches between the ABM results and the observed HSE data, the aim of the optimization process is to find solutions that minimize the total error, e, in (5).

2.3.3 *Selection-for-variation*

To convert cost function results into fitness values, the population is ranked according to e and fitnesses are assigned by interpolating exponentially between 1 (for the worst rank) and 10 (for the best rank). In order to promote diversity across the range of good parameterisations sought, we incorporate a well-known niching strategy – *fitness sharing* – into the selection process [14]. Since the performance of fitness sharing is known to be sensitive to the choice of its niche size parameter, we make use of an existing adaptive approach for setting this parameter based on guidelines for the analogous *Epanechnikov* kernel density estimator [11].

Once fitness values have been calculated, selection is performed using *stochastic universal sampling*, which is effective in minimizing undesirable sampling variation and biases [3].

2.3.4 *Variation*

Since the chosen representation is based entirely on real numbers, it is natural to adopt real-parameter variation operators for the study. We first apply a recombination operator and then a mutation operator to the candidate solutions selected for variation:

Simulated binary crossover (SBX): uses two selected solutions to produce two new solutions, drawing new values from a probability distribution [8]. The scale of the distribution is governed by the distance between the parent solutions; the shape is governed by a parameter η_c. The decision to apply SBX to parent solutions is made with probability p_c. Actual crossover operations are applied independently to each of the 13 components of the chromosome with probability 0.5. The resulting values for the components are exchanged between the new solutions with probability p_e.

Polynomial mutation: uses one selected solution to produce one new solution [9]. The decision to apply the operator is made at component-level with probability p_m. A new value is produced from a probability distribution centred over the parent value. The scale of mutation is determined by a parameter η_m.

2.3.5 *Selection-for-survival*

The use of fitness sharing in combination with quite disruptive variation operators indicates that convergence of the algorithm might be slow and this was confirmed through early empirical testing. To increase selective pressure, we therefore adopt an elitist approach for updating the population from the pool of parent, μ, and child, λ, solutions. Fitness is calculated on the pool $(\mu + \lambda)$ according to Section 2.3.3 and truncation selection is used to select the fittest N solutions to be carried forward to the next generation.

A summary of the EA configuration is given in Table 1. The algorithm was implemented in Matlab 7.7.0 (using a 64-bit floating-point encoding for the real number representation). Code is available from the authors.

3. RESULTS

In this paper we demonstrate modelling results for the 1979-1985 birth cohort in England (encoded by 220 agents), who were aged 18 to 24 in 2003, in terms of population-level frequency of drinking. In Section 3.1, we show results of the model fitting process over years 2003 to 2009. In Section 3.2, we show model predictions for 2010 and compare these to the observed drinking frequencies for that year.

3.1 Model Fitting

The convergence profile achieved by the EA is shown in Figure 3. Model fit in the early stages of the optimization process is very poor but rapid progress is made toward a level where the observed and modelled distributions should begin to look similar (a conventional chi-square test for in-

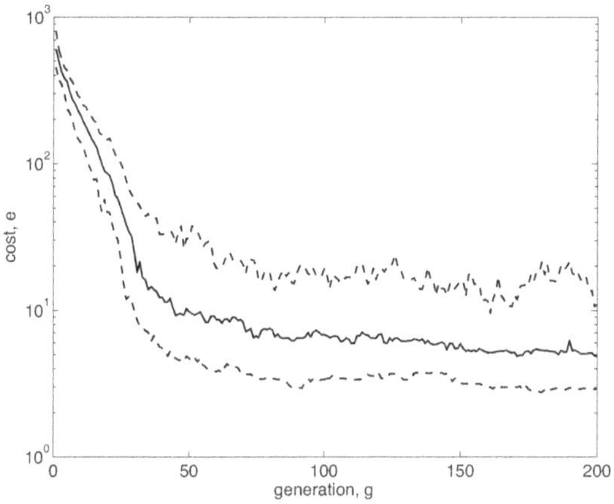

Figure 3: Convergence profile of the EA: showing 10% (broken), 50% (unbroken) and 90% (broken) deciles for $e(\mathbf{p} \in \mathcal{P}(g))$.

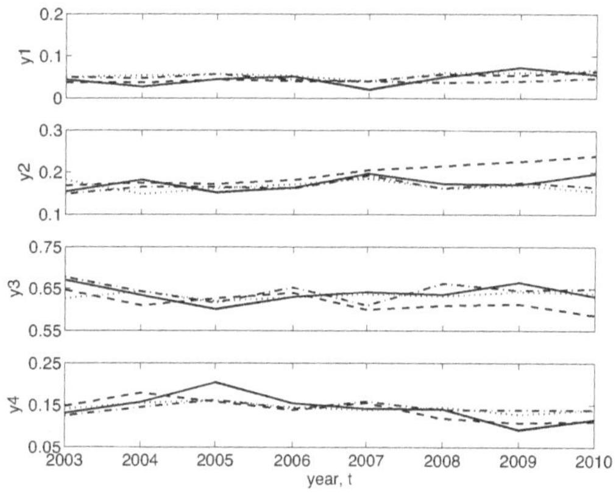

Figure 4: Time series for $\mathbf{y}(t)$ prevalence in the 1979-1985 birth cohort, covering optimization window 2003-2009 and validation year 2010: — HSE observations; ··· Model 1; – · – Model 2; – – – Model 3.

dependence at the 1% level would accept the null hypothesis for $\chi^2 \preccurlyeq 11.3$). Convergence continues at a slower rate from $g \approx 50$, with the effect of fitness sharing at maintaining diversity in the population apparent in the wide spread of performance even at later stages of the process.

In the remainder of this section, we focus on the three best candidate models (ranked by cost) returned from the optimizer at generation 200. The time series produced by each of these models is shown in Figure 4, alongside the observed time series from HSE. The main trend in frequency of drinking discernible from the HSE is the rise in the prevalence of "most days" drinking (y_4) to a peak of 20.4% in 2005, followed by a sustained reduction in prevalence to a low of 9.2% by 2009. The opposite trend occurred in the neighbouring category of "once or twice per week" drinking, with relatively static prevalences for the two categories of less frequent drinking. By inspection, all three models seem able to reproduce the observed dynamics reasonably well, particularly over the first half of the simulation window. However, none of the models capture the peak in "most days" drinking in 2005. Also, whilst Model 3 is best able to capture the decay in "most days" drinking up to 2009, it simultaneously over-predicts the prevalence in y_2 and under-predicts the prevalence in y_3 between 2007 and 2009.

The chromosomes and costs associated with the three best models are shown in Table 2. Whilst the models have similar costs (2.084, 2.322 and 2.540), they encompass quite a diverse range of cumulative logit model parameterisations, as encouraged by the niching strategy.

TPB parameters: In terms of attitudes, drinking for relaxation and social purposes (β_{a1} and β_{a3}) are consistently associated with increased odds of more frequent consumption across the models. The relative ability of these attitudes to change behaviours differs between models (e.g. for β_{a1}, a unit change in response will elicit the greatest change in drinking probabilities in Model 3 and the smallest change in Model 1). However there are fundamental differences between the models when it comes to the impact of using alcohol as a coping strategy (β_{a3}) or for hedonistic purposes (β_{a4}). In terms of subjective norms (β_{n1}), Model 1 and Model 2 associate increasing numbers of drinking partner types with increased drinking frequency, whilst Model 3 encodes the opposite. In terms of perceived behavioural control, only Model 3 indicates a positive association between number of drinking location types (β_{p2}) and drinking frequency (+2.116), which is arguably the direction of effect with the most face validity. All three models associate an increase in the number of social roles (β_{p2}) with decreased odds of engaging in more frequent drinking – with Model 3 placing the greatest emphasis on this parameter (-3.321).

Demographic parameters: Sex of respondent (β_{d1}) is identified as a key driver of drinking frequency across the three models. Whilst this result will not surprise many in the alcohol research community, the direction of effect in Model 2 (+6.015 for females) arguably lacks face validity since most of the evidence for alcohol participation levels in Western countries shows a positive association for males rather than females [31]. Increased age of respondent (β_{d2}) is associated with a small increase in odds of more frequent drinking across the models. In terms of highest educational qualification level gained, Models 1 and 3 suggest only very small (and positive) effects, whilst Model 2 suggests a strong negative association between higher educational qualifications and drinking frequency (-3.756).

Overall, despite having the loosest fit to the totality of historical data of the three models considered, Model 3 arguably has the most face validity in terms of the size and strength of the cumulative logit model coefficients. This model was also best able to reproduce the observed trend in "most days" drinking, but mistakenly over-emphasised changes across other drinking categories.

3.2 Prediction

In this section we consider the ability of the models fitted to data for 2003-2009 as predictors of macro-level drinking frequencies in 2010, denoted as $\hat{\mathbf{y}}(2010)$. Rather than focus on individual models and the face validity of their parameterisations, here we consider the final population of the EA as a whole and use it to generate a probability density estimate around the predicted variable, $\mathbf{f}(\hat{\mathbf{y}})$. Each candidate solution in $\mathcal{P}(200)$ has its own prediction for $\hat{\mathbf{y}}(2010)$. Focusing on the marginal distributions of $\mathbf{f}(\hat{\mathbf{y}})$, a histogram is constructed of the population of predictions. The contribution of each prediction to the probability density of the

Table 2: Theory of Planned Behaviour parameter estimates (values to 3 d.p.) for a microsimulation-embedded cumulative logit model (1) of drinking frequency y={`once a month;2-3 times a month;once or twice a week;most days`} for the 18-24 year old 2003 cohort in England

Type	Description	Parameter	Model 1	Model 2	Model 3
Attitude	Drinking alcohol makes me feel relaxed	β_{a1}	+0.321	+2.691	+3.584
	Drinking makes me forget my problems	β_{a2}	-2.903	-2.724	+1.710
	Drinking makes me feel more friendly and outgoing	β_{a3}	+0.445	+1.847	+0.710
	I drink to get drunk	β_{a4}	+4.882	-1.282	-4.140
	Coding for all attitudes: (0=disagree strongly,1=disagree slightly, 2=agree slightly,3=agree strongly)				
Subjective norms	Count of drinking partner types (0=1,1=2,...,8=9)	β_{n1}	+1.945	+3.372	-1.967
Perceived behavioural control	Count of drinking place types (0=1,1=2,...,8=9)	β_{p1}	-0.739	-1.480	+2.116
	Number of social roles (0,1,...,3)	β_{p2}	-0.779	-0.262	-3.321
Demographics	Sex (0=male,1=female)	β_{d1}	-7.744	+6.015	-5.940
	Age group (0=18-24,1=25-34,2=35-44,3=44-54,4=55+)	β_{d2}	+0.220	+0.095	+0.039
	Highest educational qualification *NFQ scales:* (0=entry/other,1=Level 1, 2=Level 2,3=Levels 3-5,4=Levels 6+)	β_{d3}	+0.026	-3.756	+0.040
logit intercepts	log-odds of y=once a month $\mid \mathbf{x}=0$	α_1	-9.929	-9.934	-9.951
	log-odds of $y\leq$2-3 times a month $\mid \mathbf{x}=0$	α_2	-4.060	-4.106	-2.827
	log-odds of $y\leq$once or twice per week $\mid \mathbf{x}=0$	α_3	+9.292	+9.894	+9.373
		Cost	2.084	2.322	2.540

histogram is weighted according to the ability of that model to recreate past events. Specifically, the weighting is taken as the p-value for independence between observed and modelled distributions using an average χ^2 for the time series – i.e. using Equation 5. Results are plotted in Figure 5, where the histogram has been smoothed using a normal kernel function.

The HSE observations for 2010 can be seen to lie well within the intervals predicted by the ensemble of models, and quite close to the median estimates. In particular, for "most days" drinking, the ensemble ascribes an 86% likelihood to an arrest in the trend of decreasing prevalence observed since 2005 – an outcome that did in fact occur in the HSE data for 2010. This is clearly a very different modelling estimate to what would result from a simple trend line fitted to HSE "most days" data for period 2005 to 2010. Specifically, whilst the observed prevalence increases from $y_4(2009) = 9.15\%$ to $y_4(2010) = 11.46\%$, linear and exponential trend lines predict continuing decreases in prevalence to $\hat{y}_4(2010) = 7.47\%$ and $\hat{y}_4(2010) = 8.52\%$ respectively.

4. CONCLUSION

4.1 Findings

This study is the first of its kind to build a dynamic, quantitative, model of psychological theory that aims to explain and predict change and stasis in patterns of population-level alcohol consumption. The use of a theory-driven approach allows individual models to be analysed for face validity, whilst the search for an ensemble of diverse models that can replicate history enables uncertainty intervals to be estimated for the predicted outcome.

In this paper, the proposed methodology has been demonstrated by using TPB concepts to model the dynamics of drinking frequency in the 1979-1985 birth cohort in England between 2003 and 2010. The optimizer was able to find diverse parameterisations of the model that could reproduce historical data, with the results used to generate uncertainty estimates for a one-step-ahead prediction of population drinking frequencies.

In Table 2, the finding of larger attitude and subjective norm weightings, in relation to perceived behavioural control weightings, is broadly in-line with existing TPB studies of alcohol consumption [7]. In TPB, the explanatory power of the psychological components is hypothesised to render the demographics parameters unimportant; however, in the model, sex remains an important driver of consumption behaviour. This is likely to be because, in a conventional TPB field study, the research team can carefully select the instruments used to measure the psychological components relating to the behaviour under investigation, whereas here we are limited to existing datasets with only proxy measures for these components.

The finding of a negative relationship between number of social roles and frequency of drinking in Table 2 is broadly in-line with recent empirical findings. For example, a study of 10 Western countries found that increasing numbers of social roles were associated with reduced odds of engagement in heavy drinking for both males and females, when observations were grouped across all 10 countries [19]. However our findings are somewhat stronger than those in [19] when considering that study's UK-specific analysis, wherein a statistically significant relationship was found only in males holding three roles (in comparison to no roles).

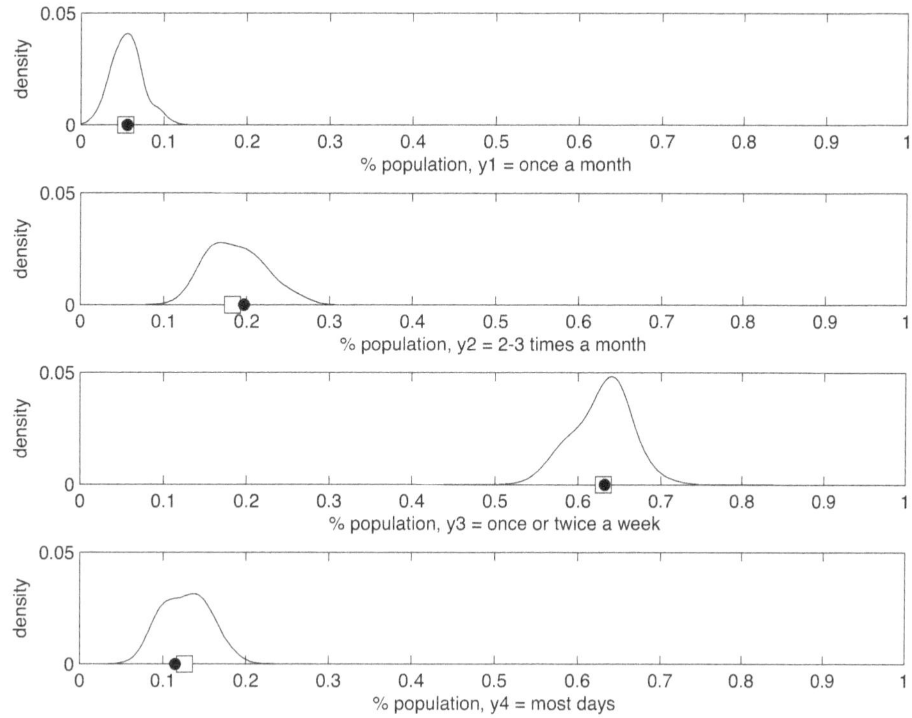

Figure 5: Marginal probability density estimates for the prediction of y(2010) based on $\mathcal{P}(200)$. Median predictions are shown as squares (□). Observations from HSE 2010 are indicated by the filled circles (•).

4.2 Limitations and Future Work

Whilst the method has generated highly promising results for one population sub-group in one country, these findings must be regarded as indicative of proof-of-principle at this stage. Further work is needed to verify if the method is reproducible on other population sub-groups both in England and in other jurisdictions. Furthermore, as yet we have taken little account of the potential effects of stochasticity, both in the ABM and the EA, on the robustness of the proposed modelling methodology. A full statistical robustness analysis is needed, with countermeasures introduced to improve robustness if this is found to be necessary. It will also be instructive to compare the method with more traditional regression approaches, as well as state-of-the-art model calibration methods, including evolutionary [27] and Bayesian [30] techniques.

From the perspective of analytical sociology [16], the generative account of how micro-level dynamics produce macro-level outcomes (i.e. the TPB microsimulation of drinking frequency) is incomplete since it does not include the social interactions that occur between individuals. Such interactions may be important for capturing the dynamics of, for example, attitude change, that may prove important for both explanation and prediction of population drinking trends. Future work will seek to introduce interaction effects into the microsimulation, e.g. adaptive models of attitudes based on either explicit or proxy measures of social connectedness between individuals.

A further limitation of the microsimulation is that it is not entirely endogenous – specifically, social role trajectories are required as exogenous inputs to the model, which in themselves may not be straightforward to predict. However, the notion of a microsimulation or ABM being able to capture all of the actions and interactions necessary to explain and predict an empirically observed social phenomenon remains something of an ideal; pragmatically, exogenous inputs (e.g. network structures) are a short-term necessity.

Future work will also examine alternative measures of consumption to be predicted by the model. Frequency of intoxication is also available in the OCJS dataset, but the outcome of greatest utility would be mean grams per day of ethanol consumed because this measure can be used directly in the existing epidemiological models that relate drinking to chronic health harms [23]. Unfortunately mean consumption is not captured by OCJS and therefore imputation will be required. We view new or enhanced population surveys that integrate, in a theory-led way, psychological and social factors with alcohol consumption (and other behaviours relevant to public health) as a priority for future funding.

In summary, we believe that the proposed methodology has the potential to be transformative in the use of complex systems methods for model-based policy appraisal, specifically in terms of alcohol, but also more widely within public health, where achieving an understanding of the dynamics of macro-level behaviour change remains a core challenge.

5. ACKNOWLEDGMENTS

This work was funded by the UK Economic and Social Research Council under grant number ES/K001760/1.

The original data creators, depositors, or copyright holders, the funders of the data collections (when different), and the UK Data Archive bear no responsibility for analyses or interpretation of the data described in this report. The BHPS, HSE and OCJS are Crown Copyright.

6. REFERENCES

[1] A. Agresti. *Categorical Data Analysis.* Wiley, New Jersey, 3rd edition, 2013.

[2] I. Ajzen. The theory of planned behavior. *Organizational Behavior and Human Decision Processes*, 50(2):179–211, 1991.

[3] J. E. Baker. Reducing bias and inefficiency in the selection algorithm. In *Proceedings of the Second International Conference on Genetic Algorithms*, pages 14–21, 1987.

[4] British Beer and Pub Association. Statistical Handbook 2013, 2013.

[5] W. Buckley. *Sociology and Modern Systems Theory.* Prentice Hall, New Jersey, 1967.

[6] D. S. Byrne. *Complexity Theory and the Social Sciences: An Introduction.* Routledge, Abingdon, 1998.

[7] R. Cooke, M. Dahdah, P. Norman, and D. P. French. How well does the theory of planned behaviour predict alcohol consumption intentions and behaviour? In *BPS Division of Health Psychology Annual Conference 2013*, 2013.

[8] K. Deb and R. B. Agrawal. Simulated binary crossover for continuous search space. *Complex Systems*, 9(2):115–148, 1995.

[9] K. Deb and M. Goyal. A combined genetic adaptive search GeneAS for engineering design. *Computer Science and Informatics*, 26(4):30–45, 1996.

[10] J. C. Duffy and C. Snowdon. *The Minimal Evidence for Minimum Pricing: The Fatal Flaws in the Sheffield Alcohol Policy Model.* ASI (Research) Ltd, London, 2012.

[11] C. M. Fonseca and P. J. Fleming. Multiobjective genetic algorithms made easy: Selection, sharing and mating restriction. In *Proceedings of the First International Conference on Genetic Algorithms in Engineering Systems: Innovation and Applications*, pages 42–52, 1995.

[12] L. A. Garrison and D. S. Babcock. Alcohol consumption amongst college students: an agent-based computational simulation. *Complexity*, 14(6):35–44, 2009.

[13] P. Giabbanelli and R. Crutzen. An agent-based social network model of binge drinking among Dutch adults. *Journal of Artificial Societies and Social Simulation*, 16(2):10, 2013.

[14] D. E. Goldberg and J. Richardson. Genetic algorithms with sharing for multimodal function optimization. In *Proceedings of the Second International Conference on Genetic Algorithms*, pages 41–49, 1987.

[15] D. M. Gorman, J. Mezic, I. Mezic, and P. J. Gruenewald. Agent-based modeling of drinking behavior: A preliminary model and potential applications to theory and practice. *American Journal of Public Health*, 96(11):2055–2060, 2006.

[16] P. Hedström. *Dissecting the Social: On the Principles of Analytical Sociology.* Cambridge University Press, Cambridge, 2005.

[17] H. D. Holder. Planning for alcohol-problem prevention through complex systems modelling: Results from *SimCom. Substance Use & Misuse*, 33(3):669–692, 1998.

[18] Home Office. Research, Development and Statistics Directorate. Offending Surveys and Research, National Centre for Social Research and BMRB. Social Research. Offending, Crime and Justice Survey, 2003 [computer file]. 3rd Edition. Colchester, Essex: UK Data Archive [distributor], August 2008. SN: 5248.

[19] S. Kuntsche, R. A. Knibbe, and G. Gmel. Social roles and alcohol consumption: A study of 10 industrialised countries. *Social Science & Medicine*, 68:1263–1270, 2009.

[20] National Centre for Social Research and University College London. Department of Epidemiology and Public Health. Health Survey for England, 2009 [computer file]. 2nd Edition. Colchester, Essex: UK Data Archive [distributor], July 2011. SN: 6732.

[21] Office of the Qualifications and Examinations Regulator. Qualifications can cross boundaries – a rough guide to comparing qualifications in the UK and Ireland. 3rd edition, 2011.

[22] R. C. Purshouse, P. S. Meier, A. Brennan, K. B. Taylor, and R. Rafia. Estimated effect of alcohol pricing policies on health and health economic outcomes in England: An epidemiological model. *Lancet*, 375:1355–64, 2010.

[23] J. Rehm, D. Bailunas, G. L. Borges, K. Graham, H. Irving, T. Kehoe, C. D. Parry, J. Patra, S. Popova, V. Poznyak, M. Roerecke, R. Room, A. V. Samokhvalov, and B. Taylor. The relation between different dimensions of alcohol consumption and burden of disease: An overview. *Addiction*, 105(5):817–843, 2010.

[24] G. Room. *Complexity, Institutions and Public Policy – Agile Decision-making in a Turbulent World.* Edward Elgar, Cheltenham, 2011.

[25] R. Room, E. Osterberg, M. Ramstedt, and J. Rehm. Explaining change and stasis in alcohol consumption. *Addiction Research and Theory*, 17(6):562–576, 2009.

[26] J. Simpura. Trends in alcohol consumption and drinking patterns: Sociological and economic explanations and alcohol policies. *Nordic Studies on Alcohol and Drugs*, 18:3–13, 2001.

[27] F. Stonedahl and U. Wilensky. Evolutionary robustness checking in the Artificial Anasazi model. In *Proceedings of the AAAI fall symposium on complex adaptive systems: resilience, robustness and evolvability*, pages 120–129, 2010.

[28] The Scottish Government. *Changing Scotland's Relationship with Alcohol: A Framework for Action.* The Scottish Government, Edinburgh, 2009.

[29] University of Essex. Institute for Social and Economic Research. British Household Panel Survey: Waves 1-18, 1991-2009 [computer file]. 7th Edition. Colchester, Essex: UK Data Archive [distributor], July 2010. SN: 5151.

[30] I. Vernon, M. Goldstein, and R. G. Bower. Galaxy formation: a Bayesian uncertainty analysis. *Bayesian Analysis*, 5(4):619–670, 2010.

[31] World Health Organization. Global status report on alcohol and health. Technical report, WHO Press, 2011.

Evolutionary Algorithms for Classification of Malware Families through Different Network Behaviors

M. Zubair Rafique, Ping Chen, Christophe Huygens, Wouter Joosen
iMinds-DistriNet, KU Leuven, 3001 Leuven, Belgium
{zubair.rafique,ping.chen,christophe.huygens,wouter.joosen}@cs.kuleuven.be

ABSTRACT

The staggering increase of malware families and their diversity poses a significant threat and creates a compelling need for automatic classification techniques. In this paper, we first analyze the role of network behavior as a powerful technique to automatically classify malware families and their polymorphic variants. Afterwards, we present a framework to efficiently classify malware families by modeling their different network behaviors (such as `HTTP`, `SMTP`, `UDP`, and `TCP`). We propose protocol-aware and state-space modeling schemes to extract features from malware network behaviors. We analyze the applicability of various evolutionary and non-evolutionary algorithms for our malware family classification framework. To evaluate our framework, we collected a real-world dataset of 6,000 unique and active malware samples belonging to 20 different malware families. We provide a detailed analysis of network behaviors exhibited by these prevalent malware families. The results of our experiments shows that evolutionary algorithms, like sUpervised Classifier System (UCS), can effectively classify malware families through different network behaviors in real-time. To the best of our knowledge, the current work is the first malware classification framework based on evolutionary classifier that uses different network behaviors.

Categories and Subject Descriptors

D.4.6 [**Security and Protection**]: Invasive software (e.g., viruses, worms, Trojan horses); H.3.4 [**Information Storage and Retrieval**]: Systems and Software—*performance evaluation (efficiency and effectiveness)*.

General Terms

Algorithms, Experimentation, Security

Keywords

Malware Classification, Network Behaviors, Machine Learning

GECCO'14, July 12–16, 2014, Vancouver, BC, Canada.

http://dx.doi.org/10.1145/2576768.2598238

1. INTRODUCTION

The classification of the diverse and massive amount of malware variants into families is one of the most challenging problem faced by the security community. A recent report by security company McAfee indicates a steep rise in distribution of malware variants, with the collection of more than 128 million samples in duration of one year [16]. Another report [10] demonstrates the same trend with the collection of 200,000 malware samples each day by security analysts. This problem has persisted for many years and is only getting worse owing to easy availability of ready-made infection vectors (e.g., exploit kits [20]) and existence of disreputable malware crafting and dissemination services [12][7].

The traditional host-based defenses, like anti-virus softwares, lag behind to contend with this enormous increase of malware. This is largely due to extensive exploitation of evasive techniques (e.g., repacking, polymorphism, and obfuscation) in malware development [26]. Furthermore, the notable prevalence of malware families – `zeroaccess` with approximately 9 million infected PCs [31], `zbot/zeus` with anti-virus detection rate of only 39.35% [32], `ransomware` the number one threat of 2013/2014 [29], and `winwebsec` an infamous fake anti-virus fraud [20] – not only shows the limitations of anti-virus softwares, but also highlights the emerging need for tools to automatically classify unknown variants of known malware families. To this end, security analysts are profoundly inclined to use behavioral attributes for malware classification [26]. Behavioral attributes are effective, as they model specific behaviors that are persistent across the variants of a particular malware family.

One of the powerful behavioral attribute to classify ever-growing malware families and their polymorphic variants is the malware network behavior. The behavior is powerful because a vast majority of real-world malware relies on network communication to perform illegal malicious activities including identity theft, on line advertisement clicks, sending Spam, launching denial of service (DoS) attacks, downloading additional malware and collection of fraudulent ransoms. In addition, inferring knowledge from network behavior (of malware variants) can enable take-downs of malicious servers, identify compromised machines [21], and establish intelligence on the criminals running the flagrant operations [20]. Last but not least, detection of malware through network behavior is more feasible than host-based techniques, facilitating detection at the network edge rather than resource-consuming installations at every end host [24]. Despite the effectiveness of this powerful behavioral attribute, malware family classification through network behavior has received negligible attention in the rich paradigm of evolutionary classification algorithms.

In this paper we performed an empirical study to analyze the applicability of different evolutionary algorithms in classification of malware variants into families using network behaviors. Our study does not focus malware family classification by assuming a single malware family or a single protocol in the malware traffic [21, 19]. In contrast, we here propose a classification framework that extracts features from different network protocols (e.g., HTTP, SMTP, UDP, TCP) exploited by variants of multiple, recent and active malware families. The extraction of features from different protocols is important, as malware families can use various protocols for different purposes (e.g., an unknown protocol on UDP to communicate with command and control (C&C) and HTTP for click-fraud [31]). We therefore use a combination of protocol-aware and state-space modelings to extract features from different network behaviors exhibited by malware samples. For our study, we selected four evolutionary and four non-evolutionary classifiers from different machine learning paradigms. These classifiers are enumerated in Table 1.

We evaluate the performance of the selected classifiers on our collection of real-world active malware samples. Our dataset contains more than 6,000 unique malware samples. These samples belong to 20 recent and active malware families. We collected the malware samples by using our customized malware-downloader tool and choosing active malware samples from [20]. We executed the collected malware samples in a controlled environment to obtain network behaviors for feature extraction and classification.

The results of our experiments show that our framework, using evolutionary classifiers (like UCS), achieves high accuracy in classifying malware samples of different families. Moreover, the processing overheads of our framework are low; as a result, it can be easily deployed for larger datasets. Finally, we make the implementation of our feature extraction tool publicly available to promote further research and allow future scholars to compare their results to ours.

The remainder of this paper is organized as follows. We present our classification framework in Section 2. We explain feature extraction schemes in Section 3. We discuss the classifiers in Section 4 and describe the evaluation strategy in Section 5. We report the results of our experiments in Section 6. Finally, we discuss the related work on malware family classification in Section 7 and then conclude the paper with an outlook to our future work in Section 8.

2. FRAMEWORK OVERVIEW

Our framework is designed to automatically learn different network behaviors of malware from the labeled binaries and extract discriminative features to classify unknown variants of known malware families. We set the following requirements for our framework: (1) it should correctly identify the unknown variants of known malware families (*malware family classification*), (2) the learning process must be robust to consolidate different network behaviors used by malware to communicate with its C&C (*multiple protocol incorporation*) and (3) the classification process should be efficient in terms of processing overheads (*real-world deployable*). Our framework is modular in nature, allows it to operate on different sets of attributes and with large variety of classification algorithms. We now discuss the different components of our system to classify malware families.

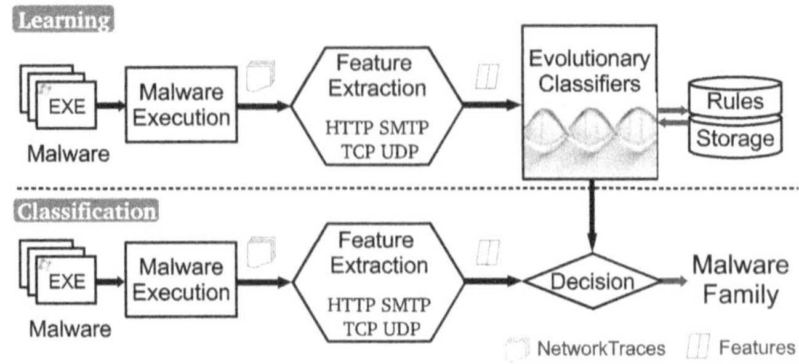

Figure 1: Architecture of malware family classification framework using different network behaviors.

Figure 1 shows the architecture of our framework. Our framework takes malicious executables as an input. These executables are marked with malware family label and can be obtained from different sources and honey-pots.

Next, the malware execution module runs each malware binary in a controlled environment. The fundamental objectives of running a malware in a controlled environment are to provoke the malicious executable to generate traffic, to gather different network behaviors such as HTTP, SMTP, TCP and UDP, and to avoid infections through network. To this end, we automatically execute malware binaries in different virtual machines (such as Virtual-box and Qemu), as provoking the malware to communicate through network usually requires executing the same malware sample numerous times in different environments. The traffic generated by executables is stored in Packet CAPture (PCAP) format. Note that malware execution is a well studied research problem [12, 20, 21] and is not the main contribution of this paper.

As network traces are obtained, our feature extraction module models the information from different network behaviors of real-world malware. We designed our framework to analyze all kind of network requests generated by the malware. We use two separate modeling schemes, (1) *protocol-aware* modeling and (2) *state-space* modeling. In the first modeling we use protocol grammars to extract fine-grained information from application protocols (e.g., HTTP, SMTP etc.). The advantage of this modeling is that we can extract distinct information from different fields of known protocol messages. In the second modeling, we use state-space features to deal with unknown protocol requests. This modeling enables us to incorporate expert knowledge from malware network behaviors that do not follow any formal protocol specifications. In the interest of optimization, we discard all requests sent towards benign endpoints by malware. Further, we use gain ratio to select discriminative features for state-space modeling of unknown protocol requests.

The classification module takes the features, from both protocol-aware and state-space modeling, as input and solves a multi-class problem to distinguish instances of different malware families. This problem is solved with the help of rules (population) stored in the rules database. In this study, we analyze the performance of the malware detection framework on wide range of classification algorithms. These algorithms are described in Section 4. The decision made by the classification module can categorize unknown variants of known malware families based on their network behaviors. It can equally be used to identify if a network message belongs to a known malware family.

```
——— Port Protocol:Payload or Request Line ———
34354 TCP:e5aac031b4dc3e40315b74084d9b39c1beb4ffb8
53     UDP:4ee3750a8a9c9e981d396c39c7047a624eb8d8f1
16471 UDP:9dc8708a28948dabc9c0d199940c89e5
80    HTTP:GET /stat2.php?w=30461&amp;i=963e6170&amp;
      a=3291195
80    HTTP:GET /56995-B8EBEDA4/counter.img?
      theme=1&amp;digits=10&amp;siteId=31226369
80    HTTP:GET /count.php?id=31226369&amp;c=1&amp;
      d=7&amp;s=0
```

Figure 2: Real-world example of single malware family (Zeroaccess) exhibiting different network behaviors.

Our malware classification approach consists of two phases. In the learning phase, network traffic obtained from malware execution (labeled with family name) is passed to the malware family classification system. The classification module of system learns its rules or evolves its population based on extracted features from network behaviors (that correspond to different protocols). For effective classification, the system can be periodically updated to accommodate changes in the network behaviors of malware families. Once the learning phase of system is terminated, it starts operating on network behaviors of malicious binaries to classify malware family based on the knowledge acquired during learning.

3. FEATURE EXTRACTION

The key intuition behind incorporating different network behaviors, exhibited by real-world malware samples, in our feature extraction process is that the patterns in requests generated by malware (when communicating with a malicious server) tend to remain consistent and are not affected by code obfuscation techniques. This is likely due in part to the considerable amount of effort required to change C&C protocol, with code changes in both malware and malicious server. At the same time, incorporating network behaviors in feature extraction process is challenging as malware families often use multiple C&C protocols. For instance, a malware family can use both `HTTP` protocol and an unknown C&C protocol built on top of `TCP` to communicate with the malicious server, and additionally even a separate protocol to perform its fraudulent actions (like `SMTP` for sending Spam or `IRC` to send bot commands).

To further illustrate this fact, we provide example of Zeroaccess, the most prevalent and active malware family [31]. Figure 2 shows six different network behaviors of Zeroaccess. The malware family uses `TCP`-based protocol on port 34354 (to communicate with malicious servers), two separate unknown `UDP`-based protocols on ports 53 and 16471 respectively (for peer-to-peer communication), and three different application protocol (`HTTP`) requests (to communicate malware affiliate-id and to perform click-fraud [31]). Since malware families can use different protocols, it is important and relevant to extract features from different protocols to achieve better accuracy. Specifically, we argue that classification scheme based on malware network behaviors should accommodate both application and unknown protocols.

As described in Section 2, we use two separate modelings to extract features from malware network behaviors. These are (1) protocol-aware modeling (for application protocol requests like `HTTP`, `SMTP` etc.) and (2) state-space modeling (for unknown protocol requests built on transport protocols i.e., `UDP` and `TCP`). We now provide details on these schemes.

```
<proto name="http">
 <field name="http.req.method" value="GET"/>
 <field name="http.req.url" value="/stat2.php"/>
 <field name="http.req.ver" value="HTTP/1.1"/>
 <field name="http.req.user_agent" value="Opera 6"/>
 - - -
 - - -
</proto>
 ---------------Feature Embedding---------------
 attribute|http.req.method|http.req.url| - -
 value    |GET            |/stat2.php  | - -
 -----------------------------------------------
```

Figure 3: Protocol-aware feature extraction example.

Protocol-aware Modeling. The main advantage of using protocol-aware modeling is the possibility to extract fine-grained information from different fields of the application protocol messages. Malware families widely use different message fields of known protocols for malicious communication. For instance, in Figure 2 the `siteId` parameter in `uri` of second last `HTTP` request is used by malware to communicate its affiliate-id [31]. Moreover, a number of malware families craft custom protocol requests, which may include peculiar field values (like a customized value of `User-Agent` header in `HTTP` [24]). Therefore, it is pertinent to incorporate information from the application protocol fields in our feature extraction process.

We use Wireshark[1] dissectors to parse requests generated by malware into the field structures of known protocols. Wireshark dissectors can be used to parse a wide range of protocols, allowing us to extract information from variety of malware network behaviors. Figure 3 shows the dissection of an `HTTP` request, initiated by malware, into the structured format and the embedding of message fields into corresponding feature space. Here, we treated each field name as attribute and field value as attribute value. Any changes in the values of particular fields shows a different crafting of C&C message. This difference indicates a network behavior of a different malware family or a different network behavior of the same malware family. Our approach is not constrained to a specific protocol (e.g., only `HTTP`) or manual incorporation of limited protocol fields (like, `http.req.method` and `http.req.url`) as in [21].

One problem of using Wireshark is that it can not automatically parse common protocols on unusual ports. For instance, it cannot automatically parse `HTTP` on the unusual `TCP` port 1435, as it only uses the destination port to select the right protocol dissector. This unusual port communication is a common practice of malware families to avoid detection and bypass firewall rules. We therefore use protocol fingerprints for each `TCP` connection made by malware during execution. These fingerprints are designed to identify application layer traffic by checking the existence of protocol keywords in the starting bytes of a payload (e.g., `GET` in `HTTP` or `EHLO` in `SMTP`). Once the known protocol is identified, we use appropriate Wireshark dissector to parse the message into the field structure.

State-space Modeling. In compare to protocol-aware modeling, state-space modeling is more challenging as it deals with the network behaviors consisting of unknown protocol requests. For such requests we extract four attributes to transform a given payload into a feature vector. These attributes are: $\langle proto, size, dest\_port, [state\_space] \rangle$. Here,

[1] `http://www.wireshark.com`

proto represents transport protocol (i.e., UDP or TCP), *size* is the number of bytes in the payload, and *dest_port* represents the destination port to which an unknown message is sent by the malware. The [*state_space*] maps the payload information of unknown request into the feature vector.

The first two features (*proto* and *size*) are useful as it is less probable that different malware families use the same transport protocol with the same message size for an unknown protocol request. The third feature *dest_port* can be effective if a particular malware family utilize the specific set of ports for unknown protocol requests (e.g., ports 16471 or 34354 in Figure 2). Finally, the [*state_space*] attributes are valuable to extract the information from the byte sequences of unknown protocol requests.

In order to extract [*state_space*], we present a payload P, of an unknown protocol message, as order of bytes $P = \{b_0, b_1, b_2 \ldots b_l\}$, where l is the length of UDP or TCP payload. Without loss of generality, we can use n-gram (joint distribution of bytes) by computing frequency of consecutive n bytes in P to model the information from the payload of unknown protocol requests. However, the major problem with n-gram is that such feature-space contains redundant information and the selection of right value of n is not trivial (i.e., if n is small, the accuracy of the system decreases whereas large values of n significantly increase the processing overheads) [23].

We therefore use a first order state-space system to incorporate the relevant information from the payloads of unknown protocol requests. The state-space uses conditional distribution rather than joint distribution, which results in small and discriminative feature-space [23]. We build our system as a set of states $\Im = \{\Im_0, \Im_1, \Im_2 ..... \Im_k\}$, where $\Im_0$ is the initial system state. We apply transformation function φ that operates on UDP or TCP protocol to transform each byte of an unknown protocol request into a system state as: $(\varphi : b_i \mapsto \Im_i \in \Im)$. With each byte b_i in payload, such that $b_i \to \Im_i$, we compute the probability of byte b_{i+1} followed by byte b_i as a state transition $t_{\Im_i, \Im_{i+1}}$. Finally, the transitions probabilities of a given P between k states are detailed in a state transition matrix as:

$$T(\Im) = \begin{bmatrix} t_{\Im_0,\Im_0} & t_{\Im_0,\Im_1} & \cdots & t_{\Im_0,\Im_k} \\ t_{\Im_1,\Im_0} & t_{\Im_1,\Im_1} & \cdots & t_{\Im_1,\Im_1} \\ \vdots & \vdots & \ddots & \ddots \\ t_{\Im_k,\Im_0} & t_{\Im_F,\Im_1} & \cdots & t_{\Im_k,\Im_k} \end{bmatrix} \quad (1)$$

The total number of states are bounded by the length l of any given unknown protocol payload. The state transitions values represent the complete formation of the unknown protocol payload for a particular malware family. Any variation in the state transition values reflects a dissimilar payload (i.e., a different crafting of unknown protocol message). We use the transition values as [*state_space*] attributes in our defined feature vector for unknown protocol requests.

Optimization. We use two kind of optimizations to make our feature space more discriminative and computationally feasible. First, we filtered all the known protocol requests sent towards the benign top 200,000 Alexa domains. This is because malware often sends requests to benign sites in order to check Internet connectivity. Including these requests, in our feature space, has little impact on classification of malware families and is obviously an additional overhead. Second, we use the gain ratio feature selection scheme to choose the most discriminative transitions in the [*state_space*].

Table 1: Classification algorithms and machine learning paradigms (Evolutionary and Non-Evolutionary).

	Algorithm	Learning Paradigm
Evolutionary	GAssist-ADI	Pittsburgh-Style GBML
	SLAVE	Genetic Fuzzy
	UCS	Michigan-Style GMBL
	XCS	Michigan-Style GMBL
Non Evolutionary	C4.5	Decision Tree Induction
	C-SVM	Support Vector Machine
	KNN	Instance Based Learning
	Naïve Bayes	Statistical Modeling

4. CLASSIFICATION

Our research analyzed the utility of evolutionary algorithms in the classification of malware families through network behaviors. In addition, we also incorporated known non-evolutionary algorithms to gain knowledge about the classification potential of algorithms in our framework. We then evaluate the effectiveness of the selected algorithms based on their classification accuracy and processing overheads (their training and testing times). Our goal is to identify the best algorithm that can accurately classify malware families using different network behavior attributes.

We have used a diverse set of well-known evolutionary and non-evolutionary classification algorithms in our classification module. Our prime driver, for selecting various classification algorithms, was an attempt to cover the various paradigms of evolutionary computing and machine learning. The paradigms and corresponding classifiers used in our study are shown in Table 1. We now briefly describe each algorithm to make the manuscript self contained. Details on these algorithms can be found in the cited references.

4.1 Evolutionary Algorithms

eXtended Classifier System (XCS). XCS is a Michigan-style classifier that derives a set of rules based on accuracy [30]. In the training phase, the input data is used to generate the initial rules. Afterwards, these initial rules are evolved into new rules using a niche Genetic Algorithm (GA) reserved in the population. The fitness of the individual (or rule) is determined based on the accuracy of each rule. The predicted payoff values for all actions are saved in prediction array. Based on the criteria for rules, some of them are also deleted from the population. The evolution of accurate generalizations and accommodation of real values makes XCS suitable to solve various real-world problems.

sUpervised Classifier System (UCS). UCS is also a Michigan style classifier and is based on accuracy [5]. UCS inherits same principle and structure of XCS where an initial population of rules is derived from training data. However, it differs from XCS as (1) it is based on a supervised learning scheme that computes fitness instead of reinforcement, (2) the GA is applied to correct the rule-set for updating its population, and (3) it does not use a prediction array. The on-line learning and evolving abilities of UCS make it useful in efficiently solving different real-world problems.

Genetic clASSIfier SysTem (GAssist). GAssist [3] is a Pittsburgh style classifier based on the approach where each individual in the population depicts a complete solution to the classification problem. It uses GA to evolve the rulesets of the population and exploits a fitness function to get a good balance between complexity and accuracy of the generated rules. The incremental learning with alternating strata (ILAS) windowing approach is used to improve the generalization of rulesets. For this study we have used the adaptive discretization intervals (ADI) rule representation.

Structural Learning Algorithm in Vague Environment (SLAVE). SLAVE is a genetic learning algorithm based on the use of fuzzy logic concepts and the genetic iterative approach [11]. The algorithm elects and gains knowledge by only one fuzzy rule in each iteration. This results in pruning of the search space for potential solutions. Next, it chooses the most suitable prior for the class by fixing a class. Finally, a series of repeated iterations outputs a full rule-set for the classification of instances. Here, the fitness of rules is computed by using completeness and consistency of the rules. The algorithm has been effectively used in several real-world applications and shows promising results [25].

4.2 Non-Evolutionary Algorithms

C4.5 Algorithm. C4.5 generates a decision-tree to interpret the class and is based on the theory of information entropy [22]. Decision trees are mostly adopted to map information about an attribute for getting outcomes of the attribute's target value using some predictive models. To generate decision-tree from training data, C4.5 uses information gain of attributes by grading a set of attributes to an individual class. It then, recursively operates on the subsets of the attributes till each of the attribute is examined or no further information can be achieved by separating the rest of attributes. Finally, the attributes with the highest information gain are chosen to build the classification model.

Support Vector Machine (SVM). SVMs build hyper planes between elements of separate classes and are based on the concept of a decision surface to solve classification problems [13]. SVM converts diverse domain knowledge with overlapping inputs into non-overlapping parametric objects by modeling the input elements to feature space using mathematical functions called kernels. The commonly used kernels in SVM are Linear, Polynomial, Radial Basis Function (RBF) and Sigmoid kernels.

Naïve Bayes Algorithm (NB). Naïve Bayes is a simple probabilistic classifier based on Bayes' theorem [27]. The classifier assumes that the features used in model building are statistically independent. Mathematically, given a feature vector $F = \{f_1, f_2, ...f_n\}$ and class C, the probability of F belongs to C is computed as $P(F/C) = \prod_{i=1}^{|F|} P(F_i/C)$. The disjoint of class conditional feature distributions implies that each distribution can be independently computed as one dimensional distribution. Naïve Bayes is notably suited for a high-dimensional feature space and has been empirically proven to be effective in various real-world applications.

K Nearest Neighbors (KNN). KNN algorithm is a non-parametric way of categorizing instances into classes based on the k closest training instances in the feature space [8]. In KNN, there is no explicit training phase and it only stores features and class information. However, the testing phase is costly (both in time and space) because an instance is classified by a majority vote of its neighbors through computing the least distance from its k nearest neighbors. The majority class of nearest instances advocates the classification of the instance under test.

Table 2: Network behavior analysis of malware families.

Family (Samples)	Reqs.	HTTP	SMTP	TCP	UDP
1.Cleaman (32)	49	100%	0%	0%	0%
2.Coinminer (3)	8	100%	0%	0%	0%
3.Cridex (72)	1,175	100%	0%	0%	0%
4.Cutwail (2)	747	40.0%	56.7%	3.3%	0%
5.Drstwex.A (45)	51	0%	0%	100%	0%
6.Foreign (6)	6	100%	0%	0%	0%
7.Malagent(8)	15	100%	0%	0%	0%
8.Onescan (9)	85	100%	0%	0%	0%
9.Qakbot-AE (11)	65	100%	0%	0%	0%
10.Ramnit (5)	22	0%	0%	100%	0%
11.Simda (20)	60	100%	0%	0%	0%
12.Spybot.bfr (1)	151	6.0%	94.0%	0%	0%
13.Spyeye (7)	27	59.3%	0%	40.7%	0%
14.Suspectcrc (10)	192	100%	0%	0%	0%
15.Waledace.C (14)	14	100%	0%	0%	0%
16.Waledace.R (29)	29	100%	0%	0%	0%
17.Webprotection (3)	17	100%	0%	0%	0%
18.Winwebsec (2541)	3,395	100%	0%	0%	0%
19.Zbot (2095)	53,568	20.0%	0%	3.6%	76.5%
20.Zeroaccess (1087)	251,874	1.3%	0%	0.3%	98.4%
Total: (6000)	311,550	6.2%	0.05%	1%	92.3%

5. EVALUATION

In this section, we present our methodology for assessing and comparing the selected machine learning algorithms. Our leading objective was to investigate the classification potential of various algorithms to categorize real-world malware samples into families. Therefore, we first present our strategy to acquire recent and active malware samples. We then provide detailed analysis on different network behaviors of the real-world malware families. Finally, we explain our experimental setup for the classification of malware samples into families using network behavior attributes.

Dataset. Our dataset contains 6,000 binaries from 20 different recent and active malware families, shown in Table 2. The dataset contains a broad range of recent malware classes such as fake anti-viruses, malware-kits, and peer-to-peer bots. All the malware families contain a high range of diversity in network behaviors with their traffic exhibiting common obfuscation techniques such as encryption and polymorphism (in IPs, domains, and payloads). The majority of malware binaries in our dataset are obtained from the publicly available `MALICIA` dataset [20]. These malware binaries are collected from different exploit kit servers from March 2012 to February 2013 (we only choose prevalent and active malware families' samples.) Apart from the `MALICIA` dataset, we also developed a malware-downloader to acquire recent malware samples from different infection vectors (such as phishing). This gives us a diverse set of recent malware samples that are not present in `MALICIA` dataset and exist in the wild.

To acquire malware from different feeds we make use of public security forums such as Malware Domain List (`MDL`) and Anti Network Virus Alliance (`ANVA`) [17]. These public forums are used by security analysts and volunteers to report and analyze malicious `URLs`. Our malware-downloader periodically visits these forums and downloads fresh malware samples by visiting the malicious `URLs`. For a downloaded sample, malware-downloader uses the same family label as mentioned in `MDL` or `ANVA` since the links leading to malware

Table 3: Qualitative analysis of HTTP attributes.

Name	Distinct	Missing	Unique	GR
http.user_agent	39	1.2%	0.02%	0.72
http.connection	3	4.0%	0%	0.60
http.accept	6	31.0%	0%	0.40
http.method	2	0%	0%	0.40
http.accept_encoding	4	54.0%	0%	0.30
http.url	3,385	0%	15.0%	0.26
http.host	2,226	0%	6.0%	0.25
http.content_type	5	72.0%	0%	0.18
http.cookie	13	98.0%	0.04%	10^{-4}
http.referer	16	94.0%	0%	10^{-4}
http.accept_language	1	90.0%	0%	0
http.authbasic	2	99.9%	0%	0
http.cache_control	1	74.0%	0%	0
http.content_encoding	1	74.0%	0%	0
http.authorization	2	99.9%	0%	0

samples reported in these forums are manually checked by experts and only verified ground-truth is reported [20].

Table 2 shows our analysis of the dataset of malware families. It presents the number of binaries for each malware family that generate network traffic, number of requests transmitted by malware of each family, as well as the % split of requests according to the network protocols for each family. We found that HTTP is the most common protocol used among malware families. However, some malware families do not completely rely on HTTP. For instance, we found that malware belonging to Ramnit solely uses an unknown binary protocol built on top of TCP. Furthermore, Cutwail and Cridex largely exploits SMTP for sending Spam, whereas Zbot and Zeroaccess heavily rely on UDP for malicious communication because of their C&C infrastructure and peer-to-peer nature. In summary, our analysis of recent and active malware samples indicates that the malware families exhibits different network behaviors during execution. Therefore, any scheme based on network behaviors should accommodate different protocols (not only HTTP [21]) to accurately classify real-world malware samples into families.

Experimental Setup. For our experiments, we have used the standard implementations of selected classifiers in an open source tool Knowledge Extraction based on Evolutionary Learning (KEEL) [2]. The classifiers are trained by using a combination of all extracted network traffic attributes. Afterwards, we used a stratified 10-fold cross validation procedure on requests belonging to different network behaviors extracted from malware dataset.

6. EXPERIMENTS AND RESULTS

In this section we demonstrate the results of our experiments. We first provide qualitative analysis of features obtained from state-space and protocol-aware modelings. This analysis is useful in measuring the effectiveness of algorithms used to classify malware samples into families. We then discuss the classification accuracy of algorithms. Finally, we provide the training and testing time analysis.

Qualitative Analysis of Features. We now analyze some of the discriminative characteristics of the attributes extracted from network behaviors of the malware dataset. We focus on the quality of the extracted attributes using protocol-aware and state-space modelings (see Section 3). Several information and theoretic measures have been used to evaluate the quality of attributes in a given dataset. For our analysis, we employ the widely used gain ratio (GR) [9] to analyze the quality of attributes extracted from the protocol-aware modeling and to select distinctive attributes obtained from the state-space modeling.

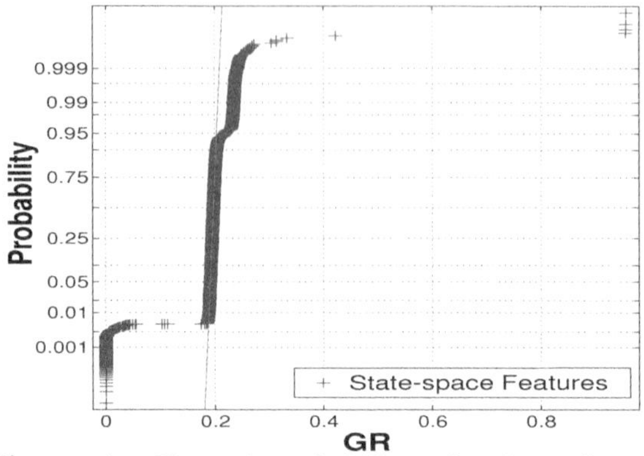

Figure 4: Normal probability plot for gain ratio of [state-space] attributes (unknown protocols).

Figure 4 shows the normal probability plot for the GR of the [*state_space*] attributes. As the value of GR ranges from 0 to 1, the values near 1 show a higher discriminative nature of computed transition probabilities and vice versa. Figure 4 shows that there are four attributes showing very high GR values. These are attributes present in UDP payload (port 16471) of Zeroaccess corresponding to the encrypted command GETL [31]. Apart from that, majority of [*state_space*] attributes have very low GR and can be redundant for classification algorithms. We therefore empirically choose only top 50 attributes with highest GR values in [*state_space*] transitions. We also tabulated our analysis on protocol-aware modeling for HTTP protocol in Table 3. Table 3 shows attribute names, distinct values of attributes in dataset, % of missing and unique values of attributes in dataset, and finally GR of each attribute. The attributes with higher GR (like http.user_agent etc.) can be regarded crucial for classification of malware families using network behaviors.

Classification Accuracy. The classification accuracy represents the percentage of correctly assigned family labels to malware binaries by using a combination of protocol-aware and state-space attributes. Table 4 shows the per family accuracy achieved by each classifier. It also shows the average accuracy attained by the particular classifier on the complete dataset (Samples).

Training Accuracy. Table 4 shows that all algorithms achieved different training accuracies for each of the 20 selected malware families. Most algorithms achieved high training accuracies for Winwebsec (18), Zbot (19), and Zeroaccess (20). This was an expected result as these families constitutes about 99% of requests generated by all malware samples in our dataset. Therefore, the average accuracy (samples) attained by a majority of the classifiers on the complete malware dataset was quite high. The only exception was SLAVE that achieved very poor training accuracy for Winwebsec (18) and Zeroaccess (20). The Michigan style UCS achieved training accuracy of 96.49% (per family) in classification of network behaviors exhibited by different malware families. The evolutionary classifiers, GAssist-ADI, SLAVE, and XCS showed poor training accuracies for the majority of malware classes. NB achieved 0% training accuracy in classifying malware belongs to Foriegn (6) and Waledace.C (15). Similarly, the non-evolutionary classifiers, C4.5 and KNN achieved 0% training accuracy in classify-

Table 4: **Classification accuracy in (%) of the selected classifiers on the malware dataset.**

	Evolutionary								Non-Evolutionary							
Classifiers	GAssist-ADI		SLAVE		UCS		XCS		C4.5		C-SVM		KNN		NB	
Malware Families	Train	Test	Train	Test	Train	Test	Train	Test	Train	Test	Train	Test	Train	Test	Train	Test
1.Cleaman	9.98	10.20	0	0	100	100	0	0	0	0	100	100	0	0	100	100
2.Coinminer	9.72	12.50	0	0	100	100	0	0	100	100	100	100	100	100	27.78	0
3.Cridex	99.92	99.83	0	0	100	100	51	51.23	100	100	100	94.55	100	100	100	100
4.Cutwail	56.85	33.30	22.22	20	94.75	88.87	1	2.56	64.44	66.67	95.19	69.88	59.75	60	65	65
5.Drstwex.A	100	100	73.33	72.92	100	100	20.70	21.57	100	100	98.04	98.04	100	100	96.08	96.08
6.Foreign	7.41	0	0	0	72.22	83.33	0	0	0	0	100	100	66.67	66.67	0	0
7.Malagent	0	0	0	0	100	73.33	0	0	0	0	100	40	100	100	100	100
8.Onescan	50.20	48.24	0	0	98.17	76.47	0	0	100	100	100	76.47	44.71	44.71	100	98.82
9.Qakbot-AE	41.71	41.54	0	0	100	95.38	0	0	100	98.46	100	95.38	99.66	100	100	100
10.Ramnit	59.26	66.67	100	100	99.07	91.67	0	0	100	100	73.15	70.83	33.33	33.33	58.33	58.33
11.Simda	5	8.33	0	0	96.85	8.33	3.33	5	100	100	100	0	63.70	63.33	100	100
12.Spybot.bfr	54.94	55.56	50	50	100	100	50	50	100	100	100	100	100	100	100	100
13.Spyeye	0	0	0	0	95.96	66.19	1.52	0	98.30	73.86	95.62	79.17	76.33	78.69	24.35	14.39
14.Suspectcrc	68.46	67.71	0	0	97.22	79.17	0.75	0	37.73	35.94	100	64.06	84.84	83.85	99.48	98.96
15.Waledace.C	0	0	0	0	82.54	64.29	0	0	0	0	100	78.57	45.24	50	0	0
16.Waledace.R	2.68	3.45	0	0	93.10	79.31	0	0	0	0	100	62.07	69.73	72.41	100	62.07
17.Webprotection	19.61	23.53	0	0	100	100	0	0	0	0	100	100	0	0	70.59	70.59
18.Winwebsec	99.98	99.88	0	0	99.97	99.35	86.64	86.72	100	99.97	100	99.82	99.91	99.85	100	100
19.Zbot	99.97	99.96	100	100	100	99.99	96.84	96.96	100	100	100	99.57	99.96	99.96	99.83	99.79
20.Zeroaccess	99.77	99.72	49.49	49.49	100	99.88	48.98	98.61	100	100	100	98.93	99.45	99.45	99.33	99.33
Avg.(per Family)	44.27	43.52	17.82	17.71	96.49	85.28	18.04	20.63	65.02	63.75	98.10	81.37	72.16	72.61	77.04	73.17
Avg.(Samples)	99.14	99.19	84.90	84.91	99.96	99.70	94.53	94.53	99.49	99.42	99.99	99.01	99.56	99.55	99.73	99.70

ing `Cleaman` (1) and `Webprotection` (17). C-SVM classifier attained highest training accuracy of 98.10% (per family).

Testing Accuracy. Table 4 shows the testing results for different malware families. The evolutionary classifier UCS achieved the best average testing results with an accuracy of 85.28% (per family). SLAVE had the lowest testing accuracy of 17.71% (per family) and as such was not an adequate algorithm in classifying malware network behaviors. GAssist-ADI and XCS were also below par and achieved a low average testing accuracy of 43.52% and 20.63% (per family) respectively. The non-evolutionary algorithms, C4.5, KNN, and NB achieved average testing accuracy of 63.75%, 72.61%, and 73.17% (per family) respectively. C-SVM was dominant among non-evolutionary classifiers and achieved testing accuracy of 81.37% (per family). However, C-SVM was not able to classify a single variant of malware family `Simda` (11) using network behavior attributes. In conclusion, the Michigan style UCS emerged as the most accurate algorithm for classifying different network behaviors of malware with the prominent accuracy results (99.70% on the complete dataset and 85.28% per family).

For the current problem, it is impossible to achieve complete coverage of malware families by using a single malware network behavior. For instance, malware families like `Drstwex.A` (5) and `Ramnit` (10) solely use `TCP` for malicious communication. Hence, the reasonable design option was to utilize both protocol-aware and state-space attributes for malware family classification. Despite achieving good accuracy on complete dataset, majority of the classifiers achieved low accuracy per family relative to the evolutionary UCS classifier (like NB achieved average accuracy of 99.70% on all malware samples and only 73.17% average accuracy per malware family). This shows that UCS has the ability to transform multi-dimensional knowledge from different malware network behaviors into accurate rules.

Training Time. The training time indicates the time taken by the classifier to build its model on given dataset. The training time is vital for frequently updating the rule-base of the classifiers on additional malware samples. Table 5 shows the time taken by the classifiers during the training phase. SLAVE had consumed more time to evolve

Table 5: Average training and testing times.

	Algorithm	Training Time	Testing Time
Evolutionary	GAssist-ADI	34.1min	0.03sec
	SLAVE	>45min	0.02sec
	UCS	8.8min	0.02sec
	XCS	3.7min	0.21sec
Non Evolutionary	C4.5	8min	0.001sec
	C-SVM	27.9min	0.001sec
	Naïve Bayes	24.5sec	0.001sec
	KNN	n/a	0.07sec

its rule as compared to other evolutionary algorithms. The Michigan style LCS (XCS and UCS) spent less time in training than the Pittsburgh style learning classifier GAssist-ADI. The lowest training time was attained by NB, which only took 24.5 seconds to build the model. KNN had no training time as it performed all computations during the testing phase.

Testing Time. As for testing time, Table 5 shows that most of the machine learning algorithms took only a fraction of a second to classify a malware family. The C4.5, C-SVM, and NB algorithms had small testing times relative to evolutionary algorithms. The Michigan style XCS had spent more time in testing as compared to all other classifiers. A higher testing time for an algorithm might cause delay in the classification of a malware family.

7. RELATED WORK

While this paper is the first to incorporate evolutionary algorithms in classification of malware families using different network behaviors, there has been an extensive work on malware classification using different techniques. A related survey of these techniques can be found in [4].

Techniques proposed for malware classification using evolutionary classifiers are based on rule learning [28], control flow graph [6], and dependency graph [15] approaches. Recently, the authors of [1] proposed a virus detection clonal algorithm based on clonal selection and genetic algorithm to detect malware. Other technique, IMAD [18] operates by extracting n-grams from the system calls made by an executable to detect malware. In contrast to these studies, our work incorporate *different* network behaviors (such as **HTTP, SMTP, UDP, TCP**) from numerous *recent and active* malware families. Also, the goal of our approach is to distinguish between instances of real-world malware families and not to distinguish between benign and malware executables.

There is also a wealth of work that does not involve evolutionary algorithms for malware classification. These studies perform malware classification by incorporating a variety of attributes such as system calls, system changes, network traffic, and screenshots [26, 7, 12]. A number of techniques that involve network-behavior attributes for malware classification using clustering are proposed in [24, 21, 14]. The major drawback of clustering methods is that they do not rely on supervised knowledge to model the information from data. This can be a hurdle in the *automatic classification* of malware and may result in inconsistent performance [26].

8. CONCLUSION

In this paper, we presented an efficient malware family classification system that models the protocol-aware and state-space features from different malware network behaviors as potential input attributes for the various classification algorithms. We performed a comprehensive study of four evolutionary and four non-evolutionary classification algorithms. A side contribution of this paper is also the collection and analysis of network behaviors exhibited by real-world malware samples. To our knowledge, this is the first investigative study of evolutionary and non-evolutionary algorithms to efficiently classify malware families using different network behaviors. The focus of our future work will be to study the classification of benign executables against known malware families using network behaviors.

Acknowledgements.

The authors would like to thank the anonymous reviewers for their insightful comments. This research is partially funded by the Research Fund KU Leuven and by the EU FP7 project NESSoS with the financial support from the Prevention of and Fight against Crime Programme of the European Union (B-CCENTRE). Opinions expressed in this material do not necessarily reflect the views of the sponsors.

9. REFERENCES

[1] S. Afaneh et al. Virus detection using clonal selection algorithm with genetic algorithm (vdc algorithm). *Applied Soft Computing*, 13(1):239 – 246, 2013.

[2] J. Alcalá-Fdez et al. KEEL: A Software Tool to Assess Evolutionary Algorithms for Data Mining Problems. *Soft Comput.*, 13(3):307–318, 2008.

[3] J. Bacardit. Analysis of the Initialization Stage of a Pittsburgh Approach Learning Classifier System. In *Proceedings of the 7th Annual Conference on Genetic and Evolutionary Computation*, pages 1843–1850. ACM, 2005.

[4] Z. Bazrafshan et al. A survey on heuristic malware detection techniques. In *Proceedings of the 5th Conference on Information and Knowledge Technology (IKT)*, pages 113–120. IEEE, 2013.

[5] E. Bernadó-Mansilla and J. M. Garrell-Guiu. Accuracy-based Learning Classifier Systems: Models, Analysis and Applications to Classification Tasks. *Evol. Comput.*, 11(3):209–238, 2003.

[6] D. Bruschi et al. Detecting Self-mutating Malware Using Control-flow Graph Matching. In *Proceedings of the Detection of Intrusions and Malware & Vulnerability Assessment*, pages 129–143. Springer, 2006.

[7] J. Caballero et al. Measuring Pay-per-Install: The Commoditization of Malware Distribution. In *USENIX Security Symposium*, 2011.

[8] T. Cover and P. Hart. Nearest neighbor pattern classification. *IEEE Trans. on Information Theory*, 13(1):21–27, 1967.

[9] T. Cover and J. A. Thomas. *Elements of information theory*, volume 306. Wiley Online, 1991.

[10] Why spam is annoying but malware is frightening. `http://blog.emsisoft.com/2013/11/13/annoying-spam/`.

[11] A. González and R. Pérez. Slave: A genetic learning system based on an iterative approach. *IEEE Trans. on Fuzzy Systems*, 7(2):176–191, 1999.

[12] C. Grier et al. Manufacturing Compromise: The Emergence of Exploit-as-a-service. In *Proceedings of the ACM Conference on Computer and Communications Security*, pages 821–832. ACM, 2012.

[13] T. Hill and P. Lewicki. *Statistics: methods and applications.* StatSoft, 2006.

[14] J. Jang et al. BitShred: Feature Hashing Malware for Scalable Triage and Semantic Analysis. In *Proceedings of the 18th ACM Conference on Computer and Communications Security*, pages 309–320. ACM, 2011.

[15] K. Kim and B.-R. Moon. Malware Detection Based on Dependency Graph Using Hybrid Genetic Algorithm. In *Proceedings of the 12th Annual Conference on Genetic and Evolutionary Computation*, pages 1211–1218. ACM, 2010.

[16] Mcafee threats report: First quarter 2013. `http://www.mcafee.com/au/resources/reports/rp-quarterly-threat-q1-2013.pdf`.

[17] Malware Domain List. `http://malwaredomainlist.com/`.

[18] S. B. Mehdi et al. IMAD: In-execution Malware Analysis and Detection. In *Proceedings of the 11th Annual Conference on Genetic and Evolutionary Computation*, pages 1553–1560. ACM, 2009.

[19] A. Mohaisen and O. Alrawi. Unveiling Zeus: Automated Classification of Malware Samples. In *Proceedings of the 22nd International Conference on World Wide Web*, pages 829–832, 2013.

[20] A. Nappa et al. Driving in the Cloud: An Analysis of Drive-by Download Operations and Abuse Reporting. In *Detection of Intrusions and Malware, and Vulnerability Assessment*, volume 7967, pages 1–20. Springer, 2013.

[21] R. Perdisci et al. Behavioral Clustering of HTTP-based Malware and Signature Generation Using Malicious Network Traces. In *Proceedings of the 7th USENIX Conference on Networked Systems Design and Implementation*, pages 26–26. USENIX Association, 2010.

[22] J. R. Quinlan. Improved use of continuous attributes in C4.5. *Journal of Art. Int. Res.*, 4:77–90, 1996.

[23] M. Z. Rafique and M. Abulaish. xMiner: Nip the Zero Day Exploits in the Bud. In *Proceedings of the 10th International Symposium on Network Computing and Applications*, pages 99–106. IEEE Computer Society, 2011.

[24] M. Z. Rafique and J. Caballero. Firma: Malware clustering and network signature generation with mixed network behaviors. In *Proceedings of the 16th International Symposium on Research in Attacks, Intrusions and Defenses*, pages 144–163. 2013.

[25] M. Z. Rafique et al. Application of Evolutionary Algorithms in Detecting SMS Spam at Access Layer. In *Proceedings of the 13th Annual Conference on Genetic and Evolutionary Computation*, pages 1787–1794. ACM, 2011.

[26] K. Rieck et al. Learning and Classification of Malware Behavior. In *Proceedings of the 5th International Conference on Detection of Intrusions and Malware, and Vulnerability Assessment*, pages 108–125. Springer-Verlag, 2008.

[27] I. Rish. An empirical study of the naive Bayes classifier. In *Workshop on Empirical Methods in Artificial Intelligence*, pages 41–46, 2001.

[28] M. Z. Shafiq et al. On the appropriateness of evolutionary rule learning algorithms for malware detection. In *Proceedings of the 11th Annual Conference on Genetic and Evolutionary Computation Conference*, pages 2609–2616. ACM, 2009.

[29] Sophos report. `http://www.sophos.com/en-us/medialibrary/PDFs/other/sophos-security-threat-report-2014.pdf`.

[30] S. Wilson. Generalization in the XCS classifier system. In *AGPC*, pages 665–674. Morgan Kaufmann, 1998.

[31] J. Wyke. The zeroaccess botnet: Mining and fraud for massive financial gain. `http://www.sophos.com/en-us/why-sophos/our-people/technical-papers/zeroaccess-botnet.aspx`.

[32] Zeus tracker. `https://zeustracker.abuse.ch/index.php`.

Multi-Objective Routing Optimisation for Battery-Powered Wireless Sensor Mesh Networks

Alma A. M. Rahat
Computer Science
University of Exeter, UK
A.A.M.Rahat@exeter.ac.uk

Richard M. Everson *
Computer Science
University of Exeter, UK
R.M.Everson@exeter.ac.uk

Jonathan E. Fieldsend
Computer Science
University of Exeter, UK
J.E.Fieldsend@exeter.ac.uk

ABSTRACT

Mesh network topologies are becoming increasingly popular in battery powered wireless sensor networks, primarily due to the extension of network range and resilience against routing failures. However, multi-hop mesh networks suffer from higher energy costs, and the routing strategy directly affects the lifetime of nodes with limited energy sources. Hence while planning routes there are trade-offs to be considered between individual and system-wide battery lifetimes. We present a novel multi-objective routing optimisation approach using evolutionary algorithms to approximate the optimal trade-off between minimum lifetime and the average lifetime of nodes in the network. In order to accomplish this combinatorial optimisation rapidly and thus permit dynamic optimisation for self-healing networks, our approach uses novel k-shortest paths based search space pruning in conjunction with a new edge metric, which associates the energy cost at a pair of nodes with the link between them. We demonstrate our solution on a real network, deployed in the Victoria & Albert Museum, London. We show that this approach provides better trade-off solutions in comparison to the minimum energy option, and how a combination of solutions over the lifetime of the network can enhance the overall minimum lifetime.

Categories and Subject Descriptors

C.2.1 [**Computer Systems Organization**]: Computer-communication networks—*network architecture and design, wireless communication*; I.2.8 [**Artificial Intelligence**]: Problem Solving, Control Methods, and Search—*Graph and tree search strategies, Heuristics methods*; G.2.2 [**Discrete Mathematics**]: Graph Theory—*Network problems, Path and circuit problems*

General Terms

Algorithms, Experimentation, Performance, Reliability

*Corresponding author.

GECCO'14, July 12–16, 2014, Vancouver, BC, Canada.
Copyright 2014 ACM 978-1-4503-2662-9/14/07 ...$15.00.
http://dx.doi.org/10.1145/2576768.2598311.

Keywords

Mesh networks, shortest path, evolutionary algorithms, multi-objective optimisation, network lifetime optimisation

1. INTRODUCTION

Wireless Sensor Networks (WSNs) consist of autonomous devices distributed over a wide area that are able to sense and periodically report environmental parameters such as temperature or humidity. They are extensively used for remote monitoring, especially in industrial and regulatory applications. Many applications require sensors to be placed far from easy access to mains power so battery-powered sensors are popular and are often necessary in such situations. However, it is also desirable that sensors can be left unattended, without battery replacement for as long as possible. In this paper we therefore investigate the use of multi-objective evolutionary algorithms to find routing schemes for *mesh* wireless sensor networks that optimally preserve the life of the network.

Many existing commercial products use an *ad hoc* topology for WSNs. Generally, these *ad hoc* networks are point to multi-point networks, in which each sensor reports directly to a central base station. Despite being a low power solution, major limitations include limited network range as each sensor node must be able to communicate directly with the base station, and the strictly rigid network structure means that networks are unable to cope with changing conditions in a dynamic radio environment, which may occur as buildings are modified or furniture is moved. As a consequence sometimes multiple base stations are required to cover a single site.

As a solution, in recent years, mesh network topologies, where data is relayed from node to node *en route* to the base station, have grown in popularity. In addition to extending the range that can be covered by using multiple hops, mesh networks provide the opportunity of using alternative routes, thus increasing resilience to radio environment changes. However, mesh networks are expensive in terms of energy consumption due to a higher overhead at each node for additional activities, namely relaying messages for other nodes and, in systems with distributed planning, calculating new routes. These additional activities can be severely detrimental to the overall life of the network before it requires servicing and battery replacement. It is desirable to maximise the average life of nodes in the network, but in addition it will usually be important to maximise the time before the battery of the shortest-lived node is exhausted. Therefore, routing optimisation in mesh networks with careful consideration of the trade-off between individual and system-wide battery lifetimes within the network, is necessary for a practical implementation.

Efficient energy usage in WSNs has attracted much research interest in recent years, especially because frequent changing of batteries is infeasible. Approaches can be divided into distributed and centralised [10]. Distributed approaches, in which responsibility for routing is distributed across the constituent nodes, involve techniques like reinforcement learning [7] and swarm intelligence [1], etc. On the other hand centralised systems, in which a centrally calculated route is broadcast to participating nodes, mostly incorporate variants of evolutionary algorithms (EAs) [11, 13, 8]. In the distributed approach, nodes need to have sufficient computational power to decide on the best path for sending data and sufficient storage for storing information about local connectivity. In comparison centralised approaches require lower computational power and lower static storage for storing route information because they only require knowledge about the node specific route information, but there is system-wide overhead incurred for gathering connectivity information and broadcasting routing information. In this paper we consider very low powered nodes each of which has limited computational power and storage. Routes are therefore computed at a mains-powered base station node.

Most current EA-based energy-aware centralised systems consider energy expense. This is the case even for multi-objective routing optimisation, where energy expense is optimised with other objectives based on factors like quality of service, bandwidth, packet loss ratio, etc. [11, 13]. However, optimising the overall energy expenditure of a network may be detrimental to the overall performance of the network, because often the goal is to prolong the lifetime of the network before batteries need replacing. Merely reducing the overall energy expenditure may place a large burden on a few nodes, resulting in the rapid exhaustion of their batteries. We therefore seek to optimise the lifetime of network nodes by modelling the charge held in their batteries and the energy expenditure at *each* node. Islam *et al.* [8], and Kamath *et al.* [9] have considered maximising only the minimum remaining lifetime among nodes. Such approaches can improve individual node specific energy state, but can be sub-optimal from system-wide perspective. We therefore seek to find the optimal trade-off between local and network-wide battery lifetimes.

In this paper, we consider a centralised approach due to the limitation of computational power and storage that a real network entails. As network longevity is our primary goal, we use a multi-objective evolutionary optimiser to simultaneously maximise the minimum lifetime of any node in the network together with the average lifetime of all nodes in the network. In practice our system also monitors packet-loss-ratio and quality-of-service performance indicators, so that re-optimisation can be invoked if performance declines, and thus permitting self-healing in dynamic radio environments. Using this procedure we are able to achieve better performance than minimum energy route and we show that using a combination of solutions over the lifetime of the network can extend minimum lifetime of the network.

In section 2 we describe the model of the system. In section 3 we present a novel search space pruning method. In section 4 we discuss the multi-objective evolutionary routing optimisation strategy. Based on this, in section 5, we demonstrate and discuss our findings in a real network deployed in the Victoria & Albert Museum, London. In section 6 we discuss how minimum lifetime of the system can be extended through re-optimisation. In section 7 we present re-optimisation as a tool to cope with the dynamism of the radio environment. Finally, the conclusions are presented in section 8.

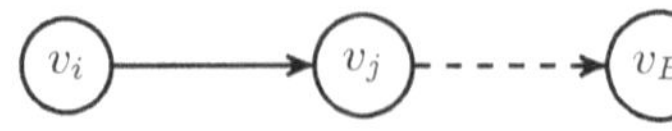

Figure 1: Route $S_i = \langle v_i, v_j, \ldots, v_B \rangle$ from v_i via v_j to the base station v_B.

2. SYSTEM MODEL AND PARETO OPTIMALITY

In this section we model the WSN and derive a multi-objective problem in order to investigate the trade-off between individual and system-wide impacts on the remaining lifetimes of nodes due to possible routing schemes in a network.

A WSN is represented as a network graph, $G = \{V, E\}$, where V is a finite set of n sensor nodes v_i plus a base station node, v_B, and E is the finite set of m edges [2, 4]. Each node must communicate with the base station, perhaps by relaying a message through one or more other nodes. In our scheme each node reports its status once every reporting cycle (e.g. once each minute).

As illustrated in Figure 1, a route from node v_i to the base station v_B is described by the sequence, $S_i = \langle v_i, v_j, \ldots, v_B \rangle$. We denote by $S_i[p]$ the pth element of the route S_i. A *routing scheme* R is a set of routes, one for each node in the network to the base station:

$$R = \{S_1, S_2, \ldots, S_n\}. \tag{1}$$

An initial mapping phase, preceding optimisation, is used to discover which other nodes the node v_i can communicate with. Communications may take place using a variety of baud rates and powers, so we assume that the most energy efficient baud rate and power combination has been discovered for each pair of nodes that can communicate; generally low power and high baud rates are most efficient in our system, but the optimisation does not rely on this. Also we assume that communication is reliable at this baud rate and power combination (given the current configuration of the physical environment in which the network is deployed).

The energy required to transmit a message from v_i to the base station is found by summing the energies required to transmit a message between each of the nodes comprising the route:

$$H_i = \sum_{p=1}^{l-1} e_{S_i[p], S_i[p+1]} \tag{2}$$

where l is the length of the route and e_{jk} is the energy required to transmit a message from v_j to v_k. Note that this generally involves energy expenditure at both the transmitting node and the receiving node, and will also involve expenditures for transmitting an acknowledgement. As noted above, we assume that the communication is reliable, but if an acknowledgement is not received from the receiver the message is resent; this additional expense is not modelled, but if a link becomes unreliable, the routing is re-optimised.

In many routing optimisation problems, such as shortest path problems, minimising a route's overall cost is desirable. The overall cost is found by summing the costs associated with each edge in the route. There are many well-known methods for minimising such costs, e.g. [5]. In this problem, however, we focus on the costs expended at the *nodes* themselves, rather than the edge costs. This is because it is energy expended at the nodes that depletes charge in the batteries and thus governs the lifetime of a node.

Let T_{ij} be the energy (charge) required at node v_i to send a message to v_j and let A_{ik} be the energy required to receive a message from v_k at v_i. Then in one reporting cycle, the energy expended at v_i in sending its own data to its downstream node $d = S_i[2]$ and relaying messages received from nodes with indices in the set $\mathcal{I}$ and sending them on to nodes with indices $\mathcal{O}$ is

$$C_i = T_{id} + \sum_{k \in \mathcal{I}} A_{ik} + \sum_{j \in \mathcal{O}} T_{ij}. \tag{3}$$

Clearly $\sum_i^n C_i = \sum_i^n H_i$ is equal to the energy cost across the whole network of sending a message from each node.

In order to calculate the lifetime remaining due to a routing scheme we require additional intrinsic information about the nodes, namely the charge Q_i remaining in the battery and the quiescent energy consumption per reporting cycle E_i due to constant micro-controller operation, sensor measurements, running an on-board display, etc. The life of the current node therefore is modelled as

$$L_i = \frac{Q_i}{(E_i + C_i)N} \tag{4}$$

where N is the number of reporting cycles per unit time. We emphasise $L_i = L_i(R)$, i.e. L_i is a function of all the routes which utilise v_i.

Our goal is to prolong the average life of the network, that is to minimise the total energy consumed, and to maximise the time before any individual node requires its battery to be recharged or changed. We therefore seek to maximise the two objective problem:

$$\text{Maximise } f_1(R) = \frac{1}{n} \sum_{i=1}^{n} L_i(R). \tag{5}$$

$$\text{Maximise } f_2(R) = \min_{i \in [1,n]} L_i(R). \tag{6}$$

In addition, it may be important to maximise the lifetime of one or more nodes v_i for $i \in U$, because, for example, they are particularly inaccessible. In this case the two-objective problem is augmented with a third objective:

$$\text{Maximise } f_3(R) = \min_{i \in U} L_i(R). \tag{7}$$

Solving this multi-objective problem may result in multiple solutions, as opposed to a single solution for single objective optimisation. In this case, there exists a set of solutions which are Pareto optimal; that is, there are no other feasible solutions available that improve performance on one objective, without a simultaneous decrease in at least in one other objective [3].

The dominance criterion is used to locate such solutions in the search space. The dominance criterion from a routing optimisation perspective is described as follows. In a multi-objective problem with D objectives, a routing scheme, R', is said to dominate another routing scheme, R, denoted $R' \succ R$, iff

$$f_i(R') \geq f_i(R) \; \forall i = 1, 2, \ldots, D, \text{ and} \tag{8}$$
$$f_i(R') > f_i(R) \text{ for some } i.$$

Hence, we seek the maximal set of feasible routes which are mutually non-dominating, which is known as the Pareto set, $\mathcal{P}$.

3. SEARCH SPACE PRUNING

The multi-objective optimisation problem described above is a combinatorial optimisation problem with, for practical WSNs, a vast number of potential solutions. It is crucial for practical implementations that the optimisation process is fast. A way to improve the speed of optimisation is to sensibly prune the search space, while retaining important potential solutions. For this purpose we deploy a novel k-shortest path based technique. Before describing the evolutionary algorithm employed, we therefore discuss the way in which solutions are represented and the search space pruned to permit an efficient approximation of the Pareto set.

The number of possible routing schemes, i.e. the search space size, depends on the number of available routes for each node in the system. For instance, in a network with n nodes excluding the base station with let the number of available loopless paths from v_i to v_B be a_i. In this case, the number of possible routing schemes, i.e. the number of combinations of routes for individual nodes that can build the routing scheme, is:

$$Z_a = \prod_{i=1}^{n} a_i. \tag{9}$$

In order to combat the potential growth in the size of the search space as the number of nodes increases we therefore limit the number of potential routes available to each node. More specifically, we attempt to search for solutions in the space defined by the k-shortest paths for each node, where the metric defining the k-shortest paths is defined below. This reflects our intuition that short paths to the base station are most likely to be energy efficient. We select from among several shortest path routes for each node because if each node were to utilise its shortest path a single node on many of them would be disproportionately burdened.

Algorithms for discovering the shortest path between two nodes in a weighted graph are well known and the shortest path can be found in $O(n \log n)$ time. However, as we noted above, the energy costs in this problem are associated with the nodes themselves rather than with the edges. We therefore weight the edges in the network graph to associate the energetic cost at the nodes with the edges connecting them. Consider the nodes v_i and v_j. We define the weight of the edge between them as:

$$w_{ij} = \frac{e_{ij}}{Q_i} + \frac{e_{ji}}{Q_j}, \tag{10}$$

where, as above, e_{ij} is the energy required to transmit a message from v_i to v_j, and Q_i and Q_j are the battery charges. It is expected that $e_{ij} = e_{ji}$. This edge weighting models the fact that a high transmission cost can be borne by nodes with a high battery charge, but transmission is relatively expensive for nodes with low battery charge because each transmission will make a larger fractional depletion of the

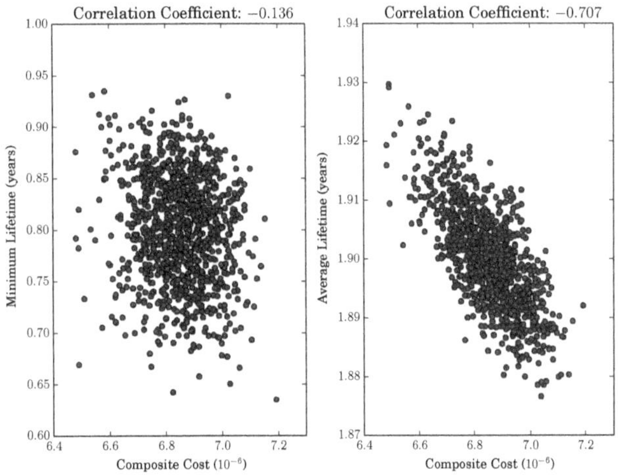

Figure 2: Correlation between objectives and composite cost. Scatter plots show *(right)* the composite cost and true average lifetime $f_1(R)$ and *(left)* minimum lifetime $f_2(R)$ for 1000 randomly generated routing schemes with random residual charges at the nodes.

charge. Likewise transmissions are free if $Q_i = \infty$ (i.e. the node is connected to mains power). Note that $Q_i / \sum_j e_{ij}$ is an estimate of the lifetime of v_i. We call the cost of a routing scheme calculated using the weights w_{ij} the *composite cost*.

As we require diversity in the search space and the possibility of load balancing among nodes, we propose to evolve solutions from among the k-shortest paths for each node calculated with the composite cost (10). A number of algorithms are available for computing the k shortest paths; see for example [12, 5]. In our implementation we have used Eppstein's algorithm [5] modified to produce only simple or loopless paths, which matches the best upper-bound time complexity for finding k-shortest simple paths [5]. We denote the mth shortest route found for node v_i by S_i^m, for $m = 1, \ldots, k$. Using this technique, the total size of the search space is no larger than k^n, although it may be smaller than this because nodes close to v_B may not have k loopless paths to v_B.

3.1 Relationship between objectives and composite cost

In order to validate the use of the composite metric for choosing candidate routes, Figure 2 presents the correlation between the objectives and composite cost for 1000 randomly chosen routing schemes with random residual charge levels Q_i at nodes for the Victoria & Albert museum network described below. There is a fairly strong negative correlation between the average battery life $f_1(R)$ and the composite cost. This indicates that routing schemes selected with low composite cost via the k-shortest paths algorithm are likely to have long average lives. On the other hand, there exists a weak negative relationship between the minimum lifetime and composite cost. This is unsurprising since the minimum lifetime depends on a *single* node in the network and is highly dependent on the interaction between routes.

Algorithm 1 Optimisation of Battery Powered Mesh Network

Inputs

T = Number of iterations
s = Size of initial archive
μ = Perturbation rate
c = Uniform crossover rate

Steps

```
A ← InitialiseArchive(s)              ▷ Initialise random archive
for i = 1 → T do
    {R1, R2} ← Select(A)              ▷ Select two parent solutions
    R' ← UniformCrossOver(R1, R2, c)
    R'' ← Perturb(R', μ)              ▷ Mutation
    A ← NonDominated(A ∪ R'')         ▷ Update archive
end for
return A                              ▷ Approximation of the Pareto set
```

4. MULTI-OBJECTIVE ROUTING OPTIMISATION

The multi-objective evolutionary algorithm used in this approach is a real-valued genetic algorithm, which maintains an unconstrained Pareto archive to reap the benefits of better convergence properties [6], but does not employ an independent search population. Algorithm 1 describes this process in more detail.

Solutions R are represented by vectors of n integers; the ith element of the solution indexes one of the k shortest paths found for node v_i. In the initialisation step, we generate at random a population from the pruned search space. This population comprises random routing schemes where the member routes are picked from the k-shortest paths for each node; thus for node v_i the shortest paths are selected from $\{S_i^m\}_{m=1}^k$. Additionally, we include in the initial population the routing scheme which uses the first shortest route for each node. The initial archive of non-dominated solutions A is the maximal non-dominated subset of this random population. At any step of the evolution, A is the current approximation of the Pareto set.

During the evolution process, we randomly select two routing schemes. These parent routing schemes are then crossed-over uniformly with a crossover rate c, resulting in the single dominating offspring. The child is then perturbed by changing routes randomly within the routing scheme, where the number of changes depends on the perturbation rate, μ. The offspring from perturbation is compared against the members in the archive: if it is not dominated by any of them then it enters the archive and any elements of A which are dominated by the new solution are removed from A. In this fashion only the non-dominated routing schemes are preserved in the archive and the archive can only approach the true Pareto set. The process of evolution continues for a fixed number of episodes (alternatively, another termination criterion, such as specified minimum dominated hypervolume, may be employed).

Once the evolution process is finished, the decision maker may manually choose the operating point using the final approximation of the Pareto front, based on the expected network longevity. The chosen routing scheme is sent to the nodes through the base station, and it then becomes the active data reporting scheme in the system.

5. ILLUSTRATION

A real network deployed in the Victoria & Albert Museum, London, is used to illustrate the proposed approach. In a controlled environment over a vast area, such as Victoria & Albert Museum, it is essential to monitor temperature and humidity in galleries and display cases for the preservation of the artefacts. Compared to wired networks, battery powered WSNs carry huge advantages in deployment cost and flexibility.

The network incorporated 30 sensor nodes and a base station, spanning five floors within an approximate area of 35000 m^2. This provides a challenging radio environment with thick, solid walls and a dynamic medium varying with the rate of passage of people in the galleries.

The connectivity map was built in an initial mapping phase in which nodes pinged each other using a range of baud rates and powers to discover the minimum energy configuration for communication between those nodes within radio range of each other.

Subspace pruning using $k = 10$ shortest paths still results in a search space of 10^{30} solutions. The initial population was built with 100 randomly chosen solutions from this subspace together with the solution consisting of the shortest route for each node. The initial archive was then found by extracting the non-dominated solutions in this population.

For optimisation purposes, we used $\mu = c = 0.1$ as the perturbation and crossover rates; these rates were chosen after a short empirical study on simulated networks, but the performance of the optimiser is relatively insensitive to their precise values. Using the dominated hypervolume measure, the Pareto set was well converged after 150, 000 iterations.

A single core Python implementation takes about 2 minutes to complete 150,000 iterations on a 2.5 GHz machine. As a consequence, the optimum routes for the new installations can be found readily, making this approach particularly feasible as part of a real system.

5.1 Baseline optimisation

Figure 3 shows the Pareto front resulting from the optimisation of the network. As the figure shows, routing schemes in the Pareto set provide the network operator with a wide range of routes trading off the average lifetime of the network against the time before any single node needs its battery replacing. We note that the optimisation has resulted in routing schemes that are substantially better, in terms of both average and minimum lifetime, than routing schemes utilising randomly chosen routes from the 10 shortest paths (I, marked with blue crosses in the figure). Indeed, the routing scheme with the longest minimum life has an average lifetime that is better than any of the solutions in the initial random population. Interestingly, the routing scheme, R_c in which each node uses its shortest path route (according to the composite cost) lies close to the Pareto front, although it is dominated by solutions in the Pareto front. We include R_c in the initial archive.

As a result of optimisation, we were able to derive the trade-off front that dominates the shortest paths routing scheme, and thus any solution from the front performs better in comparison. For example, the solution directly above R_c can provide 1 more month in the minimum lifetime, with the same average lifetime. Also, considering the left-most solution, we can get an improvement of 2.5 months in minimum lifetime at the expense of 0.5 months of average lifetime.

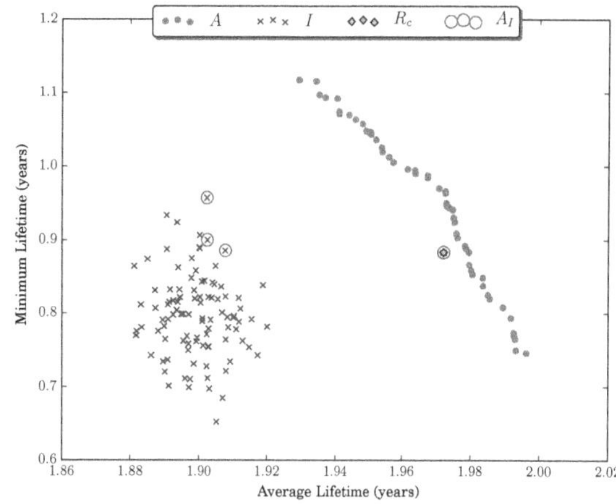

Figure 3: Baseline Optimisation. Pareto front approximation (red) and randomly generated initial solutions (blue) for the Victoria & Albert museum network. Non-dominated solutions comprising the initial archive are shown as in blue with green rings and the solution in which each node uses its shortest path based on the composite cost is shown in orange/black.

6. EXTENDING MINIMUM LIFETIME

It is of considerable practical importance to maximise the minimum lifetime of any node in the network, because the network requires no maintenance until the battery of the shortest-lived node is exhausted. Rather than using a single routing scheme for the lifetime of the network it can be advantageous to adopt a new routing scheme partway through its life which can serve to prolong the time before any single node's battery is exhausted. Rerouting of the network can be accomplished at low energy cost from the base station. To see how this can be useful, suppose that under the initial routing scheme R, a node $v^\star$ has the minimum lifetime. Now suppose that the network is optimised a second time after it has been in operation for a while. The result of this second optimisation can be a routing scheme in which $v^\star$ is very lightly loaded, prolonging its life, while a different node, v', which was lightly loaded in the first epoch, now carries a heavier load. In this way the life of $v^\star$ is extended and it may be that $v^\star$ or v' or some other node is exhausted first, but in any case the time before any single node is exhausted may be extended.

To illustrate this, we choose the routing solution with the best minimum lifetime from the Pareto front shown in Figure 3, that is, the left-most solution, which we denote by R. We simulate the operation of the network for 6 months, roughly one third of the average lifetime of the network or roughly half of the time (1.12 years) before $v^\star = v_{21}$ would be exhausted. Note that during this time, the batteries in the various nodes are discharged at different rates, so that after 6 months the residual charges $\{Q_i\}_{i=1}^n$ are unequal. Figure 4 shows the result of re-optimising the routings using these residual charges. Here A' is the new Pareto optimal front, which can be seen to dominate the original routing scheme R which is marked in blue. Note that the remaining lifetimes for R are 6 months smaller than those appearing in Figure 3 because the network has been running for 6 months.

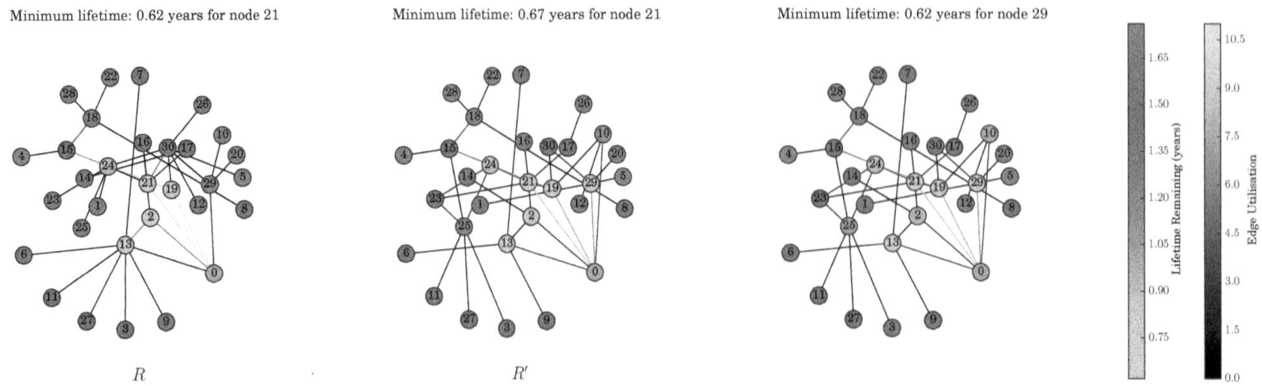

Figure 6: Network graphs. Nodes are coloured according to the remaining battery life and edges are coloured according to the utilisation of the corresponding link. *Left:* Network corresponding to the minimum lifetime solution R shown in the Figure 3. *Middle:* Network R', the best minimum life network following re-optimisation based on R after 6 months. *Right:* Routing R' showing lifetime remaining after 6 months operation, but using R' throughout.

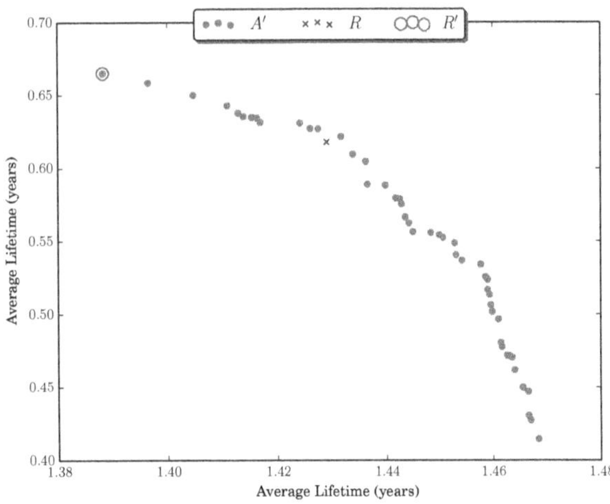

Figure 4: Re-optimised Pareto Front. The system simulated for 6 months with operating point R (blue cross). Re-optimisation with battery states after 6 months of operating R generates the Pareto front A' (red dots), with R' being the best minimum lifetime solution.

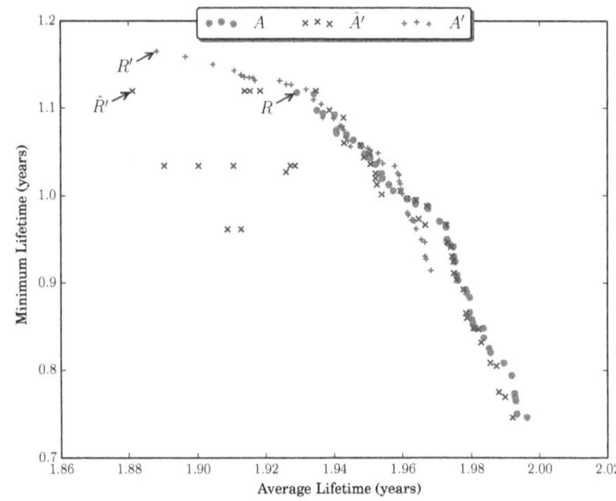

Figure 5: Comparison of overall lifetimes from one and two-stage optimisation. The Pareto front corresponding to the original optimisation is shown in red, with R being the best minimum lifetime solution from this archive A. Re-optimisation with battery states after 6 months of operating R generates the trade-off of overall lifetimes A' (green pluses), with R' being the best minimum lifetime solution. Blue crosses indicate the lifetimes of solutions from A' evaluated with the initial battery states; $\hat{R}'$ is the solution R' evaluated with the initial battery states.

We draw attention to the best minimum lifetime solution, R' from this second optimisation which has a significantly longer life than the scheme R. Thus using R for the first 6 months, followed by R' prolongs the life of the network before any battery needs changing.

To examine this further, Figure 5 compares the overall lifetimes available using the two-stage optimisation with the original lifetimes. The original Pareto front is shown in red, while the green symbols show the Pareto archive A' resulting from the second optimisation (Figure 4) with 6 months added to each objective coordinate to show the total lifetimes of the two-stage networks. Also shown, in blue and labelled $\hat{A}'$, are the routing schemes in A' re-evaluated using the batteries with charges corresponding to the initial optimisation. The $\hat{A}'$ routing schemes do not dominate the original schemes in A with one or two minor exceptions which indicate that the Pareto front is not quite fully converged.

We note that the re-optimisation was performed using k-shortest paths derived using battery charges after 6 months operation of R so a slightly different set of potential solutions was available to this optimisation.

In Figure 6 we portray network graphs corresponding to R, R', and $\hat{R}'$. The left panel of the figure illustrates the lifetimes of the nodes using the best minimum lifetime routing R from the original optimisation after it has been in use for 6 months. Nodes are coloured according to their remaining life and in this case it can be seen that node 21 has the minimum lifetime of 0.62 years. Edges are shaded according to their utilisation and, unsurprisingly, it can be seen the

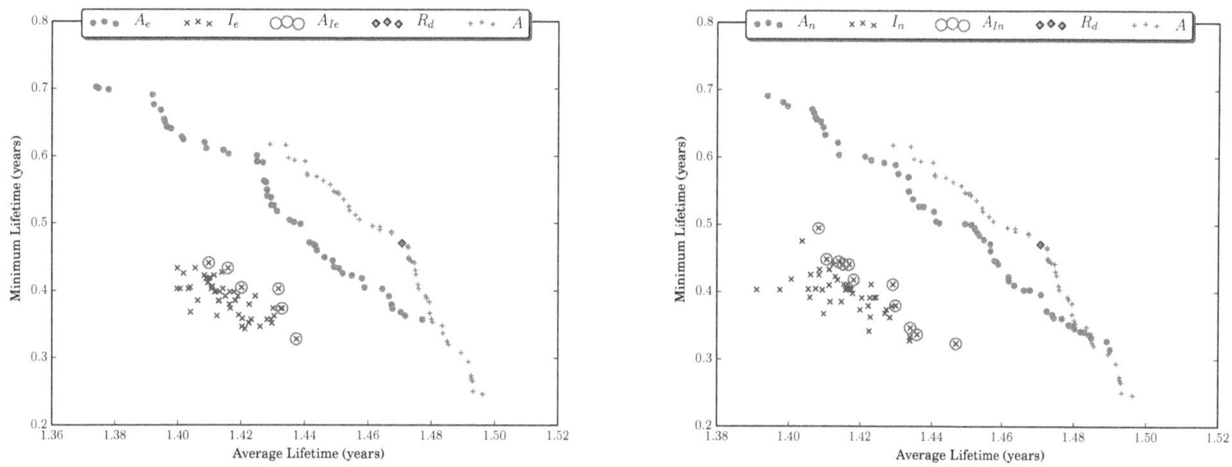

(a) Re-optimisation following deletion of edge $v_{19} \to v_B$.

(b) Re-optimisation following failure of node v_{19}.

Figure 7: Dynamic Optimisation. Average and minimum lifetimes remaining for solutions in the Pareto front after 6 months of operation (magenta pluses) using the route scheme R_d (black/orange diamond). The Pareto front resulting from re-optimisation as a result of node or edge failure is shown by red dots. The routes repaired by random selection from k shortest paths are denoted by blue crosses, and initial archive by green rings.

links to v_{21} are well used (the link $v_{21} \to v_B$ is used by 11 routes), resulting in its short life.

The network illustrated in the middle panel of Figure 6 corresponds to R', the routing scheme with the best minimum lifetime resulting from a second optimisation after 6 months based on R. As can be seen, although v_{21} is still the first node to be exhausted its life has been extended by heavier utilisation of nodes 29 and 10; in particular the $v_{21} \to v_B$ link is now used only 8 times. This redistribution of loading during the two epochs is what allows the combination of R and R' to provide superior performance to R alone. The right panel of Figure 6 shows the lifetimes remaining after 6 months using R' from the outset. Here v_{29} has the minimum life of 0.62 years which is equivalent to the minimum life v_{21} using R and no benefit is accrued from using either scheme alone. It is the combination of the two schemes that allows energy to be expended more evenly around the network, protecting different nodes in different epochs, that enables the overall minimum life of the network to be prolonged.

Clearly, this two-stage combination of routing schemes could be extended to incorporate additional epochs, although we speculate that smaller relative gains will be made as additional epochs are added. Also in the work we present here the point at which to switch from R to R' was fixed in advance of the optimisations and the second optimisation was carried out independently of the first. Current work is investigating simultaneous optimisation of two or more epoch combinations.

7. DYNAMIC OPTIMISATION

As WSNs operate in a dynamic environment, it is conceivable that over time some of the links in the routing scheme will fail. In addition nodes can disappear from the network due to hardware failure or changing requirements and new nodes can be introduced as the network is extended. Hence, it is important to detect failures and re-establish connectivity with optimal routes, thus enabling self-healing within the network.

These failures can be detected from the failure of nodes to report data within an expected period of time as indicated by the packet loss ratio. The particular edge that failed can be detected as nodes succeeding the failed link send a distress signal to the base station. In such cases, the solutions from the original Pareto front may become infeasible, as they may include the lost nodes or edges. Therefore, depending on the reliability thresholds as set by the decision maker, a re-optimisation is necessary in order to find the optimal front in this new state using the latest connectivity information. We note that the solutions from the original Pareto set contain previous knowledge of good routes which is useful for routes unaffected by the failure. These routes can be fused with newly-generated random routes in order to build the initial archive for a re-optimisation. Here we generate an initial archive for re-optimisation by replacing the affected routes from the original front with randomly selected alternatives from the available $k = 10$ shortest paths and extracting the non-dominated subset. Using this initial archive can promote subsequent rapid optimisation.

To illustrate dynamic optimisation, we select a solution R_d, which provides a good balance between minimum lifetime and average lifetime among the solutions in the original Pareto front. The network is then simulated for 6 months, and consequently R_d has a minimum lifetime of 0.47 years and an average lifetime of 1.47 years as shown in Figure 7. We noted that the node v_{19} has the minimum lifetime at this stage.

To exemplify the effects of edge failure, we delete the link between v_{19} and the base station. This edge was selected as it is common among the solutions in the original front with an average of 13 routes per solution using this link; the failure of this link therefore represents considerable damage to the network. As a result, all solutions in the original

Pareto set become infeasible. By combining the unaffected routes with random routes from 10 shortest paths, we derive an initial archive, I_e for a new optimisation. This archive is then used to optimise the network as described in section 5.1.

The Pareto fronts resulting from the re-optimisation after damage are shown in Figure 7. For both edge deletion (Figure 7a) and node failure (Figure 7b), a large portion of the new optimal front is dominated by the original front. This is unsurprising because in both cases the solution space has been significantly reduced and new optimal routes to the base station are necessarily longer than the original routes. Interestingly, however, the re-optimisation has found solutions that prolong the minimum life of the network in the way as discussed in section 6. This leads to a considerable portion of the re-estimated front being mutually non-dominating with solutions from the original Pareto front, giving the network manager considerable flexibility to choose a new operating point. We remark that because both objectives are expressed in common units (years) it is straightforward to automatically choose the new routing scheme that is closest to the original R_d using the Euclidean distance.

The utility of initialising the re-optimisation archive with solutions constructed from the original archive is evident in that, based on the hypervolume, the re-optimisation converged roughly three times as fast as an optimisation starting from random solutions, even in this case where the network was considerably damaged.

8. CONCLUSIONS

Using mesh network topologies in low power Wireless Sensor Networks poses a challenging problem of finding routes that best preserve the lifetime of individual nodes and the network as a whole. In this paper we have proposed a multi-objective evolutionary approach to approximate the optimum trade-off between local and global objectives, i.e. minimum lifetime remaining for any node and average lifetime remaining for the whole network. The potentially vast solution space is reduced by searching for routes among the approximate k-shortest paths from each node to the base station. This is made possible by associating energy costs at nodes with the edges between them using a heuristic metric. Use of the approximate k-shortest paths also provides a convenient method of representing solutions in the evolutionary optimiser.

We have shown in a real system, deployed in the Victoria & Albert Museum, that the optimiser is able to estimate the optimum trade-off between the minimum lifetime of any node in the network and the average lifetime of the network as a whole. Interestingly it was also found that the range of minimum lifetimes available can also be significantly extended by using more than one routing scheme successively. In essence this works by protecting during the first epoch nodes that will bear a heavy load in the second epoch and *vice versa*. To achieve these combined routing schemes two optimisations were required and a solution from the first optimisation must be selected as the basis for the second optimisation. Current work focuses on efficient evolutionary optimisation methods to simultaneously locate solutions for both epochs which has the potential to achieve more efficient networks.

9. ACKNOWLEDGEMENTS

This work was supported by a Knowledge Transfer Partnership awarded to the University of Exeter and The IMC Group Ltd. We would like to thank Martin Hancock (Technical Director, The IMC Group Ltd.), and Neil Lundy (Engineering Manager, The IMC Group Ltd.) for their support and contributions. We would also like to thank Boris Pretzel (Chief Scientist, Victoria & Albert Museum), and Bhavesh Shah (Scientist, Victoria & Albert Museum), for facilitating the real network test. A patent application based on this work has been made (reference number: GB 1400353.7).

10. REFERENCES

[1] S. Bashyal and G. K. Venayagamoorthy. Collaborative routing algorithm for wireless sensor network longevity. In *Intelligent Sensors, Sensor Networks and Information, ISSNIP'07.*, pages 515–520, 2007.

[2] A. W. Brander and M. C. Sinclair. A comparative study of k-shortest path algorithms. In *Proc. 11th UK Performance Eng. Workshop*, pages 370–379, 1995.

[3] C. A. C. Coello, G. B. Lamont, and D. A. V. Veldhuisen. *Evolutionary algorithms for solving multi-objective problems.* Springer, 2001.

[4] T. H. Cormen, C. E. Leiserson, R. L. Rivest, and C. Stein. *Introduction to Algorithms.* MIT Press, 2001.

[5] D. Eppstein. Finding the k shortest paths. *SIAM Journal on Computing*, 28(2):652–673, 1998.

[6] J. E. Fieldsend, R. M. Everson, and S. Singh. Using unconstrained elite archives for multiobjective optimization. *IEEE Transactions on Evolutionary Computation*, 7(3):305–323, 2003.

[7] A. Förster. Machine learning techniques applied to wireless ad-hoc networks: Guide and survey. In *Intelligent Sensors, Sensor Networks and Information, ISSNIP'07*, pages 365–370, 2007.

[8] O. Islam and S. Hussain. An intelligent multi-hop routing for wireless sensor networks. In *IEEE/WIC/ACM International Conference on Web Intelligence and Intelligent Agent Technology Workshops*, pages 239–242, 2006.

[9] S. Kamath and A. Nasipuri. Integrated load balanced and energy aware routing in large scale wireless sensor networks. In *IEEE, 30th International Performance Computing and Communications Conference (IPCCC), 2011*, pages 1–8, 2011.

[10] R. V. Kulkarni, A. Förster, and G. K. Venayagamoorthy. Computational intelligence in wireless sensor networks: A survey. *IEEE Comms Surveys & Tutorials*, 13(1):68–96, 2011.

[11] F. Xue, A. Sanderson, and R. Graves. Multi-objective routing in wireless sensor networks with a differential evolution algorithm. In *Proceedings of the 2006 IEEE International Conference on Networking, Sensing and Control, ICNSC '06*, pages 880–885, 2006.

[12] J. Y. Yen. Finding the K shortest loopless paths in a network. *Management Science*, 17:712–716, 1971.

[13] H. Yetgin, K. T. K. Cheung, and L. Hanzo. Multi-objective routing optimization using evolutionary algorithms. In *Wireless Communications and Networking Conference (WCNC)*, pages 3030–3034, 2012.

Applying GA with Local Search by Taking Hamming Distances into Consideration to Credit Erasure Processing Problems

Yuji Sato
Hosei University
3-7-2 Kajino-cho Koganei-shi
Tokyo 184-8584 JAPAN
+81-42-387-4533
yuji@k.hosei.ac.jp

Yusuke Oku
Hosei University
3-7-2 Kajino-cho Koganei-shi
Tokyo 184-8584 JAPAN
+81-42-461-6064
yusuke.oku.r6@stu.hosei.ac.jp

Masanori Fukuda
Hitachi Management Partner Corp.
2-29 Kanda-awaji-cho Chiyoda-ku
Tokyo 101-0063 JAPAN
+81-3-4541-2514
masanori.fukuda.pc@hitachi.com

ABSTRACT
Credit erasure processing refers to the process of canceling corresponding items from a list of accounts receivable by checking against a detailed statement when receiving accounts receivable and other payments. In credit erasure processing, it is sometimes necessary to perform the laborious task of searching for credited items based solely on billing data and payments received. In this paper, we define credit erasure processing as a large-scale subset sum problem, and propose a solution based on a genetic algorithm (GA). In particular, we propose improving the search precision by incorporating a local search method that takes Hamming distances into consideration. To this end, we compare the standard GA with the result of adding a simple local search to the standard GA. This is done using a set of data where the numbers of digits in the billed quantities are roughly the same, another set of data where the numbers of digits are more varied, and a set of real data. As a result, we show that the proposed method works effectively when the numbers of digits in the billed quantities are roughly the same or when the fitness score is has a somewhat higher value.

Categories and Subject Descriptors
D.0 [Computer Applications]: General

General Terms
Algorithms, Performance, Design, Economics, Experimentation.

Keywords
Credit Erasure Processing, Genetic Algorithms, Local Search.

1. INTRODUCTION
When receiving payments including accounts receivable, credit erasure processing is the process whereby the accuracy of figures such as late payments and accounts receivable is checked while eliminating corresponding items from a list of accounts receivable by checking against a detailed statement. Although payments can be simply automated on the basis of one payment per bill, it is basically almost a hundred payments and often the case that over a hundred payments are lumped together in transactions between companies in order to reduce the transfer fees. In such cases, it is not uncommon for there to be discrepancies between the billed amounts and payments received due to slight temporal shifts in collection depending on the department or the person processing the payments. Therefore, in credit erasure processing, it is necessary to obtain a breakdown of the corresponding billed amounts based on the payments received, and this can basically be defined as a particular case of a particular case of a subset sum problem [1]. It has already been shown that subset sum problems are NP-complete, and it is known that they can be solved by dynamic programming (DP) [2].

On the other hand, DP requires a large amount of memory proportional to the size of the payments received. This can sometimes make it impossible to apply DP in cases where large payments are received in transactions between companies, thus making it necessary to search for a breakdown of payments either by running an exhaustive search program or by relying on the manual labor of multiple accountants. But if an exhaustive search program is used, it could run all night without finding a solution, and if the work is done manually, then it can cause a large spike in the workload at specific times such as the end of each accounting period.

In this paper, we propose solving these issues with a method in which credit erasure processing is performed using a genetic algorithm (GA). GA methods can solve the subset sum problem (a special case of the knapsack problem) with less memory than DP, and lend themselves to fast execution in parallel many-core environments such as graphics processing units (GPUs) [3]. We also propose improving the search precision by combining this method with a local search that takes Hamming distances into consideration, and we evaluate the effectiveness of this approach.

Section 2 below presents an overview of credit erasure processing and the issues thereof. In Section 3, we propose the application of GA to credit erasure processing, and we present our basic idea of performing local searches taking Hamming distances into consideration. In Section 4, we present a GA design method for credit erasure processing. In Section 5, we present our evaluation method and test results, and finally we conclude with a discussion and summary of this study.

GECCO'14, July 12–16, 2014, Vancouver, BC, Canada.

ACM 978-1-4503-2662-9/14/07…$15.00.
http://dx.doi.org/10.1145/2576768.2598229

2. CREDIT ERASURE PROCESSING AND ITS ISSUES

Figure 1 shows an overview of credit erasure processing in Japan. Credit erasure processing refers to the process of matching up receivables with invoices in the processing of accounts receivable and debt recovery in ordinary businesses. Specifically, it is the process whereby receivables are eliminated by canceling the billing details corresponding to data on residual billing amounts when payments are received from a purchasing business. In order to reduce the transfer fees, purchasing businesses usually perform a single bank transfer to settle multiple invoices issued by the selling business. When the billed quantities and received quantities match up, credit erasure processing can be performed in itemized units, but mismatches can often arise for reasons such as the existence of a slight temporal shift in the collection of funds, depending on the department or the person processing the payments. Mismatches between billing and payments received can also arise when a payer needs to settle a single payment by splitting it into multiple invoices. Since data regarding the items that are being billed is present in itemized units, the money should be transferred in itemized units. However, the purchasing company may give no indication of which item a payment corresponds to. This is because a payer will naturally assume that because a bill has been issued, the seller company will understand the itemized correspondence. The only information available to the selling company is the amount of the received payment. Therefore, when the billed quantity does not match the received payment, it becomes necessary for the selling company to find out which item or items have not been recovered and which items have been recovered, based on the billing data and the payments received. In other words, the selling company has to solve a large-scale subset sum problem. Transactions between businesses can often involve the transfer of over a hundred bills, so in many cases an exhaustive search program can run all night without finding a solution. Furthermore, the payment amounts typically contain large numbers of digits, which makes it difficult to solve by dynamic programming as a subset sum problem, due to constraints on the memory size. This can make the execution time even longer than that of an exhaustive search. It is therefore not uncommon for automatic credit erasure processing to be abandoned and replaced with repeated manual searches by multiple accountants. Of course, even a manual search may be unable to find a solution, in which case there is no choice but to go cap in hand to a representative of the buying company and ask for a breakdown of the payments that have been made.

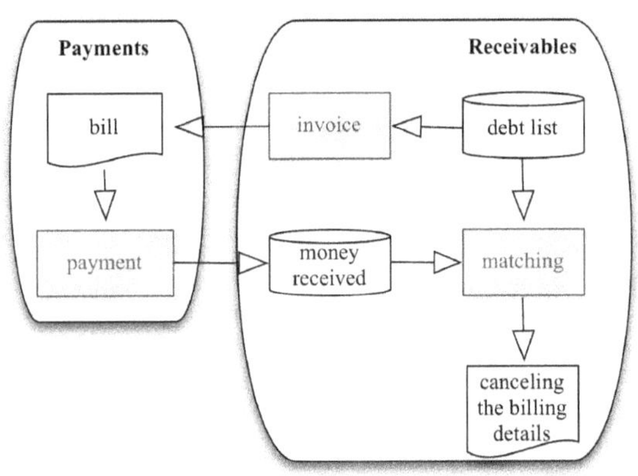

Fig. 1. Overview of credit erasure processing in Japan

3. DESIGN POLICIES AND BASIC IDEAS

3.1 Application of GA to credit erasure processing

In credit erasure processing, the total number of billed items is N, the number of payments received is k, the amount of money received is S, the number of GA entities is P, the processing time per generation is T_1, the number of generations is G, and the data is handled as int variables.

3.1.1 Performance comparison

First, we compare the execution times of an exhaustive search, DP and GA methods. For an exhaustive search, the worst-case execution time T_{ALL} is given by Equation (1) below since there are k unknowns.

$$T_{ALL} = \sum_{k=0}^{N} \binom{N}{k} = 2^N \tag{1}$$

Therefore, the execution time for an exhaustive search increases exponentially with the total number of billed items N, and depending on the value of N it is not uncommon for it to be impossible for a computer to obtain a solution even when left running for a whole day.

With DP, S searches have to be performed for each bill, and every bill has to be searched. Therefore, the DP execution time T_{DP} is given by Equation (2) below.

$$T_{DP} = N \times S \tag{2}$$

A comparison of Equations (1) and (2) shows that as the value of N increases, DP is able to obtain a solution faster than an exhaustive search. On the other hand, since the execution time is proportional to the payments received S, its performance can sometimes be worse than that of an exhaustive search when large amounts are involved, as in transactions between companies. For example, when N=30 and S=10^9, the values of T_{ALL} and T_{DP} are as follows, and DP is over 30 times slower than an exhaustive search.

$$T_{ALL}\ (N=30) = 2^{30} \approx 10^9$$

$$T_{DP}\ (N=30,\ S=10^9) = 30\times 10^9$$

With GA, processing is repeated for a number of generations until an optimal solution is obtained. Regarding the processing time per generation, the GA execution time T_{GA} is given by Equation (3).

$$T_{GA} = T_1 \times P \times G \tag{3}$$

From Equation (3), GA reaches a solution faster than an exhaustive search as the value of N increases, and since the GA execution time does not depend on the value of S, it does not suffer from the drop in performance that occurs with DP when large payments are involved. However, since the values of P and G needed to obtain an optimal solution are dependent on the value of N, evaluation by computer simulation is also required.

3.1.2 Comparison of memory size

The amounts of memory needed to run each type of program are compared below. n exhaustive search requires an array equal in length to the total number of billed items. If the array consists of int data, each cell occupies 4 bits of memory, so 4×N bits of memory are required.

On the other hand, DP requires an array equal in length to the received payments, and thus requires 4×S bits of memory.

Transactions between businesses can involve payments of billions of yen, in which case the required array size can exceed 4 GB. This has to be avoided somehow, since thee memory limit of an ordinary C compiler is just 2 GB. In DP, searches are performed while caching partial sets, so its memory requirement corresponds to a size of {No. of partial sets}×{size of a partial set}×{size of int}, as shown in Equation (4).

$$2^N \times \frac{N}{2} \times 4 \quad (4)$$

From this equation, DP requires 60 GB of memory when N has a value of 30, which would be difficult to implement in practice. It is thus difficult to apply DP to credit erasure processing unless the values of S and N are within limited ranges.

In GA on the other hand, the number of the arrays of length N that have to be stored is only $2\times P$ (including workspace provisions), so the memory requirements are as shown in Equation (5).

$$8\times N\times P \quad (5)$$

A subset sum problem is a special case of the knapsack problem, so based on a the above comparison of execution times and memory requirements, we propose an approach where evolutionary computation methods such as GA are used to fully automate credit erasure processing for business transactions involving large payments.

3.2 Proposal of local search taking Hamming distances into consideration

Figure 2 shows some examples of the shape of the search space in credit erasure processing where N=8 and k=4. Using random numbers to generate the amount of each bill as an integer of 10 to 12 digits, The horizontal axis shows the combination type (ID number), and the vertical axis shows the evaluation value normalized to a peak value of 1.0. As this figure shows, a credit erasure processing problem has a multimodal search space with a complex shape, and as the total number of billed items N increases, the number of peaks increases sharply, making it extremely difficult to search for a solution. In some cases, there can also be a combination of multiple solutions that satisfy a particular value of received payments. One might therefore consider the possibility of improving the search accuracy of GA by using methods such as niching [4].

On the other hand, in credit erasure processing where there are multiple combinations that satisfy the received payments under the same payment conditions, it is sufficient to find just one of these combinations. This is because there is no information that identifies which part of a payment corresponds to a candidate combination in the simple list of numbers constituting the received payments, so there is no way of telling which combination is correct out of multiple possibilities (besides asking the payer directly). Therefore, the improvement of search accuracy by adding a local search function is considered as a first step towards improving the GA search accuracy. In particular, in credit erasure processing where there is no large difference between the optimal solution (payments received) and a sub-optimal solution (the total amount of a combined solution with a high evaluation value), it is thought to be highly likely that the number of combined sub-optimal solutions k_q is more or less equal to the number of payments k, so we propose performing a local search to look for other combinations where the number of combinations is about the same as the sub-optimal solution. An overview of this idea is shown in Fig. 3. In Fig. 3, the chromosome's genetic loci are each made to correspond with one of the billed items and the string X_0=00000 is defined as the origin. We present a local search function whereby, during the genetic operations, three entities are created with Hamming distances $dH(X_i)$ from the origin is equal to that of the elite entity $dH(X_E)$, of which the one with the highest evaluation value is passed on to the next generation.

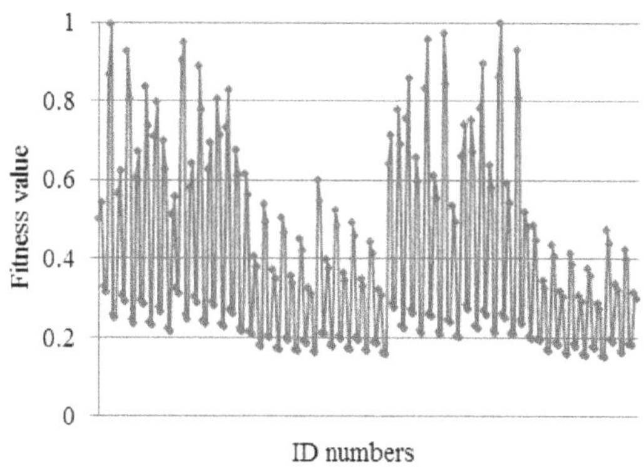

Fig. 2. Example of the shape of the search space (N=8, k=4)

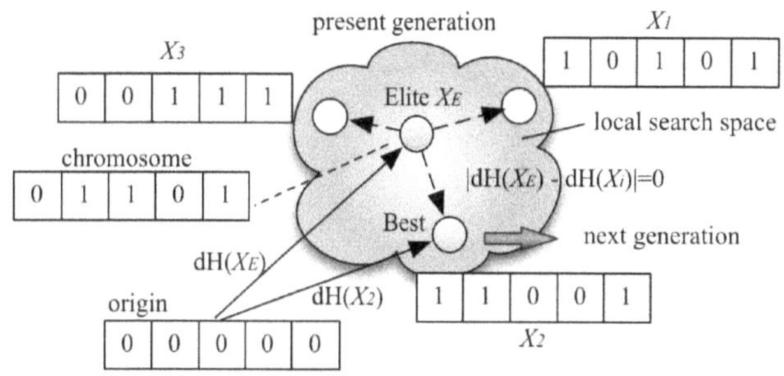

Fig.3. Examples of a local search that takes Hamming distances into account

4. DESIGN OF GA FOR CREDIT ERASURE PROCESSING

4.1 Definition of chromosome

To provide a point of reference when studying specific design methods, we first looked for other examples of evolutionary computation applied to credit erasure processing, but were unable to find any. We therefore concentrated on the fact that the number of payment items k is unknown, and started our investigation with the application of messy GA and genetic programming capable of handling variable gene lengths. However, as a result of this investigation, we noticed that if the chromosomes are defined as arrays expressing the correspondence between payments and billed items, the problem can be defined as being equivalent to applying GA to a large-scale subset sum problem. Figure 4 shows an example of a chromosome definition for credit erasure processing. By having a different genetic locus correspond to each billed item, the definition length of the chromosomes can be made equal to the number of billed items. The payments corresponding to parts of a genetic locus that have a value of 1 are regarded as having been received. In the figure, the genetic locus has a value of 1 for billed items 2, 3 and 5, so the payments corresponding to these items (\$300, \$250 and \$620, making a total of \$1170) become the received payments corresponding to this chromosome.

Using this chromosome definition method, we can solve the credit erasure processing problem by using standard GA methods.

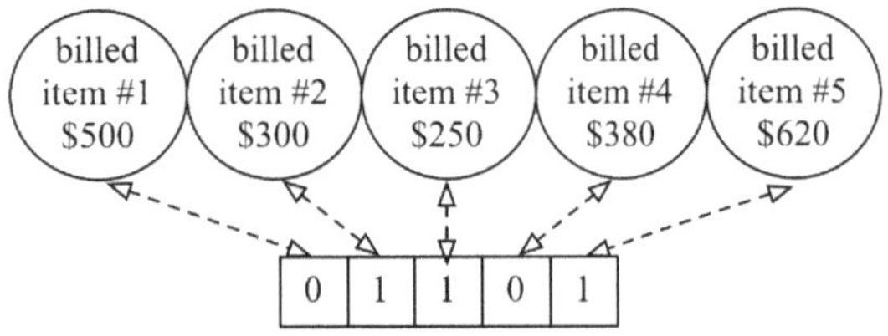

Fig.4. Chromosome configuration example for a credit erasure processing problem

4.2 Evaluation function

For the evaluation value in the genetic operations, it is valid to consider that the evaluation value becomes higher as the absolute value of the difference between the received payments and the total of the billed amounts corresponding to the chromosome becomes smaller. On the other hand, if the evaluation value is simply set to the reciprocal of the absolute value of the difference between the received payments and the total of the billed amounts, the undulation of peaks in the search space can become extremely large as shown in Figs. 2. Therefore, in this study we defined the evaluation function shown in Equation (6), which is normalized to values between 0 and 1.

$$f = \frac{S_q}{S_q + |S - S_q|} \tag{6}$$

Here, S_q is the received payment corresponding to chromosome, and S is the actual received payment. An entity that achieves an evaluation value of f=1 corresponds exactly to the received payments, and has thus reached an optimal solution.

4.3 Selection and crossover methods

Using six combinations of two selection methods (roulette selection and tournament selection) and three crossover methods (one-point crossover, two-point crossover and uniform crossover), we performed preliminary tests while varying the crossover rate, mutation rate and total number of billed items as parameters. As a result, when using a combination of roulette selection and uniform crossovers, we achieved stable convergence at the same crossover rate and mutation rate regardless of the total number of billed items N. Therefore, the following evaluation tests were performed using a combination of roulette selection and uniform crossovers.

4.4 Local search taking Hamming distances into consideration

The local search is performed after selection, crossover and mutation have been performed in the same way as in ordinary GA. Entities with the highest evaluation values found from the mutated entities and a number of local search points are subjected to genetic operations to form the next generation of entities. A local search that takes Hamming distances into consideration involves performing tests with two methods — one that searches for a difference of a Hamming distance ΔdH (= $|dH(X_E)$ - $dH(X_i)|$) of 0, and another that searches for ΔdH of 1 — and studying the validity relationship of the proposed method and the variation in the number of digits in each billed amount.

5. EVALUATION TESTS

5.1 Evaluation method

The evaluation test environment parameters and GA execution parameters are shown in Tables 1 and 2 respectively. The GA execution parameters are determined by preliminary tests when determining the choice of selection method and crossover method. Development was done using the C programming language in order to take advantage of the speed expected to become available in many-core environments such as GPUs in the future.

Table 1. Evaluation test environment

OS	Windows7
Processor	Intel(R) Core™ i5 CPU 2.40GHz
Memory (RAM)	4.00 GB
System type	64-bit operating system
Tool	Visual Studio 2008

Table 2. GA execution parameters

No. of entities	200
Crossover rate	0.6
Mutation rate	0.03
Selection method	Roulette selection
Crossover method	Uniform crossover
Mutation method	Simple mutation
No. of local search points	3

DP is limited in terms of the number of billed items N and the payments received S, and it is practically impossible to apply it to credit negation processing in businesses. Here, therefore, we start with a comparative evaluation of the execution times needed to obtain a solution with the exhaustive search and GA methods. First, to survey and investigate the effects of a local search taking Hamming distances into consideration, we compared the processing time and the number of generations needed to reach a solution when using (i) standard GA, (ii) standard GA combined with Multiple Offspring Sampling (MOS) [5] as a local search method, and (iii) standard GA combined with a local search taking Hamming distances into consideration.

There are not any bench mark problems available for credit erasure processing problems from web-site. Therefore, for a comparison of GA with an exhaustive search, we used test data consisting of numbers having from 8 to 13 digits generated with normal random numbers for each billed amount, and we performed tests in which the total number of billed items N was varied from 10 to 50. The total number of received payments k was set to a random number.

In tests to investigate the effects of a local search taking Hamming distances into consideration, we prepared two sets of data as shown in Table 3. In one set (T1), the number of digits in each billed amount was generally the same, and in the other set (T2), the number of digits was varied. Each billed amount was generated using normal random numbers. We also performed evaluations using two sets of real data R1 and R2 shown in Table 4 for which automatic credit erasure processing had previously been abandoned and replaced with manual processing. Real data R1 has a small number of payment items and the payments received also have small amounts. Real data R2 has two possible payment combination solutions, and the payments received have relatively large values.

Table 3. Test data generated randomly

	Test data T1	Test data T2
Billed amounts	11–12 digits	8–12 digits
Total num. of billed items N	30	30
Num. of payments k	20	20
Payments received S	9,933,624,267,570	3,031,005,457,546

Table 4. Real data

	Test data R1	Test data R2
Billed amounts	4–8 digits	5–8 digits
Total num. of billed items N	43	21
Num. of payments k	3	9, or 13
Payments received S	676,704	97,868,153

5.2 Test results

5.2.1 Test to compare exhaustive search with GA

Table 5 shows the results of comparing the execution times until a solution is reached by an exhaustive search and GA while varying the number of billed items N. Up to N=30, the exhaustive search was able to produce one measurement value, but for N=40 and above, the program was unable to find a solution even after running for five hours. Therefore, the theoretical worst-case values were calculated from Equation (1) based on the results obtained for N=30. GA was run 20 times and arrived at an optimal solution every time. The table shows the average of these 20 execution times. When the value of N is less than 20, the exhaustive search is sometimes faster at reaching an optimal solution, but the execution time of GA is also short enough not to cause any practical issues. When N is greater than 30, the theoretical worst-case execution time of the exhaustive search increases sharply, reaching 350 hours at N=40 and 3.6 million hours at N=50. On the other hand, the average execution time of GA for N=40 was a little over 2 minutes with a maximum value of just under 7 minutes. For N=50, the average execution time was just under 7 minutes and the maximum was just under 13 minutes. Thus, our results show that GA can find a solution about 3,000 times faster than an exhaustive search when N=40, and about 1.68 million times faster when N=50. From this table, the execution time of the exhaustive search increases exponentially as N increases, whereas the execution time of GA remains more or less proportional to N.

Table 5. Execution times of exhaustive search and GA

(N, k)	**Exhaustive search**	**GA (average)**	**GA (worst-case)**
(10, 7)	0.001s	0.001s	0.020s
(20, 14)	1.116s	0.574s	1.860s
(30, 23)	20m43s	1m	4m22s
(40,17)	350h[*1]	2m18s	6m43s
(50, 18)	360,000h[*1]	6m58s	12m50s

[*1]: approximate numbers

5.2.2 Local search taking Hamming distances into consideration

This section compares the average and maximum execution times and numbers of generations needed to reach a solution when using standard GA, standard GA combined with Multiple Offspring Sampling (GA+MOS) as a local search method, and standard GA combined with a local search taking Hamming distances into consideration. For GA combined with a local search taking Hamming distances into consideration, we performed two tests — one with the ΔdH set to zero (GA+HM0) and one with the ΔdH set to 1 (GA+HM1). The data shown in the figures and tables represents the average of 50 runs, and an optimal solution was arrived at every time.

5.2.2.1 Evaluation using test data

Table 6 shows the comparison results obtained when using test data T1 mentioned in section 4.1.

From Table 6 when MOS is added to GA as a local search method, the average execution time decreases by about 25%, and at the maximum execution time it arrives at a solution 1.3 times faster. Furthermore, with the addition of a local search that takes Hamming distances into consideration, the average execution time is reduced to about one third, and at the maximum execution time it arrives at a solution 3.8 times faster. Also, This Table shows that the addition of a local search greatly reduces the number of generations needed to reach a solution (less than a third as many generations are required).

Table 6. Comparison of execution time and number of generations (test data T1)

	Execution time (Average)	Execution time (Worst)	Generations (Average)	Generations (Worst)
GA	1.932s	13.073s	4067	27589
GA+MOS	1.476s	9.910s	1170	8001
GA+HM0	0.633s	3.931s	770	4862
GA+HM1	0.669s	4.852s	917	6449

Next, to observe the different convergence capabilities of the local search methods in more detail, Fig. 5 shows the relationship between the number of generations and the maximum evaluation value in the local search methods.

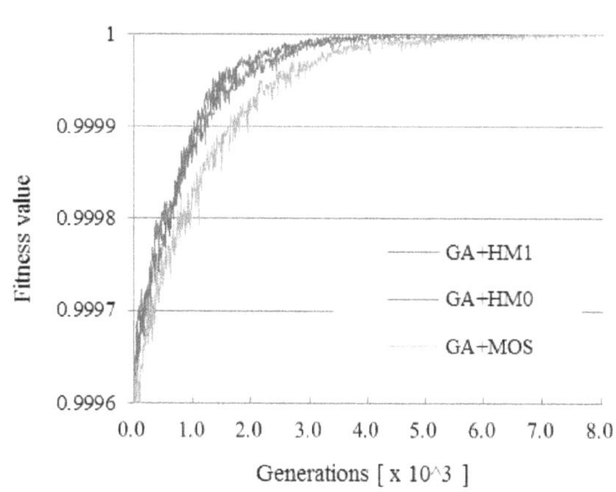

Fig. 5. Comparison of convergence with different local search methods (When using test data T1)

Table 7. Comparison of execution time and number of generations (test data T2)

	Execution time (Average)	Execution time (Worst)	Generations (Average)	Generations (Worst)
GA	257.611s	1183.169s	540299	2465368
GA+MOS	166.916s	749.061s	134553	607500
GA+HM0	102.944s	321.463s	128091	403213
GA+HM1	53.112s	277.587s	76374	400670

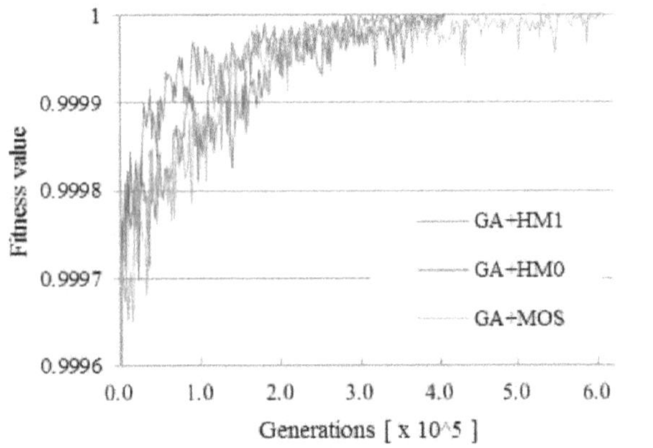

Fig. 6. Comparison of number of generations and maximum evaluation value (test data T2)

Compared with MOS, it can be seen that the local search that takes Hamming distances into consideration starts to converge earlier than the MOS method. Of the two Hamming methods, the one with the difference of the Hamming distance ΔdH set to zero arrived at a solution slightly faster.

Next, Table 7 shows the results obtained using test data T2. The average execution time was approximately a hundred times slower than in the case of test data T1 where the payments received were all of a similar order of magnitude, and the average number of generations was also about a hundred times greater.

When using test data T2, the average execution time is reduced by about 35% when MOS is added to GA as a local search method, and at the maximum execution time, a solution is reached 1.5 times faster. Furthermore, with the addition of a local search that takes Hamming distances into consideration, the average execution time is reduced to about one third, and at the maximum execution time it arrives at a solution about four times faster. Also, the tendency for the addition of a local search method to greatly reduce the number of generations needed to arrive at a solution is the same as was observed with test data T1.

Next, to observe the different convergence capabilities of local search methods in more detail, Fig. 6 shows the relationship between the number of generations and the maximum evaluation value when local search methods are added. The tendency for the local search method that takes Hamming distances into consideration to converge faster than the MOS local search method is similar to the case of test data T1, but the convergence started earlier with MOS than with the local search where the ΔdH was set to zero. In the comparison of local search methods taking Hamming distances into consideration, a solution was arrived at faster in the case where the ΔdH was set to 1.

5.2.2.2 Evaluation using real data

Table 8 shows the comparison results obtained using real data R1. To compare the convergence processes, Fig. 7 shows the relationship between the number of generations and the maximum evaluation value.

Table 8. Comparison of execution time and number of generations (real data R1)

	Execution time (Average)	Execution time (Worst)	Generations (Average)	Generations (Worst)
GA	2.928s	6.980s	4773	11733
GA+MOS	4.093s	12.550s	2531	7771
GA+HM0	0.356s	1.130s	335	1074
GA+HM1	2.162s	5.850s	2586	6982

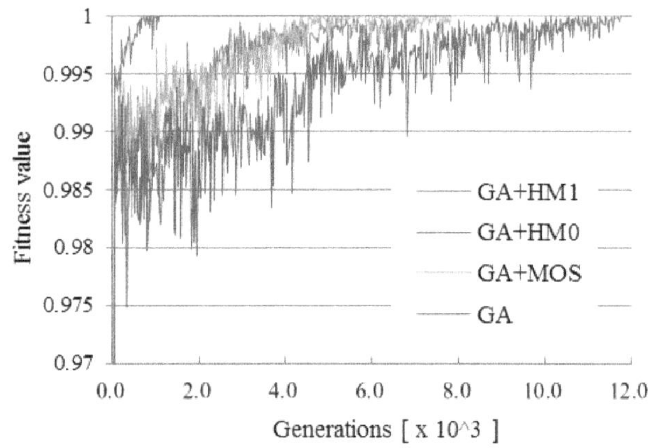

Fig. 7. Comparison of number of generations and maximum evaluation value (real data R1)

From Table 8, when MOS is added to GA as a local search method, the number of generations needed to achieve convergence was almost halved, but the average and maximum execution times both increased. When a local search taking Hamming distances into consideration was added, the number of generations until convergence and the average and maximum execution times all tended to show improvements. Also, Fig. 7 shows that the local search starts to converge much faster when the ΔdH is set to zero.

Next, Table 9 shows the results obtained using real data R2. Since the number of billed items N is small, the average execution time and the average number of generations were both reduced compared with when using real data R1.

When using real data R2, the number of generations until convergence was reduced to nearly a fifth and the average execution time was reduced by about 40% when MOS was added to GA as a local search method, but the maximum execution time increased slightly. Also, when a local search that takes Hamming distances into consideration is added, the number of generations is slightly improved compared with the use of MOS, while the average execution time and maximum execution time are both reduced to about 60%. The tendency for the addition of a local search method to greatly reduce the number of generations needed to arrive at a solution is the same as was observed with test data T1 and T2, and with real data R1.

Next, to observe the different convergence capabilities of local search methods in more detail, Fig. 8 shows the relationship between the number of generations and the maximum evaluation value in the methods where a local search was added. The tendency for the local search method that takes Hamming distances into consideration to converge faster than the MOS local search method is similar to the case of test data T1 and T2, but the convergence started slightly earlier than with MOS in the local search with the Hamming distance set to 1. In the comparison of local search methods taking Hamming distances into consideration, a solution was arrived at faster in the case where the ΔdH was set to 1.

Table 9. Comparison of execution time and number of generations (real data R2)

	Execution time (Average)	Execution time (Worst)	Generations (Average)	Generations (Worst)
GA	1.545s	4.290s	3985	10794
GA+MOS	0.841s	4.660s	864	4831
GA+HM0	0.609s	1.750s	849	2428
GA+HM1	0.408s	1.820s	694	3077

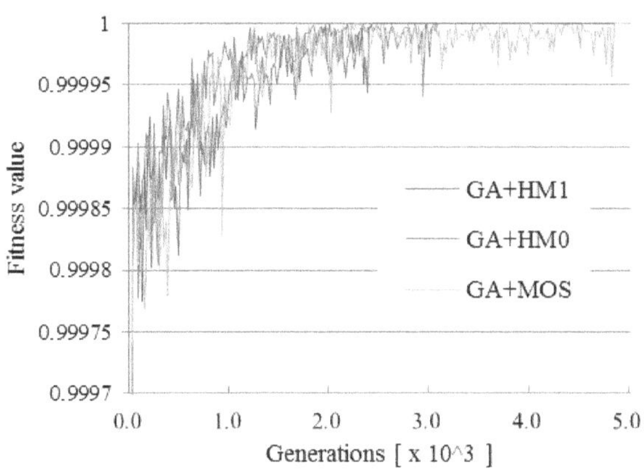

Fig. 8. Comparison of convergence with different local search methods (Real data R2)

6. DISCUSSION

In the tests of section 4.2.1, as discussed in section 3.1, the processing time of an exhaustive search increased exponentially with the total number of billed items N, but increased more or less proportionally with N in the GA methods. This is thought to be because the processing time per generation increases in proportion with N since the length of the GA array is set equal to the number of billed items N. However, since the processing time is also affected by the number of generations needed to find a solution, doubling N will cause the processing time to increase more than twofold, so it is not simply proportional to N. Furthermore, the longest execution time with GA was roughly 2 to 4 times the average execution time, and even for N=50, the execution time for GA was approximately 7 minutes on average and about 13 minutes in the worst case, which is more realistic than the exhaustive search method. Therefore, the application of GA to credit erasure processing promotes the automation of manual credit erasure processing, and is thought to be an effective way of alleviating the concentrated human workload that can arise at specific times such as at the end of the business year.

The experimental results of section 4.2.2 show that the addition of a local search function to GA is an effective way of reducing the number of generations needed to arrive at a solution, both for test data and real data. Also, the proposed local search taking Hamming distances into consideration takes longer than MOS to start converging on a solution with test data T2, but eventually converges on an optimal solution faster than MOS. Also, in the comparison of local search methods that take Hamming distances into consideration, it was found that the local search is more effective if the ΔdH is set to 0 when the billed quantities are all of a similar order of magnitude. This is thought to be because as the evaluation value increases, the number of bits with a gene locus value of "1" approaches the number of received payments k in the chromosomes corresponding to the elite entities of this generation.

In test using real data, we basically observed similar tendencies to those observed with test data. However, in tests using real data R2, the addition of a MOS function was able to reduce the number of generations needed to arrive at a solution, but the average and worst-case processing times increased. This is thought to be because when using MOS, random numbers are generated for each bit of the chromosome, so the processing time is affected by the computation time needed to judge whether or not a mutation should take place.

Next, in order to search for factors for which the efficacy of a local search taking Hamming distances into consideration was not as prominent for test data T2 (where there were varied numbers of digits in the billed quantities) and real data R2 (which had two sets of solutions) as for test data T1 or real data R1, we performed additional tests using test data T3 (where the total number of billed items N was increased to 50 and the variation of the billed quantities was increased further still), and real data R3 (where the total number of billed items was N=74) shown in Table 10.

Table 10. Additional test data

	Test data T3	Test data R3
Billed amounts	8–13 digits	3–9 digits
Total number of billed items N	50	74
Num. of payments k	18	34, or 46
Payments received S	10,415,830,407	424,744,482

Table 11 compares standard GA with GA incorporating local search functions when using test data T3, and Fig. 9 shows the relationship between the number of generations and the maximum evaluation value. Also, Table 12 compares standard GA with GA incorporating local search functions when using real data R3, and Fig. 10 shows the relationship between the number of generations and the maximum evaluation value.

As Tables 11 and 12 shows, the addition of a local search function to GA can be an effective way of hastening convergence, and compared with MOS, the proposed local search taking Hamming distances into consideration is still an effective approach. On the other hand, from Figs. 9 and 10 it can be seen that there is no pronounced difference in the speed with which the process starts converging, compared with MOS. This is thought to be because increasing the variation of the billed quantities and increasing the total number of billed items causes the search space to grow exponentially, thereby reducing the relative efficacy of local searching. To address this issue, it might be worth increasing the number of search points, but in the future it will probably be necessary to investigate improving the local search efficiency by combining this approach with techniques such as tabu search [6].

Also, this study was mainly limited to cases where N was 50 or less due to considerations of the evaluation time. In the future, it will be necessary to extend the validation by using real data including cases where N is more than 100. Furthermore, to find solutions on a practical time scale even when the total number of billed items N is large, it should be worth using a many-core environment such as a GPU to speed up the processing by making use of parallel processing. It is also important to compare the proposed method with DP based algorithms [7] to solve the credit erasure processing problems. This is left as a topic for further study.

Table 11. Comparison of execution time and number of generations (test data T3)

	Execution time (Average)	Execution time (Worst)	Generations (Average)	Generations (Worst)
GA	413.311s	1412.707s	648265	2217600
GA+MOS	867.860s	3888.307s	482185	2165045
GA+HM0	364.231s	1260.476s	381981	1355819
GA+HM1	235.597s	755.603s	256773	823025

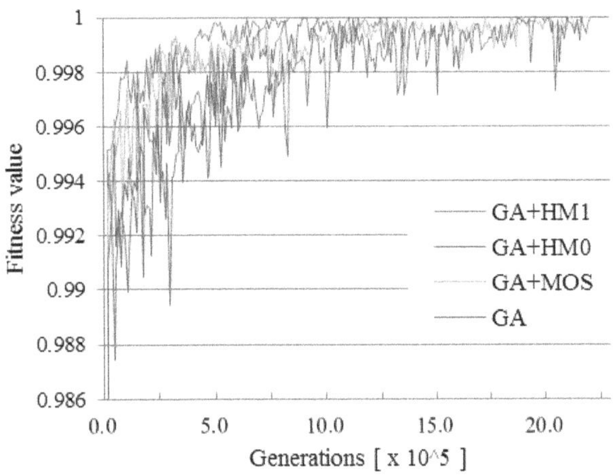

Fig. 9. Comparison of convergence with different local search methods (Test data T3)

Table 12. Comparison of execution time and number of generations (real data R3)

	Execution time (Average)	Execution time (Worst)	Generations (Average)	Generations (Worst)
GA	687.582s	2040.742s	749192	2224988
GA+MOS	468.796s	1290.153s	172407	474087
GA+HM0	223.025s	617.431s	127090	380389
GA+HM1	172.190s	455.989s	127902	339822

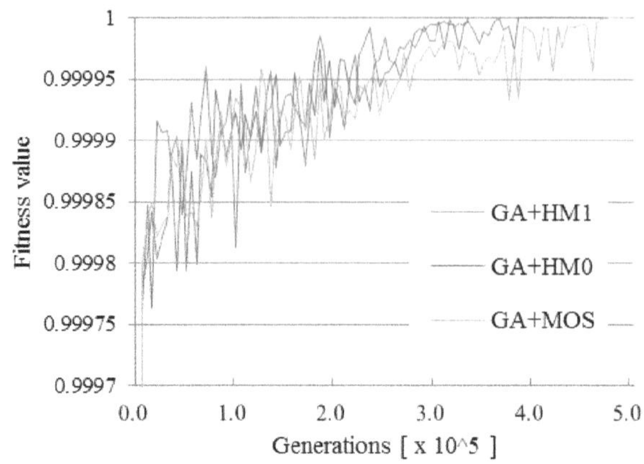

Fig. 10. Comparison of convergence with different local search methods (Real data R3)

7. CONCLUSION

In this paper, we have proposed using GA to solve credit erasure processing problems, and we have demonstrated the usefulness of this method by comparing it with exhaustive search and dynamic programming methods. In particular, we propose improving the search precision by incorporating a local search method that takes Hamming distances into consideration. To this end, we compared the standard GA with the result of adding a simple local search to the standard GA. This was done using a set of data where the numbers of digits in the billed quantities are roughly the same, another set of data where the numbers of digits are more varied, and a set of real data. As a result, we have shown that this approach is effective in cases where the billed quantities all have similar numbers of digits, or when the evaluation values are somewhat high. We also showed that it is possible to obtain correct solutions in a short amount of time when using real data for which automatic credit erasure processing had previously been abandoned and replaced with manual processing.

8. REFERENCES

[1] Wikipedia. Subset sum problem. Available via WWW: http://en.wikipedia.org/wiki/Subset_sum_problem (cited 27. 1. 2014).

[2] Cormen, T.H., Leiserson, C.E., Rivest, R.L., Stein, C. (2001). Introduction to Algorithms. The MIT Press.

[3] Sato, Y., Hasegawa, N., and Sato, M. (2011). GPU Acceleration for Sudoku Solution with Genetic Operations. In Proceedings of the 2011 IEEE Congress on Evolutionary Computation, CD-ROM.

[4] Goldberg, D. E. (2002). The Design of Innovation. Kluwer Academic Publishers.

[5] LaTorre, A. Pena, J.M., Robles, V., Muelas, S. (2008). Using Multiple Offspring Sampling to Guide Genetic Algorithms to Solve Permutation Problems. In Proceedings of the 2008 Genetic and Evolutionary Computation Conference, 1119-1120.

[6] Fred Glover (1989). "Tabu Search - Part 1". ORSA Journal on Computing 1 (2): 190–206.

[7] Martello, S., Pisinger, D., and Toth. P. (1999). Dynamic programming and strong bounds for the 0-1 knapsack problem. Management Science, 45:414–424.

Genetic Algorithm-Based Solver for Very Large Multiple Jigsaw Puzzles of Unknown Dimensions and Piece Orientation

Dror Sholomon
Dept. of Computer Science
Bar-Ilan University
Ramat-Gan 52900, Israel
dror.sholomon@gmail.com

Omid E. David
Dept. of Computer Science
Bar-Ilan University
Ramat-Gan 52900, Israel
mail@omiddavid.com

Nathan S. Netanyahu*
Dept. of Computer Science
Bar-Ilan University
Ramat-Gan 52900, Israel
nathan@cs.biu.ac.il

ABSTRACT

In this paper we propose the first genetic algorithm (GA)-based solver for jigsaw puzzles of unknown puzzle dimensions and unknown piece location and orientation. Our solver uses a novel crossover technique, and sets a new state-of-the-art in terms of the puzzle sizes solved and the accuracy obtained. The results are significantly improved, even when compared to previous solvers assuming known puzzle dimensions. Moreover, the solver successfully contends with a mixed bag of multiple puzzle pieces, assembling simultaneously all puzzles.

Categories and Subject Descriptors

I.2.10 [**Artificial Intelligence**]: Vision and Scene Understanding

General Terms

Algorithms

Keywords

Computer Vision, Genetic Algorithms, Jigsaw Puzzle, Recombination Operators

1. INTRODUCTION

Jigsaw puzzles are a popular form of entertainment, first produced around 1760 by John Spilsbury, a Londonian engraver and mapmaker. Given n different non-overlapping tiles of an image, the objective is to reconstruct the original image, taking advantage of both the shape and chromatic information of each piece. Despite the popularity and vast distribution of jigsaw puzzles, their assembly is not trivial computationally, as this problem was proven to be NP-hard [1, 7]. Nevertheless, a computational jigsaw solver may have applications in many real-world applications, such as biology [14], chemistry [20], literature [16], speech descrambling [22], archeology [2, 12], image editing [5], and the recovery of shredded documents or photographs [3, 15, 11, 6]. Regardless, as noted in [10], research of the topic may be justified solely due to its intriguing nature.

Most recently proposed solvers employ greedy strategies. Greedy algorithms are known to be problematic when encountering local optima. Moreover, such solvers rarely offer a backtrack option, i.e., a possibility to cancel a piece assignment which seemed correct at first but then turned to be globally incorrect. Hence, state-of-the-art solvers are very successful on some images, but perform poorly on others. The enormous search space of the problem, containing many local optima, seems most suitable for a genetic algorithm (GA)-based solver. The use of genetic algorithms in the field was first attempted in 2002 by Toyama *et al.* [19] but its successful performance was limited to 64-piece puzzles, probably due to the inherent difficulty in designing a crossover operator for the problem [18]. More recently, Sholomon *et al.* [18] presented another GA-based solver which can handle up to 22,755-piece puzzles. Nevertheless, their solver can handle only puzzles with (1) known piece orientations, (2) known image dimensions, and (3) pieces of a single image.

In this work we propose a novel GA-based solver, relaxing most previous assumptions. First, we assume no *a priori* knowledge regarding piece location or orientation. Second, we assume that the image dimensions (i.e., the number of row and column tiles) are unknown. Finally, we allow the input piece set to contain pieces from either a single image or from multiple images. In the case of a "mixed-bag" puzzle, the solver concurrently solves all puzzles, unmixing their pieces along the process. We set a new state-of-the-art by solving the largest and most complex puzzle ever (i.e., 22,755 pieces, which is twice the size of the current state-of-the-art without making any assumptions) and achieving the highest accuracy ever reported, even with respect to solvers that assume known image dimensions.

2. RELATED WORK

Freeman and Garder [8] were the first to tackle computationally the jigsaw problem, in 1964. Their solver handled up to 9-piece puzzles, using only piece shape. Kosiba

*Nathan Netanyahu is also with the Center for Automation Research, University of Maryland, College Park, MD 20742 (e-mail: nathan@cfar.umd.edu).

GECCO'14, July 12–16, 2014, Vancouver, BC, Canada.

http://dx.doi.org/10.1145/2576768.2598289.

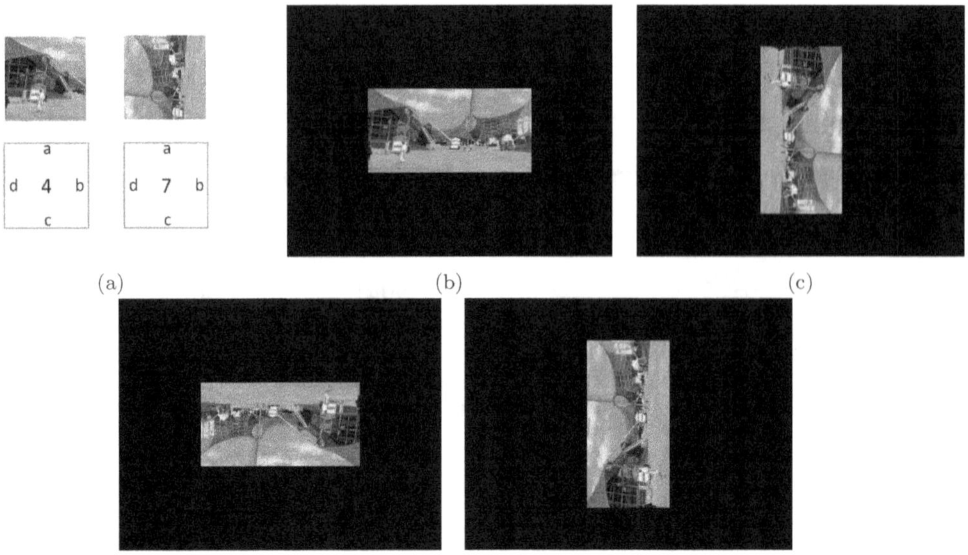

(a) (b) (c)

(d) (e)

Figure 1: Example of a relative relation assignment: (a) Pieces 4 and 7, (b)–(e) all possible image configurations of assigning the relative relation (4.b, 7.c). Note that the two pieces are always in the same relative configuration despite the different orientations.

et al. [13] were the first to facilitate the use of image content. Subsequent research has been confined to color-based square-piece puzzles, instead of the earlier shape-based variants. Cho *et al.* [4] presented a probabilistic puzzle solver that can handle up to 432 pieces, given some a priori knowledge of the puzzle (e.g., anchor pieces). Their results were improved a year later by Yang *et al.* [21], who presented a so-called particle filter-based solver. A major contribution to the field was made recently by Pomeranz *et al.* [17] who introduced, for the first time, a fully automated jigsaw puzzle solver that can handle square-piece puzzles of up to 3,000 pieces, without a priori knowledge of the image. Their solver treats puzzles with unknown piece location but with known orientation. Gallagher [9] was the first to handle puzzles with both unknown piece location and orientation, i.e., each piece might be misplaced and/or rotated by 90, 180 or 270 degrees. The latter solver was tested on 432- and 1,064-piece puzzles and a single 9,600-piece image. Sholomon *et al.* [18] successfully solved a 22,755-piece puzzle with only piece location unknown. Thus, as far as we know, current state-of-the-art algorithms can solve correctly a 22,755-piece puzzle with unknown piece location and a 9,600-piece puzzle with unknown piece location and orientation. All of the above solvers make use of the image dimensions during the solution process. We believe our work provides for the first time a solver capable of perfectly reconstructing a 22,755-piece puzzle with unknown piece location and orientation and no knowledge of the original image dimensions.

3. PUZZLE SOLVING

In its most basic form, every puzzle solver requires an estimation function to evaluate the compatibility of adjacent pieces and a strategy for placing the pieces (as accurately as possible). We propose using genetic algorithms as a piece placement strategy, aimed at achieving an optimal global score with respect to compatibilities of adjacent pieces in the resulting image. The proposed GA elements (e.g., chromosome representation, crossover operator, and fitness function) are required to tackle several non-trivial issues. First, the eventual solution needs to be valid, i.e., every puzzle piece should appear once and only once, without missing and/or duplicate pieces. Second, the resulting image dimensions should strive to meet those of the (unknown) dimensions of the original image, avoid undesirable cases (e.g., pseudo-linear configurations) which contrive to be optimal solutions. Third, in the spirit of a gradual, evolutionary improvement over time, puzzle segments assembled correctly, up to an exact location and orientation, should be tracked, inherited to child chromosomes, and undergo proper translation and rotation (see Figure 2).

(a) Original Image (b) Chromosome

Figure 2: Characteristics sought by crossover; chromosome shown correctly assembled a number of puzzle segments, most of which are incorrectly located (with respect to correct absolute location) or oriented (notice tower orientation versus flags); crossover operator should exploit correctly assembled segments and allow them to be translated and rotated in a child chromosome.

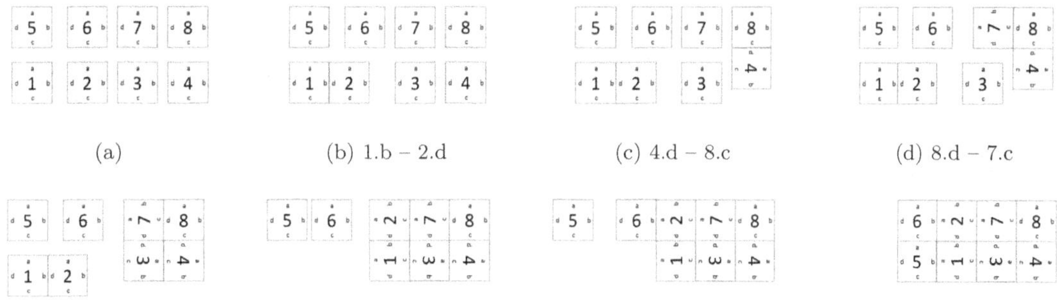

(a) (b) 1.b – 2.d (c) 4.d – 8.c (d) 8.d – 7.c

(e) 3.a – 4.c (f) 2.c – 7.a (g) 2.a – 6.b (h) 5.b – 1.a

Figure 3: Different types of relative relation assignment; each sub-caption describes the corresponding assignment made, also marked by a red line, (c) rotation of pieces, (e) explicit assignment (4.c, 3.a) leading to an implicit assignment (3.d, 7.d), and (f) merge of two piece groups, during which the entire left group is rotated. Note how in (d) the assignment (2.a, 4.c) is geometrically infeasible due to a collision between pieces 1 and 7.

3.1 Chromosome Representation

We propose for each chromosome to be equivalent to a complete solution of the jigsaw puzzle problem, i.e., a suggested placement of all the pieces. Since the image dimensions are unknown, it is not clear how to store a piece configuration in a two-dimensional array (according to piece locations and orientations), in accordance with the actual image. Instead, we store, for each chromosome, only the relative placement of neighboring pieces. Since a piece orientation is unknown, for each given piece we denote its edges as a, b, c, d, starting clockwise from a random edge. To denote the relative placement of two pieces we may say, for example, that edge $p_i.b$ (i.e., edge b of piece p_i) is placed next to edge $p_j.c$, thus encoding both the relative spatial location and orientation of the pieces. Figure 1 depicts the labeling of piece edges and their relative placement. Each chromosome is represented by an $(n \times 4)$ matrix (i.e., a matrix whose dimensions are the number of pieces times the number of piece edges), where a matrix entry $x_{i,j} (i = 1..n, j = 1..4)$ is the corresponding piece edge adjacent to $x_i.j$ (e.g., $x_i.j = p_2.c$) or *"none"*, if no edge is placed next to it (e.g., at the puzzle's boundary). This representation lends itself more easily to subsequent relative-placement evaluations and crossover operations.

3.2 Chromosome Evaluation

We use the *dissimilarity* measure below, which was presented in various previous works [17, 4, 18]. This measure relies on the premise that adjacent jigsaw pieces in the original image tend to share similar colors along their abutting edges, and thus, the sum (over all neighboring pixels) of squared color differences (over all color bands) should be minimal. Assuming that pieces p_i, p_j are represented in normalized L*a*b* space by a $K \times K \times 3$ matrix, where K is the height/width of a piece (in pixels), their dissimilarity, where p_j is "to the right" of p_i, for example, is

$$D(x_i.b, x_j.d) = \sqrt{\sum_{k=1}^{K} \sum_{ch=1}^{3} (x_i(k, K, ch) - x_j(k, 1, ch))^2}. \tag{1}$$

when ch denotes a spectral channel. Obviously, to maximize the compatibility of two pieces, their dissimilarity should be minimized.

We compute the compatibility of all possible edges for all possible pieces, summing up to 16 edges per piece pair. Notice that computing the dissimilarity between piece edges (e.g., between $p_1.b$ and $p_2.c$) is invariant to their final piece rotation. For example, assume b is the right edge of piece p_1 and c is the left edge of piece p_2, with respect to some initial piece orientation. The compatibility of $p_1.b$ to $p_2.c$ is similar whether or not the pieces are rotated, i.e., p_2 is to the right of p_1 (if the pieces are not rotated), or p_2 is below p_1 if they are rotated (clockwise) by 90 degrees. In any event, the final chromosome fitness is the sum of pairwise dissimilarities over all adjacent edges.

Representing a chromosome, as suggested, by an $(n \times 4)$ matrix, where a matrix entry $x_{i,j} (i = 1..n, j = 1..4)$ corresponds to a single piece edge, we define its fitness as:

$$\sum_{i=1}^{n} \sum_{j=1}^{4} D(p_i.j, x_{i,j}) \tag{2}$$

where D is the dissimilarity of the two given edges (edge j of piece p_i and the edge located at $x_{i,j}$). This value should, of course, be minimized.

Special care should be taken in the case of $x_{i,j} = none$, i.e., a piece edge with no adjacent pieces. Intuitively, *"none"* piece edges should be highly discouraged. In principle, only boundary pieces of the original image should contain *none* edges. Most boundary pieces should have only a single *none* edge, whereas the four corner pieces are expected to have two *none* edges each. (Ideally, no piece should have more than two *none* edges.) Assigning a dissimilarity of "0" to a *none* edge might cause the GA to converge to a non-rectangular image. On the other hand, assigning an extremely high value might lead to cases where image shape might take precedence over image content. Having tested the algorithm with many different values, we picked the dissimilarity of a *none* edge (i.e., $D(p_i.j, none)$) to be twice the average of all dissimilarities (i.e., the average of all 16 pairwise dissimilarities over all piece pairs). It appears that this measure highly encourages the GA to reach a correct reconstruction of the

(a) Generation 1 (b) Generation 2 (c) Generation 3

(d) Generation 4 (e) Generation 5 (f) Final Generation (100)

Figure 4: Solution process of a 22,755-piece puzzle (largest puzzle solved with unknown piece orientation and image dimensions): (a)–(e) Best chromosomes achieved by the GA in the first to fifth generation, and (f) final generation. Note that every chromosome (image) contains all puzzle tiles, so its image results in varying dimensions (down scaled, for display purposes). The original image was perfectly reconstructed.

original image, with respect to both image dimensions and content.

3.3 Crossover Operator

The most involved element of the proposed GA is the crossover operator. Considering the proposed representation and in light of the chosen fitness function, one can grasp the major role undertaken by the crossover operator. The operator must verify the validity of each newly created chromosome. Traditionally, this means that each puzzle piece appears once and only once in the child chromosome, and no piece is missing or duplicated. The inherent difficulty surrounding merely this condition is likely to have delayed the derivation of an effective GA-based solver for the problem. Meeting this condition still assures no validity. Since chromosomes contain only relative relations (e.g., edge $p_1.b$ is adjacent to edge $p_2.c$), the operator must also verify that all relative relation assignments result in a geometrically feasible image, i.e., that all pieces must be placed properly with no overlaps. Moreover, the operator should verify that all prospective characteristics (e.g., correctly assembled puzzle segments) discovered by the parents may be inherited by their offsprings, and allow these segments to be translated in space and rotated inside the offspring (see, e.g., Figure 2).

We propose a novel specialized crossover operator to address the aforementioned challenges. In contrast to previous works and in accordance with the chosen representation, this operator is based on relative relations of pieces edges. The assignment of a relative relation, e.g., "edge $p_1.b$ is adjacent to edge $p_2.c$", is the basic building block of the operator. An example of such an assignment can be viewed in Figure 1. To maintain consistency, each assignment is double since it immediately implies the commutative relation (i.e., that edge $p_2.c$ is adjacent to edge $p_1.b$). Each crossover consists of exactly $n-1$ double relative relation assignments, resulting in a single connected component (albeit not necessarily rectangular). Examples of such images can be viewed in Figure 4. (Note that since every chromosome contains all the puzzle pieces, its image results in varying dimensions. This is not depicted, as the figure is down scaled for display purposes.) The following paragraphs describe the complete crossover procedure. First, we describe the intrinsics of the relative relation assignment and then provide the full details of creating a child chromosome.

3.3.1 *The Relative Relation Assignment*

The crossover procedure starts with no relative relations; each puzzle piece is detached and isolated from the others. Each assignment of a relative relation between two piece edges falls inside one of three possible scenarios. The first option is for the relation to be between two detached pieces. Naturally, this is always the case of the first assignment. The double relation between the two edges is recorded and the pieces are inserted into a newly created *"piece group"*. Each such group is recorded inside a matrix, tracking the spatial relations of its pieces and verifying the geometrical validity of the represented sub-image. The second possible scenario is that one of the edges belongs to such a piece group, while the other is of a detached piece. Again, the relation is recorded and the detached piece is inserted, at the correct location, into the already existing group. Notice that by inserting a piece inside a group, implicit relations might be set, e.g., inserting a piece to the left of a piece results in it being inserted below another piece, as depicted in Figure 3. All such implicit relations are recorded at the end of the crossover operation.

Unlike the first two cases, the third case requires extra care. This is the case of the two edges originating from two different piece groups. Notice that setting a relation between two edges belonging to the same group is prohibited, since it is either redundant (the pieces already conform implicitly to the relation) or results in an invalid image. The two piece groups should then be merged to a single connected component. Unfortunately, as can be seen in Figure 5, some piece

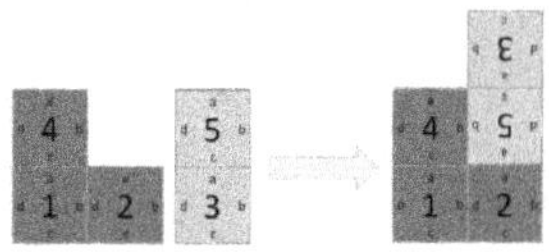

(a) Valid assignment

(b) Geometrically infeasible assignment

Figure 5: Geometrically valid and invalid relative relation assignments.

formations cannot be merged. The operator tries to merge the smaller group to the larger one, starting from the requested edge and continuing with all other recorded relations in the group. If a collision occurs between two pieces, the entire assignment of this particular relative relation is deemed illegal and is discarded, leaving the two groups disjoint. In case of a success, the new double relation is recorded and the two groups are merged into a single group. Notice that such a merge might change the orientation of all pieces inside the group being merged.

3.3.2 A Multi-Phased Algorithm

Having described the relative relation assignment, we now proceed with the assignment selection algorithm. Given two parent chromosomes, the operator initiates a multi-phased algorithm, described in Figure 6. Note that the algorithm continuously attempts to assign edges, until $n-1$ successful assignments are made. Each assignment could fail if one of the edges has already been assigned during the above group merging; otherwise, it could fail as a result of the mutation process, with some low probability. The algorithm first tries to assign all common relations, i.e., all relative relations appearing in both parents. Second, the algorithm tries to assign relations which appear in at least one of the parents and are also *best buddies*. To understand this phase, we briefly review the concept of a best-buddy piece, first introduced by Pomeranz *et al.* [17]. Two pieces are said to be best buddies if each piece considers the other as its most compatible piece, according to the dissimilarity score. We generalize this notion for piece edges, i.e., two edges are considered best-buddy edges if each edge considers the other as its most compatible edge out of all existing edges. The edges $x_i.a$ and $x_j.d$ are said to best buddies if

$$\begin{gathered}\forall e_k \in Edges,\ D(x_i.a, x_j.d) \leq D(x_i.a, e_k) \\ \text{and} \\ \forall e_p \in Edges,\ D(x_j.d, x_i.a) \leq D(x_j.d, e_p)\end{gathered} \tag{3}$$

where *Edges* is the set of all piece edges (i.e., sides a, b, c, and d of all n given pieces). Next, we introduce a greedy element. We compute, in advance, the most compatible edge for each of the $4 \times n$ edges and then try to assign most compatible edges in a random order. Finally, we try to assign two random edges until completing $n-1$ successful assignments.

Upon termination, after merging all piece groups, the crossover results in a single matrix, containing all $n-1$ pieces. The matrix records the absolute location and orientation of each piece in the resulting image. As mentioned earlier, the operator now scans the matrix, and records all relative relations created, both explicitly and implicitly, to the new chromosome. Note that this chromosome represents a geometrically valid images, containing each puzzle piece exactly once.

Until $(n-1)$ relative relations are assigned **do**

1. Try assigning all *common* relative relations.
2. Try assigning all *best-buddy* relative relations.
3. Try assigning all *most-compatible* relative relations.
4. Try assigning *random* relative relations.

Figure 6: Crossover overview

3.4 Rationale

The proposed genetic algorithm is based entirely on the concept of assigning relative relations between piece edges. This concept stems from the intuitive understanding that some puzzle segments are "easier" than others. A human solver will usually assemble first disjoint but distinct elements (e.g., animals, humans, vehicles, etc.), gradually joining them together. The assembly of more difficult parts (skies, sea, woods, and other background scenes) would be deferred to a later stage, when there are less pieces to choose from, which makes each decision easier. We mimic this behavior by allowing the solver to concurrently assemble different puzzle segments (piece groups), forcing it to merge them only at later stages. This advantage should be constructive especially in the case of puzzle pieces belonging to multiple images (i.e., a "mixed bag" of pieces), as the solver may handle each sub-image separately, as opposed to tackling the entire image of multiple excessive pieces.

Correctly assembled segments in the parents are identified either by their mutual appearance in both parents, or by a greedy consideration (due to a very high compatibility of certain edges). Only the relative relation between the edges is inherited, as the segments might be easily rotated and translated in space during the crossover procedure.

3.5 GA Parameters

We use the standard roulette-wheel selection. In each generation we start by copying the best four chromosomes. The following are the parameters used:

population size = 300
number of generations = 100
probability of not using a shared relation = 0.001

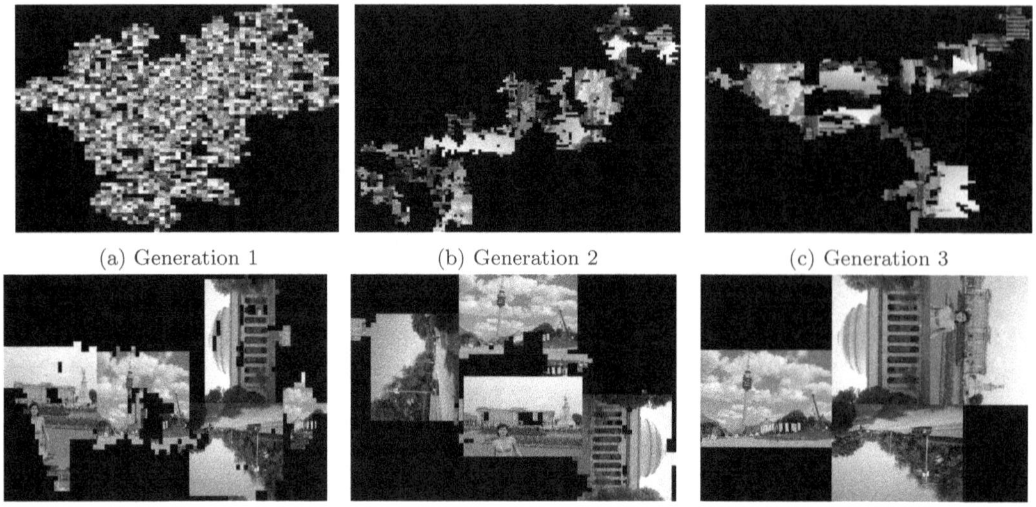

(a) Generation 1 (b) Generation 2 (c) Generation 3

(d) Generation 4 (e) Generation 5 (f) Final Generation (100)

Figure 7: Solution process of a "mixed-bag" puzzle, composed of four different 432-piece puzzles: (a)–(e) Best chromosomes achieved by the GA from first to fifth generation, and (f) final generation. All original four images were perfectly reconstructed. GA has no knowledge that given pieces belong to different images.

# Pieces	Neighbor	Perfect
432	94.88%	11
540	94.08%	8
805	94.12%	6
5,015	94.90%	7
10,375	98.03%	4

Table 1: Accuracy results under neighbor comparison on different benchmark sets. For each set we report the average accuracy obtained by the GA and number of puzzles perfectly reconstructed (out of 20).

	Neighbor	Perfect
Gallagher [9]	90.4%	9
GA	94.88%	11

Table 2: Performance comparison for puzzles with 432 pieces. Note that [9] assumes known image dimensions to improve accuracy results, while our solver does not.

4. RESULTS

To evaluate the accuracy results of each assembled image, we adopt the *neighbor comparison* measure used in all previous works, i.e., the fraction of correct pairwise piece adjacencies (with respect to the original image). In all experiments we used a standard tile size of 28×28 pixels.

We tested our solver against previously published benchmark sets [17, 18, 4] containing 20-image sets of 432-, 540-, 805-, 5,015-, and 10,375-piece puzzles. We report in Table 1 the average accuracy results per set, as well as the number of puzzles reconstructed perfectly. The results obtained for the set of 432-piece puzzles can be compared to the ones achieved by [9] on the same image set (see Table 2). We stress that the solver in [9] assumes known image dimensions to improve the accuracy results (described there as the "trimming" and "filling" stages), while ours does not. According to Table 6 in [9], their algorithm results in an average of 90.4%, i.e., we achieve a significant improvement of over 4% with less assumptions.

The largest puzzle that has been attempted so far with pieces of unknown orientation is a 9,600-piece puzzle. We attempted a 22,755-piece puzzle (i.e., more than twice larger), with unknown piece orientation and unknown image dimensions. As can be seen in Figure 4, perfect reconstruction was achieved. The solution process required a meager 3.5 hours on a modern PC (compared to 23.5 hours reported in [9] for the 9,600 piece-puzzle).

Finally, we applied the solver to "mixed-bag" puzzles, i.e., puzzles containing pieces from multiple images. Of course, the solver is unaware of the image dimensions, and of the fact that multiple images are involved. We created a mixed puzzle by combining four different 432-piece puzzles. Figure 7 depicts the gradual assembly of the puzzle until a perfect reconstruction of all four images is achieved. Next, we created another mixed puzzle by combining 16,405 pieces from seven different images; three 5,015-piece puzzles and four smaller ones. To the best of our knowledge, this is the most complex mixed-bag that has been solved, in terms of both the puzzle size and the number of mixed images. Despite containing a much larger number of pieces (relatively to single-image puzzles solved previously), the GA succeeds in fully reconstructing all the seven puzzles. Figure 8 shows the reassembled puzzles.

5. CONCLUSIONS

In this paper we presented, for the first time, a GA-based solver capable of handling puzzles with (1) pieces of unknown orientation, (2) unknown image dimensions, and (3) pieces originating from multiple images. Our solver sets a new state-of-the-art in terms of the accuracy achieved and the complexity of the puzzles handled. We improved significantly results obtained by previous works, making almost no assumptions. Specifically, we successfully tackled puzzles of more than twice the size that has been attempted before

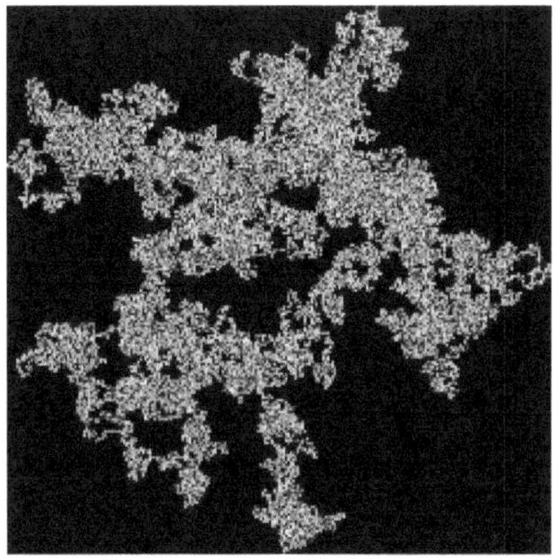

(a)

(b)

Figure 8: Perfect reconstruction of a “mixed-bag” puzzle. This puzzle is constructed of 16,405 pieces from seven different images; three 5,015-piece puzzles and four smaller puzzles. As far as we know, this is the largest and most complex mixed puzzle that has been solved, in terms of size and number of puzzles.

with the same relaxed assumptions [9]. Finally, we showed how to assemble mixed puzzles, i.e., puzzles with pieces from multiple different images. As far as we know, the mixed puzzle solved in this paper is the largest and most complex in terms of the total number of pieces and the number of mixed images.

6. REFERENCES

[1] T. Altman. Solving the jigsaw puzzle problem in linear time. *Applied Artificial Intelligence an International Journal*, 3(4):453–462, 1989.

[2] B. Brown, C. Toler-Franklin, D. Nehab, M. Burns, D. Dobkin, A. Vlachopoulos, C. Doumas, S. Rusinkiewicz, and T. Weyrich. A system for high-volume acquisition and matching of fresco fragments: Reassembling Theran wall paintings. *ACM Transactions on Graphics*, 27(3):84, 2008.

[3] S. Cao, H. Liu, and S. Yan. Automated assembly of shredded pieces from multiple photos. In *IEEE Int. Conf. on Multimedia and Expo*, pages 358–363, 2010.

[4] T. Cho, S. Avidan, and W. Freeman. A probabilistic image jigsaw puzzle solver. In *IEEE Conference on Computer Vision and Pattern Recognition*, pages 183–190, 2010.

[5] T. Cho, M. Butman, S. Avidan, and W. Freeman. The patch transform and its applications to image editing. In *IEEE Conference on Computer Vision and Pattern Recognition*, pages 1–8, 2008.

[6] A. Deever and A. Gallagher. Semi-automatic assembly of real cross-cut shredded documents. In *International Conference on Image Processing*, pages 233–236, 2012.

[7] E. Demaine and M. Demaine. Jigsaw puzzles, edge matching, and polyomino packing: Connections and complexity. *Graphs and Combinatorics*, 23:195–208, 2007.

[8] H. Freeman and L. Garder. Apictorial jigsaw puzzles: The computer solution of a problem in pattern recognition. *IEEE Transactions on Electronic Computers*, EC-13(2):118–127, 1964.

[9] A. Gallagher. Jigsaw puzzles with pieces of unknown orientation. In *IEEE Conference on Computer Vision and Pattern Recognition*, pages 382–389, 2012.

[10] D. Goldberg, C. Malon, and M. Bern. A global approach to automatic solution of jigsaw puzzles. *Computational Geometry: Theory and Applications*, 28(2-3):165–174, 2004.

[11] E. Justino, L. Oliveira, and C. Freitas. Reconstructing shredded documents through feature matching. *Forensic Science International*, 160(2):140–147, 2006.

[12] D. Koller and M. Levoy. Computer-aided reconstruction and new matches in the forma urbis romae. *Bullettino Della Commissione Archeologica Comunale di Roma*, pages 103–125, 2006.

[13] D. A. Kosiba, P. M. Devaux, S. Balasubramanian, T. L. Gandhi, and K. Kasturi. An automatic jigsaw puzzle solver. In *International Conference on Pattern Recognition*, volume 1, pages 616–618, 1994.

[14] W. Marande and G. Burger. Mitochondrial DNA as a genomic jigsaw puzzle. *Science*, 318(5849):415–415, 2007.

[15] M. Marques and C. Freitas. Reconstructing strip-shredded documents using color as feature matching. In *ACM Symposium on Applied Computing*, pages 893–894, 2009.

[16] A. Q. Morton and M. Levison. The computer in literary studies. In *IFIP Congress*, pages 1072–1081, 1968.

[17] D. Pomeranz, M. Shemesh, and O. Ben-Shahar. A fully automated greedy square jigsaw puzzle solver. In *IEEE Conference on Computer Vision and Pattern Recognition*, pages 9–16, 2011.

[18] D. Sholomon, O. E. David, and N. S. Netanyahu. A genetic algorithm-based solver for very large jigsaw puzzles. In *IEEE Conference on Computer Vision and Pattern Recognition*, pages 1767–1774, 2013.

[19] F. Toyama, Y. Fujiki, K. Shoji, and J. Miyamichi. Assembly of puzzles using a genetic algorithm. In *IEEE Int. Conf. on Pattern Recognition*, volume 4, pages 389–392, 2002.

[20] C.-S. E. Wang. *Determining molecular conformation from distance or density data*. PhD thesis, Massachusetts Institute of Technology, Dept. of Electrical Engineering and Computer Science, 2000.

[21] X. Yang, N. Adluru, and L. J. Latecki. Particle filter with state permutations for solving image jigsaw puzzles. In *IEEE Conference on Computer Vision and Pattern Recognition*, pages 2873–2880, 2011.

[22] Y. Zhao, M. Su, Z. Chou, and J. Lee. A puzzle solver and its application in speech descrambling. In *WSEAS International Conference on Computer Engineering and Applications*, pages 171–176, 2007.

On Homogenization of Coal in Longitudinal Blending Beds

Pradyumn Kumar Shukla
Karlsruhe Institute of Technology
pradyumn.shukla@kit.edu

Michael P. Cipold
J&C Bachmann GmbH
Bad Wildbad, Germany
mci@jcbachmann.de

ABSTRACT

Coal blending processes mainly use static and non-reactive blending methods like the well-known Chevron stacking. Although real-time quality measurement techniques such as online X-ray fluorescence measurements are available, the possibility to explore a dynamic adaptation of the blending process to the current quality data obtained using these techniques has not been explored. A dynamic adaptation helps to mix the coal from different mines in an optimal way and deliver a homogeneous product. The paper formulates homogenization of coal in longitudinal blending beds as a bi-objective problem of minimizing the variance of the cross-sectional quality and minimizing the height variance of the coal heap in the blending bed. We propose a cone based evolutionary algorithm to explore different trade-off regions of the Pareto front. A pronounced knee region on the Pareto front is found and is investigated in detail using a knee search algorithm. There are many interesting problem insights that are gained by examining the solutions found in different regions. In addition, all the knee solutions outperform the traditional Chevron stacking method.

Categories and Subject Descriptors

I.6.m [**Simulation and Modeling**]: Miscellaneous; J.m [**Computer Applications**]: Miscellaneous

Keywords

Multi-objective algorithms, Knees, Simulation optimization

1. INTRODUCTION AND RELATED WORK

Bulk material processing describes the handling of raw bulk materials such as minerals, coals or ores. These are mostly mined from natural source and thus are usually inhomogeneous in matters of quality parameters. Quality equalization to guarantee efficient processing can be achieved by using blending systems in the processing chain. Most systems today still implement static blending methods like the well-known Chevron stacking. There, the material is placed in the center of the stockpile while driving the stacker along the blending bed at constant speed. As the stacker is moved back and forth along the full length of the stockpile the material forms layers along the sides of the partial stockpile below. In cross section these layers form a chevron pattern.

Blending with Chevron stacking results in partially equalized quality output curves which still contain fluctuations exceeding the desired limits in many cases. Real-time quality measurement makes it possible to follow the current quality trend and react dynamically with the blending process.

This paper utilizes a particle simulation to reproduce the coal blending process virtually and allows calculation of the outcome of a possible solution during optimization. The optimization is done modifying the stacker traverse path only. This implements a method of minimal system change and thus with minimal financial and hardware effort.

Previous studies focus on analyzing and improving the coal blending efficiency; the work by Cipold. et al. [4], to the best of our knowledge, is the only one that presented a simulation based optimization of the stacker path to achieve a homogeneous coal stockpile. Kumral [8] describe a method to optimize a mineral blending system design before its construction to get the best performance. Using genetic algorithms and a multiple regression model they determine the best blending bed parameters simulating the stockpile with a simplified cell model. Pavloudakis and Agioutanis [10] use a more complex stockpile simulation approach consisting of multiple layers lying on top of each other. They assume a constant material flow and calculate the expected quality at the material output. However, their work did not focus on optimizing the blending efficiency. Bond et al. [2] describe methods to improve the efficiency of blending beds by modifying the volume of a stockpile dynamically and modifying the stacking speed while measuring the input quality with an online analyzer. They only suggest a solution with an appropriate software to control the stacker speed dynamically during the stacking to place material with recognized quality at specific locations in the blending bed but do not extend this thought in detail.

The main contributions of this paper are as follows:

- A multi-objective model of the problem that includes a realistic formulation of the objectives and a constraint violation measure is presented. (Section 3)

- A cone based algorithm, which additionally uses a utility measure to produce a biased density of solutions in good trade-off regions, is developed. (Section 4)

GECCO'14, July 12–16, 2014, Vancouver, BC, Canada.

http://dx.doi.org/10.1145/2576768.2598316.

- A detailed physics simulation and a fast simulation are used to find the optimal solutions to the multi-objective problem. (Section 5)
- Interesting insights about the problem and common principles in the obtained optimal solutions are investigated (innovization). (Section 6)
- The solutions obtained by our algorithm produce better homogenization results than Chevron stacking.

2. COAL PROCESSING AND BLENDING

Raw bulk materials such as minerals, coals or ores are mostly mined from natural resources and hence the product is usually inhomogeneous in matters of the quality parameters of interest. Typical quality parameters for coal, for example, are moisture or ash content as not burning components, sulfur content or calorific value among others [1].

In most bulk material processes a range of acceptable quality parameters can be defined for the process to work properly. The process is then adapted for the specified average quality. As the quality of the material varies over time the process is not operated in the most efficient way and the used process equipment can even take damage from too high variation even though the material meets the average quality setpoints. As an example an autoclave for coal gasification may be considered. This unit should be run at a specific heat setpoint in order to operate most efficiently. Even though the average particle size is constant during the day some minutes or even hours of smaller particles (balanced by bigger particles in the later time of the day) can cause the oven to heat up over the target setpoint. This is critical for the machines used and has to be detected, the material flow has to be reduced and the process is influenced. Even more critical situations occur if the calorific value is not longer balanced to the amount of ash in the coal. If the energy contained in the coal is not sufficient to keep the temperature above a certain limit the fluid ash will solidify which puts the autoclave out of service.

Summarized, it can be stated that the absolute average quality value is not easily controllable but also the control is not necessary as long as the process is adapted for the specified quality value but there is a requirement for a stable quality which means a low quality variance.

In the last decade a whole range of instruments has been developed to allow online determination of quality parameters like elemental composition, size distribution and other parameters of interest. These instruments are determining the parameters directly on the main stream [9] and allow the operator to create a regulated process which is adapted to the current parameter measurement. The main advantage of these instruments is the lack of the necessity to draw samples and the real-time quality determination.

The measurement instrument employed to determine the quality parameters used for the data in this paper is an online X-ray fluorescence analyzer [9]. The instrument is located over or even on the main material stream as it can be seen in Figure 1. An X-ray beam is directed onto the material surface and fluorescence radiation can be observed by a silicon drift detector. The spectra are then analyzed and the elemental composition and other desired process parameters (like moisture) can be derived. The instrument updates the current quality values every couple of seconds and is therefore usable for real-time control.

Figure 1: An online X-ray fluorescence analyzer mounted on a sled gliding over coal on a conveyor.

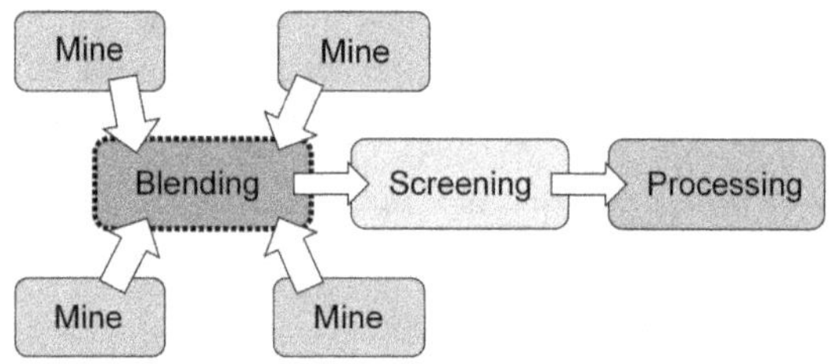

Figure 2: Illustration of coal mining and processing.

The natural deposits of coal are typically inhomogeneous and therefore in most cases the material needs to be processed in a plant. Coal is mined at places where exploration results indicate a worthwhile material extraction and then it is normally directly transported to the respective processing plant after some minor handling as illustrated in Figure 2.

Mining patterns limit the average quality and assure it does not exceed given limitations. But as layers of material are mined, the quality varies strongly. Variation levels can last for hours or days. To minimize the negative effect, which poor material would have onto the process, blending is inserted before processing. The aim is to homogenize the raw material and minimize the quality variation.

This paper here is focused on longitudinal blending beds as illustrated in Figure 3. The blending bed is an area allocated for building so-called stockpiles of raw material. The blending bed can have a typical length up to $1000m$ and a width up to $50m$. The bed is located between two rail tracks on which huge stacking and reclaiming machines move along the bed. The stacking machine is fed with the input bulk stream using a conveyor belt. The reclaimer collects the bulk material on the stockpile and feeds it to a conveyor belt moving to the plant. The stacking machine has a long arm which reaches over the middle of the blending bed where the material is deposited. The material is then stacked to stockpiles by layering it with so-called cone-shell or chevron stacking [2]. For instance, using chevron stacking, the material is layered in multiple levels. Defined by the speed of the stacking machine and the material flow the levels become

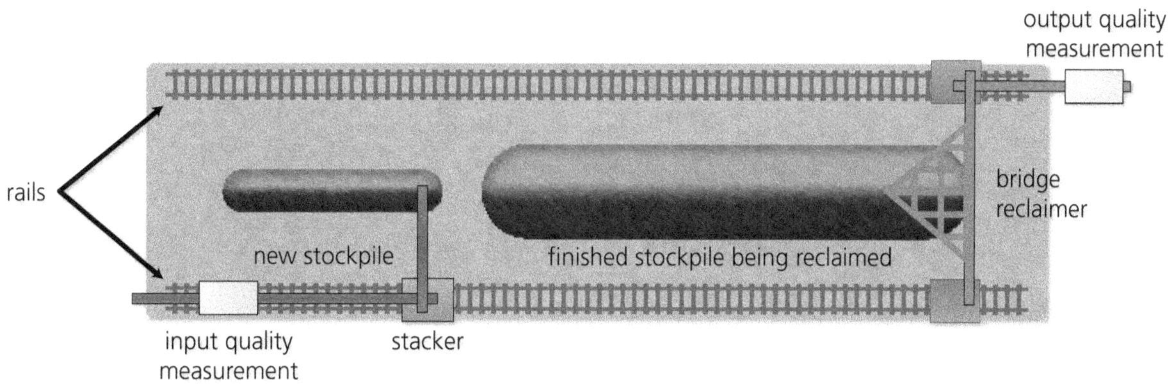

Figure 3: Illustration of a longitudinal blending bed with railed stacking and reclaiming machines.

thicker or thinner. The bridge reclaiming machine ablates the material in diagonal layers. If the stockpile was stacked using the chevron stacking method the cross sections ablated diagonally contain material of all levels. The blending result correlates mostly with the number of layers, and hence with the speed of the stacker. It is additionally influenced by the material quality curve which is illustrated in Section 6.

As standard, the necessary number of layers for a good blending result is calculated statically and optimized mainly at design time together with the general blending bed parameters [8]. In some cases the number of layers is varied by experienced operating personnel, but not directly controlled in reaction to quality variation changes.

3. MODELING AS A MULTI-OBJECTIVE OPTIMIZATION PROBLEM

The described real world system consists of multiple elements which need to be mapped into a system model first. The model consists of:

System Parameters (ϱ) are geometrical stockpile parameters, maximum stacker speed, reclaimer angle and material properties,

Quality Input (q) is the quality curve for each simulation run plotted against the total amount of material, and

Traverse Path (p) is the path along which the stacker is driving during the stockpile creation.

Given that the stacking system is unchangeable and that the quality input is fixed for each run, the optimization focuses on modifying the stacker path. For simplicity, material properties (like shape distribution of the coal particles) and weather parameters (like humidity) are not considered.

3.1 Objectives

The traverse path of the stacker is optimized for ideal material blending. The first objective here is the weighted variance of the quality at the reclaimer; this is defined as

$$F_1(\mathbf{q}, \mathbf{p}, \varrho) = \frac{n' \sum_{i=1}^{n} w_i (q_i^{\text{out}} - \overline{q}^{\text{out}})^2}{(n'-1) \sum_{i=1}^{n} w_i}, \quad (1)$$

where n is the number of cross sections ablated; w_i and q_i^{out} are the amount of material and the average material quality for Section i; n' is the number of non-empty cross sections; and $\overline{q}^{\text{out}}$ is the total average quality.

The traverse path of the stacker has a direct influence on the shape of the stockpile. This leads to the other primary objective to create a stockpile with a ridge of nearly constant height. The variance of the height is $\frac{\sum_{i=1}^{n}(h_i - \overline{h})^2}{n-1}$, where h_i is the height of cross section i, and $\overline{h}$ is the average height. From the geometry of the stockpile, it can be easily shown that the height of i-th cross section $h_i \propto \sqrt{w_i}$, and hence, the second objective function is given by

$$F_2(\mathbf{q}, \mathbf{p}, \varrho) = \frac{1}{n-1} \sum_{i=1}^{n} \left(\sqrt{w_i} - \frac{1}{n} \sum_{i=1}^{n} \sqrt{w_i} \right)^2. \quad (2)$$

For a given value of $\mathbf{q}, \mathbf{p}$, and ϱ, the values of both the above objective functions are computed from the stockpile that is formed. Simulation is used to create the stockpile.

3.2 Constraints

The constraints in this optimization problem restrict the movement of the stacker on the longitudinal blending bed. These constraints depend on the traverse path and the blending bed parameters ($\mathbf{p}$ and ϱ); these are defined next.

Position Constraint: The stacker must traverse within the stockpile region.

Speed Constraint: The given speed range is not violated.

As the stacker moves along the rails, the Position Constraint is a hard constraint. The Speed Constraint, on the other hand, is a soft constraint and it can be included as an another objective (like driving only as fast as necessary to meet a defined threshold). For simplicity, we regard the Speed Constraint as a hard constraint.

3.3 Solution Representation

This solution representation is based on position sampling and utilizes an array of real values from the interval $[0, 1]$ which correspond to the relative position in the valid traverse range of the stacking machine while creating the stockpile [4]. Hence, a solution is defined as:

$$\delta = (\delta_1, \ldots, \delta_l), \quad \delta_i \in [0, 1], l > 1. \quad (3)$$

The time t^{δ}_{slot} for driving between two positions linearly with constant velocity is calculated as described in equation 4 where t_{total} is the time to fully fill the stockpile.

$$t^{\delta}_{\text{slot}} = \frac{t_{\text{total}}}{l-1} \tag{4}$$

The position representation automatically satisfies the Position Constraint. However, the Speed Constraint can be violated if the speed exceeds the maximum speed. This is the case if $\frac{|\delta_{i+1} - \delta_i|}{v_{\max}} > t^{\delta}_{\text{slot}}$. The probability of obtaining infeasible solutions increases the smaller t^{δ}_{slot} gets. As the constraint do not depend on the quality curve $\mathbf{q}$, we can repair it using standard techniques, without having to run the simulator. To repair an infeasible solution, we use the direct correction and iterative balancing techniques from [4].

After repairing, the feasible solution produced by the evolutionary algorithm is used to run the simulation and calculate the objectives. The original infeasible solution can either be replaced by a repaired one in the population (Lamarckian technique) or remains in the population (Baldwinian technique). We investigate both Baldwininan and Lamarckian techniques in this paper. In addition, we define a constraint measure for the infeasible solutions. The measure puts a number on how far away a solution is from being feasible (degree of constraint violation). This way the solutions are sorted from feasible to infeasible to most infeasible. Feasible individuals are always preferred over infeasible individuals [5] while less infeasible individuals are preferred over more infeasible ones. The constraint measure is calculated by summing up the distance between each original position δ_i and the repaired position $r(\delta)_i$ as follows:

$$c(\delta) = \sum_{i=1}^{l} |\delta_i - r(\delta)_i|$$

We use both direct and iterative repairing methods to create feasible solutions. Repaired solutions are not written back to the population.

4. CONE UTILITY BASED GENETIC ALGORITHM

The main difficulty in a multi-objective optimization problem is to rank the solutions. Usually, the Pareto ordering is a natural relation that is used to rank the solutions. However, as the Pareto ordering is a partial order, an additional crowding or clustering measure is commonly employed to rank the Pareto non-dominated solutions. A commonly used extension of the Pareto ordering is a cone ordering as a cone ordering helps to focus on good trade-off regions of the Pareto front [5]. Moreover, using a cone based approach can also help to focus on different regions of the Pareto front.

A cone based ordering is also a partial order and hence there can be many solutions that are equally good. To differentiate among these solutions we could use an additional utility based measure that assigns a trade-off based goodness measure to each solution. This measure, together with the usual diversity measure (assumed to be crowding distance), can be used to bias the solutions in the trade-off region. Although there exist many biasing techniques we prefer to use a trade-off utility based one as trade-offs have a meaning that is easily understood by a designer (rather than other mathematical biasing measures [3])

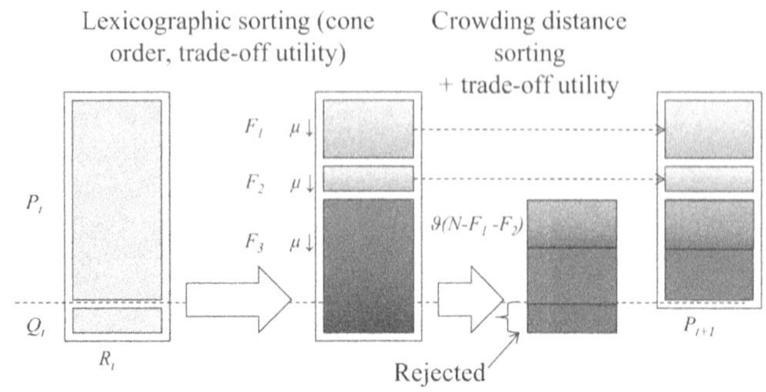

Figure 4: Illustration of CUEA. A cone partial order is used together with a trade-off based utility measure to sort the population.

In this paper, we propose and investigate a cone utility based genetic algorithm (CUEA) to solve the multi-objective problem described in Section 3. This algorithm is based on NSGA-II [5] and PKEA [11] and uses a cone based approach to focus on different regions of the Pareto front.

We assume a population size of N. At any generation t, let P_t and Q_t denote the parent and the offspring populations, respectively (in our simulation we assume $|Q_t| = 1$, a steady-state version). Let R_t be the combined population, i.e., $R_t = P_t \cup Q_t$. CUEA uses three additional parameters. The first of them $T > 0$ is a lower bound on the trade-off utility value. A second parameter $\vartheta \in [0, 1]$ is employed to ensure diversity in the population. Finally, an ordering cone $\mathfrak{C}$ needs to be specified. In order to rank the solutions in the set R_t (and create P_{t+1}) we first perform a sorting using the cone $\mathfrak{C}$ to R_t and identify different fronts: $\mathcal{F}_i$, $i = 1, 2, \ldots,$ etc.

For an arbitrary solution $\mathbf{u} \in R_t$, such that $\mathbf{u} \in \mathcal{F}_k$ for some $k \in \mathbb{N}$ ($\mathcal{F}_k$ is the k-th front in which $\mathbf{u}$ lies), let $\mu(\mathbf{u}) > 0$ be defined by

$$\mu(\mathbf{u}) = \max\left\{ \max_{\mathbf{v} \in \mathcal{F}_k} \max_{\{i: u_i > v_i\}} \min_{\{j: u_j < v_j\}} \frac{u_i - v_i}{v_j - u_j}, T \right\}. \tag{5}$$

At the end, every solution $\mathbf{u}$ has a tuple $(k, \mu(\mathbf{u}))$ and this is considered in a lexicographic way. The T parameter in Equation 5 serves as an upper trade-off bound, above which solutions are not considered relevant to the designer.

Next, we create the new parent population P_{t+1}. For this, we first set new population $P_{t+1} = \emptyset$, counter $i = 1$. Until $|P_{t+1}| + |\mathcal{F}_i| < N$, we perform $P_{t+1} = P_{t+1} \cup \mathcal{F}_i$ and $i = i + 1$. Now, we need to include $N - |P_{t+1}|$ solution more into P_{t+1} from the last front $\mathcal{F}_\ell$. For this, we sort the solutions of $\mathcal{F}_\ell$ into increasing order of their μ values and take the first $\tilde{N} := \lceil \vartheta \cdot (N - |P_{t+1}|) \rceil$ solutions into P_{t+1} from the sorted list. The $N - |P_{t+1}| - \tilde{N}$ remaining solutions are taken considering the crowding distance values (in $\mathcal{F}_\ell$).

Figure 4 shows the schematic of creating the new parent population. The sorting is based on the given cone order and the utility values in a lexicographic way. We see that the front (based on the cone ordering) cannot be fully accommodated and here, both the utility and the crowding distance values are used. The next offspring population is created from P_{t+1} using a lexicographic (rank, crowding distance) binary tournament selection, crossover and mutation operators.

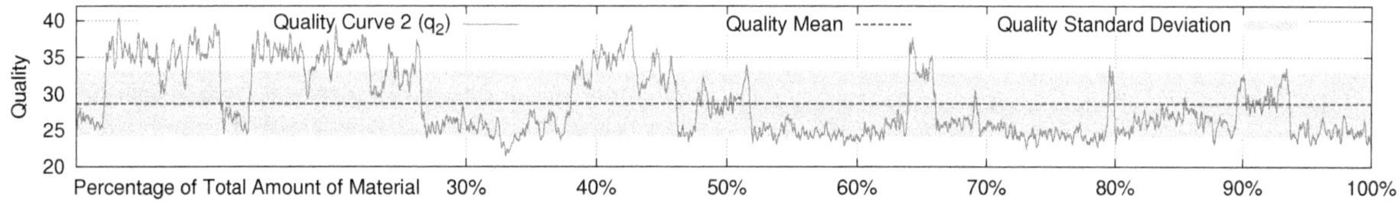

Figure 5: A quality curve from a coal processing plant in South Africa showing the variation in ash content.

5. PHYSICS SIMULATION AND EXPERIMENTAL SETUP

In contrary to the most approaches for modeling stacking and reclaiming of coal [8, 10], we proposed a physics based detailed simulation system that models the real world as close as possible by simulating the dropping, falling, rolling, and stacking of bulk materials [4]. This physics simulation, however, was regarded to be too slow to use it for optimization and thus it was replaced by a simplified fast simulation system. The physics simulation was only used to verify the optimization results generated by the simplified simulation.

For a deeper problem understanding we accelerated the detailed simulation process and ran it on modern machines (Intel Core i5-3570K, single core speed up to 3.80Ghz). The acceleration was mainly achieved by reducing the simulation complexity simulating only $60,000$ particles for a $90,000m^3$ stockpile. One simulation run takes about 25 minutes to complete which allows 100 function evaluations in 42 hours with a population size of 10.

Using the detailed simulation the stockpiles generated allow a deeper analysis of the stockpile composition. The results are closer to reality, and, in contrast to the fast simulation system, they are without integer artifacts. Furthermore, more realistic scenarios can be generated with finer granularity of simulation increasing the amount of particles simulated, allowing variable particle sizes and their effects on the stockpile building process which is an outstanding feature of this simulation system. The system itself and its integration into the standard optimization problem format allows for optimization of a highly complex problem and is an ideal example of expensive function evaluation.

Figure 5 shows one of the quality curves used in this study. The quality data was collected in a coal processing plant in South Africa. At the measuring point, coal of up to seven different mines is fed to the stockpile. The actual data used in the quality input curves for the optimization was the ash content of the coal.

The complex optimization problem is influenced by a wide range of parameters. We use three different quality input curves (denoted by Q0, Q1, and Q3) as problem instances. Except for the detailed physics simulation, each algorithmic combination is run 31 times in order to be able to give a stable statement about its performance The number of variables $l = 30$ and population size is set to 100. The maximum stacker speed is set equal to the speed necessary to place 20 layers with Chevron-stacking. The stockpile dimensions are 300 by 50 meters, the simulation detail is set to $1.5\frac{m^3}{particle}$, and we set the maximum function evaluations to be $20,000$ (except for the detailed simulation). We use the simulated binary crossover (probability 0.9; distribution index 15.0), polynomial mutation operator (probability $\frac{3.3}{variablecount=30}$; distribution index 20.0 after a limited parametric setting) and the binary tournament selection. The threshold parameter ϑ, and the trade-off parameter T were taken as 0.9 and 1.5 respectively.

We used three cones $\mathfrak{C}_1 := \{d \in \mathbb{R}^2 : d_1 \geq 0, d_2 \geq 0\}$, $\mathfrak{C}_2 := \{d \in \mathbb{R}^2 : d_1 \geq 0, d_1 + d_2 \geq 0\}$, and $\mathfrak{C}_3 := \{d \in \mathbb{R}^2 : d_2 \geq 0, d_1 + d_2 \geq 0\}$. These cones help to focus on the middle (knee) region, left (F_1 minima), and the right part (F_2 minima) of the Pareto front respectively [5].

To include problem knowledge in the algorithm, the steady state version of the CUEA algorithm was adapted to use a partially initialized population consisting of 30 solutions that are initialized with the Chevron stacking method with different speeds.

The initial population is generated as shown in Algorithm 1 by looping through m different speed levels where m is the number of Chevron initialized solutions in the initial population. For all l position variables δ_j^i of the ith solution a forward-backward motion is generated with the inner while loop where the modulo in the inner if-statement decides on the direction of movement.

Algorithm 1: Generation of Chevron stacking solutions

for $i \leftarrow 1$ *to* m **do**
  $j \leftarrow 0$
  while $j < l$ **do**
    $k \leftarrow 0$
    while $(k < i) \wedge (j < l)$ **do**
      if $\left\lfloor \frac{j}{i} \right\rfloor \equiv 0 \bmod 2$ **then**
        $\delta_j^i \leftarrow \frac{k}{i}$
      else
        $\delta_j^i \leftarrow 1 - \frac{k}{i}$
      end
      $k \leftarrow k + 1$
      $j \leftarrow j + 1$
    end
  end
end

For problem analysis and a deeper understanding, three basic experimental setups were chosen with varying subordinate parameters:

- To classify the proposed knee finding algorithm and its variations, it was run on the different problem instances and compared to *NSGA-II*, *ssNSGA-II* and *ssNSGA-II* with the same *partially initialized* population as used for CUEA.

- To evaluate the proposed algorithms combined with various repairing strategies, the algorithm was parameterized to do direct and iterative repairing either applied in the Baldwinian and Lamarckian way or used for constraint evaluation.

- To get deeper insights to the stockpile composition and problem behavior using a more realistic simulation, the detailed simulation was used with 100 function evaluations and a population size of 10 individuals.

For the coal homogenization multi-objective problem above there is no way to calculate an exact Pareto front. To get a better measure for partially calculated fronts, especially for the cone version of the CUEA algorithm, another measure has to be used. The distance to a non-dominated set describes a performance measure in which a non-dominated set of solutions is defined as a reference set. Each solution is measured against this set by first calculating the minimum distance to the reference set for each point and using the root mean square of these values as a distance measure. The reference set is obtained by grouping all ever calculated fronts and calculating the non-dominated set of these solutions which can then be used to compare the results. Equation 6 describes the set distance with $\mathbf{r}$ being the non-dominated reference set, $\mathbf{f}$ the objective values of the currently evaluated solution, $|\mathbf{r}|$, $|\mathbf{f}|$ the associated set sizes and $\mathrm{d}(\mathbf{x}, \mathbf{y})$ the Euclidean distance with equally scaled objective values as follows:

$$\mathrm{d}_{\mathrm{set}}(\mathbf{r}, \mathbf{f}) = \sqrt{\frac{1}{|\mathbf{f}|} \cdot \sum_{f^i \in \mathbf{f}} (\min_{r^i \in \mathbf{r}} \mathrm{d}(f^i, r^i))^2}. \quad (6)$$

A solution set is regarded as better than another one if the set distance (computed using Equation 6) is smaller.

Apart the above distance metric, we use the hypervolume to evaluate our algorithms. The hypervolume measures the volume of solutions that are dominated by a set of solutions, and it requires no knowledge of the exact Pareto front (which is the case for our real-world problem).

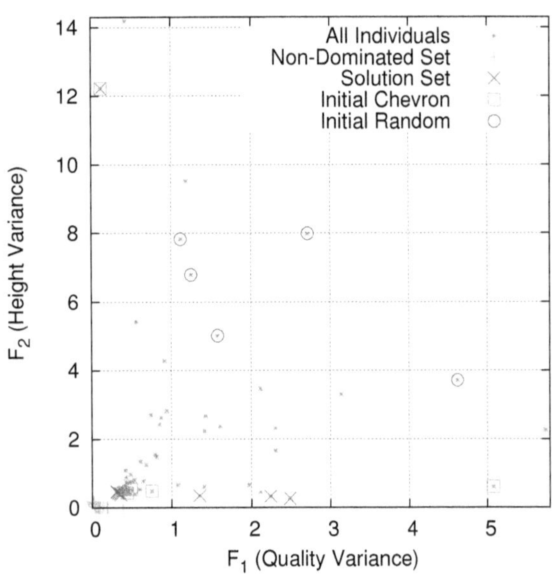

Figure 6: Illustration of an optimization run using the detailed simulation. The initial points and all intermediate points are shown. The non-dominated set computed using the fast simulator is also shown.

6. ANALYSIS

Using the detailed physics simulation and the steady state version of the CUEA algorithm focusing on the knee region together with a partially initialized population, the system was able to achieve results outperforming Chevron stacking and forming a knee region in the objective function scatter graph. The tradeoff between the height constancy and the quality stability in the output stream is clearly visible as well as the knee region (Figure 7). For better orientation the best results ever achieved in our optimization runs with the simulation system are also shown in the graph.

Figures 6 and 7 show a full scale and zoomed overview of the intermediate and final results achieved in this optimization run. The starting advantage of Chevron stacking over random solutions is clearly visible. Though the simulation was run only for 100 iterations the success of improvement of the starting population can be seen in the distribution of all individuals. Newly generated individuals are located closer to the final knee solutions in most cases.

Problem knowledge is beneficial for generic algorithms in general and we see that most of the solutions in the customized initial population generation dominate the initial random solutions (shown by circles in Figure 6). The final solutions forming the knee region are mostly static Chevron stacking solutions with little modifications which improve quality variance or height variance.

The nondominated front of this bi-objective problem is apparently a convex curve (can be seen in Figure 7). A cone based analysis of such problems is natural approach to find good trade-off solutions [14]; this also justifies the use of CUEA on this real-world problem.

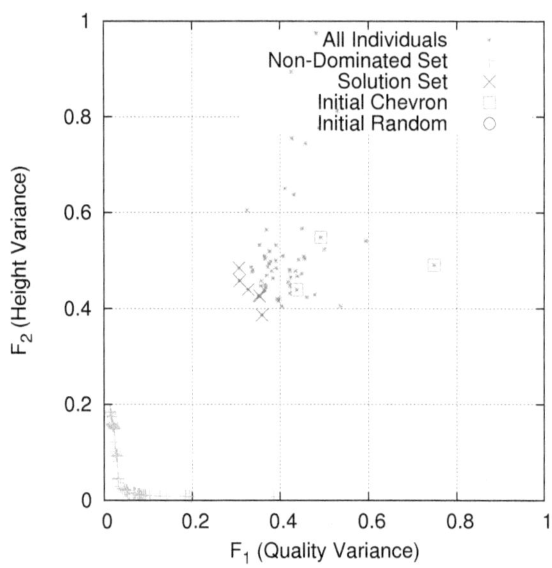

Figure 7: Enlarged illustration of the final solution sets obtained using detailed and fast simulation. One can clearly observe a pronounced knee.

Figure 8 shows the comparison of the quality variance of a random solution from the knee region of the objective space with an acceptable height variance to the quality variance of solutions generated with static Chevron stacking at different speeds. It is clearly visible that Chevron stacking is always outperformed even if it uses higher speeds than given as freedom to the optimization system. Moreover there is not always an improvement in terms of homogenization result if the speed is increased. This graph shows the clear advantage of an optimized solution compared with static stacking.

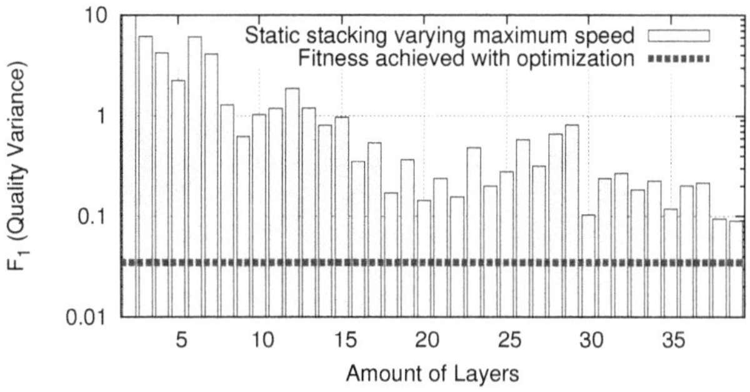

Figure 8: Illustration of a random knee solution (dotted line) in comparison to static Chevron stacking with various speeds. The quality variance in log scale (y-axis) shows a clear outperformance by the optimized solution.

Figure 9 shows the three-dimensional plot of the objective values of all solutions in fronts which were regarded for the generation of the non-dominated set in Equation 6. The z-axis of the plot indicates the average speed of each solution as a fraction of the maximum speed available. Most solutions are concentrated in a knee region, where a wide spread of speeds can be found; mainly from 0.3 to 0.7. Solutions with lowest quality variance but high height variance tend to have the highest speeds and vice versa. An important design implication of this is the following: to achieve a solution which is also good in terms of height variance the speed needs to be reduced from maximum. Such problem insights from optimized solutions are valuable (innovization); this is only possible if the problem is modeled and solved as an optimization problem, rather than adhering to a standard stacking procedure. The results from Figure 9 show not only the intuitive benefits from Chevron stacking with high speeds, but also that there is a wide range of strategic options to get results in the knee region.

Interestingly, the set of points in Figure 9 form a smooth manifold (an analytical representation of this can be computed). The reason for this is currently being investigated.

In order to compare CUEA with other standard algorithms like NSGA-II and the steady state version of NSGA-II, we executed 31 runs for all combinations of problem instances and algorithms. The results, presented in Table 1, show the advantage of CUEA over standard algorithms (algorithms using a steady state version are marked with **ss** prefix; algorithms using a partially Chevron initialized population are marked with **ini** suffix). CUEA outperforms NSGA-II in all extensions for this problem instance and all combinations of extensions in terms of hypervolume (computed using the reference point $(0.4, 0.2)$) and set distance, based on median values. The steady state algorithms show slightly better performance. Although steady state algorithms require more computation (like more sorting operations), the function evaluations (at least when using the detailed simulation) are far more expensive, and, are the most time consuming elements. Hence, these steady state algorithms are a useful choice for such optimization problems.

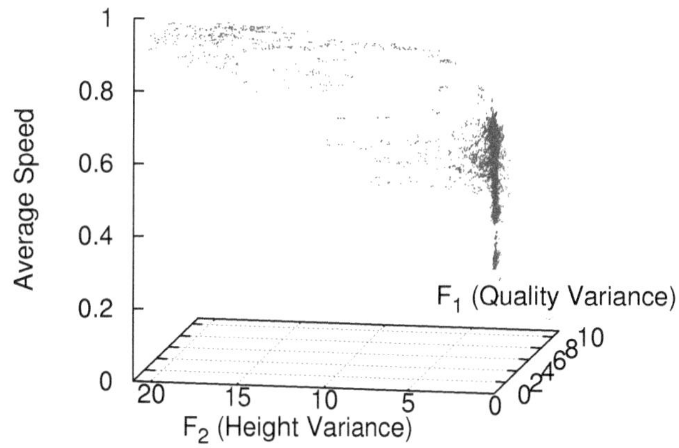

Figure 9: A 3D plot of the two objectives versus the average speed of the non-dominated solutions. Most of the knee solutions are concentrated in a central speed range. In addition, higher speeds lead to lower quality variance (F_1) but worse height variance (F_2).

Computations have shown that the standard deviation of all the algorithms are very small (stable performance) and are lie in a similar range. As the standard deviations don't offer any further insights, these are not presented in Table 1.

	Hypervolume measure			
		Quality Input Curve		
		Q0	**Q1**	**Q2**
Algorithm	**NSGA-II**	0.048	0.045	0.036
	ssNSGA-II	0.053	0.053	0.046
	ssNSGA-II-ini	0.057	0.061	0.047
	CUEA	0.060	0.054	0.051
	ssCUEA	0.060	0.059	0.056
	ssCUEAini	0.062	0.063	0.053
	Set distance measure			
Algorithm	**NSGA-II**	0.050	0.038	0.045
	ssNSGA-II	0.045	0.030	0.043
	ssNSGA-IIini	0.027	0.019	0.034
	CUEA	0.024	0.032	0.026
	ssCUEA	0.023	0.020	0.017
	ssCUEAini	0.022	0.012	0.024

Table 1: Median hypervolume (top) and distance to the non-Dominated set (bottom) values based on 31 runs of the algorithms. Whiter shades represent better values.

In direct comparison the results for the repair mechanisms (in Table 2) show the advantage of the simplest repair mechanism: the direct Baldwinian repairing. It is outperforming all other mechanisms by far. The iterative repairing usually performs worse than the direct repairing and the same is true for the Lamarckian repairing in comparison with the Baldwinian. Although the results for the Constraint Violation measure are the worst in direct comparison with other mechanisms, the difference is small. Furthermore the results are encouraging as deeper investigations have shown the quick convergence of the population towards feasible solutions generating new solutions with a high percentage being feasible and beneficial for the population.

Hypervolume measure			
	Quality Input Curve		
	Q0	Q1	Q2
Mechanism: Direct Baldwinian	0.062	0.063	0.053
Iterative Baldwinian	0.059	0.060	0.051
Direct Lamarckian	0.056	0.062	0.051
Iterative Lamarckian	0.055	0.057	0.048
Direct Constraint	0.054	0.046	0.048
Iterative Constraint	0.054	0.049	0.045
Set distance measure			
Mechanism: Direct Baldwinian	0.022	0.012	0.024
Iterative Baldwinian	0.030	0.022	0.027
Direct Lamarckian	0.034	0.012	0.036
Iterative Lamarckian	0.040	0.027	0.037
Direct Constraint	0.037	0.036	0.029
Iterative Constraint	0.032	0.038	0.033

Table 2: Median hypervolume (top) and distance to the non-Dominated set (bottom) values based on 31 runs using different repair mechanisms.

7. CONCLUSIONS

The composition of the non-dominated set shows the benefits of using cone-based algorithms where cones can be used to guide the search towards knee and extreme regions.

A new knee focusing algorithm with a biased density of solutions in good trade-off regions was proposed. We investigated various repair mechanisms and proposed a constraint violation measure. Systematic tests showed that the Baldwinian direct repairing is the most beneficial repairing method. The utilization of a distance measure to a non-dominated set was shown and is used as a more advantageous method to evaluate solution sets which are only optimal in terms of one objective.

The generation of a non-dominated set and the contributing solutions allowed insights about the benefits of the cone-based approach and insights about the speed distribution and its relation to the two objectives. The detailed simulation system was adapted to be usable from the optimization system generating results in reasonable time, allowing the results generated by the optimization system to be of higher degree of realism. The results generated by the optimization system outperform static stacking. Initializing the starting population with Chevron strategies, these can be quickly improved by the algorithm to generate much better results.

We are currently exploring the use of Parego [7] on our coal homogenization problem as Parego is designed for solving expensive multi-objective optimization problems. We are additionally employing the algorithmic framework of [12, 13] to search for robust trade-off solutions for this problem. The use of variable cone orderings [6] to simultaneously focus on different regions of the Pareto front also seems relevant.

8. ADDITIONAL AUTHORS

Additional authors: Claus Bachmann (J&C Bachmann GmbH email: cba@jcbachmann.de) and Hartmut Schmeck (Karlsruhe Institute of Technology email: schmeck@kit.edu).

9. REFERENCES

[1] J. Alderman. *Coal Blending and Optimization*, pages 52–62. Coal Age, 2012.

[2] J. Bond, R. Coursaux, and R. Worthington. Blending systems and control technologies for cement raw materials. *IEEE Industry Applications Magazine*, 6:49–59, 2000.

[3] J. Branke and K. Deb. Integrating user preferences into evolutionary multi-objective optimization. In Y. Jin, editor, *Knowledge Incorporation in Evolutionary Computation*, volume 167 of *Studies in Fuzziness and Soft Computing*, pages 461–477. Springer Berlin Heidelberg, 2005.

[4] M. Cipold, P. Shukla, C. Bachmann, K. Bao, and H. Schmeck. An evolutionary optimization approach for bulk material blending systems. In C. e. a. Coello, editor, *PPSN XII*, volume 7491 of *Lecture Notes in Computer Science*, pages 478–488. Springer, 2012.

[5] K. Deb. *Multi-objective optimization using evolutionary algorithms*. Wiley, 2001.

[6] C. Hirsch, P. Shukla, and H. Schmeck. Variable preference modeling using multi-objective evolutionary algorithms. In R. Takahashi, K. Deb, E. Wanner, and S. Greco, editors, *Evolutionary Multi-Criterion Optimization*, volume 6576 of *Lecture Notes in Computer Science*, pages 91–105. Springer, 2011.

[7] J. Knowles. Parego: a hybrid algorithm with on-line landscape approximation for expensive multiobjective optimization problems. *Evolutionary Computation, IEEE Transactions on*, 10(1):50–66, Feb 2006.

[8] M. Kumral. Bed blending design incorporating multiple regression modelling and genetic algorithms. *International Journal of Surface Mining, Reclamation and Environment*, 17:98–112, 2003.

[9] M. Laurila and C. Bachmann. X-ray fluorescence measuring system and methods for trace elements. *US Patent US 2004/0240606*, 2004.

[10] F. Pavloudakis and Z. Agioutantis. Simulation of bulk solids blending in longitudinal stockpiles. *Journal of the South African Institute of Mining and Metallurgy*, 106:229–237, 2006.

[11] P. Shukla, M. Braun, and H. Schmeck. Theory and algorithms for finding knees. In R. Purshouse, P. Fleming, C. Fonseca, S. Greco, and J. Shaw, editors, *Evolutionary Multi-Criterion Optimization*, volume 7811 of *Lecture Notes in Computer Science*, pages 156–170. Springer, 2013.

[12] P. Shukla, C. Hirsch, and H. Schmeck. A framework for incorporating trade-off information using multi-objective evolutionary algorithms. In R. Schaefer, C. Cotta, J. KoÅCodziej, and G. Rudolph, editors, *PPSN XI*, volume 6239 of *Lecture Notes in Computer Science*, pages 131–140. Springer, 2010.

[13] P. Shukla, C. Hirsch, and H. Schmeck. Towards a deeper understanding of trade-offs using multi-objective evolutionary algorithms. In C. e. a. Chio, editor, *Applications of Evolutionary Computation*, volume 7248 of *Lecture Notes in Computer Science*, pages 396–405. Springer Berlin Heidelberg, 2012.

[14] M. Wiecek. Advances in cone-based preference modeling for decision making with multiple criteria. *Decision Making in Manufacturing and Services*, 1(2), 2007.

Eco-friendly Reduction of Travel Times in European Smart Cities

Daniel H. Stolfi
LCC, University of Malaga
ETSI Informática, Campus de Teatinos
29071, Málaga, Spain
dhstolfi@lcc.uma.es

Enrique Alba
LCC, University of Malaga
ETSI Informática, Campus de Teatinos
29071, Málaga, Spain
eat@lcc.uma.es

ABSTRACT

This article proposes an innovative solution for reducing polluting gas emissions from road traffic in modern cities. It is based on our new Red Swarm architecture which is composed of a series of intelligent spots with WiFi connections that can suggest a customized route to drivers. We have tested our proposal in four different case studies corresponding to actual European smart cities. To this end, we first import the city information from OpenStreetMap into the SUMO road traffic micro-simulator, propose a Red Swarm architecture based on intelligent spots located at traffic lights, and then optimize the resulting system in terms of travel times and gas emissions by using an evolutionary algorithm. Our results show that an important quantitative reduction in gas emissions as well as in travel times can be achieved when vehicles are rerouted according to our Red Swarm indications. This represents a promising result for the low cost implementation of an idea that could engage the interest of both citizens and municipal authorities.

Categories and Subject Descriptors

I.6.3 [**Simulation and Modeling**]: Applications

Keywords

Application, evolutionary algorithm, road traffic, smart city, smart mobility, gas emissions, WiFi connections

1. INTRODUCTION

The concept of Smart Cities [3, 9] can be understood as a holistic approach to identify a city's strengths and weakness taking into account the level of development and performance in a broad range of characteristics and factors. It is common [5] to recognize six axes at work in them: i) *Smart Economy*, ii) *Smart People*, iii) *Smart Governance*, iv) *Smart Mobility*, v) *Smart Environment*, and vi) *Smart Living*. In our research we have focused on the relationship between road traffic and travel times (*Smart Mobility*), and the reduction of greenhouse gas emissions (*Smart Environment*), which results in an improvement in citizens' health and quality of life (*Smart Living*).

Road traffic is a well-known source of air pollution in urban areas [8]. Air pollution is not only an important issue for the economy, the environment, and human health, but it also damages cities' buildings and has a clear impact on our climate, since some air pollutants behave as greenhouse gases [6]. The main emissions are usually cataloged as: i) Particulate Matter (PM), ii) Nitrogen Oxides (NO_x), iii) Sulfur Dioxide (SO_2), iv) Carbon Monoxide (CO), v) Carbon Dioxide (CO_2), vi) Methane (CH_4), vii) Ground level Ozone (O_3), and viii) Hydrogen Sulfide (H_2S).

In this article we propose an effective system to manage road traffic which is capable not only of reducing travel times, but also emissions and fuel consumption in vehicles, by suggesting alternative routes so as to avoid traffic jams and contribute to more environmentally friendly driving.

Several studies have focused on reducing the gas emissions from vehicles in urban areas. In [16], the authors discuss the conflict between a reduction in travel times and gas emissions. They implement a Model Predictive Control (MPC) and propose an objective function especially built to weigh the different emission parameters as well as the traffic flow, and test them in a traffic simulator. They solve the MPC optimization problem by using a multi-start sequential quadratic programming optimization method and conclude that an improvement in the traffic flow does not necessarily guarantee reduced emission levels. This is the reason why we explicitly include here both traffic flow and emissions.

In [10], two different scenarios which model the roads within the city of Bologna and its surroundings are optimized by using different emission metrics as edge weights for the Gawron algorithm [4]. The authors observe that optimization seems to depend on the type of roads available in the area analyzed and that there are a series of interdependencies between pollutant gas emissions and road networks. We wanted to test the Red Swarm solution in different case studies to check how it behaves and observe these metrics in detail thanks to our micro-simulation of the city.

In [1], a new protocol is proposed. Called the environmentally friendly geocast protocol, it focuses on minimizing CO_2 emissions from vehicles approaching a traffic light signal. By using the information delivered by the signal, vehicles calculate their recommended environmentally friendly speed in order to avoid some actions such as stop-and-go conditions, high speeds, and high accelerations. The paper deals with

GECCO'14, July 12–16, 2014, Vancouver, BC, Canada.
Copyright 2014 ACM 978-1-4503-2662-9/14/07 ...$15.00.
http://dx.doi.org/10.1145/2576768.2598317.

just one intersection (we use extensive areas or the whole city itself) and does not reroute vehicles, as we do.

In [11], a real time traffic light control scheme for reducing vehicle CO_2 emissions is proposed. The road conditions are obtained by the wireless communication between an electronic toll collection transponder installed in vehicles and traffic lights. Vehicles send the passing requests to the traffic lights, so that the traffic control center knows the road conditions in real time and dynamically adjusts the traffic lights cycle length based on a decision tree algorithm. Despite the important reduction in CO_2 emissions achieved in this work, the authors only present the results of a simple intersection instead of a larger geographical area.

Finally, an environmental city design through land use scenarios and large-scale traffic simulation is presented in [12]. The authors evaluate the city of Yokohama in Japan as a case study with different urban forms and traffic, and analyze the relationship between them and CO_2 emissions. Although the proposed method can be a useful tool for urban planners to test some land use and transportation policies for designing sustainable cities, what we are interested in is optimizing already existing cities, taking advantage of their infrastructure (which is more realistic and affordable).

In summary, our contribution is a low-cost system which reduces travel times, fuel consumption, and greenhouse gas emissions of vehicles by suggesting alternative routes which are personalized for each single driver in the city.

The rest of this paper is organized as follows. In the next section we present the characteristics of the different geographical areas we have optimized and describe the Red Swarm architecture including the Evolutionary Algorithm (EA) and the Rerouting Algorithm (RA). In Section 3 the algorithm parameterization and experimental settings are presented. Section 4 focuses on the studies done and the discussion of the results. And finally, in Section 5, conclusions and future work are given.

2. THE RED SWARM ARCHITECTURE

The Red Swarm architecture [13] is a versatile system that takes advantage of the already existing infrastructure in modern cities such as computer-controlled traffic lights and WiFi spots combined with our software solution based on bio-inspired algorithms, with the end goal of optimizing the road traffic in a city.

A Red Swarm consists of: i) Several spots installed at traffic lights which redirect the traffic throughout the city; ii) An Evolutionary Algorithm (EA) which calculates the configuration of the spots; iii) The Rerouting Algorithm (RA) which runs in each spot and suggests alternative routes to vehicles; and iv) Smartphones, tablets or even On Board Units (OBU) installed in vehicles.

The system architecture of Red Swarm is depicted in Figure 1. It is implemented in two stages, i) The Configuration Stage, and ii) The Deployment and Use Stage.

The system configuration is calculated by the EA in the Configuration Stage by using real maps imported from OpenStreetMap into the SUMO microscopic traffic simulator [2] which interacts with TraCI (Traffic Control Interface) [15] in order to implement the changes in SUMO according to the rerouting performed by the RA.

In the Deployment and Use Stage, when a vehicle approaches a junction controlled by a Red Swarm spot, a WiFi link is established between the spot and the smartphone, tablet or OBU in the vehicle, so that the driver can inform the system of his destination. Then, the RA suggests a new route towards another spot or the final destination in real time, based on the system's configuration. This process, which is repeated for the whole journey for all the vehicles in the city, achieves an intelligent traffic distribution so as to minimize travel times, emissions, and fuel consumption.

In Figure 2 we present one example of rerouting a vehicle by using Red Swarm. When a vehicle is approaching spot RS1 via the input street ($S_{1.1}$) and connects with the WiFi spot, it could be sent to RS2 via $S_{2.1}$, to RS3 via $S_{3.1}$, or to RS4 via $S_{4.1}$ depending on the probabilities stored in the configuration. This process is repeated for each spot until the vehicle arrives at its final destination.

2.1 Case Studies

There were some initial steps taken in reducing travel times [13] and CO emissions [14] which have led us to our proposal in which we address the optimization of four affluent cities of Europe with the objective of not only reducing travel times but also greenhouse gas emissions.

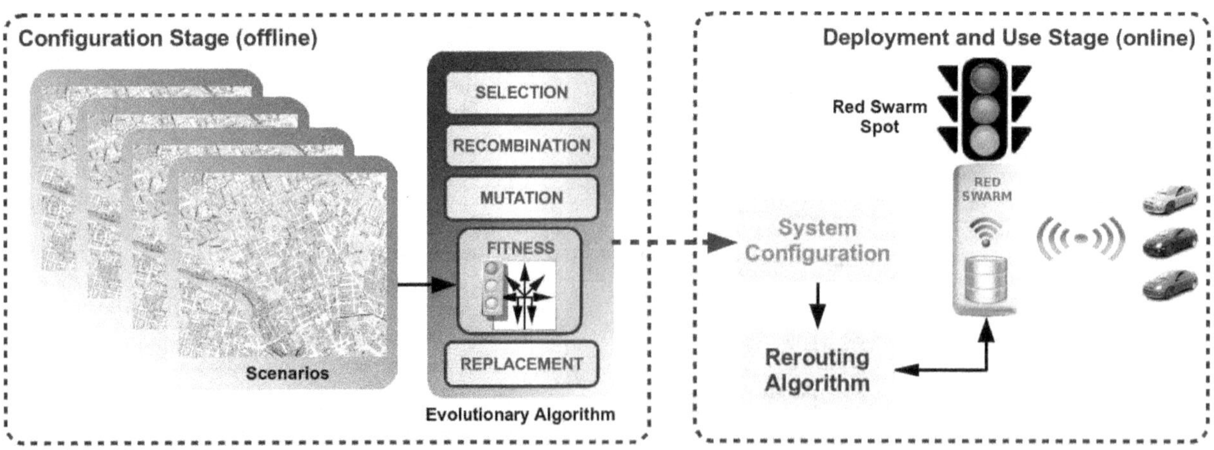

Figure 1: Red Swarm Architecture. First, it defines city scenarios and analyzes them with the EA. Second, the configuration previously calculated is applied to the spots in order to suggest alternative routes to vehicles.

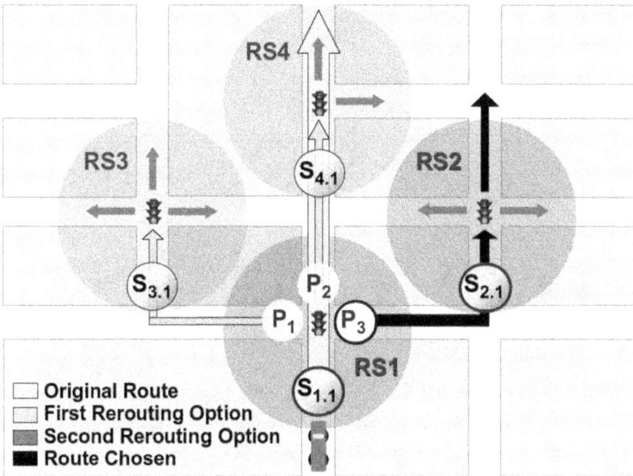

Figure 2: Rerouting of a vehicle by Red Swarm.

To build each case study we first selected four geographical areas of Malaga, Stockholm, Berlin, and Paris from OpenStreetMap. Second, we used the Java OpenStreetMap (JOSM) utility to remove extra objects such as buildings, POIs, car parks, etc., which were not useful for our experiments and may be misinterpreted by SUMO. Finally, we imported the map into SUMO by using the NETCONVERT utility and generated the vehicles' flows between each source street (the streets that let vehicles enter the zone being analyzed) and the available destinations (in this paper, we have selected as destinations only those streets by which vehicles can leave the zone being analyzed).

Each flow consists of several routes between the same origin and the different destinations (including the different routes between them), so that we avoid all vehicles driving along the same streets, which would be much too easy to optimize (just suggesting a pair of alternative routes).

These flows, generated by the DUAROUTER utility, are called the experts' solution from SUMO in this article. We have used different cost functions such as travel time but also different gas emissions, fuel consumption and noise emission in order to obtain several routes even between the same origin and destination points. In Figure 3 the process of building the scenarios is depicted.

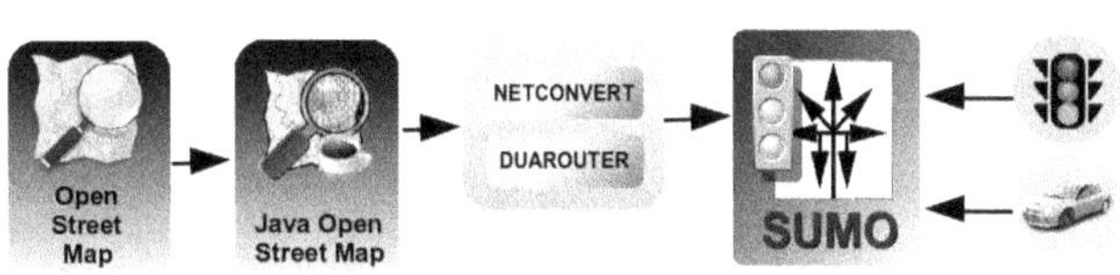

Figure 3: Real maps are obtained from OpenStreetMap, processed by using JOSM, and imported into SUMO by using NETCONVERT. Additionally, traffic flows are added by using DUAROUTER.

In order to create a more realistic approach, we have defined four different types of vehicles. Their characteristics, which are common to the four case studies, are shown in Table 1. The differences between them are the arrival probability which defines the distribution of vehicles in each scenario, the maximum speed of vehicles which is also limited by the streets' speed limit, the acceleration and deceleration rates, the vehicles' length, and the emission class from HBEFA database [7].

Table 1: Type and characteristics of vehicles.

Type	Arrival prob.	MaxSpd. (Km/h)	Accel. (m/s^2)	Decel. (m/s^2)	Length (m)	Emission class
transport	0.10	40	0.6	3.5	4.5	HDV_3_3
wagon	0.15	50	0.7	4.0	4.3	P_14_12
van	0.25	100	0.8	4.5	4.2	P_14_8
sedan	0.50	160	0.9	5.0	3.8	P_7_7

Furthermore, the scenarios of each case study are defined by the vehicle arrival probability, the driver's skill, and the flow and route chosen which defines the different traffic distributions, and in turn each scenario. We built four scenarios for the initial optimization (learning scenarios) in order to achieve a more generic solution. Then we tested the best solutions achieved in 50 different scenarios from each case study (200 scenarios tested), in order to validate them in different traffic conditions.

Table 2 shows the characteristics of each case study. In each of them, the number of vehicles is high enough to study a real city. The analysis time is the maximum time taken by vehicles to leave the area analyzed in the 50 scenarios, plus a small time margin to consider drivers' indecision. Additionally, the input streets are those where vehicles arrive at a junction controlled by a Red Swarm spot, the number of source streets and destinations are the origin and destination of the routes which are available for be assigning to vehicles when they enter the area analyzed being analyzed.

Table 2: Characteristics of the four case studies.

Case study	*Malaga*	*Stockholm*	*Berlin*	*Paris*
Analysis time (s)	2200	4000	3400	3400
# Vehicles	1200	1400	1300	1200
# Traffic lights	262	498	770	575
# Red swarm spots	10	12	10	10
# Input Streets	27	41	40	42
# Vehicle types	4	4	4	4
# Source streets	9	14	13	12
# Destinations	4	4	4	4
# Vehicle routes	169	131	122	125

In Figure 4, the four case studies analyzed are depicted including the snapshots from OpenStreetMap as well as the map imported into SUMO. The geographical characteristics of the various case studies are given below.

2.1.1 Malaga

The geographical area selected from the city of Malaga is delimited to the north by *Carretería* Street, to the south by the Mediterranean Sea, to the east by *Gutemberg* Street, and to the west by the *Guadalmedina* River, which encompasses an area of about $2.5Km^2$. We defined 169 different routes which are available to be assigned to 1200 vehicles as they enter the analyzed area depending on their source street and final destination.

2.1.2 Stockholm

For our *Stockholm* case study we defined 131 different routes to analyze the behavior of 1400 vehicles in a geo-

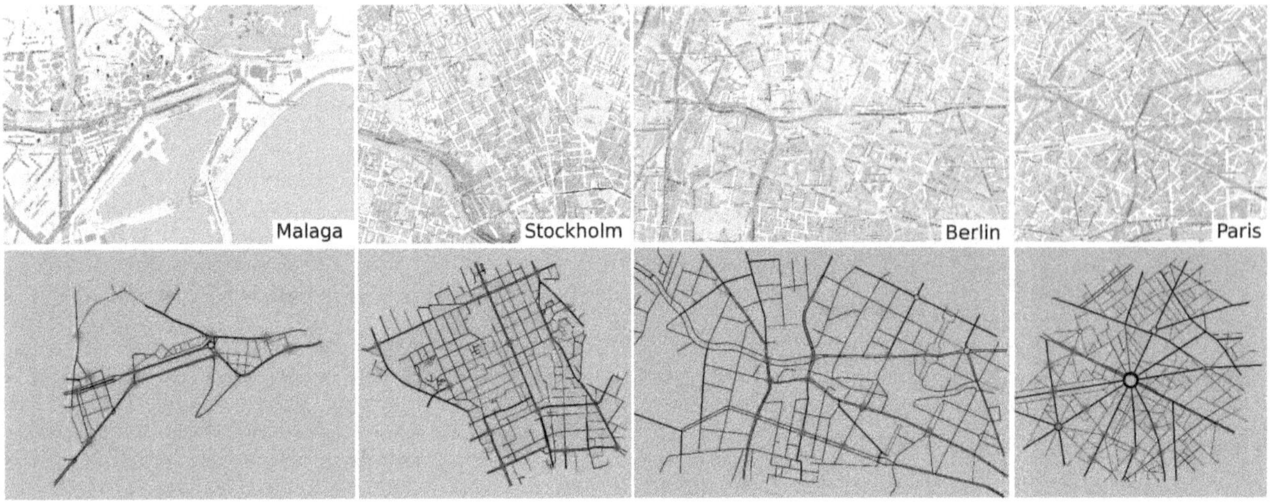

Figure 4: Case studies: *Malaga*, *Stockholm*, *Berlin*, and *Paris*, imported from OpenStreetMap (upper row) into SUMO (lower row). Note that the junctions with a Red Swarm spot are marked with a red dot.

graphical area delimited to the north by *Odengatan*, to the south by *Riddarfjärden*, to the east by *Birger Jarlsgatan*, and to the west by *Klarastrandsleden*. The total area included from Stockholm is about $2.9Km^2$.

2.1.3 Berlin

Berlin is built in the area delimited to the north by *Oranienstraße*, to the south by *Columbiadamm*, to the east by *Kottbusser Damm*, and to the west by *Potsdamer Straße*, which encompasses an area of about $7Km^2$ There are 122 different routes defined in our *Berlin* case study as well as 1300 vehicles.

2.1.4 Paris

The area chosen from the city of Paris is delimited to the north by *Avenue Villiers*, to the south by *Cours Albert 1er*, to the east by *Avenue Franklin Delano Roosevelt*, and to the west by *Boulevard Pershing* and *Boulevard Lannes*. In this case study we defined 125 different routes and we experimented with 1200 vehicles. The total area analyzed in Paris is about $5.6Km^2$.

2.2 Evolutionary Algorithm (EA)

We have designed a (10+2)-EA in order to obtain the configuration of the system which is represented by the status vector of probabilities.

2.2.1 Status Vector

The status vector, which is read by the RA to decide on the new route to suggest to vehicles, is presented in Figure 5. As we have said, it consists of the probability values which decide the next Red Swarm spot to be visited by a vehicle depending on its final destination.

Note that the probability values are arranged in chunks corresponding to the M different destinations which are part of the configuration of the N streets which are inputs to a junction controlled by a Red Swarm spot. In our experiments the destinations of vehicles are the exiting streets of each geographical area analyzed, so M and N depend directly on the case study.

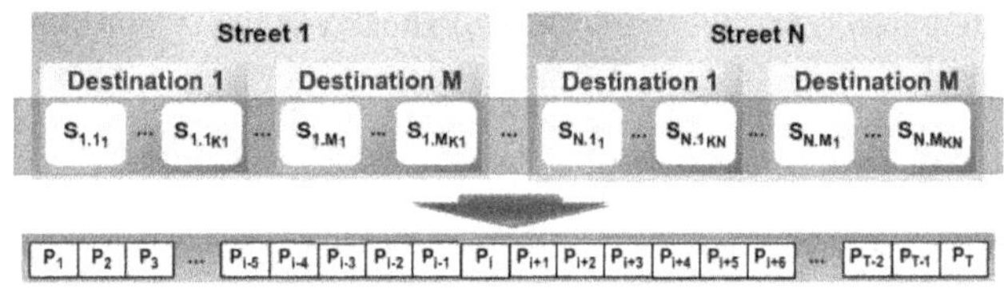

Figure 5: Solution Representation.

All in all, the status vector for the case study *Malaga* consists of 1107 real values, 2592 for *Stockholm*, 1680 for *Berlin*, and 1940 real values for *Paris*.

2.2.2 Evaluation Function

In order to minimize the average value of emissions from vehicles as well as the fuel consumption, we propose the evaluation function presented in Equation 1 which is used to calculate the fitness of each individual.

There, Θ is the total number of vehicles which enter the city, n is the number of vehicles which leave the city during the analyzed period of time, CO_i, $CO2_i$, HC_i, PM_i, and NO_i are, respectively, the emissions of Carbon Monoxide, Carbon Dioxide, Hydrocarbons, Particle Matter, and Nitrogen Oxides of vehicle i. Finally, $Fuel_i$ is the amount of fuel consumed by vehicle i during its journey. In spite of the existing correlation between these metrics we wanted to include all of them in our optimization process due to the existence of different emission classes.

$$\begin{aligned} F &= \alpha_1(\Theta - n) + \\ &+ \alpha_2\frac{1}{n}\sum_{i=1}^{n} CO_i + \alpha_3\frac{1}{n}\sum_{i=1}^{n} CO2_i + \alpha_4\frac{1}{n}\sum_{i=1}^{n} HC_i + \\ &+ \alpha_5\frac{1}{n}\sum_{i=1}^{n} PM_i + \alpha_6\frac{1}{n}\sum_{i=1}^{n} NO_i + \alpha_7\frac{1}{n}\sum_{i=1}^{n} Fuel_i \quad (1) \end{aligned}$$

Moreover, $\alpha_i, i \in [1..7]$ are the weights of each term that normalize each variable in the fitness value calculated by the function. Note that the first term of the function penalizes individuals which represent poor configurations of the Red Swarm, i.e. when there are still vehicles in the city at the end of the analysis period. Only when all vehicles end their journeys can we include the metrics from all of them in the fitness function computation and the penalization term is not present ($\Theta = n$). As we are minimizing these variables of the problem, the lower the fitness value, the better.

In our research, we have evaluated four scenarios from each case study and averaged their fitness values in order to achieve a more robust configuration as the result of the EA during the Configuration Stage.

2.2.3 Operators

The selection operator choses two individuals by using Binary Tournament to build the offspring of each generation.

For the recombination operator we have used a standard Two Point Crossover, the cross points of which are blocks of street configurations [13] (e.g. *Street 1* in Figure 5) in order to assure the summation of probabilities of each block still being equal to 1.0 after crossing.

For the mutation operator we have combined the ADOS operator (All Destinations - One Street) [13], and the ODOS operator (One Destination - One Street) [13], so that we can switch from ADOS (exploration) to ODOS (exploitation) when the minimum fitness value in the population (we are minimizing) is under a predefined threshold value (τ).

The resulting operator mutates the offspring with a probability π_1 at the beginning of the optimization process and then it changes to π_2 when the fitness of the best individual is under the threshold τ.

Finally, we have used Elitist Replacement as we are dealing with a small population ($\mu = 10$) and because we cannot afford to lose good solutions in such a complex problem. Note that by using Elitism we also ensure that the switching between ADOS and ODOS happens just once in each execution of the EA.

2.3 Rerouting Algorithm (RA)

The RA runs in each Red Swarm spot to suggest new routes to every single vehicle approaching it. In Algorithm 1 the pseudocode of the RA is presented.

First, the current street and the final destination are obtained from the data sent by the vehicle. Second, the final destination is checked to avoid rerouting a vehicle already on the last street of its itinerary, thus avoiding meaningless reroutings. If the vehicle has not yet reached its destination, all the routes from the current street to the vehicle's destination are obtained from the system's configuration.

If the final destination is not directly reachable from the current street, the algorithm obtains the next input street (belonging to another spot) which is directly reachable from the vehicle's current street so that it is sent to another Red Swarm spot. This input street is selected based on the probabilities stored in the configuration of the system.

Finally, the route from the current to the next input street is obtained and it is assigned to the vehicle in the last step of the RA. In the case that several routes are available, in this last step one of them is randomly selected.

Algorithm 1 Rerouting Algorithm

```
procedure REROUTING(vehicle)
    cur_street ← getStreet(vehicle)
    dest ← getDestination(vehicle)
    if cur_street = dest then
        route ← getCurrentRoute(vehicle)
    else
        route ← getRouteToDest(cur_street, dest)
        if route = ∅ then
            nextInStr ← getStrByProb(cur_street, dest)
            route ← getRouteToInStreet(nextInStr)
        end if
    end if
    setNewRoute(route, vehicle)
end procedure
```

3. EXPERIMENTAL SETTINGS

We again used the parameter values which achieved successful results in our previous approach [13] such as crossover probability ($P_C = 1.0$), probability of mutating an individual ($P_M = 0.75$), and probabilities of mutating a destination chunk ($\pi_1 = 0.33$, and $\pi_2 = 0.11$). Taking these values into account, we can calculate the actual mutation probabilities ($P_{M\pi_k}$) depending on the number of input streets (IS) to the spots in each case study as $P_{M\pi_k} = P_M \pi_k \frac{1}{IS}, k \in \{1, 2\}$.

Nevertheless, we adapted the rest of the parameters to each case study taking into account the values obtained from the experts' solution (Table 3).

Table 3: Experts' solution values for the four learning scenarios in each case study including the average value of travel time and emissions, fitness value, and when the last vehicle arrives at destination.

	Malaga	*Stockholm*	*Berlin*	*Paris*
Fitness	625.4	977.3	1072.9	865.0
Last arrival (s)	1997.0	3707.0	3176.0	3103.0
Travel Time (s)	537.7	1009.2	968.1	810.6
CO (mg)	7007.7	12475.8	12370.9	10478.5
CO_2 (mg)	686715.7	980807.2	1141406.6	913482.3
HC (mg)	1047.8	1802.7	1858.2	1512.2
PM (mg)	104.2	162.9	178.7	144.1
NO (mg)	4330.5	6079.8	7252.3	5681.1
Fuel (l)	272.8	388.5	453.0	362.4

We assigned to α_1 the fitness value of the experts' solution and to τ twice this value. Moreover, the values for α_2 to α_7 were calculated by normalizing the fitness function according to the values of the respective metrics from the experts' solution. Additionally, the maximum number of generations was set to 5000 and the stopping criterion used was to reach either this maximum number of generations or a number of generations (500) without any changes in the best fitness value. In Table 4 we present the complete parameterization of the EA.

Table 4: Parameters of the EA.

	Malaga	*Stockholm*	*Berlin*	*Paris*
(μ, λ)	(10, 2)			
(P_C, P_M)	(1.0, 0.75)			
(π_1, π_2)	(0.33, 0.11)			
$P_{M\pi_1}$	0.009	0.006	0.006	0.006
$P_{M\pi_2}$	0.003	0.002	0.002	0.002
τ	1300	2000	2100	1700

The experiments were conducted in 16 nodes (64 cores) equipped with an Intel Core2 Quad CPU (Q9400) @ 2.66 GHz and 4 GB of RAM which are part of the cluster of the NEO (Networking and Emerging Optimization) group.

We carried out 120 independent runs of the EA for the optimization of our case studies (four scenarios) spending a total time of about 8 days. Then, the best solution for each case study was tested against 50 different scenarios in order to analyze how our results generalize in unseen scenarios with respect to the experts' solutions.

4. EXPERIMENTS AND RESULTS

Table 5 lists the results of the optimization process performed in the four case studies in 30 independent runs, on the four different learning scenarios. There, the average value, standard deviation and maximum number of iterations, as well as the average value, standard deviation and minimum value of fitness from the 120 runs (30 per case study), are presented.

As we can see, in *Paris* the EA has converged earlier (2065.4 iterations on average) than in the rest of case studies (3008.8, 4172.7, and 3645.2 iterations on average); while the results of *Stockholm* present the largest standard deviation for the fitness value (42.5%) which denotes a lower robustness of the EA in this particular case study in comparison with the others (14.5%, 2.3%, and 2.7%).

Table 5: Number of iterations to reach the optimum and best fitness values for the four cities studied.

Case Study	# iterations			Fitness		
	Avg.	StdDev	Max.	Avg.	StdDev	Min.
Malaga	3008.8	38.3%	6034	639.0	14.5%	587.0
Stockholm	4172.7	31.3%	6418	1032.6	42.5%	864.5
Berlin	3645.2	27.4%	6162	1047.6	2.3%	1008.1
Paris	2065.4	34.4%	3985	872.3	2.7%	831.0

As we have said, we took the best solution (minimum fitness) for each city and tested it on 50 different scenarios of each case study, i.e. the best solution from the optimization of *Malaga* was tested in 50 scenarios of this case study, and the same for the rest of cities.

Table 6 presents the improvement achieved on average, over the 50 generalization scenarios, the improvements in the best of them, and the percentage of scenarios where our proposal has outperformed the experts' solution.

There, we can see an average improvement of: 7.4% (16.1% max.) in CO emissions, 0.9% (7.1% max.) in CO_2 emissions, 6.1% (16.1% max.) in HC emissions, 4.1% (16.7% max.) in PM emissions, and 0.7% (10.2% max.) in NO emissions. Furthermore, we have reduced the fuel consumption by 0.8% on average (6.8% max.) and travel times by 8.9% (17.5% max.) in all the cities analyzed.

Finally, we have reduced CO emissions in 90.5% of the 200 scenarios (50 per case study) tested, with respect to the experts' solution, CO_2 in 64.5%, HC in 89%, PM in 80%, and NO emissions in 58.5% of the scenarios tested. Additionally, we have also reduced travel times in 96% of the scenarios and the fuel consumption in 62% of them.

Looking at these results, we can see that the routes are always longer when we reroute vehicles by using Red Swarm. It is an expected characteristic of this system due to the fact that we are rerouting vehicles by alternative streets which are not part of the shortest path. It is not a negative aspect of Red Swarm, as we achieved shorter travel times, lower fuel consumption and greenhouse gas emissions because of the distributed smart rerouting decisions that emerge as a globally better swarm movement throughout the city. This yields a positive final balance both for drivers and the city.

In Figure 6 we present the box plots corresponding to the results of the 50 testing scenarios of each city. The distribution of the values confirms the improvement achieved in each metric included in the optimization process (CO, CO_2, HC, PM, NO, and $Fuel$) as well as a reduction in travel times.

Table 6: Improvement achieved on the average vehicles' travel times, gas emissions, and fuel consumption in the four case studies. Fitness values and distance traveled are also reported. Note that the best improvements of the emission-related metrics of each case study are in bold.

	Case Study	*Fitness*	*T.Time*	*CO*	CO_2	*HC*	*PM*	*NO*	*Fuel*	*Distance*
Average 50 scenarios	Malaga	0.6%	5.5%	**4.1%**	-1.5%	3.0%	0.9%	-1.8%	-1.6%	-7.9%
	Stockholm	6.9%	14.2%	**12.6%**	3.2%	11.0%	8.5%	3.0%	3.0%	-10.6%
	Berlin	4.8%	11.7%	**10.6%**	1.7%	8.7%	6.0%	1.5%	1.6%	-148.4%
	Paris	0.9%	4.1%	**2.2%**	0.2%	1.8%	1.1%	-0.1%	0.2%	-75.2%
	Average	3.3%	8.9%	7.4%	0.9%	6.1%	4.1%	0.7%	0.8%	-60.5%
Best scenario	Malaga	7.6%	12.2%	**11.3%**	4.1%	10.2%	9.9%	5.7%	4.0%	-6.0%
	Stockholm	12.2%	17.5%	16.1%	7.1%	16.1%	**16.7%**	10.2%	6.8%	-9.2%
	Berlin	9.6%	13.9%	13.2%	4.8%	13.3%	**14.5%**	7.9%	4.6%	-146.8%
	Paris	6.6%	8.9%	**11.6%**	3.8%	10.4%	5.1%	3.9%	3.8%	-72.6%
	Average	9.0%	13.1%	13.0%	5.0%	12.5%	11.5%	6.9%	4.8%	-58.7%
Scenarios Improved	Malaga	58.0%	90.0%	88.0%	24.0%	82.0%	58.0%	36.0%	22.0%	0.0%
	Stockholm	100.0%	100.0%	**100.0%**	92.0%	**100.0%**	98.0%	78.0%	92.0%	0.0%
	Berlin	100.0%	100.0%	**100.0%**	90.0%	**100.0%**	98.0%	74.0%	84.0%	0.0%
	Paris	64.0%	94.0%	74.0%	52.0%	74.0%	66.0%	46.0%	50.0%	0.0%
	Average	80.5%	96.0%	90.5%	64.5%	89.0%	80.0%	58.5%	62.0%	0.0%

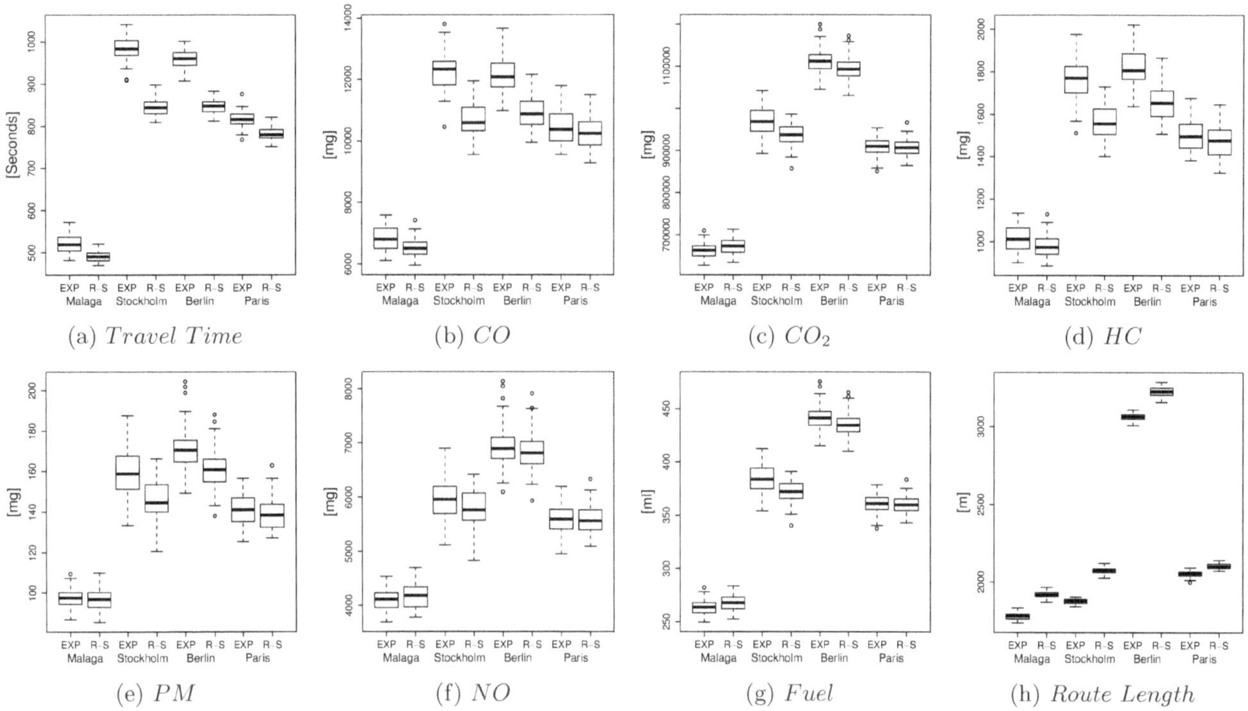

(a) *Travel Time* (b) *CO* (c) CO_2 (d) *HC* (e) *PM* (f) *NO* (g) *Fuel* (h) *Route Length*

Figure 6: Figures showing the distribution of the results in the 50 scenarios from the case studies analyzed.

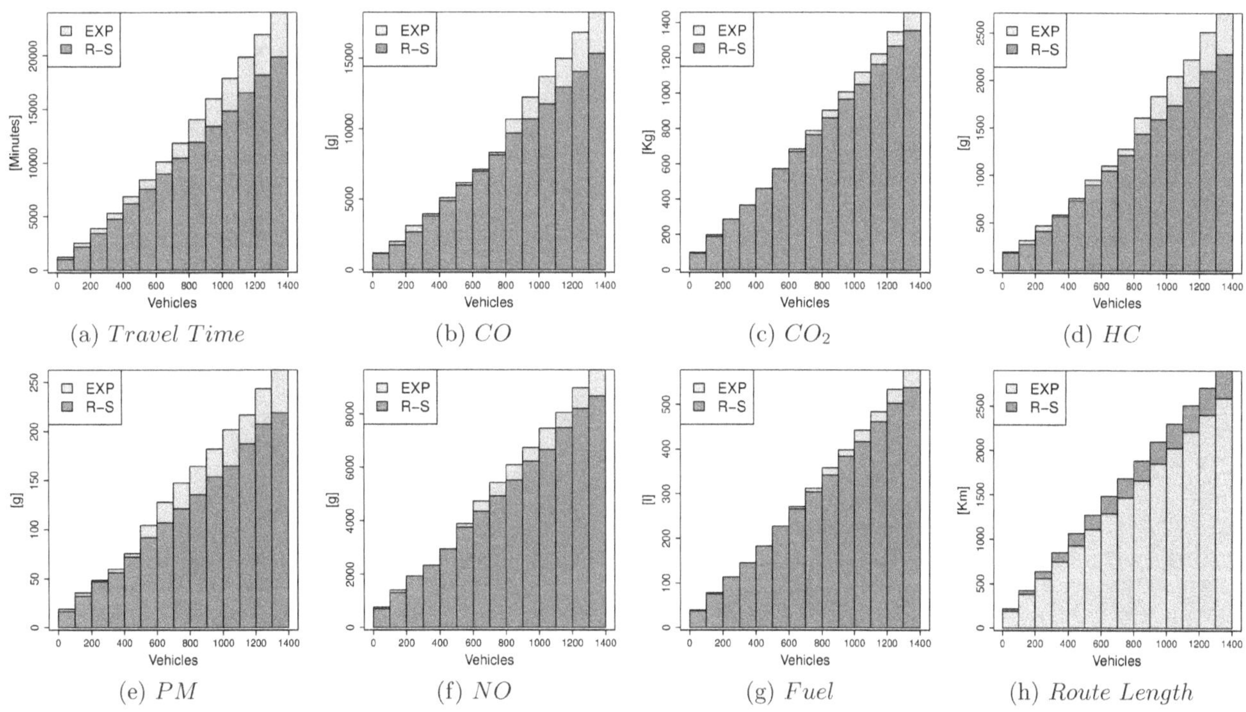

(a) *Travel Time* (b) *CO* (c) CO_2 (d) *HC* (e) *PM* (f) *NO* (g) *Fuel* (h) *Route Length*

Figure 7: Accumulated values of travel time, emissions and consumption in the best scenario of *Stockholm*.

Moreover, we can observe, the greatest improvements were achieved in CO, HC, PM, and travel times, while CO_2, NO, and $Fuel$ consumption were harder to reduce.

As we have studied the emissions from vehicles in detail, we can confirm an existing correlation (coefficients above 0.92) between PM, NO, $Fuel$, and CO_2. Additionally, our observations show that CO and HC are also correlated (0.936), as are Travel Times and Route Lengths (0.627). Contrary to common sense, where you would expect an all-to-all correlation, we have discovered just three types of correlation. We think they are somewhat connected to the four types of vehicles we are using in our studies.

Finally, Figure 7 plots the accumulated values of the different metrics from the case study *Stockholm*. We show the differences between the emissions, travel times, fuel consumption, and route lengths for the 1400 vehicles in the best scenario of that case study. We observe how Red Swarm enable vehicles to be more eco-friendly than the experts' solution in spite of the longer distances involved.

5. CONCLUSIONS

In this article we have addressed the reduction of greenhouse gas emissions, travel times and fuel consumption of road traffic in four cities of Europe: Malaga, Stockholm, Berlin, and Paris.

We have designed an effective evolutionary algorithm to optimize the scenarios which has found solutions that make all vehicles end their itineraries in the analyzed time for the 120 runs performed during the optimization process.

Our proposal has achieved average reductions of 7.4% in CO, 6.1% in HC, 4.1% in PM, and under 1% in the rest of emissions and fuel consumption. Additionally, we have shortened travel times by 8.9% on average, with an increment of route lengths (60.5%) which is a consequence of rerouting vehicles via alternative streets which are not included in the shortest path.

The results achieved, after generalizing our solution to 200 different scenarios, show that Red Swarm has worked in all of them and reduced the emissions analyzed in most of them, while travel times were shorter in 96% of these scenarios.

We noticed that the results were influenced by the different characteristics of vehicles, especially the emission class, as well as the city layout which has been favorable to Red Swarm in *Stockholm* and rather hard on *Malaga* due to the smaller geographic area analyzed in the latter.

As a matter for future work, we are testing different strategies to further improve upon our results, especially in the harder scenarios as well as implementing the rerouting by city districts so as to be able to install Red Swarm throughout the entire city. Moreover, we want to optimize different scenarios with actual traffic distributions at different times obtained from data published by the city council in order to adapt our system to the many variations

6. ACKNOWLEDGMENTS

This research is partially funded by the Ministry of Economy and Competitiveness and FEDER under contract TIN-2011-28194 (roadME `http://roadme.lcc.uma.es`). It is also partially funded by project number 8.06/5.47.4142 in collaboration with the VSB-Technical University of Ostrava.

7. REFERENCES

[1] M. Alsabaan, K. Naik, T. Abdelkader, T. Khalifa, and A. Nayak. Geocast Routing in Vehicular Networks for Reduction of CO2 Emissions. In *Information and Communication on Technology for the Fight against Global Warming*, volume 6868 of *Lecture Notes in Computer Science*, pages 26–40. Springer Berlin Heidelberg, 2011.

[2] M. Behrisch, L. Bieker, J. Erdmann, and D. Krajzewicz. SUMO - Simulation of Urban MObility: An Overview. In *SIMUL 2011: The Third International Conference on Advances in System Simulation*, pages 63–68, Barcelona, Spain, 2011.

[3] H. Chourabi, T. Nam, S. Walker, J. R. Gil-Garcia, S. Mellouli, K. Nahon, T. A. Pardo, and H. J. Scholl. Understanding Smart Cities: An Integrative Framework. *45th Hawaii International Conference on System Sciences*, pages 2289–2297, 2012.

[4] C. Gawron. *Simulation-based traffic assignment*. PhD Thesis, 1998.

[5] R. Giffinger and N. Pichler-Milanović. *Smart cities: Ranking of European Medium-sized Cities*. Number October. Centre of Regional Science, Vienna University of Technology, 2007.

[6] C. Guerreiro, F. de Leeuw, and V. Foltescu. Air quality in Europe - 2013 report. Technical report, European Environment Agency, 2013.

[7] S. Hausberger, M. Rexeis, M. Zallinger, and R. Luz. Emission Factors from the Model PHEM for the HBEFA Version 3. Technical Report I, 2009.

[8] O. Hertel, S. Jensen, M. Hvidberg, M. Ketzel, R. Berkowicz, F. Palmgren, P. Wåhlin, M. Glasius, S. Loft, P. Vinzents, O. Raaschou-Nielsen, M. Sørensen, and H. Bak. Assessing the Impacts of Traffic Air Pollution on Human Exposure and Health. In *Road Pricing, the Economy and the Environment*, Advances in Spatial Science, pages 277–299. Springer Berlin Heidelberg, 2008.

[9] R. G. Hollands. Will the real smart city please stand up? *City*, 12(3):303–320, Dec. 2008.

[10] D. Krajzewicz and P. Wagner. Large-Scale Vehicle Routing Scenarios Based on Pollulant Emissions. In *Advanced Microsystems for Automotive Applications*, pages 237–246. Springer Berlin Heidelberg, Berlin, Heidelberg, 2011.

[11] C. Li and S. Shimamoto. A real time traffic light control scheme for reducing vehicles CO2 emissions. In *Consumer Communications and Networking Conference (CCNC), 2011 IEEE*, pages 855–859, 2011.

[12] H. Mizuta, Y. Yamagata, and H. Seya. Large-scale Traffic Simulation for Low-carbon City. In *Proceedings of the Winter Simulation Conference*, WSC '12, pages 162:1–162:12. Winter Simulation Conference, 2012.

[13] D. H. Stolfi and E. Alba. Red Swarm: Smart Mobility in Cities With EAs. In *Proceeding of the Fifteenth Annual Conference on Genetic and Evolutionary Computation Conference*, GECCO '13, pages 1373–1380, New York, NY, USA, 2013. ACM.

[14] D. H. Stolfi and E. Alba. Reducing Gas Emissions in Smart Cities by Using the Red Swarm Architecture. In *Advances in Artificial Intelligence*, volume 8109 of *Lecture Notes in Computer Science*, pages 289–299. Springer Berlin Heidelberg, 2013.

[15] A. Wegener and M. Piórkowski. TraCI: An Interface for Coupling Road Traffic and Network Simulators. In *Proceedings of the 11th Communications and Networking Simulation Symposium*, CNS '08, pages 155–163, New York, NY, USA, 2008. ACM.

[16] S. K. Zegeye, B. De Schutter, H. Hellendoorn, and E. Breunesse. Reduction of Travel Times and Traffic Emissions Using Model Predictive Control. *2009 American Control Conference*, pages 5392–5397, 2009.

Evolutionary Agent-Based Simulation of the Introduction of New Technologies in Air Traffic Management

Logan Yliniemi
Oregon State University
Corvallis, OR, USA
logan.yliniemi@engr.orst.edu

Adrian Agogino
UCSC at NASA Ames
Moffett Field, CA, USA
adrian.k.agogino@nasa.gov

Kagan Tumer
Oregon State University
Corvallis, OR, USA
kagan.tumer@oregonstate.edu

ABSTRACT

Accurate simulation of the effects of integrating new technologies into a complex system is critical to the modernization of our antiquated air traffic system, where there exist many layers of interacting procedures, controls, and automation all designed to cooperate with human operators. Additions of even simple new technologies may result in unexpected emergent behavior due to complex human/machine interactions. One approach is to create high-fidelity human models coming from the field of human factors that can simulate a rich set of behaviors. However, such models are difficult to produce, especially to show unexpected emergent behavior coming from many human operators interacting simultaneously within a complex system. Instead of engineering complex human models, we directly model the emergent behavior by evolving goal directed agents, representing human users. Using evolution we can predict how the agent representing the human user reacts given his/her goals. In this paradigm, each autonomous agent in a system pursues individual goals, and the behavior of the system emerges from the interactions, foreseen or unforeseen, between the agents/actors. We show that this method reflects the integration of new technologies in a historical case, and apply the same methodology for a possible future technology.

Categories and Subject Descriptors

I.2.11 [**Distributed Artificial Intelligence**]: Multiagent Systems

General Terms

Performance, Experimentation

Keywords

Emergent Behavior; Multiagent Learning

1. INTRODUCTION

Air traffic management is an incredibly complex problem, with many layers of interacting procedures, controls, and automations, all interacting in real-time with human operators. Developing a new piece of technology to fit into this framework is a challenging process in which many unforeseen consequences. Thus, the ability to simulate new technologies within an air traffic management framework is of the utmost importance.

One approach is to create a highly realistic simulation for the entire system [13, 14], but in these cases, every technology in the system must be modeled, and their interactions must be understood beforehand. If this understanding is lacking, it may be difficult to integrate them into such a framework [16]. With a sufficiently complex system, missed interactions become a near-certainty.

Another approach is to use an evolutionary approach in which a series of simple agents evolves a model the complex behavior of the system through their interactions. Such agents have been used to gain insight into such systems as macroeconomics [3, 4, 8] and supply chain management [2]. However, the problem of defining the policies that the agents should follow is non-trivial, especially in the case where the agents may act in a heterogeneous manner: development of such agents can quickly become cyclical, with changes to one agent necessitating changes to others. These approaches are also prone to over-engineering and can quickly become too tailored to the specific problem to offer any generality or reusability.

Instead, in this work we use an evolutionary algorithm on agent policies to allow the agents to discover policies that meet certain designer-specified goals. This then trades off designer workload and required expertise for computing time. Such agents can develop both simple policies that directly meet system goals as well as more complex, emergent behaviors. We demonstrate this as a lens for examining new potential technologies by examining the historical case of the Norden Bombsight, and another situation which represents a possible future technology.

The major contributions of this work are to:

- Show that even simple behavioral models can be evolved that have predictive value in assessing technology introduction by exploring predicted outcomes of technology infusion
- Show that even with such simple evolved behavioral models, complex "emergent" behavior (not predicted or expected) may arise

The remainder of this work is organized as follows: In Section 2 we present background on evolutionary policy search and goal-based agents, as well as introducing the historical case that we use as a framework for our simulations. In Section 3 we present the domains used in this paper. In Section 4 we describe the algorithms used. In Section 5 we include the experimental parameters used for our experiments. In Section 6 we include our experimental results and Finally, in Section 7, we draw the conclusion of this work.

GECCO'14, July 12–16, 2014, Vancouver, BC, Canada.
Copyright 2014 ACM 978-1-4503-2662-9/14/07 ...$15.00.
http://dx.doi.org/10.1145/2576768.2598388.

2. BACKGROUND

This work employs an evolutionary algorithm to search for agent policies. In this section we describe these concepts and introduce the historical case of the Norden Bombsight.

2.1 Learning Agents / Multiagent System

Learning agents are autonomous actors in a system which make observations about their environment, reason based on these observations, perform actions that affect their environment, and use feedback from the environment to update their policies [15]. In a learning multiagent system, multiple agents are simultaneously performing this process. These agents exist in other agents' observations, and all actions taken affect the common environment [17].

2.2 Evolutionary Algorithms

We use an evolutionary algorithm in this work, in which agent policies are represented by neural networks. We evaluate their fitness with a calculation specific to each case that we present (Section 4). Once completed, the policies with the lowest fitness are removed from the system and replaced with slightly-modified versions of more successful policies. Over time, the population tends toward more desirable policies [1].

2.3 Agent Simulation / Goal-Based Evaluation

Romano et al. state that "Intelligent agents can act as basic building blocks of an artificial society and be used to study the emergency of the social behaviour. Agents can be autonomous, flexible, adaptable and goal-directed" [12]. This lets "Behaviours 'emerge' from the actions of these diverse units in constant motion" [12].

We take a similar approach in this work, where we merely set forth goals for the agents to achieve, and allow their collective search for good policies to lead to behaviors that emerge. In many cases these behaviors align with designer predictions, but unexpected behaviors can also emerge. In this way, the system designer need only describe the desired outcome of the system behavior, and not how the agents should go about reaching those goals.

Agent simulation has been used for modeling complex systems like macro-economics [3, 4, 8]. In these situations, simple agents interacting with the market mirror real-life observed phenomena, like the creation of "bubbles" in the market [8]. Other agent-based simulations have been used to investigate such systems as supply chains [2], network security [9], maritime piracy [7], and evacuation of dangerous environments [5, 11].

Authors investigating systems with agent-based simulation have argued for the need of simplicity in the agent representation as well [8, 9]. As LeBaron states, learning agents are put to use "that are simple enough for easier analysis and interpretation, yet rich enough to pursue many of the experiments in evolution and heterogeneity present in older, more complex frameworks" [8]. It is not the complexity of an individual agent, but rather the interaction between these agents in their shared environment, that creates the complex emergent behaviors that can be observed.

2.4 The Norden Bombsight

To assist in examining the potential effects of a new technology on a modern complex system, it is useful to consider the effects that new technologies have had on complex systems in the past. In this work we consider the well-documented historical case of the Norden Bombsight.

In World War II, the Norden Bombsight was used by the United States Army Air Force (USAAF) for their precision daylight raids over Europe. While it had a number of drawbacks (such as requiring visual contact with the desired target), it was widely adopted and used in the European theatre, with the USAAF ordering 90,000 units, and training 50,000 bombardiers to use them at a development cost of 1.5 billion USD [6].

The basic functionality of the Norden Bombsight was an analog computer that was capable of calculating the location which a bomb should be dropped to land on the sighted target, given inputs of airspeed, altitude, and crosswind velocity [6]. This bombsight offered an advantage over earlier tactics, which consisted of a visual release method without the benefit of the analytical power of the Norden. Even so, a potential problem arises: If a group of bombers in formation are attempting to release their payloads to all contact the same area, as they approach the release point, the separation of the planes will reduce to a potentially dangerous level.

In the case of the physical world, new techniques are not adopted without fully considering potential safety risks. This, combined with the fact that the 50,000 trained bombardiers had varying skill levels at the analog programming required by the Norden, resulted in the decision by 1944 that the lead bomber should be the only one using the Norden. The other bombers merely held formation with respect to the lead, and released their payload when they saw the lead bomber do so. This reduced the accuracy of the formation as a function of the size of the formation and the ability of the pilots to hold their position with respect to the bomber ahead of them, but removed the problems of separation assurance.

Though the Norden Bombsight was not as revolutionary as it was originally touted to be, nor was its use as successful as originally hoped, it still represented a new technology in an already-existing, complex system, which changed the behaviors of the actors in the system. This is our basis for including this historical example, which forms the framework for our Norden Bombsight Domain (Section 3.1) in this work.

3. DOMAINS OF STUDY

In this work we use two domains of study to show how agents can be evolved to discover emergent behavior.. The first is the Norden Bombsight Domain (Section 3.1), which models the historical example of the Norden Bombsight described in Section 2.4. The second is the "Civilian 'Cloud' Domain", a related domain which represents a possible future case of technology integration.

3.1 Norden Bombsight Domain (NBD)

In the Norden Bombsight Domain, a series of planes must cooperatively traverse a corridor from south to north, and pass as closely as possible over a single point (target location) at the far end of the corridor. The planes all travel at a constant speed. Each plane agent senses local information using the following state variables:

1. dx: X-distance from target location
2. dy: Y-distance from target location
3. V_x: X-velocity
4. V_y: Y-velocity
5. p_x: X-distance to nearest other plane
6. p_y: Y-distance to nearest other plane
7. c_x: X-distance to centroid of k nearest cloud centers
8. c_y: Y-distance to centroid of k nearest cloud centers

and each plane agent takes action by selecting the bearing that they wish to proceed toward. In the Norden Bombsight Domain, the cloud states (7 and 8) have no bearing on the goals of the planes, but they are included in the state to keep the simulations presented in this work homogeneous.

After each agent chooses an action, system dynamics described in Section 4 are then calculated, and the plane agents move to their location for the next timestep. This process is repeated until all planes exit one of the edges of the corridor or a set number of timesteps has passed. At the end of each episode, the agents in use are scored based on their performance measured on the goals set forth for them. We use the exact same agent structure in 3 separate cases, while changing the goals slightly in each case. The cases for the Norden Bombsight Domain mirror the historical case of the Norden Bombsight.

3.1.1 Case 1: Pre-Norden Bombsight

Before the integration of the Norden Bombsight, the USAAF used pilot and bombardier visual cues to identify the target, but had no precise way of calculating the ideal launch point.

We model this by making the agents' goals to (i) pass through the north end of the corridor, with no emphasis on passing over the precise target point, and (ii) maintain separation assurance with the other aircraft in flight.

3.1.2 Case 2: Full Norden Integration

With the integration of the Norden Bombsight, the USAAF had the ability to precisely identify the target location, and the Norden Bombsight itself was used as an autopilot for the plane on the final approach, where it considered only its relative position to the precise target location when giving control commands to the bomber, without considering the other planes in the formation in any way.

We model this by making each agent's goal in this case to (i) pass over the target point as precisely as possible, while ignoring any contribution from separation assurance.

3.1.3 Case 3: Norden + Separation

The USAAF eventually settled on using the Norden Bombsight on the lead bomber in the flight (with inactive backup devices on other members of the formation), while all other bombers were to maintain formation with respect to the lead plane. This had two benefits: it reduced the system to an effectively centralized controller, and removed the separation assurance problems that would have been introduced by full integration (Case 2).

We model this as a multiagent system wherein the agents still have the ability to override the autopilot for the sake of separation assurance. The agents' goals in this case are to (i) pass over the target point as precisely as possible while (ii) maintaining separation assurance with the other aircraft in flight.

3.2 Civilian "Cloud" Domain (CCD)

While the Norden Bombsight Domain allows ready comparison to historical reality, we include a second, related domain to show the general applicability of the methods used, and to remove any possible bias due to the knowledge of historical outcomes that might be present in the Norden Bombsight Domain.

In the Civilian Cloud Domain, the setup is much the same: a set of planes must traverse a corridor from south to north using the same state information as allowed in the Norden Bombsight Domain, and would ideally like to pass over a waypoint at the end of the corridor. The complication arises by the introduction of areas of the corridor that are preferably avoided. These areas may represent turbulence, storms, other incidental planes in holding patterns, or areas of poor visibility. For the ease of the reader, we collectively term all of these areas to avoid "clouds", and represent them as a single goal in the simulation.

We present three different cases in the Civilian Cloud Domain to exhibit the types of behaviors that learning agents can develop.

3.2.1 Case 4: Explicit Cloud Avoidance, No Spacing

In this case, we model a system with each plane equipped with a cloud-avoiding autopilot as it navigates through the corridor. Similar to Case 2, we define that these autopilots do not coordinate with each other in any way.

We model this by making their goals (i) to make it through the corridor to the target point successfully, while (ii) avoiding clouds. Avoiding other aircraft is not involved in their utility function.

3.2.2 Case 5: Explicit Cloud Avoidance + Spacing

In a second iteration of the Civilian Cloud Domain, we model a system in which each plane is equipped with a cloud-avoiding autopilot which *does* have the explicit goal of avoiding separation violations with other planes.

Their goals are to (i) make it through the corridor successfully, while (ii) maintaining separation assurance from other planes, and (iii) avoiding clouds.

3.2.3 Case 6: Implicit Cloud Avoidance

In our final case of the Civilian Cloud Domain, we model a system in which the cloudy areas of the airspace are able to be sensed, but avoiding clouds is not an explicit goal of the agents. However, *in this case only*, we remove their ability to sense other planes while in cloudy regions of the airspace (within 50 units of a cloud center), creating potentially dangerous conditions that are not explicitly within the utility function of the agents.

In this case, the agents' goals are to (i) make it through the corridor successfully, while (ii) maintaining separation assurance from other planes. Though the cloudy areas of the space aren't directly within the utility function, planes within the cloudy regions may experience un-sensed separation violations that occur, making the cloudy regions potentially dangerous.

4. SIMULATION DETAILS

In both simulation domains, we use the same evolutionary algorithm to execute a simulation. Certain steps do change depending on the case. The overall simulation algorithm is presented as Algorithm 1. The calculation of the utility based on the goals of the agent for each case is shown in Algorithms 2 and 3.

4.1 Simulation Algorithms

In Algorithm 1, a population of neural networks is formed, and a subset is selected to perform the first simulation. In this simulation, at each timestep each agent senses information about its surroundings into the state vector S_a, and evaluates its neural network on the state vector $(\mathcal{NN}(S_a))$, before scaling its output to be in the range $[0{:}2\pi]$. This value represents the desired heading $\hat{\theta}_a$. The actual heading for this timestep θ_a is then calculated as a weighted average between θ_a for the previous timestep and $\hat{\theta}_a$ for the current timestep, with a weighting factor ρ. In the event that θ_a and $\hat{\theta}_a$ lie on opposite sides of the $[0{:}2\pi]$ discontinuity, the smallest angle between the two is measured and used for this calculation. The plane's x- and y-location are then updated. At this point, timestep-level utilities are calculated (per $\bigstar_1$ steps in Algorithm 2 or 3).

After the final timestep, the episode-end utilities are calculated ($\bigstar_2$), and the final utility for each agent used during that simulation is calculated ($\bigstar_3$). After all agents have been used in one of the simulations, the m lowest-performing networks are removed, and m new copies of surviving networks are produced. These new networks have their weights modified with a 20% chance per link, by adding a random number drawn from a normal distribution with zero mean and standard deviation 0.2.

This process is repeated for each generation. This process is uniform across all 6 cases presented here. The only changes to the process are the steps marked $\bigstar_{\{1,2,3\}}$ and the sensing step in Case 6, in which agents cannot detect planes when they are within 50 units of a cloud center.

4.2 Goal Evaluation

The primary difference between the cases is the goals that the agents are trying to meet, and how these affect their fitness calculation. In each case, the primary goal is to traverse the corridor from south to north. To emphasize this over all other considerations, the reward for successfully exiting the corridor to the north ($u_{success}$) is multiplied by a very large number (R), such that all solutions that successfully complete this challenge will have a higher fitness than those that do not. This is a form of lexicographic ordering [10], with completion prioritized higher than all other goals, which are weighted against each other. For ease, before applying weights to the goals, they are normalized in the range [0:1], with the maximum attainable goal taking on a value of 1.

4.2.1 *Norden Bombsight Domain Goals*

Algorithm 2 lays out the goals for the first 3 cases, which are executed in the Norden Bombsight Domain. In the first case, at each timestep the separation from the nearest plane is calculated, and the separation assurance utility u_{sep} is updated. At the end of the run, the binary success measure $u_{success}$ is calculated, which is 1 if the plane successfully passes through the north end of the corridor, and 0 if the plane either does not exit the corridor within the allotted time, or exits out of one of the other sides. Finally, these two rewards are combined to form the agent's overall utility U, which is used to determine which agents will be eliminated.

In the second case, the separation calculation is replaced by a calculation for the closest distance the agent passed over the target location, leading to u_{target}. The function $dist(target)$ returns the distance to the target, scaled between 0 and 1, with 1 being the maximum possible distance to the target. This value and $u_{success}$ are the only contributions to the overall utility U in Case 2.

In the third case, both u_{sep} and u_{target} are calculated, and they are combined in the final U calculation with weights W_{sep} and W_{target}, respectively, which allows the system designer to specify the perceived tradeoff between passing directly over the target and maintaining separation assurance throughout the flight.

Algorithm 1 Simulation Process for NBD and CCD

Initialize population of n neural networks.
for $generation = 1 \rightarrow max\_generations$ **do**
  Select P neural networks not used yet this generation
  Assign one of the P neural networks to each plane
  for $simulation = 1 \rightarrow sims\_per\_gen$ **do**
    for $timestep = 1 \rightarrow max\_timesteps$ **do**
      for $a = 1 \rightarrow P$ **do**
        Sense: $S_a \leftarrow \{d_x, d_y, V_x, V_y, p_x, p_y, c_x, c_y\}$
        Choose action: $\hat{\theta}_a \leftarrow \mathcal{NN}(S_a) \in \{0,2\pi\}$
        Adjust plane heading: $\theta_a \leftarrow \theta_a + \rho * (\theta_a - \hat{\theta}_a)$
        Update x-location: $x_a \leftarrow x_a + |V|\cos(\theta_a)$
        Update y-location: $y_a \leftarrow y_a + |V|\sin(\theta_a)$
        Calculate timestep-level goal values $\bigstar_1$
      end for
    end for
    for $a = 1 \rightarrow P$ **do**
      Calculate end-of-simulation goal values $\bigstar_2$
      Calculate agent utility U $\bigstar_3$
    end for
  end for
  Remove m neural networks with lowest utility U
  Create m neural networks, identical to surviving networks
  Mutate the newly created networks
end for

4.2.2 *Civilian Cloud Domain Goals*

Algorithm 3 lays out the goals for the final 3 cases, which are executed in the Civilian Cloud Domain.

In Case 4, the goals are to proceed through the space without coming too near the cloud regions, and pass over a target. No consideration is given to the separation between airplanes.

In Case 5, we give the agents explicit utility for staying out of the cloudy regions of the airspace, with u_{cloud}, which is again aggregated into U with weight W_{cloud}.

In Case 6, we do not explicitly give utility for avoiding cloudy regions, but the agents benefit from avoiding these regions because their sensors for the nearest plane (which does form part of the utility calculation) are only effective outside of these regions: Staying outside of cloudy regions becomes an implicitly coupled goal.

5. SIMULATION SETUP

In all experiments, we use a population of $n = 110$ agents of 8-input, 6-hidden unit, 1-output neural networks that are assigned

Algorithm 2 Goals for NBD Cases

Case 1: Pre-Norden Bombsight
$\bigstar_1$: if($|p_x, p_y| < \beta$), $u_{sep} \leftarrow u_{sep} - (|p_x, p_y| - \beta)^2$
$\bigstar_2$: if($run\_success$), $u_{success} = 1$
$\bigstar_3$: $U = u_{success} * R + u_{sep}$
Case 2: Full Adoption of Norden Bombsight
$\bigstar_1$: $u_{target} = max(u_{target}, 1 - dist(target))$
$\bigstar_2$: if($run\_success$), $u_{success} = 1$
$\bigstar_3$: $U = u_{success} * R + u_{target}$
Case 3: Norden Bombsight + Separation
$\bigstar_1$: if($|p_x, p_y| < \beta$), $u_{sep} \leftarrow u_{sep} - (|p_x, p_y| - \beta)^2$
$\bigstar_1$: $u_{target} = max(u_{target}, 1 - dist(target))$
$\bigstar_2$: if($run\_success$), $u_{success} = 1$
$\bigstar_3$: $U = u_{success} * R + W_{sep} * u_{sep} + W_{target} * u_{target}$

Algorithm 3 Goals for CCD Cases

Case 4: Cloud Avoidance, No Separation Assurance
$\bigstar_1$: $u_{target} = max(u_{target}, 1 - dist(target))$
$\bigstar_1$: if($|p_x, p_y| < \beta$), $u_{sep} \leftarrow u_{sep} - (|p_x, p_y| - \beta)^2$
$\bigstar_2$: if($run\_success$), $u_{success} = 1$
$\bigstar_3$: $U = u_{success} * R + W_{cloud} * u_{cloud} + W_{target} * u_{target}$
Case 5: Cloud Avoidance with Separation Assurance
$\bigstar_1$: $u_{target} = max(u_{target}, 1 - dist(target))$
$\bigstar_1$: if($|p_x, p_y| < \beta$), $u_{sep} \leftarrow u_{sep} - (|p_x, p_y| - \beta)^2$
$\bigstar_1$: $\forall_i$ if($dist(C_i) < \beta_{cloud}$), $u_{cloud} \leftarrow u_{cloud} - dist(C_i)^{-2}$
$\bigstar_2$: if($run\_success$), $u_{success} = 1$
$\bigstar_3$: $U = u_{success} * R + W_{target} * u_{target} + W_{sep} * u_{sep} + W_{cloud} * u_{cloud}$
Case 6: Implicit Cloud Avoidance
$\bigstar_1$: if($|p_x, p_y| < \beta$), $u_{sep} \leftarrow u_{sep} - (|p_x, p_y| - \beta)^2$
$\bigstar_1$: $u_{target} = max(u_{target}, 1 - dist(target))$
$\bigstar_2$: if($run\_success$), $u_{success} = 1$
$\bigstar_3$: $U = u_{success} * R + W_{sep} * u_{sep} + W_{target} * u_{target}$

to $P = 10$ planes over $sims\_per\_gen = 11$ simulations each generation, for $max\_generations = 500$ generations. In each simulation, the policies used are randomly selected from those that have not been used in that generation.

We instruct the planes to maintain $\beta_{plane} = 15$ units of separation from each other at all times, and the planes move at a rate of 10 units per timestep. We use an effective cloud radius of $\beta_{cloud} = 50$ units. After each generation, $m = 10$ agents are removed from the population and replaced with mutated copies of more-fit agents.

The agents start at the south end of the corridor, and are directed toward a target in the center of the north end of the corridor, 1000 units away. All agents start with heading $\theta_a = \pi/2$ (North). The system dynamics are governed by the planes travelling at $|V| = 10$ units per timestep, and a heading adjustment coefficient of $\rho = 0.5$. Cases 1 and 2 involve no weights. In Cases 3-6, all weights are set to a value of 1.0 unless otherwise noted in the results.

6. RESULTS

We present the outcome of the simulation for each case presented in Section 3. The first three cases mimic the historical Norden Bombsight, while the last three cases serve as a test case, without the designer-side bias introduced by historical knowledge.

In every case we perform 30 statistical runs, and then present the simulation output for the statistical run which attained the sum of agent performance closest to the mean value across all 30 runs. We offer these plots for each of the 6 cases representing the different goal combinations that the agents were tested with (Figures 1–9).

Interpretation of Figures.

Each of the figures represents each aircraft by a distinct color-symbol combination. The lines plot out each timestep, with the symbols appearing every 10 timesteps. The planes proceed from the bottom of the figure through the top. It is important to note that if a plane travels in the x-direction, even if it appears to intersect the path created by another plane, in many cases it is in the same location many timesteps after the first plane was there.

Clouds are represented by grey circles, which represent the maximum radius at which the cloud will have effect on an agent's reward. Being closer to a cloud center is worse than being near the edge, and passing over multiple clouds simultaneously has an additional negative effect on the agent's reward.

6.1 Case 1 Results

In Case 1, the agents seek to (i) pass through the north end of the corridor, with no emphasis on passing over the target point, and (ii) maintain separation assurance with the other aircraft in flight. This represents the case in which the USAAF did not have an accurate method for determining the ideal release point for their payloads.

The agents do not show a preference to where they exit the corridor, and are only concerned with staying spaced out with respect to the other aircraft. The agents quickly converge on a solid policy: move straight forward to the end of the corridor, and perform slight corrections when too close to another plane. Other, more complex methods may exist that could be discovered by a thorough consideration of the problem by a human expert, but the simplest policies are both easier to arrive at, and tend to be the most consistent performers, resulting in this straightforward solution.

6.2 Case 2 Results

Within Case 2, the agents operate with the sole goal: (i) pass over the target point as precisely as possible, while ignoring any contribution from separation assurance. This represents a potential outcome if the USAAF were to adopt a full-scale integration of the Norden Bombsight

This leads to agent policies where the agents learn to direct themselves directly over the target location with no heed for other concerns. This means that the planes would be travelling over the target at very nearly the same time, making a very unsafe situation for all involved. This result agrees with the USAAF determination not to use the Norden Bombsight aboard all of the aircraft within the formation, and is another case where a very simple policy leads to high individual utility.

6.3 Case 3 Results

In Case 3, the agents have the two explicit goals of (i) to pass over the target point as precisely as possible while (ii) maintain-

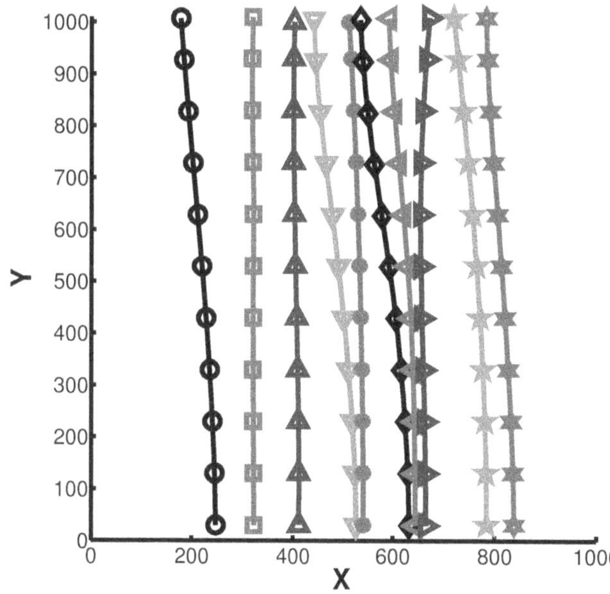

Figure 1: Case 1 — Pre-Norden Bombsight.

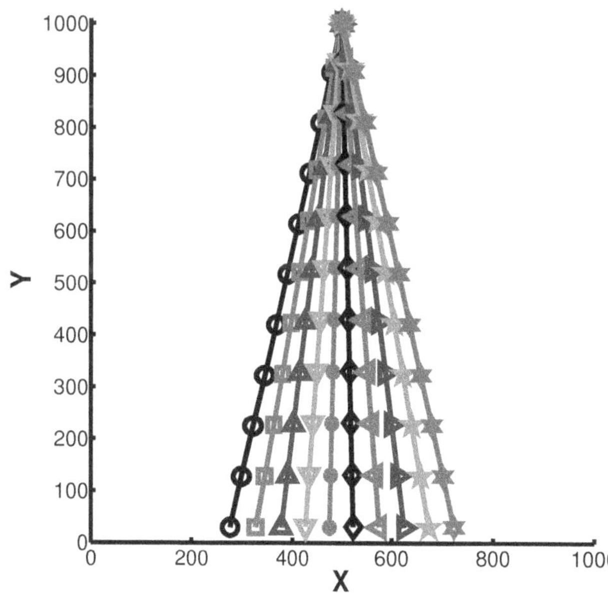

Figure 2: Case 2 — Full Norden Integration.

ing separation assurance with the other aircraft in flight. These two goals are conflicting, however, so we examine the effect of different weights on the paths chosen by the simulated aircraft. This represents a partial integration of the Norden Bombsight.

A number of interesting phenomena arise. When spacing is given a near-zero weight $W_{sep} = 0.1$ (Figure 3), the simulation reveals that the aircraft will converge to the center target point at the top of the corridor, as in Case 2. Some signs of separation concerns do appear, however, as Figure 3 shows one of the aircraft peeling off from the rest, in favor of maximizing its spacing utility over the target utility. The agents also do not converge to as tight of a group at the target point as in Case 2.

When we move the weight to consider separation $W_{sep} = 0.5$, we find that there is a tradeoff that the agents begin to make, shown by the simulation in Figure 4: there is less convergence toward the target point, and some of the agents choose to stay away from the congested center area in favor of maintaining separation assurance.

As we increase the weight for separation equal to that of the target weight $W_{sep} = 1.0$, the simulation shows that the planes favor maintaining their spacing more than passing over the center point, and spread out further. However, Figure 5 shows that the agents begin to develop a secondary strategy: they take a longer path toward the target, so that they arrive in the area at a later point in time. Notice particularly in Figure 5 the three aircraft starting at the right cross all the way behind the other planes to end up to the left of their target. This longer path takes them longer to traverse than the planes taking a more direct path, so they avoid separation violations in this way.

This is taken to the extreme when we then reduce the target weight to $W_{target} = 0.01$ and the ideal separation to a larger value

Figure 3: Case 3 — Little weight on separation.

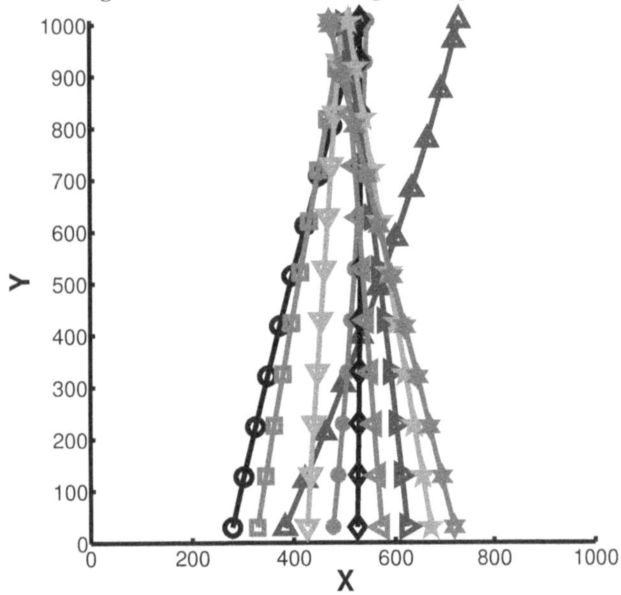

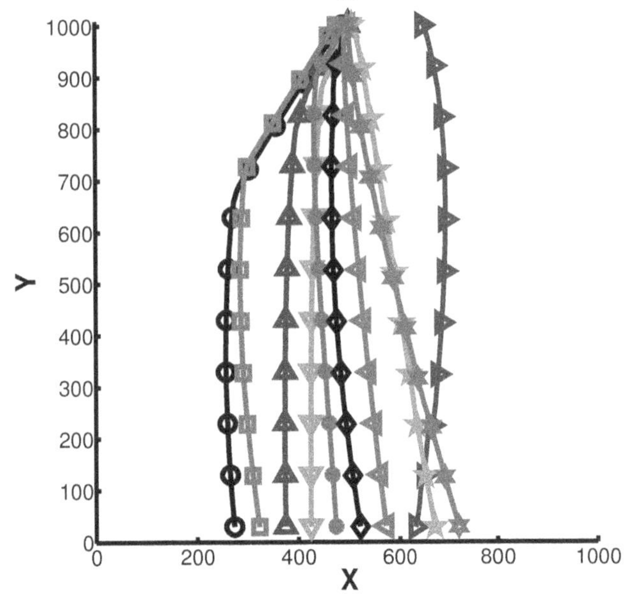

Figure 4: Case 3 — Moderate weight on separation.

Figure 5: Case 3 — Large separation weight.

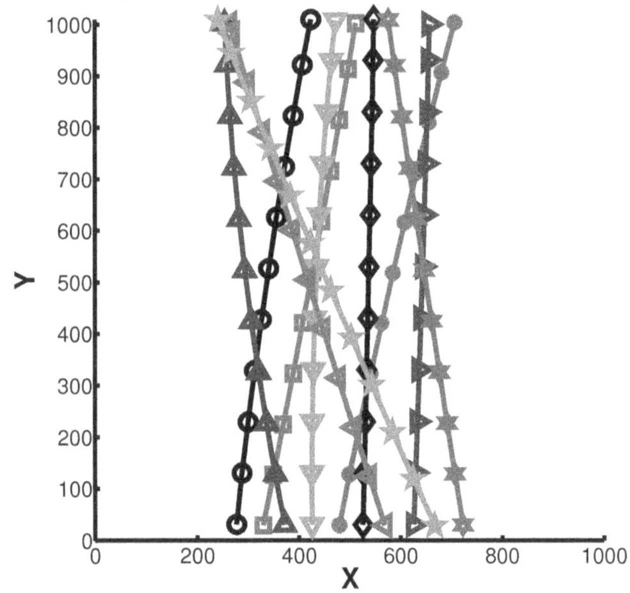

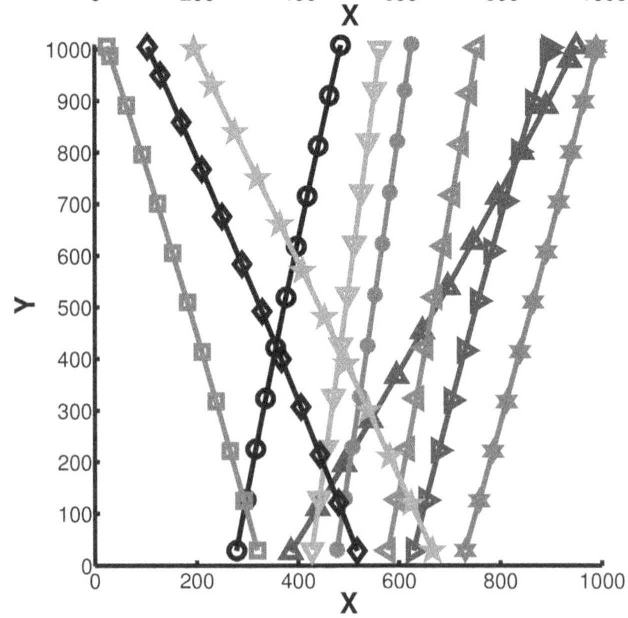

Figure 6: Case 3 — Large separation distance and weight.

$\beta_{plane} = 250$ units. With these settings, agents become solely concerned with staying in uncongested areas while traveling through the airspace. Figure 6 shows that a few of the simulated agents make large movements in the x-direction while traveling through the corridor, and the remaining agents spread out as they travel.

This strategy is a result that is not immediately apparent by inspection of the problem. Crossing behind other planes in flight is a somewhat unforeseen behavior that may not arise with hand-designed agents. The evolutionary algorithm, however, led to these policies through the agents simply seeking to maximize their utility because it was an easily accessible solution that offered improvement over more intuitive solutions.

6.4 Case 4 Results

In Case 4, we introduce the complication of clouds to avoid. This creates the agent goals for this case of (i) to make it through the corridor to the target point successfully, while (ii) avoiding clouds. Avoiding other aircraft is not involved in their utility function.

The simulation shows that the agents learning on these goals very successfully avoid the cloudy patch in the middle of the corridor, and pass near the center of the corridor end. Due to spacing being a non-concern for the agents in this case, they maintain very close distance to each other as they pass directly through the corridor.

6.5 Case 5 Results

Case 5 presents the agents with 3 goals to balance: to (i) make it through the corridor successfully, while (ii) maintaining separation assurance from other planes, and (iii) avoiding clouds.

This leads to an unexpected emergent behavior that may initially look quite disorganized, but has an underlying order. As the group of agents passes by the right side of the central cloud region, the agents peel off from the group one by one, making a complete turn before proceeding to the end of the corridor. As they turn at various points, they increase the spacing between themselves and the remainder of the formation, increasing their spacing utility, u_{sep}. In other simulations, we observed agent behaviors that were similar with a left-handed turn, as well as behaviors where the agents would split to two sub-formations performing this maneuver on either side of the cloud formation.

With even weight on all three goals, this unexpected policy of agents choosing to complete a full turn before proceeding to the end of the corridor creates a higher utility value U than a more conventional "laminar flow policy" like those seen in Figure 7. Executing the turns at different points in the corridor leads to an intermediate spreading of the planes, and also allow the agents to pass through the end of the corridor at different points in time, allowing more agents to pass closer to the center.

This type of emergent behavior manifested due to the evolutionary algorithm employed in this work, and outperformed our earlier attempts and solving the problem with rule-based agent policies. While we were subsequently able to develop hand-coded policies that were superior to the evolved policy, the concept for these policies was directly inspired by the results of the evolutionary algorithm. Furthermore, the evolutionary algorithm that developed these policies remains unchanged from the algorithm used in each of the other cases, while the superior hand-coded policies required both inspiration from the evolutionary algorithm and additional development time.

6.6 Case 6 Results

In Case 6, we remove the penalty of the cloudy regions, creating the goals of (i) make it through the corridor successfully, while (ii) maintaining separation assurance from other planes. We introduce a simulated complication due to the clouds: the agent's ability to sense other nearby planes is inhibited by the clouds, creating an implicit goal that they should avoid the cloudy areas in order to achieve their separation assurance goals. To make this case more challenging we change the allocation of clouds throughout the space so that the planes have a larger area to avoid.

The simulation reveals that the agents do learn to avoid the cloudy areas, though not quite as severely as when the goal was explicitly involved in their utility calculation. Passing through the cloudy area is not a bad decision in and of itself, but when multiple agents simultaneously choose to do so, they reduce each other's utility through the un-sensed separation violations.

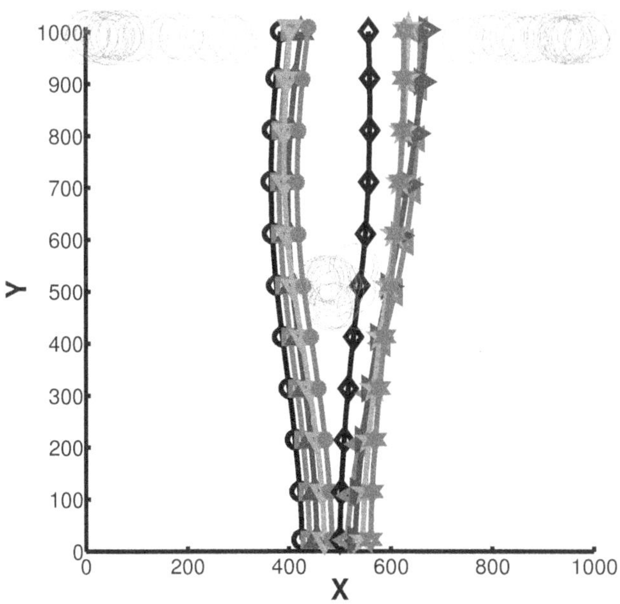

Figure 7: Case 4 — Explicit cloud avoidance.

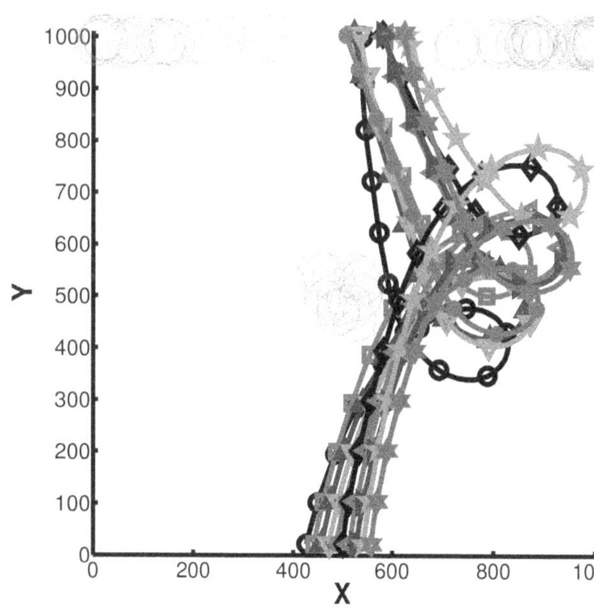

Figure 8: Case 5 — Explicit cloud avoidance and spacing.

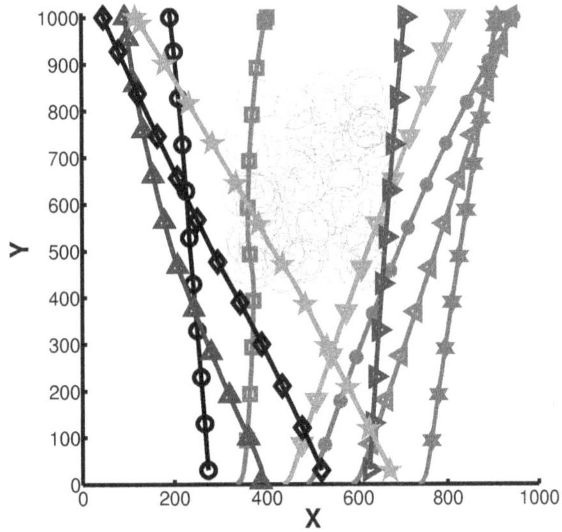

Figure 9: Case 6 — Implicit cloud avoidance.

7. CONCLUSION

In this work we have presented a method for the simulation of complex systems to predict the effects of new technology integration in air traffic management through the use of evolutionary algorithms. These evolutionary algorithms require the system designer only to specify a goal for the system, and the resultant behaviors achieve these goals in both expected and unforeseen manners.

We demonstrated the use of this technique in two domains, with the algorithm unchanged between the 6 cases tested. In the historical test cases, we arrive at the same conclusion that the historical system designers did: applying the Norden Bombsight to every bomber would be a poor idea, as many separation assurance problems would arise. Considering the separation between the planes as well as the precise location of the target is a better solution. This supports our claim that an agent-based evolutionary algorithm approach can assist in assessing the value of new technologies.

In the future technology case of the Civilian Cloud Domain, the simulation demonstrated that agents were able to balance multiple simultaneous goals for an expected outcome when we specified areas of the airspace to be avoided, in the form of clouds. When the agents also had to consider their separation from nearby planes, however, they developed a set of radical behaviors which gained higher utility than a more expected policy. This supports our claim that evolutionary algorithms may develop complex emergent behaviors, even with relatively simple agents.

Finally, the evolutionary algorithm successfully learned the implicit coupling between goals, even when one of the goals was not explicitly a part of the fitness function. In this way the agents learned to avoid the cloudy regions of the space because they negatively affected their sensing ability, even when we removed any direct consideration of the clouds from their utility function.

This type of approach — the use of agent-based evolutionary algorithms — offers the ability to analyze hypothetical cases in air traffic management before they are fully realized, and identify possibly dangerous interactions before risking human lives.

Acknowledgements.

This work was partially supported by the National Science Foundation under grant numbers CNS-0931591 and CNS-0930168.

8. REFERENCES

[1] C. A. C. Coello. Theoretical and numerical constraint-handling techniques used with evolutionary algorithms: a survey of the state of the art. *Computer methods in applied mechanics and engineering*, 191(11):1245–1287, 2002.

[2] O. Gaci and H. Mathieu. Simulation of a segregation strategy in a warehouse of dangerous goods by a multi- agent system. *IEEE Symposium on Computational Intelligence and Informatics*, 2011.

[3] M. Gallegati, G. Giulioni, and N. Kichiji. Complex dynamics and financial fragility in an agent based model. *Advances in Complex Systems*, 6(3):1–16, 2003.

[4] D. Delli Gatti, E. Gaffeo, and M. Gallegati. Complex agent-based macroeconomics: a research agenda for a new paradigm. *Journal of Economic Interaction and Coordination*, 5(2):111–135, 2010.

[5] E. Gelenbe and F-J. Wu. Large scale simulation for human evacuation and rescue. *Computers and Mathematics with Applications*, 64, 2012.

[6] M. Gladwell. The strange tale of the norden bombsight. TEDGlobal 2011, July 2011.

[7] M. Jakob, O. Vanek, O. Hrstka, and M. Pechoucek. Agents vs. pirates: Multi-agent simulation and optimization to fight maritime piracy. *AAMAS*, 2012.

[8] B. Lebaron. Heterogeneous gain learning and the dynamics of asset prices. *Journal of Economic Behavior and Organization*, 2012.

[9] J. Lin, J. Blythe, S. Clark, N. Davarpanah, N. Hughston, and M. Zyda. Unbelievable agents for large scale security simulation. *Association for the Advancement of Artificial Intelligence*, 2010.

[10] R.T. Marler and J. S. Arora. Survey of multi-objective optimization methods for engineering. *Structural and Multidisciplinary Optimization*, 26:369–395, 2004.

[11] E. Mas, A. Suppasri, F. Imamura, and S. Koshimura. Agent-based simulation of the 2011 great east japan earthquake/tsunami evacuation: An integrated model of tsunami inundation and evacuation. *Journal of Natural Disaster Science*, 34(1), 2012.

[12] D. Romano, L. Lomax, and P. Richmond. NARCSim an agent-based illegal drug market simulation. *Games Innovations Conference*, pages 101–108, 2009.

[13] M. Sierhuis, W. J. Clancey, and R. J.J. van Hoof. Brahms: A multiagent modelling environment for simulating work processes and practices. *International Journal of Simulation and Process Modelling*, 3(3):134–152, 2007.

[14] M. Sierhuis, W. J. Clancey, R. J.J. van Hoof, C. H. Seah, M. S. Scott, R. A. Nado, S. F. Blumenberg, M. G. Shatto, B. L. Anderson, A. C. Bruins, C. B. Buckley, T. E. Diegelman, T. A. Hall, D. Hood, F. F. Reynolds, J. R. Toschlog, and T. Tucker. NASA's OCA mirroring system an application of multiagent systems in mission control. *AAMAS*, 2009.

[15] R. Sutton and A. G. Barto. *Reinforcement Learning: An Introduction*. MIT Press, 1998.

[16] A. Walker and M. Wooldridge. Understanding the emergence of conventions in multiagent systems. *International Conference on Multiagent Systems*, 1995.

[17] M. Wooldridge. *An introduction to multiagent systems*. Wiley, 2002.

Tuning Multi-Objective Optimization Algorithms for Cyclone Dust Separators

Martin Zaefferer, Beate Breiderhoff, Boris Naujoks, Martina Friese, Jörg Stork, Andreas Fischbach, Oliver Flasch, Thomas Bartz-Beielstein
Cologne University of Applied Sciences
51643 Gummersbach, Germany
[firstname].[lastname]@fh-koeln.de

ABSTRACT

Cyclone separators are filtration devices frequently used in industry, e.g., to filter particles from flue gas. Optimizing the cyclone geometry is a demanding task. Accurate simulations of cyclone separators are based on time consuming computational fluid dynamics simulations. Thus, the need for exploiting cheap information from analytical, approximative models is evident. Here, we employ two multi-objective optimization algorithms on such cheap, approximative models to analyze their optimization performance on this problem. Under various limitations, we tune both algorithms with Sequential Parameter Optimization (SPO) to achieve best possible results in shortest time. The resulting optimal settings are validated with different seeds, as well as with a different approximative model for collection efficiency. Their optimal performance is compared against a model based approach, where multi-objective SPO is directly employed to optimize the Cyclone model, rather than tuning the optimization algorithms. It is shown that SPO finds improved parameter settings of the concerned algorithms and performs excellently when directly used as an optimizer.

Categories and Subject Descriptors

G.1.6 [**Mathematics of Computing**]: Optimization

General Terms

Algorithms, Experimentation

Keywords

Evolutionary Multi-objective Optimization, Parameter Tuning, Cyclone Optimization Problem

1. INTRODUCTION

Filtering dust particles from flue gas is a challenging task. Environmental consequence, governmental limitations, cost of operation, high temperature, and varying pressures increase the need for efficient filtering devices. Cyclone dust separators are frequently applied for this purpose since they combine low costs with robustness against high temperature or pressures.

The main quality indicators of a cyclone are the fraction of particles filtered from the gas, i.e. the Collection Efficiency (CE), as well as the Pressure Drop (PD). While CE reflects how well the cyclone solves its main task, PD is the main impact on operational cost. PD and CE may be conflicting, i.e., ideal PD will not coincide with ideal CE. They are heavily influenced by the choice of several geometrical design parameters, like height or diameter of a cyclone. This results into a Multi-objective Optimization (MO) problem, the so called Cyclone Optimization Problem (COP).

The quality of a cyclone may be evaluated with expensive Computational Fluid Dynamics (CFD) simulations or estimated with analytical, approximative models.

This study analyzes the performance of MO algorithms based on an analytical model of the cyclone. This allows for extensive tuning and comparisons, which may be used to parameterize algorithms used in future studies where the more expensive CFD simulations are employed.

Hence, the main goals of this study are:

- Determine performance of MO algorithms with default parameters.
- Tune the employed MO algorithms to determine good parameter settings and guarantee a fair comparison.
- Test the advantage of employing surrogate models in the MO.
- Validate results with a different model.

The remainder of this work is structured as follows. Section 2 introduces the optimization problem as well as the underlying analytical models for cyclone dust separators. Section 3 describes multi-objective optimization and related methods. After that, an empirical optimization study regarding the introduced problem is described in Sec. 4, including experimental setup as well as description and discussion of results. A final summary as well as an outlook on future research directions is given in Sec. 5.

2. CYCLONE OPTIMIZATION

2.1 Problem Description

Cyclones are frequently used devices to separate solid particles from a gas phase. Pollution and emission regulations compelled engineers to optimize the cyclone design. Cy-

GECCO'14, July 12–16, 2014, Vancouver, BC, Canada.

ACM 978-1-4503-2662-9/14/07 ...$15.00.
http://dx.doi.org/10.1145/2576768.2598260 .

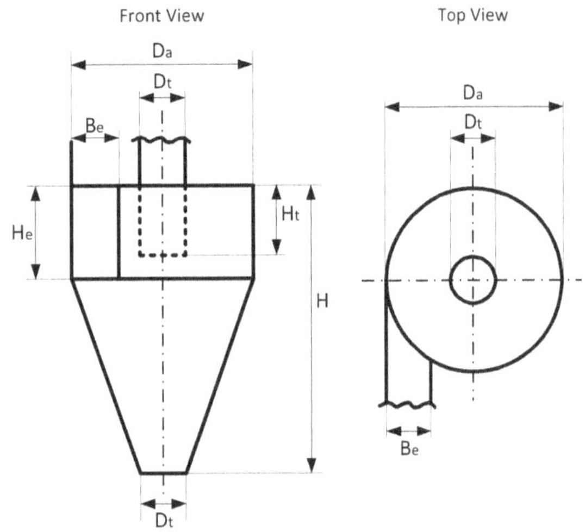

Figure 1: Schematic representation of a cyclone dust separator.

Table 1: Table of fluid, particle and geometrical parameters used in the experiments. Most values are taken from an example by Löffler [9].

Parameter	Symbol	Default	Unit
Geometrical Parameters			
Cyclone diameter	D_a	1260	mm
Cyclone height	H	2500	mm
Outlet pipe diameter	D_t	420	mm
Outlet pipe immersion	H_t	640	mm
Inlet height	H_e	600	mm
Inlet width	B_e	200	mm
Fluid/Particle Parameters			
Viscosity	μ	$18.5 \cdot 10^{-6}$	$Pa \cdot s$
Flow Rate	V_p	5000	$\frac{m^3}{h}$
Gas density	ρ_f	1.204	$\frac{kg}{m^3}$
Particle density	ρ_p	2000	$\frac{kg}{m3}$
Particle concentration	c_e	50	$\frac{g}{m^3}$
Output values			
Pressure Drop	PL	1626	Pa
Collection Efficiency	CE	0.89	–

clones exist in different shapes but the reverse flow cyclone represented in Fig.1 is the most common design in industry. The principle of cyclone separation is simple: the gas-solid mixture enters at the top section tangentially. The cylindrical body induces a spinning. Centrifugal force separates the dust from the gas stream: the dust is moved to the walls of the cylinder and down the conical section to the dust outlet while the gas exits through the outlet pipe. The efficiency of this process is mainly influenced by the geometric shape. A set of seven geometrical parameters like height or diameter allows to describe a cyclone as shown in Fig. 1. Several characteristics constitute a COP.

1. Geometric shape: Seven geometric parameters describe the cyclone as shown in Fig. 1.
2. Fluid/Gas properties: Parameters like viscosity or density describe the carrier substance
3. Particle properties: Particle composition is described by density, concentration, and size distribution

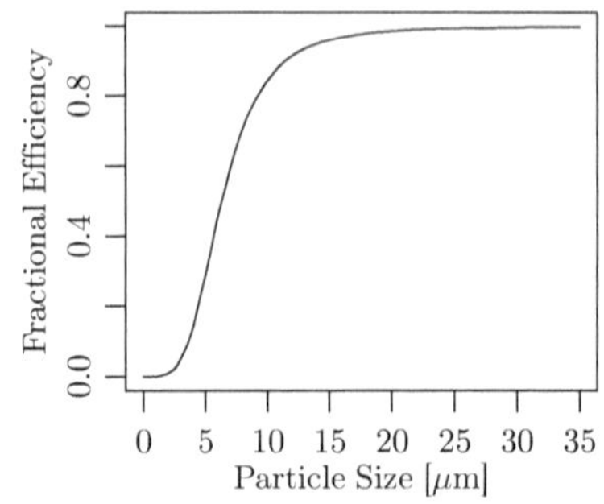

Figure 2: Fractional efficiency curve.

4. Collection Efficiency (CE): Amount of particles filtered from the gas
5. Pressure Drop (PD): Difference in pressure between inlet and outlet

The default values used in our experiments for these parameters are listed in Table 1. PD and CE are the main criteria used to evaluate cyclone performance. Both are functions of the cyclone dimensions. The goal of cyclone design is to maximize CE and to minimize PD by adjusting the geometric parameters.

2.2 Models

2.2.1 *Collection Efficiency*

Separation of particles inside a cyclone is a result of the forces acting on them. There are basically two concepts to calculate the CE of cyclones in the literature: The "equilibrium-orbit" models and the "time-of-flight" models. We use two different kinds of approaches.

The Barth model: Barth [1] developed the original "equilibrium-orbit" model. There are two forces acting on a particle rotating in the cyclone body: the centrifugal force acting towards the wall and a drag acting towards the outlet pipe. Equating these forces, Barth calculates the so called cut size x_{50}, where drag and centrifugal force are equal. Here, 50% of the particles are collected. Smaller particles are collected with lower efficiency, larger with higher efficiency. Once we have the cut size, we can fit a fractional efficiency curve through it. For high concentrations of dust, the Barth model is often corrected with an approach to model mass loading effects: the concept of a "critical load", first introduced by Muschelknautz [11]. The optimization problem based on this model will be referred to as COP1.

The model of Mothes and Löffler: Mothes and Löffler [10, 9] present a model based on differential mass balances which are formulated for four zones in the cyclone. This model is a composition of the "equilibrium-orbit" and "time-of-flight" models. "Time-of-flight" models determine whether the particle has time to reach the wall. The optimization problem based on this model will be referred to as COP2.

Both models include the main cyclone parameters and calculate a fractional efficiency curve $T(x)$ that assigns an efficiency to the particle diameter as shown in Fig. 2. Larger particles are collected more efficiently than smaller particles. The overall efficiency can be calculated by integrating the fractional efficiency curve over the particle size distribution according to:

$$E = \int_{x_{min}}^{x_{max}} T(x) q_e(x) dx = \sum_{x_{min}}^{x_{max}} T(\tilde{x_i}) \Delta Q_e(x_i) \quad (1)$$

where x_{min} is the lower bound of the particle size, x_{max} is the upper bound of the particle size, $\tilde{x}_i$ is the mean particle size, $\Delta Q_e(x_i)$ is the change in distribution of particle sizes and $q_e(x) = \frac{\Delta Q_e(x_i)}{\Delta x_i}$. In the experiments, values for $\Delta Q_e(x_i)$ are taken from an example by Löffler [9].

2.2.2 *Pressure Drop according to Muschelknautz*

PD is defined as the difference in pressure Δp between two points of a fluid carrying body. It occurs with frictional forces and relates directly to operational cost. Therefore, an exact prediction is very important. Total PD equals to:

$$\Delta p = \frac{\rho}{2} v_i^2 (\xi_{e-a} + \xi_{a-i} + \xi_{i-m}) \qquad (2)$$

where ξ_{e-a}, ξ_{a-i} and ξ_{i-m} are friction coefficients for the loss within inlet, cyclone body and outlet pipe respectively. $\frac{\rho}{2} v_i^2$ is the relationship between pressure and velocity. This model is used in both COP1 and COP2.

2.3 The Cyclone Optimization Problem

In this paper, two different COP's are solved, COP1 and COP2. Both depend on analytical models and correspond to the geometrical description in Fig. 1 as well the default parameters in Table 1. The fluid parameters are assumed to be constant for the given problems. The six geometrical parameters are to be chosen to yield optimal CE and PD, yielding a bi-objective problem. PD will be calculated as described in Sec. 2.2.2. In COP1, the CE will be calculated with the model introduced by Barth [1]. while the model by Mothes and Löffler [10, 9] is involved in COP2.

2.4 Previous Research

Ravi et al. [15] used the Non Dominated Sorting Genetic Algorithm NSGA to optimize an analytical model for cyclone dust separators by Mothes and Löffler [10, 9]. Elsayed and Lacor [5] optimized four geometrical parameters using computational fluid dynamics CFD models and a model by Barth [1]. They minimized PD only, using the response surface methodology. Pishbin and Moghiman [13] optimized seven geometry parameters with a genetic algorithm, minimizing PD and maximizing CE. They used a CFD model to construct the fitness function. The bi-objective problem was transferred to a single-objective problem using weights. Elsayed and Lacor [6] minimized PD and cut-off diameter. They used a Pareto optimization approach, utilizing a Radial Basis Function Neural Network RBFNN. A similar approach was taken by Safikhani et al. [16].

The herein presented work uses the analytical model by Barth [1] and Muschelknautz [12] to tune state-of-the-art MO algorithms. The tuned algorithms are then tested with the model by Mothes and Löffler [9]. Multi-objective Sequential Parameter Optimization [17] is compared to the tuned MO algorithms.

3. MULTI-OBJECTIVE OPTIMIZATION

A multi-objective optimization problem can be defined by a function

$$f : A \subset \mathbb{R}^n \longrightarrow \mathbb{R}^m, \quad f(x) = (f_1(x), \ldots, f_m(x)),$$

with $x \in \mathbb{R}^n$, and the feasible set A. The common way to handle multi-objective optimization problems is Pareto optimization based on the concept of Pareto-dominance. One solution $x \in A$ is said to (Pareto-) dominate ($\prec$) another solution $y \in A$, if the following holds:

$$x \prec y \quad \text{iff} \quad \forall i: \; f_i(x) \leq f_i(y) \quad \wedge \quad \exists j: \; f_j(x) < f_j(y)$$

(for $i, j \in \{1, \ldots, m\}$). Consequently, the set $\{x \in A \mid \nexists y \in A: \; y \prec x\}$ is called the Pareto-set, while the corresponding set under mapping f is called the Pareto-front.

3.1 Algorithms

Evolutionary Algorithms (EA) have become a standard tool for solving MO problems, and are here termed Evolutionary Multi-objective Optimization Algorithms (EMOA). These algorithms are based on sets of solutions. This coincides well with the challenge of finding a set of solutions in MO problems.

One of the most popular algorithms is the Non-dominated Sorting Genetic Algorithm (NSGA-II) [4]. In this algorithm, individuals are first ranked by non-dominated sorting. To select from a set of equally ranked non-dominated individuals and preserve diversity, NSGA-II employs crowding distance. Crowding distance measures the average length of a cuboid spanned by the nearest neighbors of the solution for which the measure is computed.

Whereas NSGA-II uses crowding distance as an indicator of quality, other methods use the hypervolume, i.e. the space covered by a Pareto front with respect to a predefined reference point. Maximizing the hypervolume pushes solutions towards the desired objective values. Moreover, the hypervolume rewards a high diversity of solutions, i.e. a wide spread, and a regular distribution of solutions along the border to the non-dominated area. One of the techniques employing hypervolume maximization is the S-Metric Selection EMOA (SMS-EMOA) (cf. Beume et al. [3]).

In case of expensive optimization problems, it is a standard approach to reduce the number of target Function Evaluations (FE) by shifting the load to surrogate models. Several approaches in MO employ surrogate modeling. An overview is given by Knowles and Nakayama [8].

Sequential Parameter Optimization (SPO) [2] provides a flexible framework for surrogate model based optimization. Recently, SPO has also been extended to MO [17, 18], making use of various models as well as state-of-the-art MO algorithms like SMS-EMOA and NSGA-II. Hence, multi-objective SPO (MSPO) can directly solve the COP.

3.2 Tuning

Every optimization algorithm has parameters which influence the optimization performance. Tuning these parameters towards optimal performance is thus, again, an optimization problem. Tuning may be done for several reasons. Firstly, it allows to find better parameter settings thus leading to improved algorithms which solve the problem better. Secondly, tuning may yield additional understanding of the optimization algorithms. Finally, tuned algorithms allow for a fair comparison. That is, the good/bad performance of an algorithm may not be due to fortunate/unfortunate selection of default parameter values. The last point is especially important for studies that compare different algorithms, hence very relevant for this study.

Sequential Parameter Optimization [2] is a framework for surrogate model based optimization that was initially developed for the purpose of parameter tuning of EA's but has since been applied to numerous applications. It is based on methods from Design of Experiment (DoE), Statistics and Machine Learning.

In SPO, an initial DoE is created and evaluated on the target function. The acquired data is used to build a model representing the effects and interactions of the various tuned parameters. In a sequential manner, this model is first exploited to yield new candidate solutions (i.e., parameter settings) and then updated with the data from the new candidates. This is repeated until a stopping criterion is reached, after which a report and analysis of results follows.

In this work, SPO is applied to tune the employed SMS-EMOA and NSGA-II, while MSPO is a competitor to these MO algorithms.

4. EMPIRICAL STUDY

In this empirical study, (M)SPO will be used in form of the SPO Toolbox `SPOT` R-package. This also includes an implementation of the SMS-EMOA, making use of the `emoa` R-package. The NSGA-II implementation stems from the `mco` R-package[1].

4.1 Preliminary Experiment

4.1.1 Setup

In a very first attempt to analyze behavior of the different algorithms, we perform a lengthy optimization of the target function (i.e., the cyclone model) using SMS-EMOA and NSGA-II with default parameters. The goal is to get a reasonably good approximation of the Pareto-front. This will be used to specify a target for the parameter tuning, measured by hypervolume. The default parameters of both algorithms are summarized in Table 2. These parameters are the population size μ, the distribution indexes for crossover η_c and mutation η_m as well as the probabilities for both variation operators p_c and p_m.

Table 2: Default parameters of the employed NSGA-II and SMS-EMOA implementations.

	μ	η_c	η_m	p_c	p_m
SMS-EMOA	100	15	25	0.7	0.3
NSGA-II	100	5	10	0.7	0.2

The optimization run is repeated 50 times, where each run is allowed 100 000 evaluations of the cyclone model. The reference point is chosen to be at PD 5 000 and CE zero. The upper and lower boundary of the COP are listed in Table 3. Please note, that in this work hypervolume will be measured based on the set of non-dominated solutions in an archive of all solutions found during each run, not based on the final population.

Table 3: Lower and upper boundaries of the COP. Based on an example by Löffler [9].

	Da	H	Dt	Ht	He	Be
lower	1134	2250	378	576	540	180
upper	1386	2750	462	704	660	220

4.1.2 Results and Discussion

The maximum hypervolume received from all runs was 3 843.964. Based on this, a target value for the tuning of the algorithms was defined. This was chosen to be 99.9% of the maximum hypervolume, i.e., a value of 3 843.34. Figure 3 depicts the run length distributions of the NSGA-II and SMS-EMOA runs from above. The depicted graphs show the cumulative, empirical probability of the optimization runs reaching the target value over the number of required FE.

[1]All packages are available as open source on `http://cran.r-project.org/`

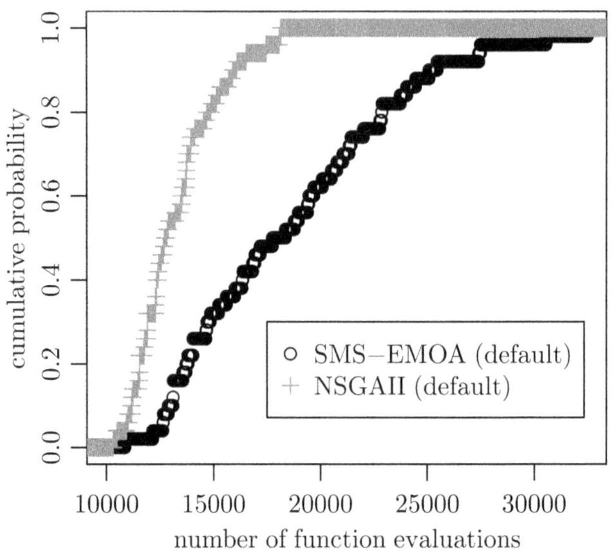

Figure 3: Run length distributons plot for target of 99.9% of hypervolume, i.e., 3 843.34

As can be seen from Fig. 3, all NSGA-II runs featuring standard parameters reached the target after about 17 000 to 18 000 FE, while all SMS-EMOA required about 30 000 FE. NSGA-II provided a much steeper slope than SMS-EMOA, which converges much slower.

The interpretation of results was twofold. On the one hand, the experiments show that both algorithms are able to reach 99.9% of the achievable hypervolume within the maximum budget. Therefore, this value was chosen as a target for the algorithm tuning. The number of FE to reach 99.9% of the achievable hypervolume is minimized. Here, the goal of the tuning is to see how much the value of 17 000 to 30 000 FE could be reduced and whether the results would be applicable for optimization based on CFD models. It is also of interest whether a tuned NSGA-II will still outperform a tuned SMS-EMOA, even though the concerned quality criterion (the hypervolume) is directly optimized by SMS-EMOA.

On the other hand, 1 000 FE or even more seem to be far too much for an optimization invoking expensive CFD models. Therefore, the question is how far, w.r.t. hypervolume, we could possibly get with a strictly limited budget of FE. This was the foundation for additional tuning experiments. Here, the budget is limited to a few hundreds FE and the achieved hypervolume is maximized.

4.2 Tuning

4.2.1 Setup

Table 4 shows the region of interest, i.e., the lower and upper boundaries between which parameters are varied during tuning. The upper boundary of μ is chosen to coincide with the smallest tuning budget, i.e., 120.

First, the algorithms were tuned to reach the previously determined target value from above, minimizing the number of required FE. This tuning task will be referred to as

Table 4: Region of interest in which parameters are tuned.

	μ	η_c	η_m	p_c	p_m
lower	3	0	0	0	0
upper	120	40	40	1	1

minimization of the required FE to reach the Target hypervolume (FTar). Additionally, both algorithms were tuned to reach a maximum hypervolume for a strictly limited budget of FE. This reflects the real world problem where only a certain budget is available for the optimization process. The budgets chosen were 120, 240, and 500 function evaluations. This second set of tuning runs will be referred to as Achieved Hypervolume maximization (AHvol). Thus, each algorithm is tuned four times, resulting into an overall number of 8 tuning runs.

SPO is utilized to tune the algorithms, but also has a large number of parameters:

- A Kriging model based on code by Forrester et al. [7] was used as a surrogate model.
- The number of algorithm runs in each tuning run are limited to 500 (for the fixed target value) and 1 000 (for the fixed budgets).
- In the initial design, each parameter setting is evaluated twice (fixed target) or four times (fixed budget).
- Each parameter setting may be re-evaluated no more than ten (fixed target) or twenty (fixed budget) times.
- In each sequential step, one new solution is evaluated on the target function and one old solution may be re-evaluated.
- The number of re-evaluations of promising solutions are increased linearly. Optimal computing budget allocation is not used.
- The initial design consists of 100 different parameter settings.
- The sequentially created models are optimized by Latin Hypercube Sampling (LHS) and Differential Evolution (DE) [14].
- The sequential step LHS evaluates 1 000 points on the model.
- The sequential step DE uses 2 000 evaluations and a population size of 50.

The larger numbers for the tuning under limited budgets is supposed to amend the higher noise level caused by small budgets.

At the end of each tuning run, resulting parameter sets are compared to default parameters. In addition to the comparison of tuned and default parameters, a model-based optimization is performed with multi-objective SPO. Here, a Kriging model is used as a surrogate for each objective. A maximum of 120 evaluations was allowed, which is a reasonably low budget for real world problems. The initial design consisted of 30 points. The surrogate is optimized with SMS-EMOA using default parameters and suggesting 10 points for evaluation in each sequential step. No repeated evaluations are performed, since the presented COP is deterministic. Note that, in contrast to NSGA-II and SMS-EMOA MSPO was not tuned.

4.2.2 *Results and Discussion*

The determined sets of tuned parameters are combined in Table 5. The suffix "Ftar" indicates parameters tuned with respect to minimum required FE to reach the 99.9% target hypervolume (case FTar from above). The results from tuning with limited budgets of 120, 240, or 500 FE are indicated by the suffix consisting of "B" and the corresponding number. Results within this table differ remarkably.

Table 5: Results of the eight tuning runs. Parameters of the best found solution are shown.

	μ	η_c	η_m	p_c	p_m
SMS-EMOA-Ftar	12.44	18.03	3.59	0.25	0.37
SMS-EMOA-B500	3.01	1.63	0.14	0.02	0.54
SMS-EMOA-B240	3.19	10.20	0.00	0.00	0.56
SMS-EMOA-B120	3.14	12.48	0.09	0.01	0.98
NSGAII-Ftar	43.04	39.09	0.11	0.45	0.25
NSGAII-B500	5.05	21.92	0.03	0.31	0.41
NSGAII-B240	3.11	17.99	0.04	0.08	0.53
NSGAII-B120	3.05	18.46	0.27	0.01	0.70

In the case of FTar, where large numbers of FE are allowed, optimal population sizes are much larger than in the case of AHvol, where the budgets are rather small. The population size is 4 times larger for SMS-EMOA and around 10 times larger for NSGA-II. Moreover, recombination plays a stronger role in case of FTar, marked by a probability of at least 0.25. For AHvol optimization, the recombination probability exceeds 0.25 in only one case, i.e. NSGA-II-B500. The mutation probability has negative correlation with the recombination probability. Thus, it is smallest where the budget is largest. It reaches nearly 100% for SMS-EMOA-B120 indicating that for smallest budgets mutation plays a much more important role than recombination.

The outlier in recombination probability (NSGA-II-B500) coincides with an unusual population size. Here, population size is five individuals, while all other AHvol cases yield an optimal population size of three individuals.

Compared to the default values, η_m was reduced remarkably, indicating that small parameter changes are preferred. On the other hand, η_c varies strongly in the given interval. The SPO Kriging model also attributed a low importance to this parameter.

Figure 4 depicts the run length distribution plots for the considered algorithms featuring standard as well as tuned parameterizations. Here, different random number generator seeds are used for initialization to prevent bias introduced by the choice of seeds during the tuning. Due to this, the results featuring standard parameterization look a bit different although they stem from the same parameterizations.

A clear improvement can be observed comparing standard and tuned parameterization. All runs with tuned parameters reach the optimization goal much earlier, i.e. SMS-EMOA after 4 100 FE compared to NSGA-II after 8 130 FE (cf. Table 7 for the concrete numbers). Interestingly, SMS-EMOA performs better than NSGA-II comparing the tuned variants, while the algorithms behave vice versa considering the standard parameterizations. Note that the slopes for cumulative probabilities for both algorithms are much larger for the tuned variants as well.

The received hypervolume values for the AHvol tuning are depicted in Table 6. Next to mean and standard deviation ("SD"), the table lists minimum and maximum values ("Min." and "Max." resp.) as well as "Mean%" being the mean percentage of achieved hypervolume. Corresponding boxplots are provided in Fig. 5. It can be observed that the

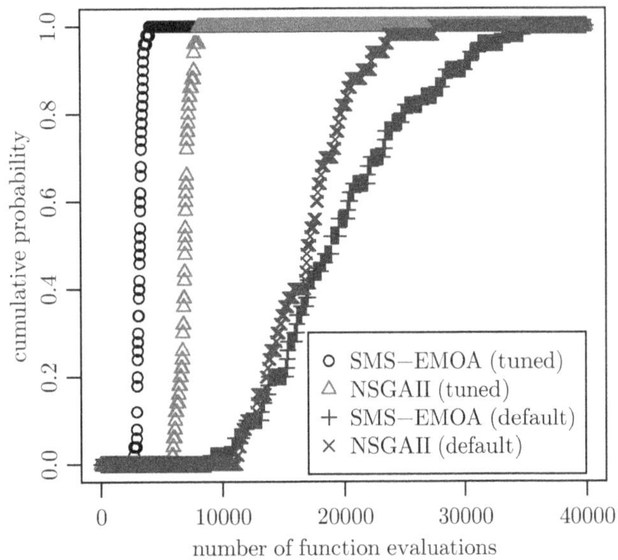

Figure 4: Run length distribution plot for target of 99.9% of hypervolume, i.e., 3 843.34. Showing results for default algorithm parameters as well as tuned to reach the target hypervolume with minimum number of function evaluations. Based on validation experiments with new random seeds.

tuned instances are significantly better than the ones featuring standard parameterizations. Moreover, the expected behavior that performance increases with increasing budget, can be retraced in the data.

Even with only 120 FE both algorithms capture about 90% of achievable hypervolume in the mean. Doubling this budget yields an increase up to 97% and having 500 FE allowed, more than 99% of hypervolume is achieved. These results can only be topped by MSPO, which is able to achieve over 99% hypervolume within only 120 FE.

Table 6: Resulting hypervolumes for default algorithm parameters (.def) as well as tuned parameters. Based on validation experiments with new random seeds on COP1.

	Min.	Mean%	Mean	Max.	SD
SMS.def.120	3517.5	64.2	3620.5	3719.5	43.2
NSG.def.120	3488.8	63.2	3614.6	3707.4	43.2
SMS.120	3687.3	87.2	3764.4	3811.9	33.1
NSG.120	3724.4	91.6	3791.7	3823.4	22.4
SMS.def.240	3574.6	74.4	3684.3	3764.4	41.9
NSG.def.240	3559.0	70.9	3662.4	3733.4	40.4
SMS.240	3802.2	97.4	3827.7	3835.7	7.1
NSG.240	3794.6	97.4	3827.7	3834.7	6.5
SMS.def.500	3688.2	84.5	3747.6	3794.2	27.2
NSG.def.500	3651.8	83.2	3739.1	3788.3	31.1
SMS.500	3834.7	99.1	3838.2	3839.6	1.1
NSG.500	3835.3	99.0	3837.5	3839.3	0.9
MSPO.120	3841.0	99.6	3841.5	3841.9	0.2

It was found that solving a COP with the considered algorithms produces a strong need for parameter tuning. Within all the received results, the performance of the tuned variants is much better than the performance of the default ones.

It turned out that a population size of three is optimal in almost all cases where a very small budget was imposed. Moreover, mutation is the more important variation operator and prefers rather small changes. Considering the case of FTar, the number of required FE was reduced to around 4 000 (from over 25 000).

If surrogate models are allowed, results further improved dramatically. MSPO proved to be the best performing algorithm in our study achieving more than 99.5% of possible hypervolume within only 120 FE.

A basic validation of results has already been performed using different random number generator seeds.To further validate our findings w.r.t. modeling, an alternative model for CE is considered, i.e., COP2. The following section will present experimental results for this second problem and compare them to COP1.

4.3 Validation

4.3.1 Setup

To validate results achieved by tuning on COP1, performance of tuned and default parameters are compared on COP2. Thus, tuned parameters are tested on a previously unseen problem instance. During validation, all algorithms are run 50 times to create statistically sound results.

Results of the two models for CE will differ. In general, the second model (COP2) does predict better CE. As the reference point remains unchanged, hypervolumes are expected to be larger for COP2. They should only be compared in terms of relative performance between algorithms, no absolute comparisons between hypervolumes of different models should be made.

4.3.2 Results and Discussion

Based on COP2, a new target hypervolume value had to be determined. A hypervolume value of 4 040.639 has been received as the maximum value. 4 039,479 represents the 99.9% target hypervolume.

Table 7: Number of FE required for all 50 of 50 runs to reach the target hypervolume (COP1: 3 843.34, COP2: 4 039.479). Based on the validation with different seeds optimizing hypervolume on COP1 as well as COP2.

	SMS.tun	SMS.def	NSG.tun	NSG.def
COP1	4100	34750	8130	27410
COP2	2830	18710	4390	18040

Table 7 summarizes the number of FE required to reach the target hypervolume. For COP2, all these values are smaller than the ones for the corresponding algorithmic variants for COP1. This reveals that COP2 may be a bit easier to solve than COP1.

Considering the influence of tuning, we were able to recapitulate the results received for COP1: the tuned variants perform much better than the ones featuring standard parameterizations. For all SMS-EMOA runs on COP2, only less than 3 000 FE were necessary to reach the target hypervolume. These results are also reflected in the corresponding run length distribution plots in Fig. 6.

Table 8 as well as Fig. 7 present the direct comparison of default and tuned parameter settings. These data supplement the results received for COP1 as presented in Table 6 and depicted in Fig. 5.

Again, the tuned variants perform much better than the ones featuring default parameters and results improve with larger budgets. For COP2, the algorithms were able to

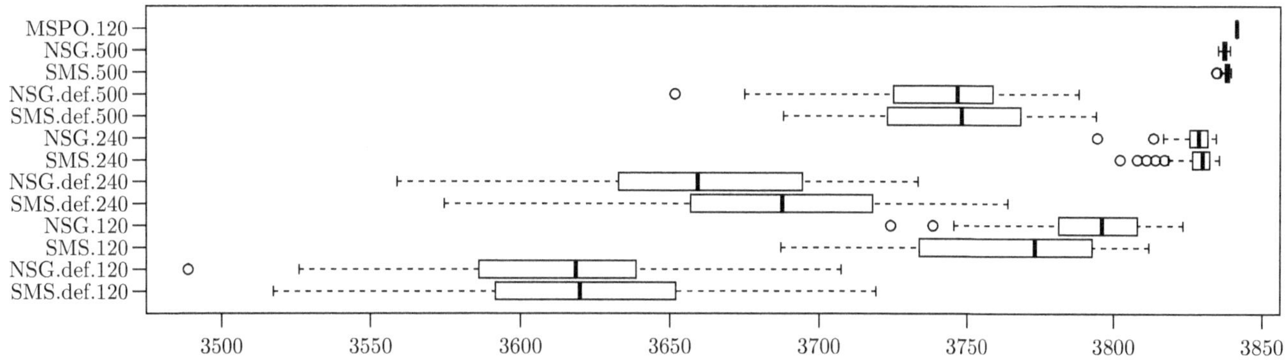

Figure 5: Boxplot of hypervolume for default algorithm parameters (.def) as well as tuned parameters on COP1. Based on validation experiments with new random seeds.

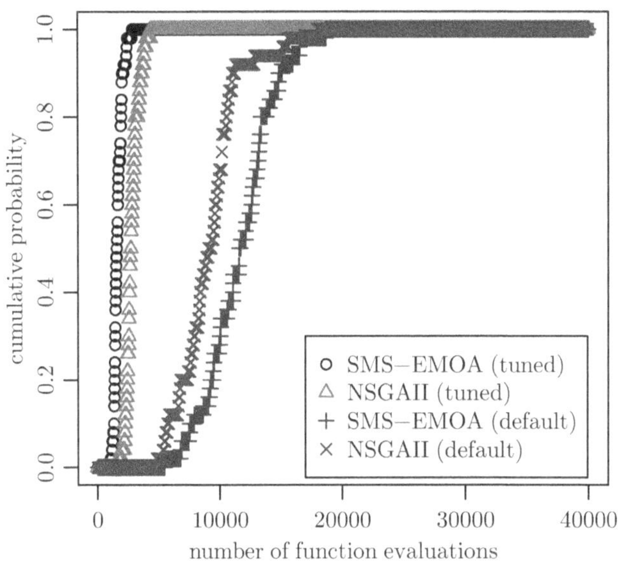

Figure 6: Rld plot for target of 99.9% of hypervolume, i.e., 4 039.479. Showing results for default algorithm parameters as well as tuned to reach the target hypervolume with minimum number of function evaluations. Based on validation experiments with COP2.

achieve around 95% of the maximum hypervolume within only 120 FE. This indicates a faster convergence on COP2 compared to COP1 as can also be observed in Table 7 and the corresponding run length distribution plots (cf. Fig. 6).

Also, for COP2, the algorithmic instances with the largest allowed budget (500 FE) were able to perform as good as the MSPO algorithm with only 120 FE. To be precise, they performed slightly better with respect to the mean values and standard deviations. Nevertheless, MSPO used much less FE and, thus, is preferable for expensive target functions.

Interestingly, NSGA-II seems to perform a bit better than SMS-EMOA when the optimization runs are limited to very small budgets. While the run length distributions indicate that SMS-EMOA performs better in the long run, NSGA-II excels for the smallest budget of 120 FE, both for COP1 and COP2

The results received for the COP were validated incorporating a different model for CE. We were able to show that optimized parameter values received for one model could be successfully transferred to the same optimization task incorporating a different model. This is a strong result for our aim to determine optimal parameter settings for industrial optimization problems. This may warrant to tune parameters with cheap models, and later apply the tuned parameters to a model where tuning would be too expensive.

Table 8: Resulting hypervolumes for default algorithm parameters (.def) as well as tuned parameters. Based on validation experiments with COP2.

	Min.	Mean%	Mean	Max.	SD
SMS.def.120	3691.6	82.3	3835.7	3929.5	47.9
NSG.def.120	3691.6	82.9	3842.7	3936.6	53.5
SMS.120	3892.0	94.7	3979.0	4029.6	34.6
NSG.120	3845.6	97.2	4007.9	4032.8	28.3
SMS.def.240	3777.2	85.5	3872.9	3954.1	42.1
NSG.def.240	3794.9	87.1	3890.7	3951.2	37.4
SMS.240	4018.4	99.3	4032.9	4038.8	5.1
NSG.240	4019.6	99.4	4033.5	4038.0	4.2
SMS.def.500	3879.0	92.1	3948.6	4025.0	34.8
NSG.def.500	3893.6	92.2	3950.4	4001.6	25.8
SMS.500	4035.6	99.8	4038.9	4039.5	0.8
NSG.500	4036.6	99.8	4038.7	4039.3	0.5
MSPO.120	4034.7	99.8	4038.6	4039.8	1.2

5. SUMMARY AND OUTLOOK

This paper investigates the cyclone (dust separator) optimization problem. After describing the problem itself, objectives, and parameters, algorithms for solving this problem are presented. These algorithms are first tested with their default parameter settings. Afterwards, the algorithms' parameters a tuned under different specifications. Firstly, a target hypervolume value is specified and the algorithms are tuned to require as few FE as possible. Secondly, very small budgets were imposed and the algorithms were tuned for a best performance w.r.t. hypervolume. Finally, results have been validated implementing an alternative model for one of the objectives.

It is found that tuned algorithm parameters perform much better than the default settings. The results for a fixed FE' budget point to a certain parameterization with a population size of three and a mutation dominated variation that promise good results for further investigations, particularly incorporating more complex simulation models.

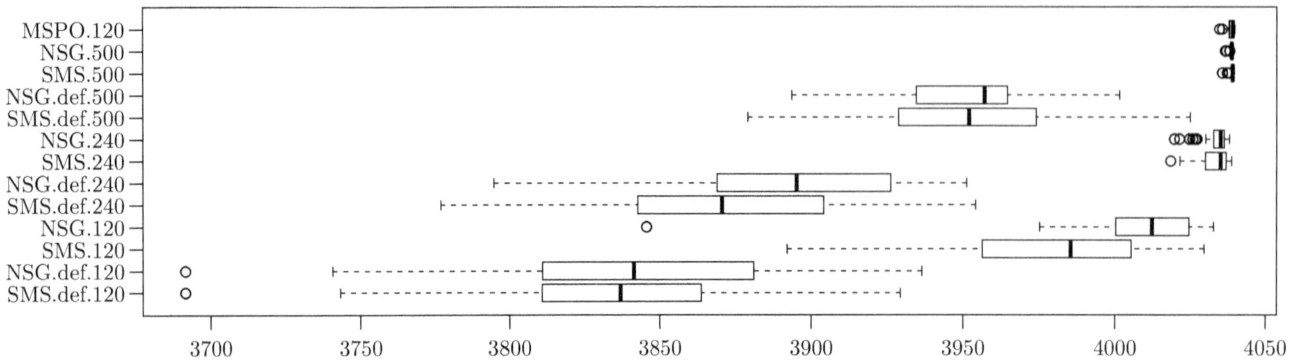

Figure 7: Boxplot of hypervolumes for default algorithm parameters (.def) as well as tuned parameters. Based on validation experiments with COP2.

Moreover, the surrogate model based MSPO approach with a very limited budget of FE performed extremely well in our comparison. Therefore, this strategy will be investigated in more detail in future research. Further research directions w.r.t. MSPO could concern the choice of model, optimization technique, or infill criteria.

Acknowledgments.
This work has been kindly supported by the Federal Ministry of Education and Research (BMBF) under the grants MCIOP (FKZ 17N0311) and CIMO (FKZ 17002X11).

6. REFERENCES

[1] W. Barth. Berechnung und Auslegung von Zyklonabscheidern auf Grund neuerer Untersuchungen. *Brennstoff-Wärme-Kraft*, 8(1):1–9, 1956.
[2] T. Bartz-Beielstein, C. Lasarczyk, and M. Preuß. Sequential parameter optimization. In B. McKay et al., editors, *Congress on Evolutionary Computation (CEC'05)*, pages 773–780. IEEE Press, Piscataway NJ, 2005.
[3] N. Beume, B. Naujoks, and M. Emmerich. SMS-EMOA: Multiobjective selection based on dominated hypervolume. *European Journal of Operational Research*, 181(3):1653–1669, 2007.
[4] K. Deb, S. Agrawal, A. Pratab, and T. Meyarivan. A Fast Elitist Non-Dominated Sorting Genetic Algorithm for Multi-Objective Optimization: NSGA-II. In M. Schoenauer et al., editors, *Parallel Problem Solving from Nature VI*, pages 849–858. Springer, Berlin, 2000.
[5] K. Elsayed and C. Lacor. Optimization of the cyclone separator geometry for minimum pressure drop using mathematical models and CFD simulations. *Chemical Engineering Science*, 65(22):6048 – 6058, 2010.
[6] K. Elsayed and C. Lacor. Modeling and Pareto optimization of gas cyclone separator performance using RBF type artificial neural networks and genetic algorithms. *Powder Technology*, 217(0):84 – 99, 2012.
[7] A. Forrester, A. Sobester, and A. Keane. *Engineering Design via Surrogate Modelling*. Wiley, Chichester UK, 2008.
[8] J. D. Knowles and H. Nakayama. Meta-modeling in multiobjective optimization. In *Multiobjective Optimization*, pages 245–284. Springer, 2008.
[9] F. Löffler. *Staubabscheiden*. Thieme, 1988.
[10] H. Mothes and F. Löffler. Motion and deposition of particles in cyclones. *German chemical engineering*, 8(4):223–233, 1985.
[11] E. Muschelknautz. Die Berechnung von Zyklonabscheidern für Gase. *Chemie Ingenieur Technik*, 44(1-2):63–71, 1972.
[12] E. Muschelknautz. *Vt-Hochschulkurs 2, mechanische Verfahrenstechnik*. Krausskopf, 1972.
[13] S. I. Pishbin and M. Moghiman. Optimization of cyclone separators using genetic algorithm. *International Review of Chemical Engineering*, 2(6):683–691, 2010.
[14] K. Price. Differential evolution: A fast and simple numerical optimizer. In *NAFIPS'96*, pages 524–525, 1996.
[15] G. Ravi, S. K. Gupta, and M. B. Ray. Multiobjective optimization of cyclone separators using genetic algorithm. *Industrial & Engineering Chemistry Research*, 39(11):4272–4286, 2000.
[16] H. Safikhani, A. Hajiloo, and M. Ranjbar. Modeling and multi-objective optimization of cyclone separators using CFD and genetic algorithms. *Computers & Chemical Engineering*, 35(6):1064 – 1071, 2011.
[17] M. Zaefferer, T. Bartz-Beielstein, M. Friese, B. Naujoks, and O. Flasch. Multi-criteria optimization for hard problems under limited budgets. In T. Soule et al., editors, *Genetic and evolutionary computation conference (GECCO'12)*, pages 1451–1452. ACM, NY, 2012.
[18] M. Zaefferer, T. Bartz-Beielstein, B. Naujoks, T. Wagner, and M. Emmerich. A case study on multi-criteria optimization of an event detection software under limited budgets. In R. C. Purshouse et al., editors, *Evolutionary Multi-Criterion Optimization (EMO'13)*, pages 756–770. Springer, Heidelberg, 2013.

Improved Heuristics for Solving OCL Constraints using Search Algorithms

Shaukat Ali
Simula Research Laboratory
Norway
shaukat@simula.no

Muhammad Zohaib Iqbal
Quest Lab, National University of Computer & Emerging Sciences, Pakistan and
SnT Luxembourg, Luxembourg
zohaib.iqbal@nu.edu.pk

Andrea Arcuri
Simula Research Laboratory
Norway
arcuri@simula.no

ABSTRACT
The Object Constraint Language (OCL) is a standard language for specifying constraints on Unified Modeling Language (UML) models. The specified constraints can be used for various purposes including verification, and model-based testing (e.g., test data generation). Efficiently solving OCL constraints is one of the key requirements for the practical use of OCL. In this paper, we propose an improvement in existing heuristics to solve OCL constraints using search algorithms. We evaluate our improved heuristics using two empirical studies with three search algorithms: Alternating Variable Method (AVM), (1+1) Evolutionary Algorithm (EA), and a Genetic Algorithm (GA). We also used Random Search (RS) as a comparison baseline. The first empirical study was conducted using carefully designed artificial problems (constraints) to assess each individual heuristics. The second empirical study is based on an industrial case study provided by Cisco about model-based testing of Video Conferencing Systems. The results of both empirical evaluations reveal that the effectiveness of the search algorithms, measured in terms of time to solve the OCL constraints to generate data, is significantly improved when using the novel heuristics presented in this paper. In particular, our experiments show that (1+1) EA with the novel heuristics has the highest success rate among all the analyzed algorithms, as it requires the least number of iterations to solve constraints.

Categories and Subject Descriptors
D.2.5 [**Software Engineering**]: Testing and Debugging

I.2.8 [**Artificial Intelligence**]: Problem Solving, Control Methods, and Search

General Terms
Algorithms, Performance, Experimentation, Theory, Verification

Keywords
UML; OCL; Search-based testing; Test data; Empirical evaluation

1. INTRODUCTION
The Object Constraint Language (OCL) [1] is a standard language to specify constraints on Unified Modeling Language (UML) models such as Class Diagrams and State Machines [2]. There are several purposes for writing constraints on the UML models, such as to give precise meaning to models and support automation. The constraints specified on the UML models may require to be solved for various applications, for example proving properties of a system and test data generation to support model-based testing. Solving complex industrial OCL constraints can be difficult due to a large number of clauses in the constraints, which might include specialized OCL operations such as *oclInState()*, *includesAll*, *forAll()* and a large number of attributes or collections of attributes used in those constraints.

To efficiently solve OCL constraints, a set of heuristics were proposed in [3, 4] based on branch distance [5] for various OCL constructs and operations to guide search algorithms including Genetic Algorithm (GA), (1+1) Evolutionary Algorithm (EA), and Alternating Variable Method (AVM). In this paper, we propose novel, improved heuristics for solving constraints on Boolean operations defined in OCL including *and*, *or*, *xor*, and *implies*. The aim is to further improve the performance of search algorithms in order to efficiently solve constraints. Our motivating assumption is that instead of solving a complicated constraint consisting of several clauses all together, we can improve the performance by solving independent clauses separately and, then, combining the results of the independent clauses to solve the complicated constraint.

We empirically evaluate the performance of the improved heuristics by conducting two sets of experiments. The first set of experiments compares the improved heuristics with existing heuristics using 28 artificial problems (constraints) carefully designed to evaluate each heuristic. The results showed that the improved heuristics significantly improve the effectiveness of all the algorithms to solve the constraints. However, GA and RS showed worse performance when compared to (1+1) EA and AVM for both improved and existing heuristics. The second set of experiments was performed on a real industrial case study of model-based robustness testing of a Video Conferencing System developed by Cisco. We evaluated our improved heuristics on 42 constraints from the industrial case study using the three search algorithms and RS. The results were consistent with the results from the artificial problems, where the novel heuristics significantly improved the performance of the search algorithms. Overall, our experiments revealed that (1+1) EA with the novel heuristics was the most efficient among all the studied algorithms.

The rest of the paper is organized as follows: Section 2 provides background information, Section 3 describes our novel heuristics, whereas Section 4 and Section 5 present the results of two empirical evaluations. Section 6 provides overall discussion on the empirical evaluations followed by describing threats to validity in Section 7.

GECCO'14, July 12–16, 2014, Vancouver, BC, Canada.

http://dx.doi.org/10.1145/2576768.2598308

We discuss related work in Section 8 and finally we conclude the paper in Section 9.

2. BACKGROUND

In [1, 6], the authors proposed and assessed novel heuristics for the application of search-based techniques, such as Genetic Algorithms (GAs), (1+1) Evolutionary Algorithm (EA), and Alternating Variable Method (AVM), to generate test data from OCL constraints. A set of heuristics were defined to guide a search algorithm to find test data that satisfy OCL constraints. The heuristics were implemented as a fitness function that is adapted from work done for code coverage (e.g., for branch coverage in C code [5]). In particular, branch distance (a function *d()*) was used as defined in [5]. The function *d()* returns *0* if the constraint is solved, a value *k* if the constraint evaluates to undefined (a special value in OCL that makes OCL a three-valued logic [1]) otherwise a positive value greater than 0 and less that *k* that heuristically estimates how far the constraint was from being evaluated to true. The work reported in [1, 6] defined various novel heuristics for calculating branch distances for various constructs and operations defined in OCL such as *includes()*, *oclInState()*, and *forAll()*.

The operations defined in OCL to combine *Boolean* clauses are *or*, *xor*, *and*, *not*, *if then else*, and *implies*. For these operations, branch distances were extended (Table I) from the ones proposed in [5], since the ones proposed in [5] work only in programming languages with two-valued Boolean logic. The operations *implies* and *xor* are syntactic sugars that usually do not appear in programming languages such as C and Java, and can be re-expressed using combinations of *and* and *or* operators. The evaluation of *d()* on a constraint composed by two clauses is specified in Table I and can simply be computed for more than two clauses recursively. In this paper, we provide improvement in calculating branch distance for these operations as we will discuss in the next section.

Table I. Branch Distance Calculation for OCL's Boolean Operations

Operation	Distance function
A	**if** A is **true** **then** d(A)=0 **else** A is **false** **then** d(A)>0 and d(A)< k **else** **then** d(A)=k
not A	**if** A is **false** **then** d(A)=0 **else** A is **true** **then** d(A)>0 and d(A)< k **else** **then** d(A)=k
A and B	numberOfUndefinedClauses + nor (d(A)+d(B))
A or B	numberOfUndefinedClauses + nor (min (d(A),d(B)))
A implies B	d(not A or B)
if A then B else C	d((A and B) or (not A and C))
A xor B	d((A and not B) or (not A and B))

3. IMPROVED BRANCH DISTANCE CALCULATION FOR LOGICAL OPERATIONS

This section presents our improved branch distance calculation for the *Boolean* operations defined in OCL. As mentioned in Section 2, in total there are six operations in OCL for *Boolean* clauses. Among them, *and*, *or*, *xor*, and *implies* are binary operations and therefore can be used to combine different constraints. Our main assumption behind defining the branch distance for these operations is that, by dividing a complex constraint into a set of small independent constraints and then solving each of them individually, we can bring significant improvement over solving the whole constraint at the same time. By independent constraint, we mean that the variables used in one constraint are not used in the other constraints belonging to the main complex constraint. Mathematically, we can say that a complicated constraint *C* consisting of *n* clauses combined using any of the *Boolean* operations (e.g., *or*, *and*) can be divided into a set *CI* of independent constraints, where $CI= \{CI_1, CI_2, ..CI_m\}$, where $m<=n$. Each CI_i is independent, if all variables *v* involved in CI_i are not used in any variable involved in CI_x, where *x* is from *1* to *m* excluding *i*. Below, we provide improved branch distance calculations for each of the *Boolean* operations defined in OCL. In this section, we show calculation of branch distance on a constraint consisting of two clauses and separated by a *Boolean* operation. However, this calculation can simply be computed for more than two clauses joined using different *Boolean* operations recursively.

3.1 Improved-and Branch Distance Calculation

In the case of *and*, since each CI_i is conjuncted, each CI_i must be solved to obtain the overall result for the complicated constraint *C*. If any CI_i was not solved, then this means that *C* was not solved successfully.

3.2 Improved-or Branch Distance Calculation

Each CI_i in this case is disjuncted and solving only one CI_i will solve *C*. To improve the performance, first we calculate branch distance for each CI_i based on a randomly generated test case. Then we select an independent constraint CI_j from *CI*, which has the minimum branch distance. After selecting CI_j, we instruct the search algorithm to only solve CI_j, thus avoiding the cost of solving and evaluating the remaining independent constraints. In this case, we need to calculate *n* branch distance calculations corresponding to *n* independent constraints in *C*, prior to solving the selected CI_j. For example, if we have a constraint A *or* B, then branch distance is calculated as follows:

If (d(A) <= d(B)) **then** Solve for *A*
else Solve for *B*

However, it could be possible that the chosen CI_j is not feasible. In such cases, if within a predefined number of fitness evaluations the fitness does not improve, then the search is re-directed toward one of the other clauses.

3.3 Improved-implies Branch Distance Calculation

The result of *implies* operation is *true* in the following two cases: (1) *false implies true/false;* (2) *true/false implies true*. To explain branch distance calculation in this case, consider a simple constraint *A implies B*, where *A* and *B* are two operands. By exploiting the definition of *implies*, we calculate branch distance as follows.

If (d(not A)<= d(B)) **then** Solve for *not A*
else Solve for *B*

Notice that we need one branch distance calculation to calculate *d(not A)* and one to calculate *d(B)* based on a randomly generated test case. This means that we need two calculations at the beginning to select either *not A* or *B*, depending on which one has the minimum distance. Later on, the selected one is solved by a search algorithm.

3.4 Improved-xor Branch Distance Calculation

The result of *xor* operator is *true* if any one of the operands is *true* and the other is *false* at the same time. In this case, by exploiting the definition of *xor*, we calculate branch distance as follows:

Considering the example: *A xor B*
If (d(A)+d(*not* B) <= d(*not* A) +d (B)) **then**

Solve for *(A and not B)* using *improved-and*

else

Solve for *(not A and B)* using *improved-and*

This means that we will calculate the branch distance for both *A and not B* and *not A and B* based on a randomly generated test case. We then make the search algorithm solve the constraint that has minimum branch distance. In this case, we need four branch distance calculations at the beginning based on a randomly generated test case to select *d(A)+d(Not B)* or *d(notA) +d (B)*.

4. EMPIRICAL EVALUATION ON ARTIFICAL PROBLEMS

4.1 Experiments Design

To empirically evaluate whether the improved heuristics (*IM*) defined in Section 3 really improve the effectiveness of a search algorithm as compared to existing heuristics, *Not IMproved* (*NIM*), we carefully defined artificial problems to evaluate each improved heuristic. For each of the four *Boolean* operations, we defined seven artificial problems covering various significant OCL operations such as *forAll*, *include*, and *one*. The model we used for the experiment consists of a very simple class diagram with one class *B*. *B* has two attributes *x* and *y* of type *Integer*. Due to space limitations, we do not provide full details of all the artificial problems used in the paper. However, the readers are requested to see the corresponding technical report, where we provide the problems in full [7].

In our experiments, we compared three search algorithms: AVM, GA, (1+1) EA, and used RS as a comparison baseline to assess the difficulty of the addressed problems [8]. AVM was selected as a representative of local search algorithms. GA was selected since it is the most commonly used global search algorithm in search-based software engineering [8]. (1+1) EA is simpler than GAs, but we found that it can be more effective for software testing problems (e.g., see [9, 10]). For GA, we set the population size to 100 and the crossover rate to 0.75, with a 1.5 bias for rank selection. We use a standard one-point crossover, and mutation of a variable is done with the standard probability 1/n, where n is the number of variables. Different settings would lead to different performance of a search algorithm, but standard settings usually perform well [11].

In this first set of experiments, we address the following research questions:

RQ1: Does *IM* improve the effectiveness of search over *NIM*?

RQ2: Among the considered search algorithms (AVM, GA, (1+1) EA), which one fares best in solving OCL constraints using *IM* and how do they compare to RS?

To compare the algorithms for *IM* and *NIM*, we followed the

Table II. Results for artificial problems for each algorithm for *IM* and *NIM**

	AVM				(1+1) EA				RS				GA			
P#	S(IM)	S(NIM)	O/A	p-value	S(IM)	S(NIM)	O/A	p-value	S(IM)	S(NIM)	O/A	p-value	S(IM)	S(NIM)	O/A	p-value
1	0.54	0.31	2	0.001	1	0.43	265	1.51E-22	0	0	*0.5*	*1*	0	0	*0.5*	*1*
2	0.95	1	*0.23*	*1.07E-07*	0.81	0.19	17	4.09E-19	0	0	*0.5*	*1*	0	0	*0.5*	*1*
3	1	1	*0.63*	*0.006*	1	0.87	*0.758*	*2.38E-05*	0	0	*0.5*	*1*	0	0	*0.5*	*1*
4	1	1	*0.59*	*0.049*	1	1	*0.972*	*5.85E-18*	0	0	*0.5*	*1*	0	0	*0.5*	*1*
5	1	1	*0.48*	*0.47*	1	1	*0.961*	*1.02E-16*	0	0	*0.5*	*1*	0	0	*0.5*	*1*
6	0	0.01	1	0.33	0.74	0.62	*0.538*	*0.04*	0	0	*0.5*	*1*	0	0	*0.5*	*1*
7	0.35	0.09	5	1.27E-05	1	1	*0.907*	*5.48E-15*	0	0	*0.5*	*1*	0	0	*0.5*	*1*
8	0.51	0.71	0.42	0.0051	1	1	*0.51*	*4.20E-02*	0.31	0.16	2	0.01	1	0.91	20	0.003
9	0.94	1	0.07	0.02	0.93	0.12	88	4.81E-34	0.14	0.18	*0.52*	*4.34E-01*	1	0.86	*0.71*	*9.86E-07*
10	1	1	*0.61*	*0.08*	1	0.86	33	7.49E-05	0.17	0.16	*0.49*	*0.8*	1	0.86	*0.68*	*1.87E-06*
11	1	1	*0.8*	*4.15E-12*	1	1	*0.544*	*3.23E-01*	1	1	*0.51*	*0.5*	1	1	*0.5*	*0.86*
12	1	1	*0.5*	*1*	1	1	*0.5*	*1*	1	1	*0.5*	*1*	1	1	*0.5*	*1*
13	0.02	0	7.51	8.20E-11	0.83	0.72	*0.421*	*7.16E-02*	0.01	0.02	*0.5*	*0.78*	1	0.99	*0.79*	*2.29E-10*
14	0.22	0.35	12.33	0.001	1	1	*0.296*	*7.40E-09*	0	0	*0.5*	*1*	0.68	0.19	8	2.53E-12
15	1	0.8	51	6.64E-07	1	1	*1*	*3.96E-18*	1	0.33	405	4.05E-28	1	0.92	18	0.006
16	1	0.99	*1*	*3.95E-18*	1	0.19	840	1.08E-37	1	0.13	1303	8.48E-43	1	0.77	61	5.71E-08
17	1	0.99	*1*	*3.87E-18*	1	0.85	36	3.46E-05	1	0.24	628	5.75E-34	1	0.82	45	3.29E-06
18	1	1	*1*	*1.55E-23*	1	1	*1*	*3.93E-18*	1	1	1	3.90E-18	1	1	1	3.90E-18
19	1	1	*1*	*3.88E-18*	1	1	*1*	*1.55E-23*	1	1	1	1.55E-23	1	1	1	1.55E-23
20	1	0	40401	2.21E-59	1	0.73	75	1.96E-09	1	0.01	13333	2.23E-57	1	0.88	28	0.0003
21	1	0.32	424	1.01E-28	1	1	*1*	*3.95E-18*	1	0	40401	2.21E-59	1	0.24	628	5.75E-34
22	1	0.78	57	1.30E-07	1	1	*0.705*	*3.29E-06*	0	0.26	0.01	4.60E-09	0	0.86	0.0008	6.91E-42
23	1	1	*0.27*	*3.43E-05*	1	0.11	1564	1.05E-44	0	0.17	0.02	7.26E-06	0	0.74	0.001	1.39E-32
24	1	0.97	*0.34*	*0.002*	1	0.9	23	0.001	0	0.18	0.02	3.29E-06	0	0.81	0.001	1.08E-37
25	1	1	*0.97*	*1.68E-14*	1	1	*0.785*	*1.13E-10*	0	1	2.48E-05	2.21E-59	0	1	2.48E-05	2.21E-59
26	0.23	1	0.001	1.11E-34	1	1	*0*	*3.96E-18*	0	1	2.48E-05	2.21E-59	0	1	2.48E-05	2.21E-59
27	1	0	40401	2.21E-59	1	0.72	79	8.25E-10	0	0.05	0.08	0.059	0	0.98	0.0001	1.14E-55
28	1	0.45	245	1.59E-21	1	1	*0.5*	*1.68E-02*	0	0	*0.5*	*1*	0	0.14	0.029	7.49E-05
M	0.81	0.71	NA		0.98	0.80	NA		0.34	0.28	NA		0.49	0.61	NA	

*M: Mean, P: Problem, S(IM): Success rate for IM, S(NIM): Success rate for NIM, O/A: Represents O, i.e., Odds Ratio if results were significant based on success rates (non-italicized) otherwise represents A, i.e., Â12 when the results are not significant based on success rates (Italics), p-value: Italicized for Mann-Whitney U and non-Italicized for Fisher's Exact test, NA: Not Applicable

guidelines defined in [12], which recommends a number of statistical procedures to assess randomized test strategies. First, we calculated the success rate for each algorithm, which is defined as the number of times a solution was found out of the total number of runs (100 in this case). These success rates are then compared using the Fisher Exact test (with a significance level of 0.05), quantifying the effect size using an odds ratio with a 0.5 correction. We chose Fisher Exact test since for each run of algorithms the result is binary, i.e., either the result is *'found'* or *'not found'* and this is exactly the situation for which the Fisher's exact test is defined. In addition to statistical significance, we used odds ratios as the results of our experiments are dichotomous. A value greater than 1 means that *IM* has more chances of success as compared to *NIM*, whereas a value of 1 means no differences.

When the differences between the success rates of *IM* and *NIM* were not significant for an algorithm, we further compared the number of iterations taken by the algorithm for *IM* and *NIM* to solve the problems. For this purpose, we used Mann-Whitney U-test [13], at a significance level of 0.05. In addition, we report effect size measurements using Vargha and Delaney's Â12 statistics, which is a non-parametric effect size measure. In our context, a value of Â12 less than 0.5 tells that *NIM* is better than *IM* in finding solutions in lesser number of iterations. A value of 0.5 tells that there is no difference between *IM* and *NIM*, whereas a value greater than 0.5 tells that *IM* is better than *NIM* in finding solutions in lesser number of iterations. In Table II, Table III, and Table IV, results for Mann-Whitney U-test and Â12 are italicized and are only shown when the differences are not significant based on success rates.

Table III. Results for artificial problems for *IM* across algorithms*

	AVM vs (1+1) EA		AVM vs RS		AVM vs GA		(1+1) EA vs RS		1+1(EA) vs GA		RS vs GA	
P#	p-value	O/A	p-value	O/A	p-value	O/A	p-value	O/A	p-value	O/A	p-value	O/A
1	3.17E-17	0.005	5.05E-21	236	5.05E-21	236	2.21E-59	40401	2.21E-59	40401	1	1
2	0.003	4	2.13E-51	3490	2.13E-51	3490	1.08E-37	840	1.08E-37	840	1	1
3	*0.11*	*0.43*	2.21E-59	40401	2.21E-59	40401	2.21E-59	40401	2.21E-59	40401	1	1
4	*3.13E-05*	*0.32*	2.21E-59	40401	2.21E-59	40401	2.21E-59	40401	2.21E-59	40401	1	1
5	*0.0005*	*0.33*	2.21E-59	40401	2.21E-59	40401	2.21E-59	40401	2.21E-59	40401	1	1
6	1.39E-32	0.001	1	1	1	1	1.39E-32	565	1.39E-32	565	1	1
7	6.16E-27	0.002	1.56E-12	109	1.56E-12	109	2.21E-59	40401	2.21E-59	40401	1	1
8	1.32E-18	0.005	0.006	2	1.32E-18	0	2.44E-29	443	1	1	2.44E-29	0.002
9	0.08	0.51	2.22E-33	87	0.02	0	2.58E-32	74	0.01	0.06	6.91E-42	0.001
10	0.13	0.59	2.64E-39	959	1	1	2.64E-39	959	1	1	2.64E-39	0.001
11	0.002	0.61	1	1	1	1	1	1	1	1	1	1
12	1	0.50	1	1	1	1	1	1	1	1	1	1
13	6.91E-36	0.005	1	2	1.14E-55	0.0001	1.90E-37	317	7.26E-06	0.02	2.23E-57	7.50E-05
14	2.08E-35	0.001	1.30E-07	58	7.19E-11	0.13	2.21E-59	40401	2.41E-11	95	1.01E-28	0.002
15	*1*	*0.5*	*1*	*0.5*	*1*	*0.5*	*1*	*0.5*	*1*	*0.5*	1	1
16	*1*	*0.5*	*1*	*0.5*	*1*	*0.5*	*1*	*0.5*	*1*	*0.5*	1	1
17	*1*	*0.5*	*1*	*0.5*	*1*	*0.5*	*1*	*0.5*	*1*	*0.5*	1	1
18	*1*	*0.5*	*1*	*0.5*	*1*	*0.5*	*1*	*0.5*	*1*	*0.5*	1	1
19	*1*	*0.5*	*1*	*0.5*	*1*	*0.5*	*1*	*0.5*	*1*	*0.5*	1	1
20	*1*	*0.5*	*1*	*0.5*	*1*	*0.5*	*1*	*0.5*	*1*	*0.5*	1	1
21	*1*	*0.5*	*1*	*0.5*	*1*	*0.5*	*1*	*0.5*	*1*	*0.5*	1	1
22	*0.03*	*0.42*	2.21E-59	40401	2.21E-59	40401	2.21E-59	40401	2.21E-59	40401	1	1
23	*0.001*	*0.39*	2.21E-59	40401	2.21E-59	40401	2.21E-59	40401	2.21E-59	40401	1	1
24	*3.15E-05*	*0.34*	2.21E-59	40401	2.21E-59	40401	2.21E-59	40401	2.21E-59	40401	1	1
25	*0.0004*	*0.32*	2.21E-59	40401	2.21E-59	40401	2.21E-59	40401	2.21E-59	40401	1	1
26	1.11E-34	0.002	5.71E-08	61	5.71E-08	61	2.21E-59	40401	2.21E-59	40401	1	1
27	*8.37E-05*	*0.37*	2.21E-59	40401	2.21E-59	40401	2.21E-59	40401	2.21E-59	40401	1	1
28	*0.005*	*0.38*	2.21E-59	40401	2.21E-59	40401	2.21E-59	40401	2.21E-59	40401	1	1

* O/A: Represents O, i.e., Odds Ratio if results were significant based on success rates (non-italicized) otherwise represents A, i.e., Â12 when the results are not significant based on success rates (Italics), p-value: Italicized for Mann-Whitney U and non-Italicized for Fisher's Exact test

4.2 Experiment Execution

We executed each of the four algorithms 100 times with both *IM* and *NIM* for the 28 problems. We let the algorithms run up to 10,000 fitness evaluations on each problem and collected data on whether the algorithms found solutions for *IM* and *NIM*. We used a PC with Intel Core Duo CPU 2.20 GHz with 4 GB of RAM, running Microsoft Windows 7 operating system for the execution of experiment.

Table IV. Results for industrial constraints for each algorithm for *IM* and *NIM**

	AVM				(1+1) EA				RS				GA			
P#	S(IM)	S(NIM)	O/A	p-value	S(IM)	S(NIM)	O/A	p-value	S(IM)	S(NIM)	O/A	p-value	S(IM)	S(NIM)	O/A	p-value
1	1	1	0.68	*5.73E-07*	1	0.5	201	4.45E-19	1	0.1	1732	1.04E-45	1	0.3	465	5.77E-30
2	1	1	*0.74*	*3.05E-05*	1	0.7	87	1.43E-10	1	0.1	1732	1.04E-45	1	0.2	789	6.51E-37
3	1	1	*0.83*	*2.20E-13*	1	0.61	129	3.54E-14	1	0.03	5599	3.91E-54	1	0.25	595	2.87E-33
4	1	1	*0.85*	*8.05E-12*	1	0.59	140	5.03E-15	1	0.01	13333	2.23E-57	1	0.19	840	1.08E-37
5	1	1	*0.75*	*1.21E-07*	1	0.68	95	2.41E-11	1	0.02	7919	1.14E-55	1	0.17	959	2.64E-39
6	1	1	*0.80*	*6.77E-10*	1	0.65	109	1.56E-12	1	0	40401	2.21E-59	1	0.14	1199	6.91E-42
7	1	1	*0.83*	*1.02E-13*	1	1	*0.34*	*0.005*	1	0.8	51	6.64E-07	1	0.7	87	1.43E-10
8	1	1	*0.73*	*2.67E-08*	1	0.8	51	6.64E-07	1	0.4	300	3.90E-24	1	0.9	23	0.001
9	1	1	*0.72*	*4.49E-06*	1	0.87	31	0.0001	1	0.42	277	4.54E-23	1	0.93	16	0.01
10	1	1	*0.71*	*6.65E-06*	1	0.83	42	7.26E-06	1	0.46	236	5.05E-21	1	0.85	36	3.46E-05
11	1	1	*0.62*	*0.008*	1	0.89	26	0.0007	1	0.26	565	1.39E-32	1	0.79	54	2.95E-07
12	1	1	*0.70*	*2.40E-06*	1	0.85	36	3.46E-05	1	0.35	371	6.16E-27	1	0.83	42	7.26E-06
13	1	1	*0.64*	*6.20E-07*	1	0.8	51	6.64E-07	1	0.1	1732	1.04E-45	1	0.4	300	3.90E-24
14	1	1	*0.72*	*3.20E-05*	1	0.7	87	1.43E-10	1	0.1	1732	1.04E-45	1	0.4	300	3.90E-24
15	1	1	*0.74*	*3.60E-07*	1	0.69	91	5.90E-11	1	0.05	3490	2.13E-51	1	0.37	340	8.62E-26
16	1	1	*0.75*	*1.54E-06*	1	0.66	104	3.91E-12	1	0.12	1423	9.76E-44	1	0.38	326	3.13E-25
17	1	1	*0.77*	*5.02E-08*	1	0.76	64	2.48E-08	1	0.06	2922	3.77E-50	1	0.17	959	2.64E-39
18	1	1	*0.70*	*1.17E-05*	1	0.69	91	5.90E-11	1	0.03	5599	3.91E-54	1	0.22	701	2.08E-35
19	1	1	*0.76*	*3.87E-08*	1	0.68	95	2.41E-11	1	0.12	1423	9.76E-44	1	0.43	266	1.51E-22
20	1	1	*0.71*	*5.96E-05*	1	0.89	26	0.0007	1	0.18	896	1.73E-38	1	0.64	114	6.13E-13
21	1	1	*0.81*	*2.19E-10*	1	0.66	104	3.91E-12	1	0.05	3490	2.13E-51	1	0.3	465	5.77E-30
22	1	1	*0.80*	*6.85E-09*	1	0.66	104	3.91E-12	1	0.02	7919	1.14E-55	1	0.31	443	2.44E-29
23	1	1	*0.00*	*3.95E-18*	0.55	1	0.01	8.93E-17	0.05	1	0.0002	2.13E-51	0.21	1	0.001	3.75E-36
24	1	1	*0.74*	*3.73E-07*	1	0.72	79	8.25E-10	1	0	40401	2.21E-59	1	0.21	743	3.75E-36
25	1	1	*0.72*	*3.82E-06*	1	0.85	36	3.46E-05	1	0.66	104	3.91E-12	1	0.94	14	0.02
26	1	1	*0.65*	*0.01*	1	0.95	*0.48*	*0.65*	1	0.92	*0.43*	*0.11*	1	0.97	*0.53*	*0.49*
27	1	1	*0.72*	*4.49E-06*	1	0.87	31	0.0001	1	0.42	277	4.54E-23	1	0.93	16	0.01
28	1	1	*0.71*	*6.65E-06*	1	0.83	42	7.26E-06	1	0.46	236	5.05E-21	1	0.85	36	3.46E-05
29	1	1	*0.62*	*0.008*	1	0.89	26	0.0007	1	0.26	565	1.39E-32	1	0.79	54	2.95E-07
30	1	1	*0.74*	*3.73E-07*	1	0.72	79	8.25E-10	1	0	40401	2.21E-59	1	0.21	743	3.75E-36
31	1	1	*0.76*	*3.87E-08*	1	0.68	95	2.41E-11	1	0.12	1423	9.76E-44	1	0.43	266	1.51E-22
32	1	1	*0.71*	*5.96E-05*	1	0.89	26	0.0007	1	0.18	896	1.73E-38	1	0.64	114	6.13E-13
33	1	1	*0.81*	*2.19E-10*	1	0.66	104	3.91E-12	1	0.05	3490	2.13E-51	1	0.3	465	5.77E-30
34	1	1	*0.80*	*6.85E-09*	1	0.66	104	3.91E-12	1	0.02	7919	1.14E-55	1	0.31	443	2.44E-29
35	1	1	*0.73*	*2.52E-07*	1	0.69	91	5.90E-11	1	0.03	5599	3.91E-54	1	0.18	896	1.73E-38
36	1	1	*0.74*	*3.73E-07*	1	0.72	79	8.25E-10	1	0	40401	2.21E-59	1	0.21	743	3.75E-36
37	1	1	*0.77*	*9.70E-09*	1	0.73	75	1.96E-09	1	0.12	1423	9.76E-44	1	0.52	186	3.85E-18
38	1	1	*0.76*	*2.48E-09*	1	0.82	45	3.29E-06	1	0.22	701	2.08E-35	1	0.66	104	3.91E-12
39	1	1	*0.74*	*3.60E-07*	1	0.69	91	5.90E-11	1	0.05	3490	2.13E-51	1	0.37	340	8.62E-26
40	1	1	*0.75*	*1.54E-06*	1	0.66	104	3.91E-12	1	0.12	1423	9.76E-44	1	0.38	326	3.13E-25
41	1	1	*0.77*	*5.02E-08*	1	0.76	64	2.48E-08	1	0.06	2922	3.77E-50	1	0.17	959	2.64E-39
42	1	1	*0.70*	*1.17E-05*	1	0.69	91	5.90E-11	1	0.03	5599	3.91E-54	1	0.22	701	2.08E-35
M	1	1	NA		0.99	0.75	NA		0.98	0.20	NA		0.98	0.48	NA	

*M: Mean, P: Problem, S(IM): Success rate for IM, S(NIM): Success rate for NIM, O/A: Represents O, i.e., Odds Ratio if results were significant based on success rates (non-italicized) otherwise represents A, i.e., Â12 when the results are not significant based on success rates (Italics), p-value: Italicized for Mann-Whitney U and non-Italicized for Fisher's Exact test, NA: Not Applicable

4.3 Experiment Results and Analysis

In this section, we will answer each of our research questions.

4.3.1 Comparision of *IM* and *NIM* for each Algorithm (RQ1)

Table II shows the results for all the algorithms for *IM* and *NIM* for 28 (P1-P28) artificial problems. P1-P7 are designed for evaluating the *improved-and* heuristic, P8-P14 for the *improved-or* heuristic, P15-P21 for the *improved-implies* heuristic, and P22-P28 for the *improved-xor* heuristic.

First we discuss the performance of AVM for *IM* and *NIM*. As we observe in Table II that for the *Boolean* operation *and* (P1-P7), *IM* is significantly better than *NIM* for four problems (P1, P3, P4, and P7) and there are no significant differences for two problems (P5-P6) between *IM* and *NIM*. In case of P2, there is no significant difference between *IM* and *NIM* in terms of success rates, but *NIM* finds the solution faster than *IM*. For the operator *or*, we observed that for three problems (P10, P11, and P13) *IM* is significantly better than *NIM*, whereas for P8, P10, and P12, there were no significant differences. However, for P9 *NIM* is significantly better than *IM*. In case of *implies* operator, *IM* was significantly better than *NIM* for all problems, either based on success rates or number of iterations. For operator *xor*, *IM* was better than *NIM* for four problems and was worse for three problems. Out of two of these three problems, there were no significant differences between *IM* and *NIM*, though *NIM* found solutions quickly. Overall, we can conclude that *IM* improved the performance of search in 18 problems. For six of the problems, there were no significant differences between *IM* and *NIM*. For four of the remaining, there were no significant differences between *NIM* and *IM* in terms of success rates, though *NIM* found solutions in lesser number of iterations.

For (1+1) EA, in the case of *and*, *IM* is significantly better than *NIM* for all the problems. For *or*, *IM* is significantly better than *NIM* for all the problems except two. For P12, there were no significant differences. For P13, *IM* has higher success rate (0.83) than *NIM* (0.72), but not significant (*p-value* = 0.08). However, in terms of number of iterations for P13, *NIM* took significantly less number of iterations. For *implies*, *IM* is significantly better than *NIM* for all problems. For *xor*, *IM* is significantly better than *NIM* for all problems, except 22, and 26 in which cases *NIM* is better. But in all these three cases P19, P22, and P26, the success rates for both *IM* and *NIM* were equal to 100%. Therefore, we can conclude that for all these operators, (1+1) EA with *IM* shows significantly better results than *NIM*, except for the problems that were either simple for the algorithm (i.e., the success rate was 100%) or for P13, where the success rate of *IM* is better, but *NIM* finds the solution faster.

For RS, in the case of *and*, success rates for both *IM* and *NIM* are 0%. For *or*, we observed that for most of the problems (P10-P14), there are no significant differences between *IM* and *NIM*. For *implies*, *IM* is significantly better than *NIM* for all problems either based on success rates or number of iterations. Similar results are observed for *xor*, where *NIM* is significantly better than *IM* (P22-P26) or there are no significant differences (P27-P28). Although, success rates are again very low for RS, i.e., less than equal to 34% as it can be seen in Table II. Therefore, we can conclude that there is no significant benefit of using *IM* rather than *NIM* for RS as for both cases, the overall success rates are very low.

For GA, in case of *and*, both *NIM* and *IM* achieved 0% success rates. In case of *or*, *IM* performed significantly better than *NIM* either in terms of success rates or number of iterations except for P11 and P12. For *implies* and *xor*, success rates for *IM* are 0% for all the problems and thus *NIM* seems to perform significantly better than *IM* for these cases.

To summarize, we can answer our RQ1 as follows: (1+1) EA with *IM* significantly improve effectiveness of solving OCL constraints for generating test data. (1+1) EA has higher average success rates with *IM* than *NIM*, i.e., 0.98 (Table II). In addition, when there were no significant differences between *IM* and *NIM*, most of the time the algorithm managed to solve constraints in significantly lesser number of iterations than *NIM* for successful runs as it can be seen in italicized Â12 values are greater than 0.5 (eight column in Table II) with p-values less than 0.05. For AVM, for more than half of the problems (18 out of 28), *IM* significantly improved the effectiveness of search and for six problems no significant differences were observed in terms of both success rates and number of iterations. For most of the remaining problems, *IM* and *NIM* have no significant differences in success rates. For RS and GA, overall we obtained very low success rates for both *IM* and *NIM*, for instance, 39% and 49% for RS and GA respectively for *NIM*.

4.3.2 Comparision of Algorithms for IM (RQ2)

Table III presents results for *IM* across each pair of algorithms for the four algorithms. For each pair, whenever Odds Ratio (O) is greater than 1, this means that the first algorithm has more chances of success than the second one. For instance in comparison of (AVM vs RS), when O>1, this means that AVM has more chances of success than RS. In Table III, a value of Â12 (*A*) less than 0.5 means that the second algorithm is better than the first one in finding solutions in lesser number of iterations. A value of Â12=0.5 means no differences and a value greater than 0.5 means that first algorithm is better than the second one.

First we discuss the performance of AVM in comparison to other algorithms. In case of AVM vs (1+1) EA, for 18 out of 28 problems (1+1) EA showed significantly better results than AVM. For the ten remaining problems, there were no significant differences between the two algorithms. For AVM vs RS, in 17 problems AVM shows significantly better results than RS (indicated in Table III by *O* values greater than 1 and p-values less than 0.05). For the remaining 11 problems, there is no difference between the two algorithms. For AVM vs GA, in the case of 16 problems, AVM showed significantly better results than GA, for the other 11 there were no significant differences, whereas for P9, RS was significantly better than GA.

Next, we discuss the comparison of (1+1) EA with the remaining algorithms (GA and RS). For (1+1) EA vs RS, in case of 19 problems, (1+1) EA shows significantly better performance than RS. For the remaining nine problems, there were no significant differences. In case of (1+1) EA vs GA, for 16 problems (1+1) EA showed significantly better performance. For the 11 problems, there were no statistically significant differences, whereas for P9, GA was significantly better than (1+1) EA.

Finally, in case of RS vs GA, for 23 problems, there were no significant differences and for the remaining five problems (P8-P10, P13, P14), GA showed significantly better performance.
Based on the above results, we can conclude that (1+1) EA with *IM* is significantly better than the other algorithms and is best suited for generating test data for OCL constraints, followed by AVM.

5. INDUSTRIAL CASE STUDY

5.1 Introduction of the Case Study

Our industrial case study is part of a project aiming at supporting automated, model-based robustness testing of a core subsystem of a video conference system (VCS) called Saturn developed by Cisco Systems, Inc, Norway. The standard behavior of the system is modeled as a UML 2.0 state machine. In addition, we modeled robustness behavior separately as aspect state machines. The robustness behavior is modeled based on different functional and non-functional properties, whose violations lead to erroneous states. Such properties can be related to the VCS or its environment such as the network and other systems interacting with the SUT. In our case study, in total we have 57 constraints and 42 out of these 57 constraints have more than one clause and thus we included them in this experiment. These constraints contain between 6 and 8 clauses and all of these clauses were conjuncted, therefore we could only evaluate the *improved-and* heuristic. We followed exactly the same design and analysis methods as for artificial problems except that we ran each algorithm for 2,000 iterations due to time limitation to execute the experiment.

5.2 Results and Analysis

5.2.1 Comparision of IM and NIM for each Algorithm (RQ1)

Table IV presents results for *IM* and *NIM* for each of the 42 constraints for all the four algorithms. We observed that mean success rates using *IM* for all the algorithms are greater than equal to 98% ; however for *NIM* mean success rates are 100%, 80%, 20%, and 50% for AVM, (1+1) EA, RS, and GA, respectively.

For AVM, for both *IM* and *NIM*, success rates are 100%, therefore, we compared *IM* and *NIM* based on number iterations to solve problems. All Â12 values are greater than 0.5 and p-values less than 0.05 suggesting that *IM* took significantly less number of iterations to solve the problems. For the rest of the three algorithms, *IM* has either significantly higher success rates than *NIM* or took significantly lower iterations to solve the problems as it can be seen in Table IV except for Problem 23.

Based on the above results we can conclude that *IM* brought significant improvement to all the algorithms.

5.2.2 Comparision of Algorithms for IM (RQ2)

The results of this research question are provided in [7] due to space limitations. In terms of *IM* across algorithms as we can observe in Table IV that success rates for all four algorithms are greater than or equal to 98%; and thus the differences in terms of success rates are not significant. Therefore, we performed comparisons based on number of iterations for each pair of algorithms as shown in Table V of supplementary file. In Table V of supplementary file, a value of Â12 less than 0.5 means that the second algorithm has higher chances of finding a solution in lesser number of iterations than the first one. A value greater than 0.5 means first algorithm is better than the second one.

For AVM vs (1+1) EA, most of Â12 values are greater than 0.5 with p-values less than 0.05 (32 out of 42) suggesting that AVM has significantly higher chances of solving constraints in lesser number of iterations than (1+1) EA. Similar results can be seen for AVM vs RS (28 out of 42) and AVM vs GA (26 out of 42) in Table V of supplementary file. For (1+1) EA vs RS, for 23 out of 42 problems, (1+1) EA took significantly less iterations than RS, whereas in nine it took significantly more iterations than RS, and no differences were observed in 10 problems. For (1+1) EA vs GA, (1+1) EA took significantly less iterations than GA for 16 problems, where (1+1) EA took significantly more iterations than GA in 13 problems, and no differences were observed for the rest of the problems. For RS vs GA, in case of 16 problems Â12 values are below 0.5 with p-values less than 0.05 suggesting RS has significantly higher chances of solving constraints with more iterations than GA. For 12 problems, RS took significantly less iterations than GA, whereas for the remaining 14 problems no significant differences were observed.

Based on the above results, we can conclude that for the industrial case study, AVM has higher chances of solving constraints with lesser number of iterations with *IM* than other algorithms.

6. OVERALL DISCUSSION

Based on the results of our empirical analyses, we recommend using (1+1) EA with *IM* for solving constraints since the effectiveness of the algorithm was better than all the other algorithms we compared, as we discussed in Section 4 based on artificial problems on which all four heuristics were applied. However, we found that AVM was the best algorithm for the industrial case study as we discussed in Section 5. Notice that, in the industrial case study, we could only evaluate the heuristic for *and* operator and, even in this case, there were no significant differences across success rates of AVM and (1+1) EA, which are 100% and 99% respectively. Based on these observations, we suggest using AVM when the constraints are conjuncted and there is limited time as it may find solutions quicker than (1+1) EA. If we are flexible with time budget (e.g., the constraints need to be solved only once, and the cost of doing that is negligible compared to other costs in the testing phase), we rather recommend running (1+1) EA for as many iterations as possible as we notice that the success rate for (1+1) EA was 99% on average for the industrial case study, whereas for the artificial problems, it has mean success rate of 98% with *IM* and AVM has 81% of average success rate (Table II).

The difference in performance between AVM and (1+1) EA has a clear explanation. AVM works like a sort of greedy local search. If the fitness function provides a clear gradient towards the global optima, then AVM will quickly converge to one of them. On the other hand, (1+1) EA puts more focus on the exploration of the search landscape. When there is a clear gradient toward global optima, (1+1) EA is still able to reach those optima in reasonable time, but it will spend some time in exploring other areas of the search space. This latter property becomes essential in difficult landscapes where there are many local optima. In these cases, AVM gets stuck and has to re-start from other points in the search landscape. On the other hand, (1+1) EA, thanks to its mutation operator, has always a non-zero probability of escaping from local optima.

7. THREATS TO VALIDITY

To reduce construct validity threats, we used search success rate measure, which is comparable across the three search algorithms (AVM, (1+1) EA, GA) and RS. Furthermore, we used the same stopping criterion for all algorithms, i.e., number of iterations, which is comparable measure across all the algorithms.

The most probable conclusion validity threat in experiments involving randomized algorithms is due to random variations. To address it, we repeated experiments 100 times to reduce the possibility that the results were obtained by chance. Furthermore, we performed Fisher exact tests to compare proportions and determine the statistical significance of the results. To determine the practical significance of the results obtained, we measured the effect size using the odds ratio of success rates across search techniques, we used Mann-Whitney U-test [13] to determine significance of results and Vargha and Delaney's Â12 statistics for report effect sizes, using the guidelines for reporting results of randomized algorithms presented in [12].

A possible threat to internal validity is that we have experimented with only one configuration setting for the GA parameters. However, these settings are in accordance with the common guidelines in the literature and our previous experience on testing problems. Parameter tuning can improve the performance of GAs, although default parameters often provide reasonable results [11].

We ran the experiments on an industrial case study to generate test data for 42 different OCL constraints, ranging from constraints having just six to eight clauses. Although the empirical analysis is based on a real industrial system, our results might not generalize to other case studies. However, such threats to external validity are common to all empirical studies. In addition to the industrial case study, we also conducted an empirical evaluation of each proposed branch distance calculation using small yet complex artificial problems to demonstrate that the effectiveness of our heuristics holds even for more complex problems.

8. RELATED WORK

A number of approaches use constraint solvers for analyzing OCL constraints for various purposes. These approaches usually translate constraints and models into a formalism (e.g., Alloy [14], temporal logic BOTL [15], FOL [16], graph constraints [17]), which can then be analyzed by a constraint analyzer (e.g., Alloy constraint analyzer [18], model checker [15], Satisfiability Modulo Theories (SMT) Solver [16], theorem prover [16]). Satisfiability Problem (SAT) solvers have also been used for evaluating OCL specifications ,e.g., for OCL operation contracts (e.g., [19]).

Some approaches are reported in the literature to solve OCL constraints and generate data that evaluate the constraints to true. The data generated can then be used as test data. Most of these approaches do not handle important features of OCL (e.g., Collections) and UML, and are based on formal constraint solving techniques, such as SAT solving (e.g., [20]), constraint satisfaction problem (CSP) (e.g., [21]), higher order logic (HOL) [22], and partition analysis (e.g., [23]). The work presented in [21] is one of the most sophisticated approaches reported so far. However, its focus is on the verification of correctness properties, though it generates an instantiation of the model as part of its process. The major limitation of the approach is that the search space is bounded and, as the bounds are raised, CSP faces a quickly increasing combinatorial explosion (as discussed in [21]). The task of determining the optimal bounds for verification is left to the user and considering that models of industrial applications can have a large number of attributes, manually finding bounds for individual attributes is often impractical.

Existing approaches for OCL constraint solving do not fully fit the needs we identified with our industrial partners. Most of the approaches are only limited to simple numerical expressions and do not handle collections, which are used widely to specify expressions that navigate over associations. These limitations are due to the high expressiveness of OCL that makes the definitions of constraints easier, but their analysis more difficult. The conversion of OCL to a SAT formula or a CSP instance can easily result in a combinatorial explosion as the complexity of the model and constraints increases (as discussed in [21]). Most of the discussed approaches listed in this section either do not support the OCL constructs present in the constraints that we have in our industrial case study or are not efficient to solve them. Hence, existing techniques based on conversion to lower-level languages seem impractical in the context of large scale, real-world systems.

9. CONCLUSION

This paper presented four new heuristics for solving OCL constraints, which are based on the process of dividing a given constraint into its independent sub constraints and solving them separately, by first focusing on the ones that are easier to solve. The new heuristics correspond to the four primary operations for OCL constraints (*and, or, implies,* and *xor*). We conducted two empirical studies, one on 28 artificial constraints and the other on 42 constraints from an industrial case study, to evaluate the performance of improved heuristics and comparing them with previously defined heuristics. For this purpose, we used three search algorithms: (1+1) Evolutionary Algorithm (EA), Genetic Algorithms (GA), and Alternating Variable Method (AVM). The results of the empirical studies show that the novel heuristics lead to significantly better performance for each algorithm, on both the artificial problems and the industrial case study. Overall, (1+1) EA with the improved heuristics showed best performance among all the algorithms and must be used in practice.

10. REFERENCES

[1] OCL. (2011). *Object Constraint Language Specification, Version 2.2*. Available: http://www.omg.org/spec/OCL/2.2/

[2] R. V. Binder, Testing object-oriented systems: models, patterns, and tools: Addison-Wesley Longman Publishing Co., Inc., 1999.

[3] S. Ali, M. Z. Iqbal, A. Arcuri, and L. Briand, "A Search-based OCL Constraint Solver for Model-based Test Data Generation," in Proceedings of the 11th International Conference On Quality Software (QSIC 2011), 2011, pp. 41-50.

[4] S. Ali, M. Z. Iqbal, A. Arcuri, and L. Briand, "Generating Test Data from OCL Constraints with Search Techniques," IEEE Trans. Softw. Eng., vol. 39, pp. 1376-1402, 2013.

[5] P. McMinn, "Search-based software test data generation: a survey: Research Articles," Softw. Test. Verif. Reliab., vol. 14, pp. 105-156, 2004.

[6] S. Ali, M. Z. Iqbal, A. Arcuri, and L. Briand, "Generating Test Data from OCL Constraints with Search Techniques," Simula Reserach Laboratory, Technical Report (2010-16)2012.

[7] S. Ali, M. Z. Iqbal, and A. Arcuri, "Empirically Evaluating Improved Heuristics for Test Data Generation from OCL Constraints using Search Algorithms," Simula Research Laboratory2012.

[8] S. Ali, L. C. Briand, H. Hemmati, and R. K. Panesar-Walawege, "A Systematic Review of the Application and Empirical Investigation of Search-Based Test Case Generation," IEEE Transactions on Software Engineering, vol. 99, 2009.

[9] A. Arcuri, "It really does matter how you normalize the branch distance in search-based software testing," Software Testing, Verification and Reliability, 2011.

[10] M. Z. Iqbal, A. Arcuri, and L. Briand, "Empirical Investigation of Search Algorithms for Environment Model-Based Testing of Real-Time Embedded Software " in International Symposium on Software Testing and Analysis (ISSTA), 2012.

[11] A. Arcuri and G. Fraser, "On Parameter Tuning in Search Based Software Engineering," presented at the International Symposium on Search Based Software Engineering (SSBSE), 2011.

[12] A. Arcuri and L. Briand., "A Practical Guide for Using Statistical Tests to Assess Randomized Algorithms in Software Engineering," presented at the International Conference on Software Engineering (ICSE), 2011.

[13] D. J. Sheskin, Handbook of Parametric and Nonparametric Statistical Procedures: Chapman and Hall/CRC, 2007.

[14] B. Bordbar and K. Anastasakis, "UML2Alloy: A tool for lightweight modelling of Discrete Event Systems," presented at the IADIS International Conference in Applied Computing, 2005.

[15] D. Distefano, J.-P. Katoen, and A. Rensink, "Towards model checking OCL," presented at the ECOOP-Workshop on Defining Precise Semantics for UML, 2000.

[16] M. Clavel and M. A. G. d. Dios, "Checking unsatisfiability for OCL constraints," presented at the In the proceedings of the 9th OCL 2009 Workshop at the UML/MoDELS Conferences, 2009.

[17] J. Winkelmann, G. Taentzer, K. Ehrig, and J. M. ster, "Translation of Restricted OCL Constraints into Graph Constraints for Generating Meta Model Instances by Graph Grammars," Electron. Notes Theor. Comput. Sci., vol. 211, pp. 159-170, 2008.

[18] D. Jackson, I. Schechter, and H. Shlyahter, "Alcoa: the alloy constraint analyzer," presented at the Proceedings of the 22nd international conference on Software engineering, Limerick, Ireland, 2000.

[19] M. Krieger and A. Knapp, "Executing Underspecified OCL Operation Contracts with a SAT Solver," presented at the 8th International Workshop on OCL Concepts and Tools., 2008.

[20] L. v. Aertryck and T. Jensen, "UML-Casting: Test synthesis from UML models using constraint resolution," presented at the Approches Formelles dans l'Assistance au Développement de Logiciels (AFADL'2003), 2003.

[21] J. Cabot, R. Claris, and D. Riera, "Verification of UML/OCL Class Diagrams using Constraint Programming," presented at the Proceedings of the 2008 IEEE International Conference on Software Testing Verification and Validation Workshop, 2008.

[22] A. D. Brucker, M. P. Krieger, D. Longuet, and B. Wolff, "A Specification-Based Test Case Generation Method for UML/OCL," presented at the Worksshop on OCL and Textual Modelling, MoDELS, 2010.

[23] L. Bao-Lin, L. Zhi-shu, L. Qing, and C. Y. Hong, "Test case automate generation from uml sequence diagram and ocl expression," presented at the International Conference on cimputational Intelligence and Security, 2007.

Surrogate-Assisted Optimisation of Composite Applications in Mobile Ad hoc Networks

Dionysios Efstathiou
Department of Informatics
King's College London, UK
name.lastname@kcl.ac.uk

Peter McBurney
Department of Informatics
King's College London, UK
peter.mcburney@kcl.ac.uk

Steffen Zschaler
Department of Informatics
King's College London, UK
szschaler@acm.org

Johann Bourcier
IRISA
University of Rennes 1, France
johann.bourcier@irisa.fr

ABSTRACT

Infrastructure-less mobile ad hoc networks enable the development of collaborative pervasive applications. Within such dynamic networks, collaboration between devices can be realised through service-orientation by abstracting device resources as services. Recently, a framework for QoS-aware service composition has been introduced which takes into account a spectrum of orchestration patterns, and enables compositions of a better QoS than traditional centralised orchestration approaches. In this paper, we focus on the automated exploration of trade-off compositions within the search space defined by this flexible composition model. For the studied problem, the evaluation of the fitness functions guiding the search process is computationally expensive because it either involves a high-fidelity simulation or actually requires calling the composite service. To overcome this limitation, we have developed efficient surrogate models for estimating the QoS metrics of a candidate solution during the search. Our experimental results show that the use of surrogates can produce solutions with good convergence and diversity properties at a much lower computational effort.

Categories and Subject Descriptors

D.2.0 [**Software Engineering**]: General

Keywords

Service composition, optimisation, surrogate models

1. INTRODUCTION

Advances in networking and hardware technology have popularised the use of powerful smart-phones and tablets, which are progressively replacing PCs for web-access [9]. These mobile devices offer a wide range of built-in sensors, fast processors, and networking capabilities. These features present great potential for creating self-configuring ecosystems of collaborating devices by forming infrastructure-less Mobile Ad hoc NETworks (MANETs) [7]. MANETs are used in various domains, such as healthcare, emergency management, and smart cities [21].

A MANET is a peer-to-peer network with no central control entity or pre-existing infrastructure. Within a MANET, data exchange is realised through multi-hop communications using intermediate nodes as relays [7]. Service Oriented Architectures (SOA) promote node-to-node collaboration in a MANET by abstracting nodes' available resources as loosely coupled software services [2]. Offered services can be called by any node participating in the network while nodes move freely and may join or leave the network at any time. One of the core ideas of SOA is the property of composability [17] where services are designed to be combined into value added structures, called service compositions. Service composition provides functionality that none of the component services could provide by themselves [24].

While the composition mechanism offers a nice programming abstraction for aggregating pieces of software, finding compositions providing the desired functionality while simultaneously exhibiting optimal Quality of Service (QoS) trade-offs is a very challenging task. In a MANET environment, nodes with heterogeneous and dynamic resources offer services with different QoS levels. There may be a large number of composite service architectures which fulfil the same functionality, but differ in their QoS such as network latency and energy consumption. Multi-Objective Evolutionary Algorithms (MOEAs) are a powerful tool for finding trade-off solutions to problems with large architectural design spaces where an exhaustive search is infeasible. The QoS metrics of interest for measuring the quality of a service composition can be used as fitness functions within a MOEA to guide the search of optimal solutions [13]. However, determining the QoS of a candidate service composition is not trivial in the case of a dynamic MANET. We can determine the QoS of a candidate composition either by simulating or actually invoking the service composition. Both approaches are computationally expensive requiring minutes or even hours for a single evaluation. This fact makes the use of such an algorithm in our problem impractical as MOEAs require a large number of fitness function evaluations before converging to a set of optimal solutions.

GECCO'14, July 12–16, Vancouver, BC, Canada.
Copyright 2014 ACM 978-1-4503-2662-9/14/07 ...$15.00.
http://dx.doi.org/10.1145/2576768.2598307 .

Current service composition optimisation approaches use synthetic fitness functions for simulating the QoS attributes of services participating in a composition [4, 26]. Others, use one-time measurements of services' QoS which are considered to remain static during the life-cycle of the composed service [22, 30]. These approaches do not take into account the computational cost for estimating the fitness functions of a composite service. On the other hand, others use a computationally expensive simulation for estimating the fitness of a solution [19] which is impractical to be integrated in the process of searching for trade-off composite services.

In this paper, we propose an efficient technique for predicting the QoS of composite applications which is crucial for supporting automated QoS-aware optimisation of composite services. Our main contributions are the following:

- We introduce low cost **surrogate models for predicting the QoS** metrics of composite services in service-based MANETs. We develop statistical models for predicting the QoS metrics of network latency, energy consumption, and success ratio.
- We present a **multi-objective surrogate-based optimisation** approach to explore trade-off composite services by **replacing the expensive** simulation-based fitness functions with **efficient surrogate models** within the evolution process of the popular NSGA-II algorithm [8]. Our experimental results show that the developed surrogates guide the NSGA-II algorithm to high quality solutions with little computational effort and by exploiting limited predictive information without the need for expensive high-fidelity simulations or real-world service invocations.

The remainder of this paper is structured as follows: In Section 2 the service composition optimisation problem is defined. Section 3 introduces our surrogate-based optimisation approach to solve this problem using the popular NSGA-II algorithm. Section 4 presents the considered use-case scenario and the research questions we seek to answer. Section 5 presents the experimental results of our study followed by Section 6 which discusses related work. Finally, Section 7 presents conclusions and future work.

2. MOTIVATION AND PROBLEM

In this section, we first describe the motivating scenario of our study and then we formulate the search problem of composing services in a distributed service-based environment.

2.1 Motivating Scenario

Due to their distributed and infrastructure-less nature, multi-hop ad hoc wireless networks are ideal for building crisis management applications [6]. Our motivating scenario considers a decision support system for improving the decision making of fire-fighters in an emergency situation such as a forest fire. In the considered scenario, fire-fighters are equipped with mobile devices which form a MANET. These devices, following SOA principles, offer their resources (e.g. application data, network and hardware components) as loosely coupled software services. Service composition promotes the collaboration between devices by composing services provided by various devices towards achieving complex applications.

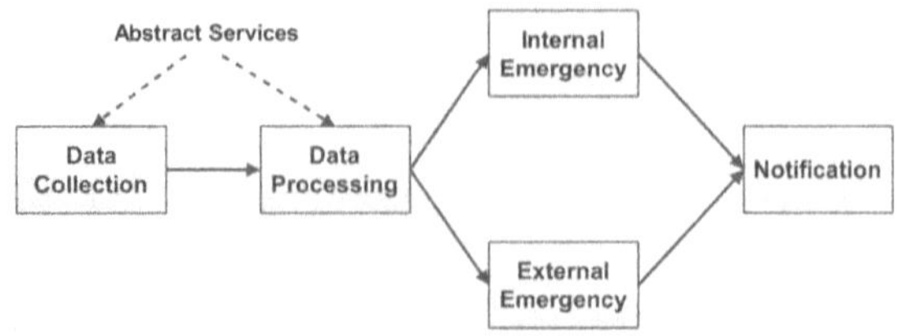

Figure 1: An example service composition plan.

For example, consider the scenario where a commanding firefighter uses a composite application comprised of five services to infer whether a firefighter is in danger and appropriate measures should be taken in time. More specifically, the commanding firefighter aggregates information about the condition of his subordinates (position, heart rate, oxygen level). This information needs to be fed to a processing service which assesses if something is going wrong. In the case of an emergency event (e.g. a firefighter has stopped moving and high levels of carbon dioxide in the blood are observed), another team in the close proximity must be notified to intervene along with a medical team which must be ready to approach. Finally, the various decisions and the situation event are logged to a central database which may respond with a set of recommended actions to be taken.

In such a dynamic and time-critical scenario where resources are limited, composite applications should exhibit QoS properties such as minimum response time and battery consumption. However, the QoS of an offered service is influenced by a variety of factors such as topology changes, user's mobility, obstacles, resource availability (e.g. battery level), and others. QoS of a composite application are highly susceptible to changes on the underlying network.

Our goal is to provide to the users of the distributed system with composite services which exhibit optimal QoS trade-offs at a small computational overhead. It is worth noting that our approach is not restricted to the presented scenario but it can be applied to others involving mobile multi-hop communication networks. Such applications can be found in the domain of *Mobile Enterprise Vision* [16].

2.2 Problem Formulation

Our problem formulation starts from the abstract plan of a composite application which describes the services to participate in the composition. Within the considered network, various nodes offer concrete services which implement the abstract services of the plan. Also, orchestrator nodes are responsible for calling services and forwarding the intermediate results to the appropriate nodes. Our goal is to produce optimal composition configurations by tuning the parameters of a service composition configuration, called Degrees of Freedom (DoF) which are the following [10]: (a) selection of concrete services, (b) partitioning of the composition into sub-orchestrations, and (c) selection of orchestrating nodes.

Def. 1. Distributed Service Orchestration Problem Given: A set of m abstract services that compose the service composition plan P, a set of n nodes participating in the network where each node provides a single concrete service and can coordinate a single orchestration, a mapping of the n available concrete services that implement the functionality of the m abstract services, and a set of q quality objectives $Q = \{Q_1, \cdots, Q_q\}$.

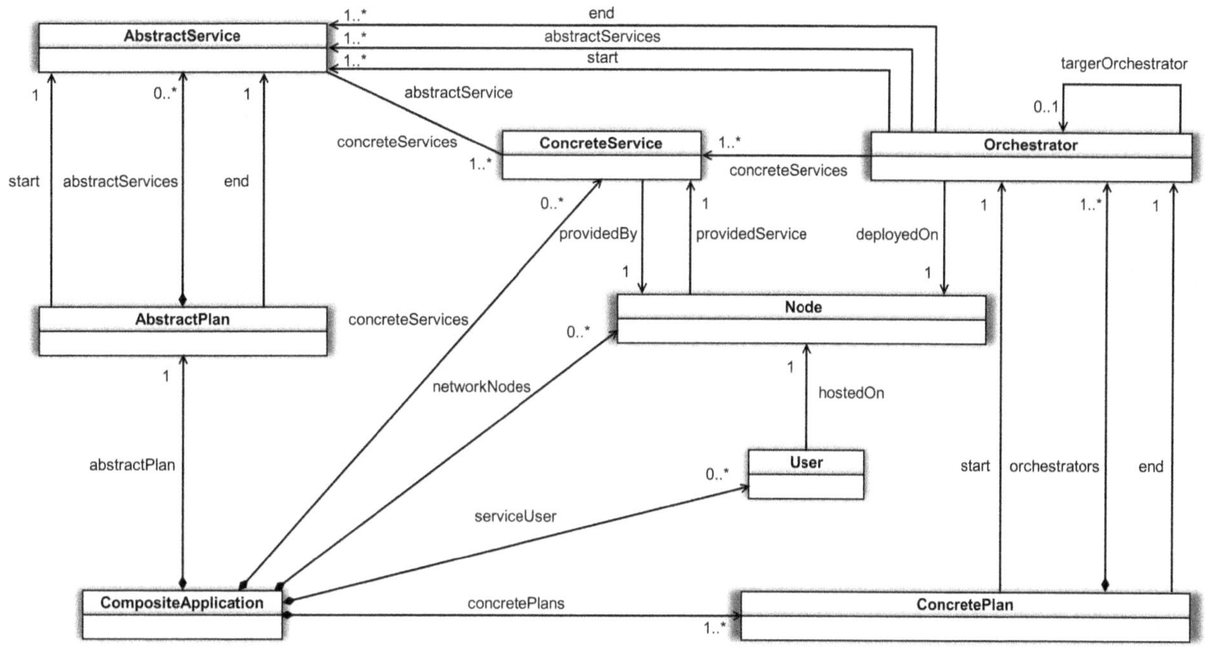

Figure 2: The composition configuration metamodel.

Problem: Find a set of service composition configurations, all of which implement the functionality described by P, but differ in their non-functional trade-offs according to Q.

Let a composite application plan P be represented as a directed graph, as shown in Fig. 1, consisting of a node set $AS = \langle AS_1, AS_1, \cdots, AS_n \rangle$ of abstract services and an edge set $DF = \langle (AS_i, AS_j) : i \neq j, 1 \leq i \leq n, 1 \leq j \leq n \rangle$ of data flow between abstract services, where AS_i is the source and AS_j the data destination.

2.3 QoS Metrics - Fitness Functions

QoS metrics of software architectures can be used as fitness functions to guide the search for optimal solutions for Search-Based Software Engineering (SBSE) problems [13]. In our study, we consider the following QoS metrics for estimating the quality of a composite service:

- *The network latency* Q_{NL} which measures the round trip time of the exchanged messages within a service composition. This metric is computed based on the network latency of successfully delivered messages.

- *The energy consumption* Q_E of a configuration, which is the energy difference observed in the nodes for realising a service composition configuration where nodes spent energy for: (a) sending/receiving data, and (b) orchestrating other services. They also spend energy for service execution, but this is independent of the configuration; therefore we can safely ignore it.

- *The success ratio* Q_{SR} is calculated as the percentage of successfully exchanged data between collaborating nodes within a composition configuration.

3. THE PROPOSED APPROACH

In this section, we describe our solution approach to the expensive optimisation service composition problem. We propose the adoption of a Search-Based Software Engineering (SBSE) [14] approach for exploring service composition configurations that exhibit quality trade-offs according to the three QoS metrics described in Section 2.3. To build a search-based approach we need to define the following two ingredients [14]: (i) a problem representation, and (ii) the appropriate fitness functions. We propose the replacement of the computationally expensive "real" simulation-based fitness functions with efficient surrogate models. The last step is to employ a search algorithm that utilises the defined fitness functions for exploring the space of candidate solutions.

3.1 Defining the Design Space

We first define the space of service composition configurations. The work in [10] showed that by taking into account multiple DoFs for tuning the quality of a composite service, a space containing solutions of higher quality than the centralised orchestration which considers only the DoF of service selection can be defined. More specifically, the authors proposed the following parameters for tuning the quality of a service composition configuration are the following: (a) service selection, (b) orchestration partitioning, and (c) orchestrator node selection. The large number of parameters affecting the performance of a configuration and their interdependencies, motivate the engineering of an automated method for design space exploration. We call a composition configuration a *solution*. The set of all candidate solutions is the set of all possible combinations of the defined DoFs.

Fig. 2 depicts our metamodel for specifying composition configurations in distributed service-based environments. The proposed metamodel abstracts away from the complexity of the underlying system and focuses only on the concepts related to the problem of distributed composition.

The *Composite Application* meta-class represents a high-level application to be realised as requested by a *User*. This high-level application is described as an *Abstract Plan* which combines a number of *Abstract Services*. An instance of *Abstract Plan* would be, for example, an abstract composition workflow such as the one depicted in Fig. 1. The connection order of the various *Abstract Services* describes the order of invocation (control flow) among the various participating services in the composition. An *Abstract Service* describes in an abstract way the functionality to be fulfilled by a concrete invocable realisation of a service which is called *ConcreteService*. As shown in our metamodel, each *Abstract Service* can be implemented by many *Concrete Services* which can be differentiated based on their provided QoS. For example, two *Concrete Services* provide the same functionality, in other words implement the same *Abstract Service*, but one may be faster than the other.

To enable the partitioning of the initial abstract workflow to sub-orchestrations, we introduce the concept of the *Orchestrator* which is responsible for composing a set of *Concrete Services* by controlling their order of execution and data flow. The *Nodes* meta-class represents a physical node that participates in the system and provides a *Concrete Service*. Another important role of a *Node* is its ability to provide an *Orchestrator*. Based on the resource-constrained nature of the studied scenario, we assume that a node can provide a single *Concrete Service* and host an *Orchestrator* at a time.

An instance of meta-class *Concrete Plan* describes a concrete realisation plan for a *Composite Application* which may be realised by more than one *Concrete Plans*. In other words, there can be many possible configurations for realising the same application which share functionality but which may differ in their provided QoS.

3.2 Computational Search

We employed the popular NSGA-II algorithm for exploring trade-off composite services which is based on two core ideas of Pareto ranking for exploiting the best solutions and crowding distance for promoting diversity within a population. To apply the NSGA-II algorithm in our problem, we have to define the following building blocks: (a) solution representation, (b) genetic operators, and (c) fitness functions, which are described in the subsections below.

3.2.1 Solution Representation

The service composition configuration chromosome constitutes a container for further chromosomes that correspond to classes shown in our metamodel (Fig. 2). The genotypes exhibit variable lengths due to the fact that the number of sub-orchestrations can be varied between one (single centralised orchestrator) and m (fully decentralised orchestration where one orchestrator is responsible for orchestrating a single abstract service).

We represent a candidate solution to our problem as a three-fold assignment of (i) concrete services to abstract services, (ii) abstract services to sub-orchestrations and (iii) network nodes to orchestrator nodes. Fig. 3(a) shows the chromosome for mapping concrete services to abstract services. The chromosome for representing a sub-orchestration is depicted in Fig. 3(b). Finally, a complete configuration can be represented as a set of sub-orchestration chromosomes as denoted by the + sign in the upper left corner of the box shown in Fig. 3(c). The grey box indicates the chromosome, while the white boxes represent the genes that compose the chromosome. The signs 1, + and ? represent the repetition of a gene or chromosome exactly once, at least once, and at most once respectively.

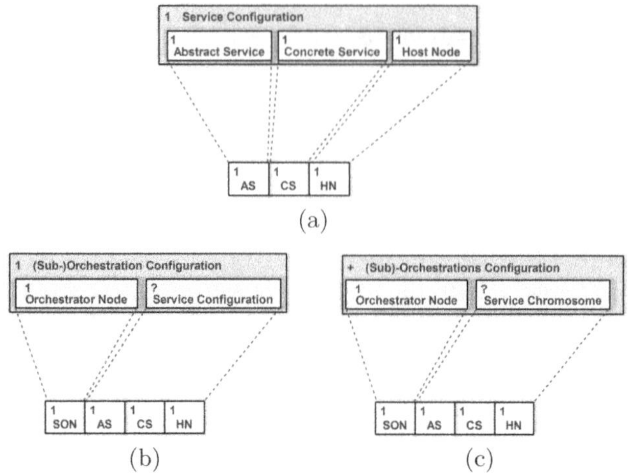

Figure 3: Chromosome representations for: (a) mapping concrete to abstract services, (b) sub-orchestrations, and (c) composition configuration.

An example chromosome representation for a complete composition configuration is depicted in Fig. 4. In this example, we have two sub-orchestrations which are hosted on nodes (SON) 2 and 4 respectively. The first sub-orchestration includes the abstract services 1 and 2, while the second orchestrates the services 3, 4 and 5. For implementing the abstract service 1 (AS), the concrete service 12 (CS) was selected which is hosted at node 2 (HN).

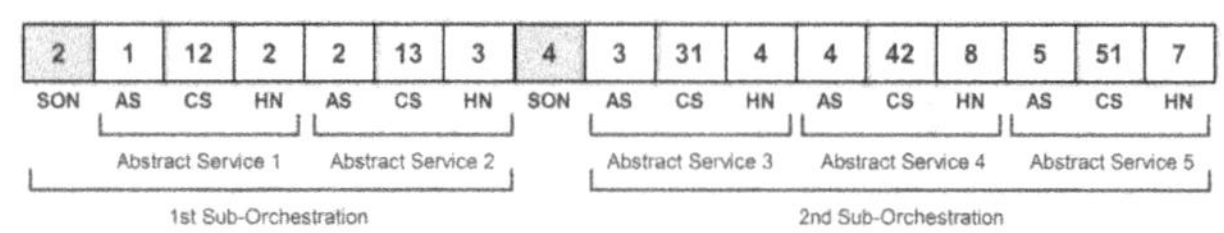

Figure 4: Example solution chromosome for a composition configuration with 2 sub-orchestrations.

3.2.2 Genetic Operators

The design of genetic operators is the second key element for constructing any MOEA. The chosen varied size representation complicates the implementation of genetic operators. For each of the three considered DoFs, we designed a pair of crossover and mutation operators, resulting to a total of 6 operators. *Crossover* ensures that features of the parents will be passed to the offspring forcing the convergence on the good solutions found so far (*exploitation*). For example, the single-point crossover for the first DoF, produces a new configuration by combining the concrete services mappings of two parents as depicted in Fig. 5.

For the second DoF, two parent configurations are combined by swapping sub-orchestrations between them. The crossover operator for the last DoF, creates an offspring by combining the list of orchestrators of the parent configura-

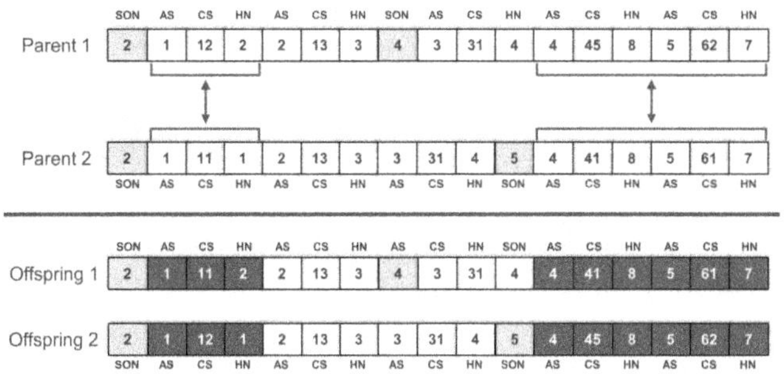

Figure 5: An example crossover operation for the first DoF.

tions. Moreover, *mutation* ensures that any possible configuration can be searched which increases the *exploration* of the space and aims at maintaining diversity by avoiding to over-bias to fittest individuals. For instance, the mutation operator for the first DoF chooses randomly a concrete service for implementing an abstract service. All the designed operators allow the modification of solutions to reach any area of the space while guaranteeing that the changed configuration is valid and conforms to our described metamodel.

3.2.3 Fitness Function

Fitness function is a quality measure of a candidate solution and guides the search process by distinguishing between better and worse solutions. For estimating the QoS metrics described in Section 2.3, we can either employ a computationally expensive experiment or simulation, or light-weight surrogate models to approximate them.

Expensive Function: As we do not have the resources for performing real-world experiments of the studied scenario, we replaced them by a less costly simulation. However, computing the QoS metrics of a candidate composition configuration by using the simulation ($\sim$ 300 seconds) is not fast enough for integrating it in an optimisation approach.

Surrogate Function: MOEAs are efficient at exploring a large and complex search space by providing several Pareto solutions in a single run at the cost of a large number of fitness function evaluations. MOEAs seem unaffordable in our problem which involves expensive fitness functions because their computational cost has a critical impact on the overall complexity of the search algorithm [13].

We have two choices for reducing the computation cost of a MOEA [18]: (a) reduce its algorithmic complexity, or (b) reduce the computational cost of the fitness function. The first approach does not seem promising because the main overhead when applying a MOEA in a real-world problem is because of the complex nature of the tackled problem. For the second approach, functional approximation [18] proposes the replacement of the expensive fitness functions with cheaper alternatives called surrogates [18, 23]. Surrogates are statistical models that are built by exploiting knowledge of already evaluated solutions (training dataset) of the real simulation or experiment-based fitness functions [19, 20]. The surrogates can be used by the MOEA to evolve the population of individuals at a smaller computational cost than that of the expensive real fitness function.

By constructing a surrogate model our goal is to predict the QoS of a composite service where service users and providers communicate over a wireless MANET. First, we need to determine the factors which may affect the QoS metrics of a composite service described in Section 2.3.

Symbol	Description
PV_1	# of hops between nodes in a composition
PV_2	# of transmitted packets in a composition
PV_3	# of hops of the longest path in a composition
PV_4	# of orchestrator nodes in a composition
PV_5	# of neighbours of each node in a composition
PV_6	# of routes between nodes in a composition
PV_7	Total distance between nodes in a composition

Table 1: Variables for predicting the QoS of composite applications.

Regression analysis [15] focuses on developing models for describing how a response variable is related to one or more predictor variables. When developing a prediction model, each predictor variable should be able to provide some information about the value of the response not already provided by any other variable.In our study, we consider the seven predictor variables ($p = 7$) shown in Table 1. These predictors are not the only ones which we could use for our study but we have chosen them for our analysis because it was comparatively easy to obtain the relevant data for them. In the last column of Table 1 we show the cost of acquiring each predictor variable. Also, we use the following approaches for creating surrogate models: (1) Linear Regression models (LR) [15], (2) Multivariate adaptive regression splines (MARS) [15], (3) Classification and Regression Trees (CART) [15], and (4) Random Forests (RF) [15].

In [11], you can find more details about how we developed the used surrogate models and more specifically the selection of their predictor variables and parameters.

4. EMPIRICAL STUDY DESIGN

We now describe our experimental case study, the metrics for the algorithms in comparison and our research questions.

4.1 Firefighting Case Study

We use a simulation-based approach for collecting our dataset for building the used surrogate models. We use the Network Simulator 3 (NS-3) [1] to simulate a service-based firefighter decision support system where firefighters of three different hierarchical levels (Group, Engine, and Team) carry devices which offer software services and cooperatively form an infrastructure-less MANET. In detail, we simulate a network of 63 mobile nodes (3 Group Leaders, 12 Engine Leaders, and 48 Team Leaders/Members) with transmission range of $45m$ distributed in a area of $500m \times 500m$. Each group follows a different mobility model because each group has a different purpose and mission to fulfil. To ensure that the network is completely configured before simulating a composition configuration we included a set-up/warm-up time of 20 seconds. For more details about the simulation scenario such as the chosen mobility, network and routing parameters, please refer to our previous work in [10].

4.2 Experimental Setting

Our prototype used the MOEA Framework[2] and the statistical environment R [25] for the various surrogate

[1] `http://www.nsnam.org/`
[2] `http://www.moeaframework.org/`

techniques. We took advantage of the elasticity provided by Amazon Elastic Compute Cloud (EC2) for executing the computationally-expensive experiments including the simulation-based fitness functions. The NSGA-II algorithm evolved a population of 96 configurations for 30 generations. After some tuning, we resulted with the following parameters for our problem: 95% crossover rate, 5% mutation rate.

4.3 Research Questions

Our experimental study was conducted to assess the applicability of surrogate models in the multi-objective service composition optimisation problem and to compare the efficiency of state of the art approaches. More specifically, we aimed to answer the following research questions:

RQ1 How does NSGA-II perform compared to random search for the studied problem?

RQ2 Can the developed cheap surrogate models replace the expensive simulation-based functions within the EA towards exploring good optimal solutions?

RQ3 What is the performance gain and loss of optimality by using a light-weight surrogate model instead of using the real expensive fitness function in our problem?

4.4 Evaluation Metrics Used

To quantitatively compare the performance of NSGA-II for the cases of the expensive and the efficient surrogates we employ three well-known quality indicators, namely Hypervolume (I_{HV}) [31], Cardinality (I_C) [31], and Spread (Δ) [8]. To compute them, we normalise fitness values and use as a reference a nadir point containing the worst possible QoS metrics for a composition configuration.

I_C of a Pareto set approximation measures the number of optimal solutions either in decision or objective space. Cardinality is very cheap to compute, but the indicator is not monotonic, or in other words, it is not compatible with the Pareto dominance relation. I_{HV} calculates the volume of the objective space which is weakly dominated by a specific Pareto set approximation. The higher the hypervolume, the better the quality of the approximation set. I_{HV} is currently the only unary indicator known to be strictly monotonic [31]. However, this advantage comes at the cost of high computational overhead which is exponential in the number of objectives. Δ is a diversity metric that measures how evenly the points in the approximation set are distributed in the objective space. A smaller spacing value indicates that the population has a better more uniform spread.

4.5 Statistical Analysis

In stochastic optimisation the relationship between quality of the resulted solutions and necessary computational resources is not fixed, but can be described by a probability density function making every statement about their performance probabilistic in nature. If we apply the same algorithm several times to the same problem, each time a different Pareto approximation may be returned. To obtain reliable conclusions about the performance of the inherently stochastic MOEAs and the quality of the generated solutions, we are forced to use statistical tools. In our experiments, we repeat each algorithm 20 times and collect the values of the corresponding quality/performance indicators.

	I_{HV} Mean	σ	I_C Mean	σ	Δ Mean	σ
Random	0.503	± 0.03	13.1	± 4.82	0.8128	± 0.12
NSGA-II	0.6669	± 0.01	30.9	± 5.5	0.6954	± 0.09

Table 2: Hypervolume (I_{HV}), Cardinality (I_C), and Spread (Δ) of random search and NSGA-II with the expensive fitness functions.

A statistical test is used to asses whether the observed differences between compared algorithms are statistically significant [1]. We use a non-parametric Mann-Whitney test to evaluate statistical significance because we have no information about the distribution of the data.

5. RESULTS AND DISCUSSIONS

Results for RQ1: To answer **RQ1** we implemented a random search algorithm which assigns random values for each of the three degrees of freedom of a candidate composite service. More specifically, we run both random search and NSGA-II by using the simulation-based expensive objective function and report the quality indicators described in Section 4.4. Finally, we compare the Pareto surfaces produced by NSGAII for both composition models in comparison.

To answer **RQ1**, we compared the quality of the Pareto solutions discovered by random search and NSGA-II. The null hypothesis (H_0) states that the approaches using a dummy random search and NSGA-II produce solutions of the same quality. H_0 is rejected by the Mann-Whitney test at 1% significance level (p-values for the three indicators $< 3.4 \cdot 10^{-8}$, $< 6 \cdot 10^{-8}$, and $< 3 \cdot 10^{-3}$ respectively).

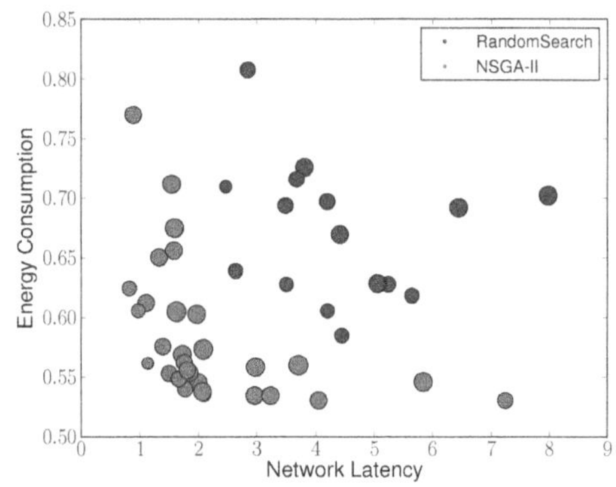

Figure 6: Pareto fronts where the size of the points represents the Success Ratio QoS dimension (the larger the point size, the higher the success ratio).

Table 2 presents the mean and standard deviation for the three quality indicators described in Section 4.4. According to the results, the quality indicators achieved by NSGA-II are significantly better than those of random search. To qualitatively support our point, we present in Fig. 6 a visualisation of the Pareto fronts achieved by the two approaches in comparison. Based on that figure we observe that the NSGA-II algorithm is able of achieving higher quality, more and better spread Pareto optimal solutions.

	I_{HV} Mean	σ	I_C Mean	σ	Δ Mean	σ	$t_{Execution}$ (seconds)	$\frac{HV_{Surrogate}}{HV_{Expensive}}$	$\frac{t_{Expensive}}{t_{Surrogate}}$
Expensive	0.6669	± 0.01	30.9	± 5.5	0.6954	± 0.09	13376.5	-	-
LR	0.6027	± 0.21	45.7	± 21.27	0.6747	± 0.06	1.4644	0.9037	9134
MARS	0.6414	± 0.02	15.9	± 4.78	0.8585	± 0.13	1.8808	0.9618	7112
CART	0.6161	± 0.02	9.4	± 1.91	0.771	± 0.09	1.9593	0.9238	6827
RF	0.6095	± 0.02	20.7	± 12.43	0.7752	± 0.14	3.0225	0.9139	4425

Table 3: Quality indicator values of simulation-based and surrogate fitness functions.

Results for RQ2: When evaluating surrogate models in the context of evolutionary computation we need to assess the ability of the developed surrogates to guide the search towards good areas of the service composition space. With regards to **RQ2**, we first run the NSGA-II algorithm with the simulation-based fitness function. Then, we replace the expensive fitness functions with the surrogate models and compute the simulation-based QoS metric values on the Pareto individuals of the last generation. In the first three columns of Table 3, we present the results for the three indicators obtained after 20 runs.

Table 3 shows that the use of the expensive fitness functions achieves the best hypervolume results as expected. Among the surrogate models, MARS achieves the highest I_{HV}. For the I_C and spread (Δ) indicators, LR achieves the best results due to its ability to assign different QoS values by doing fine-grain predictions based on slightly different predictor values. Tree-based approaches, like CART and RF, seem unable to provide fine-grain differentiation of solutions. These approaches try to handle the trade-off between building a big tree with many leaves for describing accurately a specific training set (overfitting) and generalisation of performance. LR results in Pareto fronts with many solutions but not of very good quality. The H_0 for **RQ2** states that the approaches using the expensive and surrogate functions produce Pareto solutions of the same quality is rejected by the Mann-Whitney test at 1% significance level but due to space restrictions we do not report the p-values calculated for each pair of the compared techniques.

Results for RQ3: We now study the trade-off between the accurate but expensive simulator-based fitness functions with the less accurate but computationally cheap surrogate models. To evaluate the efficiency of the various surrogate models, we present in the last three columns of Table 3: (a) the execution time ($t_{execution}$) of the various fitness functions needed to evaluate the QoS of a population of solutions within a generation of NSGA-II, (b) the quality degradation based on the hypervolume indicator of the approach using the surrogate models in relation to the best performance achieved by the accurate simulation-based fitness functions, and (c) the execution speed-up achieved by the surrogate-based approach over the one using the expensive fitness functions. Note that the one-time upfront cost of building the model is negligible and it is not reported ($<$ 5 seconds for all the models). All the experiments were executed in R using a machine with Intel Core i7 vPro with 12GB DDR3 RAM, running the Linux 3.2.0-40 kernel.

We seek an appropriate balance between the accuracy of the various surrogate models and their estimation cost. It is obvious that, due to its simplicity *LR* achieves the largest speed-up but also the worst results in terms of hypervolume. Also, MARS appears to be the best performing technique and its speed-up is comparable to the simple *LR* technique. As expected *RF* is more time-consuming than CART as it involves the construction of multiple decision trees to form an ensemble forest. It is worth noting that all of the reported model build times are small compared to the time needed for running the expensive fitness function for a single service composition configuration ($\sim$ 3 *minutes*) in the context of our studied motivating scenario.

6. RELATED WORK

The work related to our approach can be classified into two groups. The first group concerns optimising service composition by selecting the optimal set of concrete services to participate in a centralised orchestration. To achieve this, existing approaches use different techniques such as heuristics [22], genetic algorithms [3, 4], linear programming [5, 29], swarm intelligence [28], and others. However, their main limitation is that they neglect the inherent problems of centralised orchestration and try to optimise the QoS of a composite service by choosing in isolation which services to participate without considering how these services are composed together. Also, they assume that the services' QoS is known beforehand or is artificially generated without taking into account the cost of fitness function estimation.

The second group focuses on how to predict the QoS of single and composite services. Gambi *et al.* [12] proposed the use of surrogate models for building SLA protection controllers for single RESTful services. Zheng *et al.* [30] proposed a collaborative filtering approach for predicting QoS values of Web services based on past experiences of service users. Wang *et al.* [27] proposed a prediction-based approach to maintain the QoS of a composite service during execution. The authors study the service selection process and propose a probabilistic approach for modelling the reliability of services and service compositions. However, these approaches are focusing on predicting the QoS of composite services based on past QoS of the component services ignoring how these services are combined together. Also, they are based on the assumption that past QoS measurements remain static during the life-cycle of the composed service which is unrealistic for the considered dynamic environments. Finally, they focus on traditional web services offered via wired and resource-rich networks.

7. CONCLUSIONS AND FUTURE WORK

In this paper, we proposed a surrogate-assisted multi-objective optimisation approach for exploring optimal service compositions in the context of service-based MANETs. To the best of our knowledge, this is the first work to introduce the use of approximation models as fitness functions for exploring optimal service composition configurations. We explored four well-known surrogate models for predicting the QoS of service compositions which we integrated to the popular NSGA-II algorithm. The experimental results provided evidence that efficient surrogate models can guide the evolutionary search into exploring solutions of high quality.

As future work, we plan to include in our research the response time metric which depends on the processing speed and current load of the devices and the various services. For that reason, we need to include a more detailed model of the services which run on the devices of the scenario and their response time based on various processing loads.

Acknowledgements. This work has been supported by the European FP7 Marie Curie Initial Training Network "RELATE" (Grant Agreement No. 264840).

8. REFERENCES

[1] A. Arcuri and L. C. Briand. A Practical Guide for Using Statistical Tests to Assess Randomized Algorithms in Software Engineering. In *ICSE*, 2011.

[2] J. Bourcier and C. Escoffier. Implementing Home-Control Applications on Service Platform. In *4th CCNC*, 2007.

[3] M. Bozkurt. Cost-aware Pareto Optimal Test Suite Minimisation for Service-centric Systems. In *GECCO*, pages 1429–1436, 2013.

[4] G. Canfora, M. Di Penta, R. Esposito, and M. L. Villani. An Approach for QoS-Aware Service Composition Based on Genetic Algorithms. In *GECCO*, 2005.

[5] V. Cardellini, E. Casalicchio, V. Grassi, S. Iannucci, F. L. Presti, and R. Mirandola. MOSES: A Framework for QoS Driven Runtime Adaptation of Service-Oriented Systems. *TSE*, 99, 2011.

[6] T. Catarci, M. de Leoni, A. Marrella, M. Mecella, B. Salvatore, G. Vetere, S. Dustdar, L. Juszczyk, A. Manzoor, and H. L. Truong. Pervasive Software Environments for Supporting Disaster Responses. *IEEE Int. Comp.*, 12(1):26–37, 2008.

[7] S. Corson and J. Macker. Mobile Ad Hoc Networking (MANET): Routing Protocol Performance Issues and Evaluation Considerations, 1999.

[8] K. Deb, A. Pratap, S. Agarwal, and T. Meyarivan. A Fast Elitist Multi-Objective Genetic Algorithm: NSGA-II. *IEEE Trans. Evol. Comp.*, 6:182–197, 2000.

[9] T. M. T. Do, J. Blom, and D. Gatica-Perez. Smartphone Usage in the Wild: A Large-Scale Analysis of Applications and Context. In *ICMI*, pages 353–360, 2011.

[10] D. Efstathiou, P. McBurney, S. Zschaler, and J. Bourcier. Flexible QoS-Aware Service Composition in Highly Heterogeneous and Dynamic Service-Based Systems. In *WiMob*, 2013.

[11] D. Efstathiou, P. McBurney, S. Zschaler, and J. Bourcier. Efficiently Approximating the QoS of Composite Services in Mobile Ad-Hoc Networks. Technical Report TR-14-01, King's College London, January 2014. `http://www.dcs.kcl.ac.uk/staff/eustathi/papers/efstathiouTR-14-01.pdf`.

[12] A. Gambi, G. Toffetti, and M. Pezzè. Protecting SLAs with Surrogate Models. In *PESOS*, pages 71–77. ACM, 2010.

[13] M. Harman and J. Clark. Metrics Are Fitness Functions Too. In *METRICS*, 2004.

[14] M. Harman, P. McMinn, J. T. Souza, and S. Yoo. Search Based Software Engineering: Techniques, Taxonomy, Tutorial. In *Empirical Software Engineering and Verification*, volume 7007, pages 1–59. 2012.

[15] T. Hastie, R. Tibshirani, and J. Friedman. *The Elements of Statistical Learning*. Springer, 2003.

[16] HP. Enterprise Mobility Leveraging the Mobility Economy in the Enterprise. White paper, 2012.

[17] M. N. Huhns and M. P. Singh. Service-Oriented Computing: Key Concepts and Principles. *IEEE Internet Computing*, pages 75–81, 2005.

[18] Y. Jin. A Comprehensive Survey of Fitness Approximation in Evolutionary Computation. *Soft Computing*, 9(1):3–12, 2005.

[19] Y. Jin. Surrogate-Assisted Evolutionary Computation: Recent Advances and Future Challenges. *SEC*, 1(2):61–70, 2011.

[20] Y. Jin and J. Branke. Evolutionary Optimization in Uncertain Environment - A Survey. *IEEE Trans. Evol. Comput.*, 9(3):303–317, 2005.

[21] libelium. 50 Sensor Applications for a Smarter World, 2013.

[22] N. B. Mabrouk, S. Beauche, E. Kuznetsova, N. Georgantas, and V. Issarny. QoS-Aware Service Composition in Dynamic Service Oriented Environments. In *Middleware*, 2009.

[23] Y. S. Ong, P. Nair, A. Keane, and K.-W. Wong. Surrogate-Assisted Evolutionary Optimization Frameworks for High-Fidelity Engineering Design Problems. In *Knowledge Incorporation in Evolutionary Computation*, pages 307–332. 2004.

[24] M. Papazoglou and D. Georgakopoulos. Introduction: Service-Oriented Computing. *Comm. of ACM*, 46:24–28, 2003.

[25] R Core Team. *R: A Language and Environment for Statistical Computing*. R Foundation for Statistical Computing, 2013.

[26] F. Rosenberg, M. Muller, P. Leitner, A. Michlmayr, A. Bouguettaya, and S. Dustdar. Metaheuristic Optimization of Large-Scale QoS-aware Service Compositions. In *SCC*, pages 97–104, 2010.

[27] H. Wang, H. Sun, and Q. Yu. Reliable Service Composition via Automatic QoS Prediction. In *SCC*, 2013.

[28] P. Wang, K.-M. Chao, and C.-C. Lo. On Optimal Decision for QoS-Aware Composite Service Selection. *Expert Systems with Applications*, 37(1):440–449, 2010.

[29] L. Zeng, B. Benatallah, A. H.H. Ngu, M. Dumas, J. Kalagnanam, and H. Chang. QoS-Aware Middleware for Web Services Composition. *IEEE Trans. Soft. Eng.*, 30:311 – 327, 2004.

[30] Z. Zheng, H. Ma, M. Lyu, and I. King. QoS-Aware Web Service Recommendation by Collaborative Filtering. *IEEE Trans. Serv. Comp.*, 4(2):140–152, 2011.

[31] E. Zitzler, J. Knowles, and L. Thiele. Quality Assessment of Pareto Set Approximations. In *Multiobjective Optimization*, pages 373–404. 2008.

Robust Next Release Problem: Handling Uncertainty During Optimization

Lingbo Li
University College London
Malet Place, London
WC1E 6BT, UK
lingbo.li.13@ucl.ac.uk

Mark Harman
University College London
Malet Place, London
WC1E 6BT, UK
mark.harman@ucl.ac.uk

Emmanuel Letier
University College London
Malet Place, London
WC1E 6BT, UK
e.letier@ucl.ac.uk

Yuanyuan Zhang
University College London
Malet Place, London
WC1E 6BT, UK
yuanyuan.zhang@ucl.ac.uk

ABSTRACT

Uncertainty is inevitable in real world requirement engineering. It has a significant impact on the feasibility of proposed solutions and thus brings risks to the software release plan. This paper proposes a multi-objective optimization technique, augmented with Monte-Carlo Simulation, that optimizes requirement choices for the three objectives of cost, revenue, and uncertainty. The paper reports the results of an empirical study over four data sets derived from a single real world data set. The results show that the robust optimal solutions obtained by our approach are conservative compared to their corresponding optimal solutions produced by traditional Multi-Objective Next Release Problem. We obtain a robustness improvement of at least 18% at a small cost (a maximum 0.0285 shift in the 2D Pareto-front in the unit space). Surprisingly we found that, though a requirement's cost is correlated with inclusion on the Pareto-front, a requirement's expected revenue is not.

Categories and Subject Descriptors

D.2.1 [**Software Engineering**]: Requirements—*Specifications Methodologies*

General Terms

Algorithms, Measurement, Performance, Experimentation.

Keywords

Software engineering, Genetic algorithms, Multi-objective optimization, Robustness of solutions, Empirical study

GECCO'14, July 12–16, 2014, Vancouver, BC, Canada.

http://dx.doi.org/10.1145/2576768.2598334.

1. INTRODUCTION

Uncertainty is an inherent characteristic of software engineering, and cannot be avoided [25]. The uncertainties in software engineering include uncertainty about the actual implementation cost of a software project, actual revenue of implemented features, and the possibility that the resulting product achieves its expected economic performance. Underestimated or ignored uncertainties may bring risks into software projects.

Previous Multi-Objective Next Release Problem (MONRP) work was concerned with point-based estimation [11,12,23]. The limitation of point-based estimation is that uncertainty and risk are either underestimated or completely overlooked [8]. For example, a requirement engineer may estimate that the *expected cost* of a feature is £500 and *expected revenue* is £700. The *expected net-revenue* (*expected revenue − expected cost*) is £200. There is a risk that the *expected net-revenue* may be lower than a threshold assigned by decision makers due to uncertainty concerning the true revenue and cost. The development cost of the feature may exceed £500, and the revenue of the feature may lower than £700. This tendency for feature attributes to change has been regarded as one of reasons why software development is difficult and expensive [22].

In order to mitigate the impact of uncertainty, previous work on requirements engineering undertook sensitivity analysis after optimizing the Next Release Problem (NRP) [14, 16]. Sensitivity analysis was performed on solutions to investigate solutions's uncertainty. The most related work to our study is Paixão and Souza's work [20]. They formulated the uncertainty of NRP into a scenario-based framework. In their approach, the revenue of requirements have the same probability distribution: the cost of each requirement is quantified in a deterministic continuous interval format. Though this approach addresses uncertainty, it is limited by the implicit assumption that the real probability is universal.

In this paper, we adopt a search-based optimization technique with Monte-Carlo Simulation (MCS) to address uncertainty and risk in the early stages of the software engineering development process. Our approach makes explicit the trade-off between uncertainty/risk and traditional attributes of cost & revenue. It is assumed that the Probability Density Function (PDF) of features (in terms of cost and revenue) has been determined by a prior risk analysis [7]. The paper builds novel formulations of uncertainty to guide the NRP and presents robust Pareto-optimal solutions to decision makers. There are two notions of uncertainty measurement introduced: size of uncertainty region [18] and the failure possibility: the probability that actual cost exceeds a threshold. There are two definitions of robust solution considered in the paper: 1) the solution's *payoff* (in terms of cost and revenue) has narrow fluctuation range, 2) the actual cost of solution has low possibility to exceed the threshold. Each is 'robust' in the sense that it minimizes the risk associated with a requirement choice. We compute the uncertainties of variables as probability distributions, and simulate them by MCS. We measure the two kinds of robustness, and explore the Pareto-front by using multi-objective evolution algorithm. Our approach can provide the solutions that balance the trade-off among revenue, cost, and robustness in a software project.

The main contributions of this paper are the following:

1. The paper introduces two notions of uncertainty measurements for NRP: *MCNRP-US* (MCS for NRP - Uncertainty Size) and *MCNRP-R* (MCS for NRP - Risk) (Section 3). Each formulation has three objectives for optimization.

2. The paper is the first paper that addresses robust NRP by integrating the MCS into the search process itself. Previous work treats it as a post hoc computation. As a result, the decision maker has no option to *minimize* uncertainty, which is supported by our approach.

3. Results of our evaluation on 4 data sets derived from the Motorola data set [4] indicate that our approach reduces risk/uncertainty with very little change to the traditional 2D MONRP Pareto-front.

The structure of rest of the paper is organized as follows: Section 2 describes the related work in NRP, robust optimization and sensitivity analysis. Section 3 formally defines the research problem. Section 4 describes the Monte-Carlo Simulation & search algorithm used. Section 5 describes the experimental setup, algorithm configuration, evaluation methods, and research questions. Section 6 reports the results of the experiments and analyses the findings. Section 8 presents the conclusion and suggestions for future work.

2. RELATED WORK

The term NRP was introduced by Bagnall et al. [3] in 2001. The NRP aims to search the feasible and ideal solution set to balance the requests from different stakeholders. The NRP was formulated as a single-objective optimization problem by Bagnall et al. [3]. Zhang et al. [23] extended the NRP to MONRP by formulating revenue and cost as two objectives.

In terms of uncertainty analysis, researchers usually adapt quantitative analysis methods, such as uncertainty analysis [24], to evaluate the robustness of the model. Sensitivity analysis is one uncertainty analysis method. Harman et al. [16] studied the data sensitivity of NRP and MONRP by using a local sensitivity analysis approach "One-At-a-Time" [21]. This approach measured data sensitivity by perturbing variables upward or downwards to try out various what-if scenarios. To avoid potential noise from the inherent character of stochastic of the meta-heuristic algorithm, Harman et al. [14] applied an exact algorithm, a variant of the Nemhauser-Ullmann's algorithm [19], to study the precise sensitivity analysis of NRP. Al-Emran and Ruhe et al. [1, 2] applied probabilistic sensitivity analysis which integrates MCS with process simulation to study the impact of uncertainty in operational release planning and product release planning as a post-analysis.

However, Hans-Georg and Bernhard [6] indicated that it is important to investigate uncertainty *during* the process of optimization rather than using post-analysis. They proposed robust optimization [6]. Li [18] introduced a novel metric of uncertainty for guiding multi-objective optimization problem. In his work, the uncertainty of a parameter's true value was represented as an interval and the uncertainty of solutions was represented as tolerance region (uncertainty size). In 2013, Paixão and Souza used a scenario-based robust optimization framework for NRP to produce robust optimal solutions [20].

Our paper is the first paper on Search-Based Software Engineering (SBSE) [15] to introduce MCS to simulate the uncertainties of NRP as one of the objectives to guide the search to explore the robust Pareto-optimal front.

3. PROBLEM FORMULATION

In this section, we describe the definition of the NRP and the metrics that capture uncertainty in our approach.

3.1 NRP Problem

It is assumed that there is a set of stakeholders and their features in the next release of a software system. The set of stakeholders is denoted by Eq.1 and the set of possible requirements is denoted by Eq.2.

$$C = \{c_1, \cdots, c_m\} \quad (1)$$
$$R = \{r_1, \cdots, r_n\} \quad (2)$$

where m is the number of stakeholders, and n is the number of features.

In this paper, all requirements are independent of each other. During the software development, some resources (e.g., human resources and facility resources) need to be allocated to satisfy each requirement. NRP uses cost to measure the amount of resource needed to fulfill the requirement as given by Eq.3.

$$Cost = \{cost_1, \cdots, cost_n\} \quad (3)$$

There is a weight vector which reflects the degree of importance of each stakeholder for the company. The relative weight vector related to each stakeholder c ($1 \leq j \leq m$) is denoted as Eq.4:

$$Weight = \{w_1, \cdots, w_m\} \quad (4)$$

Subject to: $w_j \in [0, 1]$, and $\sum_{j=1}^{m} w_j = 1$.

It is assumed that the importance of each requirement for each stakeholder is different. Given a stakeholder, the level of satisfaction of this stakeholder is based on the requirements that are satisfied in the evolved suggestion for the next release of the software system. Based on this assump-

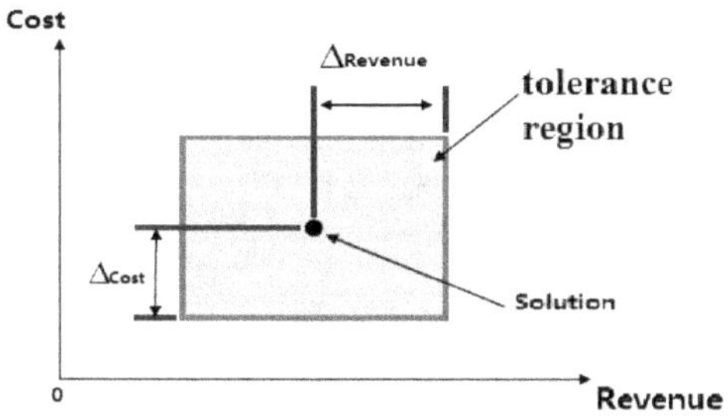

Figure 1: The tolerance region of a MONRP solution [18].

tion, each requirement r_i $(1 \leq i \leq n)$ is assigned a *value* (r_i, c_j) by each stakeholder c_j $(1 \leq j \leq m)$. The overall revenue of a given requirement r_i $(1 \leq i \leq n)$ for the company is denoted by Eq.5.

$$Revenue_i = \sum_{j=1}^{m}(w_j \cdot value(r_i, c_j)) \quad (5)$$

In NRP, the solution is presented as a decision vector $\vec{x} = \{x_1, \cdots, x_n\} \in \{0, 1\}$ to determine the requirements that are to be selected in the next release. In this vector, x_i is 1 if requirement i is selected and 0 otherwise.

3.2 Robust MONRP formulation

This paper considers two types of robustness in MONRP. These two definitions of robust solution are "reduction of the uncertainty size", and "reduction of the possibility that actual cost exceeds a threshold" (named "failure risk reduction").

3.2.1 Uncertainty Size Reduction (MCNRP-US)

Uncertainty size is used to measure the tolerance region of the solutions of multi-objective optimization problem in d dimensions (d is the number of the objectives). For example, in NRP, $\Delta cost_i$ is an acceptable fluctuation range of the cost of the ith requirement. The tolerance region consists of the confidence levels of each fitness value. The confidence level indicates the most likely fluctuation range of fitness values. Figure 1 illustrates a tolerance region for a NRP solution with cost and revenue objective functions. The shaded area is the tolerance region of the given solution. In Li's work [18], the standard deviation of each fitness value is used as confidence level. Hence, the tolerance region is composed of the standard deviation of each fitness value.

The size of tolerance region is presented by its normalized hyper-perimeter (Eq.6) and hyper-volume (Eq.7). To normalize the metric of each fitness value, we need to define fitness value referent with respect to each objective function.

$$perimeter(\vec{x}) = \sum_{k=1}^{d} \frac{2 \cdot \Delta fitness_k(\vec{x})}{referent\_fitness_k} \quad (6)$$

$$volume(\vec{x}) = \prod_{k=1}^{d} \frac{2 \cdot \Delta fitness_k(\vec{x})}{referent\_fitness_k} \quad (7)$$

where d is the number of objective functions. Therefore, all our fitness values lie in a normalized unit space. This facilitates comparison of Pareto-front using Euclidean Distance.

Besides, the weighted sum of these two metrics is defined as the *uncertainty size* and shown in Eq.8

$$Size(\vec{x}) = \alpha \cdot volume(\vec{x}) + \beta \cdot perimeter(\vec{x}) \quad (8)$$

Where $\alpha + \beta = 1$. In this work, we defined $\alpha = 0.5$ and $\beta = 0.5$.

We named this model as *MCNRP-US* (MCS for NRP-Uncertainty Size). The *MCNRP-US* consisting of the objective functions can be presented as follows (Eq.9, Eq.10, and Eq.11):

$$Maximize f_1(\vec{x}) = \sum_{i=1}^{n}(x_i \cdot Expected\_Revenue_i) \quad (9)$$

$$Minimize f_2(\vec{x}) = \sum_{i=1}^{n}(x_i \cdot Expected\_Cost_i) \quad (10)$$

$$Minimize f_3(\vec{x}) = Size(\vec{x}) \quad (11)$$

3.2.2 Failure Risk Reduction (MCNRP-R)

In our approach, the risk of a given solution is measured by the probability that the actual cost exceeds a threshold determined by the decision maker. In order to reduce the risk of budget overrun, our second approach minimizes the probability that actual cost exceeds the budget (Eq.12).

$$Risk(\vec{x}) = Pro(actual\_cost(\vec{x}) > \theta \cdot Expected\_Cost(\vec{x})) \quad (12)$$

Where θ is the percentage assigned by the decision maker (e.g., $\theta = 150\%$), and *Pro* means Probability.

This model named *MCNRP-R* (MCS for NRP-Risk). The objective functions of *MCNPR-R* are shown as Eq.9, Eq.10, and Eq.13:

$$Minimize f_3(\vec{x}) = Risk(\vec{x}) \quad (13)$$

4. OPTIMIZATION APPROACH

Our approach contains two procedures: MCS and multi-objective optimization. MCS enables us to simulate and evaluate a large number of scenarios effectively. The output of MCS process is used by the multi-objective optimization process. The multi-objective optimization is used to optimize multiple and possibly conflicting objectives simultaneously. In this paper, we adopt the NSGA-II algorithm for optimization.

Monte Carlo Simulation (MCS) [13] is a computerized mathematical technique to explore the range of possible outcomes of the model and the probability that these outcomes will occur. The principle of MCS is to sample a large number of scenarios generated by substituting the probability distributions of model parameter values. It then calculates the results of model for all scenarios.

MCS generates a "scenarios database": an $s \times n$ matrix, *Simulations*, where s is the number of scenarios and n is the number of requirements. The element $Simulations[i, j]$ denotes the value of requirement j in ith scenario. The value includes the simulated revenue and the simulated cost of a given requirement. The number of scenarios was set to $10,000$.

The well-known Non-dominated Sorting Genetic Algorithm-II (NSGA-II) was introduced by Deb et al. [9]. We use

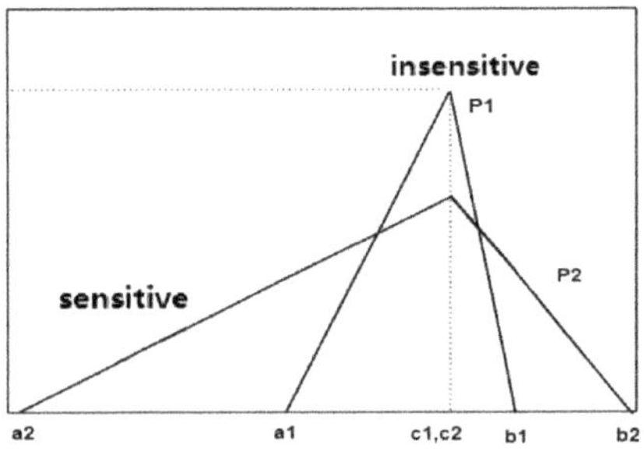

Figure 2: Illustration of the triangle probability distribution and the classification of sensitive and insensitive distributions [10]. c_1 and c_2 are the mode value of probability distribution P_1 and probability distribution P_2, respectively. a_1 and b_1 is the lowest value and highest of P_1 respectively while a_2 and b_2 is the lowest value and highest of P_2. P_1 is considered to be more 'stable' (insensitive).

NSGA-II to provide a Pareto-front that captures the trade-off between cost & revenue and risk (assessed using MCS).

5. EXPERIMENTAL SET UP

5.1 Data Sets

There are four synthetic data sets used in our experiments. The four data sets are synthetically constructed from one real project data set from Motorola [4]. The Motorola data set concerns a set of 35 requirements for hand held communication devices. Each requirement has the estimated implementation cost and expected revenue level. There is no uncertainty information for the cost and revenue of requirements. Our approaches can accept most kinds of probability distributions, such as uniform distribution, normal distribution, and discrete distribution. In this work, we simulated these uncertainties according to the "triangle probability distribution" illustrated in Figure 2.

Our four synthetic data sets represent four general scenarios (*S1* - *S4*), according to the degree of uncertainty about requirements' cost.

- ***S1*** Requirements for low cost have low probability to change (insensitive), while requirements for high cost have high probability to change (sensitive).
- ***S2*** Requirements for low cost have high probability to change (sensitive), while requirements for high cost have low probability to change (insensitive).
- ***S3*** Requirements for low cost have low probability to change (insensitive), while requirements for high cost have low probability to change (insensitive).
- ***S4*** Requirements for low cost have high probability to change (sensitive), while requirements for high cost have high probability to change (sensitive).

The ith requirement would be classified as low cost requirement if $cost_i < \frac{\sum_{j=1}^{n} cost_j}{n}$, otherwise high cost requirement, where n is the number of requirements. We define low probability as the possible change range is within 100%, while for high probability it is within 250%. The uncertainty of each cost is stochastically generated based on the above definitions. The uncertainty of revenue is randomly generated to have low probability (insensitive). A partial data of *S1* reported in Table 1.

Table 1: Illustrative fragment of *S1* data

	Cost			Revenue			
NAME	Mode	Min	Max	Mode	Min	Max	Sensitivity
REQ 1	100.00	79.42	127.91	3.00	0.65	3.32	insensitive
REQ 2	50.00	15.08	53.51	3.00	1.30	3.95	insensitive
REQ 3	300.00	270.74	1154.15	3.00	0.32	4.76	sensitive
REQ 4	80.00	52.73	105.30	3.00	1.31	5.50	insensitive
REQ 5	70.00	42.00	78.77	3.00	1.66	4.62	insensitive
REQ 6	100.00	87.34	133.04	3.00	1.01	4.19	insensitive
REQ 7	1000.00	620.75	3671.35	3.00	0.77	5.68	sensitive

5.2 Search Algorithmic Tuning

We base our algorithmic parameter & tuning on those used in previous work on MONRP [23]. We used binary encoding to represent the decision vector. The initial population size was set to 500. The algorithm was run for a maximum of 50,000 function evaluations. The genetic operators used in our approaches are tournament selection (with tournament size of 5), single-point crossover (with crossover probability 0.8) and bitwise mutation (with the mutation probability $1/n$ where n is the number of requirements). The algorithm was executed 30 times for each data set, to cater for the stochastic nature of the algorithm.

5.3 Evaluation

5.3.1 *Price of Robustness*

In order to measure such loss between the proposed robust Pareto-front and original Pareto-front with regard to cost and revenue objectives, we utilized the "reduction factor" [5] to measure the "Price of Robustness". This factor measures the distance between two fronts [16]. To compute such distance, we defined $(A_1, \cdots, A_p)$ as the $front_a$ which contains p solutions, while $(B_1, \cdots, B_q)$ denotes the q solutions in $front_b$, where p and q are the number of solutions in $front_a$ and $front_b$ respectively.

The distance from solution A to solution B is computed by the normalized objective values and Euclidean Distance. In the case of "Price of Robustness", the distance between solution A and B is defined as:

$$Dis(A, B) = \pm\sqrt{\sum_{i=1}^{d}(A\_fit_i - B\_fit_i)^2} \tag{14}$$

Where d is the number of objectives. A_fit_i and B_fit_i are the ith objectives value of A and B, respectively.

The distance from solution A to geometrically closest solution B on $front_b$ is presented as the distance from solution A to $front_b$ (Eq.15).

$$Dis(A, front_b) = Dis(A, B) \tag{15}$$

Therefore, the distance from $front_a$ to $front_b$ is the mean value of the distance from every solution on $front_a$ to $front_b$.

$$Dis(front_a, front_b) = \frac{\sum_{i=1}^{p} Dis(A_i, front_b)}{p} \tag{16}$$

5.3.2 *Probabilistic Sensitivity Analysis*

To measure the amount of robustness improvement achieved by our robust optimization approach, we performed a probabilistic sensitivity analysis. Firstly, we used the same sampling technique to simulate the uncertainties of data. After that, we adopted robustness formulations defined in our paper to calculate the robustness of Pareto-optimal solutions of traditional approach.

5.4 Research Questions

In order to evaluate the effectiveness and usefulness of the approaches, we carried out two experimental studies to assess the efficiency of the approaches and four scenarios to evaluate its usefulness. In the experiments, we compared the results obtained from our approaches with the ones obtained from MONRP, and formalized one research questions. The question is whether the proposed approaches can provide more robust solutions to decision makers with less sacrifice? This question formulated into three more detailed sub-questions (***RQ1***, ***RQ2***, and ***RQ3***).

Additionally, to aid the decision making support before preforming such professional tools, this paper also investigated the correlations between attributes of a requirement and its inclusion in solutions on the Pareto-front. This is formulated into the fourth question ***RQ4***.

RQ1 Do the proposed two kinds of robust optimization improve robustness? This question will be answered by analyzing and comparing the robustness of solutions which were generated by our approaches and the original MONRP.

RQ2 How much "Price of Robustness" would be paid for the proposed robust optimization approaches? We will answer this question by calculating the distance between the Pareto-front obtained from our approaches and those obtained from the original MONRP. The distance was used to measure the loss in *payoff*.

RQ3 How similar are the Pareto-fronts produced by our new approaches and the one produced by traditional MONRP? We computed and ranked the proportion of requirements being selected in solutions on the Pareto-front. Then we used Kendall's τ correlation coefficient to statistically investigate the degree of similarity between the rankings of requirements included in solutions on the Pareto-front to answer this question.

RQ4 Which attributes of a requirement are correlated with inclusion in solutions on the Pareto-front?

We performed an intuitive analysis to answer the ***RQ1*** and ***RQ2***, while more statistically analysis to answer the ***RQ3*** and ***RQ4***.

6. EXPERIMENTAL RESULTS & ANALYSIS

This section presents two different robust models and the results of applying these two models on four synthetic problem instances. Two experiments were conducted and the illustrations of results are presented in Figures 3 and 4 (Figures 3a, 3b, 3c, 3d, and Figures 4a, 4b, 4c, 4d), for *E1* & *E2* respectively. The two experiments, *E1* & *E2*, are described below:

Table 2: The Robustness & Comparison of the *MCNRP-US* Approach and the Traditional Approach

	S1	*S2*	*S3*	*S4*
MCNRP-US	0.1531	0.1558	0.1850	0.1290
Original Approach	0.1983	0.1599	0.1993	0.1511
Price of Robustness	0.0110	0.0201	0.0154	0.0102
Robustness Improvement	22.78%	2.54%	7.19%	14.65%

E1 The first experiment aims at evaluating the *MCNRP-US* approach and the "Price of Robustness" of this approach, when the decision maker expects to obtain robust solutions within a defined fluctuation range.

E2 The second experiment evaluates the *MCNRP-R* approach and its "Price of Robustness" for the situation in which the decision maker would like to acquire robust solutions which have a low risk of budget overrun.

In order to compare our proposed approach to the traditional MONRP approach, the Pareto-fronts of proposed approach are presented by dark black patterns and traditional ones by grey (red when viewed in colour) patterns. This selection quantitatively analysis and answer the *RQ3* and *RQ4* as well.

6.1 Experiment One (E1)

In *E1*, the *uncertainty size* of a solution is taken into account. The results of *E1* are shown in Figures 3a, 3b, 3c, and 3d corresponding to scenarios *S1*, *S2*, *S3*, and *S4*, respectively. The figures illustrate the three-dimensional Pareto surface. Each bar represents a solution on the Pareto-front. The location of each bar in the *cost-revenue* plane presents the *cost* and *revenue* of the solution respectively. The height of the bar shows the *uncertainty size* for each solution.

From the results of *E1* for *S1*, *S2*, *S3*, and *S4*, we observe that, as the overall fulfilled *cost* increases, the *uncertainty size* of solution also increases. We also observe that there are minor differences between the Pareto-fronts of *MCNRP-US* and the traditional approach in *S1* and *S4* (Figures 3a and 3d), while there are larger differences between *S2* and *S3* (Figures 3b and 3c). High cost requirements naturally have more impact on solution sensitivity than low cost requirements [16]. Requirements with high cost are stable in *S2* and *S3*, and the proposed first approach tends to select the "stable" solution rather than the solutions just have good economic performance but "unstable".

Table 2 presents the results of probabilistic sensitivity analysis for *E1*, the "*Price of Robustness*" for "*MCNRP-US*" approach, and how much robustness with regarded to *uncertainty size* improved by applying this approach.

Based on the results in this table we answer ***RQ1*** and ***RQ2*** (for *MCNRP-US*) as follows: On average, the *MCNRP-US* generates more robust solutions with respect to *uncertainty size*. The overall improvement is not large: after normalizing *cost* and *revenue*, the magnitude of standard deviation of *cost* and *revenue* is small, so the magnitude of *uncertainty size* is small. Even so, it is interesting that the robustness improvements for *S1* and *S4* (22.78% and 14.65% respectively) are better than the improvements for *S2* and *S3* (2.54% and 7.19% respectively).

Although the improvement of *MCNRP-US* is not dramatic, it pays a little as the "*Price of Robustness*". Therefore, we conclude that applying our *MCNRP-US* approach,

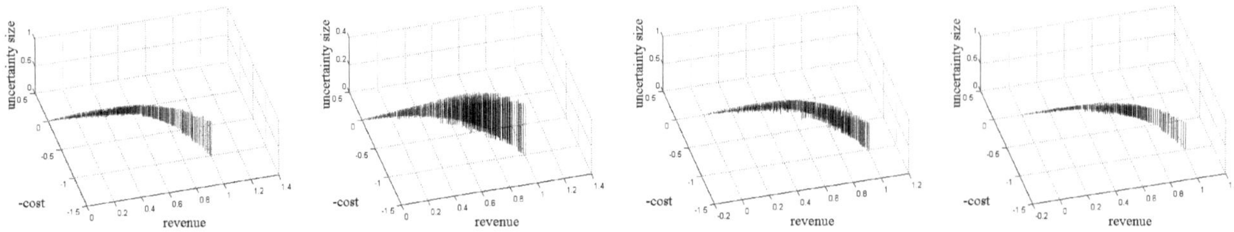

(a) The results of *E1* in *S1* (b) The results of *E1* in *S2* (c) The results of *E1* in *S3* (d) The results of *E1* in *S4*

Figure 3: The Pareto-front of *MCNRP-US* and Original Approach

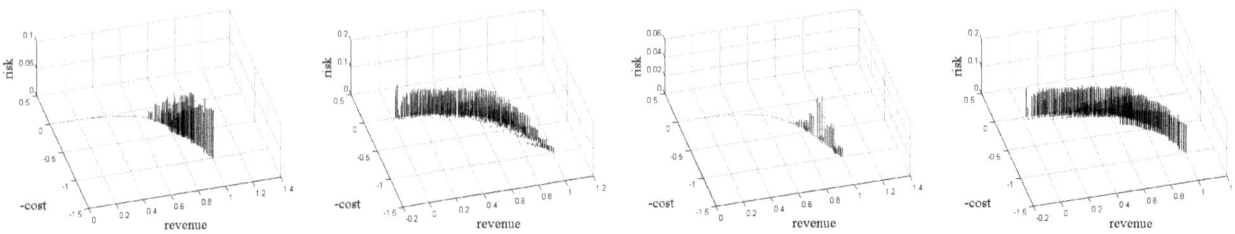

(a) The results of *E2* in *S1* (b) The results of *E2* in *S2* (c) The results of *E2* in *S3* (d) The results of *E2* in *S4*

Figure 4: The Pareto-front of *MCNRP-R* and Original Approach

Table 3: The Robustness & Comparison of the *MCNRP-R* Approach and the Traditional Approach

	S1	*S2*	*S3*	*S4*
MCNRP-R	0.0396	0.0404	0.0109	0.0591
Original Approach	0.0500	0.0755	0.0132	0.0888
Price of Robustness	0.0036	0.0253	0.0003	0.0285
Robustness Improvement	20.82%	46.49%	17.70%	33.37%

the decision maker pays a small price to obtain a more robust Pareto-front, whose solutions have smaller *uncertainty size*.

6.2 Experiment Two (E2)

The results of *E2* are plotted in Figures 4a, 4b, 4c, and 4d. In *E2*, the *risk* was considered as a third objective.

From the results of *E2* in *S1*, *S2*, *S3*, and *S4*, a general trend is observed: the degree of *risk* increases as overall *cost* increases. However, there is an interesting observation in Figure 4b. The *risk* is inversely proportional to *cost*. The reason for this phenomenon is that the *risk* is directly proportional to the stability of the probability distribution of *cost*. The more stable the probability distribution is, the lower risk there will be. In *E2*, there are some other interesting observations: According to the results, we observe that the obtained "robust" Pareto-fronts are quite close to those obtained from original MONRP in *S1* and *S3*, while there are a big gap in *S2* and *S4*. This is because the probability distribution of high *cost* is unstable in *S2* and *S4*.

Table 3 shows that the robustness with regards to risk can be noticeably improved by the *MCNRP-R* approach compared to traditional approach. Moreover, the payment (*Price of Robustness*) is low.

As an overall answer ***RQ1*** and ***RQ2*** (for MONRP-R) we find that we can achieve an improvement of at least 18% in robustness with only a little change in 2D cost-revenue Pareto-front (maximum 0.0285 in a unit space). That is, the penalization due to robustness is very small for all scenarios, which qualifies the effectiveness of *MCNRP-R* approach.

Table 4: The Correlation of Rankings of Requirements

		MONRP&R	MONRP&US	US&R
S1	τ	0.9361	0.7345	0.7311
	p-value	< 0.000	< 0.000	< 0.000
S2	τ	0.8646	0.7872	0.8756
	p-value	< 0.000	< 0.000	< 0.000
S3	τ	0.9655	0.7233	0.7311
	p-value	< 0.000	< 0.000	< 0.000
S4	τ	0.8646	0.8713	0.8387
	p-value	< 0.000	< 0.000	< 0.000

In this table, R means MONRP-R, and US means MONRP-US.

6.3 Statistical Analysis

To answer the ***RQ3*** and ***RQ4*** statistically, Kendall's τ correlation coefficient τ is used to quantitatively analyse the correlation between and within the approaches. Table 4 shows Kendall's τ correlation coefficient and corresponding p-value calculated for the relation between the paired approach (MONRP and MONRP-R, MONRP and MONRP-US, and MONRP-R and MONRP-US) with regard to each scenario. If all solutions in Pareto-front agree on a requirement to be selected, the requirement is said to be "closed" [17]. Here, we generalize this notion of "closed" decision to investigate correlations between degrees of "closedness".

The Table 4 reveals that there are existing strong correlations between the rankings of requirements produced by each approach on each scenario. All τ coefficients are greater than 0.7, and p-values are very close to zero. This confirms that

Table 5: The Correlation between the Attributes of Requirement and its Ranking

	Cost		Revenue		R/C	
MONRP	τ	$p-$Value	τ	$p-$Value	τ	$p-$Value
S1	-0.7748	< 0.000	0.0723	0.55358	0.9597	< 0.000
S2	-0.7569	< 0.000	0.1413	0.23846	0.9521	< 0.000
S3	-0.7771	< 0.000	0.074	0.54138	0.9521	< 0.000
S4	-0.7704	< 0.000	0.1346	0.26185	0.9554	< 0.000
MONRP-US	τ	$p-$Value	τ	$p-$Value	τ	$p-$Value
S1	-0.5899	< 0.000	0.0824	0.49827	0.721	< 0.000
S2	-0.6034	< 0.000	0.2336	0.049495	0.7714	< 0.000
S3	-0.5832	< 0.000	0.0924	0.44599	0.7008	< 0.000
S4	-0.6807	< 0.000	0.1765	0.14052	0.8521	< 0.000
MONRP-R	τ	$p-$Value	τ	$p-$Value	τ	$p-$Value
S1	-0.7244	< 0.000	0.1092	0.3661	0.8958	< 0.000
S2	-0.6807	< 0.000	0.1966	0.09972	0.8555	< 0.000
S3	-0.758	< 0.000	0.0924	0.44599	0.9294	< 0.000
S4	-0.674	< 0.000	0.1899	0.11213	0.8521	< 0.000

In this table, Cost is the Expected Cost, Revenue is the Expected Revenue, and R/C is the Expected *Revenue-to-Cost* Ratio.

the rankings of requirements produced by each approach are similar to each other.

Hence, the Pareto-fronts on Cost-Revenue dimension generated by each approach are similar to each other. We further observe that the correlation is stronger between MONRP and MONRP-R than MONRP and MONRP-US. This answers ***RQ3***.

In order to answer ***RQ4***, Table 5 uses Kendall's tau correlation analysis to statistically describe the correlation between the attributes of requirements and the rankings of requirements. The results reveal that, in general, the requirement's *Revenue-to-Cost* ratio and *Cost* have strong monotonic correlation with its likelihood of inclusion, while its *Revenue* is uncorrelated. The requirement's *Revenue-to-Cost* ratio is the most strongly correlated.

7. THREATS TO VALIDITY

In this paper, our approach applies a multi-objective search-based technique, which is augmented with MCS, to solve the NRP in the presence of uncertainty. We evaluated our work respecting to its construct validity, internal validity, and external validity.

7.1 Construct validity

The threat to construct validity is concerning whether our approach can deal with the real uncertainty. Our method utilizes MCS to compute the estimation uncertainties on requirements, and to produce thousands of scenarios to simulate the actual uncertain NRP parameters. In this paper, only triangle probability distribution is used to present the uncertainties, while there are sorely other kinds of uncertainties that might be used in risk analysis. Moreover, the kinds of uncertainties are used to generate the scenarios whose attributes are formed as input parameters of MONRP approach. Hence, it is straightforward to introduce other kinds of uncertainties to model the uncertainties of requirements. Our approach aims to handle the uncertainty of NRP by MCS. MCS can simulate most kinds of uncertainties. Besides, the types of uncertainties can be formed into the requirements by engineers. Therefore, we believe our approach can be extended to solve the real NRP with various uncertainties.

7.2 Internal validity

The internal validity is concerned with any possible factor that may perturb the experimental evaluations. Hence, in our experiments, we exclude other system applications, so the experimental machine only runs our application. Each experiment was repeated 30 times to cater for variations in algorithmic performance. The other potential threat to internal validity concerns the algorithm parameters tuning that could have affected the experimental results during the evaluations. Our work is based on the works of Zhang et al. [23], and the algorithm parameters have been previously studied [11] [22].

7.3 External validity

In the experimental study, we evaluated our approaches over four data sets derived from one single real world data set from Motorola. There is no uncertainty information within the Motorola data set. Therefore we simulated the four scenarios with uncertainties based on different degrees. Since we lack a real software engineering problem data set, the scale of our experiments and number of scenarios remains insufficient. More work is required to analyse different scenarios & models of uncertainty.

In our work, the experimental results did not show any critical threat to its scalability. Our implementation is able to process about $10,000$ scenarios in 15s, and each scenario consists of $50,000$ runs. The heaviest computational consumption is MCS. While the scale of problem is increasing, our methods become more complex and time consuming. A simple way to address this issue is to reduce the number of simulations. Consequently, the computation time will reduce, while the simulation error will increase. Since this paper focusses on proposing a novel approach to handle uncertainty in NRP, optimizing the performance of this approach will be an interesting further work.

8. CONCLUSIONS & FUTURE WORK

In this paper, we introduced an MCS based robust optimization approach for requirement analysis and optimization.

We introduced two notions of uncertainty measurements defined for NRP. According to the experiments upon which this paper reports, the proposed two robust MONRP approaches (*MCNRP-US* and *MCNRP-R*) overcome the limitation of the traditional MONRP approach which underestimates (or even hides) uncertainty. These allow the decision maker to choose different approaches for controlling different types of uncertainty, while retaining the performance of traditional solutions. The *MCNRP-US* offers decision makers a way to control the fluctuation range of *payoff* for solutions. The *MCNRP-R* model helps decision makers to explore solutions with lower *risk* of budget overrun.

We found that MONRP-R decisions are more closely correlated to traditional MONRP decisions regarding requirement choice, than MONRP-US. We also find that, while cost is closely correlated to inclusion of a requirement in the Pareto-front, revenue is not.

In this paper, only triangle probability distribution uncertainty has been examined. Real world requirement engineering analysis and optimization problems typically contain a mixture of types of uncertainties. Hence, future work will focus on adapting and evaluating our approach on other real world scenarios.

9. REFERENCES

[1] A. Al-Emran, P. Kapur, D. Pfahl, and G. Ruhe. Studying the impact of uncertainty in operational release planning - an integrated method and its initial evaluation. *Information and Software Technology*, 52(4):446–461, Apr. 2010.

[2] A. Al-Emran, D. Pfahl, and G. Ruhe. Decision support for product release planning based on robustness analysis. In *Proceedings of the 2010 18th IEEE International Requirements Engineering Conference (RE'10)*, pages 157–166, Washington, DC, USA, 2010. IEEE Computer Society.

[3] A. J. Bagnall, V. J. Rayward-Smith, and I. M. Whittley. The next release problem. *Information and Software Technology*, 43(14):883–890, 2001.

[4] P. Baker, M. Harman, K. Steinhofel, and A. Skaliotis. Search based approaches to component selection and prioritization for the next release problem. In *Proceedings of the 22nd IEEE International Conference on Software Maintenance (ICSM'06)*, pages 176–185, Washington, DC, USA, 2006. IEEE Computer Society.

[5] D. Bertsimas and M. Sim. The price of robustness. *Operations research*, 52(1):35–53, 2004.

[6] H.-G. Beyer and B. Sendhoff. Robust optimization–a comprehensive survey. *Computer Methods in Aplied Mechanics and Engineering*, 196(33):3190–3218, 2007.

[7] B. W. Boehm. *Software Engineering Economics.* Prentice Hall, Upper Saddle River, NJ, USA, 1st edition, 1981.

[8] A. Budzier. Why your it project may be riskier than you think. *Harvard Business Review*, 89(9):23–25, 2011.

[9] K. Deb, A. Pratap, S. Agarwal, and T. Meyarivan. A fast and elitist multiobjective genetic algorithm: NSGA-II. *Transaction on Evoluionary Computation*, 6(2):182–197, Apr 2002.

[10] J. C. Felli and G. B. Hazen. Sensitivity analysis and the expected value of perfect information. *Medical Decision Making*, 18(1):95–109, 1998.

[11] A. Finkelstein, M. Harman, S. Mansouri, J. Ren, and Y. Zhang. "Fairness analysis" in requirements assignments. In *International Requirements Engineering, 2008. RE'08. 16th IEEE*, pages 115–124, Sept 2008.

[12] D. Greer and G. Ruhe. Software release planning: an evolutionary and iterative approach. *Information and Software Technology*, 46(4):243–253, 2004.

[13] J. M. Hammersley, D. C. Handscomb, and G. Weiss. Monte carlo methods. *Physics Today*, 18:55, 1965.

[14] M. Harman, I. M.-B. Jens Krinke, J. R. Francisco Palomo-Lozano, and S. Yoo. Exact scalable sensitivity analysis for the next release problem. In *ACM Transactions on Software Engineering and Methodology, 2014.* ACM, 2014. To appear.

[15] M. Harman and B. F. Jones. Search-based software engineering. *Information and Software Technology*, 43(14):833–839, 2001.

[16] M. Harman, J. Krinke, J. Ren, and S. Yoo. Search based data sensitivity analysis applied to requirement engineering. In *Proceedings of the 11th Annual Conference on Genetic and Evolutionary Computation (GECCO'09)*, pages 1681–1688, New York, NY, USA, 2009. ACM.

[17] E. Letier, D. Stefan, and E. T. Barr. Uncertainty, risk, and information value in software requirements and architecture. *International Conference on Software Engineering*, 2014.

[18] M. Li, S. Azarm, and V. Aute. A multi-objective genetic algorithm for robust design optimization. In *Proceedings of the 2005 Conference on Genetic and Evolutionary Computation (GECCO'05)*, pages 771–778, New York, NY, USA, 2005. ACM.

[19] G. L. Nemhauser and Z. Ullmann. Discrete dynamic programming and capital allocation. *Management Science*, 15(9):494–505, 1969.

[20] M. Paixão and J. Souza. A scenario-based robust model for the next release problem. In *Proceedings of the 15th Annual Conference on Genetic and Evolutionary Computation Conference (GECCO'13)*, pages 1469–1476, New York, NY, USA, 2013. ACM.

[21] A. Saltelli, S. Tarantola, and F. Campolongo. Sensitivity analysis as an ingredient of modeling. *Statistical Science*, 15(4):377–395, 2000.

[22] Y. Zhang, E. Alba, J. J. Durillo, S. Eldh, and M. Harman. Today/future importance analysis. In *Proceedings of the 12th Annual Conference on Genetic and Evolutionary Computation (GECCO'10)*, pages 1357–1364, New York, NY, USA, 2010. ACM.

[23] Y. Zhang, M. Harman, and S. A. Mansouri. The multi-objective next release problem. In *Proceedings of the 9th Annual Conference on Genetic and Evolutionary Computation (GECCO'07)*, pages 1129–1137, New York, NY, USA, 2007. ACM.

[24] Z. Zi. Sensitivity analysis approaches applied to systems biology models. *Systems Biology, IET*, 5(6):336–346, Nov 2011.

[25] H. Ziv, D. Richardson, and R. Klösch. The uncertainty principle in software engineering. In *Proceedings of the 19th International Conference on Software Engineering (ICSE'97)*, 1997.

A Parallel Evolutionary Algorithm for Prioritized Pairwise Testing of Software Product Lines

Roberto E. Lopez-Herrejon
Johannes Kepler University
Linz, Austria
roberto.lopez@jku.at

Javier Ferrer
Universidad de Málaga,
Andalucía Tech, Spain
ferrer@lcc.uma.es

Francisco Chicano
Universidad de Málaga,
Andalucía Tech, Spain
chicano@lcc.uma.es

Evelyn Nicole Haslinger
Johannes Kepler University
Linz, Austria
evelyn.haslinger@jku.at

Alexander Egyed
Johannes Kepler University
Linz, Austria
alexander.egyed@jku.at

Enrique Alba
Universidad de Málaga,
Andalucía Tech, Spain
eat@lcc.uma.es

ABSTRACT

Software Product Lines (SPLs) are families of related software systems, which provide different feature combinations. Different SPL testing approaches have been proposed. However, despite the extensive and successful use of evolutionary computation techniques for software testing, their application to SPL testing remains largely unexplored. In this paper we present the Parallel Prioritized product line Genetic Solver (PPGS), a parallel genetic algorithm for the generation of prioritized pairwise testing suites for SPLs. We perform an extensive and comprehensive analysis of PPGS with 235 feature models from a wide range of number of features and products, using 3 different priority assignment schemes and 5 product prioritization selection strategies. We also compare PPGS with the greedy algorithm prioritized-ICPL. Our study reveals that overall PPGS obtains smaller covering arrays with an acceptable performance difference with prioritized-ICPL.

Categories and Subject Descriptors

D.2.5 [**Software Engineering**]: Testing and Debugging—*testing tools*

Keywords

Combinatorial Interaction Testing, Software Product Lines, Pairwise Testing, Feature Models

1. INTRODUCTION

A *Software Product Line (SPL)* is a family of related software systems, which provide different feature combinations [21]. The effective management and realization of *variability* – the capacity of software artifacts to vary – is crucial to reap the benefits of SPLs such as increased software reuse, faster product customization, and reduced time to market.

Because of the large number of feature combinations in typical SPLs, variability modelling poses a unique set of challenging problems for software testing. In recent years many verification and testing SPL approaches, which rely on different techniques, have been proposed (e.g. [5, 6, 8, 16]). However, and despite the extensive and successful use of evolutionary computation techniques for software testing [12, 18], their potential application to SPL testing remains largely unexplored, in particular regarding test prioritization.

In this paper we present the *Parallel Prioritized product line Genetic Solver (PPGS)*, a genetic algorithm for the generation of prioritized pairwise testing suites for SPLs. PPGS receives as input a *feature model* that denotes a set of valid feature combinations and computes a set of products that covers the desired pairs of feature combinations according to a priority scheme that assigns different priority weights to a set of products. This scheme has been sketched in [16] and it is currently successfully applied in an industrial setting. We performed a comprehensive evaluation of PPGS with 235 feature models with a wide range of number of features and number of products, using 3 different weight priority assignment methods and 5 product prioritization selection strategies. In addition, we compared PPGS with prioritized-ICPL [16], an alternative greedy algorithm implementation. For the statistical comparison analysis both algorithms were executed 30 times for each feature model and combinations of priority assignment and product prioritization which yielded a total of 79800 independent runs that required about two weeks of computation on a 64-core dedicated cluster. Our study revealed that overall PPGS obtains smaller covering arrays with an acceptable performance difference with prioritized-ICPL. However, the performance difference tends to decrease as the number of products of the feature models increase. We believe these results shed light on the potential benefits that evolutionary algorithms and other search based techniques can bring for variability modeling problems such as testing.

In summary, the contributions of our work are: *i)* Formalization of the SPL testing prioritization scheme presented in [16], *ii)* Implementation of this scheme with the evolutionary algorithm PPGS, and *iii)* Comprehensive evaluation and comparison of PPGS and the prioritized-ICPL algorithm.

GECCO'14, July 12–16, 2014, Vancouver, BC, Canada.

http://dx.doi.org/10.1145/2576768.2598305.

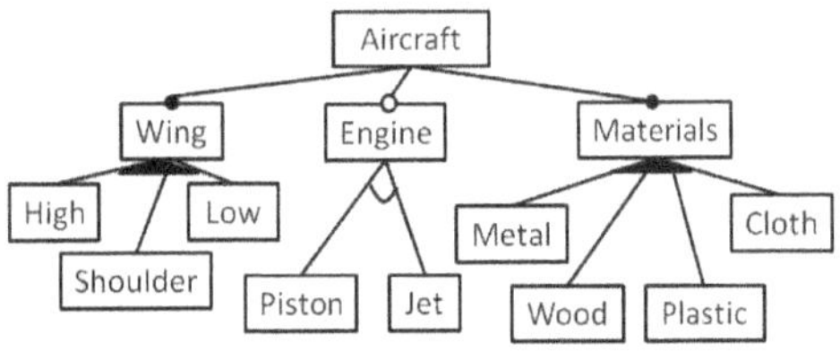

Figure 1: Aircraft SPL Feature Model

Prod	A	Wi	E	Ma	H	S	L	Pi	J	Me	Wo	Pl	C
p0	✓	✓	✓	✓	✓			✓				✓	
p1	✓	✓	✓	✓	✓			✓					✓
p2	✓	✓	✓	✓	✓				✓			✓	
p3	✓	✓	✓	✓	✓				✓				✓
p4	✓	✓		✓	✓						✓		
p5	✓	✓	✓	✓	✓			✓			✓		
p6	✓	✓	✓	✓	✓			✓		✓			
p7	✓	✓	✓	✓	✓				✓	✓			

Table 1: Sample Feature Sets of Aircraft SPL

2. FEATURE MODELS AND RUNNING EXAMPLE

Feature models have become a *de facto* standard for modelling the common and variable features (depicted as labelled boxes) of an SPL and their relationships (depicted with lines) collectively forming a tree-like structure, which denotes the set of feature combinations that the products of an SPL can have [17]. Figure 1 shows the feature model of our running example, a hypothetical SPL of aircraft machines obtained from the SPLOT repository [19]. Each feature, apart from the root, has a single parent feature and can have a set of child features. Notice here that a child feature can only be included in a feature combination of a valid product if its parent is included as well.

The root feature is always included. There are four different kinds of hierarchical feature relationships: *i) Optional features* are depicted with an empty circle and indicate that they may or may not be selected if their respective parent feature is selected. An example is feature `Engine`; *ii) Mandatory features* are depicted with a filled circle and indicate that they have to be selected whenever their respective parent feature is selected. For example, features `Wing` and `Materials`; *iii) Inclusive-or relations* are depicted as filled arcs crossing over a set of lines connecting a parent feature with its child features. They indicate that at least one of the features in the inclusive-or group must be selected if the parent is selected. An example is feature `Materials` that if selected at least one of the features `Metal`, `Wood`, `Plastic`, and `Cloth` must be selected; *iv) Exclusive-or relations* are depicted as empty arcs crossing over a set of lines connecting a parent feature with its children features. They indicate that exactly one of the features in the exclusive-or group must be selected whenever the parent feature is selected. For example, if feature `Engine` is selected, then either feature `Piston` or feature `Jet` must be selected.

Besides the parent-child relations, features can also relate across different branches of the feature model with so called *Cross-Tree Constraints (CTC)*. These constraints as well as those implied by the hierarchical relations between features are usually expressed and checked using propositional logic, for further details refer to [3].

Definition 1. *Feature List (FL) is the list of features in a feature model.*

Definition 2. *Feature Set (FS) is a 2-tuple [sel,$\overline{sel}$] where sel and $\overline{sel}$ are respectively the set of selected and not-selected features of a member product. Let FL be a feature list, thus sel, $\overline{sel} \subseteq FL$, $sel \cap \overline{sel} = \emptyset$, and $sel \cup \overline{sel} = FL$. The terms p.sel and p.$\overline{sel}$ respectively refer to the set of selected and unselected features of product p.*

Definition 3. *A feature set `fs` is valid in feature model `fm`, i.e. `valid(fs, fm)` holds, iff `fs` does not contradict any of the constraints introduced by `fm`.*

The `FL` for the Aircraft feature model is `[Aircraft, Wing, Engine, Materials, High, Shoulder, Low, Piston, Jet, Metal, Wood, Plastic, Cloth]`. For example, the feature set `p0=[{Aircraft, Wing, Engine, Materials, High, Piston, Plastic}, {Shoulder, Low, Jet, Metal, Wood, Cloth}]` is valid. As another example, a feature set with features `Piston` and `Jet` would not be valid because it violates the constraint of the exclusive-or relation which establishes that these two features cannot appear selected together in the same feature set. In our running example, the feature model denotes 315 valid feature sets. Some of them are depicted in Table 1, where for any given feature set its selected features are ticked (✓) and its unselected features are empty. In this table, we use as column labels the shortest distinguishable prefix of the feature names (e.g. `Wi` for feature `Wing`).

3. PRIORITIZED PAIRWISE COVERING ARRAYS IN SPL

In this section we provide a formal definition of the priority scheme implemented by PPGS based on the sketched description provided in [16] and its supporting code.

Definition 4. *A prioritized product `pp` is a 2-tuple [`fs`, w], where `fs` represents a valid feature set in feature model `fm` and $w \in \mathbb{R}$ represents its weight.* Let pp_i and pp_j be two prioritized products. We say that pp_i has higher priority than pp_j for test-suite generation iff pp_i's weight is greater than pp_j's weight, that is $pp_i.w > pp_j.w$.

As an example, let us say that we would like to prioritize product `p1` with a weight of 17. This would be denoted as `pp1=[p1,17]`.

Definition 5. *A pairwise configuration pc is a 2-tuple [sel, $\overline{sel}$] representing a partially configured product, defining the selection of 2 features of feature list FL, i.e. $pc.sel \cup pc.\overline{sel} \subseteq FL \wedge pc.sel \cap pc.\overline{sel} = \emptyset \wedge |pc.sel \cup pc.\overline{sel}| = 2$. We say a pairwise configuration pc is covered by feature set fs iff $pc.sel \subseteq fs.sel \wedge pc.\overline{sel} \subseteq fs.\overline{sel}$.*

Consider for example the pairwise configuration that indicates that feature `Plastic` is selected while feature `Cloth` is deselected `pc1=[{Plastic},{Cloth}]`. Notice that `pc1` is covered by products `p0` and `p2` of Table 1. Another example is pairwise configuration `pc2=[{High, Wood},{}]` with features `High` and `Wood` selected and no feature unselected. This configuration is covered by products `p4` and `p5` of Table 1. A last example is `pc3=[{},{Shoulder, Low}]`, with no selected features and `Shoulder` and `Low` as unselected features. This configuration is covered by all the products shown in Table 1. In total, for all the 315 products denoted by the feature model of Figure 1, there exist 240 valid pairwise configurations.

Definition 6. *A weighted pairwise configuration wpc is a 2-tuple [pc,w] where pc is a pairwise configuration and* $w \in \mathbb{R}$ *represents its weight computed as follows. Let PP be a set of prioritized products and* PP_{pc} *be a subset,* $PP_{pc} \subseteq PP$*, such that* PP_{pc} *contains all prioritized products in PP that cover pc of wpc, i.e.* $PP_{pc} = \{pp \in PP | pp.fs \text{ covers } wpc.pc\}$. *Then* $w = \sum_{p \in PP_{pc}} p.w$

Let us consider the following set of prioritized products from Table 1. Let `PP={[p0,17], [p1,17], [p2,15], [p3,15], [p4,13] , [p5,13], [p6,6], [p7,6]}` with pp_i = $[fs_i, w_i]$, and assume that the remaining 307 products of our feature model in Figure 1 (i.e. 315 minus 8 shown in the table) have priority weight values of 0. The weight of pairwise configuration `pc1=[{Plastic},{Cloth}]` is then `wpc1.w= pp0.w+pp2.w = 17+15 = 32`, that is, the summation of the weights of the products whose feature sets cover `pc1` with weight greater than zero, namely `p0` and `p2`. Similarly, the weight for `pc2` (`High` and `Wood` selected) is `wpc2.w= pp4.w+pp5.w = 13+13 = 26`, and for `pc3` `wpc3.w=102` computed by summing all the product weights because their feature sets all cover `pc3`. In total, the eight products shown in Table 1 generate 169 weighted pairwise configurations with value greater than zero.

Definition 7. *A prioritized pairwise covering array ppCA for a feature model fm and a set of weighted pairwise configurations WPC is a set of valid feature sets FS that covers all weighted pairwise configurations in WPC whose weight is greater than zero:* $\forall wpc \in WPC\ (wpc.w > 0 \Rightarrow \exists fs \in ppCA$ *such that fs covers* $wpc.pc)$.

Let us consider the prioritized products set `PP` just described above. The following table lists six products that together constitute a `ppCA`:

A	Wi	E	Ma	H	S	L	Pi	J	Me	Wo	Pl	C
✓	✓	✓	✓	✓			✓					✓
✓	✓	✓	✓	✓				✓			✓	
✓	✓	✓	✓	✓			✓			✓		
✓	✓	✓	✓	✓				✓	✓	✓		✓
✓	✓	✓	✓		✓		✓		✓		✓	
✓	✓		✓	✓						✓		

Notice that the first three rows correspond to products p1, p2 and p5 of Table 1. Also notice that the last three products are not part of that table even though their weights are considered zero in our running example. That is, their selection led to a ppCA with a smaller number of products than the original set. Next we describe how this pairwise prioritization scheme was implemented by PPGS.

The optimization problem we are interested in consists of finding a prioritized pairwise covering array, *ppCA*, with the minimum number of feature sets, that is: find *ppCA* with minimum $|ppCA|$. What makes the problem far from trivial is the constraints imposed to *ppCA* by Definition 7.

4. ALGORITHM DESCRIPTION

The *Parallel Prioritized product line Genetic Solver (PPGS)* is a novel constructive genetic algorithm which follows the master-slave model to parallelize the evaluation of the individuals [1]. It computes a ppCA as defined in the previous section. In each iteration, PPGS adds one new product to a partial solution until all pairwise combinations are covered. Algorithm 1 sketches the pseudocode of PPGS. It uses as inputs a feature model `FM` and the set of prioritized products for the test suite generation. At the beginning, the test suite is initialized with an empty list (Line 2) and the set of remaining pairs (`RP`) is initialized with the weighted pairwise configurations present in at least one of the given prioritized products (Line 3), as it was described in Section 3. In each iteration of the external loop (Lines 4-23) the algorithm creates a random initial population of individuals (Line 6) and enters an inner loop which applies the traditional steps of a generational evolutionary algorithm (Lines 7-20). That is, some individuals (products in our case) are selected from the population $P(t)$, recombined, and mutated. PPGS represents a product by only the list of selected features, so the operators only affect the selected features. If a generated offspring individual is not a valid product (i.e., it violates any constraint derived from the feature model), it is transformed into a valid product by applying a `Fix` operation (Line 13) provided by the FAMA tool [23].

Since the evaluation is performed in parallel in this algorithm, the fixed individuals are stored in a structure for later evaluation of them (Line 14). After we leave the inner loop (Lines 7-20), the evaluation is performed in parallel (Line 16), and finally the individuals are inserted in the offspring population Q. The fitness value of an offspring individual (Line 16) is the sum of the weights of the weighted pairwise configurations that would remain to be covered after adding the offspring solution to the test suite. Thus, this fitness function must be minimized in order to first select the product that covers weighted pairwise configurations with higher weights. Notice that, as the search progresses, the cost of computing the fitness function is reduced because every time less weighted pairwise configurations remain uncovered.

In Line 18, the best individuals of $P(t)$ and Q are kept for the next generation $P(t+1)$. The internal loop is executed until a maximum number of evaluations is reached. Then, the best individual (product) found is included in the test suite (Line 21) and `RP` is updated by removing the weighted pairwise configurations covered by the selected best solution (Line 22). Then, the external loop starts again until there is no weighted pair left in the `RP` set.

We set the configuration parameters of PPGS with values frequently observed in the literature for genetic algorithms: crossover strategy one-point with a probability of 0.8, selection strategy binary tournament, population size of 10 individuals, mutation that iterates over all selected features of an individual and replaces a feature by another randomly chosen feature with a probability of 0.1, and termination condition of 1,000 fitness evaluations and full weight coverage in the external loop.

Let us show an example of the execution of the inner loop of PPGS, assuming `RP` contains the following entries `[wpc1, wpc2, wpc3]`, where `wpc1.pc = [{Engine, Piston},{}]`, `wpc2.pc = [{Cloth}, {Plastic}]` and `wpc3.pc= [{Jet}, {Plastic}]`. Figure 2(a) shows the selected features of two valid products. PPGS applies the evolutionary operators only to the selected features. The dashed square indicates the cross-over point for the two individuals. Figure 2(b) shows the result of the crossover. Figure 2(c) illustrates mutation of the first recombined individual, the mutated element `Jet` is underlined. Notice that this product is invalid because features `Piston` and `Jet` are mutually exclusive (see Figure 1). This situation requires the application of a

Algorithm 1: Pseudocode of PPGS.

```
proc Input:feature model FM, prioritized products prods
TS ← ∅   // Initialize the test suite
RP ← weighted_pairs_to_cover(prods)
while not empty(RP) do
  t=0
  P(t) ← Create_Population() // P = population
  while evals < totalEvals do
    Q ← ∅   // Q = auxiliary population
    for i ← 1 to (PPGS.popSize / 2) do
      parents←Selection(P(t))
      offspring←Recombination(PPGS.Pc,parents)
      offspring←Mutation(PPGS.Pm,offspring)
      Fix(offspring)
      ParallelEvaluator.addSolution(offspring)
    end for
    solutions←ParallelEvaluator.evaluate();
    Insert(solutions,Q)
    P(t+1) := Replace (Q,P(t))
    t= t + 1
  end while  //internal loop
  TS ← TS ∪ best_solution(P(t))
  RemovePairs(RP, best_solution(P(t)))
end while  //external loop
return TS
end_proc
```

fix operation to provide an actual valid product shown in Figure 2(d). Once a valid product is found, the algorithm generates all its possible pairs and removes them from a copy of the `RP` set, from which the fitness value is computed as the number of pairs that remain still uncovered. In our example, `wpc2` and `wpc3` are covered by the product on Figure 2(d), thus the fitness function for this individual is `wpc3.w`, the remaining weight that has not yet been covered. The inner loop is repeated until the algorithm reaches 1,000 evaluations. Then, the best individual is removed from `RP`, the covered pairs, and the product is added to the current test suite `TS`. When there are no more weighted pairs to be covered or the maximum number of fitness evaluations has been reached, the algorithm returns its current `TS` value.

PPGS has been implemented using jMetal [7], a Java framework aimed at the development, experimentation, and study of metaheuristics for solving optimization problems. Additionally and as mentioned before, PPGS uses a framework for the analysis of feature models called FAMA [23]. This framework provides a simple, easy-to-use, and extensible programming API that supports a common and basic set of feature model operations.

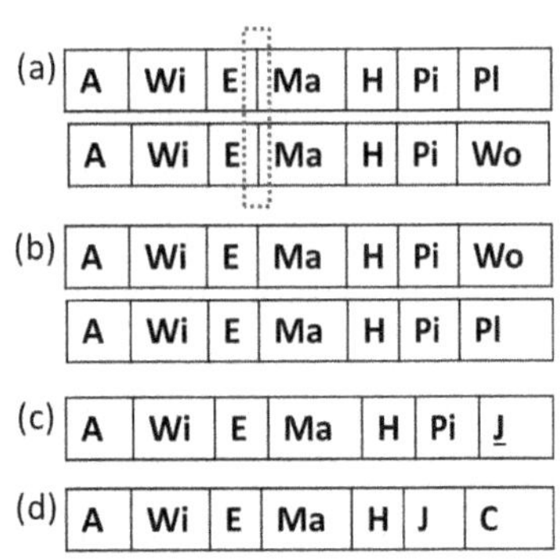

Figure 2: Evolutionary Operations

5. EVALUATION

This section describes how our evaluation was carried out. We start with the algorithm used to compare and contrast PPGS, followed by the methods employed to assign priorities, the selection of the products to prioritize, the experimental corpus of feature models, and the software and hardware infrastructure used.

5.1 Prioritized-ICPL (pICPL) Algorithm

To compare and contrast our PPGS algorithm we employed prioritized-ICPL, a greedy algorithm to generate `n`-wise covering arrays developed by Johansen et al. [16]. Prioritized-ICPL does not compute covering arrays with full coverage but rather covers only those `n`-wise combinations among features that are present in at least one of the prioritized products, as was described in Section 3. We must highlight here that the pICPL algorithm uses *data parallel execution*, supporting any number of processors. Their parallelism comes from simultaneous operations across large sets of data. For further details on prioritized-ICPL please refer to [16].

We should remark that an earlier and more well-known version of a greedy algorithm for SPL pairwise testing by the same authors Johansen et al. is also called ICPL [15]. However that version did not consider prioritization. To avoid any confusions and as a short hand notation, henceforth we will use the term pICPL to refer to prioritized-ICPL.

5.2 Weight Priority Assignment Methods

We considered three methods to assign weight values to prioritized products.

5.2.1 Measured values

For this type, the weights were derived from non-functional properties values obtained from 16 real SPL systems, from different problem domains and implemented using different technologies, that were measured with the SPL Conqueror approach [22]. This approach aims at providing reliable estimates of measurable non-functional properties such as performance, main memory consumption, and footprint. It works by performing a set of actual property measurements on different products (usually a proper subset of all the feature combinations denoted by a feature model) with different feature interaction types. The measured values are then used to compute the estimated property values for the feature combinations that were not measured. This choice of weight priority assignment allows us to emulate more realistic scenarios whereby software testers need to schedule their testing effort giving priority, for instance, to products or feature combinations that exhibit higher footprint or performance.

For our work, we use the actual values taken on the measured products considering pairwise feature interactions. Table 2 summarizes the SPL systems evaluated, their measured property (`Prop`), number of features (`NF`), number of products (`NP`), number of configurations measured (`NC`), and the percentage of prioritized products (`PP%`) used in our comparison as explained shortly.

5.2.2 Rank based values

For this second type of weight values, we selected the products to prioritize based on how dissimilar they are when compared to all other products of an SPL, and assigned them

SPL Name	Prop	NF	NP	NC	PP%
Prevayler	F	6	32	24	75.0
LinkedList	F	26	1440	204	14.1
ZipMe	F	8	64	64	100.0
PKJab	F	12	72	72	100.0
SensorNetwork	F	27	16704	3240	19.4
BerkeleyDBF	F	9	256	256	100.0
Violet	F	101	≈ 1E20	101	≈ 0.0
Linux subset	F	25	≈ 3E24	100	≈ 0.0
LLVM	M	12	1024	53	5.1
Curl	M	14	1024	68	6.6
x264	M	17	2048	77	3.7
Wget	M	17	8192	94	1.15
BerkeleyDBM	M	19	3840	1280	33.3
SQLite	M	40	≈ 5E7	418	≈ 0.0
BerkeleyDBP	P	27	1440	180	12.50
Apache	P	10	256	192	75.0

Footprint, **M**ain memory consumption, **P**erformance, **N**umber of **F**eatures, **N**umber of **P**roducts, **N**umber of **C**onfigurations, **P**ercentage of **P**rioritized products.

Table 2: Measured Values Case Studies Summary

priority weights based on their rank values. For further details please refer to the associated materials. The intuition behind this assignment choice is that by giving the same weight value to two of the most SPL-wide dissimilar products, the weight values will be more likely spread among a larger number of pairwise configurations making the covering array harder to compute. In addition, this enables us to select different percentages of the number of products for prioritization as elaborated in Subsection 5.3.

5.2.3 *Random Values*

For this type of weight values, we randomly generate weights between the minimum and maximum values obtained with the ranked based values approach.

5.3 Product Prioritization Selection

We selected the products for prioritization based on the priority assignment method. For the measured values assignment method, all the measured products were used as our prioritization products. In three cases this meant including all the products of the product line. Please refer to Table 2 for further details. For the rank based values and the random values assignment methods, a percentage of the products denoted by each individual feature model was used for product prioritization. The selected percentages are: 5%, 10%, 20%, 30%, and 50%.

5.4 Experimental Corpus

We created three groups based on both the number of products denoted by the feature models and how their priority was assigned as shown in Table 3. Group G1 was formed with 160 feature models, whose number of products ranges from 16 to 1000 products, and that were evaluated with rank based and random values. Group G2 was formed with 59 feature models, whose number of products ranged from 1000 to 80000 that were also evaluated with rank based and random values. The threshold value to divide groups G1 and G2, and the selected percentages were chosen to provide an

	G1	G2	G3	Summary
NFM	160	59	16	235
NP	16-1K	1K-80K	32- ≈3E24	16- ≈3E24
NF	10-56	14-67	6-101	6-101
WPA	RK,RD	RK, RD	M	
PP%	20,30,50	5,10,20	≈0.0 – 100	
PI	960	354	16	1330

NFM: Number Feature Models, **NP**: Number Products, **NF**: Number Features, **WPA**: Weight Priority Assignment, **RK**: Rank based, **RN**: Random, **M**: Measured, **PP%**: Prioritized Products Percentage, **PI**: Problem Instances

Table 3: Evaluation Case Studies Summary

ample variety of number of products to prioritize. Group G3 was formed with 16 feature models, with number of products ranging from 16 to ≈3E24 that were evaluated with measured values.

We obtained 16 feature models from SPL Conqueror, 5 from Johansen et al. [16], and 201 from the SPLOT website [19] (a repository for the feature model analysis research community). Thus in total we employed 222 distinct feature models. Please notice that we also incorporated 5 SPL Conqueror feature models to G1 and 8 to G2. This yields a grand total of 235 feature models to analyze. For G1 and G2 the problem instances are computed considering that for each feature model two priority assignment methods are used with three different prioritization selection percentages. For example, this yields for G1 $160 \times 2 \times 3 = 960$ instances. In total 1330 problem instances were analyzed, with two algorithms PPGS and pICPL, with 30 independent executions. This means that the data of a total of 79800 independent runs was generated and analyzed.

5.5 Hardware and Software Setup

PPGS and pICPL are non-deterministic algorithms, so we performed 30 independent runs for a fair comparison between them. As performance measures we analyzed both the number of products required to test the SPL and the time required to run the algorithm. In both cases, the lower the value the better the performance, since we want a small number of products to test the SPL and we want the algorithm to be as fast as possible. All the executions were run in a cluster of 16 machines with Intel Core2 Quad processors Q9400 (4 cores per processor) at 2.66 GHz and 4 GB memory running Ubuntu 12.04.1 LTS and managed by the HT Condor 7.8.4 cluster manager. Since we have four cores available per processor, we have executed only one task per single processor, so we have used four parallel threads in each independent execution of the analyzed algorithms. The total 79800 independent runs of our evaluation required about two weeks of computation on a 64-core dedicated cluster.

6. RESULTS AND ANALYSIS

In this work we have used two different statistical techniques to measure different aspects of the comparison.

6.1 Wilcoxon Test

In order to check if the differences between the algorithms are statistically significant or just a matter of chance, we applied the non-parametric Wilcoxon rank-sum test. We highlight in the tables the statistically significant differences with a confidence level of 95% (p-value under 0.05).

In Table 4 we summarize the results obtained for group G1, feature models with up to 1000 products. Each column corresponds to one algorithm and in the rows we show the number of products required to reach 50% up to 100% of total weighted coverage. The data shown in each cell is the mean and the standard deviation of the 30 independent runs. We highlight with a light gray background those values that are better with respect to the other algorithm with a statistically significant difference. We can observe that PPGS requires a smaller number of products to test the SPL with a significant difference when we consider a coverage level of 80% up to 99%. In the rest of the cases the differences are not statistically significant, so we cannot claim that one algorithm is better than the other. Regarding the time, pICPL is around 6 times faster than PPGS with a statistically significant difference. The time is given in milliseconds in the tables.

Cov.	PPGS	pICPL	Cov.	PPGS	pICPL
50%	$1.20_{0.40}$	$1.20_{0.40}$	96%	$4.00_{1.23}$	$4.37_{1.42}$
75%	$1.92_{0.51}$	$1.98_{0.58}$	97%	$4.38_{1.32}$	$4.71_{1.54}$
80%	$2.15_{0.59}$	$2.25_{0.68}$	98%	$4.83_{1.46}$	$5.18_{1.74}$
85%	$2.47_{0.72}$	$2.58_{0.81}$	99%	$5.58_{1.71}$	$5.87_{1.99}$
90%	$2.88_{0.86}$	$3.13_{1.03}$	100%	$7.56_{2.85}$	$7.56_{3.03}$
95%	$3.72_{1.14}$	$4.06_{1.33}$	TIME	23897_{28669}	10116_{18842}

Table 4: Mean and standard deviation of 30 indep. runs for G1 (significant differences are highlighted)

Table 5 shows the results for group G2: feature models with 1000 to 80000 products. We use the same legend and notation as for Table 4. In this case the advantage of PPGS over pICPL is larger than in the previous case. First, we can observe that PPGS is better than pICPL with statistically significant difference in all the coverage percentages except 100%. Regarding the computation time, PPGS is faster than pICPL but without statistically significant difference. From these results, the trend we can observe is that as the number of products of the SPL grows PPGS is still better in quality than pICPL while it is also better in runtime. Part of our future work is to verify if this trend holds for feature models with a larger number of products.

Cov.	PPGS	pICPL	Cov.	PPGS	pICPL
50%	$1.16_{0.36}$	$1.36_{0.83}$	96%	$4.98_{0.97}$	$5.83_{3.14}$
75%	$2.09_{0.42}$	$2.47_{1.65}$	97%	$5.55_{1.10}$	$6.43_{3.27}$
80%	$2.39_{0.52}$	$2.86_{1.79}$	98%	$6.34_{1.34}$	$7.23_{3.48}$
85%	$2.73_{0.59}$	$3.27_{2.08}$	99%	$7.66_{1.88}$	$8.59_{4.11}$
90%	$3.36_{0.76}$	$3.98_{2.38}$	100%	$14.57_{10.65}$	$13.79_{9.98}$
95%	$4.59_{0.90}$	$5.42_{3.12}$	TIME	$273728_{7.2E+5}$	$638164_{2.1E+6}$

Table 5: Mean and standard deviation of 30 indep. runs for G2(significant differences are highlighted)

Let us now focus on group G3, feature models with measured weight values. Table 6 shows the average number of products required to cover each SPL and the time for both pICPL and PPGS over the 16 models. According to the statistically significant differences the conclusions in this group of models are similar to the conclusions in the previous ones: PPGS is better in quality (lower number of products) while pICPL is faster. In detail, regarding the quality of the solutions, PPGS is better than pICPL in 68 model-coverage combinations with statistical significant difference, while pICPL is better than PPGS only in 19 model-coverage combinations. Regarding the time, pICPL is usually faster than PPGS with a statistically significant difference, with the only exception of the `SensorNetwork` model, in which they do not have statistically significant difference.

If we take a closer look at the data in the table and taking into account the statistical significant differences, we can observe that PPGS is overall better than pICPL in 8 out of the 16 models, namely: `Apache`, `BerkeleyDBF`, `BerkeleyDBP`, `LLVM`, `PkJab`, `SensorNetwork`, `Violet` and `Wget`. On the other hand, pICPL is better only for 2 models when all coverage percentages are considered: `Prevayler` and `ZipMe`. In the remaining 6 models pICPL is better for some percentages while PPGS is better for others.

As a general conclusion of this first analysis we can say that if the number of products to test is a critical aspect for the Testing Engineer, PPGS should be applied to generate these products instead of pICPL. The time required by PPGS is usually no longer than a few minutes, which is a reasonable time to generate a better quality test suite. We argue this is the most common scenario in software companies with SPLs, where carrying on each product test can require hours if not days to perform, specially if they involve complex software and hardware setups [16]. On the other hand, pICPL could be employed when the number of products to test is not a critical issue and a slightly faster generation of the test suite is preferable.

6.2 $\hat{A}_{12}$ statistic

In order to properly interpret the results of statistical tests, it is always advisable to report effect size measures. For that purpose, we have also used the non-parametric effect size measure $\hat{A}_{12}$ statistic as recommended by Arcuri and Briand [2]. Given a performance measure M, $\hat{A}_{12}$ measures the probability that running algorithm A yields higher M values than running another algorithm B. If the two algorithms are equivalent, then $\hat{A}_{12} = 0.5$. If $\hat{A}_{12} = 0.3$ entails one would obtain smaller results 70% of the time with A. Table 7 shows the $\hat{A}_{12}$ statistic to assess the practical significance of the results. In this table a value lower than 0.5 means that PPGS is better than pICPL, a value greater than 0.5 means pICPL is better than PPGS and 0.5 means a draw. At a first glance, we can see that most of the times (31), PPGS obtains smaller test suites for all percentages of coverage, meanwhile pICPL is only better than PPGS twice. We have highlighted with dark and light gray background the lowest and highest values of the table (0.2497 and 0.5157). The lowest value indicates that PPGS obtains a better test suite than pICPL for 98% of coverage in a model of G2 in more than 75% of the cases. The highest value indicates that pICPL obtains a better test suite for 100% coverage in a model of G1 with a probability near 0.5. In general, this statistic reconfirms that PPGS gets better test suites than pICPL in terms of the number of products.

7. THREATS TO VALIDITY

We identified two main threats to validity in our work. First, we used a single assignment for the parameters values of PPGS based on the authors' experience. A change in the values of these parameters could have an impact in the results of the algorithm. Thus, we can only claim that the

Model	Alg.	50%	75%	80%	85%	90%	95%	96%	97%	98%	99%	100%	TIME
Apache	PPGS	2	3	3	4	4	6	6	6	7	7	7	10394
	pICPL	2	3	3	4	5	6	7	7	7	8	8	7582
Berk.DBF	PPGS	2	4	4	5	5.97	6.97	6.97	6.97	7.97	8	8.17	11213
	pICPL	2	4	5	6	7	8	8	8	8	9	9	8152
Berk.DBM	PPGS	2	3	3	4	4.73	6.87	7.80	8.77	9.97	11.90	23.33	117607
	pICPL	2	3	3	4	6	7	8	8	10	11	21	94512
Berk.DBP	PPGS	1	2	2	3	3	4	4.83	5	5.93	7	10.60	47361
	pICPL	1	2	3	3	4	6	6	6	6	7	12	57291
Curl	PPGS	2	3	3	3.97	4.03	5.83	6	6.50	7.37	8.07	9.63	17454
	pICPL	2	3	3	4	4	6	6	6	7	7	8	6382
LinkedList	PPGS	1	2	2	2	3	4.23	5	5	6.13	7.79	13.37	60684
	pICPL	1	2	2	3	3	4	4	5	7	11	14	71151
Linux	PPGS	2	4	4	5	6	7	7.67	8	8.37	9.40	11.10	49385
	pICPL	2	4	5	5	6	8	8	8	8	9	10	30522
LLVM	PPGS	2	3	3.03	4	5	6	6	6.07	7	8	8.17	12805
	pICPL	2	3	4	4	5	6	7	7	7	8	8	9032
PKJab	PPGS	1	2	2	3	3.07	4	5	5	5	6	7	11439
	pICPL	1	2	3	3	3	5	5	6	7	8	8	4661
Prevayler	PPGS	2	3	3	3	4	5	5	5.60	6	6	6	8091
	pICPL	2	3	3	3	4	5	5	5	6	6	6	2412
S.Network	PPGS	1	3	3	3	4	5.03	5.47	6	6.97	7.87	13.97	71971
	pICPL	1	3	4	5	6	8	9	9	10	11	17	74181
SQL.Mem	PPGS	1	2.17	2.90	3.23	4.07	6.14	6.97	7.93	9.23	11.70	31.53	903118
	pICPL	1	3	4	4	5	8	8	9	11	14	28	407991
Violet	PPGS	1	1	1	2	2	2.93	3	3.07	3.30	4.53	12.83	31376054
	pICPL	1	1	1	2	2	3	3	4	4	6	15	2471691
Wget	PPGS	2	2.13	3	3.07	4	5.43	6	6.40	7	8.03	11.37	31525
	pICPL	2	3	3	4	4	6	6	7	7	9	11	19612
x264	PPGS	1.23	2.23	3	3.07	4	5.30	6	6.50	7.23	8.47	12.10	37368
	pICPL	1	2	3	3	4	5	6	7	7	9	13	13441
ZipMe	PPGS	2	3	3	4	5	6	6	7	7	7	7.03	13035
	pICPL	2	3	3	4	5	6	6	6	7	7	7	6142

Table 6: Group G3. When considering array sizes PPGS is statistically better than pICPL in 69 cases, and pICPL is better in 18 cases.

Group	50%	75%	80%	85%	90%	95%
G1	0.4985	0.4729	0.4511	0.4473	0.3785	0.3501
G2	0.4529	0.4193	0.3760	0.3726	0.3436	0.2887
G3	0.5104	0.4562	0.2844	0.3563	0.3198	0.3239
Group	**96%**	**97%**	**98%**	**99%**	**100%**	
G1	0.3410	0.3703	0.3634	0.4000	0.5157	
G2	0.2847	0.2647	0.2497	0.2595	0.4945	
G3	0.3312	0.3135	0.3927	0.3068	0.4166	

Table 7: $\hat{A}_{12}$ statistical test results for all groups. PPGS yields better test suite size values.

conclusions are valid for the combination of parameter values that we used. Second, the selection of feature models for the experiment corpus can indeed bias the results obtained. To counteract this threat, we used 3 different sources for our feature models. From them we selected a number of feature models as large as possible, with the widest ranges of both number of features and number of products. We should point out that beyond the ranges of our groups G1 and G2, the feature analysis tool FAMA that we employ for PPGS presents a performance and scalability bottleneck. Addressing these limitations is part of our future work.

8. RELATED WORK

There exists substantial literature on both search based testing and SPL testing. In this section, we briefly summarize those pieces of work closest to ours. Within the area of Search-Based Software Engineering a major research focus has been software testing [12]. A recent overview by McMinn highlights the major achievements made in the area and some of the open questions and challenges [18]. Relevant in this realm is the work by Ferrer et al. who propose a test prioritization genetic algorithm [10]. However, in clear contrast with our work their algorithm is not for SPLs but for systems without variability. Some of the very few applications of search based techniques to SPL are summarized next. Garvin et al. applied simulated annealing to combinatorial interaction testing for computing n-wise coverage for SPLs [11]. Ensan et al. propose a genetic algorithm approach for test case generation for SPLs [9]. In contrast with our work, they use as fitness function a variation of cyclomatic complexity metric adapted to feature models, their goal is not n-wise coverage and they do not consider priorities. Henard et al. propose an approach that uses a dissimilarity metric that favors individuals whose n-wise coverage varies the most from the current population thus increasing the chances of wider coverage [13]. A key difference with our work is that the prioritization is not based on assigned weights that have a perceived market or quality value. Recent surveys on SPL testing [6,8], attest the increasing relevance of the topic within the SPL community but also confirm that the latent potential of search based testing techniques remains largely untapped. Perrouin et al. propose an approach that translates t-wise coverage problems into Alloy programs and rely on its automatic instance generation to obtain covering arrays [20]. Hervieu et al. employ constraint programming for computing pairwise coverage from feature models [14]. *In sharp contrast with our work, none of these algorithms considers any prioritization criteria.*

9. CONCLUSIONS AND FUTURE WORK

In this paper we formalized a SPL testing prioritization scheme and presented its implementation with PPGS. We evaluated PPGS with 235 feature models of different characteristics using different selection criteria for product prioritization. Furthermore, we compared PPGS with greedy algorithm pICPL, a comparison that totalled 79800 independent runs. Our analysis showed that while PPGS obtains overall shorter covering arrays it exhibits a performance difference with pICPL that tends to decrease for the feature models with larger number of products. It should be noted though that the current PPGS implementation is not fine-tuned for performance, so part of our future work is to evaluate alternative representations of population individuals and evolutionary operations, and to streamline the feature model analysis support. Addressing these two limitations will extend our study to include feature models with more than 80,000 prioritized products. Also, recall that the current stopping condition of PPGS is a fixed number of evaluations. We plan to study the impact on performance of different approaches to adapt this stopping condition based on the characteristics of feature models. A starting point is the work of Bhandari et al. [4]. We believe our work sheds light on the potential of search based techniques for SPL testing.

10. ACKNOWLEDGEMENTS

This research is partially funded by the Austrian Science Fund (FWF) project P25289-N15 and Lise Meitner Fellowship M1421-N15, the Spanish Ministry of Economy and Competitiveness and FEDER under contract TIN2011-28194 and fellowship BES-2012-055967. It is also partially founded by project 8.06/5.47.4142 in collaboration with the VSB-Tech. Univ. of Ostrava and Universidad de Málaga, Andalucía Tech. We thank Martin Johansen, Øystein Haugen, and Norbert Siegmund for their help with pICPL and SPLConqueror.

11. REFERENCES

[1] E. Alba and G. Luque. *Parallel genetic algorithms*, volume 367 of *Studies in Computational Intelligence*. Springer-Verlag, 2011.

[2] A. Arcuri and L. Briand. A hitchhiker's guide to statistical tests for assessing randomized algorithms in software engineering. *Softw. Test. Verif. Reliab*, 2012.

[3] D. Benavides, S. Segura, and A. R. Cortés. Automated analysis of feature models 20 years later: A literature review. *Inf. Syst.*, 35(6):615–636, 2010.

[4] D. Bhandari, C. A. Murthy, and S. K. Pal. Variance as a stopping criterion for genetic algorithms with elitist model. *Fundam. Inform.*, 120(2):145–164, 2012.

[5] H. Cichos, S. Oster, M. Lochau, and A. Schürr. Model-based coverage-driven test suite generation for software product lines. In *MoDELS*, pages 425–439, 2011.

[6] P. A. da Mota Silveira Neto, I. do Carmo Machado, J. D. McGregor, E. S. de Almeida, and S. R. de Lemos Meira. A systematic mapping study of software product lines testing. *Information & Software Technology*, 53(5):407–423, 2011.

[7] J. J. Durillo and A. J. Nebro. jmetal: A java framework for multi-objective optimization. *Advances in Engineering Software*, 42(10):760 – 771, 2011.

[8] E. Engström and P. Runeson. Software product line testing - a systematic mapping study. *Information & Software Technology*, 53(1):2–13, 2011.

[9] F. Ensan, E. Bagheri, and D. Gasevic. Evolutionary search-based test generation for software product line feature models. In *CAiSE*, pages 613–628, 2012.

[10] J. Ferrer, P. M. Kruse, J. F. Chicano, and E. Alba. Evolutionary algorithm for prioritized pairwise test data generation. In T. Soule and J. H. Moore, editors, *GECCO*, pages 1213–1220. ACM, 2012.

[11] B. J. Garvin, M. B. Cohen, and M. B. Dwyer. Evaluating improvements to a meta-heuristic search for constrained interaction testing. *Empirical Software Engineering*, 16(1):61–102, 2011.

[12] M. Harman, S. A. Mansouri, and Y. Zhang. Search-based software engineering: Trends, techniques and applications. *ACM Comput. Surv.*, 45(1):11, 2012.

[13] C. Henard, M. Papadakis, G. Perrouin, J. Klein, P. Heymans, and Y. L. Traon. Bypassing the combinatorial explosion: Using similarity to generate and prioritize t-wise test suites for large software product lines. *CoRR*, abs/1211.5451, 2012.

[14] A. Hervieu, B. Baudry, and A. Gotlieb. Pacogen: Automatic generation of pairwise test configurations from feature models. In T. Dohi and B. Cukic, editors, *ISSRE*, pages 120–129. IEEE, 2011.

[15] M. F. Johansen, Ø. Haugen, and F. Fleurey. An algorithm for generating t-wise covering arrays from large feature models. In *SPLC (1)*, pages 46–55, 2012.

[16] M. F. Johansen, Ø. Haugen, F. Fleurey, A. G. Eldegard, and T. Syversen. Generating better partial covering arrays by modeling weights on sub-product lines. In R. B. France, J. Kazmeier, R. Breu, and C. Atkinson, editors, *MoDELS*, volume 7590 of *Lecture Notes in Computer Science*, pages 269–284. Springer, 2012.

[17] K. Kang, S. Cohen, J. Hess, W. Novak, and A. Peterson. Feature-Oriented Domain Analysis (FODA) Feasibility Study. Technical Report CMU/SEI-90-TR-21, Software Engineering Institute, Carnegie Mellon University, 1990.

[18] P. McMinn. Search-based software testing: Past, present and future. In *ICST Workshops*, pages 153–163. IEEE Computer Society, 2011.

[19] M. Mendonca. Software Product Line Online Tools(SPLOT), 2013. http://www.splot-research.org/.

[20] G. Perrouin, S. Sen, J. Klein, B. Baudry, and Y. L. Traon. Automated and scalable t-wise test case generation strategies for software product lines. In *ICST*, pages 459–468. IEEE Computer Society, 2010.

[21] K. Pohl, G. Bockle, and F. J. van der Linden. *Software Product Line Engineering: Foundations, Principles and Techniques*. Springer, 2005.

[22] N. Siegmund, M. Rosenmüller, C. Kästner, P. G. Giarrusso, S. Apel, and S. S. Kolesnikov. Scalable prediction of non-functional properties in software product lines: Footprint and memory consumption. *Information & Soft. Technology*, 55(3):491–507, 2013.

[23] P. Trinidad, D. Benavides, A. Ruiz-Cortes, S. Segura, and A. Jimenez. Fama framework. In *Software Product Line Conference, 2008. SPLC '08. 12th International*, pages 359–359, Sept.

High Dimensional Search-based Software Engineering: Finding Tradeoffs Among 15 Objectives for Automating Software Refactoring Using NSGA-III

Wiem Mkaouer, Marouane Kessentini, Slim Bechikh
University of Michigan, Dearborn, MI, USA
firstname@umich.edu

Kalyanmoy Deb
Michigan State University, USA
kdeb@egr.msu.edu

Mel Ó Cinnéide
University College Dublin, Ireland
mel.ocinneide@ucd.ie

ABSTRACT

There is a growing need for scalable search-based software engineering approaches that address software engineering problems where a large number of objectives are to be optimized. Software refactoring is one of these problems where a refactoring sequence is sought that optimizes several software metrics. Most of the existing refactoring work uses a large set of quality metrics to evaluate the software design after applying refactoring operations, but current search-based software engineering approaches are limited to using a maximum of five metrics. We propose for the first time a scalable search-based software engineering approach based on a newly proposed evolutionary optimization method NSGA-III where there are 15 different objectives to be optimized. In our approach, automated refactoring solutions are evaluated using a set of 15 distinct quality metrics. We evaluated this approach on seven large open source systems and found that, on average, more than 92% of code smells were corrected. Statistical analysis of our experiments over 31 runs shows that NSGA-III performed significantly better than two other many-objective techniques (IBEA and MOEA/D), a multi-objective algorithm (NSGA-II) and two mono-objective approaches, hence demonstrating that our NSGA-III approach represents the new state of the art in fully-automated refactoring.

Categories and Subject Descriptors

D.2 [**Software Engineering**].

General Terms

Algorithms, Reliability.

Keywords

Search-based software engineering, software quality, code smells, many-objective optimization.

1. INTRODUCTION

Search-based software engineering (SBSE) studies the application of meta-heuristic optimization techniques to software engineering problems [1]. Once a software engineering task is framed as a search problem, by defining it in terms of solution representation, objective function, and solution change operators, there are a multitude of search algorithms that can be applied to solve that problem. Search-based techniques are widely applied to solve software engineering problems such as in testing, modularization, refactoring, planning, etc. [15][13].

Based on a recent SBSE survey [15], the majority of existing work treats software engineering (SE) problems from a single-objective point of view, where the main goal is to maximize or minimize one objective, e.g., correctness, quality, etc. However, most SE problems are naturally complex in which many conflicting objectives need to be optimized such as model transformation, design quality improvement, test suite generation etc. The number of objectives to consider for most of software engineering problems is, in general, high (more than three objectives); such problems are termed *many-objective*. We claim that the reason that software engineering problems have not been formulated as many-objective problems is because of the challenges in constructing a many-objective solution. In this context, the use of traditional multi-objective techniques, e.g., NSGA-II [8], widely used in SBSE, is clearly not sufficient.

There is a growing need for scalable search-based software engineering approaches that address software engineering problems where a large number of objectives are to be optimized. Improving the scalability of SBSE approaches will increase their applicability in industry and real-world settings. Recent work in optimization has proposed several solution approaches to tackle many-objective optimization problems [17][30] using e.g., objective reduction, new preference ordering relations, decomposition, etc. However, these techniques have not yet been widely explored in SBSE [6]. To the best of our knowledge and based on recent SBSE surveys [15], only one work exists proposed by Abdel Salam et al. [26] that uses a many-objective approach, IBEA (Indicator-Based Evolutionary Algorithm) [31], to address the problem of software product line creation. However, the number of considered objectives is limited to 5.

Software refactoring is one of those software engineering problems where there are several objectives to be satisfied. Refactoring improves the design of a system by changing its internal structure without altering its external behavior [12], and is widely used to fix code smells. Code smells are known to have a negative impact on quality attributes such as flexibility or maintainability [4][29]. Software engineers often introduce code smells unintentionally during the initial design or during software development due to bad design decisions, ignorance or time pressure. Most of the existing refactoring work uses a set of more than five quality metrics to evaluate the quality of software design after applying refactoring operations. In this paper, we propose for the first time a scalable search-based software engineering approach based on NSGA-III [7] where there are 15 different objectives to optimize. Thus, in our approach, automated refactoring solutions will be evaluated using a set of 15 software quality metrics. NSGA-III is a very recent many-

GECCO'14, July 12–16, 2014, Vancouver, BC, Canada.
Copyright 2014 ACM 978-1-4503-2662-9/14/07?$15.00.
http://dx.doi.org/10.1145/2576768.2598366

objective algorithm proposed by Deb et al. [7]. The basic framework remains similar to the original NSGA-II algorithm [8], with significant changes in its selection mechanism. This paper represents the first real-world application of NSGA-III and the first scalable work that supports the use of 15 objectives to address a software engineering problem.

We implemented our approach and evaluated it on seven large open source systems and found that, on average, more than 92% of code smells were corrected. The statistical analysis of our experiments over 31 runs shows that NSGA-III performed significantly better than two other many-objective techniques (IBEA and MOEA/D), a multi-objective algorithm (NSGA-II) and two mono-objective approaches [19][23].

2. MANY-OBJECTIVE SEARCH-BASED SOFTWARE ENGINEERING

By definition, a many-objective problem is a multi-objective one but with a high number of objectives M, i.e., $M > 3$. Analytically, it could be stated as follows [5]:

$$\begin{cases} Min\ f(x) = [f_1(x), f_2(x), \ldots, f_M(x)]^T, & M > 3 \\ g_j(x) \geq 0 & j = 1, \ldots, P; \\ h_k(x) = 0 & k = 1, \ldots, Q; \\ x_i^L \leq x_i \leq x_i^U & i = 1, \ldots, n \end{cases}$$

where M is the number of objective functions and is *strictly greater* than 3, P is the number of inequality constraints, Q is the number of equality constraints, x_i^L and x_i^U correspond to the lower and upper bounds of the decision variable x_i (i.e., i^{th} component of x). A solution x satisfying the $(P+Q)$ constraints is said to be feasible and the set of all feasible solutions defines the feasible search space denoted by Ω.

In this formulation, we consider a minimization multi-objective problem (MOP) since maximization can be easily turned to minimization based on the duality principle. Over the two past decades, several Multi-Objective Evolutionary Algorithms (MOEAs) have been proposed with the hope to work with any number of objectives M. Unfortunately, It has been demonstrated that most MOEAs are ineffective in handling such type of problems. For example, NSGA-II [8], which is one of the most used MOEAs, compares solutions based on their non-domination ranks. Solutions with best ranks are emphasized in order to converge to the Pareto front. When $M > 3$, only the first rank may be assigned to every solution as almost all population individuals become non-dominated with each other. Without a variety of ranks, NSGA-II cannot keep the search pressure anymore in high dimensional objective spaces.

The difficulty faced when solving many-objective problems could be summarized as follows. Firstly, most solutions become equivalent between each other according to the Pareto dominance relation which deteriorates *dramatically* the search process ability to converge towards the Pareto front and the MOEA behaviour becomes very similar to the random search one. Secondly, a search method requires a very high number of solutions (some thousands and even more) to cover the Pareto front when the number of objectives increases. For instance, it has been shown that in order to find a good approximation of the Pareto front for problems involving 4, 5 and 7 objective functions, the number of required non-dominated solutions is about 62 500, 1 953 125 and 1 708 984 375 respectively [17]; which makes the decision making task very difficult. Thirdly, the objective space dimensionality increases significantly, which makes promising search directions very hard to find. Fourthly, the diversity measure estimation becomes very computationally costly since finding the neighbors of a particular solution in high dimensional spaces is very expensive. Fifthly, recombination operators become inefficient since population members are likely to be widely distant from each other which yields to children that are not similar to their parents; thereby making the recombination operation inefficient in producing promising offspring individuals. Finally, although it is not a matter that is directly related to optimization, the Pareto front visualization becomes more complicated, therefore making the interpretation of the MOEA's results more difficult for the user.

According to a recent survey by Harman et al. [13], most software engineering problems are multi-objective by nature. However, most of existing approaches to address software engineering problems such as model transformation, design quality improvement, test suite generation, etc. are based on a mono-objective view. Multi-objective optimization techniques have been proposed in a few works [26][24] for such problems and they satisfy up to 5 objectives. However, as with any other practical domain, most software engineering problems involve optimizing more than this number of objectives. Thus, more scalable search-based software engineering approaches will be beneficial to handle rich objective spaces. We investigate, in this paper, the applicability of many-objective techniques for the software refactoring problem where up to 15 objectives are considered to evaluate refactoring suggestions.

3. MANY-OBJECTIVE SOFTWARE REFACTORING USING NSGA-III

3.1 NSGA-III

NSGA-III is a very recent many-objective algorithm proposed by Deb et al. [7]. The basic framework remains similar to the original NSGA-II algorithm [8] with significant changes in its selection mechanism. Figure 2 gives the pseudo-code of the NSGA-III procedure for a particular generation t. First, the parent population P_t (of size N) is randomly initialized in the specified domain, and then the binary tournament selection, crossover and mutation operators are applied to create an offspring population Q_t. Thereafter, both populations are combined and sorted according to their domination level and the best N members are selected from the combined population to form the parent population for the next generation. The fundamental difference between NSGA-II and NSGA-III lies in the way the niche preservation operation is performed. Unlike NSGA-II, NSGA-III starts with a set of reference points Z^r. After non-dominated sorting, all acceptable front members and the last front F_l that could not be completely accepted are saved in a set S_t. Members in S_t/F_l are selected right away for the next generation. However, the remaining members are selected from F_l such that a desired diversity is maintained in the population. Original NSGA-II uses the crowding distance measure for selecting well-distributed set of points, however, in NSGA-III the supplied reference points (Z^r) are used to select these remaining members (cf. Figure 1). To accomplish this, objective values and reference points are first normalized so that they have an identical range. Thereafter, orthogonal distance between a member in S_t and each of the reference lines (joining the ideal point and a reference point) is computed. The member is then associated with the reference point having the smallest orthogonal distance. Next, the niche count ρ for each reference point, defined as the number of members in S_t/F_l that are associated with the reference point, is computed for further processing. The reference point having the minimum niche count is identified and the member from the last front

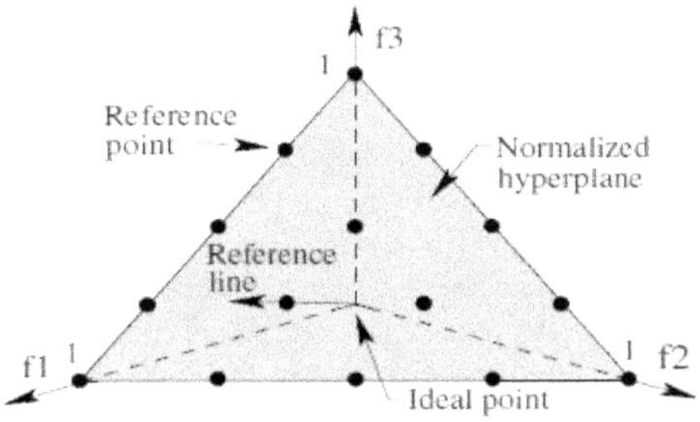

Figure 1. Normalized reference plane for a three-objective case [19].

F_l that is associated with it is included in the final population. The niche count of the identified reference point is increased by one and the procedure is repeated to fill up population P_{t+1}.

It is worth noting that a reference point may have one or more population members associated with it or need not have any population member associated with it. Let us denote this niche count as ρ_j for the j-th reference point. We now devise a new niche-preserving operation as follows. First, we identify the reference point set $J_{\min} = \{j\text{: } \mathrm{argmin}_j\ (\rho_j)\}$ having minimum ρ_j. In case of multiple such reference points, one ($j^* \in J_{\min}$) is chosen at random. If $\rho_{j^*} = 0$ (meaning that there is no associated P_{t+1} member to the reference point j^*), two scenarios can occur. First, there exists one or more members in front F_l that are already associated with the reference point j^*. In this case, the one having the shortest perpendicular distance from the reference line is added to P_{t+1}. The count ρ_{j^*} is then incremented by one. Second, the front F_l does not have any member associated with the reference point j^*. In this case, the reference point is excluded from further consideration for the current generation. In the event of $\rho_{j^*} \geq 1$ (meaning that already one member associated with the reference point exists), a randomly chosen member, if exists, from front F_l that is associated with the reference point F_l is added to P_{t+1}. If such a member exists, the count ρ_{j^*} is incremented by one. After ρ_j counts are updated, the procedure is repeated for a total of K times to increase the population size of P_{t+1} to N.

3.2 Adapting NSGA-III for the Software Refactoring Problem

3.2.1 *Problem formulation*

The refactoring problem involves searching for the best refactoring solution among the set of candidate ones, which constitutes a huge search space. A refactoring solution is a sequence of refactoring operations where the goal of applying the sequence to a software system S is typically to minimize the number of code smells in S. Usually in SBSE approaches, we use two or three metrics as objective functions for a particular multi-objective heuristic algorithm to find smells and correct them. However, in reality, there are many types of code smell and detecting the symptoms of each smell requires a particular set of metrics. Motivated by this observation, we propose in this research work to use a high number of metrics (15 metrics) where each represents a separate objective function. In this way, we obtain a many-objective (15-objective) formulation of the refactoring problem that could not be solved using standard multi-objective approaches. This formulation is given as follows:

$$Maximize\ F(x,S) = [f_1(x,S), f_2(x,S),..., f_{15}(x,S)]$$
$$subject\ to\ \ x = (x_1,..., x_n) \in X$$

NSGA-III procedure at generation *t*

Input: H structured reference points Z^s, parent population P_t
Output: P_{t+1}
Begin
$S_t \leftarrow \emptyset$, $i \leftarrow 1$;
$Q_t \leftarrow$ Variation (P_t);
$R_t \leftarrow P_t \cup Q_t$;
(F_1, F_2, ...) $\leftarrow$ Non-dominationed_Sort (R_t);
Repeat
  $S_t \leftarrow S_t \cup F_i$; $i \leftarrow i$+1;
Until $|S_t| \geq N$;
$F_l \leftarrow F_i$; /*Last front to be included*/
If $|S_t| = N$ **then**
  $P_{t+1} \leftarrow S_t$;
Else
  $P_{t+1} \leftarrow \bigcup_{j=1}^{l-1} F_j$;
  /*Number of points to be chosen from F_l*/
  $K \leftarrow N - |P_{t+1}|$;
  /*Normalize objectives and create reference set Z^r*/
  Normalize (F^M; S_t; Z^r; Z^s);
  /*Associate each member s of S_t with a reference point*/
  /*$\pi(s)$: closest reference point*/
  /*$d(s)$: distance between s and $\pi(s)$*/
  [$\pi(s)$, $d(s)$] $\leftarrow$ Associate (S_t, Z^r);
  /*Compute niche count of reference point $j \in Z^r$ */
  $\rho_j \leftarrow \sum_{s \in S_t / F_l} ((\pi(s) = j)\ ?\ 1 : 0)$;
  /*Choose K members one at a time from F_l to construct P_{t+1}*/
  Niching (K, ρ_j, $\pi(s)$, $d(s)$, Z^r, F_l, P_{t+1});
End If
End

Figure 2. Pseudocode of NSGA-III main procedure.

where X is the set of all legal refactoring sequences starting from S, x_i is the i-th refactoring operation, and $f_k(x,S)$ is the k-th metric. The 15 metrics under consideration will be detailed in the experimental study since our formulation is generic and applies to any software metrics.

3.2.2 *Solution approach*

Solution representation. As defined in the previous section, a solution consists of a sequence of n refactoring operations applied to different code elements in the source code to fix. In order to represent a candidate solution (individual/chromosome), we use a vector-based representation. Each vector's dimension represents a refactoring operation where the order of applying these refactoring operations corresponds to their positions in the vector. For each of these refactoring operations, we specify pre- and post-conditions in the style of Opdyke [12] to ensure the feasibility of their application. The initial population is generated by assigning randomly a sequence of refactorings to some code fragments. To apply a refactoring operation we need to specify which actors, i.e., code fragments, are involved/impacted by this refactoring and which roles they play in performing the refactoring operation. An actor can be a package, class, field, method, parameter, statement, or variable.

Solution variation. In each search algorithm, the variation operators play the key role of moving within the search space with the aim of driving the search towards optimal solutions. For crossover, we use the one-point crossover operator. It starts by selecting and splitting at random two parent solutions. Then, this operator creates two child solutions by putting, for the first child, the first part of the first parent with the second part of the second parent, and vice versa for the second child. This operator must ensure the respect of the length limits by eliminating randomly some refactoring operations. It is important to note that in many-objective optimization, it is better to create children that are close to their parents in order have a more efficient search process [7]. For this reason, we control the cutting point of the one-point crossover operator by restricting its position to be either belonging to the first tier of the refactoring sequence or belonging to the last tier. For mutation, we use the bit-string mutation operator that picks probabilistically one or more refactoring operations from its or their associated sequence and replaces them by other ones from the initial list of possible refactorings.

Solution evaluation. Each generated refactoring solution is executed on the system *S*. Once all required data is computed, the solution is evaluated based on the 15 metrics used as objective functions. Based on these values, the refactoring solution is assigned a non-domination rank (as in NSGA-II) and a position in the objective space allowing it to be assigned to a particular reference point based on distance calculation as previously described.

Normalization of population members. Usually objective functions (metrics) are incommensurable (i.e., they have different scales). For this reason, we used the normalization procedure proposed by Deb et al. [7] to circumvent this problem. At each generation, the minimal and maximal values for each metric are recorded and then used by the normalization procedure. Normalization allows the population members and with the reference points to have the same range, which is a pre-requisite for diversity preservation.

4. DESIGN OF THE EMPIRICAL STUDY

4.1 Research Questions

RQ1: How does NSGA-III perform compared to other many-objective (MOAE/D [30], IBEA [31]) and multi-objective (NSGA-II [8]) techniques? It is important to evaluate the performance of NSGA-III in terms of scalability when the number of considered objectives increases. In addition, it is interesting to determine if considering more metrics (objectives) improves the quality of the suggested refactoring solutions (the number of fixed code smells).

RQ2: How does NSGA-III perform compared to mono-objective refactoring approaches [19][23]? It is important to determine if considering each conflicting metric as a separate objective to optimize performs better than a mono-objective approach that aggregates all metrics in one objective. The comparison between a many-objective EA with a mono-objective one is not straightforward. The first one returns a set of non-dominated solutions while the second one returns a single optimal solution. In order to resolve this problem, for each many-objective algorithm we choose the nearest solution to the ideal point [3] (i.e., the vector composed of the best objective values among the population members) as a candidate solution to be compared with the single solution returned by the mono-objective algorithm. For both RQ1 and RQ2, we performed a qualitative evaluation where 8 PhD students in Software Engineering, with at least 2 years programming experience in Java and familiar with the evaluated open source systems, evaluated 10 operations from the best suggested refactoring solutions for each system. The operations were classified as useful (make sense semantically) or not.

RQ3: How does our many-objective formulation scale? There is a cost in allowing the developer to specify a large number of objectives. Can it be demonstrated that as the number of objectives increases, we can achieve a commensurate increase in the quality of the solutions generated? If not, then our approach is not justified.

4.2 Experimental Setup

4.2.1 Systems Studied

Our study considers the extensive evolution of different open source Java systems analyzed in the literature [19][24][21][25]. The corpus used includes releases of Apache Ant, ArgoUML, Gantt, Azureus and Xerces-J. Table 1 reports the size in terms of classes of the analyzed systems. The table also reports the number of code smells identified manually in the different systems -- more than 700 in total. Indeed, in several works [19][24][21][25], the authors asked different groups of developers to analyze the libraries to tag instances of specific code smells to validate their detection techniques. For replication purposes, they provided a corpus describing instances of different code smells including blob, spaghetti code, and functional decomposition [12]. In our study, we verified the capacity of our approach to fix classes that correspond to instances of these code smells. We used the detection rules of code smells proposed in Kessentini et al. [19] to identify the number of fixed code smells after applying the best refactoring solutions.

Table 1. Features of software systems analyzed.

Systems	*Number of classes*	*Number of code smells*
ArgoUML v0.26	1358	138
ArgoUML v0.3	1409	129
Xerces v2.7	991	82
Ant-Apache v1.5	1024	103
Ant-Apache v1.7.0	1839	124
Gantt v1.10.2	245	41
Azureus v2.3.0.6	1449	108

4.2.2 Performance Indicators

We used mainly three performance indicators to compare the different algorithms used in our experiments. These indicators are defined as follows:

- *Inverted Generational Distance (IGD):* is used as the performance metric since it has been shown to reflect both the diversity and convergence of the obtained non-dominated solutions [7]. The IGD corresponds to the average Euclidean distance separating each reference solution from its closest non-dominated one. Note that for each system we use the set of Pareto optimal solutions generated by all algorithms over all runs as reference solutions.

- *Percentage of fixed code smells (NF)* is the percentage of code smells fixed by the application of the best refactoring solution (i.e., number of fixed smells divided by the total number of code smells). The detection of code smells after applying a refactoring solution is performed using the detection rules of Kessentini et al. [19].

- *Usefulness of suggested refactorings* (UC) is the number of refactoring operations that make sense and useful divided by the total number of manually evaluated operations.

- *Computational time (CT)* is used mainly to compare the efficiency of NSGA-III with other algorithms using the same number of objectives.

4.2.3 Statistical Tests

Our experimental study is performed based on 31 independent simulation runs for each problem instance and the obtained results are statistically analyzed by using the Wilcoxon rank sum test with a 95% confidence level ($\alpha = 5\%$). The latter verifies the null hypothesis H_0 that the obtained results of two algorithms are samples from continuous distributions with equal medians, against the alternative that they are not H_1. The *p*-value of the Wilcoxon test corresponds to the probability of rejecting the null hypothesis H_0 while it is true

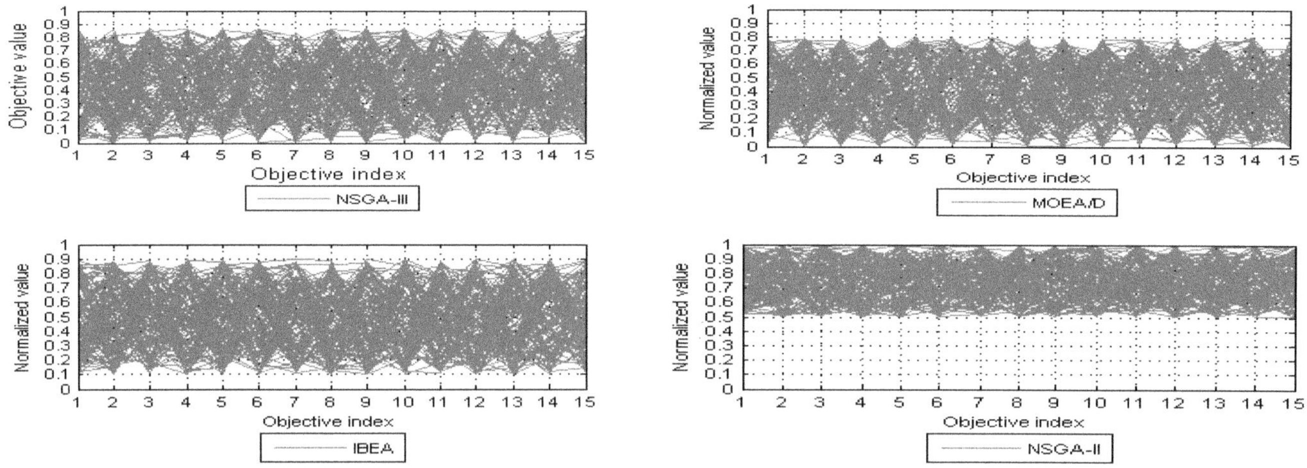

Figure 3. Value path plots of non-dominated solutions obtained by NSGA-III, MOEA/D, IBEA and NSGA-II during the median run of the 15-objective refactoring problem on ArgoUML v0.26.

(type I error). A p-value that is less than or equal to α (≤ 0.05) means that we accept H_1 and we reject H_0. However, a p-value that is strictly greater than α (> 0.05) means the opposite. In fact, for each problem instance, we compute the p-value obtained by comparing NSGA-II, IBEA, MOEA/D and mono-objective search results with NSGA-III ones.

4.2.4 Parameter Settings

Parameter setting influences significantly the performance of a search algorithm on a particular problem [1]. For this reason, for each many-objective algorithm and for each system (cf. Table 1), we perform a set of experiments using several population sizes: 91, 210, 156, 275 and 135 for respectively 3, 5, 8, 10 and 15 objectives. The maximum number of generations used is 400, 600, 750, 1000 and 1500 respectively for 3, 5, 8, 10 and 15 objectives. Each algorithm is executed 31 times with each configuration and then comparison between the configurations is done based on *IGD* using the Wilcoxon test. In order to have significant results, for each couple (algorithm, system), we use the trial and error method [1] in order to obtain a good parameter configuration. Since we are comparing different search algorithms, we classify parameters into common parameters and specific parameters. Table 2 depicts the important common parameters. We used a set of 15 quality metrics, namely Weighted Methods per Class (WMC), Response for a Class (RFC), Lack of Cohesion of Methods (LCOM), Cyclomatic Complexity (CC), Number of Attributes (NA), Attribute Hiding Factor (AH), Method Hiding Factor (MH), Number of Lines of Code (NLC), Coupling Between Object Classes (CBO), Number of Association (NAS), Number of Classes (NC), Depth of Inheritance Tree (DIT), Polymorphism Factor (PF), Attribute Inheritance Factor (AIF) and Number of Children (NOC) [10]. We selected randomly at each run some metrics from this list when the number of objectives is lower than 15. We used 23 refactoring types in our experiments, namely Add Parameter, Rename Method Encapsulate Collection/ Downcast/ Field, Collapse Hierarchy, Hide Method, Extract Class /Interface/ Method/ Subclass/ Superclass, Inline Class/ Method, Move Field/ Method, Pull Up Field/ Method, Push Down Field/ Method and Remove Parameter/ Setting Method [31].

Table 2. The setting of common parameters.

Number of objectives	Number of reference points (for NSGA-III and MOEA/D)	Population size
3	91	120
5	210	230
8	156	190
10	275	280
15	135	290

4.3 Results

Table 3 shows the median IGD and NF values of over 31 independent runs for all algorithms under comparison. All the results were statistically significant in the 31 independent simulations using the Wilcoxon rank sum test [1] with a 99% confidence level ($\alpha < 1\%$). For the 3-objective case, we see that NSGA-III and NSGA-II present similar results, and that NSGA-III provides slightly better results than IBEA and MOEA/D. For the 5-objective case, NSGA-III strictly outperforms NSGA-II and gives similar results to those of the two other multi-objective algorithms. For the 8-objective case, NSGA-III is strictly better than NSGA-II and significantly better than IBEA and MOEA/D. Additionally, IBEA seems to be slightly better than MOEA/D. It is worth noting that for problems' instances with 8 objectives or more, NSGA-II performance is dramatically degraded, which is simply denoted by the ~ symbol. For the 10- and 15-objective cases, NSGA-III is strictly better than all other algorithms. Moreover, MOEA/D seems to significantly outperform IBEA. The performance of NSGA-III could be explained by the interaction between: (1) Pareto dominance-based selection and (2) reference point-based selection, which is the distinguishing feature of NSGA-III compared to other existing many-objective algorithms. The percentage of fixed code smells using NSGA-III is better than all other algorithms in all systems in 100% of cases when more than 8 objectives are considered. It is clear from Table 3 that the percentage of fixed code smells increases as we use more quality metrics to evaluate refactoring solutions. On average, all the four algorithms NSGA-III, IBEA, MOEA/D and NSGA-II perform similarly with 3 objectives, however the percentage of fixed code smells is low in all systems. This is due to the fact that the use of only three quality metrics is not enough to evaluate the quality of the design after applying the best refactoring solution. The average percentage of fixed code smells in all systems using NSGA-III with 15 objectives on all systems is higher than 92%, which outperforms all the remaining algorithms. Thus, we can conclude that NSGA-III represents a scalable solution to find trade-offs between 15 objectives and that the use of additional objectives (metrics) improves the quality of refactoring solutions.

Figure 3 illustrates the value path plots of all algorithms regarding the 15-objective refactoring problem on ArgoUMLv0.26, the largest system used in our experiments. Similar observations were made in the remaining systems but are omitted due to space considerations. All quality metrics were normalized between 0 and 1 and all are to be minimized. We observe that NSGA-III presents the best convergence since its non-dominated solutions are the closest to the ideal point,

Table 3. Median IGD and NF values on 31 runs (best values are in bold). ~ means a large value that is not interesting to show. The results were statistically significant on 31 independent runs using the Wilcoxon rank sum test with a 99% confidence level (α < 1%).

Problem	*M*	MaxGen	NSGA-III		IBEA		MOEA/D		NSGA-II	
			NF	IGD	NF	IGD	NF	IGD	NF	IGD
ArgoUML v0.26	3	400	**69%**	**1.356×10^{-3}**	67%	1.358×10^{-3}	**69%**	1.359×10^{-3}	**67%**	**1.356×10^{-3}**
	5	600	**83%**	**3.918×10^{-3}**	79%	4.001×10^{-3}	81%	4.007×10^{-3}	54%	4.423×10^{-3}
	8	750	**86%**	**4.115×10^{-3}**	82%	4.327×10^{-3}	84%	4.331×10^{-3}	42%	~
	10	1000	**89%**	**1.727×10^{-2}**	84%	2.124×10^{-2}	87%	2.001×10^{-2}	37%	~
	15	1500	**96%**	**3.302×10^{-2}**	81%	3.826×10^{-2}	84%	3.733×10^{-2}	34%	~
Xerces v2.7	3	400	**64%**	**9.751×10^{-4}**	**64%**	9.754×10^{-4}	**64%**	9.753×10^{-4}	62%	9.752×10^{-4}
	5	600	**78%**	**7.876×10^{-3}**	76%	7.910×10^{-3}	74%	7.912×10^{-3}	56%	8.006×10^{-3}
	8	750	**84%**	**8.001×10^{-3}**	81%	8.422×10^{-3}	81%	8.428×10^{-3}	48%	~
	10	1000	**92%**	**2.115×10^{-2}**	86%	2.410×10^{-2}	86%	2.299×10^{-2}	44%	~
	15	1500	**94%**	**4.666×10^{-2}**	86%	5.198×10^{-2}	84%	4.935×10^{-2}	39%	~
ArgoUML v0.3	3	400	63%	**2.667×10^{-3}**	63%	2.668×10^{-3}	**66%**	2.668×10^{-3}	63%	**2.667×10^{-3}**
	5	600	**79%**	**4.283×10^{-3}**	76%	4.291×10^{-3}	78%	4.294×10^{-3}	51%	4.524×10^{-3}
	8	750	**91%**	**5.545×10^{-3}**	84%	5.701×10^{-3}	86%	5.716×10^{-3}	47%	~
	10	1000	**94%**	**3.339×10^{-2}**	87%	3.601×10^{-2}	89%	3.477×10^{-2}	39%	~
	15	1500	**98%**	**6.001×10^{-2}**	89%	6.554×10^{-2}	87%	6.399×10^{-2}	34%	~
Ant-Apache v1.5	3	400	**68%**	**3.854×10^{-4}**	66%	3.857×10^{-4}	66%	3.856×10^{-4}	**68%**	3.856×10^{-4}
	5	600	76%	**4.678×10^{-4}**	76%	4.702×10^{-4}	**78%**	4.709×10^{-4}	52%	5.035×10^{-4}
	8	750	**88%**	**6.111×10^{-4}**	81%	6.308×10^{-4}	83%	6.313×10^{-4}	46%	~
	10	1000	**93%**	**2.861×10^{-3}**	84%	3.008×10^{-3}	86%	2.999×10^{-3}	34%	~
	15	1500	**97%**	**5.928×10^{-3}**	82%	6.478×10^{-3}	81%	6.399×10^{-3}	31%	~
Ant-Apache v1.7.0	3	400	**61%**	**4.326×10^{-3}**	61%	4.328×10^{-3}	63%	4.329×10^{-3}	62%	4.327×10^{-3}
	5	600	**73%**	**5.612×10^{-3}**	69%	5.692×10^{-3}	71%	5.694×10^{-3}	53%	6.001×10^{-3}
	8	750	**86%**	**6.269×10^{-3}**	84%	6.516×10^{-3}	82%	6.521×10^{-3}	48%	~
	10	1000	**89%**	**4.007×10^{-2}**	87%	4.301×10^{-2}	84%	4.147×10^{-2}	37%	~
	15	1500	**92%**	**7.006×10^{-2}**	84%	7.840×10^{-2}	81%	7.688×10^{-2}	31%	~
Gantt v1.10.2	3	400	63%	**5.111×10^{-3}**	**64%**	5.113×10^{-3}	63%	5.114×10^{-3}	66%	**5.111×10^{-3}**
	5	600	**69%**	**6.601×10^{-3}**	67%	6.702×10^{-3}	**69%**	6.701×10^{-3}	54%	6.956×10^{-3}
	8	750	**88%**	**7.899×10^{-3}**	83%	8.101×10^{-3}	81%	8.116×10^{-3}	44%	~
	10	1000	**93%**	**3.333×10^{-2}**	84%	3.637×10^{-2}	86%	3.536×10^{-2}	37%	~
	15	1500	**97%**	**5.807×10^{-2}**	82%	6.202×10^{-2}	83%	6.125×10^{-2}	28%	~
Azureus v2.3.0.6	3	400	**61%**	**6.429×10^{-4}**	64%	6.432×10^{-4}	61%	6.431×10^{-4}	64%	6.431×10^{-4}
	5	600	**78%**	**6.708×10^{-4}**	72%	6.782×10^{-4}	75%	6.788×10^{-4}	47%	6.991×10^{-4}
	8	750	**84%**	**6.976×10^{-4}**	80%	7.205×10^{-4}	82%	7.212×10^{-4}	34%	~
	10	1000	**91%**	**2.745×10^{-3}**	84%	2.976×10^{-3}	87%	2.877×10^{-3}	26%	~
	15	1500	**94%**	**4.981×10^{-3}**	81%	5.508×10^{-3}	78%	5.394×10^{-3}	26%	~

i.e., the vector composed of 15 zeros. Also, MOEA/D seems to have better convergence than IBEA. However, NSGA-II is unable to progress in terms of convergence as its non-dominated solutions are situated far from the ideal vector. We conclude that although NSGA-II is the most famous multi-objective algorithm in SBSE, it is not adequate for problems involving more than 3 objectives. Based on the results we obtained for the refactoring problem, it appears that NSGA-III is a very good candidate solution for tackling many-objective SBSE problems.

We also compared the results of NSGA-III using 15 objectives and two mono-objective refactoring approaches on all seven open source systems as described in Figure 4. From the set of non-dominated solutions generated by NSGA-III, we selected the solution closest to the ideal point. NSGA-III performed better than both mono-objective algorithms in 100% of cases. In fact, since mono-objective algorithms aggregate all metrics in one objective there is a loss of information due to the conflicting nature of the used quality metrics. It is clear that mono-objective algorithms did not perform well in terms of fixing code smells whereas NSGA-III fixed on average more than 92% of them, especially in the case of large systems such as Ant Apache and Argo UML. In general, large systems contain many different types of code smells and so a large number of metrics is required to evaluate the quality of a system after applying a refactoring solution. We asked 8 PhD students in Software Engineering to manually evaluate some suggested refactorings if they are useful and semantically make sense or not. As described in Figure 5, the use of high number of metrics such as coupling and cohesion not only improve the structure by fixing code-smells but also helped our NSGA-III based algorithm to generate refactoring solutions that semantically make sense and. In all the considered systems, NSGA-III outperforms existing work in terms of semantics preservation with at least 73% of precision on every system.

4.1 Discussion

Computational time (CT):

When using optimization techniques, the most time consuming operation is the evaluation step. Thus, we studied the execution time of all many/multi-objective algorithms used in our experiments. Figure 5 shows the evolution of the running times of the different algorithms on the ArgoUMLv0.26 system, the largest system in our experiments. It is clear from this figure, that the multi-objective algorithm (NSGA-II) has similar running times for the 3- and 5-

objective cases. However, for higher numbers of objectives NSGA-III is faster than IBEA. This observation could be explained by the computational effort required to compute the contribution of each solution in terms of hypervolume. In comparison to MOEA/D, MOEA/D is slightly faster than NSGA-III since it does not make use of non-dominated sorting.

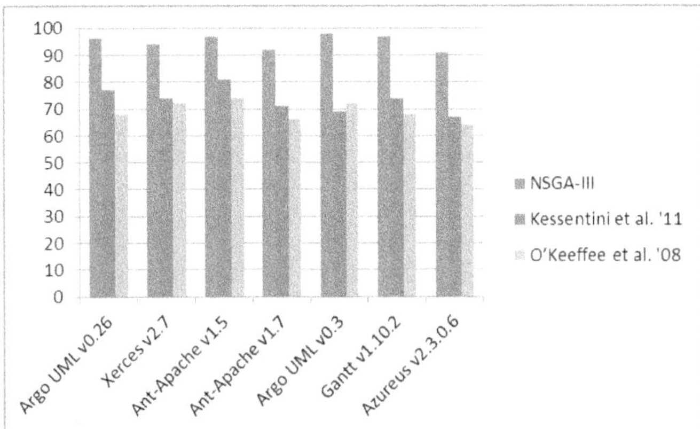

Figure 4. Median NF values on 31 independent runs using 7 systems comparing NSGA-III and two mono-objective approaches [19][23].

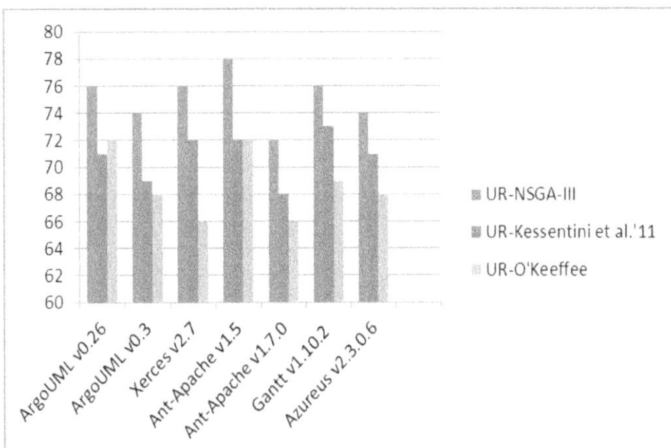

Figure 5. Median UR (semantic coherence) values on 31 independent runs using 7 systems comparing NSGA-III and two mono-objective approaches [19][23].

Quality improvements vs. number of objectives:

One of the main motivations of our work is to propose a scalable search-based software engineering approach that can address software engineering problems with a large number of objectives to be optimized. Thus, we evaluated the impact of taking into consideration a higher number of objectives (metrics) on the quality of the refactoring solutions. In fact, the symptoms of code smells can be formalized in terms of quality metrics, thus if we consider more metrics in evaluating a refactoring solution there is a better chance that more code smells are fixed. Figure 5 confirms this. The percentage of fixed code smells increases from 63% to 98% as the number of objectives/metrics increases from 3 to 15 objectives. This result allows us to affirm RQ3.

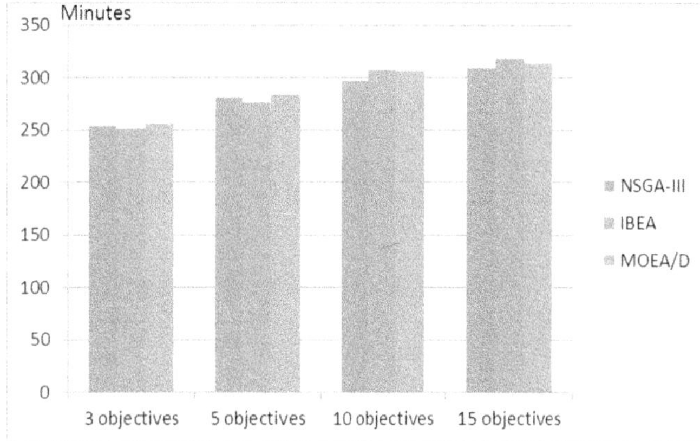

Figure 6. Median CT values on 31 independent runs using 7 systems comparing NSGA-III and two mono-objective approaches.

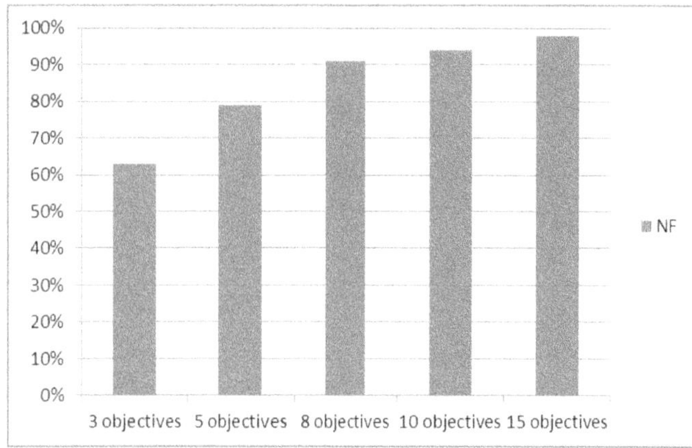

Figure 7. Median NF values on 31 independent runs using ArgoUML v 0.3 with 3, 5, 8, 10 and 15 objectives.

5. RELATED WORK

Search-based refactoring represents fully automated refactoring driven by metaheuristic search and guided by software quality metrics and used subsequently to address the problem of automating design improvement [23]. Seng et al. [27] propose a search-based technique that uses a genetic algorithm over refactoring sequences. The employed metrics are mainly related to various class level properties such as coupling, cohesion, complexity and stability. The approach was limited only to the use of one refactoring operation type, namely 'move method'. In contrast to O'Keeffe et al. [23], their fitness function is based on well-known measures of coupling between program components. Both these approaches use weighted-sum to combine metrics into a fitness function, which is of practical value but is a questionable operation on ordinal metric values. Kessentini et al. [19] also propose a single-objective combinatorial optimization using a genetic algorithm to find the best sequence of refactoring operations that improve the quality of the code by minimizing as much as possible the number of code smells detected using a set of quality metrics. Kilic et al. explore the use of a variety of population-based approaches to search-based parallel refactoring, finding that local beam search could find the best solutions. Harman and Tratt were the first to introduce the concept of Pareto optimality to search-based refactoring [14]. They use it to combine two metrics into a fitness function, namely CBO (coupling between objects) and SDMPC (standard deviation of methods per class), and demonstrate that it has several advantages over the weighted-sum approach. More recent work on multi-objective search-based refactoring is the work by Ouni et al. [24] who propose a multi-objective optimization approach to find the best sequence of refactorings using NSGA-II. The proposed approach is based on two objective functions, quality (proportion of corrected code smells) and code modification effort, to recommend a sequence of refactorings that provide the best trade-off between quality and effort.

6. CONCLUSIONS AND FUTURE WORK

This paper represents the first real-world application of NSGA-III and the first scalable work that supports the use of 15 objectives to address a software engineering problem. In our approach, refactoring solutions are evaluated using a set of 15 software quality metrics. We evaluated our approach on seven large open source systems [28][29][30][31][32]. The experimental results indicate that NSGA-III outperforms other many-objective algorithms (IBEA [31] and MOEA/D [30]), NSGA-II and mono-objective evolutionary algorithms [19][23]. As part of the future work, we plan to work on adapting NSGA-III to additional software engineering problems and we will perform more comparative studies on larger open source systems.

ACKNOWLEDGEMENT

This work was supported, in part, by the Institute for Advanced Vehicle Systems-Michigan grant and the Science Foundation Ireland grant 10/CE/I1855 to Lero - the Irish Software Engineering Research Centre.

7. REFERENCES

[1] Arcuri A. and Fraser G., 2013. *Parameter tuning or default values? An empirical investigation in search-based software engineering*, Empirical Software Engineering, 18(3).

[2] Bader, J. and Zitzler, E. 2011. Hype: An algorithm for fast hypervolumebased many-objective optimization. In *Evolutionary Computation*. vol. 19, no. 1. 45–76.

[3] Bechikh, S., Ben Said, L. and Ghédira, K. 2010. Estimating Nadir Point in Multi-objective Optimization using Mobile Reference Points. In CEC'10. 2129–2137.

[4] Brown, W. J., Malveau, R. C., Brown, W. H., and Mowbray, T. J. 1998. *Anti Patterns: Refactoring Software, Architectures, and Projects in Crisis*. John Wiley and Sons, 1st Ed.

[5] Deb, K. 2001. *Multiobjective Otpimization using Evolutionary Algorithms*. John Wiley and Sons, Ltd, New York, USA.

[6] Deb, K. and Jain H. 2012. Handling many-objective problems using an improved NSGA-II procedure. In *Proceedings of IEEE Congress on Evolutionary Computation*. 1–8.

[7] Deb, K. and Jain, H. An Evolutionary Many-Objective Optimization Algorithm Using Reference-point Based Non-dominated Sorting Approach, Part I: Solving Problems with Box Constraints. In *Proceedings of IEEE Transactions on Evolutionary Computation*. accepted.

[8] Deb, K., Pratap, A., Agarwal, S. and Meyarivan, T. 2002. A Fast and Elitist Multiobjective Genetic Algorithm: NSGA-II. *In Proceedings of IEEE Transactions on Evolutionary Computation*, vol. 6, no. 2. 182–197.

[9] di Pierro, F., Khu, S-T. and Savic, D.A. 2007. An Investigation on Preference Order Ranking Scheme for Multiobjective Evolutionary Optimization. In *Proceedings of IEEE Transactions on Evolutionary Computation*. vol. 11, no. 1. 17–45.

[10] Fenton, N. and Pfleeger, S. L. 1997. *Software Metrics: A Rigorous and Practical Approach*, 2nd ed. International Thomson Computer Press.

[11] Ferrucci, F., Harman, M., Ren, J. and Sarro, F. 2013. Not going to take this anymore: multi-objective overtime planning for software engineering projects. In ICSE '13, 462-471.

[12] Fowler, M., Beck, K., Brant, J., Opdyke, W. and Roberts, D. 1999. *Refactoring – Improving the Design of Existing Code*. 1st ed. Addison-Wesley.

[13] Harman, M. 2013. Software Engineering: An Ideal Set of Challenges for Evolutionary Computation, In GECCO '13, 1759-1760.

[14] Harman, M. and Tratt, L. 2007. Pareto optimal search based refactoring at the design level. In GECCO'07. 1106–1113.

[15] Harman, M., Mansouri, S. A. and Zhang, Y. 2012. Search-based software engineering: Trends, techniques and applications. In *ACM Computing Surveys*. vol. 45, no.1. 61 pages.

[16] Harman, M., and Jones, B., 2001. *Search Based Software Engineering*, Journal of Information and Software Technology, 43(14):833-839.

[17] Jaimes, A. L., Coello Coello, C.A. and Barrientos, J. E. U. 2009. Online Objective Reduction to Deal with Many-objective Problems. In *the 5th international conference on Evolutionary Multicriterion Optimization*. 423–437.

[18] Jain, H. and Deb, K. 2013. An Improved Adaptive Approach for Elitist Nondominated Sorting Genetic Algorithm for Many-Objective Optimization. In EMO'13, 307–321.

[19] Kessentini, M., Kessentini, W., Sahraoui, H., Boukadoum, M., and Ouni, A. 2011. Design Defects Detection and Correction by Example. In ICPC'11. 81-90.

[20] Kukkonen, S. and Lampinen, J. 2007. Ranking-Dominance and Many-Objective Optimization. In *Proceedings of IEEE Congress on Evolutionary Computation*. 3983-3990.

[21] Moha, N., Guéhéneuc, Y.-G., Duchien, L. and Le Meur, A.-F. 2009. DECOR: A Method for the Specification and Detection of Code and Design Smells. In *TSE, 2009, vol 12,*. 20–36.

[22] Ó Cinnéide, M., Tratt, L., Harman, M., Counsell, S. and Moghadam, I. H. 2012. Experimental Assessment of Software Metrics Using Automated Refactoring. In ESEM'12, 49-58.

[23] O'Keeffe, M. K. and Ó Cinnéide, M. 2008. Search-based refactoring for software maintenance. In *Journal of Systems and Software*. vol. 81, no.4. 502-516.

[24] Ouni, A., Kessentini, M., Sahraoui, H. and Boukadoum, M. 2012. Maintainability Defects Detection and Correction: A Multi-Objective Approach. *Journal of Automated Software Engineering*. vol. 20, 47-79.

[25] Palomba, F., Bavota, G., Di Penta, M., Oliveto, R., De Lucia, A. and Poshyvanyk, D. 2013. Detecting Bad Smells in Source Code Using Change History Information. In ASE 2013.

[26] Sayyad, A., Menzies, T. and Ammar, H. 2013. On the value of user preferences in search-based software engineering: a case study in software product lines. In ICSE '13. 492-501.

[27] Seng, O., Stammel, J. and Burkhart, D. 2006. Search-based determination of refactorings for improving the class structure of object-oriented systems. In GECCO'06. 1909–1916.

[28] Singh, H. K., Isaacs, A. and Ray, T. 2011. A pareto corner search evolutionary algorithm and dimensionality reduction in many-objective optimization problems. In *Proceedings of IEEE Transactions on Evolutionary Computation*. vol. 99. 1–18.

[29] Yamashita A., and Moonen, L., 2012. Do code smells reflect important maintainability aspects?, Proceedings of ICSM2012.

[30] Zhang, Q. and Li, H. 2007. MOEA/D: A Multiobjective Evolutionary Algorithm Based on Decomposition. In *Proceedings of IEEE Transactions on Evolutionary Computation*. vol. 11, no. 6. 712–731.

[31] Zitzler, E. and Künzli, S. 2004. Indicator-based selection in multiobjective search Parallel Problem Solving from Nature. In Proceedings of PPSN'04.

[32] (Refactorings in Alphabetical Order). [Online]. Available: http://www.refactoring.com/catalog/index.html

Comparing Search Techniques for Finding Subtle Higher Order Mutants

Elmahdi Omar, Sudipto Ghosh, and Darrell Whitley
Dept. of Computer Science, Colorado State University
Fort Collins, Colorado, USA
Elmahdi.omar@colostate.edu, ghosh@cs.colostate.edu, whitley@cs.colostate.edu

ABSTRACT

Subtle Higher Order Mutants (HOMs) are those HOMs that cannot be killed by existing test suites that kill all First Order Mutants (FOMs) for the program under test. Subtle HOMs simulate complex, real faults, whose behavior cannot be simulated using FOMs. However, due to the coupling effect, subtle HOMs are rare in the exponentially large space of candidate HOMs and they can be costly to find even for small programs.

In this paper we propose new search techniques for finding subtle HOMs and extend our prior work with new heuristics and search strategies. We compare the effectiveness of six search techniques applied to Java and AspectJ programs.

Our study shows that more subtle HOMs were found when the new heuristics and search strategies were used. The programming language (Java or AspectJ) did not affect the effectiveness of any search technique.

Categories and Subject Descriptors

D.2.5 [**Software Engineering**]: Testing and Debugging

General Terms

Algorithms, Experimentation

Keywords

Higher order mutation testing, search-based software engineering, software testing, genetic algorithm, local search

1. INTRODUCTION

The majority of traditional First Order Mutants (FOMs) represent trivial faults that are often easily detected. Thus, researchers use higher order mutation testing to identify the combinations of single faults that represent complex faults. Jia and Harman [4] introduced the notion of *Strongly Subsuming HOMs*, which represent the HOMs that can replace their constituent FOMs without loss of test effectiveness, and thus reduce test effort. Omar et. al. [8] introduced the notion of *subtle HOMs*, which represent the HOMs that are not killed by test suites that kill all FOMs for the program under test. *Subtle HOMs* denote cases where single faults interact (e.g., by masking each other) to produce complex faulty behavior that cannot be simulated using FOMs, and thus they can be used to improve test effectiveness.

GECCO'14, July 12–16, 2014, Vancouver, BC, Canada.
Copyright 2014 ACM 978-1-4503-2662-9/14/07 ...$15.00.
http://dx.doi.org/10.1145/2576768.2598286.

Purushothaman and Perry [10] showed that the majority of real faults not detected during testing are complex faults that cannot be simulated using FOMs. Their study reported that fixing 90% of these complex faults required making multiple changes to the source code. Because HOMs are created by making multiple syntactic changes to the source code, they can simulate such complex faults.

Subtle HOMs can be used as the basis for generating new test inputs to improve the fault detection effectiveness of existing test suites. However, the cost of finding subtle HOMs can be high even for small programs. This is because the number of candidate HOMs is exponentially large and a large majority of them are killed by test suites that kill all FOMs (coupling effect) [4, 6, 12], making the subtle ones relatively rare.

In previous work [8], we presented three search techniques, Genetic Algorithm, Local Search, and Random Search, for finding subtle HOMs. We also conducted an initial evaluation to demonstrate the ability of the search techniques to find subtle HOMs. Although all the techniques were able to find subtle HOMs, we were able to identify ways in which to improve their effectiveness based on our analysis of the generated HOMs and how each technique explored the search space of candidate HOMs.

In this paper, we introduce three improved search techniques, Guided Local Search, Restricted Random Search, and Restricted Enumeration Search for finding subtle HOMs. Guided Local Search uses a heuristic to focus on the FOM combinations that are more likely to produce subtle HOMs. Restricted Random Search uses a configurable parameter to limit the search to a region of the search space where subtle HOMs are more likely to be found. Restricted Enumeration Search enumerates all candidate HOMs in a predefined sequence starting in the region of the search space where more subtle HOMs are expected to be found.

In our previous study [8], we only used AspectJ programs to demonstrate the ability of the search techniques to find subtle HOMs. In this paper, we also included Java to determine whether or not differences in programming language constructs resulted in different levels of effectiveness.

2. SEARCH TECHNIQUES FOR FINDING SUBTLE HOMs

We first describe the objective function used by the search techniques to measure the fitness of HOMs. We summarize the previously introduced search techniques and describe the new ones. Omar et al. [8] provides a more detailed description of the previously proposed search techniques. We also briefly describe the prototype tool called HOMAJ [9] for higher order mutation testing for Java and AspectJ programs.

2.1 Objective Function

The objective function needs to identify the HOMs that have a better chance of becoming subtle HOMs if a mutated statement is added or removed. Below we provide a formal definition of the objective function.

- $F = \{f_1, \ldots, f_f\}$ is the set of all non-equivalent FOMs for the program under test.
- H is the space of all candidate HOMs. $H = \mathcal{P}(F)$.
- U is the universe of all possible test cases.
- $T = \{tc_1, \ldots, tc_t\}$ is the set of all test cases under consideration (the given test suite), $T \subset U$ and T kills all the FOMs in F.
- $h_i^n \in H$ is an HOM constructed from n FOMs, such that $h_i = \{f_{i_1}, \ldots, f_{i_n}\}$. The notation can be simplified to $h_i = h_i^n$ without confusion.
- Let $T_{h_i} \subseteq T$ denote the set of those test cases in T that kill h_i. $T_{h_i} = \emptyset$ if none of the test cases in T kill h_i.
- There are n test sets $T_{i_1}, \ldots, T_{i_n}, \forall j \in [1, \ldots, n], T_{i_j} \subseteq T$ and T_{i_j} contains all test cases that kill f_{i_j} in h_i.
- TU_i is a test set such that

$$TU_i = \bigcup_{j=1}^{n} T_{i_j}$$

Objective Function

$$fitness(h_i) = \frac{|(TU_i \cup T_{h_i})| - |(TU_i \cap T_{h_i})|}{|TU_i \cup T_{h_i}|} + subtlety(h_i) \tag{1}$$

Subtlety Function

$$subtlety(h_i) = \begin{cases} 1 & \text{if} \quad T_{h_i} = \emptyset \\ 0 & \text{otherwise} \end{cases} \tag{2}$$

To calculate the fitness of an HOM, the objective function first measures the fault detection difference between the HOM and its constituent FOMs (first term in Equation 1) and then measures its subtlety. The fault detection difference quantifies the variation between the set of test cases that kill the HOM and the union of all sets of test cases that kill the individual constituent FOMs. The subtlety value shows whether the HOM is killed by the given test set or not.

The fitness value of an HOM lies between 0 and 2. Note that a solution which has an evaluation of 2 represents a global optimum in the search space, and there are potentially many globally optimal solutions. HOMs with higher fitness values are favored in the selection process. FOMs have zero fitness value. HOMs are classified based on their fitness values as follows:

1. *Entirely Coupled HOMs* have a fitness value of 0 because there is no difference between the set of test cases that kill the HOM and the union of all sets of test cases that kill the individual constituent FOMs.
2. *Partially Coupled HOMs* have a fitness value greater than 0 but less than 1 because the set of test cases that kill the HOM and the union of all sets of test cases that kill the individual constituent FOMs are not identical but they overlap.
3. *Decoupled HOMs* have a fitness value of 1 because they are killed by a set of test cases that is totally different from the union of all sets of test cases that kill the individual constituent FOMs.
4. *Subtle HOMs* have a fitness value of 2 because they are not killed by any test case in the given test set. They represent new faulty behavior that has not been tested.

2.2 Genetic Algorithm

The Genetic Algorithm (GA) [8] takes as input the list of FOMs for the program under test along with number of crossover points, mutation rate, population size, degree of HOMs in the first population, and the number of elite HOMs that get carried over at each iteration. Each chromosome is represented as a one dimensional array of strings such that each element in the array represents a line of code (one Java/AspectJ statement) of the program under test.

The Genetic Algorithm uses *tournament selection* to implement generational replacement of the population. A certain number of HOMs with the highest fitness values are automatically carried over (copied) to the next generation. The crossover happens between two selected HOMs (parents) that are recombined to produce two HOMs (offspring).

The Genetic Algorithm mutation operator applies mutation to an existing HOM by either adding or removing an FOM. The FOMs to be added to an HOM are randomly selected from the list of FOMs for the program under test and the FOMs to be removed from an HOM are randomly selected from the HOM's constituent FOMs. All HOMs in the population are created, compiled, and executed, and then the objective function evaluates their fitness.

2.3 Local Search

The Local Search (LS) [8] technique takes as input the list of FOMs and the degree of the incumbent HOM. The incumbent HOM represents the search starting point. Local Search starts by generating an incumbent HOM using a number of randomly selected FOMs from the list of FOMs. The maximum degree of the incumbent HOM is set using a configurable parameter. After evaluating the incumbent HOM, Local Search generates all the HOMs neighboring the incumbent HOM. The neighboring HOMs are those that vary by one FOM (one step) from the incumbent HOM. A list of neighboring HOMs is maintained.

After creating and evaluating all HOMs in the neighborhood list, Local Search looks for the best neighboring HOM that has an equal or higher fitness value than the incumbent HOM. If such an HOM exists, it becomes the next incumbent HOM, and the process starts all over again. If no better HOM exists, Local Search restarts by selecting a new incumbent HOM.

2.4 Guided Local Search

The Guided Local Search (GLS) technique introduced in this paper uses the same steps as Local Search. However, Guided Local Search utilizes program structural information to help it focus on the FOM combinations that are more likely to produce subtle HOMs. When an incumbent HOM is selected and evaluated, Guided Local Search generates a smaller set of neighboring HOMs than Local Search. Guided Local Search aims to avoid creating and evaluating HOMs that are expected to be entirely coupled to their constituent FOMs.

During the early empirical studies that set the foundation for this work, we found that the majority of HOMs that have a fitness value greater than zero (partially coupled, decoupled, and subtle HOMs) are those where the mutated statements shared a common variable. For example, for the Kettle Program which is used in the empirical evaluation in this paper, we found that in 96% of HOMs with fitness value greater than zero, at least two of their mutated statements shared at least one common variable. On the other hand, 60% of the HOMs with a fitness value equal to zero, their mutated statements shared some common variables.

Although the presence of a common variable among the mutated statements in the HOM cannot guarantee that the HOM is not entirely coupled, the initial data we obtained for most subject programs motivated us to utilize this knowledge in the search process.

Guided Local Search explores only neighboring HOMs where at least two of their mutated statements share at least one common variable. That is, there exists at least one pair of mutated statements where both statements read and/or write to at least one program variable. In addition, Guided Local Search maintains a list of all second order mutants that were found and evaluated during the search process. This list contains the fitness values for the evaluated second order mutants. Guided Local Search uses this list to further refine and minimize the list of neighboring HOMs by ignoring all HOMs that contain pairs of mutated statements that share a common variable when their combination was found to result in an entirely coupled second order mutant.

2.5 Random Search

The Random Search (RS) [8] technique explores the space of all candidate HOMs by randomly selecting HOMs, one at a time, seeking out the HOMs that are not killed by the given test suite. Random Search iterates the process of generating an HOM with a set of randomly selected FOMs from the list of FOM. The degree of a generated HOM is randomly selected to allow Random Search to examine any candidate HOM in the search space. Each generated HOM is compiled and executed, its execution result is recorded, and its fitness value is calculated.

2.6 Restricted Random Search

The Restricted Random Search (RRS) technique introduced in this paper performs the same steps as the Random Search. However, in our previous study we found most of the discovered subtle HOMs were of lower degrees (less than six). Therefore, Restricted Random Search uses a configurable parameter to allow it to control the maximum degree of generated HOMs. This parameter allows Restricted Random Search to limit the search to a smaller part of the search space where subtle HOMs are more likely to be found.

2.7 Restricted Enumeration Search

The Restricted Enumeration Search (RES) technique introduced in this paper examines candidate HOMs in the search space in a predefined sequence until a defined stopping condition is met. The Restricted Enumeration Search takes as input the list of FOMs for the program under test, and then it starts by creating and evaluating mutants one at a time. It creates and evaluates all candidate second order mutants, then third order mutants and so on until a stopping condition is met.

The Restricted Enumeration Search is designed to start the search in the space of lower degree HOMs because of two reasons. First, because the space of HOMs grows exponentially (at least to a certain degree), the space of lower degree HOMs is smaller and it is easier to find subtle HOMs. Second, more subtle HOMs exist in space of lower degree HOMs because adding more faults to an HOM in general make it easier to kill.

2.8 Prototype Tool HOMAJ

We developed a prototype tool HOMAJ: Higher Order Mutation for AspectJ and Java [9]. HOMAJ automates the process of generating, compiling, and executing both first order and higher order mutants. It takes as an input the program under test along with the test suite. It then generates Java and AspectJ FOMs, and compiles and executes them against the given test suite. It starts the search process based on the selected search technique seeking out FOM combinations that are not killed by the given test suite.

The stopping condition for the search process is configured by the tester. Any of the search techniques can be stopped if it reaches the maximum number of HOMs it is allowed to generate, finds a predefined number of found subtle HOMs, or reaches a specified time interval. When the search process stops, HOMAJ presents a list of subtle HOMs that were found during the search process. A subtle HOM can possibly be an equivalent HOM. Testers need to manually inspect the subtle HOMs and identify equivalent HOMs.

The current implementation of HOMAJ allows one fault per statement. Therefore, the maximum degree of generated HOMs is restricted by the number of statements that can be mutated for the program under test.

3. EXPERIMENTAL EVALUATION

This section describes the goals of the experimental evaluation of the search techniques.

3.1 Goals

The goal was to evaluate and compare the ability of search techniques to find subtle HOMs. Therefore, we ran all the techniques with the stopping condition of generating and

Table 1: Subject Program and Test Set Characteristics

Subject program	LOC	# of classes	# of aspects	# of test cases	# Non-Equiv FOMs	# Equiv FOMs
Banking (AspectJ)	243	2	2	8	92	59
Coordinate (Java)	121	2	0	13	242	55
Kettle (AspectJ)	125	1	2	12	125	29
Movie Rental (AspectJ)	191	3	1	16	316	101
Roman (Java)	191	2	0	11	208	93
Telecom (AspectJ)	928	10	3	10	188	41

exploring a fixed number of HOMs. At the end of the execution, we compared the total number of distinct subtle HOMs found by each technique.

We also investigated how the search techniques explored the search space and how that affected their effectiveness. We investigated the growth in the number of subtle HOMs found by each search technique as the number of generated HOMs increased. We also investigated the degrees and the number of distinct HOMs generated by each technique.

3.2 Subject Programs

We used four AspectJ programs and two Java programs of different sizes. We chose AspectJ [11] programs because of the unique concepts and constructs introduced by the Aspect-Oriented Programming (AOP) paradigm. The unique constructs introduced new types of interactions between the program elements which produced new testing challenges [1, 13]. The AspectJ programs varied in size and implemented various Java and AspectJ constructs. They contained before, after, and around advices, inter-type declarations, as well as primitive and composed pointcuts. We also used two Java programs to find out if the search techniques produce different results when programs do not implement AspectJ concepts and constructs.

For each subject program, we used a test suite that covered all the statements and killed all non-equivalent FOMs. Table 1 provides information about the subject programs, their sizes, size of their test suites, and number of equivalent and non-equivalent FOMs. The Java programs have only classes and no aspects. All equivalent FOMs were manually identified and they are not included in the search process for subtle HOMs.

3.3 Experimental Configuration

We used multiple 64-bit Linux machines with Intel Core^{TM}-4x3.3G and 8Gb memory. The configuration used for each technique can affect its performance. In the early stages of this study we ran the search techniques with different configurations and finally selected the configurations that produced the highest number of subtle HOMs. The search techniques were configured the same for all subject programs as follows. For Genetic Algorithm, the number of crossover points was set at two, number of elite HOMs at 15, population size at 300, mutation rate at 0.1 of the number of mutable statements of the program, and first population degree at two. For both Local Search and Guided Local Search, the incumbent HOM degree was set at two. For Restricted Random Search, the maximum HOM degree allowed was set at six. Both Random Search and Restricted Enumeration Search did not have any configured parameters.

4. RESULTS AND ANALYSIS

To compare the ability of the search techniques to find subtle HOMs, we ran five techniques (Genetic Algorithm, Local Search, Restricted Random Search, Random Search, and Guided Local Search) 30 times per subject program with the stopping condition of generating 50,000 HOMs. Restricted Enumeration Search was run only once per subject program because it produces the same result each time. Table 2 shows the maximum, average, median, standard deviation, and minimum number of subtle HOMs found for the 30 runs per technique. Equivalent HOMs, which are treated as subtle HOMs by our objective function, are manually identified and removed. Omar et al. [8] provides more details about the treatment of equivalent HOMs.

For each subject program, all six techniques found subtle HOMs. However, Guided Local Search, Local Search, and Restricted Enumeration Search were more successful in finding the highest number of subtle HOMs than the other search techniques for all subject programs. Restricted Enumeration Search was more successful for Movie Rental and Roman programs, while Guided Local Search was more successful for all other programs.

Restricted Random Search produced better results than Random Search, which indicates that limiting the search to the space of lower degree HOMs is a good strategy because it produced a higher number of subtle HOMs. In fact, for most programs, Restricted Random Search found almost as many subtle HOMs as the Genetic Algorithm, which uses different sophisticated operators to find subtle HOMs. Although Random Search was the least successful technique because it considered every candidate HOM in the large search space at each iteration, it still managed to find subtle HOMs, which indicates subtle HOMs can be relatively easy to find.

To investigate these observations further, we analyzed the results produced by each technique. First we plotted the growth in the number of subtle HOMs over the number of generated HOMs. Figures 1 through 6 show how the average number of found subtle HOMs grew as each technique generates more HOMs. The number of generated HOMs is considered a quasi-representation of the time taken by each algorithm.

Second, we investigated the percentage of distinct HOMs generated by each techniques as shown in Table 3. For example, only 33.1% of all HOMs generated by Genetic Algorithm for Banking program are found to be distinct while 91.5% of all HOMs generated by Random Search were distinct. Restricted Enumeration Search examines each HOM once, which explains why all the HOMs were distinct.

Last, we investigated the degree of HOMs generated by each technique. Table 4 shows for each technique, the percentage of HOMs for different degrees. For example, 29% of all HOMs for the Banking program generated by Genetic Al-

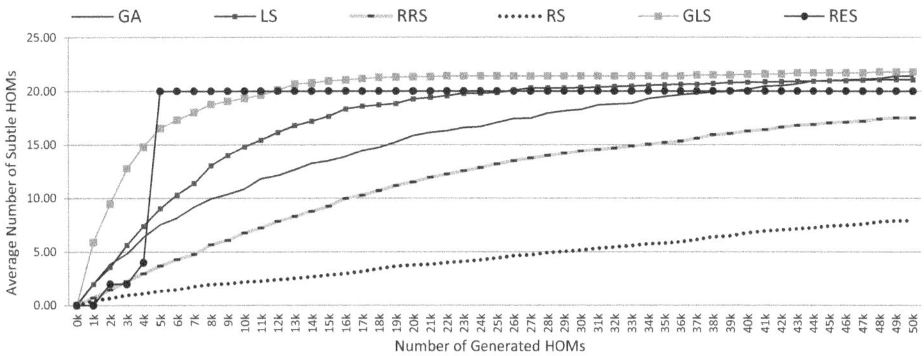

Figure 1: Growth in the average number of subtle HOMs over the number of generated HOMs for Banking

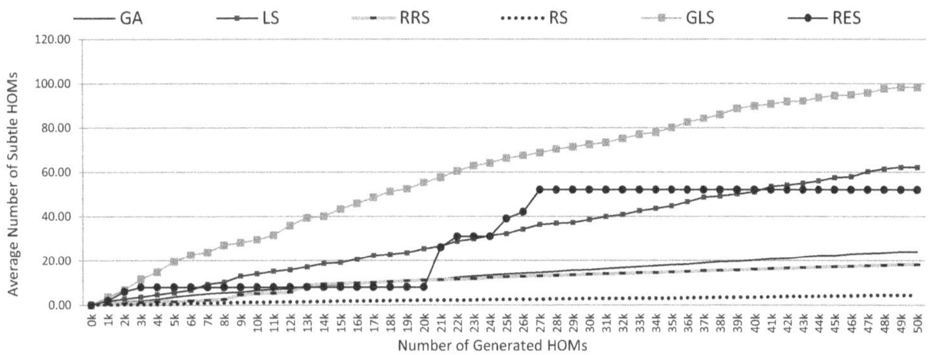

Figure 2: Growth in the average number of subtle HOMs over the number of generated HOMs for Coordinate

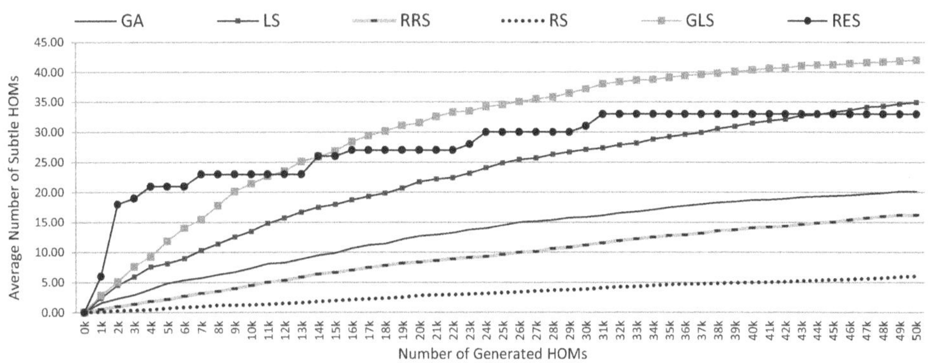

Figure 3: Growth in the average number of subtle HOMs over the number of generated HOMs for Kettle

gorithm were second order mutants. The number of second order mutants reported for Restricted Enumeration Search reflects the actual number of all candidate second order mutants. For example, there are 48,000 candidate second order mutants for the Movie Rental program (96% of 50,000). Some of the techniques can possibly generate first order mutants. For example, the Genetic Algorithm can produce an FOM when crossing over two HOMs or when mutating an HOM by removing a mutated statement. FOMs have zero fitness values and their percentages are not included in Table 4.

For the Banking program, Guided Local Search, Restricted Enumeration Search and Local Search found most of the subtle HOMs before generating 15,000 HOMs. Because the number of second order mutants for the Banking program is considerably low compared to the other programs (only 8% of 50,000 HOMs) and because the Restricted Enumeration Search examines all second order mutants before it moves to order-3 and so on, Restricted Enumeration Search was able to find a high number of subtle HOMs in the early stages of the search process. A similar pattern was observed for the Kettle program. In our previous study, the majority of the found subtle HOMs were of low degrees.

Except for the Random Search, all other techniques eventually found a comparable number of subtle HOMs for the Banking program. This indicates that subtle HOMs in general were easier to find for the Banking program. This could be because the Banking program had the smallest test set.

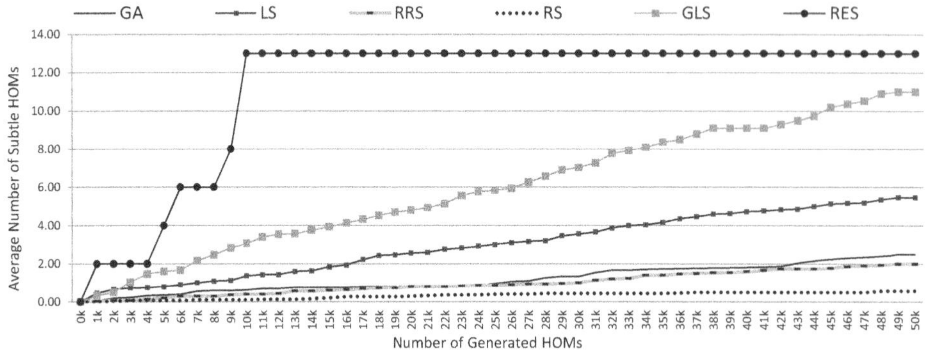

Figure 4: Growth in the average number of subtle HOMs over the number of generated HOMs for Movie

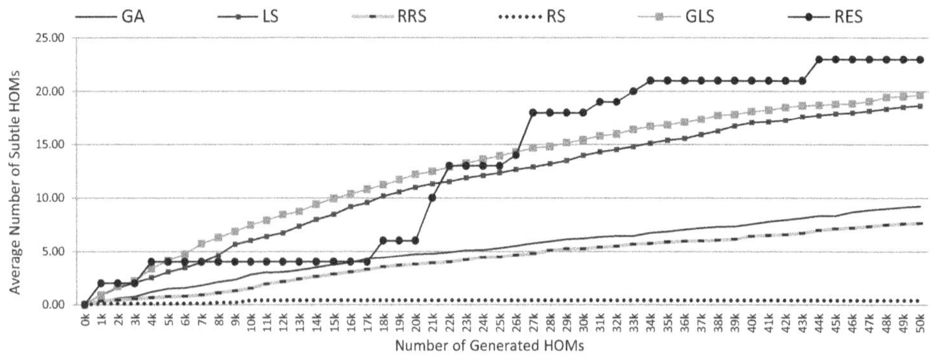

Figure 5: Growth in the average number of subtle HOMs over the number of generated HOMs for Roman

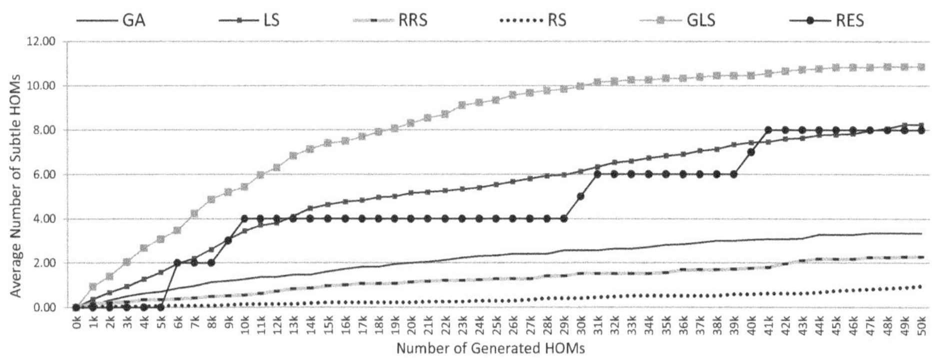

Figure 6: Growth in the average number of subtle HOMs over the number of generated HOMs for Telecom

Guided Local Search and Local Search found a higher number of subtle HOMS for the Coordinate program than all other programs even though it was the smallest in terms of size. Both Local Search and Guided Local search eventually found a higher number of subtle HOMs than Restricted Enumeration Search. The numbers of subtle HOMs found using Genetic Algorithm, Random Search, and Restricted Random Search were low compared to other search techniques.

For the Kettle program, Restricted Enumeration Search was more successful than Guided Local Search and Local Search in the early part of the search process because the Kettle program had a low number of second order mutants (only 15% of 50,000 HOMs).

For the Movie Rental program, Restricted Enumeration Search was more successful throughout the search process. Movie Rental has the highest number of second order mutants (96% of 50,000 HOMs) and Restricted Enumeration Search examined all of them and thus, it was more successful overall in finding more subtle HOMs. A similar trend can be seen for the Roman program where second order mutants represent 41% of evaluated 50,000 HOMs.

For the Roman program, Restricted Enumeration Search eventually found a higher number of subtle HOMs than Guided Local Search and Local Search. However, both Guided Local Search and Local Search were more successful than Restricted Enumeration Search in the early stages of the search process.

Table 2: Number of Subtle HOMs Found by Search Techniques

Programs	Technique	# Subtle HOMs				
		Max	Avg	Med	St.Dev	Min
Banking	GA	25	21.4	21	1.77	18
	LS	24	21.07	21	0.58	20
	RRS	20	17.5	18	1.96	11
	RS	12	7.9	8	1.99	5
	GLS	24	21.8	21	1.3	21
	RES	20	20	N/A	N/A	N/A
Coordinate	GA	33	24	24	4.19	15
	LS	98	62.2	61.5	14.03	32
	RRS	97	18.17	15	18.21	6
	RS	10	4.37	4	1.92	1
	GLS	136	98.33	102.5	22.43	52
	RES	52	52	N/A	N/A	N/A
Kettle	GA	26	20.17	20	2.42	16
	LS	50	34.93	36	5.85	23
	RRS	21	16.2	16	2.64	9
	RS	10	6	6	2.26	1
	GLS	50	42	42	3.49	37
	RES	33	33	N/A	N/A	N/A
Movie Rental	GA	5	2.5	3	1.33	0
	LS	11	5.47	5	2.83	1
	RRS	4	2	2	1.17	0
	RS	2	0.57	0	0.73	0
	GLS	19	11	11.5	4.69	4
	RES	13	13	N/A	N/A	N/A
Roman	GA	14	9.23	2.33	9	5
	LS	26	18.67	2.68	18	14
	RRS	14	7.64	2.61	8	3
	RS	2	0.4	0.7	0	0
	GLS	27	19.67	2.47	19	16
	RES	23	23	N/A	N/A	N/A
Telecom	GA	7	3.33	3	1.56	1
	LS	13	8.23	8	2.14	4
	RRS	4	2.28	2	0.96	0
	RS	2	0.96	1	0.85	0
	GLS	14	10.87	11	1.33	8
	RES	8	8	N/A	N/A	N/A

Table 4: Percentage By Degree for HOMs Generated By Search Techniques

Programs	Technique	Percentage of HOMs by Degree					
		2nd	3rd	4th	5th	6th	7th+
Banking	GA	29	22.2	17.5	12.5	8.3	10
	LS	56.1	38.8	4.8	0.2	0	0
	RRS	16.7	16.7	16.7	16.7	16.7	0
	RS	4	4	4	4	4	76
	GLS	5.8	83.2	9.8	0.6	0	0.6
	RES	8	92	0	0	0	0
Coordinate	GA	26.1	20.8	17	13.1	9.4	12.8
	LS	48.3	38.2	9.3	3.6	0.7	0
	RRS	16.9	16.6	16.5	16.6	16.6	0
	RS	4.5	4	4	3.9	4	75.2
	GLS	5.8	67.4	18.8	6.8	1.2	0.1
	RES	55	45	0	0	0	0
Kettle	GA	23.2	18.8	15.8	13	10	18.7
	LS	45.7	38.5	11.7	3.4	0.5	0.1
	RRS	16.7	16.7	16.6	16.6	16.7	0
	RS	4	4	4	4	4	76.1
	GLS	6.8	63.7	21.7	6.7	1.1	0.1
	RES	15	85	0	0	0	0
Movie Rental	GA	20.2	17	15	12.7	10.4	24.7
	LS	49.3	39.7	9.1	1.8	0.1	0
	RRS	16.7	16.7	16.7	16.7	16.6	0
	RS	4.1	4	4	4	4	75.9
	GLS	3.7	73.1	18.9	3.8	0.4	0
	RES	96	4	0	0	0	0
Roman	GA	24	20.8	17.1	13.6	9.8	14.
	LS	55.2	34.2	8.1	2.2	0.3	0
	RRS	16.9	16.8	16.6	16.5	16.1	0
	RS	4.2	4	4	4	4	75.9
	GLS	7.1	62.8	22	6.9	1.1	0.1
	RES	41.1	58.9	0	0	0	0
Telecom	GA	23.2	19.1	16.3	13.2	10.2	17.8
	LS	45.1	44.4	9.5	0.9	0.1	0
	RRS	16.7	16.7	16.7	16.7	16.7	0
	RS	4.1	4	4.1	4	4	75.8
	GLS	3.1	69.4	25	2.3	0.1	0
	RES	22	77.9	0	0	0	0

Table 3: Percentage of Distinct HOMs generated by Search Techniques

Programs	Percentage of Distinct HOMs					
	GA	LS	RRS	RS	GLS	RES
Banking	33.1	10.3	59.8	91.5	9	100
Coordinate	43.2	25	66.8	91.8	30.3	100
Kettle	33.8	13.2	60.5	92.4	15.9	100
Movie Rental	45.1	27.6	70.1	93.4	29.8	100
Roman	43.7	30.8	71.8	93.6	26.4	100
Telecom	40.1	16.3	63.9	92.8	10.2	100

For the Telecom program, Guided Local Search found a higher number of subtle HOMs than Restricted Enumeration Search during all stages of the search process. Genetic Algorithm and Restricted Random Search found less than half the number of subtle HOMs found by Local Search and Guided Local Search.

Restricted Enumeration Search by construction, can only generate distinct HOMs. Among all the other search techniques, Random Search generated the highest percentage of distinct HOMs. Although Restricted Random Search limits the search to a smaller part of the search space, it generated a higher percentage of distinct HOMs than the other search techniques. Although Guided Local Search generated the lowest percentage of distinct HOMs for most programs, it found the highest number of distinct subtle HOMs for all programs. This suggests that focusing the search on a specific set of FOM combinations can be a rewarding strategy. This also demonstrates the effectiveness of the heuristic implemented in Guided Local Search.

5. RELATED WORK

The majority of the proposed Search-Based Software Engineering testing techniques targeted test data generation for fault discovery [3]. However, other than the work presented by Harman et al. [4, 5], which is briefly described below, none of the proposed Search-Based Software Engineering testing techniques tackled similar testing goals as the techniques presented in this paper.

Jia and Harman [4] classified HOMs in terms of their coupling and subsumption relations with FOMs and introduced three search-based optimization approaches (Genetic Algorithm, Greedy Algorithm, and Hill Climbing Algorithm) for finding *Strongly Subsuming HOMs* in C programs. Unlike subtle HOMs, strongly subsuming HOMs aim to reduce testing effort and cost by reducing the total number of FOMs that need to be compiled and executed without loss of test effectiveness. Jia and Harman [4] conducted an experimental evaluation using 10 C programs. The results showed that subsuming HOMs existed in all studied programs. Although the proportions of strongly subsuming HOMs were low, the actual numbers were large. The results indicated that the Genetic Algorithm performed best in finding strongly subsuming HOMs because the subsuming HOMs were easier to generate from existing subsuming HOMs.

Langdon et al. [5] used the multi-objective Pareto optimal approach and Monte Carlo sampling Genetic Algorithms to search for HOMs that are hard-to-kill and are syntactically similar to the original program. The search algorithm produced HOMs that were harder-to-kill than their constituent FOMs and also HOMs that were constructed from single faults masking each other.

DiGiuseppe and Jones [2] presented a study of the effects of the interaction of different faults within a program. The results showed that multiple real faults could hide the impact of each other leading to fewer failures than expected. They also reported that fault obfuscation was the most prominent of all the fault interaction types.

Wedyan and Ghosh [13] presented a study of mutation testing for AspectJ programs. In the subject programs they studied, the pointcut mutants that match some of the intended join points and some of the unintended join points at the same time could only be obtained with the help of HOMs.

Omar and Ghosh [7] presented an exploratory study of higher order mutation testing in the context of AspectJ programs. They proposed four approaches to constructing higher order mutants in AspectJ programs and evaluated the approaches in terms of their ability to create higher order mutants that result in higher test effectiveness and lower test effort compared to first order mutants.

6. CONCLUSIONS AND FUTURE WORK

We presented search techniques for finding subtle HOMs. The techniques were developed based on the results and lessons learned from our previous study.

Guided Local Search used a heuristic to focus on the FOM combinations that are more likely to produce subtle HOMs. Restricted Random Search used a configurable parameter to limit the search to the region of the search space where subtle HOMs are more likely to be found. Restricted Enumeration Search enumerates all candidate HOMs in a predefined sequence starting with the region of the search space where subtle HOMs are more likely to be found.

Guided Local Search was the most successful in terms of finding the highest number of subtle HOMs for most programs that were used. Restricted Enumeration Search was the most successful for programs that have a high number of subtle second order mutants. Restricted Random Search was more successful than Random Search. The results also showed that the programming language (Java or AspectJ) did not affect the effectiveness of any search technique.

Although Guided Local Search produced the lowest percentage of distinct HOMs for most programs, it was more effective than Local Search and found the highest numbers of subtle HOMs for all the programs that were used. This demonstrates the effectiveness of the proposed heuristic and motivates us to investigate the observations further.

In the future, we will investigate the impact of different control and data flow criteria on the process of finding subtle HOMs. We will also investigate whether information about the test cases that kill each FOM can be used to help the search techniques focus on the FOM combinations that are more likely to produce subtle HOMs. We will develop new heuristics and investigate their impact on increasing the effectiveness of the search techniques. Further research is needed to develop test input generation techniques that can target subtle HOMs.

7. REFERENCES

[1] J. S. Baekken and R. T. Alexander. A candidate fault model for AspectJ pointcuts. In *International Symposium on Software Reliability Engineering*, pages 169–178, 2006.

[2] N. DiGiuseppe and J. A. Jones. Fault interaction and its repercussions. In *International Conference on Software Maintenance*, pages 3–12, 2011.

[3] M. Harman, A. Mansouri, and Y. Zhang. Search-based software engineering: Trends, techniques and applications. *ACM Computing Surveys*, 45(1):11, 2012.

[4] Y. Jia and M. Harman. Higher order mutation testing. *Information and Software Technology*, 51(10):1379–1393, 2009.

[5] W. B. Langdon, M. Harman, and Y. Jia. Efficient multi-objective higher order mutation testing with genetic programming. *Journal of Systems and Software*, 83(12):2416–2430, 2010.

[6] J. Offutt. Investigations of the software testing coupling effect. *IEEE Transactions on Software Engineering and Methodology*, 1(1):5–20, 1992.

[7] E. Omar and S. Ghosh. An exploratory study of higher order mutation testing in aspect-oriented programming. In *International Symposium on Software Reliability Engineering*, pages 1–10, 2012.

[8] E. Omar, S. Ghosh, and D. Whitley. Constructing subtle higher order mutants for Java and AspectJ programs. In *International Symposium on Software Reliability Engineering*, pages 340–349, 2013.

[9] E. Omar, S. Ghosh, and D. Whitley. Homaj: A tool for higher order mutation testing in aspectj and java. In *Workshop on Mutation Analysis*, 2014.

[10] R. Purushothaman and D. E. Perry. Toward understanding the rhetoric of small source code changes. *IEEE Transactions on Software Engineering*, 31(6):511–526, 2005.

[11] T. A. Team. AspectJ Compiler 1.6.12. http://www.eclipse.org/aspectj/. 2011.

[12] K. H. T. Wah. An analysis of the coupling effect I: single test data. *Science of Computer Programming*, 48(2âĂŞ3):119 – 161, 2003.

[13] F. Wedyan and S. Ghosh. On generating mutants for AspectJ programs. *Information and Software Technology*, 54(8):900–914, 2012.

Generating Structured Test Data with Specific Properties using Nested Monte-Carlo Search

Simon Poulding
University of York
York, YO10 5GH, UK
simon.poulding@york.ac.uk

Robert Feldt
Blekinge Institute of Technology
SE-371 79 Karlskrona, Sweden
robert.feldt@bth.se

ABSTRACT

Software acting on complex data structures can be challenging to test: it is difficult to generate diverse test data that satisfies structural constraints while simultaneously exhibiting properties, such as a particular size, that the test engineer believes will be effective in detecting faults. In our previous work we introduced GödelTest, a framework for generating such data structures using non-deterministic programs, and combined it with Differential Evolution to optimize the generation process.

Monte-Carlo Tree Search (MCTS) is a search technique that has shown great success in playing games that can be represented as a sequence of decisions. In this paper we apply Nested Monte-Carlo Search, a single-player variant of MCTS, to the sequence of decisions made by the generating programs used by GödelTest, and show that this combination can efficiently generate random data structures which exhibit the specific properties that the test engineer requires. We compare the results to Boltzmann sampling, an analytical approach to generating random combinatorial data structures.

Categories and Subject Descriptors

D.2.5 [**Software Engineering**]: Testing and Debugging; E.1 [**Data**]: Data Structures; G.1.6 [**Numerical Analysis**]: Optimization; G.2.1 [**Discrete Mathematics**]: Combinatorics

Keywords

Software Testing; Data Structures; Search-Based Software Engineering; Nested Monte-Carlo Search

1. INTRODUCTION

The verification of some types of software requires test inputs in the form of complex data structures. Examples include information retrieval programs that traverse tree-like index structures, compilers that require syntactically correct source code to test functionality beyond the lexer and parser, and web applications that consume HTML and XML inputs. Often such structures are not bounded in terms of size, and so it is not possible to exhaustively enumerate all possible structures that could be supplied to the program; instead a finite set of structures may be sampled at random.

The question then arises as to the probability distribution from which these structures should be sampled. The test engineer may have knowledge as to the particular properties that are the most effective for the type of testing being performed: for example, certain properties may increase the likelihood of detecting a fault during system testing; while for performance testing, the size of the structure may be the property of interest. The challenge is to sample data structures with the particular properties desired by the engineer without introducing other unnecessary biases that could reduce diversity and thus the fault-detecting ability of the test data.

Techniques for sampling data structures at random include analytical approaches from the field of combinatorics, stochastic grammars, and non-deterministic generating programs. An example of the first of these techniques is Boltzmann samplers [5] which are efficient at uniformly sampling data structures of a desired mean size, but lack flexibility in terms of the type of data structure to which they can be applied. In our previous work [6], we introduced the GödelTest framework that uses non-deterministic generating programs and so is more flexible than Boltzmann samplers. We applied Differential Evolution to optimize the probability distributions associated with the non-deterministic constructs in the generating program so as to sample data structures with the desired properties. This approach was more effective than that of Boltzmann samplers, but still only a relatively small proportion of the generated data structures had properties that were very close or equal to the target values.

In this paper we propose a complementary approach to optimizing GödelTest generators with the objective of efficiently generating data structures that have *exactly* the required properties. By interpreting the generation of a data structure as a single-player game, we apply Nested Monte-Carlo Search (NMCS), a search technique that has been very effective in playing such games. We show that the efficiency of GT-NMCS (the combination of GödelTest and NMCS) can be equivalent to or better than Boltzmann samplers while retaining diversity in the sampled data structures, and can be applied to a wider range of data structures.

GECCO'14, July 12–16, 2014, Vancouver, BC, Canada.
Copyright 2014 ACM 978-1-4503-2662-9/14/07 ...$15.00.
http://dx.doi.org/10.1145/2576768.2598339.

In Section 2, we describe Boltzmann samplers, the GödelTest framework, and the Nested Monte-Carlo Search algorithm. We propose how NMCS can be applied to GödelTest in Section 3. Section 4 is an empirical investigation of the utility of the GT-NMCS algorithm. We discuss related work in Section 5, and summarize our conclusions and outline future work in Section 6.

2. BACKGROUND

2.1 Boltzmann Samplers

Boltzmann samplers, developed by Duchon et al. [5], permit the random generation of combinatorial data structures in a controlled and unbiased manner.

To create a sampler, the data structure is first expressed as grammar-like rules which describe the construction of the structure from simpler structures using a small set of operators. For example, general trees—that is, trees in which each node may have any number of children—can be expressed using the recursive rule:

$$\mathcal{G} = \mathcal{Z} \cdot \mathbf{sequence}(\mathcal{G}) \tag{1}$$

where $\mathcal{G}$ represents the class of general trees, $\mathcal{Z}$ represents a single tree node, the operator $\cdot$ combines an instance of each of its two operands to form a new structure, and the operator **sequence** constructs a sequence of zero or more instances of its operand. Thus this rule specifies the construction of a general tree as a tree node (i.e. the root node) that has a sequence of zero or more subtrees that are themselves general trees.

Next, a probability distribution is assigned to each of the operators that require a choice to be made. For example, each time the operator **sequence** is encountered in the recursive rule above, a choice is made as to the number of subtrees that form the sequence. The probability distribution assigned to the **sequence** operator in a Boltzmann sampler is always a geometric distribution, but this distribution has a parameter, $0 < p \leq 1$, that controls its exact form: values of p closer to 1 favour shorter sequences.

The key feature of Boltzmann samplers is that it is relatively straightforward to calculate the parameters of the distribution associated with each operator that ensure the mean size of the generated structures has a chosen value. Moreover, when the parameters are set in this way, all structures with the same size, e.g. all general trees with 100 nodes, have the same probability of being emitted by the sampler: there is no unnecessary bias in the sampling process.

2.2 GödelTest

In the context of generating test data, Boltzmann samplers have three significant limitations. Firstly, the data structure must be expressible using the small set of operators that are supported by Boltzmann samplers; many data structures used in software, such source code or XML, cannot easily be expressed in this way. Secondly, Boltzmann samplers permit control only over the mean size of the sampled structures, but control over other properties—such as the height of a tree structure or the connectivity of a graph structure—may be necessary in order to efficiently detect faults in the software. Finally, few of the sampled structures necessarily have a size close to the mean value—the variance in the sizes can be large—and thus a sampler must often be supplemented by a potentially inefficient filtering mechanism to reject structures that are not of the desired size.

In earlier work, we developed the GödelTest framework to address these limitations [6]. GödelTest specifies the construction of the data structure using a non-deterministic program; the flexibility of such programs enables the generation of a much wider range of data structures than can Boltzmann samplers. The non-determinism may take the form of choices in the control flow of the generating program, e.g. whether or not to call a function; or choices as to the data processed, e.g. the sampling of a random integer.

```
function generator()
  node := create tree node
  add subtrees mult(generator()) to node
  return node
```

Figure 1: A GödelTest generator for general trees.

Figure 1 is an example of a GödelTest generator for general trees; the generator is described here using pseudocode[1]. In this example, **mult** is a GödelTest construct that returns an array consisting of zero or more objects created by calling the function specified as its argument (and is therefore the equivalent of the Boltzmann sampler **sequence** operator). This construct is an example of non-determinism—in this case, concerning the number of objects in the array—and so creates a *choice point*. GödelTest uses a *choice model* to resolve the non-determinism: each time a choice point is encountered during the execution of the generator program, the choice model is used to decide which choice to make. Internally, GödelTest labels each of the possible choices by a unique integer, and so the choice model supplies a single integer to identify which of the choices to make at the choice point. Figure 2 illustrates this process.

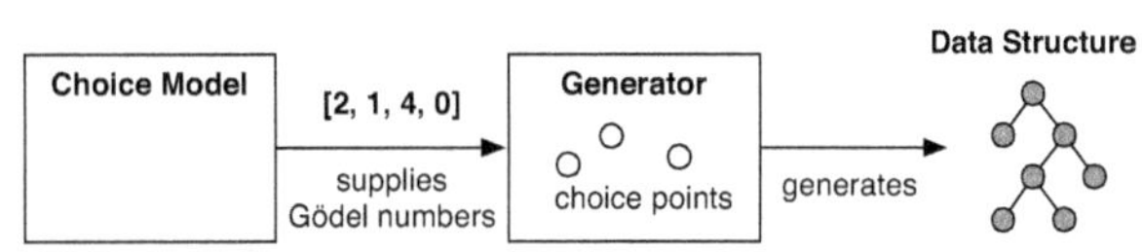

Figure 2: The GödelTest framework.

We refer to the integer supplied by the choice model as a *Gödel number*, and a single execution of a generator program is thus characterised by a sequence of Gödel numbers that we call a *Gödel sequence*. There is therefore a mapping from the set of Gödel sequences to the set of data structures that the program can generate. This mapping is a key feature of GödelTest: it enables the choice model to be abstracted from the specifics of the generating program.

In our previous work [6], the choice model was constructed in a similar manner to Boltzmann samplers: by assigning a local probability distribution to each choice point from which Gödel numbers were sampled. The parameters of the local probability distributions forming the choice model were optimized using Differential Evolution so that the generated data structures had, on average, the desired properties. We demonstrated that this a more flexible approach

[1]The GödelTest framework is not tied to a particular language: in our previous work the generating programs were written in Ruby, and for the empirical work of this paper the generators are implemented using the Julia language.

than Boltzmann samplers and thereby addressed the final two limitations described above. Firstly, the fitness metric used by the Differential Evolution (or other metaheuristic search algorithm) can be used to optimize the generator for any desirable property, not only the structure size. Secondly, by using probability distributions with more degrees of freedom, and permitting these distributions to be conditional on context information such as the recursion depth, a greater proportion of the sampled structures had properties that were closer to the desired values. Nevertheless, the proportion of sampled structures that had *exactly* the desired properties was still low. This is the motivation for the algorithm proposed in this paper: the construction of the Gödel sequence using Nested Monte-Carlo Search with the objective of satisfying the desired properties more precisely.

2.3 Nested Monte-Carlo Search

In this work we equate the generation of structured data using GödelTest to a single-player game, and use a variant of Monte-Carlo Tree Search (MCTS) that is particularly suited to this type of game: Nested Monte-Carlo Search (NMCS) proposed by Cazenave [3].

When used to play games, NMCS is applied to a *game tree*, the tree of potential game moves starting from the current game position in which nodes represent game states and edges valid moves. Figure 3 is an example of a game tree. The player has a choice of three moves: A, B, or C. If she makes move A, the next move she can make is either H, I, or J. If instead she makes move B, then no further moves are possible and the node represents a terminal state at which she has won or lost. The objective of NMCS is to determine a sequence of moves—a path in the game tree—that leads to a winning state.

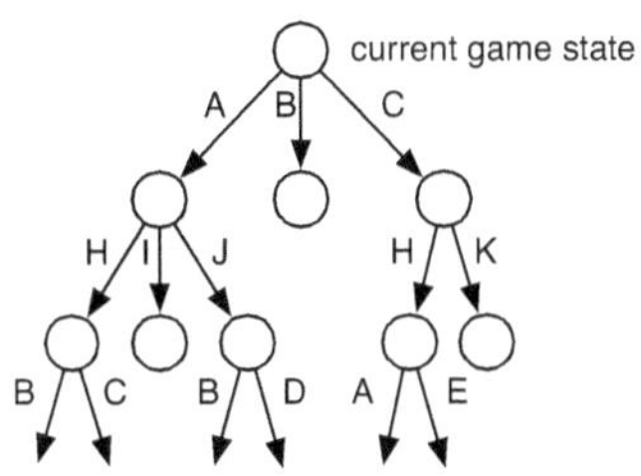

Figure 3: An example of the first three levels of a game tree. Edges are labelled by moves.

Many game-playing algorithms perform a search of the game tree that is as exhaustive as computational resources will permit. NMCS, and other variants of MTCS, take a different approach: the top-level moves are assessed by playing a relatively small number of game simulations through to conclusion. Each simulation starts with one of the top-level moves, may make a small number of deterministic moves to efficiently explore the first few levels of the game tree, but then makes all remaining moves at random until a terminal state is reached. These simulations provide an estimate of whether a given top-level move could lead to a winning state for the player. The estimate is noisy as a result of random nature of the simulation, but there is often a sufficient signal in the estimate to make an effective move choice.

At the current game state, NMCS performs one simulation of the game for each possible top-level move. This procedure is illustrated in Figure 4. At the terminal state reached by each simulation, a score is computed that is used to rank the terminal states and thus the associated top-level moves. The top-level move with the best simulation score is taken. The root of the game tree is now the state reached by taking this move, and the same procedure is applied in order to choose between top-level moves from this new root. The process repeats until no further moves are possible.

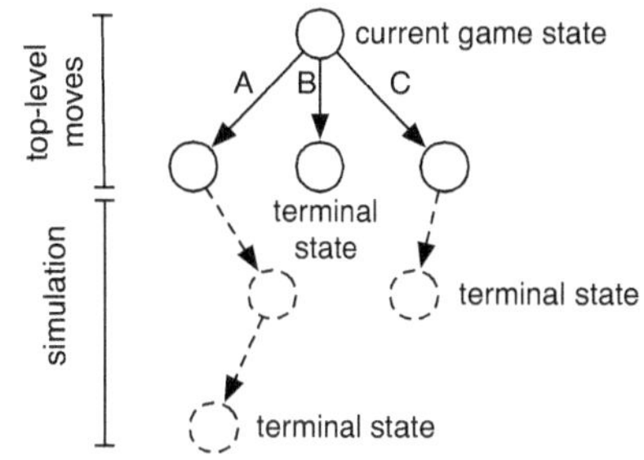

Figure 4: An illustration of Nested Monte-Carlo Search.

NMCS additionally tracks the best score, and the sequence of moves that gave rise to that score, over all the simulations performed so far. If none of the simulations at the current root state has a score greater than the tracked best score, the move from the sequence associated with the tracked best score is taken instead.

NMCS has one parameter: the nesting level which is an integer greater than or equal to 1. If the nesting level is 1, then the game simulations are random after making the first top-level move: at each step of the simulation, one of the possible moves is chosen at random, typically according to a uniform distribution. If the nesting level is greater than 1, then the game simulation itself uses NMCS—with a nesting level that is one lower—to choose moves. Figure 5 describes the NMCS algorithm in pseudocode.

3. APPLYING NMCS TO GÖDELTEST

3.1 GödelTest as a Game

Our proposal is that the generation of data structures using GödelTest can be equated to a single-player game, and that NMCS can be used to efficiently play the game to a 'winning' state that corresponds to a data structure with the desired properties. We refer to the combined algorithm as GT-NMCS.

Game states are partial Gödel sequences, and moves are the action of appending a single Gödel number to the end of the sequence. The root node is an empty Gödel sequence and a path through the game tree consists of moves that number-by-number build up a Gödel sequence. Figure 6 is an example of the first three levels of such a game tree.

To avoid a potential source of confusion, we clarify here that the game tree is *not* the same as the data structure that is being generated by GödelTest. In the empirical work of this paper, we select general trees as an example of a generated data structure since this enables a comparison with Boltzmann samplers. However GödelTest can be used to generate a wide range of data structures, and they need not be tree-like for the NMCS algorithm to be applied: a conceptual game tree exists for all GödelTest generating programs.

```
function nmcs(state, level)
  chosenSeq := empty sequence
  bestScore := -inf
  bestSeq := empty sequence
  while state is not terminal
    for each move possible from state
      state' := apply move to state
      if level == 1
        (score, seq) := random simulation from state'
      else
        (score, seq) := nmcs(state', level-1)
      end
    end
    highScore := highest score of the moves from state
    if highScore > bestScore
      bestScore := highScore
      chosenMove := move associated with highScore
      bestSeq := seq associated with highScore
    else
      chosenMove := first move in bestSeq
      bestSeq := remove first move from bestSeq
    end
    state := apply chosenMove to state
    chosenSeq := append chosenMove to chosenSeq
  end
  return (bestScore, chosenSeq)
```

Figure 5: The Nested Monte-Carlo Search algorithm, adapted from [3].

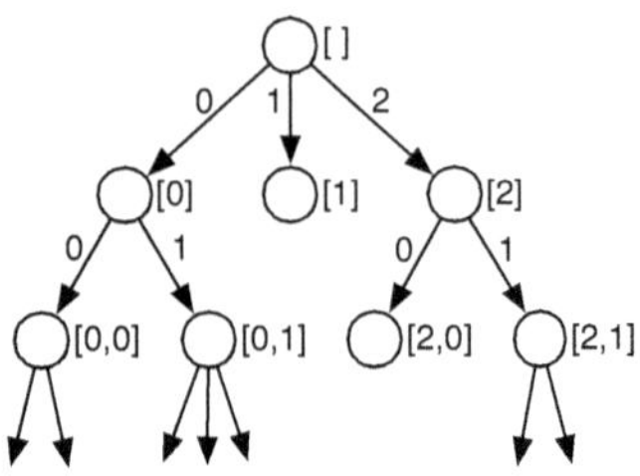

Figure 6: An example game tree for GödelTest. Edges are labelled by moves (Gödel numbers); nodes are labelled by game states (Gödel sequences).

3.2 Random Game Simulations

Normally a random game simulation in NMCS will choose moves according to a uniform distribution: each possible move has the same probability of being selected. However, this may not be the best strategy for some types of GödelTest generator: we hypothesise that the efficiency of GT-NMCS will be improved if the random simulation can incorporate domain knowledge that guides the simulation to data structures that are closer to having the desired properties. As an example, consider again the general tree generator of Figure 1: the **mult** construct is the equivalent of Boltzmann sampler **sequence** operator and so we argue that during game simulations, Gödel numbers for the **mult** choice point should be sampled from the same geometric distribution that would be used for the **sequence** operator of the general tree sampler of equation (1). Not all GödelTest generators will have an equivalent Boltzmann sampler that can be used for guidance, and so we explore the sensitivity of the GT-NMCS algorithm to the distributions used during game simulations as part of the empirical investigation of Section 4.

3.3 Choice Points with Infinite Support

Some GödelTest choice points have infinite support, i.e. there are an unlimited number of choices. The **mult** construct is an example of such a choice point: it returns an array consisting of zero or more objects and thus the associated Gödel number can be any non-negative integer. The NMCS algorithm can only assess a finite number of moves at each game state, and so we propose that at choice points with infinite support, only a small, finite subset of moves (Gödel numbers) are assessed, and this subset is chosen by random sampling from the same distribution that is used for the choice point during game simulation. The size of this finite subset becomes an additional parameter to the GT-NMCS algorithm, and we explore the effect of this parameter in the empirical investigation of Section 4.

3.4 Non-Terminating Games

Normally the GödelTest 'game' reaches a terminal state when the generating program halts, i.e. no further Gödel numbers are required in the sequence. It is possible, however, that an infeasibly long Gödel sequence may be required before reaching a terminal state or that the generating program may never halt. For example, a generator for general trees may attempt to construct trees of infinite size. For this reason, an upper limit is placed on the length of the Gödel sequence, the value of which will depend on the structures being generated. When this limit is reached no further moves are possible and thus the game state is a terminal state.

3.5 Score Function

The NMCS algorithm requires a score to be assigned to a terminal state in order to compare the state to other terminal states. In single-player games, the score is often expressed in terms of a reward of 1 if the terminal state is a winning state—which for GT-NMCS is a data structure that has exactly the properties we require—or 0 otherwise. However, we propose that the search algorithm will be more effective if the score is also able to quantify a non-winning terminal state in terms of how close the data structure's properties are to the target values.

For this reason, we use the following score function in the empirical work of this paper:

$$-\sum_{i=1}^{k} |p_i - t_i| \tag{2}$$

where the index i is over the k properties of interest, p_i is the value of the ith property for the generated data structure, and t_i is the desired target value of this property. We do not claim that this is necessarily the most effective score function—it does not, for example, weight nor normalize the contribution from each property—but we suggest it is a reasonable metric to choose for the purposes of the empirical investigation.

4. EMPIRICAL INVESTIGATION

In the following four experiments, we investigate the performance and efficacy of the GT-NMCS algorithm and demonstrate its flexibility.

4.1 Expt A: Efficiency and Parameter Settings

This experiment evaluates the efficiency of the GT-NMCS algorithm in comparison to Boltzmann samplers, and explores the effect of parameter settings on the efficiency. We use a data structure that can be generated by both GödelTest and a Boltzmann sampler: the general tree example used earlier in this paper. Since Boltzmann samplers can be tuned only for size, we specify a target property of size 100 nodes.

The Boltzmann sampler for general trees is given by equation (1) in Section 2.1. By following the analysis of Duchon et al., we determine that the **sequence** operator in this sampler should use a geometric distribution with a parameter of 0.502512 in order to sample trees with a mean size of 100.

The GödelTest generator for general trees is listed in Figure 1. As proposed in Section 3.2, the probability distribution used for the **mult** choice point is same as that for the equivalent operator in the Boltzmann sampler: i.e. a geometric distribution with a parameter of 0.502512. The GT-NMCS algorithm has two parameters when applied to this generator: the nesting level used by NMCS, and the size of the finite sample of moves used for **mult** choice point. (We additionally set an upper limit on the Gödel sequence of 250 numbers in order to avoid infinite trees; this is much larger than a sequence of 100 numbers that would be required for a tree of size 100. For the same reason, this limit is also applied to the Boltzmann sampler.)

Our measure of efficiency is the number of trees that must be constructed in order to output a tree with the target size of 100. Each tree output by the Boltzmann samplers requires only one tree to be constructed internally, but few of the outputted trees will have exactly the target size. The GT-NMCS algorithm constructs multiple trees internally for each tree that is output—one for each game simulation performed—but our intention is that a higher proportion of the outputted trees have exactly the target size. We therefore count the number of game simulations per tree outputted (or equivalently, the number of score function evaluations) made by the GT-NMCS algorithm in order to compare its efficiency to that of Boltzmann samplers.

100 trees were sampled using the GT-NMCS algorithm at different combinations of the nesting level and move sample size parameters[2]. The results are shown in Table 1[3]. The column 'Tree Constructions' is the mean number of game simulations per sample, and the column 'Success Proportion' is the proportion of sampled trees which have exactly the target size of 100. The 'Efficiency' column is calculated by dividing the mean number of tree constructions by the success proportion to give an estimate of the mean number of tree constructions required to output a tree with the target size; lower values of this estimate indicate a more efficient algorithm.

There are no additional parameters to set for the Boltzmann sampler, but since only a low proportion of the generated trees have the target size, 100,000 trees were sampled in order to provide a more accurate estimate of the sampler's efficiency. The results are shown in the final row of Table 1.

[2]We include a move sample size of 1 which might be thought to be remove all choice from the NMCS algorithm since it creates a game tree in which there is only one choice of move at every node. However, NMCS also has the alternative of choosing the move from the best move sequence found so far by the search, and so—at least for some nodes—there are effectively two move choices.

[3]The data from the experiments is available at: `http://www.cs.york.ac.uk/~smp/supplemental`.

Table 1: Expt A – Algorithm Efficiency

Nesting Level	Sample Size	Tree Constr'ns	Success Proport'n	Efficiency
1	1	32.91	23%	143.1
1	2	136.7	60%	227.8
1	4	380.3	94%	404.6
1	8	792.1	99%	800.1
1	16	1,600	100%	1,600
2	1	1,921	41%	4,684
2	2	13,620	71%	19,180
2	4	72,890	94%	77,540
3	1	60,770	41%	148,200
Boltzmann Sampler		1	0.032%	3,125

The number of tree constructions increases quickly with nesting level, but there is little increase in the success proportion for this particular generator. We speculate that a higher nesting level may be required for more complex generating programs, but for this general tree generator, a nesting level of 1 provides the best efficiency. Within a nesting level, the efficiency decreases as the move sample size increases, but we note that for all sample sizes between 1 and 16 at a nesting level of 1, the efficiency is better than that of the equivalent Boltzmann sampler.

The efficiency is assessed in terms of the number of tree constructions rather than the 'wall clock' run time in order to minimize threats to validity arising from the implementation of the respective algorithms and the noise of other processes running on the same server. With these caveats in mind, we are neverthless able to give an indication that the better efficiency of the NMCS algorithm is also reflected in the run time, although only at the lower move sample sizes. The Boltzmann sampler takes on average 0.144s to generate a tree of size 100; the NMCS algorithm takes 0.0673s, 0.0713s, 0.122s, 0.241s, and 0.482s for sample sizes of 1, 2, 4, 8, and 16 respectively at nesting level 1 on the same hardware.

4.2 Expt B: Sampling Uniformity

This experiment measures the extent to which the algorithm samples uniformly from the space of data structures with the desired properties, and how sensitive this is to the move sample size parameter. We again use general trees of size 100 as target data structure.

Many different characteristics could be used to assess how the sampled trees fill the space of all general trees of size 100. However, a particular concern is that because the GödelTest generator constructs the tree in a depth-first pre-order traversal that moves from left to right, the NMCS algorithm may introduce a bias that skews the trees to the left or to the right. Moreover, it is possible that all the trees generated by GT-NMCS are identical or very similar.

We therefore measure a characteristic of the generated trees that we term 'median coordinate', calculated using the following recursive procedure. Each node is passed an interval of the real numbers by its parent (the root node starts with the unit interval $[0, 1]$). The node is labelled with a coordinate that is the midpoint of this interval. The interval is then partitioned into subintervals of equal length, one for each of the node's children. The subintervals are then passed to the child nodes, with the interval closest to 0 being passed to the leftmost child and so on. After this procedure, nodes on the left of the tree will be labelled with coordinates closer to 0, and those on the right with coordinates closer to 1. An example is shown in Figure 7. The median coordinate of all the nodes is calculated; a median other than 0.5 indicates a skew to the left or right for an individual tree. For the example tree of Figure 7, the median coordinate is 0.375 and indeed the tree is skewed to the left.

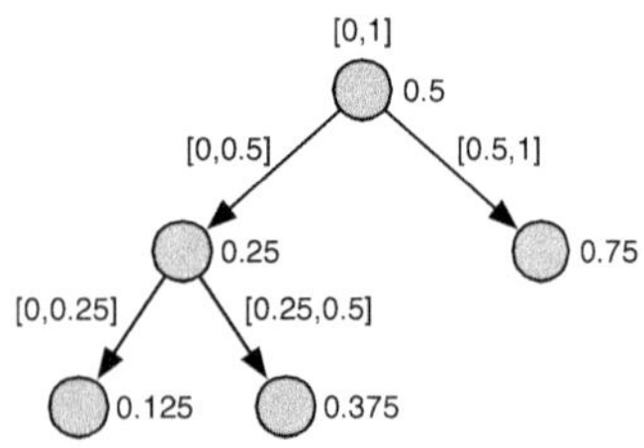

Figure 7: A tree in which the nodes are labelled by coordinate values. The intervals passed from parent to child nodes are shown on the edges.

It is not a problem if individual trees possess a skew; indeed, in a diverse sample of trees we would expect a range of skews. Instead our concern is whether the distribution of skews (measured by median coordinate) across the sample of trees generated by NMCS is consistent with uniform sampling from the space of trees of size 100. This would indicate that the the NMCS algorithm does not introduce a bias in terms of the skew *and* that it generates a diverse range of trees. We do not calculate the ideal distribution of median coordinates directly, but derive it empirically from the Boltzmann sampler which, by design, samples trees of the same size uniformly (see Section 2.1).

The empirical procedure was to generate trees of size 100 (filtering out trees of other sizes) from the Boltzmann sampler until a sample of 200 such trees was obtained. The median coordinate was calculated for each tree in the sample. The same procedure was applied to the GT-NMCS algorithm using a nesting level of 1, and move sample sizes of 1, 2, 4, 8, and 16.

The distributions of the median coordinates of the trees generated by each of the algorithms are summarised by the boxplots of Figure 8. It can be seen that the GT-NMCS algorithm using a sample size of 1 has a bias in that trees tend to be skewed to the right, but the trees generated at higher sample sizes have a distribution that is visually similar to that of the Boltzmann sampler. (The boxplot for the Boltzmann sampler suggests a small skew to the left, but we suspect this a chance occurrence as result of the finite sample size of 200 trees.)

We may quantify the similarity between the distributions using a two-sample Kolmogorov-Smirnov test; the null hypothesis is that the two samples are drawn from the same continuous probability distribution. Such a test between the Boltzmann sampler and GT-NMCS with move sample size 1 gives a p-value that is much less than 1%, indicating a statistically significant difference in the distributions. Between the Boltzmann sampler and other GT-NMCS sample sizes, the test gives p-values that are all greater than 25%. This result provides evidence that, for this generator, GT-NMCS using sample sizes of 2 and above samples trees close to uniformly from the space of trees with target size 100. We note, however, that this analysis considers only one characteristic of this space of trees.

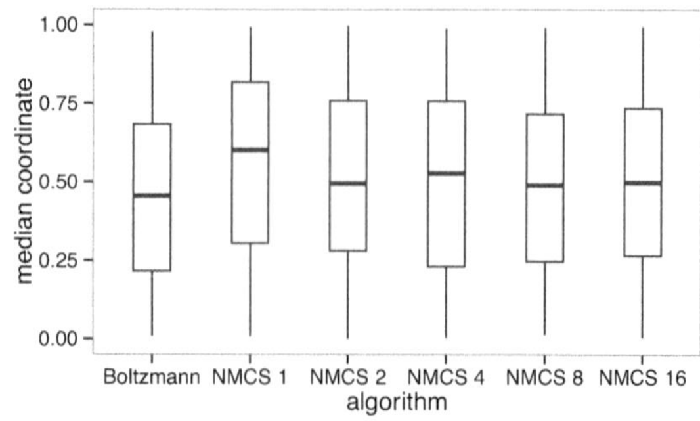

Figure 8: Boxplots summarizing the median coordinate distributions for each of the algorithms. (The number after the NMCS label indicates the move sample size.)

4.3 Expt C: Choice Point Distributions

This experiment explores the sensitivity of the algorithm to the probability distributions from which moves are sampled during game simulations.

The empirical procedure was to repeat experiments A and B for sample sizes between 1 and 16 at a nesting level of 1, while additionally varying the distribution used at the **mult** choice point in the general tree generator. The distributions investigated were geometric distributions with parameters 0.3, 0.4, 0.6, and 0.7; and a discrete uniform distribution over the integers 0 to 3.

The efficiency results are shown in Table 2 (∞ indicates that none of the 100 sampled trees had the target size of 100), and the uniformity results—as p values of Kolmogorov-Smirnov test—in Table 3. In both tables, the row for the geometric distribution with a parameter of 0.502512 (that derived using Boltzmann sampler analysis) summarises the results of experiments A and B and is included for comparison.

The results show that the efficiency of the algorithm is sensitive to the distribution used at the choice point: the efficiency is worse the further the distribution is from that derived using Boltzmann sampler analysis. However, the sensitivity of algorithm efficiency to the choice of distribution is ameliorated by larger sample sizes: at sizes 8 and 16 there is very little difference in efficiency between the Boltzmann sampler distribution and the geometric distributions with parameters 0.6 and 0.7.

The sampling uniformity is also sensitive to the distribution: relatively small deviations result in distributions of the median coordinate that are significantly different from that of the Boltzmann sampler (p-values less than 5% in table 3). There is again evidence that a higher sample size can ameliorate this sensitivity, but only for the geometric distribution with a parameter of 0.6.

4.4 Expt D: Flexibility

In this final experiment, we demonstrate the flexibility of the GT-NMCS algorithm by generating red-black trees, a data structure that cannot be expressed in the grammar of Boltzmann samplers, and by specifying more than one target property.

Red-black trees, described by Guibus and Sedgewick [8], are a form of binary tree often used in software to organise

Table 2: Expt C – Algorithm Efficiency

Distribution	Sample Size 1	2	4	8	16
geom(0.3)	∞	∞	∞	3,790	2,035
geom(0.4)	2,475	576.2	561.4	891.9	1,691
geom(0.502512)	143.1	227.8	404.6	800.1	1,600
geom(0.6)	136.1	202.6	401.1	800.1	1,600
geom(0.7)	482.0	301.7	413.8	800.6	1,600
uniform(0,3)	∞	∞	∞	1,867	1,885

Table 3: Expt C – Kolmogorov-Smirnov p-value

Distribution	Sample Size 1	2	4	8	16
geom(0.3)	N/A	N/A	N/A	0.0%	0.0%
geom(0.4)	0.0%	0.0%	0.0%	0.0%	0.0%
geom(0.502512)	0.0%	27.0%	39.3%	71.1%	32.7%
geom(0.6)	0.0%	0.0%	0.0%	6.8%	5.2%
geom(0.7)	0.0%	0.0%	0.0%	0.0%	0.0%
uniform(0,3)	N/A	N/A	N/A	0.0%	0.0%

data. They are guaranteed, by construction, to be nearly balanced—every leaf node has almost the same depth—and thereby permit efficient retrieval of the data. Each node in the tree is annotated either red or black, and the colour annotations must conform to four constraints. The first three are relatively straightforward to implement in either a grammar-based or non-deterministic program generator: the root node, the children of a red node, and leaf nodes must all be black. The fourth constraint is a property of the tree as a whole: the number of black nodes on the path from the root to a leaf node must be the same for all leaves. Enforcing this fourth constraint (without explicitly specifying the number of black nodes on the path) requires state information to be stored and retrieved during the generation process. This ability is not available in a Boltzmann sampler nor many grammar-based generators, but is possible using a non-deterministic generating program such as GödelTest.

We demonstrate this flexibility using the GödelTest generator for red-black trees shown in Figure 9 that enforces all four constraints. The argument `pcolour` is the colour of this subtree's parent node, and the argument `pbdepth` is the number of black nodes on the path from the root to this subtree's parent. The global variable `gbdepth` stores the number of black nodes that must be on the path from the root to each leaf node; this value is set by the first leaf node generated, and is -1 until then. The GödelTest **maybe** construct returns either its argument or nothing, and so the expression **maybe**('a')=='a' evaluates to either true or false. There is a choice of two Gödel numbers at a **maybe** choice point—0 and 1—and a Bernoulli distribution (a biased coin toss) is used during game simulation.

We demonstrate that GT-NMCS can generate data structures that simultaneously satisfy multiple property targets by specifying a tree size of 101 nodes *and* a tree height of 8. (Each non-leaf node in a binary tree has 2 children, and so the total number of nodes—including the root node—is odd. Since a red-black tree is nearly balanced, the possible heights are constrained to a limited range: a height of 8 is near the upper boundary of this range for tree of size 101.)

The choice point associated with the **maybe** construct has finite support and so we do not need to take a sample of moves; instead both the moves of 0 and 1 are always con-

```
global gbdepth=-1
function generator(pcolour:=red, pbdepth:=0)
  node := create tree node
  if pcolour!=red and maybe('a')=='a'
    colour node red
    bdepth := pbdepth
  else
    colour node black
    bdepth := pbdepth+1
  end
  if (gbdepth==-1 and (node is red or maybe('a')=='a'))
  or (bdepth < gbdepth)
    add subtree generator(node colour, bdepth) to node
    add subtree generator(node colour, bdepth) to node
  else if gbdepth==-1
    gbdepth := bdepth
  end
  return node
```

Figure 9: GödelTest generator for red-black trees.

sidered by the NMCS algorithm. During a random game simulation, a parameter of 0.5 is used for Bernoulli distribution associated with the **maybe** construct. We specify a nesting level of 2 in order to demonstrate the ability to generate a high proportion of the data structures with the desired properties; a nesting level of 1 has better efficiency for this particular generator but fewer of the generated structures would have exactly the desired properties.

Figure 10(a) shows the size and height of a sample of 1,000 trees generated by the GT-NMCS algorithm. (Since many trees have the same combination of size and height, a small amount of jitter is added, and the points are semi-transparent, in order to clarify the distribution.) As can be seen, all the generated trees have the desired size, and a large proportion have the desired height. Further analysis shows that 50.4% of the generated red-black trees have *both* the target size of 101 *and* the target height of 8.

We cannot generate red-black trees using a Boltzmann sampler as a comparison. Instead we use a 'random sampler': the generator of Figure 9 in which choices at the **maybe** constructs are made by random sampling from a Bernoulli distribution with a 'default' parameter of 0.5 rather than being guided by NMCS. Figure 10(b) shows the distribution of 1,000 red-black trees generated in this way. It can be seen the random sampler would generate far fewer trees of the target size and height than the GT-NMCS algorithm.

5. RELATED WORK

A number of test data generation techniques utilize non-deterministic programs of a type similar to that used by GödelTest. For example, UDITA [7] is a sophisticated Java-based framework that generates sets of test cases by exhaustively enumerating all points of non-determinism in the generating program up to a chosen bound. QuickCheck [4] is a framework for testing programs written in Haskell and a number of other languages. It facilitates the creation of custom generating programs that, in constrast to UDITA, sample test data stochastically rather than exhaustively. The generating programs of QuickCheck are therefore similar in objective to those used by GödelTest, but a key difference is that the probability distributions used by the QuickCheck generators must be optimized manually to generate test data with desirable properties, while GödelTest can perform this optimization automatically using metaheuristic search.

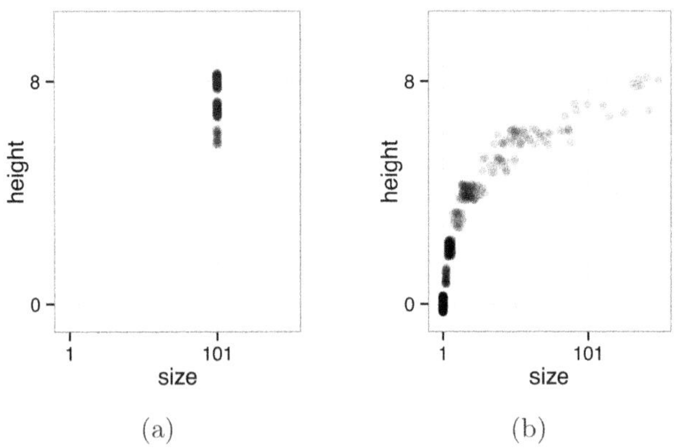

Figure 10: The size and height of 1,000 red-black trees generated by (a) the GT-NMCS algorithm; (b) a random sampler.

Similarly, a wide range of test data generation techniques utilize stochastic grammars. The algorithms described by Beyene and Andrews [1], and by Poulding et al. [9], are particularly notable in that they optimize the grammar using metaheuristic search in order to achieve coverage of the software-under-test. These grammar-based generators are inherently less flexible than non-deterministic generating programs such as GödelTest, but are potentially easier to optimize in order to satisfy target properties.

The GödelTest abstraction of choices as an integer sequence has parallels in Grammatical Evolution (GE) [10]. GE interprets an integer sequence as production rule choices in a grammar and applies evolutionary algorithms to optimize the sequence. However, GE constructs and interprets the sequences in a different way to the GT-NMCS algorithm used in this paper. The GE sequence is normally fixed-length (the sequence is re-used should more integers be required), and the integer values are not specific to the use to which they are put (the modulus is taken base the number of choices). GE optimizes the sequence as a whole, while GT-NMCS constructs an optimal sequence integer-by-integer.

NMCS and other MCTS variants have achieved great success in playing games and are often competitive with human experts [2]. We suspect that they will prove to be effective search methods for software engineering problems that can be expressed as a game tree, but as far as we are aware, this paper is the first use of such algorithms in search-based software engineering.

6. CONCLUSIONS

In this paper we proposed the application of Nested Monte-Carlo Search to our previously described GödelTest framework. We have demonstrated that for general trees, the GT-NMCS algorithm has an efficiency that is better than the equivalent Boltzmann sampler, and—with appropriate parameter settings—samples structures uniformly and so maintains diversity in the test data. However, both performance and uniform sampling are sensitive to the default distributions used during game simulations. We also demonstrated the flexibility of the framework with regards of both the type of data structure to which it can be applied and the properties of those structures that can be targeted.

As future work, we will explore the performance of the GT-NMCS algorithm on more complex data structures that require generating programs with many choice points, and investigate how the sensitivity of the algorithm to the choice of distributions during game simulation can be reduced. In addition, we would like to identify the characteristics of generating programs that determine which GT variant—GT-NMCS or GT using Differential Evolution—is the most effective for that generator.

7. ACKNOWLEDGMENTS

This work was funded by EPSRC grant EP/J017515/1, DAASE: Dynamic Adaptive Automated Software Engineering; and by The Knowledge Foundation (KKS) through the project 20130085, Testing of Critical System Characteristics (TOCSYC). The authors would like to thank Ed Powley for his feedback on a draft on this paper.

8. REFERENCES

[1] M. Beyene and J. Andrews. Generating string test data for code coverage. In *Proc. IEEE Int'l Conf. Software Testing, Verification and Validation (ICST)*, pages 270–279, 2012.

[2] C. Browne, E. Powley, D. Whitehouse, S. Lucas, P. Cowling, P. Rohlfshagen, S. Tavener, D. Perez, S. Samothrakis, and S. Colton. A survey of Monte Carlo tree search methods. *IEEE Trans. Computational Intelligence and AI in Games*, 4(1):1–43, 2012.

[3] T. Cazenave. Nested Monte-Carlo search. In *Proc. 21st Int'l Joint Conf. Artificial Intelligence (IJCAI)*, pages 456–461, 2009.

[4] K. Claessen and J. Hughes. Quickcheck: A lightweight tool for random testing of haskell programs. In *Proc. ACM SIGPLAN Int'l Conf. Functional Programming (ICFP)*, pages 268–279, 2000.

[5] P. Duchon, P. Flajolet, G. Louchard, and G. Schaeffer. Boltzmann samplers for the random generation of combinatorial structures. *Combinatorics, Probability and Computing*, 13(4-5):577–625, 2004.

[6] R. Feldt and S. Poulding. Finding test data with specific properties via metaheuristic search. In *Proc. IEEE Int'l Symp. Software Reliability Engineering (ISSRE)*, pages 350–359, 2013.

[7] M. Gligoric, T. Gvero, V. Jagannath, S. Khurshid, V. Kuncak, and D. Marinov. Test generation through programming in UDITA. In *Proc. ACM/IEEE Int'l Conf. Software Engineering (ICSE)*, volume 1, pages 225–234. ACM, 2010.

[8] L. J. Guibas and R. Sedgewick. A dichromatic framework for balanced trees. In *Proc. Annual Symp. Foundations of Computer Science*, pages 8–21, 1978.

[9] S. Poulding, R. Alexander, J. A. Clark, and M. J. Hadley. The optimisation of stochastic grammars to enable cost-effective probabilistic structural testing. In *Proc. Genetic and Evolutionary Computation Conf. (GECCO)*, pages 1477–1484, 2013.

[10] C. Ryan, J. J. Collins, and M. O'Neill. Grammatical evolution : Evolving programs for an arbitrary language. In *Proc. European Workshop on Genetic Programming (EuroGP)*, volume 1391 of *Lecture Notes in Computer Science*, pages 83–96, 1998.

On the Performance of Multiple Objective Evolutionary Algorithms for Software Architecture Discovery

Aurora Ramírez, José Raúl Romero and Sebastián Ventura

Dept. of Computer Science and Numerical Analysis, University of Córdoba
Rabanales Campus, 14071 Córdoba, Spain

{aramirez, jrromero, sventura}@uco.es

ABSTRACT

During the design of complex systems, software architects have to deal with a tangle of abstract artefacts, measures and ideas to discover the most fitting underlying architecture. A common way to structure these systems is in terms of their interacting software components, whose composition and connections need to be properly adjusted. Its abstract and highly combinatorial nature increases the complexity of the problem. In this scenario, Search-based Software Engineering (SBSE) may serve to support this decision making process from initial analysis models, since the discovery of component-based architectures can be formulated as a challenging multiple optimisation problem, where different metrics and configurations can be applied depending on the design requirements and its specific domain. Many-objective optimisation evolutionary algorithms can provide an interesting alternative to classical multi-objective approaches. This paper presents a comparative study of five different algorithms, including an empirical analysis of their behaviour in terms of quality and variety of the returned solutions. Results are also discussed considering those aspects of concern to the expert in the decision making process, like the number and type of architectures found. The analysis of many-objectives algorithms constitutes an important challenge, since some of them have never been explored before in SBSE.

Categories and Subject Descriptors

D.2.11 [**Software Engineering**]: Software Architectures; I.2.8 [**Artificial Intelligence**]: Problem Solving, Control Methods, and Search -*Heuristic methods*

Keywords

Search-based Software Engineering, component-based software architecture, multi-objective evolutionary algorithms, many-objective evolutionary algorithms

GECCO'14, July 12–16, Vancouver, BC, Canada.

ACM 978-1-4503-2662-9/14/07 ...$15.00.
http://dx.doi.org/10.1145/2576768.2598310.

1. INTRODUCTION

Software architecture modelling plays an important role in the early software conception. Frequently, software engineers have to tackle complex systems that need to satisfy multiple functional and non-functional requirements [1]. The discovery of software architectures constitutes an example of an abstract and complex problem in Software Engineering (SE). In this process, software architects have to identify highly abstract artefacts, like components and interfaces, from a previous analysis model. The resulting artefact comprises the specification of the underlying system structure, which will serve all along the software development to add later functionality, to obtain more fitting designs or to keep a proper maintenance [2].

At this stage of the project, the design abstraction hampers the decision making process, having an impact in the lack of specific metrics for measuring the quality of the resulting software designs. Metrics for architectural concepts like modularity or reusability are actually complex to be translated into quantifiable measures. Therefore, efforts have to be directed towards the conception of specific metrics [3, 4] like those already existing and commonly accepted for more concrete artefacts [5].

Software architects are often requested to choose between different metrics in order to satisfy specific requirements for the architecture under analysis [6]. Determining the most suitable subset of metrics is a non-trivial task usually accomplished by experts only guided by their own experience.

The appearance of SBSE [7], i.e. the application of metaheuristics approaches to solve tasks in Software Engineering, brings the opportunity to perform human-centered activities in the field. Ideally, it could serve to provide semiautomatic procedures that effectively create software architectures from requirements [8] or perform refactoring [9].

Since problems laid out SE usually require multiple aspects to be simultaneously considered, multi-objective evolutionary algorithms (MOEAs) have been frequently applied in SBSE [10]. However, these proposals deal with two or three predetermined objectives, where the selection of a specific MOEA is not usually set down [11]. Only a few proposals [12, 13] have considered the adequacy of a new interesting branch of algorithms, the so-called many-objectives evolutionary algorithms. Although the boundary between MOEA and many-objective approaches remains unclear in the literature, the latter are specifically designed to work on higher dimensional search spaces, where they outperforms MOEAs [14]. In this paper, we will refer indistinctly to both approaches as *multiple objective evolutionary algorithms*.

This paper analyses and discusses how to face the architectural analysis stage as a a multi-objective optimisation problem. More specifically, we address the problem of discovering component-based software architectures, focusing on the selection and tuning of several quality metrics, and its optimisation using five different implementations properly adapted to the problem domain. In this way, due to the diverse dimensions of the search space under consideration, the experimental framework proposed will allow the discussion of the suitability of many-objectives approaches when the number of objectives is increased. Some well-known MOEAs, such as SPEA2 and NSGA-II, as well as other recent proposals in many-objective evolutionary algorithms, like ϵ-MOEA, GrEA and MOEA/D, have been selected to carry out a complete study of their performance. Notice that $\epsilon-$MOEA and GrEA have been never used before in SBSE. Dealing with such a combinatorial and constrained problem is a challeging scenario, considering that these algorithms are traditionally applied to real optimisation domains.

The rest of the paper is organised as follows. Section 2 introduces the formulation of architecture discovery as a search problem, including the set of metrics to be optimised. Then, Section 3 briefly describes the main characteristics of the selected evolutionary algorithms. The experimental study, presented in Section 4, shows the obtained results from an evolutionary perspective when considering different number of objectives and setups. Results are discussed from the perspective of the decision-making process in Section 5. Finally, Section 6 outlines some conclusions and future work.

2. PROBLEM DESCRIPTION

In [15], we described the evolutionary model for the discovery of component-based software architectures. Here, due to space limitations, only the most relevant characteristics of the model are summarized.

The problem is formulated as the search of the optimal distribution of available analysis elements, i.e. classes and their relationships, to conform those highly abstract artefacts that specify the software architecture, namely components, interfaces and connectors. More specifically, a *component* is obtained from a cohesive group of classes, where the component behaviour is defined by the union of their individual behaviours. A candidate *interface* is identified from the relationships specified between classes belonging to different components. Analysing the direction of each relationship, a provided or required interface will be modelled. Finally, each *connector* is described by a pair of provided and required interfaces.

The highly combinatorial nature of the problem is reflected in two major factors: diverse architectures could be discovered for one given analysis model, and no prefixed structure is anticipated, i.e. the number of architectural artefacts is unknown a priori.

2.1 Genotype and phenotype

The genotype/phenotype mapping is illustrated in Figure 1. The representation defined has to be both comprehensible to the expert and computationally efficient. Each individual represents a complete software architecture, i.e. the phenotype. A tree structure is considered to internally handle the architecture, i.e. the genotype, allowing a hierarchical breakdown of software artefacts.

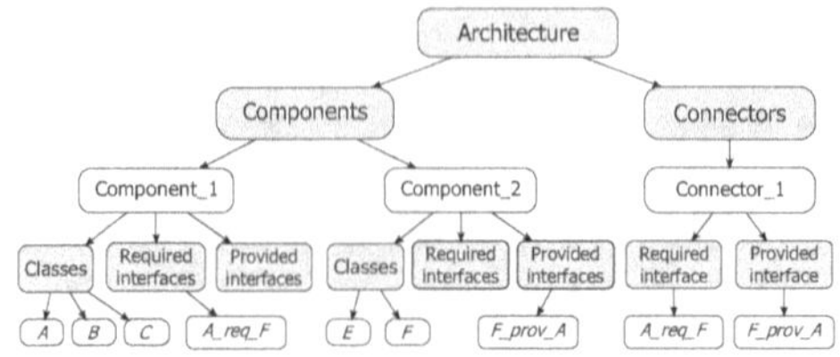

(a) Genotype

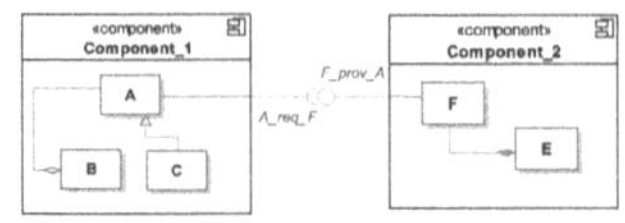

(b) Phenotype

Figure 1: Genotype/phenotype mapping

The initialisation process consists in the random distribution of classes among a number of components, also randomly selected between a minimum and a maximum value. Then, interfaces and connectors are identified from the architecture generated looking at the new relationships established between classes belonging to different components.

Every solution is subject to the following constraints: *(a)* empty components are not allowed; *(b)* each class can be added to one only component; *(c)* isolated components, i.e. those that do not specify any interface, are not permitted; and *(d)* the existence of mutually dependant components, i.e. two components where one component requires from and provides to the other, should be penalised. Constraints *(a)* and *(b)* can be arranged when the population is created and the genetic operator is applied. On the contrary, constraints *(c)* and *(d)* are gone along with the creation of the population in order to reduce the initialisation time, and promote a larger diversity of solutions. The underlying idea is that these invalid individuals will be removed from the population by means of the genetic operator and the selective pressure as the evolutionary process advances.

2.2 Genetic operator

A mutation operator is used to explore design alternatives. It can apply diverse architectural transformations, providing a variety of solutions. The selection of a specific transformation type is performed by a weighted roulette which determines those mutation procedures applicable to each selected parent. The five procedures are the following: add a component, remove a component, merge two components, split a component and move a class.

2.3 Evaluation objectives

Six different metrics related to architectural concepts have been selected and adapted for the proposed problem, providing a wide catalogue of combinations. Notice that not all of them have to be simultaneously used, but the modeller could select the most fitting metrics for the specific scenario.

Firstly, the *Intra-modular Coupling Density (ICD)* [16] establishes a trade-off between cohesion and coupling, as shown in Equation 1, and should be maximised. For each component i, the ratio between the number of internal and external relations is calculated. CI_i^{in} represents the number of interactions between classes inside the component i, whereas CI_i^{out} is the number of external relations, i.e. the number of candidate interfaces. Given that ICD_i varies in [0,1], the overall ICD can reach a maximum value of n, equal to the number of components.

$$ICD_i = \frac{CI_i^{in}}{CI_i^{in} + CI_i^{out}} \qquad ICD = \sum_{i=1}^{n} ICD_i \qquad (1)$$

A measure specifically proposed for this problem is the *External Relations Penalty (ERP)* (see Equation 2). It computes the total number of existing relationships between classes belonging to each possible pair of components, i and j. These relations are extracted from the initial analysis model in terms of generalizations (ge), associations (as), aggregations (ag) and compositions (co) between classes. Only those relationships that are not subsequently defined as interfaces are relevant to the metric. Further, a weighted sum (w_x) is considered to emphasise that some of these relationships are stronger than others. For example, dividing a generalization between a class and its subclasses into different components is more harmful to the resulting architecture than just splitting an association. The optimum value for this metric is 0, meaning that all the interactions among components occur through well-formed interfaces.

$$\begin{aligned} ERP &= \sum_{i=1}^{n}\sum_{j=1}^{n} [w_{as} \cdot n_{as_{ij}} + w_{ag} \cdot n_{ag_{ij}} + \\ &+ \; w_{co} \cdot n_{co_{ij}} + w_{ge} \cdot n_{ge_{ij}}] \end{aligned} \qquad (2)$$

The *Groups/Components Ratio (GCR)* measure is proposed for the minimisation of the number of connected groups of classes (*cgroups*) inside each component. Software architects usually search for a set of components where each is comprised by a single group of strongly related classes, determining the existence of a well-defined functionality per component. Therefore, the optimum value of the expression given in Equation 3 is 1, meaning that there is the same number of groups than components.

$$GCR = \frac{\#cgroups}{\#components} \qquad (3)$$

The following measure, *Critical Size (CS)* [3], counts the number of components that exceed a given size threshold, determined by the maximum percentage of classes contained inside of this component in relation to the total number of classes in the initial analysis model. Thus, if maintenance is a requirement requested, then smaller components would be advisable. This measure, formulated in Equation 4, varies its value in the range [0,1], n being the number of components.

$$\begin{aligned} CC_i &= \begin{cases} 1 & \text{if size}(i) > \text{threshold} \\ 0 & \text{otherwise} \end{cases} \\ CS &= \sum_{i=1}^{n} CC_i \end{aligned} \qquad (4)$$

The *Instability (Ins)* [4] measure looks for the reduction of dependencies among components. The overall instability of the system is calculated as the average of the instability of each component (Ins_i) (see Equation 5), and varies in [0,1]. AC_i is the afferent coupling of component i, i.e. the number of components that use its services, whilst EC_i is the efferent coupling, i.e. the number of external components that provide their services to component i.

$$Ins_i = \frac{EC_i}{EC_i + AC_i} \qquad Ins = \frac{1}{n}\sum_{i=1}^{n} Ins_i \qquad (5)$$

The *Encapsulation (Enc)* is inspired by the *Data Access Metric* proposed in [5]. The encapsulation of each component i, Enc_i, is determined by the ratio of its hidden classes, i.e. those that do not participate in external interactions with classes outside of the component. The total encapsulation, varies in [0,1] and should be maximised. It is calculated as the mean value of the individual encapsulation of each component.

$$Enc_i = \frac{\#inner_{classes}}{\#total_{classes}} \qquad Enc = \frac{1}{n}\sum_{i=1}^{n} Enc_i \qquad (6)$$

3. MULTIPLE OPTIMISATION WITH EVOLUTIONARY ALGORITHMS

A diversity of multi-objective and many-objective evolutionary algorithms have been selected to carry out the comparative study: SPEA2, NSGA-II, $\epsilon-$MOEA, MOEAD/D and GrEA. Their main features are detailed next.

SPEA2 (Strength Pareto Evolutionary Algorithm 2) [17] defines a fitness function for each solution based on a strength value and a density estimator technique. Then, the selection and reproduction is performed. SPEA2 also deals with an external fix-sized archive of non-dominated solutions. Individuals from both populations are selected to create the next population, performing a truncation method or filling it with dominated solutions to maintain the population size.

NSGA-II (Non-dominated Sorting Genetic Algorithm II) [18] encompasses a sorting procedure to rank the solutions in fronts, and a specific selection operator based on the crowding distance and dominance information. After the execution of the genetic operators, the replacement strategy progressively stores the solutions by fronts.

ϵ-MOEA [19] is a steady-state evolutionary algorithm which adapts the concept of Pareto dominance. The search space is divided into hypercubes and the so-called ϵ-dominance relation is defined over the resulting partitioned landscape. Then, the solution a ϵ-dominates the solution b if a belongs to better or equal hypercubes for all the objectives and, at least, to a better hypercube for one objective than b. Therefore, a more relaxed dominance relation is established, which is specially useful when the number of non-dominated solutions rapidly grows, like in high-dimensional spaces. Every hypercube has a fixed length in each dimension, named ϵ_i, and the main idea is that each has to be filled with a unique solution to promote diversity.

MOEA/D [20] is based on a decomposition strategy, so this algorithm simultaneously performs an optimisation of diverse scalar subproblems, according to their neighborhood information. MOEA/D assigns a weight vector to every individual in the population, each one being focused on the resolution of the subproblem represented by its weight vector. The *Tchebycheff* approach is used to evaluate individuals over their specific problems, computing their distance to a reference point.

Finally, GrEA (Grid-based Evolutionary Algorithm) [21] is a recent proposal, which considers the partition of the search space into hypercubes or grids. GrEA establishes the number of divisions as a parameter, instead of fixing their length as ϵ-MOEA does. Then, it constructs them adaptively considering the current objective values in the population. Inspired by NSGA-II, this algorithm also ranks the population by fronts. The authors define some grid-based metrics for measuring the crowding distance and the spread of solutions, as well as a grid-dominance relation to choose among solutions belonging to the same front. Finally, an important difference from other previous algorithms is that GrEA does not consider an archive of non-dominated solutions, but they are extracted from the final population.

4. EXPERIMENTAL FRAMEWORK

All the algorithms and the experimental framework have been written in Java. Additionally, some publicly available Java libraries have been used. SDMetrics Open Core[1] provides support for XMI parsing. Thus, the proposed approach is able to directly collect information from the analysis models created with the MagicDraw tool[2] as XMI, an specific XML-based format for model interchangeability. The preprocessing methods and the internal data structures have been implemented using the Datapro4j library[3]. The evolutionary algorithms have been coded using the JCLEC framework [22]. Experiments were run on a HPC cluster of 8 compute nodes with Rocks cluster 6.1 x64 operating system. Each node comprises two Intel Xeon E5645 CPUs with 6 cores at 2.4 GHz and 24 GB DDR memory.

Every algorithm has been executed 30 times with different random seeds. Due to space limitations, the executions have been carried out over all possible combinations of 2, 4 and 6 objectives to check the scalability of the algorithms aforementioned. Two quality indicators, hypervolume (HV) and spacing (S) have been considered to measure the evolutionary performance [23]. HV is determined by the hyper-area covered by the front in the search space, whereas S measures the spread of front. Since HV requires a search space in the range [0,1], the normalisation approach proposed in [24] has been applied. Results have been statistically validated carrying out the Friedman test, where the null hypothesis, H_0, establishes that all the algorithms perform equally well. Next, the Holm's post-hoc test is applied if H_0 is rejected with significant differences at a significance level of (1-α).

4.1 Parameter set-up

The algorithms have been configured according to the guidelines given by their respective authors and after some preliminary experimentation (see Table 1). Different values have been considered for the population size and the maximum number of evaluations, reflecting a variety of configurations for dealing with the 2-objective, 4-objective and 6-objective problems. As for the population size, the set-up proposed takes into account that MOEA/D requires a uniformly distributed set of weighted vectors for a given number of objectives, which are controlled by the H parameter as prescribed by the authors.

[1]http://www.sdmetrics.com/OpenCore.html
[2]http://www.nomagic.com/
[3]http://www.uco.es/grupos/kdis/datapro4j

Table 1: Parameter set-up

Common parameters	
Population Size	100, 120, 126
Max. Evaluations	10,000, 15,000, 20,000
Min-Max. Components	2-8
Mutator weights	
	$w_{add}=0.2$,$w_{remove}=0.3$,$w_{merge}=0.2$
	$w_{split}=0.1$,$w_{move}=0.2$
ERP metric weights	
	$w_{as}=1$,$w_{ag}=3$,$w_{co}=1$,$w_{ge}=5$
CS threshold	0.3
SPEA2 parameters	
Parents selector	Binary tournament
External population size	50
k-th neighboor	12
ϵ-MOEA parameters	
ϵ values	
	$\epsilon_{ICD}=0.25$, $\epsilon_{ERP}=5$, $\epsilon_{GCR}=0.1$
	$\epsilon_{CS}=1$, $\epsilon_{Ins}=0.05$, $\epsilon_{Enc}=0.05$
MOEA/D parameters	
Neighboorhood size (τ)	8
Max. Replacements (Nr)	2
H	99,7,4
GrEA parameters	
Number of divisions (div)	12

Six system designs have been used for the experimentation. As shown in Table 2, they present different complexity in terms of the number of classes ($\#Class$) and candidate interfaces ($\#Int$), i.e. directed relationships. The total number of relationships is divided into associations (As), dependences (De), aggregations (Ag), compositions (Co) and generalizations (Ge). Finally, notice that *Aqualush*[4] is a benchmark application used for educational purposes, whereas the rest of systems correspond to real software specifications that can be accessed from the Java Open Source Code Project [5] and the Datapro4j websites.

Table 2: Problem instances and their characteristics

Problem	*#Class*	*#Relationships*					*#Int*
		As	De	Ag	Co	Ge	
Aqualush	58	69	6	0	0	20	74
Datapro4j	59	3	4	3	2	50	12
Java2HTML	53	20	66	15	0	15	170
JSapar	46	7	33	21	9	19	80
Marvin	32	5	11	22	5	8	28
NekoHTML	47	6	17	15	18	17	46

4.2 Analysis of 2-objective problems

Table 3 shows the average rankings after applying the Friedman test over each combination of 2 objectives for every problem instance. The best rankings are shown in bold typeface; shaded cells represent significant differences. In these cases, the Holm test was also performed, writing the

[4]http://www.ifi.uzh.ch/rerg/research/aqualush.html
[5]http://java-source.net/

Table 3: Average rankings for 2-objective problems obtained from the Friedman Test ($\alpha = 0.05$)

Objectives	**SPEA2**		**NSGA-II**		**ϵ-MOEA**		**MOEA/D**		**GrEA**	
	HV	S	HV	S	HV	S	HV	S	HV	S
ICD-ERP	3.67	2.67	2.58	3.42	**1.50**	**1.33**	*4.67*	*4.67*	2.58	2.92
ICD-GCR	*4.17*	**2.33**	2.75	2.66	2.17	3.67	*4.17*	3.83	**1.75**	2.50
ICD-Ins	*4.17*	**1.50**	*3.25*	2.83	**1.17**	*4.83*	*4.17*	2.33	2.25	3.50
ICD-CS	*4.50*	2.50	*3.25*	3.25	**1.17**	4.08	*3.83*	**2.08**	2.25	3.08
ICD-Enc	*4.17*	**1.33**	2.58	*4.08*	2.17	2.17	*4.17*	2.50	**1.92**	*4.92*
ERP-GCR	**2.83**	**3.00**	3.25	**3.00**	**2.83**	**3.00**	**2.83**	**3.00**	3.25	**3.00**
ERP-Ins	**2.83**	**3.00**	3.25	**3.00**	**2.83**	**3.00**	**2.83**	**3.00**	3.25	**3.00**
ERP-CS	**2.83**	**3.00**	3.25	**3.00**	**2.83**	**3.00**	**2.83**	**3.00**	3.25	**3.00**
ERP-Enc	1.92	**2.00**	**1.67**	2.75	3.50	2.67	3.67	3.50	*4.25*	4.08
GCR-Ins	**2.83**	**3.00**	3.25	**3.00**	**2.83**	**3.00**	**2.83**	**3.00**	3.25	**3.00**
GCR-CS	**2.83**	**3.00**	3.25	**3.00**	2.83	**3.00**	**2.83**	**3.00**	3.25	**3.00**
GCR-Enc	2.75	**1.67**	**1.67**	3.75	3.33	2.00	*4.17*	3.33	3.08	*4.25*
Ins-CS	**2.83**	**3.00**	3.25	**3.00**	**2.83**	**3.00**	**2.83**	**3.00**	3.25	**3.00**
Ins-Enc	3.08	**1.00**	**1.92**	*3.75*	2.92	*3.50*	3.92	2.17	3.17	*4.58*
CS-Enc	2.83	**1.33**	**1.75**	3.17	3.50	*4.08*	*4.33*	2.83	2.58	*3.58*

ranking values in italic typeface for those algorithms lying beyond the critical threshold.

Combining objectives in pairs leads to some differences in the performance of the algorithms. MOEA/D is the only algorithm that does not obtain any significant differences. It can be noted that SPEA2 seems to take advantage of its capability to search for a diverse set of solutions, so it usually outperforms the rest of algorithms in terms of spacing. Focusing on the hypervolume, NSGA-II, ϵ-MOEA, and GrEA get the best results, showing that they are able to obtain higher quality solutions than SPEA2 and MOEA/D in most problems. In contrast, notice that obtaining good results in both hypervolume and spacing is a difficult task in this context, since some algorithms tend to promote convergence, whereas others are focused on the diversification of the Pareto set.

After scrutinising the different metric combinations, some facts are worth discussing. Those problems where *ERP* or *GCR* are used in combination with *CS*, *Ins* or *Enc* exhibit a different behaviour. Here, all the algorithms perform similarly, since all of them obtain equal spacing values and close hypervolume values. It can be explained by the fact that all the algorithms found either a unique and optimal solution or the same set of architectural solutions. In the former, the formulated problem is easily resolved. In the latter, all of them have the same troubles to deal with local optima. Nevertheless, this scenario hampers the overall decision making process, which actually pursues the generation of a variety of solutions satisfying both objectives in different ways as well as diverse kinds of architectures to be arranged for selection.

In this sense, these results show different levels of complexity when specific metrics are combined together. For example, the use of metrics like *ICD* or *Enc* seems to cancel out the optimisation of others. Thus, the dominance among solutions will be harder to achieve and the resulting Pareto front will be likely comprised of more solutions.

4.3 Analysis of 4-objective problems

Table 4 shows the results obtained in the analysis of 4-objective problems. With the increase of objectives, more differences between the algorithms can be appreciated, and some of the many-objective evolutionary algorithms become the most effective approaches. Firstly, ϵ-MOEA achieves the best ranking values for both indicators in a great number of combinations. In contrast, SPEA2 and MOEA/D continue to be the poorest algorithms in terms of hypervolume, now that they are mostly outperformed by ϵ-MOEA.

The behaviour of SPEA2 in relation to the hypervolume indicator could be expected, since its performance decreases in high-dimensional spaces. Nevertheless, good spacing values stress its ability to promote the spreading of the Pareto set. Similarly, the decomposition approach of MOEA/D is mainly focused on the search of a diversity of solutions. Hence, it explores an excessive number of directions in the search space without especially favouring any of them in the search of an appropriate convergence.

As for NSGA-II and GrEA, an interesting observation can be made. GrEA, mainly founded on NSGA-II, is specifically well suited to many-objective problems and a better performance might be expected. However, GrEA is here clearly outperformed by NSGA-II in terms of *HV* and, for some combinations of metrics, ϵ-MOEA is even statistically better. Hence, the elitism provided by the sorting method barely benefits convergence in GrEA. Regarding the spacing indicator, both algorithms obtain very similar results, characterized by poor rankings values pointing out the difficulty in obtaining a wide-spread Pareto set.

4.4 Analysis of the 6-objective problem

Finally, Table 5 presents the results obtained when all the metrics are simultaneously considered as objectives. Similarly to the 4-objective problem formulation, ϵ-MOEA is now the best algorithm in terms of hypervolume. Further, it shows significant differences with the remaining algorithms, except for NSGA-II, which has demonstrated a good scalability. On the contrary, SPEA2 is able to generate a more diverse set of solutions, outperforming the rest of algorithms in terms of scalability for the spacing indicator. Nevertheless, SPEA2 does not show significant differences with ϵ-MOEA, which is able to obtain good spacing values, and consequently to achieve a good trade-off between high-quality solutions and its spread into the Pareto front.

Table 4: Average rankings for 4-objective problems obtained from the Friedman Test ($\alpha = 0.05$)

Objectives	SPEA2		NSGA-II		ϵ-MOEA		MOEA/D		GrEA	
	HV	S	HV	S	HV	S	HV	S	HV	S
ICD-ERP-GCR-Ins	3.17	*2.33*	1.92	4.75	**1.50**	**1.83**	*4.00*	3.67	*4.42*	2.42
ICD-ERP-GCR-CS	*4.00*	*3.00*	2.25	*3.42*	**1.50**	**1.00**	*4.33*	*4.50*	2.92	*3.08*
ICD-ERP-GCR-Enc	3.17	1.83	1.92	*4.08*	**1.50**	**1.17**	*4.00*	*3.67*	*4.42*	*4.25*
ICD-ERP-Ins-CS	*4.33*	2.00	2.58	*4.42*	2.17	**1.00**	4.00	*3.67*	**1.92**	*3.92*
ICD-ERP-Ins-Enc	*4.00*	1.67	2.08	*4.08*	**1.33**	**1.33**	*3.83*	3.33	*3.75*	*4.58*
ICD-ERP-CS-Enc	*4.17*	1.83	2.08	*4.08*	**1.50**	**1.17**	*4.00*	3.00	3.25	*4.92*
ICD-GCR-Ins-CS	*4.17*	2.33	3.08	*4.08*	**1.50**	**1.00**	*4.17*	3.50	2.08	*4.08*
ICD-GCR-Ins-Enc	*4.17*	**1.33**	2.25	*3.75*	**1.17**	1.67	*4.00*	*3.67*	*3.41*	*4.58*
ICD-GCR-CS-Enc	*4.33*	2.00	2.25	*4.08*	**1.67**	**1.33**	*4.00*	3.00	2.75	*4.58*
ICD-Ins-CS-Enc	*4.17*	2.17	2.42	*4.25*	**1.67**	**1.17**	*4.17*	2.67	2.58	*4.75*
ERP-GCR-Ins-CS	**2.83**	**3.00**	3.25	**3.00**	**2.83**	3.00	**2.83**	**3.00**	3.25	**3.00**
ERP-GCR-Ins-Enc	2.33	2.00	**1.67**	*4.58*	3.17	**1.83**	3.08	3.83	*4.75*	2.75
ERP-GCR-CS-Enc	2.00	2.50	**1.75**	*4.58*	3.67	**1.17**	3.00	*3.33*	*4.58*	*3.42*
ERP-Ins-CS-Enc	2.33	2.17	**1.67**	*4.58*	3.33	**1.17**	2.92	*3.50*	*4.75*	*3.58*
GCR-Ins-CS-Enc	3.00	2.67	**1.67**	*3.75*	2.67	**1.00**	2.92	*3.17*	*4.75*	*4.42*

Table 5: Average rankings for the 6-objective problem obtained from the Friedman Test ($\alpha = 0.05$)

Objectives	SPEA2		NSGA-II		ϵ-MOEA		MOEA/D		GrEA	
	HV	S	HV	S	HV	S	HV	S	HV	S
ICD-ERP-GCR-Ins-CS-Enc	*3.83*	**1.17**	2.42	*3.58*	**1.33**	1.83	*3.50*	*4.33*	*3.92*	*4.08*

5. DISCUSSION OF RESULTS

Due to the particular nature of the problem, a further discussion of the behaviour regarding each algorithm is still required, not only from the evolutionary perspective, but also in order to analise how they could fit to the software architect's expectations. Therefore, there are other additional remarks from the experimental results that should be considered as well, since they provide relevant information for both the architectural specification and the decision support process.

Table 6 summarizes the strengths and weaknesses of each implementation. SPEA2 shows a good performance in terms of the spread of the Pareto set, providing a great variety of architectural solutions among which experts could make their selection. Additionally, SPEA2 allows better controlling the number of solutions found, since the returned archive of non-dominated solutions has a fixed size. Therefore, the software architect could select an architecture among the number of solutions he formerly considered appropriate.

Regarding NSGA-II, its scalability for 4-objective and 6-objective configurations is worth mentioning. Therefore, NSGA-II could be valid as a fitting generic choice for the discovery of software architectures on small design specifications. One weakness, also observed in GrEA, is that it could suffer from an excessive convergence and, consequently, this algorithm would not be able to obtain non-dominated solutions for most complex instances, like Java2HTML. As a consequence, for complex analysis models, a more explorative algorithm would be preferred.

A relaxed Pareto dominance, as well as a slower evolution due to the steady-state process, which allows a better trade-off between convergence and divergence, are the two main strengths of ϵ-MOEA. On the contrary, it is worth noting that, for some 2-objective problems, only one high-quality non-dominated solution is returned, which seems to point out that this algorithm may get stuck into a local optimum. This fact hampers the decision support process, since the software architect might have to cope with an incomplete analysis in terms of the diversity of architectures and the levels of optimisation achieved for the measures considered.

The decomposition approach of MOEA/D has shown a variable behaviour in the different experiments carried out. It shows a great ability to explore multiple architectural solutions. On the one hand, it has a great impact on the size of the Pareto front, being the algorithm that generates more non-dominated solutions. On the other hand, preserving this variety in the set of solutions returned is not guaranteed if the spread of the Pareto set is observed. In fact, notice that choosing one single architecture among a large set of candidates, even more when they are so similar to each other, would be a complex task for the expert.

In general, GrEA is able to obtain solutions with a higher quality than NSGA-II. Nevertheless, it has a stronger tendency to converge to certain types of architectural solutions, which could depict to an undesirable scenario for the decision support system if the architectures found do not satisfy the modeller's expectations.

As regards the specific architectural concepts, the accurate selection of the metrics to be optimised has also an important influence over the type of the solutions found and, consequently, in the compliance of non-funcional requirements. Including certain design criteria, like the cohesion by means of the *ICD* or the instability, implies that all the algorithms would tend to search for solutions comprising more components. Since this type of organisation enables a further distinction between the system function-

Table 6: Observed strengths and weaknesses of each algorithm on different dimensions of the search space

Algorithm		2-objectives	4-objectives	6-objectives	General aspects	
SPEA2	Q:	Medium/low	Low	Low	I:	No
	S:	Good	Competitive	Good	P:	Yes
	O:	Bad	Bad	Bad	T:	High
	N:	Few	Medium	Medium		
NSGA-II	Q:	Medium	Medium/low	Medium/low	I:	Yes
	S:	Competitive	Bad	Competitive	P:	No
	O:	Variable	Good	Good	T:	Medium/low
	N:	Variable	Many	Many		
ϵ-MOEA	Q:	High	High	High	I:	Yes
	S:	Competitive	Good	Competitive	P:	Yes
	O:	Good	Good	Good	T:	Very low
	N:	Few	Medium	Many		
MOEA/D	Q:	Medium	Low	Low	I:	No
	S:	Bad	Competitive	Bad	P:	Yes
	O:	Bad	Bad	Bad	T:	Medium/high
	N:	Variable	Medium	Many		
GrEA	Q:	Medium	Medium	Medium/high	I:	Yes
	S:	Competitive	Bad	Bad	P:	No
	O:	Variable	Variable	Good	T:	Medium
	N:	Variable	Variable	Many		

Q: Quality of the solutions
S: Spread of solutions
O: Trade-off between objectives
N: Number of non-dominated solutions found

I: Ability to remove invalid solutions
P: Ability to find non-dominated solutions for all instances
T: Execution time

alities, each component will encompass a well-defined set of specific services. Moreover, the more components in the system specification, the smaller they will be, which could benefit its maintenance.

On the contrary, when metrics like the encapsulation or the *ERP* are considered, the structure of the architectural solution is just the opposite. In these cases, the creation of not many components may be translated into more secure software artefacts because of the minimisation of dependences among them. Further, a structure presenting less data interchange would enable the creation of high-perfomance systems.

It is worth highlighting that, if many design criteria need to be met, not all the algorithms would reach a good trade-off. Thus, optimising some specific metric often implies heavily penalising others. For example, the optimisation of the *CS* measure is usually demoted when the *ERP* or the *Encap* metrics are also used, since they promote the minimisation of interactions among components. Then, the architectural solutions found tend to comprise at least one large component.

Regarding the 6-objective problem, the optimisation of every metric becomes a challenging task, because of the large number of conflicts among them. When combining all metrics, only ϵ-MOEA and GrEA are able to maintain good solutions in relation to the *ICD* metric. Including the *ERP* and the *GCR* within the set of metrics causes a more variable behaviour of the algorithms over the different problem instances, since they are related to specific analysis information on the original design. Finally, *Inst* and *Enc* can achieve good values for all algorithms, even when different problem instances are considered, meaning that they are less conflicting measures.

6. CONCLUDING REMARKS

This paper presents a comparative study of the performance of different multiple-objective evolutionary algorithms for software architecture discovery, an abstract problem about which many architectural decisions have to be made according to a number of requirements. The experimental framework proposed explores the ability of these algorithms for simultaneously dealing with different metrics, and draws out some ideas about how they should be selected and combined by the software architect.

Many-objective evolutionary algorithms have been adopted to address this highly combinatorial problem. It constitutes a novelty in SBSE, where classical MOEAs have been usually considered, occasionally without previously performing a comparative study of its appropriateness. The results obtained point out that many-objectives evolutionary algorithms offer interesting alternatives to further explore the resolution of complex multiple objective problems in SBSE.

Results have shown that the specific characteristics of each algorithm play an important role in the quality of the Pareto sets obtained and, consequently, in the solutions returned to the expert. In this sense, the study of the strengths of each algorithm is an important step towards their recommendation for solving an specific architectural problem.

The analysis of the results from an architectural perspective allows the expert to take advantage of other characteristics of interest beyond the sole study of the evolutionary performance. In fact, the type of architectural solutions found is mostly influenced by the set of design metrics requested, whereas the algorithm selected and the number of objectives will determine the number of solutions obtained.

Hence, this paper has contributed in identifying those determining aspects that significantly affect the semi-automatic discovery of software architectures, providing the modellers with guidelines for properly backing up their decisions along the process.

In the near future, we plan to carry on with the analysis of the most fitting evolutionary features that need to be considered when dealing with multiple design requirements. It includes extending the catalogue of metrics and algorithms, as well as considering the implementation of new problem-specific approaches.

7. ACKNOWLEDGMENTS

Work supported by the Spanish Ministry of Science and Technology, project TIN2011-22408, and FEDER funds.

8. REFERENCES

[1] L. Dobrica and E. Niemela, "A survey on software architecture analysis methods," *IEEE Trans. Softw. Eng.*, vol. 28, no. 7, pp. 638–653, 2002.

[2] S. Ducasse and D. Pollet, "Software Architecture Reconstruction: A Process-Oriented Taxonomy," *IEEE Trans. Softw. Eng.*, vol. 35, no. 4, pp. 573–591, 2009.

[3] V. L. Narasimhan and B. Hendradjaya, "Some theoretical considerations for a suite of metrics for the integration of software components," *Information Sciences*, vol. 177, no. 3, pp. 844–864, 2007.

[4] C. Sant'Anna, E. Figueiredo, A. Garcia, and C. J. Lucena, "On the Modularity of Software Architectures: A Concern-Driven Measurement Framework," in *Software Architecture*, vol. 4758 of *LNCS*, pp. 207–224, Springer Berlin Heidelberg, 2007.

[5] J. Bansiya and C. G. Davis, "A Hierarchical Model for Object-Oriented Design Quality Assessment," *IEEE Trans. Soft. Eng.*, vol. 28, no. 1, pp. 4–17, 2002.

[6] J. Bosch and P. Molin, "Software architecture design: evaluation and transformation," in *Proc. IEEE Conf. and Workshop on Engineering of Computer-Based Systems (ECBS)*, pp. 4–10, 1999.

[7] M. Harman, S. A. Mansouri, and Y. Zhang, "Search-based Software Engineering: Trends, techniques and applications," *ACM Computing Surveys*, vol. 45, no. 1, pp. 11:1–11:61, 2012.

[8] O. Räihä, K. Koskimies, and E. Makinen, "Generating software architecture spectrum with multi-objective genetic algorithms," in *Proc. 3th World Congress on Nature and Biologically Inspired Computing (NaBIC)*, pp. 29–36, 2011.

[9] A. Ouni, M. Kessentini, H. Sahraoui, and M. S. Hamdi, "The use of development history in software refactoring using a multi-objective evolutionary algorithm," in *Proc. 15th Annual Genetic and Evolutionary Computation Conference (GECCO)*, pp. 1461–1468, 2013.

[10] X. Yao, "Some Recent Work on Multi-objective Approaches to Search-Based Software Engineering," in *Proc. 5th Symp. on Search Based Software Engineering (SSBSE)*, vol. 8084, pp. 4–15, 2013.

[11] A. Sayyad and H. Ammar, "Pareto-optimal search-based software engineering (POSBSE): A literature survey," in *2nd Inter. Workshop on Realizing Artificial Intelligence Synergies in Software Engineering (RAISE)*, pp. 21–27, 2013.

[12] A. S. Sayyad, T. Menzies, and H. Ammar, "On the Value of User Preferences in Search-based Software Engineering: A Case Study in Software Product Lines," in *Proc. 2013 Inter. Conf. on Software Engineering (ICSE)*, pp. 492–501, 2013.

[13] S. Kalboussi, S. Bechikh, M. Kessentini, and L. Ben Said, "Preference-Based Many-Objective Evolutionary Testing Generates Harder Test Cases for Autonomous Agents," in *Proc. 5th Symp. on Search Based Software Engineering*, pp. 245–250, 2013.

[14] H. Ishibuchi, N. Tsukamoto, and Y. Nojima, "Evolutionary many-objective optimization: A short review," in *Proc. IEEE Congress on Evolutionary Computation (CEC)*, pp. 2419–2426, 2008.

[15] A. Ramírez, J. R. Romero, and S. Ventura, "A Novel Component Identification Approach Using Evolutionary Programming," in *Proc. 15th Annual Genetic and Evolutionary Computation Conference (GECCO)*, pp. 209–210, 2013.

[16] P. Gupta, S. Verma, and M. Mehlawat, "Optimization Model of COTS Selection Based on Cohesion and Coupling for Modular Software Systems under Multiple Applications Environment," in *Computational Science and Its Applications (ICCSA)*, vol. 7335 of *LNCS*, pp. 87–102, Springer, 2012.

[17] E. Zitzler, M. Laumanns, and L. Thiele, "SPEA2: Improving the Strength Pareto Evolutionary Algorithm," in *Proc. Conf. on Evolutionary Methods for Design, Optimisation and Control with Applications to Industrial Problems*, pp. 95–100, 2001.

[18] K. Deb, A. Pratap, S. Agarwal, and T. Meyarivan, "A fast and elitist multiobjective genetic algorithm: NSGA-II," *IEEE Transactions on Evolutionary Computation*, vol. 6, no. 2, pp. 182–197, 2002.

[19] K. Deb, M. Mohan, and S. Mishra, "Towards a Quick Computation of Well-Spread Pareto-Optimal Solutions," in *Evolutionary Multi-Criterion Optimization*, vol. 2632 of *LNCS*, pp. 222–236, Springer, 2003.

[20] Q. Zhang and H. Li, "MOEA/D: A Multiobjective Evolutionary Algorithm Based on Decomposition," *IEEE Transactions on Evoutionary Computation*, vol. 11, no. 6, pp. 712–731, 2007.

[21] S. Yang, M. Li, X. Liu, and J. Zheng, "A Grid-Based Evolutionary Algorithm for Many-Objective Optimization," *IEEE Transactions on Evolutionary Computation*, vol. 17, no. 5, pp. 721–736, 2013.

[22] S. Ventura, C. Romero, A. Zafra, J. A. Delgado, and C. Hervás, "JCLEC: a Java framework for evolutionary computation," *Soft Computing*, vol. 12, no. 4, pp. 381–392, 2008.

[23] C. A. Coello Coello, G. B. Lamont, and D. A. Van Veldhuizen, *Evolutionary Algorithms for Solving Multi-Objective Problems*. Springer, 2nd ed., 2007.

[24] F. Luna, D. L. González-Álvarez, F. Chicano, and M. A. Vega-Rodríguez, "The software project scheduling problem: A scalability analysis of multi-objective metaheuristics," *Applied Soft Computing*, vol. 15, pp. 136–148, 2014.

Applying Search Algorithms for Optimizing Stakeholders Familiarity and Balancing Workload in Requirements Assignment

Tao Yue
Simula Research Laboratory
Oslo, Norway
+47 40433125
tao@simula.no

Shaukat Ali
Simula Research Laboratory
Oslo, Norway
+47 47466831
shaukat@simula.no

ABSTRACT

During the early phase of project development lifecycle of large scale cyber-physical systems, a large number of requirements are needed to be assigned to different stakeholders from different organizations or different departments of the same organization for reviewing, clarifying and checking their conformance to industry standards and government or other regulations. These requirements have different characteristics such as various extents of importance to the organization, complexity, and dependencies between each other, thereby requiring different effort (workload) to review and clarify.

While working with our industrial partners in the domain of cyber-physical systems, we discovered an optimization problem, where an optimal solution is required for assigning requirements to different stakeholders by maximizing their familiarities to the assigned requirements while balancing the overall workload of each stakeholder. We propose a fitness function which was investigated with four search algorithms: (1+1) Evolutionary Algorithm (EA), Genetic Algorithm, and Alternating Variable Method, whereas Random Search is used as a comparison base line. We empirically evaluated their performance for finding an optimal solution using a large-scale industrial case study and 120 artificial problems with varying complexity. Results show that (1+1) EA gives the best results together with our proposed fitness function as compared to the other three algorithms.

Categories and Subject Descriptors

D.2.1 [**Software Engineering**]: Requirements/Specifications – *Methodologies and Tools.*

General Terms

Algorithms, Performance, Management, Experimentation.

Keywords

Search Based Requirements Engineering, Requirements Assignment, Search Algorithm, Experiment.

1. INTRODUCTION

Requirements play a critical role in the development of large-scale cyber-physical systems, which integrate computation, networking, and physical processes [1]. The quality of these requirements has a significant impact on almost every single activity of the project development lifecycle. Due to their inherent complexity, such systems often have a large number of requirements that have to be reviewed, clarified, and checked for their conformance to industrial standards and government or other regulations at the early phase of the project development lifecycle. These activities are often performed by a large number of stakeholders from different organization or different departments of the same organization, having different job functions such as system, software, hydraulics, mechanical and networking engineers. This leads to the situation that they often have various extents of familiarities to different requirements; therefore assigning requirements that they are most familiar with is a very important factor to assure the overall quality and productivity of a project.

However, each requirement can be characterized from different aspects such as its complexity, importance, and dependencies with other requirements. Requirements that are more important and complex, and highly depended by others typically require more effort to review, check and clarify. Therefore, the workload for performing these activities on such requirements is higher than for less important, complex and loosely depended ones. When a project manager manually assigns a set of requirements to a stakeholder, it is important to take their characteristics into account for the purpose of balancing the workload of each stakeholder for performing the relevant requirements engineering activities. To manually do so does not scale, in a real industrial context, for even an experienced project manager, when assigning a large number of requirements to many stakeholders (implying a large search/solution space), and the manual derived assignment solution might not be optimal as the process is purely based on the experience of the project manager. Therefore, we see the need for an automated solution to assist project managers to conduct the assignment with the objective of maximizing stakeholders' familiarities to requirements, while balancing the workload of each stakeholder.

According to the comprehensive review of Harman et al. [12], Search Based Software Engineering (SBSE) has been extensively investigated to address various software engineering problems spanning from requirements, testing to reengineering of a typical software development lifecycle. Particularly for requirements, SBSE has been applied for various optimization problems such as requirements selection [6], prioritization [7], and assignment [10], with different objectives such as maximizing customers'/stakeholders' satisfaction, maximize benefits/value and minimize cost. None of these work shares the same optimization objective as ours, but promisingly they

GECCO'14, July 12–16, 2014, Vancouver, BC, Canada.

http://dx.doi.org/10.1145/2576768.2598309

demonstrated the performance of applying SBSE approaches for solving various optimization problems in requirements engineering, which encouraged us to go for this direction.

In this paper, we propose and assess a fitness function for the above-mentioned optimization problem. We evaluate it in conjunction with the following search algorithms, i.e., Genetic Algorithms (GAs), (1+1) Evolutionary Algorithm (EA), Alternating Variable Method (AVM). Random Search (RS) was used as the baseline to evaluate the performance of these algorithms. An industrial case study with 135 requirements and 30 stakeholders was conducted to evaluate the performance of these algorithms together with the proposed fitness function. Results show that all the three search algorithms significantly outperformed RS, which indicates the usefulness of applying search algorithms. When comparing the performance of the three search algorithms, results show that (1+1) EA is better than AVM and AVM is better than GA. We carefully designed 120 artificial problems inspired from our industrial application with the number of requirements ranging from 50 to 1000 and the number of stakeholders ranging from 5 to 30 to test the scalability of the algorithms. Results show that the performance of (1+1) EA is not impacted with the increase in the number of requirements and stakeholders and has consistently significantly better performance than the other algorithms.

The rest of the paper is organized as follows. In Section 2, we present a formal representation of our optimization problem followed by the fitness function. In Section 3, empirical evaluation of the search algorithms on the industrial case study and artificial problems is presented, followed by an overall discussion (Section 4). Section 5 addresses the threats to validity of our empirical study. Related work is provided in Section 6 and we conclude the paper in Section 7.

2. PROBLEM REPRESENTATION AND FITNESS FUNCTION

Recall that our goal is to maximize the assignment of requirements to stakeholders according to their familiarities to the requirements, while balancing the workload of each stakeholder. In this section, we present a formal representation of the optimization problem, followed by the fitness function.

2.1 Problem Representation

A system S has a set of requirements $Req = \{R_1, R_2, R_3 \ldots R_{n_R}\}$, where n_R is the total number of requirements. S has a set of stakeholders $Stk = \{S_1, S_2, S_3 \ldots S_{n_{St}}\}$, where n_{St} is the total number of stakeholders of the system. Each stakeholder S_j from Stk has a certain familiarity value FM_{ji} for a requirement R_i from Req, which is an integer value ranging from FM_{min} to FM_{max}. A stakeholder may have no familiarity with a requirement and is assigned a value 0. For S, we have a set of such values defined as the matrix below:

$$FM = \left\{ \begin{matrix} FM_{11} & FM_{12} & \cdots & FM_{1i} & \cdots & FM_{1n_R} \\ FM_{21} & FM_{22} & \cdots & FM_{2i} & \cdots & FM_{2n_R} \\ \vdots & \vdots & \ddots & \vdots & \vdots & \vdots \\ FM_{j1} & FM_{j2} & \cdots & FM_{ji} & \cdots & FM_{jn_R} \\ \vdots & \vdots & \vdots & \vdots & \ddots & \vdots \\ FM_{n_{St}1} & FM_{n_{St}2} & \cdots & FM_{n_{St}i} & \cdots & FM_{n_{St}n_R} \end{matrix} \right\}$$

In total, we have $n_R * n_{St}$ number of FM values for the problem. In our industrial context (Section 3.1.1), FM_{min} is 1 and FM_{max} is 10. In Section 3.1.1, we also discuss how we collected these data for our industrial case study.

Each requirement R_i in Req has a complexity, an integer value from CM_{min} to CM_{max}. The complexity of each requirement can be calculated based on the application. In Section 3.1.1, we discuss how the complexity is calculated in our industrial application. Same as FM, in our industrial application, CM_{min} is 1 and CM_{max} is 10. For S, we have $CM = \{CM_1, CM_2, .., CM_{nR}\}$, and in total we have nR number of CM values, where each R_i from Req has a corresponding CM_i value in CM.

Each requirement R_i has a dependency index, which is calculated as the number of requirements in Req, on which R_i is dependent. The value of dependency index for each requirement ranges from 1 to nR. For S, we have $DP = \{DP_1, DP_2, ..., DP_{nR}\}$, and each R_i has corresponding value DP_i in DP.

In addition, each requirement R_i has an importance value, which is an integer value ranging from IM_{min} to IM_{max}. How we calculated the importance for each requirement of the industrial case study is discussed in Section 3.1.1 and it ranges from 1 to 10. For S, we have $IM = \{IM_1, IM_2, .., IM_{nR}\}$, and each requirement R_i has a corresponding value IM_i in IM.

2.2 Fitness Function

Based on the definitions provided in Section 2.1, our fitness function is presented below and it always computes a value ranging from 0 to 3, where lower the value better the fitness.

$$FS = Assign + FAM + OWL$$

$$Assign = nor(abs(((\textstyle\sum_{i=1}^{nSt} nR_i) - nR))) \quad (1)$$

$$FAM = 1- \frac{\sum_{i=i}^{nSt} \sum_{j=1}^{nR_i} \frac{FM_{ij}}{(FM_{max} - FM_{min})}}{\sum_{k=1}^{nSt} nR_k} \quad (2)$$

$$OWL = \frac{\sum_{j=1}^{nSt-1} \sum_{k=j+1}^{nSt} abs(WL_j - WL_k)}{nSt*(nSt-1)} \quad (3)$$

Our fitness function (FS) has three main parts. As shown in Formula (1), the first part calculates a value that tells how far we are from assigning all the requirements to stakeholders. nR_i returns the number of requirements assigned to i_{th} stakeholder in Stk and we sum up all the requirements. The total number obtained is then subtracted from nR (total number of requirements), which tells us how far we are from assigning all the requirements to the stakeholders. We take the absolute value to keep the distance value positive. Finally, we normalize the obtained value between from 0 to 1 using the following normalization function [3]: $nor(x) = \frac{x}{x+1}$.

Notice that we aim to make *Assign* equal to 0 meaning that all the requirements have been assigned to all the stakeholders. Doing so gives *Assign* equal weights to the other two significant parts of FS since FAM, and OWL always compute values from 0 to 1, as we will discuss below.

The second part of FS is about computing familiarity (FAM) (see Formula (2)). Part of the formula is: $\sum_{i=i}^{nSt} \sum_{j=1}^{nR_i} \frac{FM_{ij}}{(FM_{max} - FM_{min})}$, which computes the overall familiarity of each stakeholder to all the requirements assigned to her/him. Dividing it with $\sum_{k=1}^{nSt} nR_k$ gives an average familiarity value for all the stakeholders. A higher value calculated by the formula means higher familiarity and higher fitness; however in the other parts of FS a higher value means lower fitness. To make this part consistent with the rest of the parts in FS, we subtract the average value from 1. By doing so, an overall value computed by FS can be interpreted as follows: lower the value higher the fitness or in other words high familiarity and balanced workload among the stakeholders.

The third part in *FS* is to compute *Overall Work Load* (*OWL*): the overall workload assigned to each stakeholder. The formula for the computation is given in Formula (3). Recall that our objective is to balance the workload across the stakeholders while maximizing the overall familiarity (*FM*) of requirements assigned to stakeholders. WL_i computes the workload for all the requirements assigned to i_{th} stakeholder based on their complexity, dependency index, and importance. See below:

$$\mathrm{WL_i} = \frac{\sum_{j=1}^{nR_i}((\frac{CM_j}{(CM_{max}-CM_{min})}+\frac{DP_j}{nR}+\frac{IM_j}{(IM_{max}-IM_{min})})/3)}{nR_i}.$$

Notice that the requirement characteristics for calculating workload (i.e., complexity CM values, dependency index DP values, and Importance IM values) are given equal weights in our formula. *OWL* then uses these computed workload values for each stakeholder and computes how balanced is workload among the stakeholders using the formula below:

$$\sum_{j=1}^{nSt-1}\sum_{k=j+1}^{nSt} abs(WL_j - WL_k).$$

For example, suppose stakeholder 1 has workload of 0.5 and for stakeholder 2 workload is 0.4, then the overall balance of workload is 0.1 (0.5-0.4). We aim for making this as close to 0 as possible, implying that workload is balanced. Finally we divide the nominator with $nSt * (nSt - 1)$, as shown in Formula (3), to obtain average workload of each stakeholder. Recall that our aim is to minimize *OWL* or in other words to make it as close to 0 as possible.

3. EMPIRICAL EVALUATION

This section discusses the experiment design, execution, and analysis of the evaluation of the fitness function with the four search algorithms for addressing our optimization problem.

3.1 Experiment Design

The objective of our experiments is to evaluate proposed fitness function in conjunction with the selected search algorithms in terms of solving our optimization problem: maximizing the assignment of requirements to stakeholders according to their familiarities to the requirements, while balancing the workload of each stakeholder.

In these experiments, we address the following research question: ***RQ1:*** Are the search algorithms effective to solve our optimization problem, to compare with RS? ***RQ2:*** Among AVM, (1+1) EA and GA, which one fares best in solving our optimization problem? ***RQ3***: How does the combined increment of the number of stakeholders and requirements impact the performance of the search algorithms?

In our experiments, we compared four algorithms: AVM, GA, (1+1) EA, and RS. AVM was selected as a representative of local search algorithms. GA was selected as it is the most commonly used global search algorithm in search-based software engineering [2]. We selected steady state GA with a population size of 100 and a crossover rate of 0.75, with a 1.5 bias for rank selection. We used a standard one-point crossover, and mutation of a variable is done with the standard probability *1/n*, where *n* is the number of variables. Various settings would lead to different performance of an algorithm, but standard ones usually perform well [5]. (1+1) EA is simpler than GAs, but in previous software testing work we found that it can be more effective in some cases (e.g., [3]). We used RS as the baseline.

3.1.1 Industrial Case Study Design

Our industrial case study is a large-scale cyber-physical system, whose software controls and monitors the operation of electrical and mechanical instruments. The system is composed of up to hundreds of control modules and thousands of instruments, connected via communication networks.

This case study is part of a project aiming to support systematic requirements engineering of a family of control systems, with a focus on requirements analysis at the early stage of a product development lifecycle. During this stage, activities mainly conducted by domain experts from different organizations or different departments of the same organization, and focusing on product definition and analysis. When we particularly look into the requirements engineering practice, during these two phases, many domain experts are involved to perform the following activities: 1) identify and clarify ambiguous and imprecise requirements; 2) identify and add missing requirements; 3) identify and resolve conflict requirements; 4) identify infeasible or high risk requirements; 5) identify all relevant and affected documents such as design and test documents; 6) assess the impact of changes in requirements; and 7) check the conformance of requirements against various industrial standards and government and other regulations.

Considering that a project is often large-scale in industry, many requirements (including various industrial standards and government and other regulations) should be reviewed, clarified, and processed by stakeholders from different organizations or different departments of the same organization with various extents of familiarities to different requirements. More specifically, stakeholders need to perform the above-mentioned seven activities. It is therefore important to assign requirements according to stakeholders' familiarities at the same time keeping the balance of each stakeholder's workload. However, such a manual approach does not scale when the number of requirements and stakeholders is large, which is often the case for large-scale applications. This is one of the challenges our industrial partner is facing and we can see that it is a general issue for developing any large-scale cyber-physical systems.

To evaluate our search algorithms, we selected 135 requirements of a high-level system document and identified 10 stakeholders who are responsible to conduct the above-mentioned seven activities. These ten stakeholders have different responsibilities (job functions) in the organization and have various years of working experience in the organization. Therefore, one can expect that they have various extents of familiarities to the requirements to be assigned.

The organization's requirements are managed using a commercial requirements management tool. Each requirement is assigned a unique ID. Dependencies among themselves and with other documents (e.g., test artifacts) are maintained in the library. Therefore, it was not difficult for us to collect the data of requirements dependencies for running the experiment.

These requirements are classified in different ways. First, they are divided into categories according to their relevance to the key architectural components (e.g., control modules, instruments). Second, they are classified according to commonly seen requirements engineering categories such as functional requirements, non-functional requirements and safety requirements (one type of non-functional requirements). When we were collecting the data, safety requirements are considered very important. The third category is internal or external. External requirements are more important than internal requirements as any misunderstanding about external requirements will be very expensive to fix. We analyzed a control system requirements document for one project and selected in total 135 requirements for the experiment. Complexity of these requirements is measured as the number of natural language sentences contained in each requirement. We understand that we might have simplified the measurement and further investigation is needed in the future.

3.1.2 Artificial Problems Design

In addition, to empirically evaluate whether the fitness function defined in Section 2 really address our optimization problem even with large numbers of stakeholders and requirements, we carefully defined 120 artificial problems. We created artificial problems with the increasing number of requirements and stakeholders. For the number of requirements we used a range of 50 to 1000 with an increment of 50, whereas for the number of stakeholders we used a range from 5 to 30 with an increment of 5. In total we have 20 options for the number of requirements and 6 options for the number of stakeholders and in this way we defined 20*6=120 artificial problems. Note that, these artificial problems were inspired based on the industrial case study, but with a more realistic scale. For our industrial partner, they often face the problem to assign hundreds and sometimes a thousand requirements to up to 30 stakeholders for each project. For values for different factors such as familiarity, we generated them based on the actual distribution we observed from the industrial case study, for the purpose of making the artificial problems closer to real cases.

3.1.3 Dependent and Independent Variables

We have two types of dependent variables: direct and indirect dependent variables. The direct dependent variable in our context is the final fitness value (FFV) of the solution for a problem obtained after executing an algorithm with the fitness function for a certain number of generations (5000 in our experiments). Indirect dependent variables are derived from the direct dependent variable. In our analysis, we used two types of indirect dependent variables: Mean Fitness Value for each problem (MFV_p) and Mean Fitness Value for a specific number of problems (MFV_{sp}). MFV_p is a mean FFV for certain number of runs n_r (100 in our case) of a problem with an algorithm and is defined as: $MFV_p = \frac{\sum_{r=1}^{n_r} FFV_r}{n_r}$. MFV_{sp} is a mean MFV_p for a specific number of problems and is defined as: $MFV_{sp} = \frac{\sum_{p=1}^{n_{sp}} MFV_p}{n_{sp}}$, where n_{sp} is the number of problems and $1 \le n_{sp} \le 120$.

There are three factors (independent variables) that we manipulated in our experiments: four types of search algorithms with the fitness function, number of stakeholders (n_{St}) and number of requirements (n_R).

3.2 Statistical Tests

To compare the obtained results of the search algorithms, the Kruskal-Wallis test, the Wilcoxon signed-rank test and the Vargha and Delaney statistics were used, based on the guidelines presented in [3].

3.3 Experiment Execution

For the industrial case study and each of the artificial problems, we ran experiments 100 times for each of the four search algorithm for each problem. We let all the four algorithms run up to 5000 generations for each problem and collected final fitness value calculated in the 5000th generation. We used a PC with Intel Core Duo CPU 2.20 GHz with 4 GB of RAM, running Linux Ubuntu operating system for the execution of experiment.

3.4 Results and Analysis

3.4.1 Industrial Case Study

To answer RQ1 and RQ2 for the industrial case study, we compared the four algorithms based on the fitness achieved after running each algorithm for 5000 generations. Recall that we repeatedly ran each algorithm for 100 times to account for random variations and the mean fitness values used in this analysis is the average of all the 100 runs: MFV_p. We first performed the Kruskal–Wallis test. We obtained a p-value<0.0001 suggesting that there is significant difference among the four algorithms.

Second, to compare each pair of algorithms, we performed the Wilcoxon test, whose results are shown in Table 1. The first three rows show the results of the comparison of the three search algorithms with random search (RQ1). One can see that all the three algorithms significantly outperformed RA as all the p-values are less than 0.05 (our chosen significance level). Negative mean differences indicate that MFV_p of RS are higher than MFV_p for all the three search algorithms. Based on the results, we can answer our RQ1 as follows: AVM, GA and (1+1) EA are all significantly better than RS in finding an optimal solution for our problem.

To answer RQ2, we compared each pair of the search algorithms. Results are shown in the last three rows of Table 1. For each pair, p-values are greater than 0.05 suggesting that there is no significant difference between any search algorithms for finding an optimal solution for our problem. Based on these results we can answer RQ2 for our industrial problem as follows: Any of AVM, (1+1) EA and GA can find an optimal solution for our problem without significant difference.

Table 1 Results for the Wilcoxon signed-rank test at significance level of 0.05 – industrial case study

	Pair of Algorithms	Mean difference	p-value
RQ1	AVM vs RS	-2.07	**<0.0001**
	(1+1) EA vs RS	-2.07	**<0.0001**
	GA vs RS	-2.08	**<0.0001**
RQ2	AVM vs (1+1) EA	0.0004	0.9
	AVM vs GA	0.0037	0.26
	(1+1) EA vs GA	0.0033	0.35

3.4.2 Results for Artificial Problems

To answer our research questions, we compared the three search algorithms with RS based on mean fitness values achieved after 5000 generations for each algorithm and each of the 120 problems. Recall that each problem was repeated for 100 times to account for random variation.

Table 2 summarizes results of the Wilcoxon signed-rank test for RQ1. The column *A*>*B* means the number of problems out of 120 for which an algorithm *A* was significantly better than *B*, *A*<*B* means vice versa, and *A*=*B* means the number of problems for which there were no significant differences between *A* and *B* based on p-values calculated by the Wilcoxon test.

Table 3 provides the Vargha and Delaney statistics. The column

A>B means the number of problems out of 120 for which an algorithm *A* has higher chances of obtaining higher fitness value than *B*, *A<B* means vice versa, and *A=B* means the number of problems for which there were no differences between *A* and *B* as $\widehat{A}_{12}$ equals to 0.5.

3.4.2.1 Results for RQ1

To answer RQ1, we compared each search algorithm with RS, based on the mean fitness values obtained for each problem (MFV_p, $0<p<=120$). Results for RQ1 are shown in the first three rows of Table 2 and Table 3.

AVM vs RS: As we can see in Table 3, AVM performed better than RS for 107 problems but for 105 problems the results were statistically significant (Table 2). RS performed better for 13 problems as shown in the first row of Table 3, and there were no significant differences for the other two problems.

(1+1) EA vs RS: (1+1) EA performed better than RS for 120 problems (Table 3), 119 problems out of which were significantly better than RS (Table 2). There were no significant differences for one problem (Table 2).

GA vs RS: In case of GA, it performed better than RS for 55 problems (Table 3). Out of 55, for 45 problems GA was significantly better than RS (Table 2). For 65 problems there were no significant differences (Table 3).

Concluding Remarks: Based on the above results, we can answer RQ1 as follows: AVM, (1+1) EA and GA are all significantly better than RS for finding an optimal solution for our problem.

Table 2 Results for the Wilcoxon signed-rank test at significance level of 0.05– artificial problems

	Pair of Algorithms (A vs B)	A>B	A<B	A=B
RQ1	AVM vs RS	105	11	4
	(1+1) EA vs RS	119	0	1
	GA vs RS	45	0	75
RQ2	AVM vs (1+1) EA	31	55	34
	AVM vs GA	98	16	6
	(1+1) EA vs GA	108	6	6

Table 3 Results for the Vargha and Delaney $\widehat{A}_{12}$ statistics

	Pair of Algorithms (A vs B)	A>B	A<B	A=B
RQ1	AVM vs RS	107	13	0
	(1+1) EA vs RS	120	0	0
	GA vs RS	55	0	65
RQ2	AVM vs (1+1) EA	37	83	0
	AVM vs GA	100	20	0
	(1+1) EA vs GA	113	7	0

3.4.2.2 Results for RQ2

The results to answer RQ2 are presented in the last three rows of Table 2 and Table 3. These results are also based on the mean fitness values obtained for each problem (MFV_p, $0<p<=120$) for each algorithm.

AVM vs (1+1) EA: AVM performed better than (1+1) EA for 37 problems (Table 3), but for 31 problems it was significantly better than (1+1) EA (Table 2). AVM performed worse than (1+1) EA for 83 problems (Table 3) and in 55 out of these 83 problems (1+1) EA was significantly better than AVM (Table 2). There were no significant differences between the algorithms for 34 problems as shown in Table 2.

AVM vs GA: AVM performed better than GA for 100 problems (Table 3) and out of these 100 problems AVM performed significantly better than GA for 98 problems (Table 2). GA performed significantly worse than AVM for 20 problems (Table 3) and for 16 out of 20 problems results were statistically significant (Table 2). For 6 problems there were no significant differences between the algorithms as shown in Table 2.

(1+1) EA vs GA: Regarding the (1+1) EA vs GA pair, for 113 problems (1+1) EA was better than GA (Table 3); however out of these 113 problems, for 108 problems (1+1) EA was significantly better than GA (Table 2). For seven problems GA performed better than (1+1) EA as shown in Table 3, whereas there were significant differences for six out of these seven problems. In total there were no significant differences for six problems as shown in Table 2.

Concluding Remarks: Based on the above results, we can answer RQ2 as follows: (1+1) EA is better than AVM and AVM is better than GA in terms of finding optimal solutions for the artificial problems.

3.4.2.3 Results for RQ3

To answer RQ3, we plotted the mean fitness values for each algorithm with both increasing number of requirements ($\bigcup_{n_R=0,\, n_R=n_R+50}^{1000} n_R$) and increasing number of stakeholders ($\bigcup_{n_{St}=0,\, n_{St}=n_{St}+5}^{30} n_{St}$). In this case, given a fixed number of requirements and stakeholders, we have one problem corresponding to exactly one stakeholder and requirement category combination; therefore y-axis in Figure 1 is MFV_p.

The results for AVM are shown in Figure 1, from which one can see that when the number of requirements to be assigned (n_R) is less than 300, the increase in the number of stakeholders (n_{St}) has no impact on the performance of AVM. When the number of requirements is over 300, the performance of AVM for solving the problems with 5 stakeholders started to degrade, followed by the problems with 10 stakeholders, and so on.

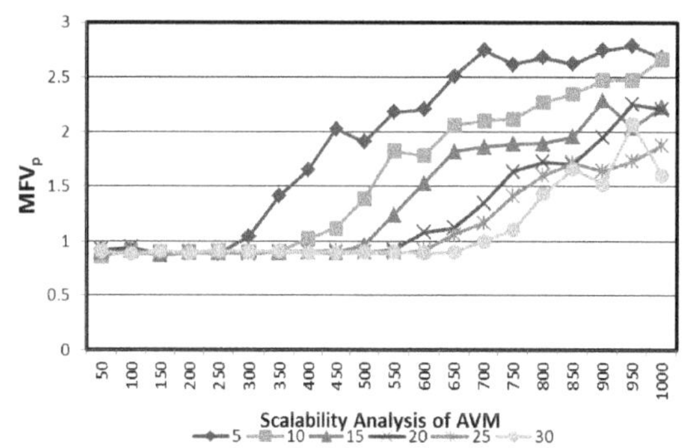

Figure 1 MFV_p with varying numbers of requirements and stakeholders – AVM

Notice that when the problems have 700 requirements to assign, the difference of the performance of AVM is large for the problems with various numbers of stakeholders, implying that at this point, the number of stakeholders plays a role of impacting the performance of AVM. However, along with the increase of the number of requirements (>700), this difference is reduced. Based on this result, we can expect that when the number of requirements is over 1000, the performance of AVM might not be significantly impacted by the number of stakeholder anymore. However, this requires further investigation with more focused experiments to confirm the phenomenon we observed. However, in general the performance of AVM is adversely affected as the problems are becoming complex.

The results for (1+1) EA are shown in Figure 2: even the increase in the numbers of requirements and stakeholders, MFV_p

do not significantly increase. This suggests that (1+1) EA has the ability to solve even complex problems with no much impact on its performance. Similar to AVM, when the number of requirements is less than 300, the performance of (1+1) EA is quite consistent for the problems with varying number of stakeholders. When the problems get complicated (with the number of requirements to assign over 300), the performance of (1+1) EA slightly degrades and it starts to be slightly impacted by the number of stakeholders, but not as much as AVM.

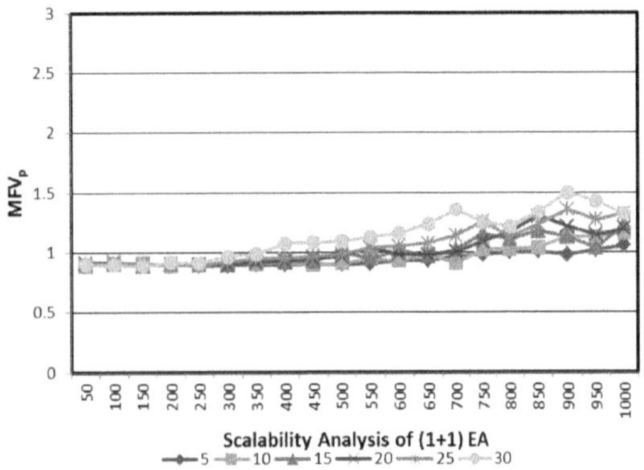

Figure 2 MFV_p with varying numbers of requirements and stakeholders – (1+1) EA

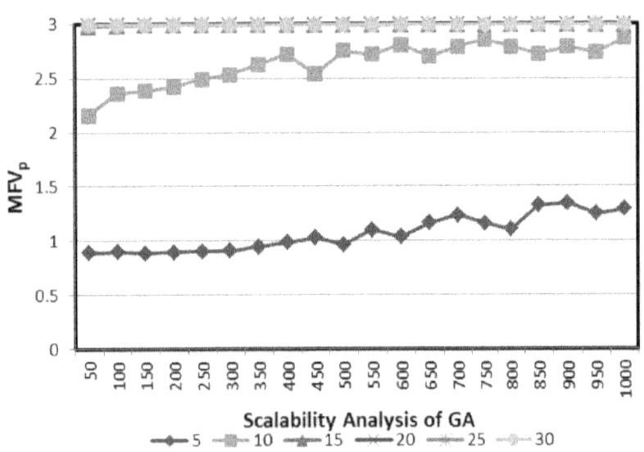

Figure 3 MFV_p with varying numbers of requirements and stakeholders – GA

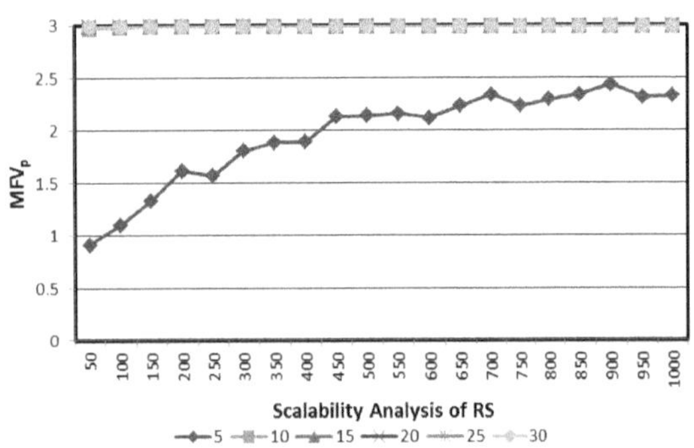

Figure 4 MFV_p with varying numbers of requirements and stakeholders – RS

For GA and RS (Figure 3 and Figure 4), MFV_p are high for the number of stakeholders over 5 regardless of the number of requirements. This implies that GA and RS cannot solve problems with the number of stakeholders over 5. Based on the above results, we can conclude that (1+1) EA has the ability to solve a wide range of problems without having its performance degraded significantly. We expect that even for more complex problems, (1+1) EA will find optimal solutions.

4. DISCUSSION

In this section, we provide an overall discussion based on the results of the experiments on the industrial case study and the artificial problems.

4.1 Performance of the Search Algorithms

We observed from the industrial case study that AVM, GA and (1+1) EA are all significantly better than RS in finding an optimal solution (RQ1), and AVM, (1+1) EA, and GA have no significant difference in terms of finding an optimal solution for our problem (RQ2).

For the experiments based on the artificial problems, we observed that AVM, (1+1) EA and GA all significantly outperformed RS for all the artificial problems (RQ1), which is consistent to what we observed from the industrial case study. For the artificial problems, (1+1) EA outperformed AVM and AVM is better than GA (RQ2). When we looked at the impact of varying numbers (50-1000) of requirements on the performance of each algorithm for the artificial problems, (1+1) EA was the best among all the four as it achieved better mean fitness values consistently and its performance does not significantly degrade along with the increase of the total number of requirements to assign in the problems, implying that (1+1) EA is the best to solve problems with large number of requirements to assign. Regarding the impact of varying numbers (5-30) of stakeholders on the performance of the search algorithms, both AVM and (1+1) EA did not show significant performance degradation. When we looked into the combined impact of both the number of stakeholders and the number of requirements on the performance of the search algorithms (RQ3), we observed that (1+1) EA is the best and has the ability to solve a wide range of problems without having its performance degraded significantly.

(1+1) EA is a global search algorithm and thus managed to find global optimal solutions as compared to AVM, which is a local search algorithm and its performance is good when problems are simpler (Figure 1). As we can see from Figure 1 that with the increased number of stakeholders and requirements, the performance of AVM decreased. This is due to the fact that with the increased numbers of stakeholders and requirements, there are more local optimal solutions and because of the nature of the working of AVM, it tends to converge to a local optimal and stuck there and consequently has to restart from other points in the search space. In contrast, for (1+1) EA due to its use of mutation operator it manages to explore the search space more exhaustively and thus always has a non-zero probability of escaping from local optimal solution (Figure 2). In case of GA (Figure 3), even though it is a global search algorithm, its performance is worse as compared to (1+1) EA. This may be because it uses only mutation for exploring the search space as compared to GA. GA relies on both mutation and crossover for exploration and exploitation of the search space. Therefore, to compare with (1+1) EA, it needs more generations to exploit (via crossover) on a specific area of the search space. Overall, it requires more generations to find a global optimal solution.

4.2 Practical Application

To apply a search-based solution in practice to solve real problems such as the one arose in our industrial case study, we need to take into account some practical issues, such as how to collect data for running a selected algorithm (in our context, (1+1) EA). In our context, such data includes 1) a set of requirements to be assigned, 2) a set of available stakeholders,

3) each stakeholder's familiarity to each requirement, 4) complexity of each requirements, 5) importance of each requirement, and 6) dependencies among the requirements. The ideal situation is that these data could be obtained automatically with as less effort as possible. However, in practice, it is not always easy or feasible to achieve this. Sometimes, it is even difficult to manually obtain these data as it really depends on the requirements engineering practice of an organization. For example, a survey might be required to obtain the familiarities of stakeholders on requirements. Below, we only discuss how we can obtain these data manually from our industrial partner and possibilities to generalize it for other contexts. In addition, we discuss the feasibility of automating the process.

Our industrial partner has a library managing all their requirements. A large portion of the requirements in the library can be reused across projects. Therefore as long as stakeholders' familiarities to these requirements are established, they can be reused. Dependencies of the requirements in the library are managed and the required information for running our algorithms can then be obtained automatically. Notice that nowadays using a requirements management is becoming a common practice in industry, especially for facilitating the development of large-scale systems requiring the collaboration of engineers across teams, departments, and even organizations. Therefore, we expect obtaining required information for applying the selected algorithm for optimizing requirements assignment seems not a problem in industry in general.

Regarding the complexity of each requirement, we currently simply count the number of natural language sentences of each requirement; hence, obtaining this information can be easily automated. Of course, one may argue that complexity of a requirement can be measured in different ways. However doing that (e.g., manually assigning values based on domain expert knowledge) needs a lot of effort and it has to be done manually. In the future, we will investigate the possibility of defining other metrics for measuring the complexity of requirements and automating the data collection process.

Importance of requirements can be also obtained automatically as our industrial partner, also a common practice in the domain with large-scale applications; requirements are classified according to their importance. Such a classification is commonly used in practice to organize requirements repositories. For example, safety requirements (one category in our industrial partner's repository) are considered as very important requirements. In conclusion, it is feasible to automatically collect required data for running the selected optimization algorithm. In the future, we plan to propose an automated solution and integrate it with well-known requirements management tools to collect data automatically, which will significantly ease the adoption of our approach in practice.

5. THREATS TO VALIDITY

To reduce construct validity threats, we chose an effectiveness measure called fitness value, which is comparable across all four search algorithms (AVM, (1+1) EA, GA and RS). Furthermore, we used the same stopping criterion for all algorithms, i.e., number of generations. This criterion is a comparable measure of efficiency across all the algorithms.

The most probable conclusion validity threat in experiments involving randomized algorithms is due to random variations. To address it, we repeated experiments 100 times to reduce the possibility that the results were obtained by chance. Furthermore, we performed the Wilcoxon test to compare the algorithms' mean fitness values of 100 runs and determine the statistical significance of the results. We chose this test since it is appropriate for the continuous data [4], thus matching our situation. To determine the practical significance of the results obtained, we measured the effect size using the $\widehat{A}_{12}$ values, which is recommended to be used in conjunction with the Wilcoxon test to better interpret the results [3].

A possible threat to internal validity is that we have experimented with only one configuration setting for the GA parameters. However, these settings are in accordance with the common guidelines in the literature and our previous experience on testing problems. Parameter tuning can improve the performance of GAs, although default parameters often provide reasonable results [5].

One common external validity threat in the software engineering experiments is about generalization of results. We ran our experiments on just one industrial case study and one may argue that the results cannot be generalized for other case studies. However, such threat to external validity is common to all empirical studies and such industrial case studies are nevertheless very rarely reported in the research literature. In addition to the industrial case study, we also conducted an empirical evaluation of our proposed fitness function using 120 artificial problems of varying complexity and our results are consistent with the results of industrial case study.

6. RELATED WORK

In [12], Harman et al. presented a comprehensive analysis and review of trends of SBSE, with a section particularly dedicated to requirements engineering. Results show that SBSE has been applied for supporting various RE activities including requirements selection and optimization (e.g., [6]), requirements assignment (e.g., [10]) and requirements prioritization (e.g., [7]), with different objectives of e.g., maximizing customers'/stakeholders' satisfaction, maximizing benefits/value and minimizing cost. Our work follows into the category of requirements assignment a difference, since we aim to maximize requirements engineers/domain experts' familiarities to their assigned requirements while keeping the balance of their workload. To the best of our knowledge, there is no work that has been done to tackle this issue.

As nicely summarized by Zhang et al. in [14], the Next Release Problem (NRP), a problem that has been mostly studied in the field, was initially formulated by Bagnall et al. [6], with the goal of finding a set of requirements that balance customer requests (according to their importance to the company) within resource constraints (limited budget), considering requirements interdependencies. Later on, the NRP problem was addressed by Greer and Ruhe [11], aiming to balance the resources required for all releases and optimizing the ordering conflicts with stakeholder priorities. More recently, in [13] and [15], two applications of SBSE to address the NRP problem were presented using multi-objective formulation.

Different approaches have been taken to address the above-mentioned problems, including Greedy Search (GS), Hill Climbing (HC), Simulated Annealing (SA), and NSGA-II. In our experiments, we evaluated (1+1) EA, AVM and GA with RS as the benchmark of the evaluation. (1+1) EA and AVM have not been studied in any of these approaches. We selected AVM as it is a representative of local search algorithms. (1+1) EA is simpler than GA, but in previous software testing work we found that it can be more effective in some cases (e.g., [3]). Therefore, in this work, we wanted to study if these search algorithms perform well in the context of search-based requirements engineering. The results of our experiments showed that they performed quietly consistently as for solving testing problems.

Based on the review of Harman et al. [12], most of the related work tested their approaches using real world cases. To roughly compare the scale of these real case studies, we use the number of requirements involved in each case study as the measure. In [8], a real case study with 32 requirements was used to evaluate their approach. Greer and Ruhe [11] evaluated their approach with a real case study having 20 requirements. In [9, 14], a real case study with 35 requirements was reported. In our empirical study, we used an industrial case study with 135 requirements, which is quite large as compared to what has been reported in the literature.

7. CONCLUSION

Due to the inherent complexity of large-scale cyber-physical systems, a large portion of effort is allocated to requirements engineering as the quality of requirements has a significant impact on almost every single down steam activity of the development lifecycle of such a system.

Based on our experience of working with industry and a systematic domain analysis we conducted in an organization developing large-scale cyber-physical systems, we observed that requirements engineering for developing such systems often involve multiple stakeholders from different organizations or different departments of the same organization. Such stakeholders need to review and clarify a large number of requirements and check their conformance to various standards and regulations for each single project. Such requirements have various extents of importance to an organization and complexity, complicated dependencies between each other. Reviewing and clarifying these requirements and checking their conformance to other documents require different expertise of stakeholders and various effort/workload required. Therefore, assigning proper requirements to stakeholders based on their familiarities to these requirements, while keeping the overall workload required, is an optimization problem. Without a systematic approach with tool support, it is infeasible to handle the assignment manually even by experienced project managers or domain experts.

To address the above-mentioned problem, in this paper, we empirically studied four search algorithms: (1+1) Evolutionary Algorithm (EA), Genetic Algorithm, Alternating Variable Method, and used Random Search as a comparison baseline, along with a newly proposed fitness function. A quite large-scale industrial case study (with 135 requirements and 10 stakeholders) was conducted and results show that all the three search algorithms significantly outperformed random search. To determine which algorithm can handle more complex problem (with for example 1000 requirements and 30 stakeholders), we created 120 artificial problems with varying complexity. Our results show that (1+1) EA gives the best results together with our proposed fitness function.

Considering that this is the first time we used search algorithms to solve our requirements assignment problem (i.e., maximizing stakeholders' familiarities while balancing the overall workload), the results we obtained are very encouraging. In the future, we plan to investigate other search algorithms and refine the fitness function by taking into account more factors such as ordering of requirements for review. We also plan to automate the process of collecting data for running the algorithms.

8. REFERENCES

[1] Cyber-Physical Systems (CPS): http://cyberphysicalsystems.org/

[2] Ali S., Briand L. C., Hemmati H. and Panesar-Walawege R. K., "A Systematic Review of the Application and Empirical Investigation of Search-Based Test Case Generation," *IEEE Transactions on Software Engineering*, vol. 99 (RapidPosts), 2009.

[3] Arcuri A., "It really does matter how you normalize the branch distance in search-based software testing," *Software Testing, Verification and Reliability*, 2011.

[4] Arcuri A. and Briand. L., "A Practical Guide for Using Statistical Tests to Assess Randomized Algorithms in Software Engineering," in *International Conference on Software Engineering (ICSE)*, 2011.

[5] Arcuri A. and Fraser G., "On Parameter Tuning in Search Based Software Engineering," in *International Symposium on Search Based Software Engineering (SSBSE)*: Springer's Lecture Notes in Computer Science (LNCS) 2011.

[6] Bagnall A. J., Rayward-Smith V. J. and Whittley I., "The next release problem," *Information and Software Technology*, vol. 43 (14), pp. 883-890, 2001.

[7] Baker P., Harman M., Steinhofel K. and Skaliotis A., "Search based approaches to component selection and prioritization for the next release problem," *Proc. Software Maintenance, 2006. ICSM'06. 22nd IEEE International Conference on*, pp. 176-185, 2006.

[8] Feather M. S. and Menzies T., "Converging on the optimal attainment of requirements," *Proc. Requirements Engineering, 2002. Proceedings. IEEE Joint International Conference on*, pp. 263-270, 2002.

[9] Finkelstein A., Harman M., Mansouri S. A., Ren J. and Zhang Y., ""Fairness Analysis" in Requirements Assignments," *Proc. International Requirements Engineering, 2008. RE'08. 16th IEEE*, pp. 115-124, 2008.

[10] Finkelstein A., Harman M., Mansouri S. A., Ren J. and Zhang Y., "A search based approach to fairness analysis in requirement assignments to aid negotiation, mediation and decision making," *Requirements Engineering*, vol. 14 (4), pp. 231-245, 2009.

[11] Greer D. and Ruhe G., "Software release planning: an evolutionary and iterative approach," *Information and Software Technology*, vol. 46 (4), pp. 243-253, 2004.

[12] Harman M., Mansouri S. A. and Zhang Y., "Search based software engineering: A comprehensive analysis and review of trends techniques and applications," *Department of Computer Science, King College London, Tech. Rep. TR-09-03*, 2009.

[13] Saliu M. O. and Ruhe G., "Bi-objective release planning for evolving software systems," *Proc. Proceedings of the the 6th joint meeting of the European software engineering conference and the ACM SIGSOFT symposium on The foundations of software engineering*, pp. 105-114, 2007.

[14] Zhang Y., Finkelstein A. and Harman M., "Search based requirements optimisation: Existing work and challenges," *Requirements Engineering: Foundation for Software Quality*, pp. 88-94, 2008.

[15] Zhang Y., Harman M. and Mansouri S. A., "The multi-objective next release problem," *Proc. Proceedings of the 9th annual conference on Genetic and evolutionary computation*, pp. 1129-1137, 2007.

Fair-Share ILS: A Simple State-of-the-art Iterated Local Search Hyperheuristic

Steven Adriaensen
Vrije Universiteit Brussel
steadria@vub.ac.be

Tim Brys
Vrije Universiteit Brussel
timbrys@vub.ac.be

Ann Nowé
Vrije Universiteit Brussel
ann.nowe@vub.ac.be

ABSTRACT

In this work we present a simple state-of-the-art selection hyperheuristic called Fair-Share Iterated Local Search (*FS-ILS*). *FS-ILS* is an iterated local search method using a conservative restart condition. Each iteration, a perturbation heuristic is selected proportionally to the acceptance rate of its previously proposed candidate solutions (after iterative improvement) by a domain-independent variant of the Metropolis condition. *FS-ILS* was developed in prior work using a semi-automated design approach. That work focused on how the method was found, rather than the method itself. As a result, it lacked a detailed explanation and analysis of the method, which will be the main contribution of this work. In our experiments we analyze *FS-ILS*'s parameter sensitivity, accidental complexity and compare it to the contestants of the CHeSC (2011) competition.

Categories and Subject Descriptors

G.1.6 [**Mathematics of Computing**]: Numerical Analysis—*Optimization*

General Terms

Algorithms, Experimentation, Performance

Keywords

Hyperheuristics, Combinatorial Optimization

1. INTRODUCTION

Many interesting combinatorial optimization problems cannot be solved in polynomial time, i.e. are NP-hard. Classical examples of such problems are MAX-SAT, the Vehicle Routing and Traveling Salesman problems. Already for relatively small instances, solving these problems can become intractable. As the problems we are interested in solving in practice are often even magnitudes larger, non-exact methods are required. One approach that recently received a lot of attention is metaheuristic optimization [10, 12]. Metaheuristic optimization methods attempt to find good solutions to a problem by iteratively trying to improve a (set of) candidate solution(s). In practice, these methods often manage to quickly find approximate solutions to otherwise intractable problems.

GECCO'14, July 12–16, 2014, Vancouver, BC, Canada.

ACM 978-1-4503-2662-9/14/07 ...$15.00.
http://dx.doi.org/10.1145/2576768.2598285.

Most research in metaheuristics is focused on problem specific techniques. This approach is motivated by the *No Free Lunch Theorem* [19], stating that on average, performance over all instances is the same for every method, therefore advocating a *made-to-measure* approach. As a consequence, metaheuristic methods are not readily applied to newly encountered problems, or even new instances of similar problems. Furthermore, the cost of developing and applying *made-to-measure* metaheuristic solutions is high, resulting in few practical applications.

Recently, there is a renewed interest in general metaheuristic search methods that attempt to solve a wide range of problems. Rather than attempting to outperform *made-to-measure* methods, these methods provide a cheap *off-the-peg* alternative. A popular approach in this renaissance are hyperheuristics [6]. A hyperheuristic combines a set of low level heuristics to solve a given problem instance. Here, low level heuristics are initialization, perturbative and recombination heuristics used in the problem instance domain. In known domains, the hyperheuristic approach can therefore leverage efficient domain-specific components used in *made-to-measure* methods. They can be applied to any domain, provided a set of low level heuristics is defined for it first. Note that the *No Free Lunch Theorem* is no argument against hyperheuristic methods as on every problem domain, the domain-specific aspects of the method (low level heuristics) differ, i.e. a different method is used.

Hyperheuristic methods can be divided in two classes. *Generation Hyperheuristics* generate (meta-)heuristics to solve a specific problem (domain); finding the combination of low-level heuristics precedes the solving of the problem (static). *Selection Hyperheuristics* iteratively select low-level heuristics to explore the search space while solving a problem (dynamic). As such, selection hyperheuristics can be viewed as domain-independent Variable Neighbourhood Search methods.

In this paper, we present Fair-Share Iterated Local Search (*FS-ILS*), a selection hyperheuristic. *FS-ILS* is an Iterated Local Search (ILS) method using a conservative restart condition. Each iteration, a perturbation heuristic is selected proportionally to the acceptance rate of the previously proposed candidate solutions (after iterative improvement) by a domain-independent variant of the Metropolis condition. One of the core design principles was simplicity and modularity, to improve reproducibility, and to encourage re-use in research and by practitioners. *FS-ILS* was obtained in [2] using a semi-automated design approach. Because [2] focused on "how" the method was found, rather than the method itself, it lacked a detailed explanation and analysis of the method, which will be the main contribution of this paper.

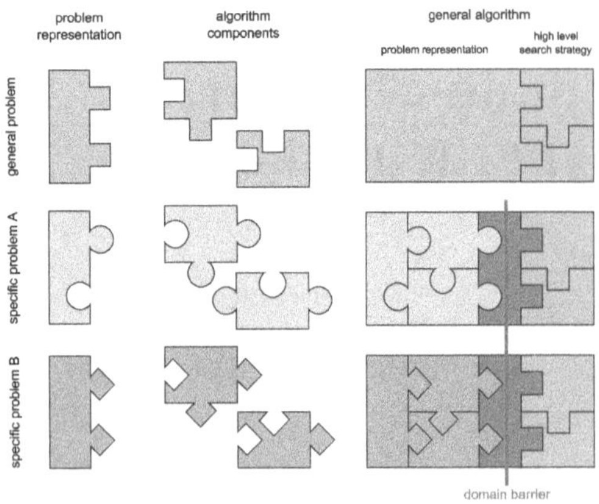

Figure 1: A graphical illustration of how a high-level search strategy can be applied to multiple problems through separation of problem specific and problem independent aspects

The remainder of the paper is organized as follows. Section 2.1 introduces the HyFlex framework. In Section 2.2 we describe *FS-ILS*, and motivate the design choices made. In Section 3 we perform experiments analysing *FS-ILS*'s parameter sensitivity and accidental complexity, and we compare it to the state-of-the-art. Section 4 discusses related research. Finally, in Section 5 we conclude.

2. METHODS

2.1 HyFlex

In the implementation and analysis of *FS-ILS*, we decided to use the HyFlex framework [15]. In this section, we motivate this decision and explain what the framework has to offer.

To evaluate general metaheuristic search strategies, we must test them on multiple instances of different problem domains. In the case of hyperheuristics, this means not only that we need benchmark problems, we also need low-level heuristics for all these domains. To avoid implementing all problem dependent aspects ourselves, we used the HyFlex framework. This framework offers a modular and flexible Java class library for developing and testing iterative general-purpose heuristic search algorithms. HyFlex currently provides 6 different problem domains: MAX-SAT, Bin Packing, Permutation Flow Shop, Personnel Scheduling, Traveling Salesman and Vehicle Routing problems. For each of these, it provides:

- A set of 10-12 benchmark instances which can be solved.
- A set of low-level heuristics: One construction heuristic and multiple perturbative and recombination heuristics.[1]
- An evaluation function, measuring the cost of a candidate solution, to be minimized.

One of HyFlex's core design principles is that all accesses to these domain-specific components must occur through a problem independent interface. Thanks to this explicit separation (i.e. the domain barrier, see Figure 1) any method using HyFlex can readily be applied to any instance of a problem domain implemented in HyFlex, without alterations.

[1]Each perturbative and recombination heuristic in addition takes two parameters: *intensity of mutation* (α) and *depth of search* β, ($0 \leq \alpha, \beta \leq 1$) In all our experiments we used $\alpha, \beta = 0.2$ (default value)

Algorithm 1 Fair-Share Iterated Local Search

function SOLVE($problem, t_{allowed}$)
  SETUP()
  INIT()
  while time()$-t_{start} < t_{allowed}$ **do**
    $t_{before} \leftarrow$ time()
    $selected \leftarrow$ PERTURBATIONSELECTION($evaluations$)
    if $selected < |llhs_{pert}|$ **then**
      $c_{proposed} \leftarrow llhs_{pert}[selected]$.apply($c_{current}$)
    else
      $c_{proposed} \leftarrow problem$.generateSolution()
    end if
    $e_{proposed} \leftarrow problem$.e($c_{proposed}$)
    LOCALSEARCH($c_{proposed}$)
    $durations[selected] \overset{+}{\leftarrow}$ time() $-t_{before} + 1$
    if $c_{proposed} \neq c_{current} \wedge$ ACCEPT() **then**
      $news[selected]$++
      $c_{current} \leftarrow c_{proposed}$
      $e_{current} \leftarrow e_{proposed}$
    end if
    $evaluations[selected] = \frac{news[selected]}{durations[selected]}$
    if RESTART() **then**
      INIT()
    end if
  end while
  return c_{best}
end function

HyFlex has been used to support the first Cross-domain Heuristic Search Challenge (CHeSC 2011). This challenge is analogous to the athletics Decathlon event, where the goal is not to excel in one event at the expense of others, but to have a good general performance on each [15]. All 20 contestants were tested on 5 instances from each of the 6 domains. To test generalization to new instances, 2 of the 5 instances used in the competition weren't available before submission, i.e. were "hidden". To test generalization to "new" domains, the Traveling Salesman and Vehicle Routing domains were hidden as well. The winner [14] was the algorithm obtaining the highest accumulated score across these 30 instances. Scores per instance were based on the ranking of median performances over 31 runs on that instance, using the pre 2010 Formula One scoring system, where the top 8 algorithms score respectively 10, 8, 6, 5, 4, 3, 2 and 1 point.

In this work we not only compare *FS-ILS* to the CHeSC contestants, we also quantify the method's performance on a problem instance relative to the median performance of the contestants on the same instance.

2.2 Fair-Share Iterated Local Search

In this section we give a detailed explanation and motivation of the design decisions made in the *FS-ILS* method. The main purpose of this section is to simplify reproduction and share the train of thought that lead to *FS-ILS*. To this purpose, we also provide the complete and unambigious pseudo-code for *FS-ILS* (Algorithms 1-7). This pseudo-code was written to be language- and HyFlex-independent, but doesn't omit any implementation details. The code's entry point is the *Solve* function, which performs optimization (minimization) on a given *problem*, for a time $t_{allowed}$, after which the best candidate solution found c_{best} is returned. First, it **initializes** the candidate solution using the construction heuristic. Next it iteratively **selects** and applies a low-level, domain-specific **perturbation heuristic**, performs **local search** on the resulting candidate solution, decides whether or not to accept the obtained candidate as new incumbent solution using an **acceptance condition**, and **restarts** if necessary.

Before discussing the specifics of these different aspects of the algorithm, we briefly discuss some **naming conventions** for the variables used in the pseudo-code. Variables named c_{foo}, e_{foo} represent candidate solution foo and its respective evaluation function value. E.g. $c_{current}$, $c_{proposed}$ are the variables representing the incumbent and proposed candidate solution respectively, while $e_{current}$ and $e_{proposed}$ refer to their respective evaluation function values. Variables named t indicate some time, e.g. t_{start} is the time at which the optimization process started. Some variables have two variants, one for a specific run (re-initialized every restart) and one for the entire optimization process. To differentiate the former from the latter we add a super-script run to the former. E.g. e^{run}_{best} is the best evaluation function value observed this run (since last restart), while e_{best} is the best evaluation function value observed over the entire optimization process (including prior runs). MAX_FLOAT is the largest floating point number (without overflow). time() returns the current wall clock time. $random$.integer and $random$.real(a,b) draw an integer or real number uniformly at random from $[a, b)$. An array a is indexed $[0, |a| - 1]$, where $|a|$ denotes the length of the array. The expression $a[0 : n] \leftarrow b$ is used to represent the initialization of an array a of length n with all elements initialized to b. Finally the assignment operator $\leftarrow$ has copy semantics.

2.2.1 Initialization

Algorithm 2 Fair-Share Iterated Local Search: Setup

```
procedure SETUP
    llhs_ls ← problem.get_llhs(GREEDY)
    llhs_pert ← problem.get_llhs(NON-GREEDY)
    wait_max ← 1
    t_start ← time()
    t_best ← +∞
    e_best ← MAX_FLOAT
end procedure
```

Algorithm 3 Fair-Share Iterated Local Search: Initialization

```
procedure INIT
    news[0 : |llhs_pert| + 1] ← 1
    durations[0 : |llhs_pert| + 1] ← 0
    evaluations[0 : |llhs_pert| + 1] ← MAX_FLOAT / (|llhs_pert|+1)
    n_impr ← 0
    wait ← 0
    t^run_start ← time()
    c_current ← problem.generateSolution()
    e_current ← problem.e(c_current)
    e^run_best ← e_current
end procedure
```

Setup (Algorithm 2) and *Init* (Algorithm 3) are auxiliary procedures that together initialize all variables. *Setup* handles all variables that are initialized once at the beginning of the optimization process, while *Init* deals with the variables that are re-initialized after each restart.

2.2.2 Perturbation Heuristic Selection

In this section we explain and motivate the hyperheuristic selection procedure used to select a perturbation heuristic (option). The relevant logic can be found in Algorithm 1 and Algorithm 4.

Algorithm 4 Fair-Share Iterated Local Search: Perturbation Heuristic Selection

```
function PERTURBATIONSELECTION(evaluations)
    norm ← 0
    for i ← 0 : |evaluations| do
        norm +← evaluations[i]
    end for
    pivot ← random.real(0,norm)
    selected ← 0
    ac ← evaluations[0]
    while ac < pivot do
        selected++
    end while
    return selected
end function
```

As options, we consider all non-greedy perturbative heuristics in the domain ($llhs_{pert}$). In HyFlex, this corresponds to the heuristics in the *mutation* and *ruin-recreate* categories. In addition, we include the construction heuristic ($problem$.generateSolution()) as a last option. We do this because some HyFlex domains, in particular the Traveling Salesman domain, lack proper explorative heuristics. Either the perturbation induced is too small to escape the local optimum, or perturbation results in a solution much worse than the initial candidate solution.

In order to decide which option to use, we assign to each a value ($evaluations$) that reflects how well it performed in the past. Each iteration, we select an option proportional to this value (a.k.a. roulette wheel selection). Before its first application, an option is assumed to be of very high quality (orders of magnitudes larger than any real quality value) to make sure every option is tried at least once.

One of the key difficulties in hyperheuristics is how to evaluate explorative heuristics, as they might only lead to improvement many steps later. Therefore, we evaluate our options based on the candidate solution obtained after local search, i.e. we evaluate the perturbation heuristic combined with the iterative improvement procedure described in Section 2.2.3.

Perturbation heuristics are the only source of diversification in the algorithm. Without sufficiently diverse proposals ($c_{proposed}$) a method risks getting stuck in local optima. Therefore, we decide to evaluate and thus select options in a non-greedy fashion. It is up to the acceptance condition (see Section 2.2.4) to decide whether or not a proposal is good, i.e. to control diversification.

Following this mindset, we started developing our hyperheuristic selection procedure starting from plain uniform selection. We found that plain uniform selection discriminates fast options. E.g. consider two options a and b, which take 1 and 10 ms respectively to generate a new candidate solution. Under uniform selection, the algorithm will spend 10 times more time on option b than it does on a. This motivated us to select options proportionally to their speed, i.e. the rate at which they generate solutions $\frac{n[i]}{durations[i]}$ where $n[i]$ is the number of applications and $durations[i]$ is the total time spent using the ith option. Using this procedure, in the limit, an equal amount of time will be spent on every option.

When an option's proposal does not lead to a new incumbent solution ($c_{current}$), either because $c_{current} = c_{proposal}$, or because the proposal is not accepted, the time spent generating it is effectively wasted. To encourage the selection of options that lead to advances in the search process, the selection procedure finally included in *FS-ILS* selects options proportional to the rate at which they generate new incumbent solutions $\frac{news[i]}{durations[i]}$ where $news[i]$ is the number of applications of the ith option that resulted in a new incumbent solution.

2.2.3 Iterative Improvement Procedure

Algorithm 5 Fair-Share Iterated Local Search: Local Search

```
function LOCALSEARCH(c)
    llhs_active ← llhs_ls
    e_c ← problem.e(c)
    while ¬llhs_active.isEmpty() do
        index ← random.integer(0,|llhs_active|)
        c ← llhs_active.apply(c)
        e_temp ← problem.e(c)
        if e_temp < e_c then
            e_c ← e_temp
            llhs_active ← llhs_ls
        else
            active.remove(index)
        end if
    end while
    return c
end function
```

In our iterative improvement procedure (Algorithm 5), we consider all greedy perturbative heuristics in the domain ($llhs_{ls}$) as options. In HyFlex, this corresponds to the heuristics in the *local search* category. Applying these heuristics can never lead to a worse candidate solution.

Each iteration of the iterative improvement procedure we select an option uniform at random. When an application of an option does not lead to improvement, it is excluded (tabu) from the selection ($active$), until some other heuristic finds improvement.

If we assume that each application of an option leads to improvement, unless we are in a local optimum for that heuristic, our iterative improvement procedure returns a candidate solution that is a local optimum for each of the options. Even though this condition is not met for all heuristics in the *local search* categories, it leads to an elegant termination point.

2.2.4 Acceptance Condition

Algorithm 6 Fair-Share Iterated Local Search: Acceptance

```
function ACCEPT
    impr ← e_current − e_proposed
    if impr > 0 then
        n_impr++
        μ_impr +← (impr − μ_impr) / n_impr
    end if
    return random.real(0,1) < e^(impr / (T*μ_impr))
end function
```

As mentioned in Section 2.2.2 the role of the acceptance condition is to control the diversification in the search process, i.e. whether or to accept a worsening proposal.[2] Never accepting worsening solutions typically results in the method getting stuck in a local optimum. While it is rare for an ILS scheme (given proper perturbation) to get stuck in a local optimum, we still risk losing a lot of time in a poor area of the search space.

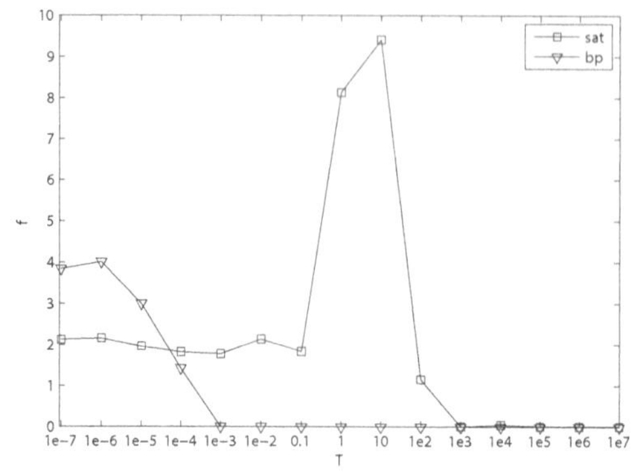

Figure 2: Performance of FS-ILS using the basic Metropolis acceptance condition with different T values.

The Metropolis acceptance condition accepts a worsening proposal with a probability $e^{\frac{e_{current}-e_{proposed}}{T}}$, where T is a positive parameter called the temperature. Under the Metropolis acceptance condition, the greater the worsening proposed, the smaller the likelihood the proposal will be accepted. Furthermore, the likelihood of accepting n times a worsening of a is equal to that of accepting a worsening of $n * a$ once. The higher the temperature, the higher the likelihood a worsening is accepted. More involved acceptance conditions vary this temperature over time (often referred to as simulated annealing [1]).

The main difficulty is choosing the temperature parameter T. Whether or not a worsening x is large is extremely domain (or even instance) dependent. E.g. in the MAX-SAT and Bin Packing domains, all evaluation function values lie in $[0, v]$ and $[0, 1]$ respectively (where v is the # variables in the formula). A worsening of 1 is the smallest possible worsening in MAX-SAT and the largest possible worsening in Bin Packing. As a consequence, any fixed temperature parameter T will either cause (nearly) all worsenings to be accepted in Bin Packing, or (nearly) no worsenings at all in MAX-SAT. Figure 2 illustrates the problem, showing the performance (f, as defined in Section 3.1.1) of *FS-ILS* using the plain Metropolis condition on the MAX-SAT and Bin Packing domains for a wide range of temperature values.

In *FS-ILS*, we use a rather crude, yet effective way to make the choice of T less domain dependent by expressing worsening in terms of mean improvement, i.e. $e^{\frac{e_{current}-e_{proposed}}{T*\mu_{impr}}}$ (Algorithm 6). Here μ_{impr} is the (moving) mean improvement in improving iterations. Thus, we normalize the amount of worsening by dividing it by a metric that is equally domain-dependent. Whereas a worsening of x in MAX-SAT can hardly be compared to the same worsening in Bin Packing, $\frac{x}{\mu_{impr}}$ will be less domain dependent and more indicative of general quality. We do keep T as the only *FS-ILS* parameter, and will perform an extensive parameter sensitivity analysis in the experimental section.

[2]Most acceptance conditions accept all improving candidate solutions. Candidate solutions of equal quality are sometimes selectively refused (e.g. tabu-search) to effectively explore plateaus in the search space.

Algorithm 7 Fair-Share Iterated Local Search: Restart

```
function RESTART
    t_elapsed ← time() − t_start
    t^run_elapsed ← time() − t^run_start
    if e_current < e^run_best then
        e^run_best ← e_current
        wait_max ←max(wait,wait_max)
        wait ← 0
        if e_current < e_best then
            c_best ← c_current
            e_best ← e_current
            t_best ← t^run_elapsed
        else if e_current = e_best then
            t_best ←min(t^run_elapsed,t_best)
        end if
    else
        wait++
    end if
    patience ← (t_allowed / t_elapsed) * wait_max
    return wait > patience ∧ (t_allowed − t_elapsed) ≥ t_best
end function
```

2.2.5 *Restart Condition*

FS-ILS is restarted after it failed to find a new best candidate solution (i.e. improve e^{run}_{best}) for a certain amount of time (Algorithm 7). This method is inspired by the fact that a lot of methods find new best solutions rather regularly. When they stop doing so we possibly have to wait a very long time for further improvement, if any (the method may be stuck). While restarting in such situation is not guaranteed to result in finding better solutions, it is often better than remaining stuck.

The hard part is how to detect that the algorithm is stuck. We propose the following heuristic, which was inspired by a method used in CHeSC contestant *VNS-TW* [11] to detect a local optimum in the ILS process. *FS-ILS* is restarted if it hasn't found improvement for $a * wait_{max}$ iterations where $wait_{max}$ is the greatest number of iterations we had to wait for a new, best solution so far. The idea is that over time, $wait_{max}$ will approximate the longest time needed to still improve.

The choice of a is crucial. On the one hand to allow $wait_{max}$ to grow it is important that a is sufficiently large (at least > 1). On the other hand however, to prevent wasting too much time later on in the search (when $wait_{max}$ is somewhat accurate) a should be as small as possible. We therefore decided to lower a hyperbolically over time: $a = \frac{t_{allowed}}{t_{elapsed}}$, where $t_{allowed}$ is the time we are allowed to optimize and $t_{elapsed}$ the time we have already spent since the beginning of the optimization. Initially, a will be extremely large, avoiding preliminary restarts; half way it is only 2, and at the end $a = 1$.

As an exception, the algorithm is not restarted when the time remaining is less than the shortest time it took to find a candidate solution as good as the best candidate solution obtained so far (t_{best}). This prevents restarts on instances on which a lot of time is required to obtain a high quality solution. E.g. given a $t_{allowed}$ of 10 minutes, when the best solution was obtained 9 minutes after initialization ($t^{run}_{elapsed}$), it is highly unlikely that a better solution is found after re-initialization.

Note that this restart condition is rather conservative and its core design concern was to prevent restarts as much as possible, and only restart when a method is obviously stuck and enough time is available to attain a solution of similar quality.

3. EXPERIMENTS

In this section, we experimentally analyze the performance of *FL-ILS*, concentrating first on its robustness to changes in its only numerical parameter. Then we analyze the accidental complexity of the method, comparing it with various simpler variants. Finally, we compare the method with the winner of the CheSC competition.

3.1 Parameter Sensitivity Analysis

3.1.1 *Setup*

The objective of the experiment described in this section is to analyze the choice of *FS-ILS*'s single (numerical) parameter T, i.e. the temperature used in its acceptance condition (see Section 2.2.4). To this purpose, we analyze *FS-ILS*'s performance using 15 different temperature values, ranging from 0.001 to 1000. In [2], T was intuitively chosen to be 0.5. To analyze the stability of this choice, 10 temperature values are chosen equidistantly in $[0.1, 1.0]$. For the sake of comparison we consider 3 further variants of *FS-ILS*

- A variant accepting all proposals (*aa*)
- A variant accepting no worsening proposals. (*anw*)
- A variant using the basic Metropolis acceptance condition with the temperature $t_i = 10^{i-7}$, $0 \leq i \leq 14$ that maximizes performance (*oracle*).

To simplify the comparison of different configurations of *FS-ILS* we want to quantify the performance of a certain configuration x. As in [2] we use the following evaluation function:

$$f(x) = \frac{1}{|P|} \sum_{\pi \in P} \frac{1}{n_{x,\pi}} \sum_{r \in R_{x,\pi}} s(r, \pi)$$

Here P is the set of benchmark instances on which x is tested. $R_{x,\pi}$ is the set of results obtained by method x over $n_{x,\pi}$ independent runs on the benchmark instance π. The scoring function s assigns points to the result of method x on an instance π as follows: A method is assigned 10, 8, 6, 5, 4, 3, 2 or $10^{(8-r)}$ points, based on the rank of its result r among the median results obtained by a set of benchmark algorithms A on π.[3] In case of ties, s returns the average of the scores for the tied ranks.

In this experiment we choose the 30 instances used in CHeSC (2011) as benchmark instances P and the 20 contestants as benchmark algorithms A. 900 tests for each configuration were performed, 30 for each instance (n_π). For each run $t_{allowed}$ is chosen such that $t_{allowed}$ time on our machine (Intel Xeon E5320 1.86GHz) corresponds to 10 minutes on the machine used during the competition.[4]

3.1.2 *Results*

Figure 3 shows the performance of *FS-ILS* with different temperature values T on all problem domains (*fs-ils*), as well as for the MAX-SAT (*fs-ils*$_{sat}$) and Bin Packing (*fs-ils*$_{bp}$) domains separately. In addition the performances of *aa*, *anw*, and the *oracle* are shown. Note that the scale of the x-axis is linear in $[0.1, 1.0]$, but logarithmic beyond.

We first have a look at the behavior of *FS-ILS* for extreme temperature values. For high temperature values *FS-ILS* accepts nearly all worsening proposals and we observe a performance similar to

[3] Ordered according to increasing cost, as determined by the domain-specific evaluation function.

[4] Using the benchmark program provided on the CHeSC(2011) website

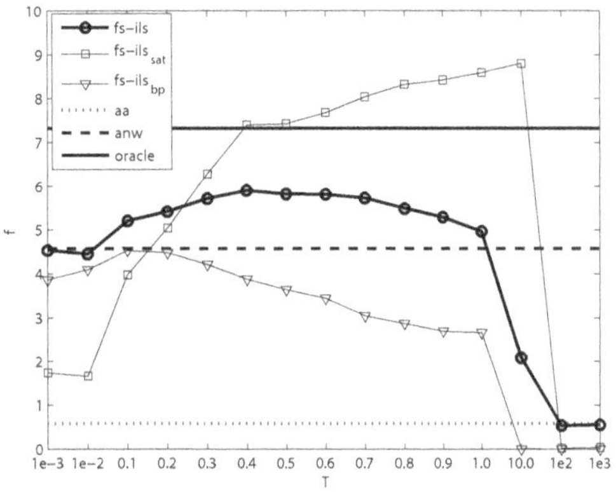

Figure 3: Performance of FS-ILS with different T values

that of *aa*. For low temperature values *FS-ILS* accepts nearly no worsening proposals and we observe a performance similar to that of *anw*.

The intuitive choice of $T = 0.5$ made in [2] seems like a good choice. Not only is it evaluated to be one of the best configurations (only 0.4 scored slightly better), this parameter choice is furthermore stable as *FS-ILS* performs similarly for similar temperature choices. Note that Figure 3 over-dramatizes the drop in performance for temperature choices beyond $[0.1, 1.0]$ because of the change in scale.

In comparing Figures 2 and 3 we find that our normalization of the Metropolis condition effectively solves the problem described in Section 2.2.2. Make no mistake, picking the best value for T is still about finding the best compromise. Some instances prefer more diversification and some less. E.g. On the MAX-SAT domain higher temperatures are preferred (10),while on the Bin Packing domain, lower temperatures are better (0.1). Furthermore, the *oracle* performs extremely well, illustrating that *FS-ILS* can be improved by making the choice of T more adaptive.

3.2 Accidental Complexity Analysis

3.2.1 Setup

The objective of the experiment described in this section is to analyze the presence of accidental complexity in *FS-ILS*, i.e. whether it can be simplified without loss of performance. To this purpose, we compare *FS-ILS* to simpler variants. We consider simpler alternatives for 4 design choices:

- The heuristic selection rule used (*SpeedNew*). Here we consider simpler variants selecting alternatives proportional to the rate at which they generate proposals (*Speed*) and variants using plain uniform selection (*Uniform*), see Section 2.2.2.
- The use of local search. Here we consider variants that do not perform local search, but use all perturbative heuristics (including the greedy) as options instead.
- The acceptance condition used (*APW*). Here we consider variants accepting only non-worsening proposals (*ANW*) and variants accepting all proposals (*AA*).
- The use of a restart condition. Here we consider variants that never restart.

Combining these simplifications gives rise to 35 simpler variants of *FS-ILS*. For each variant we perform 300 tests, 10 on each CHeSC (2011) benchmark instance to evaluate its performance. We test the significance of the differences in performance compared to *FS-ILS* using the Wilcoxon Signed-Rank test.

r	select	ls	accept	restart	f	p
1	**SpeedNew**	**yes**	**APW**	**yes**	**5.77**	**1.0**
2	SpeedNew	yes	APW	no	5.54	0.0048
3	Speed	yes	APW	yes	5.2	4.6E-5
4	Speed	yes	APW	no	4.85	2.0E-8
5	SpeedNew	yes	ANW	no	4.58	1.6E-6
6	SpeedNew	yes	ANW	yes	4.57	8.3E-7
7	Speed	yes	ANW	no	4.16	1.0E-9
8	Speed	yes	ANW	yes	3.87	4.2E-12
9	SpeedNew	no	APW	yes	3.23	3.4E-15
10	SpeedNew	no	APW	no	3.09	0.0
11	Uniform	yes	APW	no	2.99	0.0
12	Uniform	yes	APW	yes	2.96	0.0
13	Uniform	yes	ANW	yes	2.64	0.0
14	Uniform	yes	ANW	no	2.52	0.0
15	Speed	no	APW	yes	2.46	0.0
16	Speed	no	APW	no	2.42	0.0
17	Uniform	no	APW	no	2.18	0.0
18	Uniform	no	APW	yes	2.15	0.0
19	Speed	no	ANW	yes	1.84	0.0
20	Speed	no	ANW	no	1.74	0.0
21	SpeedNew	no	ANW	no	1.53	0.0
22	SpeedNew	no	ANW	yes	1.41	0.0
23	Uniform	no	ANW	yes	1.36	0.0
24	Uniform	no	ANW	no	1.35	0.0
25	SpeedNew	yes	AA	no	0.67	0.0
26	Speed	yes	AA	no	0.6	0.0
27	SpeedNew	yes	AA	yes	0.48	0.0
28	Speed	yes	AA	yes	0.48	0.0
29	Uniform	yes	AA	yes	0.41	0.0
30	Uniform	yes	AA	no	0.4	0.0
31	Uniform	no	AA	yes	0.16	0.0
32	Uniform	no	AA	no	0.12	0.0
33	SpeedNew	no	AA	yes	0.02	0.0
34	Speed	no	AA	yes	0.01	0.0
35	SpeedNew	no	AA	no	0.0	0.0
36	Speed	no	AA	no	0.0	0.0

Table 1: Comparison of FS-ILS to simpler variants

3.2.2 Results

Table 1 shows for each of the 36 configurations the design choices made, their performance (f, as defined in Section 3.1.1) and the p-value for the Wilcoxon Signed-Rank test in a pair-wise comparison with *FS-ILS*.

We find that *FS-ILS* (the best, in bold) is evaluated significantly better than its simpler variants, i.e. every design choice has a significant contribution. We note that some simplifications have a greater impact on performance than others. This allows us to measure the contribution of a certain design choice to the performance of *FS-ILS*.

The choice for speed proportional **selection** (*Speed*, *SpeedNew*) adds great value as the best configuration using uniform selection is only ranked 11th and in 20 out of 24 cases configurations using a speed proportional selection scheme outperform their version using plain uniform selection. In the 4 remaining cases the configuration has no control of diversification (*AA*), and therefore performs

r	algorithm	s_{total}	s_{sat}	s_{bp}	s_{ps}	s_{fs}	s_{tsp}	s_{vrp}
1	**FS-ILS**	**182.1**	**39.6**	20	10.5	**47**	34	**31**
2	AdapHH	162.18	28.93	**45**	9	31	**35.25**	13
3	VNS-TW	115.68	28.93	2	**39.5**	26	15.25	4
4	ML	110	10.5	8	30	31.5	10.0	20
5	PHUNTER	80.25	7.5	3	11.5	6	22.25	30
6	EPH	74.75	0	8	9.5	16	30.25	11
7	NAHH	65	11.5	19	1	18.5	10.0	5
8	HAHA	64.27	26.93	0	25.5	0.83	0.0	11
9	ISEA	59.5	3.5	28	14.5	1.5	9	3
10	KSATS-HH	53.85	19.85	8	8	0	0	18
11	HAEA	39.33	0	2	1	5.33	9	22
12	ACO-HH	32.33	0	19	0	6.33	6	1
13	GenHive	30.5	0	12	6.5	5	2	5
14	SA-ILS	21.75	0.25	0	17.5	0	0	4
15	DynILS	20	0.0	11	0	0	9	0
16	XCJ	18.5	3.5	10	0	0	0	5
17	AVEG-Nep	16.5	10.5	0	0	0	0	6
18	GISS	16.25	0.25	0	10	0	0	6
19	SelfSearch	4	0	0	1	0	3	0
20	MCHH-S	3.25	3.25	0	0	0	0	0
21	Ant-Q	0	0	0	0	0	0	0

Table 2: The results of the CHeSC 2011 competition with FS-ILS as competitor

poorly with non-greedy selection schemes. Plain uniform selection tends to be greedier than speed proportional selection as applying non-greedy heuristics tends to take less time than applying greedy ones. Configurations using *SpeedNew* outperform the version using *Speed* in 10 out of 12 cases. In the cases it does not, no local search is performed and all worsening proposals are rejected. *SpeedNew* selection becomes too greedy and fails to explore.

The use of **local search** is clearly important as the best configuration without is only ranked 9th. Furthermore, all variants using local search outperform their version not using local search.

Also, the chosen **acceptance condition** is important. The top 4 configurations use the (normalized) Metropolis acceptance condition. Furthermore, variants using this acceptance condition outperform their version accepting no worsening proposals, which in turn outperforms the version accepting all worsening proposals.

The choice for the **restart condition** is clearly the most controversial. On the one hand using the restart condition does (significantly) improve the performance of the 2 top configurations. Therefore, we decided to describe it in this paper. On the other hand, not using the restart condition is the simplification with the smallest impact and using the restart condition is in no way consistently beneficial. Therefore, one might consider omitting the restart condition, which would further simplify implementation and analysis, as there is no need for re-initialization or run-specific variables.

3.3 Comparison to State of the Art

3.3.1 Setup

The objective of the experiment described in this section is to compare the performance of *FS-ILS* to the state of the art in selection hyperheuristics. To a large extent, this has already been done in [2]. It was shown that *FS-ILS* would have won the CheSC (2011) competition if it were a contestant[5] and performs best on 3 of the 6 domains (see Table 2). To verify *FS-ILS*'s generalization to other problems, it was tested on 28 new instances (not used during its design/CHeSC). Its performance was compared to that of a publicly available implementation of *AdapHH* (the competition's winner) and was shown to be on par if not slightly better.

Currently, *FS-ILS* remains untested on 10 HyFlex instances,[6] which were excluded from [2] since no benchmark algorithms were available to evaluate its performance.[7] In this experiment we test *FS-ILS* and *AdapHH* 31 times on all 68 instances currently available in HyFlex. Rather than using some summary statistic, the comparison is done per instance, based on the median solution quality obtained. In addition we use a Mann-Whitney U test to determine whether the observed differences are significant (5% confidence).

algorithm	chesc	other	total
FS-ILS	19 (11)	20 (13)	39 (24)
=	1	4	5
AdapHH	10 (8)	14 (8)	24 (16)

Table 3: Comparison of FS-ILS to AdapHH

3.3.2 Results

Table 3 shows on how many of the HyFlex instances *FS-ILS* performs better than (or tied with) *AdapHH* (*total*), 30 of which were used during the CHeSC (2011) competition (*chesc*) and 38 that weren't (*other*). The number of significant differences are shown in brackets.

We see that neither of the methods performs best on all instances. *FS-ILS* performs better than *AdapHH* on 39 out of the 68 instances and ties for 5 instances. Furthermore, not only does it perform better for the majority (19) of the 30 *chesc* instances (on which *FS-ILS* was tested during design) it also performs better on the majority (20) of the 38 *other* instances. We find 40 of the 63 observed differences to be significant. *FS-ILS* performs significantly better than *AdapHH* on more instances than vice versa, for both *chesc* and *other* instance sets. These results provide further evidence of *FS-ILS*'s competitiveness.

4. RELATED RESEARCH

The term hyperheuristic was first used to denote a (meta-)heuristic iteratively selecting and applying heuristics from a given set of low-level heuristics in [8]. Since then a lot of research has been performed on hyperheuristics. [6] provides an extensive discussion of the origin and recent developments within the domain.

While the potential of hyperheuristics in more general problem-independent search was recognized early on [4], due to practical difficulties most methods focused on a single domain. The creation of the HyFlex framework [15] in 2010 has greatly simplified cross-domain benchmarking and has been used in the implementation of many selection hyperheuristics ever since. Most notably, HyFlex was used to support the CHeSC 2011 competition, and its winner *AdapHH* [14] can be considered state-of-the-art. Contemporary work [18] reviews 16 of the 20 CHeSC contestants and draws conclusions supporting the choices made in *FS-ILS*'s design. A downside of the HyFlex framework is that it is rather restrictive. In particular, too little information is available about candidate solutions/heuristics to properly apply reinforcement learning [9]. Various extensions to Hyflex [16, 17] have been proposed and implemented.

[5]Please note that this comparison is not entirely fair. To design FS-ILS information was used that was not available to the other contestants, i.e. the benchmark instances used during the competition and the performance of the other contestants.

[6]5 for both TSP and VRP domains

[7]For the 28 instances results for 8 benchmark algorithms were made available before the competition

Hyperheuristics follow a wide variety of designs. Traditionally they are iterative search strategies with a heuristic selection and solution acceptance stage ([3, 14]). However, other high-level search strategies have been developed recently. Iterated Local Search methods [3, 5, 7, 9] have been shown to outperform traditional search strategies in a similar setting on multiple occassions [3, 18]. Also evolutionary approaches [16], evolving a population of candidate solutions (vs. a single incumbent solution), and even (co-)evolving a population of hyperheuristics have been explored [13]. While evolutionary approaches present many interesting ideas, they tend to be complex and little evidence is provided to show they perform significantly better than simpler alternatives.

5. CONCLUSION

In this paper, we presented *FS-ILS*, a simple state-of-the-art Iterated Local Search selection hyperheuristic discovered using a semi-automated design approach [2]. We provide a detailed explanation and motivation of the design choices. In our experimental section, we first performed a parameter sensitivity analysis, showing that *FL-ILS* is largely robust to changes in its sole parameter. Subsequently we analyzed the presence of accidental complexity, showing that *FS-ILS* performs significantly better than simpler variants, motivating every design decision. Finally, we compared the performance of *FS-ILS* to that of the winner of the CHeSC competition on all HyFlex instances, providing further evidence of its competitiveness on this benchmark.

There are a vast number of metaheuristic methods. What is the value of yet another method? As a selection hyperheuristic, *FL-ILS* is an *off-the-peg* solution, and therefore readily applicable to new domains. Unlike other state-of-the-art methods, it is rather simple and therefore understandable and reproducible. E.g. using the information provided in this paper, *FS-ILS* can be reproduced in only a few hours, using about 200 lines of code.[8] In comparison, the publicly available implementation of *AdapHH* counts over 3000 lines of code.[9] These properties make *FS-ILS* an interesting starting point for future hyperheuristic research.

6. ACKNOWLEDGMENTS

The *FS-ILS* method was developed during Steven Adriaensen's master thesis, wherein Prof. Ann Nowé was promotor and Tim Brys supervisor. Currently, Steven Adriaensen and Tim Brys are funded by a Ph.D grant of the Research Foundation Flanders (FWO).

7. REFERENCES

[1] E. H. Aarts, J. H. Korst, and P. J. Van Laarhoven. Simulated annealing. *Local search in combinatorial optimization*, pages 91–120, 1997.

[2] S. Adriaensen, T. Brys, and A. Nowé. Designing reusable metaheuristic methods: A semi-automated approach. In *Evolutionary Computation (CEC), 2014 IEEE Congress on*. IEEE, 2014.

[3] E. Burke, T. Curtois, M. Hyde, G. Kendall, G. Ochoa, S. Petrovic, J. Vazquez-Rodriguez, and M. Gendreau. Iterated local search vs. hyper-heuristics: Towards general-purpose search algorithms. In *Evolutionary Computation (CEC), 2010 IEEE Congress on*, pages 1–8. IEEE, 2010.

[8] Code can be found at: https://github.com/Steven-Adriaensen/FS-ILS.

[9] To be fair, this does include some code non-essential to the optimization process. E.g. logging.

[4] E. Burke, G. Kendall, J. Newall, E. Hart, P. Ross, and S. Schulenburg. Hyper-heuristics: An emerging direction in modern search technology. *International series in operations research and management science*, pages 457–474, 2003.

[5] E. K. Burke, M. Gendreau, G. Ochoa, and J. D. Walker. Adaptive iterated local search for cross-domain optimisation. In *Proceedings of the 13th annual conference on Genetic and evolutionary computation*, pages 1987–1994. ACM, 2011.

[6] E. K. Burke, M. Hyde, G. Kendall, G. Ochoa, E. Ozcan, and R. Qu. Hyper-heuristics: A survey of the state of the art. *Journal of the Operational Research Society*, 64(12):1695–1724, 2013.

[7] C.-Y. Chan, F. Xue, W. Ip, and C. Cheung. A hyper-heuristic inspired by pearl hunting. In *Learning and Intelligent Optimization*, pages 349–353. Springer, 2012.

[8] P. Cowling, G. Kendall, and E. Soubeiga. A hyperheuristic approach to scheduling a sales summit. In *Practice and Theory of Automated Timetabling III*, pages 176–190. Springer, 2001.

[9] L. Di Gaspero and T. Urli. A reinforcement learning approach for the cross-domain heuristic search challenge. In *Proceedings of the 9th Metaheuristics International Conference (MIC 2011), Udine, Italy*, 2011.

[10] H. H. Hoos and T. Stützle. *Stochastic local search: Foundations & applications*. Morgan Kaufmann, 2004.

[11] P.-C. Hsiao, T.-C. Chiang, and L.-C. Fu. A variable neighborhood search-based hyperheuristic for cross-domain optimization problems in chesc 2011 competition. In *Fifty-Third Conference of OR Society (OR53), Nottingham, UK*, 2011.

[12] G. A. Kochenberger et al. *Handbook in Metaheuristics*. Springer, 2003.

[13] D. Meignan. An evolutionary programming hyper-heuristic with coevolution for chesc'11. In *CHeSC 2011*.

[14] M. Misir, K. Verbeeck, P. De Causmaecker, and G. Vanden Berghe. An intelligent hyper-heuristic framework for chesc 2011. In *Learning and Intelligent OptimizatioN*, 2012.

[15] G. Ochoa, M. Hyde, T. Curtois, J. Vazquez-Rodriguez, J. Walker, M. Gendreau, G. Kendall, B. McCollum, A. Parkes, S. Petrovic, et al. Hyflex: a benchmark framework for cross-domain heuristic search. *Evolutionary Computation in Combinatorial Optimization*, pages 136–147, 2012.

[16] G. Ochoa, J. Walker, M. Hyde, and T. Curtois. Adaptive evolutionary algorithms and extensions to the hyflex hyper-heuristic framework. In *Parallel Problem Solving from Nature-PPSN XII*, pages 418–427. Springer, 2012.

[17] W. Van Onsem and B. Demoen. Parhyflex: A framework for parallel hyper-heuristics.

[18] W. Van Onsem, B. Demoen, and P. De Causmaecker. Hyper-criticism: A critical reflection on todays hyper-heuristics. In *Proceedings of the 28th Anual Conference of the Operational Research Society*, volume 28, 2014.

[19] D. H. Wolpert and W. G. Macready. No free lunch theorems for optimization. *Evolutionary Computation, IEEE Transactions on*, 1(1):67–82, 1997.

A Grammatical Evolution based Hyper-Heuristic for the Automatic Design of Split Criteria

Márcio P. Basgalupp
Instituto de Ciência e Tecnologia
Universidade Federal de São Paulo
S. J. dos Campos, SP, Brazil
basgalupp@unifesp.br

Rodrigo C. Barros
Faculdade de Informática
Pontifícia Universidade Católica do Rio Grande do Sul
Porto Alegre, RS, Brazil
rodrigo.barros@pucrs.br

Tiago Barabasz
Instituto de Ciência e Tecnologia
Universidade Federal de São Paulo
S. J. dos Campos, SP, Brazil
tbarabasz@unifesp.br

ABSTRACT

Top-down induction of decision trees (TDIDT) is a powerful method for data classification. A major issue in TDIDT is the decision on which attribute should be selected for dividing the nodes in subsets, creating the tree. For performing such a task, decision trees make use of a split criterion, which is usually an information-theory based measure. Apparently, there is no free-lunch regarding decision-tree split criteria, as is the case of most things in machine learning. Each application may benefit from a distinct split criterion, and the problem we pose here is how to identify the suitable split criterion for each possible application that may emerge. We propose in this paper a grammatical evolution algorithm for automatically generating split criteria through a context-free grammar. We name our new approach ESC-GE (Evolutionary Split Criteria with Grammatical Evolution). It is empirically evaluated on public gene expression datasets, and we compare its performance with state-of-the-art split criteria, namely the information gain and gain ratio. Results show that ESC-GE outperforms the baseline criteria in the domain of gene expression data, indicating its effectiveness for automatically designing tailor-made split criteria.

Categories and Subject Descriptors

I.2.6 [**Induction and Knowledge Acquisition**]: Learning

General Terms

Algorithms

Keywords

Grammatical Evolution, Hyper-Heuristics, Split Criterion.

1. INTRODUCTION

Top-down induction of decision trees is a powerful method for data classification. Given a training dataset, decision trees are created by recursively dividing the input space such that the training data examples in each partition can be classified with increasingly smaller uncertainty. The process continues until a given stopping condition is satisfied — usually, the tree growth stops when all training data examples in a given node belong to the same class [24].

A major issue in top-down induction of decision trees is the decision on which attribute should be selected for dividing the node in subsets at each step of the recursive algorithm. For the case of *axis-parallel* decision trees (also known as *univariate*), the problem is to choose the attribute that better discriminates the input data. A decision rule based on such an attribute is thus generated, and the input data is filtered according to the outcomes of this rule. For performing such a task, decision trees make use of a *split criterion*, which is usually an information-theory based measure commonly regarded as an *impurity function*. Such a function examines heuristically the possible tests over the training dataset attributes, locally optimizing the best node splits by analyzing the estimates of the class distributions.

The rationale behind well-known split criteria such as the *information gain* [22] or the *gain ratio* [23] is that one should seek to minimize the class entropy in a given node in order to maximize the acquired gain in information. The value of entropy decreases as the probability distribution of the classes in a node become more heterogeneous. Therefore, the selected attribute is the one that generates a partition in which the examples are distributed less randomly over the classes [9].

However, each split criterion in the literature has disadvantages. For instance, the information gain tends to favor attributes with more values [15]. The χ^2 criterion [18] generates very large trees, since it favors binary attributes that lead to very narrow trees with great depth. The gain ratio criterion [23], in turn, may be undefined for some cases, and it favors attributes with highly skewed value-frequency [33]. The Gini index [5] also shares the disadvantage of being bias towards multi-valued and highly-skewed attributes.

Apparently, there is *no free-lunch* regarding decision-tree split criteria, as is the case of most things in machine learning. In the recent years, researchers have investigated hyper-heuristic approaches for developing customized solutions that can be reused in several problems. Within the machine learning literature, we can cite the work of Pappa and Freitas [21], which proposed a genetic programming based hyper-heuristic to automatically design full rule induction

GECCO'14, July 12–16, 2014, Vancouver, BC, Canada.

http://dx.doi.org/10.1145/2576768.2598327

algorithms. Similarly, the work of Barros et al. [2, 3] proposed a hyper-heuristic to automatically design full decision-tree induction algorithms. Both studies aimed at avoiding the *no free-lunch theorem* by customizing solutions to particular application domains.

Bearing in mind the strategies above-mentioned, and also the fact that each application domain may benefit from a distinct decision-tree split criterion, the problem we pose here is how to identify the suitable criterion for each possible application that may emerge. Since the manual design of tailored split criteria is unfeasible, given the huge amount of different existing applications, we propose in this paper a *grammatical evolution* (GE) based hyper-heuristic for automatically generating split criteria tailored to particular application domains.

This study goes beyond the work of Barros et al. [2, 3] considering that it proposes the automatic construction of a building block of decision-tree induction algorithms (the split criterion) instead of selecting and combining existing building blocks, enhancing the granularity level of the hyper-heuristic. Since GE is a grammar-based evolutionary algorithm, our novel method incorporates knowledge regarding the problem of finding the best split criterion in a context-free grammar. We name our approach ESC-GE (Evolutionary Split Criteria through Grammatical Evolution).

This paper is organized as follows. Section 2 describes related work in split criteria for TDIDT. Section 3 presents ESC-GE, our new approach for the automatic generation of split criteria. Section 4 details the methodology employed during the experiments, which are in turn presented in Section 5. We end this paper with our conclusions and future work suggestions in Section 6.

2. RELATED WORK

In this section, we make use of the following notation. $\mathbf{X}$ is the set of N training instances, a_i is the ith predictive attribute of $\mathbf{X}$, and y is the class vector with k rows (classes).

The most well-known split criteria in the literature are based on information-theory, following the concept of Shannon's entropy [26]. Entropy is known to be a unique function which satisfies the four axioms of uncertainty. It represents the average amount of information when coding each class into a codeword with ideal length according to its probability. Some interesting facts regarding entropy are:

- For a fixed number of classes, entropy increases as the probability distribution of classes becomes more uniform;
- If the probability distribution of classes is uniform, entropy increases logarithmically as the number of classes in a sample increases;
- If a partition induced on a set $\mathbf{X}$ by an attribute a_j is a refinement of a partition induced by a_i, then the entropy of the partition induced by a_j is never higher than the entropy of the partition induced by a_i (and it is only equal if the class distribution is kept identical after partitioning). This means that progressively refining a set in sub-partitions will continuously decrease the entropy value, regardless of the class distribution achieved after partitioning a set.

The first split criterion that arose based on entropy is the *global mutual information* (GMI) [11, 25, 28]. Ching et al. [8] propose the use of GMI as a tool for supervised discretization. They name it *class-attribute mutual information*, though the criterion is exactly the same. GMI is bounded by zero (when a_i and y are completely independent) and its maximum value is $max(\log_2 |a_i|, \log_2 k)$ (when there is a maximum correlation between a_i and y). The authors reckon this measure is biased towards attributes with many distinct values.

Information gain [7, 12, 22] is another example of measure based on Shannon's entropy, being employed in the well-known decision-tree induction algorithm ID3 [22]. The goal of information gain is to maximize the reduction in entropy due to splitting each individual node. Wilks [31] has proved that as $N \to \infty$, $2 \times N \times GMI$ (or similarly replacing GMI by information gain) approximates the χ^2 distribution. This measure is often regarded as the *G statistics* [17, 18]. Instead of using the value of this measure as calculated, we can compute the probability of such a value occurring from the χ^2 distribution on the assumption that there is no association between the attribute and the classes. The higher the calculated value, the less likely it is to have occurred given the assumption. The advantage of using such a measure is making use of the levels of significance it provides for deciding whether to include an attribute at all.

Quinlan [22] acknowledges the fact that the information gain is biased towards attributes with many values. This is a consequence of the previously mentioned particularity regarding entropy, in which further refinement leads to a decrease in its value. Quinlan proposes a solution for this matter called *gain ratio* [23]. It basically consists of normalizing the information gain by the entropy of the attribute being tested. The gain ratio compensates the decrease in entropy in multiple partitions by dividing the information gain by the attribute self-entropy. Nevertheless, the gain ratio has two deficiencies: (i) it may be undefined (*i.e.*, the value of self-entropy may be zero); and (ii) it may choose attributes with very low self-entropy but not with high gain. For solving these issues, Quinlan suggests first calculating the information gain for all attributes, and then calculating the gain ratio only for those cases in which the information gain value is above the average value of all attributes.

Several variations of the gain ratio have been proposed, such as the *normalized gain* [14] and the *average gain* [30], though the gain ratio is still considered the state-of-the-art in the split criteria literature, being employed in the well-known decision-tree induction algorithm C4.5 [23].

With respect to similar hyper-heuristic approaches, we can cite the work of Barros et al. [1–4] called HEAD-DT, which is a hyper-heuristic that automatically designs full decision-tree induction algorithms. HEAD-DT, however, does not generate novel split criteria. It simply selects from a fixed list of 15 available criteria in the literature. In a similar note, the work of Vella et al. [29] proposes a hyper-heuristic that evolves rules to allow the choice of existing split criteria. An example of rule is: "if x% of the attributes have an entropy value below a given threshold, then use the existing split criterion Y to partition the nodes in subsets". Therefore, the work of Vella et al. [29] also does not generate novel split criteria through genetic programming. To the best of our knowledge, this work is the first to propose the automatic generation of split criteria through a grammatical evolution based hyper-heuristic.

3. ESC-GE

Evolutionary Split Criteria through Grammatical Evolution (ESC-GE) is a hyper-heuristic that automatically designs split criteria for top-down decision-tree induction algorithms. Hyper-heuristics (HHs) operate on a different level of generality from metaheuristics. Instead of guiding the search towards near-optimal solutions for a given problem, a HH approach operates on the heuristic level, guiding the search towards the near-optimal heuristic that can be further applied to different application domains. HHs are therefore assumed to be problem-independent and can be easily utilized by experts and non-experts as well [20]. It can be seen as a high-level methodology which, when faced with a particular problem instance or class of instances, and a number of low-level heuristics, automatically designs a suitable combination of the provided components to effectively solve the respective problem(s) [6].

In the particular case of ESC-GE, it is considered a HH approach since it automatically designs a split criterion (mathematical function) that is problem-independent, *i.e.*, such a function can be used by a top-down decision-tree induction algorithm to split data from any classification dataset. Nevertheless, the underlying assumption of ESC-GE is that tailor-made split criteria are capable of being more effective than a single general-use split criterion. For instance, instead of using the same split criterion for all classification datasets, ESC-GE is trained with datasets that share a particular application domain, under the hypothesis that the automatically-designed split criterion that was tailored to such a domain will be more effective than traditional criteria such as the information gain and gain ratio.

ESC-GE is guided by a grammatical evolution search (GE) [19], which is considered the state-of-the-art among the available grammar-based genetic programming techniques [16]. GE tries to mimic the process of generating a protein from the genetic material of an organism. Individuals are generated by binary strings (codons) equivalent to the double helix of DNA; the integer string decoded from the binary string is the equivalent of the transcription of DNA to RNA; finally, the mapping of the integer string to the grammar production rules and the subsequent generation of a computer program (or function) is the equivalent of the translation of RNA to the sequence of amino acids that are contained within the protein molecule. Figure 1 depicts this rationale.

The remainder of this section presents the main features of ESC-GE: its grammar (Section 3.1), its genetic operators (Section 3.2), and its fitness function (Section 3.3).

3.1 Grammar

Figure 2 presents the context-free grammar employed by ESC-GE in order to generate split criteria for TDIDT. The non-terminals and terminals are detailed as follows.

Non-terminals:

- +: the sum of two scalars.
- −: the subtraction of two scalars.
- ∗: the multiplication of two scalars.
- /: the protected division of two scalars. The denominator cannot be 0 (zero).
- *log*: the protected log_{10} function over a non-zero scalar.
- *sin*: the sin function over a scalar.
- *cos*: the cos function over a scalar.

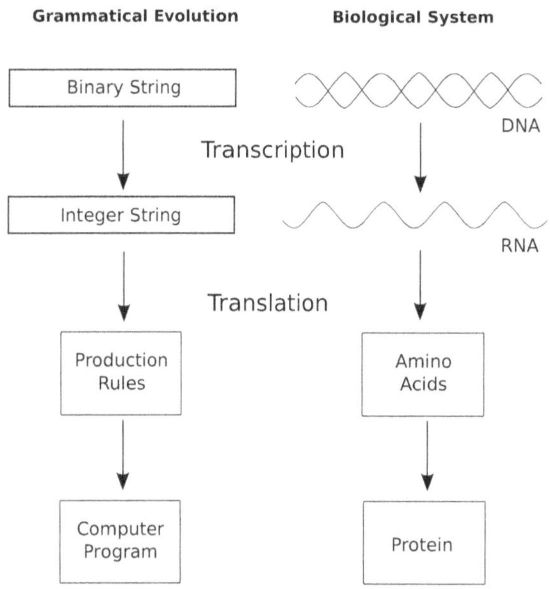

Figure 1: Comparison between the GE system and a biological genetic system. Adapted from [19].

```
1) <start>::= <esc>
2) <esc>::= (+ <esc> <esc>) | (- <esc> <esc>) | (/ <esc>
<esc>) | (* <esc> <esc> ) | (log <esc>) | (sum <vector>)
| (numClass) | (numEx) | (sin <esc>) | (cos <esc>) |
(perBagPerClass)
3) <vector> ::= (perClass) | (perBag) | (** <esc> <vec-
tor>) | (// <vector> <esc>)
```

Figure 2: Context-free grammar for generating split criteria.

- *sum*: the summation over a vector. The result is a scalar resulting from the sum of all the elements of the vector.
- ∗∗: the multiplication of a scalar and a vector. Each element of the vector is multiplied by the scalar, resulting in a new vector.
- //: similar to the (**) operator, but now resulting in a new vector in which each element is divided by the scalar. Scalars are not allowed to be 0 (zero).

Terminals:

- numEx: scalar representing the number of instances in the current node.
- perBag: vector representing the number of instances in each partition (bag) of the current node.
- perClass: vector representing the number of instances from each class of the current node.
- perBagPerClass: matrix representing the number of instances in each partition grouped by their corresponding class.

Given the grammar in Figure 2, ESC-GE evolves a function S within the following equation:

$$criterion = (1 - unknownRate) \times \sum_{p=1}^{np} \sum_{c=1}^{k} S \qquad (1)$$

where $unknownRate$ is the percentage of missing values, np is the number of partitions (bags), and k is the number of classes. Note that ESC-GE only evolves function S in Eq. 1, whereas the other terms are fixed and *criterion* should be maximized. The first term ($1 - unknownRate$) simply weights the criterion proportionally to its amount of missing values. ESC-GE avoids the further complexity of evolving the $\sum$ operators by fixing both sums over partitions and classes. The evolution of a more detailed split criterion with non-fixed $\sum$ operators is left for future work.

3.2 Genetic Operators

In the beginning of the evolutionary process, the individuals of the initial population in ESC-GE are randomly initialized. They have variable length, with a minimum size of five codons each, and a chance of 85% that new codons will be incrementally added to the individual. Each codon is comprised of 1 byte (8 bits), which is randomly generated.

To evolve the current generation of individuals, the following mutually-exclusive genetic operations can be performed: crossover, mutation, and duplication. Crossover has a chance of 90% of being performed, and both duplication and mutation have a chance of 5% of being applied. These operations are executed until all individuals of the new population are generated.

For crossover to be performed, two individuals are chosen via tournament selection. After the individuals are selected, they take part in a standard one-point crossover operation, generating two children. In the duplication process, one individual is also selected using tournament selection, and then two codons of the individual are randomly selected, copying all codons located between these two selected codons to the end of the individual. Finally, mutation requires one individual to be selected via tournament selection. This individual is traversed codon by codon, where each codon has a 10% probability of having its value replaced by a randomly-generated 8-bit value. The three operators are illustrated in Figure 3.

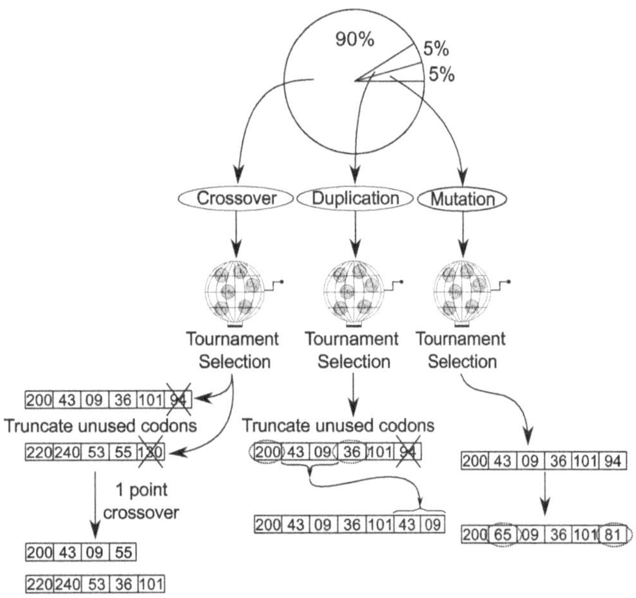

Figure 3: ESC-GE genetic operators.

3.3 Fitness Function

In ESC-GE, each individual represents a possible split criterion to be used in TDIDT. After each individual is decoded into a function, we fit such a function into the body of J48 (the Java version of C4.5) [32]. In order to computer the fitness of each individual, we evaluate the corresponding modified version of J48 in a *meta-training set*. In contrast, a *meta-test set* is used to assess the quality of the evolved split measure function, which is the best individual produced by ESC-GE. Note that there is no overlapping of instances between the meta-training and meta-test sets, which allows us to measure the generalization ability of the evolved split criterion.

The fitness evaluation process is based on [1–3], where we have multiple datasets comprising the meta-training set, and multiple (but different) datasets comprising the meta-test set. In this approach, each dataset is described by a different set of predictive attributes, so each dataset corresponds to a different classification problem.

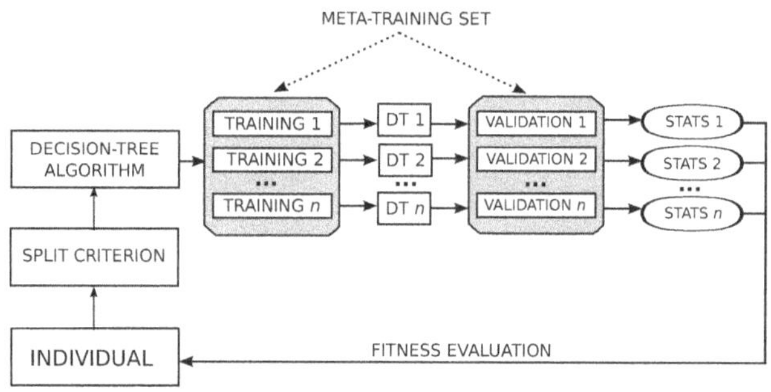

Figure 4: ESC-GE fitness evaluation.

In Figure 4, we can observe how the fitness evaluation of a split criterion occurs. First, a given individual is mapped into its corresponding split criterion, and then it is incorporated into a decision-tree induction algorithm. Next, each dataset from the meta-training set is partitioned into a training set and a validation set — typical values are 70% for training and 30% for validation [32]. The term "validation set" is used in here instead of "test set" to avoid confusion with the meta-test set, and also due to the fact that we are using the performance measure of a candidate split criterion on those validation sets to guide the evolutionary search for a better function. The same cannot be done with test sets, which are exclusively used for assessing the predictive performance of a decision-tree algorithm using the evolved function as split criterion.

After dividing each dataset from the meta-training set into "training" and "validation", we induce a decision tree for each training set available. For evaluating the predictive performance of these decision trees, we use the corresponding validation sets. Statistics regarding the predictive performance and the size of each decision tree are recorded (*e.g.*, accuracy, F-Measure, precision, recall, total number of nodes/leaves, etc.), and can be used individually or combined as the fitness function of ESC-GE. In this work, we use as fitness function the average F-Measure of the decision trees generated by a given individual for each dataset in the meta-training set. The well-known F-Measure (also known as F-score or F1 score) is the harmonic mean of precision and recall, as shown in the equations below:

$$precision = \frac{tp}{tp + fp} \quad (2)$$

$$recall = \frac{tp}{tp + fn} \quad (3)$$

$$fmeasure = 2 \times \frac{precision \times recall}{precision + recall} \quad (4)$$

$$Fitness = \frac{1}{n} \sum_{i=1}^{n} fmeasure_i \quad (5)$$

where tp (tn) is the numbers of true positives (negatives) in the validation set, fp (fn) is the numbers of false positives (negatives) in the validation set, $fmeasure_i$ is the F-Measure obtained in dataset i and n is the total number of datasets in the meta-training set.

These equations are directly applicable in the case of binary classification problems, *i.e.*, the case where a dataset has only two classes: positive and negative. Nevertheless, they can be trivially extended to multi-class problems. For instance, we can compute the value of a measure for each class — assuming each class to be the "positive" class in turn, and considering all the other classes as the "negative class" — and then compute a (weighted) average of the per-class measure.

Although accuracy is still a very popular measure of predictive performance, it is important to notice that it tends to be a misleading measure in datasets with a very unbalanced class distribution. For instance, suppose we are classifying a dataset whose class distribution is very skewed: 10% of the instances belong to the positive class and 90% to the negative class. An algorithm that always classifies instances as belonging to the negative class would achieve 90% of accuracy, even though it never predicts the positive class. In this case, assuming that the positive class is equally important to (or even more so than) the negative class, we would prefer an algorithm with a somewhat lower accuracy value, but which correctly predicts some instances as belonging to the rare positive class.

Having in mind that most datasets used in our experiments have very unbalanced class distributions, the average F-Measure is a more suitable fitness function than, say, the average accuracy, since it is well-known that the F-measure copes much better with unbalanced class-distribution problems than the accuracy measure.

4. METHODOLOGY

In this section, we present the methodology employed during the empirical analysis. We present the baseline split criteria and ESC-GE parameters in Section 4.1, whereas the public gene expression datasets are described in Section 4.2 and the statistical analysis process in Section 4.3.

4.1 Baseline Criteria and Parameters

We compare the split criterion generated by ESC-GE to well-known and widely-used entropy-based decision-tree split criteria: information gain [22], and gain ratio [23]. All the criteria employed were plugged into the J48 algorithm [32], in order to allow a fair comparison among them.

Table 1 shows the user-defined parameter values used in ESC-GE. No attempt to tune these parameter values was made. Parameter optimization is a topic left for future research.

Table 1: Configurable ESC-GE parameters.

Parameter	Value
Initialization Probability	85%
Number of Individuals	100
Minimum Individual Size	5
Number of Generations	20
Crossover Probability	90%
Duplication Probability	5%
Mutation Probability	5%
Mutation per Codon Probability	10%
Tournament Size	3
Elite	2

4.2 Datasets

The empirical analysis presented in this paper is based on 20 public datasets from the gene expression application domain [27]: alizadeh-v1, alizadeh-v2, alizadeh-v3, armstrong-v1, armstrong-v2, bittner, chen, chowdary, golub-v1, gordon, khan, lapointe-v1, lapointe-v2, liang, nutt-v3, pomeroy-v1, pomeroy-v2, ramaswamy, shipp-v1, and tomlins. In brief, microarray technology enables expression level measurement for thousands of genes in parallel, given a biological tissue of interest. Once combined, results from a set of microarray experiments produce a gene expression dataset. The datasets employed here are related to different types or subtypes of cancer, *e.g.*, patients with prostate, lung, skin, and other types of cancer. The classification task refers to labeling different examples (instances) according to their gene (attribute) expression levels.

Table 2 provides details about these datasets. They were randomly divided into two groups: A and B. Datasets belonging to A were used as the meta-training set, whereas datasets belonging to B were used as the meta-test set.

Table 2: Summary of the 20 Gene Expression datasets. For each dataset, we present the total number of instances, total number of attributes, imbalanced ratio (rate between over- and under-represented class), and total number of classes.

	Data Set	# Instances	# Attributes	IR	# Classes
	alizadeh-v3	62	2093	0.43	4
	armstrong-v1	72	1081	0.5	2
A	lapointe-v2	110	2496	0.27	4
	nutt-v3	22	1152	0.47	2
	tomlins	104	2315	0.38	5
	alizadeh-v1	42	1095	1	2
	alizadeh-v2	62	2093	0.21	3
	armstrong-v2	72	2194	0.71	3
	bittner	38	2201	1	2
	chen	179	85	0.72	2
	chowdary	104	182	0.68	2
	golub-v1	72	1868	0.53	2
B	gordon	181	1626	0.21	2
	khan	83	1069	0.38	4
	lapointe-v1	69	1625	0.28	3
	liang	37	1411	0.11	3
	pomeroy-v1	34	857	0.36	2
	pomeroy-v2	42	1379	0.4	5
	ramaswamy	190	1363	0.33	14
	shipp-v1	77	798	0.33	2

4.3 Statistical Analysis

To evaluate the statistical significance of the experimental results, we present the results of statistical tests by following the approach proposed by Demšar [10]. In brief, this approach seeks to compare multiple algorithms on multiple datasets, and it is based on the use of the Friedman test with a corresponding post-hoc test. The Friedman test is a non-parametric counterpart of ANOVA, as follows. Let R_i^j be the rank of the jth of k algorithms on the ith of N datasets. The Friedman test compares the average ranks of algorithms, $R_j = \frac{1}{N}\sum_i R_i^j$. The Friedman statistic, given by:

$$\chi_F^2 = \frac{12N}{k(k+1)}\left[\sum_j R_j^2 - \frac{k(k+1)^2}{4}\right] \tag{6}$$

is distributed according to χ_F^2 with $k-1$ degrees of freedom, when N and k are large enough.

Iman and Davenport [13] showed that Friedman's χ_F^2 is undesirably conservative and derived an adjusted statistic:

$$F_f = \frac{(N-1)\times\chi_F^2}{N\times(k-1)-\chi_F^2} \tag{7}$$

which is distributed according to the F-distribution with $k-1$ and $(k-1)(N-1)$ degrees of freedom.

If the null hypothesis of similar performances is rejected, we proceed with the Nemenyi post-hoc test for pairwise comparisons. The performance of two classifiers is significantly different if their corresponding average ranks differ by at least the critical difference

$$CD = q_\alpha\sqrt{\frac{k(k+1)}{6N}} \tag{8}$$

where critical values q_α are based on the Studentized range statistic divided by $\sqrt{2}$.

5. RESULTS AND DISCUSSION

Table 3 shows the predictive accuracy values for ESC-GE, information gain, and gain ratio. It presents the average accuracy over a 5-fold cross-validation procedure. Observe that the decision-tree induction algorithm that employs the split criterion automatically designed by ESC-GE generates trees with the best accuracy values in 10 out of 15 datasets.

Table 3: Average accuracy of J48 with its corresponding split criterion.

	ESC-GE	Info Gain	Gain Ratio
alizadeh-v1	**0.76**	0.69	0.69
alizadeh-v2	**0.95**	0.90	0.90
armstrong-v2	0.75	**0.78**	0.74
bittner	**0.76**	0.53	0.55
chen	**0.91**	0.83	0.86
chowdary	**0.91**	0.89	0.89
golub-v1	**0.93**	0.76	0.83
gordon	**0.96**	0.93	0.94
khan	0.83	0.82	**0.88**
lapointe-v1	0.70	**0.77**	0.67
liang	**0.78**	0.70	0.70
pomeroy-v1	0.79	**0.88**	**0.88**
pomeroy-v2	**0.60**	0.52	0.57
ramaswamy	0.54	0.56	**0.62**
shipp-v1	**0.79**	0.74	0.77
Number of victories	10	2	3
Average Rank	1.47	2.43	2.1

To evaluate the statistical significance of the accuracy results, we calculated the average Friedman rank for ESC-GE, information gain, and gain ratio: 1.47, 2.43, and 2.1, respectively. The average rank suggests that ESC-GE outperforms the baseline split criteria regarding predictive accuracy. The calculation of Iman's F statistic resulted in $F_f = 4.45$. Critical value of $F(k-1,(k-1)(n-1)) = F(2,28)$ for $\alpha = 0.05$ is 3.34. Since $F_f > F_{0.05}(2,28)$ $(4.45 > 3.34)$, the null-hypothesis is rejected. We proceed with a post-hoc Nemenyi test to find which method provides better results in a pairwise fashion. The critical difference $CD = 0.86$. The differences between the average rank of ESC-GE and the rank of the baseline split measures are 0.96 and 0.63, respectively. Given that the difference between ESC-GE and information gain is greater than the CD value, we can confidently argue that the performance of the split criterion evolved by ESC-GE is significantly better than the performance of information gain. Even though there is no significant difference between ESC-GE and the remaining criterion (gain ratio), we can observe that only the split criterion evolved by ESC-GE outperforms another measure with statistical significance regarding accuracy.

Table 4 shows the F-measures values for ESC-GE, information gain, and gain ratio. ESC-GE generates the best trees regarding F-Measure once again in 10 out of 15 datasets, whereas both information gain and gain ratio do it in 3 datasets. In the pomeroy-v1 dataset, the best F-Measure values are provided by both information gain and gain ratio. In terms of statistical analysis, the computed value of $F_f = 4.45$. Since $F_f > F_{0.05}(2,28)$ $(4.45 > 3.34)$, the null-hypothesis is rejected, and thus we can argue that there is significant differences among the criteria regarding F-measure. If we proceed with a post-hoc Nemenyi test, the critical difference is once again $CD = 0.86$, and we can observe that the difference between ESC-GE and information gain (0.96) is greater than CD $(0.96 > 0.86)$. It is important to notice that ESC-GE once again achieves the lowest average rank, indicating it is the most suitable option for the domain of gene expression data.

Table 4: Average F-Measure of J48 with its corresponding split criterion.

	ESC-GE	Info Gain	Gain Ratio
alizadeh-v1	**0.76**	0.69	0.69
alizadeh-v2	**0.95**	0.90	0.90
armstrong-v2	0.75	**0.78**	0.74
bittner	**0.76**	0.52	0.55
chen	**0.91**	0.83	0.86
chowdary	**0.91**	0.89	0.89
golub-v1	**0.93**	0.76	0.83
gordon	**0.96**	0.93	0.94
khan	0.83	0.82	**0.88**
lapointe-v1	0.70	**0.77**	0.67
liang	**0.76**	0.69	0.69
pomeroy-v1	0.79	**0.88**	**0.88**
pomeroy-v2	**0.57**	0.49	0.54
ramaswamy	0.54	0.57	**0.61**
shipp-v1	**0.80**	0.75	0.77
Number of victories	10	3	3
Average Rank	1.47	2.43	2.1

Figure 5 shows the Nemenyi's critical diagram, as suggested by Demšar [10]. In this diagram, a horizontal line represents the axis on which we plot the average rank values of the methods. The axis is turned so that the lowest (best) ranks are to the right since we perceive the methods on the right side as better. When comparing all the criteria

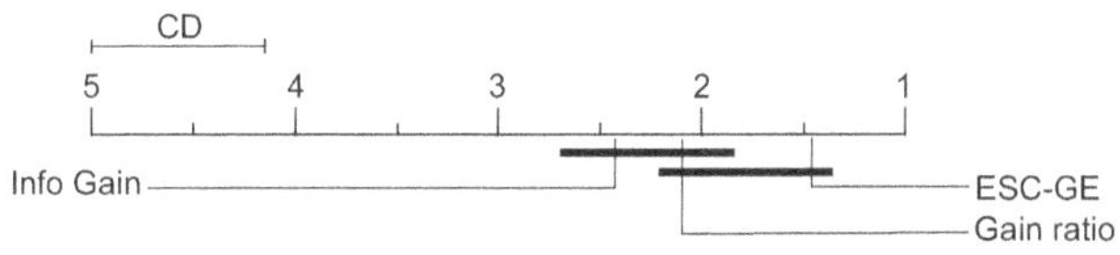

Figure 5: Critical diagram: Accuracy and F-measure.

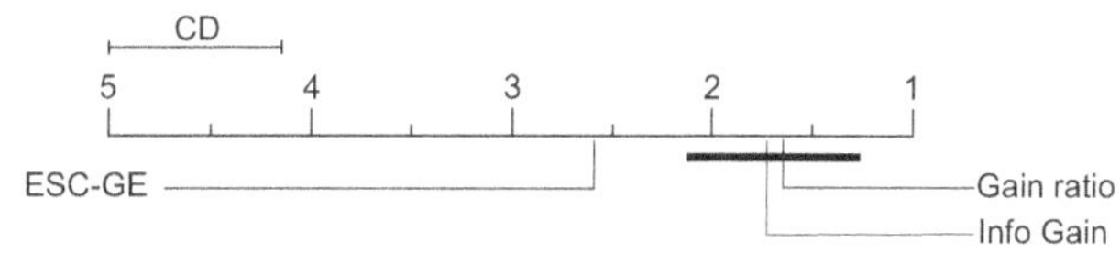

Figure 6: Critical diagram: Tree Size.

against each other, we connect the groups of criteria that are not significantly different through a bold horizontal line. We also show the critical difference given by the Nemenyi's test above the graph. Figure 5 shows both the results of accuracy and F-Measure (since the ranking values are the same). We can see that ESC-GE is connected only to gain ratio (no significant difference), though their difference is almost at the limit of the critical difference. ESC-GE is significantly better than information gain (no line connecting them), whereas gain ratio is not.

Finally, Table 5 shows the size of trees generated by J48 with the criterion evolved by ESC-GE, and also with the baseline criteria information gain and gain ratio. Results show that both information gain and gain ratio generate smaller trees in most datasets, whereas ESC-GE generates the smaller tree in only 3 datasets.

Table 5: Average tree size of J48 with its corresponding split criterion.

	ESC-GE	Info Gain	Gain Ratio
alizadeh-2000-v1	22.8	6.20	**5.80**
alizadeh-2000-v2	8.20	**5.00**	**5.00**
armstrong-2002-v2	10.2	**8.20**	9.00
bittner-2000	15.6	**6.20**	**6.20**
chen-2002	**11.2**	17.0	18.4
chowdary-2006	**9.40**	10.2	9.80
golub-1999-v1	9.80	**6.00**	6.20
gordon-2002	15.6	8.20	**7.20**
khan-2001	26.2	10.6	**9.80**
lapointe-2004-v1	14.0	10.4	**10.2**
liang-2005	5.60	**5.00**	**5.00**
pomeroy-2002-v1	12.2	**6.40**	**6.40**
pomeroy-2002-v2	70.8	**11.4**	11.6
ramaswamy-2001	**11.0**	57.2	55.4
shipp-2002-v1	17.4	**8.80**	9.40
Number of victories	3	8	8
Average Rank	2.6	1.73	1.67

Regarding the statistical analysis, the computed value of $F_f = 5.21$. Since $F_f > F_{0.05}(2, 28)$ $(5.21 > 3.34)$, the null-hypothesis is rejected. Once again, we proceed with a post-hoc Nemenyi test, and the critical difference $CD = 0.86$. The differences between the average rank of ESC-GE and the baseline split measures – information gain and gain ratio – are 0.87 and 0.93, respectively. Thus, we can assert that both gain ratio and information gain generate decision trees significantly smaller than the ones generated by ESC-GE. It is also important to note that there is no significant differences between the baseline split criteria in terms of tree size (see the critical diagram in Figure 6).

The fact that two baseline split criteria generate smaller trees than ESC-GE should not be a concern, since smaller trees are only preferable in scenarios where the predictive performance of the models is similar. The analysis previously presented clearly indicates that ESC-GE generates trees that outperform the baselines regarding predictive performance in terms of both accuracy and F-Measure. The Occam's razor assumption that among competitive hypotheses, the simpler is preferred, does not apply in this case.

The split criterion evolved by ESC-GE is presented in Eq. 9:

$$f = -N \times \sum_{p=1}^{np} \sum_{c=1}^{k} \frac{1}{(N - i_{p,c})} \times \frac{1}{i_{p,c}} \qquad (9)$$

where $i_{p,c}$ is the number of instances in partition p that belong to class c. We plan on further studying this criterion to verify its boundary values and real applicability in other domains.

6. CONCLUSION AND FUTURE WORK

In this work, we presented ESC-GE, a hyper-heuristic grammatical evolution algorithm that automatically generates split criteria for a particular application of top-down induction of decision trees. Since the human manual approach for designing tailor-made split criteria for every emerging application domain of decision trees would be unfeasible, we believe that the evolutionary search of ESC-GE constitutes a robust and efficient solution for the problem.

We performed a thorough experimental analysis in which the split criterion designed by ESC-GE was compared to state-of-the-art split criteria information gain [22] and gain ratio [23] in 20 public gene expression datasets. We assessed the performance of ESC-GE's evolved criterion through 2 different performance measures, accuracy and F-Measure, and also a complexity measure, tree size. The experimental analysis suggested that ESC-GE can generate a criterion which outperforms both information gain and gain ratio in terms of predictive performance, though generating significantly larger trees. Bearing in mind that an accurate prediction system is widely preferred over a less-accurate (but simpler) system, we believe that ESC-GE arises as an effective alternative for generating tailor-made split criteria for future applications of decision trees.

As future work, we intend to enhance ESC-GE's grammar so it can generate more complex criteria. Also, we intend to develop a multi-objective fitness function, allowing the trade-off between predictive performance and parsimony. Optimizing the evolutionary parameters of ESC-GE is also a topic left for future research.

Acknowledgment

The authors would like to thank Coordenação de Aperfeiçoamento de Pessoal de Nível Superior (CAPES), Conselho Nacional de Desenvolvimento Científico e Tecnológico (CNPq) and Fundação de Amparo à Pesquisa do Estado de São Paulo (FAPESP) for funding this research.

7. REFERENCES

[1] R. C. Barros, M. P. Basgalupp, A. C. P. L. F. de Carvalho, and A. A. Freitas. A hyper-heuristic evolutionary algorithm for automatically designing decision-tree algorithms. In *14th Genetic and Evolutionary Computation Conference (GECCO 2012)*, pages 1237–1244, 2012.

[2] R. C. Barros, M. P. Basgalupp, A. C. P. L. F. de Carvalho, and A. A. Freitas. Automatic Design of Decision-Tree Algorithms with Evolutionary Algorithms. *Evolutionary Computation*, 21(4), 2013.

[3] R. C. Barros, M. P. Basgalupp, A. A. Freitas, and A. C. P. L. F. de Carvalho. Evolutionary Design of Decision-Tree Algorithms Tailored to Microarray Gene Expression Data Sets. *IEEE Transactions on Evolutionary Computation*, in press, 2014.

[4] R. C. Barros, A. T. Winck, K. S. Machado, M. P. Basgalupp, A. C. P. L. F. de Carvalho, D. D. Ruiz, and O. S. de Souza. Automatic design of decision-tree induction algorithms tailored to flexible-receptor docking data. *BMC Bioinformatics*, 13, 2012.

[5] L. Breiman, J. H. Friedman, R. A. Olshen, and C. J. Stone. *Classification and Regression Trees*. Wadsworth, 1984.

[6] E. K. Burke, M. Hyde, G. Kendall, G. Ochoa, E. Özcan, and R. Qu. A survey of hyper-heuristics. Technical Report Computer Science Technical Report No. NOTTCS-TR-SUB-0906241418-2747, School of Computer Science and Information Technology, University of Nottingham, 2009.

[7] R. Casey and G. Nagy. Decision tree design using a probabilistic model. *IEEE Transactions on Information Theory*, 30(1):93– 99, 1984.

[8] J. Ching, A. Wong, and K. Chan. Class-dependent discretization for inductive learning from continuous and mixed-mode data. *IEEE Transactions on Pattern Analysis and Machine Intelligence*, 17(7):641–651, 1995.

[9] R. L. De Mántaras. A distance-based attribute selection measure for decision tree induction. *Machine Learning*, 6(1):81–92, 1991.

[10] J. Demšar. Statistical comparisons of classifiers over multiple data sets. *Journal of Machine Learning Research*, 7:1–30, 2006.

[11] M. Gleser and M. Collen. Towards automated medical decisions. *Computers and Biomedical Research*, 5(2):180–189, 1972.

[12] C. Hartmann, P. Varshney, K. Mehrotra, and C. Gerberich. Application of information theory to the construction of efficient decision trees. *IEEE Transactions on Information Theory*, 28(4):565– 577, 1982.

[13] R. Iman and J. Davenport. Approximations of the critical region of the friedman statistic. *Communications in Statistics*, pages 571–595, 1980.

[14] B. Jun, C. Kim, Y.-Y. Song, and J. Kim. A New Criterion in Selection and Discretization of Attributes for the Generation of Decision Trees. *IEEE Transactions on Pattern Analysis and Machine Intelligence*, 19(2):1371–1375, 1997.

[15] I. Kononenko, I. Bratko, and E. Roskar. Experiments in automatic learning of medical diagnostic rules. Technical report, Jozef Stefan Institute, Ljubljana, Yugoslavia, 1984.

[16] R. Mckay, N. Hoai, P. Whigham, Y. Shan, and M. O Neill. Grammar-based Genetic Programming: a survey. *Genetic Programming and Evolvable Machines*, 11(3):365–396, 2010.

[17] J. Mingers. Expert systems - rule induction with statistical data. *Journal of the Operational Research Society*, 38:39–47, 1987.

[18] J. Mingers. An empirical comparison of selection measures for decision-tree induction. *Machine Learning*, 3(4):319–342, 1989.

[19] M. O'Neill and C. Ryan. Grammatical evolution. *IEEE Transactions on Evolutionary Computation*, 5(4):349–358, 2001.

[20] E. Özcan, B. Bilgin, and E. E. Korkmaz. A comprehensive analysis of hyper-heuristics. *Intelligent Data Analysis*, 12(1):3–23, 2008.

[21] G. L. Pappa and A. A. Freitas. *Automating the Design of Data Mining Algorithms: An Evolutionary Computation Approach*. Springer Publishing Company, Incorporated, 2009.

[22] J. R. Quinlan. Induction of decision trees. *Machine Learning*, 1(1):81–106, 1986.

[23] J. R. Quinlan. *C4.5: programs for machine learning*. Morgan Kaufmann, San Francisco, CA, USA, 1993.

[24] L. Rokach and O. Maimon. Top-down induction of decision trees classifiers - a survey. *IEEE Transactions on Systems, Man, and Cybernetics, Part C: Applications and Reviews*, 35(4):476 – 487, 2005.

[25] I. K. Sethi and G. P. R. Sarvarayudu. Hierarchical Classifier Design Using Mutual Information. *IEEE Transactions on Pattern Analysis and Machine Intelligence*, 4(4):441–445, 1982.

[26] C. E. Shannon. A mathematical theory of communication. *BELL System Technical Journal*, 27(1):379–423, 625–56, 1948.

[27] M. Souto, I. Costa, D. de Araujo, T. Ludermir, and A. Schliep. Clustering cancer gene expression data: a comparative study. *BMC Bioinformatics*, 9(1):497, 2008.

[28] J. Talmon. A multiclass nonparametric partitioning algorithm. *Pattern Recognition Letters*, 4(1):31–38, 1986.

[29] A. Vella, D. Corne, and C. Murphy. Hyper-heuristic decision tree induction. *World Congress on Nature & Biologically Inspired Computing*, pages 409–414, 2010.

[30] D. Wang and L. Jiang. An improved attribute selection measure for decision tree induction. In *4th International Conference on Fuzzy Systems and Knowledge Discovery*, pages 654–658, 2007.

[31] S. S. Wilks. *Mathematical Statistics*. John Wiley & Sons Inc., 1962.

[32] I. H. Witten and E. Frank. *Data Mining: Practical Machine Learning Tools and Techniques with Java Implementations*. Morgan Kaufmann, October 1999.

[33] X. Zhou and T. Dillon. A statistical-heuristic feature selection criterion for decision tree induction. *IEEE Transactions on Pattern Analysis and Machine Intelligence*, 13(8):834–841, 1991.

Generic Parameter Control with Reinforcement Learning

Giorgos Karafotias
VU University
Amsterdam, Netherlands
g.karafotias@vu.nl

Agoston Endre Eiben
VU University
Amsterdam, Netherlands
a.e.eiben@vu.nl

Mark Hoogendoorn
VU University
Amsterdam, Netherlands
m.hoogendoorn@vu.nl

ABSTRACT

Parameter control in Evolutionary Computing stands for an approach to parameter setting that changes the parameters of an Evolutionary Algorithm (EA) on-the-fly during the run. In this paper we address the issue of a generic and parameter-independent controller that can be readily plugged into an existing EA and offer performance improvements by varying the EA parameters during the problem solution process. Our approach is based on a careful study of Reinforcement Learning (RL) theory and the use of existing RL techniques. We present experiments using various state-of-the-art EAs solving different difficult problems. Results show that our RL control method has very good potential in improving the quality of the solution found without requiring additional resources or time and with minimal effort from the designer of the application.

Categories and Subject Descriptors

I.2.8 [**Problem Solving, Control Methods, and Search**]: Heuristic methods, Control theory

Keywords

Evolutionary algorithms; parameter control; reinforcement learning

1. INTRODUCTION

Controlling the parameters of Evolutionary Algorithms (EA) on-the-fly has been on the research agenda of the Evolutionary Computing community since the late nineties, when Eiben et al. put the issue in the spotlight [4]. Over the last decade and a half, the field has made great progress and several good parameter control mechanisms have been invented. This progress is reviewed and related trends are identified in a recent survey [12]. However, as noted in this survey, the field suffers from the lack of generic control methods that can be applied to (m)any parameter(s). This causes *the patchwork problem*: "if one is to control more (all) parameters of an EA, then for each parameter she has to choose from a parameter specific set of existing methods and mix them into one system. Unfortunately, little is known about the joint effects of control mechanisms, thus there are no good guidelines about how to create good combinations. Therefore, the resulting mix is necessarily ad hoc and likely suboptimal."

In this paper we investigate a possible approach to mitigate this issue. Our approach is based on using reinforcement learning (RL) [21] [27]. The main idea is to use RL as a generic control mechanism that can be employed as a 'universal plugin' to adjust the values of any parameter of any EA on-the-fly.

Even though it is not common in the related parameter control literature, let us try to position this approach by discussing its possible niche, i.e., the use cases where it can (expectedly) provide an advantage. To this end, it is important to note that the performance of EAs can be greatly improved by tuning their parameters before the run. Over the last decade, this issue has received much attention and several very good parameter tuners are available, see, for instance [5] for an overview. Such tuning techniques have their niche in repetitive problems (cf. [Chap 13] in [6]) that occur with little variations and the possible extensive tuning costs are compensated by the repeatedly occurring performance benefits. On the other hand, parameter control mechanisms offer benefits in cases when tuning is not possible or not economic. For instance, in on-line evolutionary robotics or other real-time applications, where the problem can change and human intervention to adjust the EA is not feasible. Or, in case of one-off problems that need to be solved by just a few EA runs without time for tuning.

The main research question of this paper is the following:

> Can an RL-based parameter controller improve the performance of an off-the-shelf EA without the need for tailoring the controller towards the given problem?

To answer this research question we develop an RL controller and perform experiments using it as a 'plug-in' for several EAs that are tested on a number of different problems. To gain a good base for conclusions we selected good and freely available EAs with varying levels of sophistication, ranging from a straightforward ES, through some competitive GAs and ending with the highly developed IPOP CMA-ES. As for selecting the test problems, for each algorithm we chose problems from a collection for which the given EA has been developed. This guaranteed that there was no trivial gain for the controller. All together we use 4 EAs and 11 test problems, including 4 real world problems.

2. RELATED WORK

Reinforcement learning has been employed for operator selection by Sakurai et al. [18], Chen et al. [2] and Pettinger and Everson [17]. Muller et al. [16] used temporal difference learning to control the mutation step size for real valued encodings. These methods use feedback from the EA to define a state and choose actions that

GECCO'14, July 12–16, 2014, Vancouver, BC, Canada.
Copyright 2014 ACM 978-1-4503-2662-9/14/07 ...$15.00.
http://dx.doi.org/10.1145/2576768.2598360 .

set parameters, thus, model parameter control as a RL problem. However, all these methods are simplistic in their approach and further limited by the fact that they are specific to a single parameter. A reduced version of reinforcement learning, i.e. the multi-armed bandit approach, has been extensively used for adaptive operator selection (for a list of such publications refer to [12]).

The only case we are aware of where RL was used for generic parameter control is by Eiben et al. [3]. Fitness based metrics were used to define the state while actions were mapped to set any/all parameters. However, they used an unmotivated combination of on-policy and off-policy learning while the experimental results were discouraging.

3. FORMULATION OF THE PROBLEM

In this section we formulate EA parameter control as a reinforcement learning problem. We start by discussing the state of an EA, how parameter control affects it and the definition of a parameter control design. Subsequently, we map this EA parameter control design onto an RL problem.

The complete state of an EA can be defined as:

$$S_{EA} = \{G, \bar{p}\} \tag{1}$$

where G is the set of all the genomes in the population and $\bar{p}$ is the vector of current parameter values. A pair S_{EA} uniquely specifies the state of the search process for a given evolutionary algorithm (the design and specific components of the EA need not be included in the state since they are the same during the whole run) in the sense that S_{EA} fully defines the search results so far and is the only observable factor that influences the search process from this point on (though not fully defining it, given the stochastic nature of EA operators). Time is not part of S_{EA} as it is irrelevant to the state itself; it introduces an artificial uniqueness and a property that is unrelated to the evolution. Of course, state transitions are not deterministic.

The state of the EA, and in extension the outcome of the search process, can be affected by changing G or $\bar{p}$. Evolutionary operators change G; every time variation or selection is applied the genotypes in the population change. Controlling the parameters changes $\bar{p}$, thus also affecting the next state(s) of the EA. The goal of such control is to maximize the final performance (at the end of a number of available evaluations). However, the long term effects of a certain $\bar{p}$ applied cannot be known, only the current S_{EA}.

The definition of an EA parameter control method requires three components [13]: (i) the choice of parameters (including the frequency and time of updates), (ii) the observables that are derived from the search state S_{EA} and are used as input to the controller and (iii) the specific mechanism/algorithm (either static or dynamic) that maps the current observables' values to parameter values.

There is an apparent analogy between the EA parameter control problem and the full RL problem and a Markov Decision Process (MDP). The EA state observables suggest a state space, the parameters controlled and their ranges point to an action space while a dynamic control mechanism component could be implemented by a specific RL algorithm. Although this high level mapping is straightforward, the exact formulation of the RL problem is far from trivial. To define an MDP we need to define a state space, an action space, a transition function and a reward function [21] [23]. These are explained below.

The most important and challenging is the formulation of the state space. Ideally, we would like our state definition to give our process the Markov property, i.e.:

$$P(s_{t+1}, r_{t+1} | s_t, r_t, s_{t-1}, r_{t-1}, ..., s_1, r_1, s_0) = P(s_{t+1}, r_{t+1} | s_t, r_t) \tag{2}$$

Such a state definition would entirely contain all the necessary information for deciding the most appropriate action without taking into account the complete history [23].

Defining the state of the RL problem directly as S_{EA} is problematic. On one hand, using S_{EA} directly is impractical and not useful; it is unlikely such a state will be repeated, thus whatever is learned there is useless, while approximations of a state value function seem rather difficult. On the other hand, if we choose our observations to be other more compact measures derived from S_{EA} we are considering a Partially Observable MDP (PO-MDP) setting because multiple S_{EA} states can give the same observable values [20]. The alternative would be to define the state space using derived observables as its dimensions. The likely risk in this case is that the Markov property is lost and the problem becomes non-stationary. If the observables used are too simple or weak then not only the current state will not contain enough information but also the optimal actions for a state will quickly change. Furthermore, since such observables would probably be continuous, so will the state space. Prior discretization of the state space can be highly inefficient since the distribution of values of the observables cannot be known beforehand. Consequently, special techniques are required to deal with the continuous state space [8].

Regardless the exact definition of the state space, the transition function is of course unknown because of the unknown effect of parameter values and noise due to the influence of the stochastic operators on the state of the EA.

Second, we must define the actions of the RL problem that will give parameter values. There are two general options for approaching this: (i) actions that increase or decrease (or maintain) the current parameter value and (ii) actions that set a specific value to the parameter. These options pose a tradeoff. Defining actions to increase/decrease the current parameter values makes the next values dependent on the current ones. Subsequently, we should expand the state definition to include the current parameter vector or we should cope with another source of uncertainty about the current state making the PO-MDP problem described earlier stronger. On the other hand, actions that define direct values for parameters mean that the action space must be the Cartesian product of the domains of all parameters controlled. Such an action space also poses the problem of continuity since actions correspond to values of continuous parameters. However, unlike the state space, discretisation of the action space may be reasonable. Though we can expect that certain regions of parameter values may deserve more attention and finer granularity, some parameter have wide "good areas" of values (e.g. crossover rate of GAs). Even so, a reasonable amount of discretisation intervals would be required resulting in a higher number of total actions than if we used option (i), thus slowing down learning because more exploration would be required.

Finally, we define reward. According to Sutton and Barto [21] reward must indicate what we want accomplished without being biased by the designer's intuition about the "how". The difference between the previous and the current fitness would be an obvious option but it would result in disproportionate rewards: an EA tends to make large steps in the beginning even if parameters are not good while near the end very small fine-tuning improvements are very hard to achieve. This could be solved if we know the target fitness of the problem but we cannot make this assumption in general. Consequently, we try to alleviate the problem by defining reward as the ratio of the previous fitness to the current (for a minimisation problem). Since the population and offspring sizes may be among the parameters controlled, a reward should be normalised according to the effort (number of evaluations) spent for the improvement made. Thus, we make the following definition for the reward:

$$R(s_t, a_t) = C \cdot \frac{\frac{f_b^{t+1}}{f_b^t} - 1}{Evals_{t+1} - Evals_t} \quad (3)$$

where f_b^i is the best fitness at time i, $Evals_i$ is the number of evaluations spent until time i and C is a scaling constant.

A model of the reward function is not available because of the unknown effect of parameter values and the stochastic nature of the evolutionary operators.

4. A GENERIC RL CONTROLLER

In this section we present a concrete design of a generic parameter controller based on reinforcement learning to tackle the problem as defined in the previous section. First we present a concrete list of observables for defining state, subsequently the manner actions are treated and, finally, the specific algorithm used for learning.

The choice of observables that will define the state of the EA is a challenging issue as was explained in the previous section. So far there has been almost no research exploring the usefulness of different observables - the only exceptions we are aware of are by Veerapen et al. [25] and Whitacre et al. [26] - while almost all controllers found in literature use fitness and/or a form of diversity as feedback from the EA without providing any motivation or justification for this choice [12]. A systematic approach for the definition of observables was suggested by Karafotias et al. [13].

For our initial design of a generic controller we have chosen a set of simple observables that we consider appropriate and intuitively useful (since as we explained a better informed decision is impossible at the moment):

1. Genotypic diversity
2. Phenotypic diversity (when different from genotypic)
3. Fitness standard deviation
4. Fitness improvement
5. Stagnation counter

When looking at the observables, two types can be distinguished: those that measure the current state of the population (the first three items) and the ones measuring the progress made over a number of generations (the last two). As for the first type, the first two regard diversity which is generally accepted as an important descriptor of the state of an EA (see [12]). However, not only is the measurement of diversity dependent on the representation used by the EA but the concept of diversity is itself not well-defined [24]. For this paper, we conducted experiments with numeric optimisation, thus we used Euclidean distance for measuring diversity, though there are alternative options (see for example [19] and [15]). The standard deviation of fitness values in the population is used as a secondary measure of diversity and convergence. The observables measuring the progress include the fitness improvement and the stagnation counter. The fitness improvement is the only real fitness measure we use (defined the same as the reward (3)). The reason we did not include absolute fitness values is that such observables would be less useful to a non-restarting EA: states defined by absolute fitness values are not likely to occur again making anything learned from those states unusable in the future. The number of generations that have passed without any improvement is a metric that might be related to taking drastic exploratory action.

Control actions are defined as setting each controlled parameter to a certain value. To simplify our design we cope with the continuous action space by discretising parameter ranges to equal intervals. The number of discretisation intervals is the same for all parameters, regardless of the parameter's range. When the controller picks an interval to set a parameter's value, the exact value is taken uniformly randomly from within that interval. Values of symbolic parameters are treated each separately. Each action of the controller specifies the intervals for all numeric parameters and the values for all symbolic parameters. Consequently, the total number of control actions is equal to the product of the numbers of intervals/values of all parameters. Depending on the EA controlled, the number of parameters will change. The granularity of the discretisation is important here. The smaller the intervals, the more fine-grained the controller can set parameter values, but the larger the action space requiring more time to explore. The number of discretisation bins decides the number of actions; it is left as a choice for each specific application depending on the EA (i.e. how many parameters it has) and problem at hand (i.e. how long a run is possible).

The core of the controller is based on Temporal Difference (TD) learning with dynamic state space segmentation and eligibility traces. The dynamic state segmentation method used is based on the work by Uther and Veloso [22]. The controller represents states as a binary decision tree. Internal nodes are decision nodes; they segment space with an inequality on one of the observables. Leaf nodes represent actual discrete states. Each such state node S_i includes $Q(S_i, a_j)$ values and eligibility traces $e(S_i, a_j)$ for all actions a_j and a $V(S_i)$ value of the state itself. $Q(S_i, a_j)$ denotes the estimated state-action value, i.e. the expected long-term return of taking action a_j when in state S_i. These Q values are used when the controller selects actions. Eligibility traces are a way to assign credit (or blame) to actions when their influence can extend to several steps after they are taken. At each time t, every state-action pair S_i, a_j has an eligibility trace $e(S_i, a_j) \in [0, 1]$ that shows how much responsibility action a_j from state S_i is taking for the reward $R(t)$ that is presently received. The more recently action a_j was taken from state S_i the higher $e(S_i, a_j)$ is and vice versa.

At each control step (which can occur every one or more generations of the EA) the controller receives a set of observables values $\vec{o}(t)$ (as defined earlier) and a reward $R(t)$ (as defined in (3)). It derives the corresponding current discrete state by starting at the root of the state tree and traversing the decision nodes based on the observables values down to a state node $S(t)$. It then selects the current action $a(t)$ using an ϵ-greedy strategy: with probability ϵ a random action is chosen, otherwise it selects the action with the highest Q value: $a(t) = argmax_j Q(S(t), a_j)$. It then calculates the target value δ for the update of the previous action based on the reward $R(t)$ received. The target δ is derived according to the SARSA on-policy rule [21]:

$$\delta = R(t) + \gamma \cdot Q(S(t), a(t)) - Q(S(t-1), a(t-1)) \quad (4)$$

where γ is the discount rate. Before applying the δ target, the eligibility trace of the previous action is updated to one: $e(S(t-1), a(t-1)) = 1$. Subsequently, all eligible state-action pairs are updated according to target δ:

$$\begin{aligned} Q(S_i, a_j) &= Q(S_i, a_j) + \alpha_t \cdot \delta \cdot e(S_i, a_j), \\ &\forall S_i, a_j : e(S_i, a_j) > e_{min} \\ \alpha_t &= \begin{cases} \alpha_0 & R(t) = 0 \\ \alpha & otherwise \end{cases} \end{aligned} \quad (5)$$

where e_{min} is the minimum eligibility and α is the step-size parameter. The value of α decides how much influence the target δ will have on the current Q values. Because rewards (fitness improvements) tend to be zero a lot of the time, we use a different (and much lower) α_0 to avoid Q values quickly dropping to zeros.

The value of the state is updated to be the maximum action value within that state:

$$V(S_i) = maxQ(S_i, a_j) \tag{6}$$

Finally, the eligibility traces of all state-action pairs are updated:

$$e(S_i, a_j) = e(S_i, a_j) \cdot \gamma \cdot \lambda \tag{7}$$

where γ is the discount rate and λ is the trace decay parameter.

After the next action is selected and all updates are performed the state tree is updated. The state tree starts with only one root node which is a state node representing one universal state; any possible observables $\vec{o}$ will map to that state. Every time a control step is made a transition occurs from an observation and action to a reward and a new observation $T_t = (\vec{o}(t), a(t), R(t+1), \vec{o}(t+1))$. Every state maintains an archive of such transitions and at each control step the transition T_t is added to the archive of state $S(t)$. If the state's archive is larger than a threshold A_m and with probability p_s the state is checked for splitting into two new states, which means that the current node becomes an internal decision node and two new state nodes are added as its children. To convert the state node into a decision node a choice of observable and a splitting value are required to form the corresponding inequality.

The purpose of this process is to divide a state into two parts with significantly different value estimates. First, each transition in the state's archive is assigned a value equal to the reward of the transition plus the current value estimation of the state that currently corresponds to the *end* observation of the transition (the $\vec{o}(t+1)$ for T_t). Subsequently, all observables are checked as candidates for the splitting criterion. For each observable:

- Transitions in the archive are sorted according to the current observable in the transition's *starting* observation (the $\vec{o}(t)$ for T_t).
- Taking the sorted list of transitions we consider the values of the current observable. The mid-point between the observable values of every two subsequent transitions in the sorted list is a candidate for a splitting point[1]. Splitting points are only considered if they split a transition list to fractions that are larger than a A_f.
- Given the split point, the values of the transitions of the two parts form two samples. A Kolmogorov-Smirnov double test is run with these two samples and the resulting D value of the test is saved.
- The above process is repeated for all observables.

After all observables are checked, the smallest D value is taken. If it is smaller than D_{max} then the node is split at the corresponding observable and splitting point. Two new state nodes are created and their Q, V and e values are set to the values of the parent node as an initial estimation. The archive of the parent node is split according to the chosen split point and the parts are given to the corresponding children nodes. The parent node becomes a decision node with an inequality using the observable and split point derived above.

The RL controller has ten parameters due to the TD learning rule, the dynamic state tree and the eligibility traces. These parameters and their default values are shown in Table 1.

5. EXPERIMENTAL SETUP

The experiments presented in this section aim at evaluating the RL controller described earlier. To this end, we selected four different EAs (described later) and four different parameter control mechanisms: none (using the default parameter values of the given EA), PRAM [28], our RL, and a mechanism that changes parameter values randomly. In order to get results as realistic and meaningful as possible, each EA was tested with functions it was designed for or is considered competent solving.

[1]If the transitions are too many then only 100 equally spaced points are checked

Table 1: Controller Parameters

TD		State tree		Traces	
Parameter	Value	Parameter	Value	Parameter	Value
ϵ	0.1	A_m	60	λ	0.8
γ	0.8	A_f	0.2	e_{min}	0.001
α	0.9	D_{max}	0.05		
α_0	0.2	p_s	0.1		

5.1 EAs to be controlled

We decided to use algorithms and problems from the classic numeric optimisation domain which do originate from real world applications but are also widely used and understood in the research community. This also allows us to study a wide range of problems as well as the impact of the level of sophistication of the algorithm upon the performance of the RL controller. For our experiments we selected four different EAs ranging in sophistication from very simple to state-of-the-art. In particular we used:

1. A simple self-coded Evolution Strategy (ES) with real valued representation, Gaussian mutation with one σ, uniform crossover and tournament selection for both parents and survivors. The parameters controlled are the population size μ, the generation gap g (the ratio of offspring to population size), the mutation step size σ and the tournament size for survivor selection k_s (the parent tournament size is fixed to two). Being an unspecialised "naive" algorithm, the Simple ES was tested with three of the standard numeric optimisation test functions frequently used in literature: Rastrigin, Schaffer and Fletcher & Powell.

2. The Cellular GA [1] implemented for the BBOB2013[2] competition by Holtschulte and Moses [9] [3]. The parameters controlled are the choice of crossover (two-point or arithmetic), the crossover probability p_c, the choice of mutation (Gaussian, uniform, decreasing Gaussian or alternating uniform and Gaussian), the mutation rate p_m and the mutation variance m_{var}. The parent and survivor selection operators are fixed (ranking and select best) and not parameterisable. The Cellular GA was implemented for the BBOB contest thus we tested it with BBOB functions 21 through 24 (we chose the harder functions that would justify long runs and resemble the real functions tackled in one-off applications).

3. The GA MPC (GA with Multi-Parent Crossover) by Elsayed et al. [7] that was the winner of the CEC2011 competition on real world applications[4]. The parameters controlled are the population size μ, the maximum size of the parent tournament k_{max}, the randomisation probability p_r, the percentage of the population that is put in the archive f_a and the mean β_m and standard deviation β_{std} of the normal distribution used to draw the β weight used in the multi-parent crossover. The survivor selection is "select best" and involves no parameters. The GA MPC was tested with the test suite it was

[2]http://coco.gforge.inria.fr/doku.php?id=bbob-2013

[3]The source code was acquired directly from the authors

[4]http://www3.ntu.edu.sg/home/epnsugan/index_files/CEC11-RWP/CEC11-RWP.htm. The source code of GA MPC is available at the same competition page.

designed for (CEC2011); we used two problems it performed very well and two for which it performed poorly (12/13 and 7/11.8 respectively).

4. A recent CMA ES variant: the IPOP-10DDr CMA-ES by Liao and Stützle [14] that took part in the BBOB 2013 competition[5]. The parameters controlled are the backward time horizon for distribution cumulation c_c, the step size cumulation c_s, the step size damping parameter d, the mixing between rank-one and rank-mu update μ_{cov} and the recombination type (equal, linearly decreasing or super-linearly decreasing weights). The population and offspring sizes are controlled at restart by the IPOP-10DDr mechanism and cannot be changed during actual runtime. The restart conditions were kept to defaults. We used the BBOB test suite where the CMA ES variants are especially competent; we chose the same functions as the Cellular GA (for the same reason).

5.2 Control mechanisms used

Each algorithm was run in combination with four different control mechanisms. The baseline mechanism was the use of no control, that is, using static parameters set to default values as provided in the source codes or specified in the relevant publications listed above. (For our Simple ES we set parameters to "standard" values).

All algorithms were also run with the RL controller. The parameters of the RL controller were set to the default values shown in Table 1 for all experiments. The only option of the RL controller changed was the number of discretisation bins: since the number of parameters and the length of runs differ among EA and problem settings, the amount of discretisation bins was chosen for each experiment separately to yield a reasonable number of control actions.

Third, we run all algorithms with one of the few existing generic controllers, the Probabilistic Rule-driven Adaptive Model (PRAM) by Wong et al. [28]. PRAM can only handle numeric parameters, thus, any symbolic parameters were kept static to their default values when running with PRAM. For all PRAM experiments the epoch length was set to 150, 20% of which was the training phase. PRAM's step sizes were separately adjusted for each algorithm and parameter since parameter ranges differ drastically.

Finally, we also run all algorithms with their parameters being randomly varied (see [10] for the motivation). In these tests the ranges of parameters were the same as for the RL controller but values were drawn uniformly randomly.

Each algorithm/problem/control mode combination was run 30 times. Table 2 summarises the experimental setup[6] showing all algorithms, their parameters and their ranges and default values, the test problems for each algorithm, the number of action discretisation bins used for the RL controller and the step sizes of the PRAM.

6. RESULTS AND ANALYSIS

The results of all experiments are shown in Table 4. The RL controller significantly improves over the static mode in 8 out of 15 cases while it has a better best run in additional 3 cases. For PRAM these number are 6 and 0 and for random 8 and 2. The RL controller and random modes are both significantly better than static in 8 cases, in 3 of these the RL control is significantly better than random and in additional 3 it has a better best run.

[5]The source code for the (IPOP) CMA-ES was acquired from https://www.lri.fr/~hansen/cmaes_inmatlab.html. The 10DDr variation was added manually.

[6]The source code for this experiment is available for download at http://www.few.vu.nl/~gks290/resources/gecco2014.tar.gz

In several cases the performance of the EA is improved when using the RL controller compared to the static mode while there are only two cases where performance is significantly worsened with RL control. Furthermore, as we stated in Section 5, the settings of the RL controller were the same across all experiments (with the trivial exception of the number of action bins). Based on these results we can conclude that an RL-based controller can indeed improve the performance of an off-the-shelf EA with no need of tailoring to the given problem.

Looking at the results of Table 4 we can see that the RL controller has a much better effect for some EAs (notably the Simple ES) while it is not particularly advantageous for others such as the CMA-ES. One way to interpret this is by considering the margin of improvement for each algorithm when solving a specific problem, i.e. how well tailored is the algorithm to the problem at hand. The Simple ES is very crude while the Cellular GA, though more complex, is certainly not a competent numeric optimiser. Neither of them is particularly fit for the problems they are solving. On the other hand, the GA MPC is an efficient optimiser (winner of the CEC 2011 competition) but notice that it ranked low for the first two problems while it ranked first and second for the last two problems. Finally, the CMA-ES is considered the most competent numeric optimiser and consistently performs well for the BBOB competitions. Table 3 summarises[7] these observations along with a simple comparison between the static mode and the RL control. It shows that when there is margin for improvement for the specific EA/problem combination, the RL controller will exploit it.

Another factor that may contribute to the performance differences among EAs when using the RL controller is monotonicity (decided by restarting and elitism). The Simple ES is the only non-elitistic. The Cellular GA and GA MPC are elitistic and do not restart while the IPOP-10DDr CMA-ES typically restarted only four or five times per run. This is relevant if we look into the observables' values (we cannot provide graphs due to lack of space[8]). It is frequently seen that, during a run, observables will follow a monotonous increasing or decreasing curve (unless the EA restarts or is non-elitistic). This means that specific observations only occur once, thus, states do not repeat unless the EA is restarted[9]. Consequently, elitism combined with no restarting could mean that anything learned during a run is never actually used and the controller degenerates to solving a dynamic multi-armed bandit problem.

Looking at the parameter values set by the RL controller we could not discern any obvious pattern. Even when looking at one of the best performing runs for the RL control (Simple ES with the Rastrigin problem) in Figure 1 no apparent trends can be seen. However, that is not necessarily a problem considering the combined effect of multiple observables, the dynamic segmentation of the state space and the effects of exploratory actions.

For all experiments, the settings of the RL controller were fixed to the default values shown in Table 1 without making any further adjustments or tests. Though that is not enough to derive conclusions about the robustness of the RL controller, it shows that any improvements in performance reported in this paper were achieved with no additional effort for applying the RL controller to the EAs.

When comparing the performance with PRAM, the benchmark parameter controller, it can be seen that the RL controller outperforms PRAM in most cases, although for each algorithm there is

[7]Directly derived from the raw data in Table 4.

[8]All graphs are available for download at http://www.few.vu.nl/~gks290/resources/gecco2014.tar.gz

[9]Non-elitism can result in "weak" restarting with the diversity and fitness hopping to large/small values every time the best individuals do not survive.

Table 2: Experimental Setup

EA	Parameters, ranges, default values	Problems	RL Control settings	PRAM settings
Simple ES	$\mu \in [10, 80]$, $\mu = 20$ $g \in (0, 7]$, $g = 2$ $\sigma \in (0, 2]$, $\sigma = 0.8$ $k_s \in [2, 80]$, $k_s = 2$	Rastrigin, Fletcher&Powell, Schaffer, Schwefel in 10 dimensions	Action bins: 5	$s(\mu) = 8$ $s(g) = 0.25$ $s(\sigma) = 0.1$ $s(k_s) = 3$
Cellular GA	$xover \in \{2p, Ar\}$, $xover = 2p$ $p_c \in [0.6, 1]$, $p_c = 0.9$ $mut \in \{G, U, G_d, C\}$, $mut = G$ $p_m \in (0, 0.4]$, $p_m = 0.1$ $m_{var} \in (0, 0.4]$, $m_{var} = 0.2$	BBOB2013 f_{21}, f_{22}, f_{23}, f_{24} in 40 dimensions	Action bins: 4	$s(p_c) = 0.04$ $s(p_m) = 0.04$ $s(m_{var}) = 0.04$
GA MPC	$\mu \in [50, 130]$, $\mu = 90$ $k_{max} \in [3, 15]$, $k_{max} = 3$ $\beta_m \in [0.3, 1.1]$, $\beta_m = 0.7$ $\beta_{std} \in (0, 0.5]$, $\beta_{std} = 0.1$ $p_r \in (0, 0.4]$, $p_r = 0.1$ $f_a \in [0.3, 0.7]$, $f_a = 0.5$	CEC2011 f_7, $f_{11.8}$, f_{21}, f_{22}	Action bins: 4	$s(\mu) = 6$ $s(k_{max}) = 1$ $s(\beta_m) = 0.05$ $s(\beta_{std}) = 0.05$ $s(p) = 0.04$ $s(f_a) = 0.04$
IPOP-10DDr CMA ES	$c_c \in [0, 1]$, $c_c = 0.0909$ $c_s \in [0, 1]$, $c_s = 0.1375$ $d \in [1, 5]$, $d = 1.1375$ $\mu_{cov} \in [1, 20]$, $\mu_{cov} = 4.5409$ $xover \in \{E, D_l, D_{sl}\}$, $xover = D_{sl}$	BBOB2013 f_{21}, f_{22}, f_{23}, f_{24} in 40 dimensions	Action bins: 4	$s(c_c) = 0.1$ $s(c_s) = 0.1$ $s(d) = 0.5$ $s(\mu_{cov}) = 2$

a problem where PRAM has superior performance to the RL controller. Finally, it is noteworthy that random variation of parameter values had, in many cases, a positive effect on performance, even for the more complex GA MPC. Such an effect has been observed before [11],[10] and is again confirmed here.

Table 3: RL Control vs static: ++ (or --) shows that the ABF is significantly better (or worse) while + (or -) shows that ABF is not significantly different but the result of the best run is better (or worse). A 0 means no difference. Grey cells denote that the EA is particularly fit to the specific problem (see explanation in the text).

Simple ES	++	++	++	
Cellular GA	++	++	++	+
GA MPC	++	++	+	--
CMA ES	0	0	--	+

7. CONCLUSIONS

In this paper, we presented an RL-based generic parameter controller for EAs. The controller can easily be applied to any EA by simply specifying the parameters to be controlled, their ranges and the desired level of precision. We conducted experiments with four different EAs and 15 problems. The results show that the RL controller can enhance performance without the need for tweaking its parameters. A detailed analysis shows that the RL controller can exploit an existing margin of improvement, i.e. when the EA has not been fully tailored towards the particular problem at hand. Compared to two benchmark controllers (PRAM and random variation) the RL controller generally outperforms both of them. An analysis of values selected by the controller shows that, though the controller is able to improve performance, a pattern in the selection of parameter values is hard to discern. A surprising - but in retrospect logical - observation is that the EA's monotonicity can have an influence on the efficiency of the RL controller. Finally, another interesting observation is that random variation of parameter values can enhance the performance compared to static default values.

Regarding future work, we believe that a systematic exploration and evaluation of different observables is important. Currently, very little is known about the information contained in observables and their usefulness for controlling parameter values. In this work, we have selected observables that are frequently used in literature but with no underlying argumentation. Analysis of our results shows that these observables are inappropriate unless certain conditions hold (non-elitism or frequent restarts). Other future work includes the improvement of the design of the controller, an analysis of the sensitivity of the controller to its own parameters and to noise in observables as well as more rigorous testing with other EA/problem combinations.

8. REFERENCES

[1] E. Alba and B. Dorronsoro. *Cellular Genetic Algorithms*. Springer, Berlin, Heidelberg, New York, 1st edition, 2008.

[2] F. Chen, Y. Gao, Z. Chen, and S. Chen. SCGA: Controlling genetic algorithms with Sarsa(0). In *Computational Intelligence for Modelling, Control and Automation, 2005 and International Conference on Intelligent Agents, Web Technologies and Internet Commerce, International Conference on*, volume 1, pages 1177–1183, 2005.

[3] A. Eiben, M. Horvath, W. Kowalczyk, and M. Schut. Reinforcement learning for online control of evolutionary algorithms. In Brueckner, Hassas, Jelasity, and Yamins, editors, *Proceedings of the 4th International Workshop on Engineering Self-Organizing Applications (ESOA'06)*, volume 4335, pages 151–160. Springer, 2006.

[4] A. E. Eiben, R. Hinterding, and Z. Michalewicz. Parameter Control in Evolutionary Algorithms. *IEEE Transactions on Evolutionary Computation*, 3(2):124–141, 1999.

[5] A. E. Eiben and S. K. Smit. Parameter tuning for configuring and analyzing evolutionary algorithms. *Swarm and Evolutionary Computation*, 1(1):19–31, 2011.

[6] A. E. Eiben and J. Smith. *Introduction to Evolutionary Computing*. Springer, Berlin Heidelberg, 2003.

[7] S. Elsayed, R. Sarker, and D. Essam. GA with a new multi-parent crossover for solving IEEE-CEC2011 competition problems. In *Proceedings of the 2011 IEEE*

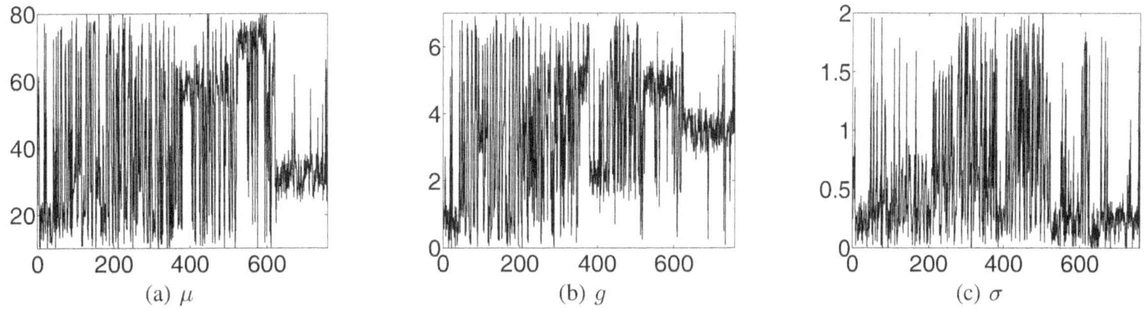

Figure 1: Parameter values over time for the best run of the Simple ES solving the Rastrigin function with RL control.

Congress on Evolutionary Computation, pages 1034–1040, New Orleans, USA, 2011. IEEE Press.

[8] H. Hasselt. Reinforcement learning in continuous state and action spaces. In Wiering and Otterlo [27], pages 207–251.

[9] N. J. Holtschulte and M. Moses. Benchmarking cellular genetic algorithms on the BBOB noiseless testbed. In *Proceeding of the Fifteenth Annual Conference Companion on Genetic and Evolutionary Computation Conference Companion*, GECCO '13 Companion, pages 1201–1208. ACM, 2013.

[10] G. Karafotias, M. Hoogendoorn, and A. Eiben. Why parameter control mechanisms should be benchmarked against random variation. In *Proceedings of the 2013 IEEE Congress on Evolutionary Computation*, pages 349–355, Cancun, Mexico, 2013. IEEE Press.

[11] G. Karafotias, M. Hoogendoorn, and A. E. Eiben. Parameter control: strategy or luck? pages 215–216, New York, NY, USA, 2013. ACM.

[12] G. Karafotias, M. Hoogendoorn, and A. E. Eiben. Parameter control in evolutionary algorithms: Trends and challenges. *IEEE Transactions on Evolutionary Computation*, to appear, 2014.

[13] G. Karafotias, S. Smit, and A. Eiben. A generic approach to parameter control. In C. Di Chio *et al*, editor, *Proceedings of EvoApplications 2012: Applications of Evolutionary Computation*, number 7248 in Lecture Notes in Computer Science, pages 366–375. Springer, Berlin, Heidelberg, New York, 2012.

[14] T. Liao and T. Stützle. Bounding the population size of IPOP-CMA-ES on the noiseless BBOB testbed. In *Proceeding of the Fifteenth Annual Conference Companion on Genetic and Evolutionary Computation Conference Companion*, pages 1161–1168. ACM, 2013.

[15] B. McGinley, J. Maher, C. O'Riordan, and F. Morgan. Maintaining healthy population diversity using adaptive crossover, mutation, and selection. *Evolutionary Computation, IEEE Transactions on*, 15(5):692 –714, 2011.

[16] S. Muller, N. Schraudolph, and P. Koumoutsakos. Step size adaptation in evolution strategies using reinforcement learning. In *2002 Congress on Evolutionary Computation (CEC'2002)*, pages 151–156, Honolulu, USA, 12-17 May 2002. IEEE Press, Piscataway, NJ.

[17] J. Pettinger and R. Everson. Controlling genetic algorithms with reinforcement learning. In W. Langdon *et al*, editor, *Proceedings of the Genetic and Evolutionary Computation Conference (GECCO-2002)*, pages 692–. Morgan Kaufmann, San Francisco, 9-13 July 2002.

[18] Y. Sakurai, K. Takada, T. Kawabe, and S. Tsuruta. A method to control parameters of evolutionary algorithms by using reinforcement learning. In *Signal-Image Technology and Internet-Based Systems (SITIS), 2010 Sixth International Conference on*, pages 74–79, 2010.

[19] S. Smit and A. E. Eiben. Population diversity index: A new measure for population diversity. In *Proceedings of the Genetic and Evolutionary Computation Conference*. ACM, 2011.

[20] M. Spaan. Partially observable markov decision processes. In M. Wiering and M. Otterlo, editors, *Reinforcement Learning*, volume 12 of *Adaptation, Learning, and Optimization*, pages 387–414. Springer Berlin Heidelberg, 2012.

[21] R. S. Sutton and A. G. Barto. *Introduction to Reinforcement Learning*. MIT Press, Cambridge, MA, USA, 1998.

[22] W. B. Uther and M. Veloso. Tree based discretization for continuous state space reinforcement learning. In *Proceedings of the fifteenth national/tenth conference on Artificial intelligence/Innovative applications of artificial intelligence*, AAAI '98/IAAI '98, pages 769–774. American Association for Artificial Intelligence, 1998.

[23] M. van Otterlo and M. Wiering. Reinforcement learning and Markov Decision Processes. In Wiering and Otterlo [27], pages 3–42.

[24] M. Črepinšek, S.-H. Liu, and M. Mernik. Exploration and exploitation in evolutionary algorithms: A survey. *ACM Comput. Surv.*, 45(3):35:1–35:33, 2013.

[25] N. Veerapen, J. Maturana, and F. Saubion. A comparison of operator utility measures for on-line operator selection in local search. In *Proceedings of the 6th international conference on Learning and Intelligent Optimization*, LION'12, pages 497–502. Springer-Verlag, 2012.

[26] J. Whitacre, T. Pham, and R. Sarker. Use of statistical outlier detection method in adaptive evolutionary algorithms. In M. Keijzer, editor, *Proceedings of the Genetic and Evolutionary Computation Conference (GECCO-2006)*, pages 1345–1352. Morgan Kaufmann, San Francisco, 2006.

[27] M. Wiering and M. Otterlo, editors. *Reinforcement Learning*, volume 12 of *Adaptation, Learning, and Optimization*. Springer Berlin Heidelberg, 2012.

[28] Y.-Y. Wong, K.-H. Lee, K.-S. Leung, and C.-W. Ho. A novel approach in parameter adaptation and diversity maintenance for genetic algorithms. *Soft Computing - A Fusion of Foundations, Methodologies and Applications*, 7:506–515, 2003.

Table 4: Results of all experiments. There are four sections, one for each algorithm. Every section includes three or four subtables with the results for each test problem. Subtables show the performance of the algorithm with that problem with four parameter modes: static default, controlled with the RL controller, controlled with PRAM, and randomly varied. Performance is shown in terms of final fitness averaged over all repeats (ABF), final fitness of the best and worst runs and the number of evaluations until the best fitness of the run is reached averaged over all repeats (AEB). In the ABF and AEB columns underlined values are significantly better than static and bold values denote the winner(s) (not significantly worse than the best). Significant difference was decided when a two-sided Kolmogorov-Smirnov test with $\alpha = 0.05$ rejected the null hypothesis that two samples came from the same distribution. All problems are minimisation.

Simple ES

	Rastrigin				Schaffer				Fletcher & Powell			
	ABF	Best	Worst	AEB	ABF	Best	Worst	AEB	ABF	Best	Worst	AEB
static	27.681	20.718	34.808	**510033**	22.036	6.934	42.749	**664785**	7935.4	1982.5	11004	**505854**
RL	**0.672**	0.039	2.423	**491921**	9.851	1.079	29.226	**579073**	**166.211**	3.424	726.75	**586305**
PRAM	11.762	2.184	32.039	**533587**	4.253	0.908	16.492	**708175**	**1022.72**	15.557	7548.2	752212
random	4.645	1.630	8.325	**591095**	**3.071**	1.982	10.527	**667068**	420.260	187.938	768.02	**575475**

Cellular GA

	BBOB f_{21}				BBOB f_{22}				BBOB f_{23}			
	ABF	Best	Worst	AEB	ABF	Best	Worst	AEB	ABF	Best	Worst	AEB
static	40.891	40.805	41.139	**973913**	-998.82	-999.08	-998.49	979100	9.062	8.573	9.472	764053
RL	40.800	40.784	40.863	998730	-999.18	-999.26	-999.05	999350	**8.486**	8.148	8.906	906923
PRAM	**40.780**	40.780	40.781	**943080**	**-999.29**	-999.49	-999.20	**900960**	9.282	8.443	9.999	**495420**
random	40.843	40.795	40.973	999210	-998.91	-999.11	-998.69	999220	8.643	8.296	9.094	923773

	BBOB f_{24}			
	ABF	Best	Worst	AEB
static	**471.809**	435.148	511.297	899713
RL	**484.621**	412.925	565.928	986693
PRAM	493.931	412.911	598.025	**502450**
random	490.169	422.008	544.902	996706

GA MPC

	CEC2011 f_7				CEC2011 $f_{11.8}$				CEC2011 f_{12}			
	ABF	Best	Worst	AEB	ABF	Best	Worst	AEB	ABF	Best	Worst	AEB
static	1.677	0.837	2.028	**100626**	1952741	1510399	2505116	**87535**	**16.300**	14.110	22.675	**149491**
RL	**0.963**	0.627	1.396	124440	**947843**	941267	955770	119430	**16.443**	12.589	20.512	149829
PRAM	1.552	0.586	1.969	**95914**	1562083	941087	3438794	**98474**	**16.213**	14.232	17.678	149968
random	**0.893**	0.584	1.219	142052	**946728**	939736	957187	132381	**16.541**	13.718	20.338	149698

	CEC2011 f_{13}			
	ABF	Best	Worst	AEB
static	**15.211**	8.609	22.207	149335
RL	19.329	14.119	26.764	**149873**
PRAM	17.342	8.861	25.672	**148652**
random	17.797	8.787	24.957	**149828**

IPOP-10DDr CMA ES

	BBOB f_{21}				BBOB f_{22}				BBOB f_{23}			
	ABF	Best	Worst	AEB	ABF	Best	Worst	AEB	ABF	Best	Worst	AEB
static	**41.390**	40.780	43.252	**163539**	**-997.666**	-999.308	-985.415	**115916**	**6.889**	6.870	6.977	**604791**
RL	**41.689**	40.780	43.252	312667	**-997.753**	-999.308	-981.711	**193861**	6.902	6.875	6.980	**673839**
PRAM	41.985	40.780	43.949	**196793**	**-997.626**	-999.308	-981.711	**184533**	6.910	6.874	6.974	**705917**
random	**41.751**	40.780	43.949	396004	**-997.876**	-999.308	-985.415	**238268**	**6.942**	6.871	7.268	**568693**

	BBOB f_{24}			
	ABF	Best	Worst	AEB
static	**131.541**	108.027	150.419	**416381**
RL	**128.907**	106.931	152.292	**483242**
PRAM	**137.570**	109.712	187.557	**594935**
random	**126.457**	107.754	153.392	561017

Evolvability Metrics in Adaptive Operator Selection

Jorge A. Soria-Alcaraz
Instituto Tecnologico de Leon
Leon, Mexico
soajorgea@gmail.com

Gabriela Ochoa
University of Stirling
Scotland, UK
goc@cs.stir.ac.uk

Martin Carpio
Instituto Tecnologico de Leon
Leon, Mexico
jmcarpio61@hotmail.com

Hector Puga
Instituto Tecnologico de Leon
Leon, Mexico
pugahector@yahoo.com

ABSTRACT

Evolvability metrics gauge the potential for fitness of an individual rather than fitness itself. They measure the local characteristics of the fitness landscape surrounding a solution. In adaptive operator selection the goal is to dynamically select from a given pool the operator to apply next during the search process. An important component of these adaptive schemes is credit assignment, whereby operators are rewarded according to their observed performance. This article brings the notion of evolvability to adaptive operator selection, by proposing an autonomous search algorithm that rewards operators according to their potential for fitness rather than their immediate fitness improvement. The approach is tested within an evolutionary algorithm framework featuring several mutation operators on binary strings. Three benchmark problems of increasing difficulty, Onemax, Royal Staircase and Multiple Knapsack are considered. Experiments reveal that evolvability metrics significantly improve the performance of adaptive operator selection, when compared against standard fitness improvement metrics.The main contribution is to effectively use fitness landscape metrics to guide a self-configuring algorithm.

Categories and Subject Descriptors

I.2.8 [**Artificial Intelligence**]: Problem Solving, Control Methods, and Search—*Heuristic methods*

General Terms

Algorithms, Design.

Keywords

Combinatorial optimization, evolutionary algorithms, evolvability, fitness landscapes, hyper-heuristics, adaptive operator selection, self-* search

GECCO'14, July 12–16, 2014, Vancouver, BC, Canada
Copyright 2014 ACM 978-1-4503-2662-9/14/07 ...$15.00.
http://dx.doi.org/10.1145/2576768.2598220.

1. INTRODUCTION

Adaptive operator selection [7, 13, 18, 21], hyper-heuristics [4] and adaptive memetic algorithms [16] are amongst recent terms describing search methodologies that autonomously configure themselves on the fly when solving a given instance of an optimisation problem. This is related to the more general topic of adaptive evolutionary algorithms [14] but is restricted here to the process of dynamically selecting (perturbation) search operators. These methods acknowledge that the usefulness of specific search operators can vary dynamically across the search process, and therefore are complementary to automatic parameter tuning or algorithm configuration tools, which use offline learning [3, 8] or meta-evolutionary algorithms [10] on a set of training instances to establish the (static) configuration to solve new instances. These two complementary types of approaches share the goal of increasing the effectiveness and generality of search methodologies, and thus reduce the role of the human expert in their design and configuration.

This article deals with adaptive operator selection (AOS) in the context of evolutionary algorithms. Two cooperating mechanisms are required in this process: *operator selection*, which defines how the next operator to be applied should be chosen according to its estimated quality; and *credit assignment*, which defines how to estimate operators quality based on the impact brought by their most recent application. The most common way of assigning credit is to account for the fitness improvement brought by the operators. That is, the fitness difference of the generated offspring with respect to a reference value, which is generally taken as the parent. Other mechanisms in the literature have considered diversity metrics for credit assignment [13, 21].

Our proposal is to use metrics based on local characteristics of the fitness landscape surrounding a solution to measure the impact of operators, and incorporate these metrics into the credit assignment mechanism. In order to measure landscape local characteristics, we consider *evolvability* metrics. Evolvability is loosely defined as the capacity to evolve, i.e. the ability of an individual to generate fitter variants than any yet existing [1, 17]. Therefore, it is more closely linked with the *potential* for fitness rather than with fitness itself; two individuals with equal fitness can have different evolvabilities [17].

Little work so far has considered the use of fitness landscape metrics to dynamically guide the search. An example is the use of neutrality and evolvability metrics to escape plateaus when solving the flow shop scheduling problem [12]. To the best of our knowledge evolvability metrics have not been implemented specifically for adaptive operator selection, although this idea may be related to the the concepts of *look ahead* [5] and *delayed reward* [22] in meta and hyper-heuristics. To prove the concept and allow comparisons, we select the algorithmic framework (high-level search strategy and relevant parameter settings) used in recent work on adaptive operator selection [7]. Three benchmark problems with binary representation are considered. Namely, the simple Onemax problem (also used in [7]), the more elaborate Royal Staircase family of functions; and a more realistic combinatorial optimisation problem, the Multiple Knapsack problem. The goal is both to determine whether operators' evolvability metrics produce a performance advantage over fitness improvement metrics, and to study the adaptive dynamics of operators selected according to each type of metric.

The next section describes evolvability and how to measure it. The proposed approach is described in section 3. Section 4 describes the empirical setup, while section 5 reports and analyses the experimental results. Finally, section 6 summarises our findings and suggests directions for future work.

2. EVOLVABILITY

Evolvability loosely refers to the capacity of an individual or population to evolve. The first formalisation of this notion is attributed to Altenberg [1] who defined evolvability as "the ability of the genetic operator/representation scheme to produce offspring that are fitter than their parents." This is clearly necessary for adaptation in natural and artificial systems and therefore relevant to adaptive operator selection. Within evolutionary algorithms, evolvability was initially considered as a measure of performance. More specifically, "as the most *local* or finest-grained scale for measuring performance in an evolutionary algorithm" [1]. Later on, Smith et al. [17] linked evolvability to the notion of fitness landscapes. They developed a notion of evolvability based on the fitness distribution of the offspring of sampled solutions. By averaging evolvability over a set of equal fitness solutions, fitness *evolvability portraits* of a landscape were constructed and shown to describe general features of ruggedness, modality, and neutrality. Moreover, the study showed that some features of the fitness evolvability portraits for real evolutionary electronics search spaces are linked to the ease of finding good solutions.

In order to use the notion of evolvability in an algorithmic setting, we need to measure it. More precisely, we are interested in measuring the evolvability of specific search operators. This is equivalent to measuring the potential of the incumbent solution from the point of view of a given operator by considering the current solution's fitness and that of its neighbourhood according to the operator. Evolvability then give us an estimate of how much we can achieve with this pair operator-solution.

As discussed in a recent survey [11], several evolvability metrics have been proposed in the literature. After a preliminary wider exploration, we selected the two best performing metrics for discrete search spaces proposed in [17]. Namely, E_a, the probability of the offspring fitness being higher or equal to the parent fitness (Equation 1); and E_b, the mean fitness of the offspring solutions (Equation 2). We follow here the notation and definitions by Smith et al. [17]. The fitness landscape can be considered as a directed graph (V, E) with vertices V (solutions) connected by edges E. There is an edge between two solutions if one is generated from the other through a single application of a given operator. Let the pair $< h, k >$ denote a solution of genotype h, and fitness value k. The set G of offspring from a parent solution $< h, k >$ is thus determined by the vertices connected to the parent vertex: $G(< h, k >) = \{g \in V : E(< h, k >) = g\}$

The fitness function F maps every solution to a single $\mathbb{R}$ value. Then, we can define a set of offspring with fitness $F(g)$ greater than a given value:

$$G_c^+(< h, k >) = \{g \in V : E(< h, k >) = g, F(g) \geq c\}$$

E_a, is the probability of the offspring fitness being higher or equal to their parent fitness. It is simply measured as the ratio between the number of offspring with fitness higher or equal to that of the parent, and the total number of offspring (when sampling this is the size of the offspring sampling size). More formally it is defined as:

$$E_a = \frac{|G_k^+(< h, k >)|}{|G(< h, k >)|} \tag{1}$$

E_b, is the mean fitness of the offspring solutions (when sampling this is the mean fitness of the sample offspring). More formally it is defined as:

$$E_b = \frac{\sum_{g \in G(< h,k >)} F(g)}{|G(< h, k >)|} \tag{2}$$

For practically calculating the evolvability metrics defined above, a sampling methodology is required. A complete enumeration of the whole neighbourhood of the incumbent solution for each available operator would require impractical computational resources. We therefore consider estimated rather that exact evolvability metrics. Sampling the search space following a uniform distribution will give equal importance to all points. As discussed in [20], many solutions in the space may not be relevant from the point of view of evolutionary search. A methodology that gives prevalence to "important" points (i.e. those with higher fitness) is desirable as they reflect the bias followed by evolutionary and other heuristic search algorithms. As suggested in [20] for calculating *fitness clouds* we use the *Metropolis-Hastings* algorithm, which extends the standard Metropolis sampling to non-symmetric stationary probability distributions.

For estimating the evolvability metrics, E_a and E_b, the Metropolis-Hastings sampling method was used to collect information about the offspring produced from the incumbent solution given a search operator. A sampling size of 7 (offsprings) was used in our experiments. This value was found empirically to produce a good balance between fast computation and good metric approximation. A larger size would produce a more accurate estimate but would take longer, impairing the use of evolvability as a competitive metric for credit assignment.

3. TECHNICAL APPROACH

We investigate the use of the evolvability metrics described above to guide the dynamic selection of mutation operators in an evolutionary algorithm. An adaptive operator selection scheme consists of two components: (i) a *credit assignment* mechanism, which associates a reward with each operator, modeling its predicted utility; and (ii) a *selection rule*, which determines the operator to be used at each time step, as a function of reward. It is within the credit assignment that evolvability metrics are introduced as described in subsection 3.1. Subsection 3.2 describes the selection rules implemented, while subsection 3.3 the high-level search strategy used.

3.1 Evolvability based credit assignment

Most credit assignment methods compute operators' credit using the fitness of the new solution compared with that of its parent [7, 18]. We use solutions' evolvability instead of their fitness values. The motivation is to have an enriched view of the operator's quality according to the local characteristics of the fitness landscape surrounding the offspring and parent solutions. We consider *extreme* values for assigning credits [7], which is based on the principle that large (but possibly infrequent) credit improvements are more effective than small frequent improvements. It rewards operators which have had a recent large positive impact, while consistent operators yielding only small improvements receive less reward. Rewards are updated as follows, when an operator *op* is selected, it is applied to the current solution. The evolvability value of this new solution is computed and the change in evolvability is added to a list of size W. Thereafter, the operator reward is updated to the maximal value in the list. Table 1 reports the value used for this parameter in our experiments, while Figure 2 gives some evidence of the suitability of the selected value. The credit assignment mechanism needs to be combined with a selection rule as described below.

3.2 Selection rule

Operator selection probabilities are calculated from their quality estimates following a selection rule. These rules maintain a probability vector $(p_i, t)_{i=1,\ldots,K}$ (where K denotes the number of operators), and use the operator's raw credit estimate to calculate probabilities. Two recent and well performing selection rules, namely, *Adaptive Pursuit* and *Dynamic Multi-Armed Bandit*, were implemented and tested in our study. An overview of these two rules is presented below. These methods introduce control parameter. The parameter settings used in our experiments are reported in Table 1.

Adaptive pursuit was originally proposed for learning automata and was adapted to operator selection in [18]. It follows a winner-takes-all strategy, selecting at each step the operator with maximal reward, increasing its selection probability, while all other operators get their probability reduced. This method has two parameters: p_{min} that indicates the minimal probability of selection for each operator, and β, the *learning rate* taken from $(0, 1]$.

The multi-armed bandit framework is commonly used in game theory for studying the *exploration vs. exploitation* dilemma. It involves N arms and a decision making-algorithm for selecting one arm at each time step with the goal of maximising the cumulative reward gathered along time. The exploration vs. exploitation balance is also relevant for heuristic search. Indeed, adaptive operator selection can be formulated using multi-armed bandits with arms corresponding to search operators [6, 7]. Specifically, the *upper confidence bound* multi-armed bandit [2] was used as it provides optimal maximisation of cumulative rewards. Two considerations were required to use this framework for adaptive operator selection. First, a scaling factor C is needed, in order to properly balance the tradeoff between exploration and exploitation. Second, the original setting is static, while adaptive operator selection is dynamic, i.e., the quality of the operators is likely to change along the different stages of the search. The multi-armed bandit framework is thus combined with the *Page-Hinkley* statistical test for detecting changes in the reward distribution, and, upon such a detection, restarting the process [7]. This combined approach is termed *dynamic multi-armed bandit*, and introduces two additional parameters associated to the *Page-Hinkley* test: γ, which controls the trade-off between false alarms and unnoticed changes; and δ, which enforces the robustness of the test when dealing with slowly varying environments.

3.3 High-level search strategy

For comparison purposes, we implemented the algorithmic framework used in recent adaptive operator selection research [7]. Namely, a standard (1+λ)-EA without recombination, where λ offspring are created from a single parent, and the best individual among the current offspring and parent becomes the parent in the next generation. The AOS module is incorporated for choosing the mutation operator to generate the next offspring as indicated in Algorithm 1.

Algorithm 1 $(1 + \lambda) - EA$ with AOS.

Require: $f : \delta \to \mathbb{R}$ fitness function, *maxGener* max number of generations, μ size of parent pool, λ size of the offspring pool

$ParentPool_0 = generatePopulation(\mu)$
for $i = 0$ until *maxGener* **do**
  initialize $OffspringPool_i = pool(\lambda)$
  for $j = 0$ until λ **do**
    $OffspringPool_i.add(AOS(ParentPool_{i-1}))$
  end for
  $ParentPool_i = Best(OffspringPool_i)$
end for
return $Best(ParentPool_i)$

4. EXPERIMENTAL SETUP

This section describes the experimental setup including test problems, algorithm variants and their parameter settings, the performance metric and statistical testing employed.

4.1 Test problems

Three benchmark problems encoded as binary strings are considered. The first benchmark function is the Onemax or counting ones problem, traditionally used in theoretical and proof of concept studies in genetic algorithms. We selected it as it was one of the benchmarks of choice in recent adaptive operator selection studies based on fitness improvement [7]. Two additional more complex test problems are also considered, as described below.

Royal staircase functions. This class of functions is related to the more familiar *Royal Road* functions [15]. They were proposed in [19] for analyzing epochal evolutionary search, that is the existence of long periods of fitness stasis punctuated by occasional fitness leaps. Although simple, Royal Staircase functions capture some essential elements found on complex problems, namely, highly degenerate genotype-to-phenotype maps, and the existence neutrality. A formal definition of the Royal Staircase class of functions is given below.

1. Genotypes are binary strings $s = s_1 s_2 \ldots s_L$, $s_i \in \{0, 1\}$, of length $L = NK$, where N is the number of blocks and K the number of bits per block.
2. Starting from the first position, the number $I(s)$ of consecutive 1s in a string is counted.
3. The fitness $f(s)$ of string s with $I(s)$ consecutive ones, followed by a zero, is $f(s) = 1 + \lfloor I(s)/K \rfloor$. The fitness is thus an integer between 1 and $N+1$, corresponding to 1 plus the number of consecutive fully-set blocks starting from the left.
4. The single global optimum is $s = 1^L$; namely, the string of all 1s.

Fixing N and K determines a particular problem or fitness landscape.

Multiple knapsack problem. The combinatorial optimisation problem described here, called the 1/0 multiple knapsack problem, follows the formulation in [9]. This problem is a generalisation of the 0/1 simple Knapsack problem where a single knapsack of capacity C, and n objects are given. Each object has a weight w_i and a profit p_i. The objective is to fill the knapsack with objects producing the maximum profit P. In other words, to find a vector $x = (x_1, x_2, \ldots, x_n)$ where $x_i \in \{0, 1\}$, such that $\sum_{i=1}^{n} w_i x_i \leq C$ and for which $P(x) = \sum_{i=1}^{n} p_i x_i$ is maximised.

The multiple version consists of m knapsacks of capacities $c_1, c_2, \ldots, c_m$ and n objects with profits $p_1, p_2, \ldots, p_n$. Each object has m possible weights: object i weighs w_{ij} when considered for inclusion in knapsack j ($1 \leq j \leq m$). Again, the objective is to find a vector $x = (x_1, x_2, \ldots, x_n)$ that guarantees that no knapsack is overfilled: $\sum_{i=1}^{n} w_{ij} x_i \leq c_j$ for $j = 1, 2, \ldots, m$; and that yields maximum profit $P(x) = \sum_{i=1}^{n} p_i x_i$.

4.2 Algorithm variants and parameter settings

The high-level search strategy is the (1+ λ)-EA (Algorithm 1) with offspring population size, $\lambda = 50$ in order to have the same high level algorithm and population size used in [7]. A common pool of mutation operators for binary representation was selected. The standard *n-flip* operator is considered, which chooses uniformly at random n bits in the current solution and flips their values (0 is changed to 1 an vice-versa). Our implementation used n values of 1, 3 and 5, as this was the choice of operators in [7].

For the Onemax problem six Adaptive Operator Selector (AOS) variants were considered by combining the three alternative credit assignment mechanisms: fitness improvement (*Fit*) and two evolvability metrics (E_a and E_b); with the two selection rules: adaptive pursuit (*ap*), and dynamic multi-armed bandits (*dmab*). These variants are identified with the pair of mechanisms separated by a hyphen. For example, E_a-*dmab* indicates a variant using credit assignment based on the evolvability metric E_a coupled with the *dmab* selection rule (see Figure 1). For the two remaining test problems, and due to space constraints, only the best performing evolvabibilty metric (E_a) and selection rule (*dmab*) are considered. This reduces the number of AOS variants to two, namely: E_a-*dmab* and *Fit-dmab*. Notice that variant *Fit-dmab*, corresponds to the algorithm proposed [7]. As a control, a variant that selects operators uniformly at random at each iteration (identified as *Random*) is also considered for all test problems.

Table 1 reports the parameter settings used in the experiments. The first 4 rows show the parameter values that are common to all the experiments. Namely, the offspring population size λ, the credit assignment window size W, the Metropolis-Hastings sampling size for calculating evolvability metrics, and the control parameter δ associated to the *dmab* rule (this value is suggested in [7]). The last 6 rows in Table 1 show the parameter values specific to each test problem. Namely, the maximum number of generations for the evolution strategy $MaxGener$, the chromosome length L, and the selection rule control parameters (C, γ for *dmab*; and β, p_{min} for *ap*). For the Onemax problem, these values follow the suggestions in [7]. For the remaining two test problems, the values were manually tuned.

Table 1: Parameter settings.

Parameter	*Onemax*	*Royal Staircase*	*M. Knapsack*
λ	50	50	50
W	30	30	30
S	7	7	7
dmab δ	0.15	0.15	0.15
$MaxGener$	1,000	10,000	5,000
L	10,000	100 to 700	50 to 105
dmab γ	100	75	80
dmab C	10	7	7.5
ap β	0.75	-	-
ap p_{min}	0.10	-	-

4.3 Performance metric and statistical testing

The performance metric is simply the value of the fitness function after the preselected fixed number of generations of the evolutionary strategy. The three test problems considered are maximisation problems. Therefore, the higher the value of the objective function at the end of the run, the better the performance of the algorithm variant. For each AOS variant and test problem instance, 33 independent runs were conducted and results are reported using descriptive statistics and box-plots summarising the performance distribution. Statistical inference (i.e. multiple comparison hypothesis testing) was used to asses the comparative performance of the AOS variants. Upon checking, our results were found to approximately follow a Normal distribution and have stable variances. Therefore, the use of parametric hypothesis testing is adequate. We used the one-way ANOVA F test (also called Omnibus test) for the Onemax problem, as there is a single factor (the AOS variant) that can explain performance differences in the unique Onemax instance considered. For the other two problems, namely, Royal Staricase and Multiple Knapksack, a two-way ANOVA F test is required as not only the AOS variant but also the specific problem instance can explain observed differences. In order to asses the statistical significance of the results, a pairwise t test is applied post-hoc to identify specific differences (if they exist) in a given pair of AOS variants. Furthermore, the *p-value* for each test is computed including a Bonferroni correction, which provides control over the so-called *family-wise* error rate. In our study the null hypothesis H_0 represents no significant performance differences between the algorithm variants. Finally, the Tukey HSD test is used to enforce t test results. All these tests were executed with the standard significance level of 0.05.

5. RESULTS AND ANALYSIS

We start by showing in Table 2 some basic descriptive statistics summarising the performance of the proposed algorithm *Ea-dmab* as compared with the state-of-the-art AOS variant *Fit-dmab* [7] and the control *Random* strategy across all the test problems. Results clearly indicate the superior performance *Ea-dmab*. The stopping condition in our experiments considers the number of generations of the of the evolutionary strategy. The calculation of evolvability through sampling, will incur in additional computational costs. However, as Table 3 indicates, running times were not greatly increased in our experiments.

Table 2: Descriptive statistics of main AOS variants across all test problems.

Onemax	Mean	Median	Std.dev	Best
Ea-dmab	**8074.12**	**8050**	**27.92**	**8200**
Fit-dmab	7832.52	7750	27.42	7957
Random	6834.53	6812	30.01	6892
R.StairCase	Mean	Median	Std.dev	Best
Ea-dmab	**16.45**	**16**	**16.03**	**19**
Fit-dmab	10.97	11	12.01	16
Random	10.78	10	13.63	15
M.Knapsack	Mean	Median	Std.dev	Best
Ea-dmab	**706600**	**718500**	**73105.9**	**863198**
Fit-dmab	495423.24	512432	77231.6	697673
Random	276634.77	269983	78332.4	35728

Table 3: Empirical running times in seconds on selected test instances.

Test Instance	Fit-dmab	E_a-dmab
$Onemax_{10,000}$	7.56	8.32
$Royal\ Staircase_{N40K5}$	7.48	12.75
$Royal\ Staircase_{N100K7}$	16.27	37.26
$Multiple\ Knapsack_{Weing7}$	0.84	1.12
$Multiple\ Knapsack_{Sento1}$	3.45	5.14

A more detailed statistical analysis of the results and the dynamic behaviour of the AOS variants is presented below for the three test problems.

5.1 Onemax

Figure 1 illustrates the magnitude and distribution of best fitness values at the end of the run for the 33 independent replicas on the Onemax instance. All the adaptive algorithms outperform the uniform random selection of operators. Clearly, the AOS variants using *dmab* outperform those using the *ap* selection rule. Within a fixed selection rule, the credit assignment mechanisms based on evolvability have the best performance, with the E_a metric consistently producing the best result. The one-way ANOVA F test, reported in Table 4, supports the existence of significant differences in the performance means given by the algorithms. A pairwise t test was also conducted with Bonferroni *p-value* corrections as shown at the bottom of Table 4. This shows evidence about the significant difference between algorithms. Specifically, we are interested in the performance of *Ea-dmab* as compared to the other AOS variants.

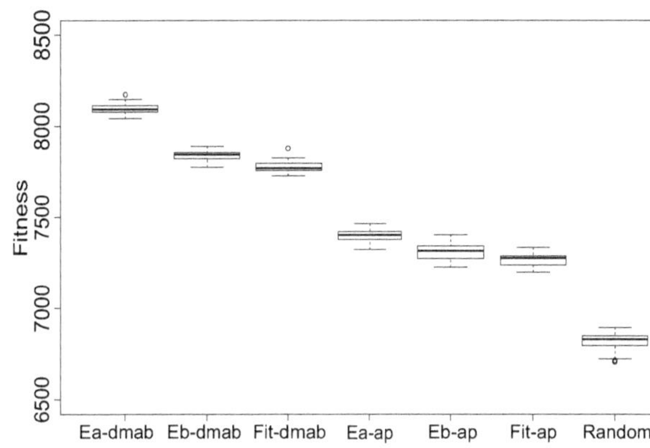

Figure 1: Onemax. Distribution of fitness values for all the AOS variants.

Table 4: Onemax. One-way ANOVA F test, and pairwise t test.

ANOVA	Df	Sum Sq	Mean Sq	F value	Pr(>F)
Algorithms	6	32928932	5488155	3748.5	1.68e-18
Residuals	217	317710	1464		
t tests	E_a-ap	E_a-$dmab$	E_b-ap	E_b-$dmab$	Fit-ap
E_a-$dmab$	**2.4e-16**	-	-	-	-
E_b-ap	1.2-16	**1.5e-17**	-	-	-
E_b-$dmab$	2e-9	**2.4e-12**	3.2e-9	-	-
Fit-ap	2.4e-8	**4.3e-18**	1.5e-09	2e-16	-
Fit-$dmab$	2.1e-16	**3.3e-16**	2.6e-16	1	4.15e-6

Figure 2 illustrates the magnitude and distribution of best fitness at the end of the run of the best performing AOS variants E_a-*dmab* and *Fit-dmab*, with different window sizes $W = \{10, 30, 50\}$. The *Random* AOS variant is also included for comparison purposes. The window size is a parameter of the extreme-value credit assignment (described in Section 3.1) indicating the memory size of previous operator's credit. Results indicate that a window size of 30 consistently produced good results, not only in the Onemax problem as illustrated in Figure 2 but in the other test problems also (not shown here due to space constraints). It seems that a small window does not give enough scope for estimating the operator's reward, while a large one maintains historic information that is no longer relevant.

Figure 3 shows the dynamic of operators' probabilities autonomously adapted through an execution for *Fit-dmab* (top) and E_a-*dmab* (bottom). The curves show a similar behaviour for both variants. A clear transition or abrupt change (most probably detected by the *dmab* mechanism) is observed around iteration 750 in both cases. The transition occurs slightly early for the fitness-based mechanism suggesting that evolvability is a more reliable indicator of change. Moreover, after the transition, the E_a based rule increases the selection probability of operator *1-flip* and decreased that of operator *3-flip* at a higher rate than the fitness based rule.

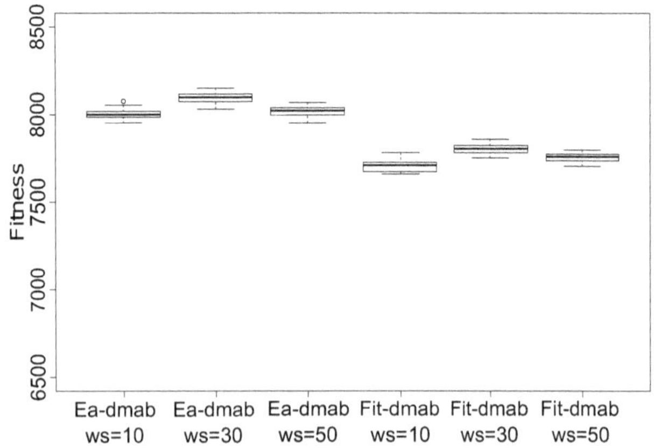

Figure 2: Onemax. Fitness distributions illustrating the effect the window size (W) parameter.

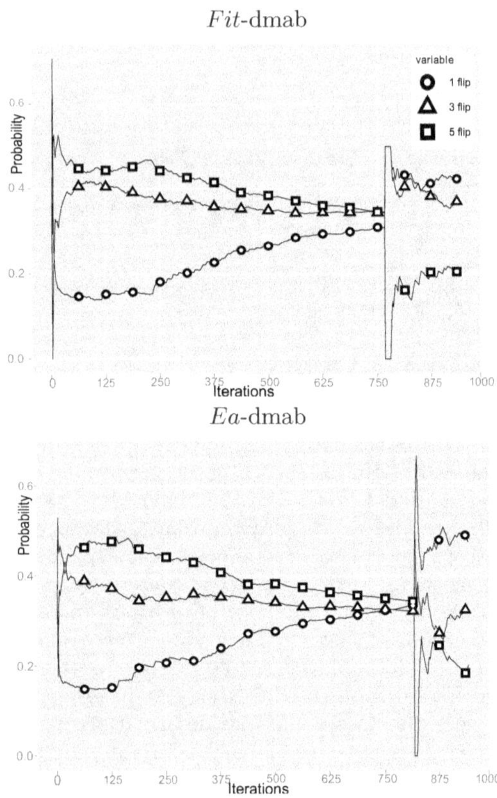

Figure 3: Onemax. Dynamic of adapted operators' probabilities over a run.

5.2 Royal Staircase

Royal Staircase functions are always unimodal, but we can increase the landscape ruggedness by decreasing the number of blocks N. Modifying the number of blocks also alters the overall shape. Four combinations of N and K were selected for the experiments in this subsection (i.e. the following <N,K> pairs: <20,5>, <40,5>, <80,5>, and <10,7>), with string lengths ($N * K$) varying from 100 to 700.

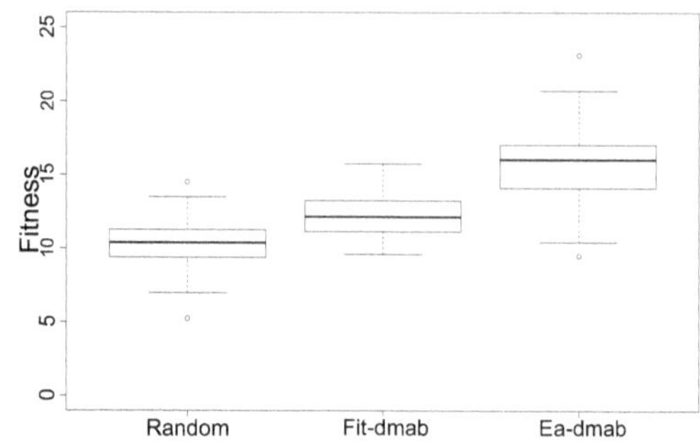

Figure 4: Royal Staircase. Post-hoc boxplot with performance distribution across all instances.

The two-way ANOVA F test combining the 4 test instances and 3 algorithm variants, reported in Table 5, supports the the existence of significant differences in the performance means of the studied AOS variants. Further analysis is required to identify which pairs of algorithms are significantly different. This is achieved with the pairwise t test with Bonferroni adjustments reported at the the middle portion of Table 5. The test supports that the E_a*-dmab* variant has significant performance differences as compared to the other variants. Finally, the Tukey HSD test with *family-wise* confidence level of 95 % (reported at the bottom of Table 5) supports this evidence. Figure 4 shows box-plots with post-hoc performance of the AOS variants. Clearly, our approach *Ea-dmab* outperforms the other variants.

Table 5: Royal Staircase. Two-way ANOVA F test, pairwise t test and Tukey HSD test.

ANOVA	Df	Sum Sq	Mean Sq	F value	Pr(>F)
Algorithm	2	950.1	475.05	42.222	**4.16e-15**
Instance	3	4990.3	1663.42	147.841	1.23e-16
Residuals	390	4388.1	11.25		
t Tests	E_a*-dmab*		*Fit-dmab*		
Fit-dmab	**2.1e-6**		-		
Random	**3.9e-8**		0.016		
TukeyHSD		diff	lwr	upr	**p adj**
Fit vs E_a		-3.03	-4.0	-2.05	**0.00**
Rand vs E_a		-3.49	-4.46	-2.52	**0.00**
Rand vs Fit		-0.46	-1.43	0.50	0.023

Figure 5 shows the dynamic of operators' learned probabilities across a run for *Fit-dmab* (top) and E_a*-dmab* (bottom) on the $N = 80, K = 5$ Royal staircase case instance. The curves show a different behaviour for both variants. The evolvability, E_a based variant (bottom plot), shows a varying selection dynamic of the tree operators, while the fitness based variant seems to converge to fixed probabilities since very early in the run.

5.3 Multiple Knapsack

Four multiple-knapsack instances, taken from the literature, were selected as test problems. These are multimodal constrained problems with sizes ranging from 50 to 105 objects and from 2 to 30 knapsacks. These (and several

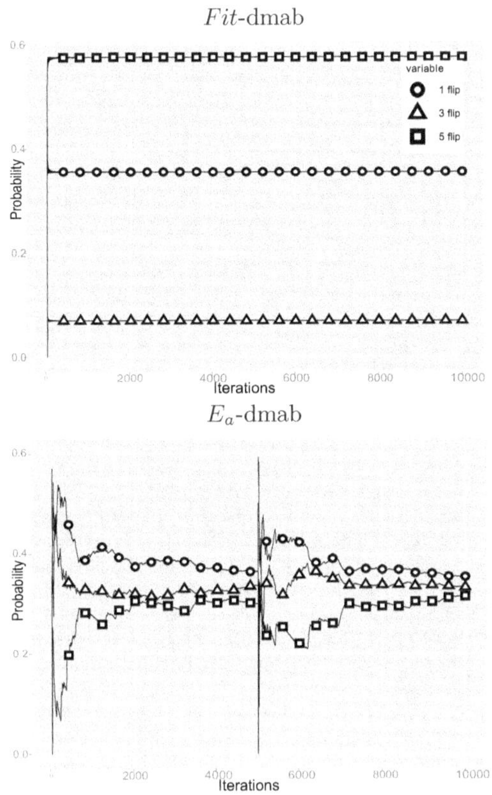

Figure 5: Royal Staircase ($N = 80, K = 5$). Dynamic of adapted operators' probabilities over a run.

other) problems are available online from the OR-library by Beasley[1].

Table 6 reports the two-way ANOVA F test (top part of the Table), and the pairwise t test with Bonferroni adjustments (middle portion of the Table). The tests support that the E_a-*dmab* variant has significant performance differences as compared to the other variants. The Tukey HSD test with *family-wise* confidence level of 95 %, also conducted and reported at the bottom of Table 6, supports this evidence. Figure 6 shows box-plots with post-hoc performance of the AOS variants. Our approach *Ea-dmab* also outperforms the other variants in the Multiple Knapsack problem.

Table 6: Multiple Knapsack. Two-way ANOVA F test, pairwise t test and Tukey HSD test.

ANOVA	Df	Sum Sq	Mean Sq	F value	Pr(>F)
Algorithm	2	6.46	3.23	9.33	**1.0-4**
Instance	3	8.42	2.80	8.11	2.2e-16
Residuals	390	1.35e10	3.46e7		
t Tests		E_a-*dmab*	*Fit-dmab*		
Fit-dmab		**3.12e-3**	-		
Random		**8.52e-5**	1.11e-2		
TukeyHSD		diff	lwr	upr	**p adj**
Fit vs Ea		-986	-2690	717	**3.27e-3**
Ran vs Ea		-3066	-4770	-1362	**8.66e-5**
Rand vs Fit		-2079	-3783	-375	0.0012

[1]The OR Library is available at `http://people.brunel.ac.uk/~mastjjb/jeb/info.html`.

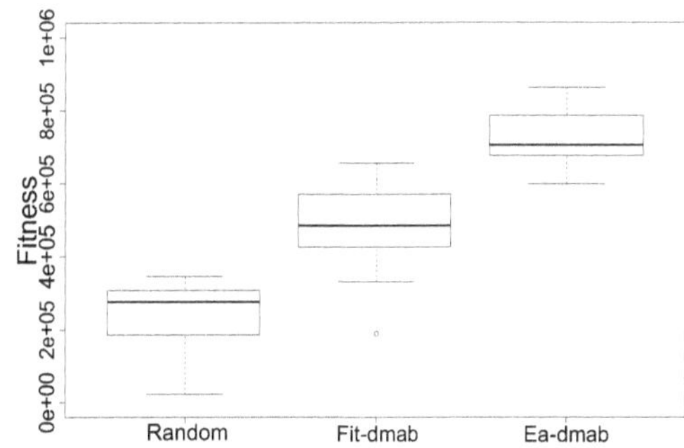

Figure 6: Multiple Knapsack. Post-hoc boxplot with performance distribution across all instances.

Figure 7 shows the dynamic of operators' learned probabilities across a run for *Fit-dmab* (top) and E_a-*dmab* (bottom) on the *Weish30* multiple knapsack instance. The curves for both plots sown a simliar overall behaviour; with the E_a based variant (bottom plot) more sharply detecting probability distribution changes. This, together with the observed improved performance, seems to indicate that the evolvabilty metric is producing a richer feedback to guide adaptive operator selection.

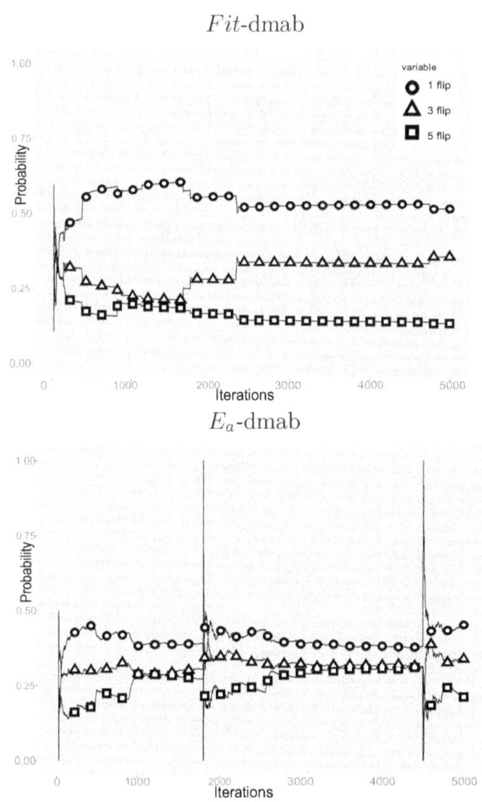

Figure 7: Multiple Knapsack ($Weish30$). Dynamic of adapted operators' probabilities over a run.

6. CONCLUSIONS

We investigated the benefits of using evolvability metrics to inform the adaptive selection of operators. Evolvability metrics are estimated using a Metropolis-Hasting algorithm, which reduces the computational complexity of their calculation. Results on binary-based combinatorial problems reveal that assigning credits to operators based on their evolvability rather than on their direct fitness improvement produces statistically significant improved results. This suggest that considering the fitness landscape local structure of combinatorial problems provides a richer picture to guide the self-configuration of heuristic search algorithms. From the two selection rules tested, the dynamic multi-armed bandit produced better performance, suggesting that it is critical to be able to detect and act upon abrupt changes in the local structure of the fitness landscape. Our research contributes to the goal of using fitness landscape local features to inform dynamic self-configuring algorithms.

Future work will test the proposed approach on real-world combinatorial optimisation problems such as educational timetabling and vehicle routing. Our study considered a standard evolution strategy with a pool of mutation operators as the high-level search strategy. It is worth stressing that adaptive operator selection methods are relevant to any heuristic search strategy or algorithmic component where a pool of search operators is available, be they mutation, recombination, memes (local searchers) or construction-destruction heuristics. This research is therefore relevant to selective hyper-heuristics, adaptive large neighbourhood search and memetic algorithms. Further work will then explore how to incorporate the proposed adaptive mechanism within other algorithmic frameworks.

Acknowledgements

This work was supported by Consejo Nacional de Ciencia y Tecnología (CONACYT) México under PhD Scholarship 311849 and the Engineering and Physical Sciences Research Council (EPSRC - grant number EP/J017515), UK.

7. REFERENCES

[1] L. Altenberg. The evolution of evolvability in genetic programming. In *Advances in Genetic Programming*, pages 47–74. MIT Press, Cambridge, MA, USA, 1994.

[2] P. Auer, N. Cesa-Bianchi, and P. Fischer. Finite-time analysis of the multiarmed bandit problem. *Machine Learning*, 47(2-3):235–256, 2002.

[3] M. Birattari, T. Stützle, L. Paquete, and K. Varrentrapp. A racing algorithm for configuring metaheuristics. In *Proceedings of the Genetic and Evolutionary Computation Conference, GECCO 2002*, pages 11–18. Morgan Kaufmann, 2002.

[4] E. K. Burke, M. Gendreau, M. Hyde, G. Kendall, G. Ochoa, E. Ozcan, and R. Qu. Hyper-heuristics: a survey of the state of the art. *Journal of the Operational Research Society (JORS)*, 64(12):1695–1724, 2013.

[5] M. Caserta, S. Schwarze, and S. Voß. A new binary description of the blocks relocation problem and benefits in a look ahead heuristic. In *Evolutionary Computation in Combinatorial Optimization*, volume 5482 of *Lecture Notes in Computer Science*, pages 37–48. Springer Berlin Heidelberg, 2009.

[6] L. Da Costa, A. Fialho, M. Schoenauer, and M. Sebag. Adaptative operator selection with dynamic multi-armed bandits. In *Proceedings of the Genetic and Evolutionary Computation Conference (GECCO 2008)*, pages 913–920. ACM, 2008.

[7] A. Fialho, L. Costa, M. Schoenauer, and M. Sebag. Dynamic multi-armed bandits and extreme value-based rewards for adaptive operator selection in evolutionary algorithms. In *Learning and Intelligent Optimization*, volume 5851 of *Lecture Notes in Computer Science*, pages 176–190. Springer Berlin Heidelberg, 2009.

[8] F. Hutter, H. Hoos, K. Leyton-Brown, and T. Stützle. Paramils: An automatic algorithm configuration framework. *Journal of Artificial Intelligence Research (JAIR)*, 36:267–306, 2009.

[9] S. Khuri, Thomas Bäck, and Jörg Heitkötter. The zero/one multiple knapsack problem and genetic algorithms. In *Proceedings of the 1994 ACM Symposium of Applied Computation*, pages 188–193. ACM Press, 1994.

[10] S. Luke and AKM K. A. Talukder. Is the meta-ea a viable optimization method? In *Proceeding of the Fifteenth Annual Conference on Genetic and Evolutionary Computation Conference*, GECCO '13, pages 1533–1540, New York, NY, USA, 2013. ACM.

[11] K. M. Malan and A. P. Engelbrecht. A survey of techniques for characterising fitness landscapes and some possible ways forward. *Information Sciences*, 241(0):148 – 163, 2013.

[12] M-E. Marmion, C. Dhaenens, L. Jourdan, A. Liefooghe, and S. Verel. On the neutrality of flowshop scheduling fitness landscapes. In *Learning and Intelligent Optimization*, volume 6683 of *Lecture Notes in Computer Science*, pages 238–252. Springer Berlin Heidelberg, 2011.

[13] J. Maturana and F. Saubion. A compass to guide genetic algorithms. In *Parallel Problem Solving from Nature, PPSN X*, pages 256–265. Springer, 2008.

[14] S. Meyer-Nieberg and H-G. Beyer. In *Parameter Setting in Evolutionary Algorithms*, volume 54 of *Studies in Computational Intelligence*, pages 47–75. Springer Berlin Heidelberg, 2007.

[15] M. Mitchell, S. Forrest, and J. H. Holland. The Royal Road for genetic algorithms: Fitness landscapes and GA performance. In *Proceedings of the First European Conference on Artificial Life. Toward a Practice of Autonomous Systems*, pages 245–254. MIT Press, Cambridge, MA, 1992.

[16] Y. S. Ong, M. H. Lim, N. Zhu, and K. W. Wong. Classification of adaptive memetic algorithms: a comparative study. *IEEE Transactions on Systems, Man, and Cybernetics, Part B*, 36(1):141–152, 2006.

[17] T. Smith, P. Husbands, P. Layzell, and M. O'Shea. Fitness landscapes and evolvability. *Evolutionary Computation*, 10(1):1–34, 2002.

[18] Dirk Thierens. An adaptive pursuit strategy for allocating operator probabilities. In *Proceedings of the 2005 conference on Genetic and evolutionary computation*, GECCO '05, pages 1539–1546, New York, NY, USA, 2005. ACM.

[19] E. van Nimwegen and J. P. Crutchfield. Optimizing epochal evolutionary search: Population-size dependent theory. Technical Report Preprint 98-06-046, Santa Fe Institute, 1998.

[20] L Vanneschi, M. Clergue, P. Collard, M. Tomassini, and S. Verel. Fitness clouds and problem hardness in genetic programming. In *Proceedings of the Genetic and Evolutionary Computation (GECCO 2004)*, volume 3103 of *Lecture Notes in Computer Science*, pages 690–701. Springer Berlin Heidelberg, 2004.

[21] N. Veerapen, J. Maturana, and F. Saubion. An exploration-exploitation compromise-based adaptive operator selection for local search. In *Genetic and Evolutionary Computation Conference, GECCO 2012*, pages 1277–1284. ACM, 2012.

[22] T. Wauters, K. Verbeeck, P. Causmaecker, and G. Berghe. Boosting metaheuristic search using reinforcement learning. In *Hybrid Metaheuristics*, volume 434 of *Studies in Computational Intelligence*, pages 433–452. Springer Berlin Heidelberg, 2013.

On the Pathological Behavior of Adaptive Differential Evolution on Hybrid Objective Functions

Ryoji Tanabe
Graduate School of Arts and Sciences
The University of Tokyo
Tokyo, Japan
rt.ryoji.tanabe@gmail.com

Alex S. Fukunaga
Graduate School of Arts and Sciences
The University of Tokyo
Tokyo, Japan
fukunaga@idea.c.u-tokyo.ac.jp

ABSTRACT

Most state-of-the-art Differential Evolution (DE) algorithms are adaptive DEs with online parameter adaptation. We investigate the behavior of adaptive DE on a class of hybrid functions, where independent groups of variables are associated with different component objective functions. An experimental evaluation of 3 state-of-the-art adaptive DEs (JADE, SHADE, jDE) shows that hybrid functions are "adaptive-DE-hard". That is, adaptive DEs have significant failure rates on these new functions. In-depth analysis of the adaptive behavior of the DEs reveals that their parameter adaptation mechanisms behave in a pathological manner on this class of problems, resulting in over-adaptation for one of the components of the hybrids and poor overall performance. Thus, this class of deceptive benchmarks pose a significant challenge for DE.

Categories and Subject Descriptors

G.1.6 [**Mathematics of Computing**]: Optimization—*Global optimization*; I.2.8 [**Artificial Intelligence**]: Problem Solving, Control Methods, and Search—*Heuristic methods*

General Terms

Algorithms

Keywords

Adaptive Differential Evolution, Parameter Control, Deception, Hybrid Functions

1. INTRODUCTION

Differential Evolution (DE) is an Evolutionary Algorithm (EA) that was primarily designed for real parameter optimization problems [11]. Despite its relative simplicity, DE has been shown to be competitive with more complex optimization algorithms, and has been applied to many practical problems [7]. As with other EAs, the search performance of DE algorithms depends on control parameter settings [6, 7, 10]. A standard DE has three main control parameters, which are the population size N, scaling factor F, and crossover rate CR. However, it is well-known that the optimal settings of these parameters are problem-dependent and parameter tuning in real-world problem is often infeasible for various reasons. Since this is a significant problem in practice, adaptive mechanisms for adjusting the DE control parameters on-line during the search process have been studied by many researchers [6, 13, 18].

It is well known that when the objective function is unimodal and nonseparable, high values of CR tend to perform well, while low values of CR tend to be effective for problems that are multimodal and separable.[1] In addition, when the objective is unimodal, moderate values of F work well, but if the objective is multimodal, high F is desirable in order to maintain diversity. Thus, adaptive DE algorithms attempt to adapt control parameters in order to match the characteristics of the objective function [6, 13, 18].

EA performance evaluations for black-box optimization are usually based on a suite of artificial benchmark problems. In recent years, benchmark sets such as the GECCO BBOB [1] and CEC2005 benchmarks [12] have been widely used in the EA community. However, it has been noted that these benchmark sets consist mostly of problems which have unrealistic, "extreme" characteristics, e.g., all of the variables are separable, or all of the variables are nonseparable [14]. Many real-world problems have more complex structure and can not be trivially characterized. For example, problems can be partially separable, where some groups of variables interact with each other but are independent of the other groups, i.e., "separability" is not a binary feature. Yet, previous standard benchmarks focused almost exclusively on such extreme benchmarks, casting some doubt on the utility of such benchmarks in predicting the performance of EAs on real-world problems. For example, real-world problems where all variables interact uniformly and completely with each other (as in the standard Rosenbrock and Rotated-Rastrigin functions) are rare. Because of this growing realization, the EA community has recently introduced benchmark sets that incorporate more complex interactions between variables [9, 14].

Hybrid objective functions [9] are a class of benchmark

GECCO'14, July 12–16, 2014, Vancouver, BC, Canada.

http://dx.doi.org/10.1145/2576768.2598322.

[1]In *separable* functions the solution vector can be decomposed as $f(\boldsymbol{x}) = \sum_{i=1}^{D} f_i(x_i)$ and can be each dimension can be optimized independently. On the other hand, nonseparable functions have dependences between variables and cannot be so easily decomposed and optimized.

functions that have been recently proposed and incorporated into the CEC2014 single-objective optimization competition test suite. In a hybrid function, the variables in a solution vector are partitioned into multiple groups, and each group is evaluated according to a different component evaluation function. The overall objective function value is the sum of the component objective values. Unlike previous benchmark functions where all variables were associated with the same search space, each group of variables are associated with a search space with characteristics that are distinct from the search spaces associated with the other variable groups.

In this paper, we show that state-of-the-art adaptive DE algorithms such as SHADE [13], JADE [18], and jDE [6] perform extremely poorly on a class of hybrid functions [9] composed of 2 components. We show, for example that a simple hybrid function which, in some sense, closely resembles the well know, trivial Sphere function, poses a serious challenge for adaptive DEs. An in-depth analysis of the failure of DEs on hybrid functions, and show extensive evidence that adaptive DEs are easily deceived by hybrid functions – they tend to quickly adapt to solve the component of the hybrid function that is easier to make progress on, and are unable to solve the other component. Thus, this study identifies a class of *adaptive-DE-hard* problems that confound adaptive DEs and poses a challenging direction for future work.

2. DIFFERENTIAL EVOLUTION

This section briefly describes DE [11]. A DE population is represented as a set of real parameter vectors $\boldsymbol{x}_i = (x_1, ..., x_D)$, $i = 1, ..., N$, where D is the dimensionality of the target problem, and N is the population size.

In each generation t, a mutant vector $\boldsymbol{v}_{i,t}$ is generated from an existing population member $\boldsymbol{x}_{i,t}$ by applying some mutation strategy. $\boldsymbol{v}_{i,t} = \boldsymbol{x}_{r_1,t} + F \cdot (\boldsymbol{x}_{r_2,t} - \boldsymbol{x}_{r_3,t})$ is rand/1 mutation strategy which is the most popular mutation strategy. The indices r_1, r_2, r_3 are randomly selected from $[1, N]$ such that they differ from each other as well as i. The parameter $F \in [0, 1]$ controls the magnitude of the differential mutation operator. After generating the mutant vector $\boldsymbol{v}_{i,t}$, it is crossed with the parent $\boldsymbol{x}_{i,t}$ in order to generate trial vector $\boldsymbol{u}_{i,t}$. Binomial Crossover, the most commonly used crossover operator in DE, is implemented as follows: For each j ($j = 1, ..., D$), if rand$[0, 1) \le CR$ or $j = j_{rand}$, $u_{j,i,t} = v_{j,i,t}$. Otherwise, $u_{j,i,t} = x_{j,i,t}$. Where, rand$[0, 1)$ denotes a uniformly selected random number from $[0, 1)$, and j_{rand} is a decision variable index which is uniformly randomly selected from $[1, D]$. $CR \in [0, 1]$ is the crossover rate.

After all of the trial vectors $\boldsymbol{u}_{i,t}, 0 \le i \le N$ have been generated, each individual $\boldsymbol{x}_{i,t}$ is compared with its corresponding trial vector $\boldsymbol{u}_{i,t}$, keeping the better vector in the population. In Section 3, we say that a generation of trial vector is successful if this replacement occurs. These process are repeated until some termination criterion is encountered.

3. STATE-OF-THE-ART ADAPTIVE DE ALGORITHMS

This section reviews three state-of-the-art adaptive DE variants, jDE [6], JADE [18], SHADE [13] that we evaluate in our experimental study. These three algorithms were selected because jDE and JADE are among the most highly cited adaptive DE algorithms, and SHADE is the hightest ranking DE method in the CEC2013 Competition on Real-Parameter Single Objective Optimization [4].

jDE [6] assigns a different set of parameter values F_i and CR_i to each $\boldsymbol{x}_i$, which is used for generating the trial vectors. Initially, the parameters for all individuals $\boldsymbol{x}_i$ are set to $F_i = 0.5$, $CR_i = 0.9$. The control parameter values of the trial vectors are inherited from their parents. However, each parameter is randomly modified (within a pre-specified range) with some probability, and modified parameters are kept for the next generation only when a trial is successful.

JADE [18] has two corresponding, adaptive variables, μ_{CR}, μ_F. The CR and F associated with each individual are generated according to a normal/Cauchy distribution with means μ_{CR}, μ_F. At the end of each generation, the values of μ_{CR}, μ_F are updated according to the CR, F pair that resulted in the generation of the successful trial vector in that generation. As the search progresses, μ_{CR}, μ_F should gradually approach the optimal values for the given problem. In addition to parameter adaptation, JADE also uses a novel mutation strategy called current-to-$p$best/1 and an external archive for storing previously generated individuals.

SHADE [13] is an adaptive DE which based on JADE algorithm, but uses a historical memory of successful parameter settings based parameter adaptation scheme. Success-history based adaptation uses a historical memory M_{CR}, M_F which stores a set of CR, F values that have performed well in the past, and generate new CR, F pairs by directly sampling the parameter space close to one of these stored pairs.

4. HYBRID FUNCTIONS

In this paper, we study a simplified, special class of hybrid functions [9] in which the number of groups is 2, i.e., each hybrid function is composed of two objective functions f, g and sum the component objectives to obtain the overall, hybrid objective value.

More specifically: Given a D-dimensional decision variable vector $\boldsymbol{x}$, in our hybrid functions $H_{f,g}$, $\boldsymbol{x}$ is partitioned into $\boldsymbol{x}^f$ ($\boldsymbol{x}^f = x_1^f, ..., x_{D_f}^f$) and $\boldsymbol{x}^g$ ($\boldsymbol{x}^g = x_1^g, ..., x_{D_g}^g$), the group of variables which will be evaluated using f, g respectively. Let $r \in [0, 1]$ be the fraction of variables assigned to component objective f. If r is set to high value, $\boldsymbol{x}^f$ is allocated to the high fraction of variables and vice versa. We ensured the integrality of D_f, D_g by setting $D_f =$ round$(D \times r)$, $D_g = D - D_f$. The D_f indices corresponding to $\boldsymbol{x}^f$ are randomly selected from $[1, D]$, and the remainder are assigned to $\boldsymbol{x}^g$.

The objective function value of a candidate individual $\boldsymbol{x}$ is $H_{f,g}(\boldsymbol{x}) = f(\boldsymbol{x}^f) + g(\boldsymbol{x}^g)$, where $f(\boldsymbol{x}^f)$ and $g(\boldsymbol{x}^g)$ are the result of evaluating $\boldsymbol{x}^f$ and $\boldsymbol{x}^g$ according to f and g, respectively. For example, if f is the Sphere function and g is the Rastrigin function, then the objective value for a candidate solution vector for the 30-dimensional ($D = 30$) hybrid function $H_{\text{Sphere,Rastrigin}}$ with $r = 0.4$ would be the sum of the results of evaluating a 12-variable Sphere function and a 18-variable Rastrigin function.

5. EXPERIMENTS

Our study uses hybrid objective functions that combine pairs of the following five, commonly used benchmark functions: Sphere, Schwefel 1.2, Rosenbrock, Rastrigin, Ackley. Table 1 shows their properties (unimodal/multimodal, separable/nonseparable). The search spaces were normalized to

Table 1: 5 basic functions for hybrid functions

Functions	Properties
Sphere	Separable, Unimodal
Schwefel 1.2	Nonseparable, Unimodal
Rosenbrock	Nonseparable, Weakly Multimodal
Rastrigin	Separable, Strongly Multimodal
Ackley	Separable, Weakly Multimodal

Table 2: 8 hybrid functions

Type of Hybrid	Hybrid Functions	Base Functions
Heterogeneous	$H_{\mathrm{Sph,Ras}}$	Sphere & Rastrigin
	$H_{\mathrm{Sph,Ack}}$	Sphere & Ackley
	$H_{\mathrm{Sch,Ras}}$	Schwefel 1.2 & Rastrigin
	$H_{\mathrm{Sch,Ack}}$	Schwefel 1.2 & Ackley
	$H_{\mathrm{Ros,Ras}}$	Rosenbrock & Rastrigin
	$H_{\mathrm{Ros,Ack}}$	Rosenbrock & Ackley
Homogeneous	$H_{\mathrm{Sph,Sch}}$	Sphere & Schwefel 1.2
	$H_{\mathrm{Ras,Ack}}$	Rastrigin & Ackley

$[-100, 100]^D$ and the global optima were shifted to a point where each dimension is uniformly selected from $[-80, 80]$. See details of these standard functions and their original feasible regions in [16].

Table 2 shows the 8 hybrid functions that we studied, which combine pairs of the 5 basic functions from Table 1. We write $H_{f,g}$ to denotes the hybrid functions constructed from f and g (e.g., $H_{\mathrm{Sph,Ras}}$ is composed of the Sphere and Rastrigin functions). The first 6 hybrid functions in Table 2, which we refer to as *heterogeneous hybrids*, combine functions whose characteristics differ significantly from each other. For example, $H_{\mathrm{Sph,Ras}}$ combines the unimodal Sphere function and the multimodal Rastrigin function. In contrast, the remaining 2 functions, which we refer to as *homogeneous hybrids*, ($H_{\mathrm{Sph,Sch}}$, $H_{\mathrm{Ras,Ack}}$) combine 2 similar functions – $H_{\mathrm{Sph,Sch}}$ combines two unimodal functions, and $H_{\mathrm{Ras,Ack}}$ combines two multimodal functions. The heterogeneous functions are studied in Section 5.1, and the homogeneous functions are studied in Section 5.2.

We studied problems with $D = 30, 50$ dimensions. The ratio of variables assigned to each component function, r (see Section 4), was varied from 0.0 to 1.0 in increments of 0.1. Each run of the DE continues until either (1) the difference between the best-so-far solution and the optimal solution $\leq$ 1e-8, in which case we treat the run as "success", or (2) the number of objective function calls exceeds $D \times 10,000$, in which case the run is treated as a "failure". On each problem, for each r, each algorithm is executed 50 times. The success rate is the number of "successes" (as defined above) divided by 50.

We evaluated three, state-of-the-art adaptive DE algorithms: SHADE [13], JADE [18] and jDE [6] (see Section 3). In addition, we also evaluate the standard DE [11] for comparison. The source code for JADE was from [2], minimally modified these programs so that it would work with our hybrid benchmark functions. The other DE's (standard DE, SHADE, and jDE) were implemented by ourselves.[2] For each algorithm, we used the control parameter values that were suggested in the cited, original papers.[3] For the standard DE, we used a typical configuration [6, 18] with population size $N = 50$ [4], rand/1/bin generation strategy, $F = 0.5$. We set CR to 0.1 and 0.9 since these values have been shown to work well for separable functions and non-separable functions respectively [10]. Below, we refer to the standard DE using CR of 0.1 and 0.9 as DE-CR0.1 and DE-CR0.9, respectively.

5.1 Results for hybrid functions with dissimilar (heterogeneous) components

Figure 1 shows the success rates of DE algorithms on the hybrid functions, $H_{\mathrm{Sph,Ras}}$, $H_{\mathrm{Sph,Ack}}$, $H_{\mathrm{Sch,Ras}}$, $H_{\mathrm{Sch,Ack}}$, $H_{\mathrm{Ros,Ras}}$, $H_{\mathrm{Ros,Ack}}$ (30, 50 dimensions) for various allocations (r) of variables among the two components.

We highlight several trends that are evident in Figure 1:

- The adaptive DE algorithms (SHADE, JADE, jDE) tend to have very high success rates when $r = 0.0$ and 1.0. That is, they are quite capable of solving the pure benchmark functions from which the hybrids are derived. The only exception is the low success rates for jDE on Schwefel 1.2 and Rosenbrock function for 50 dimensions.

- The success rates for adaptive DE algorithms tend to be high when r is close to 0, deteriorate steeply for some particular range of r (most commonly when $r = 0.5 \sim 0.9$) but recover again at $r = 1.0$, and most of the curves in Figure 1 are shaped like a "V" or "U".

- Any degradations in success rates as a function of r that are present in 30 dimensions are even more pronounced in 50 dimensions. This is expected, since problems with higher dimensionality are more difficult for DE algorithms in general.

5.1.1 Discussion

It is well known that in general, unimodal functions are easier to search than multimodal functions. Thus, on hybrid functions that combine unimodal and multimodal components ($H_{\mathrm{Sph,Ras}}$, $H_{\mathrm{Sph,Ack}}$, $H_{\mathrm{Sch,Ras}}$, $H_{\mathrm{Sch,Ack}}$), one might expect that as the multimodal component of the hybrid function increases, (i.e., fraction of variables evaluated using the multimodal Rastrigin and Ackley functions increases), the problems would become monotonically more difficult. However, our results indicate the opposite: success rates tended to be higher as the multimodal component increased, and the lowest success rates for SHADE, JADE and jDE occurred when the allocation to unimodal components (Sphere, Schwefel 1.2) were 0.8 and 0.9. A similar tendency was shown in $H_{\mathrm{Ros,Ack}}$, $H_{\mathrm{Ros,Ras}}$, which combines weakly multimodal (Rosenbrock, Ackley) and strongly multimodal (Rastrigin) functions.

[2]We used version 1.1 of SHADE, available at [3].

[3]However, for jDE, we reduced the population size to 50 because using the population size of 100 suggested in [6], since jDE did not converge within the maximum # of fitness evaluations used in this study.

[4]Although $N = 100$ is commonly used, we chose 50 for the same reason as for jDE above.

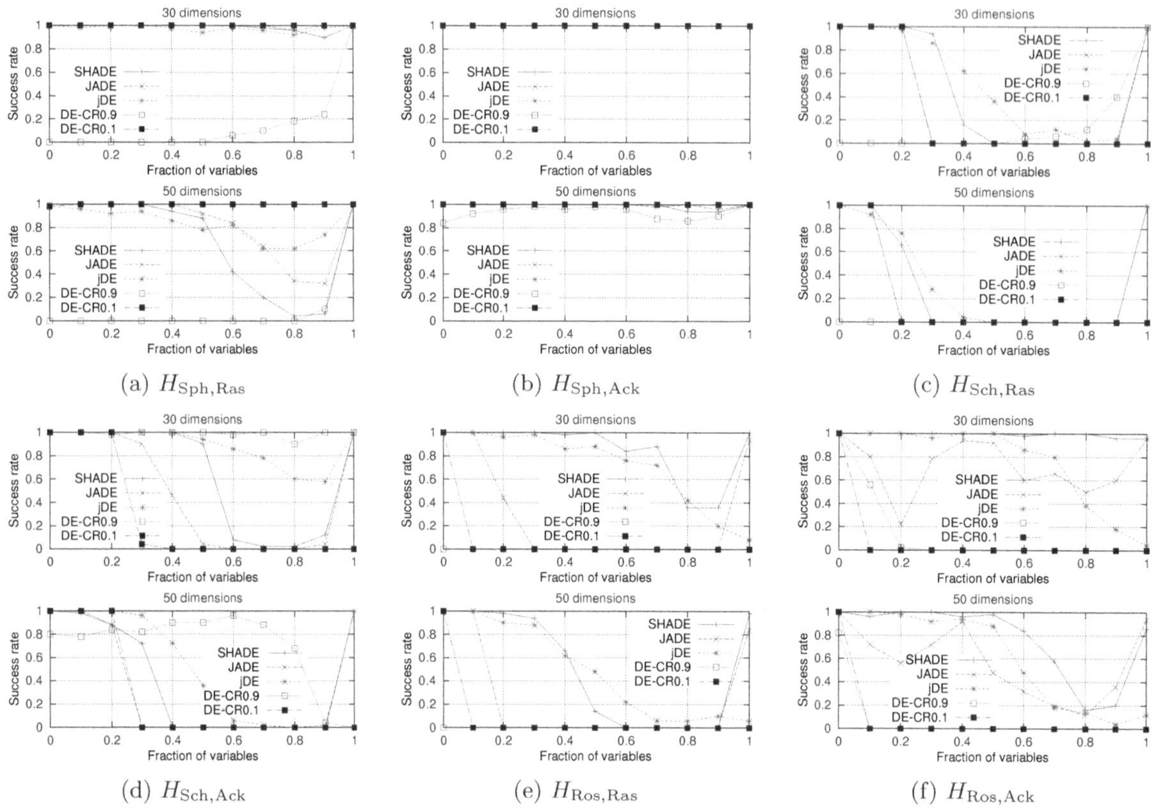

(a) $H_{\mathrm{Sph,Ras}}$ (b) $H_{\mathrm{Sph,Ack}}$ (c) $H_{\mathrm{Sch,Ras}}$

(d) $H_{\mathrm{Sch,Ack}}$ (e) $H_{\mathrm{Ros,Ras}}$ (f) $H_{\mathrm{Ros,Ack}}$

Figure 1: Performance of DE on heterogeneous hybrid functions ($H_{\mathrm{Sph,Ras}}$, $H_{\mathrm{Sph,Ack}}$, $H_{\mathrm{Sch,Ras}}$, $H_{\mathrm{Sch,Ack}}$, $H_{\mathrm{Ros,Ras}}$, $H_{\mathrm{Ros,Ack}}$). Success rate (out of 50 runs) is shown as a function of r, the fraction of variables allocated to component function f. Results for 30 and 50 dimensions are shown.

The results on the $H_{\mathrm{Sph,Ras}}$ hybrid function (Figure 1(a)) are particularly interesting: While the state-of-the-art adaptive DEs that we selected (SHADE, JADE, jDE) have been shown to perform well overall on previous benchmark suites, all of them perform extremely poorly when $r = 0.7 \sim 0.9$ – *In other words, state-of-the-art DE algorithms perform extremely poorly on a hybrid benchmark which is largely composed of the trivial Sphere function!* Furthermore, while DE is known to perform well on separable functions [8], the $H_{\mathrm{Sph,Ras}}$ function is a completely separable function that is extremely challenging for adaptive DE. This is the first such example that we are aware of. Finally (and perhaps most surprisingly), the standard DE using $CR = 0.1$ performed the best among all of the DEs evaluated on $H_{\mathrm{Sph,Ras}}$, significantly outperforming all of the sophisticated, adaptive DEs.

5.2 Results for hybrid functions with similar (homogeneous) components

Section 5.1 showed that on heterogeneous hybrid functions where the components have significantly different search space characteristics (e.g., a unimodal-multimodal hybrid), the performance of DE tended to degrade dramatically for some mixture r of the the components. Are hybrid functions, in general, extremely difficult for DE? In this section, we consider homogeneous hybrid functions where, in contrast to Section 5.1, the component functions have search space

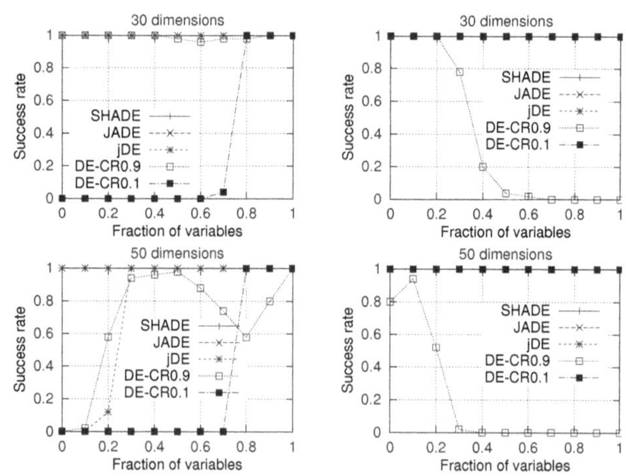

(a) $H_{\mathrm{Sph,Sch}}$ (b) $H_{\mathrm{Ras,Ack}}$

Figure 2: Performance of DE on homogeneous hybrid functions ($H_{\mathrm{Sph,Sch}}$, $H_{\mathrm{Ras,Ack}}$). Success rate (out of 50 runs) is shown as a function of r, the fraction of variables allocated to component function f. Results for 30, 50 dimensions are shown.

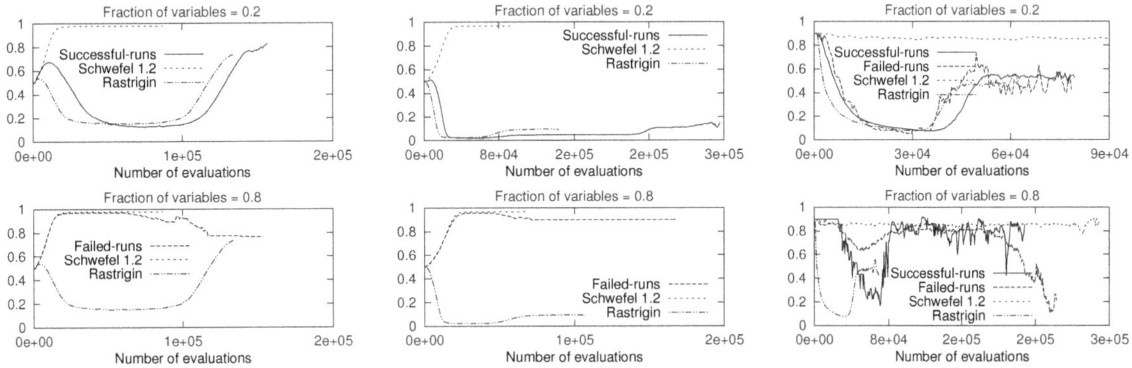

(a) SHADE (b) JADE (c) jDE

Figure 3: CR parameter adaptation history of adaptive DEs for $r = 0.2$ (top row) and $r = 0.8$ (bottom row) on $H_{\mathrm{Sch,Ras}}$ ($D = 30$).

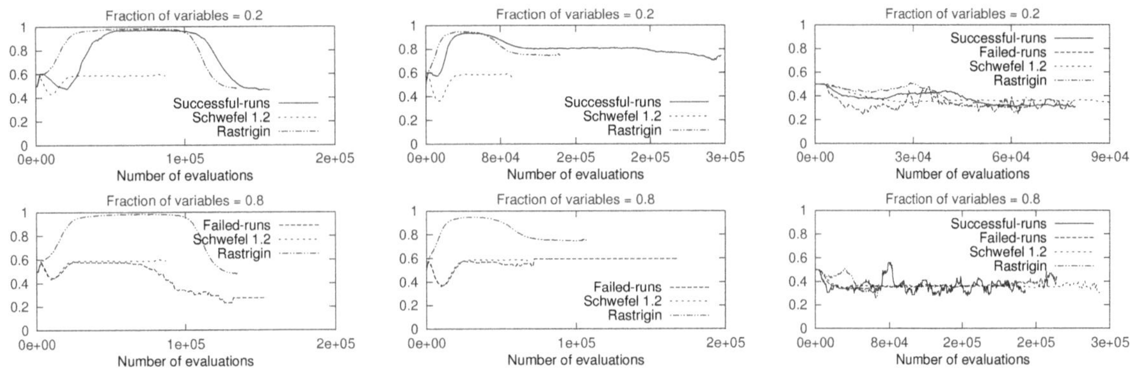

(a) SHADE (b) JADE (c) jDE

Figure 4: F parameter adaptation history of adaptive DEs for $r = 0.2$ (top row) and $r = 0.8$ (bottom row) on $H_{\mathrm{Sch,Ras}}$ ($D = 30$).

characteristics that are similar to each other. We used two hybrid functions $H_{\mathrm{Sph,Sch}}$ and $H_{\mathrm{Ras,Ack}}$. $H_{\mathrm{Sph,Sch}}$ combines two unimodal functions, and $H_{\mathrm{Ras,Ack}}$ is a hybrid of two multimodal functions.

The results for $H_{\mathrm{Sph,Sch}}$ and $H_{\mathrm{Ras,Ack}}$ in 30 and 50 dimensions are shown in Figure 2. SHADE, JADE and jDE all achieve almost perfect success rates for all values of r on $H_{\mathrm{Sph,Sch}}$ and $H_{\mathrm{Ras,Ack}}$. This result is somewhat counter-intuitive, given that solving Rastrigin and Ackley (both of which are multimodal) individually is much more difficult than solving Rastrigin and Sphere (unimodal) individually, and yet, the hybrid $H_{\mathrm{Ras,Ack}}$ seems to be much easier than the hybrid function $H_{\mathrm{Sph,Ras}}$ (Figure 1(a)), which stumps all of the adaptive DE algorithms when r is between 0.7-0.9.

This result suggests that while hybrid functions are exceptionally challenging for DE when the component functions have different search space characteristics from each other, hybrids composed of similar components such as $H_{\mathrm{Sph,Sch}}$, $H_{\mathrm{Ras,Ack}}$ do not result in difficult problems for DE.

One notable counterexample to the claim that heterogeneous hybrids are challenging is in Figure 1(b), which shows that all methods perform very well on the hybrid $H_{\mathrm{Sph,Ack}}$, regardless of r, despite the fact that Sphere is unimodal and Ackley is multimodal. However, Ackley is only weakly multimodal, and furthermore, both Sphere and Ackley are separable, so $H_{\mathrm{Sph,Ack}}$ is actually similar to a homogeneous hybrid function such as $H_{\mathrm{Sph,Sch}}$ and $H_{\mathrm{Ras,Ack}}$ and therefore does not pose a challenge for adaptive DE.

5.3 Why do adaptive DEs fail? – Analysis of adaptive DE parameter adaptation on hybrid functions

In order to understand why DE performance degrades so dramatically in the hybrid function experiments in Section 5.1, we analyze the parameter adaptation behavior for the adaptive DEs (SHADE, JADE, jDE) during the runs for the experiments in Section 5.1.[5]

Figures 3 and 4 show the adaptation of the CR, F parameters (see Section 3) by SHADE, JADE, and jDE for $r = 0.2$ (top row) and $r = 0.8$ (bottom row) on $H_{\mathrm{Sch,Ras}}$ (30 dimensions). The x-axis is the number of objective function evaluations. The y-axis shows the proxy values of CR, F

[5]We collected this parameter adaptation data by re-running the experiments described in Section 5.1 with identical random seeds used in the original experiments and saving all of the parameter adaptation histories at every generation.

values for each algorithm. Since each algorithm has a different adaptation mechanism, appropriate proxy values are shown for each mechanism: (1) for SHADE, we show the median values of the CR, F values stored in historical memory, M_{CR}, M_F, [13]; (2) for JADE, μ_{CR}, μ_F [18], the adaptive parameters for CR and F, are shown; (3) for jDE, which assigns a different CR and F to each individual i [6], the median values CR_i and F_i are shown.

Each of 50 runs (for each r, for each function, for each algorithm) was classified as Successful Runs or Failed Runs, depending on whether the run achieved the success criteria defined at the beginning of Section 5 for this study, i.e., error $\leq$ 1e-8. In cases where all 50 runs were failures or all 50 runs were successes, only one of these lines are shown.

Each figure also shows how proxy values for F and CR adapt in successful runs on pure Rastrigin and Schwefel 1.2 functions (i.e., $r = 0.0, 1.0$). The "Schwefel 1.2" and "Rastrigin" lines in Figures 3 and 4 show that on the Schwefel 1.2 function, SHADE, JADE, and jDE adapt CR to high values and F to medium values. On the other hand, for the Rastrigin function, SHADE, JADE, and jDE adapt CR to low values and F converges to high values. Thus, CR and F converge to very different values depending on the target function (Rastrigin vs. Schwefel 1.2). These results are consistent with previous work which experimentally analyzed the dynamics of DE parameter adaptation [6, 10], as well as previous results on parameter adaptation for SHADE, JADE, and jDE [6,13,18].

Now, consider the behavior of adaptive DE on $H_{\text{Sch,Ras}}$ when $r = 0.2$ (high fraction of variables allocated to the Rastrigin function). From the figures, the adaptive behavior of CR and F in SHADE and JADE very closely matches their behavior on the Rastrigin function. jDE also displays a similar tendency, albeit weaker (possibly due to the way we defined the proxy metrics as medians). On the other hand, for $r = 0.8$ (high fraction of variables allocated to Schwefel 1.2), the opposite trend can be seen, as the proxies for CR and F behave similarly to the pure Schwefel 1.2 case. This leads to the main, qualitative result of our study:

OBSERVATION 1. *When an adaptive DE is applied to a hybrid function, the parameter adaptation mechanism tends to adapt and converge the CR and F parameters so as to match the component for which initial improvements are easier. More specifically, the adaptive mechanisms target the component with larger allocation of variables.*

Observation 1 holds quite robustly for our class of hybrid functions. Trends similar to those seen in Figures 3 and 4 were observed for almost all hybrid functions we tested, for various values of r.

Since limited space prevents us from showing the equivalents of Figures 3 and 4 for all functions and all r, we instead rely on a summary, difference metric which allows to compactly summarize and visualize these trends across all of the hybrid functions, for all r.

Suppose that we run jDE on the Sphere function twice, and that runs #1 and #2 terminate after 5 and 4 generations, respectively, and that the CR-proxy values (as defined above in this section) are (0.7, 0.6, 0.5, 0.7, 0.4) for run #1 and (0.9, 0.8, 0.3, 0.5) for run #2. The average behavior of CR on these two runs is (0.8, 0.7, 0.4, 0.6, 0.4).

Further suppose that jDE is run on Rastrigin twice, with an average CR behavior of (0.4, 0.5, 0.4). The differential

Algorithm 1: Function $\delta(\overline{\boldsymbol{p}}_f, \overline{\boldsymbol{p}}_g)$ for computing the difference between two average adaptation histories

input : $\overline{\boldsymbol{p}}_f, \overline{\boldsymbol{p}}_g$: the average adaptation histories on f, g
output: δ: the average distance on overall generations between $\overline{\boldsymbol{p}}_f$ and $\overline{\boldsymbol{p}}_g$

$t_{max} = \min(|\overline{\boldsymbol{p}}_f|, |\overline{\boldsymbol{p}}_g|)$, $\delta = 0$;
for $t = 1$ **to** t_{max} **do**
  $\delta = \delta + |\overline{p}_{f,t} - \overline{p}_{g,t}|$;
$\delta = \delta / t_{max}$;

Algorithm 2: Aggregating the average distances (to obtain the data points in Figure 5)

input : $\overline{\boldsymbol{p}}_{H_{f,g}}, \overline{\boldsymbol{p}}_f, \overline{\boldsymbol{p}}_g$ on all hybrid functions
output: $\overline{\delta}_{H_{f,g},f}, \overline{\delta}_{H_{f,g},g}$: the average distance on all hybrid functions

$\overline{\delta}_{H_{f,g},f} = 0$, $\overline{\delta}_{H_{f,g},g} = 0$;
for $H_{f,g} \in \boldsymbol{I}$ **do**
  $\overline{\delta}_{H_{f,g},f} = \overline{\delta}_{H_{f,g},f} + \delta(\overline{\boldsymbol{p}}_{H_{f,g}}, \overline{\boldsymbol{p}}_f)$;
  $\overline{\delta}_{H_{f,g},g} = \overline{\delta}_{H_{f,g},g} + \delta(\overline{\boldsymbol{p}}_{H_{f,g}}, \overline{\boldsymbol{p}}_g)$;
$\overline{\delta}_{H_{f,g},f} = \overline{\delta}_{H_{f,g},f} / |\boldsymbol{I}|$, $\overline{\delta}_{H_{f,g},g} = \overline{\delta}_{H_{f,g},g} / |\boldsymbol{I}|$;

values between the CR-history on Sphere and the Rastrigin function is (0.4, 0.2, 0.0), and the distance between the CR-history over time is $(0.4 + 0.2 + 0.0)/3 = 0.2$[6]. Algorithm 1 describes the computation of average distance in general.

The distance $\delta(\overline{\boldsymbol{p}}_f, \overline{\boldsymbol{p}}_g)$ can be used as a measure of the similarity between the parameter adaptation histories $\overline{\boldsymbol{p}}_f, \overline{\boldsymbol{p}}_g$ on f and g. The smaller the value of $\delta(\overline{\boldsymbol{p}}_f, \overline{\boldsymbol{p}}_g)$, the more similar the parameter adaptation histories are, and conversely, the larger $\delta(\overline{\boldsymbol{p}}_f, \overline{\boldsymbol{p}}_g)$ is, the more different the parameter adaptation histories. Average distances among histories among a set of instances $\boldsymbol{I}$ can be computed similarly.

For example, for some particular r, suppose that $\delta(H_{\text{Sph,Ras}}$, Sphere)=0.4 and $\delta(H_{\text{Sch,Ack}}$, Schwefel 1.2) $= 0.6$. In this case, the average value of the distances is $(0.4 + 0.6)/2 = 0.5$. For the same r, if $\delta(H_{\text{Sph,Ras}}$, Rastrigin) $= 0.6$ and $\delta(H_{\text{Sch,Ack}}$, Ackley) $= 0.8$, then the average value of the distances is $(0.6 + 0.8)/2 = 0.7$. In particular, we are interested in distances between the histories on a hybrid function $H_{f,g}$ with particular r value and the histories on its component functions, $\delta(H_{f,g}, f)$ and $\delta(H_{f,g}, g)$, averaged over all instances $\overline{\delta}^r_{H_{f,g},f}$, $\overline{\delta}^r_{H_{f,g},g}$. Algorithm 2 shows the pseudocode for this overall computation for some particular r.

Figures 5 shows $\overline{\delta}^r_{H_{f,g},f}$, $\overline{\delta}^r_{H_{f,g},g}$ for both DE parameters CR (top row) and F (bottom row), averaged over all 6 of the heterogeneous hybrid functions in Table 2 according to Algorithm 2, for $r \in 0.1, ..., 0.9$. Data for both 30 and 50 dimensions are included in the SHADE and JADE figures (the similarity metric can be computed independently of dimensionality). Since jDE had a success rate of 0 on Schwefel 1.2 for 50-dimensions, we only included data for 30 dimensions. When computing the average histories for the hybrid function, we include all runs, including successful and failed runs. On the other hand, for the average histories for the

[6]If two histories have different lengths, the unmatched portions of the longer history are ignored.

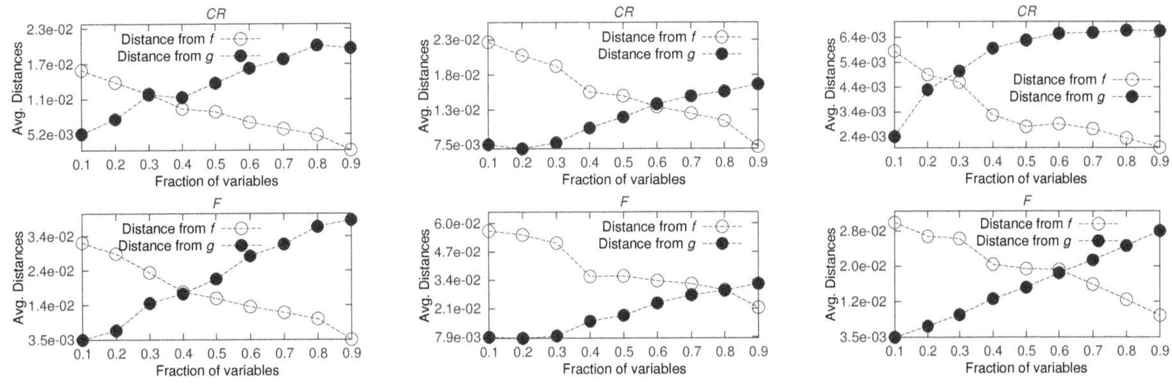

(a) SHADE (b) JADE (c) jDE

Figure 5: Average distances of parameter adaptation history of SHADE, JADE, jDE between heterogeneous hybrid functions ($H_{\mathrm{Sph,Ras}}$, $H_{\mathrm{Sph,Ack}}$, $H_{\mathrm{Sch,Ras}}$, $H_{\mathrm{Sch,Ack}}$, $H_{\mathrm{Ros,Ras}}$, $H_{\mathrm{Ros,Ack}}$) and its component function f, g.

pure component functions f and g, we used only the successful runs, because we want to compare the behavior on hybrid functions vs. the "ideal" behavior on the pure functions, and the average successful behavior is used as an approximation for this "ideal" behavior.

Figures 5 show that for all of the adaptive DEs. When r is low ($H_{f,g}$ is mostly allocated to g), the distance between the behavior on $\overline{\delta}^r_{H_{f,g},g}$ is small, which means that the parameter adaptation behavior of the DE on $H_{f,g}$ is quite similar to its parameter adaptation behavior on g. However, as r increases, $\overline{\delta}^r_{H_{f,g},g}$ grows monotonically, i.e., the DE behaves differently on the hybrid than it would on g. At the same time, as r increases, $\overline{\delta}^r_{H_{f,g},f}$ decreases, and the DE behaves more and more like it would on f. This trend can be very clearly seen for both CR and F.

From the results above, we can see that in a heterogeneous hybrid function $H_{f,g}$ composed of two component functions f, g with different search space characteristics, the proxy values for CR, F in state-of-the-art adaptive DEs behave similarly to when the DE is applied to the individual component function f or g which is allocated more variables in the hybrid function, i.e., the individual component which is most "similar" to the hybrid function.

Thus, we have shown that Observation 1 consistently holds across all 3 state-of-the-art adaptive DEs, for all of the heterogeneous, hybrid functions where pathological behavior was observed in Section 5.1.

5.3.1 Discussion

In general, most adaptive DEs that have been proposed to date, including SHADE, JADE, and jDE, operate according to the principle that if the current set of control parameter setting $S = (CR, F)$ successfully generates trial vectors that are more fit than their parents, then the next set of control parameters to be applied should be somehow based on or influenced by S. In other words, adaptive strategies tend to operate based on a meta-greedy assumption.

On our class of hybrid functions, this meta-greedy approach leads to failure. In a hybrid with 2 component functions, the component C_H with a higher fraction of variables contributes more to the objective function than the other component with lower allocation, C_L, because the overall objective value is the sum of the component objective values. Our results suggest that there is a tendency for adaptive DEs to quickly adapt to achieve good performance on C_H, neglecting C_L. After optimizing the C_H component, the adaptive DE is unable to re-adapt to so that the C_L component can be optimized.

This explains the pathological behaviors by adaptive DEs observed in Section 5.1, Figure 1(c): Although SHADE, JADE, and jDE had success rates close to 1.0 on $H_{\mathrm{Sch,Ras}}$ when $r = 0.2$, the success rate was almost 0.0 when $r = 0.8$. This is most likely due to the meta-greedy nature of the adaptive DE described above. The components of $H_{\mathrm{Sch,Ras}}$, Schwefel 1.2 and Rastrigin, differ significantly. Schwefel 1.2 is unimodal, and nonseparable, while Rastrigin is multimodal and separable, and as noted earlier, parameter settings which are appropriate for one are ineffective for the other. Figures 3 and 4 show that the DEs have adapted entirely for one or the other – this means that they have become poorly adapted for the other component.

When $r = 0.8$, the DEs have adapted to solve Schwefel 1.2, a unimodal, nonseparable function. However, these parameter settings are very poorly suited for Rastrigin, a multimodal, separable function, and it is likely that the DEs fail because their control parameters (which are adapted for a unimodal function) promote rapid descent into local minima, where the search becomes trapped.

A similar conclusion can be reached regarding the failure of adaptive DE on $H_{\mathrm{Ros,Ras}}$ in Figure 1(e). Although both Rosenbrock and Rastrigin are multimodal, Rosenbrock is nonseparable (requiring high CR values), while Rastrigin is separable (requiring low CR values), and overadaptation for one function prevents success on the other component of the hybrid objective. In general, in heterogeneous hybrid functions that include Rastrigin or Ackley, when the allocation of variables to the multimodal Rastrigin and Ackley functions are too small, the adaptive DEs can not sufficiently adapt to the multimodal component, resulting on poor success rates on the hybrid functions.

In contrast, the high success rates for $r = 0.2$ can be explained as follows. Adaptation for the multimodal Rastrigin function does not cripple the DE's ability to solve unimodal problems such as the Schwefel 1.2. Although convergence may be slowed compared to parameter settings that are tuned for a unimodal function, the lack of local minima means that the search algorithm will eventually succeed.

6. CONCLUSION

We investigated the behavior of DE on a class of hybrid functions [9], where groups of variables are assigned to different component functions. We showed that state-of-the-art adaptive DEs (SHADE [13], JADE [18], jDE [6]) all perform very poorly when the components of the hybrid functions are heterogeneous, with different search space characteristics.

The main contribution of this study is an in-depth analysis of adaptive DE control parameter behavior on hybrid functions, showing that adaptive DE fails on these hybrid functions because their parameter adaptation mechanisms are fundamentally mismatched with the structure of hybrid functions. DE control parameter adaptation tends to be "deceived" into over-adapting for one of the components of the hybrid, at the expense of adaptation for the other component.

Previous analysis of parameter adaptation in DE has been limited to plotting control parameter values [6, 18]. Our analysis of DE parameter adaptation introduces a new technique for summarizing and visualizing parameter adaptation (the parameter history distance metric described in Section 5.3) which provided a very clear understanding of when and how DE succeeds and fails in the class of hybrid functions. We believe that this kind of aggregated distance can be applied to understand the adaptive behavior of DE (and other algorithms with adaptive parameters) for other types of functions, e.g. multi-objective optimization.

This work suggests that a parameter adaptation mechanism that seeks to optimize its behavior for a single, target function is a major design limitation when faced with a hybrid objective function. Our preliminary efforts to overcome this limitation by, e.g., associating a different set of (CR, F) parameters for each variable, have not been successful so far, and this seems to be a nontrivial problem. Therefore, designing methods that are effective on hybrid objective functions is a challenging direction for future research. One possible direction would be to investigate crossover methods that explicitly seek to identify and exploit dependencies between variables in order to automatically partition and handle the components of the hybrid objective, e.g., [17].

While this study was limited to hybrid functions with 2 component functions, preliminary experiments suggest that similar issues arise on hybrids with more components, and we are currently extending this study to hybrids with 3+ components. Finally, while this study focused on understanding the difficulty that hybrid functions pose for adaptive DE, heterogeneous hybrid functions are challenging for other kinds of non-adaptive, state-of-the-art DE. CoDE, a well-known non-adaptive DE [15] also fails on these functions (see Supplemental Data [5]). Understanding the reason why hybrid functions are difficult for CoDE, as well as evaluation of hybrid functions on other classes of DE is an avenue for future work.

7. ACKNOWLEDGMENTS

This work was supported by JSPS KAKENHI Grants 2324002 and 25330253.

8. REFERENCES

[1] http://coco.gforge.inria.fr/doku.php.

[2] http://dces.essex.ac.uk/staff/qzhang.

[3] https://sites.google.com/site/tanaberyoji.

[4] http://www.ntu.edu.sg/home/EPNSugan/index_files-/CEC20-13/CEC2013.htm.

[5] Supplementary material of this paper.

[6] J. Brest, S. Greiner, B. Bošković, M. Mernik, and V. Žumer. Self-Adapting Control Parameters in Differential Evolution: A Comparative Study on Numerical Benchmark Problems. *IEEE Tran. Evol. Comput.*, 10(6):646–657, 2006.

[7] S. Das and P. N. Suganthan. Differential Evolution: A Survey of the State-of-the-Art. *IEEE Tran. Evol. Comput.*, 15(1):4–31, 2011.

[8] N. Hansen and S. Kern. Evaluating the CMA Evolution Strategy on Multimodal Test Functions. In *PPSN*, pages 282–291, 2004.

[9] J. J. Liang, B. Y. Qu, and P. N. Suganthan. Problem Definitions and Evaluation Criteria for the CEC 2014 Special Session and Competition on Single Objective Real-Parameter Numerical Optimization. Technical report, Zhengzhou University and Nanyang Technological University, 2013.

[10] J. Rönkkönen, S. Kukkonen, and K. V. Price. Real-Parameter optimization with Differential Evolution. In *IEEE CEC*, pages 506–513, 2005.

[11] R. Storn and K. Price. Differential Evolution - A Simple and Efficient Heuristic for Global Optimization over Continuous Spaces. *J. Global Optimiz.*, 11(4):341–359, 1997.

[12] P. N. Suganthan, N. Hansen, J. J. Liang, K. Deb, Y. P. Chen, A. Auger, and S. Tiwari. Problem Definitions and Evaluation Criteria for the CEC 2005 Special Session on Real-Parameter Optimization. Technical report, Nanyang Technological University, 2005.

[13] R. Tanabe and A. Fukunaga. Success-History Based Parameter Adaptation for Differential Evolution. In *IEEE CEC*, pages 71–78, 2013.

[14] K. Tang, X. Li, P. N. Suganthan, Z. Yang, and T. Weise. Benchmark Functions for the CEC'2010 Special Session and Competition on Large-Scale Global Optimization. Technical report, University of Science and Technology of China, 2010.

[15] Y. Wang, Z. Cai, and Q. Zhang. Differential Evolution With Composite Trial Vector Generation Strategies and Control Parameters. *IEEE Tran. Evol. Comput.*, 15(1):55–66, 2011.

[16] X. Yao, Y. Liu, and G. Lin. Evolutionary Programming Made Faster. *IEEE Tran. Evol. Comput.*, 3(2):82–102, 1999.

[17] M. Zhabitsky and E. Zhabitskaya. Asynchronous Differential Evolution with Adaptive Correlation Matrix. In *GECCO*, pages 455–462, 2013.

[18] J. Zhang and A. C. Sanderson. JADE: Adaptive Differential Evolution With Optional External Archive. *IEEE Tran. Evol. Comput.*, 13(5):945–958, 2009.

Analysis of Evolutionary Algorithms using Multi-Objective Parameter Tuning

Roberto Ugolotti
Dept. of Information Engineering
University of Parma, Italy
rob_ugo@ce.unipr.it

Stefano Cagnoni
Dept. of Information Engineering
University of Parma, Italy
cagnoni@ce.unipr.it

ABSTRACT

Evolutionary Algorithms (EAs) and other metaheuristics are greatly affected by the choice of their parameters, not only as regards the precision of the solutions found, but also for repeatability, robustness, speed of convergence, and other properties. Most of these performance criteria are often conflicting with one another.

In our work, we see the problem of EAs' parameter selection and tuning as a multi-objective optimization problem, in which the criteria to be optimized are precision and speed of convergence. We propose EMOPaT (Evolutionary Multi-Objective Parameter Tuning), a method that uses a well-known multi-objective optimization algorithm (NSGA-II) to find a front of non-dominated parameter sets which produce good results according to these two metrics.

By doing so, we can provide three kinds of results: (i) a method that is able to adapt parameters to a single function, (ii) a comparison between Differential Evolution (DE) and Particle Swarm Optimization (PSO) that takes into consideration both precision and speed, and (iii) an insight into how parameters of DE and PSO affect the performance of these EAs on different benchmark functions.

Categories and Subject Descriptors

I.2.8 [**Artificial Intelligence**]: Problem Solving, Control Methods, and Search—*Heuristic methods*

Keywords

Parameter Tuning; Evolutionary Algorithms; Multi-objective Optimization; Parameter Analysis

1. INTRODUCTION

The approach used most frequently when comparing different Evolutionary Algorithms (EAs) is simply to test them on several benchmark functions to extract some aggregated information, like average or median fitness, and compare them to some references. However, as happens with many real world problems, this kind of result is not the only goal of the optimization process; therefore, this is not the only "quality" measure that can be considered. For many problems (e.g. real-time optimization used in image analysis) the result is to be obtained within a limited time; in many other applications, instead of aiming at the optimum of a function, it is better to have an optimizer that robustly gives a result that is good enough, even if not the best possible. On the contrary, like in many planning or scheduling tasks, it is possible to run an optimization process several times, and then select the best result obtained in any run. In this case, an EA that is less reliable than another one, but is able to find better results once in a while might be preferable.

Therefore, it makes little sense to state that an algorithm is better than another one, if the quality criterion is not specified, especially because objectives can be conflicting.

This point of view can be taken even in the simplest situation: a single algorithm on a single problem. Considering different conditions and quality criteria, the best choice of the algorithm parameters may change. Consequently, when creating or tuning an algorithm to solve a particular problem, it is necessary to take into consideration which goals in term of robustness, precision, speed, or other quality criteria are aimed at, and the need for a trade-off is implicit.

In this paper, we propose an approach called EMOPaT (Evolutionary Multi-Objective Parameter Tuning) that can be useful in designing and tuning some commonly used EAs, like Differential Evolution (DE) or Particle Swarm Optimization (PSO)[1], according to the goals and limitations imposed by the optimization process. This work is an extension to the method we previously proposed in [23], in which PSO and DE were used as meta-optimizers to find the best PSO parameter settings, for optimizing 20 benchmark functions. We extend that approach by using a multi-objective genetic algorithm (Non-dominated Sorting Genetic Algorithm-II, NSGA-II [4]) that optimizes more than one quality criterion at the same time. In this way, the results of the tuning process is not a single set of parameters, but an entire collection of sets, which is able to generate different trade-offs between opposing goals. The EA instances we obtain, as well as their parameter values, can give useful insights into the behavior of the algorithm under investigation, suggesting good ranges of parameters and revealing how a parameter affects the quality criterion considered.

GECCO'14, July 12–16, 2014, Vancouver, BC, Canada.
Copyright 2014 ACM 978-1-4503-2662-9/14/07 ...$15.00.
http://dx.doi.org/10.1145/2576768.2598226 .

[1]PSO is not properly an EA, because it is not based on evolution. But, since there are minimal differences from an algorithmic point of view, we consider a population-based optimization method such as PSO equivalent to an EA.

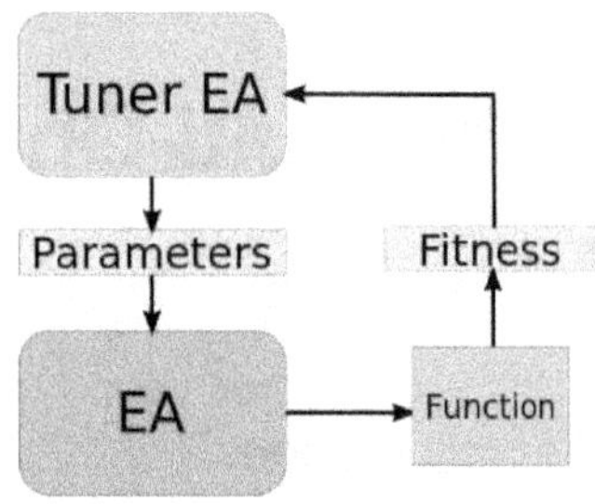

Figure 1: Scheme of a Meta-EA. The algorithm above works on the parameter space of the one below and creates instances of the latter, which are evaluated on one or more functions. The results obtained on these functions represent the quality of the algorithm at the lower level.

Generally speaking, the approach of using an EA to find good parameters for another (or the same) EA is called Meta-EA (see Figure 1). This problem (usually called automatic parameter tuning, or selection) can be seen as a complex optimization task, with many local minima, noise and no easy-to-find solutions [6]. EAs have proven over the years to be able to deal with these issues. Consequently, an evolutionary technique can be used to find a good set of parameters, using as fitness function the performance of the corresponding EA instance.

2. RELATED WORK

Several methods have been used for parameter tuning in the last years [6, 19].

According to the taxonomy presented in [6], EMOPaT can be seen as an example of meta-evolutionary algorithm. The first studies in this field are due to Mercer and Sampson [14] and Grefenstette [8] whose approaches were hampered by the limited computational power available in those years. Bäck [1] proposed a meta-algorithm that combined principles of Evolutionary Strategies and Genetic Algorithms to tune continuous and discrete parameters of a GA at the same time. More recently, some methods have tackled this problem: one of the most successful is called REVAC [15], where the population approximates the probability density function of the most promising areas of the landscape. In [20] it is shown that REVAC could find parameters able to improve the performance of the winner of the competition on the CEC 2005 test-suite. Meissner et al [13] used PSO to tune itself and applied the parameters found to neural network training; in [17], DE and PSO parameters were optimized using a simple metaheuristic called Local Unimodal Sampling.

Multi-objective meta-optimization parameter tuning has been proposed relatively few times. In [5], the authors use NSGA-II to optimize speed and precision of four different algorithms: Simulated Annealing, an Evolutionary Algorithm and two versions of the Estimation of Distribution Algorithm; however, they take into consideration only one parameter at a time, so that approach cannot be seen as a full parameter set optimization. A similar method has been proposed in [21]. The authors describe a variant of a Multi Objective EA (MOEA) called M-FETA (Multi-Function Evolutionary Tuning Algorithm), where the goals that the MOEA has to optimize are different functions, in order to find algorithms that perform well on a single function ("specialists") and on more than one ("generalists"). Finally, [2] proposes a method able to identify the best parameter settings for all possible computational budgets (number of fitness evaluations) up to a specified maximum. This is obtained using a MOEA in which a particle's fitness is the sequence of fitnesses obtained in every generation of the optimization method. Doing so, it is possible to obtain a family of parameter sets which are able to reach the best results considering different computational budgets.

3. EXPERIMENTAL SETUP

In this paper, we performed the tests taking into consideration only one function (in its basic form, no shifting and rotations involved) and two quality criteria (i.e. NSGA-II objectives) at one time. These limitations are set only in order to provide some clear examples of the possible conclusions that can be drawn using this approach, but EMOPaT can be applied to a higher number of functions and criteria. Of course, introducing more functions and criteria may raise computational and complexity issues. We selected three quality criteria, which we are going to test pairwise:

- *Q1* (Precision): best result obtained in $1E6$ fitness evaluations, averaged over N independent runs. To succeed in optimizing this criterion, an EA must be able to explore the search space, find a good solution and refine it as much as possible;
- *Q2* (Speed): number of function evaluations needed to reach a minimum fitness threshold (or goal), averaged over N independent runs. An EA that obtains good results according this criterion must move fast toward a good, even if suboptimal, solution;
- *Q3* (Speed): same as *Q2*, but more suitable for testing parallel algorithm implementations since it considers the number of generations instead of the number of function evaluations. In this way, the population size is not taken directly into consideration in the computation of the quality criterion.

We selected four commonly used benchmark functions (Sphere, Rosenbrock, Griewank and Rastrigin, see definitions in [16]) considering their 10- and 30-dimensional versions. The fitness threshold to be reached was set to 0.1 for Sphere and Griewank, 1.0 for Rosenbrock and 10.0 for Rastrigin. Each set of parameters was tested N times, with N set to 20 when problem dimension is 10 and 15 when it equals 30, and averaging the results over this number of runs. NSGA-II was run with these parameters: 60 individuals, 60 generations, $P_{mut} = 1/8$, $P_{cross} = 0.9$. Each experiment was run 10 times. All these choices, as well as choosing DE and PSO as the algorithms to investigate, are completely arbitrary and have been made just to provide an example of the potentiality of our approach.

The ranges within which DE and PSO parameters were allowed to vary are listed in Table 1. We chose ranges that are wider than the ones usually considered in literature, to see if the automatic search is able to "think outside the box", by finding parameter sets that are rarely used. To select the non-numerical parameters, such as PSO topology or DE mutation and crossover modalities, we used the approach proposed in [23]. Here, every possible option is represented

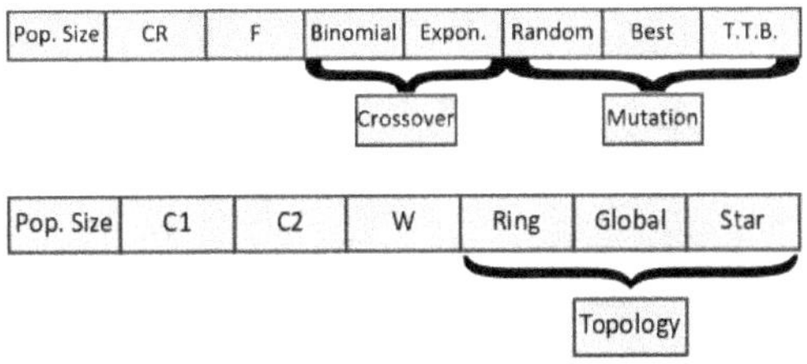

Figure 2: Representation within NSGA-II of PSO (top) and DE (bottom) instances. Non-numerical parameters are represented by a number for each available choice.

by a real value encoded in the NSGA-II individual; the option with the highest value will be selected in the generated EA (see Figure 2).

Differential Evolution	
Population Size	$[4, 300]$
Crossover Rate	$[0.0, 1.0]$
Scale Factor (F)	$[-0.5, 1.5]$
Crossover	{binomial, exponential}
Mutation	{*random*, *best*, *target-to-best*}
Particle Swarm Optimization	
Population Size	$[4, 300]$
Inertia Factor (ω)	$[-0.5, 2.0]$
ϕ_1	$[-1.0, 4.0]$
ϕ_2	$[-1.0, 4.0]$
Topology	{*ring*, *star*, *global*}

Table 1: Ranges of DE and PSO parameters allowed by the tuning algorithms. The notation is the same used in [18] for PSO and [3] for DE.

In the next two Sections, we will present some results: we will not go through a complete analysis of the results, but we will highlight some of the most evident ones, and draw some interesting conclusions.

4. SPEED VS PRECISION

In this section, we will show the results of the tests performed using *Q1* and *Q2* as the objectives (see Section 3).

From every experiment, several analyses can be performed. The following ones are the ones on which we will focus in this and in the next sections:

1. Comparison between performance of the automatically tuned versions of DE and PSO;
2. Relationship between parameters and quality criteria;
3. Range of the parameters of DE and PSO found by the NSGA-II-based optimization;
4. Comparison between the parameters we obtained and the parameters commonly used in the literature (or obtained using other techniques).

The first thing we noticed is how the Sphere function, which is a simple and unimodal function, and to a lesser extent Rosenbrock, obtained fronts usually composed by less than three, almost indistinguishable, solutions: this means that, as could have been expected, in these cases a greedy algorithm is the best choice because there is simply no tradeoff between exploration and exploitation of the search space, and a fast algorithm produces good results using a limited number of function evaluations. In other words, the two objectives of NSGA-II are not conflicting, therefore the Pareto front is reduced to a single solution. Nevertheless, as we will see in the next sections, these results can suggest some conclusions anyway.

For the remaining two functions, the first question we want to answer is if the Pareto fronts (see some examples in Figure 3) obtained by NSGA-II are significant, that is, if the parameter sets that have different locations on a front actually have different behaviors and are not just the outcome of the stochasticity of the algorithm. To clarify this point, we selected 3 solutions within each front (the two extremes and one in the middle), ran 300 tests with those combinations of parameters and compared the results obtained using statistical tests (Wilcoxon test, $p = 0.001$) on the quality values obtained for the criteria. They show that these solutions are always statistically different according to *Q1* while, in some occasions, there are no significant differences when considering *Q2* of PSO. This may suggest that the results of this algorithm are less repeatable under some circumstances.

From now on, we will focus our attention onto a single analysis at a time, and provide some results for each of them.

4.1 Comparison between DE and PSO

A straightforward analysis that can be made when running EMOPaT with two algorithms (in this case DE and PSO) is a direct comparison between the Pareto fronts obtained by optimizing their parameters. Figure 3 compares the fronts obtained for DE (in dark red) and PSO (in light blue) in the 10 runs on the Rastrigin and Griewank functions (10 and 30 dimensions). It can be seen how, in both functions, DE is better than PSO according to both objectives, since PSO generates solutions that are almost always dominated by those obtained using DE.

Moreover, Figure 3 shows that DE results for the Rastrigin function are split into two well-separated clusters. Observations of the parameter space can confirm that fitness-generated clusters can also be divided according to their parameters, which generate DE versions with small intra-cluster variability (see Figure 4).

4.2 Parameters and quality criteria

In order to show how parameters affect the quality criteria, i.e. their positions on the Pareto fronts, we selected two subsets of solutions: the first comprises the 10% of solutions with best results according to *Q1* (from now on, we will call this subset *S1*), the other the 10% with the best *Q2* (*S2*). A significant difference in the values of a parameter between the two subgroups is a reliable suggestion that such a parameter plays an important role in the algorithm. Figure 5 compares some properties of *S1* and *S2* for DE, on the Rastrigin and Griewank functions.

An interesting outcome is that the Sphere function, compared to the other two (multi-modal) ones, never selects *random* mutation, in favor of *target-to-best* and *best*. This confirms the hypothesis that *random* mutation has a less greedy behavior than the other two. Therefore, it seems possible to order the three kinds of mutations considered (see Table 1) based on increasing greediness (or decreasing

Figure 3: Pareto fronts discovered by NSGA-II (dotted dark red lines for DE, solid light blue lines for PSO) for Rastrigin (top) and Griewank (bottom) functions in ten (left) and thirty (right) dimensions. It can be seen that solutions found by DE are usually better than the ones obtained by PSO according to both metrics. Moreover, the corresponding plot shows that DE results for Rastrigin in ten dimensions, can be split into two clusters (see Figure 4). Results of Q1 below a low threshold have been clipped for visualization purposes.

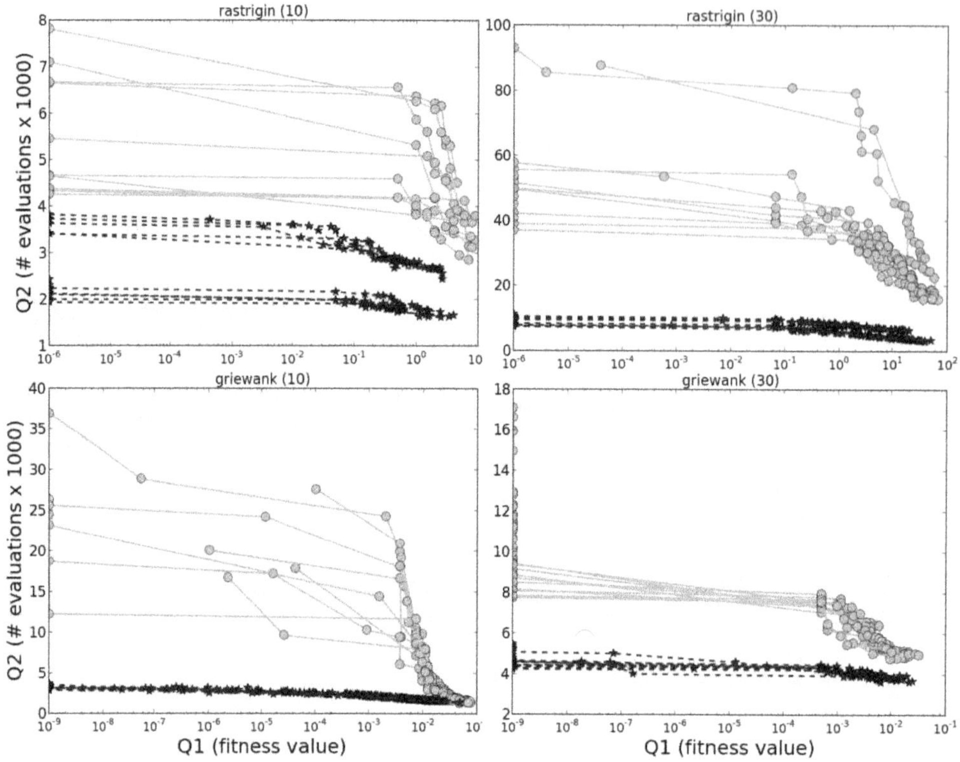

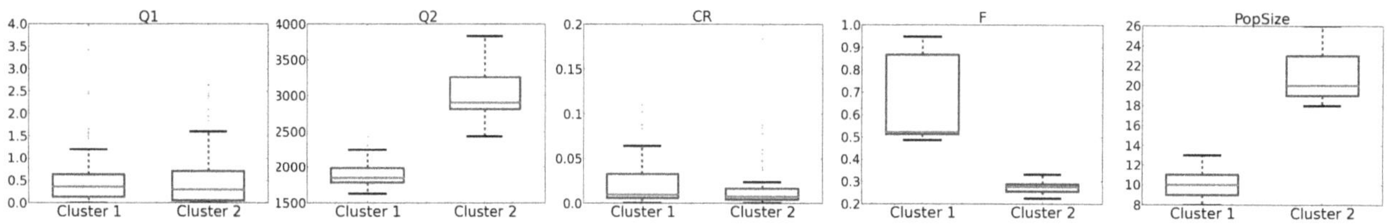

Figure 4: Figure 3 shows that the fronts found in ten independent runs of NSGA-II can be split into two clusters according to results obtained on the 10-dimensional Rastrigin function. The first two boxplots on the left show that Cluster 1 is better than Cluster 2 in *Q2*, while there are no significant differences in *Q1* according to the Wilcoxon test, using $p = 0.001$, therefore Cluster 2 can be considered a local minimum. The last three boxplots show how these results are related to the chosen parameters. Cluster 2 has larger populations, a limited range of $F \approx 0.3$ and uses mostly *random* mutation; Cluster 1 has smaller populations, larger values and variability of F and uses different mutation strategies.

precision): the greediest (therefore, the least precise) is *best*, then *target-to-best* and finally *random* mutation.

The most evident result that recurs in all experiments, for both PSO and DE, is that a direct relationship exists between population size and the position of an EA instance on the fitness front: more particles force the algorithm to waste fitness evaluations in sub-optimal zones, hampering fast convergence, but small populations are often trapped in local minima (see also [10]), making it impossible to reach good results consistently. Figure 6 shows, for the Griewank function, that *Q2* and Population Size are directly correlated for the two EAs. This result confirms the ones obtained with DE by Mallipeddi et al [11]. Moreover, DE needs a smaller population than PSO while, for both, it seems that the population size needs to be small, and the classic rules of thumb used (e.g. population size equal to 10 times the problem dimension) seem to be contradicted, in favour of more rigorous studies [7]. A similar observation can be made for F, particularly for the Griewank function: in this case the relationship is inverse, as a bigger value of F leads to a faster achievement of the fitness goal, worsening *Q1*.

4.3 Range of selected parameters

As we previously said, we allowed PSO and DE parameters to vary within a wide range to see if EMOPaT is able to find unexpected behaviors. This is certainly the case of PSO's inertia factor ω. In all the solutions in the Pareto fronts of the Rastrigin function and for several sets obtained for the Sphere and Rosenbrock functions, this value is negative, as shown in Figure 7. This has been investigated very few times in the past, but hints suggesting this possibility have already been given by automatic tuning methods [17] and systematic searches [12]. It seems that the tuning of this parameter is more influenced by the fitness landscape and less by the quality criterion considered.

Figure 5: In all boxplots and bar plots, a comparison is made between the subsets *S1* and *S2* (see Section 4.2). Each boxplot represents the distribution of the parameter represented on the y axis in the corresponding subgroup. The bar plots on the right describe the distribution of the selected mutation types for the 30-dimensional Rastrigin (top row) and Griewank (bottom) functions; from left to right Population Size, F (scale factor) and mutation type. The distribution of these three parameters is different in the two subgroups, indicating that they significantly affect DE's behavior.

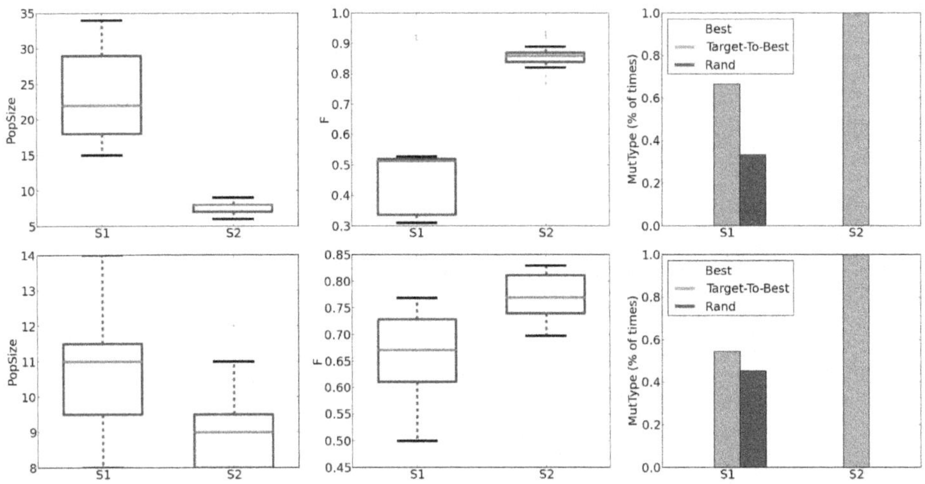

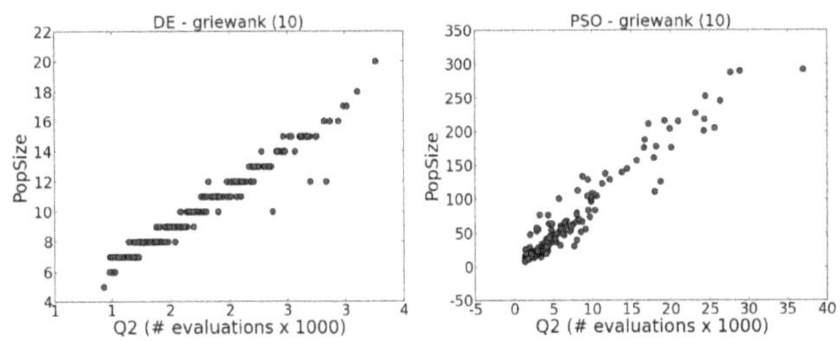

Figure 6: Population Size versus quality criterion *Q2* for DE and PSO. The relationship between the parameter and the result is clear to the naked eye, and it is confirmed by computing the Pearson coefficient, whose value is > 0.96 in all cases. From this comparison it is also noticeable that PSO needs a larger population (and consequently more fitness evaluations) to reach the same fitness as DE.

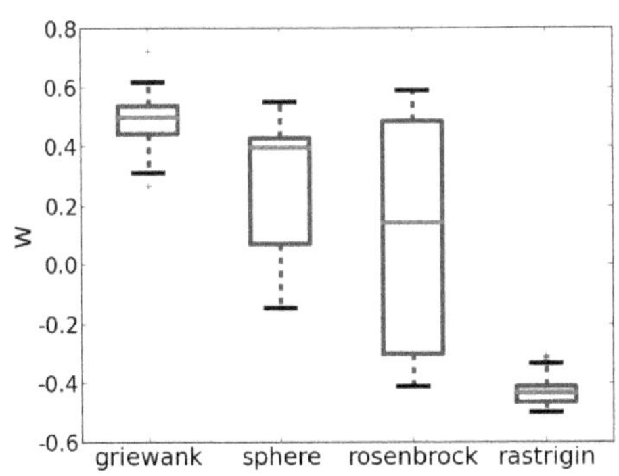

Figure 7: Values of inertia factor ω across the four benchmark functions, 10 dimensions. Negative values are often selected.

4.4 Comparison with other parameters

The last analysis regards the comparison of the results obtained by EMOPaT with other reference implementations of PSO and DE. For both metaheuristics, we selected some parameter sets available in literature, either manually or automatically tuned by the authors. The goal of this procedure is not to prove the superiority of the solutions we find, since different conditions (such as functions, quality criteria, ...) may need different parameter sets; we mainly aim at showing that the parameters we obtain, and consequently the conclusions we provide, are reliable and yield results that are comparable to the state-of-the-art.

To do so, we performed five runs with each reference (see Table 2). Each of these runs consist of N (15 or 20, see Section 3) independent executions of the function under consideration, exactly as it would have happened if these sets of parameters had been generated by NSGA-II during its evolution.

Name	Tuning	Ref.	Parameters
PSO_{M1}	Manual	[9]	Pop=60, $\phi_1 = \phi_2 = 1.496$, $\gamma = 0.730$, Global Topology
PSO_{M2}	Manual	[9]	Pop=60, $\phi_1 = \phi_2 = 1.496$, $\gamma = 0.730$, Ring Topology
DE_{M1}	Manual	[22]	Pop=50, $CR = 0.9$, $F = 0.5$, Mutation Rand, Exp. Crossover
DE_{M2}	Manual	[22]	Pop=50, $CR = 0.9$, $F = 0.5$, Mutation Rand, Bin. Crossover
PSO_{A1}	Auto	[17]	Pop=134, $\phi_1 = 1.8903$, $\phi_2 = 2.122$, $\gamma = -0.1618$, Global Topology
PSO_{A2}	Auto	[16]	Pop=125, $\phi_1 = 1.862$, $\phi_2 = 1.881$, $\gamma = 0.494$, Global Topology
PSO_{A3}	Auto	[23]	Pop=34, $\phi_1 = 1.525$, $\phi_2 = 1.881$, $\gamma = 0.443$, Global Topology
DE_{A1}	Auto	[17]	Pop=19, $CR = 0.122$, $F = 0.4983$, Mutation Rand, Bin. Crossover
DE_{A2}	Auto	[16]	Pop=48, $CR = 0.879$, $F = 0.520$, Mutation Rand, Exp. Crossover

Table 2: DE and PSO versions used as reference. The first column shows the name that is used in the paper to indicate that particular version of the EA.

Most of the settings were unable to even reach the fitness goal, especially the manually-tuned ones. Only in a few cases, some of the references obtained results comparable to the versions proposed here:

- Sphere: for 10 dimensions, DE_{A1} and PSO_{A3} provide good *Q1* with a higher *Q2*; DE_{A1} also prevails in 30 dimensions while performance of PSO_{A3} degrade;
- Rosenbrock: no comparable methods;
- Griewank: DE_{A1} is able to obtain very precise results using a higher number of function evaluations to reach the fitness goal, both in 10 and 30 dimensions;
- Rastrigin: performance of DE_{A1} are comparable to the results obtained by EMOPaT in 10 and 30 dimensions. Two versions of PSO (PSO_{A2} and PSO_{M1}) are slightly worse than those lying on the Pareto front of PSO in the 10-dimensional version (see Figure 8), but their performance degrades in 30 dimensions.

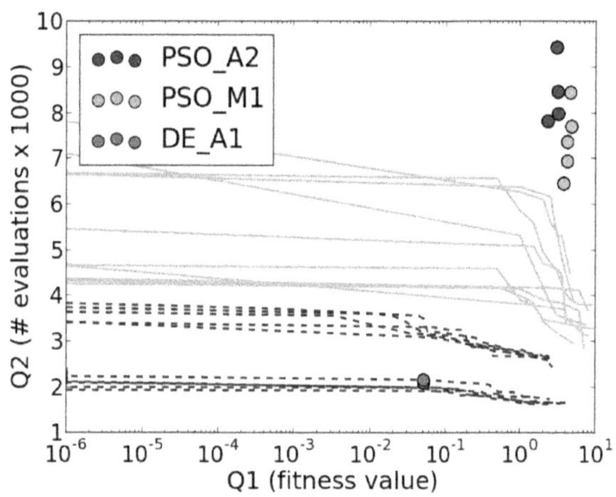

Figure 8: The reference versions of DE and PSO that are able to obtain good results on the ten-dimensional Rastrigin function. The good results of DE_{A1} are not totally unexpected, because its parameters are very similar to the ones obtained by NSGA-II, especially the ones identified as Cluster 1 in Figure 4

5. LEVEL OF PARALLELISM

One of the main benefits of EAs is their easy parallelization. In some cases, such as implementations on GPUs or on clusters, the evaluation of the fitness values of the entire population can be parallelized, in other cases (e.g. a multicore CPU) this parallelization level can be lower. Using EMOPaT with objectives *Q2* and *Q3* can be seen as a way to look at how the choice of the best parameters is affected by the level of parallelism available. We did not implement our algorithms in a distributed or parallel system, because our goal is only to prove that different levels of parallelism need different parameter sets to perform at their best.

5.1 Comparison between DE and PSO

Freed from the need to reach high precision, PSO is less dominated by DE, and in some cases is even able to reach the fitness goal in fewer iterations. Figure 9 shows some fronts, in a similar fashion as before, for all functions.

5.2 Parameters and quality criteria

Even more clearly than in the previous tests, population size is the parameter that most affects the position of a solution in the Pareto front. This factor influences other parameters as well. For instance, in DE, it is very interesting to notice how crossover rate CR and scale factor F behave similarly for almost all functions and dimensions, according to population size (and consequently, to the ratio between the quality criteria). Figure 10 shows these relationships for the Griewank and Sphere functions.

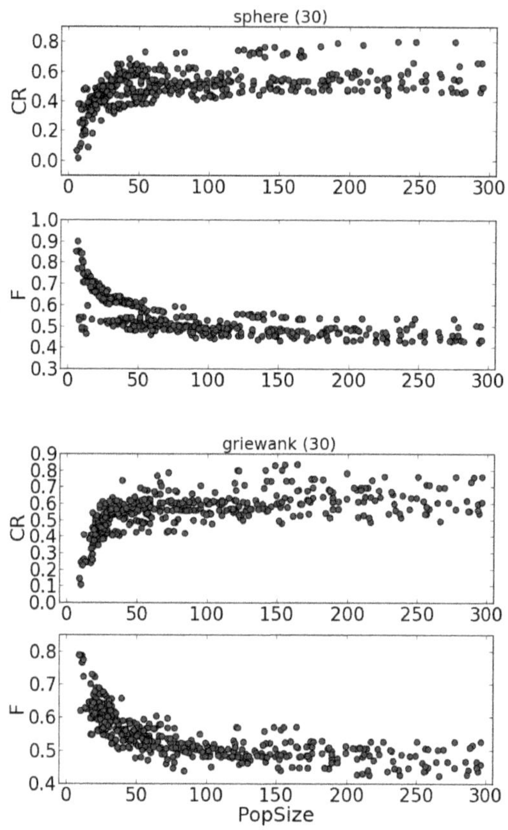

Figure 10: Population size versus crossover rate and scale factor for Sphere (top) and Griewank (bottom) functions in 30 dimensions.

A similar behavior occurs when considering PSO topology: PSO versions with small population often use *ring* topology, and when the number of elements increase, the topology switches to *global*. If we select subgroups *S2* and *S3*, as we did in the previous section, we can see that the topology distribution is very different in the two subgroups for Griewank and Rastrigin (see Figure 11), while Sphere and Rosenbrock use the *global* topology most of the times.

5.3 Range of selected parameters

Figure 12 shows that, in DE, *best* and *target-to-best*, the two greediest mutations, are selected more frequently than in the previous experiments because, even if *random* is better at reaching the global optimum in the long run, these mutation schemes converge to an acceptable solution more quickly. This result confirms the hypothesis made in Section 4.2.

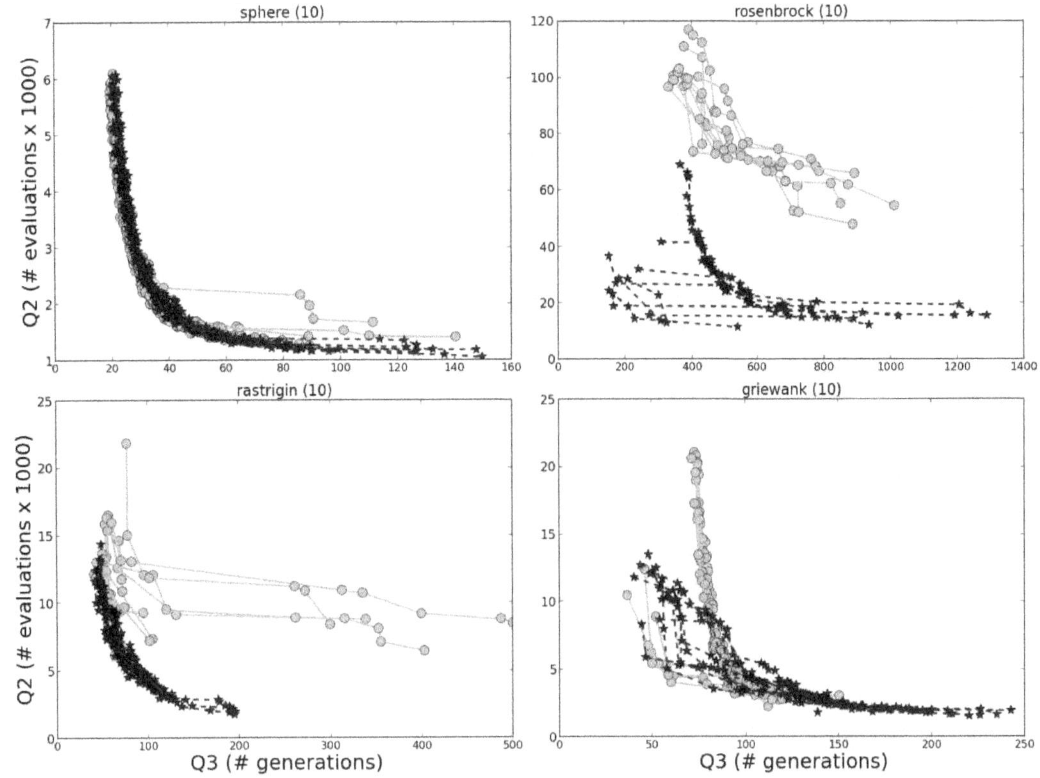

Figure 9: Pareto fronts discovered by NSGA-II (DE fronts are dotted dark red lines, PSO fronts are in light blue) for Sphere, Rosenbrock (top), Rastrigin and Griewank (bottom) functions, 10 dimensions. The two goals are the number of evaluations and generations needed to reach the fitness goal. Compared to the previous tests, PSO is more competitive with respect to DE.

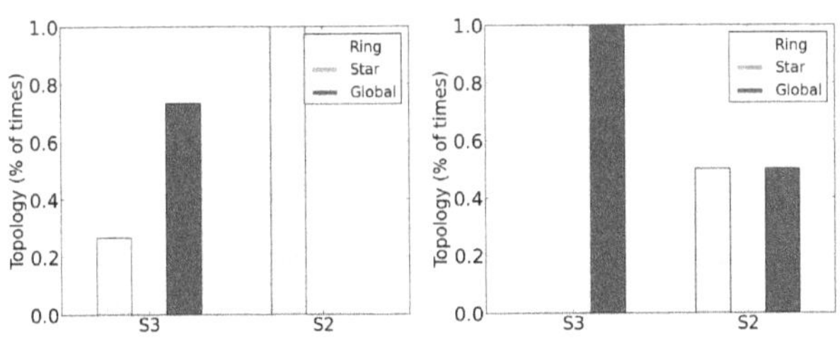

Figure 11: This figure (left for the Griewank function, right for Rastrigin) shows that the PSO versions in *S2*, that have small populations, use *ring* topology more often than the ones in *S3*, which prevalently choose *global* topology.

5.4 Comparison with other parameters

Like in Section 4.4, we repeated the tests on the reference EAs, this time taking into consideration *Q2* and *Q3*.

- Sphere: in 10 dimensions PSO_{A3} obtains results comparable to the ones on the Pareto front. It is to be noticed that this PSO version was tuned directly on a GPU, setting as termination criteria a time limit of 1 s, so the tuning procedure implicitly requested the ability to deal with parallel function evaluations;

- Rosenbrock: no reference obtains comparable results;

- Griewank: DE_{A1} is the best performing method among the reference ones, both in 10 and 30 dimensions, but it is not able to reach the performance of the versions generated by NSGA-II;

- Rastrigin: in 10 dimensions, DE_{A1}, PSO_{M1} and PSO_{A2} obtain results comparable to ours; This is valid also for DE_{A1} in 30 dimensions.

6. CONCLUSIONS AND FUTURE WORK

We proposed EMOPaT, a multi-objective parameter tuning method. EMOPaT is able to optimize an EA according to different quality criteria like robustness, speed, or others at the same time, using a multi-objective genetic algorithm.

A strength of EMOPaT is that it can be used for many purposes: in our work, rather than finding parameters that work better than the standard ones, we were able, at the same time, to extract different information, like the effect that a parameter or a design choice has on an algorithm, or the impact that this parameter has in terms of quality criteria. For instance, some of these results were unexpected and should be investigated more in depth, like the good results obtained using negative inertia factor in PSO, or the relationship between speed of convergence and scale factor F in DE or, again, the relationship between crossover rate CR and population size in DE.

In this work we limited the tests to one function and two quality criteria only, but we think that EMOPaT can be extended to more functions and quality criteria with no particular effort.

7. REFERENCES

[1] T. Bäck. Parallel optimization of evolutionary algorithms. In *Parallel Problem Solving From Nature*, pages 418–427. Spring-Verlag, 1994.

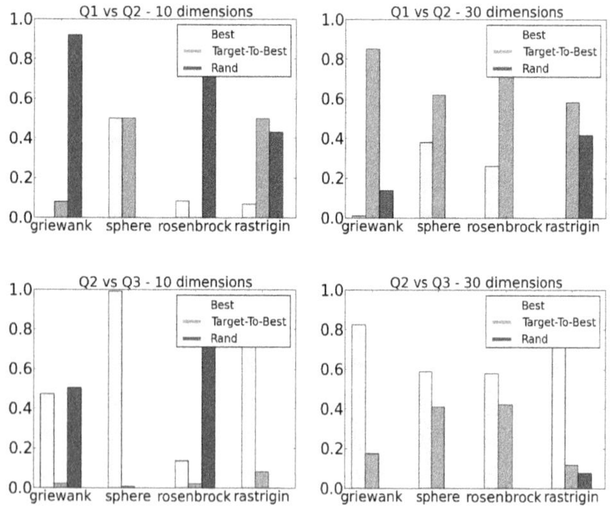

Figure 12: Frequency of mutations selected by NSGA-II using two different pairs of quality criteria (*Q1* and *Q2* in the first row, *Q2* and *Q3* in the second).

[2] J. Branke and J. A. Elomari. Meta-optimization for parameter tuning with a flexible computing budget. In *Proceedings of the Fourteenth International Conference on Genetic and Evolutionary Computation Conference*, GECCO, pages 1245–1252. ACM, 2012.

[3] S. Das and P. Suganthan. Differential Evolution: A survey of the state-of-the-art. *IEEE Transactions on Evolutionary Computation*, 15(1):4–31, 2011.

[4] K. Deb, A. Pratap, S. Agarwal, and T. Meyarivan. A fast and elitist multiobjective genetic algorithm: NSGA-II. *IEEE Transactions on Evolutionary Computation*, 6(2):182–197, 2002.

[5] J. Dréo. Using performance fronts for parameter setting of stochastic metaheuristics. In *Proceedings of the Conference Companion on Genetic and Evolutionary Computation Conference: Late Breaking Papers*, pages 2197–2200. ACM, 2009.

[6] A. E. Eiben and S. K. Smit. Parameter tuning for configuring and analyzing evolutionary algorithms. *Swarm and Evolutionary Computation*, 1(1):19 – 31, 2011.

[7] R. Gämperle, S. D. Müller, and P. Koumoutsakos. A parameter study for Differential Evolution. In *Int. Conf. on Advances in Intelligent Systems, Fuzzy Systems, Evolutionary Computation*, pages 293–298, 2002.

[8] J. Grefenstette. Optimization of control parameters for genetic algorithms. *IEEE Trans. Syst. Man Cybern.*, 16(1):122–128, 1986.

[9] J. Kennedy and M. Clerc, 2006. Online: http://www.particleswarm.info/Standard_PSO_2006.c.

[10] J. Lampinen and I. Zelinka. On stagnation of the differential evolution algorithm. In *Proceedings of MENDEL*, pages 76–83, 2000.

[11] R. Mallipeddi and P. Suganthan. Empirical study on the effect of population size on Differential Evolution algorithm. In *IEEE Congress on Evolutionary Computation*, pages 3663–3670, 2008.

[12] J. L. F. Martínez and E. G. Gonzalo. The generalized PSO: A new door to PSO evolution. *J. Artif. Evol. App.*, 2008:5:1–5:15, Jan. 2008.

[13] M. Meissner, M. Schmuker, and G. Schneider. Optimized Particle Swarm Optimization (OPSO) and its application to artificial neural network training. *BMC Bioinformatics*, 7, 2006.

[14] R. Mercer and J. Sampson. Adaptive search using a reproductive metaplan. *Kybernetes*, 7:215–228, 1978.

[15] V. Nannen and A. Eiben. A method for parameter calibration and relevance estimation in evolutionary algorithms. In *Proceedings of the 8th Annual Conference on Genetic and Evolutionary Computation*, pages 183–190, 2006.

[16] Y. Nashed, P. Mesejo, R. Ugolotti, J. Dubois-Lacoste, and S. Cagnoni. A comparative study of three GPU-based metaheuristics. In *Parallel Problem Solving from Nature*, volume 7492 of *Lecture Notes in Computer Science*, pages 398–407. Springer, 2012.

[17] M. E. H. Pedersen. Tuning and simplifying heuristical optimization. Master's thesis, University of Southampton, 2010.

[18] R. Poli, J. Kennedy, and T. Blackwell. Particle Swarm Optimization. *Swarm Intelligence*, 1(1):33–57, 2007.

[19] S. K. Smit and A. E. Eiben. Comparing parameter tuning methods for evolutionary algorithms. In *Proc. of the IEEE Congress on Evolutionary Computation*, pages 399–406, 2009.

[20] S. K. Smit and A. E. Eiben. Beating the 'world champion' evolutionary algorithm via REVAC tuning. In *Proc. of IEEE Congress on Evolutionary Computation*, pages 1–8, 2010.

[21] S. K. Smit, A. E. Eiben, and Z. Szlávik. An MOEA-based method to tune EA parameters on multiple objective functions. In *IJCCI (ICEC)*, pages 261–268, 2010.

[22] R. Storn and K. Price. Differential evolution- a simple and efficient adaptive scheme for global optimization over continuous spaces. Technical report, International Computer Science Institute, 1995.

[23] R. Ugolotti, Y. S. G. Nashed, P. Mesejo, and S. Cagnoni. Algorithm configuration using GPU-based metaheuristics. In *Proc. of the Genetic and Evolutionary Computation Conference companion*, 2013.

Online Model Racing based on Extreme Performance

Tiantian Zhang
University of Central Florida
4000 Central Florida Blvd.
Orlando, FL, USA, 32816
zhangtt@knights.ucf.edu

Michael Georgiopoulos
University of Central Florida
4000 Central Florida Blvd.
Orlando, FL, USA, 32816
michaelg@ucf.edu

Georgios C. Anagnostopoulos
Florida Institute of Technology
150 W. University Blvd
Melbourne, FL, USA, 32901
georgio@fit.edu

ABSTRACT

Racing algorithms are often used for offline model selection, where models are compared in terms of their average performance over a collection of problems. In this paper, we present a new racing algorithm variant, Max-Race, which makes decisions based on the maximum performance of models. It is an online algorithm, whose goal is to optimally allocate computational resources in a portfolio of evolutionary algorithms, while solving a particular problem instance. It employs a hypothesis test based on extreme value theory in order to decide, which component algorithms to retire, while avoiding unnecessary computations. Experimental results confirm that Max-Race is able to identify the best individual with high precision and low computational overhead. When used as a scheme to select the best from a portfolio of algorithms, the results compare favorably to the ones of other popular algorithm portfolio approaches.

Categories and Subject Descriptors

G.3 [**Probability and Statistics**]: Statistical Computing; I.2.8 [**Artificial Intelligence**]: Problem Solving, Control Methods, and Search—*Heuristic methods*; G.1.6 [**Numerical Analysis**]: Optimization—*Global Optimization*

General Terms

Algorithms, Experimentation

Keywords

Online Model Selection, Racing Algorithm, Extreme Value Theory, Algorithm Portfolio

1. INTRODUCTION

The concept of Racing Algorithms (RAs) was originally developed for model selection in machine learning. Models, broadly speaking, could refer to any algorithm, operator or learning strategy. Given an ensemble of potential models, an RA sequentially evaluates each candidate on a series of benchmark instances of a problem domain, and eliminates under-performers as soon as sufficient statistical evidence supporting their removal is accumulated. Computational resources can be devoted to exploiting promising candidates by eliminating inferior candidates as early as possible. RAs maintain a reasonable balance between model optimality and computational complexity. Furthermore, RAs have been used extensively for algorithm tuning, algorithm configuration, and hybrid algorithm development; see [3] for a pertinent exposition.

The first RA, introduced in [14] and referred to as Hoeffding Racing (HR), computes an error bound for each model using Hoeffding's inequality. The ensemble of candidate models are tested on a set of problem instances, one at a time. Next, Hoeffding's inequality is used to estimate the true error from observed errors for each candidate. A candidate is discarded once the confidence interval for its true error rises above at least one confidence interval of the remaining candidates. A parametric analogue of HR was presented in [16], namely BRACE. In BRACE, leave-one-out cross validation errors of memory-based learners are assumed to be random variables from Gaussian distributions. Bayesian statistics are employed to detect if two errors are significantly different. In [15], Bernstein's inequality was employed in the RA. Their method was shown to eliminate inferior models faster than the HR method, mainly due to the higher quality of the concentration inequality. The most popular RA is F-Race and its counterpart I/F-Race [3], which successfully transferred the idea of racing to the problem of selecting configurations of parameterized algorithms. In F-Race, a Friedman test is adopted for testing equivalence of model performance before considering pair-wise comparisons. The most recent RA is S-Race [26], a multi-objective RA, which addresses the problem of multi-objective model selection. S-Race features a non-parametric sign test and it employs Holm's step-down procedure to control the overall probability of making false rejections. The returned models are optimal in the sense of Pareto optimality. Some other examples of RA are summarized in [26].

RAs are commonly used for offline model selection. In this scenario, a subset of all available samples is chosen as a training set, and models are compared in accordance to their overall average performance on the training set. The models with the best average performance are identified by the RAs. This is a pure exploration problem, which is at risk of returning models perform poorly on previously-unseen samples. In a different scenario of solving any given problem instances, one would like to maximize the performance quality

GECCO'14, July 12–16, 2014, Vancouver, BC, Canada.

ACM 978-1-4503-2662-9/14/07 ...$15.00.
http://dx.doi.org/10.1145/2576768.2598336.

by automatically allocating most computational resources to the optimal model/solver during problem solving. This is a typical online model selection problem, for which, many algorithms have been developed and applied in a wide variety of algorithm-problem settings. In [13, 1], for instance, model selection is formulated as a Markov Decision Process, and reinforcement learning is used to find the optimal algorithm scheduling strategy. In [9, 6], multi-armed bandit algorithms are employed to find the optimal assignment of available computational resources. In online settings, the time allocation can be adapted by monitoring algorithm execution to meet a reasonable trade-off between exploration and exploitation.

Classic online model selection primarily aims at maximizing the expected cumulative or maximum rewards. However, in many practical applications involving noise-less objective functions, optimizing extrema is more pertinent or important. For example, in algorithm selection for solving a given NP-hard combinatorial optimization problem, it is highly advantageous to dynamically determine and exploit the candidate heuristics that yield the best final solution; in this case, extreme performance is the only meaningful measurement worth considering.

In this paper, an online RA, Max-Race, is introduced. To the best of our knowledge, it is the first online model selection algorithm aiming at optimizing the extreme performance quality by making the best possible use of available resources. The Max-Race algorithm performs online evaluation/racing, where model comparison and selection is performed as each problem instance is evaluated. In Max-Race, the intermediate performance of each candidate is evaluated on a regular basis, while solving the problem. The expected (or predicted) maximum performance is estimated by utilizing notions of extreme value theory. In particular, a pairwise hypothesis test is developed to identify significant difference between extreme performances of two given models. Models with inferior predicted maximum performance are gradually eliminated from the race and computational resources are increasingly invested in exploiting more promising candidate models.

The need for Max-Race is motivated by problems such as computational resources assignment in a population-based algorithm portfolio (AP). Population-based AP is an approach to automatically synthesize an ensemble of different population-based algorithms. The main motivation behind them is to enhance the overall performance of the component algorithms on any problem instance in terms of solution quality. Research on APs has gained significant attention in recent years with the booming development of powerful Evolutionary Algorithms (EAs). Recent developments on this type of problem are [21], [17] and [23]. In [21], the authors describe A Multi-algorithm Genetically Adaptive Method for Single Objective Optimization (AMALGAM-SO), which implements a self-adaptive learning strategy that automatically tunes the number of offspring each constituent algorithm will contribute to each generation. In addition, a novel elitism selection scheme is employed for generating better and diverse offspring. In [17], the authors construct a population-based algorithm portfolio (PAP), in which the constituent algorithms run in parallel with solution migration occurring at regular intervals. The share of available computational resources remains fixed. Additionally, in the AP framework proposed in [23], each algorithm runs independently without any information exchange. In each generation, however, only the algorithm with the best predicted performance in the nearest common future point is executed, while others are temporarily suspended. The prediction only depends on the past history of their performance.

Nevertheless, the existing AP approaches have certain limitations. First of all, not all combinations of algorithms perform equally well, as demonstrated via experimental results in [21, 17]. Inappropriate selection of constituent algorithms may hinder the optimization process considerably. Secondly, it is not known how to synchronize the constituent algorithms so that their performances complement each other. For example, AMALGAM-SO incorporates elitism selection and premature convergence detection along with other mechanisms to better cooperate its component algorithms. Thirdly, considerable computation time is spent on constituents with inferior performance.

In this paper, we adopt Max-Race to construct a new population-based AP approach, named Max-Race Portfolio (MRP), which follows a simple Winner-Take-All (WTA) strategy. In MRP, the algorithms in the portfolio run concurrently without any information exchange. Max-Race employs an appropriate performance measure to eliminate algorithms producing inferior solutions. The proposed methodology frees practitioners from the need to know the constituent algorithms well enough to be able to effectively combine them. It also limits waste of computational effort on under-performing algorithms. MRP is similar to the one proposed in [25], in the sense that it aborts all except one algorithm based on the best objective value obtained after a specific number of function evaluations (NFEs).

The details of Max-Race and MRP, along with a brief description of Extreme Value Theory (EVT) related concepts, are provided in Section 2. In Section 3.1, the efficiency of Max-Race is analyzed from two aspects: the prediction accuracy and achieved computational savings compared to a Brute Forth Approach (BFA), which simply executes all the constituent algorithms to completion. Finally, in Section 3.2, the performance of MRP, consisting of PSO, CPSO, jDE, JADE, SaDE and CMA-ES solvers, is compared to two baseline APs (RandEA and BestEA) and three other state-of-the-art APs (AMALGAM-SO, PAP and MultiEA) for function optimization problems. The experimental results demonstrated that Max-Race is capable of identifying the best algorithms with high likelihood and by incurring low computational cost, when exploring for models, and, hence, maximizing the quality of the final solution by making the best possible use of available resources.

2. MAX-RACE DESCRIPTION

In this paper we propose a new RA variant, named Max-Race. Max-Race is an online RA, which identifies superior models and abandons poor performing ones as the models are evaluated against each problem instance. Under certain assumptions to be elaborated on later, Max-Race tries to retain only models that achieve the best final objective value. Subsequently, Max-Race is then utilized as part of a population-based algorithm portfolio, called MRP. Without loss of generality, in this paper we regard all optimization problems as maximization problems; minimization problems can be addressed as well by maximizing the negative of an objective function.

2.1 Extreme Value Theory Concepts

The outcome of a stochastic optimizer can be viewed as an estimator of the optimum value of the objective function and, hence, is a random variable, typically, of unknown distribution. We are interested in the extreme values of this distribution as a method of assessing the peak performance of the optimizer. EVT is concerned with statistics of extreme or rare events [7]. Note that EVT concepts have been already used to study the distribution of outcomes acquired by stochastic optimizers in [12, 5, 6].

A focal result of EVT pertaining to sample maxima is analogous to that of the Central Limit Theorem and sample means. As stated in [7], the sample maximum distribution of a series of i.i.d. (independent and identically distributed) samples, after appropriate normalization, converges to a Generalized Extreme Value (GEV) distribution as the sample size approaches infinity. Let $Y = \max_{i=1,\ldots,n} X_i$, where X_i is a sequence of i.i.d. random variables with a common Cumulative Distribution Function (CDF) H, then we have

$$\lim_{n\to\infty} Pr\left\{\frac{Y-b_n}{a_n} \le y\right\} = \lim_{n\to\infty} H^n(a_n y + b_n) = G(y) \quad (1)$$

where $a_n > 0$ and b_n are normalization coefficients and the asymptotic CDF $G(y)$ has the form

$$G(y) = exp\left\{-\left[1+\tilde{\xi}\left(\frac{y-\tilde{\mu}}{\tilde{\sigma}}\right)\right]^{-1/\tilde{\xi}}\right\} \quad (2)$$

The aforementioned CDF corresponds to the so called GEV distribution with location parameter $\tilde{\mu}$, scale parameter $\tilde{\sigma} > 0$ and shape parameter $\tilde{\xi}$. Note that, depending on the value of its parameters, it specializes to one of three types of distributions: Fréchet, Weibull and Gumbel [7].

Based on Equation (1), it can be shown that, in the limit, the tail distribution of the X_i's tends to a three-parameter CDF as shown below

$$\lim_{u\to u^*} Pr\{X > x | X > u\} = F_{\xi,\mu,\sigma}(x) \quad (3)$$

where u^* is the endpoint of distribution H and

$$F_{\xi,\mu,\sigma}(x) = \begin{cases} 1-\left(1+\frac{\xi(x-\mu)}{\sigma}\right)^{-1/\xi} & for\ \xi \neq 0 \\ 1-\exp\left(-\frac{x-\mu}{\sigma}\right) & for\ \xi = 0 \end{cases} \quad (4)$$

is called the Generalized Pareto Distribution (GPD), where $\sigma > 0$, and $x \ge \mu$, when $\xi \ge 0$, and $\mu \le x \le \mu - \sigma/\xi$, if otherwise. The three parameters ξ, μ, σ are referred to as *shape*, *location* and *scale* parameters, respectively and are uniquely determined by $\tilde{\xi}, \tilde{\mu}, \tilde{\sigma}$ of the associated GEV. Similar to the GEV distribution, the GPD contains three distribution families: when $\xi > 0$, we have an ordinary Pareto distribution; when $\xi = 0$, we have an exponential distribution; and when $\xi < 0$, a short-tailed Pareto II distribution. Finally, note that the Probability Distribution Function (PDF) of the GPD is derived as

$$f_{\xi,\mu,\sigma}(x) = \frac{1}{\sigma}\left(1+\frac{\xi(x-\mu)}{\sigma}\right)^{-\frac{1}{\xi}-1} \quad (5)$$

Correspondingly, there are two basic approaches to modeling the parametric distribution of extreme values in EVT: *Block Maxima (BM)* and *Point Over Threshold (POT)*. BM is the most classical approach in EVT. In BM, the data are collected in chunks (blocks) of equal size. The distribution of the maximum of each block follows approximately a GEV distribution. However, the BM approach doesn't make efficient use of the data, since only the sample maxima of large blocks are utilized. The POT approach may utilize data better, because all observations exceeding a sufficiently high threshold are used towards GPD parameter estimation. Moreover, due to the "threshold stability" property[1] of GPD, methods based on POT are generally known to be more powerful for practical applications, such as ones in the areas of insurance, finance and environmental studies.

2.2 Modeling Model Performance via GPDs

The models considered in this paper are Evolutionary Computation (EC) algorithms, but our approach is applicable to a more general notion of what is considered as a model. EAs are population-based algorithms, where the population is a collection of samples in the decision space; these samples are updated iteratively through a guided random search. For a specific optimization problem with a bounded (global) maximum, such algorithms aim to produce a maximizer, which, hopefully, will yield the problem's global maximum. Due to the stochastic nature of EAs, the optimization outcomes could be described by their distribution. Since we are only interested in extreme outcomes, such as maxima, the intermediate outcomes can be regarded as samples along the right tail of the underlying distribution. In this framework, the POT approach is a natural choice to model the distribution of algorithm performance. In particular, the GPD approximation will be more accurate as evolution continues, because the underlying sampling distribution tends to become more stable as more samples gather close to the right endpoint. Our reported simulation results also support this thesis.

Let $gbest_t$ refer to the best objective value obtained so far (by time/iteration) t of an EA. In essence, $gbest_t$ is a sequence of random variable of a discrete time Markov chain since $gbest_t \triangleq \max\{pop_t,\ gbest_{t-1}\}$, where pop_t are samples of generation t. We assume that after some mixing time t_0, the Markov chain enters a state of equilibrium, where the collected $\{gbest_t\}$ with $t > t_0$ can be regarded as i.i.d from a stationary distribution. Therefore, we will conceptually limit ourselves to EAs with the property that the stochastic sequence $\{gbest_t\}_{t=1}^{\infty}$ has a sub-sequence $\{gbest_t\}_{t=t_o}^{\infty}$ for very large t_o, such that the aforementioned sub-sequence contains i.i.d. samples. Such an EA evolves solutions and, after the passage of many generations, its sampling distribution tends to be stationary, even if in an approximate sense.

Along this rationale, we identify $gbest_t$ after every generation, and, due to our i.i.d. assumption, we model the upper order statistics of the obtained sample by a GPD. In particular, we only consider the special case of GPD with $\xi < 0$, which has a right endpoint $\mu - \sigma/\xi$.

Figure 1 shows the merits of following a POT approach in a practical setting. The displayed data is collected from one run of CPSO [20] in the context of a multi-modal function optimization problem. However, in the POT framework, the selection of an appropriate threshold u is crucial before fitting, which involves balancing the bias and the variance of

[1]If the upper statistics of X follow a GPD for a fixed threshold level u, the conditional distribution of $X > v$ for any higher threshold $v > u$ also follows a GPD with the same ξ but a shifted σ.

parameter estimators. For example, the GPD fit in Figure 1c is not as good as the one in Figure 1b because its u, which equals to the q-quantile of s samples, is too large.

Note that several threshold selection methods are proposed in the literature [19]. However, we'll entertain fixed quantile rules as a simple choice that is justified by the threshold stability property of the GPD; specifically, the q-quantile of the sample is chosen as the threshold. The determination of a proper q value is closely related to the t_0 value in the previous discussion. As the algorithm progresses, we expect more objective values to closely cluster below the endpoint. Note that $gbest_t$ is a non-decreasing process with a fixed t_0. Accordingly, in our setting, the q value decreases exponentially with the sample size s, *viz.* $q(s) = q_0 e^{-\lambda s}$. Moreover, the quantity q_0 is chosen to be smaller than 0.9, a typical value used in POT applications, since the sample values are already maxima of some optimization process. q_0 and λ are determined empirically, based on our experimental observations, so that $q_{100} = 0.7, q_{5000} = 0.01$. After determining the threshold, the Method of Moments (MOM) [8] is adopted for estimating the GPD parameters ξ, μ and σ. MOM is computationally straightforward and the estimates are asymptotically normal, when $\xi < 0$. As shown in Figure 1a and Figure 1b, the GPD fit becomes increasingly better against the empirical distribution as evolution progresses, if the u value is properly selected. Note that the data fits better in the case of negative skewness and large magnitudes.

2.3 Max-Race Framework

RAs for classic offline model selection compare models based on their average performance. In contrast to them, Max-Race tries to identify the model with the best extreme performance for online selection.

The framework of Max-Race is similar to a typical RA procedure. The Max-Race algorithm follows a *suspend-and-resume* scheme. It starts with an ensemble of models, which are run in parallel without information exchange. For each model, the intermediate best objective value obtained is periodically recorded. Repeatedly, execution is suspended and a statistical test is performed to assess the best maximum performance of each model based on historical performance. If sufficient statistical evidence shows, that a particular model is inferior (meaning that its best maximum performance is significantly worse than all other models), it is removed from the ensemble. Execution is subsequently resumed and the whole procedure is repeated until either a pre-specified time limit is exceeded or a single model remains.

2.4 Inferring Inequivalence of Endpoints

Max-Race employs a hypothesis test to detect differences between the sample maxima of two samples. The hypothesis test is parametric and assumes that the sampled data are i.i.d stemming from a 3-parameter GPD with an upper (finite) endpoint. Testing statistical difference between endpoints has received barely any attention in the literature, probably due to the lack of practical motivations so far. Therefore, for the purposes of our work, we develop one to identify such differences between the right endpoints of two GPDs.

Given the two sets of observations $X_i, i = 1, 2, \cdots, n$ from model A and $Y_j, j = 1, 2, \cdots, m$ from model B, where $X_i \sim F_{\xi_A,\mu_A,\sigma_A}(x)$ and $Y_j \sim F_{\xi_B,\mu_B,\sigma_B}(y)$ with $\xi_A < 0, \xi_B < 0$, the null hypothesis is $H_0 : \mu_A - \frac{\sigma_A}{\xi_A} = \mu_B - \frac{\sigma_B}{\xi_B}$, indicating the equivalence of the endpoints. Correspondingly, the alternative hypothesis is $H_a : \mu_A - \frac{\sigma_A}{\xi_A} > \mu_B - \frac{\sigma_B}{\xi_B}$ assuming that the estimated endpoint for model A is larger than the one of model B. The sample maxima of the two populations are used as estimates of the corresponding endpoints. Let $U \triangleq \max\{X_1, \cdots, X_n\}$, and $V \triangleq \max\{Y_1, \cdots, Y_m\}$. Based on our earlier stated assumptions, the PDFs of U and V are provided below:

$$f_U(u) = n f_{\xi_A,\mu_A,\sigma_A}(u) F^{n-1}_{\xi_A,\mu_A,\sigma_A}(u) \tag{6}$$

and

$$f_V(v) = m f_{\xi_B,\mu_B,\sigma_B}(v) F^{m-1}_{\xi_B,\mu_B,\sigma_B}(v) \tag{7}$$

The test statistic we consider is the difference $\Delta = U - V$ between the two sample maxima, whose PDF can be shown

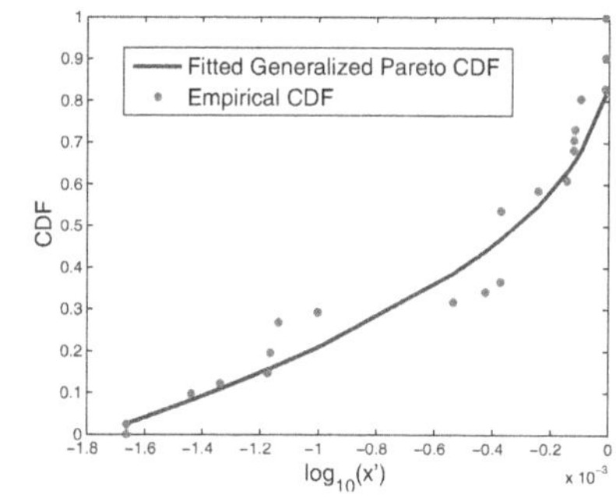

(a) $q = 0.7, s = 100$

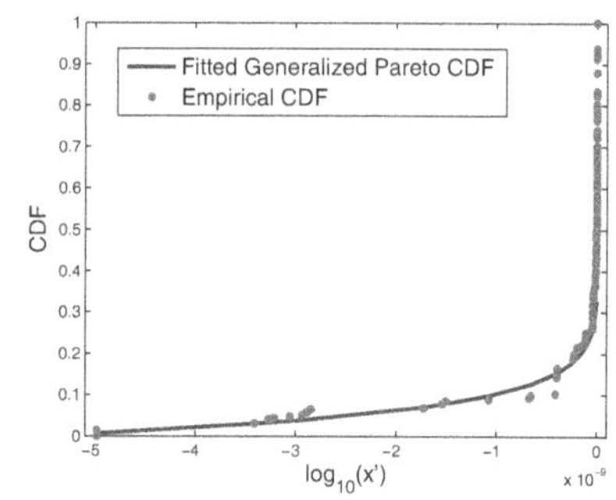

(b) $q = 0.5, s = 500$

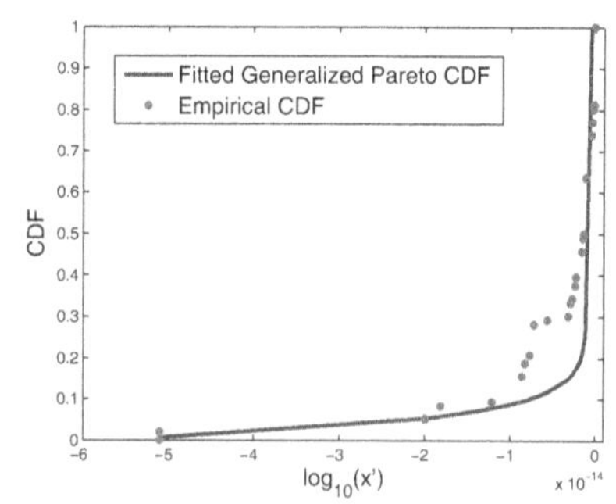

(c) $q = 0.9, s = 500$

Figure 1: GPD fit for $gbest_t$ collected from a CPSO run on a multi-modal function optimization problem. The x' shown below the x-axis represents the normalized value of x

to be

$$f_\Delta(\delta) = \int_{\mu_A}^{\mu_A - \frac{\sigma_A}{\xi_A}} f_U(u) f_V(u-\delta) du \quad (8)$$

Since the range of U is $[\mu_A, \mu_A - \frac{\sigma_A}{\xi_A}]$ and of V is $[\mu_B, \mu_B - \frac{\sigma_B}{\xi_B}]$, the range of Δ will be $[\mu_A - \mu_B + \frac{\sigma_B}{\xi_B}, \mu_A - \mu_B - \frac{\sigma_A}{\xi_A}]$. However, under H_0, the range of Δ is $[\frac{\sigma_A}{\xi_A}, -\frac{\sigma_B}{\xi_B}]$. Therefore, the probability $P(\Delta \leq d)$ under H_0 is

$$\begin{aligned} P(\Delta \leq d) &= \int_{\frac{\sigma_A}{\xi_A}}^{d} f_\Delta(\delta) d\delta \\ &= \int_0^1 F^m_{\xi_B,\mu_B,\sigma_B} \left\{ \frac{\sigma_A\left[\left(1-P^{\frac{1}{n}}\right)^{-\xi_A} - 1\right]}{\xi_A} + \mu_A - \frac{\sigma_A}{\xi_A} \right\} dP \\ &- \int_0^1 F^m_{\xi_B,\mu_B,\sigma_B} \left\{ \frac{\sigma_A\left[\left(1-P^{\frac{1}{n}}\right)^{-\xi_A} - 1\right]}{\xi_A} + \mu_A - d \right\} dP \end{aligned} \quad (9)$$

where $P = F^n_{\xi_A,\mu_A,\sigma_A}(u)$. When observing a value of d for the difference between the estimated maximum performance of model A and B, we can compute the p-value of the proposed test as follows

$$\pi(d; A, B) = P(\Delta > d) = 1 - P(\Delta \leq d) \quad (10)$$

If $\pi(d; A, B)$ is smaller than the predefined Type I error rate α, H_0 will be rejected. Since there is no closed-form expression for Equation (9), the adaptive Gaussian quadrature method for numerical integration is used to approximate the $\pi(d; A, B)$ value.

Note that the parameter values needed for calculating $\pi(d; A, B)$ are estimated from the data. The values μ_A and μ_B are first estimated using MOM. After deriving the location parameters, the original data are shifted accordingly and the values of σ_A, ξ_A, σ_B, and ξ_B under H_0 are estimated by a hybrid method consisting of Maximum Likelihood Estimation and Maximum-Goodness-of-Fit Estimation [22], since the Maximum Likelihood method is not applicable when $\xi < -1$. For a detailed description of this estimation approach, we refer the interested reader to [22].

2.5 Algorithm Portfolio based on Max-Race

The online racing framework can be easily extended to form an AP. In this subsection, we present a novel population-based AP approach hinging on Max-Race and referred to as MRP. After initialization, each candidate algorithm in MRP runs independently on its own population. For each sub-population, the *gbest* value is preserved for every generation. Once the number of new *gbest* values collected reaches N_{cs}, the component algorithms are compared, pairwise, using the test proposed in Section 2.4. Those with inferior maximum performance will be stopped once sufficient statistical evidence is presented. The portfolio execution stops when it reaches the maximal NFEs. No test is necessary if only one algorithm is left in the portfolio. Furthermore, as a multiple comparison problem, the Benjamini-Hochberg-Yekutieli procedure [2] is implemented to control the overall false discovery rate, denoted as $FDR(\cdot,\cdot)$ in Algorithm 1. It makes rejections based on given p-values and the predefined confidence level α. The output is the set of indices corresponding to the models with inferior maximum performance. Since the GPD fit becomes more accurate as more data is collected, the α value increases at a rate proportional to the sample size, and is given by

$$\alpha_s = \alpha_0 e^{-\beta(s_{max}-s)} \quad (11)$$

where s_{max} is the largest possible sample size and s is the current sample size. The values α_0 and β are chosen empirically such that $\alpha_{s_{max}} = 0.01$ and $\alpha_{s_0} = 1e-30$.

Algorithm 1 Max-Race Algorithm Portfolio

```
Initialize k sub-populations {pop_1, pop_2, ..., pop_k}
(k ≥ 2) and evaluate all the individuals
Record the best objective value in each
sub-population as gbest_0
Initialize the algorithm portfolio
P ← {A_1, A_2, ..., A_k}
while maximal NFEs is not reached do
  for each algorithm A_i ∈ Portfolio do
    Evolve pop_i for N_cs generations
    Record the best objective value obtained
    after every generation
  end for
  P_values ← ∅
  for each pair of algorithms A_i, A_j ∈ P do
    P_values ← P_values ∪ π(d; A_i, A_j)
  end for
  P ← P \ {A_k}, where k ∈ FDR(P_values, α_s)
end while
return the best objective value found
```

3. EXPERIMENTAL OUTCOMES

In this section, we assess the performance of Max-Race and its corresponding AP approach, MRP. The following suite of algorithms are used in the MRP design: PSO [27], CPSO [20], jDE [4], JADE [24], SaDE [18], and CMA-ES [11], which are popular EAs having demonstrated outstanding performance in the relevant literature. The test problems are multi-modal maximization problems with a bounded search space that are generated via a Gaussian landscape generator [10]. The boundary of the search space is set to be $[-100, 100]^D$, where D is the dimensionality of the problem. The advantage of Max-Race is illustrated in two aspects: the efficiency of Max-Race for online model selection and the competitiveness of MRP compared to other population-based APs.

3.1 Max-Race Efficiency Analysis

A simple, yet time-consuming, approach for finding the optimal algorithm is the BFA, which applies all the candidate algorithms on the problem of interest and runs them to completion. To demonstrate the efficiency of Max-Race, we compare it to BFA. Two performance metrics are specified: prediction accuracy, denoted by PA, and ratio of Max-Race to BFA running time to completion, denoted by RTR (running time ratio). PA is 1 if the algorithms with the true maximum performance are retained at the end of Max-Race execution, and 0 otherwise. RTR is calculated as the ratio of the NFEs spent by Max-Race to the NFEs spent by BFA. Ideally, PA should approach 1 and RTR should approach 0.

The efficiency of Max-Race is evaluated on 30 benchmark functions with dimensions $D = 10$ and $D = 30$. In each run, the constituent algorithms start with different sub-populations of size $5D$. In BFA, each sub-population evolves for $5000 \times 5D$ NFEs, which is large enough to ensure convergence to a solution for a variety of benchmark functions and EAs. The intermediate *gbest* values from one run of BFA are collected as pseudo-samples for simulating a run of Max-Race. In Max-Race, the statistical comparison is performed every 10 generations ($N_{cs} = 10$). For each optimization task, the average PA and RTR values over 25 runs are calculated, as well as the average number of models with maximum performance in the BFA (N_b) and the average number of models retained by the end of Max-Race (N_r). However, due to space limitations, we only report a summary of them in Table 1. As observed in Table 1, prediction accuracy is high, especially when $D = 10$. In $D = 30$, the task of identifying the best algorithm appears more challenging since the PA values decrease on average. For high-dimensional and multi-modal objective functions, the algorithms show similar performance since it is more difficult to find a good solution (see Table 2). As a result, Max-Race cannot identify the real winner. Instead, it yields the algorithm with slightly less optimal performance. Such phenomenon is reasonable because Max-Race trades off some computational effort with prediction accuracy. However, the effect of problem dimension on the performance of Max-Race deserves future investigation. In terms of RTR values, the computational burden for the Max-Race algorithm is always seen to be much lower than for the BFA algorithm.

Table 1: Summary of the comparison result between the BFA and Max-Race: PA, RTR, N_b and N_r

Dim		PA	RTR	N_b	N_r
10	max	1	0.30	3.92	1.24
	median	0.91	0.23	1.42	1.00
	min	0.80	0.22	1.04	1.00
	std	0.07	0.02	0.60	0.06
30	max	1	0.46	2.44	2.20
	median	0.83	0.41	1.28	2.00
	min	0.36	0.38	1.00	1.92
	std	0.13	0.02	0.38	0.05

Identifying the best algorithm is not necessarily the ultimate goal of online racing. Instead, the goal of Max-Race is to maximize the quality of the solution under time constraints. Therefore, we compare MRP with two baseline algorithms, namely a simple algorithm portfolio approach which randomly selects an algorithm (RandEA), and an ideal algorithm portfolio approach which always selects the best algorithm (BestEA), and we use the pseudo-samples generated from the previous experiments to do so. A maximum of $5000 \times 5D$ NFEs is allowed for MRP, RandEA and BestEA. On the basis of a paired Wilcoxon signed-rank test with significance level 0.01, MRP is better than RandEA in all cases (*i.e.*, a set of 25 runs considering a particular function to optimize). Meanwhile, BestEA only outperforms MRP significantly in 13% of the cases for $D = 30$, as shown in Table 2.

To better demonstrate how MRP performs compared to RandEA and BestEA, we estimate the density of their outcomes, 25 runs for each optimization task, from bootstrapped samples by using a kernel smoothing function. In Figure 2, we plot the density of means of the bootstrapped samples for a specific objective function (f_5 with $D = 30$). As shown, MRP accomplished nearly equal outcomes to those of BestEA and both displayed an advantage over RandEA.

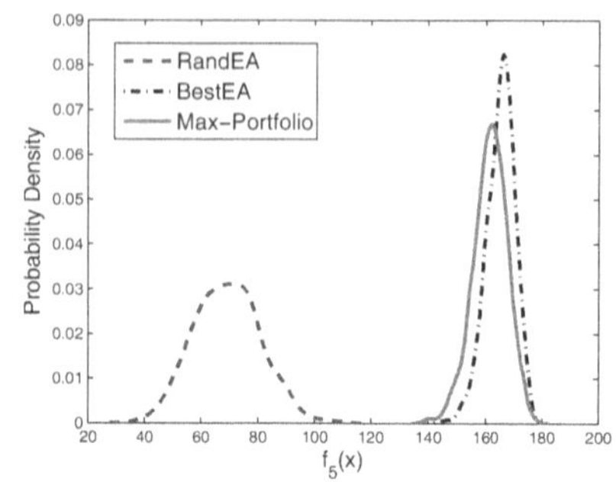

Figure 2: Bootstrap distributions of the means of final outcomes of MRP, RandEA and BestEA for f_5 with $D = 30$

Table 2: Mean values of final outcomes over 25 runs for MRP, BestEA, and RandEA; 30 problem instances for $D = 30$, with the true global maximum value of each function. If the entry is bold-faced, the associated algorithm significantly outperforms MRP. If the entry is underlined, the associate algorithm is significantly outperformed by MRP.

Probl.	MRP	BestEA	RandEA	Global Optimum
f_1	168.39	171.09	107.01	389.68
f_2	275.45	275.79	170.20	341.94
f_3	108.04	114.57	81.88	193.99
f_4	12.76	**13.61**	11.43	29.16
f_5	161.79	165.23	69.91	193.99
f_6	103.62	105.39	83.65	125.27
f_7	41.19	41.20	36.25	287.79
f_8	157.77	157.77	94.40	470.55
f_9	7.76	8.46	5.99	9.93
f_{10}	34.47	34.76	24.68	41.61
f_{11}	14.22	14.24	9.51	39.93
f_{12}	187.78	**224.36**	83.48	275.21
f_{13}	256.18	269.29	144.61	415.96
f_{14}	50.42	50.55	31.93	327.66
f_{15}	78.82	89.61	48.50	465.00
f_{16}	62.32	68.56	39.70	400.16
f_{17}	274.44	274.44	193.69	473.35
f_{18}	30.03	35.38	16.73	49.48
f_{19}	13.43	13.59	9.56	70.55
f_{20}	44.19	58.38	17.23	49.48
f_{21}	102.14	104.98	69.58	175.20
f_{22}	257.90	262.40	131.12	275.21
f_{23}	155.67	157.51	103.49	183.65
f_{24}	6.65	6.91	3.91	316.59
f_{25}	34.47	35.04	26.61	41.61
f_{26}	13.98	14.20	9.37	39.93
f_{27}	178.67	**220.17**	61.14	341.94
f_{28}	1.38	1.39	1.06	10.63
f_{29}	233.32	**265.19**	168.22	446.68
f_{30}	30.75	32.21	19.86	73.57

3.2 Comparisons of APs

To evaluate the performance of MRP, we compare it to three population-based APs: AMALGAM-SO [21], PAP [17] and Multiple Evolutionary Algorithm (MultiEA) [23], with the same constituent algorithms. Another set of 20 problem instances are generated with $D = 30$. The total population size is $5D$, which is equally divided into sub-populations, when initialized. The maximum number of NFEs is set to 3×10^5, which is commonly used in the literature. Other AP specific parameters are set according to suggested values in the respective original papers.

In Table 3, we present the results of MRP, AMALGAM-SO, PAP and MultiEA for 20 problem instances. The typical measures of merit, mean and standard deviation of the final outcomes produced over 25 runs, are reported. In addition, the Wilcoxon signed-rank test with significance level 0.01 is adopted to identify significant difference in terms of performance. In Table 3, entries are underlined to highlight algorithms that are significantly outperformed by MRP. If MRP is significantly outperformed by an algorithm, the corresponding algorithm-specific entry is highlighted in boldface. As the results show, MRP does significantly better than AMALGAM-SO, PAP and MultiEA in 13, 11, and 13 out of 20 problem instances, while it is only significantly outperformed by them in 2, 1 and 2 cases, respectively.

The overwhelming advantage of MRP confirms that applying Max-Race for online model selection is a very promising way of forming an algorithm portfolio. Given an optimization task, Max-Race is typically able to identify the ultimate winner from an ensemble of algorithms incurring much less computational overhead. MRP reflects a successful application of Max-Race, which makes the best use of computational resources for fully exploring and exploiting the search domain.

Meanwhile, the poor performance of AMALGAM-SO reveals that its success is highly dependent on synergy between the constituent algorithms. It requires a well-designed synchronization mechanism based on the characteristics of the constituent algorithms including population sharing, elitism selection, diversity control, premature convergence detection, etc. A user cannot blindly adopt the recommended settings in AMALGAM-SO's original paper for an arbitrary set of constituents, because the optimal combination of these operators needs careful tuning, which is computationally expensive.

Compared to AMALGAM-SO, PAP shows slightly better performance, since the sub-populations are only interleaved by some occasional migration of the best individual.

Among the three APs, MultiEA shares the most similar design principle as MRP: the sub-populations run independently without any interaction and only the algorithm with the best predicted performance is selected to run. However, its prediction is shortsighted in that the winner is chosen in terms of its estimated performance in the nearest common future point. And such estimation is based on bootstrapping samples collected after linear regression on the evolutionary curve. Therefore, it tends to squander time on algorithms that converge to some local maximum rapidly.

4. CONCLUSIONS

In this paper, an online Racing Algorithm (RA) is proposed, namely Max-Race. Max-Race tackles online model selection problem, aiming at optimizing the extreme performance quality by adaptively allocating available computational resources while solving a particular optimization problem instance. More specifically, Max-Race approximates the underlying distribution of model performance, measured as the best outcome obtained, via a Point Over Threshold (POT) approach rooted in Extreme Value Theory (EVT). A parametric hypothesis test based on the Generalized Pareto Distribution (GPD) is developed to identify significant difference between maximum performances of two models. The model with significant worse maximum performance will be discarded as early as possible.

The efficiency of Max-Race is evaluated by comparison to the Brute Forth Approach (BFA), a method which simply

Table 3: Mean and standard deviation (std) values of the final outcomes, out of the 25 runs, of MRP, AMALGAM-SO, PAP and MultiEA for 20 problem instances with $D = 30$

Probl.		MRP	AMALG AM-SO	PAP	MultiEA
f_1	mean	53.77	43.00	52.05	42.20
	std	2.27	4.21	4.41	3.76
f_2	mean	332.34	318.42	268.23	241.01
	std	29.42	30.87	35.42	57.40
f_3	mean	439.52	439.52	264.42	164.21
	std	1.59e-13	1.01e-05	18.87	15.57
f_4	mean	278.74	237.56	259.70	206.20
	std	26.38	22.04	18.24	35.71
f_5	mean	158.16	148.85	148.52	133.07
	std	11.10	13.50	11.26	18.17
f_6	mean	336.00	307.96	324.77	309.15
	std	22.35	27.63	19.34	26.64
f_7	mean	9.16	8.04	9.41	**10.29**
	std	1.39	4.84	5.61	**3.91**
f_8	mean	48.66	45.24	46.27	38.75
	std	2.42	7.87	5.70	10.63
f_9	mean	13.07	12.42	12.84	**15.64**
	std	1.62	1.27	1.71	**2.90**
f_{10}	mean	111.91	**119.44**	**113.46**	110.60
	std	11.94	**8.15**	**14.87**	2.23
f_{11}	mean	53.95	46.40	51.13	45.91
	std	2.11	1.13	6.12	3.66
f_{12}	mean	99.50	85.89	99.62	87.09
	std	6.49	5.53	4.79	6.51
f_{13}	mean	129.64	117.20	121.67	94.70
	std	4.06e-14	15.10	12.28	7.35
f_{14}	mean	102.98	72.97	96.67	91.69
	std	6.09	9.02	3.77	6.43
f_{15}	mean	9.94	8.47	9.10	8.20
	std	0.58	1.17	1.65	1.51
f_{16}	mean	90.15	86.58	76.50	61.23
	std	7.58	7.40	3.21	6.19
f_{17}	mean	52.78	**61.23**	43.59	50.05
	std	2.54	**4.17**	4.65	3.52
f_{18}	mean	51.64	49.34	42.64	48.85
	std	8.37	7.03	7.59	9.90
f_{19}	mean	1.51	1.11	1.23	0.83
	std	1.31	1.16	1.16	0.28
f_{20}	mean	48.48	48.23	39.52	45.85
	std	0.10	0.83	3.03	2.81

runs all the constituent algorithms to completion, for model selection. Max-Race is capable of identifying the best algorithm with high likelihood for a low computational cost. To better evaluate its performance, Max-Race is applied as a new algorithm portfolio (AP) approach, with 6 constituent algorithms: PSO, CPSO, jDE, JADE, SaDE and CMA-ES. The resulting AP, named Max-Race Portfolio (MRP), is compared to two baseline APs (RandEA and BestEA) and three other APs (AMALGAM-SO, PAP and MultiEA) on a collection of optimization problems. MRP's remarkable performance, that was experimentally demonstrated, implies that Max-Race is a promising online model selection algorithm.

5. ACKNOWLEDGEMENTS

T. Zhang acknowledges partial support from National Science Foundation (NSF) grant No. 1200566. Moreover, M. Georgiopoulos acknowledges partial support from NSF grants Nos. 0806931, 0963146, and 1161228. Finally, G. C. Anagnostopoulos acknowledges partial support from NSF grant No. 1263011. Any opinions, findings, and conclusions or recommendations expressed in this material are those of the authors and do not necessarily reflect the views of the NSF.

6. REFERENCES

[1] W. Armstrong, P. Christen, E. McCreath, and A. Rendell. Dynamic algorithm selection using reinforcement learning. *AIDM '06*, pages 18–25, 2006.

[2] Y. Benjamini and D. Yekutieli. The control of the false discovery rate in multiple testing under dependency. *The Annals of Statistics*, 29:919–1188, 2001.

[3] M. Birattari, Z. Yuan, P. Balaprakash, and T. Stützle. F-race and iterated F-race: An overview. Technical report, IRIDIA, 2011.

[4] J. Brest, S. Greiner, B. Boskovic, M. Mernik, and V. Zumer. Self-adapting control parameters in differential evolution: A comparative study on numerical benchmark problems. *IEEE Trans. on Evol. Comput.*, 10:646–657, 2006.

[5] V. A. Cicirello and S. F. Smith. Heuristic selection for stochastic search optimization: Modeling solution quality by extreme value theory. *Lect. Notes in Compu. Sc.*, 3258:197–211, 2004.

[6] V. A. Cicirello and S. F. Smith. The max K-Armed bandit: A new model of eploration applied to search heuristic selection. In *20th Natl. Conf. on Artificial Intelligence*, pages 1355–1361, 2005.

[7] S. Coles. *An Introduction to Statistical Modeling of Extreme Values.* Springer, 2001.

[8] P. de Zea Bermudez and S. Kotz. Paremeter estimation of the generalized pareto distribution - part I. *J. Stat. Plan. Inference*, 140:1353–1373, 2010.

[9] M. Gagliolo and J. Schmidhuber. Algorithm selection as a bandit problem with unbounded losses. In *LION 4 Proc. of the Learning and Intelligent Optimization Conf.*, pages 82–96, 2010.

[10] M. Gallagher and B. Yuan. A general-purpose tunable landscape generator. *IEEE Trans. on Evol. Comput.*, 10:590–603, 2006.

[11] N. Hansen, S. Müller, and P. Koumoutsakos. Reducing the time complexity of the derandomized evolution strategy with covariance matrix adaptation (CMA-ES). *Evol. Comput.*, 11:77–112, 2003.

[12] J. Hüsler, P. Cruz, A. Hall, and C. M. Fonseca. On optimization and extreme value theory. *Meth. And Comput. In Appl. Probab.*, 5:183–195, 2003.

[13] M. G. Lagoudakis and M. L. Littman. Algorithm selection using reinforcement learning. In *Proc. of the 17th Int. Conf. on Machine Learning*, pages 511–518, 2000.

[14] O. Maron and A. Moore. Hoeffding races: Accelerating model selection search for classification and function approximation. *Advances in Neural Information Processing Systems*, 6:59–66, 1994.

[15] V. Mnih, C. Szepesvári, and J. yves Audibert. Empirical bernstein stopping. In *Proc. of the 25th Int. Conf. on Machine Learning*, 2008.

[16] A. W. Moore. Efficient algorithms for minimizing cross validation error. In *Proc. of the 11th Int. Conf. on Machine Learning*, pages 190–198, 1994.

[17] F. Peng, K. Tang, G. Chen, and X. Yao. Population-based algorithm portfolios for numerical optimization. *IEEE Trans. on Evol. Comput.*, 14:782–800, 2010.

[18] A. K. Qin, V. L. Huang, and P. N. Suganthan. Differential evolution algorithm with strategy adaptation for global numerical optimization. *IEEE Trans. on Evol. Comput.*, 3:398–417, 2009.

[19] C. Scarrott and A. MacDonald. A review of extreme value threshold estimation and uncertainty quantification. *Statistical Journal*, 10:33–60, 2012.

[20] F. van den Bergh and A. Engelbrecht. A cooperative approach to particle swarm optimization. *IEEE Trans. on Evol. Comput.*, 8:225– 239, 2004.

[21] J. Vrugt, B. Robinson, and J. Hyman. Self-adaptive multimethod search for global optimization in real-parameter spaces. *IEEE Trans. on Evol. Comput.*, 13:243–259, 2009.

[22] C. Wang. A new hybrid estimation method for the generalized pareto distribution. Master's thesis, University of Calgary, 2011.

[23] S. Y. Yuen, C. K. Chow, and X. Zhang. Which algorithm should I choose at any point of the search: an evolutionary portfolio approach. In *GECCO '13 Proceeding of the Genet. and Evol. Comput. Conf.*, pages 567–574, 2013.

[24] J. Zhang and A. C. Sanderson. JADE: Adaptive differential evolution with optional external archive. *IEEE Trans. on Evol. Comput.*, 13:945–958, 2009.

[25] T. Zhang, G. Borrero, and M. Georgiopoulos. A Winner-Take-All methodology: Finding the best evolutionary algorithm for the global optimization of functions. In *GECCO'12 Proc. of the Genet. and Evol. Comput. Conf. Companion*, pages 1515–1516, 2012.

[26] T. Zhang, M. Georgiopoulos, and G. C. Anagnostopoulos. S-Race: A multi-objective racing algorithm. In *GECCO'13 Proc. of the Genet. and Evol. Comput. Conf.*, pages 1565–1572, 2013.

[27] Q. Zheng, Y. Fan, Z. Shi, and Y. Wang. Adaptive inertia weight particle swarm optimization. In *ICAISC'06 Proc. of Artificial Intelligence and Soft Computing*, volume 4029, pages 450–459, 2006.

Evolution under Partial Information

Duc-Cuong Dang
ASAP Research Group
School of Computer Science
University of Nottingham
duc-cuong.dang@nottingham.ac.uk

Per Kristian Lehre
ASAP Research Group
School of Computer Science
University of Nottingham
perkristian.lehre@nottingham.ac.uk

ABSTRACT

Complete and accurate information about the quality of candidate solutions is not always available in real-world optimisation. It is often prohibitively expensive to evaluate candidate solution on more than a few test cases, or the evaluation mechanism itself is unreliable. While evolutionary algorithms are popular methods in optimisation, the theoretical understanding is lacking for the case of partial information. This paper initiates runtime analysis of evolutionary algorithms where only partial information about fitness is available. Two scenarios are investigated. In *partial evaluation of solutions*, only a small amount of information about the problem is revealed in each fitness evaluation. We formulate a model that makes this scenario concrete for pseudo-Boolean optimisation. In *partial evaluation of populations*, only a few individuals in the population are evaluated, and the fitness values of the other individuals are missing or incorrect. For both scenarios, we prove that given a set of specific conditions, non-elitist evolutionary algorithms can optimise many functions in expected polynomial time even when vanishingly little information available. The conditions imply a small enough mutation rate and a large enough population size. The latter emphasises the importance of populations in evolution.

Categories and Subject Descriptors

F.2 [**Theory of Computation**]: Analysis of Algorithms and Problem Complexity

General Terms

Theory, Algorithms, Complexity

Keywords

Partial Evaluation, Runtime Analysis, Non-elitism

GECCO'14, July 12–16, 2014, Vancouver, BC, Canada.
Copyright 2014 ACM 978-1-4503-2662-9/14/07 ...$15.00.
http://dx.doi.org/10.1145/2576768.2598375.

1. INTRODUCTION

In the past decades, there have been a significant advances in the theoretical understanding Evolutionary Algorithms (EAs) and their behaviours in optimisation problems. A large number of results on the time-complexity of EAs have been rigorously proved [14]. In most of those analyses, it often assumes that the *true fitness* value of a solution can be received by calling an *evaluation procedure*. The time-complexity is then analysed and computed based as the number of those calls.

In real-world optimisation problems, it often happens that complete and accurate information about the quality of candidate solutions is either not available or prohibitively expensive to obtain. Optimisation problems with noise, dynamic objective function or stochastic data, generally known as *optimisation under uncertainty* [6], are examples of the unavailability. On the other hand, expensive evaluations often occur in engineering, especially in structural and engine design. For example, in order to determine the fitness of a solution, the solution has to be put in a real experiment or a simulation which may be time/resource consuming or even requiring collection and processing of a large amount of data. Such complex tasks give rise to the use the *surrogate model methods* [5] to assist EAs where a cheap and approximate procedure fully or partially replaces the expensive evaluations. The full replacement is equivalent to the case of unavailability. We summarise this kind of problem as optimisation only relying on *imprecise*, *partial* or *incomplete* information (for now) about the problem.

While EAs have been widely and successfully used in this challenging area of optimisation [5, 6], only few rigorous theoretical studies have been dedicated to fully understand the behaviours of EAs under such environments. Especially for discrete optimisation, the studies are often limited to the case of imprecise information and only extreme configuration of EAs are considered. In [2, 3], the inefficiency of $(1+1)$ EA has been rigorously demonstrated for noisy and dynamic optimisation of OneMax function. The reason behind this efficiency is that in such environments, it is very difficult for the algorithm to decide one solution is better than another, e.g. very often it will choose the wrong candidate. On the other hand, such effect could be reduced by having a population, which is not the case for $(1+1)$ EA. It has been shown in [11] that with a very large or infinite population, noise has no effect on EAs. In fact, the analysis presented in [11] is based on approximations which are not rigorous (but make sense for infinite population). Therefore, the exact order of the population size cannot be specified.

In this paper, we initiate runtime analysis of evolutionary algorithms where only partial or incomplete information about fitness is available. Two scenarios are investigated: (i) in *partial evaluation of solutions*, only a small amount of information about the problem is revealed in each fitness evaluation, we formulate a model that makes this scenario concrete for pseudo-Boolean optimisation (ii) in *partial evaluation of populations*, only a few individuals in the population are evaluated, and the fitness values of the other individuals are missing. For both scenarios, we rigorously prove that given a set of specific conditions, non-elitist evolutionary algorithms can optimise many functions in expected polynomial time even with very little information available. The conditions imply a small enough mutation rate and a large enough population size. The latter emphasises the importance of having a population and understand its required size to overcome the hazardous environment filled with incomplete/imprecise information. The remainder of the paper is organised as follows. The next section provides the generalised model of optimisation and summarises our main tool to analyse EAs with non-elitist populations which is presented in a companion paper. In Section 3, the scenario for partial evaluation of solutions is presented with specific examples of pseudo-Boolean optimisation. Partial evaluation of populations is discussed and analysed in Section 4 and finally, some conclusions are drawn.

2. ANALYTICAL TOOLS

For any positive integer n, define $[n] := \{1, 2, \ldots, n\}$. The Hamming-distance is denoted by $H(\cdot,\cdot)$. The natural logarithm is denoted by $\ln(\cdot)$, and the logarithm to the base 2 is denoted by $\log(\cdot)$. For a bitstring x of length n, define $|x|_1 := \sum_{i=1}^{n} x_i$. Given a function $f(x)$ fully defined, the generalised optimisation problem of $f(x)$ is defined as,

DEFINITION 1. *In the problem of optimising $f(x)$ knowing only $F_c(x)$ (c is a positive parameter), the evaluation of a bitstring x returns $F_c(x)$ instead of $f(x)$. For $c = 1$, $F_1(x) = f(x)$ or it is a static/classical optimisation problem, shortly called* optimising $f(x)$. *For $c < 1$, $F_c(x)$ is a random variable parameterised by c and x.*

An illustrative example of optimisation with imprecise information is the noisy case. In [3], $F_c(x)$ has probability of c of being equal to $f(x)$. Otherwise with probability $1 - c$, it is equal to the fitness of a solution randomly picked from the neighbourhood of x with radius 1 in Hamming distance. Our examples of $F_c(x)$ for optimisation with incomplete information are given in the next section. The runtime is still defined in terms of the discovery of a true optimal solution.

DEFINITION 2. *Assuming maximisation, the runtime of an algorithm $\mathcal{A}$ to optimise $f(x)$ knowing only $F_c(x)$ is considered as the number of times $F_c(x)$ being sampled by $\mathcal{A}$ until for the first time a solution x^* such that $f(x^*) = \max\{f(x)\}$ is conceived by $\mathcal{A}$.*

We focus on *when* $\mathcal{A}$ finds a true optimal solution for the first time and ignore *how* $\mathcal{A}$ recognises such an achievement. The algorithms analysed in this paper belong to the algorithmic scheme of Algorithm 1. In each step t, the algorithmic scheme generates a new population P_{t+1} based on the current one P_t. Each individual of P_{t+1} is generated

Algorithm 1 Population Selection-Variation Algorithm

Require: Finite search space $\mathcal{X}$,
  and initial population $P_0 \sim \text{Unif}(\mathcal{X}^\lambda)$.
for $t = 0, 1, 2, \ldots$ until termination condition met **do**
  for $i = 1$ to λ **do**
    Sample $I_t(i) \in [\lambda]$ according to $p_{\text{sel}}(P_t)$.
    $x := P_t(I_t(i))$.
    Sample x' according to $p_{\text{mut}}(x)$.
    $P_{t+1}(i) := x'$.
  end for
end for

independently by picking one parent from P_t using a selection mechanism, denoted by p_{sel}, then by mutating it using a variation operator, denoted by p_{mut}. For pure analytical purposes, $I_t(i)$ is used to denote the sorting index i of P_t, e.g. $P_t(I_t(i))$ returns the $\lceil i/\lambda \rceil$-ranked individual of P_t.

Note that the populations do not overlap, hence the scheme is non-elitist. It also makes sense to assume p_{sel} is *monotone* as follows. Let us denote by $p_{\text{sel}}(i \mid P)$ the probability of an individual i of P being selected by p_{sel}. A selection mechanism p_{sel} is *f-monotone* if for all $P \in \mathcal{X}^\lambda$ and pairs $i, j \in [\lambda]$ it holds that $p_{\text{sel}}(i \mid P) \geq p_{\text{sel}}(j \mid P) \iff f(P(i)) \geq f(P(j))$. We then define the *cumulative selection probability* for p_{sel} as the probability of selecting an individual with fitness at least as good as that of the γ-ranked individual. Formally,

DEFINITION 3. *The* cumulative selection probability β *associated with selection mechanism p_{sel} is defined for all $\gamma \in (0,1]$ and $P \in \mathcal{X}^\lambda$ by*

$$\beta(\gamma, P) := \sum_{y \in P} p_{sel}(y \mid P) \cdot [f(y) \geq f(P(I(\lceil \gamma\lambda \rceil)))]$$

Algorithm 1 has been investigated in a string of papers [7, 10, 8, 1]. The algorithm has exponential expected runtime when the selective pressure is low relative to the mutation rate [7, 10]. Conversely, when the cumulative selection probability is sufficiently high, it is possible to derive upper bounds on the expected runtime using a fitness-level technique [8]. The following theorem recently shown in [1] is a further improvement which provides tighter upper bounds when $\beta(\gamma) \geq \gamma(1 + \varepsilon)$ for arbitrary small $\varepsilon > 0$.

THEOREM 4 ([1]). *Given a function $f : \mathcal{X} \to \mathbb{R}$, and an f-based partition $(A_1, \ldots, A_{m+1})$, let T be the number of function evaluations until Algorithm 1 with an f-monotone selection mechanism p_{sel} obtains an element in A_{m+1} for the first time. If there exist parameters $p_0, s_1, \ldots, s_m, s_* \in (0, 1]$, and $\gamma_0 \in (0, 1)$ and $\delta > 0$, such that*

(C1) $p_{mut}\left(y \in A_j^+ \mid x \in A_j\right) \geq s_j \geq s_*$ *for all* $j \in [m]$
(C2) $p_{mut}\left(y \in A_j \cup A_j^+ \mid x \in A_j\right) \geq p_0$ *for all* $j \in [m]$
(C3) $\beta(\gamma, P)p_0 \geq (1 + \delta)\gamma$ *for all* $P \in \mathcal{X}^\lambda$ *and* $\gamma \in (0, \gamma_0)$
(C4) $\lambda \geq \dfrac{2}{a} \ln\left(\dfrac{16m}{ac\epsilon s_*}\right)$ *with* $a = \dfrac{\delta^2 \gamma_0}{2(1+\delta)}$
$\epsilon = \min\{\delta/2, 1/2\}$ *and* $c = \epsilon^4/24$

$$\text{then } \mathbf{E}[T] \leq \frac{2}{c\epsilon}\left(m\lambda(1 + \ln(1 + c\lambda)) + \frac{p_0}{(1+\delta)\gamma_0} \sum_{j=1}^{m} \frac{1}{s_j}\right).$$

In the theorem, A_j^+ is a short notation for $\cup_{k>j} A_k$. In this paper, focus on the special case of Algorithm 1 where the search space $\mathcal{X}$ is the set of bitstrings of length n, the selection operator p_{sel} is binary tournament selection, and the mutation operator p_{mut} is bitwise mutation, where each bit is flipped with probability χ/n. Note that the parameter χ is not necessarily constant with respect to n. The following simplifications and auxiliary results will be useful.

COROLLARY 5. *Given any constant $\gamma_0 \in (0,1)$, if $1/\delta \in \text{poly}(m)$ and $1/s_* \in \text{poly}(m)$ then there exists a constant b such that condition (C4) is satisfied with*

(C4') $\lambda \geq \frac{b}{\delta^2} \ln(m)$

PROOF. For γ_0 being a constant and $\delta \in (0,1)$, we remark that $1/\epsilon = O(1/\delta)$, $1/c = O(1/\delta^4)$ and $1/a = (2/\gamma_0)(1/\delta^2 + 1/\delta) = O(1/\delta^2)$. Since $1/\delta \in \text{poly}(m)$ and $1/s_* \in \text{poly}(m)$, then there must exist a constant $d > 0$ such that $m^d \geq 16m/(ac\epsilon s_*)$. Thus it suffices to choose $b := 8d/\gamma_0$ so that

$$\begin{aligned}\frac{b}{\delta^2}\ln(m) &= \frac{4d}{\gamma_0}\left(\frac{1}{\delta^2}+\frac{1}{\delta^2}\right)\ln(m)\\ &\geq \frac{4}{\gamma_0}\left(\frac{1}{\delta^2}+\frac{1}{\delta}\right)\ln\left(m^d\right) \geq \frac{2}{a}\ln\left(\frac{16m}{ac\epsilon s_*}\right)\end{aligned}$$

Then any $\lambda \geq (b/\delta^2)\ln(m)$ satisfies (C4). □

COROLLARY 6. *Given any constant $\gamma_0 \in (0,1)$, for any $\delta \in (0,1)$, the expected runtime of Algorithm 1 satisfying conditions (C1-4) is*

$$O\left(\frac{1}{\delta^5}\left(m\lambda(1+\ln(1+\delta^4\lambda)) + \sum_{j=1}^{m}\frac{1}{s_j}\right)\right).$$

PROOF. For $\delta \in (0,1)$, we have $\epsilon = \min\{\delta/2, 1/2\} = \delta/2$. Hence $2/(c\epsilon) = 48/\epsilon^5 = 1536/\delta^5$. In addition, we have $\frac{p_0}{(1+\delta)\gamma_0} \leq \frac{1}{\gamma_0}$, so by Theorem 4

$$\mathbf{E}[T] \leq \frac{1536}{\delta^5}\left(m\lambda\left(1+\ln\left(1+\frac{\delta^4\lambda}{384}\right)\right) + \frac{1}{\gamma_0}\sum_{j=1}^{m}\frac{1}{s_j}\right)$$

and the result follows. □

We also use *drift analysis* [9] to prove the inefficiency of $(1+1)$ EA under partial/incomplete information. The following theorem, which is a corollary result of Theorem 2.3 in [4], was presented in [9].

THEOREM 7 (HAJEK'S THEOREM [9]). *Let $\{X_t\}_{t\geq 0}$ be a stochastic process over some bounded state $S \in [0,\infty)$, $\mathscr{F}_t$ be the filtration generated by $X_0, ..., X_t$. Given $a(n)$ and $b(n)$ depending on a parameter n such that $b(n) - a(n) = \Omega(n)$, define $T := \min\{t | X_t \geq b(n)\}$. If there exist positive constants λ, ϵ, D such that*

(L1) $\mathbf{E}[X_{t+1} - X_t | \mathscr{F}_t, X_t > a(n)] \leq -\epsilon$
(L2) $(|X_{t+1} - X_t| | \mathscr{F}_t) \preceq Y$ *with* $\mathbf{E}\left[e^{\lambda Y}\right] \leq D$

then there exists a positive constant c such that

$$\Pr\left(T \leq e^{cn} | X_0 < a(n)\right) \leq e^{-\Omega(n)}$$

Informally, if the progress (toward state $b(n)$) becomes negative from state $a(n)$ (L1) and big jumps are very rare (L2), then $\mathbf{E}[T]$ is exponential, e.g., by Markov's inequality

$$\begin{aligned}\mathbf{E}[T | X_0 < a(n)] &\geq \Pr\left(T > e^{cn} | X_0 < a(n)\right) e^{cn}\\ &\geq \left(1 - e^{-\Omega(n)}\right) e^{cn} = e^{\Omega(n)}\end{aligned}$$

3. PARTIAL EVALUATION OF PSEUDO-BOOLEAN FUNCTIONS

We consider pseudo-Boolean functions over bitstrings of length n. It is well known that for any pseudo-Boolean function $f: \{0,1\}^n \to \mathbb{R}$, there exists a set $S := \{S_1, \ldots, S_k\}$ of k subsets $S_i \subseteq [n]$ with associated weights $w_i \in \mathbb{R}$ such that

$$f(x) = \sum_{i=1}^{k} w_i \prod_{j \in S_i} x_j. \tag{1}$$

For example, we have $k = n$ and $S_i := \{i\}$ for linear functions, in which ONEMAX is the particular case where $w_i = 1$ for all $i \in [n]$. For LEADINGONES, we also get $k = n$ and $w_i = 1$ but $S_i := [i]$. In a classical optimisation problem, full access to (S, W) is guaranteed so that $f(x)$ can be exactly determined from Equation (1).

In an optimisation problem under incomplete or partial information, the access to (S, W) is made random, so often incomplete. There are many ways to define the randomisation, however in this paper we focus on the following model.

$$F_c(x) := \sum_{i=1}^{k} w_i R_i \prod_{j \in S_i} x_j \text{ with } R_i \sim \text{Bin}(1, c) \tag{2}$$

Informally, each subset S_i has probability c of being taken into account in the evaluation. We consider classical functions, such as ONEMAX and LEADINGONES, to be the typical examples. As mentioned in the previous section, $F_c(x)$ is used instead of $f(x)$ in each *partial evaluation*.

We first have a look at the case of ONEMAX, the optimisation problem is then denoted as ONEMAX(c). Literally, each 1-bit has only probability c to be added up in fitness evaluation. We will rigorously prove that for $1/c \in \text{poly}(n)$, a population-based EA can optimise ONEMAX(c) in expected polynomial time. On the other hand, the classical (1+1) EA needs exponential time in expectation for any constant $c < 1$. For simplification, we restrict p_{sel} in our analysis to binary tournament selection. The algorithm is detailed in Algorithm 2.

Algorithm 2 EAs (2-Tournament, Partial Information)

```
1: Sample P_0 ~ Unif(X^λ), where X = {0,1}^n.
2: for t = 0,1,2,... until termination condition met do
3:   for i = 1 to λ do
4:     Sample two parents x,y ~ Unif(P_t).
5:     f_x := F_c(x) and f_y := F_c(y).
6:     if f_x > f_y then
7:       z := x
8:     else if f_x < f_y then
9:       z := y
10:    else
11:      z ~ Unif({x,y})
12:    end if
13:    Flip each bit position in z with probability χ/n.
14:    P_{t+1}(i) := z.
15:  end for
16: end for
```

Theorem 4 requires lower bounds for $\beta(\gamma)$ and δ so that the necessary condition for the mutation rate χ/n is established. The value of $\beta(\gamma)$ depends on the probability that the fitter of individual x and y is selected in lines 6–12 of

Algorithm2. Formally, for any x and y where $f(x) > f(y)$, we want to know a lower bound on the probability that the algorithm selects $z = x$.

LEMMA 8. *For any two bitstrings x and y of length n with $f(x) > f(y)$, we have $\Pr(z = x) \geq (1/2)(1 + c\Pr(X = Y))$ where X and Y are identical independent random variables following distribution $\text{Bin}(f(y), c)$.*

PROOF. Each bit of the $f(x)$ 1-bits of x has probability c being counted, so $F_c(x) \sim \text{Bin}(f(x), c)$. Similarly, we have $F_c(y) \sim \text{Bin}(f(y), c)$. Remark that $f(x) = f(y) + (f(x) - f(y))$, we can decompose $F_c(x)$ and $F_c(y)$ further. Let X, Y and Δ be independent random variables such that $X \sim \text{Bin}(f(y), c)$, $Y \sim \text{Bin}(f(y), c)$ and $\Delta \sim \text{Bin}(f(x) - f(y), c)$, then we have $F_c(x) = X + \Delta$ and $F_c(y) = Y$.

By the law of total probability,

$$\begin{aligned}
&\Pr(z = x) \\
&= \Pr(X > Y) + \Pr(X = Y)\left(\Pr(\Delta > 0) + \frac{\Pr(\Delta = 0)}{2}\right) \\
&= \Pr(X > Y) + \Pr(X = Y)\left(\Pr(\Delta \geq 0) - \frac{\Pr(\Delta = 0)}{2}\right) \\
&= \Pr(X > Y) + \Pr(X = Y)\left(1 - \frac{(1-c)^{(f(x)-f(y))}}{2}\right) \\
&\geq \Pr(X > Y) + \Pr(X = Y)\left(1 - \frac{1-c}{2}\right)
\end{aligned}$$

The inequality is due to $(1-c) \in (0, 1)$ and $f(x) - f(y) \geq 1$. Because X and Y are identical and independent, we have $\Pr(X < Y) = \Pr(X > Y)$. We also have the total probability $\Pr(X > Y) + \Pr(X = Y) + \Pr(X < Y) = 1$. The two results imply $\Pr(X > Y) = (1 - \Pr(X = Y))/2$. Put into the previous calculation of $\Pr(z = x)$,

$$\begin{aligned}
\Pr(z = x) &\geq \frac{1 - \Pr(X = Y)}{2} + \Pr(X = Y)\left(1 - \frac{1-c}{2}\right) \\
&= \frac{1}{2}(1 + c\Pr(X = Y))
\end{aligned}$$

□

COROLLARY 9. *For any two bitstrings x and y of length n with $f(x) > f(y)$, we have*

$$\Pr(z = x) \geq \frac{1}{2}\left(1 + \frac{64c/81}{6\sqrt{(n-1)c(1-c)} + 1}\right)$$

PROOF. From Lemma 8, we apply the result of Lemma 21 for $X, Y \sim \text{Bin}(n-1, c)$ (in the worst case, we have $f(y) = n - 1$) and $d = 3$ (arbitrarily chosen). □

LEMMA 10. *For any $\gamma \in (0, 1)$, the cumulative selection probability of Algorithm 2 is at least*

$$\beta(\gamma) \geq \gamma\left(1 + \frac{(1-\gamma)64c/81}{6\sqrt{(n-1)c(1-c)} + 1}\right)$$

PROOF. Without loss of generality, for any inputs x and y of the tournament selection we assume that $f(x) \geq f(y)$. Recall that $\beta(\gamma)$ is the probability of picking an individual with fitness at least equal to the fitness of the γ-ranked individual, e.g. belonging to the upper γ-portion of the population. Therefore, it suffices either x and y are picked from the portion, or at least x is picked from the portion then wins the tournament.

$$\begin{aligned}
\beta(\gamma) &\geq \gamma^2 + 2\gamma(1-\gamma)\Pr(z = x) \\
&= \gamma(1 + (1-\gamma)(2\Pr(z = x) - 1))
\end{aligned}$$

From Corollary 9, we have

$$\begin{aligned}
&2\Pr(z = x) - 1 \\
&\geq 2\left(\frac{1}{2}\left(1 + \frac{64c/81}{6\sqrt{(n-1)c(1-c)} + 1}\right)\right) - 1 \\
&= \frac{64c/81}{6\sqrt{(n-1)c(1-c)} + 1}
\end{aligned}$$

So

$$\beta(\gamma) \geq \gamma\left(1 + \frac{(1-\gamma)64c/81}{6\sqrt{(n-1)c(1-c)} + 1}\right)$$

□

COROLLARY 11. *For any $c \in (0, 1)$ and any constant $\gamma_0 \in (0, 1)$, then there exists constant $a \in (0, 1)$ such that $\beta(\gamma) \geq \gamma(1 + 2\delta)$ for all $\gamma \in (0, \gamma_0]$ where $\delta = \min\{ac, a\sqrt{c/n}\}$.*

PROOF. From Lemma 12, for all $\gamma \in (0, \gamma_0]$ we have

$$\beta(\gamma) \geq \gamma\left(1 + \frac{uc}{v\sqrt{nc} + 1}\right)$$

where $u = (1 - \gamma_0)64/81, v = 6$

If $c \leq 1/n$, then $\sqrt{nc} \leq 1$ and $\dfrac{uc}{v\sqrt{nc} + 1} \geq \left(\dfrac{u}{v+1}\right)c$.

If $c > 1/n$, then $\sqrt{nc} > 1$ and

$$\frac{uc}{v\sqrt{nc} + 1} > \frac{uc}{v\sqrt{nc} + \sqrt{nc}} = \left(\frac{u}{v+1}\right)\sqrt{\frac{c}{n}}$$

The statement now follows by choosing $a = u/(2(v+1))$. □

THEOREM 12. *Given $c \in (0, 1)$ such that $1/c \in \text{poly}(n)$, there exist constants a and b such that Algorithm 2 with $\chi = \delta/3$ and $\lambda = b\ln(n)/\delta^2$ where $\delta = \min\{ac, a\sqrt{c/n}\}$ optimises* ONEMAX(c) *in expected time*

$$\begin{cases} O\left(\dfrac{n\ln(n)}{c^7}\right) & \text{if } c \leq 1/n \text{ and} \\ O\left(\dfrac{n^{9/2}\ln(n)}{c^{7/2}}\right) & \text{if } c > 1/n. \end{cases}$$

PROOF. Remark that Corollary 11 and $1/c \in \text{poly}(n)$ imply $1/\delta \in \text{poly}(n)$, $\delta \in (0, 1)$ and $\chi < 1/3$. We then use the partition $A_j := \{x \in \{0, 1\}^n \mid |x|_1 = j\}$ to analyse the runtime. The probability of improving a solution at fitness level j by mutation is lower bounded by the probability that a single 0-bit is flipped and not the other bits,

$$(n - j)\left(\frac{\chi}{n}\right)\left(1 - \frac{\chi}{n}\right)^{n-1} > \left(1 - \frac{j}{n}\right)\left(\chi\left(1 - \frac{\chi}{n}\right)^n\right)$$

It follows from Theorem 18 and $\chi < 1/3$ that $(1 - \chi/n)^n \geq (1 - \chi) > 2/3$. Therefore, $\chi(1 - \chi/n)^n > (\delta/3)(2/3) = 2\delta/9$, and it suffices to choose the parameters $s_j := (1 - j/n)(\delta/9)$ and $s_* := \delta/(9n)$ so that (C1) is satisfied. In addition, $(1 - \chi/n)^n$ is the probability of not flipping any bit in the mutation, hence picking $p_0 = 1 - \chi$ satisfies (C2).

It now follows from Corollary 11 that for all $\gamma \in (0, \gamma_0]$

$$\begin{aligned}\beta(\gamma)p_0 &\geq \gamma(1+2\delta)(1-\chi) = \gamma(1+2\delta)(1-\delta/3)\\ &= \gamma(1-\delta/3+2\delta-2\delta^2/3) \geq \gamma(1-\delta/3+2\delta-2\delta/3)\\ &= \gamma(1+\delta)\end{aligned}$$

Therefore, (C3) is satisfied with the given value of δ. Because $1/\delta \in \text{poly}(n)$, then $1/s_* \in \text{poly}(n)$ and by Corollary 5, there exists a constant b such that condition (C4) is satisfied with $\lambda = (b/\delta^2)\ln(m)$. All conditions are satisfied, and by Corollary 6, the expected optimisation time is

$$O\left(\frac{1}{\delta^5}\left(m\lambda(1+\ln(1+\delta^4\lambda)) + \sum_{j=1}^{m}\frac{1}{s_j}\right)\right)$$

$$= O\left(\frac{1}{\delta^5}\left(\left(\frac{n\ln(n)}{\delta^2}\right)(1+\ln(1+\delta^2\ln(n))) + \frac{n}{\delta}\sum_{j=1}^{n}\frac{1}{j}\right)\right).$$

By the definition of δ, it follows that $\delta = O(1/\sqrt{n})$, so $1+\ln(1+\delta^2\ln(n)) = O(1)$. Furthermore, $\frac{n}{\delta}\sum_{j=1}^{n} 1/j = O(n\ln(n)/\delta)$ is dominated by the left term $n\ln(n)/\delta^2$. Hence, the optimisation time is $\mathbf{E}[T] = O(n\ln(n)/\delta^7)$. The theorem follows by noting that $\delta = ac$ if $c \leq 1/n$, and $\delta = a\sqrt{c/n}$ otherwise. □

We now consider the partial evaluation for LEADINGONES, so the optimisation problem LEADINGONES(c). Literally, each product $\prod_{j=1}^{i} x_j$, $i \in [n]$ has the same probability c of contributing to the fitness value in each evaluation. The following result holds for the function.

THEOREM 13. *For any $c \in (0,1)$ where $1/c \in \text{poly}(n)$, there exist constants a and b such that Algorithm 2 with $\chi = \delta/3$ and $\lambda = b\ln(n)/\delta^2$ where $\delta = \min\{ac, a\sqrt{c/n}\}$ optimises LEADINGONES(c) in expected time*

$$\begin{cases} O\left(\dfrac{n\ln(n)}{c^7}\right) & \text{if } c \leq 1/n \text{ and}\\ O\left(\dfrac{n^{9/2}\ln(n)}{c^{7/2}} + \dfrac{n^5}{c^3}\right) & \text{if } c > 1/n\end{cases}$$

PROOF. Conditions (C2)-(C4) are shown exactly as in the proof of Theorem 12. For condition (C1), use the canonical partition $A_j := \{x \in \{0,1\}^n \mid \text{LEADINGONES}(x) = j\}$. The probability of improving a solution at fitness level j by mutation is lower bounded by the probability that the leftmost 0-bit is flipped, and no other bits are flipped,

$$\left(\frac{\chi}{n}\right)\left(1-\frac{\chi}{n}\right)^{n-1} > \left(\frac{1}{n}\right)(\chi(1-\chi)) \geq \frac{2\delta}{9n}$$

We therefore choose $s_j = s_* = \delta/(9n)$ and the runtime is

$$\begin{aligned}\mathbf{E}[T] &= O\left(\frac{1}{\delta^5}\left(\left(\frac{n\ln(n)}{\delta^2}\right)(1+\ln(1+\delta^2\ln(n))) + \frac{n^2}{\delta}\right)\right)\\ &= O\left(\frac{n\ln(n)}{\delta^7} + \frac{n^2}{\delta^6}\right)\end{aligned}$$

The result now follows by noting that $\delta = ac$ if $c \leq 1/n$, and $\delta = a\sqrt{c/n}$ otherwise. □

We have shown that non-elitist EAs with populations of polynomial sizes and without elitism can optimise ONEMAX(c) and LEADINGONES(c) in expected polynomial runtime, precisely in terms of partial evaluation calls, for very small c, i.e. $1/c \in \text{poly}(n)$. Particularly, for any constant $c \in (0,1)$, the non-elitist EAs can optimise LEADINGONES(c) in $O(n^5)$ and ONEMAX(c) in $O(n^{9/2}\ln(n))$. We now show that the classical (1 + 1) EA, which is summarised in Algorithm 3, already requires exponential runtime on ONEMAX(c) for any constant $c < 1$.

Algorithm 3 (1+1) EA (Partial Information)

```
Sample x_0 ~ Unif({0,1}^n).
for t = 0, 1, 2, ... until termination condition met do
    x' := x_t.
    Flip each bit position in x' with probability 1/n.
    if F_c(x') ≥ F_c(x_t) then
        x_{t+1} := x'.
    else
        x_{t+1} := x_t.
    end if
end for
```

THEOREM 14. *For any constant $c \in (0,1)$, the expected optimisation time of (1+1) EA on ONEMAX(c) is $e^{\Omega(n)}$.*

PROOF. We use Theorem 7 with X_t as the Hamming distance from 0^n (all-zero bitstring) to x_t, so $X_t := H(0^n, x_t)$ and $b(n) := n$. The use of $F_c(x)$ implies that the algorithm can accept degraded solutions with less 1-bits than the current solution. This typically happens when all bit positions of x' are not flipped except a 1-bit then the evaluation of x' does not recognise the change, such an event is denoted by $\mathcal{E}$. To analyse $\Pr(\mathcal{E})$, let us denote the event that a specific bit position i being flipped and not the others, and $F_c(x')$ does not evaluate position i, by $\mathcal{E}_i$.

$$\Pr(\mathcal{E}_i) = (1-c)\left(\frac{1}{n}\right)\left(1-\frac{1}{n}\right)^{n-1} \geq \frac{1-c}{ne}$$

Assuming that there are currently j 1-bits in x_t, events $\mathcal{E}_i$ for those bits are non-overlapping. In addition, under the condition that one of those events $\mathcal{E}_i$ happens (so with probability $j\Pr(\mathcal{E}_i)$), we use X to denote the number of the remaining 1-bits in x_t being evaluated, and Y the number of evaluated 1-bits in x'. Indeed, X and Y are identical and independent variables following the same binomial distribution $\text{Bin}(f(x), c)$, so $\Pr(Y \geq X) \geq 1/2$. We get,

$$\Pr(\mathcal{E}) \geq j \cdot \frac{1-c}{ne} \cdot \Pr(Y \geq X) \geq \frac{j(1-c)}{2ne}$$

The drift is then

$$\mathbf{E}[X_{t+1} - X_t | \mathscr{F}_t] \leq -1 \cdot \frac{j(1-c)}{2ne} + (n-j) \cdot \frac{1}{n}$$

We have a negative drift when $\frac{j(1-c)}{2ne} \geq \frac{n-j}{n}$ or

$$j \geq \frac{n}{1+\frac{1-c}{2e}} = n\left(1-\frac{1-c}{2e+1-c}\right)$$

From that, for any constant $\epsilon \in (1-c, 2e)$, there exists $a(n) := n\left(1-\frac{1-c+\epsilon}{2e+1-c}\right)$ so that

$$\mathbf{E}[X_{t+1} - X_t | \mathscr{F}_t, X_t > a(n)] \leq -\frac{\epsilon}{2e}$$

With n sufficiently large, we have $b(n) - a(n) = \Omega(n)$ and the condition (L1) of Theorem 7 is satisfied. Condition

(L2) holds trivially due to the property of Hamming distance $|H(x_t, 0^n) - H(x_{t+1}, 0^n)| \leq H(x_t, x_{t+1}) \leq H(x_t, x')$. So

$$(|X_t - X_{t+1}| \mathscr{F}_t) \preceq Z \text{ where } Z := H(x_t, x')$$

Then $Z \sim \text{Bin}(n, 1/n)$ and $\mathbf{E}\left[e^{\lambda Z}\right] \leq e$ for $\lambda = \ln(2)$. We also remark that if each bit position of x_0 is initialised with probability $1/2$, then X_0 will be highly concentrated near $n/2 \leq a(n)$. It then follows from Theorem 7 that (1 + 1) EA requires expected exponential runtime to optimise ONEMAX(c). □

4. PARTIAL EVALUATION OF POPULATIONS

In the previous section, we have seen that EAs with populations do not need complete but only a small amount of information about the problem in each solution evaluation to discover a true optimal solution in expected polynomial runtime. One might wonder if the same thing could be true about the information containing within a population.

We first give the motivation for how such a lack of information about the population can arise. In real-life applications, the evaluation of solutions can be both time-consuming (e.g. requiring extensive simulation) and inaccurate. We associate a probability $1 - r$ with the event that the quality of a solution is not available to the algorithm. We model such a scenario in Algorithm 4 by assuming that the outcome of any comparison between two individuals is only available to the algorithm with probability r.

Algorithm 4 EAs (2-Tournament, Partially Eval. Pop.)

1: Sample $P_0 \sim \text{Unif}(\mathcal{X}^\lambda)$, where $\mathcal{X} = \{0,1\}^n$.
2: **for** $t = 0, 1, 2, \ldots$ until termination condition met **do**
3:   **for** $i = 1$ to λ **do**
4:     Sample two parents $x, y \sim \text{Unif}(P_t)$.
5:     $z := \begin{cases} \text{argmax}\{f(x), f(y)\} & \text{with probability } r \\ x & \text{otherwise} \end{cases}$
6:     Flip each bit position in z with probability χ/n.
7:     $P_{t+1}(i) := z$
8:   **end for**
9: **end for**

Unlike Algorithm 2, the algorithm in this section use complete information about the problem to evaluate solutions. However, the evaluation of individuals in the parent populations is not systematic but at random. Two individuals x and y are sampled uniformly at random from the population as parents (line 4). With probability r, the individuals are evaluated and the fitter individual is selected (line 5). Otherwise, a parent x is arbitrarily chosen without concern for the fitness value. Like before, efficient implementation is possible but that does not change the outcome of our analysis. The analysis is more straightforward compared to the previous section.

LEMMA 15. *For any $r \in (0, 1)$ and constant $\gamma_0 \in (0, 1)$, there exists a constant $a \in (0, 1)$ such that Algorithm 4 satisfies $\beta(\gamma) \geq \gamma(1 + 2\delta)$ for all $\gamma \in (0, \gamma_0)$, where $\delta = ar$.*

PROOF. An individual among the best γ-portion of the population is selected if either (i) a uniformly chosen individual is chosen as parent (with probability $1 - r$), and this individual belongs to the best γ-portion, or (ii) the tournament selection happens (with probability r), and at least one of the selected parents belongs to the γ-portion.

$$\begin{aligned} \beta(\gamma) &\geq \gamma(1 - r) + r(1 - (1 - \gamma)^2) \\ &= \gamma(1 + (1 - \gamma)r) \end{aligned}$$

So for all $\gamma \in (0, \gamma_0]$, $\beta(\gamma) \geq \gamma(1 + (1 - \gamma_0)r)$ and the statement follows by choosing $a = (1 - \gamma_0)/2$. □

The lemma can be generalised to k-tournament, however, larger tournament sizes may cause overhead in the average number of evaluations per generation. This number is a random variable following $\text{Bin}(k\lambda, r)$. Hence, we focus on $k = 2$. Similar to the previous section, we consider r small, i.e. $1/r \in \text{poly}(n)$. The following theorem holds for the runtime of ONEMAX(c).

THEOREM 16. *There exist constants a and b such that Algorithm 4 optimise* ONEMAX *under condition $r \in (0, 1)$ and $1/r \in \text{poly}(n)$, with $\chi = \delta/3$ and $\lambda = b \ln(n)/\delta^2$ where $\delta = ar$ in $O(n \ln(n)/r^7)$.*

PROOF. We use the same partition from Theorem 12 and the proof idea is similar. We first remark that by Lemma 15 and from $1/r \in \text{poly}(n)$ we have $1/\delta \in \text{poly}(n)$, $\delta \in (0, 1)$ and $\chi < 1/3$. The probability of improving a solution at fitness level j by mutation is lower bounded by

$$(n - j)\left(\frac{\chi}{n}\right)\left(1 - \frac{\chi}{n}\right)^{n-1} > \left(1 - \frac{j}{n}\right)\left(\frac{2\delta}{9}\right)$$

So we can pick $s_j := (1 - j/n)(\delta/9)$, $s_* := \delta/(9n)$ and $p_0 = 1 - \chi$ so that (C1) and (C2) are satisfied.

It now follows Lemma 15 that for all $\gamma \in (0, \gamma_0]$

$$\beta(\gamma)p_0 \geq \gamma(1 + 2\delta)(1 - \chi) = \gamma(1 + 2\delta)(1 - \delta/3) \geq \gamma(1 + \delta)$$

Therefore, (C3) is satisfied with the given value of δ. Because $1/\delta \in \text{poly}(n)$, then $1/s_* \in \text{poly}(n)$ and by Corollary 5, there exists a constant b such that condition (C4) is satisfied with $\lambda = (b/\delta^2)\ln(m)$. All conditions are satisfied, and by Corollary 6 the expected optimisation time is

$$\begin{aligned} O\left(\frac{1}{\delta^5}\left(\left(\frac{n \ln(n)}{\delta^2}\right)(1 + \ln(1 + \delta^2 \ln(n))) + \frac{n}{\delta}\sum_{j=1}^{n}\frac{1}{j}\right)\right) \\ = O\left(\frac{n \ln(n)}{\delta^7}\right) \end{aligned}$$

The result now follows by noting that $\delta = ar$. □

When the parameter r is small, the fitness function is evaluated only a few times per generation. More precisely, the fitness function is evaluated $2N$ times, where $N \sim \text{Bin}(\lambda, r)$. The proof of Theorem 4 pessimistically assumes that the fitness function is evaluated 2λ times per generation. A more sophisticated analysis which takes this into account may lead to tighter bounds than those above.

We can also use Algorithm 4 to optimise LEADINGONES. The following theorem holds for its runtime.

THEOREM 17. *There exist constants a and b such that Algorithm 4 optimise* ONEMAX *under condition $r \in (0, 1)$ and $1/r \in \text{poly}(n)$, with $\chi = \delta/3$ and $\lambda = b \ln(n)/\delta^2$ where $\delta = ar$ in $O(n \ln(n)/r^7 + n^2/r^6)$.*

PROOF. We use the same approach as the proof of Theorem 13, including the partition. So we have the same $s_j = s_* = \delta/(9n)$, and the expected runtime for any $r \in (0,1)$ with $1/r \in \text{poly}(n)$ is

$$O\left(\frac{n\ln(n)}{\delta^7}+\frac{n^2}{\delta^6}\right)=O\left(\frac{n\ln(n)}{r^7}+\frac{n^2}{r^6}\right)$$

□

Our results have shown that EAs do not need the fitness values of all individuals in their populations to efficiently optimise a function. Another interpretation is that competition between every individual before reproduction is not necessary for efficient evolution. Note that non-elitism can be considered as a way of reducing the competitiveness in populations. These observations have many analogies with evolution in biology.

5. CONCLUSIONS

We have shown by rigorous analysis the runtime of evolutionary algorithms under circumstances where only partial information about fitness is available. Two scenarios have been studied. In *partial evaluation of solutions*, only a small amount of information about the problem is revealed in each fitness evaluation. In *partial evaluation of populations*, only a few individuals in the population are evaluated, and the fitness values of the other individuals are missing. For both scenarios, we have proved that non-elitist evolutionary algorithms satisfying a set of specific conditions can optimise many functions in expected polynomial time even when very little information is available. The conditions often imply a small enough mutation rate and/or a large enough population size. The importance of populations in evolution is emphasised through the results. Future work should evaluate the advantages of populations in optimisation under imprecision and uncertainty, such as in noisy or stochastic optimisation.

Acknowledgements

The research leading to these results has received funding from the European Union Seventh Framework Programme (FP7/2007-2013) under grant agreement no 618091 (SAGE) and from the British Engineering and Physical Science Research Council (EPSRC) grant no EP/F033214/1 (LANCS).

6. REFERENCES

[1] D.-C. Dang and P. K. Lehre. Refined upper bounds on the expected runtime of non-elitist populations from fitness-levels. To appear in the Proceedings of the 16th Annual Conference on Genetic and Evolutionary Computation (GECCO'14), Vancouver, Canada, 2014.

[2] S. Droste. Analysis of the (1+1) EA for a dynamically bitwise changing OneMax. In *Proceedings of the 2003 International Conference on Genetic and Evolutionary Computation*, GECCO'03, pages 909–921, Berlin, Heidelberg, 2003. Springer-Verlag.

[3] S. Droste. Analysis of the (1+1) EA for a noisy OneMax. In *Proceedings of the 2004 International Conference on Genetic and Evolutionary Computation*, GECCO'04, pages 1088–1099, Berlin, Heidelberg, 2004. Springer-Verlag.

[4] B. Hajek. Hitting-time and occupation-time bounds implied by drift analysis with applications. *Advances in Applied Probability*, 14(3):502–525, 1982.

[5] Y. Jin. Surrogate-assisted evolutionary computation: Recent advances and future challenges. *Swarm and Evolutionary Computation*, 1(2):61–70, 2011.

[6] Y. Jin and J. Branke. Evolutionary optimization in uncertain environments - a survey. *IEEE Transactions on Evolutionary Computation*, 9(3):303–317, 2005.

[7] P. K. Lehre. Negative drift in populations. In *Proceedings of the 11th International Conference on Parallel Problem Solving from Nature*, PPSN'10, pages 244–253, Berlin, Heidelberg, 2010. Springer-Verlag.

[8] P. K. Lehre. Fitness-levels for non-elitist populations. In *Proceedings of the 13th Annual Conference on Genetic and Evolutionary Computation*, GECCO'11, pages 2075–2082, New York, NY, USA, 2011. ACM.

[9] P. K. Lehre. Drift analysis. In *Proceedings of the 14th Annual Conference Companion on Genetic and Evolutionary Computation*, GECCO'12, pages 1239–1258, New York, NY, USA, 2012. ACM.

[10] P. K. Lehre and X. Yao. On the impact of mutation-selection balance on the runtime of evolutionary algorithms. *IEEE Transactions on Evolutionary Computation*, 16(2):225–241, 2012.

[11] B. L. Miller and D. E. Goldberg. Genetic algorithms, selection schemes, and the varying effects of noise. *Evolutionary Computation*, 4:113–131, 1996.

[12] D. S. Mitrinović. *Elementary Inequalities*. P. Noordhoff Ltd, Groningen, 1964.

[13] M. Mitzenmacher and E. Upfal. *Probability and Computing: Randomized Algorithms and Probabilistic Analysis*. Cambridge University Press, 2005.

[14] P. S. Oliveto, J. He, and X. Yao. Time complexity of evolutionary algorithms for combinatorial optimization: A decade of results. *International Journal of Automation and Computing*, 4(3):281–293, 2007.

APPENDIX

THEOREM 18 (BERNOULLI'S INEQUALITY [12]). *For any integer $n \geq 0$ and any real number $x \geq -1$, it holds that $(1+x)^n \geq 1+nx$.*

THEOREM 19 (JENSEN'S INEQUALITY [12]). *For any function $f(x)$ convex in $[\alpha, \beta]$ and $a_i \in [\alpha, \beta]$ with $i \in [n]$,*

$$f\left(\frac{1}{n}\sum_{i=1}^{n} a_i\right) \leq \frac{1}{n}\sum_{i=1}^{n} f(a_i)$$

THEOREM 20 (CHEBYSHEV'S INEQUALITY [13]). *For any random variable X with finite expected value μ and finite non-zero variance σ^2, it holds that* $\Pr(|X-\mu| \geq d\sigma) \leq 1/d^2$ *for any $d > 0$.*

LEMMA 21. *Let X and Y be identical independent discrete random variables with finite expected value μ and finite non-zero variance σ^2, it holds that*

$$\Pr(X = Y) \geq \frac{(1-1/d^2)^2}{2d\sigma+1} \text{ for any } d \geq 1$$

PROOF. For any $k, \ell \in \mathbb{R}$ with $\lceil k \rceil \leq \lfloor \ell \rfloor$, we have

$$\begin{aligned}\Pr(X=Y) &= \sum_{i\in\mathbb{Z}} \Pr(X=i)^2 \geq \sum_{i=\lceil k \rceil}^{\lfloor \ell \rfloor} \Pr(X=i)^2 \\ &\geq \frac{\left(\sum_{i=\lceil k \rceil}^{\lfloor \ell \rfloor} \Pr(X=i)\right)^2}{\lfloor \ell \rfloor - \lceil k \rceil + 1} \geq \frac{\Pr(k < X < \ell)^2}{\lfloor \ell \rfloor - \lceil k \rceil + 1}\end{aligned}$$

The second last equality is due to Theorem 19 with convex function $f(x) = x^2$. It suffices to pick $k = \mu - d\sigma$ and $\ell = \mu + d\sigma$, so that by Theorem 20, we get

$$\begin{aligned}\Pr(X=Y) &\geq \frac{\Pr(|X-\mu| < d\sigma)^2}{2d\lfloor \sigma \rfloor + 1} \\ &= \frac{(1-\Pr(|X-\mu| \geq d\sigma))^2}{2d\lfloor \sigma \rfloor + 1} \geq \frac{(1-1/d^2)^2}{2d\sigma + 1}\end{aligned}$$

□

Refined Upper Bounds on the Expected Runtime of Non-elitist Populations from Fitness-Levels

Duc-Cuong Dang
ASAP Research Group
School of Computer Science
University of Nottingham
duc-cuong.dang@nottingham.ac.uk

Per Kristian Lehre
ASAP Research Group
School of Computer Science
University of Nottingham
perkristian.lehre@nottingham.ac.uk

ABSTRACT

Recently, an easy-to-use fitness-level technique was introduced to prove upper bounds on the expected runtime of randomised search heuristics with non-elitist populations and unary variation operators. Following this work, we present a new and much more detailed analysis of the population dynamics, leading to a significantly improved fitness-level technique. In addition to improving the technique, the proof has been simplified. From the new fitness-level technique, the upper bound on the runtime in terms of generations can be improved from linear to logarithmic in the population size. Increasing the population size therefore has a smaller impact on the runtime than previously thought. To illustrate this improvement, we show that the current bounds on the runtime of EAs with non-elitist populations on many example functions can be significantly reduced. Furthermore, the new fitness-level technique makes the relationship between the selective pressure and the runtime of the algorithm explicit. Surprisingly, a very weak selective pressure is sufficient to optimise many functions in expected polynomial time. This observation has important consequences of which some are explored in a companion paper.

Categories and Subject Descriptors

F.2 [**Theory of Computation**]: Analysis of Algorithms and Problem Complexity

General Terms

Theory, Algorithms, Complexity

Keywords

Runtime, Drift analysis, Non-elitism, Fitness-levels

1. INTRODUCTION

The goal of this paper is to estimate the expected runtime of algorithms covered by the scheme of Algorithm 1. Without loss of generality, we assume maximisation. The scheme defines a class of algorithms which can be instantiated by specifying the variation operator p_{mut}, and the selection mechanism p_{sel}. The general term *population selection-variation algorithm* is used to emphasise that it not only covers Evolutionary Algorithms (EAs), but also other population-based search heuristics. Here, we assume that the algorithm optimises a fitness function $f : \chi \to \mathbb{R}$, implicitly given by the selection mechanism p_{sel}. In addition, the description of p_{sel} allows the scheme to cover more possibilities than *static/classical* optimisation, e.g., optimisation under uncertainty (see [1]).

The algorithm keeps a vector $P_t \in \mathcal{X}^\lambda, t \geq 0$, of λ search points. In analogy with evolutionary algorithms, the vector will be referred to as a *population*, and the vector elements as *individuals*. Each iteration of the inner loop is called a *selection-variation* step, and each iteration of the outer loop, which counts for λ iterations of the inner loop, is called a *generation*. The initial population is sampled uniformly at random. In subsequent generations, a new population P_{t+1} is generated by independently sampling λ individuals from the existing population P_t according to p_{sel}, and perturbing each of the sampled individuals by a variation operator p_{mut}. P_{t+1} and P_t are called the *offspring* and *parent* populations at generation t. The algorithm is classified as non-elitist, because the parent and offspring populations are non-overlapping. The algorithmic scheme is restricted to *unary* variation operators, i.e., those where each individual has only one parent. Higher-arity variation operators, e.g., crossover operators, are not covered.

Algorithm 1 Population Selection-Variation Algorithm

Require: Finite state space $\mathcal{X}$,
and initial population $P_0 \sim \text{Unif}(\mathcal{X}^\lambda)$.
for $t = 0, 1, 2, \ldots$ until termination condition met **do**
  for $i = 1$ to λ **do**
    Sample $I_t(i) \in [\lambda]$ according to $p_{\text{sel}}(P_t)$.
    $x := P_t(I_t(i))$.
    Sample x' according to $p_{\text{mut}}(x)$.
    $P_{t+1}(i) := x'$.
  end for
end for

Algorithm 1 has been studied in a sequence of papers [10, 9, 8, 1]. Its running time depends critically on the balance between the selective pressure imposed by p_{sel}, and the amount of variation introduced by p_{mut} [10]. When the selective pressure falls below a certain *threshold* which depends

GECCO'14, July 12–16, 2014, Vancouver, BC, Canada.
Copyright 2014 ACM 978-1-4503-2662-9/14/07 ...$15.00.
http://dx.doi.org/10.1145/2576768.2598374.

on the mutation rate, the expected running time of the algorithm becomes exponential [9]. Conversely, if the selection pressure exceeds this threshold, it is possible to show using a *fitness-level* argument [13] that the expected running time is bounded from above by a polynomial [8]. The present paper improves this latest result in two directions: by providing more precise upper bounds on the expected runtime, as well as providing results when the selective pressure is arbitrary close to the above mentioned threshold (ie, when δ in Theorem 3 is close to 0).

Recall that fitness-levels are the simplest (and probably the oldest) ways to derive upper bounds on the expected runtime of *elitist* EAs [13]. The idea is to partition the search space $\mathcal{X}$ into so-called *fitness levels* $A_1, \ldots, A_{m+1} \subseteq \mathcal{X}$, such that for all $1 \leq j \leq m$, all the search points in fitness level A_j have inferior function value to the search points in fitness level A_{j+1} and all global optima are in the last level A_{m+1}. Due to the elitism, which means the offspring population has to compete with the best individuals of the parent population, the EA will never lose the highest fitness level found so far. If the probability of mutating any search point in fitness level A_j into one of the higher fitness levels is at least s_j, then the expected time until this occurs is at most $1/s_j$. The expected time to overcome all the inferior levels, i.e., the expected runtime, is by linearity of expectation no more than $\sum_{j=1}^{m} 1/s_j$. This simple technique can sometimes provide tight upper bounds of the expected runtime. Recently in [12], the method has been shown be efficient to derive tight lower bounds, the key idea is to estimate the number of fitness-levels being skipped on average.

Non-elitist algorithms, such as Algorithm 1, may loose the current best solution. Therefore, to guarantee the optimisation of f, a set of conditions has to be applied so that the population does not frequently fall down to lower fitness-levels. Those conditions were introduced in [8], which imply a large enough population size and a strong enough *selection pressure* relative to the variation operator. When the conditions are satisfied, [8] concludes that the runtime is bounded from above by $O(m\lambda^2 + \sum_{j=1}^{m} 1/s_j)$ assuming that values of the parameters can be fixed as constants (details are given in Section 4). The proof divides the run of the algorithm into phases. A phase is considered successful if the population does not fall to a lower fitness level during the phase. The duration of each phase conditional on the phase being successful is analysed separately using drift analysis [5]. An unconditional upper bound on the expected running time of the algorithm is obtained by taking into account the success probabilities of the phases.

The contribution of this paper is a more precise and general upper bound for the fitness-level technique of [8]. In particular, we reduce the above bound to $O(m\lambda \ln \lambda + \sum_{j=1}^{m} 1/s_j)$ and allow the parameter δ (see Theorem 3) to be arbitrary close to 0. These refinements are achieved due to a much more detailed analysis of the population dynamics.

The remainder of the paper is organised as follows. Section 2 provides a set of preliminary results that are crucial for our improvement. Our new theorem is presented with its proof in Section 3. The new results for the set of functions which was previously presented in [8] are described in Section 4. Further potential applications of the new form of the theorem are also discussed in the section. Finally, some conclusions are drawn.

2. PRELIMINARIES

For any positive integer n, define $[n] := \{1, 2, \ldots, n\}$. The indicator function is also denoted by $[X]$ for a logic statement X. The natural logarithm is denoted by $\ln(\cdot)$, and the logarithm to the base 2 is denoted by $\log(\cdot)$. For a bit-string x of length n, define $|x|_1 := \sum_{i=1}^{n} x_i$. The ordering of the elements in a population vector $P \in \mathcal{X}^\lambda$ according to decreasing f-value will be denoted $x_{(1)}, x_{(2)}, \ldots, x_{(\lambda)}$, i.e., such that $f(x_{(1)}) \geq f(x_{(2)}) \geq \cdots \geq f(x_{(\lambda)})$. For any constant $\gamma \in (0,1)$, the individual $x_{(\lceil \gamma\lambda \rceil)}$ will be referred to as the *γ-ranked individual* of the population.

Variation operators are formally represented as transition matrices $p_{\text{mut}} : \mathcal{X} \times \mathcal{X} \to [0,1]$ over the search space, where $p_{\text{mut}}(x \mid y)$ represents the probability of perturbing an individual y into an individual x. Selection operators are represented as probability distributions over the set of integers $[\lambda]$, where the conditional probability $p_{\text{sel}}(i \mid P_t)$ represents the probability of selecting individual $P_t(i)$, i.e., the i-th individual from population P_t. For notational convenience, the probability of selecting an individual $x \in P_t$ will also be denoted by $p_{\text{sel}}(x \mid P_t)$. Each individual within a generation is sampled independently from the same distribution p_{sel}. It makes sense to assume that p_{sel} is monotone with respect to an underlying fitness function $f : \mathcal{X} \to \mathbb{R}$.

DEFINITION 1 ([8]). *A selection mechanism p_{sel} is f-*monotone *if for all $P \in \mathcal{X}^\lambda$ and pairs $i, j \in [\lambda]$ it holds*

$$p_{sel}(i \mid P) \geq p_{sel}(j \mid P) \iff f(P(i)) \geq f(P(j)).$$

Informally, the *selective pressure* of a selection mechanism refers to the degree to which the selection mechanism selects individuals that have higher f-values. We define the *cumulative selection probability* of a selection mechanism p_{sel} with respect to a fitness function f as follows.

DEFINITION 2 ([8]). *The* cumulative selection probability *β associated with selection mechanism p_{sel} is defined for all $\gamma \in (0,1]$ and $P \in \mathcal{X}^\lambda$ by*

$$\beta(\gamma, P) := \sum_{y \in P} p_{sel}(y \mid P) \cdot [f(y) \geq f(x_{(\lceil \gamma\lambda \rceil)})]$$

Informally, $\beta(\gamma, P)$ is the probability of selecting an individual with fitness at least as high as that of the γ-ranked individual. We write $\beta(\gamma)$ instead of $\beta(\gamma, P)$ when β can be bounded independently of the population vector P. Recall the definition of stochastic dominance.

DEFINITION 3. *A random variable A is stochastically dominated by a random variable B, denoted by $A \preceq B$, if* $\Pr(A > x) \leq \Pr(B > x)$ *for all $x \in \mathbb{R}$.*

Equivalently, $A \preceq B$ holds if and only if $\mathbf{E}[f(A)] \leq \mathbf{E}[f(B)]$ for any non-decreasing function f. Our main tool to prove Theorem 3 is the following additive drift theorem.

THEOREM 4 (DRIFT THEOREM [5]). *Let $X_1, X_2, \ldots$ be a stochastic process over S, $d : S \to \mathbb{R}_0^+$ be a distance function on S and $\mathscr{F}_t$ be the filtration induced by $X_1, \ldots, X_t$. Define T to be the first time t such that $d(X_t) = 0$. If there exists a constant $\Delta > 0$ such that,*

1. *$\forall t \geq 0 : \Pr(d(X_t) < B) = 1$, and*
2. *$\forall t \geq 0 : \mathbf{E}[d(X_t) - d(X_{t+1}) \mid \mathscr{F}_t] \geq \Delta$,*

then $\mathbf{E}[T] \leq B/\Delta$.

The most common application of the drift theorem in evolutionary computation is to bound the expected time until the process reaches a potential of 0 (ie., $d(X_t) = 0$). The so-called *potential function* d serves the purpose of measuring the progress toward the optimum. In our case, X_t represents the number of individuals in the population who has advanced to a higher fitness level. We are interested in the time until $X_t \geq \gamma_0\lambda$, ie., until some constant fraction of the population has advanced to the higher fitness level, sometimes called the take-over time. The earlier fitness-level theorem for populations [8] used a linear potential function on the form $d(x) = C - x$, and obtained an expected progress of δX_t for some constant δ. This situation is somehow inverse to that in *multiplicative drift* [2], as we are waiting for the process X_t to reach a large value. It well known that d should be chosen such that Δ is a constant independent of X_t. In this paper, we therefore consider the potential function $d(x) = C - \ln(1+cx)$, for appropriate choices of C and c. However, in order to bound the drift with this potential function, it is insufficient to only consider the expectation of X_{t+1}. The following lemma shows that it is sufficient to exploit the fact that X_{t+1} is binomially distributed.

LEMMA 5. *If* $X \sim \text{Bin}(\lambda, p)$ *with* $p \geq (i/\lambda)(1+\delta)$ *and* $i \geq 1$ *for some* $\delta > 0$, *then*

$$\mathbf{E}\left[\ln\left(\frac{1+cX}{1+ci}\right)\right] \geq c\epsilon$$

where $\epsilon = \min\{1/2, \delta/2\}$ *and* $c = \epsilon^4/24$.

PROOF. Let $Y \sim \text{Bin}(\lambda, (i/\lambda)(1+2\epsilon))$, then $Y \preceq X$. Therefore, $\mathbf{E}\left[\ln\left(\frac{1+cX}{1+ci}\right)\right] \geq \mathbf{E}\left[\ln\left(\frac{1+cY}{1+ci}\right)\right]$ and it is sufficient to show that $\mathbf{E}\left[\ln\left(\frac{1+cY}{1+ci}\right)\right] \geq c\epsilon$ to complete the proof. We consider the two following cases.

For $i \geq 8/\epsilon^3$: let $q := \Pr(Y \leq (1+\epsilon)i)$, then by the law of total probability

$$\begin{aligned}\mathbf{E}\left[\ln\left(\frac{1+cY}{1+ci}\right)\right] &\geq (1-q)\ln\left(\frac{1+c(1+\epsilon)i}{1+ci}\right) - q\ln(1+ci)\\ &= \ln\left(1+\frac{c\epsilon i}{1+ci}\right) - q\ln\left(1+c(1+\epsilon)i\right)\end{aligned}$$

Note that $ci = (\epsilon^4/24)i \geq (\epsilon^4/24)(8/\epsilon^3) = \epsilon/3$, then

$$\frac{ci\epsilon}{ci+1} = \frac{\epsilon}{1+1/ci} \geq \frac{\epsilon}{1+3/\epsilon} = \frac{\epsilon^2}{\epsilon+3} \geq \frac{\epsilon^2}{\frac{1}{2}+3} = \frac{2\epsilon^2}{7} \quad (1)$$

We have the following based on Lemma 16 and (1)

$$\begin{aligned}\ln\left(1+\frac{c\epsilon i}{1+ci}\right) &\geq \ln(1+2\epsilon^2/7) \geq (2\epsilon^2/7)(1-\epsilon^2/7)\\ &\geq (2/7)(1-1/28)\epsilon^2 = 27\epsilon^2/98\end{aligned}$$

Using Theorem 15 with $\mathbf{E}[Y] = (1+2\epsilon)i$, and $e^x > x$

$$q \leq \exp\left(-\frac{i\epsilon^2}{2(1+2\epsilon)}\right) \leq \exp\left(-\frac{i\epsilon^2}{4}\right) < \frac{4}{i\epsilon^2}$$

We then have

$$q\ln(1+c(1+\epsilon)i) \leq qc(1+\epsilon)i \leq \left(\frac{4}{i\epsilon^2}\right)\left(\frac{\epsilon^4(1+\frac{1}{2})i}{24}\right) = \frac{\epsilon^2}{4}$$

Putting everything together, we get

$$\begin{aligned}\mathbf{E}\left[\ln\left(\frac{1+cY}{1+ci}\right)\right] &\geq \epsilon^2(27/98 - 1/4) = \frac{5\epsilon^2}{196}\\ &> \frac{1}{8}\cdot\frac{\epsilon}{24}\cdot\epsilon = \frac{1}{8}\cdot\frac{c}{\epsilon^3}\cdot\epsilon \geq c\epsilon\end{aligned}$$

For $1 \leq i \leq 8/\epsilon^3$: the condition $i \geq 1$ implies that $\mathbf{E}[Y] = (1+2\epsilon)i \geq 1+2\epsilon$, and for binomially distributed random variables we have $\mathbf{Var}[Y] \leq \mathbf{E}[Y]$, so

$$\begin{aligned}\mathbf{E}\left[Y^2\right] &= \mathbf{Var}[Y] + \mathbf{E}[Y]^2\\ &\leq \mathbf{E}[Y]^2\left(\frac{1}{\mathbf{E}[Y]}+1\right) \leq \mathbf{E}[Y]^2\left(\frac{2(1+\epsilon)}{1+2\epsilon}\right) \quad (2)\end{aligned}$$

Using Lemma 16, (2) and $ci \leq \epsilon/3$, we get

$$\begin{aligned}\mathbf{E}\left[\ln\left(\frac{1+cY}{1+ci}\right)\right] &= \mathbf{E}[\ln(1+cY)] - \ln(1+ci)\\ &\geq \mathbf{E}[cY] - \frac{\mathbf{E}\left[c^2Y^2\right]}{2} - ci\\ &\geq \mathbf{E}[cY] - \mathbf{E}[cY]^2\left(\frac{1+\epsilon}{1+2\epsilon}\right) - ci\\ &= ci(1+2\epsilon - ci(1+\epsilon)(1+2\epsilon) - 1)\\ &\geq ci\left(1+2\epsilon - \frac{\epsilon}{3}\cdot\frac{3}{2}\cdot 2 - 1\right) = ci\epsilon \geq c\epsilon\end{aligned}$$

Combining the two cases, we have, for all $i \geq 1$,

$$\mathbf{E}\left[\ln\left(\frac{1+cX}{1+ci}\right)\right] \geq \mathbf{E}\left[\ln\left(\frac{1+cY}{1+ci}\right)\right] \geq c\epsilon$$

□

We will also need the following results.

LEMMA 6 (LEMMA 18 IN [8]). *If* $X \sim \text{Bin}(\lambda, p)$ *with* $p \geq (i/\lambda)(1+\delta)$, *then* $\mathbf{E}\left[e^{-\kappa X}\right] \leq e^{-\kappa i}$ *for any* $\kappa \in (0, \delta)$.

PROOF. For the completeness of our main theorem, we detail the proof of [8] as follows. The value of the moment generating function $M_X(t)$ of the binomially distributed variable X at $t = -\kappa$ is

$$\mathbf{E}\left[e^{-\kappa X}\right] = M_X(-\kappa) = (1 - p(1-e^{-\kappa}))^\lambda$$

It follows from Lemma 18 and from $1+\kappa < 1+\delta$ that

$$p(1-e^{-\kappa}) \geq \frac{i(1+\delta)}{\lambda}\left(\frac{\kappa}{1+\kappa}\right) \geq \frac{\kappa i}{\lambda}$$

Altogether, $\mathbf{E}\left[e^{-\kappa X}\right] \leq (1-\kappa i/\lambda)^\lambda \leq e^{-\kappa i}$. □

LEMMA 7. *Let* $Y_1, Y_2, \ldots, Y_n$ *be* n *random variables where* $Y_1 \leq Y_i$ *for all* $i \in [n]$. *Then for any random variable* $Z \in [n]$, *it holds that* $\mathbf{E}[Y_Z] \geq \mathbf{E}[Y_1]$.

Particularly for the case that Z and $\{Y_i\}$ are dependent, $\mathbf{E}[Y_i] \geq \delta$ for all i does not necessarily imply that $\mathbf{E}[Y_Z] \geq \delta$. However, such a conclusion can be drawn if there is a specific Y_1 with $\mathbf{E}[Y_1] \geq \delta$ being dominated by all other Y_i as stated in the lemma.

PROOF. For any outcome ω of the sample space Ω, let $j := Z(\omega) \in [n]$. Therefore, $Y_{Z(\omega)}(\omega) = Y_j(\omega) \geq Y_1(\omega)$. Hence $(Y_Z)(\omega) \geq Y_1(\omega)$ for all $\omega \in \Omega$, and $\mathbf{E}[Y_Z] \geq \mathbf{E}[Y_1]$. □

3. A REFINED FITNESS LEVEL THEOREM

For notational convenience, define for $j \in [m]$, the set $A_j^+ := \bigcup_{i=j+1}^{m+1} A_i$, i.e., the set of search points at higher fitness levels than A_j. We have the following theorem and corollary for the runtime of non-elitist populations.

THEOREM 8. *Given a function $f : \mathcal{X} \to \mathbb{R}$, and an f-based partition $(A_1, \ldots, A_{m+1})$, let T be the number of function evaluations until Algorithm 1 with an f-monotone selection mechanism p_{sel} obtains an element in A_{m+1} for the first time. If there exist parameters $p_0, s_1, \ldots, s_m, s_* \in (0,1]$, and $\gamma_0 \in (0,1)$ and $\delta > 0$, such that*

(C1) $p_{mut}\left(y \in A_j^+ \mid x \in A_j\right) \geq s_j \geq s_*$ *for all* $j \in [m]$

(C2) $p_{mut}\left(y \in A_j \cup A_j^+ \mid x \in A_j\right) \geq p_0$ *for all* $j \in [m]$

(C3) $\beta(\gamma, P)p_0 \geq (1+\delta)\gamma$ *for all* $P \in \mathcal{X}^\lambda$ *and* $\gamma \in (0, \gamma_0)$

(C4) $\lambda \geq \frac{2}{a}\ln\left(\frac{16m}{ac\epsilon s_*}\right)$ *with* $a = \frac{\delta^2\gamma_0}{2(1+\delta)}$

$\epsilon = \min\{\delta/2, 1/2\}$ *and* $c = \epsilon^4/24$

then

$$\mathbf{E}[T] \leq \frac{2}{c\epsilon}\left(m\lambda(1+\ln(1+c\lambda)) + \frac{p_0}{(1+\delta)\gamma_0}\sum_{j=1}^{m}\frac{1}{s_j}\right)$$

The new theorem has the same form as the one in [8]. Similarly to the classical fitness-level argument, it assumes an f-based partition $(A_1, \ldots, A_{m+1})$ of the search space $\mathcal{X}$. Each subset A_j is called a *fitness level.* Condition (C1) specifies that for each fitness level A_j, the "upgrade probability", ie the probability that an individual in fitness level A_j is mutated into a higher fitness level, is lower bounded by a parameter s_j. Condition (C2) requires that there exists a lower bound p_0 on the probability that an individual will not "downgrade" to a lower fitness level. In the classical setting where p_{mut} is bitwise mutation, it suffices to let p_0 be the probability of not mutating any bits, e.g., with mutation rate χ/n, one can choose $p_0 = e^{-2\chi}$ since $e^{-2\chi} \leq \exp(-\chi(1+\chi/(n-\chi))) \leq (1-\chi/n)^n$.

Condition (C3) requires that the selective pressure (see Definition 2) induced by the selection mechanism is sufficiently strong. The probability of selecting one of the fittest $\gamma\lambda$ individuals in the population, and not downgrading the individual via mutation (probability p_0), should exceed γ by a factor of at least $1+\delta$. In applications, the parameter δ may depend on the optimisation problem.

The last condition (C4) requires that the population size λ is sufficiently large. The required population size depends on the number of fitness levels m, the selection pressure δ (c and ϵ are functions of δ), and the upgrade probabilities s_j, which are problem-dependant parameters. A population size of $\lambda = \Theta(\ln n)$, where n is the number of problem dimensions, is sufficient for many pseudo-Boolean functions.

If all the conditions (C1-4) are satisfied, then an upper bound on the expected runtime of the algorithm is guaranteed. The new theorem makes the relation between the expected runtime and the parameters, including δ, explicit. Most notably, the assumption about δ being a constant as required by the old theorem in [8] is removed. This allows the new theorem to be applied in more complex settings, such as optimisation under incomplete information or uncertainty (see eg. [1]). If δ is bounded from below by a constant, we have the following corollary.

COROLLARY 9. *In addition to (C1-4), if p_0, γ_0 and δ can be fixed as constants with respect to m, then*

$$\mathbf{E}[T] = O\left(m\lambda\ln\lambda + \sum_{j=1}^{m}\frac{1}{s_j}\right)$$

The corollary trivially holds because a, c and ϵ are constants (as being derived from the constants δ and γ_0). In that case, the first part of the runtime is reduced from $O(m\lambda^2)$ as previously stated in [8] to $O(m\lambda\ln\lambda)$. In the other word, the overhead when increasing the population size is significantly reduced compared to previous thought. We now show the proof of Theorem 8.

PROOF OF THEOREM 8. We use the following notation. The number of individuals with at least fitness j at generation t is denoted by X_t^j for $j \in [m+1]$. The current fitness level of the population at generation t is denoted by Z_t, and $Z_t = l$ iif $X_t^l \geq \lceil\gamma_0\lambda\rceil$ and $X_t^{l+1} < \gamma_0\lambda$. Note that Z_t is uniquely defined, as it is the fitness level of the γ_0-ranked individual at generation t. In addition, since we are interested in the upper bounds of the runtime, the stopping time of the process can be considered at $X_t^{m+1} \geq \gamma_0\lambda$, or equivalently $Z_t = m+1$. We also use q_j to denote the probability to generate at least one individual at fitness-level strictly better than j in the next generation, knowing that there are at least $\lceil\gamma_0\lambda\rceil$ individuals of the population at fitness-level j in the current generation. By this definition,

$$q_j = 1 - (1-\beta(\gamma_0)s_j)^\lambda \geq \frac{\beta(\gamma_0)\lambda s_j}{\beta(\gamma_0)\lambda s_j + 1} \text{ due to Lemma 18}$$

Using the following potential function, the theorem can now be proved solely relying on the additive drift argument.

$$g(t) = g_1(t) + g_2(t)$$
$$\text{with } g_1(t) = (m - Z_t)\ln(1+c\lambda) - \ln(1+cX_t^{Z_t+1})$$
$$\text{and } g_2(t) = \frac{1}{q_{Z_t}e^{\kappa X_t^{Z_t+1}}} + \sum_{j=Z_t+1}^{m-1}\frac{1}{q_j} \text{ with } \kappa \in (0,\delta)$$

The function is bounded from above by,

$$\begin{aligned} g(t) &\leq m\ln(1+c\lambda) + \sum_{j=1}^{m}\frac{1}{q_j} \\ &\leq m\ln(1+c\lambda) + \sum_{j=1}^{m}\left(1 + \frac{1}{\beta(\gamma_0)\lambda s_j}\right) \\ &= m(1+\ln(1+c\lambda)) + \frac{1}{\beta(\gamma_0)\lambda}\sum_{j=1}^{m}\frac{1}{s_j} \end{aligned}$$

At generation t, we use $R = Z_{t+1} - Z_t$ to denote the random variable describing the next progress in fitness-levels. To simplify further writing, let us put $l = Z_t$, $i = X_t^l$, $X = X_{t+1}^l$, then $\Delta = g(t) - g(t+1) = \Delta_1 + \Delta_2$ with

$$\Delta_1 = g_1(t) - g_1(t+1) = R\ln(1+c\lambda) + \ln\left(\frac{1+X_{t+1}^{l+R+1}}{1+ci}\right)$$

$$\Delta_2 = g_2(t) - g_2(t+1) = \frac{1}{q_l e^{\kappa i}} - \frac{1}{q_{l+R}e^{\kappa X_{t+1}^{l+R+1}}} + \sum_{j=l+1}^{l+R}\frac{1}{q_j}$$

Let $\mathscr{F}_t$ be the filtration induced by P_t, define $\mathcal{E}_t$ to be the event that the population in the next generation does not fall down to a lower level, $\mathcal{E}_t : Z_{t+1} \geq Z_t$, and $\bar{\mathcal{E}}_t$ the complementary event. We have,

$$\begin{aligned}
&\mathbf{E}[\Delta|\mathscr{F}_t] \\
&= (1-\Pr(\bar{\mathcal{E}}_t|\mathscr{F}_t))\mathbf{E}[\Delta|\mathscr{F}_t,\mathcal{E}_t] + \Pr(\bar{\mathcal{E}}_t|\mathscr{F}_t)\,\mathbf{E}[\Delta|\mathscr{F}_t,\bar{\mathcal{E}}_t] \\
&= \mathbf{E}[\Delta|\mathscr{F}_t,\mathcal{E}_t] - \Pr(\bar{\mathcal{E}}_t|\mathscr{F}_t)\left(\mathbf{E}[\Delta|\mathscr{F}_t,\mathcal{E}_t] - \mathbf{E}[\Delta|\mathscr{F}_t,\bar{\mathcal{E}}_t]\right)
\end{aligned}$$

We first compute the *conditional forward drift* $\mathbf{E}[\Delta|\mathscr{F}_t,\mathcal{E}_t]$. Note that R is a non-negative variable under condition $\mathcal{E}_t$ and Δ is a random variable indexed by R ($\Delta = Y_R$). We can show that $Y_{r\geq 1} \geq Y_0$ for fixed indexes.

$$\begin{aligned}
Y_0 &= \ln\left(\frac{1+cX}{1+ci}\right) + \frac{1}{q_l e^{\kappa i}} - \frac{1}{q_l e^{\kappa X}} \leq \ln\left(\frac{1+c\lambda}{1+ci}\right) + \frac{1}{q_l e^{\kappa i}} \\
Y_{r\geq 1} &= r\ln(1+c\lambda) + \ln\left(\frac{1+X_{t+1}^{l+r+1}}{1+ci}\right) \\
&\quad + \frac{1}{q_l e^{\kappa i}} - \frac{1}{q_{l+r}e^{\kappa X_{t+1}^{l+r+1}}} + \sum_{j=l+1}^{l+r}\frac{1}{q_j} \\
&\geq \ln(1+c\lambda) + \ln\left(\frac{1}{1+ci}\right) + \frac{1}{q_l e^{\kappa i}} - \frac{1}{q_{l+r}} + \sum_{j=l+1}^{l+r}\frac{1}{q_j} \\
&= \ln\left(\frac{1+c\lambda}{1+ci}\right) + \frac{1}{q_l e^{\kappa i}} + \sum_{j=l+1}^{l+r-1}\frac{1}{q_j} \\
&\geq \ln\left(\frac{1+c\lambda}{1+ci}\right) + \frac{1}{q_l e^{\kappa i}} \geq Y_0
\end{aligned}$$

It follows from Lemma 7 that $\mathbf{E}[\Delta|\mathscr{F}_t,\mathcal{E}_t] = \mathbf{E}[Y_R|\mathscr{F}_t,\mathcal{E}_t] \geq \mathbf{E}[Y_0|\mathscr{F}_t,\mathcal{E}_t]$, so we only focus on $r=0$ to lower bounding the drift. We separate two cases, $i=0$, the event is denoted by $\mathcal{Z}_t$, and $i \geq 1$ (event $\bar{\mathcal{Z}}_t$). Recall that each individual is generated independently from each other, so during $\bar{\mathcal{Z}}_t$ we have that $X \sim \mathrm{Bin}(\lambda, p)$ where $p \geq \beta(i/\lambda)p_0 \geq (i/\lambda)(1+\delta)$. The inequality is due to condition (C3). Hence by Lemma 5, it holds for $i \geq 1$ (event $\bar{\mathcal{Z}}_t$) that

$$\begin{aligned}
\mathbf{E}\left[\Delta_1|\mathscr{F}_t,\mathcal{E}_t,\bar{\mathcal{Z}}_t\right] &\geq \mathbf{E}\left[\ln\left(\frac{1+cX}{1+ci}\right)|\mathscr{F}_t,\mathcal{E}_t,\bar{\mathcal{Z}}_t\right] \geq c\epsilon \\
\mathbf{E}\left[\Delta_1|\mathscr{F}_t,\mathcal{E}_t,\mathcal{Z}_t\right] &\geq \mathbf{E}\left[\ln(1)|\mathscr{F}_t,\mathcal{E}_t,\mathcal{Z}_t\right] = 0
\end{aligned}$$

By Lemma 6, we have $e^{-\kappa i} \geq \mathbf{E}\left[e^{-\kappa X}\right]$ for $i \geq 1$, then

$$\mathbf{E}\left[\Delta_2|\mathscr{F}_t,\mathcal{E}_t,\bar{\mathcal{Z}}_t\right] \geq \frac{1}{q_l}(e^{-\kappa i} - \mathbf{E}\left[e^{-\kappa X}|\mathscr{F}_t,\mathcal{E}_t,\bar{\mathcal{Z}}_t\right]) \geq 0$$

For $i=0$, recall that $q_l = \Pr(X \geq 1|\mathscr{F}_t,\mathcal{E}_t,\mathcal{Z}_t)$, so

$$\begin{aligned}
&\mathbf{E}[\Delta_2|\mathscr{F}_t,\mathcal{E}_t,\mathcal{Z}_t] \\
&\geq \Pr(X\geq 1|\mathscr{F}_t,\mathcal{E}_t,\mathcal{Z}_t)\,\mathbf{E}\left[\frac{1}{q_l e^{\kappa i}} - \frac{1}{q_l e^{\kappa X}}|\mathscr{F}_t,\mathcal{E}_t,\mathcal{Z}_t,X\geq 1\right] \\
&\geq q_l \cdot \frac{1}{q_l}(e^{-\kappa\cdot 0} - e^{-\kappa\cdot 1}) = 1 - e^{-\kappa}
\end{aligned}$$

So the conditional forward drift is $\mathbf{E}[\Delta|\mathscr{F}_t,\mathcal{E}_t] \geq \min\{c\epsilon, 1-e^{-\kappa}\}$. Furthermore, κ can be picked in the non-empty interval $(-\ln(1-c\epsilon),\delta) \subset (0,\delta)$, so that $1-e^{-\kappa} > c\epsilon$ and $\mathbf{E}[\Delta|\mathscr{F}_t,\mathcal{E}_t] \geq c\epsilon$. Next, we compute the *conditional backward drift*, which can be done for the worst case.

$$\begin{aligned}
\mathbf{E}\left[\Delta|\mathscr{F}_t,\bar{\mathcal{E}}_t\right] &\geq -\left((m-1)\ln(1+c\lambda) + \ln(1+c\lambda) + \sum_{j=1}^{m}\frac{1}{q_j}\right) \\
&\geq -\left(m\ln(1+c\lambda) + m + \sum_{j=1}^{m}\frac{1}{\beta(\gamma_0)\lambda s_j}\right) \\
&= -m\left(1 + \ln(1+c\lambda) + \frac{1}{\beta(\gamma_0)\lambda s^*}\right)
\end{aligned}$$

The probability of not having event $\mathcal{E}_t$ is computed as follows. Recall that $X_t^l \geq \lceil\gamma_0\lambda\rceil$ and X_{t+1}^l is binomial distributed with probability of at least $\beta(\gamma_0)p_0 \geq (1+\delta)\gamma_0$, so $\mathbf{E}\left[X_{t+1}^l|\mathscr{F}_t\right] \geq (1+\delta)\gamma_0\lambda$. The event $\bar{\mathcal{E}}_t$ happens when the number of individuals at fitness level l is strictly less than $\lceil\gamma_0\lambda\rceil$ in the next generation,

$$\begin{aligned}
\Pr(\bar{\mathcal{E}}_t|\mathscr{F}_t) &= \Pr\left(X_{t+1}^l < \lceil\gamma_0\lambda\rceil|\mathscr{F}_t\right) \leq \Pr\left(X_{t+1}^l \leq \gamma_0\lambda|\mathscr{F}_t\right) \\
&= \Pr\left(X_{t+1}^l \leq \left(1-\frac{\delta}{1+\delta}\right)(1+\delta)\gamma_0\lambda|\mathscr{F}_t\right) \\
&\leq \Pr\left(X_{t+1}^l \leq \left(1-\frac{\delta}{1+\delta}\right)\mathbf{E}\left[X_{t+1}^l|\mathscr{F}_t\right]|\mathscr{F}_t\right) \\
&\leq \exp\left(-\frac{\delta^2\mathbf{E}\left[X_{t+1}^l|\mathscr{F}_t\right]}{2(1+\delta)^2}\right) \quad \text{due to Theorem 15} \\
&\leq \exp\left(-\frac{\delta^2(1+\delta)\gamma_0\lambda}{2(1+\delta)^2}\right) = e^{-a\lambda}
\end{aligned}$$

Recall condition (C4) on the population size that,

$$\begin{aligned}
\lambda \geq \frac{2}{a}\ln\left(\frac{16m}{ac\epsilon s_*}\right) &\Rightarrow \frac{8m}{ac\epsilon s_*} \leq \frac{e^{\frac{a\lambda}{2}}}{2} \leq \frac{e^{a\lambda}}{a\lambda} \quad \text{due to Lemma 19} \\
&\Rightarrow \Pr(\bar{\mathcal{E}}_t|\mathscr{F}_t) \leq e^{-a\lambda} \leq \frac{c\epsilon s_*}{8m\lambda}
\end{aligned}$$

Altogether, we have the drift of

$$\begin{aligned}
\mathbf{E}[\Delta|\mathscr{F}_t] &\geq c\epsilon - \frac{c\epsilon s_*}{8m\lambda}\left(c\epsilon + m\left(1 + \ln(1+c\lambda) + \frac{1}{\beta(\gamma_0)\lambda s_*}\right)\right) \\
&= c\epsilon - \frac{c\epsilon}{8\lambda}\left(\frac{c\epsilon s_*}{m} + s_* + s_*\ln(1+c\lambda) + \frac{1}{\beta(\gamma_0)\lambda}\right) \\
&\geq c\epsilon - \frac{c\epsilon}{8\lambda}(1+1+c\lambda+1) = c\epsilon - \frac{c\epsilon}{8\lambda}\lambda\left(c+\frac{3}{\lambda}\right) \\
&\geq \frac{c\epsilon}{2}
\end{aligned}$$

Finally, by multiplying λ with the output of Theorem 4 we have the runtime in terms of evaluations,

$$\mathbf{E}[T] \leq \frac{2}{c\epsilon}\left(m\lambda(1+\ln(1+c\lambda)) + \frac{p_0}{(1+\delta)\gamma_0}\sum_{j=1}^{m}\frac{1}{s_j}\right)$$

□

Following the proof of the theorem, we observe that for each current fitness level $j = Z_t$ the runtime of the algorithmic scheme is separated into two phases: first the algorithms waits for the generation of an *advanced* individual (with fitness $Z_t + 1$); then the γ_0-upper portion of the population is filled up with advanced individuals through harmless mutation, including replications and occasional upgradings. The algorithm is considered to have left the current fitness level when there are at least $\lceil\gamma_0\lambda\rceil$ advanced individuals in the population. The first phase is based on the probability q_j which is $1-(1-\beta(\gamma_0)s_j)^\lambda$. In fact, the lower bound for q_j is loosely estimated using a weak version of Lemma 18. So one may wonder if the true value of λ/q_j could be smaller than $1/s_j$, e.g. hypothetically improving the expected optimisation times using populations instead of the standard (1 + 1) EA. The answer is no, due to the following result.

LEMMA 10. *For any $\gamma_0, \beta(\gamma_0), s_j \in (0,1)$ and $\lambda \in N$, we have $\frac{\lambda}{1-(1-\beta(\gamma_0)s_j)^\lambda} > \frac{1}{s_j}$.*

PROOF. From the condition, we have $-\beta(\gamma_0)s_j \in (-1,0)$, it follows from Theorem 17 that $(1-\beta(\gamma_0)s_j)^\lambda \geq 1-\beta(\gamma_0)s_j\lambda$, then $\frac{\lambda}{1-(1-\beta(\gamma_0)s_j)^\lambda} \geq \frac{1}{\beta(\gamma_0)s_j} > \frac{1}{s_j}$. □

The bigger term is the expected waiting time for Algorithm 1 to generate one advanced individual. This is similar to the waiting time of a $(1+\lambda)$ EA to leave level j. So it is impossible for the new bound to improve the optimisation times, unless parallel implementations are considered. So, it is crucial to fully understand the population dynamic in the second phase to finely determine the runtime.

4. APPLICATIONS

We focus on Evolutionary Algorithms (EAs) with bitwise mutations as variation operators and consider pseudo-Boolean functions. We use the same notation χ/n as the literature to denote the probability of flipping a bit position in a bitwise mutation. As the first application, we use Theorem 8 to improve the results of [8] on static functions. The following selection mechanisms were considered in [8].

- In *tournament selection* of size $k \geq 2$, denoted as k-tournament, k individuals are uniformly sampled from the current population with replacement then the fittest one is selected. Ties are broken uniformly at random.
- In *ranking selection*, individuals are assigned ranked from 0 to 1, where the best has rank 0 and the worst has 1. Following [4], a function $\alpha : \mathbb{R} \to \mathbb{R}$ is considered a ranking function if $\alpha(x) \geq 0$ for all $x \in [0,1]$, and $\int_0^1 \alpha(x)dx = 1$. The selection mechanism chooses individuals such that the probability of selecting individuals ranked γ or better is $\int_0^\gamma \alpha(x)dx$. Note that this coincides with our definition of $\beta(\gamma)$. *Linear ranking* selection uses the ranking function $\alpha(x) := \eta(1-2x)+2x$ with $\eta \in (1,2]$.
- In *(μ,λ)-selection*, parent solutions are selected uniformly at random among the best μ out of λ individuals in the current population.
- *Fitness proportionate selection* with power scaling parameter $\nu \geq 1$ is defined for maximisation problems as follows

$$\forall i \in [\lambda] \quad p_{\text{sel}}(i \mid P_t, f) := \frac{f(P_t(i))^\nu}{\sum_{j=1}^{\lambda} f(P_t(j))^\nu}.$$

  Setting $\nu = 1$ gives the classical version.

The following lemma summarises some results of [8].

LEMMA 11. *For any constants $\delta' > 0$ and $p_0 \in (0,1)$, there exist constants $\delta > 0$ and $\gamma_0 \in (0,1)$ such that condition (C3) of Theorem 8 is satisfied for*

- *k-tournament selection with $k \geq (1+\delta')/p_0$,*
- *linear ranking selection with $\eta \geq (1+\delta')/p_0$,*
- *(μ,λ)-selection with $\lambda/\mu > (1+\delta')/p_0$,*
- *fitness proportionate selection with $\nu > \ln(2/p_0)f_{\max}$.*

PROOF. See Lemmas 5, 6, 7 and 8 in [8]. □

Selection Mechanism		Parameter
Fitness proportionate (*)		$\nu > f_{\max}\ln(2e^\chi)$
Linear ranking		$\eta > e^\chi$
k-Tournament		$k > e^\chi$
(μ,λ)		$\lambda > \mu e^\chi$
Problem	Population size	$\mathbf{E}[T]$
OneMax	$\lambda \geq c\ln n$	$O(n\lambda\ln\lambda)$
LeadingOnes	$\lambda \geq c\ln n$	$O(n\lambda\ln\lambda + n^2)$
Linear	$\lambda \geq c\ln n$	$O(n\lambda\ln\lambda + n^2)$
k-Unimodal	$\lambda \geq c\ln(nk)$	$O(k\lambda\ln\lambda + nk)$
Jump_r	$\lambda \geq cr\ln n$	$O(n\lambda\ln\lambda + (n/\chi)^r)$

Table 1: Expected runtime of Algorithm 1 with corresponding parameter settings. For clarity, all constant factors are omitted or summarised by c. (*) The result for fitness proportionate selection only holds for the OneMax function.

The lemma implies that δ and γ can be fixed as constants for bitwise mutation operators with χ being a constant by setting of the selection mechanisms correctly. In those cases, Corollary 9 provides the runtime for the following functions.

$$\text{OneMax}(x) := \sum_{i=1}^{n} x_i = |x|_1$$

$$\text{LeadingOnes}(x) := \sum_{i=1}^{n}\prod_{j=1}^{i} x_i$$

$$\text{Jump}_r(x) := \begin{cases} |x|_1 + 1 & \text{if } |x|_1 \leq n-r \text{ or } |x|_1 = n \\ 0 & \text{otherwise} \end{cases}$$

$$\text{Linear}(x) := \sum_{j=1}^{n} c_i x_i$$

We also analyse the runtime of k-Unimodal functions. Recall that a pseudo-Boolean function f is called *unimodal* if every bitstring x is either optimal, or has a Hamming-neighbour x' such that $f(x') > f(x)$. We say that a unimodal function is k-Unimodal if it has k distinct function values $f_1 < f_2 < \cdots < f_k$. Remark that LeadingOnes is a particular case of k-Unimodal with $k = n$ and OneMax is a special case of Linear with $c_i = 1$ for all $i \in [n]$. Corresponding to the new results reported in Table 1, the following theorem improves the results previously reported [8].

THEOREM 12. *Algorithm 1 with bit-wise mutation rate χ/n for any constant $\chi > 0$, and where p_{sel} is either linear ranking selection, k-tournament selection, or (μ,λ)-selection where the parameter settings satisfy column "Parameter" in the first part of Table 1 has expected runtimes as indicated in column $\mathbf{E}[T]$ in the second part, given the population sizes respecting column "Population Size" of the same part. The result of fitness proportionate selection only holds for OneMax function.*

COROLLARY 13. *Algorithm 1 with either linear ranking, or fitness proportionate or k-tournament, or (μ, λ) selection can optimise* ONEMAX *in $O(n \ln n \ln \ln n)$. With either linear ranking, or k-tournament, or (μ, λ) selection, the algorithm can optimise* LEADINGONES, LINEAR *in $O(n^2)$ and k-*UNIMODAL *with $k \leq n^d$ in $O(nk)$ for any constant $d \in \mathbb{N}$.*

PROOF. The corollary is obtained from the theorem by taking the smallest population size. It is clear that we have $O(n \ln n \ln \ln n)$ for ONEMAX and $O(n(\ln n \ln \ln n + n)) = O(n(\ln^2 n + n)) = O(n^2)$ for LINEAR and LEADINGONES. With k-UNIMODAL, because $k \leq n^d$ then $c \ln(nk) \leq c(d + 1) \ln n$. It suffices to pick $\lambda = c(d + 1) \ln n$ and the runtime is bounded by $O(k(\ln nk \ln \ln nk + n)) = O(k(\ln^2 n + n)) = O(kn)$. Remark that except for ONEMAX, the overhead of having a population of solutions is ignored for all those cases.

The proof of the theorem is similar to the one in [8], except the main tool is Corollary 9. We recall those arguments shortly as follows. The f-based partitions and upgrade probabilities are similar to the ones in [6, 7, 12]. For a LINEAR function f, without loss of generality we assume the weights $c_1 \geq c_2 \geq \cdots \geq c_n \geq 0$, then set $m = n$ and choose $A_j := \left\{x \in \{0,1\}^n \mid \sum_{i=1}^{j} c_i \leq f(x) < \sum_{i=1}^{j+1} c_i\right\}$ [6]. For ONEMAX, LEADINGONES, and k-UNIMODAL functions, with k distinct function values $f_1 < \cdots < f_k$, we set $m = k$ and use the partition [12], $A_j := \{x \in \{0,1\}^n \mid f(x) = f_j\}$.

For LINEAR functions, and for k-UNIMODAL functions (including LEADINGONES where $k = n$) it is sufficient to flip one specific bit, and no other bits to reach a higher fitness level. For these functions, we therefore choose for all j the upgrade probabilities $s_* := (\chi/n)(1 - \chi/n)^{n-1} = \Omega(1/n) =: s_j$. For ONEMAX, it is sufficient to flip one of the $n - j$ 0-bits, and no other bits to escape fitness level j. For this function, we therefore choose the upgrade probabilities $s_j := (n - j)(\chi/n)(1 - \chi/n)^{n-1} = \Omega(1 - j/n)$ and $s_* := s_{n-1}$.

For JUMP$_r$, we set $m := n - r + 1$, and choose $A_1 := \{x \in \{0,1\}^n \mid n - r \leq |x|_1 < n\}$ and $A_{j>1} := \{x \in \{0,1\}^n \mid |x|_1 = j\}$. In order to escape fitness level A_1, it is sufficient to flip at most r bits and no other bits. For fitness level $j > 1$, it suffices to flip one of $n - j$ 0-bits and no other bits. Hence, we choose the upgrade probabilities $s_1 := (\chi/n)^r(1 - \chi/n)^{n-r} = \Omega((\chi/n)^r) =: s_*$ and $s_{j>1} := (n - j)(\chi/n)(1 - \chi/n)^{n-1} = \Omega(1 - j/n)$.

By the above partitions, the first condition (C1) is satisfied. Next, we set the parameter p_0 to be a lower bound of the probability of not flipping any bits $(1 - \chi/n)^n$, if so condition (C2) is therefore satisfied. For any constant $\varepsilon > 0$, it holds for all $n > 2\chi^2/\ln(1 + \varepsilon)$ that

$$\left(1 - \frac{\chi}{n}\right)^n \geq \left[\left(1 - \frac{\chi}{n}\right)^{\frac{n}{\chi} - 1}\right]^{\chi + \frac{2\chi^2}{n}} \geq \frac{1}{(1 + \varepsilon)e^{\chi}}$$

We can set $p_0 = 1/((1+\varepsilon)e^{\chi})$ which is a constant. According to the parameter settings of Table 1 and Lemma 11 there exist constants δ and γ_0 so that (C3) is satisfied. Regarding (C4), for LINEAR functions (including ONEMAX), $m/s_* = O(n^2)$. For k-UNIMODAL functions (including LEADINGONES), $m/s_* = O(nk)$. For JUMP$_r$, $m/s_* = O(n^{r+1}/\chi^r)$. Condition (C4) is satisfied if the population size λ is set according to column "Population size" of Table 1. All conditions are satisfied, and the upper bounds in Table 1 follow. □

We now explore the possibility of using Theorem 8 for runtime analysis on uncertain, or stochastic optimisation problems. We assume that the algorithm needs to optimise a deterministic pseudo-Boolean function $f : \{0,1\}^n \to \mathbb{R}$. However, the algorithm has only access to a stochastic approximation function F, such that $F(x)$ is a random variable which represents the noisy and uncertain evaluation of $f(x)$. The approximation function F must contain some information about f. Formally, we say that F is *δ-biased* with respect to f if for all $x, y \in \{0,1\}^n$ such that $f(x) > f(y)$, it holds $\Pr(F(x) > F(y)) \geq 1/2 + \delta$.

THEOREM 14. *Let $f : \{0,1\}^n \to \mathbb{R}$ be any pseudo-Boolean function, and $F(x)$ a random variable for any $x \in \{0,1\}^n$. Consider Algorithm 1 with 2-tournament selection and bitwise mutation with mutation rate χ/n. If there exist an f-based partition $(A_1, \ldots, A_{m+1})$, and two constants $d > 0$ and D, such that*

(L1) *F is $(1/n^d)$-biased with respect to f*

(L2) $\dfrac{\chi}{n} \leq \dfrac{1}{2n(n^d + 1)}$

(L3) *(C1-2) of Theorem 8 holds with $\sum_{j=1}^{m} 1/s_j = O(n^D)$.*

then there exists some $\lambda \in \mathrm{poly}(n)$ such that the expected optimisation time when using F is in $\mathrm{poly}(n)$.

The first condition (L1) implies that the probability of selecting the fittest individual in a tournament needs only to be slightly larger than $1/2$.

PROOF. Condition (L3) implies that condition (C1) can be satisfied with $1/s_j \in \mathrm{poly}(n)$ and $1/s_* \in \mathrm{poly}(n)$. Therefore, it suffices to show that condition (C3) holds for some δ where $1/\delta \in \mathrm{poly}(n)$, because this implies that there exists a $\lambda \in \mathrm{poly}(n)$ satisfying condition (C4).

We first compute $\beta(\gamma)$, the probability of selecting an individual in the upper γ-portion of the population for the mutation. This selection event occurs when: (i) both the selected individuals are selected among the best $\gamma\lambda$ individuals in the population, or (ii) at least one of them is, and the better one of them is picked. Condition (L1) then gives,

$$\beta(\gamma) \geq \gamma^2 + 2\gamma(1 - \gamma)(1/2 + n^{-d}) = \gamma(1 + 2n^{-d}(1 - \gamma))$$

Here we can fix γ_0 to $1/2$ so that $1 - \gamma \geq 1/2$ and $\beta(\gamma) \geq \gamma(1 + n^{-d})$. We now look at p_0 which can be chosen to be exactly $(1 - \chi/n)^n$, the probability of not mutating any bit position. From condition (L2), we have the probability of not flipping any bit positions

$$\left(1 - \frac{\chi}{n}\right)^n \geq 1 - \chi \geq 1 - \frac{1}{2(n^d + 1)} = \frac{1 + (n^{-d})/2}{1 + n^{-d}} =: p_0$$

The first inequality is due to Theorem 17. Now altogether,

$$\beta(\gamma)p_0 \geq \gamma(1 + n^{-d})\left(\frac{1 + (n^{-d})/2}{1 + n^{-d}}\right) = \gamma(1 + (n^{-d})/2)$$

So δ is at least $n^{-d}/2$ where d is a constant, or $1/\delta$ is upper bounded by a polynomial of n. □

The theorem indicates that if the (1+1) EA can be shown to efficiently optimise a pseudo-Boolean function f using a fitness-level theorem, then a non-elitist EA with appropriate parameter settings may optimise the same function in expected polynomial time, using only access to an δ-biased approximation function F with $1/\delta \in \mathrm{poly}(n)$. Specific settings of noisy and uncertain approximation functions are analysed in detail in a companion paper [1].

5. CONCLUSIONS

We have presented a new version of the main theorem introduced in [8]. The new theorem offers a very general tool to analyse the expected runtime of randomised search heuristics with non-elitist populations on many optimisation problems. Sharing similarities with the classical fitness-level technique, our method is straightforward and easy-to-use. The structure of the new proof was simplified and a more detailed analysis of the population dynamics has been provided. This leads to significantly improved upper bounds for the expected runtimes of EAs on many pseudo-Boolean functions. More importantly, the new fitness-level technique makes the relationship between the selective pressure and the runtime of the algorithm explicit. Surprisingly, a very weak selective pressure is sufficient to optimise many functions in expected polynomial time. This observation has interesting consequences, e.g., optimisation under uncertainty. A very first application of this kind is discussed in our companion paper [1].

Acknowledgments

The research leading to these results has received funding from the European Union Seventh Framework Programme (FP7/2007-2013) under grant agreement no 618091 (SAGE) and from the British Engineering and Physical Science Research Council (EPSRC) grant no EP/F033214/1 (LANCS).

6. REFERENCES

[1] D.-C. Dang and P. K. Lehre. Evolution under partial information. To appear in the Proceedings of the 16th Annual Conference on Genetic and Evolutionary Computation (GECCO'14), Vancouver, Canada, 2014.

[2] B. Doerr, D. Johannsen, and C. Winzen. Multiplicative drift analysis. *Algorithmica*, 64(4):673–697, 2012.

[3] D. Dubhashi and A. Panconesi. *Concentration of Measure for the Analysis of Randomized Algorithms.* Cambridge University Press, NY, USA, 2009.

[4] D. E. Goldberg and K. Deb. A comparative analysis of selection schemes used in genetic algorithms. In *Foundations of Genetic Algorithms (FOGA I)*, pages 69–93, 1990.

[5] J. He and X. Yao. Drift analysis and average time complexity of evolutionary algorithms. *Artificial Intelligence*, 127(1):57–85, 2001. Erratum in Artif. Intell. 140(1/2): 245-248 (2002).

[6] T. Kötzing, F. Neumann, D. Sudholt, and M. Wagner. Simple max-min ant systems and the optimization of linear pseudo-boolean functions. In *Foundations of Genetic Algorithms (FOGA XI)*, pages 209–218, 2011.

[7] J. Lässig and D. Sudholt. General scheme for analyzing running times of parallel evolutionary algorithms. In *PPSN*, pages 234–243, 2010.

[8] P. K. Lehre. Fitness-levels for non-elitist populations. In *Proceedings of the 13th Annual Conference on Genetic and Evolutionary Computation*, GECCO'11, pages 2075–2082, New York, NY, USA, 2011. ACM.

[9] P. K. Lehre. Negative Drift in Populations. In *Proceedings of Parallel Problem Solving from Nature - (PPSN XI)*, volume 6238 of *LNCS*, pages 244–253. Springer Berlin / Heidelberg, 2011.

[10] P. K. Lehre and X. Yao. On the impact of mutation-selection balance on the runtime of evolutionary algorithms. *IEEE Transactions on Evolutionary Computation*, 16(2):225–241, 2012.

[11] D. S. Mitrinović. *Elementary Inequalities.* P. Noordhoff Ltd, Groningen, 1964.

[12] D. Sudholt. A new method for lower bounds on the running time of evolutionary algorithms. *IEEE Transactions on Evolutionary Computation*, 17(3):418–435, 2013.

[13] I. Wegener. Methods for the analysis of evolutionary algorithms on pseudo-boolean functions. In *Evolutionary Optimization*, volume 48, pages 349–369. Springer US, 2002.

APPENDIX

THEOREM 15 (CHERNOFF'S INEQUALITY [3]). *If $X = \sum_{i=1}^{m} X_i$, where $X_i \in \{0,1\}, i \in [m]$, are independent random variables, then* $\Pr\left(X \leq (1-\epsilon)\mathbf{E}[X]\right) \leq \exp\left(-\epsilon^2 \mathbf{E}[X]/2\right)$ *for any $\epsilon \in [0,1]$.*

LEMMA 16. *For all $x \geq 0$, $x \geq \ln(1+x) \geq x(1-x/2)$.*

PROOF. The first inequality is due to $e^x \geq 1+x$. For the next one, it is easy to see that $f(x) = \ln(1+x) - x(1-x/2)$ is non-decreasing by looking at its derivative. So $f(x) \geq f(0) = 0$ for all $x \geq 0$, or $\ln(1+x) \geq x(1-x/2)$. □

THEOREM 17 (BERNOULLI'S INEQUALITY [11]). *If $x > -1$ and $n \in \mathbb{N}$, then $(1+x)^n \geq 1+nx$.*

LEMMA 18. *For $n \in \mathbb{N}$ and $x \geq 0$, we have $1-(1-x)^n \geq 1-e^{-xn} \geq \frac{xn}{1+xn}$.*

PROOF. From $e^x \geq x+1$, it follows that $1-(1-x)^n \geq 1-e^{-nx} \geq 1-(1+x)^{-n} = 1-1/\left(1+\sum_{k=1}^{n}\binom{n}{k}x^k\right)$. For $x \geq 0$, we have $x^k \geq 0$, so it suffices to cut off the sum at any k, the result is obtained with $k=1$. □

LEMMA 19. *For all $x \in \mathbb{R}$, $e^{2x} \geq (x+1)e^x > xe^x$ and for $x > 0$, $e^{2x}/x > e^x$.*

PROOF. Multiplying e^x to $e^x - x \geq 1 > 0$ and adding xe^x to both sides give the first result, then dividing them to $x > 0$ provide the second one. □

The Impact of Random Initialization on the Runtime of Randomized Search Heuristics

Benjamin Doerr
École Polytechnique
Paris-Saclay, France

Carola Doerr
CNRS and Univ. Pierre et Marie Curie
Paris, France

ABSTRACT

It has often been observed that the expected runtime of an evolutionary algorithm with random initialization does not deviate much from the expected runtime when starting in an initial solution of average fitness. Having this information a priori would greatly simplify the runtime analysis for the algorithm using random initialization.

We prove such a result for the optimization of the OneMax test function via the two randomized search heuristics *Randomized Local Search (RLS)* and the *(1+1) Evolutionary Algorithm*. For both algorithms, we show that the expected runtime from a random initial solution deviates at most by a constant number of iterations from the expected runtime when starting with a solution having exactly $n/2$ ones.

For RLS we can precisely compute that this constant is $-1/2 \pm o(1)$. This leads to an extremely precise bound for the expected runtime. The expected number of fitness evaluations until an optimal search point is found, is $nH_{n/2} - 1/2 \pm o(1)$, where $H_{n/2}$ denotes the $(n/2)$th harmonic number when n is even, and $H_{n/2} := (H_{\lfloor n/2 \rfloor} + H_{\lceil n/2 \rceil})/2$ when n is odd.

The main technique to obtain these results is a coupling of the optimization process starting from different fitness levels. We believe this technique to be interesting also much beyond the specific results mentioned above; e.g., for the study of other optimization problems.

Categories and Subject Descriptors

F.2.2 [**Theory of Computation**]: Analysis of Algorithms and Problem Complexity—*Nonnumerical Algorithms and Problems*

Keywords

Runtime Analysis; Theory; Evolutionary Algorithms; Genetic Algorithms

GECCO'14, July 12–16, Vancouver, BC, Canada.

http://dx.doi.org/10.1145/2576768.2598359.

1. INTRODUCTION

Ever since the behavior of general-purpose randomized search heuristics is studied from a theoretical angle, the benefits of such efforts have been controversially discussed. While on the one hand it is criticized that the results are often far too theoretical and of no or little practical importance, theoreticians have always argued that studying the runtimes or the fitness-landscapes of randomized search heuristics in a mathematically rigorous manner will eventually lead to the design of better algorithms. In fact, exact runtime bounds help us understand the influence of certain parameter choices like the population size, the mutation rate, or the selection criterion. The tighter the runtime bounds are, the more can be said about these choices. Witt [14], for example, has shown that for optimizing any linear function with the $(1+1)$ EA, the best mutation rate is $1/n$. In fact, he could show that among a broader class of so-called mutation-based evolutionary algorithms the (1+1) EA using mutation probability $1/n$ is optimal [14]. A recent example showing that the hope for generating new algorithmic ideas via theoretical investigations of randomized search heuristics does indeed materialize is the genetic algorithm proposed in [3]. It is proven to outperform all existing and in fact all possible purely mutation-based evolutionary approaches on the OneMax problem. Experimental results suggest that the main idea of this algorithm, namely exploiting crossover as a means of exploration, has the potential of improving standard genetic algorithms. The work in [3] is based on findings from runtime and black-box complexity analyses.

Analyzing randomized search heuristics in a rigorous and precise manner, however, is a challenging task and often is at the limit of what is possible with the state-of-the-art tools in algorithmics. One of the main difficulties in such analyses is the large amount of randomness involved and that, in particular with random initialization and standard bit mutation, rarely but with positive probability events can occur that deviate much from the expected behavior. Such events must hence be taken into account carefully. It is therefore far beyond our current ability to analyze the runtime (number of function evaluations needed until an optimal search point is queried for the first time) of complex randomized search heuristics on relevant real-world problems. For this reason theoreticians often resort to analyzing simple search strategies on artificial problems, hoping that this gives new insight in the optimization process lead by the random searches. As has been argued before, such analyses are useful for two complementary goals: the development of new techniques for analyzing the complex random behavior of search heuristics and insight into to the behavior of such algorithms on easy parts of more complex problem spaces. An example that shows quite well how the development of new techniques can change in a few years the horizon of problems in evolutionary computation that can be rigorously analyzed is the so-called drift analysis. Drift analysis has originally been introduced in [8] and is by now one of the standard techniques for analyzing randomized search heuristics. Several versions of drift theorems exist.

Despite these efforts, two of the oldest problems in the theory of evolutionary computation remain open: the exact runtime of Randomized Local Search (RLS) and of the (1+1) Evolutionary Algorithm (EA) on ONEMAX. The best known bound for RLS is due to Witt [15]. It estimates the runtime of RLS on ONEMAX by $nH_{n/2} \pm o(n)$. Note that the proof actually gives a lower order term of $\Theta(n^{2/3})$ and note further that without greater efforts this could be reduced to $\Theta(n^{1/2+\varepsilon})$, but not further. For the $(1+1)$ EA the best known upper bound, $en\ln(n) - 0.1369n + O(1)$, is due to Doerr, Fouz, and Witt [5] and the best known lower bound, $en\ln(n) - 5.9338n - O(n\log n)$, is due to Lehre and Witt [10].

It may, at a first glance, seem surprising that determining the lower order terms for these problems are that challenging. Indeed, the "RLS on ONEMAX" problem is much related to the well-known coupon collector problem, for which very precise runtime bounds are easily derived by standard arguments. The only difference between the two problems is the random initialization of RLS.

Most randomized search heuristics are in fact initialized with a random sample—either taken uniformly at random from the search space (e.g., if not much is known about the problem at hand), or taken from a distribution that is biased towards sampling from an area of the search space in which global optima are anticipated. The random initialization is usually taken care of in runtime analysis by applying tail bound estimates (like Chernoff bounds) to the random starting point, thus showing that with reasonably large probability the initial individual lies in a certain area of the search space. This approach is often sufficient when only asymptotic results, e.g., in big-Oh notation, are sought after. However, we observe that for enhancing the state-of-the-art in runtime analysis, it has become increasingly important to derive more precise runtime bound that also provide an estimate of the lower order terms in the runtime bounds. Chernoff-type tail bounds are therefore often combined with other techniques. Indeed, this is also the approach of Witt [15] for deriving his above mentioned bound for RLS on ONEMAX. He combines the standard Chernoff-bound with a refined fitness level technique.

In this paper we contribute to the toolbox in runtime analysis by introducing a novel coupling technique. More precisely, we couple the runtime of an algorithm starting in a search point of fitness $n/2 - k$ and $n/2 + k$, respectively, with the runtime of the algorithm started on fitness level $n/2$. This method allows to compare the average runtime of a randomized search heuristic (started in a random individual) with the runtime of the same search heuristic started (deterministically) in an average initial search point. While it seems intuitive that for many problems these two runtime bounds should not deviate much, this intuition has not been quantified before, neither experimentally nor via a mathematical proof.

We use the coupling method to show that the average runtime of RLS and the $(1+1)$ EA on ONEMAX deviates from the runtime of the respective algorithm when started in an average search point (i.e., in a search point with $n/2$ ones and $n/2$ zeros) only by a constant additive term.

For RLS we compute this constant deviation precisely. Our result implies that the exact average runtime T of RLS on ONEMAX is by an additive term of $1/2$ lower than $nH_{n/2}$, which is the runtime starting from the fitness level $n/2$. Here, $H_{n/2} := \sum_{i=1}^{n/2} 1/i$ is the $(n/2)$th harmonic number when n is even, and $H_{n/2} := \frac{1}{2}H_{\lfloor n/2 \rfloor} + \frac{1}{2}H_{\lceil n/2 \rceil}$ when n is odd. Since RLS treats all strictly monotonic functions equally, this bound holds not only for ONEMAX but in fact for the runtime of RLS on any strictly monotonic function.

As mentioned above, the "RLS on ONEMAX" problem is equivalent to the coupon collector problem (cf. Section 2.1) with a random initial stake, hence this result is interesting also beyond the evolutionary computation community. Indeed, the coupon collector problem has applications in many areas of computer science, e.g., in randomized algorithms, statistics, probability theory, and distributed computing; see, e.g., [11].

For the $(1+1)$ EA, much less precise runtime estimates are known. The main reason for this is that it is difficult to compute estimates precise up to $(1 \pm o(1))$ factors for the drift of the $(1+1)$ EA started in a search point with a linear number of ones. For this reason, bounds sharp up to $o(n)$ terms are currently not in sight. Despite this, we are able to prove that the difference between starting the $(1+1)$ EA on a random search point and on a search point with $n/2$ ones is at most an additive constant. That this is possible without knowing either of these two runtimes more precise than up to $\Theta(n)$ error terms is again a strength of our coupling technique. With respect to the problem of precise bounds for the $(1+1)$ EA on ONEMAX, our result is helpful in that to gain bound sharp up to $\Theta(1)$ terms, it suffices to analyze the situation that we start the algorithm with a fixed search point having exactly $n/2$ ones.

2. RUNTIME OF RLS OPTIMIZING MONOTONIC FUNCTIONS

Randomized Local Search (RLS) is a simple hill-climbing heuristic. When used to maximize pseudo-Boolean functions $f : \{0,1\}^n \to \mathbb{R}$, RLS starts with a random initial search point $x \in \{0,1\}^n$. In each iteration it creates from x a new search point (*offspring*) y by choosing a position $j \in [n] := \{1, 2, \ldots, n\}$ uniformly at random and flipping in x the entry in the jth position. In Algorithm 1, which gives RLS in pseudocode, this *mutation step* is performed in line 2. Here and henceforth, by e_j^n we denote the binary vector of length n with all entries except for the jth one set to zero. RLS replaces x by y if and only if $f(y) \geq f(x)$, i.e., if and only if the objective value (*fitness*) of y is at least as large as the fitness of x.

A pseudo-Boolean function $f : \{0,1\}^n \to \mathbb{R}$ is called (strictly) *monotonic* if for all $x, y \in \{0,1\}^n$, we have $f(x) < f(y)$ whenever $x \leq y$ (bit-wise) and $x \neq y$. Since the selection depends only on the relative and not on absolute fitness values, RLS optimizes all monotonic functions in an identical fashion. As the particular monotonic function

Algorithm 1: Randomized Local Search for maximizing $f\colon \{0,1\}^n \to \mathbb{R}$.

Initialization: Sample $x \in \{0,1\}^n$ uniformly at random;
Optimization: **for** $t = 1, 2, 3, \ldots$ **do**
  Choose $j \in [n]$ uniformly at random and set $y \leftarrow x \oplus e_j^n$; //mutation step: flip jth bit
  if $f(y) \geq f(x)$ **then** $x \leftarrow y$; //selection step

is not important, often only the simple OneMax function $f : x \mapsto \sum_{i \in [n]} x_i$, counting the number of ones, is regarded.

Before stating the main theorem of this section, we briefly describe the connection to the well-known coupon collector problem.

2.1 Relation to the Coupon Collector Problem

The coupon collector problem ask for how many coupons, chosen independently at random from n different types, one needs to draw on average until one has a coupon of each type. It is well known and easy to prove that this number equals nH_n, where H_n denotes the nth harmonic number $H_n := 1 + \frac{1}{2} + \frac{1}{3} + \ldots + \frac{1}{n}$. The harmonic numbers are well understood. We have $H_n = \ln n + \gamma + \frac{1}{2n} \pm \Theta(n^{-2})$, where $\gamma \approx 0.5772156649\ldots$ is the Euler-Mascheroni constant. Consequently, the coupon collector needs $n \ln n + \gamma n + 1/2 \pm o(1)$ rounds to finish.

If we assume that we start the coupon collector process being already in possession of k different types of coupons, then the expected number of rounds becomes nH_{n-k}, and again the precise estimates for the harmonic numbers give very precise values for these numbers.

We now argue that a run of RLS on OneMax (or any other strictly monotonic function) naturally leads to a coupon collector process. For this, we first note that if a bit is one at some time, it never is set to zero again. Hence we can view the 1-bits as coupons to be collected. Then RLS starts with a random set of different coupon types, that is, we already have each type with probability 1/2, mutually independent among all types. In each iteration, RLS flips a random bit. If this was a 1-bit, the offspring is discarded, if this was a 0-bit, we gain a new 1-bit (coupon).

Summarizing this discussion we note the following.

Remark 1. *The expected number of iterations that RLS needs to optimize* OneMax *is exactly the number of rounds until the coupon collector process with a random initial stake finishes.*

2.2 Exact Runtime Result

Since the initial search point of RLS is a bitstring with an expected number of $n/2$ ones, one could assume that the runtime of RLS should thus be close to $nH_{n/2}$. However, it is not clear a priori that the expected runtime of RLS needs to be close to its runtime when started deterministically in a search point of fitness $n/2$. By bounding the runtime of RLS on OneMax by $nH_{n/2} \pm o(n)$, Witt [15] showed that the intuition given above is at least almost correct. In Theorem 2 we sharpen his bound further. Our result implies that the expected number of iteration until RLS finds the optimum is in fact by just $1/2 \pm o(1)$ smaller than $nH_{n/2}$.

Theorem 2. *The expected number of iterations until RLS on* OneMax *or on any other monotonic function generates an optimal search point is $1/2 \pm o(1)$ less than the average number of iterations that RLS needs to finish when started in a search point with half the bits set correctly, namely $nH_{n/2} - 1/2 \pm o(1) = n \ln(n/2) + \gamma n + 1/2 \pm o(1)$.*

2.3 Proof of Theorem 2 for Even n

We present a proof for even values of n. The case of odd n will be dealt with in Section 2.4. The main technique is coupling the two random processes of running RLS on a random search point and on one with $n/2$ ones. We compute that the difference between starting at fitness level $n/2$ compared to starting at $n/2 - a$ and $n/2 + a$ with equal probability 1/2, is only of order a^2/n (when a is sufficiently small). When comparing both processes, this difference turn up with probability $2\Pr[\mathcal{B}(n,1/2) = a]$. Hence the expected deviation of both processes is of order $\sum_a \Pr[\mathcal{B}(n,1/2) = a]a^2$, which fortunately is the (well-understood) variation of the binomial distribution.

To make things precise, let X be the random variable that describes the number of ones in the initial search point. X is binomially distributed with parameters n and success probability 1/2.

The expected number of iterations until RLS on OneMax generates an optimal search point can be written as

$$\mathrm{E}[T] = \sum_{i=0}^{n} E[T \mid X = i] \Pr[X = i] . \qquad (1)$$

By the definition of binomial distributions we have $\Pr[X = n/2 - a] = \Pr[X = n/2 + a]$ for all $a \in [n/2]$. The main idea of this proof is to show that the average runtime $1/2\,(\mathrm{E}[T \mid X = n/2 + a] + \mathrm{E}[T \mid X = n/2 - a])$ does not deviate from $\mathrm{E}[T \mid X = n/2]$ by much. Let

$$\begin{aligned}\varepsilon_a :=& 2\,\mathrm{E}[T \mid X = n/2] \\ &- (\mathrm{E}[T \mid X = n/2 + a] + \mathrm{E}[T \mid X = n/2 - a]) .\end{aligned}$$

We can rewrite (1) to

$$\mathrm{E}[T] = \mathrm{E}[T \mid X = n/2] - \sum_{a=1}^{n/2} \Pr[X = n/2 + a]\varepsilon_a . \qquad (2)$$

Consequently, it suffices to show that

$$d := \sum_{a=1}^{n/2} \Pr[X = n/2 + a]\varepsilon_a = 1/2 \pm o(1) .$$

Using the already mentioned fact that

$$E[T \mid X = k] = \sum_{i=k}^{n-1} n/(n-i) = n \sum_{i=1}^{n-k} 1/i$$

we compute

$$\begin{aligned}\varepsilon_a &= 2E[T \mid X = n/2] \\ &\quad - (\mathrm{E}[T \mid X = n/2 + a] + \mathrm{E}[T \mid X = n/2 - a]) \\ &= 2n \sum_{i=1}^{n/2} 1/i - \left(n \sum_{i=1}^{n/2-a} 1/i + n \sum_{i=1}^{n/2+a} 1/i \right) \\ &= n \left(\sum_{i=n/2-a+1}^{n/2} 1/i - \sum_{i=n/2+1}^{n/2+a} 1/i \right)\end{aligned}$$

$$= n\sum_{i=0}^{a-1}\left(\frac{1}{n/2-i}-\frac{1}{n/2+i+1}\right)$$
$$= n\sum_{i=0}^{a-1}\frac{2i+1}{(n/2-i)(n/2+i+1)}. \qquad (3)$$

Consequently,

$$\varepsilon_a \geq n\sum_{i=0}^{a-1}\frac{2i+1}{(n/2)^2+n/2} = \frac{4a^2}{n+2}$$

and thus $d \geq \sum_{a=1}^{n/2}\Pr[X=n/2+a]\frac{4a^2}{n+2}$. Fortunately,

$$\sum_{a=1}^{n/2} 2a^2 \Pr[X=n/2+a] = \mathrm{E}[(X-\mathrm{E}[X])^2] =: \mathrm{Var}[X] \quad (4)$$

is just the variance of X, which is known to equal $n/4$, so we easily obtain the lower bound

$$d \geq \frac{2\,\mathrm{Var}[X]}{n+2} = \frac{n}{2(n+2)} = 1/2 - o(1).$$

To bound the deviation d from above, using again (3) we estimate ε_a by

$$\varepsilon_a = n\sum_{i=0}^{a-1}\frac{2i+1}{(n/2-i)(n/2+i+1)}$$
$$\leq n\sum_{i=0}^{a-1}\frac{2i+1}{(n/2)^2-i^2}$$
$$\leq n\sum_{i=0}^{a-1}\frac{2i+1}{(n/2)^2-(a-1)^2}$$
$$= \frac{na^2}{n^2/4-(a-1)^2}.$$

Setting $A := \sqrt{cn\ln n}$ for a constant c to be fixed later, we split

$$d \leq \sum_{a=1}^{n/2}\Pr[X=n/2+a]\frac{na^2}{n^2/4-(a-1)^2} \qquad (5)$$
$$\leq \sum_{a=1}^{A}\Pr[X=n/2+a]\frac{na^2}{n^2/4-(A-1)^2}$$
$$- \Pr[X-n/2>A]\frac{n(n/2)^2}{n^2/4-(n/2-1)^2}.$$

We first bound the last term in this expression. Using Chernoff's bound (see, e.g., [2]), it is easy to see that

$$\Pr[X-n/2>A] \leq \exp(-2c\ln(n)) = 1/n^{2c}.$$

Furthermore,

$$\frac{n(n/2)^2}{n^2/4-(n/2-1)^2} \leq n^3.$$

Thus, for $c > 3/2$ the last term in (5) is clearly $o(1)$.

For bounding the other terms we use again fact (4) and the equality $\mathrm{Var}[X] = n/4$ to obtain

$$\sum_{a=1}^{A}\Pr[X=n/2+a]\frac{na^2}{n^2/4-(A-1)^2}$$
$$\leq \frac{n\,\mathrm{Var}[X]}{2(n^2/4-(A-1)^2)}$$
$$= \frac{n^2}{2n^2-8(A-1)^2} = 1/2+o(1).$$

Plugging this back into (5), we obtain the upper bound

$$d \leq 1/2+o(1).$$

2.4 Proof of Theorem 2 for Odd n

It remains to consider odd values of n. The computations are very similar to the ones above. We keep the notation from the proof above, but we set, for $1 \leq a \leq \lfloor n/2 \rfloor$

$$\varepsilon_a := \mathrm{E}[T \mid X=\lfloor n/2\rfloor] + \mathrm{E}[T \mid X=\lceil n/2\rceil]$$
$$-(\mathrm{E}[T \mid X=\lfloor n/2\rfloor - a] + \mathrm{E}[T \mid X=\lceil n/2\rceil + a]).$$

Similarly to (2) we have

$$\mathrm{E}[T] = 1/2\,(\mathrm{E}[T \mid X=\lceil n/2\rceil] + \mathrm{E}[T \mid X=\lfloor n/2\rfloor])$$
$$- \sum_{a=1}^{\lfloor n/2\rfloor}\Pr[X=\lfloor n/2\rfloor - a]\varepsilon_a$$

and we thus need to show that

$$\sum_{a=1}^{\lfloor n/2\rfloor}\Pr[X=\lfloor n/2\rfloor - a]\varepsilon_a = 1/2 \pm o(1).$$

Again similarly as above we bound ε_a from below

$$\varepsilon_a = n\left(\sum_{i=\lfloor n/2\rfloor-a+1}^{\lfloor n/2\rfloor} 1/i - \sum_{i=\lceil n/2\rceil+1}^{\lceil n/2\rceil+a} 1/i\right)$$
$$= n\left(\sum_{i=0}^{a-1}\frac{1}{\lfloor n/2\rfloor - i} - \frac{1}{\lceil n/2\rceil+1+i}\right)$$
$$= n\left(\sum_{i=0}^{a-1}\frac{2i+2}{(\lceil n/2\rceil-(1+i))(\lceil n/2\rceil+1+i)}\right)$$
$$\geq n\frac{a^2+a}{(\lceil n/2\rceil)^2-1} = \frac{4(a^2+a)}{n+2-3/n}$$

and from above

$$\varepsilon_a \leq \frac{4n(a^2+a)}{n^2-4a^2}.$$

The variance equals again $n/4$ and can be written as

$$\mathrm{Var}[X] = \sum_{a=0}^{\lfloor n/2\rfloor} 2\Pr[X=\lfloor n/2\rfloor - a](a+1/2)^2$$
$$= 1/2 + \sum_{a=0}^{\lfloor n/2\rfloor} 2\Pr[X=\lfloor n/2\rfloor - a](a^2+a)$$
$$= 1/2 + \sum_{a=1}^{\lfloor n/2\rfloor} 2\Pr[X=\lfloor n/2\rfloor - a](a^2+a).$$

Thus,

$$\sum_{a=1}^{\lfloor n/2\rfloor}\Pr[X=\lfloor n/2\rfloor - a]\varepsilon_a$$
$$\geq \sum_{a=1}^{\lfloor n/2\rfloor}\Pr[X=\lfloor n/2\rfloor - a]\frac{4(a^2+a)}{n+2-3/n}$$
$$= (\mathrm{Var}[X]-1/2)\frac{2}{n+2-3/n} = 1/2-o(1)$$

and

$$\sum_{a=1}^{\lfloor n/2 \rfloor} \Pr[X = \lfloor n/2 \rfloor - a]\varepsilon_a$$

$$\leq \sum_{a=1}^{\lfloor n/2 \rfloor} \Pr[X = \lfloor n/2 \rfloor - a]\frac{4n(a^2+a)}{n^2-4a^2}.$$

Splitting the sum as in the proof for even values of n shows the desired inequality $\sum_{a=1}^{\lfloor n/2 \rfloor} \Pr[X = \lfloor n/2 \rfloor - a]\varepsilon_a \leq 1/2 + o(1)$.

Remark: After preparation of this manuscript it was noted to us by Jonathan E. Rowe (University of Birmingham) that the equation

$$\frac{1}{2^n}\sum_{k=0}^{n}\binom{n}{k}H_k = H_n - \sum_{k=1}^{n}\frac{1}{k2^k}$$

was proven as Identity 14 in [13] by binomial transforms of integer sequences.

3. THE (1+1) EA OPTIMIZING ONEMAX

We now analyze the expected number of iterations that the (1+1) EA (cf. Algorithm 2) performs on OneMax until it evaluates for the first time a search point of fitness n.

The (1+1) EA differs from RLS only in the mutation step (cf. Line 3). While RLS flips in each mutation step exactly one bit, the $(1+1)$ EA flips each bit with probability $1/n$. That is, in expectation exactly one bit is flipped, but it may happen that more or less than one bit are flipped in one iteration.

Algorithm 2: The (1+1) EA for maximizing $f\colon \{0,1\}^n \to \mathbb{R}$.

---

1 **Initialization:** Sample $x \in \{0,1\}^n$ uniformly at random and query $f(x)$;
2 **Optimization:** **for** $t = 1, 2, 3, \ldots$ **do**
3   Sample $y \in \{0,1\}^n$ by flipping each bit in x with probability $1/n$ and query $f(y)$; //mutation step
4   **if** $f(y) \geq f(x)$ **then** $x \leftarrow y$; //selection step

---

It is known that the runtime of the $(1+1)$ EA on OneMax is $(1-o(1))en\ln(n)$, see, for example, [4]. Several results improving this bound have appeared. Doerr, Fouz, and Witt [5] showed that the expected runtime of the $(1+1)$ EA on OneMax is bounded from above by $en\ln(n) - 0.1369n + O(1)$ and that it is bounded from below by $en\ln(n) - O(n)$. The lower bound was made more precise by Lehre and Witt [10], who show that the expected runtime is at least $en\ln(n) - 5.9338n - O(\log n)$.

We show that the expected runtime T of the $(1+1)$ EA deviates from the expected runtime $T_{n/2}$ of the $(1+1)$ EA started in a search point of fitness $n/2$ only by a constant additive term. While this, in particular, implies that for deriving a sharp bound on T one "just" needs to determine a sharp bound for $T_{n/2}$, the latter remains to be a challenging task. As mentioned in the introduction, the main difficulty in computing a good approximation for $T_{n/2}$ is in bounding the expected fitness gain (drift) when the parent has a linear number of ones.

Theorem 3. *Let $n \in \mathbb{N}$ and $x \in \{0,1\}^n$ with $|x|_1 = \lfloor n/2 \rfloor$. The expected runtime of the $(1+1)$ EA on* OneMax *deviates from the expected runtime of the $(1+1)$ EA started in search point x only by an additive constant term.*

To prove Theorem 3, we shall again use the coupling technique comparing the two random processes, however, due to the nature of the $(1+1)$ EA, we have to overcome a number of additional difficulties, including (i) that the drift (expected change of fitness) is not know precisely for search points with a linear number of ones, and (ii) that the $(1+1)$ EA does not hit all fitness levels. While the first problem mostly forces us to work with estimates instead of precise values, it is the second problem which makes setting up the coupling much harder than in the case of RLS.

3.1 Proof of Theorem 3

To ease readability, we will assume henceforth even values of n. The case of odd n does not require any new arguments.

Here and in the following let us denote by X_0 the number of ones in the random initial search point of the $(1+1)$ EA. As for RLS, the random variable X_0 is binomially distributed with parameters n and success probability $1/2$. Let T denote the expected runtime of the $(1+1)$ EA on OneMax. For all $k \in [0..n]$ let T_k be the expected runtime of the $(1+1)$ EA started in a search point of fitness k. This expression is well-defined by the well-known following lemma, which easily follows from the *unbiasedness* of the standard bit mutation, meaning by the fact that the mutation operator treats all bit positions $j = 1, \ldots, n$ and both bit values 0 and 1 identically (see [9] for a discussion of the unbiasedness of standard bit mutation).

Lemma 4. *Let $x, y \in \{0,1\}^n$ with $|x|_1 = |y|_1$. The expected runtime of the $(1+1)$ EA started in x is the same as the expected runtime of the $(1+1)$ EA started in y.*

In the following, we speak of the (1+1) *EA started on level k* when we consider the process of the (1+1) EA that—instead of starting in a random initial search point—starts (deterministically) on a search point x with $|x|_1 = k$.

Summarizing this discussion, Theorem 3 can be expressed as $T = T_{n/2} \pm O(1)$.

We write, as in the proof of Theorem 2,

$$T = \sum_{k=0}^{n} T_k \Pr[X_0 = k] \tag{6}$$

and we show that, for $k \leq n/4$, the average of $T_{n/2-k}$ and $T_{n/2+k}$ does not deviate from $T_{n/2}$ by more than $\Theta(1 + k^2/n)$.[1] Since the events $X_0 < n/4$ and $X_0 > 3n/4$ happen only with an exponentially small probability, and since T_k can be bounded from above by $O(n \log n)$ for all k, it, roughly speaking, suffices to consider only the sum $\sum_{k=1}^{n/4} \Theta(1 + k^2/n)\Pr[X_0 = k]$. As in the proof of Theorem 2 we then exploit the fact that this expression is asymptotically equal to the variance of X_0 (which we know to be $n/4$) divided by n.

[1] In the proof of Theorem 2 we had shown that for RLS the corresponding difference is roughly $4k^2/n$. The bound for the $(1+1)$ EA is thus slightly weaker than that for RLS in that we do not compute the constant terms.

In the following, we thus concentrate our work on estimating, for $1 \le k \le n/4$, the error terms

$$\varepsilon_k := 2T_{n/2} - (T_{n/2+k} + T_{n/2-k}). \tag{7}$$

A key step in proving that $\varepsilon_k = \Theta(1 + k^2/n)$ is to show that the $(1+1)$ EA started on level $n/2 - k$ needs $\Theta(k^2/n)$ steps less to reach a bitstring of fitness at least $n/2$ than the $(1+1)$ EA started on level $n/2$ needs to sample for the first time a string of fitness at least $n/2 + k$. We will achieve this by coupling the two processes, cf. Lemma 8. But before we are ready to show this, we need a few technical statements that will facilitate this proof.

First we remind the reader of an extension of Wald's equation (Lemma 5) and of the fact that the expected progress of the $(1+1)$ EA is constant for quite a large number of steps (Lemma 6).

LEMMA 5 (EXTENSION OF WALD'S EQUATION FROM [6]). *Let T be a random variable with bounded expectation and let $X_1, X_2, \ldots$ be non-negative random variables with $\mathrm{E}[X_i \mid T \ge i] \le C$. Then $\mathrm{E}[\sum_{i=1}^{T} X_i] \le \mathrm{E}[T]C$.*

LEMMA 6 (CONSTANT PROGRESS, FOLKLORE). *Let $k = cn$ for some constant $0 \le c < 1$. Let $x \in \{0,1\}^n$ with $|x|_1 = k$, and let $m \in \{0,1\}^n$ with $\Pr[m_i = 1] = 1/n$ for all i. Then $\Pr[|x \oplus m|_1 > k] = \Theta(1)$.*

Proof. We have $|x \oplus m|_1 > |x|_1$ if $|m|_1 = 1$ and $m_j = 1$ for an index $j \in [n]$ with $x_j = 0$. The claim follows from the two facts that $\Pr[|m|_1 = 1] = (1 - 1/n)^{n-1} \ge 1/e$ and that there is a constant fraction of bits in x whose bit value is zero. □

The following statement is intuitively clear and has been proven explicitly in [12]. A previous proof for the non-strict inequality is implicit in [1].

LEMMA 7. *For $0 \le k < \ell \le n$ it holds that $T_k > T_\ell$.*

As mentioned above, we will be interested in Lemma 8 in the difference between the number of iterations needed by the $(1+1)$ EA started on level $n/2 - k$ to reach a fitness score of at least $n/2$ and the number of iterations needed by the $(1+1)$ EA started on level $n/2$ to reach a search point of fitness at least $n/2 + k$. To ease readability, we therefore denote by $T(\ell \to h)$ the expected number of fitness evaluations needed until the $(1+1)$ EA started on level ℓ has evaluated for the first time a search point of fitness *at least* h.

LEMMA 8. *If $k \le (1-\varepsilon)n/2$ for some constant $0 < \varepsilon < 1$, then $T(n/2 \to n/2 + k) = T(n/2 - k \to n/2) + O(k^2/n)$.*

Proof. We do a coupling argument. We thus describe first how we couple a run of the $(1+1)$ EA starting on level $n/2 - k$ with one starting on level $n/2$.

Let $\tilde{x}^{(0)}, \tilde{x}^{(1)}, \ldots, \tilde{x}^{(t)}$ be the trajectory of the search points of the $(1+1)$ EA started on level $n/2 - k$ until it has reached for the first time a search point of fitness at least $n/2$. Let $\tilde{m}^{(1)}, \ldots, \tilde{m}^{(t)}$ be the indicator vectors of the mutation steps. That is,

- $|\tilde{x}^{(0)}|_1 = n/2 - k$,
- $|\tilde{x}^{(i)}|_1 < n/2$ for all $j < t$ and $|\tilde{x}^{(t)}|_1 \ge n/2$, and
- $\tilde{x}^{(i+1)} = \tilde{x}^{(i)} \oplus \tilde{m}^{(i+1)}$ if $|\tilde{x}^{(i)} \oplus \tilde{m}^{(i+1)}|_1 \ge |\tilde{x}^{(i)}|_1$ and $\tilde{x}^{(i+1)} = \tilde{x}^{(i)}$ otherwise.

For $i = 0, 1, \ldots, t$ let Π_i be the set of those permutations $\pi : [n] \to [n]$ that sort search point $\tilde{x}^{(i)}$ in such a way that all the zeros are moved to the left. That is, for each $\pi \in \Pi_i$ we have $\tilde{x}^{(i)}_{\pi(1)} \ldots \tilde{x}^{(i)}_{\pi(n)} = 0^{n-|\tilde{x}^{(i)}|_1} 1^{|\tilde{x}^{(i)}|_1}$. Sample $\pi_i \in \Pi_i$ uniformly at random. This permutation is clearly independent of the mutation vector $\tilde{m}^{(i+1)}$. We set

$$x^{(i)} := \tilde{x}^{(i)}_{\pi_i(1)} \ldots \tilde{x}^{(i)}_{\pi_i(n)} = 0^{n-|\tilde{x}^{(i)}|_1} 1^{|\tilde{x}^{(i)}|_1}$$

and we sort $\tilde{m}^{(i+1)}$ by the same permutation to obtain

$$m^{(i+1)} := \tilde{m}^{(i+1)}_{\pi_i(1)} \ldots \tilde{m}^{(i+1)}_{\pi_i(n)}.$$

We now simulate a run of the $(1+1)$ EA started on level $n/2$ by fixing as starting point $y^{(0)} := 0^{n/2} 1^{\lceil n/2 \rceil}$ and setting, for $0 \le i \le t-1$, $\tilde{y}^{(i+1)} := y^{(i)} \oplus m^{(i+1)}$ and

$$y^{(i+1)} := \begin{cases} 0^{|\tilde{y}^{(i+1)}|_1} 1^{n-|\tilde{y}^{(i+1)}|_1}, & \text{if } |\tilde{y}^{(i+1)}|_1 \ge |y^{(i)}|_1; \\ y^{(i)}, & \text{otherwise.} \end{cases}$$

That is, we perform on $y^{(0)}$ the exact same mutation steps as we did on $x^{(0)}$, resorting the search points $y^{(i)}$ after the selection step. That this is a valid coupling of the $(1+1)$ EA started on level $n/2 - k$ with the one started on level $n/2$ follows from Lemma 4 and the fact that for each $i \in [t]$ we have $m^{(i)}_j = 1/n$ independently for all $j \in [n]$ (this is due to the independence of π_i from $\tilde{m}^{(i+1)}$) .

Key to proving the statement is the observation that the fitness of y increases by almost the same speed as the fitness of x. In fact, if no bit in the *difference pattern*

$$\Delta^{(i)} := \{j \in [n] \mid x^{(i)}_j \ne y^{(i)}_j\}$$

is flipped, then $|x^{(i)} \oplus m^{(i+1)}|_1 \ge |x^{(i)}|_1$ only if $|y^{(i)} \oplus m^{(i+1)}|_1 \ge |y^{(i)}|_1$ and, even more, $|x^{(i+1)}|_1 - |x^{(i)}|_1 = |y^{(i+1)}|_1 - |y^{(i)}|_1$. For convenience, let us denote these *uncritical* iterations by $\mathcal{U} \subseteq [t]$; i.e., for each $i \in \mathcal{U}$ we have $m^i_j = 0$ for all $j \in \Delta^{(i-1)}$. By $\mathcal{C} := [t] \setminus \mathcal{U}$ we denote the subset of *critical* iterations; i.e., iterations in which at least one bit of the difference pattern is flipped. The above argument shows that

$$|y^{(i)}|_1 \ge |y^{(0)}|_1 + \sum_{\ell \in \mathcal{U}} \left(|x^{(\ell)}|_1 - |x^{(\ell-1)}|_1 \right).$$

We have $|x^{(i-1)} \oplus m^{(i)}|_1 - |x^{(i-1)}|_1 \ge |y^{(i-1)} \oplus m^{(i)}|_1 - |y^{(i-1)}|_1$ always, and thus, $|x^{(i)}|_1 - |x^{(i-1)}|_1 \ge |y^{(i)}|_1 - |y^{(i-1)}|_1$. This implies

$$|x^{(i)}|_1 - |x^{(0)}|_1 \ge |y^{(i)}|_1 - |y^{(0)}|_1 \tag{8}$$

for all $i \in [t]$. In particular it holds that $|y^{(i)}|_1 \le |y^{(0)}|_1 + |x^{(i)}|_1 - |x^{(0)}|_1 < n/2 + k$ for all $i < t$ and, hence, $T(n/2 \to n/2 + k) \ge T(n/2 - k \to n/2)$.

We show that, on the other hand, the fitness increase in y is not much less that the one in x. Precisely, we show that

$$\mathrm{E}[|y^{(t)}|_1] = n/2 + k - O(k^2/n), \tag{9}$$

i.e., when the x-process has reached a search point of fitness at least $n/2$, the y-process has reached a search point of expected fitness $n/2 + k - O(k^2/n)$. Since we are in the range of constant expected progress per round (cf. Lemma 6), the expected time needed for the y-process to reach fitness level at least $n/2+k$ is thus an extra number of $O(k^2/n)$ rounds, as is claimed in the statement.

It therefore remains to prove (9). To this aim, we first show that with probability 1,

$$\left|\Delta^{(i)}\right| \leq k, i = 0, 1, \ldots, t-1; \quad (10)$$

i.e, we show that the two strings $x^{(i)}$ and $y^{(i)}$ differ in at most k bits. Since the bitstrings $x^{(i)}$ and $y^{(i)}$ are sorted such that all zeros are moved to the left, we always have $|\Delta^{(i)}| = |y^{(i)}|_1 - |x^{(i)}|_1$. Initially, we clearly have $|y^{(0)}|_1 - |x^{(0)}|_1 = k$. Rearranging (8) we see that, for $i = 0, 1, \ldots, t-1$, $|y^{(i)}|_1 - |x^{(i)}|_1 \leq |y^{(0)}|_1 - |x^{(0)}|_1 = k$.

In what follows we will show that the expected total number of bitflips that occur in the critical iterations is $O(k^2/n)$. This allows us to take a pessimistic view on these bitflips happening in iterations $i \in \mathcal{C}$ in that we can assume that all these bitflips count toward the fitness of x while they do not contribute anything to the fitness of y. That is, we exploit that

$$\mathrm{E}[|y^{(t)}|_1] \geq |y^{(0)}|_1 + |x^{(t)}|_1 - |x^{(0)}|_1 - \mathrm{E}\big[\sum_{i \in \mathcal{C}} |m^{(i)}|_1\big]. \quad (11)$$

We thus need to compute $\mathrm{E}[\sum_{i \in \mathcal{C}} |m^{(i)}|_1]$. To simplify the notation let us fix for a moment an index i, set $d := |\Delta^{(i-1)}|$, and $m := m^{(i)}$.

By the law of total probability we have

$$\begin{aligned} &\mathrm{E}[|m|_1 \mid \exists j \in \Delta : m_j = 1] \quad (12)\\ &= \frac{\mathrm{E}[|m|_1] - \mathrm{E}[|m|_1 \mid \forall j \in \Delta : m_j = 0] \Pr[\forall j \in \Delta : m_j = 0]}{\Pr[\exists j \in \Delta : m_j = 1]}. \end{aligned}$$

Since $\Pr[m_j = 1] = 1/n$ independently for all $j \in [n]$, we have $\mathrm{E}[|m|_1] = 1$, $\mathrm{E}[|m|_1 \mid \forall j \in \Delta : m_j = 0] = (n-d)/n$, and $\Pr[\forall j \in \Delta : m_j = 0] = (1-1/n)^d \geq 1-d/n$, where the latter is by Bernoulli's inequality. Using the version of Bernoulli's inequality which states that for all $a \in [0,1]$ and all positive integers r it holds that $(1-a)^r \leq 1/(1+ra)$, we also get that $\Pr[\exists j \in \Delta : m_j = 1] = 1 - (1-1/n)^d \geq d/(d+n)$. Plugging all this into (12) we get that

$$\mathrm{E}[|m|_1 \mid \exists j \in \Delta : m_j = 1] \leq 2 + d/n - d^2/n^2.$$

In particular we obtain that the conditional expectation $\mathrm{E}[|m|_1 \mid \exists j \in \Delta : m_j = 1]$ is constant. Furthermore, we clearly have—again using Bernoulli's inequality and statement (10)—that $\Pr[\exists j \in \Delta : m_j = 1] = 1 - (1-1/n)^d \leq d/n \leq k/n$. From this one would like to finish the proof by arguing that, by Lemma 6, $t = O(k)$ and that therefore

$$\begin{aligned} \mathrm{E}\big[\sum_{i \in \mathcal{C}} |m^{(i)}|_1\big] &= \sum_{i=1}^{t} \mathrm{E}[|m^{(i)}|_1 \mid i \in \mathcal{C}] \Pr[i \in \mathcal{C}] \\ &\leq O(k) \cdot O(k/n). \end{aligned}$$

Note, however, that t is a random variable. So to turn this intuition into a formal proof, we use Wald's equation from Lemma 5. We define random variables X_i, $i \in \mathbb{N}$, by letting $X_i := |m^{(i)}|_1$ if $i \in \mathcal{C}$ and $X_i := 0$ otherwise.

As argued above we have

$$\mathrm{E}[X_i \mid t \geq i] = \Pr[i \in \mathcal{C}]\, \mathrm{E}[|m^{(i)}|_1 \mid i \in \mathcal{C}] = O(k/n).$$

We can thus apply Lemma 5 and obtain

$$\mathrm{E}\big[\sum_{i \in \mathcal{C}} |m^{(i)}|_1\big] = \mathrm{E}[\sum_{i=1}^{t} X_i] \leq \mathrm{E}[t] O(k/n) = O(k^2/n).$$

Plugging this into (11) we finally get (9). □

As mentioned in the proof outline we want to show that for a large enough range of k the error term ε_k defined in (7) is $\Theta(1+k^2/n)$. The next step in showing this is the following lemma, which, intuitively, tells us that it does not matter too much whether we start in fitness level k deterministically, or whether we first run a (1+1) EA starting on a smaller fitness level and regard only the fitness evaluations that are made by the $(1+1)$ EA after having reached for the first time a search point of fitness at least k.

LEMMA 9. *Let $\ell, k \in [n]$ with $\ell \leq k < cn$ for some $c < 1$. Then $T_k = T_\ell - T(\ell \to k) + O(1)$; that is, the expected runtime of the (1+1) EA started on level k is identical up to a constant term to the expected number of fitness evaluations that the (1+1) EA started on level ℓ does after having reached for the first time a search point of fitness at least k.*

Proof. We show that in expectation the first search point of the $(1+1)$ EA started on level ℓ that has a fitness of at least k has fitness $k + O(1)$. The claim then follows from Lemmas 6 and 7.

We first prove that the expected number of bitflips that occur conditional on at least h bits flipping is less than $h+1$. In fact, by the law of total probability, we can write the expected number of bitflips that occur in a mutation step in which at least h bitflips happen as the the sum of these expected values conditioned on the fact that the ith bit is the hth bit that is flipped. That is, we write for the mutation vector m

$$\begin{aligned} \mathrm{E}[|m|_1 \mid |m|_1 \geq h] &= \sum_{i=1}^{n} \mathrm{E}[|m|_1 \mid A_i] \Pr[A_i \mid |m|_1 \geq h] \\ &= \sum_{i=1}^{n} \left(h + \frac{n-i}{n}\right) \Pr[A_i \mid |m|_1 \geq h] < h+1, \end{aligned}$$

where A_i is the event that $|\{j \in [i] \mid m_j = 1\}| = h$ and $m_i = 1$.

For computing the expected fitness of the first search point that has fitness at least k we do a similar argument. Let f be the fitness of the first search point of the $(1+1)$ EA started in level ℓ which is at least k and let f_{-1} be the fitness of the search point prior to that. Then $\mathrm{E}[f \mid f \geq k, f_{-1} < k]$ can be written as $\sum_{i=0}^{k-1} \mathrm{E}[f \mid f \geq k, f_{-1} = i] \Pr[f_{-1} = i \mid f \geq k, f_{-1} < k]$, which is less than $k+1$ by the preceding inequality. □

We are finally ready to prove Theorem 3.

Proof of Theorem 3. We recall that T denotes the expected runtime of the $(1+1)$ EA on ONEMAX. Combining (6) and (7) we see that

$$\begin{aligned} T &= \sum_{k=0}^{n} T_k \Pr[X_0 = k] \\ &= \sum_{k=0}^{n/2} \left(T_{n/2+k} + T_{n/2-k}\right) \Pr[X_0 = n/2 - k] \end{aligned}$$

$$= T_{n/2} - \sum_{k=0}^{n/2} \varepsilon_k \Pr[X_0 = n/2 - k]$$

We thus need to show that $\sum_{k=0}^{n/2} \varepsilon_k \Pr[X_0 = n/2 - k] = O(1)$. We split this sum into

$$\sum_{k=0}^{n/4} \varepsilon_k \Pr[X_0 = n/2 - k] + \sum_{k=n/4+1}^{n/2} \varepsilon_k \Pr[X_0 = n/2 - k]$$

and show for the two sums individually that they evaluate to $O(1)$.

For the last sum this is easy to see: $\Pr[X_0 < n/4] \leq \exp(-n/4)$ by Chernoff's bound (see [2] for a survey of basic tail bounds frequently used in the analysis of randomized search heuristics). It is well known also that $T_k \leq O(n \log n)$ for all $k \in [0..n]$, see, e.g., [7]. Consequently, $\varepsilon_k = O(n \log n)$ for all k. Thus,

$$\sum_{k=n/4+1}^{n/2} \varepsilon_k \Pr[X_0 = n/2 - k] \leq \Pr[X_0 < n/4] O(n \log n)$$
$$\leq \exp(-n/4) O(n \log n) = o(1).$$

Bounding $\sum_{k=0}^{n/4} \varepsilon_k \Pr[X_0 = n/2 - k]$ is the most challenging part in this proof, and it is here that we need all the technical statements proven above. As mentioned in the outline of this proof at the beginning of this section, we shall use Lemmas 8 and 9 to show that

$$\varepsilon_k = O(1 + k^2/n) \text{ for } k \leq n/4. \qquad (13)$$

From this it will follow that

$$\begin{aligned}
&\sum_{k=0}^{n/4} \varepsilon_k \Pr[X_0 = n/2 - k] \\
&= \sum_{k=0}^{n/4} O(1 + k^2/n) \Pr[X_0 = n/2 - k] \\
&= O(1) + 1/n \cdot O(\mathrm{Var}[X_0]) \\
&= O(1) + 1/n \cdot O(n/4) = O(1)\,.
\end{aligned}$$

To show (13) we first recall that by Lemma 9

$$T_{n/2} = T_{n/2+k} + T(n/2 \to n/2 + k) - O(1)$$

and

$$T_{n/2-k} = T_{n/2} + T(n/2 - k \to n/2) - O(1)\,.$$

We can thus rewrite ε_k as follows

$$\begin{aligned}
\varepsilon_k &= T_{n/2} - T_{n/2+k} - (T_{n/2-k} - T_{n/2}) \\
&= T(n/2 \to n/2 + k) - T(n/2 - k \to n/2) + O(1)\,.
\end{aligned}$$

By Lemma 8 this term evaluates to $O(1+k^2/n)$, as claimed. □

4. CONCLUSIONS

We have shown that for both RLS and the $(1+1)$ EA the average runtime does not deviate from the respective runtime of the algorithm starting in an average search point by more than an additive constant term.

From this we have derived a very precise estimate of the expected runtime of RLS on any monotonic function.

For the $(1+1)$ EA we currently lack a good estimate of the runtime when the algorithm is started deterministically in a search point of fitness $n/2$. Determining it is an interesting question that seems to be beyond the state-of-the-art techniques in runtime analysis. As a first step toward a more precise runtime estimate we suggest to compute sharp bounds for the $O(1)$-term in Theorem 3.

Another topic for future work is the derivation of precise runtime estimates for randomized search heuristics on more complex problem classes.

Acknowledgments

We thank Jonathan E. Rowe for pointing us to [13].

5. REFERENCES

[1] P. A. Borisovsky and A. V. Eremeev. Comparing evolutionary algorithms to the (1+1)-EA. *Theor. Comput. Sci.*, 403(1):33–41, 2008.

[2] B. Doerr. Analyzing randomized search heuristics: Tools from probability theory. In A. Auger and B. Doerr, editors, *Theory of Randomized Search Heuristics*, pages 1–20. World Scientific Publishing, 2011.

[3] B. Doerr, C. Doerr, and F. Ebel. Lessons from the black-box: fast crossover-based genetic algorithms. In *Proc. Gecco'13*, pages 781–788. ACM, 2013.

[4] B. Doerr, M. Fouz, and C. Witt. Quasirandom evolutionary algorithms. In *Proc. Gecco'10*, pages 1457–1464. ACM, 2010.

[5] B. Doerr, M. Fouz, and C. Witt. Sharp bounds by probability-generating functions and variable drift. In *Proc. Gecco'11*, pages 2083–2090. ACM, 2011.

[6] B. Doerr and M. Künnemann. How the (1+λ) evolutionary algorithm optimizes linear functions. In *Proc. Gecco'13*, pages 1589–1596. ACM, 2013.

[7] S. Droste, T. Jansen, and I. Wegener. A rigorous complexity analysis of the (1 + 1) evolutionary algorithm for separable functions with Boolean inputs. *Evolutionary Computation*, 6:185–196, 1998.

[8] J. He and X. Yao. Drift analysis and average time complexity of evolutionary algorithms. *Artificial Intelligence*, 127:51–81, 2001.

[9] P. K. Lehre and C. Witt. Black-box search by unbiased variation. *Algorithmica*, 64:623–642, 2012.

[10] P. K. Lehre and C. Witt. General drift analysis with tail bounds. *CoRR*, abs/1307.2559, 2013.

[11] M. Mitzenmacher and E. Upfal. *Probability and computing - randomized algorithms and probabilistic analysis*. Cambridge University Press, 2005.

[12] C. Qian, Y. Yu, and Z.-H. Zhou. On algorithm-dependent boundary case identification for problem classes. In *Proc. PPSN'12*, volume 7491 of *LNCS*, pages 62–71. Springer, 2012.

[13] M. Z. Spivey. Combinatorial sums and finite differences. *Discrete Mathematics*, 307:3130–3146, 2007.

[14] C. Witt. Tight bounds on the optimization time of a randomized search heuristic on linear functions. *Combinatorics, Probability & Computing*, 22:294–318, 2013.

[15] C. Witt. The fitness level method with tail bounds. *Information Processing Letters*, 2014. To appear. DOI: http://dx.doi.org/10.1016/j.ipl.2013.09.013.

Robustness of Populations in Stochastic Environments

Christian Gießen
Christian-Albrechts-Universität zu Kiel
24118 Kiel, Germany

Timo Kötzing
Fiedrich-Schiller-Universität Jena
07743 Jena, Germany

ABSTRACT

We consider stochastic versions of OneMax and LeadingOnes and analyze the performance of evolutionary algorithms with and without populations on these problems. It is known that the (1+1) EA on OneMax performs well in the presence of very small noise, but poorly for higher noise levels. We extend these results to LeadingOnes and to many different noise models, showing how the application of drift theory can significantly simplify *and generalize* previous analyses.

Most surprisingly, even small populations (of size $\Theta(\log n)$) can make evolutionary algorithms perform well for high noise levels, well outside the abilities of the (1+1) EA! Larger population sizes are even more beneficial; we consider both parent and offspring populations. In this sense, populations are *robust* in these stochastic settings.

Categories and Subject Descriptors

F.2 [**Theory of Computation**]: Analysis of Algorithms and Problem Complexity

General Terms

Theory, Algorithms, Performance

Keywords

Run Time Analysis, Stochastic Fitness Function, Evolutionary Algorithm, Populations, Robustness

1. INTRODUCTION

Evolutionary algorithms (EAs) are general-purpose problem solvers which can be successfully applied to a wide variety of problems with small effort. In particular, EAs are popular where no tailored solutions exist, for example because the structure of the problem is inaccessible (given as a *black box*) or where the structure of the problem is very complicated. In particular, EAs are popular in settings including uncertainties, such as noisy fitness (quality) evaluations; see [BDGG09] for a survey on examples in combinatorial optimization, but also [JB05] for an excellent survey also discussing different sources of uncertainty.

GECCO'14, July 12–16, Vancouver, BC, Canada.

ACM 978-1-4503-2662-9/14/07 ...$15.00.
http://dx.doi.org/10.1145/2576768.2598227.

We are interested in formally analyzing the performance of EAs in settings where the fitness function is probabilistic, i.e., a given search point can have different fitness values for different fitness evaluations. One way to deal with such uncertainty is to replace fitness evaluations with an average of a (large) sample of fitness evaluations and then proceed as if there was no noise. In this paper we are interested in a different approach where we accept the noise and try to analyze how much noise can be overcome by EAs without further modifications (note that this research can also be used to decide *how much* resampling is necessary for successful optimization). This was first done in [Dro04], where a noisy variant of the well-known OneMax test function was analyzed for the simplest EA, the (1+1) EA. In essence, it was shown that the (1+1) EA can deal with small noise levels, but not medium noise levels. Recently, there was a sequence of paper discussing ant colony optimization for path finding problems in the presence of uncertainty [ST12, DHK12, FK13], see also [GP96, Gut03] for early work in this area.

For this paper we are exclusively concerned with optimization problems defined on bit strings of fixed length n. In this domain we have the two well-known (static) test functions OneMax and LeadingOnes as follows. For each bit string $x \in \{0,1\}^n$ we let $\text{OneMax}(x)$ be the number of 1s in x and $\text{LeadingOnes}(x)$ is the number of consecutive 1s counting from the left until the first occurrence of a 0. The performance of various randomized search heuristics on these two *static* problems is known in detail.

We modify these test functions by adding noise. We distinguish between two general noise models: *prior noise* and *posterior noise*. In the first model we assume that the noise comes from not evaluating the search point in questions, but a noisy variant; this corresponds to the noise model used in [Dro04], where, with probability p, a bit of the search point was flipped *before* evaluation. In the second model the fitness value of a search point obtains noise *after* evaluation. For example, one can add a value drawn from a centered normal distribution (or add a value drawn from any other chosen distribution; we call such noise *additive posterior noise*). Posterior noise is essentially the model used in [GP96, ST12, DHK12, FK13].

In each case we consider the noise to be independent for different elements of the search space and for reevaluations (note that we assume that all algorithms reevaluate each search point under consideration in every iteration).

In this paper we expand on the work done in [Dro04] in three ways. First, we make the results applicable to many different noise models; second, we analyze the LEADINGONES function in noisy settings; third, we show how the use of populations can make the EA much more robust towards noise.

Regarding the generalization, we reprove the results from [Dro04] as a corollary to more general theorems which can be applied in many different settings. The proofs of these more general theorems rely heavily on *drift theory*, a modern tool which facilitates the formal analysis of randomized search heuristics significantly. Note that this tool was not available for [Dro04]. Another tool suitable for the analysis of populations was recently introduced in [Leh11] in the context of *non-elitism*, i.e. just as in the setting with noise, good solutions can get lost.

Regarding the LEADINGONES test function, we give the first formal analysis of this test function in a noisy setting.

Regarding the use of populations, the paper [PB10] gives a nice overview of several different aspects where populations (and the use of crossover operators) are beneficial for optimization of *static* fitness functions. In contrast to this, we show that populations can also be highly beneficial for the optimization of *stochastic* fitness functions, as they allow a much higher noise.

1.1 Detailed Contribution

The only algorithm we consider is the $(\mu + \lambda)$ EA, for different values of μ and λ (see Section 2 for a detailed description). We consider the (1+1) EA as an EA "without population"; this was the algorithm considered in [Dro04]. Even when we discuss EAs with populations, we only consider cases with $\mu = 1$ or $\lambda = 1$, for simplicity.

We consider optimization successful in the stochastic setting as soon as the algorithm has evaluated the best static solution (in both our cases the all-1s bit string); note that the best static solution is, in all of our models, also the solution with best expected fitness. Whenever we consider the "run time" of an algorithm, this is understood as the *expected* number of *iterations* (or generations) of the EA. In particular, population-based EAs have a higher number of fitness evaluations than iterations (also due to reevaluation of old search points).

In Section 3 we consider ONEMAX. In particular, we give a general theorem for deriving upper bounds in different noise settings (Theorem 4) and a general Theorem for deriving lower bounds (Theorem 5). As a result we completely reprove the theorems from [Dro04] (Corollary 6). These results concern prior noise where, with probability p, a (uniformly chosen) bit is flipped: The (1+1) EA is successful in this setting for values of p up to $O(\log n/n)$ away from 0 or 1 (i.e., optimizes in polynomial time), otherwise it is unsuccessful. Note that [Dro04] did not cover values of p close to 1.

As a further corollary, we show that the (1+1) EA can optimize in the presence of additive posterior noise with variance of $O(\log n/n)$ efficiently, but not, for example, in the presence of additive noise from an exponential distribution with parameter 1 (Corollary 7). This list of corollaries can easily be extended, for example to cover the case of prior noise based on mutation or similar models.

In Section 3.2 we show that populations can be much more robust towards noise. For example, a linear population is large enough to allow *arbitrary* values of p in the setting of prior bit-flip noise. Furthermore, in the case of constant p in the setting of prior bit-flip noise (a setting far outside the abilities of the (1+1) EA for efficient optimization), already a *logarithmic population size* suffices for efficient optimization. Similarly, we get robustness of small populations for posterior noise models, for example for exponentially distributed noise with constant parameter.

In Section 4, we give our results for LEADINGONES. We show that the (1+1) EA optimizes successfully in the presence of small noise, but we also give an example of higher noise levels where optimization is unsuccessful. Here again populations are helpful, even of logarithmic size.

We conclude the paper with a discussion in Section 5.

2. MATHEMATICAL PRELIMINARIES

In this paper we consider the $(\mu + \lambda)$ EA, an algorithm which bases its progress on mutation (see Algorithm 1 for a detailed description). We consider only the mutation operator which flips each bit independently with probability $1/n$. Ties in the selection of fitter individuals are broken so that individuals from the offspring population are preferred (this allows the (1+1) EA to cross plateaus and is consistent with the definition of, for example, [Dro04]); further ties are broken uniformly at random.

Algorithm 1: $(\mu + \lambda)$ EA

Let P be a set of μ uniformly chosen bit strings;
repeat
    $O \leftarrow \emptyset$;
    for $i = 1$ **to** λ **do**
        pick x u.a.r. from P;
        $O \leftarrow O \cup \{\texttt{mutate}(x)\}$;
    for $x \in P \cup O$ **do** evaluate $f(x)$;
    $P \leftarrow \mu$ f-maximal elements from $P \cup O$;
until *forever*;

Note that all references to the "run time" or the "number of steps" of an algorithm always concern the *expected first hitting time* of the optimum, as mentioned above.

2.1 Drift Theorems

We will use a variety of drift theorems to derive the theorems of this paper. *Drift*, in this context, describes the *expected change* of the best-so-far solution within one iteration with respect to some *potential*. In later proofs we will define potential functions on best-so-far solutions and prove bounds on the drift; these bounds then translate to expected run times with the use of the drift theorems from this section.

The literature knows a large number of drift theorems; this selection is not representative, but merely contains those theorems needed for this paper.

The simplest drift theorem concerns *additive drift*.

THEOREM 1 (ADDITIVE DRIFT [HY04]). *Let $(X_t)_{t\geq 0}$ be random variables describing a Markov process over a finite state space $S \subseteq \mathbb{R}$. Let T be the random variable that denotes the earliest point in time $t \geq 0$ such that $X_t = 0$. If* *there exist $c > 0$ such that*

$$E(X_t - X_{t+1}|T > t) \geq c,$$

then

$$E(T|X_0) \leq \frac{X_0}{c}.$$

We will not give the version of the *multiplicative drift theorem* for upper bounds, due to [DJW12], as it is implied by the *Variable Drift Theorem* given in [Joh10, Theorem 4.6] (independently developed in [MRC08, Section 8]); this drift theorem is applicable when the drift is not uniform across the search space; frequently one can find a uniform lower bound and use the additive drift theorem, but using the variable drift theorem will typically give much better bounds. The version of the Variable Drift Theorem that we use is due to [RS12], which removes the restriction of h being differentiable.

THEOREM 2 (VARIABLE DRIFT [RS12]). *Let $(X_t)_{t\geq 0}$ be random variables describing a Markov process over a finite state space $S \subseteq \mathbb{R}_0^+$ and let $x_{\min} := \min\{x \in S \mid x > 0\}$. Furthermore, let T be the random variable that denotes the first point in time $t \in \mathbb{N}$ for which $X_t = 0$. Suppose that there exists a monotone increasing function $h : \mathbb{R}^+ \to \mathbb{R}^+$ such that $1/h$ is integrable and*

$$E(X_t - X_{t+1} \mid X_t) \geq h(X_t)$$

holds for all $t < T$. Then,

$$E(T \mid X_0) \leq \frac{x_{\min}}{h(x_{\min})} + \int_{x_{\min}}^{X_0} \frac{1}{h(x)} dx.$$

Finally, in order to derive *lower* bounds on the run time of EAs, we use the Negative Drift Theorem.

THEOREM 3 (NEGATIVE DRIFT [OW11, OW12]). *Let $(X_t)_{t\geq 0}$ be real-valued random variables describing a stochastic process over some state space. Suppose there is an interval $[a, b] \subseteq \mathbb{R}$, two constants $\delta, \varepsilon > 0$ and, possibly depending on $\ell = b - a$, a function $r(\ell)$ satisfying $1 \leq r(\ell) = o(\ell/\log \ell)$ such that, for all $t \geq 0$, the following conditions hold.*

1. *$E(X_{t+1} - X_t \mid a < X_t < b) \geq \varepsilon$;*
2. *For all $j \geq 0$, $P(|X_{t+1} - X_t| \geq j \mid a < X_t) \leq \frac{r(\ell)}{(1+\delta)^j}$.*

Then there is a constant c such that, for $T = \min\{t \geq 0 : X_t \leq a \mid X_0 \geq b\}$, we have

$$P(T \leq 2^{c\ell/r(\ell)}) = 2^{-\Omega(\ell/r(\ell))}.$$

3. ONEMAX

In this section we present our results regarding ONEMAX. We fix a (stochastic) ONEMAX function f according to one of our models. It is easy to verify that, in each of the stochastic models we consider, there is a sequence of independent random variables $(X_k)_{k\leq n}$ such that the following holds.

- For each evaluation of f on a bit string with exactly k 1s, the return value is drawn at random $\sim X_k$ (recall that all evaluations of fitness functions are independent).
- $\forall j \leq k < n : P(X_j < X_{k+1}) \geq P(X_k < X_{k+1})$; intuitively, the larger the true difference in ONEMAX-value, the more likely this is reflected in a random ONEMAX evaluation. This simplifies some conditions.

Note that these two properties capture two important properties of the ONEMAX function: symmetry in the positions (only the number of 1s decides on the fitness, not the position), and monotonicity (the more 1s a bit string has, the higher its fitness; we need this comparison-based version, given the comparison-based definition of the (1+1) EA).

We start by giving an upper and a lower bound for the (1+1) EA in Section 3.1; in Section 3.2 we give upper bounds for population-based EAs, showing that populations are efficient for the stochastic versions of ONEMAX we consider.

3.1 (1+1) EA

Our first theorem gives an upper bound for the (1+1) EA on ONEMAX, generalizing a theorem from [Dro04].

THEOREM 4. *Suppose there is a positive constant $c < 1/9$ such that*

$$\forall k < n : P(X_k < X_{k+1}) \geq 1 - c\frac{n-k}{n}. \quad (1)$$

Then the (1+1) EA optimizes f in $\Theta(n \log n)$ steps. Furthermore, if Equation (1) holds for all $k < n - \ell$ for some $\ell > 2$, and we have

$$\forall k < n : P(X_k < X_{k+1}) \geq 1 - \frac{\ell}{n},$$

then (1+1) EA optimizes f in $n^2 + n2^{O(\ell)}$ steps.

PROOF. Let $p_k = c(n-k)/n$.

We show that there is a positive drift on the number of 1s. Let k be the number of 1s of the current search point.

Let E_0 be the event that the new search point has at least one more 1 and the comparison of old and new search point indicates correctly that the new search point is better. Let E_1 be the event that the new search point has less 1s than the current search point, and that this new search point is nonetheless accepted. Clearly, the *expected* number of 1s conditional on E_1 is at least $k - 2$. Note that $P(E_0) \geq (1-p_k)(n-k)/(en)$ and $P(E_1) \leq p_k k/n$. Thus, the expected *increase* in the number of 1s is at least

$$\begin{aligned} P(E_0) - 2P(E_1) &\geq (1 - p_k)\frac{n-k}{en} - 2p_k\frac{k}{n} \\ &\geq \frac{n-k}{en} - p_k\left(2 + \frac{n-k}{en}\right) \\ &\geq \frac{n-k}{en} - 3p_k \\ &= \frac{n-k}{n}(1/e - 3/c). \end{aligned}$$

Using $c < 1/9$ we see that $1/e - 3/c$ is a constant > 0, giving a multiplicative drift as desired.

Regarding the "furthermore" clause, we do not have sufficient drift when we use the number of 1 as the potential function. Thus, we change our potential function in a way which could also be used to show an $\exp(O(n))$ bound for optimizing the needle function with the (1+1) EA. Intuitively, this drift function takes care of the plateau of the last ℓ ONEMAX values.

We define a helper function a so that, for all $i \geq 1$,

$$a(i) = \begin{cases} \frac{i!}{\ell!}(4\ell)^{\ell-i}, & \text{if } i \leq \ell; \\ 1, & \text{otherwise.} \end{cases}$$

We now define the potential in terms of a as follows. A given search point with exactly k 0s has potential

$$g(k) = \sum_{i=1}^{k} a(i).$$

This potential function makes it particularly easy to compute the differences of the potentials of similar search points (it is a sum of successive $a(i)$). Also note that the sequence a is falling quickly for arguments $\leq \ell$, so that the sum of such elements can be bounded from above by twice its largest element. We only sketch the remaining argument. From our observations and the assumptions of the theorem one can directly compute a drift of $1/n$ towards the optimum, using almost the same arguments as in the first part of this proof (the biggest exception is that, for jumps away from the optimum, we notice that larger and larger jumps hurt us less and less, so that an expected jump of 2 away is sufficient to consider). It is easy to see that $g(n) = n + \exp(O(\ell))$, which gives the desired result. □

Now we come to our second theorem, a lower bound for the (1+1) EA on ONEMAX.

THEOREM 5. *Suppose there is $\ell \leq n/4$ and a constant $c > 16$ such that*

$$\forall k, n - \ell \leq k < n : P(X_k < X_{k+1}) \leq 1 - c\frac{n-k}{n}.$$

Then the (1+1) EA optimizes f in $2^{\Omega(\ell)}$ many steps.

PROOF. We want to show that there is a constant negative drift on the number of ones in the interval between $n-\ell$ and n; however, we will count iterations of the process only when an actual change in the number of 1s occurs (i.e., we condition on the change), as otherwise the drift would be too small (this will only yield a smaller bound than when counting all other steps as well). See also [RS12] regarding an explicit negative drift theorem in the presence of self-loops. Let $k \geq n - \ell$ be the number of 1s of the current search point. Since we do not count steps without change, it suffices to show that the drift conditional on lowering the number of 1s is at least twice the drift conditional on increasing the number of 1s (i.e., the negative drift is twice the size of the positive drift). This would yield a negative drift of at least 2/3 (this uses that we have a minimal step width of 1).

Let $p_k = c(n-k)/n$. Clearly, the negative drift is at least $p_k k/(en)$.

Let E_0 be the event that the new search point has at least one more 1 and the comparison of old and new search point indicates correctly that the new search point is better. Clearly, the *expected* number of 1s conditional on E_0 is at most $k+2$ and $P(E_0) \leq (n-k)/n$. This gives a positive drift of at most $2(n-k)/n$. Dividing the lower bound for the negative drift by the upper bound for the positive drift, we get a ratio of at least

$$\frac{p_k k}{en} \frac{n}{2(n-k)} = \frac{ck}{2en}.$$

From $k \geq 3n/4$ and $c > 16$ we get the desired bound of 2 on the ratio. As the (1+1) EA makes long jumps with sufficiently small probability, an application of the Negative Drift Theorem (Theorem 3) concludes the proof. □

Our two theorems can be used for easy corollaries, showing the optimization time of the (1+1) EA given different noise models. We first consider the noise model given in [Dro04].

COROLLARY 6 ([DRO04]). *Suppose prior noise which, with probability p, flips a bit uniformly at random. Then we have that the (1+1) EA optimizes* ONEMAX *in time*

$$\begin{cases} \Theta(n \log n), & \text{if } p \leq 1/(10n); \\ \text{polynomial}, & \text{if } p = O(\log n/n); \\ \text{superpolynomial}, & \text{if } p = \omega(\log n/n) \cap 1 - \omega(\log n/n); \\ \text{polynomial}, & \text{if } p = 1 - O(\log n/n). \end{cases}$$

PROOF. Suppose first $p \leq c/n$ for some $c \leq 1/10$ and let $k < n$. We estimate $P(X_k < X_{k+1})$ by observing that that the event $X_k \geq X_{k+1}$ requires the individual with k 1s to be evaluated to $k+1$ or the other to k. The first option has probability $\leq p(n-k)/n$, the second of $p \leq c/n$. Thus, we get the desired bound from Theorem 4.

In the case of $p \leq c \log n/n$ we similarly get the bound $P(X_k \geq X_{k+1}) \leq c \log n/n$; this is sufficient up to a distance of $c \log n$ from the optimum, which gives a polynomial bound.

Suppose $p = \omega(\log n/n) \cap 1 - \omega(\log n/n)$. Then, for all k, we estimate $P(X_k = X_{k+1})$ as $\geq p(1-p)$ (either both X_k and X_{k+1} evaluate to k or both to $k+1$). Theorem 5 gives a superpolynomial run time.

Suppose now $p = 1 - O(\log n/n)$. If X_k evaluates to $k-1$, then $X_k < X_{k+1}$. However, $P(X_k = k-1) \geq \log n/(2n)$ so that Theorem 4 gives the desired result. □

Regarding posterior noise we give the following corollary.

COROLLARY 7. *Suppose posterior noise, sampling from some distribution D with variance σ^2. Then we have that the (1+1) EA optimizes* ONEMAX *in polynomial time if $\sigma^2 = O(\log n/n)$. On the other hand, if, for example, D is exponentially distributed with parameter 1, then the (1+1) EA optimizes* ONEMAX *in superpolynomial time only.*

PROOF. We have $X_k \sim k + D$ and $X_{k+1} \sim k + 1 + D$; let D' be the difference of two independent copies of D. We have

$$P(X_k < X_{k+1}) = P(0 < X_{k+1} - X_k) = P(-1 < D').$$

The variance of the difference of two i.i.d. centered variables both with variance σ^2 is $2\sigma^2$; let D' be this difference. Now we apply Chebyshev's Inequality to see that

$$P(|D'| \geq 1) \leq 2\sigma^2.$$

Thus, for $\sigma^2 = O(\log n/n)$, the probability of being at least 1 from the mean while having a variance of $O(\log n/n)$ is $O(\log n/n)$, as sufficient for polynomial run time (see Theorem 4).

In the case of D an exponential distribution we have a constant chance of $X_k \geq k+2$ and $X_{k+1} \leq k+2$, which leads to the claimed result using Theorem 5. □

3.2 Population-Based EA

In this section we give upper bounds for a population-based EA. In particular, we consider parent populations (i.e., the $(\mu+1)$ EA). From [Wit06] we know that the $(\mu+1)$ EA needs $\Theta(\mu n + n \log n)$ iterations to optimize the *static* version of OneMax. We conjecture a similar run time for sufficiently benevolent noisy versions, but, for simplicity also for the requirements on the noise model, we only give a slightly weaker bound.

Theorem 8. *Let μ be given and, for each $k < n$, let Y_k denote the minimum over μ independent copies of X_k. If there is a positive constant $c < 1/9$ such that*

$$\forall k, n/4 < k < n : P(Y_k < X_{k+1}) \geq 1 - c\frac{n-k}{n\mu}, \quad (2)$$

then the $(\mu+1)$ EA optimizes f in $O(\mu n \log n)$ iterations.

Note that the requirement of Equation (2) might seem to get more restrictive with growing μ; however, it only gets linearly more restrictive in the fraction on the right-hand-side, while the impact of growing μ on the random variable Y_k is typically much stronger.

Proof. Let $p_k = c(n-k)/(n\mu)$.

We show that there is a positive drift on the number of ones in the current best search point. Let k be the number of 1s of the current best search point.

Let E_0 be the event that the new search point has at least one more 1 than the best one and the comparison of old and new search point indicates correctly that the new search point is better. We have $P(E_0) \geq (1-p_k)(n-k)/(e\mu n)$.

Let E_1 be the event that the new search point has less 1s than the current best search point, the best search point is unique, and that this unique search point is discarded (if the best search point is not unique, E_1 is the empty event). Clearly, the *expected* number of 1s conditional on E_1 (if $E_1 \neq \emptyset$) is at least $k-2$. We have $P(E_1) \leq p_k$. Thus, the expected *increase* in the number of 1s is at least

$$\begin{aligned} P(E_0) - 2P(E_1) &\geq (1-p_k)\frac{n-k}{e\mu n} - 2p_k \\ &= \frac{n-k}{e\mu n} - p_k\left(2 + \frac{n-k}{e\mu n}\right) \\ &\geq \frac{n-k}{e\mu n} - 3p_k. \end{aligned}$$

Using the choice of c and the definition of p_k, we see that we have sufficient multiplicative drift as desired. □

From these theorems we can again derive many corollaries regarding concrete noise models. These includes corollaries implying an exponential speedups of populations of logarithmic size, when compared with the performance of the (1+1) EA!

Corollary 9. *Suppose prior noise which, with probability p, flips a bit uniformly at random. Let $\mu \geq 5 \log n/p$. Then we have that the $(\mu+1)$ EA optimizes OneMax in time $O(\mu n \log n)$. In particular, for $p = 1/2$, we have that a population size of $\mu \geq 10 \log n$ suffices for an optimization time of $O(\mu n \log n)$.*

Proof. For $k \geq n/4$, the probability that none of μ individuals with k 1s is evaluated to $k-1$ is $\leq 1/(\mu n)$, as a simple computation shows (we omit the details of the application of the Chernoff Bound). Thus, Theorem 8 gives the desired result. □

The intuitive reason behind the previous corollary was that, regardless of the noisy evaluation of the best-so-far individual, all worse individuals have a constant chance *each* to be strictly worse.

Corollary 10. *Let any non-negative additive posterior noise be given which has a non-zero constant probability of evaluating to < 1. Then there is a constant c such that, for $\mu \geq c \log n$, the $(\mu+1)$ EA optimizes OneMax in time $O(\mu n \log n)$.*

Proof. Let D be the posterior noise and $p = P(D < 1)$ a constant $\neq 0$. The case of $p = 1$ is trivial. Let $c = -2/\log(1-p)$ and $\mu = \lceil c \log n \rceil$. We have

$P(Y_k \geq k+1) = P(D \geq 1)^\mu \leq (1-p)^{-2\log n/\log(1-p)} = n^{-2}$.

This implies the claimed result. □

Note that the last corollary applies, for example, to additive posterior noise taken from an exponential distribution with parameter 1.

4. LEADINGONES

We follow up on the section about OneMax with results for LeadingOnes. For this purpose we now fix a stochastic LeadingOnes function f according to one of our models. For each k, we let x_k^{opt} be the bit string which has only 1s, except for position $k+1$; let x_k^{pes} be the bit string with k leading ones and otherwise only 0s. In a sense, x_k^{opt} is *optimal* for a bit string with a leading ones value of k, while x_k^{pes} is pessimal. We let $(X_k^{\text{opt}})_{k \leq n}$ and $(X_k^{\text{pes}})_{k \leq n}$ be two sequences of independent random variables such that, for all $k \leq n$, $X_k^{\text{opt}} \sim f(x_k^{\text{opt}})$ and $X_k^{\text{pes}} \sim f(x_k^{\text{pes}})$. We will assume the following about f.

- For each evaluation of f on a bit string with the left-most zero at position $k+1$, the return value is drawn according to a distribution which is in between X_k^{pes} and X_k^{opt} with respect to stochastic dominance.
- $\forall j \leq k < n : P(X_j^{\text{opt}} < X_{k+1}^{\text{opt}}) \geq P(X_k^{\text{opt}} < X_{k+1}^{\text{opt}})$.
- $\forall j \leq k < n : P(X_j^{\text{pes}} < X_{k+1}^{\text{pes}}) \geq P(X_k^{\text{pes}} < X_{k+1}^{\text{pes}})$.

We show that, despite the more drastic consequences of noise, we still find sufficient conditions for efficient optimization similar to the ones we have already seen in Section 3.

We begin by giving upper and lower bounds for the (1+1) EA in Section 4.1. In Section 4.2 and Section 4.3 we show the effectiveness of parent and offspring populations, respectively, for the stochastic LeadingOnes problem by giving upper bounds.

4.1 (1+1) EA

Theorem 11. *Suppose there is a positive constant $c < 1/12$ such that*

$$\forall k < n : P(X_k^{\text{opt}} < X_{k+1}^{\text{pes}}) \geq 1 - \frac{c}{kn} \quad (3)$$

Then the (1+1) EA optimizes f in $O(n^2)$ steps.

PROOF. Let $p_k = c/(kn)$. We show that there is a positive drift on the number of leading 1 bits. Let k be the length of the prefix of the current search point consisting of 1s.

We stick to our previous notation and denote by E_0 the event that the new search point has a longer prefix consisting of 1s and the comparison of old and new search point indicates correctly that the new search point is better. Let E_1 be the event that the new search point has a smaller number of leading ones than the current search point, and that it is accepted. Conditioning on E_1 we can trivially bound the expected number of leading ones below by 0. We have $P(E_0) \geq (1-p_k)/(en)$ and $P(E_1) \leq p_k(1-e^{-1}) \leq p_k$. Therefore, the expected increase in the number of leading 1s is

$$\begin{aligned} P(E_0) - kP(E_1) &\geq \frac{(1-p_k)}{en} - kp_k \\ &\geq \frac{1}{en} - p_k\left(\frac{1}{en} + k\right) \\ &\geq \frac{1}{en} - p_k \cdot (2k) \ . \end{aligned}$$

Due to our choice of $c < 1/6$ and our definition of p_k we have a positive additive drift of $1/(2en)$ leading to an upper bound of $O(n^2)$ for the expected run time of the algorithm by applying the Additive Drift Theorem (see Theorem 1). □

It is only to be expected that noise disrupts the optimization of LEADINGONES immensely. Consequently, our following corollaries to Theorem 11 are rather weak with respect to the noise allowed (basically, the algorithm will only experience constantly many incorrect decisions during optimization, in expectation).

COROLLARY 12. *Suppose prior noise which, with probability p, flips a bit uniformly at random. Then we have that the (1+1) EA optimizes* LEADINGONES *in time $O(n^2)$ if $p \leq 1/(3n^2)$.*

PROOF. Suppose first $p \leq 1/(3n^2)$ and let $k < n$. We estimate $P(X_k^{\text{opt}} < X_{k+1}^{\text{pes}})$ by observing that the event $X_k^{\text{opt}} \geq X_{k+1}^{\text{pes}}$ requires the individual with k 1s to be evaluated to $\geq k+1$ or the other to $\leq k$. The first option has a probability of at most p/n, the second of pk/n. Hence, $P(X_k^{\text{opt}} < X_{k+1}^{\text{pes}}) \geq 1-(k+1)/(3n^3) \geq 1-1/(3n^2)$ and the desired bound follows from Theorem 11. □

Regarding posterior noise we give the following corollary.

COROLLARY 13. *Suppose posterior noise, sampling from a centered distribution D with variance σ^2. Then we have that the (1+1) EA optimizes* LEADINGONES *in $O(n^2)$ if $\sigma^2 \leq 1/(12n^2)$.*

PROOF. Note that, in this case, $X_k^{\text{opt}} \sim X_k^{\text{pes}}$, for all $k \leq n$. With the same argument as in Corollary 7 we have $P(X_k^{\text{opt}} < X_{k+1}^{\text{pes}}) \geq 1 - 2\sigma^2$. Thus, for $\sigma^2 = 1/(12n^2)$ the claim follows from Theorem 11. □

Next we give a lower bound for the (1+1) EA for the prior noise model. We will not give a general lower bound that holds for both of our models because it is very easy for the (1+1) EA to detect an inferior noisy offspring by selection if LEADINGONES is subjected to posterior noise.

THEOREM 14. *Suppose prior noise which, with probability 1/2, flips a bit uniformly at random. Then we have that the (1+1) EA optimizes* LEADINGONES *in $2^{\Omega(n)}$ steps.*

PROOF. We show that there is a constant negative drift on the number of ones in the interval between $99n/100$ and n. Let $k \geq 99n/100$ be the number of 1s of the current search point.

Let E_0 be the event that the new search point has at least one more 1 than the current search point and the comparison of old and new search point indicates that the new search point is to be accepted. The expected number of 1s conditional on E_0 is at most $k+2$ and we have a trivial bound of $P(E_0) \leq (n-k)/n \leq 1/100$.

Let E_1 be the event that the new search point differs from the old by flipping exactly one 1 in the right half of positions, and that it is accepted. We want to estimate $P(E_1)$. There are at least $49n/100$ 1s in the right half of positions, so the probability of flipping exactly one of them and no other is at least $49/(100e)$. In order to estimate the probability of accepting such an offspring, we consider two cases. First, assume that the parent has a leading ones value of at least $n/2$. Then the probability of the noisy evaluation evaluating the parent to a value $< n/2$ is at least 1/4 (by choosing to flip a bit in the left half in the evaluation), while evaluating the offspring to its true value $\geq n/2$ has a probability of at least 1/2. In total we have $P(E_1) \geq 49/(800e)$ in this case.

Second, assume that the parent has a leading ones value of $< n/2$. Then both parent and offspring have the same leading ones value; with probability 1/4 they both evaluate to their true value, which favors the offspring. Thus, in this case, we get $P(E_1) \geq 49/(400e)$. Overall we have now $P(E_1) \geq 49/(800e) > 1/50$

Thus, we have that the total (negative) drift of

$$P(E_1) - 2P(E_0) \geq 49/(800e) - 2/100$$

which gives us a constant negative drift. Since long jumps are sufficiently small (due to our choice of using the number of 1s as potential), we can apply Theorem 3 which yields our result. □

4.2 Parent Populations

THEOREM 15. *Let μ be given and, for each $k < n$, let Y_k denote the minimum over μ observed values of X_k^{opt}. If there is a positive constant $c < 1/12$ such that*

$$\forall k : n/4 < k < n \Rightarrow P(Y_k < X_{k+1}^{\text{pes}}) \geq 1 - \frac{c}{\mu k n} \ , \tag{4}$$

then the $(\mu + 1)$ EA optimizes f in $O(\mu n^2)$ steps.

Note that, due to the dependence of Y_k on μ, Equation (4) typically gets less restrictive with growing μ, just as in Theorem 8.

PROOF. Let $p_k = c/(\mu k n)$. We show that there is a positive drift on the number of leading 1 bits of a current best individual. Let k be the length of the prefix of the current search point consisting of 1s. Let E_0 be the event that a best individual is improved by at least 1 and accepted by mutation. Let E_1 be the event that the new individual has a smaller prefix consisting of 1s and that the unique best individual is dropped from the parent population. We have that $P(E_0) \geq (1-p_k)/(e\mu n)$, assuming pessimistically that there is only one best individual. On the other hand $P(E_1) \leq p_k$.

Since, conditioned on E_1, the expected number of leading ones of a best individual is trivially at least 0 we can bound the expected increase in the number of leading 1s of a best individual below by

$$\begin{aligned}P(E_0) - kP(E_1) &\geq (1-p_k)\frac{1}{e\mu n} - kp_k \\ &\geq \frac{1}{e\mu n} - p_k\left(\frac{1}{e\mu n} + k\right) \\ &\geq \frac{1}{e\mu n} - p_k(2k) \ ,\end{aligned}$$

and the last term can be bounded below by $1/(2e\mu n)$ due to our choice of $c < 1/12$ and the definition of p_k. Applying Theorem 1 yields an upper bound of $2e\mu n^2$ for the expected number of generations until the optimum is found. Taking the cost of initialization into account we have an expected run time of $\mu + 2e\mu n^2$, proving our claim. □

Theorem 15 is not strong enough to derive an upper bound for the prior noise model where a bit flip is performed with certain probability. This is because the probability that a best individual is dropped from the population is too high. Regarding posterior noise, we can still derive the following corollary.

COROLLARY 16. *Let any non-negative additive posterior noise be given which has a non-zero constant probability of evaluating to* < 1. *Then there is a constant* c *such that, for* $\mu \geq c\log n$, *the* $(\mu+1)$ *EA optimizes* LEADINGONES *in time* $O(\mu n^2)$.

PROOF. Let D be the posterior noise and $p = P(D < 1)$ a non-zero constant. Let $c = -3/\log(1-p)$ and $\mu = \lceil c \log n \rceil$. We have

$$P(Y_k < X_{k+1}) = 1 - P(D \geq 1)^{\mu} \geq 1 - (1-p)^{-3\log n/\log(1-p)} \ ,$$

and the last term equals $1 - n^{-3}$ which yields the result by applying Theorem 15. □

4.3 Offspring Populations

In this section we consider the $(1+\lambda)$ EA. The next theorem gives conditions for efficient optimization of stochastic LEADINGONES problems. The bound we give is the same as is shown for static LEADINGONES in [JDJW05].

THEOREM 17. *Let* $\lambda \geq 72\log n$ *and, for each* $k < n$, *let* Y_k *denote the maximum over* λ *observed values of* X_k^{opt} *(belonging to inferior individuals) and let* Z_k *denote the maximum over at least* $\lambda/6$ *observed values of* X_k^{pes} *(belonging to better individuals). Suppose there are positive, non-zero constants* $q < 1$ *and* $c < q/2$ *such that*

$$\forall k < n : P(Y_k < X_{k+1}^{\text{pes}}) \geq q \ , \tag{5}$$

and

$$\forall k < n : P(Y_{k-1} < Z_k) \geq 1 - \frac{c}{k(1+\frac{en}{\lambda})} \ . \tag{6}$$

Then the $(1+\lambda)$ *EA optimizes* f *in* $O(n+n^2/\lambda)$ *generations and needs* $O(n^2 + \lambda n)$ *fitness evaluations.*

PROOF. Let $p_k = c/(k(1+\frac{en}{\lambda}))$. We show that there is a positive drift on the number of leading 1 bits. Let k be the length of the prefix of the current search point consisting of 1s.

Let E_0 be the event that at least one offspring is improved by at least 1 and is correctly accepted. Let E_1 be the event that at least one offspring has a smaller prefix consisting of 1s than the current search point, and that it is still accepted. We have that $P(E_0)$ can be bounded below by

$$q\left(1 - \left(1 - \frac{1}{en}\right)^{\lambda}\right) \geq q\frac{\lambda}{en+\lambda} \ .$$

The above inequality can be shown by induction on λ, see also [He10, Theorem 1].

In order to estimate $P(E_1)$ let E_2 be the event that more than $\lambda/6$ copied offspring are created. We have

$$P(E_1) \leq P(E_1|E_2)P(E_2) + P(E_1|\overline{E_2})P(\overline{E_2}) \ .$$

Equation (6) gives us $P(E_1|E_2) \leq p_k$. By using a Chernoff bound we further get $P(\overline{E_2}) \leq e^{-\lambda/24}$. Bounding the other probabilities by 1 we obtain $P(E_1) \leq p_k + e^{-\lambda/24}$. Conditioning on E_1, the expected number of leading ones is trivially at least 0. Therefore, the expected increase in the number of leading 1s is

$$\begin{aligned}P(E_0) - kP(E_1) &\geq q\frac{\lambda}{en+\lambda} - k\left(p_k + e^{-\frac{\lambda}{24}}\right) \\ &\geq q\frac{\lambda}{en+\lambda} - k\left(p_k + \frac{1}{n^3}\right) \\ &\geq q\frac{\lambda}{en+\lambda} - 2kp_k \\ &= (q-2c)\frac{\lambda}{en+\lambda} \ .\end{aligned}$$

Due to our choice of q and $c < q/2$ we have that $q - 2c$ is a positive constant. Applying Theorem 1 yields an upper bound of $O(n + en^2/\lambda)$ for the expected number of generations. Since λ fitness evaluations are performed in each generation the expected number of fitness evaluations until an optimum is found is therefore $O(\lambda n + n^2)$. □

We give the following corollary, showing the superiority of EAs with offspring populations over the (1+1) EA, even with only small populations.

COROLLARY 18. *Let* p *be bounded away from* 0 *and* 1 *by a constant. Suppose prior noise which, with probability* p, *flips a bit uniformly at random. Then there is a constant* c *such that, for* λ *with* $c\log n \leq \lambda \leq 2c\log n$, *we have that the* $(1+\lambda)$ *EA optimizes* LEADINGONES *in time* $O(\lambda n + n^2)$.

PROOF. We give a rough sketch of the argument. We want to apply Theorem 17. It is easy to see that Equation (5) holds as, most likely, all the inferior individuals are not evaluated better than they are, and with constant probability the good individual is evaluated to its true value. Equation (6) follows since, given sufficiently many good individuals (in this case $\lambda/6$), there is a high probability that at least one of them evaluates to its true value, while all inferior individuals do not improve just as in our considerations regarding Equation (5). □

5. DISCUSSION

In this paper we consider the optimization of noisy versions of ONEMAX and LEADINGONES. The summary of the results is that populations are *necessary* for successful optimization for any substantial noise levels. The surprising result is that even very small populations (of size logarithmic in the problem size) already lead to very high robustness to noise (see Corollaries 9 and 18).

From the formal analysis we see the reason for this robustness: In a (parent) population of size μ, while the best individual might *look* bad in a given generation, there will surely be (objectively) worse individuals which also *look* worse. This holds as long as there are enough individuals in the parent populations to make sure that one of them will evaluate worse than the (objectively) best individual. For example, if a non-best individual will evaluate worse than the best individual with constant probability, a logarithmic number of non-best individuals is large enough to get very high confidence that such a bad individual is dropped. This observation probably extends to the analysis of the $(\mu + \lambda)$ EA with $\mu > 1$ *and* $\lambda > 1$.

As for offspring populations, in the $(1+\lambda)$ EA the current individual is cloned multiple times and thus hedges against bad evaluations (as long as good evaluations are sufficiently likely). This does not extend to the analysis of the $(\mu+\lambda)$ EA with $\mu > 1$ and $\lambda > 1$ in a straightforward way, as clones might be made from sub-optimal individuals.

Acknowledgements

The research leading to these results has received funding from the European Union Seventh Framework Programme (FP7/2007-2013) under grant agreement no 618091 (SAGE). The authors would like to thank Benjamin Doerr and Tobias Friedrich for many useful discussions on the topic. Furthermore, the reviewers of this paper gave a lot of helpful feedback, for which we are very grateful.

6. REFERENCES

[BDGG09] L. Bianchi, M. Dorigo, L. Gambardella, and W. Gutjahr. A Survey on Metaheuristics for Stochastic Combinatorial optimization. *Natural Computing*, 8:239–287, 2009.

[DHK12] B. Doerr, A. Hota, and T. Kötzing. Ants Easily Solve Stochastic Shortest Path Problems. In *Proc. of GECCO'12*, pages 17–24, 2012.

[DJW12] B. Doerr, D. Johannsen, and C. Winzen. Multiplicative Drift Analysis. *Algorithmica*, 64:673–697, 2012.

[Dro04] S. Droste. Analysis of the (1+1) EA for a Noisy OneMax. In *Proc. of GECCO'04*, pages 1088–1099, 2004.

[FK13] M. Feldmann and T. Kötzing. Optimizing Expected Path Lengths with Ant Colony Optimization Using Fitness Proportional Update. In *Proc. of FOGA'13*, pages 65–74, 2013.

[GP96] W. Gutjahr and G. Pflug. Simulated Annealing for Noisy Cost Functions. *Journal of Global Optimization*, 8:1–13, 1996.

[Gut03] W. Gutjahr. A Converging ACO Algorithm for Stochastic Combinatorial optimization. In *Proc. of SAGA'03*, pages 10–25, 2003.

[He10] Jun He. A Note on the First Hitting Time of $(1 + \lambda)$ Evolutionary Algorithms for Linear Functions with Boolean Inputs. In *Proc. of CEC'10*. IEEE, 2010.

[HY04] J. He and X. Yao. A Study of Drift Analysis for Estimating Computation Time of Evolutionary Algorithms. *Natural Computing*, 3:21–35, 2004.

[JB05] Y. Jin and J. Branke. Evolutionary Optimization in Uncertain Environments—A Survey. *IEEE Transactions on Evolutionary Computation*, 9:303–317, 2005.

[JDJW05] T. Jansen, K. De Jong, and I. Wegener. On the Choice of the Offspring Population Size in Evolutionary Algorithms. *Evolotionary Computation*, 13:413–440, 2005.

[Joh10] D. Johannsen. *Random Combinatorial Structures and Randomized Search Heuristics*. PhD thesis, Universität des Saarlandes, 2010. Available online at http://scidok.sulb.uni-saarland.de/volltexte/2011/3529/pdf/Dissertation_3166_Joha_Dani_2010.pdf.

[Leh11] P. K. Lehre. Fitness-levels for non-elitist populations. In *Proc. of GECCO'11*, pages 2075–2082, 2011.

[MRC08] B. Mitavskiy, J. E. Rowe, and C. Cannings. Preliminary Theoretical Analysis of a Local Search Algorithm to Optimize Network Communication Subject to Preserving the Total Number of Links. In *Proc. of CEC'08*, pages 1484–1491, 2008.

[OW11] P. Simone Oliveto and C. Witt. Simplified Drift Analysis for Proving Lower Bounds in Evolutionary computation. *Algorithmica*, 59:369–386, 2011.

[OW12] P. Oliveto and C. Witt. Erratum: Simplified Drift Analysis for Proving Lower Bounds in Evolutionary Computation. *arXiv*, abs/1211.7184, 2012.

[PB10] A. Prügel-Bennett. Benefits of a Population: Five Mechanisms That Advantage Population-Based Algorithms. *IEEE Transactions on Evolutionary Computation*, 14:500–517, 2010.

[RS12] J. E. Rowe and D. Sudholt. The Choice of the Offspring Population Size in the $(1,\lambda)$ EA. In *Proc. of GECCO'12*, pages 1349–1356, 2012.

[ST12] D. Sudholt and C. Thyssen. A Simple Ant Colony Optimizer for Stochastic Shortest Path problems. *Algorithmica*, 64:643–672, 2012.

[Wit06] C. Witt. Runtime Analysis of the $(\mu + 1)$ EA on Simple Pseudo-Boolean Functions. *Evolutionary Computation*, 14:65–86, 2006.

Concentration of First Hitting Times under Additive Drift

Timo Kötzing
Fiedrich-Schiller-Universität Jena
07743 Jena, Germany

ABSTRACT

Recent advances in drift analysis have given us better and better tools for understanding random processes, including the run time of randomized search heuristics. In the setting of multiplicative drift we do not only have excellent bounds on the *expected* run time, but also more general results showing the *concentration* of the run time.

In this paper we investigate the setting of additive drift under the assumption of strong concentration of the "step size" of the process. Under sufficiently strong drift towards the goal we show a strong concentration of the hitting time. In contrast to this, we show that in the presence of small drift a Gambler's-Ruin-like behavior of the process overrides the influence of the drift. Finally, in the presence of sufficiently strong negative drift the hitting time is superpolynomial with high probability; this corresponds to the so-called negative drift theorem, for which we give new variants.

Categories and Subject Descriptors

F.2 [**Theory of Computation**]: Analysis of Algorithms and Problem Complexity

General Terms

Theory, Algorithms, Performance

Keywords

Additive Drift, Concentration, Theory, Run Time Analysis

1. INTRODUCTION

Suppose we make a random walk on the real line starting with 0. Further suppose that, in each step of the walk, we expect to increase in value by exactly $\varepsilon > 0$; this expected increase is called a (positive) *drift*. The Additive Drift Theorem ([HY04], see Theorem 5) tells us that the *expected* time for the walk to reach some fixed value n (for the first time) is exactly n/ε (for finite search spaces). The (random) time to reach a given value for the first time is called the *first hitting time* or just *hitting time* (in this paper we will also accept overshooting). This drift theorem is based on a more general result [Haj82] and gave a new and powerful tool for the formal analysis of random processes, such as the progress of randomized search heuristics (like evolutionary algorithms and ant colony optimization).

In fact, after the publication of [HY04], the Additive Drift Theorem became more and more popular as a method to analyze the expected run time of randomized search heuristics. In order to get better bounds from a drift theorem with little effort, new drift theorems were proven, for example for drift proportional to the distance from the target (instead of uniform, as in the Additive Drift Theorem – this is called *multiplicative drift*) [DJW12]. Another very powerful family of drift theorems are the so-called *Variable Drift Theorems* (independently in [Joh10, Theorem 4.6] and [MRC08, Section 8], but see also [RS12] for a discussion and extension).

All these theorems have in common that they can be used for showing *upper* bounds on the run time of randomized algorithms. Aiming for a similarly strong tool for showing lower bounds, [OW11, OW12] derived (again from [Haj82]) a theorem which applies in case that the drift goes *away* from the target (see Theorem 6 for a precise statement and [RS12] for a powerful variant). Just as the drift theorems for upper bounds, the Negative Drift Theorem has proven to be superbly useful for the analysis of randomized search heuristics, providing an easy-to-apply tool for deriving lower bounds.

In addition to bounds on the *expected* hitting time, concentration results are also of interest. These can, for example, be directly used for statements about the concentration of the run time of an algorithm. But sometimes concentration results are necessary for deriving bounds on the expected hitting times as well: imagine, for example, an algorithm which can only be successful when n independent sub-algorithms are successful; in the analysis, one would usually need concentration results for the run time of the sub-algorithms.

For the special case of multiplicative drift, strong concentration results were given in [DG13]. In very recent work [LW13] even more general results are given, providing concentration bounds in a very general setting. In this paper, we take an approach different from that in [LW13] by focusing on the very special case of additive drift and deriving as strong as possible concentration results in this case. The advantage is that, for the theorems in this pa-

GECCO'14, July 12–16, Vancouver, BC, Canada.

ACM 978-1-4503-2662-9/14/07 ...$15.00.
http://dx.doi.org/10.1145/2576768.2598364.

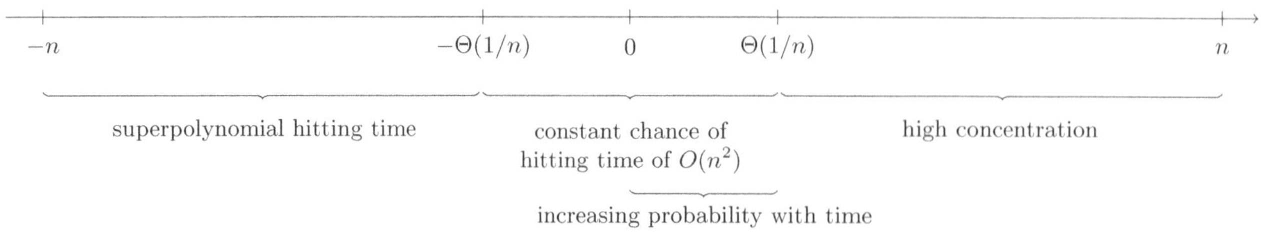

Figure 1: Intuitive regimes of additive drift. Depicted are possible values of the additive drift ε; the important change points are (up to constant factors) at $1/n$ and $-1/n$. Note that for large (superconstant) bounds on the possible jump size c of the process, the results get worse.

per, checking whether they apply is easy, and so is using the conclusion; the downside is the restricted scope.

Outside of the evolutionary computation community, a number of results also regarding positive drift are known. In particular, most of the work of this paper is based on the technique of bounded differences (basically all proofs are applications of the Azuma-Hoeffding Inequality), which is wide spread, and the applications given here are straightforward instances of these methods (see [DP09] for an introduction). A notable example where similar results regarding positive drift are shown is [Wor99] (a version of Theorem 1 can be found in its Section 4). The main purpose of the present paper is to introduce these methods to the evolutionary computation community in an easily accessible way (the Azuma-Hoeffding Inequality itself was already used in the community to derive concentration, see, for example, [DK13]).

1.1 Discussion of Results

Recall that, if we start with 0 and drift an expected amount of at most ε towards n, we have an expected time of at least n/ε to reach n. However, it is possible that n is already reached after one round with constant probability: the process might, in the first iteration, jump to the goal ($= n$) with probability $1/2$ and with the remaining $1/2$ probability it jumps to $-n$, giving an expected progress of $0 \leq \varepsilon$.[1] Similarly, one can give examples where the drift is high, but the probability to reach the goal within the expected number of steps is low.

We would like to give sufficient conditions (which hold in many cases for analyses of randomized search heuristics) under which the hitting time is concentrated around the expectation. To that end we will assume that no large jumps occur: we require that the largest possible jump is c, for some value $c > 0$. Under this condition we can derive strong results; Figure 1 gives an overview. Note the three regimes of additive drift: if it is strong, we get high concentration; if it is between about $-1/n$ and $1/n$, we get a behavior similarly to the Gambler's Ruin problem, with a constant probability of reaching n regardless of the strength of the drift due to a (sufficiently unbiased) random walk on the real line; note that this result requires a constant variance. This constant probability can be significantly boosted by allowing more time, in case of non-negative drift. Finally, for low values of drift, we get an exponential hitting time, (this is the regime of negative drift theorems). In the following we discuss these statements in more detail.

Our first theorem informs about an exponentially small probability of arriving at n significantly before the expected n/ε iterations. Note that a version of this bound was shown in [Wor99, Corollary 4.1].

THEOREM 1. *Let $(X_t)_{t\geq 0}$ be random variables over $\mathbb{R}$, each with finite expectation and let $n > 0$. With $T = \min\{t \geq 0 : X_t \geq n \mid X_0 \leq 0\}$ we denote the random variable describing the earliest point that the random process exceeds n, given a starting value of at most 0. Suppose there are $\varepsilon, c > 0$ such that, for all t,*

1. *$E(X_{t+1} \mid X_0, \ldots X_t, T > t) \leq X_t + \varepsilon$, and*
2. *$|X_t - X_{t+1}| < c$.*

Then, for all $s \leq n/(2\varepsilon)$,

$$P(T < s) \leq \exp\left(-\frac{n^2}{16c^2 s}\right).$$

Note that the first condition in the previous theorem formalizes an *additive drift of at most ε*, the second condition formalizes the bounded step width.

We see that, for example for constant c and $\varepsilon = \Omega(1/n)$, we have a superpolynomially small probability of hitting n in less than $n^2/\omega(\log n)$ iterations. Note that the bound is no longer useful (i.e. greater than 1) when $s \geq n^2$. This means that after more than n^2 steps we cannot exclude having exceeded n (at least not with this theorem). If $\varepsilon \geq 1/n$, we expected to hit n after n^2 steps anyway (due to the drift), and the bound of $s \leq n/(2\varepsilon)$ makes the bound inapplicable for values of $s \geq n^2$. As soon as we have drift of $\varepsilon < 1/n$, the drift process is intuitively more and more drowned by the random walk due to the variance (which we will consider later).

But what is now the probability of arriving significantly after the expected time? For that we need a *lower* bound on the expected progress (drift).

THEOREM 2. *Let $(X_t)_{t\geq 0}$ be random variables over $\mathbb{R}$, each with finite expectation and let $n > 0$. With $T = \min\{t \geq 0 : X_t \geq n \mid X_0 \geq 0\}$ we denote the random variable describing the earliest point that the random process exceeds n, given a starting value of at least 0. Suppose there are $\varepsilon, c > 0$ such that, for all t,*

[1]Note that iterating this idea leads to an example where, under arbitrary additive drift, the expected number of iterations until n is reached is 2, seemingly contradicting the Additive Drift Theorem; however, this iterated example requires an unbounded search space, which is ruled out by the requirements of the Additive Drift Theorem.

1. $E(X_{t+1} \mid X_0, \ldots X_t, T > t) \geq X_t + \varepsilon$, *and*

2. $|X_t - X_{t+1}| < c$.

Then, for all $s \geq 2n/\varepsilon$,

$$P(T \geq s) \leq \exp\left(-\frac{s\varepsilon^2}{16c^2}\right).$$

Thus, unless the drift is small, n will be exceeded with high probability after twice the expected number of steps. For small drift ($O(1/n)$), the bound is only meaningful for larger numbers of iterations, so that Markov's Inequality will give better bounds in this case for s close to n/ε.

If the drift is significantly negative, then we cannot hope to reach the goal in polynomial time with reasonable probability; this is the statement of the Negative Drift Theorem ([OW11, OW12], see Theorem 6). However, this theorem requires *constant* negative drift, a restriction which we replace to negative drift of essentially $\omega(1/n)$ with the following theorem. Note that a further version of such drift theorems is available in [OW13].

THEOREM 3. *Let* $(X_t)_{t\geq 0}$ *be random variables over* $\mathbb{R}$, *each with finite expectation and let* $n > 0$. *With* $T = \min\{t \geq 0 : X_t \geq n \mid X_0 \leq 0\}$ *we denote the random variable describing the earliest point that the random process exceeds* n, *given a starting value of at most* 0. *Suppose there are* c, $0 < c < n$ *and* $\varepsilon < 0$ *such that, for all* t,

1. $E(X_{t+1} \mid X_0, \ldots X_t, T > t) \leq X_t + \varepsilon$, *and*

2. $|X_t - X_{t+1}| < c$.

Then, for all $s \geq 0$,

$$P(T \leq s) \leq s \exp\left(-\frac{n|\varepsilon|}{16c^2}\right).$$

For example, for c constant and $\varepsilon = -\omega(\log(n)/n)$, this gives a superpolynomially small hitting probability for any polynomial number of steps.

Finally, we consider the case where there is only small drift $\varepsilon \in [0, 1/n]$.

THEOREM 4. *Let* $(X_t)_{t\geq 0}$ *be random variables over* $\mathbb{R}$, *each with finite expectation and let* $n > 0$. *With* $T = \min\{t \geq 0 : X_t \geq n \mid X_0 \geq 0\}$ *we denote the random variable describing the earliest point that the random process exceeds* n, *given a starting value of at least* 0. *Suppose there are* $\varepsilon, c \geq 0$ *with* $c < n$ *such that, for all* t,

1. $E(X_{t+1} \mid X_0, \ldots X_t, T > t) \geq X_t + \varepsilon$,

2. $Var(X_{t+1} - X_t \mid X_0, \ldots X_t, T > t) \geq 1$, *and*

3. $|X_t - X_{t+1}| < c$.

Then there is a constant ℓ *(independent of* n, c *and* ε*) such that, for all* $\delta > 0$,

$$P(T \leq n^2/\delta^{\ell \log(c)}) \geq 1 - \delta.$$

For example, if we have c constant and want any constant hitting probability δ, then a quadratic number of steps suffices (just as in the Gambler's Ruin problem).

1.2 Application and Open Problems

Note that all results are applicable not only for going from 0 to some n, but for drifting from any start a to any b, regardless of whether $a < b$ or $b < a$ – a simple transformation of the $(X_t)_{t\geq 0}$ shows this. Also, whenever there is no sufficiently small bound c to be used, one can condition the process on never jumping larger than some c and compute the failure probability of jumping more than this c; for example, many mutation operators can jump arbitrarily large distances (so-called *global operators*), but usually stay within some small (logarithmic) neighborhood with large probability.

The reason that we require such a bound c is that we base our results on the Azuma-Hoeffding Inequality (see Theorem 7) which requires just that. This entails also that our bounds are best when the steps of the process have a high variance (while many randomized search heuristics have step sizes of rather small variance, as compared with the range that they cover with reasonable probability). Thus, it is an *open problem* to improve the above bounds, for example by replacing the frequently occurring term c^2 by a bound on the variance of the steps of the process, or something similar. This would require finding a suitable replacement for the Azuma-Hoeffding Inequality.

2. KNOWN BOUNDS

The literature knows a large number of drift theorems; we give the two most important with respect to our setting of additive drift.

The simplest drift theorem concerns the expected hitting time under additive drift.

THEOREM 5 (ADDITIVE DRIFT [HY04]). *Let* $(X_t)_{t\geq 0}$ *be random variables describing a Markov process over a finite state space* $S \subseteq \mathbb{R}$. *Let* T *be the random variable that denotes the earliest point in time* $t \geq 0$ *such that* $X_t \geq n$. *If there exist* $\varepsilon > 0$ *such that*

$$E(X_{t+1} - X_t \mid T > t) \leq \varepsilon,$$

then

$$E(T \mid X_0) \geq \frac{X_0}{\varepsilon}.$$

If there exist $\varepsilon > 0$ *such that*

$$E(X_{t+1} - X_t \mid T > t) \geq \varepsilon,$$

then

$$E(T \mid X_0) \leq \frac{X_0}{\varepsilon}.$$

Second, the *Negative Drift Theorem* concerns adverse drift and shows a high hitting time, which can be used to derive lower bounds on the run time of algorithms.

THEOREM 6 (NEGATIVE DRIFT [OW11, OW12]). *Let* $(X_t)_{t\geq 0}$ *be real-valued random variables describing a stochastic process over some state space. Suppose there is an interval* $[a, b] \subseteq \mathbb{R}$, *two constants* $\delta, \varepsilon > 0$ *and, possibly depending on* $\ell = b - a$, *a function* $r(\ell)$ *satisfying* $1 \leq r(\ell) = o(\ell/\log \ell)$ *such that, for all* $t \geq 0$, *the following conditions hold.*

1. $E(X_{t+1} - X_t \mid a < X_t < b) \geq \varepsilon$;

2. *For all* $j \geq 0$, $P(|X_{t+1} - X_t| \geq j \mid a < X_t) \leq \frac{r(\ell)}{(1+\delta)^j}$.

Then there is a constant c such that, for $T = \min\{t \geq 0 : X_t \leq a \mid X_0 \geq b\}$, *we have*

$$P(T \leq 2^{c\ell/r(\ell)}) = 2^{-\Omega(\ell/r(\ell))}.$$

A crucial requirement of the theorem is a restriction on the jump size of the random process: the larger the step, the less likely it must be. A further important requirement is that of *constant* drift away from the target. See Corollary 15 for a comparison with the results of this paper.

For our results, we make use of the Azuma-Hoeffding Inequality for supermartingales, see [Azu67]. We give a version from [FGL12, Corollary 2.1], with scaling incorporated. For this we mention that $(X_t)_{t\geq 0}$ is a *supermartingale* if each random variable has finite expectation and, for all $t \geq 0$,

$$E(X_{t+1} \mid X_0, \ldots X_t, T > t) \leq X_t.$$

THEOREM 7 (AZUMA-HOEFFDING INEQUALITY). *Let* $(X_t)_{t\geq 0}$ *be a supermartingale such that there is c such that, for all t,* $|X_t - X_{t+1}| < c$. *Then, for all t and all x,*

$$P\left(\max_{0\leq j\leq t}(X_j - X_0) \geq x\right) \leq \exp\left(-\frac{x^2}{4c^2t}\right).$$

3. DETAILED PROOFS

In this section we give the proofs of the theorems from Section 1. The proofs for Theorems 1-3 are straightforward applications of the Azuma-Hoeffding Inequality (Theorem 7); we will discuss these in Section 3.1 on large drift (they mostly apply when the drift is $\Omega(1/n)$ in either direction). After that we will consider small drift in Section 3.2.

For this section, let $(X_t)_{t\geq 0}$ be random variables over $\mathbb{R}$, each with finite expectation. Furthermore, we let $n \in \mathbb{N}$ and let $T_{\leq} = \min\{t \geq 0 : X_t \geq n \mid X_0 \leq 0\}$ be the random variable that denotes hitting time of n (similarly, $T_{\geq} = \min\{t \geq 0 : X_t \geq n \mid X_0 \geq 0\}$). For a given ε, we say that $(X_t)_{t\geq 0}$ *has drift of at most* ε iff

$$E(X_{t+1} \mid X_0, \ldots X_t, T > t) \leq X_t + \varepsilon. \quad (1)$$

Symmetrically, we say, for a given ε, that $(X_t)_{t\geq 0}$ *has drift of at least* ε iff

$$E(X_{t+1} \mid X_0, \ldots X_t, T > t) \geq X_t + \varepsilon. \quad (2)$$

We will assume that there is c such that, for all $t \geq 0$,

$$|X_{t+1} - X_t| < c. \quad (3)$$

We call a process where Equation (3) holds *c-bounded* or *of step width at most c*.

Note that (1) is almost exactly the definition of a supermartingale (similarly, (2) corresponds to submartingales), except for the additional ε. In fact, we can derive a supermartingale in case that $(X_t)_{t\geq 0}$ has drift of at most ε by letting, for all $t \geq 0$,

$$Y_t = X_t - t\varepsilon.$$

Since $(Y_t)_{t\geq 0}$ is now a supermartingale, we can now apply the Azuma-Hoeffding Inequality (see Theorem 7). Similarly, if $(X_t)_{t\geq 0}$ has drift of at most ε, then $(-Y_t)_{t\geq 0}$ is a supermartingale.

Note that if $(X_t)_{t\geq 0}$ is c-bounded, then $(Y_t)_{t\geq 0}$ is $2c$-bounded, thanks to $|\varepsilon| \leq c$.

3.1 Large Drift

We will now use our observations to get proofs for Theorems 1-3.

THEOREM 8 (EQUIVALENT TO THEOREM 1). *Suppose that* $(X_t)_{t\geq 0}$ *has drift of at most* $\varepsilon > 0$. *Then, for all* $s \leq n/(2\varepsilon)$,

$$P(T_{\leq} < s) \leq \exp\left(-\frac{n^2}{16c^2s}\right).$$

PROOF. Let $s \leq n/(2\varepsilon)$. We apply the Azuma-Hoeffding Inequality (Theorem 7) on the supermartingale $(Y_t)_{t\geq 0}$ (which is $2c$-bounded) to see that the probability of any of the $Y_t - Y_0$ for $t \leq s$ exceeding $n/2$ is bounded from above by

$$\exp\left(-\frac{n^2}{64c^2s}\right).$$

Intuitively, we bound the probability of going half the way by random variance; as, for $s \leq n/(2\varepsilon)$, we have made at most (the other) half in expectation, this translates to the desired bound as follows. We observe that, for all $t \leq s$, $Y_t < n/2$ implies $X_t < n$ (as $s \leq n/(2\varepsilon)$). □

Similarly, we get the bound that the hitting time is reached with high probability after sufficient iterations.

THEOREM 9 (EQUIVALENT TO THEOREM 2). *Suppose that* $(X_t)_{t\geq 0}$ *has drift of at least* $\varepsilon > 0$. *Then, for all* $s \geq 2n/\varepsilon$,

$$P(T_{\geq} \geq s) \leq \exp\left(-\frac{s\varepsilon^2}{64c^2}\right).$$

PROOF. Let $s \geq 2n/\varepsilon$. We apply the Azuma-Hoeffding Inequality (Theorem 7) on the supermartingale $(-Y_t)_{t\geq 0}$ to see that the probability of $-Y_s + Y_0$ exceeding $s\varepsilon/2$ is bounded from above by

$$\exp\left(-\frac{(s\varepsilon)^2}{64c^2s}\right) = \exp\left(-\frac{s\varepsilon^2}{64c^2}\right).$$

Intuitively, we bound the probability of making only half the steps that we should have made; this is meaningful once we should have overshot by a factor of 2, i.e. for $s \geq 2n/\varepsilon$ as desired. The proof is completed by the observation that $-Y_s < s\varepsilon/2$ implies $X_s > n$ (as $s \geq 2n/\varepsilon$). □

We now use this approach to prove the theorem concerning negative drift.

THEOREM 10 (EQUIVALENT TO THEOREM 3). *Suppose that* $(X_t)_{t\geq 0}$ *has drift of at most* $\varepsilon < 0$ *and assume* $c \leq n/2$. *Then, for all* $s \geq 0$,

$$P(T_{\leq} \leq s) \leq s \exp\left(-\frac{n|\varepsilon|}{64c^2}\right).$$

PROOF. We make an analysis with phases. A phase begins when, for some t, $X_t \geq 0$ and ends when either $X_{t'} \geq n$ or $X_{t'} < 0$; in the first case we call the phase *successful*, in the second case *unsuccessful*. We will show that a phase is successful with probability at most $\exp\left(-\frac{n|\varepsilon|}{64c^2}\right)$, as then a union bound (or an application of Bernoulli's Inequality) will give the desired result, lower bounding the length of each phase with the trivial bound of 1. In order to bound the probability of a phase being successful, we use the following reasoning. Any phase starts $\leq c$. If the process does not overshoot its expectation by $n-c$ ever within $n/|\varepsilon|$ iterations, it not only did not reach n (starting from $\leq c$) but also drops below 0 (as, after $n/|\varepsilon|$ iterations, the expectation is $\leq -n$). For this we apply again the Azuma-Hoeffding Inequality (Theorem 7) and see that the probability of a phase being successful is at most

$$\exp\left(-\frac{(n-c)^2|\varepsilon|}{16c^2n}\right) \leq \exp\left(-\frac{n|\varepsilon|}{64c^2}\right),$$

where the inequality comes from $c \leq n/2$. □

3.2 Small Drift

We start with a lemma which is interesting in its own right, showing the theorem concerning negative drift (Theorem 3) to be reasonably tight. The proof of the lemma makes use of one of the result concerning the concentration of the hitting time under positive drift (Theorems 1).

LEMMA 11. *Let $b = 3072$. Then, for all n and c, the following holds. Let $k = bc^2n$. Suppose that $(X_t)_{t\geq 0}$ has a drift of at least $\varepsilon \geq -1/(4k)$, a variance in each step of at least 1 and $1 \leq c < n/2$. Let $s = 24bc^2n^2$. Then we have that, within s steps, the process does not drop below $-k$ with probability $\geq 1/2$ and*

$$P(T_{\geq} \leq s) \geq \frac{1}{2}.$$

PROOF. We give the proof for $\varepsilon \leq 0$; the case of $\varepsilon > 0$ is analogous, but easier. We let A be the event that the process does not drop below $-k$ within s steps. We first show $P(A) \geq 3/4$, after that we show that, conditional on A, the process reaches n with probability $3/4$, which will imply the claim.

For all t, we let

$$Y_t = (X_t)^2$$

and

$$\Delta_t = X_{t+1} - X_t.$$

In all of the following computations of expectation and variance the conditioning on all relevant (previous) random variables is implicitly understood but not made explicit for clarity (and brevity) of the exposition. We note that, for all t, $Var(\Delta_t) \leq 4c^2$. It suffices to show that Y_t does not reach k^2 within s steps with probability $\geq 3/4$. We want to apply Theorem 1 to $(Y_t)_{t\geq 0}$, so we compute the expected drift.

$$\begin{aligned} E(Y_{t+1}) &= E((\Delta_t + X_t)^2) \\ &= E((\Delta_t)^2 + 2\Delta_t X_t + X_t^2) \\ &= E((\Delta_t)^2) + 2E(\Delta_t)X_t + X_t^2 \\ &= Var(\Delta_t) + E(\Delta_t)^2 + 2E(\Delta_t)X_t + Y_t \\ &\leq 4c^2 + 1 + Y_t \\ &\leq 5c^2 + Y_t. \end{aligned}$$

The last inequality follows from our bound on the variance, together with our bounds on the expected drift and the value of X_t.

In order to estimate the number of steps until $(X_t)_{t\geq 0}$ reaches $-k$, we wait until the process drops below 0, and bound the time that the process $(Y_t)_{t\geq 0}$ takes to get from 0 to k^2, which, using the Additive drift theorem, has an expectation of

$$\geq k^2/(5c^2) \geq 2s$$

steps (using $b \geq 240$). It is easy to see that the process $(Y_t)_{t\geq 0}$ is $2kc$-bounded. Thus, Theorem 1 gives that $(Y_t)_{t\geq 0}$ *does* exceed k^2 within s steps starting from 0 with probability

$$\leq \exp\left(-\frac{k^4}{16 \cdot 4k^2c^2s}\right) = \exp\left(-\frac{b}{64 \cdot 24}\right) \leq 1/4$$

as desired.

Now we want to bound the probability for reaching n. To this end we let, for all $t \geq 0$,

$$Z_t = (X_t + k)^2 - k^2$$

and we condition on A. In a computation analogous to that for $(Y_t)_{t\geq 0}$ we see that

$$E(Z_{t+1}) \geq 1/2 + Z_t.$$

From the Additive Drift Theorem (Theorem 5) we now know that $(Z_t)_{t\geq 0}$ reaches $(n+k)^2 - k^2$ in an *expected* number of

$$2((n+k)^2 - k^2) = 2(2nk + n^2) \leq 6nk$$

steps. Thus, using Markov's Inequality, we get that $(Z_t)_{t\geq 0}$ reaches $(n+k)^2 - k^2$ within s steps with probability $\geq 3/4$ as desired, as $s = 4(6nk)$. □

Now we come to the last theorem of this paper.

THEOREM 12 (EQUIVALENT TO THEOREM 4). *Let $b = 3072$ just as in the preceding lemma. Suppose that $(X_t)_{t\geq 0}$ has drift of at least $\varepsilon \geq 0$, a variance in each step of at least 1 and $1 \leq c < n/2$. Then there is a constant ℓ (independent of n, c and ε) such that, for all $\delta > 0$,*

$$P(T_{\geq} \leq n^2/\delta^{\ell \log(c)}) \geq 1 - \delta.$$

PROOF. We let $k_0 = 0$ and, for all i,

$$k_{i+1} = bc^2(k_i + n) + n + k_i$$

and

$$s_i = 24bc^2(k_i + n)^2.$$

We analyze the process in an infinite series of phases, starting with phase 0. For each i, Phase $i+1$ starts as soon as Phase i ends (Phase 0 starts at time $t = 0$). Phase i ends when either the goal is reached (the process is $\geq n$), the process is $\leq -k_{i+1}$, or s_i steps passed in Phase i, whichever happens first. We call a phase *successful* if it ends with reaching the goal.

Trivially, just before the beginning of Phase i, the process is $\geq -k_i$. We want to apply Lemma 11, where the n of the Lemma corresponds to $k_i + n$ (for the application of the Lemma, we shift the process by k_i). Thus, we see that each phase is successful with probability $\geq 1/2$.

Let $\delta > 0$ and let $a > 0$ be such that $2^{a-1} \geq 1/\delta \geq 2^a$. Thus, after a phases, we have a success probability of at least $1 - \delta$ as desired. As, for all i, Phase i takes at most s_i steps, we get the desired result. □

4. COROLLARIES

In this section we will derive some useful corollaries to our theorems. We will use the terminology of the preceding section.

The first corollary is derived from Theorems 1 and 2 and gives an interval in which the hitting time is with high probability.

COROLLARY 13 (CONCENTRATION). *Suppose that $(X_t)_{t\geq 0}$ has drift of $\varepsilon = \Omega(1/n)$ and each step is bounded by c. Also suppose $X_0 = 0$ and let T be the hitting time of n. Then, for each k, there is a k' (independent of ε) such that*

$$P\left((n/\varepsilon)/(k'c^2 \log n) \leq T \leq k'(n/\varepsilon)c^2 \log n\right) \geq 1 - n^{-k}.$$

Furthermore, for all $r = \omega(c^2 \log n)$,

$$P\left((n/\varepsilon)/r \leq T \leq (n/\varepsilon)r\right) \geq 1 - n^{-\omega(1)}.$$

The next corollary is derived from Theorem 3. It shows that sufficiently negative drift gives strong (lower) bounds on the hitting time.

COROLLARY 14 (NEGATIVE DRIFT). *Suppose that $(X_t)_{t\geq 0}$ has drift of at most $\varepsilon = -\omega(c^2 \log n/n)$ and assume $c \leq n/2$. Then, for all polynomials p and all n large enough,*

$$P(T_{\leq} \leq p(n)) \leq \frac{1}{p(n)}.$$

As another corollary, we can get a statement similar to the Negative Drift Theorem ([OW11, OW12], see Theorem 6). This is not directly a corollary to Theorem 3, but a corollary to its proof (where it is easy to see that negative drift is only required in some bounded interval). Note that, in order to follow the notation of Theorem 6, the process attempts to go *down* (from b to a), so what is called a "negative drift" is a positive value (away from the goal). The constraint of boundedness is lifted by conditioning on the (very likely) event of never making a large jump.

COROLLARY 15 (NEGATIVE DRIFT II). *Suppose there is an interval $[a,b] \subseteq \mathbb{R}$, two constants $\delta, \varepsilon > 0$ and, possibly depending on $\ell = b - a$, a function $r(\ell)$ satisfying $1 \leq r(\ell) = \exp(o(\sqrt[4]{\ell}))$ such that, for all $t \geq 0$, the following conditions hold.*

1. *$E(X_{t+1} - X_t \mid a < X_t < b) \geq \varepsilon$;*
2. *For all $j \geq 0$, $P(|X_{t+1} - X_t| \geq j \mid a < X_t) \leq \frac{r(\ell)}{(1+\delta)^j}$.*

Then there is a constant c such that, for $T = \min\{t \geq 0 : X_t \leq a \mid X_0 \geq b\}$, we have

$$P(T \leq 2^{c\sqrt{\ell}}) = 2^{-\Omega(\sqrt[4]{\ell})}.$$

In comparison with the Negative Drift Theorem (Theorem 6) we see that we get only lower bounds on the hitting time ($2^{\sqrt{\ell}}$ instead of 2^{ℓ}), for the case of small $r(\ell)$, also with higher probability. However, $r(\ell)$ can increase much higher without these bounds degrading. It is not surprising that Corollary 15 works for high values of $r(\ell)$, as these high values only increase the variance logarithmically.

Acknowledgments

I would like to thank Tobias Friedrich, Benjamin Doerr and Anton Krohmer for many useful discussions on the topic of this paper; all of them also provided valuable pointers to the literature. A further source of pointers to the literature as well as many helpful comments came from the reviewers of this paper, who have proved to be very knowledgeable in this subject.

5. REFERENCES

[Azu67] Kazuoki Azuma. Weighted sums of certain dependent random variables. *Tohoku Mathematical Journal*, 19:357–367, 1967.

[DG13] Benjamin Doerr and Leslie Ann Goldberg. Adaptive drift analysis. *Algorithmica*, 65:224–250, 2013.

[DJW12] Benjamin Doerr, Daniel Johannsen, and Carola Winzen. Multiplicative drift analysis. *Algorithmica*, 64:673–697, 2012.

[DK13] Benjamin Doerr and Marvin Künnemann. How the (1+λ) evolutionary algorithm optimizes linear functions. In *Proc. of GECCO'13*, pages 1589–1596, 2013.

[DP09] Devdatt P. Dubhashi and Alessandro Panconesi. *Concentration of Measure for the Analysis of Randomized Algorithms.* Cambridge University Press, 2009.

[FGL12] Xiequan Fan, Ion Grama, and Quansheng Liu. Hoeffding's inequality for supermartingales. *Stochastic Processes and their Applications*, 122:3545–3559, 2012.

[Haj82] Bruce Hajek. Hitting-time and occupation-time bounds implied by drift analysis with applications. *Advances in Applied Probability*, 13:502–525, 1982.

[HY04] Jun He and Xin Yao. A study of drift analysis for estimating computation time of evolutionary algorithms. *Natural Computing*, 3:21–35, 2004.

[Joh10] Daniel Johannsen. *Random Combinatorial Structures and Randomized Search Heuristics.* PhD thesis, Universität des Saarlandes, 2010. Available online at http://scidok.sulb.uni-saarland.de/volltexte/2011/3529/pdf/Dissertation_3166_Joha_Dani_2010.pdf.

[LW13] Per Kristian Lehre and Carsten Witt. General drift analysis with tail bounds. *CoRR*, abs/1307.2559, 2013.

[MRC08] Boris Mitavskiy, Jonathan E. Rowe, and Chris Cannings. Preliminary theoretical analysis of a local search algorithm to optimize network communication subject to preserving the total number of links. In *Proc. of CEC'08*, pages 1484–1491, 2008.

[OW11] Pietro Simone Oliveto and Carsten Witt. Simplified drift analysis for proving lower bounds in evolutionary computation. *Algorithmica*, 59:369–386, 2011.

[OW12] Pietro Simone Oliveto and Carsten Witt. Erratum: Simplified drift analysis for proving lower bounds in evolutionary computation. *arXiv*, abs/1211.7184, 2012.

[OW13] Pietro Simone Oliveto and Carsten Witt. On the runtime analysis of the simple genetic algorithm. *Theoretical Computer Science*, 2013. In press.

[RS12] Jonathan E. Rowe and Dirk Sudholt. The choice of the offspring population size in the (1, λ) ea. In *Proc. of GECCO'12*, pages 1349–1356, 2012.

[Wor99] Nicholas C. Wormald. The differential equation method for random graph processes and greedy algorithms. In *Lectures on Approximation and Randomized Algorithms*, pages 73–155, 1999.

MMAS vs. Population-Based EA on a Family of Dynamic Fitness Functions

Andrei Lissovoi
DTU Compute, Technical University of Denmark
Kongens Lyngby, Denmark

Carsten Witt
DTU Compute, Technical University of Denmark
Kongens Lyngby, Denmark

ABSTRACT

We study the behavior of a population-based EA and the Max-Min Ant System (MMAS) on a family of deterministically-changing fitness functions, where, in order to find the global optimum, the algorithms have to find specific local optima within each of a series of phases. In particular, we prove that a (2+1) EA with genotype diversity is able to find the global optimum of the MAZE function, previously considered by Kötzing and Molter (PPSN 2012, 113–122), in polynomial time. This is then generalized to a hierarchy result stating that for every μ, a (μ+1) EA with genotype diversity is able to track a MAZE function extended over a finite alphabet of μ symbols, whereas population size $\mu - 1$ is not sufficient. Furthermore, we show that MMAS does not require additional modifications to track the optimum of the finite-alphabet MAZE functions, and, using a novel drift statement to simplify the analysis, reduce the required phase length of the MAZE function.

Categories and Subject Descriptors

F.2 [**Theory of Computation**]: Analysis of Algorithms and Problem Complexity

Keywords

Evolutionary Algorithms; Ant Colony Optimization; Dynamic Problems; Populations; Runtime Analysis

1. INTRODUCTION

Evolutionary algorithms (EAs) are a class of nature-inspired algorithms that can be applied to solve a wide variety of optimization problems. Runtime analysis of nature-inspired algorithms has advanced considerably in recent years [2, 10], though most focus on static optimization problems, where the objective is simply to find the global optimum within the least amount of steps. Many real-world optimization problems are dynamic in nature, meaning that the optimal solution to a given problem may change as the problem conditions change over time, and the algorithms therefore need to be able to not only find the optimum at some point of time, but also to *track* the optimal solution over time as the problem changes.

GECCO'14, July 12–16, 2014, Vancouver, BC, Canada.

ACM 978-1-4503-2662-9/14/07...$15.00.
http://dx.doi.org/10.1145/2576768.2598301

Application of EAs to Dynamic Optimization Problems is the subject of study in the Evolutionary Dynamic Optimization field, which in recent years has attracted lots of activity. Many applications of evolutionary algorithms on dynamic problems are considered in literature [1, 11], and there are runtime analyses building on theoretical studies of evolutionary algorithms for dynamic problems [4,7,13]. The utility of a population for tracking problems was studied in evolutionary computation by Jansen and Schellbach [7], while different mechanisms for ensuring population diversity have been considered by Oliveto and Zarges [12]. In particular, a mechanism called *genotype diversity* was proved to be inefficient on a particular dynamic problem.

In [8], Kötzing and Molter introduced a dynamic pseudo-boolean function called MAZE, the optimum of which slowly moves from the all-ones to the all-zeroes bit string in n phases where the optimum of a single bit oscillates between the two values. The paper shows that while the Max-Min Ant System is able to track the changes occurring in this fitness function and find the optimum all-zeroes string within polynomial time, a (1+1) EA loses track of the optimum and requires an exponential amount of time to find the all-zeroes optimum with high probability.

In this paper, we consider the impact of introducing a population and a simple diversity mechanism to the (1+1) EA, showing that a (2+1) EA with genotype diversity is able to track the optimum of the MAZE function. We then generalize the MAZE to a function over a finite alphabet, and prove a hierarchy result with respect to the population size. More precisely, for any μ, there is a variant of the MAZE such that a (μ+1) EA with genotype diversity will with high probability succeed in tracking the optimum, whereas population size $\mu - 1$ will with high probability make it lose track of the optimum. Finally, we return to consider the performance of the Max-Min Ant System (MMAS) Ant Colony Optimization (ACO) algorithm on the finite-alphabet version of MAZE, and conclude that MMAS, due to its pheromone memory model, is always able to successfully track the optimum in this case, even with shorter phase lengths than considered in [8]. Our proofs are based on mixing time arguments, fitness levels with tail bounds, and a new variant of a variable drift theorem, which allows for a tail bound on the probability distribution of the pheromone value in MMAS.

The paper is structured as follows. Section 2 defines the dynamic fitness function MAZE, and the (μ+1) EA with genotype diversity and MMAS algorithms generalized to larger alphabets. Section 3 proves the positive result for the simple (2+1) EA w. r. t. the classical MAZE function on bit strings. The hierarchy result for larger alphabets is proven in Section 4. Finally, Section 5 shows that MMAS is efficient in tracking the optimum for every polynomial alphabet size. We finish with some conclusions.

2. PRELIMINARIES

The MAZE dynamic fitness function defined in [8] consists of $n+1$ phases of $t_0 = kn^3 \log n$ iterations each, where k is a sufficiently large constant. During the first phase, which we will for convenience call phase 0, the function is equivalent to ONEMAX. In each subsequent phase i, the function assigns fitness values $n+2$ and $n+1$ to bit strings $0^{i-1}01^{n-i}$ and $0^{i-1}11^{n-i}$, oscillating between assigning the higher fitness value to these individuals in a 0-0-1 pattern, with 0^i1^{n-i} being favored every two iterations out of three.

The version shown below has been extended to assign fitness values to n-character strings over a finite alphabet; for $r = 1$, i.e. bit strings, it is exactly equivalent to the original MAZE. In this context, ONEMAX counts the number of literal 1 characters in the string, and the sets OPT_p and ALT_p generalize the 0-0-1 oscillation pattern.

$$\text{MAZE}(x,t) = \begin{cases} n+2 & \text{if } t > t_0 \wedge x \in \text{OPT}(t) \\ n+1 & \text{if } t > t_0 \wedge x \in \text{ALT}(t) \\ \text{ONEMAX}(x) & \text{otherwise} \end{cases}$$

$$\text{OPT}(t) = \begin{cases} \text{OPT}_{\lfloor t/t_0 \rfloor} & \text{if } t \neq 0 \mod 3 \\ \text{ALT}_{\lfloor t/t_0 \rfloor} & \text{otherwise} \end{cases}$$

$$\text{ALT}(t) = \begin{cases} \text{ALT}_{\lfloor t/t_0 \rfloor} & \text{if } t \neq 0 \mod 3 \\ \text{OPT}_{\lfloor t/t_0 \rfloor} & \text{otherwise} \end{cases}$$

$$\text{ALL}_p = \{0^{p-1}x1^{n-p} \mid x \in \{0,1,\dots,r\}\}$$
$$\text{OPT}_p = \{0^p1^{n-p}\}$$
$$\text{ALT}_p = \text{ALL}_p \setminus \text{OPT}_p$$

In this paper, we will examine how a (2+1) Evolutionary Algorithm (EA) performs on the original MAZE function, and how a (μ+1) EA performs on our finite-alphabet version. The (μ+1) EA with genotype diversity [12,14] is shown as Algorithm 1. Definition 1 extends the mutation operator mut_r to support a finite alphabet as in [3,5]; for $r = 1$, it is equivalent to the usual mutation operator of the (1+1) EA.

Several lemmas throughout this paper state that "a specific event occurs with high probability." Definition 2 provides a more formal definition of this concept.

DEFINITION 1. *Let $\Sigma = \{0,1,\dots,r\}$ be a finite alphabet. The mutation operator mut_r creates an image $y \in \Sigma^n$ from $x \in \Sigma^n$ by independently replacing each character x_i of x ($1 \leq i \leq n$) with probability $1/n$ with a symbol drawn uniformly at random from $\Sigma \setminus \{x_i\}$.*

DEFINITION 2. *An event E is said to occur with high probability if* $\text{Prob}(E) = 1 - O(n^{-c})$ *for any constant $c > 0$.*

In Section 5, we will consider how the Max-Min Ant System (MMAS) algorithm [15], shown as Algorithm 2 below, is able to track the finite-alphabet MAZE function. We use the standard choice for $\tau_{\max} = 1 - 1/n$, and set $\tau_{\min} = 1/(rn)$ to accommodate an $(r+1)$-character alphabet of the extended MAZE function.

Algorithm 1 (μ+1) EA with genotype diversity for a finite alphabet $\Sigma = \{0,1,\dots,r\}$.

Initialize $x^* = \{x_1, \dots, x_\mu\}$, st. $x_i \neq x_j$ for all $i \neq j$.
for $t \leftarrow 1,2,\dots$ **do**
  Select x_a from x^* uniformly at random.
  Let $x_t = \text{mut}_r(x_a)$.
  if $x_t \notin x^*$ **then**
    $G \leftarrow x^* \cup \{x_t\}$
    $x_{\min} \leftarrow \arg\min_{x \in G} f(x,t)$, chosen uniformly at random
    $x^* \leftarrow G \setminus \{x_{\min}\}$

Algorithm 2 The MMAS algorithm on a directed multigraph $G = (V, \mathcal{A})$, with pheromone bounds $\tau_{\min}$ and $\tau_{\max}$, and evaporation rate ρ, where $v_0, v_n \in V$ are the start and destination vertices respectively, and $\deg^+(v)$ is the outdegree of a vertex.

Initialize $\tau_a \leftarrow 1/\deg^+(v)$ for all $a = (v,v') \in \mathcal{A}$
for $t \leftarrow 1,2,\dots$ **do**
  Let x_t be an empty path.
  $p \leftarrow v_0$, $S \leftarrow \{(p,v') \in \mathcal{A} \mid v' \notin x_t\}$
  while $|S| > 0$ and $p \neq v_n$ **do**
    Pick arc $a = (p,h')$ from S with probability: $p_a = \tau_a / \sum_{s \in S} \tau_s$
    Append a to x_t
    $p \leftarrow h'$, $S \leftarrow \{(p,v') \in \mathcal{A} \mid v' \notin x_t\}$
  if $t = 1$ **or** $f(x_t,t) \geq f(x^*,t)$ **then**
    $x^* \leftarrow x_t$
  for each $a \in \mathcal{A}$ **do**
    $$\tau_a \leftarrow \begin{cases} \min(\tau_{\max}, (1-\rho)\tau_a + \rho) & \text{if } a \in x^* \\ \max(\tau_{\min}, (1-\rho)\tau_a) & \text{otherwise} \end{cases}$$

To use a path-constructing algorithm with a fitness function that assigns values to n-character strings, we use the construction graph shown in Figure 1: every n-character string $x \in \Sigma^n$ corresponds to the path from v_0 to v_n consisting of the arcs $a_{i,c}$ for which $x_i = c$, and every v_0-v_n path corresponds to some $x \in \Sigma^n$ in this fashion.

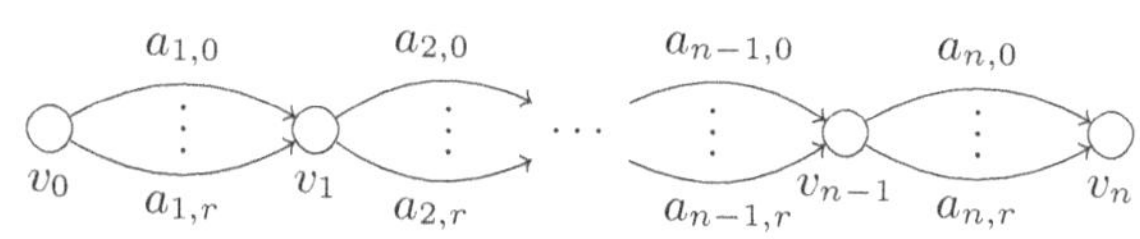

Figure 1: Construction graph used for MMAS on the finite-alphabet Maze function. There are $r+1$ edges between each pair of vertices (v_{i-1}, v_i).

Note that both algorithms re-evaluate the fitness function when selecting individuals or updating the best-so-far.

3. (2+1) EA ON MAZE

The (1+1) EA will with high probability require an exponential amount of time to find the 0^n optimum on the MAZE function, because there is at least a constant probability of ending each oscillation phase $p > 0$ with $x^* \neq 0^p1^{n-p}$, which lets the (1+1) EA revert to optimizing ONEMAX, destroying the 0 prefix constructed so far, and requiring a large mutation to recover [8]. In this section, we will show that a (2+1) EA with genotype diversity avoids this problem by being able to store both of the oscillating individuals in each phase, thereby ensuring that 0^p1^{n-p} is in the population at the start of the next phase. This ensures that at the end of the last phase, the 0^n individual is in the population with high probability.

THEOREM 3. *The (2+1) EA with genotype diversity will with high probability have the 0^n optimum in the population at the end of the last phase of the* MAZE.

To show this, we will prove that the $1^n = \text{OPT}_0$ individual is found with high probability during the initial ONEMAX phase, and the EA is then able to follow the oscillation process: if OPT_{p-1} is in the population at the beginning of phase p, OPT_p will be in the population at the end of that phase – meaning that at the end of final phase, $\text{OPT}_n = 0^n$ will be in the population.

LEMMA 4. *The (2+1) EA will discover the 1^n individual within $O(n \log n)$ iterations with high probability.*

PROOF. The fitness-based partition method can be applied: partition the possible populations into levels based on the maximum fitness value of any individual within the population. The probability of an iteration leaving the level where the highest fitness value is $n - i$ is at least $p_i \geq (1/2) \cdot (1/n) \cdot (1 - 1/n)^{n-1} \geq i/(2ne)$: i.e. that of selecting the best-valued individual in the population as the ancestor, and flipping a single zero bit. Even if the EA starts at the lowest of $n + 1$ fitness levels, it has to leave at most n levels in order to reach the level where 1^n is in the population; in expectation, this takes $E(T) \leq \sum_{i=1}^{n} \frac{1}{p_i} = 2en \log n$ iterations.

The high probability result is obtained by applying the tail bounds on fitness levels derived in [17, Theorem 2]: using $s = 50n^2 > 4\pi^2 e^2 n^2/6 \geq \sum_{i=1}^{n} \frac{1}{p_i{}^2}$, $h = 1/(2en) \leq \min p_i$, the probability that 1^n is found within $E(T) + \delta$ iterations is at least $1 - e^{-\frac{\delta}{4} \cdot \min\{\delta/s, h\}}$. Setting $\delta = 50cn \log n$, where $c > 0$, and observing that $h < \delta/s$ for sufficiently large n, yields a probability of finding 1^n within $O(n \log n)$ iterations of at least

$$1 - e^{-\frac{50cn \log n}{4} \cdot \min\left\{\frac{50cn \log n}{50n^2}, \frac{1}{2en}\right\}}$$
$$\geq 1 - e^{-\frac{50c \log n}{8e}} > 1 - n^{-2c}. \quad \square$$

LEMMA 5. *If OPT_{p-1} is in the population at the beginning of phase p, OPT_p will with high probability be in the population when phase p ends.*

PROOF. As $\text{OPT}_{p-1} \in \text{ALL}_p$, it has a fitness value of at least $n + 1$ during phase p, and therefore cannot be removed from the population. The OPT_p individual can be constructed by selecting OPT_{p-1} as the ancestor and flipping a single bit, which occurs in each iteration with probability at least $1/(2en)$. The probability of this occurring within $n^3 \log n$ iterations is at least:

$$1 - (1 - 1/(2en))^{n^3 \log n} \geq 1 - e^{-\frac{1}{2e} n^2 \log n} = 1 - n^{-\Omega(n^2)}$$

As OPT_p has a fitness value of at least $n + 1$ during phase p, when constructed, it will replace a ONEMAX-valued individual in the population, and cannot be removed from the population during phase p. $\square$

Combined, Lemma 4 and Lemma 5 prove Theorem 3.

PROOF OF THEOREM 3. By applying a union bound on the probabilities of failure during each of MAZE's $n + 1$ phases, we can conclude that the (2+1) EA finishes phase n with 0^n in the population with high probability. $\square$

4. (μ+1) EA AND THE FINITE-ALPHABET MAZE

While a (2+1) EA with genotype diversity is able to track the optimum of the original MAZE, it is interesting to consider whether there exist MAZE-like functions for which a larger population is required. In this section, we extend the MAZE function over a finite alphabet $\Sigma = \{0, 1, \ldots, r\}$, and consider a ($\mu$+1) EA with genotype diversity, where $r \in O(n)$ and $\mu < n/2$. We will build toward two results: a population of $\mu \leq r$ is insufficient to track the optimum, while $\mu > r$ is sufficient and enables the (μ+1) EA to find 0^n in polynomial time. These results are formalized in Theorems 6 and 7 below.

THEOREM 6. *If $r \geq \mu$, $r \in O(n)$, and $\mu \leq n/(2 + \epsilon)$, where $\epsilon > 0$ is an arbitrarily small constant, (μ+1) EA with genotype diversity will with high probability not find the 0^n optimum on* MAZE *within a polynomial number of iterations.*

THEOREM 7. *If $\mu, r \in O(n)$ and $r < \mu$, (μ+1) EA with genotype diversity will with high probability finish the last phase of the* MAZE *with the 0^n optimum in the population.*

As before, we need to verify that 1^n is found during the initial ONEMAX phase; this is done in Lemma 8. Then, Lemma 9 shows that if an iteration begins with one of ALL_p individuals (i.e. those with a non-ONEMAX value during that phase) in the population, the population will with high probability be saturated with ALL_p individuals before the phase is over. These two lemmas are used in both the proof of Theorem 7 and of Theorem 6.

Lemmas 10 and 11 are used for Theorem 6. The former shows that once a population of $\mu \leq r$ individuals is filled with ALL_p individuals, the probability of OPT_p being in the population is at most a constant after a small number of additional iterations; while the latter states that if a phase p begins with no ALL_p individuals in the population (i.e. OPT_{p-1} was not in the population when the phase $p - 1$ ended), the (μ+1) EA loses track of the optimum and reverts to optimizing ONEMAX. This proof strategy is partly inspired by the lower bound for the (1+1) EA on the original MAZE [8].

LEMMA 8. *The (μ+1) EA will discover the 1^n individual within $O(\mu rn \log n) = O(n^3 \log n)$ iterations with high probability.*

The method used to prove Lemma 4 can be applied to prove Lemma 8 as well: we require that the best-fitness individual in the population is chosen as the ancestor, and the mutation operator changes a single non-1 character into a 1, resulting in an individual with a higher ONEMAX value than any previously in the population.

LEMMA 9. *During phase p, once an individual from ALL_p is in the population, the population will contain $\min(\mu, r+1)$ individuals from ALL_p within $O(\mu rn \log n)$ iterations with high probability.*

PROOF. The general form of the fitness-based partition method can be applied by introducing an artificial partition on the population x^*: partition the μ-individual populations by the number of ALL_p individuals they contain, from 0 to $\min(\mu, r+1)$, observing that the number of ALL_p individuals in the population cannot be reduced during phase p. As the phase starts with a population containing at least one ALL_p individual, there are at most $\min(\mu, r+1) - 1$ "population levels" that the process may need to pass through before the population is saturated with ALL_p individuals; the time for this to happen can be bounded as a sum of geometrically distributed waiting times to leave each "level".

If $i < \min(\mu, r+1)$ is the number of ALL_p individuals in the population, the probability of a single iteration creating a new ALL_p individual (and hence moving to a higher partition) by selecting one of the i as the ancestor and performing a one-character mutation is $p_i \geq \frac{i}{\mu}\frac{r+1-i}{r}\frac{1}{en}$. Let T be the number of iterations before the population is saturated with ALL_p individuals, and $m = \min(\mu, r+1) - 1$ be the number of ALL_p individuals that need to be added to the population to achieve saturation, thus the expectation $E(T)$ is at most:

$$\sum_{i=1}^{m} \frac{\mu}{i} \frac{r}{r+1-i} en = r\mu en \sum_{i=1}^{m} \frac{1}{i(r+1-i)} = O(r\mu n)$$

Applying the tail bounds from [17, Theorem 2]: using $s = 13\mu^2 r^2 n^2 > \sum_{i=1}^{m} \frac{1}{{p_i}^2}$, $h = 1/(\mu ren) < \min p_i$, the probability that m ALL_p individuals are added to the population within $E(T)+\delta$ iterations is at least $1 - e^{-\frac{\delta}{4}\cdot\min\{\delta/s, h\}}$. Setting $\delta = 13c\mu rn \log n$, where $c > 0$, and observing that $h < \delta/s$ for sufficiently large n, yields a probability of reaching the final partition within $O(\mu rn \log n)$ iterations of at least

$$1 - e^{-\frac{13cr\mu n \log n}{4}\cdot\min\left\{\frac{13cr\mu n \log n}{13\mu^2 r^2 n^2}, \frac{1}{er\mu n}\right\}}$$
$$\geq 1 - e^{-\frac{13c \log n}{4e}} > 1 - n^{-c}$$

Thus, if an ALL_p individual exists in the population during phase p, the population will be saturated with ALL_p individuals in $O(\mu rn \log n)$ iterations with high probability. □

The following lemmas consider the situation for $\mu \leq r$, i.e. a population size too small to contain every individual in ALL_p. In this case, OPT_p can be removed from the population after being discovered. Interestingly, this happens with constant probability regardless of μ.

LEMMA 10. *If, during phase p, the population consists of μ individuals from ALL_p, and $r \geq \mu$, then after $\Omega(rn)$ iterations, the probability that OPT_p is in the population is at most a constant smaller than 1.*

PROOF. OPT_p can be replaced by an ALT_p individual that was not in the population during an iteration that favors ALT_p individuals over OPT_p. The probability p_L of OPT_p being replaced by one of $r + 1 - \mu$ ALT_p individuals not yet in the population can then be bounded:

$$p_L = \frac{r+1-\mu}{r}\frac{1}{n}\left(1 - \frac{1}{n}\right)^{n-1}$$
$$\frac{1}{rne} \leq p_L \leq \frac{1}{n}$$

The OPT_p individual can be added to the population during any iteration favoring it over the ALT_p individuals by a single-character mutation of any individual in ALT_p. The probability p_W of OPT_p being rediscovered during an iteration favoring it can be bounded:

$$p_W = \frac{1}{r}\frac{1}{n}\left(1 - \frac{1}{n}\right)^{n-1}$$
$$\frac{1}{rne} \leq p_W \leq \frac{1}{rn}$$

Consider the probability of the OPT_p individual being in the population after three additional iterations: it is greatest when the first of these three iterations favors ALT_p individuals, and the subsequent two favor OPT_p. Let p_{W3} be the probability that OPT_p is constructed during the two iterations favoring it (being added to the population if it was not already there):

$$p_{W3} = p_W + (1 - p_W) \cdot p_W$$
$$\frac{1}{rne} \leq p_W \leq p_{W3} \leq 2p_W \leq \frac{2}{rn},$$

and p_{L3} be the probability that OPT_p is replaced by an ALT_p individual and then not constructed in the two following iterations:

$$p_{L3} = p_L \cdot (1 - p_{W3})$$
$$\frac{1}{2rne} \leq \frac{1}{rne}\frac{rn-2}{rn} \leq p_{L3} \leq \frac{1}{n}\left(1 - \frac{1}{rne}\right) < \frac{1}{n},$$

where the lower bound holds for $n \geq 4$.

This behavior can be modeled in a two-state Markov chain, where the states represent having or not having OPT_p in the population, with transition probabilities p_{W3} and p_{L3}; each step of this Markov chain thus corresponds to three iterations of the (μ+1) EA. Let p_H be the probability that the OPT_p individual is in the population, and consider p_H when the Markov chain is in a steady state. Hence,

$$p_H \cdot p_{L3} = (1 - p_H) \cdot p_{W3}$$
$$\frac{1 - p_H}{p_H} = \frac{p_{L3}}{p_{W3}} \geq \frac{1}{4e}$$
$$p_H \leq \frac{1}{1 + \frac{1}{4e}} < 0.916$$

Assume, as the worst case, that the OPT_p individual is in the population when it becomes saturated with ALL_p individuals; this corresponds to starting the Markov process with $p_H = 1$. Markov chain mixing time, $t(\epsilon)$, can then be used to find the number of steps required to reduce the total variation distance to the steady state p_H to at most some ϵ (and hence the number of iterations required to reduce the probability of OPT_p being in the population to at most some constant smaller than 1), and can be upper-bounded by coupling time as in [16, Corollary 4]:

$$t(\epsilon) \leq \min\left\{t : \max_{x,y\in\Omega} P(T_{xy} > t) \leq \epsilon\right\}$$

where $T_{xy} = \min\{t : X_t = Y_t \mid X_0 = x, Y_0 = y\}$ is the coupling time, i.e. the earliest time at which the two equivalent Markov chains X_t and Y_t, initialized in different states x, y, are in the same state.

With only two states (and symmetry), the coupling time T_{xy} is greatest when the chains begin in different states. The probability that the chains remain in different states for at least t steps is then:

$$\max_{x,y\in\Omega} P(T_{xy} > t) = (p_{L3}p_{W3} + (1-p_{L3})(1-p_{W3}))^t$$

To get an upper bound on $t(\epsilon)$, an upper bound on the expression in parentheses is needed. Inserting the appropriate bounds on p_{W3} and p_{L3} yields:

$$\begin{aligned} &2p_{W3}p_{L3} + 1 - p_{L3} - p_{W3} \\ &\le \frac{4}{rn^2} + 1 - \frac{3}{2rne} \le 1 - \frac{1}{rne}\left(1.5 - \frac{4e}{n}\right) \\ &< 1 - \frac{1}{rne} \text{ (for } n \ge 22) \end{aligned}$$

$$t(\epsilon) \le \min\left\{t : \left(1 - \frac{1}{rne}\right)^t \le \epsilon\right\}$$

After e.g. $t(0.01) < 4.61rne$ steps of the Markov chain, the probability that coupling has not occurred is at most 0.01. As coupling time is an upper bound for mixing time, and each Markov chain step corresponds to three EA iterations, this means that after at most $37.60rn$ iterations, the probability that OPT_p is in the population is at most $p_H + 0.01$, and so the probability that OPT_p is not in the population is at least 0.083.

Therefore, $\Omega(rn)$ iterations after the population is saturated with ALL_p individuals, the probability that OPT_p is in the population is at most a constant. □

Lemma 10 therefore implies that there is at least a constant probability of phase $p+1$ beginning with only ALT_p individuals in the population when $r \ge \mu$. The following lemma considers the consequences of this – as OPT_p is the only individual in both ALL_p and ALL_{p+1}, this means that phase $p+1$ begins without any ALL_{p+1} individuals in the population, leaving the EA with only ONEMAX-valued individuals at the beginning of phase $p+1$.

LEMMA 11. *If at the beginning of phase $p \ge n/2+4$, the population contains only individuals from ALT_{p-1}, the $(\mu+1)$ EA will, with at least constant probability, the population at the end of phase p will consist only of 1^n and one-character mutations of 1^n.*

PROOF. The ALT_{p-1} individuals initially in the population are of the form $0^{p-2}x1^{n-p+1}$, where $x \in \Sigma \setminus \{0\}$, and have ONEMAX values of at least $n-p+1$. If any ALL_p individual (which are all of the $0^{p-1}y1^{n-p}$ form, where $y \in \Sigma$) is constructed, it will be accepted, and the optimization process will resume according to Lemma 9. If no such individual is constructed, individuals with higher ONEMAX values will continue being accepted into the population, eventually leading to the discovery of 1^n as in Lemma 8.

Until an ALL_p individual has been constructed, the probability of constructing one can be upper-bounded by the probability of a mutation changing a character at a specific position (the x in the description of ALT_p above) to a 0, i.e. $1/(rn)$.

Let a *value-improving mutation* be a mutation that produces an individual with a strictly higher ONEMAX value than the worst individual currently in the population. Note that even if a value-improving mutation occurs, the resulting individual might already be one of the $\mu-1$ other individuals in the population, in which case the population is not modified. We will now show that the probability p_I of such a mutation occurring while the minimum ONEMAX value of any individual in the population is below $n-p+4$ is at least:

$$p_I \ge \frac{n}{2}\frac{1}{n}\frac{1}{r}\left(1-\frac{1}{n}\right)^{n-1} \ge \frac{1}{2er}$$

Let $n-p+1 \le v \le n-p+3$ be the minimum ONEMAX value of an individual in the population. If the ancestor selected during an iteration has a ONEMAX value of at least $v+2$, then *any* one-character mutation will produce an individual of sufficient value to be accepted; there are $n \ge n/2$ such mutations. If the selected ancestor has a value of at most $v+1$, it contains at least $n-(n-p+4) \ge n/2$ non-1 characters, and hence at least $n/2$ one-character mutations can produce an individual with a strictly higher ONEMAX value than such an ancestor. Thus, regardless of the ancestor selection, there are at least $n/2$ possible one-character mutations leading to an acceptable fitness value.

No more than a constant fraction of those value-improving mutations can fail to be accepted due to already being in the population (as $\mu \le n/(2+\epsilon)$). This means that the probability of a value-improving mutation occurring and being accepted during a single iteration is at least $\Omega(p_I) = \Omega(1/r)$.

Consider the probability of the minimum ONEMAX value of the population rising to at least $n-p+4$ without any ALL_p individual being constructed; this requires that at most 3μ value-improving mutations to be accepted (as a value-improving mutation can only introduce an individual with the same fitness value into the population at most μ times; of course, it might also require as few as μ mutations). This occurs with at least constant probability: let A be the event that an ALL_p individual is constructed, and V be the the event that a value-improving mutation is accepted, then:

$$\text{Prob}(A \mid A \vee V) \le \frac{1/(rn)}{1/(rn) + \Omega(1/r)} = O(n^{-1})$$

$$\begin{aligned} \text{Prob}(3\mu\ V\text{s without } A) &\ge (1 - \text{Prob}(A \mid A \vee V))^{3\mu} \\ &= (1 - O(n^{-1}))^{O(n)} = \Omega(1) \end{aligned}$$

Once the minimum ONEMAX value of the population is raised to $n-p+4$, constructing an ALL_p individual requires at least three characters to be changed into a 0 simultaneously, which occurs with probability at most $1/(rn)^3$.

Thus, with at least constant probability, if phase p begins without an ALL_p individual in the population, no ALL_p individual is constructed within the $O(\mu rn \log n)$ iterations required to find the 1^n individual with high probability (per Lemma 8). Furthermore, once the 1^n individual is in the population, one-character mutations of that individual will fill the population in $O(\mu \log n)$ iterations with high probability, making construction of an ALL_p individual require a $p-2 = \Omega(n)$ character mutation. □

By combining these lemmas, it is now possible to prove Theorems 6 and 7.

PROOF OF THEOREM 6. Assume the EA successfully follows the MAZE through the first $n/2+2$ phases. Each of the remaining $\Omega(n)$ phases has at least a constant probability of not ending with the OPT_p individual in the population, causing the next phase to begin with a population filled with ALT_p individuals.

With at least a constant probability, each one the remaining phases that begin without an ALL individual will cause the EA to fill the population with one-character mutations of 1^n. Once this occurs, constructing an ALL individual (for this or any future phase) will require at least $\Omega(n)$ characters to be mutated correctly in a single iteration, which occurs with probability $(rn)^{-\Omega(n)}$.

Therefore, with probability $1 - 2^{-\Omega(n)}$, the EA will fail to track the oscillation, revert to optimizing ONEMAX, and require an exponential number of iterations to find the final 0^n optimum. □

PROOF OF THEOREM 7. Per Lemma 8, the EA is able to find the 1^n individual with high probability during phase 0. For the subsequent n oscillation phases, apply Lemma 9: if the phase begins with OPT_{p-1} (i.e. an individual from ALL_p) in the population, then the remaining individuals from ALL_p, including OPT_p will be added to the population before phase p ends with high probability. Add up the failure probabilities in these $n+1$ phases using a union bound; with high probability, none of the phases fail, and phase n ends with $\mathrm{OPT}_n = 0^n$ in the population – so the $(\mu+1)$ EA is able to find the 0^n optimum within a polynomial number of iterations with high probability when $\mu > r$. □

5. ACO ON LARGER ALPHABETS

Kötzing and Molter [8] study the case where $r = 1$, i.e., the case of bit strings, and show that MMAS with overwhelming probability will track the optimum of MAZE with oscillation phase length $t_0 = kn^3 \log n$ in polynomial time. Their proof can be summarized as follows, wherein all references to lemmas and theorems refer to the paper:

1. While a bit is oscillating, taking the total over three steps of a so-called OPT-OPT-ALT oscillation (where OPT is favored in the first two steps and ALT in the last step) there is a drift of the pheromone value on the 0-edge of the bit (i.e., the edge associated with OPT) towards its maximum. With overwhelming probability, the pheromone value will reach its upper border in $O(n^3 \log n)$ steps (Lemma 2 in their paper) provided the bit keeps oscillating so long. To obtain the bound on the probability, a multiplicative drift theorem is used, which, according to [8], "wastes a lot" since the bound on the drift obtained is additive.

2. Despite the fact that the pheromone value reaches its upper border within the oscillation phase of a bit, the multiplicative drift theorem does not imply that the pheromone value stays close to the border by the end of the oscillation phase. To prove that this is unlikely, a negative drift theorem is applied (Lemma 3), implying that it takes a large polynomial amount of time until the pheromone value drops below $1 - O((\log^2 n)/n)$.

3. The transition from "bit i oscillating" to "bit $i+1$ oscillating" is analyzed. It is shown that a string outside ALL will be best-so-far string only temporarily for at most $O(\log n)$ steps after the transition, with high probability (Lemma 3). Drift arguments towards the 0-value are applied afterwards.

4. Using an $O((n \log n)/\rho)$ bound from the literature on the time from initialization until the all-ones string with is found high probability (Lemma 5) and basically applying union bounds leads to the result (Theorem 6).

It turns out that the above analysis to a very large extent carries over to larger alphabets. Basically, one can group together all edges belonging to the non-0 entries of a character and identify the sum of their pheromone values with the pheromone on the 1-edge in the binary case. The only thing to pay attention to is the new lower bound on the pheromone values, which may increase the time to reach the upper border by a factor of r.

However, we are going to present a stronger and, as we think, more elegant analysis here. In particular, we contribute a technique that supplements the drift result from Lemma 3 in [8] with a distributional statement, which makes the application of the negative drift theorem (Lemma 4 in [8]) unnecessary. In addition, the stronger analysis allows us to work with shorter oscillation phase lengths, as detailed below.

We now present the tool by which this distributional statement is obtained. The following lemma is a variable drift theorem that is not concerned with the expected first hitting time of a set of target states but with the probability of being in this set at any time t (however, results on the hitting time can be easily obtained from this probability). It is a spin-off of the variable drift theorem with tail bounds from [9] and goes back to a statement from Hajek's paper [6] that, to the best of our knowledge, has not been applied in the running time analysis of evolutionary algorithms yet. The lemma requires a bound on the moment-generating function of a potential function g that is usually derived from the one-step drift (via the function h).

LEMMA 12. *Let $(X_t)_{t\geq 0}$, be a stochastic process, adapted to a filtration $(\mathcal{F}_t)_{t\geq 0}$, over some state space $S \subseteq \{0\} \cup [x_{\min}, x_{\max}]$, where $x_{\min} \geq 0$. Let $a, b \in \{0\} \cup [x_{\min}, x_{\max}]$, $b > a$. Let $h\colon [x_{\min}, x_{\max}] \to \mathbb{R}^+$ be such that $1/h$ is integrable on $[x_{\min}, x_{\max}]$ and define $g\colon \{0\} \cup [x_{\min}, x_{\max}] \to \mathbb{R}^{\geq 0}$ by $g(x) := \frac{x_{\min}}{h(x_{\min})} + \int_{x_{\min}}^{x} \frac{1}{h(y)}\,\mathrm{d}y$ for $x \geq x_{\min}$ and $g(0) := 0$.*
If there exist $\lambda > 0$, $\beta < 1$ and $D > 0$ such that

$$E(e^{-\lambda(g(X_t)-g(X_{t+1}))} \cdot \mathbb{1}\{X_t > a\} \mid \mathcal{F}_t) \leq \beta$$
$$\text{and } E(e^{-\lambda(g(a)-g(X_{t+1}))} \cdot \mathbb{1}\{X_t \leq a\} \mid \mathcal{F}_t) \leq D$$

then

$$\mathrm{Prob}(X_t \geq b \mid X_0) < \beta^t \cdot e^{\lambda(g(X_0)-g(b))} + \frac{1-\beta^t}{1-\beta} D e^{\lambda(g(a)-g(b))}$$

for $t > 0$.

PROOF. We use ideas implicit in in the proof of Inequality 2.6 of [6], which uses the exponential method (a generalized Chernoff bound), and argue

$$\begin{aligned}\mathrm{Prob}(X_t \geq b \mid X_0) &= \mathrm{Prob}(g(X_t) \geq g(b) \mid X_0)\\ = \mathrm{Prob}(e^{\lambda g(X_t)} \geq e^{\lambda g(b)} \mid X_0) &\leq E(e^{\lambda g(X_t) - \lambda g(b)} \mid X_0),\end{aligned}$$

where the first inequality uses that $g(x)$ is non-decreasing, the equality that $x \mapsto e^x$ is a bijection, and the last inequality is Markov's inequality. Now,

$$\begin{aligned}&E(e^{\lambda g(X_t)} \mid X_0)\\ &= E\big(e^{\lambda g(X_{t-1})} \cdot E(e^{-\lambda(g(X_{t-1})-g(X_t))} \mid \mathcal{F}_{t-1})\big)\\ &= E\big(e^{\lambda g(X_{t-1})} \cdot E(e^{-\lambda(g(X_{t-1})-g(X_t))} \cdot \mathbb{1}\{X_{t-1} > a\} \mid \mathcal{F}_t)\big)\\ &\quad + E\big(e^{\lambda g(X_{t-1})} \cdot E(e^{-\lambda(g(a)-g(X_t))} \cdot \mathbb{1}\{X_{t-1} \leq a\} \mid \mathcal{F}_t)\big)\\ &\leq \beta E(e^{\lambda g(X_{t-1})} \mid X_0) + D e^{\lambda g(a)}\end{aligned}$$

by our prerequisites; we omitted the condition on X_0 for space reasons in lines 2–4. Inductively (note that this does not assume independence of the $g(X_{t-1}) - g(X_t)$), we get

$$E(e^{\lambda g(X_t)} \mid X_0) \le \beta^t e^{\lambda g(X_0)} + \sum_{r=0}^{t-1} \beta^r D e^{\lambda g(a)},$$

altogether

$$\text{Prob}(X_t \ge b \mid X_0) \le e^{\lambda(g(X_0)-g(b))}\beta^t + \frac{1-\beta^t}{1-\beta} D e^{\lambda(g(a)-g(b))}$$

as suggested. □

The preceding lemma will be applied to show the following lemma, whose purpose is to combine Lemmas 2 and 3 from [8] and which shows that the pheromone value after a certain point of time will come close to its border and stay close with high probability. In fact, due to the strength of the lemma, we can work with an oscillation length of $\Theta(r^2n^2)$ per position, i. e., we may (but need not) redefine $t_0 := kr^2n^2$ in the MAZE function, for some constant k. By contrast, [8] needs $\Omega(n^3 \log n)$ oscillations per bit due to the application of the multiplicative drift theorem along with negative drift.

LEMMA 13. *Assume $\rho \le \frac{1}{21rn}$ and $\rho = \Omega(\frac{1}{rn})$. Consider an OPT-OPT-ALT oscillation of a single character and suppose that every iteration constructs a new solution with probability $p = (1 \pm o(1))e^{-1}$ and updates with respect to the current-best otherwise. Let τ_t denote the pheromone value belonging to entry 0 for the character after t iterations. For $t \ge C(r^2n^2 + \alpha rn)$, some sufficiently large constant $C > 0$ and all $\alpha \ge 0$ it holds*

$$\text{Prob}\left(\tau_t \le 1 - O\left(\frac{\log n}{n} + \frac{\log^2 n}{rn}\right)\right) \le e^{-\alpha} + e^{-\Omega(\log^2 n)}.$$

PROOF. Let C_t denote the indicator random variable for the event that the best-so-far entry of the character is 0. Moreover, let τ_t denote the random pheromone value of the considered edge at time t, where a time index comprises an oscillation consisting of three iterations. Following [8], we define $X_t := 1 - 1/n + \frac{21}{2}\rho - \tau_t - \frac{7}{2}\rho C_t$ as the distance from the optimum. Note that $7\rho \le X_t \le 1 - \frac{1}{n} - \frac{1}{rn} + \frac{21}{2}\rho \le 1 - \frac{1}{2n}$ since $\frac{1}{rn} \le \tau_t \le 1 - \frac{1}{n}$ and $\rho \le \frac{1}{21rn}$.

In Lemma 2 in [8], it is shown that $E(X_t - X_{t+1} \mid X_t; X_t \ge \frac{\log n}{n}) \ge c_1\rho \min\{\tau_t, 1-\tau_t\}$ for some constant $c_1 > 0$ (and large enough n); in fact they show the statement without the condition $X_t \ge \frac{\log n}{n}$, which we have to add here to compensate for the fact that the sum of pheromone values belonging to a character is not necessarily 1 but within $[1, 1 + 1/n]$. This can change the selection probabilities by a factor $1 \pm O(1/n)$, which does not affect the drift statement unless X_t is very small.

We estimate $1 - \tau_t \ge X_t - \frac{7}{2}\rho \ge \frac{X_t}{2} \ge \frac{3}{2rn}$ and $\tau_t \ge 1 - \frac{1}{n} - X_t \ge \frac{1}{2n}$. This results in a drift of at least $\frac{c_1\rho}{2rn} = \Omega(1/(r^2n^2))$ independently of X_t. We therefore set $x_{\min} := 7\rho$, $a := \frac{\log n}{n}$, $b := a + \frac{\log^2 n}{rn}$, $x_{\max} = 1$ and $h(x) := \frac{c_2}{r^2n^2}$ for some sufficiently small constant $c_2 > 0$ in Lemma 12. The choice of $h(x)$ results in $E(X_t - X_{t+1} \mid X_t; X_t \ge a) \ge h(X_t)$.

By definition, $g(x) := O(1/\rho) + (x - x_{\min})\frac{r^2n^2}{c_2} \le O(xr^2n^2)$ for $x \ge x_{\min}$. Note that $X_t - X_{t+1} \le \frac{13}{2}\rho$ since three iterations can change τ_t by at most 3ρ and $C_t \le 1$ holds. This implies $g(X_t) - g(X_{t+1}) \le c_3r^2n^2\rho$ for some constant $c_3 > 0$.

Moreover, $E(g(X_t) - g(X_{t+1}) \mid \mathcal{F}_t; X_t > a) \ge \frac{h(X_t)}{h(X_t)} = 1$. A somewhat tedious expansion of the exponential function shows for $\lambda := \frac{c_4}{rn}$, where $c_4 > 0$ is a sufficiently small constant, that

$$\begin{aligned}&E(e^{-\lambda(g(X_t)-g(X_{t+1}))} \cdot \mathbb{1}\{X_t > a\} \mid \mathcal{F}_t)\\ &\le E(e^{-\lambda(g(X_t)-g(X_{t+1}))} \mid \mathcal{F}_t; X_t > a) \le 1 - \frac{\lambda}{2} \le e^{-\lambda/2}.\end{aligned}$$

We omit some details but explain the main idea why this inequality holds. Assume $\tau_t \ge 1/2$; the other case is symmetrical. Following the analysis in [8] and inspecting the pheromone update formulas, $\text{Prob}(X_{t+1} > X_t) \le \kappa_1 X_t$, $X_t - X_{t+1} \le \kappa_2 X_t \rho$ on $X_{t+1} < X_t$, and $E(X_t - X_{t+1}) \ge \kappa_3 X_t \rho$, whence $E(g(X_t) - g(X_{t+1})) \ge \kappa_4 X_t rn$ (omitting the conditions for readability). Moreover, as already argued, $g(X_t) - g(X_{t+1}) \le \kappa_5 rn$. Here all κ_i, $1 \le i \le 5$, are constants. We get for $c_4 \le \frac{1}{\kappa_5}$ that

$$\begin{aligned}&E(e^{-\lambda(g(X_t)-g(X_{t+1}))})\\ &\le 1 - \lambda E\big(g(X_t) - g(X_{t+1})\big) + 2\lambda^2 E\big((g(X_t) - g(X_{t+1}))^2\big)\\ &\le 1 - \lambda\kappa_4 X_t rn + 2(\kappa_1 + \kappa_2)X_t(\lambda\kappa_5 rn)^2\end{aligned}$$

Choosing c_4 small enough to exploit the λ^2-factor, the last bound is still less than $1 - \frac{\lambda}{2}E(g(X_t) - g(X_{t+1}))) \le 1 - \frac{\lambda}{2}$.

We are left with the case $X_t \le a$. Pessimistically assuming the maximum change $(13/2)\rho$ of the X-values, we can bound

$$E(e^{-\lambda(g(a)-g(X_{t+1}))} \cdot \mathbb{1}\{X_t \le a\} \mid \mathcal{F}_t) \le e^{c_3c_4\rho rn} \le D$$

for some constant $D > 0$. Applying Lemma 12 with $\beta := 1 - \lambda/2$,

$$\text{Prob}(X_t \ge b) \le e^{-\frac{tc_4}{2rn} + \lambda\left(\frac{O(1)}{\rho} + \frac{r^2n^2}{c_2}\right)} + \frac{D}{\lambda/2} \cdot e^{\lambda(g(a)-g(b))}$$

since $X_0 \le 1$. Since $\lambda/\rho = O(1)$, the first exponent can be written as $-\frac{tc_4}{rn} + c_5rn$ for another constant $c_5 > 0$ (if n large enough).

Now, if $t = \frac{c_5r^2n^2}{c_4} + \frac{\alpha rn}{c_4}$ then $\text{Prob}(X_t \le b) \le e^{-\alpha} + \frac{2D}{\lambda}e^{\lambda(g(a)-g(b))}$. The second term is $O(rn) \cdot e^{-\Omega(\log^2(n))} = e^{-\Omega(\log^2(n))}$. Setting $C := \max\{\frac{c_5}{c_4}, \frac{1}{c_4}\}$, the lemma follows. □

The following lemma takes the role of Lemma 4 in [8], which analyzes the transition from position i oscillating to position $i+1$ oscillating. It applies to the case that the best-so-far solution at the end of phase i is not OPT_i despite the pheromones values favoring OPT_i. Then it is very likely that MMAS recovers, more precisely, it will sample a solution from ALL_p again before the pheromones have changed significantly. The lemma can be proven in the very same way as in [8].

LEMMA 14. *Let $\rho = \Theta(\frac{1}{rn})$. Assume for $i \in \{1, \ldots, n\}$ that the current-best solution is $0^{i-1}1^{n-i+1}$ and that the pheromones of the first $i-1$ edges belonging to 0-entries as well as the last $n-i$ edges belonging to 1-entries all are $1 - 1/n$. Finally, assume that the pheromone belonging to the i-th 0-entry is $1 - O((\log^2 n)/n)$. Then for all $c > 0$, MMAS will sample 0^i1^{n-i} within $O(\log n)$ iterations with probability $1 - O(n^{-c})$.*

Finally, Theorem 5 in [8] states a tail bound on the optimization time of classical MMAS on ONEMAX. This carries over to our enlarged search space except for that the modified lower pheromone border introduces a factor of r.

THEOREM 15. *For all $c > 0$, MMAS for the search space $\{0, \ldots, r\}^n$ optimizes* ONEMAX *in $O(nr \log(n)/\rho)$ iterations with probability $1 - O(n^{-c})$.*

Putting everything together, we obtain the following theorem, taking the role of Theorem 6 in [8]. Recall that t_0, the length of the so-called oscillation phase, is the number of iterations that a position is oscillating as OPT-OPT-ALT.

THEOREM 16. *Given any $r > 0$, choose $\rho \leq \frac{1}{21rn}$ and $\rho = \Omega(\frac{1}{rn})$. We say that MMAS tracks the optimum of the* MAZE *for the $(r+1)$-character alphabet if the best-so-far solution at the end of every oscillation phase has Hamming distance $O(1)$ to the optimum. Then for all $c > 0$ there is a constant k such that choosing $t_0 := kr^2n^2$ makes MMAS track the optimum with probability $1 - O(n^{-c})$.*

6. CONCLUSIONS

We have revisited the analysis of evolutionary algorithms and ACO on the dynamic fitness function MAZE [8]. First we have shown that a (2+1) EA with a simple population diversity mechanism is able to track the optimum, which the (1+1) EA cannot. Subsequently, we have generalized this to a hierarchy result on strings over finite alphabets, where for given μ, there exists a MAZE variant for which a population size of at least μ in a $(\mu+1)$ EA with genotype diversity is sufficient to track the optimum, whereas population size $\mu - 1$ causes the EA lose track of the optimum. Surprisingly, it turns out that a generalization of MMAS to the larger state space does not require a population and is sufficient on all functions from the hierarchy. Along the way, we have introduced a variable drift theorem dealing with tail bounds on probability distributions, which allows for a more precise and simpler analysis of the pheromone values in MMAS compared to [8]. As a subject for future research, it is interesting to study the benefits and the limitations of ACO on other dynamic problems.

7. REFERENCES

[1] Enrique Alba, Amir Nakib, and Patrick Siarry. *Metaheuristics for Dynamic Optimization.* Studies in Computational Intelligence. Springer, 2013.

[2] Anne Auger and Benjamin Doerr, editors. *Theory of Randomized Search Heuristics: Foundations and Recent Developments.* World Scientific Publishing, 2011.

[3] Benjamin Doerr and Sebastian Pohl. Run-time analysis of the (1+1) evolutionary algorithm optimizing linear functions over a finite alphabet. In *Proceedings of the Genetic and Evolutionary Computation Conference (GECCO 2012).* ACM Press, 2012. 1317-1324.

[4] Stefan Droste. Analysis of the (1+1) EA for a dynamically bitwise changing OneMax. In *Proc. of the Genetic and Evolutionary Computation Conference (GECCO 2003)*, pages 909–921. Springer, 2003.

[5] Christian Gunia. On the analysis of the approximation capability of simple evolutionary algorithms for scheduling problems. In Hans-Georg Beyer and Una-May O'Reilly, editors, *GECCO*, pages 571–578. ACM, 2005.

[6] Bruce Hajek. Hitting and occupation time bounds implied by drift analysis with applications. *Advances in Applied Probability*, 14:502–525, 1982.

[7] Thomas Jansen and Ulf Schellbach. Theoretical analysis of a mutation-based evolutionary algorithm for a tracking problem in the lattice. In *Proc. of the Genetic and Evolutionary Computation Conference (GECCO 2005)*, pages 841–848. ACM Press, 2005.

[8] Timo Kötzing and Hendrik Molter. Aco beats ea on a dynamic pseudo-boolean function. In *Parallel Problem Solving from Nature-PPSN XII*, pages 113–122. Springer, 2012.

[9] Per Kristian Lehre and Carsten Witt. General drift analysis with tail bounds. Technical Report, arXiv:1307.2559, `http://arxiv.org/abs/1307.2559`, 2013.

[10] Frank Neumann and Carsten Witt. *Bioinspired Computation in Combinatorial Optimization – Algorithms and Their Computational Complexity.* Natural Computing Series. Springer, 2010.

[11] Trung Thanh Nguyen, Shengxiang Yang, and Jürgen Branke. Evolutionary dynamic optimization: A survey of the state of the art. *Swarm and Evolutionary Computation*, 6:1–24, 2012.

[12] Pietro S. Oliveto and Christine Zarges. Analysis of diversity mechanisms for optimisation in dynamic environments with low frequencies of change. In *Proc. of the fifteenth annual conference on Genetic and Evolutionary Computation conference*, pages 837–844. ACM, 2013.

[13] Philipp Rohlfshagen, Per Kristian Lehre, and Xin Yao. Dynamic evolutionary optimisation: An analysis of frequency and magnitude of change. In *Proc. of the Genetic and Evolutionary Computation Conference (GECCO 2009)*, pages 1713–1720. ACM Press, 2009.

[14] Tobias Storch. On the choice of the parent population size. *Evolutionary Computation*, 16(4):557–578, 2008.

[15] Thomas Stützle and Holger H. Hoos. Max-min ant system. *Future Generation Comp. Syst.*, 16(8):889–914, 2000.

[16] Dirk Sudholt. Using markov-chain mixing time estimates for the analysis of ant colony optimization. In *Proceedings of the 11th workshop proceedings on Foundations of genetic algorithms*, FOGA '11, pages 139–150, New York, NY, USA, 2011. ACM.

[17] Carsten Witt. Fitness levels with tail bounds for the analysis of randomized search heuristics. *Information Processing Letters*, 114(1):38–41, 2014.

Model-Optimal Optimization by Solving Bellman Equations

Alan J. Lockett
Dalle Molle Institute for Artificial Intelligence Studies (IDSIA)
Galleria 1, 6928 Manno-Lugano, Switzerland
alan@idsia.ch

ABSTRACT

This paper analytically identifies the points chosen by the best black-box optimization methods, measured by assigning values to the history of points examined by stochastic optimization methods applied to randomly chosen but static (single) objective functions. Optimizers that make these "best" choices are called *model-optimal*. Model-optimal optimizers may not exist for a given model of static objectives but can always be approximated. If the search domain and the fitness range are both compact, or if other more abstract conditions are satisfied, it can be proven that model-optimal optimizers exist and at least one of them is deterministic. Model-optimality is studied by treating the average performance as a Bellman equation. The overall performance of an optimizer can be assessed based on the sequence of points selected for evaluation. Each choice introduces an error, and the overall performance is in every case just the sum of these errors. It might be possible to extend these results to certain stochastic or dynamic objectives, but they probably do not apply in adaptive or coevolutionary environments. The properties of model-optimality may make it possible to assess the tightness of existing bounds on average performance, and it may be possible to approximate model-optimal optimization decisions directly.

Categories and Subject Descriptors

H.4 [**Information Systems Applications**]: Miscellaneous; D.2.8 [**Software Engineering**]: Metrics—*complexity measures, performance measures*

General Terms

Theory

Keywords

model-optimal optimization, evolutionary computation, theory of optimization

GECCO'14, July 12–16, 2014, Vancouver, BC, Canada.
Copyright 2014 ACM 978-1-4503-2662-9/14/07 ...$15.00.
http://dx.doi.org/10.1145/2576768.2598306.

1. INTRODUCTION

Given a model of objective functions and a criterion to measure the performance of an optimization method, the choices made by the "best" black-box optimization methods can be stated explicitly. Performance here is determined by a function that assigns finite value to the sequence of trials generated by the method for each objective function, and the best optimization in this context is the one with the best average performance when averaged over static single objective functions sampled from a stochastic fitness model. The best optimizers for a given model are termed *model-optimal*. This paper develops the concept of model-optimality within a measure-theoretic framework by applying techniques for analyzing Bellman equations in dynamic programming. The claim applies to all bounded performance criteria and all optimization methods that have oracle access to a fixed set of information about objective evaluations, including both black-box methods and gradient-based methods. These model-optimal optimization methods may not be computable but can be approximated through sampling or by analytic expansion. Furthermore, the analytic methods of this paper may be used to establish tight lower bounds on possible performance.

The result is derived within a measure-theoretic framework for analyzing the performance of optimization methods including evolutionary algorithms [15, 14]. The optimizers considered here are roughly equivalent to Vose's *randomized search heuristics* [24, 25]. The framework also bears some similarity to the approaches used in the literature on No Free Lunch [19, 26, 2, 21, 11]. In particular, Auger and Teytaud introduced the idea of a *random fitness* similar to the concept of random objectives introduced in Section 3.1. As an aside, the No Free Lunch property can be identified as the case where all optimizers are model-optimal [16].

Section 2 introduces the concept of one-step and long-running optimizers as vector spaces. Section 3 adds the concept of random objectives and the performance duality. Model-optimal optimizers are defined in Section 4, and the implications and related results are discussed in Section 5.

2. OPTIMIZER SPACE

Any iterative optimization method works by proposing a sequence of points in the search domain with the intent of discovering the global optimum. Such a method consists of three parts: 1) a method for selecting the initial point, 2) a method for choosing the next point given the history of previously selected points, and 3) a stopping criterion. In this work, we refer to the method in points (1) and (2) together as an *optimizer*, and consider the stopping criterion as a potentially random index into the sequence generated by the optimizer. A *stochastic optimizer* is an optimizer for which the means of choosing initial and subsequent points is randomized. This randomness is modeled here using standard probability theory as developed by Kolmogorov [12], and the stochastic optimizers are embedded into a space of generalized optimizers that will enable a theoretical treatment.

2.1 Basic Notation

The domain of optimization (Ω, τ) is a Hausdorff topological space. Optimization is performed with respect to an objective function (i.e. cost function, fitness function) that maps values in Ω to some topological space (Y, τ_y). The space of all objective functions is Y^Ω. Potential optima are sampled from finite measures on the measurable space (Ω, Σ), where Σ is the Borel σ-algebra with respect to τ. The space of all finite signed measures μ on (Ω, Σ) is $ca(\Sigma)$. It is a Banach space (a complete normed vector space) under pointwise addition and multiplication with the total variation norm. A probability measure is a nonnegative measure $\mathbb{P}$ such that $\mathbb{P}(\Omega) = 1$. The set of probability measures will be denoted by $\mathcal{P}(\Sigma)$. Integrating a random variable over a probability measure is called taking the expectation, denoted by $\mathbb{E}[X] = \int_\Omega X(\omega) d\mathbb{P}(\omega)$. In some cases below, the notation $\mathbb{E}[X]$ will also be used to mean integration with respect to a finite signed measure for brevity. A basic knowledge of topology, measure theory, probability theory, and Lebesgue integration is assumed here. Details are available in the literature [17, 9, 4, 5].

Optimization histories are represented by the space of finite sequences on Ω, denoted by $\mathcal{T}_\Omega = \bigcup_{n=1}^\infty \Omega^n$. For $t \in \mathcal{T}_\Omega$, the length $|t|$ is defined as the smallest k such that $t \in \Omega^k$. The zero-length history is denoted by $\emptyset$. The fact that $\omega \in \Omega$ appears as some component of t will be written as $\omega \in t$. A history $t = (\omega_1, \ldots, \omega_n)$ may be extended by a point $\omega \in \Omega$. This extension will be written as $t \cup \omega = (\omega_1, \ldots, \omega_n, \omega)$. The space of finite sequences for sets other than Ω (e.g., $\mathcal{T}_\mathbb{N}$, $\mathcal{T}_{[0,\infty)}$) will also be used as a source for multiindices and coordinate sets.

Sequences are denoted here by parentheses, so that (ω_n) is a sequence, either finite or infinite. The set to which a sequence belongs is shown by writing $(\omega_n) \subseteq \Omega$. The restriction of a sequence (ω_n) to a sequence of consecutive elements will be abbreviated as $\omega_a^b = (\omega_n)_{n=a}^b$.

2.2 Generalized Optimizers

A *generalized optimizer* is defined as a function $\mathcal{O} : \mathcal{T}_\Omega \times Y^\Omega \to ca(\Sigma)$ [15]. Given a history $t \in \mathcal{T}_\Omega$ of points in the search domain and an objective function u, $\mathcal{O}(t, u) = \mu$ is a finite, signed measure that is sampled to produce a candidate optimum $\omega \in \Omega$. A generalized optimizer $\mathcal{O}$ will be called measurable if for all $u \in Y^\Omega$, all $t \in \mathcal{T}_\Omega$, and all Borel measurable subsets $A \subseteq \Omega^{|t|}$, the function $h_{u,A}(t) = \mathcal{O}(t, u)(A)$ is a Borel measurable function from $\Omega^{|t|}$ to the reals. A norm for optimizers is given by $||\mathcal{O}|| = \sup_{t,u} ||\mathcal{O}(t, u)||$. The set $\mathcal{MF}_\Omega$ consisting of all measurable generalized optimizers with finite norm is a Banach space on which several useful operators can be defined [15].

The set of probability-valued optimizers is given by

$$\mathcal{PF}_\Omega = \{\mathcal{O} \in \mathcal{MF}_\Omega : \mathcal{O}(t, f) \in \mathcal{P}(\Sigma) \text{ for all } t, f\}. \quad (1)$$

The set $\mathcal{PF}_\Omega$ represents the iterative stochastic optimizers in their broadest sense. Given a history t of candidate optima and an objective function u, an element $\mathcal{O} \in \mathcal{PF}$ provides a probability measure $\mathcal{O}(t, f)$ used to select the next candidate optimum. The first point $\omega_1 \in \Omega$ in an iterative optimization sequence is sampled from $\mathcal{O}(\emptyset, u)$, the second point $\omega_2 \in \Omega$ from $\mathcal{O}((\omega_1), u)$, the nth point from $\mathcal{O}((\omega_1, \ldots, \omega_{n-1}), u)$, and so on, generating an infinite sequence $(\omega_n)_{n \in \mathbb{N}}$. The stochastic process thus generated is studied in Section 2.4.

2.3 Optimizer Subspaces

The set $\mathcal{PF}_\Omega$ is too broad, and contains optimizers that can examine the entire function all at once. Thus it is necessary to restrict the class of optimizers. Given a function $I : \Omega \times Y^\Omega \to \mathcal{T}_Y$, an optimizer $\mathcal{O} \in \mathcal{MF}_\Omega$ will be said to have the *I-black-box* property if $\mathcal{O}(t, f) = \mathcal{O}(t, g)$ whenever $I(\omega, f) = I(\omega, g)$ for all $\omega \in t$. The function I is termed an *information function* for $\mathcal{O}$, since it defines the information that is used by $\mathcal{O}$ to choose the next point. The usual meaning of a black-box optimizer is recovered by setting $I(\omega, f) = (f(\omega))$. Other information functions yield distinct vector subspaces of $\mathcal{MF}_\Omega$. Gradient descent has the I-black-box property for the information function $I(\omega, f) = (f'(\omega))$. For a given I, the set of I-black-box optimizers $\mathcal{BB}_\Omega^I$ is a proper vector subspace of $\mathcal{MF}_\Omega$, and $\mathcal{BB}_\Omega^I \cap \mathcal{PF}_\Omega$ contains the stochastic optimizers in this subspace. Optimizers with the standard black-box property have previously been termed *trajectory-restricted* [15]. These subsets form the main focus of inquiry in this paper; the best possible optimizer for an evaluation in this space will be demonstrated in Section 4.

2.4 The Optimization Process

When an optimizer in $\mathcal{PF}_\Omega$ is run on a specific objective function as described at the end of Section 2.2, it generates a sequence $(\omega_n)_{n \in \mathbb{N}}$. This sequence can be described as a sample from a stochastic process, which will be termed the *optimization process*, to be written as $Z = (Z_n)_{n \in \mathbb{N}} \subseteq \Omega$.

A measure for Z can be constructed for each $u \in Y^\Omega$ using the Kolmogorov Extension Theorem, provided that the generalized optimizer has consistent full measure along each path [12, 27]; the extension is valid in particular for all of $\mathcal{PF}_\Omega$. The resulting σ-algebra on $\Omega^\mathbb{N}$ will be denoted as $\Sigma^\mathbb{N}$. Due to some issues with the construction, it is possible that $\Sigma^\mathbb{N}$ may not contain the singletons. The existence proof for a model-optimal optimizer as presented here depends on the availability of the singletons. Any of the following conditions are sufficient to make singletons $\Sigma^\mathbb{N}$-measurable (possibly after unique extension to a regular Borel-measure): 1) Ω is a metric space; 2) Ω is compact; 3) Ω is finite; 4) Ω is discrete; and 5) Ω is first-countable. These conditions are satisfied for the vast majority of spaces studied in evolutionary computation. Details on the construction of the measure for Z are given elsewhere [14].

A *long-running optimizer* $\mathcal{O}$ is a function on the space of objectives that takes values in the space of finite signed measures on $(\Omega^\mathbb{N}, \Sigma^\mathbb{N})$; that is, $\mathcal{O} : Y^\Omega \to ca(\Sigma^\mathbb{N})$. Each one-step optimizer corresponds to a long-running optimizer through its optimization process, as described in the last paragraph. The long-running optimizers also form a Banach space; this space will be denoted as $\mathcal{MF}_\Omega^\infty$. The vector operations of $\mathcal{MF}_\Omega$ and $\mathcal{MF}_\Omega^\infty$ are not consistent with each other, and so concepts such as linearity do not transfer between the spaces [15]. The subset of $\mathcal{MF}_\Omega$ consisting of long-running optimizers that produce probability distributions in $\mathcal{P}(\Sigma^\infty)$ for each objective function is denoted $\mathcal{PF}_\Omega^\infty$.

Long-running optimizers can be generated by extending one-step optimizers. It is also possible to reduce a long-running optimizer $\mathcal{O} \in \mathcal{MF}_\Omega^\infty$ to a one-step optimizer $\mathcal{O}_0 \in \mathcal{MF}_\Omega$. The reduced optimizer is unique only up to a set of zero measure in $\mathcal{O}$. So two elements of $\mathcal{MF}_\Omega$ that extend to the same long-running optimizer can differ on a set of histories that have measure zero under their long-running extension. In this paper, an element $\mathcal{O} \in \mathcal{MF}_\Omega$ will be treated as though it were simultaneously in $\mathcal{MF}_\Omega^\infty$. This identification should not cause confusion for the purposes of the present paper.

The process $Z = Z^{\mathcal{O},u}$ represents the infinite sequence of points proposed as candidate optima by an optimization method $\mathcal{O}$ in response to an objective function u. A stochastic optimizer may be thought of as a set of probability distributions over infinite sequences indexed by the objectives.

2.5 Extensions of One-Step Optimizers

Due to non-uniqueness, there are some issues with extending the subsets of $\mathcal{MF}_\Omega$ into $\mathcal{MF}_\Omega^\infty$. These issues have been discussed previously [14]; a brief explanation follows.

For the purposes of this paper, it will suffice that $\mathcal{BB}_\Omega^I \cap \mathcal{PF}_\Omega$ extends to a closed convex subset $\mathcal{BB}_\Omega^{I,\infty} \cap \mathcal{PF}_\Omega^\infty$ of $\mathcal{MF}_\Omega^\infty$, so that the results on the long-running optimizers can be transferred to the one-step optimizers. It is easy to see that every element in $\mathcal{PF}_\Omega^\infty$ can be constructed by extending an element of $\mathcal{PF}_\Omega$. However, it is possible to extend a one-step optimizer not in $\mathcal{PF}_\Omega$ to a long-running optimizer in $\mathcal{PF}_\Omega^\infty$. In this case, the one-step optimizer outside $\mathcal{PF}_\Omega$ disagrees with another optimizer inside $\mathcal{PF}_\Omega$ only on histories of measure zero in the extension.

Optimizers that differ from each other on histories that have measure zero in their extensions will be termed *equivalent*. By identifying equivalent optimizers with each other, one can obtain a bijection between the long-running and the one-step optimizers. The set of one-step optimizers in $\mathcal{MF}_\Omega$ that are equivalent to some optimizer in $\mathcal{BB}_\Omega^I$ is a vector subspace of $\mathcal{MF}_\Omega$ that extends to a vector subspace $\mathcal{BB}_\Omega^{I,\infty} \subseteq \mathcal{MF}_\Omega^\infty$. These facts justify conflating the long-running optimizers and the one-step versions together below.

3. MEASURING PERFORMANCE

The performance of an optimization method is most often measured based on an array of benchmark problems. This section defines *objective measures* to encapsulate the notion of a benchmark or problem class, and these are used to assess optimizer performance in an intuitive manner.

3.1 Objective Measures & Random Objectives

A class of optimization problems can be represented as a subset of the objective space, Y^Ω. To measure optimization performance, however, members of the class must be selected for testing somehow. By recasting Y^Ω as a measurable space, a probability measure on Y^Ω is used to select test problems.

A suitable measurable space can be found for many choices of Y and Ω. If Y is itself a measurable space together with a σ-algebra Σ_Y, the Kolmogorov Extension Theorem can be used as in Section 2.4 to construct such a σ-algebra. However, this σ-algebra may not contain the singletons, an important fact below. The singletons can be made Σ_Ω-measurable when Y is compact (e.g., if Y is the hypercube $[-M, M]^n$ for some nonnegative integer n and M finite), which covers single- and multi-objective problems.

From this point on, assume that (Y, Σ_Y) and $(Y^\Omega, \Sigma_\Omega)$ are both measurable spaces for some compatible σ-algebras Σ_Y and Σ_Ω. Then an *objective measure* is a finite signed measure on $(Y^\Omega, \Sigma_\Omega)$, that is, an element of $ca(\Sigma_\Omega)$. Such objective measures may be constructed in various ways, for example as a random combination over a finite set of objective functions, or through the definition of a consistent family of finite dimensional distributions for more general cases. When needed, F will denote a *random objective* whose distribution is given by an objective measure μ.

An underlying measure space sufficient to support both F and Z is needed. The product σ-algebra $\Sigma^\mathbb{N} \otimes \Sigma_\Omega$ makes $\Omega^\mathbb{N} \times Y^\Omega$ into a measurable space. Using the indicator function χ_A, a finite signed measure $\nu_{\mu,\mathcal{O}}$ on this space is given by

$$\nu_{\mu,\mathcal{O}}(A) = \int_{Y^\Omega} \int_{\Omega^\mathbb{N}} \chi_A((z,u))\, d\mathcal{O}(u)(z)\, d\mu(u) \tag{2}$$

for $A \in \Sigma^\mathbb{N} \otimes \Sigma_\Omega$, where μ is the objective measure for F. This measure is sufficient to support the pair (Z, F) and is used extensively below. This notation may be shortened to

$$\nu_{F,\mathcal{O}}((Z,F) \in A) = \mathbb{E}_{\nu_{F,\mathcal{O}}}[\chi_A((Z,F))], \tag{3}$$

where the set notation is abbreviated, the underlying variables z and u are implicit, and the subscript indicates the measure for the expectation, recalling that the operator $\mathbb{E}[\cdot]$ has been extended to finite signed measures.

As defined here, a random objective takes on values as a static objective function. At present, dynamic or stochastic objective functions are not considered. It is important to recognize that $F(\omega)$ does not change once it is sampled. The set of objective measures that are probabilities is $\mathcal{P}(\Sigma_\Omega)$.

3.2 Performance On a Random Objective

Random objectives were introduced as a tool for measuring performance. To this end, let $V(Z, F)$ be a random variable on the measure space $(\Omega^\mathbb{N} \times Y^\Omega, \Sigma^\mathbb{N} \otimes \Sigma_\Omega, \nu_{\mu,\mathcal{O}})$ for some random objective F corresponding to μ and some long-running optimizer $\mathcal{O} \in \mathcal{MF}_\Omega^\infty$. Then we say that the the expected value $\mathbb{E}_{\nu_{\mu,\mathcal{O}}}[V(Z,F)]$ is the *V-performance* of $\mathcal{O}$ on F. The function V will be called the *value function*, since it assigns a value to each of the histories in $\Omega^\mathbb{N}$.

If the random objective F is degenerate, i.e. $F = u$ on some set of full measure, then we may write $\phi_V(\mathcal{O}, u) = \mathbb{E}_{\mathcal{O}(u)}[V(Z,u)]$. This functional has been called a *performance criterion* [14]. As a functional on $\mathcal{MF}_\Omega$, a performance criterion is nonlinear in both arguments.

With random objectives, the V-performance is written

$$\langle \mathcal{O}, \mu \rangle_V = \mathbb{E}_{\nu_{\mu,\mathcal{O}}}[V(Z,F)], \tag{4}$$

where F is the random objective obtained by the identity function on the objective measure μ. This notation is chosen to reflect the fact that as a function from $\mathcal{MF}_\Omega^\infty \times ca(\Sigma_\Omega)$ to the reals, the V-performance is a bilinear form. Bilinearity comes from the properties of the integral in Equation 2.

Writing $\ell_{\mu,V}(\mathcal{O}) = \ell_{\mathcal{O},V}(\mu) = \langle \mathcal{O}, \mu \rangle_V$, it can be seen that $\ell_{\mu,V}$ and $\ell_{\mathcal{O},V}$ are linear functionals on $\mathcal{MF}_\Omega^\infty$ and $ca(\Sigma_\Omega)$, respectively. By a property of operator theory, a linear functional is continuous if and only if it is bounded. We are interested in the conditions when it is continuous, since in this case we will be able to prove that its extremal values are attained. The following theorem about continuity with respect to long-running optimizers can be stated quickly.

Theorem 3.1. *If V is bounded, then $\langle \mathcal{O}, \mu \rangle_V$ is bounded and continuous in both arguments.*

PROOF. We have $|V| < M < \infty$ for some M, and so $|\langle \mathcal{O}, \mu \rangle_V| < M \,||\mathcal{O}||\, ||\mu|| < \infty$; that is, $\langle \mathcal{O}, \mu \rangle_V$ is bounded and continuous.

It is not clear when the converse of Theorem 3.1 holds. If V is not bounded, it $\mathcal{O}$ and μ can be constructed so that $\langle \mathcal{O}, \mu \rangle_V$ can be made arbitrarily large. However, when one argument or the other is fixed, it may not be possible to do so. Unbounded value functions may produce continuous linear functionals in one argument or the other.

Some value functions used in practice are not bounded. The expected runtime, $V = \inf\{n : F(Z_n) < \epsilon\}$, is usually studied in the theory of evolutionary computation, and it is infinite for many algorithms and benchmarks. For practical uses, the expected runtime can be truncated by adding a cutoff time of arbitrary finite size. However, the expected runtime may fail to be continuous in general.

The expected final error is an example of a bounded value function; it is given by $V = ||F(Z_T^*) - F^*||_Y$ for a stopping time T and a global optimum F^*, where $F(Z_T^*) = \min_{n \leq T} F(Z_n)$. It is bounded if and only if Y is bounded.

The V-performance is a continuous linear functional if V is bounded. It can then be proven in this case that the optimal V-performance over $\mathcal{BB}_\Omega^I \cap \mathcal{PF}_\Omega$ is attained on some deterministic optimizer, which is summarized next.

3.3 Deterministic Optimizers Perform Best

All stochastic optimizers are outperformed or at least equaled by one or more deterministic optimizers subject to certain conditions. A brief sketch of the proof follows.

A one-step optimizer $\mathcal{O} \in \mathcal{PF}_\Omega$ is a *deterministic one-step optimizer* if there is a function $d : \mathcal{T}_\Omega \times Y^\Omega \to \Omega$ such that for all $t \in \mathcal{T}_\Omega$ and $f \in Y^\Omega$, $\mathcal{O}(t, f)(\{d(t, f)\}) = 1$. The set of such optimizers is denoted $\mathcal{DF}_\Omega$.

A set $\mathcal{DF}_\Omega^\infty$ of *deterministic long-running optimizers* can be defined similarly for an element $\mathcal{O}$ of $\mathcal{PF}_\Omega^\infty$ if there exists $d : Y^\Omega \to \Omega^\mathbb{N}$ such that for all $f \in Y^\Omega$, $\mathcal{O}(f)(\{d(f)\}) = 1$. By implication, $\mathcal{O}(f)(A) = 0$ for any set A that does not contain $d(f)$. Deterministic long-running optimizers can only be well-defined in $\mathcal{PF}_\Omega^\infty$ if $\Sigma^\mathbb{N}$ contains the singletons, as discussed in Section 2.4. When both sets of deterministic optimizers are defined, they are equivalent.

The deterministic optimizers are the extreme points of $\mathcal{PF}_\Omega$. That is, they are not contained in the interior of any line whose end points are in $\mathcal{PF}_\Omega$. The Krein-Milman theorem asserts that any convex compact set is generated by its extreme points. When $\Sigma^\mathbb{N}$ and Σ_Ω contain the singletons, the set $\mathcal{PF}_\Omega^\infty$ can be proven compact by showing that $\mathcal{MF}_\Omega^\infty$ and $ca(\Sigma_\Omega)$ are vector subspaces of each other's topological dual and applying Alaoglu's Theorem. Any convex continuous functional attains its extreme values on the extreme points of a convex set [1]. The following theorem is a consequence.

Theorem 3.2. *Suppose $\Sigma^\mathbb{N}$ and Σ_Ω contain the singletons, and let $\ell : \mathcal{MF}_\Omega^\infty \to \mathbb{R}$ be any continuous convex functional. Then ℓ attains its extreme values over $\mathcal{PF}_\Omega^\infty$ on $\mathcal{DF}_\Omega^\infty$.*

The theorem also applies to vector subspaces of $\mathcal{MF}_\Omega^\infty$ and is true of $\mathcal{BB}_\Omega^{I,\infty} \cap \mathcal{PF}_\Omega^\infty$ as well. Thus the V-performance has optimal performance that is attained by at least one deterministic I-black-box optimizer. The nature of such an optimizer is studied next.

4. MODEL-OPTIMAL OPTIMIZATION

Given a positive objective measure $\mu \in ca(\Sigma_\Omega)$ that models the evaluation environment and a value function V that codifies desirable characteristics of an algorithm, it is possible to identify exactly an optimization method that attains the optimal result with respect to the model on the value function so long as the value function is bounded and the singletons are measurable (see Section 2.4). The definition of this model-optimal optimization method is non-constructive and depends explicitly on the Axiom of Choice. This method is derived by treating optimization as a decision process with the V-performance as a Hamilton-Jacobi-Bellman equation. Model-optimal optimizers are obtained using standard techniques from dynamic programming [3].

4.1 Preliminaries

Throughout what follows, the value function V will need to be bounded. An objective measure μ is used as a source of objectives for evaluation; some theorems will require it to be non-negative. The class of optimizers under consideration is $\mathcal{BB}_\Omega^I$, where I is an information function that produces a fixed amount of information, $I : \Omega \times Y^\Omega \to Y^M$.

As above, $Z = (Z_n)_{n \in \mathbb{N}}$ is the optimization process for an I-black-box optimizer $\mathcal{O}$ on a function $u \in Y^\Omega$. This process is given its natural filtration $(\mathcal{Z}_n)$, $\mathcal{Z}_n \subseteq \Sigma^\mathbb{N}$. In addition to the optimization process, consider the information process (I_n) given by $I_n = I(Z_n, F)$ for an objective measure μ and its random objective F. Let $\mathcal{I}_n$ be the natural filtration of this process. Then the product σ-algebras $\mathcal{Z}_n \otimes \mathcal{I}_n$ and $\mathcal{Z}_n \otimes \mathcal{I}_{n-1}$ may be considered as sub-σ-algebras of $\Sigma^\mathbb{N} \otimes \Sigma_\Omega$. Therefore the conditional expectation

$$\mathbb{E}_{\nu_{\mu,\mathcal{O}}} \left[V \mid \mathcal{Z}_n \otimes \mathcal{I}_{n-1} \right] \tag{5}$$

is well-defined for $n > 1$, and it is a random variable on $\Omega^n \times Y^{M(n-1)}$. This notation can be extended to $n = 1$ by defining $\mathcal{Z}_0$ and $\mathcal{I}_0$ so that each one is just the trivial σ-algebra. In somewhat non-standard notation, we may write for $(t, y) \in \Omega^n \times Y^{M(n-1)}$,

$$\mathbb{E}_{\nu_{\mu,\mathcal{O}}} \left[V \mid \mathcal{Z}_n \otimes \mathcal{I}_{n-1} \right] (t, y). \tag{6}$$

The more standard notation is cumbersome and unclear,

$$\mathbb{E}_{\nu_{\mu,\mathcal{O}}} \left[V \mid (Z_k)_{k=1}^n = t, (I_k)_{k=1}^{n-1} = y \right], \tag{7}$$

mainly because the arguments t and y are sequences.

When optimizers have the I-black-box property, the inputs of $\mathcal{O}$ can be adjusted so that $\mathcal{O} : \mathcal{T}_{\Omega \times Y^M} \to ca(\Sigma)$. That is, $\mathcal{O}(t, y)$ for $(t, y) \in \mathcal{T}_{\Omega \times Y^M}$ is equivalent to $\mathcal{O}(t, u)$ for $(t, u) \in \mathcal{T}_\Omega \times Y^\Omega$ when $I(t_k, u) = y_k$ for all $k \leq |t|$.

The V-performance is progressively decomposable into

$$\langle \mathcal{O}, \mu \rangle_V = \sum_{k=1}^{\infty} \langle \mathcal{O}, \mu \rangle_{V_k}, \tag{8}$$

where the (V_k) are defined by $V_1 = \mathbb{E}_{\nu_{\mu,\mathcal{O}}} \left[V \mid \mathcal{Z}_1 \otimes \mathcal{I}_0 \right]$ and $V_{k+1} = \mathbb{E}_{\nu_{\mu,\mathcal{O}}} \left[V \mid \mathcal{Z}_{k+1} \otimes \mathcal{I}_k \right] - V_k$. The decomposition is progressive because each V_k only depends on the optimization process up to the kth time step and on the information process up to the $(k-1)^{th}$ time step. Thus for $t \in \Omega^k$ and $y \in Y^{k-1}$, $V_k = V_k(t,y)$, and V_k is $\mathcal{Z}_k \otimes \mathcal{I}_{k-1}$-measurable. To explain, V_1 is the expected V-performance given the initial search point, and V_{k+1} is the gain or loss in performance obtained by observing I_n and choosing Z_{n+1}. The progressive decomposition tracks the performance of the optimizer step by step, shown next.

4.2 Optimal Completion

To represent the best possible performance at any time step, for $(t,y) \in \mathcal{T}_{\Omega \times Y^M}$, define the optimal completion by

$$\hat{V}_\mu(t,y) = \inf_{\mathcal{O}} \sum_{k=|t|+1}^{\infty} \mathbb{E}_{\nu_{\mu,\mathcal{O}}}\left[V_k \mid \mathcal{Z}_n \otimes \mathcal{I}_n\right](t,y), \quad (9)$$

where the infimum is taken over $\mathcal{BB}^I_\Omega \cap \mathcal{PF}_\Omega$. This formulation assumes that low values of V are better; otherwise the supremum may be used. If $|t| = 0$ then set $y = \emptyset$, so that $\hat{V}_\mu(\emptyset,\emptyset) = \inf_{\mathcal{O}} \langle \mathcal{O}, \mu \rangle_V$. Thus $\hat{V}_\mu(\emptyset,\emptyset)$ is the optimal V-performance on μ over all I-black-box stochastic optimizers, and $\hat{V}_\mu(t,y)$ is the best performance possible once t and y have been observed. A series of theorems will now show that the optimal completion may be computed step by step. Consequently, the best choices for an optimization method may be determined one step at a time.

Theorem 4.1. *Suppose V is bounded or strictly positive. For any $\mathcal{O} \in \mathcal{BB}^I_\Omega \cap \mathcal{PF}_\Omega$, $N > 0$, and $(t,y) \in \mathcal{T}_{\Omega \times Y^M}$,*

$$\hat{V}_\mu(t,y) \le \sum_{k=|t|+1}^{|t|+N} \mathbb{E}_{\nu_{\mu,\mathcal{O}}}\left[V_k \mid \mathcal{Z}_{|t|} \otimes \mathcal{I}_{|y|}\right](t,y) + \mathbb{E}_{\nu_{\mu,\mathcal{O}}}\left[\hat{V}_\mu\left(Z_1^{|t|+N}, I_1^{|y|+N}\right) \middle| \mathcal{Z}_{|t|} \otimes \mathcal{I}_{|y|}\right](t,y). \quad (10)$$

Proof. Fix (t,y). For each $(r,w) \in \mathcal{T}_\Omega \times \mathcal{T}_{Y^M}$ with $|r| = |w| + 1 = N$, choose $\mathcal{O}^\delta_{r,w}$ so that

$$\hat{V}_\mu(t \cup r, y \cup w) + \delta > \sum_{k=|t|+|r|+1}^{\infty} \mathbb{E}_{\nu_{\mu,\mathcal{O}^\delta_{r,w}}}\left[V_k \mid \mathcal{Z}_{|t|} \otimes \mathcal{I}_{|y|}\right](t \cup r, y \cup w), \quad (11)$$

where $\cup$ represents sequence concatenation. For any $\mathcal{O}$, define $\tilde{\mathcal{O}}$ so that

$$\tilde{\mathcal{O}}(s,\ell) = \begin{cases} \mathcal{O}(s,\ell) & \text{if } |s| < |t| + N \\ \mathcal{O}^\delta_{r,w}(s,\ell) & \text{if } s << t \cup r \text{ and } \ell << y \cup w, \end{cases} \quad (12)$$

where $s << s'$ for sequences means that s is a prefix of s'. Note that $\tilde{\mathcal{O}}$ is trivially in $\mathcal{BB}^I_\Omega \cap \mathcal{PF}_\Omega$. Now then,

$$\begin{aligned} \hat{V}_\mu(t,y) &\le \sum_{k=|t|+1}^{\infty} \mathbb{E}_{\nu_{\mu,\tilde{\mathcal{O}}}}\left[V_k \mid \mathcal{Z}_{|t|} \otimes \mathcal{I}_{|y|}\right](t,y) \\ &= \sum_{k=|t|+1}^{|t|+N} \mathbb{E}_{\nu_{\mu,\tilde{\mathcal{O}}}}\left[V_k \mid \mathcal{Z}_{|t|} \otimes \mathcal{I}_{|y|}\right](t,y) \\ &\quad + \sum_{k=|t|+N+1}^{\infty} \mathbb{E}_{\nu_{\mu,\tilde{\mathcal{O}}}}\left[V_k \mid \mathcal{Z}_{|t|} \otimes \mathcal{I}_{|y|}\right](t,y). \end{aligned} \quad (13)$$

Using the properties of conditional expectation,

$$\mathbb{E}_{\nu_{\mu,\tilde{\mathcal{O}}}}\left[V_k \mid \mathcal{Z}_{|t|} \otimes \mathcal{I}_{|y|}\right] = \mathbb{E}_{\nu_{\mu,\tilde{\mathcal{O}}}}\left[\mathbb{E}_{\nu_{\mu,\tilde{\mathcal{O}}}}\left[V_k \mid \mathcal{Z}_{|t|+N} \otimes \mathcal{I}_{|y|+N}\right] \mid \mathcal{Z}_{|t|} \otimes \mathcal{I}_{|y|}\right]. \quad (14)$$

Summing on both sides, pushing the sum inside the expectation (as we may since V is positive or bounded), and applying Equation 11,

$$\sum_{k=|t|+N+1}^{\infty} \mathbb{E}_{\nu_{\mu,\tilde{\mathcal{O}}}}\left[V_k \mid \mathcal{Z}_{|t|} \otimes \mathcal{I}_{|y|}\right](t,y) < \delta + \mathbb{E}_{\nu_{\mu,\tilde{\mathcal{O}}}}\left[\hat{V}_\mu(Z_1^{|t|+N}, I_1^{yt|+N}) \mid \mathcal{Z}_{|t|} \otimes \mathcal{I}_{|y|}\right](t,y). \quad (15)$$

Plugging this back into Equation 13 and letting δ go to zero proves the theorem for $\tilde{\mathcal{O}}$. The proof is completed by observing that $\mathcal{O}$ can be replaced by $\tilde{\mathcal{O}}$ in Equation 10 without change, since it only depends on events in the σ-algebra $\mathcal{Z}_{|t|+N} \otimes \mathcal{I}_{|y|+N}$, which have identical measure under $\mathcal{O}$ and $\tilde{\mathcal{O}}$ by construction.

Theorem 4.2. *Suppose V is bounded or strictly positive. For any $\mu \in ca(\Sigma_\Omega)$, any $N > 0$, and any $(t,y) \in \mathcal{T}_{\Omega \times Y^M}$,*

$$\hat{V}_\mu(t,y) = \inf_{\mathcal{O}} \left\{ \sum_{k=|t|+1}^{|t|+N} \mathbb{E}_{\nu_{\mu,\mathcal{O}}}\left[V_k \mid \mathcal{Z}_{|t|} \otimes \mathcal{I}_{|y|}\right](t,y) + \mathbb{E}_{\nu_{\mu,\mathcal{O}}}\left[\hat{V}_\mu\left(Z_1^{|t|+N}, I_1^{|y|+N}\right) \middle| \mathcal{Z}_{|t|} \otimes \mathcal{I}_{|y|}\right](t,y) \right\}, \quad (16)$$

where the infimum is taken over $\mathcal{BB}^I_\Omega \cup \mathcal{PF}_\Omega$.

Proof. The fact that the right-hand side is an upper bound is shown in Theorem 4.1. To see that it is also a lower bound, fix $\delta > 0$ and choose $\mathcal{O}^\delta$ so that

$$\hat{V}_\mu(t,y) + \delta > \sum_{k=|t|+1}^{\infty} \mathbb{E}_{\nu_{\mu,\mathcal{O}^\delta}}\left[V_k \mid \mathcal{Z}_{|t|} \otimes \mathcal{I}_{|y|}\right](t,y). \quad (17)$$

Split this sum at $k = |t| + N + 1$ as in Equation 13. As in Equation 14, we can expand the conditional expectation to contain two conditionals. We can also push the sum inside the expectation if V is either bounded (Fubini's Theorem) or positive (Tonelli's Theorem), so that

$$\begin{aligned} &\sum_{k=|t|+N+1}^{\infty} \mathbb{E}_{\nu_{\mu,\mathcal{O}^\delta}}\left[V_k \mid \mathcal{Z}_{|t|} \otimes \mathcal{I}_{|y|}\right](t,y) \\ &= \mathbb{E}_{\nu_{\mu,\mathcal{O}^\delta}}\left[\sum_{k=|t|+N+1}^{\infty} \mathbb{E}_{\nu_{\mu,\mathcal{O}^\delta}}\left[V_k \mid \mathcal{Z}_{|t|+N} \otimes \mathcal{I}_{|y|+N}\right] \middle| \mathcal{Z}_{|t|} \otimes \mathcal{I}_{|y|} \right](t,y) \\ &\ge \mathbb{E}_{\nu_{\mu,\mathcal{O}^\delta}}\left[\hat{V}_\mu(Z_{m=1}^{|t|+N}, I_{m=1}^{|y|+N}) \middle| \mathcal{Z}_{|t|} \otimes \mathcal{I}_{|y|}\right](t,y) \end{aligned} \quad (18)$$

by the definition of $\hat{V}_\mu$. Therefore,

$$\hat{V}_\mu(t,y) > \delta + \sum_{k=|t|+1}^{|t|+N} \mathbb{E}_{\nu_{\mu,\mathcal{O}^\delta}}\left[V_k \mid \mathcal{Z}_{|t|} \otimes \mathcal{I}_{|y|}\right](t,y) + \mathbb{E}_{\nu_{\mu,\mathcal{O}^\delta}}\left[\hat{V}_\mu\left(Z_1^{|t|+N}, I_1^{|y|+N}\right) \middle| \mathcal{Z}_{|t|} \otimes \mathcal{I}_{|y|}\right](t,y). \quad (19)$$

Letting δ become arbitrarily small proves the theorem.

Corollary 4.3. *For any $\mu \in ca(\Sigma_\Omega)$, any $(t, y) \in \mathcal{T}_{\Omega \times Y^M}$, and V bounded,*

$$\hat{V}_\mu(t,y) = \inf_{\alpha \in \mathcal{P}(\Sigma)} \left\{ \int_\Omega V_{|t|+1}(t \cup \omega, y)\, d\alpha(\omega) + \int_\Omega \int_{Y^\Omega} \hat{V}_\mu\left(t \cup \omega, y \cup I(\omega, u)\right)\, d\alpha(\omega)\, d\mu(u) \right\}. \quad (20)$$

PROOF. Letting $N = 1$ in Theorem 4.2 gives $\hat{V}_\mu(t, y) =$

$$\inf_{\mathcal{O}} \left\{ \mathbb{E}_{\nu_{\mu,\mathcal{O}}} \left[V_{|t|+1} + \hat{V}_\mu\left(Z_1^{|t|+1}, I_1^{|y|+1}\right) \middle| \mathcal{Z}_{|t|} \otimes \mathcal{I}_{|y|} \right] (t, y) \right\} \quad (21)$$

Equation 21 depends on exactly one step of a deterministic optimizer $\mathcal{O}$. For each $\mathcal{O}$, there is a probability measure $\alpha_\mathcal{O} \in \mathcal{P}(\Sigma)$ such that $Z_{|t|+1}$ is distributed according to $\alpha_\mathcal{O}$ given t, y, and this measure determines $V_{|t|+1}$ as well when t, y are given. The right term under the conditional expectation likewise depends only on $\alpha_\mathcal{O}$ and μ. Thus the conditional expectations can be dropped given $\alpha_\mathcal{O}$. Further, for every measure in $\alpha \in \mathcal{P}(\Sigma)$, there is some $\mathcal{O}$ with $\mathcal{O}(t, y) = \alpha$. So the infimum can be taken over $\mathcal{P}(\Sigma)$ rather than $\mathcal{BB}_\Omega^I \cap \mathcal{PF}_\Omega$. Applying these facts yields Equation 20.

These theorems have demonstrated that the value of optimal completion at each time step does not depend on the entire definition of an optimizer, but only on its definition at one step. Because the optimal completion is the best performance possible for each history, optimal decision-making can be achieved one step at a time, discussed next.

4.3 Model-Optimal Optimization

Corollary 4.3 provides a way of minimizing the optimal completion of the V-performance without reference to a particular optimizer. The terms under the infimum in Equation 20 can be used to derive ϵ-optimal optimizers. An I-black-box optimizer $\mathcal{O}$ is *ϵ-optimal* for $\epsilon > 0$ on an objective measure μ and a bounded value function V whenever

$$\langle \mathcal{O}, \mu \rangle_V - \inf_{\mathcal{O}'} \langle \mathcal{O}', \mu \rangle_V < \epsilon, \quad (22)$$

where the infimum is taken over $\mathcal{BB}_\Omega^I \cap \mathcal{PF}_\Omega$. This difference can be computed as the sum of stepwise errors. Define a function for the term under the infimum in Equation 20,

$$\hat{V}_\mu(\omega, t, y) = V_{|t|+1}(t \cup \omega, y) + \mathbb{E}_\mu\left[\hat{V}_\mu\left(t \cup \omega, y \cup I(\omega, F)\right)\right], \quad (23)$$

and define the one-step error gain by

$$\mathrm{err}_{\mu,V}(\omega, t, y) = \hat{V}_\mu(\omega, t, y) - \hat{V}_\mu(t, y). \quad (24)$$

Then we have the following theorem.

Theorem 4.4. *For bounded V, an optimizer $\mathcal{O} \in \mathcal{BB}_\Omega^I \cap \mathcal{PF}_\Omega$ has V-performance error equal to the sum of the expected one-step error gain,*

$$\langle \mathcal{O}, \mu \rangle_V - \inf_{\mathcal{O}'} \langle \mathcal{O}', \mu \rangle_V = \sum_{k=1}^{\infty} \mathbb{E}_{\nu_{\mu,\mathcal{O}}}\left[\mathrm{err}_{\mu,V}(Z_k, Z_1^{k-1}, I_1^{k-1})\right]. \quad (25)$$

PROOF. It will be shown by induction that

$$\hat{V}_\mu(\emptyset, \emptyset) = \sum_{k=1}^{\infty} \mathbb{E}_{\nu_{\mu,\mathcal{O}}}\left[V_k - \mathrm{err}_{\mu,V}(Z_1^{k-1}, I_1^{k-1})\right], \quad (26)$$

which is equivalent to Equation 25. For the base case, the definition of err and Theorem 4.2 imply that

$$\begin{aligned} \hat{V}_\mu(\emptyset, \emptyset) &= \mathbb{E}_{\nu_{\mu,\mathcal{O}}}\left[\hat{V}_\mu(Z_1, \emptyset, \emptyset) - \mathrm{err}_{\mu,V}(Z_1, \emptyset, \emptyset)\right] \\ &= \mathbb{E}_{\nu_{\mu,\mathcal{O}}}\left[V_1(Z_1, \emptyset) + \hat{V}_\mu(Z_1, I_1) - \mathrm{err}_{\mu,V}(Z_1, \emptyset, \emptyset)\right]. \end{aligned} \quad (27)$$

Now suppose for the inductive case that $\hat{V}_\mu(\emptyset, \emptyset) =$

$$\mathop{\mathbb{E}}_{\nu_{\mu,\mathcal{O}}}\left[\sum_{k=1}^{n}\left\{V_k(Z_1^k, I_1^{k-1}) - \mathrm{err}_{\mu,V}(Z_k, Z_1^{k-1} I_1^{k-1})\right\} + \hat{V}_\mu(Z_1^n, I_1^n)\right]. \quad (28)$$

Taking the expectation in $\nu_{\mu,\mathcal{O}}$ on both sides of Equation 24, expanding $\hat{V}_\mu(\omega, t, y)$ by the definition in Equation 23, and rearranging terms obtains that $\mathbb{E}_{\nu_{\mu,\mathcal{O}}}\left[\hat{V}_\mu(Z_1^n, I_1^n)\right] =$

$$\mathop{\mathbb{E}}_{\nu_{\mu,\mathcal{O}}}\left[V_{n+1}(Z_1^{n+1}, I_1^n) + \hat{V}_\mu(Z_1^{n+1} I_1^{n+1}) - \mathrm{err}_{\mu,V}(Z_{n+1}, Z_1^n, I_1^n)\right]. \quad (29)$$

Plugging Equation 29 into Equation 28 shows that Equation 29 holds with n replaced by $n+1$, and the induction is complete. Observing that $\lim_{m \to \infty} \mathbb{E}_{\nu_{\mu,\mathcal{O}}}\left[\hat{V}_\mu(Z_1^m, I_1^m)\right] = 0$ for V bounded, it follows that $\hat{V}_\mu(\emptyset, \emptyset) =$

$$\mathbb{E}_{\nu_{\mu,\mathcal{O}}}\left[\sum_{k=1}^{\infty}\left\{V_k(Z_1^k, I_1^{k-1}) - \mathrm{err}_{\mu,V}(Z_k Z_1^{k-1}, I_1^{k-1})\right\}\right], \quad (30)$$

which is equivalent to Equation 25, proving the theorem.

Since V is bounded, the sum of the errors in Equation 25 converges for all $\mathcal{O} \in \mathcal{BB}_\Omega^I \cap \mathcal{PF}_\Omega$ and $\mu \in \mathcal{P}(\Sigma_\Omega)$. Based on the result of Theorem 4.4, it is clear that a stochastic optimizer is only ϵ-optimal if the infinite sum of the one step error gain converges to something less than ϵ. For all $\eta > 0$, define a set $\mathcal{V}_\eta[t, y]$ of η-optimal choices for ω by

$$\mathcal{V}_\eta[t, y] = \{\omega \in \Omega : \mathrm{err}_{\mu,V}(\omega, t, y) < \eta\}, \quad (31)$$

and let $\overline{\mathcal{V}}_\eta[t, y]$ be defined in the same way with $\leq$ in place of $<$. In the context of the measure $\nu_{\mu,\mathcal{O}}$, we may write $\mathcal{V}_\eta$ and $\overline{\mathcal{V}}_\eta$ to mean $\mathcal{V}_\eta\left[Z_1^{n-1}, I_1^{n-1}\right]$ and $\mathcal{V}_\eta\left[Z_1^{n-1}, I_1^{n-1}\right]$, respectively, when n is clear from the context. The next corollary summarizes the nature of an ϵ-optimal optimizer in terms of the one-step error gain.

Corollary 4.5. *An I-black-box optimizer $\mathcal{O} \in \mathcal{BB}_\Omega^I \cap \mathcal{PF}_\Omega$ is ϵ-optimal on $\mu \in ca(\Sigma_\Omega)$ and bounded V if and only if the sequence (η_n) defined by*

$$\eta_n = \mathbb{E}_{\nu_{\mu,\mathcal{O}}}\left[\mathrm{err}_{\mu,V}(Z_n, Z_1^{n-1}, I_1^{n-1})\right] \quad (32)$$

has $\sum_n \eta_n < \epsilon$, and if $\mathcal{O} \in \mathcal{DF}_\Omega$ then $Z_n \in \overline{\mathcal{V}}_{\eta_n} \setminus \mathcal{V}_{\eta_n}$ almost surely.

PROOF. The corollary is a direct consequence of the definitions and Theorem 4.4.

The meaning of these results is that an ϵ-optimal optimizer distributes its errors at each step in a way that sums below ϵ. For deterministic optimizers, something stronger has been said; an ϵ-optimal deterministic optimizer must choose all points within the set $\overline{\mathcal{V}}_{\eta_n}[t, y]$ for some sequence (η_n) with $\sum_n \eta_n < \epsilon$, except possibly on some set of histories t that have $\nu_{\mu,\mathcal{O}}$-measure zero.

Suppose now that the error ϵ is reduced to zero. If an optimizer is ϵ-optimal for all $\epsilon > 0$, then it is said to be *model-optimal* on a measure μ and a value function V. If V is bounded, then $\langle \mathcal{O}, \mu \rangle_V$ is a continuous linear functional of $\mathcal{O}$, and its extremal values over $\mathcal{BB}^I_\Omega \cap \mathcal{PF}_\Omega$ are attained on the set of I-black-box deterministic optimizers by Theorem 3.2. Equivalently, the sets $\overline{\mathcal{V}}_0[t, y]$ are non-empty for t, y with positive $\nu_{\mu,\mathcal{O}}$-measure, and there exists at least one model-optimal optimizer. In the stochastic as well as the deterministic case, Equation 32 then implies that $Z_n \in \overline{\mathcal{V}}_0$ almost surely.

Theorem 4.6. *Suppose $\Sigma^{\mathbb{N}}$ and Σ_Ω contain the singletons. For any positive $\mu \in ca(\Sigma_\Omega)$ and bounded V, there exists at least one model-optimal I-black-box optimizer $\mathcal{O} \in \mathcal{BB}^I_\Omega \cap \mathcal{PF}_\Omega$. Further, $\mathcal{O}$ is model-optimal on μ and V if and only if $Z_n \in \overline{\mathcal{V}}_0$ almost surely.*

PROOF. The existence follows from the text above. Suppose that $\mathcal{O}$ is model-optimal and that V is strictly positive. By the definition of model optimality, $\eta_n < \epsilon$ for all $\epsilon > 0$. Since μ, $\mathcal{O}$, and V are all positive, it follows from Equation 32 that $\text{err}_{\mu,V}(Z_n, Z_1^{n-1}, I_1^{n-1}) = 0$ almost surely, that is, $Z_n \in \overline{\mathcal{V}}_0$. If V is not strictly positive, then there is another V' that adds a constant factor but has the same optima, so that the claim holds for all bounded V. Conversely, any optimizer with $Z_n \in \overline{\mathcal{V}}_0$ is obviously model-optimal.

Theorem 4.6 gives both the existence and the form of a model-optimal optimizer for bounded value functions. It relies directly on the Axiom of Choice in that a model-optimal optimizer must choose one ω from each set $\overline{\mathcal{V}}_0[t, y]$. To summarize, a model-optimal optimizer makes choices so that given a history t with information sequence y,

$$\omega_{\text{opt}} \in \arg\min_{\omega \in \Omega} \min_{\substack{z \in \Omega^{\mathbb{N}} \\ t \cup \omega << z}} \mathbb{E}_\mu\left[V(z, F) \mid \mathcal{Z}_{|t|+1} \otimes \mathcal{I}_{|y|}\right](t \cup \omega, y), \tag{33}$$

where $t \cup \omega$ is sequence concatenation and $t \cup \omega << z$ indicates that $t \cup \omega$ is a prefix of z, in which the choice of ω_{opt} is not necessarily unique. A more concise expression can be stated using the one-step error gain,

$$\omega_{\text{opt}} \in \arg\min_{\omega \in \Omega} \text{err}(\omega, t, y). \tag{34}$$

Choosing points according to Equations 33 or 34 guarantees that $Z_n \in \overline{\mathcal{V}}_0$ almost surely, and a sequence of such choices is therefore model-optimal.

5. DISCUSSION AND RELATED WORK

The model-optimal optimization methods have been given in Equation 33. Related concepts are now discussed, and the possibility of explicitly computing a model-optimal method is considered along with the general limitations.

5.1 Black-box Complexity

Droste, Jansen, and Wegener [7] introduced the *black-box complexity* of a class of objective functions on a class of optimizers as the least value obtained by some optimizer for the worst expected runtime on any problem. That is,

$$\mathcal{BBC}(\mathcal{A}, \mathcal{F}) = \inf_{\mathcal{O} \in \mathcal{A}} \sup_{u \in \mathcal{F}} \mathbb{E}_{\mathcal{O}(u)}\left[V(Z, u)\right]. \tag{35}$$

Several general results have been obtained in this framework [13, 6]. The present results may be useful for determining bounds on some problems.

5.2 AIXI and Optimal Decision-Making

Hutter [10] published a theory of *universal artificial intelligence* in which a reinforcement learner named AIXI chooses actions to maximize expected future rewards averaged according to a *universal prior*. For this purpose, it is assumed that the likelihood of a particular environment is inversely proportional to the length of the shortest program computing it [23]. AIXI seeks to avoid model bias by weighting future outcomes accordingly. The formulae that result are close to Equation 33. The AIXI model only applies to discrete settings. Issues of computability are rigorously accounted for, and the model is proven computable in the limit [10]. If the results in this paper are restricted to computability, the two results may be equivalent.

5.3 Knowledge Gradients

The *knowledge gradient* was studied by Frazier et al. and Powell and Ryzhov [8, 18]. A learner is presented with multiple information sources (e.g., the search domain of an optimization problem). The knowledge gradient is the marginal value of the information gained by measuring any particular source; it is similar to the one-step error gain from Equation 24. They show that a policy that maximizes the knowledge gradient is asymptotically optimal under certain conditions [8]. The knowledge gradient is used with a Gaussian process as an objective measure. Their objective functions are stochastic in contrast to the static objectives studied here. The experimental success of the knowledge gradient methods on problems with sparse information suggests that the theory in this paper is practically applicable.

5.4 Estimating Model-Optimal Choices

If a model of the objective measure μ is available, a sampling approach can be used to approximate Equation 33 for some value functions. If the value function is the sum of weighted errors, i.e., $V(z, u) = \sum_{n=1}^{\infty} w_n \left(u(z^*) - u^*\right)$ for convergent (w_n), future errors become practically irrelevant beyond a fixed time horizon. A forest of future paths could be sampled using μ to select the point with the best expected future performance. Roulet et al. have previously used a similar Monte Carlo method and observed faster convergence times [20].

However, the model μ may not be known in advance. It must then be chosen to have properties that appear to coincide with observed optimization problems. For example, the AIXI model in particular was designed to be agnostic with respect to model uncertainty [10]. The Gaussian model used with the knowledge gradient averages out uncertainty based on the Central Limit Theorem [18].

One interesting aspect of model-optimal optimizers is that Equation 33 contains an inner optimization loop. Due to issues of infinite regress, this optimizer is likely to be uncomputable in many cases. Methods that perform an inner optimization loop have been proposed previously; the inner optimization loop can be computationally expensive [22].

5.5 Limitations of the Main Result

The model-optimality proven here has the following limitations: 1) the value function must be bounded; 2) the singletons must be measurable; 3) computability was not considered; and 4) only static objective functions were considered. The limitations are discussed in turn.

The boundedness of the value function is not a severe restriction. Because the value function is minimized, only its minimal values matter. As such it seems likely that the same results would hold if $V(z, u)$ were bounded below and had at least some finite values. This observation applies particularly to the expected runtime. The measurability of the singletons is not a serious concern, since practical objective functions often take values inside a compact set.

Regarding computability, common probability distributions cannot be computed exactly, even with a truly random source. It is therefore not clear what computability should mean for the optimizers defined in this paper. Given a definition, computable optimizers would be generate some vector subspace of $\mathcal{MF}_\Omega$. It would be interesting to know the conditions under which the model-optimal optimizers could be approximated computably. Furthermore, the fact that one can only compute with pseudorandom numbers today does not preclude the truly random computing in the future.

These model-optimal optimizers apply to static objectives. Similar results likely hold for stochastic and dynamic objective functions, although the set of optimal choices may be empty; it depends on whether the unit ball in $\mathcal{MF}_\Omega^\infty$ remains compact with these objectives. Under adaptive fitness functions, optimization may benefit from randomness. This case is particularly relevant for evolutionary algorithms.

6. CONCLUSION

A formal account has been given of the optimal choices of an optimizer for a given model of objective function behavior using bounded performance measurements. Model-optimal optimizers can be approximated by making a sequence of optimal choices at each time step. The results are general in that they apply to any probabilistic model of objective functions and to large classes of optimization methods that are defined by their access to information about the objective gained from evaluation. In particular, the results apply to black-box methods such as evolutionary algorithms and to gradient-based methods. Future studies are needed to examine the conditions under which these model-optimal optimizers can be computed or approximated as well as what kinds of models of objective behavior are suitable for general-purpose optimization.

7. REFERENCES

[1] C. C. Aliprantis and K. D. Border. *Infinite Dimensional Analysis: A Hitchhiker's Guide, 3rd Edition.* Springer, New York, New York, 2006.

[2] A. Auger and O. Teytaud. Continuous lunches are free! In *Proceedings of the 9th Annual Conference on Genetic and Evolutionary Computation (GECCO-2007)*, pages 916–922, New York, 2007. ACM Press.

[3] R. Bellman. *Dynamic Programming.* Princeton University Press, Princeton, NJ, USA, 1 edition, 1957.

[4] P. Billingsley. *Probability and Measure.* John Wiley, 1986.

[5] K. L. Chung and R. Williams. *Introduction to Stochastic Integration.* Birkhauser, Boston, MA, 1990.

[6] B. Doerr and C. Winzen. Towards a complexity theory of randomized search heuristics: Ranking-based black-box complexity. *CoRR*, abs/1102.1140, 2011.

[7] S. Droste, T. Jansen, and I. Wegener. Upper and lower bounds for randomized search heuristics in black-box optimization. *Theoretical Computer Science*, 39, 2006.

[8] P. I. Frazier, W. B. Powell, and S. Dayanik. A knowledge gradient policy for sequential information collection. *SIAM Journal on Control and Optimization*, 47(5):2410–2439, 2008.

[9] P. Halmos. *Measure Theory.* Springer-Verlag, New York, NY, 1974.

[10] M. Hutter. *Universal Artificial Intelligence: Sequential Decisions based on Algorithmic Probability.* Springer, Berlin, 2005.

[11] C. Igel. No free lunch theorems: Limitations and perspectives of metaheuristics. Springer-Verlag, 2014.

[12] A. N. Kolmogorov. *Grundbegriffe der Wahrscheinlichkeitsrechnung.* 1933.

[13] P. K. Lehre and C. Witt. Black-box search by unbiased variation. *Algorithmica*, 64(4), 2012.

[14] A. Lockett. Measure-theoretic analysis of performance in evolutionary algorithms. In *Proceedings of the 2013 IEEE Conference on Evolutionary Computation (CEC-2013).* IEEE Pres, 2013.

[15] A. Lockett and R. Miikkulainen. A measure-theoretic analysis of stochastic optimization. In *Proceedings of the 12th Workshop on Foundations of Genetic Algorithms (FOGA-2013).* ACM, 2013.

[16] A. J. Lockett. *General-Purpose Optimization Through Information Maximization.* PhD thesis, University of Texas at Austin, 2012.

[17] J. R. Munkres. *Topology.* Prentice Hall, Upper Saddle River, NJ, 2000.

[18] W. B. Powell and I. O. Ryzhov. *Optimal Learning.* John Wiley and Sons, 2012.

[19] N. Radcliffe and P. D. Surry. Fundamental limitations on search algorithms: Evolutionary computing in perspective. In *Lecture Notes in Computer Science 1000*, pages 275–291. Springer-Verlag, 1995.

[20] P. Rolet, M. Sebag, and O. Teytaud. Optimal robust expensive optimization is tractable. In *Gecco 2009*, page 8 pages, Montréal, Canada, 2009. ACM.

[21] J. E. Rowe, M. D. Vose, and A. H. Wright. Reinterpreting no free lunch. *Evolutionary Computation*, 17(1):117–129, 2009.

[22] T. Schaul, Y. Sun, D. Wierstra, F. Gomez, and J. Schmidhuber. Curiosity-Driven Optimization. In *IEEE Congress on Evolutionary Computation (CEC)*, 2011.

[23] R. J. Solomonoff. A formal theory of inductive inference. part i. *Information and Control*, 7:1–21, 1964.

[24] M. Vose. *The Simple Genetic Algorithm.* MIT Press, Cambridge, Massachusetts, 1999.

[25] M. D. Vose. Random heuristic search. *Theoretical Computer Science*, 229:103–142, 1999.

[26] D. H. Wolpert and W. G. Macready. No free lunch theorems for optimization. *IEEE Transactions on Evolutionary Computation*, 1(1):67–82, 1997.

[27] Y. Yamasaki. Kolmogorov's extension theorem for infinite measures. *Publ. RIMS, Kyoto University*, 10:381–411, 1975.

A Theoretical Analysis of Volume Based Pareto front Approximations

Pradyumn Kumar Shukla
Karlsruhe Institute of Technology
pradyumn.shukla@kit.edu

Nadja Doll
Karlsruhe Institute of Technology

Hartmut Schmeck
Karlsruhe Institute of Technology
hartmut.schmeck@kit.edu

ABSTRACT

Many multi-objective algorithms use volume based quality indicators to approximate the Pareto front. Amongst these, the hypervolume is the most widely used. The distribution of solution sets of finite size μ that maximize the hypervolume have been investigated theoretically. But nearly all results are limited to the bi-objective case. In this paper, many of these results are extended to higher dimensions and a theoretical analysis and characterization of optimal μ-distributions is done. We investigate monotonic Pareto curves that are embedded in three and higher dimensions that keep the property of the bi-objective case that only few points are determining the hypervolume contribution of a point. For finite μ, we consider the influence of the choice of the reference point and determine sufficient conditions that assure the extreme points of the Pareto curves to be included in an optimal μ- distribution. We state conditions about the slope of the front that makes it impossible to include the extremes. Furthermore, we prove more specific results for three dimensional linear Pareto fronts. It is shown that the equispaced property of an optimal distribution for a line in two dimensions does not hold in higher dimensions. We additionally investigate hypervolume in general dimensions and problems with cone domination structures.

Categories and Subject Descriptors

F.2 [**Theory of Computation**]: Analysis of Algorithms and Problem Complexity; F.m [**Theory of Computation**]: Miscellaneous

Keywords

Hypervolume indicator, cone domination, multi-objective optimization

1. INTRODUCTION

In this paper, we consider a d-dimensional optimization problem $f : X \to \mathbb{R}^d$ with d objectives $(f_1(x), \ldots, f_d(x))$ that without loss of generality are to be minimized. The aim is to search for a finite approximation of the Pareto front. The hypervolume indicator is commonly used for measuring the quality of an approximation set. For the approximation set, the hypervolume measures the volume of the dominated region that is bounded by a reference point.

A finite size approximation of the Pareto front is a long sought goal of both population based and classical scalarization techniques. The hypervolume and its variants ([2, 1, 3]) are widely used in many population based algorithms to guide the search towards an *ideal* approximation, where the goodness is measured by the hypervolume indicator value. An ideal approximation with μ points is the one that maximizes the hypervolume and has at most μ solutions; this is known as an optimal μ-distribution. By knowing how optimal μ-distributions look like, we get a better understanding of hypervolume based algorithms and can evaluate the quality of an approximation set.

The shape of the hypervolume for more than two objective functions is very complex, and it is difficult to compute, analyze, and theoretically characterize the optimal μ-distributions. Although, theoretical analysis of optimal μ-distributions have been published for two objectives but it is still an open question which of these results hold in higher dimensions. Auger et al. showed the existence, monotonicity, and density results for optimal μ-distributions for two objectives [2]. Furthermore, they proved that optimal μ-distributions in the bi-objective case are unique and equispaced for linear fronts. Some of these results have been extended to three objectives [1], and this, to the best of our knowledge, is the only work for the three objectives case.

This paper investigates theoretical results about the hypervolume indicator in three and higher dimensions. We concentrate on monotonic Pareto fronts (one-dimensional curves embedded in higher dimensions). These fronts have the property that not all other points affect the hypervolume contribution of one point and therefore, a deeper theoretical investigation can be done. We show that in nontrivial scenarios, the reference point influences the hypervolume contribution of all the points.

The main contributions of this paper are as follows:

- The hypervolume, hypervolume contribution, and necessary conditions for μ-optimality for monotonic Pareto fronts in three dimensions are derived. (Section 2)
- Results about the inclusion/exclusion of the extreme points in an optimal μ-distribution in $\mathbb{R}^d$ are presented. (Section 3)

GECCO'14, July 12–16, 2014, Vancouver, BC, Canada.
Copyright 2014 ACM 978-1-4503-2662-9/14/07 ...$15.00.
http://dx.doi.org/10.1145/2576768.2598348.

- Optimal μ-distributions for linear Pareto fronts in three dimensions are investigated. The well-known equispaced property of a linear Pareto front in two dimensions is shown *not* to hold for three dimensional Pareto fronts. (Section 4) The results also shows an undesirable property of the optimal μ-distribution; the optimal μ-distribution of a one dimensional front depends on the dimension in which it is embedded.
- Hypervolume formula for monotonic Pareto fronts in four and higher dimensions, to facilitate the use of calculus techniques for obtaining a necessary optimality condition, is derived. (Section 5)
- Theoretical results for cone and general ordering based hypervolume indicators are presented. (Section 6)

2. BASIC RESULTS

To formally define the hypervolume, we need the definition of the Minkowski sum.

DEFINITION 1. *Let $A, B \subset \mathbb{R}^d$. Then, the Minkowski sum of A and B is denoted by $\oplus$ and defined as $A \oplus B = \{a + b \,|\, a \in A \wedge b \in B\}$. The Minkowski difference (denoted by $\ominus$) is defined as $A \ominus B = \{a - b \,|\, a \in A \wedge b \in B\}$.*

For a finite approximation set $A \subset \mathbb{R}^d$, the hypervolume indicator is defined as: $I_H(A, r) := \lambda(H(A, r))$, where λ is the Lebesque measure, $H(A, r) := (A \oplus \mathbb{R}^d_+) \cap (r \ominus \mathbb{R}^d_+)$, $r \in \mathbb{R}^d$ is the reference point and $\mathbb{R}^d_+$ is the non-negative orthant. The hypervolume contribution of a point $a \in A$ is defined as $\lambda(H_a(A, r))$ with $H_a(A, r) = H(A, r) \setminus H(A \backslash \{a\}, r)$. A set of at most μ points (where $\mu \in \mathbb{N}$) that maximizes the hypervolume indicator is called optimal μ-distribution.

Let $\preceq$ denote the weak Pareto order. Hence, for $u, v \in \mathbb{R}^d$, $u \preceq v$ iff $u_i \leq v_i$ for all $i = \{1, 2, \ldots, d\}$. Let us assume that the Pareto front is a curve in $\mathbb{R}^d$ with endpoints $x, y \in \mathbb{R}^d$ and monotonic coordinate functions. We can describe such curves as $f(t) = (f_1(t), \ldots, f_d(t))^\top$, $t \in [t_{\min}, t_{\max}]$, where $f_i(t) : [t_{\min}, t_{\max}] \to \mathbb{R}$ for $i \in \{1, \ldots, d\}$ and each f_i is either monotonically increasing or decreasing. W.l.o.g. we can assume $t \in [0, 1]$ as an adequate transformation leads to that case (for $t \in [t_{\min}, t_{\max}]$ use the transformation $\phi(s) = t_{\min} + s(t_{\max} - t_{\min})$ and consider $(f \circ \phi)(s)$, $s \in [0, 1]$). For this case, we state a result that only the neighboring points influence the hypervolume contribution of a point.

THEOREM 1. *Let $f(t)$, $t \in [t_{\min}, t_{\max}]$ be a curve in $\mathbb{R}^d$ with each objective monotonic and let $A_t = \{t_1, \ldots, t_\mu\}$ describe an ordered set of distinct points on f with $|A_t| = \mu$. Let the points be non-dominated (i.e., $f(t_i) \npreceq f(t_j)$ for each distinct index i and j). Then, the hypervolume contribution of a point $f(t_i)$ with $t_i \in A_t$, $i \in \{1, \ldots, \mu\}$ can only be a function of its neighboring points on the curve, i.e. $f(t_{i-1})$ and $f(t_{i+1})$ if they exist, and possibly the reference point r.*

PROOF. We prove that for points on f with $t > t_i$ only the first following point $f(t_{i+1})$ (and possibly r) influences the hypervolume contribution of $a := f(t_i)$. The other case ($t < t_i$) can be proven in the same way.

Let $b := f(t_{i+1})$, $c := f(t)$ with $t > t_{i+1}$ and let z be an arbitrary point which is dominated by a and dominates the reference point, i.e. $a \preceq z$ and $z \preceq r$. These are all points that are possibly part of the hypervolume contribution. Hence, to prove the theorem, we have to show the following: *If $a \preceq z$ and $c \preceq z$ then $b \preceq z$.* This means that if a point is excluded from being part of the hypervolume contribution of a because it is also dominated by another point c with $t > t_i$, then also the direct neighbor b dominates this point. As $a \preceq z$, $a_j \leq z_j \,\forall j \in \{1, \ldots, d\}$ and as $c \preceq z$, $c_j \leq z_j \,\forall j \in \{1, \ldots, d\}$. Now we use the monotonicity in each coordinate. For all $j \in \{1, \ldots, d\}$ with f_j increasing we have $b_j \in [a_j, c_j]$ and therefore $b_j \leq c_j \leq z_j$. For all decreasing objectives we get $b_j \in [c_j, a_j]$ and therefore $b_j \leq a_j \leq z_j$. Together, this results in $b_j \leq z_j \forall j \in \{1, \ldots, d\}$, i. e. $b \preceq z$.

For $i = 1$ and $i = \mu$, only one neighbor on the curve exists and hence, the hypervolume contribution is only influenced by this neighbor and possibly the reference point. □

For two objectives, Auger et al. have shown ([2]) that only the contributions of the extreme points are depending on the reference point whereas the other points are only influenced by their neighbors on the curve. We will show later (Proposition 1) that for three and higher dimensions, the reference point influences the contributions of *all* the points.

For f describing the Pareto front, this result makes the examination of sets A_t easier and allows us to formulate optimality conditions by maximizing the hypervolume contribution of a point. A concrete formula for the hypervolume contribution H_i of $f(t_i)$, $i \in \{2, \ldots, \mu-1\}$ will be a function of t_i, t_{i-1} and t_{i+1} and the reference point r.

The position of a point $f(t_i)$ between its neighbors only influences the hypervolume that is exclusively dominated by this point, i.e. its hypervolume contribution, whereas the remaining hypervolume stays the same. So if we can increase the hypervolume contribution by shifting t_i, the whole hypervolume will increase. Because of that, we can use a Greedy approach to find and investigate optimal μ-distributions: In an optimal μ-distribution, the hypervolume contribution of each point has to be maximal. So if an optimal μ-distribution exists, we can formulate a condition to maximize H_i, $i \in \{2, \ldots, \mu - 1\}$ assuming the other points to be fixed. This optimality condition will again be a function of t_i, t_{i-1} and t_{i+1} and the reference point r.

To formulate such a condition, we first need to calculate the hypervolume and the hypervolume contribution in higher dimensions. We now restrict the investigation to the case of three objective functions. The Pareto front can then be described as $f(t) = (f_1(t), f_2(t), f_3(t))^\top$, $t \in [t_{\min}, t_{\max}]$. Without loss of generality, we can assume f_1 and f_2 to be increasing and f_3 to be decreasing. If two f_i are decreasing and one increasing, we can change the direction how the curve is passed through. This means that we can use $f(t_{\max} - t)$, $t \in [0, t_{\max} - t_{\min}]$ to get two increasing and one decreasing function. Furthermore, we can rearrange the functions such that f_1 and f_2 are the increasing ones. Either f_1 or f_2 might be constant, but at least two out of $\{f_1, f_2, f_3\}$ must be non-constant and have different monotonicity. Otherwise, there will be dominated points on f and hence, f will not describe a Pareto front.

For such a front, we can provide a concrete formula for the hypervolume contribution of a point $f(t_i)$. As proven in Theorem 1, this is a function of t_{i-1}, t_i, t_{i+1}, and the reference point r. For the sake of readability we use a, b, c instead of $f(t_{i-1}), f(t_i), f(t_{i+1})$.

PROPOSITION 1. *Let $f(t) = (f_1(t), f_2(t), f_3(t))^\top$, where $t \in [t_{\min}, t_{\max}]$, f_1, f_2 increasing, f_3 decreasing describe the Pareto front. Moreover, r denotes the reference point and let*

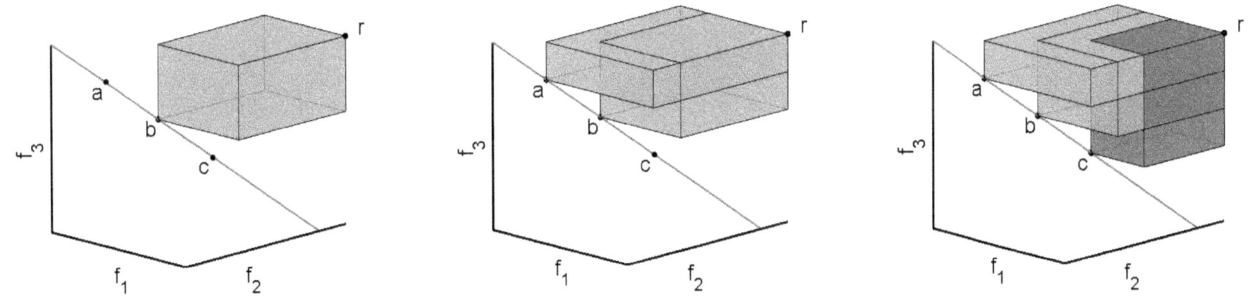

Figure 1: Stepwise construction of the hypervolume contribution H_i of point b. First, the considered volume is cut from above by the preceding point a. Afterwards, the following point c cuts out a rectangular box.

a, b, c be consecutive points on f with corresponding t-values $t_{i-1} < t_i < t_{i+1}$. Then the hypervolume contribution of b is given by

$$\begin{aligned} H_i &= (a_3 - b_3)[(c_1 - b_1)(r_2 - b_2) + (r_1 - c_1)(c_2 - b_2)] \\ &= (f_3(t_{i-1}) - f_3(t_i))[(f_1(t_{i+1}) - f_1(t_i))(r_2 - f_2(t_i)) \\ &\quad +(r_1 - f_1(t_{i+1}))(f_2(t_{i+1}) - f_2(t_i))]. \qquad (1) \end{aligned}$$

If there exists no such point a (c), i.e. b is the point with the smallest t-value (largest t-value) in the considered set, replace a_i by r_i (c_i by r_i) in the formula.

PROOF. We will prove the formula for the hypervolume contribution by constructing the space exclusively dominated by b from the whole set of points that are dominated by b. Because of Proposition 1, we only have to look at the direct neighbors a and c when computing the hypervolume contribution of b. The set of points that are dominated by b and which themselves dominate the reference point r is the cuboid $B := [b_1, r_1] \times [b_2, r_2] \times [b_3, r_3]$ (see first part of Figure 1) and equivalently for a this is $A := [a_1, r_1] \times [a_2, r_2] \times [a_3, r_3]$. Since $a_1 < b_1$ and $a_2 < b_2$, the whole cuboid B is overlapped by A when the value of the third coordinate is greater than a_3. So $B^* := [b_1, r_1] \times [b_2, r_2] \times [b_3, a_3]$ is left to be part of the hypervolume contribution of b (see second part of Figure 1). As dominated points of c, we get accordingly $C := [c_1, r_1] \times [c_2, r_2] \times [c_3, r_3]$ where $c_3 < b_3$. So C overlaps a part of B^* over the whole 3-axis and removes the cuboid $[c_1, r_1] \times [c_2, r_2] \times [b_3, a_3]$ from B^* (see last part of Figure 1). It remains only H_b which consists of two cuboids: $[b_1, c_1] \times [b_2, r_2] \times [b_3, a_3]$ and $[b_1, r_1] \times [b_2, c_2] \times [b_3, a_3]$ where the part $[b_1, c_1] \times [b_2, c_2] \times [b_3, a_3]$ overlaps and therefore has to be subtracted. This leads to

$$\begin{aligned} H_i &= \lambda([b_1, c_1] \times [b_2, r_2] \times [b_3, a_3] \cup [b_1, r_1] \times [b_2, c_2] \times [b_3, a_3]) \\ &= (c_1 - b_1)(r_2 - b_2)(a_3 - b_3) + (r_1 - b_1)(c_2 - b_2)(a_3 - b_3) \\ &\quad -(c_1 - b_1)(c_2 - b_2)(a_3 - b_3) \\ &= (a_3 - b_3)[(c_1 - b_1)(r_2 - b_2) + (r_1 - c_1)(c_2 - b_2)]. \end{aligned}$$

The case when there exists no point a means that B isn't cut from above in the first step which leads to the formula $H_i = (r_3 - b_3)[(c_1 - b_1)(r_2 - b_2) + (r_1 - c_1)(c_2 - b_2)]$. If there is no point c, the cuboid $[c_1, r_1] \times [c_2, r_2] \times [b_3, a_3]$ won't be removed from B^* in the second step which results in $H_i = (r_1 - b_1)(r_2 - b_2)(a_3 - b_3)$. Both cases are equal to the formula with replaced a_i and c_i, respectively. □

As a consequence of Proposition 1, we can get a necessary condition for an optimal μ-distribution. Every point must be chosen that way that it maximizes its hypervolume contribution. We have seen that the value of the hypervolume contribution only depends on the reference point and the neighboring points and will be zero by converging to one of the neighbors. So an inner maximum must exist and by assuming f to be differentiable on $(t_{\min}, t_{\max})$, we can set the derivative of Equation 1 to zero to get the necessary optimality condition.

PROPOSITION 2. *Let $f(t) = (f_1(t), f_2(t), f_3(t))^\top$, where $t \in [t_{\min}, t_{\max}]$, f_1, f_2 increasing, f_3 decreasing describe the Pareto front and let r be the reference point. If $t_1, \ldots t_\mu$ denote the t-values of an optimal μ-distribution, then for all t_i, $i \in \{2, \ldots, \mu - 1\}$*

$$\begin{aligned} &- f_3'(t_i)[(f_1(t_{i+1}) - f_1(t_i))(r_2 - f_2(t_i)) + (r_1 - f_1(t_{i+1})) \\ &(f_2(t_{i+1}) - f_2(t_i))] - f_1'(t_i)(r_2 - f_2(t_i))(f_3(t_{i-1}) - f_3(t_i)) \\ &- f_2'(t_i)(r_1 - f_1(t_i))(f_3(t_{i-1}) - f_3(t_i)) = 0. \qquad (2) \end{aligned}$$

The corresponding formula in the two-dimensional case is $H_i'(x_i) = -x_{i+1}f'(x_i) - f(x_{i-1}) + f(x_i) + x_i f'(x_i)$. By comparing this formula to the necessary condition in the three-dimensional case, we discover the following difference. Whereas the formula in the two-dimensional case is an equation of the consecutive points, the reference point is included in the formula in 2. This means that the reference point influences the optimal position of every point whereas in $\mathbb{R}^2$ case changing the reference point only changes the hypervolume contribution of the first and the last point.

One may wonder that if a one dimensional plane curve Pareto front for a three objective problem is detected (say during a simulation run using a population based algorithm), one could just compute the two dimensional hypervolumes on the plane where the line and the origin $(0, 0, 0)^\top$ lie. After all, for algorithmic (selection) purposes just the relative magnitudes of the hypervolume contributions play a role. The next example shows that, even in such simple situations, the order of points corresponding to their hypervolume contributions in three dimensions might be different than the order considering their two dimensional hypervolume contributions. Hence, even for plane fronts for a three objective problem, it makes a difference whether two dimensional or three dimensional hypervolume is considered.

EXAMPLE 1. *Let us consider three points a, b, c on the plane $x = y$ with coordinates $a = (0.1332, 0.1332, 0.8116)^\top$,*

$b = (0.2515, 0.2515, 0.6443)^\top$, *and* $c = (0.4394, 0.4394, 0.3786)^\top$. *If we consider the reference point* $r = (1/\sqrt{2}, 1/\sqrt{2}, 1)^\top$, *the hypervolume contribution of the points are* 0.0229, 0.0227, *and* 0.0190 *respectively. Changing the coordinate system to a two dimensional coordinate system on the plane* $x = y$ *(via a linear transformation), we obtain the points* $\hat{a} = (0.1884, 0.8116)^\top$, $\hat{b} = (0.3557, 0.6443)^\top$, $\hat{c} = (0.6214, 0.3786)^\top$ *and* $\hat{r} = (1, 1)^\top$. *The two dimensional hypervolume of the points* $\hat{a}, \hat{b}$ *and* $\hat{c}$ *is* 0.0315, 0.0445 *and* 0.1006 *respectively. We see that the order of the hypervolumes contributions is now reversed.*

3. CHOICE OF THE REFERENCE POINT IN THREE DIMENSIONS

As the reference point is contained in the necessary condition, the choice of the reference point influences the optimal μ-distributions. This section provides results how the reference point should be chosen to ensure that the extreme points of the Pareto front, $f(t_{\min})$ and $f(t_{\max})$, are included in an optimal μ-distribution and in which cases this is never possible (detailed proofs are as available as a supplementary material). We assume that $\mu \in \mathbb{N}$ and $\mu \geq 2$ and the blanket assumption described next.

Blanket Assumption for Section 3 The function $f : [t_{\min}, t_{\max}] \to \mathbb{R}^3$, is such that f_1, f_2 is strictly increasing, f_3 is strictly decreasing, f_i is continuous on $[t_{\min}, t_{\max}]$ and differentiable on $(t_{\min}, t_{\max})$ for $i = 1, 2, 3$.

3.1 Inclusion of the Point $f(t_{\min})$

The first theorem states a result for t_1 and how the reference point can be chosen to make sure that $t_1 = t_{\min}$.

THEOREM 2. *Let* $f_1'(t)$ *and* $f_2'(t)$ *be monotonically decreasing and* $f_1'(t_{\min}) + f_2'(t_{\min}) < \infty$. *If* $\lim_{t \to t_{\min}} |f_3'(t)| < \infty$ *and*

$$\mathcal{R}_3 = \sup_{t \in [t_{\min}, t_{\max})} \{-f_3'(t)(t_{\max} - t) + f_3(t)\}$$

is finite, the extreme point $(f_1(t_{\min}), f_2(t_{\min}), f_3(t_{\min}))$ *is contained in an optimal* μ*-distribution if the reference point* $r = (r_1, r_2, r_3)$ *satisfies* $r_3 > \mathcal{R}_3$.

The next theorem states the conditions under which the point $f(t_{\min})$ will never be included in an optimal distribution. This theorem gives a similar result to [1, Theorem 2] but for a different class of Pareto fronts. Whereas in [1] Pareto fronts of the type $f(x, y, z) = 0$ were investigated, we show a result for monotonic curves. A monotonic curve cannot always be written in the form $f(x, y, z) = 0$ and hence the following theorem is an addition to existing results.

THEOREM 3. *Let* $f_1'(t_{\min}) + f_2'(t_{\min}) < \infty$. *If* $\lim_{t \to t_{\min}} -f_3'(t) = +\infty$, *the extreme point* $(f_1(t_{\min}), f_2(t_{\min}), f_3(t_{\min}))$ *will never be included in an optimal* μ*-distribution.*

Next we investigate a limiting case where either $f_1(t)$ or $f_2(t)$ are constant functions. For this, let $f_2(t) = c$ be a constant function. In this case, the 3d-problem turns into a 2d-problem as the value of f_2 doesn't depend on t and therefore doesn't influence the optimal μ-distribution. Hence, the result about the inclusion of extreme points should be the same as in two dimensions. To confirm this, we need a different notation of the curve.

In case of a curve with monotonic coordinate functions, we can rewrite the parametric representation by setting $f_1(t) = x$ and $f_i(t) = f_i(f_1^{-1}(x)) = \tilde{f}_i(x)$, $i > 1$ since f_1 has an inverse function. If f_1 is monotonic increasing, f_1^{-1} is increasing and therefore. $\tilde{f}_i(x)$, $i > 1$ is increasing/decreasing if and only if $f_i(t)$ is increasing/decreasing. So instead of $f(t) = (f_1(t), f_2(t), f_3(t))^\top, t \in [t_{\min}, t_{\max}], f_1, f_2$ increasing, f_3 decreasing, we now formulate $f(x) = (x, \tilde{f}_2(x), \tilde{f}_3(x))^\top, x \in [x_{\min}, x_{\max}], x_{\min} = f_1(t_{\min}), x_{\max} = f_1(t_{\max}), \tilde{f}_2$ increasing, $\tilde{f}_3$ decreasing. In this notation, we can reformulate Theorem 2 and Theorem 3 together in Theorem 4. We do not prove this here as the proof could be done in exactly the same way.

THEOREM 4. *Let* $f(x) = (x, \tilde{f}_2(x), \tilde{f}_3(x))$ *and additionally let* $\tilde{f}_2'(x_{\min}) < \infty$. *If* $\lim_{x \to x_{\min}} \left|\tilde{f}_3'(x)\right| < \infty$, *let*

$$\mathcal{R}_3 = \sup_{x \in [x_{\min}, x_{\max})} \{-\tilde{f}_3'(x)(x_{\max} - x) + \tilde{f}_3(x)\}.$$

When $\tilde{f}_2'(x)$ *is decreasing and* $\mathcal{R}_3$ *is finite, the extreme point* $(x_{\min}, \tilde{f}_2(x_{\min}), \tilde{f}_3(x_{\min}))$ *is contained in an optimal* μ*-distribution if the reference point* $r = (r_1, r_2, r_3)$ *satisfies* $r_3 > \mathcal{R}_3$. *Moreover, if* $\lim_{x \to x_{\min}} -\tilde{f}_3'(x) = +\infty$, *the extreme point* $(x_{\min}, \tilde{f}_2(x_{\min}), \tilde{f}_3(x_{\min}))$ *is never included in the optimal* μ*-distributions.*

If $\tilde{f}_2(x)$ is constant, then $\tilde{f}_2'(x) = 0$ and hence the assumptions $\tilde{f}_2'(x)$ decreasing and $\tilde{f}_2'(x_{\min}) < \infty$ are fulfilled. Just the assumption $\tilde{f}_2$ strictly increasing must be turned into $\tilde{f}_2$ increasing which includes constant. As expected the result is exactly the same as in the 2-dimensional case which was stated by Auger et al. [2, Theorem 2], where $\tilde{f}_3$ is corresponding to f.

3.2 Inclusion of the Point $f(t_{\max})$

Similarly to Theorem 2 and Theorem 3, we can formulate theorems for the inclusion of the point $(f_1(t_{\max}), f_2(t_{\max}), f_3(t_{\max}))$ in an optimal μ-distribution.

THEOREM 5. *Let* $f_3'(t)$ *be increasing and* $f_3'(t_{\max}) < \infty$. *If* $\lim_{t \to t_{\max}} |f_i'(t)| < \infty$ *for* $i = 1, 2$, *let for arbitrary* $\varrho \in (0, 1)$

$$\mathcal{R}_1 = \sup_{t \in (t_{\min}, t_{\max}]} \{(f_1'(t)(t - t_{\min}))/\varrho + f_1(t)\},$$

$$\mathcal{R}_2 = \sup_{t \in (t_{\min}, t_{\max}]} \{(f_2'(t)(t - t_{\min}))/(1 - \varrho) + f_2(t)\}.$$

When $\mathcal{R}_i$, $i = 1, 2$ *are finite, the extreme point* $(t = t_{max})$ *is contained in an optimal* μ*-distribution if the reference point* $r = (r_1, r_2, r_3)$ *satisfies* $r_1 > \mathcal{R}_1$ *and* $r_2 > \mathcal{R}_2$.

In contrast to results for the bi-objective case, we need a trade-off parameter ϱ in the definitions of $\mathcal{R}_1, \mathcal{R}_2$ in Theorem 5 to take care of two increasing functions. To make sure that the extreme is included in the 3d case we have to assure that the hypervolume is above a certain value and as two functions are increasing in the 3d case, this value depends on both functions. The ϱ parameter describes the trade-off between these functions.

THEOREM 6. *Let $f_3'(t_{\max}) < \infty$. If $\lim_{t\to t_{\max}} f_1'(t) = \infty$ or $\lim_{t\to t_{\max}} f_2'(t) = \infty$, the point $(f_1(t_{\max}), f_2(t_{\max}), f_3(t_{\max}))$ will never be included in an optimal μ-distribution.*

Again, as a limiting case, we can easily show that if $f_2(t)$ is a constant function, it will lead to the same result as in the two dimensional case (cf. [2, Theorem 3]).

3.3 Examples

We can apply the results from Theorem 2 and 3 as well as Theorem 5 and 6 to concrete functions and calculate the values, how r must be chosen to assure that the endpoints of the curve will be included in an optimal μ-distribution. Table 1 shows the resulting values for a rewritten form of the test problem DTLZ5, for a line and for functions where one extreme is not included because the slope of the corresponding coordinate function is infinite. Choosing r_i above the values in the table makes sure that the extremes are included, $\mathcal{R}_i = \infty$ means that we cannot find such an r_i. So if $\mathcal{R}_1 = \infty$ or $\mathcal{R}_2 = \infty$, the point $f(t_{\max})$ will never be included in an optimal μ-distribution and if $\mathcal{R}_3 = \infty$, the point $f(t_{\min})$ will never be included in an optimal μ-distribution.

function	ϱ	$\mathcal{R}$
$f = \left(\frac{\sin t}{\sqrt{2}}, \frac{\sin t}{\sqrt{2}}, \cos t\right)^\top, t \in [0, \frac{\pi}{2}]$	$\frac{1}{2}$	$(1.4, 1.4, 1.4)^\top$
	$\frac{1}{4}$	$(2.1, 1.1, 1.4)^\top$
$f = (0,0,1)^\top + t(2,3,-1)^\top, t \in [0,1]$	$\frac{1}{2}$	$(6, 9, 2)^\top$
	$\frac{1}{4}$	$(10, 7, 2)^\top$
$f = (t^2, t^2, 1-\sqrt{t})^\top, t \in [0,1]$	$\frac{1}{2}$	$(5, 5, \infty)^\top$
	$\frac{1}{4}$	$(9, \frac{11}{3}, \infty)^\top$
$f = (2t, 1-\sqrt{1-t}, 1-t^2), t \in [0,1]$	$\frac{1}{2}$	$(6, \infty, \frac{4}{3})^\top$
	$\frac{3}{4}$	$(\frac{14}{3}, \infty, \frac{4}{3})^\top$

Table 1: Exemplary functions with corresponding $\mathcal{R}$-values that result from Theorem 2 and 3 and Theorem 5 and 6 for different values of λ. The values of DTLZ5 (first row) are calculated numerically.

4. OPTIMAL DISTRIBUTIONS FOR LINES IN THREE DIMENSIONS

When we consider the special case of a line in $\mathbb{R}^3$ as a Pareto front, we get more explicit results. A line with endpoints x and y can be described as $tx + (1-t)y$, $t \in [0,1]$ or equivalently $y + t(x-y), t \in [0,1]$. Therefore, $f_1 = y_1 + tz_1, f_2 = y_2 + tz_2$ and $f_3 = y_3 + tz_3$ where $z_i = x_i - y_i$.

Proposition 1 stated a formula for the hypervolume contribution of a point and this formula is also applicable for a line as a Pareto front. As it is only depending on the neighboring points and the reference point, we can compute the position of a point b between its neighboring points a and c that maximizes the hypervolume contribution of this point. As b lies on the line between a and c, replacing it by $(1-t)a + tc$, $t \in [0,1]$ in Equation 1 yields:

$$\begin{aligned} H_b &= (a_3 - b_3)[(c_1 - b_1)(r_2 - b_2) + (r_1 - c_1)(c_2 - b_2)] \\ &= (a_3 - ((1-t)a_3 + tc_3))[(c_1 - ((1-t)a_1 + tc_1))(r_2 - \\ &\quad ((1-t)a_2 + tc_2)) + (r_1 - c_1)(c_2 - ((1-t)a_2 + tc_2))] \\ &= (1-t)t\gamma(\alpha - t\beta), \end{aligned}$$

where $\alpha = (r_1 - c_1)(c_2 - a_2) + (c_1 - a_1)(r_2 - a_2)$, $\beta = (c_1 - a_1)(c_2 - a_2)$, and $\gamma = a_3 - c_3$. The resulting optimization problem is $\max_t H_b$, $t \in [0,1]$ and hence the necessary condition $\frac{\mathrm{d}H_b}{\mathrm{d}t} = 0$ for an optimal μ-distribution becomes:

$$\begin{aligned} (\gamma\alpha - 2t\gamma\alpha) - (2\gamma\beta t - 3\gamma\beta t^2) &= 0 \\ \Leftrightarrow 3\beta t^2 - 2t(\alpha + \beta) + \alpha &= 0 \qquad (\gamma \neq 0). \end{aligned} \tag{3}$$

LEMMA 1. *In case of a line in $\mathbb{R}^3$ as a Pareto front, an equispaced optimal μ-distribution is only possible when the line is parallel to the x_2/x_3 or the x_1/x_3 plane, respectively, i.e. equal to the 2d-case with just adding one axis.*

PROOF. By setting $t = \frac{1}{2}$ in the necessary condition $3\beta t^2 - 2t(\alpha + \beta) + \alpha = 0$, we get that $\frac{3}{4}\beta - \beta = 0$ and therefore $\beta = 0$. So either $a_1 = c_1$ or $a_2 = c_2$ which means that either $z_1 = 0$ or $z_2 = 0$ and hence the line is parallel to the plane spanned by the axes x_2, x_3 or x_1, x_3, respectively. □

REMARK 1. *The result from Lemma 1 shows that in contrast to the bi-objective case, an equispaced solution is only possible for $a_1 = c_1$ or $a_2 = c_2$ in the scenario described above. Moreover from Equation 3, we see that endpoints and the reference point influence the optimal μ-distribution.*

We next investigate which values of t can be attained by solving Equation 3. It turns out that we can specify an interval in which t lies.

THEOREM 7. *Let a and c be two points in $\mathbb{R}^3$ with $a_1 < c_1, a_2 < c_2, a_3 > c_3$ and let r be the reference point with $a, c \preceq r$. Let $b = (1-t^*)a + t^*c$, $t^* \in [0,1]$ be the point on the line from a to c with maximal hypervolume contribution. Then for t^*, it holds that $t^* \in \left[\frac{1}{3}, \frac{1}{2}\right]$.*

PROOF. The general solution of the necessary condition 3 is

$$t_{1,2} = \frac{1}{3}(1 + \alpha/\beta \pm \sqrt{(\alpha/\beta)^2 - \alpha/\beta + 1}). \tag{4}$$

As the second derivative of the formula for the hypervolume contribution equals $6\beta t - 2(\alpha + \beta)$, a maximum occurs for $t < \frac{1}{3}(\frac{\alpha}{\beta} + 1)$ since the second derivative is then smaller than zero. Therefore, the solution with "$-$" in front of the root in Equation 4 is the right one. So $t^* = \frac{1}{3}(1 + \alpha/\beta - \sqrt{(\alpha/\beta)^2 - \alpha/\beta + 1})$. We know that the reference point fulfills $r_1 \geq c_1$ and $r_2 \geq c_2$ and can conclude $\frac{r_2 - a_2}{c_2 - a_2} \geq 1 \Rightarrow \frac{\alpha}{\beta} \geq 1$. This implies that

$$\begin{aligned} \sqrt{(\alpha/\beta)^2 - \alpha/\beta + 1} &\leq \sqrt{(\alpha/\beta)^2} = \alpha/\beta \\ \Rightarrow t^* &\geq \frac{1}{3}(1 + \alpha/\beta - \alpha/\beta) = \frac{1}{3}. \end{aligned}$$

Therefore, the lower bound of t^* is $\frac{1}{3}$ and it is attained for $r_1 = c_1, r_2 = c_2$ as then $\frac{\alpha}{\beta} = 1$. Hence, $t^* = \frac{1}{3}(1+1-1) = \frac{1}{3}$.

To find the upper bound, we estimate the values x that can be attained by $\alpha/\beta - \sqrt{(\alpha/\beta)^2 - \alpha/\beta + 1}$. As $t^* \in [0,1]$, possible x-values lie in the interval $[-1, 2]$. Moreover,

$$\alpha/\beta - \sqrt{(\alpha/\beta)^2 - \alpha/\beta + 1} = x \Leftrightarrow \alpha/\beta = (x^2 - 1)/(2x - 1).$$

As $\frac{\alpha}{\beta} \geq 1$, only values of x which lead to $\frac{x^2-1}{2x-1} \geq 1$ are relevant. This is the case for $x \in [0, \frac{1}{2})$ and for $x \geq 2$. Thus, the upper bound for x is $\frac{1}{2}$ which leads to the value $t^* \leq \frac{1}{3}(1+\frac{1}{2}) = \frac{1}{2}$. As shown in Lemma 1, the upper bound is attained for $a_1 = c_1$ or $a_2 = c_2$. $\square$

Furthermore, we can reformulate the constraints for r in Theorem 2 and Theorem 5 for lines in a general form.

COROLLARY 1. *Let $y + t(x - y), t \in [0, 1]$ describe a line with $x, y \in \mathbb{R}^3$ where $x_3 - y_3 < 0$ and $x_i - y_i > 0$, $i = 1, 2$. The extremes x and y are included in an optimal μ-distribution if the reference point r satisfies $r_1 > \mathcal{R}_1$, $r_2 > \mathcal{R}_2$ and $r_3 > \mathcal{R}_3$ where $\mathcal{R}_1 = y_1 + (x_1 - y_1)\left(1 + \frac{1}{\varrho}\right)$, $\mathcal{R}_2 = y_2 + (x_2 - y_2)\left(1 + \frac{1}{1-\varrho}\right)$, and $\mathcal{R}_3 = 2y_3$, with any $\varrho \in (0, 1)$.*

PROOF. A line as described in the corollary always fulfills the conditions of Theorem 5 and Theorem 2. All coordinate functions $y_i + tx_i$ are continuous and differentiable. Furthermore, their derivative equals x_i and is constant and therefore monotonic. Hence, all conditions of Theorem 5 and Theorem 2 are satisfied and we can get the requirements for r that ensure that the extremes are included. By replacing $f_i(t)$ with $y_i + t(x_i - y_i)$ and rearranging the terms, we get

$$\mathcal{R}_1 = \sup_{t \in (0,1]} \left\{ y_1 + (x_1 - y_1)\left(1 + \frac{1}{\varrho}\right) t \right\} \quad (5)$$

$$\mathcal{R}_2 = \sup_{t \in (0,1]} \left\{ y_1 + (x_1 - y_1)\left(1 + \frac{1}{1-\varrho}\right) t \right\} \quad (6)$$

$$\mathcal{R}_3 = \sup_{t \in [0,1)} \{ y_3 + (x_3 - y_3)(2t - 1) \} \quad (7)$$

and taking the suprema yields $\mathcal{R}_i$, $i = 1, 2, 3$ as stated. $\square$

By choosing ϱ between 0 and 1 and a concrete line, we get different values for $\mathcal{R} = (\mathcal{R}_1, \mathcal{R}_2, \mathcal{R}_3)^\top$. In Figure 2, the resulting values for possible ϱ are visualized. An exemplary line is given by the black curve and the top right curve shows the values for $\mathcal{R}$. The figure on the right shows the projection of the two curves onto the x_1x_2-plane. All points that are dominated by the top right (parabolic) curve in three dimensions could be chosen as a reference point to assure to include the endpoints of the line in an optimal μ-distribution. In the two dimensional scenario, [2, Theorem 6] gives the lower bound for the reference point so as to ensure that extremes are always in any μ-distribution. The lower bound in this case is just a point, whilst in our three dimensional scenario it is a curve. This is due to the trade-off parameter ϱ.

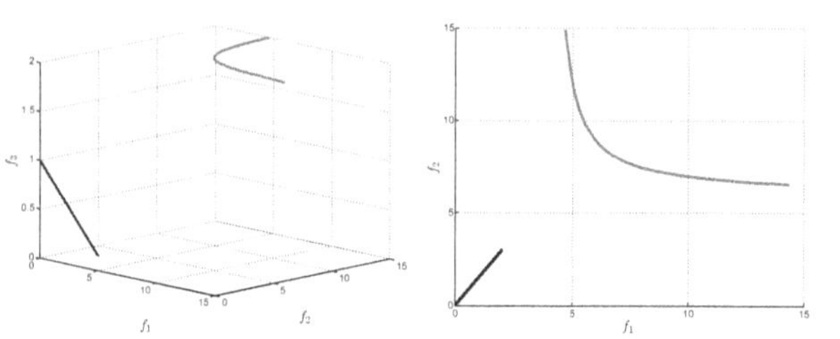

Figure 2: A plot of $\mathcal{R} = (\mathcal{R}_1, \mathcal{R}_2, \mathcal{R}_3)^\top$ for different values of ϱ for a three dimensional linear front.

5. ANALYTICAL FORMULA IN GENERAL DIMENSIONS

It is desirable to transfer the presented results of the previous sections also to higher dimensional spaces. The challenge here is to find explicit formulas for the hypervolume and even more challenging for the hypervolume contribution in higher dimensions. Without those formulas, we cannot theoretically analyze the hypervolume indicator.

Whereas the hypervolume in a three-dimensional space is the sum of rectangular cuboids and thus similar to bi-objective case (sum of rectangles), the situation gets more complex in higher dimensions. There, the shape of the hypervolume is depending on the number of increasing and decreasing functions. It turns out that the form of summing up rectangular cuboids is only preserved if all functions are increasing and only one function is decreasing, or vice versa. Otherwise, the shape of the hypervolume is still based on the summation of d-dimensional cuboids, but the boxes have a more complex shape and overlap in some areas so that the formula has to be adjusted.

In the next theorem, a formula for the hypervolume of monotonic curves with an arbitrary number of increasing and decreasing functions as a Pareto front in $\mathbb{R}^d$ is presented. The formula enables us to calculate the hypervolume in higher dimensions in a faster and more efficient way. Furthermore, we can apply techniques of calculus to get information about optimal μ-distributions and all other aspects. For the sake of readability, the points are directly entitled by x^1 to x^μ instead of using $f(t_1)$ to $f(t_\mu)$.

THEOREM 8. *Let $f(t) = (f_1(t), \ldots, f_d(t))^\top, t \in [0, 1]$ be a curve in $\mathbb{R}^d$ such that $f_1, \ldots, f_{d-l}$ are strictly increasing and $f_{d-l+1}, \ldots, f_d$ are strictly decreasing with $0 < l < d$, (i.e., there are $d - l$ increasing and l decreasing functions). Let $x^1, \ldots, x^\mu$ be consecutive points on the curve. Then the hypervolume enclosed by these points can be computed by:*

$$I_H(\{x^1, \ldots, x^\mu\}, r) = \prod_{j=1}^{d} (r_j - x_j^1) + \sum_{i=2}^{\mu} \left(\sum_{k=1}^{l} \left[\left(\prod_{j=1}^{d-k} (r_j - x_j^i)\right)(x_{d-k+1}^{i-1} - x_{d-k+1}^i) \prod_{j=d-k+2}^{d} (r_j - x_j^{i-1}) \right] \right)$$

PROOF. The formula in the theorem contains a number of d-dimensional boxes (or volume elements). To prove that the formula is correct, the following three properties must be shown:

P1: The interior of the (d-dimensional) boxes is disjoint.

P2: Each dominated point that dominates r is included in at least one box.

P3: All points in the boxes are dominated points.

We have to look at the following boxes: For $i = 1$, we have the Box $[x_1^1, r_1] \times \ldots \times [x_d^1, r_d]$ and for $i \in \{2, \ldots, \mu\}$, $k \in \{1, \ldots, l\}$, we have the Boxes $i.k$: $[x_1^i, r_1] \times \ldots \times [x_{d-k}^i, r_{d-k}] \times [x_{d-k+1}^i, x_{d-k+1}^{i-1}] \times [x_{d-k+2}^{i-1}, r_{d-k+2}] \times \ldots \times [x_d^{i-1}, r_d]$.

We next show that P1,P2, and P3 hold.

Proof of P1.: Boxes $i.k$ and $j.k$ are disjoint for all $i, j \in \{2, \ldots, d\}, i \neq j$, $k \in \{1, \ldots, l\}$ because of disjoint $(d-k+1)$-values: Assume there is a point p which lies in the interior of two Boxes $i.k$ and $j.k$. Then, $p_{d-k+1} \in (x_{d-k+1}^i, x_{d-k+1}^{i-1})$ and $p_{d-k+1} \in (x_{d-k+1}^j, x_{d-k+1}^{j-1})$. Let w.l.o.g. $i > j$. Then, as

f_{d-k+1} is decreasing, $x^i_{d-k+1} < x^{i-1}_{d-k+1} \leq x^j_{d-k+1} < x^{j-1}_{d-k+1}$ and hence, the two intervals are disjoint which leads to a contradiction. Therefore, no such point p exists and the interior of Box $i.k$ and $j.k$ is disjoint.

Analogously, we can prove:

Boxes $i.k$ and $i.m$ are disjoint for $i \in \{2, \ldots, d\}, k, m \in \{1, \ldots, l\}, k > m$ because of disjoint $(d-m+1)$-values (Box $i.k$: $p_{d-m+1} \in (x^{i-1}_{d-m+1}, r_{d-m+1})$ and Box $i.m$: $p_{d-m+1} \in (x^i_{d-m+1}, x^{i-1}_{d-m+1})$).

Boxes $i.k$ and $j.m$ are disjoint for $i, j \in \{2, \ldots, d\}, i > j$, $k, m \in \{1, \ldots, l\}, k > m$ because of disjoint $(d-k+1)$-values (Box $i.k$: $p_{d-k+1} \in (x^i_{d-k+1}, x^{i-1}_{d-k+1})$ and Box $j.m$: $p_{d-k+1} \in (x^j_{d-k+1}, r_{d-k+1})$).

Boxes $i.k$ and $j.m$ are disjoint for $i, j \in \{2, \ldots, d\}, i < j$, $k, m \in \{1, \ldots, l\}, k > m$ because of disjoint $(d-m+1)$-values (Box $i.k$: $p_{d-m+1} \in (x^{i-1}_{d-m+1}, r_{d-m+1})$ and Box $j.m$: $p_{d-m+1} \in (x^j_{d-m+1}, x^{j-1}_{d-m+1})$).

Boxes 1 and $i.k$ are disjoint for $i \in \{2, \ldots, d\}, k \in \{1, \ldots, l\}$ because of disjoint $(d-k+1)$-values (Box 1: $p_{d-k+1} \in (x^1_{d-k+1}, r_{d-k+1})$ and Box $i.k$: $p_{d-k+1} \in (x^i_{d-k+1}, x^{i-1}_{d-k+1})$). Hence, all boxes are disjoint.

Proof of P2.: Let p be a point that dominates r and is dominated by at least one x^i. Let x^j be that one of those dominating points with the smallest t-value, i.e. $x^j \preceq p$ but $x^k \npreceq p$ for $k < j$, especially $x^{j-1} \npreceq p$. This means $x^j_s \leq p_s \, \forall s \in \{1, \ldots, d\}$ and therefore $x^k_s \leq p_s \, \forall s \in \{1, \ldots, d-l\}$, $k < j$ since $f_1, \ldots, f_{d-l}$ are increasing.

Since $x^{j-1} \npreceq p$, there exists at least one and at most d coordinates $u \in \{d-l+1, \ldots, d\}$ where $x^{j-1}_u > p_u$. Let v be the largest coordinate with $x^{j-1}_v > p_v$. From that, we get

1) $x^j_u \leq p_u$, for $u < v$
2) $x^j_u \leq p_u < x^{j-1}_u$, for $u = v$
3) $x^j_u < x^{j-1}_u \leq p_u$, for $u > v$

and therefore, p is in Box $[x^j_1, r_1] \times \ldots \times [x^j_{v-1}, r_{v-1}] \times [x^j_v, x^{j-1}_v] \times [x^{j-1}_{v+1}, r_{v+1}] \times \ldots \times [x^{j-1}_d, r_d]$, i.e. Box $j.(d-v+1)$.

Proof of P3.: In each box each coordinate is dominated by the smallest value in this coordinate that appears in the box. For Box 1, this is $(x^1_1, \ldots, x^1_d) = x^1$, so each point in Box 1 is dominated by x^1. For Box $i.k$, this is $(x^i_1, \ldots, x^i_{d-k}, x^i_{d-k+1}, x^{i-1}_{d-k+2} \ldots x^{i-1}_d) = \tilde{x}$. So each point in Box $i.k$ is dominated by $\tilde{x}$. Since $f_{d-k+2}, \ldots, f_d$ are decreasing, $x^i_n < x^{i-1}_n$ for $n \in \{d-k+2, \ldots, d\}$. Hence, $x^i \preceq \tilde{x}$. This means each point in Box $i.k$ is also dominated by x^i. □

Applying a similar approach, one could obtain a formula for the hypervolume contribution in d-dimensions. We can then apply calculus techniques to get information about optimal μ-distributions and other aspects that were considered in this paper. The complexity of these investigations increases with the complexity of the hypervolume formula.

6. EXTENSIONS TO CONE BASED DOMINATION STRUCTURES

Many multi-objective optimization problems use a cone based domination concept. A nonempty set $C \subseteq \mathbb{R}^d$ is called a cone if $c \in C \Rightarrow \lambda c \in C$ for all $\lambda \geq 0$. A cone C is convex if $C + C \subset C$. A cone C is called pointed if it satisfies that $C \cap (-C) = \{\mathbf{0}\}$ where $\mathbf{0}$ is the zero vector in $\mathbb{R}^d$. The non-negative orthant of $\mathbb{R}^d$, $\mathbb{R}^d_+$ is also a closed, convex and pointed cone. Let $\preceq_C$ denote the weak cone order induced by the cone C. Hence, for $u, v \in \mathbb{R}^d$, $u \preceq_C v$ iff $v - u \in C$. Based on cones, we found two approaches to defining hypervolume indicators.

6.1 Cone Based Hypervolume

The cone based hypervolume indicator [3] was defined recently. For a finite approximation set $A \subset \mathbb{R}^d$ and a closed, convex and pointed cone $\mathcal{C}$, the cone hypervolume indicator is defined as:

$$CI_H(A, r) = \lambda(CH(A, r)) = \lambda((A \oplus \mathcal{C}) \cap (r \ominus \mathcal{C})),$$

where λ is the Lebesque measure, $r \in \mathbb{R}^d$ is the reference point. The cone based hypervolume contribution is defined in the usual way. Figure 3 shows the cone based hypervolume indicator for six Pareto-optimal points, out of which

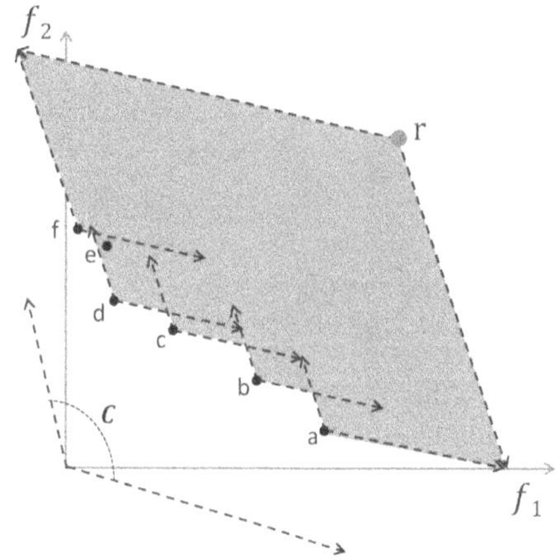

Figure 3: An illustration of *cone based hypervolume*. r is the reference point, $\mathcal{C}$ is the cone, and the shaded area is the cone based hypervolume. The Pareto front consists of the points a, b, c, d, e, f. The point e is cone dominated by d and hence e has no cone based hypervolume contribution.

The theorem that only the neighboring points on the curve influence the hypervolume contribution of a point can be extended for the case of lines to the cone based scenario.

THEOREM 9. *Let $f(t)$, $t \in [t_{\min}, t_{\max}]$ be a* line *in $\mathbb{R}^d$ with each objective monotonic and let $A_t = \{t_1, \ldots, t_\mu\}$ describe an ordered set of distinct points on f with $|A_t| = \mu$. Let the points be C non-dominated (i.e., $f(t_i) \npreceq_C f(t_j)$ for each distinct index i and j). Then, the hypervolume contribution of a point $f(t_i)$ with $t_i \in A_t$, $i \in \{1, \ldots, \mu\}$ is only influenced by its neighboring points on the curve, i.e. $f(t_{i-1})$ and $f(t_{i+1})$ if they exist, and possibly the reference point r.*

PROOF. The proof idea is similar to the proof of Theorem 1. Let $a := f(t_i)$, $b := f(t_{i+1})$, $c := f(t)$ with $t > t_{i+1}$ and let z be an arbitrary point which is cone dominated by a and cone dominates the reference point, i.e. $a \preceq_C z$ and $z \preceq_C r$. We have to show that if $a \preceq_C z$ and $c \preceq_C z$ then

$b \preceq_C z$. Using linearity and convexity

$$\begin{aligned} z - b &= z - (\delta a + (1-\delta)c), \quad \text{for some } \delta \in (0,1) \\ &= \delta(z-a) + (1-\delta)(z-c) \\ &= \delta c^1 + (1-\delta)c^2 \quad \text{for some } c^1, c^2 \in C \\ &\in C \end{aligned} \tag{8}$$

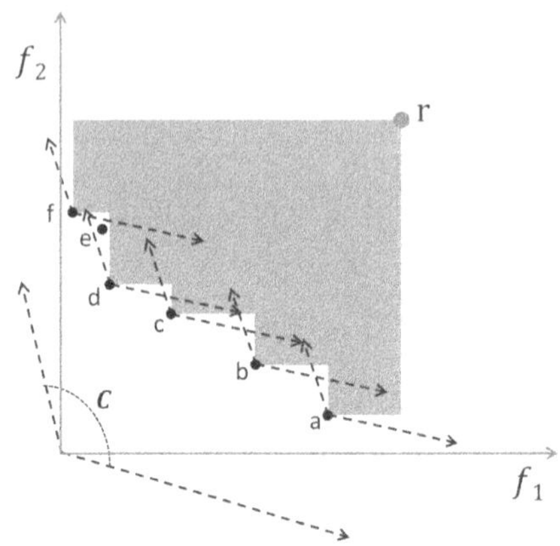

Figure 4: An illustration of general ordering based hypervolume. r is the reference point, C is the cone, and the shaded area is the *general ordering based hypervolume*. The Pareto front consists of the points a, b, c, d, e, f. The point e is cone dominated by d and hence e has no general ordering based hypervolume contribution.

For the case of polyhedral cones, we can obtain more results. For this, let $\mathcal{A}$ be the $d \times d$ matrix that defines the polyhedral cone, i.e., $C := \{u \in \mathbb{R}^d : \mathcal{A}d \geq 0\}$. From [3] and from [4, Lemma 2.3.4], we know that the set of cone efficient solutions is the same as the set of (Pareto) efficient points of the transformed objective $\mathcal{A}f$. Hence, if C is polyhedral, we can obtain results similar to the theoretical results from Sections 2-6 of this paper, by working in the (linearly) transformed objective space.

6.2 General Ordering Based Hypervolume

In the case of general ordering relation (cone or non-cone based), a different way of calculating hypervolumes is proposed in [5]. Given an ordering relation that we assume to be a cone C, this hypervolume measure in [5] is defined as the hypervolume (according to the Pareto cone) of exactly those solutions that are optimal w.r.t. C. In other words, the hypervolume contribution of cone dominated points is *set* to zero, the other points have a hypervolume contribution according to the Pareto cone.

The theoretical results from Sections 2-6 of this paper can easily be reformulated in the case of this cone based hypervolume measure (in the sense of [5]). For this, we just need to remove the dominated elements (according to the underlying ordering relation) beforehand (see Figure 4). If we assume a cone based ordering and a linear front (whereby front is according to the Pareto cone) then either the entire line is cone optimal or just an endpoint is cone optimal. Hence, the results for linear fronts also hold if the entire line consist only of points that are optimal w.r.t. the cone ordering relation.

7. CONCLUSIONS AND OUTLOOK

This paper presented results about the hypervolume indicator in case of three and more objective functions. We have seen that the choice of the reference point can determine if the extremes of the Pareto front are included (or not) in an optimal μ-distribution. Especially for linear fronts, we got insights in the shape of optimal μ-distributions and achieved the surprising result that an equispaced solution is not possible in a proper three-dimensional problem. We have also seen that investigation become much more complex when the number of objective functions increases. The formula for the hypervolume in the general case of d objective functions (Theorem 8) hints at the growing complexity of such investigations.

We are currently exploring results about uniqueness of the optimal μ-distribution, for both Pareto, polyhedral and nonpolyhedral general cones. Furthermore, it would be interesting to examine if the results could be generalized for the weighted hypervolume indicator [7] or other trade-off based indicators [6].

8. REFERENCES

[1] A. Auger, J. Bader, and D. Brockhoff. Theoretically investigating optimal μ-distributions for the hypervolume indicator: First results for three objectives. In R. Schaefer, C. Cotta, J. KoÅĆodziej, and G. Rudolph, editors, *PPSN*, pages 586–596. Springer, 2010.

[2] A. Auger, J. Bader, D. Brockhoff, and E. Zitzler. Theory of the hypervolume indicator: Optimal μ-distributions and the choice of the reference point. In *FOGA*, pages 87–102. ACM, 2009.

[3] M. Emmerich, A. Deutz, J. Kruisselbrink, and P. Shukla. Cone-based hypervolume indicators: Construction, properties, and efficient computation. In R. Purshouse, P. Fleming, C. Fonseca, S. Greco, and J. Shaw, editors, *EMO*, volume 7811 of *Lecture Notes in Computer Science*, pages 111–127. Springer, 2013.

[4] Y. Sawaragi, H. Nakayama, and T. Tanino. *Theory of multiobjective optimization*, volume 176. Academic Press Inc., Orlando, FL, 1985.

[5] P. Shukla and M. Braun. Indicator based search in variable orderings: Theory and algorithms. In R. e. a. Purshouse, editor, *Evolutionary Multi-Criterion Optimization*, volume 7811 of *Lecture Notes in Computer Science*, pages 66–80. Springer, 2013.

[6] P. Shukla, C. Hirsch, and H. Schmeck. A framework for incorporating trade-off information using multi-objective evolutionary algorithms. In R. Schaefer, C. Cotta, J. KoÅĆodziej, and G. Rudolph, editors, *PPSN XI*, volume 6239 of *Lecture Notes in Computer Science*, pages 131–140. Springer, 2010.

[7] E. Zitzler, D. Brockhoff, and L. Thiele. The hypervolume indicator revisited: On the design of pareto-compliant indicators via weighted integration. In S. Obayashi, K. Deb, C. Poloni, T. Hiroyasu, and T. Murata, editors, *EMO*, pages 862–876. Springer, 2007.

Gaussian Mixture Model of Evolutionary Algorithms

Bo Song
Dept. of Electrical and Electronic Engineering
The University of Hong Kong, Hong Kong
bsong@hku.hk

Victor O. K. Li
Dept. of Electrical and Electronic Engineering
The University of Hong Kong, Hong Kong
vli@eee.hku.hk

ABSTRACT

This paper proposes a novel finite Gaussian mixture model to study the population dynamics of evolutionary algorithms on continuous optimization problems. While previous research taking on a dynamical system view has established the transition equation between the density functions of consecutive populations, the equation usually does not have closed-form solutions and can only be applied to very few optimization problems. In this paper, we address this issue by approximating both the population density function of each generation and the objective function by finite Gaussian mixtures. We show that by making such approximations the transition equation can be solved exactly and key statistics, such as the expected mean and the variance of fitness values of the population, can be calculated easily. We also prove that by choosing appropriate values of the parameters, the L^1-norm error between our model and the actual population density function can be made arbitrarily small, up until a predefined generation. We present experimental results to show that our model is useful in simulating and examining the dynamics of evolutionary algorithms.

Categories and Subject Descriptors

F.2.1 [**ANALYSIS OF ALGORITHMS AND PROBLEM COMPLEXITY**]: Numerical Algorithms and Problems; I.2.8 [**ARTIFICIAL INTELLIGENCE**]: Problem Solving, Control Methods, and Search—*Heuristic methods*; G.1.6 [**NUMERICAL ANALYSIS**]: Optimization

General Terms

Algorithms; Theory

Keywords

Evolutionary Algorithm; Population Dynamics; Gaussian Mixture

GECCO'14, July 12–16, 2014, Vancouver, BC, Canada.

http://dx.doi.org/10.1145/2576768.2598252 .

1. INTRODUCTION

Despite the efficiency and effectiveness of evolutionary algorithms at solving difficult optimization problems, the understanding of the underlying evolutionary processes and the behavior of these algorithms remain incomplete. Among the many theoretical analyses of evolutionary algorithms, the dynamical systems modelling approach is a primary and influential one. The idea is to consider the state space of all possible populations, and the stochastic evolution of the populations from one generation to the next is characterized by the transition matrix of a Markov chain. Equivalently, as a distribution of the population states corresponds to a probability density function determining the probability that each individual occurs in the population (henceforth denominated as population density function), the evolution of the algorithm can also be characterized by a difference equation (transition equation) between population density functions of consecutive generations. The transition equation describes exactly how the population evolves as the evolutionary algorithm progresses. In order to obtain simple forms of the transition equation and derive analytical results, an assumption that the evolutionary algorithm has infinite population size is often made, and properties regarding the transient and asymptotic behavior of the evolutionary algorithms are analyzed. In addition, given the initial population density function, it is possible to simulate and visualize the trajectories of key statistics of the algorithm such as the expected average fitness value and the expected mean center of the population on certain optimization problems, by recursively applying the transition equation.

Research efforts adopting a dynamical system view have been fruitful. Here we mention the fundamental monographs of Vose [13], Beyer [1], and the survey of Reeves and Rowe [10]. Usually, the research starts with the most general forms of population density functions (or population vectors as used in [10, 13]) and objective (fitness) functions. Then, the transition equation is derived by modeling the effects of various operators on the population, such as that of mutation and fitness proportional selection. Though under the infinite population size assumption the transition equation often has simple forms and general properties can be derived from the transition matrix of the Markov chain, the problem with this approach is that given particular optimization problems, it is usually impossible to construct the transition matrix in practice, and to solve the transition equation analytically. In other words, the transition equation cannot be applied recursively to simulate the running of the evolutionary algorithms generation by generation.

To resolve this issue, one major approach is to introduce the framework of statistical mechanics [10,11]. The idea is that instead of using *microscopic* descriptions of population dynamics to describe precisely what happens to the population density function after each iteration, use *macroscopic* descriptions where key statistics of interest such as the average fitness value of the population become the target to be modeled and analyzed. For example, if the average fitness value is taken as the key statistic to describe a population, the first step of a statistical mechanics analysis is likely to be modelling the probability distribution of average fitness values over all possible populations in each generation. Then, by truncating a representation of this distribution (such as moments or cumulants) to a certain number of terms, a transition equation of the preserved terms can be derived and readily solved. The benefit of this approach is that by characterizing population dynamics by a few statistics, the scale of the model is greatly reduced, thus simulation and visualization of the dynamics of the system are possible. Also, most of the time the key statistics in the model are closely related to the properties of interest. Therefore, this level of description seems sufficient. However, the drawback of this approach is that the key statistics do not contain all the information to describe a population and truncating transformations of probability distributions further discards information, additional approximation errors are introduced. Besides, in general, the transition equation of the preserved terms is usually difficult to derive, and other principles such as the principle of maximum entropy or other modelling assumptions are needed to derive it. In fact, only a few discrete optimization problems have been successfully analyzed by this approach [10].

In this paper, we propose a different approach. We are concerned mainly with continuous optimization problems, and the target model to be approximated is the general model introduced by [8,9]. This model studies the dynamics of simple evolutionary algorithms with infinite population size, and the transition equation of the model is a microscopic level description of the evolution of the population density functions. Instead of using statistical mechanics to simulate the evolution of the system, we propose a novel finite Gaussian mixture model to solve the transition equation approximately. The key to our model is that both the objective function and the population density functions are approximated by finite Gaussian mixtures. Due to the nice properties of Gaussian functions, such approximations guarantee that the transition equation can be solved analytically and the solution is also a Gaussian mixture. Moreover, key statistics of interest such as the expected mean and the variance of fitness values of the population can also be easily calculated from the population density functions of Gaussian mixtures. Regarding the accuracy of our method, we prove that our framework works for nearly arbitrary continuous objective functions, and given a predefined generation number k and a tolerance level ϵ, by choosing appropriate parameter values, the L^1-norm error of our method can be less than ϵ up until the kth generation. We simulate our model running on low dimensional multimodal optimization problems and visualize and compare the simulation results with results obtained from actually running the algorithm. The experimental results show that our method can predict the behavior of evolutionary algorithms with fair accuracy. To the best of our knowledge, our effort is the first in adopting approximation techniques other than statistical mechanics and function transforms to study the population dynamics of evolutionary algorithms.

The rest of this paper is organized as follows. In Section 2 we provide a review on research efforts directly related to our work. In Section 3 we describe our Gaussian mixture model. The analysis of the L^1-norm error is presented in Section 4. Experimental results are presented in Section 5. Finally, in Section 6 we conclude the paper and suggest possible future work.

2. RELATED WORK

As our method is different from traditional approaches, we draw our inspirations from diverse sources. It is our understanding that the greatest difficulty in calculating an infinite population model in the general case lies in the fact that the fitness function can be of any form. This mandates that in order to solve the transition equation analytically and iterate it recursively, the approximation framework must assume "compatible" forms of both the fitness function and population density functions. In this regard, the research of [14,15] is illuminating. Though the crux of these papers is not to devise an approximation framework as in this one, in the analysis the authors directly applied the Walsh transform (the Fourier transform for binary representations) to mixing matrix (or population density function in this context) and at some point to the fitness functions. However, as we are more concerned with evolutionary algorithms on continuous optimization problems and it usually incorporates operators that directly use Gaussian functions, it is more natural and simpler to approximate the fitness function and population density functions as Gaussian mixtures.

There are also a few studies on population dynamics of evolutionary algorithms solving specific problems. Among them [3] is similar to this work in that it also assumes a specific form of population density functions. The population density functions are described by probabilistic graphical models in their research. For the symbolic regression problem considered in that paper, this representation is natural and exact. However, our study differs from that paper in that the latter is mainly an empirical study which does not consider transition functions explicitly and the graphical model is learned from experimental results.

Though to our knowledge we are the first to use Gaussian mixtures to study population dynamics of evolutionary algorithms, in other fields such as estimation and filtering theory, Gaussian mixtures have been used to study dynamical systems. Among them we mention [12], which seems most relevant to our study. That study is concerned with evolving state probability density functions of nonlinear dynamical systems. Its main contribution is in proposing two novel schemes to update the weights of components of Gaussian mixtures as system uncertainty propagates. However, unlike this paper their study assumes that the number of components in the Gaussian mixture remains the same all the time, which seems unrealistic for modelling evolutionary algorithms and also introduces additional error. Besides, the approximation and propagation error of density functions is not considered in their research.

With respect to the L^1-norm error of the model, the first part of our proof is based entirely on the fundamental results of [4–6]. Basically, the study of [6] proves that Gaussian mixtures can approximate any functions in L^p, $p \in [1, +\infty)$

with arbitrarily small L^p-norm error, while the study of [4,5] gives a more detailed analysis on the error of approximations with regard to parameter values. In particular, [5] is an application of the general results in the field approximate approximations introduced by the Swedish mathematician Vladimir Maz'ya (see [4] for a more recent survey).

3. THE GAUSSIAN MIXTURE MODEL

3.1 Notations and Preliminaries

In this paper, a function a of x is commonly denoted as $a(x)$, and a is used when there is no risk of confusion. Random variables and random vectors are represented in ***boldface***. The expectation and variance of $a(\boldsymbol{x})$ with $\boldsymbol{x} \sim f(x)$ are denoted as $E_f a(\boldsymbol{x})$ and $Var_f a(\boldsymbol{x})$, respectively, or $E_{\boldsymbol{x}} a(\boldsymbol{x})$ and $Var_{\boldsymbol{x}} a(\boldsymbol{x})$ if the distribution is clear in the context. Notice that if a maps $\boldsymbol{x}$ into a vector, $Var_{\boldsymbol{x}} a$ is actually the covariance matrix of $a(\boldsymbol{x})$.

The multidimensional Gaussian function or multivariate normal distribution with parameters μ, Σ is denoted as

$$f_N(\mu, \Sigma)(x) = \frac{1}{(2\pi)^{\frac{d}{2}} |\Sigma|^{\frac{1}{2}}} \exp\left[-\frac{1}{2}(x-\mu)^T \Sigma^{-1}(x-\mu)\right]$$

where $\mu \in \mathbb{R}^d$ is the mean vector and the symmetric positive definite matrix $\Sigma \in \mathbb{R}^{d\times d}$ is the covariance matrix. A finite Gaussian mixture in $\mathbb{R}^d$ with m components is a function $h : \mathbb{R}^d \mapsto \mathbb{R}$ with the form

$$h(x) = \sum_{i=1}^{m} \pi_i f_N(\mu_i, \Sigma_i)(x) \tag{1}$$

where π_i is called the weight of component i. Notice that in the paper we are using the term "finite Gaussian mixture" to mean any function with the form (1). If the finite Gaussian mixture represents a probability density function, it is also required that $\pi_i > 0$ and $\sum_{i=1}^{m} \pi_i = 1$.This requirement is often omitted if the context is clear.

We use Euclidean norm for vectors and denote it as $\|\cdot\|$, and the L^p norm for functions is denoted as $\|\cdot\|_p$ where $p \in [1, +\infty]$. For any two functions $a, b : \mathbb{R}^d \mapsto \mathbb{R}$, denote $(a * b)(x)$ or $a * b$ as the d-dimensional convolution of a and b, i.e.

$$(a * b)(x) = \int_{\mathbb{R}^d} a(y) b(x-y) dy$$

Throughout the paper the continuous optimization problem has the following form

$$\max g(x) \text{ s.t. } x \in \mathbb{R}^d$$

where $g : \mathbb{R}^d \mapsto \mathbb{R}$ is the objective function or the so-called fitness function. We further assume that

$$0 < g_{\min} \leqslant g(x) \leqslant g_{\max} < \infty \tag{2}$$

where $g_{\min}$ and $g_{\max}$ are the known lower and upper bounds, respectively. Note that by (2) $g \in L^\infty$.

The simple evolutionary algorithm considered in this paper includes only mutation and fitness proportional selection. It is similar to the algorithm analyzed in [8]. However, we restrict the mutation operator to be adding an independent multivariate normal random vector $\boldsymbol{w} \sim f_N(\mu_w, \Sigma_w)$ to each individual in the population. In fact it is also the most commonly used mutation operator for continuous optimization problems. The pseudo-code of the algorithm is shown in Algorithm 1.

Algorithm 1: The Simple Evolutionary Algorithm

```
Input: population size N; initial population density
       function f_0
set k = 0; sample N individuals x_0^1, x_0^2, ..., x_0^N
  identically and independently according to f_0;
while stopping criteria is not satisfied do
  | (Selection) choose y_k^i from x_k^1, x_k^2, ..., x_k^N such that
  | Pr{y_k^i = x_k^j} = g(x_k^j) / sum_{l=1}^N g(x_k^l) for all i, j = 1, 2, ..., N;
  | (Mutation) sample x_{k+1}^i from the distribution of
  | random vector y_k^i + w for all i = 1, 2, ..., N;
  | k = k + 1;
end
```

In this paper the population density function of generation k is denoted as f_k. In particular, f_0 is the density function of the first population and it depends on how the initial population is constructed. To simplify the analysis of approximation errors we further assume that

$$f_0 \text{ is continuous with compact support} \tag{3}$$

The key result of [8] is the large sample theory proof of the transition function between f_k and f_{k+1} as $N \to \infty$. It also serves as the target of approximation in our research. To reframe it in this context, this theorem reads as follows.

Theorem 1 (Qi & Palmieri [8]). *Let f_k be the population density function of the kth generation, $k = 0, 1, 2, \ldots$, and the objective function $g(x)$ satisfy (2). For the simple evolutionary algorithm as in Algorithm 1, as $N \to \infty$ the population density function f_{k+1} satisfies*

$$f_{k+1}(x) = \frac{f_k(x) \cdot g(x)}{\int_{\mathbb{R}^d} f_k(y) g(y) dy} * f_N(\mu_w, \Sigma_w)(x) \tag{4}$$

The transition equation (4) in Theorem 1 can be divided into two parts. The effects of fitness proportional selection constitute the first part. If we denote

$$f'_k(x) = \frac{f_k \cdot g}{\int_{\mathbb{R}^d} f_k(y) g(y) dy} \tag{5}$$

then f'_k is the population density function after selection. Similarly, the effect of mutation is expressed by

$$f_{k+1}(x) = f'_k * f_N(\mu_w, \Sigma_w) \tag{6}$$

As can be seen from (4), because g can be any real-valued function, it is highly probable that (4) cannot be analytically solved. Moreover, even if f_{k+1} can be obtained by substituting g and f_k into (4), it is not likely that subsequent population density functions starting from f_{k+2} can all be obtained by substituting g and its predecessors. It is for this reason that the approximations of g and f_k should have "compatible" forms.

3.2 The Gaussian Mixture Model

The core of our research is to use finite Gaussian mixtures to approximate g and f_k, so that the transition function (4) is analytically solvable and the solution is also in Gaussian mixture form.

3.2.1 Approximation of Fitness Function g and Initial Population Density Function f_0

This section explains the method to approximate the fitness function g and the initial population density function f_0 with finite Gaussian mixtures. The idea is to sample function values on a lattice in a region of interest, and then interpolate the function with Gaussian kernels. The approach coincides with [6] and [5] and we describe it in our context.

Consider an arbitrary continuous function $u \in L^p : \mathbb{R}^d \mapsto \mathbb{R}$ for some $p \in [1, +\infty]$. The approximation procedure requires two parameters $D > 0$ and $h > 0$ to control the sampling granularity and an additional parameter $r > 0$ to control the region of sampling. The formula of interpolation reads as

$$\hat{u}(x) = \sum_{z \in \mathbb{Z}^d, hz \in [-r,r]^d} h^d \cdot u(hz) \cdot f_N(hz, \frac{Dh^2}{2} I_d) \quad (7)$$

where I_d is the d-dimensional identity matrix. Basically this procedure samples the region $[-r, r]^d$ with step size h and interpolates each sample with the Gaussian function $f_N(0, \frac{Dh^2}{2} I_d)$. The result $\hat{u}$ has $(\lfloor \frac{2r}{h} \rfloor + 1)^d$ components.

Note that in (7), if $\hat{u}$ is constructed by sampling and interpolating the whole region of $\mathbb{R}^d$, the Gaussian mixture $\hat{u}$ will have infinite number of components. Therefore, to make $\hat{u}$ a finite mixture the parameter r is introduced.

To approximate f_0, because f_0 has a compact support, r_{f_0} can be a value such that *supp*$(f_0) \subset [-r_{f_0}, r_{f_0}]^d$ where *supp*$(\cdot)$ denote the support of a function. In practice however, it may happen that f_0 does not have a compact support. In that case, we suggest a method of assigning r_{f_0} for practical use. For f_0, given a threshold $0 < \epsilon < 1$ we choose r_{f_0} such that

$$\int_{\mathbb{R}^d \setminus [-r_{f_0}, r_{f_0}]^d} |f_0(x)| dx < \epsilon \int_{\mathbb{R}^d} |f_0(x)| dx = \epsilon$$

The idea is to choose r_{f_0} such that the sampling region covers most "masses" of f_0. Such r_{f_0} can always be obtained because $\|f_0\|_1$ is 1.

As g is in L^∞, there is no general way to derive r_g. For practical use however, it is possible to derive a region of interest either from prior knowledge or from previous runs of the algorithm. For example, if prior knowledge is available that the global maximum is likely to be within a region S where $r_s = \max_{x \in S} \|x\|$ is known, we can set r_g to be $\max(r_{f_0}, r_s)$.

After r_g and r_{f_0} are fixed, given the parameter values of D and h we can approximate g and f_0 according to formula (7). The error of approximation with regard to parameters D and h will be analyzed in Section 4. In fact, it is more convenient to organize the expressions of approximated functions into standard representations of Gaussian mixtures. From now on we will use the notations that the Gaussian mixture approximation of g is

$$\hat{g}(x) = \sum_{i=1}^{n} c_i f_N(\mu_i, \Sigma_i) \quad (8)$$

and the Gaussian mixture approximation of the kth population density function $f_k, k = 0, 1, 2, \ldots$ is

$$\hat{f}_k(x) = \sum_{i=1}^{m_k} \pi_{ki} f_N(\mu_{ki}, \Sigma_{ki}) \quad (9)$$

3.2.2 Approximation of Transition Equation

By approximating g and f_0 by $\hat{g}$ and $\hat{f}_0$, an approximated dynamical system is constructed. The input to the system is $\hat{g}$ and $\hat{f}_0$, and the evolution of the system follows the transition equation

$$\hat{f}_{k+1}(x) = \frac{\hat{f}_k \cdot \hat{g}}{\int_{\mathbb{R}^d} \hat{f}_k(y) \hat{g}(y) dy} * f_N(\mu_w, \Sigma_w) \quad (10)$$

.

The idea is that evolving the real system (with g and f_0 as its input and (4) as the transition equation) and obtaining its population dynamics is difficult, while evolving the approximated system and observing its population dynamics $\hat{f}_k$ and key statistics such as $E_{\hat{f}_k} \hat{g}$ is easy. The transition equation of the approximated system needs not change from (4) as they are both modeling the same operators, and the error is only introduced by the approximations of g and f_0. In this section, we explain how the approximated dynamical system evolves and calculate the approximated population density function $\hat{f}_k$ by solving the transition equation (10). The key result is presented in Theorem 2 which gives a recursive equation between $\hat{f}_k$ and $\hat{f}_{k+1}$.

Theorem 2. *Let $\hat{g}$ and $\hat{f}_k$ be the approximated fitness function and the population density function of the kth generation, respectively, $k = 0, 1, 2, \ldots$, and assume that $\hat{g}$ and $\hat{f}_k$ are Gaussian mixtures with known coefficients as represented in (8) and (9). Then for the transition function (10) the population density function $\hat{f}_{k+1}$ is also a Gaussian mixture and has the following form*

$$\hat{f}_{k+1} = \frac{\sum_{i=1}^{m_k} \sum_{j=1}^{n} \pi_{ki} c_j \tilde{c}_{ij} f_N(\tilde{\mu}_{ij} + \mu_w, \tilde{\Sigma}_{ij} + \Sigma_w)}{\sum_{i=1}^{m_k} \sum_{j=1}^{n} \pi_{ki} c_j \tilde{c}_{ij}} \quad (11)$$

where

$$\begin{aligned} \tilde{c}_{ij} &= f_N(\mu_j, \Sigma_{ki} + \Sigma_j)(\mu_{ki}) \\ \tilde{\Sigma}_{ij} &= (\Sigma_{ki}^{-1} + \Sigma_j^{-1})^{-1} \\ \tilde{\mu}_{ij} &= (\Sigma_{ki}^{-1} + \Sigma_j^{-1})^{-1} (\Sigma_{ki}^{-1} \mu_{ki} + \Sigma_j^{-1} \mu_j) \end{aligned} \quad (12)$$

Proof. Similar to (5) and (6), we consider the effects of selection and mutation separately. The approximated population density function after selection is

$$\hat{f}'_k(x) = \frac{\hat{f}_k \cdot \hat{g}}{\int_{\mathbb{R}^d} \hat{f}_k(y) \hat{g}(y) dy} = \frac{\hat{f}_k \cdot \hat{g}}{E_{\hat{f}_k} \hat{g}} \quad (13)$$

Consider $\hat{f}_k \cdot \hat{g}$ only. By using the fact (8.1.8 in [7]) that

$$f_N(\mu_a, \Sigma_a) \cdot f_N(\mu_b, \Sigma_b) = c f_N(\mu_c, \Sigma_c)$$

where

$$\begin{aligned} c &= f_N(\mu_b, \Sigma_a + \Sigma_b)(\mu_a) \\ \Sigma_c &= (\Sigma_a^{-1} + \Sigma_b^{-1})^{-1} \\ \mu_c &= (\Sigma_a^{-1} + \Sigma_b^{-1})^{-1} (\Sigma_a^{-1} \mu_a + \Sigma_b^{-1} \mu_b) \end{aligned}$$

$\hat{f}_k \cdot \hat{g}$ can be calculated as

$$\begin{aligned}\hat{f}_k\hat{g} &= \sum_{i=1}^{m_k}\sum_{j=1}^{n}\pi_{ki}c_j f_N(\mu_{ki},\Sigma_{ki}) f_N(\mu_j,\Sigma_j)\\ &= \sum_{i=1}^{m_k}\sum_{j=1}^{n}\pi_{ki}c_j\tilde{c}_{ij} f_N(\tilde{\mu}_{ij},\tilde{\Sigma}_{ij}) \qquad (14)\end{aligned}$$

where $\tilde{c}_{ij}$, $\tilde{\mu}_{ij}$ and $\tilde{\Sigma}_{ij}$ satisfies (12). Also by (14)

$$E_{\hat{f}_k}\hat{g} = \sum_{i=1}^{m_k}\sum_{j=1}^{n}\pi_{ki}c_j\tilde{c}_{ij} \qquad (15)$$

Combining (13), (14) and (15) we get

$$\hat{f}_k'(x) = \frac{\sum_{i=1}^{m_k}\sum_{j=1}^{n}\pi_{ki}c_j\tilde{c}_{ij} f_N(\tilde{\mu}_{ij},\tilde{\Sigma}_{ij})}{\sum_{i=1}^{m_k}\sum_{j=1}^{n}\pi_{ki}c_j\tilde{c}_{ij}} \qquad (16)$$

Now the effect of mutation can be characterized as

$$\hat{f}_{k+1}(x) = \hat{f}_k' * f_N(\mu_w,\Sigma_w) \qquad (17)$$

Substituting (16) into (17) and taking into account the fact (8.1.4 in [7]) that

$$f_N(\mu_a,\Sigma_a) * f_N(\mu_b,\Sigma_b) = f_N(\mu_a+\mu_b,\Sigma_a+\Sigma_b)$$

(11) can be easily verified and the proof is complete. □

Theorem 2 states that if $\hat{f}_k$ is a Gaussian mixture of m_k components, then $\hat{f}_{k+1}$ is also a Gaussian mixture and it has $m_k \cdot n$ components. Notice that it is the selection operator that increases the number of components, and for the mutation operator the component number remains the same. It can be conceived that for the approximated dynamical system, the population density function of the kth generation has $m_0 \cdot n^k$ components. As it grows exponentially, we simply limit the number of components in the mixture by discarding components with least weights in our implementation.

3.2.3 *Key Statistics*

In this section we show that key statistics of interest of the approximated dynamical system can also be derived from Gaussian mixture population density functions. In fact, in the proof of Theorem 2 the expected average fitness value of the population $E_{\hat{f}_k}\hat{g}$ is already calculated in (15). To be complete it is also included in the result.

Theorem 3. *Let $\hat{g}$ and $\hat{f}_k$ be the approximated fitness function and the population density function of kth generation as in Theorem 2, respectively. Then*

$$E_{\hat{f}_k}\hat{g} = \sum_{i=1}^{m_k}\sum_{j=1}^{n}\pi_{ki}c_j\tilde{c}_{ij} \qquad (18)$$

$$Var_{\hat{f}_k}\hat{g} = \sum_{\gamma=1}^{m_k}\sum_{\alpha=1}^{n}\sum_{\beta=1}^{n}\pi_{k\gamma}c_\alpha c_\beta d_{\alpha\beta} + \Big(\sum_{i=1}^{m_k}\sum_{j=1}^{n}\pi_{ki}c_j\tilde{c}_{ij}\Big)^2 \qquad (19)$$

$$E_{\hat{f}_k}\boldsymbol{x} = \bar{\mu} \qquad (20)$$

$$Var_{\hat{f}_k}\boldsymbol{x} = \sum_{i=1}^{m_k}\pi_{ki}\Sigma_{ki} + \sum_{i=1}^{m_k}\pi_{ki}(\mu_{ki}-\bar{\mu})(\mu_{ki}-\bar{\mu})^T \qquad (21)$$

where

$$\begin{aligned}\tilde{c}_{ij} &= f_N(\mu_j,\Sigma_{ki}+\Sigma_j)(\mu_{ki})\\ d_{\alpha\beta} &= f_N(\mu_\beta,\Sigma_\alpha+\Sigma_\beta)(\mu_\alpha) \qquad (22)\\ \bar{\mu} &= \sum_{i=1}^{m_k}\mu_{ki}\end{aligned}$$

Proof. (18) is already proved. For $Var_{\hat{f}_k}\hat{g}$, noticing that

$$Var_{\hat{f}_k}\hat{g} = E_{\hat{f}_k}\hat{g}^2 - (E_{\hat{f}_k}\hat{g})^2$$

and taking into account that $\hat{g}^2$ is also a Gaussian mixture with n^2 components, (19) can be proved by taking a similar approach to the one used in Theorem 2.

The remaining two equations are properties of finite Gaussian mixtures. The proof of (20) is straightforward and thus omitted. For (21), consider a random variable $\boldsymbol{s}$ following a discrete distribution that

$$\Pr(\boldsymbol{s}=i) = \pi_{ki}, i = 1,2,\ldots,m_k$$

Define a d-dimensional random vector $\boldsymbol{Y}$ following the conditional distribution that

$$(\boldsymbol{Y}|\boldsymbol{s}=i) \sim f_N(\mu_{ki},\Sigma_{ki})$$

It is known that the distribution of $\boldsymbol{Y}$ is equivalent to the distribution of $\boldsymbol{x}$ and they all follow the same Gaussian mixture distribution $\hat{f}_k$. By adopting the law of total covariance that

$$Var_{\hat{f}_k}\boldsymbol{Y} = E_{\boldsymbol{s}}(Var_{\boldsymbol{Y}|\boldsymbol{s}}\boldsymbol{Y}) + Var_{\boldsymbol{s}}(E_{\boldsymbol{Y}|\boldsymbol{s}}\boldsymbol{Y}) \qquad (23)$$

and calculating the two terms in (23), (21) can be proved. □

Theorem 3 gives expressions of the expected average fitness value and the variance of fitness values of the population as well as the expected mean center and the covariance matrix of the population. Though our approximated model is a microscopic description, these statistics can still be calculated with ease due to the nice properties of Gaussian mixtures. Moreover, by explicitly yielding an expression of population density function of each generation, our model provides more details of the dynamics of evolutionary algorithms than statistical mechanics methods.

4. APPROXIMATION ERROR ANALYSIS

In this section we study the L^1-norm error between the approximated population density function and the real one. More precisely, we are mostly concerned with $\|f_k - \hat{f}_k\|_1$ for $k = 0,1,2,\ldots$, where f_k and $\hat{f}_k$ are specified in Theorem 1 and Theorem 2, respectively. The analysis is on the ideal case that the number of components in a finite Gaussian mixture can be arbitrarily large, i.e. the approximation system has infinite memory. As a result, the error of truncating mixtures in implementation is not considered here. As expounded in Section 3, the approximation error stems from the interpolation of f_0 and g. Approximating f_0 introduces the error $\|f_0 - \hat{f}_0\|_1$. Then, as the two systems evolve according to the transition equations (4) and (10) respectively, the approximation error propagates and amplifies under the influence of g and $\hat{g}$. Therefore, to analyze the error of the whole system, the errors of initially approximating f_0 and g as well as the amplification effect of the transition equations must be analyzed first.

4.1 Approximation Errors of f_0 and g

This section analyzes the approximation errors of f_0 and g. The key result in this section is entirely based on [6] and [4,5]. Due to the high degree of technicality in these papers it is both impractical and unnecessary to include all details of proofs in this paper. Therefore key theorems relevant to our research are included and the implications for our research are discussed.

Theorem 4 (Park & Sandberg [6]). *Let $K : \mathbb{R}^r \mapsto \mathbb{R}$ be an integrable bounded function such that K is continuous almost everywhere and $\int_{\mathbb{R}^r} K(x)dx \neq 0$. Then the family S_K is dense in L^p for every $p \in [1, \infty)$ where S_K consists of functions $q : \mathbb{R}^r \mapsto \mathbb{R}$ represented by*

$$q(x) = \sum_{i=1}^{M} \omega_i \cdot K\left(\frac{x - z_i}{\sigma}\right) \tag{24}$$

where $\sigma > 0$, $M \in \mathbb{N}$, $\omega_i \in \mathbb{R}$ and $z_i \in \mathbb{R}^r$.

Theorem 4 is the main result in [6]. It proves that under certain mild conditions (bounded, integrable and continuous almost everywhere) the function family S_K can approximate any function in L^p with arbitrarily small L^p-norm error. If we take the function $f_N(0, I_d)$ as K, apparently it satisfies the conditions in Theorem 4. Therefore the family $S_{f_N(0,I_d)}$ is dense in L^p. By merging constants into ω_i, $S_{f_N(0,I_d)}$ consists of functions of the form

$$q(x) = \sum_{i=1}^{M} \omega_i \cdot f_N(z_i, \sigma^2 I_d) \tag{25}$$

Therefore we have

Corollary 1. *The family of Gaussian mixtures of functions in the form of (25) is dense in L^p with $p \in [1, +\infty)$.*

Comparing (7) with (25), it can be seen that $\hat{u}$ is in $S_{f_N(0,I_d)}$ and $\hat{u}$ corresponds to an instance of (25) where the values of z_i, ω_i, σ and M are decided by r, h, D and $u(\cdot)$. In fact, though Corollary 1 states that the family $S_{f_N(0,I_d)}$ has the ability to universally approximate any functions in L^p, it does not necessarily prove that the approximation formula (7) can achieve the same goal. After carefully examining the proof of Theorem 4 in [6] however, we found that the authors in fact proved Theorem 4 by first proving that formula (7) is able to universally approximate any continuous functions with compact support in L^p as $\sqrt{D}h \to 0$, though this fact was not presented as a lemma or a theorem in the paper. Combining this fact with the fact that f_0 is continuous with compact support and is in L^1, we have

Theorem 5. *Let f_0 be the density function of the first population and satisfy (3). Then there exist appropriate values of r, D and h for f_0 such that by applying formula (7) to f_0 the approximation error $\|f_0 - \hat{f}_0\|_1$ can be arbitrarily small.*

For the approximation of g, because g satisfies (2), g is in L^∞ and does not have compact support. Therefore, the reasoning leading to Theorem 5 is not applicable to g. In this regard, [4,5] provides further analysis. Based on Lemma 2.1 in [5] and its related discussions we formulate one relevant result as a theorem and discuss its implications.

Theorem 6 (Maz'ya & Schmidt [5]). *For any function $u \in C^2(\mathbb{R}^n) \cap W^2_\infty(\mathbb{R}^n)$ it holds that*

$$\begin{aligned} |u(x) - \tilde{u}(x)| \leqslant{} & |u(x)| \sum_{v \in \mathbb{Z}^n \setminus \{0\}} \exp(-D\pi^2\|v\|^2) \\ & + Dh\pi \sum_{|\boldsymbol{\alpha}|=1} |\partial^{\boldsymbol{\alpha}} u(x)| \sum_{v \in \mathbb{Z}^n \setminus \{0\}} |v^{\boldsymbol{\alpha}}| \exp(-D\pi^2\|v\|^2) \\ & + (\sqrt{D}h)^2 \sum_{|\boldsymbol{\alpha}|=2} \rho_{\boldsymbol{\alpha}} \|\partial^{\boldsymbol{\alpha}} u\|_\infty \end{aligned} \tag{26}$$

where

$$\tilde{u}(x) = (\pi D)^{-\frac{n}{2}} \sum_{m \in \mathbb{Z}^n} u(hm) \exp\left(-\frac{\|x - hm\|^2}{Dh^2}\right) \tag{27}$$

and

$$\rho_{\boldsymbol{\alpha}} = \frac{1}{\boldsymbol{\alpha}!} \left\| D^{-n/2} \sum_{m \in \mathbb{Z}^n} \left| \left(\frac{\cdot - m}{\sqrt{D}}\right) \eta\left(\frac{\cdot - m}{\sqrt{D}}\right) \right| \right\|_\infty \tag{28}$$

In Theorem 6, $\boldsymbol{\alpha}$ is a multi-index $(\alpha_1, \alpha_2, \ldots, \alpha_n) \in \mathbb{Z}^n_{\geqslant 0}$ and $|\boldsymbol{\alpha}| = \alpha_1 + \cdots + \alpha_n$, $x^{\boldsymbol{\alpha}} = x_1^{\alpha_1} \cdots x_n^{\alpha_n}$, $\boldsymbol{\alpha}! = \alpha_1! \cdots \alpha_n!$ and $\partial^{\boldsymbol{\alpha}} u(x) = \frac{\partial^{|\boldsymbol{\alpha}|}}{\partial {x_1}^{\alpha_1} \cdots \partial {x_n}^{\alpha_n}} u(x)$. The Sobolev space W^N_p, $p \in [1, +\infty]$ and $N \in \mathbb{N}$ consists of functions in L^p whose generalized derivatives up to order N also belong to L^p. C^N consists of continuous functions whose generalized derivatives up to order N exist and are all continuous.

To see the relevance of Theorem 6 to our research, first note that $\tilde{u}$ in (27) is equivalent to $\hat{u}$ in (7) when $r = +\infty$. Secondly, as $u \in W^2_\infty$, $\|u\|_\infty$ and $\|\partial^{\boldsymbol{\alpha}} u\|_\infty, |\boldsymbol{\alpha}| = 1, 2$ are all finite. Therefore the terms related to u in (26) can all be bounded by constants. As a consequence, if D is fixed and $h \to 0$, the second and third terms in (26) vanish and the remaining term or the so-called saturation error is $\|u(x)\|_\infty \sum_{v \in \mathbb{Z}^n \setminus \{0\}} \exp(-D\pi^2\|v\|^2)$. It can be seen that this term can be arbitrarily small when $D \to +\infty$. Combining these facts, it can be concluded that $\|u - \tilde{u}\|_\infty$ can be arbitrarily small if the values of h and D are chosen appropriately.

For the approximation error of $\hat{u}$, it is proved in chapter 2.3.2 of [4] that $\|\tilde{u} - \hat{u}\|_\infty$ can be arbitrarily small by choosing appropriate values of r in (7) when D and h are all fixed. Because $\|u - \hat{u}\|_\infty \leqslant \|u - \tilde{u}\|_\infty + \|\tilde{u} - \hat{u}\|_\infty$, combining this fact with all previous reasoning it can be concluded that $\|u - \hat{u}\|_\infty$ can be arbitrarily small if the values of D, h and r are chosen appropriately. In summary, we have

Theorem 7. *Let $g \in C^2 \cap W^2_\infty$ be the objective function. Then there exist appropriate values of r, D and h for g such that by applying formula (7) to g the approximation error $\|g - \hat{g}\|_\infty$ can be arbitrarily small.*

4.2 Propagation Error

In this section we analyze the amplification effects of transition functions on approximation errors. More specifically, assume the error of the kth generation $\|f_k - \hat{f}_k\|_1$ is known, we want to derive an upper bound for $\|f_{k+1} - \hat{f}_{k+1}\|_1$.

Theorem 8. *Let g and $\hat{g}$ be the real and approximated fitness functions and f_k and $\hat{f}_k$ be the real and approximated population density functions of the kth generation, $k = 0, 1, 2, \ldots$. Assume that g satisfies (2) and $\|f_k - \hat{f}_k\|_1$ and $\|g - \hat{g}\|_\infty$ are known. Then*

$$\|f_{k+1} - \hat{f}_{k+1}\|_1 \leqslant \frac{2g_{\max}}{g_{\min}} \|f_k - \hat{f}_k\|_1 + \frac{2\|g - \hat{g}\|_\infty}{g_{\min}} \tag{29}$$

Furthermore, if $\|f_0 - \hat{f}_0\|_1$ is known, it holds that

$$\|f_k - \hat{f}_k\|_1 \leqslant \alpha^k \|f_0 - \hat{f}_0\|_1 + \|g - \hat{g}\|_\infty \cdot \frac{1-\alpha^k}{1-\alpha}\beta \quad (30)$$

where $\alpha = \frac{2g_{\max}}{g_{\min}}$ and $\beta = \frac{2}{g_{\min}}$.

Proof. To be concise we denote $\int_{\mathbb{R}^d} a(x)b(x)dx$ as $\int ab$. Adopting the notations in the proof of Theorem 2, we consider the effects of selection and mutation separately.

To analyze the effect of selection, first note that as g satisfies (2) and the Gaussian mixtures $\hat{f}_k, \hat{g} > 0$ are continuous functions,

$$0 < g_{\min} \leqslant \int f_k g = \left| \int f_k g \right| = \int |f_k g|$$

and

$$0 < \int \hat{f}_k \hat{g} = \left| \int \hat{f}_k \hat{g} \right| = \int \left| \hat{f}_k \hat{g} \right|$$

The L^1-norm difference after selection is

$$\begin{aligned}
\left\| f'_k - \hat{f}'_k \right\|_1 &= \left\| \frac{f_k g}{\int f_k g} - \frac{\hat{f}_k \hat{g}}{\int \hat{f}_k \hat{g}} \right\|_1 \\
&= \frac{\left\| \int \hat{f}_k \hat{g} \cdot \left(f_k g - \hat{f}_k \hat{g} \right) + \hat{f}_k \hat{g} \cdot \left(\int \hat{f}_k \hat{g} - \int f_k g \right) \right\|_1}{\int f_k g \int \hat{f}_k \hat{g}} \\
&\leqslant \frac{\int \hat{f}_k \hat{g} \cdot \left\| f_k g - \hat{f}_k \hat{g} \right\|_1 + \int \hat{f}_k \hat{g} \cdot \left| \int \hat{f}_k \hat{g} - \int f_k g \right|}{\int f_k g \int \hat{f}_k \hat{g}} \\
&\leqslant \frac{2 \left\| f_k g - \hat{f}_k g + \hat{f}_k g - \hat{f}_k \hat{g} \right\|_1}{\int f_k g} \\
&\leqslant \frac{2}{\int f_k g} \left(\left\| g(f_k - \hat{f}_k) \right\|_1 + \left\| \hat{f}_k (g - \hat{g}) \right\|_1 \right) \\
&\leqslant \frac{2}{g_{\min}} \left(g_{\max} \left\| f_k - \hat{f}_k \right\|_1 + \|g - \hat{g}\|_\infty \right)
\end{aligned}$$

In the proof we used the Minkowski inequality $\|a + b\|_1 \leqslant \|a\|_1 + \|b\|_1$, Hölder's inequality $\|ab\|_1 \leqslant \|a\|_1 \|b\|_\infty$ and the inequality $\int a \leqslant \int |a|$.

To analyze the effect of mutation, first we denote $h = f_N(\mu_w, \Sigma_w)$. Obviously $\|h\|_1 = 1$. The L^1-norm difference after mutation is

$$\begin{aligned}
\left\| f_{k+1} - \hat{f}_{k+1} \right\|_1 &= \left\| f'_k * h - \hat{f}'_k * h \right\|_1 = \left\| (f'_k - \hat{f}'_k) * h \right\|_1 \\
&\leqslant \left\| f'_k - \hat{f}'_k \right\|_1 \|h\|_1 \text{ by Young's inequality} \\
&= \left\| f'_k - \hat{f}'_k \right\|_1
\end{aligned}$$

Combining the two inequalities, the proof of (29) is complete. (30) is obtained by expanding (29) recursively until $\|f_0 - \hat{f}_0\|_1$.

□

4.3 Overall Error

By applying Theorem 5 and Theorem 7, the initial approximation errors $\|f_0 - \hat{f}_0\|_1$ and $\|g - \hat{g}\|_\infty$ can be arbitrarily small. As a consequence, if k is fixed in (30), $\|f_k - \hat{f}_k\|_1$ can be arbitrarily small. Therefore the error introduced by the Gaussian mixture model can be arbitrarily small up to a predefined generation k. This result is summarized in the following theorem.

Theorem 9. *Let f_0 be the density function of the first population and satisfy (3), and $g \in C^2 \cap W^2_\infty$ be the objective function and satisfy (2). Then given a threshold $0 < \epsilon < 1$ and a generation number $k \in \mathbb{N}$, there exist appropriate values of r, D and h for f_0 and g, respectively such that by applying formula (7) to them and evolving the two systems according to Theorem 1 and Theorem 2, the approximation error $\|f_l - \hat{f}_l\|_1 < \epsilon$ for all $l \in \mathbb{N}, l \leqslant k$.*

5. EXPERIMENTAL RESULTS

In this section we apply the finite Gaussian model on a simple low dimensional optimization problem to illustrate the usefulness of the model in predicting the behavior of evolutionary algorithms. In the experiment the solution space is $\mathbb{R}^2$ and the objective function under consideration is an isotropic Gaussian mixture with two components

$$g(x) = c_1 f_N(\mu_1, \Sigma) + c_2 f_N(\mu_2, \Sigma)$$

where $\begin{pmatrix} c_1 \\ c_2 \end{pmatrix} = \begin{pmatrix} 50000 \\ 40000 \end{pmatrix}, \mu_1 = \begin{pmatrix} 2.5 \\ 2.5 \end{pmatrix}, \mu_2 = \begin{pmatrix} -2.5 \\ -2.5 \end{pmatrix}$ and $\Sigma = \begin{pmatrix} 2 & 1 \\ 1 & 2 \end{pmatrix}$. Though the problem is simple it is sufficient to illustrate our proposed approach. Besides, we mention that in general finding the maximum or all modes of a multidimensional Gaussian mixture is not an easy task [2].

The initial population density function f_0 is a Gaussian function with $\mu_{f_0} = (0, -2.5)$ and $\Sigma_{f_0} = 64I_2$. We evolve the Gaussian mixture model according to Theorem 2 for 50 generations. We also run Algorithm 1 with population size of 100, 1000, 10000 and 100000 to solve this problem once respectively. The mutation vector $\boldsymbol{w}$ follows $f_N(0, I_2)$, and the stopping criteria of the algorithm is the iteration number reaching 50. The expected average fitness value $E_{\hat{f}_k}\hat{g}$ and the expected population mean center $E_{\hat{f}_k}\boldsymbol{x}$ are calculated for each generation, and they are compared with the values observed by running the real algorithm. To facilitate calculation we set the component number limit to be 2^{15}, i.e. we preserve the largest 2^{15} components in the calculation. The simulation results are depicted in Figure 1 and Figure 2.

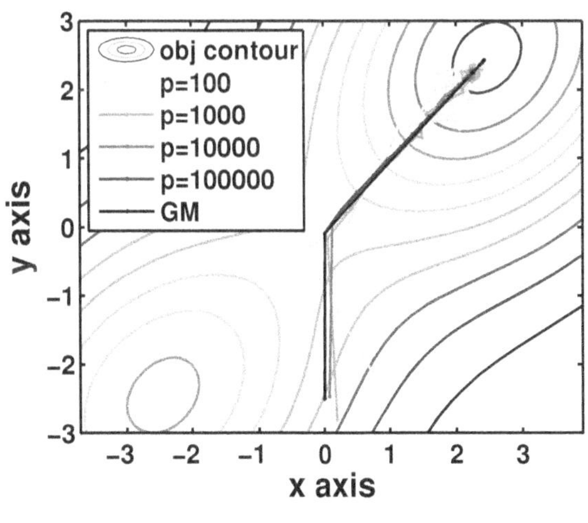

Figure 1: Trajectories of population mean center predicted by our proposed approximation and observed from running the real algorithm

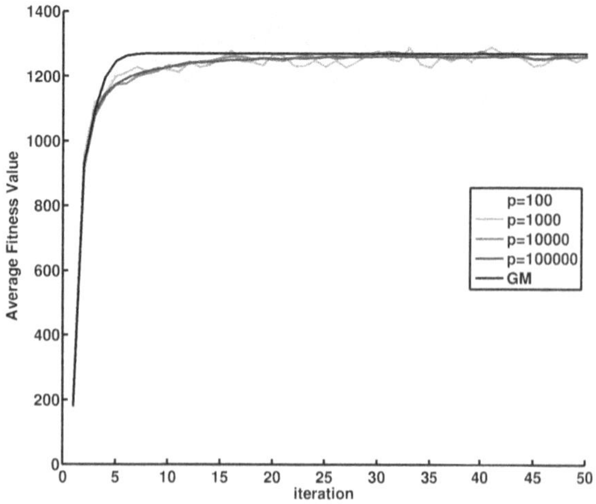

Figure 2: Comparison of average fitness values predicted by our proposed approximation with observed values from running the real algorithm

In Figure 1 the line in black (marked GM) is the trajectory of predicted population mean center calculated by $E_{\hat{f}_k}\boldsymbol{x}$, while lines in other colors (marked $p = 100$, 1000, 10000, and 100000) are the real population means observed by running the algorithm with different population sizes. Similarly, in Figure 2 we depict average fitness values of our prediction and that of real observations versus iteration number, respectively. From both figures it can be seen that our model can predict key statistics of evolutionary algorithm with fair accuracy, and as the population size grows, the error becomes smaller. This is due to the fact that our model is aimed at predicting the behavior of evolutionary algorithms with infinite population size. Since in the experiment f_0 and g are both Gaussian mixtures, the error comes from the finite population effect and the truncation of Gaussian mixtures during the calculation.

6. CONCLUSION

In this paper we propose a novel finite Gaussian mixture model to approximate the behavior of simple evolutionary algorithms. Our model is conceptually straightforward yet it has many nice properties. In the model the transition function can be easily iterated and key statistics of interest can be calculated by simple formula. As it also yields explicit expressions of population density functions, it can provide more insight into the dynamics of evolutionary algorithms than traditional approaches. In addition, based on [4–6], we proved that in theory our model can approximate the dynamics of simple evolutionary algorithm with arbitrarily small error. The experimental result illustrated the effectiveness and usefulness of the model.

For future work, it is possible to extend this research in many directions. Firstly, the errors due to finite population in real algorithm and the truncation of mixtures in the implementation can be analyzed. Secondly, to simplify things, the crossover operator is not considered in this paper. However, it would not be too difficult to apply our model on elementary crossover operators. Last but not least, the truncation method in the implementation is a very elementary method. It is possible to adopt more advanced mixture component number reduction algorithms in our framework to cope with more complex problems.

7. REFERENCES

[1] H.-G. Beyer. *The Theory of Evolution Strategies.* Springer, Berlin, 2001.

[2] M. Carreira-Perpinan. Mode-finding for mixtures of Gaussian distributions. *IEEE Transactions on Pattern Analysis and Machine Intelligence*, 22(11):1318–1323, 2000.

[3] E. Hemberg, C. Berzan, K. Veeramachaneni, and U.-M. O'Reilly. Introducing graphical models to analyze genetic programming dynamics. In *Proceedings of the Twelfth Workshop on Foundations of Genetic Algorithms XII*, FOGA XII '13, pages 75–86, 2013.

[4] V. Maz'ya. *Approximate approximations.* American Mathematical Society, Providence, R.I., 2007.

[5] V. Maz'ya and G. Schmidt. On approximate approximations using Gaussian kernels. *IMA Journal of Numerical Analysis*, 16(1):13–29, 1996.

[6] J. Park and I. W. Sandberg. Universal approximation using radial-basis-function networks. *Neural Computation*, 3(2):246–257, 1991.

[7] K. B. Petersen and M. S. Pedersen. The matrix cookbook. `http://www2.imm.dtu.dk/pubdb/p.php?3274`, Nov 2012. Version 20121115.

[8] X. Qi and F. Palmieri. Theoretical analysis of evolutionary algorithms with an infinite population size in continuous space. Part I: Basic properties of selection and mutation. *IEEE Transactions on Neural Networks*, 5(1):102–119, 1994.

[9] X. Qi and F. Palmieri. Theoretical analysis of evolutionary algorithms with an infinite population size in continuous space. Part II: Analysis of the diversification role of crossover. *IEEE Transactions on Neural Networks*, 5(1):120–129, 1994.

[10] C. R. Reeves and J. E. Rowe. *Genetic Algorithms - Principles and Perspectives : A Guide to GA Theory.* Kluwer Academic Publishers, Boston, 2003.

[11] J. L. Shapiro. Statistical mechanics theory of genetic algorithms. In L. Kallel, B. Naudts, and A. Rogers, editors, *Theoretical Aspects of Evolutionary Computing*, Natural Computing Series, chapter 5, pages 87–108. Springer Berlin Heidelberg, 2001.

[12] G. Terejanu, P. Singla, T. Singh, and P. D. Scott. Uncertainty propagation for nonlinear dynamic systems using Gaussian mixture models. *Journal of Guidance, Control, and Dynamics*, 31(6):1623–1633, 2008.

[13] M. D. Vose. *The Simple Genetic Algorithm : Foundations and Theory.* MIT Press, Cambridge, Mass., 1999.

[14] M. D. Vose and A. H. Wright. The simple genetic algorithm and the Walsh transform: Part I, theory. *Evolutionary Computation*, 6(3):253–273, 1998.

[15] M. D. Vose and A. H. Wright. The simple genetic algorithm and the Walsh transform: Part II, the inverse. *Evolutionary Computation*, 6(3):275–289, 1998.

Superpolynomial Lower Bounds for the (1+1) EA on Some Easy Combinatorial Problems

Andrew M. Sutton
Fakultät für Mathematik und Informatik
Friedrich-Schiller-Universität Jena
07743 Jena, Germany
andrew.sutton@uni-jena.de

ABSTRACT

The (1+1) EA is a simple evolutionary algorithm that is known to be efficient on linear functions and on some combinatorial optimization problems. In this paper, we rigorously study its behavior on two easy combinatorial problems: finding the 2-coloring of a class of bipartite graphs, and constructing satisfying assignments for a class of satisfiable 2-CNF Boolean formulas. We prove that it is inefficient on both problems in the sense that the number of iterations the algorithm needs to minimize the cost functions is superpolynomial with high probability.

Our motivation is to better understand the influence of problem instance structure on the runtime character of a simple evolutionary algorithm. We are interested in what kind of structural features give rise to so-called metastable states at which, with probability $1 - o(1)$, the (1+1) EA becomes trapped and subsequently has difficulty leaving. Finally, we show how to modify the (1+1) EA slightly in order to obtain a polynomial-time performance guarantee on both problems.

Categories and Subject Descriptors

F.2 [**Theory of Computation**]: Analysis of Algorithms and Problem Complexity

General Terms

Theory, Algorithms, Performance

Keywords

Runtime Analysis; Lower Bounds

1. INTRODUCTION

Randomized search heuristics such as evolutionary algorithms are techniques for function optimization that are often applied to complex problems. These algorithms are usually deployed in situations in which problem-specific knowledge is incomplete or missing and the structure of the problem is not well-defined, changes dynamically, or is not completely accessible to the algorithm designer.

On the other hand, it is often very useful to study the behavior of randomized search heuristics on problems with well-understood structure in order to better understand their principles. For example, a large amount of progress has been made for linear pseudo-Boolean functions culminating in the recent work by Witt [14] who proved the (1+1) EA requires $en \ln n + O(n)$ steps in expectation and with high probability to find the extremum of any linear pseudo-Boolean function. This bound is tight up to lower order terms, and for a subclass of linear functions (ONEMAX-like functions), is only a polylogarithmic factor slower than the corresponding black-box complexity.

The study of certain randomized search heuristics applied to easy linear functions has illuminated several fundamental properties of these algorithms as well as cultivated the development of new proof techniques [3] and new efficient algorithms [2]. Inspired by these successes, we want to commute this approach into the realm of combinatorial problems with easily understood structure and study the influence of such structure on algorithm behavior. In particular, we are interested in natural, computationally easy problems for which the (1+1) EA is provably inefficient. Our main focus is to better understand the structural properties of problems that pose challenges to evolutionary algorithms.

The (1+1) EA is already known to exhibit inefficient behavior on some easy combinatorial problems. Giel and Wegener [5] proved that the (1+1) EA takes exponential time in expectation to find the maximum matching on a class of bipartite graphs. Neumann, Reichel, and Skutella [8] showed that the (1+1) EA takes superpolynomial time with high probability to find the minimum cut in a weighted, digraph and proved that a multi-objective evolutionary algorithm runs in polynomial time. Sudholt [12] proved that the expected runtime of the $(\mu + \lambda)$ EA applied to the Ising model on binary trees is bounded below by $2^{\Omega(n)}$, but that a simple genetic algorithm using crossover with a population size of two could solve the problem in expected polynomial time.

This paper is organized as follows. In the remainder of this section, we introduce the algorithm and basic analytical framework for the paper. In Section 2, we analyze the runtime of the (1+1) EA searching for a 2-coloring of a bipartite graph and provide tail bounds that prove with high probability the evolutionary algorithm needs at least a superpolynomial number of iterations in the worst case. In Section 3, we prove a similar result for the (1+1) EA searching

GECCO'14, July 12–16, 2014, Vancouver, BC, Canada.

ACM 978-1-4503-2662-9/14/07 ...$15.00.
http://dx.doi.org/10.1145/2576768.2598278

for a satisfying assignment to a satisfiable Boolean 2-CNF formula. In Section 4 we show that the (1+1) EA can be adapted slightly by changing the fitness function and mutation operator to take advantage of domain-specific information, and that this adaptation results in a polynomial-time performance guarantee for both problems. We conclude the paper in Section 5.

1.1 Preliminaries

We consider the minimization of nonlinear pseudo-Boolean functions $f\colon \{0,1\}^n \to \mathbb{R}$ where f measures the cost of candidate solutions (encoded as length-n bitstrings) to a combinatorial problem. For a bitstring $x \in \{0,1\}^n$, we will denote the i-th element in x as $x[i]$. The (1+1) EA, illustrated in Algorithm 1 for minimizing f, is a simple evolutionary algorithm employing a unit population size, uniform mutation, and truncation selection.

Algorithm 1: (1+1) EA.

Choose $x \in \{0,1\}^n$ uniformly at random;
repeat *forever*
  $y \leftarrow x$;
  Flip each bit $y[i]$ with probability $1/n$;
  if $f(y) \leq f(x)$ **then** $x \leftarrow y$

We regard a run of Algorithm 1 as an infinite stochastic process $\{x^{(t)} : t \in \mathbb{N}\}$, where $x^{(t)} \in \{0,1\}^n$ denotes the candidate solution generated in iteration t of the algorithm. The *optimization time* T of an algorithm is the random variable

$$T = \inf\{t \in \mathbb{N} : \ f(x^{(t)}) \text{ is minimal}\}.$$

In the following, we will be primarily interested in tail bounds for T. In other words, we want to derive the probability that T exceeds some value $g(n)$.

2. COLORING BIPARTITE GRAPHS

Given a graph $G = (V, E)$ and a set $[k] = \{1, 2, \ldots, k\}$, a *coloring* of G is a mapping $\chi\colon V \to [k]$. We are interested in finding a coloring χ that minimizes the set of monochromatic edges $\{(u,v) \in E : \chi(u) = \chi(v)\}$. We say a graph G is k-colorable if there exists a k-coloring $\chi^\star$ such that

$$\{(u,v) \in E : \chi^\star(u) = \chi^\star(v)\} = \emptyset.$$

Note that a graph is 2-colorable if and only if it is bipartite, and in this case the problem of finding a 2-coloring with no monochromatic edges is in P. Obviously, a 2-coloring of a bipartite graph can be found in time linear to the size of the graph by depth-first search. In this section, we will introduce a class of pathological instances of bipartite graphs that the (1+1) EA fails to solve efficiently with high probability.

We construct a graph $G = (V, E)$ on $|V| = n$ vertices as follows. Let $0 < \epsilon < 1/2$ be an arbitrary real constant. Without loss of generality, let $m = n^{2\epsilon}/4 - 1/2$ and $k = \Theta(n^{1-2\epsilon})$ be integers. A *block* is a subgraph $G_i = (V_i, E_i)$ where $|V_i| = 4m + 2 = n^{2\epsilon}$ and $|E_i| = 2m^2 + 2m + 1$.

The vertex set V_i is composed of five mutually disjoint sets $\{A_i, B_i, C_i, D_i, \{u_i, v_i\}\}$ where $|A_i| = |B_i| = |C_i| = |D_i| = m$. The subgraph induced by $A_i \cup B_i$ is isomorphic to the complete bipartite graph $K_{m,m}$. Similarly, the subgraph induced by $C_i \cup D_i$ is also isomorphic to $K_{m,m}$. We construct the remaining $2m + 1$ edges to form a cutset between these two complete bipartite subgraphs. We add (u_i, v_i) to E_i, and an edge between u_i and every vertex in B_i, as well as an edge between v_i and every vertex in C_i. Clearly G_i is bipartite (see Figure 1 for a diagram).

We now construct G by taking a sequence of $k = \Theta(n^{1-2\epsilon})$ blocks $G_1, G_2, \ldots, G_k$ and attaching G_i to G_{i+1} for all $1 \leq i < k$ by adding arbitrary edges between vertices in D_i and A_{i+1} subject to the constraint that the maximum degree of the subgraph of G induced by $A_{i+1} \cup D_i$ is one (see Figure 2).

The set of all 2-colorings of G is isomorphic to $\{0,1\}^n$, and, as is typical with evolutionary algorithms, we consider each candidate solution as a bitstring $x \in \{0,1\}^n$. The pseudo-Boolean fitness function $f\colon \{0,1\}^n \to \mathbb{N}$ counts the number of monochromatic edges in a coloring, i.e.,

$$f(x) = |\{(u,v) \in E : x[u] = x[v]\}|. \tag{1}$$

Here $x[u]$ is the element of the bitstring corresponding to vertex u. Obviously, a 2-coloring corresponding to x is optimal if and only if $f(x) = 0$. We want to analyze the performance of Algorithm 1 minimizing f on the graph G. The main result of this section is that, with high probability, the (1+1) EA optimizing the pseudo-Boolean fitness function defined in Equation (1) fails to find a 2-coloring for G in time bounded by any polynomial of n.

Theorem 1. *Let G be a bipartite graph as defined above for any real constant $0 < \epsilon < 1/2$ with $n > 18^{\frac{1}{2\epsilon}}$. With probability $1 - o(1)$, the (1+1) EA does not find a feasible 2-coloring of G in $2^{\Omega(n^\epsilon)}$ steps.*

Before proving Theorem 1, we will need a few definitions and technical lemmas. We will use the following result to obtain tight bounds on the probabilities of specific events.

Lemma 1. *Let $1 \leq h(n) < n$ be an integer function of n. Then*

$$\frac{h(n)}{en} \leq 1 - \left(1 - \frac{1}{n}\right)^{h(n)} \leq \frac{h(n)}{n}.$$

PROOF. For the lower bound, we have

$$\frac{1-(1-1/n)^{h(n)}}{1/n} = \frac{1-(1-1/n)^{h(n)}}{1-(1-1/n)},$$

which is equal to the sum of the first $h(n)$ terms of a geometric series:

$$\sum_{j=0}^{h(n)-1} (1-1/n)^j \geq h(n)(1-1/n)^{n-1} \geq h(n)/e.$$

The upper bound follows from Bernoulli's inequality. □

Definition 1. *For a block G_i, we say that a 2-coloring x of G is* deceptive *for G_i if the following five conditions hold.*

1. $x[u_i] = x[v_i] = 0$.
2. $|\{v \in A_i : x[v] = 0\}| > m/2$,
3. $|\{v \in B_i : x[v] = 1\}| > m/2$,
4. $|\{v \in C_i : x[v] = 1\}| > m/2$,
5. $|\{v \in D_i : x[v] = 0\}| > m/2$,

For brevity, we will sometimes in this case say x is deceptive *when G_i is clear from context.*

Definition 2. *Let $\delta\colon \{0,1\}^n \times 2^V \to \mathbb{N}$ count the deviation of the majority color from $|U|/2$ in a set $U \subseteq V$ under a*

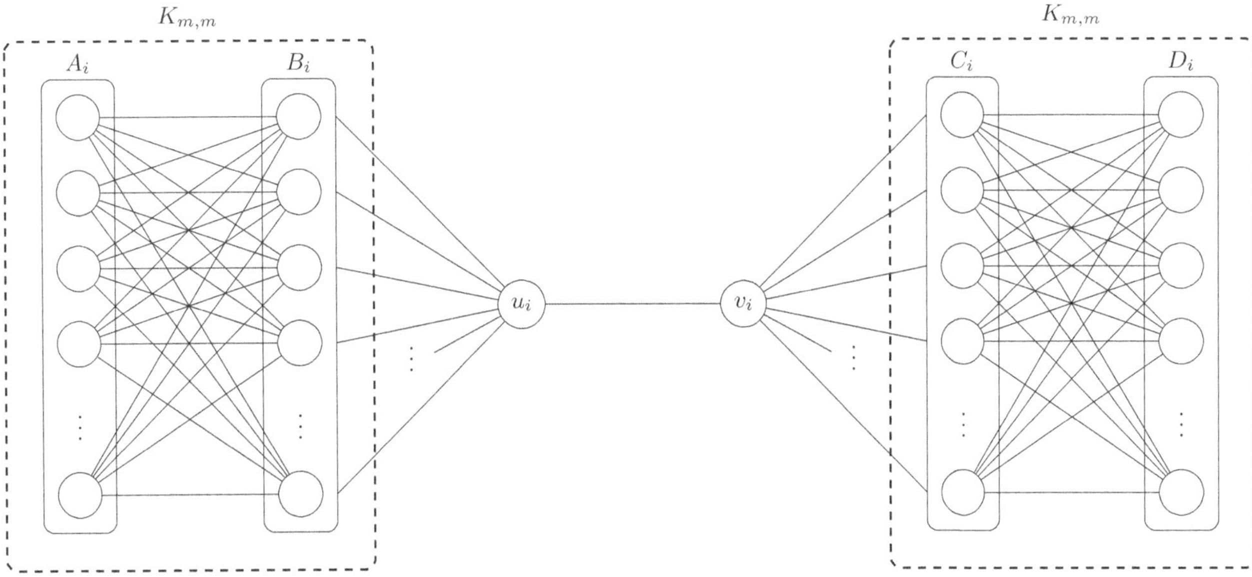

Figure 1: Bipartite block subgraph $G_i = (V_i, E_i)$.

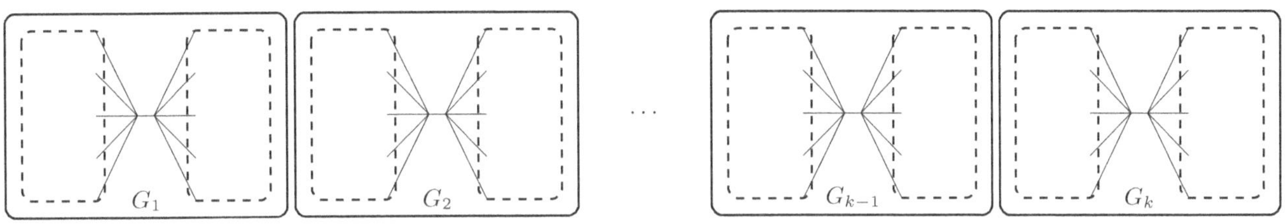

Figure 2: A bipartite graph G constructed by connecting a sequence of $k = \Theta(n^{1-2\epsilon})$ blocks.

particular coloring. That is, for a 2-coloring x and a subset $U \subseteq V$,

$$\delta(x, U) = \max_{z \in \{0,1\}} |\{v \in U : x[v] = z\}| - |U|/2.$$

Let G_i be a block. For each $U \in \{A_i, B_i, C_i, D_i\}$ we define a function

$$\psi_U(x) = \begin{cases} \delta(x, U) & \text{if } x \text{ is deceptive for } G_i; \\ 0 & \text{otherwise.} \end{cases}$$

We define the following block potential function *with respect to G_i.*

$$\varphi_i(x) = \psi_{A_i}(x) + \psi_{B_i}(x) + \psi_{C_i}(x) + \psi_{D_i}(x).$$

Informally, a coloring is called deceptive for a block G_i because it lies in the basin of attraction of a so-called *metastable state* where the only monochromatic edge in the block is (u_i, v_i) (see Figure 3). This metastable state is an attractor for the dynamics of the (1+1) EA, and we formalize this in the following lemma that ensures that the stochastic process described by the (1+1) EA has a positive drift toward this metastable state.

Lemma 2. *Let $x^{(t)}$ be the coloring found in iteration t of the (1+1) EA. Suppose $x^{(t)}$ is deceptive for a block G_i, and let P be the event that mutation changes the color of some vertices in G_i in iteration t. Suppose that*

$$\sqrt{m}/5 \leq \psi_U(x^{(t)}) \leq \sqrt{m}/4$$

for each $U \in \{A_i, B_i, C_i, D_i\}$. Then there exists a positive constant c such that

$$\mathrm{E}\left(\varphi_i(x^{(t+1)}) - \varphi_i(x^{(t)}) \;\middle|\; P\right) > 4c.$$

PROOF. We first show that, under the claimed conditions, there exists a positive constant c such that the expectation of $\psi_{A_i}(x^{(t+1)}) - \psi_{A_i}(x^{(t)})$ conditioned on P is at least c. Let y be the offspring created by uniform mutation in iteration t of the (1+1) EA. By the selection process, $x^{(t+1)} = y$ if and only if $f(y) \leq f(x^{(t)})$, otherwise $x^{(t+1)} = x^{(t)}$. Define the random variable $Z = Z_{t+1} = \psi_{A_i}(x^{(t+1)}) - \psi_{A_i}(x^{(t)})$ and let I_P be the indicator random variable for event P.

In this proof, we will rely heavily on the law of total probability and partition the probability space based on the following events (along with their complements). Let Q_1 be the event that in iteration t, mutation does not change the color of any vertices in $V \setminus A_i$. Let Q_2 be the event that the block remains deceptive after mutation and selection.

We first consider the event $Q_1 \cap Q_2$. Since $x^{(t)}$ is deceptive for G_i, the majority of vertices in A_i are labeled 0 by $x^{(t)}$. Furthermore, each vertex in A_i labeled 1 is adjacent to at least $m/2 + \sqrt{m}/5$ vertices labeled 1 in B_i, and adjacent to at most $m/2 - \sqrt{m}/5$ vertices labeled 0 in B_i, and at most one vertex in D_{i-1} possibly labeled 0.

Under event Q_1, if the majority color in A_i is strictly reduced by mutation, the resulting coloring y has strictly more monochromatic edges, and thus y will not be accepted. Thus, $Q_1 \subseteq Q_2$ and so $Q_1 \cap Q_2 = Q_1$ and it suffices to bound

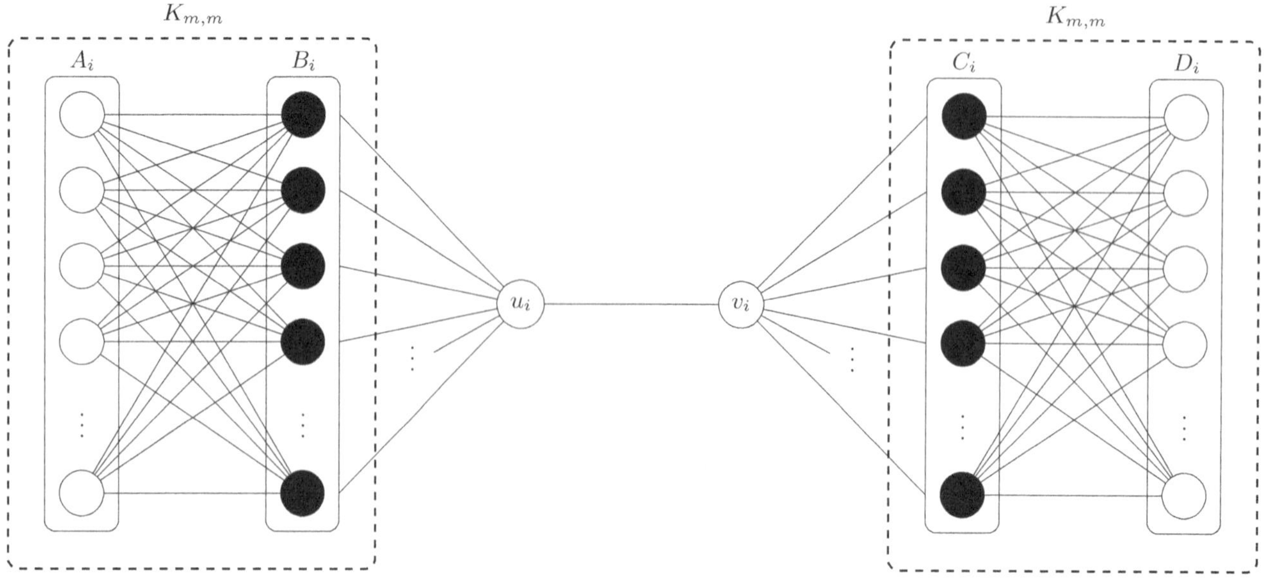

Figure 3: A metastable state for a block G_i. Deceptive colorings for G_i lie in this state's basin of attraction, i.e., the stochastic process drifts toward this metastable state in the region of deceptive colorings for G_i.

$E(Z \mid Q_1)$. There are $m-(m/2+\psi_{A_i}(x^{(t)}))$ vertices labeled 1 by $x^{(t)}$. The probability that exactly one of these vertices changes color under mutation is at least $1/(en)$. Each such event contributes to the expectation of Z under Q_1. Since a reduction in majority color will not be accepted under Q_1, by linearity of expectation and the assumed bounds on ψ_{A_i},

$$E(Z \mid Q_1 \cap Q_2) = E(Z \mid Q_1) \geq (m/2-\sqrt{m}/4)/(en).$$

We now examine the event $\overline{Q_1} \cap Q_2$. In this case, vertices outside A_i are allowed to change, and the vertices of majority color in A_i might be lost after selection because a change in $V \setminus A_i$ is so favorable that it masks any loss of fitness coming from A_i. However, under this event the expected number of vertices that change color in A_i can be no worse than the expected change under pure mutation (i.e., ignoring any effect of selection). Under mutation, the probability a single vertex in A_i changes color is no more than $1/n$, so by linearity of expectation, this is at least

$$\left(m-\left(\frac{m}{2}+\psi_{A_i}(x^{(t)})\right)\right)/n-\left(\frac{m}{2}+\psi_{A_i}(x^{(t)})\right)/n.$$

Due to the assumption that $\psi_{A_i}(x^{(t)}) \leq \sqrt{m}/4$, this is bounded below by

$$E(Z \mid \overline{Q_1} \cap Q_2) \geq -\frac{\sqrt{m}}{2n}.$$

Applying the law of total probability, we can write

$$\begin{aligned} E(Z \mid Q_2) &= E(Z \mid Q_1 \cap Q_2)\Pr(Q_1) \\ &\quad + E(Z \mid \overline{Q_1} \cap Q_2)(1-\Pr(Q_1)) \\ &\geq \frac{(m/2)-\sqrt{m}/4}{en}\Pr(Q_1) - \frac{\sqrt{m}}{2n}(1-\Pr(Q_1)) \\ &\geq \frac{(m/2)-\sqrt{m}/4}{e^2 n} - \frac{\sqrt{m}}{2n} \end{aligned}$$

since $\Pr(Q_1) = (1-1/n)^{n-m} \geq 1/e$. Again, by the law of total probability,

$$E(Z) = E(Z \mid Q_2)(1-\Pr(\overline{Q_2})) + E(Z \mid \overline{Q_2})\Pr(\overline{Q_2}).$$

The block can only go non-deceptive after mutating at least $\sqrt{m}/5$ bits, so $\Pr(\overline{Q_2}) \leq e^{-\Omega(\sqrt{m}\log m)}$. Thus,

$$E(Z) \geq \frac{(m/2)-\sqrt{m}/4}{e^2 n} - \frac{\sqrt{m}}{2n} - e^{-\Omega(\sqrt{m}\log m)}.$$

To complete the proof, we must condition the expectation on the event P. If event P has not occurred, no change is possible inside the block and Z must be zero. Stated more formally, for an element ω of the probability space, $Z(\omega)=0$ if $\omega \in \overline{P}$ and so we have $Z = ZI_P$. By definition,

$$E(Z \mid P) = E(ZI_P)/\Pr(P) = E(Z)/\Pr(P).$$

Since $\Pr(P) = 1-\Pr(\overline{P}) = 1-(1-1/n)^{4m+2}$, by applying Lemma 1, we can tightly bound the probability of P,

$$(4m+2)/(en) \leq \Pr(P) \leq (4m+2)/n,$$

and thus

$$E(Z \mid P) \geq \frac{2m-\sqrt{m}}{16e^2 m + 8e^2} - \frac{e\sqrt{m}}{8m+4} - e^{-\Omega(\sqrt{m}\log m)}.$$

It follows that, for n sufficiently large, there exists a positive constant c such that

$$E(Z|P) = E\left(\psi_{A_i}(x^{(t+1)}) - \psi_{A_i}(x^{(t)}) \;\middle|\; P\right) > c.$$

Using symmetric arguments, the expected differences for ψ_{B_i}, ψ_{C_i}, and ψ_{D_i} are also all bounded below by c. The claim for the block potential function φ_i then follows by linearity of expectation. □

We have therefore proved that the drift (conditioned on P) of the stochastic process $\{\varphi_i(x^{(t)}) : t \in \mathbb{N}\}$ is strictly positive for a set of colorings in the deceptive region for G_i. Figure 4 illustrates the situation. This lemma formalizes the concept that for colorings deceptive for a block G_i, in expectation the (1+1) EA is attracted to the metastable state for G_i.

Definition 3. *For a block G_i, we say a deceptive 2-coloring x of G is* bad *for G_i if the following five conditions hold.*

1. $x[u_i] = x[v_i] = 0$.
2. $|\{v \in A_i : x[v] = 0\}| \geq m/2 + \sqrt{m}/4$,
3. $|\{v \in B_i : x[v] = 1\}| \geq m/2 + \sqrt{m}/4$,
4. $|\{v \in C_i : x[v] = 1\}| \geq m/2 + \sqrt{m}/4$,
5. $|\{v \in D_i : x[v] = 0\}| \geq m/2 + \sqrt{m}/4$,

We sometimes say that such a coloring is bad *when G_i is clear from context.*

Lemma 3. *Let $U \subseteq V$ be a subset of m vertices where $m > 4$. In any uniformly random coloring of U, at least $m/2 + \sqrt{m}/4$ vertices in U are colored 0 (1) with probability at least $\frac{1}{15e} > 1/41$.*

PROOF. Let X be the random variable that counts the number of vertices in U colored 0 (1) in a uniformly random coloring of V. Since X is distributed binomially, we have the following lower bound for any $0 < t < m/8$ (derived explicitly in [6, Proposition 7.3.2 on page 46] and follows as a special case of a result due to Feller [4]).

$$\Pr(X \geq \mathrm{E}(X) + t) \geq \frac{1}{15} e^{-16t^2/m}.$$

The claim holds by substituting $\mathrm{E}(X) = m/2$ and $t = \sqrt{m}/4 < m/8$. □

Lemma 3 gives a lower bound on the probability that, in a uniformly random 2-coloring, there is a majority of vertices of a certain color in a subset of size m, and that this majority deviates from $m/2$ by at least $\sqrt{m}/4$. This immediately provides the following bound on the probability that the initial random 2-coloring is bad for any block.

Lemma 4. *Let $G_i = (V_i, E_i)$ be an arbitrary block of G. With at least constant probability, the initial uniformly random 2-coloring is bad for G_i.*

PROOF. Since $\{A_i, B_i, C_i, D_i, \{u_i, v_i\}\}$ form a partition of V_i, the five events in Definition 3 are mutually independent, and it suffices to show their joint probability is bounded below by a constant. Clearly, event (1), i.e., the event in which $x[u_i] = x[v_i] = 0$ in the initial coloring $x \in \{0,1\}^n$, occurs with probability 1/4. By Lemma 3, the probability of each of events 2–5 is at least 1/41. By independence, the joint probability of the five events is $\Omega(1)$. □

We are now ready to prove the main result of this section.

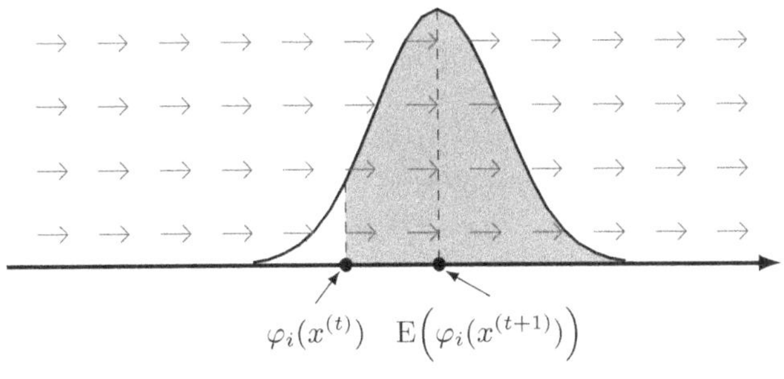

Figure 4: Drift of block potential function φ_i on a coloring deceptive for G_i.

PROOF OF THEOREM 1. Clearly, every feasible 2-coloring of G must be non-deceptive for all blocks so a necessary condition for every feasible 2-coloring $x^\star$ is that $\varphi_i(x^\star) = 0$ for every $i \in \{1, 2, \ldots, k\}$. If at any time during the execution of the (1+1) EA a block is bad, the algorithm must change the color of at least $\Omega(\sqrt{m})$ vertices to make it non-deceptive.

Suppose that $x^{(1)}$ is bad with respect to block G_i. We consider the restriction of the stochastic process $\{x^{(t)} : t \in \mathbb{N}\}$ consisting only of steps in which there is a mutation that changes vertices in G_i. The drift of φ_i in this process is exactly the conditional drift from the claim of Lemma 2. We now appeal to the simplified negative drift theorem [10, 9]. The first condition of the simplified negative drift theorem is given by Lemma 2. The second condition of the theorem follows naturally since the EA uses uniform mutation, and thus the argumentation at the beginning of Section 4 of [9] carries over. Thus, with with probability $1 - o(1)$, the EA needs $2^{\Omega(\sqrt{m})} = 2^{\Omega(n^\epsilon)}$ steps in this restricted process to reduce the potential of a bad block since $m = \Theta(n^{2\epsilon})$. Since the restricted process to solve the bad block can only be faster than the optimization time of the EA (in which there can only be additional steps where nothing occurs within the block), it follows that with high probability the EA needs at least superpolynomial time to solve any bad blocks.

Finally, by Lemma 4, with probability $p = \Omega(1)$ the initial uniformly random coloring is already bad for an arbitrary block. Consequently, with probability at least $1 - (1-p)^k = 1 - o(1)$ there is at least one bad block in the initial coloring. The asymptotic expression follows from the fact that $k = \Theta(n^{1-2\epsilon})$. Thus, with high probability, the EA must first fix a bad block, and this takes superpolynomial time with high probability. Since all bad blocks must be fixed before a feasible 2-coloring is found, the claim follows. □

3. SATISFIABLE 2-CNF FORMULAS

Boolean satisfiability is an important combinatorial problem with extensive theoretical and practical relevance. A Boolean formula in r-conjunctive normal form (r-CNF) is a set of disjunctive clauses on a set of n Boolean variables in which each clause is a set of at most r literals (a variable or its negation). A formula is said to be *satisfiable* if there is an assignment to the variables such that all clauses in the formula evaluate to true. If there is no such assignment, the formula is said to be *unsatisfiable*.

For $r \geq 3$, the problem of deciding the satisfiability of r-CNF formulas is already NP-complete. However, when $r = 2$, there is a linear time deterministic algorithm [1] for solving the decision problem, and a randomized local search heuristic that can identify satisfiable formula in quadratic time [7, 11]. Typically, randomized search heuristics cannot identify unsatisfiable formulas and so we usually consider them as randomized algorithms with one-sided error.

In this section we study the performance of the (1+1) EA on satisfiable 2-CNF formulas. The set of assignments to n Boolean variables $\{v_1, v_2, \ldots, v_n\}$ is isomorphic to $\{0,1\}^n$, the set of length-n bitstrings. Given a bitstring $x \in \{0,1\}^n$, we assign variable v_i the value *true* if and only if $x[i] = 1$ and v_i the value *false* if and only if $x[i] = 0$. A literal ℓ is satisfied by an assignment $x \in \{0,1\}^n$ if $\ell = v_i$ and $x[i] = 1$, or $\ell = \overline{v_i}$ and $x[i] = 0$.

We call a literal *negative* if it is an instance of a negated variable, otherwise, it is *positive*. A clause is satisfied by x

if at least one of its literals is satisfied by x. Given an assignment x, we use the standard fitness function for Boolean satisfiability that counts the number of unsatisfied clauses under x, that is,

$$f(x) = |\{C \in F : C \text{ is not satisfied by } x\}|. \tag{2}$$

Thus, the satisfying assignments of F are exactly the zeros of f. We now show by a straightforward reduction that the result in Section 2 also carries over to 2-CNF formulas.

Let $G = (V, E)$ be a graph on n vertices. We construct a 2-CNF formula consisting of n variables $v_1, v_2, \ldots v_n$ with $2|E|$ clauses as follows. For every edge $(v_i, v_j) \in E$ we add the clauses $(v_i \vee v_j)$ and $(\overline{v_i} \vee \overline{v_j})$. For any assignment, at most one of these clauses is violated, and one is violated if and only if $x[i] = x[j]$. Thus the fitness of x calculated by the coloring fitness function defined in Equation (1) is equivalent to the fitness defined by the number of unsatisfied clauses in Equation (2) for the corresponding formula. The next Lemma follows as an immediate consequence.

Lemma 5. *Let $G = (V, E)$ be a bipartite graph. Then the 2-CNF formula constructed using the above process is satisfiable.*

Moreover, the equivalence immediately implies that there are also hard 2-CNF formulas for the (1+1) EA. In particular, this result entails the following theorem.

Theorem 2. *Let F be a Boolean formula constructed by reduction from the bipartite graph G in Section 2. By Lemma 5, F is satisfiable. With probability $1-o(1)$, the (1+1) EA does not find a satisfying assignment to F in $2^{\Omega(n^\epsilon)}$ steps.*

4. DESIGNING AN EFFICIENT EA

In this section we show how to slightly modify the evolutionary algorithm listed in Algorithm 1 to run in expected polynomial time on every bipartite graph, and every satisfiable 2-CNF formula. To achieve this, we leave the black-box setting and introduce problem-specific information into the runtime environment of the evolutionary algorithm. We focus on the case of satisfiable 2-CNF formulas and then implicitly rely on the equivalence stated in Section 3. We modify Algorithm 1 in two ways. First, we change the representation slightly so that in each iteration the algorithm works on a subformula induced by the unsatisfied clauses. Second, we employ a nonuniform mutation rate that takes into consideration the number of unsatisfied clauses in which each variable appears (cf. Algorithm 2). We show that these modifications to Algorithm 1 result in an upper bound of $O(n^2\sqrt{m})$ on the expected time to solve every satisfiable 2-CNF formula with n variables and m clauses. We remark that these modifications result in the EA behaving closer to the conflict-directed random walk algorithm for satisfiable 2-CNF formulas discovered independently by Papadimitriou [11] and McDiarmid [7].

Let F be a Boolean formula with m clauses and n variables. For any assignment $x \in \{0,1\}^n$, we denote the unsatisfied subformula induced by x as

$$F[x] = \{C \in F : C \text{ is not satisfied under } x\}.$$

Let $\gamma_i(x)$ count the clauses in $F[x]$ that contain the i-th variable v_i. For the fitness function, we use a subscript to denote the formula, e.g., $f_{F[x]}(y)$ is the number of clauses in the induced subformula $F[x]$ that are not satisfied by y.

Algorithm 2: Modified (1+1) EA.

```
Choose x ∈ {0,1}^n uniformly at random;
repeat forever
    y ← x;
    Flip each bit y[i] with probability γ_i(x)/(|F[x]|+1);
    if f_{F[x]}(y) ≤ f_{F[x]}(x) then x ← y
```

Theorem 3. *Let F be a satisfiable 2-CNF formula on n variables with m unique clauses. Algorithm 2 finds a satisfying assignment for F in expected time bounded by $O(n^2\sqrt{m})$.*

PROOF. Let $x^\star$ be a satisfying assignment to F. We examine the stochastic process $\{X_t : t \in \mathbb{N}\}$ on $\{0, 1, \ldots, n\}$ where

$$X_t = \begin{cases} |\{x^{(t)}[i] \neq x^\star[i] : i \in \{1,\ldots,n\}\}| & \text{if } F[x^{(t)}] \neq \emptyset; \\ 0 & \text{otherwise.} \end{cases}$$

Thus X_t is zero only if $x^{(t)}$ is a satisfying assignment, otherwise X_t is the Hamming distance between $x^\star$ and the candidate solution of the (1+1) EA in iteration t. Let $T \in \{0, 1, 2, \ldots\} \cup \{\infty\}$ be a random variable defined as $T = \inf\{t \in \mathbb{N} : X_t = 0\}$. T therefore measures the number of iterations until the (1+1) EA finds any satisfying assignment. In the following, we make the implicit assumption that no other satisfying assignment is found before $x^\star$, which could only result in a faster process.

Denote the filtration $\mathscr{F}_{t-1} := X_1, \ldots, X_{t-1}$. Let $\Delta_t = X_t - X_{t-1}$. We first show that there exists a $\sigma^2 = \Omega(1/\sqrt{m})$ such that $\mathrm{E}(\Delta_t^2 \mid \mathscr{F}_{t-1}) \geq \sigma^2$. We will later apply this fact to derive an asymptotic bound on the expectation of T. For any $t > 1$, let $x = x^{(t-1)}$ be the candidate solution during iteration $t-1$ of the (1+1) EA. Note that the selection operation in Algorithm 2 is actually superfluous since it is impossible to generate a disimproving move with respect to $F[x]$. Thus Δ_t measures the change in Hamming distance to $x^\star$, provided that no other satisfying assignment has been found. Let $Z_i \in \{0,1\}$ for $i \in \{1,\ldots,n\}$ be the set of Bernoulli random variables that take on the value 1 if and only if the i-th bit of x flips. Thus, letting n' denote the number of distinct variables in $F[x]$ and m' the number of clauses in $F[x]$,

$$\Delta_t = \sum_{i=1}^{n'} Z_i(1-2d_i), \text{ where } d_i = \begin{cases} 1 & \text{if } x^{(t-1)}[i] = x^\star[i]; \\ 0 & \text{otherwise.} \end{cases}$$

We have

$$\mathrm{E}(\Delta_t^2 \mid \mathscr{F}_{t-1}) \geq \mathrm{Var}(\Delta_t) = \sum_{i=1}^{n'} \mathrm{Var}(Z_i(1-2d_i))$$

since each bit is flipped independently. Furthermore, $(1-2d_i) \in \{-1, 1\}$ depends only on $x^{(t-1)}$ and $x^\star$, and so, given $\mathscr{F}_{t-1}$, is a constant with respect to Δ_t. Since $\mathrm{Var}(aX) = a^2\mathrm{Var}(X)$,

$$\begin{aligned} &= \sum_{i=1}^{n'} \mathrm{Var}(Z_i) = \sum_{i=1}^{n'} \frac{\gamma_i(x)}{m'+1}\left(1 - \frac{\gamma_i(x)}{m'+1}\right) \\ &\geq \frac{n'}{m'+1}\left(1 - \frac{1}{m'+1}\right) \geq \frac{n'}{2(m'+1)}. \end{aligned}$$

In any set of m' distinct clauses, there must be at least $\sqrt{m'}/2$ distinct variables. Setting $\sigma^2 = \sqrt{m'}/(4m'+4) = \Omega(1/\sqrt{m})$ since $m' \le m$, we have the claimed bound on $\mathrm{E}(\Delta_t^2 \mid \mathscr{F}_{t-1})$.

We now show that, using the modified mutation and selection operators of Algorithm 2,

$$\mathrm{E}(\Delta_t \mid \mathscr{F}_{t-1}) \le 0. \qquad (3)$$

Each unsatisfied clause C in $F[x]$ contains a literal ℓ that *must* be set incorrectly since C is satisfied by $x^\star$. Let S be the set of variables in $F[x]$ corresponding to such literals. Let R denote the set of remaining variables in $F[x]$. Flipping any variable in S moves the solution closer to $x^\star$. On the other hand, flipping a variable in R *might* move the solution further from $x^\star$. Thus we have

$$\Delta_t \le |\{\text{bits in } R \text{ that flip}\}| - |\{\text{bits in } S \text{ that flip}\}|.$$

By definition, each clause contains at least one variable from S and the sum of $\gamma_i(x)$ over $i \in S$ (resp., $i \in R$) counts at least half (resp., at most half) of the $2m'$ literals in $F[x]$. Thus,

$$\mathrm{E}(|\{\text{bits in } S \text{ that flip}\}|) = \sum_{i\in S} \gamma_i(x)/(m'+1) \ge \frac{m'}{(m'+1)}$$

$$\mathrm{E}(|\{\text{bits in } R \text{ that flip}\}|) = \sum_{i\in R} \gamma_i(x)/(m'+1) \le \frac{m'}{(m'+1)},$$

and Inequality (3) holds. We define the random variable $Y_t = X_t^2 - aX_t - bt$ where $a = 2n$ and $b = \sigma^2$.

$$\mathrm{E}(Y_t \mid \mathscr{F}_{t-1}) = \mathrm{E}((X_{t-1}+\Delta_t)^2 - a(X_{t-1}+\Delta_t) - bt \mid \mathscr{F}_{t-1}),$$

and since, for any function g, $\mathrm{E}(g(X_{t-1}) \mid \mathscr{F}_{t-1}) = g(X_{t-1})$,

$$\begin{aligned} &= X_{t-1}^2 - aX_{t-1} - bt + (2X_{t-1} - a)\mathrm{E}(\Delta_t \mid \mathscr{F}_{t-1}) \\ &\quad + \mathrm{E}(\Delta_t^2 \mid \mathscr{F}_{t-1}) \\ &= Y_{t-1} - b + (2X_{t-1} - a)\mathrm{E}(\Delta_t \mid \mathscr{F}_{t-1}) \\ &\quad + \mathrm{E}(\Delta_t^2 \mid \mathscr{F}_{t-1}) \\ &\ge Y_{t-1}. \end{aligned}$$

The final inequality comes from the fact that $(2X_{t-1} - a)\mathrm{E}(\Delta_t \mid \mathscr{F}_{t-1}) \ge 0$ and $\mathrm{E}(\Delta_t^2 \mid \mathscr{F}_{t-1}) - b \ge 0$. Therefore, the sequence $\{Y_t\}$ is a submartingale with respect to the sequence $\{X_t\}$, and by the Optional Stopping Theorem [13, Theorem 10.10] $\mathrm{E}(Y_T) \ge E(Y_1)$. Therefore,

$$\mathrm{E}(X_T^2) - 2n\mathrm{E}(X_T) - \sigma^2 E(T) \ge X_1^2 - 2nX_1$$

and since $X_T^2 = X_T = 0$ and $0 \le X_1 \le n$,

$$\mathrm{E}(T) \le (2nX_1 - X_1^2)/\sigma^2 \le n^2/\sigma^2 = O(n^2\sqrt{m}),$$

which follows by the asymptotic bound on σ^2. □

Thus, the modified (1+1) EA can solve every satisfiable 2-CNF formula in expected polynomial time. Moreover, by Lemma 5, the modified algorithm can also find the 2-coloring of any bipartite graph in expected polynomial time. We point out that the modified (1+1) EA is not necessarily a good practical algorithm. First, as mentioned in the proof of Theorem 3, the selection step is not even necessary since disimproving offspring technically cannot be created. Furthermore, the bound on the runtime is a factor of $\sqrt{m}$ worse than Papadimitriou's conflict-directed random walk algorithm for 2-SAT. This factor arises because the probability of flipping a bit depends now on m so the variance of each mutation operation can no longer be bounded below by a positive constant. However, the goal of this section was simply to demonstrate that a slight modification to an evolutionary algorithm that allows it to use a small amount of domain knowledge can mean the difference between polynomial and superpolynomial performance.

5. CONCLUSION

Understanding the influence of problem structure on algorithm performance is important to the design and analysis of algorithms. In this paper, we have rigorously studied the performance of the (1+1) EA on two combinatorial problems that are known to be solvable in polynomial time. For each problem, we identified structural aspects that make it difficult to solve by the (1+1) EA, and showed that there are classes of instances on which the evolutionary algorithm needs a superpolynomial number of iterations to find an optimal solution with probability $1 - o(1)$. We then show how to modify the (1+1) EA to guarantee expected polynomial-time behavior on both problems.

Acknowledgements

The research leading to these results has received funding from the European Union Seventh Framework Programme (FP7/2007-2013) under grant agreement no. 618091 (SAGE), and from the Air Force Office of Scientific Research, Air Force Materiel Command, USAF, under grant no. FA9550-11-1-0088. The U.S. Government is authorized to reproduce and distribute reprints for Governmental purposes notwithstanding any copyright notation thereon. The author would also like to thank an anonymous GECCO reviewer for identifying an error in an earlier version of Lemma 2 and for pointing out the reduction from 2-coloring to 2-satisfiability.

6. REFERENCES

[1] Bengt Apsvall, Michael F. Plass, and Robert Endre Tarjan. A linear time algorithm for testing the truth of certain quantified Boolean formulas. *Information Processing Letters*, 8(3):121–123, 1979.

[2] Benjamin Doerr, Carola Doerr, and Franziska Ebel. Lessons from the black-box: Fast crossover-based genetic algorithms. In *Proceedings of the Genetic and Evolutionary Computation Conference (GECCO)*, pages 781–788. ACM, 2013.

[3] Benjamin Doerr, Daniel Johannsen, and Carola Winzen. Multiplicative drift analysis. *Algorithmica*, 64(4):673–697, 2012.

[4] William Feller. Generalization of a probability limit theorem of Cramér. *Transactions of the American Mathematical Society*, 54(3):361–372, 1943.

[5] Oliver Giel and Ingo Wegener. Evolutionary algorithms and the maximum matching problem. In Helmut Alt and Michel Habib, editors, *Proceedings of the Symposium on Theoretical Aspects of Computer Science (STACS)*, volume 2607 of *Lecture Notes in Computer Science*, pages 415–426. Springer, 2003.

[6] Jiří Matoušek and Jan Vondrák. The probabilistic method (lecture notes), March 2008. `http://kam.mff.cuni.cz/~matousek/prob-ln.ps.gz`.

[7] Colin McDiarmid. A random recolouring method for graphs and hypergraphs. *Combinatorics, Probability & Computing*, 2:363–365, 1993.

[8] Frank Neumann, Joachim Reichel, and Martin Skutella. Computing minimum cuts by randomized search heuristics. *Algorithmica*, 59(3):323–342, 2011.

[9] Pietro S. Oliveto and Carsten Witt. Erratum: Simplified drift analysis for proving lower bounds in evolutionary computation. `arXiv:1211.7184 [cs.NE]`.

[10] Pietro S. Oliveto and Carsten Witt. Simplified drift analysis for proving lower bounds in evolutionary computation. *Algorithmica*, 59(3):369–386, 2011.

[11] Christos H. Papadimitriou, Alejandro A. Schäffer, and Mihalis Yannakakis. On the complexity of local search. In *Proceedings of the Annual ACM Symposium on Theory of Computing (STOC)*, pages 438–445. ACM, 1990.

[12] Dirk Sudholt. Crossover is provably essential for the Ising model on trees. In *Proceedings of the Genetic and Evolutionary Computation Conference (GECCO)*, pages 1161–1167. ACM, 2005.

[13] David Williams. *Probability with Martingales.* Cambridge Mathematical Textbooks. Cambridge University Press, 1991.

[14] Carsten Witt. Tight bounds on the optimization time of a randomized search heuristic on linear functions. *Combinatorics, Probability and Computing*, 22(2):294–318, 2013.

Runtime Analysis to Compare Best-Improvement and First-Improvement in Memetic Algorithms

Kuai Wei
Dept. Computer Science, University of Auckland
Private Bag 92019, Auckland, New Zealand
kuai@cs.auckland.ac.nz

Michael J. Dinneen
Dept. Computer Science, University of Auckland
Private Bag 92019, Auckland, New Zealand
mjd@cs.auckland.ac.nz

ABSTRACT

In recent years, the advantage afforded by using multiple local searches in a Memetic Algorithm (MA) to solve one problem (a single fitness function), has been verified in many successful experiments. These experiments also give the observation that the local search operator that gives the best results in an MA on the same fitness function for solving a NP-hard problem is instance specific. This paper will provide a theoretical evidence for this observation. In this paper, we will formalize the (1+1) Restart Memetic Algorithms applying two different local searches, the first-improvement and the best-improvement, respectively. We will then run them on a single fitness function to solve the Clique Problem. We then show that there are two families of graphs such that, for the first family of graphs, MAs with one local search drastically outperform MAs with the other local search, and vice versa for the second family of graphs. Our study explains why using multiple local searches can outperform using a single local search in Memetic Algorithms.

Categories and Subject Descriptors

F.2.2 [**Theory of Computation**]: Analysis of Algorithms and Problem Complexity—*Nonnumerical Algorithms and Problems*

Keywords

Memetic algorithms, local search, maximum clique, analysis

1. INTRODUCTION

A Memetic Algorithm (MA) is a meta-heuristic algorithm which combines an Evolutionary Algorithm (EA) with local search algorithms. It is generally believed that MAs are successful because they inherit both the exploratory search ability of evolutionary algorithms and the neighborhood search ability of local search methods. There are many successful experimental studies in the literature, but theoretical progress lags far behind the experimental approach.

GECCO'14, July 12–16, Vancouver, BC, Canada.

ACM 978-1-4503-2662-9/14/07 ...$15.00.
http://dx.doi.org/10.1145/2576768.2598386.

The first runtime analysis on MAs was studied by Sudholt in 2006 [15], in which the (1+1) MA, (1+1) EA and the randomized local search were compared. MAs and EAs both apply mutations and recombinations, and the runtime analysis of these operations have been studied a lot in EAs. Therefore, theoretical analyses of MAs have mainly focused on the impact of the local searches. For example, Sudholt, in 2008 [16], analyzed the (1+1) MA with variable-depth search to overcome local optima on three binary combinatorial problems: Mincut, Knapsack, and Maxsat; and in 2009 [17], he showed that changing the depth of local searches or the frequency of applying local searches in MAs will change the performance from polynomial to super-polynomial. Furthermore, the interaction of mutations and local searches has attracted much attention. For example, Dinneen and Wei [4], in 2013, analyzed a dynamic mutation with two different local searches on some artificially created functions; they also analyzed a (1+1) Adaptive MA on the clique problem and showed that, for any local optimum that is hard to escape, the (1+1) Adaptive MA is expected to overcome the local optima super-polynomially faster than the basic (1+1) EA [3]; and a further study in [18] showed that hybridizing the dynamic mutation approach with local searches greatly enhances the algorithm's ability to escape local optima. More details of runtime analysis on EAs and MAs can be found in surveys [1], [7], [11], [12].

Theoretical studies of MAs have attracted many more researchers. The results of these studies explain the success of some experiments. For example, an adaptive mutation approach in an MA [2] gained success in experiments, and a theoretical evidence was studied in [4]. However, there are still many experimental approaches that lag theoretical evidences to explain their success. In particular, one trend in experimental research is to use multiple local searches in MAs to solve a single problem (one fitness function). In 2001, Krasnogor and Smith [8] did experiments and showed that even for a single problem class (TSP), the local search operator that gives the best results in an MA is entirely instance specific. Then, in 2005, Krasnogor and Smith [9] presented a taxonomy of memetic algorithms that provided a functional framework for using multiple local searches. This trend is also known as the multimeme algorithm [10], where each local search is a meme that is used adaptively or self-adaptively (see a survey in [13]). Furthermore, Coevolving Memetic Algorithms have been studied that coevolve the local search operators together with the mainstream population [14]. Essentially all of these approaches use multiple local searches in MAs to solve a single problem.

This trend of using multiple local searches created new challenges in the runtime analysis of MAs. A few theoretical studies show that, on one fitness function, MAs with one local search drastically outperform MAs with another local search, but the results are reversed when the same algorithms are applied to a different function [4], [5], [15], [16]. However, these studies are insufficient to explain why the local search operator that gives the best results in an MA for the same problem is instance specific, which is the aim of this paper. Our theoretical evidences also show that, if the best local search for the problem instance is unknown, then using multiple local searches can outperform using a single local search in MAs.

The paper is structured as follows. In Section 2, we will formalize the fitness function $f_{\texttt{OPL}}$ for the Clique Problem, then propose the (1+1) Restart Memetic Algorithm (RMA), and two local searches, the Best-Improvement Local Search (BILS) and the First-Improvement Local Search (FILS). Next, in Section 3, we will construct a family of graphs (G_1), and show that, to solve the Clique Problem on the graph family G_1, the (1+1) RMA with the BILS is expected to take a polynomial number of fitness evaluations, but the (1+1) RMA with the FILS is expected to take a super-polynomial number of fitness evaluations. In Section 4, we will construct another family of graphs (G_2) and show the opposite. Finally, a conclusion will be given in Section 5.

2. ALGORITHM DEFINITIONS

2.1 The Clique Problem

A *clique* of a graph is a subset of vertices from this graph such that every two vertices in the subset are connected by an edge. The *Clique Problem* is the NP-hard problem of finding the largest size of a clique in a graph. There are many possible usable fitness functions for solving the Clique Problem (see [19] for more details). However, due to the focus of this paper, which is to compare different local searches, we simply use the following fitness function $f_{\texttt{OPL}}$ for the Clique Problem.

For a given graph $G = (V = \{v_1, v_2, ..., v_n\}, E)$, a bit string $x = (x_1, x_2, ..., x_n) \in \{0,1\}^n$ defines a clique potential solution (an induced subgraph) where $x_i = 1$ represents that the vertex v_i is selected. We say x represents a clique if each selected vertex in x is connected to all other selected vertices in x, i.e. $\{(v_i, v_j) \mid x_i = x_j = 1 \text{ and } i \neq j\} \subseteq E$.

Definition 1. The fitness function $f_{\texttt{OPL}}$ (`ONES`, `P[otential] V[ertices]`, `LACKEDGES`) is defined as follows:

$$f_{\texttt{OPL}}(x) = \begin{cases} \texttt{ONES}(x) + \texttt{PV}(x)/n, & \text{if x represents a clique,} \\ -\texttt{LACKEDGES}(x), & \text{otherwise,} \end{cases}$$

where $\texttt{ONES}(x)$ is the number of ones in x; $\texttt{PV}(x)$ is the number of zeros in x such that, when each of these zeros is flipped individually, a larger clique is obtained. And $\texttt{LACKEDGES}(x)$ is the number of missing edges such that the subgraph becomes a clique.

A maximum clique for a graph G is a global optimal solution x that maximizes $f_{\texttt{OPL}}(x)$.

2.2 Algorithms to be analyzed

For completeness we list the foundational algorithms used in our study (e.g. the first two algorithms also used for our companion paper [19]).

Algorithm 2. (1+1) RMA.

1. Set the number of generations $\texttt{gen} := 0$, $x = 0^n$.
2. $y := x$. Flip every bit in y with probability $1/n$.
3. $z := \texttt{LocalSearch}(y)$.
4. If $f(z) \geq f(x)$ then $x := z$.
5. $\texttt{gen} := \texttt{gen} + 1$.
6. If $\texttt{gen} = \lambda$ then go to step 1.
7. Stop if any stopping criterion is met, otherwise, go to step 2.

Note that the algorithm will restart in every λ generations. We will analyze the impact of λ on the algorithm's ability to find a global optimal solution. The local search $\texttt{LocalSearch}(y)$ can have many variations. We will analyze a *Best-Improvement Local Search* (BILS), which uses a steepest ascent pivot rule, and a *First-Improvement Local Search* (FILS), which uses a greedy pivot rule.

Algorithm 3. Best-Improvement Local Search (BILS). For a given string $x \in \{0,1\}^n$:

1. $\texttt{BestNeighborSet} :=$
$$\left\{ \begin{array}{l} y \mid f(y) > f(x), \texttt{Hamming}(x,y) = 1, \text{ and} \\ \forall z \text{ with } \texttt{Hamming}(x,z) = 1 : f(y) \geq f(z) \end{array} \right\}.$$
2. Stop and return x if $\texttt{BestNeighborSet} = \emptyset$.
3. x is randomly chosen from $\texttt{BestNeighborSet}$.
4. Go to step 1.

Note, $\texttt{Hamming}(x,y)$ is the number of different bits between x and y. It is easy to see that the BILS will stop on the fitness function $f_{\texttt{OPL}}$ within $2n^2$ fitness evaluations [19].

The FILS randomly generates a permutation to represent the sequence of bits to search and executes the flipping as soon as the fitness evaluation improves.

Algorithm 4. First-Improvement Local Search (FILS). For a given string $x = (x_1, x_2, \cdots, x_n) \in \{0,1\}^n$:

1. Generate a random permutation $\texttt{Per}$ of length n.
2. $i := 0$, $\texttt{NoBetterCount} := 0$.
3. $y := \texttt{flip}(x, \texttt{Per}[i])$.
4. If $f(y) > f(x)$ then $x := y$, $\texttt{NoBetterCount} := 0$.
5. $\texttt{NoBetterCount} := \texttt{NoBetterCount} + 1$.
6. $i := (i+1) \bmod n$.
7. Stop if $\texttt{NoBetterCount} = n$. Otherwise, go to step 3.

Here $\texttt{flip}(x, \texttt{Per}[i])$ denotes that the $\texttt{Per}[i]$-th bit in x is flipped, and $\texttt{Per}[i]$ is the i-th number in the permutation $\texttt{Per}$.

Example 5. Suppose the bit string $x = (0,0,0,0)$, and $\texttt{Per} = (3,2,1,4)$. So the FILS will first check a possible flipping for the third bit in x to get $x' = (0,0,1,0)$. If $f(x') > f(x)$ then $x := x'$. This check sequence follows $\texttt{Per}$ in a cyclic fashion. That is, after checking the fourth bit in x, the FILS will restart checking the third bit in x.

Note that the FILS moves to the first neighbor solution that improves the fitness, so it will stop on the fitness function $f_{\texttt{OPL}}$ within $3n$ fitness evaluations. Note that the FILS will first check all n bits within the first n fitness evaluations and flip some of them from ones to zeros in order to find a clique; then it will use at most n fitness evaluations to flip some bits from zeros to ones in order to find a local optimum; lastly, it will use n fitness evaluations to find out that there is no better neighbors and stop.

In the rest of this paper, we will use (1+1) RMA_BILS to denote that the (1+1) RMA is using the BILS as the local search, and (1+1) RMA_FILS to denote that the (1+1) RMA is using the FILS as the local search.

3. A FAMILY OF GRAPHS ON WHICH THE (1+1) RMA_BILS OUTPERFORMS THE (1+1) RMA_FILS

In this section, we will use the family of graphs G_1, which we have studied in [19], to show that the (1+1) RMA_BILS is expected to find the maximum clique on any graph of the family G_1 within a polynomial number of fitness evaluations, while the (1+1) RMA_FILS is expected to take a super-polynomial number of fitness evaluations to find the maximum clique on any graph of the family G_1.

Definition 6. The graph $G_1(t)$ has $n = t(2t+2)$ vertices for the variable t. We separate all vertices into $(2t+2)$ disjoint sets $V_0, V_1, \ldots, V_{2t+1}$ such that $V_i \cap V_j = \emptyset$ and $|V_i| = t$ for $0 \le i \le 2t+1$, $0 \le j \le 2t+1$ and $i \ne j$. We use $v_{i,k}$ to refer the k-th vertex in V_i $(0 \le k \le t-1)$. To make it easier to understand the edge set E, we first assume it is a complete graph, and then delete edges according to the following rules:

1. Delete the edge between $v_{i,k}$ and $v_{j,k}$ for all variables i, j, k with $\lfloor i/2 \rfloor \ne \lfloor j/2 \rfloor$, $0 \le k \le t-1$, $0 \le i \le 2t+1$ and $0 \le j \le 2t+1$.
2. Delete the edge between $v_{i,t-1}$ and $v_{j,t-1}$ for all variables i, j with $2 \le i \le 2t+1$ and $\lfloor i/2 \rfloor = \lfloor j/2 \rfloor$.
3. Delete the edge between $v_{1,k}$ and $v_{j,l}$ for all variables j, k, l with $2 \le j \le 2t+1$, $0 \le k \le t-1$, $0 \le l \le t-1$ and $k \equiv (l-1) \bmod t$.

Now we fill all vertices from the sets $V_0, V_1, \ldots, V_{2t+1}$ into a $(2t+2)$-by-t matrix with each set V_i being the i-th row vector, as shown in Figure 1. Hence, $v_{i,j}$ is the vertex in row i and column j. We use $V(x)$ to denote the set of vertices x has chosen, recall $x = (x_1, x_2, \ldots, x_n)$. Then we use $v_{i,k}(x) = 1$ (a solid circle in Figure 1) to denote that $v_{i,k} \in V(x)$, and $v_{i,k}(x) = 0$ (a hollow circle in Figure 1) otherwise.

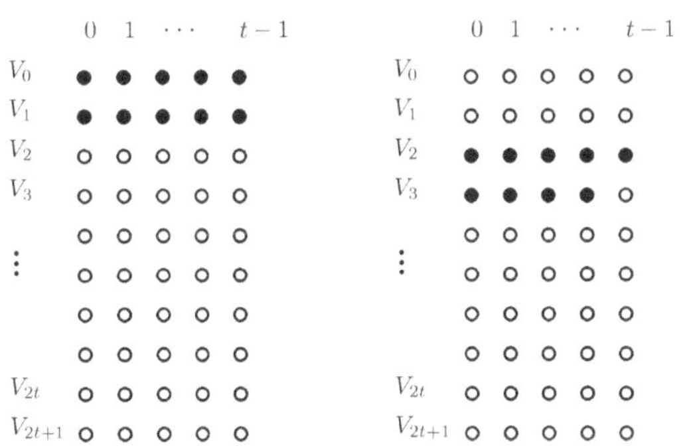

The global optimum $V_0 \cup V_1$ A local optimum in $V_2 \cup V_3$

Figure 1: Two examples of the $(2t+2)$-by-t matrix for $G_1(t)$ where the left is the global optimum and the right is a local optimum.

Some properties of the graph $G_1(t)$ are now mentioned.

Claim 7. *([19]) For the graph $G_1(t)$, if the bit string x represents a clique, $V(x)$ has at most two vertices in each column, i.e. $\forall k, 0 \le k \le t-1 : \sum_{i=0}^{2t+1} v_{i,k}(x) \le 2$.*

Claim 8. *([19]) For the graph $G_1(t)$, if the bit string x represents a maximal clique, $V(x)$ contains at least one vertex in each column, i.e. $\forall k, 0 \le k \le t-1 : \sum_{i=0}^{2t+1} v_{i,k}(x) \ge 1$. Furthermore, $V(x)$ contains at least t vertices, i.e. $|V(x)| \ge t$.*

Claim 9. *([19]) The only maximum clique of the graph $G_1(t)$ is $V_{global} = V_0 \cup V_1$, which contains $2t$ vertices.*

Theorem 10. *For any λ with $\lambda = \Theta(1)$, the (1+1) RMA_BILS is expected to find the maximum clique of the graph $G_1(t)$ within $O(n^2)$ fitness evaluations.*

Proof. In this proof, we say a bit string is on the *Path* if it is 0^n, or it represents a clique that only contains vertices in $V_0 \cup V_1$.

Part 1. According to Algorithm 2, since the algorithm starts with $x = 0^n$, and the mutation probability is $1/n$, the probability that the mutation does not flip any bits is $(1-1/n)^n$, which approaches $1/e$ as n increases. Thus, within $\Theta(1)$ restarts, we expect to have a mutation that gets a bit string y, with $y = 0^n$, which is on the *Path*. Furthermore, the algorithm will restart after each λ mutations and BILSs, where each BILS will stop within $2n^2$ fitness evaluations (see the analysis after Algorithm 3). Therefore, we expect to have a mutation to find the bit string of 0^n within $O(n^2)$ fitness evaluations.

Part 2. We claim that, apart from the maximum clique bit string, for any bit string z on the *Path*, the best neighbors of z must be on the *Path* as well (we will prove this in the next paragraphs). Therefore, once the BILS finds a bit string on the *Path*, the BILS will keep adding vertices from $V_0 \cup V_1$ until it finds the maximum clique of $V_0 \cup V_1$. Also, we expect to have a mutation to find a clique on the *Path* within $O(n^2)$ fitness evaluations (see Part 1). Overall, the (1+1) RMA_BILS is expected to find the maximum clique of the graph $G_1(t)$ within $O(n^2)$ fitness evaluations.

Now we show that, apart from the maximum clique bit string, for any bit string z on the *Path*, the best neighbors of z must be on the *Path*. We prove this by assuming that there exists a bit string z' that is one of the best neighbors of z and that is not on the *Path*, and then showing that there exists a bit string z'', that is also a neighbor of z, yet has a larger fitness value than z', thus z' does not exist.

Firstly, according to the assumption, z' is obtained by adding a vertex from $\bigcup_{i=2}^{2t+1} V_i$ to z, and this added vertex (say $v_{i,k}$) is the only vertex in z' that is in $\bigcup_{i=2}^{2t+1} V_i$. Also note that z does not contain any vertex in column k, otherwise z' cannot be a better neighbor of z due to Rule 1 in Definition 6. Therefore, we claim $\mathtt{PV}(z') \le \mathtt{PV}(z) - 2t - 2$. This is because there are at least $2t+2$ vertices in $\mathtt{PV}(z)$ but not in $\mathtt{PV}(z')$. In detail, these $2t+2$ vertices are:

1. The flipped vertex $v_{i,k}$.
2. One vertex $v_{1,(k-1) \bmod t}$ due to Rule 3 in Definition 6.
3. $2t$ vertices of $v_{j,k}$ for all $0 \le j \le 2t+1$ and $\lfloor i/2 \rfloor \ne \lfloor j/2 \rfloor$ due to Rule 1 in Definition 6.

Secondly, let z'' be a neighbor of z that adds the vertex $v_{0,k}$, this means:

1. z'' must be a better neighbor of z. This is because a), the vertex $v_{0,k}$ must not be chosen by z, otherwise z' can not be a better neighbor of z; and b), the vertex $v_{0,k}$ is connected to all vertices in z since they are in $V_0 \cup V_1$, which is the maximum clique due to Claim 9.

2. $\texttt{PV}(z'') = \texttt{PV}(z) - 2t - 1$. This is because there are exactly $2t+1$ vertices in $\texttt{PV}(z)$, but not in $\texttt{PV}(z'')$. These $2t+1$ vertices are a) the flipped vertex $v_{0,k}$, and b) $2t$ vertices from $\bigcup_{j=2}^{2t+1}\{v_{j,k}\}$ due to Rule 1 in Definition 6.

Thus, we have a bit string z'' that is a better neighbor of z, and has a larger fitness value than z'. This conflicts with our assumption that z' is one of the best neighbors of z. □

We now introduce the Global Gambler's Ruin that we will use to prove Theorem 12.

Theorem 11. *Global Gambler's Ruin (Happ et al. [6]) Let $X_0, X_1, X_2, \ldots$ be random variables describing a Markov process over the state space $\mathbb{N}_0$. For constants $a, b \in \mathbb{R}$ with $0 \leq a < b \leq 1$ let the random variable T denote the earliest point in time $p \geq 0$ that satisfies $X_p \leq an$.*

If there exist constants $\delta > 1$ and $C > 0$ such that the three conditions

1. *$P[X_0 \geq bn] = 1 - 2^{-\Omega(n)}$,*
2. *$P[X_{p+1} - X_p = j \mid X_p] \geq \delta^j \cdot P[X_{p+1} - X_p = -j \mid X_p]$ for all $j \geq 1$, $p \geq 0$, and $an < X_p < bn$,*
3. *$\sum_{j\geq 1} \delta^j \cdot P[X_{p+1} - X_p = -j \mid X_p] \leq C$ for all $p \geq 0$ and $X_p \geq bn$*

hold then $T \geq \delta^{(1/3)(b-a)n}$ with probability $1 - 2^{-\Omega(n)}$.

The theorem above shows that if the three conditions hold, then the first hitting time T is exponential with a probability exponentially close to one.

Theorem 12. *For any static or dynamic variable λ, the probability of the (1+1) RMA_FILS finding the maximum clique of the graph $G_1(t)$ within a polynomial number of fitness evaluations is super-polynomially (to n) close to zero.*

Proof. We prove the theorem by showing that from the start, or from each restart, the (1+1) RMA_FILS is expected to become trapped in a local optimal solution and take a super-polynomial number of fitness evaluations to find the global optimal solution. In detail, our proof consists of three parts, with each part having a failure probability super-polynomially close to zero.

Part 1. Let y be the first bit string found by the algorithm, after the start or each restart, that represents a clique. We claim that $V(y)$ is has a constant number of vertices in $V_0 \cup V_1$ with a probability super-polynomially close to one.

Since the algorithm starts or restarts with $x = 0^n$, and the mutation probability is $1/n$, the bit string after the mutation has a constant number of ones in $V_0 \cup V_1$ with a probability super-polynomially close to one (we will show this in the next paragraph). This bit string either a) represents a clique, then Part 1 is true; b) is 0^n, then the local search will flip one bit from zero to one to find a clique, hence, Part 1 is true; or c) does not represent a clique, then the local search will keep flipping bits from ones to zeros until the bit string represents a clique, hence, Part 1 is true.

Now we show that from 0^n, the mutation with a mutation probability $1/n$ flips a constant number of ones in $V_0 \cup V_1$ with a probability super-polynomially close to one. Suppose the above statement fails, i.e., the mutation flips $p = \omega(1)$ bits in $V_0 \cup V_1$. Since there are $2t$ vertices in $V_0 \cup V_1$, and $n = t(2t+2)$, the probability of this event occurring is

$$\binom{2t}{p}\frac{1}{n^p}\left(1 - \frac{1}{n}\right)^{2t-p} \leq \frac{c}{p!}\left(\frac{2t}{n}\right)^p,$$

for a constant c. This probability is super-polynomially close to zero since $p = \omega(1)$ and $n = t(2t+2)$.

Part 2. Assume Part 1 has succeeded. Let z be the first bit string found by the algorithm, after start or each restart, that represents a local optimal clique. We claim that the number of vertices in $V(z)$ that are also in $V_0 \cup V_1$ is $O(\log t)$ with a probability super-polynomially close to one.

Recall that the FILS will check neighbors according to its permutation array, and moves to its neighbor immediately if that neighbor improves the fitness value. Besides, for any column k with $0 \leq k \leq t-1$, due to $|\bigcup_{j=2}^{2t+1}\{v_{j,k}\}| = t|\{v_{0,k}, v_{1,k}\}| = 2t$, the probability of the FILS checking a vertex in $\{v_{0,k}, v_{1,k}\}$ before checking any other vertices in the same column is $1/(t+1)$. Thus, if adding any vertex $v_{i,k}$ ($0 \leq i \leq 2t+1$) from the column k to the current clique creates a larger clique, then the probability of the FILS adding a vertex from $\bigcup_{j=2}^{2t+1}\{v_{j,k}\}$ is t times the probability of the FILS adding a vertex from $\{v_{0,k}, v_{1,k}\}$.

Given above, and because there are t columns in the graph, if we for now ignore the consequences of Rule 3 in Definition 6, then with a probability super-polynomially close to one, there are at most $\log t$ columns of which z includes vertices from $V_0 \cup V_1$. This can be shown by assuming that z has $p = \Omega(\log t)$ columns that include vertices from $V_0 \cup V_1$. Then the probability of this result occurring is:

$$\binom{t}{p}\left(\frac{1}{t}\right)^p\left(1 - \frac{1}{t}\right)^{t-p} < \frac{1}{ep!} < \frac{1}{2^{cp}},$$

for any constant c, which is super-polynomially close to zero since $p = \Omega(\log t)$.

Now we take Rule 3 in Definition 6 into consideration. Before the FILS reaches the local optimal z, there may exist a column k, $0 \leq k \leq t-1$, such that the current clique contains the vertex $v_{1,k}$, but does not contain any vertices in the next column $(k+1) \bmod t$. Thus adding any vertex from $\bigcup_{i=2}^{2t+1}\{v_{i,(k+1) \bmod t}\}$ will not improve the fitness, but adding any vertex from $\{v_{0,(k+1) \bmod t},\ v_{1,(k+1) \bmod t}\}$ will improve the fitness. Consequently, the FILS will choose to add a vertex from $\{v_{0,(k+1) \bmod t},\ v_{1,(k+1) \bmod t}\}$ to the clique no matter the sequence of the random permutation. After the FILS has added the vertex $v_{1,(k+1) \bmod t}$ to the clique, it might keep influencing the column $(k+2) \bmod t$ in which the FILS can only add vertices from $\{v_{0,(k+2) \bmod t}, v_{1,(k+2) \bmod t}\}$, and then the column $(k+3) \bmod t$, and so on.

However, we claim that if a clique includes a vertex from V_1, but does not include any vertices in the next $\mu = \omega(1)$ columns, then the probability of the FILS adding vertices from $V_0 \cup V_1$ in the next μ columns is super-polynomially close to zero (we will show this in the next paragraph). Thus, since we only expect to have at most $\log t$ vertices chosen from $V_0 \cup V_1$ when we ignore Rule 3 in Definition 6, then adding this rule is only expected to result in an increase of a constant factor of the number of vertices from $V_0 \cup V_1$, which is overall $O(\log t)$.

Now we show that if a clique includes a vertex from $v_{1,k}$, but does not include any vertices in the next $\mu = \omega(1)$ columns, then the probability of the FILS adding vertices from $V_0 \cup V_1$ in the next μ columns is super-polynomially close to zero. Let us assume by contradiction, i.e., there exists a column k, and the FILS will keep adding vertices from $V_0 \cup V_1$ in the columns $(k+1) \bmod t, (k+2) \bmod t, \cdots, (k+\mu) \bmod t$ for any $\mu = \omega(1)$. We now show that this probability is super-polynomially close to zero. Note, for our assumption to succeed, the random permutation array needs to guide the FILS to check the vertex $v_{1,(k+1) \bmod t}$ before checking all vertices that are in the bottom $2t$ rows and also in the next μ columns, i.e., from $\bigcup_{i=2}^{2t+1} \bigcup_{j=(k+2) \bmod t}^{(k+\mu) \bmod t} \{v_{i,j}\}$. The probability of getting this exact permutation array is $1/2t(\mu-1)$. Otherwise, if the FILS checks any vertex from $\bigcup_{i=2}^{2t+1} \bigcup_{j=(k+2) \bmod t}^{(k+\mu) \bmod t} \{v_{i,j}\}$ first, it will find out that adding this vertex to the clique will improve the fitness. Since the FILS moves every time it finds a better neighbor, our assumption fails. Meanwhile, the permutation array needs to guide the FILS to check the vertex $v_{1,(k+2) \bmod t}$ before checking all vertices that are in the bottom $2t$ rows and also in the next $\mu-1$ columns, i.e., from $\bigcup_{i=2}^{2t+1} \bigcup_{j=(k+3) \bmod t}^{(k+\mu) \bmod t} \{v_{i,j}\}$, and so on. In other words, for each variable l with $1 \le l < \mu$, the permutation array needs to guide the FILS to check the vertex $v_{1,(k+l) \bmod t}$ before checking all vertices that are in $\bigcup_{i=2}^{2t+1} \bigcup_{j=(k+l+1) \bmod t}^{(k+\mu) \bmod t} \{v_{i,j}\}$. The probability of this permutation array occurring is:

$$\frac{1}{2t(\mu-1)} \frac{1}{2t(\mu-2)} \cdots \frac{1}{2t} = \frac{1}{(2t)^{\mu-1}(\mu-1)!},$$

which is super-polynomially close to zero since $\mu = \omega(1)$ and $n = t(2t+2)$.

Part 3. Assume Part 2 has succeeded. After z is found, the (1+1) RMA_FILS will either a) restart (the next restart will find another z that represents a clique with $O(\log t)$ vertices in $V_0 \cup V_1$ as well), or b) cannot find the maximum clique within a polynomial number of fitness evaluations with a probability super-polynomially close to one.

We now apply Theorem 11 to prove this part. Let X_p denote the number of columns in which the current clique contains vertices in $\bigcup_{i=2}^{2t+1} V_i$ at time p. Note that $0 \le X_p \le t$ and $n = t(2t+2)$. According to Claim 8, the current clique, which is a local optimum, contains at least one vertex in each column, then the target state is $X_T = 0$ (note that when a local optimum does not contain any vertex in the bottom $2t$ rows, it is the maximum clique of $V_0 \cup V_1$). Let $a = 1/4$ and $b = 1/2$. Since z only has $O(\log t)$ vertices in $V_0 \cup V_1$ (Part 2 has succeeded), z has more than $(1/2)t$ columns that include vertices in $\bigcup_{i=2}^{2t+1} V_i$. Therefore, $X_0 \ge (1/2)t$, and so Condition 1 of Theorem 11 is met.

Then we analyze Condition 2 of Theorem 11. Suppose the current state $X_p \in (an, bn)$. Let $\delta = 2$. Then we show that $P[X_{p+1} - X_p = j \mid X_p] \ge \delta^j \cdot P[X_{p+1} - X_p = -j \mid X_p]$.

We start with an example that only jumps one step, i.e., $j = 1$ (see Figure 2). Suppose a column includes two vertices in $\bigcup_{i=2}^{2t+1} V_i$ at state X_p, and then at state X_{p+1}, it includes vertices in $V_0 \cup V_1$. To achieve this goal, i.e., $X_{p+1} - X_p = -1$, the mutation and the FILS need to remove the two selected vertices that are in $\bigcup_{i=2}^{2t+1} V_i$, and also add the two vertices that are in $V_0 \cup V_1$ (see an example of $X_p \to X_{p+1}^1$ in Figure 2). On the other hand, suppose a column includes two vertices in $V_0 \cup V_1$ at state X_p, and then at state X_{p+1}, it includes vertices in $\bigcup_{i=2}^{2t+1} V_i$. To achieve this goal, i.e., $X_{p+1} - X_p = 1$, the mutation and the FILS need to remove the two selected vertices that are in $V_0 \cup V_1$, and also add a pair of two vertices from $\bigcup_{i=2}^{2t+1} V_i$ in the same column. Note that the addition operation has t choices (see an example of $X_p \to \{X_{p+1}^2, X_{p+1}^3, X_{p+1}^4, X_{p+1}^5, X_{p+1}^6\}$ in Figure 2). In the example of Figure 2 where $t = 4$, there are t cliques that can achieve $X_{p+1} - X_p = 1$, while only one clique that can achieve $X_{p+1} - X_p = -1$. Furthermore, the probabilities of achieving each of these cliques are the same since they all need to change the same number of bits.

Besides, note that $X_p \in (an, bn)$, which indicates that, in the state X_p, there are more columns that can achieve the negative drift of $X_{p+1} - X_p = 1$ than columns that can achieve the positive drift of $X_{p+1} - X_p = -1$. Therefore, $P[X_{p+1} - X_p = 1 \mid X_p] \ge t \cdot P[X_{p+1} - X_p = -1 \mid X_p] > \delta \cdot P[X_{p+1} - X_p = -1 \mid X_p]$.

Similarly, since $X_p \in (an, bn)$, and the size of the bottom $2t$ rows is t times the size of the top two rows, we can see that the total number of cliques that can achieve $X_{p+1} - X_p = j$ is t^j times the total number of cliques that can achieve $X_{p+1} - X_p = -j$. In addition, the probabilities of achieving each of these cliques are the same. Therefore, $P[X_{p+1} - X_p = j \mid X_p] \ge \delta^j \cdot P[X_{p+1} - X_p = -j \mid X_p]$. for all $j \ge 1$, $p \ge 0$, $\delta = 2$ and $X_p \in (an, bn)$.

Lastly, we analyze Condition 3 of Theorem 11. Note that for each column that undergoes a positive drift or a negative drift, the mutation needs to flip at least one bit in that column (note that the graph is dense according to the deleting edge rules in Definition 6). Therefore, to jump j steps towards the target state, i.e., $X_{p+1} - X_p = -j$, the mutation needs to flip at least j bits. Then we say that the probability of $X_{p+1} - X_p = -j$ is at most the mutation flips at least j bits, i.e., $\sum_{q=j}^{n} \binom{n}{q} \cdot (1/n)^q (1 - 1/n)^{n-q} \le \sum_{q=j}^{n} 1/(q!)$. Therefore, $\sum_{j \ge 1} \delta^j P[X_{p+1} - X_p = -j \mid X_p] \le \sum_{j \ge 1} j \cdot \delta^j/(j!) = \sum_{j \ge 1} j \cdot 2^j/(j!)$, which is a constant (note that $j!$ grows faster than 4^j when $j > 4$).

Overall, with $a = 1/4$, $b = 1/2$, $\delta = 2$ and $C = \sum_{j \ge 1} j \cdot 2^j/(j!)$, then the three conditions in Theorem 11 hold. By applying Theorem 11, $T \ge 2^{(1/12)t}$ with probability $1 - 2^{-\Omega(t)}$. Hence, the probability that the algorithm finds the maximum clique within a polynomial number of fitness evaluations is super-polynomially close to zero. □

4. A FAMILY OF GRAPHS ON WHICH THE (1+1) RMA_FILS OUTPERFORMS THE (1+1) RMA_BILS

In this section, we will use the family of graphs G_2, which we studied in [19], to show that the (1+1) RMA_FILS is expected to find a maximum clique within a polynomial number of fitness evaluations, while the (1+1) RMA_BILS is expected to find a maximum clique within a super-polynomial number of fitness evaluations.

Definition 13. The graph $G_2(t)$ has the same number of vertices as the graph $G_1(t)$, but the edge connections are different. It has $n = t(2t+2)$ vertices for the variable t. We separate all vertices into $(2t+2)$ disjoint sets $V_0, V_1, \ldots, V_{2t+1}$ such that $V_i \cap V_j = \emptyset$ and $|V_i| = t$ for $0 \le i \le 2t+1$, $0 \le j \le 2t+1$ and $i \ne j$. We use $v_{i,k}$ to refer the k-th vertex in V_i $(0 \le k \le t-1)$. To make it easier to understand the edge set E, we first assume it is a complete graph, and then delete edges according to the following rules:

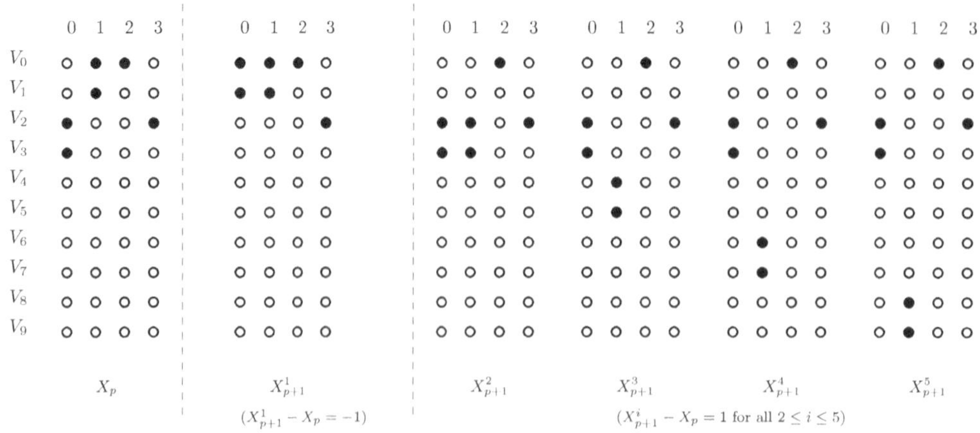

Figure 2: Examples of the X^1_{p+1} where $X^1_{p+1} - X_p = -1$ and all X^i_{p+1}s where $X^i_{p+1} - X_p = 1$ for $2 \le i \le 4$.

1. Delete the edge between $v_{i,k}$ and $v_{j,k}$ for all variables i, j, k with $0 \le k \le t-1$, $0 \le i \le 2t+1$, $0 \le j \le 2t+1$ and $\lfloor i/2 \rfloor \ne \lfloor j/2 \rfloor$.
2. Delete the edge between $v_{0,t-1}$ and $v_{1,t-1}$.
3. Delete the edge between $v_{i,k}$ and $v_{j,l}$ for all variables i, j, k, l with $2 \le i \le 2t+1$, $2 \le j \le 2t+1$, $\lfloor i/2 \rfloor = \lfloor j/2 \rfloor$, $0 \le k \le t-1$, $0 \le l \le t-1$ and $k \ne l$.
4. Delete the edge between $v_{1,k}$ and $v_{j,l}$ for all variables j, k, l with $2 \le j \le 2t+1$, $0 \le k \le t-1$, $0 \le l \le t-1$ and $k \equiv (l-1) \bmod t$.
5. Delete the edge between $v_{1,k}$ and $v_{j,l}$ for all variables j, k, l with $2 \le j \le 2t+1$, $0 \le k \le t-1$ and $l \in \{k - k \bmod \lfloor \log t \rfloor, k + \lfloor \log t \rfloor - k \bmod \lfloor \log t \rfloor\}$ where $0 \le l \le t-1$.

Like we did for the graph $G_1(t)$, we can visualize the graph $G_2(t)$ as a $(2t+2)$-by-t matrix with each set V_i being the i-th row vector, as shown in Figure 3.

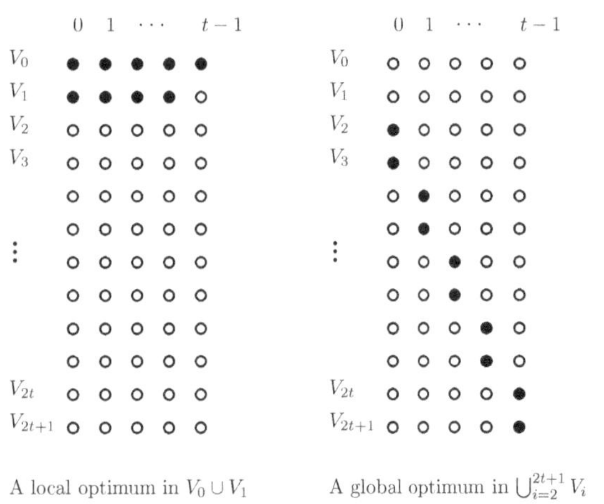

Figure 3: Two examples of the $(2t+2)$-by-t matrix for $G_2(t)$, where the left is a local optimum and the right is a global optimum.

Claim 14. *([19]) For the graph $G_2(t)$, if the bit string x represents a clique, $V(x)$ has at most two vertices in each column, i.e. $\forall k, 0 \le k \le t-1 : \sum_{i=0}^{2t+1} v_{i,k}(x) \le 2$.*

Claim 15. *([19]) For the graph $G_2(t)$, if the bit string x represents a maximal clique, $V(x)$ contains at least one vertex in each column, i.e. $\forall k, 0 \le k \le t-1 : \sum_{i=0}^{2t+1} v_{i,k}(x) \ge 1$. Furthermore, $V(x)$ contains at least t vertices, i.e. $|V(x)| \ge t$.*

Claim 16. *([19]) For the graph $G_2(t)$, if the bit string x represents a maximal clique, then for each row V_i with $2 \le i \le 2t+1$, $V(x)$ contains at most one vertex in V_i, i.e., $\forall i, 2 \le i \le 2t+1 : |V(x) \cap V_i| \le 1$.*

Claim 17. *([19]) For any bit string x that represents a maximal clique of the graph $G_2(t)$, if $V(x)$ does not contain any vertices in $V_0 \cup V_1$, then it contains $2t$ vertices and is a maximum clique. Otherwise, $V(x)$ contains less than $2t$ vertices.*

Definition 18. For the graph $G_2(t)$ and a maximum clique x, a section is called *hard-to-escape* if a) it contains $\lfloor \log t \rfloor$ consecutive columns, that starts from a column k_1 with $k_1 \bmod \lfloor \log t \rfloor = 0$; and b) x contains exact two vertices in $V_0 \cup V_1$ from each column of this section.

Claim 19. *([19]) For each* hard-to-escape *section in Definition 18, if the mutation and the following local search wants to find another clique of which the clique size is not decreased, but has less vertices in $V_0 \cup V_1$ in this section, then the only way is to remove all vertices in $V_0 \cup V_1$ in this section, and add the same number of vertices in $\bigcup_{i=2}^{2t+1} V_i$ in this section. Furthermore, the probability to achieve this jump is super-polynomially close to zero.*

Theorem 20. *For any λ with $\lambda = \Theta(1)$, the (1+1) RMA_FILS is expected to find a maximum clique of the graph $G_2(t)$ within $O(n^{1.5})$ fitness evaluations.*

Proof. Part 1. Same as the proof of Part 1 for Theorem 10, we know that, within $\Theta(1)$ restarts, we expect to have a mutation that produces the bit string 0^n. Also, because we will restart the algorithm after each $\lambda = \Theta(1)$ generations, and the FILS will take at most $3n$ fitness evaluations in each generation (see Algorithm 4), we expect to have a mutation that does not flip any bits within $O(n)$ fitness evaluations.

Part 2. Proceeding from Part 1, i.e. the FILS starts from the bit string 0^n, now we look at the probability of the FILS finding a local optimal clique that does not contain any vertices in $V_0 \cup V_1$, which is also a maximum clique, according to Claim 17.

Note that the FILS will keep checking neighbors according to the permutation array, then moving to the first neighbor that improves fitness value. Also, according to Claim 15, when the FILS finds a local optimal clique, this clique must contain at least one vertex in each column. Therefore, if we look at each column, and focus on the first vertex in the column that the FILS will add to the current clique, there must exist a sequence of columns $C = (c_1, c_2, \ldots, c_t)$, such that the FILS will first add one vertex from the column c_1 to the current clique, then add another vertex from the column c_2 to the current clique, and so on. Note that in each column k, $|\bigcup_{i=2}^{2t+1}\{v_{i,k}\}| = t|\{v_{0,k}, v_{1,k}\}| = 2t$. Hence, in the first column (c_1), the probability of the permutation array guiding the FILS to add a vertex from $V_0 \cup V_1$ to the current clique is $1/(t+1)$. That is to say, in the column c_1, the probability of the permutation array guiding the FILS to add a vertex from $\bigcup_{i=2}^{2t+1} V_i$ to the current clique is $1 - 1/(t+1) = t/(t+1)$. Also note that, if the FILS has added any vertex from $\bigcup_{i=2}^{2t+1} V_i$ in the column c_1 to the clique, then, in the column c_2, there are two vertices from $\bigcup_{i=2}^{2t+1} V_i$ that are disconnected with the current clique, due to Rule 3 in Definition 13. Therefore, in the column c_2, the number of vertices from $\bigcup_{i=2}^{2t+1} V_i$ that can be added to the current clique to get a larger clique will be decreased to $2t - 2$. Meanwhile, the number of vertices from $V_0 \cup V_1$ in the column c_2 that can be added to the current clique to get a larger clique will still be at most two. Thus, the probability of the random permutation array guiding the FILS to add a vertex from $\bigcup_{i=2}^{2t+1} V_i$ in the column c_2 to the current clique is at least $(t-1)/t$. And so on, in the column c_i, if the current clique does not contain any vertices in $V_0 \cup V_1$, i.e. there are $i-1$ columns from which the current clique contains vertices in $\bigcup_{i=2}^{2t+1} V_i$, then, the probability of the random permutation array guiding the FILS to add a vertex from $\bigcup_{i=2}^{2t+1} V_i$ in the column c_i to the current clique is at least $(t-i+1)/(t-i+2)$. Overall, the probability of the random permutation array guiding the FILS to find a local optimal clique that does not contain any vertices in $V_0 \cup V_1$ is at least $\frac{t}{t+1}\frac{t-1}{t}\cdots\frac{1}{2} = 1/(t+1)$.

Therefore, if we have $O(t)$ mutations that all produce the bit string 0^n, the FILS is expected to find a local optimal clique that does not contain any vertices in $V_0 \cup V_1$, which is a maximum clique due to Claim 17. Also, according to Part 1, we expect to have a mutation that produces the bit string 0^n within $O(n)$ fitness evaluations. Hence, the (1+1) RMA_FILS is expected to find a maximum clique within $O(tn)$ fitness evaluations, which is $O(n^{1.5})$ since $n = t(2t+2)$. □

Theorem 21. *For any static or dynamic variable λ, the probability of the (1+1) RMA_BILS finding a maximum clique of the graph $G_2(t)$ within a polynomial number of fitness evaluations is super-polynomially close to zero.*

Proof. We prove this by showing that, from the start or from each restart, the algorithm is expected to become trapped in a local optimal clique and take a super-polynomial number of fitness evaluations to find a global optimal clique. In detail, our proof consists of three parts, with each part having a failure probability super-polynomially close to zero.

Part 1. Let y be the first bit string found by the algorithm after the start or each restart that represents a clique. We claim that $V(y)$ has no more than $\log n$ vertices with a probability super-polynomially close to one. The proof is similar to the proof of Part 1 for Theorem 12, so we only need to show that, from 0^n, no more than $\log n$ bits are flipped with a probability super-polynomially close to one. Suppose the above statement fails, i.e., the mutation flips $p = \Omega(\log n)$ bits, the probability of this event occurring is:

$$\binom{n}{p}\left(\frac{1}{n}\right)^p\left(1-\frac{1}{n}\right)^{n-p} \le \frac{1}{ep!}\frac{n(n-1)\cdots(n-p+1)}{n^p} < \frac{1}{ep!} < \frac{1}{2^{cp}},$$

for any constant c. This probability is super-polynomially close to zero since $p = \Omega(\log n)$.

Part 2. Assume Part 1 has succeeded, let z be the first bit string found by the algorithm after the start or each restart that represents a local optimal clique. We claim that z has at most $\log n$ vertices in $\bigcup_{i=2}^{2t+1} V_i$ with a probability super-polynomially close to one.

After y is found, the BILS will keep checking the current string's neighbors, then moving to one of the best neighbors. Since $V(y)$ only contains no more than $\log n$ vertices, there are still $\Theta(t)$ columns from which y has not chosen any vertices. Let us call them *un-chosen columns*. Furthermore, among these *un-chosen columns*, we call a column a *negative column* if $V(z)$ contains a vertex from $V_0 \cup V_1$ in this column due to the fact that it is moving further away from all global optimal cliques. Alternatively, if $V(z)$ contains a vertex from $\bigcup_{i=2}^{2t+1} V_i$ in an *un-chosen column*, we call it a *positive column*. We claim that, when the BILS reaches z, there is at most one *positive column* while all other *un-chosen columns* will be *negative columns* (we will show this in the next paragraph). And for each *negative column*, the BILS will not add any vertices from $\bigcup_{i=2}^{2t+1} V_i$ in this column to the clique due to Rule 1 in Definition 13. Also, the *positive column* can have at most two vertices from $\bigcup_{i=2}^{2t+1} V_i$, due to Claim 14. Thus, $V(z)$ is expected to contain at most $\log n$ vertices in $\bigcup_{i=2}^{2t+1} V_i$.

Now we show that when the BILS reaches z, there is at most one *positive column* while all other columns will be *negative columns*. We assume that there is more than one *positive column*, then we can select any two *positive columns* of column k and l ($k \neq l$), and show a contradiction. First, let $v_{i,k}$ be the first vertex in the column k that the BILS will add to the clique, and let $v_{j,l}$ be the first vertex in the column l that the BILS will add to the clique. Since the column k and the column l are both *positive columns*, we know $2 \le i \le 2t+1$ and $2 \le j \le 2t+1$. Furthermore, let us assume that the BILS will add the vertex $v_{i,k}$ before adding the vertex $v_{j,l}$. Let x be the bit string before the BILS adds the vertex $v_{i,k}$, and x' be the bit string after the BILS adds the vertex $v_{i,k}$ to x. Also, let s be the number of vertices in the column k that are in $\mathtt{PV}(x)$, i.e. $s = |\{v_{p,k} \mid 0 \le p \le (2t+1) \text{ and } \forall v \in V(x) \to \{v_{p,k}, v\} \in E\}|$. Then we say $\mathtt{PV}(x') \le \mathtt{PV}(x) - s - 1$ due to the fact that there are at least $s+1$ vertices in $\mathtt{PV}(x)$, but not in $\mathtt{PV}(x')$. In detail, these $s+1$ vertices are:

1. $s-1$ vertices in the column k. This is because the vertex $v_{i,k}$ is connected to only one vertex in the same column, thus all other vertices would not be in $\mathtt{PV}(x')$. Note the vertex $v_{i,k}$ is in $\mathtt{PV}(x)$, but not in $\mathtt{PV}(x')$.

2. 2 vertices in the column l. These two vertices are $v_{i,l}$ and $v_{i',l}$, with $\lfloor i/2 \rfloor = \lfloor i'/2 \rfloor$ and $i \neq i'$. This is because a) the vertices $v_{i,l}$ and $v_{i',l}$ are not connected to the vertex $v_{i,k}$, due to Rule 3 in Definition 13, hence, they are not in $\mathtt{PV}(x')$; and b) $v_{i,l}$ and $v_{i',l}$ must be in $\mathtt{PV}(x)$. We prove this by assuming that $v_{i,l}$ or $v_{i',l}$ is not in $\mathtt{PV}(x)$, and show a contradiction. If $v_{i,l}$ or $v_{i',l}$ is not in $\mathtt{PV}(x)$ because of Rule 3 in Definition 13, then the vertex $v_{i,k}$ should not be in $\mathtt{PV}(x)$ as well. Hence, the BILS will not add the vertex $v_{i,k}$ to x. Or if $v_{i,l}$ or $v_{i',l}$ is not in $\mathtt{PV}(x)$ because of Rule 4 or Rule 5 in Definition 13, then the column l can not be a *positive column*. Therefore, $v_{i,l}$ and $v_{i',l}$ must be in $\mathtt{PV}(x)$.

Meanwhile, we claim that another solution x'', of which $V(x'') = V(x) \cup \{v_{0,k}\}$, has a larger fitness value than x' (we will show this later). And we know that x'' is a neighbor of x. Therefore, the BILS will not move to x', which contradicts our assumption. (Recall that the BILS only moves to one of the best neighbors of the current solution).

Firstly, x'' must represent a clique. This is because $V(x)$ does not contain any vertices in the column k, and $v_{0,k}$ is connected to all vertices in other columns. Therefore, adding the vertex $v_{0,k}$ into x still represents a clique. Thus $\mathtt{ONES}(x'') = \mathtt{ONES}(x')$. Secondly, according to the edge rules in Definition 13, the vertex $v_{0,k}$ is connected to all vertices that are not in the column k. Thus, for all vertices in other columns, if they are in $\mathtt{PV}(x)$, then they will still be in $\mathtt{PV}(x'')$ as well. This means that $\mathtt{PV}(x'') \geq \mathtt{PV}(x) - s > \mathtt{PV}(x')$. Hence, x'' has a larger fitness value than x'.

Part 3. Assume Part 2 has succeeded, there are $t - \log t$ columns from which the current local optimal clique has vertices from $V_0 \cup V_1$. Therefore, there are $\omega(1)$ *hard-to-escape* sections of Definition 18. Then, due to Claim 19, the probability of the algorithm finding a maximum clique within a polynomial number of fitness evaluations is super-polynomially close to zero. □

5. CONCLUSIONS

This paper provided the theoretical evidence for the experimental observation that the local search operator that gives the best results in an MA on the same fitness function is entirely instance specific. In detail, we have formalized a (1+1) Restart Memetic Algorithm and two local searches, BILS and FILS, and run them on the fitness function $f_{\mathtt{OPL}}$ to solve the Clique Problem. We then constructed two families of graphs, G_1 and G_2, and showed that, for the first family of graphs G_1, the (1+1) RMA_BILS drastically outperforms the (1+1) RMA_FILS, and vice versa for the second family of graphs G_2. This indicates that an MA with multiple local searches can outperform MAs with a single local search in some instances of the Clique Problem.

6. REFERENCES

[1] A. Auger and B. Doerr, *Theory of Randomized Search Heuristics: Foundations and Recent Developments.* World Scientific Publishing Co., Inc., 2011.

[2] M. J. Dinneen, Z. Y. Lin, and K. Wei, "An intelligent self-adjusting memetic algorithm for solving course scheduling problems," in *3rd International Conference on Information Science and Engineering (ICISE)*, vol. 1, 2011, pp. 140–144.

[3] M. J. Dinneen and K. Wei, "A (1+1) adaptive memetic algorithm for the maximum clique problem," in *Proceedings of Congress on Evolutionary Computation*, CEC'13, vol. 1. IEEE, June 2013, pp. 1626–1634.

[4] ——, "On the analysis of a (1+1) adaptive memetic algorithm," in *Proceedings of Memetic Computing, MC2013.* IEEE, 2013, pp. 24–31.

[5] C. GieBen, "Hybridizing evolutionary algorithms with opportunistic local search," in *Proceeding of the Fifteenth Annual Conference on Genetic and Evolutionary Computation Conference*, GECCO'13. ACM, 2013, pp. 797–804.

[6] E. Happ, D. Johannsen, C. Klein, and F. Neumann, "Rigorous analyses of fitness-proportional selection for optimizing linear functions," in *Proceedings of the 10th Annual Conference on Genetic and Evolutionary Computation*, GECCO'08. ACM, 2008, pp. 953–960.

[7] T. Jansen, *Analyzing Evolutionary Algorithms: The Computer Science Perspective*, Natural Computing Series. Springer, 2013.

[8] N. Krasnogor and J. Smith, "Emergence of profitable search strategies based on a simple inheritance mechanism," in *Proceedings of the 2001 Genetic and Evolutionary Computation*, GECCO'01, N. Krasnogor, Ed. ACM, 2001, pp. 432–439.

[9] ——, "A tutorial for competent memetic algorithms: model, taxonomy, and design issues," *IEEE Transactions on Evolutionary Computation*, vol. 9, no. 5, pp. 474–488, 2005.

[10] F. Neri, J. Toivanen, G. L. Cascella, and Y.-S. Ong, "An adaptive multimeme algorithm for designing HIV multidrug therapies," *IEEE/ACM Transactions on Computational Biology and Bioinformatics*, vol. 4, no. 2, pp. 264–278, Apr. 2007.

[11] F. Neumann and C. Witt, *Bioinspired Computation in Combinatorial Optimization: Algorithms and Their Computational Complexity*, 1st ed. Springer-Verlag, 2010.

[12] P. S. Oliveto, J. He, and X. Yao, "Time complexity of evolutionary algorithms for combinatorial optimization: A decade of results," *International Journal of Automation and Computing*, vol. 4, no. 3, pp. 281–293, 2007.

[13] Y.-S. Ong, M.-H. Lim, N. Zhu, and K.-W. Wong, "Classification of adaptive memetic algorithms: a comparative study," *Trans. Sys. Man Cyber. Part B*, vol. 36, no. 1, pp. 141–152, Feb. 2006.

[14] J. E. Smith, "Coevolving memetic algorithms: A review and progress report," *Trans. Sys. Man Cyber. Part B*, vol. 37, no. 1, pp. 6–17, Feb. 2007.

[15] D. Sudholt, "On the analysis of the (1+1) memetic algorithm," in *Proceedings of the 8th Annual Conference on Genetic and Evolutionary Computation*, GECCO'06. ACM, 2006, pp. 493–500.

[16] ——, "Memetic algorithms with variable-depth search to overcome local optima," in *Proceedings of the 10th Annual Conference on Genetic and Evolutionary Computation*, GECCO'08. ACM, 2008, pp. 787–794.

[17] ——, "The impact of parametrization in memetic evolutionary algorithms," *Theoretical Computer Science*, vol. 410, no. 26, pp. 2511–2528, 2009.

[18] K. Wei and M. J. Dinneen, "Hybridizing the dynamic mutation approach with local searches to overcome local optima," in *Proceedings of Congress on Evolutionary Computation*, CEC'14. IEEE, July 2014, World Congress on Computaitonal Intelligence. To appear.

[19] ——, "Runtime analysis comparison of two fitness functions on a memetic algorithm for the clique problem," in *Proceedings of Congress on Evolutionary Computation*, CEC'14. IEEE, July 2014, World Congress on Computational Intelligence. To appear.

Author Index

www.ingramcontent.com/pod-product-compliance
Lightning Source LLC
LaVergne TN
LVHW080108011026
849160LV00013B/1055